The New College
LATIN & ENGLISH
Dictionary

THIRD EDITION

by
JOHN C. TRAUPMAN, Ph.D.
St. Joseph's University, Philadelphia

AMSCO SCHOOL PUBLICATIONS, INC.,
a division of Perfection Learning®

The New College Latin & English Dictionary, Third Edition

Cover Design by Meghan Shupe
Cover photograph: Looking Up at Dome in St. Peter's Basilica,
    Vatican City, Rome, Italy by FOTOSEARCH
Composition by Dom Roberti

When ordering this book, please specify:
either 13494 or LATIN DICTIONARY

Please visit our Web sites at:
www.amscopub.com and *www.perfectionlearning.com*

ISBN 978-1-56765-433-2

Published by Amsco School Publications, Inc., a division of
Perfection Learning®, by arrangement with the copyright owners.

Printed in the United States of America

4 5 6 7 8 9 10   18 17 16 15

Contents

PREFACE TO THE THIRD EDITION

This totally revised and expanded edition, with over 70,000 words and phrases, in addition to all the features of the second edition, reflecting the increased interest in oral Latin, includes many neologisms in the **English–Latin** section in order to deal with subjects such as house and furniture, daily activities, health and physical fitness, classroom activities, sports and other leisure activities, modern means of transportation, and modern technology, such as computers. This dictionary also provides a wide range of historical, mythological, and geographical names as they would have been known in ancient times. Where appropriate, the modern geographical name is provided, e.g., Brundisium (*modern Brindisi*).

Since current Latin textbooks use the consonantal *i* in place of the *j*, this edition has also adopted the consonantal *i*. Variant spellings of Latin words are provided within the entries. In the Latin–English section, long vowels in closed syllables are indicated by a macron. The transitive and intransitive functions of verbs have been clearly presented, with the transitive uses always preceding the intransitive uses. Illustrative phrases within the entries are all translated and arranged in alphabetical order.

The level of usage of Latin words and phrases is faithfully reflected in the level of usage of the English transitions, so that, if the Latin word is colloquial, slang, or vulgar, the English translation corresponds.

The author gratefully acknowledges the kind support of Henry Brun, President, and of John Aliano, Foreign Languages Director, of Amsco School Publications. Special thanks are due to Dr. Dominic M. Roberti, chemistry professor turned desktop publisher, who gave much helpful advice; he is responsible for the page design and typesetting of this book. The author also wishes to express his thanks to Dr. James McDonough for his critical comments and to Steven Earl Heinsz and Gary Varney for pointing out various typographical errors.

Abbreviations

abbr . . . . .abbreviation
abl . . . . . .ablative
acc . . . . . .accusative
adj . . . . .adjective
adjl . . . . .adjectival
adv . . . . .adverb
advl . . . . .adverbial
anat . . . . .anatomy
archit . . . .architecture
astr . . . . .astronomy
bot . . . . . .botany
c. . . . . . . .circa, about
cf. . . . . . . .confer, compare
cent. . . . . .century
coll . . . . . .colloquial
com . . . . .commerce
comp . . . .comparative
conj . . . . .conjunction
d. . . . . . . .died
dat . . . . . .dative
defect . . . .defective verb
dim. . . . . .diminutive
E. . . . . . . .East(ern)
eccl . . . . .ecclesiastical
educ . . . . .education
euphem . .euphemism
esp. . . . . .especially
expr. . . . .expressed
f . . . . .feminine noun
fem . . . . . .feminine
fig . . . . . .figurative
fin . . . . . .finance
Ē . . . . . . .floruit, flourished
fpl . . . . . .feminine plural
            noun
fut . . . . . .future
gen . . . . . .genitive

geog . . . . .geography
geol . . . . .geology
gram . . . .grammar
hum . . . . .humorous
imperf . . .imperfect
impers . . .impersonal verb
impv . . . . .imperative
indecl . . . .indeclinable
indef . . . . .indefinite
indic . . . . .indicative
inf . . . . . .infinitive
interj . . . .interjection
interrog . .interrogative
intr . . . . . .intransitive
leg . . . . . .legal
lit . . . . . .literal
loc . . . . . .locative
m . . . . . . .masculine noun
masc . . . .masculine
math . . . .mathematics
med . . . . .medicine
mf . . . . . .masculine or femi-
            nine noun
mil . . . . . .military
mpl . . . . .masculine plural
            noun
mus . . . . .music
n . . . . . . .neuter noun
N. . . . . . .North(ern)
naut . . . . .nautical
neg. . . . . .negative
neut . . . . .neuter
nom . . . . .nominative
npl . . . . . .neuter plural noun
opp . . . . .opposite of
p . . . . . . .participle
pass . . . . .passive

pej . . . . . .pejorative
perf . . . . .perfect
phil . . . . .philosophy
pl . . . . . . .plural
poet . . . . .poetry
pol . . . . . .politics
pp . . . . . .past participle
pref . . . . .prefix
prep . . . . .preposition
pres . . . . .present
pron . . . . .pronoun
pros . . . . .prosody
prov . . . . .proverb
refl . . . . . .reflexive
rel . . . . . .relative
relig . . . . .religion
rhet . . . . .rhetoric
s . . . . . . .substantive
S. . . . . . .South(ern)
singl . . . . .singular
sl . . . . . . .slang
s.o. . . . . . .someone
s.th. . . . . .something
subj . . . . .subjunctive
suf . . . . . .suffix
superl . . . .superlative
theat . . . . .theater
topog . . . .topography
tr . . . . . . .transitive verb
usu. . . . . .usually
vbl . . . . . .verbal
v defect . .defective verb
v impers . .impersonal verb
vulg . . . . .vulgar
w. . . . . . . .with
W. . . . . . .West(ern)

A Guide to the Dictionary

The main entry, its inflected forms, spelling variants, and illustrative phrases are set in boldface. Part-of-speech labels are set in italics.

Centered periods within entry words indicate division points at which inflectional elements are to be added, without regard to syllabification, e.g.,

ord·ō -inis = ordō, ordinis

Compound words are generally given in their assimilated forms, e.g., **accurrō** rather than **adcurrō**. Cross-references are provided as guides for those using texts which employ the unassimilated forms, e.g.,

adc- = acc-

sēpiō *see* **saepio**

Spelling variants are indicated in bold type in parentheses after the part-of-speech abbreviation, e.g.,

affīnit·ās -ātis *f* (**adf-**) affinity, connection; relationship by marriage

However, nouns with both Greek and Latin endings are shown in full, e.g.,

troch·us *or* **troch·os -ī** *m* hoop

Tened·os *or* **Tened·us   -ī** *f* Tenedos *(island off the coast of Troy)*

Adjectives of three endings, whether of the first and second or of the third declension, are shown with three endings; adjectives with a single ending are shown in the nominative, followed by the genitive ending, e.g.,

curv·us -a -um *adj* curved

simil·is -is -e *adj* similar

dīlig·ens -entis *adj* careful; diligent

When constructions are provided, cases are not shown with the most common prepositions

ab, ad, ex, *or* **cum**. For all other prepositions, the case that the preposition governs is shown, e.g.,

stō stāre stetī statum *intr* to stand; *(w.* **ex)** to consist of; *(w. abl or* **in** *+ abl)* to depend on; *(w.* **per** *+ acc)* to be due to, thanks to

Synonymous meanings are separated by commas; distinct meanings are separated by semicolons. When a grammatical construction applies to several distinct meanings, thus extending beyond semicolons, the distinct meanings are numbered, e.g.,

perfugiō *intr (w.* **ad** *or* **in** *+ acc)* **1** to flee to for refuge; **2** to desert to; **3** to have recourse to

Discriminations between two or more meanings of an entry word are often shown by means of English words in parentheses, coming before or after the English meaning, e.g.,

argūt·us -a -um *adj* bright, smart *(person);* rustling *(leaves);* babbling *(brook);* chirping *(bird, cricket);* pungent *(smell);* expressive *(eyes, gestures)*

aspect·ō -āre -āvī -ātus *tr* (**ads-**) to look at, gaze at; *(of a place)* to face; to obey *(orders)*

However, words in parentheses, but not in italics, coming before or after a meaning are optional additions to the word in the target language, e.g.,

avuncul·us -ī *m* (maternal) uncle

abi·es -etis *f* fir (tree)

Level of usage of Latin words, indicated by the abbreviations *(coll)* for "colloquial," *(sl)* for "slang," and *(vulg)* for "vulgar," is reflected in the level of usage of the English translation of the Latin word, e.g.,

1

admutil·ō -āre *tr* to clip close; *(coll)* to clip, cheat

ab·eō -īre -īvī *or* **-iī itum** *vi* to go away, depart; **abi in malam rem!** *(sl)* go to hell!

cole·ī -ōrum *mpl (vulg)* balls

Subject labels are given in italics and listed in alphabetical order, e.g.,

concurs·us -ūs *m* a running together, concourse; *(astr)* conjunction; *(gram)* juxtaposition *(of letters); (leg)* joint-right; *(mil)* charge, clash

When an entry word is a proper noun, the proper noun is not repeated in English if the form is the same in Latin and in English; but when the proper noun has two possible endings, the form used in English is provided, e.g.,

Eurīpid·ēs -is *m* Athenian tragic playwright *(480-406 B.C.)*

Eurōp·a -ae *or* **Eurōp·ē -ēs** *f* Europa *(daughter of the Phoenician king Agenor)* ‖ (continent of) Europe

Substantives formed from adjectives are generally listed under the adjectives from which they are derived and are separated by vertical parallel bars, e.g.,

dialectic·us -a -um *adj* logical ‖ *m* logician ‖ *f* logic ‖ *npl* dialectics

Proper nouns derived from adjectives or from common nouns are subsumed, in short entries, under the adjective and common noun respectively, e.g.,

daedal·us -a -um *adj* skillful, artistic; intricately constructed ‖ **Daedal·us -ī** *m* builder of the Labyrinth in Crete

Tarquini·us -a -um *adj* Tar-quinian ‖ *m* Tarquinius Priscus *(fifth king of Rome, c. 616-579 B.C.)* ‖ Tarquinius Superbus *(seventh and last king of Rome, c. 534-510 B.C.)*

cast·or -ōris *m* beaver ‖ **Castor** *son of Tyndareus, twin brother of Pollux*

Vertical parallel bars are used to separate different parts of speech of the entry word, for instance, pronominal adjectives from pronouns, e.g.,

alt·er -era -erum *adj* one *(of two);* a second, the second; the next ‖ *pron* one *(of two),* the one, the other; a second one

Vertical parallel bars are used to separate past participles, when occurring as separate entries, from adjectives and substantives derived from them, e.g.,

impens·us -a -um *pp of* **impendo** ‖ *adj* high, costly, expensive; ‖ *f see* **impensa** ‖ *n* high price

Vertical parallel bars are used to separate nouns in the singular from nouns in the plural when the plural of the nouns carries a special meaning, e.g.,

aed·es *or* **aed·is -is** *f* room; apartment; shrine, temple ‖ *fpl* house, home

Vertical parallel bars are used to separate common nouns from proper nouns, e.g.,

urs·a -ae *f* she-bear ‖ **Ursa Major** *(astr)* Great Bear; **Ursa Minor** *(astr)* Little Bear

Vertical parallel bars are used to separate verb functions. Transitive *(tr),* reflexive *(refl),* passive (with intransitive sense) *(pass),* intransitive *(intr),* and impersonal *(v impers)* functions of verbs with their dependent constructions are clearly differentiated and are presented in the fixed order as listed above, e.g.,

ēmer·gō -gěre -sī -sus *vt* to raise *(from the water)* ‖ *refl or pass* to rise ‖ *intr* to emerge; to rise *(in power)*

Illustrative phrases are provided at the end of entries in strict alphabetical order. However, when a Latin phrase illustrates a specific meaning, for instance, when the main entry is a prefix suffix, or preposition, the phrase is placed immediately after that meaning and introduced by a colon, e.g.,

-i·cō -āre *vbl suff* **1** used to form verbs from adjectives: **claudicāre** to be lame, to limp; **2** used to form verbs from other verbs: **fodicāre** to stab *(from* **foděre)**

For the sake of clarity, optional variants in illustrative phrases are placed in parentheses, e.g.,

vera et falsa *(or* **vera a falsis) dijudicare** to distinguish truth from falsehood

Vowel lengths are not shown on words within an entry except when clarity demands them, e.g.

succīdere [sub + caedere] to cut down (in order to distinguish it from **succĭdere [sub + cadere]** to collapse)

adversā viā up the road

nullā condicione by no means

de industriā on purpose

When a noun may be either masculine or feminine, the abbreviations are written together, but when a noun is generally, say, masculine but only rarely feminine or neuter, the rarer gender is shown in parentheses, e.g.,

serp·ens -entis *mf* serpent

pampin·us -ī *m (f)* vine shoot

sāl salis *m (n)* salt

Past participles are listed as separate entries when difference in form from the first person singular present indicative warrants such listing, provided they fall alphabetically more than one word before or after their verb, e.g.,

vīs·us -a -um *pp of* **video**

Similarly, the perfect form of a verb is listed as a separate entry in its alphabetical position, e.g.,

trīvī *perf of* **tero**

On the Latin-English side, the twofold purpose in marking the quantity of vowels is

1. to indicate accentuation of words
2. to provide the basis for scansion of Classical Latin verse

Thus, all vowels that are long by nature and occur in open syllables are marked, whereas vowels in closed syllables, whether long or short by nature, are not marked, since the syllable in either case is long. However, since a vowel followed by a mute and a liquid can be open or closed, its quantity is marked when it is long.

On the English-Latin side, Latin vowels are marked to distinguish:

1. words otherwise spelled alike: **lēvis** (smooth), **lěvis** (light)
2. the ablative singular from the nominative singular of nouns of the first declension whenever the distinction is not clear from the context
3. the infinitive of verbs of the second conjugation from the infinitive of verbs of the third conjugation
4. the genitive singular and nominative and accusative plural from the nominative singular of the fourth declension whenever the distinction is not clear from the context

On the English-Latin side, a boldface dash represents the vocabulary entry, e.g.,

awake *adj* vigil, vigilans; **to be —** vigilare

3

Pronunciation

Vowels

CLASSICAL METHOD	ECCLESIASTICAL METHOD
ă *a* in ago: **compărō**	
ā *a* in father: **imāgō**	
ĕ *e* in pet: **propĕrō**	
ē *a* in late: **lēnis**	Generally the same as the Classical
ĭ *i* in hit: **ĭdem**	Method. However, in practice the different values of the vowels are frequently not
ī *ee* in keen: **amīcus**	rigidly adhered to.
ŏ *o* in often: **mŏdus**	
ō *o* in hope: **nōmen**	
ŭ *u* in put: **ŭt**	
ū *u* in rude: **ūtor**	
ў *ü* in German Hütte: **mўrta**	
ȳ *ü* in German über: **Tȳdeus**	

Diphthongs

CLASSICAL METHOD	ECCLESIASTICAL METHOD
ae *y* in by: **c*ae*cus**	ae *a* in late: **c*ae*cus**
au *ow* in now: **n*au*ta**	au as in Classical Method
eī *ey* in they: **h*eī***	ei as in Classical Method
eū *eu* in feud: **Orph*eū*s**	eu *eu* in Italian neutro: ***eu*ge**
oē *oi* in oil: **c*oē*pit**	oe *a* in late: **c*oe*pit**
uī *uey* in gluey: **c*uī*;** after **q**, *wee* in **week: qui**	ui same as Classical Method

Consonants

CLASSICAL METHOD	ECCLESIASTICAL METHOD
b English b	b English b
c always *c* in can: **cīvis, cantō, cedō**	c before **e, i, ae,** or **oe** = *ch* in cherry: **celsus, civis, caelum, coepit,** but before other letters, *c* in can: **cantō, actus**
d English d	d English d
f English f	f English f
g always *g* in go: **gallīna, genus, grātus, gula**	g before **e** or **i** = *g* in gentle: **genus, regīna,** but before other letters except **g** and **n** (see under Consonant Groups) = *g* in go: **gallīna, grātus, gula, rogō**
h English h	h English h

4

j	*y* in yes: *j*am, *j*ungō	j	as in Classical Method
k	English k, but unaspirated	k	English k
l	English l	l	English l
m	English m, but in verse final **m** before an initial vowel or **h** in the following word was presumably not pronounced	m	English m
n	English n	n	English n
p	English p, but unaspirated	p	English p
q	English q	q	English q
r	trilled r as in the Romance languages	r	as in Classical Method
s	always *s* in sing: mi*s*er, mor*s*	s	*s* in sing: **salūs,** but when standing between two vowels or when final and preceded by a voiced consonant = *z* in dozen: mi*s*er, mor*s*
t	English t, but unaspirated	t	as in Classical Method
u	*w* in wine, when unaccented, preceded by q, sometimes by s, and sometimes by g, and followed by a vowel: q*ui*·a, s*uā*·vis (but s*u*·ō·rum), dis·tin·g*u*ō (but ex·i·gŭ·*us*)	u	in Classical Method
v	*w* in wine: *v*ī*v*ō	v	English v
x	*x* (= ks) in six: e*x*trā	x	*x* (as ks) in six: pa*x*; but in words beginning with **ex** and followed by a vowel, **h,** or **s,** = *x* (as **gz**) in exhaust: e*x*audī, e*x*hālō, e*x*solvō
z	*dz* in adze: *z*ōna	z	as in Classical Method

Consonant Groups

	CLASSICAL METHOD		ECCLESIASTICAL METHOD
bs	*ps* in apse: o*bs*idō, ur*bs*	bs	bs in obsession: o*bs*idō, but in the final position = **bs** (= **bz**) in observe: ur*bs*
bt	*pt* in captain: o*bt*inēre	bt	*bt* in obtain: o*bt*inēre
cc	*kk* in bookkeeper: e*cc*īdō, o*cc*āsum, o*ccl*ūdō	cc	before **e** or **i** = *tch* in catch: e*cc*īdō; but before other letters = *kk* in bookkeeper; o*cc*āsum, o*ccl*ūdō
ch	*ch* in chaotic: pul*ch*er	ch	as in Classical Method
gg	*gg* in leg guard: a*gg*er	gg	before **e** or **i** = *dj* in adjourn: a*gg*er; but before other letters = *gg* in leg guard: a*gg*rĕgō
gn	*ny* in canyon: di*gn*us	gn	as in Classical Method
gu	see consonant **u**	gu	as in Classical Method
ph	*p-h* in top-heavy: *ph*ōca	ph	*ph* in phoenix: *ph*ōca
qu	see consonant **u**	qu	as in Classical Method

sc *sc* in scope: *sci*ō, *sc*ūtum

su see consonant **u**

th *t* in take: *th*eātrum

ti *ti* in English patio: nā*ti*ō

sc before **e** or **i** = *sh* in **sh**in: a**sc**endō, **sci**ō; but before other letters = **sc** in scope: *sc*andō, *sc*ūtum

su as in Classical Method

th as in Classical Method

ti when preceded by **s, t,** or **x,** or when followed by a consonant = *ti* in English patio: hos*ti*a, admix*ti*ō, for*ti*ter; but when unaccented, followed by a vowel, and preceded by any letter except **s, t,** or **x** = *tzy* in ritzy: nā*ti*ō, pre*ti*um

Syllabification

1. Every Latin word has as many syllables as it has vowels or diphthongs: **ae·ger, fī·li·us, Bai·ae**

2. When a word is divided into syllables:

   a) a single consonant between two vowels goes with the following syllable (**h** is regarded as a consonant; **ch, ph, th, qu,** and sometimes **gu** and **su** are regarded as single consonants)*; **a·ger, ni·hil, a·qua, ci·hor·rē·um**

   b) the first consonant of a combination of two or more consonants goes with the preceding vowel: **tor·men·tum, mit·tō, mon·strum**

   c) a consonant group consisting of a mute (**b, c, d, g, p, t**) followed by **l** or **r** is generally left undivided and goes with the following vowel: **pā·trēs, a·cris, du·plex.** In Classical poetry this combination is often treated like any other pair of consonants: **pāt·rēs, ac·ris, dup·lex**

   d) prefixes form separate syllables even if the division is contrary to above rules: **ab·est, ob·lā·tus, abs·ti·nē·ō, ab·stō**

3. A syllable ending in a vowel or diphthong is called *open;* all others are called *closed*

4. The last syllable of a word is called the *ultima;* the next to last is called the *penult;* the one before the penult is called the *antepenult*

---

* The double consonant **x** goes with the preceding vowel: **dix·it**

Quantity of Vowels

1. A vowel is *long* (**lēvis**) or *short* (**lĕvis**) according to the length of time required for its pronunciation

2. A vowel is long:

   a) before **ns, nf,** (and perhaps **gn**): **ingēns, īnfāns, (māgnus)**

3. A vowel is short (with some rare exceptions):

   a) before another vowel or **h: dĕa, trăhō**

   b) generally before **nd** and **nt: amăndus, amănt**

4. Diphthongs are long: **causa**

6

Quantity of Syllables

1. Syllables are distinguished as *long* or *short* according to the length of time required for their pronunciation
2. A syllable is long:

   a) if it contains a long vowel or a diphthong: vē·nī scrī·bō, caus·ae (such a syllable is said to be *long by nature*)

   b) if it contains a short vowel followed by x, z, or any two consonants except a mute (b, d, g, p, t, c) followed by l or r: sax·um, gaz·a, mit·tō, cur·sor (such a syllable is said to be *long by position,* but the vowel is pronounced *short*)
3. A syllable is short:

   a) if it contains a short vowel followed by a vowel or by a single consonant (h is regarded as a consonant; ch, ph, th, qu, and sometimes gu and su are regarded as single consonants): me·us, ni·hil, ge·rit, a·qua

   b) if it contains a short vowel followed by a mute (b, d, g, p, t, c) plus l or r, but it is sometimes long in verse: flă·grans, ba·ră·thrum, ce·lĕ·brō (such a syllable is said to be *common*)

NOTE: In this dictionary, on the Latin-English side, long vowels are marked except before x, z, or two or more consonants unless the two consonants are a mute plus a liquid (e.g., pātris). The short penult of the infinitive of verbs of the third conjugation is marked with a breve (e.g., vincĕre) to distinguish it from the long penult of the infinitive of verbs of the second conjugation (e.g., vidēre). In addition, the short syllable of words is marked to contrast it with the long syllable of otherwise homographs, e.g., concīdĕre (to kill) and concĭdĕre (to collapse); ănus (old woman) and ānus (anus, rectum).

Accent

1. Words of two syllables are accented on the first syllable: om′nēs, tan′gō, ge′rit
2. Words of more than two syllables are accented on the penult if it is long: a·mī′cus, re·gun′tur, and on the antepenult if the penult is short: fa·mi′lĭ·a, ge′rĭ·tur
3. These rules apply to words with enclitics appended (-ce, -dum, -met, -ne, -que, -ve): vos′met, lau·dat′ne, de′ă·que (nominative), dē·a′que (ablative)
4. In the second declension, the contracted genitive and the contracted vocative of nouns in -ius and the contracted genitive of those in -ium retain the accent of the nominative: Vir·gĭ′lī, in·gĕ′nī
5. Certain words which have lost a final -e retain the accent of the complete forms: il·līc′ for il·lī′ce, tan·tōn′ for tan·tō′ne
6. Certain compounds of faciō, in which a feeling for the individuality of the components was preserved, retain the accent of the simple verb: be·ne·fă′cit

Guide to Latin Grammar

Nouns

FIRST DECLENSION SINGULAR			SECOND DECLENSION SINGULAR	
rosa *f*	sonus *m*		puer *m*	ager *m*
rose	*sound*		*boy*	*field*
NOM	rosa	sonus	puer	ager
GEN	rosae	sonī	puerī	agrī
DAT	rosae	sonō	puerō	agrō
ACC	rosam	sonum	puerum	agrum
ABL	rosā	sonō	puerō	agrō

FIRST DECLENSION PLURAL			SECOND DECLENSION PLURAL	
NOM	rosae	sonī	puerī	agrī
GEN	rosārum	sonōrum	puerōrum	agrōrum
DAT	rosīs	sonīs	puerīs	agrīs
ACC	rosās	sonōs	puerōs	agrōs
ABL	rosīs	sonīs	puerīs	agrīs

SECOND DECLENSION SINGULAR

	vir *m*	dōnum *n*	servos *m*	fīlius *m*	ingenium *n*
	man	*gift*	*servant*	*son*	*talent*
NOM	vir	dōnum	servos	fīlius	ingenium
GEN	virī	dōnī	servī	fīl·iī *or* -ī	ingen·iī *or* -ī
DAT	virō	dōnō	servō	fīliō	ingeniō
ACC	virum	dōnum	servom	fīlium	ingenium
ABL	virō	dōnō	servō	fīliō	ingeniō

SECOND DECLENSION PLURAL

	virī	dōna	servī	fīliī	ingenia
NOM	virī	dōna	servī	fīliī	ingenia
GEN	virōrum	dōnōrum	servōrum	fīliōrum	igeniōrum
DAT	virīs	dōnīs	servīs	fīliīs	ingeniīs
ACC	virōs	dōna	servōs	fīliōs	ingenia
ABL	virīs	dōnīs	servīs	fīliīs	ingeniīs

NOTES (a) The vocative singular of **-us** nouns ends in **-e: amīce**. The vocative singular (and sometimes the genitive singular) of **-ius** nouns ends in **-ī: fīlī, Tiberī**. But the vocative of **deus** is **deus**.

          (b) The earlier inflection of masculine nouns of the second declension, down to Caesar and Cicero, followed the pattern of **servos**.

Third Declension Masculine/Feminine Nouns Singular

	rēx m *king*	**mīles** m *soldier*	**prīnceps** *m chief*	**māter** f *mother*
NOM	rēx	mīles	prīnceps	māter
GEN	rēgis	mīlitis	prīncipis	mātris
DAT	rēgī	mīlitī	prīncipī	mātrī
ACC	rēgem	mīlitem	prīncipem	mātrem
ABL	rēge	mīlite	prīncipe	mātre

Third Declension Masculine/Feminine Nouns Plural

NOM	rēgēs	mīlitēs	prīncipēs	mātrēs
GEN	rēgum	mīlitum	prīncipum	mātrum
DAT	rēgibus	mīlitibus	prīncipibus	mātribus
ACC	rēgēs	mīlitēs	prīncipēs	mātrēs
ABL	rēgibus	mīlitibus	prīncipibus	mātribus

Third Declension Masculine/Feminine Nouns Singular

	hostis *m enemy*	**custōs** *m guard*	**vigil** m *fireman*	**nox** f *night*
NOM	hostis	custōs	vigil	nox
GEN	hostis	custōdis	vigilis	noctis
DAT	hostī	custōdī	vigilī	noctī
ACC	host·em *or* -im	custōdem	vigilem	noctem
ABL	host·e *or* -ī	custōde	vigile	nocte

Third Declension Masculine/Feminine Nouns Plural

NOM	hostēs	custōdēs	vigilēs	noctēs
GEN	hostium	custōdum	vigilum	noctium
DAT	hostibus	custōdibus	vigilibus	noctibus
ACC	host·ēs *or* -īs	custōdēs	vigilēs	noctēs
ABL	hostibus	custōdibus	vigilibus	noctibus

Third Declension Neuter Nouns Singular

	nōmen n *name*	**caput** n *head*	**opus** n *work*	**iter** n *road*	**mare** n *sea*	**animal** n *animal*	**cor** n *heart*
NOM	nōmen	caput	opus	iter	mare	animal	cor
GEN	nōminis	capitis	operis	itineris	maris	animālis	cordis
DAT	nōminī	capitī	operī	itinerī	marī	animālī	cordī
ACC	nōmen	caput	opus	iter	mare	animal	cor
ABL	nōmine	capite	opere	itinere	marī	animālī	corde

Third Declension Neuter Nouns Plural

NOM	nōmina	capita	opera	itinera	maria	animālia	corda
GEN	nōminum	capitum	operum	itinerum	marium	animālium	—
DAT	nōminibus	capitibus	operibus	itineribus	maribus	animālibus	cordibus
ACC	nōmina	capita	opera	itinera	maria	animālia	corda
ABL	nōminibus	capitibus	operibus	itineribus	maribus	animālibus	cordibus

NOTES (a) Masculine and feminine i-stem nouns, such as **hostis,** regularly end in -is in the nominative singular, and always have **-ium** in the genitive plural. The accusative singular ends in **-em** *or* **-im**, and the ablative in **-e** *or* **-ī**, and the accusative plural in **-ēs** *or* **-īs**.

(b) A number of monosyllabic nouns with mute stems (like **cor**) lack the genitive plural.

9

FOURTH DECLENSION SINGULAR			FIFTH DECLENSION SINGULAR	
fructus *m*	**manus** *f*	**genū** *n*	**diēs** *m*	**rēs** *f*
fruit	*hand*	*knee*	*day*	*thing*
NOM fructus	manus	genū	diēs	rēs
GEN fructūs	manūs	genūs	diēī	reī
DAT fructuī	manuī	genū	diēī	reī
ACC fructum	manum	genū	diem	rem
ABL fructū	manū	genū	diē	rē

FOURTH DECLENSION PLURAL			FIFTH DECLENSION PLURAL	
NOM fructūs	manūs	genua	diēs	rēs
GEN fructuum	manuum	genuum	diērum	rērum
DAT fructibus	manibus	genibus	diēbus	rēbus
ACC fructūs	manūs	genua	diēs	rēs
ABL fructibus	manibus	genibus	diēbus	rēbus

NOTES Nouns of the fourth declension are mostly masculine nouns. The following nouns in **-us** are feminine: **acus** needle; **domus** house; **manus** hand; **porticus** colonnade; **tribus** tribe; **īdūs** *(pl)* Ides; also most names of trees, such as **quercus** oak.

(b) All fifth-declension nouns are feminine, except **diēs** *m* "day" and **merīdiēs** *m* "midday, noon." But **diēs** is sometimes feminine in the singular, especially in phrases indicating a fixed time, and regularly when used of time in general, e.g., **constitūtā diē** "on the appointed day"; **longa diēs** "a long time."

Greek Nouns

FIRST DECLENSION

Greek nouns that end in **-ē** are feminine; those that end in **-ās** and **-ēs** are masculine. In the plural, when found, they are declined like regular Latin nouns of the first declension.. In the singular they are declined as follows:

	Aenēās m	Anchīsēs m	Pēnelopē f	Persēs m
	Aeneas	*Anchises*	*Penelope*	*Persian*
NOM	Aenēās	Anchīsēs	Pēnelopē	Persēs
GEN	Aenēae	Anchīsae	Pēnelopēs	Persae
DAT	Aenēae	Anchīsae	Pēnelopae	Persae
ACC	Aenē·am *or* -ān	Anchīs·ēn, -am	Pēnelopēn	Pers·ēn *or* -am
ABL	Aenēā	Anchīs·ē *or* -ā	Pēnelopē	Pers·ē *or* -ā
VOC	Aenē·ā *or* -a	Anchīs·ē *or* -ā *or* -a	Pēnelopē	Pers·ē *or* -a

SECOND DECLENSION

Greek nouns of the second declension end in **-os** *or* **-ōs** and are masculine or feminine; those ending in **-on** are neuter. In the plural, when found, they are declined like regular Latin nouns. They are mostly proper names and are declined as follows in the singular:

	Lesbos *f*	Athōs *m*	Īlion *n*	Panthūs *m*
	Lesbos	*Athos*	*Ilium*	*Panthus*
Nom	Lesb·ōs or -us	Ath·ōs or -o	Īli·on or -um	Panthūs
Gen	Lesbī	Ath·ō or -ōnis	Īliī	Panthī
Dat	Lesbō	Athō	Īliō	Panthō
Acc	Lesb·on or -um	Ath·ōn or -ōnem	Īli·on or -um	Panthūn
Abl	Lesbō	Ath·ō or -ōne	Īliō	Panthō
Voc	Lesbō	Athōs	Īli·on or -um	Panthū

THIRD DECLENSION SINGULAR

	hērōs *m* hero	basis *f* base	nāïs *f* naiad	tigris *mf* tiger	lampas *f* torch
NOM	hērōs	basis	nāïs	tigris	lampas
GEN	hērōïs *or* -idos	bas·eōs	nāïd·os *or* -is	tigr·is *or* -idis	lampados
DAT	hērōï	basī	nāïdī	tigrī	lampadī
ACC	hērōa	bas·in *or* -ida *or* -im	nāïda	tigr·in *or* -idem	lampada
ABL	hērōë	basī	nāïde	tigr·ī *or* -ide	lampade

THIRD DECLENSION PLURAL

NOM	hērōes	basēs	nāïdes	tigrēs	lampades
GEN	hērōum	bas·eōn *or* -ium	nāïdum	tigrium	lampadum
DAT	hērōïbus	basibus	nāïdibus	tigribus	lampadibus
ACC	hērōas	basīs *or* -eîs	nāïdas	tigr·īs *or* -idas	lampadas
ABL	hērōïbus	basibus	nāïdibus	tigribus	lampadibus

THIRD DECLENSION PROPER NAMES

NOM	Dīdō	Capys	Paris	Orpheûs
GEN	Dīdōnis *or* Dīdūs	Capyos	Paridis	Orph·eī *or* -eōs
DAT	Dīdōnī *or* Dīdō	Capyī	Paridī	Orph·eō *or* -eī
ACC	Dīdō *or* Dīdōnem	Capyn	Parid·em *or* -im *or* -in	Orphe·um *or* -a
ABL	Dīdōne *or* -ō	Capyë	Paridē *or* Parī	Orphcō
VOC	Dīdō	Capy	Pari	Orpheû

NOM	Periclēs	Simoïs	Atlās	Selīnūs
GEN	Pericl·īs *or* -ī	Simoënt·is *or* -os	Atlantis	Selīnuntis
DAT	Pericl·ī *or* -i	Simoëntī	Atlantī	Selīnuntī
ACC	Pericl·em *or* -ea *or* -ēn	Simoënta	Atlanta	Selīnuntā
ABL	Pericle	Simoënte	Atlante	Selīnunte
VOC	Pericl·ēs *or* -ē	Simoïs	Atlā	Selīnūs

NOTES   (a) The regular Latin forms may be used for most of the above.

         (b) Most stems in id- *(nom:* -is), as **tigris**, often have also the forms of i-stems: *gen:* -idis *or* -idos *or* -is; *acc:* -idem *or* -ida *or* -im *or* -in; *abl:* -ide *or* -ī. However, most feminine proper names have *acc* -idem *or* -ida, *abl:* -ide, — not -im *or* -ī.

         (c) Stems in **ant-, ent-,** and a few in **unt-** follow the model of **Simoïs, -entis, Atlās, -antis** and **Selīnūs -untis.**

         (d) Many Greek names, of the third declension in Latin, pass over into the first declension in the plural, as, **Hyperid·ae -ārum,** etc.

         (e) Many names in -ēs belonging to the third declension have also genitive in -ī, e.g., **Pericl·ēs -is *or* -ī.**

         (f) Greek names in -eûs, like **Orpheûs,** have forms of the second and third declensions.

         (g) Greek nouns of the third declension end in -es in the nominative plural, as **Phryges** Phrygians, and end in -as in the accusative plural, as **Phrygas** Phrygians.

Pronouns
Personal Pronouns

ego *I*   **tu** *you*   **is** *he*   **ea** *she*   **id** *it*

SINGULAR

	1st Pers	2nd Pers	3rd Pers		
NOM	ego	tū	is	ea	id
GEN	meī	tuī	ēius	ēius	ēius
DAT	mihi *or* mī	tibi	ī	eī	eī
ACC	mē	tē	eum	eam	id
ABL	mē	tē	eō	eā	eō

PLURAL

	1st Pers	2nd Pers	3rd Pers		
NOM	nōs	vōs	eī *or* iī	eae	ea
GEN	nostrum	vestrum	eōrum	eārum	eōrum
	nostrī	vestrī			
DAT	nōbīs	vōbīs	eīs	eīs	eīs
ACC	nōs	vōs	eōs	eās	ea
ABL	nōbīs	vōbīs	eīs	eīs	eīs

NOTES   (a)   The forms **nostrum** and **vestrum** are used partitively, e.g., **ūnusquisque nostrum** each one of us; otherwise, the forms **nostrī** and **vestrī** are used, e.g., **meminit vestrī** he remembered you.

(b)   The form **mī** is sometimes used in poetry instead of **mihi**.

Reflexive Pronouns
SINGULAR

	1st Pers	2nd Pers	3rd Pers
NOM	——	——	——
GEN	meī	tuī	suī
DAT	mihi	tibi	sibi
ACC	mē	tē	sē *or* sēsē
ABL	mē	tē	sē *or* sēsē

NOTES   The reflexive of the third person serves for *all genders* of both singular and plural. Thus, **suī** may mean "of himself," "of herself," "of itself," or "of themselves;" **sibi** may mean "to himself," "to herself," or "to themselves," etc.

(b)   All of the reflexive pronouns can serve as reciprocal pronouns, e.g., **inter sē culpant** they blame each other (one another).

PLURAL

	1st Pers	2nd Pers	3rd Pers
NOM	——	——	——
GEN	nostrī	vestrī	suī
DAT	nōbīs	vōbīs	sibi
ACC	nōs	vōs	sē *or* sēsē
ABL	nōbīs	vōbīs	sē *or* sēsē

12

Demonstrative Pronouns

hic this (one)   **haec** this (one)   **hoc** this (one)

SINGULAR

	masc	*fem*	*neut*
NOM	hīc	haec	hōc
GEN	hūius	hūius	hūius
DAT	huic	huic	huic
ACC	hunc	hanc	hōc
ABL	hōc	hāc	hōc

PLURAL

	masc	*fem*	*neut*
NOM	hī	hae	haec
GEN	hōrum	hārum	hōrum
DAT	hīs	hīs	hīs
ACC	hōs	hās	haec
ABL	hīs	hīs	hīs

ille that (one)   **illa** that (one)   **illud** that (one)

SINGULAR

	masc	*fem*	*neut*
NOM	ille	illa	illud
GEN	illīus	illīus	illīus
DAT	illī	illī	illī
ACC	illum	illam	illud
ABL	illō	illā	illō

PLURAL

	masc	*fem*	*neut*
NOM	illī	illae	illa
GEN	illōrum	illārum	illōrum
DAT	illīs	illīs	illīs
ACC	illōs	illās	illa
ABL	illīs	illīs	illīs

NOTES   (a)   **Iste, ista, istud** ("that") is declined like **ille.**

          (b)   **Ille** and **iste** appear in combination with the demonstrative particle **-c,** shortened from **-ce** (giving the sense "that there") in the following forms:

SINGULAR

	masc	*fem*	*neut*
NOM	illic	illaec	illuc *or* illoc
ACC	illunc	illanc	illuc *or* illoc
ABL	illōc	illāc	illōc

PLURAL

	masc	*fem*	*neut*
NOM	——	——	illaec
ACC	——	——	illaec

13

	masc	*fem*	*neut*
NOM	istic	istaec	istuc *or* istoc
ACC	istunc	istanc	istuc *or* istoc
ABL	istōc	istāc	istōc

PLURAL

	masc	*fem*	*neut*
NOM	——	——	istaec
ACC	——	——	istaec

īdem the same	**eadem** the same	**idem** the same

SINGULAR

	masc	*fem*	*neut*
NOM	īdem	eadem	idem
GEN	ēiusdem	ēiusdem	ēiusdem
DAT	eīdem	eīdem	eīdem
ACC	eundem	eandem	idem
ABL	eōdem	eādem	eōdem

PLURAL

	masc	*fem*	*neut*
NOM	eīdem *or* iīdem	eaedem	eadem
GEN	eōrundem	eārundem	eōrundem
DAT	eīsdem *or* īsdem	eīsdem *or* īsdem	eīsdem *or* īsdem
ACC	eōsdem	eāsdem	eadem
ABL	eīsdem *or* īsdem	eīsdem *or* īsdem	eīsdem *or* īsdem

Intensive Pronouns

ipse -self	**ipsa** -self	**ipsum** -self

SINGULAR

	masc	*fem*	*neut*
NOM	ipse	ipsa	ipsum
GEN	ipsīus	ipsīus	ipsīus
DAT	ipsī	ipsī	ipsī
ACC	ipsum	ipsam	ipsum
ABL	ipsō	ipsā	ipsō

PLURAL

	masc	*fem*	*neut*
NOM	ipsī	ipsae	ipsa
GEN	ipsōrum	ipsārum	ipsōrum
DAT	ipsīs	ipsīs	ipsīs
ACC	ipsōs	ipsās	ipsa
ABL	ipsīs	ipsīs	ipsīs

Relative Pronouns

quī who, that   **quae** who, that   **quod** which, that

SINGULAR

	masc	*fem*	*neut*
NOM	quī	quae	quod
GEN	cūius	cūius	cūius
DAT	cui	cui	cui
ACC	quem	quam	quod
ABL	quō	quā	quō

PLURAL

	masc	*fem*	*neut*
NOM	quī	quae	quae
GEN	quōrum	quārum	quōrum
DAT	quibus	quibus	quibus
ACC	quōs	quās	quae
ABL	quibus	quibus	quibus

NOTE (a) The interrogative adjective **quī, quae, quod** (what? what kind of? which?), is declined throughout like the relative pronoun.

Interrogative Pronouns

quis who?   **quid** what?

	masc & fem	*neut*
NOM	quis	quid
GEN	cūius	cūius
DAT	cui	cui
ACC	quem	quid
ABL	quō	quō

NOTES The rare form of the plural follows the declension of the relative pronoun.

(b) **Quī** is sometimes used for **quis** in indirect questions.

(c) **Quis,** when modifying words denoting persons, is sometimes an adjective: **quis homō** = what man? whereas **quī homō** = what sort of man?

(d) The pronoun **quis** and the pronominal adjective **quī** may be strengthened by adding **-nam**, e. g., **quisnam** just who? exactly who?; **quidnam** just what?, exactly what?; **quīnam, quaenam, quodnam** of exactly what kind?

15

Indefinite Pronouns

aliquis somone   **aliqua** someone   **aliquid** something

Singular

	masc	*fem*	*neut*
Nom	aliquis (aliquī)	aliqua	aliquid (aliquod)
Gen	alicūius	alicūius	alicūius
Dat	alicui	alicui	alicui
Acc	aliquem	aliquam	aliquid (aliquod)
Abl	aliquō	aliquā	aliquō

Plural

	masc	*fem*	*neut*
Nom	aliquī	aliquae	aliqua
Gen	aliquōrum	aliquārum	aliquōrum
Dat	aliquibus	aliquibus	aliquibus
Acc	aliquōs	aliquās	aliqua
Abl	aliquibus	aliquibus	aliquibus

Notes   (a)   The indefinite adjective **aliquī** "some" is declined in the same way as the indefinite pronoun **aliquis** "someone" except in the three cases indicated above in parentheses: nominative masculine singular, neuter nominative singular, and neuter accusative singular.

          (b)   **Quis** is used instead of **aliquis** after **nē, sī, nisi,** and **num,** e.g., **sī quis** "if anyone."

quīdam, quaedam a certain person   **quiddam** a certain thing

Singular

	masc	*fem*	*neut*
Nom	quīdam	quaedam	quiddam
Gen	cūiusdam	cūiusdam	cūiusdam
Dat	cuidam	cuidam	cuidam
Acc	quendam	quandam	quiddam
Abl	quōdam	quādam	quōdam

Plural

	masc	*fem*	*neut*
Nom	quīdam	quaedam	quaedam
Gen	quōrundam	quārundam	quōrundam
Dat	quibusdam	quibusdam	quibusdam
Acc	quōsdam	quāsdam	quaedam
Abl	quibusdam	quibusdam	quibusdam

Notes   (a)   The corresponding pronomimal adjective differs only in these forms: **quoddam** for **quiddam.**

          (b)   There are two indefinite relative pronouns: **quīcumque** and **quisquis** "whoever." **Quīcumque** declines only the first part; **quisquis** declines both but has only **quisquis, quidquid,** and **quōquō** in common use.

16

Adjectives

First and Second Declensions Singular

	bonus good			tener tender		
	masc	*fem*	*neu*	*masc*	*fem*	*neut*
Nom	bonus	bona	bonum	tener	tenera	tenerum
Gen	bonī	bonae	bonī	tenerī	tenerae	tenerī
Dat	bonō	bonae	bonō	tenerō	tenerae	tenerō
Acc	bonum	bonam	bonum	tenerum	teneram	tenerum
Abl	bonō	bonā	bonō	tenerō	tenerā	tenerō

First and Second Declensions Plural

	masc	*fem*	*neu*	*masc*	*fem*	*neut*
Nom	bonī	bonae	bona	tenerī	tenerae	tenera
Gen	bonōrum	bonārum	bonōrum	tenerōrum	tenerārum	tenerōrum
Dat	bonīs	bonīs	bonīs	tenerīs	tenerīs	tenerīs
Acc	bonōs	bonās	bona	tenerōs	tenerās	tenerā
Abl	bonīs	bonīs	bonīs	tenerīs	tenerīs	tenerīs

First and Second Declensions Singular

	sacer sacred		
	masc	*fem*	*neut*
Nom	sacer	sacra	sacrum
Gen	sacrī	sacrae	sacrī
Dat	sacrō	sacrae	sacrō
Acc	sacrum	sacram	sacrum
Abl	sacrō	sacrā	sacrō

First and Second Declensions Plural

	masc	*fem*	*neut*
Nom	sacrī	sacrae	sacra
Gen	sacrōrum	sacrārum	sacrōrum
Dat	sacrīs	sacrīs	sacrīs
Acc	sacrōs	sacrās	sacra
Abl	sacrīs	sacrīs	sacrīs

Nine Irregular Adjectives

alter the other............................*see below*
alius another...............................*see below*
nūllus none........................same as tōtus
neuter neither.....................same as uter
sōlus alone.........................same as tōtus
tōtus whole.............................*see below*
ūllus any............................same as tōtus
ūnus one............................same as tōtus
uter which (of two)?...............*see below*

First and Second Declension Irregular Adjectives

They are declined in the singular as follows (the plural is regular):

	masc	*fem*	*neut*	*masc*	*fem*	*neut*
Nom	alius	alia	aliud	alter	altera	alterum
Gen	alterīus	alterīus	alterīus	alterīus	alterīus	alterīus
	alīus	alīus	alīus			
Dat	aliī	aliī	aliī	alterī	alterī	alterī
Acc	alium	aliam	aliud	alterum	alteram	alterum
Abl	aliō	aliā	aliō	alterō	alterā	alterō

		masc	*fem*	*neut*	*masc*	*fem*	*neut*
Nom	uter	utra	utrum	tōtus	tōta	tōtum	
Gen		utrīus	utrīus	utrīus	tōtīus	tōtīus	tōtīus
Dat		utrī	utrī	utrī	tōtī	tōtī	tōtī
Acc		utrum	utram	utrum	tōtum	tōtam	tōtum
Abl		utrō	utrā	utrō	tōtō	tōtā	tōtō

THIRD DECLENSION ADJECTIVES OF THREE ENDINGS: SINGULAR

alacer lively

	masc	*fem*	*neut*
NOM	alacer	alacris	alacre
GEN	alacris	alacris	alacris
DAT	alacrī	alacrī	alacrī
ACC	alacrem	alacrem	alacre
ABL	alacrī	alacrī	alacrī

THIRD DECLENSION ADJECTIVES OF THREE ENDINGS: PLURAL

	masc	*fem*	*neut*
NOM	alacrēs	alacrēs	alacria
GEN	alacrium	alacrium	alacrium
DAT	alacribus	alacribus	alacribus
ACC	alacr·ēs *or* -īs	alacr·ēs *or* -īs	alacria
ABL	alacribus	alacribus	alcribus

THIRD DECLENSION ADJECTIVES OF TWO ENDINGS: SINGULAR

fortis brave   **fortior** braver

	masc & fem	*neut*	*masc & fem*	*neut*
NOM	fortis	forte	fortior	fortius
GEN	fortis	fortis	fortiōris	fortiōris
DAT	fortī	fortī	fortiōrī	fortiōrī
ACC	fortem	forte	fortiōrem	fortius
ABL	fortī	fortī	fortiō·re *or* -rī	fortiō·re *or* -rī

THIRD DECLENSION ADJECTIVES OF TWO ENDINGS: PLURAL

	masc & fem	*neut*	*masc & fem*	*neut*
NOM	fortēs	fortia	fortiōrēs	fortiōra
GEN	fortium	fortium	fortiōrum	fortiōrum
DAT	fortibus	fortibus	fortiōribus	fortiōribus
ACC	fort·ēs *or* -īs	fortia	fortiōr·ēs *or* -īs	fortiōra
ABL	fortibus	fortibus	fortiōribus	fortiōribus

THIRD DECLENSION ADJECTIVES OF ONE ENDING: SINGULAR

audax bold   **potens** powerful   **vetus** old

	masc & fem	*neut*	*masc & fem*	*neut*	*masc & fem*	*neut*
NOM	audāx	audāx	potēns	potēns	vetus	vetus
GEN	audācis	audācis	potentis	potentis	veteris	veteris
DAT	audācī	audācī	potentī	potentī	veterī	veterī
ACC	audācem	audāx	potentem	potēns	veterem	vetus
ABL	audācī	audācī	potentī	potentī	vetere	vetere

THIRD DECLENSION ADJECTIVES OF ONE ENDING: PLURAL

	masc & fem	*neut*	*masc & fem*	*neut*	*masc & fem*	*neut*
NOM	audācēs	audācia	potentēs	potentia	veterēs	vetera
GEN	audācium	audācium	potentium	potentium	veterum	veterum
DAT	audācibus	audācibus	potentibus	potentibus	veteribus	veteribus
ACC	audāc·ēs -īs	audācia	potentēs	potentia	veterēs	vetera
ABL	audācibus	audācibus	potentibus	potentibus	veteribus	veteribus

Comparison of Irregular Adjectives

Positive	Comparative	Superlative
bonus, *good*	mel**ior**, *better*	opt**imus**, *best*
exter, *external*	exter**ior**, *outer*	extr**ēmus**, *outermost*
frūgī, *thrifty*	frūgāl**ior**, *thriftier*	frūgāl**issimus**, *thriftiest*
magnus, *big*	mā**ior**, *bigger*	max**imus**, *biggest*
malus, *bad*	pē**ior**, *worse*	pess**imus**, *worst*
multus, *bad*	pl**ūs**, *more*	plūr**imus**, *most*
nēquam, *worthless*	nēqu**ior**, *worse*	nēqu**issimus**, *worst*
posterus, *following*	poster**ior**, *later*	postr**ēmus**, post**umus**, *last*
superus, *upper*	super**ior**, *higher*	supr**ēmus**, summ**us**, *highest*
——————	dēter**ior**, *worse*	dēter**rimus**, *worst*
——————	īnfer**ior**, *lower*	īnf**imus**, īm**us**, *lowest*
——————	inter**ior**, *inner*	int**imus**, *innermost*
——————	ōc**ior**, *swifter*	ōc**issimus**, *swiftest*
——————	pot**ior**, *preferable*	pot**issimus**, *most important*
——————	pr**ior**, *former*	prī**mus**, *first*
——————	prop**ior**, *nearer*	prox**imus**, *nearest*
falsus, *false*	——————	fals**issimus**, *most false*
fīdus, *faithful*	——————	fīd**issimus**, *most faithful*
novus, *new*	(recent**ior**), *more recent*	nov**issimus**, *latest, newest*
parvus, *small*	min**or**, *smaller*	minimus, *smallest*
sacer, *sacred*	——————	sacer**rimus**, *most sacred*
vetus, *old*	(vetust**ior**), *older*	veter**rimus**, *oldest*

NOTES (a) For the declension of the comparative degree, see **fortior, fortius** above.

(b) Adjectives in **-er** form the superlative by adding **-rimus** to the nominative of the positive. The comparative is regular. Thus:

ācer, *sharp*	ācr**ior**, *sharper*	ācer**rimus**, *sharpest*
celer, *swift*	celer**ior**, *swifter*	celer**rimus**, *swiftest*
miser, *wretched*	miser**ior**, *more w.*	miser**rimus**, *most w.*

(c) Five adjectives in **-ilis** form the superlative by adding **-limus** to the stem of the positive. The comparison is regular. Thus:

facilis, *easy*	facil**ior**, *easier*	facil**limus**, *easiest*
difficilis, *difficult*	difficil**ior**, *more d.*	difficil**limus** *most d.*
similis, *similar*	simil**ior**, *more s.*	simil**limus**, *most s.*
dissimilis, *unlike*	dissimil**ior**, *more u.*	dissimil**limus**, *most u.*
humilis, *low*	humil**ior**, *lower*	humil**limus**, *lowest*

Adverbs

Comparison of Irregular Adverbs

bene, *well*	mel**ius**, *better*	opt**imē**, *best*
diū, *long*	diūt**ius**, *longer*	diūt**issimē**, *longest*
magnopere, *greatly*	mag**is**, *more*	max**imē**, *most*
male, *badly*	pē**ius**, *worse*	pess**imē**, *worst*
multum, *much*	pl**ūs**, *more*	plūr**imum**, *most*
nēquiter, *worthlessly*	nēqu**ius**, *more w.*	nēqu**issimē**, *most w.*
nūper, *recently*	——————	nūper**rimē**, *most r.*
parum, *little*	min**us**, *less*	min**imē**, *least*
prope, *near*	prop**ius**, *more c.*	prox**imē**, *most c.*
saepe, *often*	saep**ius**, *oftener*	saep**issimē**, *most o.*
secus, *otherwise*	sēt**ius**, *less*	——————
——————	pot**ius**, *rather*	pot**issimum**, *especially*
	pr**ius**, *previously*	prī**mum**, *first*

19

First Conjugation Verbs

Principal parts: amō   *I love, am loving*

Principal parts: | amō | *I love, am loving*
| amāre | *to love*
| amāvī | *I loved, I have loved*
| amātus | *(having been) loved*

Indicative Mood

	Active Voice		*Passive Voice*
Singular	*Plural*	*Singular*	*Plural*

PRESENT

amō	amāmus	amor	amāmur
amās	amātis	amā·ris *or* -re	amāminī
amat	amant	amātur	amantur

IMPERFECT

amābam	amābāmus	amābar	amābāmur
amābās	amābātis	amābā·ris *or* -re	amābāminī
amābat	amābant	amābātur	amābantur

FUTURE

amābō	amābimus	amābor	amābimur
amābis	amābitis	amābe·ris *or* -re	amābiminī
amābit	amābunt	amābitur	amābuntur

PERFECT

amāvī	amāvimus	amātus sum	amātī sumus
amāvistī	amāvistis	amātus es	amātī estis
amāvit	amāvē·runt *or* -re	amātus est	amātī sunt

PLUPERFECT

amāveram	amāverāmus	amātus eram	amātī erāmus
amāverās	amāverātis	amātus erās	amātī erātis
amāverat	amāverant	amātus erat	amātī erant

FUTURE PERFECT

amāverō	amāverimus	amātus erō	amātī erimus
amāveris	amāveritis	amātus eris	amātī eritis
amāverit	amāverint	amātus erit	amātī erunt

Subjunctive Mood

Active Voice		Passive Voice	
Singular	*Plural*	*Singular*	*Plural*

PRESENT

amem	amēmus	amer	amēmur
amēs	amētis	amē·ris *or* -re	amēminī
amet	ament	amētur	amentur

IMPERFECT

amārem	amārēmus	amārer	amārēmur
amārēs	amārētis	amārē·ris *or* -re	amārēminī
amāret	amārent	amārētur	amārentur

PERFECT

amāverim	amāverimus	amātus sim	amātī sīmus
amāveris	amāveritis	amātus sīs	amātī sītis
amāverit	amāverint	amātus sit	amātī sint

PLUPERFECT

amāvissem	amāvissēmus	amātus essem	amātī essēmus
amāvissēs	amāvissētis	amātus essēs	amātī essētis
amāvisset	amāvissent	amātus esset	amātī essent

Imperative Mood

Active Voice		Passive Voice	
Singular	*Plural*	*Singular*	*Plural*

PRESENT

amā *(2nd pers)*	amāte *(2nd pers)*	amāre *(2nd pers)*	amāminī *(2nd pers)*

FUTURE

amātō *(2nd pers)*	amātōte *(2nd pers)*	amātor *(2nd pers)*	———
amātō *(3rd pers)*	amantō *(3rd pers)*	amātor *(3rd pers)*	amantor *(3rd pers)*

Infinitive	Participle	Infinitive	Participle

PRESENT

amāre	am·āns, -antis	amārī	———

PERFECT

amāvisse	———	amātus esse	amātus

FUTURE

amātūrus esse	amātūrus	amātum īrī	amandus *(gerundive)*

	Gerund	Supine	
GEN	amandī	———	
DAT	amandō	———	
ACC	amandum	amātum	
ABL	amandō	amātū	

21

Second Conjugation Verbs

Principal parts:	moneō	I advise, am advising
	monēre	to advise
	monuī	I advised, have advised
	monitus	(having been) advised

Indicative Mood

	Active Voice		*Passive Voice*	
Singular	*Plural*		*Singular*	*Plural*

PRESENT

moneō	monēmus		moneor	monēmur
monēs	monētis		monē·ris *or* -re	monēminī
monet	monent		monētur	monentur

IMPERFECT

monēbam	monēbāmus		monēbar	monēbāmur
monēbās	monēbātis		monēbā·ris *or* -re	monēbāminī
monēbat	monēbant		monēbātur	monēbantur

FUTURE

monēbō	monēbimus		monēbor	monēbimur
monēbis	monēbitis		monēbe·ris *or* -re	monēbiminī
monēbit	monēbunt		monēbitur	monēbuntur

PERFECT

monuī	monuimus		monitus sum	monitī sumus
monuistī	monuistis		monitus es	monitī estis
monuit	monuē·runt *or* -re		monitus est	monitī sunt

PLUPERFECT

monueram	monuerāmus		monitus eram	monitī erāmus
monuerās	monuerātis		monitus erās	monitī erātis
monuerat	monuerant		monitus erat	monitī erant

FUTURE PERFECT

monuerō	monuerimus		monitus erō	monitī erimus
monueris	monueritis		monitus eris	monitī eritis
monuerit	monuerint		monitus erit	monitī erunt

Subjunctive Mood

	Active Voice		Passive Voice
Singular	*Plural*	*Singular*	*Plural*

PRESENT

moneam	moneāmus	monear	moneāmur
moneās	moneātis	moneā·ris *or* -re	moneāminī
moneat	moneant	moneātur	moneantur

IMPERFECT

monērem	monērēmus	monērer	monērēmur
monērēs	monērētis	monērē·ris *or* -re	monērēminī
monēret	monērent	monērētur	monērentur

PERFECT

monuerim	monuerimus	monitus sim	monitī sīmus
monueris	monueritis	monitus sīs	monitī sītis
monuerit	monuerint	monitus sit	monitī sint

PLUPERFECT

monuissem	monuissēmus	monitus essem	monitī essēmus
monuissēs	monuissētis	monitus essēs	monitī essētis
monuisset	monuissent	monitus esset	monitī essent

Imperative Mood

	Active Voice		Passive Voice
Singular	*Plural*	*Singular*	*Plural*

PRESENT

monē *(2nd pers)*	monēte *(2nd pers)*	monēre *(2nd pers)*	monēminī *(2nd pers)*

FUTURE

monētō *(2nd pers)*	monētōte *(2nd pers)*	monētor *(2nd pers)*	———
monētō *(3rd pers)*	monentō *(3rd pers)*	monētor *(3rd pers)*	monentor *(3rd pers)*

Infinitive	Participle	Infinitive	Participle

PRESENT

monēre	mon·ēns, -entis	monērī	———

PERFECT

monuisse	———	monitus esse	monitus

FUTURE

monitūrus esse	monitūrus	monitum īrī	monendus *(gerundive)*

Gerund		Supine	
GEN	monendī	———	
DAT	monendō	———	
ACC	monendum	monitum	
ABL	monendō	monitū	

23

Third Conjugation Verbs

Principal parts:	regō	I rule, am ruling
	regere	to rule
	rēxī	I ruled, have ruled
	rēctus	(having been) ruled

Indicative Mood

| | Active Voice | | Passive Voice | |
Singular	Plural	Singular	Plural

PRESENT

regō	regimus	regor	regimur
regis	regitis	rege·ris *or* -re	regiminī
regit	regunt	regitur	reguntur

IMPERFECT

regēbam	regēbāmus	regēbar	regēbamur
regēbās	regēbātis	regēbā·ris *or* -re	regēbāminī
regēbat	regēbant	regēbātur	regēbantur

FUTURE

regam	regēmus	regar	regēmur
regēs	regētis	regēr·is *or* -re	regēminī
reget	regent	regētur	regentur

PERFECT

rēxī	rēximus	rēctus sum	rēctī sumus
rēxistī	rēxistis	rēctus es	rēctī estis
rēxit	rēxē·runt *or* -re	rēctus est	rēctī sunt

PLUPERFECT

rēxeram	rēxerāmus	rēctus eram	rēctī erāmus
rēxerās	rēxerātis	rēctus erās	rēctī erātis
rēxerat	rēxerant	rēctus erat	rēctī erant

FUTURE PERFECT

rēxerō	rēxerimus	rēctus erō	rēctī erimus
rēxeris	rēxeritis	rēctus eris	rēctī eritis
rēxerit	rēxerint	rēctus erit	rēctī erunt

Subjunctive Mood

	Active Voice		Passive Voice
Singular	*Plural*	*Singular*	*Plural*

PRESENT

regam	regāmus	regar	regāmur
regās	regātis	regā·ris *or* -re	regāminī
regat	regant	regātur	regantur

IMPERFECT

regerem	regerēmus	regerer	regerēmur
regerēs	regerētis	regerē·ris *or* -re	regerēminī
regeret	regerent	regerētur	regerentur

PERFECT

rēxerim	rēxerimus	rēctus sim	rēctī sīmus
rēxeris	rēxeritis	rēctus sīs	rēctī sītis
rēxerit	rēxerint	rēctus sit	rēctī sint

PLUPERFECT

rēxissem	rēxissēmus	rēctus essem	rēctī essēmus
rēxissēs	rēxissētis	rēctus essēs	rēctī essētis
rēxisset	rēxissent	rēctus esset	rēctī essent

Imperative Mood

	Active Voice		Passive Voice
Singular	*Plural*	*Singular*	*Plural*

PRESENT

| rege *(2nd pers)* | regite *(2nd pers)* | regere *(2nd pers)* | regiminī *(2nd pers)* |

FUTURE

| regitō *(2nd pers)* | regitōte *(2nd pers)* | regitor *(2nd pers)* | ——— |
| regitō *(3rd pers)* | reguntō *(3rd pers)* | regitor *(3rd pers)* | reguntor *(3rd pers)* |

nfinitive	Participle	Infinitive	Participle

PRESENT

| regere | reg·ēns, -entis | regī | — |

PERFECT

| rēxisse | — | rēctus esse | rēctus |

FUTURE

| rēctūrus esse | rēctūrus | rēctum īrī | rēgendus *(gerundive)* |

	Gerund		Supine
GEN	regendī		———
DAT	regendō		———
ACC	regendum		rēctum
ABL	regendō		rēctū

Third Conjugation Verbs in -*io*

Principal parts:

capiō	*I take, am taking*	
capere	*to take*	
cēpī	*I took, have taken*	
captus	*(having been) taken*	

Indicative Mood

Active Voice		*Passive Voice*	
Singular	*Plural*	*Singular*	*Plural*

PRESENT

capiō	capimus	capior	capimur
capis	capitis	cape·ris *or* -re	capiminī
capit	capiunt	capitur	capiuntur

IMPERFECT

capiēbam	capiēbāmus	capiēbar	capiēbāmur
capiēbās	capiēbātis	capiēbā·ris *or* -re	capiēbāminī
capiēbat	capiēbant	capiēbātur	capiēbāntur

FUTURE

capiam	capiēmus	capiar	capiēmur
capiēs	capiētis	capiē·ris *or* -re	capiēminī
capiet	capient	capiētur	capientur

PERFECT

cēpī	cēpimus	captus sum	captī sumus
cēpistī	cēpistis	captus es	captī estis
cēpit	cēpē·runt *or* -re	captus est	captī sunt

PLUPERFECT

cēperam	cēperāmus	captus eram	captī erāmus
cēperās	cēperātis	captus erās	captī erātis
cēperat	cēperant	captus erat	captī erant

FUTURE PERFECT

cēperō	cēperimus	captus erō	captī erimus
cēperis	cēperitis	captus eris	captī eritis
cēperit	cēperint	captus erit	captī erunt

Subjunctive Mood

Active Voice		Passive Voice	
Singular	*Plural*	*Singular*	*Plural*

PRESENT

capiam	capiāmus	capiar	capiāmur
capiās	capiātis	capiā·ris *or* -re	capiāminī
capiat	capiant	capiātur	capiantur

IMPERFECT

caperem	caperēmus	caperer	caperēmur
caperēs	caperētis	caperē·ris *or* -re	caperēminī
caperet	caperent	caperētur	caperentur

PERFECT

cēperim	cēperimus	captus sim	captī sīmus
cēperis	cēperitis	captus sīs	captī sītis
cēperit	cēperint	captus sit	captī sint

PLUPERFECT

cēpissem	cēpissēmus	captus essem	captī essēmus
cēpissēs	cēpissētis	captus essēs	captī essētis
cēpisset	cēpissent	captus esset	captī essent

Imperative Mood

Active Voice		Passive Voice	
Singular	*Plural*	*Singular*	*Plural*

PRESENT

cape *(2nd pers)*	capite *(2nd pers)*	capere *(2nd pers)*	capiminī *(2nd pers)*

FUTURE

capitō *(2nd pers)*	capitōte *(2nd pers)*	capitor *(2nd pers)*	————
capitō *(3rd pers)*	capiuntō *(3rd pers)*	capitor *(3rd pers)*	capiuntor *(3rd pers)*

nfinitive	Participle	Infinitive	Participle

PRESENT

capere	cap·iēns, -entis	capī	————

PERFECT

cēpisse	————	captus esse	captus

FUTURE

captūrus esse	captūrus	captum īrī	capiendus *(gerundive)*

Gerund		Supine	
GEN	capiendī		————
DAT	capiendō		————
ACC	capiendum		captum
ABL	capiendō		captū

27

Fourth Conjugation Verbs

Principal parts: audiō   *I hear, am hearing*
                      audīre   *to hear*
                      audīvī   *I heard, have heard*
                      audītus   *(having been) heard*

Indicative Mood

Active Voice		Passive Voice	
Singular	*Plural*	*Singular*	*Plural*
PRESENT			
audiō	audīmus	audior	audīmur
audīs	audītis	audī·ris *or* -re	audīminī
audit	audiunt	audītur	audiuntur
IMPERFECT			
audiēbam	audiēbāmus	audiēbar	audiēbāmur
audiēbās	audiēbātis	audiēbā·ris *or* -re	audiēbāminī
audiēbat	audiēbant	audiēbātur	audiēbantur
FUTURE			
audiam	audiēmus	audiar	audiēmur
audiēs	audiētis	audiē·ris *or* -re	audiēminī
audiet	audient	audiētur	audientur
PERFECT			
audīvī	audīvimus	audītus sum	audītī sumus
audīvistī	audīvistis	audītus es	audītī estis
audīvit	audīvēr·unt *or* -re	audītus est	audītī sunt
PLUPERFECT			
audīveram	audīverāmus	audītus eram	audītī erāmus
audīverās	audīverātis	audītus erās	audītī erātis
audīverat	audīverant	audītus erat	audītī erant
FUTURE PERFECT			
audīverō	audīverimus	audītus erō	audītī erimus
audīveris	audīveritis	audītus eris	audītī eritis
audīverit	audīverint	audītus erit	audītī erunt

Subjunctive Mood

	Active Voice		Passive Voice
Singular	*Plural*	*Singular*	*Plural*

PRESENT

audiam	audiāmus	audiar	audiāmur
audiās	audiātis	audiā·ris *or* -re	audiāminī
audiat	audiant	audiatur	audiantur

IMPERFECT

audīrem	audīrēmus	audīrer	audīrēmur
audīrēs	audīrētis	audīrē·ris *or* -re	audīrēminī
audīret	audīrent	audīrētur	audīrentur

PERFECT

audīverim	audīverimus	audītus sim	audītī sīmus
audīveris	audīveritis	audītus sīs	audītī sītis
audīverit	audīverint	audītus sit	audītī sint

PLUPERFECT

audīvissem	audīvissēmus	audītus essem	audītī essēmus
audīvissēs	audīvissētis	audītus essēs	audītī essētis
audīvisset	audīvissent	audītus esset	audītī essent

Imperative Mood

	Active Voice		Passive Voice
Singular	*Plural*	*Singular*	*Plural*

PRESENT

audī *(2nd pers)*	audīte *(2nd pers)*	audīre *(2nd pers)*	audīminī *(2nd pers)*

FUTURE

audītō *(2nd pers)*	audītōte *(2nd pers)*	audītor *(2nd pers)*	———
audītō *(3rd pers)*	audiuntō *(3rd pers)*	audītor *(3rd pers)*	audiuntor *(3rd pers)*

Infinitive	Participle	Infinitive	Participle

PRESENT

audīre	audi·ēns, -entis	audīrī	———

PERFECT

audīvisse	———	audītus esse	audītus

FUTURE

audītūrus esse	audītūrus	audītum īrī	audiendus *(gerundive)*

Gerund	Supine

GEN	audiendī	———
DAT	audiendō	———
ACC	audiendum	audītum
ABL	audiendō	audītū

Conjugation of *sum*

Principal parts:

sum	*I am*
esse	*to be*
fuī	*I was, have been*
futūrus	*about to be*

Indicative Mood

Singular	Plural
PRESENT	
sum	sumus
es	estis
est	sunt
IMPERFECT	
eram	erāmus
erās	erātis
erat	erant
FUTURE	
erō	erimus
eris	eritis
erit	erunt
PERFECT	
fuī	fuimus
fuistī	fuistis
fuit	fuē·**runt** *or* **-re**
PLUPERFECT	
fueram	fuerāmus
fuerās	fuerātis
fuerat	fuerant
FUTURE PERFECT	
fuerō	fuerimus
fueris	fueritis
fuerit	fuerint

Subjunctive Mood

Singular	Plural
PRESENT	
sim	sīmus
sīs	sītis
sit	sint
IMPERFECT	
essem	essēmus
essēs	essētis
esset	essent
PERFECT	
fuerim	fuerīmus
fuerīs	fuerītis
fuerit	fuerint
PLUPERFECT	
fuissem	fuissēmus
fuissēs	fuissētis
fuisset	fuissent

Imperative Mood

Singular	Plural
PRESENT	
es *(2nd pers)*	este *(2nd pers)*
FUTURE	
estō *(2nd pers)*	estōte *(2nd pers)*
estō *(3rd pers)*	suntō *(3rd pers)*

Infinitive   Participle

PRESENT	
esse	———
PERFECT	
fuisse	———
FUTURE	
futūrus esse	futūrus

Conjugation of *volō, nōlō, mālō*

Principal parts:

volō	*I wish*	velle	*to wish*	voluī	*I wished*
nōlō	*I do not wish*	nōlle	*to be unwilling*	nōluī	*I did not wish*
mālō	*I prefer*	mālle	*to prefer*	māluī	*I preferred, have preferred*

Indicative Mood

PRESENT	volō	nōlō	mālō
	vīs	nōn vīs	māvīs
	vult	nōn vult	māvult
	volumus	nōlumus	mālumus
	vultis	nōn vultis	māvultis
	volunt	nōlunt	mālunt
IMPERFECT	volēbam	nōlēbam	mālēbam
FUTURE	volam	nōlam	mālam
PERFECT	voluī	nōluī	māluī
PLUPERFECT	volueram	nōlueram	mālueram
FUTURE PERFECT	voluerō	nōluerō	māluerō

Subjunctive Mood

PRESENT	velim	nōlim	mālim
	velīs	nōlīs	mālīs
	velit	nōlit	mālit
	velīmus	nōlīmus	mālīmus
	velītis	nōlītis	mālitis
	velint	nōlint	mālint
IMPERFECT	vellem	nollem	mallem
PERFECT	voluerim	nōluerim	māluerim
PLUPERFECT	voluissem	nōluissem	māluissem

Imperative Mood

PRESENT	nōlī; nōlīte *(2nd pers)*
FUTURE	nōlītō; nōlītōte *(2md pers)*
	nōlītō; nōluntō *(3rd pers)*

Infinitive

PRESENT	velle	nōlle	mālle
PERFECT	voluisse	nōluisse	māluisse

Participle

PRESENT	vol·ēns, -entis	nōl·ēns, -entis	————

31

Conjugation of *eo*

Principal parts: eō   *I go, am going*
                       īre   *to go*
                       īvī *or* iī   *I went*
                       itum (est)   *people went*

Indicative Mood

	Singular	Plural
PRESENT	eō	īmus
	īs	ītis
	it	eunt
IMPERFECT	ībam	ībāmus
FUTURE	ībō	ībimus
PERFECT	īvī *or* iī	īvimus *or* iimus
PLUPERFECT	īveram *or* ieram	īverāmus *or* ierāmus
FUTURE PERFECT	īverō *or* ierō	īverimus *or* ierimus

Subjunctive Mood

PRESENT	eam	eāmus
IMPERFECT	īrem	irēmus
PERFECT	īverim *or* ierim	īverīmus *or* ierīmus
PLUPERFECT	īvissem *or* iissem	īvissēmus *or* iissēmus

Imperative Mood

PRESENT	ī *(2nd pers)*	īte *(2nd pers)*
FUTURE	ītō *(2nd pers)*	ītōte *(2nd pers)*
	ītō *(3rd pers)*	euntō *(3rd pers)*

Infinitive / Participle

	Infinitive	Participle
PRESENT	īre	iēns, euntis
PERFECT	īvisse *or* isse	———
FUTURE	itūrus esse	itūrus
	eundum *(gerundive)*	

Gerund / Supine

	Gerund	Supine
GEN	eundī	———
DAT	eundō	———
ACC	eundum	itum
ABL	eundō	itū

Conjugation of *fio*

Principal parts:

fīō	*I am made, become*
fierī	*to be made, become*
factus sum	*I was made, became*

Indicative Mood

	Singular	*Plural*
PRESENT	fīō	fīmus
	fīs	fītis
	fit	fīunt
IMPERFECT	fīēbam	fīēbāmus
FUTURE	fīam	fīēmus
PERFECT	factus sum	factī sumus
PLUPERFECT	factus eram	factī erāmus
FUTURE PERFECT	factus erō	factī erimus

Subjunctive Mood

PRESENT	fīam	fiāmus
IMPERFECT	fierem	fierēmus
PERFECT	factus sim	factī sīmus
PLUPERFECT	factus essem	factī essēmus

Imperative Mood

Singular	*Plural*
fī	fīte

Infinitive / Participle

	Infinitive	**Participle**
PRESENT	fierī	———
PERFECT	factus esse	factus
FUTURE	factum īrī	faciendus *(gerundive)*

Roman Numerals

	Cardinal	Ordinal	
1	ūnus, ūna, ūnum	prīmus	I
1	ūnus, ūna, ūnum	prīmus	I
2	duo, duae, duo	secundus	II
3	trēs, tria	tertius	III
4	quattuor	quārtus	IV
5	quīnque	quīntus	V
6	sex	sextus	VI
7	septem	septimus	VII
8	octō	octāvus	VIII
9	novem	nōnus	IX
10	decem	decimus	X
11	ūndecim	ūndecimus	XI
12	duodecim	duodecimus	XII
13	tredecim	tertius decimus	XIII
14	quattuordecim	quārtus decimus	XIV
15	quīndecim	quīntus decimus	XV
16	sēdecim	sextus decimus	XVI
17	septendecim	septimus decimus	XVII
18	duodēvīgintī	duodēvīcēsimus	XVIII
19	ūndēvīgintī	ūndēvīcēsimus	XIX
20	vīgintī	vīcēsimus	XX
21	vīgintī ūnus	vīcēsimus prīmus	XXI
	ūnus et vīgintī		
22	vīgintī duo	vīcēsimus secundus	XXII
	duo et vīgintī		
30	trīgintā	trīcēsimus	XXX
40	quadrāgintā	quadrāgēsimus	XL
50	quīnquāgintā	quīnquāgēsimus	L
60	sexāgintā	sexāgēsimus	LX
70	septuāgintā	septuāgēsimus	LXX
80	octōgintā	octōgēsimus	LXXX
90	nōnāgintā	nōnāgēsimus	XC
100	centum	centēsimus	C
101	centum ūnus	centēsimus prīmus	CI
	centum et ūnus		
200	ducentī, -ae, -a	ducentēsimus	CC
300	trecentī, -ae, -a	trecentēsimus	CCC
400	quadringentī, -ae, -a	quadringentēsimus	CCCC
500	quīngentī, -ae, -a	quīngentēsimus	D
600	sēscentī, -ae, -a	sēscentēsimus	DC
700	septingentī, -ae, -a	septingentēsimus	DCC
800	octingentī, -ae, -a	octingentēsimus	DCCC
900	nōngentī, -ae, -a	nōngentēsimus	DCCCC
1,000	mīlle	mīllēsimus	M
2,000	duo mīlia	bis mīllēsimus	MM
10,000	decem mīlia	deciēs mīllēsimus	CCIƆƆ
100,000	centum mīlia	centiēs mīllēsimus	CCCIƆƆƆ

NOTES   (a)   -ēnsimus and -iēns are often written in the numerals instead of -ēsimus and -iēs.

            (b)   The declension of ūnus, ūna, ūnum is indicated under "Nine Irregular Adjectives," p. 17.

Declension of duo and tres

	masc	fem	neut	masc	fem	neut
NOM	duo	duae	duo	trēs	trēs	tria
GEN	duōrum	duārum	duōrum	trium	trium	trium
DAT	duōbus	duābus	duōbus	tribus	tribus	tribus
ACC	duōs, duo	duās	duo	trēs (trīs)	trēs (trīs)	tria
ABL	duōbus	duōbus	duōbus	tribus	tribus	tribus

LATIN – ENGLISH

A

A, a *(supply* littera*) f* first letter of the Latin alphabet; letter name: **a**

A. *abbr* **Aulus** *(Roman first name, praenomen); (leg)* **Absolvō** I acquit; *(pol)* **Antīquō** I vote "no" *(on the bill)*

-ā *advl suf* forms adverbs which are also used as prepositions, *e.g.,* **suprā** above

-a *masc suf* indicating occupation or profession, *e.g.:* **agricola** one who tills a field, farmer; **scrība** one who writes, scribe

ā *or* **āh** *interj* ah!

ā- *or* **ab- abs-** *pref (before initial* **f** *becomes* **au-:** **auferre** to take away; *before* **p** *becomes* **as-:** **asportāre** to take away, carry off, *with the sense of:* **1** from, away, away from: **abdūcere** to lead away; **2** off: **abscīdere** to cut off; **3** at a distance: **abesse** to be at a distance, be absent; **4** completely, thoroughly: **abūtī** to use up, exhaust by using; **5** the absence of what the noun implies: **āmēns** demented; **6** a more remote degree of relationship: **abnepōs** great-great-grandson

ā *or* **ab** *prep (w. abl)* **1** *(of agency)* by, at the hands of: **ā Caesare in servitūtem redāctus** reduced to slavery by Caesar; **2** *(of time)* since, from, after: **ā puerō** since childhood; **ā somnō** after a sleep; **3** *(of space)* from, away from: **ā castrīs perfuga** a deserter from the camp; **4** *(named)* after: **oppidum ā Latīnī fīliā appellātum** a town named after the daughter of Latinus; **5** on: **ā dextrō latere** on the right side; **6** in: **ā tergō** in the rear; **ab ūnā parte corporis** in one part of the body; **7** *(of cause, motive)* out of, from: **ab singulārī amōre** out of unparalleled love; **8** *(designating an office):* **ab epistulīs** secretary; **ā ratiōnibus** accountant; **9** *(in respect to):* **dolēre ab stomachō** to have a stomachache (to ache in respect to the stomach); **10** on the side of: **ab senātū stāre** to side with the Senate (to stand on the side of the Senate)

abāctus *pp of* **abigō**

abac·us -ī *m* cupboard; game board; abacus *(calculator);* panel; tray

abaliēn·ō -āre -āvī -ātus *tr* to alienate, estrange; to sell; to separate; **alicūius animum ā sē abaliēnāre** to turn s.o. else's attention away from oneself

Abantiad·ēs -ae *m* descendant of Abas

Ab·ās -antis *m* 12th king of Argos, father of Acrisius, and grandfather of Perseus

abav·us -ī *m* great-great-grandfather *(a grandfather's grandfather)*

Abdēr·a -ōrum *npl or* **Abdēr·a -ae** *f* town in S. Thrace, notorious for the alleged stupidity of its people

abdicāti·ō -ōnis *f* abdication, renunciation, resignation; disowning; disinheriting

abdic·ō -āre -āvī -ātus *tr* to abdicate, renounce, resign; to disinherit **‖** *refl* **sē magistrātū abdicāre** to resign from office

ab·dīcō -dīcere -dīxī -dictus *tr (in augury)* to disapprove of, forbid

abditē *adv* secretly, privately

abdit·us -a -um *adj* hidden, secret; secluded; abstruse; **abditus ā cōnspectū** hidden from view

ab·dō -dere -didī -ditus *tr* to hide; to remove, withdraw; to banish; to plunge *(e.g., a sword)* **‖** *refl* to hide; **in litterīs sē abdere** to bury oneself in literature

abdōm·en -inis *n* abdomen, belly; *(fig)* gluttony, greed

ab·dūcō -dūcere -dūxī -ductus *tr* to lead away, take away; to withdraw *(troops);* to seduce; to alienate; *(w. ab)* to distinguish from; **animum abdūcere** to distract attention

Abell·a -ae *f* town in Campania, abounding in filbert nuts

ab·eō -īre -iī -itum *intr* to go away, depart; to disappear: **ab oculīs** *(or* **ē cōnspectū)** **abīre** to disappear from sight; to pass away, die; *(of time)* to pass, elapse; to change, be changed; to retire; **abī in malam rem!** *(sl)* go to hell!

abequit·ō -āre -āvī *intr* to ride off

aberrāti·ō -ōnis *f* wandering; escape, relief

aberr·ō -āre -āvī -ātum *intr* to wander, go astray; to get lost; to make a mistake, go wrong; to do wrong; to digress; *(of a stream)* to overflow; *(w. ab)* **1** to disagree with; **2** to get one's mind off *(e.g., sadness);* **3** to deviate from; **4** to differ from

abesse *inf of* **absum**

abhinc *adv (w. acc or abl of time)* ago; **abhinc annōs centum** a hundred years ago

abhorr·eō -ēre -uī *intr* to shrink back; *(w. ab)* **1** to be averse to; **2** to be inconsistent with; **3** to differ from; **4** to be free from

ab·iciō -icere -iēcī -iectus *tr* to throw away, throw down; to push away; to understate; to belittle, slight; to give up; to humble, debase; to cow, reduce to despair; to sell cheaply, sacrifice; to express carelessly *or* perfunctorily; to discard; to cease to wear, take off; to expose *(a child to die);* to leave *(a corpse)* unburied; to turn down *(an offer);* to give up *(practices, intentions, attitudes);* **animam**

(or **vītam) abicere** to give up (this) life; **arma abicere** to throw down one's arms ‖ *refl* to throw oneself down, fall down; **sē ad pedēs alicūius abicere** to throw oneself down at s.o.'s feet; **sē in herbā abicere** to fall down on the grass

abiectē *adv* negligently; unworthily

abiect·us -a -um *adj* dejected, downhearted; undistinguished; unimportant; despicable; groveling

abiēgn·us -a -um *adj* fir, made of fir wood

abi·ēs -etis *f* fir (tree); ship; spear; writing tablet

ab·igō -igere -ēgī -āctus *tr* to drive away, get rid of; to banish, expel; to dispel

abit·a -ūs *m* departure; outlet; end

abiūdic·ō -āre -āvī -ātus *tr* to take away *(by judicial decree);* to reject

ab·iungō -iungere -iūnxī -iūnctus *tr* to unyoke; to detach ‖ *refl (w.* **ab)** to detach oneself from, give up *(an activity);* **sē ab hōc refrāctāriolō dīcendī genere abiungere** to give up this quibbling style of speaking

abiūr·ō -āre -āvī -ātus *tr* to deny under oath

ablātīv·us -a -um *adj & m* ablative

ablāt·us -a -um *pp of* **auferō**

ablēgāti·ō -ōnis *f* sending off; banishment

ablēg·ō -āre -āvī -ātus *tr* to send away; to remove, banish; to dismiss, get rid of

abligū(r)r·iō -īre -īvī *or* **-iī** *tr* to eat up; *(coll)* to gobble up, waste, squander

abloc·ō -āre -āvī -ātus *tr* to lease, rent out

ab·lūdō -lūdere -lūsī lūsum *intr* to be out of tune; to be unlike; *(w.* **ab)** to differ from, fall short of

ab·luō -luere -luī -lūtus *tr* to wash away, cleanse, remove; to flush *(a toilet); (poet)* to bathe, refresh

abneg·ō -āre -āvī -ātus *tr* to refuse, turn down

abnep·ōs -ōtis *m* great-great-grandson

abnept·is -is *f* great-great-granddaughter

abnoct·ō -āre -āvī *intr* to spend the night, stay out all night

abnōrm·is -is -e *adj* irregular, unorthodox

ab·nuō -nuere -nuī *tr* to refuse *(to do s.th.);* to deny *(an assertion, allegation, one's guilt);* to repudiate responsibility for *(a crime);* to reject, refuse *(an offer);* to refuse to grant *(e.g., an interview);* to refuse to submit to *(authority);* to forbid, rule out *(e.g., hope);* to decline *(battle);* to refuse to perform *(a duty, task);* to disown *(children); (w.* **acc & inf)** to forbid *(the occurrence of an event);* **nōn abnuere** to admit, not to deny ‖ *intr* to say "no"; *(w.* **dē** + *abl)* to say "no" to; **dē societāte haud abnuērunt barbarī** the barbarians did not say "no" to (the idea of) an alliance

abnūt·ō -āre *intr* to keep saying "no" *(with a nod)*

abol·eō -ēre -ēvī -itus *tr* to abolish, efface; to destroy, obliterate; to banish from the mind, efface the memory of; to allow *(a practice)* to lapse, drop; to prohibit, ban; to put an end to *(an institution);* to rescind *(a law);* **abolēre memoriam** *(w. gen)* to blot out the memory of *(s.th. unpleasant);* **abolēre reum** *(leg)* to give up prosecuting a defendant

abol·ēscō -ēscere -ēvī *intr* to decay, vanish, die out; *(of things)* to be forgotten; *(of a memory)* to fade

aboliti·ō -ōnis *f* abolition, rescinding *(of a law, sentence);* amnesty

aboll·a -ae *f* cloak; *(fig)* wearer of a cloak, soldiers, philosophers

abōminand·us -a -um *adj* ill-omened; detestable, abominable

abōmin·or -ārī -ātus sum *tr* to loathe, detest; to seek to avert *(e.g., a bad omen, destruction)* by prayer

aborīgin·ēs -um *mpl* aborigines, original inhabitants, natives

ab·orior -orīrī -ortus sum *intr* to miscarry; to fail; *(of stars, etc.)* to set

aborti·ō -ōnis *f* miscarriage, abortion

abortīv·us -a -um *adj* prematurely born ‖ *n* drug causing abortion

abort·us -ūs *m* miscarriage; **abortum facere** to have *or* to cause a miscarriage

ab·rādō -rādere -rāsī -rāsus *tr* to scrape off, shave; *(fig)* to squeeze out, extort

ab·ripiō -ripere -ripuī -reptus *tr* to take away by force, kidnap; to seize *(as booty);* to squander; *(of the wind)* to blow, drive *(off course);* to rescue *(from a bad situation);* **abripere mordicus** to bite off ‖ *refl* to hurry away, get away

ab·rōdō -rōdere -rōsī -rōsus *tr* to gnaw off

abrogāti·ō -ōnis *f* repeal

abrog·ō -āre -āvī -ātus *tr* to repeal, annul

abroton·um -ī *n* **(hab-)** southernwood *(aromatic medicinal plant)*

ab·rumpō -rumpere -rūpī -ruptus *tr* to break off; to tear, sever; to burst apart *(e.g., the clouds);* to rupture *(a body part);* to put an end to, cut short ‖ *refl (w.* **abl)** to dissociate oneself from

abruptē *adv* abruptly; rashly

abrupti·ō -ōnis *f* breaking off *(of relations);* divorce

abrupt·us -a -um *pp of* **abrumpō** ‖ *adj* abrupt, steep ‖ *n* precipice

abs- *pref see* **ā-, ab-, abs-**

abs *prep (w. abl, confined almost exclusively to the combination* **abs tē)** by, from

abs·cēdō -cēdere -cessī -cessum *intr* **(aps-)** to go away, depart; to vanish; to retire *(from* *work);* to desist; *(w. dat)* to cease to support; *(of feelings, illness)* to pass; *(of heavenly bodies)* to move farther away; *(mil)* to retreat; **nōn abscēdere ā corpore** not to leave the body *(of a deceased person)*

abscessi·ō -ōnis *f* diminution, loss

abscess·us -ūs *m* departure; absence; remoteness

abs·cīdō -cīdere -cīdī -cīsus *tr* (aps-) to cut off, chop off; to cut short; to destroy *(hope);* to banish *(from the mind)*

ab·scindō -scindere -scidī -scissus *tr* to tear off, break off; to renounce; to divide

abscīs·us -a -um *pp of* **abscīdō** ‖ *adj* steep, precipitous; concise; abrupt

abscissus *pp of* **abscindō**

absconditē *adv* secretly; obscurely; profoundly

abscondit·us -a -um *adj* concealed, secret; abstruse, profound

abscon·dō -dere -dī *or* **-didī -ditus** *tr* to hide; to keep secret, conceal; to lose sight of, leave behind; to shroud (in darkness); *(w.* **in** + *acc)* to plunge *(weapon)* into ‖ *refl & pass* to hide

abs·ens -entis *pres p of* **absum** ‖ *adj* absent; in spite of being absent; non-existent; **mē absente** in my absence; **praesēns absēns** whether present or absent

absenti·a -ae *f* (aps-) absence; non-appearance in court

absil·iō -īre -(i)ī *intr* to jump away

absimil·is -is -e *adj (w. dat)* unlike

absinth·ium -(i)ī *n* wormwood *(plant yielding bitter extract, used in flavoring wine)*

abs·is -idis *f* (aps-) vault, arch, orbit *(of a star)*

ab·sistō -sistere -stitī *intr* to stand back, retire, withdraw, depart; to cease

absolūtē *adv* absolutely, perfectly, completely

absolūti·ō -ōnis *f* exhaustiveness, completeness; perfection; acquittal; release *(from an obligation)*

absolūtōri·us -a -um *adj* of acquittal, granting acquittal

absolūt·us -a -um *adj* perfect, complete, unqualified

absol·vō -vere -vī -ūtus *tr* (aps-) to release, set free; to detach; to acquit; to get *(s.o.)* acquitted; *(of single juror)* to vote for the acquittal of; to complete, finish *(task, transaction, book);* to put the finishing touches to *(an operation);* to pay off, discharge *(an account, debt);* (w. gen or abl of the charge) to prove *(s.o.)* innocent of; **verbō** *(or* **paucīs** *or* **breviter) absolvere** to sum up, put in a nutshell

abson·us -a -um *adj* (aps-) discordant, harsh *(sound);* unpleasant, jarring; *(w. dat or abl)* inconsistent with

absor·beō -bēre -buī *(or* **-psī) -ptus** *tr* (aps-) to swallow, devour; to absorb; to engross; to engulf

absque *prep* (aps-) *(w. abl)* without, apart from, but for: **absque mē foret** had it not been for me; **absque ūnā hāc foret** but for this one thing

abstēmi·us -a -um *adj* abstemious, temperate; sober

abster·geō -gēre -sī -sus *or* **absterg·ō -ere** *tr* (aps-) to wipe off, wipe dry; to expel, banish; **flētum abstergēre** to wipe away tears

absterr·eō -ēre -uī -itus *tr* (aps-) to scare away; to deter

abstin·ēns -entis *adj* temperate; forbearing; chaste; *(w. gen or abl)* showing restraint in respect to, not greedy for

abstinenter *adv* with restraint, incorruptibly

abstinenti·a -ae *f* restraint, self-control; integrity; *(w. gen or abl)* **1** restraint in respect to; **2** abstinence from

abs·tineō -tinēre -tinuī -tentus *tr* (aps-) to withold, keep away, hold back; to restrain ‖ *refl (w. abl or* **ab**) to refrain from, keep oneself from ‖ *intr* to abstain, refrain; *(w. gen, abl or w.* **ab**, *w. inf, w.* **quīn** *or* **quōminus)** to refrain from

abst·ō -āre *intr* (aps-) to stand at a distance, stand aloof

abstra·hō -here -xī -ctus *tr* (aps-) to pull away, draw away, remove; to detach; to split; to deduct, subtract; to distract, divert; to exclude, except

abstrū·dō -dere -sī -sus *tr* (aps-) to push away; to conceal, suppress ‖ *pass* to be concealed *(by intervening object)*

abstrūs·us -a -um *pp of* **abstrūdō** (aps-) ‖ *adj* hidden, concealed, secret; profound, abstruse; reserved *(person);* secluded

abstulī *perf of* **auferō**

absum abesse āfuī āfutūrus *intr* to be away, be absent, be distant; to be missing; to be unsuitable, be inappropriate; to be wanting; *(w. abl or* **ab**) to be removed from, keep aloof from, be disinclined to; *(w.* **ab**) **1** to be different from; **2** to be inconsistent with; **3** to be free from; **4** to be unsuitable for, be unfit for; *(w. dat)* to be of no help to; **ab hōc cōnsiliō abesse** to have no part in this strategy; **ā culpā abesse** to be free of guilt; **ā perīculīs abesse** to avoid dangers; **lēgātōs haud procul āfuit quīn violārent** they came close to outraging the ambassadors; **nōn multum aberat ab eō quīn** he was not far from, he was almost on the point of; **tantum aberat ā bellō, ut** he was so averse to war that

absūm·ō -ere -psī -ptus *tr* to take away, diminish; to consume, use up, waste; to exhaust; to destroy; to spend *(time);* to cause the death of, carry off ‖ *pass (w.* **in** + *acc)* to disappear into

absurdē *adv* (aps-) out of tune; absurdly

absurd·us -a -um *adj* (aps-) out of tune; absurd, illogical, senseless, silly

Absyrt·us -ī *m* brother of Medea and son of Aeëtes, the king of Colchis

abund·āns -antis *adj* abundant, overflowing; affluent; more than enough; *(of rivers)* in flood; *(w. gen or abl)* abounding in, rich in

abundanter *adv* abundantly; profusely

abundanti·a -ae *f* abundance; affluence; lavishness; profusion

abundē *adv* abundantly, amply

abūsi·ō -ōnis *f* incorrect use *(of words)*

abūsque *prep (w. abl)* all the way from

ab·ūtor -ūtī -ūsus sum *intr (w. abl)* 1 to use up; 2 to misuse, abuse; alicūius patientiā abūtī to try s.o.'s patience

Abȳd·os *or* Abȳd·us -ī *f* town on the Hellespont

ac *conj (usually before consonants)* and, and also, and moreover; *(connecting a more emphatic sentence element)* and in particular, and what is more; *(connecting a sentence element which strengthens or corrects the first element)* and in fact; *(in comparisons)* than, as

Acadēmi·a -ae *f* Academy *(where Plato taught);* Platonic philosophy; Cicero's villa near Puteoli

Acadēmic·us -a -um *adj* Academic ‖ *m* Academic philosopher ‖ *npl* Cicero's treatise on Academic philosophy

acalanth·is -idis *f* goldfinch *(bird)*

acanth·us *or* acanth·os -ī *m (bot)* acanthus *(plant on whose leaves the architectural ornament of capitals of Corinthian columns was patterned)*

Acarnāni·a -ae *f* district in N.W. Greece

Acast·us -ī *m* son of Pelias

ac·cēdō -cēdere -cessī -cessum *tr* (adc-) to come up to, approach ‖ *intr* to approach; *(w. ad)* to come up to, approach; *(w. dat or ad)* 1 to agree with, approve of, to go along with; 2 to be like, resemble; *(w. ad or in + acc)* to enter upon, undertake; accēdit ut *or* quod there is the additional fact that

acceler·ō -āre -āvī -ātus *tr* to speed, quicken ‖ *intr* to hurry

accen·dō -dere -dī -sus *tr* to light *(a fire, lamp);* to set on fire; to arouse *(emotions);* to aggravate *(conditions);* to work up, incite *(people);* to raise *(prices);* to light up, brighten; accēnsa lūmina lamp-lighting time, dusk

accēns·eō -ēre -uī -us *tr* to regard; to assign *(as attendant)*

accēns·us -a -um *pp of* accendō ‖ *adj* on fire

accēns·us -ī *m* attendant, orderly ‖ *mpl* rear-echelon troops

accent·us -ūs *m* accent, intonation

accepti·ō -ōnis *f* accepting, receiving

accept·ō -āre -āvī -ātus *tr* to accept, receive *(regularly);* to be given *(a name)*

accept·or -ōris *m* recipient; approver

acceptr·īx -īcis *f* recipient *(female)*

accept·us -a -um *pp of* accipiō ‖ *adj* welcome, pleasing, acceptable ‖ *n* receipt; credit side *(in account books);* acceptum facere *(or* ferre) to treat *(a debt)* as paid off; acceptum fierī *(w. dat)* to be set down to the credit of; acceptum referre *(w. dat)* to set down to the credit side, have *(him, her, etc.)* to thank for

accersō *or* arcess·ō -ere -īvī *or* -iī -ītus *tr* to call, summon; to bring, procure

accessi·ō -ōnis *f* approach; addition, increase; additional payment, bonus; intensification; appendage, accessory; addition to one's resources; accessiōnem facere to make progress, gain ground; accessiō temporis *(leg)* extra time *(added to possessorship)*

access·us -ūs *m* act of approaching, approach; attack; rising *(of heavenly bodies);* blowing *(of the wind);* going at, tackling *(a task);* right to approach, access; entry, way in, passage; accessus et recessus aestuum flow and ebb of the tide

Accher·ūns -untis *mf* lower world

ac·cī·dō -cīdere -cīdī -cīsus *tr* to cut down; to impair, weaken; to decimate

ac·cidō -cidere -cidī *intr* to happen, occur, come to pass; *(w. dat of person affected)* to happen to, befall; *(w. adv)* to turn out; *(w. abl of cause)* to happen as the result of; *(w. dat)* to strike *(s.o. as), e.g.:* hōc tibi īnsolentia praeter opīniōnem accidēbat this struck you as exceptional insolence; *(w. in + acc)* 1 to fall upon; 2 to be applicable to; *(w. dat or ad)* to fall at *(e.g., s.o.'s feet);* aurēs *(or* auribus *or* ad aurēs) accidere *(w. gen)* to reach the ears of; accidit ut *(w. subj or* quod *w. indic)* it happens that; sī quid mihi acciderit if anything should happen to me

ac·cingō -cingere -cīnxī -cīnctus *tr* to gird; to gird up, tuck up *(one's clothing)* ‖ refl and pass *(w. abl)* to arm oneself with, equip oneself with; accingī *or* sē accingere *(w. dat or* ad *or* in + *acc)* to prepare oneself for, to enter upon, to undertake; ferrō accingī to put on the sword

ac·ciō -cīre -cīvī -cītus *tr* to call, send for, invite; mortem sibi accīre to commit suicide

ac·cipiō -cipere -cēpī -ceptus *tr* to take, receive, accept; to welcome, entertain; to hear, learn, understand; to interpret, explain; to undertake *(a task);* to assume *(a responsibility);* to take *(medicine, food);* to incur *(a wound, loss);* to accept *(a post, office);* to borrow *(money);* to approve of, agree to; to have room for, accommodate; to welcome, entertain; to accept as valid, admit; to learn, hear, be told of; to infer, conclude; *(geol)* to let in *(the sea);* **accipere dareque** to exchange; **āctiōnem accipere** *(leg)* to be granted a hearing; **auribus accipere** to hear, learn by listening; **initium** *(or* **orīginem** *or* **ortum) accipere** to begin; **fīnem accipere** to come to an end

accipi·ter -tris *m* hawk

accīs·us -a -um *pp of* **accīdō** ‖ *adj* impaired, ruined; troubled, disordered

accītus *pp of* **acciō**

accīt·us -ūs *m* summons, call

Acc·ius -(i)ī *m* Roman tragic poet *(170–85? B.C.)*

acclāmāti·ō -ōnis *f* **(adc-)** shout *(of approval or disapproval)*

acclām·ō -āre -āvī -ātus *tr* to hail, acclaim ‖ *intr* to shout *(in approval); (w. dat)* to shout at

acclār·ō -āre -āvī *tr* **(adc-)** to clarify

acclīnāt·us -a -um *adj* prostrate; sloping; *(w. dat)* **1** leaning on; **2** inclined toward, disposed to

acclīn·ō -āre -āvī -ātus *tr* **(adc-)** *(w. dat or in + acc)* to lean *or* rest *(s.th.)* against ‖ *refl (w. ad) (fig)* to be inclined toward

acclīv·is -is -e *adj* **(adc-)** sloping upwards, uphill, steep

acclīvit·ās -ātis *f* **(adc-)** slope, ascent

accol·a -ae *mf* **(adc-)** neighbor

ac·colō -colere -coluī -cultus *tr* **(adc-)** to dwell near

accommodātē *adv* **(adc-)** suitably, fittingly; comfortably

accommodāti·ō -ōnis *f* **(adc-)** adjustment; compliance, accommodation

accommodāt·us -a -um *adj* **(adc-)** *(w. dat or ad)* fit for, adapted to, suitable for

accommod·ō -āre -āvī -ātus *tr* **(adc-)** *(w. dat or ad)* to adjust *or* adapt *or* apply *(s.th.)* to ‖ *refl (w. ad)* to apply *or* devote oneself to

accommod·us -a -um *adj* **(adc-)** *(w. dat)* fit for, adapted to, suitable for

accrē·dō -dere -didī -ditum *intr* **(adc-)** *(w. dat)* to believe, put faith in, trust

accr·ēscō -ēscere -ēvī -ētum *intr* **(adc-)** to grow larger, increase; to be added

accrēti·ō -ōnis *f* **(adc-)** increase

accubiti·ō -ōnis *f* **(adc-)** reclining *(at meals)*

accub·ō -āre *intr* to lie nearby; to recline at table; *(w. dat)* to lie near

accūd·ō -ere *tr* **(adc-)** to coin

ac·cumbō -cumbere -cubuī -cubitum *intr* **(adc-)** to take one's place at table; *(w. cum)* to lie down with

accumulātē *adv* **(adc-)** abundantly

accumulāt·or -ōris *m* **(adc-)** hoarder

accumul·ō -āre -āvī -ātus *tr* **(adc-)** to heap up, accumulate, amass; to load, overwhelm

accūrātē *adv* **(adc-)** carefully, accurately, exactly, meticulously

accūrāti·ō -ōnis *f* **(adc-)** carefulness, accuracy

accūrāt·us -a -um *adj* **(adc-)** careful, accurate, exact; studied

accūr·ō -āre -āvī -ātus *tr* **(adc-)** to take care of, attend to; *(w. subj,* **ut, nē)** to see to it (that, that not)

ac·currō -currere -currī *or* **-cucurrī -cursum** *intr* **(adc-)** to run up; *(w. ad or in + acc)* to run (up) to

accurs·us -ūs *m* **(adc-)** running, concourse; *(mil)* attack, charge

accūsābil·is -is -e *adj* reprehensible

accūsāti·ō -ōnis *f* accusation; *(leg)* (bill of) indictment

accūsātīv·us -a -um *adj & m* accusative

accūsāt·or -ōris *m* accuser, prosecutor; informant

accūsātōriē *adv* like an accuser, as a prosecutor

accūsātōri·us -a -um *adj* accuser's, prosecutor's

accūsātr·īx -īcis *f* accuser *(female)*

accūsit·ō -āre -āvī -ātus *tr* to keep on accusing

accūs·ō -āre -āvī -ātus *tr* to accuse; to prosecute; to reproach, blame; *(w. gen of the charge or w.* **dē** *+ abl)* to accuse of

ā·cer -cris -cre *adj* sharp, pointed; alert, vigilant; shrewd; energetic, active; excited, eager, enthusiastic; strict, stern, hard; pinched, sharp *(features);* strong *(drink);* fierce, sharp *(bite);* bright, vivid *(color);* strong, pungent *(odor);* strong, bitter *(taste);* wild, savage *(animal);* fierce, relentless *(enemy);* violent *(storm);* biting *(cold);* strong, high *(wind);* swift *(river);* intense *(hunger, pain);* drastic *(remedy);* strong, powerful *(incentive);* serious, critical *(situation); (coll)* huge, terrific; **nāribus ācer** keen-scented

ac·er -eris *n* maple tree; maple wood

acerbē *adv* bitterly, harshly

acerbit·ās -ātis *f* bitterness, harshness, sharpness, sourness; distress, painful experience; ill-feeling, bitterness; satirical quality *(of writing)*

acerb·ō -āre -āvī -ātus *tr* to embitter; to exacerbate; to render *(s.th.)* disagreeable

acerb·us -a -um *adj* bitter, harsh, sour *(flavor, taste);* unripe, green *(fruit);* cruel, hostile, pitiless *(enemy);* harsh *(speech, remark);* untimely, premature *(death);* bitter *(feelings; cold);* rough *(winter);* strict, severe *(person in authority); (in a weakened sense)* troublesome, disagreeable

acern·us -a -um *adj* maple

acerr·a -ae *f* incense box

acersecom·ēs -ae *m* young man

acervātim *adv* in heaps; briefly
acerv·ō -āre -āvī -ātus *tr* to heap *or* pile up
acerv·us -ī *m* heap, pile; multitude; *(in logic)* sorites
acēscō acēscere acuī *intr* to turn sour
Acest·ēs -ae *m* king of Sicily
acētābul·um -ī *n* vinegar bottle
acēt·um -ī *n* sour wine, vinegar; *(fig)* sharp tongue
Achaemen·ēs -is *m* first king of Persia, great-grandfather of Cyrus
Achaemenid·ēs -ae *m* follower of Ulysses who was left behind in Sicily
Achaemeni·us -a -um *adj (poet)* Persian; Parthian
Achae·us -a -um *adj & m* Achaean; Greek
Achai·a *or* **Achāï·a -ae** *f* province in N. part of Peloponnesus on Gulf of Corinth; Greece
Achāï·cus -a -um *adj & m* Achaean; Greek
Achāt·ēs -ae *m* companion of Aeneas ‖ river in Sicily
Achelō·is -idis *f* daughter of Acheloüs; a Siren; a water nymph
Acheloï·us -a -um *adj* of the river Acheloüs; of Acheloüs *(the river god); descended from* Acheloüs
Achelō·üs -ī *m* river in N.W. Greece, flowing between Aetolia and Acarnania; god of this river
Acher·ōn -ontis *or* **Acher·ūns -untis** *m (f) or* **Acher·os -ī** *m* Acheron *(river in Hades); god* of this river; lower world; river in Epirus; river in S. Italy
Acheruntic·us -a -um *adj* of Acheron, of the lower world; **senex Acherunticus** old man with one foot in the grave
Acherūsi·us -a -um *adj* of the river Acheron, of the lower world
Achill·ās -ae *m* Egyptian who murdered Pompey
Achill·ēs -is *or* **-ī** *or* **-eī** *m* Greek warrior, son of Peleus and Thetis
Achillē·us -a -um *adj* of Achilles
Achillīd·ēs -ae *m* son *or* descendant of Achilles *(esp. his son Pyrrhus)*
Achīv·us -a -um *adj* Achaean, Greek
Acīdali·a -ae *f* Venus
acid·us -a -um *adj* sour, tart; *(of sound)* harsh, shrill; sharp, keen; pungent; unpleasant, disagreeable
aci·ēs -ēī *f* sharpness, sharp edge; keenness of vision; glance; eyesight, eye; pupil *(of the eye);* mental power; battle line, battle array; battlefield; battle; debate
acīnac·ēs -is *m* scimitar *(used by the Persians, Medes, and Scythians)*
acin·um -ī *n or* **acin·us -ī** *m* berry; grape; seed in the berry
acipēns·er -eris *or* **acipēns·is -is** *m* sturgeon

Āc·is -idis *m* son of Faunus, loved by Galatea, changed after his death into a river in Sicily
acl·ys -ydis *f* small javelin
aconīt·um -ī *n (bot)* wolfsbane; strong poison
ac·or -ōris *m* sour taste, sourness
acqui·ēscō -ēscere -ēvī -ētum *intr* **(adqu-)** to become quiet; to rest; to die; *(w. abl, dat, or in + abl)* **1** to find rest in; **2** to acquiesce in, be content with; **3** find pleasure in, rejoice in
acquī·rō -rere -sīvī -sītus *tr* **(adqu-)** to acquire, obtain, gain, win
Acrae·us -a -um *adj (title of Jupiter and Juno)* on the heights, on high
Acrag·ās -antis *m* town on S.W. coast of Sicily *(poetic and Greek for Agrigentum)*
acrātophor·um -ī *n* vessel for holding unmixed wine
acrēdul·a -ae *f* bird *(species unknown; perhaps owl or nightingale)*
ācricul·us -a -um *adj* irritable, peevish
ācrimōni·a -ae *f* sharpness, pungency; irritation; energy
Ācrisiōn·ē -ēs *f* daughter of Acrisius *(Danaë)*
Ācrisiōnē·us -a -um *adj* of Acrisius
Ācrisiōniad·ēs -ae *m* descendant of Acrisius *(Perseus)*
Ācris·ius -(i)ī *m* king of Argos, father of Danaë, grandfather of Perseus
ācriter *adv* sharply, keenly; clearly, in a distinctive manner; closely, attentively; with vigor, with enthusiasm; severely; vehemently; bitterly, hard
ācroām·a -atis *n* entertainment; comic actor; actor
ācroās·is -is *f* public lecture; recital
Ācrocerauni·a -ōrum *npl* promontory in Epirus on the Adriatic Sea
Ācrocorinth·us -ī *f* citadel of Corinth
Ācr·ōn -ōnis *m* a king of the Caeninenses *(killed by Romulus)*
Ācrot·a -ae *m* a king of Alba *(brother of Romulus Silvius)*
act·a -ae *f* seashore; seaside resort; beach party
āct·a -ōrum *npl see* **āctum**
Actae·ōn -onis *m* grandson of Cadmus, changed into a stag and devoured by his own dogs
Actae·us -a -um *adj* Attic, Athenian; **Actaea virgō** Athena
āctāri·us -ī *m* registrar of state documents; shorthand writer
Actē -ae *f* early name of Attica
Actiac·us -a -um *adj* of Actium; celebrating the victory of Actium
Acti·as -adis *fem adj* Attic
ācti·ō -ōnis *f* doing, performance, action, activity; proceedings; act, deed; proposal, measure; delivery *(of orator or actor);* plot, action *(of play); (leg)* suit, right to bring a suit;

grātiārum āctiō expression of gratitude; nātūrālēs āctiōnēs physiological functions

āctit·ō -āre -āvī -ātus *tr* to do *(repeatedly);* to plead *(cases regularly);* to act *(often)* in *(plays)*

Acti·um -ī *n* promontory in Epirus *(where Octavian defeated Antony and Cleopatra in 31 B.C.)*

āctiuncul·a -ae *f* short law-court speech

āctīv·us -a -um *adj* practical *(philosophy); (gram)* active

Act·or -oris *m* companion of Aeneas

āct·or -ōris *m* doer, performer; agent, manager; actor, player; herdsman; *(leg) (with or without* causae) 1 defense counsel; 2 prosecutor; āctor summārum cashier, accountant

āctuāriol·um -ī *n* small, fast boat

āctuāri·us -a -um *adj* swift ‖ *m* stenographer ‖ *f* swift passenger ship *(having both sails and oars)*

āct·um -ī *n* act, deed; transaction ‖ *npl* great deeds, exploits, achievements; official records *(of events; of business transacted by the Senate, emperors, etc.);* decrees *(of a magistrate, general, etc.);* ācta diurna day-by-day record of events; ācta Herculis labors of Hercules; ācta mittere to publish the news

āctuōsē *adv* actively, energetically

āctuōs·us -a -um *adj* active, energetic

āct·us -a -um *pp of* agō ‖ *adj* finished, past

āct·us -ūs *m* act, performance; physical movement; driving *(of cattle or wagon);* right of way; cow path; wagon track; path, course *(of sun);* linear land measure *(120 ft.);* sequence *(of numbers);* drawing *(of breath);* transaction *(of business);* performance *(of a play);* act *(of a play);* delivery *(of a speech);* dēdūcere in āctus to dramatize; in āctū esse to be active

āctūtum *adv* instantly, immediately

acul·a *or* aquol·a -ae *f* small stream

aculeāt·us -a -um *adj* prickly; *(of insects)* having a sting; *(fig)* stinging, barbed

acule·us -ī *m* sting, proboscis *(of insects);* barb *(of arrow);* spike; sharp point; sarcasm; aculeum ēmittere *(fig)* to shoot one's wad, spend all one's money

acūm·en -inis *n* point, sharpness; sting *(of insects);* cunning; clever trick; ingeniī acūmen mental acumen

acuō acuere acuī acūtus *tr* to sharpen, make pointed; to whet; to tune *(musical instruments);* to stir emotionally; to stimulate; to quicken *(one's pace);* to accent *(syllable)*

ac·us -ūs *f* needle, pin; hairpin; curling iron; ab aciā et acū in great detail; acū rem tangere to hit the nail on the head

acūtē *adv* acutely, sharply, keenly

acūtul·us -a -um *adj* somewhat sharp, rather subtle

acūt·us -a -um *pp of* acuō ‖ *adj* sharp, pointed; shrill *(sound);* keen *(senses, mind);* shrewd, intelligent *(person);* piercing *(cold);* fiercely hot *(sun);* nimble *(movement);* pungent *(smell, taste);* subtle *(distinction)*

ad- *pref* 1 at: adclāmāre *(or* acclāmāre) to shout at; 2 toward, aiming at: adīre to go toward; 3 bringing things together: adstringere *(or* astringere) to tie up; 4 toward a purpose: adiūrāre to swear to, swear by; 5 of increase or addition: addere to add; 6 of intensity: adamāre to love deeply

ad *prep (w. acc) (of space)* to, toward, at, near; *(often w.* ūsque) reaching to, as far as; for the purpose of, to; according to; in consequence of; with respect to; compared with; at the house of, with; in the company of; before *(judge, magistrate); (of time)* toward, about, until, at, on, by; *(with numbers)* about, almost; ad Capuam toward Capua, in the direction of Capua; ad diem on the right day, promptly; ad extrēmum to the very end; ad haec *or* ad hōc besides; ad locum on the spot; ad manum on hand, available; ad omnia in all directions; to crown all; ad praesēns for the moment; ad prīma to the highest degree; ad summam in short; ad summum at most; ad tempus on time, in time; ad ultimum utterly; ad ūnum one and all; ad unguen exactly, to the tee; ad verbum word for word; ad vesperum toward evening

adācti·ō -ōnis *f* administering *(an oath)*

adāctus *pp of* adigō

adāct·us -ūs *m* bringing together; snapping *(of jaws)*

adaequē *adv* equally

adaequ·ō -āre -āvī -ātus *tr* to make level; to equal, match, come up to the level of; *(fig)* to put on the same level; adaequāre solō to level to the ground ‖ *intr* to be on the same level, be equal; *(of votes)* to be equally divided *(for acquittal and for condemnation); (w. dat)* to be level with; *(w. abl)* to be on a par with, be equal to *(in some respect)*

adamantē·us -a -um *adj* made of steel

adamantin·us -a -um *adj* hard as steel, adamantine; saxa adamantina diamonds

adam·ās -antis *m* adamant; steel; diamond; anything inflexible

adambul·ō -āre *intr (w. dat or* ad) to walk beside, walk up to

adam·ō -āre -āvī -ātus *tr* to love deeply; to fall in love with; to take a fancy to

adaper·iō -īre -uī -tus *tr* to uncover, throw open; to open up; to disclose to view, make visible; to open wide *(mouth, door);* to uncover *(head as sign of respect); (med)* to loosen *(bowels)*

adapertil·is -is -e *adj* that can be opened

adapert·us -a -um *adj* open *(door, flower)*

adaptāt·us -a -um *(w. dat)* adjusted to

adapt·ō -āre -āvī -ātus *tr* to adapt, modify; *(w. dat)* to fit to

adaqu·ō -āre *tr* to water **‖** *intr* to fetch water

adauctus *pp of* **adaugeō**

adauct·us -ūs *m* further growth, increase

adau·geō -gēre -xī -ctus *tr* to increase; to increase the number of; to exaggerate; *(w. abl)* to crown with

adaugēsc·ō -ere *intr* to begin to grow

adbib·ō -ere -ī *tr* to begin to drink; to listen attentively to

adbīt·ō -ere *intr* to approach

adc- = acc-

addec·et -ēre *v impers* it is proper

addēns·eō -ēre *or* **addēns·ō -āre** *tr* to close *(ranks)*

ad·dīcō -dīcere -dīxī -dictus *tr (w. dat)* 1 *(leg)* to assign *(property)* to; 2 to give custody of *(debtor)* to *(creditor)*; 3 to sell *(by sale or auction)* to; 4 to award *(prizes, provinces)* to; 5 to ascribe to *(author)*; 6 to condemn, doom to **‖** *refl & pass (w. dat)* to give one's support to **‖** *intr (in augury)* to be favorable

addict·us -a -um *adj (w. dat)* addicted to, a slave of; *(w. inf)* bound to *(do s.th.)* **‖** *mf* person enslaved for debt or theft

ad·discō -discere -didicī *tr* to learn in addition

additāment·um -ī *n* addition, increase

ad·dō -dere -didī -ditus *tr* to add; to give additionally; to add by way of exaggeration; to increase; to quicken *(one's pace)*; to impart; to insert; to put *(into a container)*; *(w. dat)* 1 to attach to, fit onto; 2 to serve *(a drink)* to; 3 to give to, confer on, inflict on; 4 to attribute to; 5 to intensify *(feelings);* **manūs in vincula addere** to tie one's hands

addoc·eō -ēre -uī *tr* to teach in addition, teach new *(skills, etc.)*

addubit·ō -āre -āvī -ātus *tr* to call into doubt **‖** *intr* to begin to feel doubt; to hesitate

ad·dūcō -dūcere -dūxī -ductus *tr* to lead up, bring up; to bring with one, bring along; to import; to bring up *(reinforcements);* to lead *(the mind to);* to introduce *(arguments);* to draw together, wrinkle; to induce; to sail *(a ship to);* to bring *(water to a town);* to shut *(door);* to shorten *(rein);* to draw back *(bowstring);* to bend *(bow); (of time, conditions)* to bring on; *(leg)* to prosecute, bring to trial; **(in iūdicium) addūcere** to take to court

adduct·us -a -um *adj* drawn tight, strained; narrow, tight *(place);* strict, serious *(character)*

ad·edō -edere *or* **-ēsse -ēdī -ēsus** *tr* to nibble at; to eat up; to waste; *(of fire)* to scorch; *(of water)* to erode

adempti·ō -ōnis *f* a taking away; confiscation

ademptus *pp of* **adimō**

adeō *adv* to such a degree, so; even, indeed, truly; very, extremely; for that matter; *(following pronouns and numerals, to give emphasis)* precisely, exactly; quite, just, chiefly; *(at the beginning of sentence)* thus far, to such an extent; *(w.* **ut** + *subj)* to the end that; *(w.* **nē** + *subj)* to the end that ... not; *(w.* **dum, donec,** *etc.)* to the point of time when; **adeō nōn** much less

ad·eō -īre -iī *or* **-īvī -itus** *tr* to approach; to attack; to consult; to visit; to undertake, set about, undergo; to consult *(an oracle)* **‖** *intr* to go up, come up; *(w.* **ad)** 1 to go up to, approach; 2 to enter upon, undertake, set about; 3 to meet *(danger);* **ad rem pūblicam adīre** to go into politics

ad·eps -ipis *mf* fat; corpulence

adepti·ō -ōnis *f* obtaining, acquisition

adeptus *pp of* **adipīscor**

adequit·ō -āre -āvī -ātum *intr* to ride up; *(w. dat or* **ad)** to ride up to, ride toward

adesse *inf of* **adsum**

adēsse *inf of* **adedō**

adēsur·iō -īre -īvī *intr* to be very hungry

adēsus *pp of* **adedō**

adf- = aff-

adfuī *perf of* **adsum**

ad·haereō -haerēre -haesī -haesum *intr (w. dat, abl,* **ad** *or in* + *acc)* 1 to cling to, stick to; 2 to keep close to, hang on to; 3 *(anat)* to be attached to; 4 *(of land)* to be contiguous with, be near; **laterī adhaerēre** to stick to *(a person's)* side; **memoriae adhaerēre** to stick in one's memory

adhae·rēscō -rēscere -sī -sum *intr* to stick; to falter; *(w. dat, abl,* **in** + *abl, or* **ad)** 1 to stick to, cling to; 2 to be devoted to; 3 to correspond to, accord with; 4 *(of weapons)* to become lodged in; 5 to run aground on

adhaesi·ō -ōnis *f* clinging, adhesion

adhaes·us -ūs *m* clinging, adhesion

Adherb·al -alis *m* son of Micipsa *(king of Numidia),* murdered by Jugurtha; Carthaginian general in the 2nd Punic War

adhib·eō -ēre -uī -itus *tr* to stretch out *(hands);* to apply *(remedies, fetters, treatment);* to administer *(medicine);* to call in *(as advisor, witness, expert);* to cite *(an authority); (w. abl)* to supply *(s.o.)* with; **animum adhibēre** *(w. dat)* to turn one's attention to; **fidem adhibēre** *(w. dat)* to lend credence to; *(w. adv)* to treat; *(w.* **ad)** to invite *(to a meal);* **‖** *refl* to conduct oneself, behave

adhinn·iō -īre -iī *or* **-īvī -ītus** *tr* to whinny after; to lust after ‖ *intr* (*w. dat or* **ad** *or* **in** + *acc*) **1** to whinny after; **2** to lust after, crave; **3** to chuckle in delight at

adhortāti·ō -ōnis *f* exhortation, encouragement; pep talk

adhortāt·or -ōris *m* fan, supporter

adhort·or -ārī -ātus sum *tr* to cheer on, encourage

adhūc *adv* thus far, hitherto; till now; as yet, still; besides, in addition, moreover; to a greater degree, still further; (*w. numerals*) besides; **nihil adhūc** nothing as yet

adiac·eō -ēre -uī *tr* to adjoin ‖ *intr* (*w. dat or* **ad**) to lie near; to border

ad·iciō -icere -iēcī -iectus *tr* to add; to increase; (*w. dat or* **ad**) **1** to hurl (*weapon, insults*) at; **2** to add (*s.th.*) to; **3** to turn (*eyes, attention*) to; (*w.* **in** + *acc*) to hurl (*weapon*) at

adiecti·ō -ōnis *f* addition; annexation

adiectīv·us -a -um *adj* adjectival ‖ *n* adjective

ad·igō -igere -ēgī -āctus *tr* to drive (*cattle*); to move up (*siege engine*); to assemble (*ships*); to hurl (*weapon*); to inflict (*wound*); to plunge (*weapon*) into; **aliquem iūs iūrandum adigere** to have s.o. swear allegiance; **prōvinciam in verba sua et Pompēiī iūs iūrandum adigere** to have the province swear allegiance to himself and Pompey

ad·imō -imere -ēmī -emptus *tr* (*w. dat of separation*) to take away from; **alicui vītam** (*or* **lībertātem**) **adimere** to deprive s.o. of life *or* liberty

adipātus -a -um *adj* fatty, greasy; gross, bombastic ‖ *n* pastry (*made in fat*)

ad·ipīscor -ipīscī -eptus sum *tr* to get, obtain; to arrive at, reach; to inherit; to win (*victory*); **mortem adipīscī** to commit suicide

aditiāl·is -is -e *adj* inaugural

aditi·ō -ōnis *f* a going to

aditus *pp of* **adeō**

adit·us -ūs *m* doorway, entrance, passage; extent to which a door is opened, opening; approach; arrival; access; entrance; right of entry, admittance; right to hold (*an office*); audience, interview; beginning, commencement; chance, opportunity; hostile approach, attack; chance of attacking, an "opening"; **prīmus aditus** first encounter (*with a person*)

adiūdic·ō -āre -āvī -ātus *tr* to adjudge, award; to ascribe, assign

adiūment·um -ī *n* help, support

adiūnct·a -ōrum *npl* attendant circumstances; **ad nōmina adiūncta** epithets, nicknames

adiūncti·ō -ōnis *f* joining, union; addition; (*rhet*) repetition

ad·iungō -iungere -iūnxī -iūnctus *tr* (*w. dat*) **1** to yoke *or* harness (*animal*) to; **2** to add

(*ingredients*) to; **3** to ascribe (*qualities*) to; **4** to bestow (*praise, honor*) on; (*w. dat or* **ad**) **1** to add, attach (*s.th.*) to; **2** to apply, direct (*mind, attention, etc.*) to; **uxōrem adiungere** to get married ‖ *refl* (*w. dat*) to join

adiūr·ō -āre -āvī -ātus *tr* to swear to; to swear by ‖ *intr* to swear

adiūtābil·is -is -e *adj* helpful

adiūt·ō -āre -āvī -ātus *tr* to help ‖ *intr* (*w. dat*) to be of assistance to

adiūt·or -ōris *m* helper, assistant; aide, adjutant, deputy; supporting actor

adiūtōr·ium -(i)ī *n* help, support

adiūtr·īx -īcis *f* helper (*female*)

ad·iuvō -iuvāre -iūvī -iūtus *tr* to help; to encourage; to keep (*the fire*) going; (*med*) to relieve; (*w.* **ad** *or* **in** + *acc*) to contribute to ‖ *v impers* it helps, it is advantageous, it is useful

adl- = **all-**

admātūr·ō -āre *tr* to bring to maturity, ripen; to speed up, expedite

ad·mētior -mētīrī -mēnsus sum *tr* (*w. dat*) to measure (*s.th.*) out to

Admēt·us -ī *m* king of Pherae in Thessaly, husband of Alcestis

admigr·ō -āre *intr* (*w.* **ad**) to move to

adminicul·ō -āre -āvī -ātus *tr* to prop up

adminicul·um -ī *n* prop, support, stake, pole; rudder; aid; assistant

adminis·ter -trī *m* assistant; server, waiter

administr·a -ae *f* assistant, handmaid; waitress

administr·ō -āre -āvī -ātus *tr* to administer, direct, manage, run; to rule; to execute (*orders*); to govern (*a province*); to conduct (*a war*) ‖ *intr* to manage

administrāti·ō -ōnis *f* handling, administration, management, government; method of dealing with ‖ *fpl* administrative functions *or* duties; administrative qualities

administrāt·or -ōris *m* administrator, director, manager

admīrābil·is -is -e *adj* admirable, wonderful; strange, surprising; **admīrābile est** it is remarkable

admīrābilit·ās -ātis *f* admiration, wonder; wonderfulness

admīrābiliter *adv* admirably; astonishingly

admīrāti·ō -ōnis *f* admiration, wonder; surprise

admīrāt·or -ōris *m* admirer

admīr·or -ārī -ātus sum *tr* to admire, wonder at; to be surprised at

admī·sceō -scēre -scuī -xtus *tr* to mix in, add; to involve, implicate; to join, mingle; (*w. dat, w.* **ad** *or* **in** + *acc or* **cum**) to add (*s.th.*) to; to mix *or* mix up (*s.th.*) with ‖ *refl* to get involved

admissār·ius -(i)ī *m* stallion; (*fig*) stud

admissi·ō -ōnis *f* audience, interview
admiss·um -ī *n* fault, crime
ad·mittō -mittere -mīsī -missus *tr* to let in, admit; to allow; to let loose; to listen to; to put at a gallop; to let *(water, hair)* flow; to allow; to commit *(error, crime)*; **facinus in sē admittere** to commit a fault, error, crime; **ad animum admittere** to consider; **auribus** *(or* **ad aurēs) admittere** to listen to ‖ *intr (in augury)* to be propitious
admīxti·ō -ōnis *f* admixture
admīxtus *pp of* admīsceō
admoderātē *adv* appropriately
admodum *adv* to the limit; very, quite, fully; *(w. numbers)* just about; *(w. negatives)* at all; *(in answers)* quite so, yes
admoen·iō -īre -īvī -ītus *tr* to besiege
admol·ior -īrī -ītus sum *tr* to pile up; **manūs admolīrī** *(w. dat)* to lay violent hands on ‖ *intr (w.* **ut** + *subj)* to struggle to
admon·eō -ēre -uī -itus *tr* to admonish, remind, suggest; to warn; *(w. acc or gen)* to recall
admoniti·ō -ōnis *f* admonition, reminder, suggestion
admonit·or -ōris *m* reminder, one who admonishes
admonit·um -ī *n* advice, warning, suggestion
admonit·us -ūs *m* advice; suggestion; warning; command *(given to an animal);* **admonitū** *(w. gen)* at the suggestion of
admord·eō -ēre *(no perf)* **admorsus** *tr* to bite at; *(fig)* to fleece
admōti·ō -ōnis *f* moving, movement
ad·moveō -movēre -mōvī -mōtus *tr* to move up, bring up, bring near; to lead on, conduct; to promote, advance; to employ *(fear, flattery); (w. dat or* **ad) 1** to move or bring *(s.th.)* to; **2** to apply *(s.th.)* to; **3** to direct *(attention, etc.)* to; **aurem admovēre** to give heed; **calcar** *(or* **stimulum) admovēre** *(w. dat)* to spur
admūg·iō -īre *intr (w. dat)* to bellow to
admurmurāti·ō -ōnis *f* murmuring
admurmur·ō -āre -āvī -ātum *intr* to murmur *(in approval or disapproval)* ‖ *impers pass* **admurmurātum est** people murmured
admutil·ō -āre -āvī -ātus *tr* to clip close; *(coll)* to clip, cheat *(of money)*
adn- = ann-
ad·oleō -olēre *intr* to smell
ad·oleō -olēre -oluī -ultus *tr* to burn *(ritually);* to make burnt sacrifices to, worship; to cremate; to light *(pyre);* to destroy by fire, burn; **adolēre altāria dōnīs** to pile the altar high with gifts; **flammīs adolēre penātis** *(fig)* to light the hearth; **honōrēs adolēre** *(dat)* to make burnt offerings to
adolēsc·ēns -entis *m* young man ‖ *f* young lady

adol·ēscō -ēscere -ēvī **adultum** *intr* (adul-) to grow up; to become mature; to increase; *(of habits, etc.)* to become established
Adōn·is -is *or* -idis *m* son of Cinyras *(king of Cyprus),* loved by Venus, killed by a wild boar
adoper·iō -īre -uī -tus *tr* to cover up; to close
adopert·us -a -um *adj* covered; veiled; hiding; shut, closed; *(poet)* clothed
adopīn·or -ārī -ātus sum *tr* to suppose, conjecture further
adoptāti·ō -ōnis *f* adoption *(into a family)*
adopti·ō -ōnis *f* adoption *(into a family)*
adoptīv·us -a -um *adj* adoptive
adopt·ō -āre -āvī -ātus *tr* to adopt; to select; to graft *(plants)*
ad·or -ōris *or* -oris *n* spelt *(hardy European type of wheat)*
adōrāti·ō -ōnis *f* adoration, worship
adōre·a -ae *f (a gift of grain as)* reward for valor; praise, glory
adōre·us -a -um *adj* of spelt, of wheat
ad·orior -orīrī -ortus sum *tr* to rise up against, attack; to attempt; to undertake
adōrn·ō -āre -āvī -ātus *tr* to adorn; to equip, get ready
adōr·ō -āre -āvī -ātus *tr* to implore, entreat; to ask for; to adore, worship
adp- = app-
adq- = acq-
adr- = arr-
ad·rādō -rādere -rāsī -rāsus *tr* to shave close
Adrast·us -ī *m* king of Argos, father-in-law of Tydeus and Polynices
Adri- = Hadri-
adsc- = āsc-
adsi- = assi-
adso- = asso-
adsp- = asp-
adst- = ast-
adsu- = assu-
ad·sum -esse -fuī -futūrus *intr* to be present; to appear; *(of conditions)* to exist; *(of time, events)* to be at hand; to be of assistance; *(of an assembly)* to convene; *(w. dat)* **1** to share in, participate in; **2** to assist, stand by; **3** *(leg)* to serve as attorney to; **4** *(of gods)* to look favorably on; **adesse animō** *(or* **animīs)** to pay attention; to cheer up; **adest illī corporis pulchritūdō** he has a handsome physique
adt- = att-
adūlāti·ō -ōnis *f* flattery; fawning, cringing
adūlāt·or -ōris *m* flatterer
adūlātōri·us -a -um *adj* flattering
adulēsc·ēns -entis *m* (adol-) young man ‖ *f* young lady
adulēscenti·a -ae *f* (adol-) youth, young people
adulēscentul·a -ae *f* girl

adulēscentul·us -ī *m* boy

adūl·ō -āre *tr* to fawn on *(like a dog)*

adūl·or -ārī -ātus sum *tr* to fawn on ‖ *intr (w. dat)* to kowtow to

adult·er -era -erum *adj* adulterous, unchaste; cross-bred *(plants);* debased *(coinage);* **adultera clāvis** skeleton key ‖ *m* lover, adulterer ‖ *f* adulteress

adulterīn·us -a -um *adj* adulterous; counterfeit

adulter·ium -(i)ī *n* adultery; adulteration

adulter·ō -āre -āvī -ātus *tr* to defile, corrupt; to adulterate; to counterfeit; to falsify *(documents)* ‖ *intr* to commit adultery

adult·us -a -um *adj* grown, mature, adult

adumbrātim *adv* in outline

adumbrāti·ō -ōnis *f* sketch, outline

adumbrāt·us -a -um *adj* shadowy, sketchy; spurious

adumbr·ō -āre -āvī -ātus *tr* to shade; to obscure *(truth);* to sketch; to counterfeit

aduncit·ās -ātis *f* curvature

adunc·us -a -um *adj* curved, hooked

adurg·eō -ēre *tr* to be in hot pursuit of

ad·ūrō -ūrere -ūssī -ūstus *tr* to scorch, singe; to cause a burning sensation in, to burn; to nip, freeze; to desiccate; *(med)* to cauterize

adūsque *prep (w. acc)* all the way to, right up to

adūsti·ō -ōnis *f* burning; *(med)* burn; heatstroke

adūst·us -a -um *pp of* **adūrō** ‖ *adj* scorched; **nivibus adūstus** frostbitten; **sōle adūstus** sunburned

advectīci·us -a -um *adj* imported, foreign

advect·iō -ōnis *f* transportation

advect·ō -āre *tr* to import

advectus *pp of* **advehō**

advect·us -ūs *m* importation

adve·hō -here -xī -ctus *tr* to convey; to ship; to import ‖ *pass* to ride; **equō advehī (ad** *or* **in** + *acc)* to ride to; **nāvī advehī (in** + *acc)* to sail to

advēl·ō -āre *tr* to veil; to wreathe

adven·a -ae *mf* stranger, foreigner

ad·veniō -venīre -vēnī -ventum *intr* to arrive; *(of periods of time, events)* to draw near, approach, be imminent; *(w.* **ad** *or* **in** + *acc, or acc of limit of motion)* to arrive at, come to, reach; *(w. dat) (of possession)* to come into the hands of; *(pres p)* at *or* upon my (your, his, her, etc.) arrival; **advenientem īlicō ad cēnam addūxī** immediately upon his arrival I took him to dinner

adventīci·us -a -um *adj* foreign; imported; extraneous; unusual; migratory *(birds);* **cēna adventīcia** reception; **ex adventīciō** from an extraneous source

advent·ō -āre -āvī -ātum *intr* to keep coming closer; to turn up *(at a place); (of tide)* to come in; *(of time, events)* to draw near

advent·or -ōris *m* visitor, guest; customer

advent·us -ūs *m* arrival, approach; visit; (official) visitation

adversāri·us -a -um *adj* (-vors-) *(w. dat)* turned toward, opposed to, opposite ‖ *mf* adversary ‖ *npl* journal, notebook, memoranda; assertion *(of opponent)*

adversātr·īx -īcis *f* (-vors-) opponent *(female)*

adversi·ō -ōnis *f* directing

advers·ō -āre -āvī -ātus *tr* (-vors-) to turn, direct; **animum adversāre** to direct attention; *(w.* **nē)** to be careful not to

advers·or -ārī -ātus sum *intr* (-vors-) to put up opposition; to be unfavorable; *(w. dat)* **1** to oppose, resist; **2** to be incompatible with; **3** to be inconsistent with

adversum *or* **adversus** *adv* (-vors-) in the opposite direction ‖ *prep (w. acc)* facing, opposite, toward; in the direction of; in the opposite direction to, against; compared with, in comparison with; to the disadvantage of; *(after verbs expressing hostile intent)* to meet, face; compared with; contrary to; in the eyes of; in criticism of; in reply to, in response to; **adversus clīvum (** *or* **collem)** uphill

advers·us -a -um *adj* (-vors-) opposite, in front; facing; unfavorable; hostile; *(astr)* diametrically opposite; **adversā viā** up the road; **adversō flūmine** upstream; **frontibus adversīs** head-on; **rēs adversae** misfortunes, adversities; **ventus adversus** head wind ‖ *n* trouble, adversity, misfortune; the opposite; **ex adversō** *(w. dat)* opposite to; **in adversum** forwards; to meet face to face; *(of several things)* in the opposite direction; **in adversum subīre** to go uphill; **per adversum** in the opposite direction

adver·tō -tere -tī -sus *tr* (-vor-) *(w. acc or dat or in* + *acc)* **1** to turn *or* direct *(s.th.)* toward; **2** to steer *(ship)* toward; **animōs (** *or* **aurēs** *or* **oculōs) advertere** to attract attention; **animum advertere** *(w. dat or* **ad)** to pay attention to, heed, observe ‖ *intr* to land; *(w.* **in** + *acc)* to punish

advesper·āscit -āscere -āvit *v impers* evening approaches

advigil·ō -āre -āvī -ātum *intr* to be vigilant, keep watch; *(w. dat)* to keep watch over, bestow attention on; *(w.* **prō** + *abl)* to watch out for

advocāt·a -ae *f* supporter *(female)*

advocāti·ō -ōnis *f* legal assistance; legal counsel; the bar; period of time allowed to procure legal assistance; delay, adjournment

advocāt·us -ī *m* helper, supporter; *(leg)* attorney

advoc·ō -āre -āvī -ātus *tr* to call; to convoke; to invoke; to invoke the help of; to invite *(to a meal);* to consult; to cite; *(leg)* to adjourn

advol·ō -āre -āvī -ātum *intr (w. dat or* **ad) 1** to fly toward; **2** to rush at; **3** *(mil)* to swoop down on

advol·vō -vere -vī -ūtus *tr (w. dat or* **ad)** to roll *(s.th.)* to *or* toward **ǁ** *refl* **sē advolvere ad genua** *(or* **genibus)** *(w. gen)* to fall prostrate before

advor- = adver-

adyt·um -ī *n* sanctuary; *(fig)* tomb

Aeacidēi·us -a -um *adj* of the descendants of Aeacus; **Aeacidēia rēgna** Aegina

Aeacid·ēs -ae *m* descendant of Aeacus

Aeac·us *or* **Aeac·os -ī** *m* king of Aegina, father of Peleus, Telamon, and Phocus, and judge of the dead

aed·ēs *or* **aed·is -is** *f* room, apartment; shrine, temple **ǁ** *fpl* house; **in ūnīs aedibus** in one house

aedicul·a -ae *f* chapel, shrine; small room, closet; small house **ǁ** *fpl* small house

aedificāti·ō -ōnis *f* constructing, building; structure, building

aedificātiuncul·a -ae *f* tiny building

aedificāt·or -ōris *m* builder, architect; **aedificātor mundī** creator of the world

aedific·ium -(i)ī *n* building, edifice

aedific·ō -āre -āvī -ātus *tr* to build; **locum aedificāre** to erect buildings on a site **ǁ** *intr* to erect a building

aedīlici·us -a -um *adj* aedile's **ǁ** *m* ex-aedile

aedīl·is -is *m* (**ēd-**) aedile *(Roman magistrate charged with the supervision of public buildings, markets, grain supply, games, and theatrical productions);* magistrate in Italian and other towns; **aedīlis cereālis** aedile in charge of the grain supply

aedīlit·ās -ātis *f* aedileship

aedis *see* **aedēs**

aeditu·us *or* **aeditim·us** *or* **aeditum·us -ī** *m* sacristan

Aedu·ī -ōrum *mpl* (**Haed-**) Gallic tribe occupying the territory between the Saône and the Loire

Aeëtae·us -a -um *adj* of Aeëtes

Aeët·ēs *or* **Aeët·ās** *or* **Aeët·a -ae** *m* Aeëtes *(king of Colchis and father of Medea)*

Aeëti·as -adis *f* daughter of Aeëtes *(Medea)*

Aegae·us -a -um *adj* (**Aegē·us**, **Ēgē·us**) Aegean **ǁ** *n* Aegean Sea

Aegāt·ēs -um *fpl* Aegatian Islands *(three islands off the W. coast of Sicily where the Carthaginians were defeated, thus ending the First Punic War in 241 B.C.)*

ae·ger -gra -grum *adj* sick; *(w. abl of cause or* **ex)** sick from; diseased; weary, exhausted; depressed; depraved *(character, mind);* labored *(breathing, words);* corrupt *(institutions)* **ǁ** *mf* patient

Aeg·eus -eï *m* king of Athens and father of Theseus

Aegīd·ēs -ae *m* son of Aegeus *(Theseus)*

Aegīd·ae -ārum *mpl* descendants of Aegeus

Aegīn·a -ae *f* island off Attica **ǁ** mother of Aeacus

aeg·is -idis *f* shield of Minerva and of Jupiter; aegis, protection

Aegisth·us -ī *m* son of Thyestes and murderer of Agamemnon

aegrē *adv* painfully; with difficulty; reluctantly; hardly, scarcely; **aegrē esse alicui** *or* **aegrē facere alicui** to annoy s.o.; to hurt s.o.; **aegrē ferre** *(or* **patī)** to take (it) hard; to resent

aegr·eō -ēre *intr* to be sick

aegrēsc·ō -ere *intr* to become sick; to get worse; to be distressed

aegrimōni·a -ae *f* distress, trouble

aegritūd·ō -inis *f* sickness; sorrow

aegr·or -ōris *m* illness

aegrōtāti·ō -ōnis *f* sickness, disease; sorrow

aegrōt·ō -āre -āvī -ātum *intr* to be sick; **animō aegrōtāre** to be mentally ill

aegrōt·us -a -um *adj* sick; love-sick

Aegypti·us -a -um *adj* of Egypt, Egyptian

Aegypt·us -ī *f* Egypt **ǁ** *m* mythical king of Egypt, whose 50 sons married the 50 daughters of his brother Danaüs

aelinon *interj* exclamation of sorrow, said to signify "alas for Linus"

aelin·os -ī *m* a dirge

Aëll·ō -ūs *f* one of the Harpies; a swift dog

Aemiliān·us -a -um *adj* of the Aemilian gens; Scipio Aemilianus Minor, son of L. Aemilius Paulus

Aemili·us -a -um *adj* name of a Roman clan *(nomen), esp.* Lucius Aemilius Paulus, who defeated Perseus at Pydna in 168 B.C.; **Via Aemilia** road from Ariminum to Placentia

Aemilius Macer a poet from Verona, friend of Vergil and Ovid

Aemoni·a -ae *f* (**Hae-**) Thessaly

aemul·a -ae *f* rival *(female);* rival city

aemulāti·ō -ōnis *f* emulation, rivalry

aemulāt·or -ōris *m* rival, imitator

aemulāt·us -ūs *m* emulation, rivalry

aemul·or -ārī -ātus sum *or* **aemul·ō -āre** *tr* to emulate, rival **ǁ** *intr (w. dat or* **cum)** to be jealous of

aemul·us -a -um *adj (w. gen or dat)* **1** jealous of, striving after; **2** *(of things)* similar to, comparable to **ǁ** *m* rival **ǁ** *f* rival

Aenari·a -ae *f* island on the Campanian coast, where Aeneas made landfall *(modern Ischia)*
Aenead·ēs -ae *m* descendant of Aeneas; Trojan; Roman; Augustus
Aenē·ās -ae *m* son of Venus and Anchises, and hero of Vergil's epic
Aenē·is -idis *or* **-idos** *f* the *Aeneid*
aēne·um *or* **ahēne·um** *or* **aēn·um -ī** *n* bronze vessel, cauldron, pot
aēne·us *or* **ahēne·us** *or* **a(h)ēn·us -a -um** *adj* bronze; hard as bronze; bronze-colored
Aenīd·ēs -ae *m* son of Aeneas *(Ascanius)*
aenigm·a -atis *n* enigma, riddle, puzzle
aēni·pēs -pedis *adj* bronze-footed
aēnum *see* **aēneum**
aēnus *see* **aēneus**
Aeoli·a -ae *f* realm of Aeolus *(king of winds); group of islands off Sicily*
Aeolid·ēs -ae *m* a descendant of Aeolus *(esp. his sons Sisyphus and Athamas)*
Aeoli·ī -ōrum *or* **Aeol·ēs -um** *mpl* Aeolians *(in N.W. Asia Minor)*
Aeol·is -idis *or* **-idos** *f* Aeolia *(N.W. part of Asia Minor)*
Aeol·us -ī *m* god of winds *(son of Jupiter, ruler of the Aeolian islands)*
aequābil·is -is -e *adj* equal; alike; consistent, uniform; fair, impartial
aequābilit·ās -ātis *f* equality; uniformity; impartiality
aequābiliter *adv* evenly, equally; uniformly
aequaev·us -a -um *adj* of the same age, coeval
aequāl·is -is -e *adj* equal; of equal importance; even, level; of the same age; contemporary; symmetrical; affecting all equally, universal, general; *(of conditions, etc.)* comparable; uniform *(in consistency, shape, color, content, style);* homogeneous; *(of natural phenomena)* regular, continuous; *(of weather)* settled; equally balanced *(contest); (w. dat)* level with, on a level with, on a par with; *(w. ad)* equally disposed to ‖ *mf* comrade; contemporary
aequālit·ās -ātis *f* equality *(of age, status, merit);* regularity; evenness; smoothness
aequāliter *adv* equally; evenly
aequanimit·ās -ātis *f* calmness, patience; kindness; impartiality
aequāti·ō -ōnis *f* equal distribution
aequē *adv* equally; justly, fairly; **aequē ... ac** *or* **atque** *or* **et** just as if; **aequē ... quam** as ... as, in the same way as
Aequ·ī -ōrum *mpl* a people of central Italy
aequilībrit·ās -ātis *f* balance
aequilībr·ium -(i)ī *n* horizontal position; equilibrium
aequinoctiāl·is -is -e *adj* equinoctial
aequinoct·ium -(i)ī *n* equinox

aequiperābil·is -is -e *adj (w. dat or* **cum)** comparable to
aequiper·ō -āre -āvī -ātus *tr* (**-par-**) to compare; to equal, rival, come up to; *(w. dat, w.* **ad** *or* **cum)** to compare *(s.th.)* to ‖ *intr (w. dat)* to become equal to, be equal to
aequit·ās -ātis *f* evenness; conformity; symmetry; equity; calmness; **animī aequitās** equanimity, calmness
aequ·ō -āre -āvī -ātus *tr* to make level; to smooth (out); to equalize; to equal, match, rival; to reach as high *(or* as deep) as; to keep pace with; to balance *(scales); (w. dat)* to liken to; **gradūs aequāre** to keep pace; **solō aequāre** to raze to the ground; **sortēs aequāre** to shake up the lots fairly
aequ·or -oris *n* level surface; plain; sea
aequore·us -a -um *adj* of the sea, marine
aequ·us -a -um *adj* level, even, flat, smooth; on a level *(with),* as tall *or* as high *(as);* fairminded, impartial, just, reasonable; evenly balanced; *(of laws, treaties)* giving equal rights, fair; *(of persons)* on an equal footing, equal *(in strength, etc.); (of qualities)* matching, equal, alike; *(of love)* reciprocated; *(of verse)* regular, uniform; *(of movement)* steady, calm; *(of the mind)* calm, resigned; *(of things)* favorable, advantageous; *(w. dat)* **1** inclined toward; **2** sympathetic to, favorable to; **3** content with; **aequā mente** with calmness, patiently; **aequa pars** a half; **aequā parte** on a basis of equality; **aequī facere** to regard as immaterial, regard as a matter of indifference; **aequīs manibus** *(of battles)* equally balanced; **aequō animō** with calmness, patiently; **aequō campō** *(mil)* on a level field *(offering advantage to neither side);* **aequō fronte** *(mil)* in a straight line, in line; **aequō Mārte** *(of battles)* evenly balanced; **aequō pede** on even terms, on an equal footing; **aequum est** it is right (that); **aequum solō pōnere** to raze to the ground; **ex īnferiōre locō loquitur sīve ex aequō sīve ex superiōre** whether he speaks before the judges on the bench or in the Senate, or from the rostra ‖ *n* level, plain; justice, fairness; **ex aequō** from the same level; *(fig)* equally
ā·ēr -eris *m* air; atmosphere; climate; sky; weather; mist
aerāment·um -ī *n* bronze utensil
aerāri·us -a -um *adj* copper, bronze; of mines; financial, fiscal ‖ *m* coppersmith; low-class Roman citizen ‖ *f* mine; smelting furnace ‖ *n* treasury; funds contained in the treasury; *(specifically)* public treasury at Rome, kept in the temple of Saturn in the Forum; **aerārium mīlitāre** treasury for veterans' benefits; **aerārium sānctius** a reserve fund *(to be touched only in an emergency)*

aerāt·us -a -um *adj* copper, bronze; rich
aere·us -a -um *adj* bronze; bronze-armored; bronze-beaked *(ships)*
āēre·us -a -um *adj see* **āērius**
aerif·er -era -erum *adj* carrying (bronze) cymbals
aerip·ēs -edis *adj* bronze-footed
āēri·us -a -um *adj* aerial, lofty; airy; air-borne; **āērium mel** dew
Āërop·ē -ēs *or* **Āërop·a -ae** *f* Aërope *(wife of Atreus, mother of Agamemnon and Menelaus)*
aerūginōs·us -a -um *adj* rusty
aerūg·ō -inis *f* copper rust, verdigris; money; corroding passion, envy, greed
aerumn·a -ae *f* trouble; distress; task; labor *(of Hercules)*
aerumnābil·is -is -e *adj* distressing
aerumnōs·us -a -um *adj* full of troubles, distressed; causing distress, calamitous
aes aeris *n* copper, bronze; bronze object; armor; statue; utensil; trumpet; money, cash; bronze coin, a copper; inscribed bronze tablet; payment; reward; **aes album** *(or* **candidum)** brass; **aes aliēnum** debt; **aes et lībra** *(leg)* (symbolical) copper coin and scales *(used in transactions over property, emancipation of slaves, etc.);* **aes mīlitāre** military pay; **in meō aere sum** I am free of debt
Aeschin·ēs -is *m* famous Athenian orator and opponent of Demosthenes ‖ Milesian orator contemporary of Cicero ‖ follower of Socrates
Aeschyl·us -ī *m* Athenian tragic poet *(525–456 B.C.)*
Aesculāp·ius -(i)ī *m* god of medicine
aesculēt·um -ī *n* **(ēsc-)** oak forest
aescule·us -a -um *adj* oak
aescul·us -ī *f* **(ēsc-)** Italian oak
Aeserni·a -ae *f* town in Samnium
Aesernīn·us -a -um *adj* of Aesernia
Aes·ōn -onis *m* Aeson *(father of Jason)*
Aesonid·ēs -ae *m* son of Aeson *(Jason)*
Aesoni·us -a -um *adj* of Aeson, of Jason
Aesōp·us -ī *m* Aesop
aest·ās -ātis *f* summer; summer heat, summer weather
aestif·er -era -erum *adj* sultry; *(of a constellation)* that brings on the hot weather
aestimābil·is -is -e *adj* valuable
aestimāti·ō -ōnis *f* **(-tum-)** appraisal, assessment; esteem; worth, value; **lītis** *(or* **lītium)** **aestimātiō** *(leg)* assessment of damages *or* penalty; **possessiōnum et rērum aestimātiō** real estate appraisal
aestimāt·or -ōris *m* appraiser
aestim·ō -āre -āvī -ātus *tr* **(-tum-)** to appraise, rate, value, estimate; to esteem highly; to judge; to consider, think; *(w. gen or abl of value)* to consider worth; **lītem (lītēs) aestimāre** *(leg)* to assess the damages; **magnī** *(or* **parvī) aestimāre** to consider *(s.th. or s.o.)* worth much *(or* little)
aestīv·a -ōrum *npl* summer camp; campaign season, campaign; summer pastures; cattle
aestīvē *adv* scantily *(clad)*
aestīv·ō -āre -āvī -ātum *intr* to spend the summer
aestīv·us -a -um *adj* summer; **occāsus aestīvus** northwest; **oriēns aestīvus** northeast
aestuār·ium -(i)ī *n* estuary, lagoon; marsh; air shaft
aestu·ō -āre -āvī -ātum *intr* to boil, seethe; to burn, glow; to undulate, swell; to be tossed, heave; to waver; to be in heat, be all worked up
aestuōsē *adv* hotly, impetuously
aestuōs·us -a -um *adj* sultry; billowy; raging, seething; passionate; wavering
aest·us -ūs *m* agitation, anxiety, restlessness; glow, heat, sultriness; surge, billows; tide; **minuente aestū** at low tide
aet·ās -ātis *f* lifetime, age; period of life; generation; passage of time; age group; era; **aetātem agere** to spend one's life; **aetātem exigere** to live out one's life; **id** *(or* **hōc) aetātis** at this time of life; **media** *(or* **cōnstāns,** *or* **firmāta) aetās** middle age; **prōvecta aetās** old age
aetātul·a -ae *f* tender age
aeternit·ās -ātis *f* eternity; immortality; *(of things)* durability; courtesy title of the Emperor
aeternō *adv* forever
aetern·ō -āre *tr* to perpetuate, immortalize
aeternum *adv* forever; constantly
aetern·us -a -um *adj* eternal, everlasting, immortal; imperishable; durable; permanent, enduring a lifetime; *(of events)* remembered for ever; **in aeternum** forever
aeth·ēr -eris *m* upper air *(opp:* **āēr); sky, heaven; upper world *(opp:* Hades)
aetheri·us -a -um *adj* ethereal, heavenly; of the upper world; **ignēs aetheriī** inspiration
Aethiopi·a -ae *f* Ethiopia
Aethi·ops -opis *m* Ethiopian; black man; *(poet)* Egyptian
aethr·a -ae *f* pure air, serene sky; air, sky, heavens
Aethr·a -ae *f* wife of Aegeus and mother of Theseus ‖ daughter of Oceanus and mother of Hyas ‖ wife of Hyperion
Aetn·a -ae *or* **Aetn·ē -ēs** *f* Mt. Etna
Aetnae·us -a -um *adj* of Etna; **frātrēs Aetnaeī** the Cyclopes
Aetōli·a -ae *f* district in N.W. Greece
Aetōlic·us *or* **Aetōli·us -a -um** *adj* Aetolian

Aetōl·us -a -um adj of Aetolia, Aetolian; of Diomedes; of Meleager, like those of Meleager; of Tydeus **II** mpl Aetolians
aevit·ās -ātis f age, lifetime
aev·um -ī n or **aev·us -ī** m age, lifetime, life; time, period; generation; eternity; **ad hōc aevī** hitherto; **aevō** (or **aevīs**) for ages; **aevum agere** (or **agitāre, dēgere, exigere**) to spend one's life; **ex ineunte aevō** from one's earliest years; **in** (or **per**) **(omne) aevum** forever; **prīmum aevum** early youth
Ā·fer -fra -frum adj African; **Āfer turbō** S.W. Wind **II** m African **II** Publius Terentius Afer (i.e., Terence, playwright, d. 159 B.C.) **II** mpl Africans; inhabitants of the Roman province of N. Africa
affābil·is -is -e adj (adf-) affable; kind
affābilit·ās -ātis f (adf-) affability
affabrē adv (adf-) skillfully, ingeniously
affatim or **ad fatim** adv (adf-) sufficiently, enough
affātur (adf-) see **affor**
affātus pp of **affor**
affāt·us -ūs m (adf-) address, discourse
affectāti·ō -ōnis f (adf-) disposition, state of mind; affectation, conceit
affectāt·or -ōris m (adf-) (w. gen) aspirant to
affectāt·us -a -um adj (adf-) affected
affecti·ō -ōnis f (adf-) frame of mind, mood; feeling; attitude, point of view; inclination, partiality; affection
affect·ō -āre -āvī -ātus tr (adf-) to grasp; to strive after, aim at, aspire to (power); to try to win over; to affect, feign; (w. inf) to aim to; **dextrā affectāre** to lay one's hand on, seize; **iter** (or **viam**) **affectāre** to set out on a journey; **spem affectāre** to cherish a hope
affectus pp of **afficiō** (adf-)
affect·us -a -um adj (adf-) furnished, provided; gifted; weakened, sick; affected, moved, touched
affect·us -ūs m (adf-) state, disposition, mood; feeling, emotion; affection
afferō afferre attulī allātus tr (adf-) to bring; to carry, convey; to report, announce; to introduce; to quote; to apply, employ, exert, exercise; to produce, cause, occasion; to impart; to allege; to assign; to contribute; to help; to offer for sale; **auxilium** (or **opem**) **afferre** to bring help; **causam afferre** (w. gen or dat) to be the cause of; **in iūdicium causam afferre** to prefer charges; **manūs afferre** (w. dat) to lay violent hands on, attack
af·ficiō -ficere -fēcī -fectus tr (adf-) to treat, handle, manage; to influence, move; to attack, afflict; to impair; (w. adv) to treat (in a certain way); (abl and verb may be rendered by the English verb corresponding to

the Latin abl): **cruce afficere** to crucify; **honōribus afficere** to honor; **suppliciō afficere** to punish
af·fīgō -fīgere -fīxī -fīxus tr (adf-) (w. dat or ad) to fasten, attach, nail to; to apply (as a remedy); **animō affīgere** to impress on the mind
af·fingō -fingere -fīnxī -fictus tr (adf-) to form, fashion besides; to make up, invent (in a bad sense); (w. dat) **1** to attach, affix, add, join, contribute (s.th.) to; **2** to connect with, associate with; **3** to ascribe to, impute to
affīn·is -is -e adj (adf-) adjoining, neighboring; related by marriage; (w. dat or ad) taking part in, privy to, associated with; subject to (an affliction) **II** mf neighbor; in-law
affīnit·ās -ātis f (adf-) affinity, connection; relationship by marriage
affirmātē adv (adf-) with solemn assurance, positively
affirmāti·ō -ōnis f (adf-) affirmation, assertion, declaration; emphasis
affirm·ō -āre -āvī -ātus tr (adf-) to strengthen; to confirm, encourage; to assert
affīx·us -a -um pp of **affīgō** (adf-) **II** adj (w. dat) **1** (of guards, attendants) assigned to; **2** attached to, devoted to; **3** intent on
afflāt·us -ūs m (adf-) blast, breeze; breath; inspiration
affl·eō -ēre tr (adf-) to weep at
afflīctāti·ō -ōnis f affliction
afflīct·ō -āre -āvī -ātus tr (adf-) to strike repeatedly; (of storms) to toss about; to shatter, damage; to trouble, distress, torment; (mil) to harass **II** refl & pass to be troubled
afflīct·or -ōris m (adf-) subverter
afflīct·us -a -um adj (adf-) damaged, shattered; downhearted; vile
af·flīgō -flīgere -flīxī -flīctus tr (adf-) to knock down; to batter; to injure, damage; to distress, afflict; (fig) to crush
affl·ō -āre -āvī -ātus tr (adf-) to blast (w. heat, lightning); (w. dat) **1** to breathe on, blow on; **2** to impart to **II** intr (of winds) to blow; (of smells) to be wafted; to blow favorably **II** pass (of sounds or smells) to carry toward
afflu·ēns -entis adj (adf-) flowing; affluent; abounding, numerous
affluenter adv (adf-) lavishly, abundantly
affluenti·a -ae f (adf-) flow; abundance; extravagance
afflu·ō -ere -xī -xum intr (adf-) (w. dat or ad) **1** to flow to or toward, glide by; **2** to flock to; (w. abl) to abound in
af·for -fārī -fātus sum tr (adf-) (of this defective verb, the chief forms in use are pres indic **affātur, affāminī, affantur;** pres impv **affāre;** inf **affārī;** pp **affātus**) to address, accost **II** pass to be destined

affore = **adfutūrus esse** (*fut inf of* **adsum**)
afforem = **adessem** (*imperf subj of* **adsum**)
afformīd·ō -āre *intr* (**adf-**) to get scared
afful·geō -gēre -sī *intr* (**adf-**) to shine, beam; to dawn; to appear; (*w. dat*) to shine on
af·fundō -fundere -fūdī -fūsus *tr* (**adf-**) (*w. dat*) 1 to pour, sprinkle (*s.th.*) on; 2 to send *or* dispatch (*s.o.*) to ‖ *refl & pass* (*w. dat*) to prostrate oneself before
aflu·ō -ere -xī *intr* (**abf-**) to flow away; to be abundant; (*w. abl*) to abound in; (*w.* **ex**) to issue from, come from
āfore = **āfutūrus esse** (*fut inf of* **absum**)
āforem = **abessem** (*imperf subj of* **absum**)
Afrāni·us -a -um *adj* Roman clan name (*nomen*), *esp.* Lucius Afranius (*comic poet*) ‖ Lucius Afranius (*one of Pompey's generals*)
Āfric·a -ae *f* originally the district of Carthage, made a Roman province after the 3rd Punic War in 146 B.C.; continent of Africa; (*fig*) inhabitants of Africa
Āfricān·us -a -um *adj* African ‖ *m* Roman honorary name (*agnomen*) conferred upon the two Scipios
Āfric·us -a -um *adj* African ‖ *m* S.W. wind
āfuī *perf of* **absum**
āfutūrus *fut p of* **absum**
Agamēmn·ōn -onis *m* king of Mycenae, son of Atreus and Aërope, brother of Menelaus, murdered by his wife Clytemnestra
Agamēmnonid·ēs -ae *m* son of Agamemnon (*i.e., Orestes*)
Agamēmnoni·us -a -um *adj* of Agamemnon, descended from Agamemnon
Aganipp·ē -ēs *f* fountain on Mt. Helicon sacred to the Muses
agās·ō -ōnis *m* stable boy; driver; lackey
Agathocl·ēs -is *m* king of Sicily, son of a potter, famous for his war with Carthage over the possession of Sicily (*361–287 B.C.*)
Agāv·ē -ēs *f* wife of Echion, king of Thebes, and mother of Pentheus
agedum *interj* come on!; well!
agell·us -ī *m* little field, plot
agēm·a -atis *n* (*mil*) honor guard
Agēn·or -oris *m* son of Belus, king of Phoenicia, father of Cadmus and Europa, and ancestor of Dido
Agēnorid·ēs -ae *m* descendant of Agenor (*esp. Cadmus, Perseus*)
ag·ēns -entis *pres p of* **agō** ‖ *adj* powerful, striking ‖ *mpl* secret police (*under the Empire*)
a·ger -grī *m* (arable) land, (tilled) field (*opp:* **campus** = untilled, open land); ground; soil; farm, estate; territory, land, district; country (*opp:* **urbs**); **ager pūblicus** state-owned land; **in agrum** in depth (*opp:* **in fronte** in frontage) ‖ *mpl* countryside

agg·er -eris *m* rubble; soil; rampart; breakwater; dike, dam; fortification; ramp; pile, heap, collection; ridge, mound, hill; funeral pyre; — **rīpae** bank (*of river);* — (**viae**) causeway
agger·ō -āre -āvī -ātus *tr* to pile up, fill up; to amass; to increase; (*fig*) to stimulate, intensify
ag·gerō -gerere -gessī -gestus *tr* (**adg-**) to bring forward; to pile up; (*w. dat*) to heap (*accusations, benefits*) on
aggest·us -ūs *m* (**adg-**) accumulation; terrace
agglomer·ō -āre -āvī -ātus *tr* (**adg-**) to gather together ‖ *refl & intr* to gather
agglūtin·ō -āre -āvī -ātus *tr* (**adg-**) to glue, paste; to solder ‖ *refl* (*w.* **ad**) to stick close to
aggravēsc·ō -ere *intr* (**adg-**) to grow heavy; (*of diseases*) to get worse
aggrav·ō -āre -āvī -ātus *tr* (**adg-**) to weigh down; to make (*conditions*) worse, aggravate; to increase the force of (*a blow);* (*fig*) to burden, oppress
ag·gredior -gredī -gressus sum *tr* (**adg-**) to approach; to address; to attack; (*w. inf*) to undertake to ‖ *intr* (*w.* **ad**) (*fig*) to tackle
aggreg·ō -āre -āvī -ātus *tr* (**adg-**) to assemble; (*w.* **in** *acc*) include (in); to implicate; (*leg*) (*w. dat*) to lump together with ‖ *refl & pass* to flock together; (*w. dat or* **ad**) to join
aggressi·ō -ōnis *f* (**adg-**) attack; (*rhet*) introduction
aggressus *pp of* **aggredior** (**adg-**)
agil·is -is -e *adj* agile, nimble, quick; busy, active; easily moved, mobile
agilit·ās -ātis *f* agility, nimbleness, quickness; activity; mobility
agitābil·is -is -e *adj* mobile
agitāti·ō -ōnis *f* motion, movement, agitation; activity; waving (*of arms*)
agitāt·or -ōris *m* driver; charioteer
agit·ō -āre -āvī -ātus *tr* to set in motion; to drive on, impel; to hunt; to scour (*for game);* to brandish, wave (*weapon);* to pursue (*an objective);* to shake (*reins);* to drive (*vehicle);* to ride (*horse);* to tend (*flocks);* to urge, support, insist on; to practice (*justice, a trade*); to exercise (*the body*); to engage in (*conversation*); to enjoy (*peace, fame*); to observe, celebrate; to obey, carry out; to spend, pass (*time);* to toss, disturb; to distress; to stimulate, arouse (*the mind, emotions);* to deride, insult; to criticize; to discuss; to cherish (*hope);* **sēcum** (*or* **animō** *or* **mente**) **agitāre** to think about, consider, ponder; (*w. indirect question*) to debate (*in one's mind*) ‖ *intr* to live, spend one's life
Āglaur·ōs -ī *f* daughter of Cecrops
agm·en -inis *n* herd, flock, troop, crowd; body, mass; army column; procession; retinue, escort; course, flow (*of a stream);* movement

(of oars); **agmen claudere** *(or* **cōgere)** to bring up the rear; **agmen dūcere** to form the van; **agmen prīmum** the van; **agmine** *(or* **ūnō agmine** *or* **agmine factō)** in marching formation; in a body

agn·a -ae *f* lamb *(female)*

ag·nāscor -nāscī -nātus sum *intr* to be born subsequently *(after the father has made his will);* **testāmentum agnāscendō rumpitur** a will is broken by the subsequent birth (of a son)

agnāti·ō -ōnis *f* blood relationship *(on the father's side)*

agnāt·us -ī *m* relative *(on the father's side)*

agnell·us -ī *m* little lamb

agnīn·a -ae *f* mutton, lamb

agniti·ō -ōnis *f* recognition, acknowledgement, admission; knowledge

ag·nōscō -nōscere -nōvī -nitus *tr* to recognize, identify; to acknowledge; to own up to, admit to

agn·us -ī *m* lamb

agō agere ēgī āctus *tr* to drive, lead, conduct; to chase, hunt; to drive away, steal; to spend *(time);* to do; to manage, administer, carry on; to transact; to discuss; to play, act the part of; to plead *(a case);* to exercise, practice; to hold *(an office);* to celebrate *(triumph);* to work at, be busy on; to have in mind, plan; to push *(siege works)* forward; to emit *(smoke, flames);* to trace *(one's descent);* (*fig*) to dispel *(fear, hunger, etc.);* to spend, pass *(time, life);* *(of plants)* to put forth *(roots, sprouts);* to drive *(chariot);* to sail *(ship);* to construct *(anything linear: rampart, tunnel);* **agere fūrtī** to accuse of theft *or* robbery; **agere reum** to indict a defendant; **aliud** *(or* **aliam rem) agere** not to attend to one's business; **animam agere** to breathe one's last; **grātiās agere** to thank; **in crucem agere** to crucify; **iter** *(or* **cursum) agere** to make one's way; **nūgās agere** to act foolishly; **praedam** *(or* **bovēs) agere** to rustle cattle; **prīmās partēs agere** to play the lead role; **proelium agere** to do battle; **quid agis?** how do you do? **quō agis?** what's your point?; **satis agere** to have more than enough to do; **spūmās agere** to foam *(at the mouth)* ‖ *refl* to go, come; to grow; to behave, comport oneself ‖ *pass* to be done, happen, occur, come to pass; to be involved, be at stake; **bene agitur** things turn out well; **quid agitur?** what's going on? ‖ *intr* to take action, act; to be busy; to bargain; to live, dwell; *(theat)* to act; **age!** come on!; *(in assent)* O.K., very well; **bene (male) agere cum aliquō** to treat s.o. well (badly); **cum populō** *(or* **ad populum) agere** to address the people; **quō tū agis?** where are you off to?

-**āg·ō -inis** *fem suf* mostly formed from verbs in -**āre: imāgō** image; also from other sources: **cartilāgō** cartilage

ag·ōn -ōnis *m* contest

agrāri·us -a -um *adj* agrarian, land ‖ *mpl* land-reform party

agrest·is -is -e *adj* rustic, country; boorish; wild, uncultivated *(plants);* savage; uncivilized ‖ *m* peasant, rustic

agricol·a -ae *m* farmer, peasant

Agricol·a -ae *m* Gnaeus Julius Agricola *(father-in-law of Tacitus)*

agricultūr·a -ae *f* agriculture

Agrigent·um -ī *n* city on S. coast of Sicily *(modern Agrigento)*

agripet·a -ae *m* colonist, settler

Agripp·a -ae *m* Marcus Vipsanius Agrippa *(son-in-law of Augustus, husband of Julia, and father of Agrippina)*

Agrippīn·a -ae *f* Vipsania Agrippina *(daughter of Agrippa, wife of Tiberius and mother of Drusus, d. A.D. 20)* ‖ Vipsania Agrippina Major *(wife of Germanicus and mother of Caligula, d. A.D. 33)* ‖ Julia Agrippina Minor *(daughter of the previous Agrippina and Germanicus, and mother of Nero, murdered by Nero in A.D. 59)*

āh *interj (denoting various feelings: distress, pity, regret; surprise, joy; contempt; entreaty)* ah!, ha!, oh!

aha *interj (denoting surprise, irony)* aha!

ai *interj (denoting grief)* ah!

Āi·āx -ācis *m* son of Telamon *(king of Salamis)* ‖ son of Oïleus *(king of the Locri)*

āin = **aisne** *(see* **āiō)**

āiō *tr & intr (used mainly in pres and imperf indic; opp:* **negō)** I say; I say yes, I say so; I assert, tell relate; **ain** (= **aisne) tandem?** *(or* **ain tū?** *or* **ain tūte** *or* **ain vērō?)** *(coll) (expressing surprise)* do you really mean it?, you don't say!, really?

-**al -ālis** *neut suf* forms neuter nouns: **animal** animal; **cubital** elbow cushion

āl·a -ae *f* wing; armpit; squadron *(of cavalry);* flank *(of battle line);* reef *(of a sail)*

alabas·ter -trī *m,* **alabastr·um -ī** *n* perfume box

ala·cer *or* **ala·cris -cris -cre** *adj* lively, brisk; quick; eager; active; cheerful

alacrit·ās -ātis *f* liveliness, briskness; quickness; eagerness; cheerfulness

alap·a -ae *f* slap; ceremonius slap given to a slave at emancipation

ālār·is -is -e *adj (mil)* consisting of auxiliary cavalry

ālāri·us -a -um *adj* consisting of auxiliary troops ‖ *mpl* auxiliaries, allies

ālāt·us -a -um *adj* winged

alaud·a -ae *f* lark

Alb·a -ae *f* town *(also called Alba Longa)* founded by Ascanius

Albān·ī -ōrum *mpl* inhabitants of Alba Longa

Albān·um -ī *n* Alban estate; Alban wine

albāt·us -a -um *adj* dressed in white

alb·eō -ēre -uī *intr* to be white

albēsc·ō -ere *intr* to turn white, whiten; to dawn; *(of hair)* to turn grey

albic·ō -āre -āvī -ātum *or* **albic·or -ārī -ātus sum** *intr* to be white, be whitish

albid·us -a -um *adj* white, whitish

Albi·ōn -ōnis *f* Britain

albitūd·ō -inis *f* whiteness

Albul·a -ae *f* earlier name of the Tiber River

albul·us -a -um *adj* whitish

alb·um -ī *n* white; record, list, register; white tablet: **1** = the Annales Maximi *(the record of the year's event, kept by the Pontifex Maximus;* **2** the tablet on which the edicts of the praetor were posted in public; **3** list or register of names, e.g., of senators or jurors, etc.

Albune·a -ae *f* fountain at Tibur; nymph of that fountain

alb·us -a -um *adj* flat white; bright, shining, clear *(sky, light, sun, etc.);* favorable; clad in white; light-skinned, fair; whitened, made white; favorable, auspicious; grey *(hair);* pale *(from fear, sickness);* **album opus** stucco work; **albus āterne sit nēscīre** not to know a person from Adam *(literally, not to know whether he is white or black)* ‖ *m* white man

Alcae·us -ī *m* Greek lyric poet from the Island of Lesbos *(fl. 610 B.C.)*

alcēd·ō -inis *f* kingfisher, halcyon

alcēdōni·a -ōrum *npl* halcyon days; *(fig)* deep calm, tranquillity

alc·ēs -is *f* elk

Alcēst·is -is *or* **Alcēst·ē -ēs** *f* Alcestis *(loyal wife of Admetus, king of Pherae, who gave up her life to save the life of her husband; she was rescued by Hercules and given back to Admetus)*

Alc·ēus -eī *and* **-eos** *m* father of Amphitryon and grandfather of Hercules

Alcibiad·ēs -ae *or* **-is** *or* **-ī** *m* Athenian politician, disciple of Socrates *(450?–404 B.C.)*

Alcīd·ēs -ae *m* descendant of Alceus *(esp. Hercules)*

Alcimed·ē -ēs *f* wife of Aeson and mother of Jason

Alcino·üs -ī *m* king of the Phaeacians, who entertained Ulysses

Alcitho·ē -ēs *f* daughter of Minyas of Thebes, changed into a bat for ridiculing Bacchic rites

Alc(u)mēn·a -ae *or* **Alcmēn·ē -ēs** *f* Alcmene *(wife of Amphitryon and mother of Hercules by Jupiter)*

alcy·ōn -onis *f* (hal-) halcyon *(bird believed to build its nest on the sea)*

Alcyon·ē -ēs *or* **Alcyon·a -ae** *f* (Hal-) Alcyone *(daughter of Aeolus and wife of Cyex both of whom were changed into halcyons)* ‖ wife of Meleager ‖ one of the Pleiades

āle·a -ae *f* dice game; gambling; die; risk, gamble; **āleā lūdere** to gamble; **iacta ālea est** the die is cast

āleāri·us -a -um *adj* gambling

āleāt·or -ōris *mf* gambler

āleātōri·us -a -um *adj* gambling

ālēc *see* **allēc**

Ālect·ō -ūs *f* one of the three Furies

āle·ō -ōnis *m* gambler

āl·es -itis *adj* winged ‖ *mf* winged creature, bird ‖ *m* poet; Cupid ‖ *f* augury, omen

alēsc·ō -ere *intr* to grow up

Alexan·der -drī *m* Paris *(son of Priam and Hecuba)* ‖ Alexander the Great *(son of Philip II and Olympias, and king of Macedonia, 356–323 B.C.)* ‖ son of Perseus *(king of Macedonia)* ‖ a tyrant of Pherae in Thessaly ‖ a king of Epirus

Alexandrē·a -ae *f* **(-drī·a)** Alexandria (Greek city of N. Egypt, founded by Alexander the Great)

Alexandrīn·us -a -um *adj* Alexandrine; characteristic of Alexandria *(i.e., luxurious)*

alg·a -ae *f* seaweed

alg·ēns -entis *adj* cold; **algēns toga** thin toga

alg·eō -ēre ālsī *intr* to be cold; to feel cold; to endure cold; *(fig)* to be left out in the cold

al·gēscō -gēscere ālsī *intr* to catch a cold

algid·us -a -um *adj* cold

Algid·us -a -um *adj* of Mt. Algidus ‖ *m* mountain in Latium, S. of Tusculum

alg·or -ōris *m* cold; fit of shivering

alg·us -ūs *m* the cold

ali- *a stem meaning* else, different, other, *e.g.,* **alius;** *but when combined with* **quis, quam, cubi,** *etc., is translated* some or other, *e.g.,* **aliquis** someone or other, **alicubi** somewhere or other

aliā *adv* by another way

aliās *adv* at another time, at other times; previously; subsequently; in other circumstances, otherwise; apart from this, in any case, besides; all the same, nevertheless; **aliās ... aliās** at one time ... at another, sometimes ... sometimes

āliāt·um -ī *n* food flavored with garlic

alibī *adv* elsewhere; otherwise, in other respects; in another passage *(in a book, speech);* **alibī ... alibī** in one place ... in another, here ... there; **alibī aliter** differently in different places; **alius alibī** one in one place, another in another

alic·a -ae *f* emmer *(type of wheat)*

alicāri·us -a -um *adj* of emmer ‖ *f* prostitute

ali·cubi *adv* somewhere or other; anywhere (at all); occasionally

ālicul·a -ae *f* light cape

ali·cunde *adv* from somewhere; from someone else

aliēnāti·ō -ōnis *f* transfer *(of property)*; alienation; aversion; **aliēnātiō mentis** insanity

aliēnigen·a -ae *m* foreigner, stranger *(born in another country)*

aliēn·ō -āre -āvī -ātus *tr* to transfer, sell; to give up *(children)* for adoption; to alienate, set at variance; to treat as an enemy; to remove, separate; to drive mad; **ā sēnsū aliēnāre** to deprive of feeling; **paene aliēnātā mentc** almost driven mad **‖** *pass* to fall into s.o. else's hands; *(mil)* to fall into the enemy's hands; *(w.* **ab)** to recoil from

aliēn·us -a -um *adj* another's; foreign; contrary; hostile; strange; unsuitable; incongruous, inconsistent; inconvenient; **aliēnum est** it is out-of-place, it is amiss **‖** *m* stranger, foreigner **‖** *n* another's property; foreign soil **‖** *npl* another's affairs

ālif·er *or* **ālig·er -era -erum** *adj* winged, wearing wings

alimentāri·us -a -um *adj* **(alum-)** relating to welfare

aliment·um -ī *n* **(alum-)** nourishment, food, provisions; fuel **‖** *npl* means of livelihood; alms

alimōni·a -ae *f or* **alimōn·ium -(i)ī** *n* nourishment, food; support; cost of living

aliō *adv* to another place, elsewhere; to another topic; to another policy; for another purpose; **aliō ... aliō** in one direction ... in another; **alius aliō** one in one direction, another in another

aliōquī(n) *adv* otherwise, in other respects, for the rest; apart from these considerations; besides; in general; in any case

aliōrsum *or* **aliōvorsum** *adv* **(-sus)** in another direction; in a diffcrent manner; in a different sense

ālip·ēs -edis *adj* wing-footed, swift-footed

alipt·ēs *or* **alipt·a -ae** *m* wrestling trainer, rubdown man

aliquā *adv* somehow; to some extent

aliquam *adv* to some degree; **aliquam multī** fairly many

aliquamdiū *adv* **(-quan-)** for some time; for a considerable distance

aliquandō *adv* sometime or other, once; at any time, ever; now and then; for once, now; finally, now at last; someday *(in the future)*

aliquantill·um -ī *n* a bit

aliquantisper *adv* for a while

aliquantō *adv* somewhat, to some extent, a little, rather

aliquantulum *adv* somewhat

aliquantul·us -a -um *adj* little **‖** *n* a small amount

aliquantum *adv* somewhat, a little, rather

aliquant·us -a -um *adj* considerable **‖** *n* a certain amount *(of);* a certain degree *(of);* a bit, a part

aliquātenus *adv* for some distance; to a certain extent; in some respects, partly; up to a point

ali·quī -qua -quod *adj* some; *(after a negative,* **sī,** *etc.)* any at all

aliquid *adv* to some extent

ali·quid -cūius *pron* something, anything; something important; **ad aliquid esse** *(of a term)* to be relative; **aliud aliquid** something else; **aliquid vīnī** some wine; **est aliquid** *(w. inf)* it is something to **‖** *adv* to some degree

ali·quis -cūius *pron* someone, somebody, anyone; someone important

aliquō *adv* to some place, somewhere

aliquot *indecl adj* some, several

aliquotiēns *adv* several times

aliquōvorsum *adv* in one direction or another

aliter *adv* otherwise, else; **aliter ... aliter** in one way ... in another; **aliter atque aliter** now in one way, now in another; **aliter esse** *or* **aliter sē habēre** to be different; **nōn** *(or* **haud) aliter quam** *(or* **ac) sī** just as if

alitus *pp of* **alō**

aliubi *adv* elsewhere; **aliubi ... aliubi** here ... there

āl·ium -(i)ī *n* **(all-)** garlic

aliunde *adv* from another place; **aliunde ... aliunde** from one place ... from another; **alius aliunde** one from one place, another from another

ali·us -a -ud *adj* (*gen singl is generally* **alterīus;** *dat:* **alterī**) another, other, different; *(w.* **ac, atque, et, nisi, quam)** other than **‖** *pron* another; **aliī ... aliī** some ... others; **alius ... alius** one . . . another, the one ... the other; **alius atque alius** first one person, then another; **alius ex aliō** one after another

al·lābor -lābī -lāpsus sum *intr* **(adl-)** to glide toward, slide toward, slip; *(of liquids)* to flow toward, approach; *(of missiles)* to fly toward, go sailing toward

allabōr·ō -āre *intr* **(adl-)** to work hard

allacrim·ō -āre *intr* **(adl-)** to weep

allāps·us -ūs *m* **(adl-)** slithering

allātr·ō -āre -āvī -ātus *tr* **(adl-)** to bark at; *(fig)* to revile; *(of sea)* to break against

allāt·us -a -um *pp of* **afferō (adf-)**

allaudābil·is -is -e *adj* praiseworthy

allaud·ō -āre *tr* **(adl-)** to praise highly

all·ēc -ēcis *n* **(hall-)** fish sauce

allēcti·ō -ōnis *f* **(adl-)** promotion, advancement

allect·ō -āre *tr* **(adl-)** to allure, entice

Allect·ō -ūs *f* (**Ālec-**) Alecto *(one of the three Furies)*

allēgāti·ō -ōnis *f* (**adl-**) intercession; allegation

allēgāt·us -ūs *m* (**adl-**) prompting, instigation **‖** *mpl* deputies

allēg·ō -āre -āvī -ātus *tr* (**adl-**) to commission; to deputize; to put up; to dispatch; to allege; to instigate; *(w. dat)* to lay *(prayers)* before

al·legō -legere -lēgī -lēctus *tr* (**adl-**) to select; to appoint *(to an office)*

allēgori·a -ae *f* allegory

allevāment·um -ī *n* (**adl-**) alleviation

allevāti·ō -ōnis *f* lifting; alleviating, easing

allev·ō -āre -āvī -ātus *tr* (**adl-**) to lift up, raise; to alleviate; to comfort; to lighten

Alli·a -ae *f* tributary of the Tiber where the Gauls defeated the Romans in 390 B.C.

allice·faciō -facere -fēcī -factus *tr* to entice, allure

al·liciō -licere -lexī -lectus *tr* (**adl-**) to attract; to bring on *(sleep);* to attract the attention of; to win over

allī·dō -dere -sī -sus *tr* (**adl-**) *(w. dat or ad or in + acc)* to dash *(s.th.)* against **‖** *pass* to be shipwrecked

Alliēns·is -is -e *adj* of the Allia River; of the battle at the Allia River

allig·ō -āre -āvī -ātus *tr* (**adl-**) to bind; to bandage *(wounds);* to tie up; to grip firmly; to hold together; to freeze solid; to curdle *(milk);* to curb, restrict; to fetter; to hinder, detain; to involve, implicate; *(w. ad)* to bind *(s.th.)* to; *(of laws)* to be binding on

al·linō -linere -lēvī -litus *tr* (**adl-**) to smudge; *(w. dat)* to smear *(s.th.)* on

all·ium -(i)ī *n* (**āli**) garlic

Allobrog·ēs -um *mpl* Gallic tribe in Gallia Narbonensis

allocūti·ō -ōnis *f* (**adl-**) address; pep talk

alloqu·ium -(i)ī *n* (**adl-**) address; conversation; reassuring words

allo·quor -quī -cūtus sum *tr* (**adl-**) to speak to, address; to invoke *(gods);* to console, comfort

allubēsc·ō -ere *intr* (**adl-**) to be lovely

allūc·eō -ēre -xī *intr* (**adl-**) *(w. dat)* to be a light for

allūdi·ō -āre *intr* (**adl-**) to play, frolic

allū·dō -dere -sī -sus *tr* (**adl-**) to play with **‖** *intr* to play, joke; *(of waves) (w. dat)* to lap; *(w. dat or ad)* to allude playfully to

allu·ō -ere -ī *tr* (**adl-**) *(of rivers, the sea)* to flow past, lap, touch; *(of water)* to touch, wet *(a part of the body)*

alluvi·ēs -ēī *f* (**adl-**) pool *(left by flood waters);* silt

alluvi·ō -ōnis *f* (**adl-**) flood; alluvial land

alm·us -a -um *adj* nourishing; kind, gracious; bountiful *(earth)*

aln·us -ī *f* alder tree; *(fig)* ship

al·ō -ere -uī -tus *or* **-itus** *tr* to nurse, breastfeed; to feed, nourish; to promote the growth of; to raise *(children, animals);* to support *(family, etc.);* *(of places, employment)* to provide a livelihood for; to foment *(discord);* to encourage; to promote the interests of; to increase; to strengthen

alo·ē -ēs *f (bot)* aloe *(whose bitter juice was used as a purgative);* bitterness

Alō·eus -eī *m* a son of Poseidon and Canace

alogi·a -ae *f* folly, nonsense

Alōïd·ae -ārum *mpl* the giants Otus and Ephialtes *(sons of Poseidon and Iphimedeia, the wife of Aloeus)*

Alp·ēs -ium *fpl* the Alps

alpha *indecl n* alpha *(first letter of the Greek alphabet)*

Alphē·us *or* **Alphī·us** *or* **Alphē·os -ī** *m* Alpheus *(chief river of the Peloponnesus)*

Alpic·us -a -um *adj* Alpine

Alpīn·us -a -um *adj* Alpine

alsī *perf of* **algeō** *and* **algēscō**

als(i)·us -a -um *adj* chilly, cold

altār·ia -ium *npl* altar; altars, high altars; burnt-offerings

altē *adv* high, on high, highly; from a great height; deeply, far, remotely; intensely, profoundly

alt·er -era -erum *adj* one *(of two);* a second, the second, the next **‖** *pron* one *(of two),* the one, the other; a second one, the second one, the next one; anyone else; another *(one's fellow man);* **alter ... alter** the one ... the other, the former ... the latter; **ūnus et** *(or* **aut) alter** one or two

alterās *adv* at another time

altercāti·ō -ōnis *f* altercation, dispute, argument; *(phil)* debate

altercāt·or -ōris *m* disputant, debater

alterc·ō -āre *or* **alterc·or -ārī -ātus sum** *intr* to argue, wrangle; to argue back and forth *(in court)*

alternīs *adv* by turns, alternately

altern·ō -āre -āvī -ātus *tr* to do by turns; to alternate, arrange in alternating order; to exchange **‖** *intr* to alternate

altern·us -a -um *adj* one after another, alternate; mutual; every other; **alternā vice** *(or* **alternīs vicibus)** alternately; in turn, successively; **in alternum** for one another, reciprocally; **īre per alternās vicēs** to go back and forth

alteru·ter -tra -trum *(fem also* **altera utra;** *neut also* **alterum utrum)** *adj* one *(of two),* either, one or the other **‖** *pron* one, either one, one or the other

Althae·a -ae *f* wife of Oeneus, king of Calydon, and mother of Meleager

alticīnct·us -a -um *adj* energetic
altil·is -is -e *adj* fattened, fat; *(fig)* rich ‖ *f* fattened fowl
altison·us -a -um *adj* sounding from on high; sublime
altiton·āns -antis *adj* thundering on high
altitūd·ō -inis *f* height; depth; *(fig)* profundity *(of mind);* loftiness *(of style);* **ad** *or* **in altitūdinem** vertically ‖ *fpl* the heights
altiusculē *adv* rather high
altiuscul·us -a -um *adj* rather high
altivol·āns -antis, altivol·us -a -um *adj* high-flying
alt·or -ōris *m* foster father
altrim secus *adv* on the other side
altrīnsecus *adv* on the other side
altr·īx -īcis *f* foster mother; wet nurse; *(of the earth)* nourisher; motherland
altrōvorsum *adv* (**-sus**) on the other hand
alt·us -a -um *adj* high; tall; deep; profound *(wisdom);* deep, loud *(sound);* intense *(heat, cold);* thick *(fog);* high-born, ancient *(lineage)* ‖ *n* high seas, the deep; heaven; **ab altō** from on high, from heaven; **ex altō** far-fetched; **ex altō petere** (*or* **repetere**) to go far afield for
ālūcin·or -ārī -ātus sum *intr* (**hāl-, allūc-**) to ramble on; to rave; to daydream
alumn·a -ae *f* foster daughter
alumn·us -ī *m* foster son
alūt·a -ae *f* soft leather; shoe; purse
alv(e)ār·ium -(i)ī *n* beehive
alveol·us -ī *m* bowl, basin; bathtub; river bed; game board
alve·us -ī *m* hollow; tub; bathtub; riverbed; hull of boat; game board; beehive
alv·us -ī *f (m)* belly, bowels, stomach; womb; rectum; boat; beehive; **alvum purgāre** (*or* **solvere**) to move the bowels; **alvus fūsa** (*or* **cita**) diarrhea
am- *pref see* **ambi-**
amābil·is -is -e *adj* lovable, lovely, attractive; delightful
amābilit·ās -ātis *f* attractiveness
amābiliter *adv* lovingly, delightfully
Amalthē·a -ae *f* nymph who fed infant Jupiter with goat's milk ‖ Cumaean sibyl
āmandāti·ō -ōnis *f* sending away
āmand·ō -āre -āvī -ātus *tr* (**amend-**) to send away
am·āns -antis *adj* loving, affectionate; **amāns patriae** patriotic ‖ *mf* lover
amanter *adv* lovingly, affectionately
āmanuēns·is -is *m* secretary
amārac·us -ī *mf and* **amārac·um -ī** *n* marjoram *(aromatic plants whose leaves are used as seasoning)*
amarant·us -ī *m* amaranth *(imaginary flower that never fades)*

amārē *adv* bitterly
amāriti·ēs -ēī *f* bitterness
amāritūd·ō -inis *f* bitterness; tang; sadness
amār·or -ōris *m* bitterness
amār·us -a -um *adj* bitter, pungent, tangy; shrill; brackish; **nux amāra** almond
Amaryll·is -idis *f* conventional name for a shepherdess
amāsi·ō -ōnis *m* lover
amāsiuncul·a -ae *f* darling
amāsiuncul·us -ī *m* lover
amās·ius -(i)ī *m* lover
amāt·a -ae *f* loved one
Amāt·a -ae *f* mother of Lavinia
Amath·ūs -untis *f* town in Cyprus
Amathūsiac·us -a -um *adj* of Amathus
Amathūsi·us -a -um *adj* of Amathus ‖ *f* Venus
amāti·ō -ōnis *f* love affair
amāt·or -ōris *m* lover; friend; **amātor patriae** patriot
amātorcul·us -ī *m* poor little lover
amātōriē *adv* lovingly
amātori·us -a -um *adj* erotic, love ‖ *n* love charm
amātr·īx -īcis *f* mistress, girlfriend
Amāz·ōn -onis *or* **Amāzon·is -idis** *f* Amazon
Amāzonic·us -a -um *adj* Amazonian
Amāzoni·us -a -um *adj* Amazonian
amb- *pref see* **ambi-**
ambact·us -ī *m* vassal
ambāg·ēs -is *f* a winding, labyrinth; double talk; roundabout way; digression; ambiguity, obscurity; **per ambāgēs** enigmatically
amb·edō -ēsse -ēdī -ēsus *tr* to eat up; to waste, squander; *(of fire)* to char
ambestr·īx -īcis *f* gluttonous woman
ambi- *pref (before vowels usually* **amb-;** *before consonants* **ambi-, am-, an-**) around
ambig·ō -ere *tr* to go around, avoid; to call into question, debate ‖ *intr* to waver, hesitate, be undecided; to argue, debate, wrangle ‖ *v impers* **ambigitur** it is uncertain
ambiguē *adv* indecisively; ambiguously; in an untrustworthy manner
ambiguit·ās -ātis *f* ambiguity
ambigu·us -a -um *adj* wavering, changeable; uncertain; disputed; unreliable, untrustworthy; ambiguous, dark, obscure ‖ *n* doubt, uncertainty; paradox
amb·iō -īre -īvī *or* **-iī -itus** *tr* to go the round of; to go around, encircle; to throng; to go round, go past; to embrace; to include; *(pol)* to campaign for ‖ *intr* to move in an orbit; to rotate
ambiti·ō -ōnis *f* ambition *(in good and bad sense);* popularity; flattery; partiality, favoritism; pomp, ostentation; *(pol)* campaigning *(by lawful means)*

ambitiōsē *adv* ambitiously; ostentatiously; from a desire to please

ambitiōs·us -a -um *adj* winding; publicity-conscious; ambitious; ostentatious; eager for popularity

ambit·us -ūs *m* winding, revolution; circuit, circumference, border; orbit; ostentation; circumlocution; *(pol)* illegal campaign practices, bribery; **ambitus verbōrum** *(or* **ōrātiōnis)** phrase; *(rhet)* rounded and balanced sentence, period

ambiv·ium -(i)ī *n* road junction

amb·ō -ae -ō *adj (dat & abl:* **ambōbus, ambābus;** *acc:* **ambō** *&* **ambōs)** both, two ‖ *pron* both, the two

Ambraci·a -ae *f* district of Epirus

Ambraciēns·is -is -e *adj* of Ambracia

Ambraciōt·ēs -ae *m* an Ambracian

Ambraci·us -a -um *adj* of Ambracia

ambrosi·a -ae *f* ambrosia *(food of the gods; imaginary healing plant)*

ambrosi·us -a -um *adj* (-e·us) ambrosial, divine

ambūbāi·a -ae *f* Syrian singer and courtesan ‖ *(bot)* wild endive

ambulācr·um -ī *n* walk, avenue

ambulāti·ō -ōnis *f (act; place)* walk

ambulātiuncul·a -ae *f* short walk; small promenade

ambulāt·or -ōris *m* stroller *(person);* idler, loafer; peddler

ambulātōri·us -a -um *adj* movable

ambul·ō -āre -āvī -ātus *tr* to traverse, travel ‖ *intr* to walk, take a walk; to march; to travel; to strut; *(of things)* to extend, run; **bene ambulā!** bon voyage!

amb·ūrō -ūrere -ūssī -ūstus *tr* to burn up; to scorch, char; to scald; to cremate; *(of cold)* to numb, nip

ambūstulāt·us -a -um *adj* half-roasted

ambūstus *pp of* **ambūrō** ‖ *n* a burn

amell·us -ī *m (bot)* wild aster *(plant having daisylike flowers of various colors)*

ām·ēns -entis *adj* insane; foolish, stupid

āmenti·a -ae *f* insanity; folly

āment·ō -āre -āvī -ātus *tr* (amm-) to fit *(a javelin)* with a strap

āment·um -ī *n* (amm-) strap, thong

Ameri·a -ae *f* town in Umbria, noted for its osiers *(modern Amelia)*

Amerīn·us -a -um *adj* of Ameria; produced in Ameria ‖ *m* Amerian

am·es -itis *m* pole for fowler's net; fence rail

amethystināt·us -a -um *adj* dressed in violet-blue

amethystin·us -a -um *adj* violet-blue; set with amethysts ‖ *npl* violet-blue garments

amethyst·us -ī *f* amethyst

amfrāctus *see* anfrāctus

amīc·a -ae *f* girlfriend, lady friend; mistress

amīcē *adv* in a friendly way

am·iciō -icīre -icuī *or* -īxī -ictus *tr* to wrap around; to cover, clothe, wrap

amīciter *adv* in a friendly way

amīciti·a -ae *f* friendship; alliance, ties of friendship *(between nations);* **amīcitiam comparāre** *(or* **contrahere, iungere, facere)** cum *(w. abl)* to form an alliance *(or* league of friendship) with; **amīcitiam gerere** to carry on a friendship; **amīcitiam dīrumpere** to break off a friendship, sever ties of friendship; **in amīcitiā esse** to be on terms of friendship

amīciti·ēs -ēī *f see* amīcitia

amictori·um -ī *n* wrap

amictus *pp of* **amiciō**

amict·us -ūs *m* wrap, cloak; clothing; fashion *(in dress),* style *(in dress);* headdress used in worship

amīcul·a -ae *f* girlfriend, mistress

amīcul·um -ī *n* wrap, mantle ‖ *npl* clothing

amīcul·us -ī *m* dear friend; pal, buddy

amīc·us -a -um *adj* friendly; supportive; favorable, congenial; helpful; dear, welcome; **amīcus reīpūblicae** patriotic ‖ *m* friend; lover; partisan, supporter; companion, disciple; **amīcus reīpūblicae** patriot ‖ *f see* amīca

āmigr·ō -āre *intr* to move (away)

Amilcar *see* **Hamilcar**

āmissi·ō -ōnis *f* loss

āmissus *pp of* **āmittō**

āmiss·us -ūs *m* = āmissiō

amit·a -ae *f* aunt *(father's sister; mother's sister is* **mātertera); magna amita** great aunt

Amitern·um -ī *n* town in the Sabine district, birthplace of Sallust

ā·mittō -mittere -mīsī -missus *tr* to lose; to let slip, miss; to let go, release; to let fall, drop; **animam** *(or* **spīritum) āmittere** to lose one's life; **fidem āmittere** to break one's word; **spē āmissā** having given up hope

amm- = **adm-**

amment·ō -āre *see* **āmentō**

amment·um -ī *n* (āmen-) strap

Amm·ōn *or* **Hamm·ōn -ōnis** *m* an Ethiopian god, identical with Jupiter and represented as a ram

amnicol·a -ae *mf* riverside plant

amnicul·us -ī *m* brook

amn·is -is *m (f)* river; river water; **adversō amnī** upstream; **secundō amnī** downstream

am·ō -āre -āvī -ātus *tr* to love, like, be fond of; to fall in love with; **amābō (tē)** *(coll)* please ‖ *intr* to be in love

amoenē *adv* charmingly, pleasantly

amoenit·ās -ātis *f* charm

amoen·us -a -um *adj* charming, pleasant *(esp. to sight)* ‖ *npl* pleasant places āmōl·ior -īrī *tr* to remove; to put aside, put away; to get rid of, shake *(a person)*; to put out of the way, dispose of *(a person)*; to refute ‖ *refl* to remove oneself, clear out

amōm·um -ī *n (bot)* spice plant; spice obtained from this plant

am·or -ōris *m* love; affection; object of affection, love; liking, fondness, attachment; strong desire, yearning; love song; Cupid; *(w. in + acc,* ergā *+ acc)* affection for, love of; amor patriae patriotism ‖ *mpl* love affair

āmōti·ō -ōnis *f* removal

ā·moveō -movēre -mōvī -mōtus *tr* to remove; to withdraw, put away; to lay aside *(suspicion, etc.);* to get rid of; to banish; to deprive of rights; to dispel *(fear);* to steal; ex animō āmovēre to put out of one's mind ‖ *refl* to retire, withdraw

Amphiarā·üs -ī *m* famous Greek seer, son of Oecle(u)s *(or* Apollo) and Hypermestra, one of the Seven against Thebes

Amphiarēïad·ēs -ae *m* descendant of Amphiaraüs, his son Alcmaeon

amphiboli·a -ae *f* ambiguity, double meaning

Amphictyon·es -um *mpl* the representatives of the confederated Greek states who met in Thermopylae, later at Delphi

Amphilochi·a -ae *f* small district at the E. end of the Ambracian Gulf

Amphiloch·us -ī *m* son of Amphiaraüs, and founder of Argos Amphilochium *(the chief town of Amphilochia)*

Amphī·ō(n) -onis *m* son of Zeus and Antiope, twin brother of Zethus, and husband of Niobe

Amphīoni·us -a -um *adj* of Amphion

Amphipol·is -is *f* town in Macedonia near the mouth of the Strymon

amphitheātr·um -ī *n* amphitheater

Amphitrīt·ē -ēs *f* wife of Neptune; *(fig)* the sea

Amphitry·ō(n) *or* Amphitru·ō -ōnis *m* husband of Alcmena

Amphitryōniad·ēs -ae *m* Hercules

amphor·a -ae *f* amphora; liquid measure *(c. 7 gallons)*

ampl·a -ae *f* opportunity

amplē *adv* amply; grandly, splendidly

am·plector -plectī -plexus sum *tr* to embrace, hug; to cling to; to accept gladly, welcome; to comprise, extend over, cover, include; to encircle *(enemy forces);* to grasp, grip; to understand; *(of serpent)* to coil itself around; *(mil)* to occupy

amplex·ō -āre *or* amplex·or -ārī -ātus sum *tr* to embrace; to welcome; to cling to, grasp; to espouse, cherish

amplex·us -ūs *m* circuit; embrace, caress; coil *(of snake)*

amplificāti·ō -ōnis *f* extension, enlargement; *(rhet)* amplification

amplificāt·or -ōris *m* amplifier, enhancer

amplificē *adv* splendidly

amplific·ō -āre -āvī -ātus *tr* to enlarge, extend, widen; to increase; to extol; *(rhet)* to enlarge upon, develop

ampli·ō -āre -āvī -ātus *tr* to widen, enlarge; to enhance; to postpone *(judgment);* to adjourn *(court in order to gather more evidence);* to magnify, glorify; *(leg)* to postpone *(trial)*

ampliter *adv* splendidly; fully, very

amplitūd·ō -inis *f* width, size, bulk, extent; greatness, dignity, importance; high rank; *(rhet)* amplification, development

amplius *adv* any further, any more, any longer; besides; further, more, longer; more than *(without quam);* amplius centum cīvēs Rōmānī *(without quam)* more than a hundred Roman citizens; amplius hōc what is more, in addition; amplius ūnō diē one day longer; nec amplius no longer; nēmō amplius no one else; nihil amplius nothing else; quid amplius (quam) what else (than) ‖ *n* more, a larger amount *or* number; amplius negōtī more trouble

ampliusculē *adv* rather more freely

ampl·us -a -um *adj* ample, large, wide, spacious; strong, great, powerful; grand, imposing; eminent, prominent, illustrious; amplissimō genere nātus born from an eminent family; amplissimus *(as title for persons of high office)* his Eminence; amplissimus ōrdō senatorial rank; amplus ōrātor a powerful speaker; parum amplus *(w. dat)* insufficiently large (for); spēs ampla high hopes; vīrēs amplae great strength

Ampsanct·us -ī *m* valley and lake in Samnium with toxic exhalations, regarded as an entrance to the lower world

ampull·a -ae *f* bottle, flask; *(fig)* bombast

ampullār·ius -(i)ī *m* bottle-maker

ampull·or -ārī -ātus sum *intr* to be bombastic

amputāti·ō -ōnis *f* pruning

amput·ō -āre -āvī -ātus *tr* to lop off, prune; to curtail, shorten; amputāta loquī to speak disconnectedly

Amūl·ius -(i)ī *m* king of Alba Longa, brother of Numitor, and granduncle of Romulus and Remus

amurc·a -ae *f* dregs of oil

Amycl·ae -ārum *fpl* town in Laconia, the birthplace of Castor and Pollux

Amyclae·us -a -um *adj* of Amyclae

Amyclīd·ēs -ae *m* Hyacinthus *(worshiped at Amyclae)*

amygdal·a -ae *f* almond tree

amygdal·um -ī *n* almond

amyst·is -idis *f* drinking bottoms up

an *conj (introducing the second or further part of a multiple question, direct or indirect)* or, or whether; **haud sciō an** I am inclined to think, probably

anabathr·a -ōrum *npl* bleachers

Anacre·ōn -ontis *m* lyric poet of Teos *(fl 540 B.C.)*

anadēm·a -atis *n* headband

anaglypt·a -ōrum *npl* work in bas-relief

anagnōst·ēs -ae *m* reader, reciter

analect·a -ae *m* slave who cleaned up the crumbs after a meal

analectr·is -idis *f* shoulder pad *(to improve the figure)*

analogi·a -ae *f* ratio; *(gram)* analogy *(similarity in inflection and derivatives of words); (phil)* method of reasoning from similar cases

anancaec·um -ī *n* large cup that must be emptied "bottoms up"

anapaest·us -a -um *adj (pros)* anapestic ‖ *m* anapest (◡ ◡ —) ‖ *n* poem in anapestic meter; anapestic line *or* passage

Anāp·us -ī *m* river in Sicily

an·as -atis *f* duck

anaticul·a -ae *f* **(anet-)** *(sometimes as term of endearment)* duckling

anatīn·us -a -um *adj* **(anet-)** duck's

anatocism·us -ī *m* compound interest

Anaxagor·ās -ae *m* Greek philosopher, teacher of Pericles and Euripides *(500?–428 B.C.)*

Anaximan·der -drī *m* Greek philosopher of Miletus *(610–547 B.C.)*

Anaximen·ēs -is *m* Greek philosopher of Miletus *(fl 544 B.C.)*

an·ceps *or* **ancip·es -cipitis** *adj* two-headed, facing in two directions; exposed on both sides; two-edged; twin-peaked; amphibious; of doubtful allegiance, untrustworthy; unreliable, unpredictable; *(of a person)* undecided, wavering; *(of a battle)* fought on two fronts; *(of enemies)* attacking on both sides; *(of dangers, evils)* arising from two sources, double, twofold; *(of roads)* leading in two directions; *(of battles)* indecisive; *(of words)* ambiguous; *(of situations)* hazardous, critical ‖ *n* danger, peril

Anchīs·ēs -ae *m* son of Capys, lover of Venus, and, by her, father of Aeneas

Anchīsē·us -a -um *adj* of Anchises

Anchīsiad·ēs -ae *m* son of Anchises *(Aeneas)*

ancīl·e -is *n* small figure-eight shield *(esp. one of twelve such kept by the Salii in the shrine of Mars and carried in religious processions)*

ancill·a -ae *f* slave girl

ancillār·is -is -e *adj* having the status of a slave girl

ancillul·a -ae *f* little slave girl

Ancōn·a -ae *f* seaport in N. Picenum

ancor·a -ae *f* **(anch-)** anchor

ancorāl·e -is *n* anchor cable

ancorāri·us -a -um *adj* of an anchor

Anc·us Mārci·us -ī *m* the fourth king of Rome

Ancȳr·a -ae *f* Ankara, capital of Galatia

andabat·a -ae *m* blindfolded gladiator

And·ēs -ium *fpl* village near Mantua, birthplace of Vergil

Andri·us -a -um *adj* of the Greek island of Andros ‖ *mpl* people of Andros ‖ *f* woman from Andros

Androge·ōs -ō *or* **Androge·ōn -ōnos** *or* **Androge·us -ī** *m* Androgeüs *(son of Minos and Pasiphaë, whose death Minos avenged by attacking Athens)*

androgyn·us -ī *m* *or* **androgynē -ēs** *f* hermaphrodite

Andromach·ē -ēs *or* **Andromach·a -ae** *f* Andromache (Hector's wife)

Andromed·a -ae *or* **Andromed·ē -ēs** *f* daughter of Cepheus and Cassiope, rescued from a sea monster by Perseus

andr·ōn -ōnis *m* corridor

Andronīc·us -ī *m* Livius Andronicus *(fl 241 B.C., first epic and dramatic poet of Latin literature)*

Andr·os *or* **Andr·us -ī** *f* Aegean island

ānell·us -ī *m* little ring

anēt(h)·um -ī *n* *(bot)* dill *(aromatic herb whose seeds and leaves were used as seasoning)*

-āne·us -a -um *adjl suf* chiefly from nouns denoting a place: **circumforāneus** connected with (the business of) the forum

anfrāct·us -ūs *m* curve *(of road, seashore);* spiral, coil; *(astr)* orbit; *(rhet)* circumlocution

angell·us -ī *m* small angle, small corner

angin·a -ae *f* tonsillitis; throat infection

angiport·us -ūs *m* *or* **angiport·um -ī** *n* alley

ang·ō -ere *tr* to choke, strangle; to distress; to tease; to trouble

ang·or -ōris *m* strangling, suffocation; anguish, distress

anguicom·us -a -um *adj* snake-haired

anguicul·us -ī *m* small snake

anguif·er -era -erum *adj* snaky, having snakes in place of hair, snake-haired; *(of places)* snake-infested

anguigen·a -ae *m* offspring of a dragon; Theban

anguill·a -ae *f* eel

anguine·us -a -um *adj* snaky; serpent-like

anguīn·us -a -um *adj* snaky

anguip·ēs -edis *adj* serpent-footed

angu·is -is *mf* snake, serpent ‖ **Anguis** *m* Dragon, Serpent, Hydra *(constellations)*

Anguiten·ēns -entis *m* Ophiuchus *(constellation)*

angulār·is -is -e *adj* angular

angulāt·us -a -um *adj* **(angl-)** angular

angul·us -ī *m* angle, corner; nook, recess; **ad parēs angulōs** *(or* **rēctīs angulīs)** at right angles

angustē *adv* within narrow limits; closely; hardly, scarcely; briefly, concisely

angusti·ae -ārum *fpl* narrow place; defile; narrow passage, strait; shortage, scarcity, want, deficiency; difficulty, tight spot; limitations; distress, straits; narrow-mindedness; poverty of vocabulary; **angustiae spīritūs** shortness of breath

angusticlāvi·us -a -um *adj* wearing a tunic with a narrow purple stripe *(a sign of equestrian rank)*

angust·ō -āre -āvī -ātus *tr* to narrow down; to reduce in size *or* amount; to choke

angust·us -a -um *adj* narrow, close; short, brief *(time);* scanty *(means);* tight *(reins);* difficult, critical; narrow-minded; base, mean; short, limited *(time, money, supplies);* curt *(style)* **ǁ** *n* a confined space; narrowness; critical condition, danger; **in angustum addūcere** *(or* **cōgere, conclūdere, dēdūcere)** to narrow down, compress, reduce

anhēlāti·ō -ōnis *f* panting

anhēlit·us -ūs *m* panting, difficulty in breathing, puffing; breath, breathing; vapor; **anhēlitum recipere** to catch one's breath; **vīnī anhēlitus** breath that reeks of wine

anhēl·ō -āre -āvī -ātus *tr* to breathe out, to pant after **ǁ** *intr* to pant, puff; to exhale; *(of fire, sea)* to roar

anhēl·us -a -um *adj* panting

anicul·a -ae *f* little old lady

Aniē(n)s·is -is -e *or* **Aniēn·us -a -um** *adj* of the Anio *(Tiber tributary)*

anīl·is -is -e *adj* of an old woman; **anīlēs fābulae** old wives' tales

anīlit·ās -ātis *f* old age *(of women)*

anīliter *adv* like an old woman

anim·a -ae *f* air, wind, breeze; breath; breath of life, life; soul *(as principle of life, opposed to* **animus** *as principle of thought and feelings);* spirit, ghost; **animam agere** to gasp for breath; **animam dūcere** to draw a breath; **animam ēdere** *(or* **efflāre** *or* **ēmittere** *or* **exspīrāre)** to breathe one's last; **animam trahere** to struggle to breathe

animadversi·ō -ōnis *f* attention, observation; mention; remark; criticism; punishment

animadvers·or -ōris *m* observer

animadver·tō -tere -tī -sus *tr* (**-vort-**) to pay attention to, attend to; to notice, observe, realize; to criticize; to punish

anim·al -ālis *n* animal; living creature

animāl·is -is -e *adj* consisting of air; animate, living **ǁ** *mfn* living creature, animal

anim·āns -antis *adj* living, animate **ǁ** *mfn* living thing; animal

animāti·ō -ōnis *f* the bestowal of life; *(fig)* living being

animāt·us -a -um *adj* courageous; inclined, disposed; *(w.* **ergā** *or* **in** + *acc)* disposed toward

anim·ō -āre -āvī -ātus *tr* to make alive, animate; to encourage

animōsē *adv* courageously; eagerly

animōs·us -a -um *adj* courageous; energetic; violent *(wind, fire);* spunky *(horse);* *(w. causal abl)* proud of

animul·a -ae *f* little soul, little life

animul·us -ī *m* darling; **mī animule** my darling

anim·us -ī *m* (*cf* **anima**) intellect, understanding; mind; state of mind; thought, reason; memory; knowledge; sense, consciousness; *(mostly in the abl)* judgment, opinion; imagination; heart, feelings, passions; spirit, courage, morale; disposition, character; pride, haughtiness; will, purpose, desire, inclination; pleasure, delight; confident hope; **aequō animō** patiently, calmly; **animī causā** for amusement; **animō libentī** gladly; **animum advertere** *(w. dat)* *or* **adiungere** *or* **adhibēre** *or* **applicāre** *or* **attendere** *or* **intendere** to apply the mind to, turn attention to, pay attention to: **animus aeger** sick feeling; **bonō animō esse** to take heart, be of good cheer; **commūnī animō** unanimously; **compos animī** in control of oneself; **ex animō** from the bottom of the heart, sincerely; **ex animō effluere** to slip one's mind; **ex animī tuī sententiā** in your opinion; **animīs fingite** imagine; **in animō habēre** *or* **esse** *(w. inf)* to have in mind to, intend to; **impos, inops animī** lacking self-control; **meō quidem animō** at least in my opinion; **ūnō animō** unanimously

Ani·ō -ōnis *m* tributary of the Tiber

Ani·us -ī *m* king and priest on Delos

ann- = adn-

Ann·a -ae *f* sister of Dido **ǁ** **Anna Perenna** goddess of the returning year

annāl·is -is -e *adj* lasting a year, annual; **lēx annālis** law fixing the minimum age for holding public offices **ǁ** *mpl* annals, chronicle

annat·ō -āre -āvī -ātum *intr* (**adn-**) *(w. dat or* **ad)** to swim to

anne *conj (alternate form of* **an)** or, or whether

anne·ctō -ctere -xuī -xus *tr* (**adn-**) *(w. dat or* **ad)** to tie, connect, annex *(s.th.)* to; *(w. dat)* to apply *(s.th.)* to

annex·us -ūs *m* connection

annicul·us -a -um *adj* (**-ucul-**) one year old; lasting only one year

annī·tor -tī -sus *or* **-xus sum** *intr* **(adn-)** to try one's hardest; to give support; *(w. dat or w.* **ad)** to lean on; *(w.* **ut** *or inf)* to strive to

anniversāri·us -a -um *adj* employed annually, renewed annually; occurring every year, growing every year; *(of games, festivals, sacrifices)* celebrated annually, annual

ann·ō -āre -āvī -ātum *intr* **(adn-)** *(w. dat, w.* **ad,** *w.* **acc** *of limit of motion)* to swim to *or* toward; *(w. dat)* to swim along with

annōn *conj* or not; **suntne dī annōn?** are there gods or not?

annōn·a -ae *f* year's crop; grain; price of grain; cost of living; high price; **annōna cāra** high prices

annōs·us -a -um *adj* aged, old

annotāti·ō -ōnis *f* **(adn-)** notation, remark

annōtin·us -a -um *adj* last year's, a year old

annot·ō -āre -āvī -ātus *tr* **(adn-)** to note *(in writing),* put on record; to observe, notice; to comment on; to register, designate

annumer·ō -āre -āvī -ātus *tr* **(adn-)** *(w. dat)* to count out *(money)* to; *(w. dat or* **in** + *acc)* to add *(s.th.)* to, include *(s.o.)* among

annūnti·ō -āre -āvī -ātus *tr* **(adn-)** to announce, make known, bring the news, proclaim

an·nuō -nuere -nuī -nūtus *tr* **(adn-)** to designate by a nod; to indicate, declare; *(w. dat)* to promise, grant *(s.th.)* to ‖ *intr* to nod assent; *(w. dat)* to nod assent to, be favorable to, smile on

ann·us -ī *m* year; season; age, time of life; year of office; year's produce, crops; circuit *(e.g., of a planet);* **ad annum** for the coming year, a year from now; **annō** *(advl phrase)* a year ago, last year; **annō exeunte** *(or* **annō plēnō)** at the end of the year; **annum** *(or* **in annum)** for a year; **annus meus (tuus,** *etc.)* my (your, *etc.)* year of office; my (your, *etc.)* birthday; **annus solidus** a full year; **per annōs** year by year

annu·us -a -um *adj* lasting a year; annual, yearly ‖ *npl* yearly pay, pension

an·quīrō -quīrere -quīsīvī -quīsītus *tr* to search carefully; to examine, inquire into; *(w. gen or abl of the charge)* to accuse *(s.o.)* of ‖ *intr* to hold an inquest

āns·a -ae *f* handle; *(fig)* opportunity

ānsāt·us -a -um *adj* having handles; **homō ānsātus** man with arms akimbo

āns·er -eris *m* goose *(male),* gander

Āns·er -eris *m* a poet, friend of the triumvir Antonius

Antae·us -ī *m* Libyan giant, son of Earth, killed by Hercules ‖ name of a Carthaginian general

ante *adv* before, previously, in the past; in front; forwards; **ante ... quam** before; **annō**

ante a year ago; **multīs annīs ante** many years before that

ante- *pref (used in the senses of the adv)*

ante *prep (w. acc)* **1** before, in front of: **ante urbis portās** before the city gates; **2** before *(in time):* **ante diem** before the due date, too early; *(in dates):* **ante diem quārtum Īdūs Mārtiās** *(instead of* **quārtō diē ante Īdūs Mārtiās)** *or abbr* **a.d. IV Id. Mart.** three days before the Ides of March; **ante tempus** before time, prematurely; **3** *(in preference, choice)* more than, above; **ante omnia** first of all; above all

anteā *adv* before, previously, formerly; **iam anteā** already in the past

anteāct·us -a -um *adj (of time)* that has passed

anteambul·ō -ōnis *m* one who runs before *(to clear the way),* blocker

ante·capiō -capere -cēpī -ceptus *tr* to receive beforehand; to take possession of beforehand, preoccupy; to anticipate

ante·cēdō -cēdere -cessī -cessus *tr* precede; to outdo, surpass ‖ *intr (w. dat)* **1** to have precedence over; **2** to excel, surpass

antecell·ō -ere *tr* to surpass ‖ *intr (w. dat) (w. abl of respect or* **in** + *abl)* to surpass *(s.o.)* in

antecessi·ō -ōnis *f* antecedent cause

antecess·or -ōris *m (mil)* scout ‖ *mpl* advance guard

antecurs·or -ōris *m (mil)* scout ‖ *mpl* vanguard

ante·eō -īre -īvī *or* **-iī** *tr* to precede; to surpass; to anticipate, prevent ‖ *intr* to precede; to take the lead; *(w. dat)* **1** to go before; **2** to surpass

ante·ferō -ferre -tulī -lātus *tr* to prefer; to anticipate

antefīx·um -ī *n* antefix *(image, statue, etc., affixed to roofs and gutters of temples or homes)*

ante·gredior -gredī -gressus sum *tr* to precede

antehab·eō -ēre -uī *tr* to prefer

antehāc *adv* before now, formerly, previously; before that (time)

antelātus *pp of* **anteferō**

antelogi·um -ī *n* introduction, prologue

antelūcān·us -a -um *adj* pre-dawn

antemerīdiān·us -a -um *adj* before noon

ante·mittō -mittere -mīsī -missus *tr* to send out ahead

Antemn·ae -ārum *fpl* ancient town in Latium

Antemnāt·ēs -ium *mpl* the people of Antemnae

antenn·a *or* **antemn·a -ae** *f* yardarm, sail yard, sail

Antēn·or -oris *m* Trojan founder of Patavium *(Padua)*

Antēnore·us -a -um *adj* Patavian, Paduan

Antēnorid·ēs -ae *m* descendant of Antenor; native of Patavium *(Padua)*

anteoccupāti·ō -ōnis *f (rhet)* anticipation of an opponent's arguments, objection

antepart·um -ī *n* (-pert-) thing *or* property acquired in the past

ante·pēs -pedis *m* forefoot

antepīlān·ī -ōrum *mpl* front ranks *(soldiers drawn up in the first two lines of a battle formation)*

antepoll·eō -ēre *tr* to surpass in strength **||** *intr (w. dat)* to be superior to *(s.o.)* in strength

ante·pōnō -pōnere -posuī -positus *tr* to place *or* station in front of; to place before *(in time);* to prefer, esteem more highly; *(w. dat)* to give *(a person)* preference over *(another);* to serve *(food);* to put *(a word, prefix, or letter)* before *(a word)*

antepot·ēns -entis *adj* very wealthy

antequam *or* ante ... quam *conj* before; sooner ... than

anteri·or -ōris *adj* anterior; previous *(time); (of place)* in front

Anter·ōs -ōtis *m* avenger of unrequited love *(son of Venus and Mars)*

ant·ēs -ium *mpl* rows *(of vines, soldiers, etc.)*

antesignān·us -ī *m* soldier fighting in front of the standards to defend them; leader, prominent man, protagonist

ante·stō *or* anti·stō -stāre -stitī *intr* to excel; *(w. dat)* to be superior to

antest·or -ārī -ātus sum *tr (leg)* to call as witness

antetulī *perf of* anteferō

ante·veniō -venīre -vēnī -ventus *tr* to come before, arrive ahead of; to anticipate, thwart; to surpass **||** *intr* to arrive first; to become more distinguished; *(w. dat)* **1** to anticipate; **2** to get ahead of; **3** to be better than, surpass

antever·tō -tere -tī -sus *tr* (-vort-) to go *or* come before; to anticipate; to prefer **||** *intr* to act first; to go out first, set out first; *(w. dat)* to outweigh

antevol·ō -āre *intr* to dash out ahead

Antiānus -a -um *adj* of Antium *(very ancient coastal town in Latium)*

Antiās -ātis *adj* of Antium **||** *mpl* people of Antium

Antiātīnus -a -um *adj* of Antium

Anticat·ō -ōnis *m* title of the books which Caesar wrote in answer to Cicero's panegyric *Cato*

anticipāti·ō -ōnis *f* preconception

anticip·ō -āre -āvī -ātus *tr* to anticipate; to have a preconceived idea of; **viam anticipāre** to take the lead *(in a race)*

antīc·us -a -um *adj* front, foremost

Anticyr·a -ae *f* name of several Greek towns famous for their hellebore *(used to cure insanity)*

antideā, antideō, antidhāc *adv* old forms for anteā, anteō, antehāc

antidot·um -ī *n or* antidot·os *or* antidot·us -ī *f* antidote

Antigon·ē -ēs *or* Antigon·a -ae *f* Antigone *(daughter of Oedipus* **||** *daughter of Laomedon, changed into a stork)*

Antigon·us -ī *m* Greek name, *esp.* one of the generals of Alexander the Great **||** Antigonus Doson

Antiloch·us -ī *m* son of Nestor

Antiochī·a -ae *f* (-chē·a) Antioch *(chief city of Syria)*

Antioch·us -ī *m* name of seven kings of Syria **||** Academic philosopher, teacher of Cicero and Brutus

Antiop·a -ae *or* Antiop·ē -ēs *f* Antiope *(mother, by Jupiter, of Amphion and Zethus)*

Antipa·ter -trī *m* a general and successor of Alexander the Great, father of Cassander **||** his grandson, son of Cassander, and son-in-law of Lysimachus **||** name of several philosophers

Antiphat·ēs -ae *m* king of the Laestrygonians **||** son of Sarpedon, killed by Turnus

antiquāri·us -a -um *adj & m* antiquarian

antīquē *adv* in former times; in the good old style

antīquit·ās -ātis *f* antiquity; the ancients; the good old days

antīquitus *adv* in former times, of old; from ancient times; in the old style

antīqu·ō -āre -āvī -ātus *tr* to reject *(law, bill) (the letter A was used = Antiquo, I vote against the bill)*

antīqu·us -a -um *adj* (-tic-) old, ancient; old-fashioned, venerable; long-standing *(friendship);* located *or* lying in front **||** *mpl* ancients, ancient authors **||** *n* antiquity; old custom

antisophist·ēs -ae *m (rhet)* opponent in argument

antist·ēs -itis *m* high-priest *(of temple or deity);* authority *(of an art, philosophical school)* **||** *f* high-priestess

Antisthen·ēs -is *or* -ae *m* pupil of Socrates and founder of Cynic philosophy *(455?–360 B.C.)*

antistit·a -ae *f* high-priestess

antithet·on -ī *n (rhet)* antithesis

Ant·ium -(i)ī *n* coastal town in Latium *(modern Anzio)*

antli·a -ae *f* pump; treadmill

Antōni·us -a -um *adj* Roman clan name *(nomen), esp.* Marcus Antonius *(orator, consul in 99 B.C.)* **||** Marcus Antonius *(triumvir, consul in 44 B.C.)*

antr·um -ī *n* cave, cavern, grotto; *(fig)* hollow *(of a tree)*

Anūb·is -is *or* **-idis** *m* jackal-headed Egyptian god of hunting

ānulār·ius -(i)ī *m* ring maker

ānulāt·us -a -um *adj* wearing a ring

ānul·us -ī *m* ring, signet ring

-ān·us -a -um *adjl suf* 1 from common nouns: **urbānus** of the city; 2 from place names: **Rōmānus** from *or* of Rome, Roman; 3 from personal names: **Claudiānus** of Claudius, Claudian

ān·us -ī *m* anus, rectum; ring

an·us -ūs *f* old woman; *(pej)* hag

anxiē *adv* uneasily

anxiet·ās -ātis *f* anxiety, worry; meticulousness

anxif·er -era -erum *adj* disquieting, worrisome

anxitūd·ō -inis *f* anxiety, worry

anxi·us -a -um *adj* worried, anxious, uneasy; meticulous

Anx·ur -uris *m* & *n* coastal town of Latium *(modern Terracina)*

Anyt·us -ī *m* one of Socrates' three accusers

Āonid·ēs -um *fpl* Muses *(named after the section of Boeotia, called Aonia, where Mt. Helicon is located)*

Āoni·us -a -um *adj* Boeotian; Theban; of the Muses; of Helicon; poetic ‖ *f* Boeotia

Aorn·os -ī *m* Lake Avernus *(meaning: having no birds)*

apage *interj* go!; scram!

Apamē·a -ae *f* name of several towns in Asia Minor, *esp.* that in Syria and that in Phrygia

apēliōt·ēs -ae *m* east wind

Apell·ēs -is *m* Greek painter *(fl 4th cent. B.C.)*

Āpennīnicol·a -ae *m* **(App-)** inhabitant of the Apennines

Āpennīnigen·a -ae *adj (masc only)* **(App-)** born on the Apennines

Āpennīn·us -a -um *adj* **(App-)** Apennine ‖ *m* Apennine Mountains

a·per -prī *m* wild boar; meat of wild boar as food

aper·iō -īre -uī -tus *tr* to open, uncover, lay bare, disclose, reveal; to prove, demonstrate; to explain; to recount; to cut open, split; to usher in *(a new year);* to introduce *(a subject); (mil)* to spread out *(forces); (topog)* to bring into view; **locum aperīre** *(w. dat)* to open the way to, afford an opportunity for ‖ *refl (of flowers)* to open; to come into view

apertē *adv* openly, frankly, candidly

apert·ō -āre *tr* to bare

apert·us -a -um *pp of* **aperiō** ‖ *adj* bare, uncovered, exposed; without decks; clear *(style);* frank, candid; plain, evident; accessible, unobstructed ‖ *n* open space; **in apertō**

in the open; **in apertō esse** to be clear, evident, well known, notorious

ap·ex -icis *m* point, tip; top, summit; conical flamen's hat; cap, crown; crowning glory; long mark over a vowel, macron

ap(h)eliōt·ēs -ae *m* the E. wind

aphract·us -ī *f or* **aphract·um -ī** *n* cargo ship without a deck

Aphrodīsi·a -ōrum *npl* festival in honor of Aphrodite

aphronit·um -ī *n* washing soda, sodium carbonate

apiār·ius -iī *m* beekeeper

apiastr·um -ī *n* a variety of balm

Apīc·ius -iī *m* gourmet of the lst cent. A.D.

apicul·a -ae *f* little bee

apin·ae -ārum *fpl* trifles, nonsense

ap·is -is *f (gen pl:* **-um** & **-ium)** bee

Āp·is -is *or* **-idis** *m* Egyptian sacred bull

ap·īscor -īscī -tus sum *tr* to pursue; to get, reach, gain; to get, obtain; *(lit & fig)* to grasp; to get hold of; **lītem apīscī** to win a lawsuit

ap·ium -iī *n* celery; parsley

aplustr·e -is *or* **aplustr·um -ī** *n (naut)* curved ornamental stern

Apoclēt·ī -ōrum *mpl* select committee *(of Aetolian League)*

apodytēr·ium -(i)ī *n* dressing room *(of a bath)*

apolactiz·ō -āre *tr* to kick aside; to scorn

Apollinār·is -is -e *adj* of Apollo; **lūdī Apollinārēs** games in honor of Apollo, instituted after the victory at Cannae ‖ *n* place sacred to Apollo

Apoll·ō -inis *m* son of Jupiter and Latona, twin brother of Diana, god of the sun, divination, archery, healing, poetry, and music

Apollodōr·us -ī *m* rhetorician, teacher of Augustus

Apollōni·a -ae *f* name of several cities: on the S. coast of Illyricum; on the S. coast of the Black Sea; in Crete

apolog·us -ī *m* story, fable

Apon·us -ī *m* warm spring near Padua

apophorēt·a -ōrum *npl* presents for departing house guests

apoproēgmen·a -ōrum *npl* things that have been rejected

aposphrāgism·a -atis *n* device on signet ring, seal

apothēc·a -ae *f* warehouse, storeroom

apparātē *adv* **(adp-)** sumptuously

apparāti·ō -ōnis *f* **(adp-)** preparation

apparāt·us -a -um *adj* **(adp-)** getting *or* making ready, preparing; providing; well supplied; splendid

apparāt·us -ūs *m* equipment, apparatus, gear; equipping, organization; armaments; stock, store; rhetorical devices; pomp, display, magnificence

appār·ēns -entis *adj* **(adp-)** visible

appāreō -ēre -uī -itum *intr* **(adp-)** to appear, become visible, be visible; to be seen, show oneself, show up; to materialize, take shape; to appear, look *(e.g., unhappy);* to be perceptible *(to the senses);* to be clearly ... , be seen to be; *(of facts)* to be clear, be evident, be obvious; *(w. dat)* **1** to wait on, serve; **2** to obey *(laws);* **nec caput nec pēs appāret mihi** I can make neither head nor tail of it; **nūsquam appārēre** to have disappeared **‖** *v impers* it is evident, it is clear; **ut appāret** apparently

appāriti·ō -ōnis *f* **(adp-)** attendance, service; provision **‖** *fpl* household servants

appārit·or -ōris *m* servant; attendant *(of public official, e.g., aide, lictor, secretary)*

appar·ō -āre -āvī -ātus *tr* **(adp-)** to prepare; to provide; to organize *(weddings, public games, war);* *(w. inf or* **ut)** to get ready to **‖** *refl (w.* **in** *+ acc)* to prepare oneself for, equip oneself for

appellāti·ō -ōnis *f* **(adp-)** addressing; *(w.* **ad)** appeal to *(in general; to higher authority);* naming, calling by name; designation, name, title; pronunciation; *(gram)* common noun

appellāt·or -ōris *m (leg)* one who appeals, appellant

appell·ō -āre -āvī -ātus *tr* **(adp-)** to speak to, address, accost; to appeal to, call on, beseech; to make overtures to, approach; to invoke *(god as witness);* to demand payment of; to call up *(to pay a debt or obligation);* to recognize (as), style officially; to name, call; to mention by name, use the name of, mention; to pronounce; to designate, term, call; to demand payment of; *(leg)* to sue; **imperātōrem appellāre** to hail as "Imperator" **‖** *intr* to appeal

ap·pellō -pellere -pulī -pulsus *tr* **(adp-)** *(w. dat or* **ad)** **1** to drive *(s.th.)* to; **2** to move *(military equipment, personnel)* to; **3** to steer *(ship)* to **‖** *pass (w.* **ad)** *(of a ship)* to put in at **‖** *intr (of a ship)* to land

appendicul·a -ae *f* small addition

append·ix -icis *f* addition, appendage; related topic; hanger-on; *(anat)* appendix

appen·dō -dere -dī -sus *tr* **(adp-)** to hang; to weigh; to pay out; *(fig)* to weigh, consider

Appenn- = **Āpenn-**

appet·ēns -entis *adj* **(adp-)** greedy; *(w. gen)* eager for, craving

appetenter *adv* **(adp-)** greedily, avidly

appetenti·a -ae *f* **(adp-)** *(w. gen)* the craving for, desire for; **cibī appetentia** appetite (for food)

appetīti·ō -ōnis *f* **(adp-)** grasping; desire; appetite; *(w. gen)* **1** the craving for; **2** the reaching out for; **appetītiō nātūrālis** *(or* ex

nātūrā *or* **animī)** instinctive desire, appetite *(for),* impulse *(toward)*

appetīt·us -ūs *m* **(adp-)** desire, appetite *(esp. natural or instinctive)* **‖** *mpl* the appetites, passions *(opp:* **ratiō** reason)

appet·ō -ere -īvī *or* **-iī -ītus** *tr* **(adp-)** to try to reach; to lay hold of; to strive after, aim for; to seek the friendship of; to court; to make for, head for; to attack, assault; to have an appetite for *(food);* to tackle *(a job)* **‖** *intr (of events)* to approach, draw near

Appiān·us -a -um *adj* of Appia, a town in Phrygia **‖** of Appius Claudius the decemvir **‖** *m* Appian of Alexandria *(historian of the 2nd cent. A.D.)*

Appi·as -adis *f* a nymph of the Appian fountain, near the temple of Venus Genetrix **‖** title of Venus

Appiet·ās -ātis *f* the rank *or* status of an Appius

apping·ō -ere *tr* **(adp-)** to paint; to write *(s.th.)* in addition *(to a verbal picture)*

Appi·us -a -um *adj* Appian; **aqua Appia** Appian Aqueduct *(built by Appius Claudius Caecus);* **via Appia** Appian Way *(road between Rome and Capua, built by the same man)* **‖** *m* Roman first name, *esp.* of the Claudian clan: Appius Claudius Crassus *(consul and decemvir in 451 B.C.)* **‖** Appius Claudius Caecus *(censor in 312 B.C.)* **‖** Appius Claudius Caudex *(consul in 264 B.C.)* **‖** Appius Claudius Pulcher *(consul in 54 B.C., censor in 50 B.C.)* **‖** **Appī Forum** town in Latium on the Appian Way

applau·dō -dere -sī -sus *tr* **(adp-)** to strike, slap; **terrae applaudere** to dash to the ground **‖** *intr* to applaud

applicāti·ō -ōnis *f* **(adp-)** application

applicāt·us -a -um *adj* **(adp-)** *(w.* **ad)** inclined to; *(w. dat)* lying close to, attached to

applicit·us -a -um *adj* **(adp-)** *(w. dat)* adjacent to

applic·ō -āre -āvī *or* **-uī -ātus** *or* **-itus** *tr* **(adp-)** to bring into close contact; *(w. dat or* **ad)** **1** to apply, attach, add, join *(s.th.)* to; **2** to steer *(ship)* toward; **3** to apply *(mind, attention)* to; *(w.* **ad)** to place *(geographically)* near to **‖** *refl* to lean (against); to sit down (on); *(w.* **ad)** to devote oneself to, apply oneself to **‖** *intr (of ships)* to put in *(at),* land

applōdō *see* **applaudō**

applōr·ō -āre -āvī *intr* **(adpl-)** to lament

ap·pōnō -pōnere -posuī -positus *tr* **(adp-)** to serve *(food);* *(w. dat or* **ad)** to put or lay *(s.th.)* near, at, *or* beside; *(w. dat)* **1** to set *(food)* before; **2** to appoint, assign *(s.o.)* to; **3** to reckon *(s.th.)* as; **modum appōnere** *(w. dat)* set a limit to

apporrēct·us -a -um *adj* (**adp-**) stretched out near *or* beside

apport·ō -āre -āvī -ātus *tr* (**adp-**) to carry, bring (to); to bring along, bring with one; to import; to present *(a play);* to bring in its train, cause; *(w. dat)* to carry *(s.th.)* to

apposc·ō -ere *tr* to demand in addition

appositē *adv* (**adp-**) appropriately

apposit·us -a -um *pp of* **appōnō** ‖ *adj (w.* **ad)** suited to; *(w. dat)* situated near, bordering on

appōt·us -a -um *adj* (**adp-**) drunk

apprec·or -ārī -ātus sum *tr* (**adp-**) to pray to, worship

apprehen·dō *or* **appren·dō -dere -dī -sus** *tr* (**adp-**) to grasp, seize, take hold of; to arrest; to take up *(topic); (mil)* to occupy

apprīmē *adv* (**adp-**) chiefly, especially; very

ap·primō -primere -pressī -pressus *tr* (**adp-**) *(w. dat)* to press *(s.th.)* close to

approbāti·ō -ōnis *f* (**adp-**) approbation, approval; proof; decision

approbāt·or -ōris *m* (**adp-**) one who seconds *or* approves

approbē *adv* (**adp-**) very well

approb·ō -āre -āvī -ātus *tr* (**adp-**) to approve; to prove; to prove *(statement)* true

apprōmitt·ō -ere *tr* (**adp-**) to promise in addition

apprōn·ō -āre -āvī -ātus *refl* (**adp-**) to lean forward

approper·ō -āre -āvī -ātus *tr* (**adp-**) to hasten, speed up ‖ *intr* to hurry

appropinquāti·ō -ōnis *f* (**adp-**) approach

appropinqu·ō -āre -āvī *intr* (**adp-**) to approach; *(w. dat or* **ad)** to come near, approach

appugn·ō -āre -āvī -ātus *tr* (**adp-**) to fight, attack

appulsus *pp of* **appellō**

appuls·us -ūs *m* (**adp-**) landing; approach; influence, impact

aprīcāti·ō -ōnis *f* sunbathing

aprīc·or -ārī -ātus sum *intr* to sunbathe

aprīc·us -a -um *adj* sunny ‖ *n* sunny spot; sunshine, light of day

Aprīl·is -is -e *adj* of April; **mēnsis Aprīlis** April ‖ *m* April *(second month of the old calendar until 153 B.C.)*

aprūgn·us -a -um *adj* of a wild boar

aps = abs

apsinth·ium -(i)ī *n* (**abs-**) *(bot)* wormwood *(yielding a bitter abstract used in flavoring wine)*

apsūmēd·ō -inis *f* a devouring

aptē *adv* closely; suitably

apt·ō -āre -āvī -ātus *tr* to fasten, fit, adjust; to make ready, equip

apt·us -a -um *adj* tied, bound, fastened; fitted together; suitable, adapted; neat, orderly, in

good order, in good condition; handy, convenient; *(w. abl)* provided with; *(w.* **ex** *or adv)* following from, dependent on; *(w.* **ad** *or* **in** + *acc)* **1** equipped for, ready for; **2** efficient at, good at; **3** convenient for; **4** useful for; **5** favorable for; **causae inter sē aptae** connected causes

apud *prep (w. acc)* at, by, near, among; at the house of; in *(a building, town);* in the care of, in the hands of, in possession of; before, in the presence of; in the writings of; (with influence) over; **apud gentēs** *(or* **hominēs)** in the whole world; **apud mē (tē)** in my (your) care; at my (your) house; **apud mēnsam** at table; **apud prīncipia** on parade; **apud sē esse** to be in one's right mind

Āpūli·a -ae *f* region in S.W. Italy

Āpūlic·us -a -um *adj* Apulian

Āpūl·us -a -um *adj* Apulian

aqu·a -ae *f* water; rain, rainfall; aqueduct; **aquā et ignī interdīcere** to outlaw *(literally, to keep (away) from water and fire);* **aquam praebēre** *(w. dat)* to entertain *(guests)* ‖ *fpl* spa, baths

aquaeduct·us -ūs *m* aqueduct

aquāliculus -ī *m* potbelly

aquāl·is -is -e *adj* water ‖ *mf* washbasin

aquāri·us -a -um *adj* of water ‖ *m* water-conduit inspector ‖ *n* water supply

Aquār·ius -(i)ī *m (astr)* Aquarius *(constellation and sign of the zodiac)*

aquātic·us -a -um *adj* growing in water; watery, moist, humid ‖ *npl* well-watered places; marshes

aquātil·is -is -e *adj* living *or* growing in water, aquatic; watery

aquāti·ō -ōnis *f* fetching water; water hole

aquāt·or -ōris *m* water carrier

aquil·a -ae *f* eagle *(bird; Roman legionary standard); (fig)* legion; gable *(of house)*

Aquilēi·a -ae *f* town in Venetia at head of the Adriatic

aquil·ex -egis *m* water finder, dowser; water conduit inspector

aquilif·er -erī *m* standard-bearer

aquilīn·us -a -um *adj* eagle's

aquil·ō -ōnis *m* north wind; North

aquilōni·us -a -um *adj* northerly

aquil·us -a -um *adj* swarthy

Aquīn·ās -ātis *adj* of Aquinum ‖ *m* citizen of Aquinum

Aquīn·um -ī *n* town of the Volsci, birthplace of Juvenal

Aquītāni·a -ae *f* province in S.W. Gaul

aquol·a *or* **acul·a -ae** *f* (**aquu-**) brook; small amount of water

aqu·or -ārī -ātus sum *intr* to fetch water

aquōs·us -a -um *adj* well-watered; rainy; humid; *(med)* dropsical

aquul·a -ae f brook
ār·a -ae f altar; altar tomb; (fig) sanctuary (of protection) **ǁ Āra** (astr) Altar (constellation)
arabarch·ēs -ae m customs officer in Egypt
Arab·ī -ōrum mpl Arabs
Arabi·a -ae f Arabia
Arabic·us or **Arabi·us** or **Arab·us -a -um** adj Arabian
Arab·s -is m Arab
Arachn·ē -ēs f Lydian girl whom Minerva changed into a spider
arāne·a -ae f spider; cobweb
arāneol·a -ae f small spider
arāneol·us -ī m small spider
arāneōs·us -a -um adj full of cobwebs; resembling cobwebs
arāne·us -a -um adj spider's **ǁ** m spider **ǁ** n spider web
Ar·ar -aris (acc: **Ararim**) m Rhone tributary (modern Saône)
arāti·ō -ōnis f cultivation, tilling; agriculture; arable land
arātiuncul·a -ae f small plot; small farm
arāt·or -ōris m farmer **ǁ** adj plow
arātr·um -ī n plow
Arāt·us -ī m Greek author, from Soli in Cilicia, of poem on astronomy (fl 270 B.C.)
Arax·ēs -is m river in Armenia **ǁ** river in S. Persia, now Iran
arbi·ter -trī m eyewitness, spectator; judge; (leg) arbitrator (with wider discretionary power than a **iūdex**); ruler, director, controller
arbitr·a -ae f eyewitness
arbitrāriō adv uncertainly
arbitrāri·us -a -um adj discretionary; arbitrary
arbitrāt·us -ūs m decision; inclination, pleasure, choice; **arbitrātū** (w. gen) at the discretion of; (leg) according to the decision of (an official arbitrator); **arbitrātū meō, tuō** (coll) to my (your) heart's content
arbitr·ium -(i)ī n (process of) arbitration (before an arbitrator); independent judgment; settlement (of a matter); mastery, power, control; wishes, desires; whim, caprice; **ad arbitrium nostrum** as much as we please; **meī arbitriī est** it is in my power; **suī arbitriī esse** to be one's own master; **suō arbitriō** on one's own initiative
arbitr·ō -āre -āvī -ātus tr to think, judge; (w. a predicate) to consider **ǁ** pass (of a dispute) to be settled
arbitr·or -ārī -ātus sum tr & intr to decide or judge (as an arbitrator); to consider, judge, think; to reckon, suppose, imagine; to infer; to be a witness of; to award as an arbiter; (w. inf) to think it proper

arb·or or arb·ōs -oris f tree; mast, oar, ship; gallows; **arbor Iovis** oak tree; **arbor Palladis** olive tree; **arbor Phoebī** the laurel; **Herculea arbor** the poplar
arborēt·um -ī n plantation of trees
arbore·us -a -um adj of a tree; tree-like
Arbuscul·a -ae f Arbuscula (actress in the time of Cicero)
arbuscul·a -ae f small tree, sapling
arbust·us -a -um adj wooded, planted with trees **ǁ** n orchard; vineyard planted with trees **ǁ** npl trees
arbute·us -a -um adj of arbutus
arbut·um -ī n wild strawberry (fruit of arbutus)
arbut·us -ī f arbutus, strawberry tree
arc·a -ae f chest, cupboard; money box (also the money itself), safe, coffer; coffin; prison cell
Arcadi·a -ae f district in central Peloponnesus, famed for its pastoral beauty
Arcadic·us or **Arcadi·us -a -um** adj Arcadian
arcānō adv in secret; in confidence
arcān·us -a -um adj secret, concealed; private; trustworthy (friend) **ǁ** n secret; sacred mystery
Arc·as -adis m inhabitant of Arcadia, Arcadian **ǁ** Arcas (son of Callisto by Jupiter, eponymous hero of Arcadia) **ǁ** Mercury (who was born on Mt. Cyllene in Arcadia)
arc·eō -ēre -uī tr to shut up, enclose; to keep out (rain, cold); to keep at a distance, keep off; to hinder, prevent; to control, govern; to prevent, stop; (w. abl) to protect from, rescue from
arcer·a -ae f ambulance
Arcesil·ās -ae or **Arcesilā·üs -ī** m philosopher of the 3rd cent. B.C., founder of the Middle Academy
arcessīt·us -a -um pp of **accessō** (**accers-**) **ǁ** adj foreign; far-fetched; self-inflicted (death)
arcessīt·us -ūs m call, summons
arcess·ō or accers·ō -ere -īvī or -iī -ītus tr to send for, summon; to raise (money); to drag in (gratuitously); to induce (sleep, tears); to bring upon oneself (troubles); to derive; to import; (leg) to arraign
archetyp·us -a -um adj original, autograph **ǁ** n original
Archiloch·us -ī m Greek iambic and elegaic poet of Paros (c. 714–676 B.C.)
archimagīr·us -ī m chef
Archimēd·ēs -is or **-ī** m Greek scientist of Syracuse (287?–212 B.C.)
archipīrāt·a -ae m pirate captain
architect·ō -āre -āvī -ātus tr to design
architect·ōn -onis m architect
architect·or -ārī -ātus sum tr to design; to build; (fig) to devise

architectūr·a -ae *f* architecture
architect·us -ī *m* architect; designer, deviser
arch·ōn -ontis *m* archon *(a chief magistrate of Athens)*
Archyt·ās -ae *m* Pythagorean philosopher *(from Tarentum)* of the 4th cent. B.C.
arcisell·ium -(i)ī *n* chair *(with rounded back)*
arciten·ēns -entis *adj* holding a bow; **dea arcitenēns** Diana **‖ Arcitenēns** *m* Apollo; *(astr)* Sagittarius *(constellation and sign of the zodiac)*
Arctophyl·ax -acis *m (astr)* Boötes *(constellation)*
arct·os -ī *m* North Pole; North; north wind; night **‖ Arctos** *m (astr)* the Great and Little Bear *(double constellation)*
arctūr·us -ī *m (astr)* brightest star in Boötes
arcuāt·us -a -um *adj* bow-shaped; covered *(carriage)*
arcul·a -ae *f* small box *(for perfumes, jewels)*
arculār·ius -(i)ī *m* maker of small jewel boxes
arcu·ō -āre -āvī -ātus *tr* to curve
arc·us -ūs *m* bow; rainbow; curve; arch; triumphal arch; one of the five zones of the sky; halo *(of the sun)*
ardeli·ō -ōnis *m* busybody, meddler
arde·a -ae *f* heron **‖ Ardea** town in Latium
Arde·ās -ātis *adj* of Ardea **‖** *mpl* the people of Ardea
Ardeātīn·us -a -um *adj* of Ardea
ārd·ēns -entis *adj* blazing, burning, hot, fiery; gleaming; intense *(emotions);* zealous, eager; high *(fever);* bright *(colors, stars)*
ārdenter *adv* ardently, passionately; eagerly
ārdeō ārdēre ārsī ārsūrus *tr* to be in love with **‖** *intr* to be on fire, burn, blaze; to flash, glow; to smart, burn; *(of countries)* to be in turmoil; *(of corpses)* to be cremated; *(of seas)* to be rough
ārdēsc·ō -ere *intr* to catch fire; to gleam, glitter; *(of passions)* to become more intense, flare up
ārd·or -ōris *m* heat, flame; flashing, brightness; heat *(of passions);* loved one, flame
Arduenn·a -ae *f* forest in the N. of Gaul *(Ardennes)*
ardu·us -a -um *adj* steep, high; uphill; erect; difficult; *(of hopes)* difficult to realize **‖** *n* height; difficulty; **in arduum** *(or* **per arduum)** upwards, uphill; high into the air
āre·a -ae *f* open space; forecourt *(of temple);* park, playground; building site; threshing floor; bald spot
āre·faciō -facere -fēcī -factus *tr* to dry up
Arelāte *indecl n* town in S. Gaul *(Arles)*
arēna *see* **harēna**
ār·ēns -entis *adj* dry, parched; parching *(thirst)*
ār·eō -ēre *intr* to be dry; to be thirsty
Areopagīt·ēs -ae *m* member of the Areopagus

Arēopag·us -ī *m* criminal court in Athens; hill where this court met
Ar·ēs -is *m* Greek god of war *(counterpart of Mars)*
ār·ēscō -ēscere -uī *intr* to become dry; to wither; *(of streams)* to run dry
aretālog·us -ī *m* teller of tall tales
Arethūs·a -ae *f* nymph pursued by river god Alpheus in the Peloponnesus and changed into a fountain **‖** fountain in Syracuse
Argē·ī -ōrum *mpl* figures of men made of straw and thrown annually into the Tiber in place of earlier human sacrifices
argentāri·us -a -um *adj* silver; silvery; financial; banker's **‖** *m* banker **‖** *f* banking; bank; silver mine
argentāt·us -a -um *adj* silver-plated; *(hum)* concerned with money
argenteol·us -a -um *adj* (-tiol-) silver
argente·us -a -um *adj* silver, silvery; *(hum)* of money **‖** *m* silver coin
argent·um -ī *n* silver; silver plate; money, cash; **argentum bīgātum** silver coin stamped with a two-horse chariot; **argentum signātum** silver coin; **argentum vīvum** mercury, quicksilver
Argē·us *or* **Argei·us** *or* **Argī·us -a -um** *adj* Argive; Greek
Arg·ī -ōrum *mpl or* **Argos** *n (only nom and acc)* Argos *(town in N.E. Peloponnesus)*
Argīlēt·um -ī *n (also* **Argī lētum)** district in Rome between the Quirinal and Capitoline Hills
argill·a -ae *f* potter's clay
Arginūs(s)·ae -ārum *fpl* group of three islands off the coast of Asia Minor, the scene of an Athenian naval victory in 406 B.C.
argīt·is -idis *f* vine with white grapes
Argīv·us -a -um *adj* Argive; Greek
Arg·ō -ūs *(acc & abl:* **Argō)** *f* Jason's ship
Argolic·us -a -um *adj* Argive; Greek
Argol·is -idis *adj (fem only)* Argive **‖** Argive woman **‖** the Argolid *(district around Argos)*
Argonaut·ae -ārum *mpl* Argonauts
Argos *n (only nom & acc)* Argos *(see* **Argī)**
Argō·us -a -um *adj* of the Argo
argūmentāti·ō -ōnis *f* argumentation; proof
argūment·or -ārī -ātus sum *tr* to adduce as proof; to support by arguments; *(w.* **dē** + *abl)* to conclude from **‖** *intr* to adduce arguments, argue
argūment·um -ī *n* evidence, proof; argument; theme, plot; topic, subject; motif *(of artistic representation);* **ex argūmentō** from the facts of the case
arg·uō -uere -uī -ūtus *tr* to prove; to reveal, betray; to accuse, charge, impeach *(person);* to find fault with *(thing);* to denounce as wrong; to prove guilty, convict

Arg·us -ī *m* many-eyed monster set over Io and killed by Mercury

argūtāti·ō -ōnis *f* creaking

argūtē *adv* shrewdly

argūti·ae -ārum *fpl* subtlety; sophistry; wit

argūt·ō -āre -āvī *tr* to say childishly

argūt·or -ārī -ātus sum *intr* to chatter

argūtul·us -a -um *adj* somewhat subtle

argūt·us -a -um *adj* clearcut, bright, distinct; piercing; bright, smart, witty *(person);* clearvoiced, melodious; rustling *(leaves);* babbling *(brook);* chirping *(birds, crickets);* pungent *(smell);* expressive *(eyes, gestures)*

argyrasp·is -idis *adj* wearing a silver shield

-āri·a -ae *fem suf* forms nouns 1 denoting a place: **argentāria** a bank; 2 a female agent: **librāria** female secretary

Ariadn·a -ae *or* **Ariadn·ē** -ēs *f* Ariadne *(daughter of King Minos; she extricated Theseus from the Labyrinth)*

Arīci·a -ae *f* town in Latium on the Via Appia

āridul·us -a -um *adj* somewhat dry

ārid·us -a -um *adj* dry, parched; withered; meager; dry *(style)*

ari·ēs -etis *m* ram; battering ram; bulwark *(used as breakwater);* **ariete crebrō** with constant ramming ‖ **Ariēs** Aries *(sign of Zodiac)*

ariet·ō -āre -āvī -ātus *tr* to batter, ram; **inter sē arietārī** to collide ‖ *intr* to collide; to trip; *(w.* **in** + *acc)* to ram against

Ariobarzān·ēs -is *m* king of Cappadocia

Arī·ōn -onis *m* early Greek poet and musician, rescued from drowning by a dolphin

Ariovist·us -ī *m* king of Germanic tribe

-ār·is -is -e *adjl suf* collateral with **-ālis** but used when the stem contains an **l**: **cōnsulāris** consular

arist·a -ae *f* ear of grain

Aristae·us -ī *m* son of Apollo and Cyrene *(said to have taught man beekeeping and to have been the first to plant olive trees)*

Aristarch·us -ī *m* Alexandrine critic and scholar *(fl 156 B.C.);* stern critic

Aristīd·ēs -ae *m* Athenian politician and general in the time of Persian Wars, famous for his honesty ‖ author from Miletus

aristolochi·a -ae *f (bot)* birthwort *(plant believed to aid in childbirth)*

Aristophan·ēs -is *m* Greek comic playwright *(c. 450?–385? B.C.)*

Aristotel·ēs -is *or* -ī Aristotle *(384–322 B.C.)*

arithmētic·us -a -um *adj* of numbers ‖ *f or npl* arithmetic

āritūd·ō -inis *f* dryness

-ār·ium -(i)ī *n suf* denoting a place, *e.g.,* **armāmentārium** place for keeping arms, arsenal

-ār·ius -(i)ī *m suf* denoting "dealer in," *e.g.,* **librārius** bookseller

arm·a -ōrum *npl* armor, defensive arms *(opp* **tēla** weapons to throw or thrust); war, warfare; camp life; armed men, troops; equipment, tools; utensils; nature's arms *(teeth, claws, etc.);* **ab armīs dēcēdere** *or* **discēdere** to lay down one's arms, stop fighting; **ad arma adīre** *(or* **venīre**) to resort to military force; **arma capere** (**movēre, sūmere,** *etc.*) to take up arms; **arma cōnferre cum** to clash with; **arma ferre contrā** *or* **in** *(w. acc)* to fight against; **arma īnferre** *(dat)* to make war on; **arma pōnere** *(or* **dēpōnere**) to lay down one's arms; **arma vēnātōria** hunting gear; **in armīs** *(or* **sub armīs**) under arms, mobilized; **levia arma** light-armed troops; *(applied to the wings made by Daedalus)* **umerīs arma** equipment for his shoulders

armamax·a -ae *f* a Persian travel carriage for women

armāment·a -ōrum *npl* ship's gear; equipment

armāmentār·ium -(i)ī *n* arsenal, armory

armāriol·um -ī *n* small cabinet, chest, closet

armār·ium -(i)ī *n* cupboard, chest; bookcase; safe

armātūr·a -ae *f* outfit, equipment; armor; light-armed troops

armāt·us -a -um *adj* armed; equipped ‖ *m* armed man, soldier

armāt·us -ūs *m* armor; **gravis armātī** heavy-armed troops

Armeni·a -ae *f* (-min-) country in N.E. Asia Minor

Armeniac·um -ī *n* apricot

Armeniac·us -ī *f* apricot tree

Armeni·us -a -um *adj* Armenian; **prūnum Armenium** apricot ‖ *m* an Armenian

armentāl·is -is -e *adj* of the herd

armentār·ius -(i)ī *m* herdsman

arment·um -ī *n* herd *(of oxen, horses, stags, sea monsters)*

armif·er -era -erum *adj* arms-bearing, armed, warlike; **deus armifer** Mars; **dea armifera** Minerva

armig·er -era -erum *adj* armed; producing warriors; *(of a field sown with dragon's teeth)* producing armed men ‖ *m* armed man; bodyguard; armor-bearer ‖ *f* armor-bearer *(female);* **Iovis armigera** Jove's armor-bearer *(i.e., the eagle)*

armill·a -ae *f* armlet, bracelet

armillātus -a -um *adj* wearing a bracelet

Armilūstr·um -ī *n* ceremony of purifying arms

armipot·ēns -entis *adj* powerful in arms, valiant

armison·us -a -um *adj* reverberating with arms

arm·ō -āre -āvī -ātus *tr* to arm; to rouse to arms; to equip *(ships)* for war
arm·us -ī *m* shoulder, shoulder blade, upper arm; flank *(of animal)*
Arniēns·is -is -e *adj* name of one of the tribes in Rome
ar·ō -āre -āvī -ātus *tr* to plow, till
Arpīn·ās -ātis *adj* of Arpinum **ǁ** *mpl* inhabitants of Arpinum
Arpīn·um -ī *n* town in Latium, birthplace of Marius and Cicero
arq- = arc-
arquāt·us -a -um *adj* jaundiced
arr- = adr-
arrab·ō -ōnis *m* down payment, deposit; **arrabō amōris** token of love; **centum dēnāriōs arrabōnī dare** to make a down payment of one hundred denarii
arrēct·us -a -um *pp of* **arrigō ǁ** *adj* upright; steep
arrēp·ō -ere -sī *intr* (adr-) *(w. dat or* ad) to creep toward, steal up on
Arrēt·ium -(i)ī *n* town in Etruria, known for its pottery
arrēxī *perf of* arrigō
arrī·deō -dēre -sī -sus *tr* (adr-) to smile at **ǁ** *intr (w. dat)* **1** to smile at, smile on; **2** to laugh with; **3** to be favorable to; **4** to please
ar·rigō -rigere -rēxī -rēctus *tr* (adr-) to erect; to arouse, excite; to prick up *(ears);* **animum arrigere** to arouse courage; **in digitōs arrēctus** on tiptoe; **oculī arrēctī** staring eyes
ar·ripiō -ripere -ripuī -reptus *tr* (adr-) to snatch, seize eagerly; to get hold of; to obtain, acquire; to head eagerly for *(destination);* to jump at *(a chance, excuse); (of disease)* to attack; to assail, attack suddenly; *(fig)* to grasp quickly; *(leg)* to arrest, arraign
arrīsī *perf of* arrideō
arrō·dō -dere -sī -sus *tr* (adr-) to gnaw at, nibble away part of
arrog·āns -antis *adj* (adr-) arrogant
arroganter *adv* (adr-) arrogantly
arroganti·a -ae *f* (adr-) arrogance; presumption
ar·rogō -āre -āvī -ātus *tr* (adr-) to question; to lay claim to, arrogate; to claim to possess; to assign, attribute
arrōsī *perf of* arrōdō
arrōsus *pp of* arrōdō
Arrūn·s -tis *m* Etruscan proper name, traditionally given to the younger sons
ars artis *f* skill; craft, trade; craftsmanship; art; work of art; invention, device; trick, stratagem; *(mil)* tactic; profession, occupation; method, way, manner, means; artificial means, artificiality; science; theory *(opp:* ūsus practice); manual, textbook; **arte** cunningly; **bonae** *(or* līberālēs) **artēs** liberal arts; **ex arte** systematically; **istae artēs** evil practices, bad habits

Arsac·ēs -is *m* first king of the Parthians; title of his successors
ārsī *perf of* ārdeō
Artaban·us -ī *m* name of several Parthian kings
artē *adv* closely, tightly; *(to love)* deeply, dearly; *(to sleep)* soundly
Artem·is -idis *f* Greek counterpart of Diana
artēri·a -ae *f* windpipe; artery
arthrītic·us -a -um *adj* arthritic
articulātim *adv* piecemeal; *(to speak)* articulately, distinctly
articul·ō -āre *tr* to articulate
articul·us -ī *m* joint, knuckle; finger; toe; limb; point of time, juncture; *(gram)* single word *(of a sentence); (gram)* clause; *(gram)* (definite, indefinite) article; *(gram)* pronoun, pronominal adjective; **in articulō temporis** in the nick of time
artif·ex -icis *adj* (-tuf-) skilled, ingenious, professional; creative, productive; cunning; skillfully made, cunningly wrought; *(w. gen, ad or in + acc)* skilled in, expert in; broken, trained *(horse)*
artif·ex -icis *m* craftsman, artist, master, professional; performer, actor, musician; author *(of book);* originator, contriver; *(w. gen or* ad *or in + abl)* expert in
artificiōsē *adv* skillfully; systematically
artificiōs·us -a -um *adj* skillful, ingenious, accomplished; artificial
artific·ium -(i)ī *n* skill, talent; work of art; trade, profession; cleverness, cunning; theory
arti·us -a -um *adj* sound in mind and body
art·ō -āre -āvī -ātus *tr* (arct-) to pack closely; to compress, contract; to limit; to tighten
artolagan·us -ī *m* pancake *(made of meal, pepper, wine, milk, oil, lard)*
artopt·a -ae *m* bread pan; baker
artu·a -ōrum *npl* limbs
art·us -a -um *adj* close, tight; confined, restricted; narrow; dense; firm; scanty, small; needy; parsimonious, stingy; strict; sound *(sleep)* **ǁ** *n* narrow space; tight spot, difficulty; **in artum colligere** to summarize
art·us -ūs *m* joint; limb
ārul·a -ae *f* small altar
arund·ō -inis *f* reed; shaft, arrow; pipe, flute; pen; fishing rod; hobby-horse; *(in weaving)* comb
arvīn·a -ae *f* grease
arv·us -a -um *adj* arable, plowed **ǁ** *n* arable land, soil, land; plain; region; grain
arx arcis *f* citadel; fortress, stronghold; place of refuge; hilltop, peak; *(fig)* mainstay, protection; summit, pinnacle; **arcem facere ē cloācā** *(prov)* to make mountains out of

molehills; **arx caelī** height of heaven; **arx corporis** head; **Rōmae septem arcēs** seven hills of Rome

-ās *advl suf:* **aliās** elsewhere

ās assis *m* pound *(divisible into 12 ounces);* bronze coin, penny; jugerum *(c. 3/5 of an acre);* undivided estate; **hērēs ex asse** sole heir; **nōn assis facere** not to give a hoot about

-ās -ātis *adjl suf* **1** originally used in ethnic adjectives from the names of Italian towns: **Arpīnās** of *or* connected with Arpinum; **2** extended to other stems to form adjectives and substantives: **optimās** aristocratic; **optimātēs** artistocrats

Ascan·ius -(i)ī *m* son of Aeneas and Creusa and founder of Alba Longa

ascen·dō -dere -dī -sus *tr* **(ads-)** to climb; to mount *(horse);* to board *(ship)* ‖ *intr* to climb up, ascend; *(of voice, river)* to rise; *(w.* **ad** *or* **in** + *acc)* to climb, climb up to; *(w.* **super** *or* **suprā** + *acc)* to rise above, surpass; **per gradūs ascendere** to climb the stairs

ascēnsi·ō -ōnis *f* climbing up, ascent

ascēns·us -ūs *m* **(ads-)** ascent; means of ascending, approach; step, degree; flight of stairs; *(fig)* climb, rise

asci·a -ae *f* ax, hatchet; mason's trowel; **sub asciā** while still under construction

asc·iō -īre *tr* **(ads-)** to associate with oneself

asc·īscō -īscere -īvī -ītus *tr* **(ads-)** to adopt; to approve *(a bill);* to assume, arrogate; to select, to receive, admit *(as ally, citizen, etc.);* to hire; *(w.* **in** + *acc)* to admit *(to citizenship, the senate);* **inter patriciōs ascīscere** to admit to the patrician order

ascīt·us -a -um *adj* acquired *(as opposed to innate)*

Asclēpiad·ēs -is *m* famous doctor of Prusa in Bithynia, who practised in Rome and was a friend of Crassus *(d. 40 b.c.)*

āscop·a -ae *f* small leather pouch

Ascr·a -ae *f* birthplace of Hesiod in Boeotia, near Mt. Helicon

Ascrae·us -a -um *adj* of Ascra; **Ascraeus poēta** *or* **senex** Hesiod

ascrī·bō -bere -psī -ptus *tr* **(ads-)** to add *(by writing);* to impute, ascribe; to enroll, register; to reckon, number, class

ascrīptīci·us -a -um *adj* **(ads-)** enrolled, registered

ascrīpti·ō -ōnis *f* **(ads-)** addition *(in writing)*

ascrīptīv·us -ī *m* **(ads-)** *(mil)* reserve

ascrīpt·or -ōris *m* **(ads-)** supporter

Asc(u)l·um -ī *n* chief town of Picenum in N. Italy

Asculān·us -ī *m* inhabitant of Asculum

asell·a -ae *f* ass *(female)*

asell·us -ī *m* ass, donkey

Āsi·a -ae *f* Asia; Asia Minor *(modern Turkey);* kingdom of Troy

Āsiān·us -a -um *adj & m* Asian

Āsiātic·us -a -um *adj* connected with Asia or the East *(esp. Asia Minor and the Roman province of Asia);* **mare Āsiāticum** Carpathian Sea

asīl·us -ī *m* horsefly, gadfly

asin·a -ae *f* ass

asināri·us -a -um *adj* connected with asses; **via asināria** a road S.E. of Rome ‖ *m* ass-driver

asin·us -ī *m* ass; *(coll)* ass, fool

Ās·is -idis *f* Asia; Asia Minor

Āsi·us -a -um *f* of Asia, of Asia Minor

Āsōp·us *or* **Āsōp·os -ī** *m* a river in Boeotia, personified as the father of Aegina

asōt·us -ī *m* playboy, rake

asparag·us -ī *m* asparagus

aspargō *see* **aspergō**

aspectābil·is -is -e *adj* visible

aspect·ō -āre -āvī -ātus *tr* **(ads-)** to look at, gaze at; to look with respect at; *(of a place)* to face; to obey *(orders)*

aspectus *pp of* **aspiciō**

aspect·us -ūs *m* **(ads-)** look, sight, glance; sense of sight; eyes, expression in the eyes, look; range of vision, view; appearance, aspect; sight, vision; **prīmō aspectū** at first sight; **sub oculōrum aspectum cadere** to come into view; **ūnō aspectū** at a glance

aspell·ō -ere *tr* to drive away

asp·er -era -erum *(aspr·īs = asper·īs) adj* rough, uneven; harsh, severe, stormy *(climate);* grating, hoarse *(sound);* pungent, strong *(odor);* rough, hard; unkind, cruel, bitter, rude *(character);* austere, rigid *(person);* wild, fierce *(animal);* rough, annoying, adverse *(circumstances);* embossed *(cup, etc.);* craggy; rugged *(style)*

asperē *adv* roughly; harshly, sternly, severely

asper·gō -gere -sī -sus *tr* **(ads-)** **(-spar-)** to sprinkle, scatter; to taint; *(w. dat)* to sprinkle *(s.th.)* on

asperg·ō -inis *f* **(ads-)** **(-spar-)** sprinkling; spray

asperit·ās -ātis *f* unevenness, roughness; severity, fierceness; difficulty, trouble

āspernāti·ō -ōnis *f* disdain

āspern·or -ārī -ātus sum *tr* to disdain, spurn, reject

asper·ō -āre -āvī -ātus *tr* to make rough *or* uneven, roughen; to exasperate; to make worse

aspersi·ō -ōnis *f* sprinkling

aspiciō aspicere aspexī aspectus *tr* **(ads-)** to catch sight of, spot; to look at; to inspect, look over; to look *(a person)* in the eye; to visit; to consider; to picture

aspīrāti·ō -ōnis *f* (ads-) breathing; exhalation; *(gram)* aspiration *(making an h sound)*
aspīr·ō -āre -āvī -ātum *intr* to breathe, blow; *(w. dat or ad or in + acc)* to aspire to, desire to reach *or* obtain, come near to obtaining; *(w. dat)* to favor; *(w. ad)* to rival; *(w. acc & dat)* to instil *(e.g., love)* in
asp·is -idis *f* asp *(poisonous snake of N. Africa)*
asportātiō -ōnis *f* removal
asport·ō -āre -āvī -ātus *tr* to carry away, remove; *(of vehicles)* to haul away
asprēt·a -ōrum *npl* rough terrain
Assarac·us -ī *m* king of Troy, son of Tros, and grandfather of Aeneas
assecl·a -ae *m* (ads-) hanger-on
assectāti·ō -ōnis *f* (ads-) (political) support
assectāt·or -ōris *m* (ads-) attendant, companion; disciple; devotee; *(pol)* supporter
assect·or -ārī -ātus sum *tr* (ads-) to follow closely; to escort; to be an adherent of, follow
assecul·a -ae *m* (ads-) hanger-on
assēnsi·ō -ōnis *f* (ads-) approval, applause; agreement, belief ‖ *fpl* expressions of approval
assēns·or -ōris *m* (ads-) backer, supporter
assēns·us -ūs *m* (ads-) assent, approval; agreement; belief
assentāti·ō -ōnis *f* (ads-) assent, agreement; flattery
assentātiuncul·a -ae *f* (ads-) bit of flattery
assentāt·or -ōris *m* (ads-) yes-man
assentātōriē *adv* (ads-) flatteringly
assentātr·īx -īcis *f* (ads-) flatterer *(female)*
assen·tiō -tīre -sī -sum *or* assen·tior -tīrī -sus sum *intr* (ads-) to agree; *(w. dat)* assent to, agree with, approve
assent·or -ārī -ātus sum *intr* (ads-) to agree always; *(w. dat)* 1 to agree always with; 2 to humor
asse·quor -quī -cūtus sum *tr* (ads-) to pursue, go after; to catch up to, reach; to gain, obtain, procure; to achieve, attain, win *(wisdom, citizenship, etc.)*; to come up to, equal, match; to comprehend, understand
ass·er -eris *m* pole; joist, rafter; pole on which a litter was carried
asser·ō -ere -uī -tus *tr* (ads-) to set free, liberate *(slave)*; to protect, defend; to claim, appropriate; in servitūtem asserere to claim *(s.o.)* as one's slave
as·serō -serere -sēvī -situs *tr* (ads-) *(w. dat)* to plant *(s.th.)* close to
asserti·ō -ōnis *f* (ads-) declaration of civil status
assert·or -ōris *m* (ads-) defender, protector, champion; *(leg)* claimant *(who claims a person as his slave)*
asserv·iō -īre -īvī *or* -iī *intr* (ads-) *(w. dat)* to apply oneself to

asserv·ō -āre -āvī -ātus *tr* (ads-) to preserve; keep *(records)*; to watch; to keep in custody; *(mil)* to guard
assessi·ō -ōnis *f* (ads-) company (legal) support, standing by
assess·or -ōris *m* (ads-) adviser; *(leg)* counselor
assess·us -ūs *m* (ads-) legal assistance
assevēranter *adv* (ads-) emphatically
assevērāti·ō -ōnis *f* (ads-) assertion; emphasis; earnestness; firmness; *(rhet)* emphasizing particle *(e.g., eheu)*
assevēr·ō -āre -āvī -ātus *tr* (ads-) to assert emphatically; *(of things)* to give clear evidence of; to be serious about ‖ *intr* to be serious
as·sideō -sidēre -sēdī -sessus *tr* (ads-) to sit near; *(mil)* to besiege ‖ *intr* to sit nearby; *(w. dat)* 1 to sit near, stand by, take care of, keep *(s.o.)* company; 2 to be busily engaged in; 3 *(of places)* to be situated close to; 4 to attend to, mind; 5 to resemble; 6 *(mil)* to encamp near; 7 *(mil)* to set up a blockade against
as·sīdō -sīdere -sēdī *intr* (ads-) to sit down; *(of birds)* to land, alight
assiduē *adv* (ads-) assiduously, continually
assiduit·ās -ātis *f* (ads-) constant presence; persistence, frequent recurrence
assiduō *adv* (ads-) continually
assidu·us -a -um *adj* (ads-) constantly present; persistent, incessant; tireless, busy; restless *(sea)* ‖ *m* taxpayer; rich man
assignāti·ō -ōnis *f* (ads-) allotment *(of land)*
assign·ō -āre -āvī -ātus *tr* (ads-) to mark out, allot, assign *(land)*; *(w. dat)* 1 to confer *(honors)* on; 2 to ascribe to, impute to; 3 to attribute to; 4 to entrust to the care of
as·siliō -silīre -siluī -sultum *intr* (ads-) to jump; *(w. dat)* 1 to jump upon, leap at; 2 *(mil)* to make a sudden assault on; *(w. ad)* 1 to jump to; 2 to have recourse to
assimil·is -is -e *adj* (ads-) *(w. gen or dat)* similar to, like
assimiliter *adv* (ads-) in like manner
assimulāti·ō -ōnis *f* (ads-) similarity; comparison; pretense
assimulāt·us -a -um *adj* (ads-) similar; counterfeit
assimul·ō -āre -āvī -ātus *tr* (ads-) (-mil-) to pretend; to resemble, imitate; *(w. dat)* to compare to
as·sistō -sistere -titī *intr* (ads-) to stop; to stand nearby; *(w. ad)* to stand at *or* near; *(w. dat)* to assist, defend; *(mil)* *(w. in + acc)* to take up a position against; *(leg)* to assist in court; *(leg)* *(w. dat)* to assist, defend
assitus *pp of* asserō
assol·eō -ēre *intr* (ads-) to be usual
asson·ō -āre *intr* (ads-) *(w. dat)* to echo

assūctus *pp of* assūgō sucked in

assūdēsc·ō -ere *intr* (ads-) (-āsc-) to break out into a sweat

assuē·faciō -facere -fēcī -factus *tr* (ads-) to train; *(w. dat or* ad *or inf)* to accustom *(s.o.)* to, get *(s.o.)* used to

assu·ēscō -ēscere -ēvī -ētus *tr* (ads-) *(w. dat)* to accustom *(s.o.)* to, make *(s.o.)* familiar with ‖ *intr (w. dat,* ad, *or w. inf)* to become used to; *(w. dat)* to become intimate with

assuētūd·ō -inis *f* (ads-) habit, custom; intimacy

assuēt·us -a -um *pp of* assuēscō ‖ *adj* accustomed, customary, usual; *(w. abl)* trained in; *(w. dat,* ad *or* in + *acc or inf)* accustomed to, used to; *(w. dat)* intimate with

assū·gō -gere -xī -ctus *tr* (ads-) to suck in

assul·a -ae *f* splinter, chip, shaving

assulātim *adv* into splinters

assult·ō -āre -āvī -ātus *tr* (ads-) to assault ‖ *intr (w. dat)* to jump at, jump to

assult·us -ūs *m* (ads-) assault

assūm·ō -ere -psī -ptus *tr* (ads-) to take in addition, add; to adopt; to usurp; to claim, assume; to employ, hire; to derive, borrow; to gain, acquire *(qualities);* to take *(food, drink, bait);* to take along *(as companion);* sibi assūmere to lay claim to

assūmpti·ō -ōnis *f* (ads-) assumption; adoption; acquisition; claim; *(in logic)* minor premise; *(rhet)* taking up *(of a point)*

assūmptīv·us -a -um *adj* (ads-) resting on external evidence, extrinsic

assu·ō -ere *tr* (ads-) *(w. dat)* to sew *(e.g. patch)* on

assur·gō -gere -rēxī -rēctum *intr* (ads-) to stand up; to rise; to increase, swell; *(of hair)* to stand on end; *(w. dat)* to rise out of respect for

ass·us -a -um *adj* roasted; dry *(sunbathing without anointing)* ‖ *n* roast

assūxī *perf of* assūgō

Assyri·a -ae *f* Assyria

Assyri·us -a -um *adj* Assyrian ‖ *mpl* Assyrians

ast *conj (old form of* at) but

Astart·ē -ēs *f* Syro-Phoenician goddess, counterpart of Venus

Asteri·a -ae *f* sister of Leto, who was metamorphosed into a quail at Delos

astern·ō -ere *tr* (ads-) to strew ‖ *pass* to prostrate oneself

astic·us -a -um *adj* city, urban

astipulāt·or -ōris *m* (ads-) legal assistant; supporter, adherent

astipul·or -ārī -ātus sum *intr* (ads-) *(w. dat)* to side with

astit·uō -uere -uī -ūtus *tr* to place near; *(w. ad)* to make *(s.o.)* stand near

ast·ō -āre -itī *intr* (ads-) to stand erect, stand up; to stand nearby, stand by; *(w. dat)* 1. to stand by; 2. to assist; astā! stand still!, stop!

Astrae·a -ae *f* goddess of justice

Astrae·us -a -um *adj* of Astraeus; frātrēs Astraeī the winds ‖ *m* a Titan, husband of Aurora and father of the winds

astrep·ō -ere -uī *tr* (ads-) *tr* to assail *(with shouts)* ‖ *intr* to shout in support; *(w. dat)* to applaud

astrictē *adv* (ads-) concisely; strictly

astrīct·us -a -um *pp of* astringō ‖ *adj* drawn together, tight; stingy; concise

astrif·er -cra -erum *adj* starry

astr·ingō -ingere -īnxī -īctus *tr* (ads-) to tighten, bind fast; to obligate; to restrain; to freeze; to pledge; *(fig)* to numb; *(fig)* to compress, abridge; to occupy *(attention);* to embarrass; to implicate *(in a crime);* fidem astringere to give one's word; inter sē astringere to fasten together

astrologi·a -ae *f* astronomy; astrology

astrolog·us -ī *m* astronomer; astrologer

astr·um -ī *n* star; constellation ‖ *npl* stars; sky, heaven

astr·uō -uere -uxī -uctus *tr* (ads) to build as an additional structure; nōbilitātem alicui astruere to add nobility to s.o.

astu *indecl n the* city *(i.e., Athens)*

astup·eō -ēre -uī *intr (w. dat)* to be amazed at, be enthralled by

ast·us -ūs *m* cunning; trick

astūtē *adv* slyly

astūti·a -ae *f* cunning, slyness; astuteness; astūtiae sly tricks

astūt·us -a -um *adj* clever, astute; *(usu. pej)* cunning

Astyag·ēs -is *m* king of Media and grandfather of Cyrus; an enemy of Perseus changed by him into a stone by means of the head of Medusa

Astyan·ax -actis *m* son of Hector and Andromache

asyl·um -ī *n* refuge, asylum

at *conj* but; *(in a transition)* but on the other hand; *(in anticipation of an opponent's objection)* but, it may be objected; *(in an ironical objection)* but really, but after all; *(after a negative clause, to introduce a qualification)* but at least; at contrā but on the contrary; at tamen but at least

Atābul·us -ī *m* sirocco, S.E. wind

Atalant·a -ae *or* Atlant·ē -ēs *f* daughter of King Schoeneus, defeated by Hippomenes in a footrace ‖ daughter of Iasius and participant in the Calydonian boar hunt

atat *(or* attat) *interj (expressing surprise or fear)* aha!, uhoh!

atav·us -ī *m* great-great-great-grandfather; ancestor

Ātell·a -ae *f* Campanian town

Ātellān·a -ae *f* comic farce *(originated in Atella)*

ā·ter -tra -trum *adj* flat black *(different from* **niger** glossy black)*; dark; gloomy; malicious; poisonous; unlucky, ill-omened

Atham·ān -ānis *m* inhabitant of Athamania

Athamāni·a -ae *f* district in Epirus

Athamantē·us -a -um *adj* of Athamas *(referring to Phrixus or Palaemon)*

Atham·ās -antis *m* king of Thessaly, father of Helle and Phrixus by Nephele, and of Learchus and Melecertes by Ino

Athēn·ae -ārum *fpl* Athens

Athēniēns·is -is -e *adj* Athenian

Athēnodōr·us -ī *m* Stoic philosopher, teacher of Augustus

athe·os -ī *m* atheist

āthlēt·a -ae *m* athlete; boxer; wrestler

āthlēticē *adv* athletically; like an athlete

āthlētic·us -a -um *adj* athletic **‖** *f* athletics

Ath·ōs *or* **Athō** *or* **Ath·ōn** *(no gen) m* mountain on the peninsula of Acte in Chalcidice

Ātīn·a -ae *f* town in Latium **‖** town in Lucania (now Basilicata)

Ātīn·ās -ātis *m* of Atina **‖** *mpl* the people of Atina

Atl·ās -antis *m* Atlas *(giant supporting the sky, son of Iapetus and Clymene)* **‖** Mt. Atlas *(on N.W. coast of Africa)*

Atlantē·us -a -um *adj* Atlantic

Atlantiad·ēs -ae *m* grandson of Atlas (Mercury) **‖** great-grandson of Atlas (Hermaphroditus)

Atlantic·us -a -um *adj* Atlantic

Atlant·is -idis *or* **-idos** *f* daughter *or* female descendant of Atlas

atom·os -ī *f* atom *(an indivisible element)*

atque *conj (used before vowels and "h" and sometimes consonants; see* **ac***)* and, and also, and besides; *(in adding a more important word)* and indeed, and in particular

atquī *conj* but yet, and yet; however, rather, and yet

ātrāment·um -ī *n* ink; **ātrāmentum sūtōrium** black shoe polish

ātrāt·us -a -um *adj* dressed in black *(for mourning)*

Atr·eūs -eī *m* son of Pelops, brother of Thyestes, father of Agamemnon and Menelaus

ātricol·or -ōris *adj* black

Atrīd·ēs -ae *m* descendant of Atreus

ātriēns·is -is *m* butler

ātriol·um -ī *n* small hall, anteroom

ātrit·ās -ātis *f* blackness

ātrīt·us -a -um *adj* blackened

ātr·ium -(i)ī *n* atrium *(first main room of Roman house)*; hall *(of temple or public building)* **‖** *npl* house; palace

atrōcit·ās -ātis *f* hideousness; fierceness, brutality, cruelty; severity, rigor

atrōciter *adv* atrociously, horribly; cruelly

Atrop·os -ī *f* one of the three Fates whose function it was to cut the thread of human life

atrōt·us -a -um *adj* invulnerable

atr·ōx -ōcis *adj* atrocious, horrible; hideous; frightful; cruel, fierce; harsh, stern, unyielding, grim

attāctus *pp of* **attingō**

attāct·us -ūs *m* **(adt-)** touch, contact

attag·ēn -ēnis *m* woodcock *(game bird)*

attagēn·a -ae *f* woodcock *(game bird)*

Attalic·us -a -um *adj* of Attalus; Pergamean; rich, splendid; covered with gold brocade **‖** *npl* gold brocade

Attal·us -ī *m* king of Pergamum

attamen *conj* but still, but yet

attat *or* **attatae** *interj* uhoh!

attegi·a -ae *f* hut, cottage

attemperātē *adv* **(adt-)** on time, at the right time; in the nick of time

attempt·ō -āre -āvī -ātus *tr* **(adt-)** to attempt; to test; to tempt, try to seduce; to call into question; to attack

atten·dō -dere -dī -tus *tr* **(adt-)** to notice, mark; to pay attention to, mind, consider; **animō attendere** to listen to; **animum attendere** to pay attention; **aurēs attendere** to listen closely **‖** *intr* to pay attention, listen

attentē *adv* **(adt-)** attentively

attenti·ō -ōnis *f* attention

attentō *see* **attemptō**

attent·us -a -um *pp of* **attendō ‖** *adj* attentive; careful; frugal; industrious

attenuātē *adv* plainly, in a plain style

attenuāt·us -a -um *adj* weak, weakened; shortened, brief; over-refined, affected; plain, bald *(style)*

attenu·ō -āre -āvī -ātus *tr* **(adt-)** to weaken; to thin; to lessen, diminish; to impoverish **‖** *pass* to become thinner, shrink

at·terō -terere -trīvī -trītus *tr* **(adt-)** to rub (against), wear away, wear out; to reduce in dimensions, diminish; to impair *(faculties, qualities);* to reduce *(military forces);* to weaken, exhaust; to waste, fritter away; to destroy **‖** *pass* **atterī** to lose face by being outdone

attest·or -ārī -ātus sum *tr* **(adt-)** to attest

attex·ō -ere -uī -tus *tr* **(adt-)** to add *(by weaving);* to add on

Atth·is -idis *f* Attica

Attic·a -ae *f* district of Greece, with Athens as its capital

Atticē *adv* in the Athenian style

Atticiss·ō -āre *tr & intr* to speak in the Athenian (Attic) manner

Attic·us -a -um *adj* Attic, Athenian ‖ *m* Titus Pomponius Atticus *(friend of Cicero, 109–32 B.C.)* ‖ *f* daughter of Atticus

attigō *see* **attingō**

at·tineō -tinēre -tinuī -tentus *tr* **(adt-)** to hold tight, hold on to, hold back; to reach for ‖ *intr (w. ad)* to pertain to, relate to, refer to, concern; **quod ad mē attinet** as far as I am concerned

at·tingō -tingere -tigī -tāctus *tr* **(adt-)** to touch, come in contact with; to reach, arrive at; to touch *(food),* taste; to touch, lie near, border; to touch upon, mention lightly; to touch, strike, attack; to touch, affect; to undertake, engage in; to take in hand, manage; to resemble; to concern, belong to

Att·is -idis *m* priest of Cybele

attoll·ō -ere *tr* **(adt-)** to lift up, raise; to erect; to stir up *(dust, sea);* to cause *(river)* to rise; to hold aloft, carry; to exalt; to uplift; to extol; **īrās atollere** to rouse anger ‖ *refl & pass* to rise; to appear; to grow

atton·deō -dēre -dī -sus *tr* **(adt-)** to clip, shave, shear; to prune; to crop; *(fig)* to fleece, cheat, clip

attonit·us -a -um *adj* **(adt-)** thunderstruck, stunned, dazed, astonished; inspired; frantic, frenzied

atton·ō -āre -uī -itus *tr* **(adt-)** to strike with lightning; to drive crazy; to shock

attorqu·eō -ēre *tr* **(adt-)** to wind up *(before hurling),* hurl up

at·trahō -trahere -trāxī -trāctus *tr* **(adt-)** to attract; to drag in; to cause to happen, bring on; to draw toward oneself; to bend *(a bow);* to draw up *(the feet);* to contract, draw together

attrect·ō -āre -āvī -ātus *tr* **(adt-)** to touch, handle; to appropriate to oneself

attrepid·ō -āre *intr* **(adt-)** to hobble along

attrib·uō -uere -uī -ūtus *tr* **(adt-)** to allot, assign; to appoint *(to a post);* to put under the command of; to attribute; to bestow, give; to impose *(taxes)*

attribūti·ō -ōnis *f* **(adt-)** *(gram)* predicate; *(leg)* transference of a debt *(to another person, obligating him)*

attribūt·um -ī *n* **(adt-)** *(gram)* predicate

attrīt·us -a -um *pp of* **atterō** ‖ *adj* worn away, wasted; thin; hardened

au *interj* ouch!

au·ceps -cupis *m* fowler, bird trapper; poulterer; spy, eavesdropper

auctār·ium -(i)ī *n* addition, overweight *(in a purchase)*

auctific·us -a -um *adj* increasing

aucti·ō -ōnis *f* increase; auction; **auctiōnem cōnstituere** *or* **facere** to hold an auction; **auctiōnem prōscrībere** to advertise an auction

auctiōnāri·us -a -um *adj* auction

auctiōn·or -ārī -ātus sum *intr* to hold an auction

auctit·ō -āre *tr* to keep increasing

auct·ō -āre *tr* to increase; *(w. abl)* to bless with *(children)*

auctor -ōris *m* originator, author; writer, historian; reporter, harbinger *(of news);* acknowledged expert, authority *(for statement or theory);* proposer *(of a law);* supporter, backer; vendor, seller; progenitor *(of a clan, family, race);* founder *(of city);* model, example; adviser, counselor; teacher; guarantor, security; leader, statesman; source, thrower, dealer *(of missile, wound, death);* **auctor esse (w. ut, nē + subj)** to advocate, advise; to move that, propose that; **faenoris auctor** lender; **mē auctōre** on my initiative, at my suggestion; **pecūniae auctor** person responsible for or owing a sum of money; **rērum omnium auctor parēnsque** the Creator *(literally, the author and parent of all things);* **sine auctōre** anonymous

auctōrāment·um -ī *n* contract; pay

auctōrit·ās -ātis *f* origination, source, cause; view, opinion, judgment; advice, encouragement; power, authority, weight, influence; prestige; leadership; importance, significance, worth, consequence; example, model, precedent; authority *(for establishing a fact);* document, record; decree *(of senate);* right of ownership, title

auctōr·ō -āre -āvī -ātus *or* **auctōr·or -ārī** *tr* to hire out, sell ‖ *refl & pass* to hire oneself out

auct·us -a -um *pp of* **augeō** ‖ *adj* blessed *(with children, good omens)*

auct·us -ūs *m* increase, growth; abundance, prosperity

aucup·ium -(i)ī *n* fowling; trap; eavesdropping; **aucupia verbōrum** quibbling

aucup·ō -āre -āvī -ātus *or* **aucup·or -ārī -ātus sum** *tr* to lie in wait for, watch for; to chase, strive after, catch ‖ *intr* to trap birds

audāc(i)ter *adv* boldly

audāci·a -ae *f* boldness, courage, daring; recklessness, effrontery, audacity; bold deed ‖ *fpl* adventures

aud·āx -ācis *adj* bold, daring; reckless

aud·ēns -entis *adj* bold, daring

audenti·a -ae *f* boldness, daring

audeō audēre ausus sum *tr* to dare, risk; **vix ausim** *(old perf subj active)* **crēdere** I could scarcely dare to believe ‖ *intr* to dare, be bold

audi·ēns -entis *m* hearer, listener ‖ *mpl* audience

audienti·a -ae *f* hearing, attention; **audientiam facere** to command attention, command silence

aud·iō -īre -īvī *or* -**iī -ītus** *tr* to hear, listen to; to be taught by, learn from; to grant; to accept, agree with, yield to; to obey; to be called, be named; to be reported, be regarded

audīti·ō -ōnis *f* hearsay, rumor

audīt·ō -āre -āvī *tr* to hear

audīt·or -ōris *m* hearer; student

audītōr·ium -(i)ī *n* lecture hall; the audience

audīt·us -ūs *m* hearing, sense of hearing; hearsay

auferō auferre abstulī ablātus *tr* to take away, bear off; to remove, withdraw; to steal; to sweep away, kill, destroy; to gain, obtain; to learn, understand; to mislead; to lead into a digression; to abduct; to captivate; **pedēs auferre** to go away || *pass* **ē cōnspectū auferrī** to disappear from sight || *refl* to go away

Aufid·us -ī *m* river in Apulia

au·fugiō -fugere -fūgī *tr* to shun, flee from || *intr* to run away, escape

Aug·ē -ēs *f* mother of Telephus by Hercules

Augē·ās -ae *m* king of Elis, whose stables were cleaned by Hercules

au·geō -gēre -xī -ctus *tr* to increase, enlarge, augment, spread; to magnify; to exalt; to exaggerate; to emphasize; to enrich; to honor, advance, promote; to reinforce; to feed *(flame);* to raise *(voice);* to endow

augēsc·ō -ere *intr* to begin to grow; to become larger, increase; to prosper; *(of river)* to rise

aug·ur -uris *mf* augur *(priest who foretold future by observing birds);* seer

augurācul·um -ī *n* place of augury *(later known as the* **arx***)*

augurāl·is -is -e *adj* augural, augur's || *n* area in a Roman camp where the general took the auguries

augurāti·ō -ōnis *f* prophesying

augurātō *adv* after taking the auguries

augurāt·us -a -um *adj* consecrated after taking the auspices

augurāt·us -ūs *m* office of augur

augur·ium -(i)ī *n* observation of omens, interpretation of omens, augury; sign, omen; prophecy; foreboding

auguri·us -a -um *adj* of augurs; **iūs augurium** the right to take auguries

augur·ō -āre -āvī -ātus *or* **augur·or -ārī -ātus sum** *tr* to consult by augury; to consecrate by augury; to predict, prophesy; to conjecture, imagine || *intr* to act as augur; to take auspices

August·a -ae *f* title of wife, mother, grandmother, daughter, or sister of the emperor

Augustāl·is -is -e *adj* of Augustus; **sodālēs Augustālēs** priests of deified Augustus || *npl* games in honor of Augustus

Augustān·us -a -um *adj* of Augustus, Augustan; of an emperor, imperial || *mpl* knights appointed by Nero

augustē *adv* reverently, solemnly

Augustiān·ī -ōrum *mpl* Nero's claque in the theater

Augustīn·us -a -um *adj* of Augustus

august·us -a -um *adj* august, sacred, venerable; majestic

August·us -a -um *adj* Augustan, imperial; **mēnsis Augustus** August || *m* honorary cognomen of Octavius Caesar after 27 B.C. and of subsequent emperors

aul·a -ae *f* inner court, hall *(of house);* palace; royal court; people of the royal court, the court; royal power

aulae·um -ī *n (more frequently used in the pl)* bed coverings; canopy; curtain *(which was let down below the stage when the play began, and was raised again when the play ended; hence,* **aulaea premuntur** *or* **aulaeum mittitur** the curtain is lowered *(i.e., the performance is beginning);* **aulaeum tollitur** the curtain is raised *(i.e., the play is over)* || *npl* curtain; tapestries

aulic·us -a -um *adj* courtly, princely || *m* courtier

Aul·is -is *or* -**idis** *f* port in Boeotia from which Greeks sailed for Troy

auloed·us -ī *m* singer accompanied by reed pipe

aur·a -ae *f* breeze; breath of air, wind; air, atmosphere; heights, heaven; upper world; odor, exhalation; daylight, publicity; **ad aurās ferre** to make known, publicize; **ad aurās venīre** to come to the upper world; **aura aurī** the gleam of gold; **auram captāre** to sniff the air; **aura populāris** popular favor; **aurās fugere** to hide; **aura speī** breath of hope; **sub aurās** to light, into the air; into the open air

aurāri·us -a -um *adj* gold, golden || *f* gold mine

aurāt·us -a -um *adj* made of gold; gold-plated; golden; glittering; **aurāta pellis** the Golden Fleece

Aurēli·us -a -um *adj* Roman clan name *(nomen), esp.* Marcus Aurelius *(Roman Emperor A.D. 161–180)* || named after an Aurelius, *esp.* Via Aurelia *(running along the Etruscan coast to the Maritime Alps)*

aureol·us -a -um *adj* gold, golden; splendid; very precious

aure·us -a -um *adj* gold, golden; gilded, gilt; beautiful, magnificent; brilliant || *m* gold coin

auricom·us -a -um *adj* golden-haired; with golden foliage

auricul·a -ae *f* (**ōr-**) outer ear; earlobe; *(leg)* **auriculam tangere** *or* **appōnere** to agree to be a witness

aurif·er -era -erum *adj* producing *or* containing gold; *(of trees)* bearing golden apples

aurif·ex -icis *m* (**auru-**) goldsmith

aurīg·a -ae *mf* (**ōr-**) charioteer; *(fig)* pilot **‖ Aurīga** *m* Auriga *(constellation)*

aurīgāti·ō -ōnis *f* chariot-driving

aurigen·a -ae *m* offspring of gold *(i.e., Perseus)*

aurig·er -era -erum *adj* gold-bearing; gilded

aurīg·ō -āre -āvī -ātum *intr* to drive a chariot; to compete in a chariot race

aur·is -is *f* ear; **aurem admovēre** to listen; **auribus servīre** to flatter; **aurēs adhibēre** to pay attention; **in aurem dextram** *(or in* **aurem utramvīs) dormīre** to sleep soundly, be unconcerned; **in** *or* **ad aurem** *or* **in aure dīcere, admonēre,** *etc.* to whisper in the ear

aurīscalp·ium -(i)ī *n (med)* earpick, probe

aurītul·us -ī *m* "little long-ears" *(i.e., an ass)*

aurīt·us -a -um *adj* long-eared; attentive; nosey; **testis aurītus** witness by hearsay only **‖** *m* rabbit, hare

aurōr·a -ae *f* dawn, daybreak; the East **‖ Aurora** goddess of dawn

aur·um -ī *n* gold; color of gold, golden luster; gold cup; gold necklace; gold jewelry; gold plate; golden fleece; gold money; Golden Age

Aurunc·a -ae *f* town in Campania, birthplace of the poet Lucilius

Aurunc·us -a -um *adj* of Arunca **‖** *mpl* people of Arunca

auscultāti·ō -ōnis *f* obedience; a listening

auscultāt·or -ōris *m* listener

auscult·ō -āre -āvī -ātus *tr* to listen to; to overhear **‖** *intr (w. dat)* to obey, listen to

ausim *see* **audeō**

Auson·es -um *mpl* Ausonians *(ancient inhabitants of central Italy)*

Ausoni·a -ae *f (poet)* Italy

Ausonid·ae -ārum *mpl (poet)* Italians

Ausoni·us -a -um *adj (poet)* Ausonian, Italian **‖** *mpl (poet)* Ausonians, Italians

ausp·ex -icis *mf* augur, soothsayer; *(fig)* guide, director, protector **‖** *mpl* witnesses *(at a marriage ceremony)*

auspicātō *adv* after taking the auspices; auspiciously

auspicāt·us -a -um *adj* consecrated *(by auguries);* auspicious, lucky

auspic·ium -(i)ī *n (often used in the plural)* auspices *(from behavior of birds or chickens);* right to take the auspices; sign, omen; command, leadership, authority; inaugura-

tion; **auspicia incerta** ambiguous auspices; **auspicium habēre** to have the right to take auspices; **auspicium facere** *(of birds)* to give a sign; **pullārium in auspicium mittere** to send the keeper of chickens to take the auspices; **tuīs auspiciīs** under your command *(or* leadership)

auspic·ō -āre -āvī *intr* to take the auspices

auspic·or -ārī -ātus sum *tr* to inaugurate, make a ceremonial beginning of; to enter upon **‖** *intr* to take auspices; to make a start

aus·ter -trī *m* south wind; the South

austērē *adv* austerely, severely

austērit·ās -ātis *f* austerity

austēr·us -a -um *adj* austere, stern, harsh *(person);* pungent *(odor);* harsh *(taste);* drab, dark *(color);* serious *(talk);* gloomy, hard *(circumstances);* dry *(wine)*

austrāl·is -is -e *adj* southern; **cingulus** *(or* **regiō** *or* **ōra) austrālis** torrid zone

austrīn·us -a -um *adj* southerly, from the south; southern

aus·us -a -um *pp of* **audeō ‖** *n* daring attempt, enterprise, venture; outrage

aut *conj* or; *(correcting what precedes)* or rather, or else; *(adding emphatic alternative)* or at least; **aut ... aut** *(introducing two or more logically exclusive alternatives)* either ... or; **ūnus aut alter** one or two

autem *conj (regularly follows an emphatic word)* but, on the other hand, however; *(in transitions)* now

autheps·a -ae *f* cooker *(utensil)*

autograph·us -a -um *adj* written with one's own hand, autograph

Autolyc·us -ī *m* father of Anticlea, maternal grandfather of Ulysses

automat·on *or* **automat·um -ī** *n* automaton

automat·us -a -um *adj* automatic, spontaneous, voluntary

Automed·ōn -ontis *m* charioteer of Achilles; a charioteer

Autono·ē -ēs *f* daughter of Cadmus, wife of Aristaeus, and mother of Actaeon

autumnāl·is -is -e *adj* autumnal, fall

autumn·us -a -um *adj* autumn **‖** *m* autumn

autum·ō -āre -āvī -ātus *tr* to assert, state, say; *(w. acc & inf)* to say that

auxiliār·is -is -e *adj* auxiliary **‖** *mpl* auxiliary troops, auxiliaries

auxiliāri·us -a -um *adj* auxiliary

auxiliāt·or -ōris *m* helper

auxiliāt·us -ūs *m* help, aid

auxili·or -ārī -ātus sum *intr (w. dat)* **1** to give help to; **2** *(of things)* to be helpful to, be of use to; **3** *(med)* to relieve, heal, cure

auxil·ium -(i)ī *n* help; *(med)* relief, remedy; **auxiliō esse** *(w. dat)* to be of assistance to **‖** *npl* auxiliary troops; reinforcements

avārē *adv* greedily

avāriter *adv* greedily

avāriti·a -ae *f* avarice, greed; gluttony

avār·us -a -um *adj* greedy, avaricious; *(w. gen)* eagerly desirous of, greedy for

avē! *see* **aveō**

āve·hō -here -xi -ctus *tr* to haul away ‖ *pass* to ride off; to sail away

ā·vellō -vellere -vellī *(or* -**vulsī** *or* -**volsī)** -**vulsus** *(or* -**volsus)** *tr* to pull *or* pluck away; to tear off; to separate, remove ‖ *refl & pass (w. ab)* to tear oneself away from, withdraw from

avēn·a -ae *f* oats; reed, stem, stalk, a straw; shepherd's pipe

Aventīn·us -a -um *adj* Aventine ‖ *m & n* Aventine Hill *(one of the Seven Hills of Rome)* ‖ *m* son of Hercules

av·eō *or* **hav·eō -ēre** to desire, long for, crave; *(w. inf)* to long to ‖ *intr* to say goodbye; **avē!**, **avēte!** hello!, farewell!, goodbye!; **aliquem avēre iubeō** I send greetings to s.o.

Avernāl·is -is -e *adj* of Lake Avernus

Avern·us -a -um *adj* birdless; of Lake Avernus ‖ *m* Lake Avernus *(near Cumae, reputed entrance to the underworld)*

āverr·ō -ere -ī *tr* to sweep away

āverrunc·ō -āre *tr* to avert

āversābil·is -is -e *adj* abominable

āvers·or -ārī -ātus sum *tr* (**-vor-**) to repulse, reject, refuse; to shun, avoid; to send away ‖ *intr* to turn away *(in displeasure, shame, contempt)*

āvers·or -ōris *m* embezzler

āvers·us -a -um *pp of* **āvertō** ‖ *adj* turned back, reversed; rear, in the rear; *(of blows)* coming from the rear; distant, remote; out-of-the-way; disinclined, alienated, unfavorable, hostile; *(w. dat or ab)* averse to, hostile to, opposed to, estranged from ‖ *n* the back part, the back; **in āversum** backwards ‖ *npl* the back; hinterland

ā·vertō -vertere -vertī -versus *tr* (**-vor-**) to turn away, avert; to embezzle, misappropriate; to divert, distract; to alienate ‖ *refl* to retire ‖ *intr* to withdraw, retire

avi·a -ae *f* grandmother; old wives' tale

āvi·a -ōrum *npl* wasteland

aviāri·us -a -um *adj* of birds, bird ‖ *n* aviary; haunt of wild birds

avidē *adv* eagerly, greedily

avidit·ās -ātis *f* eagerness, longing; avarice

avid·us -a -um *adj* eager, earnest; greedy; voracious, gluttonous; *(w. gen or dat or in acc)* eager for

av·is -is *f* bird; sign, omen; **avis alba** *(or* **rāra)** rarity

avīt·us -a -um *adj* grandfather's; ancestral; *(wine)* old

āvi·us -a -um *adj* pathless; out-of-the-way, lonely; untrodden; wandering, straying; going astray

āvocāment·um -ī *n* diversion, recreation, hobby

āvocāti·ō -ōnis *f* distraction

āvoc·ō -āre -āvī -ātus *tr* to call away; to divert, remove, withdraw; to amuse; to distract *(attention);* to interrupt *(work)*

āvol·ō -āre -āvī -ātum *intr* to fly away; to dash off

āvulsus *pp of* **āvellō**

avuncul·us -ī *m* (maternal) uncle; **avunculus magnus** granduncle

av·us -ī *m* grandfather; forefather

-āx -ācis *suf* implying tendency, ability: **capāx** ability to hold, **dīcāx** tendency to talk, **pertināx** tendency to hold on

Axen·us -ī *m* Black Sea

axici·a -ae *f* pair of scissors

āxill·a -ae *f* armpit

ax·is -is *m* axle; wagon, chariot; the earth's axis; north pole; vault of heaven; region, climate, country; board, plank

B

B, b *(supply* littera*) f* second letter of the Latin alphabet; letter name: **be**

babae *interj* great!, wonderful!

Babyl·ō -ōnis *m* Babylonian; rich man

Babyl·ōn -ōnis *f* city on the Euphrates River

Babylōni·a -ae *f* country between Tigris and Euphrates

Babylōnic·a -ōrum *npl* Babylonian tapestry

Babylōniēns·is -is -e *adj* Babylonian

Babylōni·us -a -um *adj* Babylonian ‖ *mpl* Babylonians

bāc·a -ae *f* berry; olive; fruit; pearl

bācāt·us -a -um *adj* adorned with pearls; **monīle bācātum** pearl necklace

bacc·ar -aris *n* cyclamen *(plant with showy white, pink, or red flowers)*

Bacch·a -ae *f* Bacchante *(female member of the orgiastic cult of Bacchus)*

bacchābund·us -a -um *adj* raving

Bacchān·al -ālis *n* site sacred to Bacchus ‖ *npl* Bacchanalian orgies

bacchant·ēs -(i)um *fpl* Bacchantes

bacchāti·ō -ōnis *f* orgy, revelry

Bacchē(i)·us, Bacchic·us, Bacchi·us -a -um *adj* Bacchic

bacch·or -ārī -ātus sum *intr* to celebrate the rites of Bacchus; to revel, rage, run wildly about; *(of a place)* to be the scene of Bacchanalian orgies; *(of a rumor)* to run wild

Bacch·us -ī *m* god of wine; *(fig)* vine, wine

baceol·us -a -um *adj (coll)* nutty

bācif·er -era -erum *adj* bearing berries; bearing olives

bacill·um -ī *n* small staff, wand; lictor's staff

Bactr·a -ōrum *npl* Bactra *(capital of Bactria, a province of Parthia)*

Bactriān·us -a -um *adj* Bactrian ‖ *mpl* Bactrians

Bactri·us -a -um *adj* Bactrian

bacul·um -ī *n or* **bacul·us -ī** *m* a cane; (lictor's) staff; scepter

badiz·ō -āre *intr* to go, walk

Baeticāt·us -a -um *adj* dressed in clothes of Baetican wool

Baetic·us -a -um *adj* of the Baetis river ‖ *mpl* the people of Baetica ‖ *f* Baetica *(Roman province in S. Spain, modern Andalusia)*

Baet·is -is *m* river in Spain *(modern Guadalquivir)*

Baeturi·a -ae *f* part of the province of Baetica

Bagō·ās -ae *m* eunuch *(used to guard women's quarters)*

Bagrad·a -ae *m* river in N. Africa *(modern Majerda)*

Bāi·ae -ārum *fpl* resort town at N. end of Bay of Naples ‖ villa at Baiae

Bāi·ānus -a -um *adj* of Baiae

bāiul·ō -āre *tr* to carry, bear

bāiul·us -ī *m* porter

bālaen·a *or* **ballaen·a -ae** *f* (**bālēn-**) whale

balanāt·us -a -um *adj* anointed with balsam; embalmed

balan·us -ī *mf* acorn; date; balsam; type of shellfish

balatr·ō -ōnis *m* jester, buffoon

bālāt·us -ūs *m* bleating *(of sheep)*

balb·us -a -um *adj* stammering, stuttering ‖ **Balbus** *m* Roman family name, *cognomen, esp. Lucius Cornelius Balbus (a supporter of Caesar, defended by Cicero in 56 B.C.)*

balbūt·iō *or* **balbutt·iō -īre** *tr & intr* to stammer, stutter; to babble

Baliāric·us -a -um *adj* (**Bale-**) Balearic

Baliār·is -is -e *adj* (**Bale-**) Balearic; **Baliārēs īnsulae** Balearic Islands *(Majorca and Minorca)*

baline·um -ī *n* bath

ballēna *see* **bālaena**

Balli·ō -ōnis *m* actor playing the worthless fellow; worthless fellow

ballist·a -ae *f* (**bālis-**) artillery piece *(for hurling stones and other missiles)*

ballistār·ium -(i)ī *n* artillery emplacement

balne·ae -ārum *fpl* (**balin-**) baths

balneāri·us -a -um *adj* (**balin-**) of a bath ‖ *npl* baths

balneāt·or -ōris *m* (**balin-**) bath superintendent

balneol·ae -ārum *fpl* baths

balneol·um -ī *n* small bath

balne·um -ī *n* (**balin-**) *(pl also:* **balne·ae -ārum**) bathroom; public baths; bathing, taking a bath

bāl·ō -āre -āvī -ātum *intr* to bleat

balsam·um -ī *n* fragrant gum of the balsam tree ‖ *npl* balsam *(used as perfume)*

balte·us -ī *m or* **balte·um -ī** *n* belt; shoulder strap; woman's belt

bal·ūx -ūcis *f* gold dust

Bandusi·a -ae *f* pleasant fountain on Horace's Sabine farm

Bantīn·us -a -um *adj* of the town of Bantia in Apulia

baptistēr·ium -(i)ī *n* swimming pool

barāthr·um -ī *n* abyss, chasm, pit; lower world; maw, stomach *(of a greedy man)*

barb·a -ae *f* beard *(of man or animals);* **barbam dēmittere** to grow a beard; **barbam vellere** to tuck on the beard *(as a sign of insult)*

barbar·a -ae *f* foreign woman

barbarē *adv* in a foreign language; savagely; *(of diction, etc.)* rudely

barbari·a -ae *or* **barbari·ēs -ēī** *f* foreign country; strange land; rudeness, lack of culture; barbarity, brutality

barbaric·us -a -um *adj* barbarian; barbaric; foreign, outlandish

barbariēs *see* **barbaria**

barbarism·us -ī *m* barbarism *(error in pronunciation or expression)*

barbar·us -a -um *adj* foreign; barbarous ‖ *mf* foreigner; barbarian ‖ *n* barbarism

barbātul·us -a -um *adj* wearing a short beard

barbāt·us -a -um *adj* bearded; adult; old-time ‖ *m* old-timer

barbig·er -era -erum *adj* bearded

barbit·os -ī *m (f)* lyre; lute; music of the lute

barbul·a -ae *f* short beard

Barc·a -ae *m* name of Carthaginian family to which Hamilcar, Hannibal, and Hasdrubal belonged

Barcae·ī -ōrum *mpl* the people of Barce *(city of Cyrenaica)*

barcal·a -ae *m* simpleton

Barcīn·us -a -um *adj* of the Barca family, Barcan

Bardae·ī -ōrum *mpl* Illyrian tribe

Bardaïc·us -a -um *adj* (**Var-**) Bardaean; **Bardaïcus calceus** a soldier's boot

bard·us -a -um *adj* stupid, dull

bār·is -idos *f* flat-bottomed boat

barīt·us -ūs *m* (**barr-**) the war cry of the Germans

Bār·ium -(i)ī *n* coastal town in Apulia *(modern Bari)*

bār·ō -ōnis *m* dunce, blockhead

barrīt·us -ūs *m* trumpeting *(of elephants);* war cry

barr·us -ī *m* elephant

bāscaud·a -ae *f* basin *(of British origin)*

bāsiāti·ō -ōnis *f* kissing; kiss

bāsiāt·or -ōris *m* one who kisses

basilic·a -ae *f* basilica, courthouse

basilicē *adv* royally

basilic·us -a -um *adj* royal; splendid **ǁ** *n* princely robe

bāsi·ō -āre -āvī -ātus *tr* to kiss

bāsiol·um -ī *n* little kiss, peck

bas·is -is *f* base, support; pedestal; base *(of a triangle)*

bās·ium -(i)ī *n* kiss

Bassar·eūs -eī *m* Bacchus

Bassaric·us -a -um *adj* of Bacchus

Bassar·is -idos *f* Bacchante

Bastarn·ae -ārum *mpl* **(Bat-)** Germanic tribe close to the mouth of the Danube

bā(t)tu·ō -āre *tr* to beat, pound; *(vulg)* to screw **ǁ** *intr* to fence

Batāv·us -a -um *adj* of the Batavi, Batavian **ǁ** *mpl* people of Lower Germany *(modern Holland)*

batioc·a -ae *f* drinking cup

batiol·a -ae *f* drinking vessel

Bat·ō -ōnis *m* Illyrian rebel leader

Battiad·ēs -ae *m* inhabitant of Cyrene *(esp.* the poet Callimachus)

Batt·us -ī *m* legendary founder of Cyrene

Bauc·is -idis *f* wife of Philemon

Baul·ī -ōrum *mpl* town between Baiae and Misenum

baxe·a -ae *f* kind of sandal

beātē *adv* happily **ǁ** *interj* great!; bravo!

beātit·ās -ātis *f* happiness

beātitūd·ō -inis *f* happiness

beātul·us -a -um *adj (of a deceased person)* of blessed memory

beāt·us -a -um *adj* happy; prosperous; fertile; abundant; wealthy, rich; sumptuous **ǁ** *mpl* the blessed (people) **ǁ** *n* happiness

Bebryci·a -ae *f* territory of the Bebryces in Asia Minor

Bebryci·us -a -um *adj* of Bebrycia *or* of the Bebryces

Bēdriāc·um -ī *n* **(Bētr-)** village between Mantua and Cremona

Belg·ae -ārum *mpl* inhabitants of N. Gaul

Belgic·us -a -um *adj* of the Belgae; **Gallia Belgica** N. part of the province of Gallia Comata, occupied by the Belgae

Belg·ium -iī *n* country of the Belgae

Bēlīd·ēs -ae *m* descendant of Belus

Bēlīd·ēs -um *fpl* Danaids *(descendants of Belus)*

bellāri·a -ōrum *npl* sweets, dessert

bellāt·or -ōris *adj (masc only)* warlike; **bellātor equus** war horse **ǁ** *m* warrior, fighter

bellātōri·us -a -um *adj* warlike

bellātr·īx -īcis *f* warrior *(female)*

bellē *adv* prettily, nicely, well; **bellē esse** to have a nice time; **bellē est** all is well *(of health);* **cētera bellē** the rest is all right; **sē bellē habēre** to be in good health

Belleroph·ōn -ontis *or* Bellerophont·ēs -ae *m* slayer of Chimaera and rider of Pegasus

Bellerophontē·us -a -um *adj* of Bellerophon

belliātul·us -a -um *adj* pretty little

belliāt·us -a -um *adj* pretty

bellicōs·us -a -um *adj* warlike

bellic·us -a -um *adj* war, military; warlike, fierce **ǁ** *n* bugle; bugle call

bellig·er -era -erum *adj* warring, warlike; war

belliger·ō -āre -āvī -ātum *or* belliger·or -ārī -ātus sum *intr* to fight a war, be at war, fight

bellipot·ēns -entis *adj* mighty *or* valiant in war **ǁ** *m* Mars

bell·ō -āre -āvī -ātum *or* bell·or -ārī -ātus sum *intr* to wage war, be at war; to fight

Bellōn·a -ae *f* **(Duell-)** goddess of war

bellul·us -a -um *adj* pretty, cute

bell·um -ī *n* **(duell-)** war; warfare; **bellī** *(loc)* at war, abroad; **bellī domīque** at home and abroad, on the war front and the home front; **bellō** *or* **in bellō** in war, in times of war; **bellum administrāre** to conduct a war *(as a general);* **bellum agere** *or* **gerere** to fight a war, wage war; **bellum compōnere** to settle a war *(by diplomacy);* **bellum cōnficere** *or* **perficere** to bring an end to the war *(by victory);* **bellum dēnūntiāre** *or* **dīcere** to declare war; **bellum dūcere** *or* **trahere** to drag out, protract a war; **bellum īnferre alicui** to go to war with someone; **bellum movēre** to stir up a war

bell·us -a -um *adj* pretty; fine, nice

bēlu·a -ae *f* beast, brute, monster

bēluāt·us -a -um *adj* embroidered with figures of beasts

bēluōs·us -a -um *adj* full of monsters

Bēl·us -ī *m* Baal **ǁ** king of Tyre and father of Dido **ǁ** king of Egypt, father of Danaüs and Aegyptus

Bēnāc·us -ī *m* lake near Verona *(modern Lago di Garda)*

bene *adv* well; thoroughly, very, quite; elegantly; **bene ambulā!** bon voyage!; **bene audīre** to be well spoken of; **bene dīcere** to speak well, sensibly, correctly, to the point; **bene dīcite!** hush!; **bene emere** to buy at a bargain; **bene esse** *(w. dat)* to be well with, to be doing all right; **bene est** it's O.K.; **bene ferre** to put up with in good spirits; **bene habet** it's O.K.; **bene sum** *or* **mihi bene est** I am content; **bene sentīre dē** (+ *abl*) to have sound views about; **bene spērāre** to be optimistic; **bene vēndere** to sell at a good price; **satis bene** fairly well; **sē bene habēre** to be happy, be content; to do well; ‖ *interj* (*w. acc or dat*) (*in drinking to health*) here's to you!

benedicē *adv* with friendly words, kindly

benedī·cō -cere -xī -ctus *intr* (*w. dat*) to speak well of, praise; (*eccl*) to bless

bene·faciō -facere -fēcī -factus *tr* to do (*s.o.*) a service, confer a benefit on; **multa ergā** (+ *acc*) **benefacere** to do many kindnesses to

beneficenti·a -ae *f* beneficence, kindness

beneficiāri·ī -ōrum *mpl* soldiers exempt from menial tasks

benefic·ium -(i)ī *n* (**benif-**) kindness, favor, benefit, service; help, support; promotion; right, privilege; **beneficiō** (*w. gen*) thanks to; **beneficium accipere et reddere** to receive and return a favor

benefic·us -a -um *adj* generous, liberal, obliging

Benevent·um -ī *n* town in Samnium in S. Italy (*modern Benevento*)

benevolē *adv* (**beniv-**) kindly

benevol·ēns -entis *adj* (**beniv-**) kind-hearted, benevolent, obliging

benevolenti·a -ae *f* (**beniv-**) benevolence, kindness, goodwill; favor

benevol·us -a -um *adj* (**beniv-**) kind, benevolent ‖ *m* well-wisher

benignē *adv* kindly, courteously; mildly; generously, liberally; **benignē!** (*both in accepting and declining an offer*) thank you!; much obliged!; no, thank you!

benignit·ās -ātis *f* kindness, friendliness, courtesy; generosity

benign·us -a -um *adj* kind-hearted; mild; liberal; favorable; bounteous

be·ō -āre -āvī -ātus *tr* to make happy; to bless; to enrich; to refresh

Berecynt(h)i·us -a -um *adj* Berecyntian; epithet of Cybele

Berecynt·us -ī *m* mountain in Phrygia sacred to Cybele *or* Magna Mater

Berenīc·ē -ēs *f* female name, *esp.* the daughter of the Jewish King Agrippa I; **crīnis Berenīcēs** "hair of Berenice" (*constellation, named after the wife of Ptolemy Euergetes*)

bēryll·us -ī *m* beryl (*precious stone*)

bēs bē(s)sis *m* two thirds; **bēs alter** one and two thirds; **faenus bēssibus** interest at ⅔% per month *or* 8% per year

bēsāl·is -is -e *adj* comprising two-thirds

Bess·ī -ōrum *mpl* a people of Thrace

Bessic·us -a -um *adj* of the Bessi

bēsti·a -ae *f* beast, wild beast

bēstiāri·us -a -um *adj* of wild beasts ‖ *m* wild-beast fighter

bēstiol·a -ae *f* insect

bēt·a -ae *f* beet

bēta *indecl n* beta (*second letter of the Greek alphabet*)

bētāce·us -a -um *adj* of a beet

bētiz·ō -āre *intr* to be listless

bi- *pref* consisting of, having, measuring two of the things named, *e.g.*: **bimar·is -is -e** situated between two seas

bibliopōl·a -ae *m* bookseller

bibliothēc·a -ae *f* library; study (*room*)

bibliothēcār·ius -(i)ī *m* librarian

bib·ō -ere -ī *tr* to drink; to visit, live near (*river*); (*fig*) to take in, absorb ‖ *intr* to drink; to guzzle

bibul·us -a -um *adj* fond of drinking; absorbent; thirsty; (*of ears*) eager to hear

bi·ceps -cipitis *adj* two-headed; twin-peaked

biclīn·ium -(i)ī *n* table for two

bicol·or -ōris *adj* two-colored, of two colors

bicorn·is -is -e *adj* two-horned; two-pronged

bicorp·or -oris *adj* double-bodied

bid·ēns -entis *adj* with two teeth; with two points; two-pronged ‖ *m* hoe, mattock; sacrificial animal; sheep

bident·al -ālis *n* place struck by lightning

Bidīn·us -a -um *adj* of Bidis (*town in Sicily*)

bīdu·um -ī *n* two-day period; two days

bienn·ium -(i)ī *n* two-year period; two years; **in** (*or* **per**) **biennium** for two years

bifāriam *adv* on both sides, twofold; in two parts; in two ways; in two directions

bifāri·us -a -um *adj* double, twofold

bif·er -era -erum *adj* bearing (fruit *or* flowers) twice (a year)

bifid·us -a -um *adj* split in two, forked, cloven

bifor·is -is -e *adj* having two doors; having two holes *or* openings; (*of sound*) double, coming from double pipes

bifōrmāt·us -a -um *adj* double, having two forms

bifōrm·is -is -e *adj* double, having two forms

bifr·ōns -ontis *adj* two-faced

bifurc·us -a -um *adj* two-pronged ‖ *n* crotch

bīg·ae -ārum *fpl* two-horse chariot; team of horses

bīgāt·us -a -um *adj* (*of a coin*) stamped with the image of a two-horse chariot

biiug·is -is -e *or* **biiug·us -a -um** *adj* two-horse

Bilbil·is -is *f* town in Hispania Tarraconensis, birthplace of Martial

bilībr·a -ae *f* two pounds

bilībr·is -is -e *adj* two-pound

bilingu·is -is -e *adj* two-tongued; bilingual; deceitful, two-faced

-bil·is -is -e *adjl suf* denoting ability, *e.g.*: **terribilis** able to frighten

bīl·is -is _f_ bile; wrath; **bīlis ātra** melancholy; insanity; **bīlem movēre** _(w. dat)_ to get _(s.o.)_ angry

bil·īx -īcis _adj_ with a double thread _or_ wire

bilūstr·is -is -e _adj_ lasting for two lustra _(i.e., ten years)_

bimar·is -is -e _adj_ situated between two seas

bimarīt·us -ī _m_ bigamist

bimāt·er -ris _adj_ having two mothers, twice-born _(Bacchus)_

bimembr·is -is -e _adj_ half-man, half-beast ‖ _m_ centaur

bimēstr·is -is -e _adj_ two-month-old; lasting two months

bīmul·us -a -um _adj_ two-year-old

bīm·us -a -um _adj_ two-year-old; lasting two years

bīn·ī -ae -a _adj_ two by two, two each; two at a time; two _(per day, year, etc.);_ a set of, a pair of; double, twofold; **inter bīna castra** between the two camps

binoct·ium -(i)ī _n_ period of two nights

binōmin·is -is -e _adj_ having two names

Bi·ōn -ōnis _f_ Greek philosopher, noted for his sharp sayings

Biōnē·us -a -um _adj_ typical of Bion, satirical

bipalm·is -is -e _adj_ two palms long _or_ broad

bipartītō _adv see_ **bipertītō**

bipat·ēns -entis _adj_ opening in two directions

bipedāl·is -is -e _adj_ two-foot (long, broad, _or_ high)

bipennif·er -era -erum _adj_ wielding a two-edged ax

bipenn·is -is -e _adj_ two-edged ‖ _f_ two-edged ax

bipertītō _adv_ (**-part-**) in two parts; **bipertītō esse** to be divided

bipertīt·us -a -um _adj_ (**-part-**) divided into two parts, bipartite

bip·ēs -edis _adj_ two-footed, biped

birēm·is -is -e _adj_ two-oared; with two banks of oars ‖ _f_ ship with two banks of oars

bis _adv_ twice; doubly; **bis tantō** _or_ **tantum** twice as much

Bīsalt·ae -ārum _mpl_ a people of Macedonia

Bīsalt·is -is _f_ Theophane, daughter of Bisaltes _(changed by Neptune into a crane)_

Biston·es -um _mpl_ fierce tribesmen in Thessaly

bisulc·us -a -um _adj_ split; forked; cloven

Bīthȳni·a -ae _f_ a district, later a Roman province, on the N.W. coast of Asia Minor

Bīthȳnic·us -a -um _or_ **Bīthȳn·us -a -um** _adj_ Bithynian

bīt·ō -ere _intr_ to go

bitūm·en -inis _n_ asphalt, pitch

bivi·us -a -um _adj_ two-way ‖ _n_ crossroads, intersection

blaes·us -a -um _adj_ lisping; slurring

blandē _adv_ flatteringly; coaxingly, seductively, charmingly

blandidic·us -a -um _adj_ smooth-spoken, using flattering words

blandiloquentul·us -a -um _or_ **blandiloqu·us -a -um** _adj_ smooth, smooth-tongued

blandīment·um -ī _n_ flattery, compliment; charm

blandi·or -īrī -ītus sum _intr_ _(w. dat)_ **1** to flatter; **2** to coax; **3** to allure; **4** to charm, please; **5** _(of dogs)_ to fawn on; _(w._ **ut** + _subj)_ to coax, persuade with blandishments to ‖ _refl (w. dat)_ to delude oneself

blanditer _adv_ flatteringly

blanditi·a -ae _or_ **blanditi·ēs -ēī** _f_ flattery, compliment; charm

bland·us -a -um _adj_ smooth; flattering; fawning; alluring, charming, winsome, pleasant

blater·ō -āre -āvī -ātus _tr_ to utter _(in a babbling way)_ ‖ _intr_ to babble

blat·iō -īre to talk foolishly, babble

blatt·a -ae _f_ cockroach; _(insect)_ bookworm; clothes-moth

blenn·us -ī _m_ _(coll)_ idiot, blockhead

blite·us -a -um _adj_ silly; tasteless ‖ _n_ worthless stuff, trash

blit·um -ī _n_ tasteless vegetable _(kind of spinach)_

boāri·us -a -um _adj_ (**bov-**) cattle; **forum boārium** cattle market

Boc(c)h·us -ī _m_ king of Mauretania, who betrayed Jugurtha to the Romans ‖ king of Mauretania in the time of Julius Caesar

Boeb·ē -ēs _f_ lake in Thessaly

Boeōti·a -ae _f_ district N. of Attica

Boeōti·us -a -um _or_ **Boeōt·us -a -um** _adj_ Boeotian ‖ _mpl_ Boeotians

bōi·a -ae _f_ collar _(worn by criminals)_

Boi·ī -ōrum _mpl_ Celtic people who migrated from Gaul into N. Italy

bōlēt·us -ī _m_ mushroom

bol·us -ī _m_ throw _(of the dice);_ cast _(of the net);_ _(fig)_ haul, piece of good luck, gain; choice morsel

bombax _interj_ _(of surprise)_ strange!; indeed!

bomb·us -ī _m_ booming; buzzing, humming

bombȳcin·us -a -um _adj_ silk, silken ‖ _npl_ silk clothes

bomb·ȳx -ȳcis _m_ silkworm; silk; silk garment

Bon·a De·a -ae _f_ Roman goddess of chastity and fertility, worshipped by women

bonit·ās -ātis _f_ goodness, integrity, good behavior; excellence, high quality _(of things)_

Bonn·a -ae _f_ city in Lower Germany _(modern Bonn)_

Bonōni·a -ae _f_ city of Cisalpine Gaul _(modern Bologna)_

Bonōniēns·is -is -e _adj_ of Bologna

bon·us -a -um *adj* good; *(morally)* good; cheerful *(face);* sound, valid, well-founded *(arguments);* pretty, shapely; *(w. dat)* good for; *(w. ad)* good at; *(w. dat or ad)* good, kind toward; **bona aetās** prime of life; **bonae artēs** liberal arts, liberal education; **bonae reī esse** to be wealthy; **bonae rēs** good things, desirable things; wealth; **bonae vīrēs** full strength; **bona fōrma** good appearance; **bone vir!** sir!; my good fellow!; **bonō animō esse** *(or* **bonum animum habēre)** to be of good cheer, be in a good mood; to be well-disposed; **bonō modō** in moderation; **bonō perīculō** with little risk; **bonum est** *(w. inf)* it is good to; **bonus ā tempestātibus** free from storms, fine; **bonus stomachus** good humor; **cum bonā pāce** *(w. gen)* with the full consent of; **(cum) bonā veniā tuā** with your kind permission; **virī bonī** decent citizens; *(pol)* conservatives ‖ *mpl* decent people; brave men; *(pol)* conservatives ‖ *n* good thing, good; **bonō esse alicui** to be good for s.o., be profitable to s.o.; **cui bonō?** for whose benefit? ‖ *npl* goods, property

bo·ō -āre *or* **-ere** *intr* to bawl; to bellow, roar

Boōt·ēs -ae *m* Boötes *(constellation)*

bore·ās -ae *m* north wind; the North ‖ **Boreās** god of the north wind

borē·us -a -um *adj* north, northern

Borysthen·ēs -is *m* Scythian river *(modern Dnieper)*

bōs bovis *m (gen pl:* **boum** *or* **bovum; dat & abl pl:* **bōbus** *or* **būbus)** ox, bull ‖ *mpl* cattle ‖ *f* cow

Bosp(h)or·us *or* **Bosp(h)or·os -ī** *m* strait between Thrace and Asia Minor, connecting Propontis and Black Sea

botell·us -ī *m* small sausage

botul·us -ī *m* a black pudding

bovīl·e -is *n* ox stall, cow stable

Bovill·ae -ārum *fpl* town in Latium on the Appian Way, about 12 miles S. of Rome

bovill·us -a -um *adj* cattle

brabeut·a -ae *m* umpire

bracchiāl·is -is -e *adj* of the arm

bracchiol·um -ī *n* dainty arm

bracch·ium -(i)ī *n* arm, lower arm; *(cf.* **lacertus** *the upper arm);* claw; branch; tendril; arm of the sea; *(naut)* yardarm

brāc·ae -ārum *fpl* pants, trousers

brācāt·us -a -um *adj* wearing trousers; foreign, barbarian; effeminate

brācil·is -is -e *adj (esp. of a tunic)* to be worn with trousers

bracte·a -ae *f* **(bratt-)** gold leaf; gold foil

bracteol·a -ae *f* **(bratt-)** very thin gold leaf

brassic·a -ae *f* cabbage

bratt- = bract-

Brenn·us -ī *m* Celtic chieftain who captured Rome about 390 B.C. ‖ Galatian chieftain who invaded Greece in 279 B.C.

brevī *adv* briefly, in a few words; shortly, in a short time; **brevī ante (post)** shortly before (afterwards)

breviār·ium -(i)ī *n* abridgment, summary

brevicul·us -a -um *adj* rather short

breviloqu·ēns -entis *adj* concise, of few words

breviloquenti·a -ae *f* conciseness

brevi·ō -āre -āvī -ātus *tr* to shorten; to abbreviate; to pronounce *(a syllable)* short

brev·is -is -e *adj* short, little; low; stunted *(trees); (of depth)* shallow; brief; transient; short-lived; compressed, concise *(style);* small *(amounts, weights);* modest, simple; small, narrow, confined *(space);* **ad** *(or* **in) breve tempus** for (only) a short time ‖ *f (gram)* short syllable ‖ *n* a short space of time; **ad** *(or* **in) breve** for (only) a short time; **brevī** in a few words, briefly; in a short time, soon; for (only) a short time; after a lapse of a short space of time; **brevī ante** shortly before; **brevī post** shortly after; **in brevī** in a few words, briefly ‖ *npl* shallow water, shallows

brevit·ās -ātis *f* brevity; smallness; shortness; stunted size *(of trees);* short period of time; shortness of life; *(pros)* short quantity; *(rhet)* conciseness, terseness

breviter *adv* for (only) a short time; within a short space of time, quickly; in (only) a few words, briefly; to (only) a short distance; *(pros)* short

Brigant·es -um *mpl* a people of N. Britannia

Brīsē·is -idos *f (acc:* **Brīsēida)** slave and concubine of Achilles

Britann·ī -ōrum *mpl* Britons

Britanni·a -ae *f* **(Britt-)** Britain

Britannic·us -a -um *adj* British ‖ *m* surname of the emperor Claudius after his victory in Britain; name taken by Germanicus, son of Claudius and Messalina

Britann·us -a -um *adj* British

Brit(t)·ō -ōnis *m* Briton

Brixi·a -ae *f* town in Cisalpine Gaul *(modern Brescia)*

brocch·us -a -um *adj* buck-toothed

Brom·ius -(i)ī *m* epithet of Bacchus "the roaring god"

Bront·ēs -ae *m* Brontes *(a Cyclops)*

brūm·a -ae *f* winter solstice, shortest day; (dead of) winter; winter's cold

brūmāl·is -is -e *adj* wintry

Brundis·ium -(i)ī *n* port in S.E. Italy on the Adriatic Sea *(modern Brindisi)*

Bruti·ī -ōrum *mpl* inhabitants of Apulia, the toe of Italy brūt·us -a -um *adj* heavy, unwieldy; dull, stupid

Brūt·us -ī *m* Roman family name, *cognomen, esp.* Lucius Iunius Brutus *(drove out Tarquinius Superbus)* ‖ Marcus Iunius Brutus *(one of the murderers of Julius Caesar)*

būbīl·e -is *n* cow stable

būb·ō -ōnis *mf* owl

būb(u)l·us -a -um *adj* ox, bull's, cow's; **corius būbulus** oxhide, oxhide whip; **oculus būblus** bull's-eye

būbul·a -ae *f* beef

bubulcit·or -ārī *intr* to tend cattle, be a herdsman; to ride herd

bubulc·us -ī *m* herdsman

būcaed·a -ae *m (coll)* flogged slave

buc(c)ul·a -ae *f* little cheek; visor

bucc·a -ae *f* cheek; loudmouth; trumpeter; parasite; mouthful; **dīcere quidquid in buccam venerit** to say whatever came into his head

buccell·a -ae *f* small mouthful; morsel

bucc·ō -ōnis *f (coll)* fathead

bucculent·us -a -um *adj* having fat cheeks; loud-mouthed

būcer(i)·us -a -um *adj* horned

būcin·a -ae *f (curved)* trumpet *(used to proclaim the watches of the day and night; also used for summoning a public meeting);* war trumpet; shepherd's horn; Triton's trumpet shell

būcināt·or -ōris *m* trumpeter

būcin·us -ī *m* trumpeter

būcolic·us -a -um *adj* pastoral, bucolic ‖ *npl* pastoral poetry, bucolics

būcul·a -ae *f* heifer

būf·ō -ōnis *m* toad

-bul·a -ae *fem suf* forms feminine nouns denoting instrument or agent, *e.g.:* **fībula** safety pin

bulb·us -ī *m* bulb; onion

būl·ē -ēs *f (Greek)* council, senate

būleut·a -ae *m* councilor

būleutēr·ium -(i)ī *n* meeting place of a Greek council

bull·a -ae *f* bubble; boss, stud, knob; amulet; locket *(hung around neck of children)*

bullāt·us -a -um *adj* inflated, bombastic; studded; wearing a bulla *(i.e., still a child)*

bull·iō -īre *intr* to bubble, boil

bullul·a -ae *f* little bubble

-bul·um -ī *neut suf* denoting instrument or place, *e.g.:* **vēnābulum** hunting instrument, spear; **stabulum** place for cattle to stand, stable

būmast·us -a -um *adj* having large grapes

būr·a -ae *or* būr·is -is *f* curved handle of plow

Busīr·is -idos *or* -idis *m* king of Egypt who sacrificed strangers and was killed by Hercules

būstirap·us -ī *m* tomb robber

būstuāri·us -a -um *adj* of a tomb, of a pyre; **gladiātor būstiārius** gladiator who fought at a tomb in honor of the dead

būst·um -ī *n* pyre; grave mound, tomb; *(pej) (applied to a person)* ruination

būte·ō -ōnis *m* buzzard

Būt(h)rōt·um (·on) -ī *n or* Būt(h)rōt·os -ī *f* town on the coast of Epirus

buxēt·um -ī *n* plantation of boxwood trees

buxif·er -era -erum *adj* producing boxwood trees

bux·um -ī *n (bot)* boxwood tree; *(object made of the hard wood of the boxwood tree):* (spinning) top, comb, writing tablet, flute

bux·us -ī *f* boxwood tree

Bybl·is -idis *f* daughter of Miletus and Cyaneë, changed into a fountain

Byrs·a -ae *f* (Bur-) citadel of Carthage

Byzant·ium -(i)ī *n* city on the Bosporus, later named Constantinople *(modern Istanbul)*

Byzanti·us -a -um *adj* Byantine ‖ *mpl* Byzantines

C

C, c *(supply* littera) *f* third letter of the Latin alphabet; letter name: ce

C *abbr* centum (one hundred)

C. *abbr* Gāius *(Roman first name, praenomen)*

caballīn·us -a -um *adj* horse's; **fōns caballīnus** *(pej)* "nag's spring" *(i.e., Hippocrene)*

caball·us -ī *m* horse, nag; packhorse; riding horse; **Gorgoneus caballus** Pegasus *(sprung from the blood of the Gorgon Medusa)*

Cabīr·us -ī *m* deity worshiped on Lemnos and Samothrace *(e.g., Bacchus)*

cacātur·iō -īre -īī *intr (vulg)* to want *or* need to shit

cachinnāti·ō -ōnis *f* horselaugh

cachinn·ō -āre -āvī -ātum *intr* to laugh loud, roar *(with laughter)*

cachinn·us -ī *m* loud laugh; *(fig)* rippling *(of waves)*

cac·ō -āre -āvī -ātus *tr & intr (vulg)* to shit

cacoēth·es -is *n* malignant, incurable disease; *(fig)* itch; **cacoēthes scrībendī** an itch to write

cacozēli·a -ae *f* bad taste *(in style)*

cacozēl·os -on *adj (of style)* in bad taste

cacul·a -ae *m (sl)* soldier's slave, "dog robber"

cacūm·en -inis *n* point, tip, top, peak; young shoot; extrēmum cacūmen outer limit
cacūmin·ō -āre -āvī -ātus *tr* to point, make pointed
Cāc·us -ī *m* giant son of Vulcan, living on the Aventine Hill and slain by Hercules
cadāv·er -eris *n* corpse, carcass
cadāverōs·us -a -um *adj* cadaverous, ghastly
Cadmē·is -idos *adj* (*fem only*) of Cadmus ‖ *f* daughter of Cadmus
Cadmē·us -a -um *adj* Cadmean, Theban; Tyros Cadmēa Tyre, home city of Cadmus ‖ *f* citadel of Thebes
Cadm·us -ī *m* son of Phoenician king Agenor, brother of Europa, and founder of the citadel of Thebes; Cadmī terra Phoenicia
cadō cadere cecīdī cāsum *intr* to fall, sink, drop; to be slain, die, be sacrificed; to happen, occur, turn out, come to pass; to belong, refer, be suitable, apply; to flag, decline, decay; to vanish, fail, cease; to derive (*from a source); (of parts of the body*) to fall out, be shed; (*of heavenly bodies*) to sink, set; (*of wind, sea, noise*) to die down; (*of words*) to fall from one's lips; (*of efforts*) to come to nothing; (*w.* in + *acc*) 1 to come upon, arrive at by chance; 2 to fall upon (*the enemy); 3* to coincide with (*a time, period); 4* to fall due on (*a date); 5* to be consistent *or* compatible with, fit; 6 (*of words, clauses*) to end, terminate in (*e.g., a long syllable); 7* to fall into (*a category); (w.* ad *or* in + *acc*) to lapse into, degenerate into; apte cadere ad to be exactly adapted to; causā cadere (*leg*) to lose one's case, be convicted; (*fig*) to be in the wrong; fōrmulā cadere to lose one's case on a technicality; hūc cadere to fall so low; numerōsē cadere to sound rhythmical
cādūceāt·or -ōris *m* herald
cādūce·us -ī *m* herald's staff, caduceus
cādūcif·er -era -erum *adj* with herald's staff
cādūc·us -a -um *adj* falling; fallen; inclined to fall, tottery, unsteady; frail, perishable, transitory; (*of hopes, words*) futile; (*of persons*) destined to die, doomed; (*of fire*) likely to go out; (*of streams*) likely to dry up; (*of vines*) drooping; (*leg*) lapsed, without heir; (*mil*) fallen in battle
cadurc·um -ī *n* coverlet; (*fig*) marriage bed
cad·us -ī *m* (large) jar, keg (*mostly of clay*)
Cadūsi·ī -ōrum *mpl* the people of Cadusia (*near the Caspian Sea*)
caecigen·us -a -um *adj* born blind
Caecili·us -a -um *adj* Roman clan name, nomen
caecit·ās -ātis *f* blindness; caecitās animī moral blindness; caecitās mentis mental blindness, lack of discernment

caec·ō -āre -āvī -ātus *tr* to blind; to obscure the judgment of; astū caecāre (*fig*) to pull the wool over (*s.o.'s*) eyes
Caecub·um -ī *n* Caecuban wine (*from Caecubum in S. Latium*)
Caecul·us -ī *m* son of Vulcan and founder of Praeneste
caec·us -a -um *adj* blind; invisible; vague, random, aimless; uncertain, unknown; unsubstantiated; blinding; obscure, mysterious; dark, gloomy; concealed, disguised; unforeseeable (*dangers*); diē caecō emere to buy on credit (*i.e., to buy with no definite date of payment*)
caed·es -is *f* murder, slaughter, massacre; bloodshed, gore; the slain
caedō caedere cecīdī caesus *tr* to hack at; to chop; to strike, beat; to fell; to cut off, cut to pieces; to cut through, sever; to kill, murder; to crack, smash, break; to use up, consume; (*hum*) to devour; sermōnēs caedere to exchange chitchat
caedu·us -a -um *adj* ready for felling
caelām·en -inis *n* engraving, bas-relief
caelāt·or -ōris *m* engraver
caelāt·um -ī *n* engraved work
caelātūr·a -ae *f* engraving
cael·ebs -ibis *adj* (-eps) unmarried, single (*whether bachelor or widower); (of trees*) not supporting vines
cael·es -itis *adj* heavenly ‖ *mpl* gods
caelest·is -is -e *adj* heavenly, celestial; supernatural, divine ‖ *mf* deity; godlike person ‖ *npl* heavenly bodies
caelibāt·us -ūs *m* celibacy
caelicol·a -ae *mf* denizen of heaven (*god or goddess*)
caelif·er -era -erum *adj* supporting the sky
Caelimontān·us -a -um *adj* located on the Caelian Hill
caelipot·ēns -entis *adj* powerful in heaven
caelit·ēs -um *mpl* gods in heaven
Caeli·us -a -um *adj* Roman clan name (*nomen*)
Caeli·us Mōns (*gen:* Caeliī Montis) *m* Caelian Hill (*in Rome*)
cael·ō -āre -āvī -ātus *tr* to engrave in relief, emboss; to carve; to cast; to fashion, compose; to adorn
cael·um -ī *n* engraver's chisel
cael·um -ī *n* sky, heaven(s); air, climate, weather; universe, world; caelum apertum (*or* patēns) the open air; in caelō esse to be in seventh heaven; positiō caelī (*geog*) latitude
caement·um -ī *n* (cēm-) (*also used in pl*) crushed stone
Caen·eûs -eī *or* -eos *m* child of Elatus, born a girl, but changed by Neptune into a boy

Caenīn·a -ae *f* ancient city of Latium *(defeated by Romulus)*

Caen·is -idis *f* child of Elatus, born a girl but changed into a boy

caenōs·us -a -um *adj* filthy, muddy

caen·um -ī *n* (**cēn-**) filth, mud, slime; *(applied to persons) (sl)* scum

caep·a *or* **cēp·a -ae** *f or* **caep·e** *or* **cēp·e -is** *n* onion

Caepi·ō -ōnis *m* Roman family name *(cognomen), esp.* in the *gens Servilia*

Caer·e -itis *or* **-ētis** *n* city in Etruria *(modern Cerveteri)*

Caer·es -itis *or* **-ētis** *adj* of Caere; **dignus Caerite cērā** *i.e.,* without voting rights **‖** *mpl* the people of Caere

Caerētān·us -a -um *adj* of Caere

caerimōni·a -ae *f* rite, ceremony; sanctity; awe, reverence **‖** *fpl* rites, ceremonies; practices

caerul·a -ōrum *npl* blue expanse *(of the sky);* blue waters *(of the sea)*

caerul(e)·us -a -um *adj* blue; blue-eyed; dark-blue; greenish-blue; dark

Caes·ar -aris *m* Gaius Julius Caesar *(102?–44* B.C.*)* **‖** honorary title of Octavian and succeeding emperors **‖** cognomen of various members of the imperial family

Caesarē·a -ae *f* name of several towns, *esp.* two in Palestine, one in Cappadocia, and one in Mauretania

Caesare·us -a -um *or* **Caesariān·us -a -um** *adj* connected with Julius Caesar; connected with Augustus; imperial

Caesariān·us -i *m* soldier *or* supporter of Julius Caesar; supporter *or* servant of the Roman emperor

caesariāt·us -a -um *adj* long-haired

caesari·ēs -ēī *f* long, flowing hair

caesīci·us -a -um bluish, dark-blue

caesim *adv* by chopping, by cutting; with a slashing blow; *(rhet)* in short clauses, in a clipped style

caesi·us -a -um *adj* bluish-grey; blue-eyed; grey-eyed; cat-eyed **‖ Caesius** Roman clan name *(nomen)*

Caes·ō -ōnis *m* (**Kaes-**) Roman first name *(praenomen)*

caesp·es -itis *m* sod, turf; grass; altar of sod; rampart made of turf; mound of earth *(esp. as the covering of a grave)*

caest·us -ūs *m* (**cēst-**) boxing glove

caes·us -a -um *pp of* **caedō ‖** *npl:* **inter caesa et porrēcta** *(fig)* at the eleventh hour *(literally, between the victim being slain and offered)*

caetr·a -ae *f* (**cēt-**) short Spanish shield

caetrāt·us -a -um *adj* armed with a shield **‖** *mpl* soldiers armed with a shield; Greek peltasts

Caïc·us -ī *m* (**Cay-**) river in Mysia

Cāiēt·a -ae *f* nurse of Aeneas **‖** town on the coast of Latium

cai·ō -āre *tr* to beat, thrash

Cāïus *see* **Gāius**

Cala·ber -bra -brum *adj* Calabrian

Calabri·a -ae *f* region of S.E. Italy

Cala·is -is *m* *(winged)* son of Boreas and Orithyia, and brother of Zetes

calamāri·us -a -um *adj* for holding pens

Calam·is -idis *m* Greek sculptor of the 5th cent. B.C.

calamis·ter -trī *m* curling iron

calamistrāt·us -a -um *adj* curled *(with a curling iron)*

calamistr·um -ī *n* curling iron

calamit·ās -ātis *f* calamity, disaster; *(mil)* defeat

calamitōsē *adv* disastrously

calamitōs·us -a -um *adj* disastrous; liable to disaster; blighted *(fields);* hit by disaster, ill-starred **‖** *m* victim of a disaster

calam·us -ī *m* reed; stalk, shoot *(of a plant);* pen *(for writing on paper, as opposed to* **stilus** *of metal or bone for writing on wax);* arrow; fishing rod; lime rod *(smeared at top with lime to catch birds);* vine prop; *(mus)* reed pipe; *(collectively or pl)* Panpipes

calathīsc·us -ī *m* small wicker basket

calath·us -ī *m* wicker basket; vessel for holding cheese *or* curdled milk; wine bowl

Cālāti·a -ae *f* town in Campania

calāt·or -ōris *m* (**kal-**) servant; priest's attendant

calautic·a -ae *f* type of woman's headdress

calc·ar -āris *n* spur; *(fig)* stimulus

calceāment·um -ī *n* footwear, shoe

calceār·ium -(i)ī *n* shoe allowance

calceāt·or -ōris *m* shoemaker

calceāt·us -ūs *m* footwear, shoes

calce·ō -āre -āvī -ātus *tr* to put shoes on; to shoe *(animals)*

calceolār·ius -(i)ī *m* shoemaker

calceol·us -ī *m* small shoe, half-boot; slipper

calce·us -ī *m* shoe; **calceī mulleī** *(or* **patriciī)** red shoes worn by senators who had held curule office; **calceōs mūtāre** *(fig)* to become a senator *(from the shoes that senators wore);* **calceōs poscere** to leave the table *(literally, to call for one's shoes)*

Calc(h)·ās -antis *m* Calchas *(Greek seer at Troy)*

Calc(h)ēd·ōn -ōnis *f* Calchedon *(town on the Asiatic side of the Bosphorus, opposite Byzantium)*

calci- *see* **calce-**

calcitr·ō -āre -āvī -ātum *intr* to kick; to be recalcitrant, kick up one's heels

calcitr·ō -ōnis *m* kicker; blusterer

calc·ō -āre -āvī -ātus *tr* to trample; to trample on; to tread *(grapes)*; to set foot on; to tread on accidentally, trip upon; *(fig)* to spurn; **viam calcāre** to tread a path

calculāt·or -ōris *m* arithmetic teacher; accountant, bookkeeper

calcul·us -ī *m* pebble, stone; kidney stone; counter of an abacus; piece *(used in games);* **calculus albus** white pebble *(of acquittal);* **calculōs** *(or* **calculum) pōnere** *(or* **subdūcere)** to make a calculation *(esp. gains or losses);* **calculus āter** black pebble *(of condemnation);* vote, decision, sentence; **parem calculum pōnere cum** to return an equivalent gift to

calda, caldārius, caldus *see* **calid-**

cal(e)·faciō -facere -fēcī -factus *tr* to warm, heat; to rouse, excite, anger

Calēdoni·a -ae *f* Caledonia, Scotland

calefact·ō -āre -āvī -ātus *tr* to warm, heat

calefierī *pass inf of* **calefaciō**

Calend- *see* **Kalend-**

Calēn·us -a -um *adj* of Cales *(in Campania)* ‖ *n* wine from Cales

cal·eō -ēre -uī *intr* to be warm, be hot; to feel warm; to glow; to be flushed *(with wine);* to be hot *(with lust);* to be busy, have one's hands full; to be yet new, be fresh ‖ *impers* **calētur** *(of the weather)* it is hot

Cal·ēs -ium *fpl* Campanian town famous for its wine

cal·ēscō -ēscere -uī *intr* to get warm, get hot; to become excited *(with love)*

caliandrum *see* **caliendrum**

calidē *adv* promptly, quickly

calid·us -a -um *adj* **(cald-)** warm, hot; eager, rash; hot-headed; hasty; intoxicating *(wine);* high *(fever);* cold *(cash)* ‖ *f* warm water ‖ *n* hot drink; heat

caliendr·um -ī *n* **(-lian-)** wig *(for women)*

calig·a -ae *f* army boot; *(fig)* military service

caligāt·us *or* **caligāri·us -a -um** *adj* wearing army boots ‖ *m (mil)* private

cālīginōs·us -a -um *adj* misty, foggy

cālīg·ō -āre *tr* to veil in darkness, obscure; to make dizzy ‖ *intr* to be dark, be gloomy; to steam, reek; to be wrapped in mist *or* darkness; to be blind, grope

cālīg·ō -inis *f* darkness; mist, fog; dark smoke; gloom; obscurity; mental blindness; dizziness

caligul·a -ae *f* small army boot

Caligul·a -ae *m* nickname given by soldiers to Emperor Gaius, son of Germanicus, when he was a small boy

cal·ix -icis *m* cup, goblet; cooking pot; *(fig)* wine

Callaec·ī -ōrum *mpl* a people in the N.W. corner of Spain

callaïn·us -a -um *adj* turquoise

call·eō -ēre -uī *tr* to know by experience; to have skill in; *(w. inf)* to know how to, be able to ‖ *intr* to grow hard, be calloused; *(fig)* to be thick-skinned, be callous; *(w. abl)* to be experienced in, be skilled in

callidē *adv* skillfuly; well; cunningly

callidit·ās -ātis *f* skill, dexterity; shrewdness; cunning ‖ *fpl* clever tricks

callid·us -a -um *adj* expert, adroit, skillful; ingenious, clever; cunning, wily; *(w. gen, dat, or* **in** + *abl)* experienced in; *(w. inf)* skilled at

Callimach·us -ī *m* Alexandrine poet and grammarian *(fl c. 270 B.C.)*

Calliop·ē -ēs *or* **Calliop(ē)·a -ae** *f* Calliope *(Muse of epic poetry)*

Callirrho·ē -ēs *f* daughter of the River Acheloüs, and second wife of Alcmaeon ‖ a famous spring in Athens

call·is -is *mf* rough footpath ‖ *mpl* mountain pasturage; cattle trails

Callistō -ūs *(dat:* **-ō)** *f* daughter of Lycaon *(king of Arcadia),* changed into a she-bear and then into the constellation Ursa Major

callōs·us -a -um *adj* thick-skinned, calloused; solid, hard

call·um -ī *n or* **call·us -ī** *m* hard skin; *(lit & fig)* callousness; **callum obdūcere dolōrī** to produce insensibility to grief

cal·ō -āre -āvī -ātus *tr* **(kal-)** to proclaim; to convoke *(only in religious matters)*

cāl·ō -ōnis *m* soldier's slave,"dog-robber"; drudge

cal·or -ōris *m* warmth, heat; glow; passion, love; fire, zeal, impetuosity; fever

Calp·ē -ēs *f* Gibraltar

Calpurni·us -a -um *adj* name of a plebeian clan ‖ *f* Calpurnia *(wife of Julius Caesar)*

calt(h)·a -ae *f (bot)* marigold

caltul·a -ae *f (woman's)* yellow slip *(tied below the breasts)*

calumni·a -ae *f* **(kal-)** false accusation, malicious charge; frameup; conviction for malicious prosecution; false statement, misrepresentation; trickery; pretext; sham; **calumniam** *or* **dē calumniā iūrāre** to swear that one is not making a false accusation

calumniāt·or -ōris *m* malicious accuser; shyster

calumni·or -ārī -ātus sum *tr* to accuse fasely; to misinterpret, misrepresent; to blame unjustly; to find fault with ‖ *intr* to make a false accusation; to practice legal chicanery

calv·a -ae *f* bald head, scalp; skull

calvit·ium -(i)ī *n,* **calviti·ēs -ēī** *f* baldness
calv·us -a -um *adj* bald
cal·x -cis *f* heel; (back of the) hoof; *(fig)* foot, kick; **calcibus caedere** to kick
cal·x -cis *f* lime, limestone; pebble *(used in games);* finish line, goal; **ad calcem pervenīre** to reach the goal; *(prov)* **ad carcerēs ā calce revocārī** to have to do a thing all over again *(lit:* to be called back to the starting gate from the finish line)
Calyd·ōn -ōnis *or* **-ōnos** *f* town in Aetolia, site of the boar hunt led by Meleager
Calydōn·is -idos *adj (fem only)* Calydonian ‖ *f* Calydonian woman *(Deianira, the sister of Maleager)*
Calydōni·us -a -um *adj* Calydonian
Calyps·ō -ūs *f* nymph *(daughter of Atlas)* who entertained Ulysses on the island of Ogygia
camara *see* **camera**
camell·a -ae *f* drinking cup
camēl·us -ī *m* camel
Camēn·a -ae *f* Muse; poem; poetry
camer·a -ae *f* **(-mar-)** vault, arched roof, arch; flat boat with arched covering
Camerīn·um -ī *n* town in Umbria
Camill·a -ae *f* Volscian female warrior, ally of Turnus against Aeneas
Camill·us -ī *m* Marcus Furius Camillus, who liberated Rome from the Gauls in 390 B.C.
camīn·us -ī *m* fireplace; furnace, forge; vent of subterranean fires; **oleum addere camīnō** *(prov)* to pour oil on the fire
cammar·us -ī *m* **(gam-)** lobster
Campāni·a -ae *f* region on E. coast of central Italy below Latium
Campān·us -a -um *adj* Campanian
campes·ter *or* **campes·tris -tris -tre** *adj* flat, level; overland *(march); (of city)* situated in a plain; *(of army)* fighting in a plain; *(of sports, elections)* held in the Campus Martius ‖ *n* loincloth ‖ *npl* flat lands
camp·us -ī *m* open field *(opp:* **ager** tilled field); flat space, plain; level surface; *(fig)* field of action, subject of debate; **Campus Mārtius** Field of Mars *(near the Tiber, used for sports, elections, military exercises)*
cam·ur *or* **cam·urus -ura -urum** *adj* crooked; concave
Canac·ē -ēs *f* daughter of Aeolus, who committed incest with her brother Macareus
canāl·is -is *mf* pipe, conduit; gutter, open drain; channel *(of a river; of the sea);* flow *(of language)*
cancell·ī -ōrum *mpl* railing, grating; barrier *(at sports, public events);* boundaries, limits; **intrā cancellōs** in a confined space
can·cer -crī *m* crab; the South; tropical heat; *(med)* cancer ‖ **Cancer** *(astr)* Cancer, the Crab *(sign of the zodiac)*

cande·faciō -facere -fēcī -factus *tr* to make white; to make white-hot
candēl·a -ae *f* candle, taper; waxed cord
candēlābr·um -ī *n* candlestick, candelabrum; lampstand
cand·ēns -entis *adj* white, shining, glistening; white-hot *(iron)*
cand·eō -ēre -uī *intr* to be shiny white, glitter, shine; to be white-hot
cand·ēscō -ēscere *intr* to become white, begin to glisten; to get white-hot
candidātōri·us -a -um *adj* of a candidate, candidate's
candidāt·us -a -um *adj* clothed in white ‖ *m* candidate
candidē *adv* in dazzling white; clearly, simply, sincerely
candidul·us -a -um *adj* white, gleaming
candid·us -a -um *adj (cf* **albus** flat white) shiny white, white, bright, dazzling, gleaming, sparkling; lucky, favorable, happy; fair *(complexion);* candid, frank *(person);* bright, cheerful *(mood, circumstances);* clear, bright *(day); (of winds)* bringing clear weather; white, silvery *(poplar, hair);* clear, unaffected *(style);* **candidus līmes** Milky Way; **candida sententia** vote of acquittal
cand·or -ōris *m* whiteness, brightness, radiance; fair complexion; candor, sincerity, kindness; clarity *(of style)*
can·ēns -entis *pres p of* **canō**
cān·ēns -entis *adj* grey, white
cān·eō -ēre -uī *intr* to be grey
cānēsc·ō -ere *intr* to turn grey; to grow old; *(of discourse)* to become dull
cān·ī -ōrum *mpl* grey hair(s)
canīcul·a -ae *f* small dog ‖ **Canīcula** *(astr)* Canicula, Sirius, Dog Star
canīn·us -a -um *adj* canine; snarling, spiteful; **canīna littera** the letter R
can·is -is *mf* dog; *(pej)* skunk; worst throw *(in dice)* ‖ **Canis** *m (astr)* Canis Major *or* Sirius
canistr·um -ī *n* wicker basket *(for bread, flowers, etc.)*
cāniti·ēs -ēī *f* greyness; *(fig)* grey hair; *(fig)* old age
cann·a -ae *f* reed; reed pipe, flute
cannab·is -ae *f or* **cannab·um -ī** *n* hemp, marijuana; hempen rope
Cann·ae -ārum *fpl* town in Apulia where Hannibal defeated the Romans in 216 B.C.
Cannēns·is -is -e *adj* of Cannae
canō canere cecinī cantus *tr* to sing; to sing of; to speak in a singsong tone; to sing of; to prophesy, predict; *(mil)* to blow, sound; **signa** *(or* **classicum) canere** to sound the signal for battle ‖ *intr* to sing; *(w. abl)* to play *(a musical instrument); (of birds)* to sing; *(of roosters)* to crow; *(of frogs)* to croak; **receptuī**

canere to sound the retreat; **surdīs canere** to preach to deaf ears; **tībiā canere** to play the flute

Canōp·us -ī *m* town on W. mouth of the Nile

can·or -ōris *m* tune, sound, melody, song; tone *(of instruments)*

canōr·us -a -um *adj* melodious, musical; singsong, jingling ‖ *n* melody

Canta·ber -brī *m* Cantabrian; **Cantabr·ī -ōrum** *mpl* the people of Cantabria in N. Spain

Cantabri·a -ae *f* district in N. Spain

cantām·en -inis *n* incantation, spell

cantāt·or -ōris *m* singer

cant(h)ērīn·us -a -um *adj* of a horse

cant(h)ēr·ius -(i)ī *m* gelding; eunuch

canthar·is -idis *f* beetle; Spanish fly

canthar·us -ī *m* wide-bellied drinking vessel with handles, tankard

canth·us -ī *m* iron rim; wheel

cantic·um -ī *n* song; aria in Roman comedy; singing tone *(in an orator's delivery)*

cantilēn·a -ae *f* old song; *(coll)* gossip; **cantilēnam eandem canere** *(fig)* to harp on the same old theme

canti·ō -ōnis *f* singing; incantation, spell, charm

cantit·ō -āre -āvī -ātus *tr* to keep on singing *or* playing

Cant·ium -(i)ī *n* district of Britain *(modern Kent)*

cantiuncul·a -ae *f* catchy tune

cant·ō -āre -āvī -ātus *tr* to sing; to sing of, celebrate; to harp on, keep repeating; to drawl out; to predict; *(of birds)* to sing, crow, warble; *(of actor)* to play the part of ‖ *intr* to sing; *(w. abl)* to play *(a musical instrument); (of instruments)* to sound; to drawl; *(of rooster)* to crow; **ad surdās aurēs cantāre** *(fig)* to preach to deaf ears

cant·or -ōris *m* singer; poet; eulogist; actor, player; musician

cantr·īx -īcis *f* singer, player, musician *(female)*

cant·us -ūs *m* song, tune, melody; incantation; magic spell; prediction; poetry

cān·us -a -um *adj* grey; white; grey-haired; old; age-old *(things);* whitened, foam-capped *(sea); (of trees, plants)* covered with silvery foliage

Canusīn·a -ae *f* garment made of Canusian wool

Canus·ium -(i)ī *n* Greek town in Apulia *(modern Canosa)*

capācit·ās -ātis *f* capacity

Capan·ēus -ēī *m* one of the "Seven against Thebes," killed by lightning

cap·āx -ācis *adj* capacious, spacious, wide, roomy; *(of mind)* able to grasp, receptive; *(w.*

gen, dat or inf) big enough for; *(w. gen)* **1** capable of, capable of holding; **2** susceptible of; **3** capable of understanding; **capāx nāvium** navigable

capēd·ō -inis *f* cup, bowl *(used in sacrifices)*

capēduncul·a -ae *f* small cup *or* bowl *(used in sacrifices)*

capell·a -ae *f* she-goat, nanny goat ‖ *(astr)* **Capella** *(star in the constellation Auriga)*

Capēn·a -ae *f* a town of the Veientians in Etruria *(now San Martino)*

Capēn·ās -ātis *adj* of Capena ‖ **Capēnātēs** inhabitants of Capena

Capēn·us -a -um *adj* of Capena; **Porta Capēna** *(gate in the Servian Wall marking the start of the Via Appia, now the Porta San Sabastiano)*

ca·per -prī *m* he-goat, billy goat

caperr·ō -āre -āvī -ātus *tr & intr* to wrinkle

capess·ō -ere -īvī *or* **-iī -ītus** *tr* (**-iss-**) to try to reach, make for; to seize, get hold of, snatch at; to take up, engage in; **arma capessere** to take up arms, go to war; **cursum** *(or* **viam)** **capessere** to take the road (to); **flammam capessere** to catch fire; **iūssa capessere** to execute orders; **poenās capessere** to exact punishment; **rem pūblicam capessere** to engage in politics ‖ *refl & intr* to go

Caphēr·eus -eī *m* (**-phar-**) rocky promontory at the S.E. end of Euboea

capillāment·um -ī *n* wig, toupeé

capillār·e -is *n* hair oil

capillāt·us -a -um *adj* long-haired

capill·us -ī *m* hair *(of the head); (single)* hair; *(of plants)* fibers; hair, fur *(of animals)*

capiō capere cēpī captus *(archaic fut:* **capsō)** *tr* to take hold of, grasp; to occupy; to take up *(arms);* assume *(office);* to put on *(clothes, armor);* to catch, capture; to catch *(fish);* to bag *(game);* to captivate, charm; to cheat, mislead, seduce, delude; to trap; to defeat, overcome; to keep under control; to be able to hold, have room for; to convince; to reach, arrive at, land at; to exact *(tribute, penalty);* to extort, accept as a bribe; to take, obtain, enjoy, reap *(profit, advantage);* to reap, gather *(crops);* to cherish, cultivate, adopt *(habits, etc.);* to form, come to, reach *(conclusions, plans, thoughts, resolutions, purposes);* to take, derive, draw, obtain *(examples, proofs, instances);* to receive, experience *(impressions, feelings); (of feeling)* to come over; to suffer, be subjected to *(injury);* to hold, contain, be large enough for; to comprehend, grasp; **animō capere** to grasp, get, understand; **cōnsilium capere** to form a plan; **fidem capere** to be credible; **finem capere** to come to an end; **fugam capere** to take to flight; **honōrem capere** to assume an office;

initium capere to begin; īnsulam, portum capere reach the island, harbor *(by ship);* prīncipium capere to make a beginning, begin; rādīcem capere to take root; quiētem capere to get some rest; somnum capere to go to sleep; ūsū capere to acquire, inherit **ll** *refl* sē nōn capere not to contain oneself, not to control oneself

cap·is -idis *f* bowl *(with one handle, used in sacrifices)*

capistr·ō -āre -āvī -ātus *tr* to put a halter on, muzzle

capistr·um -ī *n* halter, muzzle

capit·al *or* capit·āle -ālis *n* capital offense; crime punishable by death

capitāl·is -is -e *adj* relating to the head *or* life; *(leg)* affecting a person's life *or* civil status; *(of crime)* punishable by death, punishable by loss of civil rights; dangerous, deadly, fatal; mortal *(enemy);* first-class, fine

capitāliter *adv* with bitter hostility

capit·ō -ōnis *m (coll)* bighead

Capitōlīn·us -a -um *adj* Capitoline **ll** *m* Capitoline Hill **ll** *mpl* persons in charge of the Capitoline games **ll** *n see* Capitōlium

Capitōl·ium -(i)ī *n* the Capitol *(temple of Jupiter on the summit of Mons Tarpeius);* the Capitoline Hill *(including temple and citadel);* citadel *(of any city)*

capitulātim *adv* briefly, summarily

capitul·um -ī *n* small head; *(as term of endearment)* dear fellow; end, point *(of an instrument, pole, etc.)*

Cappadoci·a -ae *f* country in E. Asia Minor between Cilicia and Pontus

Cappadoc·us -a -um *adj* Cappadocian

Cappad·ox -ocis *m* inhabitant of Cappadocia; *(pej)* Asiatic

cappar·is -is *f* pickled flower bud of the caper plant *(prickly shrub)*

capr·a -ae *f* she-goat **ll** Capra *(astr)* star in the constellation Auriga

capre·a -ae *f* wild she-goat; Capr(e)ae Palūs Goat's Pool *(in Campus Martius, site of Circus Flaminius)*

Capre·ae -ārum *fpl* Isle of Capri

capreol·us -ī *m* chamois, roebuck; rafter

Capricorn·us -ī *m (astr)* Capricorn

caprific·us -ī *f* wild fig tree

caprigen·us -a -um *adj* of goats; caprigenum pecus herd of goats

caprimulg·us -ī *m* country bumpkin *(literally, goat milker)*

caprīn·us -a -um *adj* goat; dē lānā caprīnā rīxārī *(fig)* to fight over nothing

caprip·ēs -edis *adj* goat-footed *(poetic epithet of rural dieties)*

caps·a -ae *f* container, holder, box, case *(esp. for scrolls)*

capsō *see* capiō

capsul·a -ae *f* small box

capt·a -ae *f* captive *(female)*

captāti·ō -ōnis *f* hunt, quest; captātiō verbōrum verbalism

captātor -ōris *m* seeker; legacy hunter; aurae populāris captātor publicity hound

capti·ō -ōnis *f* trick, fraud; loss, disadvantage; verbal quibble

captiōsē *adv* slyly, trickily

captiōs·us -a -um *adj* tricky, deceptive; sophistical; harmful, disadvantageous

captiuncul·a -ae *f* quibble, sophism

captīvit·ās -ātis *f* captivity; capture

captīv·us -a -um *adj* captured; captive; prisoner's; caught *(in hunting, fishing)* **ll** *mf* prisoner-of-war

capt·ō -āre -āvī -ātus *tr* to try to catch; to keep reaching for; to chase after; to strive after, long for, desire earnestly; to try to find; to try to trap, lure; to catch *(fish);* to try to get the better of *(in an argument);* to adopt *(plan);* to try to cause *(laughter, response in others);* to watch for *(an opportunity);* to begin *(conversation);* aure *(or* auribus) captāre to try to hear, listen in on, eavesdrop on; cēnam captāre to sponge a meal

captūr·a -ae *f* capture; quarry, kill; catch *(in fishing)*

capt·us -a -um *pp of* capiō **ll** *adj* captive; oculīs et auribus captus blind and deaf; mente captus crazy

capt·us -ūs *m* grasping, taking; capacity, potentiality

Capu·a -ae *f* chief city of Campania

capūd·ō -inis *f* primitive sacrificial vessel

capulār·is -is -e *adj (sl)* with one foot in the grave

capul·us -ī *m* coffin; hilt, handle

cap·ut -itis *n* head; top, summit; point; principal point, main item; essential thing, matter of prime importance; end *(of anything, esp. when rounded or resembling a head, e.g., of a pole);* source *(of river);* beginning *(of a road);* root *(of plant);* top *(of tree, poppy);* head, leader; prime mover, ring-leader; individual, person *(e.g.,* caput līberum free person; chief city, capital *(of a country, etc.);* main point *(of discourse);* chapter, heading; substance, summary; beginning, first part *(of a speech, action; initial letter, beginning of a word or sentence);* main course; *(com)* capital; *(fin)* principal; *(leg)* life, civil status; capitis accūsāre to accuse of a capital crime; capitis damnāre to condemn to death; capitis rēs matter of life and death; caput dēmittere to hang one's head; dīminūtiō capitis loss of civil rights; dīminūtiō capitis maxima condemnation to death *or* slavery;

dīminūtiō capitis media loss of citizenship; dīminūtiō capitis minima change of status *(as by adoption, marriage);* suprā caput esse to be imminent

Cap·ys -yos *m* son of Assaracus and father of Anchises ‖ companion of Aeneas ‖ eighth king of Alba Longa

carbase·us -a -um *adj* linen, canvas

carbas·us -a -um *adj* linen ‖ *f* sail, canvas; awning; linen cloth ‖ *npl* linen clothing

carb·ō -ōnis *m* charcoal; piece of charcoal used in writing, drawing, marking; *(fig)* something worthless

carbōnār·ius -(i)ī *m* charcoal burner *(person),* collier

carbuncul·us -ī *m* (live) coal, ember; garnet; *(med)* carbuncle, tumor

carc·er -eris *m* prison; prisoners; *(coll)* jailbird ‖ *mpl* starting gate *(at racetrack);* ad carcerēs ā calce revocārī to start over from scratch *(literally, to be called back from the chalk line, i.e., finish line, to the starting gate)*

carcerāri·us -a -um *adj* prison

carchēs·ium -(i)ī *n* drinking cup; masthead *(of ship)*

cardiac·us -a -um *adj* suffering from heartburn ‖ *m* dyspeptic

card·ō -inis *m* (kar-) pivot and socket; hinge; turning point; axis, pole; boundary; region, district *(of a country);* the earth *(as pivot of the universe);* cardō extrēmus old age; cardō rērum critical juncture; cardō summus zenith *(of the sky)*

cardu·us -ī *m* thistle

cārē *adv* at a high price, dearly

cārect·um -ī *n* a bed of sedge *(reed grass, having solid rather than hollow stems)*

car·eō -ēre -uī *intr (w. abl or gen)* 1 to be without; 2 to miss; 3 to be free from *(trouble, pain, blame);* 4 to keep away from, be absent from; 5 to abstain from; 6 to fail to achieve, be denied; 7 to go without

cār·ex -icis *f* sedge, reed grass *(having solid rather than hollow stems)*

Cāri·a -ae *f* district in S.W. Asia Minor

cari·ēs -ēī *f* decaying; decay, rot; shriveling up

carīn·a -ae *f* keel; ship ‖ Carīnae *fpl* the Keels *(district in Rome between the Esquiline and Caelian Hills)*

carīnār·ius -(i)ī *m* dyer of yellow

cariōs·us -a -um *adj* rotten, decayed; crumbly; wrinkled *(old age)*

cār·is -idis *f* shrimp

cārit·ās -ātis *f* dearness, costliness, high price, high cost of living; affection

carm·en -inis *n* song, tune; poem; poetry; lyric poetry; incantation; oracular utterance; ritual formula; legal formula; adage

Carment·a -ae *or* Carment·is -is *f* Roman goddess, mother of Evander

Carmentāl·is -is -e *adj* of Carmenta; Porta Carmentālis gate in the Servian Wall in Rome

Carment·is -is *f see* Carmenta

carnār·ium -(i)ī *n* meat hook

carnār·ius -(i)ī *m* butcher, dealer in meat

Carnead·ēs -is *m* Greek Academic philosopher of the 2nd cent. B.C.

Carneadē·us -a -um *adj* characteristic of Carneades

carnif·ex -icis *m* (carnu-) executioner, hangman; murderer, butcher; scoundrel

carnificīn·a -ae *f* (carnu-) execution; *(fig)* torture

carnific·ō -āre -āvī -ātus *tr* to execute, butcher; to mutilate

car·ō -nis *or* carn·is -is *f* meat; carō būbula beef; carō ferīna venison; carō pūtida carrion; *(fig)* rotten egg

Carpathi·us -a -um *adj* of the island of Carpathus *(between Crete and Rhodes);* Carpathius senex (vātēs) Proteus

carpatin·a -ae *f* rough-leather shoe

carpent·um -ī *n* two-wheeled covered carriage *(used esp. by women)*

carp·ō -ere -sī -tus *tr* to pluck, pick; to carp at, pick on; to enjoy, make use of; to crop *(grass); (mil)* to harass; to cut to pieces; to card *(wool); (of wild animals)* to tear at; aurās vītālēs carpere to breathe the breath of life; diem carpere to make the most of the present; gȳrum carpere to go in a circle; iter *(or* viam) carpere to make one's way, travel; pēnsum *(or* vellera) carpere to spin

carptim *adv* piecemeal, separately; selectively; at different times; at various points; gradually

carpt·or -ōris *m* carver *(at table)*

carrūc·a -ae *f* four-wheeled carriage

carr·us -ī *m,* carr·um -ī *n* Gallic type of wagon

Carthae·us -a -um *adj* of Carthaea *(town on the Greek island of Ceos)*

Carthāginiēns·is -is -e *adj* (Kar-) Carthaginian

Carthāg·ō -inis *f* (Kar-) Carthage *(city in N. Africa, founded in 9th cent. B.C.)*

Carthēi·us -a -um *adj see* Carthaeus

caruncul·a -ae *f* scrap of meat

cār·us -a -um *adj* dear, expensive; dear, loving, affectionate

Cār·us -ī *m* Roman family name *(cognomen)*

cas·a -ae *f* cottage, cabin, hut; play house

Casc·a -ae *m* Roman family name *(cognomen),* esp. Gaius and Publius Servilius Casca Longus *(two of Caesar's assassins)*

cāsc·us -a -um *adj* old-time, primitive

cāseol·us -ī *m* small piece of cheese
cāse·us -ī *m* cheese
casi·a -ae *f* wild cinnamon tree; fragrant shrub
Caspi·a -a -um *adj* Caspian; mare Caspium Caspian Sea; sinus Caspius Caspian Sea; Caspiae pylae (*or* portae) name of passes in the Caucasus mountains S. of the Caspian Sea
Cassandr·a -ae *f* prophetic daughter of Priam and Hecuba, believed by no one
cass·ēs -ium *see* cassis
cassid·a -ae *f* metal helmet
Cassiop·ē -ēs *or* Cassiopē·a -ae *f* wife of Cepheus and mother of Andromeda, afterwards changed into a constellation
cass·is -idis *f* metal helmet (*cf* galea leather helmet)
cass·is -is *m (often pl)* hunting net, snare; spider web; cassēs alicui tendere to set a trap for s.o.
cassiter·um -ī *n* tin
Cass·ius -(i)ī *m* name of a Roman clan (*nomen*), *esp.* Gaius Cassius Longinus (*one of Caesar's murderers*)
cass·ō -āre *intr* to totter
cass·us -a -um *adj* empty, hollow; (*fig*) groundless, pointless; (*w. abl*) deprived of, devoid of, without; cassus lūmine without life; in cassum (*also as one word:* incassum) to no purpose, pointlessly
Castali·a -ae *f* spring at Delphi, associated with Apollo and the Muses
Castal·is -idis *adj (fem only)* Castalian; sorōrēs Castalidēs Muses ‖ *f* Muse
Castali·us -a -um *adj* of Castalia, of Apollo, of the Muses, of the Delphic oracle, Castalian
castane·a -ae *f* chestnut tree; chestnut
castē *adv* chastely, purely, spotlessly; virtuously; devoutly
castellān·us -a -um *adj* of a fortress ‖ *mpl* occupants of a fortress, garrison
castellātim *adv* one fortress after another; castellātim dissipātī (troops) stationed in various fortresses
castell·um -ī *n* fort, fortress; castle; (*fig*) stronghold, refuge; small reservoir *or* center of distribution on an aqueduct
castēri·a -ae *f* rower's quarters (*on a ship*)
castīgābil·is -is -e *adj* punishable
castīgāti·ō -ōnis *f* correction, punishment; censure, reproof
castīgāt·or -ōris *m* castigator
castīgātōri·us -a -um *adj* reproving
castīgāt·us -a -um *adj* small, delicate (*breast*)
castīg·ō -āre -āvī -ātus *tr* to correct, make right; to reprove, find fault with; to restrain, hold in check
castimōni·a -ae *f* purity, morality; chastity; ceremonial purification

castit·ās -ātis *f* chastity, purity
cast·or -oris *m* beaver ‖ Castor Castor (*son of Tyndareus, twin brother of Pollux, brother of Helen and Clytemnestra, and patron of sailors*); aedes (*or* templum) Castoris temple of Castor (and Pollux)
castore·um -ī *n* strong-smelling secretion of beavers (*used in medicine*)
castr·a -ōrum *npl* camp; day's march; the service, army life; (*pol*) party; (*phil*) school; bīna castra two camps; castra facere (*or* munīre *or* pōnere) to construct a camp; castra habēre to be encamped; castra movēre to break camp; castra ūnā one camp
castrēns·is -is -e *adj* camp, military; characteristic of soldiers; corōna castrēnsis crown conferred on first soldier to enter an enemy's camp
castr·ō -āre -āvī -ātus *tr* to castrate
castr·um -ī *n* fort, fortress ‖ *npl see* castra
cast·us -a -um *adj* chaste, pure, innocent; (*of places*) free from crime; holy, sacred
casul·a -ae *f* little hut, little cottage
cās·us -ūs *m* falling; fall, downfall, overthrow, end; chance, event, occurrence; occasion, opportunity; adventure; emergency; misfortune, accident; plight; eventuality, possible situation, contingency; death; fate; (*gram*) case; nōn cōnsultō sed cāsū not on purpose but accidentally
cataclysm·os -ī *m* deluge
catafract- *see* cataphract-
catagraph·us -a -um *adj* print (*dress*)
catamīt·us -ī *m* catamite ‖ Catamītus Ganymede
cataphag·ās -ae *m* glutton
cataphract·ēs -ae *m* coat of mail
cataphract·us -a -um *adj* clad in mail
cataplūs *m (nom only)* putting into port, ship's arrival
catapult·a -ae *f* catapult
catapultāri·us -a -um *adj* catapulted, shot (*from a catapult*)
cataract·a *or* catarract·a -ae *or* catar-(r)(h)act·ēs -ae *f* rapids, cataract; sluice; portcullis
cataractri·a -ae *f (fictitious)* spice
catast·a -ae *f* platform on which slaves were displayed for sale
catē *adv* skillfully, wisely
catēi·a -ae *f* javelin
catell·a -ae *f* puppy (*female*); small chain (*worn by women*)
catell·us -ī *m* puppy; small chain
catēn·a -ae *f* chain; series; curb, restraint ‖ *fpl* chains, fetters
catēnāt·us -a -um *adj* chained
caterv·a -ae *f* crowd, throng, band, mob; troop (*of actors*); (*mil*) troop

catervāri·us -a -um *adj* in a crowd
catervātim *adv* in groups; in companies; in herds
cathedr·a -ae *f* armchair, cushioned seat; sedan chair; teacher's chair
Catilīn·a -ae *m* Lucius Sergius Catiline *(leader of conspiracy in 63 B.C.)*
catīll·ō -ōnis *m* plate licker
catīll·ō -āre -āvī -ātum *intr* to lick the plate
catīll·us -ī *m or* catill·um -ī *n* (small) plate
catīn·us -ī *m* plate, bowl, dish
Cat·ō -ōnis *m* Marcus Porcius Cato *(model of Roman aristocratic conservatism, 239–149 B.C.)* ‖ Marcus Porcius Cato Uticensis *(grandson of the former, arch-enemy of Julius Caesar, 95–45 B.C.)*
Catull·us -ī *m* Gaius Valerius Catullus *(lyric and elegiac poet of Verona, 86–54 B.C.)* ‖ a mime writer
catul·us -ī *m* puppy; cub ‖ Catulus Roman family name *(cognomen), esp.* Quintus Lutatius Catulus *(consul in 78 B.C.)*
cat·us -a -um *adj* clever; sly
Caucasi·us -a -um *adj* of the Caucasus; portae Caucasiae pass through the Caucasus Mountains
Caucas·us -ī *m* Caucasus Mountains
caud·a -ae *f* tail (cōd-) *(of an animal);* tail-end; *(vulg)* penis; caudam iactāre *(w. dat)* to flatter; caudam movēre to wag the tail; caudam trahere *(to have a tail stuck on)* to be mocked
caude·us -a -um *adj* wooden
caud·ex -icis *m* (cōd-) trunk *(of tree);* block *(of wood to which one was tied for punishment);* book, tablet; ledger; *(coll)* blockhead
caudicāl·is -is -e *adj* wood-splitting
Caudīn·us -a -um *adj* of Caudium, Caudine; Furculae Caudīnae Caudine Forks *(where Romans suffered a great defeat at the hands of Samnites in 321 B.C.)*
Caud·ium -(i)ī *n* town in Samnium *(near which was the mountain pass where the Romans were defeated)*
caul·ae -ārum *fpl* fence; sheepfold; opening, hole; caulae corporis *(anat)* pores
caulicul·us -ī *m* small stalk; small cabbage
caul·is -is *f* stalk, stem; cabbage
caup·ō -ōnis *m* innkeeper
caupōn·a -ae *f* inn, tavern; innkeeper *(female);* retail shop
caupōni·us -a -um *adj* of an inn *or* shop
caupōn·or -ārī -ātus sum *tr* to trade in, traffic in
caupōnul·a -ae *f* small inn; small shop
Caur·us *or* Cor·us -ī *m* the northwest wind
caus·a *or* causs·a -ae *f* cause, grounds, motive, reason; good reason, just cause; pretext, pretense; inducement, occasion; side, party, fac-

tion; condition, situation, position; responsibility, blame; *(leg)* case, trial, plea; *(med)* case, symptoms; *(rhet)* matter of discussion, subject matter; matter, business, concern; causā *(postpositive) (w. gen)* for the sake of, because of; animī causā for the sake of amusement; causae amīcitiae ties of friendship; causae necessitūdinis friendly relations; causam agere *(or* dīcere *or* ōrāre) to plead a case; causam cognōscere *(of a judge)* to examine a case; in causā esse to be responsible; meā causā for my sake; as far as I am concerned, for all I care; nōn sine causā with good reason; ob hanc causam because of this; per causam *(w. gen)* under the pretense of; valētūdinis causā for reasons of (poor) health; vestrā causā in your interests
causāri·us -a -um *adj* sick; missiō causāria *(mil)* medical discharge ‖ *m* soldier with medical discharge
causi·a -ae *or* cause·a -ae *f* wide-brimmed Macedonian hat
causidic·us -ī *m* lawyer; *(pej)* shyster
causific·or -ārī -ātus sum *intr* to make excuses
caus·or -ārī -ātus sum *tr* to give as an excuse, pretend
caussa *see* causa
causul·a -ae *f* poor reason; *(leg)* petty lawsuit
cautē *adv* cautiously, carefully; without risk
cautēl·a -ae *f* precaution, caution
caut·ēs -is *f* (cōt-) *(usu. pl)* rock, crag, cliff; *(fig)* hard-heartedness
cautim *adv* warily, cautiously
cauti·ō -ōnis *f* caution, wariness; guarantee, provision; *(leg)* bond, bail; mea *(or* mihi) cautiō est I must see to it, I must take care
caut·or -ōris *m* wary person; *(leg)* bondsman
caut·us -a -um *pp of* caveō ‖ *adj* cautious, careful; safe, secure
cavaed·ium -(i)ī *n* inner court of a Roman house
cave·a -ae *f* cavity; enclosure for animals: cage, den, hole, stall, beehive; auditorium *(of a theater);* prīma cavea section of auditorium for nobility; ultima cavea section for lower classes
caveō cavēre cāvī cautus *tr* to guard against, beware of; to keep clear of; to stipulate, decree, order; to guarantee; cavē canem! beware of the dog! ‖ *intr* to be careful, look out, be on one's guard; *(w. abl or* ab) to be on one's guard against; *(w. ab)* to get a guarantee from; *(w. dat)* 1 to guarantee, give a guarantee to; 2 to provide for, take care of; cavē tangere (= nōlī tangere)! do not touch! ‖ *impv with subj* 1 *without* nē take care not to, don't; 2 *with* ut take care to

cavern·a -ae *f* hollow; cavity *(in tooth);* cavern; hole; den, lair; hold *(of ship);* **caverna caelī** vault of the sky
cavill·a -ae *f* jeering, scoffing
cavillāti·ō -ōnis *f* banter, scoffing; quibbling
cavillāt·or -ōris *m* scoffer; quibbler
cavill·or -ārī -ātus sum *tr* to scoff at, mock, criticize, satirize ‖ *intr* to scoff, jeer; to quibble
cav·ō -āre -āvī -ātus *tr* to hollow out, excavate, dig a hole in; to pierce, run through
cav·us -a -um *adj* hollow, hollowed; concave, vaulted; deep-channeled *(river)* ‖ *m & n* depression; cave, cavern; burrow, hole *(of an animal);* hole, cavity, hollow; aperture, perforation; **cavum aedium** inner court of a house
-ce demonstrative enclitic appended to pronouns and adverbs (like colloquial English *here, there,* with *this* or *that);* **hīce** *(for* **hicce)** this *(here);* **huiūsce** of this *(here);* (when followed by the enclytic **-ne,** the form becomes **-ci: hīcine, sīcine)**
Cē·a *or* **Cī·a -ae** *or* **Cē·os -ī** *f* Ceos *(Greek island in the Cyclades)*
Cecropi·a -ae *f* Athens, the citadel of Athens
Cecropid·ēs -ae *m* descendant of King Cecrops; **Cecropidae** Athenians
Cecrop·is -idis *or* **idos** *f* female descendant of Cecrops; Aglauros; Procne; Philomela; Athenian woman
Cecropi·us -a -um *adj* of Cecrops; Athenian
Cecr·ops -opis *m* first king of Athens
cēd·ēns -entis *adj* unresisting
cedo *(pl:* **cette)** *(old impv)* give here, hand over, bring here; let's hear, tell, out with; look at; **cedo dum!** all right! **cedo ut īnspiciam** let me have a look
cēdō cēdere cessī cessus *tr* to grant, concede, yield, give up ‖ *intr* to go, move, walk, walk along; to go away, depart, withdraw; *(usu. w.* **vītā)** to pass away, die; *(of time)* to pass; *(of events)* turn out; *(w. dat)* **1** to befall, fall to the lot of; **2** to yield to, submit to, give in to; **3** to be inferior to; **4** to comply with, conform to, obey; *(w.* **in** + *acc)* **1** to result in; **2** to be changed into, become; *(w.* **prō** + *abl)* **1** to pass for; **2** to be the equivalent of; **3** to be the price of; **bonīs** *(or* **possessiōnibus) alicui cēdere** to give up *or* cede one's property to s.o.; **forō cēdere** to go bankrupt
cedr·us -ī *f* cedar; cedarwood; cedar-wood oil
Celaen·ō -ūs *f* daughter of Atlas and one of the Pleiades ‖ one of the Harpies ‖ greedy woman
cēlāt·um -ī *n* secret
cele·ber -bris -bre *adj* crowded, populous, frequented; well-attended; famous; well-known,

common, usual; solemn, festive; numerous, repeated, frequent
celebrāti·ō -ōnis *f* large assembly; festival, celebration; widespread use ‖ *fpl* throngs
celebrāt·us -a -um *adj* crowded, populous; much-frequented; celebrated, famous; solemn, festive; common, current
celebrit·ās -ātis *f* crowd; large assembly; publicity; frequency; fame
celebr·ō -āre -āvī -ātus *tr* to frequent; to crowd, fill; to inhabit; to celebrate, observe; to honor, worship; to escort, attend; to practice, exercise; to announce, publicize; **sermōne celebrāre** to discuss
cel·er -eris -ere *adj* fast; agile, quick; hurried; rash, hasty; passing quickly
celere *adv* quickly
Celer·ēs -um *mpl* mounted bodyguards of Roman kings
celerip·ēs -edis *adj* swift-footed ‖ *m* race horse
celerit·ās -ātis *f* speed; quickness; excessive speed
celeriter *adv* quickly; soon, early
celer·ō -āre -āvī *tr* to quicken, speed up ‖ *intr* to be quick, rush, hurry
celeum·a -atis *n* boatswain's call *(giving time to the rowers)*
Cele·us -ī *m* king of Eleusis and father of Triptolemus
cell·a -ae *f* storeroom; silo; small room; *(coll)* hole-in-the-wall, poor man's apartment; sanctuary *(of temple where statue stood);* cell *(of beehive);* cubicle *(in a bathing establishment or in a brothel);* porter's room
cellāri·us -a -um *adj* of a storeroom ‖ *m* one in charge of the storeroom
cellul·a -ae *f* **(-ola)** small storeroom; small room; porter's lodge; slave's room
cēl·ō -āre -āvī -ātus *tr* to hide, conceal; to keep secret, keep quiet about; to conceal the identity of; *(w. acc of thing and acc of person from whom one conceals)* to keep *(s.o.)* in the dark about *(s.th.),* hide *(s.th.)* from *(s.o.)* ‖ *refl & pass* to pass out of view; **cēlārī dē** *(w. abl)* to be kept in ignorance of
cel·ox -ōcis *adj* swift, quick ‖ *f* light, fast boat
cels·us -a -um *adj* high, lofty, towering, prominent; erect; lofty *(thoughts);* high *(rank);* proud; *(of head)* held high; tall *(animals, person, trees, buildings)*
Celt·ae -ārum *mpl* Celts
Celtib·ēr -ērī *mpl* a Celtiberian ‖ *mpl* Celtiberians *(early people of central Spain)*
cēn·a -ae *f* dinner; dish, course; **ad cēnam invītāre** *or* **vocāre** to invite to dinner; **caput cēnae** main dish; **cēnam appōnere** to serve dinner; **in cēnā** for dinner; **inter cēnam** at table, during dinner

cēnācul·um -ī *n* dining room *(usually on the upper floor);* upper floor, attic; attic apartment

cēnātic·us -a -um *adj* dinner

cēnāti·ō -ōnis *f* dining room

cēnātōri·a -ōrum *npl* formal wear; dinner apparel

cēnāt·us -a -um *pp of* cēnō having dined; stuffed from feasting

cēnit·ō -āre *intr* to dine often

cēn·ō -āre -āvī -ātus *tr* to dine on, eat ‖ *intr* to dine, eat dinner

cēns·eō -ēre -uī -us *tr* to think, believe, suppose, imagine, expect; to esteem, appreciate, value; *(of senator)* to propose, move, vote; to recommend; to suggest, advise; *(of the Senate and other bodies and supreme magistrates)* to decide, resolve; *(of the censor)* to estimate, rate, assess, tax; to register *(possessions); (w. abl)* to measure by; cēnseō *(in replies)* I think so; quid cēnsēs? what is your opinion? *(formula used by the presiding magistrate to invite a senator to express his opinion)* ‖ *pass (w. abl)* to be valued for, have one's reputation based on; *(as deponent)* to reckon, count (as)

cēnsi·ō -ōnis *f* tax assessment; punishment *(imposed by the censor)*

cēns·or -ōris *m* censor *(one of two magistrates who took the census and exercised general control over morals);* severe judge of morals; critic

cēnsōri·us -a -um *adj* of the censors; subject to censure; rigid, stern; fūnus cēnsōrium public funeral; homō cēnsōrius ex-censor; lēx cēnsōria contract *(drawn up by censors)* for leasing buildings; opus cēnsōrium a fault *or* crime punished by the censors

cēnsūr·a -ae *f* office of censor, censorship; censure, criticism

cēns·us -ūs *m* census; register of the census; income bracket; wealth, property; rich presents; cēnsum agere *(or* habēre*)* to hold a census; cēnsū prohibēre to exclude from citizenship; in cēnsum referre to register in the census list

centaurē·um -ī *n* (-i·um, -i·on) centaury *(herb)*

Centaurē·us -a -um *adj* of Centaurs

Centaur·us -ī *m* Centaur *(half-man, half-horse); (astr)* Centaurus *(a constellation)*

centēn·ī -ae -a *adj* one hundred each; deciēns centēna mīlia passuum ten hundred thousand *(one million)* paces, one thousand miles

centēsim·us -a -um *adj* hundredth ‖ *f* hundredth part, one percent; *(com)* 1% monthly, 12% annually

centi·ceps -cipitis *adj* hundred-headed

centiēs *adv* (-iēns) a hundred times; *(fig)* a good many times

centiman·us -a -um *adj* hundred-handed

cent·ō -ōnis *f* patchwork, quilt

centr·um -ī *n* center

centum *indecl adj* hundred

centumgemin·us -a -um *adj* hundredfold

centumpl·ex -icis *adj* hundredfold

centumpond·ium -(i)ī *n* hundred pounds, hundred-pound weight

centumvirāl·is -is -e *adj* of the centumvirs

centumvir·ī -ōrum *mpl* panel of one hundred *(jurors chosen annually to try civil suits under a quaestor, esp. concerning inheritances)*

centuncul·us -ī *m* piece of patchwork; blanket *(made of patchwork)*

centuri·a -ae *f (mil)* company, century *(nominally 100 soldiers); (pol)* century, voting division; unit of land *(100 heredia, 200 jugera, i.e., c. 133 acres)*

centuriātim *adv (mil, pol)* by companies *or* centuries

centuriāt·us -a -um *adj (mil, pol)* divided into companies *or* centuries; comitia centuriāta centuriate assembly *(legislative body that met in the Campus Martius to elect high magistrates, decree war, etc.)*

centuriāt·us -ūs *m* rank of centurion; division into centuries

centuri·ō -āre -āvī -ātus *tr* to divide into centuries *or* companies

centuri·ō -ōnis *m* centurion *(commander of an infantry company)*

centuriōnāt·us -ūs *m* rank of centurion; revision of the list of centurions

centuss·is -is *m* copper coin, worth about one dollar

cēnul·a -ae *f* light dinner

cēnum *see* caenum

Ceōs *see* Cēa

cēpa *or* cēpe *see* caepa

Cephallāni·a -ae *f* Greek island in the Ionian Sea

Cephal·us -ī *m* husband of Procris, whom he accidentally killed

Cēphē·is -idos *f* daughter of Cepheus *(Andromeda)*

Cēphēi·us -a -um *adj* descended from Cepheus

Cēphēn·es -um *mpl* a people of Ethiopia

Cēphēn·us -a -um *adj* of the Cephenes, Ethiopian

Cēph·eūs -eī *m* king of the Cephenes *(Ethiopia),* father of Andromeda

Cēphīs·os -ī *m* Cephissus *(river in Attica; river in Phocis)*

cēr·a -ae *f* wax; writing tablet *(covered with wax);* wax seal; wax bust of an ancestor; cell *(of beehive);* **prīma cēra** first page

Ceramb·us -ī *m* herdsman, changed into a beetle

Ceramīc·us -ī *m* cemetery of Athens

cērār·ium -(i)ī *n* fee for affixing a seal

cerast·ēs -ae *m* horned serpent

ceras·um -ī *n* cherry

ceras·us -ī *f* cherry tree; cherry

cērāt·us -a -um *adj* waxed ‖ *n* wax-salve *(made of wax and oil)*

Cerber·us -ī *m* three-headed dog guarding entrance to lower world

cercopithēc·us -ī *m* long-tailed monkey

cercūr·us -ī *m* swift-sailing ship

cerd·ō -ōnis *m* (common) laborer

Cereāl·is -is -e *adj* of Ceres; of grain; **arma Cereālia** utensils for grinding and baking ‖ *npl* festival of Ceres *(April 10)*

cerebrōs·us -a -um *adj* hot-headed

cerebr·um -ī *n* brain; head, skull; hot temper; *(fig)* brains

Cer·ēs -eris *f* goddess of grain and fruits and mother of Proserpina; grain, wheat; bread; food

cēre·us -a -um *adj* of wax, waxen; wax-colored; soft, pliant ‖ *m* taper

cērinth·a -ae *f* wax flower

cērin·us -a -um *adj* wax-colored

Cermal·us -ī *m* (**Germ-**) part of the Palatine Hill in Rome

cernō cernere crēvī crētus *tr* to sift; to distinguish, make out, see; to understand, see; to decide, decree, determine; **hērēditātem cernere** to accept an inheritance formally; **vītam cernere** to decide a question of life or death

cernu·us -a -um *adj* leaning forward; headfirst

cērōm·a -atis *n* wrestler's oil; *(fig)* wrestler

cērōmatic·us -a -um *adj* smeared with oil, oily, greasy

cerrīt·us -a -um *adj* possessed by Ceres, crazy, frenzied

certām·en -inis *n* contest, match; rivalry; *(mil)* battle, combat

certātim *adv* with a struggle, in rivalry

certāti·ō -ōnis *f* contest; rivalry, discussion, debate

certē *adv* surely, certainly; of course; *(in answers)* certainly; *(to restrict an assertion)* at least

certō *adv* for sure; in fact, really; **certō scīre** to know for sure

cert·ō -āre -āvī -ātus *tr* to contest ‖ *pass* to be fought over ‖ *intr (w.* dē + *abl)* to fight over, struggle for; *(w.* cum) to fight with, struggle with, compete with; *(w. inf)* to strive to; *(leg)* to debate

cert·us -a -um *adj* certain, sure; fixed; regular; specific, particular, definite; faithful, trusty; unerring; unwavering; **certiōrem facere** to inform; **certum est mihi** *(w. inf)* I am determined to ‖ *n* certainty; **certum habēre** to regard as certain; **prō certō** for sure; **prō certō habēre** to be assured, regard as certain

cērul·a -ae *f* piece of wax; crayon; **cērula miniāta** "red pencil" *(of a critic)*

cēruss·a -ae *f* ceruse, white paint

cērussāt·us -a -um *adj* painted white

cerv·a -ae *f* doe

cervīc·al -ālis *n* pillow, cushion

cervīcul·a -ae *f* slender neck

cervīn·us -a -um *adj* of a stag

cerv·īx -īcis *f (often in plural with same meaning as singular)* neck, nape; **in cervīcibus nostrīs esse** *(fig)* to be on our necks; **ā cervīcibus nostrīs āvertere** *(fig)* to get *(s.o.)* off our necks; **cervīcibus sustinēre** to shoulder *(responsibility)*

cerv·us -ī *m* stag, deer; *(mil)* palisade

cessāti·ō -ōnis *f* cessation; letup; delay; idleness, inactivity

cessāt·or -ōris *m* loafer

cessāt·us -a -um *adj* having been in abeyance; *(of land)* having been left fallow; spent in idleness

cessi·ō -ōnis *f (leg)* surrendering

cess·ō -āre -āvī -ātum *intr* to cease; to let up, slack off, become remiss; to be idle, do nothing; to lie fallow; to fail, not function; *(w. inf)* to hesitate to, be slow to; *(of things)* to stop, give out; *(of things)* to be at rest, be motionless; *(of things)* to be neglected, remain unused; *(w. abl or* ab) to be free of, be clear of, be wanting in; *(leg)* to fail to take action, default; *(leg)* to fail to appear in court

cessus *pp of* cēdō

cest·os *or* cest·us -ī *m* brassière

cestrosphendon·ē -ēs *f* artillery piece for hurling stones

cētār·ium -(i)ī *n* fish pond

cētār·ius -(i)ī *m* fishmonger; fisherman

cētē *see* cētus

cētera *adv* otherwise, in all other respects, for the rest

cēterōquī(n) *adv* otherwise, in all other respects, for the rest

cēterum *adv* but, still; for the rest, otherwise; however that may be

cēter·(us) -a -um *adj (nom singl masc not in use)* the other, the remaining, the rest of ‖ *pron masc pl & fem pl* the others, all the rest, everybody else ‖ *n* the rest; **dē cēterō** for the rest; otherwise; for the future; **in cēterum** in the future

Cethēg·us -ī *m* Gaius Cornelius Cethegus *(fellow conspirator of Catiline)*

cette *see* cedo

cēt·us *or* cēt·os -ī *(nom & acc npl:* cētē) *m* large sea animal: whale, shark, dolphin, seal; sea-monster

ceu *conj (in comparisons)* as, just as; *(in comparative conditions)* as if, just as if; ceu cum as when

cēv·eō -ēre *intr (cf.* crīsō) *(of a male) (sl)* to move the hips, shake it up

Cē·ȳx -ȳcis *m* king of Trachis, changed into a kingfisher *(bird)*

Chaerōnē·a -ae *f* town in Boeotia where Philip of Macedon defeated the Greeks in 338 B.C.

Chalcidic·us -a -um *adj* of Chalcis *(in Euboea);* of Cumae *(in Italy)*

Chaldae·us -a -um *adj* Chaldean ‖ *m* astrologer, fortuneteller

chalybēi·us -a -um *adj* of steel, steel

Chalyb·es -um *mpl* people of Pontus in Asia Minor noted as steel-workers and iron-workers

chal·ybs -ybis *m* steel; iron

Chāon·es -um *mpl* tribe in Epirus

Chāoni·us -a -um *adj* Chaonian; of Epirus ‖ *f* Chaonia *(in Epirus)*

Cha·os -ī *n* chaos, the unformed world; ā Chaō from the beginning of the world

char·a -ae *f* wild cabbage (?)

Charit·ēs -um *fpl* the Graces

Char·ōn -ōntis *m* ferryman of the lower world

chart·a -ae *f* sheet of papyrus, paper; thin sheet of metal ‖ *fpl (fig)* writings

chartul·a -ae *f* sheet of papyrus, slip of paper; note

Charybd·is -is *f* whirlpool between Italy and Sicily *(regarded as a female monster); (fig)* cruel person

Chatt·ī -ōrum *mpl* Germanic tribe

Chauc·ī -ōrum *mpl* Germanic tribe

Chēl·ae -ārum *fpl (astr)* the Claws *(of the constellation Scorpio); (astr)* Libra

chelydr·us -ī *m* poisonous water snake

chelys *(gen not in use; acc:* chelyn) *f* tortoise; lyre

cheragr·a -ae *f* arthritis in the hand

Cheronēs·us -ī *f* (Cherson-) a peninsula, *esp.* Cheronēsus Thrācia the Chersonese *(now Gallipoli)*

chīliarch·ēs -ae *or* chīliarch·us -ī *m* commander of 1,000 men; Persian chancellor *(highest office next to the king)*

Chimaer·a -ae *f* fire-breathing female monster, with lion's head, goat's body, and dragon's tail

Chimaerifer·a -ae *adj (fem only) (of Lycia)* that produced the Chimaera

Chi·os *or* Chi·us -ī *f* Chios *(Greek island off the coast of Ionia)*

chīrograph·um -ī *n* (-graf-) one's handwriting; autograph; manuscript; written promise; falsum chīrographum forgery

Chīr·ō(n) -ōnis *m* Chiron *(Centaur, tutor of Hercules, Achilles, etc.); (astr)* Chiron *(constellation)*

chīronom·ōn -untos *adj* gesticulating ‖ *mf* gesticulator

chīronom·os -ī *m* pantominist

chīrūrgi·a -ae *f* surgery

chīrūrgic·us -ī *m* surgeon

chīrūrg·us -ī *m* surgeon

Chi·us -a -um *adj & mf* Chian ‖ *n* Chian wine ‖ *npl* Chian cloth

chlamydāt·us -a -um *adj* wearing a military cape

chlam·ys -ydis *f* Greek military cape; gold-brocaded cape

Choeril·us -ī *m* incompetent panegyrist of Alexander the Great

chorāg·ium -(i)ī *n* stage properties

chorāg·us -ī *m* theatrical producer

choraul·ēs -ae *m* flute player *(who accompanied the choral dance)*

chord·a -ae *f* string *(of musical instrument);* cord, rope

chore·a -ae *f* dance

chore·us -ī *m* trochee (— ᴗ)

chorocitharist·ēs -ae *m* one who accompanied a chorus on the cithara

chor·us -ī *m* chorus; choir

Chrem·ēs -ētis *or* -is *or* -ī *m* miserly old character in plays of Terence

Christiān·us -ī *m* Christian

Christ·us -ī *m* Christ

Chrȳsē·ïs -idis *or* -idos *f* Agamemnon's slave girl, daughter of Chryses

Chrȳs·ēs -ae *m* priest of Apollo

Chrȳsipp·us -ī *m* famous Stoic philosopher *(290–210 B.C.)*

chrȳsolith·os -ī *m* chrysolite, topaz

chrȳs·os -ī *m* gold

cibāri·us -a -um *adj* of food; common, coarse *(food for slaves)* ‖ *npl* rations, provisions, food allowance

cibāt·us -ūs *m* food; feed, fodder

cib·ō -āre -āvī -ātus *tr* to feed

cibōr·ium -(i)ī *n* chalice

cib·us -ī *m* food; feed; meal; nutriment; fuel; cibum capere to take food, eat food, eat a meal

cicād·a -ae *f* cicada; harvest fly

cicātrīcōs·us -a -um *adj* scarred, covered with scars

cicātr·īx -īcis *f* scar

cicc·us -ī *m* core of pomegranate; *(sl)* junk

cic·er -eris *m* chickpea; testicle

Cicer·ō -ōnis *m* Cicero *(Marcus Tullius Cicero, orator and politician, 106–43 B.C.)* ‖

Quintus Tullius Cicero *(his brother, 102–43 B.C.)* ‖ Marcus Tullius Cicero *(his son, consul in 30 B.C.)*

cichorē·um *or* **cichōri·um** -ī *n* endive

cicima(li)ndr·um -ī *n* comic name for an imaginary seasoning

Cicon·es -um *mpl* Thracian tribe

cicōni·a -ae *f* stork

cic·ur -uris *adj* tame

cicūt·a -ae *f* hemlock tree; hemlock poison; pipe, flute *(carved from hemlock wood)*

-cīd·a -ae *m* *suf* denoting one who cuts *or* kills *(e.g., **lapicīda** stonecutter; **mātricīda** murderer of one's mother)*

cidar·is -is *f* tiara *(of Persian king)*

cieō ciēre cīvī citus *tr* to set in motion, move; to stir up, rouse up, muster; to call for, send for; to summon for help; to invoke, appeal to; to bring about; to cause, make; **lacrimās ciēre** to shed tears; **strāgem ciēre** to wreak havoc

Cilici·a -ae *f* country and Roman province in S.E. Asia Minor

cilic·ium -(i)ī *n* rug *or* blanket of goat's hair

Cilici·us -a -um *adj* Cilician ‖ *n* garment made of goat's hair

Ciliss·a -ae *f* Cilician woman

Cil·ix -icis *adj* & *m* Cilician

-cill·um -ī *neut* *suf* forms diminutives: **corcillum** little heart

-cill·us -ī *masc* *suf* forms diminutives from diminutives: **penicillus** (small) painter's brush

Cim·ber -brī *m* Cimbrian ‖ Roman family name *(cognomen)*

Cimbr·ī -ōrum *mpl* Germanic tribe that invaded Gaul and Italy at the end of the 2nd cent. B.C. and was defeated by Marius

Cimbric·us -a -um *adj* Cimbrian

cīm·ex -icis *m* bedbug; *(pej)* vermin

Cimmeri·ī -ōrum *mpl* people in the Crimea ‖ mythical people living in perpetual darkness in caves between Baiae and Cumae

cinaedic·us -a -um *adj* lewd

cinaed·us -ī *m* catamite; homosexual

cincinnāt·us -a -um *adj* curly-haired ‖ **Cincinnātus** *m* Lucius Quinctius Cincinnatus *(Roman war hero, appointed dictator in 458 B.C.)*

cincinn·us -ī *m* a curl, lock of curled hair; *(rhet)* artificial expression

Cinci·us -a -um *adj* name of a Roman gens *(nomen);* L. Cincius Alimentus *(Roman historian of the Second Punic War)*

cīncticul·us -ī *m* small belt *or* sash

cīnctūr·a -ae *f* belt, sash

cīnctus *pp* of **cingō**

cīnct·us -ūs *m* tucking up; belt, sash; **cīnctus Gabinius** Gabinian style of wearing the toga

(usually employed at religious festivals; it was tucked up, its corner drawn over the left shoulder and under the right arm)

cīnctūt·us -a -um *adj* wearing a belt *or* sash; old-fashioned

Cine·ās -ae *m* a friend of King Pyrrhus, who advised Pyrrhus to make peace with the Romans

cinefact·us -a -um *adj* reduced to ashes

cinerār·ius -(i)ī *m* hairdresser

cin·gō -gere cīnxī cīnctus *tr* to surround, encircle; to escort; to enclose *(a space);* to wreathe *(head);* to tuck up *(garment); (mil)* to cover, protect ‖ *pass* to get dressed; to form a circle; **cingī in proelia** to gear up for battle; **ferrum cingī** to put on one's sword; **Hispānō gladiō cingitur** he puts on a Spanish sword

cingul·a·ae *f* belt; sash; girth; sword belt; chastity belt

cingul·um -ī *n* belt; sword belt; sash; girdle; chastity belt

cingul·us -ī *m* zone *(of the earth)*

cinīfl·ō -ōnis *m* hairdresser

cin·is -eris *m (f)* ashes; ruin, death

-cin·ium -(i)ī *neut* *suf* denoting activity or profession *(e.g., **latrōcinium** robbing, robbery)*

Cinn·a -ae *m* Lucius Cornelius Cinna *(notorious consul 87–84 B.C.)*

cinnamōm·um *or* **cinnam·um** -ī *n* cinnamon ‖ *npl* cinnamon sticks

cīnxī *perf* of **cingō**

Cinyr·ās -ae *m* father of Myrrha, and, by her, also father of Adonis

cipp·us -ī *m* stake, post, pillar; gravestone; *(mil)* palisade

circā *adv* around, round about; all around, in the vicinity ‖ *prep (w. acc)* around, surrounding, about, in the neighborhood of, near; through; attending, escorting; concerning, in respect to; *(of time)* around, about, toward; *(w. numbers)* about, nearly, almost

Circa *see* **Circē**

Circae·us -a -um *adj* of Circe

circāmoer·ium -(i)ī *n* area on both sides of a city wall

Circ·ē -ēs *or* **Circ·a** -ae *f* Circe *(famous witch, daughter of Sol and Perse)*

circēns·is -is -e *adj* of the racetrack ‖ *mpl* races

circin·ō -āre -āvī -ātus *tr* to make round; to circle

circin·us -ī *m (geometer's)* compass

circiter *adv* about, nearly, approximately ‖ *prep (w. acc)* about, near

circlus *see* **circulus**

circ(u)l·us -ī *m* circle, circuit; ring, hoop; social circle; *(astr)* orbit

circueō *see* **circumeō**

circuitiō *see* **circumitiō**

circuit·us -ūs *m* circuit; going around, revolution; detour; circumference; beating around the bush; *(rhet)* period

circulātim *adv* in groups

circulāt·or -ōris *m* peddler; itinerant performer

circulātr·īx -īcis *f* peddler *(female);* itinerant performer *(female)*

circul·or -ārī -ātus sum *intr* to gather a crowd around oneself; to stroll about

circum *adv* about, all around ‖ *prep (w. acc)* around, about; in the neighborhood of

circum- *suf* around, about: circumstāre to stand around

circu(m)iti·ō -ōnis *f* going around; patrolling; beating around the bush

circum·agō -agere -ēgī -āctus *tr* to turn around; to turn *(e.g., a wheel);* to sway ‖ *refl* & *pass* to turn around; *(of feelings)* to change; to change *(in form);* to go out of one's way; *(of time)* to pass, roll around

circumar·ō -āre -āvī *tr* to plow around

circumcaesūr·a -ae *f* contour, outline

circumcī·dō -dere -dī -sus *tr* to cut around, trim; to cut short; to cut down on *(expenses);* to abridge, shorten; to circumcise

circumcircā *adv* all around

circumcīs·us -a -um *pp of* circumcīdō ‖ *adj* steep, inaccessible; abridged

circumclū·dō -dere -sī -sus *tr* to shut in, enclose; *(mil)* to surround; *(fig)* circumvent

circumcol·ō -ere *tr* to live near

circumcurs·ō -āre -āvī *tr* & *intr* to run around

circum·dō -dare -dedī -datus *tr* to surround, enclose, encircle; *(w. dat)* to place *or* put *(s.th.)* around

circumdū·cō -cere -xī -ctus *tr* lead around, draw around; *(w. double acc)* to lead *(s.o.)* around to; aliquem omnia praesidia circumdūcere to lead s.o. around to all the garrisons

circumductī·ō -ōnis *f* perimeter; *(w. gen)* cheating out of; *(rhet)* period

circum·eō -īre -īvī *or* -iī -itus *tr* to go around, go around to, visit, make the rounds of; to surround, encircle, encompass; to circumvent, deceive, cheat ‖ *intr* to go around, make a circuit

circumequit·ō -āre *tr* to ride around *(on horseback)*

circumerr·ō -āre -āvi *tr* & *intr* to wander around, prowl around

circum·ferō -ferre -tūlī -lātus *tr* to carry around, hand around; to publicize, spread around; to purify; oculōs circumferre to glance about ‖ *pass* to revolve

circumfle·ctō -ctere -xī -xus *tr* to turn around, wheel about

circumfl·ō -āre *tr* to blow around; *(fig)* to buffet

circumflu·ō -ere -xī *tr* to flow around; to surround; to overflow ‖ *intr* to be overflowing, abound

circumflu·us -a -um *adj* flowing around; surrounded *(by water)*

circumforāne·us -a -um *adj* strolling about from market to market, itinerant; around the forum

circumfrem·ō -ere -uī *intr* to groan all around

circum·fundō -fundere -fūdī -fūsus *tr* to pour around; to surround, cover, envelop ‖ *refl* & *pass* to crowd around; *(w. dat)* to cling to

circumgem·ō -ere *tr* to growl around *(e.g., a sheepfold)*

circumgest·ō -āre *tr* to carry around

circum·gredior -gredī -gressus sum *tr* to surround *(esp. to attack)*

circumiac·eō -ēre *intr (w. dat)* to lie near, border on, be adjacent to

circumiect·us -a -um *adj* surrounding, encompassing, taking in

circumiect·us -ūs *m* an encompassing

circum·iciō -icere -iēcī -iectus *tr* to throw *or* place around; to surround; *(w. dat)* to throw *(s.th.)* around *(s.o. or s.th.);* fossam circumicere to dig a trench all around

circumitus *see* circuitus

circumlāt·us -a -um *pp of* circumferō

circumlav·ō -āre *or* -ere *tr* to wash around, wash the sides of

circumlīg·ō -āre -āvī -ātus *tr* to bind; *(w. dat)* to tie *(s.th.)* to

circum·linō -linere (-lēvī) -litus *tr* to smear all over, to anoint; to cover; *(fig)* to clothe

circumlu·ō -ere *tr* to flow around

circumluvi·ō -ōnis *f* island *(formed by a river flowing in a new channel)*

circum·mittō -mittere -mīsī -missus *tr* to send around

circummūg·iō -īre *intr* to moo around

circummūn·iō -īre -īvī -ītus *tr* (-moen-) to fortify *(with wall, moat, etc.)*

circummūnīti·ō -ōnis *f* investment *(of town);* circumvallation

circumpadān·us -a -um *adj* situated along the Po River

circumpend·eō -ēre *intr* to hang around

circumplaud·ō -ere *tr* to applaud from every direction

circumple·ctor -ctī -xus sum *tr* to embrace; to surround

circumplic·ō -āre -āvī -ātus *tr* to wind up; to coil around; *(w. dat)* to wind *(s.th.)* around

circum·pōnō -pōnere -posuī -positus *tr (w. dat)* to place *or* set *(s.th.)* around

circumpōtāti·ō -ōnis *f* round of drinks

circumrēt·iō -īre *tr* to snare

circumrō·dō -dere -sī -sus *tr* to nibble all around; to hesitate to say; to slander

circumsaep·iō -īre -sī -tus *tr* (**-sēp-**) to fence in, enclose

circumscind·ō -ere *tr* to strip off

circumscrī·bō -bere -psī -ptus *tr* to draw a line around, mark the boundaries of; to limit, circumscribe; to set aside; to defeat the purpose of; to trap, defraud

circumscrīptē *adv* concisely; *(rhet)* in periodic style

circumscrīpti·ō -ōnis *f* encircling; circle; limits, boundary; outline, definition; cheating; *(rhet)* periodic sentence

circumscrīpt·or -ōris *m* cheat

circumscrīpt·us -a -um *pp of* **circumscrībō ‖** *adj* restricted; concise; *(rhet)* periodic, rounded-off

circumsec·ō -āre -uī -tus *tr* to cut around; to circumcise

circum·sedeō -sedēre -sēdī -sessus *tr* to beset, besiege, blockade

circumsēpiō *see* **circumsaepiō**

circumsessi·ō -ōnis *f* blockading

circum·sīdō -sīdere -sēdī -sessus *tr* to besiege, surround, invest

circumsil·iō -īre *tr & intr* to hop around

circum·sistō -sistere -stetī *tr* to stand around, surround

circumson·ō -āre -uī *tr* to make resound, cause to re-echo ‖ *intr* to resound everywhere; *(w. dat)* to resound to

circumson·us -a -um *adj* noisy

circumspectātr·īx -īcis *f* spy *(female)*

circumspecti·ō -ōnis *f* looking around; circumspection, caution

circumspect·ō -āre *tr* to watch for, search carefully for; to catch sight of ‖ *intr* to keep looking around, look around anxiously

circumspect·us -a -um *pp of* **circumspiciō ‖** *adj* well-considered, guarded *(words);* circumspect, cautious

circumspect·us -ūs *m* consideration; commanding view; contemplation

circum·spiciō -spicere -spexī -spectus *tr* to look around at, survey; to catch sight of; to consider, examine ‖ *refl* to think highly of oneself ‖ *intr* to be circumspect, be cautious, be on the watch

circumstant·ēs -ium *mpl* bystanders

circum·stō -stāre -stetī *tr* to surround, envelop; *(of terror, etc.)* to grip ‖ *intr* to stand around

circumstrep·ō -ere -uī -itus *tr* to shout at on all sides, surround with noise *or* shouts

circumsurg-ēns -entis *adj (of mountains)* rising all around

circumtent·us -a -um *adj* tightly covered

circumter·ō -ere *tr* to rub shoulders with, crowd around

circumtext·us -a -um *adj* with embroidered border

circumton·ō -āre -uī *tr* to crash around, thunder around

circumtōns·us -a -um *adj* clipped *or* trimmed all around

circumvā·dō -dere -sī *tr* to attack on every side; *(of terror)* to grip

circumvag·us -a -um *adj* flowing around, encircling

circumvall·ō -āre -āvī -ātus *tr* to blockade ‖ *refl* to form a blockade

circumvecti·ō -ōnis *f* carting around *(of merchandise);* circular course, revolution *(of sun)*

circumvect·ō -āre -āvī -ātus *tr* to carry around ‖ *pass* to travel around, sail around

circumve·hor -hī -ctus sum *tr* to ride around (to), sail around (to), travel around (to); to travel past

circumvēl·ō -āre *tr* to envelop, cover

circum·veniō -venīre -vēnī -ventus *tr* to enclose, surround; to go around to; to distress, beset; to circumvent, cheat; to prosecute *or* convict unjustly

circumver·tō -tere -tī -sus *tr* (**-vor-**) to turn *(s.th.)* around ‖ *pass* to turn around; **rota circumvertitur axem** the wheel revolves around its axle

circumvest·iō -īre *tr* to clothe

circumvinc·iō -īre *tr* to tie up

circumvīs·ō -ere *tr* to look around, glare around at

circumvolit·ō -āre -āvī *tr & intr* to fly around, dash about, rove around; to hover around

circumvol·ō -āre -āvī *tr* to fly around, dart around ‖ *intr* to hover about, hover over, flit about

circumvol·vō -vere -vī -ūtus *tr* to wind, roll around ‖ *refl & pass (w. dat or acc)* to revolve around, wind oneself around

circ·us -ī *m* circle; racetrack; *(astr)* orbit

Circ·us Flāmini·us -ī *m* racetrack built by Gaius Flaminius Nepos in the Campus Martius in 220 B.C.

Circ·us Maxim·us -ī *m* oldest racetrack in Rome, between the Palatine and Aventine Hills

cirrāt·us -a -um *adj* curly-haired

Cirrh·a -ae *f* (**Cyrr-**) town near Delphi, sacred to Apollo

Cirrhae·us -a -um *adj* of Cirrha; of Apollo

cirr·us -ī *m* lock, curl; forelock

Cirt·a -ae *f* town in Numidia

Cirtēns·ēs -ium *mpl* inhabitants of Cirta

cis- *pref* used in the sense of the preposition

cis *prep (w. acc)* on this side of *(on the Roman side of); (of time)* within

Cisalpīn·us -a -um *adj* Cisalpine *(on the Roman side of the Alps)*

cis·ium -(i)ī *n* gig *(light, two-wheeled carriage)*

Cisp·ius -(i)ī *m* **(Cesp-)** one of the summits of the Esquiline Hill

Cisrhenān·us -a -um *adj* dwelling on the W. side of the Rhine

Cissē·is -idis *f* daughter of Cisseus *(i.e., Hecuba)*

Ciss·eūs -eī *m* king of Thrace and father of Hecuba

cist·a -ae *f* box, chest *(esp. of wicker, for clothes, money, books, etc.);* ballot box

cistell·a -ae *f* small box

cistellātr·īx -īcis *f* female slave in charge of the money box

cistellul·a -ae *f* small box

cistern·a -ae *f* cistern, reservoir

cistophor·us -ī *m* Asiatic coin *(with a representation of a bearer of the cista of Dionysus on it)*

cistul·a -ae *f* small box

citātim *adv* quickly, hurriedly

citāt·us -a -um *adj* rapid, speedy; *(of limbs)* moved quickly; *(of pace, actions)* quick, speedy; *(of bowels)* loose; **citātō equō** at full gallop

citāt·us -ūs *m* impulse

citeri·or -or -us *adj* on this side, near *(to Rome);* earlier; *(nearer to the present)* later, more recent; more down-to-earth, nearer home; *(w. abl)* earlier than

Cithaer·ōn -ōnis *m* Greek mountain range dividing Attica from Boeotia

cithar·a -ae *f* lyre

citharist·a -ae *m* lyre player

citharistri·a -ae *f* lyre player *(female)*

cithariz·ō -āre *intr* to play the lyre

citharoed·us -ī *m* singer *(playing the lyre)*

citim·us -a -um *adj* (lying) nearest

citius *adv* sooner, rather; **dictō citius** no sooner said than done; **sērius aut citius** sooner or later

cito *adv* quickly; soon

cit·ō -āre -āvī -ātus *tr* to excite, rouse; to call, summon; to call to witness, appeal to; to arouse, produce; to cite *(as an authority)*

citrā *adv* on this side, on the near side; **citrā cadere** to fall short ‖ *prep (w. acc)* **1** on this side of, on the near side of: **citrā mare** on this side of the sea, in Italy; **2** *(of time)* since, before: **citrā Trōiāna tempora** before the Trojan period; **3** just short of, less than, except: **peccāvī citrā scelus** I committed a fault just short of a crime; **4** regardless of *(e.g., a person's wishes):* **citrā senātūs**

populīque auctōritātem regardless of *or* without regard for the authority of the senate and the people

citre·us -a -um *adj* of citrus wood

citrō *adv* to this side, this way; **ultrō (et) citrō** *(or* **citrō ultrōque)** to and fro, up and down; mutually

citr·um -ī *n* wood of the citron tree; table *(made of citron wood)*

citr·us -ī *f* citron tree

cit·us -a -um *pp of* **cieō** ‖ *adj* quick

cīvic·us -a -um *adj* civil; civilian; suitable for one as a civilian; **corōna cīvica** civic crown *(given to war hero for saving s.o.'s life)*

cīvīl·is -is -e *adj* civil, civic; civilian; forensic, legal; political; unassuming; **iūs cīvīle** private *or* civil law; civil rights; **ratiō cīvīlis** political science; **rēs cīvīlis** *(or* **cīvīlēs)** politics; **vir cīvīlis** statesman, politician

cīvīlit·ās -ātis *f* politics; courtesy

cīvīliter *adv* like a citizen; as an ordinary citizen should; politely

cīv·is -is *mf* citizen; fellow citizen; private citizen

cīvit·ās -ātis *f* state; community; city; citizenship

clād·ēs -is *f* disaster; loss; *(mil)* defeat, carnage; destruction; ruins; *(of person)* scourge, destroyer

clam *adv* secretly, privately; stealthily; **clam habēre aliquem** to keep s.o. in the dark ‖ *prep (w. abl or acc)* without the knowledge of; **neque clam mē est** nor is it unknown to me; **clam patre** without the father's knowledge

clāmāt·or -ōris *m* loudmouth

clāmitāti·ō -ōnis *f* bawling, racket

clāmit·ō -āre -āvī -ātus *tr & intr* to cry out, yell, to keep yelling

clām·ō -āre -āvī -ātus *tr* to shout, yell; to proclaim; to call upon ‖ *intr* to shout

clām·or -ōris *m* shout; acclamation; applause; battle cry; noise; wailing

clāmōsē *adv* with a shout, loudly

clāmōs·us -a -um *adj* yelling, noisy; loud-barking *(dog)*

clanculum *adv* secretly; privately ‖ *prep (w. acc)* unknown to

clandestīnō *adv* secretly

clandestīn·us -a -um *adj* clandestine

clang·ō -ere *intr (of eagle)* to scream

clang·or -ōris *m* clang, noise; blast *(of trumpet);* cry, scream *(of bird);* baying *(of dog)*

clārē *adv* clearly; out loud; brightly; with distinction, honorably; **clārē legere** to read aloud

clār·eō -ēre *intr* to be clear, be distinct, be bright; to be evident; to be famous

clār·ēsco -ēscere -uī *intr* to become clear, become distinct; to become bright; to become famous; *(of sound)* to get loud

clārigāti·ō -ōnis *f* reparation; fine

clārig·ō -āre -āvī -ātum *intr* to demand satisfaction, demand reparation

clārison·us -a -um *adj* clear-sounding

clārit·ās -ātis *f* loudness; clarity; brightness; distinction, renown

clāritūd·ō -inis *f* brightness; fame

Clari·us -a -um *adj* of the island of Claros, *esp.* as epithet of Apollo

clār·ō -āre -āvī -ātus *tr* to clarify, explain; to light up, illuminate; to make famous

Clar·os -ī *f* town in Asia Minor famous for a temple and oracle of Apollo

clār·us -a -um *adj* loud; clear, bright; plain, manifest; famous; notorious; **clāra lūx** broad daylight; **clārior lūce** clearer than daylight; **vir clārissimus** gentleman of the Senate

classiāri·us -a -um *adj* naval ‖ *mpl* marines

classicul·a -ae *f* flotilla

classic·us -a -um *adj* first-class, belonging to the highest class of citizens; classical; naval ‖ *m* trumpeter who summoned the *comitia centuriata* ‖ *mpl* marines, sailors ‖ *n* battle signal; bugle call; **classicum canere** to sound the bugle *(to begin battle; to announce a capital trial or an execution)*

class·is -is *f* fleet; *(social)* class; grade, class *(of pupils);* band, group; **classī** with a fleet, at sea; in a naval battle

clāt(h)rāt·us -a -um *adj* barred

clāt(h)r·ī -ōrum *mpl* bars; railings

claud·eō -ēre *or* claud·ō -ere *intr* to be lame, to limp; to falter; to be imperfect

Claudiān·us -a -um *adj* connected with members of the Claudian clan, *esp.* the Emperor Claudius

claudicāti·ō -ōnis *f* limping

claudic·ō -āre *intr* to be lame, to limp; to incline to one side; to be halting, be defective; to be deficient, fall short

Claud·ius -(i)ī *m* Appius Claudius Caecus *(censor in 312 B.C. and builder of the Appian Way and Appian aqueduct)* ‖ the Roman Emperor Claudius *(Tiberius Claudius Nero Germanicus, reigned 41–54 A.D.)*

clau·dō -dere -sī -sus *tr* to shut, close; to bring to a close, conclude; to shut up; to lock up, imprison; *(mil)* to blockade, hem in; to limit; to cut off, block; to keep secret, suppress *(feelings, thoughts);* **agmen claudere** to bring up the rear; **numerīs** *(or* **pedibus) claudere** to put into verse; **trānsitum claudere** to block traffic

claud·us -a -um *adj* **(clōd-)** lame, limping; crippled, imperfect, defective; wavering; untrustworthy

claustell·um -ī *n* **(clos-)** keyhole

claustr·a -ōrum *npl* lock, bolt, bar; gate; dam, dike; barrier, barricade; cage, den; fortress; defenses

clausul·a -ae *f* close, conclusion *(of a letter, speech, argument; of a transaction);* clause *(in a law or document);* end *(of a word, of a line of verse); (rhet)* close of a periodic sentence with particular regard to its rhythm

claus·us -a -um *pp of* **claudō** ‖ *adj* closed, inaccessible *(place); (of a person)* impervious to feelings; shut, locked up; enclosed *(in a container)* ‖ *n* enclosure

Claus·us -ī *m* a Sabine chief, reputed ancestor of the *gens Claudia* ‖ *mpl* members of the *gens Claudia*

clāv·a -ae *f* cudgel, club

clāvār·ium -iī *n* soldier's allowance for shoe nails

clāvāt·or -ōris *m* club-bearer

clāvicul·a -ae *f* tendril; key; pivot

clāvig·er -era -erum *adj* carrying a club; carrying keys ‖ *m* club bearer *(Hercules);* key bearer *(Janus)*

clāv·is -is *f* key; hook *(for rolling a hoop);* **clavīs adimere uxōrī** to take the keys away from a wife, get a divorce

clāv·us -ī *m* nail; rivet; rudder, helm; purple stripe *(worn on the tunic, broad for senators and their sons, narrow for equites);* **clāvō** *(or* **clāvō trabālī) figere** to nail; *(fig)* to nail down, clinch; **clāvum rēctum tenēre** to keep a steady course; **clāvus annī** beginning of the year; **clāvus trabālis** spike *(large nail)*

clēm·ēns -entis *adj* gentle, mild, kind, compassionate; mild, calm *(weather)*

clēmenter *adv* gently, mildly, kindly, compassionately; at an easy pace; **collēs clēmenter assurgentēs** gently rising hills

clēmenti·a -ae *f* mildness, clemency, compassion

Cle·on -ōnis *m* rhetorician from Halicarnassus

Cleōn·ae -ārum *fpl* small town in Argolis near Nemea

Cleopatr·a -ae *f* daughter of Ptolemy Auletes and queen of Egypt *(d. 31 B.C.)*

clep·ō -ere -sī -tus *tr* to steal, swipe

clepsydr·a -ae *f* water clock; *(fig)* time *(allotted to speakers);* **clepsydram dare** *(w. dat)* to give *(s.o.)* the floor; **clepsydram petere** to ask to have the floor

clept·ēs *or* ·a -ae *m* thief

clīban·us -ī *m* oven; bread plate

cli·ēns -entis *m* client *(e.g., ex-slave protected by a former owner acting as patron);* follower, retainer; vassal ‖ *mpl* clients *(the citizens of an Italian or other city in their relationship to their Roman patronus)*

client·a -ae *f* client *(female)*

clientēl·a -ae f clientele; patronage, protection; clientship *(the relationship of a provincial city or a foreign people to their Roman patronus);* vassalage || *fpl* allies, dependants
clientul·us -ī m *(as term of contempt)* just a poor client
clīnām·en -inis n swerve
clīnāt·us -a -um *adj* bent, inclined, sunk
clīnic·us -ī m clinical physician *(who tends patients at their bedside)*
Clī·ō -ūs f Muse of history
clipeāt·us -a -um *adj* armed with a *(round)* shield
clipe·um -ī n or clipe·us -ī m round bronze shield; medallion; disc *(of sun)*
clītell·ae -ārum *fpl* packsaddle
clītellāri·us -a -um *adj* carrying a packsaddle
clīvōs·us -a -um *adj* hilly; steep
clīv·us -ī m sloping ground, incline, hill; slope, pitch; *(fig)* uphill struggle; **adversus clīvum** uphill; **prīmī clīvī** foothills
Clīv·us Sac·er *(gen:* Clīv·ī Sac·rī) m Sacred Incline *(part of the Via Sacra ascending the Capitoline Hill, also called* Clīvus Capitōlīnus)
cloāc·a -ae f sewer, drain; **cloāca maxima** main sewer *(draining the area of the Roman Forum)*
Cloācīn·a -ae f Venus *(the "purifier")*
Clōdi·a -ae f sister of the notorious tribune Clodius
Clōdiān·us -a -um *adj* Clodian, of the Clodian faction
Clōd·ius -(i)ī m Publius Clodius Pulcher *(notorious tribune of the plebs, enemy of Cicero, killed in 52 B.C.)*
Cloeli·a -ae f Roman girl who was given as hostage to Porsenna and escaped by swimming the Tiber back to Rome
Clōthō *(gen not in use; acc:* Clōthō) f one of the three Fates
clu·eō -ēre or clu·eor -ērī *intr* to be spoken of as, be known for; **ut nōmen cluet** as the word implies
clūn·is -is *mf* buttock || *mpl* & *fpl* buttocks; hind quarters *(of an animal)*
clūr·a -ae f ape
clūrīn·us -a -um *adj* of apes
Clūs·ium -(i)ī n chief Etruscan town
Clūs·ius -(i)ī m Janus
Clymen·ē -ēs f mother of Phaëthon
clyst·ēr -ēris m an injection; *(fig)* syringe
Clyt(a)em(n)estr·a -ae f Clytemnestra *(wife of Agamemnon, sister of Helen, Castor, and Pollux, and mother of Electra, Iphigenia, and Orestes)*
Cn. *abbr* Gnaeus *(Roman first name, praenomen)*

Cnid·os or Cnid·us -ī f town in Caria, famous for the worship of Venus *(modern Knossis)*
Cnōss·us (Gnōss·us or -os) -ī f town in Crete, capital of King Minos
Cnōssi·us -a -um (Gnōs-) of Cnossus
coacervāti·ō -ōnis f accumulation
coacerv·ō -āre -āvī -ātus *tr* to gather into a heap; to accumulate; to make *(by heaping up)*
coac·ēscō -ēscere -uī *intr* to become sour; *(fig)* to go sour
coācti·ō -ōnis f collection *(of money);* abridgment
coāct·ō -āre *tr* to force
coāct·or -ōris m collector *(of money, taxes);* **agminis coāctōrēs** rearguard elements
coāct·us -a -um *pp of* cōgō || *adj* forced, unnatural, hypocritical || n felt cloth || *npl* felt cloak
coāct·us -ūs m coercion, compulsion
coaedific·ō -āre -āvī -ātus *tr* to build *(a town);* to build up *(an area),* fill with buildings
coaequ·ō -āre -āvī -ātus *tr* to level off; to treat as equal, equate
coagmentāti·ō -ōnis f union; joint
coagment·ō -āre -āvī -ātus *tr* to join together; to glue, cement together; to construct; to fit *(words)* together
coagment·um -ī n joint
coāgul·um -ī n rennet *(curdled milk taken from the stomach of young mammals);* curds
coal·ēscō -ēscere -uī -itum *intr* (cōl-) to grow together, coalesce; *(of wounds)* to close; to become unified; to grow firm, take root; to become established, thrive
coangust·ō -āre -āvī -ātus *tr* (conang-) to contract, compress; to limit, restrict
coarct- *see* coart-
coargu·ō -ere -ī *tr* to bring out into the open *(usu. s.th. undesirable);* to prove conclusively, demonstrate; to refute, prove wrong or guilty; *(w. gen of the charge)* to prove *(s.o.)* guilty of
coartāti·ō -ōnis f crowding together; tightening
coart·ō -āre -āvī -ātus *tr* to narrow, make narrower; to crowd together, confine; to pack *(e.g., the Forum);* to shorten; to abridge
coax·ō -āre *intr* *(of frogs)* to croak
Cōcal·us -ī m mythical king of Sicily who protected Daedalus
Coccēi·us -a -um *adj* Roman clan name *(nomen), esp.* Marcus Cocceius Nerva, emperor A.D. 96–98
coccināt·us -a -um *adj* dressed in scarlet
coccin(e)·us -a -um *adj* scarlet || *npl* scarlet clothes; scarlet coverlets
cocc·um -ī n scarlet dye, scarlet
coc(h)le·a -ae f snail
coc(h)leār·(e) -is n spoon

cocilendr·um -ī *n* an imaginary magical seasoning

cocl·es -itis *m* person blind in one eye **‖ Cocles** Horatius Cocles *(commonly called Horatio and famous for defending the Pons Sublicius against Porsenna's army)*

coctil·is -is -e *adj* baked; brick

coct·or -ōris *m* cook

coct·us -a -um *pp of* **coquō ‖** *adj* cooked; roasted; baked *(bricks);* ripe; *(fig)* mild **‖** *n* cooked food

coc·us -ī *m* **(coqu-)** cook

Cōcȳt·us -ī *m* river (of wailing) of the lower world

Cōdēt·a -ae *f* piece of ground in the Campus Martius

cōd·ex -icis *m* **(caud-)** trunk *(of tree);* block *(of wood to which one was tied for punishment);* book, tablet; ledger; *(coll)* blockhead

cōdicill·ī -ōrum *mpl* **(-cell-)** fire logs; set of writing tablets; note; petition to the emperor; rescript from the emperor; supplement to a will, codicil

Codr·us -ī *m* last king of Athens

coēgī *perf of* **cōgō**

coel- *see* **cael-**

Coel·ē -ēs *adj (fem only)* **Coelē Syria** "Hollow Syria" *(the S. part of Syria, esp. the region between Lebanon and Antilebanon);* **Coelē Thessalia** the plain of Thessaly

co·emō -emere -ēmī -emptus *tr* to buy up

coēmpti·ō -ōnis *f* fictitious sale of an estate; marriage *(contracted by fictitious sale of contracting parties)*

coēmptiōnāl·is -is -e *adj* of a marriage by fictitious sale

coen- *see* **caen-**

co·eō -īre -iī -itus *tr* **societātem coīre** to form an alliance **‖** *intr* to come together; to meet, assemble; to be united, combine; to mate, copulate; to have sexual intercourse; to congeal, curdle; to agree; to conspire; to clash *(in combat); (of wounds)* to close

coep·ī -isse -tus *(v. defect) tr & intr* to have begun

coept·ō -āre -āvī -ātus *tr* to begin eagerly; *(w. inf)* to try to **‖** *intr* to make a beginning

coept·um -ī *n* undertaking, enterprise

coept·us -ūs *m* beginning; undertaking

coëpulōn·us -ī *m* dinner guest

coërc·eō -ēre -uī -itus *tr* to enclose, confine, hem in; to limit; to restrain, check, control, keep in order

coërciti·ō -ōnis *f* physical restraint, coercion; inflicting of summary punishment by a magistrate; right to inflict summary punishment

coët·us -ūs *m* coming together, meeting; crowd, company; gang; combination

Coē·us -ī *m* Titan, father of Latona

cōgitātē *adv* deliberately, carefully

cōgitāti·ō -ōnis *f* thinking, deliberating; reflection; thought, plan, idea; reasoning power, imagination

cōgitāt·us -a -um *adj* well-considered, deliberate **‖** *npl* thoughts, ideas

cōgit·ō -āre -āvī -ātus *tr* to consider, ponder, reflect on; to imagine; *(w. inf)* to intend to **‖** *intr* to think

cognāti·ō -ōnis *f* relationship by birth; agreement, resemblance, affinity; relatives, family

cognāt·us -a -um *adj* related by birth; related, similar, akin **‖** *mf* relative

cogniti·ō -ōnis *f* learning, acquiring knowledge; knowledge; notion, idea; recognition; *(w. gen)* knowledge of, acquaintance with; *(leg)* inquiry, hearing, trial

cognit·or -ōris *m* attorney; defender, protector; witness

cognitūr·a -ae *f* the duty of an attorney

cognit·us *pp of* **cognōscō ‖** *adj* acknowledged, known; familiar

cognit·us -ūs *m* act of getting to know; **dignus cognitū** worth knowing; **iucundus cognitū** pleasant to know

cognōm·en -inis *n* surname, family name *(e.g.,* **Caesar;** *a second* **cognōmen,** *called* **agnōmen** *by later grammarians, was given as an honorary name to a person for some achievement, e.g.,* **Āfricānus);** additional title of a god *(e.g.,* **Iupiter Feretrius);** nickname; derived name *(esp. of places);* **ā duce Tarpeiā mōns est cognōmen adeptus** the hill took its name from Tarpeia *(the enemy's)* guide

cognōment·um -ī *n* family name; name

cognōmināt·us -a -um *adj* synonymous; surnamed

cognōmin·is -is -e *adj* like-named, with the same name

cognōmin·ō -āre -āvī -ātus *tr* to give *(s.o.)* a surname *or* nickname

cogn·ōscō -ōscere -ōvī -itus *tr* to become acquainted with, get to know, learn; to recognize, identify; to inquire into, investigate; *(mil)* to reconnoiter; **cognōvisse** to know

cōgō cōgere coēgī coāctus *tr* to gather together, collect; to assemble; to round up; to gather *(crops);* to collect, raise *(money, taxes);* to force, compel; to pressure; to exact, extort; to infer, conclude; to prove conclusively; to compress *(into a mass);* to abridge; to shorten, restrict in time; to form *(e.g., wrinkles by contraction);* to thicken, condense, curdle; **agmen cōgere** to bring up the rear; **in ōrdinem cōgere** to bring to order, bring back into line

cohaer·ēns -entis *adj* adjoining, continuous; consistent; harmonious

cohaerenti·a -ae *f* organic structure

cohae·reō -rēre -sī -sum *intr* to stick *or* cling together, cohere; to be consistent, be in agreement; *(w.* **cum) 1** to be closely connected with; **2** to be in harmony with; **3** to be consistent with; **inter sē cohaerēre** to be consistent

cohaerēsc·ō -ere cohaesī *intr* to stick together, cohere; to adhere

cohēr·ēs -ēdis *mf* joint-heir

cohib·eō -ēre -uī -itus *tr* to hold together, hold close; to confine; to clothe; to keep *(information, etc.)* secret, suppress; to check the growth of *(e.g., power);* to withold *(assent);* to hold back, repress *(emotions);* to check, stop *(an action, etc.); (w. acc & inf)* to prevent **‖** *refl* to remain, stay *(in a place);* to exercise self-restraint

cohonest·ō -āre *tr* to honor, pay respect to; to make respectable

cohorr·ēscō -ēscere -uī *intr* to shiver all over

cohor·s -tis *f* barnyard; retinue, escort; *(mil)* cohort *(comprising 3 maniples or 6 centuries and forming one-tenth of a legion, or 600 men)*

cohortāti·ō -ōnis *f* encouragement

cohorticul·a -ae *f* small cohort

cohort·or -ārī -ātus sum *tr* to encourage, cheer up, urge on

coïti·ō -ōnis *f* meeting; encounter; conspiracy; coalition

coït·us -ūs *m* meeting; junction, meeting place; sexual intercourse

col- *pref* see con-

-col·a -ae *masc suf* denotes a person who inhabits, tills, or worships: **amnicola** one who dwells near the river; **agricola** one who tills the field; **Iūnōnicola** one who worships Juno

colaph·us -ī *m* a punch

Colchic·us, Colch·us -a - um *adj* Colchian, of Colchis

Colch·is -idis *f* country on E. end of the Black Sea **‖** Colchian woman, Medea

cōle·ī -ōrum *mpl (vulg)* balls; **sī cōleōs habērēmus** if we had the balls *(i.e., if we dared assert ourselves)*

col·ēns -entis *p of* **colō ‖** *adj (w. gen)* devoted to

cōl·is -is *m* stalk; cabbage

collabāsc·ō -ere *intr* **(conl-)** to waver, totter

collabefact·ō -āre *tr* **(conl-)** to shake hard

collabe·fīō -fierī -factus sum *intr* **(conl-)** to collapse, be ruined; to sink down

collā·bor -bī -psus sum *intr* **(conl-)** to fall down, collapse; to sink

collacrimāti·ō -ōnis *f* **(conl-)** weeping

collacrim·ō -āre -āvī -ātus *tr* **(conl-)** to cry bitterly over **‖** *intr* to cry together

collacte·a -ae *f* **(-ti·a)** foster sister

collār·e -is *n or* **collār·is -is** *m* collar

Collāti·a -ae *f* old town in Latium

Collātīn·us -ī *m* husband of Lucretia

collāti·ō -ōnis *f* **(conl-)** bringing together; contribution of money, collection, fund; comparison; *(gram)* comparison; **collātiō prīma** comparative; **collātiō secunda** superlative

collāt·or -ōris *m* **(conl-)** contributor

collātus *pp of* **cōnferō**

collaudāti·ō -ōnis *f* **(conl-)** warm praise

collaud·ō -āre -āvī -ātus *tr* **(conl-)** to praise highly

collax·ō -āre *tr* to loosen

collēct·a -ae *f* **(conl-)** contribution of money

collēctāne·us -a -um *adj* **(conl-)** collected from various sources

collēctīci·us -a -um *adj* **(conl-)** hastily gathered

collēcti·ō -ōnis *f* **(conl-)** gathering; recapitulation; inference; *(phil)* syllogism

collēctus *pp of* **colligō** (to collect)

collēct·us -ūs *m* collection

collēg·a -ae *m* **(conl-)** colleague *(in office);* associate; fellow member

collēg·ium -(i)ī *n* **(conl-)** association in office; official body, board, college; guild, corporation; club, society

collībert·us -ī *m* **(conl-)** fellow ex-slave

collib·uit *or* **collub·uit -uisse -itum** *v impers* **(conl-)** it pleases

collī·dō -dere -sī -sus *tr* **(conl-)** to smash to pieces, crush; to strike together; to cause to clash, set at variance **‖** *pass* to be at variance, conflict; *(of teeth)* to chatter

colligāti·ō -ōnis *f* **(conl-)** binding together, connection

collig·ō -āre -āvī -ātus *tr* **(conl-)** to tie together, connect; to stop, restrain, check

col·ligō -ligere -lēgī -lēctus *tr* **(conl-)** to pick up; to gather together, collect; to attain, acquire *(esp. by natural processes);* to compile *(in a book);* to build (up) *(a reputation);* to hitch up, tuck up *(clothing);* to furl *(sails);* to gather in *(the reins);* to harvest *(fruit, crops);* to summarize, sum up; to contract, compress, concentrate; to acquire gradually, amass; to infer, conclude, gather; *(of numbers, totals)* to amount to; to enumerate; **animum** *(or* **mentem) colligere** to compose oneself; **ignēs colligere** to catch fire; **vāsa colligere** *(mil)* to gather up one's gear, break camp **‖** *refl & pass* to pull oneself together; to amount to; *(of winds, clouds, dust)* to gather; *(of anger)* to build up

collīne·ō -āre -āvī -ātus *tr* **(-ni·ō) (conl-)** to aim, direct **‖** *intr* to hit the mark

col·linō -linere -lēvī -litus *tr* **(conl-)** to smear; to defile

Collīn·us -a -um *adj* of the Quirinal Hill; **Collīna Porta** Colline Gate *(near the Quirinal Hill)*

colliquefact·us -a -um *adj* (**conl-**) melted, dissolved

coll·is -is *m* hill

collocāti·ō -ōnis *f* (**conl-**) arrangement; giving in marriage

collocāt·us -a -um *adj* (**conl-**) *(geog)* located, lying

colloc·ō -āre -āvī -ātus *tr* (**conl-**) to place *(in a particular place);* to put in order, arrange; to station, deploy *(troops);* to give in marriage; to lodge, quarter; to occupy, employ; to spend, invest *(money);* to bestow; *(w.* **in** + *acc or abl)* to devote *(time, energy)* to; **in tūtō** *(or* **in tūtum) collocāre** to make safe ‖ *pass* to occur, be found

collocuplēt·ō -āre -āvī -ātus *tr* (**conl-**) to enrich

collocūti·ō -ōnis *f* (**conl-**) conversation; debate, discussion; conference

colloqu·ium -(i)ī *n* (**conl-**) conversation; discussion, conference; interview

collo·quor -quī -cūtus sum *tr* (**conl-**) to talk to ‖ *intr (w.* **cum**) talk with, converse with; *(w. acc* & *inf)* to say in conversation (that)

collubet *see* **collibet**

collūc·eō -ēre *intr* (**conl-**) to shine brightly, be entirely illuminated; *(fig)* to glitter

colluctāti·ō -ōnis *f* (**conl-**) struggling

colluct·or -ārī -ātus sum *intr* (**conl-**) *(w.* **cum**) to wrestle *(with)*

collū·dō -dere -sī -sum *intr* (**conl-**) to play together; to be in collusion; *(w. dat)* to play with

coll·um -ī *n or* **coll·us -ī** *m* neck; bottleneck, neck of a flask

col·luō -luere -luī -lūtus *tr* (**conl-**) to wash out, rinse; to wash away

collūsi·ō -ōnis *f* (**conl-**) collusion

collūs·or -ōris *m* (**conl-**) playmate; fellow gambler

collūstr·ō -āre -āvī -ātus *tr* (**conl-**) to light up; to survey, inspect; *(in painting)* to represent in bright colors

collutulent·ō -āre *tr* (**conl-**) to soil, defile

colluvi·ō -ōnis *or* **colluvi·ēs -ēī** *f* (**conl-**) sewage; dregs; impurities; impure mixture; turmoil; rabble

collyb·us -ī *m* (**collu-**) conversion of currency; rate of exchange

collȳr·a -ae *f* pasta, noodles, macaroni

collȳric·us -a -um *adj* **iūs collȳricum** noodle soup

colō colere coluī cultus *tr* to till *(the soil);* to cultivate *(friendship, other ties);* to live in, inhabit; *(of gods)* to care for, guard, protect; to honor, revere, worship; to adorn, dress; to

follow, practice *(religion);* to observe *(laws, customs);* to experience, live *(one's life);* **ārās colere** to bow down before the altars; **sacra colere** to perform the sacred rites

colocāsi·a -ae *f* lotus, water lily

colōn·a -ae *f* peasant woman

colōni·a -āe *f* colony; *(coll)* town; settlers, colonists; **colōniam dēdūcere** *(or* **mittere)** to send out settlers

colōnic·us -a -um *adj* colonial

colōn·us -ī *m* farmer; colonist, settler

Coloph·ōn -ōnis *m* city in Ionia, one of the "birthplaces" of Homer

col·or *or* **col·ōs -ōris** *m* color, tint; external condition; complexion; tone, style; luster; grace; colorful pretext

colōrāt·us -a -um *adj* colored, tinted; tanned; swarthy; trumped up

colōr·ō -āre -āvī -ātus *tr* to color; to tan; *(fig)* to give a certain tone to

colossē·us -a -um *adj* colossal

coloss·us *or* **coloss·os -ī** *m* colossus *(any large statue of a Roman emperor, made to rival the orginal Colossus)* ‖ **Colossus Rhodī** the Colossus of Rhodes

colostr·a -ae *f or* **colostr·ūm -ī** *n* (**-lust-**) first milk after childbirth, colostrum

colu·ber -brī *m* snake, adder

colubr·a -ae *f* snake, adder *(female)*

colubrif·er -era -erum *adj* snaky, wearing snakes *(of Medusa)*

colubrīn·us -a -um *adj* cunning, wily

cōl·um -ī *n* strainer

columb·a -ae *f* pigeon, dove *(female)*

columb·ar -āris *n* pigeonhole

columbār·ium -(i)ī *n* pigeonhole; niche in a sepulcher

columbīn·us -a -um *adj* of a dove *or* pigeon ‖ *m* little dove

columb·us -ī *m* pigeon, dove

columell·a -ae *f* small column, pillar

colum·en -inis *n* height, summit, peak; roof; ridgepole; head, leader; *(fig)* "crown," "jewel"; *(fig)* cornerstone *(of an argument); (fig)* very embodiment *(of a quality);* **summum columen** highest point *(of an orbit)*

column·a -ae *f* column, pillar; support; waterspout; *(vulg)* (big) penis; **columnae Herculis** *(or* **Hesperiae)** the Pillars of Hercules; **columna Maenia** whipping post *(in the Forum for thieves and slaves and to which debtors were summoned for trial);* **Prōteī columnae** the Pillars of Proteus, the "borders of Egypt" ‖ *fpl* portico; bookshop

columnār·ium -(i)ī *n* tax on house pillars

columnār·ius -(i)ī *m* debtor *(convicted at the* **Columna Maenia**)

columnāt·us -a -um *adj* supported by pillars; **ōs columnātum** *(fig)* the head supported by one's arms

colurn·us -a -um *adj* of hazelwood

col·us -ī *or* **-ūs** *mf* distaff

colūte·a -ae *f* pod-like kind of fruit

cōlyphi·a -ōrum *npl* choice cuts of meat, loin cuts

com- *pref see* **con-**

com·a -ae *f* hair *(of head)*; mane; fleece; foliage; grass; *(poet)* rays

com·āns -antis *adj* hairy; long-haired; plumed *(helmet)*; leafy; **comāns stella** comet

cōmarch·us -ī *m* village chief

comāt·us -a -um *adj* long-haired; leafy; **Gallia Comāta** Gaul other than the province existing after the conquest by Caesar

combib·ō -ere -ī *tr* **(conb-)** to drink up; to absorb; to swallow, engulf; to repress, conceal *(tears)*; to absorb *(knowledge)*

combib·ō -ōnis *m* **(conb-)** drinking partner

com·būrō -būrere -būssī -būstus *tr* **(conb-)** to burn up, consume; *(fig)* to ruin

combūstus *pp of* **combūrō**

com·edō -edere *(or* **-ēsse)** **-ēdī -ēsus** *(or* **-ēstus)** *tr* to eat up, consume; to squander **‖** *refl* to pine away; *(fig)* to feast one's eyes on

com·es -itis *mf* companion; fellow traveler; associate, partner; attendant; staff member; concomitant

comēsse *see* **comedō**

comēstus *pp of* **comedō**

comēsus *pp of* **comedō**

comēt·ēs -ae *m* comet

cōmicē *adv* like a comedy

cōmic·us -a -um *adj* of comedy, comic; **cōmicum aurum** stage money **‖** *m* actor, playwright *(of comedy)*

cōminus *see* **comminus**

cōm·is -is -e *adj* polite; kind, friendly; *(w. dat or* **ergā** *or* **in** + *acc)* kind toward

cōmissābund·us -a -um *adj* riotous; drunken; boozing

cōmissāti·ō -ōnis *f* drinking party

cōmissāt·or -ōris *m* reveler

cōmiss·or -ārī -ātus sum *intr* to carouse, make merry

cōmit·ās -ātis *f* politeness, kindness

comitāt·us -a -um *adj* **(by)** accompanied *(w. abl)*; **comitātior** accompanied by a larger following, better attended

comitāt·us -ūs *m* escort, retinue; court *(of emperor, king)*; company *(traveling together)*, caravan

cōmiter *adv* politely; kindly

comitiāl·is -is -e *adj* of the assembly; **diēs comitiālis** day on which the comitia could transact business; **morbus comitiālis** epilep-

sy *(so called because its occurrence could cause an assembly to be adjourned)*

comitiāt·us -ūs *m (pol)* assembly

comit·ium -(i)ī *n* comitium, assembly place, voting place **‖** *npl* popular assembly; elections; **comitia habēre** to hold elections

comit·ō -āre -āvī -ātus *or* **comit·or -ārī -ātus sum** *tr* to accompany; to escort; to share *(a fate)*; to attend *(a funeral)*; *(of ancestral busts)* to be carried at *(a funeral)* **‖** *intr (w. dat)* to be present with, attend

comm·a -atis *n (gram)* phrase, part of a line

commacul·ō -āre -āvī -ātus *tr* to spot; to stain, defile

commanip(u)lār·is -is *m* army buddy

commarīt·us -ī *m* fellow husband

commeāt·us -ūs *m* passage; traffic; convoy; *(mil)* furlough; *(mil)* lines of communication; *(mil)* supplies; **in commeātū esse** to be on furlough

commedit·or -ārī *tr* to practice hard; to imitate

com·mēiō -mēiere -mī(n)xī mī(n)ctus *tr (sl)* to wet, pee

commemin·ī -isse *(v. defect) tr & intr* to remember well

commemorābil·is -is -e *adj* memorable

commemorāti·ō -ōnis *f* **(conm-)** reminder; recollection, remembrance

commemor·ō -āre -āvī -ātus *tr* **(conm-)** to remember; to bring up, mention, relate

commendābil·is -is -e *adj* commendable

commendātīci·us -a -um *adj* of recommendation, of introduction

commendāti·ō -ōnis *f* recommendation; commendation, praise; approval, esteem; excellence

commendāt·or -ōris *m* backer

commendātr·īx -īcis *f* backer *(female)*

commendāt·us -a -um *adj* recommended; acceptable, suitable

commend·ō -āre -āvī -ātus *tr* to entrust; to recommend; to commit *(to writing, posterity)*; to commend **‖** *refl (w. dat)* to devote oneself to

commentāriol·um -ī *n* notebook; essay

commentār·ium -(i)ī *n or* **commentār·ius -(i)ī** *m* **(conm-)** notebook, diary, journal; record, register; textbook; (collection of) notes; **ā commentāriīs** official in charge of records

commentāti·ō -ōnis *f* careful study; treatise, commentary; textbook; *(rhet)* argument

commentīci·us -a -um *adj* thought-out; imaginary, fictitious

comment·or -ārī -ātus sum *tr* to think over, consider; to contrive, make up; to write, compose; to discuss; to practice, prepare *(a speech)*

comment·or -ōris *m* inventor, deviser

comment·us -a -um *pp of* **comminīscor** ‖ *adj* fictitious, invented, pretended ‖ *n* invention; fabrication; contrivance, device

comme·ō -āre -āvī -ātum *intr* to come and go; to back and forth; to travel repeatedly; *(of water)* to pass, flow; to travel around; to commute; to pass *(from one state to another)*

commerc·ium -(i)ī *n* trade, commerce; dealing, business; communication, correspondence; exchange *(of goods)*, trafficking; goods, merchandise; sexual intercourse; *(leg)* right to engage in trade, commercial rights; *(w. gen)* right to buy and sell *(a commodity)*, *e.g.:* **commercium agrī** right to buy and sell land; **commericium bellī** ransom; **commercium epistulārum** correspondence; **commercium linguae** common language *(shared by various tribes)*; **iūs commerciī** trading rights

commerc·or -ārī -ātus sum *tr* (**conm-**) to purchase

commer·eō -ēre -uī -itus *or* **commer·eor -ērī -itus sum** *tr* (**conm-**) to deserve fully, merit; to be guilty of

com·mētior -mētīrī -mēnsus sum *tr* (**conm-**) to measure; *(w. cum)* to measure *(s.th.)* in terms of

commēt·ō -āre -āvī *intr* to go often, come and go

commīctus *pp of* **commingō**

commigr·ō -āre -āvī -ātum *intr* to move, migrate

commīlit·ium -(i)ī *n* military comradeship

commīlit·ō -ōnis *m* army buddy

commināti·ō -ōnis *f* violent threat

com·mingō -mingere -mīnxī -mīctus *tr (sl)* to pee on; to wet *(bed);* **commīctum caenum** *(sl)* dirty skunk

com·minīscor -minīscī -mentus sum *tr* to think up, contrive; to fabricate *(lie);* to state falsely, pretend, allege

commin·or -ārī -ātus sum *tr* to threaten, make a threat of

commin·uō -uere -uī -ūtus *tr* to lessen considerably; to smash, shatter; *(fig)* to crush, humiliate

comminus *adv* hand to hand; near at hand; **comminus cōnferre signa** to engage in hand-to-hand combat

commi·sceō -scēre -scuī -xtus *tr* to mix together; to confuse; to unite, bring together; *(w. cum)* to discuss with

commiserāti·ō -ōnis *f (rhet)* appeal for compassion *or* pity

commiserēsc·ō -ere *intr (w. gen)* to feel pity for ‖ *v impers* **mē commiserēscit ēius** I pity him

commiser·or -ārī -ātus sum *tr* to feel sympathy for ‖ *intr (rhet)* to try to evoke sympathy

commīsī *perf of* **committō**

commissi·ō -ōnis *f* commencement

commissūr·a -ae *f* connection; joint

commiss·us -a -um *pp of* **committō** ‖ *n* offense, crime; secret, trust; undertaking; thing confiscated

commītig·ō -āre *tr* (**conm-**) to soften up

com·mittō -mittere -mīsī -missus *tr* (**conm-**) to bring together; to join together, make continuous, connect, combine; to cause to compete, match *(for a fight, etc.);* to begin, commence *(games);* to undertake; to commit *(crime),* do *(s.th. wrong);* to incur *(penalty);* to bring about, effect; to give up, forfeit, hand over; to engage in *(battle, war);* *(w. dat)* **1** to take *(a person or matter)* before *(s.o.)* for a verdict, decision, *or* approval; **2** to entrust *(a person or thing)* to *(s.o.);* **hostēs pugnae (or proeliō) committere** to engage the enemy; **memoriae committere** to commit to memory; **omnēs inter sē committere** to set all at variance with one another; **proelium (or pugnam) committere** to go into action, engage the enemy ‖ *refl (w.* **in** + *acc)* to venture into ‖ *intr* to commit an offense, break the law

commodē *adv* properly, appropriately; neatly; adequately, satisfactorily; at the right moment; conveniently, readily; helpfully, obligingly; tastefully; comfortably

commodit·ās -ātis *f* timeliness, right time; proportion, symmetry; convenience, comfort; pleasantness, kindness; *(rhet)* aptness of expression

commodō *adv* suitably, conveniently

commod·ō -āre -āvī -ātus *tr* to adjust, adapt; to bestow, supply, lend, give; **aurem (or aurēs) commodāre** to lend an ear; **manum commodāre** to lend a helping hand ‖ *refl* **mihi tē commodāre** to put yourself at my disposal ‖ *intr* to be obliging; *(w. dat)* to be accommodating to, help

commodulē *or* **commodulum** *adv* nicely, conveniently

commodum *adv* at a good time; in the nick of time; **commodum cum** just at the time when

commod·um -ī *n* convenience; opportunity; profit, advantage; privilege; loan; pay, reward; **commodō tuō** at your convenience; **ex commodō (or per commodum)** *(w. gen)* at the convenience of

commod·us -a -um *adj* convenient, suitable, fit; timely; opportune, good *(time);* comfortable; advantageous; agreeable, obliging, pleasant *(person);* good *(health);* **quod commodum est** just as you please

Commod·us -ī *m* Roman Emperor *(son of Marcus Aurelius, reigned A.D. 180-192)*

commōl·ior -īrī -ītus sum *tr* to set in motion, move with effort

commōnstr·ō -āre -āvī -ātus *tr* to point out; to show where *(a person, thing, place)* is

commone·faciō -facere -fēcī -factus *tr* to call to mind; *(w. acc of person and gen of thing)* to remind *(s.o.)* of

common·eō -ēre -uī -itus *tr* to remind, warn; *(w. gen or* dē + *abl)* to remind *(s.o.)* of

commoniti·ō -ōnis *f* reminder

commorāti·ō -ōnis *f* stay; delay *(rhet)* dwelling on a point

com·morior -morī -mortuus sum *intr (w. dat or* cum) to die with

commor·or -ārī -ātus sum *tr* to stop, detain ‖ *intr* to linger, stay, stop off; **in sententiā commorārī** to stick to an opinion

commōti·ō -ōnis *f* motion; commotion; **animī commōtiō** excitement

commōtiuncul·a -ae *f* slight agitation

commōt·us -a -um *adj* excited, nervous; deranged *(mind);* angry; impassioned; *(rhet)* lively *(style)*

com·moveō -movēre -mōvī -mōtus *tr* to stir up, shake; to disturb, upset; to excite, shake up; to arouse, provoke; to generate, produce; *(fig)* to touch, move; to influence; to impress; to cause, start *(a war, battle);* to dislodge *(an enemy);* to call in *(a debt)*

commūn·e -is *n* common property; community; **in commūne 1** publicly; **2** for the good of all; **3** jointly; **4** in general terms

commūnicāti·ō -ōnis *f* sharing; *(rhet)* deliberating with the audience

commūnic·ō -āre -āvī -ātus *or* commūnic·or -ārī -ātus sum *tr* to share; to unite, link; to impart, communicate; to discuss together; to plan together

commūn·iō -īre -īvī *or* -iī -ītus *tr* (-moen-) to fortify; to build and fortify; *(fig)* to strengthen, fortify

commūni·ō -ōnis *f* sharing; kinship, association

commūn·is -is -e *adj* (conm-) common, joint; common, ordinary; public; universal, general; familiar; courteous; democratic; *(of arguments)* applicable to either side; **commūnis est coniectūra** it is open to conjecture; **commūnis est aestimātiō** it is a matter of opinion; **loca commūnia** public places; **locī commūnēs** general topics; **sēnsus commūnis** civic *or* public spirit ‖ *n see* **commūne** ‖ *npl* the common good; *(poet)* common lot

commūnit·ās -ātis *f* sharing, partnership, joint possession; social ties, fellowship, togetherness; affability

commūniter *adv* in common

commūnīti·ō -ōnis *f* road building; *(fig)* preparation, introduction

commurmur·ō -āre *or* commurmur·or -ārī -ātus sum *intr* to murmur, grumble

commūtābil·is -is -e *adj* changeable, subject to change; interchangeable

commūtāti·ō -ōnis *f* change, alteration; shift; exchange; reversal

commūtāt·us -ūs *m* change

commūt·ō -āre -āvī -ātus *tr* to change, alter; to interchange, exchange; to barter; to give in exchange; *(w. abl or* cum) to exchange *(s.th.)* for; **verba commūtāre** to exchange words, talk

cōm·ō -ere -psī -ptus *tr* to set, do, braid *(the hair);* to adorn, deck out

cōmoedi·a -ae *f* comedy

cōmoedicē *adv* as in comedy

cōmoed·us -a -um *adj* of comic actors ‖ *m* comic actor

comōs·us -a -um *adj* with long hair; hairy; leafy

compacīscor *see* compecīscor

compācti·ō -ōnis *f* framework

compāct·us -a -um *pp of* compingō ‖ *adj* compact, well-built ‖ *n* compact

compāg·ēs -is *f* construction; joint, seam; structure, framework; *(anat)* joint

compāg·ō -inis *f* (conp-) (act of) fastening; connection; framework, structure

comp·ār -aris *adj* (conp-) similar, alike; equal; *(w. dat)* matching, resembling ‖ *mf* buddy; playmate; perfect match; spouse

comparābil·is -is -e *adj* (conp-) comparable, similar

comparātē *adv* (conp-) comparatively

comparāti·ō -ōnis *f (from* compar- + ō) comparison; relative position *(of planets); (gram)* comparative degree; *(rhet)* argument based on the law of probability; **ex comparātiōne** *(w. gen)* in comparison with; **comparātiō prō portiōne** proportion

comparāti·ō -ōnis *f (from* con- + parō) preparation; acquisition, procuring, obtaining, provision *(by purchasing or otherwise);* arrangement, settlement

comparātīv·us -a -um *adj* (conp-) comparative; *(gram)* that is in the comparative degree

compār·eō -ēre -uī *intr* (conp-) to be visible, be plain, be evident; to appear; to be at hand, be present

compar·ō -āre -āvī -ātus *tr (from* compar- + ō) to unite; to match, pit; to align; to estimate; to compare *(with or to);* to point out by way of comparison

compar·ō -āre -āvī -ātus *tr (from* con- + parō) to prepare, make preparations for; to purchase; to plan, devise; to put together, get together, provide; to match; to set up *(courts,*

a body of laws); to procure, get, collect; to appoint; to establish, institute; to raise *(troops);* to compose *(writings);* **comparāre inter sē** *(esp. of consuls)* to arrange, settle
compās·cō -cere — -tus *tr & intr* **(conp-)** to feed together
compāscu·us -a -um *adj* **(conp-)** of public grazing; **compāscuus ager** public pasture land
compect·us -a -um *adj* in agreement **‖** *n* agreement, compact; **(dē) compectō** by previous agreement
comped·iō -īre — -ītus *tr* **(conp-)** to shackle
compedīt·us -a -um *pp of* **compediō ‖** *adj* shackled **‖** *m* shackled slave
compēgī *perf of* **compingō**
compellāti·ō -ōnis *f* **(conp-)** rebuke; *(rhet)* addressing, apostrophizing
compell·ō -āre -āvī -ātus *tr* **(conp-)** to address, speak to; to call upon, appeal to; to challenge; *(w. predicate adj)* to call *(s.o., e.g., disloyal, etc.);* to rebuke, call to account; *(leg)* to arraign
com·pellō -pellere -pulī -pulsus *tr* **(conp-)** to drive together, round up; to crowd together; to compel, drive; *(of wind, waves)* to drive, push, force; *(w. in + acc)* to drive *(s.o.)* into; *(w.inf or ut + subj)* to compel *(s.o.)* to *(do s.th.);* to coerce, constrain; to reduce by force *(to some state or condition);* to clench *(teeth);* to localize, concentrate *(fighting)*
compendiāri·us -a -um *adj* **(conp-)** short, abridged; **via compendiāria** shortcut
compend·ium -(i)ī *n* **(conp-)** careful weighing; saving *(of money);* profit; shortening, abridging; shortcut; **compendium facere** *(w. gen)* to save oneself the trouble of; **compendī fierī** to be brief; **compendiō servīre** to serve one's own private interests
compēnsāti·ō -ōnis *f* compensation
compēns·ō -āre -āvī -ātus *tr* **(conp-)** to compensate for, make up for; to balance mentally
comper·cō -cere -sī *tr* **(conp-)** to save up, hoard; *(w. inf)* to refrain from
comperendināti·ō -ōnis *f or* **comperendināt·us -ūs** *m* **(conp-)** *(leg)* two-day adjournment
comperendin·ō -āre -āvī -ātus *tr* **(conp-)** to adjourn *(court)* for two days; to put off *(defendant)* for two days
comper·iō -īre -ī -tus *or* **comper·ior -īrī -tus sum** *tr* **(conp-)** to find out, discover, learn; **compertum habeō** *or* **compertum mihi est** I know for certain
compern·is -is -e *adj* **(conp-)** having thighs close together
compert·us -a -um *pp of* **comperiō ‖** *adj* ascertained; well authenticated; *(w. gen)* convicted of; **compertum habeō** I have verified;

nihil compertī no certainty; **prō compertō** *(to regard)* as certain; **rēs comperta** *(or* **compertae)** reliable information
comp·ēs -edis *f* **(conp-)** *(usu. pl)* shackles *(for the feet),* fetters; bond *(of love)*
compēsc·ō -ere -uī *tr* **(conp-)** to confine, restrain; to imprison; to close, block *(entrances);* to check the movement of, steady; to stop, restrain *(activity of any kind);* to calm *(a storm);* to control *(a person);* to subdue, quell, crush *(an enemy, a mutiny);* to curb *(one's tongue, one's words);* to stifle *(feelings, fears, laughter);* to quench *(thirst);* to allay *(hunger);* **compēsce dīcere iniūstē!** stop speaking unfairly!; **compēsce digitō labellum!** put your finger to your lip! *(to indicate silence)*
competīt·or -ōris *m* **(conp-)** competitor; rival claimant *(to the throne);* rival bidder *(at an auction); (pol)* fellow candidate
competītr·īx -īcis *f* **(conp-)** competitor *(female)*
compet·ō -ere -īvī *or* **-iī -ītum** *intr* **(conp-)** to come together, meet; *(of events)* to coincide; to be adequate, be suitable; *(w. ad)* to be capable of **‖** *v impers* **sī competit** if it is convenient; *(w. ut)* if it happens that
compīlāti·ō -ōnis *f* **(conp-)** plundering burglary; *(of a collection of documents)* compilation
compīl·ō -āre -āvī -ātus *tr* **(conp-)** to pillage; to plagiarize
com·pingō -pingere -pēgī -pāctus *tr* **(conp-)** to put together, construct; to compose; to lock up, put *(in jail)*
compitāl·ia -ium *npl* **(conp-)** festival of the Lares at crossroads, celebrated twice annually at the crossroads with flowers
compitālici·us -a -um *adj* **(conp-)** of the crossroads
compitāl·is -is -e *adj* **(conp-, compet-)** associated with the festival at the crossroads
compit·um -ī *n* **(conp-)** crossroads; *(fig)* crucial decision
complac·eō -ēre -uī *or* **-itum** *intr* **(conp-)** *(w. dat)* to suit just fine
complān·ō -āre -āvī -ātus *tr* **(conp-)** to level; to raze
comple·ctor -ctī -xus sum *tr* **(conp-)** to embrace, hug; to display affection for, display esteem for; to clasp *(the right hand); (of sleep)* to hold in its embrace; *(fig)* to embrace, take up *(a cause, a course of action);* to grip, grasp, cling to; to encircle, surround, enclose; to comprise; to take in, include within its limits *(an area); (of power, reputation, knowledge)* to extend over, embrace; to involve, associate, include *(in a relationship, class, activity);* to include, cover *(in a book or speech);* to state in a con-

cise manner, sum up; to grasp, understand; **animō** *(or* **mente) complectī** to comprehend, take in; **memoriā complectī** to keep in mind

complēment·um -ī *n* **(conp-)** complement, completion

compl·eō -ēre -ēvī -ētus *tr* **(conp-)** to fill, fill up; to fill with sound, make resound; to supply, furnish; to complete; to impregnate; to bring *(a legion)* to full strength; *(mil)* to man

complēt·us -a -um *adj* **(conp-)** complete, perfect

complexi·ō -ōnis *f* **(conp-)** combination, collection, group; *(rhet)* summary; **complexiō verbōrum** a connected series of words, period, sentence

complex·us -ūs *m* **(conp-)** embrace; *(fig)* love, affection; close combat; mental grasp; grouping *(of words);* envelopment

complicāt·us -a -um *adj* **(conp-)** complicated

complic·ō -āre -āvī *(or* **-uī) -ātus** *(or* **-itus)** *tr* **(conp-)** to fold up

complō·dō -dere -sī -sus *tr* **(conp-)** to clap *(the hands)* together

complōrāti·ō -ōnis *f or* **complōrāt·us -ūs** *m* **(conp-)** wailing, lamentation

complōr·ō -āre -āvī -ātus *tr* **(conp-)** to mourn (together *or* deeply)

complūr·ēs -ēs -a *or* **-ia** *adj* **(conp-)** several, a fair number of

complūriēns *adv* **(-iēs) (conp-)** several times, a good many times

complūscul·ī -ae -a *adj* **(conp-)** several

compluv·ium -(i)ī *n* **(conp-)** compluvium *(quadrangular, inward-sloping central part of the roof of a Roman house to direct rain to a pool below, called* impluvium*)*

com·pōnō -pōnere -posuī -positus *tr* **(conp-)** to put together, join; to place *(things together);* to store up, hoard; to lay aside, put away; to build; to compose, write; to arrange, settle, agree upon; to match; to match up *(pairs);* to compare; to treat as comparable; to balance *(e.g., deeds with words);* to lay out *(the dead);* to put in an urn; to bury; to arrange in order, lay out; to arrange systematically; to arrange properly, adjust; to deploy *(troops);* to arrange, plan, organize *(a plan of action);* to make up, fabricate *(a false report, story);* to reconcile; to concoct, contrive; to quell *(a revolt);* to subdue *(rebels);* to calm, soothe, appease *(a person);* to reconcile *(estranged friends);* to settle *(disputes, problems, affairs);* **bellum compōnere** to end a war *(by coming to terms);* **in maestitiam compositus** putting on the appearance of sadness; **vultum compōnere** to put on a false front

comport·ō -āre -āvī -ātus *tr* **(conp-)** to bring together, bring in, collect, accumulate

comp·os -otis *adj* **(conp-)** *(w. gen or abl)* in possession of, master of, having control over; **compos animī** *(or* **mentis)** sane; **compos suī** self-controlled; **compos vōtī** having one's prayer answered

compos(i)tūr·a -ae *f* **(conp-)** structure

compositē *adv* **(conp-)** in an orderly manner; *(of actions)* deliberately; **compositē dīcere** to speak logically

compositi·ō -ōnis *f* **(conp-)** putting together, fitting together, connecting, arranging, composition; matching *(of gladiators, etc.);* reconciliation *(of friends);* orderly arrangement *(of words)*

compositō *adv* **(conp-)** by prearrangement

composit·or -ōris *m* **(conp-)** an arranger; writer

composit·us -a -um *pp of* **compōnō** ‖ *adj* compound *(words, etc.);* composite, blended; orderly, tidy; calm *(sea);* composed, calm ‖ *n* compound medication; **dē** *(or* **ex) compositō** by agreement, as agreed ‖ *npl* law and order, settled situation

compōtāti·ō -ōnis *f* **(conp-)** drinking party

compot·iō -īre -īvī -ītus *tr* **(conp-)** *(w. acc of person and abl of thing)* to make *(s.o.)* master of ‖ *pass (w. abl)* to attain

compōt·or -ōris *m*, **compōtr·īx -īcis** *f* **(conp-)** drinking partner

comprāns·or -ōris *m* **(conp-)** dinner companion, fellow guest

comprecāti·ō -ōnis *f* **(conp-)** public supplication

comprec·or -ārī -ātus sum *tr* **(conp-)** to pray earnestly to, implore, invoke; *(w. acc of thing)* to pray for; *(w. ut + subj)* to pray that

comprehen·dō -dere -dī -sus *or* **compren·dō -dere -dī -sus** *tr* **(conp-)** to bind together, unite; to hold together *(e.g., w. ropes);* to take hold of, grasp; to catch; to attack; to arrest; to capture; to occupy; to detect; to comprehend; to express; to describe, recount; **animō** *(or* **mente) comprehendere** to apprehend, appreciate; **ignem comprehendere** to catch fire; **memoriā comprehendere** to remember; **numerō comprehendere** to count, enumerate

comprehēnsibil·is -is -e *adj* **(conp-) (-dibilis)** comprehensible, intelligible

comprehēnsi·ō *or* **comprēnsi·ō -ōnis** *f* **(conp-)** seizing; arrest; comprehension, perception; combining; *(rhet)* period

comprendō *see* **comprehendō**

compressi·ō -ōnis *f* **(conp-)** pressing closely; embrace; *(rhet)* compression

compress·or -ōris *m* rapist

compress·us -ūs *m* **(conp-)** compression; embrace; rape

com·primō -primere -pressī -pressus *tr* (conp-) to press together, compress; to close; to embrace; to check, curb; to keep back, suppress, withhold, conceal; to rape; to hold *(one's breath);* **compressīs manibus sedēre** to sit on folded hands, not lift a finger; **ōrdinēs comprimere** to close ranks

comprobāti·ō -ōnis *f* (conp-) full approval

comprobāt·or -ōris *m* (conp-) enthusiastic approver

comprob·ō -āre -āvī -ātus *tr* (conp-) to approve, sanction, acknowledge; to prove, establish, verify; to confirm; to justify

comprōmiss·um -ī *n* (conp-) *(leg)* compromise *(agreement between the parties to abide by the arbitrator's decision)*

comprō·mittō -mittere -mīsī -missum *intr* (conp-) *(leg)* to compromise *(to agree to abide by the arbitrator's decision)*

comptiōnāl·is -is -e *adj (of worn-out goods)* suitable to be sold in batches

cōmpt·us -a -um *pp of* **cōmō** ‖ *adj (of hair)* set, neatly arranged; *(of person)* dressed up; *(of speech, writing)* polished

cōmpt·us -ūs *m* hairdo

compulī *perf of* **compellō**

compulsus *pp of* **compellō**

compun·gō -gere compūnxī compūnctus *tr* (conp-) to puncture, prick; to tattoo; to prod

comput·ō -āre -āvī -ātus *tr* (conp-) to compute, count

computrēsc·ō -ere *intr* (conp-) to rot

Cōm·um -ī *n* Como *(town N. of Po River, modern Como)*

con- *pref (also:* **co-, col-, com-, cor-**) **1** together: **coniungere** to join together; **2** up, completely, fully: **cōnsūmere** to use up; **concrēdere** to trust completely; **3** with: **cōnspīrāre** to plot with *(s.o.);* **4** hard: **conicere** to throw hard, fling

cōnām·en -inis *n* effort, struggle; support; *(often pl)* endeavor, attempt

cōnāt·um -ī *n* effort; venture

cōnāt·us -ūs *m* effort; endeavor; thrust *(with weapon)*

concac·ō -āre -āvī -ātus *tr (vulg)* to soil, shit

concaed·ēs -ium *fpl* log barricade

concale·faciō -facere -fēcī -factus *tr* to warm up, heat

concal·ēscō -ēscere -uī *intr* to grow quite warm; to glow *(e.g., with love)*

concall·ēscō -ēscere -uī *intr* to grow hard; *(fig)* to become insensitive

concamerāt·us -a -um *adj* vaulted

Concān·us -ī *m* one of a Spanish tribe that drank horse's blood

concastīg·ō -āre -āvī -ātus *tr* to dress down; to chastise, punish

concav·ō -āre *tr* to curve, bend

concav·us -a -um *adj* concave, hollow; deepsunken *(eyes);* deep *(valley)*

con·cēdō -cēdere -cessī -cessus *tr* to give up; to pardon, overlook; to grant ‖ *intr* to go away; to withdraw, retire; to pass away, die; *(w. dat)* **1** to yield to, succumb to; **2** to submit to, comply with; **3** to make allowances for, pardon; **4** to be inferior to; *(w. in + acc)* to pass over to, be merged into; **fātō** *(or* **nātūrae** *or* **vītā) concēdere** to die

concelebr·ō -āre -āvī -ātus *tr* to frequent; to fill; to pursue *(studies);* to enliven; to celebrate; to publish, proclaim

concēnāti·ō -ōnis *f* dinner party

concenti·ō -ōnis *f* singing together, sing-along, harmony

concenturi·ō -āre *tr* to assemble by centuries *(groups of hundreds);* *(fig)* to marshal

concent·us -ūs *m* concert; harmony; shouting in unison; blending

concepti·ō -ōnis *f* conception; *(leg)* formula

concept·us -a -um *pp of* **concipiō** ‖ *adj* **concepta verba** formula

concept·us -ūs *m* conception; embryo, fetus

concerp·ō -ere -sī -tus *tr* to tear up, tear to shreds; *(fig)* to cut up, revile

concertāti·ō -ōnis *f* wrangling

concertāt·or -ōris *m* rival

concertātōri·us -a -um *adj* controversial

concert·ō -āre -āvī -ātus *tr* to quarrel over; to rival ‖ *intr* to fight, quarrel

concessi·ō -ōnis *f* concession; admission *(of guilt with a plea for mercy)*

concess·ō -āre -āvī *intr (w. inf)* to cease to, stop *(doing s.th.)*

concess·us -a -um *pp of* **concēdō** ‖ *adj* allowable, lawful ‖ *n* concession

concess·us -ūs *m* permission; **concessū Caesaris** with Caesar's permission

conch·a -ae *f* clam, oyster, mussel, murex; clamshell, oyster shell; pearl; purple dye; trumpet *(of Triton);* vessel *(for ointments, etc.);* vulva

conch·is -is *f* bean

conchīt·a -ae *m* clam digger

conchul·a -ae *f* a small shellfish

conchȳliāt·us -a -um *adj* purple

conchȳl·ium -(i)ī *n* shellfish, clam, oyster; murex; purple dye, purple ‖ *npl* purple garments

concī·dō -dere -dī -sus *tr* to cut up, cut to pieces, kill; to beat severely; *(fig)* to demolish *(w. arguments);* *(rhet)* to chop up *(sentences)*

concid·ō -ere -ī *intr* to collapse; to fall *(in battle);* *(fig)* to decline, fall, fail, decay, perish; *(of winds)* die down

con·cieō -ciēre -cīvī -cītus *or* **con·ciō -cīre -cīvī -cītus** *tr* to assemble; to shake; *(fig)* to stir up

conciliābul·um -ī *n* public meeting place
conciliāti·ō -ōnis *f* union, bond; conciliating; inclination, bent
conciliāt·or -ōris *m* mediator; agent
conciliātrīcul·a -ae *f* madame *(of a brothel);* dear matchmaker
conciliātr·īx -īcis *f* matchmaker; promoter *(of relationships)*
conciliāt·us -a -um *adj (w. ad)* endeared to, disposed toward
conciliāt·us -ūs *m* union, joining
concili·ō -āre -āvī -ātus *tr* to bring together, unite; to win over; to bring about *(by mediation);* to acquire, win
concil·ium -(i)ī *n* popular assembly *(esp. that of the plebs in Rome);* private meeting; council; union; association; a hearing in council; deliberation, debate; *(pol)* a league of states; **in ūnō conciliō** together
concin·ēns -entis *adj* harmonious
concinnē *adv* nicely, daintily
concinnit·ās -ātis *or* **concinnitūd·ō -inis** *f* elegance; excessive refinement; symmetry *(of style)*
concinn·ō -āre -āvī -ātus *tr* to prepare for use, make ready; to repair; to touch up; to make up, concoct; to give rise to; to make, drive *(e.g., insane);* **lacrumentem concinnās tuam uxōrem** you are making your wife cry
concinn·us -a -um *adj* symmetrical; elegant; courteous, nice; polished
concin·ō -ere -uī *tr* to sing of; to prophesy ‖ *intr* to sing *or* play together; *(fig)* to agree
conciō *see* **concieō**
concipil·ō -āre -āvī -ātus *tr* to seize and carry off
con·cipiō -cipere -cēpī -ceptus *tr* to take in, absorb; to imagine, think; to understand, perceive; to conceive; to produce, form; *(of things)* to contain, hold; to contract *(disease);* to catch *(fire);* to entertain *(hope);* to frame *(in formal language);* to announce *(in formal language);* *(w. abl, adv,* **ab, ex)** to draw, derive from *(a source);* to utter solemnly; **verba concepta** solemn utterance
concīsē *adv* concisely
concīsi·ō -ōnis *f (rhet)* dividing a sentence into short phrases
concīs·us -a -um *pp of* **concīdō** ‖ *adj* cut up, cut short, terse; minute, very small
concitātē *adv* vigorously, vividly
concitāti·ō -ōnis *f* rapid movement; excitement; disturbance, riot
concitāt·or *or* **concit·or -ōris** *m* instigator, ring-leader; rabble-rouser
concitāt·us -a -um *adj* excited; rapid
concit·ō -āre -āvī -ātus *tr* to stir up, rouse, urge; to spur on *(horses, etc.);* to agitate, stir up, disturb; to awaken; to summon, assemble; to galvanize into action; to infuriate; to bring about, cause, occasion
concitor *see* **concitātor**
conclāmāti·ō -ōnis *f* loud shouting, yell; acclamation
conclāmit·ō -āre *intr* to keep on shouting, keep on yelling
conclām·ō -āre -āvī -ātus *tr* to shout, yell; to call to *(for help);* to call repeatedly by name, bewail *(the dead);* to exclaim; **iam conclāmātum est** *(coll)* all's lost; **vāsa conclāmāre** *(mil)* to give the signal to pack up; **ad arma conclāmāre** to sound the call to arms
conclāv·e -is *n* room; public restroom
conclū·dō -dere -sī -sus *tr* to shut up, enclose; to include, comprise; to round off, conclude *(speech, letter);* to end rhythmically; to deduce, conclude
conclūsē *adv (rhet)* in a rhythmical cadence
conclūsi·ō -ōnis *f* conclusion; *(mil)* blockade; *(rhet)* summation
conclūsiuncul·a -ae *f* false conclusion
conclūs·us -a -um *pp of* **conclūdō** ‖ *adj* confined, restricted
concol·or -ōris *adj* of the same color
concomitāt·us -a -um *adj* escorted
conco·quō -quere -xī -ctus *tr* to cook thoroughly; to boil down; to digest; to stomach, put up with; to cook up, concoct *(ideas);* to weigh seriously; to ripen ‖ *intr* to digest one's food
concordi·a -ae *f* harmony, concord
concorditer *adv* harmoniously
concord·ō -āre -āvī -ātum *intr* to be of one mind; to be in harmony, agree
concor·s -dis *adj* of the same mind, agreeing, harmonious
concoxī *perf of* **concoquō**
concrēbr·ēscō -ēscere -uī *intr* to grow strong
concrē·dō -dere -didī -ditus *tr* to entrust; to confide *(a secret)*
concrem·ō -āre -āvī -ātus *tr* to burn to ashes, burn down
concrep·ō -āre -uī *intr* to rattle, creak, grate, clash, sound, make noise; **digitīs concrepāre** to snap the fingers ‖ *tr* to cause to sound *or* to rattle
con·crēscō -crēscere -crēvī -crētum *intr* to grow together; to congeal; to curdle; to clot; to stiffen; to take shape, grow, increase
concrēti·ō -ōnis *f* condensing, congealing; matter, substance
concrēt·us -a -um *pp of* **concrēscō** ‖ *adj* grown together, compounded; solid, hard; frozen; matted; condensed, dense; curdled; inveterate, ingrained; dim *(light)* ‖ *n* hardness; solid matter
concrēvī *perf of* **concrēscō**

concrīmin·or -ārī -ātus sum *intr* to make bitter charges

concruci·ō -āre *tr* to torture

concubīn·a -ae *f* concubine

concubīnāt·us -ūs *m* free love

concubīn·us -ī *m* catamite, homosexual

concubit·us -ūs *m* reclining together; sexual intercourse

concubi·us -a -um *adj* concubiā nocte at bedtime ‖ *n* intercourse

conculc·ō -āre -āvī -ātus *tr* trample under foot; to despise, treat with contempt

con·cumbō -cumbere -cubuī -cubitum *intr* to sleep together; *(w.* cum*)* to sleep with, have intercourse with

concup·īscō -īscere -īvī *or* -iī -ītus *tr* to long for; to strive for

concūr·ō -āre *tr* to take good care of

concur·rō -rere -rī -sum *intr* to run together, flock together; to unite; to strike one another, crash; to happen at the same time, coincide; *(mil)* to clash; *(w.* ad*)* to have recourse to; *(of jaws)* to snap together; *(of facts, statements)* to agree

concursāti·ō -ōnis *f* running together, assembly; rushing about; *(mil)* skirmish

concursāt·or -ōris *m* skirmisher

concursi·ō -ōnis *f* concourse; *(gram)* collocation *(of vowels); (rhet)* repetition for emphasis

concurs·ō -āre -āvī -ātus *tr* to run around to; domōs concursāre to run from house to house ‖ *intr* to rush around excitedly, dash up and down; *(mil)* to skirmish

concurs·us -ūs *m* a running together; concourse, assembly; combination; collision *(of atoms); (astr)* conjunction; *(gram)* juxtaposition *(of letters); (leg)* joint right; *(mil)* charge, clash

concussi·ō -ōnis *f* shaking; earthquake

concuss·us -ūs *m* shaking, shock

concu·tiō -tere -ssī -ssus *tr* to bang together; to convulse; to shake; to shatter; to harass, upset, shock; to stir up; to wave *(weapon, hand);* to weaken, shake *(authority, confidence)*

condal·ium -(i)ī *n* (slave's) ring

condec·et -ēre *v impers* it is quite becoming

condecor·ō -āre -āvī -ātus *tr* to adorn; to grace

condemnāt·or -ōris *m* accuser; *(leg)* prosecutor

condemn·ō -āre -āvī -ātus *tr* to condemn, doom; to blame; *(leg)* to prosecute successfully, convict, sentence

condēns·ō -āre -āvī -ātus *tr* to pack together

condēns·us -a -um *adj* crowded, packed

condici·ō -ōnis *f* contract, arrangement; stipulation, terms, condition; state, situation, circumstances; state of health; legal status; rank,

place; marriage contract, marriage; prospective marriage partner, good match; nature, character; choice, option; eā condiciōne ut on the condition that; in condiciōne manēre to stick to an agreement; nūllā condiciōne by no means; sub condiciōne conditionally; vītae condiciō living conditions

condī·cō -cere -xī -ctus *tr* to talk over, arrange together; (ad) cēnam condīcere *(w. dat)* to make a dinner engagement with

condignē *adv* very worthily

condign·us -a -um *adj (w. abl)* fully deserving of, fully worthy of

condīment·um -ī *n* seasoning, spice

cond·iō -īre -īvī *or* -iī -ītus *tr* to season; to pickle, preserve; to embalm; *(fig)* to give zest to

condiscipul·a -ae *f* schoolmate *(female)*

condiscipulāt·us -ūs *m* companionship at school

condiscipul·us -ī *m* schoolmate

con·discō -discere -didicī *tr* to learn thoroughly, learn by heart

condīti·ō -ōnis *f* seasoning; method of preserving *(food)*

condit·or -ōris *m* founder, builder; originator *(of a practice; of a product);* organizer; creator; *(as honorary title)* preserver; author, writer

condīt·or -ōris *m* seasoner

conditōr·ium -(i)ī *n* coffin; tomb

condīt·us -a -um *pp of* condiō ‖ *adj* seasoned, spicy; elegant *(style)*

condit·us -a -um *pp of* condō ‖ *adj* concealed, secret; sunken *(eyes)*

condīxī *perf of* condīcō

con·dō -dere -didī -ditus *tr* to build, found; to write, compose; to establish *(a practice, institution);* to store up, hoard; to preserve; to keep safe; to plunge *(a weapon);* to drown out *(a sound);* to put *(in prison, chains);* to put an end to *(a day)*

condoce·faciō -facere -fēcī -factus *tr* to train well

condoc·eō -ēre -uī -tus *tr* to teach thoroughly

condol·ēscō -ēscere -uī *intr* to begin to ache, get very sore; *(fig)* to feel grief

condōnāti·ō -ōnis *f* donation

condōn·ō -āre -āvī -ātus *tr* to give, present; to permit; to deliver over *(to enemy, for punishment);* to adjudge; *(w. double acc)* to make *(s.o.)* a present of *(s.th.); (w. acc of thing and dat of person)* to forgive, pardon *(s.o. an offense)*

condorm·iō -īre *intr* to sleep soundly

condorm·īscō -īscere -īvī *or* -iī *intr* to fall soundly asleep

condūcibil·is -is -e *adj* advantageous, profitable; *(w.* ad *or* in + *acc)* just right for

condū·cō -cere -xī -ctus *tr* to bring together, collect, assemble; to connect, unite; to rent; to borrow; to induce, bribe; to employ, hire; to contract for, undertake a contract in connection with *(buildings, etc.)* ‖ *intr* to be of use; *(w. dat)* 1 to be useful to, be of use to; 2 to be profitable to; 3 to be fitting for; 4 to be conducive to; *(w. ad or in + acc)* to be conducive to

conductīci·us -a -um *adj* mercenary; rented *(house)*

conducti·ō -ōnis *f* bringing together; recapitulation; the taking of a lease, renting

conduct·or -ōris *m* contractor; lessee, tenant

conduct·us -a -um *pp of* condūcō ‖ *mpl* hired men; mercenaries ‖ *n* rented apartment, rented house; lease, contract

conduplicāti·ō -ōnis *f* doubling; *(hum)* embrace

conduplic·ō -āre -āvī -ātus *tr* to double; **corpora conduplicāre** to embrace

condūr·ō -āre -āvī -ātus *tr* to harden

cond·us -ī *m* storeroom manager

cōne·ctō -ctere -xuī -xus *tr* **(conn-)** to tie; to connect, join, link; to state as a conclusion; **nōdum cōnectere** to tie a knot

cōnexi·ō -ōnis *f* logical conclusion

cōnexuī *perf of* cōnectō

cōnex·us -a -um *pp of* cōnectō ‖ *adj* linked; related, associated; interdependent; **per affīnitātem cōnexus** *(w. dat)* related by marriage to ‖ *n* logical connection, necessary consequence

cōnex·us -ūs *m* connection

cōnfābul·or -ārī -ātus sum *tr* to discuss ‖ *intr* to have a talk, chat

cōnfarreāti·ō -ōnis *f* solemn marriage ceremony before the Pontifex Maximus and ten witnesses

cōnfarre·ō -āre -āvī -ātus *tr* to marry with solemn rites; to contract *(marriage)*

cōnfātāl·is -is -e *adj* bound by the same fate

cōnfecti·ō -ōnis *f* preparation; completion; conclusion, end; compiling; mastication

cōnfect·or -ōris *m* finisher, executor; destroyer

cōnfer·ciō -cīre — -tus *tr* to stuff, cram, pack together; to stuff full

cōn·ferō -ferre -tulī -lātus *or* collātus *tr* to bring together; to contribute *(money, etc.);* to condense, compress; to assemble *(ideas, plans, etc.);* to discuss, talk over; to bear, convey, direct; to devote, apply; to confer, bestow, give, lend, grant; to ascribe, impute, assign; to postpone; *(w. in + acc)* to change *(s.o. or s.th.)* into; to compare, contrast; **capita cōnferre** to put heads together, confer; **gradum cōnferre cum** to walk together with; **lītēs cōnferre** to quarrel; **pedem cum**

pede cōnferre** to fight toe to toe; **sermōnēs cōnferre cum** to engage in conversation with; **signa cōnferre** to begin fighting ‖ *refl (w. in + acc)* 1 to go to, head for; 2 to have recourse to; 3 to join *(a group, etc.)*

cōnfertim *adv (mil)* shoulder to shoulder

cōnfert·us -a -um *pp of* cōnferciō ‖ *adj* crowded, packed, thick, dense; *(mil)* shoulder to shoulder

cōnfervēfac·iō -ere *tr* to make glow, make melt

cōnfer·vēscō -vēscere -buī *or* -vuī *intr* to begin to boil

cōnfessi·ō -ōnis *f* confession, acknowledgment; admission of guilt; token, proof

cōnfess·us -a -um *pp of* cōnfiteor ‖ *adj* acknowledged, incontrovertible ‖ *m* confessed criminal ‖ *n* admission; **ex cōnfessō** admittedly, beyond doubt; **in cōnfessum venīre** to be generally admitted

cōnfestim *adv* immediately, suddenly

cōnfici·ēns -entis *adj* productive, efficient; *(w. gen)* 1 productive of; 2 efficient in ‖ *npl (w. gen)* sources of

cōn·ficiō -ficere -fēcī -fectus *tr* to make, manufacture, process, refine; to do, perform, accomplish; to carry out, discharge; to celebrate *(a rite, festival);* to make ready, prepare; to complete, execute, fulfill; to bring about, cause; to bring together, collect; to secure, obtain; to use up, wear out, exhaust; to finish off, destroy, kill; to run through, waste *(money, inheritance);* to chew *(food);* to digest *(food);* to spend, pass *(time);* to compose, write; to set down in writing, record; to demonstrate; to cover *(a distance); (of grief, worry)* to overwhelm

cōnficti·ō -ōnis *f* fabrication

cōnfictus *pp of* cōnfingō

cōnfīd·ēns -entis *adj* trustful; self-confident; presumptuous, smug

cōnfīdenter *adv* confidently; smugly

cōnfīdenti·a -ae *f* confidence; self-confidence, smugness

cōnfīdentiloqu·us -a -um *adj* speaking confidently

cōnfī·dō -dere -sus sum *intr* to have confidence, be confident; *(w. dat)* to confide in, rely on, trust, believe

cōnfī·gō -gere -xī -xus *tr* to fasten, join together; to pierce, transfix; *(fig)* to paralyze

cōn·fingō -fingere -fīnxī -fictus *tr* to make up, fabricate

cōnfīn·is -is -e *adj* having common boundaries, adjoining; *(fig)* akin

cōnfīn·ium -(i)ī *n* common boundary, frontier; border; *(fig)* borderline ‖ *npl* limits, confines

cōnfīnxī *perf of* cōnfingō

cōn·fīō -fierī *intr* to be accomplished; to occur, happen; *(w.* **ex)** to be made from

cōnfirmāti·ō -ōnis *f* confirmation, encouragement; verification; *(rhet)* presentation of evidence

cōnfirmāt·or -ōris *m* guarantor

cōnfirmāt·us -a -um *adj* resolute, confident, courageous; established, well-attested

cōnfirmit·ās -ātis *f* firmness; stubbornness

cōnfirm·ō -āre -āvī -ātus *tr* to strengthen; to establish on a firm basis; to develop *(mind, character);* to reinforce; to sanction, ratify; to encourage; to corroborate; to assert positively; *(w.* acc *&* inf*)* to prove that; to prove the existence of; to give assurances of, affirm; *(mil)* to strengthen *(a position)* ‖ *refl* to recover, gain strength ‖ *pass* to become mature

cōnfisc·ō -āre -āvī -ātus *tr* to deposit in a treasury; to confiscate *(for the public treasury)*

cōnfīsi·ō -ōnis *f* confidence

cōnfisus *pp of* **cōnfīdō**

cōn·fiteor -fitērī -fessus sum *tr* to confess, acknowledge, admit; to reveal ‖ *intr* to confess; *(poet)* to admit defeat

cōnfīxī *perf of* **cōnfīgō**

cōnfīxus *pp of* **cōnfīgō**

cōnflagrāti·ō -ōnis *f* conflagration; eruption *(of a volcano)*

cōnflagr·ō -āre -āvī -ātum *intr* to burn, be on fire; to be burnt down; *(fig)* to be utterly destroyed

cōnflīcti·ō -ōnis *f* conflict

cōnflīct·ō -āre -āvī -ātus *tr* (*usu.* used in the passive*)* to strike down; to ruin; to afflict, torment; to buffet

cōnflīct·or -ārī -ātus sum *intr* to struggle, wrestle

cōnflīct·us -ūs *m* clash, collision

cōnflī·gō -gere -xī -ctus *tr* to knock together, beat, clap ‖ *intr* to clash, fight, battle; *(w.* **cum)** to come into conflict with, clash with; *(w.* **adversus** + *acc or* **contrā** + *acc)* to fight against; **inter sē cōnflīgere** to collide with one another

cōnfl·ō -āre -āvī -ātus *tr* to kindle, ignite; to inflame *(passions);* to melt down *(metals);* to raise *(army, money, etc.);* to concoct *(a lie);* to run up *(debt);* to bring about, cause; to hatch *(plot);* to organize *(riot)*

cōnflu·ēns -entis *adj* flowing together; flowing into; **ā cōnfluente Rhodānō** from the confluence of the Rhone *(with the Arar)*

cōnflu·ēns -entis *m (often pl)* confluence

cōnflu·ō -ere -xī *intr* to flow together; *(fig)* to flock together, come in crowds; *(of things)* to gather

cōn·fodiō -fodere -fōdī -fossus *tr* to dig up *(soil);* to stab; *(fig)* to harm

cōnfore = cōnfutūrum esse to be about to happen

cōnfōrmāti·ō -ōnis *f* shape, form; fashion; idea, notion; arrangement *(of words);* expression *(in voice); (rhet)* figure of speech

cōnfōrm·ō -āre -āvī -ātus *tr* to shape, fashion, put together; to describe, delineate; to train, educate; to bring into harmony

cōnfoss·us -a -um *pp of* **cōnfodiō** ‖ *adj* full of holes, punctured

cōnfrāctus *pp of* **cōnfringō**

cōnfragōs·us -a -um *adj* rough, rugged ‖ *npl* rugged terrain

cōnfrem·ō -ere -uī *intr* to grumble

cōnfric·ō -āre *tr* to rub vigorously; to massage

cōn·fringō -fringere -frēgī -frāctus *tr* to smash, crush; to ruin, undo ‖ *pass (of ships)* to be wrecked

cōn·fugiō -fugere -fūgī *intr* to flee, take refuge, run for help; *(w.* **ad) 1** to have recourse to; **2** to appeal to

cōnfug·ium -(i)ī *n* place of refuge, sanctuary, shelter

cōnfulg·eō -ēre -sī *intr* to glitter, sparkle

cōn·fundō -fundere -fūdī -fūsus *tr* to pour together, blend, mingle; to mix up, jumble together, confuse, bewilder; to spread, diffuse

cōnfūsē *adv* in confusion

cōnfūsi·ō -ōnis *f* mixing, blending; confusion, mixup; **cōnfūsiō ōris** blush

cōnfūs·us -a -um *pp of* **cōnfundō** ‖ *adj* confused; troubled *(look)*

cōnfūt·ō -āre -āvī -ātus *tr* to keep from boiling over; to repress, stop; to confute

cōnfu·tuō -tuere -tuī -tūtus *tr (vulg)* to screw; **quidquid puellārum cōnfutuere** to screw any and every girl

congel·ō -āre -āvī -ātus *tr* to cause to freeze up, harden; to curdle; *(fig)* to chill; **in lapidem congelāre** to petrify ‖ *intr* to freeze, freeze up; to become hard; to become inactive

congemināti·ō -ōnis *f* doubling

congemin·ō -āre -āvī -ātus *tr* to double

congem·ō -ere -uī -itus *tr* to deplore deeply ‖ *intr* to gasp, sigh, groan

con·ger -grī *m* eel

congeri·ēs -ēī *f* heap, pile

con·gerō -gerere -gessī -gestus *tr* to bring together; to heap up, build up; to build, erect; to keep up, multiply; to repeat *(arguments);* *(w.* **in** + *acc)* **1** to shower *(weapons)* on; **2** to heap *(curses, favors)* upon

congerr·ō -ōnis *m* playmate

congestīci·us -a -um *adj* piled up

congestus *pp of* **congerō**

congest·us -ūs *m* heap, mass

congiāl·is -is -e *adj* holding a gallon

congiāri·us -a -um *adj* holding a gallon ‖ *n* gift of one gallon *(e.g., of olive oil apiece to the people);* bonus *(to the army);* gift of money *(to the people);* gift, donation

cong·ius -(i)ī *m* liquid measure *(about 6 pints)*

conglaci·ō -āre -āvī *intr* to freeze up

conglīsc·ō -ere *intr* to blaze up

conglobāti·ō -ōnis *f* massing together

conglob·ō -āre -āvī -ātus *tr* to make round, form into a ball; to mass together

conglomer·ō -āre -āvī -ātus *tr* to roll up; to group together, crowd together ‖ *refl (w.* **in** + *acc)* to crowd into

conglūtināti·ō -ōnis *f* gluing together; *(fig)* combining *(of words)*

conglūtin·ō -āre -āvī -ātus *tr* to glue, cement; *(fig)* to unite closely, to cement

congraec·ō -āre -āvī -ātus *tr* to squander like a Greek

congrātulāti·ō -ōnis *f* congratulations

congrātul·or -ārī -ātus sum *intr* to offer congratulations; *(of several persons)* to express their joy

con·gredior -gredī -gressus sum *tr* to meet, accost, address; to engage ‖ *intr* to come together, meet; *(w.* **cum) 1** to meet with; **2** to associate with; **3** to fight against

congregābil·is -is -e *adj* gregarious

congregāti·ō -ōnis *f* flocking together, congregation, union, association

congreg·ō -āre -āvī -ātus *tr* to herd together; to assemble; to group together ‖ *pass* to flock together; **parēs cum paribus facillimē congregantur** *(prov)* birds of a feather flock together

congressi·ō -ōnis *f* meeting, conference

congressus *pp of* **congredior**

congress·us -ūs *m* meeting, association, society; union, combination; hostile encounter; fight; sexual intercourse

congru·ēns -entis *adj* coinciding, corresponding; suitable; consistent; self-consistent, uniform

congruenter *adv* consistently; *(w.* **dat** *or* **ad)** in conformity with; **congruenter nātūrae vīvere** to live in conformity with nature

congruenti·a -ae *f* consistency; similarity; good proportion

congru·ō -ere -ī *intr* to coincide; to correspond, agree, be consistent; *(w.* **ad** *or* **cum)** to correspond to, agree with, be consistent with; *(w.* **dat** *or* **in** + *acc)* to agree with

congru·us -a -um *adj* agreeing, corresponding

coniecti·ō -ōnis *f* hurling, barrage *(of missiles);* conjecture; guesswork; interpretation *(of dreams, etc.);* prophecy; **coniectiōnem facere** to draw a conclusion

coniect·ō -āre -āvī -ātus *tr* **(cōiect-)** to conjecture, infer

coniect·or -ōris *m* interpreter of dreams, seer

coniectr·īx -īcis *f* interpreter of dreams, seeress

coniectūr·a -ae *f* **(cōiect-)** conjecture, guess; inference; interpretation

coniectūrāl·is -is -e *adj* conjectural

coniect·us -ūs *m* throwing together; crowding together; connecting; heap, crowd, pile; throwing, hurling; turning, directing *(eyes);* casting *(a glance);* barrage *(of stones, missiles);* **ad** *(or* **intrā)** **tēlī coniectum venīre** to come within range of a weapon

cōnif·er *or* **cōnig·er -era -erum** *adj* coniferous

con·iciō -icere -iēcī -iectus *tr* **(cō·iciō)** to hurl, cast; to pile together; to conclude, infer; to conjecture; to interpret ‖ *refl* **sē in fugam** *(or* **in pedēs) conicere** to take to one's heels

cōnī·tor -tī -xus sum *or* **-sus sum** *intr* to make a great effort, struggle, exert oneself; *(w.* **in** + *acc)* to struggle toward, try to reach

coniugāl·is -is -e *adj* conjugal

coniugāti·ō -ōnis *f (gram)* etymological relationship *(of words)*

coniugāt·or -ōris *m* uniter *(said of Hymen, god of marriage)*

coniugiāl·is -is -e *adj* marriage

coniug·ium -(i)ī *n* union *(e.g., of body and soul);* marriage, wedlock; mating *(of animals); (fig)* spouse

coniug·ō -āre -āvī -ātus *tr* to join in marriage; to form *(a friendship);* **verba coniugāta** *(gram)* cognates

coniūnctē *adv* conjointly; at the same time; hypothetically; in intimacy

coniūnctim *adv* jointly

coniūncti·ō -ōnis *f* combination, union; association, connection; friendship, intimacy; marriage; relationship *(by blood or marriage);* sympathy, affinity; *(gram)* conjunction

coniūnct·us -a -um *adj (w.* **dat** *or* **abl)** bordering on, near; *(w.* **dat** *or* **abl** *or* **cum) 1** connected with; **2** agreeing with, conforming with ‖ *n* connection

coniun·gō -gere coniūnxī coniūnctus *tr* to join together; to unite in making *(war);* to join in marriage; to unite *(by bonds of friendship); (w.* **dat)** to add *(e.g., words)* to *(e.g., a letter)*

con·iūnx -iugis *m* **(-iux)** spouse, husband ‖ *mpl* married couple ‖ *f* spouse, wife; fiancée; bride; the female *(of animals)*

coniūrāti·ō -ōnis *f* plot, conspiracy; alliance

coniūrāt·us -a -um *adj* bound together by an oath, allied, associated; *(mil)* sworn in ‖ *mpl* conspirators

coniūr·ō -āre -āvī -ātum *intr* to take an oath together; to plot, conspire coniux *see* coniūnx

cōn·īveō -īvēre -īvī *or* -īxī *intr* (conn-) to close the eyes; to blink; *(of sun, moon)* to be eclipsed; to be drowsy; *(w.* in + *acc)* to connive at, overlook

conj- = coni-

conl- = coll-

conm- = comm-

Con·ōn -ōnis *(acc:* -ōna) famous Athenian admiral *(fl c. 400 B.C.)* ‖ famous mathematician and astronomer of Samos *(fl c. 230 B.C.)*

cōnōpī·um -ī *n* (-pē·um) mosquito net; bed with net, canopy bed

cōn·or -ārī -ātus sum *tr* to try

conquassāti·ō -ōnis *f* severe shaking, disturbance

conquass·ō -āre -āvī -ātus *tr* to shake hard; *(fig)* shatter, upset, disturb

conque·ror -rī -stus sum *tr* to complain bitterly about, deplore ‖ *intr* to complain bitterly

conquesti·ō -ōnis *f* complaining, complaint; *(rhet)* appeal for sympathy; *(w. gen, w.* dē + *abl or* adversus + *acc)* complaint about

conquest·us -ūs *m* loud complaint

conqui·ēscō -ēscere -ēvī -ētum *intr* to rest, take a rest; to go to sleep; to find rest, find recreation; to keep quiet, remain inactive; to slacken; to lie dormant; to stop, pause

con·quīnīscō -quīnīscere -quexī *intr* to crouch down, squat

conquī·rō -rere -sīvī *or* -siī -sītus *tr* to search for, look for; to procure, bring together, collect; *(fig)* to go after *(e.g., pleasures)*

conquīsīti·ō -ōnis *f* search *(in order to bring together or obtain),* procuring, collection; *(mil)* recruitment, draft

conquīsīt·or -ōris *m* (-quist-) recruiting officer

conquīsīt·us -a -um *pp of* conquīrō ‖ *adj* select, choice

conr- = corr-

cōnsaep·iō -īre -sī -tus *tr* (-sēp-) to fence in, enclose

cōnsaept·um -ī *n* (-sēp-) enclosure

cōnsalūtāti·ō -ōnis *f* exchange of greetings

cōnsalūt·ō -āre -āvī -ātus *tr* to greet *(as a group),* greet cordially ‖ *intr* inter sē cōnsalūtāre to greet one another, exchange greetings

cōnsān·ēscō -ēscere -uī *intr* to heal up; to recover

cōnsanguine·us -a -um *adj* related by blood ‖ *m* brother ‖ *mpl* relatives ‖ *f* sister

cōnsanguinit·ās -ātis *f* blood relationship; cōnsanguinitāte propinquus closely related

cōnsauci·ō -āre -āvī -ātus *tr* to wound severely

cōnscelerāt·us -a -um *adj* wicked, depraved, criminal; *(fig)* rotten to the core

cōnsceler·ō -āre -āvī -ātus *tr* to stain with guilt, dishonor, disgrace

cōnscen·dō -dere -dī cōnscēnsus *tr* to climb up, ascend; to climb *(tree);* to mount *(horse, chariot);* to board *(ship);* aequor nāvibus cōnscendere to go to sea ‖ *intr* to climb up; to climb aboard

cōnscēnsi·ō -ōnis *f* embarkation; in nāvēs cōnscēnsiō boarding the ships

cōnscienti·a -ae *f* joint knowledge; consciousness, knowledge; conscience; scruples; remorse

cōn·scindō -scindere -scidī -scissus *tr* to tear up, tear to pieces; *(fig)* to tear apart, abuse

cōnsc·iō -īre -īvī *tr* to have on one's conscience

cōnsc·īscō -īscere -īvī *or* -iī -ītus *tr* to decree, decide on; *(w.* sibi) to inflict on oneself; sibi mortem cōnscīscere to decide on suicide

cōnsci·us -a -um *adj* cognizant, conscious, aware; *(w. gen or dat)* having knowledge of, privy to ‖ *mf* partner; accomplice; confidant(e), confederate

cōnscre·or -ārī -ātus sum *intr* to clear the throat

cōnscrī·bō -bere -psī -ptus *tr* to enlist, enroll; to write up, compose; to prescribe

cōnscrīpti·ō -ōnis *f* record

cōnscrīpt·us -a -um *pp of* cōnscrībō ‖ *m* senator; patrēs cōnscrīptī gentlemen of the Senate ‖ *n (leg)* deposition

cōnsec·ō -āre -uī -tus *tr* to cut up into small pieces, dismember

cōnsecrāti·ō -ōnis *f* consecration; deification *(of emperors)*

cōnsecr·ō -āre -āvī -ātus *tr* to consecrate; to dedicate to the gods below, doom to destruction; to immortalize; to hallow; to deify

cōnsectāri·us -a -um *adj* conclusive

cōnsectāti·ō -ōnis *f* eager pursuit

cōnsectātr·īx -īcis *f* eager pursuer

cōnsecti·ō -ōnis *f* cutting up

cōnsect·or -ārī -ātus sum *tr* to follow eagerly, go after; to chase, hunt; to overtake; to imitate, follow

cōnsecūti·ō -ōnis *f* effect, consequences; *(rhet)* order, sequence

cōnsen·ēscō -ēscere -uī *intr* to grow old, grow old together; to become grey; to become obsolete; to waste away, fade, decline; to degenerate

cōnsēnsi·ō -ōnis *f* agreement, unanimity; harmony; plot

cōnsēns·us -ūs *m* agreement, unanimity; harmony; plot; cōnsēnsū with one accord; in cōnsēnsum vertere to become a general custom

cōnsentāne·us -a -um *adj (w. dat or* cum) 1 agreeing with; 2 according to, in accord with;

3 proper for; **cōnsentāneum est** it is reasonable ‖ *npl* concurrent circumstances

cōnsenti·ēns -entis *adj* unanimous

cōnsen·tiō -tīre -sī -sus *tr* to agree on; to consent to; **bellum cōnsentīre** to agree on war, vote for war ‖ *intr* to agree; *(w. inf)* **1** to agree to; **2** to plot to; *(w.* **cum)** **1** to agree with; **2** *(pej)* to plot with, conspire with; **3** *(of things)* to fit in with, be consistent with, harmonize with

cōnsēp- = **cōnsaep-**

cōnsequ·ēns -entis *adj* reasonable; corresponding; logical; suitable ‖ *n* consequence, conclusion

cōnsequenter *adv* consequently

cōnsequenti·a -ae *f* consequence; natural sequence; **per cōnsequentiās** consequently

cōnse·quor -quī -cūtus sum *tr* to follow, follow up, pursue, go after; to catch up with, catch; to reach, attain to; to arrive at; *(fig)* to follow, copy, imitate; to obtain, get, acquire; to understand; *(of speech)* to do justice to; *(of time)* to come after, follow; to result from

cōnser·ō -ere -uī -tus *tr* entwine, tie, join, string together; **manum** *(or* **manūs)** **cōnserere** to fight hand-to-hand; **proelium** *(or* **pugnam) cōnserere** to begin to fight

con·serō -serere -sēvī -situs *tr* to sow, plant

cōnsertē *adv* in close connection

cōnserv·a -ae *f* fellow slave *(female)*

cōnservāti·ō -ōnis *f* preservation

cōnservāt·or -ōris *m* preserver, defender

cōnservātr·īx -īcis *f* protectress

cōnservit·ium -(i)ī *n* fellowship in slavery

cōnserv·ō -āre -āvī -ātus *tr* to keep safe, preserve, maintain; to act in accordance with, observe; *(fig)* to keep intact

cōnserv·us -ī *m* fellow slave

cōnsess·or -ōris *m* neighbor *(one who sits next to another at a feast, assembly, court of justice, public games)*

cōnsess·us -ūs *m* a sitting together, an assembly, a court, an audience

cōnsīderātē *adv* deliberately, with caution

cōnsīderāti·ō -ōnis *f* consideration, examination

cōnsīderāt·us -a -um *adj* cautious; well-considered, deliberate

cōnsīder·ō -āre -āvī -ātus *tr* to inspect, examine; to consider, reflect on

cōnsīd·ium -(i)ī *n* court of justice

cōn·sīdō -sīdere -sēdī *or* **-sīdī -sessum** *intr* to sit down, be seated; to hold sessions, be in session; to settle, stay *(in residence);* to settle, sink; *(fig)* to sink; to subside, calm down; *(mil)* to encamp, take up a position; **cōnsīdere in** *(+ abl) (of a bird)* to land on

cōnsign·ō -āre -āvī -ātus *tr* to seal, sign; to certify, vouch for; to record *(in a sealed document);* to put on record

cōnsil·ēscō -ēscere -uī *intr* to fall silent; to become still, calm down

cōnsiliāri·us -a -um *adj* counseling ‖ *m* counselor, consultant; cabinet member *(of an emperor)*

cōnsiliāt·or -ōris *m* counselor

cōnsiliō *adv* intentionally

cōnsili·or -ārī -ātus sum *intr* to deliberate; to give advice

cōnsil·ium -(i)ī *n* consultation, deliberation; advice; council; council of war; plan, stratagem; measure; decision; purpose, intention; policy; judgment, wisdom, discretion, sense; *(emperor's)* cabinet; **cōnsiliō** *(or* **cōnsiliīs) alicūius** on s.o.'s instructions; **cōnsilium capere** *(or* **inīre** *or* **suscipere)** to form a plan, come to a decision; **cōnsilium mihi est** *(w. inf)* I intend to; **in cōnsiliō esse** to be available for consultation; **nōn est cōnsilium mihi** *(w. inf)* I don't mean to; **prīvātō cōnsiliō** for one's own purpose

cōnsiluī *perf of* **cōnsilēscō**

cōnsimil·is -is -e *adj* quite similar; *(w. gen or dat)* just like

cōnsip·iō -ere *intr* to be sane

cōn·sistō -sistere -stitī *intr* to come to a stop, stop, pause, halt; *(w.* **cum)** to talk with; to take a stand; to stand still; to grow hard, become solid, set; *(of ships)* to come to anchorage, to ground; *(of travelers)* to halt on a journey; to be firm, be steadfast, endure; to be, exist; to come into existence; to continue in existence, remain; to occur, take place; *(mil)* to take up a position, be posted, make a stand; *(w. abl or in + abl)* **1** to consist of; **2** to depend on; **3** to be based on; **4** to base one's case on; *(w. abl, w.* **in** *+ abl, w.* **dē** *or* **ex** *+ abl)* to be comprised of; **cōnstitit** *(w. acc & inf)* it is a fact that

cōnsiti·ō -ōnis *f* sowing, planting

cōnsit·or -ōris *m* sower, planter

cōnsitūr·a -ae *f* sowing, planting

cōnsōbrīn·a -ae *f* first cousin *(female)*

cōnsōbrīn·us -ī *m* first cousin

cōnsoc·er -erī *m* (a joint) father-in-law

cōnsociāti·ō -ōnis *f* association

cōnsoci·us -a -um *adj* shared

cōnsoci·ō -āre -āvī -ātus *tr* to join in *(plans, activities);* to share ‖ *intr* to enter into a partnership

cōnsōlābil·is -is -e *adj* consolable

cōnsōlāti·ō -ōnis *f* consolation, comfort; encouragement; allaying

cōnsōlāt·or -ōris *m* comforter

cōnsōlātōri·us -a -um *adj* comforting; **litterae cōnsōlātōriae** letter of condolence

cōnsōlor -ārī -ātus sum *tr* to console, comfort; to reassure, soothe, encourage; to relieve

cōnsomni·ō -āre -āvī *tr* to dream about

cōnson·ō -āre -uī *intr* to sound together, ring, resound, reecho; *(w. dat or* cum) to harmonize with, agree with; inter sē cōnsonāre to agree, be in accord

cōnson·us -a -um *adj* harmonious

cōnsōp·iō -īre -īvī *or* -ītus *tr* to put to sleep

cōnsor·s -tis *adj* having a common lot; common; shared in common ‖ *mf* partner ‖ *m* brother ‖ *f* sister

cōnsorti·ō -ōnis *f* partnership; association; fellowship

cōnsort·ium -(i)ī *n* community of goods; partnership; participation; *(w. gen)* partnership in

cōnspect·us -a -um *pp of* cōnspiciō ‖ *adj* visible; in full sight; conspicuous, striking

cōnspect·us -ūs *m* look, sight, view; (sense of) sight; mental view; appearance on the scene; cōnspectū in mediō before all eyes

cōnsper·gō -gere -sī -sus *tr* to sprinkle; to splatter

cōnspiciend·us -a -um *adj* worth seeing; distinguished

cōnspicill·um -ī *n* lookout (post)

cōn·spiciō -spicere -spexī -spectus *tr* to look at attentively, observe, fix the eyes on; to catch sight of, spot; to look at with admiration; to face *(e.g., the Forum)* ‖ *pass* to be conspicuous, be noticed, be admired; to attract attention

cōnspic·or -ārī -ātus sum *tr* to catch sight of, spot, see; *(in a passive sense)* to be conspicuous

cōnspicu·us -a -um *adj* visible, in sight; conspicuous, striking, remarkable, distinguished

cōnspīrāti·ō -ōnis *f* agreement, unanimity, harmony; plot

cōnspīrāt·us -a -um *adj* conspiring, conspiratorial

cōnspīr·ō -āre -āvī -ātum *intr* to act in harmony; to agree; to conspire

cōnspōns·or -ōris *m* co-guarantor

cōn·spuō -spuere -spuī -spūtus *tr* to spit on

cōnspurc·ō -āre -āvī -ātus *tr* to defile, mess up; to defile sexually

cōnspūt·ō -āre -āvī -ātus *tr* to spit on

cōnstabil·iō -īre -īvī *or* -iī -ītus *tr* to stabilize, put on a firm basis

cōnst·āns -antis *adj* constant, uniform, steady, fixed, stable, regular, invariable, persistent; consistent; *(fig)* faithful, trustworthy

cōnstanter *adv* constantly, steadily, uniformly, invariably; consistently

cōnstanti·a -ae *f* constancy, steadiness, firmness, perseverance; consistency, harmony; steadfastness; self-possession

cōnsternāti·ō -ōnis *f* consternation, dismay, alarm; disorder, disturbance; mutiny; wild rush, stampede

cōnstern·ō -āre -āvī -ātus *tr* to shock; to startle; to stampede; to derange; *(w.* ad *or* in + *acc)* to drive *(by fear, etc.)* to *(some action)*

cōn·sternō -sternere -strāvī -strātus *tr* to spread, cover; to pave; to thatch; cōnstrāta nāvis ship with deck

cōnstīp·ō -āre -āvī -ātus *tr* to pack together, crowd together

cōnstit·uō -uere -uī -ūtus *tr* to set up, erect; settle *(e.g., people in a place);* to establish; to settle on, fix *(date, price, penalty);* to moor *(a ship);* to arrange, organize; to designate, appoint, assign; to decide, arbitrate, decree, judge; *(mil)* to station, post, deploy; *(w. inf)* to decide to

cōnstitūti·ō -ōnis *f* constitution, nature; disposition; regulation, ordinance; definition; *(rhet)* issue, point of discussion

cōnstitūt·us -a -um *pp of* cōnstituō ‖ *adj* ordered, arranged; bene cōnstitūtum corpus good constitution ‖ *n* agreement, arrangement; appointment

cōn·stō -stāre -stitī *intr* to stand together; to agree, correspond; to stand firm, be constant; to stand still; to be in existence; *(com)* to tally, be correct; *(w. abl of price)* to cost; ratiō cōnstat the account tallies, is correct ‖ *v impers* it is a fact, it is known; nōn mihi satis cōnstat I have not quite made up my mind; satis cōnstat it is an established fact, all agree

cōnstrāt·us -a -um *adj* paved; *(ship)* with deck ‖ *n* platform; deck *(of ship);* flooring

cōn·stringō -stringere -strīnxī -strictus *tr* to tie together, tie up; to chain; *(fig)* to restrain, inhibit, control; to limit, confine; to limit in time; to knit *(the brow);* to tone up *(the body); (rhet)* to condense

cōnstructi·ō -ōnis *f* building, construction; arrangement *(of words)*

cōnstru·ō -ere -xī -ctus *tr* to heap up; to construct; to arrange in a group; *(gram)* to construct

cōnstuprāt·or -ōris *m* rapist

cōnstupr·ō -āre -āvī -ātus *tr* to rape

cōnsuā·deō -dēre -sī -sus *tr* to advocate ‖ *intr* *(w. dat)* to try to persuade

Cōnsuāl·ia -ium *npl* feast of Consus *(ancient Italic god of fertility, celebrated on August 21 and December 15)*

cōnsuās·or -ōris *m* adviser

cōnsūcid·us -a -um *adj* very juicy

cōnsūd·ō -āre -āvī *intr* to sweat profusely

cōnsuē·faciō -facere -fēcī -factus *tr* to accustom, inure

cōnsu·ēscō -ēscere -ēvī -ētus *tr* to accustom, inure ‖ *intr* to become accustomed; *(w. inf)* to become accustomed to, get used to; *(w.* **cum)** to cohabit with

cōnsuēti·ō -ōnis *f* sexual intercourse

cōnsuētūd·ō -inis *f* custom, habit; usage, idiom; social ties; sexual intercourse; **ad cōnsuētūdinem** *(w. gen)* according to the custom of; **(ex) cōnsuētūdine** from habit; **prō meā cōnsuētūdine** as is my habit; **ut fert cōnsuētūdō** as is usual

cōnsuēt·us -a -um *pp of* cōnsuēscō ‖ *adj* customary

cōn·sul -sulis *m* consul *(one of the two highest magistrates of the Roman Republic);* **cōnsul dēsignātus** consul-elect; **cōnsulem creāre** *(or* **dīcere,** *or* **facere)** to elect a consul; **cōnsul ōrdinārius** regular consul *(who entered office in January 1);* **cōnsul suffectus** substitute consul *(chosen in the course of the year to fill a vacancy)*

cōnsulār·is -is -e *adj* consular; **aetās cōnsulāris** minimum legal age to be consul *(42 years);* **comitia cōnsulāria** consular elections; **vir cōnsulāris** a man of consular rank ‖ *m* ex-consul

cōnsulāriter *adv* like a consul, in a manner worthy of a consul

cōnsulāt·us -ūs *m* consulship; **cōnsulātum gerere** to hold the consulship; **cōnsulātum petere** to run for the consulship; **sē cōnsulātū abdicāre** to resign from the consulship

cōnsul·ō -ere -uī -tus *tr* to consult; to consider; to advise *(s.th.),* offer as advice; **bonī (optimī) cōnsulere** to think well (very highly) of ‖ *intr* to deliberate, reflect; *(w. dat)* to look after; *(w.* **ad** *or* **in** + *acc)* to reflect on, take into consideration; *(w.* **in** + *acc)* to take measures against; *(w.* **dē** + *abl)* to pass sentence on

cōnsultāti·ō -ōnis *f* mature deliberation, consideration; consulting; inquiry; subject of consultation

cōnsultē *adv* deliberately, with due deliberation, prudently

cōnsultō *adv* deliberately, on purpose

cōnsult·ō -āre -āvī -ātus *tr* to reflect on, consider maturely; to ask *(s.o.)* for advice, consult ‖ *intr* to deliberate; *(w. dat)* to look after, take care of; **in medium** *(or* **in commūne)** **cōnsultāre** to look after the common good

cōnsult·or -ōris *m* counselor, consultant; advisee, client

cōnsultr·īx -īcis *f* protectress

cōnsult·um -i *n see* cōnsultus

cōnsult·us -a -um *pp of* cōnsulō ‖ *adj* skilled, experienced ‖ *m* expert; **iūris cōnsultus** legal expert, attorney ‖ *n* deliberation, considera-

tion; decree, decision; response *(from an oracle);* **bene cōnsultum** a good measure; **male cōnsultum** an ill-advised measure; **senātūs cōnsultum** decree of the Senate

cōnsummāt·us -a -um *adj* consummate, perfect

cōnsumm·ō -āre -āvī -ātus *tr* to sum up; *(of numbers)* to add up to; to finish, accomplish, perfect; to complete *(public works)*

cōnsūm·ō -ere -psī -ptus *tr* to consume, use up, exhaust; to devour; to wear out; to waste

cōnsūmpti·ō -ōnis *f* consumption; wasting

cōnsūmpt·or -ōris *m* consumer; spendthrift

con·suō -suere -suī -sūtus *tr* to sew up

cōnsur·gō -gere -rēxī -rēctum *intr* to stand up; to rise in a body; *(w.* **ad** *or* **in** + *acc)* to aspire to

cōnsurrēcti·ō -ōnis *f* rising up, standing up in a body

Cōns·us -ī *m* ancient Italic deity of agriculture and fertility

cōnsusurr·ō -āre -āvī *intr* to whisper to one another

contābē·faciō -facere -fēcī -factus *tr* to wear out; to waste *(fig)* to run *(s.o.)* down

contāb·ēscō -ēscere -uī *intr* to waste away

contabulāti·ō -ōnis *f* flooring; floor, story

contabul·ō -āre -āvī -ātus *tr* to cover with boards; to construct with multiple stories; to bridge, span

contāct·us -a -um *pp of* contingō

contāct·us -ūs *m* touch, contact; contagion; *(fig)* infection

contāg·ēs -is *f* touch, contact

contāgi·ō -ōnis *f* touching; touch, contact; contagion, infection

contāg·ium -(i)ī *n* touch, contact; contagion; moral contamination

contāmināt·us -a -um *adj* contaminated, polluted; vile

contāmin·ō -āre -āvī -ātus *tr* to contaminate, pollute; to adulterate; to defile, desecrate; to ruin, spoil

contechn·or -ārī -ātus sum *intr* to devise plots; to think up tricks

conte·gō -gere -tēxī contēctus *tr* to cover up; to hide; to protect; to put a roof on; to bury

contemer·ō -āre -āvī -ātus *tr* to defile

contem·nō -nere -psī -ptus *tr* to regard with contempt, look down on, despise; to treat with contempt; to pay no attention to, disregard; to have nothing to do with

contemplāti·ō -ōnis *f* viewing, surveying; contemplation, consideration

contemplāt·or -ōris *m* contemplator, observer

contemplāt·us -ūs *m* contemplation

contempl·ō -āre -āvī -ātus *or* **contempl·or -ārī -ātus sum** *tr* to observe, survey, gaze on, contemplate

contemptim *adv* contemptuously; fearlessly

contempti·ō -ōnis *f* scorn; contempt; disregarding, belittling

contempt·or -ōris *m* despiser

contemptr·īx -īcis *f* despiser *(female)*

contempt·us -a -um *pp of* **contemnō** ‖ *adj* contemptible

contempt·us -ūs *m* contempt; **contemptuī esse** to be an object of contempt

conten·dō -dere -dī -tus *tr* to stretch, draw tight; to tune *(instrument);* to aim, shoot, hurl; to strain, exert; to assert, hold, allege; to compare, contrast; **cursum** *(or* **iter) contendere** to make one's way ‖ *intr* to exert oneself; to contend, compete, fight; to dispute, argue; to travel, march; to match, contrast; *(w.* **dē** + *abl)* to demand from; *(w. inf)* to be in a hurry to; *(w.* **in** + *acc)* to rush to, head for; *(w.* **ad)** to strive for, aspire to; *(w.* **cum) 1** to contend with, argue with; **2** to fight with

contentē *adv (from* **contendō)** vehemently, vigorously, earnestly

contentē *adv (from* **contineō)** in a restricted way, sparingly. scantily

contenti·ō -ōnis *f* stretching, tension; exertion, effort; competition; quarrel; contrast, comparison, antithesis; *(gram)* comparison of adjectives; *(rhet)* crescendo; **in contentiōnem venīre** *or* **vocārī** *(or* **in contentiōne pōnī)** to become the subject of a dispute

content·us -a -um *pp of* **contendō** ‖ *adj* tense, strained; energetic

content·us -a -um *pp of* **contineō** ‖ *adj* content, satisfied

contermin·us -a -um *adj* neighboring; *(w. dat)* adjacent to

con·terō -terere -trīvī -trītus *tr* to grind to powder, pulverize, crush; to wear out; *(fig)* to wear down; *(fig)* to trample on; to expunge, wipe out; to waste *(time, effort);* to exhaust *(topic)*

conterr·eō -ēre -uī -itus *tr* to scare the life out of

contest·or -ārī -ātus sum *tr* to call to witness; *(fig)* to prove, attest; **lītem contestārī** to open a lawsuit by calling witnesses

contex·ō -ere -uī -tus *tr* to weave together; to make by joining, devise, build; to link, join *(words);* to compose *(writings);* to dream up

contextē *adv* in a coherent manner

context·us -a -um *pp of* **contexō** ‖ *adj* interwoven; coherent; continuous, uninterrupted

context·us -ūs *m* joining together; coherence; continuity, connection; structure; plan, course

contic·ēscō -ēscere *or* **contic·īscō -īscere -uī** *intr* to become quite still, fall completely silent; to keep silence; *(fig)* to abate, cease

conticinn·um -ī *n* silence of the night; **conticinnō** in the evening

conticīscō *see* **conticēscō**

contignāti·ō -ōnis *f* floor, story

contign·ō -āre -āvī -ātus *tr* to lay a floor on

contigu·us -a -um *adj* contiguous, touching, adjoining, within reach; *(w. dat)* bordering on, near

contin·ēns -entis *adj* continuous, unbroken; homogeneous; adjacent, close; next, immediately following; successive *(days);* self-controlled, moderate; restrained; *(w. dat)* contiguous with, adjacent to; *(w.* **cum)** bordering on ‖ *f* interior *(of a country);* mainland ‖ *n* main point *(of argument);* **ex continentī** *(or* **in continentī)** without delay

continenter *adv* in unbroken succession; without interruption; *(sitting)* close together; moderately

continenti·a -ae *f* repression; self-control

con·tineō -tinēre -tinuī -tentus *tr* to hold *or* keep together; to keep within bounds, confine; to contain, comprise, include; to control, repress

con·tingō -tingere -tigī -tāctus *tr* to come into contact with; to touch, border on; to reach, attain; to infect; to contaminate; *(fig)* to touch, affect ‖ *intr* to happen, turn out, come to pass; *(w. dat)* to touch, border on ‖ *v impers* it happens, turns out; *(w. dat)* it befalls, happens to

continuāti·ō -ōnis *f* unbroken series, succession; *(rhet)* period

continuō *adv* immediately; right from the first; without more ado; continuously; necessarily

continu·ō -āre -āvī -ātus *tr* to make continuous, join together, connect; to extend *(in time or space);* to continue, carry on, draw out, prolong; to pass, occupy *(time)* ‖ *pass (w. dat)* **1** to be contiguous with, adjacent to; **2** to follow closely upon ‖ *intr* to continue, last

continu·us -a -um *adj* continuous, unbroken; successive; **diēs continuōs quīnque** (for) five days in a row

conti·ō -ōnis *f* meeting, rally; public meeting *(of the people or soldiers);* speech, pep talk; **contiōnem habēre** to give a speech; to give a pep talk

contiōnābund·us -a -um *adj* haranguing, holding forth *(like a demogogue)*

contiōnāl·is -is -e *adj* like in assembly; demogogic

contiōnāri·us -a -um *adj* mob-like

contiōnāt·or -ōris *m* demogogue
contiōn·or -ārī -ātus sum *intr* to hold forth at
a rally, to harangue; to come to a rally **ǁ** *tr (w.
acc & inf)* to say at a rally (that)
contiuncul·a -ae *f* small rally
contoll·ō -ere *tr* gradum contollere to step up
(to a person)
conton·at -āre *v impers* it is thundering loudly
contor·qeō -quēre -sī -tus *tr* to twist, whirl; to
throw hard; to twist *(words)* around
contortē *adv* intricately
contortiōn·ēs -um *fpl* intricacies *(of language)*
contort·or -ōris *m* perverter; contortor lēgum
shyster
contortul·us -a -um *adj* terribly complicated
contortuplicāt·us -a -um *adj* all tangled up
contort·us -a -um *pp of* contorqueō **ǁ** *adj*
involved, intricate
contrā *adv* in opposition, opposite, in front,
face to face; in turn, in return; on the other
hand; on the other side; reversely, in the
opposite way, the other way; on the contrary,
conversely; contrā atque *(or* ac) contrary to,
otherwise than; contrā dīcere to reply; to
raise objections; contrā dīcitur the objection
is raised; contrā ferīre to make a counterattack; contrā quam fās est contrary to divine
law; contrā quam senātus cōnsuluisset contrary to what the Senate would have decided;
quīn contrā nay on the contrary
contrā *prep (w. acc)* 1 opposite, opposite to,
facing, toward: contrā septentriōnēs facing
north; 2 *(in a hostile sense)* against, with, in
opposition to: contrā patriam exercitum
dūcere to lead an army against one's country; 3 injurious to, unfavorable to: quod
contrā sē ipsum sit dīcere to say what is
against one's own interests; 4 in defiance of:
contrā senātum profīcīscī to depart in defiance of the Senate; 5 in violation of: contrā
iūs gentium in violation of international law;
6 contrary to, the reverse of contrā
exspectātiōnem omnium contrary to universal expectation; contrā spem contrary to
hope, unexpectedly; 7 in comparison with:
nunc contrā istum librum faveō ōrātiōnī
quam nūper dedī now in comparison with
that book I prefer the speech which I recently gave *(you)*
contracti·ō -ōnis *f* contraction; shortening *(of
syllable);* contractiō animī depression; contractiō nervōrum cramp
contractiuncul·a -ae *f* slight mental depression
contract·us -a -um *pp of* contrahō **ǁ** *adj* contracted; narrow, limited *(place);* brief; pinch-
ing *(poverty);* limited in scope; parsimonious; terse *(style)*
contract·us -ūs *m* contraction

contrā·dīcō -dīcere -dīxī -dictum *tr* to contradict **ǁ** *intr (w. dat)* 1 to contradict; 2 to speak
against, oppose
contrādicti·ō -ōnis *f* objection, refutation
con·trahō -trahere -trāxī -tractus *tr* to draw
together; to contract; to collect, assemble; to
shorten, narrow, abridge; to lessen; to wrinkle; to bring about, accomplish, cause, produce, incur; to conclude *(a bargain);* to transact *(business);* to settle *(an account);* to complete *(business arrangements)*
contrāposit·um -ī *n* antithesis
contrāriē *adv* in opposite directions; in a different way
contrari·us -a -um *adj* opposite; contrary,
conflicting; hostile, antagonistic; from the
opposite direction; reciprocal, mutual; *(w.
dat)* opposed to, contrary to **ǁ** *n* the opposite,
the contrary, the reverse; antithesis;
contrāriō on the contrary; e(x) contrāriō on
the contrary; on the opposite side; in
contrāriās partes in opposite directions; in
contrāria versus changed into its opposite;
in contrārium in the opposite direction
contrectābiliter *adv* (-tract-) appreciably, tan-
gibly
contrectāti·ō -ōnis *f* (-tract-) handling, touching; fondling, caressing
contrect·ō -āre -āvī -ātus *tr* (-tract-) to touch,
handle; *(sl)* to fondle; *(sl)* to have sexual
intercouse with; to deal with *(a subject)*
contrem·īscō -īscere -uī *tr* to shudder at **ǁ** *intr*
to tremble all over; to waver
contrem·ō -ere -uī *intr* to tremble all over; to
quake
contrib·uō -uere -uī -ūtus *tr* to bring together,
enroll together; to associate, unite, incorporate; to contribute, add
contrīst·ō -āre -āvī -ātus *tr* to sadden; to cast
gloom over, darken, cloud
contrīt·us -a -um *pp of* conterō **ǁ** *adj* worn
out; common, trite
contrōversi·a -ae *f* controversy, quarrel, dispute; debate; civil lawsuit, litigation; subject
of litigation; contradiction; question
contrōversiōs·us -a -um *adj* controversial
contrōvers·us -a -um *adj* disputed, controversial; questionable, undecided
contrucīd·ō -āre -āvī -ātus *tr* to cut down,
massacre; *(sl)* to make a mess of
contrū·dō -dere -sī -sus *tr* to push hard; to
crowd together
contrunc·ō -āre -āvī -ātus *tr* to hack to pieces
contubernāl·is -is *m* army buddy; junior staff
officer; *(coll)* husband *(of slave);* personal
attendant; companion, colleague **ǁ** *f* wife *(of
slave)*
contubern·ium -(i)ī *n* sharing the same tent;
wartime friendship; army tent; serving as a

junior staff officer; concubinage; marriage *(among slaves);* hovel *(of slave couple)*

contudī *perf of* **contundō**

contu·eor -ērī -itus sum *tr* to look intently at; to catch sight of; to be within sight of *(a place)*

contuit·us *or* **contūt·us -ūs** *m* sight, observation, gaze

contumāci·a -ae *f* insubordination, defiance; *(leg)* contempt

contumāciter *adv* defiantly

contum·āx -ācis *adj* insubordinate, defiant

contumēli·a -ae *f* mistreatment; outrage; abuse; insult, affront

contumēliōsē *adv* abusively; outrageously

contumēliōs·us -a -um *adj* insulting, outrageous, humiliating; abusive, rude

contumul·ō -āre -āvī -ātus *tr* to bury

con·tundō -tundere -tudī -tūsus *tr* to crush, grind, pound; to bruise; *(fig)* to crush, subdue; to baffle; to outdo *(performance)*

conturbāti·ō -ōnis *f* disorder; dismay, consternation

conturbāt·or -ōris *m* a bankrupt person

conturbāt·us -a -um *adj* confused, distracted, in confusion

conturb·ō -āre -āvī -ātus *tr* to confuse, throw into confusion; to disturb; to upset *(plans);* **ratiōnēs** *(or* **ratiōnem) conturbāre** to be bankrupt **‖** *intr* to go bankrupt

cont·us -ī *m* pole

contūsus *pp of* **contundō**

cōnūbiāl·is -is -e *adj* conjugal

cōnūb·ium -(i)ī *n* intermarriage; right to intermarry; marriage; **iūs cōnūbiī** right to intermarry

cōn·us -ī *m* cone; apex *(of helmet)*

convad·or -ārī -ātus sum *tr* to subpoena

conval·ēscō -ēscere -uī *intr* to grow strong, thrive; to convalesce; *(fig)* to improve; *(leg)* become valid

convall·is -is *f* valley

convās·ō -āre -āvī -ātus *tr* to pack, pack up

convect·ō -āre -āvī -ātus *tr* to gather

convect·or -ōris *m* fellow passenger

conve·hō -here -xī -ctus *tr* gather, bring in *(esp. the harvest);* to convey, ship

con·vellō -vellere -vellī -vulsus *tr* (**-vols-**) to tear away, pull off, pluck, wrest; to tear to pieces, dismember; to break, shatter; *(fig)* to turn upside down, subvert, overthrow; **convellere signa** to break camp

conven·ae -ārum *mpl or fpl* strangers; refugees, vagabonds, the homeless

conveni·ēns -entis *adj* agreeing, harmonious, consistent; appropriate; *(w. dat or* **cum)** consistent with, appropriate to; *(w.* **ad)** appropriate for, suitable for

convenienter *adv* consistently; suitably; *(w.* **cum** *or* **ad)** in conformity with

convenienti·a -ae *f* agreement, accord, harmony; conformity

con·veniō -venīre -vēnī -ventus *tr* to meet, go to meet; to interview; *(leg)* to sue; **Rēgulus convēnit mē in praetōris officiō** Regulus met me at the installation of a praetor **‖** *intr* to come together, meet, gather; to make an agreement; to coincide; to converge; to unite, combine; to come to an agreement, agree; to fit; *(w.* **ad)** to fit *(as a shoe fits the foot);* *(w. dat or* **cum** *or* **ad** *or* **in** + *acc)* to be applicable to, appropriate to; **bene convenīre** to be on good terms; to fit well; **in mātrimōnium cum virō convenīre** *(of a bride)* to get married; **virō in manum convenīre** *(of a bride)* to come under the control of her husband **‖** *v impers* it is fitting; it is proper; it is agreed; **bene convenit nōbīs** we get along well; **convenit inter cōnsulēs** there is agreement between the consuls

conventīci·us -a -um *adj* coming together, met by chance **‖** *n* fee paid for attending the assembly

conventicul·um -ī *n* small gathering; small meeting place

conventi·ō -ōnis *f* assembly; agreement, contract

convent·um -ī *n* contract, agreement

convent·us -ūs *m* gathering, assembly; congress; district court; company, corporation; agreement; **ex conventū** by agreement; of one accord; **conventum agere** to hold court

converber·ō -āre -āvī -ātus *tr* to beat soundly, bash

conver·rō -rere -rī -sus *tr* (**-vorr-**) to sweep out; to brush thoroughly; *(fig)* to scoop up *(e.g., an inheritance)*

conversāti·ō -ōnis *f* familiarity, close association *(with people);* **conversātiō parit contemptum** *(prov)* familiarity breeds contempt

conversi·ō -ōnis *f* rotation; cycle; transposition; inversion; alteration; political change, upheaval; *(rhet)* repetition of word at end of clause; *(rhet)* balancing of phrases; *(rhet)* period

convers·ō -āre -āvī -ātus *tr* to turn around **‖** *refl* to revolve

conver·tō -tere -tī -sus *tr* (**-vor-**) to rotate; to turn back, reverse; *(fig)* to turn, direct *(attention, laughter);* to convert, transform; to translate; to turn upside down; to convulse, shake; to turn *(e.g., horse)* around; to shift, transfer; to transpose, invert *(an arrangement);* to turn aside, divert; to distract *(the mind);* to repulse *(attackers);* **ad sē** *(or* **in sē) convertere** to attract *(e.g., attention);* **in fugam convertere** to put to flight; **signa con-**

vertere to face about; **terga convertere** to turn tail **II** *refl* to turn around; *(mil)* to retreat **II** *intr* to return; to change, turn; *(w.* in + *acc)* to be changed into, turn into
convest·iō -īre *tr* to clothe, cover
convex·us -a -um *adj* rounded off; arched, convex; concave; sloping down **II** *n* vault, arch, dome
convīciāt·or -ōris *m* heckler
convīci·or -ārī -ātus sum *intr* to jeer; *(w. dat)* to heckle, jeer at
convīc·ium -(i)ī *n* noise, chatter; wrangling; jeers, heckling, abuse; cry of protest; reprimand, **aliquem convīciīs cōnsectārī** to heckle s.o.; **convīcium habēre** *(coll)* to catch hell
convicti·ō -ōnis *f* socializing, association, companionship; companions
convict·or -ōris *m* bosom pal
convict·us -ūs *m* socializing, association
con·vincō -vincere -vīcī -victus *tr* to refute, prove wrong; *(leg)* to convict; to prove, demonstrate clearly; **dēvōtiōnem convincere** *(of a god)* to grant a request
convīs·ō -ere -ī -us *tr* to examine, search; to go to visit
convīv·a -ae *m (f)* guest; dinner guest
convīvāl·is -is -e *adj* convivial, festive
convīvāt·or -ōris *m* host; master of ceremonies
convīv·ium -(i)ī *n* banquet, dinner party; party; **convīvium agitāre** *(coll)* to throw a party; **convīvium dare** to give a party **II** *npl* dinner guests
convī·vō -vere -xī -ctum *intr* to live together; to live at the same time; *(w.* **cum***)* to dine with
convīv·or -ārī -ātus sum *intr* to feast together, have a party
convocāti·ō -ōnis *f* calling together
convoc·ō -āre -āvī -ātus *tr* to convoke
convol·ō -āre -āvī -ātum *intr* to flock together
convol·vō -vere -vī -ūtus *tr* to roll together; to roll up *(scroll);* to fasten together, interweave; to wrap; **terga convolvere** *(of snakes)* to wiggle **II** *refl* to roll along; to go in a circle
convom·ō -ere -uī -itus *tr* to vomit all over
convortō *see* **convertō**
convulner·ō -āre -āvī -ātus *tr* **(-vol-)** to wound seriously
convuls·us -a -um *pp of* **convellō**
coöper·iō *or* **cōperi·ō -īre -uī -tus** *tr* **(cōp-)** to cover; to overwhelm
coöptāti·ō -ōnis *f* **(cōp-)** coöptation *(election of a colleague by incumbents)*
coöpt·ō -āre -āvī -ātus *tr* **(cōp-)** to coöpt
coör·ior -īrī -tus sum *intr* to rise (all together *or* all at once; to be born; to originate; to appear suddenly; *(of war)* to break out; *(mil)* to go on the attack
coört·us -ūs *m* rising, originating

Co·os *or* **Co·us -ī** *f* small island in the Aegean, famous for its wine and fine linen *(modern Kos)*
cōp·a -ae *f* barmaid
cophin·us -ī *m* basket
cōpi·a -ae *f* abundance, supply, store; plenty; multitude, large number; wealth, prosperity; opportunity, means; command of language, fluency; *(w. gen)* power over; *(w. dat)* access to; **cōpia dīcendī** *(or* **verbōrum***)* command of language, large vocabulary, richness of expression; **prō cōpiā** as one's circumstances allow **II** *fpl* troops, armed forces; provisions, supplies
cōpiol·ae -ārum *fpl* small contingent of troops
cōpiōsē *adv* abundantly; *(rhet)* fully, at length, eloquently
cōpiōs·us -a -um *adj* plentiful; well-supplied; rich; eloquent, fluent; *(w. abl)* abounding in, rich in
cop·is -idis *f* small, curved sword
cōpō *see* **caupō**
cōp·s -is *adj* rich, well-supplied; *(of the chest)* swelling *(with pride)*
copt·a -ae *f* crisp cake
cōpul·a -ae *f* cord, string, rope, leash; *(fig)* tie, bond
cōpulāti·ō -ōnis *f* coupling, joining; union; combining *(of words)*
cōpulāt·us -a -um *adj* closely connected; compound, complex; close, intimate *(relationship)*
cōpul·ō -āre -āvī -ātus *tr* to couple, join; *(fig)* to unite; *(w. dat or* **cum***)* to couple with, join to, combine with **II** *refl & pass* to unite *(for practical purposes)*
cōpul·or -ārī -ātus sum *tr* to join, clasp; **dextrās copulārī** to shake hands
coqu·a -ae *f* cook *(female)*
coquīn·ō -āre -āvī -ātum *intr* to be a cook
coquīn·us -a -um *adj* of cooked and baked food
co·quō -quere -xī -ctus *tr* to cook; to fry, roast, boil, bake; to brew; to bake *(bricks, bread);* to fire *(pottery);* to smelt *(ore);* to season *(lumber);* to burn, parch; to ripen; to digest *(food);* to disturb, worry; to concoct, dream up; to hatch *(plots)*
coqu·us *or* **coc·us -ī** *m* cook
cor cordis *n* heart *(as the seat of the emotions, as the seat of wisdom);* mind, judgment; dear friend; **aliquid cordī habēre** to take s.th. to heart; **cordī esse** *(w. dat)* to please, be dear to, be agreeable to; **cor habēre** to have common sense; **sī vōbīs nōn fuit cordī** *(w. acc & inf)* if it was not to your liking that **II** *npl* friends, souls
coracīn·us -ī *m* dark-colored species of fish

cōram *adv* in person, personally; publicly, openly; in someone's presence, face to face ‖ *prep (coming before or after abl)* before, in the presence of, face to face with, before the eyes of

corb·is -is *m (f)* wicker basket

corbīt·a -ae *f* slow-sailing merchant ship

corbul·a -ae *f* small basket

corcōta *see* crocōta

corcōtāri·us -a -um *adj* concerned with saffron-colored clothes

corcul·um -ī *n* little heart; sweetheart; poor fellow; the Wise *(name given to Publius Scipio Nasica)*

Corcȳr·a -ae *f* island off coast of Epirus, sometimes identified with Scheria, the island of Alcinoüs

cordātē *adv* wisely, prudently

cord·āx -ācis *m* trochaic meter; indecent dance

cordol·ium -(i)ī *n* heartache

Cordub·a -ae *f* town in S. Spain *(modern Cordova)*

cordȳl·a -ae *f* baby tuna

Corfīn·ium -(i)ī *n* town in central Italy, center of the Social War

coriandr·um -ī *n (bot)* coriander *(aromatic herb, used as seasoning)*

Corinn·a -ae *f* Greek lyric poetess *(fl c. 500 B.C.)*

Corinthiac·us -a -um *or* Corinthiēns·is -is -e *adj* Corinthian

Corinthi·us -a -um *adj* Corinthian; aes Corinthium alloy of gold, silver, and copper used in expensive jewelry ‖ *mpl* Corinthians ‖ *npl* costly Corinthian products

Corinth·us *or* Corinth·os -ī *f* Corinth

Coriolān·us -ī *m* Gnaeus Marcius Coriolanus *(notorious Roman general who led the Volsci against Rome)*

cor·ium -(i)ī *n or* cor·ius -(i)ī *m* skin, hide; leather; bark; peel, rind; *(sl)* one's hide; coriō suō lūdere *(sl)* to risk one's own hide; corium alicūius petere *(sl)* to be after s.o.'s hide

Cornēli·us -a -um *adj* Roman clan name *(nomen)* and tribal name; lēx Cornēlia a law proposed by any member of the Cornelian clan *(esp. Sulla)*

corneol·us -a -um *adj* made of horn; *(fig)* hard, tough

corne·us -a -um *adj* of horn; of cornel wood; of the cornel tree

cornic·en -inis *m* horn blower

cornīc·or -ārī -ātus sum *tr (sl)* to croak, say in a croaking voice ‖ *intr* to caw

cornīcul·a -ae *f* poor little crow

corniculār·ius -(i)ī *m* soldier decorated with horn-shaped medal for bravery; adjutant to a centurion

cornicul·um -ī *n* (cornu-) little horn; *(mil)* horn-shaped decoration

cornig·er -era -erum *adj* horned

cornip·ēs -edis *adj* hoofed

corn·īx -īcis *f* crow; *(pej)* old crow

corn·ū -ūs *or* corn·um -ī *n* horn *(of animals, insects);* drinking vessel *(made from a horn);* funnel *(made from a horn);* horn, trumpet; lantern; oil cruet; hoof; bill *(of bird);* horn *(of moon);* tip *(of a bow);* branch *(of river);* arm *(of lake);* tongue *(of land);* crest socket *(of helmet);* roller end *(of scroll);* *(mil)* wing, flank; cornua addere *(w. dat)* to give courage to, add strength to; cornua sūmere to gain strength; cornū cōpiae cornucopia; cornū Indicum ivory

corn·um -ī *n* cornel cherry; spear

corn·us -ī *f* cornel cherry tree; dogwood tree; spear, shaft, javelin

coroll·a -ae *f* small garland

corollār·ium -(i)ī *n* garland; gilt wreath *(given as reward to actors);* gift, tip

corōn·a -ae *f* crown, garland; circle of bystanders; *(mil)* cordon of besiegers; *(mil)* ring of defense; corōna cīvica decoration for a saving a life; corōna mūrālis decoration for being the first to scale an enemy wall; corōna nāvālis decoration for naval victory; corōna obsidiālis decoration for breaking a blockade; sub corōnā vēndere to sell *(captives)* as slaves; sub corōnā vēnīre *(of captives)* to be sold at auction ‖ Corōna *(astr)* Ariadne's crown, Corona Borealis

corōnāri·us -a -um *adj* for a crown; aurum corōnārium gold collected in the provinces for a victorious general's crown

Corōnē·a -ae *f* town in Boeotia

Corōn·eūs -eī *m* king of Phocis, whose daughter was changed into a crow

Corōnīd·ēs -ae *m* Aesculapius, son of Coronis

Corōn·is -idis *f* mother, by Apollo, of Aesculapius

corōn·is -idis *f* symbol for showing the end of a book, colophon

corōn·ō -āre -āvī -ātus *tr* to crown, wreathe; to enclose, encircle, shut in

corpore·us -a -um *adj* physical, of the body, bodily; corporeal, substantial; of flesh

corpulent·us -a -um *adj* corpulent, stout

corp·us -oris *n* body; matter, substance; flesh; plumpness; trunk *(of tree);* corpse; person, individual; frame, structure, framework; community; corporation; society, union, guild; particle, grain; sum *(of money);* *(literary)* corpus; *(in geometry)* a solid; corporis *(w. noun)* body, bodily, physical; corporis custōs bodyguard; corpus reīpūblicae the body politic; tōtō corpore with all one's strength

corpuscul·um -ī *n* puny body; particle, atom; *(coll)* little fellow

corrā·dō -dere -sī -sus *tr* **(conr-)** to scrape together, rake up; *(coll)* to scrape *(money)* together

correcti·ō -ōnis *f* **(conr-)** correction, improvement, amendment; rhetorical restatement

correct·or -ōris *m* **(conr-)** corrector, reformer

correct·us -a -um *pp of* **corrigō ‖** *adj* improved, correct

corrēp·ō -ere -sī -tum *intr* **(conr-)** to creep, slink; **in dūmēta corrēpere** *(coll)* to beat around the bush, indulge in jargon

correptē *adv* **(conr-)** with a short vowel *or* syllable

correptius *adv* **(conr-)** more briefly; **correptius exīre** to end in a short vowel

correptus *pp of* **corripiō (conr-) ‖** *adj* short *(syllable, vowel)*

corrēxī *perf of* **corrigō**

corrīd·eō -ēre *intr* **(conr-)** to laugh out loud

corrigi·a -ae *f* shoelace

cor·rigō -rigere -rēxī -rēctus *tr* **(conr-)** to straighten out; to smooth out; to correct, improve, reform; to make up for *(delay);* to make the best of

cor·ripiō -ripere -ripuī -reptus *tr* **(conr-)** to take hold of, snatch up; to seize *(a person);* to seize unlawfully; *(of a current)* to carry off; to steal, carry off; to enrapture, sweep off one's feet; to attack suddenly; to speed up, rush; to shorten, contract; to abridge *(a literary work);* to reproach; to cut short *(period of time); (gram)* to pronounce *(a word)* with a short syllable, pronounce *(a syllable)* short; **arma corripere** to go to war; **gradum corripere** to pick up the pace; **igne** *(or* **flammā) corripere** to ignite, set on fire; **in sē corripere** to absorb **‖** *refl* to bestir oneself, jump up, hurry off

corrōbor·ō -āre -āvī -ātus *tr* **(conr-)** to strengthen, invigorate; *(fig)* to fortify, encourage; *(mil)* to reinforce **‖** *refl & pass* to become mature

cor·rōdō -rōdere -rōsī -rōsus *tr* **(conr-)** to gnaw, chew up

corrog·ō -āre -āvī -ātus *tr* **(conr-)** to go asking for, collect, drum up, solicit; to invite, summon

corrōsus *pp of* **corrōdō**

corrūg·ō -āre -āvī -ātus *tr* **(conr-)** to wrinkle; **nārēs corrūgāre** *(w. dat)* to turn up one's nose at

cor·rumpō -rumpere -rūpī -ruptus *tr* **(conr-)** to burst, to break to pieces, smash; to destroy completely, ruin, waste; to mar; to corrupt; to adulterate; to falsify, tamper with; to bribe; to seduce

corru·ō -ere -ī *tr* **(conr-)** to shatter, wreck, ruin **‖** *intr* to fall down, tumble, sink; *(fig)* to fall, fail, sink

corruptē *adv* **(conr-)** corruptly, perversely; in a lax manner

corruptēl·a -ae *f* **(conr-)** corruption; seduction; bribery; corrupting influence

corrupti·ō -ōnis *f* **(conr-)** corruption, ruining, breaking up; corrupt condition

corrupt·or -ōris *m or* **corruptr·īx -īcis** *f* **(conr-)** corrupter, seducer, briber

corrupt·us -a -um *pp of* **corrumpō (conr-) ‖** *adj* corrupt, spoiled, bad, ruined

Corsic·a -ae *f* Corsica

cort·ex -icis *m (f)* bark, shell, hull, rind; cork; **nāre sine cortice** to swim without a cork life preserver; *(fig)* to be on one's own

cortīn·a -ae *f* kettle, caldron; tripod; *(fig)* vault of heaven

corulus *see* **corylus**

cōrus *see* **caurus**

corūsc·ō -āre -āvī *tr* to shake, wave, brandish **‖** *intr* to flit, flutter; to oscillate; to tremble; to flash, gleam

corūsc·us -a -um *adj* oscillating, vibrating, tremulous; flashing, gleaming, glittering

corv·us -ī *m* raven; *(mil)* grapnel

Corybant·ēs -ium *mpl* the Corybantes *(priests of goddess Cybele)*

Corybanti·us -a -ium *adj* of the Corbyantes

Coryb·ās -antis *m* priest of Cybele

Cōrycid·es -um *fpl* **nymphae Cōrycides** the Muses

Cōryci·us -a -um *adj* of the Corycian mountain-caves on Mt. Parnassus

cōryc·us -ī *m* punching bag

corylēt·um -ī *n* cluster of hazel trees

coryl·us -ī *f* **(-rul-)** hazel tree

corymbif·er -era -erum *adj* wearing *or* carrying clusters of ivy berries **‖** *m* Bacchus

corymb·us -ī *m* cluster *(esp. of ivy berries)*

coryphae·us -ī *m* leader, head

cōrȳt·os *or* **cōrȳt·us -ī** *m* quiver

cōs- = **cōns-**

cōs cōtis *f* whetstone

cosmēt·a -ae *f* slave girl in charge of the wardrobe

cosmic·os -ē -on *adj* worldly, fashionable

cosm·os -ī *m* the universe, cosmos **‖** a chief magistrate of Crete

cost·a -ae *f* rib; *(fig)* side, wall

cost·um -ī *n* perfume

cothurnāt·us -a -um *adj* wearing buskins; suitable to tragedy, tragic

cothurn·us -ī *m* high boot; hunting boot; buskin *(worn by tragic actors);* subject of tragedy; tragedy; lofty style of Greek tragedy

cōtīd- = **cottīd-**

cottab·us -ī *m* game which consisted of flicking drops of wine on a bronze vessel

cottan·a -ōrum *npl* (**-on·a**) Syrian figs

cottīdiānō *adv* (**cōt-, quōt-**) daily

cottīdiān·us -a -um *adj* (**cōt-, quōt-**) daily; everyday, ordinary

cottīdiē *adv* (**cōt-, quōt-**) daily

coturn·īx -īcis *f* quail

Cot·ys -yis *m* name of several Thracian kings

Cotỹtt·ō -ūs *f* Thracian goddess of orgiastic rites

Cotytti·a -ōrum *npl* festival of Cotytto

Cō·us -a -um *adj* Coan, of Cos **‖** *n* Coan wine **‖** *npl* Coan garments

Coüs *see* **Coos**

covinnār·ius -(i)ī *m* soldier who fought from a chariot

covinn·us -ī *m* war chariot (*of Britons and Belgae, with scythes attached to the axles*); coach (*for travel*)

cox·a -ae *f* hip; haunch (*of an animal*)

coxend·īx -īcis *f* hip; hipbone

crābr·ō -ōnis *m* hornet; **irritāre crābrōnēs** (*fig*) to stir up a hornet's nest

cramb·ē -ēs *f* cabbage; **crambē repetīta** warmed-over cabbage; (*fig*) same old story, hackneyed writing

Crant·or -ōris *m* Greek Academic philosopher (*fl 300 B.C.*)

crāpul·a -ae *f* drunkenness; hangover; **crāpulam obdormīre** to sleep off a hangover

crāpulāri·us -a -um *adj* for getting rid of a hangover

crās *adv* tomorrow

crassē *adv* thickly; rudely, confusedly; dimly

crassitūd·ō -inis *f* thickness, density; dregs

crass·us -a -um *adj* thick, dense; stout, plump; (*fig*) dense, dull

Crass·us -ī *m* Lucius Licinius Crassus (*famous orator, d. 90 B.C.*) **‖** Marcus Licinius Crassus Dives (*triumvir*) (*112?–53 B.C.*)

crāstin·us -a -um *adj* tomorrow's; **diē crāstinī** (*old abl form*) tomorrow **‖** *n* tomorrow; **in crāstinum differre** to put off till tomorrow

crāt·ēr -ēris *m* or **crātēr·a -ae** *f* mixing bowl; bowl; crater of a volcano **‖ Crātēr** *m* (*astr*) Bowl (*a constellation*)

crāt·is -is *f* wickerwork; lattice work; harrow; ribs of shield; crisscross structure; cage; (*anat*) rib cage; (*mil*) faggots (*for filling trenches*)

creāti·ō -ōnis *f* election, appointment; procreation (*of children*)

creāt·or -ōris *m* creator; procreator; father; founder; one who appoints

creātr·īx -īcis *f* creatress; mother

crē·ber -bra -brum *adj* numerous, crowded; repeated; frequent; luxuriant, prolific (*growth*)

crēbr·ēscō -ēscere -uī *intr* to increase; to become frequent; to become widespread; to gain strength

crēbrit·ās -ātis *f* frequency; density

crēbrō *adv* repeatedly, frequently, again and again; thickly, densely

crēdibil·is -is -e *adj* credible, trustworthy; convincing, plausible; likely; **crēdibile est** (*w. acc & inf*) it is probable that

crēdibiliter *adv* credibly

crēdit·or -ōris *m* creditor, lender

crēd·ō -ere -idī -itus *tr* to lend, loan; to entrust; to believe, accept as true; to believe in; to think, suppose, imagine; (*w. predicate adj*) to believe to be, regard as **‖** *intr* (*w. dat*) to believe, put faith in, have trust *or* confidence in; **crēdās** one would imagine, you can imagine; **crēde mihi** (*to give assurance*) believe me; **crēdō** (*in replies*) I think so; (*parenthetical*) I suppose **‖** *refl* (*w. dat*) to entrust oneself to **‖** *v impers* **satis crēditum est** it is believed on good evidence

crēdulit·ās -ātis *f* credulity, trustfulness

crēdul·us -a -um *adj* credulous, trustful; gullible; (*w. dat or in + acc*) trusting in

crem·ō -āre -āvī -ātus *tr* to burn; to burn alive; (*of fire*) to consume; to cremate; (*w. dat*) to offer as a burnt offering to

Cremōn·a -ae *f* town in N. Italy

Cremōnēns·is -is -e *adj* of Cremona

crem·or -ōris *m* thick broth; gravy; thickened juice

cre·ō -āre -āvī -ātus *tr* to create; to produce; to elect *or* appoint (*to office*); to cause, occasion; to beget, bear

Cre·ōn -ontis *or* **Cre·ō -onis** *or* **-ōnis** *m* Creon (*brother of Jocasta and brother-in-law of Oedipus*) **‖** Creon (*king of Corinth who gave his daughter in marriage to Jason*)

crep·er -era -erum *adj* dark; (*fig*) obscure, uncertain, doubtful

crepid·a -ae *f* slipper, sandal

crepidāt·us -a -um *adj* wearing sandals *or* slippers

crepīd·ō -inis *f* base, pedestal; pier; dike; curb, sidewalk

crepidul·a -ae *f* small sandal *or* slipper

crepitācill·um -ī *n* small rattle

crepit·ō -āre -āvī -ātum *intr* to make noise, rattle, creak, chatter, rumble, rustle; (*of flames*) to crackle

crepit·us -ūs *m* noise, rattle, creak, chatter, rumble, rustle, crackle; (*vulg*) fart; **crepitum ventris ēmittere in convīviō** (*vulg*) to let a fart at a dinner party; **crepitus digitōrum** snap(ping) of the fingers

crep·ō -āre -uī *tr* to rattle; to talk noisily about, rattle on about **‖** *intr* to make noise, rattle, crackle, creak, chatter, rustle; (*of the stom-*

ach) to rumble; *(of doors)* to creak; *(of flames)* to crackle; *(vulg)* to fart

crepundi·a -ōrum *npl* toy rattle; **in crepundiīs** in earliest childhood

crepūscul·um -ī *n* twilight; dimness, obscurity **‖** *npl* darkness

Crēs Crētis *m* a Cretan; Cretan dog

crēscō crēscere crēvī crētum *intr* to come into being, arise; to grow, grow up; to increase *(in size, amount, numbers, length, quantity, dimensions);* to swell; to expand; *(of rivers)* to rise; *(of period of time)* to advance, progress; to prosper, thrive; to become great; to swell with pride; **crēscunt nōbīs animī** our spirits rise; **diē crēscente** as the day progressed

Crēsi·us -a -um *adj* Cretan

Cress·a -ae *adj (fem only)* Cretan; of chalk **‖** *f* Cretan woman; Ariadne

crēt·a -ae *f* whitish clay; clayey soil; chalk; finish line *(in a chariot race);* **crēta figulāris** *(or* **figlīna)** potter's clay; **crēta fullōnia** fuller's earth; **crēta sūtōria** shoe polish

Crēt·a -ae *or* **Crēt·ē -ēs** *f* Crete; *(fig)* the Cretans

Crētae·us -a -um *adj* Cretan

Crētān·ī -ōrum *mpl* Cretans

crētāt·us -a -um *adj* whitened with chalk *(feet of slaves about to be auctioned off);* dressed in white *(as candidate)*

Crētēns·is -is -e *adj & m* Cretan **‖** *n* Cretan wine

crēte·us -a -um *adj* of chalk, of clay, clayey

Crētic·us -a -um *adj* Cretan **‖** *m (pros)* Cretic (foot) (— ‿ —)

crēti·ō -ōnis *f (leg)* formal acceptance of an inheritance; *(leg)* terms laid down for making the declaration of acceptance

Crēt·is -idis *adj (fem only)* Cretan

crētōs·us -a -um *adj* clayey

crētul·a -ae *f* white clay

crēt·us -a -um *pp of* **cernō** *and of* **crēscō ‖** *adj (w. abl or* **ab** *or* **dē)** sprung from

Creūs·a -ae *f* daughter of Priam and wife of Aeneas **‖** daughter of Creon (king of Corinth), and wife of Jason **‖** mother of Ion

crībr·um -ī *n* sieve; **imbrem in crībrum gerere** *(prov)* to swim against the tide *(literally, to carry rain water in(to) a sieve)*

crīm·en -inis *n* indictment; reproach; guilt; crime; **esse in crīmine** to be arraigned; **in crīmen addūcī** *(or* **pōnī** *or* **venīre** *or* **vocārī)** to be indicted; *(of actions)* to be called into question

crīmināl·is -is -e *adj (leg) (opp.* **cīvīlis)** criminal

crīmināti·ō -ōnis *f* indictment; accusation; slander

crīmināt·or -ōris *m* accuser

crīmin·ō -āre *or* **crīmin·or -ārī -ātus sum** *tr* to indict, accuse; to slander; to complain of; to denounce

crīminōsē *adv* by way of accusation, accusingly; slanderously

crīminōs·us -a -um *adj* accusatory, reproachful; shameful

crīnāl·is -is -e *adj* for the hair; **acus crīnālis** hairpin **‖** *n* hairpin

crīn·is -is *m (f)* hair *(of the head);* lock of hair; tail of a comet

crīnīt·us -a -um *adj* long-haired; **crīnīta dracōnibus ōra** *(Medusa's)* snake-haired head; **crīnītae angue sorōrēs** snake-haired sisters; **stella crīnīta** *(or* **sidus crīnītum)** comet

crīs·ō -āre -āvī -ātum *intr (sl) (of a woman)* to wiggle the buttocks, shake it up *(cf.* **ceveō)**

crīsp·āns -antis *adj* curly; wrinkled

crīsp·ō -āre -āvī -ātus *tr* to curl, wave *(hair);* to wave, brandish *(weapons)*

crīspul·us -a -um *adj* having short curly hair

crīsp·us -a -um *adj* curled, waved; curly-headed; wrinkled; tremulous, quivering

crist·a -ae *f* cockscomb; crest, plume

cristāt·us -a -um *adj* crested, plumed

critic·a -ōrum *npl* literary criticism

critic·us -ī *m* critic

croce·us -a -um *adj* of saffron; yellow, golden

crocin·um -ī *n* saffron oil *(used as perfume)*

crōc·iō *or* **grōc·iō -īre** *intr* to croak

crocodīl·us -ī *m* **(-dill-)** crocodile

crocōt·a -ae *f* saffron-colored dress *(worn by women and transvestites)*

crocōtāri·us -a -um *adj* of saffron-colored clothes

crocōtul·a -ae *f* saffron-colored dress

croc·us -ī *m or* **croc·um -ī** *n* saffron; saffron color; saffron oil

Croes·us -ī *m* king of Lydia, famous for his wealth *(590?–546 B.C.)*

crotalistri·a -ae *f* castinet dancer

crotal·um -ī *n* castanet

Crotō(n) -ōnis *or* **Crotōn·a -ae** *f* Crotona *(town in S. Italy)*

cruciābilitāt·ēs -um *fpl* torments

cruciābiliter *adv* with torture

cruciāment·um -ī *n* torture

cruciāt·us -ūs *m* torture; mental torment; instrument of torture

cruci·ō -āre -āvī -ātus *tr* to put on the rack, torture; *(fig)* to torment **‖** *refl or pass* to suffer mental anguish

crūdēl·is -is -e *adj* cruel, hardhearted; *(w.* **in** *+ acc)* cruel toward

crūdēlit·ās -ātis *f* cruelty

crūdēliter *adv* cruelly

crūd·ēscō -ēscere -uī *intr* to become fierce; *(of battle, disease)* to get rough crūdit·ās -ātis *f* indigestion

crūd·us -a -um *adj* bloody, bleeding; uncooked *(food);* raw *(meat; wound);* unripe, green *(fruit);* untanned *(hide);* undigested *(food);* suffering from indigestion; hoarse; hardy, vigorous *(old age);* coarse, rude; fierce, wild, savage

cruent·ō -āre -āvī -ātus *tr* to bloody, stain with blood; *(fig)* to wound

cruent·us -a -um *adj* gory, blood-stained; bloodthirsty; blood-red

-cr·um -ī *neut suf* denoting place or instrument: **ambulācrum** a walk, avenue; **involūcrum** wrapper, envelope

crumēn·a -ae *f* (-mīn-) purse, pouch; *(fig)* money supply

crumill·a -ae *f* small purse

cru·or -ōris *m* blood, gore ‖ *mpl* bloodshed, murder

cruppellāri·ī -ōrum *mpl* warriors in full armor

crūrāl·is -is -e *adj* of the shin; **fāsciae crūrālēs** puttees

crūricrepid·a -ae *m (hum) (of one who has chains rattling around his legs)* "rattle-legs"

Crūrifrag·ius -(i)ī *m (comic slave name)* "Broken-shins"

crūs crūris *n* leg; shin; upper support of a bridge

crūscul·um -ī *n* little leg

crusm·a -atis *n* tune

crūst·a -ae *f* crust, shell; peel, rind; inlaid work

crūstul·um -ī *n* cookie

crūst·um -ī *n* pastry

Crustumīnus -a -um *adj* of Crustumerium *or* Crustumium *(town in the Sabine district of Italy)*

crux crucis *f* cross; crucifixion; torment; tormentor; **ī in malam crucem!** *(coll)* go hang yourself!

crypt·a -ae *f* (cru-) underground passage, covered gallery; tunnel; crypt

cryptoportic·us -ūs *f* covered walk

crystallīn·us -a -um *adj* (crus-) made of crystal ‖ *npl* crystal vases

crystall·us -ī *f or* crystall·um -ī *n* (crus-) crystal

cub·āns -antis *adj* lying down; low-lying

cubiculāri·us -a -um *adj* bedroom ‖ *m* chamberlain

cubicul·um -ī *n* bedroom; room; emperor's box in the theater *or* circus; **ā cubiculō** (imperial) chamberlain

cubīl·e -is *n* bed, couch; marriage bed; lair, nest, hole; kennel

cubit·al -ālis *n* elbow cushion

cubitāl·is -is -e *adj* of the elbow; one cubit long *(i.e., 17 to 21 inches)*

cubit·ō -āre -āvī -ātum *intr* to lie down, be in the habit of lying down; *(w.* **cum)** to go to bed with, have intercourse with

cubit·um -ī *n* elbow; forearm; cubit; **cubitum pōnere** *(fig)* to sit down to dinner

cubitūr·a -ae *f* reclining, lying down

cubit·us -ūs *m* lying down; sexual intercourse

cub·ō -āre -uī *or* -āvī -itum *intr* to lie, lie down; to recline at table; to lie in bed; to take one's rest, sleep; to be confined to bed; *(of bones)* to rest; *(of roof)* to slope; *(of towns)* to lie on a slope; *(w.* **cum)** to have intercourse with

cub·us -ī *m* cube; lump

cucull·us -ī *m* cowl, hood

cucūl·us -ī *m* cuckoo; *(pej)* ninny

cucum·a -ae *f* large kettle *(for cooking)*

cucum·is -is *or* -eris *m* cucumber

cucurbit·a -ae *f* gourd; *(sl)* dolt, dummy; *(med)* cupping glass

cūd·ō -ere *tr* to strike, beat, pound; to thresh; to forge; to coin, stamp

cūi·ās *or* cūi·ātis -ātis *interrog pron* from what country?; **Scīpiō eum percontātus est quis et cūiās esset** Scipio asked who he was and from what country he came

cuicuimodī *or* quoiquoimodī *adj* of any kind, of whatever sort

cūius *(gen of* **quī, quae, quod, quis, quid)** *pron (interrog)* whose, of whom ‖ *(interrog)* whose?

cūiusnam *(gen of* **quisnam, quidnam)** *pron (interrog)* just whose, exactly whose?

cūiuscemodī, cūiusmodī *adj* which kind of?

-cul·a -ae *fem suf* forms diminutives: **uxorcula** dear wife

culcit·a -ae *f* mattress, feather tick; cushion, pillow

culcitell·a *or* culcitul·a -ae *f* small cushion

cūleus *see* **culleus**

cul·ex *or* cul·ix -icis *mf* gnat

culīn·a -ae *f* kitchen; cuisine

culle·us -ī *m* (cūle-) leather bag *(for holding liquids);* leather sack *(in which criminals were sewn and drowned);* *(sl)* scrotum

culm·en -inis *n* peak; summit; stalk; *(fig)* pinnacle, height; **fabae culmen** bean stalk

culm·us -ī *m* stalk, stem; straw, thatch; hay

culp·a -ae *f* fault, blame; sense of guilt; imperfection, fault, defect; *(poet)* cause of blame; **in culpā esse** *(or* **versārī)** to be at fault

culpit·ō -āre *tr* to blame

culp·ō -āre -āvī -ātus *tr* to blame, reproach; to find fault with, complain of

cult·a -ōrum *npl* standing crops; grain fields

cultē *adv* elegantly, tastefully

cultell·us -ī *m* small knife

cul·ter -trī *m* knife; razor; plowshare

culti·ō -ōnis *f* cultivation, tilling

cult·or -ōris *m* tiller, cultivator, planter, farmer; inhabitant; supporter; worshipper

cultrār·ius -(i)ī *m* one who slew the victim

cultr·īx -īcis *f* cultivator *(female)*; worshipper *(female)*; inhabitant *(female)*

cultūr·a -ae *f* tilling, cultivating; agriculture; cultivation *(e.g., of the mind, important friendships)*

cult·us -a -um *pp* of **colō** ‖ *adj* tilled, cultivated; neat, prim; refined, civilized, cultured

cult·us -ūs *m* tilling, cultivation; care, tending *(of flocks)*; training, education; culture, refinement, civilization; high style of living; luxury; style of dress, fancy clothes; fancy outfit; worship, reverence; cult; management *(of a household)*; **cultus corporis** personal grooming; **cultus vītae** standard of living

culull·us -ī *m* drinking cup, goblet

-cul·um -ī *neut suf* **1** denoting places: **cubiculum** place for sleeping; **2** denoting instruments: **curriculum** small chariot

cūl·us -ī *m (sl)* ass, anus

-cul·us -ī *masc suf* **1** forming diminutives: **pisciculus** little fish; **2** nouns ending in -ō, -ōnis and -ō -inis take the form -un- before the suffix -culus: **sermunculus** small talk; **homunculus** little man, puny person

cum *prep (w. abl)* **1** *(accompaniment)* with, together with; **2** *(time)* at the same time with, at the time of, at, with; **3** *(circumstance, manner, etc.)* with, under, in, in the midst of, among, in connection with; **cum eō quod** *or* **cum eō ut** on the condition that; **cum pāce** peacefully; **cum prīmā lūce** at dawn; **cum prīmīs** especially, particularly; **mēcum** at my house; with me

cum, quum, *or* **quom** *conj* when, at the time when; whenever; while, as; since, now that, because; although; **cum maximē** just when; especially when, just while; just then; **cum prīmum** as soon as; **cum ... tum** both . . . and, not only ... but also, while ... so too; **praesertim cum** *or* **cum praesertim** especially since; **quippe cum** since of course; **utpote cum** seeing that

Cūm·ae -ārum *fpl* town near Naples, residence of its famous Sibyl

Cūmae·us -a -um *adj* Cumaean

Cūmān·us -a -um *adj* Cumaean ‖ *n* Cicero's estate near Cumae

cūmātil·is -is -e *adj* sea-blue

cumb·a *or* **cymb·a -ae** *f* boat

cumer·a -ae *f* bin

cumīn·um -ī *n* cumin *(medicinal plant, said to produce paleness)*

cummi *indecl n or* **cumm·is -is** *f* **(gumm-)** gum

cumque, cunque, *or* **quomque** *adv* at any time

-cumque *suf added to relative pronouns and pronominal adverbs:* **quīcumque** whoever; **ubicumque** wherever

cumulātē *adv* completely, abundantly

cumulāt·us -a -um *adj* heaped; abundant, vast, great; *(w. gen or abl)* abounding in

cumul·ō -āre -āvī -ātus *tr* to heap up, pile up; accumulate; to fill up, overload; to increase, augment; *(fig)* to crown

cumul·us -ī *m* heap, pile; increase; *(fig)* finishing touch, crown; *(fig)* peak, pinnacle; **summus cumulus** highest point

cūnābul·a -ōrum *npl* cradle

cūn·ae -ārum *fpl* cradle; *(poet)* nest

cunctābund·us -a -um *adj* hesitant

cunct·āns -antis *adj* hesitant, slow to act; clinging

cunctanter *adv* hesitantly, slowly

cunctāti·ō -ōnis *f* hesitation, reluctance, delay

cunctāt·or -ōris *m* dawdler, slow-poke, procrastinator ‖ **Cunctātor** Quintus Fabius Maximus Cunctator *(cautious general who constantly avoided battles with Hannibal, d. 203 B.C.)*

cunct·or -ārī -ātus sum *intr* to hesitate, delay, linger; to be in doubt; **cunctātū brevī** after a moment's hesitation

cūnct·us -a -um *adj* all together, the whole, all, entire

-cund·us -a -um *adjl suf* denoting a tendency: **īrācundus** inclined toward anger, irascible

cuneātim *adv* in the form of a wedge, in tight formation

cuneāt·us -a -um *adj* wedge-shaped

cune·ō -āre -āvī -ātus *tr* to fasten with a wedge; *(fig)* to wedge in, squeeze in

cuneol·us -ī *m* small wedge; pin

cune·us -ī *m* wedge; wedge-form section of seats in the theater; *(mil)* troops formed in shape of wedge

cunīculōsus -a -um *adj* full of rabbits

cunīcul·us -ī *m* rabbit; burrow, hole; tunnel; water conduit, channel; *(mil)* mine

cunil·a -ae *f (bot)* savory *(aromatic plant used as seasoning)*

cunn·us -ī *m (vulg)* cunt

cunque *see* **cumque**

cūp·a -ae *f* vat

cūpēd- = cuppēd-

cupidē *adv* eagerly

Cupīdine·us -a -um *adj* Cupid's, charming, alluring

cupidit·ās -ātis *f* eagerness, longing, desire; passion, lust; ambition; greed; object of one's desire

cupīd·ō *or* **cūpēdō** *or* **cuppēdō -inis** *mf* eagerness, desire; carnal desire, lust; greed ‖ **Cupīdō** *m* Cupid, son of Venus

cupid·us -a -um adj eager; lecherous; ambitious; (w. gen) desirous of, longing for, fond of, enthusiastic about

cupi·ēns -entis adj eager, enthusiastic; (w. gen) desirous of, longing for, fond of, enthusiastic about

cupienter adv eagerly

cup·iō -ere -īvī or **-iī -ītus** tr to wish, be eager for, long for, desire

cupīt·or -ōris m daydreamer

cuppēdenār·ius -(i)ī m pastry baker

cuppēdi·a -ōrum npl or **cūpēdi·a -ae** f sweets; delicacies; sweet tooth

cuppēdinār·ius -(i)ī m (**cūpēd-**) confectioner

cuppēd·ō -inis f see **cupīdō**

cupp·es -edis adj fond of sweets; gluttonous

cupressēt·um -ī n cypress grove

cupresse·us -a -um adj cypress

cupressif·er -era -erum adj cypress-bearing

cupress·us -ī or **-ūs** f cypress tree

cūr or **quor** adv why

cūr·a -ae f care, concern, worry; carefulness, attention, pains; heartache; object of concern; sweetheart; task, reponsibility, post; administration, management, charge; trusteeship, care; guardian, keeper; study, reflection; literary effort, study, literary work; (w. gen) eagerness for, anxiety about, zeal for; (med) treatment; (med) cure; **in cūrā esse** (w. dat) to be a matter of concern to, be dear to; **in cūrā habēre** to hold dear, care dearly about; **cūrā** purposely; **cūrae esse** (w. dat) to be of concern to; to be dear to; **cūrae habēre** to hold dear

cūrābil·is -is -e adj troublesome; needing medical treatment

cūral·ium -(i)ī n coral

cūrāti·ō -ōnis f management, administration; office; (med) treatment

cūrātius adv more carefully

cūrāt·or -ōris m superintendent, manager; (leg) guardian

cūrātūr·a -ae f care, attention; superintendence

cūrāt·us -a -um adj well cared-for; anxious, sollicitous, earnest

curculi·ō -ōnis m (**gurg-**) weevil; (vulg) penis

curculiuncul·us -ī m little weevil; (fig) trifle

Cur·ēs -ium mpl ancient Sabine town

Cūrēt·es -um mpl people of Crete who attended Jupiter at his birth

cūri·a -ae f senate building; meeting of the senate; curia, ward (one of the 30 wards into which Romulus had divided the people)

cūriāl·is -is -e adj belonging to a ward **‖** m ward member

cūriātim adv by wards

cūriāt·us -a -um adj composed of wards; passed by the assembly of wards; **comitia cūriāta** assembly of wards, curiate assembly

cūri·ō -ōnis m ward boss; **cūriō maximus** chief ward boss

cūriōsē adv carefully; curiously

cūriōsit·ās -ātis f curiosity, inquisitiveness

cūriōs·us -a -um careful, diligent; curious, inquisitive; careworn

cur·is or **quir·is -ītis** f spear

cūr·ō -āre -āvī -ātus tr to take care of, look after, attend to, trouble oneself about; to worry about; to take charge of, see to; to procure; to provide for the payment of, settle up; to attend to (the body with food, washing, etc.); (med) to treat; (med) to cure; **cūrā ut** see to it that; (at end of letter) **cūrā ut valeās** take care of yourself; **cutem cūrāre** to look after one's appearance

curriculō adv at full speed, on the double

curricul·um -ī n race; lap; racetrack; racing chariot; (fig) career

currō currere cucurrī cursus tr to run over, skim over, traverse **‖** intr to run, dash; to sail; to move quickly, flow along; to fly; (of night, day) to pass

curr·us -ūs m chariot, car; war chariot; triumphal car; triumph; racing chariot; (poet) plow wheel; (poet) ship

cursim adv on the double, quickly

cursit·ō -āre -āvī intr to keep running around, run up and down; to vibrate

curs·ō -āre -āvī intr to run around, run up and down

curs·or -ōris m runner, racer; courier; errand boy

cursūr·a -ae f running; haste, speed

curs·us -ūs m running, speeding, speed; trip; course, direction; suitable time or weather for travel; rapid movement, flow; progress; **magnō cursū** at top speed; **cursus honōrum** political career

Curt·ius -a -um adj Roman clan name (nomen), esp. Quintus Curtius Rufus (who wrote a history of Alexander the Great's campaigns) **‖ Lacus Curtius** area of the Roman Forum that was once a pond

curt·ō -āre -āvī -ātus tr to shorten; (hum) to circumcise

curt·us -a -um adj shortened; gelded, castrated; (hum) circumcised; broken; defective

curūl·is -is -e adj official, curule; **aedīlis curūlis** patrician aedile; **sella curūlis** curule chair, official chair (inlaid with ivory, used by consuls, praetors, and patrician aediles)

curvām·en -inis n curve, bend

curvātūr·a -ae f curvature; **curvātūra rotae** rim of a wheel

curv·ō -āre -āvī -ātus *tr* to curve, bend, arch; *(fig)* to affect, move, stir
curv·us -a -um *adj* curved, bent; crooked; concave, arched; hollow, winding *(stream, shore); (fig)* crooked ‖ *n* wrong, crookedness
-c·us -a -um *adjl suf formed from nouns:* **bellicus** warlike
cusp·is -idis *f* point; bayonet; spearhead; spear, javelin; trident; scepter; sting *(of a scorpion)*
custōdēl·a -ae *f* charge, custody *(of a person or thing)*
custōdi·a -ae *f* protection, safekeeping, defense; preservation *(of a practice, etc.);* place for safekeeping; watch, care; sentry, guard; sentry post; custody, confinement, prison; prisoner, *(collectively)* prisoners; **custōdiam agitāre** to be on guard; **in lībera custōdiā** under surveillance, under house arrest
custōd·iō -īre -īvī *or* **-iī -ītus** *tr* to guard, watch over, protect, defend; to hold in custody; to keep an eye on; to keep carefully, preserve; **memoriā custōdīre** to keep in mind
cust·ōs -ōdis *m* guard; guardian; watchman; protector; jailer; *(mil)* sentinel; **custōs corporis** bodyguard ‖ *mpl* garrison ‖ *f* guardian; protectress; container
cutīcul·a -ae *f* (thin external) skin, cuticle
cut·is -is *f* skin; **cutem cūrāre** to look after one's appearance; *(fig)* to look after one's own skin
Cyan·ē -ēs *f* a spring in Syracuse; nymph who was changed into that spring
cyathiss·ō -āre -āvī *intr* to ladle out wine
cyath·us -ī *m* ladle; liquid measure *(half pint)*
cybae·a -ae *f* merchant ship
Cybel·ē -ēs *f* (**Cybēbē**) Phrygian goddess of fertility, worshipped in Rome as Ops *or* Magna Mater ‖ mountain of Phrygia
Cybelēi·us -a -um *adj* of Cybele
Cybel·us -ī *m* mountain in Phrygia
cyb·ium -(i)i *n* young tuna
cycladāt·us -a -um *adj* wearing a formal gown
Cyclad·es -um *fpl* Cyclades *(group of islands, roughly forming a circle, in the Aegean Sea)*
cycl·as -adis *f* woman's formal gown
cyclic·us -a -um *adj* cyclic; **poēta cyclicus** cyclic poet *(one of a group of poets treating epic sagas revolving around the Trojan War)*
Cyclōpi·us -a -um *adj* Cyclopean
Cycl·ōps -ōpis *m* one-eyed giant of Sicily, *esp.* Polyphemus
cycn·us -ī *m* (**cyg-**) swan; *(fig)* poet ‖ **Cycnus** king of the Ligurians, changed into a swan, and placed among the stars as a constellation ‖ son of Neptune
Cyd·ōn -ōnis *adj* Cydonian, of Cydonea *(a city on the N. coast of Crete)* ‖ *m* inhabitant of Cydonea

Cydōnae·us -a -um *adj* (**-ē·us**) Cydonian; *(esp. as poetic epithet for arrows)* Cretan
Cydōne·a -ae *f* city on the N. coast of Crete
Cydōni·us -a -um *adj* Cretan ‖ *n* quince
cygnus *see* **cycnus**
cylindr·us -ī *m* cylinder; roller *(for rolling the ground);* cylindrical jewel
Cyllēn·ē -ēs *or* **-ae** *f* mountain in Arcadia where Mercury was said to have been born
Cyllēn·us *or* **Cyllēni·us -a -um** *adj* of Mt. Cyllene ‖ *m* Mercury
cymb·a -ae *f* (**cum-**) boat
cymbal·um *or* **cymbal·on -ī** *n* (*usu. pl, esp. as used in the worship of Cybele*) cymbal; *(fig)* tedious speaker
cymb·ium -(i)ī *n* small cup
Cynicē *adv* like the Cynics
Cynic·us -a -um *adj* Cynic, relating to the Cynic philosophy ‖ *m* Cynic philosopher, *esp.* Diogenes, its founder *(412–323 B.C.)*
cynocephal·us -ī *m* dog-headed ape
Cynosūr·a -ae *f (astr)* Cynosure *(the constellation Ursa Minor)*
Cynthi·us -a -um *adj* of Mt. Cynthus; Cynthian ‖ *m* Apollo ‖ *f* Diana
Cynth·us -ī *m* low mountain on Delos, where Latona is said to have given birth to Apollo and Diana
cypariss·us -ī *f* cypress tree
cypress·us -ī *or* **-ūs** *f* cypress tree; box made of cypress
Cypri·us -a -um *adj* Cypriote; **aes Cyprium** copper ‖ *f* Venus
Cypr·us *or* **Cyp·ros -ī** *f* Cyprus *(island off S. coast of Asia Minor)*
Cypsel·us -ī *m* despot of Corinth *(reigned 655–625 B.C.)*
Cyrēnae·us -a -um *or* **Cyrēnaic·us -a -um** *or* **Cyrēnēns·is -is -e** *adj* of Cyrene
Cyrēn·ē -ēs *f or* **Cyrēn·ae -ārum** *fpl* chief city of Greek settlement in N.E. Africa
Cyrē·us -a -um *adj* of Cyprus
Cyrnē·us -a -um *adj* Corsican
Cyrn·os -ī *f* Greek name for Corsica
Cyr·us -ī *m* father of Cambyses and founder of the Persian monarchy in 559 B.C. *(d. 529 B.C.)* ‖ Cyrus the Younger, son of Darius Nothus, whose famous march against his brother Artaxerxes is recorded by Xenophon *(d. 401 B.C.)*
Cyt·ae -ārum *fpl* town in Colchis, reputed birthplace of Medea
Cytae·is -idis *f* Medea
Cythēr·a -ōrum *npl* island off the S. coast of the Peloponnesus, famous for the worship of Venus
Cytherē·is -idis *f* Venus
Cytherēi·us -a -um *adj* Cytherean; **hērōs Cythereïus** Aeneas ‖ *f* Venus

Cytherē·us -a -um *adj* Cytherean ‖ *f* Venus
cytis·us -ī *mf or* **cytis·um -ī** *n* clover
Cytōriāc·us -a -um *adj* of Cytorus, Cytorian; **pecten Cytōriācus** comb made of boxwood
Cytōr·us *or* **Cytōr·os -ī** *m* mountain in Paphlagonia, famous for its boxwood
Cȳzicēn·us -a -um *adj* of Cyzicus
Cyzic·um -ī *n or* **Cyzic·us** *or* **Cyzic·os -ī** *f* town on S. coast of Propontis

D

D, d *(supply* littera*)* *f* fourth letter of the Latin alphabet; letter name: **de**
D *abbr* **quīngentī** five hundred
D. *abbr* **Decimus** *(Roman first name, praenomen)*
Dāc·ī -ōrum *mpl* Dacians
Dāci·a -ae *f* Roman province on the lower Danube *(roughly modern Romania)*
Dācic·us -a -um *adj* Dacian ‖ *m* gold coin struck under Domitian, conqueror of Dacia
dactylic·us -a -um *adj (pros)* dactylic
dactyliothēc·a -ae *f* ring case
dactyl·us -ī *m (pros)* dactyl (— ◡ ◡)
daedal·us -a -um *adj* skillful, artistic; intricately constructed ‖ **Daedal·us -ī** *m* builder of the Labyrinth in Crete and the first person to construct wings and fly
Damascēn·us -a -um *adj* of Damascus ‖ *npl* plums from Damascus
Damasc·us *or* **Damasc·os -ī** *f* city in Syria
damm·a *or* **dām·a -ae** *f* deer; venison
damnāti·ō -ōnis *f* condemnation; *(w. gen of the crime)* conviction on the charge of; **damnātiō ambitūs** conviction on illegal campaign practices; **condemnātiō pecūniae** a fine
damnātōri·us -a -um *adj (leg)* guilty *(verdict)*
damnāt·us -a -um *adj (leg)* found guilty; hateful, damn
damnific·us -a -um *adj* harmful
damnigerul·us -a -um *adj* injurious
damn·ō -āre -āvī -ātus *tr (leg)* to find guilty, convict; to sentence, condemn; to secure the condemnation of; to offer as a sacrifice, doom to the gods below; to pass judgment on *(a case); (w. dat of the aggrieved person)* to deliver by judicial sentence to, award *(s.o. s.th.); (w. abl)* to fine *(s.o.)* in the amount of; *(w. gen or abl)* to find fault with for; *(w. gen or abl of the charge)* to find *(s.o.)* guilty of; **aliquem vōtī damnāre** to condemn s.o. to the amount he has vowed; **capite** *(or* **capitis)* **damnāre** to condemn to death; **dē māiestāte damnāre** to find guilty of treason; **exiliō**

damnārī to be sentenced to exile; **vōtī damnāre** to oblige *(s.o.)* to fulfill a vow
damnōsē *adv* ruinously, with great loss
damnōs·us -a -um *adj* damaging, destructive; prodigal; **canēs damnōsī** crap *(worst throw of dice)*
damn·um -ī *n* loss, damage, harm; fine; defect; *(w. gen)* forfeiture of; *(mil)* losses; **damnum explēre** *(or* **sarcīre)** to make good a loss; **damnum facere** to incur a loss; to cause loss *(to another);* **nātūrae damnum** a natural defect
Dana·ē -ēs *f* daughter of Acrisius and mother, by Zeus, of Perseus
Danaïd·es -um *fpl* fifty daughters of Danaüs
Dana·üs -ī *m* Danaüs *(son of Belus and brother of Aegyptus and king of Argos)* ‖ *mpl* Greeks
danīst·a -ae *m* moneylender, banker
danīstic·us -a -um *adj* moneylending, banking
danō *see* **dō**
Dānuv·ius -(i)ī *m* (**Dānub-**) Upper Danube *(opp:* **Hister** = Lower Danube)
Daphn·ē -ēs *f* nymph *(daughter of the river-god Peneus, pursued by Apollo and changed into a laurel tree)*
Daphn·is -idis *(acc:* **-im** *or* **-in)** *m* handsome young Sicilian shepherd, inventor of pastoral poetry
dapin·ō -āre *tr* to serve *(food)*
dap·s -is *f* ceremonial feast; feast; banquet; feed *(for animals)*
dapsil·is -is -e *adj* sumptuous, costly
Dardanid·ēs -ae *m* descendant of Dardanus; Trojan; Roman
Dardan·is -idis *or* **-idos** *adj (fem only)* Trojan
Dardan·us -a -um *adj* Dardanian, Trojan; Roman *(descendant of Aeneas)* ‖ *m* son of Jupiter and ancestor of the Trojan race ‖ *mpl* Illyrian tribe; a people of Asia Minor
Dārē·us *or* **Dārī·us -ī** *m* Darius *(521–485 B.C., Persian king whose generals were defeated by the Greeks at Marathon in 490 B.C.)* ‖ Darius Nothus *(424–405 B.C., son of Artaxerxes I)* ‖ Darius Codomanus *(last king of Persia, reigned 336–331 B.C.)*
datāri·us -a -um *adj* to be handed out, to be given away
datātim *adv* by giving *or* tossing from hand to hand *(in games)*
dati·ō -ōnis *f* giving, allotting; transfer *(e.g., of property)*
datīv·us -a -um *adj & m (gram)* dative
dat·ō -āre -āvī -ātus *tr* to keep giving
dat·or -ōris *m* giver; *(in playing ball)* passer
dat·us -ūs *m* giving
Daul·is -idis *f* town in Phocis, famous for the fable of Procne and Philomela

Daun·us -ī *m* mythical king of Apulia, the father of Turnus

dē- (de- before vowels and **h)** *pref* indicating: **1** motion down from or away: **dēpendēre** to hang down; **2** removal, deprivation: **dēspolīre** to despoil; **3** left behind: **dērelinquere** to leave behind; **4** reversal of process: **deonerāre** to unload; **5** completely, to the end: **dēpugnāre** to fight it out, fight to the finish; **6** down, from the right path or state or norm: **dēfōrmis** ugly; **7** intensity: **deamāre** to love passionately

dē *prep (w. abl)* **1** (*of space*) down from, from, away from, out of; **2** (*of origin*) from, of, descended from: **Priamī dē stirpe Diōrēs** Diores of Priam's lineage; **3** (*of separation*) from among, out of: **noctem dē diē facere** to make night out of day; **4** (*in partitive sense*) of, out of: **dīmidium dē praedā dare** to give half of the booty; **5** (*of time*) immediately after; **diem dē diē** day after day; **6** (*of reference*) about, on, concerning, of, in respect to: **ōrātiō dē domō suā** a speech concerning his own home; **7** according to, in imitation of: **castae dē mōre puellae** like a chaste girl (*literally, according to the manner of a chaste girl*); **8** (*of cause*) for, on account of, because of: **quā dē causā** for that reason, wherefore; **9** (*of which s.th. is made*) **templum dē marmore** a marble temple, a temple (made) of marble; **10** (*indicating persons over whom victory is gained*) over: **dē Samnitibus triumphāvit** he held a triumph for his victory over the Samnites; **11** (*indicating change*) from, out of: **dē templō carcerem facere** to make a prison out of a temple; **dē imprōvīsō** unexpectedly; **dē industriā** on purpose, intentionally; **dē integrō** afresh, all over again; **dē nocte** (*or* **dē vigiliā**) at night; **dē novō** anew

de·a -ae (*dat & abl pl:* **deābus**) *f* goddess

dealb·ō -āre -āvī -ātus *tr* to whiten, whitewash

deambulāti·ō -ōnis *f* strolling, walking about, walk, stroll

deambul·ō -āre -āvī -ātum *intr* to go for a walk

deam·ō -āre -āvī -ātus *tr* to love passionately; to be much obliged to

dearm·ō -āre -āvī -ātus *tr* to disarm

deartu·ō -āre -āvī -ātus *tr* to tear limb from limb, dismember

deasci·ō -āre -āvī -ātus *tr* to smooth with an ax; (*fig*) to cheat, con

dēbacch·or -ārī -ātus sum *intr* to rant and rave

dēbellāt·or -ōris *m* conqueror

dēbell·ō -āre -āvī -ātus *tr* to fight it out with, wear down, subdue **‖** *intr* to fight it out to the end; to bring a war to an end

dēb·eō -ēre -uī -itus *tr* to owe; to be responsible for; (*w. inf*) **1** to have to, be obliged to; **2** to be destined to; **dēbeō abīre** I ought to leave **‖** *pass* (*w. dat*) to be due to

dēbil·is -is -e *adj* crippled, frail, feeble; ineffective

dēbilit·ās -ātis *f* lameness; debility, weakness, feebleness

dēbilitāti·ō -ōnis *f* disabling, enfeebling

dēbilit·ō -āre -āvī -ātus *tr* to disable; to debilitate, weaken; to unnerve; (*fig*) to paralyze

dēbiti·ō -ōnis *f* debt

dēbit·or -ōris *m* debtor; person under obligation

dēbit·um -ī *n* debt; obligation

dēblater·ō -āre -āvī -ātus *tr & intr* to blurt out

dēcant·ō -āre -āvī -ātus *tr* to repeat monotonously; to reel off **‖** *intr* to sing on to the end; to stop singing

dē·cēdō -cēdere -cessī -cessum *intr* to withdraw, depart, clear out; to retreat; to make way, make room, yield; to disappear; to die; to abate, subside, cease; to go wrong; (*w. dat*) to give in to; (*w.* **dē** + *abl*) to give up, abandon, relinquish

decem *indecl adj* ten

Decem·ber -bris -bre *adj* December, of December; **mēnsis December** (month of) December (*tenth month of the Roman calendar until 153 B.C.*) **‖** **Decem·ber -bris** *m* December

decemiug·is -is *m* ten-horse chariot

decemped·a -ae *f* ten-foot measuring rod

decempedāt·or -ōris *m* surveyor

decempl·ex -icis *adj* tenfold

decemprīm·ī *or* **decem prīm·ī -ōrum** *mpl* tenman council (*governing Italic towns*)

decemscalm·us -a -um *adj* ten-oared

decem·vir -virī *m* decemvir (*member of a board of ten*)

decemvirāl·is -is -e *adj* decemviral; **lēgēs decemvirālēs** laws passed by the decemviri

decemvirāt·us -ūs *m* decemvirate

decemvir·ī -ōrum *mpl* board of ten (*appointed in Rome at different times and for various purposes: maintaining Sibylline books, distribution of land; codifying the XII Tables; deciding whether a person was free or slave*); **decemvirī sacrīs faciundīs** commission for attending to religious matters

decenn·is -is -e *adj* ten-year

dec·ēns -entis *adj* decent, proper, becoming; handsome, pretty

decenter *adv* decently, properly

decenti·a -ae *f* decency, propriety

dē·cernō -cernere -crēvī -crētus *tr* to sift, separate; to decide, determine, settle; to resolve, decree, vote; to decide by combat; to fight, combat **‖** *intr* to contend, compete, struggle;

to put forward a proposal; *(w.* **dē** *or* **prō +** *abl)* to fight over, fight for *(in court)*

dēcerp·ō -ere -sī -tus *tr* to tear off, break off; to gather *(fruit, grapes);* to pick *(flowers);* to derive *(e.g., benefits, satisfaction);* **aliquid dē gravitāte dēcerpere** to detract somewhat from dignity

dēcertāti·ō -ōnis *f* decisive struggle

dēcert·ō -āre -āvī -ātum *intr* to fight it out, decide the issue

dēcessi·ō -ōnis *f* withdrawing; retirement, departure *(from a province);* decrease; disappearance

dēcess·or -ōris *m* retiring official; predecessor *(opp:* **successor)**

dēcess·us -ūs *m* withdrawal; retirement *(of an official from a province);* decease, death

dec·et -ēre -uit *(used only in inf and 3rd sing & pl) tr* to befit; to lend grace to; to adorn ‖ *v impers (w. inf)* it is proper for *(s.o.)* to; *(w. dat & inf)* it is proper *or* right for *(s.o.)* to

dē·cidō -cidere -cidī *intr* to fall down; to die; to drop; to sink; *(of things)* to fail, go wrong; to end up, land; *(of plants)* to wilt

dē·cīdō -cīdere -cīdī -cīsus *tr* to cut off, cut away; to cut down; to cut short, terminate; to settle *(a matter);* **pennās dēcīdere** *(w. dat) (fig)* to clip *(s.o.'s)* wings ‖ *intr (w.* **cum)** to come to terms with

deciēns *adv* **(-iēs)** ten times; **deciēns centēna mīlia** *(or simply* **deciēns)** a million; **bis deciēns** two million

decimānus *see* **decumānus**

decimum *adv* for the tenth time

decim·us -a -um *adj* **(-cum-)** the tenth; **cum decimō** tenfold; **cum decimō effēcit ager** the field produced a tenfold return

dē·cipiō -cipere -cēpī -ceptus *tr* to deceive, cheat; to dupe, mislead; to frustrate, disappoint; to escape the notice of; **aliquem labōrum dēcipere** to make s.o. forget his troubles

dēcīsi·ō -ōnis *f* settlement

dēcīsum *pp of* **dēcīdō**

Dec·ius -(i)ī *m* Publius Decius Mus *(father and son, who gave their lives to save the Roman army)*

dēclāmāti·ō -ōnis *f* practice in public speaking; practice speech; theme *(in a practice speech)*

dēclāmāt·or -ōris *m* student of public speaking, declaimer

dēclāmātōri·us -a -um *adj* rhetorical

dēclāmit·ō -āre -āvī -ātus *tr* to plead *(cases)* ‖ *intr* to practice public speaking

dēclām·ō -āre -āvī -ātus *tr* to recite ‖ *intr* to practice public speaking, declaim

dēclārāti·ō -ōnis *f* declaration, disclosure, announcement; **dēclārātiō amōris** an expression of affection

dēclār·ō -āre -āvī -ātus *tr* to make clear, make evident, disclose; to proclaim, announce officially; to show, prove, demonstrate; to mean, express, signify; to declare *(e.g., s.o. consul)*

dēclīnāti·ō -ōnis *f* deviation, swerve; inclination; avoidance; digression; *(gram)* declension

dēclīn·ō -āre -āvī -ātus *tr* to deflect; to parry, avoid; *(gram)* to decline, conjugate ‖ *intr* to deviate; to digress

dēclīv·e -is *n* slope; **per dēclīve** downwards

dēclīv·is -is -e *adj* sloping, steep, down-hill

dēclīvit·ās -ātis *f* sloping terrain

dēcoct·a -ae *f* cold beverage *(invented by Nero)*

dēcoct·or -ōris *m* a bankrupt person

dēcoct·us -a -um *pp of* **dēcoquō** ‖ *adj* luscious; ripe; over-ripe; mellow, over-sweet *(style)*

dēcoll·ō -āre -āvī -ātus *tr* to behead

dēcōl·ō -āre -āvī *intr* to drain away, come to naught, fail

dēcol·or -ōris *adj* off-color, faded; dark-skinned; degenerate, depraved

dēcolōr·ō -āre -āvī -ātus *tr* to discolor, stain, deface; to disgrace

dēco·quō -quere -xī -ctus *tr* to boil down, boil thoroughly; to bring to ruin; to digest *(food)* ‖ *intr* to go bankrupt

dec·or -ōris *m* beauty, grace, elegance, charm; ornament

decōrē *adv* beautifully, gracefully; suitably, properly

decor·ō -āre -āvī -ātus *tr* to beautify, adorn, embellish; to decorate, honor

decōr·us -a -um *adj* beautiful, graceful; glorious, noble; suitable, proper ‖ *n* grace; propriety

dēcoxī *perf of* **dēcoquō**

dēcrepit·us -a -um *adj* decrepit, broken down, worn out

dē·crēscō -crēscere -crēvī -crētum *intr* to grow less, become fewer, diminish, fade; *(of time)* to grow shorter; *(of water)* to subside, go down

dēcrēt·us -a -um *pp of* **dēcernō** ‖ *n* decree, decision; principle

decum·a -ae *f* **(-cim-)** one-tenth; tithe, land tax; largess to the people

decumān·us -a -um *adj* **(-cim-)** paying tithes; of the tenth legion, of the tenth cohort; subject to the 10% tax; **porta decumāna** main gate of Roman camp on the side turned away from the enemy ‖ *m* tax collector ‖ *mpl* men of the tenth legion ‖ *f* tax collector's wife

decumāt·ēs -ium *pl adj* subject to tithes

dē·cumbō -cumbere -cubuī *intr* to lie down; to recline at table; to fall *(in battle)*

decuri·a -ae *f* decury *(unit in Roman government consisting of ten families);* group of ten *(organized for work, recreation, etc.);* panel *(from which jury members were selected);* social club, society

decuriāti·ō -ōnis *f or* **decuriāt·us -ūs** *m* dividing into decuries

decuri·ō -āre -āvī -ātus *tr (fig)* to divide into groups; *(pol)* to divide into groups of ten

decuri·ō -ōnis *m* squad leader *(in the cavalry or navy in charge of ten men);* councilman *(of a municipality or colony);* chief chamberlain

dē·currō -currere -(cu)currī -cursus *tr* to run down, hurry down *(e.g., a path);* to travel over *(a course),* to cover *(a distance);* to make straight for; to turn to *(s.o.)* for help; to pass through *(life);* to run through *(mentally, in a speech),* discuss, treat **‖** *intr* to run down; to run for exercise, jog; *(of liquids)* to run down, flow down; *(of terrain)* to slope down; *(of rivers, ships)* to run down to the sea; *(of ships, travelers)* to come to land; to travel downstream; *(mil)* to run through a drill, carry out maneuvers, parade **‖** *v impers* **eō dēcursum est ut** it got to the point where

dēcursi·ō -ōnis *f* raid; *(mil)* drill, maneuvers, dress parade

dēcurs·us -ūs *m* running down; downward course; *(mil)* maneuvers; *(mil)* dress parade; *(mil)* attack from higher ground; *(rhet)* the flow *(of a sentence, verse);* **dēcursiō honōrum** completion of a political career

dēcurtāt·us -a -um *adj* cut down, cut off short, mutilated; clipped *(style)*

dec·us -oris *n* beauty, glory, honor, dignity; virtue, worth; source of glory **‖** *npl* achievements

dēcuss·ō -āre -āvī -ātus *tr* to divide crosswise *(in the form of an X)*

dēcu·tiō -tere -ssī -ssus *tr* to shake off, beat off, strike down; to chop off *(head);* to break down *(wall with battering ram)*

dēdec·et -ēre -uit *v impers* it ill befits; *(w. inf)* it is a disgrace to

dēdecor·ō -āre -āvī -ātus *tr* to disgrace, dishonor; to make a sham of

dēdecōr·us -a -um *adj* disgraceful, dishonorable, unbecoming

dēdec·us -oris *n* disgrace, dishonor, shame; vice, crime, outrage; *(mil)* disgraceful defeat; **dēdecorī esse** *(w. dat)* to be a source of disgrace to; **dēdecus admittere** to incur disgrace; **per dēdecus** disgracefully

dēdicāti·ō -ōnis *f* dedication, consecration

dēdic·ō -āre -āvī -ātus *tr* to dedicate, consecrate, set aside; to declare *(property in a census return)*

dēdign·or -ārī -ātus sum *tr* to disdain, look down on; *(w. double acc)* to scorn *(s.o.)* as; **aliquem marītum dēdignārī** to regard s.o. as an unworthy husband

dē·discō -discere -didicī *tr* to unlearn, forget

dēditīc·ius -(i)ī *m* prisoner-of-war

dēditi·ō -ōnis *f* surrender; **aliquem in dēditiōnem accipere** to accept the surrender of s.o.

dēdit·us -a -um *pp of* **dēdō ‖** *adj (w. dat)* given to, devoted to; addicted to; *(w. in + acc)* absorbed in **‖** *mpl* prisoners-of-war

dēd·ō -ere -idī -itus *tr* to give up, surrender; to devote; to apply; to abandon; **dēditā operā** on purpose; **necī** *(or* **ad necem) dēdere** to put to death

dēdoc·eō -ēre -uī -tus *tr* to cause to forget; *(w. inf)* to teach *(s.o.)* not to

dēdol·eō -ēre -uī *intr* to feel pain no more

dēdol·ō -āre -āvī -ātus *tr* to hew into shape

dēdū·cō -cere -xī -ctus *tr* to lead *or* draw down; to launch *(ship);* to accompany, escort; to lead out *(colonists to new colony);* to conduct *(bride to husband),* give *(bride)* away; to evict; to subtract, deduct; to summon *(as witness);* to divert; to mislead; to derive *(name);* to compose *(poetry);* to comb out *(hair);* to draw out *(thread in spinning);* to lure *(into a trap);* (leg) to arraign; *(pol)* to install *(in a position of authority);* **rem hūc** *(or* **eō) dēdūcere ut** to bring things to the point that

dēducti·ō -ōnis *f* draining *(of water);* settling of colonists; subtraction, deduction; inference; *(leg)* eviction; **ratiōnis dēductiō** line of reasoning; **sine ūllā dēductiōne** in full

dēduct·or -ōris *m* escort

dēduct·us -a -um *pp of* **dēdūcō ‖** *adj* drawn down; bent inwards, concave; lowered, modest; subtle, well-wrought *(poem);* **nāsus dēductus** pug nose

deërr·ō -āre -āvī -ātum *intr* to go astray, wander away, get lost; to stray; to go wrong

dēfaec·ō -āre -āvī -ātus *tr* to remove the dregs of, strain; *(fig)* to clear up

dēfatīgāti·ō -ōnis *f* (**-fet-**) exhaustion

dēfatīg·ō -āre -āvī -ātus *tr* (**-fet-**) to exhaust

dēfatīscor *see* **dēfetīscor**

dēfecti·ō -ōnis *f* failure; defection, desertion; weakening, exhaustion; *(astr)* eclipse; *(gram)* ellipsis; **dēfectiō animī** mental breakdown; **in dēfectiōne esse** to be in revolt

dēfect·or -ōris *m* defector, deserter

dēfect·us -a -um *pp of* **dēficiō ‖** *adj* weak, worn out

dēfect·us -ūs *m* failing, failure; desertion, defection; *(astr)* eclipse

dēfen·dō -dere -dī -sus *tr* to defend, protect, guard; to repel, beat off, avert; to keep off *(the cold, heat);* to answer *(a charge);* to support, uphold *(argument);* to play the part of *(a character); (leg)* to defend; *(w. dat)* to ward off *(s.th. harmful)* from; **sōlstitium pecorī dēfendere** to ward off the noonday heat from the flock, protect the flock from the noonday heat

dēfēnsi·ō -ōnis *f* defense

dēfēnsit·ō -āre -āvī -ātus *tr* to defend (often); **causās dēfēnsitāre** to be a lawyer

dēfēns·ō -āre -āvī -ātus *tr* to defend, protect

dēfēns·or -ōris *m* defender, protector; champion *(leg)* defense lawyer; *(leg)* guardian

dēfēnsus *pp of* **dēfendō**

dē·ferō -ferre -tulī -lātus *tr* to bring *or* carry down; to carry away; to drive *(ship)* off course; to offer, confer, grant; to inform against, indict; to give an account of; to announce, report; to recommend; to register; **aliquem ad aerārium dēferre** to recommend s.o. for a monetary reward; **ad cōnsilium dēferre** to take into consideration

dēfer·vēscō -vēscere -v(u)ī *or* **-buī** *intr* to stop boiling, cool off; *(fig)* to calm down

dēfess·us -a -um *adj* weary, tired

dēfetīgō *see* **dēfatīgō**

dē·fetīscor -fetīscī -fessus sum *intr* (-fat-) to get tired; *(w. inf)* to tire of

dē·ficiō -ficere -fēcī -fectus *tr* to fail, disappoint; to desert, abandon **‖** *intr* to fail, be a failure; *(of supplies, etc.)* to run low, run out; *(of strength, morale)* to fail, sink; *(of sun, moon)* to be eclipsed; *(of a family line, race)* to become extinct; *(of fire)* to die out; *(w. dat or* **ad***)* to be insufficient for; *(com)* to be bankrupt; *(mil, pol)* to defect; *(pol)* to secede

dēfī·gō -gere -xī -xus *tr* to fix, fasten down; to drive down; to fix, concentrate *(eyes, attention);* to root to the spot, astound; to bewitch; **in terrā dēfīgere** to stick *or* plant *or* set *(s.th.)* up in the ground; to stick *(weapon into s.o.)*

dēfing·ō -ere dēfīnxī *tr* to form, mold; to disfigure

dēfīn·iō -īre -īvī *or* **-iī -ītus** *tr* to mark out the limits of *(a place);* to limit, restrict; to define; to fix, determine, appoint; to bring to a finish, put an end to; to assign, prescribe

dēfīnītē *adv* precisely

dēfīnīti·ō -ōnis *f* boundary; *(fig)* marking out, prescribing; definition

dēfīnītīv·us -a -um *adj* definitive, explanatory; decisive

dēfīnīt·us -a -um *pp of* **dēfīniō ‖** *adj* definite, precise

dēfīnxī *perf of* **dēfingō**

dē·fīō -fierī *intr* to fail, be lacking, be in short supply

dēflagrāti·ō -ōnis *f* conflagration

dēflagr·ō -āre -āvī -ātus *tr* to burn down **‖** *intr* to burn down; to perish, be destroyed; *(of passions)* to cool off

dē·flectō -flectere -flexī -flexus *tr* to deflect, bend aside, turn away, divert; *(fig)* to modify, twist; to bend *(a bow);* to lead astray **‖** *intr* to digress, deviate

dēfl·eō -ēre -ēvī -ētus *tr* to cry bitterly for; to lament; to mourn as lost **‖** *intr* to cry bitterly

dēfloccāt·us -a -um *adj (hum)* bald

dēflocc·ō -āre -āvī -ātus *tr* to rub the nap off *(cloth); (fig)* to fleece

dēflōr·ēscō -ēscere -uī *intr* to shed blossoms; *(fig)* to fade, droop

dēflu·ō -ere -xī -xum *intr* to flow *or* float down; to glide down; to slide, fall; to drain off, run dry; to vanish, pass away, cease; to go out of style; *(w.* **ab***)* to be descended from

dē·fodiō -fodere -fōdī -fossus *tr* to dig down; to hollow out; to bury, conceal

dēfore = **dēfutūrum esse** *fut inf of* **dēsum**

dēfōrmāti·ō -ōnis *f* configuration; disfigurement

dēfōrm·is -is -e *adj* shapeless; misshapen, disfigured, ugly; degrading; degraded; humiliating; unbecoming

dēfōrmit·ās -ātis *f* deformity, ugliness, hideousness; vileness; lack of good taste *(in writing)*

dēfōrmiter *adv* without grace; shamefully

dēfōrm·ō -āre -āvī -ātus *tr* to form from a pattern; to sketch, delineate; to deform, disfigure, mar

dēfossus *pp of* **dēfodiō**

dēfraud·ō *or* **dēfrūd·ō -āre -āvī -ātus** *tr* to defraud, rob; to cheat; **animum (or sē or genium suum) dēfraudāre** to deny oneself some pleasure

dēfrēnāt·us -a -um *adj* unbridled

dēfric·ō -āre -uī -tus *or* **-ātus** *tr* to rub down; to brush *(teeth); (fig)* to satirize

dē·fringō -fringere -frēgī -frāctus *tr* to break off, break to pieces

dēfrūdō *see* **dēfraudō**

dēfrut·um -ī *n* new wine

dē·fugiō -fugere -fūgī *tr* to run away from, avoid, shirk; to evade *(e.g., authority, law)* **‖** *intr* to run off

dēfūnct·us -a -um *pp of* **dēfungor ‖** *adj* finished; dead

dē·fundō -fundere -fūdī -fūsus *tr* to pour out; to empty

dēfun·gor -gī dēfūnctus sum *intr (w. abl)* **1** to perform, carry out; **2** to finish, be done with; **3** to have done with, get rid of; **dēfūnctus**

honōribus having ended a public career; **dēfūnctus iam sum** I'm safe now; **dēfungī (vītā)** to die; **quasi dēfūnctus rēgis imperiō** as if carrying out the king's order; **suā morte dēfūnctus est** he died a natural death

dēfūsus *pp of* **dēfundō**

dēfutūt·us -a -um *adj (vulg)* worn out from excessive sex

dēgen·er -eris *adj* degenerate; unworthy; ignoble

dēgener·ō -āre -āvī -ātus *tr* to disgrace, dishonor; to fall short of ‖ *intr* to degenerate; *(w.* **ad** *or in + acc)* to sink to

dēger·ō -ere *tr* to carry off

dēg·ō -ere *tr* to spend, pass *(time);* to spend one's time in ‖ *intr* to spend one's time, live

dēgrandin·at -āre *v impers* it is hailing hard

dēgrav·ō -āre — -ātus *tr* to weigh down; *(fig)* to burden, distress, inconvenience, overpower

dē·gredior -gredī -gressus sum *intr* to march down, go down, walk down, descend; *(from a standard)* to depart; **ad pedēs dēgredī** to dismount

dēgrunn·iō -īre *intr* to grunt loud

dēgust·ō -āre -āvī -ātus *tr* to taste; *(fig)* to taste, sample, try, experience; *(of weapon)* to graze

dehinc *adv* from here, from now on, after this; then, next; hereafter

dehīsc·ō -ere *intr* to part, divide, gape, yawn; to develop a crack; *(w.* **in** *+ acc)* to split open and reveal

dehonestāment·um -ī *n* blemish, disfigurement, dishonor, disgrace

dehonest·ō -āre -āvī -ātus *tr* to dishonor, disgrace

dehort·or -ārī -ātus sum *tr* to dissuade, discourage; **multa mē dehortantur ā vōbīs** many things tell me to keep my distance from you

Dēianīr·a -ae *f* daughter of Oeneus and wife of Hercules

dē·iciō -icere -iēcī -iectus *tr* (**dē·ji-**) to throw down, fling down; to kill *(sacrificial victim); (of winds)* to drive off course; to depose, fire *(from office);* to lower *(eyes);* to banish *(feelings); (leg)* to evict; *(mil)* to dislodge; *(w. abl or* **dē** *+ abl)* to deprive *(s.o.)* of, prevent *(s.o.)* from obtaining, rob *(s.o.)* of; **ā rē pūblicā oculōs dēicere** to take one's eyes off the government; **dē gradū** *(or* **dē locō** *or* **dē statū)** **dēicere** to throw off balance; **mente suā dēiectus** driven out of one's mind; **sortem dēicere** to cast a lot *(into an urn)*

dēiecti·ō -ōnis *f* (**dējec-**) *(leg)* eviction

dēiect·us -a -um *pp of* **dēiciō** ‖ *adj* (**dējec-**) low, depressed, sunken *(place);* downhearted, depressed, despondent

dēier·ō -āre -āvī -tum *tr & intr* (**dējer-**) to swear solemnly

dein *see* **deinde**

deinceps *adv* one after another, in succession, in order; without interruption; *(of time)* from now on, from then on, after that, after this, next; *(of space)* beyond that; **et deinceps** and so on

deinde *or* **dein** *adv (of place)* from that place, from there; *(of time)* then, thereafter, thereupon, afterwards; *(in enumerating facts, presenting arguments)* secondly, in the next place

Dēïphob·us -ī *m* son of Priam and Hecuba, and husband of Helen after Paris' death

dē·iungō -iungere -iūnxī -iūnctus *tr* (**dējun-**) to unyoke; to sever

dēiūrō *see* **dēierō**

dēiuv·ō -āre *tr* (**dējuv-**) to refuse to help

dēj- = dēi-

dēlā·bor -bī -psus sum *intr* to slip down, fall down, sink; to glide down, float down; *(of water)* to flow down; *(fig)* to stoop, condescend; *(w.* **ad**) to be inclined toward, be partial to; *(w.* **in** *+ acc)* to sneak in among

dēlacer·ō -āre -āvī -ātus *tr* to tear to pieces

dēlāment·or -ārī -ātus sum *tr* to grieve deeply for

dēlass·ō -āre -āvī -ātus *tr* to tire out, weary

dēlāti·ō -ōnis *f* reporting; informing, denouncing; **nōminis dēlātiō** indicting a person

dēlāt·or -ōris *m* reporter; *(leg)* informant

dēlātus *pp of* **dēferō**

dēlēbil·is -is -e *adj* able to be obliterated

dēlectābil·is -is -e *adj* delightful; delicious

dēlectāment·um -ī *n* delight; amusement, pastime, hobby

dēlectāti·ō -ōnis *f* delight, pleasure, amusement; satisfaction

dēlect·ō -āre -āvī -ātus *tr* to delight; to amuse, charm; to attract, allure; **dēlectārī** *(w. abl)* delight in ‖ *v impers* **mē īre dēlectat** I like to go, I enjoy going

dēlēct·us -ūs *m* choosing, choice; *(mil)* recruitment; *(mil)* recruits

dēlēgāti·ō -ōnis *f* *(leg)* assignment to a third party of a creditor's interest in a debt

dēlēg·ō -āre -āvī -ātus *tr* to assign, appoint *(s.o. to a task);* to ascribe *(credit, blame);* to transfer *(ownership of property)*

dēlēnific·us -a -um *adj* soothing, ingratiating

dēlēniment·um -ī *n* allurement, bait; solace, comfort

dēlēn·iō -īre -iī -ītus *tr* (**-līn-**) to soothe, calm down, console, appease; to allure, win over

dēlēnīt·or -ōris *m* charmer

dēl·eō -ēre -ēvī -ētus *tr* to destroy; to annihilate; to overthrow; to extinguish; to raze; to blot out, erase; to put an end to, abolish

dēlētr·īx -īcis _f_ destroyer _(female)_
Dēliac·us -a -um _adj_ Delian, of Delos
dēlīberābund·us -a -um _adj_ deep in thought
dēlīberāti·ō -ōnis _f_ considering, weighing; deliberation, consultation; **habet rēs dēlībe-rātiōnem** the matter requires thought
dēlīberātīv·us -a -um _adj_ deliberative; requiring deliberation
dēlīberāt·or -ōris _m_ thoughtful person
dēlīberāt·us -a -um _adj_ resolved upon, determined
dēlīber·ō -āre -āvī -ātus _tr_ to weigh, think over; to resolve; to consult _(an oracle)_ ‖ _intr_ to deliberate; _(w._ **dē** + _abl)_ to think over; _(w._ **cum)** to consult
dēlīb·ō -āre -āvī -ātus _tr_ to sip, take a sip of; to taste, take a taste of, nibble at; to take away, subtract, remove; to touch on _(subject)_
dēlibr·ō -āre -āvī -ātus _tr_ to strip the bark off
dēlibūt·us -a -um _adj_ anointed; defiled, smeared, stained; steeped
dēlicātē _adv_ delicately; luxuriously
dēlicāt·us -a -um _adj_ delicate, dainty, tender; pampered; frivolous; fastidious, squeamish; self-indulgent; luxurious ‖ _mf_ favorite
dēlici·a -ae _f_ darling, pet
dēlici·ae -ārum _fpl_ delight, pleasures; sweetheart, darling; pet, favorite; comforts, luxuries; ornaments; mannerisms, airs; **dēliciās facere** to enjoy oneself; to have fun _(at s.o. else's expense);_ **dēliciās facere** _(w. dat) (sl)_ to play around with _(a girl);_ **esse in dēliciīs** _(w. dat)_ to be the pet _or_ favorite of; **habēre in dēliciīs** to have as a pet _or_ favorite
dēliciol·ae -ārum _fpl_ darling
dēlic·ium -(i)ī _n_ darling; pet
dēlic·ō -āre _tr_ (**-qu·ō**) to make clear
dēlict·um -ī _n_ fault, offense, wrong; defect _(in a thing)_
dēlicu·us -a -um _adj_ (**-liqu-**) lacking, missing
dēlig·ō -āre -āvī -ātus _tr_ (**-leg-**) to tie up, fasten; _(med)_ to bandage
dē·ligō -ligere -lēgī -lēctus _tr_ to pick off; to pick out, choose, select; to gather; _(mil)_ to draft; _(mil)_ to hold a draft in _(a place)_
dēlin·g(u)ō -g(u)ere -xī _tr_ to lick off; to have a lick of
dēlīni- = dēlēni-
dēlin·ō -ere — -itus _tr_ to smudge
dē·linquō -linquere -līquī -lictus _tr_ _(w. neut pron)_ to commit _(an offense);_ **māiōra dēlinquere** to commit greater wrongs; **sī quid dēlīquerō** if I commit some offense ‖ _intr_ to be missing; to be wanting, fall short; to do wrong, commit an offense
dē·liquēscō -liquēscere -licuī _intr_ to melt, dissolve; to pine away
dēliqui·ō -ōnis _f_ failure; _(w. gen)_ failure to get; _(astr)_ eclipse

dēliqu·ium -(i)ī _n_ failure
dēliquō _see_ **dēlicō**
dēlīrāment·um -ī _n_ nonsense, delusion, absurdity
dēlīrāti·ō -ōnis _f_ silliness, folly, madness; infatuation; dotage
dēlīr·ō -āre _intr_ to be off the beam, be crazy; to rave
dēlīr·us -a -um _adj_ crazy, silly; senseless; in dotage
dēlit·ēscō -ēscere -uī _intr_ (**-tīsc-**) to conceal oneself, lie hidden, lurk
dēlītig·ō -āre _intr_ to rant, have it out
Dēli·us -a -um _adj_ Delian, of Delos, of Apollo ‖ _m_ Apollo
Dēl·os -ī _f_ sacred island in the Cyclades, where Apollo and Diana were born
Delph·ī -ōrum _mpl_ town in Phocis, in Central Greece, famous for the shrine and oracle of Apollo ‖ people of Delphi
Delphic·us -a -um _adj_ of Delphi; of Apollo ‖ _f_ three-legged table
delphīn·us -ī _or_ **delph·īn -īnis** _m_ dolphin ‖ **Delphīnus** _(astr)_ Dolphin _(constellation)_
Delph·is -idis _f_ Delphic priestess of Apollo
delta _indecl n_ delta _(letter of the Greek alphabet)_ ‖ **Delta** the Delta _(of the Nile River)_
Deltōt·on -ī _n_ _(astr)_ the Triangle _(constellation)_
dēlūbr·um -ī _n_ shrine, sanctuary
dēluct·ō -āre -āvī _or_ **dēluct·or -ārī -ātus sum** _intr_ to wrestle
dēlūdific·ō -āre -āvī -ātus _tr_ to make fun of
dēlū·dō -dere -sī -sus _tr_ to fool, con
dēlumb·is -is -e _adj_ lame
dēlumb·ō -āre _tr_ to lame in the loins; _(fig)_ to weaken
dēmad·ēscō -ēscere _intr_ to become drenched, become wet; to be moistened
dēmand·ō -āre -āvī -ātus _tr_ to hand over, entrust
dēmān·ō -āre -āvī _intr_ to run down
dēmarch·us -ī _m_ demarch _(chief of a village in Attica);_ _(fig)_ tribune of the people
dēm·ēns -entis _adj_ demented, out of one's mind; senseless, reckless
dēmēns·us -a -um _pp of_ **dēmētior** ‖ _n_ ration, allowance
dēmenter _adv_ insanely
dēmenti·a -ae _f_ insanity; folly
dēment·iō -īre _intr_ to be insane
dēmer·eō -ēre -uī -itus _or_ **dēmer·eor -ērī -itus sum** _tr_ to earn, merit, deserve; to serve well, do a service to, win the favor of
dēmer·gō -gere -sī -sus _tr_ to sink; to plunge, dip; to bury ‖ _pass (of heavenly bodies)_ to set
dēmessus _pp of_ **dēmetō**
dēmēt·ior -īrī -mēnsus sum _tr_ to measure out

dē·metō -metere -messuī -messus *tr* to mow, reap, harvest; to pick *(flowers, fruit);* to cut off

Dēmētr·ius -(i)ī *m* Demetrius Poliorcetes, son of Antigonus, and king of Macedonia ‖ Demetrius of Phaleron, famous orator and politician at Athens

dēmigrāti·ō -ōnis *f* emigration

dēmigr·ō -āre -āvī -ātum *intr* to migrate, emigrate, move, depart; *(fig)* to pass on, die

dēmin·uō -uere -uī -ūtus *tr* to make smaller, lessen, diminish; to deduct; *(w. abl)* to deprive of; *(w.* dē + *abl)* to deduct from; **capite dēminuere** to deprive of civil rights

dēminūti·ō -ōnis *f* lessening, diminution, abridging; *(leg)* right of disposing of property; **capitis dēminūtiō** loss of civil rights; **prōvinciae dēminūtiō** shortening of term of office

dēmīr·or -ārī -ātus sum *tr* to be surprised at, be amazed at

dēmissē *adv (opp:* **altē)** low; humbly, modestly; abjectly

dēmissīci·us -a -um *adj* allowed to hang down, flowing; *(of clothes)* ankle-length

dēmissi·ō -ōnis *f* letting down, sinking, lowering; **dēmissiō animī** low morale

dēmiss·us -a -um *pp of* **dēmittō** ‖ *adj* low, low-lying *(place);* drooping *(lips, etc.);* bent *(head);* flowing, long *(hair); (of clothes)* hanging down, full-length; *(fig)* downhearted, dejected; *(fig)* poor, humble; *(w. abl)* descended from

dēmītig·ō -āre *tr* to calm down

dē·mittō -mittere -mīsī -missus *tr* to drop, let drop, let sink; to lower; to dip; to sink *(a well);* to bring downstream; to shed *(blood);* to land *(ship);* to let down *(hair);* to grow *(beard);* to move down *(troops from a higher place);* **animum** *(or* **mentem) dēmittere** to become discouraged; **dēmittere aurēs ad** to deign to listen to ‖ *refl* to descend, go down; to stoop, bend down; *(fig)* to plunge into; *(geog)* to slope downwards ‖ *pass* to descend, go down

dēmiurg·us -ī *m* **(dāmi-)** magistrate in a Greek state

dēm·ō -ere -psī -ptus *tr* to take away, remove, withdraw; *(w. dat or abl or* **ab** *or* dē + *abl)* to take away from, remove from, subtract from, withhold from; **vincla pedibus dēmere** to remove the fetters

Dēmocrit·us -ī *m* philosopher from Abdera in Thrace and founder of the atomic theory *(born c. 460 B.C.)*

dēmōl·ior -īrī -ītus sum *tr* to demolish, pull down

dēmōlīti·ō -ōnis *f* demolishing

dēmōnstrāti·ō -ōnis *f* pointing out; explanation; description

dēmōnstrātīv·us -a -um *adj* showy

dēmōnstrāt·or -ōris *m* one who points out, indicator

dēmōnstr·ō -āre -āvī -ātus *tr* to point out clearly; to state precisely, explain, describe; to mention, speak of; to demonstrate, prove, establish

Dēmopho·ōn -ontis *m* son of Theseus and Phaedra

dēmor·ior -ī -tuus sum *tr* to be dying for ‖ *intr* to die; to die off; to become extinct

dēmor·or -ārī -ātus sum *tr* to delay, detain; to hinder, block ‖ *intr* to wait

Dēmosthen·ēs -is *or* -ī *m* greatest Greek orator *(384–322 B.C.)*

dē·moveō -movēre -mōvī -mōtus *tr* to remove, move away; to dispossess, expel; to oust

dēmptus *pp of* **dēmō**

dēmūgīt·us -a -um *adj* bellowing, lowing

dēmul·ceō -cēre -sī *tr* to stroke lovingly, pet

dēmum *adv* at last, finally; not till then; *(to give emphasis)* precisely, exactly, just; *(to give assurance)* in fact, certainly, to be sure, as a matter of fact; **decimō dēmum annō** not till the tenth year; **modo dēmum** only now, not until now; **nunc dēmum** now at last, not until now; **post dēmum** not until afterwards; **tum dēmum** then finally, not until then

dēmurmur·ō -āre *tr* to grumble through *(e.g., a performance)*

dēmūtāti·ō -ōnis *f* transformation

dēmūt·ō -āre -āvī -ātus *tr* to change; to make worse ‖ *intr* to fail; to change one's mind

dēnār·ius -iī *m* denarius *(about $1);* money

dēnārr·ō -āre -āvī -ātus *tr* to recount in detail

dēnās·ō -āre *tr* to bite the nose off *(s.o.'s face)*

dēnat·ō -āre *intr* to swim downstream

dēneg·ō -āre -āvī -ātus *tr* to deny, refuse, turn down ‖ *intr* to say no

dēn·ī -ae -a *adj* in sets of ten, ten each, in tens; tenth

dēnicāl·is -is -e *adj* purifying from death; **fēriae dēnicālēs** purification service *(after death in the household)*

dēnique *adv* finally, at last; in short, in a word; *(for emphasis)* just, precisely; *(ironical)* of course; **octāvō dēnique mēnse** not till after the eighth month; **tum dēnique** then at last, only then, not till then

dēnōmin·ō -āre -āvī -ātus *tr (w.* **ab** *or* **ex)** to name after

dēnōrm·ō -āre *tr* to make crooked *or* irregular; to disfigure, spoil

dēnot·ō -āre -āvī -ātus *tr* to mark down, specify; to take careful note of; to observe closely

dēns dentis *m* tooth; ivory; point, prong; fluke; *(of an elephant)* tusk; **albīs dentibus dērīdēre aliquem** *(prov)* to laugh heartily at s.o.; **dēns Indus** elephant's tusk

dēnsē *adv* closely, thickly, in quick succession, repeatedly

dēnseō *see* **dēnsō**

dēnsit·ās -ātis *f* closeness; thickness

dēns·ō -āre -āvī -ātus *or* **dēns·eō -ēre** *tr* to thicken; to press close together; to close *(ranks);* to condense

dēns·us -a -um *adj* dense, close, thick, crowded; frequent, repeated; intense *(love, cold);* concise *(style)*

dentāl·ia -ium *npl* plow beam

dentāt·us -a -um *adj* toothed; serrated; *(of paper)* polished smooth

dentifrangibul·us -a -um *adj (hum)* tooth-breaking ‖ *m* thug ‖ *n* fist

dentifric·ium -(i)ī *n* tooth powder

dentileg·us -ī *m (hum)* toothpicker *(one who picks up teeth after they have been knocked out)*

dent·iō -īre *intr* to teethe

dentiscalp·ium -(i)i *n* toothpick

dēnū·bō -bere -psī -ptum *intr (of a woman)* to marry beneath her rank; to go through a mock marriage

dēnūd·ō -āre -āvī -ātus *tr* to strip naked, strip bare; to expose, leave unprotected; *(fig)* to lay bare

dēnumer·ō -āre -āvī -ātus *tr* to pay *(money)* in full

dēnūntiāti·ō -ōnis *f* intimation; warning, threat; announcement, proclamation; **senātūs dēnūntiātiō** Senate ordinance; **testimōniī dēnūntiātiō** summons to testify

dēnūnti·ō -āre -āvī -ātus *tr* to intimate; to give notice of; to announce officially; to give official warning to; to warn, threaten; *(mil)* to report to; **dēnūntiāre testimōnium** *(w. dat)* to give *(s.o.)* a summons to testify

dēnuō *adv* anew, once more, all over again; **dēnuō alius** yet another

deoner·ō -āre *tr* to unload

deopt·ō -āre *tr* to choose

deorsum *adv* **(-sus)** downwards, down; *(of position)* down below, underneath

deōscul·or -ārī -ātus sum *tr* to shower with kisses

dēpāct·us -a -um *adj* fastened down

dēparc·us -a -um *adj* very stingy

dēpacīscor *see* **dēpecīscor**

dē·pāscō -pāscere -pāvī -pāstus *or* **dē·pāscor -pāscī -pāstus sum** *tr* to eat up; to feed on; to graze on; to feed the cattle on *(grass, etc.);* to consume, to destroy, waste; *(fig)* to prune off *(excesses in style);* **altāria dēpāscere** to consume the flesh on the altar

dēpec·īscor -īscī -tus sum *tr* **(-pac-)** to agree on, come to terms on; to bargain for

dēpe·ctō -ctere — -xus *tr* to comb out; *(fig)* to flog

dēpeculāt·or -ōris *m* embezzler

dēpecūl·or -ārī -ātus sum *tr* to embezzle; to steal

dē·pellō -pellere -pulī -pulsus *tr* to drive off, drive away; to drive out; to avert; *(mil)* to dislodge; *(w.* **quīn** *or w.* **ab** *or* **dē** + *abl)* to deter from, dissuade from, wean from ‖ *intr* to deviate

dēpend·eō -ēre -ī *intr* to hang down; *(w. abl)* to be derived from; *(w.* **ab** *or* **dē** + *abl)* to depend on; *(w.* **ex)** to hang down from

dēpen·dō -dere -dī -sus *tr* to pay up; to pay *(penalty)*

dēper·dō -dere -didī -ditus *tr* to lose completely; to ruin, destroy

dēper·eō -īre -iī *tr* to be hopelessly in love with ‖ *intr* to go to ruin, perish; to be lost, be finished; **dēperiī!** I'm done for!

dēpexus *pp of* **dēpectō**

dēpilāt·us -a -um *adj* plucked; *(fig)* swindled, gypped

dē·pingō -pingere -pīnxī -pictus *tr* to paint, portray; to embroider; *(fig)* to portray, describe, represent

dēplan·gō -gere -xī *tr* to beat one's breast in mourning over; to grieve over, cry one's heart out over

dēplex·us -a -um *adj* grasping, gripping firmly

dēplōrābund·us -a -um *adj* complaining bitterly; sobbing

dēplōr·ō -āre -āvī -ātus *tr* to cry over, mourn; to despair of ‖ *intr* to cry bitterly, take it hard

dēplu·it -ere -it *v impers* it is raining hard, is pouring down

dē·pōnō -pōnere -posuī (-posīvī) pos(i)tus *tr* to put down, put aside; to get rid of; to bet; to deposit; *(w.* **apud** + *acc)* to entrust to, commit to the care of; **bellum dēpōnere** to give up war; **imperium dēpōnere** to relinquish power

dēpopulāti·ō -ōnis *f* ravaging, pillaging

dēpopulāt·or -ōris *m* marauder

dēpopul·ō -āre -āvī -ātus *or* **dēpopul·or -ārī -ātus sum** *tr* to ravage, pillage, lay waste; *(of diseases)* to ravage; *(fig)* to wreck, destroy

dēport·ō -āre -āvī -ātus *tr* to carry down; to carry away; to bring home, win *(victory);* to transport; to banish

dē·poscō -poscere -poposcī *tr* to demand; to require, call for; to request earnestly; to challenge

dēposit·us -a -um *pp of* **dēpōnō** ‖ *adj* despaired of ‖ *n* deposit *(as down-payment; for safekeeping);* **dēpositī agere** to sue for breach of trust; **dēpositī damnāre** to convict of breach of trust

dēprāvātē *adv* perversely

dēprāvāti·ō -ōnis *f* distorting; *(fig)* distortion; perversity, perversion

dēprāv·ō -āre -āvī -ātus *tr* to make crooked, distort; to pervert, corrupt, seduce; to misrepresent

dēprecābund·us -a -um *adj* imploring

dēprecāti·ō -ōnis *f* supplication, averting by prayer; invocation, earnest entreaty; *(w. gen)* intercession against *(danger, etc.)*

dēprecāt·or -ōris *m* intercessor; *(w. gen)* champion of

dēprec·or -ārī -ātus sum *tr* to pray against, avert by prayer; to pray for, beg for; to intercede on behalf of; to plead in excuse **‖** *intr* to pray; to make an entreaty

dēprehen·dō -dere -dī -sus *or* **dēpren·dō -dere -dī -sus** *tr* to get hold of; to arrest; to catch, intercept; to surprise, catch in the act; to detect, discover; to perceive, understand; to embarrass

dēprehēnsi·ō -ōnis *f* detection

dēpress·us -a -um *pp of* **dēprimō ‖** *adj* low *(voice);* low-lying *(land)*

dē·primō -primere -pressī -pressus *tr* to depress, weigh down; to plant deep; to dig *(e.g., trench);* to sink *(ship)* **‖** *pass* to sink

dēproeli·or -ārī *intr* to fight it out, battle fiercely

dēprōm·ō -ere -psī -ptus *tr* to take down; to bring out, produce; **pecūniam ex arcā dēprōmere** to get the money out of the safe

dēproper·ō -āre *tr* to make in a hurry **‖** *intr* to hurry

deps·ō -ere -uī -tus *tr* to knead; *(vulg)* to feel up

dēpud·et -ēre -uit *v impers* **eum dēpudet** he is unashamed, has lost all sense of shame

dēpūg·is -is *adj* (**-pȳg-**) *(masc & fem only)* with thin buttocks

dēpugn·ō -āre -āvī -ātum *intr* to fight hard; to fight it out **‖** *v impers (pass)* **dēpugnātum est** they fought hard

dēpulsī *perf of* **dēpellō**

dēpulsi·ō -ōnis *f* averting; *(rhet)* defense

dēpuls·ō -āre *tr* to push aside; **dē viā dēpulsāre** to push out of the way

dēpuls·or -ōris *m* averter

dēpulsus *pp of* **dēpellō**

dēpung·ō -ere *tr* to mark off *(in an account by punching holes)*

dēpurg·ō -āre -āvī -ātus *tr* to clean (out) thoroughly

dēput·ō -āre -āvī -ātus *tr* to prune; to reckon, consider

dēpȳgis *see* **dēpūgis**

dēque *adv* down, downwards

dērād·ō -ere -rāsī -rāsus *tr* to shave off; to scrape off

dērēct·us -a -um *pp of* **dērigō;** *see* **dīrēctus**

dērelicti·ō -ōnis *f* neglect

dēre·linquō -linquere -līquī -lictus *tr* to leave behind, abandon

dērepente *adv* suddenly, all of a sudden

dērēp·ō -ere -sī *intr* to crawl down

dēreptus *pp of* **dēripiō**

dērī·deō -dēre -sī -sus *tr* to deride **‖** *intr* to laugh it off *(i.e., get off scot-free)*

dērīdicul·us -a -um *adj* quite ridiculous, absurd **‖** *n* derision; absurdity; **dērīdiculō esse** to be the butt of ridicule

dērig·ēscō -ēscere -uī *intr* to grow stiff, grow rigid; to curdle

dērigō *see* **dīrigō**

dē·ripiō -ripere -ripuī -reptus *tr* to tear off; to remove; to seize; to tear down, pull down

dērīs·or -ōris *m* scoffer

dērīs·us -ūs *m* derision

dērīvāti·ō -ōnis *f* diverting *(of streams);* divergence of sense; derivation *(of words)*

dērīv·ō -āre -āvī -ātus *tr* to draw off, divert; to derive

dērō·dō -dere — -sus *tr* to nibble away at

dērog·ō -āre -āvī -ātus *tr* to propose to repeal *(a law)* in part; to restrict, modify; to take away

dērōs·us -a -um *adj* gnawed away, nibbled

dēruncin·ō -āre -āvī -ātus *tr* to plane off; *(fig)* to rip off

dēru·ō -ere -ī *tr* to throw down, demolish; *(w. dē + abl)* to detract from

dērupt·us -a -um *adj* rough, steep **‖** *npl* crevasses, crags

dēsaev·iō -īre -(i)ī -ītum *intr* to rage furiously, vent one's rage; to run wild

dēsalt·ō -āre -āvī -ātus *tr* to dance; **canticum dēsaltāre** to dance a number

dēscen·dō -dere -dī -sum *intr* to climb down, descend, come down; to dismount; to fall, sink; to sink in, penetrate; to go down *(to the forum);* *(fig)* to go down, sink down, penetrate; *(fig)* to lower oneself, stoop, yield; *(mil)* to march down

dēscēnsi·ō -ōnis *f* descent; sailing down; **dēscēnsiō Tiberīna** sailing down the Tiber

dēscēns·us -ūs *m* climbing down, descent; slope

dēsc·īscō -īscere -īvī *or* **-iī -ītum** *intr* to revolt, defect; *(fig)* to depart, deviate; *(w. ab)* to deviate from, break allegiance with, revolt from; **ā mē dēsciī** I abandoned my own principles; **in mōnstrum dēscīscere** to degenerate into a monster

dēscrī·bō -bere -psī -ptus *tr* to write out, transcribe, copy; to describe, portray, design, sketch

dēscrīptē *see* dīscrīptē
dēscrīpti·ō -ōnis *f* copy; diagram, plan; transcript; description; **dēscrīptiō crīminis** indictment
dēscrīptus *pp of* dēscrībō
dēsec·ō -āre -uī -tus *tr* (-sic-) to cut off
dēser·ō -ere -uī -tus *tr* to desert, abandon, forsake; *(leg)* forfeit
dēsert·or -ōris *m* deserter
dēsert·us -a -um *pp of* dēserō ‖ *adj* deserted; uninhabited ‖ *npl* wilderness, desert
dēserv·iō -īre *intr (w. dat)* to be a slave to, serve devotedly
dēs·es -idis *adj* sitting down, sitting at ease; lazy, idle; apathetic, listless
dēsicc·ō -āre *tr* to dry up; to drain
dē·sideō -sidēre -sēdī *intr* to sit idle, remain inactive
dēsīderābil·is -is -e *adj* desirable
dēsīderāti·ō -ōnis *f* missing, feeling the absence, yearning; **dēsīderātiō voluptātum** yearning for pleasures
dēsīder·ium -(i)ī *n* longing, missing, feeling of loss; want, need, desire; request, petition; **ex dēsīderiō labōrāre** to be homesick; **mē dēsīderium tenet** *(w. gen)* I miss, am homesick for
dēsīder·ō -āre -āvī -ātus *tr* to miss, long for; to call for, require; *(mil)* to lose *(men)* in combat ‖ *pass* to be lost, be missing, be a casualty
dēsidi·a -ae *f* idleness, inactivity; laziness; apathy
dēsidiābul·um -ī *n (coll)* place to lounge, hangout
dēsidiōsē *adv* idly
dēsidiōs·us -a -um *adj* idle, lazy; causing idleness *or* laziness; spent in idleness
dē·sīdō -sīdere -sēdī *or* -sīdī *intr* to sink; to subside; to settle down; *(of morals)* to deteriorate; **in īmō dēsīdere** to settle at the bottom
dēsignāti·ō -ōnis *f* specification; layout; appointment; election
dēsignātor *see* dissignātor
dēsign·ō -āre -āvī -ātus *tr* to mark out, point out, designate; to outline; to define, trace; *(of words)* to denote, indicate; to earmark; to appoint, elect; **cōnsul dēsignātus** consul-elect
dē·siliō -silīre -siluī *or* -silīvī *or* -siliī -sultum *intr* to jump down; to dismount
dē·sinō -sinere -sīvī *or* s(i)ī -situs *tr* to give up, abandon, finish with; *(w. inf)* to stop *(doing s.th.)*; **furere dēsinere** to stop raging ‖ *intr* to stop, come to a stop, end; to stop speaking; *(w. gen)* to cease from; *(w. in + acc)* to end in; **similiter dēsinere** to have similar endings
dēsipi·ēns -entis *adj* foolish, silly
dēsipienti·a -ae *f* foolishness
dēsip·iō -ere *intr* to be silly, fool around

dē·sistō -sistere -stitī *intr* to stop, desist; to get stuck, stick; *(w. abl or w.* **ab** *or* **dē** + *abl)* to desist from, abandon, give up *(an action begun)*; **dēsistere ā dēfēnsiōne** to give up the defense
dēsitus *pp of* dēsinō
dēsōl·ō -āre -āvī -ātus *tr* to leave desolate, leave empty; to strip *(of inhabitants)*; to leave alone, forsake, abandon; **dēsōlātus** left in the lurch; *(w. abl)* deprived of
dēspect·ō -āre *tr* to look down on, overlook, command a view of; *(fig)* to look down on, despise
dēspect·us -a -um *pp of* dēspiciō ‖ *adj* contemptible
dēspect·us -ūs *m (with* **in** + *acc)* commanding view of; contempt,
dēspēranter *adv* dispairingly, hopelessly
dēspērāti·ō -ōnis *f* desperation, despair
dēspērāt·us -a -um *adj* desperate, hopeless; despaired of
dēspēr·ō -āre -āvī -ātus *tr* to despair of ‖ *intr* to despair, give up hope; *(w.* **dē** + *abl)* to despair of
dēspicāti·ō -ōnis *f* contempt ‖ *fpl* feelings of contempt
dēspicāt·us -a -um *adj* despicable; **aliquem dēspicātum habēre** to hold s.o. in contempt
dēspicāt·us -ūs *m* contempt
dēspici·ēns -entis *adj* contemptuous; *(w. gen)* contemptuous of
dēspicienti·a -ae *f* contempt
dē·spiciō -spicere -spexī -spectus *tr* to despise, look down on ‖ *intr* to look down; *(w.* **in** + *acc)* to look down on, have a view of
dēspic·or -ārī -ātus sum *tr* to despise, disdain
dēspoliāt·or -ōris *m* robber, plunderer
dēspoli·ō -āre -āvī -ātus *tr* to strip, rob, plunder
dēspon·deō -dēre -dī -sus *tr* to pledge, promise solemnly; to promise in marriage; **animum** *(or* **animōs)** **dēspondēre** to lose heart, despair
dēspōns·ō -āre *tr* to betroth
dēspōns·us -a -um *pp of* dēspondeō
dēspūm·ō -āre -āvī -ātus *tr* to skim (off); to work off *(i.e., digest)* ‖ *intr* to stop foaming
dēspu·ō -ere *tr* to spit out, spit down; to avert by spitting; *(fig)* to reject ‖ *intr* to spit on the ground *(to avert evil, etc.)*
dēsquām·ō -āre -āvī -ātus *tr* to scale *(fish)*; *(fig)* to peel off
dēstill·ō -āre -āvī -ātus *tr* to drip, distill ‖ *intr* to drip, trickle down
dēstimul·ō -āre *tr* to goad on
dēstināti·ō -ōnis *f* designation; nomination; purpose, intention; **locus dēstinātiōnis** destination

dēstināt·us -a -um *adj* obstinate; fixed, determined; **animus mortī dēstinātus** a mind set on death; **dēstinātum est mihi** (*w. inf*) I have made up my mind to; **locus dēstinātus** destination ‖ *n* design, intention; mark (*aimed at*); **ex dēstinātō** according to plan

dēstin·ō -āre -āvī -ātus *tr* to lash down, secure; to fix, determine, resolve; to earmark; to appoint, designate; to arrange the purchase of; to aim at ‖ *intr* to make up one's mind ‖ *v impers* **dēstinātum mihi est** I have made up my mind

dēstit·uō -uere -uī -ūtus *tr* to set apart; to set down, place; to forsake; to leave high and dry, betray, desert; (*w.* **ab**) to rob of, leave destitute of

dēstitūti·ō -ōnis *f* forsaking, abandonment; disappointment

dēstrict·us -a -um *pp of* **dēstringō** ‖ *adj* severe, rigid

dē·stringō -stringere -strīnxī -strictus *tr* to strip; to unsheathe; to give (*s.o.*) a rubdown; to brush gently against, skim; (*of weapon*) to graze; (*fig*) to criticize, satirize

dēstructi·ō -ōnis *f* pulling down (*e.g., of walls*); destruction, demolition; refutation

dēstru·ō -ere -xī -ctus *tr* to pull down, demolish; (*fig*) to ruin

dēsubitō *or* **dē subitō** *adv* suddenly

dēsūdāsc·ō -ere *intr* to begin to sweat all over

dēsūd·ō -āre -āvī -ātum *intr* to sweat; (*w. dat*) (*fig*) to sweat over

dēsuē·fiō -fierī -factus sum *intr* (*w.* **ab**) to become unused to, get away from

dēsu·ēscō -ēscere -ēvī -ētum *intr* (*w. inf*) to become unaccustomed to, get away from

dēsuētūd·ō -inis *f* disuse, lack of use

dēsuēt·us -a -um *pp of* **dēsuēscō** ‖ *adj* unused, out of use, obsolete; out of practice; (*w. dat*) unused to, unfamiliar with

dēsult·or -ōris *m* circus rider (*who leaps from one horse to another*); **amōris dēsultor** fickle lover, "butterfly"

dēsultōri·us -a -um *adj* of a circus rider; **equus dēsultōrius** show horse

dēsultūr·a -ae *f* jumping down

dē·sum -esse -fuī -futūrus *intr* to fall short, fail; to fail in one's duty; to be absent, be missing; (*w. dat*) **1** to be absent from, be missing from; **2** to fail to support; **sibi dēesse** to sell oneself short; **temporī dēesse** (*or* **occāsiōnī temporis**) **dēesse** to pass up the opportunity

dēsūm·ō -ere -psī -ptus *tr* to pick out, choose; to undertake; **sibi hostem dēsūmere** to take on an enemy

dēsuper *adv* from above

dēsur·gō -gere -rēxī -rēctum *intr* to rise; **cēnā dēsurgere** to get up from the table; (*euphem*) to go to the toilet, leave the room

dē·tegō -tegere -tēxī -tēctus *tr* to detect, uncover, expose, lay bare; to reveal, disclose, betray

dēten·dō -dere — -sus *tr* to loosen; to strike (*a tent*)

dētentus *pp of* **dētineō**

dēter·geō -gēre -sī -sus *or* **dēter·gō -gere** to wipe off, wipe away; (*fig*) to wipe clean

dēteri·or -or -us *adj* inferior, worse, poorer; lower in value; weaker

dēterius *adv* worse

dētermināti·ō -ōnis *f* boundary; conclusion, end

dētermin·ō -āre -āvī -ātus *tr* to bound, limit; (*rhet*) to conclude (*sentence, period*)

dē·terō -terere -trīvī -trītus *tr* to rub away, wear away; to wear out; to lessen, weaken, detract from; **calcēs alicūius dēterere** to tread on s.o.'s heels

dēterr·eō -ēre -uī -itus *tr* to deter, frighten away, discourage; (*w. abl or* **ab** *or* **dē** + *abl, or w.* **nē, quīn,** *or* **quōminus** *w. subj*) to deter (*s.o.*) from, discourage (*s.o.*) from

dētersus *pp of* **dētergeō**

dētestābil·is -is -e *adj* detestable

dētestāti·ō -ōnis *f* detestation; curse; (*leg*) formal renunciation

dētest·or -ārī -ātus sum *tr* to curse; to invoke (*the gods*) to avert; to plead against; to detest; (*w.* **in** + *acc*) to call (*e.g., vengeance*) upon; **invidiam dētestārī** to avert jealousy, avoid unpopularity

dētex·ō -ere -uī -tus *tr* to weave, finish weaving; (*fig*) to finish (off)

dē·tineō -tinēre -tinuī -tentus *tr* to hold back, keep back; to hold up, detain; to occupy, keep busy; (*w.* **ab** *or* **dē** + *abl*) to keep back from; (*w. abl or* **in** + *abl*) to occupy (*day, mind*) with, keep (*s.o.*) busy with

dēton·deō -dēre -dī -sus *tr* to cut off, shear off; (*fig*) to strip off

dēton·ō -āre -uī *intr* to stop thundering; (*of Jupiter*) to thunder down

dētōnsus *pp of* **dētondeō**

dētor·queō -quēre -sī -tus *tr* to twist *or* bend aside; to twist out of shape; to turn aside; to turn, direct; to avert (*eyes*); to divert, pervert; to distort, misrepresent (*words*)

dētracti·ō -ōnis *f* (-trect-) taking away, wresting; removal; (*rhet*) ellipsis

dētractō *see* **dētrectō**

dētract·or -ōris *m* detractor

dē·trahō -trahere -trāxī -tractus *tr* to drag down, drag away, pull down, pull away; to remove, withdraw; to deprive, rob, strip; to induce to come down (*e.g., an enemy from a*

strong position); to disparage, detract, slander; *(w. dat or* dē *+ abl)* to rob *(s.o.)* of
dētrectāti·ō -ōnis *f* drawing back, avoidance; mīlitiae dētrectātiō draft dodging
dētrectāt·or -ōris *m* detractor; shirker
dētrect·ō -āre -āvī -ātus *tr* (-trac-) to draw back from, shirk, decline, reject; to disparage; to demean; mīlitiam dētrectāre to dodge the draft
dētrīmentōs·us -a -um *adj* detrimental
dētrīment·um -ī *n* detriment, loss, harm; dētrīmentum accipere *(or* capere) to incur a loss; dētrīmentum īnferre *(or* afferre) to cause harm *or* loss
dētrītus *pp of* dēterō
dētrīvī *perf of* dēterō
dētrū·dō -dere -sī -sus *tr* to push down, push away, push off; to postpone; *(mil)* to dislodge; *(leg)* to evict; aliquem dē suā sententiā dētrūdere to get s.o. to change his mind
dētrunc·ō -āre -āvī -ātus *tr* to cut off, lop off; to mutilate; to behead
dētulī *perf of* dēferō
dēturb·ō -āre *tr* to beat down, tear down, strike down; to eject, expel, dispossess; *(mil)* to dislodge; aliquem dē sānitāte dēturbāre to drive a person mad
dēturp·ō -āre *tr* to disfigure
Deucali·ōn -ōnis *m* son of Prometheus who, together with his wife Pyrrha, survived the Deluge
deūn·x -cis *m* eleven-twelfths; hērēs ex deūnce heir to eleven-twelfths
de·ūrō -ūrere -ussī -ūstus *tr* to burn up, destroy; *(of frost)* to nip
de·us -ī *(nom pl:* deī, dī *or* diī; *gen pl:* deōrum *or* deum; *dat and abl pl:* deīs, dīs *or* diīs; *vocative sg:* deus) *m* god, deity ‖ *mpl (of people in high places)* the powers that be; dī bonī! good heavens!; dī hominēsque all the world; dī meliōra! Heaven forbid!; dīs volentibus with the help of the gods; dī tē ament! bless your little heart!
deūstus *pp of* deūrō
de·ūtor -ūtī *intr (w. abl)* to mistreat
dēvast·ō -āre -āvī -ātus *tr* to devastate
dēve·hō -here -xī -ctus *tr* to carry down, carry away, carry off, ship off ‖ *pass* to ride down; to sail down
dēvellō dēvellere dēvellī *or* dēvolsī dēvulsus *or* dēvolsus *tr* to pluck
dēvēl·ō -āre *tr* to unveil
dēvener·or -ārī -ātus sum *tr* to worship; to avert by prayer
dē·veniō -venīre -vēnī -ventum *intr* to come down, arrive; *(w. acc of extent of motion or w.* ad *or* in *+ acc)* to arrive at, reach; *(w.* ad) to happen to, befall

dēverber·ō -āre -āvī -ātus *tr* to thrash soundly
dēverb·ium -(i)ī *n* spoken parts of a play, unaccompanied by music
dēvers·or -ārī -ātus sum *intr* to stay as a guest; *(w.* apud *+ acc)* to stay at the house of
dēvers·or -ōris *m* (vor-) guest
dēversōriol·um -ī *n* small inn
dēversōri·us -a -um *adj* (-vor-) of an inn, fit to stay at; taberna dēversōria inn ‖ *n* inn
dēverticul·um -ī *n* (-vort-) side road; detour; digression; refuge; inn, tavern; *(coll)* dive; *(fig)* loophole
dēver·tō -tere -tī -sum *or* dēver·tor -tī -sus sum *intr* (-vort-) to turn aside, turn away; to stay as guest, spend the night; *(w.* ad *or* apud *+ acc)* to stay with, stay at the house of; *(w.* ad) to have recourse to
dēvex·us -a -um *adj* inclining, sloping, steep; *(w.* ad) prone to, inclined to
dē·vinciō -vincīre -vīnxī -vīnctus *tr* to tie up, clamp; *(fig)* to obligate, unite closely ‖ *refl* sē vīnō dēvincīre *(coll)* to get tight on wine
dē·vincō -vincere -vīcī -victus *tr* to beat decisively, trounce
dēvīnctus *pp of* dēvinciō ‖ *adj (w. dat)* strongly attached to
dēvītāti·ō -ōnis *f* avoidance
dēvīt·ō -āre -āvī -ātus *tr* to avoid
dēvi·us -a -um *adj* out of the way; off the beaten track; living apart, solitary, sequestered; inconsistent ‖ *npl* wilderness
dēvoc·ō -āre -āvī -ātus *tr* to call down; to call off; to recall; to call away; to allure; deōs ad auxilium dēvocāre to invoke the gods for help
dēvol·ō -āre -āvī -ātum *intr* to fly down; to fly away; to rush down, rush away
dēvol·vō -vere -vī -ūtus *tr* to roll down; *(w.* dē *+ abl);* to roll down from ‖ *pass* to roll down, go tumbling down; *(w.* ad) to fall back on
dēvor- = dēver-
dēvor·ō -āre -āvī -ātus *tr* to devour, gulp down; to consume, waste; *(of sea)* to engulf, swallow up; to swallow, mumble *(words);* to repress *(tears);* to bear with patience
dēvorti·a -ōrum *npl* side roads, detour
dēvōti·ō -ōnis *f* self-sacrifice; cursing; outlawing; incantation, spell; capitis *(or* vītae) dēvōtiō sacrifice of one's life
dēvōt·ō -āre -āvī -ātus *tr* to bewitch, jinx
dēvōt·us -a -um *pp of* dēvoveō ‖ *adj* devoted, faithful; accursed; *(w. dat)* 1 devoted to; 2 addicted to
dē·voveō -vovēre -vōvī -vōtus *tr* to devote, vow, sacrifice, dedicate; to mark out, doom, destine; to curse; to bewitch ‖ *refl* sē (dīs) dēvovēre to devote onself to death
dēvulsus *pp of* dēvellō

dext·āns -antis *m* five-sixths
dextell·a -ae *f* little right hand; right-hand man
dex·ter -tera -terum *or* **-tra -trum** *adj* right, on the right side; handy, dexterous; lucky, propitious, favorable; opportune, right ‖ *f* right hand, right side, the right; **ā dextrā laevāque** to the right and left, right and left, everywhere; **dextrā** with the right hand; *(fig)* with valor; **dextrā** *(w. gen or acc)* to the right of; **dextrae iungere dextram** to shake hands; **dextram dare** *(or* **tendere)** to give a pledge of friendship
dexterē *or* **dextrē** *adv* dexterously, skillfully; **dextrē fortūnā ūtī** *(fig)* to play the cards right
dexterit·ās -ātis *f* dexterity; readiness to help
dextrōrsum *or* **dextrōrsus** *or* **dextrōversum** *adv* (**-vor-**) to the right, toward the right side
dī *see* **deus**
Dī·a -ae *f* ancient name of the island of Naxos ‖ mother of Mercury
diabathrār·ius -(i)ī *m* shoemaker
diadēm·a -atis *n* diadem
diadēmāt·us -a -um *adj* wearing a diadem, wearing a crown
diaet·a -ae *f* room; suite *(of rooms);* cabin *(of ship);* annex *(to the main building);* *(med)* regimen *(proper exercise, etc.)*
dialecticē *adv* logically
dialectic·us -a -um *adj* dialectical, logical ‖ *m* dialectician, logician ‖ *f* logic, dialectics ‖ *npl* dialectics
dialect·os -ī *f* dialect
Diāl·is -is -e *adj* of Jupiter; of Jupiter's high priest; **apex Diālis** high priest's miter; **flāmen Diālis** high priest of Jupiter
dialog·us -ī *m* dialogue, conversation; literary composition in the form of a dialogue
Diān·a *or* **Diān·a -ae** *f* Diana *(Roman goddess, identified with Artemis);* *(fig)* Diana's temple; *(fig)* moon; **īrācunda Diāna** lunacy
Diāni·us -a -um *adj* Diana's ‖ *n* enclosure sacred to Diana
diāri·a -ōrum *npl* daily ration
dibaph·us -ī *f* crimson robe; official robe *(of a magistrate or augur)*
dic·a -ae *f (leg)* lawsuit, case, judicial proceedings; **dicam alicuī impingere** to hit s.o. with a lawsuit; **dicam scrībere** *(w. dat)* to sue s.o.; **dicās sortīrī** to select a jury
dicācit·ās -ātis *f* sarcasm
dicācul·us -a -um *adj* witty, sharp; sarcastic
dicāti·ō -ōnis *f* declaration of intent of becoming a citizen
dic·āx -ācis *adj* witty, sharp; sarcastic
dichorē·us -ī *m (pros)* double trochee
dici·ō -ōnis *f* jurisdiction; sway, authority, control, rule, dominion, sovereignty; **in** *(or* **sub) dicaōne esse** *(w. gen)* to be under the control

of, be subject to, be under the jurisdiction of; **in dicōnem redigere** *(w. gen)* *or* **dicōnī subicere** *(w. gen)* to bring *(s.o.)* under the control of
dicis causā *or* **grātiā** *adv* for show, for the sake of appearances
dic·ō -āre -āvī -ātus *tr* to dedicate, consecrate; to deify; to inaugurate; to set apart, devote; *(w. dat)* to devote *(e.g., time, energy, self)* to
dīcō dīcere dīxī dictus *tr* to say; to tell, relate; to indicate, mention, specify, point out; to nominate, appoint; to fix, set *(day, date);* to speak, deliver, recite; to pronounce, utter, articulate; to call, name; to assert, state; to describe; to predict; *(w. double acc)* to appoint *(s.o.)* as; **causam dīcere** to plead *or* defend a case; **diem dīcere** *(w. dat)* to set a date for; **facētē dictum!** well put!; **sententiam dīcere** to express an opinion; **testimōnium dīcere** to give evidence
dicrot·a -ae *f* bireme
dicrot·um -ī *n* bireme
Dictae·us -a -um *adj* of Mt. Dicte, Dictaean, Cretan
dictamn·us *or* **dictamn·os -ī** *f (bot)* dittany *(aromatic plant, believed to have magical powers)*
dictāt·a -ōrum *npl* lessons, rules; dictation
dictāt·or -ōris *m* dictator *(emergency magistrate in Rome, legally appointed for a maximum six-month term);* chief magistrate *(of Italic town)*
dictātōri·us -a -um *adj* of a dictator
dictātr·īx -īcis *f* mistress of ceremonies
dictātūr·a -ae *f* dictatorship
Dict·ē -ēs *f* mountain in Crete, the alleged birthplace of Jupiter
dicti·ō -ōnis *f* saying, speaking, uttering; diction, style; conversation; oracular response, prediction; **dictiō causae** pleading of a case; **dictiō testimōnī** right to give testimony; **iūris dictiō** administration of justice; jurisdiction
dictit·ō -āre -āvī -ātus *tr* to keep saying, to state emphatically; **causās dictitāre** to practice law
dict·ō -āre -āvī -ātus *tr* to reiterate, say repeatedly; to dictate; to compose; to suggest, remind
dict·us -a -um *pp of* **dīcō** ‖ *n* saying, word, statement; witticism; maxim, proverb; prediction; order, instruction; promise, assurance; derisive remark; **dicta dīcere** to make (witty *or* cutting) remarks; **dictīs manēre** to stick to one's promises
Dictynn·a -ae *f* Cretan goddess Britomartis, identified with Diana
-dicus -a -um *adjl suf;* **-dic·us -ī** *masc suf* denotes one who speaks: **vēridicus** saying

the truth; **causidicus** one who pleads cases, lawyer

dī·dō *or* **dis·dō** **-dere** **-didī** **-ditus** *tr* to publicize, disseminate; to distribute, hand out

Dīd·ō **-ūs** *or* **-ōnis** *(acc:* **Dīdō** *or* **Didōn)** *f* daughter of Tyrian king Belus, and foundress and queen of Carthage

dīdū·cō **-cere** **-xī** **-ctus** *tr* to draw apart, open; to part, sever, separate, split; to undo, untie; to divide, distribute; to scatter, disperse; to untie *(knot);* to break up *(friendships);* to deploy *(forces);* to digest *(food);* to open wide *(mouth); (in mathematics)* to divide; **animus dīductus** *(w. abl)* the mind torn between *(alternatives)*

dīducti·ō **-ōnis** *f* separation into parts, distribution

diēcul·a **-ae** *f* a little while

diērēct·us **-a** **-um** *adj (coll)* finished, done for; **ābī** *(or* **ī) diērēctus!** *(sl)* go straight to blazes!

di·ēs **-ēī** *m (but occasionally feminine when referring to a fixed day or time in general)* day; time, period, space of time, interval; daylight; light of day; anniversary; daybreak; season; **dē diē** by day; **diē** in the daytime; **diem dīcere** *(w. dat)* to impeach, bring an accusation against; **diem ex diē** from day to day, day after day; **diem noctemque** day and night; **diēs meus** my birthday; **in diem** for the moment; for a future day; **in diēs** (more and more) every day; **longō diē** throughout the long day; **multō dēnique diē** not till late in the day; **postrīdiē ēius diēī** the day after that; **post tertium ēius diēī** two days after that

Diēspi·ter **-tris** *m* Jupiter

diffām·ō **-āre** **-āvī** **-ātus** *tr* to spread the bad news of; to defame, slander

differenti·a **-ae** *f* difference, diversity; distinguishing characteristic; specific difference, species

differit·ās **-ātis** *f* difference

differō differre distulī dīlātus *tr* to carry in different directions; to scatter, disperse; to publicize; to postpone; to put *(a person)* off; to humor; to get rid of; to bewilder; to disquiet **‖** *intr* to differ, be different; *(w. ab)* to differ from **‖** *v impers* there is a difference; **multum differt** there is a great difference

differt·us **-a** **-um** *adj* stuffed; crowded, overcrowded

difficile *adv* with difficulty

difficil·is **-is** **-e** *adj* difficult, hard; surly; hard to manage; hard to please

difficiliter *adv* with difficulty, barely

difficult·ās **-ātis** *f* difficulty, hardship, trouble, distress; surliness; poverty, financial embarrassment

difficulter *adv* with difficulty, barely; grudgingly

diffīd·ēns **-entis** *adj* diffident, lacking in confidence; anxious, nervous

diffīdenter *adv* without confidence, distrustfully

diffīdenti·a **-ae** *f* diffidence, mistrust, distrust

diffī·dō **-dere** **-sus sum** *intr (w. dat)* to distrust; to despair of; *(w. acc & inf)* to have no confidence that; *(w. inf)* to expect not to

dif·findō **-findere** **-fidī** **-fissus** *tr* to split, divide; **diem diffindere** *(fig)* to put off the day of the trial

diffing·ō **-ere** *tr* to form differently, remodel; to alter

diffissus *pp of* **diffindō**

diffit·eor **-ērī** *tr* to disavow, disown

diffl·ō **-āre** **-āvī** **-ātus** *intr* to blow away; to disperse

difflu·ō **-ere** **-xī** **-ctum** *intr* to flow in different directions, flow away; to dissolve, melt away, disappear; *(w. abl)* to wallow in *(e.g., luxury)*

dif·fringō **-fringere** **-frēgī** **-frāctus** *tr* to shatter, break apart, smash

dif·fugiō **-fugere** **-fūgī** *intr* to flee in different directions; to disperse; to disappear

diffug·ium **-(i)ī** *n* dispersion

diffundit·ō **-āre** *tr* to pour out, scatter; to waste

dif·fundō **-fundere** **-fūdī** **-fūsus** *tr* to pour out; to scatter, diffuse, spread, extend; to bottle *(wine);* to give vent to; to cheer up, gladden

diffūsē *adv* diffusely; fully

diffūsil·is **-is** **-e** *adj* diffusive

diffūs·us **-a** **-um** *pp of* **diffundō** **‖** *adj* extending over a wide area; extensive *(writings);* diffuse, expansive *(speech)*

diffutūt·us **-a** **-um** *adj (vulg)* exhausted by too much sex

dī·gerō **-gerere** **-gessī** **-gestus** *tr* to distribute in all directions; to spread about, disperse, divide; to arrange; to interpret

dīgesti·ō **-ōnis** *f* arrangement; *(rhet)* enumeration

dīgestus *pp of* **dīgerō**

digitul·us **-ī** *m* little finger

digit·us **-ī** *m* finger; inch *(one sixteenth of a Roman foot);* toe; **digitīs concrepāre** to snap the fingers; **digitō ūnō attingere** to touch lightly, touch tenderly; **digitum intendere ad** to point the finger at; **digitum tollere** to make a bid; **digitus index** index finger; **digitus medius** *(or* **īnfāmis** *or* **obscēnus)** middle finger; **digitus minimus** little finger; **digitus pollex** thumb; **digitus quārtus** ring finger; **in digitōs arrēctus** on tiptoe; **prīmus** *(or* **prīmōris** *or* **prior) digitus** fingertip

dīgladi·or **-ārī** **-ātus sum** *intr* to fight in a gladiatorial contest

dignāti·ō -ōnis *f* esteem, respect; dignity, honor; rank, status, social position

dignē *adv* worthily

dignit·ās -ātis *f* worth, worthiness; dignity; authority, rank, reputation, distinction, majesty; self-respect; dignitary; political office

dign·ō -āre -āvī -ātus *or* **dign·or -ārī -ātus sum** *tr (w. abl)* to think worthy of; *(w. inf)* to think fit to; *(w. double acc)* to think *(s.o.)* worthy of being *(e.g., a son)*

dīgnōsc·ō *or* **dīnōsc·ō -ere** *tr* to distinguish, know the difference; *(w. abl)* to distinguish *(s.o.)* from; **dominum ac servum dīgnōscere** to know the difference between master and slave

dign·us -a -um *adj* worthy, deserving; fit, adequate, suitable, deserved, proper; *(w. abl)* worthy of

dīgre·dior -dī -ssus sum *intr* to move apart, separate; to deviate; to digress

dīgressi·ō -ōnis *f* parting, separation; deviation; digression

dīgressus *pp of* **dīgredior**

dīgress·us -ūs *m* departure; digression

dīiūdicāti·ō -ōnis *f* decision

dīiūdic·ō -āre -āvī -ātus *tr* to decide, settle; **vēra et falsa** *(or* **vēra ā falsīs) dīiūdicāre)** to distinguish between truth and falsehood

dī·lābor -lābī -lāpsus sum *intr* to fall apart, break up; *(of ice)* to melt; to disperse; to decay; *(of time)* to slip by; *(of water)* to flow in different directions

dīlacer·ō -āre -āvī -ātus *tr* to tear to pieces

dīlāmin·ō -āre *tr* to split in two; to crack *(nuts)*

dīlani·ō -āre -āvī -ātus *tr* to tear to pieces

dīlapid·ō -āre -āvī -ātus *tr* to demolish *(a structure of stone); (coll)* to squander

dīlāpsus *pp of* **dīlābor**

dīlarg·ior -īrī -ītus sum *tr* to hand out generously, lavish

dīlāti·ō -ōnis *f* postponement, delay; *(leg)* adjournment

dīlāt·ō -āre -āvī -ātus *tr* to dilate, stretch, broaden, extend, enlarge; *(fig)* to amplify, spread, extend; to drawl out

dīlāt·or -ōris *m* procrastinator, slowpoke

dīlātus *pp of* **differō**

dīlaud·ō -āre *tr* to praise enthusiastically

dīlēct·us -a -um *pp of* **dīligō** ‖ *adj* beloved, dear

dīlēct·us -ūs *m* selection; *(mil)* selective service, draft; draftees; recruitment; **dīlēctum habēre** to conduct a draft; **legiōnēs ex novō dīlēctū cōnficere** to bring the legions to full strength with new draftees

dīlīd·ō -ere *tr* to smash to pieces

dīlig·ēns -entis *adj* careful, accurate; exacting, strict; thrifty; industrious; *(w. gen)* **1** obser-

vant of; **2** devoted to, fond of; *(w. ad or in + acc)* **1** careful in, careful to; **2** conscientious about

dīligenter *adv* carefully, diligently; thoroughly, well, in detail

dīligenti·a -ae *f* care, diligence, industry, attentiveness; economy, frugality; *(w. gen)* regard for

dī·ligō -ligere -lēxī -lēctus *tr* to esteem; to like; to value, appreciate; to love

dīlōrīc·ō -āre -āvī -ātus *tr* to tear open

dīlūc·eō -ēre *intr* to be clear, be evident; *(w. dat)* to be obvious to

dī·lūcēscō -lūcēscere -lūxī *intr* to get light, dawn

dīlūcidē *adv* clearly, distinctly

dīlūcid·us -a -um *adj* clear, distinct, plain, evident

dīlūcul·um -ī *n* daybreak, dawn

dīlūd·ium -(i)ī *n* intermission *(between plays, games, etc.)*

dīl·uō -uere -uī -ūtus *tr* to wash away; to break up, separate; to dilute; to get rid of *(worries, annoyances);* to atone for; to explain

dīluvi·ēs -ēī *f* flood, deluge

dīluvi·ō -āre *tr* to flood, inundate

dīluv·ium -(i)ī *n* flood, deluge

dimach·ae -ārum *mpl* (Macedonian) soldiers who fight either on foot or on horseback

dīmān·ō -āre *intr* to flow in different directions; *(fig)* to spread around

dīmēnsi·ō -ōnis *f* measurement, dimensions

dī·mētior -mētīrī -mēnsus sum *tr* to measure out; to count off

dīmēt·ō -āre *or* **dīmēt·or -ārī** *tr* to measure *or* mark off

dīmicāti·ō -ōnis *f* fight, combat, struggle; contest, rivalry

dīmic·ō -āre -āvī -ātus *intr* to contend, fight, struggle; **dē capite** *(or* **dē vītā) dīmicāre** to fight for one's life

dīmidi·a -ae *f* half

dīmidiāt·us -a -um *adj* half, in half

dīmid·ium -(i)i *n* half; **dīmidiō longior** twice as long; **dīmidium mīlitum quam** half as many soldiers as

dīmidi·us -a -um *adj* half; broken (in two); **dīmidius patrum, dīmidius plēbis** half patrician, half plebeian; **parte dīmidiā auctus** twice as large

dīmi·nuō -nuere -nuī -nūtus *tr* to shatter

dīmissi·ō -ōnis *f* dismissal; sending out; *(mil)* discharge

dī·mittō -mittere -mīsī -missus *tr* to send away, let go; to dismiss *(an assembly);* to spread; to set free, release; to let off; to scatter, distribute; to let go of, let loose; to abandon; to let go, let slip, forgo *(a chance, an opportunity);* to divorce *(a wife); (fin)* to settle *(a debt); (fin)* to pay off *(a creditor); (mil)* to discharge *(a soldier),* disband *(an army)*

dimminuō *see* **dīminu·ō**

dī·moveō -movēre -mōvī -mōtus *tr* to move apart, part, separate; to disperse, scatter; to dismiss; to lure away

Dindymēn·ē -ēs *f* Cybele *(named after Dindymus, a mountain in Phrygia sacred to Cybele)*

Dindym·us *or* **Dindym·os -ī** *m* Mt. Dindymus *(in Phrygia)*

dīnōscō *see* **dignōscō**

dīnumerāti·ō -ōnis *f* enumeration, counting up

dīnumer·ō -āre -āvī -ātus *tr* to enumerate, count up; to count out, pay

diōbolār·is -is -e *adj* costing two obols *(about 2¢)*

Diodot·us -ī *m* Stoic philosopher and tutor of Cicero *(d. 59 B.C.)*

dioecēs·is -is *or* **-eōs** *f* district; governor's jurisdiction

dioecēt·ēs -ae *m* treasurer; secretary of revenue

Diogen·ēs -is *m* Ionic philosopher *(5th cent. B.C.)* ‖ Cynic philosopher from Sinope, in Pontus *(412?–323 B.C.)*

Diomēd·ēs -is *m* son of Tydeus and king of Argos, and hero at Troy

Diō(n) -ōnis *m* Dion *(brother-in-law of the elder Dionysius, the tyrant of Syracuse, and a pupil and friend of Plato's)*

Diōn·ē -ēs *or* **Diōn·a -ae** *f* mother of Venus

Dionȳsi·a -ōrum *npl* festival of Dionysus

Dionȳs·ius -(i)ī *m* tyrant of Syracuse *(430–367 B.C.)* ‖ Dionysius the Younger *(397–330? B.C.)*

Dionȳs·us *or* **Dionȳs·os -ī** *m* Greek god of wine and fertility, equated with Bacchus

diōt·a -ae *f* two-handled wine jar

Diphil·us -ī *m* Greek comic writer of Sinope, used by Plautus

diplōm·a -atis *n* travel pass *(to travel free on the Imperial post);* certificate

dips·as -adis *f* poisonous snake whose bite provokes thirst

Dipyl·on -ī *n* N.W. gate at Athens

dipyr·us -a -um *adj* twice burned

Dīr·a -ae *f* Fury *(goddess of revenge)*

dīr·ae -ārum *fpl* bad omens; curses

Dircae·us -a -um *adj* Dircean, Boeotian; **cycnus Dircaeus** Boeotian swan *(Pindar, lyric poet from Boeotia)*

Dirc·ē -ēs *f* famous spring in Boeotia

dīrēctē *adv* **(dēr-)** in a straight line

dīrēctō *adv* **(dēr-)** in a straight line; directly, without intervening procedures

dīrēct·us *or* **dērēct·us -a -um** *pp of* **dīrigō** ‖ *adj* straight, direct; level; upright, vertical, perpendicular; *(fig)* direct, straightforward, simple; **in dīrēctum** *(or* **per dīrēctum)** in a

straight line; **in dīrēctō** on a straight stretch *(of road)*

diremptus *pp of* **dirimō**

dirempt·us -ūs *m* separation

dīrepti·ō -ōnis *f* plundering, pillaging ‖ *fpl* acts of pillage; a scramble for a share

dīrept·or -ōris *m* plunderer

dīreptus *pp of* **dīripiō**

dirib·eō -ēre -uī -itus *tr* to sort *(votes taken out of the ballot box)*

diribiti·ō -ōnis *f* sorting *(of votes)*

diribit·or -ōris *m* sorter *(of ballots)*

diribitōr·ium -iī *n* sorting room

dīrigō dīrigere dīrēxī dīrēctus *tr* **(dē-)** to direct; to put in order, arrange, line up, straighten out; to level *(a surface);* to construct *(roads, tunnels, along a given line); (mil)* to deploy

dir·imō -imere -ēmī -emptus *tr* to take apart; to part, separate, divide; to break off, disturb, interrupt; to separate, dissolve; to put off, delay; to break off, end, bring to an end; to nullify, bring to naught

dī·ripiō -ripere -ripuī -reptus *tr* to tear apart, tear to pieces; to lay waste, pillage; to loot, rob; to steal; to snatch away; to whip out *(sword);* to run after, compete for the company of *(person)*

dīrit·ās -ātis *f* frightfulness; dire event

dī·rumpō -rumpere -rūpī -ruptus *tr* to break to pieces, smash, shatter; to break off *(friendship);* to sever *(ties)* ‖ *pass* to burst *(w. laughter, envy, etc.)*

dīru·ō -ere -ī -tus *tr* to pull apart, demolish, destroy, overthrow; to scatter; to bankrupt; *(mil)* to break up *(enemy formation)*

dīr·us -a -um *adj* dire, awful, fearful; ominous, ill-omened; dreadful; cruel, relentless, fierce; **temporibus dīrīs** in the reign of terror; **venēna dīra** deadly poisons ‖ *fpl & npl* ill-boding portents, unlucky signs

dīrutus *pp of* **dīruō**

dīs dītis *adj* rich; fertile; generous; expensive; *(w. abl)* abounding in ‖ **Dīs Dītis** *m* Pluto *(king of the lower world)*

dis- *pref* (unchanged before initial **c p t s**; **dī-** before **b d g l m n r**, consonantal **u** and sometimes **i**; **dif-** before **f**; **dir-** *(by rotacism)* before vowels and **h** *(with rare exceptions);* it commonly signifies **1** separation or dispersion or both: **diffugere** to flee in different directions, disperse; **discēdere** to draw apart; **2** the reversal of a previous process: **disiungere** to disunite, disperse; **3** a negative sense: **displicēre** to displease, not please

di(s)iūnctē *adv* in separate words, separately

di(s)iūncti·ō -ōnis *f* separation, alienation; divination; variation; dilemma; *(rhet)* asyndeton

(*succession of phrases or clauses without conjunction*)

di(s)iūnct·us -a -um *adj* separate, distinct; distant, remote; disjointed, disconnected, incoherent; logically opposed **‖** *npl* opposites

di(s)iun·gō -gere -xī -ctus *tr* to unyoke; to sever, divide, part, remove; to separate; to alienate

dis·cēdo -cēdere -cessī -cessum *intr* to go away, depart; to separate, be severed; to disperse, be dissipated, disappear; to split open, come apart; (*of wife*) to separate (*from husband*); to deviate, swerve; to pass away, cease; (*mil*) to march off, break camp; (*mil*) to come off (*victorious, etc.*); (*w. abl*) **1** to forsake (*e.g., friends*); **2** to deviate from, swerve from; (*w.* **ex** *or* **dē** + *abl*) to depart from; (*w.* **ad**) to depart for; (*w.* **in** + *acc*) to vote for; **ā vītā discēdere** to die; **discēdere in Catōnis sententiam** to vote for Cato's proposal; **ut discēdātur ab** apart from

disc·ēns -entis *m* learner, apprentice, trainee

disceptāti·ō -ōnis *f* dispute, difference of opinion; discussion, debate

disceptāt·or -ōris *m*, **disceptātr·īx -īcis** *f* arbitrator

discept·ō -āre -āvī -ātus *tr* to debate, dispute, discuss, treat; to decide, settle **‖** *intr* to act as judge, arbitrate; to argue; to be at stake

dis·cernō -cernere -crēvī -crētus *tr* to separate, mark off, divide; to keep apart; to distinguish between; to discern, make out

discerp·ō -ere -sī -tus *tr* to mangle, mutilate; (*fig*) to tear apart (*with words, arguments*)

discessi·ō -ōnis *f* separation, division; divorce; (*in the Senate*) division, formal vote; **discessiō sine ūllā varietāte** unanimous vote

discess·us -ūs *m* separation, parting; departure; banishment; marching off

discid·ium -(i)ī *n* parting; discord, disagreement; divorce

discīd·ō -ere -ī *tr* to cut up

discīnct·us -a -um *pp of* **discingō ‖** *adj* without a belt; dissolute, loose; effeminate, voluptuous

di·scindō -scindere -scidī -scissus *tr* to tear apart, tear open, rend; **amīcitiās discindere** to break off the ties of friendship

dis·cingō -cingere -cīnxī -cīnctus *tr* to take off; to loosen; to disarm

disciplīn·a -ae *f* instruction, training, teaching, education; learning, knowledge, science; discipline, branch of study, subject; custom, habit; system; **mīlitāris disciplīna** basic training; **reīpūblicae disciplīna** statesmanship

discipul·a -ae *f* pupil (*female*)

discipul·us -ī *m* pupil; disciple, follower

discissus *pp of* **discindō**

disclū·dō -dere -sī -sus *tr* to keep apart, shut off; to seal up, seal off; to assign

discō discere didicī *tr* to learn; to get to know, become acquainted with; to be told (*e.g., the truth*); (*w. inf*) to learn how to

discobol·us -ī *m* discus-thrower

discol·or -ōris *adj* of a different color; of different colors; (*w. dat*) different from

discondūc·ō -ere *intr* to be unprofitable, be prejudicial

disconven·iō -īre *intr* to disagree; to be inconsistent **‖** *v impers* there is disagreement

discordābil·is -is -e *adj* discordant, disagreeing

discordi·a -ae *f* discord, dissension, disagreement; mutiny

discordiōs·us -a -um *adj* prone to discord, mutinous

discord·ō -āre *intr* to quarrel, disagree; (*w. dat or ab*) **1** to be be out of harmony with; **2** to be opposed to

discor·s -dis *adj* discordant; at variance; contradictory, inconsistent; warring (*winds, etc.*); (*w. abl*) inconsistent with, different from

discrepanti·a -ae *f* discrepancy, dissimilarity, difference

discrepāti·ō -ōnis *f* disagreement, dispute

discrepit·ō -āre *intr* to be completely different

discrep·ō -āre -āvī *or* **-uī** *intr* to be different in sound, sound different; to be out of tune; to disagree; to be different, vary; to be inconsistent; to be disputed; (*w. dat or abl or* **ab** *or* **cum**) **1** to disagree with; **2** to be different from; **3** to be inconsistent with **‖** *v impers* there is a difference of opinion, it is a matter of dispute, it is undecided

discrī·bō -bere -psī -ptus *tr* to distribute, divide; to classify; to assign, apportion; (*w.* **in** + *acc*) to distribute among, divide among

discrīm·en -inis *n* dividing line; interval, intervening space, division, distance, separation; discrimination, difference, distinction; critical moment, turning point; crisis, jeopardy, peril, danger, risk; decision, determination; decisive battle; difference in pitch; part (*in the hair*); **rēs in discrīmine est** the situation is at a critical stage; **parvum discrīmen lētī** narrow escape from death

discrīmin·ō -āre -āvī -ātus *tr* to divide, separate; to apportion

discrīptē *adv* in an orderly way, lucidly, distinctly

discrīpti·ō -ōnis *f* distribution, classification

discrīpt·us -a -um *pp of* **discrībō ‖** *adj* well-arranged, sorted, classified

discruci·ō -āre -āvī -ātus *tr* to torture; to distress, torment

discumbō discumbere discubuī discubitum *intr (of several)* to take their places at the table; *(of several)* to go to bed

discup·iō -ere *tr (coll)* to want badly; *(w. inf) (coll)* to be dying to

dis·currō -currere -cucurrī *or* **-currī -cursum** *intr* to run in different directions, scamper about, run up and down, dash around

discurs·us -ūs *m* running up and down, running about; *(mil)* pincer movement

disc·us -ī *m* discus

discussus *pp of* **discutiō**

discu·tiō -tere -ssī -ssus *tr* to knock apart; to smash to pieces, shatter; to shake off; to break up, disperse *(an assembly, gathering);* to dispel *(danger, sleep);* to frustrate, bring to naught; to suppress, destroy

disertē *adv* clearly, eloquently

disertim *adv* clearly, distinctly

disert·us -a -um *adj* fluent, eloquent; clear

dis·iciō -icere -iēcī -iectus *tr* to drive apart, scatter; to tear to pieces; to ruin; to frustrate, wreck; *(mil)* to break up *(enemy formation)*

disiect·ō -āre -āvī -ātus *tr* to toss about

disiect·us -a -um *pp of* **disiciō** ‖ *adj* scattered; dilapidated

disiect·us -ūs *m* scattering

disj- = disi-

dispālēsc·ō -ere *intr* to be spread abroad, get around

dispāl·or -ārī -ātus sum *intr* to wander around; to straggle, stray off

dis·pandō pandere — -pānsus *tr* (-pen-) to stretch out, extend; to expand

dis·pār -paris *adj* different, unlike; unequal; ill-matched

disparāt·us -a -um *adj* separate, distinct; negatively opposite *(e.g., sapere et nōn sapere* to be wise and not to be wise)

disparil·is -is -e *adj* dissimilar, different

dispariliter *adv* differently

dispar·ō -āre -āvī -ātus *tr* to separate; to make different ‖ *intr* to be different

dispartiō, dispartior *see* **dispertiō**

dispectus *pp of* **dispiciō**

dis·pellō -pellere -pulī -pulsus *tr* to dispel, drive away; to disperse

dispend·ium -(i)ī *n* expense, cost; loss *(as result of a transaction)*

dispendō *see* **dispandō**

dis·pennō -pennere — -pessus *tr* to stretch out, extend; to expand

dispēnsāti·ō -ōnis *f* weighing out, doling out; management, superintendence, administration; office of treasurer

dispēnsāt·or -ōris *m* household manager, chief butler; cashier; treasurer

dispēns·ō -āre -āvī -ātus *tr* to weigh out, pay out; to distribute, manage *(household stores);* to regulate, manage

dispercut·iō -ere *tr* to knock out; **cerebrum dispercutere** *(w. dat)* to knock *(s.o.'s)* brains out

disper·dō -dere -didī -ditus *tr* to spoil, ruin; to squander

disper·eō -īre -iī *intr* to go to ruin; to go to waste; to be undone, perish; **disperiī!** *(coll)* I'm finished!; **dispeream sī** *(coll)* I'll be darned if

disper·gō -gere -sī -sus *tr* (**sparg-**) to scatter about, disperse; to splatter; to distribute, scatter *(e.g., men)* without organization; to spread, extend *(war, rumor, etc.)*

dispersē *adv* here and there; occasionally

dispersus *pp of* **dispergō**

dispers·us -ūs *m* dispersal

dispert·iō -īre -īvī *or* **-iī -ītus** *or* **dispert·ior -īrī -ītus sum** *tr* to distribute, divide; to assign *(e.g., gates, areas)* as posts to be guarded

dispertīti·ō -ōnis *f* distribution, sharing

dispessus *pp of* **dispandō**

di·spiciō -spicere -spexī -spectus *tr* to see clearly, make out, distinguish, detect; to look into, consider carefully, perceive, discover; to reflect on ‖ *intr* to see clearly

displic·eō -ēre -uī -itum *intr* to be unpleasant, be displeasing; *(w. dat)* to displease; **sibi displicēre** to be dissatisfied with oneself; to be in a bad mood

dis·plōdō -plōdere — -plōsus *tr & intr* to burst apart

dis·pōnō -pōnere -posuī -positus *tr* to place here and there; to distribute; to arrange, set in order; to station, post, assign; to adjust; to dispose; **diem dispōnere** to arrange the day's schedule

dispositē *adv* orderly, methodically

dispositi·ō -ōnis *f* orderly arrangement, development *(of a theme)*

dispositūr·a -ae *f* order, arrangement

disposit·us -a -um *pp of* **dispōnō** ‖ *adj* well-arranged; methodical, orderly

disposit·us -ūs *m* order, orderly arrangement

dispud·et -ēre -uit *v impers (w. inf)* it's a great shame to

dispulsus *pp of* **dispellō**

dis·pungō -pungere -pūnxī -pūnctus *tr* to check, audit, balance *(accounts)*

disputāti·ō -ōnis *f* argument, discussion

disputāt·or -ōris *m* disputant

disput·ō -āre -āvī -ātus *tr* to dispute, discuss; *(com)* to estimate; to examine, treat, explain ‖ *intr* to argue, argue one's case

disquīr·ō -ere *tr* to examine closely

disquīsīti·ō -ōnis *f* inquiry, investigation

disrumpō *see* **dīrumpō**

dissaep·iō -īre -sī -tus *tr* to partition, fence off

dissaept·um -ī *n* partition, barrier

dissāvi·or *or* **dissuāvi·or -ārī** *tr* to kiss passionately

dissec·ō -āre -uī -tus *tr* to cut up, dissect

dissēmin·ō -āre -āvī -ātus *tr* to disseminate

dissēnsi·ō -ōnis *f* difference of opinion, disagreement; dissension; conflict, incompatibility

dissēns·us -ūs *m* dissension, discord

dissentāne·us -a -um *adj* disagreeing, dissenting; conflicting; contrary

dissen·tiō -tīre -sī -sum *intr* to dissent, disagree; to differ, be in conflict, be inconsistent; *(w. dat or* **ab** *or* **cum**) to differ with; *(w.* **ab**) to differ from, be opposed to

disserēn·at -āre -āvit *v impers* it is clearing up

disser·ō -ere -uī -tus *tr* to discuss; to examine; to arrange **‖** *intr (w.* **dē** + *abl)* to discuss

dis·serō -serere -sēvī -situs *tr* to scatter; to sow here and there; to stick in the ground at intervals

disserp·ō -ere *intr* to creep around; to spread gradually

disserti·ō -ōnis *f* severance, a disconnecting

dissert·ō -āre -āvī -ātus *tr* to discuss

dissertus *pp of* **disserō** *(to discuss)*

dis·sideō -sidēre -sēdī *intr* to be distant, be remote; to live far apart; to disagree; to differ, be unlike; *(of garment)* to be on crooked; *(w.* **ab** *or* **cum**) to disagree with

dissignāti·ō -ōnis *f* arrangement

dissignāt·or -ōris *m* (**dēsig-**) master of ceremonies; usher *(at theater);* undertaker, mortician

dissign·ō -āre -āvī -ātus *tr* to regulate; to arrange; to contrive

dissil·iō -īre -uī *intr* to fly apart, burst, split, break up; to be dissolved

dissimil·is -is -e *adj* dissimilar, different; *(w. gen or dat or w.* **atque** *or* **ac**) different from

dissimiliter *adv* differently

dissimilitūd·ō -inis *f* difference

dissimulābiliter *adv* furtively

dissimulanter *adv* secretly, slyly

dissimulanti·a -ae *f* faking, hiding

dissimulāti·ō -ōnis *f* dissimulation; Socratic irony; pretended ignorance

dissimulāt·or -ōris *m* dissembler, faker

dissimul·ō -āre -āvī -ātus *tr* to conceal, disguise; to keep secret; to pretend not to see, ignore

dissipābil·is -is -e *adj* (**dissu-**) that may be dissipated

dissipāti·ō -ōnis *f* (**dissu-**) dispersal, dissipation; distribution

dissip·ō *or* **dissup·ō -āre -āvī -ātus** *tr* to scatter, disperse; to demolish, overthrow; to squander, dissipate; to circulate, spread; to drive away *(worries); (mil)* to break up *(enemy formation)*

dissitus *pp of* **disserō** *(to scatter)*

dissociābil·is -is -e *adj* incompatible; irreconcilable

dissociāti·ō -ōnis *f* separation

dissoci·ō -āre -āvī -ātus *tr* to dissociate, separate; to ostracize; to set at variance; to divide into factions; to detach

dissolūbil·is -is -e *adj* dissoluble, separable

dissolūtē *adv* disconnectedly, loosely; carelessly

dissolūti·ō -ōnis *f* dissolution, breakup; abolition; destruction; refutation; looseness, dissoluteness; *(rhet)* asyndeton

dissolūt·us -a -um *adj* disconnected, loose; careless, negligent, remiss; loose, dissolute **‖** *n (rhet)* asyndeton

dissol·vō -vere -vī -ūtus *tr* to dissolve, melt; to dismantle; to disband; to make to disappear; to free, release; to loosen, undo; to solve *(problem);* to break up; to pay *(debt);* to refute; to weaken, wear out; to put an end to, do away with; to refute *(argument);* **animam dissolvere** to die; **lēgem dissolvere** to rescind a law; **poenam dissolvere** to pay the penalty

disson·us -a -um *adj* discordant, jarring, confused *(sounds); (w. abl)* differing from, different from

dissor·s -tis *adj* having a different fate; *(w.* **ab**) unshared by

dissuā·deō -dēre -sī -sus *tr* to advise against; to dissuade **‖** *intr* to argue against an idea

dissuāsi·ō -ōnis *f* dissuasion; *(w. gen)* opposition to, objection to

dissuās·or -ōris *m* opponent

dissuāvior *see* **dissāvior**

dissult·ō -āre *intr* to fly apart, burst

dissu·ō -ere -uī -tus *tr* to take the stitches out of, undo

dissupō *see* **dissipō**

distaed·et -ēre *v impers (w. gen)* it makes *(one)* tired of; **mē distaedet loquī** I'm sick and tired of talking

distanti·a -ae *f* distance, remoteness; difference, diversity

disten·dō *or* **disten·nō -dere -dī -tus** *tr* to stretch apart, stretch out; to distend; to cause to swell *or* bulge; to fill to capacity; to distract; to perplex **‖** *pass* to swell; to bulge

distent·us -a -um *pp of* **distendō ‖** *adj* distended **‖** *pp of* **distineō ‖** *adj* busy, occupied, distracted

distermin·ō -āre -āvī -ātus *tr* to serve as a boundary between, separate by a boundary, divide, limit

distich·on -ī *n (pros)* couplet

dīstīnctē *adv* distinctly, clearly

dīstīncti·ō -ōnis *f* distinction, differentiation, discrimination; distinctive quality *(of a thing);* difference; punctuation mark; division, paragraphing

dīstīnct·us -a -um *pp of* dīstinguō **||** *adj* distinct, separate; studded, adorned; varied, diversified; lucid *(speaker);* eminent

dīstīnct·us -ūs *m* distinction, difference

dis·tineō -tinēre -tinuī -tentus *tr* to keep apart, separate; to detain, hold back, hinder; to employ, engage; to divert; to put off, delay; to keep divided; to stand in the way of; to distract

dīstin·guō -guere dīstīnxī dīstīnctus *tr* to mark off; to distinguish; to specify; to set off *(w. colors, gold, etc.);* to punctuate

dīst·ō -āre *intr* to stand apart, be separate, be distant; to differ; *(w. dat or* ab*)* to differ from; *(w. abl)* to be separated by *(a period of time)* **||** *v impers* there is a difference, it makes a difference

distor·queō -quēre -sī -tus *tr* to twist, distort; to curl *(lips);* to roll *(eyes);* cogitātiōnem distorquēre to rack one's brains

distorti·ō -ōnis *f* twisting; contortion

distort·us -a -um *pp of* distorqueō **||** *adj* distorted, misshapen, deformed; perverse

distracti·ō -ōnis *f* pulling apart; dividing; discord, dissension

distract·us -a -um *adj* severed; rarefied; distracted, perplexed

dis·trahō -trahere -trāxī -tractus *tr* to pull *or* drag apart, separate forcibly; to tear away, drag away, remove; to distract; to sever; to alienate; to prevent, frustrate; to end, settle *(e.g., disputes);* to sell retail; to sell *(land)* in lots

distrib·uō -uere -uī -ūtus *tr* to distribute

distribūtē *adv* methodically

distribūti·ō -ōnis *f* distribution, apportionment, division

dīstrict·us -a -um *adj* drawn in opposite directions; distracted; busy, engaged

dī·stringō -stringere -strīnxī -strictus *tr* to draw apart; to distract, draw attention to

distrunc·ō -āre -āvī -ātus *tr* to cut in two, hack apart

distulī *perf of* differō

disturbāti·ō -ōnis *f* demolition

disturb·ō -āre *tr* to throw into confusion; to demolish; to break up *(a marriage);* to frustrate

dītēsc·ō -ere *intr* to get rich

dīthyrambic·us -a -um *adj (pros)* dithyrambic

dīthyramb·us -ī *m* dithyramb *(song in honor of Bacchus)*

dīti·ae -ārum *fpl* riches

dīt·ō -āre -āvī -ātus *tr* to enrich, make rich **||** *pass* to get rich

diū *adv* by day, in the daytime; long, for a long time; in a long time; diū noctūque by day and by night; iam diū this long; satis diū long enough

diurn·us -a -um *adj* of the day, by day, day, daytime; daily, of each day; day's, of one day; mērum diurnum daytime drinking **||** *n* account book **||** *npl* record, journal, diary

dī·us *or* dīv·us -a -um *adj* godlike, divine; divinely inspired; having the brightness of day

diūtīnē *adv* for a long time

diūtīn·us -a -um *adj* long, lasting, long-lasting

diūtissimē *adv* for a very long time; longest; iam diūtissimē long long ago

diūtius *adv* longer, still longer; paulum diūtius a little too long

diūturnit·ās -ātis *f* length of time, long duration; durability

diūturn·us -a -um *adj* long, long-lasting; chronic

dīv·a -ae *f* goddess

dīvāric·ō -āre -āvī -ātus *tr* to stretch out, spread **||** *pass* to stand *or* sit with legs apart

dī·vellō -vellere -vellī -vulsus *or* -volsus *tr* to tear apart; to tear away; to untie; to wrest, remove, separate; to estrange

dīvēnd·ō -ere -idī -itus *tr* to sell retail

dīverber·ō -āre -āvī -ātus *tr* to split; to batter; to zip through, fly through

dīverb·ium -(i)ī *n (theat)* dialogue

dīversē *adv* (-vor-) in different directions, differently

dīversit·ās -ātis *f* distance; diversity; difference; difference of opinion; difference of method; direct opposite; inconsistency; *(w. gen or* int + *acc)* difference between

dīvers·us -a -um *adj* (-vor-) in different directions; *(of roads)* running *or* leading in different directions; moving from opposite directions, converging; facing *or* turned in two *(or more)* directions; *(w.* ab*)* leading away from; situated at a distance from each other, apart, separate; distant, remote; opposite; of the opposing side *(in war),* hostile; unsettled, irresolute; dissimilar, distinct; inconsistent; different *(from one another in quality, quantity, purpose, degree, effect, etc.);* *(w. dat or* gen *or* ab *or* quam*)* different from, the reverse of **||** *mpl* individuals **||** *n* opposite direction, different quarter, opposite side, opposite view; ex dīversō from a different direction; on opposite sides; from *or* on the opposing side; in contrast, on the other hand; on the contrary; from a different point of view, in turn; in reverse, vice versa; in dīversum in a different direction; for a different reason; to a different effect; vice versa; **per dīversum** crosswise **ǁ** *npl* different parts; **in dīversa** in different directions; **per dīversa** for different reasons

dīver·tō -tere -tī -sum *intr* (**-vor-**) to go different ways; to turn off; to stop off, stay

dīv·es -itis *adj* rich; costly; precious, sumptuous; plentiful; *(w. gen or abl)* rich in, abounding in

dīvex·ō -āre -āvī -ātus *tr* to ravage; to harass

dīvidi·a -ae *f* worry, trouble; nuisance; dissension, antagonism

dī·vidō -videre -vīsī -vīsus *tr* to divide; to distribute, share; to break up, destroy; to arrange, apportion; to separate, distinguish; to segregate, keep apart; to accompany *(songs with music);* **dīmidium dīvidere** to go halves *(w. s.o.);* **sententiam dīvidere** to break down a proposal *(so as to vote on each part separately)*

dīvidu·us -a -um *adj* divisible; divided, separated; forked

dīvīnāti·ō -ōnis *f* clairvoyance; forecasting, predicting, divination; *(leg)* selection of the most suitable prosecutor

dīvīnē *adv* through divine power; prophetically; divinely, gorgeously

dīvīnit·ās -ātis *f* divinity, godhead; prophetic power, clairvoyance; excellence

dīvīnitus *adv* from heaven, from god; providentially; prophetically; divinely, in a godlike manner; excellently

dīvīn·ō -āre -āvī -ātus *tr* to divine, predict; to guess

dīvīn·us -a -um *adj* divine, heavenly; divinely inspired, prophetic; godlike; gorgeous, excellent; **dīvīnum iūs** natural law; **dīvīnum iūs et hūmānum** natural and positive law; **dīvīnum scelus** sacrilege; **rem dīvīnam facere** to worship; to sacrifice; **rēs dīvīna** rite; **rēs dīvīnae** religious affairs, religion; celestial matters **ǁ** *m* prophet **ǁ** *npl* divine matters; religious duties; **dīvīna hūmānaque** things divine and human, the whole world; **dīvīna hūmānaque agere** to perform religious and secular duties

dīvīsi·ō -ōnis *f* division, distribution

dīvīs·or -ōris *m* distributor; agent hired by a candidate to give out bribes

dīvīs·us -a -um *pp of* **dīvidō ǁ** *adj* separate, distinct

dīvīs·us -ūs *m* division, distribution; **facilis dīvīsuī** easily divided

dīviti·ae -ārum *fpl* riches; richness *(of soil);* costly things

dīvolg- = dīvulg-

dīvor- = dīver-

dīvort·ium -(i)ī *n* divorce; fork *(of road or river);* **dīvortium facere cum** to divorce *(a woman)*

dīvulgāt·us -a -um *adj* common, widespread

dīvulg·ō -āre -āvī -ātus *tr* to divulge, spread among the people; to publish *(book);* to publicize, advertise

dīvulsus *pp of* **dīvellō**

dīv·us *or* **dī·us -a -um** *adj* divine, deified **ǁ** *m* god, deity; title applied to dead emperors **ǁ** *n* sky; the open; **sub dīvō** out in the open; **sub dīvum rapere** to bring out into the open

dō dare dedī datus (**danit** = **dat; danunt** = **dant; dāne** = **dāsne; duim, duis, duit** = **dem, dēs det;** *(in Plautus:* **dane** = **dāsne; datin** = **datisne; dabin** = **dabisne; duās** = **dēs)** *tr* to give; to offer, dedicate; to pay out *(money);* to confer; to permit, grant; to give up, hand over; to communicate, tell; to ascribe, impute, assign; to cause, make; to furnish, afford, present; to admit; to administer *(medicine);* to utter, give expression to, announce; **amplexūs dare** to embrace; **comoediam dare** to present a comedy; **concilium** (*or* **contiōnem**) **dare** to allow a private person to address the assembly; **cōnspectum dare** to make visible; **damnum dare** to cause damage; **fābulam dare** to present a play; **iūs** (*or* **iūra**) **dare** to give laws, give a constitution, administer justice; **lētō** (*or* **mortī**) **dare** to send *(s.o.)* to *(his)* death; **lēgem dare** to enact a law; **litterās dare** to mail a letter; **locum dare** *(w. dat)* to make way for; **manūs dare** to surrender; **nōmen dare** to enlist; **operam dare** *(w. dat)* to pay attention to, devote attention to, look out for; **palam dare** to make clear; **poenam** (*or* **poenās** *or* **supplicium**) **dare** to pay the penalty; **satis dare** *(w. dat)* to give satisfaction to, satisfy; **senātum dare** to allow a private person to address the Senate; **spatium dare** to make room; **terga dare** to take to one's heels; **vēlum dare** to set sail; **veniam dare** to grant pardon; **vēnum dare** to put up for sale **ǁ** *refl* to present oneself; to plunge, rush; **sē dare mīlitem** (*or* **mīlitiae**) to enlist in the service

doc·eō -ēre -uī -tus *tr* to teach, instruct; to give instructions to; to tell, inform *(s.o. of a fact);* *(w. double acc)* to teach *(s.o. s.th.);* **fābulam docēre** to produce a play, put on a play

dochm·ius -iī *m (pros)* dochmiac foot *(consisting of iamb and cretic)* (˘ — — ˘ —)

docil·is -is -e *adj* easily taught, teachable; ready to listen

docilit·ās -ātis *f* aptitude for learning

doctē *adv* skillfully; learnedly; cleverly

doct·or -ōris *m* teacher

doctrīn·a **-ae** *f* teaching, instruction, education, training; lesson; erudition, learning; science; **doctrīnā** on principle

doct·us **-a** **-um** *pp of* **doceō** ‖ *adj* learned, skilled, experienced, trained; clever, shrewd; *(w. abl or ad or* **in** + *abl)* skilled in, clever at

document·um **-ī** *or* **docum·en** **-inis** *n* (**doci-**) example, model, pattern; object lesson, warning; proof, evidence

Dōdōn·a **-ae** *f* town in Epirus, famous for the oracular oak tree sacred to Jupiter; *(fig)* the oak grove in Dodona

Dōdōnae·us **-a** **-um** *adj* of Dodona

Dōdōn·is **-idis** *adj (fem only)* of Dodona

dōdr·āns **-antis** *m* three-fourths; **hērēs ex dōdrante** heir to three-fourths of an estate

dōdrantāri·us **-a** **-um** *adj* **tabulae dōdrantāriae** account books connected with the Valerian Law of 86 B.C., which reduced debts by three-fourths

dogm·a **-atis** *n* doctrine, tenet

Dolabell·a **-ae** *m* Roman family name *(cognomen)* in the *gens Cornelia, esp.* Publius Cornelius Dolabella, Cicero's son-in-law *(d. 43 B.C.)*

dolābr·a **-ae** *f* pickax, mattock

dol·ēns **-entis** *adj* painful, smarting; distressing; grieving

dolenter *adv* painfully; with sorrow

dol·eō **-ēre** **-uī** **-itūrus** *tr* to give pain to, hurt ‖ *intr* to feel pain; to hurt, be sore, ache, smart; to grieve, be sorry, be hurt; take offense; *(w. dat)* to give pain to, afflict; **caput mihi dolet** I have a headache

dōliār·is **-is** **-e** *adj (coll)* fat, tubby

dōliol·um **-ī** *n* small barrel

dōl·ium **-iī** *n* large earthenware barrel

dol·ō **-āre** **-āvī** **-ātus** *tr* to chop; to beat up, drub; *(fig)* to hack out *(e.g., a poem)*

dol·ō **-ōnis** *m* pike *(having a wooden shaft and a short iron point);* topsail

Dol·ōn **-ōnis** *m* Dolon *(Trojan spy)*

Dolop·es **-um** *mpl* tribe of Thessaly

dol·or **-ōris** *m* pain, ache; grief, distress; indignation, resentment, chagrin; pathos; object of grief; **capitis dolor** headache; **dentium dolor** toothache; **esse dolōrī** *(w. dat)* to be a cause of grief or resentment to

dolōsē *adv* shrewdly, slyly

dolōs·us **-a** **-um** *adj* wily, cunning

dol·us **-ī** *m* trick; deceit, cunning; **dolus malus** *(leg)* malice aforethought, fraud

domābil·is **-is** **-e** *adj* able to be tamed

domesticātim *adv* at home, by the use of one's domestics

domestic·us **-a** **-um** *adj* of the house *or* home; domestic, household; familiar, private, personal; native, of one's own country; **bellum**

domesticum civil war ‖ *mpl* members of the household, one's staff

domī *see* **domus**

domicēn·ium **-(i)ī** *n* a meal at home

domicil·ium **-(i)ī** *n* residence, home

domin·a **-ae** *or* **domn·a** **-ae** *f* lady of the house; mistress, owner; lady; sweetheart; wife; *(as a title of courtesy)* Ma'am

domin·āns **-antis** *adj* ruling, dominant; **nōmen domināns** word in its literal sense, normal word ‖ *m* ruler

domināti·ō **-ōnis** *f* mastery; tyranny, despotism; dominion, kingdom ‖ *fpl* control; supremacy; rulers

domināt·or **-ōris** *m* arbitrary ruler, lord

dominātr·īx **-īcis** *f* ruler, mistress

domināt·us **-ūs** *m* absolute rule, sovereignty; ownership; mastery

dominic·us **-a** **-um** *adj* master's; mistress's; owner's; belonging to the emperor ‖ **Dominic·a** **-ae** *f (eccl)* the Lord's day, Sunday

domin·ium **-(i)ī** *n* rule, dominion; ownership; banquet, feast

domin·or **-ārī** **-ātus sum** *intr* to be master, be lord, have dominion; to domineer; *(w.* **in** + *acc or abl)* to lord it over, dominate

domin·us **-ī** *m* owner, proprietor; employer; master, ruler, lord; tyrant; commander; lover; manager *(of a troupe); (as a courtesy title)* Sir; *(as imperial title)* His Imperial Highness; **convīvī dominus** host ‖ **Dominus** *(eccl)* the Lord

domiport·a **-ae** *f* house-carrier *(snail)*

Domitiān·us **-ī** *m* Domitian *(Titus Flavius Domitianus, son of Vespasian and Roman emperor, 81–96 A.D.)*

domit·ō **-āre** **-āvī** *tr* to train, break in

domit·or **-ōris** *m* tamer; conqueror

domitr·īx **-īcis** *f* tamer *(female)*

domit·us **-a** **-um** *adj* house-bound, kept at home

domit·us **-ūs** *m* taming

dom·ō **-āre** **-uī** **-itus** *tr* to tame, break in; to domesticate; to master, subdue, vanquish, conquer

dom·us **-ūs** *or* **-ī** *(dat:* **domō** *or* **domuī;** *abl* **domō** *or* **domū;** *loc:* **domī,** *rarely* **domō** *or* **domuī;** *gen pl:* **domōrum** *or* **domuum)** *f* house, home; mansion, palace; family, household; school *(of philosophers);* building *(of any sort);* seat *(an activity);* **domī** at home; by one's own resources; **domī mīlitiaeque** at home and in the field; in peace and in war; **domī meae** at my home; **domī tuae** at your home; **domō** from home; from the house; from one's own resources; at home; **domum** *(to one's)* home; *(coll)* into one's pocket

dōnābil·is -is -e *adj* worthy of a gift
dōnār·ium -(i)ī *n* gift repository of a temple; sanctuary; altar; votive offering
dōnāti·ō -ōnis *f* donation
dōnātīv·um -ī *n* (*mil*) bonus
dōnec (*also* **dōnicum**) *conj* while; as long as; until
dōn·ō -āre -āvī -ātus *tr* to present, grant; to condone, excuse; to forgive, let off; to give up, sacrifice; **aliquem cīvitāte dōnāre** to present s.o. with citizenship; **cīvitātem alicui dōnāre** to bestow citizenship on s.o.
dōn·um -ī *n* gift, present; votive offering, sacrifice; **ultima dōna** funeral rites, obsequies
dorc·as -adis *f* gazelle
Dōr·ēs *or* **Dōr·īs -um** *mpl* Dorians (*one of the four Hellenic tribes inhabiting the Peloponnese in the classical period; also, the inhabitants of Doris in N. Greece*)
Dōricē *adv* in the Dorian dialect
Dōric·us -a -um *adj* Doric ‖ *mpl* the Dorians
Dōr·is -idis *or* **-idos** *adj* (*fem only*) Dorian, Doric ‖ *f* district in N. Greece ‖ the S.W. tip of Caria with its offshore islands ‖ a sea-goddess, wife of Nereus and mother of fifty sea nymphs
Dōri·us -a -um *adj* Dorian
dorm·iō -īre -īvī *or* **-iī -ītum** *intr* to sleep; to fall asleep; to be idle, be unconcerned
dormītāt·or -ōris *m* night-prowler
dormīt·ō -āre -āvī *intr* to be sleepy, be drowsy; to nod, fall asleep
dormīt·or -ōris *m* sleeper
dormītōri·us -a -um *adj* for sleeping; **cubiculum dormītōrium** bedroom
dors·um -ī *n or* **dors·us -ī** *m* back; ridge; reef; ridge (*of a mountain*)
doryphor·os *or* **doryphor·us -ī** *m* spearman
dōs dōtis *f* dowry; endowment
Dossenn·us -ī *m* hunchback, clown (*well-known character in early Italic comedy*)
dōtāl·is -is -e *adj* of a dowry, given as a dowry, dotal
dōtāt·us -a -um *adj* endowed; **dōtātissimus** richly endowed
dōt·ō -āre -āvī -ātus *tr* to endow
drachm·a *or* **drachum·a -ae** *f* drachma (*Greek coin approximately the value of a denarius, c. $1*)
drachumiss·ō -āre *intr* to work for a drachma a day
drac·ō -ōnis *m* dragon; huge serpent ‖ **Dracō** Draco (*Athenian lawgiver, notorious for his severity, c. 621 B.C.*); (*astr*) Dragon (*constellation*)
dracōnigen·us -a -um *adj* sprung from (the teeth of) a dragon; **urbs dracōnigena** Thebes
drāpet·a -ae *m* runaway slave
drauc·us -ī *m* athlete

drom·as -adis *m* dromedary, camel
drom·os -ī *m* parade ground
drōp·ax -acis *m* hair-remover
Druid·ēs -um *or* **Druid·ae -ārum** *mpl* Druids (*priests and sages of the Gauls and Britons*)
Drūsill·a -ae *f* Livia Drusilla (*second wife of Augustus and mother of Tiberius, 58 B.C.–A.D. 29*) ‖ sister of Caligula ‖ daughter of Caligula, murdered in infancy
Drūs·us -ī *m* Livius Drusus (*tribune of the people with Gaius Gracchus in 122 B.C.*) ‖ Marcus Livius Drusus (*former's son, famous orator and tribune of the people in 91 B.C.*) ‖ Nero Claudius Drusus (*son of Livia, brother of Tiberius, 38 B.C.–A.D. 9*)
dry·as -adis *f* dryad (*wood nymph*)
Dryop·ē -ēs *f* mother of Amphissus by Apollo ‖ mother of Tarquinius
Dryop·es -um *mpl* a people of Epirus
dubiē *adv* doubtfully; **haud dubiē** undoubtedly, indubitably
dubitābil·is -is -e *adj* doubtful
dubitanter *adv* doubtingly, hesitantly
dubitāti·ō -ōnis *f* doubt, uncertainty; wavering, hesitancy; hesitation, delay; (*rhet*) pretended embarrassment (*to win over sympathy*)
dubit·ō -āre -āvī -ātus *tr* to doubt; to consider, ponder, wonder about ‖ *intr* to be doubtful, be in doubt, be uncertain, be perplexed; to deliberate; to waver, hesitate, delay
dubi·us -a -um *adj* wavering, doubtful, dubious, uncertain; precarious, critical; adverse, difficult; dim (*light*); overcast (*sky*); indecisive (*battle*); **haud prō dubiō habēre** to regard as beyond doubt; **in dubium venīre** to come into question; **in dubium vocāre** to call into question; **procul dubiō** undoubtedly
ducāt·us -ūs *m* military leadership, command
ducēnāri·us -a -um *adj* receiving an annual salary of 200,000 sesterces (*c. $50,000*)
ducēn·ī -ae -a *adj* two hundred each
ducentēsim·a -ae *f* half-percent tax
ducent·ī -ae -a *adj* two hundred
ducentiēns *adv* (**-iēs**) two hundred times
dūcō dūcere dūxī ductus *tr* to lead, guide, direct, conduct; to command; to march; to draw, pull; to draw out, prolong; to pass, spend (*time*); to stall (*s.o.*); to pull at (*oars*); to mislead, take in, fool; to draw, attract; to draw (*lots*); to draw in, breathe in; to sip, drink; to trace; to construct, form, fashion, shape; to run, build (*a wall or ditch or rampart or road from one point to another*); to drive (*vehicles*); to assume, get (*a name*); (*of a man*) to marry; to calculate, compute; to regard, consider, hold, account; to derive, trace (*lineage*); to spin (*wool*); (*of a road*) to lead, take (*s.o.*); **dūcere triumphum** to hold

a triumph; **id parvī dūcere** to consider it of little importance; **initium** *(or* **ratiōnem)** **dūcere** to take account *(of)*, pay attention *(to);* **prīncipium dūcere** *(w.* **ab)** to start from, originate from, trace to, e.g.: **bellī initium ā fame dūcere** to trace the beginning of the war to hunger; **uxōrem dūcere** *(of the groom)* to get married, take a wife

ductil·is -is -e *adj (of a river)* that is led along a course

ductim *adv* in a continuous stream

ductit·ō -āre -āvī -ātus *tr* to take home, marry *(a woman);* to lead on, trick

duct·ō -āre -āvī -ātus *tr* to lead; to draw; to accompany, escort

duct·or -ōris *m* leader, commander, general; guide; pilot

duct·us -ūs *m* drawing, conducting; line, row; leadership, command; **aquae ductus** aqueduct; **ōris ductus** facial expression

dūdum *adv* a short time ago; just now; once, formerly; **cum dūdum** just as; **haud dūdum** not long ago, just now; **iam dūdum** for some time; **iam dūdum eum exspectō** I have been waiting for him a long time; **quam dūdum** how long; **ut dūdum** just as

Duill·ius *or* **Duīl·ius -(i)ī** *m* Duilius *(Roman consul who won Rome's first naval victory, off Sicily, in 260 B.C.)*

duim, duis duit *see* **dō**

dulcēd·ō -inis *f* sweetness; pleasantness, charm, delightfulness

dulc·ēscō -ēscere *intr* to become sweet

dulciāri·us -a -um *adj* **pīstor dulciārius** confectioner, pastry baker

dulcicul·us -a -um *adj* rather sweet

dulcif·er -era -erum *adj* full of sweetness, sweet

dulc·is -is -e *adj* sweet; pleasant, delightful; dear, affectionate, kind

dulciter *adv* sweetly; pleasantly

dulcitūd·ō -inis *f* sweetness

dūlicē *adv* like a slave

Dūlich·ium -iī *n* **or** **Dūlichi·a -ae** *f* Dulichium *(island in the Ionian Sea)*

Dūlich·ius -(i)ī *m* Ulysses

dum *adv* up to now, yet, as yet; now; **age dum!** *(pl:* **agite dum!)** come now!; all right!; **nēmō dum** no one (as) yet; **nōn dum** not yet

dum *conj* while; as long as; until; provided that, if only; **dum modo** *or* **dummodo** provided that, if only; **exspectābam dum redīret** I was waiting for him to return

dūmēt·um -ī *n* thicket, underbrush

dummodo *conj* provided that

dūmōs·us -a -um *adj* overgrown with bushes, bushy

dumtaxat *adv (with numbers)* up to, at most, not exceeding; *(with small numbers)* only,

just; not less than, at least; *(limiting a statement)* at any rate, at least, strictly speaking; up to a point **II** *conj* provided that, as long as; **nōn dumtaxat … sed** not just … but also

dūm·us -ī *m* bush, bramble

du·o -ae -o *(dat & abl pl:* **duōbus, duābus, duōbus;** *masc acc pl:* **duo** *or* **duōs)** *adj* two

duodeciēns *adv* **(-ciēs)** twelve times

duodecim *indecl adj* twelve

duodecim·us -a -um *adj* **(-cum-)** twelfth

duodēn·ī -ae -a *adj* twelve each, twelve, apiece; a dozen; **duodēnīs assibus** at 12%

duodēquadrāgēsim·us *adj* thirty-eighth

duodēquadrāgintā *indecl adj* thirty-eight

duodēquīnquāgēsim·us -a -um *adj* forty-eighth

duodēquīnquāgintā *indecl adj* forty-eight

duodētrīciēns *adv* **(-ciēs)** twenty-eight times

duodētrīgintā *indecl adj* twenty-eight

duodēvīcēn·ī -ae -a *adj* eighteen each

duodēvīgintī *indecl adj* eighteen

duoetvīcēsimān·ī -ōrum *mpl* soldiers of the twenty-second legion

duoetvīcēsim·us -a -um *adj* **(-cens-)** twenty-second

duovirī *see* **duumvirī**

dupl·a -ae *f* a double amount of money; double the price

dupl·ex -icis *adj* twofold, double; divided into two; in double rows; double, twice as big; twice as long; complex, compound; two-faced, double-dealing, false

duplicār·ius -iī *m* soldier receiving double pay

dupliciter *adv* doubly; in two ways; into two categories

duplic·ō -āre -āvī -ātus *tr* to double up, bend over; to double *(in size, length, quantity)*

dupl·us -a -um *adj* double, twice as much, twice as large **II** *f see* **dupla II** *n* double the price; **in duplum** twice the amount; **in duplum īre** to pay twice as much

dupond·ius -(i)ī *m* **or** **dupond·ium -(i)ī** *n* two-as coin *(worth c. 2¢)*

dūrābil·is -is -e *adj* durable, lasting

dūracin·us -a -um *adj* having a hard berry

dūrām·en -inis *n* hardness

dūrate·us -a -um *adj* wooden

dūrē *or* **dūriter** *adv* hard, sternly, rigorously, roughly; stiffly, awkwardly

dūr·ēscō -ēscere -uī *intr* to grow hard, harden; to become solid

dūrit·ās -ātis *f* hardness, toughness; harshness

dūriter *see* **dūrē**

dūriti·a -ae *or* **dūriti·ēs -ēī** *f* hardness; austerity; strictness, harshness, rigor; oppressiveness; insensibility, callousness

dūriuscul·us -a -um *adj* somewhat hard, rather harsh

dūr·ō -āre -āvī -ātus *tr* to harden, solidify; *(fig)* to harden, inure, toughen up; to make insensible; to dull, blunt **ǁ** *intr* to be tough, be inured; to become hard; *(of liquids)* to become solid; to endure, last, hold out; to continue unchanged, remain; *(of food)* to keep; *(of hills)* to continue unbroken, extend

dūr·us -a -um *adj* hard; lasting; rough *(to the senses);* tough, hardy; rough, rude, uncouth; shameless, brazen; harsh, cruel; callous, insensitive; severe, oppressive; parsimonious

duum·vir *or* duo·vir *or* **II**·vir -virī *m* duumvir *(member of a board of two)* *(see* **duumvirī)**

duumvirāt·us -ūs *m* duumvirate, office of duumvir

duumvir·ī -ōrum *or* duovir·ī *or* **II**·virī -ōrum *mpl* two-man board; **duumvirī ad aedem faciendam** two-man board for the construction of a temple; **duumvirī iūrī dīcundō** two-man board of colonial magistrates; pair of judges; **duumvirī nāvālēs** two-man board to equip the navy; **duumvirī perduelliōnis** criminal court *(to try cases of treason);* **duumvirī sacrōrum** two-man board in charge of the Sibylline books

dux ducis *m* *(f)* general; guide; leader, head, ringleader; driver *(of chariot);* captain *(of ship),* commander *(of naval force);* **dux gregis** shepherd

Dymant·is -idos *f* daughter of Dymas *(Hecuba)*

Dym·ās -antis *m* father of Hecuba

dynam·is -is *f* store, plenty

dynast·ēs -ae *m* ruler, (Eastern) prince

Dyrr(h)ach·ium -(i)ī *n* Adriatic port in Illyria, serving as landing place for those sailing from Italy to Greece

dysenteri·a -ae *f* dysentery

dyspepsi·a -ae *f* indigestion

E

E, e *(supply* littera) *f* fifth letter of the Latin alphabet; letter name: **e**

-ē *advl suf* forms adverbs from adjectives: **clārē** clearly; but in prosody, **bene, male**

ē- *pref see* ex-

ē *prep* of, out of, from *(see* **ex)**

eā *adv* there; that way

ea ēius *pron* she

eādem *adv* the same way, by the same route; at the same time; likewise, by the same token

eāpropter *adv* therefore

eapse = ipsa *(old feminine emphatic form of* ipse)

eātenus *adv* so far; *(followed by* **quod** *or* **ut)** so far … as (that)

eben·us -ī *f* ebony tree, ebony

ēbib·ō -ere -ī -itus *tr* to drink up, drain; *(of things)* to absorb, swallow up; to spend on drinks

ebiscum *see* hibiscum

ēbīt·ō -ere *intr* to go out

ēbland·ior -īrī -ītus sum *tr* to coax out, obtain by flattery

Eborāc·um -ī *n* **(Ebur-)** town in Britain *(modern York)*

eborāt·us -a -um *adj* **(ebur-)** adorned with ivory

ēbriet·ās -ātis *f* drunkenness

ēbriol·us -a -um *adj* tipsy

ēbriōsit·ās -ātis *f* habitual drunkenness, heavy drinking

ēbriōs·us -a -um *adj* addicted to drinking **ǁ** *mf* drunkard

ēbri·us -a -um *adj* drunk; drunken *(acts, words),* of a drunk; *(fig)* intoxicated *(e.g., w. love, power)*

ēbull·iō -īre -iī *or* -īvī *tr* to babble about; **animam ēbullīre** *(coll)* to give up the ghost **ǁ** *intr* to bubble up

ebul·um -ī *n or* ebul·us -ī *f (bot)* dwarf elder *(small tree having clusters of white flowers and red or blackish berry-like fruit)*

eb·ur -oris *n* ivory; ivory object *(e.g., statue, flute, scabbard);* elephant's tusk; elephant; curule chair *(of a magistrate, ornamented with ivory)*

eburāt·us -a -um *adj* inlaid with ivory

eburneol·us -a -um *adj* made of ivory

eburne·us *or* eburn·us -a -um *adj* ivory; white as ivory; **dentēs eburneī** tusks; **ēnsis eburneus** sword with ivory hilt

ec- *pref (prefixed to interrogatives with intensive or indefinite force, e.g.,* **ecquis** *is there anyone who?)*

ēcastor *interj (used mainly by women)* by Castor!

ecca, eccam, eccās *see* ecce

ecce *interj* see!, look!, look here! here!; *(followed by accusative in early literature; also followed by nominative from time of Cicero on)* **ecce mē!** here I am!; **ecce nōs!** here we are!; *(colloquially combined with the pronouns* **is, ille, iste: ecca!** *(i.e.,* **ecce + ea)** *(fem sing)* here she is!; *(neut pl)* here they are!; **eccam!** *(i.e.,* **ecce + eam)** here she is!; **eccilla** *or* **eccistam!** there she is!; **eccillum** *or* **eccum!** here he is!; **eccōs!** here they are!; *(calling attention to something non-visual)* mark this!; *(in vivid narrative, introducing a surprising event)* lo and behold!

eccerē *interj* there!

eccheum·a -atis *n* pouring out

eccill- *see* **ecce**

eccist- *see* **ecce**

ecclēsi·a -ae *f* Greek assembly of the people; *(eccl)* church, congregation

eccōs *interj see* **ecce**

eccum *interj see* **ecce**

ecdic·us -ī *m* public prosecutor; public defender

ecf- = eff-

echidn·a -ae *f* viper **‖ Echidna** Hydra; **Echidna Lernaea** Lernaean Hydra **‖** monstrous mother of Cerberus, half woman and half serpent

Echidnē·us -a -um *adj* of Echidna; **canis Echidnēus** Cerberus

Echīnad·es -um *fpl* cluster of small islands off Acarnania

echīn·us -ī *m* sea urchin; hedgehog; dishpan

Echī·ōn -onis *m* hero who sprang from the dragon's teeth sown by Cadmus, married Agave, and became father of Pentheus **‖** an argonaut

Echīonid·ēs -ae *m* Pentheus, son of Echion

Echīoni·us -a -um *adj* Cadmean, Theban

Ēch·ō -ūs *(acc:* **-ō** *or* **-ōn)** *f* nymph who was changed by Hera into an echo

eclog·a -ae *f* literary selection; eclogue

eclogāri·ī -ōrum *mpl* excerpted literary passages

ecquandō *adv* ever, at any time; *(in indirect questions)* whether ever

ecqu·ī -ae *(or* **-a) -od** *interrog adj* any at all, really any

ecquī *conj (in indirect questions)* whether

ec·quid -cūius *pron* anything at all; *(in questions)* whether, if at all

ec·quis -cūius *pron* any at all, anyone at all; *(in indirect questions)* whether anyone

ecquō *adv* anywhere

ecule·us -ī *m* foal, colt; small equestrian statue; torture rack; hobbyhorse

edācit·ās -ātis *f* gluttony

ed·āx -ācis *adj* gluttonous; *(fig)* devouring, destructive

ēdent·ō -āre -āvī -ātus *tr (sl)* to knock the teeth out of

ēdentul·us -a -us *adj* toothless, old

edepol *interj* by Pollux!, gad!

eder·a *or* **heder·a -ae** *f* ivy

ē·dīcō -dīcere -dīxī -dictus *tr* to proclaim; to decree; to appoint

ēdicti·ō -ōnis *f* edict, decree

ēdict·ō -āre -āvī -ātus *tr* to proclaim, publish

ēdict·um -ī *n* edict, proclamation; edict of a praetor listing rules he would follow in his capacity as judge

ē·discō -discere -didicī *tr* to learn by heart, learn thoroughly

ēdisser·ō -ere -uī -tus *tr* to explain in detail, analyze fully

ēdissert·ō -āre -āvī -ātus *tr* to explain fully, explain in detail

ēditīci·us -a -um *adj* set forth, proposed; **iūdicēs ēditīciī** panel of jurors *(subject to challenge by defendant)*

ēditi·ō -ōnis *f* statement, account; publication; edition *(of book); (leg)* declaration *(of the form of judicial procedure to be followed)*

ēdit·us -a -um *adj* high; raised, rising; *(fig)* exalted; **locus ēditus** height, hill **‖** *n* height; ordinance; **ex ēditō** from a height; **in ēditō** on a hill; *(fig)* on a pedestal

edō edere *(or* **ēsse) ēdī ēsus** *tr* to eat; *(fig)* to devour, consume, destroy; **pugnōs edere** *(sl)* to to be hit with a fist, cast a knuckle sandwich

ēd·ō -ere -idī -itus *tr* to give out, put forth, bring forth, emit; to give birth to, bear; to publish; to tell, announce, disclose; to show, display, produce, perform; to bring about, cause; to bring forward *(witnesses); (leg)* to give the defendant notice of; **animam ēdere** to give up the ghost

ēdoc·eō -ēre -uī -tus *tr* to teach thoroughly; to instruct clearly; to inform; to show clearly; *(w. double acc)* to teach *(s.o. s.th.)* well

ēdol·ō -āre -āvī -ātus *tr* to hew out: *(fig)* to hew into shape

ēdom·ō -āre -uī -itus *tr* to conquer thoroughly; to overcome *(vices, difficulties)*

Ēdōn·ī -ōrum *or* **Ēdōn·es -um** *mpl* Thracian tribe noted for its heavy drinking

Ēdōn·is -idis *adj (fem only)* Edonian **‖** *f* Bacchante

Ēdōn·us -a -um *adj* Edonian

ēdorm·iō -īre -īvī *or* **-iī -ītus** *tr* to sleep off; to sleep through *(e.g., a lecture);* **crāpulam ēdormīre** to sleep off a hangover **‖** *intr* to sleep soundly

ēdormīsc·ō -ere *tr* to sleep off *(a hangover)*

ēducāti·ō -ōnis *f* raising *(of children, animals, plants)*

ēducāt·or -ōris *m* fosterer; foster father

ēducātr·īx -īcis *f* foster mother; nurse

ēduc·ō -āre -āvī -ātus *tr* to bring up, raise *(children, animals, plants);* to produce *(fruit, grain)*

ēdū·cō -cere -xī -ctus *tr* to draw out, to take away; to build high, raise, erect *(tower);* to drain off *(liquids);* to draw *(sword);* to spend *(time);* to lead out *(army);* to raise *(children, animals, plants);* **in iūs ēdūcere** to take to court

edūl·ia -ium *npl* eatables

edūl·is -is -e *adj* edible, eatable

ēdūr·ō -āre *intr* to last, endure

ēdūr·us -a -um *adj* hard, tough; *(fig)* tough

Ēēti·ōn -ōnis *m* father of Andromache and king of Thebe in Cilicia

effarciō *see* **efferciō**

effāt·us -a -um *pp of* **effor** ‖ *adj* solemnly pronounced ‖ *n* pronouncement; axiom, proposition

effecti·ō -ōnis *f* accomplishment, performance; efficient cause

effectīv·us -a -um *adj* effective; practical

effect·or -ōris *m,* **effectr·īx -īcis** *f* producer, author

effect·us -a -um *pp of* **efficiō** ‖ *adj* finished, complete ‖ *n* effect

effect·us -ūs *m* effecting; completion; effect, result; **ad effectum addūcere** to bring to completion; **cum effectū** in fact, actually; **effectū** in effect, to all intents and purposes; **sine effectū** without a decisive result

effēmināte *adv* effeminately

effēmināt·us -a -um *adj* (**ecf-**) effeminate

effēmin·ō -āre -āvī -ātus *tr* (**ecf-**) to make a woman of; to represent as a woman, regard as female; to emasculate ‖ *pass* to become unmanly

efferāt·us -a -um *adj* wild, savage

effer·ciō *or* **effarciō -cīre -sī -tus** *tr* (**ecfer-, ecfar-**) to stuff; to fill in *(e.g., a ditch)*

efferit·ās -ātis *f* wildness, barbarism

effer·ō -āre -āvī -ātus *tr* (**ecf-**) to make wild, brutalize; to exasperate

efferō efferre extulī ēlātus *tr* (**ecf-**) to carry out, bring out, bring forth; to utter, express, to publish, spread *(news);* to carry out for burial, bury; to produce, bear; to name, designate; to lift up, raise; to promote, advance; to bring out, expose; to praise, extol; to sweep off one's feet; *(w.* **ex**) to copy out *(of some text);* **in lūcem efferre** *(of fields)* to produce *(crops);* **gressum** *(or* **pedem) efferre** to go forth ‖ *refl* to arise; to be haughty, be conceited ‖ *pass (fig)* to be carried away

effert·us -a -um *pp of* **efferciō** ‖ *adj* chockfull, crammed, bulging

effer·us -a -um *adj* very wild, savage

efferv·eō -ēre *or* **efferv·ō -ere** *intr* to boil over; *(of bees, etc.)* to come pouring out; *(of volcano)* to erupt

efferv·ēscō -ēscere -ī *intr* to boil, boil over; to burst forth; to get all worked up; to seethe; to rage; *(of words) (fig)* to become heated

effēt·us -a -um *adj* worn out, spent; vain, delusive; *(w. gen)* incapable of

efficācit·ās -ātis *f* efficiency

efficāciter *adv* efficiently, effectively

effic·āx -ācis *adj* efficient, effective, efficacious

effici·ēns -entis *adj* efficient, effective; **rēs efficientēs** *(phil)* efficient causes

efficienter *adv* efficiently

efficienti·a -ae *f* efficiency, efficacy, influence

ef·ficiō -ficere -fēcī -fectus *tr* (**ecf-**) to bring about, bring to pass, effect, cause, produce; to make, form; to construct; to finish, complete, accomplish; to show, prove; *(w.* **ut**) to bring it about that; to carry out *(an order); (of component parts)* to constitute; to cover *(a distance in travel); (of numbers)* to amount to, add up to; *(of a field)* to produce, yield; to compose *(a speech, an essay);* *(w. double acc)* to elect *(s.o., e.g., consul)* ‖ *pass* to follow; **ita efficitur ut** thus it follows that

effictus *pp of* **effingō**

effigi·ēs -ēī *or* **effigi·a -ae** *f* effigy, likeness, semblance; opposite number; copy, imitation; image; statue, figure, portrait; ghost, phantom

ef·fingō -fingere -fīnxī -fictus *tr* (**ecf-**) to mold, form, fashion; to imitate; to wipe out, wipe clean; to represent, portray; to imagine

effiō *pass of* **efficiō**

efflāgitāti·ō -ōnis *f* urgent demand

efflāgitāt·us -ūs *m* insistence

efflāgit·ō -āre *tr* to demand, insist on; to pester *(s.o. with requests)*

effl·āns -antis *pres p of* **efflō** & *adj* dying; deadly, fatal

efflīctim *adv* (**ecf-**) passionately

ef·flī·gō -flīgere -flīxī -efflīctus *tr* (**ecf-**) to strike dead, exterminate

effl·ō -āre -āvī -ātus *tr* (**ecf-**) to breathe out; **animam efflāre** to expire

efflōr·ēscō -ēscere -uī *intr* (**ecf-**) to bloom, blossom forth; *(fig)* to flourish

efflu·ō -ere -xī *intr* (**ecf-**) to flow out, flow forth, run out; to slip away, drop out, disappear; *(of rumor)* to get out, circulate; *(of secret)* to leak out; **ex animō** *(or* **memoriā) effluere** to slip one's mind

effluv·ium -(i)ī *n* outlet

ef·fodiō -fodere -fōdī -fossus *tr* (**ecf-, exf-**) to dig up; to gouge out *(eyes);* to hollow out; to root out; to make *(by digging);* to erase; **humum** *(or* **terram) effodere** to dig a hole in the ground

ef·for -fārī -fātus sum *tr* (**ecf-**) to say out loud, tell; *(in augury)* to mark off, consecrate *(an area)* ‖ *intr* to speak out

effossus *pp of* **effodiō**

effrēnāte *adv* (**ecf-**) without restraint, out of control

effrēnāti·ō -ōnis *f* impetuosity

effrēnāt·us -a -um *adj* (**ecf-**) unbridled; *(fig)* unbridled, unrestrained

effrēn·us -a -um *adj* unbridled; *(fig)* uncontrolled

ef·fringō -fringere -frēgī -frāctus *tr* (**ecf-**) to break open, smash, break off; to break down *(door)* ef·fugiō -fugere -fūgī *tr* (ecf-, exf-) to escape; to keep away from *(a person or place);* to avoid; to escape the grasp of, slip out of *(the hands);* to escape the notice of ‖ *intr* to escape, slip away; *(w. abl or w.* **ab** *or* **ex)** to escape from

effug·ium -(i)ī *n* escape, flight; means of escape; avoidance

efful·geō -gēre -sī *or* effulg·ō -ere *intr* to shine forth, gleam, flash, glitter; *(fig)* to shine forth

effult·us -a -um *adj* propped up, supported

ef·fundō -fundere -fūdī -fūsus *tr* (ecf-) to pour out, pour away; to emit; to utter *(sounds);* to allow *(rain water)* to run off; to shed *(tears);* to hurl, shower *(weapons);* (w. **in** + *acc*) to shower *(praises)* on; *(of the stomach)* to throw up; to give up, let go, abandon, resign; to knock down, overturn *(walls, buildings);* to produce in abundance; to lavish, waste *(money, energy);* *(of tree)* to spread out *(branches);* to empty out *(bags, etc.);* to give vent to, pour out ‖ *refl & pass* to come pouring out; *(of rain)* to pour down; *(of a river)* (w. **ab)** to begin to flow from, have its source at; **super rīpam effundī** to overflow its banks

effūsē *adv* far and wide; at random, in disorder; lavishly; immoderately

effūsi·ō -ōnis *f* (ecf-) outpouring, rushing out; shedding; effusion; profusion, lavishness, extravagance ‖ *fpl* excesses

effūs·us -a -um *pp of* **effundō** ‖ *adj* spread out, extensive; *(of troops)* thinly spread out *(over a large area);* straggly, disorderly; relaxed, loose; disheveled; lavish; unrestrained; immoderate; *(w.* **in** + *acc)* very prone to *(some weakness),* passionately devoted to *(some cause);* **effūsissimīs habēnīs** at full speed

effūt·iō -īre -īvī *or* -iī -ītus *tr & intr* to blab, babble

effut·uō -uere -uī -ūtus *tr* (ecf-) *(vulg)* to wear out through excessive sex

ēgelid·us -a -um *adj* tepid; cool

eg·ēns -entis *adj* needy, poor; *(w. gen)* in need of, needing

egēn·us -a -um *adj* needy, destitute; *(w. gen or abl)* in need of, needing

eg·eō -ēre -uī *intr* to be needy, suffer want; *(w. gen)* **1** to be in need of; **2** to lack, be without; **3** to want, desire, miss

Ēgeri·a -ae *f* nymph whom King Numa visited at night for advice

ē·gerō -gerere -gessī -gestus *tr* to carry out, take away, remove; to discharge, vomit, emit; to express *(grief)*

egest·ās -ātis *f* need, want, poverty; *(w. gen)* lack of

ēgesti·ō -ōnis *f* squandering

ēgestus *pp of* **ēgerō**

ego *pron* I

egomet *pron* I personally, I and nobody else

ē·gredior -gredī -gressus sum *tr* to go beyond, pass; to quit; *(fig)* to surpass ‖ *intr* to go out, come out; to march out; to disembark, land; to go up, climb; *(fig)* to digress

ēgregiē *adv* exceptionally, singularly, uncommonly, splendidly

ēgregi·us -a -um *adj* exceptional, uncommon; distinguished, illustrious; **vir ēgregius** *(title given under the Empire to officials of equestrian rank)* the honorable ...

ēgressus *pp of* **ēgredior**

ēgress·us -ūs *m* way out, exit; departure; disembarking, landing; mouth *(of river);* digression ‖ *mpl* comings and goings

ēgurgit·ō -āre *tr* to pour out, lavish

ehem *interj (expressing pleasant surprise)* ha!, aha!

ēheu *interj (expressing pain)* oh!

eho *interj (often expressing rebuke)* look here!, see here!; whoa!; **eho dum!** look here now!

ei *interj* **hei** *(expressing fear or dismay)* ah!; *(expressing pain)* ouch!

ēia *or* hēia *interj (expressing joy or surpise)* ah!; ah ha!; good!; *(expressing haste)* quick!, come on!; **ēia age** come on!, up then!; be quick!; **ēia vērō** *(ironic)* nonsense!; oh sure!; oh yeah!

ēiacul·or -ārī -ātus sum *tr* to squirt ‖ *refl (of water, etc.)* to squirt

ēiciō ēicere ēiēcī ēiectus *tr* to throw out, drive out, put out, eject, expel; to banish; to utter; to run aground; to reject, disapprove; to boo *(s.o.)* off the stage ‖ *refl (of passions)* to come to the fore, break out ‖ *pass* to be stranded

ēiectāment·a -ōrum *npl* refuse; jetsam

ēiecti·ō -ōnis *f* ejection; banishment, exile

ēiect·ō -āre -āvī -ātus *tr* to spout forth; to keep throwing up *(e.g., blood)*

ēiect·us -ūs *m* emission

ēier·ō āre -āvī -ātus *tr* (ēiūr-) to refuse under oath, abjure, forswear; to deny under oath; to resign, abdicate; to disown, abandon

ēiulāti·ō -ōnis *f* lamenting

ēiulāt·us -a -um *adj* wailing

ēiul·ō -āre *intr* (hēi-) to wail, lament

ēiūrō *see* ēierō

ēiusdemmodī *see* modus

ēj- = ēi-

-ēl·a, -ell·a -ae *fem suf* forms diminutives chiefly from verbs: **querēla** complaint *(from* **querī** to complain)*

ēlā·bor -bī -psus sum *intr* to glide off; to slip away, escape; to pass away, disappear; *(w. abl or super + acc)* to glance off ēlabōrāt·us -a -um *adj* studied, overdone; elaborate, finished

ēlabōr·ō -āre -āvī -ātus *tr* to work out, elaborate; to produce ‖ *intr* to make a great effort, take great pains; *(w. inf)* to strive to

ēlāmentābil·is -is -e *adj* very mournful, pathetic

ēlangu·ēscō -ēscere -ī *intr* to slow down, slacken, let up

ēlāpsus *pp of* ēlābor

ēlātē *adv* proudly

ēlāti·ō -ōnis *f* elation, ecstasy

ēlātr·ō -āre *tr* to bark out

ēlāt·us -a -um *pp of* efferō ‖ *adj* high, elevated; exalted; haughty, proud

ē·lavō -lavāre -lāvī -lautus *or* -lōtus *tr* to wash out; *(coll)* to clean out, rob ‖ *intr* to be cleaned out, be wrecked; ēlavāre bonīs *(coll)* to be broke

Ele·a -ae *f* town in Lucania in S. Italy *(modern Velia)*, birthplace of Eleatic philosophy

Eleāt·ēs -ae *m* inhabitant of Elea *(e.g., Zeno)*

Eleātic·ī -ōrum *mpl* Eleatics, Eleatic philosophers *(Parmenides and Zeno)*

ēlecebr·a -ae *f* (exl-) snare; seductress

ēlēctē *adv* tastefully

ēlēctil·is -is -e *adj* choice, dainty

ēlēcti·ō -ōnis *f* choice, selection

ēlēct·ō -āre *tr* to select, choose; to wheedle out, coax out *(a secret)*

Ēlectr·a -ae *f* daughter of Agamemnon and Clytemnestra ‖ Pleiad, daughter of Atlas and mother of Dardanus

ēlectr·um -ī *n* amber; gold-silver alloy ‖ *npl* amber beads

ēlēct·us -a -um *pp of* ēligō ‖ *adj* select, choice; *(mil)* elite

ēlēct·us -ūs *m* choice

ēleg·āns -antis *adj* elegant; choosy; fine, choice, select; *(pej)* dainty

ēleganter *adv* elegantly, tastefully

ēleganti·a -ae *f* elegance, refinement, taste, propriety; *(pej)* daintiness

elegē·um -ī *n* (gīum) elegiac poem

eleg·ī -ōrum *mpl* elegiac verses

elegī·a -ae *f* (-gē·a *or* -gēi·a) elegy

Elel·eūs -eī *m* (epithet of) Bacchus

elementāri·us -a -um *adj* engaged in learning the rudiments; senex elementārius old schoolteacher

element·um -ī *n* first principle, element; atom, particle; letter of the alphabet ‖ *npl* rudiments, elements; beginnings; ABC's

elench·us -ī *m* (pear-shaped) pearl ‖ *mpl* criticisms

elephantomach·a -ae *m* fighter mounted on an elephant

elephant·us -ī *or* eleph·ās -antis *m* elephant; *(fig)* ivory

Ēlē·us -a -um *adj* of Elis *(in the Peloponnese)*

Eleus·īn -īnis *f* Eleusis *(town in Attica, sacred to Demeter, the Roman Ceres)*

Eleusīn·us -a -um *adj* Eleusinian; Eleusīna Māter Demeter *or the Roman* Ceres

eleutheri·a -ae *f* freedom, liberty

ēlev·ō -āre -āvī -ātus *tr* to lift up, raise; to alleviate; to lessen; to make light of, disparage

Ēli·as -adis *adj* (fem only) Elian, Olympic

ēlic·iō -ere -uī -itus *tr* to elicit, draw out; to lure out, entice; to conjure up

ēlicitus *pp of* ēliciō

Ēlic·ius -(i)ī *m* (epithet of) Jupiter

ēlī·dō -dere -sī -sus *tr* to knock out, strike out, tear out, force out; to shatter, smash to pieces, crush; to force out, stamp out

ē·ligō -ligere -lēgī -lēctus *tr* (-leg-) to pluck out; to pick out, choose

ēlīmin·ō -āre *tr* to carry outside; to spread abroad

ēlīm·ō -āre -āvī -ātus *tr* to file; to finish off, perfect

ēlingu·is -is -e *adj* speechless; *(fig)* inarticulate; *(rhet)* dull, flat, insipid

ēlingu·ō -āre *tr* to tear out *(s.o.'s)* tongue

Ēl·is -idis *f* town and district on the W. coast of the Peloponnesus in which Olympia is located

-ēl·is -is -e *adjl suf* formed from nouns and adjectives: crūdēlis cruel

Eliss·a *or* Elīs·a -ae *f* Dido

ēlīsus *pp of* ēlīdō

ēl·ix -icis *m* drainage ditch

ēlix·us -a -um *adj* boiled; *(sl)* soused

-ell·a -ae *fem suf* forms diminutives: cistella a little box

ellam = ecce + illam there she is!

elleborōs·us -a -um *adj* crazy

ellebor·us -ī *m or* ellebor·um -ī *n* (hell-) hellebore *(plant used to cure mental illness)*

ellips·is -is *f* ellipsis

ellum = ecce + illum there he is!

-ell·us -ī *masc suf* forms diminutives: agellus small plot

ēloc·ō -āre -āvī -ātus *tr* to lease out, rent out

ēlocūti·ō -ōnis *f* style of speaking, elocution, delivery

ēlog·ium -(i)ī *n* saying, maxim; inscription; epitaph; codicil *(in a will);* criminal record

ēloqu·ēns -entis *adj* eloquent

ēloquenter *adv* (used in comp & supl degree) eloquently

ēloquenti·a -ae *f* eloquence

ēloqu·ium -(i)ī *n* eloquence

ēlo·quor -quī -cūtus sum *tr* to speak out, declare; to divulge, tell ‖ *intr* to speak, give a speech

ēlōtus *pp of* ēlavō

ēlū·ceō -cēre -xī *intr* to shine forth; to glitter

ēluct·or -ārī -ātus sum *tr* to struggle out of, struggle through *(e.g., deep snow);* to surmount *(difficulties)* ‖ *intr* to force a way out

ēlūcubr·ō -āre -āvī -ātus *or* ēlūcubr·or -ārī -ātus sum *tr* to compose by lamplight

ēlū·dō -dere -sī -sus *tr* to elude, parry, avoid; to escape, shun; to delude, deceive; to make fun of; to get the better of, outmaneuver ‖ *intr* to end the game; to behave outrageously with impunity, have free play *(for outrageous conduct)*

ēlū·geō -gēre -xī *tr* to mourn for ‖ *intr* to cease to mourn

ēlumb·is -is -e *adj* (-bus -a -um) having a dislocated hip; bland *(style)*

ē·luō -luere -luī -lūtus *tr* to wash off, wash clean; to wash away; to rinse out; *(fig)* to wash away, get rid of ‖ *intr (coll)* to lose one's property, be cleaned out

ēlūsus *pp of* ēlūdō

ēlūt·us -a -um *pp of* ēluō ‖ *adj* watery, insipid; weak

ēluvi·ēs -ēī *f* inundation, overflow; sewage; ravine

ēluvi·ō -ōnis *f* deluge

Elvīn·a -ae *f* (Hel-) epithet of Ceres

Ēlys·ium -iī *n* realm of the blessed in the lower world

Ēlysi·us -a -um *adj* Elysian

em *interj* (hem) *(in offering some object or fact to s.o., often followed by a dat)* here (there) you are!

emācit·ās -ātis *f* fondness for shopping, mania for buying

ēmad·ēscō -ēscere -uī *intr* to become soaked

ēmancipāti·ō -ōnis *f* (-cup-) emancipation; transfer of property

ēmancipāt·us -a -um *adj* transferred; sold

ēmancip·ō -āre -āvī -ātus *tr* (-cup-) to transfer; to declare *(a son)* free and independent, emancipate; to surrender, abandon

ēmān·ō -āre -āvī -ātum *intr* to flow down; to trickle out, leak out; to become known ‖ *v impers* ēmānābat *(w. acc & inf)* word got out that

Ēmathi·a -ae *f* Macedonia; Thessaly, Pharsalus

Ēmath·is -idis *adj (fem only)* Macedonian ‖ *fpl* the Pierides

Ēmathi·us -a -um *adj* Macedonian, Thessalian, Pharsalian

ēmātūr·ēscō -ēscere -uī *intr* to begin to ripen; to soften; *(fig)* to mellow

em·āx -ācis *adj* fond of shopping; *(fig) (of a prayer)* bargaining with the gods, haggling

emblēm·a -atis *n* mosaic; inlay

embol·ium -(i)ī *n* interlude; insertion *(in literary work)*

ēmendābil·is -is -e *adj* capable of correction

ēmendātē *adv* faultlessly, pefectly

ēmendāti·ō -ōnis *f* emendation

ēmendāt·or -ōris *m,* ēmendātr·īx -īcis *f* corrector, reformer

ēmendāt·us -a -um *adj* faultless

ēmendīc·ō -āre -āvī -ātus *tr* to get by begging

ēmend·ō -āre -āvī -ātus *tr* to emend, correct; to reform, improve, revise; to atone for

ēmēnsus *pp of* ēmētior

ēment·ior -īrī -ītus sum *tr* to falsify, fabricate, feign ‖ *intr* to tell a lie

ēmerc·or -ārī -ātus sum *tr* to buy up; to obtain through bribery

ēmer·eō -ēre -uī -itus *or* ēmer·eor -ērī -itus sum *tr* to earn; to lay under obligation, do *(s.o.)* a favor; *(mil)* to serve out *(term of service)* ‖ *intr* to serve out one's time in the army

ēmer·gō -gere -sī *tr* to raise *(from the water)* ‖ *refl & pass* to raise oneself up, rise ‖ *intr* to emerge; to rise *(in power);* to extricate oneself; *(w. ex)* to get clear of

ēmerit·us -a -um *pp of* ēmereō ‖ *adj (mil)* discharged; *(fig)* ready to be let out to pasture ‖ *m* veteran

ēmersus *pp of* ēmergō

emetic·a -ae *f* an emetic

ē·mētior -mētīrī -mēnsus sum *tr* to measure out; to traverse, travel over; to live through; to impart

ēmet·ō -ere *tr* to mow down; *(w. abl)* to reap from

ēmi- = hēmi-

ēmic·ō -āre -uī -ātum *intr* to dart out, dash out; *(of liquids)* to spurt out; *(of flame)* to shoot out; *(fig)* to stand out, be conspicuous

ēmigr·ō -āre -āvī -ātum *intr* to move out, depart; ē vītā ēmigrāre to pass on

ēmināti·ō -ōnis *f* threatening, blustering

ēmin·ēns -entis *adj* projecting, prominent, high; eminent

ēminenti·a -ae *f* projection, prominence; *(in painting)* highlights, foreground

ēmin·eō -ēre -uī *intr* to stand out, project; to be conspicious; *(in paintings)* to be highlighted, stand out against a background

ēmin·or -ārī *tr* to threaten

ēminus *adv* at long range, at a distance; from afar

ēmīr·or -ārī -ātus sum *tr* to be greatly surprised at, stand aghast at

ēmissār·ium -(i)ī *n* drain, outlet

ēmissār·ius -(i)ī *m* scout, spy

ēmissīci·us -a -um *adj* spying; oculī ēmissīciī prying eyes

ēmissi·ō -ōnis *f* discharge, hurling, shooting; releasing, letting off

ēmissus *pp of* ēmittō

ēmiss·us -ūs *m* emission, sending forth; hurling, shooting

ē·mittō -mittere -mīsī -missus *tr* to send out; to hurl, shoot; to let go, let slip, let loose, drop, release, let out; to publish; to allow to escape; to emancipate, set at liberty; to utter; to pass up *(opportunity);* animam ēmittere to give up the ghost **ll** *refl & pass (w.* **ex)** to break out of

emō emere ēmī emptus *tr* to buy; *(w. gen or abl of price)* to buy *(s.th.)* at; to pay for; to gain, obtain; to bribe; **bene emere** to buy at a bargain; **in diem emere** to buy on credit; **male emere** to pay dearly for; **percussōrem emere** to hire a killer

ēmoder·or -ārī *tr* to moderate

ēmodul·or -ārī *tr* to sing the praises of, celebrate in song

ēmōl·ior -īrī -ītus sum *tr* to accomplish with great effort

ēmoll·iō -īre -īvī *or* -iī -ītus *tr* to soften; to make mild; to enervate

ēmol·ō -ere — *tr* to grind up

ēmolument·um -ī *n* effort, exertion; reward; achievement, success; profit; advantage, benefit

ēmon·eō -ēre *tr* to admonish earnestly

ēmor·ior -ī -tuus sum *intr* to die; to die off; *(of a fire)* to die down, go out; *(of river)* to peter out; *(fig)* to die out

ēmortuāl·is -is -e *adj* of death

ēmortuus *pp of* ēmorior

ē·moveō -movēre -mōvī -mōtus *tr* to **(exm-)** to move out, remove, expel; to dislodge; to shake *(e.g., foundations of a wall)*

Empedocl·ēs -is *or* -ī *m* philosopher of Sicily who is said to have jumped into the crater of Mt. Etna *(444 B.C.)*

emphas·is -is *f* emphasis, stress

empīric·us -ī *m* empiricist *(physician who relies on experience rather than on scientific theory)*

empor·ium -(i)ī *n* market town; trade mart, market, shopping center

emptī·ō -ōnis *f* buying, purchase; thing purchased, purchase

emptit·ō -āre -āvī -ātus *tr* to be in the habit of buying, buy *(regularly)*

empt·or -ōris *m,* emptr·īx -īcis *f* purchaser, customer

empt·um -ī *n* a purchase

emptus *pp of* emō

ēmūg·iō -īre *tr* to bellow out

ēmul·geō -gēre — -sus *tr* to drain off *(milk);* to drain *(a swamp)*

ēmūnct·us -a -um *adj* refined; snobbish; **nāris ēmūnctae esse** to have discriminating tastes

ē·mungō -mungere -mūnxī -mūnctus *tr* to wipe the nose of; *(fig)* to swindle; *(w. abl)* to cheat *(s.o.)* of **ll** *refl & pass* to blow one's nose

ēmūn·iō -īre -īvī *or* -iī -ītus *tr* to build up; to fortify; to make a road through *(woods)*

ēn *interj (in questions)* really?; *(in commands)* come on!; *(to call attention)* hey!

ēnārrābil·is -is -e *adj* explainable, describable, intelligible

ēnārrāti·ō -ōnis *f* description; analysis

ēnārr·ō -āre -āvī -ātus *tr* to explain in detail; to describe; to interpret

ēnāscor ēnāscī ēnātus sum *intr* to grow out, sprout, arise; to be born

ēnat·ō -āre -āvī -ātum *intr* to swim away, escape by swimming; *(fig)* to get away with it

ēnātus *pp of* ēnāscor

ēnāvig·ō -āre -āvī -ātus *tr* to sail across, traverse **ll** *intr* to sail away; *(fig)* to escape

encaust·us -a -um *adj* burnt in, painted in encaustic *(i.e., with molten wax as paint)*

Encelad·us *or* Encelad·os -ī *m* one of the giants whom Jupiter buried under Mount Etna

endrom·is -idis *f* athlete's bathrobe

Endymi·ōn -ōnis *m* handsome young man with whom Luna fell in love and who was doomed to everlasting sleep on Mt. Patmos; any handsome young man

ēnec·ō *(or* ēnicō) -āre -uī *(or* -āvī) -tus *(or* -ātus) *tr* to kill, kill off; to exhaust, wear out; *(coll)* to kill, pester to death

ēnervāt·us -a -um *adj* without sinews, without muscles; without energy

ēnerv·is -is -e *or* ēnerv·us -a -um *adj* weak, feeble

ēnerv·ō -āre -āvī -ātus *tr* to weaken, enervate, render impotent

ēnicō *see* ēnecō

enim *conj* namely, for instance; yes, indeed, certainly; for; you know; in fact, to be sure; *(in replies)* of course, no doubt; for, because

enimvērō *adv* yes indeed, to be sure, certainly; *(ironically)* of course

Enīp·eūs -eī *m* tributary of the River Peneus in Thessaly

ēnīsus *pp of* ēnītor

ēnit·eō -ēre -uī *intr* to shine out, sparkle; to be conspicuous

ēnit·ēscō -ēscere *intr* to begin to shine, begin to brighten; to become conspicuous

ēnī·tor -tī -sus *or* -xus sum *tr* to work one's way up, climb; to give birth to **ll** *intr* to exert oneself, make an effort; *(w. inf)* to struggle to, strive to

ēnīxē *adv* strenuously, earnestly

ēnīx·us -a -um *pp of* ēnītor **ll** *adj* strenuous, earnest

Enni·us -(i)ī *m* father of Latin literature, writer of tragedy, comedy, epic, and satire *(239–169 B.C.)*

Ennosigae·us -ī *m* *(epithet of Neptune)* Earthshaker

ēn·ō -āre -āvī -ātum *intr* to swim out, swim away, escape by swimming

ēnōdātē *adv* without knots; clearly

ēnōdāti·ō -ōnis *f* solution, explanation

ēnōd·is -is -e *adj* without knots; clear

ēnōd·ō -āre -āvī -ātus *tr* to explain, clarify

ēnorm·is -is -e *adj* abnormal; enormous; shapeless, irregular; ill-fitting *(clothes);* extravagant *(style)*

ēnormit·ās -ātis *f* enormity; irregular shape

ēnōt·ēscō -ēscere -uī *intr* to become known

ēnot·ō -āre -āvī -ātus *tr* to take notes of, note down

ēnsicul·us -ī *m* little sword

ēnsif·er *or* **ēnsig·er -era -erum** *adj* with a sword, wearing a sword

-ēns·is -is -e *adjl suf* forms adjectives mainly from words denoting places: **Athēniēnsis** Athenian, from Athens

ēns·is -is *m* sword

enterocēl·ē -ēs *f* hernia of the intestines

enterocēlic·us -a -um *adj* suffering from an intestinal hernia

entheāt·us -a -um *adj* filled with divine frenzy

enthe·us -a -um *adj* inspired; inspiring, that fills with divine frenzy

enthȳmēm·a -atis *n* thought, reflection; *(phil)* condensed syllogism

ēnū·bō -bere -psī *intr (of a woman)* to marry outside her rank

ēnucleātē *adv* precisely

ēnucleāt·us -a -um *adj* precise, to the point; straightforward, simple *(style);* fine-drawn *(arguments)*

ēnucle·ō -āre -āvī -ātus *tr (fig)* to examine carefully; to weigh *(one's decision)*

ēnumerāti·ō -ōnis *f* enumeration

ēnumer·ō -āre -āvī -ātus *tr* to count up; to count out, pay out; to recount, detail, enumerate

ēnūntiāti·ō -ōnis *f* announcement; *(in logic)* assertion; proposition; *(gram)* pronunciation *(of a word or syllable)*

ēnūnti·ō -āre -āvī -ātus *tr* to disclose, reveal, betray; to say, assert, express; to proclaim publicly; *(gram)* to pronounce *(a word or syllable)*

ēnūpti·ō -ōnis *f* right of a woman to marry outside her clan

ēnūtr·iō -īre -īvī *or* **-iī -ītus** *tr* to nourish, raise, bring up

Enȳ·ō -us *f* Greek goddess of war; *(fig)* war

eō *adv* there, to that place; to that end, to that purpose; so far, to such an extent, to such a pitch; on that account, for that reason, with that in view; **eō erō brevior** I will be all the briefer; **eō magis** all the more; **eō maximē**

quod especially because; **eō quō** to the place to which; **quō … eō** the … the … ; **quō plūs potestis, eō moderātius imperiō ūtī dēbētis** the more power you have, the more moderately you ought to use that power; **eō quod** because; **eō … ut** to such an extent … that

eō īre īvī *or* **iī itum** *intr* to go; to walk, sail, ride; *(of time)* to pass; *(of events)* to go on, happen, turn out; *(of things)* to give way; *(mil)* to march; *(w. abl)* to stem from; **in sententiam īre** *(pol)* to vote for a bill

eōdem *adv* to the same place, purpose, *or* person

Ēōs *(nom only)* *f* Dawn *(the Latin Aurora, daughter of Hyperion and Theia or Euryphaëssa)*

Ēō·us -a -um *adj* of the dawn; Eastern, oriental ‖ *m* morning star; dawn; an oriental

Ēō·us -ī *m* morning star ‖ inhabitant of the East ‖ one of the horses of the sun ‖ dawn

Epamīnōnd·ās -ae *m* famous Theban general who defeated the Spartans in two great battles *(c. 371 B.C.)*

epaphaeres·is -is *f* a second close clip *(of the hair)*

Epaph·us -ī *m* son of Jupiter and Io

ēpāst·us -a -um *adj* eaten up

Epē·us *or* **Epī·us -ī** *m* builder of the Trojan horse

ephēb·us -ī *m (Greek)* young man

ephēmer·is -idis *or* **-idos** *f* diary; journal

Ephes·us *or* **Ephes·os -ī** *f* city on the coast of Asia Minor with famous temple of Diana

ephippiāt·us -a -um *adj* riding a saddled horse

ephipp·ium -iī *n* saddle

ephor·us -ī *m* ephor *(Spartan magistrate)*

Ephyr·a -ae *or* **Ephyr·ē -ēs** *f* ancient name of Corinth

Epicharm·us -ī *m* Sicilian Greek writer of early comedy *(530?–440 B.C.)*

epichys·is -is *f* wine ladle

epicōp·us -a -um *adj* furnished with oars; **phasēlus epicōpus** rowboat

epicroc·us -a -um *adj* thin yellow *(garment)* ‖ *n* thin yellow garment

Epicūr·us -ī *m* Greek philosopher, born on Samos *(342–270 B.C.)*

epic·us -a -um *adj* epic ‖ **Epic·ī -ōrum** *mpl* epic poets

epidīctic·us -a -um *adj* showy

epidipn·is -idis *f* a dessert

epigramm·a -atis *or* **-atos** *n* inscription; epitaph; short poem, epigram

epilog·us -ī *m* epilogue, peroration

epimēni·a -ōrum *npl* month's rations

Epimēth·eūs -eī *m* son of Iapetus and brother of Prometheus

epinīc·ion -iī *n* victory song

epiraed·ium -(i)ī *n* horse-drawn carriage

Ēpīrōt·ēs -ae *m* native of Epirus

Ēpīr·us *or* Ēpīr·os -ī *f* district of N.W. Greece

epistol·ium -(i)ī *n* note

epistul·a -ae *f* (-tol-) letter; ab epistulīs *(in apposition)* secretary

epistulār·is -is -e *adj* (-tol-) concerned with letters; chartae epistulārēs writing paper, stationery

epitaph·ium -(i)ī *n* eulogy

epithalam·ium -(i)ī *n* wedding song

epithēc·a -ae *f* addition, increase

epitom·a -ae *or* epitom·ē -ēs *f* epitome, abridgment

epitȳr·um -ī *n* olive salad

epoch·ē -ēs *f* suspension of judgment

ep·ops -opis *m* hoopoe *(an Old World bird having a fanlike crest and a slender downward-curving bill)*

epos *(nom & acc only; pl:* opē) *n* epic

ēpōt·us -a -um *adj* (exp-) drunk dry, drained to the dregs; *(fig)* swallowed up, absorbed

epul·ae -ārum *fpl* courses, dishes; sumptuous meal; epulae rēgum dinner fit for a king

epulār·is -is -e *adj* at dinner, of a dinner; sermō epulāris talk at dinner, table talk

epulāti·ō -ōnis *f* banqueting

epul·ō -ōnis *m* dinner guest; Trēsvirī *(or* Septemvirī) Epulōnēs college of priests who superintended the state dinner to the gods

epul·or -ārī -ātus sum *tr* to feast on ‖ *intr* to attend a dinner; *(w. abl)* to feast on

epul·um -ī *n* banquet, feast

equ·a -ae *f* mare

Equ·es -itis *m* knight; capitalist *(member of Roman middle class);* equestrian order, bourgeoisie

equ·es -itis *m* rider; trooper, cavalryman; cavalry ‖ *mpl* cavalry

eques·ter *or* equest·ris -tris -tre *adj* equestrian; cavalry; middle-class

equidem *adv* truly, indeed, in any event; of course, to be sure; *(w. first person)* for my part, as far as I am concerned

equīn·us -a -um *adj* horse's

equīri·a -ōrum *npl* (equirr-) horse races *(held annually in the Campus Martius in honor of Mars)*

equitāt·us -ūs *m* cavalry

equit·ō -āre -āvī -ātum *intr* to ride, ride a horse

equule·us -ī *m* foal, colt; small equestrian statue; torture rack

equ·us -ī (equos *and* equom *in pre-Augustan period,* ecus *and* ecum *from Aug. period to end of 1st cent.* A.D., equus *and* equum *after that) m* horse; equīs virīsque *(or* equīs virīs) *(fig)* with might and main; equō merēre to serve in the cavalry; equō vehī to ride a

horse; equus bipēs sea horse; in equō mounted ‖ *mpl* chariot

er·a *or* her·a -ae *f* lady of the house

ērādīc·ō -āre -āvī -ātus *tr* (exr-) to uproot; to destroy utterly

ērā·dō -dere -sī -sus *tr* to scratch out, erase, obliterate

eran·us -ī *m* mutual insurance society *(in Greece)*

Erāt·ō *(nom and voc only) f* Muse of erotic poetry; Muse

Eratosthen·ēs -is *m* Alexandrine geographer, poet, and philosopher *(276–196 B.C.)*

erc- *see* herc-

Ereb·us -ī *m* god of darkness, son of Chaos and brother of Night; lower world

Erechthē·us -a -um *adj* of Erechtheus; *(poet)* Athenian

Erechth·eūs -eī *m* king of Athens, son of Hephaestus ‖ grandson of former and son of Pandion

Erechthīd·ae -ārum *mpl* descendants of Erechtheus; *(poet)* Athenians

ērēct·us -a -um *pp of* ērigō ‖ *adj* erect, upright; noble, elevated, lofty; haughty; attentive, alert, tense; resolute, courageous

ērēp·ō -ere -sī *tr* to crawl through *(a field);* to crawl up *(a mountain)* ‖ *intr* to crawl out

ērepti·ō -ōnis *f* robbery

ērept·or -ōris *m* robber

ēreptus *pp of* ēripiō

Eretri·a -ae *f* city on the island of Euboea, birthplace of the philosopher Menedemus

Eretriac·ī -ōrum *mpl* philosophers of the school of Menedemus

ergā *(prep) (w. acc)* to, toward; against; next to

ergastul·um -ī *n* prison *(on a large estate where unruly slaves were kept);* chain gang

ergō *adv* therefore, consequently; *(resumptive)* well then, I say, as I was saying; *(w. imperatives)* then, now

ergō *prep (w. preceding gen)* for the sake of, in consequence of; illīus ergō for his sake

Erichthon·ius -iī *m* king of Athens ‖ son of Dardanus, father of Tros, and king of Troy

ēric·ius -(i)ī *m* hedgehog; *(mil)* beam with iron spikes

Ēridan·us -ī *m* Greek name of the river Padus *(modern Po); (astr)* constellation

erifug·a -ae *m* runaway slave

ē·rigō -rigere -rēxī -rēctus *tr* to set up straight, straighten out *(e.g., tree);* to set up, erect; to cheer up, encourage; to arouse, excite; *(mil)* to deploy troops on a slope ‖ *refl & pass* to raise oneself, get up

Ērigon·ē -ēs *f (astr)* Virgo *(constellation)*

erīl·is -is -e *or* herīl·is -is -e *adj* master's, mistress's

Erīn·ys -yos *f* Fury; *(fig)* frenzy

Eriphȳl·a -ae *or* **Eriphȳl·ē -ēs** *f* wife of the seer Amphiaraus; a treacherous wife

ē·ripiō -ripere -ripuī -reptus *tr* to snatch away, pull out, tear out; to deliver, rescue; to rob; *(w. dat or w.* **ab** *or* **ex)** to take away from, rescue from **‖** *refl* to escape

-ern·us -a -um *adjl suf* forms adjectives denoting times: **hestiernus** yesterday's

ērogāti·ō -ōnis *f* expenditure, outlay, payment

ērogit·ō -āre *tr* to try hard to find out

ērog·ō -āre -āvī -ātus *tr* to allocate, expend; to bequeath; *(w.* **in** + *acc)* **1** to allocate to, spend on; **2** to bequeath to

Er·ōs -ōtis *m* Love, Cupid, Eros

errābund·us -a -um *adj* wandering, straggling

errātic·us -a -um *adj* erratic, wandering; **stella errātica** planet

errāti·ō -ōnis *f* wandering

errāt·um -ī *n* error, mistake

errāt·us -ūs *m* roving, wandering about

err·ō -āre -āvī -ātum *intr* to wander, roam; to lose one's way, stray; to waver; to err, make a mistake, be mistaken; *(w.* **in** + *abl)* to be mistaken about

err·ō -ōnis *m* vagrant, vagabond

err·or -ōris *m* wandering; wavering, uncertainty; error; cause of error, deception; maze, winding, intricacy

ērubēscendus -a -um *adj* enough to make one blush, shameful

ērub·ēscō -ēscere -uī *tr* to blush at; to be ashamed of; to respect **‖** *intr* to grow red, redden; to blush

ērūc·a -ae *f (bot)* cole *(type of cabbage)*

ēruct·ō -āre -āvī -ātus *tr* to belch, vomit; to talk drunkenly about

ērud·iō -īre -iī *or* **-īvī -ītus** *tr* to educate, teach, instruct; *(w. double acc)* to teach *(s.o. s.th.)*

ērudītē *adv* learnedly

ērudīti·ō -ōnis *f* instructing, instruction; erudition, learning

ērudītul·us -a -um *adj* somewhat experienced, somewhat skilled

ērudīt·us -a -um *adj* educated, learned, accomplished

ēruī *perf of* **ēruō**

ē·rumpō -rumpere -rūpī -ruptus *tr* to cause to break out; to give vent to; **īram in hostēs ērumpere** to vent one's wrath on the enemy **‖** *intr* to burst out, break out

ēru·ō -ere -ī -tus *tr* to uproot, dig out; to tear out, gouge out *(eyes);* to undermine, demolish, destroy; to draw out, elicit; to churn up *(sea);* to plow up

ērupti·ō -ōnis *f* eruption; *(bot)* sprouting; *(mil)* sortie

ēruptus *pp of* **ērumpō**

er·us *or* **her·us -ī** *m* master of the house, head of the family; lord, owner; *(coll)* boss

ērutus *pp of* **ēruō**

erv·um -ī *n (bot)* vetch *(cultivated for its edible seeds)*

Erycīn·us -a -um *adj* of Mt. Eryx *(in N.W. Sicily);* of Venus; Sicilian **‖** *f* Venus

Erymanth·is -idos *f* Callisto *(changed first into a bear and then into a constellation)*

Erymanth·us -ī *m* mountain range in Arcadia, where Hercules killed a boar

Erythē·a -ae *f* small island in the Bay of Gades, home of the giant Geryon

erythīn·us -ī *m* red mullet *(fish)*

Er·yx -ycis *or* **Eryc·us -ī** *m* Eryx *(mountain on N.W. coast of Sicily, famous for its temple to Venus)* **‖** son of Venus and Butes, half-brother of Aeneas

ēsc·a -ae *f* dish; food; bait

ēscāri·us -a -um *adj* of food; of bait **‖** *npl* dishes, courses

ēscen·dō -dere -dī -sus *tr & intr* to climb, climb up; to sail up

ēscēnsi·ō -ōnis *f* climbing up; hostile raid *(from the coast)*

ēscēns·us -ūs *m* ascent

-ēsc·ō -ere *vbl suf* formed from nouns and adjectives, with inchoative force: **senēscere** to begin to be old, get old

ēsculent·us -a -um *adj* edible **‖** *npl* edibles, foodstuffs

ēsculētum *see* **aesculētum**

ēsculus *see* **aesculus**

-ēsim·us *or* **-ēnsim·us -a -um** *suf* used to form ordinal numbers from 20 to 1000

ēsit·ō -āre -āvī -ātus *tr* (essi-) to be used to eating

Ēsquili·ae -ārum *fpl* Esquiline Hill

Ēsquilīn·us -a -um *adj* Esquiline **‖** *f* Esquiline gate

Ēsquili·us -a -um *adj* Esquiline

esse *inf of* **sum** to be; **ēsse** *inf of* **edō** to eat

essedār·ius -(i)ī *m* soldier *or* gladiator fighting from a chariot

essed·um -ī *n* Gallic war chariot; light traveling carriage

essenti·a -ae *f* essence

essitō *see* **ēsitō**

-ess·ō -ere -īvī *or* **-iī -ītus** *vbl suf* with conative force: **capessere** to try to catch, snatch at, catch at eagerly, strive for

essuri·ō -ōnis *m* a hungry man

ēstr·īx -īcis *f* glutton *(female)*

ēsuriāl·is -is -e *adj* (ess-) of hunger

ēsur·iō -īre *tr* (ess-) to be hungry for **‖** *intr* to be hungry

ēsuri·ō -ōnis *m* a hungry man

ēsurīti·ō -ōnis *f* hunger

ēsus *pp of* **edō**

ēs·us -ūs *m* eating; **ēsū** in the eating

et *adv* besides, also; even, I mean

et *conj* and; *(for emphasis)* and even, yes and; *(antithetical)* however, but; **et ... et** both ... and, not only ... but also

etenim *conj* for, and as a matter of fact

etēsi·ae -ārum *mpl (fpl)* periodic winds *(on the Aegean Sea)*; monsoons

ēthic·ē -ēs *f* ethics

ēthologi·a -ae *f* portrayal of character

ētholog·us -ī *m* impersonator

etiam *adv & conj* also, and also, besides, likewise; *(of time)* yet, as yet, still, even now; *(in affirmation)* yes, yes indeed, certainly, by all means; *(emphatic)* even, rather; *(w. emphatic imperatives)* but just; **etiam atque etiam** again and again

etiamnunc *or* etiamnum *adv* even now, still

etiamsī *conj* even if, although

etiamtum *or* etiamtunc *adv* even then, till then, still

Etrūri·a -ae *f* district N. of Rome

Etrusc·us -a -um *adj* Etruscan, of Etruria **‖** *mpl* the Etruscans

etsī *conj* even if, although

-ēt·um -ī *neut suf* formed mainly from names of plants to denote the place where they grow: **rosētum** rose bed

etymologi·a -ae *f* etymology

eu *interj (sometimes ironic)* fine!, great!

Euān *or* Euhān *m* cult title of Bacchus, cult cry

eu·āns *or* euh·āns -antis *adj* crying Eu(h)an *(Bacchic cry)*

euax *interj* hurray!

Euboe·a -ae *f* Greek island off E. coast of Attica and Boeotia

Euēn·us -ī *m* a king of Aetolia, father of Marpessa **‖** river in Aetolia

euge *or* eugepae *interj* terrific!

euhāns *see* euāns

Euhēmer·us -ī *m* Greek writer who attempted to prove that all ancient myths were basically historical events *(c. 316 B.C.)*

Euh·ius -iī *m* Bacchus

Euhoe *or* Euoe *interj* ecstatic cry of revelers at festival of Bacchus

Euius *see* Euhius

Eumenid·ēs -um *fpl* Eumenides *or* Erinyes *or* Furies *(goddesses of vengeance)*

eunūch·us -ī *m* eunuch

Euoe *see* Euhoe

Euphorb·us -ī *m* brave Trojan warrior whose soul Pythagoras asserted had transmigrated to himself

Euphrāt·ēs -is *or* -ae *or* -ī *m* Euphrates River

Eupol·is -idis *or* -is *m* Athenian comic playwright *(446?–411 B.C.)*

Eurīpid·ēs -is *m* Athenian tragic playwright *(485–405 B.C.)*

eurīp·us -ī *m* channel; trench running between the arena and the seats in the Circus Maximus **‖ Eurīpus** strait between Boeotia and Euboea

Eurōp·a -ae *or* Eurōp·ē -ēs *f* Europe **‖** Europa, daughter of Agenor and mother of Sarpedon, Rhadamantus, and Minos by Jupiter, who, in the shape of a bull, carried her off to Crete

Eurōt·ās -ae *m* chief river of Laconia in S. Greece, on which Sparta stood

Eur·us -ī *m* S.E. wind; east wind; wind

Eurydic·ē -ēs *f* wife of Orpheus

Eurysth·eūs -eī *m* king of Argos who imposed the Twelve Labors on Hercules

Euryt·is -idos *f* daughter of Eurytus, king of Oechalia *(i.e., Iole)*

-e·us -a -um *adjl suf* formed from nouns, usually to denote material: **ligneus** (made) of wood, wooden

euschēmē *adv* gracefully

Euterp·ē -ēs *f* Muse *(later associated with the reed pipe)*

Euxīn·us Pont·us -ī *m* Black Sea

ēvā·dō -dere -sī -sus *tr* to pass, pass by; to pass through, escape **‖** *intr* to go out; to turn out to be, become, prove to be; to get away; to climb; **quō ēvādis?** *(fig)* what's your point?

ēvag·or -ārī -ātus sum *tr* to stray beyond, transgress **‖** *intr (fig)* to spread; *(mil)* to maneuver

ēval·ēscō -ēscere -uī *intr* to grow strong; to increase; *(of a word or expression)* to gain currency; *(w. inf)* to be able to; *(w.* in + *acc)* to develop into

ēvalid·us -a -um *adj* very strong

Evan·der *or* Evan·drus -drī *m* Evander *(Arcadian who founded Pallanteum at the foot of the Palatine Hill)*

ēvān·ēscō -ēscere -uī *intr* to vanish, pass away, die away; to be forgotten; *(of liquids)* to evaporate

ēvānid·us -a -um *adj* vanishing

ēvast·ō -āre -āvī -ātus *tr* to devastate, wreck completely

ēvāsus *pp of* ēvādō

ēve·hō -here -xī -ctus *tr* to carry out; to spread abroad; to lift up, raise **‖** *pass* to ride, sail, drift

ē·vellō -vellere -vellī *or* -vulsī -vulsus *tr* to pluck out; to eradicate; to extract *(teeth)*

ē·veniō -venīre -vēnī -ventum *intr* to come out, come forth; to come to pass, happen; to turn out, result, end **‖** *v impers* it happens

ēvent·um -ī *n* event, occurrence; result, effect, consequence; fortune; experience

ēvent·us -ūs *m* happening; outcome, event; lot, fate; issue, consequence, result; occurrence, accident; good fortune, success

Evēn·us -ī *m* river in Aetolia
ēverber·ō -āre -āvī -ātus *tr* to hit hard; to beat
 up
ēverricul·um -ī *n* broom; dragnet
ēver·rō -rere -rī -sus *tr* to sweep out; *(fig)* to
 clean out, strip
ēversi·ō -ōnis *f* overthrow, subversion,
 destruction
ēvers·or -ōris *m* destroyer
ēversus *pp of* ēverrō *and of* ēvertō
ēver·tō -tere -tī -sus *tr* (-vor-) to overturn, turn
 upside down; to overthrow; to expel; to subvert, destroy, ruin
ēvestīgāt·us -a -um *adj* tracked down
ēvictus *pp of* ēvincō
ēvid·ēns -entis *adj* evident, visible, plain,
 clear, obvious
ēvidenter *adv* plainly, obviously
ēvidenti·a -ae *f* obviousness; evidence; *(rhet)*
 vividness
ēvigil·ō -āre -āvī -ātus *tr* to watch through *(the
 night);* to work through the night writing
 (e.g., books) ‖ *intr* to be wide-awake; *(fig)* to
 be on one's toes
ēvīl·ēscō -ēscere -uī *intr* to depreciate, become
 worthless
ē·vinciō -vincīre -vīnxī -vīnctus *tr* to tie up; to
 crown, wreathe
ē·vincō -vincere -vīcī -victus *tr* to conquer
 completely, trounce; to prevail over
ēvīnctus *pp of* ēvinciō
ēvirāt·us -a -um *adj* effeminate
ēvir·ō -āre -āvī -ātus *tr* to castrate, emasculate
ēviscer·ō -āre -āvī -ātus *tr* to disembowel, gut,
 eviscerate; to mangle
ēvītābil·is -is -e *adj* avoidable
ēvītāti·ō -ōnis *f* avoidance
ēvīt·ō -āre -āvī -ātus *tr* to avoid, escape
ēvocāt·ī -ōrum *mpl* veterans called up again,
 reenlisted veterans
ēvocāt·or -ōris *m* recruiter
ēvoc·ō -āre -āvī -ātus *tr* to call out, summon;
 to challenge; to evoke, excite, stir; *(mil)* to
 call up *(for service)*
ēvolgō *see* ēvulgō
ēvol·ō -āre -āvī -ātum *intr* to fly out, fly away;
 to rush out; *(fig)* to soar
ēvolsi·ō -ōnis *f* extraction
ēvolūti·ō -ōnis *f* unrolling a scroll; *(fig)* reading
ēvol·vō -vere -vī -ūtus *tr* to roll out, unroll,
 unfold; to spread; to read, study; to disclose;
 to free, extricate; to repel; to evolve, develop
ēvom·ō -ere -uī -itus *tr* to vomit, spew out,
 disgorge
ēvulg·ō -āre -āvī -ātus *tr* (-vol-) to divulge,
 make public
ēvulsi·ō -ōnis *f* extraction
ēvulsus *pp of* ēvellō

ex- or ē- *pref* (ex- normally before vowels, c, q,
 p, s, t; s is sometimes absorbed, e.g.,
 expectāre; x is dropped in ēscendere,
 ēpotāre; e- before g, b, d, r, l, m, n, i, u; with
 f, ff- is commonly formed, also ecf-) 1 out:
 exīre to go out; 2 away: ēfugere to run away;
 3 well, thoroughly: ēdiscere to learn thoroughly, learn by heart; 4 hard, up:
 ēverberāre to beat hard, beat up; 5 *(negative,
 deprivation)* -less, un-: exsanguis unbloody;
 exos boneless; 6 up: exaggerāre to pile up
ex *or* ē *prep (w. abl)* 1 *(of space)* out of, from:
 ex conciliō īre to come out of the assembly;
 2 *(of space)* down from: sē ex altissimō
 praecipitāre to jump down from a great
 height; 3 *(of space)* up from: ē lectō surgere
 to get up from his bed; 4 *(of time)* from,
 from … onward, following, since: ex eō *(or
 ex illō or ex quō)* from that time on, ever
 since then; 5 *(of time)* right after: ex imbre
 right after the rain; 6 *(of material of which
 s.th. consists)* of: statua ex aurō a statue of
 gold; 7 *(of parentage, racial origin)* by, from:
 trēs fīliōs ex eā generāvit he had three children by her; 8 *(of cause or origin)* from,
 through, by, on account of, by reason of: ex
 aere aliēnō commōtus upset because of his
 debts; 9 *(derivation of a word)* from, after:
 appellāta est ex virō virtus "manliness" is
 derived from "man"; 10 *(in partitive sense)*
 of, out of, from among: paucōs ex suīs
 dēperdidit he lost few of his own men; 11
 (indicating extent): cōpiae ex parte dēlētae,
 ex parte captae troops partly destroyed,
 partly captured; 12 *(indicating repetition)*
 after: bella ex bellīs serere to sow the seeds
 of war after war; diēs ex diē day after day; 13
 (indicating recovery) ex vulnere refectus
 recovered from a wound; 14 *(indicating point
 from which action is performed)* from: ex
 equō pugnāre to fight from a horse *(i.e., on
 horseback);* ex itinere pugnāre to fight en
 route; 15 *(indicating conformity)* after,
 according to, in conformity with: ex
 cōnsuētūdine cōtīdiānā according to their
 daily habit; 17 *(w. verbs of learning)* from: ex
 litterīs tuīs intellēxī I understood from your
 letter
e(x)sangu·is -is -e *adj* bloodless; pale; feeble;
 causing paleness
exacerb·ō -āre -āvī -ātus *tr* to exasperate,
 enrage; to exacerbate, make worse
exācti·ō -ōnis *f* driving out, expulsion;
 demanding; exaction, collection; supervision
 (of public works)
exāct·or -ōris *m* expeller; collector; supervisor
exāct·us -a -um *pp of* exigō ‖ *adj* exact, precise

exac·uō -uere -uī -ūtus *tr* to sharpen; to stimulate, spur, inflame

exadversum *or* **exadversus** *adv* (**-vor-**) on the opposite side **‖** *prep (w. dat or acc)* across from, right opposite

exaedificāti·ō -ōnis *f* construction

exaedific·ō -āre -āvī -ātus *tr* to finish building, build, construct; *(fig)* to complete

exaequāti·ō -ōnis *f* leveling; uniformity

exaequ·ō -āre -āvī -ātus *tr* to level, make level; *(fig)* to equal, regard as equal **‖** *pass (w. dat)* to be put on the same level with

exaestu·ō -āre -āvī -ātum *intr* to seethe, boil; to ferment

exaggerāti·ō -ōnis *f* exaltation; *(rhet)* intensification *(by repetition or piling up);* **animī exaggerātiō** broadening of the mind

exagger·ō -āre -āvī -ātus *tr* to pile up; to enlarge; to enhance

exagitāt·or -ōris *m* critic

exagit·ō -āre -āvī -ātus *tr* to stir up, keep on the move; to scare away; to criticize, satirize; to irritate; to arouse *(feelings)*

exagōg·a -ae *or* **exagōgē -ēs** *f* exportation

exalb·ēscō -ēscere -uī *intr* to turn pale

exām·en -inis *n* swarm; crowd; tongue of a scale; weighing, consideration

exāmin·ō -āre -āvī -ātus *tr* to weigh, balance; to examine **‖** *intr* to swarm

examussim *adv* exactly

exancl·ō -āre -āvī -ātus *tr* to draw off, drain; to go through *(e.g., a war)*

exanimāl·is -is -e *adj* dead, lifeless; deadly

exanimāti·ō -ōnis *f* breathlessness; terror, panic

exanim·is -is -e *or* **exanim·us -a -um** *adj* breathless, terrified; lifeless; fainting

exanim·ō -āre -āvī -ātus *tr* to knock the breath out of; to tire, weaken; to deprive of life, kill; to scare out of one's wits; to dishearten; to agitate

exanimus *see* **exanimis**

exār·dēscō -dēscere -sī -sum *intr* to catch fire; *(lit & fig)* to flare up

exār·ēscō -ēscere -uī *intr* to become quite dry, dry up

exarm·ō -āre -āvī -ātus *tr* to disarm

exar·ō -āre -āvī -ātus *tr* to plow up; to raise, produce; to write *(on wax with a stylus),* write down, note; to furrow, wrinkle; **frontem rūgīs exarāre** to knit one's brows

exasper·ō -āre -āvī -ātus *tr* to make rough, roughen; to exasperate; to make worse

exauctōr·ō -āre -āvī -ātus *tr (mil)* to discharge; *(mil)* to give a dishonorable discharge to

exaud·iō -īre -īvī *or* **-iī -ītus** *tr* to hear clearly; to discern; to perceive, understand; to listen to; to grant

exaug·eō -ēre *tr* to increase greatly

exaugurāti·ō -ōnis *f* deconsecration

exaugur·ō -āre -āvī -ātus *tr* to deconsecrate

exauspic·ō -āre -āvī *intr (w.* **ex**) *(hum)* to come out of *(e.g., chains)* with good auspices

exb- = **ēb-**

exballist·ō -āre *tr* to finish off, batter down the defenses of

exbibō *see* **ēbibō**

exc- = **exsc-**

excaec·ō -āre -āvī -ātus *tr* to blind; to block up *(a river, pipe);* to dim, darken

excalceāt·us -a -um *adj* unshod, barefoot; *(of an actor)* not wearing the buskin, acting in comedy **‖** *mpl* comic actors

excalce·ō -āre *tr* **excalceāre pedēs** take off the shoes

excandēscenti·a -ae *f* mounting anger, outburst of anger

excand·ēscō -ēscere -uī *intr* to grow white hot; to burst into a rage, flare up, reach a pitch *(of emotion)*

excant·ō -āre -āvī -ātus *tr* to charm away

excarnific·ō -āre -āvī -ātus *tr* (**-nu-**) to tear to pieces, torture to death; to torment *(mentally)*

excav·ō -āre -āvī -ātus *tr* to hollow out

ex·cēdō -cēdere -cessī -cessus *tr* to exceed, pass, surpass **‖** *intr* to go out, go away, withdraw, depart, disappear; to die; **ē mediō (or ē vītā) excēdere** to depart this life

excell·ēns -entis *adj* excellent, superior

excellenter *adv* excellently

excellenti·a -ae *f* excellence, superiority; **per excellentiam** par excellence

excell·ō -ere -uī *intr* to excel; *(w. dat or* **super** + *acc)* to be superior to, surpass; *(w. abl or* **in** + *abl)* to be superior in, excel in

excelsē *adv* high, loftily

excelsit·ās -ātis *f* loftiness

excels·us -a -um *adj* high, lofty; tall; eminent **‖** *n* height, high ground; high social status; **in excelsō aetātem** *(or* **vītam**) **agere** to be in the limelight

excepti·ō -ōnis *f* exception, restriction, limitation; *(leg)* objection raised by a defendant against an accuser's statement; *(leg)* a limiting clause

except·ō -āre -āvī -ātus *tr* to catch; to pick up

exceptus *pp of* **excipiō**

ex·cernō -cernere -crēvī -crētus *tr* to sift out, separate

excerp·ō -ere -sī -tus *tr* to pick out, extract, to choose; to gather; to leave out, omit

excerpt·um -ī *n* excerpt

excess·us -ūs *m* departure; death; digression

excetr·a -ae *f* water-snake; spiteful woman

excidi·ō -ōnis *f* destruction

excid·ium -(i)ī *n* destruction, overthrow; cause of destruction ex·cīdō -cīdere -cīdī -cīsus *tr* to cut out, cut off, cut down; to raze, demolish; *(fig)* to banish, eliminate

ex·cidō -cidere -cidī *intr* to fall out; *(of an utterance)* to slip out; to pass away, perish; to degenerate; to disappear; to be forgotten; *(w.* in + *acc)* to degenerate into; *(w. abl or* ex) 1 to be deprived of, lose; 2 to forget, miss; *(w. dat or* dē + *abl)* 1 to fall from; 2 to escape from *(lips);* ē memoriā excidere to slip one's mind

excieō *see* exciō

exc·iō -īre -īvī *or* -iī -ītus *or* -itus *or* exci·eō -ēre *tr* to call *(s.o.)* out, summon; to awaken; to disturb; to frighten; to stir up, excite; to produce, occasion

ex·cipiō -cipere -cēpī -ceptus *tr* to take out, remove; to rescue; to exempt; to take, receive, catch, capture; to follow, succeed to; to intercept; to be exposed to; to incur; to welcome; to take up eagerly; to listen to, overhear; to except, make an exception of; to reach *(a place);* to mention in particular; to take on, withstand

excīsi·ō -ōnis *f* destruction

excīsus *pp of* excīdō

excitāt·us -a -um *adj* excited, lively, vigorous; loud

excit·ō -āre -āvī -ātus *tr* to wake up, rouse; to raise, stir up; to erect, construct, produce; to cause, occasion; *(fig)* to arouse, awaken, inspire, stimulate, enliven, encourage; to startle

excītus *or* excitus *pp of* exciō

excīvī *pp of* exciō

exclāmāti·ō -ōnis *f* exclamation

exclām·ō -āre -āvī -ātus *tr & intr* to exclaim, shout, yell

exclū·dō -dere -sī -sus *tr* to exclude, shut out, shut off; to remove, separate; to hatch; *(coll)* to knock out *(an eye);* to prevent

exclūsi·ō -ōnis *f* exclusion

exclūsus *pp of* exclūdō

excoctus *pp of* excoquō

excōgitāti·ō -ōnis *f* thinking up, inventing, contriving

excōgitāt·us -a -um *adj* carefully thought up; choice

excōgit·ō -āre -āvī -ātus *tr* to think up, devise, contrive

ex·colō -colere -coluī -cultus *tr* to tend, cultivate, work carefully; to refine, ennoble, perfect, improve; to adorn; to worship

ex·coquō -coquere -coxī -coctus *tr* to cook out, boil away; to dry up; to bake thoroughly; to temper *(steel)*

excor·s -dis *adj* senseless, silly

excrēment·um -ī *n* excretion *(spittle, urine, etc.);* excrement

excreō *see* ex(s)creō

ex·crēscō -crēscere -crēvī -crētum *intr* to grow out; to grow up, rise up

excruciābil·is -is -e *adj* deserving torture

excruci·ō -āre -āvī -ātus *tr* to torture, torment

excubi·ae -ārum *fpl* standing guard; sentry; watchfire

excubit·or -ōris *m* sentry

excub·ō -ere -uī -itum *intr* to sleep out of doors; to be attentive, be on the alert; *(mil)* to stand guard

excū·dō -dere -dī -sus *tr* to beat out, strike out; to hammer out; to forge; to hatch *(eggs);* *(fig)* to hammer into shape, write up

exculc·ō -āre -āvī -ātus *tr* to kick out; to tread down on; to stomp

excultus *pp of* excolō

excūrāt·us -a -um *adj* carefully attended to

ex·currō -currere -cucurrī *or* -currī -cursum *intr* to run out, dash out; *(mil)* to sally forth, make an incursion; to project, extend; *(fig)* to fan out, expand

excursi·ō -ōnis *f* sally, sortie; excursion, short trip *(away from a place);* journey, expedition; digression; outset, opening *(of a speech)*

excurs·or -ōris *m* skirmisher; emissary; courier

excurs·us -ūs *m* sortie, raid, charge; expedition, short trip *(away from a place);* journey; digression; *(geog)* projection

excūsābil·is -is -e *adj* excusable

excūsātē *adv* excusably, without blame

excūsāti·ō -ōnis *f* excuse

excūsāt·us -a -um *adj* free from blame, exempt

excūs·ō -āre -āvī -ātus *tr* to free from blame, excuse; to except; to make excuses for, apologize for; to allege in excuse, plead as an excuse ‖ *refl* to apologize

excussus *pp of* excutiō

excūsus *pp of* excūdō

excu·tiō -tere -ssī -ssus *tr* to shake out, shake off, shake loose; to knock out *(e.g., teeth);* *(of a horse)* to throw; to shake out *(a garment);* to jilt, give the cold shoulder to; to toss, throw, shoot; to search; to examine, investigate; to discover; *(fig)* to shake off

exd- = ēd-

exdorsu·ō -āre *tr* to fillet *(fish)*

exec- *see* exsec-

ex·edō -ēsse *or* -edere -ēdī -ēsus *tr* to eat up, consume; to destroy; to prey on; to make hollow; to wear away, corrode; to emaciate

exedr·a -ae *f (semi-circular recess in a wall for sitting, often used for lectures)* sitting room; lecture hall

exedr·ium -(i)ī *n* small sitting room

exempl·ar *or* exempl·āre -āris *n* copy; transcript; likeness; pattern, model, ideal

exemplār·is -is -e *adj* following a model ‖ *n* copy; transcript

exempl·um -ī *n* sample, example, typical instance; precedent; pattern, make, character; model, pattern *(of conduct);* object lesson; warning; copy; transcript; portrait

exemptus *pp of* **eximō**

exenter·ō -āre -āvī -ātus *tr* (**int-**) to disembowel, gut; *(fig)* to empty *(a purse)*

ex·eō -īre -īvī *or* **-iī -itus** *tr* to pass beyond, cross; to ward off, avoid; *(fig)* to exceed ‖ *intr* to go out, go forth; to go away, withdraw, depart, retire; to march out; to disembark; to pour out, gush out, flow out; to escape, be freed; to pass away, perish; *(of time)* to run out; to get out, become public; to burgeon forth; *(of hills)* to rise

exeq- = exseq-

exerc·eō -ēre -uī -itus *tr* to exercise, train; to keep *(s.o.)* busy, keep *(s.o.)* going; to supervise; to cultivate, work *(the soil);* to occupy *(the mind);* to practice *(medicine, patience, skills, etc.);* to carry into effect; to annoy, bother; to worry; to last through *(e.g., winter);* to levy, collect *(taxes);* to use *(instruments, materials);* to wield *(power, authority);* to run *(a business, a shop);* to carry on *(investigation);* (*mil*) to drill, train; **aleam exercēre** to gamble; **causidicōs exercēre** to keep the lawyers busy; **faenus exercēre** to lend money at interest; **imperium exercēre** to wield power; **iūstitiam exercēre** to administer justice; **lēgem exercēre** to enforce a law; **medicīnam exercēre** to practice medicine; **negōtium exercēre** to run a business; **quaestiōnem dē sicāriīs exercēre** to conduct prosecutions for murder; **studia līberālia exercēre** to pursue liberal arts; **tabernam exercēre** to run a shop; **vectīgālia exercēre** to levy taxes, collect taxes ‖ *refl* to exercise, do exercises

exercitāti·ō -ōnis *f* exercise, practice, experience, training; cultivation; *(w. gen)* practice in

exercitāt·us -a -um *adj* experienced, trained, disciplined; troubled

exercit·ium -(i)ī *n* exercise, training, practice; written exercise; proficiency

exercit·ō -āre -āvī -ātus *tr* to keep in training, train, exercise; to habituate; to trouble

exercit·or -ōris *m* trainer

exercit·us -a -um *pp of* **exerceō** ‖ *adj* disciplined; experienced; trying, tough; troubled, harassed

exercit·us -ūs *m* army; infantry; army of followers; swarm, flock, multitude; *(pol)* assembly of the people

exerō *see* **exserō**

exēs·or -ōris *m* corrosive factor, underminer

exēsus *pp of* **exedō**

exf- *see* **eff-**

exhālāti·ō -ōnis *f* exhalation, vapor

exhāl·ō -āre -āvī -ātus *tr* to exhale, give off; **animam** (*or* **vītam**) **exhālāre** to breathe one's last ‖ *intr* to exhale; to steam

exhau·riō -rīre -sī -stus *tr* to draw out, empty; to drain, exhaust; to deplete; to take away, remove; to drain dry; to bring to an end; to undergo, endure; to carry out *(task);* to discuss fully

exhērēd·ō -āre -āvī -ātus *tr* to disinherit

exhēr·ēs -ēdis *adj* disinherited

exhib·eō -ēre -uī -itus *tr* to hold out; to present, produce; to display, exhibit; to cause, occasion; to render, make

exhilar·ō -āre -āvī -ātus *tr* to cheer up

exhorr·ēscō -ēscere -uī *tr* to shudder at ‖ *intr* to be terrified

exhortāti·ō -ōnis *f* encouragement ‖ *fpl* words of encouragement

exhort·or -ārī -ātus sum *tr* to encourage, exhort

ex·igō -igere -ēgī -āctus *tr* to drive out, push out, thrust out, expel; to demand, exact, collect; to require; to pass, spend, complete *(life, time);* to finish, conclude; to ascertain; to weigh, consider, estimate; to examine; to test; to dispose of

exiguē *adv* slightly, sparingly, barely; briefly

exiguit·ās -ātis *f* shortness, smallness; meagerness, scantiness, scarcity

exigu·us -a -um *adj* slight, small, meager, scanty, poor, paltry, inadequate; a little, a bit of ‖ *n* a bit, a small amount

exiliō *see* **exsiliō**

exīl·is -is -e *adj* thin, small, meager, feeble; *(in wealth)* poor; dreary; depleted *(ranks);* worthless; insincere; *(rhet)* dry, flat, jejune *(style)*

exīlit·ās -ātis *f* thinness; meagerness; dreariness

exīliter *adv* concisely; drearily; parsimoniously; jejunely

exilium *see* **exsilium**

exim *see* **exinde**

eximiē *adv* exceptionally

eximi·us -a -um *adj* excepted; exempt; choice, select; special, exceptional

ex·imō -imere -ēmī -emptus *tr* to take out, take away, remove; to exempt; to free, release, let off; to make an exception of; to waste, lose *(time);* to banish *(worries)*

exin *see* **exinde**

exinān·iō -īre -īvī *or* **-iī -ītus** *tr* to empty; to drain, dry up; to weaken; to strip; *(fig)* to clean out, fleece

exinde *or* **exim** *or* **exin** *adv* from that place, from that point; *(in enumerating)* after that, next, then, furthermore; *(of time)* from that point, after that, then; accordingly

existimāti·ō -ōnis *f* (-tum-) opinion, view, judgment, favorable opinion; appraisal; decision, verdict; reputation, good name; *(com)* credit; **vulgī existimātiō** public opinion; **existimātiō tibi est** it is for you to judge

existimāt·or -ōris *m* critic, judge

existim·ō -āre -āvī -ātus *tr* (-tum-) to form an opinon of, judge, consider, regard; to think, suppose; **in hostium numerō existimāre** to regard as an enemy

existō *see* **exsistō**

exitiābil·is -is -e *adj* deadly, fatal

exitiāl·is -is -e *adj* deadly, fatal

exiti·ō -ōnis *f* going out, exit

exitiōs·us -a -um *adj* deadly, destructive

exit·ium -(i)ī *n* destruction, ruin; cause of destruction; death

exit·us -ūs *m* going out, exit, departure; way out, outlet; end, close, conclusion; **ad exitum addūcere** to bring to a close

exl- = ēl-

exlecebra *see* **ēlecebra**

ex·lēx -lēgis *adj* without law, exempt from the law; lawless

exm- = ēm-

exo- = exso-

exobsecr·ō -āre -āvī -ātus *tr* (exops-) to beg earnestly, entreat

exocul·ō -āre -āvī -ātus *tr* to knock the eyes out of

exod·ium -(i)ī *n* finale; farce *(presented after the main feature)*

exol·ēscō -ēscere -ēvī -ētum *intr* (exs-) to decay, fade; to become obsolete; to grow up, become an adult

exolēt·us -a -um *adj* full-grown ‖ *m (fig)* male prostitute

exoner·ō -āre -āvī -ātus *tr* to unload; to empty; *(fig)* to relieve, free

exoptābil·is -is -e *adj* highly desirable, long-awaited

exoptāt·us -a -um *adj* longed-for, welcome, desired

exopt·ō -āre -āvī -ātus *tr* to long for, wish earnestly for, desire greatly

exōrābil·is -is -e *adj* accessible, sympathetic

exōrābul·a -ōrum *npl* enticements, bait, entreaties

exōrāt·or -ōris *m* successful petitioner

exōr·dior -dīrī -sus sum *tr* & *intr* to begin, start, commence

exōrd·ium -(i)ī *n* beginning, start, commencement; origin; introduction

exor·ior -īrī -tus sum *intr* to come out, come forth, rise, appear; to begin, arise, be caused, be produced

exōrnāti·ō -ōnis *f* embellishment

exōrnāt·or -ōris *m* embellisher

exōrn·ō -āre -āvī -ātus *tr* to fit out, furnish, equip, provide, supply; to adorn, embellish, decorate, set off

exōr·ō -āre -āvī -ātus *tr* to prevail upon, win over; to gain *or* obtain by entreaty; to appease

ex·ors -ortis *see* **exsors**

exōrs·us -a -um *pp of* **exōrdior** ‖ *npl* beginning, commencement; introduction, preamble

exōrs·us -ūs *m* beginning, commencement; introduction

exortus *pp of* **exorior**

exort·us -ūs *m* rising; the East

ex·os -ossis *or* **exoss·is -is -e** *adj* boneless

exōscul·or -ārī -ātus sum *tr* to kiss lovingly, kiss tenderly

exoss·ō -āre -āvī -ātus *tr* to bone, take the bones out of

exōstr·a -ae *f* movable stage; **in exōstrā** in public

exōs·us -a -um *adj* hating, detesting; hateful

exōtic·us -a -um *adj* foreign; exotic; **Graeca exōtica** Magna Graecia *(S. Italy)*

exp- = exsp-

expall·ēscō -ēscere -uī *tr* to turn pale at, dread ‖ *intr* to turn pale

expalliāt·us -a -um *adj* robbed of one's cloak

expalp·ō -āre -āvī -ātus *tr* to coax out

ex·pan·dō -dere -dī -sus *or* **-passus** *tr* to spread out, unfold, expand

expassus *pp of* **expandō**

expatr·ō -āre -āvī -ātus *tr* to squander

ex·pavēscō -pavēscere -pāvī *tr* to panic at ‖ *intr* to panic

expect- = exspect-

expecūliāt·us -a -um *adj* stripped of one's savings

exped·iō -īre -īvī *or* **-iī -ītus** *tr* to untie, unwrap; to unfetter; to extricate *(a person from a confined position);* to disentangle; to get ready; to clear for action; to clear *(roads of obstacles);* to solve, clear up *(problems);* to settle *(a debt);* to get *(s.o.)* out of *(troubles);* to put in order, arrange, settle, adjust, set right; to explain, clear up; to disclose; to recount, relate; to supply, provide; to accomplish, achieve ‖ *refl* to prepare oneself, get ready ‖ *intr* to be useful, be profitable; to set out *(on a military expedition);* to turn out *(in a certain manner); (w. dat)* to be useful to ‖ *v impers (w. inf)* it is useful to, is good to

expedītē *adv* freely, nimbly; quickly, expeditiously; unambiguously

expedīti·ō -ōnis *f* (military *or* naval) expedition, campaign; special mission; *(rhet)* proof by elimination

expedīt·us -a -um *adj* unencumbered, unhampered, unobstructed; ready, prompt; ready at hand, convenient; agile; *(of roads)* easy to travel, fast; quick *(mind); (mil)* light-armed; **in expedītō** in readiness, at hand; without hindrance

ex·pellō -pellere -pulī -pulsus *tr* to drive out, expel; to disown

expen·dō -dere -dī -sus *tr* to weigh out; to pay out, pay down, lay out, expend; to rate, estimate; to ponder, consider; to pay *(penalty)*

expēns·us -a -um *adj* paid out, spent **II** *n* payment, expenditure

expergē·faciō -facere -fēcī -factus *tr* to awaken, wake up; to arouse

exper·gīscor -gīscī -rēctus sum *intr* to wake up; to be alert

experg·ō -ere -ī -itus *tr* to wake up

experi·ēns -entis *adj* enterprising, active; *(w. gen)* ready to undergo

experienti·a -ae *f* test, trial, experiment; experience, practice; effort

experīment·um -ī *n* test, experiment, proof; experience; person serving as a test, test-case

exper·ior -īrī -tus sum *tr* to test, try, prove; to experience, endure, find out; to try to do, attempt; to measure strength with **II** *intr* to go to court

experrēctus *pp of* **expergīscor**

exper·s -tis *adj (w. gen)* **1** having no share in, having no part in; **2** devoid of, free from, without

expert·us -a -um *pp of* **experior II** *adj* tried, tested, proved; *(w. gen)* experienced in

expetess·ō -ere *tr* to desire, long for

expet·ō -ere -īvī *or* **-iī -ītus** *tr* to ask for, demand; to exact *(penalty);* to ask about; to aim at, head for; to desire, long for **II** *intr (w. in + acc)* to befall; to fall upon, assail

expiāti·ō -ōnis *f* expiation, atonement; satisfaction; purification

expictus *pp of* **expingō**

expīlāti·ō -ōnis *f* pillaging, ransacking, looting

expīlāt·or -ōris *m* plunderer, looter

expīl·ō -āre -āvī -ātus *tr* to plunder, rob, ransack; to plagiarize

ex·pingō -pingere -pīnxī -pictus *tr* to paint; to depict

expi·ō -āre -āvī -ātus *tr* to purify; to atone for, expiate; to avenge; to appease; to avert *(a curse, bad omen)*

expīrō *see* **exspīrō**

expisc·or -ārī -ātus sum *tr* to go fishing for *(information)*

explānātē *adv* plainly, clearly

explānāti·ō -ōnis *f* explanation; clear pronunciation

explānāt·or -ōris *m* interpreter

explānāt·us -a -um *adj* plain

explān·ō -āre -āvī -ātus *tr* to explain, make clear; to flatten out; to pronounce distinctly

explaudō *see* **explōdō**

explēment·um -ī *n* filling, stuffing

expl·eō -ēre -ēvī -ētus *tr* to fill up; to complete; to satisfy *(desires);* to make good *(losses);* to fulfill, perform, accomplish, discharge

explēti·ō -ōnis *f* satisfying, fulfillment

explēt·us -a -um *adj* full, complete, perfect

explicātē *adv* clearly, plainly

explicāti·ō -ōnis *f* unfolding, uncoiling; analysis; interpretation

explicāt·or -ōris *m,* **explicātr·īx -īcis** *f* explainer, interpreter

explicāt·us -a -um *adj* plain, clear-cut, straightforward

explicāt·us -ūs *m* unfolding, explanation, interpretation

explicit·us -a -um *adj* disentangled; simple, easy

explic·ō -āre -āvī *(or* **-uī) -ātus** *(or* **-itus)** *tr* to unfold, unroll; to spread out; to loosen, undo; to set free; to arrange, adjust, settle; to exhibit; to explain; to display

ex·plōdō -plōdere -plōsī -plōsus *tr* **(-plaud-)** to drive off the stage *(by clapping);* to boo; to disapprove of, discredit

explōrātē *adv* after careful examination; for sure, for certain

explōrāti·ō -ōnis *f* exploration, examination

explōrāt·or -ōris *m* scout, spy

explōrāt·us -a -um *adj* sure, certain; safe, secure; *(w. abl)* clear of; **explōrātum** *(or* **prō explōrātō) habēre** to know for sure

explōr·ō -āre -āvī -ātus *tr* to explore, investigate; to probe, search; to test, try, try out; *(w. acc & inf)* to ascertain that; *(w. ut, nē)* to ensure (that; that not); *(mil)* to reconnoiter

explōsi·ō -ōnis *f* driving off the stage, booing

expol·iō -īre -īvī *or* **-iī -ītus** *tr* to polish; to finish *(a building e.g., with plaster); (fig)* to embellish, adorn, refine

expolīti·ō -ōnis *f* polishing, finishing off, embellishing

expolīt·us -a -um *adj* polished, lustrous; refined

ex·pōnō -pōnere -posuī -positus *or* **-postus** *tr* to put out, bring out (into the open); to expose *(children to die);* to leave in an exposed position; to display, exhibit; to make available; to reveal; to publish; to exhibit; to relate; to explain; to offer, tender; to set on shore, land; to send *(s.o.)* sprawling; *(w. dat or* **ad** *or* **adversus** + *acc)* to expose to

expor·rigō *or* **expor·gō -rigere -rēxī -rēctus** *tr* to stretch out, spread (out); **exporge frontem!** *(coll)* quit frowning! **II** *refl (geog)* to extend, reach

exportāti·ō -ōnis *f* exportation

export·ō -āre -āvī -ātus *tr* to carry out; to export

ex·poscō -poscere -poposcī *tr* to demand, beg, insist upon; to demand the surrender of; *(w. double acc)* to ask *(s.o.)* for *(s.th.)*

expositīci·us -a -um *adj* foundling

expositi·ō -ōnis *f* exposing; *(rhet)* statement, description, explanation

exposit·us -a -um *pp of* **expōnō** ‖ *adj* frank; affable; plain, trite

expostulāti·ō -ōnis *f* insistent demand; complaint

expostul·ō -āre -āvī -ātus *tr* to demand, insist on; to complain of; *(w.* **cum** *of person)* to complain about *(s.th.)* to *(s.o.)* ‖ *intr (w.* **cum)** to lodge a complaint with

expostus *pp of* **expōnō**

expōtus *see* **ēpōtus**

express·us -a -um *adj* distinct, clear, express; *(w.* **ad)** closely modeled on

ex·primō -primere -pressī -pressus *tr* to press out, squeeze out; to extort; to press upwards, raise; to model, form, portray; to stamp *(a design on a surface);* to represent; to imitate, copy; *(w.* **ad)** to model on *(a pattern);* to describe; to express; to translate; to pronounce, articulate; **exprimere in melius** to improve on

exprobrāti·ō -ōnis *f (w. gen)* reproach arising from

exprobr·ō -āre -āvī -ātus *tr* to reproach, find fault with; *(w. dat)* to cast *(s.th.)* up to, put the blame for *(s.th.)* on ‖ *intr (w. dat)* to complain to

exprōm·ō -ere -psī -ptus *tr* to bring out, fetch out *(from storage);* to give vent to; to disclose, display, exhibit; to utter, express, state; to bring into play, put to use

expugnābil·is -is -e *adj* vulnerable to attack

expugnāci·or -or -us *adj* more potent

expugnāti·ō -ōnis *f* assault; *(w. gen)* assault on; ruin

expugnāt·or -ōris *m* attacker; **expugnātor pudīcitiae** rapist

expugn·ō -āre -āvī -ātus *tr* to assault, storm; to break into, plunder *(a home);* to defeat; *(fig)* to overcome, sweep aside *(conditions, purposes); (fig)* to achieve, accomplish; *(fig)* to extort, wrest, gain; to persuade, overcome the resistance of

expulsi·ō -ōnis *f* expulsion

expuls·ō -āre -āvī -ātus *tr* to drive out, expel

expuls·or -ōris *m* expeller

expulsus *pp of* **expellō**

expultr·īx -īcis *f* expeller *(female)*

ex·pungō -pungere -pūnxī -pūnctus *tr* to expunge; *(fin)* to cancel *(a debt),* check off the list as paid

expuō *see* **exspuō**

expūrgāti·ō -ōnis *f* (-pūrig-) justification, excuse; cleansing

expūrg·ō -āre -āvī -ātus *tr* (-pūrig-) to cleanse, purify; to cure; to vindicate; to excuse, justify

expūtēsc·ō -ere *intr* to rot away

exput·ō -āre -āvī -ātus *tr* to prune, lop off; to consider; to figure out

exquīrō exquīrere exquīsīvī exquīsītus *tr* (-quaer-) to look into, ask about; to look for; to search, examine, check into; to find out; **pretium exquīrere** to work out a price

exquīsītē *adv* carefully, accurately; exquisitely

exquīsīt·us -a -um *pp of* **exquīrō** ‖ *adj* carefully considered; meticulous; choice, exquisite

exr- = ēr-

exrādīcitus *adv* utterly

exsar·ciō -cīre -sī -tus *tr* (exser-) to patch up, mend

exsati·ō -āre -āvī -ātus *tr* to satisfy fully

exscindō exscindere exscidī exscissus *tr* to annihilate, demolish; to exterminate *(a people)*

exscre·ō -āre -āvī -ātus *tr* to cough up, spit out

exsculp·ō -ere -sī -tus *tr* to carve out; to scratch out, erase; *(fig)* to extort

exsec·ō *or* **exsic·ō -āre -uī -tus** *tr* to cut out, cut away, cut off; to castrate; to deduct

exsecrābil·is -is -e *adj* accursed; bitter, merciless, deadly; amounting to execration

exsecrāti·ō -ōnis *f* curse, execration; solemn oath

exsecrāt·us -a -um *adj* accursed, detestable

exsecr·or -ārī -ātus sum *tr* to curse ‖ *intr* to take a solemn oath

exsecti·ō -ōnis *f* cutting out

exsecūti·ō -ōnis *f* execution, performance; administration *(of a province);* development *(of a subject)*

exsecūtus *pp of* **exsequor**

exsequi·ae -ārum *fpl* funeral procession; funeral service; **exsequiās īre** to attend a funeral

exsequiāl·is -is -e *adj* funeral; **carmina exsequiālia** dirges

exse·quor -quī -cūtus sum *tr* to follow out; to accompany to the grave; to perform, execute, carry out; to follow up, investigate; to pursue, go after; to avenge, punish; to say, tell, relate; to describe; to enumerate, go through; *(rhet)* to develop *(a topic);* **verbīs exsequī** to enumerate

exser·ō -ere -uī -tus *tr* to untie, disconnect; to stretch out *(one's arms);* to stick out *(one's tongue);* to bare, uncover

exsert·ō -āre -āvī -ātus *tr* to keep on stretching *or* sticking out

exsertus *pp of* **exserō** ‖ *adj* uncovered, bare; protruding

exsībil·ō -āre -āvī -ātus *tr* to hiss off the stage

exsiccāt·us -a -um *adj* dry, uninteresting

exsicc·ō -āre -āvī -ātus *tr* to dry up; to drain dry

exsicō *see* exsecō

exsil·iō -īre -uī *intr* to jump out; to be startled; exsilīre gaudiō to jump for joy

exsil·ium -(i)ī *n* exile; place of exile

ex·sistō -sistere -stitī -stitum *intr* to come out, come forth; to appear, emerge; to exist, be; to arise, proceed; to turn into; to be visible ‖ *v impers* it follows as a consequence

exsol·vō -vere -vī -ūtus *tr* to loosen, untie; to release, set free; to discharge, pay; to keep, fufill; to satisfy *(hunger);* to break open, wound; to solve; to explain; to throw off, get rid of; to repay, requite; to give out *(awards, punishment)*

exsomn·is -is -e *adj* sleepless

exsor·beō -bēre -psī *tr* to absorb; to suck up, drain; to gulp down; to exhaust; *(fig)* to gobble up *(wealth, etc.)*

exsor·s -tis *adj* without lots; chosen specially; *(w. gen)* having no share in, free from

exspati·or -ārī -ātus sum *intr* to go *or* wander off course; to flow away from its course; to digress; to expatiate

exspectābil·is -is -e *adj* expected, anticipated

exspectāti·ō -ōnis *f* expectation, anticipation, suspense; exspectātiōnem facere to cause suspense

exspectāt·us -a -um *adj* expected, awaited, desired

exspēs *adj (only in nom sing)* hopeless, without hope

exspīrāti·ō -ōnis *f* breathing out, exhalation

exspīr·ō -āre *tr* to breathe out, exhale, emit ‖ *intr* to be exhaled; to expire, breathe one's last; *(fig)* to come to an end, cease

exsplend·ēscō -ēscere -uī *intr* to glitter, shine; to become conspicuous

exspoli·ō -āre -āvī -ātus *tr* to strip; to pillage

exsp·uō -uere -uī -ūtus *tr* to spit out; *(fig)* to banish *(e.g., cares)*

exstern·ō -āre -āvī -ātus *tr* to startle, scare; to terrify; to stampede

exstīll·ō -āre -āvī *intr* to drip, trickle out; to melt

exstimulāt·or -ōris *m* instigator

exstimul·ō -āre -āvī -ātus *tr* to goad; *(fig)* to stir up

exstīncti·ō -ōnis *f* extinction

exstīnct·or -ōris *m* extinguisher; suppressor; destroyer

ex·stinguō -stinguere -stīnxī -stīnctus *tr* to extinguish, put out; to destroy, kill; to abolish, annul ‖ *pass* to die, die out; to be forgotten

exstirp·ō -āre -āvī -ātus *tr* to pull up by the roots, extirpate, root out, eradicate

exst·ō -āre exstitī *intr* to stand out, protrude, project; to stand out, be prominent, be conspicuous; to be visible; to appear; to exist, be extant

exstrūcti·ō -ōnis *f* erection, construction

ex·struō -struere -strūxī -strūctus *tr* to pile up; to build, erect, construct

exsūct·us -a -um *pp of* exsūgō ‖ *adj* dried up

exsūd·ō -āre -āvī -ātus *tr* to sweat over; to exude ‖ *intr* to ooze out

exsū·gō -gere -xī -ctus *tr* to suck out; *(fig)* to draw out *(moisture)*

exs·ul -ulis *mf* exile, refugee

exsul·ō -āre -āvī *intr* to be an exile, be a refugee

exsultāti·ō -ōnis *f* exultation, jumping for joy

exsultim *adv* friskily

exsult·ō -āre -āvī *intr* to jump up; to frisk about; *(of horses)* to rear, prance; *(of heart)* to throb; to exult, rejoice, jump for joy; to revel, run riot; to boast; *(of speech)* to jump around

exsuperābil·is -is -e *adj* conquerable

exsuperanti·a -ae *f* superiority

exsuper·ō -āre -āvī -ātus *tr* to surmount; to tower above; to exceed; to be too strong for, overpower; to outdo; to outlive ‖ *intr* to rise; to be superior, excel, to be conspicuous; to gain the upper hand; *(of flames)* to shoot up

exsurd·ō -āre -āvī -ātus *tr* to deafen; to dull *(the senses)*

exsur·gō -gere -rēxī *intr* to get up, rise, stand up; to swell; *(fig)* to recover strength; forās ex(s)urgere to get up and go out

exsaev·iō -īre *intr* to lose its fury

exsangu·is -is -e *adj* bloodless; pale; feeble; causing paleness

exsaturābil·is -is -e *adj* appeasable

exsatur·ō -āre -āvī -ātus *tr* to satisfy completely, glut

exscē- = ēscē-

exscrī·bō -bere -psī -ptus *tr* to write down; to write out in full; to copy; *(fig)* to take after, resemble

exsign·ō -āre -āvī -ātus *tr* to mark down exactly, write down in detail

exspect·ō -āre -āvī -ātus *tr* to await, wait for, look out for; to hope for, anticipate, long for, expect ‖ *intr* to wait with anticipation

exsper·gō -gere — -sus *tr* to sprinkle, scatter

exstrūct·um -ī *n* platform

exsuscit·ō -āre -āvī -ātus *tr* to rouse from sleep; to fan *(fire);* to excite, stir up

ext·a -ōrum *npl* vital organs *(heart, lungs, liver, spleen)*

extāb·ēscō -ēscere -uī *intr* to waste away; to pine away; to disappear

extār·is -is -e *adj* used for cooking the sacrificial victim; sacrificial

extemplō *adv* immediately, right away; on the spur of the moment

exten·dō -dere -dī -tus *or* **-sus** *tr* to stretch out, spread out, extend; to enlarge, increase; to widen; to prolong, continue; to pass, spend; to exert, strain; **labellum extendere** to pout *(literally, to extend the lip);* **vīrēs omnēs imperiī extendere** to do everything in one's power **‖** *refl* to exert oneself **‖** *pass* to stretch out, extend; to be stretched out at full length

extent·ō -āre -āvī -ātus *tr* to exert, strain

extent·us -a -um *pp of* **extendō ‖** *adj* extensive, wide; level; **per fūnem extentum īre** to walk a tightrope

extenuāti·ō -ōnis *f* belittlement

extenuāt·us -a -um *adj* thinned, reduced; trifling; weak, faint

extenu·ō -āre -āvī -ātus *tr* to thin out; to lessen; to detract from

exter *or* **exter·us -a -um** *adj* exterior, outward; foreign, strange; **mare exterum** the ocean *(as opposed to the Mediterranean Sea)* **‖** *m* foreigner

exterebr·ō -āre -āvī -ātus *tr* to bore out; to extort

exter·geō -gēre -sī -sus *or* **exter·gō -gere** *tr* to wipe out, wipe away; to wipe clean; *(fig)* to clean out

exteri·or -or -us *adj* exterior, outer

exterius *adv* on the outside

extermin·ō -āre -āvī -ātus *tr* to drive out, banish; to put aside, put away; to dismiss *(from the mind)*

extern·us -a -um *adj* external, outward; foreign, strange **‖** *m* foreigner, stranger, foreign enemy **‖** *npl* foreign goods

ex·terō -terere -trīvī -trītus *tr* to rub out, wear away; *(fig)* to crush

exterr·eō -ēre -uī -itus *tr* to terrify; *(w. abl)* to frighten out of

extersī *perf of* **extergeō**

extersus *pp of* **extergeō**

exters·us -ūs *m* the wiping

exterus *see* **exter**

extex·ō -ere -uī -tus *tr* to unweave; *(fig)* to cheat

extim·ēscō -ēscere -uī *tr* to become terribly afraid of, dread **‖** *intr (w.* **dē** + *abl)* to become panicky over

extim·us -a -um *adj* outermost, farthest, most remote

extisp·ex -icis *m* soothsayer *(who makes predictions by inspecting the entrails of animals)*

extispic·ium -(i)ī *n* the examination of vital organs as a means of divination

extoll·ō -ere *tr* to lift up; to erect; to postpone; to extol, praise; to raise, exalt; to keep raised, hold up; to beautify; **animōs extollere** to

raise the morale **‖** *refl* & *pass (of heavenly bodies)* to rise

extor·queō -quēre -sī -tus *tr* to wrench, wrest; to dislocate; to extort

extorr·is -is -e *adj* driven out of one's country, banished, exiled

extorsī *perf of* **extorqueō**

extort·or -ōris *m* extortionist

extort·us -a -um *pp of* **extorqueō ‖** *adj* deformed

extrā *adv* outside, on the outside; from the outside; **extrā quam** except in the case that; **extrā quam sī** unless **‖** *prep (w. acc)* 1 outside, outside of: **extrā nostrum ōrdinem** outside our class; **extrā ōrdinem** outside the usual order, extraordinarily, exceptionally; **extrā sortem** by direct appointment *(literally, outside the casting of lots);* 2 beyond (the limits of): **extrā meum fundum** beyond (the limits of) my farm; **extrā tēlī iactum** beyond the range of the weapon, out of range; 3 beyond the scope of, not subject to: **extrā lēgēs** beyond the scope of the laws, not subject to the laws; 4 free from, without: **extrā modum** immoderately, abnormally *(literally, without measure);* **extrā numerum** not in meter; off-key; **extrā numerum es mihi** *(fig)* you don't count in my eyes; 5 apart from, except: **omnēs extrā mē** everyone except me; 6 aside from: **extrā iocum** all joking aside

ex·trahō -trahere -trāxī -tractus *tr* to pull out, drag out; to draw *(water)* out; to pull up *(to higher ground);* to prolong; to waste *(time);* to extricate, rescue; to remove; to tow *(a ship)* out

extrāne·us -a -um *adj* extraneous, external, irrelevant; foreign **‖** *mf* stranger; foreigner

extrāōrdināri·us -a -um *adj* extraordinary

extrāri·us -a -um *adj* outward, external; unrelated *(by family ties)*

extrēm·a -ōrum *npl* extremities, last measures, last resort; end *(e.g., of life, of strip of land);* *(mil)* rear elements

extrēmit·ās -ātis *f* extremity, end

extrēmō *adv* finally, at last

extrēmum *adv* finally, at last; for the last time

extrēm·us -a -um *adj* extreme, outermost, on the end; latest, last, hindmost; the last part of, end of; the tip of, the edge of; *(of degree)* utmost, extreme; lowest; **ad extrēmum** at last; at the end; utterly; **extrēma aetās** advanced old age; **extrēma cauda** tip of the tail; **extrēmā līneā amāre** to love at a distance; **extrēma manus** final touches; **extrēmīs digitīs attingere** to touch lightly; to hold tenderly; to touch lightly on; **extrēmō tempore** finally; **extrēmus ignis** flickering flame; **in extrēmō** in mortal danger, in a crisis; **in extrēmō librō secundō** at the end of the second book ‖ *n* end; limit; edge; tip; bottom; extremity; conclusion

extrīc·ō -āre -āvī -ātus *or* **extrīc·or -ārī -ātus sum** *tr* to extricate; to clear up; to obtain with difficulty

extrīnsecus *adv* from the outside, from abroad; outside, on the outside

extrītus *pp of* **exterō**

extrīvī *perf of* **exterō**

extrū·dō -dere -sī -sus *tr* to push out; to eject, expel, drive out; to keep out *(e.g., the sea with dikes)*

extum·eō -ēre -uī *intr* to swell up

ex·tundō -tundere -tudī -tūsus *tr* to beat out, hammer out; to fashion; to devise; to extort

exturb·ō -āre -āvī -ātus *tr* to drive out, chase out, drive away; to divorce; to knock out; to disturb, upset; **mātrimōniō exturbāre** to divorce *(a woman)*

exūber·ō -āre -āvī -ātum *intr* to grow luxuriantly; to abound

exul *see* **exsul**

exulcer·ō -āre -āvī -ātus *tr* to make sore; to aggravate; to exasperate; to wound the feelings of

exulō *see* **exsulō**

exulul·ō -āre -āvī -ātus *tr* to invoke with cries ‖ *intr* to howl, ululate

exūnctus *pp of* **exungō**

exund·ō -āre -āvī *intr* to gush up, well up; to overflow; **in lītora exundāre** to wash ashore

ex·ungō -ungere -ūnxī -ūnctus *tr* to rub down with oil

ex·uō -uere -uī -ūtus *tr* to take off, pull off; to shake off; to undress; to strip; to deprive *(of possessions);* to release; to cast aside, cast off; to bare

exurg·eō -ēre *tr* to squeeze out

ex·ūrō -ūrere -ūssī -ūstus *or* **-ūssus** *tr* to burn out; to burn up; to burn down; to dry up; to consume, destroy; to purge away; *(fig)* to inflame; **vīvum** *(or* **vīvam)** **exūrere** to burn alive

exūssus *pp of* **exūrō**

exūsti·ō -ōnis *f* conflagration

exūst·us -a -um *pp of* **exūrō**

exūtus *pp of* **exuō** ‖ *adj* bare; **ūnum pedem exūtus** with one foot bare

exuvi·ae -ārum *fpl* spoils *(stripped from an enemy, such as armor);* souvenir; hide, skin; slough *(of snake);* clothing; symbols of the gods *(e.g., lightning bolt, scepter, etc., carried in procession)*

exuv·ium -(i)ī *n* spoils

F

F, f *(supply* littera) *f* sixth letter of the Latin alphabet; letter name: **ef**

fab·a -ae *f* fava, lima bean

fabāl·is -is -e *adj* bean; **stipulae fabālēs** bean stalks

fābell·a -ae *f* short story; fable; play

fa·ber -bra -brum *adj* skilled ‖ *m* craftsman; skilled worker; smith; carpenter; builder; **faber aerārius** coppersmith; **faber ferrārius** blacksmith; **faber marmoris** marble worker; **faber nāvālis** ship builder; **faber sandapilārum** maker of (cheap) coffins; **faber tignārius** carpenter

Fab·ius -(i)ī *m* Quintus Fabius Maximus Cunctator *(see* **cunctātor**)

fabrē *adv* skillfully

fabrē·faciō -facere -fēcī -factus to build, construct; to forge

fabrēfact·us -a -um *adj* constructed by craftsmen

fabric·a -ae *f* craft, trade, industry; workshop; workmanship; process of building, construction, production; **fabricam fingere** *(w.* ad) *(coll)* to pull a trick on

fabricāti·ō -ōnis *f* construction; structure

fabricāt·or -ōris *m* builder, producer, creator, architect

fabric·or -ārī -ātus sum *or* **fabric·ō -āre -āvī -ātus** *tr* to make, build, construct, produce; to forge; to prepare, form; to coin *(words)*

fabrīl·is -is -e *adj* craftsman's, carpenter's, smith's, builder's, sculptor's; skilled ‖ *npl* tools

fābul·a -ae *f* story, tale; talk, conversation; conversation piece; small talk; gossip; affair, matter; myth, legend; drama, play; dramatic poem; **fābula est** *(w.* acc & *inf)* legend has it that, the story goes that; **fābulae!** *(coll)* baloney!; **fābulam dare** *(or* docēre) to present a play; **fābulam nārrāre** to tell a story; **lupus in fābulā!** *(coll)* speak of the devil!; **quae haec est fābula?** *(coll)* what's that you are saying?

fābulār·is -is -e *adj* legendary; **historia fābulāris** mythology

fābulāt·or -ōris *m* story-teller; writer of fables

fābul·or -ārī -ātus sum *tr* to say, invent ‖ *intr* to talk, chat, gossip

fābulōs·us -a -um *adj* legendary; incredible; fictitious, mythical ‖ *n* myth, legend

fābul·us -ī *m* small bean

facess·ō -ere -īvī *or* **-iī -ītus** *tr* to do eagerly, perform, accomplish; to bring on, cause, create; **negōtium alicui facessere** to cause s.o. trouble; *(leg)* to bring a case against s.o.; **rem facessere** *(leg)* to sue ‖ *intr* to go away, depart, take off; *(lit & fig)* to retire; **cubitum facessere** to go to sleep

facētē *adv* facetiously, humorously, wittily, amusingly, brilliantly

facēti·ae -ārum *fpl* clever thing, clever talk, witticism, humor

facēt·us -a -um *adj* witty, humorous; fine, elegant; brilliant

faci·ēs -ēī *f* face; look, facial expression; appearance; make, form, shape, outline; nature, character; pretense, pretext; **ā faciē** in the face, in front; **in faciē** *(w. gen)* in the presence of; **in faciem** *(w. gen)* so as to give the appearance of; into the presence of; **prīmā faciē** at first sight

facile *adv* easily, without trouble; unquestionably, far, by far; generally; quite, fully; promptly, readily, willingly; pleasantly, well; **nōn facile** hardly

facil·is -is -e *adj* easy; nimble; convenient, suitable; ready, quick; easygoing, good-natured; favorable; prosperous; gentle *(breeze)*; easily borne, slight *(loss)*; tame, obedient *(animals)*; **ex** *(or* **ē)** **facilī** easily; **facile est** *(w. inf)* it is easy to; **facile est dē** (+ *abl)* it does not matter about; **facilis vīctū** well-to-do, well-off; **facilius est ut** it is more likely that; **in facilī esse** to be easy

facilit·ās -ātis *f* facility, ease, easiness; readiness; fluency; aptitude; good nature; courteousness; levity

faciliter *adv (pedantic for* **facile)**

facinorōs·us -a -um *adj & m* **(-ner-)** criminal; wicked

facin·us -oris *n* deed, act; event; crime, outrage; criminal

faciō facere fēcī factus (faxim = fēcerim; faxō = fēcerō) *tr* to make; to do, perform; to fashion, frame, create; to build, erect; to produce, compose; to produce *(young)*; to bring about, cause, occasion; to acquire, get, gain; to incur, suffer; to render, grant, give, confer; to assert, say, represent, depict; to choose, appoint; to follow, practice; to regard, prize, value; **aliquem certiōrem facere dē** (+ *abl)* to inform s.o. about; **cōpiam facere** *(w. dat)* to afford *(s.o.)* the opportunity; **diēs facere** to spend days; **fac ita esse** suppose it were so, granted that it is so; **fidem facere** to give one's word; **grātiam facere** to grant pardon, excuse; **grātum (pergrātum) facere** *(w. dat)* to do s.o. a (great) favor; **pecūniam** *(or* **stipendium) facere** to make money, earn money; **pretium facere** to name the price; **prōmissum facere** to fulfill a promise; **sacra facere** to sacrifice, offer sacrifice; **verba facere** to speak; **viam facere** *(w. dat)* to make way for **‖** *intr* to do, act; to take part, take sides; *(w. dat or* **ad)** to be satisfactory for, be fit for, do for;

(of medicines) to work; *(w.* **ad)** to be effective in dealing with; **suā causā** *(or* **suā rē) facere** to act in one's own interests; *(euph. for relieving oneself; supply* **aquam)** to pee

facteon = faciendum

facti·ō -ōnis *f* doing; making; party, faction; partisanship; band, group; troupe *(of actors)*; social set, association; **quae haec factiō est?** *(coll)* what's this all about?

factiōs·us -a -um *adj* busy; well-connected; belonging to a faction; factious, subversive, revolutionary

factit·ō -āre -āvī -ātus *tr* to keep doing, keep making; to practice *(e.g., trade)*; *(w. double acc)* to declare *(s.o.)* to be *(e.g., heir)*

fact·or -ōris *m* maker; perpetrator *(of crime)*; **factōrēs et datōrēs** pitchers and catchers *(in ballgame)*

factū *abl sing. masc.* **facilis factū** easy to do

fact·us -a -um *pp of* **faciō ‖** *n* deed, act; accomplishment, exploit; misdeed; **bonum factum!** *(formula of good omen)* knock on wood!; **dictum factum** no sooner said than done

facul·a -ae *f* little torch

facult·ās -ātis *f* opportunity; feasibility; ability, capacity, skill; material resources; *(of things)* power, potency; supply *(of money, ships, men)*; convenience; *(w. gen)* **1** power over; **2** skill in; **facultās ingeniī** expertise **‖** *fpl* talents; resources

fācundē *adv* eloquently

fācundi·a -ae *f* eloquence

fācundit·ās -ātis *f* eloquence

fācund·us -a -um *adj* eloquent

faece·us -a -um *adj* foul

faecul·a -ae *f* **(fēc-)** wine lees *(when dried, used as medicine or spice)*

faenebr·is -is -e *adj* **(fēn-)** *(fin)* of interest; lent at interest

faenerāti·ō -ōnis *f* **(fēn-)** lending at interest, investment

faenerātō *adv* with *or* at interest

faenerāt·or -ōris *m* **(fēn-)** money lender, investor

faener·or -ārī -ātus sum *or* **faener·ō -āre -āvī -ātus** *tr* **(fēn-)** to lend at interest; to invest *(money)*; to finance; to ruin *(e.g., a province)* through high interest rates **‖** *intr* to yield interest, bring profit

faene·us -a -um *adj* made of hay

faenicul·um -ī *n* fennel *(used as seasoning or medicine)*

faenīl·ia -ium *npl* **(fēn-)** hayloft

faenisec·a -ae *m* **(fēn-)** reaper, farmer

faen·um -ī *n* **(fēn-)** hay; **faenum habet in cornū** *(sl)* he's crazy *(literally, he has hay on his horns)*

faen·us -oris *n* **(fēn-)** interest; debt *(as result of heavy interest)*; capital; *(fig)* profit, gain, advantage; **faenore** at interest; **in faenore** on loan

faenūscul·um -ī *n* (**fēn-**) a little interest

fae·x -cis *f* wine lees, dregs; sediment; slag; impure mixture; *(fig)* scum

fāgine·us *or* **fāgin·us** *or* **fāge·us** -a -um *adj* beech

fāg·us -ī *f* beech tree

fal·a *or* **phal·a** -ae *f* movable wooden siege tower; scaffold; curtain towers in the Circus

falāric·a -ae *f* (**phal-**) incendiary missile

falcār·ius -(i)ī *m* sickle maker

falcāt·us -a -um *adj* fitted with scythes; sickle-shaped, curved

falcif·er -era -erum *adj* scythe-bearing

falc·ō -ōnis *m* pigeon-toed person

Faleri·ī -ōrum *mpl* city of Etruria

Falern·us -a -um *adj* Falernian; **ager Falernus** district in N. Campania, famous for its wine ‖ *n* Falernian wine

Falisc·us -a -um *mpl* Faliscan ‖ *mpl* a people of S. E. Etruria

fallāci·a -ae *f* deception, deceit, trick

fallācit·ās -ātis *f* deceptiveness

fallāciter *adv* deceptively; falsely

fall·āx -ācis *adj* deceptive, deceitful; spurious, false

fall·ēns -entis *adj* deceptive

fallō fallere fefellī falsus *tr* to cause to fall, trip; to lead into error, mislead; to deceive, trick, dupe, cheat; to fail to live up to, disappoint; to while away *(time)*; to escape the clutches of; to escape the notice of, slip by; in disguise; *(poet)* to swear falsely by; **faciem alicūius fallere** to impersonate s.o.; **fidem fallere** to break one's word; **oculōs fallere** to be invisible; **opīniōnem fallere** *(w. gen)* to fail to live up to the expectations of ‖ *pass* **nisi** *(or* **nī**) **fallor** unless I'm mistaken ‖ *intr* to go unnoticed ‖ *v impers* **mē fallit** I am mistaken

falsār·ius -(i)ī *m* forger

falsē *adv* falsely

falsidic·us -a -um *adj* speaking falsely, lying

falsific·us -a -um *adj* acting dishonestly

falsiūri·us -a -um *adj* swearing falsely

falsiloqu·us -a -um *adj* lying

falsimōni·a -ae *f* trick, deception

falsipar·ēns -entis *adj* bastard

falsō *adv* mistakenly, wrongly, erroneously; falsely, deceitfully

fals·us -a -um *adj* false, untrue; mistaken, wrong, erroneous; lying, deceitful; vain, groundless, empty; spurious, sham, fictitious ‖ *n* error; lying; lie, falsehood; perjury

fal·x -cis *f* sickle; pruning hook, pruning knife; *(mil)* hook for pulling down walls

fām·a -ae *f* talk, rumor, report, news; saying, tradition; *(w. gen)* reputation *(for)*; fame,

renown, name; infamy, notoriety; public opinion

famēlic·us -a -um *adj* famished

fam·ēs -is *f* hunger; starvation; famine; fasting; *(fig)* craving; *(rhet)* bald style, poverty of expression

fāmigerāti·ō -ōnis *f* rumor

fāmigerāt·or -ōris *m* gossip, rumormonger

famili·a -ae *or* -ās *f* household slaves, domestics; gang of slaves; retinue of servants; household; house, family; family estate; sect, school; **familia gladiātōrum** stable of gladiators; **familiam dūcere** to head a sect; **pater familiās** head of the family

familiār·is -is -e *adj* domestic, family, household; familiar, intimate; private, personal *(as opposed to public); (in augury)* one's own *(part of the sacrificial animal);* **rēs familiāris** one's private property, estate, patrimony ‖ *m* servant, slave; acquaintance; close friend

familiārit·ās -ātis *f* close friendship, intimacy; familiarity; *(of things)* close relationship

familiāriter *adv* in the manner of a close friend; thoroughly; as if at home, in a familiar manner; familiarly

fāmōs·us -a -um *adj* much talked of; famous, renowned; infamous; slanderous, libelous; **carmen fāmōsum** lampoon

famul·a -ae *f* maid, slave-girl

famulār·is -is -e *adj* of slaves, servile

famulāt·us -ūs *m* slavery, servitude

famul·or -ārī -ātus sum *intr* to be a slave; *(w. dat)* to serve

famul·us -a -um *adj* servile ‖ *m* servant, attendant; slave ‖ *f see* **famula**

fānātic·us -a -um *adj* belonging to a temple; fanatic, enthusiastic, inspired; frantic ‖ *mf* temple attendant

fand·us -a -um *adj* that may be spoken

fān·um -ī *n* shrine, sanctuary; temple

fār farris *n* spelt *(type of wheat);* coarse meal, grits; sacrificial meal; bread; dog biscuit ‖ *npl* grain

far·ciō -cīre -sī -tus *tr* to stuff; to fatten *(birds for table); (w.* **in** *+ acc)* to cram into ‖ *refl* to gorge oneself

farfar·us *or* **farfer·us** -ī *m* coltsfoot *(plant w. heart-shaped leaves)*

-fāriam *advl suf* forms multiplicative adverbs denoting -sided: **multifāriam** many-sided

farīn·a -ae *f* flour; powder; *(fig)* character, quality

farrāg·ō -inis *f* mash *(for cattle); (fig)* medley, hodgepodge

farrāt·us -a -um *adj* filled with grain, made with grain

fart·is -is *f* stuffing, filling; mincemeat; **fartim facere ex hostibus** to make mincemeat of the enemy

fart·or -ōris *m* fattener of poultry

far·tus -us -a -um *pp of* **farciō** ‖ *adj* well-fed; crammed, gorged, stuffed

fās *indecl* *n* divine law; sacred duty, divine will, fate; right; natural law; **fās est** it is right, it is lawful; it is permissible; **fās tibi est** you have the right; **omne fās est fīdere** there is every reason to trust

fāsci·a -ae *f* bandage; bra; diaper; headband, fillet; wisp of cloud

fāsciātim *adv* in bundles

fāscicul·us -ī *m* small bundle

fāscin·ō -āre -āvī -ātus *tr* to cast an evil eye on, bewitch, jinx; to envy

fāscin·um -ī *n or* **fāscin·us -ī** *m* evil eye; jinx; witchcraft; charm, amulet; *(vulg)* penis

fāsciol·a -ae *f* ribbon; headband

fāsc·is -is *m* bundle, pack, parcel; fagot; load, burden; baggage ‖ *mpl* fasces *(bundle of rods and ax, carried before high magistrates by lictors as symbols of authority);* high office, supreme power, consulship

fassus *pp of* **fateor**

fāst·ī -ōrum *mpl* calendar, almanac; annals; register of higher magistrates ‖ **Fāstī** poem by Ovid

fastīd·iō -īre -īvī *or* **-iī -ītus** *tr* to despise, snub, turn up the nose at ‖ *intr* to feel disgust, feel squeamish; to be snobbish, be haughty

fastīdiōsē *adv* fastidiously, squeamishly; disdainfully, snobbishly

fastīdiōs·us -a -um *adj* fastidious, squeamish; disdainful, snobbish; refined, delicate; nauseating

fastīd·ium -(i)ī *n* fastidiousness, distaste, squeamishness, disgust, loathing; snobbishness, haughtiness; **(in) fastīdiō esse** to be repugnant; **in fastīdium īre** to become repugnant

fastīgātē *adv* sloped, at an angle

fastīgāt·us -a -um *adj* rising to a point; sloping down

fastīg·ium -(i)ī *n* gable; pediment; roof; ceiling; slope; height, elevation; top, edge; depth, depression; completion; rank, dignity; main point, heading; highlight *(of a story, etc.)*

fastīg·ō -āre -āvī -ātus *tr* to make pointed; to taper; to cause to slope, incline ‖ *refl & pass* to taper; to narrow

fastōs·us -a -um *adj* disdainful; *(fig)* magnificent

fāst·us -a -um *adj (of day)* lawful *(for transaction of business);* **diēs fāstus** court day ‖ *mpl see* **fāstī**

fast·us -ūs *m* contempt; arrogance, haughtiness ‖ *mpl* arrogant deeds

Fāt·a -ōrum *npl* the Fates

fātāl·is -is -e *adj* fateful, destined, preordained; fatal, deadly; **deae fātālēs** the Fates

fātāliter *adv* by fate, by destiny

fateor fatērī fassus sum *tr* to admit, acknowledge, confess; to profess, declare; **fatendī modus** *(gram)* the indicative mood ‖ *intr* to admit guilt, confess; to say yes; *(w. inf)* to agree to

fātican·us -a -um *adj* **(-cin-)** prophetic

fātidic·us -a -um *adj* prophetic

fātif·er -era -erum *adj* fatal, deadly

fatīgāti·ō -ōnis *f* fatigue

fatīg·ō -āre -āvī -ātus *tr* to fatigue, weary, tire out; to wear down; to worry, torment, bother; to pray to constantly

fātiloqu·a -ae *f* prophetess

fatīsc·ō -ere *or* **fatīsc·or -ī** *intr* to split, crack, give way; *(fig)* to become exhausted, wear out, grow weary

fātū *abl sing* *m* in the telling; **haud mollis fātū** not easy to tell

fatuē *adv* foolishly

fatuit·ās -ātis *f* silliness

fāt·um -ī *n* divine utterance, oracle; fate, destiny, doom; calamity; ruin; death; *(fig)* cause of death, cause of ruin; **ad fāta novissima** to the last; **fātō fūnctus** dead; **fātō obīre** to meet death; **fātum est** it is fated; **fātum prōferre** to put off fate, prolong life ‖ *npl* what fate has in store, the future

fātus *pp of* **for**

fatu·us -a -um *adj* silly, foolish; clumsy; tasteless *(food)* ‖ *m* fool; jester

fauc·ēs -ium *(poet: abl singl:* **fauce**) *fpl* throat; gullet; neck; strait, channel; pass, gorge; mouth *(of river);* entrance *(to harbor, home, building, cave, lower world);* jaws, maw *(of wild animals);* crater *(of volcano);* neck *(of vase, jar);* **faucēs premere** *(w. gen)* to throttle s.o.

Faun·us -ī *m* king of Latium, father of Latinus and worshiped as the Italian Pan ‖ *mpl* Fauns, woodland spirits

faustē *adv* favorably, auspiciously

faustit·ās -ātis *f* fertility; good fortune, happiness

Faustul·us -ī *m* shepherd who rescued and raised Romulus and Remus

faust·us -a -um *adj* auspicious, favorable; lucky ‖ **Faustus** personal name *(agnomen)* of the son of the dictator Sulla

faut·or *or* **favit·or -ōris** *m,* **fautr·īx -īcis** *f* patron, supporter, fan

fave·a -ae *f* favorite girl, pet slave girl

faveō favēre fāvī fautum *intr (w. dat)* to be favorable to, favor, support, side with; *(w. inf)* to be eager to; **favēre linguīs** *(or* **ōre**) to observe a reverential silence

favill·a -ae *f* ashes, embers; *(fig)* spark, beginnings

favitor *see* **fautor**

Favōn·ius -(i)ī *m* West Wind *(also called Zephyrus)*

fav·or -ōris *m* favor, support; applause; appreciation *(shown by applause)*

favōrābil·is -is -e *adj* popular

favōrābiliter *adv* in order to win popularity

fav·us -ī *m* honeycomb **‖** *mpl* honey

fax facis *f* torch; wedding torch, wedding; funeral torch, funeral; meteor, shooting star, comet; firebrand; fire, flame; guiding light; instigator; flame of love; stimulus, incitement; cause of ruin *or* destruction; **dīcendī facēs** fiery eloquence; **dolōrum facēs** pangs of grief

faxim, faxō *see* **faciō**

febrīcul·a -ae *f* slight fever

febrīculōs·us -a -um *adj* fever-ridden; prone to fevers

febr·is -is *f* fever

Februa·a -ōrum *npl* Roman festival of purification and expiation, celebrated on February 15

Februāri·us -a -um *adj & m* February *(twelfth month of the Roman calendar until the reform of 153 B.C.)*

febru·um -ī *n* purification

fēcundit·ās -ātis *f* fertility, fruitfulness; *(rhet)* overstatement

fēcund·ō -āre -āvī -ātus *tr* to fertilize

fēcund·us -a -um *adj* fertile, fruitful; abundant, rich; fertilizing; *(w. gen or abl)* rich in, abounding in

fefellī *perf of* **fallō**

fel fellis *n* gallbladder; gall, bile; bitterness, animosity; poison

fēl·ēs *or* **fēl·is -is** *f* cat

fēlicit·ās -ātis *f* fertility; luck, piece of luck; felicity, happiness

fēlīciter *adv* fruitfully, abundantly; luckily; happily; sucessfully; favorably; *(ellipsis)* **fēlīciter (tibi ēveniat)**! good luck!

fēlis *see* **fēlēs**

fēl·īx -īcis *adj* fruit-bearing; fruitful, fertile; favorable, auspicious; lucky; happy; successful; well-aimed

fellāt·or -ōris *m,* **fellātr·īx -īcis** *f* one who practices oral sex

fell·ō -āre -āvī -ātus *tr* to practice oral sex with **‖** *intr* to practice oral sex

fēmell·a -ae *f* girl, young lady

fēmin·a -ae *f* female; woman

femināl·ia -ium *npl* stockings *(to cover the thighs)*

fēmine·us -a -um *adj* woman's; effeminate, unmanly

fēminīn·us -a -um *adj* female; *(gram)* feminine

fem·ur -oris *or* **-inis** *n* thigh

fēn- = faen-

fenestr·a -ae *f* window; hole *(for earrings);* *(fig)* window of opportunity; *(fig)* loophole; *(mil)* breach *(in a wall);* window *(of the soul)*

-fer -fera -ferum *adjl suf* denotes bearing, carrying, or bringing: **cōnifer** bearing cones

fer·a -ae *f* wild beast, wild animal; sea monster; **magna minorque ferae** the Great and Little Bear

ferāciter *adv* fruitfully

ferācius *adv* more fruitfully

Fērāl·ia -ium *npl* **(Fer-)** memorial service of the dead, celebrated on February 17th or 21st

fērāl·is -is -e *adj* associated with death *or* the dead; funeral; deadly, fatal, gloomy, dismal; **pāpiliō fērālis** funerary butterfly *(symbolizing the soul)*

fer·āx -ācis *adj* fertile, fruitful; *(w. gen)* productive of

fercul·um -ī *n* food tray; dish; course; float *(for carrying spoils in a victory parade or cult images in a religious procession)*

fercul·us -ī *m* litter bearer

ferē *or* **fermē** *adv* approximately, nearly, almost, about, just about; generally, as a rule, usually; *(w. negatives)* practically; **haud ferē** *(or* **nōn ferē)** hardly ever; **nēmō ferē** practically no one

ferentār·ius -(i)ī *m* light-armed soldier; eager helper

Feretr·ius -(i)ī *m* epithet of Jupiter on the Capitoline Hill

feretr·um -ī *n* litter, bier

fēri·ae -ārum *fpl* holidays, vacation; *(fig)* leisure

fēriāt·us -a -um *adj* vacationing, taking it easy; dressed for the holiday; unemployed; **diēs fēriātus** holiday, day off

fericulum = ferculum

ferīn·us -a -um *adj* of wild animals; brutish; **carō ferīna** venison; **vīta ferīna** life in the wild **‖** *f* venison

fer·iō -īre *tr (the forms of the perf and pp are supplied by* **percutiō**) to strike, hit, shoot, knock; to kill; to slaughter, sacrifice *(an animal);* to coin; *(fig)* to strike, reach, affect; *(fig)* to cheat, trick; **cornū ferīre** to butt; **foedus ferīre** to conclude a treaty; *(fig)* to strike a bargain; **secūrī ferīre** to behead; **verba ferīre** to coin words

ferit·ās -ātis *f* wildness, fierceness

fermē *see* **ferē**

ferment·um -ī *n* yeast; beer; *(fig)* anger; *(fig)* cause of anger

ferō ferre tulī *or* **tetulī lātus** *tr* to bear, carry; to bear, produce; to bear, endure; to lead, drive, conduct, direct; to bring, offer; to receive, acquire, obtain, win; to carry off, plunder, ravage; to manifest, display; to make known, report, say, tell; to call; to propose, bring forward; to allow, permit; to cause, create; to set in motion; to call, name; *(of circumstances, etc.)* to suggest; *(in accounting)* to enter; to carry *(e.g., a ward in an election);* **aditum ferre** to approach; **aegrē ferre** to be annoyed at; to take it hard; **caelō supīnās manūs ferre** to raise the hands heavenward in prayer; **crīmina ferre in** *(w. acc)* to bring charges against; **cursum** *(or* **iter)** **ferre** to go, proceed, pursue a course; **hunc inventōrem artium ferunt** they call him the inventor of the arts; **in oculīs ferre** *(fig)* to have before one's eyes, have on one's mind; **iūdicem ferre** *(w. dat)* to propose a judge to *(i.e., to go to court with);* **laudibus ferre** to extol; **lēgem ferre** to propose a bill; **molestē ferre** to be annoyed at; **ōre ferre** to show *(by one's looks);* **ōsculum ferre** *(w. dat)* to give *(s.o.)* a kiss; **pedem** *(or* **pedēs) ferre** to come, go, move, get going; **prae sē ferre** to display, manifest; **repulsam ferre** to experience defeat *(at polls);* **respōnsum ferre** to get an answer; **sententiam ferre** to pass judgment; to cast a vote; **signa ferre** *(mil)* to begin marching; **suffrāgium ferre** to cast a vote, cast a ballot; **ventrem ferre** to be pregnant ‖ *refl* to go, proceed; to rush, flee; *(of rivers)* to flow; **sē ferre obviam** *(w. dat)* to rush to meet ‖ *pass (of things)* to be carried along; to extend; *(of sounds)* to carry ‖ *intr* to say *(e.g., ut ferunt* as people say, as they say); to allow, permit *(e.g., sī occāsiō tulerit* if the occasion permit); to lead *(e.g., iter ad oppidum ferēbat* the road led to the town)

ferōci·a -ae *f* fierceness, ferocity; fighting spirit; pride, presumption

ferōc·iō -īre *intr* to rampage

ferōcit·ās -ātis *f* fierceness, ferocity; aggressiveness; presumption

ferōciter *adv* ferociously, aggressively; defiantly, arrogantly

Fērōni·a -ae *f* early Italic goddess of groves and springs, and patroness of ex-slaves

fer·ōx -ōcis *adj* fierce, ferocious; warlike; defiant; arrogant

ferrāment·um -ī *n* tool, implement

ferrāri·us -a -um *adj* iron, of iron; **faber ferrārius** blacksmith; **officīna** *(or* **taberna) ferrāria** blacksmith shop ‖ *m* blacksmith ‖ *fpl* iron mines; iron works

ferrātil·is -is -e *adj* fit to be chained

ferrāt·us -a -um *adj* iron-plated; iron-tipped; in chains; in armor; **calx ferrāta** spur ‖ *mpl* soldiers in armor

ferre·us -a -um *adj* iron, of iron; cruel, hardhearted; firm, unyielding; armored; inex-

orable, inflexible *(fate, laws);* **ferreus somnus** death

ferricrepin·us -a -um *adj (coll)* clanking with chains

ferriter·ium -(i)ī *n (coll)* brig *(jail)*

ferriter·us -ī *m (coll)* glutton for punishment

ferritrīb·āx -ācis *adj (coll)* chainsore *(from dragging chains)*

ferrūgine·us -a -um *adj* rust-colored, dark, dusky

ferrūg·ō -inis *f* rust, verdigris; dark-red; dark color; gloom

ferr·um -ī *n* iron; tool, implement; iron object: sword, dart, arrowhead, ax, plowshare, crowbar, spade, scissors, stylus, curling iron, *(surgical)* knife; gladiatorial fight; **ferrō atque ignī** with fire and sword; **ferrō dēcernere** to decide by force of arms; **ferrum sūmere** to resort to arms

ferrūm·en -inis *n* adhesive, cement

fertil·is -is -e *adj* fertile, fruitful; productive; fertilizing; life-giving; profitable, lucrative; *(w. gen, dat, or abl)* productive of

fertilit·ās -ātis *f* fertility

ferul·a -ae *f* reed, stalk; rod, whip

fer·us -a -um *adj* wild; uncultivated, untamed; savage, uncivilized; rude, cruel, fierce; wild, bleak *(place)* ‖ *m* wild beast; wild horse; lion; stag ‖ *f* wild beast, wild animal

fervē·faciō -facere -fēcī -factus *tr* to heat, boil

ferv·ēns -entis *adj* seething, burning, hot; red-hot *(iron); (of mind)* in turmoil; *(fig)* hot, heated, violent, impetuous, ardent; **fervēns īra oculīs** anger sparkling in the eyes

ferventer *adv (fig)* heatedly, impetuously

ferv·eō -ēre ferbuī *or* **ferv·ō -ere -ī** *intr* to boil, seethe, steam; to foam; to swarm; to be busy, bustle about; *(fig)* to burn, glow, rage, rave; **fervet opus** the work goes on at a feverish pace

fervēsc·ō -ere *intr* to become boiling hot, grow hot, begin to boil

fervid·us -a -um *adj* boiling, seething, hot; fermenting *(grapes);* hot, highly spiced; *(fig)* hot, fiery, violent, impetuous, hot-blooded

fervō *see* **ferveō**

ferv·or -ōris *m* heat; boiling; fermenting; fever; raging *(of the sea); (fig)* heat, vehemence, ardor, passion

Fescenni·a -ae *f* town in Etruria

Fescennīn·us -a -um *adj* Fescennine ‖ *mpl* Fescennine verses *(coarse, boisterous form of dramatic dialogue)*

fess·us -a -um *adj* tired out, worn out; weakened *(by wounds, disease, etc.); (fig)* demoralized, depressed; *(w. abl)* weary of, sick of

festīnanter *adv* quickly

festīnāti·ō -ōnis *f* hurry, haste

festīnātō *adv* hurriedly

festīn·ō -āre -āvī -ātus *tr* to perform, *(or* make *or* do) without delay; to move *(s.th.)* quickly; to accelerate; **iūssa festīnāre** to carry out orders promptly **||** *intr* to rush, hurry; to bustle; to be in a hurry; *(w. inf)* to be anxious to, lose no time in

festīn·us -a -um *adj* hasty, speedy

fēstīvē *adv* gaily; *(coll)* humorously; *(coll)* delightfully, neatly, nicely

fēstīvit·ās -ātis *f* festivity, gaiety, fun; *(rhet)* humor, liveliness *(of speaker, speech)*

fēstīv·us -a -um festal, of a holiday *or* festival; merry, jolly; humorous

festūc·a -ae *f* (**fīs-**) stalk; rod *(with which slaves were tapped when freed)*

fēst·us -a -um *adj* festive, joyous, in holiday mood; **diēs fēstus** holiday **||** *n (often plural in singular sense)* holiday, festival; **fēstum agere** to observe a holiday

fētiāl·is -is -e *adj* negotiating, diplomatic; fetial, of the fetial priests **||** *m* fetial *(member of a college of priests who performed the ritual in connection with declaring war and making peace)*

fētid·us -a -um *adj* (**foet-**) fetid, stinking

fētūr·a -ae *f* breeding, bearing; offspring, young

fēt·us -a -um *adj* pregnant, breeding; fruitful, teeming, productive

fēt·us -ūs *m* childbirth; laying *(of eggs); (of plants)* producing, bearing; offspring, young; fruit, produce; *(fig)* product *(of mind or imagination)*

fī *interj (at a bad smell)* phew!

fi·ber -brī *m* beaver

fibr·a -ae *f* fiber, filament; lobe *(of liver, lungs)* **||** *fpl* entrails

fībul·a -ae *f* clasp, safety pin, brooch; barrette; clamp; bolt, peg; chastity clamp *(worn through the prepuce to prevent sexual intercourse)*

fīcedul·a -ae *f* (**-cēd-**) beccafico, fig-pecker *(small songbird)*

fictē *adv* falsely, fictitiously

fictil·is -is -e *adj* clay, earthen **||** *n* jar; clay statue **||** *npl* earthenware

ficti·ō -ōnis *f* forming, formation; disguising; supposition; fiction

fict·or -ōris *m* shaper, sculptor, molder; attendant of priest who kneaded the sacrificial cake

fictr·īx -īcis *f* maker, molder *(female)*

fictūr·a -ae *f* shaping, fashioning

fict·us -a -um *pp of* **fingō** **||** *adj* false, fictitious; insincere *(person, character, emotions);* false *(witness);* **vox ficta** falsehood **||** *n* falsehood; pretense; fiction

fīcul·a -ae *f* little fig

fīculn(e)·us -ā -um *adj* of a fig tree

fīc·us -ī *or* **-ūs** *f* fig; fig tree; **prīma fīcus** early autumn **||** *fpl* hemorrhoids

fīdēcommiss·um -ī *n* (**fidēī-**) trust fund

fidēlē *adv* faithfully

fidēli·a -ae *f* earthen pot, bucket; **duo parietēs dē eādem fidēliā dealbāre** *(prov)* to kill two birds with one stone *(literally, to whitewash two walls with one bucket)*

fidēl·is -is -e *adj* faithful, loyal; trustworthy, true, sure; safe *(ship, port, advice, etc.); (w. dat or* **ad**) faithful to **||** *m* confidant

fidēlit·ās -ātis *f* fidelity, loyalty

fidēliter *adv* faithfully, loyally; securely, certainly

Fīdēn·ae -ārum *fpl* Fidenae *(ancient town near Rome, once the rival of Rome)*

Fīdēn·ās -ātis *adj* of Fidenae, against Fidenae **||** *mpl* people of Fidenae

fid·ēns -entis *adj* self-confident; bold; *(w. gen)* confident in

fīdenter *adv* confidently; boldly

fīdenti·a -ae *f* self-confidence; assurance; boldness

fid·ēs -eī *f* trust, faith, reliance, confidence; credence, belief; trustworthiness, conscientiousness, honesty; promise, assurance; word, word of honor; protection, guarantee; safe conduct; confirmation, proof; *(com)* credit; **bonae fideī** in good faith; **bonā fidē** *(or* **ex bonā fide**) in good faith; really, genuinely; **dē fide malā** in bad faith; **Dī vostram fidem!** for heaven's sake!; **fidē dēcēdere** to cease to be loyal; **fideī causā** as proof of *(one's)* trustworthiness; **fidem dare** to give one's word; **fidem alicūius dēcipere** to deceive s.o. through (misplaced) trust, betray s.o.'s trust; **fidem facere** *(w. dat)* **1** to convince; **2** to place trust in; **fidem fallere** to break one's word; **fidem firmāre** to make good one's word, back up one's promise; **fidem habēre** to be credible, be believed, have credibility; **fidem habēre** *(w. dat)* to have confidence in, give credence to; **fidem obsecrāre** to beg for support *or* protection; **fidem obligāre** to pledge one's word, make a solemn promise, guarantee one's loyalty; **fidem obstringere** *(w. dat)* to pledge one's word to; **fidem praestāre** *(or* **servāre** *or* **tenēre** *or* **retinēre**) to keep one's word; **fidem sequī** *(w. gen)* to seek the protection of; **fidēs pūblica** promise of immunity; safe conduct; **in fidem accipere** to take under one's protection; **in fidē manēre** to remain loyal; **meā (tuā) fidē** on my *(your)* word; **optimā fidē** with the utmost honesty; **prō fidem deum!** for heaven's sake!; **rēs fidēsque** capital and credit

fid·ēs -is *f* string *(of musical instrument)* **||** *fpl* stringed instrument, lyre; *(fig)* lyric poetry; **fidibus canere** to play the lyre; **fidibus dis-**

cere to learn to play the lyre; **fidibus scīre** to know how to play the lyre

fidī *perf of* **findō**

fidic·en -inis *m* lyre player; *(fig)* lyric poet

fidicin·a -ae *f* lyre player *(female)*

fidicul·a -ae *f* small lyre **||** *fpl* torture rack

Fīd·ius -(i)ī *m* epithet of Jupiter; **medius fidius!** honest to goodness!, so help me God!

fīdō fīdere fīsus sum *intr (w. dat or abl)* to trust, confide in, put confidence in

fīdūci·a -ae *f* trust, confidence, reliance; self-confidence; trustworthiness; security; guarantee; *(w. gen)* confident hope of; *(leg)* deposit, pledge, security; **fīdūciā** *(w. gen)* with reliance on

fīdūciāri·us -a -um *adj* held in trust, fiduciary; of a trustee

fīd·us -a -um *adj* trusty, dependable; certain, sure, safe; *(w. dat)* loyal to; **fīdō animō esse** to be steadfast; **male fīdus** *(w. dat)* treacherous (to *or* for)

figlīn·us -a -um *adj* (**figul-**) potter's

figment·um -ī *n* figment; unreality

fīgō fīgere fīxī fīxus *tr* to fix, fasten, affix, attach, nail; to drive in; to pierce; to erect, set up; to build; to put up, hang up, post; **crucī** *(or* **in cruce) fīgere** *(or simply* **fīgere)** to crucify; **dicta animō fīgere** to let the words sink in; **lūmine fīgere** *(poet)* to stare at

figulār·is -is -e *adj* potter's

figul·us -ī *m* potter; bricklayer

figūr·a -ae *f* figure, shape, form; phantom, host; nature, kind; figure of speech; *(gram)* form *(of a word by inflexion)*

figūrāti·ō -ōnis *f* forming; form, shape; description, sketch

figūrāt·us -a -um *adj* figurative

figūr·ō -āre -āvī -ātus *tr* to shape, form, mold, fashion; to train; *(w. in + acc)* to transform into; *(rhet)* to embellish *(a speech)* with rhetorical figures

fīlātim *adv* thread by thread

fīli·a -ae *f* (*dat & abl pl:* **fīliābus)** daughter

filicāt·us -a -um *adj* engraved with fern patterns

fīliol·a -ae *f* little daughter, dear daughter

fīliol·us -ī *m* little son, dear son

fīl·ius -(i)ī *m* son; **terrae fīlius** a nobody

fil·ix -icis *f* fern

fīl·um -ī *n* thread; string, cord; wick; fillet; figure, shape *(of a woman);* build *(of a person);* texture, quality, style *(of speech); (fig)* character; **fīla lyrae** strings of a lyre; **fīlō pendēre** to hang by a thread, be in a precarious situation

fimbri·ae -ārum *fpl* fringe, edge, border *(esp. if separated into shreds)*

fim·us -ī *m* dung, manure; mire

findō findere fīdī fissus *tr* to split **||** *refl & pass* to fork, split

fingō fingere fīnxī fictus *tr* to shape, form; to mold, model *(in clay, wax);* to arrange *(esp. the hair),* trim; to imagine, suppose, think; to contrive, invent; to pretend, feign; to train, influence *(s.o.)* to be; to compose *(poetry);* to disguise *(looks);* to trump up *(charges); (w. double acc)* to represent as, depict as; **ars fingendī** sculpture; **linguā fingere** to lick **||** *refl* to pretend to be; *(w. ad)* **1** to adapt oneself to; **2** to be subservient to

fīni·ēns -entis *m* horizon

fīn·iō -īre -īvī *or* **-iī -ītus** *tr* to limit; *(fig)* to set bounds to, limit, restrain; to mark out, fix, determine; to put an end to, finish, complete **||** *pass* **&** *intr* to come to an end

fīn·is -is *m (f)* boundary, border, limit; end; purpose, aim; extreme limit, summit, highest degree; starting point; goal; death; **eādem fīnī** within the same period; **fīne** *(w. gen)* up to, as far as; **fīnem facere** *(w. gen or dat)* to put an end to; **in fīne** in conclusion; **quā fīne** *(or* **quā fīnī)** up to the point where; up to what point?; **quem ad fīnem** how long, to what extent **||** *mpl* boundaries, country, territory, land

fīnītē *adv* to a limited degree; specifically

fīnitim·us -a -um *adj* (**-tum-**) neighboring, bordering; *(w. dat)* **1** bordering on; **2** *(fig)* bordering on, akin to **||** *mpl* neighbors

fīnīt·or -ōris *m* surveyor

fīnīt·us -a -um *pp of* **fīniō ||** *adj* limited; *(rhet)* rhythmical

fīō fierī factus sum *intr* to come into being, arise; to be made; to be done; to become, get; to happen, occur; *(of events, festivals, etc.)* to take place, be held; *(of physical phenomena)* to arise, develop; *(w. gen of price)* to be valued at; *(in arithmetic)* to equal; **fīat** so be it; **fierī nōn potest quīn** it is inevitable that; **fierī potest ut** it is possible that; **ita fit ut** *(or* **quō fit ut)** thus it happens that; **plūrimī fierī** to be valued highly; **quid fīet?** *(w. dat)* what's going to happen to?; **quoad fīat** as far as is possible **||** *v impers* a sacrifice is being offered

firmām·en -inis *n* prop, support

firmāment·um -ī *n* prop, support; mainstay; main point

firmāt·or -ōris *m* promoter

firmē *adv* firmly, steadily

firmit·ās -ātis *f* firmness, stability; strength

firmiter *adv* firmly, tight,; securely, safely; resolutely

firmitūd·ō -inis *f* firmness, strength, durability; vigor; stability; **memoriae firmitūdō** unfaltering memory firm·ō -āre -āvī -ātus *tr* to strengthen, support, reinforce; to encourage; to assure; to fortify; to put *(laws, institutions)* on a firm footing, establish; to guarantee; to assert, affirm; to substantiate, vouch for *(a statement or its veracity);* aliquem in sē *(or* sibi) firmāre to make sure of the loyalty of; animum firmāre to get up one's courage; fidem firmāre to make good one's word, back up one's promise; gradum firmāre to walk resolutely; oculōs *(or* vultum) firmāre to look determined **‖** *refl* to brace oneself

firm·us -a -um *adj* firm, strong; stable; hardy, sound *(health);* solid, substantial *(food);* steadfast, trusty; lasting

fiscāl·is -is -e *adj* fiscal, of the imperial treasury

fiscell·a -ae *f* small basket

fiscin·a -ae *f* wicker basket, wickerwork; cum porcīs cum fiscinā *(fig)* lock, stock, and barrel *(literally, with pigs and with wicker basket)*

fisc·us -ī *m* basket; money box; imperial treasury *(distinct from state treasury:* aerārium); state revenues

fissil·is -is -e *adj* easily split; split

fissi·ō -ōnis *f* dividing, splitting

fiss·us -a -um *pp of* findō **‖** *adj* cloven, divided **‖** *n* split

fistūca *see* festūca

fistul·a -ae *f* pipe, tube; water pipe; hollow reed; flute; *(med)* fistula

fistulāt·or -ōris *m* one who plays a shepherd's pipe

fistulāt·us -a -um *adj* provided with pipes

fīsus *pp of* fīdō

fīx·us -a -um *pp of* fīgō **‖** *adj* fixed, immovable; irrevocable; *(w. abl)* fitted with

flābellifer·a -ae *f* female slave who waved a fan

flābellul·um -ī *n* small fan

flābell·um -ī *n* fan

flābil·is -is -e *adj* of air

flābr·a -ōrum *npl* gusts of wind; breezes, winds

flacc·eō -ēre *intr* to be flabby; to lose heart; *(of a speech)* to get dull

flacc·ēscō -ēscere -uī *intr* to become flabby; to wither, droop

flaccid·us -a -um *adj* flaccid, flabby; weak, feeble

flacc·us -a -um *adj* flabby

flagell·ō -āre -āvī -ātus *tr* to whip

flagell·um -ī *n* whip; scourge; riding crop; young shoot, sucker; tentacle *(of polyp);* pang *(of conscience)*

flāgitāti·ō -ōnis *f* demand

flāgitāt·or -ōris *m* persistent demander

flāgitiōsē *adv* shamefully, disgracefully

flāgitiōs·us -a -um *adj* shameful, disgraceful, scandalous

flāgit·ium -(i)ī *n* shame, disgrace, scandal; good-for-nothing

flāgit·ō -āre -āvī -ātus *tr* to demand; *(w. double acc, or w.* ab) to demand *(s.th.)* of *(s.o.)*

flagr·āns -antis *adj* blazing, flaming, hot; shining, glowing, glittering; ardent, hot, vehement, eager

flagranter *adv* vehemently, ardently

flagranti·a -ae *f* blaze, glow; passionate love; flāgitī flagrantia utter disgrace

flagritrib·a -ae *m (coll) (said of a slave)* victim of constant whipping, whipping boy

flagr·ō -āre -āvī *tr* to burn with love for **‖** *intr* to blaze, be on fire; *(w. abl)* **1** to glow with, flare up in; **2** to be the victim of *(e.g., envy)*

flagr·um -ī *n* whip; whipping

flām·en -inis *m* flamen *(priest of a specific deity);* flāmen Diālis priest of Jupiter

flām·en -inis *n* gust, gale; breeze

flāminic·a -ae *f* wife of a flamen; priestess

Flāminīn·us -ī *m* Titus Quintus Flamininus *(consul of 198 B.C, and conqueror of Philip V of Macedon at Cynoscephalae in 197 B.C.)*

flāmin·ium -(i)ī *n* office of flamen, priesthood

Flāminī·us -a -um *adj* Flaminian; via Flāminia road leading N. from Rome to Ariminum **‖** *m* Gaius Flaminius *(conqueror of Insubrian Gauls in 223 B.C., and builder of the Circus Flaminius and Flaminian road)*

flamm·a -ae *f* flame, fire, blaze; star; torch; burning fever; glow, passion; sweetheart; danger; flare-up *(of violence);* flammam adicere *(or* suggerere) *(w. dat)* to fan the flames of; flammam concipere to catch fire; in flammā in flames, ablaze

flammār·ius -(i)ī *m* maker of bridal veils

flammeol·um -ī *n (flame-colored)* bridal veil

flamm·ēscō -ere *intr* to become inflamed, become fiery

flamme·us -a -um *adj* flaming, fiery; flashing *(eyes);* flame-colored **‖** *n (flame-colored)* bridal veil

flammif·er -era -erum *adj* fiery

flamm·ō -āre -āvī -ātus *tr* to set on fire; *(fig)* to get *(s.o.)* all excited **‖** *pass* to glow, flame

flammul·a -ae *f* little flame

flāt·us -ūs *m* blowing, breathing, breath; breeze, wind; flātum ēmittere *(sl)* to break wind **‖** *mpl* haughtiness, arrogance

flāv·ēns -entis *adj* yellow, golden

flāv·eō -ēre *intr* to be yellow, be blond(e)

flāv·ēscō -ere *intr* to become yellow, become golden-yellow

Flāvi·us -a -um *adj* Flavian; gēns Flāvia Flavian clan *(to which the emperors Vespasian, Titus, and Domitian belonged)*

flāv·us -a -um *adj* yellow; blond; reddish-yellow, golden ‖ *m* gold coin
flēbil·is -is -e *adj* pitiful, pathetic, deplorable; tearful
flēbiliter *adv* tearfully, mournfully
fle·ctō -ctere -xī -xus *tr* to bend, curve; to turn, wheel about, turn around; to wind, twist; to curl *(hair);* to direct, avert, turn away *(eyes, mind, etc.);* to double, sail around *(a cape);* to inflect *(voice);* to change *(mind);* to persuade, move, appease; to handle *(reins, tiller);* to guide, steer; **animum** *(or* **mentem) flectere** to give way, bend; **viam** *(or* **iter) flectere** *(w.* **ad)** to make one's way toward, head toward; **vultum flectere** to change one's expression ‖ *refl & pass (geog)* to wind, curve ‖ *intr* to turn; to go
flēmin·a -um *npl* swollen ankles
fl·eō -ēre -ēvī -ētus *tr* to cry for, mourn (for) ‖ *intr* to cry
flēt·us -ūs *m* crying ‖ *mpl* tears
flexanim·us -a -um *adj* moving, touching, persuasive
flexī *perf of* **flectō**
flexibil·is -is -e *adj* flexible; shifty
flexil·is -is -e *adj* flexible, pliant
flexiloqu·us -a -um *adj* ambiguous
flexi·ō -ōnis *f* bending, turning; winding *(path);* inflection *(of voice)*
flexip·ēs -edis *adj* creeping *(ivy)*
flexuōs·us -a -um *adj* winding
flexūr·a -ae *f* bending, winding
flex·us -a -um *pp of* **flectō** ‖ *adj* curved, twisting; involved, obscure *(language);* modulated *(voice); (of a syllable)* having a circumflex
flex·us -ūs *m* bending, curving, turning, winding; bend, curve; shift, change, transition; curling *(of hair);* inflection *(of voice)*
flīct·us -ūs *m* clashing, banging together, collision
flō flāre flāvī flātus *tr* to blow; to breathe, exhale; to coin *(money);* to play *(flute, songs)* ‖ *intr* to blow; to breathe
flocc·us -ī *m* tuft of wool; down; **floccī facere** *(or* **pendere)** to think little of, not give a hoot about
Flōr·a -ae *f* goddess of flowers *(honored on April 28-May 3)*
Flōrāl·ia -ium *npl* festival of Flora *(on April 28)*
Flōrālici·us -a -um *adj* of the Floralia
Flōrāl·is -is -e *adj* connected with Flora *or* her festival
flōr·ēns -entis *adj* blooming; prosperous; flourishing; illustrious; strong, powerful; vivid *(speaker); (w. abl)* in the prime of, at the height of
flōr·eō -ēre -uī *intr* to blossom, bloom; *(of wine)* to foam, froth, ferment; *(of arts)* to

flourish; to be prosperous, be eminent; *(w. abl)* **1** to abound in; **2** to swarm with, be filled with; **aetāte flōrēre** to be in one's prime
flōr·ēscō -ēscere -uī *intr* to begin to bloom; to increase in renown
flōre·us -a -um *adj* flowery; made of flowers
flōridul·us -a -um *adj* flowery; pretty; in the bloom of youth
flōrid·us -a -um *adj* flowery; covered with flowers; fresh, pretty; florid *(style)*
flōrif·er -era -erum *adj* flowery
flōrileg·us -a -um *adj (of bees)* going from flower to flower
flōs flōris *m* flower; bud, blossom; best *(of anything);* prime *(of life);* youthful beauty; innocence, chastity; crown, glory; aroma *(of wine);* best period, heyday, zenith; *(rhet)* literary ornament
flōscul·us -ī *m* little flower; flower, pride, glory; *(rhet)* literary ornament
flūctifrag·us -a -um *adj* surging, wave-breaking *(shore)*
flūctig·er -era -erum *adj* wave-borne
flūctuāti·ō -ōnis *f* wavering, vacillation
flūctu·ō -āre -āvī -ātus *or* **flūctu·or -ārī -ātus sum** *intr* to fluctuate, undulate, wave; to be restless; to waver, vacillate
flūctuōs·us -a -um *adj* rough *(sea)*
flūct·us -ūs *m* wave; flowing, undulating; turbulence, commotion; disorder, unrest; **flūctus in simpulō** *(prov)* tempest in a teacup
flu·ēns -entis *adj* loose, flowing; *(morally)* loose; smooth, fluent *(speech, composition)*
fluent·a -ōrum *npl* flow, stream, river
fluenter *adv* like a wave
fluid·us -a -um *or* **flūvid·us -a -um** *adj* flowing, fluid; soft; relaxing
fluit·ō -āre *intr* to float, swim; to sail; to toss about; to hang loose, flap; to be uncertain, waver; to stagger; *(of fluids)* to flow
flūm·en -inis *n* flowing, stream; river; *(fig)* flood *(e.g., of tears, words);* **flūmine adversō** upstream; **secundō flūmine** downstream
flūmine·us -a -um *adj* river
flu·ō -ere -xī -xum *intr* to flow; to run down, drip; to overflow; to fall gradually, sink, drop, slip; to droop; to pass away, vanish, perish; *(of time)* to slip by; *(of plans)* to proceed, develop; to melt; to be fluent; to be monotonous; *(w.* **ab** *or* **ex) 1** to spring from, arise from, proceed from; **2** *(of words)* to be derived from; *(of crowds)* to stream, flock; *(of branches)* to spread; *(of clothes, hair)* to hang loosely, flow; *(phil)* to be in a state of transition *or* flux
fluviātil·is -is -e *adj* river, found in rivers; **equus fluviātilis** hippopotamus; **fluviātilēs nāvēs** river boats

flūvidus *see* **fluidus**
fluv·ius -(i)ī *m* river; running water; stream
fluxī *perf of* **fluō**
flux·us -a -um *adj* flowing, loose; careless; loose, dissolute; frail, weak; transient, perishable
fōcāl·e -is *n* scarf
fōcil·ō -āre -āvī -ātus *tr* to warm, revive; *(fig)* to foster, cherish
fōcul·um -ī *n* stove
focul·us -ī *m* brazier; *(fig)* fire
foc·us -ī *m* hearth, fireplace; brazier; funeral pile; altar; *(fig)* home, family
fodic·ō -āre -āvī -ātus *tr* to poke, nudge
fodiō fodere fōdī fossus *tr* to dig, dig out; *(fig)* to prod
foecund- = fēcund
foedē *adv* foully, cruelly, shamefully
foederāt·us -a -um *adj* federated, allied
foedifrag·us -a -um *adj* treaty-breaking, treacherous
foedit·ās -ātis *f* foulness, hideousness
foed·ō -āre -āvī -ātus *tr* to make filthy, foul up; to make hideous, disfigure; to mutilate, mangle; to ravage savagely *(land);* to darken, dim *(light);* to pollute, defile; to disgrace
foed·us -a -um *adj* foul, filthy, disgusting; horrible, shocking
foed·us -eris *n* treaty, charter; league; compact, agreement; law; **aequō foedere** on equal terms, mutually; **foedere certō** by fixed law; **foedere pactō** by fixed agreement; **foedus īcere** to conclude a treaty; **foedus rumpere** to break a treaty
foen- = faen-
foet·eō -ēre *intr* **(faet-, fēt-)** to stink
foetid·us -a -um *adj* **(faet-, fēt-)** fetid, stinking
foet·or -ōris *m* **(faet-, fēt-)** stink, stench
foetu- = fētu-
foliāt·us -a -um *adj* leafy **‖** *n* perfume *(made from aromatic leaves)*
fol·ium -(i)ī *n* leaf; petal; **folium recitāre Sibyllae** *(coll)* to tell the gospel truth *(literally, to read aloud the leaf of the Sibyl)*
follicul·us -ī *m* small bag, sack; shell, skin; eggshell; large inflated ball
foll·is -is *m* bag, sack; punching bag; inflated ball; bellows; moneybag; puffed-out cheeks
follīt·us -a -um *adj* enclosed in a sack
fōment·um -ī *n* compress, dressing; *(fig)* remedy, solace, alleviation
fōm·es -itis *m* tinder
fōns fontis *m* spring, fountain; spring water, water; stream; headwaters, source *(of river);* *(fig)* source, origin
fontān·us -a -um *adj* spring
fonticul·us -ī *m* little spring, little fountain
for fārī fātus sum *tr & intr* to say, speak

forābil·is -is -e *adj* vulnerable; *(w. abl)* vulnerable to
forām·en -inis *n* hole, opening; socket; pore; stop *(in musical pipe)*
forās *adv (w. verbs implying motion)* out, outside, out of doors; *(w. verbs of selling, lending)* into the hands of outsiders; *(w. verbs of publishing)* into the light of day; **vocātus ad cēnam forās** invited out to dinner; **forās cēnāre** to eat out
forc·eps -ipis *f* tongs; tweezers; pliers; clippers; claw *(of a crab)*
ford·a -ae *f* pregnant cow
fore = futūr·us -a -um esse to be about to be
forem = essem
forēns·is -is -e *adj* of the Forum, in the Forum; public *(as opp. to domestic);* forensic, of the lawcourts *(because the lawcourts were located in the Forum)* **‖** *npl* street clothes
forf·ex -icis *f* scissors; tongs, forceps
forficul·ae -ārum *fpl* scissors
foric·a -ae *f* public toilet
forīs *adv* outside, out of doors; outside the Senate, among the people; among strangers, in public life; abroad, in foreign countries; from outside, from abroad; **ā forīs** from outside; **forīs cēnāre** to eat out; **forīs esse** to be bankrupt
for·is -is *f* door; entrance, opening **‖** *fpl* double doors; **in foribus** in the doorway
fōrm·a -ae *f* form, shape, figure; beauty, good looks; image; mold, stamp; shoemaker's last; vision, apparition, phantom; species, form, nature, sort, kind; outline, design, sketch; plan; map
fōrmāl·is -is -e *adj* formal
fōrmāment·um -ī *n* shape
fōrmāt·or -ōris *m* shaper, creator
fōrmātūr·a -ae *f* fashioning, shaping
Formi·ae -ārum *fpl* town on S. coast of Latium
formīc·a -ae *f* ant
formīcīn·us -a -um *adj* ant-like
formīdābil·is -is -e *adj* terrifying, formidable
formīd·ō -āre -āvī -ātus *tr* to dread **‖** *intr* to be afraid
formīd·ō -inis *f* fear, terror; *(religious)* dread, awe; bogy; threats
formīdolōsē *adv* **(-dul-)** dreadfully, terribly
formīdolōs·us -a -um *adj* **(-dul-)** formidable, alarming; fearful, frightened
fōrm·ō -āre -āvī -ātus *tr* to form, shape, mold, build; *(w. in + acc)* to transform into, make into; to make, produce, invent; to imagine; to shape, direct; to instruct; to depict, represent; *(gram)* to inflect
fōrmōsē *adv* beautifully, gracefully
fōrmōsit·ās -ātis *f* beauty, good looks

fōrmōs·us -a -um *adj* shapely, beautiful, handsome, good-looking
fōrmul·a -ae *f* nice shape, beauty; list, register; legal position; formula; contract, agreement; rule, regulation; pattern, type; charter *(of a government); (leg)* regular form of judicial procedure; *(leg)* provisions *(of a law); (phil)* principle; **fōrmula quaestiōnis** the rule of evidence; **fōrmulam accipere** to be sued; **fōrmulam ēdere** *(or* **intendere** *or* **scrībere)** to bring an action, bring suit
fornācāl·is -is -e *adj* of an oven
fornācul·a -ae *f* small oven
forn·āx -ācis *f* oven, furnace; kiln; forge
fornicāti·ō -ōnis *f* arch, vaulting
fornicāt·us -a -um *adj* arched
forn·ix -icis *m* arch, vault; arcade; brothel
fornus *see* **furnus**
for·ō -āre -āvī -ātus *tr* to bore, pierce
fors *adv* perhaps, chances are
for·s -tis *f* chance, luck, accident; **forte** by chance, accidentally, by accident; perhaps; **vīdistīne forte eum?** did you happen to see him?
forsan *or* **forsit** *or* **forsitan** *adv* perhaps
fortasse *or* **fortassis** *adv* perhaps
forte *see* **fors**
forticul·us -a -um *adj* quite bold, rather brave
fort·is -is -e *adj* brave, courageous; strong, mighty, powerful; resolute, steadfast, firm; loud, noisy *(sounds); (of cities)* rich in resources *or* manpower; decent, honorable *(conduct);* drastic *(remedies);* vigorous *(speakers);* strong, potent *(medicine, wine)*
fortiter *adv* bravely, boldly; strongly, vigorously, firmly; justifiably
fortitūd·ō -inis *f* fortitude, bravery, courage; strength; resolution
fortuītō *adv* fortuitously, by chance, accidentally; haphazardly
fortuīt·us -a -um *adj* fortuitous, accidental; random, haphazard
fortūn·a -ae *f* chance, luck, fate, fortune; good luck, prosperity; bad luck, misfortune; lot; opportunity; circumstances; state, rank, position; property, goods, fortune; **fortūnae mandāre** to leave to chance; **fortūnam alicūius sequī** to follow s.o.'s leadership; **fortūnam suam sequī** to follow one's star; **fortūnam temptāre** *(or* **perīclitārī)** to tempt fate; **in fortūnā positus esse** *(or* **fortūnae subiectus esse)** to be left to chance, be dependent on luck; **per fortūnās!** *(in earnest entreaties)* for heaven's sake! ‖ *fpl* riches, fortune
fortūnātē *adv* happily; prosperously; successfully
fortūnāt·us -a -um *adj* fortunate, lucky, prosperous; happy; rich

fortūn·ō -āre -āvī -ātus *tr* to make happy, make prosperous; to bless
forul·ī -ōrum *mpl* bookshelves
For·um Appiī *(gen:* **Forī Appiī)** *n* town in Latium on the Via Appia
for·um -ī *n* forum, civic center; shopping center, mall, marketplace; market town; trade, commerce; public life, public affairs; jurisdiction; popular assembly; the bar, the courts; game board; **ad forum dēdūcere** to escort *(a young man)* to the Forum to assume the toga of manhood; **cēdere forō** to go bankrupt; **extrā suum forum** beyond his jurisdiction; **Forum Boārium** cattle market; **Forum Olitōrium** produce market; **Forum Piscātōrium** fish market; **Forum Rōmānum** Roman Forum; **in forō** outside one's home, in public; **forum agere** to hold court; **forum attingere** to enter public life; **in forō versārī** to be engaged in business
for·us -ī *m* gangway; tier of seats; tier of a beehive; **forī** bleachers
foss·a -ae *f* ditch, trench; moat; canal; **fossam dēprimere** to dig a ditch
fossi·ō -ōnis *f* digging
foss·or -ōris *m* digger; *(fig)* lout
fossūr·a -ae *f* digging
fossus *pp of* **fodiō**
fōtus *pp of* **foveō**
fove·a -ae *f* small pit; *(lit & fig)* pitfall
foveō fovēre fōvī fōtus *tr* to warm, keep warm; to refresh, soothe; to bathe; to massage; to freshen *(breath);* to nurse *(wounds);* to fondle, caress; to cherish *(hope);* to foster, nurture; to take the side of; to support, encourage; to pamper
frāct·us -a -um *pp of* **frangō** ‖ *adj* interrupted, irregular; weak, feeble
frāg·a -ōrum *npl* strawberries
fragil·is -is -e *adj* fragile, brittle; crackling; frail, flimsy; unstable; impermanent, uncertain
fragilit·ās -ātis *f* fragility; frailty
fraglō *see* **flagrō**
fragment·um -ī *n* fragment, remnant
frag·or -ōris *m* crash, noise, uproar, din; applause; clap of thunder
fragōs·us -a -um *adj* broken, uneven, rough; crashing, roaring
frāgr·ō *or* **fragl·ō -āre -āvī** *intr* to smell sweet, be fragrant; to reek
frame·a -ae *f* German spear
frangō frangere frēgī frāctus *tr* to break to pieces, smash to pieces, shatter; to grind, crush *(grain);* to curl *(hair);* to make *(waters)* choppy; to violate, break *(treaty, law, promise); (fig)* to break down, overcome, crush, dishearten, humble; to repress *(feelings);* to weaken, soften; to inflict a crushing blow on

(a nation); (esp. of old age) to exhaust, wear out; to break the force of; to move, touch; **diem merō frangere** to break up the day with wine; **iter frangere** to force a way; **nāvem frangere** to wreck a ship ‖ *pass* to suffer shipwreck; to relent

frātell·us -ī *m* little brother

frā·ter ·tris *m* brother; cousin; *(euphem) (homosexual)* sex partner; **frāter germānus** full brother; **frāter patruēlis** first cousin *(on father's side)*

frātercul·us -ī *m* little brother

frāternē *adv* like a brother

frāternit·ās -ātis *f* brotherhood

frātern·us -a -um *adj* fraternal; brotherly; brother's

frātricīd·a -ae *m* murderer of a brother, fratricide

fraudāti·ō -ōnis *f* swindling

fraudāt·or -ōris *m* swindler, cheat

fraud·ō -āre -āvī -ātus *tr* to swindle, cheat, defraud; to embezzle; *(w. abl)* to cheat *(s.o.)* out of

fraudulenti·a -ae *f* dishonesty

fraudulent·us -a -um *adj* fraudulent, dishonest; deceitful, treacherous

frau·s -dis *f* fraud, deception, trickery; error, delusion; offense, crime; harm, damage; *(person)* fraud, cheat; **sine fraude** without harm to oneself, unscathed; without risk of punishment, with impunity; **fraudem lēgī facere** to violate the law

fraxine·us -a -um *adj* made of ash wood

fraxin·us -a -um *adj* of ash wood

fraxin·us -ī *f* ash tree; spear *(made of ash wood)*

frēgī *perf of* **frangō**

fremibund·us -a -um *adj* (**-meb-**) roaring

fremid·us -a -um *adj* growling

fremit·us -ūs *m* roar, growl, rumble, hum; din, noise; grumbling, muttering; loud buzz of approval

frem·ō -ere -uī -itus *tr* to grumble at, complain loudly about; to demand angrily, clamor for; to declare noisily ‖ *intr* to roar, growl, snort, howl; to grumble; to resound

frem·or -ōris *m* roaring, grumbling; murmuring

frend·ō -ere -uī *intr* to gnash the teeth; **dentibus frendere** to gnash the teeth

frēnī *see* **frēnum**

frēn·ō -āre -āvī -ātus *tr* to bridle, curb; *(fig)* to curb

frēn·um -ī *n or* **frēn·a -ōrum** *npl or* **frēn·ī -ōrum** *mpl* reins; bridle, bit; *(fig)* curb, control, restraint; *(poet)* riding *(on horseback);* **frēna** *(or* **frēnōs** *or* **frēnum) accipere** *(or* **patī)** to take the bit, learn obedience; **frēna** *(or* **frēnōs) dare** *(or* **effundere** *or* **immittere** *or* **laxāre** *or* **remittere)** to loosen the reins; **frēna (ab)rumpere** to snap the reins, bolt; **frēna** *(or* **frēnōs) tenēre** *(or* **moderārī)** *(w. gen)* to hold the reins of, be in control of; **in frēnīs** *(or* **sub frēnō)** under control

frequ·ēns -entis *adj* crowded, packed, filled; in crowds, numerous; frequent, repeated, usual, common; full, plenary *(Senate session); (of persons)* constant, regular; *(may be rendered adverbially)* often, frequently, *e.g.:* **frequēns et audīvī et adfuī** I was often at your side and heard you speak; *(w. abl)* **1** crowded with; **2** densely covered with; **frequēns emporium** well-stocked market; **frequēns est** *(w. inf)* it is a common practice to

frequentāti·ō -ōnis *f* piling up, concentration

frequenter *adv* in crowds, in large numbers; frequently, in quick succession; commonly, widely; **frequenter habitārī** *(or* **colī)** to be densely populated

frequenti·a -ae *f* crowd; crowded assembly, large attendance; dense mass; populousness; populous district; crowded-ness; abundance; multitude; population; frequency; conscientious performance *(of duties);* **frequentia vehiculōrum** heavy traffic

frequent·ō -āre -āvī -ātus *tr* to crowd, people, populate; *(w. abl)* to pack with, stock with, crowd with; to assemble in a crowd; to crowd around *(a person);* to attend *(e.g., games)* in large numbers; to sue frequently; to say over and over again; to do often, repeat; to use frequently; to frequent, resort to; to visit often; to celebrate, observe *(festival, ceremony);* to attend *(a meeting, school, lecture);* to appear on *(the stage);* to inhabit *(a place)* ‖ *pass* to become crowded

fretēns·is -is -e *adj* **mare fretēnse** Strait of Messina *(between Italy and Sicily)*

fret·um -ī *n* strait, channel; sea, the deep; waters; *(fig)* seething flood

frēt·us -a -um *adj* *(w. dat or abl)* relying on, confident of, depending on; *(w. acc & inf)* confident that

fret·us -ūs *m* strait

fric·ō -āre -uī -tus *or* **-ātus** *tr* to rub; to chafe; to rub down, massage

frictus *pp of* **fricō**

frictus *pp of* **frīgō**

frīgefact·ō -āre *tr* to cool

frīg·eō -ēre *intr* to be cold, be chilly; to freeze; *(fig)* to be numbed, be lifeless, be dull; *(fig)* to get a cool reception, get the cold shoulder; *(of words)* to fall flat; *(of an old man)* to lack vigor; to have nothing to do, be idle

frīger·ō -āre *tr* to cool off

frīgēsc·ō -ere frīxī *intr* to become cold, become chilled; to become lifeless; *(of a speech)* to fall flat

frīgid·a -ae *f* cold water

frīgidāri·us -a -um *adj* cooling

frīgidē *adv* feebly; coolly

frīgidul·us -a -um *adj* rather cold; rather faint

frīgid·us -a -um *adj* cold, cool; numbed, dull, lifeless; indifferent, unimpassioned; flat, insipid, trivial ‖ *f* cold water

frīg·ō frīgere frīxī frīctus *tr* to roast, fry

frīg·us -oris *n* cold, coldness, chill, coolness; frost; cold of winter, winter; coldness of death, death; chill, fever; shudder, chill; cold region; cold reception; coolness, indifference; slowness, inactivity ‖ *npl* cold spell

frigutt·iō -īre *intr* to stutter

fringill·a -ae *f* a songbird

fri·ō -āre -āvī -ātus *tr* & *refl* & *pass* to crumble

fritill·us -ī *m* dice box

frīvol·us -a -um *adj* frivolous, trifling, worthless, sorry, pitiful ‖ *npl* trifles

frīxī *perf of* **frīgēscō** *and* **frīgō** *and* **frīgeō**

frondāt·or -ōris *m* pruner

frond·eō -ēre *intr* to have leaves; *(of places)* to be green with trees

frondēsc·ō -ere *intr* to get leaves

fronde·us -a -um *adj* leafy

frondif·er -era -erum *adj* leafy

frondōs·us -a -um *adj* full of leaves, leafy

frōn·s -dis *f* foliage; leafy bough, green bough; chaplet, garland

frōn·s -tis *f* forehead, brow; front end, front; face, look; façade; vanguard; exterior, appearance; outer end of a scroll; sense of shame; **ā fronte** in front; **frōns firma** *(fig)* a bold front; **frōns prīma** front line; **frontem contrahere** *(or* **addūcere** *or* **cōnstringere** *or* **obdūcere)** to frown; **frontem ferīre** to tap oneself on the forehead *(in annoyance)*; **frontem remittere** *(or* **exporrigere)** to smooth the brow, cheer up, relax; **frontis tenerae vidērī** to seem to blush *(literally, to seem to be of sensitive brow); in fronte (in measuring land)* in breadth, in frontage; **salvā fronte** without shame; **tenuis frōns** low forehead

frontāl·ia -ium *npl* frontlet *(ornament for forehead of horse)*

front·ō -ōnis *m* person with bulging forehead

frūctuāri·us -a -um *adj* productive; subject to land tax

frūctuōs·us -a -um *adj* fruitful, productive

frūctus *pp of* **fruor**

frūct·us -ūs *m* fruit, produce; proceeds, profit, income, return, revenue; enjoyment, satisfaction; benefit, reward, results, consequence

frūgāl·is -is -e *adj* thrifty, frugal

frūgālit·ās -ātis *f* frugality, economy; temperance; honesty; worth

frūgāliter *adv* frugally, economically; temperately

frūgēs *see* **frūx**

frūgī *indecl adj* frugal; thrifty; temperate; honest; worthy; useful; proper; **frūgī esse** to do the right thing

frūgif·er -era -erum *adj* fruitful, productive, fertile; profitable

frūgifer·ēns -entis *adj* fruitful

frūgileg·us -a -um *adj (of ants)* food-gathering

frūgipar·us -a -um *adj* fruitful

fruitus *pp of* **fruor**

frūmentāri·us -a -um *adj* of grain, grain; grain-producing; of provisions; **rēs frūmentāria** *(mil)* supplies, quartermaster ‖ *m* grain dealer; *(mil)* forager

frūmentāti·ō -ōnis *f (mil)* foraging

frūmentāt·or -ōris *m* grain merchant; *(mil)* forager

frūment·or -ārī -ātus sum *intr (mil)* to forage

frūment·um -ī *n* grain; wheat ‖ *npl* grain fields; crops

frūn·īscor -īscī -ītus sum *tr* to enjoy

fruor fruī frūctus sum *or* **fruitus sum** *tr* to enjoy; ‖ *intr (w. abl)* **1** to enjoy, delight in; **2** to enjoy the company of; **3** *(law)* to have the use and enjoyment of

frūstillātim *adv* in bits

frūstrā *adv* in vain, uselessly, for nothing; without reason, groundlessly; **frūstrā discēdere** to go away disappointed; **frūstrā esse** to be mistaken; **frūstrā habēre** to have *(s.o.)* confused

frūstrām·en -inis *n* deception, error

frūstrāti·ō -ōnis *f* deception; frustration

frūstrāt·us -ūs *m* deception; **frūstrātuī habēre** *(coll)* to take for a sucker

frūstr·or -ārī -ātus sum *or* **frūstr·ō -āre** *tr* to deceive, trick; to disappoint; to frustrate

frūstulent·us -a -um *adj* full of crumbs

frūst·um -ī *n* crumb, bit, scrap; **frūstum puerī** *(coll)* whippersnapper

frutect·um *or* **fruticēt·um -ī** *n* thicket, shrubbery ‖ *npl* bushes

frut·ex -icis *m* shrub, bush; stem, trunk; *(coll)* blockhead

fruticētum *see* **frutectum**

frutic·ō -āre -āvī *or* **frutic·or -ārī** *intr* to sprout; to become bushy; *(fig) (of hair)* to become bushy

fruticōs·us -a -um *adj* bushy, overgrown with bushes

frūx frūgis *f* *or* **frūg·ēs -um** *fpl* produce; crops; grain; vegetables; bread, meal; barley meal *(for sacrifice);* fruits, benefit; *(singl)* morality, honesty; **ad frūgem bonam sē recipere** to turn over a new leaf; **bonae frūgī**

esse to be honest, be thrifty; **expers frūgis** worthless; **frūgem facere** to do the decent thing

fūcāt·us -a -um *adj* artificial *(color);* dyed, colored, painted; phony

fūc·ō -āre -āvī -ātus *tr* to dye, tint; to apply makeup to; to disguise, falsify

fūcōs·us -a -um *adj* painted, colored; artificial, spurious

fūc·us -ī *m* (red) paint; rouge; drone; bee-glue; disguise; pretense, deceit; **sine fūcō ac fallāciīs** without mincing words

fūdī *perf of* **fundō**

fue *or* **fu** *interj* phui!

fug·a -ae *f* flight, escape; avoidance; exile; speed, swift passage; disappearance; *(w. gen)* avoidance of, escape from; **fugae sēsē mandāre** *(or* **fugam capere** *or* **fugam capessere** *or* **fugam facere** *or* **sē in fugam cōnferre** *or* **sē in fugam conicere** *or* **sēsē in fugam dare)** to flee; **in fugam cōnferre** *(or* **in fugam conicere** *or* **in fugam dare** *or* **in fugam impellere)** to put to flight; **fugam petere** to look for a means of escape

fugācius *adv* more cautiously, with one eye on flight

fug·āx -ācis *adj* apt to flee, fleeing; shy, timid; swift; transitory; *(w. gen)* shy of, shunning, avoiding, steering clear of, averse to

fugi·ēns -entis *adj* fleeing, retreating; *(w. gen)* avoiding, averse to

fugiō fugere fūgī fugitus *tr* to escape, escape from, get away from; to run away from, shun, avoid; to succeed in avoiding; to vanish from; to be repelled by; to leave *(esp. one's country);* to be averse to, dislike; to escape the notice of, be unknown to; **fuge** *(w. inf)* do not ... !; **fugere cōnspectum** *(w. gen)* to keep out of sight of; **fūgit mē ratiō** I made a mistake; **fūgit mē scrībere** it slipped my mind to write **‖** *intr* to flee, escape, run away; to go into exile; to vanish; to pass away, perish; to begin to decay; *(w. ab)* to keep away from, shrink from; *(of things)* to slip out of one's grasp *or* control

fugit·āns -antis *adj* fleeing; *(w. gen)* averse to

fugitīv·us -a -um *adj & m* runaway, fugitive

fugit·ō -āre *tr* to run away from, shun **‖** *intr* to run away

fug·ō -āre -āvī -ātus *tr* to put to flight, rout, drive away, chase away; to exile, banish; to avert

fulcīm·en -inis *n* support, prop

ful·ciō -cīre -sī -tus *tr* to prop up, support; to sustain, strengthen; **pedibus fulcīre** to tread

fulcr·um -ī *n* bedpost; couch leg; *(fig)* bed, couch

ful·geō -gēre -sī *or* **fulg·ō -ere** *intr* to gleam, flash, blaze, shine, glare; to be conspicuous, be illustrious

fulgid·us -a -um *adj* flashing, shining

fulgō *see* **fulgeō**

fulg·or -ōris *m* flash; flash of lightning, lightning; brightness; splendor, glory; *(astr)* meteor; *(astr)* bright star; **fulgor lūnae** moonlight

fulg·ur -uris *m* flash of lightning; place struck by lightning

fulgurāl·is -is -e *adj* of lightning; *(books)* on lightning

fulgurāt·or -ōris *m* interpreter of lightning

fulgurīt·us -a -um *adj* struck by lightning

fulgur·ō -āre -āvī -ātum *tr* to lighten, send lightning **‖** *v impers* it is lightning

fulic·a -ae *or* **ful·ix -icis** *f* waterfowl *(perhaps the coot)*

fūlīg·ō -inis *f* soot *(used as a cosmetic, in paint, in medications, in ink)*

fulix *see* **fulica**

full·ō -ōnis *m* fuller *(person who shrank, beat, pressed, cleaned, and whitened cloth with chalk)*

fullōni·a -ae *f* fuller's craft, fulling

fullōnic·a -ae *f* fuller's craft, fulling; fuller's shop

fullōni·us -a -um *adj* fuller's

fulm·en -inis *n* thunderbolt, lightning bolt; *(fig)* bolt out of the blue; **fulmine ict·us -a -um** struck by lightning

fulment·a -ae *f* heel

fulmine·us -a -um *adj* of lightning, lightning; shiny, sparkling, flashing

fulmin·ō -āre -āvī -ātum *intr (said of Jupiter)* send lightning;; *(fig)* to flash; *(fig)* to spread disaster **‖** *impers* it is lightning

fulsī *perf of* **fulciō** *and* **fulgeō**

fultūr·a -ae *f* support, prop

fultus *pp of* **fulciō**

fulv·us -a -um *adj* yellow, yellowish brown, reddish yellow, tawny; strawberry-blond

fūme·us -a -um *adj* smoky, murky

fūmid·us -a -um *adj* smoky, full of smoke; smoking; steaming

fūmif·er -era -erum *adj* smoking

fūmific·ō -āre -āvī *intr* to smoke; to burn incense

fūmific·us -a -um *adj* smoking, steaming

fūm·ō -āre -āvī *intr* to smoke, fume; to steam; to reek

fūmōs·us -a -um *adj* smoky; grimy from smoke; smoked *(food)*

fūm·us -ī *m* smoke; fume; steam, vapor **‖** *mpl* clouds of smoke

fūnāl·e -is *n* taper of wax-soaked rope; chandelier, candelabrum

fūnambul·us -ī *m* tightrope walker

fūncti·ō -ōnis *f* performance

fūnct·us -a -um *pp of* fungor **‖** *adj* dead **‖** *mpl* the dead

fund·a -ae *f* sling; pebble *(used in a sling);* dragnet

fundām·en -inis *n* foundation; **fundāmina pōnere** to lay the foundations

fundāment·um -ī *n* foundation; *(fig)* basis, ground, beginning; **ā fundāmentīs** utterly; **fundāmenta agere** *(or* **iacere** *or* **locāre)** to lay the foundation(s)

fundāt·or -ōris *m* founder

fundāt·us -a -um *adj* well-founded, established

Fund·ī -ōrum *mpl* Fundi *(town in Latium)*

fundit·ō -āre -āvī -ātus *tr* to sling, hurl with a sling; *(fig)* to sling *(e.g., words)* around

fundit·or -ōris *m* slinger

funditus *adv* from the bottom, utterly, entirely

fund·ō -āre -āvī -ātus *tr* to found; to put on a firm basis, establish; to secure, make fast **‖** *pass (w. abl)* to be based on

fundō fundere fūdī fūsus *tr* to pour, pour out; to smelt *(metals);* to cast *(in metal);* to pour in streams, shower, hurl; to pour out, empty; to spread, extend, diffuse; to bring forth, bear, yield in abundance; to throw to the ground, bring down; to give up, lose, waste; to pour out *(words); (mil)* to pour in *(troops); (mil)* to rout

fund·us -ī *m* bottom; farm; estate; *(leg)* sanctioner, authority

fūnebr·is -is -e *adj* funeral, funerary; deadly, murderous

fūnerāt·us -a -um *adj* done in, killed; **prope fūnerātus** almost sent to *(one's)* grave

fūnere·us -a -um *adj* funerary, mourning; deadly, fatal

fūner·ō -āre -āvī -ātus *tr* to bury; to bring *(s.o.)* to his grave, kill

fūnest·ō -āre -āvī -ātus *tr* to defile with murder, desecrate

fūnest·us -a -um *adj* funereal, mourning; lamentable; polluted *(through contact with a corpse);* deadly, fatal, calamitous; sad, dismal, mournful

fungīn·us -a -um *adj* of a mushroom

fun·gor -gī fūnctus sum *tr* to perform, execute; **diem** *(or* **vītam) fungī** to die **‖** *intr (w. abl)* **1** to perform, execute, discharge, do; **2** to busy oneself with, be engaged in; **3** to finish complete; *(w.* **prō** + *abl)* to act as; **fātō** *(or* **morte** *or* **vītā** *or* **officiō) fungī** to die

fung·us -ī *m* mushroom, fungus; candle snuffer; *(fig)* clown

fūnicul·us -ī *m* cord

fūn·is -is *m* rope, cable, cord; rigging; **fūnem redūcere** *(fig)* to change one's mind; **per extentum fūnem īre** *(lit & fig)* to walk a tightrope; **sequī potius quam dūcere fūnem tortum** to follow the lead rather than to lead

fūn·us -eris *n* funeral, funeral rites, burial; corpse; death; murder; havoc, ruin, destruction; **sub fūnus** on the brink of the grave **‖** *npl* shades of the dead

fūr fūris *mf* thief; *(fig)* rogue

fūrācissimē *adv* just like a thief

fūr·āx -ācis *adj* thievish

furc·a -ae *f* fork; fork-shaped prop *(for supporting vines, bleachers, etc.);* pillory *(used to punish slaves); (topog)* defile, pass

furcif·er -erī *m* rogue, rascal

furcifer·a -ae *f* rascal *(female)*

furcill·a -ae *f* pitchfork; **furcillā extrūdī** *(coll)* to be given the bum's rush

furcill·ō -āre -āvī -ātus *tr* to support, prop up

furcul·a -ae *f* fork-shaped prop **‖** *fpl* narrow pass, defile; **Furculae Caudīnae** Caudine Forks *(mountain pass in Samnium where Roman army was trapped in 321 B.C. and made to pass under the yoke)*

furenter *adv* furiously

furf·ur -uris *m* chaff; bran

furi·a -ae *f* frenzy, madness, rage; remorse; madman **‖ Furia** Fury *(one of the three goddesses of vengeance: Megaera, Tisiphone, and Alecto)*

furiāl·is -is -e *adj* frenzied, frantic, furious; infuriated; of the Furies

furiāliter *adv* frantically

furibund·us -a -um *adj* frenzied, frantic, mad; inspired

fūrīn·us -a -um *adj* of thieves

furi·ō -āre -āvī -ātus *tr* to drive mad, infuriate

furiōsē *adv* in a rage, in a frenzy

furiōs·us -a -um *adj* frenzied, frantic, mad, furious; maddening

furn·us -ī *m* **(for-)** oven; bakery

fur·ō -ere *intr* to be out of one's mind; to rush furiously around; to rage, rave

fūr·ō -ārī -ātus sum *tr* to steal, pilfer; to plagiarize; to obtain by fraud **‖** *refl* to steal away

fur·or -ōris *m* madness, rage, fury, passion; furor, excitement; prophetic frenzy, inspiration; passionate love

fūrtific·us -a -um *adj* thievish

fūrtim *adv* secretly; imperceptibly

fūrtīvē *adv* secretly, stealthily

fūrtīv·us -a -um *adj* stolen; secret, hidden, furtive

fūrt·um -ī *n* theft, robbery; trick; secret action, intrigue; secret love; **fūrtum facere** to steal **‖** *npl* intrigues; secret love affair; stolen goods

fūruncul·us -ī *m* petty thief

furv·us -a -um *adj* black, dark, gloomy, eerie; **diēs furvus** unlucky day

fūscin·a -ae *f* trident

fūsc·ō -āre -āvī -ātus *tr* to darken, blacken

fūsc·us -a -um *adj* dark; dim, ill-lit *(room);* hoarse *(voice);* dark-skinned, swarthy; low, muffled *(sound)*

fūsē *adv* widely, extensively; in great detail; loosely, roughly

fūsil·is -is -e *adj* molten, liquid

fūsi·ō -ōnis *f* outpouring, effusion

fūst·is -is *m* club; stick; beating to death *(as military punishment)*

fūstitudin·us -a -um *adj (hum)* whip-happy

fūstuār·ium -(i)ī *n* beating to death *(as military punishment)*

fūs·us -a -um *pp of* **fundō** ‖ *adj* spread out; broad, wide; diffuse *(style)*

fūs·us -ī *m* spindle

fūtātim *adv* frequently, abundantly

futtilē *adv* uselessly, in vain

futtil·is -is -e *adj* **(fūtil-)** brittle; futile, worthless; trifling

futtilit·ās -ātis *f* **(fūtil-)** futility, uselessness

fut·uō -uere -uī -ūtus *tr (vulg)* to have intercourse with, screw *(a woman)*

futūr·us -a -um *adj* coming, future; impending, imminent; **tempus futūrum** *(gram)* future tense ‖ *n* the future; **in futūrum** for the future ‖ *npl* future events, the future

futūti·ō -ōnis *f (vulg)* sex, screwing

futūt·or -ōris *m (vulg)* sex partner

futūtr·īx -īcis *adj (fem only) (vulg)* lecherous ‖ *f* sex partner *(female)*

G

G, g *(supply* littera) *f* seventh letter of the Latin alphabet; letter name: **ge**

gabat·a -ae *f* plate, dish

Gabi·ī -ōrum *mpl* Gabii *(ancient town just outside Rome)*

Gabīni·us -a -um *adj* of the Gabinian clan

Gabīn·us -a -um *adj* of Gabii ‖ *mpl* the people of Gabii

Gād·ēs *or* **Gād·īs -ium** *fpl or* **Gād·is -is** *f* Cadiz *(in S. Spain)*

Gādītān·us -a -um *adj* of Gades ‖ *mpl* the people of Gades ‖ *fpl* dancing girls from Gades ‖ *n* dance by Gades dancing girls

gaes·um -ī *n* **(gēs-)** Gallic spear

Gaetūl·us -a -um *adj* Gaetulian, African ‖ *mpl* a people in N.W. Africa along the Sahara Desert

Gāï·a -ae *f* Gaia *(archaic feminine form of Gaius, surviving in ritual and legal language as a name for any woman)*

Gā·ïus -iī Gaius *(Roman praenomen; the names of Gaius and Gaia were formally* given to the bridegroom and bride respectively at the wedding ceremony)

Galat·ae -ārum *mpl* Galatians *(a people of central Asia Minor)*

Galatē·a -ae *f* sea nymph loved by Acis and Polyphemus

Galati·a -ae *f* Galatia *(Roman province in Asia Minor)*

Galb·a -ae *m* Roman emperor *(A.D. 68–69)*

galbane·us -a -um *adj* of galbanum

galban·um -ī *n* galbanum *(resinous sap of a Syrian plant)*

galbe·us -ī *m* armband *(worn as ornament or for medical purposes)*

galbināt·us -a -um *adj* dressed in chartreuse

galbin·us -a -um *adj* chartreuse; yellowish; *(fig)* effeminate ‖ *npl* chartreuse clothes

gale·a -ae *f* helmet *(usu. of leather)*

galeāt·us -a -um *adj* helmeted, wearing a helmet

gale·ō -āre *tr* to equip with a helmet

galēricul·um -ī *n* leather cap; toupee

galērīt·us -a -um *adj* wearing a leather cap

galēr·um -ī *n or* **galēr·us -ī** *m* leather cap; ceremonial cap *(worn by pontifices, flamines, etc.);* wig

gall·a -ae *f* gallnut *(nutlike growth on a plant)* ‖ *f* Gallic woman

Gall·ī -ōrum *mpl* Gauls *(inhabitants of modern France, Belgium, and N. Italy)*

Galli·a -ae *f* Gaul

Gallicān·us -a -um *adj* Gallic

gallicin·ium -(i)ī *n* cockcrow, daybreak

Gallic·us -a -um *adj* Gallic; belonging to the priests of Cybele; **canis Gallicus** a breed of hunting dog ‖ *f* Gallic shoe

gallīn·a -ae *f* chicken, hen; *(as term of endearment)* chick

gallīnāce·us -a -um *adj* of domestic fowl; **gallus gallīnāceus** rooster; **lac gallīnāceum** *(hum)* hen's milk *(i.e., an impossible thing)*

gallīnār·ius -(i)ī *m* poultry farmer; one who looks after the poultry used in augury

Gallograec·ī -ōrum *mpl* Galatians *(Celts who migrated from Gaul to Asia Minor in 3rd cent. B.C.)*

Gall·us -a -um *adj* Gallic ‖ *m* a Gaul; priest of Cybele; Galatian

gall·us -ī *m* rooster, cock

gāne·a -ae *f or* **gāne·um -ī** *n* low-class restaurant, dive; gluttonous eating

gāne·ō -ōnis *m* glutton

gāneum *see* **gānea**

Gangarid·ae -ārum *mpl* an Indian people near the Ganges

Gang·ēs -is *m* Ganges River

Gangētic·us -a -um *adj* Indian

gann·iō -īre *intr* to snarl

gannīt·us -ūs *m* snarling

Ganymēd·ēs -is *m* Ganymede *(handsome boy carried off to Olympus by an eagle to become the cupbearer of the gods and catamite of Zeus)*

Ganymēdē·us -a -um *adj* of Ganymede

Garamant·ēs -um *mpl* tribe in N. Africa

Garamant·is -idos *adj (fem only) (poet)* African

Gargān·us -ī *m* mountain in S.E. Italy

Gargar·a -ōrum *npl* a peak in the Ida mountain range in the Troad; town in that region

garr·iō -īre -īvī *tr* to chatter, prattle; **nūgās garrīre** to talk nonsense ‖ *intr* to chatter, chat; *(of frogs)* to croak

garrulit·ās -ātis *f* talkativeness; chattering

garrul·us -a -um *adj* garrulous, talkative; blabbing; *(of birds)* chattering; *(time)* for chattering

gar·um -ī *n* fish sauce

gaud·ēns -entis *adj* cheerful

gaudeō gaudēre gavīsus sum *tr* to rejoice at; **gaudium gaudēre** to feel joy ‖ *intr* to rejoice, be glad; *(w. abl)* to be glad about, feel pleased at, delight in; **in sē gaudēre** *(or in* **sinū) gaudēre** to be secretly glad

gaud·ium -(i)ī *n* joy, gladness, delight; cause of joy, source of delight; **gaudium nūntiāre** to announce good news; **mala mentis gaudia** gloating

gaul·us -ī *m* bucket

gausap·a -ae *f or* **gausap·e -is** *or* **gausap·um -ī** *n* coarse woolen cloth; felt; shaggy beard

gāvīsus *pp of* **gaudeō**

gāz·a -ae *f* royal treasure; treasure, riches

gelasīn·us -ī *m* dimple

gelidē *adv* coldly; indifferently

gelid·us -a -um *adj* cold, icy, frosty; ice-cold, stiff, numbed ‖ *f* ice-cold water

gel·ō -āre -āvī -ātus *tr & intr* to freeze

Gelōn·ī -ōrum *mpl* Scythian tribe

gel·u -ūs *n or* **gel·um -ī** *n* cold; frost; ice; chill, coldness *(of death, old age, fear)*

gemebund·us -a -um *adj* groaning

gemellipar·a -ae *f* mother of twins

gemell·us -a -um *adj & m* twin

gemināti·ō -ōnis *f* doubling; repetition

gemin·ō -āre -āvī -ātus *tr* to double; to join, unite; to pair; to do repeatedly ‖ *intr* to become double

gemin·us -a -um *adj* twin; paired, double, twofold, two, both; similar ‖ *m* twin

gemit·us -ūs *m* sigh, groan

gemm·a -ae *f* bud; gem, jewel; jeweled goblet; signet ring, signet; eye *(of a peacock's tail);* literary gem; pebble *(for marking days);* a piece in a game-board

gemm·āns -antis *adj* adorned with gems; decorated

gemmāt·us -a -um *adj* set with gems, jeweled

gemme·us -a -um *adj* set with jewels, jeweled; brilliant, glittering, sparkling

gemmi·fer -fera -ferum *adj* containing gems; gem-producing

gemm·ō -āre -āvī -ātum *intr* to sprout, bud; to sparkle

gem·ō -ere -uī -itus *tr* to sigh over, lament ‖ *intr* to sigh, groan, moan; to creak

Gemōni·ae -ārum *fpl* steps on the Aventine slope from which the corpses of criminals were thrown into the Tiber River

gen·a -ae *f* cheek; cheekbone; eyelid ‖ *fpl* cheeks; region about the eyes, eyes; sockets of the eyes

geneālog·us -ī *m* genealogist

gen·er -erī *m* son-in-law; daughter's fiancé; brother-in-law

generāl·is -is -e *adj* general, universal

generāliter *adv* in general, generally

generāsc·ō -ere *intr* to be generated

generātim *adv* by species, by classes; in general, generally

generāt·or -ōris *m* producer, father

gener·ō -āre -āvī -ātus *tr* to beget, procreate, father; *(of places, of the body)* to produce; to engender, arouse *(emotions)*

generōsē *adv* with dignity, nobly

generōsit·ās -ātis *f* good breeding, nobility of stock

generōs·us -a -um *adj* of good stock, high-born, noble; noble-minded; high-spirited

genes·is -is *f* birth; horoscope

genesta *see* **genista**

genetīv·us -a -um *adj* (-nit-) inborn, innate; *(gram)* genitive ‖ *m (gram)* genitive case

genetr·īx -īcis *f* (-nit-) mother, ancestress

geniāl·is -is -e *adj* nuptial, bridal; genial; joyous, merry, festive

geniāliter *ad* merrily

geniculāt·us -a -um *adj* knotted, having knots, jointed

genist·a -ae *f* (-nest-) broom plant

genitābil·is -is -e *adj* productive

genitāl·is -is -e *adj* generative, productive; of birth; **diēs genitālis** birthday ‖ *n* genital organ

genitāliter *adv* fruitfully

genitīvus *see* **genetīvus**

genit·or -ōris *m* father; creator; source, cause

genitrīx *see* **genetrīx**

genitūr·a -ae *f* horoscope

genitus *pp of* **gignō**

gen·ius -iī *m* guardian spirit *(of person, place, or thing);* (hum) personification of all natural appetites, natural inclination; talent, wit

gen·ō -ere *see* **gignō**

gēn·s -tis *f (Roman)* clan, extended family *(sharing the same nomen and, theoretically, the same ancestor);* stock; tribe; nation, people; country; class, set, race; species; breed; descendant, offspring; *(poet)* herd, flock, hive **ll** *fpl* the peoples of the world; rest of the world *(apart from the Romans)*, foreign nations; **longē gentium abīre** to be far, far away; **minimē gentium** by no means; **ubi gentium** where in the world

gentic·us -a -um *adj* tribal; national

gentīlici·us -a -um *adj* of a Roman clan, of the extended family

gentīl·is -is -e *adj* family, hereditary; tribal; national **ll** *m* clansman, kinsman

gentīlit·ās -ātis *f* clan relationship

gen·ū -ūs *n* knee; **genibus minor** kneeling; **genibus nīxus** on one's knees; **genuum iūnctūra** knee joint; **sē advolvere ad genua** *(w. gen)* to prostrate oneself before

genuāl·ia -ium *npl* garters

genuī *perf of* **gignō**

genuīn·us -a -um *adj* innate, natural

genuīn·us -a -um *adj* of the cheek; jaw, of the jaw **ll** *mpl* back teeth

-gen·us -a -um *adjl suf* forms adjectives meaning "born of": **caeligenus** heaven-born

gen·us -eris *n* race, descent, lineage, breed, stock, family; noble birth; tribe; nation, people; descendant, offspring, posterity; kind, sort, species, class; rank, order, division; fashion, style, way; matter, respect; genus; sex; *(gram)* gender; **aliquid id genus** *(acc of respect instead of gen of quality)* something of that sort; **genus hūmānum** *(or* **genus hominum)** the human race, mankind; **in omnī genere** in every respect; **suī generis** in a class of its *(her, his, their)* own, unique

geōgraphi·a -ae *f* geography

geōmetr·ēs -ae *m* geometer, mathematician

geōmetri·a -ae *f* geometry

geōmetric·us -a -um *adj* geometrical **ll** *f* geometry **ll** *npl* geometry

geōrgic·us -a -um *adj* agricultural **ll** *npl* Georgics *(poems on farming by Vergil)*

ger·ēns -entis *adj (w. gen)* managing, running *(e.g., a business)*

germānē *adv* sincerely

Germān·ī -ōrum *mpl* Germans

Germāni·a -ae *f* Germany

Germānic·us -a -um *adj* Germanic **ll** *m* cognomen of Tiberius's nephew and adoptive son *(15 B.C.–A.D. 19)*

germānit·ās -ātis *f* brotherhood, sisterhood *(relationship between brothers and sisters of the same parents; relationship between colonies of the same mother-city)*

germān·us -a -um *adj* having the same parents; brotherly, sisterly; genuine, real, true **ll** *m* full brother **ll** *f* full sister

germ·en -inis *n* sprout, shoot; bud; embryo

germin·ō -āre -āvī -ātus *tr* to put forth, grow *(hair, wings, etc.)* **ll** *intr* to sprout

gerō gerere gessī gestus *tr* to bear, carry *(in one's hands); (of things)* to have in it, contain; to bear *(fruit);* to bear, carry *(in the womb);* to wear *(clothing);* to hold *(consulship, etc.);* to spend, pass *(time);* to bring; to display, exhibit; to entertain *(feelings);* to assume; to carry on, manage; to govern, regulate, administer; to carry out, transact, do, accomplish; **bellum gerere** to fight a war, carry on a war; **cōnsulātum gerere** to hold the consulship; **dum ea geruntur** while that was going on; **mōrem gerere** *(w. dat)* to gratify; **persōnam gerere** *(w. gen)* to play the part of; **rem gerere** to run a business, conduct an affair; **rēs prosperē gerere** *(mil)* to conduct a successful campaign **ll** *refl* to behave, conduct oneself; *(w. prō + abl)* to claim to be for; **sē medium gerere** to remain neutral

ger·ō -ōnis *m* porter

gerr·ae -ārum *fpl* trifles; *as interj* nonsense!

gerulifigul·us -ī *m* accomplice; *(w. gen)* accomplice in

gerul·us -ī *m* porter

Gēry·ōn -onis *or* **Gēryon·ēs -ae** *m* Geryon *(three-headed monster of Spain that was slain by Hercules)*

gessī *perf of* **gerō**

gestām·en -inis *n* load; article(s) worn; load, pack, burden; vehicle, litter **ll** *npl* ornaments; accouterments; arms

gestāti·ō -ōnis *f* ride *(on horseback, in litter, in vehicle);* drive *(place),* walk *(place)*

gestāt·or -ōris *m* bearer, carrier

gest·iō -īre -īvī *or* **-iī** *intr* to be delighted, be thrilled; to be eager; *(w. inf)* to be itching to, long to

gesti·ō -ōnis *f* performance

gestit·ō -āre -āvī *tr* to be in the habit of carrying *or* wearing

gest·ō -āre -āvī -ātus *tr* to bear, wear, carry; to take for a ride *(in a litter, in a vehicle, on horseback);* to spread, blab, tell; to cherish, harbor *(thoughts)* **ll** *pass* to ride, drive, sail *(esp. for pleasure)*

gest·or -ōris *m* tattler

gestuōs·us -a -um *adj* gesturing; suggestive

gest·us -a -um *pp of* **gerō** **ll** *adj* **rēs gestae** deeds, accomplishments **ll** *n* business; deed

gest·us -ūs *m* gesture; gesticulation, gestures; posture, bearing, attitude

Get·ae -ārum *mpl* Thracian tribe on the Lower Danube

Geticē *adv* in Getic, in the Getic language

Getic·us -a -um *adj* of the Getae; Thracian

gibb·us -ī *m or* **gibb·a -ae** *f* hump

Gigant·ēs -um *mpl* Giants *(race of gigantic size that tried to storm heaven and were placed under various volcanoes)*

gignō gignere genuī genitus *or* **gen·ō -ere** *tr* to beget, bear, produce; to cause, occasion; to give rise to, bring about; to create, begin ‖ *pass* to be born; *(of faculties, parts of the body)* to be produced; *(w. abl)* to be born of, spring from; *(phil)* to come into being

gilv·us -a -um *adj* pale-yellow; **equus gilvus** palomino

gingīv·a -ae *f* gum *(of mouth)*

-gintā *indecl suf* forms numerals from 30 to 90

glabell·us -a -um *adj* bald; smooth

gla·ber -bra -brum *adj* bald; smooth ‖ *m* young slave, favorite slave

glaciāl·is -is -e *adj* icy, frozen

glaci·ēs -ēī *f* ice

glaci·ō -āre -āvī -ātus *tr* to turn into ice, freeze ‖ *intr* to congeal, harden

gladiāt·or -ōris *m* gladiator; ruffian; assassin ‖ *mpl* gladiatorial combat, gladiatorial show; **gladiātōrēs dare** *(or* **ēdere)** to stage a gladiatorial show

gladiātōri·us -a -um *adj* gladiatorial; **mūnus gladiātōrium** gladiatorial show ‖ *n* gladiator's pay

gladiātūr·a -ae *f* gladiatorial profession

gladiol·us -ī *m* small sword; *(bot)* gladiola

glad·ius -(i)ī *m* sword; murder, death; **gladium ēdūcere** *(or* **stringere)** to draw the sword; **gladium recondere** to sheathe the sword; **iūs** *(or* **potestās) gladiī** right to try and punish at capital crime *(granted by emperor to provincial governors)*

glaeb·a -ae *f* **(glēb-)** lump of earth, clod; soil, land; lump, piece

glaebul·a -ae *f* **(glēb-)** small lump; bit of land, small farm

glaesum *see* **glēsum**

glandif·er -era -erum *adj* acorn-bearing

gland·ium -(i)ī *n* delicate kernel *(esp. of pork)*

glān·s -dis *f* acorn, beechnut, chestnut; pellet, bullet *(for a sling); (anat)* head of the penis

glāre·a -ae *f* gravel

glāreōs·us -a -um *adj* full of gravel, gravelly

glaucōm·a -atis *(acc fem singl:* **glaucumam)** *n* cataract; **glaucumam ob oculōs obicere** *(w. dat)* to throw dust into *(s.o.'s)* eyes

glau·cus -a -um *adj* grey-green, greyish; bright, sparkling ‖ **Glauc·us -ī** *m* leader of the Lycians in the Trojan War ‖ fisherman of Euboea who was changed into a sea deity ‖ son of Sisyphus

glēb- = glaeb-

glēs·um *or* **glaes·um -ī** *n* amber

glī·s -ris *m* dormouse *(small, furry-tailed Old World rodent resembling a small squirrel in appearance and habits)*

glīsc·ō -ere *intr* to grow, swell up, spread, blaze up; to grow, increase

globōs·us -a -um *adj* spherical, round

glob·us -ī *m* ball, sphere, globe; crowd, throng, gathering; clique

glomerām·en -inis *n* ball, globe

glomer·ō -āre -āvī -ātus *tr* to form into a ball; to gather up, roll up; to collect, gather together, assemble ‖ *refl & pass* to gather, assemble

glom·us -eris *n* ball of yarn

glōri·a -ae *f* glory, fame; pride; feeling of pride; source of pride, pride and joy; false pride, vanity, boasting; glorious deed; thirst for glory, ambition

glōriāti·ō -ōnis *f* boasting, pride

glōriol·a -ae *f* bit of glory

glōri·or -ārī -ātus sum *tr (only w. neuter pron as object)* to boast about; **haec glōriārī** to boast about this, be proud of this; **idem glōriārī** to make the same boast, be proud of the same thing ‖ *intr* to be proud; to boast; *(w. abl or w.* **dē** *or in + abl)* to take pride in, boast about; *(w.* **adversus** *+ acc)* to boast *or* brag to *(s.o.)*

glōriōsē *adv* gloriously, proudly; boastfully, pompously

glōriōs·us -a -um *adj* glorious, illustrious; eager for glory, ambitious; boastful; proud

glossēm·a -atis *n* word to be glossed

glūb·ō -ere *tr* to peel, skin

glūt·en -inis *n* glue

glūtināt·or -ōris *m* bookbinder

glūtin·ō -āre -āvī -ātus *tr* to glue together; *(med)* to close *(wounds)*

glutt·iō -īre -īvī *or* **-iī -ītus** *tr* **(glūt-)** to gulp down

glutt·ō -ōnis *m* glutton

Gnae·us *or* **Gnē·us -ī** *m* Roman first name *(praenomen, abbreviated Cn.)*

gnār·us -a -um *adj* skilled, expert; known, familiar; *(w. gen)* having knowledge of, familiar with, expert in, experienced in

gnāta *see* **nāta**

gnātus *see* **nātus**

gnōbilis *see* **nōbilis**

Gnō(s)s·us -ī *f* Cnossos *(ancient capital of Crete and residence of King Minos)*

gnōscō *see* **nōscō**

Gnōsi·a -ae *or* **Gnōsi·as -adis** *or* **Gnōs·is -idis** *f* Ariadne *(daughter of King Minos of Cnossos)*

gnōtus *see* **nōtus**

gōb·ius -(i)ī *m* **(cōb-)** goby *(small fish)*

Gorgi·ās -ae *(acc:* **-am** *and* **-ān)** *m* famous orator and sophist from Sicily *(480–c.390 B.C.)*

Gorg·ō -ōnis f Gorgon *(one of three daughters of Phorcys and Ceto: Stheno, Medusa, and Euryale)*
Gorgone·us -a -um *adj* Gorgonian; **Gorgoneus equus** Pegasus; **Gorgoneus lacus** the spring Hippocrene *(on Mt. Helicon)*
grabāt·us -ī m cot; army cot
Gracch·us -ī m Roman family name *(cognomen);* Tiberius Sempronius Gracchus *(social reformer, and tribune in 133* B.C.*)* ‖ Gaius Sempronius Gracchus *(younger brother of Tiberius and tribune in 123* B.C.*)*
gracil·is -is -e *adj* slim, slender; thin, skinny; poor; slight, insignificant; plain, simple *(style)*
gracilit·ās -ātis f slenderness; thinness, leanness, meagerness
grācul·us -ī m **(gracc-)** jackdaw *(glossy, black European bird resembling the crow)*
gradātim *adv* step by step, gradually, little by little
gradāti·ō -ōnis f flight of steps; tiers of seats *(in theater); (rhet)* series of propositions of ascending emphasis
gradior gradī gressus sum *intr* to go, walk, step
Grādīv·us *or* **Gradīv·os -ī** m epithet of Mars
grad·us -ūs m step, pace, walk, gait; step, degree, grade, stage; approach, advance, progress; status, rank; station, position; step, rung, stair; footing, stance; **concitō gradū** on the double; **dē gradū deicere** *(fig)* to throw off balance; **gradum celerāre** *(or* **corripere)** to pick up the pace; **gradum cōnferre** *(mil)* to come to close quarters; **gradūs ferre** *(mil)* to charge; **plēnō gradū** on the double; **per gradūs** by degrees; **per gradūs ascendere** to climb the stairs; **suspēnsō gradū** on tiptoe
Graecē *adv* Greek, in Greek; **Graecē discere (legere, loquī, scīre)** to learn (read, speak, know) Greek
Graeci·a -ae f Greece; **Magna Graecia** Greek cities along the coast of S. Italy, including Sicily
graeciss·ō -āre *intr* to ape the Greeks; to speak Greek
graec·or -ārī *intr* to go Greek, act like a Greek, live it up
Graecul·us -a -um *adj (pej)* Greek through and through, hundred-percent Greek ‖ *mf (pej)* Greekling, dirty little Greek
Graec·us -a -um *adj & mf* Greek ‖ *n* Greek, Greek language
Grāiugen·a -ae m Greek *(by birth)*
Grāi·us -a -um *adj* Greek ‖ *mpl* Greeks
grall·ae -ārum *fpl* stilts
grallāt·or -ōris m stilt walker
grām·en -inis n grass; meadow, pasture; plant, herb

grāmine·us -a -um *adj* grassy, of grass
grammatic·us -a -um *adj* grammatical, of grammar ‖ m teacher of literature and language; philologist ‖ f & npl grammar; philology
grammatist·a -ae m elementary school teacher
grānāri·a -ōrum *npl* granary
grandaev·us -a -um *adj* old, aged
grandēsc·ō -ere *intr* to grow, grow big
grandicul·us -a -um *adj* rather large; pretty tall
grandif·er -era -erum *adj* productive, producing large crops
grandiloqu·us -ī m big talker
grandin·at -āre v *impers* it is hailing
grand·iō -īre *tr* to enlarge, increase
grand·is -is -e *adj* full-grown, grown up, tall; large, great; aged; important; powerful, strong; lengthy *(book, speech);* intense *(emotions);* proud, noble *(words, sentiments);* grand, lofty *(style);* dignified *(person);* loud, strong *(voice);* heavy *(debt);* dignified *(speaker);* **aevō** *(or* **aetāte) grandis** advanced in years, elderly
grandit·ās -ātis f grandeur
grand·ō -inis f *(m)* hail, hailstorm
grānif·er -era -erum *adj (of an ant)* grain-carrying
grān·um -ī n small particle, grain; seed; kernel; stone *(in fruit);* **grānum piperis** peppercorn
graphiār·ium -(i)i n case for holding a stylus, "pencil box"
graphicē *adv* in the manner of a painter; vividly, graphically; *(coll)* perfectly, properly, thoroughly
graphic·us -a -um *adj* artistic; *(coll)* exquisite, first-class
graph·ium -(i)ī n stylus
grassāt·or -ōris m tramp; bully, hoodlum; mugger, prowler, thug
grassātūra -ae f waylaying, mugging
grass·or -ārī -ātus sum *intr* to advance, press on; to prowl; to run riot, rage; *(w.* **adversus** *or* **in** + *acc)* to attack, waylay, mug
grātē *adv* willingly, with pleasure; gratefully
grātēs *(gen not in use) fpl* thanks, gratitude; **grātēs agere** *(w. dat)* to thank; **grātēs habēre** *(w. dat)* to feel grateful toward
grāti·a -ae f grace, charm, pleasantness, loveliness; influence, prestige; popularity; love, friendship; service; favor, kindness; thanks, gratitude; cause, reason, motive; **cum grātiā** *(w. gen)* to the satisfaction of; with the approval of; **eā grātiā ut** for the reason that; **exemplī grātiā** for example; **grātiā** *(w. gen) (postpositive)* for the sake of, on account of; **grātiam facere** *(w. dat of person and gen of thing)* pardon *(s.o.)* for *(a fault);* **grātiās**

agere *(w. dat)* to thank; **grātiās habēre** *(w. dat)* to be grateful to; **in grātiam** *(w. gen)* in order to win the favor of, in order to please; **in grātiam habēre** to regard *(s.th.)* as a favor; **meā grātiā** for my sake; **quā grātiā?** why?

Grāti·ae -ārum *fpl* Graces *(Aglaia, Euphrosyne, and Thalia)*

grātificāti·ō -ōnis *f* kindness, favor

grātific·or -ārī -ātus sum *tr* to give up, surrender, sacrifice ‖ *intr (w. dat)* 1 to do *(s.o.)* a favor; 2 to gratify, please *(s.o.)*; 3 to humor *(s.o.)*

grātiōs·us -a -um *adj* popular, influential; obliging

grātīs *adv* gratis, free, for nothing

grāt·or -ārī -ātus sum *intr* to rejoice; to express gratitude; *(w. dat)* to congratulate; **invicem inter sē grātārī** to congratulate one another

grātuītō *adv* gratuitously, gratis, for nothing; for no particular reason

grātuīt·us -a -um *adj* done for mere thanks, gratuitous, free, spontaneous; voluntary; unprovoked

grātulābund·us -a -um *adj* congratulating

grātulāti·ō -ōnis *f* congratulation; rejoicing, joy; public thanksgiving

grātulāt·or -ōris *m* well-wisher

grātul·or -ārī -ātus sum *intr* to be glad, rejoice; *(w. dat)* 1 to congratulate; 2 to render thanks to

grāt·us -a -um *adj* pleasing, pleasant, agreeable, welcome; thankful, grateful; deserving thanks, earning gratitude; popular ‖ *n* favor; **grātum (et acceptum) habēre** *(w. dat)* to be grateful to **grātum facere** *(w. dat)* to do *(s.o.)* a favor

gravanter *adv* reluctantly

gravātē *adv* with difficulty; unwillingly, grudgingly

gravātim *adv* with difficulty; unwillingly

gravēdinōs·us -a -um *adj* prone to catch colds, susceptible to colds

gravēd·ō -inis *f* cold, head cold

graveol·ēns -entis *adj* stinking

gravēsc·ō -ere *intr* to grow heavy; *(fig)* to get worse

gravidit·ās -ātis *f* pregnancy

gravid·ō -āre -āvī -ātus *tr* to impregnate

gravid·us -a -um *adj* loaded, filled, full; pregnant; *(w. abl)* teeming with

grav·is -is -e *adj* heavy, weighty; burdensome; grave, serious; troublesome, oppressive, painful, harsh, hard, severe, unpleasant; indigestible *(food)*; important, influential; venerable, dignified; grave, serious; pregnant; hostile; relentless; obnoxious *(person)*; exorbitant *(prices)*; low, deep *(voice)*; flat *(note)*;

harsh, bitter, offensive *(smell, taste)*; impressive *(speech)*; stormy *(weather)*; labored *(breathing)*; oppressive *(heat)*; unhealthy *(climate, place, season)*; dangerous *(animal, person)*; *(mil)* heavy-armed

gravit·ās -ātis *f* weight; severity, harshness; seriousness; importance; dignity, influence, authority; pregnancy; violence, vehemence; offensiveness *(of smell)*; unhealthfulness *(of climate, place, season)*

graviter *adv* heavily, ponderously; hard, violently, vehemently; severely, harshly; unpleasantly; sadly, sorrowfully; with dignity, with propriety, with authority; *(to feel)* deeply; *(to smell)* offensive; *(to speak)* impressively; **graviter ferre** to take *(s.th.)* hard

grav·ō -āre -āvī -ātus *tr* to weigh down, load (down); to be burdensome to, be oppressive to; to aggravate; to increase

grav·or -ārī -ātus sum *tr* to feel annoyed at, object to; to refuse, decline; to bear with reluctance, regard as a burden ‖ *intr* to feel annoyed

gregāl·is -is -e *adj* of the herd *or* flock; common; **mīles gregālis** a private; **sagulum gregāle** a private's uniform ‖ *mpl* comrades, companions

gregāri·us -a -um *adj* of the flock *or* herd; common, ordinary; **mīles gregārius** a private ‖ *m (mil)* a private

gregātim *adv* in flocks, in herds, in crowds

grem·ium -(i)ī *n* lap, bosom; womb

gressus *pp of* **gradior**

gress·us -ūs *m* step; course, way

gre·x -gis *m* flock, herd; swarm; school *(of fish)*; company, group, crowd, troop, set, clique, gang; theatrical cast, troupe

gruis *see* **grūs**

grunn·iō -īre -īvī *or* **-iī -ītum** *intr* **(grund-)** to grunt

grunnīt·us -ūs *m* grunt, grunting

gru·ō -ere *intr (of a crane)* to honk

grū·s *or* **gru·is -is** *mf* crane

grȳps grȳpis *m* griffin *(fabled monster having the head and wings of an eagle and the body of a lion)*

gubernāc(u)l·um -ī *n* rudder, tiller, helm ‖ *npl (fig)* helm

gubernāti·ō -ōnis *f* navigation

gubernāt·or -ōris *m* navigator, pilot, helmsman; ruler, governor, director

gubernātr·īx -īcis *f* directress

gubern·ō -āre -āvī -ātus *tr* to steer, navigate, pilot; to direct, govern

gul·a -ae *f* gullet, throat; palate, appetite; gluttony

gulōs·us -a -um *adj* appetizing, dainty; fond of fine foods

gurg·es -itis *m* abyss, gulf, whirlpool; waters, flood, depths, sea; spendthrift

gurguli·ō -ōnis *m* gullet; windpipe

gurgust·ium -(i)ī *n* dark hovel; (*fig*) hole in the wall

gustātōr·ium -(i)ī *n* appetizer

gustāt·us -ūs *m* sense of taste; flavor, taste

gust·ō -āre -āvī -ātus *tr* to taste; (*fig*) to enjoy; to overhear **‖** *intr* to have a snack

gust·us -ūs *m* tasting; flavor, taste; appetizer; small portion, taste

gutt·a -ae *f* drop; spot, speck

guttātim *adv* drop by drop

guttāt·us -a -um *adj* spotted

guttul·a -ae *f* tiny drop

gutt·ur -uris *n (m)* gullet, throat, neck **‖** *npl* throat, neck

gūt·us -ī *m* (**gutt-**) cruet, flask

Gy·ās -ae *m* hundred-armed giant

Gȳg·ēs -is *or* **-ae** *m* king of Lydia (*reigned 716–678 B.C.*)

gymnasiarch·us -ī *m* manager of a gymnasium

gymnas·ium -(i)ī *n* gymnasium

gymnastic·us -a -um *adj* gymnastic

gymnic·us -a -um *adj* gymnastic

gymnosophist·ae -ārum *mpl* Hindu Stoics

gynaecē·um -ī *or* **gynaecī·um -ī** *n* women's apartment in a Greek house

gynocōnit·is -idis *f* women's apartment in a Greek house

gypsāt·us -a -um *adj* covered with gypsum, white with gypsum

gyps·ō -āre -āvī -ātus *tr* to whiten with gypsum (*the feet of slaves put up for auction*); to plaster up

gyps·um -ī *n* gypsum; plaster of Paris; (*fig*) figure of plaster

gȳr·us -ī *m* circle, cycle, ring; (*astr*) orbit, course; a place where horses are trained; **in gȳprōs īre** to go in circles; **in gȳrum** in a circle; all around

H

H, h (*supply* littera) *f* eighth letter of the Latin alphabet; letter name: **ha**

ha *interj* expression of joy, satisfaction, *or* laughter

habēn·a -ae *f* strap **‖** *fpl* reins; (*fig*) reins of government; **habēnae rērum** reins of state; **habēnās addūcere** (*or* **dare** *or* **effundere** *or* **immittere**) (*w. dat*) to give free rein to; **habēnās premere** to tighten the reins; **immissīs habēnīs** at full speed

hab·eō -ēre -uī -itus *tr* to have; to hold; to possess; to own; to keep, retain, detain; to have

at one's disposal, have available; to have on one's side, have in one's favor; to control, have under one's control; to involve, entail; to have knowledge of (*facts, information*); to afford, give (*e.g., pleasure*); to have on, wear (*clothes*); to treat, handle, use; (*of a vessel*) to hold, contain; to be made up of, consist of; (*of feelings*) to beset, come over, grip; to hold, conduct (*meeting, inquiry, census*); to deliver, give (*speech*), give (*a talk*); to keep, observe (*a law, edict, practice*); (*of owner, inhabitant*) to occupy, inhabit; to pronounce, utter (*words*); to spend, live (*life, youth*); to hold, manage, govern, wield; to hold, think, consider, believe; to occupy, engage, busy; to occasion, produce, render; to know, be informed of, be acquainted with; to take, accept, endure, bear; **animō habēre** (*w. inf*) to have in mind to, intend to; **certum habēre** to regard as certain; **comitia habēre** to hold an assembly; to hold elections; **contiōnem habēre** to hold a meeting *or* rally; **grātiam habēre** to be grateful; **in animō habēre** to have on one's mind, have in mind; **iūstum habēre** (*w. inf*) to have a duty to; **locum priōrem habēre** to have the lead (*in a race*); **melius habēre** (*w. inf*) to think it better to; **necesse habēre** (*w. inf*) to have an obligation to; **parum habēre** (*w. inf*) to think it a minor matter to; **parum habēre violāsse** to think nothing of having violated; **prō certō habēre** to regard it as certain; **prō explōrātō habēre** to regard it as an established fact; **rūs mē nunc habet** I am now in the country; **sēcum habēre** to have with one *or* in one's possession, have in one's company; **sēcum** (*or* **sibi**) **habēre** to keep (*s.th.*) to oneself, keep secret **‖** *refl* (*w. adv*) to be, feel (*well, etc.*); **bene vōs habētis** you are doing fine; **mē male habeō** I'm doing lousy; **quō pactō tē habēs?** how are you doing?; **sīc rēs sē habet** that's the situation, that's the way things are; **singulōs ut sēsē habēret rogitāns** asking each and every one how he was doing **‖** *intr* (*w. adv or abl*) to be, live, dwell (*in a place*); **habet!** (*said of gladiator receiving fatal wound*) he's had it!; **hīc ego habeō** I live here **‖** *v impers* **bene habet** (that's) fine!, O.K. then!; **sīc habet** that's how it is

habil·is -is -e *adj* handy; easy to handle; suitable, convenient; active; (*of vehicles*) easy to control

habilit·ās -ātis *f* aptitude

habitābil·is -is -e *adj* fit to live in

habitāti·ō -ōnis *f* residence; (cost of) rent

habitāt·or -ōris *m* inhabitant; occupant, tenant (*of house, apartment*)

habit·ō -āre -āvī *tr* to live in, inhabit **‖** *intr* to dwell, live habitūd·ō -inis *f* condition, appearance; bearing

habitur·iō -īre *tr* to like to have

habit·us -a -um *pp of* habeō **‖** *adj* in good physical condition; **corpulentior et habitior vidērī** to look stouter and in better physical condition

habit·us -ūs *m* condition *(of the body);* physical make-up, build, looks, form, shape; circumstances; style, style of dress; character, quality; disposition, state of feeling; posture

hāc *adv* this way, in this way

hāctenus *adv* to this place, thus far; until now, hitherto, so far; to this extent, so much; *(in writing)* to this point; **haec hāctenus** enough of this

Hadri·a -ae *f* (Adr-) Adriatic Sea

Hadriac·us -a -um *adj* Adriatic

Hadriān·us -a -um *adj* (Adr-) Adriatic **‖** *m* Hadrian *(Roman emperor,* A.D. *117–138)*

Hadriātic·us -a -um *adj* Adriatic

haec hōrum *(neut pl of* hoc) *adj & pron* these

haec hūius *(older form:* haece; *gen:* huiūsce) *(fem of* hic) *adj* this; the present, the actual; the latter; *(occasionally)* the former; **haec … haec** one … another **‖** *pron* this one, she; the latter; *(occasionally)* the former; **haec … haec** one … another one; **haecine (haec** *w. interrog enclitic* -ne) is this … ?

haece *see* haec

haecine *see* haec

Haed·ī -ōrum *mpl (astr)* the Kids *(pair of stars in the constellation Auriga)*

haedili·a -ae *f* little goat

haedill·us -ī *m (term of endearment)* little goat

haedīn·us -a -um *adj* kid's, goat's

haedul·us -ī *m* little kid, little goat

haed·us -ī *m* young goat, kid

Haemōni·a -ae *f* Thessaly

Haem·us *or* Haem·os -ī *m* mountain range in N. Thrace

hae·reō -rēre -sī -sum *intr* to cling, stick; to hang around, linger, stay, remain fixed, remain in place; to be rooted to the spot; to come to a standstill, stop; to be embarrassed, be at a loss, hesitate, be in doubt; *(w. dat or abl or w.* in + *abl)* **1** to cling to, stick to, be attached to; **2** to loiter in, hang around in, waste time in *(a place) or* at *(an activity);* **3** to adhere to, stick by *(an opinion, purpose);* **4** to gaze upon; **5** to keep close to; **in terga** *(or* tergīs *or* in tergīs) **hostium haerēre** to keep on the enemy's tail

haerēsc·ō -ere *intr* to stick together

haeres·is -is *f* philosophical school

haesitābund·us -a -um *adj* hesitating, faltering

haesitanti·a -ae *f* hesitancy

haesitāti·ō -ōnis *f* hesitation, indecision

haesitāt·or -ōris *m* hesitator

haesit·ō -āre -āvī -ātum *intr* to get stuck; to hesitate; to stammer; to be undecided, be at a loss

hahae, hahahahae *interj* expression of joy, satisfaction, *or* laughter

halagor·a -ae *f* salt market

hāl·āns -antis *adj* fragrant

hāl·ēc *or* (h)all·ēc -ēcis *n* (·ex) fish sauce; fish soup

haliaeët·os -ī *m* osprey *(large hawk that preys on fish, also called fish hawk)*

hālit·us -ūs *m* breath; steam, vapor

hal(l)ūcin·ō -āre *or* hālūcin·or -ārī -ātus sum *tr* to say in a distracted state **‖** *intr* to have hallucinations; to daydream; to ramble

hāl·ō -āre *tr* to exhale **‖** *intr* to be fragrant

halopant·a -ae *m* scoundrel

halōs·is -is *(acc:* -in) *f* capture

halt·ēr -ēris *m* weight held in the hand by an athlete

hālūcinor *see* hal(l)ūcinō

ham·a *or* am·a -ae *f* bucket

Hamādry·as -adis *(dat pl:* Hamādryasin) *f* wood nymph

hāmātil·is -is -e *adj* with hooks

hāmāt·us -a -um *adj* hooked

Hamilc·ar -aris *m* Carthaginian general in the First Punic War, surnamed Barca, and father of Hannibal *(d. 228* B.C.)

hāmiōt·a -ae *f* fisher(man)

Hamm·ō(n) *or* Amm·ōn -ōnis *m* Ammon *(Egyptian god, represented as a ram, who had a famous oracle in Libya and was identified with Jupiter Ammon);* **ultimus Ammon Āfrōrum** deepest Africa

hāmul·us -ī *m* small hook

hām·us -ī *m* hook, fishhook; barb

Hannib·al -alis *m* son of Hamilcar Barca and famous general in the Second Punic War *(240–182* B.C.)

har·a -ae *f* pen, coop, stye

(h)arēn·a -ae *f* sand; seashore, beach; arena **‖** *fpl* desert

harēnāri·a -ae *f* sandpit

harēnōs·us -a -um *adj* sandy

hariol·a -ae *f* fortuneteller *(female)*

hariol·or -ārī -ātus sum *intr* to foretell the future; to talk gibberish

hariol·us -ī *m* fortuneteller

harmoni·a -ae *f* harmony **‖ Harmonia** wife of Cadmus, founder and first king of Thebes

harpag·ō -āre -āvī -ātus *tr (coll)* to hook *(to steal)*

harpag·ō -ōnis *m* hook; harpoon; grappling hook; greedy person

Harpalyc·ē -ēs *f* Thracian princess, raised as a warrior

harpast·um -ī *n* handball

harp·ē -ēs *f* sickle; scimitar

Harpȳi·a -ae *f* harpy *(creature with head of a woman and body of a bird)*

harundif·er -era -erum *adj* reed-bearing

harundine·us -a -um *adj* of reeds

harund·ō -inis *f* reed; cane; fishing rod; pen; shepherd's pipe; shaft, arrow; fowler's rod; weaver's comb; **harundō Indica** bamboo

harusp·ex -icis *m* soothsayer *(interpreter of internal organs, prodigies, and lightning)*

haruspic·a -ae *f* soothsayer *(female)*

haruspicīn·us -a -um *adj* of divination **‖** *f* the art of divination

haruspic·ium -(i)ī *n* divination

Hasdrub·al -alis *m* brother of Hannibal *(d. 207 B.C.)* **‖** son-in-law of Hamilcar Barca *(d. 221 B.C.)*

hast·a -ae *f* spear *(weapon; spear stuck into ground at public auction; symbol of the centumviral court, which dealt with cases of property and inheritance);* **sub hastā vēndere** to sell at auction

hastāt·us -a -um *adj* armed with a spear **‖** *mpl* soldiers in the first line of a Roman battle formation

hastīl·e -is *n* shaft; spear; rod

hau *or* **au** *interj* oh!, ow!, ouch!

haud *or* **haut** *or* **hau** *adv* hardly; not, not at all, by no means

hau(d)quāquam *adv* by no means whatsoever, not at all

hau·riō -rīre -sī -stus *tr* to draw, draw up, draw out; to drain, drink up; to spill, shed *(blood); (of water)* to swallow up, engulf; *(of flames)* to devour; to consume, use up *(resources);* to scoop up; to hollow out; to derive; *(fig)* to have one's fill of; *(fig)* drink in

haustr·um -ī *n* scoop *(on a water-wheel)*

haustus *pp of* **hauriō**

haust·us -ūs *m* drawing *(of water);* drinking, swallowing; drink, draft; handful; stream *(of blood)*

haut *see* **haud**

haveō *see* **aveō**

hebdom·as -adis *f* week; a group of seven; fever occurring at seven-day intervals

Hēb·ē -ēs *f* goddess of youth, daughter of Juno, and cupbearer of the gods

heben·us -ī *f* ebony tree, ebony

heb·eō -ēre *intr* to be blunt, be dull; *(of light)* to grow dim; *(of anger)* to die down; *(fig)* to be sluggish, be inactive

heb·es -etis *adj* blunt, dull; faint, dim; dull, obtuse, stupid

hebēsc·ō -ere *intr* to grow blunt, grow dull; to become faint *or* dim; to lose vigor

hebet·ō -āre -āvī -ātus *tr* to blunt, dull, dim

Hebr·us -ī *m* principal river in Thrace

Hecat·ē -ēs *f* goddess of magic and witchcraft, identified with Diana

hecatomb·ē -ēs *f* hecatomb *(public sacrifice of 100 oxen to the gods)*

Hect·or -oris *m* son of Priam and Hecuba, husband of Andromache

Hecub·a -ae *or* **Hecub·ē -ēs** *f* (**-cab-**) wife of Priam (*after the destruction of Troy, she became a slave and was metamorphosed into a dog)*

heder·a -ae f ivy

hederig·er -era -erum *adj* wearing ivy

hederōs·us -a -um *adj* overgrown with ivy

hēdycr·um -ī *n* perfume

hei, hēia *see* **ei, ēia**

Helen·a -ae *or* **Helen·ē -ēs** *f* Helen of Troy *(wife of Menelaus, sister of Clytemnestra, Castor, and Pollux)*

Helen·us -ī *m* prophetic son of Priam and Hecuba

Hēliad·es -um *fpl* daughters of Helios and sisters of Phaëthon, who were changed into poplar trees and whose tears were changed into amber

helic·a -ae *f* spiral

Helicā·ōn -onis *m* the son of Antenor and founder of Patavium *(modern Padua)*

Helicāoni·us -a -um *adj* of Helicaon *(i.e., of Patavium)*

Helic·ē -ēs *f (astr)* Big Bear *(constellation Ursa Major); (poet)* northern regions

Helic·ōn -ōnis *m* mountain in Boeotia sacred to Muses and Apollo

Helicōniad·es *or* **Helicōnid·es -um** *fpl* Muses

Helicōni·us -a -um *adj* of Helicon

hēliocamīn·us -ī *m* sun-room

Hell·as -adis *or* **-ados** *f* (mainland of) Greece

Hell·ē -ēs *f* daughter of Athamas and Nephele who, while riding the golden-fleeced ram, fell into the Hellespont *(= Helle's Sea)* and drowned

hellebor- = ellebor-

Hell·ēn -ēnis *m* son of Deucalion, and king of Thessaly, from whom the Greeks were said to have been called Hellenes

Hellespont·us -ī *m* Hellespont *(modern Dardanelles)*

hellu·ō -ōnis *m* glutton; squanderer

hellu·or -ārī -ātus sum *intr* to be a glutton

hel·ops *or* **ell·ops -opis** *m* highly prized fish *(perhaps the sturgeon)*

helvell·a -ae *f* delicious herb

Helvēti·us -a -um *adj* Helvetian **‖** *mpl* Helvetians *(a people of ancient Switzerland)*

helv·us -a -um *adj* pale-yellow

hem *interj (expression of surprise)* well!

hēmerodrom·us -ī *m* courier

hēmicill·us -ī *m (pej)* mule, ass

hēmicycl·ium -(i)ī *n* semicircle of seats

hēmīn·a -ae *f* half a sextarius *(half a pint)*
hendecasyllab·ī -ōrum *mpl (pros)* hendecasyl-labics *(verses with eleven syllables)*
hēpatiāri·us -a -um *adj* of the liver
heptēr·is -is *f* galley *(perhaps)* with seven banks of oars
Hēr·a -ae *f* Greek goddess, identified with Juno
hera *see* **era**
Hēraclē·a -ae *f* name of numerous towns *(esp. a part of Lucania on the Siris River and, in Sicily, a town between Lilybaeum and Agrigentum)* ‖ epic poem on the subject of Hercules
Hēraclīt·us -ī *m* early Greek philosopher of Ephesus who believed fire to be the primary element *(fl 513 B.C.)*
Hērae·a -ōrum *npl* festival in honor of the Greek goddess Hera
herb·a -ae *f* blade; stalk; herb; plant; grass, lawn; **adhūc tua messis in herbā est** *(prov)* don't count your chickens before they are hatched *(literally, your harvest is still on the stalk);* **herba mala** weed
herbēsc·ō -ere *intr* to sprout
herbe·us -a -um *adj* grass-green
herbid·us -a -um *adj* grassy; full of weeds
herbif·er -era -erum *adj* grassy, grass-produc-ing; made of herbs; bearing magical herbs
herbigrad·us -a -um *adj (of a snail)* that crawls on the grass
herbōs·us -a -um *adj* grassy; made with herbs; resembling vegetation
herbul·a -ae *f* small plant
hercīsc·ō -ere *intr* to divide an inheritance
herct·um -ī *n* inheritance
hercle *or* **hercule** *or* **ercle** *interj (used for emphasis or to express strong feeling, nor-mally used by the male sex only)* by Hercules!
Herculānēns·is -is -e *adj* of Herculaneum ‖ *m* district of Herculaneum ‖ *mpl* inhabitants of Herculaneum
Herculāne·um -ī *n* town on the Bay of Naples, destroyed by the volcano of Mt. Vesuvius in A.D. 79
Hercul·ēs -is *or* **-ī** *or* **-eī** *m* son of Jupiter and Alcmena, husband of Deianira
Herculēs *or* **Herc(u)le** *interj* by Hercules! *(see* **hercle)**
Herculē·us -a -um *adj* of Hercules
Hercyni·us -a -um *adj* Hercynian, of Hercynia *(a region of the forest-covered mountains extending from the Rhine to the Carpathians)*
here *see* **herī**
hērēdipet·a -ae *m* legacy hunter
hērēditāri·us -a -um *adj* of an inheritance; inherited, hereditary

hērēdit·ās -ātis *f* inheritance; hereditary suc-cession; **hērēditās sine sacrīs** an inheritance without encumbrances
hērēd·ium -(i)ī *n* inherited estate
hēr·ēs -ēdis *m* heir *(to an estate, throne);* **hērēs ex dōdrante** heir to three-quarters of an estate; *(w. ordinal numbers, indicating order of succession):* **hērēs Pelopis tertius** Pelop's heir third in order of succession *(i.e., Agamemnon)* ‖ *f* heiress
herī *or* **here** *adv* yesterday
herif-, herīl- = **erif-, erīl-**
Hermaphrodīt·us -ī *m* son of Hermes and Aphrodite who combined with the nymph Salmacis to become one bisexual person
Hermathēn·a -ae *f* a herm *(i.e., a quadrangu-lar pillar)* with a bust of Athena
Herm·ēs -ae *m* Greek god identified with Mercury; herm *(quadrangular pillar with the bust of Hermes, or later, of other gods)*
Hermion·ē -ēs *or* **Hermion·a -ae** *f* Hermione *(daughter of Helen and Menelaus and wife of Orestes)*
Herm·us -ī *m* gold-rich river in the Greek dis-trict of Aeolis
Hērodot·us -ī *m* father of Greek history, born at Halicarnassus on coast of Asia Minor *(484–425 B.C.)*
hērōïc·us -a -um *adj* heroic, epic
hērōïn·a -ae *f* demigoddess, heroine
hērō·is -idis *f* demigoddess, heroine
hēr·ōs -ōis *m* hero *(mythological figure; a man with heroic qualities)*
hērō·us -a -um *adj* heroic, epic ‖ *m* dactylic hexameter; a dactyl
Hersili·a -ae *f* wife of Romulus
herus *see* **erus**
Hēsiod·us -ī *m* Hesiod *(early Greek poet from Boeotia, 8th cent. B.C.)*
Hēsion·ē -ēs *or* **Hēsion·a -ae** *f* Hesione *(daughter of Laomedon, king of Troy, whom Hercules rescued from a sea monster)*
Hesperi·a -ae *f* the land of the evening star *(i.e., Italy and Spain)*
Hesperid·es -um *fpl* daughters of Hesperus who guarded the golden apples beyond Mount Atlas
Hesper·us *or* **Hesper·os -ī** *m* evening star
hestern·us -a -um *adj* yesterday's
hetairi·a -ae *f* secret society
hetairic·ē -ēs *f* Macedonian mounted guard
heu! *interj (expression of pain or dismay)* oh!, ah!
heus! *interj (to draw attention)* say there!, hey!
hexame·ter -tra -trum *adj (pros)* hexameter, having six metrical feet *(applied esp. to dactylic hexamter)* ‖ *mpl* verse in this meter
hexaphor·um -ī *n* litter carried by six men

hexēr·is -is *f* ship *(perhaps)* with 6 banks of oars

hiāt·us -ūs *m* opening; open mouth; mouthing, bluster; basin *(of a fountain); (w. gen)* greedy desire for; chasm; *(pros)* hiatus

Hibēr·es -um *mpl* Spaniards ‖ tribe south of the Caucasus

Hibēri·a -ae *f* Iberian peninsula *(Greek name for Spain)*

Hibēric·us -a -um *adj* Spanish

hībern·a -ōrum *npl (mil)* winter quarters; winter-quartering

hībernācul·a -ōrum *npl* winter bivouac; winter residence

Hiberni·a -ae *f* Ireland

hībern·ō -āre -āvī -ātum *or* hībern·or -ārī -ātus sum *intr* to spend the winter; to stay in winter quarters; *(fig)* to hibernate

hībern·us -a -um *adj* winter, in winter, wintry; designed for winter use

Hibēr·us -ī *m* river in Spain *(modern Ebro)*

hibīsc·um -ī *n (bot)* hibiscus *(plant w. large, showy flowers)*

hibrid·a -ae *mf* (hyb-) hybrid, mongrel, halfbreed

hic hūius *(older form:* hice hūiūsce) *adj* this; the present, the actual; the latter; *(occasionally)* the former; hic ... hic one ... another ‖ *pron* this one, he; this man; myself, yours truly *(i.e., the speaker or writer);* the latter; *(occasionally)* the former; *(in court)* the defendant, my defendant; hic ... hic one ... another; hicine (hic + *interrog* enclitic -ne) is this ... ?

hīc *adv* here, in this place; at this point; in this affair, in this particular

hice *see* hic

hicine *see* hic

hiemāl·is -is -e *adj* winter, wintry; stormy

hiem·ō -āre -āvī -ātum *intr* to spend the winter; to be wintry, be cold, be stormy

Hiemps·ala -alis *m* name of several N. African kings, *esp.* a grandson of Massinisa and cousin of Jugurtha, by whom he was killed

hiem·s *or* hiem·ps -is *f* winter; cold; storm

Hier·ō(n) -ōnis *m* Hieron *(ruler of Syracuse and patron of philosophers and poets, d. 466 B.C.)* ‖ Hieron *(ruler of Syracuse, in Sicily, and friend of the Romans in First Punic War, 306?–215 B.C.)*

Hierosolym·a -ae *f or* Hierosolym·a -ōrum *npl* Jerusalem

hiet·ō -āre *intr* to keep yawning

hilarē *adv* cheerfully, merrily

hilar·is -is -e *adj* cheerful, merry

hilarit·ās -ātis *f* cheerfulness

hilaritūd·ō -inis *f* cheerfulness

hilar·ō -āre -āvī -ātus *tr* to cheer up

hilarul·us -a -um *adj* cheerful little

hilar·us -a -um *adj* cheerful, merry

hill·ae -ārum *fpl* smoked suasage

Hīlōt·ae -ārum *mpl* Helots *(serfs of the Spartans)*

hīl·um -ī *n (usu. after a neg.)* the least bit

hinc *adv* from here, from this place; on this side, here; for this reason; from this source; after this, from now on, henceforth; *(partitive)* of this, of these; hinc illinc from one side to the other

hinn·iō -īre -iī *intr* to whinny, neigh

hinnīt·us -ūs *m* neighing

hinnule·us -ī *m* fawn, young deer

hi·ō -āre -āvī *tr* to mouth, sing with mouth wide open ‖ *intr* to open, be open; to gape; to yawn; to make eyes *(in surprise or greedy anticipation); (rhet)* to be disjointed

hippagōg·os -ī *f* ship for transporting horses

Hipparch·us -ī *m* son of Pisistratus, tyrant of Athens, slain in 514 B.C.

Hippi·ās -ae *m* son of Pisistratus *(tyrant of Athens),* and tyrant of Athens himself *(527–510 B.C.)*

hippocentaur·us -ī *m* centaur

Hippocrat·ēs -is *m* founder of scientific medicine *(c. 460–380 B.C.)*

Hippocrēn·ē -ēs *f* spring on Mt. Helicon, sacred to the Muses and produced when the hoof of Pegasus hit the ground there

Hippodam·ē -ēs *or* Hippodamē·a *or* Hippodamī·a -ae *f* Hippodamia *(daughter of Oenamaüs, king of Elis, and wife of Pelops)* ‖ Hippodamia *(daughter of Adrastus and wife of Pirithoüs)*

hippodrom·os -ī *m* racetrack

Hippolyt·ē -ēs *or* Hippolyt·a -ae *f* Hippolyte *(Amazonian wife of Theseus)* ‖ wife of Acastus, king of Magnesia

Hippolyt·us -ī *m* (Ipp-) son of Theseus and Hippolyte

hippoman·es -is *n* discharge of a mare in heat; membrane of the head of a new-born foal

Hippomen·ēs -ae *m* young man who competed with Atalanta in a race and won her as his bride

Hippōn·ax -actis *m* Greek satirist *(fl 540 B.C.)*

hippotoxot·ae -ārum *mpl* mounted archers

hippūr·us -ī *m* goldfish

hīr·a -ae *f* empty gut

hircīn·us -a -um *adj* (-quīn-) goat, of a goat

hircōs·us -a -um *adj* smelling like a goat

hirc·us -ī *m* (-qu·us) goat

hirne·a *or* hirni·a -ae *f* jug

hirsūt·us -a -um *adj* hairy, hirsute, shaggy; bristly; prickly; rude

Hirt·ius -(i)ī *m* Aulus Hirtius *(consul in 43 B.C. and author of the eighth book of Caesar's Memoirs on the Gallic War)*

hirt·us -a -um *adj* hairy, shaggy; uncouth

hirūd·ō -inis _f_ leech, bloodsucker
hirundinīn·us -a -um _adj_ swallow's
hirund·ō -inis _f_ swallow _(bird)_
hīsc·ō -ere _tr_ to murmur, utter **II** _intr_ to (begin to) open, gape, yawn; to open the mouth; to split open
Hispān·ī -ōrum _mpl_ Spaniards
Hispāni·a -ae _f_ Spain
Hispāniēns·is -is -e _adj_ Spanish
hispid·us -a -um _adj_ hairy, shaggy; rough, rugged _(terrain)_
His·ter -trī _m_ Lower Danube _(also applied to the whole river)_
histori·a -ae _f_ history; account, story; theme _(of a story)_
historic·us -a -um _adj_ historical **II** _m_ historian
histric·us -a -um _adj_ theatrical
histri·ō -ōnis _m_ actor
histriōnāl·is -is -e _adj_ theatrical; histrionic
histriōni·a -ae f dramatics, art of acting
hiulcē _adv_ with frequent hiatus
hiulc·ō -āre _tr_ to split open
hiulc·us -a-um _adj_ split, split open; open, gaping; with hiatus
hōc hūius _(old form:_ hōce; _gen:_ hūiūsce) _(neut of_ hic) _adj_ this; the present, the actual; the latter; _(occasionally)_ the former **II** _pron_ this one, it; the latter; _(occasionally)_ the former; _(w. gen)_ this amount of, this degree of, so much; hōc erat quod this was the reason why; hōc est that is, I mean, namely; hōcine (hōc + _interrog enclitic_ -ne) is this … ?; hōc facilius all the more easily
hōce _see_ hōc
hōcine _see_ hōc
hodiē _adv_ today; nowadays; still, to the present; at once, immediately; hodiē māne this morning; numquam hodiē _(coll)_ never at all
hodiern·us -a -um _adj_ today's; hodiernus diēs this day, today
holit·or -ōris _m_ grocer
holitōri·us -a -um _adj_ vegetable
hol·us -eris _n_ vegetable; _(collectively)_ vegetables; holus ātrum cabbage-like plant growing on the seashore
holuscul·um -ī _n (pej)_ vegetables
Homērē·us -a -um _or_ Homēri·us -a -um _adj_ Homeric
Homēric·us -a -um _adj_ Homeric
Homēr·us -ī _m_ Homer
homicīd·a -ae _m_ murderer
homicīd·ium -(i)ī _n_ homicide, murder, manslaughter
hom·ō -inis _mf_ human being, man, person, mortal; mankind, human race; fellow; fellow creature; member of a military force; mī homō! my good man! **II** _mpl_ people; inter hominēs esse to be alive; to see the world

homull·us -ī _or_ homunci·ō -ōnis _or_ homuncul·us -ī _m_ poor guy
honest·a -ae _f_ lady
honestāment·um -ī _n_ ornament
honest·ās -ātis _f_ good reputation, respectability; sense of honor, respect; beauty, grace; integrity; decency **II** _fpl_ respectable persons, decent people
honestē _adv_ honorably, respectably, decently; honestly, fairly; honestē genitus (_or_ nātus) high-born
honest·ō -āre -āvī -ātus _tr_ to honor, dignify; to grace, adorn; to put a good face on
honest·us -a -um _adj_ honored, respected; honorable, decent, respectable; handsome; well-born, of high rank **II** _n_ a virtue, a good
hon·or _or_ hon·ōs -ōris _m_ honor, esteem; (high) position, office, post; mark of honor, reward, prize, acknowledgment; recompense, fee; offering, sacrifice, rites _(to the gods or the dead);_ grace, beauty, charm; glory, fame, reputation; honor mortis (_or_ sepultūrae) funeral rites; honōris causā out of respect, with all respect; in honōre esse to meet general approval; praefārī honōrem to begin with an apology; pugnae honor military glory; tempus honōris term of office
honōrābil·is -is -e _adj_ honorable, respectable
honōrār·ium -(i)ī _n_ honorarium, fee
honōrāri·us -a -um _adj_ complimentary, honorary; summa (pecūnia) honōrāria sum of money contributed by a magistrate to the treasury on entering office
honōrātē _adv_ with honor, honorably
honōrāt·us -a -um _adj_ honored, respected; in high office; honorable, respectable; honōrātum habēre to hold in honor
honōrificē _adv_ honorably, respectfully
honōrific·us -a -um _adj_ conferring honor, complimentary
honōr·ō -āre -āvī -ātus _tr_ to honor, respect; to embellish, decorate
honōr·us -a -um _adj_ conferring honor, complimentary; deserving honor
honōs _see_ honor
hoplomach·us -ī _m_ heavy-armed gladiator
hōr·a -ae _f_ hour; time; season; ad hōram on time, punctually; hōrās quaerere to ask what time it is; in diem et hōram continually; in hōram vīvere to live from hand to mouth; quota hōra est? what time is it? **II** _fpl_ hours; time; clock; hōrās īnspicere to look at the clock; hōrās quaerere ab aliquō to ask s.o. the time; omnibus hōrīs at all hours, at all times; omnium hōrārum suited to all occasions; quotās hōrās nūntiāre to say what time it is, tell the time
Hor·a -ae _f_ wife of Quirinus _(i.e., of deified Romulus),_ called Hersilia before her death

Hōr·ae -ārum *fpl* Hours *(daughters of Jupiter and Themis, who kept watch at the gates of heaven)*

hōrae·us -a -um *adj* pickled; seasoned; in season

Horāt·ius -(i)ī *m* Horace *(Quintus Horatius Flaccus, poet, 65–8 B.C.)* ‖ Horatio *(Horatius Cocles, defender of the bridge across the Tiber in the war with Porsenna)*

horde·um -ī *n* **(ord-)** barley

hōri·a -ae *f* fishing boat

hōriol·a -ae *f* small fishing boat

horiz·ōn -ontos *m* horizon

hornō *adv* this year, during this year

hornōtin·us -a -um *adj* this year's

hōrn·us -a -um *adj* this year's

hōrolog·ium -iī *n* clock, water clock, sundial

hōrōscop·us *or* **hōrōscop·os -ī** *m* horoscope; eastern horizon

horrend·us -a -um *adj* horrendous, horrible; awesome

horr·ēns -entis *adj* dreadful, awful

horr·eō -ēre -uī *tr* to dread; to shudder at, shrink from; to be amazed at; to regard *(gods, etc.)* with awe ‖ *intr* to stand on end, stand up straight; to get gooseflesh; to shiver, tremble; to bristle; to look frightful, look unkempt; to have a gloomy character

horr·ēscō -ēscere -uī *tr* to dread, become terrified at ‖ *intr* to stand on end; *(of the sea)* to become rough; to begin to shake *or* shiver; to start, be startled

horre·um -ī *n* barn, shed; silo, granary; wine cellar; storehouse *(of bees),* beehive

horribil·is -is -e *adj* horrible, terrifying; amazing; rough, uncouth

horridē *adv* roughly, rudely; harshly

horridul·us -a -um *adj* rather shaggy; somewhat shabby; *(rhet)* somewhat unsophisticated *(style)*

horrid·us -a -um *adj* shaggy, prickly; bristly *(pig);* choppy *(sea);* disheveled *(appearance);* rugged, wild *(terrain);* rude, uncouth *(manner);* horrible; shivering *(from cold)*

horrif·er -era -erum *adj* causing shudders; freezing, chilling; terrifying

horrificē *adv* awfully, in a frightening way

horrific·ō -āre -āvī *tr* to make rough, ruffle; to terrify, frighten

horrific·us -a -um *adj* frightful, terrifying

horrison·us -a -um *adj* frightening *(sound),* frightening to hear

horr·or -ōris *m* bristling; shivering, shuddering; horror, dread; awe, reverence; chill; thrill

hōrsum *adv* this way

hortām·en -inis *n* injunction; encouragement; incentive

hortāment·um -ī *n* encouragement

hortāti·ō -ōnis *f* exhortation, encouragement

hortāt·or -ōris *m* backer, supporter, rooter; instigator

hortāt·us -ūs *m* encouragement, cheering, cheer

Hortēns·ius -(i)ī *m* Quintus Hortensius *(lawyer and friendly competitor of Cicero, 114–50 B.C.)*

hort·or -ārī -ātus sum *tr* to encourage, cheer, incite, instigate; to give a pep talk to *(soldiers)*

hortul·us -ī *m* little garden

hort·us -ī *m* garden; garden used by Epicurus as a place of teaching; *(fig)* philosophical system ‖ *mpl* park

hosp·es -itis *m* host, entertainer; guest, visitor; friend; stranger, foreigner

hospit·a -ae *f* hostess; guest, visitor; friend; stranger, foreigner; **hospita nāvis** foreign ship

hospitāl·is -is -e *adj* host's; guest's; hospitable ‖ *npl* guest room

hospitālit·ās -ātis *f* hospitality

hospitāliter *adv* hospitably, as a guest

hospit·ium -(i)ī *n* hospitality; ties of hospitality, friendship; welcome; guest room; lodging; inn

hospit·or -ārī -ātus sum *intr* to be put up *(as a guest)*

hosti·a -ae *f* victim, sacrificial animal; **hostia māior** full-grown victim

hostiāt·us -a -um *adj* bringing sacrificial victims

hostic·us -a -um *adj* hostile, of the enemy; foreign ‖ *n* enemy territory

hostific·us -a -um *adj* hostile, bitter

hostīl·is -is -e *adj* enemy, hostile

hostīliter *adv* like an enemy, in a hostile manner

Hostīl·ius -(i)ī *m* Tullus Hostilius *(third king of Rome)*

hostīment·um -ī *n* compensation

host·iō -īre *tr* to get even with ‖ *intr* to get even

host·is -is *mf* (public) enemy; stranger

hūc *adv* here, to this place; to this point, so far; to such a pitch; for this purpose; **hūc atque illūc** here and there, in different directions; **hūcine? (hūc +** *interrog enclitic)* so far?

hui! *interj* wow!

hūius(ce)modī *adj (indecl)* of this sort, this kind of

hūmānē *adv* like a human being; politely, gently, with compassion

hūmānit·ās -ātis *f* human nature; humanity; kindness, compassion, human feeling; courtesy; culture, refinement, civilization

hūmāniter *adv* like a human being; reasonably; gently, with compassion

hūmānitus *adv* humanly; humanely, kindly, compassionately

hūmān·us -a -um *adj* of a human being, human; humane, kind, compassionate; courteous; cultured, refined, civilized

humāti·ō -ōnis *f* burial

hūme- = ūme-

hūmid- = ūmid-

humil·is -is -e *adj* low, low-lying, low-growing; short *(in stature)*; humble; lowly, poor, obscure; insignificant; petty, unimportant; small-minded, cheap; humiliated, humbled

humilit·ās -ātis *f* lowness, lack of stature; lowliness, insignificance; small-mindedness; humiliation; humility, subservience

humiliter *adv* low, deeply; abjectly

hum·ō -āre -āvī -ātus *tr* to bury

hum·us -ī *f* ground, earth, soil; land, region, country; **humī** on *(or* in) the ground

hyacinthin·us -a -um *adj* of the hyacinth; crimson

hyacinth·us *or* **hyacinth·os -ī** *m* hyacinth ‖ **Hyacinth·us** *or* **Hyacinth·os -ī** *m* Hyacinth *(Spartan youth who was accidentally killed by Apollo and from whose blood hyacinths sprang)*

Hyad·es -um *fpl* Hyades *(group of 7 stars in the head of the constellation Taurus whose rising indicated rain)*

hyaen·a -ae *f* hyena

hyal·us -ī *m* glass; **color hyalī** glass-green color

Hyantē·us -a -um *adj* Boeotian

Hy·ās -antis *m* son of Atlas; **sīdus Hyantis** the Hyades

Hybl·a -ae *or* **Hybl·ē -ēs** *f* Sicilian town on the slopes of Mt. Aetna, famous for its honey

Hyblae·us -a -um *adj* of Hybla; **Hyblaeus liquor** honey

hybrid·a -ae *mf* hybrid, mongrel, half-breed

Hydasp·ēs -is *m* tributary of the Indus River

Hȳdr·a -ae *f* Hydra *(seven-headed water snake killed by Hercules)* ‖ monster guarding the gate to the lower world *(mother of Cerberus)* ‖ *(astr)* Hydra *or* Anguis *(constellation)*

hydraulic·us -a -um *adj* hydraulic

hydraul·us -ī *m* water organ

hydri·a -ae *f* water jug, urn

Hydrocho·us -ī *m (astr)* Aquarius

hydrōpic·us -a -um *adj* dropsical

hydr·ops -ōpis *m* dropsy

hydr·us *or* **hydr·os -ī** *m* water snake; snake; dragon

Hygī·a -ae *f* goddess of health

Hȳlae·us -ī *m* centaur who wounded Milanion, the lover of Atalanta

Hyl·ās -ae *m* favorite of Hercules who was carried off by the nymphs

Hyll·us -ī *m* son of Hercules and husband of Iole

Hym·ēn -enis *or* **Hymenae·us** *or* **Hymenae·os -ī** *m* Hymen *(god of marriage);* wedding ceremony; wedding; wedding song

Hymett·us *or* **Hymett·os -ī** *m* mountain in E. Attica, famous for its honey and marble

Hypan·is -is *m* river in Sarmatia *(modern River Bug)*

hyperbat·on -ī n *(rhet)* transposition of words *or* clauses

hyperbol·ē -ēs *f* hyperbole

Hyperbore·ī -ōrum *mpl* people in the land of the midnight sun

Hyperī·ōn -onis *or* **-onos** *m* son of Titan and Earth, father of the Sun

Hypermestr·a -ae *or* **Hypermestr·ē -ēs** *f* only one of the 50 daughters of Danaüs who did not kill her husband on her wedding night

hypocaust·um *or* **hypocaust·on -ī** *n* sub-floor heating chamber

hypodidascal·us -ī *m* assistant teacher

hypomnēm·a -atis *n* note, reminder

hypothēc·a -ae *f (fin)* collateral

Hypsipyl·ē -ēs *f* queen of Lemnos at the time of the Argonauts

Hyrcāni·a -ae *f* country on S.E. side of the Caspian Sea

Hyrcān·us -a -um *adj* of Hyrcania; **mare Hyrcānum** Caspian Sea

hysteric·us -a -um *adj* having a gynecological ailment

I

I, i *(supply* littera) *f* ninth letter of the Latin alphabet; letter name: **i**

-i·a -ae *fem suf* forms abstract nouns from adjectives: **audācia** boldness *(from* **audāx** bold)

Iacch·us -ī *m* Bacchus; wine

iac·eō -ēre -uī -itum *intr* to lie, lie down; to recline *(at table);* to lie ill, be sick; to rest; to lie dead, to have fallen *(in battle); (of structures, cities)* to lie in ruins; to linger, stay *(in a place); (of places)* to lie, be stituated; *(of places)* to be low-lying, lie low; *(of fields)* to lie idle; *(of prices)* to be low; *(of persons)* to feel low, be despondent; *(of the eyes, face)* to be downcast; *(of hair)* to hang loose; *(of the sea)* to be calm; *(of duties, responsibilities)* to be neglected; to lie prostrate, be powerless; *(of arguments)* to fail, be refuted; to be low in s.o.'s opinion; **amīcī iacentem animum incitāre** to cheer up a friend's despondent mood; **animī mīlitum iacent** the morale of

the soldiers is low; **Brundisī iacēre** to linger in Brundisi; **in orbem iacēre** *(of a group of islands)* to lie in a circle, form a circle; **iacēre cum** to have sexual intercourse with; **mihi ad pedēs iācere** to lie prostrate at my feet
iaciō iacere iēcī iactus *tr* to throw, cast, fling; to toss *(head, limbs);* to hurl *(charges, insults);* to lay *(foundations);* to build, establish, set, found, construct; to emit, produce *(heat, light, sparks);* to sow, scatter *(seed);* to throw down; to throw away; to mention, utter, declare, intimate; **contumēliam in aliquem iacere** to hurl the charge of defiance at s.o., charge s.o. with defiance; **fundāmenta iacere** to lay the foundations; **vōcēs iaciuntur** words are uttered ‖ *refl* to leap; to rush, burst
iact·āns -antis *adj* boastful, showing off; proud
iactanter *adv* boastfully; ostentatiously; arrogantly
iactanti·a -ae *f* bragging; ostentation
iactāti·ō -ōnis *f* tossing to and fro; swaying; shaking; writhing; bragging, showing off; **iactātiō animī** agitation; **iactātiō corporis** gesticulation; **iactātiō maritima** seasickness
iactāt·us -ūs *m* tossing, waving
iactit·ō -āre *tr* to display, show off
iact·ō -āre -āvī -ātus *tr* to throw, hurl; to toss about, shake; to wave, brandish; to throw away, throw out; to throw overboard; to throw aside, reject; to disturb, disquiet, stir up; to make restless, cause to toss; to consider, discuss; to throw out, mention; to brag about, show off ‖ *refl* to boast, show off, throw one's weight around ‖ *pass* to toss, rock
iactūr·a -ae *f* throwing away, throwing overboard; loss, sacrifice
iactus *pp of* **iaciō**
iact·us -ūs *m* toss, throw, cast
iaculābil·is -is -e *adj* missile
iaculāti·ō -ōnis *f* hurling
iaculāt·or -ōris *m* thrower, hurler; light-armed soldier; spearman; hunter
iaculātr·īx -īcis *f* huntress
iacul·or -ārī -ātus sum *tr* to throw; to shoot at; *(fig)* to aim at, strive after
iacul·us -a -um *adj* throwing, casting ‖ *n* dart, javelin; casting net
iāiūn- = iēiūn-
Iālysi·us -a -um *adj* of Jalysos, a town on the island of Rhodes
Iālys·us -ī *m* son of the god Helios, and eponym of the town Jalysos ‖ famous portrait of Jalysus by Protogenes
iam *adv (in the present)* now, already; *(in the past)* already, by then, by that time; *(in the future)* very soon, right away; *(in transition)*

now, next, moreover; *(for emphasis)* actually, precisely, quite; *(in conclusion)* then surely; **iam ante(ā)** even before that; **iam dūdum** long ago, long since; **iam inde** immediately; **iam inde ab** all the while from, continuously from; **iam iam** *(for emphasis or emotive effect)* at last, now finally **iam … iam** at one time … at another; first … then; **iamiamque** at any time now, now all but … ; **iam nunc** even now; **iam prīdem** long since; **iam prīmum** to begin with, first of all; **iam tum** even then, even at that time; **quid iam?** *(coll)* what (is the matter) now?
iambē·us -a -um *adj (pros)* iambic
iamblc·us -a -um *adj (pros)* iambic
iamb·us -ī *m (pros)* iamb (ᴗ —); iambic trimeter *(consists of three double feet, i.e., of six iambic feet);* iambic poem; iambic poetry
Iānicul·um -ī *n* Roman hill on right bank of the Tiber
Iānigen·a *adj (masc & fem only)* born of Janus
iānit·or -ōris *m* doorman, porter
iānitr·īx -īcis *f* portress
ianthin·us -a -um *adj* violet ‖ *n* the color violet ‖ *npl* violet clothes
iānu·a -ae *f* door; doorway, entrance; *(fig)* entrance, approach, gateway; **iānua lētī** gateway of death, gateway to the lower world
Iānuāri·us -a -um *adj* of Janus; **mēnsis Iānuārius** January *(first month, after 153 B.C., of the Roman year)* ‖ *m* January
iān·us -ī *m* covered passage, arcade; **iānus īmus, iānus medius, iānus summus** bottom archway, middle archway, top archway *(three archways on the east side of the Forum, where money changers and merchants conducted their business)* ‖ **Iānus** Janus *(old Italic deity, represented as having two faces)* ‖ temple of Janus *(at the bottom of the Argiletum in the Forum)* ‖ **Iānus Geminus** *(or* **Iānus Quirīnus** *or* **Iānus Quirīnī)** shrine of Janus in the Forum consisting of an archway, with doors at the ends that were closed in times of peace
Iāpyd·es -um *mpl (-pud-)* an Illyrian tribe
Iāpydi·a -ae *f* country in the N. part of Illyria
Iāpygi·a -ae *f* Greek name for part of S.E. Italy, including some or all of Calabria and Apulia
Iāp·yx -ygis *adj* Iapygian ‖ *m* son of Daedalus who ruled in S. Italy ‖ wind that blew from Apulia to Greece
Iāp·yx -ygis *or* **-ygos** *adj* Iapygian ‖ *m* son of Daedalus, who gave his name to Iapygia ‖ river in Apulia ‖ the W.N.W. wind, which favors the crossing from Italy to Greece
Iarb·a(s) -ae *m* Iarbas *(king of the Gaetulians in N. Africa, whom Dido rejected as a suitor)*
Iarbīt·a -ae *m* Mauretanian, Moor

Iardan·is -idis f daughter of Jardanus, king of Lydia (i.e., Omphale)
Iās·ō(n) -onis m Jason (son of Aeson, leader of the Argonauts, and husband of Medea)
Iāsoni·us -a -um adj Jason's
iasp·is -idis or -idos f jasper
Iās·us -ī f town on the coast of Caria
iātralipt·ēs -ae m masseur
Iāz·yx -ygis m member of a people dwelling near the Danube
ibi or ibī adv there, in that place; then, on that occasion; therein
ibidem or ibīdem adv in the same place, just there; in the place already mentioned, therein, thereon; at that very moment, there and then; at the same time; in the same matter
īb·is -is or -idis f ibis (bird sacred to the Egyptians)
Īcariōt·is -idis adj of Penelope ‖ f Penelope (daughter of Icarius)
Īcari·us -a -um adj of Icarus, Icarian; of the Icarian Sea; Canis Īcarius (astr) Dog Star; ‖ m father of Penelope ‖ n Icarian Sea
Īcar·us -ī m son of Daedalus, who, on his flight from Crete with his father, fell into the sea
ichneum·ōn -onis m ichneumon (Egyptian rat that eats crocodile eggs)
īcī perf of īcō
-ici·us -a -um adjl suf 1 used to form adjectives from nouns denoting officers, relationships, etc.: tribūnicius tribunician; patricius patrician; 2 denoting the time of birth, of a birthday: nātālicius of the time of birth, belonging to a birthday; 3 used to form adjectives from past participles: expositicius exposed, foundling; 4 used to form adjectives from nouns denoting materials: latericius brick, of brick (from later brick)
īc·ō -ere -ī -tus tr to hit, strike, shoot; to sting, bite; foedus īcere to conclude a treaty
-icō vbl suf 1 used to form verbs from adjectives: claudicāre to be lame, to limp (from claudus lame, limping); 2 used to form verbs from other verbs: fodicāre to stab (from fodere to stab, dig)
īc·ōn -onis f image
īconic·us -a -um adj giving an exact image
icteric·us -a -um adj jaundiced
ict·is -idis f weasel
ictus pp of īcō
ict·us -ūs m stroke, blow, hit; cut; sting, bite; wound; range; (musical or metrical) beat; (fig) shock, blow; sub ictum within range
id adv for that reason, therefore
id ēius (neut of is) adj this, that, the aforesaid ‖ pron it; a thing, the thing; ad id for that purpose; aliquid id genus s.th. of that sort, s.th. like that; cum eō ut on condition that, with the stipulation that; ēo plūs the more; ex eō

from that time on; as a result of that, consequently; id cōnsilī some sort of plan, some plan; id temporis at that time; of that age; in id to that end; in eō esse to depend on it; in eō esse ut to be so far gone that, to get to the point where
Īd·a -ae or Īd·ē -ēs f Mt. Ida (mountain range near Troy) ‖ Mt. Ida (mountain in Crete where Jupiter was brought up)
Īdae·us -a -um adj Idaean, of Mt. Ida (in Crete or near Troy)
Īdal·ium -(i)ī n city in Cyprus dear to Venus
idcircō adv on that account, for that reason, therefore
īdem eadem idem adj the same, the very same, exactly this; (often equivalent to a mere connective) also, likewise ‖ pron the same one
identidem adv again and again, continually; over and over again
ideō adv therefore
idiōt·a -ae m layman, amateur; private individual
īdōl·on -ī n apparition, ghost
idōneē adv suitably
idōne·us -a -um adj suitable, fit, proper; (w. dat or w. ad or in + acc) fit for, capable of, suited for, convenient for, sufficient for
Īd·ūs -uum fpl Ides (15th day of March, May, July, and October, and 13th day of the other months; interest, debts, and tuition were often paid on the Ides)
iec·ur -oris or -ineris or -inoris n liver; (as the seat of emotions) anger, lust
iecuscul·um -ī n little liver
iēiūnē adv (fig) dryly
iēiūniōs·us -a -um adj (iāiūn-) (hum) abounding in hunger, hungry
iēiūnit·ās -ātis f (iāiūn-) fasting; dryness (of style);
iēiūn·ium -(i)ī n fasting, fast; hunger, leanness
iēiūn·us -a -um adj (iāiūn-) fasting; hungry; thin; insignificant, paltry; poor (land); jejune (style)
iēns euntis pres p of eō
-iēns or -iēs advl suf forming numerals and adjectives to denote a number of times: centiēns a hundred times; totiēns so many times, so often
-iēns·is -is -e adjl suf used to form ethnic adjectives from place names: Carthaginiēnsis Carthaginian
ientācul·um -ī n (iāien-) breakfast
ient·ō -āre -āvī intr to eat breakfast
igitur adv then, therefore, accordingly; (resumptive after parenthetical matter) as I was saying; (in summing up) so then, in short
ignār·us -a -um adj ignorant, unaware, inexperienced; unsuspecting; senseless; unknown, strange, unfamiliar; (w. gen) unaware of, unfamiliar with, ignorant of

ignāvē *adv* listlessly, lazily
ignāvi·a -ae *f* listlessness, laziness; cowardice
ignāviter *adv* listlessly, lazily
ignāv·us -a -um *adj* listless, lazy, idle, inactive; relaxing; cowardly; unproductive, useless
ignēsc·ō -ere *intr* (**-nis-**) to catch fire, become inflamed, burn; *(fig)* to flare up
igne·us -a -um *adj* of fire, on fire, fiery; red-hot; fiery, ardent *(person)*
ignicul·us -ī *m* small fire, little flame; sparkle; *(lit & fig)* spark
ignif·er -era -erum *adj* fiery
ignigen·a -ae *m* son of fire *(epithet of Bacchus)*
ignip·ēs -edis *adj* fiery-footed
ignipot·ēns -entis *adj* lord of fire *(epithet of Vulcan)*
ign·is -is *m* fire; watch fire, fire signal; torch; lightning, bolt of lightning; funeral pyre; star; brightness, glow, splendor; *(fig)* fire, rage, fury, love, passion; flame, sweetheart; agent of destruction, fanatic ‖ *mpl* love poems
ignōbil·is -is -e *adj* unknown, obscure, insignificant, undistinguished; low-born, ignoble
ignōbilit·ās -ātis *f* obscurity; humble birth
ignōmini·a -ae *f* ignominy, dishonor, disgrace; *(mil)* dishonorable discharge; **ignōminiā afficere** to dishonor, disgrace; **ignōminia senātūs** public censure imposed by the Senate
ignōminiōs·us -a -um *adj* disgraced; ignominious, disgraceful, shameful ‖ *m (person)* disgrace
ignōrābil·is -is -e *adj* unknown
ignōranti·a -ae *f* ignorance
ignōrāti·ō -ōnis *f* ignorance
ignōr·ō -āre -āvī -ātus *tr* to not know, be ignorant of, be unfamiliar with; to be unaware of, know nothing about; to fail to recognize; to mistake, misunderstand; to ignore, disregard, take no notice of
ignōsc·ēns -entis *adj* forgiving, indulgent
ig·nōscō -nōscere -nōvī -nōtum *intr (w. dat)* to pardon, forgive, excuse; *(w. dat of person and acc of the offense)* to pardon, forgive, excuse *(s.o. a fault)*
ignōt·us -a -um *adj* unknown, unfamiliar, strange; inglorious; unnoticed; low-born, ignoble; vulgar; ignorant
īl·ex -icis *f* holm oak *(European evergreen oak with foliage resembling that of a holly)*
Īli·a -ae f Rhea Silvia *(daughter of Numitor and mother of Romulus and Remus)*
īl·ia -ium *npl* flank, side *(of the body extending from the hips down to the groin)* guts, intestines; belly, groin, private parts
Īliac·us -a -um *adj* Trojan
Īli·as -adis *f Iliad;* Trojan woman

īlicet *adv (ancient form for adjourning an assembly)* you may go; *(expressing dismay)* it's all over!, finished!; at once, immediately
īlicō *adv* on the spot, right then and there, immediately
īlign(e)·us -a -um *adj* of holm oak, oaken
Īl·ios -iī *f* Ilium, Troy
Īlithȳi·a -ae *f* goddess who aided women in childbirth
Īl·ium -iī *n or* **Īl·ion -iī** *n of* **Īl·ios -iī** *f* Ilium, Troy
Īli·us -a -um *adj* of Ilium, Trojan
illā *adv* that way
ill·a -īus *adj fem* that; that famous ‖ *pron* that one, she
illabefact·us -a -um *adj* (inl-) unbroken, uninterrupted; unimpaired
illā·bor -bī -psus sum *intr* (inl-) to flow; to sink, fall; to fall in, cave in; to slip; *(w. dat or w. ad or in + acc)* to flow into, enter into, penetrate
illabōr·ō -āre *intr* (inl-) *(w. dat)* to work at, work on
illāc *adv* that way
illacessīt·us -a -um *adj* (inl-) unprovoked
illacrimābil·is -is -e *adj* (inl-) unlamented, unwept; inexorable
illacrim·ō -āre -āvī *or* **illacrim·or -ārī -ātus sum** *intr* (inl-) *(w. dat)* to cry over
ill·aec *(acc: -anc; abl: -āc) adj fem* that ‖ *pron* she
illaes·us -a -um *adj* (inl-) unharmed
illaetābil·is -is -e *adj* (inl-) sad, melancholy
illāpsus (inl-) *pp of* **illābor**
illaque·ō -āre -āvī -ātus *tr* (inl-) to trap, entangle
illātus (inl-) *pp of* **īnferō**
illaudāt·us -a -um *adj* (inl-) unworthy of praise, unpraised
ill·e -īus *adj masc* that; that famous; the former; **ille aut ille** this or that, such and such ‖ *pron* that one; he; the former one
illecebr·a -ae *f* (inl-) attraction, allurement
illecebrōs·us -a -um *adj* (inl-) alluring, seductive
illēct·us -a -um *adj* (inl-) unread
illectus (inl-) *pp of* **illiciō**
illect·us -ūs *m* (inl-) allurement
illepidē *adv* (inl-) inelegantly, rudely
illepid·us -a -um *adj* (inl-) inelegant, lacking refinement
illēvī *perf of* **illinō**
ill·ēx -ēgis *adj* (inl-) lawless
ill·ex -icis *mf* (inl-) lure, decoy
illexī *perf of* **illiciō**
illībāt·us -a -um *adj* (inl-) undiminished, unimpaired, intact
illīberāl·is -is -e *adj* (inl-) stingy
illīberālit·ās -ātis *f* (inl-) stinginess

illīberāliter *adv* (inl-) stingily

ill·ic *(acc:* -unc; *abl:* -ōc) *adj masc* that ‖ *pron* he

illīc *adv* there, in that place; in that matter, therein

il·liciō -licere -lexī -lectus *tr* (inl-) to allure, attract; to seduce, mislead

illicitāt·or -ōris *m* (inl-) hired bidder *(one who bids at an auction to make others bid higher)*

illicit·us -a -um *adj* (inl-) unlawful, illicit

illī·dō -dere -sī -sus *tr* (inl-) to smash to pieces, crush; *(w. dat or w.* **ad** *or* **in** + *acc)* to smash *(s.th.)* against

illig·ō -āre -āvī -ātus *tr* (inl-) to attach, connect; to tie, bind; to oblige, obligate; to impede; to involve, tie up

illim *adv* from there

illīm·is -is -e *adj* unmuddied, clear

illinc *adv* from there; on that side

il·linō -linere -lēvī -litus *tr* (inl-) to cover; to smear; *(w. dat)* to smear *or* spread *(s.th.)* on, cake *(s.th.)* on

illiquefact·us -a -um *adj* (inl-) melted

illīsī *perf of* **illīdō**

illīsus *pp of* **illīdō**

illi(t)terāt·us -a -um *adj* (inl-) uneducated, illiterate

illitus *pp of* **illinō**

illō(c) *adv* there, at that place; at that point

illōt·us *or* **illaut·us -a -um** *adj* (inl-) unwashed, dirty

ill·ūc *(acc;* -ūc; *abl* -ōc) *adj neut* that ‖ *pron* it

illūc *adv* to that place, in that direction; to that person, to him, to her; to that matter; to that point

illūc·eō -ēre *intr* (inl-) *(w. dat)* to shine on

illū·cēscō -cēscere -xī *intr* (inl-) to grow light, dawn; to begin to shine

ill·ud -īus *adj neut* that; the former ‖ *pron* it

illū·dō -dere -sī -sus *tr* (inl-) to make fun of, ridicule; to waste, fritter away *(time, life)* ‖ *intr (w. dat) (coll)* to play around with *(sexually)*

illūminātē *adv* (inl-) clearly

illūmin·ō -āre -āvī -ātus *tr* (inl-) to illuminate, light up, make bright; to illustrate

illūsī *perf of* **illūdō**

illūsi·ō -ōnis *f* (inl-) irony

illūstr·is -is -e *adj* (inl-) bright, clear, brilliant; plain, distinct, evident; distinguished, famous, illustrious, noble

illūstr·ō -āre -āvī -ātus *tr* (inl-) to light up, illuminate; to make clear, clear up, explain; to make famous; to embellish

illūsus *pp of* **illūdō**

illuvi·ēs -ēī *f* (inl-) filth, dirtiness; mud; inundation; *(of a person) (pej)* scum

illūxī *perf of* **illūcēscō**

Illyric·us -a -um *adj* Illyrian ‖ *n* Illyria

Illyri·us -a -um *adj & m* Illyrian ‖ *f* Illyria *(on the E. coast of the Adriatic Sea)*

Īl·us -ī m son of Tros, father of Laomedon, and founder of Ilium ‖ Ascanius

-im *advl suf*

imāgināri·us -a -um *adj* imaginary

imāginātiōn·ēs -um *fpl* imaginings

imāgin·or -ārī -ātus sum *tr* to imagine

imāg·ō -inis *f* image, likeness, picture, bust; bust of ancestor; ghost, vision; echo; appearance, semblance, shadow; mental picture, concept, thought, idea; figure of speech, simile, metaphor

imbēcillit·ās -ātis *f* (inb-) weakness, feebleness; helplessness

imbēcill·us -a -um *adj* (inb-) weak, feeble; helpless; *(of medicine)* ineffective

imbell·is -is -e *adj* (inb-) anti-war; unwarlike; peaceful, quiet; ineffective *(weapon); (pej)* unfit for war, soft

im·ber -bris *m* rain, rainstorm; *(lit & fig)* shower; rain cloud; rainwater; water *(in general);* snowstorm; hail-storm; flood of tears; **maximus imber** very heavy downpour

imberb·is -is -e *or* **imberb·us -a -um** *adj* (inb-) beardless

imbib·ō -ere -ī *tr* (inb-) to imbibe, drink in; **(animō) imbibere** to absorb, form *(e.g., an opinion)*

imbīt·ō -ere *tr* (inb-) to enter

imbr·ex -icis *f* (fluted) tile, gutter tile

imbric·us -a -um *adj* rainy

imbrif·er -era -erum *adj* rainy, bringing rain

im·buō -buere -buī -būtus *tr* to wet, soak; to dip; to moisten; to stain, taint, infect; to imbue, fill, steep; to instruct; *(w.* **ad***)* to introduce to

imitābil·is -is -e *adj* imitable, capable of being imitated

imitām·en -inis *n* imitation, copy; image, likeness

imitāment·um -ī *n* imitation ‖ *npl* pretense

imitāti·ō -ōnis *f* imitation; mimicking, copying; copy, counterfeit

imitāt·or -ōris *m,* **imitātr·īx -īcis** *f* imitator

imitāt·us -a -um *adj* fictitious, copied

imit·or -ārī -ātus sum *tr* to imitate, copy; to portray; to ape

immad·ēscō -ēscere -uī *intr* (inm-) to become wet

immāne *adv* (inm-) savagely

immān·is -is -e *adj* (inm-) huge, enormous, monstrous; inhuman, savage

immānit·ās -ātis *f* (inm-) vastness, enormity; savageness, cruelty

immānsuēt·us -a -um *adj* (inm-) untamed, savage, wild

immātūrit·ās -ātis *f* (inm-) immaturity; prematureness; overanxiousness immātūr·us -a -um *adj* (inm-) immature; unripe; premature

immedicābil·is -is -e *adj* (inm-) incurable

immem·or -oris *adj* (inm-) forgetful, forgetting; negligent, heedless; **immemor patriae** forgetting (one's) country

immemorābil·is -is -e *adj* (inm-) not worth mentioning; untold

immemorāt·a -ōrum *npl* (inm-) novelties, things hitherto untold

immēnsit·ās -ātis *f* (inm-) immensity ‖ *fpl* immense stretches

immēns·us -a -um *adj* (inm-) immense, unending, immeasurable, huge ‖ *n* infinity, infinite space

immer·ēns -entis *adj* (inm-) undeserving, innocent

immer·gō -gere -sī -sus *tr* (inm-) to immerse, dip, plunge; to overwhelm, drown; *(w. in + acc)* to dip *(s.th.)* into ‖ *refl (w. in + acc)* 1 to plunge into; 2 to insinuate oneself into

immeritō *adv* (inm-) undeservedly, innocently

immerit·us -a -um *adj* (inm-) undeserving, innocent; undeserved; **immeritō meō** through no fault of mine

immersābil·is -is -e *adj* (inm-) unsinkable

immersī *perf of* immergō

immersus *pp of* immergō

immētāt·us -a -um *adj* (inm-) unmeasured, undivided

immigr·ō -āre -āvī -ātum *intr* (inm-) to immigrate; *(w. in + acc)* 1 to move into; 2 to invade

immin·eō -ēre *intr* (inm-) to project, stick out; to be near, be imminent; to threaten, menace; *(w. dat)* 1 to look out over, overlook *(a view)*; 2 to hover over, loom over, threaten; *(w. dat or in + acc)* to be intent on, be eager for

immin·uō -uere -uī -ūtus *tr* (inm-) to lessen, curtail; to weaken, impair; to infringe upon, encroach upon, violate, subvert, destroy

imminūti·ō -ōnis *f* (inm-) lessening; mutilation; *(rhet)* understatement

im·mīsceō -mīscēre -mīscuī -mīxtus *tr* (inm-) to mix in, intermix, blend; *(fig)* to mix up, confuse; **manūs manibus immīscēre** *(of boxers)* to mix it up ‖ *refl & pass (w. dat)* 1 to join, join in with, mingle with, get lost in *(e.g., a crowd)*; 2 to blend with, disappear in *(e.g., the night, a cloud)*

immiserābil·is -is -e *adj* (inm-) unpitied

immisericorditer *adv* (inm-) unmercifully

immisericor·s -dis *adj* (inm-) merciless

immīsī *perf of* immittō

immissi·ō -ōnis *f* (inm-) letting *(e.g., saplings)* grow

immissus *pp of* immittō

immīt·is -is -e *adj* (inm-) unripe, sour, green *(fruit);* sour *(wine);* harsh; rude; cruel, ruthless, pitiless

im·mittō -mittere -mīsī -missus *tr* (inm-) to send *(to or into);* to steer *(a ship);* to guide *(a horse);* to insert; to let in, let go in, admit; to let go of, let drop; to let fly, throw; to let *(death, ills)* loose *(on);* to direct the flow of *(water, air, etc., into or against);* **habēnās immittere** to slacken the reins ‖ *refl & pass* to go *(into);* to leap *(into);* *(geog)* to extend *(to, into)*

immīxtus (inm-) *pp of* immīsceō

immō *or* immo *adv (in contradiction or correction of preceding words)* nay, on the contrary, or rather, more precisely; *(in confirmation of preceding words)* quite so, yes indeed; **immō vērō** yes and in fact

immōbil·is -is -e *adj* (inm-) motionless, unshaken; immovable; fixed, unalterable; clumsy, unwieldy

immoderātē *adv* (inm-) immoderately

immoderāti·ō -ōnis *f* (inm-) lack of moderation, excess

immoderāt·us -a -um *adj* (inm-) unmeasured, limitless; immoderate, uncontrolled, excessive

immodestē *adv* (inm-) immoderately, shamelessly

immodesti·a -ae *f* (inm-) lack of self-control; excesses; insubordination

immodest·us -a -um *adj* (inm-) immoderate, uncontrolled

immodicē *adv* (inm-) excessively

immodic·us -a -um *adj* (inm-) huge, enormous; immoderate, excessive; *(w. gen or abl)* given to, excessive in

immodulāt·us -a -um *adj* (inm-) unrhythmical

immolāti·ō -ōnis *f* (inm-) sacrifice

immolāt·or -ōris *m* (inm-) sacrificer

immōlīt·us -a -um *adj* (inm-) constructed, erected ‖ *npl* buildings

immol·ō *or* inmol·ō -āre -āvī -ātus *tr* (inm-) to sprinkle the feet of *(the victim)* with coarse flour in preparation for sacrifice; to immolate, sacrifice

immor·deō -dēre — -sus *tr* to bite into; *(fig)* stimulate

immor·ior -ī -tuus sum *intr* (inm-) *(w. dat)* to die in, die upon; *(fig)* to get sick over

immor·or -ārī -ātus sum *intr* (inm-) *(w. dat)* to dwell upon

immors·us -a -um *adj* (inm-) bitten into; excited, stimulated

immortāl·is -is -e *adj* (inm-) immortal

immortālit·ās -ātis *f* (inm-) immortality

immortāliter *adv (coll)* (inm-) infinitely, eternally

immortuus (inm-) *pp of* immorior

immōt·us -a -um *adj* (**inm-**) unmoved, immovable; unshaken, undisturbed, steadfast
immūg·iō -īre -īvī *or* **-iī -ītum** *intr* (**inm-**) to bellow; to roar
immulg·eō -ēre *tr* (**inm-**) to milk
immunditi·a -ae *f* (**inm-**) dirtiness, filth
immund·us -a -um *adj* (**inm-**) dirty, filthy
immūn·iō -īre -īvī *or* **-iī** *tr* (**inm-**) to reinforce, fortify
immūn·is -is -e *adj* (**inm-**) without duty *or* office; tax-exempt; free, exempt; pure, innocent; *(w. abl or* **ab***)* free from, exempt from; *(w. gen)* **1** free of, free from; **2** devoid of, without; **3** having no share in
immūnit·ās -ātis *f* (**inm-**) immunity, exemption; exemption from tribute
immūnīt·us -a -um *adj* (**inm-**) unfortified; unpaved *(road)*
immurmur·ō -āre *intr* (**inm-**) to grumble; *(w. dat) (of the wind)* to whisper among
immūtābil·is -is -e *adj* (**inm-**) immutable, unchangeable; changed
immūtābilit·ās -ātis *f* (**inm-**) immutability
immūtāti·ō -ōnis *f* (**inm-**) exchange, substitution; *(rhet)* metonymy
immūtāt·us -a -um *adj* (**inm-**) unchanged
immūt·ō -āre -āvī -ātus *tr* (**inm-**) to change, alter; to substitute
impācāt·us -a -um *adj* (**inp-**) unsubdued
impāctus *pp of* **impingō**
impall·ēscō -ēscere -uī *intr* (**inp-**) *(w. abl)* to turn pale at
imp·ār -aris *adj* (**inp-**) uneven, odd *(numbers);* uneven *(in size or length);* unlike *(in color or appearance);* unequal; unfair; ill-matched; crooked; *(w. dat)* **1** not a match for, inferior to; **2** unable to cope with
imparāt·us -a -um *adj* (**inp-**) unprepared
impariter *adv* (**inp-**) unequally
impāst·us -a -um *adj* (**inp-**) unfed, hungry
impati·ēns -entis *adj* (**inp-**) impatient; *(w. gen)* **1** impatient with; **2** unable to endure, unable to take *(e.g., the heat);* **impatiēns īrae** unable to restrain one's anger
impatienter *adv* (**inp-**) impatiently; intolerably
impatienti·a -ae *f* (**inp-**) *(w. gen)* inability *or* unwillingness to endure
impavidē *adv* (**inp-**) fearlessly
impavid·us -a -um *adj* (**inp-**) fearless, undismayed
impedīment·um -ī *n* (**inp-**) impediment, hindrance; difficulty ‖ *npl* baggage; mule train
imped·iō -īre -īvī *or* **-iī -ītus** *tr* (**inp-**) to entangle; to hamper, hinder; to entwine, encircle; to clasp, embrace; to block *(road);* to hinder, prevent; to embarrass; *(w.* **nē, quīn,** *or* **quōminus***)* to prevent *(s.o.)* from
impedīti·ō -ōnis *f* (**inp-**) hindrance ‖ *fpl* cases of obstruction

impedīt·us -a -um *adj* (**inp-**) hampered; obstructed, blocked; difficult, intricate; impassable; busy, occupied
impēgī (**inp-**) *perf of* **impingō**
im·pellō -pellere -(pe)pulī -pulsus *tr* (**inp-**) to strike against, strike; to reach *(the ears);* to push, drive, drive forward, impel, propel; to urge, persuade; to stimulate, induce; to force, compel; to put to rout; to swell *(sails)*
impend·eō -ēre *intr* (**inp-**) to be near, be at hand, be imminent, threaten; *(w. dat)* to hang over; *(w. dat or* **in** *+ acc)* to hover over, loom over
impendiōs·us -a -um *adj* (**inp-**) extravagant, free-spending
impend·ium -(i)ī *n* (**inp-**) expense, cost, outlay; interest *(paid out);* loss
impen·dō -dere -dī -sus *tr* (**inp-**) to weigh out, pay out; to expend, devote, apply, employ; *(w.* **in** *+ acc)* **1** to spend *(money)* on; **2** to expend *(effort)* on; **3** to pay *(attention)* to
impenetrābil·is -is -e *adj* (**inp-**) impenetrable
impēns·a -ae *f* (**inp-**) expense, cost, outlay; waste; contribution; **impēnsam facere** to incur an expense; **meīs impēnsīs** at my expense
impēnsē *adv* (**inp-**) at a high cost, expensively; with great effort
impēns·us -a -um *pp of* **impendō** ‖ *adj* high, costly, expensive; strong, vehement; earnest ‖ *n* high price
imper·āns -antis *m* (**inp-**) master, ruler
imperāt·or -ōris *m* (**inp-**) commander, general; commander in chief; emperor; director; master, ruler
imperātōri·us -a -um *adj* (**inp-**) of a general, general's; imperial
imperātr·īx -īcis *f* (**inp-**) controller, mistress
imperāt·um -ī *n* (**inp-**) command, order
impercept·us -a -um *adj* (**inp-**) unperceived, unknown
imperc·ō -ere *intr (w. dat)* (**inp-**) to spare, take it easy on
impercuss·us -a -um *adj* (**inp-**) noiseless
imperdit·us -a -um *adj* (**inp-**) not killed, unscathed
imperfect·us -a -um *adj* (**inp-**) unfinished; imperfect; undigested *(food)*
imperfoss·us -a -um *adj* (**inp-**) unpierced, not stabbed
imperiōs·us -a -um *adj* (**inp-**) masterful, commanding; imperial; magisterial; tyrannical, overbearing, domineering, imperious
imperītē *adv* (**inp-**) unskillfully, clumsily; in an ignorant manner
imperīti·a -ae *f* (**inp-**) inexperience, awkwardness, ignorance
imperit·ō -āre -āvī -ātus *tr & intr* (**inp-**) to command, rule, govern

imperīt·us -a -um *adj* **(inp-)** inexperienced, unfamiliar, ignorant, unskilled; *(w. gen)* inexperienced in, unacquainted with, ignorant of
imper·ium -(i)ī *n* **(inp-)** supreme administrative power *(exercised by the kings, subsequently by certain magistrates and provincial governors, and later by Roman emperors);* absolute authority *(in any sphere);* dominion, sway, government; empire; command, order; right to command; authority; exercise of authority; military commission, military command; mastery; sovereignty; realm, dominion; public office, magistracy; term of office
imperiūrāt·us -a -um *adj* **(inp-)** sacrosanct
impermiss·us -a -um *adj* **(inp-)** forbidden
imper·ō -āre -āvī -ātus *tr* **(inp-)** to requisition, give orders for, order, demand; *(w. acc of thing and dat of source demanded from)* to demand *(e.g., hostages)* from **ll** *intr* to be in command, rule, be master; *(w. dat)* to give orders to, order, command, govern, master, exercise control over; *(gram)* to express a command
imperterrit·us -a -um *adj* **(inp-)** undaunted, fearless
impert·iō -īre *tr* **(inp-)** *(w. dat)* to impart, communicate, bestow, assign, direct *(s.th.)* to, share *(s.th.)* with; *(w. acc of person and abl of thing)* to present *(s.o.)* with
imperturbāt·us -a -um *adj* **(inp-)** unperturbed, unruffled
impervi·us -a -um *adj* **(inp-)** impassable; *(w. dat)* impervious to
impete *(abl singl)* *m* with an assault, with a charge
impetibil·is -is -e *adj* **(inp-)** intolerable
impet·ō -ere *tr* **(inp-)** to make for; to attack
impetrābil·is -is -e *adj* **(inp-)** obtainable; successful
impetrāti·ō -ōnis *f* **(inp-)** obtaining one's request
impetr·iō -īre *tr* **(inp-)** to try to obtain through favorable omens
impetr·ō -āre -āvī -ātus *tr* **(inp-)** to obtain, procure *(by asking);* to achieve, accomplish, bring to pass
impet·us -ūs *m* **(inp-)** attack, assault; rush; impetus; impetuosity, vehemence, vigor; violence, fury, force; wide expanse *(of sea, sky);* *(w. gen)* sudden burst of; *(w. inf or* **ad)** impulse to *(do s.th.);* **animī impetus** impulse, urge; **omnī impetū** with all one's might
impex·us -a -um *adj* **(inp-)** uncombed, unkempt, tangled
impiē *adv* **(inp-)** wickedly
impiet·ās -ātis *f* **(inp-)** impiety, irreverence, lack of respect; disloyalty

impi·ger -gra -grum *adj* **(inp-)** diligent, active, energetic
impigrē *adv* **(inp-)** energetically, actively
impigrit·ās -ātis *f* **(inp-)** energy, activity
im·pingō -pingere -pēgī -pāctus *tr* **(inp-)** *(w. dat or* **in** + *acc)* **1** to fasten to; **2** to pin against, force against, dash against; **3** to press *or* force *(s.th.)* on; **4** to fling at
impi·ō -āre -āvī -ātus *tr* **(inp-)** to make disrepectful **ll** *refl* to act disrespectfully
impi·us -a -um *adj* **(inp-)** impious, godless, irreverent, disrespectful; disobedient; disloyal; wicked, unscrupulous; **Tartara impia** Tartarus, the abode of the impious
implācāt·us -a -um *adj* **(inp-)** implacable, inexorable, insatiable
implacid·us -a -um *adj* **(inp-)** restless; rough, wild
impl·eō -ēre -ēvī -ētus *tr* **(inp-)** to fill up; to satisfy; to fatten; to make pregnant; to enrich; to cover with writing, fill up *(a book);* to discharge, execute, implement; to complete, end; to occupy, take up *(time);* to make up, amount to; to fulfill, satisfy *(wishes, hopes, prophecies, appetites)*
implex·us -a -um *adj* **(inp-)** entwined; involved
implicāti·ō -ōnis *f* **(inp-)** interweaving; network; **implicātiō reī familiāris** financial embarrassment
implicāt·us -a -um *adj* **(inp-)** involved, intricate
implicīsc·or -ī *intr* **(inp-)** to become confused
implicitē *adv* **(inp-)** intricately
implicitus *pp of* **implicō ll** *adj* confused; **implicitus morbō** disabled by sickness
implic·ō -āre -āvī -ātus *or* **-āre -uī -itus** *tr* **(inp-)** to entwine, wrap; to intertwine; to involve; to envelop; to embrace, clasp, grasp; to connect, join, unite; to implicate; to kindle *(a fire)* **ll** *refl* **sē dextrae implicāre** to clasp *(s.o.'s)* right hand **ll** *pass* to be intimately associated; to be embroiled
implōrāti·ō -ōnis *f* **(inp-)** imploring
implōr·ō -āre -āvī -ātus *tr* **(inpl-)** to implore, appeal to; *(w. double acc)* to beg *(s.o.)* for; *(w.* **ab)** to ask for *(s.th.)* from
impl·uit -uere -uit *or* **-ūvit -ūtum** *intr* **(inp-)** *(w. dat)* to rain on
implūm·is -is -e *adj* **(inp-)** featherless, unfledged; without wings
impluviāt·us -a -um *adj* **(inpl-)** square, shaped liked an impluvium
impluv·ium -(i)ī *n* **(inp-)** impluvium, rain basin *(square basin built into the floor of the atrium to hold rain water; (rarely =* **compluvium:** *square opening in the roof of the atrium of a Roman house to get rid of smoke and let in light and air)*

impolītē *adv* **(inp-)** simply, without fancy words
impolīt·us -a -um *adj* **(inp-)** unpolished, rough; lacking culture; *(of materials)* in the crude state
impollūt·us -a -um *adj* **(inp-)** unsullied
im·pōnō -pōnere -posuī -positus *or* **-postus** *tr* **(inp-)** to impose; *(w. dat or* **in** + *acc)* to place on, lay on, set on; *(w. dat or* **super** + *acc)* to build *(house, bridge, city)* on; *(w. dat or* **ad)** to station *(soldiers)* in *or* at; *(w. dat or* **ad** *or* **in** + *acc)* to apply *(remedies)* to; *(w. dat)* **1** to place *(s.o.)* in command *or* control of, put *(s.o.)* in charge of; **2** to put *(garments)* on *(s.o.);* **3** to impose *(taxes, terms, laws, responsibilites, limits, etc.)* on; **4** to inflict *(wounds, blows, punishment)* on; *(w. dat, w.* **in** + *acc,* **in** + *abl, or* **suprā** + *acc)* to place, put, set, lay *(s.th. or s.o.)* on **‖** *intr (w. dat)* **1** to impose upon; **2** to trick, cheat
import·ō -āre -āvī -ātus *tr* **(inp-)** to bring in, import; to introduce; to bring about, cause; *(w. dat)* to inflict *(damage, trouble)* on
importūnit·ās -ātis *f* **(inp-)** importunity, rudeness, insolence; unfitness
importūn·us -a -um *adj* **(inp-)** inconvenient; unsuitable, out of place; troublesome, annoying; lacking consideration for others, rude, ruthless; stormy *(weather);* grim *(looks);* ill-omened
importuōs·us -a -um *adj* **(inp-)** without a harbor
imp·os -otis *adj* **(inp-)** out of control; *(w. gen)* not having control of; **impos animī** *(or* **mentis** *or* **suī)** out of one's mind
impositus (inp-) *pp of* **impōnō ‖** *adj* situated, located
impossibil·is -is -e *adj* **(inp-)** impossible
impostus *pp of* **impōnō**
imposuī *perf of* **impōnō**
impot·ēns -entis *adj* **(inp-)** impotent, powerless; lacking self-control, uncontrollable, wild, violent; *(w. gen)* having no control over; **impotēns suī** *(or* **animī)** out of one's mind
impotenter *adv* **(inp-)** impotently, weakly; without self-control, lawlessly, intemperately
impotenti·a -ae *f* **(inp-)** weakness, helplessness; lack of self-control, violence, fury, lawlessness
impraesentiārum *adv* **(inp-)** for the present, under present circumstances
imprāns·us -a -um *adj* **(inp-)** without breakfast *or* lunch, fasting
imprecāti·ō -ōnis *f* **(inp-)** the calling down of curses, imprecation
imprec·or -ārī -ātus sum *tr* **(inp-)** to call down *(a curse);* to invoke
impressī *perf of* **imprimō**

impressi·ō -ōnis *f* **(inp-)** pressure; attack, charge; rhythmical beat; emphasis; impression *(on the mind)*
impressus *pp of* **imprimō**
imprīmīs *or* **in prīmīs** *adv* **(inp-)** in the first place; chiefly, especially
im·primō -primere -pressī -pressus *tr* **(inp-)** to press down; to impress, imprint, stamp *(a seal, marks, patterns);* to thrust, drive in *(esp. weapons);* to plant *(the feet, kisses); (fig)* to impress; **animum quasi cēram imprimere** to impress the mind like wax
improbāti·ō -ōnis *f* **(inp-)** disapproval; *(leg)* discrediting *(of a witness)*
improbē *adv* **(inp-)** badly, wickedly, wrongfully; recklessly; persistently
improbit·ās -ātis *f* **(inp-)** wickedness, depravity; roguishness
improb·ō -āre -āvī -ātus *tr* **(inp-)** to disapprove of, condemn, blame, reject
improbul·us -a -um *adj* **(inp-)** somewhat impudent, naughty
improb·us -a -um *adj* below standard, inferior; bad, shameless; rebellious, unruly; restless, indomitable, self-willed; cruel, merciless; disloyal, ill-disposed; *(of language)* offensively rude
improcēr·us -a -um *adj* **(inp-)** undersized
imprōdict·us -a -um *adj* **(inp-)** not postponed
imprompt·us -a -um *adj* **(inp-)** slow
improperāt·us -a -um *adj* **(inp-)** unhurried
impropri·us -a -um *adj* **(inp-)** *(gram)* improper, incorrect
improsp·er -era -erum *adj* **(inp-)** unfortunate
improsperē *adv* **(inp-)** unfortunately
imprōvidē *adv* **(inp-)** without foresight, thoughtlessly
imprōvid·us -a -um *adj* **(inp-)** not foreseeing, not anticipating; *(w. gen)* indifferent to
imprōvīs·us -a -um *adj* **(inp-)** unexpected; **dē imprōvīsō** *(or* **ex imprōvīsō** *or* **imprōvīsō)** unexpectedly **‖** *npl* emergencies
imprūd·ēns -entis *adj* **(inp-)** not foreseeing, unsuspecting; off one's guard; inconsiderate; foolish, imprudent; *(w. gen)* **1** unaware of, ignorant of; **2** heedless of; **3** not experienced in
imprūdenter *adv* **(inp-)** without foresight, thoughtlessly, unintenionally; foolishly, imprudently
imprūdenti·a -ae *f* **(inp-)** thoughtlessness; ignorance, imprudence
impūb·ēs -eris *or* **impūb·is -is -e** *adj* **(inp-)** youthful, young, underage; beardless *(cheeks);* innocent, chaste, celibate, virgin; **annī impūbēs** childhood years
impud·ēns -entis *adj* **(inp-)** shameless
impudenter *adv* **(inp-)** shamelessly, impudently; immodestly

impudenti·a -ae *f* **(inp-)** shamelessness, impudence; immodesty
impudīciti·a -ae *f* immodesty, lewdness, shamelessness
impudīc·us -a -um *adj* **(inp-)** immodest, lewd, shameless
impugnāti·ō -ōnis *f* **(inp-)** assault, attack
impugn·ō -āre -āvī -ātus *tr* **(inp-)** to assault, attack; *(fig)* to impugn; *(w. acc & inf)* to assert in opposition *(that)*
impulsi·ō -ōnis *f* **(inp-)** pressure; impulse
impuls·or -ōris *m* **(inp-)** instigator
impulsus *pp of* **impellō**
impuls·us -ūs *m* **(inp-)** blow, impact, shock; impulse; instigation, incitement
impūnē *adv* **(inp-)** with impunity, unpunished, scot-free; safely, unscathed
impūnit·ās -ātis *f* **(inp-)** impunity
impūnītē *adv* **(inp-)** with impunity
impūnīt·us -a -um *adj* **(inp-)** unpunished; unrestrained; safe
impūrāt·us -a -um *adj* **(inp-)** filthy
impūrē *adv* **(inp-)** impurely
impūrit·ās -ātis *f* **(inp-)** impurity
impūriti·ae -ārum *fpl* **(inp-)** filth
impūr·us -a -um *adj* **(inp-)** impure; unclean, filthy
imputāt·us -a -um *adj* **(inp-)** unpruned, untrimmed
imput·ō -āre -āvī -ātus *tr* **(inp-)** to charge to someone's account, enter in an account; *(w. dat)* **1** to charge to; **2** to ascribe to; **3** to give credit for *(s.th.)* to; **4** to put the blame for *(s.th.)* on
īmul·us -a -um *adj* cute little
īm·us -a -um *adj* deepest, lowest; last; the bottom of, the foot of, the tip of ‖ *n* bottom, depth; **ab īmō** utterly; **ab īmō ad summum** from top to bottom; **ex īmō** utterly, completely ‖ *npl* lower world
in- *pref* **(n** is assimilated to following **l, m,** and **r; becomes m** before **b** and **p; disappears** before **gn) 1** combines, usu. with verbs, in the local or figurative senses of the preposition, e.g., **inaedificāre** to build in *(a place); also with intensive force, e.g.,* **increpāre** to make a loud noise; **2** *inchoative:* **īnsūdāre** to begin to sweat, break out in a sweat; **3** *negative or privative pref, e.g.:* **incognitus** unknown
in *prep (w. abl)* **1** in, on, upon; **2** among; **3** at; **4** before; **5** under; **6** *(of time)* during, within, in, at, in the course of, on the point of; **7** in case of; **8** in relation to; **9** subject to; **10** affected by; **11** engaged in, involved in; **12** over: **pōns in flūmine** a bridge over a river ‖ *(w. acc)* **1** into; **2** up to, as far as *(a point of space or time);* **3** *(indicating person toward whom feelings are directed)* toward, to, for; **4** until; **5** about, respecting; **6** *(w. verbs of*

opposition or hostility) against; **7** for, with a view to; **8** according to, after; *(w. verbs of sending, traveling)* to *(a country, city);* **9** *(w. verbs of spending)* on; **10** *(w. verbs of distributing)* among
inaccess·us -a -um *adj* inaccessible
inac·ēscō -ēscere -uī *intr* to turn sour
Īnachid·ēs -ae *m* descendant of Inachus *(esp.* Perseus and Epaphus)
Īnach·us or **Īnach·os -ī** *m* first king of Argos and father of Io
inacuī *perf of* **inacēscō**
inadsc- = ināsc-
inadt- = inatt-
inadūst·us -a -um *adj* unburned, unsinged
inaedific·ō -āre -āvī -ātus *tr* to build on, build as an addition, erect, construct; to wall up, barricade; *(w.* in + *abl)* to build *(s.th.)* on top of
inaequābil·is -is -e *adj* uneven
inaequābiliter *adv* unevenly, unequally
inaequāl·is -is -e *adj* uneven, unequal; unlike; changeable, inconstant
inaequālit·ās -ātis *f* unevenness
inaequāliter *adv* unevenly
inaequāt·us -a -um *adj* unequal
inaequ·ō -āre -āvī -ātus *tr* to level off
inaestimābil·is -is -e *adj* inestimable; invaluable; valueless
inaestu·ō -āre *intr* to seethe; to flare up
inaffectāt·us -a -um *adj* unaffected, natural
inamābil·is -is -e *adj* hateful, revolting
inamārēsc·ō -ere *intr* to become bitter
inambitiōs·us -a -um *adj* unambitious
inambulāti·ō -ōnis *f* walking about, strutting about
inambul·ō -āre -āvī *intr* to walk up and down; to stroll about
inamoen·us -a -um *adj* unpleasant
ināni·ae -ārum *fpl* emptiness
inānilogist·a -ae *m* chatterbox
inānīment·um -ī *n* empty space
inanim·us -a -um *adj* inanimate
inān·is -is -e *adj* empty, void; deserted, abandoned, unoccupied; hollow; worthless, idle; lifeless, unsubstantial; penniless; unprofitable; groundless ‖ *n* empty space, vacuum; emptiness; worthlessness
inānit·ās -ātis *f* empty space, emptiness; uselessness, worthlessness
ināniter *adv* uselessly, vainly
inarāt·us -a -um *adj* untilled, unplowed
inār·dēscō -dēscere -sī *intr* to catch fire, burn, glow
inārēsc·ō -ere *intr* to become dry, dry up
inārsī *perf of* **inārdēscō**
ināscēns·us -a -um *adj* not climbed
inassuēt·us -a -um *adj* unaccustomed

inattenuāt·us -a -um *adj* undiminished; unappeased

inaud·āx -ācis *adj* timid

inaud·iō -īre -īvī *or* **-iī -ītus** *tr* **(indau-)** to hear, learn, get wind of

inaudīt·us -a -um *adj* unheard-of, unprecedented; unusual; without a court hearing

inaugurātō *adv* after taking the auspices

inaugur·ō -āre -āvī -ātus *tr* to inaugurate, consecrate, install ‖ *intr* to take the auspices

inaurāt·us -a -um *adj* gilded, gilt, gold-plated

inaur·ēs -ium *fpl* earrings

inaur·ō -āre -āvī -ātus *tr* to goldplate, gild; to line the pockets of *(s.o.)* with gold

inauspicātō *adv* without consulting the auspices

inauspicāt·us -a -um *adj* undertaken without auspices; unlucky

inaus·us -a -um *adj* unattempted

inb- = imb-

incaedu·us -a -um *adj* uncut, unfelled

incal·ēscō -ēscere -uī *intr* to get warm, get hot; to get excited

incalfac·iō -ere *tr* to warm, heat

incallidē *adv* unskillfully

incallid·us -a -um *adj* unskillful; stupid, simple, clumsy

incand·ēscō -ēscere -uī *intr* to become white; to get white-hot

incantāt·us -a -um *adj* enchanted

incān·us -a -um *adj* grown grey

incassum *adv* in vain

incastīgāt·us -a -um *adj* unscolded, unpunished

incautē *adv* incautiously, recklessly

incaut·us -a -um *adj* incautious, inconsiderate, thoughtless, reckless; unforeseen, unexpected; unguarded

in·cēdō -cēdere -cessī -cessum *intr* to go, walk, move; to step, stride, strut; to proceed; to come along, happen, occur, appear, arrive; to advance, go on; *(of troops)* to march, advance

incelebrāt·us -a -um *adj* unheralded

incēnāt·us -a -um *adj* supperless

incendiārius -(i)ī *m* agitator; arsonist

incend·ium -(i)ī *n* fire; heat

incen·dō -dere -dī -sus *tr* to light, set on fire, burn; to light up, make bright; *(fig)* to inflame, fire up, excite, enrage

incēn·is -is -e *adj* dinnerless

incēnsi·ō -ōnis *f* burning

incēns·us -a -um *adj* not registered *(w. the censor)*

incēnsus *pp of* **incendō**

incepti·ō -ōnis *f* inception, beginning; undertaking

incept·ō -āre -āvī -ātus *tr* to begin; to undertake

incept·or -ōris *m* beginner, originator

incept·us -a -um *pp of* **incipiō** ‖ *n* beginning; undertaking, attempt, enterprise; subject, theme

in·cernō -cernere -crēvī -crētus *tr* to sift

incēr·ō -āre -āvī -ātus *tr* to wax, cover with wax, coat with wax

incertē *adv* uncertainly

incertō *adv* uncertainly

incert·ō -āre -āvī -ātus *tr* to render doubtful, make uncertain

incert·us -a -um *adj* uncertain; vague, obscure; doubtful; unsure, hesitant ‖ *n* uncertainty, insecurity; contingency; **in incertum** for an indefinite time

incessī *perf of* **incēdō**

incess·ō -ere -ī *or* **-īvī** *or* **-uī** *tr* to fall upon, assault; to reproach, accuse, attack

incess·us -ūs *m* walk, gait, pace; trampling; invasion, attack; advance; procession

incestē *adv* impurely, sinfully; indecently

in·cidō -cidere -cidī -cāsum *intr* to happen, occur; *(w.* **ad** *or* **in** *+ acc)* to fall into, fall upon; *(w.* **in** *+ acc)* **1** to come upon unexpectedly, fall in with; **2** to attack; *(w.* **dat** *or* **in** *+ acc)* **1** to occur to *(mentally);* **2** to fall on *(a certain day);* **3** to befall, happen to; **4** to agree with

incī·dō -dere -dī -sus *tr* to carve, engrave, inscribe; to cut, sever; *(fig)* to cut into, cut short, put an end to, break off, interrupt

incīl·e -is *n* ditch, trench

in·cingō -cingere -cīnxī -cīnctus *tr* to drape; to wreathe; to invest, surround

incin·ō -ere *tr* to sing; to play

incipessō *see* **incipissō**

in·cipiō -cipere -cēpī -ceptus *tr* & *intr* to begin, start

incipiss·ō -ere *tr* to begin

incīsē *or* **incīsim** *adv* in short phrases

incīsi·ō -ōnis *f* incision; *(rhet)* short phrase

incīsus *pp of* **incīdō**

incitāment·um -ī *n* incentive

incitāti·ō -ōnis *f* inciting, rousing; speed

incitāt·us -a -um *adj* rapid, speedy; **equō incitātō** at full gallop

incit·ō -āre -āvī -ātus *tr* to incite, urge on, spur on, drive on; to stimulate; to inspire; to stir up, arouse; to increase; **currentem incitāre** *(fig)* to spur a willing horse ‖ *refl* to rush

incit·us -a -um *adj* rapid, swift; immovable; **ad incita** *(or* **ad incitās) adigere** to bring to a standstill

inclāmit·ō -āre -āvī -ātus *tr* to cry out against, revile, abuse

inclām·ō -āre -āvī -ātus *tr* to call out to; to invoke; to shout at, scold, revile ‖ *intr* to yell

inclār·ēscō -ēscere -uī *intr* to become famous

inclēm·ēns -entis *adj* harsh, unmerciful; violent *(movement)*
inclēmenter *adv* harshly; rudely
inclēmenti·a -ae *f* harshness, cruelty
inclīnāti·ō -ōnis *f* leaning; inclination, tendency, bias; change; *(gram)* inflection
inclīnāt·us -a -um *adj* inclined, prone; sinking; low, deep; *(gram)* inflected
inclīn·ō -āre -āvī -ātus *tr* to bend, turn; to turn back, drive back, repulse; to shift *(e.g., blame);* to change; *(gram)* to inflect *(nouns or verbs)* ‖ *refl & pass* to lean, bend, turn; to change *(esp. for the worse)* ‖ *pass (mil)* to fall back ‖ *intr* to bend, turn, lean, dip, sink; to change, deteriorate; to change for the better
inclit·us -a -um *adj* famous
inclū·dō -dere -sī -sus *tr* to shut in, confine, lock up; to include; to insert; to block, shut off, obstruct; to restrain, control; to close, end *(e.g., a day)*
inclūsi·ō -ōnis *f* locking up, confinement
inclut·us -a -um *adj* famous
incoct·us -a -um *pp of* **incoquō** ‖ *adj* uncooked, raw; undigested
incōgitābil·is -is -e *adj* thoughtless, inconsiderate
incōgit·āns -antis *adj* unthinking, thoughtless
incōgitanti·a -ae *f* thoughtlessness
incōgitāt·us -a -um *adj* thoughtless, inconsiderate
incōgit·ō -āre -āvī -ātus *tr* to think up
incognit·us -a -um *adj* not investigated; unknown, unrecognized, unidentified, incognito; unparalleled
incohāt·us *or* **inchoāt·us -a -um** *adj* only begun, unfinished, imperfect; temporary *(structure)*
incoh·ō -āre -āvī -ātus *tr* to begin
incol·a -ae *mf* inhabitant; resident alien
incol·ō -cre -uī *tr* to live in, inhabit, occupy ‖ *intr* to live, reside
incolum·is -is -e *adj* unharmed, safe and sound, unscathed, alive; *(w. abl)* safe from
incolumit·ās -ātis *f* safety
incomitāt·us -a -um *adj* unaccompanied
incommendāt·us -a -um *adj* unprotected
incommodē *adv* at the wrong time; inconveniently; annoyingly; improperly; unfortunately
incommodestic·us -a -um *adj (coll)* ill-timed, inconvenient
incommodit·ās -ātis *f* inconvenience; unsuitableness; disadvantage
incommod·ō -āre -āvī -ātum *intr (w. dat)* to inconvenience, be inconvenient for, be annoying to
incommod·us -a -um *adj* inconvenient; troublesome, tiresome, annoying; disadvanta-

geous, unfavorable; unpleasant, disagreeable ‖ *n* inconvenience, discomfort; disadvantage; misfortune, trouble; *(med)* ailment; *(mil)* setback, disaster
incommūtābil·is -is -e *adj* unchangeable
incomparābil·is -is -e *adj* unequaled, incomparable
incompert·us -a -um *adj* unknown, undetermined; forgotten
incompositē *adv* in disorder
incomposit·us -a -um *adj* disordered, poorly arranged, poorly written; clumsy, awkward *(movements);* disorganized *(troops)*
incomprehēnsibil·is -is -e *adj* incomprehensible
incompt·us -a -um *adj* unkempt, messy; untidy; simple, unstudied; unpolished *(writing, speech)*
inconcess·us -a -um *adj* forbidden, unlawful
inconcili·ō -āre -āvī -ātus *tr* to deceive, trick; to rob, fleece
inconcinn·us -a -um *adj* clumsy, awkward; absurd
inconcuss·us -a -um *adj* unshaken
inconditē *adv* confusedly
incondit·us -a -um *adj* unorganized, disorderly, confused; irregular; rough, undeveloped *(style);* raw *(jokes)*
incōnsīderātē *adv* thoughtlessly
incōnsīderāt·us -a um *adj* thoughtless
incōnsōlābil·is -is -e *adj* inconsolable; *(fig)* incurable
incōnst·āns -antis *adj* inconsistent, fickle, shifty
incōnstanter *adv* inconsistently
incōnstanti·a -ae *f* inconsistency, fickleness
incōnsultē *adv* indiscreetly
incōnsult·us -a -um *adj* indiscreet, ill-advised; not consulted
incōnsult·us -ūs *m* lack of consultation; **incōnsultū meō** without consulting me
incōnsumpt·us -a -um *adj* unconsumed
incontāmināt·us -a -um *adj* untainted
incontent·us -a -um *adj* loose, untuned *(string)*
incontin·ēns -entis *adj* intemperate
incontinenter *adv* without self-control, intemperately
incontinenti·a -ae *f* lack of self-control
inconveni·ēns -entis *adj* unsuitable, dissimilar
inco·quō -quere -xī -ctus *tr* to boil *(in or with);* to dye; to imbue
incorrēct·us -a -um *adj* uncorrected
incorruptē *adv* honestly, fairly
incorrupt·us -a -um *adj* intact, unspoiled, untainted; uncorrupted; not open to bribes, incorruptible; chaste; genuine, authentic
incoxī *perf of* **incoquō**

increb(r)·esco -escere -ui *intr* to grow; to rise; to increase; to spread

incredibil·is -is -e *adj* incredible

incredibiliter *adv* incredibly

incredul·us -a -um *adj* incredulous

increment·um -i *n* growth, increase; increment, addition; addition to the family, offspring

increpit·o -are -avi -atus *tr* to scold, rebuke

increp·o -are -ui -itus *or* -avi -atus *tr* to cause to make noise, cause to ring; to rattle; *(of Jupiter)* to thunder at; to scold, rebuke; to protest against; *(of sounds)* to strike *(the ears); (w. acc & inf)* to say reproachfully that, to remark indignantly that ‖ *intr* to make noise; to snap, rustle, rattle, clash; to speak angrily; *(of a bow)* to twang; *(of flying object)* to whiz, whir; **suspicio tumultus increpat** the suspicion of a riot sounds the alarm

incr·esco -escere -evi *intr* to grow, increase; *(w. dat or abl)* to grow in *or* upon

incretus *pp of* incerno

increvi *perf of* incerno *and* incresco

incruentat·us -a -um *adj* unbloodied

incruent·us -a -um *adj* bloodless, without bloodshed

incrust·o -are -avi -atus *tr* to coat, cover with a coat, encrust

incub·o -are -ui -itum *intr (w. dat)* 1 to lie in *or* upon; 2 to lean on; 3 to brood over; 4 to watch jealously over

incu·do -dere -di -sus *or* -ssus *tr* to indent by hammering; to emboss

inculc·o -are -avi -atus *tr* to impress, inculcate; *(w. dat)* to force *(s.th.)* upon

inculpat·us -a -um *adj* blameless

inculte *adv* uncouthly, roughly

incult·us -a -um *adj* untilled, uncultivated; neglected, slovenly; rough, uneducated, uncivilized ‖ *npl* desert, wilderness, the wilds

incult·us -us *m* neglect; dirt, squalor

in·cumbo -cumbere -cubui -cubitum *intr (w. dat or in + acc)* 1 to lean on *or* against; 2 to lie down on *(bed, couch);* 3 to bend to *(the oars);* 4 to light on, fall on; 5 *(fig)* to press upon, burden, oppress, weigh down; 6 to apply oneself to, take pains with; 7 to pay attention to; *(w. ad or in + acc)* to be inclined toward, lean toward

incunabul·a -orum *npl* baby clothes; *(fig)* cradle, infancy; birthplace; origin, source

incurat·us -a -um *adj* neglected; uncured

incuri·a -ae *f* carelessness, negligence

incuriose *adv* carelessly

incurios·us -a -um *adj* careless, unconcerned, indifferent; neglected

in·curro -currere -curri *or* -cucurri -cursus *tr* to attack ‖ *intr (w. dat or in + acc)* 1 to run

into, rush at, charge, attack; 2 to invade; 3 to extend to; 4 to meet, run into; 5 to fall on, coincide with

incursi·o -onis *f* incursion, invasion, raid; attack; collision

incurs·o -are -avi -atus *tr* to attack; to invade ‖ *intr (w. dat or in + acc)* 1 to attack; 2 to run into, bump against; 3 to strike, meet *(e.g., the eyes);* 4 to affect, touch, move

incurs·us -us *m* attack; invasion, inroad, raid; collision, impact

incurv·o -are -avi -atus *tr* to bend

incurv·us -a -um *adj* bent, crooked

inc·us -udis *f* anvil

incusati·o -onis *f* accusation

incus·o -are -avi -atus *tr* to blame, find fault with, accuse

incussi *perf of* incutio

incussus *pp of* incutio

incuss·us -us *m* shock

incustodit·us -a -um *adj* unguarded; unconcealed; imprudent

incus·us -a -um *pp of* incudo ‖ *adj* forged; embossed; **lapis incusus** indented millstone

incu·tio -tere -ssi -ssus *tr* to throw; to produce; *(w. dat or in + acc)* to strike *(s.th.)* on *or* against; *(w. dat)* 1 to strike into, instill in; 2 to throw at, to fling upon; **metum incutere** *(w. dat)* to strike fear into; **scipione in caput alicuius incutere** to beat s.o. over the head with a stick

indagati·o -onis *f* investigation, search

indagat·or -oris *m,* indagatr·ix -icis *f* investigator

indag·o -are -avi -atus *tr* to track down, hunt; to investigate, explore

indag·o -inis *f* dragnet; **indagine agere** to ferret out

indaudio *see* inaudio

inde *adv* from there; from that source, therefrom; from that time on, after that, thereafter; then; from that cause

indebit·us -a -um *adj* that is not owed, not due

indec·ens -entis *adj* unbecoming, improper, indecent

indecenter *adv* improperly, indecently

indec·eo -ere *tr* to be improper for ‖ *intr (w. dat)* to be inappropriate to

indeclinat·us -a -um *adj* unchanged, constant

indec·or -oris *or* indecor·is -is -e *adj* disgraceful, dishonorable; cowardly

indecore *adv* indecently, improperly

indecor·o -are -avi -atus *tr* to disgrace

indecor·us -a -um *adj* unsightly

indefens·us -a -um *adj* undefended

indefess·us -a -um *adj* tireless; not tired

indeflet·us -a -um *adj* unwept

indeiect·us -a -um *adj* undemolished

indelebil·is -is -e *adj* indestructible, indelible

indēlībāt·us -a -um *adj* undiminished
indemnāt·us -a -um *adj* unconvicted
indēplōrāt·us -a -um *adj* unwept
indēprēns·us -a -um *adj* undetected
indeptus *pp of* **indipīscor**
indēsert·us -a -um *adj* unforsaken
indēspect·us -a -um *adj* unfathomable
indēstrīct·us -a -um *adj* unscathed
indētōns·us -a -um *adj* unshorn
indēvītāt·us -a -um *adj* unavoidable, unerring (e.g., arrow)
ind·ex -icis *m* index, sign, mark; indication, proof; title (of book); informer, spy; index finger
Indi·a -ae *f* India
Ind·ī -ōrum *npl* Indians, people of India
indicāti·ō -ōnis *f* setting the price; statement, declaration
indīc·ēns -entis *adj* not speaking; **mē indīcente** without a word from me
indic·ium -(i)ī *n* information, disclosure, evidence; indication, proof; permission to give evidence; reward for giving evidence; **indiciō esse** to give evidence; to be an indication *or* proof; **indicium afferre** (or **dēferre**) to adduce evidence; **indicium facere** to give away a secret; to give an indication *or* warning
indic·ō -āre -āvī -ātus *tr* to point out; to reveal, disclose; to betray, inform against; to put a price on ‖ *intr* to give evidence
in·dīcō -dīcere -dīxī -dictus *tr* to proclaim, announce, publish; to summon, convoke; to impose (a fine); **bellum indīcere** to declare war; **diem indīcere** to set a date
indict·us -a -um *adj* unsaid; **causā indictā** without a hearing
Indic·us -a -um *adj* Indian ‖ *m* Indian ‖ *n* indigo
indidem *adv* from the same place; from the same source, from the same thing
indiffer·ēns -entis *adj* (morally) indifferent; unconcerned, indifferent
indigen·a -ae *adj masc & fem* native
indig·ēns -entis *adj* indigent; (w. gen) in need of
indigenti·a -ae *f* indigence, need; craving
indig·eō -ēre -uī *intr* (w. gen or abl) **1** to need, be in need of; **2** to require; (w. gen) to crave, desire
indig·es -etis *adj* indigenous, native ‖ *m* native god; national hero
indīgest·us -a -um *adj* unarranged, disorderly, confused, in confusion
indignābund·us -a -um *adj* highly indignant
indign·āns -antis *adj* indignant; (w. gen) resentful of

indignāti·ō -ōnis *f* indignation, displeasure; provocation, occasion for indignation ‖ *fpl* expressions of indignation
indignē *adv* unworthily; undeservedly; shamefully, outrageously; **indignē ferre** (or **patī**) to be indignant at
indignit·ās -ātis *f* unworthiness; indignation; indignity, shameful treatment; enormity, shamelessness
indign·or -ārī -ātus sum *tr* to be indignant at, displeased at, angry at, offended by
indign·us -a -um *adj* unworthy, undeserving; undeserved; shameful, scandalous; (w. abl) **1** unworthy of; **2** not deserving; **3** not worth; (w. gen) unworthy of, undeserving of; **indignum!** shame!
indig·us -a -um *adj* needy, indigent; (w. gen or abl) in need of
indīlig·ēns -entis *adj* careless
indīligenter *adv* carelessly
indīligenti·a -ae *f* carelessness
ind·ipīscor -ipīscī -eptus sum *or* **indipīsc·ō -ere** *tr* to obtain, get; to win, acquire ‖ *intr* (w. dē + abl) to gain one's point about
indīrept·us -a -um *adj* unplundered
indīscrēt·us -a -um *adj* closely connected, inseparable; used indiscriminately; indistinguishable; **indīscrētum est** it makes no difference
indisertē *adv* ineloquently
indisert·us -a -um *adj* without eloquence
indisposit·us -a -um *adj* confused, disordered
indissolūbil·is -is -e *adj* imperishable, indestructible
indistīnct·us -a -um *adj* indistinct; applied without distinction
inditus *pp of* **indō**
indīvidu·us -a -um *adj* indivisible; inseparable; equal, impartial ‖ *n* atom, indivisible particle
in·dō -dere -didī -ditus *tr* to put, place; to introduce; to impart, give; (w. in + acc) to put *or* place (s. th.) into *or* on, insert into
indocil·is -is -e *adj* slow to learn; impossible to teach; untrained, ignorant
indoctē *adv* unskillfully
indoct·us -a -um *adj* untaught, untrained; ignorant, uninformed
indolenti·a -ae *f* freedom from pain; insensibility to pain
indol·ēs -is *f* inborn quality, natural quality; nature, character; natural ability, talent; (w. gen) natural capacity for, natural tendency toward
indol·ēscō -ēscere -uī *intr* to feel sorry; to feel resentment
indomābil·is -is -e *adj* untamable
indomit·us -a -um *adj* untamed, wild; indomitable; unrestrained; unmanageable

indorm·iō -**īre** -**īvī** *or* -**iī** -**ītum** *intr* to fall asleep; to grow careless; *(w. dat or abl or in + abl)* **1** to fall asleep at *or* on; **2** to fall asleep over; **3** to become careless about

indōtāt·us -**a** -**um** *adj* without dowry; poor; without funeral rites; **ars indōtāta** *(rhet)* unadorned style

indubitābil·is -**is** -**e** *adj* indubitable

indubitāt·us -**a** -**um** *adj* undoubted

indubit·ō -**āre** *intr (w. dat)* to begin to distrust, begin to doubt

indubi·us -**a** -**um** *adj* undoubted, certain

indūci·ae *or* **indūti·ae** -**ārum** *fpl* armistice, truce

in·dūcō -**dūcere** -**dūxī** -**ductus** *tr* to lead in, bring in; to introduce; to induce; to seduce; to overlay, drape, wrap, cover; to put on, clothe; to strike out, erase; to repeal, cancel; to present, exhibit; *(theat)* to stage, put on; to mislead, delude; *(w. in + acc)* **1** to lead to, lead into, lead against; **2** to bring into, introduce into; **3** to enter into *(account books)*; *(w. dat or super + acc)* to put *(item of apparel, esp. shoes)* on, spread *(s.th.)* over, wrap *(s.th.)* around, draw *(s.th.)* over; **animūm** *(or in animum)* **indūcere** to make up one's mind, convince oneself, be convinced, conclude, suppose, imagine

inducti·ō -**ōnis** *f* bringing in, introduction, admission; resolution, determination; intention; induction, generalization; **animī inductiō** inclination; **errōris inductiō** deception

induct·or -**ōris** *m (hum) (referring to a whip)* persuader

induct·us -**a** -**um** *pp of* **indūco** ‖ *adj* alien, adventitious

induct·us -**ūs** *m* inducement

indūcul·a -**ae** *f* slip, petticoat

indulg·ēns -**entis** *adj* indulgent, lenient; *(w. dat or in + acc)* lenient toward, kind toward

indulgenter *adv* indulgently, leniently, kindly

indulgenti·a -**ae** *f* indulgence, leniency, kindness

indul·geō -**gēre** -**sī** -**sus** *tr (w. dat)* to grant, concede *(s.th.)* to; **veniam indulgēre** *(w. dat)* to make allowances for ‖ *refl* **sibi indulgēre** to be self-indulgent, take liberties ‖ *intr (w. dat)* **1** to be lenient toward, be kind to, be tender to; **2** to yield to, give way to; **3** to indulge in, be addicted to; **4** to make allowance for; **5** *(of deities, fate, etc.)* to look favorably on, show kindness to; **6** to take pleasure in; **7** to devote oneself to *(an activity)*

ind·uō -**uere** -**uī** -**ūtus** *tr* to put on *(e.g., a tunic)*; to cover, wrap, clothe, array; to envelop; to engage in; to assume, put on; to assume the part of; to involve; *(w. dat)* to put *(e.g., a tunic)* on *(s.o.)*

indup· = **imp-**

indūr·ēscō -**ēscere** -**uī** *intr* to become hard, harden

indūr·ō -**āre** -**āvī** -**ātus** *tr* to harden

indūruī *perf of* **indūrēscō**

Ind·us -**a** -**um** *adj* Indian ‖ *m* Indian; Ethiopian; mahout

indusāri·us -**ī** *m* maker of women's underwear

indusiāt·us -**a** -**um** wearing underwear

industri·a -**ae** *f* industry, diligence; **dē** *(or* **ex)** **industriā** diligently; **industriā** *(or* **dē** *or* **ex industriā** *or* **ob industriam)** on purpose, deliberately

industriē *adv* industriously, diligently

industri·us -**a** -**um** *adj* industrious, diligent, painstaking

indūti·ae *or* **indūci·ae** -**ārum** *fpl* armistice, truce

indūt·us -**a** -**um** *pp of* **induō**

indūt·us -**ūs** *m* putting on, wearing

induvi·ae -**ārum** *fpl* clothes

inebri·ō -**āre** -**āvī** -**ātus** *tr* to make drunk; *(fig)* to fill *(e.g., the ear with gossip)*

inedi·a -**ae** *f* fasting; starvation

inēdit·us -**a** -**um** *adj* not made known, unknown, unpublished

inēleg·āns -**antis** *adj* inelegant, undistinguished

inēleganter *adv* without style, poorly; without clear thought

inēluctābil·is -**is** -**e** *adj* inescapable

inēmor·ior -**ī** *intr (w. dat)* to die at the sight of

inempt·us -**a** -**um** *adj* unpurchased; without ransom

inēnārrābil·is -**is** -**e** *adj* indescribable

inēnārrābiliter *adv* indescribably

inēnōdābil·is -**is** -**e** *adj* inexplicable

in·eō -**īre** -**īvī** -**iī** -**itus** *tr* to enter; to enter upon, undertake, form; to begin, engage in; **ab ineunte pueritiā** from earliest boyhood; **cōnsilium inīre** to form a plan; **in cōnsilium inīre ut** *(or* **quā** *or* **quemadmodum)** to plan how to *(do s.th.)*; **ineunte vēre** at the beginning of spring; **inīre numerum** *(w. gen)* to go into an enumeration of, enumerate; **inīre ratiōnem** *(w. gen)* to form an estimate of; **inīre ratiōnem ut** *(or* **quā** *or* **quemadmodum)** to consider, find out, *or* figure out how to *(do s.th.)*; **viam inīre** to begin a trip; to find a way, devise a means

ineptē *adv* foolishly, absurdly, inappropriately, pointlessly

inepti·a -**ae** *f* foolishness ‖ *fpl* nonsense; trifles

inept·iō -**īre** *intr* to be absurd, make a fool of oneself

inept·us -**a** -**um** *adj* foolish, silly; inept, awkward, absurd; unsuitable, out of place; tactless, tasteless

inerm·is -is -e *or* inerm·us -a -um *adj* unarmed, defenseless; undefended; toothless *(gums);* harmless; peaceful

inerr·āns -antis *adj* not wandering, fixed

inerr·ō -āre -āvī *intr* to wander about

iner·s -tis *adj* unskilled, incompetent; inactive, sluggish; weak, soft, helpless; stagnant, motionless; ineffective; dull, insipid; numbing *(cold);* expressionless *(eyes);* uneventful, leisurely *(time)*

inerti·a -ae *f* lack of skill, ignorance, rudeness; inactivity; laziness

inērudīt·us -a -um *adj* uneducated; crude, inconsiderate

inēsc·ō -āre -āvī -ātus *tr* to bait; *(fig)* to bait, trap; to gorge

inēvect·us -a -um *adj* mounted

inēvītābil·is -is -e *adj* inevitable, inescapable

inexcīt·us -a -um *adj* unexcited, calm

inexcūsābil·is -is -e *adj* without excuse; admitting no excuse

inexercitāt·us -a -um *adj* untrained

inexhaust·us -a -um *adj* unexhausted, not wasted; inexhaustible

inexōrābil·is -is -e *adj* inexorable, relentless; unswerving, strict

inexperrēct·us -a -um *adj* unawakened

inexpert·us -a -um *adj* untried, untested; novel; *(w. abl or adversus or in + acc)* inexperienced in, unaccustomed to

inexpiābil·is -is -e *adj* inexpiable, not to be atoned for; irreconcilable, implacable

inexplēbil·is -is -e *adj* insatiable

inexplēt·us -a -um *adj* unsatisfied, unfilled

inexplicābil·is -is -e *adj* inextricable; inexplicable, baffling; impassable *(road);* involved, unending *(war);* incurable *(disease)*

inexplōrātō *adv* without reconnoitering

inexplorāt·us -a -um *adj* unexplored; unfamiliar; not investigated

inexpugnābil·is -is -e *adj* impregnable, unassailable; invincible

inexspectāt·us -a -um *adj* unexpected, unforeseen

inexsuperābil·is -is -e *adj* insuperable, insurmountable

inextīnct·us -a -um *adj* unextinguished; insatiable

inextrīcābil·is -is -e *adj* inextricable

īnfabrē *adv* unskillfully

īnfabricāt·us -a -um *adj* unshaped, untrimmed, unwrought

īnfacētē *adv* boorishly

īnfacēti·ae -ārum *fpl* crudities

īnfacēt·us -a -um *adj* not witty, not funny, dull, stupid

īnfācund·us -a -um *adj* ineloquent

īnfāmi·a -ae *f* bad reputation; disrepute, disgrace; scandal; *(w. gen)* stigma of; *(pol)* pub-

lic disgrace *(involving loss of some civil rights)*

īnfām·is -is -e *adj* infamous, notorious, disreputable, disgraceful; disgraced; *(w. in + acc or abl)* suspected of misconduct with; **īnfāmis digitus** middle finger *(used in obscene gestures)*

īnfām·ō -āre -āvī -ātus *tr* to defame, dishonor, disgrace; to smear *(esp. groundlessly)* **‖** *pass (w. in + acc)* to be suspected of misconduct with

īnfand·us -a -um *adj* unspeakable, shocking

īnf·āns -antis *adj* speechless, unable to speak; baby, infant, young; childish, silly; *(fig)* tongue-tied **‖** *mf* infant

īnfanti·a -ae *f* infancy; childishness; inability to speak; lack of eloquence; young children

īnfar- = īnfer-

īnfatu·ō -āre -āvī -ātus *tr* to make a fool of

īnfaust·us -a -um *adj* ill-omened, unpropitious; unfortunate

īnfect·or -ōris *m* dyer

īnfect·us -a -um *pp of* īnficiō **‖** *adj* not made, not done, undone, unfinished; unwrought *(metals);* unachieved; infeasible; **foedere īnfectō** without concluding a treaty; **rē īnfectā** without achieving the objective

īnfēcundit·ās -ātis *f* unfruitfulness

īnfēcund·us -a -um *adj* unfruitful

īnfēlīcit·ās -ātis *f* bad luck, misfortune

īnfēlīciter *adv* unhappily; unluckily; unsuccessfully

īnfēlīc·ō -āre *tr* to make unhappy

īnfēl·īx -īcis *adj* unfruitful; unhappy; unfortunate, unlucky; causing misfortune, ruinous; ill-omened; pessimistic

īnfēnsē *adv* with hostility, aggressively

īnfēns·ō -āre -āvī -ātus *tr* to antagonize; to make dangerous **‖** *intr* to be hostile

īnfēns·us -a -um *adj* hostile, antagonistic; dangerous; *(w. dat or in + acc)* **1** hostile to; **2** dangerous to

īnfer·a -ōrum *npl* lower world

īnfer·ciō -cīre -sī -ctus *tr* (-far-) to stuff, cram

īnfer·ī -ōrum *mpl* the dead; the world below

īnferi·ae -ārum *fpl* rites and offerings to the dead

īnferi·or -or -us *adj* lower, farther down; *(fig)* inferior; subsequent; later, more recent *(period);* *(w. abl or in + abl)* inferior, worse in *(some respect)*

īnferius *adv* lower, at a lower level; too low; at a later stage

īnfernē *adv* below, beneath

īnfern·us -a -um *adj* lower; infernal, of the lower world **‖** *mpl* the shades below **‖** *npl* the lower world

īnferō īnferre intulī illātus *tr* to bring in, carry in; to import; to introduce; to bring forward, adduce, produce; *(w. dat)* to cause *(injury, death, delay)* to; to bury, inter; *(w.* in + *acc)* to reduce to; *(w. dat)* to pay *(money)* to *(e.g., the treasury);* **arma** *(or* **bellum)** **īnferre** *(w. dat)* to make war on; **gradum** *(or* **pedem** *or* **signa) īnferre** to advance *(usually to attack);* **conversa signa īnferre** *(w. dat)* to turn around and attack; **facēs** *(or* **ignem) īnferre** *(w. dat)* to set fire to; **honōrēs īnferre** to offer a sacrifice; **manūs īnferre** *(w. dat)* to lay hands on; **nōmen in tabulās īnferre** to enter one's name in the records ‖ *refl & pass* to enter'; to rush in *or* on; to go, march, charge, plunge; **sē in perīculum īnferre** to expose oneself to danger ‖ *intr* to infer, conclude

īnfer·us -a -um *adj* lower; southern ‖ *mpl* the dead

īnferv·eō -ēre *intr* to come to a boil

īnfervēsc·ō -ere *intr* to simmer, come to a boil, start to boil

īnfestē *adv* hostilely, violently

īnfest·ō -āre -āvī -ātus *tr* to annoy, harass, bother; to attack; to damage; *(of diseases, pests)* to infest

īnfest·us -a -um *adj* hostile, antagonistic; aggressive, warlike; troubled *(times, conditions); (of weapons)* poised to strike; *(of armies)* taking the offensive; *(of things)* harmful, troublesome; *(of places)* threatened, exposed to danger, insecure; *(w. abl)* **1** dangerous *or* unsafe because of; **2** infested with

īnficēt- = **īnfacēt-**

īn·ficiō -ficere -fēcī -fectus *tr* to dip, dye, tint; to infect; to stain; to corrupt, spoil; to imbue, instruct; *(fig)* to poison, infect

īnfidēl·is -is -e *adj* unfaithful, untrue, disloyal

īnfidēlit·ās -ātis *f* infidelity, disloyalty

īnfidēliter *adv* disloyally

īnfidī *perf of* **īnfindō**

īnfid·us -a -um *adj* untrustworthy, treacherous

īn·fīgō -fīgere -fīxī -fīxus *tr* to drive in, nail, thrust; to imprint, fix, impress; *(w. dat)* **1** to drive into, thrust into; **2** to impale on; **3** to imprint on *or* in; **4** to fasten to, attach to

īnfimātis *see* **īnfumātis**

īnfim·us -a -um *(superl of* **īnferus)** *adj* **(-fum-)** lowest, last; worst; humblest; **ab īnfimō colle** at the foot of the hill; **īnfimum mare** the bottom of the sea ‖ *n* bottom

īn·findō -findere -fidī -fissus *tr (w. dat)* to cut *(e.g., furrows)* into

īnfinit·ās -ātis *f* endlessness, infinity; *(phil)* the Infinite

īnfinītē *adv* without bounds, without end, infinitely; without exception

īnfinīti·ō -ōnis *f* boundlessness, infinity

īnfinīt·us -a -um *adj* unlimited, boundless; without end, endless, infinite; countless; indefinite

īnfirmāti·ō -ōnis *f* invalidation; refutation

īnfirmē *adv* weakly, faintly, feebly

īnfirmit·ās -ātis *f* weakness, feebleness; infirmity; inconstancy

īnfirm·ō -āre -āvī -ātus *tr* to weaken, enfeeble; to refute, disprove; to annul

īnfirm·us -a -um *adj* weak, faint, feeble; infirm, sick; trivial; inconstant

īnfissus *pp of* **īnfindō**

īnfit *v defect* he, she, it begins

īnfiti·ae -ārum *fpl* denial; **īnfitiās īre** *(w. acc)* to deny, refuse to acknowledge as true; to disown, repudiate

īnfitiāl·is -is -e *adj* negative

īnfitiāti·ō -ōnis *f* denial

īnfitiāt·or -ōris *m* repudiator

īnfiti·or -ārī -ātus sum *tr* to deny, repudiate, disown; to contradict

īnfīxī *perf of* **īnfīgō**

īnfīxus *pp of* **īnfīgō**

īnflammāti·ō -ōnis *f* setting on fire; *(med)* inflammation; **animī īnflammātiō** inspiration; **īnflammātiōnem īnferre** *(w. dat)* to set on fire

īnflamm·ō -āre -āvī -ātus *tr* to set on fire, kindle, light up; *(med)* to inflame; *(fig)* to excite

īnflāti·ō -ōnis *f* swelling up; flatulence, gas; **habet īnflātiōnem faba** beans cause gas

īnflātius *adv* rather pompously

īnflāt·us -a -um *adj* blown up, inflated; swollen; haughty; turgid *(style)*

īnflāt·us -ūs *m* puff, blast; inspiration

īnfle·ctō -ctere -xī -xus *tr* to bend, curve, bow; to tilt, slant; to turn aside; to change *(course);* to influence; to inflect, modulate *(voice)* ‖ *refl & pass* to curve; to change course; to turn around; *(of a person)* to change

īnflēt·us -a -um *adj* unwept

īnflexī *perf of* **īnflectō**

īnflexibil·is -is -e *adj* inflexible

īnflexi·ō -ōnis *f* bending; modification, adaptation

īnflexus *pp of* **īnflectō**

īnflex·us -ūs *m* curve, bend, winding

īnflī·gō -gere -xī -ctus *tr (w. dat)* **1** to strike *(s.th.)* against, smash *(s.th.)* against; **2** to inflict *(wound)* on; **3** to bring *(e.g., disgrace)* to

īnfl·ō -āre -āvī -ātus *tr (of wind)* to blow on; to blow *(horn),* play *(flute); (of a deity)* to inspire; to inflate, fill with conceit; to puff up *(cheeks);* to fill *(sails);* to distend, bloat; to amplify *(sound);* to inflate *(price)*

īnflu·ō -ere -xī *intr (w.* in + *acc)* **1** to flow into; **2** *(fig)* to spill over into, stream into, pour into; **3** *(of words, ideas)* to sink into, penetrate

in·fodiō -fodere -fōdī -fossus *tr* to dig; to bury

īnfōrmāti·ō -ōnis *f* formation *(of an idea)*; sketch; idea

īnfōrm·is -is -e *adj* unformed, shapeless; ugly, hideous

īnfōrm·ō -āre -āvī -ātus *tr* to form, shape; to sketch *(in words)*, give an idea of; to instruct, educate

īnfor·ō -āre -āvī -ātus *tr* to bring into court

īnfortūnāt·us -a -um *adj* unfortunate

īnfortūn·ium -(i)ī *n* misfortune; *(euphem. for punishment)* trouble

īnfossus *pp of* **īnfodiō**

īnfrā *adv* below, underneath; down south; down the coast; downstream; lower down *(on the page or in the work)*; below the surface; later **‖** *prep (w. acc)* **1** below, beneath, under; **2** inferior *(in quality, rank, etc.)* to; **3** smaller than; **4** lower *(in number)* than; **5** beneath the dignity of, degrading to; **6** submissive to; **7** south of; **īnfrā et suprā Ephesum** south and north of Ephesus; **8** after, later than; **9** falling short of *(a target)*

īnfrācti·ō -ōnis *f* breaking; **animī īnfrāctiō** discouragement

īnfrāct·us -a -um *pp of* **īnfringō ‖** *adj* broken; disjointed *(words)*; weakened; humble, subdued *(tone)*; **īnfrāctōs animōs gerere** to feel down and out

īnfragil·is -is -e *adj* unbreakable, indestructible; vigorous *(voice)*

īnfrēgī *perf of* **īnfringō**

īnfrem·ō -ere -uī *intr* to growl, bellow, roar; to rage

īnfrēnāt·us -a -um *adj* unbridled

īnfrend·eō -ēre *or* **īnfrend·ō -ere** *intr* to grit the teeth; **dentibus īnfrendere** to grit the teeth, gnash the teeth

īnfrēn·is -is -e *or* **īnfrēn·us -a -um** *adj* unbridled

īnfrēn·ō -āre -āvī -ātus *tr* to bridle; to harness; *(fig)* to curb

īnfrēnus *see* **īnfrēnis**

īnfrequ·ēns -entis *adj* uncrowded, not numerous; poorly attended; thinly populated; unusual, infrequent *(words)*; inconstant; irregular; *(mil)* undermanned; below strength; *(mil)* absent without leave

īnfrequenti·a -ae *f* small number, scantiness; poor attendance; emptiness; depopulated condition *(of a place)*

in·fringō -fringere -frēgī -frāctus *tr* to break; to break in; to bend; to break up *(sentences)*; to impair, affect adversely; to subdue; to weaken, break down; to cause to relent; to foil *(an action)*; to render null and void

īnfr·ōns -ondis *adj* leafless

īnfructuōs·us -a -um *adj* unfruitful; pointless

īnfūcāt·us -a -um *adj* painted over

īnfūdī *perf of* **īnfundō**

īnful·a -ae *f* bandage; fillet *(worn by priests, by sacrificial victims; displayed as a sign of submission)*; festoon *(hung on doorposts at a wedding)*

īnfumāt·is -is *m* (**īnfim-**) one of the lowest *(in rank)*

īnfumus *see* **īnfimus**

īn·fundō -fundere -fūdī -fūsus *tr* to pour in, pour on, pour out; *(w. dat or* in + *acc)* **1** to pour into, pour upon; **2** to administer to; **3** to shower *(gifts)* upon; **4** to rain *(missiles)* upon; **5** to stretch out *(the body)* upon; **6** to instil *(ideas, feelings)* in **‖** *refl & pass (w. dat)* to spread out on, relax on

īnfusc·ō -āre -āvī -ātus *tr* to darken, obscure; to stain, corrupt, sully

īnfūs·us -a -um *pp of* **īnfundō ‖** *adj* diffused; permeating; fallen *(snow)*; crowded; **coniugis īnfūsus gremiō** relaxing on the lap of his spouse; **īnfūsīs humerō capillīs** with his hair streaming over his shoulders

ingemin·ō -āre -āvī -ātus *tr* to redouble; to repeat; **ingemināre vōcēs** to call repeatedly; **ignēs ingemināre** to flash repeatedly **‖** *intr* to increase in intensity, get worse

ingem·īscō -īscere -uī *intr* (**-ēsc-**) to groan, heave a sigh; *(w. dat or* in + *abl)* to groan over, sigh over

ingem·ō -ere -uī *tr* to groan over, sigh over **‖** *intr* to groan, moan; *(w. dat)* to sigh over

ingener·ō -āre -āvī -ātus *tr* to engender, generate, produce; *(fig)* to implant

ingeniāt·us -a -um *adj* naturally endowed, talented

ingeniōsē *adv* ingeniously

ingeniōs·us -a -um *adj* ingenious, clever, talented; *(w. dat or* ad) naturally suited to

ingenit·us -a -um *adj* inborn, natural

ingen·ium -(i)ī *n* innate quality; nature, temperament, character; bent, inclination; mood; natural ability, talent, intellect; bright person; gifted writer; skill, ingenuity; clever device

ing·ēns -entis *adj* huge, vast; great, mighty, powerful; a great amount of, a great number of; very important, momentous; proud, haughty, heroic *(character)*; *(w. abl)* outstanding in; **ingēns pecūnia** a lot of money

ingenuē *adv* liberally; frankly

ingenuī *perf of* **ingignō**

ingenuit·ās -ātis *f* noble birth; noble character; frankness

ingenu·us -a -um *adj* native, indigenous; natural; free-born; like a freeman, noble; ingenuous, frank

in·gerō -gerere -gessī -gestus *tr* to carry in, throw in, heap; to ingest *(food, drink, esp. in* *large amounts);* to hurl, shoot *(missiles);* to pour out *(angry words);* to heap *(abuse);* to rain *(blows); (w. dat)* to force *(unwelcome things)* on *(s.o.);* to say repeatedly

in·gignō -gignere -genuī -genitus *tr* to cause *(plants)* to grow; *(fig)* to implant *(qualities, etc.)*

inglōri·us -a -um *adj* inglorious, without glory, inconspicuous

ingluvi·ēs -ēī *f* crop, maw; gluttony

ingrātē *adv* unpleasantly; unwillingly; ungratefully

ingrātific·us -a -um *adj* ungrateful

ingrātiīs *or* ingrātīs *f abl pl* unwillingly, against one's will; against another's will; *(w. gen or poss adj)* against the wishes of

ingrāt·us -a -um *adj* unpleasant, unwelcome; ungrateful; receiving no thanks, unappreciated; thankless

ingravēsc·ō -ere *intr* to get heavier; to become pregnant; *(of troubles)* to grow worse; to become more serious; to become weary; to become dearer *(in price); (of prices)* to become inflated; to become more important

ingre·dior -dī -ssus sum *tr* to enter; to undertake; to begin; to walk in, follow *(footsteps)* ‖ *intr* to go in, enter; to go, walk, walk along; to begin, commence; to begin to speak; *(mil)* to go to the attack; *(w.* in + *acc)* 1 to go into, enter; 2 to enter upon, begin, take up, undertake; *(w. dat)* to walk on; in rem pūblicam ingredī to enter politics

ingressi·ō -ōnis *f* entering; walking; gait, pace; beginning

ingress·us -ūs *m* entry; walking; gait; beginning; *(mil)* inroad

ingru·ō -ere -ī *intr* to come, come on, rush on; *(of war)* to break out; *(of rain)* to pour down; *(w. dat or* in + *acc)* to fall upon, attack

ingu·en -inis *n* groin; swelling, tumor ‖ *npl* private parts

ingurgit·ō -āre -āvī -ātus *tr* to pour in; to gorge, stuff ‖ *refl* to stuff oneself; *(w.* in + *acc)* 1 to steep oneself in; 2 to devote oneself to

ingustāt·us -a -um *adj* untasted

inhabil·is -is -e *adj* clumsy, unhandy, unwieldy; *(w. dat or* ad) unfit for

inhabitābil·is -is -e *adj* uninhabitable

inhabit·ō -āre -āvī -ātus *tr* to inhabit, occupy ‖ *intr (w. dat or* in + *abl)* to live in

inhae·reō -rēre -sī -sum *intr* to stick, cling, adhere; to be inherent; *(w. dat, w.* ad *or* in + *acc)* 1 to cling to; 2 to be closely connected with; 3 to gaze upon

inhae·rēscō -rēscere -sī *intr* to begin to stick, become attached; to become stuck; to become fixed *(in the mind)*

inhal·ō -āre -āvī -ātus *tr (w. dat)* to breathe *(e.g., bad breath)* on *(s.o.)*

inhib·eō -ēre -uī -itus *tr* to hold back, curb, check, control; to use, employ, apply; to inflict *(punishment);* retrō nāvem *(or* nāvem rēmīs) inhibēre to back up the ship ‖ *intr* to row backwards, backwater; rēmīs inhibēre to backwater

inhibiti·ō -ōnis *f* backing up

inhi·ō -āre -āvī -ātus *tr* to gape at; to pore over; to cast longing eyes at ‖ *intr* to stand open-mouthed, be amazed; *(w. dat)* to be eager for

inhonestē *adv* dishonorably, disgracefully; dishonestly

inhonest·ō -āre -āvī -ātus *tr* to dishonor, disgrace

inhonest·us -a -um *adj* dishonorable, disgraceful, shameful; indecent; ugly, degrading

inhonōr·us -a -um *adj* defaced

inhorr·eō -ēre -uī *intr* to stand on end, bristle

inhorr·ēscō -ēscere -uī *intr* to stand on end, bristle; to vibrate; to shiver, tremble, shudder

inhospitāl·is -is -e *adj* inhospitable, unfriendly

inhospitālit·ās -ātis *f* inhospitality

inhospit·us -a -um *adj* inhospitable

inhūmānē *adv* inhumanly; rudely; heartlessly

inhūmānit·ās -ātis *f* inhumanity; churlishness, stinginess; heartlessness

inhūmāniter *adv* impolitely; heartlessly

inhūmān·us -a -um *adj* uncivilized; ill-bred, discourteous; heartless, brutal

inhumāt·us -a -um *adj* unburied

inibi *or* inibī *adv* there, in that place; near at hand

in·iciō -icere -iēcī -iectus *tr* to throw, inject; to hurl, discharge *(missiles);* to impose, apply; to inspire, infuse; to cause, occasion; to furnish *(a cause);* to bring up, mention *(a name); (w. dat)* to put *(e.g., a cloak)* on *(s.o.);* manicās alicui inicere to put handcuffs on s.o.; manum inicere *(w. dat)* 1 to lay hands on; 2 take possession of ‖ *refl (w. dat or* in + *acc)* 1 to throw oneself into, rush into, expose oneself to; 2 to fling oneself down on; 3 *(of the mind)* to turn itself to, concentrate on, reflect on

inimīc·a -ae *f (personal)* enemy *(female)*

inimīcē *adv* with hostility, in an unfriendly way

inimīciti·a -ae *f* unfriendliness, enmity ‖ *fpl* feuds

inimīc·ō -āre -āvī -ātus *tr* to make into enemies, set at odds

inimīc·us -a -um *adj* unfriendly, hostile; harmful ‖ *m (personal)* enemy; inimīcissimus suus his bitterest *(personal)* enemy ‖ *f (personal)* enemy *(female)*

inīquē *adv* unequally, unevenly; unfairly

iníquit·ās -ātis *f* unevenness; inequality; disadvantage; unfairness

iníqu·us -a -um *adj* uneven, unequal; not level, sloping; unfair; adverse, harmful; dangerous, unfavorable; prejudiced; excessive; impatient, discontented; **iníquō animō** impatiently, unwillingly **ll** *m* enemy, foe

initi·ō -āre -āvī -ātus *tr* to initiate, begin; to initiate *(into mysteries)*

init·ium -(i)ī *n* entrance; beginning **ll** *npl* elements; first principles; sacred rites, sacred mysteries

initus *pp of* ineō

init·us -ūs *m* entrance; beginning

iniūcundit·ās -ātis *f* unpleasantness

iniūcundius *adv* rather unpleasantly

iniūcund·us -a -um *adj* unpleasant

iniūdicāt·us -a -um *adj* undecided

iniun·gō -gere iniūnxī iniūnctus *tr* to join, attach, fasten; *(w. dat)* 1 to join to, attach to, fasten to; 2 to inflict on; 3 to impose *(e.g., taxes)* on

iniūrāt·us -a -um *adj* not under oath

iniūri·a -ae *f* injustice, wrong, outrage; insult, affront; harshness, severity; revenge; injury, damage, harm; ill-gotten goods; **iniūriā** unjustly, undeservedly, innocently; **per iniūriam** unjustly; outrageously

iniūriōsē *adv* unjustly, wrongfully

iniūriōs·us -a -um *adj* unjust, wrongful; insulting; harmful

iniūri·us -a -um *adj* unjust, wrong

iniūr·us -a -um *adj* unjust

iniūssū *(abl only) m* without orders; **iniūssū meō** without my orders

iniūss·us -a -um *adj* unasked, unbidden, voluntary

iniūstē *adv* unjustly

iniūstiti·a -ae *f* injustice

iniūst·us -a -um *adj* unjust

inl- = ill-

inm- = imm-

innābil·is -is -e *adj* unswimmable

in·nāscor -nāscī -nātus sum *intr (w. dat)* 1 to be born in; 2 *(of plant life)* grow in *or* on; *(w.* **in** + *abl)* 1 to originate in; 2 *(of plant life)* to grow in; 3 *(of minerals)* to occur in, be native to

innat·ō -āre -āvī *tr* to swim **ll** *intr (w. dat)* to swim around in, float on; *(w.* **in** + *acc)* to swim into

innāt·us -a -um *pp of* innāscor **ll** *adj* innate, inborn, natural

innāvigābil·is -is -e *adj* unnavigable

in·nectō -nectere -nexuī -nexus *tr* to entwine; to tie, fasten together; to join, attach, connect; *(fig)* to devise, invent, plan

innī·tor -tī -xus sum *or* -sus sum *intr (w. abl)* to lean on, rest on, be supported by

inn·ō -āre *tr* to swim; to sail, sail over **ll** *intr (w. abl)* 1 to swim in, float on; 2 to sail on; 3 *(of the sea)* to wash against *(a shore)*

innoc·ēns -entis *adj* harmless; innocent; upright; unselfish; *(w. gen)* innocent of

innocenter *adv* innocently, blamelessly; harmlessly

innocenti·a -ae *f* innocence; integrity; unselfishness

innocuē *adv* harmlessly; innocently

innocu·us -a -um *adj* harmless, innocuous; innocent; unharmed

innōt·ēscō -ēscere -uī *intr* to become known; to become notorious

innov·ō -āre -āvī -ātus *tr* to renew, restore **ll** *refl (w.* **ad** + *acc)* to return to

innoxi·us -a -um *adj* harmless; safe; innocent; unhurt; *(w. gen)* innocent of

innub·a -ae *adj (fem only)* unmarried

innūbil·us -a -um *adj* cloudless

innū·bō -bere -psī *intr (of a girl) (w. dat)* to marry into *(a family)*

innumerābil·is -is -e *adj* innumerable

innumerābilit·ās -atis *f* countless number

innumerābiliter *adv* in countless ways; countless times

innumerāl·is -is -e *adj* innumerable

innumer·us -a -um *adj* countless

in·nuō -nuere -nuī -nūtum *intr* to give a nod; *(w. dat)* to nod to

innūpt·a -ae *adj (fem only)* unmarried **ll** *f* unmarried girl, maiden

innūtr·iō -īre -īvī *or* -iī -ītus *tr (w. abl)* to bring up in

Īn·ō -ūs *f* daughter of Cadmus and Harmonia, wife of Athamas and mother of Learchus and Melicertes

inoblīt·us -a -um *adj* unforgetful

inobrut·us -a -um *adj* not overwhelmed

inobservābil·is -is -e *adj* unnoticed

inobservanti·a -ae *f* inattention

inobservāt·us -a -um *adj* unobserved

inoccidu·us -a -um *adj* never setting

inodōr·us -a -um *adj* odorless

inoffēns·us -a -um *adj* unobstructed, uninterrupted, unhindered; unimpaired; smooth *(path)*

inofficiōs·us -a -um *adj* irresponsible; unobliging; **testāmentum inofficiōsum** a will passing over the relatives

inol·ēns -entis *adj* odorless

inol·ēscō -ēscere -ēvī *tr* to implant **ll** *intr* to become inveterate; *(w. dat)* to grow in, develop in

inōmināt·us -a -um *adj* ill-starred, inauspicious

inopi·a -ae *f* lack, want, need, poverty; scarcity; helplessness; *(rhet)* barrenness *(of style)*; *(rhet)* lack of subject matter

inopīn·āns -antis *adj* unsuspecting, taken by surprise, off one's guard

inopīnanter *adv* unexpectedly

inopīnātō *adv* unexpectedly, by surprise

inopīnāt·us -a -um *adj* unexpected, unsuspected, surprising **‖** *n* surprise; **ex inopīnātō** by surprise, unexpectedly

inopīn·us -a -um *adj* unexpected

inopiōs·us -a -um *adj (hum) (w. gen)* in need of

in·ops -opis *adj* without means *or* resources; poor, needy, destitute; helpless, weak, forlorn; *(rhet)* bald *(style);* poor *(expression);* deficient in vocabulary; pitiful, contemptible; *(w. gen)* destitute of, stripped of, without; *(w. abl)* lacking in, deficient in, poor in

inōrāt·us -a -um *adj* not presented; **rē inōrātā** without presenting one's case

inōrdināt·us -a -um *adj* disordered

inōrnāt·us -a -um *adj* unadorned; unheralded; *(rhet)* plain *(style)*

inp- = **imp-**

inquam *v defect (the following forms are found: pres:* **inquam, inquis, inquit, inquimus, inquiunt;** *imperfect:* **inquiēbat;** *fut:* **inquiēs, inquiet;** *perfect:* **inquiī, inquisti;** *persent subj:* **inquiat;** *impv:* **inque** *or* **inquitō)** to say; *(after one or more words of direction quotation, e.g.,* **dēsilite, inquit, mīlitēs et** ... "jump down, fellow soldiers," he says, " and ... "); *(in emphatic repetition, e.g.,* **tuās, tuās inquam suspiciōnēs** ... your suspicions, yes I say yours ...); **inquit** it is said, one says, they say

inqui·ēs -ētis *adj* restless

inquiēt·ō -āre -āvī -ātus *tr* to disquiet, disturb

inquiēt·us -a -um *adj* restless, unsettled

inquilīn·us -ī *m* tenant, lodger

inquinātē *adv* filthily

inquināt·us -a -um *adj* filthy, foul

inquin·ō -āre -āvī -ātus *tr* to mess up, defile, contaminate

in·quīrō -quīrere -quīsīvī *or* **-quīsiī -quīsītus** *tr* to search for, inquire into, examine, pry into **‖** *intr* to hold an investigation; to hold a preliminary hearing

inquīsīti·ō -ōnis *f* search, inquiry, investigation; preliminary hearing; *(w. gen)* search for, inquiry into, investigation of

inquīsīt·or -ōris *m* inspector, examiner; spy; *(leg)* investigator

inquīsīt·us -a -um *pp of* **inquīrō ‖** *adj* not investigated, unexamined

inquīsīvī *perf of* **inquīrō**

inquit *see* **inquam**

inquiunt *see* **inquam**

inr- = **irr-**

īnsalūbr·is -is -e *adj* unhealthy, unhealthful

īnsalūtāt·us -a -um *adj* ungreeted

īnsānābil·is -is -e *adj* incurable

īnsānē *adv* insanely, madly

īnsāni·a -ae *f* insanity, madness, frenzy; rapture; mania; excess; **ad īnsāniam** to the point of madness

īnsān·iō -īre -īvī *or* **-iī -ītum** *intr* to be insane; to be absurd; to be wild, rave; *(w.* **in** + *acc)* to be crazy about

īnsānit·ās -ātis *f* insanity

īnsānum *adv (coll)* exceedingly, very

īnsān·us -a -um *adj* insane, crazy; absurd, foolish; excessive, extravagant; monstrous, outrageous; inspired; maddening

īnsatiābil·is -is -e *adj* insatiable; voracious; that cannot cloy

īnsatiābiliter *adv* insatiably

īnsatiet·ās -ātis *f* insatiable desire

īnsaturābil·is -is -e *adj* insatiable

īnsaturābiliter *adv* insatiably

īnscen·dō -dere -dī -sus *tr* to climb up; to get up on *(horse, chariot)* **‖** *intr* to climb up; **in arborem īnscendere** to climb a tree; **in currum īnscendere** to climb into a chariot; **in nāvem īnscendere** to board a ship

īnscēnsi·ō -ōnis *f* mounting; **in nāvem īnscēnsiō** embarkation

īnscēnsus *pp of* **īnscendō**

īnsci·ēns -entis *adj* unaware; silly, ignorant, stupid

īnscienter *adv* ignorantly; inadvertently

īnscītē *adv* ignorantly, unskillfully

īnscīti·a -ae *f* ignorance; inexperience; lack of skill; neglect

īnscīt·us -a -um *adj* ignorant; stupid

īnsci·us -a -um *adj* unaware; ignorant, silly, stupid

īnscrī·bō -bere -psī -ptus *tr* to inscribe; to ascribe; to title *(a book); (w. dat)* **1** to assign, attribute to; **2** to apply to; **3** to address *(a letter)* to; *(w. dat or* **in** + *abl)* to write *(s.th.)* on *or* in; **aedēs vēnālēs** *(or* **mercēde) īnscrībere** to advertise a house for sale

īnscrīpti·ō -ōnis *f* inscribing; branding *(of slaves);* inscription; title *(of book)*

īnscrīpt·us -a -um *pp of* **īnscrībō ‖** *adj* unwritten; *(of a book)* entitled **‖** *n* inscription; brand *(mark);* title *(of a book)*

īnsculp·ō -ere -sī -tus *tr* to cut, carve, engrave; *(w. dat or abl or* **in** + *abl)* to cut, carve, *or* engrave on; **in animō** *(or* **in mente) īnsculpere** to imprint on the mind

īnsectāti·ō -ōnis *f* hot pursuit

īnsectāt·or -ōris *m* persecutor

īnsect·or -ārī -ātus sum *or* **īnsect·ō -āre** *tr* to pursue, chase, attack; to heckle, harass

īnsect·us -a -um *adj* indented, notched; **animālia īnsecta** insects **‖** *n* insect

īnsecūtus *pp of* **īnsequor**

īnsēdābiliter *adv* unquenchably

īnsēdī *perf of* īnsideō *and* īnsīdō

īnsen·ēscō -ēscere -uī *intr (w. dat)* to grow old amidst, grow old over; *(of the moon)* to wane

īnsēnsil·is -is -e *adj* imperceptible

īnsepult·us -a -um *adj* unburied

īnsequ·ēns -entis *adj* next, following, succeeding

īnse·quor -quī -cūtus sum *tr* to follow (immediately behind); to succeed, follow up; to attack, go for; to persecute; to catch up with; to reproach; to strive after ‖ *intr* to follow, come next; to pursue the point; *(w. inf)* to proceed to

īnser·ō -ere -uī -tus *tr* to insert; to introduce; to include *(in a book, speech);* to involve; to join, enroll, associate; to mingle, blend; **manūs īnserere** *(w. dat)* to lay hands on, seize; **oculōs īnserere** *(w. in + abl)* to look into *(e.g., s.o.'s heart)*

īn·serō -serere -sēvī -situs *tr* to sow, plant; to graft on *(a cutting);* to graft a cutting on *(a tree); (lit & fig)* to implant; **singulōs hortōs cūiusque generis surculīs serere** to plant each garden with one kind of cutting

īnsert·ō -āre -āvī -ātus *tr* to insert

īnserv·iō -īre -īvī *or* -iī -ītus *tr* to serve, obey ‖ *intr* to be a slave, be a subject; *(w. dat)* **1** to serve, be subservient to; **2** to be subject to; **3** to be devoted to; **4** to pay attention to

īnsessus *pp of* īnsideō *and* īnsīdō

īnsēvī *perf of* īnserō (to plant)

īnsībil·ō -āre -āvī -ātum *intr (of the wind)* to whistle (in *or* among)

in·sideō -sidēre -sēdī -sessus *tr* to hold, occupy ‖ *intr* to sit down; to settle down; to be deep-seated; *(w. abl or in + abl)* **1** to sit on; **2** to settle down on *or* in; **3** *(fig)* to be fixed in, be stamped in

īnsidi·ae -ārum *fpl* ambush; plot, trap; **īnsidiās dare** *(or* **collocāre** *or* **parāre** *or* **struere)** *(w. dat)* to lay a trap for

īnsidiāt·or -ōris *m* soldier in ambush; *(fig)* plotter, subversive

īnsidi·or -ārī -ātus sum *intr (w. dat)* **1** to lie in wait for; **2** to plot against; **3** to watch for, be on the lookout for *(e.g., opportunity)*

īnsidiōsē *adv* insidiously, by underhand means

īn·sīdō -sīdere -sēdī -sessus *tr* to occupy, keep possession of, possess ‖ *intr* to sink in, penetrate; *(of diseases)* to become deep-seated; *(w. dat)* to settle in *or* on; *(w. in + abl)* to become fixed in, become imbedded in; *(of a bird)* to land on

īnsign·e -is *n (s.th. worn or carried as an indication of rank or status)* insignia, mark; coat of arms; signal; honor, distinction; brilliant passage, gem; *(mil)* decoration, medal ‖ *npl* insignia, regalia, uniform; outer trappings

īnsign·iō -īre -īvī *or* -iī -ītus *tr* to make conspicuous, distinguish, mark

īnsign·is -is -e *adj* conspicuous, distinguished; prominent, eminent, extraordinary, singular

īnsignītē *adv* notably, extraordinarily

īnsigniter *adv* remarkably

īnsignīt·us -a -um *adj* marked, conspicuous, clear, glaring; distinguished, striking, notable

īnsil·ia -ium *npl* treadle *(of a loom)*

īnsil·iō -īre -uī *or* -īvī *tr* to jump up on, mount ‖ *intr (w. dat)* to jump on; *(w.* **in** *+ acc)* **1** to jump into *or* on(to); **2** to mount; **3** to climb aboard

īnsimulāti·ō -ōnis *f* allegation *(of a crime);* charge, accusation

īnsimul·ō -āre -āvī -ātus *tr* to allege; to charge, accuse

īnsincēr·us -a -um *adj* adulterated; not genuine, insincere

īnsinuāti·ō -ōnis *f (rhet)* winning sympathy *(in a speech)*

īnsinu·ō -āre -āvī -ātus *tr* to bring in secretly, sneak in ‖ *refl (w.* **inter** *+ acc)* to wriggle in between, work one's way between *or* among; **sē īnsinuāre in familiārītātem** *(w. gen)* to ingratiate oneself with

īnsipi·ēns -entis *adj* foolish

īnsipienter *adv* foolishly

īnsipienti·a -ae *f* foolishness

īn·sistō -sistere -stitī *tr* to stand on, trample on; to set about, keep at *(a task, etc.);* to follow, chase after; **iter** *(or* **viam)** **īnsistere** to pursue a course ‖ *intr* to stand, stop, come to a stop; to pause; *(w. dat)* **1** to tread on the heels of, pursue closely; **2** to press on with; **3** to dwell upon; *(w. dat or* **in** *+ abl)* to persist in; *(w.* **ad** *or* **in** *+ acc)* **1** to keep at, keep after, keep the pressure on; **2** pursue vigorously

īnsiti·ō -ōnis *f* grafting; grafting time

īnsitīv·us -a -um *adj* grafted; *(fig)* spurious

īnsit·or -ōris *m* grafter *(of trees)*

īnsit·us -a -um *pp of* īnserō ‖ *adj* inborn, innate; incorporated

īnsociābil·is -is -e *adj* incompatible

īnsōlābiliter *adv* unconsolably

īnsol·ēns -entis *adj* unaccustomed, unusual; immoderate, excessive; extravagant; insolent; *(w. gen or* **in** *+ abl)* **1** unaccustomed to; **2** inexperienced in; **in aliēnā rē īnsolēns** free with someone else's money

īnsolenter *adv* unusually; excessively; insolently

īnsolenti·a -ae *f* unusualness, novelty, strangeness, inexperience; affectation; insolence, arrogance

īnsolēsc·ō -ere *intr* to become proud, become insolent; to become elated

īnsolid·us -a -um *adj* soft

īnsolit·us -a -um *adj* unaccustomed; inexperienced; unusual, strange, uncommon **ǁ** *n* the unusual

īnsomni·a -ae *f* insomnia

īnsomn·is -is -e *adj* sleepless

īnsomn·ium -(i)ī *n* sleeplessness; dream; vision in a dream *or* trance

īnson·ō -āre -uī *intr* to make noise; to sound, resound, roar; **calamīs īnsonāre** to play the reed pipe; **flagellō īnsonāre** to crack the whip; **pennīs īnsonāre** to flap the wings

īns·ōns -ontis *adj* innocent; harmless

īnsōpīt·us -a -um *adj* sleepless

īnsop·or -ōris *adj* sleepless

īnspeciōs·us -a -um *adj* homely

īnspecti·ō -ōnis *f* inspection

īnspect·ō -āre -āvī -ātus *tr* to look at, view, observe, examine **ǁ** *intr* to look on; **īnspectante Rōsciō** with Roscius looking on, under the eyes of Roscius

īnspectus *pp of* īnspiciō

īnspēr·āns -antis *adj* not hoping, not expecting

īnspērāt·us -a -um *adj* unhoped for, unexpected, unforeseen; unwelcome; **(ex) īnspērātō** unexpectedly

īnsper·gō -gere -sī -sus *tr* to sprinkle on

īn·spiciō -spicere -spexī -spectus *tr* to inspect, look into, examine; to look at, watch; to consider; to comprehend, grasp; to investigate; to look at, consult *(books);* to look into *(the mirror)* **ǁ** *intr* (w. **in** + *acc)* to look into

īnspīc·ō -āre -āvī -ātus *tr* to make pointed

īnspīr·ō -āre -āvī -ātus *tr* to inspire, infuse, enkindle **ǁ** *intr (w. dat)* to blow on, breathe on

īnspoliāt·us -a -um *adj* undespoiled

īnsp·uō -uere -uī -ūtus *tr* to spit on **ǁ** *intr (w. dat)* to spit on

īnspūt·ō -āre -āvī -ātus *tr* to spit on

īnstābil·is -is -e *adj* unstable, unsteady; not remaining still; *(fig)* changeable

īnst·āns -antis *adj* present; immediate, threatening, urgent

īnstanter *adv* vehemently, insistently

īnstanti·a -ae *f* presence; earnestness, insistence; concentration

īnstar *indecl n* image, likeness, appearance, resemblance; *(w. gen)* like, equal to, as large as, worth, as good as; **ad īnstar** *(w. gen)* according to the standard of

īnstaurāti·ō -ōnis *f* renewal, repetition

īnstaurātīv·us -a -um *adj* begun anew, repeated

īnstaur·ō -āre -āvī -ātus *tr* to set up; to renew, repeat, start all over again *(esp. games and celebrations because of alleged bad omens in the initial event);* to repay, requite

īn·sternō -sternere -strāvī -strātus *tr* to cover; to lay *(a floor, deck)*

īnstīgāt·or -ōris *m,* īnstīgātr·īx -īcis *f* instigator, ringleader

īnstīg·ō -āre -āvī -ātus *tr* to instigate, goad on, stimulate, incite

īnstill·ō -āre -āvī -ātus *tr (w. dat)* to pour *(s.th.)* on, instill *(s.th.)* in

īnstimulāt·or -ōris *m* instigator

īnstimul·ō -āre -āvī -ātus *tr* to stimulate, urge on, goad on

īnstinct·or -ōris *m* instigator

īnstinct·us -a -um *adj* aroused, fired up; infuriated; inspired

īnstipul·or -ārī -ātus sum *intr* to bargain

īnstit·a -ae *f* border, flounce; band, ribbon; *(fig)* lady

īnstitī *perf of* īnsistō *and* īnstō

īnstiti·ō -ōnis *f* standing still

īnstit·or -ōris *m* salesman, huckster

īnstit·uō -uere -uī -ūtus *tr* to set, fix, plant; to set up, erect, establish; to arrange; to build, make, construct; to prepare; to provide, furnish; to institute, organize, set up; to appoint, designate; to undertake, begin; to control, direct, govern; to teach, train, instruct, educate; *(w. inf)* to decide to

īnstitūti·ō -ōnis *f* arrangement; custom; instruction, education; **mōrum īnstitūtiō** established custom **ǁ** *fpl* principles of education

īnstitūt·um -ī *n* plan, program; practice, custom, usage; precedent; principle; decree, regulation, stipulation, terms; purpose, intention; **ex īnstitūtō** according to custom, by convention **ǁ** *npl* teachings, precepts, principles of education

īn·stō -stāre -stitī *tr* to follow, pursue; to work hard at; to menace, threaten **ǁ** *intr* to be at hand, approach, be impending; to insist; *(w. dat or in + abl)* to stand on *or* in; *(w. dat)* **1** to be close to; **2** to be on the heels of, pursue closely; **3** to harass

īnstrātus *pp of* īnsternō

īnstrāvī *perf of* īnsternō

īnstrēnu·us -a -um *adj* lethargic

īnstrep·ō -āre -uī -itum *intr* to creak, rattle

īnstructi·ō -ōnis *f* construction; array, formation; instruction

īnstructius *adv* with better preparation

īnstruct·or -ōris *m* supervisor; preparer

īnstruct·us -a -um *pp of* īnstruō **ǁ** *adj* equipped, furnished; prepared, arranged; instructed, versed

īnstruct·us -ūs *m* equipment; *(rhet)* stock-in-trade *(of an orator)*

īnstrūment·um -ī *n* instrument, tool, utensil; equipment; dress, outfit; repertory, stock-in-trade; means, supply, provisions; *(leg)* document, deed, instrument

īnstru·ō -ere -xī -ctus *tr* to build up, construct; to furnish, prepare, provide, fit out; to instruct; *(mil)* to deploy

īnsuās·um -ī *n* dark-orange color

īnsuāv·is -is -e *adj* unpleasant, disagreeable

īnsūd·ō -āre -āvī *intr* to sweat, break a sweat; *(w. dat)* to drip sweat on

īnsuēfact·us -a -um *adj* accustomed

īnsu·ēscō -ēscere -ēvī -ētus *tr* to accustom, familiarize **‖** *intr (w. dat, w.* **ad** *or w.* inf) to get used to

īnsuēt·us -a -um *adj* unusual; *(w. gen or dat, w.* **ad** *or w.* inf) unused to

īnsuēvī *perf of* **īnsuēscō**

īnsul·a -ae *f* island; apartment building

īnsulān·us -ī *m* islander

īnsulār·ius -(i)ī *m* superintendent *(of an apartment building)*

īnsulsē *adv* in poor taste; insipidly, absurdly

īnsulsit·ās -ātis *f* lack of taste; silliness, absurdity

īnsuls·us -a -um *adj* unsalted, without taste; coarse, tasteless, insipid; silly, absurd; bungling **‖** *fpl* silly creatures *(i.e., women)*

īnsult·ō -āre -āvī -ātus *tr* to insult, scoff at, taunt; *(of votaries)* to dance about in **‖** *intr* to jump, gambol, prance; to gloat; *(w. abl)* **1** to jump in, cavort in, gambol on, jump upon; **2** to gloat over; *(w. dat or in + acc)* **1** to scoff at; **2** to gloat over

īnsultūr·a -ae *f* jumping on *or* in

īn·sum -esse -fuī *intr* to be there, exist; *(w. dat or in + acc)* **1** to be in, be on; **2** to be implied in, be contained in, belong to

īnsūm·ō -ere -psī -ptus *tr* to spend, devote, waste; *(w. dat or in + acc)* to devote to, apply to; *(w. abl or in + abl)* to expend on; **operam īnsūmere** *(w. dat)* to devote effort to, waste effort on

īn·suō -suere -suī -sūtus *tr* to sew up; *(w. dat)* **1** to sew up in; **2** to embroider *(s.th.)* on

īnsuper *adv* above, overhead, on top; from above; moreover, besides, in addition **‖** *prep (w. acc)* above, over, over and above; *(w. abl)* in addition to, besides

īnsuperābil·is -is -e *adj* insurmountable; unconquerable

īnsur·gō -gere -rēxī -rēctum *intr* to rise, stand up, stand high, tower; to rise, increase, grow, grow intense; to rise to power; *(of language)* to soar; *(w. dat)* **1** to rise up against; **2** to strain at *(e.g., oars)*

īnsusurr·ō -āre -āvī -ātus *tr (w. dat)* to whisper *(s.th.)* to; **īnsusurrāre in aurem** *(w. gen)* to whisper in *(s.o.'s)* ear; **sibi cantilēnam īnsusurrāre** to hum a tune to oneself **‖** *intr* to whisper; *(of wind)* to blow gently

intāb·ēscō -ēscere -uī *intr* to melt away gradually, dissolve gradually; *(fig)* to waste away, pine away

intāctil·is -is -e *adj* intangible

intāct·us -a -um *adj* untouched; uninjured, intact; unpolluted; untried; unmarried, virgin, chaste

intāct·us -ūs *m* intangibility

intāmināt·us -a -um *adj* unsullied

intēct·us -a -um *pp of* **integō ‖** *adj* uncovered; naked; open, frank

integell·us -a -um *adj* fairly pure *or* chaste; in fair condition

inte·ger -gra -grum *adj* whole, complete, intact; unhurt, unwounded; healthy, sound; new; fresh; pure, chaste; untouched, unaffected; unbiased; unattempted; unconquered; unbroken *(horse);* not worn, unused; inexperienced; virtuous, honest, blameless; healthy, sane; *(mil)* having suffered no losses; **ab** *(or* **dē** *or* **ex) integrō** anew, all over again; **in integrum restituere** to restore to a former condition; to pardon; **integrum alicui esse** *(w. inf)* to be in someone's power to

in·tegō -tegere -tēxī -tēctus *tr* to cover up; to protect

integrāsc·ō -ere *intr* to start all over again

integrāti·ō -ōnis *f* renewal, new beginning

integrē *adv* wholly, entirely; honestly; correctly

integrit·ās -ātis *f* soundness; integrity; innocence; purity, chastity

integr·ō -āre -āvī -ātus *tr* to make whole; to heal, repair; to renew, begin again; to refresh, reinvigorate

integument·um -ī *n* covering; lid; wrapping; protection

intellēctus *pp of* **intellegō**

intellēct·us -ūs *m* intellect; perception; comprehension, understanding

intelleg·ēns -entis *adj* intelligent; *(w. gen)* appreciative of; *(w.* **in** + *abl)* versed in

intellegenter *adv* intelligently

intellegenti·a -ae *f* intelligence; understanding, knowledge; perception, judgment, discrimination, taste; skill; concept, notion; *(w. gen)* knowledge of, understanding of; *(w.* **in** + *abl)* judgment in

intel·legō -legere -lēxī -lēctus *tr* to understand, perceive, comprehend; to realize, recognize; to have an accurate knowledge of, be an expert in **‖** *intr (in answers)* I understand, I get it

intemerāt·us -a -um *adj* undefiled, pure, chaste; pure, undiluted

intemper·āns -antis *adj* intemperate, without restraint; lewd

intemperanter *adv* intemperately

intemperanti·a -ae *f* intemperance, lack of self-control; extravagance; *(w. gen)* unrestrained use of

intemperāri·ae -ārum *fpl* wild outbursts; wildness

intemperātē *adv* intemperately

intemperāt·us -a -um *adj* excessive

intemperi·ēs -ēī *f* wildness, excess; outrageous conduct, excesses; **intemperiēs aquārum** heavy rain; **intemperiēs caelī** stormy weather

intempestīvē *adv* at a bad time, at the wrong time

intempestīv·us -a -um *adj* untimely; unseasonable *(weather);* poorly timed

intempest·us -a -um *adj* unseasonable; dark, dismal; unhealthy; **nox intempesta** dead of night

intemptāt·us -a -um *adj* (-tent-) unattempted, untried

inten·dō -dere -dī -tus *or* **-sus** *tr* to stretch, stretch out, extend, spread out; to stretch, bend *(e.g., a bow);* to aim, shoot *(weapon);* to spread *(sails);* *(of winds)* to fill *(sails);* to cover *(e.g., with festoons);* to increase, magnify, intensify; to intend; to urge, incite; to aim at, intend; to assert, maintain; to raise *(voice);* to stretch *(truth);* to direct, turn, focus *(mind, attention);* to pitch *(tent);* **cursum** *(or* **iter) intendere** to direct one's course ‖ *intr (w.* **in** + *acc)* **1** to direct one's effort to, apply oneself to; **2** to turn to

intentātus *see* **intemptātus**

intentē *adv* intently, attentively

intenti·ō -ōnis *f* stretching, straining; tension, tautness; attention; effort, exertion; aim, intention; accusation; *(leg)* statement of the charge

intent·ō -āre -āvī -ātus *tr* to stretch out; to aim, direct; to threaten; to brandish threateningly; **arma Latīnīs intentāre** to threaten the Latins with war; **manūs intentāre in** *(w. dat or* **in** *(w. acc)* to shake hands with; **oculōs intentāre** *(w. dat)* to fix one's gaze on, gaze at

intent·us -a -um *pp of* **intendō** ‖ *adj* tense, taut; intent, attentive; eager; tense, nervous; strict *(discipline);* vigorous *(speech)*

intent·us -ūs *m* stretching out, extending *(of the palms)*

intep·eō -ēre -uī *intr* to be lukewarm

intep·ēscō -ēscere -uī *intr* to get warm, be warmed

inter- *pref* with one of the senses of the preposition

inter *prep (w. acc)* **1** between, among, amidst; **2** during, within, in the course of; **inter cēnam** during dinner; **inter haec** during these events, in the meantime; **inter tālia**

opera during such frenetic activites; **3** *(in classifying)* among, in, with; **inter sē** each other, one another, mutually

interaestu·ō -āre *intr* to retch

interāment·a -ōrum *npl* framework of a ship

Interamn·a -ae *f* town in Latium on the Liris River ‖ town in Umbria, birthplace of Tacitus

interārēsc·ō -ere *intr* to dry up

interātim *adv* meanwhile

interbib·ō -ere *tr* to drink up

interbīt·ō -ere *intr* to come to nothing

intercalār·is -is -e *adj* intercalary, added *(to the calendar)*

intercal·ō -āre -āvī -ātus *tr* to intercalate, add *(to the calendar)*

intercapēd·ō -inis *f* interruption, break, pause

inter·cēdō -cēdere -cessī -cessum *intr* to come *or* go in between; *(of time)* to intervene, pass, occur; to act as an intermediary; to intercede; *(of tribunes)* to exercise the veto; *(w. dat)* **1** to veto, protest against; **2** to interfere with, obstruct, hinder

intercepti·ō -ōnis *f* interception

intercept·or -ōris *m* embezzler

interceptus *pp of* **intercipiō**

intercessi·ō -ōnis *f* intercession, mediation; *(tribune's)* veto

inter·cīdō -cīdere -cīdī -cīsus *tr* to cut through, sever; to cut off, cut short; to cut the seals of, tamper with *(documents)*

inter·cidō -cidere -cidī *intr* to fall short, miss the mark; to happen in the meantime; to drop out, be lost

intercin·ō -ere *tr* to interrupt with song *or* music

inter·cipiō -cipere -cēpī -ceptus *tr* to intercept; to trap *(animals);* to draw *(water illegally from the aqueduct);* to steal, usurp *(rights, honors);* to interrupt, cut off, cut short *(a conversation);* to appropriate; to misappropriate; to receive by mistake *(e.g., poison);* *(mil)* to cut off *(the enemy);* *(mil)* to capture; *(mil)* to be struck by *(e.g., spear intended for another)*

intercīsē *adv* piecemeal

intercīsus *pp of* **intercīdō**

interclū·dō -dere -sī -sus *tr* to shut off, shut out, cut off; to stop, block up; to hinder, prevent; to blockade, shut in; to cut off, intercept; to separate, divide

interclūsi·ō -ōnis *f* stopping; parenthetical matter; **animae interclūsiō** shortwindedness

interclūsus *pp of* **interclūdō**

intercolumn·ium -(i)ī *n* space between columns, intercolumniation

inter·currō -currere -cucurrī -cursum *intr* to intervene, mediate; to mingle; to rush in

intercurs·ō -āre -āvī -ātum *intr* to crisscross; **inter sē intercursāre** to crisscross each other

intercurs·us -ūs *m* intervention

interc·us -utis *adj* between the skin and flesh; **aqua intercus** dropsy

inter·dīcō -dīcere -dīxī -dictus *tr* to forbid, prohibit ‖ *intr* to issue a prohibition, issue an injunction; **aquā et ignī interdīcere** *(w. dat)* to outlaw *(s.o.)*, banish *(s.o.) (literally, to prohibit s.o. from receiving water and fire)*

interdicti·ō -ōnis *f* prohibiting; **aquae et ignī interdictiō** banishment

interdict·um -ī *n* prohibition; contraband; injunction *(by praetor or pro-magistrate)*

interdictus *pp of* **interdīcō**

interdiū *or* **interdiūs** *adv* by day, in the day-time

interdīxī *perf of* **interdīcō**

inter·dō -dare -dedī -datus *tr* (·**duō**) to place between, place at intervals, interpose; **ciccum** *(or* **floccum** *or* **nihil) interduim** *(sl)* I don't give a hoot

interduct·us -ūs *m* (inter)punctuation

interdum *adv* sometimes, now and then, occasionally; meanwhile

interdu·ō *see* **interdō**

intereā *adv* meanwhile, in the interim; anyhow, nevertheless

interemptus *pp of* **interimō**

inter·eō -īre -iī -itum *intr* to die; to be done for, be finished, perish, be lost; to become extinct

interequit·ō -āre -āvī -ātus *tr* to ride between *(e.g., the ranks or columns)* ‖ *intr* to ride *(on horseback)* in between

interfāti·ō -ōnis *f* interruption

interfecti·ō -ōnis *f* killing

interfect·or -ōris *m*, **interfectr·īx -īcis** *f* killer, murderer

inter·ficiō -ficere -fēcī -fectus *tr* to kill; to destroy

inter·fīō -fierī *intr* to be destroyed

inter·fluō -fluere -flūxī *tr* to flow between ‖ *intr* to flow in between

inter·fodiō -fodere -fōdī -fossus *tr* to pierce, penetrate

inter·for -fārī -fātus sum *tr & intr* to interrupt

interfug·iō -ere *intr* to slip in between

interfulg·eō -ēre *intr (w. abl)* to shine amid *or* among

interfūs·us -a -um *adj* spread here and there; *(w. acc)* flowing between

interiac·eō -ēre *intr (w. dat)* to lie between

interiaciō *see* **intericiō**

interibi *adv* in the meantime

inter·iciō -icere -iēcī -iectus *tr* to interpose; *(w. dat or* inter + *acc)* **1** to throw *or* set *(s.th.)* between; **2** to intermingle *(s.th.)* with, intermix *(s.th.)* with

interiecti·ō -ōnis *f (gram)* interjection; *(rhet)* parenthetical remark *or* phrase

interiect·us -a -um *pp of* **intericiō** ‖ *adj (w. dat or* inter + *acc)* set *or* lying between

interiect·us -ūs *m* interposition; interval

interim *adv* meanwhile; for the moment; sometimes; however, anyhow

inter·imō -imere -ēmī -emptus *tr* to do away with, abolish; to kill

interi·or -or -us *adj* inner, interior; internal; inner side of; more remote *(places, peoples, esp. far from the seacoast)*; secret, private; deeper, more profound; more intimate, more personal, more confidential

interiti·ō -ōnis *f* ruin, destruction; *(violent or untimely)* death

interit·us -ūs *m* ruin; *(violent or untimely)* death; dissolution *(of institutions, society, material things)*; extinction

inter·iungō -iungere -iūnxī -iūnctus *tr* to join together; to clasp

interius *adv* on the inside; inwardly; in the middle; too short; *(to listen)* closely; more deeply

inter·lābor -lābī -lāpsus sum *intr* to glide in between, flow in between

inter·legō -legere -lēgī -lēctus *tr* to pick *or* pluck here and there

inter·linō -linere -lēvī -litus *tr* to smear; to daub in the gaps *(of a structure)*; to tamper with *(a document; to falsify it)*

interlo·quor -quī -cūtus sum *intr* to interrupt

interlū·ceō -ēre -xī *intr* to shine through; to be lightning now and then; to be transparent; to be plainly visible

interlūni·a -ōrum *npl* new moon

interlu·ō -ere *tr* to flow between; to wash

intermēnstru·us -a -um *adj* of the new moon ‖ *n* new moon

intermināt·us -a -um *adj* endless

intermin·or -ārī -ātus sum *tr (w. dat)* to threaten *(s.o.)* with *(s.th.)* ‖ *intr* to threaten

inter·mīsceō -mīscēre -mīscuī -mīxtus *tr* to intermingle

intermissi·ō -ōnis *f* intermission, pause, interruption; interval of time; *(leg)* adjournment

inter·mittō -mittere -mīsī -missus *tr* to interrupt, break off, suspend; to omit, neglect; to leave gaps in, leave unoccupied, leave undefended; to allow *(time)* to pass ‖ *intr* to pause, stop

intermīxtus *pp of* **intermīsceō**

inter·morior -morī -mortuus sum *intr* to die suddenly; to faint

intermortu·us -a -um *adj* dead; unconscious; *(fig)* half-dead

intermundi·a -ōrum *npl* outer space

intermūrāl·is -is -e *adj* intermural, between two walls internāt·us -a -um *adj (w. dat)* growing among *or* between

internecīn·us -a -um *adj* internecine, exterminating, of extermination

interneci·ō -ōnis *f* massacre

internecīv·us -a -um *adj* exterminating; **bellum internecīvum** war of extermination

internec·ō -āre -āvī -ātus *tr* to exterminate

internect·ō -ere *tr* to intertwine

internit·eō -ēre *intr* to shine out

internōd·ium -(i)ī *n (anat)* space between two joints

inter·nōscō -nōscere -nōvī -nōtus *tr* to distinguish, pick out; *(w.* **ab***)* to distinguish *(one thing)* from *(another)*

internūnti·ō -āre *intr* to exchange messages

internūnt·ius -(i)ī *m,* **internūnti·a -ae** *f* messenger, courier; mediator, go-between

intern·us -a -um *adj* internal; civil, domestic

in·terō -terere -trīvī -trītus *tr* to rub in; to crumble up

interpellāti·ō -ōnis *f* interruption

interpellāt·or -ōris *m* interrupter; petitioner

interpell·ō -āre -āvī -ātus *tr* to interrupt, break in on; to disturb, obstruct; to raise an objection; to accost with a request

interpol·is -is -e *adj* patched up, touched up, made like new

interpol·ō -āre -āvī -ātus *tr* to refurbish, touch up; to make like new

inter·pōnō -pōnere -posuī -positus *tr* to insert, interpose, intersperse; to add as an ingredient; to include *(in a speech or book);* to introduce, bring into play; to introduce as witness *or* participant; to admit *(a person);* to let *(time)* pass; to alter, falsify *(writings);* to allege, use as a pretext; *(w.* **inter** *+ acc)* to place between; **auctōritātem interpōnere** to assert one's authority, exert one's influence; **fidem interpōnere** to give one's word; **fidem suam in eam rem interpōnere** to give his word in that matter; **operam** *(or* **studium***)* **interpōnere** to apply effort ‖ *refl v* to interfere; to intervene in order to veto; *(w. dat or* **in** *+ acc)* to interfere with, meddle with, get mixed up with ‖ *pass (of time)* to elapse in the meantime, intervene; to lie between; *(of writing)* to contain insertions

interpositi·ō -ōnis *f* insertion; introduction; inclusion; parenthetical statement

interposit·us -ūs *m* interposition

interpositus *pp of* **interpōnō**

interpr·es -etis *mf* mediator, negotiator; middleman, broker; interpreter; expounder; translator

interpretāti·ō -ōnis *f* interpretation, explanation; meaning; translation

interpret·or -ārī -ātus sum *tr* to interpret, construe; to infer, conclude; to decide; to translate

inter·primō -primere -pressī -pressus *tr* to squeeze; **faucēs interprimere** to choke

interpūncti·ō -ōnis *f* punctuation

interpūnct·um -ī *n* pause *(between words and sentences);* punctuation mark

interpūnct·us -a -um *adj* well-divided; *(w. abl)* interspersed with

inter·pungō -pungere -pūnxī -pūnctus *tr* to divide *(words)* with punctuation, punctuate; to intersperse

interqui·ēscō -ēscere -ēvī *intr* to rest awhile; to pause awhile

interrēgn·um -ī *n* interregnum *(time between the death of one king and election of another or similar interval between consuls)*

inter·rēx -rēgis *m* interrex, regent

interrit·us -a -um *adj* undaunted

interrogāti·ō -ōnis *f* question; interrogation; cross-examination; argument developed by question and answer

interrogāt·um -ī *n* question; **ad interrogātum respondēre** to answer the question

interrog·ō -āre -āvī -ātus *tr* to ask, question; to interrogate, cross-examine; to sue; to seek information from; **cāsus interrogandī** *(gram)* genitive case; **sententiam interrogāre** to ask *(a senator's)* opinion; **lēge** *(or* **lēgibus***)* **interrogāre** *(leg)* to arraign, indict ‖ *intr* to ask a question, ask questions; to argue, reason

interrumpō interrumpere interrūpī interruptus *tr* to break apart, break in half; to break up, smash; to divide, scatter; to interrupt, break off

interruptē *adv* with interruptions

interruptus *pp of* **interrumpō**

intersaep·iō -īre -sī -tus *tr* to fence off, ēnclose; to stop up, close, cut off

inter·scindō -scindere -scidī -scissus *tr* to tear apart, tear down; to cut off, separate

interscrī·bō -bere -psī -ptus *tr* to write *(s.th.)* in between

interser·ō -ere -uī *tr* to interpose, insert; *(w. dat)* to add *(s.th.)* to

interspīrāti·ō -ōnis *f (rhet)* breathing pause, correct breathing *(in delivering a speech)*

interstīnct·us -a -um *adj* blotchy, spotted

interstin·guō -guere -xī -ctus *tr* to spot, blotch; to extinguish

interstring·ō -ere *tr* to squeeze; to strangle

inter·sum -esse -fuī *intr* to be present, assist, take part; to differ; to be of interest; *(w. dat)* **1** to be present at, attend; **2** take part in; *(w.* **in** *+ acc)* to be present at ‖ *v impers* there is a difference; it makes a difference; it is of importance; it is of interest; *(w.* **inter** *+ acc or* in + *abl*) there is a difference between; *(w. gen or with fem of poss pronouns* **meā, tuā, nostrā,** *etc.)* it makes a difference to, it is of importance to, it concerns (me, you, us, etc.); *(w. gen of value, e.g.,* **magnī, permagnī, tantī,** *or w.* adv **multum, plūrimum, maximē**) it makes a (great, very great, such a great) difference, it is of (great, very great, such great) concern; **nē minimum quidem interest** there is not the slightest difference; **nihil omnīnō interest** there is no difference whatever

intertext·us -a -um *adj* interwoven

intertra·hō -here -xī -ctus *tr (w. dat)* to take *(s.th.)* away from

intertrīment·um -ī *n* wear and tear; loss, wastage

interturbāti·ō -ōnis *f* confusion, turmoil

interturb·ō -āre -āvī *tr* to confuse

intervall·um -ī *n* interval, space, distance; gap, opening; interval of time, spell; pause; break, intermission; contrast, difference *(in degree, quality, etc.);* **ex intervallō** at *or* from a distance; after a while; at intervals; **ex intervallīs** at intervals; **longo intervallō** after a long while, much later; **per intervallum** *(or* **intervalla)** at intervals

inter·vellō -vellere -vulsī -vulsus *tr* to pluck here and there

inter·veniō -venīre -vēnī -ventus *tr* to interfere with **‖** *intr* to happen along, come on the scene; to intervene, intrude; to happen, crop up; *(w. dat)* to interfere with, interrupt, put a stop to, come in the way of, oppose, prevent

intervent·or -ōris *m* intruder, untimely visitor

intervent·us -ūs *m* intervention; intrusion; mediation

interver·tō -tere -tī -sus *tr* (**-vort-**) to divert, embezzle

intervīs·ō -ere -ī -us *tr* to drop in on; to visit from time to time

intervolit·ō -āre -āvī *intr* to flit about

intervom·ō -ere -uī -itus *tr (w.* **inter** + *acc)* to throw up amongst

intervulsus *pp of* **intervellō**

intestābil·is -is -e *adj* infamous, notorious; detestable, shameful

intestātō *adv* intestate

intestāt·us -a -um *adj* intestate; unconvicted by witnesses

intestīn·us -a -um *adj* internal **‖** *n* alimentary canal; intestine; **intestīnum tenue** small intestine

intexī *perf of* **integō**

intex·ō -ere -uī -tus *tr* to interweave, interlace; to weave; to embroider; to surround, envelop

intib·um -ī *n* (**inty-**) endive

intimē *adv* intimately, cordially

intim·us -a -um *adj* (**-tum-**) innermost; deepest, most abstruse, most profound; most secret, most intimate **‖** *m* close friend

in·tingō -tingere -tīnxī -tīnctus *tr* to dip, soak; to color *(w. cosmetics)*

intolerābil·is -is -e *adj* intolerable; irresistible

intolerand·us -a -um *adj* intolerable

intoler·āns -antis *adj* intolerable; *(w. gen)* unable to stand, unable to put up with

intoleranter *adv* intolerably, immoderately, excessively

intoleranti·a -ae *f* impatience

inton·ō -āre -uī -itus *tr* to thunder forth **‖** *intr* to thunder

intōns·us -a -um *adj* unshorn, untrimmed; long-haired; rude

intor·queō -quēre -sī -tus *tr* to twist, turn, roll; *(w.* **circum** + *acc)* to wrap *(s.th.)* around; *(w. dat or* **in** + *acc)* to hurl *(e.g., spear)* at

intort·us -a -um *adj* twisted; tangled; *(fig)* crooked

intrā *adv* on the inside, inside, within; inward

intrā *prep (w. acc)* **1** inside, within; **intrā parietēs** within the walls, at home, privately; **intrā sē** to oneself, privately; by oneself, alone; in one's own country, at home; **2** inside *(a period of time),* within, during, in the course of, in less than; **intrā hōs diēs** within these (last few) days; **3** within the limits of, without passing beyond, on this side of, short of *(a certain point);* **modicē hoc facere aut etiam intrā modum** to do this with moderation and even keep on the safe side of moderation; **intrā tēlī iactum prōgredī** to come within range; **intrā (et) extrā** inside and out, on both sides

intrābil·is -is -e *adj* approachable

intractābil·is -is -e *adj* intractable, unmanageable; formidable

intractāt·us -a -um *adj* untamed; unbroken *(horse);* unattempted

intrem·īscō -īscere -uī *intr* to begin to tremble

intrem·ō -ere -uī *intr* to shake, tremble, shiver

intrepidē *adv* calmly, intrepidly

intrepid·us -a -um *adj* calm, intrepid, not nervous; untroubled

intric·ō -āre -āvī -ātus *tr* to entangle, involve

intrīnsecus *adv (opp:* **extrīnsecus**) on the inside; to the inside, inwards

intrīt·us -a -um *adj* not worn away; *(fig)* not worn out

intrō *adv* inwards, inside, in

intr·ō -āre -āvī -ātus *tr & intr* to enter; to penetrate

intrō·dūcō -dūcere -dūxī -ductus *tr* to bring in, lead in; to introduce; to raise *(a subject, point)*

intrōducti·ō -ōnis *f* introduction

intrō·eō -īre -īvī *or* **-iī -itum** *tr & intr* to enter intrō·ferō -ferre -tulī -lātus *tr* to carry in; *(w.* in + *acc)* to carry into; **pedem intrōferre** *(w.* in + *acc)* to set foot in

intrō·gredior -gredī -gressus sum *intr* to step inside

introit·us -ūs *m* entrance; hostile entry; invasion; beginning, prelude

introlātus *pp of* intrōferō

intrō·mittō -mittere -mīsī -missus *tr* to let in, admit; to send in; to introduce

intrōrsum *adv* (-sus) inwards, toward the inside; *(fig)* inwardly

intrō·rumpō -rumpere -rūpī -ruptus *tr* to break in, enter by force

intrōspect·ō -āre *tr* to look in on

intrō·spiciō -spicere -spexī -spectus *tr* to look into; to look at, regard; *(fig)* to look into, examine **‖** *intr (w.* in + *acc) (lit & fig)* to look into, inspect

intub·um -ī *n* endive

intu·eor -ērī -itus sum *or* intu·or -ī *tr* to look at, gaze at; to consider, take into consideration; to look up to, have regard for; to keep an eye on; to examine visually, inspect **terram intuērī** to look down at the ground

intum·ēscō -ēscere -uī *intr* to swell up, rise; *(of voice)* to grow louder; *(of river)* to rise, become swollen; to become angry; to get a big head, swell with pride

intumulāt·us -a -um *adj* unburied

intuor *see* intueor

inturbid·us -a -um *adj* undisturbed, quiet

intus *adv* inside, within; at home, in; to the inside; from within

intūt·us -a -um *adj* unsafe; unprotected, unguarded, defenseless

inul·a -ae *f* elecampane *(tall, coarse plant with yellow flowers)*

inult·us -a -um *adj* unavenged; unpunished

inumbr·ō -āre -āvī -ātus *tr* to shade; to cover

inundāti·ō -ōnis *f* inundation, flood

inund·ō -āre -āvī -ātus *tr* to inundate, flood **‖** *intr* to overflow; **sanguine inundāre** to run red with blood

in·ungō (in·unguō) -ungere -ūnxī -ūnctus *tr* to anoint

inurbānē *adv* impolitely, rudely

inurbān·us -a -um *adj* impolite; unsophisticated, rude, rustic

inur·geō -gēre -sī *intr* to butt

in·ūrō -ūrere -ūssī -ūstus *tr* to burn in, brand, imprint; *(w. dat)* **1** to brand upon, imprint upon, affix to; **2** to inflict upon

inūsitātē *adv* unusually, strangely

inūsitāt·us -a -um *adj* unusual, strange, uncommon, extraordinary

inūstus *pp of* inūrō

inūtil·is -is -e *adj* useless; unprofitable; impractical; injurious, harmful

inūtilit·ās -ātis *f* uselessness; harmfulness

inūtiliter *adv* uselessly; harmfully

invā·dō -dere -sī -sus *tr* to come *or* go into, enter; to enter upon, undertake, attempt; to invade, attack, rush upon; *(fig)* to seize, take possession of **‖** *intr* to come *or* go in; to invade; *(w.* in + *acc)* **1** to invade; to assail; **2** to seize; **3** to get possession of; **4** to rush to embrace

inval·ēscō -ēscere -uī *intr* to grow stronger; *(fig)* to increase in power; to grow in frequency; to predominate

invalid·us -a -um *adj* weak; feeble; dim *(light, fire);* inadequate; ineffectual

invāsī *perf of* invādō

invāsus *pp of* invādō

invecti·ō -ōnis *f* importation, importing; arrival by boat

in·vehō -vehere -vēxī -vectus *tr* to carry in, bring in, ship in *(by cart, horse, boat, etc.); (w. dat)* to bring *(e.g., evils)* upon **‖** *refl (w. acc or* in + *acc)* to rush against, attack **‖** *pass* to ride, drive, sail; *(w. acc or* in + *acc)* **1** to ride into, sail into; **2** to attack; **3** to inveigh against, attack *(w. words);* **invehī equō** to ride a horse; **invehī nāve** to sail

invēndibil·is -is -e *adj* unsaleable

in·veniō -venīre -vēnī -ventus *tr* to come upon, find, come across, discover; to find out, to invent, devise; to learn, ascertain; to get, reach, earn

inventi·ō -ōnis *f* inventiveness; inventing; invention

invent·or -ōris *m,* inventr·īx -īcis *f* inventor, author, discoverer

invent·us -a -um *pp of* inveniō **‖** *n* invention, discovery

invenust·us -a -um *adj* having no sex appeal; homely, unattractive; unlucky in love

inverēcund·us -a -um *adj* disrespectful, immodest, shameless

inverg·ō -ere *tr (w. dat or* in + *acc)* to pour upon

inversi·ō -ōnis *f* inversion *(of words);* irony; allegory

invers·us -a -um *pp of* invertō **‖** *adj* turned upside down; turned inside out; **manus inversa** back of the hand

inver·tō -tere -tī -sus *tr* to invert, turn upside down, upset, reverse, turn inside out; to transpose, reverse; to pervert, abuse, misrepresent; to use ironically

invesperāsc·it -ere *v impers* evening is approaching, twilight is falling

investīgāti·ō -ōnis *f* investigation; search

investīgāt·or -ōris *m* investigator

investīg·ō -āre -āvī -ātus *tr* to track, trace, search after; to investigate, search into, search after

inveter·āscō -āscere -āvī *intr* to begin to grow old, get old; to become fixed, become established; to become rooted, grow inveterate; to become obsolete

inveterāti·ō -ōnis *f* chronic illness

inveterāt·us -a -um *adj* inveterate, long-standing

invēxī *perf of* **invehō**

invicem *or* **in vicem** *adv* in turn, taking turns, one after another, alternately; mutually, each other; **dēfatigātīs invicem integrī succēdunt** fresh troops take turns in relieving the exhausted troops

invict·us -a -um *adj* unconquered; invincible

invid·ēns -entis *adj* envious, jealous

invidenti·a -ae *f* envy, jealousy

invideō -vidēre -vīdī -vīsus *tr* to envy, be jealous of **‖** *intr* (*w. dat*) to envy, begrudge; (*w. dat of person and abl of cause or* **in** + *abl*) to begrudge (*s.o. s.th.*), to envy (*s.o.*) because of (*s.th.*)

invidi·a -ae *f* envy, jealousy; unpopularity; **invidiae esse** (*w. dat*) to be the cause of envy to; **invidiam habēre** to be unpopular

invidiōsē *adv* spitefully; so as to bring unpopularity on an opponent

invidiōs·us -a -um *adj* envious; spiteful; envied; enviable, causing envy

invid·us -a -um *adj* envious, jealous; (*w. dat*) hostile to, unfavorable to

invigil·ō -āre -āvī -ātum *intr* to be alert, be on one's toes; (*w. dat*) to be on the lookout for, keep an eye on, pay attention to, watch over; (*w.* **prō** + *abl*) to watch over

inviolābil·is -is -e *adj* inviolable; invulnerable, indestructible

inviolātē *adv* inviolately

inviolāt·us -a -um *adj* inviolate, unhurt; inviolable

invīsitāt·us -a -um *adj* unusual, strange; not seen before, unknown

invīs·ō -ere -ī -us *tr* to visit, go to see; to look into, inspect; to look after; to catch sight of

invīs·us -a -um *pp of* **invideō ‖** *adj* unseen; hated, detested; hostile

invītāment·um -ī *n* attraction, allurement, inducement

invītāti·ō -ōnis *f* invitation; challenge

invītāt·us -ūs *m* invitation

invītē *adv* unwillingly, against one's wishes

invīt·ō -āre -āvī -ātus *tr* to invite; to entertain; to summon, challenge; to ask, request; to allure, attract; to encourage, court

invīt·us -a -um *adj* reluctant, unwilling, against one's will; **invītā Minervā** against one's better judgment, against the grain

invi·us -a -um *adj* without roads, trackless, impassable **‖** *npl* rough terrain

invocāti·ō -ōnis *f* invocation

invocāt·us -a -um *adj* unbidden

invoc·ō -āre -āvī -ātus *tr* to invoke, call upon; to call out (*name of one's girlfriend in rolling dice*); to pray for; to address (*with an honorific title*)

involāt·us -ūs *m* flight

involgō *see* **invulgō**

involit·ō -āre -āvī *intr* (*w. dat*) (of long hair) to trail over

invol·ō -āre -āvī -ātus *tr* to swoop down on, pounce on **‖** *intr* to swoop down; (*w.* **in** + *acc*) to swoop down on

involūcr·um -ī *n* wrapper; cover; envelope; (*fig*) cover-up, front

involūt·us -a -um *adj* complicated

invol·vō -vere -vī -ūtus *tr* to wrap up; to involve, envelop; to cover completely, overwhelm; (*w. dat or* **in** + *acc*) to pile (*s.th.*) on **‖** *refl* (*w. dat*) (*fig*) to get all wrapped up in

involvol·us -ī *m* caterpillar (*which rolls up the leaves it infests*)

invulg·ō -āre -āvī -ātus *tr* (-**vol**-) to reveal, publicize **‖** *intr* to give public evidence

iō *interj* (*expressing joy*) ho!; hurray!; (*expressing pain*) ah!; (*in a sudden call*) yo!

Ī·ō -ūs *or* **-ōnis** *f* (*acc & abl:* **Īō**) Io (*daughter of Argive King Inachus, loved by Jupiter, changed into a heifer because of fear of Juno, and driven by Juno over the world*)

Iocast·a -ae *or* **Iocast·ē -ēs** *f* Jocasta (*wife of Laius, and mother as well as wife of Oedipus*)

iocāti·ō -ōnis *f* jesting, humor

iocineris *gen of* **iecur**

ioc·or -ārī -ātus sum *or* **ioc·ō -āre** *tr* to say in jest **‖** *intr* to joke, crack a joke, be joking

iocōsē *adv* humorously, as a joke, jokingly

iocōs·us -a -um *adj* humorous, funny; fond of jokes

ioculār·is -is -e *adj* humorous, funny

ioculāri·us -a -um *adj* ludicrous

ioculāt·or -ōris *m* joker

iocul·or -ārī -ātus sum *intr* to joke

iocul·us -ī *m* joke; **ioculō** as a joke, in fun

ioc·us -ī *m* (*pl:* **ioc·ī -ōrum** *mpl,* **ioc·a -ōrum** *npl*) joke; laughing stock; child's play; **iocō remōtō** all joking aside; **per iocum** as a joke

Īolā·us -ī *m* son of Iphicles and companion of Hercules

Īol·ē -ēs *f* daughter of Eurytus, who fell in love with Hercules

Īōn·es -um *mpl* Ionians (*Greek inhabitants of the W. coast of Asia Minor*)

Īōnic·us -a -um *adj* Ionic **‖** *m* Ionic dancer **‖** *npl* Ionic dance

Īōni·us -a -um *adj* Ionian **‖** *f* Ionia (*coastal district of Asia Minor*) **‖** *n* Ionian Sea (*off W. coast of Greece*)

īōta *indecl n* iota (*ninth letter of the Greek alphabet*)

Īphianass·a -ae f Iphigenia

Īphigenī·a -ae f daughter of Agamemnon and Clytemnestra, who was to have been sacrificed at Aulis but was saved by Artemis

Īphit·us -ī m Argonaut, son of Eurytus and Antiope

ips·a -īus or **-ius** adj self, very, just, mere, precisely; in person; by herself, alone; of her own accord ‖ pron she herself; lady of the house

ips·e or **ips·us -īus** or **-ius** adj self, very, just, mere, precisely; in person; by himself, alone; of his own accord ‖ pron he himself; master; host

ipsim·a -ae f (coll) boss

ipsim·us -ī m (coll) boss

ips·um -īus or **-ius** adj self, very, just, mere, precisely; by itself, alone; of itself, spontaneously; **nunc ipsum** just then ‖ pron it itself, that itself; **ipsum quod** ... the very fact that

ipsus see **ipse**

īr·a -ae f wrath, resentment

īrācundē adv angrily; passionately

īrācundi·a -ae f quick temper; anger, wrath, passion, violence; resentment

īrācund·us -a -um adj hot-tempered, irritable; angry; resentful

īrāsc·or -ārī intr to get angry, fly into a rage; (w. dat) to get angry with

īrātē adv angrily

īrāt·us -a -um adj irate, angry, enraged; (w. dat) angry at

īrōnī·a -ae f irony

irrās·us -a -um adj unshaven

irrationāl·is -is -e adj (inr-) irrational

irrau·cēscō -cēscere -sī intr (inr-) to become hoarse

irredivīv·us -a -um adj (inre-) irreparable

irred·ux -ucis adj (inre-) one-way (road)

irreligāt·us -a -um adj (inre-) not tied

irreligiōsē adv (inr-) impiously, blasphemously

irreligiōs·us -a -um adj (inr-) irreligious, impious

irremeābil·is -is -e adj (inr-) from which there is no return, one-way

irreparābil·is -is -e adj (inr-) irretrievable; irreparable (damage)

irrepert·us -a -um adj (inr-) undiscovered, not found

irrēp·ō -ere -sī -tum intr (inr-) to creep in; (fig) to sneak in; (w. ad or in + acc) to creep toward or into; (fig) to sneak up on

irreprehēns·us -a -um adj (inr-) blameless

irrequiēt·us -a -um adj (inr-) restless

irresect·us -a -um adj (inr-) untrimmed

irresolūt·us -a -um adj (inr-) not loosened, still tied, unrelaxed

irrēt·iō -īre -īvī or **-iī -ītus** tr (inr-) to net, trap in a net

irretort·us -a -um adj (inr-) not turned back; **oculō irretortō** without one backward glance

irrever·ēns -entis adj (inr-) irreverent, disrespectful

irreverenter adv (inr-) irreverently, disrespectfully

irreverenti·a -ae f (inr-) irreverence, disrespect

irrevocābil·is -is -e adj (inr-) irrevocable; implacable, relentless

irrevocāt·us -a -um adj (inr-) not called back, not asked back

irrī·deō -dēre -sī -sus tr (inr-) to ridicule, laugh at ‖ intr to laugh, joke; (w. dat) to laugh at

irrīdiculē adv (inr-) with no sense of humor

irrīdicul·um -ī n (inr-) laughing stock

irrigāti·ō -ōnis f (inr-) irrigation

irrig·ō -āre -āvī -ātus tr (inr-) to irrigate, water; to inundate; (fig) to diffuse; (fig) to flood, steep, soak

irrigu·us -a -um adj (inr-) wet, soaked, well-watered; refreshing

irrīsī (inr-) perf of **irrīdeō**

irrīsi·ō -ōnis f (inr-) ridicule, mockery

irrīs·or -ōris m (inr-) reviler, mocker

irrīsus (inr-) pp of **irrīdeō**

irrīs·us -ūs m (inr-) mockery, derision; laughing stock, object of derision

irrītābil·is -is -e adj (inr-) easily excited; easily enraged, irritable; sensitive

irrītām·en -inis n (inr-) incentive; provocation

irrītāment·um -ī n (inr-) incentive; provocation

irrītāti·ō -ōnis f (inr-) incitement; irritation, provocation; stimulant

irrīt·ō -āre -āvī -ātus tr (inr-) to provoke, annoy; to incite; to excite, stimulate; to bring on (a calamity, etc.)

irrit·us -a -um adj (inr-) not valid, null and void; futile, pointless, useless; unsuccessful (person)

irrogāti·ō -ōnis f (inr-) imposition (e.g., of a fine)

irrog·ō -āre -āvī -ātus tr (inr-) to impose, inflict; to object to (proposals)

irrōr·ō -āre -āvī -ātus tr (inr-) to moisten with dew; to sprinkle, water; **aquam capitī irrōrāre** to sprinkle water on (s.o.'s) head

irruct·ō -āre intr (inr-) to belch

ir·rumpō -rumpere -rūpī -ruptus tr (inr-) to rush into, break down ‖ intr to rush in; (w. dat or in + acc) **1** to rush into, rush through; **2** (fig) to intrude upon

irru·ō -ere -ī intr (inr-) to rush in, force one's way in; (w. dat or in + acc) **1** to rush into; **2**

to rush on; **3** to invade, attack; **irruere in odium** (*w. gen*) to incur the anger of
irrūpī (**inr-**) *perf of* **irrumpō**
irrupti·ō -ōnis *f* (**inr-**) bursting in; forcible entry; (*mil*) incursion; assault
irrupt·us -a -um (**inr-**) *pp of* **irrumpō** ‖ *adj* unbroken
is ēius (*see also* **ea** *and* **id**) *adj* this, that, the said, the aforesaid ‖ *pron* he; **is quī** he who, the person who, the one who
Ismari·us -a -um *adj* of Mt. Ismarus in Thrace; Thracian
ista *see* **iste**
istāc *adv* that way
istāctenus *adv* thus far
istaec *see* **istic**
ist·e -a -ud *adj* that of yours; this, that, the very, that particular; such, of such a kind; that terrible, that despicable ‖ *pron* that one; (*in court*) your client
Isthm·us *or* **Isthm·os -ī** *m* Isthmus of Corinth
istīc *adv* there, in that place; herein; on this occasion
ist·ic -aec -oc *or* -**uc** *adj* that, that of yours; (*in form of questions:* **isticine** *and* **istūcine**) ‖ *pron* the one, that one
istinc *adv* from there; from your side; from what you have
istīusmodī *or* **istīmodī** *or* **istīus modī** *or* **istī modī** *adj* that kind of; **istīusmodī scelus** that kind of crime
istō *adv* where you are; therefore; in that matter
istōc *adv* there, to where you are
istōrsum *adv* in that direction, that way
istūc *adv* there, to that place, to where you are, that way; **istūc veniam** I'll come to that matter
istūcine *see* **istic**
istud *see* **iste**
ita *adv* thus, so, in this manner, in that way; (*of natural consequence*) thus, accordingly, therefore, under these circumstances; (*in affirmation*) yes, true, exactly; (*in questions*) really?, truly?; **ita ... ut** (*in comparisons*) just as ... so; (*introducing contrast*) whereas ... at the same time; (*as adversative*) although ... nevertheless; (*introducing result clauses*) so *or* in such a way that; (*as correlatives*) both ... and, both ... as well as; (*in restriction*) on the condition that, insofar as, on the assumption that; (*of degree*) to such a degree ... that, so much ... that, so ... that; **nōn ita** not very, not especially; **quid ita?** how so?, what do you mean?
Ītali·a -ae *f* Italy
Ītalic·us -a -um *adj* Italic
Ītal·is -idis *adj* Italian ‖ *fpl* Italian women
Ītali·us -a -um *adj* Italian ‖ *f see* **Ītalia**

Ītal·us -a -um *adj* Italian
itaque *adv* and so, and thus, accordingly, therefore, consequently
item *adv* likewise, besides, moreover
it·er -ineris *n* journey, trip; walk; march; day's march; day's journey; route; right of way; duct, passage; method, course, way, road; **ex** (*or* **in**) **itinere** en route, on the way; **iter facere** to take a trip; to travel; to make way; (*mil*) to march; **iter flectere** to change course; **iter patefacere** to clear a way; **iter terrestre** overland route; **itinere** en route; **maximīs itineribus** by marching at top speed
iterāti·ō -ōnis *f* repetition
iter·ō -āre -āvī -ātus *tr* to repeat, renew; to plow again
iterum *adv* again, a second time; **iterum atque iterum** repeatedly, again and again
Ithac·a -ae *or* **Ithac·ē -ēs** *f* Ithaca (*island off W. coast of Greece in the Ionian Sea and home of Odysseus*)
itidem *adv* in the same way
itin- *see* **iter**
iti·ō -ōnis *f* going
it·ō -āre -āvī *intr* to go
it·us -ūs *m* going; departure
It·ys -yos *m* son of Tereus and Procne, who was killed by Procne and served up as food to Tereus
iu- = **iu-**
iub·a -ae *f* mane; crest
iub·ar -aris *n* radiance, brightness; sunshine
iubāt·us -a -um *adj* crested
iubeō iubēre iussī iussus *tr* to order;; to bid, ask, tell; to prescribe (*a task*); to designate, appoint; (*med*) prescribe; (*pol*) to order, decree, ratify; **iubē frātrem tuum salvēre** (*in letters*) best regards to your brother; say good-bye to your brother
iūcundē *adv* pleasantly, delightfully
iūcundit·ās -ātis *f* pleasantness, delight, enjoyment ‖ *fpl* favors
iūcund·us -a -um *adj* pleasant, delightful, agreeable
Iūdae·us -a -um *adj* Jewish ‖ *mf* Jew ‖ *f* Judea, Palestine
Iūdaïc·us -a -um *adj* Jewish; of Judea; (*mil*) stationed in Judea
iūd·ex -icis *m* judge; juror; arbitrator; umpire; critic, scholar; **iūdex mōrum** censor; **mē iūdice** in my judgment
iūdicāti·ō -ōnis *f* judicial investigation; (*fig*) judgment, opinion
iūdicāt·us -a -um *adj* decided, determined ‖ *n* condemned person ‖ *n* judicial decision, judgment; precedent; fine; **iūdicātum facere** to carry out a decision; **iūdicātum solvere** to pay a fine
iūdicāt·us -ūs *m* judgeship

iūdiciāl·is -is -e *adj* judicial, forensic
iūdiciāri·us -a -um *adj* judiciary
iūdic·ium -(i)ī *n* trial, court; sentence; jurisdiction; opinion, decision; faculty of judging, judgment, good judgment, taste, tact, discretion; criterion; **ad iūdicium īre** to go to court; **in iūdiciō esse** to be under investigation; **in iūdicium dēdūcere** *(or* **vocāre)** to take to court; **in iūdicium venīre** to come before the court; **iūdicium agere** to conduct a trial; **iūdicium dare** *(or* **reddere)** *(of a praetor)* to grant an action; **iūdicium facere (in +** *acc)* to pass judgment against; **iūdicium tenēre** *(or* **vincīre)** to win a case; **iūdicium prīvātum** civil suit; **iūdicium pūblicum** criminal trial; **meō iūdiciō** in my judgment; **suō iūdiciō** intentionally; **suprēma iūdicia** last will and testament
iūdic·ō -āre -āvī -ātus *tr* to judge; to examine; to sentence, condemn; to form an opinion of; to conclude; to declare, proclaim; *(w. dat of person and acc of the offense)* to convict *(s.o.)* of; *(w. gen)* to find *(s.o.)* guilty of; *(w. dat of person and gen of the offense)* to convict *(s.o.)* of
iugāl·is -is -e *adj* yoked together; nuptial
iugāti·ō -ōnis *f* tying up
iūger·um -ī *n* jugerum *(land measure, about ⅔ of an acre)*
iūg·is -is -e *adj* continuous, perennial, inexhaustible
iūgl·āns -andis *f* walnut tree; walnut
iugōs·us -a -um *adj* hilly
Iugul·ae -ārum *fpl (astr)* Orion's Belt *(3 stars in the constellation Orion)*
iugul·ō -āre -āvī -ātus *tr* to cut the throat of, kill, murder; to destroy; to silence
iugul·um -ī *n,* **iugul·us -ī** *m* throat
iug·um -ī *n* yoke, collar; pair, team; crossbar *(of loom);* thwart *(of boat);* common bond, union; wedlock; pair, couple; mountain ridge; *(mil)* yoke *(consisting of a spear laid crosswise on two upright spears, under which the conquered had to pass)* ‖ *npl* heights
Iugurth·a -ae *m* king of Numidia *(160–104 B.C.)*
Iūli·a -ae *f* aunt of Julius Caesar and wife of Marius ‖ daughter of Julius Caesar and wife of Pompey *(d. 54 B.C.)* ‖ daughter of Augustus by Scribonia *(39 B.C.–A.D. 14)*
Iūli·us -a -um *adj* Julian; of July; **mēnsis Iūlius** July ‖ *m* Roman first name *(praenomen);* July
Iūl·us -ī *m* son of Aeneas *(also called Ascanius)*
iūment·um -ī *n* beast of burden, horse, mule
iunce·us -a -um *adj* of reeds; slim, slender
iuncōs·us -a -um *adj* overgrown with reeds

iūnctim *adv* side by side; in succession
iūncti·ō -ōnis *f* joining, combination, union
iūnctūr·a -ae *f* joining, uniting, joint, juncture; connection, relationship; combination
iūnct·us -a -um *pp of* **iungō** ‖ *adj* connected, associated, united, attached
iunc·us -ī *m* reed
iungō iungere iūnxī iūnctus *tr* to join, join together, unite, connect; to yoke, harness; to couple, pair, mate; to bridge *(a river);* to bring together, associate, ally; to add; to compose *(poems);* to combine *(words)*
iūni·or -ōris *adj (mas & fem only)* younger ‖ *mpl* younger men *(esp. of military age, between 17 and 46 years)*
iūniper·us -ī *f* juniper
Iūni·us -a -um *adj* June, of June; **mēnsis Iūnius** June ‖ *m* Roman first name *(praenomen);* June
iūn·ix -īcis *f* heifer
Iūn·ō -ōnis *f* daughter of Saturn and wife and sister of Jupiter *(commonly identified with Hera);* woman's tutelary deity *(corresponding to a male's* **genius); Iūnō Lūcīna** goddess of childbirth *(applied to Juno and Diana);* **Iūnō īnferna** name of Proserpina *(queen of the lower world);* **Iūnōnis avis** peacock; **Iūnōnis stella** planet Venus
Iuppiter *(or* **Diēspiter) Iovis** *m* son of Saturn, brother and husband of Juno, and chief god of the Romans *(commonly identified with Zeus)*
iūrāt·or -ōris *m* judge; assistant censor
iūrāt·us -a -um *adj* being under oath; having given one's word
iūre *adv* rightfully; with good reason, deservedly; correctly
iūrecōnsult·us -ī *m* **(iūris-)** legal expert
iūreperītus *see* **iūrisperītus**
iurg·ium -(i)ī *n* quarrel ‖ *npl* reproaches, abuse
iurg·ō -āre -āvī -ātus *tr* to scold ‖ *intr* to quarrel
iūridiciāl·is -is -e *adj* juridical
iūriscōnsult·us -ī *m* **(iūre-)** legal expert, lawyer
iūrisdicti·ō -ōnis *f* administration of justice; jurisdiction
iūrisperīt·us -ī *m* **(iūre-)** legal expert, lawyer
iūr·ō -āre -āvī -ātus *tr* to swear; to swear by, attest, call to witness; to swear to, attest; to promise under oath, vow ‖ *intr* to swear, take an oath; *(w. in +* *acc)* **1** to swear allegiance to; **2** to swear to observe *(the laws, etc.);* **3** to conspire against; **in haec verba iūrāre** to swear according to the prescribed form; **in verba alicūius iūrāre** to swear allegiance to s.o.; **iūrāre calumniam** to swear that the accusation is not false

iūs iūris *n* juice, broth, gravy

iūs iūris *n* law, the laws *(as established by society and custom rather than statute law);* legal system, right, justice; law court; legal right, authority, permission; prerogative; jurisdiction; **in iūs īre** to go to court; **iūra dare** to prescribe laws, administer justice; **iūre** by right, rightfully; **iūs cīvīle** civil law; **iūs dīcere** to sit as judge, hold court; **iūs gentium** law available to aliens as well as to citizens; international law; **iūs patrium** the power of life or death over one's children; **iūs praetōrium** principles of law contained in a praetor's edict; **iūs pūblicum** constitutional law; **meī iūris** subject to my control; **prō iūre suō** without exceeding one's rights, at will, freely; in one's own right; **suī iūris** *(or* **suō iūre)** legally one's own master; **summum iūs** strict letter of the law

iūsiūrandum *or* iūs iūrandum *(gen:* iūr·isiūrand·ī *or* iūr·is iūrand·ī) *n* oath; **aliquem iūreiūrandō adigere** to bind s.o. with an oath, have s.o. take an oath

iūssū *(abl only) m* by order; **meō iūssū** by my order

iūss·us -a -um *pp of* iubeō ‖ *n* order, command, bidding

iūstē *adv* justly, rightly

iūstific·us -a -um *adj* righteous

iūstiti·a -ae *f* justice, fairness

iūstit·ium -(i)ī *n* suspension of legal business, legal holiday; period of mourning; *(fig)* standstill

iūst·us -a -um *adj* just, fair; justified, wellfounded; formal; in due order, according to protocol, regular ‖ *n* justice; due measure; **plūs quam iūstō** more than due measure, too much ‖ *npl* rights, one's due; regular tasks, formalities; ceremonies, due ceremony; funeral rites, obsequies

Iūturn·a -ae *f* nymph, sister of Turnus, the king of the Rutuli

iūtus *pp of* iuvō

iuvenāl·is -is -e *adj* youthful; juvenile ‖
  Iuvenālis *m* Juvenal *(Decimus Junius Juvenalis, Roman satirist in the time of Domitian and Trajan, c. A.D. 62–142)*

iuvenc·us -a -um *adj* young ‖ *m* bullock; young man ‖ *f* heifer; girl

iuven·ēscō -ēscere *intr* to grow up; to become young again

iuvenīl·is -is -e *adj* youthful; juvenile; cheerful

iuvenīliter *adv* youthfully, boyishly

iuven·is -is -e *adj* young ‖ *m* young man *(between the ages of 20 and 45);* warrior ‖ *f* young lady

iuven·or -ārī -ātus sum *intr* to act like a kid

iuvent·a -ae *f* youth

iuvent·ās -ātis *f or* iuvent·ūs -ūtis *f* youth, prime of life, manhood; *(collectively)* young people, the young, youth

iuv·ō iuvāre iūvī iūtus *tr* to help; *(of terrain)* to give *(one)* an advantage; to back up *(an opinion);* to benefit, do good to; to please, delight ‖ *v impers (w. inf)* it helps to; **iuvat mē** it delights me, I am glad, I am relieved

iūxtā *adv* nearby, in close proximity; alike, in like manner, equally; *(w.* **ac, atque, et, quam,** *or* **cum)** as well as, just the same as ‖ *prep (w. acc)* **1** close to, near to, next to; **2** next to, immediately after; **3** near, bordering on; **4** next door to

iūxtim *adv* near; equally

Ixīone·us -a -um of Ixion

Ixī·ōn -onis *or* -onos *m* Ixion *(king of the Lapiths, who was tied to a wheel by Jupiter for trying to seduce Juno and sent flying into Tartarus)*

Ixīonid·ēs -ae *m* son of Ixion *(esp.* Pirithous)

Ixīoni·us -a -um *adj* of Ixion

J

Note: Following contemporary practice, the letter j *has been replaced by the letter* i *in this dictionary.*

K

K, k *(supply* littera) *f* tenth letter of the Latin alphabet; letter name: **ka**

K. *abbr* **Kaeso** *(Roman first name, praenomen)*

Kalend·ae -ārum *fpl* **(Cal-)** Kalends *(first day of the Roman month);* **ad Kalendās Graecās solvere** to pay on the Greek Kalends *(i.e., never, since there were no Greek Kalends);* **trīstēs Kalendae** gloomy Kalends *(because interest was due on the Kalends)*

Kalendār·ium -(i)ī *n* account book, ledger

Karthāginiēns·is -is -e *adj* **(Carth-)** Carthaginian

Karthāg·ō -inis *f* **(Carth-)** Carthage

L

L, l *(supply* littera) *f* eleventh letter of the Latin alphabet; letter name: **el**

L *abbr* the number 50

L. *abbr* **Lūcius** *(Roman first name, praenomen)*

labāsc·ō -ere *intr* to wave, totter; to give in, yield

lābēcul·a -ae *f* blemish, stain *(of disgrace)*

labe·faciō -facere -fēcī -factus *tr* to cause to totter; to shake, weaken; *(fig)* to cause to waver, shake; *(fig)* to undermine *(authority, power)*

labefactāti·ō -ōnis *f* loosening

labefact·ō -āre -āvī -ātus *tr* to shake, loosen, make unsteady; to undermine the authority of; to undermine *(loyalty, etc.)*

labe·fīō -fierī *pass of* labefaciō

labell·um -ī *n* cute lip

lābell·um -ī *n* small basin

labeōs·us -a -um *adj* thick-lipped

lāb·ēs -is *f* fall, falling down; stroke, blow; disaster; cause of disaster; blot, stain; blemish, defect; disgrace, discredit; *(geol)* subsidence, landslide; **lābem dare** to collapse

labi·a -ae *f and* labi·um -ī *n* (thick) lip; **aliquem labiīs ductāre** *(prov)* to lead s.o. by the nose

Labīcān·us -a -um *adj* of the town of Labici; **Via Labīcāna** a road entering Rome from the S.E. ‖ *n* territory of the Labici

Labīc·ī -ōrum *mpl* small town about 15 miles S.E. of Rome ‖ *mpl* the Labicans

Labiēn·us -a -um *adj* Roman clan name *(nomen), esp.* Titus Labienus *(Caesar's officer who defected to Pompey, d. 45 B.C.)*

labiōs·us -a -um *adj* thick-lipped

lab·ium -(i)ī *n and* labi·a -ae *f* (thick) lip

lab·ō -āre -āvī *intr* to totter, wobble; to waver, hesitate, be undecided; to fall to pieces, go to ruin

lābor lābī lāpsus sum *intr* to glide, slide, slip; to fall, sink; to slip away, disappear, escape; *(of time)* to slip by, pass; *(of liquids, rivers)* to flow; *(of the sun)* to sink down; *(of day)* to decline; *(of style)* to run smoothly; *(of words)* to slip out; *(of a building)* to collapse; *(fig)* to fade; *(fig)* to fall into error, go wrong; **memoriā lābī** to have a lapse of memory; **mente lābī** to go out of one's mind

lab·or *or* lab·ōs -ōris *m* effort, exertion; work, labor; trouble, distress, suffering; cause of distress; wear and tear; product of work, production; drudgery; **lūnae** *(or* sōlis*)* **labōrēs** eclipse of the moon *(or* sun*)*

labōrif·er -era -erum *adj* struggling, hard-working

labōriōs·us -a -um *adj* laborious; full of troubles, troublesome; energetic, industrious, hard-working

labōr·ō -āre -āvī -ātus *tr* to work at; to make by toil; to produce *(grain, etc.); (w. internal acc)* to be worried about, be concerned about, *e.g.:* **hoc hominēs timent, hoc labōrant** people fear this, they are worried about this;

nihil labōrō dē īis I am not concerned about them; nihil labōrō, nisi ut salvus sīs my only concern is that you are O.K. *(literally, I am concerned as to nothing except that you be well)* ‖ *intr* to work, perform physical work; to suffer, be troubled; to exert oneself; *(w. abl of cause or* ab *or* ex*)* **1** to suffer *(physical pain)* from, *e.g.:* (ā) **stomachō** *(or* ex **stomachō) labōrāre** to have stomach trouble; ē **dolōre labōrāre** to suffer pain; ē **rēnibus labōrāre** to have kidney problems; **labōrantēs uterō puellae** pregnant girls, girls in labor *(i.e., in giving birth);* **2** to be distressed at, be anxious about, be worried about, be in trouble because of: **labōrat dē aestimātiōne suā** he is anxious *or* worried about his reputation; **ex aere aliēnō labōrāre** to be heavily in debt, be in trouble because of debt; ē **dolōre labōrāre** to be afflicted with grief; **ex īnscientiā labōrāre** to suffer from ignorance; **cūius manū sit percussus, nōn labōrō** I do not concern myself about whose hand struck him; *(w.* in + *abl)* **1** to be in trouble over, be in danger because of, *e.g.:* **in rē familiārī valdē labōrāre** to be in deep trouble over personal finances, be in deep financial trouble; **2** to take pains with, exert oneself on behalf of, *e.g.:* **multō plūs est in reliquā causā labōrandum** much greater pains must be taken with the rest of the case *or* lawsuit; *(w.* in + *acc)* to strive for, work for, *e.g.:* **in dīvitiās luxuriamque labōrāre** to strive for wealth and luxury; *(w. inf or* ut + *subj)* to strive to, try to, take pains to, make an effort to, *e.g.:* **labōrābat ut reliquās cīvitātēs adiungeret** he tried to annex the rest of the communities; *(w.* dē + *abl)* to be anxious about, be worried about; **lūna labōrat** *(astr)* the moon is in eclipse; **silvae labōrantēs** the groaning forests; **suīs labōrantibus succurrere** to help his own people in difficulty

labōs *see* labor

lābr·um -ī *n* basin, tub, bathtub

labr·um -ī *n* lip; edge

labrūsc·a -ae *f* wild vine

labrūsc·um -ī *n* wild grape

labyrinthē·us -a -um *adj* labyrinthine

labyrinth·us -ī *m* labyrinth, maze *(esp. that built by Daedalus on Crete)*

lac lactis *n* milk; milky sap of plants

Lacaen·a -ae *f* Spartan woman

Lacedaem·ō(n) -onis *f* Sparta

Lacedaemōni·us -a -um *adj* Spartan

lac·er -era -erum *adj* mangled, lacerated; *(of things)* badly damaged

lacerāti·ō -ōnis *f* laceration, tearing, mangling

lacern·a -ae *f* mantle, cloak

lacernāt·us -a -um *adj* cloaked, wearing a cloak

lacer·ō -āre -āvī -ātus *tr* to lacerate, tear, mangle; to batter, damage; to rack *(w. pain);* to slander, abuse; to waste *(time);* to wreck *(a ship); (fig)* to murder *(a song, speech)*

lacert·a -ae *f* lizard *(female)*

lacertōs·us -a -um muscular

lacert·us -ī *m* lizard; upper arm

lacert·us -a -um *adj* muscular **‖** *m* upper arm; muscle; lizard **‖** *mpl* muscles, brawn **‖** *f* lizard *(female)*

lacess·ō -ere -īvī *or* **-iī -ītus** *tr* to provoke, exasperate; to challenge; to move, arouse

Laches·is -is *f* one of the three Fates

lacini·a -ae *f* flap *(of a garment)*

Lacīn·ium -(i)ī *n* promontory in Bruttium with a temple to Juno

Lac·ō(n) -ōnis *m* Spartan; Spartan dog

Lacōni·a -ae *f* district of the Peloponnesus of which Sparta was the chief city

Lacōnic·us -a -um *adj* Spartan **‖** *n* sweat bath, sauna

lacrim·a -ae *f* (-rum-) tear(drop); *(bot)* gumdrop *(from plant)* **‖** *fpl* tears; dirge

lacrimābil·is -is -e *adj* worthy of tears, deplorable

lacrimābund·us -a -um *adj* tearful, about to break into tears

lacrim·ō -āre -āvī -ātus *tr* (-rum-) to cry for, shed tears over **‖** *intr* to cry, shed tears

lacrimōs·us -a -um *adj* crying, tearful; causing tears, bringing tears to the eyes

lacrimul·a -ae *f* teardrop, little tear; *(fig)* crocodile tear

lacrum- = lacrim-

lact·āns -antis *adj* milk-giving

lactāri·us -a -um *adj* milky

lact·ēns -entis *adj* unweaned, still breast-feeding; milky, juicy, tender; full of milk **‖** *m* suckling

lacteol·us -a -um *adj* milk-white

lact·ēs -ium *fpl* small intestines; *(as a dish)* chitterlings; **laxae lactēs** empty stomach

lactēsc·ō -ere *intr* to turn to milk

lacte·us -a -um *adj* milky, full of milk; milk-colored, milk-white; **lacteus orbis** *or* **lactea via** the Milky Way

lact·ō -āre -āvī -ātus *tr* to cajole, induce

lactūc·a -ae *f* lettuce

lacūna -ae *f* ditch, hole, pit; pond, pool; *(fig)* hole, gap

lacūn·ar -āris *n* paneled ceiling

lacūn·ō -āre -āvī -ātus *tr* to panel

lacūnōs·us -a -um *adj* sunken; pitted

lac·us -ūs *m* vat; tank, pool, reservoir, cistern; lake

lae·dō -dere -sī -sus *tr* to knock, strike; to hurt; to rub open; to wound; to break *(promise,*

pledge); to harm *(reputation, interests);* to offend, outrage, violate; *(w.* **ad)** to smash *(s.th.)* against; *(poet)* to mar

laen·a -ae *f* lined upper garment *(worn by the flamens and by persons of distinction)*

Lāërt·ēs -ae *m* father of Odysseus

laesī *perf of* **laedō**

laesi·ō -ōnis *f* attack, provocation

Laestrȳg·ōn -onis *or* **-onos** *m* Laestrygonian *(one of the mythical races of cannibals in Italy, founders of Formiae)*

Laestrȳgoni·us -a -um *adj* Laestrygonian, of Formiae

laes·us -a -um *pp of* **laedō** **‖** *adj* harmed; **rēs laesae** adversity

laetābil·is -is -e *adj* cheerful, glad

laet·āns -antis *adj* joyful, glad

laetāti·ō -ōnis *f* rejoicing, joy

laetē *adv* joyfully, gladly

Lāërt·ēs -ae *(acc:* **-ēn)** *m* father of Odysseus

Lāërtiad·ēs -ae *m* son of Laërtes *(Odysseus)*

laetific·āns -antis *adj* joyous

laetific·ō -āre -āvī -ātus *tr* to gladden, cheer up **‖** *pass* to rejoice

laetific·us -a -um *adj* joyful, cheerful

laetiti·a -ae *f* joyfulness, gladness, exuberance

laet·or -ārī -ātus sum *intr* to rejoice, be glad

laet·us -a -um *adj* glad, cheerful, rejoicing; happy; fortunate, auspicious; fertile, rich *(soil);* smiling *(grain);* sleek, fat *(cattle);* bright, cheerful *(appearance);* cheering, welcome *(news)*

laevē *adv* awkwardly

laev·us -a -um *adj* left, on the left side; awkward, stupid; ill-omened; lucky, propitious **‖** *f* left hand, left side **‖** *n* the left **‖** *npl* the area on the left

lagan·um -ī *n,* **lagan·us -ī** *m* pancake

lagēna *see* **lagoena**

lagē·os -ī *f* a Greek variety of vine

Lāgē·us -a -um *adj* of Lagus *(i.e., of the Ptolemies),* Egyptian

lagoen·a *or* **lagōn·a** *or* **lagēn·a** *or* **lagūn·a -ae** *f* bottle

lagō·is -idis *f* grouse

lagōna *see* **lagoena**

lagūna *see* **lagoena**

laguncul·a -ae *f* flask

Lāg·us -ī *m* Ptolemy I, King of Egypt

Lāïad·ēs -āe *m* son of Laius *(Oedipus)*

Lāï·us -ī *m* Laius *(father of Oedipus)*

lall·ō -āre *intr* to sing a lullaby

lām·a -ae *f* swamp, bog

lamber·ō -āre *tr* to tear to pieces

lamb·ō -ere -ī *tr* to lick, lap; *(of a river)* to lap, flow by; *(of ivy)* to cling to

lāment·a -ōrum *npl* lamentation

lāmentābil·is -is -e *adj* pitiable; doleful; mournful, sorrowful

lāmentāri·us -a -um *adj* sorrowful, pitiful
lāmentāti·ō -ōnis *f* lamentation
lāment·or -ārī -ātus sum *tr* to lament **ǁ** *intr* to lament, wail, cry
lami·a -ae *f* witch, sorceress
lāmin·a *or* **lammin·a** *or* **lāmn·a -ae** *f* plate, thin sheet *(of metal or wood);* blade; *(coll)* cash; peel, shell
lamp·as -adis *or* **-ados** *f* torch; brightness; light *(of the sun, moon, stars);* meteor; lamp; *(w. numerals)* day
Lam·us -ī *m* king of the Laestrygonians **ǁ** son of Hercules and Omphale
lān·a -ae *f* wool; working in wool, spinning; **lāna aurea** golden fleece; **lānam trahere** to card wool; **lānās dūcere** to spin wool; **rīxārī dē lānā caprīnā** *(prov)* to fight over nothing *(literally, to fight over goat wool)*
lānār·ius -(i)ī *m* wool worker
lānāt·us -a -um *adj* woolly **ǁ** *fpl* sheep
lance·a -ae *f* lance, spear
lancin·ō -āre -āvī -ātus *tr* to squander
lāne·us -a -um *adj* woolen; soft
langue·faciō -facere -fēcī -factus *tr* to make tired
langu·ēns -entis *adj* languid, drooping, listless
langu·eō -ēre *intr* to be tired, be weary; to be weak, be feeble *(from disease);* to be sick; *(fig)* to be listless; to be without energy; *(of water)* to be sluggish; *(of plants)* to droop, wilt
langu·ēscō -ēscere -uī *intr* to become weak, grow faint; to become listless; to decline, decrease; to relax
languidē *adv* weakly; slugglishly
languidul·us -a -um *adj* languid, wiltėd, drooping *(plants)*
languid·us -a -um *adj* weak, faint; weary; languid, sluggish; listless; lazy; drooping, wilting *(plants)*
langu·or -ōris *m* weakness, faintness, languor; listlessness, sluggishness; apathy; idleness
laniāt·us -ūs *m* mangling **ǁ** *mpl* mental anguish
laniēn·a -ae *f* butcher shop
lānific·ium -(i)ī *n* weaving
lānific·us -a -um *adj* spinning, weaving, of spinning, of weaving
lānig·er -era -erum *adj* fleecy **ǁ** *m* sheep *(ram)* **ǁ** *f* sheep *(ewe)*
lani·ō -āre -āvī -ātus *tr* to tear to pieces, mangle
lanist·a -ae *m* gladiator trainer, fencing master; *(pej)* ringleader
lānit·ium -(i)ī *n* wool
lan·ius -(i)ī *m* butcher; *(pej)* executioner, butcher
lantern·a -ae *f* (**lāt-**) lantern
lanternār·ius -(i)ī *m* guide

lānūg·ō -inis *f* down *(of plants, on cheeks)*
Lānuv·ium -(i)ī *n* town in Latium on the Appian Way
lān·x -cis *f* dish, platter; pan *(of a pair of scales);* **aequā lance** impartially
Lāöco·ōn -ontis *m* son of Priam and priest of Apollo, who, with his two sons, was killed by sea serpents
Lāömedontē·us *or* **Lāömedonti·us -a -um** *adj* Trojan
Lāömedontiad·ēs -ae *m* son of Laomedon *(Priam)* **ǁ** *mpl* Trojans
lapath·um -ī *n* or **lapath·us -ī** *f* sorrel *(plant)*
lapicīd·a -ae *m* stonecutter, quarry worker
lapicīdīn·ae -ārum *fpl* stone quarry
lapidāri·us -a -um *adj* stone; **lātomiae lapidāriae** stone quarry **ǁ** *m* stonecutter
lapidāti·ō -ōnis *f* throwing stones, stoning
lapidāt·or -ōris *m* stone thrower
lapide·us -a -um *adj* of stones, stone, stony; **lapideus imber** shower of meteoric stones; **lapideus sum** *(fig)* I am petrified
lapid·ō -āre -āvī -ātus *tr* to throw stones at, stone **ǁ** *v impers* it is raining stones
lapidōs·us -a -um *adj* full of stones, stony; hard as stone; gritty *(bread)*
lapill·us -ī *m* small stone, pebble; precious stone, gem; piece, counter *(in a game);* voting pebble
lap·is -idis *m* stone; milestone; platform; boundary stone, landmark; tombstone; precious stone, gem, pearl; stone statue; marble table; **lapidēs loquī** to speak harsh words
Lapith·ae -ārum *mpl* mountain tribe in Thessaly that fought the centaurs
lapp·a -ae *f* bur *(prickly head or seed vessel of certain plants)*
lāpsi·ō -ōnis *f* sliding, slipping; *(fig)* tendency
lāps·us -ūs *m* falling, fall, sliding, slipping, gliding, flow, flight; blunder, slip; fall from favor; lapse *(of time);* course *(of the stars);* **lāpsus rotārum** rolling wheels
laqueār·ia -ium *npl* paneled ceiling
laqueāt·us -a -um *adj* paneled, having a paneled ceiling
laque·us -ī *m* noose; snare; *(fig)* snare, trap **ǁ** *mpl* subtleties
Lār Laris *(gen plur:* **Larum** *or* **Larium)** *m* tutelary deity, household god; hearth, home **ǁ** *mpl* hearth, home, house, household, family
lard·um -ī *n* bacon
Lārenti·a -ae *f (also* **Acca Lārentia)** wife of Faustulus who reared Romulus and Remus
largē *adv* liberally, generously; in large numbers, in large quantities; to a great extent *or* degree
largific·us -a -um *adj* bountiful
largiflu·us -a -um *adj* gushing
largiloqu·us -a -um *adj* talkative

larg·ior -īrī -ītus sum *tr* to give generously, bestow freely; to lavish; to confer; to grant, concede; to condone, overlook; *(w. dat)* to overlook in favor of: **rogō ut amōrī nostrō plūsculum, quam concedat vēritās, largiāre** I beg you to overlook a little more than truth would allow, in favor of our affection (for each other) ‖ *intr* to give bribes, engage in bribery; *(of time, conditions)* to allow

largit·ās -ātis *f* generosity, bounty

largiti·ō -ōnis *f* generosity; bribery

largīt·or -ōris *m* generous donor; spendthrift; briber

larg·us -a -um *adj* abundant, plentiful, large, much; generous; bountiful, profuse

lārid·um -ī *n* bacon

Lāriss·a -ae *f* (-rīs-) town in Thessaly on the Peneus River, famous for its beauty

Lārissae·us -a -um *adj* (-rīs-) of Larissa

Lār·ius -(i)ī *m* Lake Como

Lar·s -tis *m* first name *(praenomen)* of Etruscan origin, *usu.* given to the eldest son

larv·a -ae *f* mask; ghost; *(pej)* devil

larvāt·us -a -um *adj* bewitched

lasan·um -ī *n or* **lasan·us** -ī *m* chamber pot

lāsarpīcif·er -era -erum *adj* producing asafetida *(used as an anti-spasmodic)*

lāscīvi·a -ae *f* frisking, playfulness; lewdness, sexual freedom; fun

lāscīvibund·us -a -um *adj* frisky

lāscīv·iō -īre -iī -ītum *intr* to frolic, be frisky; to run riot, run wild; to be in heat

lāscīv·us -a -um *adj* playful, frisky; brash, impudent; licentious; horny; luxuriant *(growth)*

lāserpīc·ium -(i)ī *n* silphium *(plant yielding asafetida, used as an anti-spasmodic)*

lassitūd·ō -inis *f* tiredness, lassitude

lass·ō -āre -āvī -ātus *tr* to tire out, exhaust

lassul·us -a -um *adj* somewhat tired

lass·us -a -um *adj* tired, exhausted

lātē *adv* widely, extensively; profusely; **lātē longēque** far and wide; **lātē patēre** to cover a wide field, have wide application

latebr·a -ae *f* hiding place, hideaway, hideout; *(fig)* loophole

latebricol·a -ae *mf* person who hangs around dives and brothels

latebrōsē *adv* secretly

latebrōs·us -a -um *adj* full of holes; hidden, secret; porous

lat·ēns -entis *adj* hidden, secret

latenter *adv* in secret

lat·eō -ēre -uī *intr* to hide, lie hidden; to lurk; to be out of sight, be invisible; to lie below the surface; to keep out of sight, sulk; to live a retired life, remain in obscurity, remain unknown; to escape notice; to be in safety; to avoid a summons, lie low; to be obscure; to take shelter

lat·er -eris *m* brick, tile; brickwork; **laterem lavāre** *(prov)* to waste effort *(literally, to wash sun-dried bricks of clay);* **laterēs dūcere** to make bricks

laterām·en -inis *n* earthenware

latercul·us -ī *m* small brick; tile; biscuit

laterici·us -a -um *adj* brick, of brick ‖ *n* brickwork

lātern·a -ae *f* (lant-) lantern

latēsc·ō -ere *intr* to hide

lat·ex -icis *m* liquid, fluid; water; spring; wine; oil

latibul·um -ī *n* hiding place, hideout, lair, den; *(fig)* refuge

lāticlāvi·us -a -um *adj* having a broad crimson stripe *(distinctive mark of senators, military tribunes of the equestrian order, and of sons of distinguished families)* ‖ *m* senator; nobleman

lātifund·ium -(i)ī *n* large estate, ranch

Latīnē *adv* Latin, in Latin; in proper Latin; in plain Latin; **Latīnē docēre** to teach Latin; **Latīnē loquī** to speak Latin; to speak correct Latin; *(coll)* to talk turkey; **Latīnē reddere** to translate Latin; **Latīnē scīre** to understand Latin

Latīnit·ās -ātis *f* pure Latin, Latinity; Latin rights and privileges

Latīn·us -a -um *adj* Latin; possessing Latin rights and privileges ‖ *m* Latinus *(king of Latium, who gave his daughter Lavinia in marriage to Aeneas)* ‖ *mpl* the Latins, people of Latium ‖ *f* Latin (language) ‖ *n* Latin (language); **in Latīnum convertere** to translate into Latin

lāti·ō -ōnis *f* bringing, rendering; formal proposal *(of a law);* **suffrāgiī lātiō** the franchise

latitāti·ō -ōnis *f* lying in concealment

latit·ō -āre -āvī *intr* to keep hiding oneself; to be concealed, hide, lurk; to lie low *(in order to avoid a summons)*

lātitūd·ō -inis *f* breadth, width; latitude; size, extent; wide area; richness of expression; **lātitūdō verbōrum** drawl; **in lātitūdine** *(or* **per lātitūdinem)** horizontally; **in lātitūdinem** in width

Lati·us -a -um *adj* of Latium, Latin, Roman ‖ *n* Latium *(district in W. central Italy, in which Rome is situated);* **iūs Latiī** *(or* **iūs Latium)** Latin political rights and privileges

lātius *adv* of late

Lātō·is -idis *f* daughter of Latona *(Diana)*

lātom- = **lautom-**

Lātōn·a -ae *f* mother of Apollo and Diana *(equated with the Greek goddess Leto)*

Lātōnigen·a -ae *mf* child of Latona *(Apollo, Diana)*

Lātōni·us -a -um *adj* of Latona ‖ *f* Diana

lāt·or -ōris *m* bringer, bearer; proposer *(of a law)*

Lātō·us -ī *m* son of Latona *(Apollo)*

lātrāt·or -ōris *m* barker; dog

lātrāt·us -ūs *m* barking

lātrīn·a -ae *f* washroom; toilet

lātr·ō -āre -āvī -ātus *tr* to bark at, snarl at ‖ *intr* to bark; *(fig)* to rant

latr·ō -ōnis *m* mercenary; robber, bandit, brigand; *(of animal or hunter)* predator; *(in chess)* pawn

latrōcin·ium -(i)ī *n* military service *(as a mercenary)*; brigandage, banditry, vandalism, piracy; robbery, highway robbery; villany, outrage; band of robbers

latrōcin·or -ārī -ātus sum *intr* to serve as a mercenary; to be a bandit, be a pirate

latruncul·us -ī *m* small-time bandit; piece *(on a battle-game board)*

lātumi·ae -ārum *fpl* stone quarry; prison

lāt·us -a -um *adj* wide, broad; extensive; widespread; drawling *(pronunciation);* in **lātum** in width; **lātus clāvus** broad vertical crimson stripe on the tunic of men of the senatorial class

lat·us -eris *n* side, flank; body, person; lungs; lateral surface; coast; *(mil)* flank; **ā latere** *(mil)* on the flank; **ā latere** *(w. gen)* 1 at the side of, in the company of; 2 from among the friends of; **apertō latere** *(mil)* on the exposed flank; **in latus cubāre** to lie on one's side; **latere tēctō** scot-free; **latus dare** to expose oneself; **latus tegere** *(w. gen)* to walk by the side of, to escort

lātus *pp of* **ferō**

latuscul·um -ī *n* small side

laudābil·is -is -e *adj* laudable

laudābiliter *adv* laudably

laudāti·ō -ōnis *f* commendation; eulogy, panegyric, funeral oration; *(in court)* testimony by a character witness

laudāt·or -ōris *m* praiser; eulogist, panegyrist; *(leg)* character witness

laudāt·us -a -um *adj* praiseworthy, commendable, excellent

laud·ō -āre -āvī -ātus *tr* to praise, commend; to name, quote, cite; to pronounce the funeral oration over, eulogize

laure·a -ae *f* laurel tree; laurel branch; laurel crown, bay wreath; triumph

laureāt·us -a -um *adj* laureate, laureled, crowned with laurel; **litterae laureātae** communiqué announcing victory

Laur·ēns -entis *adj* Laurentian, of Laurentum

Laurent·ēs -um *mpl* Laurentians *(people of Laurentum, a town in Latium)*

Laurentīn·us *or* **Laurenti·us** -a -um *adj* Laurentian

laureol·a -ae *f* little laurel crown; triumph

laure·us -a -um *adj* laurel, of laurel ‖ *f see* **laurea**

lauricom·us -a -um *adj* laurel-covered *(mountain)*

laurif·er -era -erum *or* **laurig·er** -era -erum *adj* producing laurels; crowned with laurels

laur·us -ī *or* -ūs *f* laurel tree, bay; laurel branch; triumph

lau·s -dis *f* praise, commendation; fame, glory; reputation; approval; praiseworthy deed; merit, worth; **laus est** *(w. inf or ut w. subj)* it is praiseworthy to ‖ *fpl* eulogy; praises; **laudibus ferre** *(or* **efferre** *or* **tollere) in** *(or* **ad) caelum** to praise to the skies

Laus·us -ī *m* son of Numitor and brother of Rhea Silvia ‖ son of Mezentius, killed by Aeneas

lautē *adv* sumptuously, splendidly

lauti·a -ōrum *npl* state banquet *(given to foreign ambassadors and state guests)*

lautiti·a -ae *f* luxury, high living

lautumi·ae *or* **lātomi·ae** *or* **lātumi·ae** -ārum *fpl* stone quarry *(esp. used as a prison)*

laut·us -a -um *adj* expensive, elegant, fine; well-heeled; refined, fashionable

lavābr·um -ī *n* bath

lavāti·ō -ōnis *f* washing, bathing, bath; bathing kit

Lāvīni·us -a -um *adj* Lavinian, of Lavinium ‖ *n* town in Latium founded by Aeneas ‖ *f* wife of Aeneas

lav·ō lavāre *(or* **lavere)** **lāvī lautum** *(or* **lavātum** *or* **lōtum)** *tr* to wash, bathe; to wet, drench; to wash away ‖ *refl & pass & intr* to wash, wash oneself, bathe

laxāment·um -ī *n* relaxation, respite, letup, mitigation

laxāt·us -a -um *adj* loose, extended *(e.g., ranks)*

laxē *adv* loosely, widely; freely

laxit·ās -ātis *f* roominess; extent, width; freedom of movement

lax·ō -āre -āvī -ātus *tr* to extend, widen, expand; to spread out, scatter; to open up *(passage, hole);* to undo; to loose *(bonds, bolts, doors);* to untie; to relax *(body, mind);* to slacken; to mitigate; *(fig)* to release, relieve; to unstring *(bow)* ‖ *refl* to increase in size, spread out ‖ *pass* to relax ‖ *intr (of prices)* to go down

lax·us -a -um *adj* roomy, wide; loose, slack; prolonged, extended *(time);* far off, distant *(date);* low *(price);* loose-hanging *(clothes);* wide-open *(door);* gaping *(joints, holes);* *(fig)* relaxed, easygoing

le·a -ae *f* lioness

leaen·a -ae *f* lioness

Lēan·der -drī m youth of Abydos who swam across the Hellespont every night to his girlfriend

Learch·us -ī m son of Athamas and Ino, killed by his mad father

leb·ēs -ētis m cauldron

lectic·a -ae f litter

lectīcār·ius -(i)ī m litter bearer

lectĭcul·a -ae f small litter; small bier

lēcti·ō -ōnis f selection; reading, reading aloud; perusal; **lēctiō senātūs** revision of the Senate roll (by censors)

lectisterniāt·or -ōris m slave who arranged the seating at table

lectistern·ium -(i)ī n ritual feast (at which images of the gods were placed on couches at the table)

lēctĭt·ō -āre -āvī -ātus tr to read and reread; to like to read

lēctiuncul·a -ae f light reading

lēct·or -ōris m reader (esp. a slave who read aloud to his master)

lectul·us -ī m cot; small bed, small couch, settee; humble bier

lēct·us -a -um pp of **lēgo** ‖ adj select, choice, special, elite

lect·us -ī m bed; couch; dining couch; bier; **lectus geniālis** marriage bed (placed in the atrium)

Lēd·a -ae f mother of Helen, Clytemnestra, Castor, and Pollux

lēgāti·ō -ōnis f embassy, mission, legation; members of an embassy; work or report of work of a mission; nominal staff appointment; command of a legion; **lēgātiō lībera** junkct

lēgāt·um -ī n bequest, legacy

lēgāt·us -ī m deputy, representative; commander (of a legion); commander-in-chief; ambassador, envoy; adjutant (of a consul, proconsul, or praetor); **lēgātus Augustī** governor of an imperial province;

lēgī perf of **lego** (to read)

lēgif·er -era -erum adj lawgiving

legi·ō -ōnis f legion (divided into 10 cohorts and numbering between 4,200 and 6,000 men); army, active service

legiōnāri·us -a -um adj legionary ‖ m legionary soldier

lēgirup·a -ae or **lēgirupi·ō -ōnis** m lawbreaker

lēgitimē adv legitimately, lawfully; properly

lēgitim·us -a -um adj legitimate; lawful; regular, right, just, proper; genuine; professional (boxers, gladiators) ‖ npl legal formalities

legiuncul·a -ae f under-manned legion

lēg·ō -āre -āvī -ātus tr to commission; to send on a public mission, despatch; to delegate, deputize; to bequeath, will; (fig) to entrust

lego legere lēgī lēctus tr to read, peruse; to recite, read aloud; to gather, collect, pick; to pick out, choose; to pick one's way through, cross; to sail by, coast along; to pick up, steal; to pick up (news, rumor); **fīla legere** to wind up the thread of life; **senātum legere** to read off the Senate roll

lēgulē·ius -(i)ī m pettifogger

legūm·en -inis n leguminous plant; vegetable; pulse; bean

lemb·us -ī m cutter, yacht (built for speed), speedboat

lemm·a -atis n theme, subject matter; epigram

Lemnicol·a -ae m inhabitant of Lemnos (i.e., Vulcan)

lēmniscāt·us -a -um adj heavily decorated with combat ribbons

lēmnisc·us -ī m ribbon which hung down from a victor's wreath

Lemni·us -a -um adj Lemnian ‖ m Lemnian (i.e., Vulcan) ‖ mpl the people of Lemnos

Lemn·os or **Lemn·us -ī** f large island in the N. Aegean Sea

Lemur·ēs -um mpl ghosts

Lemūri·a -ōrum npl night festival, held on May 9th, 11th, 13th to drive ghosts from the house

lēn·a -ae f madame (of brothel)

Lēnae·us -a -um adj Bacchic; **laticēs Lēnaeī** wine ‖ m Bacchus

lēnē adv gently

lēnīm·en -inis n consolation

lēnīment·um -ī n alleviation

lēn·iō -īre -īvī or **-iī -ītus** tr to soothe, alleviate, calm ‖ intr to calm down

lēn·is -is -e adj mild, gentle, soft, smooth; calm; gentle (slope); weak, mild (medicine); quiet (sleep); mellow (wine); tolerable, moderate (conditions); kind (person)

lēnit·ās -ātis f mildness, gentleness, softness, smoothness; tenderness, clemency

lēniter adv mildly, gently, softly, smoothly; quietly, calmly; halfheartedly; (of style) smoothly

lēnitūd·ō -inis f mildness, gentleness, softness, smoothness

lēn·ō -ōnis m pimp, brothel keeper

lēnōcin·ium -(i)ī n pimping, pandering; allurement; alluring makeup; sexy clothes; flattery

lēnōcin·or -ārī -ātus sum intr to be a pimp; (w. dat) **1** to play up to, pander to; **2** to stimulate, promote

lēnōni·us -a -um adj pimp's

lēn·s -tis f lentil

lentē adv slowly; indifferently, half-heartedly; calmly, leisurely, deliberately

lentēsc·ō -ere intr to get sticky; (fig) to soften, weaken lentīscif·er -era -erum *adj (of a region)* producing mastic trees

lentīsc·us -ī *f* mastic tree *(small evergreen tree that yields an aromatic resin called mastic);* toothpick *(made of mastic wood)*

lentitūd·ō -inis *f* slowness; insensibility, apathy, dullness

lent·ō -āre -āvī -ātus *tr* to bend *(under strain)*

lentul·us -a -um *adj* somewhat slow

lent·us -a -um *adj* sticky, clinging; pliant, limber; slow, sluggish; lingering; irresponsive, reluctant, indifferent, backward; slow-moving; tedious; at rest, at leisure, lazy; calm, unconcerned

lēnul·us -ī *m* little pimp

lēnuncul·us -ī *m* young pimp

lēnuncul·us -ī *m* small boat, skiff

le·ō -ōnis *m* lion ‖ Leō *(astr)* Leo *(constellation and sign of the zodiac)*

Leōnid·ās -ae *m* king of Sparta *(who fell at Thermopylae after a gallant stand in 480 B.C.)*

leōnīn·us -a -um *adj* lion's, of a lion

Leontīn·ī -ōrum *mpl* town in E. Sicily

lep·as -adis *f* limpet *(shellfish)*

lepidē *adv* charmingly, pleasantly, neatly; *(as affirmative answer)* yes; *(of approval)* great!

lepid·us -a -um *adj* charming, delightful, nice, neat; witty, amusing *(writings, remarks)*

lep·ōs *or* lep·or -ōris *m* pleasantness, charm, attractiveness

lep·us -oris *m* hare ‖ Lepus *(astr)* Lepus, the Hare *(constellation)*

lepūscul·us -ī *m* little hare

Lern·a -ae *f* marsh near Argos, where Hercules slew the Hydra

Lernae·us -a -um *adj* Lernaean

Lesbi·us -a -um *adj* of Lesbos, Lesbian ‖ *f* fictitious name given by Catullus to his mistress Clodia ‖ *n* Lesbian wine

Lesb·os *or* Lesb·us -ī *f* large island in the N. Aegean, birthplace of Alcaeus and Sappho

less·us *(gen does not occur; acc:* lessum*) m* loud wailing

lētāl·is -is -e *adj* lethal, fatal, mortal

Lēthae·us -a -um *adj* of Lethe; infernal; causing drowsiness

lēthargic·us -ī *m* lazy fellow

lētharg·us -ī *m* lethargy

Lēth·ē -ēs *f* Lethe *(river of forgetfulness in lower world)*

lētif·er -era -erum *adj* deadly, fatal; **locus lētifer** mortal spot

lēt·ō -āre -āvī -ātus *tr* to kill

lēt·um -ī *n* death; ruin, destruction; **lētō dare** to put to death

Leuc·as -adis *f* "White Island," island off W. Greece

leucasp·is -idis *adj* armed with a white shield

Leucipp·us -ī *m* philosopher, teacher of Democritus, and one of the founders of Atomism *(5th cent. B.C.)*

Leuctr·a -ōrum *npl* small town in Boeotia where Epaminondas defeated the Spartans in 371 B.C.

levām·en -inis *n* alleviation, comfort, consolation

levāment·um -ī *n* alleviation, comfort, consolation

levāti·ō -ōnis *f* lightening, easing; relief, comfort; lessening, mitigation

levicul·us -a -um *adj* somewhat vain

levidēns·is -is -e *adj* poor, inferior

levifīd·us -a -um *adj* untrustworthy

lev·is -is -e *adj* light, not heavy; light-armed; lightly dressed; easily digested; thin, poor *(soil);* nimble; flitting; slight, small; unimportant, trivial; unfounded *(rumor);* easy, simple; mild; gentle, easygoing; capricious, unreliable, fickle; lacking authority; lacking power; unsubstantial, thin; **in levī habēre** to make light of

lēv·is -is -e *adj* smooth; slippery; hairless, beardless; delicate, tender; effeminate; smooth *(style)*

levisomn·us -a -um *adj* light-sleeping

levit·ās -ātis *f* lightness; mobility, nimbleness; levity, frivolity; *(fig)* shallowness

lēvit·ās -ātis *f* smoothness; *(fig)* fluency

leviter *adv* lightly; slightly, a little, somewhat; easily, without difficulty; nimbly

lev·ō -āre -āvī -ātus *tr* to lift up, raise; to lighten, relieve, ease; to console, comfort; to lift off, remove; to lessen, weaken; to release, free; to take away; to avert; to restore, refresh

lēv·ō -āre -āvī -ātus *tr* to make smooth, polish; to soothe

lēv·or -ōris *m* smoothness

lēx lēgis *f* motion, bill; law, statute; rule, regulation; principle, precept; condition, stipulation; **ad lēgem** neatly; **eā lēge ut** with the stipulation that, on condition that; **lēge** *(or* **lēgibus)** legally; **lēge agere** to go to court, take legal action; **lēgem abrogāre** to repeal a law; **lēgem dērogāre** to amend a bill *or* law; **lēgem ferre** to propose a bill; **lēgem iubēre** *(of the assembly)* to sanction a law; **lēgem perferre** to get a bill *or* law passed; **lēgēs** constitution; **lēgēs pācis** terms of peace; **sine lēgibus** without restraint, without control

lībām·en -inis *n* libation; firstfruits

lībāment·um -ī *n* libation; firstfruits

lībāti·ō -ōnis *f* libation

lībell·a -ae *f* small silver coin, one tenth of a denarius *(c. 10¢);* small sum; *(carpenter's)* level; **ad lībellam** to a tee, exactly; **hērēs ex lībellā** heir to one tenth of the estate

libell·us -ī *m* booklet, pamphlet; notebook; journal, diary; program; handbill, advertisement; petition; answer to a petition; letter; written accusation, indictment; libel; satirical verse

lib·ēns -entis *adj* **(lub-)** willing, ready, glad; merry, cheerful; **libentī animō** willingly

libenter *adv* **(lub-)** willingly, gladly, with pleasure

li·ber -brī *m* book, work, treatise; catalog, list, register; letter, rescript; bark *(of a tree)*

līb·er -era -erum *adj* free; open, unoccupied; unrestricted; unprejudiced; outspoken, frank; uncontrolled, unrestricted; *(of states or municipalities)* independent, autonomous; exempt; free of charge; *(w. abl or ab)* free from, exempt from; *(w. gen)* free of **‖** *mpl see* **līberī**

Līb·er -erī *m* Italian fertility god, later identified with Bacchus; wine

Līber·a -ae *f* Proserpina **‖** Ariadne *(the wife of Bacchus)*

Līberāl·ia -ium *npl* festival of Liber *(held on March 17, at which young men received the toga virilis)*

līberāl·is -is -e *adj* relating to freedom, relating to civil status, of free citizens; worthy of a freeman, honorable, gentleman's; courteous; liberal, generous; handsome

līberālit·ās -ātis *f* courtesy, politeness; liberality, generosity; grant, gift

līberāliter *adv* like a freeman, nobly; liberally *(e.g., educated);* courteously; liberally, generously

līberāti·ō -ōnis *f* liberation, freeing; release *(from debt); (leg)* acquittal

līberāt·or -ōris *m* liberator

līberē *adv* freely; frankly; ungrudgingly; like a freeman, liberally

līber·ī -ōrum *or* **-um** *mpl* children; sons; **iūs trium līberōrum** a privileged status granted by the *Lex Papia Poppaea* of A.D. 9 to fathers of three or more children *(occasionally extended to others)*

līber·ō -āre -āvī -ātus *tr* to free, set free, release; to acquit; to cancel, get rid of *(e.g., debts);* to pay for, cover *(an expense);* to exempt; to manumit; to cross *(threshold);* to draw *(a sword);* to clear *(positions of hostile forces); (w. abl or w. ab or ex)* to free from, release from, acquit of; **fidem līberāre** to keep one's promise; **nōmina līberāre** to cancel debts; **prōmissa līberāre** to fulfill promises **‖** *refl* to pay up a debt

lībert·a -ae *f* freedwoman, ex-slave

lībert·ās -ātis *f* liberty, freedom; status of a freeman; political freedom; freedom of speech, freedom of thought; frankness

lībertīn·us -a -um *adj* of the status of a freedman **‖** *m* freedman, ex-slave **‖** *f* freedwoman, ex-slave

lībert·us -ī *m* freedman, ex-slave

lib·et -ēre -uit *or* **libitum est** *v impers* **(lub-)** *(w. dat)* it pleases, it is pleasant for, is agreeable to, is nice for *(s.o.); (w. inf)* it is nice, pleasant to *(do s.th.);* **mihi libet** I feel like, want; **quī libet** any you like to mention; **sī lubet** if you please; **ut lubet** as you please

libīdin·or -ārī -ātus sum *intr* to gratify lust

libīdinōsē *adv* willfully; arbitrarily

libīdinōs·us -a -um *adj* **(lub-)** willful; arbitrary; lustful, lecherous

libīd·ō -Inls *f* **(lub-)** desire, longing, inclination, pleasure; will, willfulness, arbitrariness, caprice, fancy; lust, sexual desire; rut, heat; **ad** *(or* per) **libīdinem** *(w. gen)* at the pleasure of; **ex libīdine** arbitrarily; **libīdinem habēre in** *(w. abl)* to be fond of, take pleasure in

libīt·a -ōrum *npl* will, pleasure

Libitīn·a -ae *f* burial goddess; implements for burial; grave; death

līb·ō -āre -āvī -ātus *tr* to taste, sip; to pour as a libation, offer, consecrate; to touch lightly, barely touch, graze; to spill, waste; to extract, collect, compile

lībr·a -ae *f* balance, scales; plummet; level; pound *(of 12 ounces)*

lībrāment·um -ī *n* weight; balance, ballast; level surface, horizontal plane; gravity

lībrāri·a -ae *f* forelady *(who weighed out wool for slaves to spin)*

lībrāriol·us -ī *m* copyist, scribe

lībrāri·us -a -um *adj* book, of books; **taberna librāria** bookstore **‖** *m* copyist, scribe, secretary; bookseller **‖** *n* bookcase

lībrāt·us -a -um *adj* weighing a pound

lībrāt·or -ōris *m* surveyor

lībrāt·us -a -um *adj* horizontal, level; poised; well-aimed

lībrīl·is -is -e *adj* one-pound

lībrit·or -ōris *m* artilleryman

lībr·ō -āre -āvī -ātus *tr* to balance; to poise, level, hurl, launch; to sway

līb·um -ī *n* *or* **līb·us -ī** *m* cake *(usu. used in sacrficial offerings);* **lībum nātāle** birthday cake

Liburni·a -ae *f* district of Illyria between Istria and Dalmatia

Liburn·us -a -um *adj* Liburnian **‖** *mf* Liburnian **‖** *f* Liburnian galley

Liby·a -ae *or* **Liby·ē -ēs** *f* Libya *(general term for all of N. Africa)*

Libyc·us -a -um *adj* Libyan, N. African

Lib·ys -yos *adj* of N. Africa, N. African **‖** *m* N. African

Libyss·us -a -um *adj* N. African

Libystīn·us *or* **Liby·us -a -um** *adj* Libyan; N. African

Libyst·is -idis *adj (fem only)* N. African

lic·ēns -entis *adj* free, unrestrained; licentious; forward, pushy, bold

licenter *adv* freely, without restraint; licentiously; boldly

licenti·a -ae *f* license, freedom; unruly behavior, lawlessness; outspokenness; licentiousness; free imagination; *(w. gen of gerund)* freedom to *(do s.th.)*; **lūdendī licentia** (unrestricted) freedom to play

lic·eō -ēre -uī *intr* to be for sale; *(w. abl or gen of price)* to cost, fetch

lic·eor -ērī -itus sum *tr* to bid on, bid for, make an offer for ‖ *intr* to bid

lic·et -ēre -uit *or* **-itum est** *v impers* it is permitted, it is lawful; *(w. dat & inf)* it is all right for *(s.o.)* to; **licet** *(to express assent)* yes, O.K.; **mihi licet** I may, I can *(often w. neut. pron as subject):* **sī tibi hoc licitum est** if you are allowed to do this; *(w. the force of a conjunction, w. subj)* although, granting that

Lich·ās -ae *m* companion of Hercules

līch·ēn -ēnos *m* lichen *(resin used to cure skin diseases);* ringworm *(a skin disease)*

licitāti·ō -ōnis *f* bidding *(at auction);* haggling

licitāt·or -ōris *m* bidder

licit·or -ārī -ātus sum *tr* to bid for

licit·us -a -um *adj* permissible, lawful, legitimate ‖ *n* lawful action

lict·or -ōris *m* lictor *(attendant and bodyguard of a magistrate)*

li·ēn -ēnis *m* spleen

liēnōs·us -a -um *adj* splenetic

ligām·en -inis *n* string, tie; bandage

ligāment·um -ī *n* bandage

lignār·ius -(i)ī *m* carpenter

lignāti·ō -ōnis *f* gathering of lumber

lignāt·or -ōris *m* woodcutter, lumberjack

ligneol·us -a -um *adj* wooden

ligne·us -a -um *adj* wooden; woody; tough, wiry *(person)*

lign·or -ārī -ātus sum *intr* to gather wood

lign·um -ī *n* wood; *(also pl)* firewood *(as opp. to* **māteria** = lumber for building); stump; log, plank; writing tablet; tree; stone *(of olive, fruit); (various objects made of wood):* spearshaft, money box, writing tablet, wooden mask, boat; **in silvam ligna ferre** *(prov)* to carry coals to Newcastle *(literally, to carry logs into the woods);* **mōbile lignum** puppet

lig·ō -āre -āvī -ātus *tr* to tie, tie up, bandage; to close *(a deal);* to draw tight, knot; to cement *(an alliance);* to unite in harmony; *(w. dat or* **ad***)* to tie to

lig·ō -ōnis *m* mattock, hoe; farming

ligul·a *or* **lingul·a -ae** *f* shoe strap; flap; *(geog)* tongue of land

Lig·ur *or* **Lig·us -uris** *mf* Ligurian

ligū(r)rīti·ō -ōnis *f* constant hankering for food

Liguri·a -ae *f* Liguria *(district along the N.W. coast of Italy)*

ligūr(r)·iō -īre -īvī *or* **-iī -ītus** *tr* to lick; to pick at, eat daintily; *(fig)* to be dying for; *(fig)* to sponge on

Ligus *see* **Ligur**

Ligusc·us *or* **Ligustic·us** *or* **Ligustīn·us -a -um** *adj* Ligurian

ligustr·um -ī *n (bot)* privet *(widely used for hedges)*

līl·ium -(i)ī *n (bot)* lily; *(mil)* trench lined with sharp stakes

līm·a -ae *f* file; *(fig)* revision, polishing; **līmae labor** *(fig)* the work of polishing

līmātius *adv* in a more polished style

līmātul·us -a -um *adj* refined, sensitive *(judgment)*

līm·āx -ācis *mf* snail

limbulāri·us -a -um *adj* hem; **textōrēs limbulāriī** tassel makers, hemmers

limb·us -ī *m* fringe, hem, tassel

līm·en -inis *n* lintel, threshold; doorway; entrance; outset, beginning; starting gate *(at racetrack);* house, home

līm·es -itis *m* country trail; path; road along a boundary; boundary, frontier; *(fig)* limit; boundary marker; channel *(of river);* course *(of life);* track, trail *(of a shooting star);* line of color, streak

līm·ō -āre -āvī -ātus *tr* to file; *(fig)* to polish, refine; to file down, take away from, lessen; to get down to *(the truth)*

līmōs·us -a -um *adj* muddy; growing in mud

limpid·us -a -um *adj* limpid, clear

līmul·us -a -um *adj* squinting

līm·us -a -um *adj* squinting; sidelong

līm·us -ī *m* ceremonial apron *(trimmed with purple and worn by priests at sacrifice)*

līm·us -ī *m* mud; dirt, grime

līne·a -ae *f* line; string, thread; fishing line; plumb line; outline; boundary line, limit; **ad līneam** *(or* **rēctā līneā***)* in a straight line; vertically; horizontally; **extrēmā līneā amāre** to love at a distance; **līneās trānsīre** to go out of bounds

līneāment·um -ī *n* line; characteristic, feature; outline ‖ *npl* lineaments, lines *(of the face)*

līne·ō -āre -āvī -ātus *tr* to make straight, make perpendicular

līne·us -a -um *adj* flaxen, linen

lingō lingere līnxī līnctus *tr* to lick; to lap up

lingu·a -ae *f* tongue; speech, language, dialect; eloquence; utterance; style *(of s.o.'s speech); (of animals)* note, song, bark; *(geog)* tongue of land; **favēte linguīs!** observe a sacred silence!; **linguam comprimere** *(or* **tenēre***)* to hold one's tongue; **linguā prōmptus** insolent, cheeky; **utraque lingua** both languages *(Greek and Latin)*

lingul·a -ae *f* shoe strap; flap; *(geog)* tongue of land

lingulāc·a -ae *mf* gossip, chatterbox

līnig·er -era -erum *adj* wearing linen

linō linere lēvī *or* **līvī litus** *tr* to smear; to erase; to cover, coat; *(fig)* to mess up

linquō linquere līquī *tr* to leave, forsake; to depart from; to leave alone; to leave in a pinch **||** *pass* to faint; **animō linquī** to faint **||** *v impers* **linquitur** *(w.* **ut)** it remains to *(do s.th.)*

linteātus -a -um *adj* canvas

linte·ō -ōnis *f* linen-weaver

linteol·um -ī *n* small linen cloth

lin·ter -tris *f* skiff; vat, tank

linte·us -a -um *adj* linen **||** *n* linen; linen cloth; canvas, sail; kerchief

lintricul·us -ī *m* small boat

līn·um -ī *n* flax; linen; thread; rope, line; fishing line; net; linen dress

Lin·us *or* **Lin·os -ī** *m* son of Apollo and instructor of Orpheus and Hercules

Lipar·a -ae *or* **Lipar·ē -ēs** *f* Lipara *(island off the N. coast of Sicily)* **||** *fpl* the Aeolian Islands *(modern Lipari Islands)*

Liparae·us -a -um *or* **Liparēns·is -is -e** *adj* of Lipara

lipp·iō -īre -īvī *or* **-iī -ītum** *intr* to have sore eyes; *(of eyes)* to burn

lippitūd·ō -inis *f* running eyes, inflammation of the eyes

lipp·us -a -um *adj* with sore eyes; burning *(eyes); (fig)* half-blind

liquām·en -inis *n* fish sauce

lique·faciō -facere -fēcī -factus *(pass:* **lique·fiō -fierī -factus sum)** *tr* to melt; to dissolve; to decompose; to waste, weaken

liqu·ēns -entis *adj* clear, limpid; flowing, gliding

liqueō liquēre liquī *or* **licuī** *intr* to be liquid; to be clear **||** *v impers* it is clear, is apparent, is evident; **liquet mihi** *(w. inf)* I am free to; **nōn liquet** *(leg)* it is not clear *(legal formula used by a hung jury)*

liquēscō liquēscere licuī *intr* to melt; to decompose; to grow soft, grow effeminate; to become clear; *(fig)* to melt away

liquidē *adv* clearly

liquidiuscul·us -a -um *adj* gentler

liquidō *adv* clearly, plainly, certainly

liquid·us -a -um *adj* liquid, fluid, flowing; clear, transparent; evident; pure *(pleasure);* clear *(voice);* calm *(mind)* **||** *n* liquid, water; clearness, certainty

liqu·ō -āre -āvī -ātus *tr* to melt, dissolve; to strain, filter

līqu·or -ī *intr* to flow; to melt; *(fig)* to waste away; **in lacrimās līquī** to dissolve into tears

liqu·or -ōris *m* fluidity; liquid, fluid; sea

Līr·is -is *m* river between Latium and Campania

līs lītis *f (old form:* **stlīs stlītis)** matter of dispute; quarrel, dispute; wrangling; *(leg)* lawsuit, litigation; *(leg)* charge, accusation; **līs capitis** criminal charge; **lītem aestimāre** *(or* **taxāre)** to assess damages; **lītem intendere** *(or* **lītem īnferre)** *(w. dat)* to bring a suit against, sue *(s.o.)*

litāti·ō -ōnis *f* successful sacrifice *(i.e., obtaining of favorable omens from a sacrifice)*

litatō *adv* with favorable omens

lītera *see* **littera**

Lītern·um -ī *n* town on the coast of Campania

litic·en -inis *m* trumpeter

lītigāt·or -ōris *m (leg)* litigant

lītigiōs·us -a -um *adj* litigious; quarrelsome; disputed

lītig·ium -(i)ī *n* quarrel, dispute

lītig·ō -āre -āvī -tum *intr* to squabble; *(leg)* to go to court

lit·ō -āre -āvī -ātus *tr* to propitiate; to offer by way of atonement; to atone for; **litandum est** atonement must be made **||** *intr* to obtain favorable omens from a sacrifice; *(of a sacrifice)* to give favorable omens; *(w. dat)* to appease, propitiate

lītorāl·is -is -e *adj* shore, of the shore

lītore·us -a -um *adj* at *or* along the seashore

litter·a *or* **līter·a -ae** *f* letter *(of the alphabet);* handwriting; **ad litteram** verbatim; **littera salūtāris** *(leg) (i.e.,* **A = absolvō)** vote of acquittal; **littera tristis** *(leg) (i.e.,* **C = condemnō)** vote of guilty **||** *fpl* epistle, letter, dispatch; edict, ordinance; literature, books, literary works; book learning, liberal education, scholarship; branch of learning; records, account; inscription; **in litterās dīgerere** to arrange in alphabetical order; **litterās discere** to learn to read and write; **litterās scīre** to know how to read and write, be literate

litterāri·us -a -um *adj* of reading and writing; **lūdus litterārius** elementary school

litterātē *adv* legibly, in a clear handwriting; literally; learnedly

litterāt·or -ōris *m* elementary-school teacher; schoolmaster

litterātūr·a -ae *f* writing; alphabet; grammar; writings, literature

litterāt·us -a -um *adj* learned, scholarly; liberally educated; devoted to literature; *(of time)* devoted to studies; marked *or* inscribed with letters **||** *m* man of culture; teacher of literature; scholar

litterul·a -ae *f* small letter **||** *fpl* short letter, note; slight literary endeavors; ABC's litūr·a -ae *f* erasure; erased passage; correction; smudge, smear

līt·us -oris *n* seashore, beach, coast; riverbank; lītus arāre *(prov)* to waste effort *(literally, to plow the shore)*

litus *pp of* linō

litu·us -ī *m* cavalry trumpet, clarion; *(fig)* signal; augur's wand *(a crooked staff carried by an augur);* lituus meae profectiōnis signal for my departure

līv·ēns -entis *adj* livid; black-and-blue

līv·eō -ēre *intr* to be black-and-blue, be livid; to be envious; *(w. dat)* to be jealous of

līvēsc·ō -ere *intr* to turn black-and-blue

Līvi·a -ae *f* second wife of Augustus and mother of Tiberius and Drusus (58 B.C.–A.D. 29)

līvidul·us -a -um *adj* inclined to be jealous, somewhat envious

līvid·us -a -um *adj* leaden *(in color);* blue; black-and-blue; jealous, envious, spiteful

Līv·ius -(i)ī *m* Livy *(Titus Livius Patavinus, historian, 58 B.C.–A.D. 17)* ‖ Livius Andronicus *(a Greek who was the first to write Latin poetry, both tragedies and comedies; his first drama was staged in 240 B.C.; he also translated the Odyssey into Saturnian verse)*

līv·or -ōris *m* leaden color; bluish color; black-and-blue mark; jealousy, envy, spite

lix·a -ae *m* peddler *(around a camp),* camp follower

locār·ius -(i)ī *m* ticket broker, scalper *(one who buys up theater seats as an investment)*

locāti·ō -ōnis *f* arrangement, placement; renting out, contract, lease

locāt·or -ōris *m* lessor

locāt·um -ī *n* lease, contract

locell·us -ī *m* small box

locit·ō -āre *tr* to lease out

loc·ō -āre -āvī -ātus *tr* to place, put, set, lay; to establish, constitute, set; to lay *(foundations);* to station *(troops);* to rent out, lease; to contract for; to invest *(effort);* to lend at interest; to farm out *(taxes);* locāre in mātrimōnium *(or* nūptiīs *or* nūptum*) (w. dat)* to give in marriage *(to s.o.)*

locul·us -ī *m* little place, spot; pocket; drawer

locupl·ēs -ētis *adj* rich; *(w. abl)* rich in, well supplied with; reliable, responsible; locuplēs ōrātiōne *(or* in dīcendō*)* esse to be a polished speaker

locuplēt·ō -āre -āvī -ātus *tr* to make rich, enrich; to embellish *(a building)*

loc·us -ī *(pl:* loc·ī -ōrum *mpl* passages, verses; loc·a -ōrum *npl* physical places) *m* place; site; spot; locality, district; seat; town, village; period (of time); opportunity, room, occasion; situation, position; category; rank, degree; birth; office, post; passage *(in a*

book); topic, subject, point, division; *(mil)* post, station; *(in astrology)* house; adhūc locōrum until now; ad id locōrum until then; ex aequō locō dīcere to speak in the Senate; to hold a conversation; ex *(or* dē*)* locō superiōre dīcere to speak from the Rostra; ex locō īnferiōre dīcere to speak before a judge, speak in court; inde locī since then; in eō locī in such a condition; in locum *(w. gen)* in place of, as a substitute for, instead of; intereā locī meanwhile; loca *(vulg)* female genitals; locī commūnēs general topics; public places, parks; locō *(w. gen)* in stead of, in place of; locō *(or* in locō*)* at the right time; on the spot; locō cēdere to give way, yield; locō movēre to dislodge; to dislocate *(a limb);* locum dare to make way; locum habēre to be valid, be applicable, hold good; locum facere to clear the way; locum mūtāre to change one's residence, move; locus pūblicus public building, public square; mentem (meam, tuam, ēius) locō movēre *(or* pellere*)* to drive (me, you, him) out of (my, your, his) mind; nullō locō under no circumstances; posteā locī afterwards; post id locōrum afterwards; stare locō to stand still; ubicumque locī whenever

lōcust·a -ae *f* locust

Lōcust·a -ae *f* (Lūc-) woman notorious as poisoner in the time of Claudius and Nero

locūti·ō -ōnis *f* speech; way of speaking; expression; word; pronunciation

locūtus *pp of* loquor

lōd·ix -īcis *f* blanket

logic·us -a -um *adj* logical ‖ *npl* logic

log·os *or* log·us -ī *m* word; witticism ‖ *mpl* mere words, empty talk

lōlīgō *see* lollīgō

lol·ium -(i)ī *n* darnel *(type of grass)*

lollīg·ō -inis *f* (lōl-) squid

lollīguncul·a -ae *f* small squid

lōment·um -ī *n* a face cream *(for cleansing skin)*

Londīn·ium -(i)ī *n* London

longaev·us -a -um *adj* aged

longē *adv* far, far off, a long way off; away, distant; out of reach; long, for a long period; *(to speak)* at greater length; *(w. comparatives)* far, by far, much; longē lātēque far and wide

longinquit·ās -ātis *f* length, extent; remoteness, distance; length, duration

longinqu·us -a -um *adj* long, extensive; far off, distant, remote; from afar, foreign; long, prolonged, continued, tedious; e(x) longinquō from far away; in longinquō far away

longitūd·ō -inis *f* length; in longitūdinem 1 lengthwise, in length; 2 to an immoderate

length, too far; **3** for the distant future; **longitūdine** (or **per longitūdinem**) lengthwise
longiūscul·us -a -um adj pretty long
longur·ius -(i)ī m long pole
long·us -a -um adj long; spacious; tall (person); protracted; tedious; **longa nāvis** battleship; **longum est** (w. inf) it would take too long to **‖** n length; **in** (or **per**) **longum** for a long while; **nē longum faciam** to make a long story short
loquācit·ās -ātis f talkativeness
loquāciter adv long-windedly; at length, in detail
loquācul·us -a -um adj rather talkative
loqu·āx -ācis adj loquacious, talkative
loquēl·a -ae f (**-quell-**) speech; word, expression
loqu·ēns -entis adj articulate
loquit·or -ārī -ātus sum intr to chatter away
loquor loquī locūtus sum tr to say; to talk of, speak about; to tell, tell of, mention; (fig) to declare, show, indicate **‖** intr to speak; to rustle, murmur; **Latīnē loquī** to speak Latin; (coll) to talk turkey; **male loquī** to speak abusively
lōrār·ius -(i)ī m slave driver
lōrāt·us -a -um adj tied with thongs
lōre·us -a -um adj made of strips of leather; **vostra faciam latera lōrea** (coll) I'll cut your hide to ribbons
lōrīc·a -ae f breastplate; parapet; **librōs mūtāre lōrīcīs** to exchange books for arms
lōrīcāt·us -a -um adj wearing a breastplate, mail-clad
lōrip·ēs -edis adj bowlegged
lōr·um -ī n strip of leathter, thong, strap; dog's leash; whip, scourge; leather badge **‖** npl reins
Lōt·is -idis f a nymph who changed into a lotus tree to escape the advances of Priapus
Lōtophag·ī -ōrum mpl Lotus-eaters
lōt·os or **lōt·us -ī** f lotus (fabulous plant bringing forgetfulness to those who eat its fruit); flute (of lotus wood)
lōtus see **lautus**
Lu·a -ae f cult partner of Saturn (to whom captured arms were dedicated)
lub- = lib-
lubenti·a -ae f pleasure
lūbric·ō -āre -āvī -ātus tr to oil, grease, make smooth
lūbric·us -a -um adj slippery; smooth; slimy; (of streams) gently flowing, gliding; deceitful, tricky; precarious, ticklish (situations, undertakings) **‖** n precarious situation, critical period; unstable condition; **in lūbricō pōnī** to be placed in a dangerous situation; **in lūbricō versārī** to be in a precarious situation
Lūc·a bōs (gen: **Lūc·ae bovis**) f elephant

Lūcāni·a -ae f district in S.W. Italy
Lūcān·us -a -um adj Lucanian **‖** m Lucanian **‖** Lucan (Marcus Annaeus Lucanus, epic poet, condemned to death by Nero, A.D. 39–65)
lūc·ar -āris n funds allocated for public games (derived from a forest tax)
lucell·um -ī n slight profit
lū·ceō -cēre -xī intr to shine, be light, glow, glitter, be clear; (fig) to be clear, be apparent, be conspicuous **‖** v impers it is light, day is dawning
Lūcer·ēs -um mpl (**Luc-**) one of the three original Roman tribes
lucern·a -ae f oil lamp; (fig) midnight oil; **ad lucernam** after dark; **ante lucernās** before nightfall; **vīnum et lucernae** wine and lamps (i.e., evening festivities)
lūcēscō lūcēscere lūxī intr (**-cīsc-**) to begin to shine **‖** v impers it is getting light
Lūci·a -ae f female name
lūcidē adv clearly, distinctly
lūcid·us -a -um adj shining, bright, clear; lucid
lūcif·er -era -erum adj shiny
Lūcif·er -erī m (astr) morning star **‖** (astr) planet Venus **‖** son of Aurora and Cephalus
lūcifug·us -a -um adj light-shunning; avoiding the public eye, sulking
Lūcil·ius -(i)ī m Gaius Lucilius (first Roman satiric poet, c. 180–102 B.C.)
Lūcīn·a -ae f goddess of childbirth; childbirth
lūcīscō see **lūcēscō**
Lūc·ius -(i)ī m Roman first name (praenomen; abbr: L.)
Lucmō see **Lucumō**
Lucrēti·a -ae f wife of Collatinus, who, having been raped by Sextus Tarquinius, committed suicide in 509 B.C.
Lucrēt·ius -(i)ī m Spurius Lucretius (father of Lucretia and consul in 509 B.C.) **‖** Lucretius (Titus Lucretius Carus, philosophical poet, 94?–55? B.C.)
lucrificābil·is -is -e or **lucrific·us -a -um** adj profitable
lucrifug·a -ae m person not interested in profit, spendthrift
Lucrīn·us -a -um adj Lucrine; **Lacus Lucrīnus** Lucrine Lake (near Baiae, famous for its oysters)
lucripet·a -ae m profiteer
lucr·or -ārī -ātus sum tr to gain, win (as profit) **‖** intr (w. ex) to profit from
lucrōs·us -a -um adj profitable
lucr·um -ī n profit, gain; wealth; greed, love of gain; **lucrī facere** to gain for oneself; to make profit; **lucrī fierī** to be gained; **lucrō esse** (w. dat) to be advantageous to (s.o.); **pōnere in lucrō** (or **in lucrīs**) to regard as gain; **vīvere dē lucrō** to be lucky to be alive

luctām·en -inis *n* wrestling; struggle, effort
luct·āns -antis *adj* reluctant
luctāti·ō -ōnis *f* wrestling; struggle, effort
luctāt·or -ōris *m* wrestler
lūctific·us -a -um *adj* causing sorrow, calamitous
lūctison·us -a -um *adj* sad-sounding
luct·or -ārī -ātus sum *or* **luct·ō -āre** *intr* to wrestle; *(w.* **cum)** to struggle with, grapple with; *(w. inf)* to struggle to
lūctuōsē *adv* so as to cause sadness
lūctuōsius *adv* more pitifully
lūctuōs·us -a -um *adj* causing sorrow, sorrowful; sad, feeling sad
lūct·us -ūs *m* sorrow, mourning, grief, distress; signs of sorrow, mourning clothes; source of grief
Luc(u)m·ō -ōnis *m* Etruscan personal name
lūcubrāti·ō -ōnis *f* working by lamp light; evening gossip
lūcubr·ō -āre -āvī -ātus *tr* to compose at night ‖ *intr* to burn the midnight oil
lūculentē *adv* splendidly, well; *(to beat)* soundly; *(to sell)* at an excellent price
lūculenter *adv* brilliantly, smartly
lūculent·us -a -um *adj* bright, brilliant; excellent, fine; good-looking
Lūcull·us -ī *m* Lucius Licinius Lucullus *(Roman general and politician, 117–56 B.C.)*
lūc·us -ī *m* sacred grove; woods
lūdi·a -ae *f* actress; gladiator *(female)*
lūdibr·ium -(i)ī *n* toy, plaything; derision; object of derision, butt of ridicule; frivolous behavior; sham, pretense; *(fig)* sucker; **lūdibriō esse** *(w. dat)* to be made a fool of by *(s.o.),* be taken in by *(s.o.);* **lūdibriō habēre** to take *(s.o.)* for a sucker ‖ *npl* outrages, insults
lūdibund·us -a -um *adj* playful, playing around, having fun; without effort, without danger; carefree
lūdi·cer -cra -crum *adj* for sport, in sport; *(theat)* of the stage, dramatic, acting; **lūdicra ars et scaena tōta** dramatic art and the stage in general; **lūdicra exercitātiō** sports; **lūdicra rēs** drama; **lūdicrās partēs sustinēre** *(theat)* to play a dramatic role, act on the stage; **lūdicrum praemium** sports award; ‖ *n* sport, game; toy; show, public game; stage play
lūdificābil·is -is -e *adj* used in mockery
lūdificāti·ō -ōnis *f* ridiculing, mocking; fooling, tricking
lūdificāt·or -ōris *m* mocker
lūdificāt·us -ūs *m* mockery
lūdific·ō -āre -āvī -ātus *or* **lūdific·or -ārī -ātus sum** *tr* to make a fool of, take for a sucker; to fool, trick
lūdi·ō -ōnis *m or* **lūd·ius -(i)ī** *m* actor

lū·dō -dere -sī -sus *tr* to play; to spend *(time)* in play; to lose *(money)* in gambling; to amuse oneself with, do for amusement, practice as a pastime; to imitate, mimic, do a take-off on, ridicule; to tease, tantalize; to deceive, delude; **operam lūdere** to waste one's efforts; ‖ *intr* to play; to have fun; to jest, joke; to frolic; *(sl)* to play around, make love; **aleā lūdere** to play dice; **pilā lūdere** to play ball
lūd·us -ī *m* play, game, sport, pastime, diversion; mere child's play; joke, fun; *(sl)* playing around, fooling around, lovemaking; school; public show, public game; **āmōtō lūdō** all joking aside; **in lūdum īre** *and* **itāre** to go to school; **lūdum alicui dare** *(w. dat)* to allow s.o. to enjoy himself; **lūdum frequentāre** to attend school; **lūdus gladiātōrius** gladiatorial school; **lūdus (litterārius, litterārum)** (elementary) school; **per lūdum** as a joke, for fun ‖ *mpl* public games, public exhibition; games, tricks; **lūdōs facere** *(or* **lūdōs reddere)** *(w. dat)* **1** to play tricks on; **2** to put on a show for; **3** to make fun of; **lūdōs sibi facere** to amuse oneself; **lūdī circēnsēs** festival of public games, contests, *or* theatrical shows held at the racetrack; **lūdī magister** school teacher; **lūdī magnī** special votive games; **lūdī plēbēiī** games given annually by the plebeian aediles on Nov. 4-17; **lūdī Rōmānī** games given annually by the curule aediles on Sept. 4-19; **lūdī scaenicī** public events held in the theater, plays
luell·a -ae *f* expiation, atonement
lu·ēs -is *f* infection, contagion, plague, pestilence; calamity
Lugdūnēns·is -is -e *adj* of Lyons
Lugdūn·um -ī *n* Lyons *(town in E. Gaul)*
lū·geō -gēre -xī -ctus *tr* to mourn, lament, deplore ‖ *intr* to mourn, be in mourning; to be in mourning clothes
lūgubr·ia -ium *npl* mourning clothes
lūgubr·is -is -e *adj* mourning; doleful; disastrous
lumbifrag·ium -(i)ī *n* physical wreck
lumbrīc·us -ī *m* earthworm; *(as a term of reproach)* worm, creep
lumb·us -ī *m* loin ‖ *mpl* loins; genitals
lūm·en -inis *n* light; lamp, torch; brightness, sheen, gleam; daylight; light of the eye, eye; light of life, life; window, window light; luminary, celebrity; glory, pride; *(leg) (usu. pl)* the amount of light falling on a building to which the owner is entitled; *(rhet)* strong point *(of an argument); (rhet)* brilliant phrase *or* expression; **ad lūmina prīma** until lamp-lighting time, until dusk; **lūmen adferre** *(w. dat)* to shed light on *(a subject);* **lūmen vītāle** light enjoyed by living creatures; life; **lūmina**

āmittere to go blind; **lūminibus captus** blind; **sub lūmina prīma** around dusk, just before dusk
lūminōs·us -a -um *adj* luminous, dazzling; *(fig)* bright, conspicuous
lūn·a -ae *f* moon; month; night; crescent *(worn as an ornament by senators on their shoes);* **ad lūnam** by moonlight; **lūna labōrāns** moon in eclipse, eclipse of the moon; **lūna minor** waning moon; **nova lūna** new moon
Lūn·a -ae *f* town in N. Etruria near modern Carrara
lūnār·is -is -e *adj* lunar, of the moon
lūnāt·us -a -um *adj* crescent-shaped
lūn·ō -āre -āvī -ātus *tr* to make crescent-shaped, curve
lūnul·a -ae *f* little crescent *(ornament worn by women)*
lu·ō -ere -ī *tr* to wash; to cleanse, purge; to set free, let go; to pay *(debt, penalty);* to pay as a fine; to suffer, undergo; to atone for, expiate; to satisfy, appease; to avert by expiation *or* punishment; **poenās luere** to suffer a punishment *(by way of expiation)*
lup·a -ae *f* she-wolf; flirt, prostitute
lupān·ar -āris *n* brothel
lupāt·us -a -um *adj* jagged *(like wolf's teeth)* ‖ *npl* jagged bit *(for spunky horses)*
Luperc·al -ālis *n* shrine on the Palatine Hill sacred to Pan
Lupercāl·ia -ium *npl* Lupercalia *(festival of Lycaean Pan, celebrated in February)*
Luperc·us -ī *m* Pan
lupill·us -ī *m (bot)* small lupine
lupīn·us -a -um *adj* wolf's, lupine ‖ *m & n (bot)* lupine *(plant having clusters of flowers of various colors)*
lup·us -ī *m* wolf; *(fish)* pike; jagged bit *(for horse);* grapnel
lurc(h)·ō -ōnis *m* glutton
lūrid·us -a -um *adj* pale-yellow, wan, ghastly, lurid; causing paleness
lūr·or -ōris *m* sallowness, sickly yellow color
-lus -la -lum *suf* forming diminutives, e.g., **lapillus** pebble, **agellus** little field, plot, **homunculus** little man
lūscini·a -ae *f* nightingale
lūsciniol·a -ae *f* little nightingale
lūscin·ius -(i)ī *m* nightingale
lūsciōs·us *or* **lūscitiōs·us -a -um** *adj* partly blind
lūsc·us -a -um *adj* one-eyed
lūsī *perf of* **lūdō**
lūsi·ō -ōnis *f* play, game
Lūsitān·ī -ōrum *mpl* Lusitanian
Lūsitāni·a -ae *f* Lusitania *(modern Portugal and W. part of Spain)*
lūsit·ō -āre *intr* to like to play

lūs·or -ōris *m* player; gambler; humorous writer; joker
lūstrāl·is -is -e *adj* lustral, propitiatory; quinquennial
lūstrāti·ō -ōnis *f* purification, lustration; wandering, traveling
lūstr·ō -āre -āvī -ātus *tr* to purify; to travel over, traverse; to check, examine; to go around, encircle; to light up, make bright, illuminate; to scan *(with the eyes);* to consider, review; to survey; *(mil)* to review *(troops)*
lustr·or -ārī -ātus sum *intr* to frequent brothels
lustr·um -ī *n* haunt, den, lair; wilderness; brothel; sensuality
lūstr·um -ī *n* purificatory sacrifice, lustration; lustrum, period of five years; period of years; **ingēns lūstrum** a century
lūsus *pp of* **lūdō**
lūs·us -ūs *m* play, game, sport, amusement; playing around *(amorously);* **lūsum lūdere** to play a game
lūteol·us -a -um *adj* yellowish
lūte·us -a -um *adj* golden-yellow, yellow, orange
lute·us -a -um *adj* of mud, of clay; muddy; dirty, grimy; (morally) dirty, filthy
lutit·ō -āre *tr* to splatter with mud; *(fig)* to throw mud at
lut·ō -āre -āvī -ātus *tr* to cover with mud, daub; *(fig)* to smear
lutulent·us -a -um *adj* muddy; dirty; *(fig)* filthy; turbid *(style)*
lūt·um -ī *n* yellow pigment, yellow
lut·um -ī *n* mud, mire; clay; **in lutō esse** *(or* **haerēre)** *(fig)* to be in a pickle; **prō lutō esse** to be dirt-cheap
lūx lūcis *f* light; light of day, life; daylight; public view, publicity; the public, the world; light of hope, encouragement; glory; elucidation; **lūce** *(or* **lūcī)** by daylight, in the daytime; **lūx aestīva** summer; **lūx brūmālis** winter; **(cum) prīmā lūce** at daybreak
lux·ō -āre -āvī -ātus *tr* to dislocate *(a limb)*
lux·or -ārī -ātus sum *intr* to live riotously, have a ball
luxuri·a -ae *or* **luxuri·ēs -ēī** *f* luxuriance; luxury, extravagance, excess, sumptuousness
luxuri·ō -āre -āvī -ātum *or* **luxur·ior -ārī -ātus sum** *intr* to grow luxuriantly; to luxuriate; *(of the body)* to swell up; *(of animals)* to be frisky; to lead a wild life
luxuriōsē *adv* luxuriously, voluptuously
luxuriōs·us -a -um *adj* luxuriant; exuberant; extravagant; voluptuous; highly fertile *(land)*
lux·us -ūs *m* luxury, extravagance, excess; splendor, pomp, magnificence
Lyae·us -a -um *adj* Bacchic ‖ *m* Bacchus; wine

Lycae·us -a -um *adj* Lycaean *(esp. applied to Pan);* **Mōns Lycaeus** Mount Lycaeus *(mountain in Arcadia where Jupiter and Pan were worshiped)*

Lycā·ōn -onis *m* king of Arcadia, whose daughter Callisto was changed into a she-bear and transferred to the sky as the Great Bear

Lycāon·is -idis *f* daughter of Lycaon *(i.e., Callisto)*

Lycāoni·us -a -um *adj* descended from Lycaon of Arcadia; **axis Lycāonia** North Pole *(where Callisto as the Great Bear is located)*

lychnūch·us -ī *m* lamp stand; **lychnūchus pēnsilis** chandelier

lychn·us -ī *m* lamp, chandelier

Lyci·a -ae *f* country in S. Asia Minor

Lycī·um -ī *n* **(Lycē-)** the Lyceum *(gymnasium near Athens where Aristotle taught)* ‖ Lyceum *(name given by Cicero to the gymnasium in his Tusculan villa)*

Lyci·us -a -um *adj* of Lycia, Lycian ‖ *mpl* Lycians

Lycomēd·ēs -is *m* king of the Greek island of Scyros, father of Deidamia

Lycophr·ōn -onis *or* **-onos** *m* Alexandrine poet, noted for his obscure style *(born c. 320 B.C.)*

Lycōr·is -idis *or* **-idos** *f* name under which the poet Gallus wrote about his mistress Cytheris

Lycorm·ās -ae *m* old name for the Aetolian river Evenus

Lycti·us -a -um *adj* Cretan, of Lyctos *(a town in Crete)*

Lycurgē·us -a -um *adj* Lycurgan *(resembling the orator Lycurgus, noted for his relentlessness as prosecutor)*

Lycurgīd·ēs -ae *m* son of the Arcadian king Lycurgus *(i.e., Ancaeus, killed by the Calydonian boar)*

Lycurg·us -ī *m* traditional founder of the Spartan constitution ‖ Athenian orator, contemporary with Demosthenes *(born c. 396 B.C.)* ‖ son of Dryas and king of the Edones, who persecuted Bacchus and his worshipers

Lyc·us -ī *m* king of Thebes and husband of Dirce ‖ name of numerous rivers in Asia Minor, *esp.* a tributary of the Menander

Lȳdi·a -ae *f* country in W. Asia Minor

Lȳdi·us -a -um *adj* Lydian

Lȳd·us -a -um *adj* Lydian ‖ *mf* Lydian; Etruscan

lygd·os -ī *f* marble from Paros

lymph·a -ae *f* water nymph; *(poet)* water

lymphātic·us -a -um *adj* frenzied

lymphāt·us -a -um *adj* frenzied, frantic

lymph·ō -āre *tr* to drive crazy ‖ *pass* to be in a state of frenzy

Lyncest·is -idis *adj (fem only)* of the Lycestae, a people of W. Macedonia

Lync·ēus -ēī *m* Argonaut, famed for his sharp eyesight ‖ son of Aegyptus and husband of Hypermestra

Lyncē·us -a -um *adj* of Lynceus the Argonaut; keen-sighted, Lynceus-like

Lyncīd·ēs -ae *m* descendant of Lynceus, husband of Hypermestra *(esp. his great-grandson Perseus)*

lyn·x -cis *or* **-cos** *mf* lynx

lyr·a -ae *f* lyre; *(fig)* lyric poetry ‖ **Lyra** *(astr)* Lyra *(constellation)*

Lyrcē·us -a -um *adj* of Mt. Lyrceum on the borders of Arcadia and Argolis

lyric·us -a -um *adj* of the lyre; lyric ‖ *m* lyric poet ‖ *npl* lyric poetry

Lyrnēs·is -idis *or* **-idos** *f* Briseis *(Achilles' slave girl from Lyrnesos, a town in Phrygia)*

Lȳsan·der -drī *m* Spartan general and statesman *(d. 395 B.C.)*

Lȳsi·ās -ae *m* Athenian orator *(c. 459–c. 380 B.C.)*

Lȳsimach·us -ī *m* bodyguard of Alexander the Great, who later became King of Thrace

M

M, m *(supply* littera) *f* twelfth letter of the Latin alphabet; letter name: **em**

M *abbr* **mīlle** one thousand

M. *abbr* **Marcus** *(Roman first name, praenomen)*

M'. *abbr* **Manius** *(Roman first name, praenomen)*

Macarē·is -idos *f* daughter of Macareus *(i.e., Isse)*

Macar·ēus -ēī *or* **-eos** *m* son of Aeolus *(who lived in incest with his sister Canace)*

macc·us -ī *m* clown *(in Atellan farces)*

Maced·ō -onis *m* Macedonian

Macedoni·a -ae *f* Macedonia

Macedonic·us -a -um *adj* Macedonian

Macedoniēns·is -is -e *adj* Macedonian

Macedoni·us -a -um *adj* Macedonian

macellār·ius -(i)ī *m* grocer

macell·um -ī *n* grocery store; *(fig)* groceries

mac·eō -ēre *intr* to be lean, to be skinny

ma·cer -cra -crum *adj* lean; skinny; poor *(soil);* scraggly *(plants);* lean *(meat)*

Ma·cer -crī *m* Gaius Licinius Macer *(Roman historian and orator, d. 66 B.C.)* ‖ Gaius Licinius Macer Calvus *(son of the latter, and orator and poet, 82–46 B.C.)* ‖ Marcus Aemilius Macer *(poet and friend of Vergil and Ovid)* māceri·a -ae *f* brick *or* stone wall; garden wall

mācer·ō -āre -āvī -ātus *tr* to soften, tenderize; to weaken, wear down; to soak; to worry, annoy, torment ‖ *refl & pass* to fret, worry

macēsc·ō -ere *intr* to grow thin; *(of fruit)* to shrivel

machaer·a -ae *f* (**macch-**) (single-edged) sword

machaerophor·us -ī *m* soldier armed with a single-edged sword

Machā·ōn -onis *m* famous physician of the Greek army in the Trojan War and son of Aesculapius

Machāoni·us -a -um *adj* of Machaon; *(fig)* medical

māchin·a -ae *f* large mechanism, machine; crane, derrick; pulley, windlass, winch; revolving stage; siege engine; platform on which slaves were exhibited for sale (= **catasta**); cage, pen; *(fig)* scheme, stratagem

māchināment·um -ī *n* contrivance, device; *(mil)* siege engine;

māchinār·ius -(i)ī *m* crane operator

māchināti·ō -ōnis *f* mechanism; machine; trick; art of making machines; *(mil)* field piece

māchināt·or -ōris *m* engineer, machinist; *(fig)* contriver

māchin·or -ārī -ātus sum *tr* to engineer, design, contrive; to scheme

māchinōs·us -a -um *adj* containing a mechanism

maci·ēs -ēī *f* leanness, thinness; barrenness; poverty *(of soil; of style)*

macilent·us -a -um *adj* skinny

macrēsc·ō -ere *intr* to grow thin

macritūd·ō -inis *f* leanness

macrocoll·um -ī *n* large-size sheet of paper

mactābil·is -is -e *adj* deadly

mactāt·us -ūs *m* sacrifice

mactē *interj* well done!; good luck!; bravo!; *(w. gen, acc, or abl)* hurrah for; **mactē virtūte estō**! bless you for your excellence!; well done!

mact·ō -āre -āvī -ātus *tr* to glorify, honor; to slay *(sacrificially)*, sacrifice; to kill, slaughter, put to death; to destroy, overthrow, ruin; to trouble; *(w. abl)* to afflict *or* punish with

mact·us -a -um *adj* glorified; struck, smitten

macul·a -ae *f* spot, stain; mesh *(of net)*; *(fig)* blemish, defect

macul·ō -āre -āvī -ātus to spot, stain, pollute; *(fig)* defile, dishonor, disgrace

maculōs·us -a -um *adj* spotted; stained; *(fig)* defiled, dishonored, filthy; **maculōsī senātōrēs** rotten senators

made·faciō -facere -fēcī -factus *(pass: made·fīō -fierī -factus sum)* *tr* to wet, moisten, drench, soak

mad·ēns -entis *adj* wet, moist; flowing *(hair);* melting *(snow);* reeking *(w. blood)*

mad·eō -ēre -uī *intr* to be wet, be moist, be soaked, be drenched; to drip; to flow; *(coll)* to be soused; to be full, overflow

mad·ēscō -ēscere -uī *intr* to become wet, become moist; *(coll)* to get soused

madidē *adv* drunkenly

madid·us -a -um *adj* wet, moist, drenched; dyed, steeped; *(coll)* drunk, soused

mad·or -ōris *m* moisture

maduls·a -ae *m (coll)* souse, drunkard

Maean·der *or* Maean·dros *or* Maean·drus -drī *m* river in Asia Minor, famous for its winding course; winding; winding border; devious course

Maecēn·ās -ātis *m* Gaius Cilnius Maecenas *(adviser to Augustus and friend of Vergil and Horace, d. 8 B.C.)*

maen·a -ae *f* sprat *(fish)*

Maenal·is -idis *adj* of Mt. Maenalus, Arcadian; **Maenalis ursa** Callisto *(who was changed into the Great Bear)*

Maenal·us *or* Maenal·os -ī *m or* Maenal·a -ōrum *npl* Mt. Maenalus *(in Arcadia, sacred to Pan)*

Maen·as -adis *f* Bacchante; frenzied woman

Maeni·us -a -um *adj (name of a Roman clan)* Maenian; **Maenia Columna** pillar in the Forum at which the **triumvirī capitālēs** held court and at which thieves, slaves, and debtors were tried and flogged

Maeon·es -um *mpl* Maeonians *(ancient name of the Lydians)*

Maeoni·a -ae *f* E. part of Lydia; *(from the alleged ancestry of its people)* Etruria

Maeonid·ēs -ae *m* native of Maeonia; Homer *(believed to have been born in Lydia);* an Etruscan

Maeon·is -idis *adj (fem only)* Lydian ‖ *f* Maeonian woman *(esp. Arachne or Omphale)*

Maeoni·us -a -um *adj* Lydian; Homeric; Etruscan ‖ *f see* **Maeonia**

Maeōt·ae -ārum *mpl* a Scythian people on Lake Maeotis *(Sea of Azov)*

Maeōt·is -idis *adj* Maeotic; Scythian; **Maeōtis lacus** Sea of Azov

Maeōti·us -a -um *adj* Maeotian, of the Maeotae *(a Scythian people)*

maer·eō -ēre *tr* to mourn for, grieve for ‖ *intr* to mourn, grieve

maer·or -ōris *m* mourning, grief

maestē *adv* mournfully, sadly

maestiter *adv* mournfully, sadly

maestiti·a -ae *f* sadness, sorrow, grief; gloom; dullness *(of style)*

maestitūd·ō -inis *f* sadness

maest·us -a -um *adj* mourning, sad, gloomy

Maev·ius -(i)ī *m* poetaster often ridiculed by Vergil and Horace

māgāl·ia -ium *npl* huts

mag·ē -ēs *f* magic

mage *see* **magis**

magic·us -a -um *adj* magic; **artēs magicae** magic

magis *or* **mage** *adv* more, to a greater extent, in a higher degree, rather; **eō magis** (all) the more; **magis … atque** rather … than; **magis aut minus** more or less; **magis est ut, quod** it is more the case that; **magis magisque** more and more; **magis … quam** rather … than; **nōn magis … quam** not so much … as

magis·ter -trī *m* chief, master, director; teacher; adviser, guardian; ringleader, author; *(in apposition with noun in the gen)* expert; *(keeper of animals)* shepherd, herdsman; **magister equitum** *(title of dictator's second-in-command)* Master of the Cavalry; **magister mōrum** censor; **magister sacrōrum** chief priest; **magister vīcī** ward boss; **nāvis magister** ship's captain

magister·ium -(i)ī *n* directorship, presidency, superintendence; control, governance; instruction; **magisterium mōrum** censorship

magistr·a -ae *f* directress, mistress; instructress, teacher

magistrāt·us -ūs *m* magistracy; magistrate, official; military command

magmentār·ium -(i)ī *n* receptacle for a part of the sacrificial animal

magnanimit·ās -ātis *f* magnanimity; high ideals; bravery

magnanim·us -a -um *adj* magnanimous, noble, big-hearted; brave

magnāri·us -a -um *adj* wholesale; **magnārius negōtiātor** wholesale dealer

magn·ēs -ētis *adj* magnetic; **magnēs lapis** magnet

Magn·ēs -ētis *adj* of Magnesia, Magnesian

Magnēsi·a -ae *f* district in E. Thessaly on the Aegean Sea ‖ city in Caria near the Menander River ‖ city in Lydia near Mt. Sipylus

magnēsi·us -a -um *adj* magnetic; **saxum magnēsium** lodestone

magnidic·us -a -um *adj* talking big

magnificē *adv* magnificently, splendidly; pompously

magnificenti·a -ae *f* magnificence, grandeur, splendor; pompousness

magnific·ō -āre -āvī -ātus *tr* to make much of

magnific·us -a -um *adj* magnificent, splendid; sumptuous; proud

magniloquenti·a -ae *f* pompous language, braggadocio; *(rhet)* lofty style

magniloqu·us -a -um *adj* (-loc-) sublime; bragging

magnitūd·ō -inis *f* magnitude; size; large quantity, large number; vastness, extent; greatness; importance; power, might; high station, dignity, high rank; dignity of character; length *(of time)*; intensity *(of storm, etc.)*; strength, loudness *(of voice)*

magnopere *or* **magnō opere** *adv* greatly, very much; particularly; strongly, earnestly, heartily

magn·us -a -um *(comp:* **māior;** *superl:* **maximus)** *adj* big, large; important; great; distinguished; impressive; complete, utter, full, pure; high, powerful *(in rank)*; long *(time)*; high *(price)*; loud *(voice)*; heavy *(rain)*; advanced *(age)*; noble *(character)*; **magna itinera** forced marches; **Magna Māter** Cybele; **magnō cāsū occidere** to happen by pure chance; **mare magnum** the ocean; **vir magnō iam nātū** a man advanced in years ‖ *n* great thing; great value; boast, proud claim; **magnī (pretiī) aestimāre** *(or* **magnī habēre)** to value highly, have a high regard for; **magnō emere (vēndere)** to buy (sell) at a high price; **magnum spīrāre** to be proud

Māg·ō -ōnis *m* brother of Hannibal

mag·us -a -um *adj* magic; **artēs magae** magic ‖ *m* magician; learned man *(among the Persians)*

māiāl·is -is *m* castrated hog; *(as term of abuse)* swine

māiest·ās -ātis *f* majesty, dignity, grandeur; sovereign power, sovereignty; authority; *(as a crime of diminishing the majesty of the Roman people)* high treason; **māiestās laesa** *(or* **imminūta)** high treason

māi·or -or -us *(comp of* **magnus)** *adj* bigger, larger; greater; more important; **annōs nātū māior quadrāgintā** forty years older; **in māius ferre** to exaggerate; **māiōris (pretiī)** at a higher price; **māior nātū** older ‖ *mpl see* **māiōrēs** ‖ *npl* worse things, worse sufferings

māiōr·ēs -um *mpl* ancestors, forefathers

Māi·us -a -um *adj & m* May ‖ *f* daughter of Atlas and Pleione and mother of Mercury by Jupiter

māiuscul·us -a -um *adj* somewhat greater; a little older

māl·a -ae *f* cheekbone, upper jaw ‖ *fpl* cheeks; *(fig)* jaws *(e.g., of death)*

malaci·a -ae *f* calm at sea, dead calm

malaciss·ō -āre -āvī -ātus *tr* to soften (up)

malac·us -a -um *adj* soft; luxurious

male *adv (comp:* **pēius;** *superl:* **pessimē)** badly, wrongly; wickedly, cruelly, maliciously; unfortunately, unsuccessfully; awkwardly; excessively, extremely, very much; *(w. adjectives having a bad sense)* terribly, awfully; **male accipere** to treat roughly; **male audīre** to be ill spoken of; **male dīcere** (w. dat) to say nasty things to; **male existimāre dē** (w. abl) to have a bad opinion of; **male emere** to buy at a high price; **male facere** (w. dat) to treat badly, treat cruelly; **male factum!** (coll) too bad!; **male ferre** to take (it) hard; **male fīdus** unsafe; **male grātus** ungrateful; **male habēre** to harass; **male metuere** to be terribly afraid of; **male perdere** to ruin utterly; **male sānus** insane; **male vēndere** to sell at a loss; **male vīvere** to be a failure in life

mal(e)fact·um -ī n wrong, injury

maledic·āx -ācis adj abusive, foul-mouthed

maledicē adv abusively, slanderously

maledīc·ēns -entis adj abusive, foul-mouthed

male·dīcō -dīcere -dīxī -dictum intr (w. dat) to speak ill of, abuse, slander; **2** to say nasty things to

maledicti·ō -ōnis f abusive language, abuse

maledictit·ō -āre -āvī intr (w. dat) to keep saying nasty things to

maledict·um -ī n insult, taunt

maledic·us -a -um adj abusive, foul-mouthed; slanderous

male·faciō -facere -fēcī -factum intr to do wrong; (w. dat) to injure, do wrong to

malefact·or -ōris m malefactor, troublemaker

maleficē adv mischievously

maleficenti·a -ae f harm, wrong, mischief

malefic·ium -(i)ī n evil deed, crime, offense; harm, injury, wrong, mischief; **maleficium admittere** (or **committere**) to commit a crime

malefic·us -a -um adj wicked, vicious, criminal ‖ m mischief-maker

malesuād·us -a -um adj seductive

malevol·ēns -entis adj malevolent, spiteful, malicious ‖ mf spiteful person

malevolenti·a -ae f malevolence, spitefulness, ill will

malevol·us -a -um adj malevolent, spiteful, nasty

Māliac·us -a -um adj Malian, of Malis; **sinus Māliacus** Malian Gulf (in S. Thessaly, modern Gulf of Zeitouni)

Māliēns·is -is -e adj of Malis (a district of S. Thessaly)

mālifer -a -um apple-bearing

malignē adv spitefully; jealously; grudgingly; scantily, poorly

malignit·ās -ātis f spite, malice, jealously; stinginess

malign·us -a -um adj spiteful, malicious, jealous; stingy; (fig) unproductive (soil); scanty (light)

maliti·a -ae f malice, ill-will, bad behavior ‖ fpl devilish tricks

malitiōsē adv wickedly; craftily

malitiōs·us -a -um adj malicious, crafty, wicked, devilish

malleol·us -ī m small hammer, small mallet; fiery arrow

malle·us -ī m hammer, mallet; **malleus ferreus** pole-ax (for slaughtering sacrificial animals)

mālō or **māvolō mālle māluī** tr to prefer; **pecūniam quam sapientiam mālle** to prefer money to wisdom; (w. inf) to prefer to (do s.th.); (w. acc & inf, w. ut) to prefer that ‖ intr (w. dat) to incline toward, be more favorably disposed to

malobathr·um -ī n malobathrum oil (used as perfume)

māl·um -ī n apple; **aureum mālum** quince; **fēlīx mālum** lemon; **mālum Persicum** peach; **mālum Pūnicum** (or **mālum grānātum**) pomegranate; **mālum silvestre** crab apple

mal·um -ī n evil, ill; harm; punishment; disaster; hardship; trouble; (as a term of abuse): **quī, malum, istī sunt?** who the heck are they?

mal·us -a -um adj bad; ill, evil; ugly; unpatriotic; adverse, unfavorable; unsuccessful; harmful; inappropriate, misplaced; insulting, abusive (words); humble (birth); **ī in malam rem!** (sl) go to hell!; **mala aetās** old age; **rēs mala** trouble ‖ n see **malum**

māl·us -ī f apple tree

māl·us -ī m mast (of ship); pole

malv·a -ae f mallow (used as food or mild laxative)

Mām·ers -ertis m Mars

Māmertīn·ī -ōrum mpl inhabitants of Messana who precipitated the First Punic war

mamill·a -ae f breast, teat

mamm·a -ae f breast (of a woman); dug (of an animal); (baby talk) mummy, mamma

mammeāt·us -a -um adj large-breasted

mammōs·us -a -um adj large-breasted, chesty

mānābil·is -is -e adj penetrating (cold)

manc·eps -ipis m purchaser; contractor

mancip·ium -(i)ī n (-cup-) formal purchase; possession, right of ownership; slave; **mancipiō accipere** to take possession of; **mancipiō dare** to turn over possession of; **rēs mancipī** possessions (basic to running a farm e.g., land, slaves, livestock, farm implements); **rēs nec mancipī** possessions (other than those needed to run a farm)

mancip·ō -āre -āvī -ātus tr (-cup-) to sell, transfer

manc·us -a -um adj crippled, maimed; (fig) defective, weak

mandāt·um -ī n command, order, commission ‖ npl instructions

mandāt·us -ūs m command, order

mand·ō -āre -āvī -ātus *tr* to hand over; to commit, entrust; to command, order, enjoin; to commission; to delegate *(authority)*; to prescribe, specify; **humō aliquem mandare** to bury s.o.; **memoriae** *(or* **animō) mandāre** to commit to memory, record ‖ *refl* **sē fugae mandāre** to run away

man·dō -dere -dī -sus *tr* to chew; to champ; to eat, devour; **humum mandere** *(fig)* to bite the dust

mandr·a -ae *f* stable, stall; column of pack animals *or* cattle; checkerboard

mandūc·us -ī *m* mask representing a glutton

māne *indecl n* morning ‖ *adv* in the morning; **bene māne** early in the morning; **crās māne** tomorrow morning; **herī māne** yesterday morning; **hodiē māne** this morning; **postrīdiē ēius diēī māne** the following morning

man·eō -ēre -sī -sus *tr* to wait for, await ‖ *intr* to stay, remain; to stop off, pass the night; to last, endure, continue, persist; to be left over; **in condiciōne manēre** to stick to an agreement; **in sententiā manēre** to stick to an opinion

mān·ēs -ium *mpl* spirits of the dead; lower world; mortal remains

mang·ō -ōnis *m* slave dealer; pushy salesman

manic·ae -ārum *fpl* handcuffs; grappling hook; long sleeves; gloves

manicāt·us -a -um *adj* long-sleeved

manicul·a -ae *f* little hand

manifestē *adv* plainly, distinctly

manifestō *adv* red-handed; plainly, manifestly, evidently

manifest·ō -āre -āvī -ātus *tr* to reveal; to make known; to clarify

manifest·us -a -um *adj* manifest, plain, clear, distinct; exposed, brought to light, detected, caught; *(w. gen)* caught in, convicted of; *(w. inf)* known to

manipl = manipul-

manip(u)l·us -ī *m* handful *(esp. of hay); (coll)* gang; *(mil)* maniple, company *(three of which constituted a cohort)*

manipulār·is -is -e *adj (mil)* of a maniple *or* company; **mīles manipulāris** private

manipulātim *adv (mil)* by companies

Manl·ius -(i)ī *m* Marcus Manlius Capitolinus *(consul in 392 B.C., who, in 389 B.C. saved the Capitoline from the invading Gauls)* ‖ Titus Manlius Torquatus *(consul in 340 B.C., famous for his military discipline)*

mannul·us -ī *m* little pony

mann·us -ī *m* pony

mān·ō -āre -āvī -ātus *tr* to pour out; to shed *(tears)* ‖ *intr* to drip, trickle; *(w. abl)* to drip with; to leak; to flow, pour; to stream; *(of rumors)* to spread, circulate; *(of secrets)* to leak out; *(fig)* to be derived, emanate

mānsi·ō -ōnis *f* staying; stopover

mānsit·ō -āre -āvī *intr* to stay on

mānsuē·faciō -facere -fēcī -factus *(pass:* **mānsuē·fīō -fierī -factus sum)** *tr* to tame; to civilize

mānsu·ēs -is *or* **-ētis** *adj* tame, mild

mānsu·ēscō -ēscere -ēvī -ētus *tr* to tame ‖ *intr* to become tame; *(fig)* to become gentle; to relent; to grow less harsh

mānsuētē *adv* gently, mildly

mānsuētūd·ō -inis *f* mildness, gentleness

mānsuēt·us -a -um *adj* tame; mild, gentle

mānsus *pp of* **mandō** *and* **maneō**

mantēl·e -is *n* hand towel; napkin; tablecloth

mantēl·ium -(i)ī *n* hand towel; napkin

mantell·um -ī *n* **(-tēl-)** mantle

mantic·a -ae *f* knapsack

Mantinē·a -ae *f* town in Arcadia, where the Spartans were defeated by the Thebans in 362 B.C.

manticin·or -ārī -ātus sum *intr* to prophesy

mant·ō -āre *tr* to wait for ‖ *intr* to stay, remain, wait

Mant·ō -ūs *f* prophetic daughter of Tiresias

Mantu·a -ae *f* town in N. Italy, birthplace of Vergil

manuāl·e -is *n* wooden case for a book

manuāl·is -is -e *adj* that can be held in hand, hand-sized *(e.g., rocks)*

manubi·ae -ārum *fpl* money derived from the sale of booty; *(coll)* proceeds from robbery, loot

manubiāl·is -is -e *adj* obtained from the sale of booty

manubiāri·us -a -um *adj (coll)* bringing in the loot

manūbr·ium -(i)ī *n* handle; hilt

manufestāri·us -a -um *adj* **(mani-)** plain, obvious

manule·a -ae *f* long sleeve

manuleār·ius -(i)ī *m* sleeve maker

manuleāt·us -a -um *adj* long-sleeved

manūmissi·ō -ōnis *f* manumission, freeing *(of a slave)*

manū·mittō -mittere -mīsī -missus *tr* to manumit, set free *(a slave)*

manupret·ium -(i)ī *n* workman's pay, wages; *(fig)* pay, reward

man·us -ūs *f* hand; band, gang, company; force, violence, close combat; finishing touch; handwriting; work; workmanship; trunk *(of elephant);* twigs *(of a tree); (leg)* power of a husband over his wife and children; *(med)* surgery; **ad manum** close at hand, within easy reach; **ad manum habēre** to have at hand, have in readiness; **ad manum venīre** to come within reach; **ad**

manūs pervenīre to resort to fighting; **aequā manū** (*or* **aequīs manibus**) on even terms; **ā manū servus** secretary; **dē manū** personally; **ē manū** at a distance, from a distance; **in manibus esse** (*gen*) to be in the power of; be under the jurisdiction of; **inter manūs** under one's hand, in one's arms; **inter manūs habēre** to have in hand, be busied with; **manibus pedibusque** (*fig*) with might and main; **manū** by hand, artificially; in deed; by force; (*mil*) by force of arms; **manū (ē)mittere** to set (*a slave*) free; **manū factus** manmade; **manum committere** (*or* **cōnserere** *or* **cōnferre**) to begin to fight; **manum dare** to lend a hand; **manum inicere** (*w. dat*) to lay hands on, arrest; **manūs dare** (*or* **manūs dēdere**) to surrender; **manus extrēma** (*or* **summa** *or* **ultima**) finishing touches; **manus (ferrea)** grappling iron; **manū tenēre** to know for sure; **media manus** a go-between; **per manūs** by hand; by force; from hand to hand, from mouth to mouth, from father to son; **plēnā manū** generously; **prae manibus** (*or* **prae manū**) at hand, in readiness; **sub manū** (*or* **sub manum**) at hand, near; immediately, promptly; **suspēnsā manū** reluctantly

mapāl·ia -ium *npl* African huts; (*fig*) a mess

mapp·a -ae *f* napkin; flag (*used in starting races at the racetrack*)

Marath·ōn -ōnis *f* site in E. Attica of the victory of Miltiades over the Persians (*490 B.C.*)

Marathōni·us -a -um *adj* of Marathon

Marcell·us -ī *m* Roman family name (*cognomen*) in the gens Claudia; Marcus Claudius Marcellus (*nephew of Augustus, 43–23 B.C.*)

marc·eō -ēre *intr* to wither, droop, shrivel; to be weak, be feeble; be decrepit, be run-down; to slack off

marcēsc·ō -ere *intr* to begin to wither, begin to droop; to become weak, become run-down; to become lazy

marcid·us -a -um *adj* withered, droopy; groggy

Marc·ius -(i)ī *m* Ancus Marcius (*fourth king of Rome*)

marcul·us -ī *m* small hammer

Mārc·us -ī *m* Roman first name (*praenōmen*)

mar·e -is *n* sea; saltwater; **mare caelō mīscēre** to raise a huge storm; (*fig*) to have all hell break loose; **mare īnferum** Tyrrhenian Sea; **mare magnum** the ocean; **mare nostrum** Mediterranean Sea; **mare superum** Adriatic Sea; **trāns mare** overseas, abroad

Mareōt·a -ae *f* town and lake near Alexandria in Egypt

Mareōtic·us -a -um *adj* Mareotic; Egyptian

margarīt·a -ae *f or* **margarīt·um -ī** *n* pearl

margin·ō -āre -āvī -ātus *tr* to furnish with a border; to curb (*a street*)

marg·ō -inis *f* margin, edge, border; frontier; bank (*of a stream*); **margō cēnae** side-dishes

Mariān·ī -ōrum *mpl* partisans of Marius

Marīc·a -ae *f* nymph of Minturnae, mother of Latinus

marīn·us -a -um *adj* sea, marine; seagoing

marisc·a -ae *f* a fig; **tumidae mariscae** the piles

marīt·a -ae *f* wife

marītāl·is -is -e *adj* marital, nuptial; matronly, of a married woman

maritim·us -a -um *adj* (**-tum-**) sea, of the sea; seafaring, maritime; (*fig*) changeable (*like the sea*); **ōra maritima** seacoast ‖ *npl* seacoast

marīt·ō -āre -āvī -ātus *tr* to provide with a husband *or* wife, marry; to train (*a vine to a tree*) ‖ *pass* to get married

marīt·us -a -um *adj* matrimonial, nuptial ‖ *m* husband ‖ *f* wife

Mar·ius -(i)ī *m* Gaius Marius (*conqueror of Jugurtha and of the Cimbri and Teutons, and seven times consul, 157–86 B.C.*)

marm·or -oris *n* marble; marble statue, marble monument; marble vessel; milestone; smooth surface of the sea ‖ *npl* marble pavement

marmore·us -a -um *adj* marble, made of marble; marble-like

Mar·ō -ōnis *m* cognomen of Vergil

marr·a -ae *f* hoe, weeding hook

Mārs Mārtis *m* god of war and father of Romulus and Remus; battle, war; engagement; (*astr*) Mars; **aequō Mārte** on an equal footing, in an even battle; **stella** (*or* **sīdus**) **Mārtis** (*astr*) the planet Mars; **suō Mārte** by his own exertions, independently

Mars·ī -ōrum *mpl* Marsians (*a people of S. central Italy, regarded as tough warriors*)

marsupp·ium -(i)ī *n* purse, pouch

Marsy·ās *or* **Marsy·a -ae** *m* satyr who challenged Apollo with the flute and was flayed alive upon his defeat ‖ statue of Marsyas in the Roman Forum

Mārtiāl·ēs -ium *mpl* college of priests of Mars; troops of the **legiō Mārtia** (*Martian legion*)

Mārtiāl·is -is *m* Martial (*Marcus Valerius Martialis, famous for his epigrams, c. A.D. 40–120*)

Mārticol·a -ae *m* worshiper of Mars

Mārti·us -a -um *adj* Martian, of Mars; sacred to Mars; descended from Mars; of March; **mēnsis Mārtius** March (*third month of the year after the year 153 B.C., originally the first month*) ‖ *m* March

mās maris *adj* male, masculine; manly, brave ‖ *m* male

māsculīn·us -a -um *adj* male, masculine

māscul·us -a -um *adj* male, masculine; manly, vigorous ‖ *m* male

mass·a -ae *f* mass, lump; *(coll)* chunk of money; bulk, size; heavy weight *(used in exercising)*

Massaget·ae -ārum *mpl* a nomadic tribe of Scythia

Massic·us -a -um *adj* Massic ‖ *m* Mt. Massicus *(between Latium and Campania, famous for its wine)* ‖ *n* Massic wine

Massili·a -ae *f* Greek Colony on S. coast of Gaul *(modern Marseilles)*

Massyl·ī -ōrum *mpl* tribe of E. Numidia

mastīgi·a *or* **mastīgi·ās -ae** *m* rascal *(whip-needer)*

mastrūc·a -ae *f* sheepskin; *(pej)* ninny

mastrūcāt·us -a -um *adj* dressed in a sheep-skin coat

masturbāt·or -ōris *m* masturbator

masturb·or -ārī -ātus sum *intr* to masturbate

matar·a -ae *or* **matar·is -is** *f* Celtic javelin

matell·a -ae *f* chamber pot

matelli·ō -ōnis *m* small pot

mā·ter -tris *f* mother; matron; foster mother; *(in addressing an old woman)* ma'am; *(of animals)* dam; cause, origin, source; mother-land, native land; native city; **Magna Māter** Cybele; **māter familiās** lady of the house

mātercul·a -ae *f* little mother, poor mother

māt·erfamiliās -risfamiliās *f* lady of the house, mistress of the household

māteri·a -ae *or* **māteri·ēs -ēī** *f* matter, stuff, material; lumber *(for building);* fuel; subject, subject matter, theme, topic; cause, source; occasion, opportunity; capacity, natural ability; disposition

māteriār·ius -(i)ī *m* lumber merchant

māteriāt·us -a -um *adj* built with lumber; **male materiātus** built with poor lumber

māteriēs *see* **māteria**

māteri·or -ārī -ātus sum *intr* to gather wood

mātern·us -a -um *adj* maternal, mother's, of a mother

māterter·a -ae *f* aunt, mother's sister; **mātert-era magna** grandaunt, grandmother's sister

mathēmatic·a -ae *or* **mathēmatic·ē -ēs** *f* mathematics; astrology

mathēmatic·us -a -um *adj* mathematical, of arithmetic, of geometry ‖ *m* mathematician; astrologer

Matīn·us -ī *m* mountain in Apulia near Horace's birthplace, famous for honey

mātricīd·a -ae *m* murderer of one's mother

mātricīd·ium -(i)ī *n* murder of one's mother, matricide

mātrimōn·ium -(i)ī *n* matrimony, marriage; **in mātrimōnium accipere** to marry *(a man);* **in mātrimōnium dare** *(or* **collocāre)** to give in marriage; **in mātrimōnium dūcere** to marry *(a woman)*

mātrim·us -a -um *adj* having a mother still living

mātrōn·a -ae *f* married woman, matron, wife; lady

Mātrōnāl·ia -ium *npl* festival celebrated by married women on March 1 in honor of Mars

mātrōnāl·is -is -e *adj* matronly, wifely, womanly

matt·a -ae *f* straw mat

matul·a -ae *f* pot; chamber pot; *(pej)* block-head

mātūrātē *adv* promptly

mātūrē *adv* at the right time; in good time, in time; at an early date; at an early age; quickly; prematurely

mātūr·ēscō -ēscere -uī *intr* to get ripe, ripen, mature

mātūrit·ās -ātis *f* ripeness, maturity; harvest season; the proper time; *(fig)* maturity, height, perfection

mātūr·ō -āre -āvī -ātus *tr* to ripen, bring to maturity; to speed up, hasten; *(w. inf)* to be too quick in doing ‖ *intr* to hurry; **mātūrātō opus est** there is no time to lose

mātūr·us -a -um *adj* ripe, mature, full-grown; opportune, at the right time; *(of winter, etc.)* early, coming early; advanced in years; marriageable; mellow

Mātūt·a -ae *f* goddess of the dawn

mātūtīn·us -a -um *adj* morning, early; **diēs mātūtīnus** early part of the day; **tempora mātūtīna** morning hours

Mauritāni·a -ae *f* country of N.W. Africa

Maur·us -a -um *adj* Moorish; African

Maurūsi·us -a -um *adj* Moorish, Mauretanian

Māvor·s -tis *m* Mars; warfare; *(astr)* Mars

Māvorti·us -a -um *adj* Martian, of Mars; war-like, martial ‖ *m* Meleager *(son of Mars)*

maxill·a -ae *f* jaw

maximē *adv* (**-xum-**) very, most, especially, particularly; just, precisely, exactly; *(in sequences)* in the first place, first of all; *(in affirmations)* by all means, certainly, yes; **immo maximē** certainly not; **nūper maximē** just recently; **quam maximē** as much as possible; **tum cum maximē** at the precise moment when; **tum maximē** just then; **ut maximē … ita maximē** the more … so much the more

maximit·ās -ātis *f* magnitude

maxim·us -a -um *(superl of* **magnus)** *adj* (**-xum-**) biggest, largest; tallest; most important, leading, chief; highest, utmost; greatest *(in amount, number, value, power, or reputation); (with or without* **nātū)** oldest; **maximā vōce** at the top of one's lungs

mazonom·um -ī *n* serving dish

meāmet = meā, *abl fem sing of* meus, *strengthened by* -met
meāpte = meā, *abl fem sing of* meus, *strengthened by* -pte
meāt·us -ūs *m* motion, movement; course, channel
mecastor *interj* by Castor! *(used by women)*
mēchanic·us -ī *m* mechanic, engineer
mēcum = cum mē
mēd = mē *(archaic form of acc and abl)*
medd·ix -icis *m* (mēd-) magistrate *(among the Oscans);* meddix tuticus chief magistrate
Mēdē·a -ae *f* daughter of Aeëtes, the king of Colchis, and wife of Jason
Mēdē·is -idos *adj* magical
med·ēns -entis *m* doctor
med·eor -ērī *tr* to heal **ǁ** *intr (w. dat)* to heal, cure; *(w.* adversus *or* contrā + *acc)* to be good for *(e.g., a cold, headache)*
Mēd·ī -ōrum *mpl* Medes; Parthians; Persians
Mēdi·a -ae *f* country of the Medes S. of the Caspian Sea
mediān·us -a -um *adj* central **ǁ** *n* central part, middle
mediast(r)īn·us -ī *m* servant *(without any specific skill)*
mēdic·a -ae *f* alfalfa
medicābil·is -is -e *adj* curable
medicām·en -inis *n* medicine, medication; drug, antidote; remedy; tincture; cosmetic; *(fig)* remedy
medicāment·um -ī *n* medicine, medication; potion; *(fig)* relief, antidote; *(rhet)* embellishment
medicāt·us -a -um *adj* healing, having healing powers; imbued with magical substances
medicāt·us -ūs *m* magic charm
medicīn·a -ae *f* medicine *(medication; science of medicine);* remedy; doctor's office; *(w. gen) (fig)* cure for, remedy for; medicīnam exercēre *(or* facere) to practice medicine
medicīn·us -a -um *adj* of medicine
medic·ō -āre -āvī -ātus *tr* to medicate, cure; to dye; to poison
medic·or -ārī -ātus sum *tr* to cure **ǁ** *intr (w. dat)* to heal, cure
medic·us -a -um *adj* medical; healing **ǁ** *m* doctor, surgeon **ǁ** *f* physician *(female),* midwife
Mēdic·us -a -um *adj* Median, of the Medes
medīdi·ēs -ēī *f (early form of* merīdiēs) noon; south
mediē *adv* moderately
mediet·ās -ātis *f* the mean; middle
medimn·um -ī *n or* medimn·us -ī *m* bushel *(containing six modii or* "pecks")
mediocr·is -is -e *adj* of medium size, medium, average, ordinary; undistinguished; mediocre; narrow, small; intermediate

mediocrit·ās -ātis *f* moderate size *or* amount; middle course, mean; moderation; mediocrity **ǁ** *fpl* moderate passions
mediocriter *adv* moderately, fairly; not particularly, not very, not much; calmly; with moderation; *(w. neg.)* in no slight degree, considerably, extraordinarily
Mediolānēns·is -is -e *adj* of Milan
Mediolān·um -ī *n* Milan
medioxum·us -a -um *adj (coll)* in the middle, intermediate
meditāment·um -ī *n* practice, drill, exercise *(in school, in the army)*
meditātē *adv* intentionally
meditāti·ō -ōnis *f* reflection, contemplation; practice; rehearsal; *(w. gen)* reflection on
meditāt·us -a -um *adj* premeditated
mediterrāne·us -a -um *adj* inland **ǁ** *n* interior *(of a country)*
medit·or -ārī -ātus sum *tr* to think over, reflect on; to practice, rehearse; to have in mind, intend; to plan, design **ǁ** *refl* to practice, train **ǁ** *intr* to prepare one's speech, rehearse; *(w.* dē + *abl)* to reflect on, think about;
meditull·ium -(i)ī *n* the interior *(of a country);* middle, center
medi·us -a -um *adj* middle, central, the middle of, in the middle; intermediate; moderate; intervening *(time);* middling, ordinary, common; undecided, neutral, ambiguous; diēs medius *(or* lūx media, sōl medius) midday; the south; in mediā viā in the middle of the road; media pars half; medium mare the high seas **ǁ** *n* the middle part, center; the general public; intervening space; intermediate stage; dē *(or* ē) mediō from the scene; in mediō in mid-course; within reach; in mediō positus made available to all; in mediō pōnere to disclose; in medium on behalf of the general public; for the common good; in medium prōferre to make public; in medium *(or in* mediō) relinquere to leave undecided; mediō temporis in the meanwhile
medius fidius *interj* so help me God!; honest to God!
mēd·ix -icis *see* meddix
medull·a -ae *f* marrow; *(fig)* middle **ǁ** *fpl (fig)* heart; īmīs medullīs in the innermost heart, deep within one's heart
medullitus *adv* with all one's heart
medullul·a -ae *f* ānseris medullula goose down
Mēd·us -a -um Mede, of the Medes **ǁ** *m* son of Aegeus and Medea, the eponymous hero of the Medes
Medūs·a -ae *f* one of the three Gorgons, whose look turned people to stone

Medūsae·us -a -um *adj* Medusan; equus Medūsaeus Pegasus

Megaer·a -ae *f* one of the three Furies

Megalēns·ia *or* Megalēs·ia -ium *npl* festival of Cybele, celebrated on the 4th of April

Megalēns·is -is -e *adj* of the Magna Mater *or* Cybele; lūdī Megalēnsēs games in honor of Cybele

Megar·a -ae *f or* Megar·a -ōrum *npl* town near Athens on the Saronic Gulf ‖ Greek town in Sicily

Megar·a -ae *f* wife of Hercules, whom he killed in a fit of madness

Megarē·us *or* Megaric·us -a -um *adj* of Megara, Megarean

megistān·es -um *mpl* grandees

meherc(u)le *or* mehercules *interj* by Hercules!

mēi·ō -ere *intr (coll)* to pee

mel mellis *n* honey; meum mel *(as term of endearment)* my honey ‖ *npl* drops of honey

melancholic·us -a -um *adj* melancholy

melandry·um -ī *n* piece of salted tuna

Melanipp·a -ae *f or* Melanipp·ē -ēs *f* Melanippe *(daughter of Aeolus or Desmon, the mother of two children by Neptune)*

Melanth·ius -(i)ī *m* goatherd of Ulysses

melcul·um -ī *n (term of endearment)* little honey

Melea·ger *or* Melea·gros -grī *m* Meleager *(son of King Oeneus of Calydon and participant in the famous Calydonian boar hunt)*

Meleagrid·es -um *fpl* sisters of Meleager who were changed into birds

mēl·ēs -is *f* badger

Melicert·a -ae *or* Melicert·ēs -ae *m* Melicertes *(son of Ino and Athamas, who was changed into a sea-god, called Palaemon by the Greeks and Portunus by the Romans)*

melic·us -a -um *adj* musical, melodious; lyric

melilōt·os -ī *m* clover-like plant

melimēl·a -ōrum *npl* honey apples

mēlīn·a -ae *f* (mell-) leather pouch

Mēlīn·um -ī *n* pigment; Melian white *(from Melos)*

meli·or -or -us *(comp of bonus) adj* better; kinder, more gracious; melius est *(w. inf, w. acc & inf)* it is (would be) preferable to, that

melisphyll·um -ī *n* balm *(herb of which bees are fond)*

Melit·a -ae *or* Melit·ē -ēs *f* Malta; a sea nymph

Melitēns·is -is -e *adj* Maltese

melius *(comp of bene) adv* better

meliusculē *adv* pretty well

meliuscul·us -a -um *adj* a little better

mell·a -ae *f* mead *(mixture of honey and water)*

mellicul·us -a -um *adj* sweet as honey

melli·fer -fera -ferum *adj* producing honey

mellific·ō -āre *intr* to make honey

mellill·a -ae *f (term of endearment)* little honey

mellīn·a -ae *f* (mēlī-) leather pouch *(made from the skin of a badger)*

mellin·a -ae *f* sweetness, delight

mellīt·us -a -um *adj* honeyed; sweet as honey

mel·os -eos *n or* mel·um -ī *n or* mel·os -ī *m* song, tune

Melpomen·ē -ēs *f* Muse of tragic poetry

membrān·a -ae *f* membrane, skin; slough *(of a snake);* parchment; film

membrānul·a -ae *f* small piece of parchment

membrātim *adv* limb by limb; singly, piecemeal; in short sentences

membr·um -ī *n* member, organ, limb, genital; part, division *(of a thing);* apartment, room; *(gram)* clause; *(rhet)* small section of a speech *or* literary work

mēmet *pron (emphatic form of mē)* me

memin·ī -isse *(imperative:* mementō; mementōte) *tr* to remember ‖ *tr (w. gen)* to remember, be mindful of

Memn·ōn -onis *m* son of Tithonus and Aurora, king of the Ethiopians, killed by Achilles ‖ statue in Egypt *(actually of Amenhotep III)*

Memnonid·es -um *fpl* birds that rose from the pyre of Memnon

Memnoni·us -a -um *adj* Memnonian; Oriental; Moorish; black

mem·or -oris *adj* mindful, remembering having a good memory; careful, thoughtful; observant; *(w. gen)* mindful of, remembering

memorābil·is -is -e *adj* memorable, remarkable

memorand·us -a -um *adj* worth mentioning, notable

memorāt·us -ūs *m* mention

memori·a -ae *f* memory; remembrance; period of recollection, time, lifetime; a memory, past event, history; historical account; in memoriā habēre to bear in mind; in memoriā redīre *(or* regredī) to recollect; in memoriā indūcere *(or* redigere) to call to mind; in memoriam *(w. gen)* in memory of; memoriā *(w. gen)* in the time of; memoriā tenēre to keep in mind; to remember; memoriae causā as a reminder; memoriae mandāre *(or* trādere) to commit to memory; memoriae prōdere to hand down to posterity; paulō suprā hanc memoriam not long ago; post hominum memoriam within the memory of man; superiōre memoriā in earlier times

memoriāl·is -is -e *adj* for memoranda

memoriol·a -ae *f* poor memory

memoriter *adv* from memory, by heart

memor·ō -āre -āvī -ātus *tr* to mention, bring up; to name, call ‖ *intr (w.* dē + *abl)* to speak of

Memph·is -is *or* -idos *f* capital city of Pharaonic Egypt

Memphītic·us -a -um *adj* Egyptian
Menan·der *or* **Menan·dros -drī** *m* Greek playwright of Attic New Comedy *(342–291 B.C.)*
Menandrē·us -a -um *adj* of Menander
mend·a -ae *f* fault, blemish; slip of the pen
mendāciloqui·or -or -us *adj* more false
mendāc·ium -(i)ī *n* lie
mendāciuncul·um -ī *n* white lie, fib
mend·āx -ācis *adj* mendacious, lying, false **||** *m* liar
mendīcit·ās -ātis *f* begging
mendīc·ō -āre -āvī -ātus *or* **mendīc·or -ārī -ātus sum** *tr* to beg, beg for **||** *intr* to beg, be a beggar
mendīcul·us -a -um *adj* beggarly
mendīc·us -a -um *adj* needy, poverty-stricken; paltry *(meal)* **||** *m* beggar
mendōsē *adv* faultily, carelessly
mendōs·us -a -um *adj* full of physical defects; full of faults, faulty, incorrect, erroneous; blundering
mend·um -ī *n* defect, fault; blunder *(esp. in writing)*
Menelā·us -ī *m* son of Atreus, brother of Agamemnon, and husband of Helen
Menēn·ius -(i)ī *m* Menenius Agrippa *(told the plebs the fable of the belly and the limbs, 494 B.C.)*
Menoec·eūs -eī *or* **-eos** *m* son of Theban king Creon, who hurled himself off the city walls to save the city
Menoetiad·ēs -ae *m* son of Menoetius *(i.e., Patroclus)*
Menoet·ius -(i)ī *m* one of the Argonauts and father of Patroclus
mēn·s -tis *f* mind, intellect; frame of mind, attitude; will, inclination; understanding, reason; thought, opinion, intention, plan; courage, boldness; passion, impulse; **addere mentem** to give courage; **captus mente** crazy; **dēmittere mentem** to lose heart; **in mentem venīre** to come to mind; **mentis suae esse** to be in one's right mind
mēns·a -ae *f* table; meal, course, dinner; guests at table; counter; bank; sacrificial table, altar; **mēnsa secunda** dessert
mēnsār·ius -(i)ī *m* banker; treasury official; **triumvirī mēnsāriī** board of three treasury officials
mēnsi·ō -ōnis *f* measure, measuring; *(pros)* quantity *(of a syllable)*
mēns·is -is *(gen pl:* **mēnsium** *or* **mēnsum)** *m* month; **prīmō mēnse** at the beginning of the month
mēns·or -ōris *m* surveyor
mēnstruāl·is -is -e *adj* for a month

mēnstru·us -a -um *adj* monthly; lasting for a month **||** *n* rations for a month; month's term of office; monthly payment
mēnsul·a -ae *f* small table
mēnsūr·a -ae *f* measuring, measurement; standard of measure; amount, size, proportion, capacity, extent, limit, degree; **mēnsūra duōrum digitōrum** a pinch *(e.g., of salt)*
mēnsus *pp of* **metior**
ment·a *or* **menth·a -ae** *f* mint
menti·ēns -entis *m (phil)* sophism, fallacy
menti·ō -ōnis *f* mention; **mentiōnem facere** *(w. gen or* **dē** *+ abl)* to make mention of; **mentiōnēs serere** *(w. ad)* to throw hints to
ment·ior -īrī -ītus sum *tr* to invent, fabricate; to feign, imitate, fake **||** *intr* to lie; to act deceitfully
Ment·or -oris *m* friend of Ulysses **||** Greek silversmith of 4th cent. B.C.; *(fig)* a work by Mentor
mentul·a -ae *f (vulg)* penis, dick
ment·um -ī *n* chin
me·ō -āre -āvī -ātum *intr* to go, pass
mēopte *pron (emphatic form of* **mē)** me, me myself
mephīt·is -is *f* sulfurous fumes
merāc(u)l·us -a -um *adj* pretty pure
merāc·us -a -um *adj* undiluted, pure
mercābil·is -is -e *adj* buyable
merc·āns -antis *m* merchant
mercāt·or -ōris *m* merchant, dealer
mercātōri·us -a -um *adj* mercantile, trading, business; **nāvis mercātōria** merchant ship
mercātūr·a -ae *f* commerce, trade, trading; purchase **||** *fpl* goods, wares
mercāt·us -ūs *m* market, marketplace; fair; trade, traffic
mercēdul·a -ae *f* poor pay; low rent
mercennāri·us *or* **mercēnāri·us -a -um** *adj* hired, paid, mercenary **||** *m* common laborer
merc·ēs -ēdis *f* pay, wages; bribe; reward, recompense; cost; price; payment *(esp. for effort, pain, misfortune);* injury, detriment; stipulation, condition; retribution, punishment; rent, income, interest; **ūnā mercēde duās rēs assequī** *(prov)* to kill two birds with one stone *(literally, to buy two things for the price of one)*
mercimōn·ium -(i)ī *n* merchandise, goods, wares
merc·or -ārī -ātus sum *tr* to purchase **||** *intr* to trade, buy and sell
Mercuriāl·is -is -e *adj* of Mercury **||** *mpl* corporation of merchants in Rome
Mercur·ius -(i)ī *m* Mercury *(son of Jupiter and Maia, messenger of the gods, patron of commerce, diplomacy, gambling, etc.); (astr)* Mercury; **sīdus** *(or* **stella)** **Mercuriī** the planet Mercury

merd·a -ae *f* droppings, excrement

merend·a -ae *f* lunch, snack

mer·eō -ēre -uī -itus *or* **mer·eor -ērī -itus sum** *tr* to deserve, merit, be entitled to; to win, gain *(glory, fame, reproach);* to earn *(money);* **merēre pecūniam ut** to accept money on condition that; **stipendia** *(or* **stipendium) merēre** *(mil)* to serve ‖ *intr* to serve; to serve in the army; *(w.* **dē** + *abl)* to serve, render service to, do a favor for; **bene dē rē pūblicā mērere** *(or* **merērī)** to serve one's country well; **dē tē meruī** I have done you a favor, I have treated you well; **equō merēre** to serve in the cavalry

meretrīciē *adv* like a prostitute

meretrīci·us -a -um *adj* prostitute's

meretrīcul·a -ae *f* cute little wench; *(pej)* the little wench

meretr·īx -īcis *f* prostitute, hooker

merg·ae -ārum *fpl* pitchfork; device for reaping

merg·es -itis *f* sheaf of wheat

mer·gō -gere -sī -sus *tr* to dip, plunge, sink; to flood, inundate, engulf, swallow up; to swamp, overwhelm; to bury; to drown ‖ *refl* to dive ‖ *pass* to sink; *(of heavenly bodies)* to go down; to drown; to go bankrupt

merg·us -ī *m* seagull

merīdiān·us -a -um *adj* midday, noon; southern, southerly

merīdiāti·ō -ōnis *f* siesta

merīdi·ēs -ēī *m* midday, noon; south; **ab merīdiē** in the south; **spectāre ad merīdiem** to face south

merīdi·ō -āre -āvī *or* **merīdi·or -ārī -ātus sum** *intr* to take a siesta

Mērion·ēs -ae *m* charioteer of Idomeneus of Crete in the Trojan War

meritō *adv* deservedly, rightly

merit·ō -āre -āvī -ātus *tr* to earn regularly

meritōri·us -a -um *adj* rented, hired ‖ *npl* rented lodgings

merit·us -a -um *adj* deserved, just, right, proper, deserving; guilty ‖ *n* service, favor, kindness; merit, worth; blame, fault, offense; **meritum reddere** to return a favor

merobib·us -a -um *adj* drinking unmixed wine

Merop·ē -ēs *f* one of the Pleiades, daughter of Atlas and Pleione

Merop·s -is *m* king of Ethiopia, husband of Clymene, and reputed father of Phaëthon

mer·ops -opis *m* bee-eater *(bird)*

mers·ō -āre -āvī -ātus *tr* to keep dipping *or* plunging; to drown; *(fig)* to engulf ‖ *pass (w. dat)* to plunge into

mersus *pp of* **mergō**

merul·a -ae *f* blackbird

mer·us -a -um *adj* pure, unmixed, undiluted; *(fig)* nothing but, mere ‖ *n* (undiluted) wine

mer·x -cis *f* merchandise, wares; **mala merx** *(fig)* a bad lot

Messallīn·a -ae *f* Valeria Messallina *(wife of Claudius and mother of Britannicus)* ‖ Statilia Messalina *(wife of Nero)*

Messān·a -ae *f* town in N.E. Sicily *(modern Messina)*

Messāpi·us -a -um *adj* of Messapia, of Calabria ‖ *f* town and district of Messapia in S.E. Italy

mess·is -is *f (acc:* **messem** *or* **messim)** harvest; harvest time; **adhūc tua messis in herbā est** *(prov)* don't count your chickens before they are hatched *(literally, your harvest is still on the stalk, i.e., in early stages of growth)*

mess·or -ōris *m* reaper, mower

messōri·us -a -um *adj* reaper's

messuī *perf of* **metō**

messus *pp of* **metō**

mēt·a -ae *f* marker for measuring a lap at a racetrack; haystack; *(fig)* goal, end; *(fig)* turning point

metall·um -ī *n* metal ‖ *npl* mine

metamorphōs·is -is *f* transformation

metaphor·a -ae *f* metaphor

mētāt·or -ōris *m* planner; **mētātor urbis** city planner

Metaur·us -ī *m* river in Umbria

Metell·us -ī *m* Roman family name *(cognomen);* Quintus Caecilius Metellus Numidicus *(commander of the Roman forces against Jugurtha, 109–107 B.C.)*

Mēthymn·a -ae *f* town on the Island of Lesbos

metīculōsus *see* **metūculōsus**

mētior mētīrī mēnsus sum *tr* to measure; to traverse, travel; to judge, estimate; *(w. dat)* to measure *(s.th.)* out to, distribute *(s. th.)* among; *(w. abl)* to judge *(s.o.)* by the standard of

metō metere messuī messus *tr* to reap, mow, gather, harvest; *(fig)* to mow down *(e.g., with the sword);* **ut sementem fēceris, ita et metēs** *(prov)* as you sow, so shall you reap

mēt·or -ārī -ātus sum *tr* to measure off; to lay out *(e.g., a camp)*

metrēt·a -ae *f* liquid measure *(about nine gallons)*

metūculōs·us -a -um *adj* **(metīc-)** fearful; scary; awful

metu·ēns -entis *adj* afraid, anxious

met·uō -uere -uī -ūtus *tr* to fear, be afraid of ‖ *intr* to be afraid, be apprehensive

met·us -ūs *m* fear, anxiety; **in metū esse** to be in a state of alarm; to be an object of concern

me·us -a -um *adj* my ‖ *pron* mine; **meā inter-est** it is of importance to me; **meum est** *(w. inf)* it is my duty to; **meus est** *(coll)* I've got him, he's mine

Mezent·ius -(i)ī *m* Etruscan ruler of Caere, slain by Aeneas

mī = mihi

mīc·a -ae *f* crumb, morsel

Micips·a -ae *m* son of Masinissa and king of Numidia *(148–118 B.C.)* ‖ *mpl (fig)* Numidians, N. Africans

mic·ō -āre -uī *intr* to vibrate, quiver; to twinkle, sparkle, flash

mictur·iō -īre *intr* to have to urinate

Mid·ās -ae *m* king of Phrygia, at whose touch everything turned to gold *(8th cent. B.C.)*

migrāti·ō -ōnis *f* moving, changing residence; migration; *(fig)* metaphorical use

migrō -āre -āvī -ātus *tr* to move, transport; *(fig)* to violate *(a law)* ‖ *intr* to move, change residence; migrate; *(fig)* to change, turn

mīl·es -itis *m* soldier; infantryman; private; *(fig)* army

Mīlēsi·us -a -um *adj* Milesian, of Miletus

Mīlēt·us -ī *f* town on W. coast of Asia Minor ‖ *m* founder of the town of Miletus

mīl·ia -ium *npl* thousands; *see* mīlle

mīliār·ium -(i)ī *n* milestone

mīlitār·is -is -e *adj* military

mīlitāriter *adv* in a military manner, like a soldier

mīlitāri·us -a -um *adj* soldierly, military

mīliti·a -ae *f* army; war; the military; military discipline; mīlitiae in war, on the battlefield, in the army; mīlitiae domīque abroad and at home, on the war front and on the home front

mīlit·ō -āre -āvī -ātum *intr* to be a soldier, do military service

mīl·ium -(i)ī *n* millet *(a food grain)*

mīlle *(indecl) adj* thousand; mīlle hominēs a thousand people ‖ mīlia *npl (declinable noun) (gen:* mīlium*)* thousands; *(w. gen):* duo mīlia hominum two thousand people; duo mīlia passuum two miles *(literally, two thousands of paces)*

mīllēsim·us *or* mīllēnsim·us -a -um *adj* thousandth

mīliār·ium -(i)ī *n* milestone; mīliārium aureum golden milestone *(set up by Augustus in the forum to indicate distances to various places in the Empire)*

mīlliēns *or* mīlliēs *adv* a thousand times; innumerable times

Mil·ō -ōnis *m* Titus Annius Papinianus Milo *(defended by Cicero on a charge of having murdered Clodius in 52 B.C.)*

Miltiad·ēs -is *m* Athenian general victorious at Marathon *(490 B.C.)*

mīlvīn·us *or* mīluīn·us -a -um *adj* rapacious *(as a kite)*

mīlv·us *or* mīlv·os *or* mīlu·us -ī *m* kite *(bird of prey);* flying gurnard *(fish); (astr)* mistakenly taken by Ovid as a constellation

mīm·a -ae *f* actress *(of mimes)*

Mimallon·es -um *fpl* Bacchantes

Mimallon·is -idis *f* a Bacchante

Mim·ās -antis *m* one of the Giants

mīmicē *adv* like a mime actor

mīmic·us -a -um *adj* suitable for the mime, farcical

Mimnerm·us -ī *m* Greek elegiac poet of Colophon on the W. coast of Asia Minor *(fl 630 B.C.)*

mīmul·a -ae *f* miserable little actress

mīm·us -ī *m* mime, farce; actor *(of a mime); (fig)* farce

min·a -ae *f* Greek unit of weight, equal to 100 drachmas, or 100 Roman denarii; Greek coin *(about 100 denarii, i.e., about $100)*

mināci·ae -ārum *fpl* threats

mināciter *adv* threateningly

min·ae -ārum *fpl* threats; projecting points of a wall

minanter *adv* threateningly

mināti·ō -ōnis *f* a threatening

min·āx -ācis *adj* threatening, menacing; projecting, jutting out

min·eō -ēre *intr* to project, jut out

Minerv·a -ae *f* goddess of wisdom and of the arts and sciences, identified with Athena; *(fig)* skill, genius; spinning and weaving; invītā Minervā against one's better judgment

mingō mingere mīnxī *or* mīxī mīnctum *or* mīctum *intr* (coll) to urinate

miniān·us -a -um *adj* vermilion

miniātul·us -a -um *adj* reddish

minimē *or* minumē *adv* least of all, least, very little; by no means, certainly not, not in the least; *(w. numerals)* at least; minimē gentium *(coll)* by no means

minim·us *or* minum·us -a -um *(superl of parvus) adj* smallest, least, very small; slightest, very insignificant; least important; youngest; shortest *(time);* minimus nātū youngest ‖ *n* the least, minimum; lowest price; minimō emere to buy at a very low price; minimō prōvocāre to provoke on the flimsiest pretext

mini·ō -āre -āvī -ātus *tr* to color red, paint red

minis·ter -trī *m* servant, attendant, helper; waiter; agent, subordinate, tool

minister·ium -(i)ī *n* activity of a servant *or* attendant, service, attendance; task, duty; office, ministry; occupation, work; agency, instrumentality ‖ *npl* servants

ministr·a -ae *f* servant, attendant, helper; waitress; handmaid

ministrāt·or -ōris *m or* ministrātr·īx -īcis *f* assistant, helper

ministr·ō -āre -āvī -ātus *tr* to serve, wait on; to tend; to execute, carry out *(orders); (w.*

dat) to hand out *(s.th.)* to; *(w. abl)* to supply *(s.o. or s.th.)* with

minitābund·us -a -um *adj* threatening, menacing

minit·ō -āre *or* **minit·or -ārī -ātus sum** *tr* to make threats of *(e.g., war); (w. acc of thing and dat of person)* to threaten to bring *(e.g., evil, harm)* upon, hold *(s.th.)* threateningly over *(s.o.)* ‖ *intr* to jut out, project; to be menacing, make threats; *(w. dat)* to threaten

min·or -or -us *(comp of* **parvus)** *adj* smaller, less; shorter *(time);* inferior; less important; *(w. abl)* **1** *(of time)* too short for; **2** inferior to; **3** unworthy of; *(w. inf)* unfit to, incapable of; **dīmidiō minor quam** half as small as; **minor capitis** deprived of civil rights; **minōrēs facere fīliōs quam** to think less of the sons than of; **minor nātū** younger ‖ *mpl* descendants, posterity ‖ *n* less; **minōris emere** to buy at a lower price; **minus praedae** less booty

mīn·or -ārī *intr* to jut, project; *(w. dat)* to threaten; *(w. dat of person and acc of thing)* to threaten *(s.o.)* with; *(w. acc & inf)* to threaten that ...

Mīn·ōs -ōis *or* **-ōnis** *m* son of Zeus and Europa, king of Crete, husband of Pasiphaë, and, after his death, judge in the lower world

Mīnōtaur·us -ī *m* monstrous offspring of Pasiphaë, half man and half bull, kept in the Labyrinth

minum- = **minim-**

min·uō -uere -uī -ūtus *tr* to diminish, lessen, reduce; to weaken, lower; to modify *(plans);* to settle *(controversies);* to limit *(authority);* to offend against, try to cheapen *(e.g., the majesty of the Roman people)* ‖ *intr* to diminish, abate, ebb; **minuente aestū** at ebbtide

minus *adv* less; not; by no means, not at all

minuscul·us -a -um *adj* smallish

minūt·al -ālis *n* hash, hamburger

minūtātim *adv* piecemeal; bit by bit

minūtē *adv* in a small-minded way

minūtul·us -a -um *adj* tiny

minūt·us -a -um *adj* small, minute; petty, narrow-minded

Miny·ae -ārum *mpl* descendants of Minyas, *esp.* the Argonauts

Miny·ās -ae *m* king of Thessaly

mīrābil·is -is -e *adj* remarkable, extraordinary, amazing, wonderful

mīrābiliter *adv* amazingly

mīrābund·us -a -um *adj* astonished, wondering

mīrācul·um -ī *n* wonder, marvel; surprise; amazement; *(pej)* freak; **septem mīrācula** the seven wonders *(of the ancient world)*

mīrand·us -a -um *adj* fantastic

mīrāti·ō -ōnis *f* astonishment, wonder

mīrāt·or -ōris *m,* **mīrātr·īx -īcis** *f* admirer

mīrē *adv* surprisingly, strangely; uncommonly; wonderfully; **mīrē quam** it is strange how, strangely

mīrificē *adv* wonderfully

mīrific·us -a -um *adj* causing wonder, wonderful; fascinating

mīrimodīs *adv* in a strange way

mirmill·ō -ōnis *m* gladiator *(who fought with Gallic arms)*

mīr·or -ārī -ātus sum *tr* to be amazed at, be surprised at; to look at with wonder, admire

mīr·us -a -um *adj* amazing, surprising, astonishing; wonderful; **mīrum est** *(w. acc & inf)* it is surprising that; **est mīrum quam** *(or* **mīrum quantum)** it is amazing how, it is amazing to what extent

mīscellāne·a -ōrum *npl* (**mīscill-**) hash, hodgepodge

mīsceō mīscēre mīscuī mīxtus *tr* to mix, blend, mingle; to combine, associate, share; to give and take; to mix up, confuse, turn upside down; to mix, prepare, brew; to fill *(with confused noise, etc.);* to unite sexually; **arma** *(or* **manūs** *or* **proelium** *or* **proelia) mīscēre** to join battle

misell·us -a -um *adj* poor little

Mīsēn·um -ī *n* promontory and town on the northern end of the Bay of Naples

mis·er -era -erum *adj* poor, pitiful; wretched, miserable, unhappy; sorry, worthless

miserābil·is -is -e *adj* miserable, pitiable; piteous

miserābiliter *adv* pitiably; piteously

miserand·us -a -um *adj* pitiful; deplorable

miserāti·ō -ōnis *f* pity, compassion, sympathy; appeal for sympathy

miserē *adv* wretchedly, miserably, unhappily; pitifully; desperately

miser·eō -ēre -uī -itum *or* **miser·eor -ērī -itus sum** *intr (w. gen)* to pity, feel sorry for, sympathize with ‖ *v impers (w. acc of person who feels pity and gen of object of pity), e.g.,* **miseret** *(or* **miserētur) mē aliōrum** I feel sorry for the others

miserēsc·ō -ere *intr* to feel pity, feel sympathetic; *(w. gen)* to pity, feel sorry for ‖ *v impers (w. acc of person who feels pity and gen of object of pity), e.g.,* **mē miserēscit virī** I feel sorry for the man, I pity the man

miseri·a -ae *f* pitiful condition, misery, distress, trouble

misericordi·a -ae *f* pity, sympathy, compassion; mercy

misericor·s -dis *adj* sympathetic, merciful

miseriter *adv* sadly

miser·or -ārī -ātus sum *tr* to deplore; to pity ‖ *intr* to feel pity

mīsī *perf of* **mittō**

missicul·ō -āre -āvī -ātus *tr* to keep sending
missil·is -is -e *adj* missile, flying **ǁ** *npl* missiles
missi·ō -ōnis *f* release, liberation; sending off, dispatching; military discharge; dismissal from office; **missiō cum ignōminiā** dishonorable discharge; **sine missiōne** without letup, to the death
missit·ō -āre -āvī -ātus *tr* to keep sending
missus *pp of* mittō
miss·us -ūs *m* letting go, throwing, hurling; sending
mītēsc·ō -ere *intr* to grow mild; to grow mellow, become ripe; *(fig)* to get soft; *(fig)* to become gentle, become tame; *(of feelings)* to become less intense, abate, cool off
Mithr·ās -ae *m* Mithra(s) *(sun-god of the Persians)*
Mithridāt·ēs -is *m* Mithridates the Great *(king of Pontus from 120 to 63 B.C.)*
Mithridātē·us *or* Mithridātic·us -a -um *adj* Mithridatic
mītigāti·ō -ōnis *f* mitigation
mītig·ō -āre -āvī -ātus *tr* to mellow, ripen; to soften; to calm down, appease; to make more tolerable, alleviate; to tone down *(a statement);* to soothe, mollify *(feelings);* to civilize
mīt·is -is -e *adj* mellow, ripe, soft; calm, placid; mild, gentle
mitr·a -ae *f* miter, turban
mittō mittere mīsī missus *tr* to send; to let fly, throw, hurl, launch; to emit, shed; to let out, utter; to let go of, drop; to free, release; to discharge, dismiss; to pass over in silence; to send for, invite; to pass up, forego; to dedicate *(a book);* to yield, produce; to export; to forget, dismiss *(from the mind);* **sanguinem mittere** to bleed; **sanguinem prōvinciae mittere** *(fig)* to bleed a province dry; **sub lēgēs orbem mittere** to subject the world to laws; **vōcēs mittere** to utter words
mītul·us -ī *m* limpet *(kind of mussel)*
mīxtim *adv* promiscuously
mīxtūr·a -ae *f* mixing, blending
mīxtus *pp of* mīsceō
Mnēmosyn·ē -ēs *f* mother of the Muses
mnēmosyn·on -ī *n* souvenir
mōbil·is -is -e *adj* mobile, movable, portable; nimble, active; shifty, changing; impressionable, excitable
mōbilit·ās -ātis *f* mobility; agility, quickness; shiftiness, fickleness
mōbiliter *adv* quickly, rapidly
mōbilit·ō -āre -āvī -ātus *tr* to impart motion to, endow with motion
moderābil·is -is -e *adj* moderate
moderām·en -inis *n* control
moderanter *adv* under control
moderātē *adv* with moderation

moderātim *adv* gradually
moderāti·ō -ōnis *f* controlling, control, regulation; curbing, checking; guidance; moderation, self-control
moderāt·or -ōris *m or* moderātr·īx -īcis *f* controller, director, guide
moderāt·us -a -um *adj* controlled, well-regulated, orderly, restrained
moder·ō -āre -āvī -ātus *or* moder·or -ārī -ātus sum *tr* to control, direct, guide **ǁ** *intr (w. dat)* **1** to moderate, restrain; **2** to allay, mitigate
modestē *adv* with moderation, discreetly; modestly
modesti·a -ae *f* moderation, restraint; discretion; modesty, sense of shame, sense of honor, dignity; propriety; mildness *(of weather)*
modest·us -a -um *adj* moderate, restrained; modest, discreet; orderly, obedient
modiāl·is -is -e *adj* containing a *modius* or peck
modicē *adv* moderately, with restraint; in an orderly manner; only slightly
modic·us -a -um *adj* moderate; small; modest, unassuming; ordinary; puny, trifling
modificāt·us -a -um *adj* regulated *(in length),* measured
mod·ius -(i)ī *m* modius, peck *(one-sixth of a medimnus or bushel);* **plēnō modiō** in full measure
modo *adv* only, merely, simply; *(of time)* just now, just recently, lately; presently, in a moment; **modo ... deinde** *(or* **tum, posteā, interdum)** first ... then, at one time ... next time; **modo ... modo** now ... now, sometimes ... sometimes, at one moment ... at another; **nōn modo ... sed etiam** *(or* **vērum etiam)** not only ... but also **ǁ** *conj* if only, provided that
modulātē *adv* according to measure, in time; melodiously
modulāt·or -ōris *m* director, musician
modul·or -ārī -ātus sum *tr* to regulate the time of, measure rhythmically; to modulate; to sing; to play
modul·us -ī *m* small measure; small stature; unit of measurement
mod·us -ī *m* measured amount, quantity; standard of measurement, unit of measurement, measure; time, rhythm; size, extent, length; due *or* proper measure, limit, boundary; rule, regulation; way, manner, style, mode; kind, form, type; *(gram)* voice *(of a verb); (mus)* measure, beat, note, tone; *(poet)* verse, poetry, meter; *(rhet)* rhythmic pattern; **ad modum** *(or* in modum) in time, rhythmically; **ad modum** *(w. gen) or* in modum *(w. gen)* in the manner of, like; **cūiusdam modī**

of a certain kind, a certain kind of; **cūiusdam modī pugna** a certain kind of fight; **cum modō** with restraint, moderately; **ēius modī homō** that kind of person; **ex Tūscō modō** in the Etruscan manner *or* style; **hūius modī homō** this kind of person; **modō** moderately; **modum adhibēre** (*or* **cōnstituere** *or* **facere** *or* **impōnere** *or* **pōnere** *or* **statuere**) to impose a limit, set bounds; **nullō modō** in no way, not at all; **omnī modō** in every case; **praeter** (*or* **suprā**) **modum** excessively; **prō modō** (*w. gen*) in proportion to; **quem ad modum** how; **quemnam ad modum** just how; **quid modī?** what limit?; **quōnam modō** just how; **sine modō** without restraint **‖** *mpl* tune, melody, song; poetry, poems

moech·a -ae *f* adulteress

moechiss·ō -āre *tr* to commit adultery with

moech·or -ārī -ātus sum *intr* to have an affair, commit adultery

moech·us -ī *m* adulterer

moen·ia -ium *npl* town walls, ramparts, fortifications; fortified town; castle, stronghold; defenses

moeniō *see* **mūniō**

moerus *see* **mūrus**

Moes·ī -ōrum *mpl* people of the Lower Danube basin

Moesi·a -ae *f* Moesia (*Roman province S. of the Danube and extending to the Black Sea*)

mol·a -ae *f* millstone; mill; flour **‖** *fpl* mill

molār·is -is *m* millstone; molar (*tooth*)

mōl·ēs -is *f* mass, bulk, pile; massive structure; dam, mole, pier; mass (*of people, etc.*); burden, effort, trouble; calamity; might, greatness

molestē *adv* with annoyance; with difficulty, with trouble; **molestē ferre** to be annoyed at, be disgruntled at, barely stand *or* tolerate

molesti·a -ae *f* annoyance, nuisance, trouble; worry; affectation (*of style*)

molest·us -a -um *adj* annoying, troublesome, distressing; labored, affected (*style*)

mōlīm·en -inis *n* great exertion, great effort; attempt, undertaking

mōlīment·um -ī *n* great exertion, great effort

mōl·ior -īrī -ītus sum *tr* to do with great effort, strain at, exert oneself over; to get rid of; to wield, heave, hurl (*missiles*); to wield (*a weapon, an instrument*); to get (*a ship*) under way; to get (*a vehicle*) moving; to rouse (*bodies of men*) to action; to work hard at; to build, erect (*usu. huge constructions*); to displace, shift from its position; to undertake, attempt; to perform; to cause, occasion **‖** *intr* to exert oneself, struggle, take great pains; to make one's way (*w. effort*), proceed

mōlīti·ō -ōnis *f* building, erection; (the action of) shifting *or* moving; **rērum mōlītiō** the creation

mōlīt·or -ōris *m* builder; contriver, schemer

mōlītr·īx -īcis *f* contriver (*female*)

mōlītus *pp of* **mōlior**

molitus *pp of* **molō ‖** *adj* ground, milled

mollēsc·ō -ere *intr* to become soft; to become gentle; to become effeminate

mollicul·us -a -um *adj* tender, dainty

moll·iō -īre -īvī *or* **-iī -ītus** *tr* to make soft, soften; (*fig*) to soften, mitigate; to demoralize

mollip·ēs -edis *adj* tender-footed

moll·is -is -e *adj* soft; springy; flexible; flabby; mild, calm; easy; gentle (*slope*); sensitive, impressionable; tender, touching; weak, effeminate; amatory (*verses*); changeable, untrustworthy

molliter *adv* softly; gently, smoothly; effeminately; voluptuously; patiently, with fortitude

molliti·a -ae *or* **molliti·ēs -ēī** *f* softness; flexibility; tenderness; sensitivity; weakness, irresolution; effeminacy, voluptuousness

mollitūd·ō -inis *f* softness; flexibility; susceptibility

mol·ō -ere -uī -itus *tr* to grind

Moloss·us -a -um *adj* Molossian **‖** *m* Molossian hound **‖** *mpl* Molossians (*a people of Epirus*)

mōl·y -yos *n* magic herb

mōm·en -inis *n* movement, motion; momentum

mōment·um -ī *n* movement, motion; alteration; turn, critical time; moment; impulse; momentum; influence; importance; motive

Mon·a -ae *f* Isle of Anglesey

monēdul·a -ae *f* jackdaw (*bird*)

mon·eō -ēre -uī -itus *tr* to call to mind, remind, advise, point out; to warn; to foretell; to teach; to inform

monēr·is -is *f* galley

Monēt·a -ae *f* Juno Moneta (*in whose temple on the Capitoline Hill money was coined*); mint; coin, money; stamp, die (*for money*)

monētāl·is -is -e *adj* of the mint **‖** *m* superintendent of the mint

monīl·e -is *n* necklace

monim- = monum-

monit·a -ōrum *npl* warnings; prophecies; precepts

moniti·ō -ōnis *f* reminder; warning

monit·or -ōris *m* reminder; counselor; teacher; prompter

monit·us -ūs *m* reminder; warning **‖** *mpl* promptings, warnings

monogramm·us -a -um *adj* sketchy, shadowy; unsubstantial, hollow

monopod·ium -(i)ī *n* table with a single central leg

monotrop·us -a -um *adj* single, alone

mōn·s -tis *m* mountain; hill; mountain range; mass, heap; montīs aurī pollicērī *(prov)* to make wild promises *(literally, to promise mountains of gold);* summus mōns mountaintop **||** *mpl* hill country, the hills

mōnstrāti·ō -ōnis *f* pointing out

mōnstrāt·or -ōris *m* displayer, demonstrator

mōnstr·ō -āre -āvī -ātus *tr* to show, point out; to make known; to demonstrate, teach; to indicate, suggest; to appoint, designate **||** *intr* to show the way

mōnstr·um -ī *n* sign, portent, wonder; warning; monster, monstrosity; atrocity; monstrous event

mōnstruōsē *adv* unnaturally

mōnstruōs·us -a -um *adj* unnatural, monstrous, strange

montān·us -a -um *adj* mountain, of a mountain; mountainous **||** *mpl* hill-dwellers *(esp. of the seven hills of Rome)* **||** *npl* mountainous regions

monticol·a -ae *m* mountaineer

montivag·us -a -um *adj* wandering over the mountains

montōs·us *or* montuōs·us -a -um *adj* mountainous

monument·um -ī *n* reminder; monument, memorial; literary work, book; history; record *(written or oral);* token of identification **||** *npl* recorded tradition; annālium monumenta annals; litterārum monumenta literary record, document

Mopsopi·us -a -um *adj* Athenian **||** *f* Athens; *(ancient name for)* Attica

mor·a -ae *f* delay; pause; spell, period of time; stop-off; haud morā without hesitation; in morā esse to be a hindrance; in morā habēre to allow to be a hindrance; mora est it will take too long; moram afferre to present difficulties, waste time; moram facere to obstruct; to cause delay

mor·a -ae *f (mil)* division *(of the Spartan army of from 300 to 700 men)*

mōr·a -ae *f* fool

mōrāl·is -is -e *adj* moral

morāt·or -ōris *m* obstructionist; loiterer; *(in court)* lawyer who spoke only to gain time

mōrāt·us -a -um *adj* -mannered, -natured; in character; *(of a thing)* natured; bene mōrātus well-mannered, civilized; male mōrātus ill-mannered, rude; mīrābiliter mōrātus est he is a strange creature

morbid·us -a -um *adj* sickly; causing sickness, unwholesome

morbōs·us -a -um *adj* sickly; sex-crazy, horny; morbōsus in *(w. acc)* mad about

morb·us -ī *m* sickness, disease, ailment; fault, vice; distress; in morbum cadere *(or* in morbum incidere)* to fall sick

mordācius *adv* more bitingly; *(fig)* more radically

mord·āx -ācis *adj* biting, snapping; *(fig)* sharp, stinging, caustic; snarling; pungent, tart

mordeō mordēre momordī morsus *tr* to bite; to eat, devour; to grip; *(of cold)* to nip; *(of words)* to cut, hurt

mordic·ēs -um *mpl* bites; incisor teeth

mordicus *adv* by biting, with the teeth; *(fig)* tightly, doggedly

mōrē *adv* foolishly

mōrēt·um -ī *n* salad

moribund·us -a -um *adj* dying, at the point of death; mortal; deadly

mōriger·ō -āre *or* mōriger·or -ārī -ātus sum *intr (w. dat)* 1 to humor, pamper; 2 to yield to; 3 to comply with

mor·ior -ī -tuus sum *intr* to die; *(fig)* to decay, pass away, die out; *(of fires)* to die out; *(of flowers)* to wither, die off; moriar nisi *(coll)* hope to die if … not

morm·ȳr -ȳris *f* Pontic fish

mor·or -ārī -ātus sum *tr* to delay, detain; to entertain, hold the attention of; to hinder, prevent; nihil morārī *(w. acc)* 1 to disregard, care nothing for, not value; 2 to have nothing against, have nothing to say against **||** *intr* to delay, linger, loiter; to stay, remain; to wait; quid moror? *(or* quid multīs morer?)* why should I drag out the point?; to make a long story short

mōrōsē *adv* morosely, crabbily

mōrōsit·ās -ātis *f* moroseness, crabbiness

mōrōs·us -a -um *adj* morose, crabby; fastidious, particular; *(fig)* stubborn *(disease)*

Morph·eús -eos *(acc: -ea) m* god of dreams

mors mortis *f* death; destruction; corpse; bloodshed; morte commūnī of natural causes; mortem obīre *(or* oppetere)* to meet death; mortem *(or* mortī)* occumbere to die; mortem sibi cōnscīscere to commit suicide *(literally, to decide on death for oneself);* mortis honōs burial; mortis poena death penalty

mors·a -ōrum *npl* bits, little pieces

morsiuncul·a -ae *f* peck, kiss

morsus *pp of* mordeō

mors·us -ūs *m* bite; pungency; grip; corrosion; gnawing pain; sting; vicious attack

mortāl·is -is -e *adj* mortal, subject to death; human; transient; man-made **||** *m* mortal, human being

mortālit·ās -ātis *f* mortality; mortals, mankind

morticīn·us -a -um *adj & m* carrion

mortif·er *or* mortif·erus -era -erum *adj* lethal, deadly, fatal

mortiferē *adv* mortally
mortuāl·ia -ium *npl* dirges
mortu·us -a -um *adj* dead, deceased; withered, decayed; scared to death; over and done with; half-hearted, feeble ‖ *m* dead person ‖ *mpl* the dead
mōrul·us -a -um *adj* dark, blackberry-colored
mōr·um -ī *n* black mulberry
mōr·us -a -um *adj* foolish ‖ *mf* fool
mōr·us -ī *f* black mulberry tree
mōs mōris *m* custom, usage, practice; caprice, mood; nature; manner; fashion, style; rule, regulation, law; **dē mōre** *(or* **ex mōre)** according to custom; **mōre** in the customary manner; **mōre** *(or* **in mōrem** *or* **dē mōre)** *(w. gen)* in the manner of, like; **mōrem gerere** *(w. dat)* to humor *(s.o.),* to indulge *(s.o. or one's feelings);* **mōs māiōrum** tradition; **nullō mōre** *(or* **sine mōre)** without restraint, wildly; lawlessly; **suprā mōrem** more than is usual ‖ *mpl* morals; character; behavior; customs; laws; **ex meīs mōribus** according to my wishes
Mōs·ēs *or* **Moys·ēs -is** *m* Moses
mōti·ō -ōnis *f* motion, movement
mōtiuncul·a -ae *f* slight attack of fever
mōt·ō -āre -āvī -ātus *tr* to keep moving
mōtus *pp of* **moveō**
mōt·us -ūs *m* motion, movement; gesture; dancing; change *(e.g., of fortune);* impulse, inspiration; passion; revolt, riot; tactical move; *(rhet)* figure of speech; **in mōtū** active; **in mōtū esse** to be in a state of flux; **mōtus animī** emotion; **mōtūs mentis** thought process; **mōtus pedum** activity; **mōtus terrae** earthquake
mov·ēns -entis *adj* active; restless, shifting; **rēs moventēs** movable property *(e.g., clothes, furniture)* ‖ *npl* motives
moveō movēre mōvī mōtus *tr* to move; to stir, shake, disturb; to cause, occasion, promote; to begin; to undertake; to trouble, torment; to touch, influence, affect; to throw into political turmoil; to eject, expel *(from office, post);* to degrade; to remove, take away; to dislodge *(the enemy);* to shake, cause to waver; to plow; to strum, play *(a musical instrument);* to dissuade; to exert, exercise; to turn over in the mind, ponder; **aliquem locō movēre** to dislodge s.o.; **arma** *or* **bellum movēre** to bring on a war, begin a war; **senātū movēre** to remove from the Senate roll; **signa movēre** to begin a march; **ventrem movēre** to move the bowels; **vōcem movēre carmine** to raise the voice in song ‖ *refl* to move; to dance; *(of heavenly bodies)* to rise; *(of riots)* to break out; **sē ex locō movēre** to budge from the spot ‖ *pass & intr* to move; to shake,

quake, throb ‖ *intr* to move off, depart; *(of buds)* to sprout, come out
mox *adv* soon, presently; hereafter; next, then; later on
Moys·ēs -is *m* Moses
mūcid·us -a -um *adj* sniveling, snotty; moldy, musty
Mūc·ius -(i)ī *m* Roman clan name *(nomen);* Gaius Mucius Cordus Scaevola *(tried to kill Porsenna and, when caught, deliberately burned his right hand)*
mucr·ō -ōnis *m* sharp point, sharp edge; tip; sword; edge, boundary; keenness
mūc·us -ī *m* **(mucc-)** mucus, snot
mūgient·ēs -ium *mpl* oxen
mūg·il *or* **mūg·ilis -ilis** *m* gray mullet *(a sea fish)*
mūgīn·or -ārī -ātus sum *intr* to dilly-dally
mūg·iō -īre -īvī *or* **-iī -ītum** *intr* to moo, bellow, low; to roar, rumble; *(of a bugle)* to blast, sound
mūgīt·us -ūs *m* mooing, bellowing; roaring, rumbling
mūl·a -ae *f* mule
mul·ceō -cēre -sī -sus *or* **mul(c)tus** *tr* to stroke, pet; to stir gently; to soothe, alleviate; to appease; to gladden, delight
Mulcib·er -erī *or* **-eris** *m* Vulcan; *(fig)* fire
mulc·ō -āre -āvī -ātus *tr* to beat up, cudgel; to mistreat, injure; to worst *(in battle)*
mulctr·a -ae *f* milk pail
mulctrār·ium -(i)ī *or* **mulctr·um -ī** *n* milk pail
mul·geō -gēre -sī -sus *or* **-ctus** *tr* to milk
muliebr·is -is -e *adj* woman's, womanly, feminine; womanish, effeminate; *(of deities)* presiding over the lives of women; *(gram)* feminine; **pars muliebris** *(or* **partēs muliebrēs)** female sexual organs ‖ *npl* female sexual organs; **virī muliebria patiuntur** men play the role of women *(i.e., let themselves be used as catamites)*
muliebriter *adv* like a woman; effeminately
muli·er -eris *f* woman; wife
mulierāri·us -a -um *adj* woman's ‖ *m* womanizer, wolf
muliercul·a -ae *f* little *(or* weak *or* foolish) woman; sissy
mulierōsit·ās -ātis *f* weakness for women
mulierōs·us -a -um *adj* woman-crazy
mūlīn·us -a -um *adj* mulish
mūli·ō -ōnis *m* mule driver
mūliōni·us -a -um *adj* mule driver's
mullul·us -ī *m* little mullet *(fish)*
mull·us -ī *m* red mullet *(fish)*
mulsī *perf of* **mulceō** and **mulgeō**
muls·us -a -um *pp of* **mulceō** *and of* **mulgeō** ‖ *adj* honeyed, sweet as honey ‖ *f (term of*

endearment) honey **ll** *n* mead *(wine mixed with honey)*

multa *adv* much, very; earnestly

mult·a -ae *f* fine; penalty; loss of money; **multam certāre** to contest a fine; **multam committere** to incur a fine; **multam dīcere** *(w. dat of person and acc of the fine)* to fine *(s. o. a certain amount);* **multam subīre** to incur a fine, be fined

mult·a -ōrum *npl* many things; much; **nē multa** in short

multangul·us -a -um *adj* having many angles, many-angled

multātīci·us -a -um *adj* of a fine; **multātīcia pecūnia** fine

multāti·ō -ōnis *f* fine, penalty

multēsim·us -a -um *adj* trifling, negligible

mult·ī -ōrum *mpl* many men, many; multitude, mass, common people

multibib·us -a -um *adj* fond of drinking, heavy-drinking

multicav·us -a -um *adj* porous

multīci·a -ōrum *npl* diaphanous garments

multifāriam *adv* in many places

multifid·us -a -um *adj* divided into many parts; splintered *(wood); (of a river)* having many tributaries

multifōrm·is -is -e *adj* multiform, manifold

multifor·us -a -um *adj* many-holed; *(flute)* having many stops

multigen·er -eris *or* **multigen·us -a -um** *adj* of many kinds, various

multiiug·is -is -e *or* **multiiug·us -a -um** *adj* many yoked together; many tied together; *(fig)* various

multiloqu·āx -ācis *adj* talkative

multiloqu·ium -(i)ī *n* talkativeness

multiloqu·us -a -um *adj* talkative

multimodīs *adv* in many ways

multiplex -icis *adj* with many folds; winding, serpentine; manifold; many; *(in comparisons)* many times as great, far greater; varied, complicated; versatile, changeable, many-sided; sly, cunning **ll** *n* manifold return

multiplicābil·is -is -e *adj* manifold, many

multipliciter *adv* in various ways

multiplic·ō -āre -āvī -ātus *tr* to multiply, increase, enlarge; to have *(or* use *or* practice) on many occasions

multipot·ēns -entis *adj* mighty, powerful

multitūd·ō -inis *f* great number, multitude, crowd, throng; rabble, common people; population

multivol·us -a -um *adj* passionate

multō *adv (w. comparatives)* much, far, by far, a great deal; **multō aliter ac** much different from; **multō ante** long before; **multō post** long after; **nōn multō secus fierī** to turn out just about the same

mult·ō -āre -āvī -ātus *tr* to punish; to fine

multum *adv* much, a lot, greatly, very; often, frequently; *(w. comparatives)* much, far; **multum valēre** to have considerable influence

mult·us -a -um *(comp:* (**plūs) plūrēs, plūra;** *superl:* **plūrimus)** *adj* many a, much, great; abundant, considerable, extensive; tedious, long-winded; full, numerous, thick, loud, heavy; constant; **ad multum diēm** till late in the day; **multā nocte** late at night; **multō diē** late in the day; *(with plural nouns)* many **ll** *mpl see* **multī ll** *n* much; **multī** of great value, highly; **multī facere** to think highly of, make much of; **multum est** it is of great importance; **multum temporis** a great deal of time, much time **ll** *npl see* **multa**

mūl·us -ī *m* mule

Mulvi·us -a -um *adj* Mulvian; **Mulvius pōns** Milvian bridge *(across the Tiber, above Rome on the Via Flaminia)*

Mumm·ius -(i)ī *m* Lucius Mummius Achaicus *(conqueror of Corinth, 146 B.C.)*

mundān·us -a -um *adj* of the world **ll** *m* world citizen

mundē *or* **munditer** *adv* neatly, cleanly

munditi·a -ae *or* **munditi·ēs -ēī** *f* neatness, cleanliness; elegance; politeness; refinement of language

mundul·us -a -um *adj* trim, neat

mund·us -a -um *adj* neat, clean, nice; fine, smart, sharp, elegant; choice *(words)* **ll** *m* neat person; world, earth, universe; heavens; mankind; beauty aids; **in mundō** ready, in store; **mundus caelī** firmament

mūnerār·ius -(i)ī *m* producer of gladiatorial shows

mūnerigerul·us -ī *m* bearer of presents

mūner·ō -āre -āvī -ātus *or* **mūner·or -ārī -ātus sum** *tr* to reward, honor, present; *(w. acc of thing and dat of person)* to present *(s.th.)* to

mūni·a -ōrum *npl* official duties *or* functions

mūnic·eps -ipis *mf* citizen of a municipality; fellow citizen, fellow countryman

mūnicipāl·is -is -e *adj* municipal; *(pej)* provincial

mūnicipātim *adv* by municipalities

mūnicip·ium -(i)ī *n* municipality, town *(whose people were Roman citizens, but otherwise autonomous)*

mūnificē *adv* generously

mūnificenti·a -ae *f* generosity

mūnific·ō -āre -āvī -ātus *tr* to treat generously

mūnific·us -a -um *adj* generous; splendid

mūnīm·en -inis *n* defense

mūnīment·um -ī *n* defense, protection, fortification, rampart; *(fig)* shelter, defense, safeguard

mūn·iō -īre -īvī *or* -iī -ītus *tr* (moen-) to defend with a wall, wall in; to fortify, strengthen, defend, protect, secure; to build *(road);* to provide with a road; *(fig)* to guard, shelter, protect, support

mūn·is -is -e *adj* obliging, ready to be of service

mūnīti·ō -ōnis *f* building, fortifying, defending; fortification, rampart, trenches, lines; mūnītiō flūminum bridging of rivers; mūnītiō viae road construction

mūnīt·ō -āre *tr* to open up *(a road)*

mūnīt·or -ōris *m* builder *(of fortifications)*

mūnīt·us -a -um *pp of* mūniō **‖** *adj* well-fortified, well-protected; *(fig)* safe, protected

mūn·us -eris *n* (moen-) service, function, duty; gift; favor, kindness; tax, duty; public entertainment, gladiatorial show; tribute *(to the dead),* rite, sacrifice; public office; in mūnere *(or* mūnere *or* prō mūnere) as a gift

mūnūscul·um -ī *n* small gift

mūraen·a -ae *f* moray *(eel-like fish)*

mūrāl·is -is -e *adj* wall, of a wall; wall-destroying; wall-defending

mūr·ex -icis *m* murex, mollusk *(yielding purple dye);* purple dye, purple; jagged rock; spiked trap *(as defense against cavalry attack)*

muri·a -ae *or* muri·ēs -ēī *f* brine *(used for pickling)*

muriātic·um -ī *n* pickled fish

mūricīd·us -ī *m* (murr-) mouse killer; *(fig)* coward

murmill·ō -ōnis *m* gladiator *(with Gallic arms, who fought against an opponent who used a net)*

murm·ur -uris *n* murmur, murmuring; buzz, hum; roar, crash; growling, grumbling; rumbling; hubbub

murmurill·um -ī *n* low murmur

murmur·ō -āre -āvī -ātus *tr* to murmur against **‖** *intr* to mutter, grumble; to rumble, roar

murr·a -ae *f* fluorspar *(mineral from which expensive vases were made)*

murr·a *or* murrh·a *or* myrrh·a -ae *f* myrrh tree; myrrh

murre·us -a -um *adj* made of fluorspar

murre·us -a -um *adj* (myrrh-) myrrh-colored, reddish-brown

murt- = myrt-

mūr·us -ī *m* wall; city wall(s); dike; rim *(of dish or pot); (fig)* defender, champion

mūs mūris *m* mouse; rat

Mūs·a -ae *f* Muse *(patron goddess of poetry, song, dance, literature, etc.);* poem, song; talent; poetic inspiration

Mūsae·us -ī *m* pre-Homeric bard in the time of Orpheus

Mūsae·us *or* Mūsē·us -a -um *adj* of the Muses, musical, poetic **‖** *n* institute of philosophy and research at Alexandria

mūsc·a -ae *f* fly; *(fig)* nosey person

mūscār·ium -(i)ī *n* fly swatter

mūscipul·a -ae *f or* mūscipul·um -ī *n* mousetrap

mūscōs·us -a -um *adj* mossy

mūscul·us -ī *m* little mouse; muscle; *(mil)* mantelet

mūsc·us -ī *m* moss

mūsic·a -ae *or* mūsic·ē -ēs *f or* mūsic·a -ōrum *npl* music; art of music *(including poetry)*

mūsicē *adv* pleasantly, elegantly

mūsic·us -a -um *adj* relating to the Muses; musical; melodious, tuneful; poetic; *(of a person)* expert in music **‖** *mf* musician

mussit·ō -āre -āvī -ātus *tr* to bear in silence **‖** *intr* to be silent; to mutter, grumble

muss·ō -āre -āvī -ātus *tr* to bear in silence; to brood over **‖** *intr* to mutter, murmur; to hesitate; *(of bees)* to hum

mustāce·us -ī *m or* mustāce·um -ī *n* wedding cake *(baked with must and set on laurel leaves)*

mustēl·a -ae *f* (-tell-) weasel

mustēlīn·us -a -um *adj* (-tell-) of a weasel

muste·us -a -um *adj* fresh; *(of a book)* in the early stages

must·um -ī *n* fresh grape juice, must; vintage

mūtābil·is -is -e *adj* changeable; fickle

mūtābilit·ās -ātis *f* mutability; fickleness

mūtāti·ō -ōnis *f* mutation, change; exchange, interchange; translation; mūtātiō animī change of heart

mutil·ō -āre -āvī -ātus *tr* to chop off, lop off, crop; to mutilate; to reduce; to rob

mutil·us -a -um *adj* mutilated; maimed; having chopped-off horns

Mutin·a -ae *f* town of N. Central Italy, S. of the Po *(modern Modena),* where Decimus Brutus was besieged by Antony *(44–43 B.C.)*

Mutinēns·is -is -e *adj* of Mutina

mūtiō *see* muttiō

mūtitiō *see* muttitiō

mūt·ō -āre -āvī -ātus *tr* to change, shift; to alter; to exchange, interchange, barter, sell; to modify, transform; to vary; to change for the better; to change for the worse; *(w.* in + *acc)* to change *(s.th. or s.o.)* into; *(w.* abl *or w.* cum *or* prō + *abl)* to exchange *or* substitute *(s.th. or s.o.)* for; mūtāre fidem to change allegiance, change sides; mūtāre latus to roll over *(in bed); (of fish)* to flip over ‖ *pass* to change; *(w.* in + *acc)* to change into; *(w. abl)* to change in respect to: **silvae foliīs mūtantur** the forests change their leaves ‖ *intr* to change; **mūtāre in melius** *(or* **pēius)** to change for the better *(or* for the worse) ‖ *v impers* **nōn mūtat** it makes no difference

mutt·iō -**īre** -**īvī** -**ītus** *tr* **(mūt-)** to mutter, mumble

muttiti·ō *f* **(mūt-)** muttering

mutt·ō *or* **mūt·ō** -**ōnis** *m (vulg)* penis

mūtuē *adv* mutually; in turn

mūtuit·or -**ārī** *tr* to wish to borrow

mutūniat·us -**a** -**um** *adj (vulg)* having a large penis

mūtuō *adv* mutually, in return

mūtu·or -**ārī** -**ātus sum** *tr* to borrow; to obtain, get; to derive

mūt·us -**a** -**um** *adj* mute; dumb, speechless; silent, still, noiseless; **mūta persōna** non-speaking actor ‖ *npl* dumb animals

mūtu·us -**a** -**um** *adj* mutual, reciprocal, interchangeable; borrowed, lent ‖ *n* loan; reciprocity; **aliquid mūtuum accipere** *(or* **sūmere)** to borrow s.th.; **aliquid mūtuum dare** *(w.* **cum)** to lend s.th. to *(s.o.);* **mūtuās pecūniās sūmere ab** to borrow money from; **mūtuum argentum rogāre ab** to ask *(s.o.)* for a loan of cash; **mūtuum facere cum aliquō** to reciprocate s.o.'s feelings ‖ *npl (w. advl sense)* mutually, reciprocally; **in mūtua** toward each other; **per mūtua** with one another

Mycēn·ae -**ārum** *fpl or* **Mycēn·ē** -**ēs** *f* Mycenae *(city of King Agamemnon in Argolis)*

Mycēn·is -**idis** *f* Mycenaean girl *(i.e., Iphigenia)*

Mygdon·es -**um** *mpl* a people of Thrace, some of whom later migrated to Phrygia

Mygdoni·us -**a** -**um** *adj* Phrygian

myopar·ōn -**ōnis** *m* galley

myrīc·a -**ae** *or* **myrīc·ē** -**ēs** *f* tamarisk

Myrmidon·es -**um** *mpl* Myrmidons *(people of Thessaly whom Achilles led in battle)*

Myr·ōn -**ōnis** *m* famous Greek sculptor *(5th cent. B.C.)*

myropōl·a -**ae** *m* perfumer

myropōl·ium -**(i)ī** *n* perfume shop

myrrh- = **murr-**

myrtēt·um -**ī** *n* **(mur-)** myrtle grove

myrte·us -**a** -**um** *adj* **(mur-)** myrtle; crowned with myrtle

Myrtō·um Mar·e *(gen:* **Myrtōī Maris)** *n* Myrtoan Sea *(between the Peloponnesus and the Cyclades)*

myrt·um -**ī** *n* myrtle berry

myrt·us -**ūs** *or* -**ī** *f* myrtle tree

Mȳsi·us -**a** -**um** *adj* Mysian ‖ *f* Mysia *(country in N.W. Asia Minor)*

myst·a *or* **myst·ēs** -**ae** *m* priest of the mysteries of Ceres; an initiate

mystagōg·us -**ī** *n* initiator; tourist guide

mystēr·ium -**(i)ī** *n* **(mist-)** secret religion, secret service, secret rite; divine mystery; secret; **mystēria facere** to hold service; **mystēria Rōmāna** festival of Bona Dea

mystic·us -**a** -**um** mystic

Mytilēn·ae -**ārum** *fpl or* **Mytilēn·ē** -**ēs** *f* Mytilene *(chief city of the island of Lesbos)*

Mytilēnae·us -**a** -**um** *or* **Mytilēnēns·is** -**is** -**e** *adj* of Mytilene

N

N, n *(supply* littera) *f* thirteenth letter of the Latin alphabet; letter name: **en**

N. *abbr* **Numerius** *(Roman first name, praenomen);* **Nōnae** the Nones; **Nummus** coin

Nabatae·us -**a** -**um** *adj* Nabataean; Eastern ‖ *mpl* Nabataeans *(a people of N. Arabia)*

nabl·ia -**ium** *npl* Phoenician harp

nactus *pp of* **nancīscor**

Naeviān·us -**a** -**um** *adj* of Naevius

Naev·ius -**(i)ī** *m* Gnaeus Naevius *(early Roman dramatic and epic poet, c. 270–200 B.C.)*

Nāï·as -**adis** *or* **Nā·is** -**idis** *or* -**idos** *f* Naiad, water nymph

nam *conj* for; for in that case; *(affirmative)* yes, to be sure; *(transitional)* now, but now, on the other hand

namque *conj* for in fact, for no doubt, for surely

nan·cīscor -**cīscī** **nānctus sum** *or* **nactus sum** *tr* to get, obtain; to come across, find; to arrive at; to experience, meet with; to contract *(a disease)*

nān·us -**ī** *m* dwarf, midget

Napae·ae -**ārum** *fpl* dell nymphs

nāp·us -**ī** *m* turnip

Narb·ō -**ōnis** *m* Narbonne *(city in S. Gaul, from which the province of Narbonese took its name)*

Narbōnēns·is -**is** -**e** *adj* Narbonese

narciss·us -**ī** *m (bot)* narcissus ‖ **Narcissus** son of Cephisus and the nymph Liriope, who was changed into a narcissus ‖ powerful freedman of Claudius

nard·um -**ī** *n or* **nard·us** -**ī** *f* nard, spikenard *(fragrant ointment)*

nār·is -**is** *f* nose; **homō acūtae nāris** *(or* **ēmūnctae nāris)** a man of keen perception; **homō nāris obēsae** dimwit *(literally, thick-*

nosed man) ‖ *fpl* nostrils, nose; **nārēs corrūgāre** to cause (*s.o.*) to turn up his nose; **nāribus dūcere** to smell; **nāribus ūtī** (*w.* ad) to turn up the nose at, ridicule

Narni·a -ae *f* town in Umbria

Narniēns·is -is -e *adj* of Narnia

nārrābil·is -is -e *adj* to be told

nārrāti·ō -ōnis *f* narrative

nārrātiuncul·a -ae *f* anecdote

nārrāt·or -ōris *m* narrator

nārrāt·um -ī *n* account, narrative

nārrāt·us -ūs *m* narrative, tale

nārr·ō -āre -āvī -ātus *tr* to tell, relate, narrate, recount; to describe, tell about ‖ *intr* to speak, tell; **bene nārrāre** (*w.* dē + *abl*) to tell good news about (*s.o.*); **male nārrāre** (*w.* dē + *abl*) to tell bad news about (*s.o.*); **tibi nārrō** (*coll*) I'm telling you, I assure you; **quam tū mihi nunc nāvem nārrās?** (*coll*) now, what's this ship you're talking about?

narthēc·ium -(i)ī *n* medicine chest

nārus *see* **gnārus**

Nāryci·us -a -um *adj* of Narycum (*birthplace of Ajax, son of Oileus*)

nāscor nāscī nātus sum *intr* (gn-) to be born; to begin, originate, spring forth, proceed; to be produced; (*of plants*) to grow; (*of rocks, minerals*) to be found, occur; (*astr*) to rise

Nāsīc·a -ae *m* Roman honorary name (*agnomen*) Publius Cornelius Scipio Nasica (*consul in 191 B.C.*)

Nās·ō -ōnis *m* Ovid (*Publius Ovidius Naso, Roman poet, 43 B.C.–A.D. 17*)

nass·a -ae *f* wicker trap (*for catching fish*); (*fig*) trap

nassitern·a -ae *f* large watering pot

nāsturc·ium -(i)ī *n* (*bot*) watercress

nās·us -ī *m* or **nās·um -ī** *n* nose; sense of smell; sagacity; scorn; satirical wit; spout, nozzle

nāsūtē *adv* sarcastically

nāsūt·us -a -um *adj* big-nosed; sarcastic, satirical

nāt·a *or* **gnāt·a -ae** *f* daughter

nātālici·us -a -um *adj* birthday; natal, congenital; **diēs nātālicius** birthday ‖ *f* birthday party ‖ *n* birthday present

nātāl·is -is -e *adj* of birth, natal, congenital; **diēs nātālis** birthday ‖ *m* birthday; foundation day (*of city, temple, etc.*) ‖ *mpl* birth, origin, parentage; **nātālibus suīs restituere** (*or* **reddere**) to confer the status of a free-born citizen on (*one born into slavery*)

nat·āns -antis *adj* swimming; swimming in the sea, marine ‖ *mf* fish

natāti·ō -ōnis *f* swimming, swim

natāt·or -ōris *m* swimmer

nat·ēs -ium *fpl see* **natīs**

nāti·ō -ōnis *f* tribe, nation, people; race, stock; (*pej*) breed

nat·is -is *f* buttock, rump ‖ *fpl* buttocks, rear end

nātīv·us -a -um *adj* born; inborn, innate, original; native, local; produced by nature, natural; primitive (*words*)

nat·ō -āre -āvī -ātus *tr* to swim (across) ‖ *intr* to swim, float; to flow; to overflow; (*of eyes*) to be glassy; (*of birds*) to fly, glide; to waver, fluctuate; to hover; to move to and fro

nātr·īx -īcis *f* water snake

nātūr·a -ae *f* nature, natural constitution; character, temperament; ability; distinctive feature *or* characteristic; naturalness (*in art*); order of the world, course of things; element, substance; sex organs; **in nātūrā** (*or* **in rērum nātūrā**) **esse** to be the natural choices, to be the alternatives; **nātūrā** (*or* **per nātūram**) naturally; **nātūra flūminis** the natural course of the river; **nātūra rērum** (physical) nature; **suā nātūrā** of its own accord

nātūrāl·is -is -e *adj* natural; by birth, one's own (*father, son, etc.*); produced by nature; according to nature

nātūrāliter *adv* naturally, by nature

nāt·us *or* **gnāt·us -a -um** *pp of* **nāscor** ‖ *adj* born; (*w.* dat *or* ad *or* in + *acc*) born for, made for, naturally suited to, fit for; (*w.* annōs) at the age of ... , ... years old, *e.g.,* **annōs vīgintī nātus** at the age of twenty, twenty years old; **nōn amplius nōvem annōs nātus** no more than nine years old; **prō rē nātā** (*or* **ē rē nātā**) under the existing circumstances, as matters stand; **rēs nāta** the situation, the way things are ‖ *m* son ‖ *mpl* children ‖ *f* daughter

nauarch·us -ī *m* ship's captain, skipper

nauclēric·us -a -um captain's ‖ *m* ship owner, captain

nauclēr·us -ī *m* ship's captain

naucul·or -ārī -ātus sum *intr* to go boating, go sailing

nauc·um -ī *n* trifle; (*mostly in gen. of value with a negative*) **nōn naucī esse** to be good for nothing; **nōn naucī habēre** to regard as worthless

naufrag·ium -(i)ī *n* shipwreck; wreck, ruin, destruction; wreckage; (*fig*) shattered remains; **naufragium facere** to be shipwrecked; (*of things*) to be lost ‖ *npl* remnants, shattered remains; **naufragia Caesaris amīcōrum** the remnants of Caesar's friends

naufrag·ō -āre -āvī *intr* to suffer shipwreck

naufrag·us -a -um *adj* shipwrecked, of the shipwrecked; causing shipwreck, dangerous to shipping; (*fig*) ruined ‖ *m* shipwrecked person

naul·um -ī *n* fare, passage money
naumachi·a -ae *f* simulated naval engagement *(staged as an exercise or for amusement)*
naumachiār·ius -(i)ī *m* person taking part in a mock sea fight
Naupact·us -ī *f* town on the N. shore of the Gulf of Corinth
Naupliad·ēs -ae *m* son of Nauplius *(Palamedes)*
Naupl·ius -(i)ī *m* king of Euboea who wrecked the Greek fleet to avenge the death of his son Palamedes
nause·a -ae *f* seasickness; vomiting, nausea; **nausea fluēns** vomiting
nause·ō -āre -āvī *tr* to make *(s.o.)* throw up; *(fig)* to belch forth, throw up, utter ‖ *intr* to be seasick; to vomit; to feel squeamish, feel disgust; to cause disgust
nauseol·a -ae *f* slight squeamishness
Nausica·a -ae *f* daughter of Alcinoüs, king of the Phaeacians
naut·a *or* **nāvit·a -ae** *m* sailor, seaman, mariner; captain
naute·a -ae *f* nausea; bilge water
nautic·us -a -um *adj* nautical, sailor's ‖ *mpl* sailors, seamen
nāvāl·is -is -e *adj* naval, of ships, of a ship; **castra nāvālia** camp for the protection of ships; **fōrma nāvālis** shape of a ship ‖ *n* tackle, rigging ‖ *npl* dock, dockyard, shipyard; rigging
nāvē *adv* industriously
nāvicul·a -ae *f* small ship
nāviculāri·us -a -um *adj* of a small ship ‖ *m* skipper; ship owner ‖ *f* shipping business
nāvifrag·us -a -um *adj* dangerous, treacherous, causing shipwreck
nāvigābil·is -is -e *adj* navigable
nāvigāti·ō -ōnis *f* sailing, navigation, voyage
nāvig·er -era -erum *adj* navigable
nāvig·ium -(i)ī *n* ship; boat
nāvig·ō -āre -āvī -ātus *tr* to sail across, navigate ‖ *intr* to sail, put to sea; *(fig)* to swim
nāv·is -is *f* ship; *(astr)* Argo *(constellation);* **nāvem appellere** *(or* **nāvem terrae applicāre)** to land a ship; **nāvem dēdūcere** to launch a ship; **nāvem solvere** to set sail; **nāvem subdūcere** to beach a ship; **nāvī** *(or* **nāvibus)** by ship, by sea; **nāvis aperta** ship without a deck; **nāvis longa** battleship; **nāvis mercātōria** merchant vessel; **nāvis onerāria** transport, cargo ship; **nāvis praetōria** flagship; **nāvis tēcta** ship with a deck
nāvit·a -ae *m see* **nauta**
nāvit·ās -ātis *f* energy, zeal
nāviter *adv* energetically, zealously, actively, busily; utterly, completely
nāv·ō -āre *tr* to do *or* perform energetically, conduct *or* carry out with vigor; **operam**

nāvāre to act energetically; **operam nāvāre** *(w. dat)* to render assistance to
nāv·us -a -um *adj* (gn-) energetic, busy
Nax·os -ī *f* largest island of the Cyclades in the Aegean Sea
-ne *enclitic (introducing a question and added to the first important word of a clause; it does not imply anything about the expected answer); (introducing an alternative in a question)* Or ... ?; *(in indirect questions)* whether; *(introducing a double or multiple indirect question)* whether
nē *interj (nearly always with a personal or demonstrative pronoun)* indeed, certainly, surely; **nē ego homo īnfēlīx fuī** I was indeed an unhappy man ‖ *adv* not; **nē ... quidem** *(to negate emphatically the words placed between)* not even; **nē timēte!** do not fear! ‖ *conj* that not, lest; so as to prevent *(s.th. from happening);* much less, let alone; **nē dīcam** not to mention; **nē mentiar** to tell the truth; **nē multa** *(or* **nē multīs)** to make a long story short ‖ *conj (after verbs and nouns denoting fear)* that
nebul·a -ae *f* mist, fog, vapor; cloud *(of dust, smoke); (fig)* darkness, obscurity
nebul·ō -ōnis *m* loafer, good-for-nothing
nebulōs·us -a -um *adj* foggy
nec *or* **neque** *adv* not ‖ *conj* nor, and not; **nec ... et** not only ... but also; **nec ... nec** *(or* **neque ... neque)** neither ... nor; **nec nōn (et)** *(introducing an emphatic affirmative)* and certainly, and besides
necdum *or* **neque dum** *conj* and not yet, nor yet
necessāriē *or* **necessāriō** *adv* necessarily, of necessity
necessāri·us -a -um *adj* necessary, indispensable, needful, requisite; inevitable; pressing, urgent; connected by blood or friendship, related, closely connected ‖ *mf* relative, kinsman; friend ‖ *npl* necessities
necesse *indecl adj* necessary; unavoidable, inevitable; requisite; **necesse esse** to be necessary; **necesse habēre** to regard as necessary, regard as inevitable
necessit·ās -ātis *f* necessity, inevitability; compulsion, urgency; requirement; privation, want; relationship, connection, friendship
necessitūd·ō -inis *f* necessity, need, want, distress; relationship, bond, connection, friendship ‖ *fpl* ties of friendship; relatives, friends, personal connections
necessum *indecl adj* necessary, requisite; inevitable
necne *conj* or not
nec·ō -āre -āvī -ātus *tr* to kill, murder
necopīn·āns -antis *adj* unaware
necopīnātō *adv* unexpectedly, by surprise

necopīnāt·us -a -um *adj* unexpected; **ex necopīnātō** unexpectedly

necopīn·us -a -um *adj* unexpected; unsuspecting; careless, off-guard

nect·ar -aris *n* nectar *(drink of the gods);* nectar *(term for honey, milk, wine, poetry, sweetness)*

nectare·us -a -um *adj* of nectar, sweet *(or* delicious*)* as nectar

nectō nectere nexuī *or* **nexī nexus** *tr* to tie, connect, fasten together, join; to weave; to clasp; to imprison; to fetter; to devise, contrive; *(fig)* to attach

nēcubi *conj* lest anywhere, so that nowhere

nēcunde *conj* lest from anywhere

nēdum *conj (after an expressed or implied negative)* much less, still less; *(after an affirmative)* not to say, much more

nefand·us -a -um *adj* unspeakable, heinous

nefāriē *adv* wickedly, foully

nefāri·us -a -um *adj* nefarious, heinous, criminal **‖** *n* crime, foul deed

nefās *indecl n* crime, wrong, wickedness; act contrary to divine law, sin; criminal, monster; **fās atque nefās** right and wrong; **nefās est** *(w. inf)* it is a crime to; **per omne fās ac nefās** by hook or by crook **‖** *interj* shocking!, dreadful!

nefāst·us -a -um *adj* forbidden, unlawful; impious, irreligious; criminal; **diēs nefāstus** holiday **‖** *n* outrage

negāti·ō -ōnis *f* denial

negit·ō -āre -āvī *tr* to keep denying; to turn down, refuse repeatedly

neglēcti·ō -ōnis *f* (nec-) neglect

neglēctus (nec-) *pp of* **neglegō ‖** *adj* neglected, despised, slighted

neglēct·us -ūs *m* (nec-) neglect

negleg·ēns -entis *adj* (nec-) negligent, careless, indifferent

neglegenter *adv* (nec-) carelessly

neglegenti·a -ae *f* (nec-) negligence, carelessness, neglect; **epistulārum neglegentia** failure to write

neg·legō -legere -lēxī -lēctus *tr* (nec-) to be unconcerned about; to neglect, disregard, overlook; to do without; to slight; to make light of; *(w. inf)* to fail to

neg·ō -āre -āvī -ātus *tr* to deny; *(w. acc & inf)* to say that ... not **‖** *refl* to refuse one's services **‖** *intr* to say no; to refuse; *(w. dat)* to say no to, turn down *(regarding marriage or sexual favors, dinner invitation, etc.)*

negōtiāl·is -is -e *adj* business

negōti·āns -antis *m* business man

negōtiāti·ō -ōnis *f* business, trade; business deal; business establishment

negōtiāt·or -ōris *m* businessman; banker; salesman, dealer

negōtiol·um -ī *n* minor matter

negōti·or -ārī -ātus sum *intr* to conduct business; to do banking; to trade; **homō negōtiāns** businessman

negōtiōs·us -a -um *adj* business; busy; **diēs negōtiōsus** workday

negōt·ium -(i)ī *n* business; occupation, employment; matter, thing, affair; situation, difficulty; trouble; banking, money-lending; trade, commerce; **dare negōtium alicui ut** to give s.o. the job of; **in magnō negōtiō habēre** *(w. inf)* to make a point of; **negōtium gerere** to conduct business; **negōtium suum** private affairs; **nōn negōtium est quīn** there is nothing to do but; **quid negōtī est?** what's the matter?; **quid negōtī tibi est?** what business is it of yours?; **suum negōtium agere** *or* **gerere** to mind one's own business **‖** *npl* commercial activities, business transactions; lawsuits

Nēl·eus -eī *or* **-eos** *m* king of Pylos and father of Nestor

Nēlīd·ēs -ae *m* descendant of Neleus

Neme·a -ae *or* **Neme·ē -ēs** *f* Nemea *(town in Argolis, where Hercules slew a lion and founded the Nemean games)*

Neme·a -ōrum *npl* Nemean games *(held every two years at Nemea)*

Nemeae·us -a -um *adj* Nemean

Nemes·is -eōs *f* goddess of vengeance

nēm·ō -inis *mf* no one, nobody; a person of no consequence, a nobody; **nēmō alius** no one else; **nēmō dum** no one yet; **nēmō nōn** every; **nēmō quisquam** nobody at all; **nēmō ūnus** no single person, no one by himself; **nōn nēmō** someone, many a one, a few

nemorāl·is -is -e *adj* sylvan

nemorēns·is -is -e *adj* of a grove; of Diana's grove

nemoricultr·īx -īcis *f* denizen *(female)* of the forest

nemorivag·us -a -um *adj* roaming the woods

nemorōs·us -a -um *adj* wooded; covered with foliage

nempe *adv (in confirmation or in sarcasm)* of course, naturally; *(in questions)* do you mean?

nem·us -oris *n* cluster of trees; grove; sacred grove

nēni·a -ae *f* (naen-) funeral song; doleful song; incantation; ditty

neō nēre nēvī nētus *tr* to spin; to weave

Neoptolem·us -ī *m* the son of Achilles *(also called Pyrrhus)*

nep·a -ae *f* scorpion; crab; *(astr)* Scorpio

Nephelē·is -idos *f* Helle *(daughter of Nephele and Athamas)*

nep·ōs -ōtis *m* grandson; nephew; descendant; spendthrift, playboy; **sērī nepōtēs** distant descendants **‖** **Nepōs** Cornelius Nepos

(Roman biographer and friend of Cicero, c. 100–25 B.C.)
nepōtul·us -ī *m* little grandson
nept·is -is *f* granddaughter; descendant *(female)*
Neptūni·us -a -um *adj* of Neptune
Neptūn·us -ī *n* Neptune *(god of the sea and brother of Jupiter)*
nēquam *(comp:* nēquior; *superl:* nēquissimus) *indecl adj* worthless, bad, good for nothing; naughty; nēquam facere to be naughty
nēquāquam *adv* by no means, not at all
neque *see* nec
nequedum *see* necdum
nequ·eō -īre -īvī *or* -iī -ītum *intr (w. inf)* to be unable to, be incapable of; *(w.* quīn) to be unable to keep oneself from; nequit *(w.* quīn) it is impossible to
nēqui·or -or -us *(comp of* nēquam) *adj* worse, more worthless
nēquīquam *or* nēquicquam *adv* pointlessly, for nothing, to no purpose; without good reason; with impunity
nēquissim·us -a -um *(superl of* nēquam) *adj* worst, most worthless
nēquiter *adv* wickedly; wrongly, with poor results; worthlessly; *(in playful use)* naughtily
nēquiti·a -ae *or* nēquiti·ēs -ēī *f* worthlessness, vileness, wickedness; naughtiness
Nērē·is -idis *f* Nereid, sea nymph *(one of the fifty daughters of Nereus)*
Nēr·eus -eī *or* -eos *m* son of Oceanus and Tethys, and husband of Doris, and father of the Nereids; sea
Nērīnē -ēs *f* daughter of Nereus
Nēriti·us -a -um *adj* of Neritus; dux Nēritius Ulysses; Nēritia ratis ship of Ulysses
Nērit·os *or* Nērit·us -ī *m* island near Ithaca
Ner·ō -ōnis *m* Nero Claudius Caesar *(A.D. 38–68; reigned A.D. 54–68)*
Nerōniān·us -a -um *adj* Nero's, Neronian
Nerv·a -ae *m* Marcus Cocceius Nerva *(A.D. 30–98; reigned A.D. 96–98)*
nervōsē *adv* strongly, vigorously
nervōs·us -a -um *adj* sinewy, brawny, muscular
nerv·us *or* nerv·os -ī *m* sinew, tendon, muscle; string, wire; bowstring; thong; strap; leather covering of a shield; *(vulg)* penis; prison **||** *mpl* power, vigor, strength, nerve, force, energy; nervī bellī pecūnia money, the sinews of war; nervī coniūrātiōnis the force *(i.e., the leaders)* behind the conspiracy
nēsc·iō -īre -īvī *or* -iī -ītus *tr* not to know, be ignorant of, be unacquainted with; *(w. inf)* not to know how to, be unable to; nēsciō modo somehow or other; nēsciō quandō

sometime or other; nēsciō quid something or other; nēsciō quis someone or other
nēsci·us -a -um *adj* unaware, ignorant; unknown; *(w. gen or* dē + *abl)* ignorant of, unaware of; *(w. inf)* not knowing how to, unable to, incapable of; *(w. acc & inf)* unaware that, not knowing that
Ness·us -ī *m* centaur who was slain by Hercules with a poisoned arrow for trying to molest his wife
Nest·or -oris *m* son of Neleus, king of Pylos, and wise counselor of the Greeks at Troy
Nestorid·ēs -ae *m* son of Nestor *(i.e., Antilochus)*
neu *see* nēve
neu·ter -tra -trum *adj* neither *(of two);* neuter; of neither sex **||** *pron* neither one *(of two)*
neutiquam *or* ne utiquam *adv* on no account, in no way
neutrāl·is -is -e *adj (gram)* neuter
neutrō *adv* to neither side, in neither direction
neutrubi *adv* in neither the one place nor the other
nēve *or* neu *conj* or not, and not; nēve ... nēve *(or* neu ... neu) neither ... nor
nex necis *f* death; violent death, murder, slaughter; necem (sibi) cōnscīscere to decide to commit suicide *(literally, to decide on death for oneself);* necī *(or* ad necem) dare *(or* mittere) to put to death
nexil·is -is -e *adj* plaited, intertwined
nex·um -ī *n* slavery for debt; voluntary servitude for debt
nex·us -a -um *pp of* nectō **||** *m* bondman *(person who has pledged his person as security for a debt)*
nex·us -ūs *m* bond; tie *(of kinship, etc.);* legal obligation; grip *(in wrestling);* embrace; combination **||** *mpl* coils *(of snake);* knotty problem
nī *adv* not; quid nī? why not? **||** *conj (in prohibition or negative purpose)* that not; *(in negative condition)* if not, unless
nīcētēr·ium -(i)ī *n* prize *(of victory)*
nict·ō -āre -āvī -ātum *or* nict·or -ārī -ātus sum *intr* to blink; to wink; *(w. dat)* to wink at
nīdāment·um -ī *n* material for a nest
nīd·or -ōris *m* steam, vapor, smell
nīdul·us -ī *m* small nest
nīd·us -ī *m* nest; nestlings, brood; pigeonhole *(fig)* home **||** *mpl* nestlings, brood
ni·ger -gra -grum *adj* black; dark; swarthy; dismal; unlucky, ill-omened; bad *(character);* malicious
nigr·āns -antis *adj* black, dusky
nigr·ēscō -ēscere -uī *intr* to grow black, grow dark
nigr·ō -āre -āvī -ātus *tr* to blacken **||** *intr* to be black

nigr·or -ōris *m* blackness, darkness

nihil *or* **nīl** *indecl n* nothing; *(w. partitive gen)* no, not a bit of *(e.g.,* **nihil cibī** no food); **nihil agere** to do nothing, sit still; **nihil aliud** nothing else; **nihil bonī** no good, not a bit of good; **nīl est** *(in replies)* it is pointless, it's no good; **nihil dum** nothing so far; **nihil est** it doesn't matter; **nihil est mihi cum** I have nothing to do with; **nihil est quod** *(or* **cūr** *or* **quamobrem)** there is no reason why; **nihil est ubi** *(or* **quō)** there is no place where *(or* to which); **nihil quicquam** nothing whatever; **nōn nihil** a considerable amount, quite a lot; to a considerable extent

nihilōminus *adv* nevertheless, just the same; no less

nihil·um *or* **nīl·um -ī** *n* nothing; **ad nihilum venīre** to come to nothing; **dē nihilō** for nothing, for no reason; **nihilī facere** *(or* **pendere)** to consider as worthless; **nihil** *(w. comparatives or words expressing difference, e.g.:* **nihil cārius** nothing dearer); **nihilō minus** nonetheless, nevertheless; **prō nihilō putāre** *(or* **dūcere** *or* **habēre)** to regard as worthless, disregard

nīl *see* **nihil**

Nīliac·us -a -um *adj* Nile, of the Nile; Egyptian

nīlum *see* **nihilum**

Nīl·us -ī *m* Nile; god of the Nile; a type of conduit

nimbāt·us -a -um *adj* light, frivolous

nimbif·er -era -erum *adj* stormy

nimbōs·us -a -um stormy, rainy

nimb·us -ī *m* rain cloud, storm cloud; cloud; rainstorm, heavy shower; shower, spray; *(fig)* storm; *(fig)* dense crowd

nimiō *adv* far, much; **nimiō plūs** far more, much more

nīmīrum *adv* no doubt, certainly sure; *(ironically)* of course

nimis *adv* very, very much, too much; **nōn nimis** not particularly

nimium *adv* too, too much; very much; **nimium quam** *(or* **nimium quantum)** very much indeed, ever so much, very; **nimium quam es barbarus** you are as uncouth as can be; **nōn nimium** not particularly, not very much

nimi·us -a -um *adj* very much; very great; too great, extraordinary, excessive; extravagant, intemperate; over-eager; over-confident; *(w. gen or abl of respect)* intemperate in, going overboard about; *(w. dat)* too much for, too strong for; **nimiō opere** to excess ‖ *n* excess

ning(u)it ningere ninguit *or* **nīnxit** *v impers* it is snowing

ningu·ēs -ium *fpl* snow flakes; snow; snowdrifts

Nin·os *or* **Nin·us -ī** *m* king of Assyria, legendary founder of Nineveh; Nineveh

Niob·a -ae *or* **Niob·ē -ēs** *f* Niobe *(daughter of Tantalus and wife of Amphion; she was turned into a weeping mountain)*

Nīr·eūs -eī *or* **-eos** *m* second-handsomest Greek at Troy *(after Achilles)*

Nīsē·is -idis *f* daughter of Nisus, Scylla

nisi *conj* unless, if not; except; **nisi sī** unless, if not; **nisi quia** *(or* **quod)** except that

Nīs·us -ī *m* king of Megara and father of Scylla ‖ friend of Euryalus *(in the Aeneid)*

nīsus *pp of* **nītor**

nīs·us *or* **nīx·us -ūs** *m* pressure, effort; labor pains; soaring, flight; posture; **nīsū immōtus eōdem** immobile in the same posture

nītēdul·a -ae *f* dormouse *(squirrel-like rodent)*

nit·ēns -entis *adj* shining, bright, sparkling; brilliant; beautiful, glamorous; sleek *(cattle);* prosperous, thriving; illustrious, outstanding

nit·eō -ēre -uī *intr* to shine, gleam, glisten; to be glamorous; to glow with health; *(of animals)* to be sleek; *(of style)* to be brilliant; *(of fields, plants)* to be luxuriant

nit·ēscō -ēscere -uī *intr* to become shiny, become bright; to begin to glow *(with health or beauty);* to grow sleek; *(of plants)* to begin to thrive

nitidē *adv* brightly

nitidiusculē *adv* somewhat more sprucely

nitidiuscul·us -a -um *adj* a little more shiny

nitid·us -a -um *adj* shining, bright; glowing, radiant, handsome *(with health or beauty);* spruce, well-groomed, glamorous; glossy, lustrous *(hair);* sleek *(animals);* luxuriant, lush *(plants, fields);* cultivated, refined; elegant *(style)*

nitor nītī nīxus sum *(usually in the literal sense)* or **nīsus sum** *(usually in the figurative sense)* *intr* to make an effort, struggle, strain, strive; to be in labor; to push forward, advance, climb, fly; to contend, insist; *(w. abl or* **in** *+ acc)* to lean on, support oneself on; *(w. abl or* **in** *+ abl)* to depend on, rely on, trust to; *(w.* **ad**) to aspire to; *(w. inf)* to try to, endeavor to, struggle to

nit·or -ōris *m* brightness, sheen; luster; glamour, beauty; healthy glow; elegance *(of style);* dignity *(of character)*

nitr·um -ī *n* soda, potash; cleanser

nivāl·is -is -e *adj* snowy; covered with snow; cold, wintry; *(fig)* cold, chilly

nive·us -a -um *adj* snowy, covered with snow; snow-white; cooled with snow

nivōs·us -a -um *adj* snowy

nix nivis *f* snow ‖ *fpl (fig)* grey hair

nix·or -ārī -ātus sum *intr* to struggle hard; *(w. abl)* to lean on, rest on

nīxus *pp of* **nītor**

nīx·us -ūs *see* nīsus

nō nāre nāvī *intr* to swim, float; to sail; to fly; *(of eyes)* to be glazed

nōbil·is -is -e *adj* known, familiar; noted; notable, remarkable, noteworthy; famous; notorious; noble; thoroughbred; fine, excellent; *(w. abl of cause)* famous for, noted for; **nōbile est** *(w. acc & inf)* it is well-known that **ǁ** *m* notable, nobleman, aristocrat

nōbilit·ās -ātis *f* fame, renown; noble birth; nobility; the nobility, the nobles; excellence

nōbiliter *adv* with distinction

nōbilit·ō -āre -āvī -ātus *tr* to make generally known, call attention to; to make famous; to make notorious

noc·ēns -entis *adj* harmful; *(w. abl)* guilty of **ǁ** *m* guilty person, criminal

noc·eō -ēre -uī -itum *intr* *(w. dat)* to harm, injure; **haud ignārus nocendī** well aware of the mischief

nocīv·us -a -um *adj* harmful, injurious

noctif·er -erī *m* evening star *(night-bringer)*

noctilūc·a -ae *f* moon *(she who shines by night)*

noctivag·us -a -um *adj (esp. of heavenly bodies)* wandering at night

noctū *adv* by night, at night

noctu·a -ae *f* owl *(night bird)*

noctuābund·us -a -um *adj* traveling by night

noctuīn·us -a -um *adj* of owls

nocturn·us -a -um *adj* nocturnal, of night, at night, by night, night

noctuvigil·us -a -um *adj* awake at night

nocu·us -a -um *adj* harmful

nōd·ō -āre -āvī -ātus *tr* to tie in a knot, knot

nōdōs·us -a -um *adj* knotty

nōd·us -ī *m* knot; knot *(in wood)*; node *(in stem of grass or plant)*; bond, tie; obligation; knotty point, problem, difficulty; coil *(of serpent)*; check, restraint; **igneus nōdus** fireball

Nōl·a -ae *f* town of Campania E. of Naples *(where Augustus died)*

nōlō nōlle nōluī *tr (w. inf)* to be unwilling to, wish not to, refuse to **ǁ** *intr* to be unwilling; *(2nd person imperative w. inf to form negative command)* do not ... : **nōlī** *(pl:* **nōlīte)** **tangere** do not touch!

Nom·as -adis *or* -ados *mf* nomad; Numidian

nōm·en -inis *n* name; clan *(or* middle) name *(e.g., Julius, as distinct from the praenomen, or first name, e.g., Gaius, and the cognomen, or family name, e.g., Caesar);* good name, reputation; title; stock; race; bond, claim, debt; debtor; pretext, pretense, excuse; authority; sake, behalf; reason, cause; responsibility; heading, category; entry *(of a loan, etc., in a ledger); (gram)* noun; **aetātis nōmine** on the pretext of age; on account of age; **eō nōmine** on that account; **nōmen**

alicūius accipere *(or* recipere) *(of a presiding judge)* to consent to hear the case against s.o.; **nōmen dare** *(or* ēdere *or* profitērī) to enlist *(in the army; as a colonist);* **nōmen dēferre** *(w. gen)* to bring an accusation against, accuse *(s.o.);* **nōmen dissolvere** *(or* **nōmen expedīre** *or* **nōmen solvere)** *(com)* to liquidate an account, pay off a debt; **nōmen Latīnum** those with Latin rights; **nōmen Rōmānum** the Roman people; **nōmina facere** *(com)* to enter a business transaction in a ledger; **nōmina magna** big shots, celebrities; **nōmina sua exigere** to collect one's debt; **nōmine** *(w. gen)* by the authority of, in the name of; on the pretext of; in the guise of; **nōn rē sed nōmine** not in reality but in name only; **oppidum nōmine Nōla** a town named Nola; **per nōmen** *(w. gen)* on the pretext of; in the guise of; **sub nōmine** *(w. gen)* by the authority of, in the name of; **suō nōmine** on one's own responsibility, independently; **ūnō nōmine** in a word

nōmenclāt·or -ōris *m* name-caller *(slave who accompanied his master and discreetly identified those whom they met, esp. during a political campaign)*

Nōment·um -ī *n* town in Latium on the Sabine border

nōminātim *adv* by name, expressly

nōmināti·ō -ōnis *f* nomination for office; name, term

nōminātīv·us -a -um *adj & m (gram)* nominative

nōminit·ō -āre -āvī -ātus *tr* to name, call, term

nōmin·ō -āre -āvī -ātus *tr* to name, call by name; to mention by name; to make famous; to nominate for office; to denounce, arraign

nomism·a -atis *n* coin; coinage; voucher, token

nōn *adv* not; no; by no means; **nōn iam** no longer

Nōn. *abbr* Nōnae

Nōnacrīn·us -a -um *adj* of Nonacris; **virgō** *(i.e., Callisto)*

Nōnacr·is -is *f* mountain and town in Arcadia

Nōnacri·us -a -um *adj* of Nonacris; **hērōs Nōnacrius** *(i.e., Evander)*

Nōn·ae -ārum *fpl* Nones *(the ninth day before the Ides, and so the fifth day in all months, except March, May, July, and October, in which the Nones occurred on the seventh)*

nōnāgēnsim·us -a -um *adj* (-gēs-) ninetieth

nōnāgiēns *adv* (-giēs) ninety times

nōnāgintā *indecl adj* ninety

nōnān·us -a -um *adj* of the ninth legion **ǁ** *m* soldier of the ninth legion

nōnāri·a -ae *f* prostitute

nōndum *adv* not yet

nōngent·ī -ae -a *adj* nine hundred

nōnne *adv (interrog particle in questions expecting a positive answer)* is it not?; *(in indirect questions)* whether not; **nōnne vidēs?** you see, don't you?, don't you see?; **quaeritur nōnne īre statim velīs** the question is whether you do not wish to go at once

nōnnūll·us -a -um *adj* some, a certain amount of; many a ‖ *pl* some, not a few

nōnnumquam *adv* (**-nunq-**) sometimes

nōnnūsquam *adv* in some places

nōn·us -a -um *adj* ninth ‖ *f* ninth hour

nōn·us decim·us -a -um *adj* nineteenth

Nōric·us -a -um *adj* of Noricum ‖ *n* Noricum *(Roman province between the Danube and the Alps)*

nōrm·a -ae *f (carpenter's)* square; *(fig)* standard, norm of behavior

nōs *pron* we; us *(at times used in place of* **ego,** *esp. in letter writing)*

nōscit·ō -āre -āvī -ātus *tr* to examine closely, observe; to know, recognize

nōscō nōscere nōvī nōtus *tr* (**gn-**) to get to know, become acquainted with, learn; to recognize; to examine, inquire into; to approve of; **nōvisse** to have become acquainted with, *(and therefore)* to know

nōsmet *pron (emphatic form of* **nōs**) we ourselves; us ourselves

nos·ter -tra -trum *adj* our, our own ‖ *pron* ours; **noster** our friend; **nostrī** our men, our soldiers, our side, our friends

nostrās -ātis *adj* born *or* produced in our country, native, of our country, indigenous

not·a -ae *f* note; mark; sign; letter, character; punctuation mark; brand *(of wine);* marginal note, critical mark; tattoo marks, brand; distinctive mark, distinctive quality; stamp *(on coin);* stigma; nickname; black mark *(against one's name);* reproach, disgrace; nod, sign, beck; sign of the zodiac; **in notam alicūius** so as to humiliate s.o.; **per notās scrībere** to write in code ‖ *fpl* letters of the alphabet; shorthand notes; memoranda

notābil·is -is -e *adj* notable, noteworthy, memorable; conspicuous

notābiliter *adv* notably, remarkably, perceptibly

notār·ius -(i)ī *m* stenographer; secretary

notāti·ō -ōnis *f* notation, mark; black mark *(of censor);* choice; observation; etymology

notāt·us -a -um *adj* noted, distinguished

nōt·ēscō -ēscere -uī *intr* to become known

noth·us -a -um *adj* bastard, illegitimate; mongrel, crossbreed; spurious; *(of the moon's light)* reflected

nōti·ō -ōnis *f* acquaintance; *(fig)* notion, idea; *(leg)* investigation

nōtiti·a -ae *or* **nōtiti·ēs -ēī** *f* acquaintance, knowledge; awareness; fame; notion, conception; familiarity *(w. things);* **nōtitia eī cum Perseō est** he is familiar with Perseus; **nōtitiam fēminae habēre** to have sex with a woman

nōt·ō -āre -āvī -ātus *tr* to mark; to mark out; to note, observe; to write down; to record; to take down in shorthand; to mark critically; to brand; to indicate, denote; to reproach; to indicate by a sign; *(of things)* to be a sign of; to mention *(in a speech or writing)*

nōt·or -ōris *m* guarantor

nōt·us -a -um *pp of* **nōscō** ‖ *adj* known, well-known; notorious; familiar, customary; **nōtum est** *(w. acc & inf)* it is common knowledge that; **nōtum facere** *(w. acc & inf)* to make it known that; **nōtum habēre** *(w. acc & inf)* to be informed that ‖ *m* an acquaintance; one who knows

novācul·a -ae *f* razor

novāl·is -is *f or* **novāl·e -is** *n* field plowed for the first time, reclaimed land; cultivated field; fallow land; crops

novātr·īx -īcis *f* innovator *(female)*

novē *adv* newly, in an unusual manner

novell·us -a -um *adj* new, fresh, young; newly acquired

novem *indecl adj* nine

Novem·ber *or* **Novem·bris -bris -bre** *adj* November; **mēnsis November** *(9th month of the Roman calendar until 153 B.C.)* ‖ **Novem·ber -bris** *m* November

novemdecim *indecl adj* (**noven-**) nineteen

novendiāl·is -is -e *adj* (**novem-**) nine-day; occurring on the ninth day; **cinerēs novendiālēs** *(fig)* ashes not yet cold ‖ *n* nine-day festival *(to mark the appearance of an omen);* funeral feast *(held nine days after death)*

novēn·ī -ae -a *adj* in groups of nine, nine each, nine

novēnsil·ēs -ium *mpl* new gods *(introduced from abroad)*

noverc·a -ae *f* stepmother

novercāl·is -is -e *adj* stepmother's, of a stepmother; like a stepmother

novīci·us -a -um *adj* new, brand new; recently imported *(slaves);* recently discovered *(things); (pej)* new-fangled

noviēns *or* **noviēs** *adv* nine times

novissimē *adv* of late, very recently

novissim·us -a -um *adj* latest, last, final; most recent; most extreme, utmost; **novissimum agmen** *(mil)* the rear; **novissima verba** parting words ‖ *mpl (mil)* rear guard ‖ *npl* the worst

novit·ās -ātis *f* newness, novelty; innovation; rareness, strangeness, unusualness; unexpectedness; recently acquired rank *(condition of* *being a* **novus homō); novitās rērum** revolution

nov·ō -āre -āvī -ātus *tr* to make new, renew, renovate; to repair; to refresh; to change; to coin *(words);* **rēs renovāre** to bring about a revolution

nov·us -a -um *adj* new; young; fresh; novel; unexpected; strange, unusual, unheard-of; recent, modern; unused; inexperienced; renewed, revived, as good as new; newly recuited *(soldiers);* inexperienced; subversive *(plans, activities);* fallow *(field);* newly arrived *(in a place);* **novae tabernae** new shops *(on N. side of the Forum);* **novus homō** self-made man *(first man of a family to reach a curule office);* **rēs nova** a new development; **rēs novae** revolution

nox noctis *f* night; night activity; sleep; death; darkness, blindness; mental darkness, ignorance; gloom; **ad multam noctem** till late at night; **nocte** *(or* **dē nocte)** at night, by night; **noctem et diem** night and day; **sub noctem** at nightfall ‖ *fpl* **noctēs et diēs** night and day, continually

nox·a -ae *f* harm, injury; offense; fault, guilt, responsibility; **in noxā esse** to be guilty of wrongdoing; **noxae** *(or* **ad** *or* **in** + *acc)* **dēdere** to hand *(s.o.)* over for punishment; **noxā** *(or* **noxīs) solūtus** *(of a slave in a formula of sale)* guilty of no prior injurious conduct

noxi·us -a -um *adj* harmful, noxious; guilty; *(w. gen)* guilty of ‖ *f* harm, damage, injury; blame, guilt; fault; offense; **in noxiā esse** to be at fault

nūbēcul·a -ae *f* little cloud; gloomy expression

nūb·ēs -is *f or* **nūb·is -is** *m* cloud; gloom; veil

nūbif·er -era -erum *adj* cloudy; cloud-capped; cloud-bringing *(wind)*

nūbigen·a -ae *adj (masc only) (of the Centaurs, whom Ixion fathered on a cloud-image of Hera; of Phrixus, son of the cloud-goddess Nephele)* born of clouds

nūbil·is -is -e *adj* marriageable

nūbil·us -a -um *adj* cloudy; cloud-bringing *(wind);* troubled; gloomy, melancholy

nūbō nūbere nūpsī -nūptum *intr (of a woman)* to marry; *(w. dat)* to marry *(a man);* to be married to *(a man)* ‖ *refl* to get married

Nūceri·a -ae *f* town in Campania

Nūcerīn·us -a - um *adj* of Nuceria

nucifrangibul·um -ī *n (coll)* nutcracker *(i.e., teeth)*

nucle·us -ī *m* nut; kernel, stone *(of fruit)*

nudius [*contraction for* **nunc dius (diēs)**] *adv* it is now the ... day since, *e.g.,* **nudius tertius** it is now the third day since *(by Roman reckoning, the day before yesterday);* **nudius diēs dedī ad tē epistulam** it is now the third

day since I mailed you a letter; ago, *e.g.,* **nudius tertius decimus** thirteen days ago *(twelve days ago by our reckoning, since the Romans counted both the first and last day)*

nūd·ō -āre -āvī -ātus *tr* to strip, bare; to lay bare, uncover; to explain; to strip *(a person of office or rank);* to empty *(a building)* of all its occupants; *(mil)* to leave undefended; *(w. abl)* to divest of; **terga nūdāre** to expose their backs *(to attack)*

nūd·us -a -um *adj* nude, naked; lightly clothed; bare, empty; defenseless; poor, needy; mere, simple, sole, only; *(w. gen or abl or w. ab)* bare of, without, stripped of, deprived of

nūg·a -ae *m (sl)* a nut, joker

nūg·ae -ārum *fpl* nonsense, baloney; trivia; trash, junk; a good-for-nothing, a nobody; **nūgae** *(or* **nūgās)!** nonsense!; baloney!; **nūgae sunt** it's no use; **nūgās agere** to waste one's effort

nūgāt·or -ōris *m* joker; fibber; babbler; braggart

nūgātōri·us -a -um *adj* worthless, useless, nonsensical; frivolous

nūg·āx -ācis *adj* nonsensical; frivolous

nūgigerul·us -ī *m* dealer in women's apparel

nūg·or -ārī -ātus sum *intr* to talk nonsense; *(w. dat)* to tell tall stories to

nūll·us -a -um *adj* no; *(coll)* not, not at all; non-existent; of no account ‖ *pron* none

num *adv (of time, used only w.* **etiam)** now, *e.g.,* **etiam num** now, even, now, still ‖ *adv (interrog particle expecting negative answer)* surely not, really, actually, *e.g.,* **num ista est nostra culpa?** is that really our fault?; that isn't our fault, is it? ‖ *conj (in indirect questions)* whether

Num. *abbr* **Numerius** *(Roman first name, praenomen)*

Num·a -ae *m* Numa Pompilius *(second king of Rome)*

numcubi *interrog adv* at any time, ever?

numell·a -ae *f* shackle, restrainer

nūm·en -inis *n* nod; will, consent; divine will; divine power; divine majesty; divinity, deity, godhead

numerābil·is -is -e *adj* easily counted, few in number

numerāt·um -ī *n* cold cash

numerāt·us -a -um *adj* counted out, paid down; in cold cash

numerō *adv* at the right time, just now; too soon

numer·ō -āre -āvī -ātus *tr* to number; to count; to pay out, pay down *(money);* to consider; to enumerate, mention; to relate, recount; to reckon as one's own, possess, own; *(w.* **in** + *abl or* **inter** + *acc)* to count

among, include in *(a category); (w.* **in** + *acc)* to allocate to; *(w. pred. adj)* to treat as, class as; **Senātum numerāre** to count the Senate *(to see whether a quorum is present)*
numerōsē *adv* rhythmically
numerōs·us -a -um *adj* numerous; rhythmical
numer·us -ī *m* number; mere cipher; class, category; rank, position; estimation, regard; portion *(of work),* part, function; *(often w.* **suus)** the proper number, the full number, full complement; *(gram)* number; *(mil)* division, troop; *(mus, rhet)* rhythm, meter, verse; *(mus)* tune; *(pros)* quantity, measure; **ad numerum** *(or* **in numerum)** *(mus, pros, rhet)* rhythmically, in time; **aliquō (nūllō) numerō esse** to be of some (no) account; **extrā numerum** *(mus)* off beat, out of time; **in numerō esse** to be included in a group; **in numerō habēre** *(w. gen)* to be regarded as, be ranked among; **nūllō numerō esse** to be of no account; **nūmerō** at the right time, just now; too soon, too early; **numerō hūc advenīs ad prandium** you are arriving here too early for lunch; **suum numerum nāvium habēre** to have one's full complement of ships; **super** *(or* **suprā) numerum** not attached to the regular staff ‖ *mpl* mathematics, arithmetic; astronomy; notes of the scale; melody; **ad numerōs** *(mus, pros)* rhythmically, in time; **in numerīs esse** to be on active duty; **omnibus numerīs perfectus** perfect in every detail
Numid·a -ae *m* Numidian
Numidi·a -ae *f* Numidia *(country of N. Africa; Roman province, extending W. and S. of Carthage)*
Numidic·us -a -um *adj* Numidian
Numit·or -ōris *m* king of Alba, brother of Amulius, father of Ilia *(or* Rhea Silvia), and grandfather of Romulus and Remus
nummāri·us -a -um *adj* financial; *(pej)* mercenary, venal
nummāt·us -a -um *adj* rich; **bene nummātus** well-to-do, well-off
nummulār·ius -(i)ī *m* money changer
nummul·ī -ōrum *mpl* petty cash, small change
numm·us -ī *m* coin; cash, money; sesterce *(small silver coin, worth about a dime);* small sum, trifle; **in nummīs habēre** to have in cash
numquam *adv* **(nun-)** never; **nōn numquam** sometimes
numquid *adv (to introduce direct question):* **numquid meministī?** do you remember?; *(to introduce an indirect question)* whether
nunc *adv* now; nowadays, today; now, in view of this, but as matters now stand; **nunc ipsum** at this very moment; **nunc ... nunc** at one time ... at another, once ... once

nuncupāti·ō -ōnis *f* name, title; public pronouncing *(of vows);* nomination *(to some position)*
nuncup·ō -āre -āvī -ātus *tr* to name, call; to take *(a vow)* publicly; to appoint *(as heir);* to utter the name of, invoke; to address *(a person)*
nūndin·ae -ārum *fpl* market day *(occurring regularly at intervals of eight days, i.e., every ninth day by Roman reckoning);* marketplace; market town; mart
nūndināl·is -is -e *adj* market
nūndināti·ō -ōnis *f* marketing, trading
nūndin·or -ārī -ātus sum *tr* to traffic in; to buy ‖ *intr* to hold a market, attend a market; to trade; to gather in crowds
nūndin·um -ī *n* market time; **inter nūndinum** the time between two market periods; **trīnum nūndinum** a sequence of three market periods *(i.e., 24 days)*
nunq- = numq-
nūnti·a -ae *f* messenger *(female)*
nūntiāti·ō -ōnis *f* announcement *(by an augur)*
nūnti·ō -āre -āvī -ātus *tr* to bring word of; to announce, declare; to report *(omens);* to give warning of *(some future event);* **gaudium nūntiāre** to bring good news; **salūtem nūntiāre** to send greetings
nūnti·us -a -um *adj* bringing news, announcing ‖ *m* messenger, courier; message, news; order, injunction; **nūntium remittere** *(w. dat)* to send a letter of divorce to, to divorce *(a wife)* ‖ *n* message, communication
nūper *adv* recently; in modern times
nūper·us -a -um *adj* recent
nūpt·a -ae *f* bride, wife
nūpti·ae -ārum *fpl* marriage, wedding
nūptiāl·is -is -e *adj* nuptial, wedding
nur·us -ūs *f* daughter-in-law; young lady, young married woman
nūsquam *adv* nowhere; on no occasion; for nothing, to nothing; **nūsquam alibi** nowhere else; **nūsquam esse** not to exist; **nūsquam gentium** nowhere in the world; **plēbs nūsquam aliō nāta, quam ad serviendum** the plebs, born for nothing else than to serve
nūt·ō -āre -āvī -ātus *intr* to keep nodding; to sway to and fro, totter; to waver
nūtrīcāt·us -ūs *m* breast-feeding
nūtrīc·ius -(i)ī *m (child's)* guardian
nūtrīc·ō -āre -āvī -ātus *or* **nūtrīc·or -ārī -ātus sum** *tr* to breast-feed, nurse; to nourish, promote the growth of *(plants, animals);* to rear, bring up, support; to take care of, attend to; to cherish, cultivate
nūtrīcul·a -ae *f* nanny; wet-nurse; *(of persons or things)* fosterer

nūtrīm·en -inis *n* nourishment

nūtrīment·um -ī *n* nourishment ‖ *npl* upbringing *(of a child)*

nūtr·iō -īre -īvī *or* -iī -ītus *or* nūtrior nūtrīrī nūtrītus sum *tr* to breast-feed, suckle; to support with food, nourish; to feed *(animals, plants, fire);* to build up *(resources);* to take care of, attend to *(the skin, hair);* to bring up *(a child);* to raise *(animals, crops);* to give rise to, foster, promote *(a condition, feeling);* to treat *(a wound, sick person);* to look after *(material things);* to deal gently with *(faults, people at fault)*

nūtrīt·or -ōris *m* one who feeds

nūtr·īx -īcis *f* nurse ‖ *fpl* the breasts

nūt·us -ūs *m* nod; hint, intimation; nod of assent; will, pleasure; command; gravitation, gravitational pull; **nūtus et renūtus** nod of assent and nod of dissent

nux nucis *f* nut; nut tree; almond tree; **nucēs relinquere** *(fig)* to put away childish things; **nux abellāna** *(or* **avellāna)** hazelnut; **nux castanea** chestnut; **nux Graeca** (sweet) almond; **nux iuglāns** walnut; **nux pīnea** pine cone

Nyctē·is -idis *f* Antiope *(daughter of Nycteus, wife of Lycus (king of Thebes) and mother of Amphion and Zethus)*

Nyct·eūs -eī *or* -eos *m* father of Antiope

nymph·a -ae *or* nymph·ē -ēs *f* nymph; bride; mistress; *(fig)* water *(cf.* lympha)

Nȳs·a -ae *f* legendary mountain on which Bacchus was alleged to have been born *(usually located in India)*

Nȳsae·us *or* Nȳsi·us -a -um *adj* of Nysa, Nysaean

Nȳs·eūs -eī *or* -eos *m* Bacchus

Nȳsigen·a -ae *m* native of Nysa

O

O, o *(supply* littera) *f* fourteenth letter of the Latin alphabet; letter name: **o**

ō *interj* oh!

Ōapet·us -ī *m* a Titan, father of Prometheus, Epimetheus, and Atlas

Ōari·ōn -ōnis *m* Orion

Ōas·ius -(i)ī *m* son of Jupiter and Electra and brother of Dardanus

Oax·ēs *or* Oax·is -is *m* river in Crete

ob- *pref (also* oc-, of-, og-, op-; the **b** is lost in **ōmittō** and **operiō)** conveying the sense of: **1** movement toward a meeting: **obeō** to go to meet; **2** covering a surface: **oblimō** to cover with mud; **obdūcō** to cover the surface of; **3** protecting: **obdūcō** to draw *or* place as a protection *or* obstacle; **4** of overwhelming: **opprimō** to oppress; **5** counterbalancing: **oppōnō** to set off against by way of balance; **6** confrontation: **obstō** *(w. dat)* to stand in the way of, obstruct; **7** surprise or the unexpected: **obveniō** *(w. dat)* to fall to the lot of; **8** pleasant effect: **oblectō** to delight, entertain; **9** hostility: **obtrectō** to mistreat, disparage; **10** assault: **occīdō** to kill

ob *prep (w. acc)* **1** before, in front of: **ob oculōs** *(or* **ob ōs)** before one's eyes, right in front of s.o., under s.o.'s very nose; **2** on account of, because of, for: **quam ob rem** for which reason, accordingly, wherefore; **quās ob causās** for what reasons, why; **3** for the sake of, in the interest of: **ob rem pūblicam** for the sake of the country; **4** as a reward *or* punishment for, in return for: **ob mendācium tuum** in punishment for your lie; **5** *(in connection with bribes)* in payment for: **ob tua ēdicta pecūniae dabantur** you were given money *(i.e., bribes)* in payment for your edicts; **6** in connection with: **ob rem** to the purpose, usefully, profitably; **ob suam partem** on one's own account

obaerāt·us -a -um *adj* deeply in debt ‖ *m* debtor

obambul·ō -āre -āvī -ātus *tr* to prowl all over, prowl about *(e.g., the city)* ‖ *intr* to walk about; to wander; to prowl about; *(w. dat)* to prowl about near; *(w.* **ante** + *acc)* to wander around in front of

obarm·ō -āre -āvī -ātus *tr* to arm *(against)*

obar·ō -āre -āvī -ātus *tr* to plow up, plow over

obb·a -ae *f* decanter, beaker

obbrūt·ēscō -ēscere -uī *intr* to grow dull

obc- = occ-

ob·dō -dere -didī -ditus *tr* to set before; to fasten *(a bolt);* to close, lock *(a door);* to expose

obdorm·iō -īre -īvī *or* -iī -ītum *intr* to fall asleep

obdorm·īscō -īscere *intr* to fall fast asleep

ob·dūcō -dūcere -dūxī -ductus *tr (w.* **ad**) to lead *(troops)* toward or against; to extend in front as a barrier *or* protection; to fasten *(bolt);* to obstruct, block; to screen, protect; to cover the surface of; to close *(the curtains);* to veil, envelop; to swallow; to put on *(clothes);* to bring forward as an opposing candidate; to pass *(time);* to dig *(ditch); (w. dat of thing protected)* to draw *or* place *(s.th.)* over; *(w. dat or* **ad**) to pit *(s.o. or s.th.)* against; **tenebrās obdūcere** *(w. dat)* to cast darkness over

obducti·ō -ōnis *f* veiling, covering

obduct·ō -āre *tr* to introduce as a rival

obduct·us -a -um *pp of* obdūcō ‖ *adj* cloudy; gloomy; **obductus cicātrīx** a closed scar

obdūr·ēscō -ēscere -uī *intr* to grow hard, harden; to become insensitive; **Gorgonis vultū obdūrēscere** to become petrified *(literally, to grow hard at the sight of the Gorgon)*

obdūr·ō -āre -āvī -ātum *intr* to stick it out

ob·eō -īre -īvī *or* **-iī -itus** *tr* to go to meet; to travel, travel to, travel across; to wander through, traverse, encircle; to visit; to run over, review, enumerate *(in a speech);* to undertake, engage in; **diem ēdictī** *(or* **diem** *or* **diem suum** *or* **diem extrēmum** *or* **mortem) obīre** to meet one's death ‖ *intr* to go; to pass away, die; to fade, disappear; *(of heavenly bodies)* to set

obequit·ō -āre -āvī -ātum *intr* to ride up *(on horseback); (w. dat)* to ride up to

oberr·ō -āre -āvī -ātum *intr* to ramble about, wander around; *(w. abl)* **1** to wander among; **2** to make a mistake on *or* at

obēs·us -a -um *adj* obese; swollen; crude, coarse

ob·ex -icis *mf* bar, bolt; barrier, barricade

obf- = off-

obg- = ogg-

obhae·rēscō -rēscere -sī *intr* to get stuck

obiac·eō -ēre -uī *intr (w. dat)* to lie before, lie at

obiectāti·ō -ōnis *f* reproach

obiect·ō -āre -āvī -ātus *tr* to oppose; to expose, endanger; to throw in the way; to cause *(delay); (w. dat)* **1** to impute to, throw up *(faults)* to; **2** to bring a charge of *(e.g., madness)* against, fling *(charges, abuse)* at; *(w. dat & acc & inf)* to throw a hint to *(s.o.)* that

obiect·us -a -um *pp of* **obiciō** ‖ *adj* lying in the way, lying in front; *(w. dat)* **1** opposite; **2** exposed to ‖ *npl* charges

obiect·us -ūs *m* interposition; obstacles, hindrance; protection; *(w. gen)* protection afforded by

ob·iciō -icere -iēcī -iectus *tr* to hold up as an example; to bring up, cite *(before an opponent as a ground for disapproval or condemnation),* throw up in one's face; to set up as a defense, use as a barrier *or* defense; to bar, shut *(the gates to prevent entry by an enemy);* to throw in, use, deploy *(troops); (w. dat)* **1** to throw *or* set *(e.g., food, fodder)* before; **2** to expose *(people)* to *(the wild beasts);* **3** *(coll)* to toss *or* hand out *(money)* to; **4** to put *(a bandage)* on *(a part of the body);* **5** to turn *(a ship)* so as to face *(e.g., a hostile shore);* to set up as a defense against; **6** to hold out *(false hopes, incentives, temptations)* to; **7** to throw up *(faults, weaknesses, etc.)* to, lay *(faults)* to one's charge; **hī exercituī Caesaris luxuriem obiciēbant** they were charging Caesar's army with extravagance; **8**

to subject *(s.o.)* to *(danger, misfortune);* **9** to bring up, throw in *(troops)* against; **exceptiōnem obicere** to raise an objection; **interdum metus animō obicitur** at times fear crosses my mind; **portās obicere** to bar the gates; **religiōnem obicere** to raise the matter of religious scruples *(as a hindrance to some action);* **signum obicere** to raise an omen as an objection *(to some action)* ‖ *refl (w. dat)* to expose oneself to; **turba oculīs meīs modo sē obiēcit** a crowd just came into view ‖ *pass (w. dat)* to happen to, befall, occur to; *(geog) (w. dat)* to be located near *or* opposite (to)

obīr·āscor -āscī -ātus sum *intr (w. dat)* to get angry with

obiter *adv* on the way, as one goes along; *(fig)* in passing, incidentally

obitus *pp of* **obeō**

obit·us -ūs *m* approach, visit; death, passing; ruin, downfall; *(astr)* setting

obiūrgāti·ō -ōnis *f* scolding, rebuke

obiūrgāt·or -ōris *m* critic

obiūrgātōri·us -a -um *adj* reproachful

obiūrgit·ō -āre -āvī -ātus *tr* to keep on scolding

obiūrg·ō -āre -āvī -ātus *tr* to scold, rebuke, reprimand; to correct; to deter

oblangu·ēscō -ēscere -ī *intr* to taper off

oblātrātr·īx -īcis *f* nagging woman

oblātus *pp of* **offerō**

oblectām·en -inis *n* delight

oblectāment·um -ī *n* delight, amusement, pastime

oblectāti·ō -ōnis *f* delight, amusement; attraction; *(w. gen)* diversion from

oblect·ō -āre -āvī -ātus *tr* to delight, amuse, entertain, attract; to spend *(time)* pleasantly ‖ *refl* to amuse oneself, enjoy oneself

oblēvī *perf of* **oblinō**

ob·līdō -līdere -līsī -līsus *tr* to rush; to squeeze *(the throat),* strangle

obligāti·ō -ōnis *f* binding, pledging; obligation

obligāt·us -a -um *adj* obliged, under obligation; *(w. dat)* owed by right to, due to

oblig·ō -āre -āvī -ātus *tr* to tie up, bandage; to bind, obligate, put under obligation, make liable; to hamper; to earmark; to embarrass; to mortgage *(property); (w dat)* to pledge to, devote to; **fidem obligāre** to pledge one's word, make a solemn promise; to guarantee one's loyalty ‖ *refl* to bind oneself, pledge oneself ‖ *pass* to be liable; *(w. abl)* **1** to be guilty of; **2** to be obliged to, compelled to

oblīm·ō -āre -āvī -ātus *tr* to cover with mud; to dissipate, squander

ob·linō -linere -lēvī *or* **līvī -itus** *tr* to smear, daub, coat; to seal up *(jar); (fig)* to sully, sully the reputation of; *(fig)* to overload

oblīquē *adv* sideways; zigzag; *(fig)* indirectly

oblīqu·ō -āre -āvī -ātus *tr* to turn aside, twist, shift, slant; to avert *(eyes)*

oblīqu·us -a -um *adj* slanting, crosswise, sideways; zigzag; from the side; indirect *(language);* sly; envious; downhill *(road);* **oblīquus oculus** disapproving look; envious look **‖** *n* side; **ab** *(or* **ex) oblīquō** from the side, at an angle, obliquely; **in oblīquum** at an angle, sideways; **per oblīquum** diagonally across

oblīsī *perf of* **oblīdō**

oblīsus *pp of* **oblīdō**

oblit·ēscō -ēscere -uī *intr* to hide, disappear

oblitter·ō -āre -āvī -ātus *tr* (**-līt-**) to erase; to cancel; *(fig)* to blot out; **nōmina oblitterāre** to cancel debts

oblituī *perf of* **oblitēscō**

oblitus *pp of* **oblinō**

oblītus *pp of* **oblīvīscor**

oblīvi·ō -ōnis *f* oblivion; forgetting; forgetfulness

oblīviōs·us -a -um *adj* forgetful, oblivious; *(wine)* causing forgetfulness

oblī·vīscor -vīscī -tus sum *tr* to forget **‖** *intr* to forget; *(w. gen)* to forget, neglect, disregard, be indifferent to

oblīv·ium -(i)ī *n* forgetfulness, oblivion

oblocūt·or -ōris *m* one who contradicts

oblong·us -a -um *adj* oblong

ob·loquor -loquī -locūtus sum *intr (w. dat)* **1** to interrupt; **2** to rail at; **3** to accompany *(musically)*

obluct·or -ārī -ātus sum *tr (w. dat)* to struggle with, fight against

oblūdi·ō -āre *intr* to make a fool of oneself

oblūd·ō -ere *tr* to play jokes on

obmōl·ior -īrī -ītus sum *tr* to make a barricade of; to block up *(a gap)*

obmurmur·ō -āre -āvī -ātum *intr (w. dat)* to roar in answer to

obmūt·ēscō -ēscere -uī *intr* to become silent, hush up; to cease

obnāt·us -a -um *adj (w. dat)* growing on *(e.g., a river bank)*

ob·nītor -nītī -nīxus sum *intr* to strain, struggle, put on the pressure; *(w. dat)* **1** to press against, lean against; **2** to resist, oppose

obnīxē *adv* with all one's might; obstinately

obnīx·us -a -um *pp of* **obnītor ‖** *adj* steadfast, firm, obstinate

obnoxiē *adv* guiltily; submissively

obnoxiōsius *adv* more slavishly

obnoxiōs·us -a -um *adj* submissive

obnoxi·us -a -um *adj* submissive, servile, obedient; weak, timid; *(w. dat)* **1** subservient to; **2** at the mercy of; **3** exposed to *(harm, danger, storms, etc.);* **4** indebted to, under obligation to; **5** legally liable to, answerable to; **obnoxium est** *(w. inf)* it is dangerous to

ob·nūbō -nūbere -nūpsī -nūptus *tr* to veil, cover *(the head)*

obnūntiāti·ō -ōnis *f* announcement *(of omens)*

obnūnti·ō -āre -āvī -ātum *intr* to make an announcement; to make an announcement that the omens are adverse; to announce bad news

oboedi·ēns -entis *adj* obedient; *(w. dat or ad)* obedient to; **dictō oboediēns** obedient to the command

oboedienter *adv* obediently

oboedienti·a -ae *f* (**-bēd-**) obedience

oboed·iō -īre -īvī *or* **-iī -ītum** *intr (w. dat)* **1** to obey, listen to; **2** *(of things)* to respond to

obol·eō -ēre -uī *tr* to smell of **‖** *intr* to smell, stink

obor·ior -īrī -tus sum *intr* to rise. rise up, appear; *(fig) (of thoughts, sudden events)* occur, spring up

obp- = opp-

obrēp·ō -ere -sī -tus *tr* (**opr-**) to creep up on, sneak up on **‖** *intr* to creep up; *(w. dat)* **1** to creep up on, sneak up on, take by surprise; **2** to trick, cheat; *(w. in + acc)* to steal over; **obrēpere ad honōrēs** to worm one's way into high positions

obrēpt·ō -āre -āvī -ātum *intr* (**opr-**) to sneak up

obrēt·iō -īre -īvī *or* **-iī -ītus** *tr* to entangle

obrig·ēscō -ēscere -uī *intr* to stiffen; to freeze

obrōd·ō -ere *tr* to gnaw at

obrog·ō -āre -āvī -ātum *intr (w. dat)* to supersede

obru·ō -ere -ī -tus *tr* to cover up, cover, hide, bury; to overwhelm, overthrow; to sink, cover with water, swamp; to overflow; to overpower, surpass, obscure, eclipse **‖** *intr* to fall to ruin

obruss·a -ae *f* test, proof

obrutus *pp of* **obruō**

obsaep·iō -īre -sī -tus *tr* (**-sēp-**) to fence in; to block *(road); (fig)* to block

obsatur·ō -āre -āvī -ātus *tr* to cloy **‖** *pass (w. gen)* to have more than enough of

obscaen- = obscēn-

obscaev·ō -āre -āvī -ātum *intr (w. dat)* to augur well for; to augur ill for

obscēnē *adv* (**-scaen-**) obscenely

obscēnit·ās -ātis *f* (**-scaen-**) obscenity

obscēn·us -a -um *adj* (**-scaen-**) obscene, indecent; dirty; filthy; ominous **‖** *m* sexual pervert; foul-mouthed person **‖** *npl* sexual *or* excretory parts *or* functions, private parts

obscūrāti·ō -ōnis *f* obscuring, darkening; disappearance

obscūrē *adv* indistinctly, dimly; in an under-hand manner; cryptically; imperceptibly; **obscūrē ferre** to conceal, keep secret
obscūrit·ās -ātis *f* obscurity
obscūr·ō -āre -āvī -ātus *tr* (ops-) to obscure, darken; to cover, hide; to suppress; to veil *(words); (of love)* to blind
obscūr·us -a -um *adj* (ops-) obscure; dark, shady; dim, indistinct, dimly seen, shadowy; barely visible; not openly expressed, unpublicized; obscure, unintelligible; secret; reserved; vague, uncertain; gloomy **II** *n* the dark, darkness; obscurity; **in obscūrō est** it is not clear, it is doubtful
obsecrāti·ō -ōnis *f* (ops-) entreaty; public supplication of the gods
obsecr·ō -āre -āvī -ātus *tr* (ops-) to entreat, appeal to, implore; **fidem obsecrāre** to beg for protection *or* support; **tē obsecrō** I beseech you; please
obsecund·ō -āre -āvī -ātum *intr* (ops-) *(w. dat)* to comply with, humor
obsecūtus *pp of* obsequor
obsēp- = obsaep-
obsequ·ēns -entis *adj* (ops-) compliant, obedient; indulgent, gracious *(gods); (w. dat)* obedient to
obsequenter *adv* (ops-) compliantly
obsequenti·a -ae *f* (ops-) compliance, deference
obsequiōs·us -a -um *adj* (ops-) compliant, deferential
obsequ·ium -(i)ī *n* (ops-) compliance, indulgence; obedience, allegiance
ob·sequor -sequī -secūtus sum *intr* (ops-) *(w. dat)* 1 to comply with, yield to, give in to; 2 to gratify, humor; 3 to pay respect to
obser·ō -āre -āvī -ātus *tr* (ops-) to bolt, lock up
ob·serō -serere -sēvī -situs *tr* (ops-) to sow *or* plant thickly; to fill, cover
observābil·is -is -e *adj* perceptible; capable of being guarded against
observ·āns -antis *adj* attentive; *(w. gen)* 1 respectful of; 2 attentive to; 3 careful about
observanti·a -ae *f* regard, respect; *(w. gen or* in + *acc)* regard for, respect for
observāti·ō -ōnis *f* (ops-) observation; caution, care; observance, usage, practice; remark, observation; safeguarding, protection
observāt·or -ōris *m* observer
observit·ō -āre -āvī -ātus *tr* to watch carefully, note carefully
observ·ō -āre -āvī -ātus *tr* to watch; to watch out for *(dangers, opportunities);* to watch for *(to ensnare);* to take careful note of; to guard; to observe, keep, obey, comply with; to pay attention to, pay respect to; to regard as important *or* authoritative; to keep to *(a*

date); (w. predicate) to regard as, accept as; to adopt *(a course of action); (w. ut)* to follow *(such a course of action)* that
obs·es -idis *mf* (opses) hostage; guarantee, pledge; bail
obsessi·ō -ōnis *f* blockade
obsess·or -ōris *m* (ops-) frequenter, regular visitor; blockader
ob·sideō -sidēre -sēdī -sessus *tr* (ops-) to sit near *or* at, remain by *or* near; to frequent; to block, choke; to occupy, fill; to look out for, watch closely; to keep guard over; *(mil)* to besiege, blockade
obsidiāl·is -is -e *adj (mil)* for breaking a blockade
obsidi·ō -ōnis *f (mil)* blockade, siege
obsid·ium -(i)ī *n* (ops-) *(mil)* blockade, siege; status of hostage
ob·sīdō -sīdere -sēdī -sessus *tr* to take possession of, occupy *(so as to bar passage); (mil)* to besiege, blockade
obsignāt·or -ōris *m* sealer; witness; **obsignātor testāmentī** witness to a will
obsign·ō -āre -āvī -ātus *tr* (ops-) to seal, to sign and seal; *(fig)* to stamp
ob·sistō -sistere -stitī -stitum *intr* (ops-) *(w. dat)* 1 to stand in the way of, block; 2 to resist, oppose; 3 to disapprove of, forbid
obsitus (ops-) *pp of* obserō (to sow) **II** *adj (w. abl)* overgrown with, covered with
obsole·faciō -facere -fēcī -factus *tr (pass:* obsole·fīō -fierī -factus sum) to degrade, lower the dignity of
obsol·ēscō -ēscere -ēvī -ētum *intr* to go out of style, become obsolete; to fade away; to suffer degradation; *(of reputation)* to become tarnished; *(of persons)* to sink into obscurity
obsolētē *adv* shabbily
obsolēt·us -a -um *adj* out of date, obsolete; worn out; shabby, threadbare; soiled, dirty; low, poor; *(of language)* hackneyed, trite
obsōnāt·or -ōris *m* (ops-) shopper *(for groceries)*
obsōnāt·us -ūs *m* (ops-) shopping *(for groceries)*
obsōn·ium -(i)ī *n* (ops-) shopping; groceries **II** *npl* groceries; pension
obson·ō -āre -āvī -ātum *intr (w. dat)* to drown out
obsōn·ō -āre -āvī -ātus *or* obsōn·or -ārī -ātus sum *tr* (ops-) to shop for *(groceries);* **famem obsōnāre** to work up an appetite **II** *intr* to go shopping; to provide food; *(w.* dē + *abl)* to provide a feast for
obsorb·eō -ēre -uī *tr* (ops-) to gulp down
obstanti·a -ōrum *npl* obstacles, obstructions
obstetr·īx -īcis *f* (ops-) midwife
obstinātē *adv* resolutely, with determination; obstinately, stubbornly

obstināti·ō -ōnis *f* determination; obstinacy, stubbornness

obstināt·us -a -um *adj* determined, fixed; obstinate, stubborn

obstin·ō -āre -āvī -ātus *tr* (ops-) to set one's mind on, persist in ‖ *intr (w.* **ad)** to persist in

obstipēscō *see* **obstupēscō**

obstīp·us -a -um *adj* bent, bent forwards, bowed; **capite obstīpō stare** to stand with bowed head

obstit·us -a -um *adj* slanting, oblique

ob·stō -stāre -stitī -stātum *intr* (ops-) to stand in the way, raise opposition; *(w. dat)* **1** to stand in the way of, block the path of; **2** to block the view of, stand in front of; **3** to oppose, object to, resist, obstruct; **4** to constitute a boundary to; *(w.* **nē** *or* **quīn** *or* **quōminus** *or* **cūr nōn)** to prevent *(s.o.)* from

obstrep·ō -ere -uī -itus *tr* (ops-) to fill with noise, drown out ‖ *intr* to make a racket, make noise; *(w. dat)* **1** to shout at, drown out, interrupt with shouts; **2** *(of the sea)* to resound against

ob·stringō -stringere strīnxī obstrictus *tr* (ops-) to tie a rope tightly around *(a neck);* *(w.* **ob** + *acc)* to tie onto; to tie up, shut in, confine; *(fig)* to involve, put under obligation *(by an agreement, oath);* to pledge, promise *(s.th.);* **fidem obstringere** *(w. dat)* to pledge one's word to; **in verba alicūius obstringere** to have *(s.o.)* swear loyalty to s.o. ‖ *refl & pass (w. abl)* **1** to get involved in; **2** to be guilty of

obstructi·ō -ōnis *f* obstruction

obstructus *pp of* **obstruō**

obstrū·dō -dere -sī -sus *tr* (obt-) to gulp down; *(w. dat)* to force *(s.th.)* upon, thrust *(s.th.)* upon

obstru·ō -ere -xī -ctus *tr* (ops-) to pile up, block up, stop up; *(w. dat)* to block *or* close *(e.g., a road)* against

obstrūsus *pp of* **obstrūdō**

obstupe·faciō -facere -fēcī -factus *tr* to stun, astonish, strike dumb, daze; *(of drinks)* to stupefy; to paralyze *(emotions, etc.)*

obstup·ēscō -ēscere -uī *intr* (-stip-) to be astounded, be stunned, be paralyzed; to be struck with awe *or* wonder; *(of the body)* to become numb

obstupid·us -a -um *adj* (ops-) struck dumb, stunned, dazed, astounded

ob·sum -esse -fuī *or* **offuī -futūrus** *intr (w. dat)* **1** to be opposed to, be against; **2** to be prejudicial to; **3** to be harmful to; **nihil obest dīcere** there is no harm in saying

ob·suō -suere -suī -sūtus *tr* to sew on; to sew up

obsurd·ēscō -ēscere -uī *intr* to become deaf; *(fig)* to turn a deaf ear

ob·tegō -tegere -tēxī -tēctus *tr* (opt-) to cover up *(w. clothing);* to protect; to conceal, screen; to keep secret

obtemperāti·ō -ōnis *f (w. dat)* obedience to, submissiveness to

obtemper·ō -āre -āvī -ātum *intr* (opt-) *(w. dat)* to comply with, be submissive to, obey, follow

obten·dō -dere -dī -tus *tr* (opt-) to spread, stretch out; to offer as an excuse; to envelop; to conceal; to allege ‖ *pass (w. dat)* to lie opposite; **obtentā nocte** under cover of darkness

obtent·us -ūs *m* (opt-) screen, cover; pretext, pretense

ob·terō -terere -trīvī -trītus *tr* to trample on, trample down, crush; *(fig)* to trample on, degrade, destroy, crush

obtestāti·ō -ōnis *f* calling to witness; solemn invocation; solemn appeal

obtest·or -ārī -ātus sum *tr* (opt-) to call as witness; to make an appeal to, implore, entreat

obtex·ō -ere -uī -tus *tr* to cover, veil

obtic·eō -ēre -uī *intr* (opt-) to be silent

obtic·ēscō -ēscere -uī *intr* (opt-) to fall silent; to be dumbstruck

ob·tineō -tinēre -tinuī -tentus *tr* (opt-) to hold on to, keep up, persist in; to possess; to maintain, preserve, uphold; to remain in charge of; to retain military control of; to achieve *(a goal),* gain *(one's point);* to secure *(rights);* to win *(one's case);* to secure *(one's rights);* to cover, extend over; to constitute; to comprise; *(of conditions)* to prevail over; to hold *(a rank, position; an opinion);* **auctōritātem obtinēre** *(w. gen)* to have the authority of; **locum obtinēre** *(w. gen)* to fulfill the function of; **rem obtinēre** to be successful, be victorious; **vim obtinēre** *(w. gen)* to have the force of ‖ *intr* to carry the day, get one's way, succeed; *(of an opinion, report)* to be generally accepted

ob·tingō -tingere -tigī *intr* (opt-) to happen, occur; *(w. dat)* to happen to, befall

obtorp·ēscō -ēscere -uī *intr* (opt-) to become numb, become stiff; to become insensible

obtor·queō -quēre -sī -tus *tr* (opt-) to twist; to restrain with a noose

obtrectāti·ō -ōnis *f* (opt-) detraction, disparagement

obtrectāt·or -ōris *m* (opt-) detractor

obtrect·ō -āre -āvī -ātus *tr* (opt-) to treat spitefully, mistreat, disparage; to carp at ‖ *intr (w. dat)* to detract from, disparage

obtrītus *pp of* **obterō**

obtrīvī *perf of* **obterō**

obtrūdō *see* **obstrūdō**

obtrunc·ō -āre -āvī -ātus *tr* (opt-) to cut off, cut down; *(in battle)* to cut down, kill

ob·tueor -tuērī -tuitus sum *or* optu·or -ī *tr* (opt-) to gaze at, gaze upon; to see clearly

ob·tundō -tundere -tudī -tūsus *or* -tūnsus *tr* (opt-) to beat, beat on, thump on; to blunt; *(fig)* to pound away at, stun; to deafen; to annoy

obturb·ō -āre -āvī -ātus *tr* (opt-) to throw into disorder; *(fig)* to disturb, confuse, distract

ob·turgēscō -turgēscere -tursī *intr* to begin to swell

obtūr·ō -āre -āvī -ātus *tr* (opt-) to block up, plug up; **aurēs obtūrāre** to refuse to listen; **ōs alicūius obtūrāre** to shut s.o. up

obtūs·us *or* obtūns·us -a -um *pp of* **obtundō** ‖ *adj* dull; blunt; husky, coarse *(voice); (of utterances)* obtuse; *(of actions)* blunt, lacking in refinement

obtūt·us -ūs *m* (opt-) stare, gaze

obumbr·ō -āre -āvī -ātus *tr* to overshadow, shade; to darken, obscure; to cover, screen

obunc·us -a -um *adj* hooked

obūst·us -a -um *adj (of a stake)* having an end burned to a point; hardened in the fire; nipped *(by cold)*

obvāg·iō -īre *intr* to bawl

obvall·ō -āre -āvī -ātus *tr* to fortify *(with a rampart)*

ob·veniō -venīre -vēnī -ventum *intr* to come up, happen, come one's way; *(w. dat)* 1 to fall to *(s.o.'s)* lot; 2 to come to *(s.o.'s)* notice

obvers·or -ārī -ātus sum *intr* to make an appearance, show oneself; *(fig)* to appear *(before one's eyes, mind)*

obvers·us -a -um *adj (w. ad)* 1 turned toward, facing; 2 inclined to; *(w. dat)* engaged in ‖ *m* opponent

ob·vertō -vertere -vertī -versus *tr* (-vor-) *(w. dat or ad)* to turn *(s.th.)* toward *or* in the direction of; *(w. in + acc)* to turn *(e.g., soldiers)* to face *(e.g., the enemy)* ‖ *pass (w. ad)* to turn toward

obviam *or* ob viam *adv (w. dat)* 1 to meet, in order to meet, in the way of; 2 *(fig)* opposed to; **effundī obviam** *(w. dat)* to pour *or* rush out to meet; **obviam esse** *(w. dat)* 1 to meet; 2 to oppose, resist; 3 to be at hand, be handy; **obviam īre** *(or* **obviam prōcēdere)** *(w. dat)* 1 to go to meet; 2 to face up to *(dangers);* **obviam obsistere** *(w. dat)* to stand in the way of; **obviam prōdīre** *(or* **proficīscī** *or* **prōgredī)** *(w. dat)* to go to meet; **obviam venīre** *(w. dat)* to come *or* go to meet

obvigilāt·um -ī *n* vigilance

obvi·us -a -um *adj* in the way; exposed, open; accessible *(person);* ready, at hand; *(w. dat)* 1 to meet, so as to meet; 2 opposed to; 3

exposed to, open to; **obvius esse** *(w. dat)* to meet, encounter

obvol·vō -vere -vī -ūtus *tr* to wrap up, cover up

occaec·ō -āre -āvī -ātus *tr* (obc-) to blind; to darken, obscure; to hide; *(of fear)* to numb

occall·ēscō -ēscere -uī *intr* (obc-) to become thick-skinned, become callused; *(fig)* to become callous, become insensitive

occan·ō -ō -uī *intr (mil)* to sound the charge

occāsi·ō -ōnis *f* opportunity, good time, right moment, chance; pretext; *(mil)* surprise, raid; **ex occāsiōne** at the right time; **occāsiōnem āmittere** to lose the opportunity; **occāsiōnem arripere** to seize the opportunity; **per occāsiōnem** *(or* **occāsiōnēs)** at the right time

occāsiuncul·a -ae *f* nice little opportunity

occās·us -ūs *m* setting; sunset; the West; *(fig)* downfall, ruin, death

occāti·ō -ōnis *f* harrowing, breaking up of the soil

occāt·or -ōris *m* harrower

oc·cēdō -cēdere -cessī -cessum *intr* to go up; **obviam occēdere** *(w. dat)* to go to meet

occent·ō *or* occant·ō -āre -āvī -ātus *tr* (obc-) to serenade; to satirize in verse

occept·ō -āre -āvī -ātus *tr* to begin

occid·ēns -entis *m* the setting sun; the West; **vīta occidēns** the twilight of life

occīdi·ō -ōnis *f* massacre, annihilation; **occīdiōne occīdere** to massacre

oc·cidō -cidere -cidī -cāsum *intr* to fall, fall down; *(of the sun)* to set; to fall, be slain; *(of hope, etc.)* to fade; *(of species)* to become extinct, die out; *(fig)* to be ruined, be done for; **occidī!** *(coll)* I'm done for!

oc·cīdō -cīdere -cīdī -cīsus *tr* to kill; to murder; to knock down; to bring about the ruin of; *(fig)* to be the death of; to pester to death

occidu·us -a -um *adj* setting; western; *(fig)* sinking, fading, dying

occill·ō -āre -āvī -ātus *tr* to smash

oc·cinō -cinere -cecinī *or* -cinuī *or* occan·ō -ere -uī *intr* to sing inauspiciously, sound ominous

oc·cipiō -cipere -cēpī -ceptus *tr & intr* (-cup-) to begin

occipit·ium -(i)ī *or* occip·ut -itis *n* back of the head

occīsi·ō -ōnis *f* murder, killing

occīs·or -ōris *m* murderer, killer

occīsus *pp of* occīdō

occlāmit·ō -āre -āvī -ātus *tr* to shout at ‖ *intr* to shout, yell

occlū·dō -dere -sī -sus *tr* (obc-) to close up, shut up, lock up; to close access to *(buildings);* to restrain

occ·ō -āre -āvī -ātus *tr* to harrow, break up *(the soil)*
occub·ō -āre *intr* to lie; to rest; **crūdēlibus umbrīs occubāre** to lie dead in the cruel lower world
occulc·ō -āre -āvī -ātus *tr* to trample down
occul·ō -ere -uī -tus *tr* to cover; to cover up, hide
occultāti·ō -ōnis *f* concealment, hiding
occultāt·or -ōris *m* one who conceals
occultē *adv* secretly, in secret
occult·ō -āre -āvī -ātus *tr* to hide, conceal; to suppress, keep *(facts, information)* secret **ǁ** *refl & pass* to hide
occult·us -a -um *pp of* **occulō ǁ** *adj* hidden, secret; clandestine; recondite *(expressions);* invisible *(forces of nature);* reserved *(person)* **ǁ** *n* concealment; secret; **ex occultō** from a concealed position; **in occultō** in hiding; **per occultum** without being observed, secretly
oc·cumbō occumbere occubuī occubitus *tr* to meet *(death)* **ǁ** *intr* to fall dying; *(w. dat or abl)* to meet *(death);* **occumbere per** *(w. acc)* to die at the hands of
occupāti·ō -ōnis *f* occupation, employment, business; business engagement, task, job; occupying *(of a town);* preoccupation, concentration, close attention
occupāt·us -a -um *adj* occupied, busy, engaged
occup·ō -āre -āvī -ātus *tr* to occupy; to seize; to grasp, grab; to win, gain; to attack, strike down; to outstrip, overtake; to fill up, occupy *(a space);* to assume *(title, position);* to invest; to loan, lend, invest *(money);* to head for, reach; to forestall; to take by surprise; to take the lead over *(competitor);* *(w. inf)* to be the first to
oc·currō -currere -currī *or* **-cucurrī -cursum** *intr* **(obc-)** to run up; *(w. dat)* **1** to run up to, run to meet, hurry to meet; **2** to rush against, attack; **3** to resist, oppose, counteract; **4** to meet, answer, reply to, object to; **5** to relieve, remedy; **6** to occur to, suggest itself to, present itself to; **7** run into, run up against, get involved in; **8** to encounter
occursāti·ō -ōnis *f* hustle and bustle; excited welcome; officiousness
occurs·ō -āre -āvī -ātus *tr* **(obc-)** to run to meet **ǁ** *intr (w dat)* **1** to run to meet, come to meet, meet; **2** to attack, charge, oppose; **3** *(of thoughts)* to occur to
occurs·us -ūs *m* meeting; *(w. gen)* running into *(s.o. or s.th.)*
Ōceanīt·is -idis *or* **-idos** *f* ocean nymph, daughter of Oceanus

ōcean·us -ī *m* ocean **ǁ Ōceanus** Oceanus *(son of Uranus and Ge and father of the river gods and ocean nymphs)*
ocell·us -ī *m* eye; gem; darling
ōcim·um -ī *n* basil *(seasoning)*
ōcin·um -ī *n* fodder *(possibly clover)*
ōci·or -or -us *adj* swifter, quicker
ōcius *adv (superl:* **ōcissimē)** more swiftly, more quickly; sooner; more easily; immediately, on the spot; *(w. abl)* rather than; **ōcius sērius** sooner or later; **quam ōcissime** as quickly as possible
ocre·a -ae *f* greave, shin guard
ocreāt·us -a -um *adj* wearing shin guards
octaphoros *see* **octōphoros**
octāv·a -ae *f* one-eighth; eighth hour of the day *(i.e., 2:00 p.m.)*
Octāvi·a -ae *f* sister of Augustus, wife of Gaius Marcellus, and later of Marc Antony *(64–11 B.C.)* **ǁ** daughter of Claudius and wife of Nero *(murdered in A.D. 62)*
Octāv·ius -(i)ī *m* Gaius Octavius *(Augustus, who, upon adoption by Julius Caesar, became Gaius Julius Caesar Octavianus, 63 B.C.–A.D. 14)*
octāvum *adv* for the eighth time
octāv·us -a -um *adj* eighth; **octāva pars** one-eighth **ǁ** *f see* **octāva ǁ** *n* **cum octāvō efficere** to produce an eightfold yield
octāv·us decim·us -a -um *adj* eighteenth
octiēns *or* **octiēs** *adv* eight times
octingentēsim·us -a -um *adj* eight hundreth
octingent·ī -ae -a *adj* eight hundred
octip·ēs -edis *adj* eight-footed
octiplicāt·us -a -um *adj* eightfold
octō *indecl adj* eighteen
Octō·ber -bris -bre *adj* October, of October; **mēnsis Octōber** October *(8th month of the Roman calendar until 153 B.C.)* **ǁ Octō·ber -bris** *m* October
octōdecim *indecl adj* eighteen
octōgē(n)sim·us -a -um *adj* eightieth
octōgēnāri·us -a -um *adj & m* octogenarian
octōgēn·ī -ae -a *adj* eighty each
octōgiē(n)s *adv* eighty times
octōiug·is -is -e *adj* eight-horse
octōn·ī -ae -a *adj* eight at a time, eight each
octōphor·os -os -on *adj* **(octa-)** carried by eight men **ǁ** *n* litter carried by eight men
octupl·us -a -um *adj* eightfold **ǁ** *n* eightfold fine
octuss·is -is *m* copper coin, worth about eight cents
oculāt·us -a -um *adj* having eyes; exposed to view, conspicuous; **oculātus testis** eyewitness
ocule·us -a -um *adj* many-eyed
oculissim·us -a -um *adj (hum)* dearest

oculitus *adv (to love s.o.)* like one's own eyes, dearly

ocul·us -ī *m* eye; eyeball; eye, bud *(in plants);* sight, vision; mind's eye; **aequīs oculīs** contentedly; **alterō oculō captus** blind in one eye; **ante oculōs** in full view; *(fig)* obvious; **ante oculōs pōnere** to imagine; **ex oculīs abīre** to go out of sight, disappear; **in oculīs** in view, in public, in the limelight; **in oculīs ferre** *(or* **gestāre)** to hold dear, value; **oculōs adicere** *(w.* **ad)** to eye; to covet; **oculōs dēicere ab** to take one's eyes off; *(fig)* to lose sight of; **oculōs pāscere** *(w. abl)* to feast one's eyes on; **sub oculīs** *(w. gen)* in the presence of, under the very nose of

ōdī odisse ōsus sum *tr* to have taken a dislike to, dislike, hate, be disgusted with

odiōsē *adv* hatefully; unpleasantly

odiōsic·us -a -um *adj (hum)* odious, unpleasant, annoying

odiōs·us -a -um *adj* odious, unpleasant, annoying

od·ium -(i)ī *n* dislike, aversion, hatred; object of hatred, nuisance; dissatisfaction, disgust; offensive conduct, insolence; **odiō esse** *(w. dat)* to be hateful to, be disliked by, be hated by ‖ *npl* feelings of hatred

od·or *or* **od·ōs -ōris** *m* odor, smell, scent; stench; pleasant smell, fragrance; perfume; inkling, suggestion, hint ‖ *mpl* perfume

odōrāti·ō -ōnis *f* smell, smelling

odōrāt·us -a -um *adj* fragrant, scented

odōrāt·us -ūs *m* smell, smelling; sense of smell

odōrif·er -era -erum *adj* fragrant

odōr·ō -āre -āvī -ātus *tr* to make fragrant

odōr·or -ārī -ātus sum *tr* to sniff at, scent; to aspire to, aim at; to be sniffing after, search for, investigate; to get a smattering of

odōr·us -a -um *adj* smelly; fragrant; keen-scented

odōs *see* **odor**

Odrys·ae -ārum *mpl* a people of the Thracian interior

Odrysi·us -a -um *adj & m* Thracian

Odyssē·a *or* **Odyssī·a -ae** *f* the *Odyssey*

Oea·ger *or* **Oea·grus -grī** *m* Oeager *(king of Thrace and father of Orpheus)*

Oeagri·us -a -um *adj* Thracian

Oea·gus -grī *m* king of Thrace and father of Orpheus

Oebalid·ēs -ae *m* male descendant of Oebalus *(see* **Oebalus)** ‖ *mpl* Castor and Pollux

Oebali·us -a -um *adj* Spartan; Tarentine; Sabine ‖ *f* Tarentum *(Spartan colony in S. Italy, modern Taranto)*

Oebal·us -ī *m* king of Sparta, father of Tyndareus, and grandfather of Helen, Clytemnestra, Castor, and Pollux

Oedip·ūs -odis *or* **-ī** *m* Oedipus

Oen·eùs -eī *or* **-eos** *m* king of Calydon, husband of Althaea, and father of Meleager and Dejanira

Oenīd·ēs -ae *m* descendant of Oeneus; Meleager; Diomedes

Oenoma·ǖs -ī *m* king of Pisa in the Peloponnesus and father of Hippodamia

oenophor·um -ī *n* wine-bottle basket

Oenopi·a -ae *f* ancient name of Aegina

oenopōl·ium -(i)ī *n* wine shop

Oenōtri·us -a -um *adj* Oenotrian, Italic ‖ *f* ancient name of S.E. Italy; Italy

oestr·us -ī *m* horsefly, gadfly; fancy, inspiration

oesyp·um -ī *n* **(-sop-)** lanolin

Oet·a -ae *or* **Oet·ē -ēs** *f* Mt. Oeta *(in S. Thessaly, on which Hercules died)*

Oetae·us -a -um *adj* Oetean ‖ *m* Hercules

ofell·a -ae *f* small chunk of meat

off·a -ae *f* lump; dumpling; lump, swelling

offectus *pp* of **officiō**

offen·dō -dere -dī -sus *tr* to bump, bump against, stub, strike, hit; to hit upon, come upon, meet with, bump into, stumble upon, find; to offend, shock; to annoy, disgust; to hurt *(feelings);* to injure *(reputation);* **nihil offendere** to suffer no damage, receive no injury ‖ *intr* to blunder, make a mistake; to give offense, be offensive; to fail, take a loss, be defeated, come to grief; to run aground; *(w. dat or* **in** *+ abl)* to hit against, bump against; *(w. dat)* to give offense to; *(w.* **in** *+ acc)* to take offense at; **terrae offendere** to run aground

offēns·a -ae *f* offense, affront; displeasure, resentment, hatred; crime; **offēnsā** *(w. gen)* out of hatred for

offēnsi·ō -ōnis *f* stubbing; tripping, stumbling; obstacle; setback, mishap; detriment; affront, outrage ‖ *fpl* offensive acts; feelings of displeasure

offēnsiuncul·a -ae *f* slight mishap

offēns·ō -āre -āvī -ātus *tr & intr* to bump

offēns·us -a -um *pp* of **offendō** ‖ *adj* offensive, odious; *(w. dat)* offended at, displeased with

offēns·us -ūs *m* bump; shock; offense

offerō offerre obtulī oblātus *tr* to offer, bring forward, present, show; to cause; to confer, bestow; to inflict; to deliver, hand over ‖ *refl (w. adj)* to show oneself to be; *(w. dat)* **1** to meet, encounter; **2** to expose oneself to *(e.g., danger);* **3** to give oneself up to *(an authority);* **4** to offer one's services to, volunteer for ‖ *refl & pass (esp. of an apparition)* to appear; *(of an idea)* to suggest itself

offerūment·a -ae *f (said humorously of a blow or welt)* present

officīn·a *or* **opificīn·a -ae** *f* shop, workshop, factory; office; artist's studio; training school

of·ficiō -ficere -fēcī -fectum *intr* (*w. dat*) **1** to get in the way of, interfere with, oppose; **2** to obstruct, hinder; **3** to be detrimental to

officiōsē *adv* obligingly, courteously

officiōs·us -a -um *adj* ready to serve, obliging; dutiful; officious

offic·ium -(i)ī *n* service, favor, kindness, courtesy; obligation, duty; function, part; social obligation, social call, social visit; ceremony; ceremonial observance, attendance; official duty; employment, business, job; sense of duty, conscience; allegiance; **officiō togae virīlis interesse** to attend the ceremony of the assuming of the manly toga

of·fīgō -fīgere -fīxī -fīxus *tr* to fasten down, nail down, drive in

offirmāt·us -a -um *adj* determined

offirm·ō -āre -āvī -ātus *refl & intr* to steel oneself, be determined

offlect·ō -ere *tr* to turn (*s.th.*) around

offrēnāt·us -a -um *adj* curbed

offrēn·ō -āre -āvī -ātus *tr* (*fig*) to curb

offūci·a -ae *f* cosmetic; (*fig*) trick, deception

offul·geō -gēre -sī *intr* (*w. dat*) to shine on

of·fundō -fundere -fūdī -fūsus *tr* to pour out; to cover; to fill; to eclipse **‖** *pass* (*w. dat*) to pour out over, spread over

oggann·iō -īre -īvī *or* **-iī -ītus** *tr or intr* to growl

ogger·ō -ere *tr* to bring, offer

Ogyg·ēs -is *or* **Ogyg·us -ī** *m* mythical king of Thebes, in whose reign the Deluge allegedly occurred

Ogygi·us -a -um *adj* Theban; **Ogygius deus** Theban god (*i.e., Bacchus*)

oh *interj* oh!

ōhē *or* **ohē** *interj* whoa!

Oïl·eus -eī *or* **-eos** *m* king of Locris in N. Greece and father of Ajax the archer

ole·a -ae *f* olive; olive tree

oleāgin·us -a -um *adj* olive, of an olive tree

oleāri·us -a -um *adj* oil, of oil **‖** *m* oil merchant

oleas·ter -trī *m* oleaster, wild olive tree

Ōleni·us -a -um *adj* of Olenus (*town in Achaia and Aetolia*); Achaian, Aetolian

ol·ēns -entis *adj* smelling; fragrant; smelly, stinking; musty

ol·eō -ēre -uī *tr* to smell of, smell like; (*fig*) to betray **‖** *intr* to smell; (*w. abl*) to smell of

ole·um -ī *n* olive oil, oil; (*fig*) palestra; **oleum addere camīnō** (*prov*) to pour oil on the fire; **oleum et operam perdere** to waste time and effort

ol·faciō -facere -fēcī -factus *tr* to smell

olfact·ō -āre -āvī -ātus *tr* to sniff at

olid·us -a -um *adj* smelly

ōlim *adv* once, once upon a time; at the time; for a good while; someday (*in the future*), hereafter; now and then, at times; ever, at any time

olit- = holit-

olīv·a -ae *f* olive; olive tree; olive wreath; olive branch; olive staff

olīvēt·um -ī *n* olive grove

olīvi·fer -fera -ferum *adj* producing olives, olive-growing

olīv·um -ī *n* olive oil; ointment; (*fig*) palestra

oll·a -ae *f* pot, jar

olle *or* **ollus = ille**

ol·or -ōris *m* swan

olōrīn·us -a -um *adj* swan

olus *see* **holus**

Olympi·a -ae *f* Olympia (*region in Elis, in the Peloponnesus, where the Olympic games were held*)

Olympi·a -ōrum *npl* Olympic games

Olympiac·us -a -um *adj* Olympic

Olympi·as -adis *or* **-ados** *f* Olympiad (*period of 4 years between Olympic games, starting in 776 B.C., according to which the Greeks reckoned time*) **‖** Olympias (*wife of Philip V of Macedon and mother of Alexander the Great*)

Olympic·us -a -um *adj* Olympic, of the games held at Olympia

Olympionīc·ēs -ae *m* Olympic victor

Olympi·us -a -um *adj* Olympian (*cult title of Zeus*); (*of games*) Olympic, held at Olympia; (*of temple*) dedicated to Olympian Zeus

Olymp·us -ī *m* Mt. Olympus (*on the boundary of Macedonia and Thessaly, regarded as the home of the gods*)

omās·um -ī *n* tripe

ōm·en -inis *n* omen (*good or bad*); foreboding; **ōmen accipere** to believe an event to be an omen; **prīma ōmina** first marriage; (**procul**) **ōmen abestō!** (*or* **quod ōmen dī āvertant!**) God forbid!

ōment·um -ī *n* fatty membrane covering the bowels; the bowels

ōmināt·or -ōris *m* diviner

ōmin·or -ārī -ātus sum *tr* to foretell, predict, forebode

ōminōs·us -a -um *adj* ominous

ōmīsī *perf of* **ōmittō**

ōmiss·us -a -um *pp of* **ōmittō ‖** *adj* remiss, negligent, heedless

ōmittō ōmittere ōmīsī ōmissus *tr* to let go; to let go of, let fall, drop; to give up, abandon; to omit, pass over; to overlook, disregard; to release from custody; to allow to escape; to discard

omnigen·us -a -um *adj* (*also indecl*) every kind of

omnimodīs *or* **omnimodō** *adv* by all means, wholly

omnīnō *adv* altogether, entirely, wholly; *(w. numerals)* in all; *(in generalizations)* in general; *(in concessions)* no doubt, to be sure, yes, by all means; **haud omnīnō** *(or* **nōn omnīnō)** not quite, not entirely; absolutely not, not at all; not expressly; **omnīnō nēmō** absolutely no one

omnipar·ēns -entis *adj* all-producing *(earth)*

omnipot·ēns -entis *adj* omnipotent

omn·is -is -e *adj* all, every; every kind of; the whole ‖ *mpl* all, everybody ‖ *n* the universe ‖ *npl* all things, everything; all nature; all the world

omnitu·ēns -entis *adj* all-seeing

omnivag·us -a -um *adj* roaming everywhere

omnivol·us -a -um *adj* all-craving

Omphal·ē -ēs *f* Lydian queen who bought Hercules as a slave for a year

ona·ger *or* **ona·grus -grī** *m* wild ass

onāg·os -ī *m* ass-driver

Onchēsmīt·ēs -ae *m* wind blowing from Onchesmus *(harbor in Epirus)*

onerāri·us -a -um *adj* carrying freight; **iūmenta onerāria** beasts of burden; **onerāria** *(or* **nāvis onerāria)** freighter, transport

oner·ō -āre -āvī -ātus *tr* to load, load down, burden; *(fig)* to overload, oppress; *(fig)* to pile on, aggravate

onerōs·us -a -um *adj* onerous, burdensome, oppressive; heavy

on·us -eris *n* burden; load; freight, cargo; trouble; tax burden; fetus, embryo; **onerī esse** *(w. dat)* to be a burden to

onust·us -a -um *adj* loaded down, burdened; filled, full

on·yx -ychis *mf* onyx; onyx box

opācit·ās -ātis *f* shade, shadiness

opāc·ō -āre -āvī -ātus *tr* to shade, make shady

opāc·us -a -um *adj* shady; dark, obscure ‖ *npl* **opāca locōrum** shady places; **opāca viārum** dark streets

opell·a -ae *f* light work; small effort

oper·a -ae *f* effort, pains, exertion; work; care, attention; service, assistance; leisure, spare time; laborer, workman, artisan; a day's work *(by one person);* **operae esse** *(or* **operae pretium esse)** to be worthwhile; **operam dare** to take pains, exert oneself, be busied, pay attention, give attention, apply oneself; **operam fūnerī dare** to attend a funeral; **operam magistrō dare** *(or* **reddere)** to attend a teacher's lectures, study under a teacher; **operam lūdere** *(or* **perdere)** to waste one's time and effort; **operam sermōnī dare** to listen to a conversation; **operam tōnsōrī dare** to go see a barber, get

a haircut; **operā meā (tuā,** *etc.)* through my (your, *etc.)* agency, thanks to me (you, *etc.)*

operāri·us -a -um *adj* working; working for hire ‖ *m* workman ‖ *f* working woman

opercul·um -i *n* lid, cover

operīment·um -ī *n* lid, cover

oper·iō -īre -uī -tus *tr* to cover, cover up; to shut; to hide; to clothe; to bury; to bury with a shower of missiles

oper·or -ārī -ātus sum *intr* to work hard, take pains; *(w. dat)* **1** to work hard at, be busied with, be engaged in; **2** to perform *(religious services);* **3** to attend; **4** to worship

operōsē *adv* with great effort, at great pains

operōs·us -a -um *adj* active, busy, painstaking; troublesome, difficult, elaborate; efficacious, powerful *(drugs)*

opertus *pp of* **operiō** ‖ *adj* closed; hidden; secret ‖ *n* secret; secret place; **in opertō** inside, in secret ‖ *npl* depth; veiled oracles

operuī *perf of* **operiō**

opēs *see* **ops**

ophīt·ēs -ae *m* serpentine *(type of marble)*

Ophiūsi·us -a -um *adj* Cyprian ‖ *f* old name of Cyprus

ophthalmi·ās -ae *m* a type of fish

ophthalmic·us -ī *m* eye-doctor

Opic·us -a -um *adj* Oscan; boorish; ignorant *(esp. of Latin),* uncultured

opif·er -era -erum *adj* helpful

opif·ex -icis *m* maker, creator; craftsman, mechanic

opificīn·a -ae *f* workshop

opific·ium -(i)ī *n* work

ōpili·ō -ōnis *m* shepherd

opīmē *adv* splendidly; richly

opīmit·ās -ātis *f* prosperity

opīm·us -a -um *adj* fat, plump; fertile, fruitful; rich, enriched; abundant, plentiful; sumptuous, splendid; lucrative; noble; **spolia opīma** armor stripped from one general by another on the field of battle

opīnābil·is -is -e *adj* conjectural, imaginary

opīnāti·ō -ōnis *f* mere opinion, conjecture, supposition, hunch

opīnāt·us -a -um *adj* supposed, imagined

opīnāt·us -ūs *m* supposition

opīni·ō -ōnis *f* opinion; conjecture, guess, supposition; expectation; general impression; estimation; rumor; reputation, bad reputation; **amplius opīniōne** beyond expectation, beyond all hopes; **celerius opīniōne** sooner than expected; **hāc opīniōne ut** under the impression that; **in opīniōne esse** *(w. acc & inf)* to be of the opinion that; **praebēre opīniōnem timōris** to convey the impression of fear; **praeter opīniōnem** contrary to expectation, sooner than expected; **ut opīniō mea est** as I suppose opīn·ō -āre *or* opīn·or -ārī -ātus sum *tr* to suppose, imagine, conjecture ‖ *intr (parenthetical)* to suppose, imagine

opiparē *adv* splendidly, sumptuously

opipar·us -a -um *adj* splendid, sumptuous, ritzy

opisthograph·us -a -um *adj* written on the back; **in opisthographō** on the reverse side of a document

opitul·or -ārī -ātus sum *intr (w. dat)* to bring help to, assist

oport·et -ēre -uit *v impers* it is right, it is proper; **mē abīre oportet** I ought to go, I should go

op·pangō -pangere -ēgī -pāctus *tr* to affix, imprint

oppect·ō -ere *tr* to comb off; *(coll)* to pluck, pick at, eat

oppēdō -ere *intr (vulg) (w. dat)* **1** to fart at; **2** *(fig)* to deride, mock

opper·ior -īrī -tus sum *tr* to wait for; *(w.* **num)** to wait and see whether ‖ *intr* to wait

oppet·ō -ere -īvī *or* -iī -ītus *tr* to meet, encounter *(prematurely)* ‖ *intr* to meet death, die

oppidān·us -a -um *adj* of a town, in a town; *(pej)* provincial ‖ *mpl* townspeople

oppidō *adv* absolutely, quite; *(as affirmative answer)* exactly, extremely; **oppidō quam breve intervallum** an extremely short distance

oppidul·um -ī *n* small town

oppid·um -ī *n* town

oppigner·ō -āre -āvī -ātus *tr* to pledge

oppīl·ō -āre -āvī -ātus *tr* to shut up, shut off

oppl·eō -ēre -ēvī -ētus *tr* to fill up, fill completely

op·pōnō -pōnere -posuī -positus *tr* to put, place, station; to oppose; to expose, lay bare, open; to wager; to mortgage; to bring forward, adduce, allege; to reply, object; to compare; **currum oppōnere** to block a rival's chariot

opportūnē *adv* at the right time

opportūnit·ās -ātis *f* opportunity, chance *(to do s.th.);* right time, opportuneness; advantage; suitability, fitness, convenience

opportūn·us -a -um *adj* opportune, suitable, convenient; advantageous, useful; exposed; **tempore opportūnissimō** in the nick of time

oppositi·ō -ōnis *f* opposition

opposit·us -a -um *pp of* **oppōnō** ‖ *adj* opposite; *(w. dat)* opposite, across from

oppressi·ō -ōnis *f* force, violence, violent seizure; suppression, overthrow

oppressiuncul·a -ae *f* slight pressure

oppressus *pp of* **opprimō**

oppress·us -ūs *m* pressure

op·primō -primere -pressī -pressus *tr* **(obp-)** to press down, weigh down; to pressure, put pressure on; to shut; to overwhelm; to put down, quell; to sink *(ship);* to subvert, overthrow, crush, overpower; to conceal, suppress; to catch

opprobrāment·um -ī *n* disgrace, scandal

opprobr·ium -(i)ī *n* **(obp-)** disgrace, scandal, reproach; cause of disgrace; taunt, abuse, abusive word

opprobr·ō -āre -āvī -ātus *tr* **(obp-)** to throw up *(s.th.)* to *(s.o. as a reproach)*

oppugnāti·ō -ōnis *f* **(opr-)** assault; *(fig)* attack, accusation

oppugnāt·or -ōris *m* **(obp-)** assailant

oppugn·ō -āre -āvī -ātus *tr* to assault, attack, storm; *(fig)* to attack, assail

ops- = obs-

ops opis *f* power, might; help, aid; influence, weight; **nōn opis est nostrae** it is not in our power; **ope meā** with my help; **opem ferre** *(w. dat)* to bring help to, help ‖ *fpl* wealth, resources, means; military *or* political resources; *(ex)* **summīs opibus** with all one's might ‖ **Ops** *(goddess of abundance (sister and wife of Saturn and mother of Jupiter)*

optābil·is -is -e *adj* desirable

optāti·ō -ōnis *f* wishing, wish

optātō *adv* according to one's wish

optāt·us -a -um *adj* longed-for, desired, welcome ‖ *n* wish, desire

optigō *see* **obtegō**

optim·ās -ātis *m* **(-tum-)** aristocrat ‖ *mpl* aristocracy, aristocratic party

optimē *(superl of* **bene)** *adv* **(-tum-)** very well; thoroughly; best; most opportunely, just in time

optim·us -a -um *(superl of* **bonus)** *adj* **(-tum-)** very good, best; excellent; most beneficial, most advantageous; *(of a legal title)* most valid, having the soundest basis; **in optimam partem** most favorably; **optimā fide** with the utmost honesty; **optimum est** *(w. inf)* it is best to; **optimum factū est** *(w. inf)* the best thing to do is to; **ut optimus maximusque** *(leg) (of property)* in its optimum condition *(i.e., free from all encumbrances)*

opti·ō -ōnis *f* option, choice ‖ *m* helper, assistant; *(mil)* adjutant

optīv·us -a -um *adj* chosen

opt·ō -āre -āvī -ātus *tr* to choose, select; to pray for; to wish for, desire

optum- = optim-

opul·ēns -entis *adj* opulent, rich

opulentē *or* opulenter *adv* richly

opulenti·a -ae *f* opulence, wealth; resources; power

opulentit·ās -ātis *f* opulence; power

opulent·ō -āre -āvī -ātus *tr* to make rich, enrich

opulent·us -a -um *adj* opulent, rich; sumptuous; powerful

op·us -eris *n* work; product of work: structure, building; literary work, composition, book; work of art, workmanship; deed, achievement; literary genre; occupation, employment; what a person is expected to do, function, business; *(w. gen) (poet)* a thing the size of; *(mil)* offensive works, siege works; *(mil)* defensive works, fortifications; **dulce opus peragere** to perform one's pleasant business *(i.e., sexual intercourse);* **in opere** at work; **magnō opere** greatly, to a great extent; **māiōre (summō) opere** to a greater (the greatest) extent; **opere** *(w. gen)* through the agency of; **quantō opere** how much, how greatly; **tantō opere** so much, so greatly; **operis alicūius esse** to be s.o.'s doing; **opus est** *(w. dat of person in need and abl of person or thing needed)* to need, *e.g.,* **opus est mihi duce** I need a leader; **suī operis esse** to be part of one's business

opuscul·um -ī *n* little work, minor work, small job

-or -ōris *m suf* forms nouns denoting **1** abstracts, *e.g.:* **candor** whiteness; **amor** love; **2** doer of the action of the verb, *e.g.,* **amātor** lover

ōr·a -ae *f* boundary, border, edge; coastline; coast; region, district; cable, hawser; *(fig)* people of the coast, people of the region; division of the world; **ōra maritima** seacoast ‖ *fpl* region, land; **ōrae extremae** the most distant lands, farthest shores; **ōrae lūminis** *(or* **ōrae superae)** the upper world

ōrāc(u)l·um -ī *n* oracle; prophesy

ōrāri·us -a -um *adj* coasting; **nāvis ōrāria** coasting vessel, coaster

ōrāt·a -ōrum *npl* prayer, requests

ōrāti·ō -ōnis *f* faculty of speech; speech, language; style of speech, manner of speaking, style, expression; oration, speech; theme, subject; prose; eloquence; dialect; imperial rescript; **ōrātiōnem habēre** to give a speech; **ōrātiō solūta** *(or* **ōrātiō prōsa)** prose; **pars ōrātiōnis** part of speech

ōrātiuncul·a -ae *f* short speech, insignificant speech

ōrāt·or -ōris *m* orator, speaker; suppliant; spokesman

ōrātōriē *adv* oratorically

ōrātōri·us -a -um *adj* orator's, oratorical

ōrātr·īx -īcis *f* suppliant *(female)*

ōrāt·us -ūs *m* request

orb·a -ae *f* orphan

orbāt·or -ōris *m* murderer *(of s.o.'s children or parents)*

Orbil·ius -(i)ī *m* Lucius Orbilius Pupillus *(Horace's teacher in Venusia)*

orb·is -is *m* circle; disk, ring; orbit *(of heavenly bodies);* quoit; hoop; wheel; spinning wheel; potter's wheel; round shield; eye socket, eye; globe, earth, world, universe; region, territory, country; circuit, round; rotation; cycle, period; zodiac; *(rhet)* balance; **magnus orbis** a year; **orbis caelī** vault of heaven; **Orbis Lacteus** Milky Way; **orbis lūminis** eye; **orbis noster** our section of the world; **orbis oculī** eyeball; **orbis terrae** *(or* **terrārum)** earth, world, universe

orbit·a -ae *f* rut; *(astr)* orbit; *(fig)* routine

orbit·ās -ātis *f* childlessness, widowhood, orphanhood

orbitōs·us -a -um *adj* full of ruts

orb·ō -āre -āvī -ātus *tr* to bereave of parents, father, mother, children, husband, *or* wife; to strip, rob, deprive; to make destitute

orb·us -a -um *adj* bereaved, bereft; destitute; orphaned, fatherless; childless; widowed; *(w. gen or abl or* **ab)** bereft of, without ‖ *mf* orphan

orc·a -ae *f* vat

Orcad·es -um *fpl* islands N. of Scotland *(modern Orkneys)*

orch·as -adis *f* a kind of olive

orchestr·a -ae *f* senatorial seats *(in the theater);* orchestra *(area in front of the Greek stage where the chorus sang and danced)*

Orc·us -ī *m* lower world; Pluto *(king of the lower world);* death

orde- = horde-

ōrdināri·us -a -um *adj* ordinary, usual, regular; normally elected *(consul)*

ōrdinātim *adv* in order, in good order; in succession; regularly

ōrdināti·ō -ōnis *f* orderly arrangement; orderly government

ōrdināt·us -a -um *adj* regular; appointed

ōrdin·ō -āre -āvī -ātus *tr* to set in order, arrange, regulate; to govern, rule; to record chronologically

ōrdior ōrdīrī ōrsus sum *tr* to begin, undertake; to describe ‖ *intr* to begin; to begin to speak

ōrd·ō -inis *m* line, row; series; row of seats *(in theater);* order, methodical arrangement; order, class; social standing, rank, position; *(mil)* line, file *(of soldiers),* company, century; command of a company *or* century; **amplissimus ōrdō** senatorial order; **ex ōrdine** in succession, without a break; **extrā ōrdinem** extraordinarily, especially, uncommonly; **in ōrdine** *(mil)* in regular order, in battle array; **in ōrdinem cōgere** *(or* **redigere)** to put *(s.o.)* in his place, tell *(s.o.)* off; **ōrdine** *(or* **in ōrdine** *or* **per ōrdinem)** in order, in sequence; in a straight line; in detail;

with regularity, regularly **ll** *mpl* officers of a company; promotions

Orē·as -adis *or* **-ados** *f* Oread *(mountain nymph)*

Orest·ae -ārum *mpl* tribe on the borders of Macedonia and Epirus

Orest·ēs -is *or* **-ae** *m* son of Agamemnon and Clytemnestra

Orestē·us -a -um of Orestes

orex·is -is *f* craving, appetite

organic·us -ī *m* organist

organ·um -ī *n* instrument, implement; musical instrument; water organ; organ pipe; **organum hydraulicum** water organ

orgi·a -ōrum *npl* Bacchic revels; orgies

orichalc·um -ī *n* copper ore; brass

ōricill·a -ae *f* little ear; lobe

ori·ēns -entis *m* rising sun, morning sun; morning; day; land of the rising sun, Orient, the East; **ab oriente** in the East

orīg·ō -inis *f* origin, source, beginning, start; birth, lineage, descent; race, stock, family; founder, progenitor; derivation *(of a word)*

Ōrī·ōn -ōnis *or* **-ōnos** *m* giant hunter, killed by Diana and turned into a constellation; *(astr)* Orion

orior orīrī ortus sum *intr* to rise; to get up; to become visible, appear; to be born, originate, be descended; to proceed, begin, start; *(of a spring, river)* to rise; *(of living creatures)* to come into existence, be born; *(of plants)* to come up, sprout; *(of events)* to arise, crop up; **homō ā sē ortus** a self-made man

Ōrīthȳi·a -ae *f* daughter of Erechtheus, king of Athens

oriund·us -a -um *adj* descended; *(w. abl)* originating from, originally from *(a place)*

ōrnāment·um -ī *n* equipment, trappings, apparatus; ornament, decoration; trinket, jewel; *(fig)* distinction; pride and joy; *(rhet)* rhetorical device

ōrnātē *adv* ornately, elegantly

ōrnātr·īx -īcis *f* hairdresser *(female)*

ōrnāt·us -ūs *m* equipment; apparel, outfit; furniture; decoration, ornament; preparation; *(rhet)* rhetorical embellishment

ōrn·ō -āre -āvī -ātus *tr* to equip, fit out, furnish; to outfit, dress; to set off, decorate, adorn; to show *(s.o.)* respect; *(w. abl)* **1** to honor with; **2** *(of things)* to give distinction to, enhance

orn·us -ī *f (bot)* mountain ash

ōr·ō -āre -āvī -ātus *tr* to beg, entreat, implore, plead with; to ask for; *(w. double acc)* to ask *(s.o.)* for; *(leg)* to plead *(a case)* **ll** *intr* to plead, beg, pray; *(w.* **cum***)* to plead with, argue with

Orōd·ēs -is *m* name of several eastern kings, *esp.* Orodes II of Parthia, whose general defeated Crassus at Carrhae *(53 B.C.)*

Oront·ēs -is *or* **-ae** *m* chief river of Syria **ll** companion of Aeneas

Orontē·us -a -um *adj* from the River Orontes, Syrian

Orph·eūs -eī *or* **-eos** *m* famous musician and poet, husband of Eurydice

Orphē·us *or* **Orphic·us -a -um** *adj* Orphic

ōrs·us -a -um *pp of* **ōrdior ll** *npl* beginnings; utterance, words; attempt

ōrs·us -ūs *m* beginning; attempt, undertaking

orthographi·a -ae *f* spelling

ortus *pp of* **orlor**

ort·us -ūs *m* rising; sunrise, daybreak; the East; birth *(of living creatures);* origin; source; **sōlis ortus** sunrise; the East; beginning, dawning *(of a period)*

Ortygi·a -ae *or* **Ortygi·ē -ēs** *f* Ortygia *(old name of Delos)* **ll** Ortygia *(island in the port of Syracuse in Sicily)* **ll** Ortygia *(old name of Ephesus)*

Ortygi·us -a -um *adj* of Ortygia, Delian; Syracusan

or·yx -ygis *m* gazelle

oryz·a -ae *f* rice

ōs ōris *n* mouth; beak; voice, speech; expression; lip, face, countenance, look; sight, presence *(of a person);* impudence; mask; opening, orifice, front; **favēte ōre!** observe a respectful silence!; **habēre aliquid in ōre** to be talking about s.th. continually; **in ōra hominum venīre** to become a household name; **in ōre omnium esse** to be on the lips of all; **in ōs aliquem laudāre** to praise s.o. to his face; **ōs amnis** mouth of a river; **ōs dūrum** hardened look *or* expression, big mouth; **ōs laedere** *(w. dat)* to insult s.o. to his, her face; **ōs oblinere** *(w. dat)* to hoodwink *(s.o.);* **ōs ostendere** to show one's face; **ōs timidum** expression of fear; **ōs vēnae** opening in a blood vessel; **per ōra ferrī** to go from mouth to mouth; **per** *(or* **praeter)* **ōra nostra** before our eyes; **summō ōre** just with the lips; **tria Dianae ōra** the three forms of Diana; **ūnō ōre** unanimously

os ossis *n* bone; marrow, innermost parts; kernel *(of a nut);* stone *(of fruit)* **ll** *npl* bones; skeleton; **ossa legere** to collect the bones *(from a pyre)*

ōsc·en -inis *mf* foreboding bird *(a bird of augury from whose note auguries were taken, e.g., crow, raven, owl)*

ōscill·um -ī *n* small mask

ōscit·āns -antis *adj* yawning; *(fig)* indifferent, bored

ōscit·ō -āre -āvī -ātus *or* **ōscit·or -ārī -ātus sum** *intr* to gape; to yawn

ōsculāti·ō -ōnis f kissing
ōscul·or -ārī -ātus sum tr to kiss; (fig) to make a fuss over
ōscul·um -ī n kiss; mouth, lips (usually, puckered for a kiss); breve ōsculum peck
Ōsc·us -a -um adj Oscan ‖ mpl Oscans (ancient people of Campania and Samnium)
Ōs·ī -ōrum mpl people of Germany on the Danube
Osīr·is -is or -idis m Egyptian god, husband of Isis
ōs·or -ōris m hater
Oss·a -ae f mountain in N.E. Thessaly
osse·us -a -um adj bony
osten·dō -dere -dī -tus or -sus tr to hold out for inspection; to show, exhibit, display, expose; to stretch out, stretch forth; to bring to one's attention; to expose; to reveal, disclose; to declare, make known; to represent in art; ōs ostendere to show one's face ‖ refl to show oneself, appear; sē optimē ostendere to appear very friendly
ostentāti·ō -ōnis f display; ostentation, showing off; mere show, pretense
ostentāt·or -ōris m show-off
ostent·ō -āre -āvī -ātus tr to show, exhibit; to show off, display, parade, boast of; to declare, point out, set forth
ostent·um -ī n portent, prodigy
ostent·us -ūs m display, show; ostentuī for appearances
Ōsti·a -ae f or Ōsti·a -ōrum npl Ostia (port town at mouth of Tiber)
ōstiār·ium -(i)ī n tax on doors
ōstiār·ius -(i)ī m doorman
ōstiātim adv from door to door
ōst·ium -(i)ī n door; entranceway; entrance, mouth
ostre·a -ae f or ostre·um -ī n oyster
ostreāt·us -a -um adj covered with oyster shells; (fig) black-and-blue
ostreōs·us -a -um adj abounding in oysters
ostri·fer -fera -ferum adj producing oysters, oyster-bearing
ostrīn·us -a -um adj purple
ostr·um -ī n purple dye; purple; purple garment, purple coverlet
-ōs·us -a -um adjl suf (formed chiefly from nouns) abounding in, rich in, full of: ostreōsus abounding in oysters
ōsus pp of ōdī
ōsūrus fut p of ōdī
Oth·ō -ōnis m Marcus Salvius Otho (Roman emperor in A.D. 69) ‖ Lucius Roscius Otho (author of the law of 67 B.C. reserving 14 rows in theaters for the equestrian order)
Othr·ys -yos m mountain range in S. Thessaly
ōtiol·um -ī n bit of leisure
ōti·or -ārī -ātus sum intr to take it easy

ōtiōsē adv at leisure; leisurely, without haste; calmly, fearlessly
ōtiōs·us -a -um adj at leisure, relaxing, having nothing to do; free from official obligations; quiet, calm; undisturbed; unconcerned, indifferent, neutral; passionless; having no practical use, useless; superfluous, unnecessary; leading a peaceful existence; (of land) unoccupied, vacant ‖ m private person (not holding public office); civilian, non-combatant
ōt·ium -(i)ī n leisure, free time, relaxation; freedom from public affairs, retirement; peace, quiet; peaceful relations (with another country); ease, idleness, inactivity; calm weather; respite, lull; (in) ōtiō (or per otium) at leisure, undisturbed; in ōtium venīre to retire, go into retirement
ov·āns -antis adj joyful, jubilant
ovāti·ō -ōnis f ovation, minor triumph (in which the victor went on foot rather than driving a chariot)
ovāt·us -a -um adj triumphal, of an ovation
Ovid·ius -(i)ī m Ovid (Publius Ovidius Naso, Latin poet, born at Sulmo, 43 B.C.–A.D. 17)
ovīl·e -is n sheepfold; voting enclosures in the Campus Martius
ovīlis -is -e adj sheep, of sheep
ovill·a -ae f mutton, lamb
ovill·us -a -um adj sheep, of sheep
ov·is -is f sheep; wool; simpleton, ninny
ov·ō -āre -āvī -ātum intr to rejoice; to hold a celebration; to celebrate a minor triumph
ōv·um -ī n egg ‖ npl wooden balls used to mark the laps at the racetrack
oxycomin·a -ōrum npl pickled olives
oxygar·um -ī n fish sauce containing vinegar

P

P, p (supply littera) f fifteenth letter of the Latin alphabet; letter name: pe
P. abbr Pūblius (Roman first name, praenomen)
pābulāti·ō -ōnis f foraging
pābulāt·or -ōris m forager
pābul·or -ārī -ātus sum intr to forage; to feed, graze; (coll) to make a living
pābul·um -ī n feed, fodder; pasturage; grass; (fig) nourishment, fuel
pācāl·is -is -e adj of peace, peaceful
pācāt·us -a -um adj peaceful, quiet, calm; (of people) living in peace; of peacetime; pacified (euphemism for conquered); pācātae rāmus olīvae the olive branch, symbolic of peace; vīcī male pācātī villages not completely pacified ‖ n peaceful countryside

Pachȳn·um -ī *n or* **Pachȳn·os -ī** *f* S.E. point of Sicily

pācif·er -era -erum *adj* peace-bringing, peaceful; *(of olive and laurel)* symbolizing peace

pācificāti·ō -ōnis *f* pacification

pācificāt·or -ōris *m* peacemaker

pācificātōri·us -a -um *adj* peace-making

pācific·ō -āre -āvī -ātus *tr* to pacify, appease ‖ *intr* to make peace, conclude peace

pācific·us -a -um *adj* peace-making; peaceable

pac·īscor -īscī -tus sum *tr* to bargain for, agree upon; to stipulate; to barter; to become engaged to ‖ *intr* to come to an agreement, strike a bargain, make a contract; *(w. inf)* to agree to, pledge oneself to

pāc·ō -āre -āvī -ātus *tr* to pacify, soothe; to reclaim *(land by war)*

pact·a -ae *f* fiancée; bride

pacti·ō -ōnis *f* pact, contract, agreement; treaty, terms; condition, stipulation; collusion; *(leg)* settlement *(in a dispute);* **pactiō nūptiālis** marriage contract

Pactōl·us *or* **Pactōl·os -ī** *m* river in Lydia famous for its gold

pact·or -ōris *m* contractor, party *(in a contract);* negotiator

pact·um -ī *n* pact, contract, agreement; way, manner; **aliquō pactō** somehow; **ex pactō** according to the contract; **hōc pactō** in this way; **in pactō manēre** to stick to an agreement; **quō pactō** in what way

pact·us -a -um *pp of* **pacīscor** *and* **pangō** ‖ *adj* agreed, settled, determined, stipulated; **coniunx pacta** the betrothed, fiancée

Pācuv·ius -(i)ī *m* Marcus Pacuvius *(c. 220–133 B.C., Roman tragic poet, native of Brundisium and nephew of Ennius)*

Pad·us -ī *m* Po River *(in N. Italy)*

Padūs·a -ae *f* one of the mouths of the Po River

pae·ān -ānis *m* hymn to Apollo; paean, hymn of praise, victory song ‖ **Paeān** epithet of Apollo as god of healing

paedagōg·ium -iī *n* (pēd-) training school for pages

paedagōg·us -ī *m* (pēd-) slave in charge of school children; *(fig)* guide, leader

paedīc·ō -āre -āvī -ātus *tr* (pēd-) to have homosexual relations with *(boys)*

paedīc·ō -ōnis *m* (pēd-) homosexual, pedophile

paed·or -ōris *m* (ped-) filth

pael·ex -icis *f* (pēl-, pell-) concubine, mistress

paelicāt·us -ūs *m* (pēl-) concubinage

Paelign·ī -ōrum *mpl* (Pēl-) a people of central Italy

paene *adv* nearly, almost

paenīnsul·a -ae *f* peninsula

paenitend·us -a -um *adj* regrettable

paenitenti·a -ae *f* (poen-) repentance, regret

paenit·eō -ēre -uī paenitūrus *tr* (poen-) to cause to regret; to displease ‖ *intr (w. gen)* to regret ‖ *v impers (w. acc of person), e.g.,* **mē paenitet** I am sorry; *(w. acc of person and gen of thing), e.g.,* **mē paenitet cōnsilī** I regret the idea, am dissatisfied with the plan; *(w. acc of person and inf or* **quod***), e.g.,* **eōs paenitet animum tuum offendisse** *(or* **eōs paenitet quod animum tuum offenderint)** they regret having offended your feelings

paenul·a -ae *f* travel coat; raincoat

paenulāt·us -a -um *adj* wearing a traveling coat *or* raincoat

pae·ōn -ōnis *m (pros)* metrical foot containing one long and three short syllables *(first paeonic:* — ◡ ◡ ◡; *second paeonic:* ◡ — ◡ ◡; *third paeonic:* ◡ ◡ — ◡; *fourth paeonic:* ◡ ◡ ◡ —)

Paeon·es -um *mpl* a people inhabiting Paeonia

Paeoni·a -ae *f* Paeonia *(the country N. of Macedonia)*

paeōni·us -a -um *adj* healing, medicinal; **herba paeōnia** peony

Paestān·us -a -um *adj* of Paestum

Paest·um -ī *n* town in Lucania in S. Italy, famous for its roses

paetul·us -a -um *adj* slightly squint-eyed

paet·us -a -um *adj* squinting, squint-eyed; leering ‖ **Paetus** *m* Roman family name *(cognomen)*

pāgān·us -a -um *adj* of a village, rustic; ignorant ‖ *m* villager, peasant; *(pej)* yokel

Pagas·a -ae *f or* **Pagas·ae -ārum** *fpl* town on the E. coast of Thessaly from which the *Argo* set sail

Pagasae·us -a -um *adj* Pagasean ‖ *m* Jason

pāgātim *adv* by villages, village by village, in every village

pāgell·a -ae *f* small page *or* sheet

pāgin·a -ae *f* page; *(poet)* piece of writing; **in īmā pāginā** at the bottom of the page

pāginul·a -ae *f* small page *or* sheet

pāg·us -ī *m* village; canton, province; country people, villagers

pāl·a -ae *f* spade

palaestr·a -ae *f* palaestra, wrestling school, gymnasium; school of rhetoric; rhetorical training; school; wrestling; exercise; brothel

palaestricē *adv* as at the palaestra

palaestric·us -a -um *adj* of the palaestra, gymnastic ‖ *f* gymnastics

palaestrīt·a -ae *m* wrestling coach; director of a palaestra

palam *adv* openly, publicly, plainly; **palam esse** to be public, be well known; **palam facere** to make public, disclose ‖ *prep (w.*

abl) before, in the presence of, face to face with

Palātīn·us -a -um *adj* Palatine; imperial

Palāt·ium -(i)ī *n* Palatine Hill; palace; a temple on the Palatine

palāt·um -ī *n or* **palāt·us -ī** *m (anat)* palate; *(fig)* taste; *(fig)* literary taste

pale·a -ae *f* chaff

paleār·ia -ium *npl* dewlap *(fold of skin that hangs from the neck of a bovine animal)*

Pal·ēs -is *f* Italic goddess of shepherds and flocks

Palīc·ī -ōrum *mpl* twin sons of Jupiter and the nymph Thalia

Palīl·is -is -e *adj* of Pales ‖ *npl* feast of Pales *(celebrated April 21)*

palimpsest·um -ī *n* palimpsest *(parchment from which writing has been erased and new writing put on)*

Palinūr·us -ī *m* pilot of Aeneas who fell overboard and drowned ‖ promontory named after Palinurus

paliūr·us *or* **paliūr·os -ī** *mf (bot)* Christ's thorn *(a plant)*

pall·a -ae *f* ladies' long outdoor dress *(counterpart of the male's toga); male outer garment (restricted to non-Romans);* tragic actor's costume

pallac·a -ae *f* concubine

Pallacīn·a -ae *f* section of Rome near the Circus Flaminius

Palladi·us -a -um *adj* of Pallas, associated with Pallas Athene *(Minerva)* ‖ *n* statue of Pallas; Palladium *(Trojan statue of Pallas allegedly stolen by Odysseus and said subsequently to have been brought to Rome, since the safety of the city depended on it)*

Pallantē·um -ī *n* city in Arcadia, the home of Pallas ‖ city founded by Evander in Italy where Rome later stood

Pallantē·us -a -um *adj* of Pallas *(great-grandfather of Evander)*

Pall·as -adis *or* **-ados** *f* Athene; olive oil, oil; olive tree; Palladium *(Trojan statue of Pallas)*

Pall·ās -antis *m* great-grandfather of Evander ‖ son of Evander ‖ son of Pandion and brother of Aegeus ‖ father of Minerva

pall·ēns -entis *adj* pale; chartreuse, yellowish; sick-looking; dim *(light)*

pall·eō -ēre -uī *intr* to be pale, look pale; to have a pale *(greenish or yellowish)* color; to fade; to be dim; *(w. dat)* to grow pale over, worry about

pall·ēscō -ēscere -uī *tr* to turn pale at ‖ *intr* to turn pale; to turn yellow; to fade, grow dim

palliāt·us -a -um *adj* wearing a Greek cloak; **fābula palliāta** Latin play with Greek setting and characters

pallidul·us -a -um *adj* somewhat pale

pallid·us -a -um *adj* pallid, pale; grey-green, yellow-green, chartreuse

palliolātim *adv* in a mantle

palliolāt·us -a -um *adj* wearing a pallium

palliol·um -ī *n* short cloak; hood

pall·ium -(i)ī *n* pallium *(rectangular material worn mainly by men, esp. Greek men, as an outer garment);* bed cover, couch cover

pall·or -ōris *m* pallor, pale complexion; **pallōrem dūcere** to turn pale

pallul·a -ae *f* small outer garment *(see* **palla***)*

palm·a -ae *f* palm of the hand, hand; palm tree, date; palm branch; palm wreath; palm of victory, first prize; victory; victor *(carrying a palm);* oar, oar blade

palmār·is -is -e *adj* excellent, deserving of the palm *or* prize ‖ *n* masterpiece

palmāri·us -a -um *adj* prize-winning, excellent ‖ *n* masterpiece

palmāt·us -a -um *adj* embroidered with palm-branch design; **tunica palmāta** embroidered tunic *(with palm-branch design, worn by a general)*

palm·es -itis *m* vine shoot, vine branch, vine; branch, twig *(of any tree)*

palmēt·um -ī *n* palm grove

palmi·fer -fera -ferum *adj* producing palms, palm-bearing

palmōs·us -a -um *adj* full of palm trees

palmul·a -ae *f* oar blade; date *(fruit of the palm tree)*

pāl·or -ārī -ātus sum *intr* to roam about, wander aimlessly

palpāti·ō -ōnis *f* stroking ‖ *fpl* flatteries

palpāt·or -ōris *m* flatterer

palpebr·a -ae *f* eyelid

palpit·ō -āre -āvī *intr* to throb, palpitate, quiver

palp·ō -āre -āvī -ātus *or* **palp·or -ārī -ātus sum** *tr* to stroke, pat; to wheedle, coax; to flatter ‖ *intr (w. dat)* **1** to coax; **2** to flatter

palp·us -ī *m* palm of the hand; coaxing, flattery

palūdāment·um -ī *n* general's cloak

palūdāt·us -a -um *adj* wearing a general's cloak

palūdōs·us -a -um *adj* swampy

palumb·ēs -is *mf* pigeon, dove

pāl·us -ī *m* stake, post; wooden sword *(used in practice)*

pal·ūs -ūdis *f* swamp, marsh; sedge

palus·ter *(or* **-tris) -tris -tre** *adj* swampy, marshy; growing in a swamp; used *or* located in a swamp ‖ *npl* swamp, marshland

pampine·us -a -um *adj* of vine tendrils, made of vine leaves; **odor pampineus** bouquet of wines

pampin·us -ī *m (f)* vine shoot, tendril; vine leaf; tendril *(of any kind)*

Pān Pānos *(acc:* **Pāna)** *m* Pan *(Greek god of flocks, shepherds, and woods, often identified with Faunus)*

panacē·a -ae *f or* **pan·ax -acis** *m or* **panac·ēs -is** *n* panacea, cure-all

Panaetōlic·us -a -um *adj* Pan-Aetolian

pānār·ium -(i)ī *n* breadbox; breadbasket; food basket; picnic basket

Panchāï·a -ae *f* region in Arabia famous for its frankincense

panchrest·os -os -on *adj* good for everything, universally useful; **panchreston medicāmentum** *(hum)* briberȳ *(the cure-all medication)*

pancraticē *adv (coll)* fine, splendidly; **pancraticē valēre** to get along splendidly

pancrat·ium *or* **pancrat·ion -iī** *n* contest which included the skills of boxing and wrestling

Pandar·us -ī *m* famous Lycian archer in the Trojan army ‖ companion of Aeneas, killed by Turnus

pandicul·or -ārī -ātus sum *intr (of a person while yawning)* to stretch

Pandī·ōn -onis *or* **-onos** *m* king of Athens and father of Procne and Philomela

Pandīoni·us -a -um *adj* of Pandion

pan·dō -dere -dī pānsus *or* **pāssus** *tr* to spread out, extend, expand, unfold; to open, lay open, throw open; to open up *(a road);* to make *(a place)* accessible, open *(a building);* to reveal, make known, publish; *(mil)* to deploy

pand·us -a -um *adj* curved

pangō pangere pānxī *or* **pepegī** *or* **pēgī pāctus** *tr* to fasten, fix, drive in; to fix, set *(boundaries);* to settle *(a matter);* to agree upon, determine; to write, compose, celebrate, record; to promise in marriage; to provide; **indūtiās pangere cum** to conclude an armistice with

pānice·us -a -um *adj* made of bread; **mīlitēs pāniceī** *(coll)* Breadville brigade *(humorous coinage applied to bakers)*

pānicul·a -ae *f* tuft

pānic·um -ī *n* Italian millet *(cereal grass, raised for its seed or small grains to be used as food)*

pān·is -is *m* bread; loaf of bread; **pānem coquere** to bake bread; **pānis cibārius** coarse bread; **pānis secundus** stale bread

Pānīsc·us -ī *m* little Pan

pannicul·us -ī *m* rag

Pannoni·a -ae *f* Pannonia *(country of Lower Danube in the area of modern Austria)*

Pannoni·us -a -um *adj* Pannonian

pannōs·us -a -um *adj* tattered, threadbare; dressed in rags

pannūce·us *or* **pannūci·us -a -um** *adj* ragged; shriveled, wrinkled

pann·us -ī *m* patch; rag

Panop·ē -ēs *or* **Panopē·a -ae** *f* a sea nymph

pāns·a -ae *adj (masc & fem only)* flatfooted ‖ **Pānsa** *m* Roman family name *(cognomen, esp.* Gaius Vibius Pansa *(cos. 43 B.C.)*

pānsus *pp of* **pandō**

panthēr·a -ae *f* panther

Panthoid·ēs -ae *m* son of Panthus, *(i.e., Euphorbus, a Trojan warrior)*

Panth·us -ī *m* priest of Apollo at Troy and father of Euphorbus

pantic·ēs -um *mpl* guts; sausages

papae *interj (in delight)* great!, wonderful!; *(in pain)* ouch!; *(in astonishment)* wow!

pāp·as -ae *or* **-atis** *m* papa *(baby-talk for pedagogue)*

papāv·er -eris *n (m)* poppy; poppyseed

papāvere·us -a -um *adj* of poppies

Paphi·ē -ēs *f* Paphian goddess *(Venus); (poet)* heterosexual love

Paphi·us -a -um *adj* of Paphos

Paph·os -ī *f* town in S.W. Cyprus sacred to Venus ‖ *mf* child of Pygmalion

pāpili·ō -ōnis *m* butterfly; moth

papill·a -ae *f* nipple, teat; breast

papp·ō -āre *tr* to eat *(soft food)*

papp·us -ī *m* hairy seed *(of certain plants)*

papul·a -ae *f* pimple

papȳrif·er -era -erum *adj* papyrus-producing

papȳr·us -ī *f or* **papȳr·um -ī** *n* papyrus

pār paris *adj* equal, like, on a par, equally matched, well-matched; suitable, adequate; of equal size; *(w. dat or* **cum)** equal to, comparable to, similar to, as large as; *(w. limiting abl, w.* **ad** *or in + acc)* equal, similar, alike in; **pār est** it is right, it is proper; **pār proelium** even *or* indecisive battle; **ut pār est** *(used parenthetically)* as is only right ‖ *m* companion; equal, mate, spouse; **parēs cum paribus facillimē congregantur** *(prov)* birds of a feather flock together ‖ *n* pair, couple, the like; **pār parī** tit for tat

parābil·is -is -e *adj* available

parasīt·a -ae *f* parasite *(female)*

parasītas·ter -trī *m* poor parasite

parasītāti·ō -ōnis *f* sponging

parasītic·us -a -um *adj* parasitical

parasīt·or -ārī -ātus sum *intr* to be a parasite, sponge, freeload

parasīt·us -ī *m* parasite, sponger, freeloader

parātē *adv* with preparation; carefully; readily, promptly

parāti·ō -ōnis *f* preparing; procuring, acquisition

paratragoed·ō -āre *intr* to talk in the tragic style, be melodramatic, ham it up

parātus 300 pars

parāt·us -a -um *adj* prepared, ready; ready at hand, available; furnished, equipped; learned, well-versed, skilled; *(w. dat or* ad**) 1** ready for; **2** equipped for; *(w. inf)* prepared to, ready to; *(w. abl or* in + *abl)* versed in, experienced in

parāt·us -ūs *m* preparation; equipment, outfit; clothing, apparel; *(food at dinner table)* spread

Parc·a -ae *f* goddess of Fate, Fate

parcē *adv* sparingly, thriftily; moderately, with restraint; stingily; rarely

parcēprōm·us -ī *m* stingy person

parcō parcere pepercī parsūrus *tr* to spare, use sparingly ‖ *intr* to be sparing, economize; *(w. dat)* **1** to spare, use carefully; **2** to show mercy to, take it easy on; **3** to show consideration for; **4** to abstain from, refrain from; *(w. inf)* to cease to

parc·us -a -um *adj* thrifty, economical, frugal; stingy; moderate, conservative; slight, little, scanty, paltry *(thing given)*

pard·us -ī *m* leopard

pār·ēns -entis *adj* obedient, submissive ‖ *mpl* subjects

par·ēns -entis *m* parent, father; ancestor, grandparent; founder; inventor; parēns patriae father of one's country ‖ *mpl* ancestors ‖ *f* parent, mother; mother country; mother city

parentāl·is -is -e *adj* parental; diēs parentālis memorial day ‖ *npl* festival in honor of dead ancestors and relatives

parent·ō -āre -āvī -ātum *intr* to hold a memorial service in honor of dead parents *or* relatives; *(w. dat)* **1** to offer sacrifice to *(the dead);* **2** to avenge *(dead person with the death of another person);* **3** to appease, satisfy

pār·eō -ēre -uī -itum *intr* to appear, be visible, be evident, be at hand; *(w. dat)* **1** to obey, be obedient to; **2** to comply with; **3** to be subject to, be subservient to; **4** to yield to, gratify, satisfy *(pleasures, etc.);* **5** to fulfill *(promises)*

pari·ēs -etis *m* wall *(inner or outer wall of house or other building);* intrā parietēs in private, at home, under one's own roof

parietin·ae -ārum *fpl* tumble-down walls; *(lit & fig)* ruins

Parīl·ia -ium *npl* (Palīl-) festival of Pales *(April 21)*

paril·is -is -e *adj* equal, like; aetās parilis same age, like age

Parīl·is -is -e *adj* (Palīl-) connected with Pales *or* her festival

pariō parere peperī partus *tr* to bear, bring forth, give birth to; *(of animals)* to produce, spawn, lay *(eggs); (of countries, of the earth)* to produce, be a source of; *(of things)* to give rise to; *(fig)* to create, devise, cause, accomplish; to acquire

Par·is -idis *m* son of Priam and Hecuba ‖ pantomime actor in the reign of Nero ‖ pantomime actor in the reign of Domitian

pariter *adv* equally, in like manner, as well, alike; at the same time, at one and the same time, together; side by side; evenly, uniformly; in equal quantity *or* degree; at once; pariter ac *(or* atque *or* ut) as well as; pariter ac sī just as if; pariter cum together with, at the same time as

parit·ō -āre *tr (w. inf)* to get ready to

Par·ium *or* Par·ion -iī *n* town of the Troad near the entrance to the Propontis *(modern Kemer)*

Pari·us -a -um *adj* Parian, of Paros

parm·a -ae *f* small round shield

parmāt·us -a -um *adj* armed with a small, round shield, light-armed

parmul·a -ae *f* small round shield

Parnās·is -idis *or* Parnāsi·us -a -um *adj* of Parnassus, Parnassian

Parnās·us *or* Parnās·os -ī *m* mountain forming the backdrop to Apollo's shrine at Delphi

par·ō -āre -āvī -ātus *tr* to prepare, make ready, provide, furnish; to get, procure; to purchase; to acquire, gather ‖ *refl* to get ready ‖ *intr* to get ready, make preparations, make arrangements; *(w. dat or* ad) to get ready for

paroch·a -ae *f* room and board *(which provincials had to provide for traveling Roman officials)*

paroch·us -ī *m* official host *(provided accommodations for traveling Roman dignitaries)*

parops·is -idis *f* dish; dessert dish

Par·os *or* Par·us -ī *f* Greek island of the Cyclades, famous for its white marble

parr·a -ae *f* owl

Parrhas·is -idis *or* -idos *f* Arcadian woman; Callisto *(as Ursa Major)*

Parrhasi·us -a -um *adj* Arcadian; Parrhasia virgō Callisto *(as Ursa Major)* ‖ *f* district in Arcadia

parricīd·a -ae *mf* parricide *(murderer of one's parent or close relative);* assassin of a high magistrate; murderer; traitor, outlaw

parricīd·ium -(i)ī *n* parricide *(murder of a parent or close relative);* murder; assassination; high treason

par·s -tis *f* part, portion, share, section; fraction; side, direction, region; part, function, duty; part of body, member *(esp. genital organs);* ab omnī parte in every respect; ā parte partly; exiguā parte in a slight degree; ex alterā parte on the other hand; ex parte partly; ex eā parte *(or* in eam partem) quātenus to the extent that; in eam partem in that direction; in that sense; **in parte** *(or* **in partem)** partly, in part; in such a manner; **in parte alicūius rēī esse** to form part of s.th., be included in s.th.; **in pēiōrem partem rapere** to put a worse construction on; **in utramque partem** in both directions; **magnā ex parte** to a great degree; **māior pars populī** the majority; **maximam partem** for the most part; **minor pars populī** a minority; **pars dīmidia (tertia, quārta,** *etc.)* one half (one-third, one-fourth, *etc.);* **pars … pars, pars … aliī** some … others; **pars ōrātiōnis** *(gram)* part of speech; **parte** in part, partly; **prō meā parte** to the best of my ability; **prō parte** in part, partially; **prō parte sēmisse** half and half; **prō ratā parte** in a fixed proportion; **prō suā parte** *(or* **prō virīlī parte)** to the best of one's ability ‖ *fpl* part, role; task, function; character; political party; pieces, fragments; scraps *(esp. of food);* **omnibus partibus** in all respects; **partēs obscēnae** privates, private parts; **per partēs** *(or* **partibus)** (so much) at a time, in stages; **trēs partēs** three-fourths; **tuae partēs sunt** the task *(or* decision) devolves on you

parsimōni·a -ae *f* parsimony, thrift

Parthā·ōn -onis *m* king of Calydon, the son of Agenor and Epicaste and father of Oeneus

Parthāoni·us -a -um *adj* of Parthaon; Calydonian

parthenic·ē -ēs *f (bot)* chamomile *(plant with white flowers, used medicinally and as tea)*

Parthenopae·us -ī *m* one of the Seven against Thebes, the son of Meleager and Atalanta

Parthenop·ē -ēs *f* ancient name of Naples *(named after the Siren Parthenope who was supposedly buried there)*

Parthi·a -ae *f* Parthia *(country located S.E. of the Caspian Sea)*

Parthic·us -a -um *adj* Parthian; honorary title of several Roman Emperors

Parth·us -a -um *adj* & *m* Parthian

partic·eps -ipis *adj (w. gen)* sharing in, taking part in ‖ *m* partner, confederate; *(w. gen)* partner in

particip·ō -āre -āvī -ātus *tr* to make *(s.o.)* a partner; to share *(s.th.)*

particul·a -ae *f* bit, particle, grain

partim *adv* partly, in part, to some extent; for the most part; *(w. gen or* **ex)** some of; **partim … partim** some … others, partly. . . partly

part·iō -īre -īvī -ītus *or* **part·ior -īrī -ītus sum** *tr* to share; to distribute, apportion, divide

parti·ō -ōnis *f* bringing forth, producing

partītē *adv* with proper divisions

partīti·ō -ōnis *f* division, distribution, sharing; classification; *(rhet)* division of a speech

partitūd·ō -inis *f* bearing *(of young)*

partur·iō -īre -īvī *tr* to teem with; to be ready to produce; to bring forth, yield; *(fig)* to brood over ‖ *intr* to be in labor

part·us -a -um *pp of* **pariō** ‖ *adj* acquired ‖ *n* acquisition; gain; store

part·us -ūs *m* giving birth; birth; young, offspring; embryo; *(fig)* beginnings

parum *adv* & *indecl n* a little, too little, insufficiently; **parum est** it is not enough; **parum habēre** to regard as unsatisfactory; **satis ēloquentiae sapientiae parum** enough eloquence but too little wisdom

parumper *adv* for a little while, just for a moment

parvit·ās -ātis *f* smallness

parvul·us -a -um *adj* (**-vol-**) tiny; slight, petty; young ‖ *n* childhood, infancy; **ā parvulīs** from childhood, from infancy; **ā parvulō** from childhood on

parv·us -a -um *(comp:* **minor;** *superl:* **minimus)** *adj* small, little, puny; short; young; brief, short *(time);* slight; insignificant, unimportant; low, cheap *(price)* ‖ *n* a little, trifle; childhood, infancy; **ā parvīs** *(or* **ā parvō)** from childhood, from infancy; **parvī esse** to be of little importance; **parvī facere** *(or* **aestimāre** *or* **habēre** *or* **dūcere)** to think little of, care little for; **parvī pretiī** of little worth; **parvī rēfert** it makes little difference, it matters little; **parvō** at a low price; **parvō animō esse** to be small-minded

pāsceol·us -ī *m* moneybag

pāscō pāscere pāvī pāstus *tr* to feed; to be food for; to pasture, keep, raise *(animals); (of land)* to provide food for; to cultivate, cherish; to feed *(fire; flames of passion);* to pile up *(debts);* to grow *(beard);* to lay waste, ravage *(fields);* to use *(land)* as pasturage; to feast *(the eyes, the mind)* ‖ *refl* & *pass* to support oneself; *(w. abl)* to get rich on, grow fat on ‖ *pass (of animals)* to graze; to feed; *(w. abl)* **1** to feast on, thrive on; **2** to gloat over ‖ *intr* to feed, graze

pāscu·us -a -um *adj* grazing, pasture ‖ *n* pasture

Pāsipha·ē -ēs *or* **Pāsipha·a -ae** *f* Pasiphaë *(daughter of Helios, sister of Circe, wife of Minos, and mother of Phaedra, Ariadne, and the Minotaur)*

pass·er -eris *m* sparrow; flounder; **passer marīnus** ostrich *(because imported from overseas)*

passercul·us -ī *m* little sparrow

passim *adv* here and there; all over the place; at random, without order, indiscriminately

passit·ō -āre *intr (of a starling)* to sing

passīv·us -a -um *adj (gram)* passive

pāssus *pp of* **pandō** ‖ *adj* spread out, extended, open; disheveled; *(of grapes and other fruits*

spread out in the sun) dried, dry **ǁ** *f* raisin **ǁ** *n* raisin wine
passus *pp of* **patior**
pāss·us -ūs *m* step, pace; footstep, track; **mīlle pāssūs** thousand paces, a mile; **tria mīlia pāssuum** three miles
pastill·us -ī *m* lozenge
pāsti·ō -ōnis *f* pasture, grazing
pāst·or -ōris *m* shepherd
pāstōrāl·is -is -e *adj* pastoral
pāstōrici·us -a -um *or* **pāstōri·us -a -um** *adj* shepherd's, pastoral
pāstus *pp of* **pāscō**
pāst·us -ūs *m* the feeding of animals; pasture; fodder, feed
patagiār·ius -(i)ī *m* fringe maker
patagiāt·us -a -um *adj (tunic)* with fringes
Patar·a -ae *f or* **Patar·a -ōrum** *npl* town in Lycia with an oracle of Apollo
Patar·ēus -eī *or* **-eos** *m* Apollo
Patavīn·us -a -um *adj* of Patavium
Patav·ium -(i)ī *n* city in N. Italy, birthplace of Livy *(modern Padua)*
pate·faciō -facere -fēcī -factus *(pass:* **pate·fīō -fierī)** *tr* to uncover, reveal; to open *(gates, windows, buildings, containers, etc.)*; to throw open; to open up, make accessible; to bring to light; to disclose; *(mil)* to deploy; *(mil) (w. dat)* to expose to *(attack)*
patefacti·ō -ōnis *f* disclosure
patell·a -ae *f* pan, dish, plate
pat·ēns -entis *adj* open, accessible; extensive; exposed; evident
patentius *adv* more openly; more clearly
pat·eō -ēre -uī *intr* to stand open, be open; to be accessible; to be exposed; to open, stretch out, extend; to be clear, be plain, be well-known; to be attainable, be free; *(of the mind)* to be open, be receptive; *(of wounds)* to gape; **lātē patēre** to have wide application, cover a wide field
pa·ter -tris *m* father; **pater cēnae** host; **pater familiās** head of the family; **quārtus pater** great-great-grandfather **ǁ** *mpl* forefathers; patricians; senators; **patrēs cōnscrīptī** gentlemen of the Senate
pater·a -ae *f* flat dish, saucer *(used esp. in making libations)*
paterfamiliās, *gen:* **patrisfamiliās** *m* head of the family
patern·us -a -um *adj* father's, paternal, fatherly; ancestral; of a native country, native
pat·ēscō -ēscere -uī *intr* to be opened, be open; to stretch out, extend; to be disclosed, be divulged, become evident; *(mil)* to be deployed
pathic·us -a -um *adj* lustful
patibil·is -is -e *adj* tolerable; sensitive

patibulāt·us -a -um *adj* fastened to a yoke *or* gibbet, pilloried
patibul·um -ī *n* pillory *(fork-shaped yoke to which criminals were fastened);* fork-shaped gibbet
pati·ēns -entis *adj* hardy, tough; hard; stubborn, unyielding; patient, tolerant; *(w. gen or ad)* able to endure, inured to, able to take; **amnis patiēns nāvium** navigable river
patienter *adv* patiently
patienti·a -ae *f* patience, endurance; resignation; submissiveness; sexual submission
patin·a -ae *f* dish, pan
patināri·us -a -um *adj* of pans; in a pan; **struēs patināria** pile of dishes
patior patī passus sum *tr* to experience, undergo, suffer; to put up with, allow; to submit to *(sexually);* **aegrē patī** to resent, be displeased with
patrāt·or -ōris *m* perpetrator
patrāt·us -ī *adj (masc only)* **pater patrātus** plenipotentiary senator *(sent on a foreign mission)*
patri·a -ae *f* native land, native city, home
patricē *adv* like a patrician
patriciāt·us -ūs *m* status of patrician
patrici·us -a -um *adj & m* patrician
patrimōn·ium -(i)ī *n* patrimony, inheritance
patrim·us -a -um *adj* having a father still living
patriss·ō -āre *intr* to take after one's father
patrīt·us -a -um *adj* father's, inherited from one's father
patri·us -a -um *adj* father's, of a father, fatherly; ancestral; traditional, hereditary; native **ǁ** *f see* **patria**
patrō -āre *tr* to bring about, effect, achieve, perform; to finish, conclude; **bellum patrāre** to bring a war to an end; **iūs iūrandum patrāre** to take an oath *(confirming a treaty);* **pācem patrāre** to conclude a peace; **prōmissa patrāre** to fulfill promises **ǁ** *intr* to reach a sexual climax
patrōcin·ium -(i)ī *n* patronage, protection; legal defense, legal representation
Patrocl·us -ī *m* son of Menoetius and friend of Achilles, killed by Hector
patrōn·a -ae *f* legal protectress, patroness; defender; safeguard
patrōncin·or -ārī -ātus sum *intr* to be a patron, afford protection; *(w. dat)* to serve *(s.o.)* as patron, protect, defend
patrōn·us -ī *m* legal protector, patron; advocate *(in court);* defender
patruēl·is -is -e *adj* on the father's side, cousin's; **frāter patruēlis** cousin; **soror patruēlis** cousin *(female)* **ǁ** *m* cousin

patru·us -a -um *adj* of a *(paternal)* uncle ‖ *m* father's brother, paternal uncle; **patruus magnus** great-uncle, granduncle

patul·us -a -um *adj* open, standing open; spreading, spread out, broad

pauc·ī -ae -a *adj* few ‖ *pron masc pl* few, a few; the select, elite; **inter paucōs** *(or* in **paucās** *or* in **pauca** *or* in **paucīs**) *(in connection with an adj)* among a few, especially, unusually, uncommonly ‖ *pron neut pl* a few things, a few words; **paucīs** in a few words, briefly

pauciloqu·ium -(i)ī *n* reticence

paucit·ās -ātis *f* paucity, scarcity, small number

paucul·ī -ae -a *adj* just a few, very few ‖ *npl* few words

paul(l)ātim *adv* little by little, gradually, by degrees; a few at a time

paul(l)isper *adv* for a little while

paul(l)ō *adv (as abl of degree of difference in comparisons)* a little, somewhat; **paulō ante** a little earlier; **paulō post** a little later

paul(l)ulō *adv* somewhat, a little; cheaply, at a low price

paul(l)ulum *adv* somewhat, a little

paul(l)ul·us -a -um *adj* very little ‖ *n* very little, a bit; **paullulum pecūniae** a bit of money, very little money

paul(l)um *adv* a little, to some extent

paul(l)·us -a -um *adj* small, little ‖ *n* a bit, trifle; **post paulum** after a bit

Paul·us -ī *m* Lucius Aemilius Paulus Macedonicus *(conqueror of Macedonia at Pydna in 168 B.C.)*

paup·er -eris *adj* poor *(financially);* scanty, meager; *(w. gen)* poor in ‖ *mf* pauper

paupercul·us -a -um *adj* poor little

pauperi·ēs -ēī *f* poverty

pauper·ō -āre -āvī -ātus *tr* to impoverish; *(w. abl)* to rob *(s.o.)* of

paupert·ās -ātis *f* poverty

paus·a -ae *f* pause, intermission, stop, end; **pausam dare** *(or* **facere**) to make a pause, take a break; **pausam facere** *(w. dat)* put an end to

pauxillātim *adv* little by little

pauxillisper *adv* bit by bit

pauxillulum *adv* a little, a bit ‖ *n (w. gen)* a bit of

pauxillul·us -a -um *adj* tiny

pauxill·us -a -um *adj* very little, tiny ‖ *n* small amount

pavefact·us -a -um *adj* frightened

paveō pavēre pāvī *tr* to be scared of, be terrified at ‖ *intr* to be terrified, tremble with fear

pavēsc·ō -ere *tr* to get scared of ‖ *intr* to begin to be alarmed

pāvī *perf of* **pāscō** *and of* **paveō**

pavidē *adv* in panic

pavid·us -a -um panicky, alarmed, trembling with fear, startled; with beating heart, nervous; causing alarm

pavīment·ō -āre *tr* to pave

pavīment·um -ī *n* pavement; floor

pav·iō -īre -īvī *or* -**iī** -**ītus** *tr* to strike, beat

pavit·ō -āre *tr* to be panicky over ‖ *intr* to quake with fear, be scared to death; to shiver *(w. fever)*

pāv·ō -ōnis *or* **pāv·us -ī** *m* peacock

pav·or -ōris *m* panic, terror, dread; dismay; quaking, shivering; **pavōrem inicere** *(w. dat)* to strike terror into

pāx *interj* quiet, enough!

pāx pācis *f* peace; peace treaty; reconciliation; compact, agreement; harmony, tranquility; favor, pardon *(from the gods);* **cum bonā pāce** with full consent; **pāce tuā** with your leave, with your permission

pecc·āns -antis *m* offender, sinner

peccāt·um -ī *n* fault, mistake, slip; moral offense, sin

pecc·ō -āre -āvī -ātum *intr* to make a mistake, blunder; to make a slip in speaking; to be wrong; to sin

pecorōs·us -a -um *adj* rich in cattle

pect·en -inis *m* comb; plectrum; rake; pubic bone; pubic region; scallop *(as seafood)*

pectō pectere pex(u)ī pexus *or* **pexitus** *tr* to comb; to card *(wool); (hum)* to thrash

pect·us -oris *n* breast, chest; heart, feeling; soul, conscience; mind, understanding; person, character; **dē summō pectore dīcere** to say off-hand; **tōtō pectore** heart and soul

pecū *(gen not in use; pl:* **pecua**) *n* flock, herd; **squamōsum pecū** *(hum)* school of fish ‖ *npl* farm animals; cattle; pastures

pecuāri·us -a -um *adj* **(pequ-)** of sheep, of cattle; **rēs pecuāria** livestock ‖ *m* cattleman, cattle breeder, rancher ‖ *f* livestock ‖ *npl* herds of cattle, herds of sheep

pecūlāt·or -ōris *m* embezzler

pecūlāt·us -ūs *m* **(peq-)** embezzlement

pecūliār·is -is -e one's own, as one's own private property; special; exceptional, singular

pecūliāriter *adv* especially

pecūliāt·us -a -um *adj* well off

pecūli·ō -āre -āvī -ātus *tr* to provide with personal property

pecūl·ium -(i)ī *n* personal property *or* savings *(of a slave or a son under his father's control)*

pecūni·a -ae *f* money; property, possessions

pecūniāri·us -a -um *adj* pecuniary, financial, money

pecūniōs·us -a -um *adj* rich, well-off; profitable

pec·us -oris *n* cattle, herd, flock; sheep; head of cattle; livestock; **pecus equīnum** stud; *(pej)* cattle

pec·us -udis *f* head of cattle; beast; sheep; domestic animal; land animal *(as opposed to birds and fish); (pej)* brute, beast, swine

pedāl·is -is -e *adj* one-foot-long

pedār·ius -(i)ī *m* senator of lower standing *(who lets others step all over him)*

pedāt·us -ūs *m* one of the three formal stages in issuing an ultimatum

ped·es -itis *m* infantryman, footsoldier; pedestrian; **equitēs peditēsque** all Roman citizens

pedes·ter *or* **pedes·tris -tris -tre** *adj* infantry; pedestrian; on land, by land; written in prose; prosaic, plain

pedetem(p)tim *adv* by feeling one's way, step by step, slowly, cautiously

pedic·a -ae *f* foot chain, fetter; trap, snare

pedīculōs·us -a -um *adj* lousy, full of lice

pēd·is -is *mf* louse

pedisequ·a -ae *f* attendant, handmaid

pedisequ·us -ī *m* attendant

peditastell·us -ī *m* poor infantryman

peditāt·us -ūs *m* infantry

pēdit·um -ī *n (vulg)* fart

Pedi·us -a -um *adj* name of a Roman clan *(nomen) (esp. Quintus Pedius, Caesar's nephew);* **lēx Pedia** law providing a trial for Caesar's murderers

Ped·ō -ōnis *m* Roman family name *(cognomen), esp.* Albinovanus Pedo, a poet and friend of Ovid

pēdō pēdere pepēdī pēditum *intr (vulg)* to fart

ped·um -ī *n* shepherd's crook

Pēgase·us *or* **Pēgasēī·us -a -um** *adj* of Pegasus, Pegasean

Pēgas·is -idis *or* -idos *adj (fem only)* of Pegasus *(with reference to Hippocrene)* **‖** *f* fountain nymph **‖** *fpl* Muses

Pēgas·us *or* **Pēgas·os -ī** *m* winged horse that sprang from the blood of Medusa

pegm·a -atis *n* bookcase; scaffold

pēierātiuncul·a -ae *f* petty oath

pēierāt·us -a -um *adj* (-iūr-) offended by false oaths; **iūs pēierātum** false oath

pēier·ō -āre -āvī -ātus *tr* (-iūr-) to swear falsely by **‖** *intr* to swear a false oath; *(coll)* to lie

pēierōs·us -a -um *adj* (-iūr-) perjured

pēi·or -or -us *(comp of* malus) *adj* worse

pēius *(comp of* male) *adv* worse

pelagi·us -a -um *adj* of the sea

pelag·us -ī *n* sea, open sea

pēlam·is -idis *or* **pēlam·ys -ydis** *f* young tuna

Pelasg·ī -ōrum *mpl* aborigines of Greece; *(poet)* certain early inhabitants of Italy; *(poet)* Greeks *(opp:* Trojans); *(poet)* Argives *(opp:* Thebans)

Pēl·eūs -eī *or* -eos *m* king of Thessaly, son of Aeacus, husband of Thetis, and father of Achilles

Pēli·a -adis *adj (fem only)* of Mt. Pelion

Pēli·as -adis *adj (fem only)* of Mt. Pelion, from Mt. Pelion

Peli·ās -ae *m* king of Iolcos in Thessaly and uncle of Jason

Pēlīd·ēs -ae *m* descendant of Peleus; Achilles; Neoptolemus

Pēl·ion -(i)ī *n* mountain in E. Thessaly

Pēli·us *or* **Pēliac·us -a -um** *adj* of Mt. Pelion

Pell·a -ae *or* **Pell·ē -ēs** *f* Pella *(city in Macedonia, birthplace of Alexander the Great)*

pellāci·a -ae *f* charm, allurement

Pellae·us -a -um *adj* of *or* from Pella; **Pellaeus iuvenis** Alexander

pell·āx -ācis *adj* seductive, alluring

pellecti·ō -ōnis *f* perusal

pel·liciō -licere -lexī *or* **licuī -lectus (per-)** *tr* to captivate, allure, entice, coax

pellicul·a -ae *f* small *or* thin hide, skin

pelli·ō -ōnis *m* furrier

pell·is -is *f* skin, hide; leather; felt; tent; shield cover; **dētrahere pellem** to expose one's true character *(literally, to take off one's hide);* **ossa ac pellis** mere skin and bones

pellīt·us -a -um *adj* clothed in skins; wearing a leather coat

pellō pellere pepulī pulsus *tr* to push, beat, strike, knock; to beat *(drum, chest);* to knock at *(door);* thrust; to drive, impel; to rouse, stimulate; to drive away, eject, expel; to banish; to repel, drive back, rout; to strum *(lyre, etc.);* to affect, impress, strike; to stomp *(the earth)*

pellūc- = **perlūc-**

Pelopēi·as -ados *or* **Pelopē·us -a -um** *adj* Pelopian, of Pelops; Mycenaean; Phrygian

Pelopē·is -idos *f* descendant of Pelops *(female)*

Pelopid·ae -ārum *mpl* descendants of Pelops

Peloponnēns·is -is -e *adj* (-nnēs-) Peloponnesian

Peloponnēsiac·us *or* **Peloponnēsi·us -a -um** *adj* Peloponnesian

Peloponnēs·us *or* **Peloponnēs·os -ī** *f* Peloponnesus *(modern Morea)*

Pel·ops -opis *m* son of Tantalus, father of Atreūs and Thyestes, and grandfather of Agamemnon and Menelaüs

pelōr·is -idos *m* large mussel

Pelōr·us *or* **Pelōr·os -ī** *m* N.E. promontory of Sicily *(modern Cape Faro)*

pelt·a -ae *f* small leather shield

peltast·a (·ēs) -ae *m* soldier armed with a small leather shield

peltāt·us -a -um *adj* armed with a small leather shield

Pēlūs·ium -(i)ī *n* city on the E. mouth of the Nile

pelv·is -is *f* basin, shallow bowl

penāri·us -a -um *adj* for storing food; **cella penāria** pantry

Penāt·ēs -ium *mpl* Penates, household gods; Penates of the State; hearth; house; home *(also applied to a nest, a hive, a temple)*

penātig·er -era -erum *adj* carrying the household gods

pendeō pendēre pependī *intr* to hang (down), be suspended; to hang loose; to be flabby; to be weak; to be in suspense, be uncertain, hesitate; to hang around, loiter; to hang in the air, hover, float; to overhang; *(of plants)* to droop; *(w. abl or* **ab, dē,** *or* **ex** + *abl)* **1** to hang down from, hang by; **2** to depend on, be dependent upon; **3** to be based on, hinge on; **4** to result from; **5** to hang onto; *(w.* **in** + *abl)* to be poised on, hover in, hover over; **animī pendēre** to be in suspense, be perplexed; **pendēre ab ōre** *(w. gen)* to hang on *(s.o.'s)* words, listen with rapt attention to; **pendēre ex vultū** *(w. gen)* to gaze intently at *(s.o.'s)* face

pendō pendere pependī pēnsus *tr* to weigh, weigh out; to pay, pay out; to ponder, consider, value, esteem; **floccī pendere** to think little of; **magnī (parvī) pendere** to think much (little) of; **poenās pendere** to pay the penalty; **supplicia pendere** to suffer punishment

pendul·us -a -um *adj* hanging, hanging down; doubtful, uncertain

Pēnē·is -idos *or* **Pēnēi·us -a -um** *adj* of the Peneus River *(in Thessaly)*

Pēnelop·a -ae *or* **Pēnelop·ē -ēs** *f* Penelope *(daughter of Icarius and Periboea and wife of Odysseus)*

penes *prep (w. acc of person only)* in the possession of, in the power of, belonging to, resting with; at the house of, with; **penes sē esse** to be in one's senses, be in one's right mind

penetrābil·is -is -e *adj* penetrating, piercing; penetrable

penetr·āl·e -is *n see* **penetrālis**

penetrāl·is -is -e *adj* penetrating, piercing; inner, internal, interior ‖ *n* inner part, innermost recess *(of a building);* inner shrine *(of a temple);* shrine of the Penates; house, home ‖ *npl* the interior, center; inner chambers; sanctuary; *(geog)* the interior, hinterlands

penetr·ō -āre -āvī -ātus *tr* to penetrate, enter; to cross *(river);* **pedem penetrāre intrā** *(w. acc)* to set foot inside ‖ *refl* to go; **forās sē penetrāre** to go outside ‖ *intr* to penetrate, enter; *(w. ad)* to go as far as, go all the way to, reach, gain entrance to; *(w.* **in** + *acc)* to enter, penetrate

Pēnē·us *or* **Pēnī·os -ī** *m* the Peneüs River *(largest river in Thessaly)* ‖ river god, the father of Cyrene and Daphne

pēnicill·us -ī *m or* **pēnicill·um -ī** *n* paint brush; sponge

pēnicul·us -ī *m* brush; sponge; little penis

pēn·is -is *m* tail; penis; *(fig)* lechery

penitē *adv* deep down inside

penit·us -a -um *adj* inner, inward

penitus *adv* internally, inside, deep within, deeply; from within; thoroughly, through and through; heartily

penn·a -ae *f* feather; wing; flight

pennāt·us -a -um *adj* feathered

pennig·er -era -erum *adj* winged, feathered

pennipot·ēns -entis *adj* able to fly

pennul·a -ae *f* little wing

pēnsil·is -is -e *adj* hanging; supported on arches; suspended in mid-air

pēnsi·ō -ōnis *f* payment *(esp. by installments),* installment; rent money; compensation

pēnsit·ō -āre -āvī -ātus *tr* to pay; to weigh, ponder, consider ‖ *intr* to be taxable

pēns·ō -āre -āvī -ātus *tr* to weigh out; to weigh, ponder, consider, examine; to compare, contrast; to pay; to atone for; to repay, compensate, requite

pēns·um -ī *n* work quota; duty, task; consideration, scruple; **nihil pēnsī habēre** *(or* **dūcere)** to have no scruples; **pēnsī esse** *(w. dat)* to be of value to, be of importance to; **pēnsī habēre** *(or* **dūcere)** to value, consider of importance

pēnsus *pp of* **pendō**

pentēr·is -is *f* galley, quinquereme

Penthesilē·a -ae *f* Amazon warrior queen, killed by Achilles at Troy

Penth·eus -eī *or* **-eos** *m* king of Thebes, son of Echion and Agave, grandson of Cadmus

pen·um -ī *n or* **pen·us -ūs** *f (m) or* **pen·us -oris** *n* food, provisions *(in the pantry)*

pēnūri·a -ae *f* want, need, dearth

pen·us -ūs *f (m) see* **penum**

pependī *perf of* **pendeō** *and of* **pendō**

pepercī *perf of* **parcō**

peperī *perf of* **pariō**

pepl·um -ī *n or* **pepl·us -ī** *m* robe for the statue of Athena

pepulī *perf of* **pellō**

-per *advl suf* denoting the duration or the number of times, *e.g.:* **paulisper** for a little while

per- *pref* conveying the idea of: **1** through: **perfringere** to break through; **2** intensive force: **perfacile** very easy; **3** throughly, to the end: **perficere** to complete; **perlegere** to read through to the end; **perdomāre** to tame thoroughly; **4** of going in the wrong direction: **pervertere** to turn the wrong way; **perfidia**

treachery *(a trust, gone in the wrong direction)*

per *prep (w. acc) (of space)* through; all over *(an area, space)*, throughout; along *(a linear direction); (of time)* through, during, for, in the course of, over a period of; *(of agency)* through, by, by means of, at the hands of; *(of means or manner)* through, by, under pretense of; *(w. refl pron)* for one's *or* its own sake, on its own account, by: **multiplicāre VI per IIII fit XXIIII** multiplying 6 by 4 gives 24; **per causam** on the grounds *(that);* **per manūs trādere** to pass from hand to hand; **per mē** as far as I am concerned; **per mē stat** it is due to me *(that),* it is my fault *(that);* **per omnia** in all respects, throughout; **per speciem** on the pretext *(of);* **per omnēs deōs iūrāre** to swear by all the gods; **per sē** in itself, by itself *(or* himself, herself, *etc.);* **per tempus** at the right time; **per Tiberim** along the Tiber

pēr·a -ae *f* pouch *(bag slung over the shoulder for carrying the day's provisions)*

perabsurd·us -a -um *adj* completely absurd

peraccommodāt·us -a -um *adj* very convenient

perā·cer -cris -cre *adj* very sharp

peracerb·us -a -um *adj* very harsh, very sour

peracēsc·ō -ere *intr* to turn completely sour

perācti·ō -ōnis *f* conclusion; last act *(of a play)*

perāctus *pp of* **peragō**

peracūtē *adv* very acutely

peracūt·us -a -um *adj* very sharp; very clear *(voice, intellect)*

peradulēsc·ēns -entis *adj* very young

peradulēscentul·us -ī *m* very young man

peraequē *adv* quite equally, uniformly; in all cases, invariably; **omnēs peraequē** all alike

peragit·ō -āre -āvī -ātus *tr* to harass

per·agō -agere -ēgī -āctus *tr* to carry through to the end, complete, accomplish; to pierce; to travel through; to harass, disturb, trouble; to describe, relate, go over; to work, till, cultivate *(the soil);* to fulfill *(hopes, promises);* to live out *(a period of time);* to come to the end of *(of period of time);* to treat *(a subject)* thoroughly; to use up *(resources);* to deliver *(a speech); (leg)* to prosecute to a conviction; **partēs peragere** to play the part

peragrāti·ō -ōnis *f* traveling

peragr·ō -āre -āvī -ātus *tr* to travel through, travel, traverse **ǁ** *intr (fig)* to spread, penetrate

peram·āns -antis *adj (w. gen)* very fond of

peramanter *adv* very lovingly

perambul·ō -āre -āvī -ātus *tr* to walk through; to walk about in; to travel about in, tour

peramīcē *adv* in a very friendly way

peram·ō -āre -āvī -ātus *tr* to show a great liking for

peramoen·us -a -um *adj* very pleasant, very charming

perampl·us -a -um *adj* very large; very spacious

perangustē *adv* very narrowly

perangust·us -a -um *adj* very narrow

perantīqu·us -a -um *adj* very ancient, very old

perapposit·us -a -um *adj* very suitable, very appropriate

perardu·us -a -um *adj* very difficult

perargūt·us -a -um *adj* very clear; very sharp, very witty

perarmāt·us -a -um *adj* heavily armed

perar·ō -āre -āvī -ātus *tr* to plow through; to furrow; to write on *(a wax tablet);* to inscribe

pērātim *adv* bag by bag, bag after bag

perattentē *adv* very attentively

peraudiend·us -a -um *adj* that must be heard to the end

perbacch·or -ārī -ātus sum *tr* to carouse through *(e.g., the night)*

perbeāt·us -a -um *adj* very happy

perbellē *adv* very prettily

perbene *adv* very well

perbenevol·us -a -um *adj* very friendly, very well-disposed

perbenīgnē *adv* very kindly

perbib·ō -ere -ī *tr* to drink up, drink in, imbibe; *(of plants)* to be well watered

perbīt·ō -ere *intr* to perish, die

perbland·us -a -um *adj* very attractive, very charming

perbon·us -a -um *adj* very good, excellent

perbrev·is -is -e *adj* very short, very brief; **perbrevī** *(or* **perbrevī tempore)** in a very short time

perbreviter *adv* very briefly

perc·a -ae *f* perch *(fish)*

percalefact·us -a -um *adj* warmed through and through

percal·ēscō -ēscere -uī *intr* to become quite hot

percall·ēscō -ēscere -uī *tr* to become thoroughly versed in **ǁ** *intr* to become very hardened

percār·us -a -um *adj* very dear; very costly

percaut·us -a -um *adj* very cautious

percelebr·ō -āre -āvī -ātus *tr* to make widely known **ǁ** *pass* to be quite famous

percel·er -eris -ere *adj* very rapid

perceleriter *adv* very rapidly

per·cellō -cellere -culī -culsus *tr* to knock down, beat down, overthrow; to scare to death; to ruin; to send scurrying; *(lit & mil)* to hit hard

percēns·eō -ēre -uī *tr* to count up; to review, survey; to travel all through *(a country)*

percepti·ō -ōnis *f* comprehension; reaping, harvesting ‖ *fpl* concepts

percept·us -a -um *pp of* **percipiō** ‖ *n* rule, principle

percī·dō -dere -dī -sus *tr* to smash to pieces

perci·eō -ēre *or* **perc·iō -īre -īvī** *or* **-iī -ītus** *tr* to stir up, set in motion; to excite

per·cipiō -cipere -cēpī -ceptus *tr* to get a good hold of; to catch; to occupy, seize; to gather in, harvest, reap; *(of the senses)* to take in, perceive, feel; *(of feelings)* to get hold of, get the better of, come over *(s.o.)*; to learn, know, comprehend, perceive

percit·us -a -um *pp of* **percieō** *and of* **perciō** ‖ *adj* aroused, provoked; impetuous, excitable

percoctus *pp of* **percoquō**

percol·ō -āre -āvī -ātus *tr* to strain, filter

percolō -colere -coluī -cultus *tr* to reverence, revere, worship; to beautify; to crown, complete

percōm·is -is -e *adj* very courteous

percommodē *adv* very conveniently; very well; very suitably

percommod·us -a -um *adj* very convenient, very comfortable; very suitable

percontāti·ō -ōnis *f* thorough investigation

percontāt·or -ōris *m* inquisitive fellow; interrogator

percont·or -ārī -ātus sum *tr* to question, investigate, interrogate; *(w. double acc)* to ask *(s.o. s.th.)*

percontum·āx -ācis *adj* very defiant

per·coquō -quere -xī -ctus *tr* to cook thoroughly; to heat thoroughly; to ripen; to scorch, blacken

percrēb(r)·ēscō -ēscere -uī *tr* to become widespread; to get to be widely believed

percrep·ō -āre -uī *intr* to resound, ring

percruci·or -ārī -ātus sum *intr* to be tormented

perculsus *pp of* **percellō**

percult·us -a -um *pp of* **percolō** ‖ *adj* decked out; *(coll)* all dolled up

percupid·us -a -um *adj (w. gen)* very fond of

percup·iō -ere -iī -ītūs *tr* to desire greatly; *(w. inf)* to be very eager to, be dying to

percūriōs·us -a -um *adj* very curious

percūr·ō -āre -āvī -ātus *tr* to treat successfully, heal

percurrō percurrere per(cu)currī percursus *tr* to run through, run along, run over, pass over, speed over; *(fig)* to scan briefly, look over; *(in a speech)* to treat in succession, go over, run over; *(of feelings)* to run through, penetrate, pierce ‖ *intr* to run fast, hurry along; *(w. ad)* to dash to; *(w. per + acc)* **1** to run through *or* across, travel through; **2** *(fig)* to run through, mention quickly, treat in succession

percursāti·ō -ōnis *f* traveling; a tour

percursi·ō -ōnis *f* quick survey

percurs·ō -āre -āvī -ātum *tr & intr* to roam about

percussi·ō -ōnis *f* hitting, striking; snapping *(of fingers); (mus)* beat, time

percuss·or -ōris *m* assassin

percussus *pp of* **percutiō**

percuss·us -ūs *m* impact; striking

percu·tiō -tere -ssī -ssus *tr* to beat *or* hit hard; to strike *(w. lightning, sword, etc.); (of snakes)* to bite; to knock at *(door);* to strum *(lyre, etc.);* to smash; to pierce, stab, run through; to shoot; to kill; to shock, make a deep impression on; to astound; to dig *(ditch);* to coin *(money);* to trick, cheat; **fustī percutere** to beat to death; **secūrī percutere** to behead

perdecōr·us -a -um *adj* very pretty

perdēlīr·us -a -um *adj* very silly, quite irrational; quite crazy

perdeps·ō -ere -uī *tr* to knead thoroughly; *(sl)* to feel up *(sexually)*

Perdicc·ās -ae *m* founder of the Macedonian monarchy ‖ Perdiccas II, King of Macedonia from 454 to 413 B.C. ‖ Perdiccas III *(d. 359 B.C.)* ‖ distinguished general of Alexander the Great *(d. 321 B.C.)*

perdifficil·is -is -e *adj* very difficult

perdifficiliter *adv* with great difficulty

perdign·us -a -um *adj (w. abl)* quite worthy of

perdīlig·ēns -entis *adj* very diligent, very conscientious

perdīligenter *adv* very diligently, very conscientiously

per·discō -discere -didicī *tr* to learn thoroughly, learn by heart

perdisertē *adv* very eloquently

perditē *adv* recklessly, desperately

perdit·or -ōris *m* destroyer

perdit·us -a -um *adj* ruined, done-for; degenerate; infamous; reckless, incorrigible, hopeless; lost

perdit·us -ūs *m* ruination

perdiū *adv* for a very long time

perdiūturn·us -a -um *adj* protracted, long-lasting

perdīv·es -itis *adj* very rich

perd·īx -īcis *mf* partridge ‖ Perdīx Perdix *(nephew of Daedalus; Perdix was changed into a partridge)*

per·dō -dere -didī -ditus *tr* to wreck, ruin, destroy; to waste, squander; to lose; **perdere operam** to waste one's efforts

perdoc·eō -ēre -uī -tus *tr* to teach thoroughly

perdoctē *adv* very skillfully

perdoct·us -a -um *pp of* **perdoceō** ‖ *adj* very learned, very skillful

perdol·eō -ēre -uī -itum *intr* to be annoyed; to be a cause of annoyance

perdolēsc·ō -ere *intr* to become hurt, become annoyed

perdom·ō -āre -uī -itus *tr* to tame completely, subdue, subjugate

perdormīsc·ō -ere *intr* to sleep on, keep on sleeping

per·dūcō -dūcere -dūxī -ductus *tr* to lead, guide *(to a destination);* to bring *(to court); (of roads)* to lead *(to); (of a pimp)* to take *(s.o.)* to *(s.o. else's bed);* to cover, spread; to prolong, drag out; to induce; to seduce; *(w. ad)* **1** to lead, guide, escort to; **2** to build, run *(wall, ditch, road, etc.)* to; **3** to prolong, drag out, continue *(s.th.)* to *or* until; **4** to win over to, convince of

perduct·ō -āre -āvī -ātus *tr* to lead, guide

perduct·or -ōris *m* guide; pimp

perdūdum *adv* long long ago

perduelli·ō -ōnis *f* treason

perduell·is -is *m* enemy

perdūr·ō -āre -āvī -ātum *intr* to last, hold out

per·edō -edere *or* **-ēsse -ēdī -ēsus** *tr* to eat up, devour; *(of things)* to eat away

perēgī *perf of* **peragō**

peregrē *adv* abroad, away from home; from abroad; **peregrē abīre** *(or* **peregrē exīre)** to go abroad

peregrīn·a -ae *f* foreign woman

peregrīnābund·us -a -um *adj* traveling around, touring

peregrīnāti·ō -ōnis *f* living abroad; foreign travel, touring; *(of animals)* roaming, ranging

peregrīnāt·or -ōris *m* traveler *(abroad),* tourist

peregrīnit·ās -ātis *f* foreign manners, outlandish ways; alien status

peregrīn·or -ārī -ātus sum *intr* to live abroad; to travel abroad; *(fig)* to be a stranger

peregrīn·us -a -um *adj* foreign; strange; alien, exotic; outlandish; *(fig)* strange; *(fig)* inexperienced; **amōrēs peregrīnī** love affairs with foreign women; **praetor peregrīnus** praetor who tried cases involving disputes between foreigners and Roman citizens; **terror peregrīnus** fear of a foreign enemy ‖ *mf* foreigner, alien

perēleg·āns -antis *adj* very elegant

perēleganter *adv* very elegantly

perēloqu·ēns -entis *adv* very eloquent

peremn·is -is -e *adj* **auspicia peremnia** auspices taken before crossing a river

peremptus *pp of* **perimō**

perendiē *adv* the day after tomorrow

perendin·us -a -um *adj* **diēs perendinus** the day after tomorrow

perenn·is -is -e *adj* perennial, continual, everlasting

perenniserv·os -ī *m* slave for life

perennit·ās -ātis *f* continuance, perpetuity

perenn·ō -āre *intr* to last

pērenticīd·a -ae *m (hum)* purse snatcher

per·eō -īre -iī -itum *intr* to pass away, pass on, die; to go to waste, perish, be destroyed; to be lost, be ruined, be undone; to be desperately in love, pine away; *(of snow)* to melt away; *(of iron)* to rust away; **periī!** *(coll)* I'm finished!, I'm washed up!

perequit·ō -āre -āvī -ātus *tr* to ride through *(on horseback)* ‖ *intr* to ride around *(on horseback)*

pererr·ō -āre -āvī -ātus *tr* to roam around, wander through; to survey, look *(s.o.)* over ‖ *intr* to roam all around

perērudīt·us -a -um *adj* very learned, erudite

perēsus *pp of* **peredō**

perexcels·us -a -um *adj* very high up

perexiguē *adv* very sparingly

perexigu·us -a -um *adj* tiny; insignificant; very short *(day)*

perexpedīt·us -a -um *adj* readily available

perfacētē *adv* very wittily

perfacēt·us -a -um *adj* very witty

perfacile *adv* very easily

perfacil·is -is -e *adj* very easy

perfamiliār·is -is -e *adj* very close, intimate ‖ *mf* very close friend

perfectē *adv* completely; perfectly

perfecti·ō -ōnis *f* completion; perfection

perfect·or -ōris *m* finisher, perfecter; **dīcendī perfector** stylist

perfect·us -a -um *pp of* **perficiō** ‖ *adj* complete, finished; perfect; *(gram)* perfect; **praeteritum perfectum** perfect tense

per·ferō -ferre -tulī -lātus *tr* to carry through; to endure to the end, bear with patience, put up with; to drive home *(a weapon);* to deliver *(message),* bring news of; to cause *(news)* to reach; to keep up *(an attitude, activity)* to the end; *(of things)* to be capable of accommodating; *(pol)* to get *(a law)* passed

per·ficiō -ficere -fēcī -fectus *tr* to complete, finish, bring to an end; to accomplish, carry out, execute; to perfect; to cause; *(w. ut, nē)* to bring it about (that, that not)

perfic·us -a -um *adj* that completes *or* perfects

perfidē *adv* dishonestly

perfidēl·is -is -e *adj* completely trustworthy

perfidi·a -ae *f* treachery, perfidy

perfidiōsē *adv* treacherously

perfidiōs·us -a -um *adj* treacherous, false

perfid·us -a -um *adj* treacherous, false; untrustworthy, dishonest, sneaky ‖ *m* a sneak

perfī·gō -gere -xī -xus *tr* to pierce

perflābil·is -is -e *adj* airy; invisible

perflāgitiōs·us -a -um *adj* utterly disgraceful, utterly scandalous

perflāt·us -ūs m draft
perfl·ō -āre -āvī -ātus tr to blow across, blow through; to blow throughout (a period) ‖ intr to blow hard, blow continuously
perfluctu·ō -āre -āvī -ātus tr to surge through
perflu·ō -ere -xī intr to flow along; to leak all over; (w. per) to flow through
per·fodiō -fodere -fōdī -fossus tr to dig through; to pierce, stab
perfor·ō -āre -āvī -ātus tr to bore through, pierce; to make by boring
perfortiter adv very bravely
perfoss·or -ōris m borer; parietum perfossor burglar (literally, one who bores through walls)
perfossus pp of perfodiō
perfrāctus pp of perfringō
perfrem·ō -ere intr to snort loud
perfrequ·ēns -entis adj very crowded, overcrowded
perfric·ō -āre -uī -tus and -ātus tr to rub hard, rub all over; ōs perfricāre to rub away blushes, put on a bold front
perfrīgefac·iō -ere tr (fig) to send a chill over, make shudder
per·frīgēscō perfrīgēscere perfrīxī intr to become chilled; to catch a bad cold
perfrīgid·us -a -um adj ice-cold
per·fringō -fringere -frēgī -frāctus tr to break through; to break into; to break to pieces, smash; to break down (a door); (fig) to break up (conspiracy); (fig) to break (the law); (med) to fracture
per·fruor -fruī -frūctus sum intr (w. abl) 1 to enjoy fully; 2 to perform gladly
perfug·a -ae m military deserter; political turncoat; refugee
per·fugiō -fugere -fūgī intr (w. ad or in + acc) 1 to flee to for refuge; 2 to desert to; 3 to have recourse to
perfug·ium -(i)ī n place of refuge, shelter, sanctuary; way of escape; (fig) an escape; excuse, defense; means of protection or safety
perfūncti·ō -ōnis f performance, performing, discharge
perfūnctus pp of perfungor
per·fundō -fundere -fūdī -fūsus tr to drench, bathe; to flood; to sprinkle; to dye; (of river) to flow through; (of sun) to drench (w. light, color); (fig) to fill, steep, inspire ‖ refl & pass to bathe, take a bath
per·fun·gor -fungī -fūnctus sum tr to enjoy ‖ intr (w. abl) 1 to perform, discharge, fulfill; 2 to endure, undergo; 3 to get rid of; 4 to be finished with, be done with; 5 to enjoy
perfur·ō -ere intr to rage wildly, rage on and on
perfūsus pp of perfundō

Pergam·a -ōrum npl or Pergam·um -ī n Pergamum (citadel of Troy), Troy
Pergame·us -a -um adj Trojan ‖ f Pergamea (name given by Aeneas to his city on Crete) ‖ mpl Trojans
Pergam·os -ī f or Pergam·um -ī n or Pergam·on -ī n Pergamum (city of Mysia famous for its library and temple of Aesculapius)
pergaud·eō -ēre intr to be very glad
pergn·ōscō -ōscere -ōvī tr to be well-acquainted with
per·gō -gere -rēxī -rēctus tr to go on interruptedly with, continue; (w. inf) to continue to; iter pergere to go on one's way ‖ intr to go straight on, continue, proceed; (w. ad) 1 to make one's way toward; 2 to pass on to, proceed to (esp. a topic); perge modo! go on now!, now get going!
pergraec·or -ārī intr (coll) to go completely Greek, have a ball
pergrand·is -is -e adj very large, huge; pergrandis nātū very old
pergraphic·us -a -um adj perfectly drawn
pergrāt·us -a -um adj very pleasant ‖ n distinct pleasure; pergrātum mihi fēceris sī you would be doing me a very great favor if
pergrav·is -is -e adj very heavy; very important; very impressive
pergraviter adv very seriously
pergul·a -ae f open porch (used for business, as a school, as a brothel)
perhib·eō -ēre -uī -itus tr to present; to assert, regard, maintain; to call, name; to adduce, cite; testimōnium perhibēre to bear witness
perhīlum adv very little
perhonōrificē adv with all due respect, very respectfully
perhonōrific·us -a -um adj very complimentary; very respectful
perhorr·ēscō -ēscere -uī tr to begin to shudder at; to develop a terror of ‖ intr to begin to tremble violently
perhūmāniter adv very kindly
perhūmān·us -a -um adj very kind
Pericl·ēs -is m famous Athenian statesman (495–429 B.C.)
perīclitāti·ō -ōnis f test, experiment
perīclit·or -ārī -ātus sum tr to test, put to the test, try; to jeopardize; to risk ‖ intr to be in danger, be in jeopardy; to run a risk; (w. abl) to be in danger of losing (life, reputation, etc.); capite perīclitārī to risk one's life
perīc(u)l·um -ī n danger, peril, risk; trial, attempt; experiment, test; literary venture; (leg) case, trial, lawsuit, legal record, sentence; perīculum facere to run the risk; try it out; (w. gen) to test, put to the test (e.g., s.o.'s loyalty); perīculum facere ex aliīs to learn

from the mistakes of others; **perīculum intendere** *(w. dat)* to expose *(s.o.)* to danger, endanger *(s.o.);* **volō perīculum facere an** I want to see whether

perīculōsē *adv* dangerously

perīculōs·us -a -um *adj* dangerous, risky, perilous

perīdōne·us -a -um *adj* very suitable; *(w. dat or* **ad)** well-adapted to, well-suited to

Perillē·us -a - um *adj* of Perillus

Perill·us -ī *m* Athenian sculptor who made for the tyrant Phalaris a bronze bull in which to roast people alive

perillūstr·is -is -e *adj* very clear; very illustrious, very distinguished

perimbēcill·us -a -um *adj* very weak, very feeble

per·imō -imere -ēmī -emptus *tr* to take away completely; to destroy; to kill

perimpedīt·us -a -um *adj* rough *(terrain);* full of obstacles

perincommodē *adv* very inconveniently

perincommod·us -a -um *adj* very inconvenient

perinde *adv* in the same manner, equally, just as, quite as; *(w.* **ac, atque, ut, prout,** *or* **quam)** just as; *(w.* **ac sī, quasi, tamquam,** *or* **quamsi)** just as if; **nōn perinde** not particularly, not as much as one would expect

perindulg·ēns -entis *adj* very tender; *(w.* **ad)** very tender toward

perīnfirm·us -a -um *adj* very weak

peringeniōs·us -a -um *adj* very gifted

perinīqu·us -a -um *adj* very unfair; very upset, very annoyed; very impatient; very reluctant; **perinīquō animō patī** *(or* **ferre)** to be quite upset at, be very reluctant about

perīnsign·is -is -e *adj* very remarkable

perinvīt·us -a -um *adj* very unwilling

period·us -ī *f (rhet)* complete sentence, period *(a group of words organically related in grammar and sense)*

peripatētic·us -a -um *adj* Peripatetic, Aristotelian **ǁ** *mpl* Peripatetics, Aristotelians

peripetasmat·a -um *npl* curtains, drapes

Periph·ās -antis *m* king of Attica, changed into an eagle by Zeus

periphras·is -is *f (acc:* -in) circumlocution

perīrāt·us -a -um *adj* very angry; *(w. dat)* very angry with

periscel·is -idis *f* anklet

peristrōm·a -atis *n* carpet; bedspread

peristȳl·ium -(i)ī *or* **peristȳl·um** *or* **peristȳl·on -ī** *n* peristyle *(inner court surrounded by a colonnade)*

perītē *adv* skillfully, expertly

perīti·a -ae *f* experience, practical knowledge, skill; *(w. gen)* experience in, familiarity with, knowledge of

perīt·us -a -um *adj (w. gen or abl, w.* **in** + *abl or* **ad)** experienced in, skillful in, expert in *or* at, familiar with; *(w. inf)* skilled in, expert at, *e.g.,* **perītus cantāre** skilled in singing; **iūris perītus** expert in the law, legal adviser, lawyer

periūcundē *adv* very pleasantly

periūcund·us -a -um *adj* very pleasant

periūr·ium -(i)ī *n* perjury; false oath; false promise

periūrō -āre *tr* **(-ier-)** to swear falsely by **ǁ** *intr* to swear a false oath, commit perjury; *(coll)* to lie

periūr·us -a -um *adj* **(-ier-)** perjured, oathbreaking; *(coll)* lying

per·lābor -lābī -lāpsus sum *intr* to glide along, skim across *or* over; *(w.* **per** + *acc)* **1** to slip through; **2** to slip along, glide along; *(w.* **ad)** to come, move, glide, *or* slip toward; *(w.* **in** + *acc)* to glide into, slip into

perlaet·us -a -um *adj* very glad, most joyful

perlāpsus *pp of* **perlābor**

perlātē *adv* very extensively

perlat·eō -ēre -uī *intr* to be completely hidden

perlātus *pp of* **perferō**

perlecebr·ae -ārum *fpl* enticement

perlēcti·ō -ōnis *f* thorough perusal

per·legō -legere -lēgī -lēctus *tr* to scan, survey thoroughly, to read through; to recount *(in a speech)*

perlepidē *adv* very nicely

perlev·is -is -e *adj* very light; very slight

perleviter *adv* very lightly; very slightly

perlib·ēns -entis *adj* **(-lub-)** very willing

perlibenter *adv* **(-lub-)** very gladly, very willingly

perlīberāl·is -is -e *adj* very well-bred, very genteel

perlīberāliter *adv* very generously

perlib·et -ēre *v impers* **(lub-)** **perlibet mē** *(w. inf)* I should very much like to

perliciō *see* **pelliciō**

perlit·ō -āre -āvī -ātus *tr* to sacrifice *(in order to get a favorable omen);* **ǁ** *intr* **bove perlitāre** to sacrifice an ox *(to obtain a favorable omen)*

perlongē *adv* a long way off

perlonginqu·us -a -um *adj* **(-os -a -om)** very long; very tedious

perlong·us -a -um *adj* very long; very tedious

perlub- = **perlib-**

per·lūceō -lūcēre *intr* **(pell-)** to shine clearly, be bright; to be clearly visible; to be transparent; to be clear, be intelligible

perlūcidul·us -a -um *adj* transparent

perlūcid·us -a -um *adj* **(pell-)** very bright; transparent

perlūctuōs·us -a -um *adj* very sad

per·luō **-luere** **-luī** **-lūtus** *tr* to wash thoroughly; to wash off; to bathe

perlūstr·ō **-āre** **-āvī** **-ātus** *tr* to traverse; to scan, survey, review

permade·faciō **-facere** **-fēcī** **-factus** *tr* to soak through and through, drench

permad·ēscō **-ēscere** **-uī** *intr* to become drenched

permagn·us **-a** **-um** *adj* very big; very great; very important ‖ *n* great thing; **permagnō** at a very high price, very dearly; **permagnum aestimāre** *(w. inf)* to think it quite something to

permānanter *adv* pervasively

permānāsc·ō **-ere** *intr (of a report)* to leak out

perman·eō **-ēre** **-sī** **-sum** *intr* to last, continue, hold out, remain, persist; *(of the voice)* to remain steady; **permanēre esse** to continue to be

permān·ō **-āre** **-āvī** **-ātus** *tr* to seep through, penetrate ‖ *intr* to penetrate; *(w.* **ad** *or* **in** + *acc)* **1** to seep through to; **2** to seep into, penetrate; **3** *(fig)* to reach, extend to, penetrate

permānsi·ō **-ōnis** *f* persistence, continuance

permarīn·us **-a** **-um** *adj* seagoing

permātūr·ēscō **-ēscere** **-uī** *intr* to become fully ripe

permediocr·is **-is** **-e** *adj* completely normal, very moderate

permeditāt·us **-a** **-um** *adj* well-rehearsed, well-trained

permēiō **-mēiere** **-mī(n)xī** **-ī(n)ctus** *tr (sl)* to soak with urine, urinate all over

permēnsus *pp of* **permētior**

perme·ō **-āre** **-āvī** **-ātus** *tr* to go through, cross over, cross ‖ *intr (w.* **in** + *acc)* to penetrate; *(w.* **per** + *acc)* to penetrate, permeate

Permēss·us **-ī** *m* river in Boeotia sacred to Apollo and the Muses

per·mētior **-mētīrī** **-mēnsus sum** *tr* to measure exactly; to travel over, traverse; to pass right through *(a period of time)*; **permētīrī oculīs** to take stock of, eye appraisingly

per·mingō **-mingere** **-minxī** **-mī(n)ctus** *tr (sl)* to soak with urine, urinate all over

permīr·us **-a** **-um** *adj* very surprising, truly amazing

per·mīsceō **-mīscēre** **-mīscuī mīxtus** *tr* to mix together, blend thoroughly, intermingle; to unite *(by marriage); (fig)* to involve, embroil; *(fig)* to mix up, confuse, treat as identical; to throw into confusion ‖ *pass (w.* **cum**) to combine with; *(w. abl or* **ex**) to consist of, be made up of

permissi·ō **-ōnis** *f* permission; unconditional surrender; *(as rhetorical device)* concession

permiss·us **-a** **-um** *pp of* **permittō** ‖ *n* permission

permiss·us **-ūs** *m* permission, leave

permitiāl·is **-is** **-e** *adj* destructive

permiti·ēs **-ēī** *f* wasting away; ruin; *(of persons)* source of ruin, ruination

per·mittō **-mittere** **-mīsī** **-missus** *tr* to let through, let go through; to hurl; to give up, surrender; to concede, relinquish; to let loose, let go; to let, permit, allow, grant; *(w. dat)* to surrender *(s.th.)* to, entrust *(s.th.)* to, grant *(s.th.)* to; *(w.* **in** + *acc)* to send flying at, hurl at

permīxtē *or* **permīxtim** *adv* confusedly; indiscriminately

permīxti·ō **-ōnis** *f* mixture; confusion, bedlam

permīxt·us **-a** **-um** *pp of* **permīsceō** ‖ *adj* confused; promiscuous; composite

permodest·us **-a** **-um** *adj* very modest, very moderate

permolestē *adv* with much trouble; **permolestē ferre** to be quite annoyed at

permolest·us **-a** **-um** *adj* very troublesome, very annoying

permol·ō **-ere** *tr* to grind up; **aliēnās uxōrēs permolere** *(sl)* to have sex with other men's wives

permōti·ō **-ōnis** *f* excitement; **animī permōtiō** *(or* **mentis permōtiō**) deep emotion

per·moveō **-movēre** **-mōvī** **-mōtus** *tr* to stir up, churn up *(the sea);* to move deeply, make a deep impression on; to excite, agitate, upset; to influence, induce

permul·ceō **-cēre** **-sī** **-sus** *tr* to stroke, pet; to soothe, calm down, relax; to smoothe out *(one's hair);* to charm, delight; to appease

permultō *adv* by far, much, far

permultum *adv* very much; **permultum ante** very often before; **permultum interest** it makes a world of difference

permult·us **-a** **-um** *adj* very much; *(w. pl nouns)* very many ‖ *n* a lot, much

permūn·iō **-īre** **-īvī** *or* **-iī** **-ītus** *tr* to fortify thoroughly; to finish fortifying

permūtāti·ō **-ōnis** *f* interchange; exchange; bartering; substitution, switch; reversal *(of an arrangement);* turning upside down, revolution; alternation, transformation

permūt·ō **-āre** **-āvī** **-ātus** *tr* to change *or* alter completely, transform; to interchange; to remit by bill of exchange; to reverse *(an order, arrangement);* to turn topsy-turvy *(w. abl or* **cum** *or* **prō** + *abl)* **1** to exchange for, replace with; **2** to receive in exchange for; **3** to acquire at the price of; **4** to substitute for

pern·a **-ae** *f* ham

pernecessāri·us **-a** **-um** *adj* very necessary; very closely related ‖ *m* close friend; close relative

pernecesse *indecl neut adj* very necessary, indispensable

perneg·ō -āre -āvī -ātus *tr* to deny flatly; to turn down flat

per·neō -nēre -nēvī -nētus *tr (of the Fates)* to spin out

perniciābil·is -is -e *adj* ruinous

pernici·ēs -ēī *f* ruin, destruction, disaster; pest, curse; cause of ruin

perniciōsē *adv* perniciously, ruinously

perniciōs·us -a -um *adj* pernicious, ruinous

pernīcit·ās -ātis *f* agility, nimbleness, swiftness

pernīciter *adv* nimbly, swiftly

perni·ger -gra -grum *adj* jet black; very dark *(eyes)*

pernimium *adv* much too much

pern·īx -īcis *adj* agile, nimble, swift, quick, speedy

pernōbil·is -is -e *adj* very famous

pernoct·ō -āre -āvī -ātum *intr* to spend the night

per·nōscō -nōscere -nōvī -nōtus *tr* to examine thoroughly; to become fully acquainted with, get accurate knowledge of

pernōt·ēscō -ēscere -uī *intr* to become generally known

per·nox -noctis *adj* all-night; **lūna pernox** full moon

pernumer·ō -āre -āvī -ātus *tr* to count up

pēr·ō -ōnis *m* clodhopper *(worn by peasants and soldiers)*

perobscūr·us -a -um *adj* very obscure; very vague

perō·dī -disse -sus *tr* to detest, loathe

perodiōs·us -a -um *adj* very annoying

perofficiōsē *adv* with attention, with great devotion; very politely

pērōnāt·us -a -um *adj* wearing clodhoppers

peropportūnē *adv* very conveniently, most opportunely

peropportūn·us -a -um *adj* most opportune, very convenient, well-timed

peroptātō *adv* very much in accordance with one's wishes

peroptāt·us -a -um *adj* greatly desired, longed-for

peropus *indecl n* great need; **peropus est** *(w. acc & inf)* it is essential that

perōrāti·ō -ōnis *f* peroration, summation

perōrnāt·us -a -um *adj* very flowery *(speech)*

perōrn·ō -āre -āvī -ātus *tr* to enhance the prestige of

perōr·ō -āre -āvī -ātus *tr* to bring *(a case, discussion)* to a close ‖ *intr* to bring a speech to a close; *(leg)* to wind up a case, give the summation

perōs·us -a -um *adj* hating, detesting; hated, hateful

perpāc·ō -āre -āvī -ātus *tr* to silence completely; to pacify thoroughly

perparcē *adv* most stingily

perparvul·us -a -um *adj* tiny

perparv·us -a -um *adj* very small

perpāst·us -a -um *adj* well-fed

perpauc·ī -ae -a *adj* very few ‖ *npl* very few words

perpaucul·ī -ae -a *adj* very few

perpaulum *adv* somewhat, slightly

perpaul·um -ī *n* small bit

perpaup·er -eris *adj* very poor

perpauxill·um -ī *n* little bit

perpave·faciō -facere -fēcī -factus *tr* to frighten the daylights out of

per·pellō -pellere -pulī -pulsus *tr* to push hard; to urge strongly, force; to drive all the way

perpendicul·um -ī *n* plumb line; **ad perpendiculum** perpendicularly

perpen·dō -dere -dī -sus *tr* to weigh carefully, consider; to value, judge

perperam *adv* incorrectly, wrongly; by mistake

Perpern·a *or* **Perpenn·a -ae** *m* Roman family name *(cognomen),* esp. Marcus Perperna Vento, partisan and later murderer of Sertorius

perp·es -etis *adj* continuous, uninterrupted

perpessi·ō -ōnis *f* endurance

per·petior -petī -pessus sum *tr* to endure, put up with, stand; to allow, permit

perpetr·ō -āre -āvī -ātus *tr* to accomplish, go through with, carry out, perform; to perpetrate, commit; to fulfill *(a promise); (w.* ut*)* to bring it about that

perpetuē *adv* constantly

perpetuit·ās -ātis *f* perpetuity

perpetuō *adv* constantly; forever

perpetu·ō -āre -āvī -ātus *tr* to perpetuate

perpetu·us -a -um *adj* perpetual, continuous; general, universal; whole; **quaestiōnēs perpetuae** standing courts; permanent committees ‖ *n* **in perpetuum** continuously; forever

perplac·eō -ēre *intr (w. dat)* to please immensely

perplexābil·is -is -e *adj* perplexing, puzzling

perplexābiliter *adv* perplexingly

perplexē *or* **perplexim** *adv* confusedly, unintelligibly

perplex·or -ārī *intr* to cause confusion

perplex·us -a -um *adj* intricate, complicated; ambiguous; muddled, mistaken; baffling *(words)*

perplicāt·us -a -um *adj* entangled

perplu·ō -ere *intr (of roof, etc.)* to let the rain in; *(of rain)* to come in

perpol·iō -īre -īvī *or* **-iī -ītus** *tr* to bring to a high polish; *(fig)* to polish up, perfect

perpolīt·us -a -um *adj* highly polished, refined

perpopul·or -ārī -ātus sum *tr* to ravage, devastate

perpōtāti·ō -ōnis *f* heavy drinking; drinking party

perpōt·ō -āre -āvī -ātus *tr* to drink up ‖ *intr* to drink heavily, carouse

per·primō -primere -pressī -pressus *tr* to press hard, squeeze hard

perpropinqu·us -a -um *adj* very near ‖ *m* close relative

perprūrīsc·ō -ere *intr* to begin to itch all over

perpugn·āx -ācis *adj* very belligerent

perpul·c(h)er -c(h)ra -c(h)rum *adj* very beautiful, very handsome

perpulsus *pp of* **perpellō**

perpurg·ō -āre -āvī -ātus *tr* to cleanse thoroughly, clean up; *(fig)* to clear up

perpusill·us -a -um *adj* puny

perput·ō -āre -āvī -ātus *tr* to prune back hard; to explain in detail

perquam *adv* very, extremely

per·quīrō -quīrere -quīsīvī *or* **-quīsiī -quīsītus** *tr* to search carefully for; to examine carefully

perquīsītius *adv* more accurately, more critically

perquīsit·or -ōris *m* enthusiast

perrārō *adv* very rarely

perrār·us -a -um *adj* very rare

perrecondit·us -a -um *adj* recondite

perrēctus *pp of* **pergō**

perrēp·ō -ere -sī *tr* to creep through; to crawl along *(the ground)*

perrept·ō -āre -āvī *tr* to creep through, sneak through ‖ *intr* to creep around

perrēxī *perf of* **pergō**

Perrhaeb·us -a -um *adj* of Perrhaebia *(a mountainous region of N. Thessaly)* ‖ *m* inhabitant of Perrhaebia

perrīdiculē *adv* most absurdly

perrīdicul·us -a -um *adj* utterly absurd

perrogāti·ō -ōnis *f* passage *(of a law)*

perrog·ō -āre *tr* to ask for in turn; to question in turn; **sententiās perrogāre** to poll the opinions *(in the senate)*

per·rumpō -rumpere -rūpī -ruptus *tr* to break through, force one's way through; to break in two, shatter, smash; to offend against, violate ‖ *intr* to break through, make a breakthrough

Pers·a -ae *or* **Pers·ē -ēs** *f* Perse, a daughter of Oceanus, wife of the sun, and mother of Circe, Perses *(father of Hecate)*, Aeëtes, and Pasiphaë *(wife of King Minos)*

Pers·a *or* **Pers·ēs -ae** *m* Persian

persaepe *adv* very often

persalsē *adv* very wittily

persals·us -a -um *adj* very witty

persalūtāti·ō -ōnis *f* round of greetings, greeting all in turn

persalūt·ō -āre -āvī -ātus *tr* to salute one after another

persanctē *adv* very solemnly

persapi·ēns -entis *adj* very wise

persapienter *adv* very wisely

perscienter *adv* very skillfully

per·scindō -scindere -scidī -scissus *tr* to tear to pieces; to split

perscīt·us -a -um *adj* very clever, very smart

per·scrībō -scrībere -scrīpsī -scrīptus *tr* to write out; to describe fully, give in detail; to finish writing; to record, register; to enter *(into an account book)*; to write out in full *(as opposed to abbreviating)*; **pecūniam perscrībere** to write a check for *(a certain sum of money)*

perscrīpti·ō -ōnis *f* entry, official record; check, payment by check

perscrīpt·or -ōris *m* bookkeeper, accountant

perscrīptus *pp of* **perscrībō**

perscrūt·or -ārī -ātus sum *tr* to search *or* examine thoroughly, scrutinize

Pers·ē -ēs *f see* **Persa** *f*

persec·ō -āre -uī -tus *tr* to dissect; to cut through; to lance *(a boil)*

persect·or -ārī -ātus sum *tr* to follow eagerly, investigate

persecūti·ō -ōnis *f* pursuit; *(leg)* right to sue; *(leg)* prosecution, suing

persecūtus *pp of* **persequor**

per·sedeō -sedēre -sēdī -sessum *intr* to remain seated

persēgn·is -is -e *adj* very slow-moving, very sluggish

Persē·is -idis *or* **-idos** *adj (fem only)* of Persa; of Perseus ‖ *f* daughter of Persa *(Hecate, Circe)* ‖ **Persa**

persen·tiō -tīre -sī -sus *tr* to perceive clearly, to feel deeply

persentīsc·ō -ere *tr* to become fully conscious of; to begin to feel deeply

Persephon·ē -ēs *f* daughter of Demeter and Zeus and queen of the lower world *(named Proserpina by the Romans)*

persequ·ēns -entis *adj* pursuing; *(w. gen)* given to the pursuit *or* practice of

perse·quor -quī -cūtus sum *tr* to follow persistently, follow up; to be in hot pursuit of, be on the heels of; to chase after, catch up to; to follow verbatim; to imitate, copy; to take vengeance on; to follow out, execute; to describe, explain; *(leg)* to prosecute

Pers·ēs *or* **Pers·a -ae** *or* **Pers·eūs -eī** *or* **-eos** *m* Perseus *(last king of Macedonia, conquered by Aemilius Paulus at Pydna in 169 B.C.)*

Pers·eūs -eī *or* **-eos** *m* son of Jupiter and Danaë, and slayer of Medusa ‖ *see* **Persēs**

Persē·us *or* **Persēī·us -a -um** *adj* of Perseus *(son of Jupiter and Danaë)*

persevēr·āns -antis *adj* persevering, persistent, relentless

persevēranter *adv* persistently

persevēranti·a -ae *f* perseverance

persevēr·ō -āre -āvī -ātus *tr* to persist in ‖ *intr* to persevere

persevēr·us -a -um *adj* very strict

Persi·a -ae *or* **Pers·is -idis** *or* **-idos** *f* Persia

Persic·us -a -um *adj* Persian; *(fig)* luxurious, soft; of Perseus *(king of Macedonia);* **mālum Persicum** peach ‖ *mpl* Persians ‖ *f* peach tree ‖ *n* peach ‖ *npl* Persian history

per·sīdō -sīdere -sēdī *intr* to sink down; *(w. ad or in + acc)* to penetrate

persign·ō -āre -āvī -ātus *tr* to record in detail *(articles in an inventory)*

persimil·is -is -e *adj* very similar; *(w. gen or dat)* very similar to

persimpl·ex -icis *adj* very simple

Pers·is -idis *or* **-idos** *adj (fem only)* Persian ‖ *f* Persia; Persian woman

Pers·ius -(i)ī *m* Persius *(Aulus Persius Flaccus, satirist in the reign of Nero, A.D. 34–62)*

persōll·a -ae *f* little mask; *(pej)* you ugly little thing!

persōl·us -a -um *adj* all alone

per·solvō -solvere solvī -solūtus *tr* to solve; to explain; to pay up, pay in full; to pay *(a penalty);* to fulfill *(a vow);* to carry out *(a duty);* to render *(thanks);* to offer *(sacrifice);* *(w. gen)* to pay the penalty for *(a crime);* *(w. dat)* to pay *(the penalty)* at the hands of; to solve *(a problem, riddle);* **ab omnibus eī poenae persolūtae sunt** punishment was inflicted on him by all; **dēbitum nātūrae persolvere** to pay one's debt to nature *(i.e., to die);* **honōrem dīs persolvere** to offer sacrifices to the gods; **grātēs dīs persolvere** to render thanksgiving to the gods; **grātiam dīs persolvere** to render thanks to the gods; **iūsta persolvere** to pay honors to the dead; **poenās dīs hominibusque persolvere** to suffer punishment at the hands of gods and men; **vectīgālia persolvere** to pay taxes; **vōta persolvere** to fulfill vows

persōn·a -ae *f* mask; part, character; pretense; personality; person; *(gram)* person; *(leg)* the person involved in a case; **ab** *(or* **ex** *or* **in)** **suā persōnā** *(acting, speaking)* in one's own name, on one's own behalf; **in persōnā** *(w. gen)* in the case of, in the instance of; **mea persōna** my personality *or* character; **persōnae fictiō** personification; **persōna mūta** a character with no speaking part

persōnāl·is -is -e *adj* personal

persōnāliter *adv* personally

persōnāt·us -a -um *adj* wearing a mask, masked; *(fig)* under false pretenses, putting on a front; **pater persōnātus** the father in the play; **persōnāta fābula** a play in which actors wear masks; **persōnātus histriō** an actor wearing a mask

person·ō -āre -uī -ātus *tr* to make *(a place)* resound; to shout out; to sing loudly, belt out *(a song);* **aurem personāre** to make the ear ring ‖ *intr* to resound, reecho; *(of a musician w. abl. of instrument)* to play loudly on *(e.g., the lyre); (of a singer)* to sing loudly; **citharā personāre** to produce loud music on the lyre

perspargō *see* **perspergō**

perspectē *adv* intelligently

perspect·ō -āre -āvī -ātus *tr* to examine carefully; to watch steadily ‖ *intr* to look all around, have a look around

perspect·us -a -um *pp of* **perspiciō** ‖ *adj* well-known, clear, evident; **rēs penitus perspectae** matters clearly understood

perspecul·or -ārī -ātus sum *tr* to explore thoroughly; *(mil)* to reconnoiter

persper·gō -gere -sī -sus *tr* **(-spar-)** to sprinkle; to strew *(w. flowers)*

perspexī *perf of* **perspiciō**

perspic·āx -ācis *adj* sharp-sighted; keen, penetrating, perspicacious

perspicienti·a -ae *f* clear perception

per·spiciō -spicere -spexī -spectus *tr* to see through; to look through; to look closely at, look over, examine, inspect, observe; to discern, ascertain; to prove

perspicuē *adv* clearly

perspicuit·ās -ātis *f* clarity

perspicu·us -a -um *adj* clear; transparent; clearly visible, conspicuous; plain, evident; lucid *(expression)*

perspīr·ō -āre *intr* to blow steadily

perspissō *adv* very slowly

persternō -sternere -strāvī -strātus *tr* to pave *(a road)* along its full length

perstimul·ō -āre -āvī -ātus *tr* to stimulate; to continue to stir up

per·stō stāre -stitī -stātum *intr* to stand firm, hold one's ground; to remain standing; to remain unchanged, last; to be firm, persevere, hold out; *(of soldiers)* to continue under arms; *(of things)* to remain stationary; *(w. inf)* to continue obstinately to *(do s.th.)*

perstrātus *pp of* **persternō**

perstrep·ō -ere -uī *intr* to make a loud noise, make a lot of noise

perstringō perstringere perstrīnxī perstrictum *tr* to tie, tie up; to make unfavorable mention of; *(of sounds)* to grate on; to blunt, deaden *(the senses);* to dazzle *(the eyes);* to deafen *(the ears);* *(of a weapon)* to graze; to glance over; to touch lightly on; to wound

(s.o.'s) feelings, offend; **Crassus meīs litterīs perstrictus est** Crassus was offended by *(or* took offense at) my letter; **horror ingēns spectantēs perstrīnxit** a deep shudder came over the onlookers
perstudiōsē *adv* enthusiastically
perstudiōs·us -a -um *adj (w. gen)* very fond of, enthusiastic about, very interested in
persuā·deō -dēre -sī -sum *intr (w. dat)* to persuade, convince; **sibi persuāsum habēre** to have oneself convinced
persuāsi·ō -ōnis *f* convincing; conviction, belief
persuāstr·īx -īcis *f* seductress
persuāsum *pp of* **persuādeō**
persuās·us -ūs *m* persuasion
persubtīl·is -is -e *adj* of very fine texture; very subtle, very ingenious
persult·ō -āre -āvī -ātus *tr* to prance about; to scour *(woods)* ‖ *intr* to gambol, prance, run around
per·taedet -taedēre -taesum est *v impers (w. acc of person = subject in English and gen. of thing = object in English)* to be weary of, be sick and tired of, be bored with, *e.g.,* **mē hūius negōtiī pertaedet** I am sick and tired of this business
per·tegō -tegere -tēxī -tēctus *tr* to cover up, cover completely; to roof over
pertempt·ō -āre -āvī -ātus *tr* (-tent-) to test thoroughly; to sound *(s.o.)* out; to consider well; *(fig)* to fill, pervade; **gaudia pertemptant pectus** joy fills *(their)* hearts
perten·dō -dere -dī -sus *or* -tus *tr* to press on with, continue, carry out ‖ *intr* to press on, continue, persevere, keep going
pertenu·is -is -e *adj* very thin, very slight, very small, very fine
perterebr·ō -āre -āvī -ātus *tr* to bore through
perter·geō -ēre -sī -sus *tr* to wipe off; *(of air)* to brush lightly against
perterre·faciō -facere -fēcī -factus *tr* to scare the life out of
perterr·eō -ēre -uī -itus *tr* to frighten, terrify; *(w. ab)* to frighten *(s.o.)* away from
perterricrep·us -a -um *adj* terrible-sounding, rattling frightfully
pertex·ō -ere -uī -tus *tr* to bring to an end, go through with, accomplish; to complete the composition of *(a speech, writing)*
pertic·a -ae *f* pole; rod, staff; ten-foot measuring pole; *(fig)* measure
pertimefact·us -a -um *adj* thoroughly frightened
pertim·ēscō -ēscere -uī *tr* to be alarmed at, become afraid of ‖ *intr* to become very frightened *or* alarmed
pertināci·a -ae *f* stubbornness; perseverance, determination

pertināciter *adv* stubbornly, tenaciously; through thick and thin
pertin·āx -ācis *adj* very tenacious; persevering, steadfast; stubborn
pertin·eō -ēre -uī *intr* to reach, extend; *(w. per + acc)* to pervade; **2** reach; *(w. ad)* **1** to extend, to reach; **2** to pertain to, relate to, concern; **3** to apply to, be applicable to, suit, be suitable to; **4** to be conducive to; **5** to belong to; **quod pertinet** *(w. ad)* as regards
perting·ō -ere *tr* to get as far as, reach ‖ *intr* to extend; **collis in inmēnsum pertingēns** a hill extending a very long distance
pertoler·ō -āre -āvī -ātus *tr* to put up with, endure to the end
pertorqu·eō -ēre *tr* to twist, distort
pertractātē *adv* in a trite manner
pertractāti·ō -ōnis *f* handling, treatment
pertract·ō -āre -āvī -ātus *tr* to handle; *(fig)* to treat systematically; to examine in detail
per·trahō -trahere -trāxī -tractus *tr* to drag along; to drag by force *(to s.th. unpleasant);* to lure, lead on *(an enemy);* to tow
pertrect- = **pertract-**
pertrīst·is -is -e *adj* very sad; very stern
pertulī *perf of* **perferō**
pertumultuōsē *adv* very excitedly, hysterically
per·tundō -tundere -tudī -tūsus *tr* to punch a hole through, perforate
perturbātē *adv* in confusion
perturbāti·ō -ōnis *f* confusion, disorder; riot; distress, agitation; strong emotion
perturbātr·īx -īcis *f* disturbing element
perturbāt·us -a -um *adj* disturbed, troubled, excited, alarmed; embarrassed
perturb·ō -āre -āvī -ātus *tr* to throw into confusion, confuse; to disturb; to embarrass; to upset; to alarm
perturp·is -is -e *adj* downright shameful
pertūs·us -a -um *pp of* **pertundō** ‖ *adj* perforated; tattered *(clothes)*
pērul·a -ae *f* small satchel
per·ung(u)ō -ung(u)ere -ūnxī -ūnctus *tr* to anoint thoroughly
perurbān·us -a -um *adj* very polite; very sophisticated ‖ *m* snob
per·ūrō -ūrere -ūssī -ūstus *tr* to burn up; to consume; to inflame, rub sore; to scorch; *(of cold)* to nip, bite; *(fig)* to fire, inflame
Perusi·a -ae *f* town in Etruria *(modern Perugia)*
Perusīn·us -a -um *adj* of Perusia ‖ *mpl* inhabitants of Perusia ‖ *n* an estate in Perusia
perūssī *perf of* **perūrō**
perūstus *pp of* **perūrō**
perūtil·is -is -e *adj* very useful
per·vādō -vādere -vāsī -vāsus *tr* to pass through, go through; to pervade ‖ *intr* to spread; to penetrate; *(w. ad or in + acc)* **1** to

go as far as, spread to; **2** to reach, arrive at; **3** to penetrate; *(w.* **per** + *acc)* to spread through *or* over

pervagāt·us -a -um *adj* widespread, prevalent, well-known; general, common; of widespread application

pervag·or -ārī -ātus sum *tr* to spread through *or* over, pervade ‖ *intr* to wander all over, range about; *(w.* **ad) 1** to spread to, extend to; **2** to be known as far as

pervag·us -a -um *adj* wandering about

perval·eō -ēre *intr (of a magnet)* to retain (its) power

pervariē *adv* in various versions

pervast·ō -āre -āvī -ātus *tr* to devastate

pervāsus *pp of* **pervādō**

perve·hō -here -xī -ctus *tr* to bring, carry, convey; to bring *(e.g, supplies)* through ‖ *pass* to ride, drive, sail; **in portum pervehī** to sail into port, reach port

pervell·ō -ere -ī *tr* to pull hard; to pinch hard; to excite, arouse; to cause to twinge; *(fig)* to disparage; **aurem alicui pervellere** to pull s.o.'s ear *(as a reminder)*

per·veniō -venīre -vēnī -ventus *tr* to come to, reach ‖ *intr* to come up; to arrive; *(w.* **ad** *or* **in** + *acc)* **1** to arrive at, reach; **2** *(fig)* to attain to

pervēn·or -ārī *tr* to search through, scour *(e.g., all the city)*

perversāriō *adv* (**-vors-**) in a wrong-headed way, wrongly

perversē *adv* (**-vors-**) wrongly, perversely

perversit·ās -ātis *f* perversity, unreasonableness; distortion

pervers·us -a -um *adj* (**-vors-**) turned the wrong way, awry, crooked; cross-eyed; *(fig)* crooked, wrong, perverse; *(fig)* spiteful, malicious

per·vertō -vertere -vertī -versus *tr* (**-vort-**) to overturn, upset, knock down; to invert the order of; to cause to face in the opposite direction; to bend out of shape, distort; to misrepresent, falsify *(statements);* to divert to an improper use, misuse, abuse; to undo, destroy; to pervert, spoil

pervesperī *adv* late in the evening

pervestīgāti·ō -ōnis *f* thorough search, examining, investigation

pervestīg·ō -āre -āvī -ātus *tr* to track down; to examine in detail; *(fig)* to trace, detect

pervet·us -eris *adj* very old, ancient

pervetust·us -a -um *adj* very ancient

pervexī *perf of* **pervehō**

perviam *adv* **perviam facere** to make accessible

pervicāci·a -ae *f* persistence; *(pej)* stubbornness; **pervicācia in hostem** obstinate resistance to the enemy

pervicācius *adv* more stubbornly

pervic·āx -ācis *adj* persistent, determined; *(pej)* headstrong, stubborn

pervīcī *perf of* **pervincō**

pervictus *pp of* **pervincō**

per·videō -vidēre -vīdī -vīsus *tr* to look over, survey; to see through; to examine, investigate; to realize, perceive fully

pervig·eō -ēre -uī *intr* to continue to thrive

pervig·il -ilis *adj* wide-awake, ever watchful

pervigilāti·ō -ōnis *f* religious vigil

pervigil·ium -(i)ī *n* all-night vigil

pervigil·ō -āre -āvī -ātus *tr* to spend *or* pass *(nights, days)* without sleep ‖ *intr* to stay awake all night, keep an all-night vigil

pervīl·is -is -e *adj* very cheap

per·vincō -vincere -vīcī -victus *tr* to defeat completely, completely get the better of; to outdo; to outbid; to convince; to prove ‖ *intr* to win, succeed; to carry a point; *(w.* **ut)** to succeed in, bring it about that; **nōn pervīcit ut referrent cōnsulēs** he did not succeed in having the consuls make a formal proposal

pervīsus *pp of* **pervideō**

pervi·us -a -um *adj* crossable, passable; open at both ends; perforated; accessible; open to entreaty ‖ *n* passage

per·vīvō -vīvere -vīxī *intr* to live on, go on living

pervolgō *see* **pervulgō**

pervolit·ō -āre -āvī -ātus *tr & intr* to fly about, flit about

pervol·ō -āre -āvī -ātus *tr* to fly through, fly about, flit about; to dart through, pass quickly over ‖ *intr* to fly about, flit about; *(w.* **in** + *acc)* to fly through to, arrive at, reach

per·volō -velle -voluī *tr* to wish very much; **tē quam prīmum pervelim vidēre** I'd like very much to see you as soon as possible

pervolūt·ō -āre -āvī -ātus *tr* to turn over often, read through *(a scroll)*

per·volvō -volvere -volvī -volūtus *tr* to roll *(s.o.)* over; to keep reading, read through *(a scroll)* ‖ *refl* to roll around ‖ *pass* to be busy

pervor- = **perver-**

pervulgāt·us -a -um *adj* (**-vol-**) widely known, very common

pervulg·ō -āre -āvī -ātus *tr* (**-vol-**) to make known, make public, publicize; to frequent ‖ *refl* to prostitute oneself

pēs pedis *m* foot *(of body, of table, of couch; in verse);* rope at lower part of a sail, sheet; **ad pedēs dēscendere** to dismount *(in order to fight on foot);* **ad pedēs pugna** an infantry fight; **aequīs pedibus lābī** to sail on an even keel; **ante pedēs** in plain view; **in pedēs** feet first; **pede dextrō** *(or* **fēlīce** *or* **secundō)** auspiciously *(the right foot being associated with good omens);* **pedem cōnferre** to come to close quarters; **pedem ferre** to come; to go; **pedem pōnere** *(w.* in + *abl)* to set foot in; **pedem referre** to step back, retreat; **pedēs tollere** to lift the legs *(for sexual intercourse);* **pedibus** on foot; **pedibus claudere** to set to verse, put in meter; **pedibus īre in sententiam** *(w. gen)* to vote in favor of the proposal of; **pedibus itur in sententiam** the proposal is put to a vote; **pedibus merēre** *(or* **pedibus merērī)** to serve in the infantry; **pedibus vincere** to win a footrace; **plānō pede** on level ground; **pugna ad pedēs** infantry battle; **sē in pedēs conicere** *(or* **sē in pedēs cōnferre** *or* **sē in pedēs dare** *or* **sē pedibus dare)** to take to one's heels; **servus ā pedibus** footman; **sub pedibus** under one's sway

pessimē *(superl of* **male)** *adv* **(-sum-)** worst; most wickedly; most unfortunately; by a stroke of bad luck

pessim·us -a -um *(superl of* **malus)** *adj* **(-sum-)** worst; most villainous; most distressing

Pessin·ūs -ūntis *m* Galatian town on the borders of Phrygia, famous for its cult of Cybele

pessul·us -ī *m* bolt *(of a door)*

pessum *adv* down, to the ground, to the bottom; **pessum dare** *(or* **pessumdare** *as one word)* to send to the bottom, sink, drown, ruin, destroy; **pessum īre** to go down, sink, go to pot, go to the dogs

pestif·er -era -erum *adj* pestilential; destructive, pernicious, disastrous ‖ *m* troublemaker

pestiferē *adv* disastrously

pestil·ēns -entis *adj* pestilential, unhealthful; *(fig)* disastrous

pestilenti·a -ae *f* pestilence, plague; unhealthful atmosphere *or* climate

pestilit·ās -ātis *f* pestilence, plague

pest·is -is *f* contagious disease; plague; death, destruction; instrument of death *or* destruction; *(of persons)* troublemaker, anarchist, subversive

petasāt·us -a -um *adj* wearing a hat; *(fig)* ready to travel

petas·ō -ōnis *m* ham, leg of pork

petasuncul·us -ī *m* little ham

petas·us -ī *m* broad-rimmed hat

petaur·um -ī *n* springboard

Petēli·a -ae *f* town in Bruttium, besieged by Hannibal

petess·ō -ere *tr* **(-tiss-)** to be eager for, pursue; **pugnam petessere** to be spoiling for a fight

petīti·ō -ōnis *f* attack, blow, thrust, aim; petition, request, application; *(leg)* claim, suit, suing, right to sue; *(pol)* candidacy, political campaign; **petītiōnī sē dare** to become a candidate

petīt·or -ōris *m* applicant; *(leg)* plaintiff; *(pol)* political candidate

petītr·īx -īcis *f (leg)* plaintiff *(female)*

petītur·iō -īre *intr (pol)* to be eager for office

petīt·us -a -um *pp of* **petō** ‖ *adj* **longē petītus** far-fetched ‖ *n* request

pet·ō -ere -īvī *or* **-iī -ītus** *tr* to make for, head for; to attack; to strive after; to aim at; to demand, require, exact; to ask for; to claim, lay claim to, sue for; to beg, entreat; to look for, go in search of, search for; to run after, chase *(girls);* to go and fetch; to obtain; to draw *(a sigh);* to run for *(office);* to refer to, relate to; *(w. dat or* ad *or* in + *acc)* to demand *(s.o. or s.th.) (for a specific purpose), e g.,* **custōdem in vincula petere** to demand that the watchdog be chained; **astra petere** to mount to the stars; **terram petere** to fall to the earth

petorrit·um -ī *n* **(-tōri-)** open four-wheeled carriage *(of Celtic origin)*

Petosīr·is -idis *m* Egyptian astrologer; *(fig)* a great astrologer, mathemtician

Petr·a -ae *f* Petra *(name of several towns, esp. the chief town of Arabia Petraea)*

petr·a -ae *f* rock, crag

Petrēi·us -ī *m* Roman clan name *(nomen), esp.* Marcus Petreius *(legate of Gaius Antonius against Catiline and later of Pompey in the Civil War)*

Petrīn·um -ī *n* place near Sinuessa on the border between Latium and Campania ‖ estate in this area

petr·ō -ōnis *m* castrated ram; *(pej)* yokel

Petrōn·ius -(i)ī *m* Petronius Arbiter *(author and master of cermonies at the court of Nero)*

petul·āns -antis *adj* petulant, brash, smartalecky; *(of sexual behavior)* horny

petulanter *adv* brashly, rudely

petulanti·a -ae *f* petulance, brashness; *(of speech)* rudeness; *(of sexual behavior)* horniness

petulc·us -a -um *adj* butting, apt to butt

Peuceti·a -ae *f* Peucetia *(S. section of Apulia)*

Peuceti·us -a -um *adj* of Peucetia

pexī *perf of* **pectō**

pex·us -a -um *pp of* **pectō** ‖ *adj* neatly combed; new, still having the nap on

P(h)thīōtic·us -a -um *adj* of Phthia *(native country of Achilles in Thessaly)*

Phaeāc·es -um *mpl* Phaeacians *(people living on a utopian island, according to the Odyssey)*

Phaeāc·ia -a -um *adj* Phaeacian ‖ *f* Phaeacia *(sometimes identified with Corcyra and ruled by King Alcinoüs)*

Phaeāc·us -a -um *adj* Phaeacian

Phae·āx -ācis *m* Phaeacian ‖ *m* Phaeacian; well-fed man

Phaedr·a -ae _f_ daughter of Minos and wife of Theseus

Phaedr·us -ī _m_ one of the Socratic circle, who gave his name to a dialogue of Plato ‖ Epicurean philosopher of Athens, who taught Cicero ‖ writer of fables, freedman of Augustus

Phaesti·as -adis _or_ **-ados** _adj (fem only)_ a woman of Phestum

Phaesti·us -a -um _adj_ of Phestum

Phaest·um -ī _n_ town in S. Crete

Phaët(h)·ōn -ontis _or_ **-ontos** _m_ son of Helios, who was killed by Zeus while driving his father's chariot

Phaët(h)ontiad·es -um _fpl_ sisters of Phaëthon, who were turned into trees

Phaëthonte·us -a -um _adj_ of Phaëthon

Phaëthont·is -idis _or_ **-dos** _adj (fem only)_ of Phaëthon ‖ _fpl_ sisters of Phaëthon

Phaëthūs·a -ae _f_ the eldest sister of Phaëthon

pha·ger -grī _m_ fish _(sea-bream?)_

phalang·a -ae _f_ wooden roller _(for moving ships and siege engines)_

phalangīt·ae -ārum _mpl_ soldiers belonging to a Macedonian phalanx

phal·anx -angis _f_ phalanx _(compact body of heavy-armed men in battle formation first developed by the Macedonians)_

phalāric·a -ae _f_ **(fal-)** firebrand, fiery missile _(shot by a catapult or thrown by hand)_

Phalar·is -idis _m_ a tyrant of Agrigentum on S. coast of Sicily, notorious for the bronze bull in which he roasted his victims _(c. 570–554 B.C.)_

phaler·ae -ārum _fpl_ military medals; medallions _(worn by horses on the forehead and chest)_

phalerāt·us -a -um _adj_ wearing medals, decorated; ornamental

Phalēr·eūs -eī _or_ **-eos** _m_ Demetrius of Phalerum _(Athenian statesman)_

Phalēric·us -a -um _adj_ of Phaleron

Phalēr·um -ī _n_ Athenian harbor

phantasm·a -atis _n_ phantom, ghost

Pha·ōn -ōnis _f_ legendary Lesbian, reputed lover of Sappho

pharetr·a -ae _f_ quiver

pharetrāt·us -a -um _adj_ carrrying a quiver

Phari·us -a -um _adj_ of Pharos, Pharian; _(poet)_ Egyptian

pharmaceutri·a -ae _f_ witch, sorceress

pharmacopōl·a -ae _m_ druggist; _(pej)_ quack

Pharnac·ēs -is _m_ Pharnaces I _(king of Pontus and grandfather of Mithridates, died c. 169 B.C.)_ ‖ Pharnaces II _(son of Mithridates the Great, easily defeated by Caesar at Zela in 47 B.C.)_

Phar·os _or_ **Phar·us -ī** _f (m)_ Pharos _(island lying off Alexandria)_; lighthouse _(built on the_

E. tip of Pharos by Ptolemy II Philadelphus); a lighthouse _(in general); (poet)_ Egypt

Pharsālic·us -a -um _adj_ of Pharsalus

Pharsāli·us -a -um _adj_ Pharsalian ‖ _f_ Pharsalia _(district of Thessaly)_

Pharsāl·os _or_ **Pharsāl·us -ī** _f_ town in Thessaly near which Caesar defeated Pompey _(48 B.C.)_

phasēl·us _or_ **phasēl·os -ī** _mf_ kidney bean; light passenger ship

Phāsiac·us -a -um _adj_ of the River Phasis in Colchis; Colchian

phāsiān·a -ae _f_ pheasant _(female)_

phāsiān·us -ī _m_ pheasant _(male)_

Phāsi·as -ados _adj (fem only)_ Colchian ‖ _f_ Medea

Phās·is -idis _or_ **-idos** _m_ river in Colchis

phasm·a -atis _n_ specter, ghost

Phēgēi·us -a -um _adj_ of Phegeus, king of Psophis in Arcadia, the father of Alphesiboea

Phēm·ius -(i)ī _m_ minstrel of Ithaca

Phene·us _or_ **Phene·os -ī** _m or_ **Phene·on -ī** _n_ a town and stream with subterranean channels in Arcadia

Pher·ae -ārum _fpl_ city in Thessaly, home of Admetus

Pherae·us -a -um _adj_ of Pherae

Pherecl·ē·us -a -um _adj_ of Phereclus _(the builder of Paris' ship)_

phial·a -ae _f_ saucer

Phīdiac·us -a -um _adj_ of Phidias

Phīdi·ās -ae _m_ Greek sculptor and friend of Pericles _(fl 440 B.C.)_

Philaen·ī -ōrum _mpl_ two Carthaginian brothers who agreed to be buried alive to establish the frontier between Carthage and Cyrene

Philamm·ōn -ōnis _m_ legendary musician, son of Apollo

philēm·a -atis _n_ kiss

Philēm·ō(n) -onis _m_ Philemon _(pious rustic who was changed into an oak tree while his wife Baucis was changed into a linden tree)_

Philippēns·is -is -e _adj_ of Philippi ‖ _mpl_ the people of Philippi

Philippē·us -a -um _adj_ of Philip II of Macedon _(esp. as epithet of gold coins minted by Philip)_

Philipp·ī -ōrum _mpl_ city in Macedonia where Octavian and Antony defeated Brutus and Cassius _(42 B.C.)_

Philippic·ae -ārum _fpl_ Philippics _(series of vitriolic speeches directed at Antony by Cicero)_

Philippopol·is -eos _f_ city in Thessaly on the right bank of the Hebrus River

Philipp·us -ī _m_ name of several kings of Macedon _(esp. Philip II, father of Alexander, c. 382–336 B.C.)_

Philist·us -ī _m_ historian, from Syracuse _(d. 356 B.C.)_

philiti·a *or* **phīditi·a -ōrum** *npl* public meals at Sparta
Philoctēt·ēs -ae *m* Greek warrior who was abandoned by the Greek army on the island of Lemnos
philologi·a -ae *f* love of study; study of literature
philolog·us -a -um *adj* learned, scholarly ‖ *m* scholar
Philomēl·a -ae *f* daughter of Pandion; she and her sister Procne were changed into nightingales
Phil·ō(n) -ōnis *m* Philo (*Academic philosopher and teacher of Cicero*)
philosoph·a -ae *f* philosopher (*female*)
philosophē *adv* philosophically
philosophi·a -ae *f* philosophy
philosoph·or -ārī -ātus sum *intr* to pursue philosophy; to philosophize, moralize
philosoph·us -a -um *adj* philosophical ‖ *m* philosopher
philtr·um -ī *n* love potion
philyr·a -ae *f* inner bark of the lime tree (*from which bands for chaplets were made*)
Philyr·a -ae *f* nymph, the mother of Chiron by Saturn
Philyrēi·us -a -um *adj* of Philyra; of Chiron; **hērōs Philyrēius** Chiron
Philyrid·ēs -is *m* son of Philyra (*i.e., Chiron*)
phīm·us -ī *m* dice box
Phīnēi·us -a -um *adj* of Phineus
Phīn·eūs -ēī *or* **-eos** *m* king of Thrace, plagued by the Harpies
Phīnid·ēs -ae *m* descendant of Phineus
Phlegeth·ōn -ontis *m* river of fire in the lower world
Phlegethont·is -idis *adj* (*fem only*) of Phlegethon
Phlegr·a -ae *f* a country of Macedonia, later called Pelle (*where the Giants were said to have been struck by lightning in battle with the gods*)
Phlegrae·us -a -um *adj* of Phlegra
Phlegy·ae -ārum *mpl* a people of Thessaly
Phlegy·ās -ae *m* king of the Lapiths, son of Ares, and father of Ixion
Phlī·ūs -ūntis *f* city of N.E. Peloponnesus
phōc·a -ae *or* **phōc·ē -ēs** *f* seal
Phōcae·a -ae *f* Ionian city on the coast of Asia Minor
Phōcaeēns·is -is -e *adj* of Phocaea ‖ *mpl* the people of Phocaea
Phōcae·us -a -um *adj* of Phocaea ‖ *mpl* the people of Phocaea
Phōcaïc·us *or* **Phōci·us -a -um** *adj* Phocian
Phōc·is -idis *or* **-idos** *f* region of central Greece containing the oracle of Delphi
Phoeb·as -adis *f* prophetess, priestess of Apollo

Phoeb·ē -ēs *f* Phoebe (*moon goddess, the sister of Phoebus, identified with Diana*); night
Phoebēi·us -a -um *adj* of Phoebus (*as sun-god and as god of prophecy, music, and healing*); of Aesculapius; **āles Phoebēius** the raven; **anguis Phoebēius** the snake of Aesculapius
Phoebē·us -a -um *adj* of Phoebus
Phoebigen·a -ae *m* son of Phoebus (*i.e., Aesculapius*)
Phoeb·us -ī *m* Apollo as sun-god; sun
Phoenīc·a -ae *or* **Phoenīc·ē -ēs** *f* Phoenicia
Phoenīc·es -um *mpl* Phoenicians
phoenīcopter·us -ī *m* flamingo
Phoeniss·a -ae *f* Phoenician woman (*esp. Dido*)
Phoen·īx -īcis *or* **-īcos** *m* Phoenician ‖ son of Amyntor and companion of Achilles ‖ son of Agenor and brother of Cadmus
phoen·ix -icis *or* **-īcos** *m* phoenix (*a bird said to live 500 years and from whose ashes a young phoenix would be born*)
Phol·us -ī *m* name of a Centaur
phōnasc·us -ī *m* voice teacher
Phorc·is -idos *f* daughter of Phorcus; Medusa ‖ *fpl* the Graeae
Phorc·us -ī *m* son of Neptune and father of Medusa and the other Gorgons and the Graeae
Phorcȳn·is -idis *or* **-idos** *f* Medusa
Phormi·ō -ōnis *m* Athenian admiral (*died c. 428 B.C.*) ‖ Peripatetic philosopher who lectured Hannibal on military science
Phraāt·ēs -ae *m* king of Parthia
phrenēs·is -is *f* frenzy, delirium
phrenētic·us -a -um *adj* frenetic, frantic, delirious
Phrix·us *or* **Phrix·os -ī** *m* Phrixus (*son of Athamas and Nephele and brother of Helle, with whom he fled to Colchis, riding the ram with a golden fleece*)
phronēs·is -is *f* wisdom
Phryg·es -um *mpl* Phrygians
Phrygi·a -ae *f* a country comprising part of the central and W. Asia; (*poet*) Troy
phrygi·ō -ōnis *m* (**fryg-**) embroiderer
Phrygi·us -a -um *adj & mf* Phrygian; Trojan
Phrȳn·ē -ēs *f* Athenian courtesan who offered to rebuild Thebes when it was destroyed by Alexander the Great
Phry·x -gis *or* **-gos** *adj* Phrygian (*often w. reference to Troy or the Trojans*)
Phthī·a -ae *f* home of Achilles in Thessaly
Phthī·as -adis *f* woman from Phthia
Phthīōt·a -ae *or* **Phthīōt·ēs -ae** *m* native of Phthia
phthis·is -is *f* tuberculosis
Phthī·us -a -um *adj* of Phthia
phȳ *interj* (*to express disdain*) bah!
phylac·a -ae *f* prison

Phylac·ē -ēs *f* city of Thessaly, where Protesilaus was king
Phylacē·is -idos *adj (fem only)* of Phylace, *or* of Phylacus, the founder of Phylace
Phylacēi·us -a -um *adj* of Phylace *or* Phylacus; **coniūnx Phylacēia** Laodamia *(wife of Protesilaus)*
Phylacid·ēs -ae *m* descendant of Phylacus, son of Diomede *(esp. Protesilaus)*
phylarch·us -ī *m* tribal chief, emir
Phyllēi·us -a -um *adj* of the city of Phyllus in Thessaly; **Phyllēius iuvenis** Caeneus
Phyll·is -idis *or* -idos *f* daughter of King Sithon of Thrace, who was changed into an almond tree ‖ stock female name in poetry
physic·a -ae *or* **physic·ē -ēs** *f* natural science
physicē *adv* scientifically
physic·us -a -um *adj* natural, physical, belonging to natural philosophy *or* physics ‖ *m* natural philosopher, physicist ‖ *npl* natural science
physiognōm·ōn -onis *m* physiognomist *(one who judges people's character by their appearance)*
physiologi·a -ae *f* natural science
piābil·is -is -e *adj* expiable
piāculār·is -is -e *adj* expiatory; demanding expiatory rites ‖ *npl* expiatory sacrifices
piācul·um -ī *n* propitiatory sacrifice, victim; atonement, expiation; remedy; crime, sacrilege; punishment
piām·en -inis *n* atonement
pīc·a -ae *f* magpie, jay
picāri·a -ae *f* place where pitch is made
pice·a -ae *f* pine tree, spruce
Pīc·ēns -entis *adj* Picene, of Picenum
Pīcentīn·us -a -um *adj* of Picenum; of Picentia *(town in S. Campania)*
Pīcēn·um -ī *n* distinct on the Adriatic coast of central Italy
Pīcēn·us -a -um *adj & m* Picene ‖ *n see* **Pīcēnum**
pice·us -a -um *adj* made of pitch; pitch-black
pic·ō -āre -āvī -ātus *tr* to tar, coat with pitch
pict·or -ōris *m* painter ‖ **Pictor** Quintus Fabius Pictor *(earliest Roman historian, who wrote a history of Rome in Greek, fl 225 B.C.)*
pictūr·a -ae *f* painting; (art of) painting; embroidery
pictūrāt·us -a -um *adj* painted; embroidered
pict·us -a -um *pp of* **pingō** ‖ *adj* painted; embroidered *(in color);* **tābula picta** a painting
pīc·us -ī *m* woodpecker; griffin ‖ **Pīcus** *(son of Saturn and grandfather of Latinus; Picus was changed by Circe into a woodpecker)*
piē *adv* dutifully; affectionately
Pīeri·a -ae *f* district of S. E. Macedonia
Pīeri·ae -ārum *fpl* the Muses

Pīer·is -idos *f* daughter of Pieros; Muse ‖ *fpl* the nine Muses
Pīeri·us -a -um *adj* Pierian; poetic; musical ‖ *f see* **Pīeria** ‖ *fpl* the Muses
Pīer·os *or* **Pīer·us -ī** *m* Pieros *(King of Emathia, or Macedonia, who named his nine daughters after the Muses; they were defeated in a contest with the Muses and were changed into birds)*
piet·ās -ātis *f* sense of responsibility, sense of duty; devotion, piety; *(of gods)* due regard *(for human beings);* kindness, tenderness; loyalty to the gods and country; *(w dat or adversus or ergā or in + acc)* respect for, devotion to, loyalty to
pi·ger -gra -grum *adj* apathetic, slow, lazy; reluctant, unwilling; numbing *(cold);* slow-moving, tedious *(war, etc.);* backward, slow, dull
pig·et -ēre -uit *or* **-itum est** *v impers* it irks, pains, annoys; *(w. gen of cause of feeling),* e.g.: **piget stultitiae meae** I am irked by my own foolishness; *(w. inf),* e.g.: **illa mē composuisse piget** I regret having written those verses
pigmentār·ius -(i)ī *m* paint dealer
pigment·um -ī *n* pigment, paint, color; coloring *(of style)*
pignerāt·or -ōris *m* mortgagee
pigner·ō -āre -āvī -ātus *tr* to mortgage; to pawn; *(fig)* to pledge
pigner·or -ārī -ātus sum *tr* to take as a pledge, accept in good faith; to lay claim to; to assure
pign·us -eris *or* **-oris** *n* pledge, security, guarantee; hostage; mortgage; income from mortgages; wager, stake; *(fig)* pledge, assurance ‖ *npl* children
pigrē *adv* slowly, sluggishly
pigriti·a -ae *or* **pigriti·ēs -ēī** *f* sluggishness, laziness
pigr·ō -āre -āvī *or* **pigr·or -ārī** *intr* to be slow, be sluggish, be lazy
pīl·a -ae *f (vessel for pounding)* mortar; pillar; pier; funerary monument *(w. cavity for mortal remains)*
pil·a -ae *f* ball; ball game; globe; ballot *(used by jury);* **mea pila est** the ball is mine, I've won; **pilā lūdere** to play ball
pīlān·us -ī *m* soldier in the third rank in battle
pīlāt·us -a -um *adj* armed with javelin
Pīlāt·us -ī *m* Pontius Pilate *(prefect of Judea, A.D. 26–36)*
pīlent·um -ī *n* ladies' carriage
pilleāt·us -a -um *adj* (**pīl-**) wearing a felt skullcap *(as a symbol of freed status)*
pilleol·us -ī *m* (small felt) skullcap
pille·um -ī *n or* **pille·us -ī** *m or* **pīle·um -ī** *n* felt cap *or* hat *(worn by Romans at festivals, esp. at the Saturnalia, and given to a slave*

when freed as a symbol of his freedom); freedom

pilōs·us -a -um *adj* hairy

pīl·um -ī *n* javelin

Pīlumn·us -ī *m* primitive Italic deity

pīl·us -ī *m* maniple *or* company of the triarii; company of veteran reserves; **prīmī pīlī centuriō** chief centurion of a legion; **prīmus pīlus** chief centurion *(of the triarii and therefore of the legion)*

pil·us -ī *n* hair; **nōn pilī facere** to not care a whit for

Pi(m)plē(i)·us -a -um *adj* of Pimpla ‖ *f* the spring at Pimpla

Pimpl·a -ae *f* town and spring in Pieria sacred to the Muses

Pimplē·a -ae *or* **Pi(m)plē·is -idis** *or* **idos** *f* Muse

pīn·a -ae *f* a bivalve shellfish

pinacothēc·a -ae *f* art gallery

Pīnāri·us -a -um *adj* name of a patrician clan at Rome, concerned with the cult of Hercules

Pindaric·us -a -um *adj* Pindaric

Pindar·us -ī *m* Pindar *(Greek lyric poet from Thebes in Boeotia, 519–438 B.C.)*

Pind·us -ī *m* mountain range separating Thessaly from Macedonia, connected with the Muses

pīnēt·um -ī *n* pine forest

pīne·us -a -um *adj* pine, of pine

pingō pingere pīnxī pictus *tr* to draw, paint; to embroider; to depict, represent, portray; to stain, color; to decorate; *(rhet)* to embellish

pingu·e -is *n* fat

pinguēsc·ō -ere *intr* to get fat; to become fertile

pingu·is -is -e *adj* fat; fatty, greasy; *(of lamps)* full of oil; *(of torches)* full of pitch; juicy; full-bodied *(wine);* rich, full *(sound);* rich, fertile *(land);* fat, sleek *(cattle);* thick *(in dimension);* strong *(words); (of altars)* caked with fat and blood; dense; stupid, dull; clumsy *(writing);* quiet, comfortable *(life, home, retreat);* **crūra lutō pinguia** legs caked with mud

pīnif·er *or* **pīnig·er -era -erum** *adj* pine-producing, pine-covered

pinn·a -ae *f* feather; wing; flight; fin; feathered arrow; pinnacle, battlement

pinnāt·us -a -um *adj* feathered, winged

pinnig·er -era -erum *adj* winged; feathered; having fins

pinnip·ēs -edis *adj* wing-footed

pinnipot·ēns -entis *adj* able to fly

pinnirap·us -ī *m* crest-snatcher *(gladiator who tried to get the crest of his opponent's helmet)*

pinnul·a -ae *f* little wing

pīnotēr·ēs -ae *m* hermit crab

pīnsit·ō -āre *tr* to pound (continually)

pīns·ō -ere pīnsī *or* **pīnsuī pīnsitus (pīs-)** to beat; to pound; **flāgrō pīnsere** to scourge, whip

pīn·us -ūs *or* **-ī** *f* pine tree, fir tree; pine forest; ship; torch; wreath of pine

pi·ō -āre -āvī -ātus *tr* to appease by sacrifice, propitiate; to honor with religious rites, worship; to purify with religious rites; to atone for, expiate; to avert

pip·er -eris *n* pepper

pīpil·ō -āre *intr* to chirp

pipinn·a -ae *f* childish term for the penis

pīpi·ō -āre *intr* to chirp

pīpul·um -ī *n* or **pīpul·us -ī** *m* shrieking, yelling

Pīrae·ēus *or* **Pīrae·us -ī** *m or* **Pīrae·a -ōrum** *npl* Piraeus *(principal harbor of Athens)*

Pīrae·us -a -um *adj* of Piraeus ‖ *mpl* inhabitants of Piraeus

pīrāt·a -ae *m* pirate

pīrātic·us -a -um *adj* pirate ‖ *f* piracy; **pīrāticam facere** to practice piracy

Pīrēn·ē -ēs *or* **Pīrēn·a -ae** *f* Pirene *(spring on the citadel of Corinth near which Bellerophon caught Pegasus)*

Pīrēn·is -idos *adj (fem only)* of the spring of Pirene

Pīritho·üs -ī *m* son of Ixion and king of the Lapiths

pir·um -ī *n* pear

pir·us -ī *f* pear tree

Pīs·a -ae *f or* **Pīs·ae -ārum** *fpl* Pisa *(capital of Pisatis in Elis on the Alpheus River)*

Pīs·ae -ārum *fpl* Pisa *(ancient city of N. Etruria, alleged to have been founded by the people of Greek Pisa)*

Pīsae·us -a -um *adj* of Pisa ‖ *f* Hippodamia

Pīsān·us -a -um *adj* of Pisa *(in Etruria)*

Pisaur·um -ī *n* city in Umbria on the Adriatic coast *(modern Pisaro)*

piscāri·us -a -um *adj* fish; of fishing; **forum piscārium** fish market

piscāt·or -ōris *m* fisherman; fishmonger

piscātōri·us -a -um *adj* fishing; fish

piscāt·us -ūs *m* fishing; fish *(as food; (fig)* good haul

piscicul·us -ī *m (lit & fig)* little fish

piscīn·a -ae *f* fish pond; swimming pool

piscīnār·ius -(i)ī *m* person fond of swimming pools *or* of fish ponds

pisc·is -is *m* fish ‖ **Piscēs** *mpl (astr)* Pisces *(constellation)*

pisc·or -ārī -ātus sum *intr* to fish

piscōs·us -a -um *adj* full of fish

pisculent·us -a -um *adj* well-stocked with fish

Pisid·a -ae *m* Pisidian *(inhabitant of Pisidia, referred to in contempt for the alleged addiction of the Pisidians to augury)*

Pisidi·a -ae *f* region in S. Asia Minor
Pīsistratid·ae -ārum *mpl* sons of Pisistratus *(Hippias & Hipparchus)*
Pīsistrat·us -ī *m* enlightened tyrant of Athens *(560–527 B.C.)*
Pīs·ō -ōnis *m* Roman family name *(cognomen)* of the Calpurnian clan ‖ Gnaeus Calpurnius Piso *(consul 7 B.C., accused of the murder of Germanicus in A.D. 19)* ‖ Gaius Calpurnius Piso *(alleged leader of the conspiracy against Nero in A.D. 65)*
pīsō *see* pīnsō
pīstill·um -ī *n or* pīstill·us -ī *m* pestle
pīst·or -ōris *m* miller; baker
Pistōriēns·is -is -e *adj* of Pistorium *(town in Etruria)*
pīstōri·us -a -um *adj* baker's; opus pīstōrium pastry
pīstrill·a -ae *f* small mill; small bakery
pīstrīn·a -ae *f* flour mill; bakery
pīstrīnēns·is -is -e *adj* of *or* belonging to a bakery
pīstrīn·um -ī *n* flour mill; bakery; drudgery
pistr·is -is *or* pistr·īx -īcis *f* sea monster; whale, shark; swift ship; *(astr)* the Whale *(constellation)*
pīs·um -ī *n* pea
pithēc·ium -(i)ī *n* little monkey
Pitthē·is -idos *f* daughter of Pittheus *(i.e., Aethra)*
Pitth·eūs -eī *or* -eos *m* king of Troezen and father of Aethra, the mother of Theseus
Pitthē·us *or* Pitthēi·us -a -um *adj* of Pittheus
pītuīt·a -ae *f* phlegm; rheum; head cold
pītuītōs·us -a -um *adj* full of phlegm, phlegmatic
pity·ōn -ōnis *m* woods of pine trees
pi·us -a -um *adj* conscientious, dutiful; godfearing, godly, holy; fatherly, motherly, brotherly, sisterly; affectionate; patriotic; good; sacred, holy *(objects connected with religion)*
pix picis *f* pitch, tar ‖ *fpl* chunks of pitch
plācābil·is -is -e *adj* easily appeased; pacifying, appeasing
plācābilit·ās -ātis *f* readiness to forgive, conciliatory disposition
plācām·en -inis *n* means of appeasing, peaceoffering
plācāment·um -ī *n* means of appeasing, peaceoffering
plācātē *adv* calmly, quietly
plācāti·ō -ōnis *f* pacifying, propitiating
plācāt·us -a -um *adj* calm, quiet; appeased, reconciled
plac·ēns -entis *adj* pleasing
placent·a -ae *f* flat cake
placenti·a -ae *f* agreeableness

Placenti·a -ae *f* town on the river Po *(modern Piacenza)*
plac·eō -ēre -uī -itum *intr (w. dat)* to please, satisfy, give pleasure to, be acceptable to; sibi placēre to be pleased with oneself ‖ *v impers* it seems right, seems proper; it is settled, is agreed; it is resolved, is decided; eīs placitum est ut cōnsīderārent they decided to consider; senātuī placuit the senate decided
placidē *adv* calmly, gently, quietly
placid·us -a -um *adj* calm; gentle; quiet, peaceful; tame *(animal)*
placit·ō -āre *intr* to be very pleasing
placit·us -a -um *adj* pleasing, acceptable; agreed upon ‖ *n* principle, belief, tenet; ultrā placitum laudāre to praise excessively
plāc·ō -āre -āvī -ātus *tr* to calm, quiet; to appease; to reconcile
plāg·a -ae *f* blow; wound, gash, welt; *(fig)* blow
plag·a -ae *f* region, tract, zone; hunting net; mesh of a net; curtain; *(fig)* trap
plagiār·ius -(i)ī *m* plunderer; kidnapper; plagiarist
plāgig·er -era -erum *adj* covered with welts
plāgigerul·us -a -um *adj* covered with welts
plāgipatid·ēs -ae *m* whipping boy
plāgōs·us -a -um *adj* quick to use the rod
plagul·a -ae *f* curtain
plagūsi·a -ae *f* a kind of shellfish
plānctus *pp of* plangō
plānct·us -ūs *m* beating
plānē *adv* clearly, distinctly; legibly; completely, quite; certainly, to be sure
plan·gō -gere plānxī plānctus *tr* to strike, beat; to beat *(head, breast as sign of grief);* to lament, bewail; *(fig)* to wring the hands ‖ *pass* to beat one's breast; *(of bird)* to flap its wings ‖ *intr* to wail
plang·or -ōris *m* striking, beating; beating of the breast, wailing
plāniloqu·us -a -um *adj* outspoken
plānip·ēs -edis *m* barefooted actor *(in the role of a slave)*
plānit·ās -ātis *f* distinctness
plāniti·ēs -ēī *or* plāniti·a -ae *f* flat surface, level ground, plain
plant·a -ae *f* sprout, shoot, young plant, seedling; *(anat)* sole
plantār·ia -ium *npl* cuttings, slips
plantār·ium -(i)ī *n* seedbed *(for starting seedlings)*
plān·us -a -um *adj* flat, level, even; plain, clear ‖ *n* level ground; plain; dē plānō easily; ē plānō out of court
plan·us -ī *m* tramp; con man
plasm·a -atis *n* phoney accent

Platae·ae -ārum *fpl* Plataea *(town in Boeotia where the Greeks defeated the Persians in 479 B.C.)*

Plataeēns·is -is -e *adj* of Plataea ‖ *mpl* Plataeans

platale·a -ae *f* spoonbill *(waterfowl)*

platan·ōn -ōnis *m* grove of plane trees

platan·us -ī *or* **-ūs** *f* plane tree

plate·a *or* **platē·a -ae** *f* street

Plat·ō(n) -ōnis *m* Plato *(Greek philosopher, 429–348 B.C.)*

Platōnic·us -a -um *adj* Platonic ‖ *mpl* Platonists

plau·dō -dere -sī -sus *tr* (**plōd-**) to slap, clap, beat ‖ *intr* to clap, beat, flap; applaud; *(w. dat)* to applaud, approve of; **ālīs plaudere** to flap the wings; **manibus plaudere** to clap the hands

plausibil·is -is -e *adj* deserving of applause

plaus·or *or* **plōs·or -oris** *m* applauder

plaustr·um -ī *n* (**plos-**) wagon, cart; **plaustrum percellere** *(fig)* to upset the applecart ‖ **Plaustrum** *(astr)* the Great Bear *(constellation)*

plausus *pp of* **plaudō**

plaus·us -ūs *m* clapping, flapping; applause

Plautīn·us -a -um *adj* of Plautus

Plauti·us -a -um *adj* of Plautus

Plaut·us -ī *m* Plautus *(Titus Maccius Plautus, Roman writer of comedies, born in Umbria, c. 254–184 B.C.)*

plēbēcul·a -ae *f* rabble

plēbēi·us -a -um *adj* plebeian, of the common people; common, low, vulgar ‖ *m* plebeian

plēbicol·a -ae *m* democrat; demagogue

plēbis(s)cīt·um -ī *n* decree of the assembly of the plebeians

plēbs *or* **plēps plēbis** *or* **plēb·ēs -ēī** *f* the plebeians, common people; the masses, proletariat

plectil·is -is -e *adj* plaited, braided

plēct·ō -ere *tr* to beat; to punish

plectō plectere plexī *or* **plexuī plexus** *tr* to plait, braid

plēctr·um -ī *n* plectrum; *(fig)* lyre

Plēï·as -adis *or* **-ados** *f* Pleiad ‖ *fpl* Pleiades *(seven daughters of Atlas and Pleione, who were placed among the stars)*

Plēïon·ē -ēs *f* daughter of Oceanus and Tethys, wife of Atlas, and mother of the Pleiades

Plēmyr·ium -(i)ī *n* headland at the S. end of the Bay of Syracuse

plēnē *adv* fully, completely

plēn·us -a -um *adj* full; stout, plump; pregnant; filled, satisfied, full; packed *(street, theater, etc.);* strong, loud *(voice);* full-length, unabridged, uncontracted; complete, entire; plentiful; advanced *(years);* complete; *(w. abl or gen)* full of

ple·ō -ēre *tr* to fill

plērumque *adv* generally, mostly, for the most part; often, frequently

plēr·usque -aque -umque *adj* a very great part of, the greater part of, most; a good many; **plērīque omnēs** nearly all ‖ *mpl* most people, the majority ‖ *n* the greatest part

Pleur·ōn -ōnis *f* a city in Aetolia

-pl·ex -icis *adj suf usu., formed from numerals, equivalent to the English "-fold," e.g.:* **centumplex** hundredfold

plex·us -a -um *pp of* **plectō** ‖ *adj* plaited

plicātr·īx -īcis *f* woman who folds clothes, folder

plic·ō -āre -āvī *or* **-uī -ātus** *or* **-itus** *tr* to fold, wind, coil up

Plīn·ius -(i)ī *m* Pliny the Elder *(Gaius Plinius Secundus, author of a work on natural history, d. A.D. 79)* ‖ Pliny the Younger *(Gaius Plinius Caecilius Secundus (his nephew), author of Letters and Panegyric to Trajan, A.D. 61–114)*

plīpi·ō -āre *intr (of a hawk)* to caw

plōdō *see* **plaudō**

plōrabil·is -is -e *adj* dismal

plōrātill·us -a -um *adj* tearful

plōrāt·or -ōris *m* mourner

plōrāt·us -ūs *m* wailing, crying

plōr·ō -āre -āvī -ātus *tr* to cry over ‖ *intr* to cry aloud, wail

plōstell·um -ī *n* small cart

plōstr·um -ī *n* wagon

ploxen·um -ī *n* (**-xin-**) wagon body

pluit pluere pluit *v impers (tr)* it is raining *(stones, blood, etc.)* ‖ *v impers (intr)* it is raining; *(w. abl)* it is raining *(stones, etc.);* **sanguine pluit** it rained blood

plūm·a -ae *f* down, soft feather; *(collectively)* down, feathers

plūmātil·e -is *n* dress embroidered with feathers

plūmāt·us -a -um *adj* covered with feathers

plumbe·us -a -um *adj* lead, of lead, leaden; oppressive *(weather);* dull *(blade);* cheap *(wine);* stupid

plumb·um -ī *n* lead; pellet *(for a sling);* pipe; ruler *(for drawing lines);* **plumbum album** *(or* **candidum)** tin

plūme·us -a -um *adj* downy; filled with down; like feathers

plūmip·ēs -edis *adj* with feathered feet

plūm·ō -āre -āvī -ātum *tr* to cause to be covered with feathers

plūmōs·us -a -um *adj* feathered, covered with feathers; *(fig)* feathery

plūrāl·is -is -e *adj (gram)* plural

plūrāliter *adv (gram)* in the plural

plūr·ēs -ēs -a *adj* more; several; too many; **plūribus (verbīs)** at great length, in greater detail **‖** *mpl* most people, the majority; the dead, "the majority" **‖** *npl* more things

plūrifāriam *adv* extensively, in many places

plūrimum *adv* (-rum-) very much, especially, commonly, generally, mostly; **plūrimum valēre** to be most powerful, have the greatest influence

plūrim·us -a -um *(superl of* **multus)** *adj* (-rum-) many a; most; very much; very many; very great, very intense; very powerful, very violent; **plūrimam salūtem dare** to send warmest greetings **‖** *mpl* most people, a very great number of people **‖** *n* a great deal; **plūrimī facere** to think very highly of, think a great deal of; **plūrimī vēndere** to sell at a very high price; **quam plūrimō vēndere** to sell at the highest possible price; **quam plūrimum** as much as possible

plūs *adv* more; **multō plūs** much more; **plūs minus** more or less; **paulō plūs** a little more

plūs plūris *(comp of* **multus)** *adj* more **‖** *n* more, too much; **plūs animī** more courage; **plūs nimiō** much too much; **plūs plūsque** more and more; **plūris esse** *(gen of value)* to be of more value, be worth more, be higher, be dearer; **plūris aestimāre** *(or* **facere** *of* **putāre** *or* **habēre)** to regard more highly, think more highly of **‖** *npl* more things; **quid plūra?** why say more?, in short, needless to say

plūscul·us -a -um *adj* a little more, somewhat more **‖** *n* a little more

plute·us -ī *m or* **plute·um -ī** *n* barrier, screen; low wall; parapet; headboard *or* footboard of bed *or* couch; *(fig)* couch; *(fig)* dining couch; bier; lectern; bookcase; *(mil)* movable mantlet *or* shed used to protect soldiers in siege works

Plūt·ō(n) -ōnis *m* Pluto *(king of the lower world, husband of Proserpina, and brother of Jupiter and Neptune)*

Plūtōni·us -a -um *adj* of Pluto

pluvi·a -ae *f* rain

pluviāl·is -is -e *adj* rain, of rain, rainy

pluvi·us -a -um *adj* rain, of rain, rainy; **pluvia aqua** rain water; **pluvius arcus** rainbow **‖** *f* rain

pōcill·um -ī *n* small drinking cup

pōc(u)l·um -ī *n* drinking cup; drink, draft; **pōculum (dūcere** *or* **exhaurīre)** to drain a cup

poda·ger -gra -grum *adj* suffering from sore feet

podagr·a -ae *f* arthritis

podagrōs·us -a -um *adj* arthritic

Podalīri·us -ī *m* legendary physician, son of Aesculapius

pōd·ex -icis *m (sl)* ass, behind

pod·ium -(i)ī *n* balcony; box seat *(for the emperor)*

Poeantiad·ēs -is *m* son of Poeas, Philoctetes

Poeanti·us -a -um *adj* of Poeas **‖** *m* Philoctetes

Poe·ās *or* **Poe·āns -antis** *m* father of

poēm·a -atis *n (dat & abl pl:* **poēmātibus** *or* **poēmatīs)** poem; poetry

poēmat·ium -(i)ī *n* short poem

poen·a -ae *f* punishment; penalty, fine; compensation, recompense, retribution, satisfaction; hardship, loss, pain; *(in games)* penalty; **poenam (or poenās) dare** *(or* **dēpendere, pendere, persolvere, reddere, solvere, suscipere, sufferre)** to pay the penalty; **poenam (or poenās) capere** *(or* **exigere, persequī, petere, repetere, repōscere)** to exact a penalty, demand satisfaction; **poena mortis** death penalty

Poenici·us -a -um *adj* Punic, Carthaginian

Poenīn·ī -ōrum *mpl* the Pennine Alps *(from Mont Blanc to Monte Rosa)*

poeniō *see* **pūniō**

Poenul·us -ī *m* little Phoenician *(i.e., Zeno the Stoic)*

Poen·us -a -um *adj* Phoenician; Carthaginian **‖** *m* Carthaginian *(esp. Hannibal)*

poēs·is -is *f* art of poetry; poetry, poems

poēt·a -ae *m* poet; playwright; *(fig)* person of great skill, artist

poētic·a -ae *or* **poētic·ē -ēs** *f* art of poetry; poetics

poēticē *adv* poetically

poētic·us -a -um *adj* poetic

poētri·a -ae *f* poetess

poētr·is -idis *or* **-idos** *f* poetess

pol *interj* by Pollux!; Gads!; really, indeed; **certō pol** most assuredly

Polem·ōn -ōnis *m* Platonic philosopher, disciple of Xenocrates and teacher of Zeno

Polemōnē·us -a -um *adj* professing the philosophy of Polemon

polent·a -ae *f* pearl barley

polentāri·us -a -um *adj* caused by eating barley

pol·iō -īre -īvī *or* **-iī -ītus** *tr* to polish; to smooth; *(fig)* to polish

polītē *adv* in a polished manner, with taste, smoothly, elegantly

polītic·us -a -um *adj* political

polīt·us -a -um *adj (lit & fig)* polished, smooth

poll·en -inis *n or* **poll·is -inis** *mf* flour

poll·ēns -entis *adj* strong, powerful

pollenti·a -ae *f* might, power

poll·eō -ēre *intr* to be strong, be powerful; to be capable, be able; to have influence; *(of medicines)* to be efficacious; **in rē pūblicā plūrimum pollēre** to have tremendous influence in politics

poll·ex -icis *m* thumb; big toe; **pollicem premere** to press the thumb *(against the index finger to indicate approval);* **pollicem vertere** to turn the thumb down *(to indicate disapproval)*
pollic·eor -ērī -itus sum *tr* to promise
pollicitāti·ō -ōnis *f* promise
pollicit·or -ārī -ātus sum *tr* to keep promising
pollicit·us -a -um *pp of* **polliceor ‖** *n* promise
pollināri·us -a -um *adj* flour
pollīnct·or -ōris *m* mortician, undertaker
pol·lingō -lingere -līnxī -līnctus *tr* to prepare *(a corpse),* lay out
Polli·ō -ōnis *m* Gaius Asinius Pollio *(orator, poet, historian, and patron of literature, 76 B.C.–A.D. 4)*
poll·is -inis *mf* (fine) flour
pol·lūceō -lūcēre -lūxī -lūctus *tr* to offer up *(as a sacrifice);* to serve *(food, a meal)*
pollūcibiliter *adv* sumptuously
pollūctūr·a -ae *f* sumptuous dinner
pol·luō -luere -luī -lūtus *tr* to pollute; to violate; to dirty, soil
Poll·ūx *or rarely* **Poll·ūcēs -ūcis** *m* Pollux *(son of Tyndareus and Leda, twin brother of Castor, and patron of boxers)*
pol·us -ī *m* pole *(either end of the axis on which the heavenly spheres were believed to revolve);* star; sky; heaven; **polus austrālis** South Pole; **polus superior** North Pole
Polyb·ius -iī *m* Greek historian and friend of Scipio Aemilianus *(c. 203–120 B.C.)*
Polyclīt·us -ī *m* **(-clēt-)** Polycletus *(Greek sculptor of Argos, fl c. 452–412 B.C.)*
Polycrat·ēs -is *m* ruler of Samos in the 6th cent. B.C., patron of the arts and close friend of Anacreon
Polydam·ās -antos *m* **(Pōl-)** Trojan warrior, son of Panthus and friend of Hector
Polydōrē·us -a -um *adj* of Polydorus
Polydōr·us -ī *m* youngest son of Priam and Hecuba, murdered by Polymester, king of Thrace
Polyhymni·a -ae *f* one of the Muses; Muse of lyric poetry
Polymēst·or -oris *m* king of Thracian Chersonese, husband of Ilione (the daughter of Priam), and murderer of Polydorus
Polynīc·ēs -is *m* son of Oedipus and Jocasta, and brother of Eteocles, Antigone, and Ismene, and leader of the Seven against Thebes
Polyphēm·us -ī *m* son of Neptune and one of the Cyclopes
pōlyp·us -ī *m* polyp *(sea animal; tumor)*
Polyxen·a -ae *or* **Polyxen·ē -ēs** *f* Polyxena *(daughter of Priam and Hecuba whom Pyrrhus, son of Achilles, sacrificed at his father's tomb)*

Polyxeni·us -a -um *adj* of Polyxena
pōmāri·us -a -um *adj* fruit, of fruit trees ‖ *m* fruit vendor ‖ *n* orchard
pōmēr·ium -(i)ī *n* **(-moer-)** space kept free of buildings inside and outside a city wall
pōmif·er -era -erum *adj* fruit-bearing
Pōmōn·a -ae *f* Roman goddess of fruit
pōmōs·us -a -um *adj* loaded with fruit
pomp·a -ae *f* solemn procession; parade; retinue; pomp, ostentation
Pompēi·a *or* **Pompēi·a -ae** *f* Julius Caesar's second wife, the daughter of Quintus Pompeius Rufus *(consul in 88 B.C.)* ‖ a daughter of Pompey, who married Faustus Cornelius Sulla
Pompēiān·us -a -um *adj* Pompeian ‖ *mpl* inhabitants of Pompeii ‖ soldiers *or* followers of Pompey
Pompēi·ī -ōrum *mpl* city about 10 miles S. of Naples, destroyed by Vesuvius in A.D. 79
Pompēi·us -ī *m* Gnaeus Pompeius Strabo *(father of the the triumvir)* ‖ Pompey the Great *(Gnaeus Pompeius Magnus, Roman general and politician, 106–48 B.C.)* ‖ Sextus Pompeius Magnus *(his younger son, killed in 35 B.C.)*
Pompil·ius -(i)ī *m* Numa Pompilius *(second king of Rome and traditional founder of Roman state religion)*
pompil·us -ī *m* pilot-fish
Pompōniān·us -a -um *adj* of a member of the Pomponian clan
Pompōn·ius -(i)ī *m* Lucius Pomponius *(of Bononia, a writer of Atellan farces (c. 109–32 B.C.)* ‖ Titus Pomponius Atticus *(the friend and correspondent of Cicero (109–32 B.C.)* ‖ Publius Pomponius Secundus *(writer of dramatic verse)*
Pomptīn·us -a -um *adj* Pomptine; **Pomptīnae palūdēs** Pomptine Marshes *(in Latium near the seacoast)*
pōm·um -ī *n* fruit; fruit tree
pōm·us -ī *f* fruit tree
ponder·ō -āre -āvī -ātus *tr (lit & fig)* to weigh; to ponder, consider
ponderōs·us -a -um *adj* weighty, massive; *(fig)* dignified
pondō *indecl n* pound, pounds; *(in advl sense)* in weight; *(where specific number of pounds is given, the numeral is usually expressed in the neuter:* **argentī pondō bīna sēlībrās in mīlitem praestāre** to offer two and a half pounds of silver per soldier); **aurī quīnque pondō** five pounds of gold; **duo pondō saxum** a two-pound rock; **quot pondō tēd esse cēnsēs nūdum?** how many pounds do you think you weigh nude?

pond·us -eris *n* weight; mass; burden; importance; stability of character **‖** *npl* balance, equilibrium

pōne *adv* behind, after, back **‖** *prep (w. acc)* behind; **ī tū pōne mē** walk behind me

pōnō pōnere posuī pos(i)tus *tr* to put, set, place; to put down, put aside; to pitch *(camp);* to station, post *(troops);* to lay *(foundation, keel);* to build, found *(town, colony, building);* to plant *(tree); (of trees)* to shed leaves; to serve *(food);* to stage *(a play);* to lay down *(arms);* to take off *(clothes, ornaments);* to cut *(beard, hair, fingernails);* to arrange, smooth *(the hair);* to take *(steps);* to deposit *(money);* to bet *(money);* to lend *(money)* at interest; to set aside, store; to lay out, spend *(time, effort, etc.);* to file *(legal claim);* to lay down *(rule, law);* to stage *(a play);* to yield up *(life, breath);* to get rid of, drop; to esteem, value; to classify; to appoint *(to specific position);* to calm *(sea);* to lay *(egg);* to fix *(penalty, price);* to offer *(award);* to depict *(in art);* to assume, suppose; to quote, cite; to state *(in writing or speech);* to pose, ask *(question);* to spend *(time, money, energy);* to give as security; to give *(a name);* to lay out for burial; *(w.* **in** *+ abl)* to base *or* stake *(upon);* **fīnem pōnere** *(w. dat)* to put an end to; **genū pōnere** to kneel down; **in locō** *(or* **locō** *or* **in numerō) pōnere** to place in a class *or* category; **in mediō pōnere** to make accessible to all; **modum pōnere** *(w. dat)* to limit, set bounds to **‖** *intr (of snow)* to fall; *(of wind)* to drop, stop; to be neutral

pōn·s -tis *m* bridge; gangway; drawbridge; deck; **pōns in flūmine** a bridge over the river

Ponti·ae -ārum *fpl* island in the Tuscan Sea S. of Circeii

ponticul·us -ī *m* small bridge

Pontic·us -a -um *adj* Pontic, of Pontus *(region around the Black Sea);* **mare Ponticum** Black Sea; **nux Pontica** hazelnut; **rādīx Pontica** rhubarb

pontif·ex -icis *m* (**-tuf-**) pontiff, pontifex, priest *(one of a board of 15);* **pontifex maximus** chief pontiff

pontificāl·is -is -e *adj* pontifical

pontificāt·us -ūs *m* pontificate

pontific·us -a -um *adj* pontifical

pont·ō -ōnis *m* ferry

Pont·us -ī *m* Euxine *or* Black Sea; region around the Black Sea **‖** Pontus *(kingdom of Mithridates, between Bithynia and Armenia, after 63 B.C. a Roman province)*

pont·us -ī *m* sea; sea water

pop·a -ae *m* priest's assistant *(who slew the victim)*

popan·um -ī *n* sacrificial cake

popell·us -ī *m* rabble, mob

popīn·a -ae *f* low-class restaurant, dive; food sold at a low-class restaurant

popīn·ō -ōnis *m* diner at a low-class restaurant

popl·es -itis *m* hollow of the knee; knee; **duplicātō poplite** on bended knee; **contentō poplite** with a stiff knee

Pōplicola *see* **Pūblicola**

popōscī *perf of* **pōscō**

poppysm·a -atis *n* smacking of the lips *(to indicate satisfaction)*

populābil·is -is -e *adj* destructible

populābund·us -a -um *adj* ravaging

populār·is -is -e *adj* of the people, people's; approved by the people, popular; favoring the people, democratic; demagogic; of the same country, native; common, coarse **‖** *mf* fellow countryman; party member; fellow member, associate; *(w. gen)* partner *or* associate in **‖** *mpl* people's party, democrats **‖** *npl* general-admission seats

populārit·ās -ātis *f* courting popular favor; fellow citizenship

populāriter *adv* like the people; like a demagogue, to win popular favor; **populāriter loquī** to use slang

populāti·ō -ōnis *f* ravaging

populāt·or -ōris *m,* **populātr·īx -īcis** *f* ravager, destroyer

populāt·us -ūs *m* devastation

pōpule·us -a -um *adj* of poplars, poplar

pōpulif·er -era -erum *adj* poplar-bearing

pōpuln(e)us -a -um *adj* of poplar

popul·ō -āre -āvī -ātus *or* **popul·or -arī -ātus sum** *tr* to ravage, devastate, lay waste; *(fig)* to pillage, ruin, spoil

pōpul·us -ī *f* poplar tree

popul·us -ī *m* the people *(as political community);* nation; public; crowd; citizens *(as opposed to soldiers),* civilians; region, district

por- *pref* giving the sense of "forth," *e.g.:* **portendō** to stretch forth

porc·a -ae *f* sow

porcell·a -ae *f* little sow, suckling pig

porcell·us -ī *m* little hog, suckling pig

Porci·a -ae *f* daughter of Cato Uticensis, married first to Marcus Bibulus, consul in 59 B.C., and afterwards to Marcus Brutus, the assassin of Julius Caesar

porcīnār·ius -(i)ī *m* pork seller

porcīn·us -a -um *adj* hog's, pig's **‖** *f* pork

Porc·ius -(i)ī *m* Cato *(Marcus Porcius Cato the Censor 235–149 B.C.)* **‖** Cato Uticensis *(Marcus Porcius Cato Uticensis (95–46 B.C.)*

porcul·a *or* **porculēn·a -ae** *f* little sow

porcul·us -ī *m* little pig

porc·us -ī *m* pig, hog

porgō *see* **porrigō**

porphyrētic·us -a -um *adj* made of porphyry *(a purple-streaked marble)*
porphyri·ō -ōnis *f* type of waterfowl
Porphyri·ōn -ōnis *m* one of the Giants who fought against the gods
Porphyr·ius -(i)i *m* Porphyry *(Neo-Platonic philosopher, born* A.D. *233, who edited the works of Plotinus)*
porrēcti·ō -ōnis *f* extending, stretching out
porrēct·us -a -um *pp of* **porrigō** *and* **porriciō** ‖ *adj* stretched out, extended, extensive, long; protracted; laid out, dead; *(fig)* widespread ‖ *npl* offerings
por·riciō -ricere -rēxī -rēctus *tr* to offer up; **Inter caesa et porrēcta** *(prov)* at the last moment, at the eleventh hour *(literally, between the slaughtering and the offering)*
porrīg·ō -inis *f* dandruff
por·rigō -rigere -rēxī -rēctus *tr* to reach out, stretch out, extend; to stretch out *(in sleep or death)*; to offer, present, hand; to lengthen *(a syllable)* ‖ *refl & pass* to extend
Porrim·a -ae *f* cult name of the birth-goddess Antevorta
porrō *adv* forwards; farther on, on; far off, at a distance; long ago; in the future, hereafter; again, in turn; next, furthermore, moreover, on the other hand
porr·um -ī *n or* **porr·us -ī** *m* leek; chive
Porsenn·a *or* **Porsēn·a** *or* **Porsinn·a -ae** *m* Lars Porsen(n)a *(king of Clusium in Etruria who sided with Tarquin in a war against Rome)*
port·a -ae *f* city-gate; gate; entrance; outlet; camp-gate *(of which there were always four:* **praetōria,** **prīncipālis,** **decumānus,** **quaestōria)**
portāti·ō -ōnis *f* carrying
porten·dō -dere -dī -tus *tr* to indicate, foretell, portend, predict
portentific·us -a -um *adj* abnormal
portentōs·us -a -um *adj* abnormal, unnatural; monstrous
portent·um -ī *n* portent, omen, sign; monstrosity, monster; fantasy, far-fetched fiction; *(as term of contempt)* monster
portentus *pp of* **portendō**
porthm·eūs -eī *or* **-eōs** *m* ferryman *(i.e., Charon)*
porticul·a -ae *f* small portico
portic·us -ūs *f* portico, colonnade; *(mil)* gallery *(formed by placing vineae end to end);* Stoicism
porti·ō -ōnis *f* portion, share; ratio, proportion; installment, payment; **prō portiōne** proportionately, relatively
portīscul·us -ī *m* gavel *(used to keeping time for rowers)*

portit·or -ōris *m* customs officer; ferryman, boatman
port·ō -āre -āvī -ātus *tr* to carry; to bring
portōr·ium -(i)ī *n* port-duty, customs duty; tax *(on peddlers)*
portul·a -ae *f* small gate
Portūn·us -ī *m* tutelary deity of harbors
portuōs·us -a -um *adj* having good harbors
port·us -ūs *m* port, harbor; haven, refuge; mouth of a river
pōsc·a -ae *f* sour drink
pōscō pōscere popōscī *tr (weaker than* **flāgitō)** to ask, request, beg, demand; to ask for in marriage; *(at auction)* to bid for; *(of things)* to require, demand, need, call for, make necessary; *(w.* **ab)** to ask for *(s.th.)* from, demand *(s.th.)* of; *(w. double acc)* to demand *(s.th.)* of *(s.o.),* ask *(s.o.)* for *(s.th.)*
pōsi·a -ae *f* **(paus-)** unripe olive
Posīd·ēs -ae *m* favorite freedman of the Emperor Claudius
Posīdōn·ius -(i)ī *m* Stoic philosopher at Rhodes, teacher of Cicero *(135–51* B.C.*)*
positi·ō -ōnis *f* putting, placing, setting; position, posture; situation
posit·or -ōris *m* builder
positūr·a -ae *f* posture; formation
posit·us -a -um *pp of* **pōnō** ‖ *adj* situated, located; stretched out, lying down
posit·us -ūs *m* position, site; arrangement; *(gram)* position *(of a syllable)*
possessi·ō -ōnis *f* possession; getting possession, occupation; estate
possessiuncul·a -ae *f* small estate
possess·or -ōris *m* possessor, occupant; *(leg)* defendant
possibil·is -is -e *adj* possible
pos·sideō -sidēre -sēdī -sessus *tr* to possess, occupy; to have, own; to dwell in, live in; *(fig)* to take hold of; *(poet)* to take up *(space)* with one's bulk
pos·sīdō -sīdere *tr* to take possession of, occupy, seize
possum posse potuī *intr* to be able; **multum (plūs, plūrimum) posse** to have much (more, very great) influence; **nōn possum quīn exclāmem** I can't help shouting out; **quantum** *(or* **ut) fierī potest** as far as is possible
post *older* **poste** *adv (of place)* behind, back, backwards; *(of time)* later, afterwards; *(of order)* next; **aliquantō post** somewhat later; **multīs post annīs** many years later ‖ *prep (w. acc) (of place)* behind; *(of time)* after, since
post- *pref used in the senses of the adverb*
posteā *adv* afterwards, after this, after that, hereafter, thereafter
posteāquam *conj (also as two words)* after; ever since, from the time that

posteri·or -or -us *adj* later, next, following; latter, posterior; inferior; hind *(e.g., legs)*
posterit·ās -ātis *f* the future, afterages, posterity, later generations; offspring *(of animals);* **in posteritātem** in the future
posterius *adv* later, at a later date
poster·us -a -um *adj* following, ensuing, next, subsequent, future **‖** *mpl* future generations, posterity, descendants **‖** *n* future time; next day; consequence; **in posterum** until the next day; for the future
post·ferō -ferre *tr* to treat as less important, esteem less; to sacrifice
postgenit·us -a -um *adj* born later **‖** *mpl* later generations
posthab·eō -ēre -uī -itus *tr* to consider of secondary importance; to slight, neglect; *(w. dat)* to think *(s.th.)* less important than
posthāc *adv* hereafter, in the future
posthinc *or* **post hinc** *adv* from here, next
posthōc *or* **post hōc** *adv* after this, afterwards
postibi *adv* afterwards, then
postīcul·um -ī *n* small building in the rear, outhouse
postīc·us -a -um *adj* rear, back **‖** *n* back door; *(coll)* rear, rear end
postid *adv* then, afterwards
postideā *adv* afterwards, after that
postilēn·a -ae *f* rump; buttocks
postili·ō -ōnis *f* sacrifice demanded by the gods to make up for a previous omission in sacrifice
postillā(c) *adv* afterwards
post·is -is *m* doorpost; door **‖** *mpl* double doors
postlīmin·ium -(i)ī *n* right to return home and resume one's former rank and privileges after exile or capture; recovery, restoration
pos(t)merīdiān·us -a -um *adj* afternoon
postmerīdiē *adv* in the afternoon
postmodo *or* **postmodum** *adv* after a bit, a little later, afterwards
postpart·or -ōris *m* successor, heir
post·pōnō -pōnere -posuī -positus *tr* to consider of secondary importance; to postpone; *(w. dat)* to consider *(s.th.)* of less importance than, set *(s.th.)* aside in favor of; **omnibus rēbus postpositīs** laying aside everything
postprīncip·ium -(i)ī *n* *(also written as two words)* sequel; **postprīncipia** *(mil)* second line of battle
postput·ō -āre -āvī -ātus *tr* *(also written as two words)* to consider of secondary importance; *(w. prae + abl)* to consider *(s.th.)* less important than
postquam *conj* after, when
postrēmō *adv* at last; finally
postrēmum *adv* for the last time, last of all
postrēm·us -a -um *(superl of* **posterus***) adj* last; latest, most recent; last in line, rear; least

important; lowest, worst **‖** *n* the end; **ad postrēmum** in the end, finally; in the last place
postrīdiē *adv* on the day after, on the following day; **postrīdiē māne** the next morning **‖** *prep (w. gen), e.g.,* **postrīdiē ēius diēī** on the day after that; *(w. acc), e.g.,* **postrīdiē lūdōs** on the day after the games
postrīduō *adv* on the day after
postscaen·ium -(i)ī *n* backstage
post·scrībō -scrībere -scrīpsī -scrīptus *tr (w. dat)* to add *(e.g., a name)* to; **Tiberī nōmen suō postscrībere** to add the name of Tiberius to his own
postulāti·ō -ōnis *f* demand, request, desire; complaint; *(leg)* application for permission to present a claim
postulāt·or -ōris *m* one who makes demands; plaintiff
postulāt·um -ī *n* demand; request; claim
postulāt·us -ūs *m* petition, request
postul·ō -āre -āvī -ātus *tr* to demand, claim; to look for as due, expect; *(of things)* to require; *(leg)* to arraign, prosecute; *(leg)* to apply for *(a writ from the praetor to prosecute)*
Postumi·us -a -um *adj* Roman clan name *(nomen), esp.* Aulus Postumius Tubertus *(father-in-law of Cincinnatus)* **‖** Gaius Postumius *(a soothsayer consulted by Sulla)*
postum·us -a -um *adj* last, latest-born; born after the father's death
Postum·us -ī *m* Roman first name *(praenomen),* subsequently in use as a family name *(cognomen)*
postus *pp of* **pōnō**
Postvert·a -ae *f* goddess presiding over breech births
posuī *perf of* **pōnō**
pōtāti·ō -ōnis *f* drinking; drinking party
pōtāt·or -ōris *m* drinker; a drunk
pot·ēns -entis *adj* capable; mighty, powerful, strong; efficacious, potent; influential; *(w. gen)* **1** capable of, equal to, fit for; **2** having power over; **3** presiding over; **4** having obtained *(one's wish);* **5** having carried out *(an order)*
potentāt·us -ūs *m* political power, rule, dominion
potenter *adv* powerfully, mightily, effectually, vigorously; according to one's ability
potenti·a -ae *f* force, power; political power *(esp. unconstitutional power in contrast to* **potestās***)*
potēr·ium -iī *n* goblet
potest·ās -ātis *f* power, ability, capacity; efficacy, force; public authority, rule, power, sway, dominion, sovereignty, empire; magisterial power, magistracy, office; possibility, opportunity *(to choose, decide),* discretion,

power of choice; permission; person in office, magistrate, ruler; property, quality

Pothīn·us -ī *m* minister of Ptolemy XIII of Egypt, who ordered the assassination of Pompey the Great

potin *or* **potin'** = **potisne** can you?

pot·iō -īre -īvī -ītus *tr (w. acc and gen)* to put *(s.o.)* under the power of

pōti·ō -ōnis *f* drinking; drink, draught; magic potion

pōtiōnāt·us -a -um *adj (w. abl)* having been given a drink of

pot·ior -īrī -ītus sum *tr* to acquire, get possession of ‖ *intr (w. abl)* to acquire, get possession of, become master of, get hold of

poti·or -or -us *(comp of* **potis)** *adj* more powerful; more precious; better, preferable, superior; more important; *(w. gen)* having greater control over

potis *or* **pote** *indecl adj* able, capable; possible

potissimum *adv* chiefly, especially

potissim·us -a -um *adj* chief, principal, most important

pōtit·ō -āre -āvī -ātus *tr* to drink (habitually)

pōtiuncul·a -ae *f* a little drink

potius *adv* rather, more, by preference; **potius quam** more than, rather than

Potni·as -ados *adj (fem only)* of Potniae *(a Boeotian village)*

pōt·ō -āre -āvī -ātus *or* **-us** *tr* to drink; to absorb ‖ *intr* to drink

pōt·or -ōris *m* drinker; a drunk

pōtr·īx -īcis *f* drinker *(female)*

pōtulent·us -a -um *adj* drinkable; tipsy ‖ *npl* drinks

pōt·us -a -um *pp of* **pōtō** ‖ *adj* having drunk; drunken, intoxicated

pōt·us -ūs *m* drinking; a drink

prae *adv* before, in front; in preference ‖ *prep (w. abl)* **1** *(in its literal sense, usu. w. refl pron, in certain phrases)* before, in front of: **prae sē** in front of oneself, publicly, openly, plainly; **prae sē ferre** to display, manifest, profess; **prae manū** at hand; **2** compared with, in comparison with: **Gallīs prae magnitūdine corporum suōrum brevitās nostra contemptuī est** in comparison with the size of their own bodies the Gauls hold our shortness of stature in contempt; **3** by reason of, in consequence of, because of, for: **prae laetitiā lacrimāre** to weep for joy; **nec loquī prae maerōre potuit** he could not speak because of his grief; **4** in consequence of, out of: **prae pudōre** out of shame; **prae timōre** out of fear

prae- *pref* indicating **1** position in front, ahead: **praecēdere** to go in front, go ahead; **2** position in the end: **praeūrere** to burn at the extremity; **praeacuere** to sharpen to a point;

3 temporal precedence: **praedīcere** to tell in advance; **4** with adjectives, pre-eminence in the quality concerned: **praeacūtus** very sharp; **5** rank: **praeesse** to be in charge; **praetor** one in charge; **6** protection: **praesidium** defense, protection

praeac·uō -uere -uī -ūtus *tr* to sharpen to the point

praeacūt·us -a -um *adj* very sharp; pointed

praealt·us -a -um *adj* very high; very deep

praeb·eō -ēre -uī -itus *tr* to hold out, offer, present; to supply, give; to exhibit, represent, show; to give up, yield, surrender; to cause, occasion; to permit, allow; **praebēre aurem** *(or* **aurēs)** *(w. dat)* to listen to; **praebēre exemplum** to set an example; **praebēre suspiciōnem** to cause suspicion ‖ *refl* to show oneself, behave; to offer oneself as

praebib·ō -ere -ī -itus *tr (w. dat)* to drink *(e.g., a toast)* to

praebit·or -ōris *m* supplier

praecalid·us -a -um *adj* very hot

praecalv·us -a -um *adj* very bald

praecant·ō -āre -āvī -ātus *tr* (-cen-) to cast a spell over ‖ *intr (w. dat)* to recite a spell over

praecantr·īx -īcis *f* witch, enchantress

praecān·us -a -um *adj* prematurely gray

prae·caveō -cavēre -cāvī -cautus *tr* to take precautions against, guard against, try to avoid ‖ *intr* to take precautions, be on one's guard; *(w. dat)* to look out for, look after; *(w. abl)* to guard against, be on one's quard against

prae·cēdō -cēdere -cessī -cessus *tr* to precede, go out before, lead; to surpass ‖ *intr* to excel; *(w. dat)* to be superior to

praecell·ēns -entis *adj* excellent, outstanding, preeminent

praecell·ō -ere *tr* to surpass, outdo ‖ *intr* to distinguish oneself, excel; to take precedence; *(w. dat)* **1** to rule over; **2** to surpass

praecels·us -a -um *adj* towering

praecenti·ō -ōnis *f* singing before a sacrifice; prelude

praecentō *see* **praecantō**

praecentus *pp of* **praecinō**

praecēpī *perf of* **praecipiō**

praeceps *adv* headfirst

praec·eps -ipitis *adj* headfirst; downhill, steep, precipitous; sinking *(sun);* swift, rushing, violent; hasty, rash, inconsiderate; dangerous ‖ *n* edge of a cliff, cliff; *(fig)* brink; danger; **in praeceps** *(or* **per praeceps)** headlong, straight downward; **in praecipiti** on the edge; *(fig)* on the brink of disaster

praecepti·ō -ōnis *f* preconception; precept, rule; instruction; *(leg)* receiving *(of an inheritance)* in advance *(of the general partition of an estate)*

praecept·or **-ōris** *m*, **praceptr·īx** **-īcis** *f* teacher, tutor

praecept·um **-ī** *n* instruction, bit of advice; rule; maxim; order, direction

praecerp·ō **-ere** **-sī** **-tus** *tr* to pick beforetime; *(w. dat) (fig)* to snatch away from

praecī·dō **-dere** **-dī** **-sus** *tr* to lop off, cut off; to cut short; to cut, cut through; to damage, mutilate; to break off, end suddenly *(a speech, etc.)*; to end, destroy *(hopes, etc.)*; to refuse, decline

prae·cingō **-cingere** **cīnxī** **-cīnctus** *tr* to gird; to surround, ring; to dress ‖ *pass* to be surrounded, be ringed; **altius praecīnctus** with tunic tucked up higher; *(fig)* more energetic(ally); **ēnse cingī** to wear a sword; **male cīnctus** improperly dressed; **rēcte cinctus** properly dressed

prae·cinō **-cinere** **-cinuī** **-centus** *tr* to predict; *(w. dat)* to predict *(s.th.)* to ‖ *intr* to make predictions; *(w. dat)* to sing or play before or at *(e.g., sacrifice, dinner, etc.)*

prae·cipiō **-cipere** **-cēpī** **-ceptus** *tr* to take in advance, occupy in advance; to receive in advance; to grasp beforehand, anticipate; to teach, instruct, direct, advise, order, bid, warn; to prescribe; **aliquantulum viae** *(or temporis)* **praecipere** *(or* **iter praecipere)** to get a headstart; **animō** *(or* **cogitātiōne) praecipere** to imagine beforehand, reckon on, anticipate, expect; **artem nandī praecipere** to give swimming instructions; **gaudium praecipere** to rejoice in advance; **oculīs praecipere** to see beforehand, get a preview of; **opīniōne praecipere** to suspect; **pecūniam mūtuam praecipere** to get an advance loan

praecipitanter *adv* at top speed

praecipit·ō **-āre** **-āvī** **-ātus** *tr* to throw down headfirst; to hasten, hurry, precipitate ‖ *refl* to throw oneself down, throw oneself headfirst, jump down, dive; to sink ‖ *intr* to rush headfirst, rush at top speed, rush thoughtlessly; to fall, sink; to be ruined

praecipuē *adv* especially, chiefly

praecipu·us **-a** **-um** *adj* special, peculiar, particular; chief, principal; distinguished, excellent, extraordinary ‖ *n* excellence, superiority ‖ *npl* outstanding *or* important elements; **praecipua rērum** highlights

praecīsē *adv* briefly, concisely; absolutely

praecīs·us **-a** **-um** *pp of* **praecīdō** ‖ *adj* abrupt, precipitous; rugged, rough; brief, shortened *(speech)*; clipped *(words)*

praeclārē *adv* very clearly; excellently; *(to express agreement)* very good, excellent

praeclār·us **-a** **-um** *adj* very clear; very nice; splendid, noble, distinguished, excellent; famous; notorious

praeclū·dō **-dere** **-sī** **-sus** *tr* to shut, shut off, obstruct, bar the way of; to hinder, impede, stop; to preclude *(an action, event)*; **portās cōnsulī praeclūdere** to shut the gates in the consul's face; **vōcem praeclūdere alicui** to shut s.o. up, hush s.o. up

praec·ō **-ōnis** *m* crier, herald; auctioneer; *(fig)* eulogist

praecōgit·ō **-āre** **-āvī** **-ātus** *tr* to premeditate

praecognit·us **-a** **-um** *adj* known beforehand, foreseen

prae·colō **-colere** **-coluī** **-cultus** *tr* to cultivate prematurely; *(fig)* to embrace prematurely

praecomposit·us **-a** **-um** *adj* arranged beforehand; studied, self-conscious

praecōni·us **-a** **-um** *adj* of a public crier; of an auctioneer ‖ *n* crier's office; proclamation, announcement; praising, praise

praecōnsūm·ō **-ere** **-psī** **-ptus** *tr* to spend *or* use up beforehand

praecontrect·ō **-āre** *tr* to consider in advance

praecoqu·is **-is** **-e** *adj* premature; precocious

praecordi·a **-ōrum** *npl* midriff; lower chest; chest; diaphragm; insides, stomach; breast, heart *(as seat of emotions)*; *(poet)* body

praecor·rumpō **-rumpere** **-rūpī** **-ruptus** *tr* to bribe in advance

prae·cox **-cocis** *adj* premature; early, precocious

praecupid·us **-a** **-um** *adj (w. gen)* very fond of

praecurrent·ia **-ium** *npl* antecedents

prae·currō **-currere** **-(cu)currī cursus** *tr* to precede, anticipate; to outdo, surpass ‖ *intr* to run out ahead, take the lead; *(w.* **ante** + *acc)* to run out ahead of; *(w. dat)* to outdo

praecursi·ō **-ōnis** *f* previous occurrence; *(mil)* skirmish; *(rhet)* warmup *(of the audience)*

praecurs·or **-ōris** *m* forerunner; spy; *(mil)* scout; *(mil)* advance guard

praecursōri·us **-a** **-um** *adj* sent in advance

prae·cutiō **-cutere** *tr* to wave, brandish in front

praed·a **-ae** *f* booty, spoils, plunder; prey; *(of fish)* catch; *(in hunting)* the game; prize, profit; **praedae esse** *(w. dat)* to fall prey to; **vocāmus in partem praedamque Iovem** we invite Jupiter to share the game

praedābund·us **-a** **-um** *adj* pillaging, plundering, marauding

praedamn·ō **-āre** **-āvī** **-ātus** *tr* to condemn beforehand; **spem praedamnāre** to give up hope too soon

praedāti·ō **-ōnis** *f* plundering

praedāt·or **-ōris** *m* marauder, looter, vandal; hunter; greedy man

praedātōri·us **-a** **-um** *adj* marauding, looting; graspy, greedy

praedāt·us **-ūs** *m* robbery

praedēlass·ō **-āre** *tr* to tire out, weaken beforehand

praediāt·or -ōris *m* real-estate dealer
praediātōri·us -a -um *adj* concerned with real-estate; **iūs praediātōrium** *(leg)* mortgage law
praedicābil·is -is -e *adj* praiseworthy, laudable
praedicāti·ō -ōnis *f* announcement, publication; praise, commendation
praedicāt·or -ōris *m* eulogist
praedic·ō -āre -āvī -ātus *tr* to announce; to report; to assert, state; to praise, recommend
prae·dīcō -dīcere -dīxī -dictus *tr* to mention beforehand *or* earlier; to prearrange; to predict; to order beforehand, command beforehand
praedicti·ō -ōnis *f* prediction
praedict·um -ī *n* prediction, prophecy; command, order; **velut ex praedictō** as if by prearrangement
praediol·um -ī *n* small estate, small farm
praedisc·ō -ere *tr* to learn beforehand, find out in advance
praedisposit·us -a -um *adj* previously arranged
praedit·us -a -um *adj* gifted; *(w. abl)* endowed with, provided with, furnished with
praed·ium -iī *n* estate, farm; collateral *(consisting of land);* **praedium urbānum** *(whether in town or in the country)* building site
praedīv·es -itis *adj* very rich
praedīvīn·ō -āre -āvī -ātus *tr* to know in advance, have a presentiment of
praed·ō -ōnis *m* robber; pirate
praedoct·us -a -um *adj* instructed beforehand
praed·or -ārī -ātus sum *tr* to raid, plunder, loot, rob; *(fig)* to rob, ravish; **amōrēs alicūius praedārī** to steal s.o.'s sweetheart away ‖ *intr* to plunder, loot, make a raid; *(w. ex)* to prey on, profit by, take advantage of, *e.g.,* **ex alterīus īnscientiā praedārī** to prey on *or* take advantage of another's ignorance
prae·dūcō -dūcere -dūxī -ductus *tr* to run *or* construct *(trench, wall)* out in front *(as a defense)*
praedulc·is -is -e *adj* very sweet; *(fig)* very satisfying *(honor, reward)*
praedūr·us -a -um *adj* very tough *(skin);* tough, brawny
praeēmin·eō *or* **praemin·eō -ēre** *tr* to surpass, excel ‖ *intr* to project, stick out
prae·eō -īre -īvī *or* **-iī** *tr* to lead, precede; to read out, dictate, lead *(prayers)* ‖ *intr* to go out ahead, take the lead; *(w. dat)* to walk in front of
praefāti·ō -ōnis *f* preface, introduction; formula
praefātus *pp of* **praefor**
praefectūr·a -ae *f* supervision, superintendence; office of prefect, superintendency;

government of a district; prefecture *(Italian city governed by a Roman prefect);* territory of a prefecture, district
praefect·us -ī *m* prefect, supervisor, superintendent; commander; governor; *(w. gen or dat)* supervisor of, commander of, prefect *or* governor of; satrap; **praefectus classis** admiral; **praefectus praetōriō** commander of the imperial bodyguard
prae·ferō -ferre -tulī -lātus *tr* to hold out, carry in front; *(w. dat or* **quam**) to prefer *(one thing)* to *(another);* to anticipate; to display, reveal, betray; to offer, present; to offer as a model ‖ *refl & pass (w. dat)* to surpass ‖ *pass* to ride past, ride by, march past; to outflank
praefer·ōx -ōcis *adj* very defiant; impetuous
praeferrāt·us -a -um *adj* iron-tipped; *(coll)* chained *(slave)*
praefervid·us -a -um *adj (lit & fig)* boiling
praefestīn·ō -āre -āvī -ātus *tr* to hurry past; *(w. inf)* to be in a big hurry to
praefic·a -ae *f* hired mourner *(female)*
prae·ficiō -ficere -fēcī -fectus *tr* to put *(s.o.)* in charge; *(w. double acc)* to appoint *(s.o.)* as; *(w. dat)* to put *(s.o.)* in charge of, set *(s.o.)* over, appoint *(s.o.)* to command
praefīd·ēns -entis *adj* too trustful; overconfident; *(w. dat)* too trustful of; **hominēs sibi praefīdentēs** overconfident people
praefī·gō -gere -xī -xus *tr* to fix, fasten, set up in front, fasten on the end; *(w. abl)* to tip with; *(w. in + abl)* to impale on; **capistrīs praefīgere** to muzzle
praefin·iō -īre -īvī *or* **-iī -ītus** *tr* to determine in advance; to prescribe, appoint; to limit
praefīnītō *adv* in the prescribed manner
praefiscinē *or* **praefiscinī** *or* **praefascinē** *adv* so as to avoid bad luck; meaning no offense
praefīxī *perf of* **praefīgō**
praefix·us -a -um *pp of* **praefīgō** ‖ *adj* cuspidibus praefīxus** pointed; **ferrō praefīxus** iron-tipped
praeflōr·ō -āre -āvī -ātus *tr* to deflower beforehand; *(fig)* to tarnish
praeflu·ō -ere *tr & intr* to flow by
praefōc·ō -āre -āvī -ātus *tr* to suffocate; to block *(windpipe, road)* ‖ *pass* to choke
prae·fodiō -fodere -fōdī -fossus *tr* to bury beforehand; to dig in front of; **portās praefodere** to dig trenches in front of the gates
prae·for -fārī -fātus sum *tr* to say beforehand, utter in advance, preface; to address in prayer beforehand; to fortell; to invoke ‖ *intr* to pray beforehand; *(w. dat)* to pray before
praefrāctē *adv* obstinately
praefrāct·us -a -um *pp of* **praefringō** ‖ *adj* determined reolute; abrupt
praefrīgid·us -a -um *adj* very cold

prae·fringō -fringere -frēgī -frāctus *tr* to break off at the tip; to break to pieces, smash
praeful·ciō -cīre -sī -tus *tr* to prop up, support in front; *(w. dat)* to use *(s.o.)* as a prop *or* support for
praeful·geō -gēre -sī *intr* to shine forth, glitter, sparkle
praegelid·us -a -um *adj* very cold
praegest·iō -īre *intr* to be very eager
praegn·āns -antis *or* **praegn·ās -ātis** *adj* pregnant; *(w. abl)* full of, swollen with
praegracil·is -is -e *adj* lanky
praegrand·is -is -e *adj* huge; very great; very powerful
praegrav·is -is -e *adj* very heavy; weighed down; very troublesome
praegrav·ō -āre -āvī -ātus *tr* to weigh down; to outweigh; *(fig)* to burden
prae·gredior -gredī -gressus sum *tr* to go in advance of, go ahead of; to go by, go past; *(fig)* to outstrip **‖** *intr* to walk out in front; *(w. dat)* to precede, lead
praegressi·ō -ōnis *f* procession; *(fig)* precedence
praegress·us -ūs *m* prior occurrence
praegustāt·or -ōris *m* taster, sampler
praegust·ō -āre -āvī -ātus *tr* to taste beforehand, sample, get a sample of
praehib·eō -ēre -uī -itus *tr* to offer, furnish, supply; to utter, speak; **operam praehibēre** to offer help
praeiac·eō -ēre *tr* to lie before, be located in front of **‖** *intr (w. dat)* to lie before
praeiūdicāt·us -a -um *adj* decided beforehand; prejudiced; **opīniō praeiūdicata** prejudice **‖** *n* prejudged matter; prejudice; **id prō praeiūdicātō ferre** to take it as a foregone conclusion
praeiūdic·ium -(i)ī *n* preliminary hearing; prejudice; presumption; precedent, example
praeiūdic·ō -āre -āvī -ātus *tr* to decide beforehand, prejudge **‖** *intr (w. dat of disadvantage)* to be prejudicial to
prae·iuvō -iuvāre -iūvī *tr* to help in advance
prae·lābor -lābī -lāpsus sum *tr & intr* to glide along, glide, by, float by
praelamb·ō -ere *tr* to lick beforehand
praelarg·us -a -um *adj* very ample
praelātus *pp of* **praeferō**
praelaut·us -a -um *adj* plush
praelēcti·ō -ōnis *f* lecture
prae·legō -legere -lēgī -lēctus *tr* to lecture on; to sail past
praelig·ō -āre -āvī -ātus *tr* to tie up; *(w. dat)* to tie *(s.th.)*
praelong·us -a -um *adj* very long; very tall
prae·loquor -loquī -locūtus sum *tr* to make *(a speech)* before s.o. else; to say by way of

preface; *(leg)* to present *(a case)* first; **‖** *intr* to speak first
prae·lūceō -lūcēre -lūxī *tr (fig)* to enkindle *(hope)* **‖** *intr (w. dat)* 1 to throw light on; 2 to outshine, outdo, surpass; 3 to light the way for
praelūsi·ō -ōnis *f* prelude
praelūstr·is -is -e *adj* magnificent
praemandāt·a -ōrum *npl (leg)* warrant for arrest
praemand·ō -āre -āvī -ātus *tr* to recommend beforehand; to order in advance
praemātūrē *adv* too soon, prematurely
praemātūr·us -a -um *adj* premature
praemedicāt·us -a -um *adj* protected by drugs *or* charms
praemeditāti·ō -ōnis *f* premeditation, prior consideration
praemedit·or -ārī -ātus sum *tr* to think over beforehand; to practice; to practice on *(e.g., a lyre)*; **mala praemeditāta** premeditated crimes
praemerc·or -ārī -ātus sum *tr* to buy in advance
praemetu·ēns -entis *adj* apprehensive, anxious
praemetuenter *adv* anxiously; cautiously
praemetu·ō -ere *tr* to fear beforehand **‖** *intr (w. dat)* to be apprehensive about
praemin·eō -ēre *tr* to surpass, exceed **‖** *intr* to stand out prominently
prae·mittō -mittere -mīsī -missus *tr* to send out ahead, send in advance **‖** *intr* to send word
praem·ium -(i)ī *n* prize, reward, recompense; exploit *(worthy of reward)*; gift, bribe
praemolesti·a -ae *f* apprehension, presentiment of trouble
praemōl·ior -īrī *tr* to prepare beforehand, work at in advance
praemon·eō -ēre -uī -itus *tr* to forewarn; to warn of; to foreshadow, presage, predict
praemonit·us -ūs *m* premonition, forewarning
praemōnstrāt·or -ōris *m* guide
praemōnstr·ō -āre -āvī -ātus *tr* to point out the way to, guide, direct; to predict
praemor·deō -dēre -dī *or* **-sī -sus** *tr* to bite the tip off *(s.th.)*; *(fig)* to crib, pilfer
praemor·ior -ī -tuus sum *intr* to die too soon, die prematurely
praemūn·iō -īre -īvī -ītus *tr* to fortify in front; to protect, secure **‖** *intr (fig) (of a lawyer)* to prepare one's defenses
praemūnīti·ō -ōnis *f (rhet)* preparation, conditioning *(of the minds of the hearers)*
praenārr·ō -āre -āvī -ātus *tr* to relate beforehand
praenat·ō -āre -āvī *tr & intr* to float past, flow by

praenāvig·ō -āre -āvī -ātum *tr* & *intr* to sail by

Praenest·e -is *n* (*f*) ancient town in Latium (*c. 20 miles S.E. of Rome, modern Palestrina*)

Praenestīn·us -a -um *adj* & *m* Praenestine

praenit·eō -ēre -uī *intr* (*w. dat*) 1 to outshine; 2 to appear more attractive to

praenōm·en -inis *n* first name

prae·nōscō -nōscere -nōvī *tr* to find out beforehand

praenōti·ō -ōnis *f* innate idea, preconception

praenūbil·us -a -um *adj* heavily clouded; dark, gloomy

praenūnti·a -ae *f* harbinger, omen

praenūnti·ō -āre -āvī -ātus *tr* foretell

praenūnti·us -a-um *adj* foreboding ‖ *m* forecaster, harbinger, omen

praeoccupāti·ō -ōnis *f* seizing beforehand, advance occupation

praeoccup·ō -āre -āvī -ātus *tr* to occupy before another; to preoccupy; to anticipate, prevent

praeol·et -ēre *or* **praeol·it -ere** *v impers* a smell is emitted, there is a strong smell; **praeolit mihi quō tū velīs** I scent your wishes before you express them

praeopt·ō -āre -āvī -ātus *tr* to prefer

praepand·ō -ere *tr* to spread, extend; (*fig*) to reveal

praeparāti·ō -ōnis *f* preparation

praeparāt·us -a -um *adj* prepared, supplied, furnished, ready ‖ *n* stores; **ex ante praparātō** from the stores; (*fig*) by previous arrangement

praepar·ō -āre -āvī -ātus *tr* to get ready, prepare, prepare for; to gather together; to furnish beforehand; to plan in advance

praepedīment·um -ī *n* impediment

praeped·iō -īre -īvī *or* **-(i)ī -ītus** *tr* to shackle, chain; to hinder, obstruct, hamper; to embarrass

praepend·eō -ēre *intr* to hang down in front

praep·es -etis *adj* (*of birds of omen*) flying straight ahead, of good omen; winged, swift of flight ‖ *mf* bird of good omen; bird, large bird

praepilāt·us -a -um *adj* tipped with a ball; **missile praepilātum** blunted missile

praepingu·is -is -e *adj* very fertile

praepoll·eō -ēre -uī *intr* to be very powerful; to be superior; (*w. dat*) to surpass in power

praeponder·ō -āre -āvī -ātus *tr* to outweigh; to regard as superior ‖ *intr* to weigh more

prae·pōnō -pōnere -posuī -positus *tr* (*w. dat*) 1 to place, set, put (*s.th.*) in front of *or* before (*s.o.*); 2 to serve (*s.o. food*); 3 to entrust (*s.o.*) with; 4 to put (*s.o.*) in charge of *or* in command of; 5 to prefer (*s.o. or s.th.*) to, to give priority to

praeport·ō -āre -āvī -ātus *tr* to carry before oneself

praepositi·ō -ōnis *f* preference; prefixing; (*gram*) preposition

praeposit·um -ī *n* preferable thing (*i.e., s.th. short of absolute good*)

praeposit·us -a -um *pp of* **praepōnō** ‖ *adj* preferred, preferable ‖ *m* prefect, commander ‖ *n* that which is desirable, a desirable good

praeposterē *adv* out of the proper order

praeposter·us -a -um *adj* inverted, in the wrong order; badly timed; topsy-turvy; preposterous

praeposuī *pref of* **praepōnō**

praepot·ēns -entis *adj* very powerful; (*w. gen*) in full control of

praeproperanter *or* **praeproperē** *adv* very quickly, too fast

praeproper·us -a -um *adj* very quick; overhasty, sudden

praepūt·ium -(i)ī *n* foreskin

praequam *conj* in comparison to; **nihil hōc est, praequam aliōs sumptūs facit** this is nothing in comparison to the other expenses that he runs up

praequest·us -a -um *adj* complaining beforehand; **multa praequestus** having first voiced many complaints

praeradi·ō -āre *tr* to outshine

praerapid·us -a -um *adj* very swift

praereptus *pp of* **praeripiō**

praerig·ēscō -ēscere -uī *intr* to become very stiff

prae·ripiō -ripere -ripuī -reptus *tr* to snatch away, carry off; to anticipate, forestall; to count on too soon, presume upon; (*w. dat*) to snatch from

prae·rōdō -rōdere -rōsī -rōsus *tr* to bite the end of, nibble at; **digitōs praerōdere** to bite the fingernails

praerogātīv·us -a -um *adj* asked before others; (*pol*) voting first, privileged; **ōmen praerogātīvum** omen to vote first ‖ *f* (*pol*) first tribe *or* century to vote; (*pol*) vote of the first tribe *or* century to vote; (*pol*) previous election; sure sign, omen

praerōsī *perf of* **praerōdō**

praerōsus *pp of* **praerōdō**

prae·rumpō -rumpere -rūpī -ruptus *tr* to break off, tear away (*s.th.*) in front

praerupt·us -a -um *adj* broken off, broken up; rough (*terrain*); steep; hasty, impetuous; (*of an utterance*) cut short ‖ *n* precipice, steep place; (*fig*) dangerous undertaking

praes *adv* at hand, now

prae·s -dis *m* bondsman, surety; collateral

praesaep· = praesēp·

praesāgāti·ō -ōnis *f* power of knowing the future, presentiment

praesāg·iō -īre -īvī *or* -iī *or* praesāg·ior -īrī *tr* to have forebodings of, feel beforehand; to forebode, portend

praesāgīti·ō -ōnis *f* presentiment, strange feeling; prophetic power

praesāg·ium -(i)ī *n* presentiment, prophetic instinct; portent; prediction

praesāg·ō -āre -āvī *tr* to have a presentiment of

praesāg·us -a -um *adj* prophetic

praesc·iō -īre -īvī -ītus *tr* to know beforehand

praesc·īscō -īscere -(i)ī *tr* to find out *or* learn beforehand

praesci·us -a -um *adj* prescient, having foreknowledge; praescius ventūrī foreseeing the future

prae·scrībō -scrībere -scrīpsī -scrīptus *tr* to prefix in writing; to describe beforehand; to determine in advance, prescribe, ordain; to dictate; to outline, map out; to put forward as an excuse

praēscrīpti·ō -ōnis *f* heading, title; preface; pretext; rule, law; limit, restriction

praēscrīpt·um -ī *n* regulation, rule; boundary line; route

praesec·ō -āre -uī -tus *tr* to cut off; to cut away; to pare *(nails)*

praesegmin·a -um *npl* clippings

praes·ēns -entis *adj* present, in person, face to face; at hand; existing, contemporary; prompt, immediate, instant; impending; efficacious, powerful, effective; influential; resolute; *(of a god)* ready to help, propitious; *(of payment)* in cash; in praesēns tempus for the present; in rem prasentem venīre to come to the very spot; (in) rē praesentī on the spot; praesēns pecūnia cold cash; praesentī diē on the day in question; sermō praesēns a face-to-face talk ‖ *n* present time; ad *(or* in) praesēns for the present; in praesentī on the spot; in the present case; on the present occasion

praesēnsī *perf of* praesentiō

praesēnsi·ō -ōnis *f* presentiment; preconception

praesēnsus *pp of* praesentiō

praesentāne·us -a -um *adj (of a poison)* having an immediate effect

praesentāri·us -a -um *adj* paid in cash on the spot

praesenti·a -ae *f* presence; efficacy, effect; animī praesentiā presence of mind; resolution; in praesentiā at present, in the present state of affairs; in praesentiā esse to be present, be available; in praesentiam for the present

praesen·tiō -tīre -sī -sēnsus *tr* to feel beforehand, to realize in advance, have strange feelings about

praesēp·e -is *n or* praesēp·ēs -is *f* (-saep-) stall, stable; crib, manger; *(coll)* brothel; *(coll)* lodgings, room

praesēp·iō -īre -sī -tus *tr* (-saep-) to fence in, barricade

praesertim *adv* especially, particularly; praesertim cum especially because

praeserv·iō -īre *intr (w. dat)* to serve *(s.o.)* as a slave

praes·es -idis *m* guard, guardian, protector, defender; president, superintendent; captain, pilot; governor *(of a province)* ‖ *f* guardian, protectress

praesid·ēns -entis *m* president, ruler

prae·sideō -sidēre -sēdī *tr* to guard, protect, defend; to command, be in command of ‖ *intr* to be in charge, be in command; *(w. dat)* 1 to watch over, guard, protect; 2 to preside over, direct, manage; 3 to command

praesidiāri·us -a -um *adj* on garrison duty

praesid·ium -(i)ī *n* protection, defense; assistance; *(mil)* guard, garrison; *(mil)* garrison post, defensive position; *(naut)* convoy; praesidium agitāre to stand guard

praesignific·ō -āre -āvī -ātus *tr* to indicate in advance, foretoken

praesign·is -is -e *adj* outstanding

praeson·ō -āre -uī *tr & intr* to sound beforehand

praesparg·ō -ere *tr* to strew, scatter

praestābil·is -is -e *adj* excellent, outstanding; of outstanding importance

praest·āns -antis *adj* outstanding

praestanti·a -ae *f* excellence, preëminence, superiority

praestantissimē *adv* exceptionally well

praestern·ō -ere *tr* to strew in front

praest·es -itis *m* guardian, protecting deity

praestīgi·ae -ārum *fpl* sleight of hand; juggling; tricks; illusion

praestīgiāt·or -ōris *m,* praestīgiātr·īx -īcis *f* juggler; magician; imposter

praestin·ō -āre -āvī -ātus *tr* to buy, shop for, bargain for

praesti·tuō -tuere -tuī -tūtus *tr* to fix *or* set up beforehand; to prescribe

praestitus *pp of* praestō

praestō *adv* at hand, ready, present, here; praestō esse *(w. dat)* 1 to be on hand for, attend, serve, be helpful to, aid; 2 to be in the way of, resist, oppose

prae·stō -stāre -stitī -stitus *(fut participle:* praestātūrus) *tr* to be superior to, outdo; to show, exhibit, give evidence of, display; to answer for, be responsible for, take upon oneself; to perform, discharge, fulfill; to keep, maintain, retain; to present, offer, supply; fidem praestāre to keep one's word; impetūs populī praestāre to be responsible for popular outbreaks; **nihil praestāre** to be answerable for nothing; **officia praestāre** to perform duties; **sociōs salvōs praestāre** to keep the allies safe; **terga hostī praestāre** to show one's back to the enemy, retreat; **virtūtem praestāre** to display courage **ǁ** *refl* to show oneself, behave **ǁ** *intr* to stand out, be outstanding, be preëminent **ǁ** *v impers* it is preferable, it is better

praestōl·or -ārī -ātus sum *or* **praestōl·ō -āre** *tr* to wait for, expect **ǁ** *intr (w. dat)* to wait for, await

prae·stringō -stringere -strīnxī -strictus *tr* to draw together, constrict, squeeze; to graze; *(fig)* to touch lightly on; to blunt *(an edge);* to blind, dazzle *(the eyes);* to dazzle, baffle; to throw into the shade

praestru·ō -ere -xī -ctus *tr* to build up, to block up, stop up; to build up *(e.g., confidence)* beforehand

praes·ul -ulis *or* **praesultāt·or -ōris** *m* dancer *(at the head of a religious procession)*

praesult·ō -āre -āvī -ātum *intr (w. dat)* to dance in front of, jump around in front of

prae·sum -esse -fuī -futūrus *intr* to preside; **in prōvinciā praeesse** to govern a province; *(w. dat)* **1** to preside over, be in charge of, be in command of; **2** to be preëminent in; **3** to govern *(a province)*

prae·sūmō -sūmere -sumpsī -sumptus *tr* to take in advance; to anticipate, presume, take for granted

praesumpti·ō -ōnis *f* anticipation; presumption; *(rhet)* anticipation *(of an opponent's objections)*

praesūt·us -a -um *adj* sewn up; covered

praetempt·ō -āre -āvī -ātus *tr* to try out in advance, test in advance; to grope for

praeten·dō -dere -dī -tus *tr* to hold *or* stretch in front of oneself; to present; to offer an an excuse, give as pretext, allege, pretend; *(w. dat)* to hold *(e.g., a toga)* in front of *(e.g., the eyes)* **ǁ** *pass (of places) (w. dat)* to lie to the front of *or* opposite

praetent·ō -āre *tr* to allege

praetep·ēscō -ēscere -uī *intr (of love)* to glow, grow warm

praeter *adv* by, past

praeter *conj* besides, other than **ǁ** *prep (w. acc)* **1** *(of place)* past, by, along, before, in front of: **praeter castra cōpiās suās dūcere** to lead his troops past *or* in front of the camp; **2** beyond in degree, surpassing: **praeter spem** beyond hope, unexpectedly; **3** despite, contrary to: **praeter speciem** despite appearances; **praeter cōnsuētūdinem** contrary to normal usage, contrary to custom; **4** in addition to, as well as, besides: **praeter haec** besides this, moreover; **praeter id quod** in

addition to the fact that; **5** except, but, other than: **nunc quidem praeter nōs nēmō est** now there's really no one but us; **6** exclusive of, except for: **praetōrēs quotannīs praeter paucōs locuplētātī sunt** the praetors with few exceptions were getting rich every year

praeter- *pref* by, past

praeterag·ō -ere *tr (w. double acc)* to drive *(e.g., a horse)* past *(a place)*

praeterbīt·ō -ere *tr & intr* to go by *or* past

praeter·dūcō -dūcere -dūxī -ductus *tr* to lead by, conduct past

praevēreā *adv (also written as two words)* besides, moreover; hereafter, thereafter

praeter·eō -īre -īvī *or* **-iī -itus** *tr* to go past, pass by; to skip, pass over in silence; to escape the notice of; to go beyond; to surpass **ǁ** *intr* to go by

praeterequit·āns -antis *adj* riding by *(on horseback)*

praeter·ferō -ferre -tulī -lātus *tr (w. double acc)* to carry *or* take *(s.o.)* past *(s.th.)* **ǁ** *pass* to move by *(a place)*

praeterflu·ō -ere *tr & intr* to flow by

praeter·gredior -gredī -gressus sum *tr* to march by, go past; to surpass **ǁ** *intr* to march by, go past

praeterhāc *adv* in addition

praeterit·us -a -um *pp of* **praetereō** **ǁ** *adj* past, bygone, former; *(gram)* **(tempus) praeteritum** past tense

praeter·lābor -lābī -lāpsus sum *tr & intr* to glide by, slip past

praeterlātus *pp of* **praeterferō**

praeterme·ō -āre *tr & intr* to go past

praetermissi·ō -ōnis *f* leaving out, omission; passing over, neglecting; *(w. gen)* omission of

praeter·mittō -mittere -mīsī -missus *tr* to let pass, let go by; to leave undone; to pass over, omit, disregard, overlook, neglect

praeternāvig·ō -āre *tr* to sail past

prae·terō -terere -trīvī *tr* to wear down in front *(by rubbing)*

praeterquam *or* **praeter quam** *conj* except that; **praeterquam quī** apart from a person who; **praeterquam quod** apart from the fact that; *(w. illipsis)* **num quō crīmine is esset accūsātus praeterquam venēnī?** had he ever been charged with any crime except that of poisoning?; **praeterquam bis** except on two occasions

praetertulī *perf of* **praeterferō**

praetervecti·ō -ōnis *f* passing by; sailing past; riding by

praeter·vehor -vehī -vectus sum *tr & intr* to pass by *or* past; to ride by; to sail by; to march by

praetervol·ō -āre *tr & intr* to fly by; *(of opportunity)* to slip by; to escape

praetex·ō -ere -uī -tus *tr* to border, edge, fringe; to adorn in front; *(fig)* to cloak, conceal, disguise; to use as a pretext, allege, pretend

praetext·a -ae *f* crimson-bordered toga *(worn by higher magistrates and by freeborn boys and possibly girls);* tragedy; **praetextās docēre** to put on tragedies

praetextāt·us -a -um *adj* wearing the toga praetexta *(crimson-bordered toga);* underage, juvenile; **mōrēs praetextātī** loose morals

praetext·um -ī *n* adornment, glory; pretext, cloak

praetext·us -a -um *pp of* **praetexō** ‖ *adj* bordered; wearing the crimson-bordered toga; **fābula praetexta** Roman tragic drama ‖ *f see* **praetexta** ‖ *n* pretext, pretense, excuse

praetext·us -ūs *m* show, appearance; pretext

praetim·eō -ēre *intr* to be apprehensive

praetīnct·us -a -um *adj* previously dipped

praet·or -ōris *m* praetor *(judicial magistrate, accompanied by six lictors); (during early days of the Republic)* chief magistrate, chief executive; *(in Italian municipalities)* chief magistrate; **praetor peregrīnus** praetor who had jurisdiction over cases involving a Roman and a foreigner; **praetor urbānus** *(or* **urbis)** praetor with jurisdiction over cases involving Roman citizens; **prō praetōre** magistrate with extended governorship, or other persons ranked as such

praetōriān·us -a -um *adj* praetorian, belonging to the emperor's bodyguard; **mīles praetōriānus** a praetorian guard ‖ *mpl* praetorian guard

praetōrici·us -a -um *adj* received from the praetor *(at public games)*

praetōri·us -a -um *adj* of the commander in chief, of the commander *or* general; praetor's; propraetor's; **cohors praetōria** general's bodyguard; **comitia praetōria** praetorial elections; **nāvis praetōria** flagship; **porta praetōria** camp gate nearest the general's tent; **turba praetōria** crowd around the praetor ‖ *n* general's quarters, headquarters; official residence of the governor in a province; council of war; emperor's bodyguard; palace, mansion

praetor·queō -quēre -sī -tus *tr* to twist beforehand; to strangle first

praetract·ō -āre *tr* to consider in advance

praetrepid·ō -āre *intr* to tremble in anticipation

praetrepid·us -a -um *adj* very nervous, trembling

praetrīvī *perf of* **praeterō**

praetrunc·ō -āre -āvī -ātus *tr* to cut off; to lop off the tip of

praetulī *perf of* **praeferō**

praetūr·a -ae *f* praetorship; propraetorship

Praetūtiān·us -a -um *adj* of the Praetutii *(a people of Picenum)*

praeumbr·āns -antis *adj* casting a shadow; *(fig)* overshadowing

praeūst·us -a -um *adj* burnt at the tip, hardened by fire at the point; frostbitten

praeut *conj* as compared with, when compared with

praeval·ēns -entis *adj* exceptionally powerful, exceptionally strong

praeval·eō -ēre -uī *intr* to be stronger, have more power; to have greater influence; to have the upper hand

praevalid·us -a -um *adj* unusually strong, unusually powerful, imposing; too strong

praevāricāti·ō -ōnis *f (leg)* collusion

praevāricāt·or -ōris *m (leg)* prosecutor in collusion with the defense

praevāric·or -ārī -ātus sum *intr (leg) (of an attorney)* to act in collusion with his opposite to secure a particular outcome to a trial

praevār·us -a -um *adj* very crooked; very knock-kneed

prae·vehor -vehī -vectus sum *tr (of a river)* to flow by ‖ *intr* to ride in front, ride by; to sail by

prae·veniō -venīre -vēnī -ventus *tr* to come before, precede, get the jump on, anticipate; to prevent ‖ *intr* to come before, precede

praeverb·ium -(i)ī *n (gram)* prefix

praeverr·ō -ere *tr* to sweep *(the ground)* before

praever·tō -tere -tī -sus *or* **prae·vertor -vertī -versus sum** *tr* **(-vort-)** to go before, precede, outrun, outstrip; to turn to first, attend to first; to prefer; to come before, anticipate; to prevent; to preoccupy, surprise; *(w. dat or* **prae** + *abl)* to prefer *(s.o. or s.th.)* to ‖ *intr (w. dat or* **ad)** to go first to, turn to first, attend to first

prae·videō -vidēre -vīdī -vīsus *tr* to foresee

praeviti·ō -āre -āvī -ātus *tr* to taint *or* pollute beforehand

praevi·us -a -um *adj* going before, leading the way

praevol·ō -āre -āvī *intr* to fly out in front

pragmatic·us -a -um *adj* experienced, worldly-wise ‖ *m* legal adviser

pran·deō -dēre -dī -sus *tr* to eat for breakfast, eat for lunch ‖ *intr* to have breakfast, have lunch

prand·ium -(i)ī *n* breakfast; lunch

prānsit·ō -āre *intr* to usually eat breakfast *or* lunch

prāns·or -ōris *m* guest at lunch

prānsōri·us -a -um *adj* suitable for lunch
prāns·us -a -um *pp of* **prandeō ‖** *adj* having had breakfast *or* lunch, after eating; well-fed; **prānsus pōtus** having been wined and dined
prasināt·us -a -um *adj* wearing a green outfit
prasiniān·us -ī *m* fan of the green faction *(at the racetrack)*
prasin·us -a -um *adj* (bright) green; **factiō prasina** the Greens *(one of the stables of horses at the racetrack)*
prātēns·is -is -e *adj* meadow, growing in a meadow
prātul·um -ī *n* small meadow
prāt·um -ī *n* meadow; *(fig)* broad expanse of the sea **‖** *npl* meadow grass
prāvē *adv* crookedly; improperly, wrongly, badly, poorly; **prāvē factī versūs** poorly written verses
prāvit·ās -ātis *f* crookedness, distortion; impropriety, irregularity; perverseness, depravity
prāv·us -a -um *adj* crooked, distorted, deformed; irregular, improper, wrong, bad; perverse, vicious
Praxitel·ēs -ī *or* **-ūs** *or* **-ae** *m* Athenian sculptor *(4th cent. B.C.)*
Praxitelī·us -a -um *adj* of Praxiteles
precāriō *adv* upon request
precāri·us -a -um *adj* obtained by prayer; dependent on another's will, uncertain, precarious
precāti·ō -ōnis *f* prayer; **precātiōnēs facere** to say prayers
precāt·or -ōris *m* intercessor, suppliant
precēs = *pl of* **prex**
preci·ae -ārum *fpl* grapevine
prec·or -ārī -ātus sum *tr* to entreat, supplicate, pray to; to pray for; to wish for; *(w. double acc)* to pray to *(s.o.)* for; *(w. acc of thing and abl of person)* to request *(s.th.)* from; *(w.* **prō** + *abl)* to entreat *(e.g., the gods)* on behalf of; *(w.* **ut, nē)** to pray that, pray that not; **longum Augustō diem precārī** to wish Augustus long life **‖** *intr* to pray; *(w.* **ad)** to pray to, *e.g.,* **dī ad quōs precantur** the gods to whom they pray; **male precārī** to curse, utter curses
prehen·dō *or* **pren·dō -dere -dī -sus** *tr* to take hold of, grasp, seize; to detain; to arrest; to catch, surprise; to reach, arrive at; to grasp, understand; *(w.* **in** + *abl)* to catch a person in the act of; *(mil)* to occupy
prēl·um -ī *n* wine press, oil press; clothes press
premō premere pressī pressus *tr* to press, squeeze; to lie down on *(the ground)*; *(of things)* to be on top of, rest on; to bury *(in the ground)*; to trample on; to get on top of, have sex with *(a woman)*; to hug *(the shore)*; to suppress, hide; to cover, crown; to press hard, bear down on; to weigh down, burden; to put

emphasis on *(a point of argument)*; to chase, attack; to weigh down, load; to press together, close; to choke, throttle; to block *(an entranceway)*; to keep shut up, prevent from escaping; to curb, stop *(movement, an action, a process)*; to depress, lower; to submerge, sink; to drown out *(a noise)*; *(of sleep, death)* to overcome, overpower; *(of darkness)* to cover, hide; to mark, impress; to prune; to pressure, urge, importune; to degrade, humble, disparage; to abridge, condense, compress *(words, thoughts)*; to press *(wine, oil)*; to subjugate; *(geog)* to hem in, surround; **forum premere** to frequent the forum, walk about in the forum; **oculōs premere** to close the eyes *(of a dead person)*; **pollicem premere** to give the good luck sign *(by pressing the thumb against the index finger)*; **vestīgia premere** *(w. gen)* **1** to follow hard upon the tracks of; **2** *(fig)* to follow in *(s.o.'s)* tracks; **vōcem premere** to fall silent **‖** *refl* & *pass* to lower oneself *(in dignity)*, stoop **‖** *refl* to huddle together
prēnsāti·ō -ōnis *f (pol)* campaign
prēns·ō *or* **prehēns·ō -āre -āvī -ātus** *tr* to take hold of, clutch at, grab; to buttonhole **‖** *intr (pol)* to campaign
prēnsus *pp of* **prendō**
pressē *adv* distinctly, with articulation; concisely; accurately, simply
pressī *perf of* **premō**
pressi·ō -ōnis *f* pressure *(exerted by the fulcrum of a lever)*; fulcrum
press·ō -āre -āvī -ātus *tr* to press, exert pressure on; to weigh down
pressūr·a -ae *f* pressure
press·us -a -um *pp of* **premō ‖** *adj* closed, shut tight; compact, dense; low *(sound)*, subdued *(voice)*; tight *(embrace)*; deliberate *(pace)*; concise *(style)*; **bāsia pressa** one kiss after another; **cōpia lactis pressī** a supply of cheese
press·us -ūs *m* pressure; expression *(of the face)*
pretiōsē *adv* at great cost, expensively
pretiōs·us -a -um *adj* precious, valuable; expensive; extravagant
pret·ium -(i)ī *n* price; value, worth; reward, return, recompense; bribe; pay, wages; ransom; **ad pretium redigere** to put a price on; **in pretiō esse** to be prized; to be held in high esteem; **in pretiō habēre** to prize, hold in high esteem; **pretiō meō (tuō)** at my (your) expense; **pretium cūrae esse** to be worth the trouble; **pretium facere** to set a price; **pretium habēre** to have value, be worth something; **pretium operae esse** to be worth the effort, be worthwhile

prex precis *f (usu. pl)* prayer; request; intercession; curse, imprecation
Priamē·is -idos *f* daughter of Priam (*Cassandra*)
Priamēï·us -a -um *adj* of Priam
Priamid·ēs -ae *m* son of Priam
Priam·us -ī *m* Priam (*son of Laomedon, husband of Hecuba, father of Hector, Paris, Cassandra, etc., king of Troy*)
Priāp·us -ī *m* son of Dionysus and Aphrodite, god of gardens and vineyards, and protector of flocks
prīdem *adv* formerly, previously; once (*in the past*); long ago; **haud ita prīdem** not so long ago, not long before; **iam prīdem** long ago; **quam prīdem?** for how long?; how long ago?
prīdiān·us -a -um *adj* of the day before
prīdiē *adv* the day before
Priēn·ē -ēs *f* coastal town in Ionia, opposite Miletus
prīm·a -ōrum *npl* first part, beginning; first principles *or* elements; **cum prīmīs** among the first, especially; chiefly; first of all; **in prīmīs** above all, chiefly, particularly, especially
prīm·ae -ārum *fpl* lead, first rank, highest place, highest importance; **prīmās dare** (*w. dat*) to attach supreme importance to
prīmaev·us -a -um *adj* youthful
prīmān·ī -ōrum *mpl* soldiers of the first legion
prīmāri·us -a -um *adj* first in rank; first-rate
prīmē *adv* to the highest degree
prīmigen·us -a -um *adj* first-born
prīmipīlār·is -is *m* ranking centurion of a legion
prīmipīl·us -ī *m* ranking centurion of a legion
prīmiti·ae -ārum *fpl* first fruits; (*fig*) beginnings; **ā prīmitiīs** from the beginning, thoroughly
prīmitus *adv* originally, at first; for the first time
prīmō *adv* first, in the first place; at first, at the beginning
prīmord·ium -(i)ī *n* origin, beginning; commencement; beginning of a new reign
prīmōr·is -is -e *adj* first, leading; the front of, the beginning of; tip of; first, earliest; front (*teeth, battle line*); principal; basic; leading (*men*); **digitulī prīmōrēs** fingertips; **in labrīs prīmōribus** on the tip of one's tongue; **prīmoris manus** wrist ‖ *mpl* leaders, chiefs, nobles; (*mil*) front ranks
prīmulum *adv* for the first time; at first, first of all
prīmul·us -a -um *adj* very first
prīmum *adv* first, in the first place, before all else; at first; for the first time; **cum prīmum** (*or* **ubi prīmum** *or* **ut prīmum**) as soon as;

prīmum dum in the first place; **quam prīmum** as soon as possible
prīmumdum *adv* in the first place
prīm·us -a -um *adj* first; foremost; principal; distinguished; nearest; basic, fundamental; first-class; the earliest stages; the front of; front (*teeth*); the tip of, end of; **prīmā fronte** (*or* **faciē**) outwardly, at first glance; **prīmās partēs agere** to play the lead role; **prīmī pedēs** forefeet; **prīmīs digitīs** with *or* at the fingertips; **prīmō annō** at the beginning of the year *or* season; **prīmō quoque tempore** at the very earliest opportunity; **prīmus in prōvinciam introiit** he was the first to enter the province; **prīmus quisque** the very first, the first possible; each in turn ‖ *mpl* leading citizens ‖ *fpl see* **prīmae** ‖ *n* beginning; front; **ā prīmō** from the first; **in prīmō** in the beginning; (*mil*) at the head of the column ‖ *npl see* **prīma**
prīnc·eps -ipis *adj* first; earliest; original; leading, in front; foremost, chief ‖ *m* leader, chief; emperor; (*mil*) maniple, company; (*mil*) captain, company commander, centurion; (*mil*) rank of centurion; **prīnceps prīmus** a centurion ranking second among the six centurions of a legion ‖ *mpl* (*mil*) soldiers of the second line (*between the* **hastātī** *and the* **triāriī**), second line
prīncipāl·is -is -e *adj* first, foremost; original, primitive; chief, principal; of the emperor; **via prīncipālis** (*mil*) main street (*of a camp*); **porta prīncipālis** (*mil*) main gate (*of a camp*)
prīncipāt·us -ūs *m* first place; post of commander in chief; principate; rule, sovereignty; origin, beginning; **prīncipātum tenēre** to occupy first place, be in the lead
prīncipi·a -ōrum *npl* first principles; foundations; (*mil*) front line, front-line troops; (*mil*) headquarters
prīncipiāl·is -is -e *adj* initial
prīncipiō *adv* in the beginning, at first
prīncip·ium -(i)ī *n* beginning, start; starting point; origin; beginner, originator; basis; premise; (*pol*) first to vote; (*pol*) right to vote first; **ā prīncipiō** in the beginning, at first; **dē prīncipiō** right from the start; **prīncipium capere** (*or* **sūmere** *or* **exōrdīrī**) to begin; **prīncipium dūcere ab** to originate with ‖ *npl* foundations; (*mil*) headquarters; (*mil*) the second line in order of battle; (*phil*) rudimentary particles of matter, elements
pri·or -or -us (*gen:* **-ōris**) *comp; no positive exists*) *adj* previous, preceding, prior, former; more fundamental, basic; better, superior, preferable; (*of kings, rulers*) the elder; **in priōrem partem** in a forward direction; **priōrēs partēs agere** to play a more important role ‖ *mpl* forefathers, ancestors,

ancients **ll** *fpl (only acc)* lead, preference **ll** *npl* earlier events

prīscē *adv* in the old-fashioned style

prīsc·us -a -um *adj* old, ancient; old-time, old-fashioned; former, previous

Prīsc·us -ī *m* Roman family name *(cognomen), esp.* Lucius Tarquinius Priscus *(the fifth king of Rome)* **ll** Quintus Servilius Priscus Fidenas *(conqueror of the Veientes and Fidenates in 435 B.C.)* **ll** Helvidius Priscus *(prominent Stoic under Nero and Vespasian)*

prīstīn·us -a -um *adj* former, earlier; pristine, primitive, original; preceding, previous, yesterday's **ll** *n* **in prīstīnum restituere** to restore to its former condition

pristr·is -is *(acc:* **-im** *or* **-in)** *f or* **pistr·īx -īcis** *f* sea monster; whale, shark; swift ship; *(astr)* the Whale *(constellation)*

prius *adv* earlier, before, previously, sooner, first; sooner, rather

priusquam *conj (also written as two words)* before

prīvātim *adv* privately, in private; as a private citizen; at home

prīvāti·ō -ōnis *f* removal, negation

prīvāt·us -a -um *adj* private; personal, individual, peculiar; isolated; ordinary *(language)* **ll** *m* private citizen; civilian; subject *(of a ruler)* **ll** *n* privacy, retirement; private property, private land; **ex prīvātō** out of one's own pocket; **in prīvātō** in private; **in prīvātum** for private use

Prīvern·ās -ātis *adj* of Privernum **ll** *mpl* the people of Privernum

Prīvern·um -ī *n* Latin town founded by the Volscians

prīvigna -ae *f* stepdaughter

prīvign·us -ī *m* stepson **ll** *mpl* stepchildren

prīvilēg·ium -(i)ī *n* privilege, special right; *(pol)* special bill directed against *or* in favor of an individual

prīv·ō -āre *tr (w. abl)* **1** to deprive of, rob of; **2** to release from, relieve of, free from

prīv·us -a -um *adj* every, each, single; own, private; *(w. gen)* deprived of

prō *adv* (w. **quam** *or* **ut**) just as, according as **ll** *prep (w. abl)* before, in front of; in the presence of; for, on behalf of, in favor of, in the service of, on the side of; instead of, for, in lieu of; just as, the same as, for; in proportion to; according to; in comparison with; by virtue of; in name of; **esse prō** *(w. abl)* to be as good as, be the equivalent of; **esse** *(or* **stāre prō** + *abl)* to be on the side of *(s.o.);* **prō certō habēre** to regard *(s.th.)* as certain; **prō eō** just the same; **prō eō atque** *(or* **ac)** just as, the same as; **prō eō quod** in view of the fact that; **prō eō quantum** in proportion to, according as; **prō eō ut** instead of being

the case that; **prō hērēde** in his capactiy as heir; **prō occīsō relictus** left for dead; **prō rōstrō ōrātiōnem habēre** to speak from the rostrum; **prō sē quisque** each one for himself, individually; **prō sententiā dīcere** to state as his opinion; **prō testimōniō dīcere** to state by way of evidence; **prō vallō carrōs obiciunt** they put their wagons in the way to serve as a barricade; **utrum prō ancillā mē habēs an fīliā?** do you regard me as a maid or a daughter? **ll** *interj* oh!; **prō dī immortālēs!** oh, heavens above!

prō- (prō-, prod-) *pref* **1** forward movement: **prōgredī** to go forward; **2** downward movement: **prōclīvis** downhill; **3** action in front: **prōtegere** to cover in front; **4** bringing into the open: **prōdere** to bring out, publish; **5** priority in time: **prōvidēre** to see beforehand; **6** advantage: **prōdesse** *(w. dat)* to be advantageous, be good for

proāgor·us -ī *m* mayor *(in some Greek provincial towns in Sicily)*

proauct·or -ōris *mf* early ancestor

proavi·a -ae *f* great-grandmother

proavīt·us -a -um *adj* great-grandfather's, ancestral

proav·us -ī *m* great-grandfather; ancestor, forefather

probābil·is -is -e *adj* worthy of approval, commendable, acceptable; pleasing, agreeable; probable, plausible, likely

probābilit·ās -ātis *f* probability

probābiliter *adv* probably

probāti·ō -ōnis *f* approval, approbation; criterion, test; proof

probāt·or -ōris *m* approver, supporter, backer

probāt·us -a -um *adj* approved, acceptable; tried, tested, good; esteemed

probē *adv* correctly, well, satisfactorily; thoroughly, very, very much; **haud probē** not really, no; **pereō probē** *(coll)* I'm absolutely a goner

probit·ās -ātis *f* probity, uprightness, honesty, goodness; sexual purity; good behavior

problēm·a -atis *m (rhet)* difficult question for debate, problem

prob·ō -āre -āvī -ātus *tr* to approve, commend, esteem; to make good, represent as good, make acceptable; to pronounce judgment on; to pronounce approval of; to make credible, prove, show, demonstrate; to test, try, inspect; **probāre prō** *(w. abl)* to pass *(s.o.)* off as **ll** *pass* **probārī prō** *(w. abl)* to pass for, be taken for

probosc·is -idis *f* snout; trunk *(of an elephant)*

probriperlecebr·ae -ārum *fpl* temptations

probrōs·us -a -um *adj* scandalous, shameful, abusive

probr·um -ī *n* abuse, invective, reproach; shameful act; lewdness, indecency; shame, disgrace; charge of disgraceful conduct

prob·us -a -um *adj* good, honest, upright, virtuous, decent; *(coll)* real, proper, downright

Prob·us -ī *m* Roman family name *(cognomen)*, *esp.* Marcus Valerius Probus *(grammarian of the 1st cent.* A.D.*)*

Proc·a *or* **Proc·ās -ae** *m* Proca *(king of Alba Longa and father of Numitor and Amulius)*

procācit·ās -ātis *f* brashness

procāciter *adv* brashly

proc·āx -ācis *adj* brash

prō·cēdō -cēdere -cessī -cessum *intr* to proceed, go forward, advance; to make progress; to come out *(in public)*, show oneself, appear; to come forth, arise; *(of time)* to pass, elapse; to turn out, result, succeed; to continue

procell·a -ae *f* violent wind, squall, hurricane, storm; *(fig)* violence, commotion, storm; *(mil)* violent charge

prōcell·ō -ere *tr* to throw down ‖ *refl* **sē procellere in mēnsam** to flop down at the table

proc·er -eris *m* chief, noble

procellōs·us -a -um *adj* gusty, stormy

prōcērē *adv* far

procer·ēs -um *mpl* leading men *(of a society, etc.)*; leaders *(of a profession, art)*

prōcērit·ās -ātis *f* height, tallness; length ‖ *fpl* the different heights *(e.g., of trees)*

prōcērius *adv* farther, to a greater extent, more

prōcēr·us -a -um *adj* tall *(person, tree)*; long *(neck, beak)*; lofty *(idea)*; *(pros)* long; **palmae prōcērae** open palms

prōcessī *perf of* **prōcēdō**

prōcessi·ō -ōnis *f* advance

prōcess·us -a -um *pp of* **prōcēdō** ‖ *adj* advanced *(age)*

prōcess·us -ūs *m* advance, progress

Prochyt·a -ae *or* **Prochyt·ē -ēs** *f* small island off the Campanian coast *(modern Procida)*

proc·ī -ōrum *mpl* class of leading citizens under the Servian constitution

prō·cidō -cidere -cidī *intr* to fall forwards, fall over, fall down, fall prostrate

prōcīnctū *(abl only)* *m* **in prōcīnctu** ready for combat, on red alert

prōclāmāt·or -ōris *m* loudmouth

prōclām·ō -āre -āvī -ātus *tr* to yell out; to exclaim; *(w. acc & inf)* to cry out that ‖ *intr* to yell; to practice public speaking

Procl·ēs -is *m* one of the first pair of kings to reign at Sparta, together with Eurysthenes

prōclīn·ō -āre -āvī -ātus *tr* to bend, bend forward; **rēs prōclīnāta** critical situation, crisis

prōclīv·e -is *n* slope, descent; **in prōclīvī esse** to be easy

prōclīvī *adv* downhill; effortlessly

prōclīv·is -is -e *or* **prōclīv·us -a -um** *adj* sloping down; sloping forward; downhill; easy; *(w.* **ad***)* inclined to, disposed to, ready for; *(of years, seasons)* declining; *(fig)* going downhill, insecure; *(w.* **ad***)* inclined to

prōclīvit·ās -ātis *f* proclivity, tendency, predisposition

prōclīviter *adv* readily; easily, effortlessly

prōclīvius *adv* more rapidly

prōclīv·us *see* **prōclīvis**

Procn·ē -ēs *f* **(Prog-)** Procne *(daughter of Pandion, sister of Philomela, wife of Tereus, and mother and murderess of Itys; she was changed into a swallow)*; swallow

proc·ō -āre *or* **proc·or -ārī** *tr* to require, demand

prōcōns·ul *(and* **prō cōnsule***)* **-ulis** *m* viceconsul, proconsul; governor of a province; military commander

prōcōnsulār·is -e *adj* proconsular

prōcōnsulāt·us -ūs *m* proconsulship, proconsulate

prōcrāstināti·ō -ōnis *f* procrastination

prōcrāstin·ō -āre -āvī -ātus *tr* to put off till the next day, postpone ‖ *intr* to procrastinate

prōcreāti·ō -ōnis *f* procreation

prōcreāt·or -ōris *m* procreator; creator ‖ *mpl* parents

prōcreātr·īx -īcis *f* mother

prōcre·ō -āre -āvī -ātus *tr* to procreate, beget; to produce

prōcrēsc·ō -ere *intr* to spring forth, be produced; to continue to grow, grow up

Procr·is -is *or* **-idis** *f* Procris *(wife of Cephalus, who mistook her for a wild beast and shot her with bow and arrow)*

Procrūst·ēs -ae *m* Procrustes *(notorious robber in Attica who stretched his victims to the length of his bed or mutilated them if they were too tall)*

prōcub·ō -āre -uī *intr* to lie stretched out

prō·cūdō -cūdere -cūsī -cūsus *tr (lit & fig)* to hammer out, forge

procul *adv* at a distance, in the distance; far away, a great way off; from a distance, from far; **haud procul āfuit quīn lēgātōs violārent** they came close to outraging the ambassadors; **nōn procul ab** not far from

prōculc·ō -āre -āvī -ātus *tr* to trample upon, trample down

Proculēi·us -ī *m* Roman clan name *(nomen)*, *esp.* Gaius Proculeius *(friend of Augustus and literary patron)*

prōcumbō prōcumbere prōcubuī prōcubitum *intr* to fall down, sink down; to lean forward, bend over, be broken down; to lie down; *(fig)* to go to ruin; *(topog)* to extend, spread

prōcūrāti·ō -ōnis *f* attention; *(w. gen)* 1 concern for, care for; 2 responsibility for, charge over; 3 management of, administration of; 4 procuratorship of; 5 expiation of
prōcūrāt·or -ōris *m* procurator, manager, administrator; agent, deputy; governor of a (minor) province
prōcūrātr·īx -īcis *f* superintendent *(female)*
prōcūr·ō -āre -āvī -ātus *tr* to look after, attend to; to administer *(as procurator);* to have charge of; to avert by sacrifice; to expiate ‖ *intr* to serve as procurator
prō·currō -currere -(cu)currī -cursum *intr* to run out ahead, dash forward; to jut out, project
prōcursāti·ō -ōnis *f* sally, charge
prōcursātōr·ēs -um *mpl* skirmishers
prōcurs·ō -āre *intr* to keep charging out; to continue to skirmish
prōcurs·us -ūs *m* sally, charge
prōcurv·us -a -um *adj* curving forwards; curving, winding *(shore)*
proc·us -ī *m* suitor; gigolo ‖ *mpl* class of leading citizens in the Servian constitution; impudentēs procī shameless candidates
Procy·ōn -ōnis *m (astr)* Lesser Dog Star *(the constellation Canis Minor)*
prōdāctus *pp of* prōdigō
prōdeambul·ō -āre *intr* to go out for a walk
prōd·eō -īre -iī -itum *intr* to go out, come out, go forth, come forth; *(of plants)* to come out; to appear in public; to come forward *(in the assembly or court);* to appear *(on stage);* to go ahead, advance; in proelium prōdīre to go into battle; obviam prōdīre *(w. dat)* to go out to meet *(s.o.);* (e.g., *of a cliff)* to jut out, project
prō·dīcō -dīcere -dīxī -dictus *tr* to set *(a date)* beforehand *(for some activity);* praetor reō atque accūsātōribus diem prōdīxit *(leg)* the praetor announced the date of the trial to the defendant as well as the plaintiffs
prōdictāt·or -ōris *m* vice-dictator
Prodic·us -ī *m* sophist of Ceos, contemporary with Socrates
prōdigē *adv* lavishly
prōdigenti·a -ae *f* extravagance; prōdigentia opum wasting of resources
prōdigiāl·is -is -e *adj* marked with prodigies
prōdigiāliter *adv* to a fantastic degree
prōdigiōs·us -a -um prodigious; freakish
prōdig·ium -(i)ī *n* prodigy, portent; unnatural crime, monstrous crime; monster, freak
prōd·igō -igere -ēgī -āctus *tr* to squander, waste
prōdig·us -a -um *adj* wasteful; lavish, openhanded; *(w. gen)* free with; animae prōdigus free with *or* careless with one's life; herbae

prōdigus locus spot with luxurious growth of grass
prōditi·ō -ōnis *f* betrayal, treason; prōditiōnem agere *(w. dat)* to commit treason against, betray
prōdit·or -ōris *m* betrayer, traitor
prō·dō -dere -didī -ditus *tr* to bring out, bring forth, produce; to reveal, disclose; *(of a writer, esp. w.* memoriā *or* memoriae *or ad* memoriam) to record, relate, report, hand down, transmit; to proclaim; to appoint; to give up, surrender; to forsake, betray; to prolong; *(w. dat)* 1 to betray to; 2 to reveal to
prōdoc·eō -ēre *tr* to teach publicly
prodrom·us -ī *m* forerunner; northerly winds *(that precede the Etesian winds)*
prō·dūcō -dūcere -dūxī ductus *tr* to bring out, bring forth; to produce; to promote, advance; to bring to light; to bring into the world; to raise, bring up; to educate; to drag out, protract; to lengthen *(a syllable);* to lead on, induce; to put off, adjourn; to put *(a slave)* up for sale; to produce, perform *(on the stage); (leg)* to bring to court
prōduct·a -ōrum *npl* preferable things, preferences
prōductē *adv* long; prōductē litteram dīcere to pronounce the letter *or* vowel long
prōducti·ō -ōnis *f* lengthening
prōduct·ō -āre *tr* to drag out
prōduct·us -a -um *pp of* prōdūcō ‖ *adj* lengthened, prolonged, long
proēgmen·on -ī *n* preference
proeliār·is -is -e *adj* battle, of battle
proeliāt·or -ōris *m* combatant
proeli·or -ārī -ātus sum *intr* to battle
proel·ium -(i)ī *n* battle, combat, fight; proelium committere *or* facere *or* inīre *or* sūmere to go into action, begin to battle ‖ *npl* fighting men, warriors
Proetid·es -um *fpl* daughters of Proetus, who were driven mad by Hera and imagined that they were cows
Proēt·us -ī *m* Proëtus, king of Argos *or* Tiryns, twin-brother of Acrisius
profān·ō -āre -āvī -ātus *tr* to profane
profān·us -a -um *adj* unconsecrated, ordinary; impious; ill-omened
profātur *(3rd singl)* profārī profātus est *tr* to say, declare ‖ *intr* to speak out
prōfēcī *perf of* prōficiō
profecti·ō -ōnis *f* setting out, departure; source *(of money)*
profectō *adv* really, actually
prōfectus *pp of* prōficiō
profectus *pp of* proficīscor
prōfect·us -ūs *m* progress, advance; success; profit

prō·ferō -ferre -tulī -lātus *tr* to bring forward, advance, bring out; to extend, enlarge; to put off, postpone; to produce, discover, invent; to make known, publish; to express; to mention, cite, quote; **in medium** (*or* **in lūcem**) **prōferre** to publish, disclose; **pedem prōferre** to advance; **rēs prōferre** (*leg*) to declare a recess; **signa prōferre** (*mil*) to march forward

professi·ō -ōnis *f* public acknowledgment, profession, declaration; registration (*at which property, etc., was declared*); profession, business

profess·or -ōris *m* professor, teacher

professōri·us -a -um *adj* professorial; professional, expert

professus *pp of* profiteor

profēst·us -a -um *adj* non-holiday, ordinary; diēs profēstus workday

prō·ficiō -ficere -fēcī -fectum *intr* to make progress, make headway, advance; to have success; to be useful, do good, help, be conducive; **nihil prōficere** to do no good

pro·ficīscor -ficīscī -fectus sum *intr* to set out, start, go, depart; to originate, proceed, arise

pro·fiteor -fitērī -fessus sum *tr* to declare publicly, acknowledge, confess, profess; to offer freely, promise, volunteer; to follow as a profession, practice (*e.g., law*); to make a declaration of, register (*property, etc., before a public official*); **indicium profitērī** to volunteer evidence, testify freely; **nōmen profitērī** to put one's name in as a candidate; **sē adiūtōrem profitērī** (*w.* ad) to volunteer to help (*s.o.*) ‖ *intr* to make a confession, make an admission; to be a professor, be a teacher

prōflīgāt·or -ōris *m* big spender

prōflīgāt·us -a -um *adj* profligate

prōflīg·ō -āre -āvī -ātus *tr* to knock to the ground, knock down; to defeat; to bring to an end, do away with, finish off; to ruin, crush; to degrade, debase

prōfl·ō -āre -āvī -ātus *tr* to breathe out

prōflu·ēns -entis *adj* flowing along; fluent (*speech*) ‖ *f* running water

prōfluenter *adv* easily, effortlessly, fluently

prōfluenti·a -ae *f* fluency

prōflu·ō -ere -xī *intr* to flow out; to flow along; (*fig*) to proceed; **gravēdō prōfluit** the head cold results in a runny nose

prōfluv·ium -(i)ī *n* flow

pro·for -fārī -fātus sum *tr* to say, declare ‖ *intr* to speak out

prōfūdī *perf of* prōfundō

pro·fugiō -fugere -fūgī -fugitūrus *tr* to run away from, escape from ‖ *intr* to run away, escape; (*w.* ad) to take refuge with, take refuge at the house of

profug·us -a -um *adj* fugitive; banished, exiled; nomadic ‖ *m* refugee

pro·fundō -fundere -fūdī -fūsus *tr* to pour, pour out; to shed (*blood, tears*) freely; to utter; to give vent to; to spend freely, squander; **animam** (*or* **spīritum**) **prōfundere** to breathe one's last; **vītam prō patriā prōfundere** to give one's life for one's country ‖ *refl & pass* to come pouring out; to sprout

profund·us -a -um *adj* deep; boundless, vast; dense (*forest, cloud*); high; infernal; (*fig*) bottomless, boundless ‖ *n* depth; the deep, deep sea; abyss

profūsē *adv* in disorder, haphazardly, helter-skelter; extravagantly

profūsi·ō -ōnis *f* profusion

profūs·us -a -um *pp of* prōfundō ‖ *adj* extravagant, lavish, profuse; excessive, expensive

prōgen·er -erī *m* granddaughter's husband

prōgener·ō -āre -āvī -ātus *tr* to beget, give birth to; to produce

prōgeni·ēs -ēī *f* offspring, progeny; line, family; lineage, descent

prōgenit·or -ōris *m* progenitor

prō·gignō -gignere -genuī -genitus *tr* to beget, produce

prōgnāriter *adv* precisely, exactly

prōgnāt·us -a -um *adj* (*w. abl or* ab *or* ex) born of, descended from ‖ *m* child; grandson

Prognē *see* Procnē

prognōstic·on *or* prognōstic·um -ī *n* sign of the future, prognostic ‖ *npl* signs of the weather

prō·gredior -gredī -gressus sum *intr* to go forward, march forward; to advance; to go on, make headway, make progress; to go forth, go out

prōgressi·ō -ōnis *f* progress, advancement; increase, growth; (*rhet*) climax

prōgressus *pp of* progredior

prōgress·us -ūs *m* progress, advance; march (*of time or events*)

prōh *interj* oh!; **prōh dī immortālēs!** oh, heavens above!

pro(h)oemi·or -ārī *intr* to make an introduction *or* preface

pro(h)oem·ium *or* pro(h)ēm·ium -(i)ī *n* introduction, preface; prelude; (*fig*) prelude (*e.g., to a fight*)

prohib·eō -ēre -uī -itus *tr* to hold back, check, hinder, prevent, avert, keep off; to prohibit; to preclude; to keep away; to defend, protect; (*w.* nē, quōminus, *or in negative contexts* quīn) to keep (*s.o.*) from (*doing s.th.*)

prohibiti·ō -ōnis *f* prohibition

prōiēcī *perf of* prōiciō

prōiectīci·us -a -um *adj* exposed, abandoned (*child*)

prōiecti·ō -ōnis _f_ stretching out; **prōiectiō bracchiī** stretching out of the arm

prōiect·us -a -um _pp of_ **prōiciō** ‖ _adj_ jutting out; prostrate, stretched out; abject, contemptible; downcast; _(w._ **ad)** prone to

prōiect·us -ūs _m_ projection, extension

prō·iciō -icere -iēcī -iectus _tr_ to throw down; to throw away, abandon, forsake; to fling from oneself as unwanted, discard; to hold out, extend; to banish, exile; to neglect, desert; to blurt out; to give up, sacrifice; to put off, delay; to throw overboard; _(w._ in + acc _or_ ad) to abandon to _(a fate),_ expose to; **proicere in exilium** to drive out, banish ‖ _refl_ to throw oneself, plunge; to rush; _(w._ in + acc) to give way to _(a feeling, tears, habit);_ **sē prōicere ad pedēs** _(w. gen)_ to throw oneself at the feet of; **sē prōicere ex nāve** to jump overboard; **sē prōicere in Forum** to rush into the Forum; **sē prōicere in muliebrēs flētūs** to give way to unmanly weeping ‖ _pass (geog)_ to extend; _(of a promontory)_ to jut out ‖ _intr_ to jut out

proïnde _or_ **proïn** _(or_ **proin** _as monosyllable) adv_ so then, consequently, accordingly; equally; likewise; **proïnde atque** _(or ac or ut or quam)_ just as, exactly as; **proïnde atque sī** _(or ac sī or quasi)_ just as if

prō·lābor -lābī -lāpsus sum _intr_ to glide forward, slip _or_ move forward; to fall forwards, fall on one's face; to slip out; _(of words)_ to slip out, escape; to be led on, led astray _(by fear, greed, etc.);_ _(fig)_ to fail, go to ruin, collapse; **prōlābī per equī caput** to go flying over the head of the horse

prōlāpsi·ō -ōnis _f_ slipping

prōlāpsus _pp of_ **prōlābor**

prōlāti·ō -ōnis _f_ extension _(of territory);_ adducing, mentioning _(of precedents);_ citing _(of examples);_ delay, postponement

prōlāt·ō -āre _tr_ to extend; to put off, delay

prōlātus _pp of_ **prōferō**

prōlect·ō -āre -āvī -ātus _tr_ to lure

prōl·ēs -is _f_ offspring, progeny, children; descendants; race, stock; child; young man

prōlētār·ius -(i)ī _m_ proletarian ‖ _mpl_ proletariat

prōli·ciō -cere _tr_ to entice, bring out, lead on; to incite

prōlixē _adv_ freely, wildly, readily, cheerfully, willingly

prōlix·us -a -um _adj_ long, freely growing, wild _(beard, hair, etc.);_ favorable _(circumstances)_

prōlocūtus _pp of_ **prōloquor**

prōlog·us -ī _m_ prologue _(of a play);_ actor who gives the prologue

prōlo·quor -quī -cūtus sum _tr & intr_ to speak out

prōlub·ium -(i)ī _n_ desire, inclination, yen

prōlū·dō -dere -sī -sum _tr_ to be a prelude to ‖ _intr_ to practice; _(of boxers)_ to spar, shadow-box

prō·luō -luere -luī -lūtus _tr_ to wash out, flush, wash off; _(of water)_ to wash away; to wet, drench; to wash clean, wash out

prōlūsi·ō -ōnis _f_ practice fight, dry run; sparring

prōlūtus _pp of_ **prōluō**

prōluvi·ēs -ēī _f_ flood; discharge, excrement

prōmercāl·is -is -e _adj_ sold in the open market

prōmer·eō -ēre -uī -itus _or_ **prōmer·eor -ērī -itus sum** _tr_ to deserve, merit, earn ‖ _intr_ to be deserving; _(w._ dē + abl) to deserve the gratitude of; **bene dē multīs prōmerēre** _(or_ **prōmererī)** to deserve the full gratitude of many people

prōmerit·um -ī _n_ favor; reward, due; merit; guilt; **bene (male) prōmeritum** a good (bad) turn

Prōmēth·eūs -eī _or_ **-eos** _m_ son of Iapetus and Clymene, brother of Epimetheus, and discoverer of use of fire, which he taught to men

Prōmēthē·us -a -um _adj_ Promethean, of Prometheus

Prōmēthīd·ēs -ae _m_ son of Prometheus, Deucalion _(who, with his wife Pyrrha, survived the Deluge)_

prōmin·ēns -entis _adj_ prominent, projecting ‖ _n_ headland

prōmin·eō -ēre -uī _intr_ to jut out, stick out, stick up; _(of persons)_ to lean out, bend forward; _(w._ in + acc) to reach down to, reach out for

prōmīscam _or_ **prōmīscē** _or_ **prōmīscuē** _adv_ in common; without distinction; all at the same time _or_ in the same place

prōmīsc(u)·us -a -um _adj_ promiscuous, haphazard, indiscriminate; in common, open to all; common

prōmissi·ō -ōnis _f_ promise

prōmiss·or -ōris _m_ one who promises _or_ guarantees

prōmiss·us -a -um _adj_ allowed to grow, long ‖ _n_ promise; prediction

prō·mittō -mittere -mīsī -missus _tr_ to send forth; to let _(e.g., hair)_ grow; to promise, guarantee; to predict as certain; to give hope of; **ad cēnam** _(or_ **ad aliquem) prōmittere** to accept an invitation to dinner _(or_ to s.o.'s home); **damnī īnfectī prōmittere** to guarantee compensation for damage done; **prōmittere (in mātrimōnium)** to promise _(one's daughter)_ in marriage ‖ _refl (w._ ad) to have expectations of attaining; **sibi prōmittere** to promise oneself, look forward to, count on

prōm·ō -ere -(p)sī -ptus *tr* to bring out, draw out; to produce *(arguments);* to bring to light, reveal; to bring out, express *(ideas, emotions)*

prōmon·eō -ēre *tr* to warn openly

prōmontōr·ium -(i)ī *n* promontory, cape

prōmōt·a -ōrum *npl* second choice

prō·moveō -movēre -mōvī -mōtus *tr* to move *(s.th.)* forward, cause to advance; to enlarge, extend; to effect, accomplish; to encourage, egg on; to promote *(to higher office);* to bring to light, reveal; to postpone; **gradum** *(or* **pedem) prōmovēre** to step forward; **nihil prōmovēre** to accomplish nothing, do no good, make no progress ‖ *intr* to make headway

promptārius *see* **promptuārius**

promptē *adv* readily; willingly; fluently

prompt·ō -āre *tr* to give out, distribute; to be treasurer of

promptuāri·us -a -um *adj* of a storehouse, storage; **cella promptuāria** *(coll)* jail, cooler ‖ *n* storeroom, cupboard

prompt·us -a -um *pp of* **prōmō** ‖ *adj* at hand, readily available; easy; glib *(tongue);* brought to light, evident; bold, enterprising; *(w. dat or ad or in + acc)* **1** readily inclined to; **2** ready *or* prepared for; *(w.* **in** *+ abl)* quick at; *(w.* **adversus** *+ acc)* ready for, prepared against; *(w. inf)* ready to, quick to; **promptum est** *(w. inf)* it is an easy matter to

prompt·us -ūs *m* **in promptū 1** within easy reach, at one's disposal *or* command; **2** in full view, in a prominent position; **3** within one's powers *or* capabilities; **4** at one's command; **in promptū esse** to be obvious; **in promptū gerere** *(or* **habēre** *or* **ponere)** to display

prōmulgāti·ō -ōnis *f (pol)* promulgation, official publication *(of a proposed law)*

prōmulg·ō -āre -āvī -ātus *tr* to promulgate, to publish, publicize

prōmuls·is -idis *f* hors d'oeuvres

prōmuntur·ium *or* **prōmontōr·ium -(i)ī** *n* promontory, cape

prōm·us -ī *m* butler

prōmūtu·us -a -um *adj (fin)* on credit, advanced as a loan

prōnē *adv* downwards; slantwise

pronep·ōs -ōtis *m* great-grandson

pronept·is -is *f* great-granddaughter

pronoe·a -ae *f* divine providence

prōnōm·en -inis *n (gram)* pronoun; *(gram)* demonstrative pronoun

prōnub·a -ae *f* matron of honor *(who conducted the bride to the husband's home);* *(of Juno, Bellona, Tisiphone)* patroness of marriage

prōnūntiāti·ō -ōnis *f* proclamation, declaration; verdict; pronunciation *(of words);* proposition *(in logic);* *(rhet)* delivery

prōnūntiāt·or -ōris *m* narrator

prōnūntiāt·um -ī *n* proposition *(in logic)*

prōnūnti·ō -āre -āvī -ātus *tr* to proclaim, announce; to express *(opinion, judgment);* to pronounce *(words);* to hold out, promise *(rewards)* publicly; to recite, deliver; to narrate, relate; **sententiam prōnūntiāre** *(pol)* to announce a motion *(for discussion in the Senate),* to put a motion to a vote ‖ *intr (theat) (of an actor)* speak one's lines

prōnūper *adv* quite recently

prōnur·us -ūs *f* grandson's wife

prōn·us -a -um *adj* leaning, inclined, bending, stooping, bent over, bent forwards; swift, rushing, dashing, moving swiftly along; sloping, steep *(hill, road);* sinking, setting *(sun, etc.);* downhill; easy; *(w. dat or ad or in + acc)* inclined toward, disposed toward, prone to; *(w. dat)* inclined to favor *(e.g., a winner)* ‖ *n* downward tendency, gravity ‖ *npl* slopes

propāgāti·ō -ōnis *f* propagation, reproduction; prolongation; transmission *(to posterity);* **nōminis propāgātiō** perpetuation of the name

propāgāt·or -ōris *m* one who extends *(s.th.)* in time; **propāgātor prōvinciae** grantor of an extended provincial command

propāg·ō -āre -āvī -ātus *tr* to produce *(plants)* from slips; to produce *(offspring);* to propagate *(race, religion);* to extend *(territory);* to prolong *(a period, life);* to cause *(a family name, tradition)* to endure, hand down *(to posterity)*

propāg·ō -inis *f* slip *(from which a plant is propagated);* offspring, progeny; race, line; descendants

prōpalam *adv* openly, publicly

prōpatul·us -a -um *adj* open ‖ *n* open space; **in prōpatulō habēre** to display

prope *(comp:* **propius;** *superl:* **proximē)** *adv* near, nearby; *(of time)* near, at hand; *(of degree)* nearly, almost, practically, just about; *(w.* **ab** *+ abl)* close by, near to; *(of time)* toward, about; **prope est cum** the time has come when ‖ *prep (w. acc)* near, near to; **prope diem** very soon, any day now

propediem *adv* very soon, any day now

prō·pellō -pellere -pulī -pulsus *tr* to propel, drive forward; to push over, overturn, upset; to drive away, drive out; to banish, expel

propemodo *or* **propemodum** *adv* nearly, practically, almost

prōpen·deō -dēre -dī -sum *intr* to hang down; *(w.* **in** *+ acc)* to be inclined to, be favorably disposed to

prōpēnsē *adv* readily, willingly

prōpēnsi·ō -ōnis *f* propensity, inclination

prōpēns·us -a -um *pp of* **prōpendeō** ‖ *adj* weighty; approaching; inclined; ready, will-

ing; *(w. dat, w.* **ad** *or* **in** + *acc)* favorably disposed to, partial to; **prōpēnsō animō** with ready mind, willingly; **prōpēnsus in alteram partem** inclined toward the other point of view
properanter *adv* hastily, quickly
properanti·a -ae *f* haste
properāti·ō -ōnis *f* haste
properātō *adv* hastily, speedily
properāt·us -a -um *adj* hurried, hasty, speedy **||** *n* speed; **properātō opus est** speed is required
properē *adv* hastily, in haste, quickly; without hesitation
properip·ēs -edis *adj* quick-moving, quick-footed
proper·ō -āre -āvī -ātus *tr* to speed up; to prepare hastily, do in haste **||** *intr* to be quick; to go *or* move quickly
Propert·ius -(i)ī *m* Sextus Aurelius Propertius *(Latin elegiac poet, native of Umbria, c. 50–15 B.C.)*
proper·us -a -um *adj* quick, speedy
prōpex·us -a -um *adj* combed forward
prophēt·a -ae *m* prophet
propīn *n (only nom and acc in use)* apéritif
prōpīnāti·ō -ōnis *f* toast
prōpīn·ō -āre -āvī -ātus *tr* to drink *(e.g., a cup of wine)* as a toast; to drink a toast to *(s.o.);* *(w. dat)* **1** to drink *(e.g., a cup of wine as a toast)* to; **2** to pass on *(a cup)* to
propinqu·a -ae *f* relative *(female)*
propinquē *adv* near at hand
propinquit·ās -ātis *f* proximity, nearness, vicinity; relationship, affinity; friendship
propinqu·ō -āre -āvī -ātus *tr* to bring on; to hasten **||** *intr* to approach; *(w. dat)* to draw near to, approach
propinqu·us -a -um *adj* near, neighboring; *(of time)* near, at hand; closely related; *(w. dat)* akin to; **in spē propinquā missiōnis** in the hope of an early discharge; **nūlla propinqua spēs** no hope for the near future; **spēs propinquī reditūs** hope for an early return **||** *mf* relative **||** *n* neighborhood; **in propinquō** in the vicinity; *(of time, events)* near at hand, in the offing
propi·or -or -us *adj* nearer, closer; *(of time)* earlier; later, more recent; more closely related, more like, more nearly resembling; more imminent; more intimate, closer *(tie);* of more importance, of more concern; *(of battle)* fought at close range; shorter *(route);* *(w. dat)* **1** nearer to, closer to; **2** closer to *(in resemblance),* more like; **3** to be favorably disposed to; *(w. acc or w.* **ab** + *abl)* closer to **||** *npl* closer side *(e.g., of a river);* more recent events

propiti·ō -āre -āvī -ātus *tr* to propitiate, appease
propiti·us -a -um *adj (w. dat)* **1** propitious toward; **2** favorably disposed toward
propnigē·um *or* **propnigē·on -ī** *n* sweat room *(of a bath)*
Prōpoētid·es -um *fpl* Cyprian girls who denied the divinity of Venus, becoming the first prostitutes, subsequently turned to stone
propōl·a -ae *f* retailer, huckster
prōpollu·ō -ere *tr* to further pollute
prō·pōnō -pōnere -posuī -positus *tr* to put *or* place forward, expose to view, display; to propose, suggest; to imagine; to offer, propose; to say, report, relate, publish; to threaten; to denounce; to design, determine, intend
Propontiac·us -a -um *adj* of the Propontis
Propont·is -idis *or* **-idos** *f* Propontis, Sea of Marmora
prōporrō *adv* furthermore; wholly
prōporti·ō -ōnis *f* proportion, symmetry; *(gram)* analogy
prōport·ō -āre *tr* to cite
prōpositi·ō -ōnis *f* proposition; intention, purpose; theme; basic assumption *(in logic)*
prōposit·us -a -um *pp* of **prōpōnō ||** *adj* exposed, open; accessible; impending, at hand **||** *n* intention, purpose; main point, theme; first premise *(in logic);* **mihi prōpositum** it is my intention, it is my plan; **prōpositum habēre** to have as one's object
prōpraet·or -ōris *m* propraetor *(ex-praetor as governor of a province)*
propriē *adv* in the strict sense; properly; strictly for oneself, personally; peculiarly, especially
propriet·ās -ātis *f* property, peculiarity, quality
prōprītim *adv* specifically, properly
propri·us -a -um *adj* own, very own; special, peculiar, individual, particular, personal; lasting
propter *adv* near, near at hand
propter *prep (w. acc)* near, close, next to; on account of, because of, for the sake of; through, by means of; **propter quod** wherefore
proptereā *or* **propter eā** *adv* for that reason, therefore, on that account; **proptereā quod** for the very reason that
prōpudiōs·us -a -um *adj* shameful
prōpud·ium -(i)ī *n* shameful act; *(said of a person)* disgrace, vile wretch, skunk
prōpugnācul·um -ī *n* rampart, battlement; defense; *(fig)* safeguard
prōpugnāti·ō -ōnis *f* defense, vindication; protection
prōpugnāt·or -ōris *m* defender, champion

prōpugn·ō -āre -āvī -ātus *tr* to defend ‖ *intr* to come out and fight; to fight a defensive action, repel an assault; *(fig)* to put up a defense

prōpulsāti·ō -ōnis *f* repulse; warding off *(of danger)*

prōpuls·ō -āre -āvī -ātus *tr* to drive off, repel; *(fig)* to ward off, repel

prōpulsus *pp of* prōpellō

Propylae·a -ōrum *npl* Propylaea *(monumental gateway, esp. the entrance to the Athenian Acropolis)*

prōquaest·or -ōris *m* proquaestor *(magistrate who, after his quaestorship in Rome, was associated as a financial officer with a proconsul in the administration of a province)*

prōquam *or* prō quam *conj* just as, according as

prōr·a -ae *f* prow; *(fig)* ship; **mihi prōra et puppis est** my intention from first to last is *(literally, it is prow and stern to me)*

prōrēp·ō -ere -sī -ptum *intr* to creep ahead, crawl out

prōrēt·a -ae *m* lookout man at the prow

prōreus *m (nom only)* look-out man at the prow

prō·ripiō -ripere -ripuī -reptus *tr* to drag forth, drag out; to rush ‖ *refl* to rush, dash

prōrogāti·ō -ōnis *f* extension *(of a term of office);* putting off

prōrog·ō -āre -āvī -ātus *tr* to extend, prolong; to put off, postpone

prōrs·a *or* prōs·a -ae *f* prose

prōrsum *or* prōsum *adv* forwards, straight ahead; *(as an intensive)* altogether, absolutely; *(w. negatives)* absolutely, at all, *e.g.,* **prōrsum nihil** absolutely nothing, nothing at all

prōrsus *or* prōsus *adv* forward; straight *(to the destination); (intensifying a word, phrase, etc., which it may either precede or follow)* altogether, absolutely; *(w. a negative)* absolutely, at all; *(emphasizing the second and stronger of two related terms)* more than that, even; *(connecting a clause or sentence with what precedes)* in fact, all in all; *(in summing up)* in short, in a word; *(w. demonstrative pron or adv, emphasizing correspondence)* exactly, just

prō·rumpō -rumpere -rūpī -ruptus *tr* to make *(s.th.)* burst forth; to give vent to; to emit ‖ *pass* to rush forth, rush out ‖ *intr* to rush forth; *(of vapors, etc.)* to burst forth; *(of news)* to come out; *(mil)* to make an attack

prōru·ō -ere -ī -tus *tr* to overthrow, demolish ‖ *intr* to rush forth; to tumble

prōrupt·us -a -um *pp of* prōrumpō ‖ *adj* unrestrained

prōs·a -ae *(or* prōsa ōrātiō) *f* prose

prōsāpi·a -ae *f* stock, race, line

prōscaen·ium -(i)ī *n* (-scēn-) stage

prō·scindō -scindere -scidī -scissus *tr* to plow up, break up; *(fig)* to criticize harshly, cut to pieces

prōscrī·bō -bere -psī -ptus *tr* to publish in writing; to proclaim, announce; to advertise *(for sale, etc.);* to confiscate *(property);* to punish with confiscation; to proscribe, outlaw *(people)*

prōscrīpti·ō -ōnis *f* advertisement; proscription, political purge; notice of confiscation; notice of outlawry

prōscrīptur·iō -īre *intr* to be eager to hold a proscription *or* purge

prōscrīpt·us -a -um *pp of* prōscrībō ‖ *m* outlaw

prōsec·ō -āre -uī -tus *tr* to cut off *(esp. parts of a sacrificial victim)*

prōsecūtus *pp of* prōsequor

prōsed·a -ae *f* prostitute

prōsēmin·ō -āre -āvī -ātus *tr* to sow, scatter about, plant; to propagate, raise

prō·sentiō -sentīre -sēnsī *tr* to sense *or* realize beforehand, get wind of

prō·sequor -sequī -secūtus sum *tr* to escort, attend; to pursue *(enemy);* to chase; follow; to follow up *(actions, words);* to go on with, continue *(a topic);* to describe in detail; to follow, imitate; to honor, reward *(with);* to send *(s.o.)* on his *or* her way with gifts; *(of events)* to occur after, succeed

prōser·ō -ere *tr* to stick out *(e.g., the tongue)*

Prōserpin·a -ae *f* daughter of Ceres and carried off by Pluto to become queen of the lower world

prōserp·ō -ere *intr* to creep *or* crawl forwards, creep along

proseuch·a -ae *f* synagogue

prōsil·iō -īre -uī *or* -īvī *or* -iī *intr* to jump forward, jump up; to jump to one's feet; *(of blood)* to spurt; *(of sparks)* to shoot out, fly; to dash

prōsoc·er -erī *m* wife's grandfather; husband's grandfather

prosōdi·a -ae *f* the tone *or* accent of a syllable, prosody

prosōpopoei·a -ae *f* impersonation

prōspect·ō -āre -āvī -ātus *tr* to view, look out at, gaze upon; *(of places)* to look toward, command a view of, face; to look for, hope for; *(w. indir. ques.)* to look to see *(what, whether)*

prōspectus *pp of* prōspiciō

prōspect·us -ūs *m* distant view; view; faculty of sight; a sight *(thing seen)*

prōspecul·or -ārī -ātus sum *tr* to look out for, watch for ‖ *intr* to look around, reconnoiter

prosper *see* prosperus

prosperē *adv* favorably, luckily, as desired, successfully

prosperit·ās -ātis *f* success, good fortune, prosperity; **prosperitās valētūdinis** good health

prosper·ō -āre *tr* to cause to succeed, make happy

prosp·erus *or* **prosp·er -era -erum** *adj* successful, fortunate, lucky, favorable, prosperous

prōspicienti·a -ae *f* foresight, precaution

prō·spiciō -spicere -spexī -spectus *tr* to see in the distance; to spot; to command a view of; to watch for; to look out for, provide for; to foresee **||** *intr* to look forward; to look into the distance, have a view; to be on the lookout, exercise foresight; *(w.* **in** + *acc)* to command a view of, overlook; **ex superiōribus in urbem prōspicere** to have a view of the city from a vantage point; **parum prōspiciunt oculī** the eyes are nearsighted

prō·sternō -sternere -strāvī -strātus *tr* to throw to the ground, knock down; *(of sickness)* to strike down; to wreck, ruin, overthrow, subvert; to demean **||** *refl* to debase oneself; **sē prōsternere ad pedēs** *(w. gen)* to throw oneself at the feet of, fall down before

prōstibil·is -is *f* prostitute

prōstibul·um -ī *n* prostitute

prōstit·uō -uere -uī -ūtus *tr* to expose for sale; to prostitute

prōstitūt·a -ae *f* prostitute

prō·stō -stāre -stitī -stitum *intr* to project, stick out; *(of wares)* to be set up for sale; to prostitute oneself, be a prostitute

prōstrātus *pp of* **prōsternō**

prōstrāvī *perf of* **prōsternō**

prōsubig·ō -ere *tr* to dig up in front

prōsum *adv see* **prōrsum**

prō·sum -desse -fuī -futūrus *intr* to be useful, do good, be profitable; *(w. dat)* to be good for, do *(s.o.)* good; **multum prōdesse** to do a lot of good

Prōtagor·ās -ae *m* Greek sophist, contemporary of Socrates, born at Abdera *(c. 485–415 B.C.)*

prō·tegō -tegere -tēxī -tēctus *tr* to cover in front, cover up; to cover with a roof; to shelter, protect; *(fig)* to cover, defend, protect

prōtēl·ō -āre -āvī -ātus *tr* to chase away

prōtēl·um -ī *n* team of oxen in tandem; row, series

prōten·dō -dere -dī -tus *tr* to stretch forth, stretch out, extend

prōtent·us -a -um *pp of* **prōtendō ||** *adj* extended

prōtenus *see* **prōtinus**

prō·terō -terere -trīvī -trītus *tr* to wear down; to rub out; to trample down, trample under foot; *(fig)* to trample upon, rub out, crush

prōterr·eō -ēre -uī -itus *tr* to scare away

protervē *adv* brashly, brazenly

protervit·ās -ātis *f* brashness

proterv·us -a -um *adj* brash, brazen

Prōtesilāē·us -a -um *adj* of Protesilaus

Prōtesilā·us -ī *m* first Greek casualty in the Trojan War, husband of Laodamia

Prōt·eus -eī *or* **-eos** *m* a god of the sea with power to assume various forms

prothȳmē *adv* willingly, readily

prothȳmi·a -ae *f* willingness, readiness

prōtinam *adv* immediately

prōtinus *or* **prōtenus** *adv* straight on, forward, farther on; continuously, right on, without pause; on the spot

prōtoll·ō -ere *tr* to stretch out *(hand);* to put off, postpone

prōtoprāxi·a -ae *f (fin)* priority *(among creditors receiving payment)*

prō·trahō -trahere -trāxī -tractus *tr* to drag forward, drag out; to produce; to reveal, bring to light

prōtrītus *pp of* **prōterō**

prōtrīvī *perf of* **prōterō**

prōtrū·dō -dere -sī -sus *tr* to push forwards, push out; to postpone

prōturb·ō -āre -āvī -ātus *tr* to drive ahead, drive on in confusion; to drive away, repel; to knock down

prouït *(or* **prout,** scanned as one syllable) *conj* as, just as; in so far as, in as much as; *(introducing alternatives)* **prout ... ita** according to whether ... or

prōvect·us -a -um *adj* advanced; **aetāte prōvectus** advanced in years; **nox prōvecta erat** the night had been far advanced

prōve·hō -here -xī -ctus *tr* to carry forwards; to transport, convey; to lead, lead on; to promote, advance, raise **||** *pass* to ride, drive, move, *or* sail ahead

prō·veniō -venīre -vēnī -ventum *intr* to go on, proceed; to succeed; to come out, appear; *(of plants, seeds)* to come out, come up, grow; to come about, happen

prōvent·us -ūs *m* result, outcome; success; yield, produce; harvest

prōverb·ium -iī *n* proverb

prōvexī *perf of* **prōvehō**

prōvid·ēns -entis *adj* prudent

prōvidenter *adv* prudently, with foresight

prōvidenti·a -ae *f* foresight, foreknowledge; precaution; **prōvidentia deōrum** divine providence

prō·videō -vidēre -vīdī -vīsus *tr* to see in the distance; to see coming; to foresee; to provide for; to provide against, guard against, avert, avoid; to look after, look out for, care for; to prepare, make ready; *(w.* **ut)** to see to it that ‖ *intr* to exercise forethought, take precautions; *(w. dat or* **dē** + *abl)* to look after, care for ‖ *v impers* **prōvīsum est** care was taken

prōvid·us -a -um *adj* foreseeing; prudent, cautious; provident; *(w. gen)* providing for

prōvinci·a -ae *f* province; sphere of administration *or* jurisdiction; office, duty, charge; public office, commission, command, administration; sphere of action

prōvinciāl·is -is -e *adj* provincial, of a province; in a province; **bellum prōvinciāle** war in a province; **molestia prōvinciālis** annoyance of administering a province ‖ *m* provincial

prōvinciātim *adv* province by province

prōvīsi·ō -ōnis *f* foresight; precaution; *(w. gen)* precaution against

prōvīsō *adv* with forethought

prōvīs·ō -ere *tr* to go out to see; to be on the lookout for

prōvīs·or -ōris *m* lookout *(person);* provider

prōvīsū *m (abl only)* by looking forward; *(w. objective gen)* **1** by foreseeing *(e.g., danger);* **2** by providing, providing for

prōvīsus *pp of* **prōvideō**

prō·vīvō -vīvere -vīxī *intr* to live on, go on living

prōvocāti·ō -ōnis *f* challenge; *(leg)* appeal

prōvocāt·or -ōris *m* challenger; a type of gladiator

prōvoc·ō -āre -āvī -ātus *tr* to challenge *(a person, a statement);* to provoke; to exasperate; to stir, stimulate; **bellum prōvocāre** to provoke a war; **beneficiō prōvocātus** touched *or* stirred by an act of kindness; **in aleam prōvocāre** to challenge to a game of dice; **prōvocāre maledictīs** to provoke *or* exasperate with nasty remarks ‖ *intr (leg)* to appeal; *(leg) (w.* **ab)** to appeal from the decision of *(a magistrate); (leg) (w.* **ad)** to appeal to *(a higher authority)*

prōvol·ō -āre -āvī *intr* to fly out, rush out, dash out

prōvol·vō -vere -vī -ūtus *tr* to roll forward, roll along; to roll over, overturn; to humble; to ruin ‖ *refl* to prostrate oneself, fall down, grovel

prōvom·ō -ere *tr* to vomit, throw up

prōvōrsus *adv* straight ahead

prōvulg·ō -āre -āvī -ātus *tr* to make publicly known

prox *interj (comic representation of a fart):* **dum ēnītor, prox!** iam paene inquīnāvī **pallium** as I struggle to my feet, bang! I darn near soiled my clothes

proxenēt·a -ae *m* business agent

proximē *adv* **(-umē)** *(superl of* **prope)** *(of place)* nearest, next; *(of time)* most recently, just recently; *(w. acc)* **1** close to, next to, at the side of; **2** very much like, resembling; *(w. dat) (of place)* next to; **proximē atque** almost as much as, nearly the same as; **proximē Pompēium sedēbam** I was sitting next to Pompey; **quam proximē** *(w. dat or acc)* as close as possible to

proximit·ās -ātis *f* proximity, vicinity; resemblance, similarity; close relationship

proximō *adv* very *(or* just) recently

proxim·us -a -um *adj* **(-xum-)** nearest, next; adjoining; living nearby, living next door; readiest at hand; *(of time)* immediately preceding, previous, most recent, following, latest, last; just mentioned; closely related; *(of affections)* closely devoted; *(of cause)* immediate, proximate; *(of an argument)* relevant; very like *(in character, resemblance);* nearest *(in degree);* next *(in rank, worth),* second-best; next in order; most direct *(route);* **proximum est ut** (+ *subj)* it is most likely that; the next point is that; the next thing is to ‖ *m* close relative, next of kin; heir next in succession; friend, intimate; next-door neighbor ‖ *n* neighborhood; the house next door; the recent past; **dē proximō** aptly, very closely; **ex proximō** from the readiest source; close by; **in proximō** within easy reach; close at hand; **in proximum** for the following day

prūd·ēns -entis *adj* foreseeing; conscious, aware; skilled, skillful, experienced; prudent, discreet, sensible, intelligent; *(w. gen or abl or w.* **in** + *abl)* **1** aware of, conscious of; **2** familiar with; **3** skilled in, experienced in, versed in ‖ *m* expert; *(leg)* jurist

prūdenter *adv* prudently, cautiously; skillfully

prūdenti·a -ae *f* foreseeing; prudence, discretion, good sense; **prūdentia iūris pūblicī** *(leg)* knowledge of *or* experience in constitutional law

pruīn·a -ae *f* frost; winter; **pruīnae** a covering of frozen snow

pruīnōs·us -a -um *adj* frosty

prūn·a -ae *f* live coal

prūnice·us -a -um *adj* made of plum-tree wood

prūniti·us -a -um *adj* of plum-tree wood

prūn·um -ī *n* plum

prūn·us -ī *f* plum tree

prūrīg·ō -inis *f* itch, tickle; yen

prūr·iō -īre *intr* to itch, tickle; to have an itch; to be sexually aroused; *(w.* **in** + *acc)* to be itching for

Prūsi·ās *or* **Prūsi·a -ae** *m* Prusias *(name of several kings of Bithynia, esp. Prusias Cholus, d. about 182 B.C., with whom Hannibal took refuge after his defeat)*

prytanē·um *or* **prytanī·um -ī** *n* town hall *(in some Greek cities where the Prytanes, or magistrates, held meetings and dined)*
prytan·is -is *m* magistrate *(in some Greek states)*
psall·ō -ere -ī *intr* to play the cithara
psaltēr·ium -(i)ī *n* cithara *(form of harp)*
psalt·ēs -ae *m* cithara-player, citharist
psaltri·a -ae *f* citharist *(female)*
Psamath·ē -ēs *f* a sea nymph, wife of Aeacus and mother of Phocus ‖ daughter of the Argive King Crotopus
psec·as -adis *f* female slave who perfumed her lady's hair; typical name of maidservants
psell·us -a -um *adj* faltering in speech
psēphism·a -atis *n* *(pol)* plebiscite of the Greek assembly
Pseudocat·ō -ōnis *m* a make-believe Cato
Pseudol·us -ī *m* "Little Liar" *(title of a play by Plautus)*
pseudomen·os *or* **pseudomen·us -ī** *m* *(phil)* fallacious syllogism
Pseudophilipp·us -ī *m* "False Philip" *(i.e., Andriscus, who claimed to be the son of Perseus of Macedon and was defeated by the Romans in 148 B.C.)*
pseudothyr·um -ī *n* hidden door
psīlocitharist·a -ae *m* one who plays the lyre without singing in accompaniment
psithi·us -a -um *adj* psithian *(the name of a type of vine)* ‖ *fpl* grapes
psittac·us -ī *m* parrot
Psōph·is -idos *f* town in Arcadia to the S. of Mt. Erymanthus
Psȳch·ē -ēs *f* girlfriend of Cupid, made immortal by Jupiter
psychomantī·um *or* **psychomantē·um -ī** *n* place of séance
-pte *enclitic (added to pronouns, usu. w. poss adj and esp. in abl)* self, own; **sonitū suōpte titinant aurēs** the ears are ringing (with their own sound)
ptisanār·ium -(i)ī *n* gruel
Ptolemae·us -ī *m* Ptolemy *(name of a series of thirteen Egyptian kings descended from Lagus, one of Alexander the Great's generals)*
Ptolomae·um -ī *n* name of a gymnasium ‖ tomb of the Ptolemies
pūb·ēns -entis *adj* full of sap, succulent, vigorous
pūber *see* **pūbēs**
pūbert·ās -ātis *f* puberty; manhood; sign of maturity; beard; physical signs of puberty
pūb·ēs -is *f* pubic hair; private parts; puberty; adult population, manpower; throng
pūb·ēs *or* **pūb·er -eris** *adj* grown up, adult; downy, covered with down ‖ *mpl* grown-ups, men

pūb·ēscō -ēscere *intr* to reach the age of puberty, arrive at maturity; *(of plants)* to grow up, ripen; *(of meadows, fields)* to be clothed, covered *(e.g., with flowers)*
pūblic·a -ae *f* prostitute
pūblicān·us -a -um *adj* of public revenues ‖ *m* revenue agent, publican, tax collector ‖ *f* public prostitute
pūblicāti·ō -ōnis *f* confiscation; disclosure
pūblicē *adv* publicly; officially, on behalf of the state, for the state; at public expense; generally, universally; **pūblicē dīcere** to speak officially
pūblicitus *adv* at public expense, at the expense of the state; publicly
Pūblici·us -a -um *adj* Publician *(Roman clan name, nomen);* **Clīvus Pūblicius** Publician Slope *(road leading up to the Aventine Hill)*
pūblic·ō -āre -āvī -ātus *tr* to confiscate; to throw open to the general public; to prostitute
Pūblicol·a -ae *m* **(Popl-)** Publius Valerius Publicola *(regarded as one of the first consuls, fl 509 B.C.)*
pūblic·us -a -um *adj* public, of the people, common; of the state, state, national; ordinary, vulgar; general; **causa pūblica** affair of national importance; *(leg)* federal case *(i.e., criminal case);* **id bonō pūblicō facere** to do it for the public good; **pūblica ācta** the public record, the official gazette; **rēs pūblica** state, government, politics, public life, country; **rem pūblicam inīre** to enter politics ‖ *m* public official ‖ *n* public, publicity; public property; national treasury; federal revenue; **dē pūblicō** at public expense; **in pūblicō** in public, publicly; **in pūblicum prōdīre** to go out in public; **in pūblicum redigere** to hand over to the national treasury ‖ *f* prostitute
pudend·us -a -um *adj* shameful, scandalous; **pars pudenda** genitals ‖ *npl* genitals
pud·ēns -entis *adj* modest, bashful
pudenter *adv* modestly, bashfully
pud·eō -ēre -uī *or* **puditum est** *tr* to make ashamed, put to shame ‖ *intr* to be ashamed ‖ *v impers (w. acc of person and gen or abl of cause of feeling), e.g.,* **mē tuī pudet** I am ashamed of you
pudibund·us -a -um *adj* modest, bashful
pudīcē *adv* chastely, modestly, decently; in a subdued style
pudīciti·a -ae *f* chastity, purity
pudīc·us -a -um *adj* chaste, pure
pud·or -ōris *m* shame, sense of shame, decency, modesty; sense of honor, propriety; cause for shame, disgrace; blush
puell·a -ae *f* girl; girlfriend, sweetheart; young wife
puellār·is -is -e *adj* young girl's, girlish, youthful

puellāriter *adv* girlishly
puellul·a -ae *f* little girl; little sweetheart
puell·us -ī *m* little boy, lad; catamite
pu·er *also* **pu·erus -erī** *m* boy, lad; servant, slave *(regardless of age);* page; bachelor; **ā puerīs** *(or* **ā puerō)** from childhood on; **ex puerīs excēdere** to outgrow childhood
puerāsc·ō -ere *intr* to approach boyhood
puercul·us -ī *m* little son
puer(i)ti·a -ae *f* childhood; boyhood
puerīl·is -is -e *adj* boyish, childish, youthful, puerile
puerīliter *adv* like a child, childishly
puerper·a -ae *f* woman in labor; woman who has given birth
puerper·ium -(i)ī *n* childbirth, delivery, giving birth
puerper·us -a -um *adj* easing labor pains, helping childbirth
puertia *see* **pueritia**
puerul·us -ī *m* little boy; little slave
pūg·a *or* **pȳg·a -ae** *f* rear, buttocks
pug·il -ilis *m* boxer
pugilāti·ō -ōnis *f* boxing
pugilātōri·us -a -um *adj* boxing; **follis pugilātōrius** punching bag
pugilāt·us -ūs *m* boxing match
pugilicē *adv* like a boxer
pugillār·is -is -e *adj* hand-size ‖ *mpl & npl* set of tablets; notebook
pūgi·ō -ōnis *m* dagger
pūgiuncul·us -ī *m* small dagger
pugn·a -ae *f* fistfight, brawl; fight, combat, battle
pugnācit·ās -ātis *f* pugnacity, aggressiveness
pugnāciter *adv* aggressively
pugnācul·um -ī *n* fortress
pugnant·ēs -ium *mpl* fighters, warriors
pugnant·ia -ium *npl* contradictions, inconsistencies
pugnāt·or -ōris *m* fighter, combatant
pugnātōri·us -a -um *adj* used in fighting; **arma pugnātōria** combat weapons
pugn·āx -ācis *adj* pugnacious, scrappy, aggressive; quarrelsome; dogged
pugne·us -a -um *adj* of the fist; **hospitiō pugneō accipere** *(hum)* to welcome s.o. with a reception of fists; **merga pugnea** *(hum)* punch reaper
pugn·ō -āre -āvī -ātus *tr* to fight; **clāra pugna ad Perusiam pugnāta est** a brilliant battle was fought at Perusia; **proelia, bella pugnāre** to fight battles, wars ‖ *intr* to fight; to contend, dispute; *(w. dat or* **cum)** **1** to fight, fight against, struggle with, oppose; **2** to contradict
pugn·us -ī *m* fist
pul·c(h)er -c(h)ra -c(h)rum *adj* beautiful, fair, handsome

pulchell·us -a -um *adj* cute little
Pul·cher -chrī *m* Roman family name *(cognomen)* in the Claudian clan, *esp.* Publius Clodius Pulcher *(tribune of 58 B.C.)*
pulchrē *adv* beautifully, attractively; thoroughly; perfectly; *(in gloating or irony)* nicely; *(as exclamation)* fine!; **pulchrē mihi est** I am fine
pulchritūd·ō -inis *f* **(pulcr-)** beauty; excellence, attractiveness
pūlē·ium -(i)ī *n (bot)* pennyroyal, mint; *(fig)* fragrance, pleasantness
pūl·ex *or* **pūl·ix -icis** *m* flea
pullār·ius -(i)ī *m* keeper of the sacred chickens
pullāt·us -a -um *adj* wearing black, in black, in mourning
pullul·ō -āre -āvī -ātus *intr* to sprout; *(of animals)* to produce young
pull·us -a -um *adj* dark-grey, dark, blackish; mourning; **toga pulla** mourning toga ‖ *n* dark-grey garment
pull·us -ī *m* young *(of animals)*, foal, offspring, chick; favorite boy, catamite; sprout, shoot ‖ *mpl* chickens *(used in divination)*
pulmentār·ium -(i)ī *n* relish, appetizer
pulment·um -ī *n* relish; appetizer; food
pulm·ō -ōnis *m* lung
pulmōne·us -a -um *adj* of the lungs, pulmonary
pulp·a -ae *f* lean meat; *(pej)* flesh *(man's carnal nature)*
pulpāment·um -ī *n* meat; game
pulpit·um -ī *n* platform; stage; podium
pulp·ō -āre *intr* to make the sound of a vulture
puls **pultis** *f* pulse, porridge, mush
pulsāti·ō -ōnis *f* knock
puls·ō -āre -āvī -ātus *tr* to batter, keep hitting; to knock at; to strum *(lyre);* to beat on, strike against; *(fig)* to jolt ‖ *intr* to throb
pulsus *pp of* **pellō**
puls·us -ūs *m* push, pushing; beat, beating, striking, stamping; blow, stroke; trampling; *(fig)* impression, influence
pultāti·ō -ōnis *f* knocking *(at door)*
Pultiphagōnid·ēs -ae *m (humorous patronymic)* son of Porridge-eater
pultiphag·us -ī *m* porridge eater
pult·ō -āre *tr* to knock at *(a door);* to beat
pulvere·us -a -um *adj* dust, of dust; dusty; fine as dust; raising dust
pulverulent·us -a -um *adj* dusty; raising dust; covered with dust
pulvill·us -ī *m* small cushion
pulvīn·ar -āris *n* cushioned couch; sacred couch for the images of the gods; seat of honor
pulvīnār·ium -(i)ī *n* cushioned seat of a god; *(naut)* dry dock
pulvīn·us -ī *m* pillow, cushion; seat of honor

pulv·is -eris *m* (*f*) dust, powder; scene of action, arena, field; effort, work
pulviscul·us -ī *m* fine dust; fine powder
pūm·ex -icis *m* (*f*) pumice (*esp. used to polish books and also used as a depilatory*); lava
pūmice·us -a -um *adj* pumice; lava
pūmic·ō -āre -āvī -ātus *tr* to polish with pumice
pūmili·ō -ōnis *m* midget, dwarf; pygmy
pūmil·ius -(i)ī *m* dwarf, pygmy
pūmil·us -a -um *adj* of short stature, dwarf
pūnctim *adv* with the point, with the pointed end
pūnct·um -ī *n* prick, puncture; point; spot, dot; moment; (*gram*) clause, phrase; (*math*) point; (*pol*) vote, ballot (*dot made on wax tablet to indicate vote*); **pūnctō temporis eōdem** at the same instant; **pūnctum temporis** moment, point in time, instant
pungō pungere pupugī *or* **pepugī pūnctus** *tr* to prick, puncture, dent; to sting, bite; to cause (*a wound*); to stab; (*fig*) to sting, annoy, disturb
Pūnicān·us -a -um *adj* Punic, Carthaginian, in the Carthaginian style
Pūnicē *adv* (**Poen-**) Punic, in the Punic language
pūnice·us -a -um *adj* (**poen-**) reddish, scarlet, crimson **ǁ Pūniceus** (**Poen-**) Punic, Carthaginian
Pūnic·us -a -um *adj* (**Poen-**) Punic, Carthaginian; red, crimson, reddish, pink; **Pūnicum mālum** (*or* **pōmum**) pomegranate **ǁ** *n* pomegranate
pūn·iō -īre -īvī *or* **-iī -ītus** *or* **pūn·ior -īrī -ītus -sum** *tr* (*older form:* **poen-**) to punish; to avenge **ǁ** *intr* to inflict punishment
pūnīti·ō -ōnis *f* punishment
pūnīt·or -ōris *m* avenger
pūp·a -ae *f* doll, puppet; girl, kid
pūpill·a -ae *f* orphan girl, ward; minor; (*anat*) pupil
pūpillār·is -is -e *adj* of an orphan, belonging to an orphan
pūpill·us -ī *m* orphan boy, ward
Pūpini·us -a -um *adj* **ager Pūpinius** a barren district between Rome and Tusculum
Pūpi·us -a -um *adj* Roman clan name (*nomen*), *esp.* Publius Pupius (*a tragedian*)
pupp·is -is (*acc sing usu.* **puppim**) *f* stern; ship; (*coll*) back; **ā puppī** astern
pūpul·a -ae *f* little girl, kid; (*anat*) pupil, eye
pūpul·us -ī *m* little boy, kid
pūp·us -ī *m* boy, child, kid
pūrē *adv* clearly, brightly; plainly, simply; chastely, purely
purgām·en -inis *n* dirt, filth; means of expiation, purification

purgāment·a -ōrum *npl* offscourings, dirt, filth, garbage; (*term of abuse*) trash, garbage
purgāti·ō -ōnis *f* cleansing, cleaning, cleanup; justification
purgāt·us -a -um *adj* cleansed, clean, pure
purg·ō -āre -āvī -ātus *tr* to cleanse, clean; to clear, clear away, remove; to clear of a charge; to excuse, justify; to refute; to purify ritually; to purge (*the body*) **ǁ** *refl & pass* (*of water, the sky*) to become clear
pūrific·ō -āre -āvī -ātus *tr* to purify
pūriter *adv* purely, cleanly; **vītam pūriter agere** to lead a clean life
purpur·a -ae *f* purple dye (*ranging in shade from blood-red to deep violet*); purple, deep-red, royal purple, crimson; royal-purple cloth; royal-purple robe; royalty; consular diginity; imperial dignity
purpurāri·us -a -um *adj* (royal) purple; relating to the purple dyeing *or* to the selling of purple cloth
purpurāsc·ō -ere *intr* to turn purple
purpurāt·us -a -um *adj* wearing royal purple **ǁ** *m* courtier
purpure·us -a -um *adj* purple, crimson, royal purple (*and various shades as applied to roses, poppies, grapes, lips, flesh, blood, wine, dawn, sun at sunrise, hair*)
purpurissāt·us -a -um *adj* rouged
purpuriss·um -ī *n* rouge; red dye
pūr·us -a -um *adj* pure, clear, clean; cleared, cleansed; cleansing, purifying; chaste; plain, naked, unadorned, natural; plain (*toga*), without crimson border; faultless (*style*); (*leg*) unconditional, absolute; (*leg*) subject to no religious claims **ǁ** *n* clear sky
pūs pūris *n* pus; (*fig*) venom, malice
pusill·us -a -um *adj* petty, puny **ǁ** *n* bit, trifle
pūsi·ō -ōnis *m* little boy
pūsul·a *or* **pussul·a** *or* **pūstul·a -ae** *f* pimple; blister
pūsulāt·us *or* **pūstulāt·us -a -um** *adj* refined, purified (*silver*)
putām·en -inis *n* shell (*of nuts, eggs, turtles*); peel (*of fruit*)
putāti·ō -ōnis *f* pruning
putāt·or -ōris *m* pruner
pute·al -ālis *n* low wall (*around a well or sacred spot*), stone enclosure; **puteal Libōnis** stone enclosure in Roman Forum near which much business was transacted
puteāl·is -is -e *adj* of a well
pūtē·faciō -facere -fēcī -factus *tr* to cause to rot; to cause to crumble
pūt·eō -ēre -uī *intr* to stink; to be rotten
Puteolān·us -a -um *adj* of Puteoli
Puteol·ī -ōrum *mpl* Puteoli (*commercial city on the coast of the Bay of Naples, modern Pozzuoli*)

pu·ter *or* pu·tris -tris -tre *adj* putrid, rotting; crumbling; flabby

pūt·ēscō -ēscere -uī *intr* to become rotten

pute·us -ī *m* well; pit; dungeon

pūtidē *adv* disgustingly; affectedly

pūtidiūscul·us -a -um *adj* rather tedious

pūtid·us -a -um *adj* stinking, rotten; worn-out *(brain);* rotten *(person);* offensive *(words, actions);* unnatural, disgusting *(style)*

putill·us -a -um *adj* tiny

put·ō -āre -āvī -ātus *tr* to trim, prune; to think, ponder, consider, judge; to suppose, imagine; to reckon, estimate, value; to believe in, recognize *(gods);* to clear up, settle *(accounts);* magnī putāre to think highly of; prō certō putāre to regard as certain ‖ *intr* to think, imagine, suppose

pūt·or -ōris *m* stench; rottenness

putre·faciō -facere -fēcī -factus *tr* to rot; to cause to crumble, soften

putrēsc·ō -ere *intr* to become rotten, get moldy

putrid·us -a -um *adj* rotten; flabby

putris *see* puter

put·us -a -um *adj (ancient word for* pūrus *and usu. used in combination with* pūrus) pure, bright, perfectly pure; splendid; unmixed; unmitigated; certum pondus argentī pūrī putī a certain weight of perfectly pure silver ‖ *m* boy

pyct·a *or* pyct·ēs -ae *m* boxer

Pydn·a -ae *f* Pydna *(city in Macedonia near which Aemilius Paulus defeated Perseus, king of Macedonia, 169 B.C.)*

pyel·us -ī *m* bathtub

pȳg·a -ae *f* rear, buttocks

pȳgarg·us -ī *m* kind of antelope with white rump

Pygmae·ī -ōrum *mpl* Pygmies *(a dwarfish race, esp. in Africa, said to have been constantly at war with cranes, by whom they were always defeated)*

Pygmae·us -a -um *adj* of the Pygmies; avis Pygmaeus a crane

Pygmali·ōn -ōnis *or* -ōnos *m* son of Belus and brother of Dido ‖ king of Cyprus who fell in love with a statue

Pylad·ēs -ae *or* -is *m* son of Strophius and friend of Orestes

Pyladē·us -a -um *adj* worthy of Pylades

Pyl·ae -ārum *fpl* Thermopylae

Pylaemen·ēs -is *m* king of the Paphlagonians and ally of Priam

Pylaïc·us -a -um of Thermopylae

Pyli·us -a -um *adj* of Pylos ‖ *m* Nestor

Pyl·os -ī *f* Pylos *(home of Nestor in S.E. Peloponnesus)*

pyr·a -ae *f* pyre

pȳram·is -idis *or* -idos *f* pyramid; cone

Pȳram·us -ī *m* neighbor and boyfriend of Thisbe

Pȳrēnae·us -a -um *adj* of the Pyrenees

Pȳrēn·ē -ēs *f (geog)* the Pyrenees

Pyrēn·eûs -eī *m* king of Thrace who tried to rape the Muses

pyrethr·um -ī *n* Spanish camomile *(medicinal plant)*

Pyrgēns·is -is -e adj of (the town of) Pyrgi

Pyrg·ī -ōrum *mpl* town on the coast of Etruria

Pyriphlegeth·on -ontos *m* one of the rivers of the lower world *(= Phlegethon)*

pyrōp·us -ī *m* bronze

Pyrrh·a -ae *f* daughter of Epimetheus, wife of Deucalion, and survivor of the Deluge

Pyrrhi·as -adis *adj (fem only)* of (the town of) Pyrrha in Lesbos

Pyrrh·ō(n) -ōnis *m* Pyrrho *(philosopher of Elis, contemporary of Aristotle and founder of the school of Skepticism, c. 360–270 B.C.)*

Pyrrhōnē·us -a -um *adj* of the school founded by Pyrrho

Pyrrh·us -ī *m* son of Achilles and founder of Epirus *(also called Neoptolemus)* ‖ king of Epirus who invaded Italy against the Romans in 280 B.C. *(319–272 B.C.)*

Pȳthagor·ās -ae *m* Greek philosopher and mathematician *(6th cent. B.C.)* ‖ a servant of Nero

Pȳthagorē·us *or* Pȳthagoric·us -a -um *adj* Pythagorean

Pȳthi·a -ae *f* Pythia *(priestess of Apollo at Delphi)*

Pȳthi·as -adis *f* typical name for a slave girl in comedy

Pȳthic·us -a -um *adj* Pythian, Delphic

Pȳthi·us -a -um *adj* Pythian, Delphic ‖ *m* Apollo ‖ *f* Pythia *(priestess of Apollo at Delphi)* ‖ *npl* Pythian games *(held in honor of Apollo every four years at Delphi)*

Pȳth·ō -ūs *f* ancient name of Delphi *or* its oracle

Pȳth·ōn -ōnis *or* -ōnos *m* dragon slain by Apollo near Delphi

pȳtism·a -atis *n* mouthful of wine *(spat out after tasting)*

pȳtiss·ō -āre *tr* to spit out *(wine after tasting it)*

pyx·is -idis *or* -idos *f* powder box, cosmetic box

Q

Q, q *(supply* littera) *f* sixteenth letter of the Latin alphabet; letter name: qu

Q. *abbr* Quīntus *(first name, praenomen)*

quā *adv (interrog)* by which road?, which way? in which direction?, by which route?, where?; by what means?, how? ‖ *(rel)* where; to the extent that; in so far as; in as much as; in the manner in which, as ‖ *(indef)* by any route, by any way; by any chance, in any way; **quā … quā** partly … partly, both … and

quācumque *adv* (**-cunq-**) wherever; by whatever way, in whatever way; by whatever means, howsoever

quādam tenus *adv* to a certain point, only so far and no farther

quadr·a -ae *f* (square) dining table; square crust; square bit, cube *(of cheese, etc.)*; (square) slice *(of bread, cake)*

quadrāgēn·ī -ae -a *adj* forty each

quadrāgēsim·us -a -um *adj* (**-gēnsi-**) fortieth ‖ *f* one-fortieth; 2½% tax

quadrāgiēs *adv* (**-giēns**) forty times

quadrāgintā *indecl adj* forty

quadr·āns -antis *m* one-fourth, a quarter; penny *(smallest coin, worth one sixth of Roman* **as**); quarter of a pound; quarter pint *(quarter of a* **sextārius**); **quadrante lavātum īre** to take a bath for a penny *(usual price of a bath)*

quadrant·al -ālis *n* five-gallon jar

quadrantāri·us -a -um *adj* quarter; **mulier quadrantāria** two-bit wench *(woman who sells herself for a pittance;* **tabulae quadrantāriae** record of debts reduced to a fourth

quadrāt·us -a -um *adj* square; stocky *(build);* 90-degree *(angle);* compact *(style);* cube, cubic ‖ *n* square; square object; cube

quadri- *pref* consisting of, having four of the things named

quadrīdu·um -ī *n* four-day period; **in quadrīduō** within four days; **quadrīduō** for a period of four days; within the next four days; **quadrīduō ante (post)** four days before (after)

quadrienn·ium -(i)ī *n* four-year period, four years

quadrifāriam *adv* in four directions; in four ways; in four places; in fours

quadrifid·us -a -um *adj* split into four parts

quadrīg·a -āe *f or* **quadrīg·ae -ārum** *fpl* four-horse team *(running four abreast);* four-horse chariot

quadrīgāri·us -a -um *adj* connected with chariot racing

quadrīgār·ius -(i)ī *m* chariot racer

quadrīgāt·us -a -um *adj (of a coin)* stamped with the image of a four-horse chariot

quadrīgul·ae -ārum *fpl (figurine of a)* four-horse chariot

quadriiug·is -is -e *or* **quadriiug·us -a -um** *adj* drawn by a four-horse team *(yoked abreast);*

(of horses) yoked four abreast ‖ *mpl* four-horse team

quadrilībr·is -is -e *adj* four-pound

quadrīmul·us -a -um *adj* only four years old

quadrīm·us -a -um *adj* four-year-old

quadringēnāri·us -a -um *adj* consisting of four hundred men each

quadringēn·ī -ae -a *adj* four hundred each

quadringentēsim·us -a -um *adj* four-hundredth

quadringent·ī -ae -a four hundred

quadringentiē(n)s *adv* four hundred times

quadripertītō *adv* in four parts, in four divisions

quadripertīt·us -a -um *adj* four-fold

quadrirēm·is -is -e *adj* having four banks of oars *(or possibly with four rowers to every bench)* ‖ *f* quadrireme

quadriv·ium -(i)ī *n* crossroads

quadr·ō -āre -āvī -ātus *tr* to make square; to complete; *(rhet)* to round out, give rhythmic finish to *(a speech)* ‖ *intr* to make a square; to be exact; *(of accounts)* to agree, come out right, tally; *(w. dat or* **in** *+ acc)* to suit, fit

quadr·um -ī *n* square; **in quadrum redigere sententiam** *(rhet)* to balance a sentence *(by changing word order)*

quadruped·āns -antis *adj* galloping ‖ *mpl* horses

quadruped·us -a -um *adj* galloping

quadrup·ēs -edis *adj* four-footed; on all fours ‖ *mf* quadruped

quadruplāt·or -ōris *m* informer *(who received* ¼ *of the forfeiture);* corrupt judge

quadrupl·ex -icis *adj* quadruple, fourfold

quadruplic·ō -āre -āvī -ātus *tr* to quadruple, multiply by four

quadrupl·or -ārī -ātus sum *intr* to be an informer, be a whistleblower

quadrupl·us -a -um *adj* quadruple, fourfold ‖ *n* four times the amount

quaerit·ō -āre -āvī -ātus *tr* to keep looking for; to keep asking

quae·rō -rere -sīvī *or* **-siī -sītus** *tr* to look for, search for; to try to get; to get, obtain; to try to gain, earn, acquire; to miss, lack; to require, demand, call for; to ask, interrogate; to examine, investigate; to plan, devise, aim at; *(w. inf)* to try to, wish to; *(w.* **ab** *or* **dē** *or* **ex** *+ abl)* to ask *(s.th.)* of or from *(s.o.)* ‖ *intr* to hold an examination; *(w.* **dē** *+ abl)* to ask about; **quid quaeris?** *(introducing a short, clinching remark)* what more can I say?; **sī quaeris** *(or* **sī quaerimus**) to tell the truth

quaesīti·ō -ōnis *f (leg)* questioning under torture

quaesīt·or -ōris *m (leg)* judge *(praetor or other official who presided over a criminal trial)*

quaesīt·us -a -um *pp of* **quaerō** ‖ *adj* select, special; far-fetched; artificial, affected ‖ *npl* gains, earnings, acquisitions, store

quaes·ō -ere *tr* to try to obtain; to beg, ask for, request ‖ *intr* to carry out a search; **quaesō** *(usually parenthetical)* please; *(w. direct questions)* please tell me; *(in exclamations)* just look!; take note!

quaesticul·us -ī *m* slight profit

quaesti·ō -ōnis *f* inquiry, investigation, questioning, examination; *(leg)* judicial investigation, criminal trial, court of inquiry, court; *(leg)* questioning under torture, third degree; *(leg)* question, subject of investigation, case; *(leg)* court record; *(w. dē + abl of the nature of the charge)* court investigating a charge of *(e.g., forgery)*; **in quaestiōne versārī** to be under investigation; **quaestiō extraōrdināria** investigation by a special board; **quaestiō inter sīcāriōs** murder trial, court investigating a murder; **quaestiō perpetua** standing court; **quaestiōnī pracesse** to preside over a case; **servōs in quaestiōnem dare** *(or* **ferre)** to hand over slaves for questioning under torture

quaestiuncul·a -ae *f* minor *or* trivial question; small problem, puzzle

quaest·or -ōris *m* quaestor *(serving, at various periods as: financial officer; treasury official; public prosecutor of criminal offenses; aide to a provincial governor; army paymaster; personal aide to the emperor);* **prō quaestōre** acting quaestor, vice-quaestor

quaestōri·us -a -um *adj* quaestor's, of a quaestor; employed in a quaestor's office; qualified for the rank of quaestor; having quaestorian rank *(i.e., having held the office of quaestor);* **ager quaestōria** conquered land sold on behalf of the state treasury; **porta quaestōria** the gate nearest the quaestor's tent *(perhaps* **porta decumāna)** ‖ *m* ex-quaestor ‖ *n* quaestor's tent in a camp; quaestor's residence in a province

quaestuōs·us -a -um *adj* profitable, productive; acquiring wealth; eager to make a profit, acquisitive; good at money-making; enriched, wealthy

quaestūr·a -ae *f* quaestorship; *(fig)* public funds

quaest·us -ūs *m* gain, profit; acquisition; way of gaining a livelihood, job, occupation, business, trade; income; *(fig)* benefit, advantage; **ad quaestum** for profit, to make a profit; **in quaestū esse** to be profitable; **in quaestū habēre** to derive profit from; **pecūniam in quaestū relinquere** to deposit money at interest; **quaestuī rem pūblicam habēre** to use public office for personal profit; **quaes-**

tum facere to make money, make a living; **quaestūs facere** to make gains

quālibet *adv* **(-lub-)** anywhere, everywhere; in any way, as you please

quāl·is -is -e *adj* what sort of, what kind of; of such a kind, such as, as; *(w. quotations and citations)* as, as for example; **in hōc bellō, quāle** in this war, the likes of which; **quālis erat!** what a man he was!

quāl·iscumque -iscumque -ecumque (-cunque) *adj* of whatever kind; of any kind whatsoever, any at all; **hominēs, quālēscumque sunt** people, no matter what kind they are; **quāliscumque** *(or* **quālecumque) est** such as it is, for what it is worth

quāl·islibet -islibet -elibet *adj* of whatever kind, of whatever sort

quāl·isnam -isnam -enam *adj* just what kind of

quālit·ās -ātis *f* quality, nature; property, characteristic; high quality; *(gram)* mood *(of a verb)*

quāliter *adv* as, just as

quāl·us -ī *m or* **quāl·um -ī** *n* wicker basket, straw basket

quam *adv (in questions and exclamations)* how, how much; *(in comparisons)* as, than; *(with superlatives)* as ... as possible, *e.g.,* **quam celerrimē** as fast as possible; **quam plūrimō vēndere** to sell at the highest price possible; **quam prīmum** as soon as possible; *(indicating numerical proportion)* **dīmidium (duplex,** *etc.)* **quam** half as much as (twice as much as, *etc.); (as the correlative of* **tam)** the ... the: **quam magis id reputō, tam magis ūror** the more I think it over, the madder I get; *(after verbs of preferring)* than: **praestat nēminī imperāre quam alicui servīre** it is preferable to rule over no one than to be a slave to someone

quamdiū *or* **quam diū** *interrog & rel adv* how long ‖ *conj* as long as

quamlibet *adv* **(-lub-)** as much as you please

quamobrem *or* **quam ob rem** *adv* for what reason, why; for which reason, wherefore, why

quamquam *conj* although

quamvīs *adv (with adj or adv)* however, no matter how; ever so; **illa quamvīs rīdicula essent** no matter how funny they were ‖ *conj* although

quānam *adv* by what route *or* way

quandō *adv (in questions)* when, at what time; *(indefinite, after* **sī, nē, num)** ever, at any time ‖ *conj* when, because, since

quandōcumque *adv* **(-cunque)** at some time or other, someday ‖ *conj* whenever; as often as, no matter when

quandōque *adv* at some time, at one time or other, someday ‖ *conj* whenever; as often as; since

quandōquidem *conj* in as much as, whereas, seeing that

quantill·us -a -um *interrog adj* how much?, how little?

quantit·ās -ātis *f* quantity; size

quantō *adv* by how much, how much; **quantō … tantō** the … the: **quantō longior nox est, tantō brevior diēs fit** the longer night is, the shorter the day becomes

quantopere *or* **quantō opere** *adv* by how much, how much; with how great effort, how carefully

quantulum *adv* how little; **quantulum interest utrum** how little difference it makes whether

quantul·us -a -um *adj* how great, how much, how little, how small, how insignificant

quantuluscumque quantulacum quantulumcumque *adj* however small, however unimportant

quantum *adv* as much as, so much as, as great an extent; how much, how far, to what extent; *(w. comparatives)* the more, the greater; **quantum in mē fuit** as much as I could, to the best of my ability; **quantum maximā vōce potuit** at the top of his voice; **quantum potest** as much *(or* fast, quickly, soon, long, *etc.)* as possible

quantumcumque *adv* as much as; however much, however little; to whatever degree, as far as

quantumlibet *or* **quantum libet** *adv* however much

quantumvīs *adv (also written as two words)* however; **quantumvīs rūsticus** however unsophisticated, although unsophisticated

quant·us -a -um *adj (interrogative or exclamatory)* how great, how much, of what size, of what importance, of what worth ‖ *n* **in quantum** to whatever extent, as far as; **quantī** *(gen of price)* how much, how high, how dearly, at what price; **quantō** *(abl of price)* at what price, for how much; **quantum frūmentī** how much grain ‖ *pl* how many

quant·uscumque -acumque -umcumque *adj* however great; of whatever size; however small; however trifling; however important *(or* unimportant); **quantīcumque** at whatever price, at whatever cost

quant·uslibet -alibet -umlibet *adj* however great; ever so great

quantusquantus quantaquanta quantumquantum *adj (also written as two words)* however big, however great, of whatever degree ‖ *n* however much, whatever

quant·usvīs -avīs -umvīs *adj* of whatever size; amount, degree, *etc.,* you wish; however big, however great, no matter how great

quāpropter *adv* wherefore, why

quāquā *adv* by whatever route, in whatever way

quāquam *adv* in any way; anywhere

quārē *or* **quā rē** *adv* by what means, how; in what way, from what cause, why; whereby; wherefore; **nec quid nec quārē** without why or wherefore

quart·a -ae *f* a fourth, one quarter

Quart·a -ae *f* female first name *(praenomen)*

quartadecumān·ī -ōrum *mpl* **(-decim-)** *mpl* soldiers of the 14th legion

quartān·us -a -um *adj* occurring every fourth day ‖ *f* quartan fever ‖ *mpl* soldiers of the 4th legion

quartār·ius -(i)ī *m* quarter pint

quartō *adv* for the fourth time

quartum *adv* for the fourth time; in the fourth place, fourthly

quart·us -a -um *adj* fourth

quart·us decim·us -a -um *adj* fourteenth

quasi *adv* as it were, so to speak; about, nearly, almost; allegedly ‖ *conj* on the charge that; as would be the case if; *(expressing the supposed reason for an action)* on the grounds that; *(introducing a hypothetical situation after verbs of asserting or supposing)* saying that, believing that, to the effect that: **spārsit rūmōrem, quasi … bellum gerere nōn possit** he spread a rumor to the effect that he could not fight a war

quasill·um -ī *n or* **quasill·us -ī** *m* small basket

quassāti·ō -ōnis *f* (violent) shaking

quass·ō -āre *tr* to keep shaking, keep tossing, keep waving; to batter, shatter, smash to pieces; *(fig)* to shake, weaken ‖ *intr (of the head)* to keep on shaking

quass·us -a -um *pp of* **quatiō** ‖ *adj* shattered, broken; quavering *(voice);* chopped *(wood)*

quate·faciō -facere -fēcī -factus *tr* to shake; *(fig)* to weaken

quātenus *adv* how far, to what point; as far as, till when, how long; to what extent; **est quātenus** there is an extent to which ‖ *conj* as far as; insofar as, in as much as, seeing that, since, as

quater *adv* four times

quater deciē(n)s *adv* fourteen times

quatern·ī -ae -a *adj* four together, four in a group, four each

quatiō quatere *(no perf)* **quassus** *tr* to shake, cause to tremble, cause to vibrate; to brandish, wave about; to beat, strike, drive; to batter, crush; *(fig)* to touch, move, affect; *(fig)* to plague, harass

quattuor *indecl adj* four

quattuordecim *indecl adj* fourteen

quattuor·vir -virī *m* member of a board of four *(one of the four chief magistrates of a municipium; member of a committee of four at Rome)*

quattuorvirāt·us -ūs *m* membership on the board of four

quāvīs *adv* anyway you like, in any possible way

quax·ō -āre *intr (of frogs)* to croak

-que *enclitic conj* and; **-que … -que** *(mostly poetical)* both … and; **terrā marīque** on land and on sea

-que *suf used in the formation of certain adverbs and conjunctions, e.g.:* **itaque** and so, therefore; *esp. to give indefinite force to relative pronouns and adverbs, e.g.,* **quandōque** at some time or other, someday

quemadmodum *or* **quem ad modum** *adv* in what way, how **‖** *conj* just as, as

qu·eō -īre -īvī *or* **-iī -itum** *intr* to be able; *(w. inf)* to be able to

quercēt·um -ī *n* oak forest

querce·us -a -um *adj* oak, of oak

querc·us -ūs *f* oak tree; oak-leaf crown *(awarded to a soldier who saved a citizen in battle);* acorns

querēl·a -ae *f* **(-ell-)** complaint; grievance, protest; difference of opinion

queribund·us -a -um *adj* full of complaints; whining *(voice)*

querimōni·a -ae *f* complaint, grievance; elegy

querit·or -ārī *intr* to keep complaining

quern·us -a -um *adj* oak, of oak

queror querī questus sum *tr* to complain of, complain about; to lament **‖** *intr* to complain; *(of birds)* to sing, warble, sing sadly, coo mournfully

querquētulān·us -a -um *adj (as name of various places and deities associated with oaks)* oak, covered with oak trees; **Mōns Querquētulānus** Oak Hill *(an old name for the Caelian Hill in Rome;* **Porta Querquētulāna** Oak Gate *(probably between the Caelian and the Esquiline Hills)*

querquēt·um -ī *n* oak forest

querul·us -a -um *adj* complaining, full of complaints, querulous; plaintive; warbling, cooing

questi·ō -ōnis *f* complaining

questus *pp of* **queror**

quest·us -ūs *m* complaint; plaintive note *(of the nightingale)*

quī *adv* how; why; at what price; whereby; in some way, somehow

quī quae *or* **qua quod** *adj (interrog)* which, what, what kind of; *(indef)* any **‖** *pron (rel)* who, that; *(indef, after* **sī, nisi, num, nē)** anyone

quia *conj* because

quianam *adv (interrog)* why in fact?, just why?

quicquam cūiusquam *pron* anything

quicque cūiusque *pron* each (one)

quīcum *(old abl of* **quī** *and* **cum)** *pron* with whom, with which

quīcumque quaecumque quodcumque *(also* **-cunque, -quomque)** *pron & adj (rel & indef)* whoever, whosoever, everyone who, whatever, whatsoever, everything ever

quid *adv* how?; why? **quid agis?** how do you do?; **quid plūra?** why say more?

quid cūius *pron (interrog)* what?; *(w. gen)* what kind of?: **quid mulieris uxōrem habēs?** what sort of woman do you have as your wife?; *(indef, after* **sī, nisi, num, nē)** anything

quīdam quaedam quiddam *pron* a certain one, a certain person, a certain thing

quīdam quaedam quoddam *adj* a certain; *(to soften an expression)* a kind of, what one might call

quidem *adv (emphasizing the word before it)* indeed, in fact; *(qualifying or limiting)* at least, at any rate; *(concessive)* it is true; of course; all right; *(exemplifying)* for example; **nē … quidem** *(emphasizing the intervening word)* not even, *e.g.,* **nē tū quidem** not even you

quidnam *adv* why in the world

quidnam cūiusnam *pron (interrog)* just what?

quidnī *adv* why not?

quidpiam *adv* in some respect

quidpiam cūiuspiam *pron* anything, something

quidquid *adv* to whatever extent, the further

quidquid *or* **quicquid** *(gen and dat not in use; abl:* **quōquō)** *pron* whatever, whatsoever, everything which; **per quidquid deōrum** by all the gods

quīdum *adv* how so?

qui·ēs -ētis *f* quiet, rest, peace; calm, lull; neutrality; sleep; dream; sleep of death, death

qui·ēscō -ēscere -ēvī -ētum *intr (contracted forms:* **quiēsse** = **quiēvisse; quiērunt** = **quiēvērunt; quiēram** = **quiēveram)** to rest, keep quiet, be inactive; to fall asleep; to sleep, be asleep; to lie still, be still, be undisturbed; to say no more, be quiet; *(of the dead)* to find rest; to pause, make a pause; *(of a person)* to be calm, remain calm, be unruffled; *(of physical forces, of conditions)* to die down, subside, be still; *(of things)* to cease to operate; to be neutral, keep neutral, take no action; to refrain from violence, make no disturbance, remain peaceful; *(of troops)* to make no move; *(w. inf)* to cease to, stop; to

take no steps to, omit to; *(w.* ab + *abl)* to be free from
quiētē *adv* quietly, calmly
quiēt·us -a -um *adj* at rest, resting, free from exertion, inactive; quiet; peaceful, undisturbed; natural; calm; still, silent; idle **‖** *npl* period of peace
quīlibet quaelibet quidlibet (-lubet) *pron* anyone, any you wish, no matter who, anything, anything you wish, no matter what, everything
quīlibet quaelibet quodlibet (-lubet) *adj* any, any at all, any you wish
quīn *adv (Interrog)* why not, *(corroborative)* in fact, as a matter of fact **‖** *conj* so that not, without; **facere nōn possum, quīn ad tē mittam librum** I can't help sending you the book; **nūllō modō intrōīre possem, quīn vidērent mē** I just couldn't walk in without their seeing me; *(after verbs of preventing, opposing)* from: **mīlitēs aegrē sunt retentī quīn oppidum oppugnārent** the soldiers could barely be kept from assaulting the town; *(after verbs of hesitation, doubt, suspicion):* **nōn dubitō quīn** I do not doubt that; *(esp. representing a nominative of a relative pronoun with a negative)* that ... not: **nēmō aspicere potest quīn dīcat** no one can look on without saying; **nēmō est quīn velit** there is no one who does not wish
quīnam quaenam quodnam *adj* which, what, just which, just what
quīnavīcēnāri·us -a -um *adj* of twenty-five; **lēx annōrum quīnavīcēnāria** the law prohibiting those under twenty-five years of age from making contracts
Quīnctili·us -a -um *adj* the name of a Roman gens *(nomen),* esp. Quinctilius Varus *(proconsul of Syria, later commander of the Romans in Germany, defeated by Armenius* A.D. *9)* **‖** Quinctilius Varus *(poet of Cremona, a friend of Horace and a relative of Vergil)*
Quīncti·us -a -um *adj* the name of a Roman gens *(nomen),* esp. Lucius Quinctius Cincinnatus *(called on his farm to become dictator in 458* B.C.*)* **‖** Titus Quinctius Flamininus *(consul in 198* B.C., *who "liberated" Greece from Macedonia)* **‖** Publius Quinctius *(represented by Cicero in his first case, in 81* B.C.*)*
quīnc·ūnx -ūncis *m* five-twelfths; 5% *(interest);* the figure five *(as arranged on dice or cards)*
quīndeciē(n)s *adv* fifteen times
quīndecim *indecl adj* fifteen
quīndecimprīm·ī -ōrum *mpl* executive board of fifteen *(magistrates of a municipality)*
quīndecimvirāl·is -is -e *adj* of the board of fifteen

quīndecimvīr·ī -ōrum *mpl* board of fifteen; **quīndecimvīrī Sibyllīnī** board of fifteen in charge of the Sibylline Books
quīngēnāri·us -a -um *adj* of five hundred each, consisting of five hundred *(men, pounds, etc.)*
quīngēn·ī -ae -a *adj* five hundred each
quīngentēsim·us -a -um *adj* five-hundredth
quīngent·ī -ae -a *adj* five hundred
quīngentiē(n)s *adv* five hundred times
quīn·ī -ae -a *adj* five each; **quīnī dēnī** fifteen each; **quīnī vīcēnī** twenty-five each
quīnquāgēn·ī -ae -a *adj* fifty each
quīnquāgēsim·us -a -um *adj* fiftieth **‖** *f* 2% tax
quīnquāgintā *indecl adj* fifty
Quīnquātr·ūs -uum *fpl or* **Quīnquātr·ia -ium** *npl* festival in honor of Minerva *(celebrated from March 19 to 23 esp. by the trades and professions under her patronage);* **quīnquātrūs minōrēs** *(or* **minusculae)** festival of Minerva *(held on June 13)*
quīnque *indecl adj* five
quīnquennāl·is -is -e *adj* quinquennial, occurring every five years; five-year, lasting five years
quīnquenn·is -is -e *adj* five-year-old
quīnquenn·ium -(i)ī *n* five-year period, five years
quīnqueped·al -ālis *n* five-foot ruler
quīnquepertīt·us -a -um (-part-) *adj* fivefold, divided into five parts
quīnqueprīm·ī -ōrum *mpl* five-man board of magistrates
quīnquerēm·is -is -e *adj* having five banks of oars **‖** *f* quinquereme
quīnque·vir -virī *m* member of a five-man board *(created at various times for various purposes)*
quīnquevirāt·us -ūs *m* membership on a board of five
quīnquiē(n)s *adv* five times
quīnquipl·ex -icis *adj* fivefold; **cēra quīnquiplex** tablet consisting of five sheets
quīnquiplic·ō -āre -āvī -ātus *tr* to multiply by five
Quīnt·a -ae *f* woman's name *(praenomen)*
quīntadecimān·ī -ōrum *mpl* **(-decum-)** soldiers of the 15th legion
quīntān·us -a -um *adj* of the fifth **‖** *mpl* members of the fifth legion **‖** *f* camp street running between the 5th and 6th maniple and the 5th and 6th squadron of cavalry *(used as a market street of the camp)*
Quīntiliān·us -ī *m* Quintilian *(Marcus Fabius Quintilianus, orator and professor of rhetoric,* A.D. *c. 35–95)*
Quīntīl·is *or* **Quīnctīl·is -is -e** *adj & m* July *(fifth month of the old Roman calendar until*

153 B.C.; renamed **Iūlius** *after the Julian reform of the calendar*)
Quīnt·ius *or* **Quīnct·ius -(i)ī** *m* name of a Roman gens *(nomen)*
quīntō *or* **quīntum** *adv* for the fifth time
quīnt·us -a -um *adj* fifth **‖ Quīntus** *m* Roman first name *(praenomen)*
quīnt·us decim·us -a -um *adj* fifteenth
quippe *adv* of course, naturally, obviously, by all means **‖** *conj* since, for; **quippe quī** since he *(is, was, will be one who)*, inasmuch as he; **multa Caesar questus est quippe quī vīdisset …** Caesar complained a lot since he had seen …
quippiam = **quidpiam**
quippinī *adv* why not?; of course, to be sure
Quirīnāl·is -is -e *adj* of Quirinus *(i.e., Romulus);* **collis Quirīnālis** Quirinal Hill *(one of the seven hills of Rome)* **‖** *npl* festival in honor of Romulus *(celebrated on February 17)*
Quirīn·us -a -um *adj* of Quirinus **‖** *m* Quirinus *(epithet of Romulus after his deification, of Janus, of Augustus, and of Antony)*
Quir·īs -ītis *m* Roman citizen; inhabitant of Cures *(Sabine town)* *(after the union of the Sabines and Romans, the Romans called themselves* **Quirītēs** *in their peace-time capacity. They were styled on all solemn occasions* **Populus Rōmānus Quirītēs(que);** *in later times it was distorted into* **Populus Rōmānus Quirītēs)**
quirītāti·ō -ōnis *f* shrieking, shriek
quirītāt·us -ūs *m* shriek, scream
Quirītēs -ium *mpl (pl form of* **Quirīs**) *(see* **Quirīs**) Roman citizens; **iūs Quirītium** legal rights enjoyed by Roman citizens
quirīt·ō -āre *tr & intr* to shriek, scream
quīs = **quibus**
quis cūius *pron (interrog)* who, which one; *(indef)* anyone
quisnam quaenam *(see* **quidnam**) *pron (interrog)* who, just who
quispiam cūiuspiam *pron* someone
quispiam quaepiam quodpiam *adj* any
quisquam cūiusquam *pron* anyone
quisque cūiusque *pron* each, each one, everybody, everyone; **doctissimus quisque** everyone of great learning, all the most learned; **optimus quisque** all the best ones
quisque quaeque quodque *or* **quidque** *or* **quicque** *adj* each
quisquili·ae -ārum *fpl or* **quisquili·a -ōrum** *npl* refuse, scraps, trash, junk; **quisqiliae!** baloney!
quisquis *(gen and dat not in use; abl:* **quōquō**) *pron* whoever, whosoever; everyone who; everyone, each

quīvīs quaevīs quidvīs *pron* anyone at all, anyone you please; **quīvīs ūnus** any one person
quō *adv (interrog)* where?, to what place?; what for?, to what purpose?; *(after* **sī, nisi,** *or* **nē**) to any place, anywhere; **quō … eō** the … the; **quō magis … eō magis** the more … the more **‖** *conj* where, to which place; whereby, wherefore; *(replacing* **ut** *when the clause contains a comparative)* in order that, so that
quoad *adv* how far; to what extent; by what time, how soon; how long; **est modus quoad** there is a limit up to which **‖** *conj* as long as; until, until such time as; as far as; *(w.* **ēius** *in the phrase:* **quoad ēius (facere) possum** as far as *(i.e.,* as well as) I can
quōcircā *adv* for which reason, wherefore, therefore, that's the reason
quōcumque (-cunque, -quomque) *adv* to whatever place, wherever
quod *conj* because; as for the fact that; the fact that; insofar as; as far as; **quod sī** *(or* **quodsī)** but if
quōdammodo *or* **quōdam modō** *adv* in a way
quoi = **cui**
quoiquoimodī *see* **cuicuimodī**
quōius = **cūius**
quoivīsmodī *see* **cuivīsmodī**
quōlibet *adv* anywhere you please, anywhere at all
quom *see* **cum**
quōminus *conj* that not; *(after verbs of hindering)* from, *e.g.,* **dēterrēre aliquem quōminus aliquid habeat** to keep s.o. from having s.th.
quōmodo *adv (interrog)* how, in what way; *(rel)* just as, as
quōmodocumque *adv* in whatever way, however
quōmodonam *interrog adv* where?, whereto?; to what purpose?, to what end?
quōnam *interrog adv* where on earth?, just where(to)? **quōnam ūsque** just how much longer? to what possible degree? to what conceivable end?
quondam *adv* once, at one time, formerly; at times, once in a while; someday, one day *(in the future)*
quoniam *conj* because, seeing that, now that
quōpiam *adv* at any place, anywhere
quōquam *adv* to any place; in any direction, anywhere
quoque *adv (always succeeds the word it emphasizes)* too
quōquō *adv* to whatever place, wherever
quōquōmodo *adv* in whatever way, however
quōquōversum *adv* (-vōrsum, -sus) in every direction, every way

quōrsum *interrog & rel adv* (**-sus**) in what direction, whereto; to what end, why

quot *indecl adj (interrog)* how many; *(correlative)* as many; **quot Kalendīs** every first of the month; **quot mēnsibus** every month

quotannīs *adv* every year

quotcumque *indecl adj* however many

quotēn·ī -ae -a *adj* how many each

quotīdiān·us -a -um *adj* (**cōt-, cott-**) daily

quotīdiē *adv* (**cōt-, cott-**) daily

quotiē(n)s *adv (interrog)* how many times; *(correlative)* as often as, whenever

quotiē(n)scumque *or* **quotiē(n)scunque** *adv* as often as, however often, whenever

quotquot *indecl adj* however many; **quotquot annīs** every year; **quotquot mēnsibus** every month

quotum·us -a -um *adj* which in number, which in order

quot·us -a -um *adj* which, what; what a small, what a trifling; **quota hōra est?** what time is it?; **quota pars** (*or* **portiō**) what part, what portion; **quotus quisque** how few?; **quotus quisque philosophōrum invenitur** how few of the philosophers are found *or* how rarely is one of the philosophers found?

quot·uscumque -acumque -umcumque *adj* just what, just which

quō ūsque *or* **quoūsque** *adv* how far, how long, till when; to what degree

quōvīs *adv* to any place whatsoever, anywhere; **quōvīs gentium** anywhere in the world

quum = cum *(conj)*

qūr *or* **quūr** *see* **cūr**

R

R, r *(supply* littera) *f* seventeenth letter of the Latin alphabet; letter name: **er**

rabidē *adv* rabidly, madly; furiously

rabid·us -a -um *adj* rabid, mad; furious, raving, uncontrolled

rabi·ēs *(gen not in use) f* madness; *(fig)* rage, anger, fury, wild passion; ferocity *(of animals);* rabies

rabiōsē *adv* furiously, madly

rabiōsul·us -a -um *adj* half-mad, rather rabid

rabiōs·us -a -um *adj* rabid *(animal);* mad; frenzied, furious, raving

rabō -ōnis *m (shortened form of* **arrabō**) token payment, down payment, deposit

rabul·a -ae *m* ranting lawyer

racēmif·er -era -erum *adj* clustered; covered with grape clusters

racēm·us -ī *m* cluster, bunch *(esp. of grapes); (fig)* wine

radi·āns -antis *adj* shining, beaming, radiant

radiāt·us -a -um *adj* spoked; having rays, radiant

rādīcitus *adv* by the roots, root and all; *(fig)* completely, utterly

rādīcul·a -ae *f* small root; radish

radi·ō -āre *or* **radi·or -ārī** *intr* to radiate, shine

radiōs·us -a -um *adj* radiant

rad·ius -(i)ī *m* stake, stick; spoke; ray, beam; *(in weaving)* shuttle; radius *(of a circle);* measuring rod; elongated olive

rād·īx -īcis *f* root; radish; foot *(of hill or mountain);* base, foundation; basis, origin

rā·dō -dere -sī -sus *tr* to scrape, scratch; to shave; to scratch out, erase; to graze, touch in passing; to strip off; *(of wind)* to lash

raed·a -ae *f* (**rēd-**) four-wheeled carriage, coach

raedār·ius -(i)ī *m* coach driver

Raetic·us -a -um *adj* (**Rhaet-**) Rhaetian

Raeti·us -a -um *adj* (**Rhaet-**) Rhaetian ‖ *f* Rhaetia *(Alpine country between Germany and Italy)*

Raet·us -a -um *adj & m* (**Rhaet-**) Rhaetian

rall·us -a -um *adj* thin, threadbare

rāmāl·ia -ium *npl* brushwood, undergrowth

rāment·a -ae *f or* **rāment·um -ī** *n* chip, shaving

rāmes *see* **rāmex**

rāme·us -a -um *adj* of branches, of boughs

rām·ex -icis *m or* **ram·es -itis** *m* rupture; blood vessel of the lung ‖ *mpl* lungs

Ramn·ēs *or* **Ramnēns·ēs -ium** *mpl* one of the three original Roman tribes; *(fig)* blue bloods

rāmōs·us -a -um *adj* having many branches, branching; branch-like

rāmul·us -ī *m* twig

rām·us -ī *m* branch, bough; branch *(of an antler);* genealogical branch

rān·a -ae *f* frog; **rāna quaxat** the frog croaks

ranc·ēns -entis *adj* putrid, stinking

rancid·us -a -um *adj* stinky, rank; rather disgusting

rancid·us -a -um *adj* rancid, rank, stinking; disgusting

ranc·ō -āre *intr (of a tiger)* roar

rānuncul·us -ī *m* little frog, tadpole

rapācid·a -ae *m (humorous patronymic)* son of a thief

rapācit·ās -ātis *f* rapacity, greediness

rap·āx -ācis *adj* rapacious, grasping, greedy for plunder; insatiable

raphan·us -ī *m* radish

rapidē *adv* rapidly; *(to burn)* fiercely

rapidit·ās -ātis *f* rapidity, velocity, swiftness, rush

rapid·us -a -um *adj* tearing away, seizing; fierce, consuming, white-hot *(fire);* rapid, swift, rushing, impetuous
rapīn·a -ae *f* rapine, pillage; prey
rap·iō -ere -uī -tus *tr* to seize and carry off; to snatch, tear, pluck; to drag off; to hurry, drive, cause to rush; to carry off by force, ravish; to ravage, lay waste; to lead on hurriedly; **flammam rapere** to catch fire; **in iūs rapere** to haul off to court **‖** *refl* to hurry, dash, take off
raptim *adv* hurriedly; suddenly
rapti·ō -ōnis *f* abduction, ravishing
rapt·ō -āre *tr* to seize and carry off; to abduct, kidnap; to drag away; to drag along; to plunder; **in iūs raptāre** to haul off to court
rapt·or -ōris *m* plunderer, robber; abductor
rapt·um -ī *n* plunder, loot
rapt·us -a -um *pp of* **rapiō ‖** *n* plunder, loot
rapt·us -ūs *m* snatching away; looting, robbery; abduction, kidnapping
rāpul·um -ī *n* little turnip
rāp·um -ī *n* turnip
rārē *adv* rarely; sparsely; loosely
rārē·faciō -facere -fēcī -factus *tr* to rarefy, thin out
rārē·fīō -fierī -factus sum *intr* to become less solid, rarefy
rārēsc·ō -ere *intr* to grow thin, lose density, become rarefied; to grow wider, widen out, open up; to become fewer; to disappear, die away
rārit·ās -ātis *f* looseness of texture; thinness; small number; sparseness; infrequency; rarity
rārō *adv* rarely, seldom
rār·us -a -um *adj* wide apart, of loose texture; thin; scattered, far apart; scarce, sparse; few; uncommon, rare; unusual; *(mil)* in open rank
rāsī *perf of* **rādō**
rāsil·is -is -e *adj* shaved smooth, scraped, polished
rāsit·ō -āre -āvī -ātus *tr* to shave (regularly)
rastell·us -ī *m* rake *(usu. of wood)*
rastr·um -ī *(pl: rastr·ī -ōrum mpl) n* rake; mattock
rāsus *pp of* **rādō**
rati·ō -ōnis *f* calculation, computation, reckoning, account; register; matter, affair, business, transaction; consideration, respect; grounds; guiding principle; scheme, system, method; procedure; theory, doctrine; science; relation, connection, reference; fashion, way, style; reasoning, reason, judgment, understanding, reasonableness; order, law, rule; view, opinion; *(w. gen)* a reason for; **(lībertus) ā ratiōnibus** bookkeeper, accountant; **fūgit tē ratiō** *(coll)* you're off your rocker; **nōn erat ratiō āmittere ēiusmodī occāsiōnem** there was no reason to pass up that kind of oppor-

tunity; **parēs ratiōnēs facere cum** to square accounts with; **populāris rātiō** popular cause; **prō ratiōne** proportionately; according to the rule, properly; **propter ratiōnem** *(w. gen)* out of regard for; **ratiō aerāria** rate of exchange; **ratiō atque ūsus** theory and practice; **ratiō cōnstat** the account tallies; **ratiō itineris** itinerary; **ratiōne** with good reason; according to the rules, properly; **ratiōnem cōnferre** *(or* **dēferre** *or* **referre)** *(w. gen)* to render *or* give an account of, account for; **ratiōnem (dē)dūcere** to make a calculation, reckon; **ratiōnem habēre cum** to have to do with; **ratiōnem inīre** *(or* **reddere** *or* **tenēre)** to calculate, make a calculation; to embark on a scheme; **ratiō vītae** pattern of life, life style
ratiōcināti·ō -ōnis *f* exercise of the reasoning powers, reasoning; theory, theorizing; deduction, inference
ratiōcinātīv·us -a -um *adj* concerned with reasoning, syllogistic
ratiōcināt·or -ōris *m* accountant
ratiōcin·or -ārī -ātus sum *tr & intr* to calculate, reckon; to reason, argue, conclude, infer
ratiōnāl·is -is -e *adj* rational; theoretical; dialectical
ratiōnār·ium -(i)ī *n* financial survey
rat·is -is *f* raft; *(poet)* ship, craft **‖** *fpl* pontoons
ratiuncul·a -ae *f* small account; trifling reason; petty argumentation
rat·us -a -um *pp of* **reor ‖** *adj* reckoned, calculated; fixed, established, settled, certain, sure; approved; **prō ratā parte** *(or* **prō ratā)** in proportion, proportionately; **ratum facere** *(or* **efficere)** to confirm, ratify, approve; **ratum habēre** *(or* **dūcere)** to consider valid, regard as certain *or* sure
raucison·us -a -um *adj* hoarse-sounding
rauc·us -a -um *adj* raucous, hoarse; screaming, strident; scraping; deep, deep-voiced
raud·us -eris *n* (rōd-, rūd-) copper coin; lump
rauduscul·um -ī *n* (rōd-, rūd-) bit of money
Ravenn·a -ae *f* Ravenna *(port and naval base)*
rāv·iō -īre *intr* to be hoarse
rāv·is -is *f* hoarseness
rāv·us -a -um *adj* greyish
re- *pref (also* **red-)** *denoting* **1** movement back, in reverse: **revocāre** to call back; **2** reversal of an action, un-: **retegere** to uncover; **3** restoration: **revalēscere** to recover again; **4** response: **respondēre** to respond; **rescrībere** to answer *(in writing);* **5** opposition: **rebellāre** to rebel; **6** separation: **removēre** to remove; **7** repeated action: **replēre** to refill; **reïterāre** repeat again and again
re·a -ae *f* defendant; guilty woman
Rēa *see* **Rhēa**
rēapse *adv* **(-abs-)** in fact, actually, really

Reāt·e -is *n* Sabine town
Reātīn·us -a -um *adj* of Reate
rebellāti·ō -ōnis *f* rebellion
rebellātr·īx -īcis *adj (fem only)* rebellious;
  rebellātrīx Germānia rebellious Germany
rebelli·ō -ōnis *f* rebellion
rebell·is -is -e *adj* rebellious **‖** *mpl* rebels
rebell·ium -(i)ī *n* rebellion
rebell·ō -āre -āvī -ātum *intr* to rebel
rebell·us -a -um *adj* reddish
rebīt·ō -ere *intr* to go back
rebo·ō -āre *tr* to make reecho **‖** *intr* to reecho,
  bellow back
recalcitr·ō -āre *intr* to kick back
recal·eō -ēre *intr* to get warm again; *(of a
  river)* to run warm *(e.g., w. blood)*
recal·ēscō -ēscere -uī *intr* to grow warm again
recal·faciō -facere -fēcī *tr* to warm up again
recalv·us -a -um *adj* bald in front, with receding hairline
recand·ēscō -ēscere -uī *intr* to grow white; *(w.
  dat)* to grow hot, glow in response to
recanō *see* **recinō**
recant·ō -āre -āvī -ātus *tr* to recant; to charm
  back, charm away **‖** *intr* to reecho
reccidō *see* **recidō** *(to fall back)*
re·cēdō -cēdere -cessī -cessum *intr* to go back;
  to go away, withdraw, recede; to give
  ground, fall back; to depart; to vanish; to
  stand back, be distant
recell·ō -ere *intr* to recoil
recēns *adv* just, recently, lately
rec·ēns -entis *adj* recent, fresh, young; newly
  arrived, just arrived; modern; fresh; rested;
  recentissimus latest **‖** *npl* recent events
recēns·eō -ēre -uī -sus *tr* to count, enumerate,
  number, survey; to recount, go over again,
  retell; *(mil)* to review; *(pol) (of a censor)* to
  revise the roll of, review, enroll
recēnsi·ō -ōnis *f* revision
recēnsus -us -ūs *m* review; census; valuation *(of
  property)*
recēpī *perf of* **recipiō**
receptācul·um -ī *n* receptacle, container;
  reservoir; place of refuge, shelter; hiding
  place
recepti·ō -ōnis *f* reception
recept·ō -āre *tr* to take back; to welcome frequently into the home, entertain; to tug at **‖**
  refl to beat a hasty retreat
recept·or -ōris *m or* **receptr·īx -īcis** *f* shelter-
  er; concealer
recept·us -a -um *pp of* **recipiō ‖** *n* obligation
recept·us -ūs *m* taking back, recantation; way
  of escape; refuge; return; *(mil)* retreat;
  (signum) **receptuī canere** to sound the
  retreat
recessī *perf of* **recēdō**

recessim *adv* backwards
recess·us -ūs *m* retreat, withdrawal; departure;
  secluded spot, retreat; inner room, central
  chamber; recess; background
recharmid·ō -āre *ref* to stop being a
  Charmides *(character in Roman comedy)*
recidīv·us -a -um *adj* recurring, returning;
  rebuilt
re·cidō -cidere -cidī -cāsum *or* **reccid·ō -ere**
  intr to fall back; to jump back, recoil; to suffer a relapse; *(fig)* to fall back, sink, relapse;
  to turn out, result; *(w. ad or in + acc)* to pass
  to, be handed over to
recī·dō -dere -dī -sus *tr* to cut back, cut off, cut
  away, cut down; to abridge, cut short
re·cingō -cingere -cīnxī -cīnctus *tr* to loosen,
  undo, take off
recin·ō -ere *tr* to repeat, reecho **‖** *intr* to sound
  a warning
reciper- = recuper-
re·cipiō -cipere -cēpī -ceptus *tr* to keep back,
  keep in reserve; to withdraw, bring back,
  carry back; to retake, recover, regain; to take
  in, accept, receive, welcome; to gain, collect,
  take in, make *(money);* to take up, assume,
  undertake; to guarantee, pledge; *(mil)* to
  retake, recapture, seize, take, occupy; **ad sē**
  (or **in sē) recipere** to take upon oneself, take
  the responsibility for, promise, guarantee **‖**
  refl to get hold of oneself again, regain composure, recover, come to again; to retreat,
  escape; **sē recipere** *(w. ad or* **in** + *acc)* to
  retreat to, escape to, find refuge in
reciproc·ō -āre -āvī -ātus *tr* to move back and
  forth; to turn back; to back up *(e.g., a ship)*,
  reverse the direction of; to reverse, convert *(a
  proposition)* **‖** *intr (of the tide)* to ebb and
  flow, rise and fall
reciproc·us -a -um *adj* ebbing and flowing,
  going backwards and forwards
recīsus *pp of* **recīdō**
recitāti·ō -ōnis *f* reading aloud, recitation
recitāt·or -ōris *m* reader, reciter
recit·ō -āre -āvī -ātus *tr* to read out, read
  aloud, recite; to name in writing, appoint,
  constitute; **senātum recitāre** to take roll call
  in the Senate
reclāmāti·ō -ōnis *f* cry of disapproval; shout of
  protest
reclāmit·ō -āre *intr* to voice disapproval; *(w.
  dat)* to protest against
reclām·ō -āre -āvī -ātus *tr* to protest **‖** *intr* to
  raise a protest, shout objections; to reverberate; *(w. dat)* to express disapproval to, contradict
reclīn·is -is -e *adj* reclining, leaning back
reclīn·ō -āre -āvī -ātus *tr* to bend back, lean
  back, rest; *(w. ab)* to distract *(s.o.)* from **‖** *refl*
  to lean

reclū·dō -dere -sī -sus *tr* to open; to lay open, disclose; to draw *(sword);* to break up *(the soil)*

recoctus *pp of* recoquō

recōgit·ō -āre -āvī -ātum *tr* to consider, think over ‖ *intr (w.* dē + *abl)* to think again about, reconsider

recogniti·ō -ōnis *f* formal inspection

reco·gnōscō -gnōscere -gnōvī -gnitus *tr* to call to mind again, review; to recognize; to look over, examine, inspect, investigate; to certify, authorize

recol·ligō -ligere -lēgī -lēctus *tr* to gather again, gather up, collect; tē recollige! get hold of yourself!; take heart! ‖ *refl* to pull oneself together

re·colō -colere -coluī -cultus *tr* to till again, cultivate once more; to honor again; to call to mind, think over, consider; to practice again, resume

recomment·or -ārī -ātus sum *tr* to remember, recall

recomminīsc·or -ī *tr* to call to mind again, recall

recomposit·us -a -um *adj* rearranged

reconciliāti·ō -ōnis *f* winning back again, reestablishment, restoration; reconciliation

reconciliāt·or -ōris *m* reconciler; pācis reconciliātor restorer of peace

reconcili·ō -āre -āvī -ātus *tr* to bring back, regain, recover; to restore, reestablish; to win over again, conciliate; to bring together again, reconcile

reconcinn·ō -āre *tr* to set right again, repair

recondit·us -a -um *adj* hidden, concealed; recondite, abstruse, profound; reserved *(person)*

recon·dō -dere -didī -ditus *tr* to put back again; to put away, hoard; to hide, conceal; to plunge *(sword);* to close *(eyes)* again; to store up *(in the mind)*

reconfl·ō -āre *tr* to rekindle

reco·quō -quere -xī -ctus *tr* to cook, boil, *or* bake again; to recast, remold

recordāti·ō -ōnis *f* recollection, remembrance

record·or -ārī -ātus sum *tr & intr* to recall, recollect, remember

recoxī *perf of* recoquō

recre·ō -āre -āvī -ātus *tr* to recreate, restore, renew; *(fig)* to revive, refresh

recrep·ō -āre *intr* to reecho

re·crēscō -crēscere -crēvī *intr* to grow again; to be renewed

recrūd·ēscō -ēscere -uī *intr (of a wound)* to open up again; *(of a revolt)* to break out again

rēctā *adv* by a direct route, straight

rēctē *adv* in a straight line; rightly, correctly; suitably, properly, well; quite; *(in answers)* good, very good; quite right; *(in evasive answers)* well, right, it's all right; *(in politely*

declining an offer, like benignē) no, thank you.

rēcti·ō -ōnis *f* direction, controlling

rēct·or -ōris *m* guide, controller; rider, driver *(of an animal);* leader; master; pilot; tutor; *(mil)* commander; *(naut)* helmsman, pilot; *(pol)* ruler, governor

rēct·us -a -um *pp of* regō ‖ *adj* in a straight line, straight, direct; correct, right, proper, appropriate; just, upright, conscientious, virtuous; standing erect; *(impartial)* judge; straight-forward *(expression);* sheer *(cliff);* aere rēctō cantāre to play a reed pipe; cāsus rēctus *(gram)* nominative case; fūnis rēctus tightrope; rēctīs oculīs with eyes not lowered, without flinching ‖ *n* right; uprightness, rectitude, virtue; in rēctum in a straight line; in a vertical position *or* direction, vertically; straight forward

recub·ō -āre *intr* to lie on one's back, lie down, rest

rēcul·a -ae *f* little thing

recultus *pp of* recolō

re·cumbō -cumbere -cubuī *intr* to lie down (again); to recline *(esp. at table);* to sink down *(e.g., in a swamp);* to fall; *(of fog)* to settle down

recuperāti·ō -ōnis *f* recovery

recuperāt·or -ōris *m* (-cip-) recoverer; *(leg)* arbiter *(member of a bench of from 3 to 5 men who expedited cases needing speedy decisions)*

recuperātōri·us -a -um *adj* (-cip-) of the special court for summary civil suits

recuper·ō -āre -āvī -ātus *tr* (-cip-) to regain, recover, get back; to win over again

recūr·ō -āre -āvī -ātus *tr* to restore, refresh, restore to health

recur·rō -rere -rī -sum *intr* to run back, hurry back; to return *(to the starting point of a cycle);* to recur, come back *(to the mind);* *(of a process)* to run in the opposite direction; to revert *(to a former condition);* *(w.* ad) to have recourse to

recurs·ō -āre *intr* to keep running back; to keep recurring

recurs·us -ūs *m* return; retreat

recurv·ō -āre -āvī -ātus *tr* to curve, bend back

recurv·us -a -um *adj* curving, curved, bent, crooked

recūsāti·ō -ōnis *f* refusal; *(leg)* objection, protest; *(leg)* counterplea

recūs·ō -āre -āvī -ātus *tr* to raise objections to, reject, refuse; *(w. inf)* to be reluctant to, refuse to ‖ *intr* to raise an objection; to make a rebuttal

recuss·us -a -um *adj* reverberating

recu·tiō -tere -ssī -ssus *tr* to strike *(so as to cause to resound)*

recutīt·us -a -um *adj* raw *(skin, from being rubbed);* circumcised

red- *see* **re-**

redāctus *pp of* **redigō**

redambul·ō -āre *intr* to walk back

redam·ō -āre *tr* to love in return

redārdēsc·ō -ere *intr* to blaze up again

redargu·ō -ere -ī *tr* to disprove, refute, contradict; to disprove the existence of

redauspic·ō -āre *intr* to take the auspices again

red·dō -dere -didī -ditus *tr* to give back, return, restore, replace; to repay; to repeat *(words);* to recite, rehearse *(words);* to produce *(a sound);* to ascribe, attribute; to translate; to utter in response; to render, make; to give as due, pay, grant, deliver; to reflect, reproduce, imitate; **animam ā pulmōnibus reddere** to exhale *(lit: to give back a breath from the lungs);* **causam reddere** to give a reason *or* explanation; **conūbia reddere** to grant intermarriage rights; **iūdicium reddere** to administer justice; to grant a trial; **iūra reddere** to administer justice; **litterās reddere** to deliver a letter; **morbō nātūrae dēbitum reddere** to die of disease; **poenās reddere** to suffer punishment; **quī tē nōmine reddet** who will bear your name; **ratiōnem reddere** to render an account *(financial or other);* **reddere hostī clādem** to pay back the enemy for the massacre; **tālia eī reddere** to answer him in words such as this; **veniam reddere** *(w. dat)* to forgive; **verbum prō verbō reddere** to translate word for word; **vītam reddere** to die ‖ *refl* to return

redempti·ō -ōnis *f* ransoming; bribing; revenue collection

redempt·ō -āre *tr* to ransom (repeatedly)

redempt·or -ōris *m* contractor; revenue agent

redemptūr·a -ae *f* undertaking of public contracts

redemptus *pp of* **redimō**

red·eō -īre -iī -itum *intr* to go back, come back, return; *(of a speaker)* to return *(to the theme);* *(w. ad)* **1** to return to, revert to; **2** to fall back on, have recourse to; **3** to be reduced to; **4** *(of power, inheritances, etc.)* to revert to, devolve upon; **ad sē redīre** to come to again, regain consciousness; to control oneself

redhāl·ō -āre *tr* to exhale

redhib·eō -ēre -uī -itus *tr (of a vendor)* to take back *(a defective purchase);* *(of a purchaser)* to return *(a defective purchase)*

red·igō -igere -ēgī -āctus *tr* to drive back, lead back, bring back; to call in, collect, raise, make *(money);* to gather in *(crops);* to repel *(the enemy);* to reduce *(in quantity, number, or to a condition);* to force, compel, subdue;

(w. double acc) to render, make; *(w. in or sub + acc)* to bring under the power of; **ad vānum et irritum redigere** to make meaningless; to make null and void; **in memoriam redigere** to remember, recall; **in ōrdinem redigere** to bring into line; **in prōvinciam redigere** to reduce to the status of a province; **in potestātem redigere** *(w. gen)* to bring under the control of; **in pūblicum** *(or* **in aerārium) redigere** to turn over *(money)* to the public treasury

redimīcul·um -ī *n* band, chaplet, fillet; chain, fetter

redim·iō -īre -iī -ītus *tr* to crown, wreathe; to surround, encircle

red·imō -imere -ēmī -emptus *tr* to buy back; to ransom, redeem; to buy off, ward off, avert; to pay for, compensate for, atone for; *(com)* to get by contract, collect under contract

redintegrāti·ō -ōnis *f* renewal; repetition

redintegr·ō -āre *tr* to make whole again, restore, revive, refresh; *(mil)* to bring to full strength

redipīsc·or -ī *tr* to get back

rediti·ō -ōnis *f* return

redit·us -ūs *m* return; *(fig)* restoration; *(astr)* orbit, revolution; *(fin)* revenue, proceeds, return; **(in) reditū esse** to yield a return

redivia *see* **reduvia**

redivīv·us -a -um *adj* second-hand

redol·eō -ēre -uī *tr* to smell of, smell like ‖ *intr* to smell, be redolent

redōn·ō -āre -āvī -ātus *tr* to restore, give back again; to give up, abandon

redorm·iō -īre *intr* to go back to sleep (again)

re·dūcō -dūcere -dūxī -ductus *tr* to lead back, bring back; to draw back; to revive *(a practice);* to escort *(an official, as mark of honor, to his home);* to remarry *(after a separation);* to restore to normal, restore to a previous condition; to withdraw *(troops);* *(leg)* to make retrospective; **gradum redūcere** to draw back; **in grātiam redūcere** to restore to favor; **in memoriam redūcere** to recall; **rem hūc redūcere** ut to make it possible that

reducti·ō -ōnis *f* restoration

reduct·or -ōris *m* restorer

reduct·us -a -um *pp of* **redūcō** ‖ *adj* remote, secluded, aloof

redunc·us -a -um *adj* bent backwards, curved backwards

redundanti·a -ae *f* excess; redundancy

redund·ō -āre -āvī -ātum *tr* to cause to overflow; **aqua redundāta** the overflow ‖ *intr* to overflow; to be too numerous, be too large; *(of writers)* to be excessive; to be soaked *(e.g., w. blood);* *(w. abl)* to abound in; *(w. ex or dē + abl)* to stream from, overflow with

reduvi·a *or* **redivi·a -ae** *f* hangnail
red·ux -ucis *adj* (**redd-**) guiding back, rescuing; that brings back home *(esp. a soldier on a foreign mission);* brought back, restored
redūxī *perf of* **redūcō**
refecti·ō -ōnis *f* restoration, repairing; regaining one's strength; convalescence
refectus *pp of* **reficiō**
refell·ō -ere -ī *tr* to refute, disprove
refer·ciō -cīre -sī -tus *tr* (**refarc-**) to stuff, cram, choke, crowd
refer·iō -īre *tr* to strike back
referō referre rettulī relātus *tr* to bring back, carry back; to give back, return, restore; to pay back, repay; to (re)echo *(a sound);* to renew, revive, repeat; to direct, focus, turn *(mind, attention);* to present again, represent; to say in turn, reply; to announce, report, relate, tell; to note down, enter, register, record; to consider, regard; to refer, attribute, ascribe; to bring up, spit out, vomit; **gradum referre** to go back, retreat; **grātiam referre** to do a return favor; **grātiās referre** to return thanks, show gratitude; **pedem referre** to go back, retreat; **pedēs fertque refertque** he walks up and down; **ratiōnēs referre ad aerārium** to make an accounting to the treasury; **vestīgia referre** to retrace footsteps ‖ *refl* to go back, return ‖ *intr (pol)* to make a motion, make a proposal; **ad senātum referre** *(w. dē + abl)* to bring before the Senate the matter of, make a proposal to the Senate about
rē·fert -ferre *v impers* it is of importance, it is of consequence, it concerns; **meā (tuā, nostrā) rēfert** it is of importance *or* of advantage to me (you, us); **nōn rēfert utrum** it makes no difference whether; **parvī rēfert** *(w. inf)* it is of little importance, of little advantage to; **quid rēfert?** what's the difference?; **quid rēfert ad mē?** what's the difference to me?
refert·us -a -um *pp of* **referciō** ‖ *adj* packed, crammed, stuffed; crowded; full, replete, chuck-full
referv·eō -ēre *intr* to boil over, bubble over
refervēsc·ō -ere *intr* to begin to boil *or* bubble
refibul·ō -āre *tr* to unpin
re·ficiō -ficere -fēcī -fectus *tr* to rebuild, repair, restore; to revive *(hope, etc.);* to refresh, invigorate; to get *(e.g., money)* back again; to reappoint, re-elect
refī·gō -gere -xī -xus *tr* to unfasten, undo; to take down *(posters, etc.);* to annul *(laws)*
refing·ō -ere *tr* to refashion
refīxus *pp of* **refīgō**
reflāgit·ō -āre *tr* to demand again, ask back
reflāt·us -ūs *m* headwind

re·flectō -flectere -flexī -flexus *tr* to bend back *or* backwards, turn around, turn away; *(fig)* to turn back, bring back, change
refl·ō -āre -āvī -ātus *tr* to breathe out again ‖ *intr* to blow in the wrong direction
reflu·ō -ere *intr* to flow back, run back; to overflow
reflu·us -a -um *adj* ebbing, receding
refocill·ō -āre -āvī -ātus *tr* to rewarm; to revive
refōrmāt·or -ōris *m* reformer
reformīdāti·ō -ōnis *f* dread
reformīd·ō -āre -āvī -ātus *tr* to dread, stand in awe of; to shrink from, shun
refōrm·ō -āre -āvī -ātus *tr* to reshape, remold, transform
re·foveō -fovēre -fōvī -fōtus *tr* to warm again; to restore, revive, refresh
refrāctāriol·us -a -um *adj* a bit refractory, somewhat stubborn
refrāctāri·us -a -um unruly
refrāctus *pp of* **refringō**
refrāg·or -ārī -ātus sum *or* **refrāg·ō -āre** *intr* *(w. dat)* to oppose, resist, thwart
refrēn·ō -āre -āvī -ātus *tr* to curb, restrain, keep down, control
refric·ō -āre -uī -ātus *tr* to rub open, scratch open; to irritate, reopen *(a wound);* *(fig)* to exasperate; *(fig)* to renew ‖ *intr* to break out again
refrīger·ō -āre -āvī -ātus *tr* to cool, cool off, chill; to refresh; to weary, exhaust ‖ *pass* to grow cool; to grow weary
re·frīgēscō -frīgēscere -frīxī *intr* to grow cool, become cool; *(fig)* to lose force, flag, abate, fail, grow dull, grow stale; *(fig)* to fall flat
re·fringō fringere -frēgī -frāctus *tr* to break open, break down; to tear off *(clothes);* *(fig)* to break, check, destroy, put an end to
re·fugiō -fugere -fūgī *tr* to run away from; to avoid ‖ *intr* to run away, escape; to disappear
refug·ium -(i)ī *n* place of refuge; recourse
refug·us -a -um *adj* receding, vanishing ‖ *m* fugitive, refugee
reful·geō -gēre -sī *intr* to gleam, reflect *(light),* glitter
re·fundō -fundere -fūdī -fūsus *tr* to pour back, pour out ‖ *pass* to flow back; to overflow
refūtāti·ō -ōnis *f* refutation
refūtāt·us -ūs *m* refutation
refūt·ō -āre -āvī -ātus *tr* to repress, suppress; to refute, disprove
rēgāliol·us -ī *m* wren
rēgāl·is -is -e *adj* regal, kingly; royal
rēgāliter *adv* royally; despotically
regel·ō -āre -āvī -ātus *tr* to cool off, air; to thaw, unfreeze, warm

re·gerō -gerere -gessī -gestus *tr* to carry back, throw back; *(fig)* to throw back *(remarks)*

rēgi·a -ae *f* palace; court *(royal or imperial establishment);* capital; *(in camp)* king's tent; regia *(originally the house of King Numa in the Roman Forum and later the residence of the Pontifex Maximus)*

rēgiē *adv* royally; despotically

Rēgiēns·is -is -e *or* **Rēgīn·us -a -um** *adj* **(Rhēg-)** of Rhegium ‖ *mpl* inhabitants of Rhegium *(in Bruttium in S. Italy)*

rēgific·us -a -um *adj* fit for a king

Rēgill·um -ī *n or* **Rēgill·ī -ōrum** *mpl* Sabine town from which the Fabian clan is said to have come

Rēgill·us -ī *m* family name *(cognomen)* in the Aemilian clan ‖ name of a small lake south of Gabii *(now dried up)* where the Romans defeated the Latins in 496 B.C.

regim·en -inis *n* steering *(of a ship);* steering oar; control *(of a horse);* direction, control *(of public and private affairs)*

rēgīn·a -ae *f* queen

Rēgīn·us -a -um (Rhēg-) of Rhegium *(in Bruttium)* ‖ *mpl* inhabitants of Rhegium

regi·ō -ōnis *f* straight line, line, direction; boundary, boundary line; region, area, quarter, neighborhood; ward *(of Rome);* district, province *(of a country);* department, sphere; geographical position; **ā rēctā regiōne** in a straight line; **dē rēctā regiōne dēflectere** to veer off the straight path; **ē regiōne** in a straight line, directly; *(w. gen or dat)* in the opposite direction to, exactly opposite; **rēctā regiōne** by a direct route

regiōnātim *adv* by districts

rēgi·us -a -um *adj* king's, royal, regal; like a king, worthy of a king, magnificent ‖ *mpl* king's troops ‖ *f see* **rēgia**

reglūtin·ō -āre *tr* to unglue

rēgnāt·or -ōris *m* ruler, sovereign

rēgnātr·īx -īcis *adj (fem only)* reigning, imperial

rēgn·ō -āre -āvī -ātum *intr* to reign; to be supreme, hold sway; to dominate; to rule the roost, play (the part of a) king; *(w. gen)* to be king of; *(w. in + acc)* to rule over

rēgn·um -ī *n* monarchy, royal power, kingship; absolute power, despotism; supremacy, control, direction, sovereignty; kingdom, realm; domain, estate

regō regere rēxī rēctus *tr* to keep in a straight line; to keep on a proper course; to guide, conduct; to guide *(morally);* to manage, direct; *(mil)* to command; *(pol)* to rule, govern; **imperium regere** to exercise dominion, rule supreme; **regere fīnīs** *(leg)* to mark out the limits

re·gredior -gredī -gressus sum *intr* to step *or* go back; to come back, return; *(mil)* to march back, retreat

regressi·ō -ōnis *f (mil)* withdrawl; *(rhet)* repetition

regress·us -ūs *m* return; retreat

rēgul·a -ae *f* ruler *(for drawing straight lines or measuring);* rod, bar; rule, standard, model, principle *(in conduct, language)*

rēgul·us -ī *m* petty king; prince ‖ **Rēgulus** Marcus Atilius Regulus *(Roman general who refused to let himself be ransomed in the First Punic War)* ‖ Marcus Aquilius Regulus *(an informer under Nero, later a successful advocate)*

regust·ō -āre -āvī -ātus *tr* to taste again; *(fig)* to delve again into *(e.g., literature)*

re·iciō -icere -iēcī -iectus *tr* to throw back; to throw over one's shoulders; to beat back, repel; to reject; to refer, direct, assign; to postpone; *(leg) (of judges)* to challenge, overrule; **rem reicere** *(w. ad)* to refer the matter *(to s.o. for decision);* **potestās reiciendī** *(leg)* right to challenge

reiect·a -ōrum *npl (phil)* things which, while not absolutely bad, should be avoided

reiectāne·us -a -um *adj* to be rejected

reiecti·ō -ōnis *f* rejection; *(leg)* challenging; **reiectiō iūdicum** challenging potential jury members

reiectus *pp of* **reiciō**

re·lābor -lābī -lāpsus sum *intr* to slide *or* glide back; to sink down *(upon a couch);* *(of rivers)* to flow back; to sail back; *(fig)* to return

relangu·ēscō -ēscere -ī *intr* to faint; to be relaxed, relax; to weaken

relāti·ō -ōnis *f* report *(made by a magistrate to the Senate or the emperor);* repetition; **relātiō crīminis** *(leg)* responding to a charge

relāt·or -ōris *m (pol)* proposer of a motion in the Senate

relātus *pp of* **referō**

relāt·us -ūs *m* official report; narration; recital

relaxāti·ō -ōnis *f* relaxation; easing off, mitigation

relax·ō -āre -āvī -ātus *tr* to stretch out, widen, open; to loosen, open; to release, set free; to relax; to cheer up; to mitigate ‖ *pass* to relax

relēctus *pp of* **relegō**

relēgāti·ō -ōnis *f* banishment; sending into retirement

relēg·ō -āre -āvī -ātus *tr* to send away, remove; to send into retirement, retire; to banish; to relegate; to shift *(blame, responsibility);* to give back

re·legō -legere -lēgī -lēctus *tr* to collect again, gather up; to travel over, sail over again; to go over, review *(in thought, in a speech);* to reread

relentēsc·ō -ere *intr* to slack off, cool off

relev·ō -āre -āvī -ātus *tr* to lighten; to lift up *or* raise again; *(fig)* to relieve, ease the pain of; to lessen in force; to soothe

relicti·ō -ōnis *f* abandonment

relictus *pp of* **relinquō ‖** *adj* abandoned, forsaken

relicuus *see* **reliquus**

relīd·ō -ere *tr* to dash back *(in the direction from which s.th. came)*

religāti·ō -ōnis *f* tying back *or* up

religi·ō -ōnis *f* religion; religious scruple, sense of right, conscience; misgivings; reverence, awe; sanctity, holiness; sect, cult; mode of worship; object of veneration, sacred object, sacred place; divine service, worship, ceremonies; religious practice, ritual; *(pej)* taboo; superstition; manifestation of divine sanction; *(w. gen)* scruple about, scrupulous regard for

religiōsē *adv* religiously, reverently, piously; scrupulously, conscientiously, carefully, exactly

religiōs·us -a -um *adj* religious, reverent, pious, devout; scrupulous, conscientious, exact, precise, accurate; superstitious; sacred, holy, consecrated; subject to religious claims, under religious liability

relig·ō -āre -āvī -ātus *tr* to tie back, tie up; to moor *(ship);* to untie, unfasten; to bind *(with a wreath, ribbon)*

re·linō -linere -lēvī *tr* to unseal, uncork

re·linquō -linquere -līquī -lictus *tr* to leave behind, not take along; to bequeath; to let remain; to leave alive; to forsake, abandon, leave in the lurch; to relinquish, resign; to leave unmentioned; **in mediō** *(or* **in medium) relinquere** to leave *(a question)* open; **locum integrum relinquere** to leave the place untouched

reliqu·ī -ōrum *mpl* the rest, the others; the survivors; posterity

reliqui·ae -ārum *fpl* remains, remnants, leftovers

reliqu·us -a -um *adj (also* **-cuus)** remaining, left over, left; subsequent, future *(time);* outstanding *(debt)* **‖** *mpl see* **reliquī ‖** *n* remainder, rest, residue; **in reliquum** in the future, for the future; **nihil reliquī facere** to leave nothing undone, leave no stone unturned; **reliquum est** *(w. inf or* **ut)** it only remains to; **reliquum aliquid facere** *(or* **aliquid reliquī facere)** to leave s.th. behind, neglect s.th.

rellig- = **relig-**

relliq- = **reliq-**

relū·ceō -cēre -xī *intr* to reflect light, gleam, shine out, blaze

relū·cēscō -cēscere -xī *intr* to grow bright again, clear

reluct·or -ārī -ātus sum *intr* to fight back, put up a struggle, resist; to be reluctant

remacrēsc·ō -ere *intr* to shrink and become thin

remaledīc·ō -ere *intr* to return abuse

remand·ō -ere *tr* to chew again

reman·eō -ēre -sī -sum *intr* to stay behind; to remain, continue *(in a certain state)*

remān·ō -āre *intr* to flow back

remānsi·ō -ōnis *f* staying behind

remed·ium -(i)ī *n* remedy, cure

remēnsus *pp of* **remētior**

reme·ō -āre -āvī -ātus *tr* to retrace, relive **‖** *intr* to go back, come back, return

re·mētior -mētīrī -mēnsus sum *tr* to remeasure; to retrace, go back over

rēm·ex -igis *m* rower, crew member; **rēmigēs -um** *mpl* crew

Rēm·ī -ōrum *mpl* a people of Gaul *(near modern Rheims)*

rēmigāti·ō -ōnis *f* rowing

rēmig·ium -(i)ī *n* rowing; oars; oarsmen, rowers; **rēmigium ālārum** *(poet)* flapping of wings

rēmig·ō -āre -āvī *intr* to row

remigr·ō -āre -āvī -ātum *intr* to move back; **domum remigrāre** to move back home

reminīsc·or -ī *tr* to call to mind, remember **‖** *intr* to remember; *(w. gen)* to be mindful of, be conscious of, remember

re·mīsceō -mīscēre — -mixtus *tr* to mix up, intermingle; **vērīs falsa remīscēre** to mix in lies with the truth

remissē *adv* mildly, gently

remissi·ō -ōnis *f* release; easing, letting down, lowering; relaxing *(of muscles);* relaxation, recreation; mildness, gentleness; submissiveness; abating, diminishing; remission *(of debts)*

remiss·us -a -um *adj* relaxed, loose, slack; mild, gentle; remiss; easy-going, indulgent; gay, merry, light; low, cheap *(price);* **remissiōre ūtī genere dīcendī** to speak in a lighter vein

re·mittō -mittere -mīsī -missus *tr* to send back; to release; to slacken, loosen; to emit, produce, let out, give off; to return, restore; to reecho *(a voice);* to give up, reject, resign, concede; to relax, relieve *(the mind);* to pardon; to remit, *(penalty, debt, obligation);* *(w. inf)* to stop *(doing s.th.);* **frontem** *(or* **ōs** *or* **vultum) remittere** to relax the tense expression; **loquī remittere** to stop speaking; **nihil remittere** to spare no effort; **repudium remittere** to send a notice of divorce **‖** *intr (of wind, rain)* to let up, slack off

remīxtus *pp of* **remīsceō**

remōlior 367 reparō

remōl·ior -īrī -ītus sum *tr* to push *or* move back *or* away, heave back
remollēsc·ō -ere *intr* to soften again; to weaken
remoll·iō -īre -īvī -ītus *tr* to soften
remor·a -ae *f* hindrance, delay
remorāmin·a -um *npl* hindrances, delays
remor·deō -dēre -dī -sus *tr* to bite back; to attack in return; to worry, nag
remor·or -ārī -ātus sum *tr* to hinder, delay, hold back ‖ *intr* to loiter, linger, delay, stay behind
remōtē *adv* at a distance, far away
remōti·ō -ōnis *f* withdrawal; removal, elimination *(of a condition); remōtiō crīminis the shifting of a charge
remōt·us -a -um *adj* removed, out of the way, far off, remote, distant; *(fig)* remote, apart, separate; dead; *(w. ab)* 1 removed from, separate from, apart from; 2 clear of, free from; iocō remōtō all joking aside
re·moveō -movēre -mōvī -mōtus *tr* to move back, withdraw; to put away; to remove; to shroud, veil; *(fig)* to put out of sight, set aside, abolish; aliquem ā vītā removēre to kill s.o. ‖ *refl* to withdraw, retire
remūg·iō -īre *intr* to bellow back; *(fig)* to reecho, resound
remul·ceō -cēre -sī -sus *tr* to stroke, smooth back; caudam remulcēre to put the tail between the legs *(in fear)*
remulc·um -ī *n* towline, towrope
Remul·us -ī *m* a king of Alba Longa
remūnerāti·ō -ōnis *f* remuneration, recompense, reward
remūner·or -ārī -ātus sum *or* remūner·ō -āre *tr* to repay, remunerate
Remūri·a -ōrum *npl* (Le-) festival held in May to appease the spirits of the dead
remurmur·ō -āre *tr* & *intr* to murmur in reply
rēm·us -ī *m* oar; ad rēmōs dare to assign *(s.o.)* as rower; rēmī corporis *(fig)* hands and feet *(of a swimmer);* rēmīs by rowing; rēmīs incumbere to lean to the oars
Rem·us -ī *m* twin brother of Romulus, killed by him
renārr·ō -āre *tr* retell
re·nāscor -nāscī -nātus sum *intr* to be born again; to rise again, spring up again, be restored; to reappear; to recur
renāvig·ō -āre *intr* to sail back
ren·eō -ēre *tr* to unravel, undo
rēn·ēs -(i)um *mpl* kidneys
renīd·ēns -entis *adj* beaming, glad
renīd·eō -ēre *intr* to reflect (light), glitter, shine; to smile, grin all over; to beam with joy
renīdēsc·ō -ere *intr* to grow bright, gleam, begin to glitter

renī·tor -tī *intr* to fight back, put up a struggle, resist
ren·ō -āre -āvī *intr* to swim back, float back
rēn·ō -ōnis *m* (rhē-) reindeer skin *(used for clothing)*
renōd·ō -āre -āvī -ātus *tr* to tie back in a knot; to untie
renovām·en -inis *n* renewal, new form
renovāti·ō -ōnis *f* renovation, renewal; revision; *(fin)* compound interest
renov·ō -āre -āvī -ātus *tr* to make new again; to renovate, repair, restore; to plow up *(a fallow field);* to reopen *(a wound);* to revive *(an old custom, etc.);* to start *(a battle)* all over again; to refresh *(the memory);* to repeat, keep repeating, reaffirm; faenus renovāre in singulōs annōs *(fin)* to compound the interest on a yearly basis
renumer·ō -āre -āvī -ātus *tr* to count over again, recount; to pay back, repay
renūntiāti·ō -ōnis *f* formal *or* official report, announcement
renūnti·ō -āre -āvī -ātus *tr* to report; to announce; to retract *(a promise, statement);* to renounce *(an alliance, a friendship);* to reject; to call off *(a previous engagement);* *(w. dat)* to call off *(e.g., friendship, association, luncheon)* with *(s.o.);* *(w. double acc)* to announce *or* declare *(s.o.)* elected as; *(w. acc & inf)* to bring back word that; lēgātiōnem renūntiāre *(of an ambassador)* to give an account of an embassy; repudium renūntiāre to break off an engagement, send a letter of divorce; sibi renūntiāre to say to oneself, remind oneself ‖ *intr* to take back a message; *(w. dat)* to withdraw from, renounce, give up
renūnt·ius -(i)ī *m* reporter
renu·ō -ere -ī *tr* to nod refusal to, turn down, decline, say no to, reject ‖ *intr* to shake the head in refusal; *(w. dat)* to say no to, deny *(a charge)*
renūt·ō -āre -āvī *intr* to refuse emphatically
reor rērī ratus sum *tr* to think, deem; to reckon, calculate; *(w. acc & inf)* to think that; *(w. acc & adj as objective complement)* to regard *(s.th.)* as ‖ *intr* to think, suppose
repāgul·a -ōrum *npl* bolts, bars; *(fig)* restraints, regulations, rules, limits
repand·us -a -um *adj* curved backwards, concave; *(shoes)* with turned-up toes
reparābil·is -is -e *adj* capable of being repaired, reparable, retrievable
reparc·ō -ere repersī *intr* *(w. dat)* to be sparing with, take it easy on
repar·ō -āre -āvī -ātus *tr* to get again, acquire again; to recover, retrieve, make good; to restore, renew; to repair; to recruit *(a new

army); **vīna merce reparāre** to get wine in exchange for wares, barter for wine

repastināti·ō -ōnis *f* the act of turning *(the ground)* over again for planting

repastin·ō -āre -āvī -ātus *tr* to turn *(the ground)* over again for planting

re·pectō -pectere -pexī -pexus *tr* to comb back; to comb again

repellō repellere reppulī repulsus *tr* to drive back, push back, repel; to reject; to remove; to refute

repen·dō -dere -pendī -pēnsus *tr* to repay, pay back; to ransom; *(fig)* to repay in kind, requite, recompense, reward; to compensate for; to balance, balance out; **magna rependere** to pay back in full

rēp·ēns -entis *pres p of* **rēpō**

rep·ēns -entis *adj* sudden, unexpected; completely new

repēnsus *pp of* **rependō**

repente *adv* suddenly, all of a sudden; unexpectedly

repentīnō *adv* suddenly; unexpectedly, without warning

repentīn·us -a -um *adj* sudden, unexpected; hasty, impetuous

reperc·ō -ere *intr (w. dat)* **1** to be sparing with; **2** to refrain from

repercussī *perf of* **repercutiō**

repercuss·us -a -um *pp of* **repercutiō ‖** *adj* rebounding; reflected, reflecting; echoed, echoing

repercuss·us -ūs *m* reverberation, echo, repercussion; reflection

reper·cutiō -cutere -cussī -cussus *tr* to make *(s.th.)* rebound, make reverberate, make reflect

reperiō reperīre repperī repertus *tr* to find, discover; to find again; to get, procure, win; to find out, ascertain, realize; to invent, devise

repertīci·us -a -um *adj* newly discovered

repert·or -ōris *m* discoverer, inventor, author

repert·us -a -um *pp of* **reperiō ‖** *npl* discoveries, inventions

repetīti·ō -ōnis *f* repetition; *(w. in + acc)* going back to; *(rhet)* anaphora

repetīt·or -ōris *m* claimant

repet·ō -ere -īvī *or* **-iī -ītus** *tr* to head back to, try to reach again, return to; to aim at again; to fetch back; to attack again; to persecute again; to demand anew; to demand back, claim, demand in compensation, retake; to trace back, retrace; to trace in thought, think over, recall, recollect; to repeat, undertake again, resume, renew; **animō** *(or* **memoriā)** **repetere** to recall; **lēx dē pecūniīs** *(or* **rēbus) repetundīs** law on extortion *(literally, law concerning recovering money or property);*

memoriam repetere to recall the memory; **pecūniam repetere** to sue for the recovery of money; **poenam** *(or* **poenās) repetere** to demand satisfaction; **rēs repetere** to sue for the recovery of property; **reus pecūniārum repetundārum** guilty of extortion **‖** *intr (w. ad)* to head back to

repetund·ae -ārum *fpl* money extorted; extortion; **repetundārum arguī** to be charged with extortion; **repetundārum tenērī** to be held on an extortion charge

repexus *pp of* **repectō**

repl·eō -ēre -ēvī -ētus *tr* **(reppl-)** to refill, replenish; to fill to the brim; to make up for, replace, compensate for; *(mil)* to recruit, bring *(an army)* to full strength

replēt·us -a -um *pp of* **repleō ‖** *adj* filled, full; *(of the body)* well-filled out; *(w. abl or gen)* **1** full of; **2** fully endowed with

replicāti·ō -ōnis *f* folding back, rolling back, rolling up; reflex action

replic·ō -āre -āvī -ātus *tr* to fold back, turn back; to unfold

rēp·ō -ere -sī *intr* to crawl, creep

re·pōnō -pōnere -posuī -positus *or* **-postus** *tr* to put back, set back, lay *(e.g., the head)* back; to replace; to restore; to substitute; to lay out, stretch out *(the body);* to lay aside, store, keep, preserve; to renew, repeat; to place, class; to repay, requite; **in scēptra repōnere** to reinstate in power; **membra repōnere** *(w. ab or in + abl)* to stretch out on *(e.g., a bed);* **sē in cubitum repōnere** to rest on one's elbow; **spem repōnere** *(w. in + abl)* to put one's hopes in *or* on, count on

report·ō -āre -āvī -ātus *tr* to bring back; to report; **victōriam reportāre** to win a victory

repōsc·ō -ere *tr* to demand back; to ask for, claim, require, demand

repos(i)t·us -a -um *pp of* **repōnō ‖** *adj* out-of-the-way, remote

repositōr·ium -(i)ī *n* large serving dish

repost·or -ōris *m* restorer

repostus *pp of* **repōnō**

repōti·a -ōrum *npl* second round of drinks, seconds

repperī *perf of* **reperiō**

reppulī *perf of* **repellō**

repraesentāti·ō -ōnis *f* vivid presentation; *(fin)* cash payment

repraesent·ō -āre -āvī -ātus *tr* to present again, show, exhibit, display, depict; to do immediately, accomplish instantly; to rush, speed up *(e.g., plans);* to anticipate; to pay in cash; to apply *(medicines)* immediately

reprehen·dō *or* **repren·dō -dere -ī -sus** *tr* to hold back; to restrain, check; to blame, find fault with, criticize; to refute; *(leg)* to prosecute, convict, condemn

repre(hē)nsi·ō -ōnis *f* checking, check; finding fault, blame, criticism, rebuke; *(rhet)* refutation; *(rhet)* self-correction

reprehēns·ō -āre *tr* to hold back (continually *or* eagerly *or* strongly)

reprehēns·or -ōris *m* critic, censurer

reprendō *see* **reprehendō**

reprēnsō *see* **reprehēnsō**

repress·or -ōris *m* one who represses, restrainer

re·primō -primere -pressī -pressus *tr* to hold back, keep back; to restrain, limit, confine, curb, repress, suppress ‖ *refl* to control oneself; *(w.* **ab**) to refrain from

reprōmissi·ō -ōnis *f* counter promise, promise in return

reprō·mittō -mittere -mīsī -missus *tr* to promise in return ‖ *intr (leg) (w. dat)* to make a counter-promise to *(s.o.)*

rept·ō -āre -āvī -ātum *intr* to crawl around

repudiāti·ō -ōnis *f* repudiation; refusal, rejection; refusal to approve a policy

repudi·ō -āre -āvī -ātus *tr* to repudiate, scorn; to refuse, reject; to jilt; to divorce

repudiōs·us -a -um *adj* objectionable, offensive

repud·ium -(i)ī *n* repudiation, separation, divorce; **repudium renūntiāre** *(or* **remittere)** *(w. dat)* to send a letter of divorce to

repuerāsc·ō -ere *intr* to become a child again; to behave childishly

repugn·āns -antis *adj* contradictory, inconsistent ‖ *npl* contradictions, inconsistencies

repugnanter *adv* reluctantly

repugnanti·a -ae *f* contradiction, inconsistency; conflicting demands; incompatibility

repugn·ō -āre -āvī -ātum *intr* to fight back; *(w. dat)* **1** to oppose, offer opposition to, fight against, be against; **2** to disagree with, be inconsistent with, be incompatible with; *(w.* **contrā** + *acc)* to fight against

repuls·a -ae *f* defeat at the polls; rebuff, cold shoulder; **repulsa cōnsulātūs** defeat in running for the consulship; **repulsam ferre** to suffer a defeat, lose an election

repuls·āns -antis *adj* throbbing; reechoing

repuls·us -a -um *pp of* **repellō** ‖ *adj* rejected, spurned

repuls·us -ūs *m* reverberation, echo

repung·ō -ere *tr* to goad again

repurg·ō -āre -āvī -ātus *tr* to clean again; to purge away, remove

reputāti·ō -ōnis *f* rethinking, reconsideration, review; subject of thought, reflection

reput·ō -āre -āvī -ātus *tr* to think over, reflect upon, reconsider; to count back, calculate

requi·ēs -ētis *f* rest, relief; relaxation; break, pause, intermission; recreation, amusement, hobby; *(w. gen)* rest from

requi·ēscō -ēscere -ēvī -ētus *tr* to put to rest, quiet down, calm down ‖ *intr* to rest, take a rest; to come to rest, stop, end; to relax; to find peace, be consoled, find relief; to rest, lie quietly, sleep; *(of the dead)* to rest, sleep

requiēt·us -a -um *adj* rested up

requīrit·ō -āre *tr* to keep asking for; to be on a constant lookout for

re·quīrō -quīrere -quīsīvī *or* **-quīsiī -quīsītus** *tr* to look for, search for, hunt for; to miss; to ask; to ask for, demand, require; *(w.* **ab** *or* **dē** + *abl)* to ask *or* demand *(s.th.)* from *or* of

requīsītum -ī *n* a need

rēs reī *or* **rēī** *f* thing; matter, affair; object; cirumstance; event, occurrence; deed; condition, case; reality, truth, fact; property, possessions; wealth; estate, effects; benefit, advantage, interest, profit; business affair, transaction; cause, reason, motive, ground; historical event; theme, topic, subject matter; *(leg)* case, suit; *(mil)* operation, campaign, battle; *(pol)* state, government, politics; **ab rē** contrary to interests, disadvantageous, useless; **ad rem pertinēre** to be relevant to the matter at hand; **ex rē** according to circumstances, according to the situation; **ex rē istīus** for his good; **ex rē pūblicā** for the common good, in the public interest; **ex tuā rē** to your advantage; **in rē** *(or* **rē ipsā** *or* **rē vērā)** in fact, in reality; **in rē praesentī** on the spot; **in rem** for the good, useful, advantageous; **in rem praesentem** on the spot; **nīl ad rem est** *(frequently with ellipsis of* **est)** it is not to the point, it is irrelevant; **ob eam rem** for that reason; **ob rem** to the purpose, for the good, advantageous; **prō rē** according to circumstances; **quae rēs?** what's that? what are you talking about?; **rē** in fact, in practice, in reality, actually, really; **rem agere** *(leg)* to conduct a case; **rem gerere** *(mil)* to conduct a military operation; **rem solvere** to settle a matter; **rēs capitālis** *(or* **rēs capitis)** *(leg)* a case involving the death penalty *or* loss of civil rights; **rēs familiāris** private property; **rēs frūmentāria** grain situation; grain supply; foraging; **rēs iūdiciāria** administration of justice, department of justice; **rēs mihi tēcum est** I have some business with you; **rēs pecuāria et rūstica** livestock; **rēs rūstica** agriculture; **rēs pūblica** state, government, politics, public life, commonwealth, country; **rēs sit mihi cum hīs** let me handle them; **rēs solī** real property, real estate *(as contrasted with* **rēs mōbilis);** **rēs uxōria** marriage; dowry; **rēs Veneris** sexual intercourse, love making ‖ *fpl* physical phenomena; property; affairs, public affairs; **rērum** *(w. superl adj)* the best in the world: **rērum facta est pulcherrima Rōma** Rome became the most beautiful city in the world; **rērum potīrī** to get control of the government; **rērum scrīptor** historian, annalist; **rēs gestae** exploits, accomplishments, military achievements; **rēs novae** revolution; **rēs Persicae** Persian history, Parthian history; **rēs populī Rōmānī perscrībere** to write (in full) a history of the Roman people; **rēs prōlātae** business adjourned *(for the holiday);* **rēs pūblicās inīre** to enter politics; **rēs secundae** prosperity; **summa rērum** world; universe; **tibi rēs tuās habē** *(formula for divorce)* take your things and go!

resacr·ō *or* **resecr·ō -āre** *tr* to ask again for; to free from a curse

resaevi·ō -īre *intr* to go wild again

resalūtāti·ō -ōnis *f* a greeting in return

resalūt·ō -āre -āvī -ātus *tr* to greet in return

resān·ēscō -ēscere -uī *intr* to heal again

resar·ciō -cīre -sī -tus *or* **-sus** *tr* to patch up; to repair; to make good *(a loss)*

re·scindō -scindere -scidī -scissus *tr* to tear off; to cut down; to tear open; to rescind, repeal; *(fig)* to expose

re·scīscō -scīscere -scīvī *or* **-sciī -scītus** *tr* to find out, learn, ascertain

re·scrībō -scrībere -scrīpsī -scrīptus *tr* to write back in reply; to rewrite, revise; to enlist, enroll; to pay back, repay ‖ *intr* to write a reply

rēscrīpt·um -ī *n* imperial rescript

resec·ō -āre -uī -tus *tr* (**-sic-**) to cut back, cut short; to reap; *(fig)* to trim, curtail; **ad vīvum resecāre** to cut to the quick

resecr·ō *see* **resacrō**

resectus *pp of* **resecō**

resecūtus *pp of* **resequor**

resēmin·ō -āre *tr* to sow again; *(poet)* to reproduce

re·sequor -sequī -secūtus sum *tr* to reply to, answer

reser·ō -āre -āvī -ātus *tr* to unlock, unbar, open; to disclose; to begin *(a year)*

reserv·ō -āre -āvī -ātus *tr* to reserve, hold back; to spare; to hold on to; to store

res·es -idis *adj* remaining, left over; lazy, idle, inactive; slow, sluggish; calm

re·sideō -sidēre -sēdī *intr* to sit down, settle back; to sink down, settle, subside; to calm down

re·sīdō -sīdere -sēdī *or* **-sīdī** *intr* to sit down; *(of a person lying down)* to sit up; *(of birds)* to perch; *(after rising or climbing)* to fall back, sink back; *(of things)* to come to rest, lodge; *(of colonists)* to settle; *(of water)* to go down, subside; *(of swellings)* to go down, shrink; *(of natural features)* to dip (down); *(of wind, flame, rain)* to die down; *(of a per-*

son) to quiet down; *(of activity, condition)* to diminish in intensity, abate; *(mil)* to encamp

residu·us -a -um *adj* remaining, left; in arrears, outstanding *(money)* ‖ *n* the remainder, the rest

resign·ō -āre -āvī -ātus *tr* to unseal, open; to disclose; to give up, resign; to annul, cancel; to destroy *(confidence)*

resil·iō -īre -uī *or* **-iī** *intr* to spring back, jump back; to recoil; to contract

resīm·us -a -um *adj* turned-up, snub

rēsīn·a -ae *f* resin *(secreted by various trees, used to preserve and season wine, used as a depilatory, etc.)*

rēsināt·us -a -um *adj* rubbed with resin, resined

resip·iō -ere *tr* to taste of, taste like, have the flavor of

resip·īscō -īscere -īvī *or* **-iī** *or* **-uī** *intr* to come to one's senses

resist·ēns -entis *adj* firm, tough

re·sistō -sistere -stitī *intr* to stand still, stop, pause; to stay, stay behind, remain; to resist, put up resistance; to rise again; *(w. dat)* **1** to be opposed to, resist; **2** to reply to

resolūt·us -a -um *adj* loose, limp; effeminate

re·solvō -solvere -solvī -solūtus *tr* to untie, unfasten, undo; to open; to dissolve, melt, thaw; to relax *(the body);* to stretch out *(the limbs);* to unravel; to cancel; to dispel; to unnerve, enervate; to release, set free

resonābil·is -is -e *adj* resounding, answering *(echo)*

reson·āns -antis *adj* echoing

reson·ō -āre -āvī *tr* to repeat, reecho, resound with, make ring ‖ *intr* to resound, ring, reecho; *(w. **ad**)* to resound in answer to

reson·us -a -um *adj* resounding, re-echoing

resorb·eō -ēre *tr* to suck in, swallow again

respargō *see* **respergō**

respect·ō -āre *tr* to look back on; to keep an eye on, care for; to have regard for, respect; to gaze at, look at ‖ *intr* to look back; to look around

respectus *pp of* **respiciō**

respect·us -ūs *m* backward glance, looking back; looking around; refuge; respect, regard, consideration; **respectum habēre** *(w. dat or* **ad**) to have respect for

resper·gō -gere -sī -sus *tr* (**-spar-**) to sprinkle, splash, spray; to defile

respersi·ō -ōnis *f* sprinkling, splashing

respersus *pp of* **respergō**

re·spiciō -spicere -spexī -spectus *tr* to look back at, see behind oneself; to look around for; to look back upon *(the past, etc.);* to look at, gaze at; to regard, contemplate, consider; to notice; to look after, take care of, see to; to respect **ǁ** *intr* to look back; to look around; *(w.* **ad)** to look at, gaze at

respīrām·en -inis *n* respiration, breathing; exhalation; letup, rest, pause *(to catch one's breath),* breathing space

respīrāti·ō -ōnis *f* respiration, breathing; breathing pause; *(fig)* exhalation, emission of vapor

respīrāt·us -ūs *m* respiration

respīr·ō -āre -āvī -ātus *tr* to breathe, breathe out, exhale **ǁ** *intr* to breathe, take a breath, breathe again; to recover *(from fright, etc.); (of combat, passions, etc.)* to slack off, die down, subside; **ā continuīs clādībus respīrāre** to catch one's breath again after continuous disasters; **ā metū respīrāre** to recover from a shock

resplend·eō -ēre *intr* to glitter

respon·deō -dēre -dī -sus *tr* to answer; to say in reply; to say in refutation; **ficta respondēre** to make up answers; **hōc quod rogō respondē** answer my question; **multa respondēre** to give a lengthy reply; **pār parī respondēre** to give tit for tat; **verbum verbō respondēre** to answer word for word **ǁ** *intr* to answer, reply; *(of officials, seers, priests)* to give an official *or* formal reply; to echo; to satisfy the claims *(of a creditor); (leg)* to answer a summons to appear in court; *(of lawyers)* to give an opinion, give legal advice; *(of priests)* to give a response *(from a god); (w. dat)* **1** to answer, reply to; **2** to match, balance, correspond to, be equal to; **3** to resemble; **4** to measure up to; **amōrī amōre respondēre** to return love for love; **nōminibus respondēre** to pay off debts

respōnsi·ō -ōnis *f* response, answer, reply; refutation; *(rhet)* **sibi ipsī respōnsiō** a reply to one's own arguments

respōnsit·ō -āre -āvī *intr* to give professional legal advice

respōns·ō -āre *intr* to answer, reply; to reecho; *(w. dat)* **1** to answer to, agree with; **2** to resist, defy; **3** to talk back to *(in disobedience)*

respōns·or -ōris *m* respondent

respōns·us -a -um *pp of* **respondeō ǁ** *n* answer, response; oracular response; *(leg)* professional advice; **respōnsum auferre** *(or* **ferre)** *(w. ab)* to receive an answer from; **respōnsum referre** to deliver an answer

rēspūblica reīpūblicae *f* state, government, politics, public life, commonwealth, country; **rempūblicam inīre** to enter politics; *(see also* **rēs pūblica** *under* **rēs)**

respu·ō -ere -ī *tr* to spit out; to cast out, eject, expel; to refuse, to reject

restagn·ō -āre *intr* to form pools; to run over, overflow; to be inundated

restaur·ō -āre -āvī -ātus *tr* to restore, rebuild; to renew, take up again

resticul·a -ae *f* thin rope, cord

restīncti·ō -ōnis *f* quenching

restin·guō -guere -xī -ctus *tr* to quench, extinguish, put out; to snuff out; to exterminate, destroy

resti·ō -ōnis *f* rope dealer; *(hum)* roper *(person who is whipped with ropes)*

restipulāti·ō -ōnis *f* counterclaim

restipul·or -ārī -ātus sum *tr* to stipulate in return **ǁ** *intr* to make a counterclaim

rest·is -is *f (acc:* **restem** *or* **restim)** rope

restit·ō -āre *intr* to stay behind, lag behind; to keep offering resistance

restitr·īx -īcis *f* a stay-at-home *(female)*

resti·tuō -tuere -tuī -tūtus *tr* to set up again; to restore, rebuild, reconstruct; to renew, reestablish, revive; to bring back, restore, reinstate; to give back, return, replace; to restore, repair, remedy; to reenact *(a law);* to reverse; to revoke, undo, cancel, make void; to make good, compensate for, repair

restitūti·ō -ōnis *f* restoration; reinstatement, pardon; recall *(from exile)*

restitūt·or -ōris *m* restorer, rebuilder

restitūtus *pp of* **restituō**

re·stō -stāre -stitī *intr* to stand firm, stand one's ground, resist; to stay behind, stay in reserve; to be left over **ǁ** *v impers (w. inf or* **ut)** it remains to *(do s.th.)*

restrictē *adv* sparingly; exactly, precisely

restrict·us -a -um *pp of* **restringō ǁ** *adj* tied back, tight; stingy; moderate, strict, stern

re·stringō -stringere -strīnxī -strictus *tr* to tie *(the hands, arms)* behind one; to draw tight, tie; to tighten; to draw back the cover from *(s.th. concealed); (of dogs)* to show *(the teeth); (fig)* to restrain; *(fig)* to restrict the activity of

resūd·ō -āre *intr* to sweat, ooze

result·ō -āre *intr* to rebound; to resound, reverberate

resūm·ō -ere -psī -ptus *tr* to resume; to recover *(strength)*

resu·ō -ere -uī -ūtus *tr* to undo the stitching of

resupīn·ō -āre -āvī -ātus *tr* to throw *(s.o.)* on his back, throw over, throw down; *(coll)* to knock for a loop; to break down *(door)*

resupīn·us -a -um *adj* lying on the back; bent back, thrown back; leaning backward; proud *(gait)*

resur·gō -gere -rēxī -rēctum *intr* to rise again; to appear again

resūscit·ō -āre *tr* to resuscitate

retardāti·ō -ōnis *f* retardation

retard·ō -āre -āvī -ātus *tr* to retard, slow down, hold back, delay; to keep back, check, hinder **ǁ** *intr* to lag behind

retax·ō -āre *tr* to rebuke
rēt·e -is *n* net; *(fig)* trap
re·tegō -tegere -tēxī -tēctus *tr* to uncover; to unclothe, expose; to open; to reveal, make visible; to disclose *(secrets)*
retempt·ō -āre -āvī -ātus *tr* to attempt again, try again; to test again
reten·dō -dere -dī -tus *or* -sus *tr* to release from tension, unbend, relax
retenti·ō -ōnis *f* holding back; slowing down; withholding *(assent)*
retent·ō -āre *tr* to hold back, hold tight; to attempt again; to retain the loyalty of; to keep *(feelings)* in check
retentus *pp of* retendō *and* retineō
retēxī *perf of* retegō
retex·ō -ere -uī -tus *tr* to unravel; to cancel, reverse, annul, undo; to weave anew; to renew, repeat; to correct, revise; to retract *(words)*
rēti·a -ae *f* net
rētiār·ius -(i)ī *m* net-man *(gladiator who tried to entangle his opponent in a net)*
reticenti·a -ae *f* reticence; *(rhet)* abrupt pause; poena reticentiae punishment for suppression of truth
retic·eō -ēre -uī *tr* to be silent about, suppress, keep secret ‖ *intr* to be silent, keep silent; *(w. dat)* to make no answer to
rēticulāt·us -a -um *adj* covered with a net; net-shaped, reticulate
rēticul·um -ī *n* small net; hair net; mesh-work bag *(for protecting bottles); racket (for playing ball)*
retinācul·a -ōrum *npl* cable, rope
retin·ēns -entis *adj (w. gen)* clinging to, sticking to
retinenti·a -ae *f* retention
re·tineō -tinēre -tinuī -tentus *tr* to hold back, keep back; to restrain; to keep, retain; to hold in reserve; to preserve, maintain, uphold; to hold, engross *(attention);* to detain, delay
retinn·iō -īre *intr* to ring again, ring out, tinkle in response
reton·ō -āre *intr* to resound
retor·queō -quēre -sī -tus *tr* to twist *or* bend back; to hurl back *(weapons);* mentem retorquēre to change the mind; oculōs retorquēre *(w. ad)* to look back wistfully at
retorrid·us -a -um *adj* parched, dried out, withered; wily, shrewd
retortus *pp of* retorqueō
retractāti·ō -ōnis *f* holding back, hesitation; sine retractātiōne without hesitation
retractāt·us -a -um *adj* revised
retract·ō *or* retrect·ō -āre *tr* to rehandle, take in hand again, undertake once more, take up once more; to reexamine, review; to revise ‖ *intr* to refuse, decline; to be reluctant

retract·us -a -um *adj* remote, distant
retra·hō -here -xī -ctus *tr* to draw back, withdraw, pull back; to bring to light again, make known again; *(fig)* to drag away, remove
retrectō *see* retractō
retrib·uō -uere -uī -ūtus *tr* to hand back; to repay
retrō *adv* backwards, back; to the rear; behind, on the rear; in the past, formerly, back, past; in return; on the contrary, on the other hand; in reverse order *(of words);* counting back to an earlier date, retrospectively; *(w. reference to reasoning)* back to first principles
retro·agō -agere -ēgī -āctus *tr* to drive backward; to reverse the order of, invert; to repeat backwards
retrō·cēdō -dere -cessī -cessum *intr* to move backward; to withdraw, retire
retrōrsum *adv* (-sus) back, backwards, in reverse; in reverse order
retrū·dō -dere — -sus *tr* to push back; to hide, conceal
retundō retundere retudī *(or* rettudī) retūnsus *(or* retūsus) *tr* to pound back; to dull, blunt; *(fig)* to deaden, weaken, repress, restrain
retūns·us *or* retūs·us -a -um *pp of* retundō ‖ *adj* blunt, dull; *(fig)* dull
re·us -ī *m (either of the two parties involved in litigation)* defendant, the accused, plaintiff; convict, criminal, culprit; *(w. gen)* person charged with; in reōs recipere *(or* referre) to list among the accused; reum agere to try a defendant; reum facere to indict, bring a defendant to trial; reum postulāre to prosecute, force to face a trial
reval·ēscō -ēscere -uī *intr* to regain one's strength, recover; to become valid again
re·vehō -vehere -vexī -vectus *tr* to carry back, bring back ‖ *pass* to ride back, drive back; to sail back; *(fig)* to go back *(e.g., to an earlier period)*
re·vellō -vellere -vellī -vulsus *tr* to pull out, pull back, tear off, tear out; to tear up *(the ground),* dig up; *(fig)* to unmask *(deception)*
revēl·ō -āre -āvī -ātus *tr* to unveil, uncover
re·veniō -venīre -vēnī -ventum *intr* to come again, come back, return
rēvērā *adv* in fact, actually
reverber·ō -āre -āvī -ātus *tr* to beat back; to repel
reverend·us -a -um *adj* venerable, awe-inspiring; deserving respect
rever·ēns -entis *adj* reverent, respectful
reverenter *adv* respectfully
reverenti·a -ae *f* reverence, respect
rever·eor -ērī -itus sum *tr* to revere, respect, stand in awe of

reversi·ō -ōnis *f* (**-vor-**) turning back *(before reaching one's destination);* recurrence

revert·ō -ere -ī *or* **re·vertor -vertī -versus sum** *intr* (**-vor-**) to turn back, turn around, come back, return; *(in speaking)* to return, revert

revictus *pp of* **revincō**

revid·eō -ēre *tr* to go back to see

re·vinciō -vincīre -vīnxī -vīnctus *tr* to tie back, tie behind, tie up

re·vincō -vincere -vīcī -victus *tr* to conquer in turn; to refute, convict of falsehood; *(w. acc or gen of the charge)* to convict *(s.o.)* of

revīnctus *pp of* **revinciō**

revir·ēscō -ēscere -uī *intr* to become green again; to grow young again; to grow again, grow strong again, revive

revīs·ō -ere *tr* to revisit; to look back to see ‖ *intr* to come *or* go back; *(w. ad)* **1** to look at again, look back at; **2** to return to, revisit

re·vīvīscō -vīvīscere -vīxī *intr* (**-ēscō**) to come back to life, be restored to life, revive; *(fig)* to recover, gain strength

revocābil·is -is -e *adj* capable of being recalled; **nōn revocābilis** irrevocable

revocām·en -inis *n* recall

revocāti·ō -ōnis *f* calling back, recall; calling away; retraction

revoc·ō -āre -āvī -ātus *tr* to call back, recall; to call off, withdraw *(troops);* to call back *(a performer)* for an encore; to bring back to life, revive; *(leg)* to arraign again; to regain *(strength, etc.);* to resume *(career, studies);* to revoke, retract; to check, control; to cancel; *(w. ad)* to refer, apply, subject, submit *(s.o. or s.th.)* to

revol·ō -āre -āvī *intr* to fly back

revolsus *see* **revulsus**

revolūbil·is -is -e *adj* able to be rolled back; **nōn revolūbilis** irrevocable *(fate)*

revol·vō -vere -vī -ūtus *tr* to roll back, unroll, unwind; to retravel; to unroll, read over, read again *(a scroll);* to reexperience; to go over, think over ‖ *pass* to revolve; to come around again, recur, return

revom·ō -ere -uī *tr* to throw up again, disgorge

revor- = rever-

revorr·ō -ere *tr* to sweep back

revulsus *pp of* **revellō**

rēx rēgis *m* king; patron; queen bee

Rhadamanth·us *or* **Rhadamanth·os -ī** *m* son of Jupiter, brother of Minos, and one of the three judges in the lower world

Rhaet·ī -ōrum *mpl* people of Rhaetia

Rhaeti·a -ae *f* Alpine country between Germany and Italy

Rhamn·ūs -untos *f* Attic deme famous for its statue of Nemesis

Rhamnūsi·us -a -um *adj* of the deme of Rhamnus; **Rhamnūsia virgō** the goddess worshiped at Rhamnus *(i.e., Nemesis)*

rhapsōdi·a -ae *f* Homeric lay, selection from Homer; **rhapsōdia secunda** second book *(of Homer)*

Rhe·a -ae *f* Cybele

Rhe·a Silvi·a -ae *f* daughter of Numitor and mother of Romulus and Remus by Mars, the god of war

rhēd- = raed-

Rhēg·ium -(i)ī *n* (*also* **Rēg-**) town at the toe of Italy

Rhēnān·us -a -um *adj* of *or* on the Rhine

rhēn·ō -ōnis *f* reindeer skin *(used as clothing)*

Rhēn·us -ī *m* the Rhine

Rhēs·us -ī *m* Thracian king who fought as an ally of Troy

rhēt·or -oris *m* rhetorician, teacher of rhetoric; orator

rhētoric·a -ae *or* **rhētoric·ē -ēs** *f* rhetoric, public speaking

rhētoric·a -ōrum *npl* treatise on rhetoric

rhētoricē *adv* rhetorically, in an oratorical manner

rhētoric·us -a -um *adj* rhetorician's, rhetorical; **doctōrēs rhētoricī** professors of rhetoric; **librī rhētoricī** textbooks on rhetoric

rhīnocer·ōs -ōtis *or* **-ōtos** *m* rhinoceros; vessel made of a rhinoceros's tusk; **puerī nāsum rhīnocerōtis habent** the children turn up their noses

rhō *indecl* *n* rho *(seventeenth letter of the Greek alphabet)*

Rhodan·us -ī *m* the Rhone River

Rhodiēns·is -is -e *or* **Rhodi·us -a -um** *adj* Rhodian, of Rhodes ‖ *mpl* Rhodians

Rhodop·ē -ēs *f* mountain range in Thrace

Rhodopēi·us -a -um *adj* Thracian

Rhod·os *or* **Rhod·us -ī** *f* Rhodes *(island off the S.W. coast of Asia Minor)*

Rhoetē·us -a -um *adj* Trojan; of the promontory of Rhoeteum; **Rhoetēus ductor** Aeneas; **Rhoetēum profundum** sea near the promontory of Rhoeteum ‖ *n* promontory on the Dardanelles near Troy

rhomb·us -ī *m* magic wheel; turbot *(fish)*

rhomphae·a -ae *f* long javelin

rhythmic·us -a -um *adj* rhythmical ‖ *m* teacher of prose rhythm

rhythm·os *or* **rhythm·us -ī** *m* rhythm; symmetry

rhyt·ion -iī *n* conical cup *or* urn

rīc·a -ae *f* veil *(worn by Roman women at sacrifice)*

rīcīn·ium -(i)ī *n* short mantle with a cowl

rict·um -ī *n* snout; wide-open mouth

rict·us -ūs *m* snout; wide-open mouth; rīsū rictum dīdūcere to break into a broad grin **ǁ** *mpl* jaws, gaping jaws

rīdeō rīdēre rīsī rīsus *tr* to laugh at, ridicule; to smile upon **ǁ** *intr* to laugh; to smile, grin; *(w. dat or* ad) to smile at, laugh at

rīdibund·us -a -um *adj* laughing

rīdiculāri·us -a -um *adj* funny, laughable **ǁ** *npl* jokes

rīdiculē *adv* jokingly, humorously; ridiculously

rīdiculōs·us -a -um *adj* funny, amusing; ridiculous

rīdicul·us -a -um *adj* funny, amusing, laughable; ridiculous, silly **ǁ** *m* joker, clown **ǁ** *n* joke

rig·ēns -entis *adj* rigid, stiff

rig·eō -ēre -uī *intr* to be stiff, be rigid; to be numb; to stand on end, stand erect; to stand stiff; to be unmoved by entreaties

rig·ēscō -ēscere -uī *intr* to grow stiff, become numbed; to stiffen, harden; to stand on end

rigid·a -ae *f (vulg)* penis in erect state

rigidē *adv* rigorously, severely

rigid·us -a -um *adj* rigid, stiff, hard, inflexible; stern, severe; rough, rude; erect *(penis)*

rig·ō -āre *tr* to wet, moisten, water; to conduct, convey *(water)*

rig·or -ōris *m* stiffness; numbness; cold; hardness; sternness

rigu·us -a -um *adj* constantly flowing, irrigating; well-watered, irrigated; **ǁ** *npl* irrigated areas, flood plain; irrigation ditches

rīm·a -ae *f* crack; chap *(in the skin); (in a law)* loophole; rīmās agere to cause cracks to develop; rīmās dūcere to develop cracks

rīm·or -ārī -ātus sum *tr* to lay open, tear open; to pry into, search, examine; to search for *(facts);* to rummage about for; to ransack; nāribus rīmārī to sniff at; oculīs rīmārī to scrutinize

rīmōs·us -a -um *adj* full of cracks; leaky

ringor ringī *intr* to open the mouth wide; to show the teeth; to snarl; *(fig)* to be snappy

rīp·a -ae *f* river bank; aequoris rīpa seashore

Ripae·us -a -um *adj (also* Rhip-) of the Rhipean mountains; mōns R(h)ipaeus legendary mountain range in the extreme north

rīpul·a -ae *f* riverbank

rīsc·us -ī *m* chest, trunk

rīsiōn·ēs -um *fpl* laughs

rīs·or -ōris *m* scoffer; teaser

rīs·us -ūs *m* laugh, laughter, smile; laughingstock; rīsum continēre to keep from laughing; rīsum movēre *(w. dat)* to make *(s.o.)* laugh; rīsūs captāre to try to make people laugh, try to get a laugh

rīte *adv* according to religious usage; duly, justly, rightly, fitly; in the usual way, customarily

rīt·us -ūs *m* rite, ceremony; custom, habit, way, manner, style; rītū *(w. gen)* in the manner of, like; pecudum rītū like cattle

rīvāl·is -is *m* one who uses the same stream, neighbor; one who uses the same mistress, rival

rīvālit·ās -ātis *f* rivalry

rīvul·us *or* rīvol·us -ī *m* brook

rīv·us -ī *m* brook, stream; artificial watercourse, channel; flow *(of water in the aqueducts)*

rīx·a -ae *f* brawl, fight; squabble

rīx·or -ārī -ātus sum *intr* to brawl, come to blows, fight; to squabble

rōbīginōs·us -a -um *adj* (rub-) rusty; envious

rōbīg·ō -inis *f* rust; blight, mildew; film *(on teeth),* tartar

rōbore·us -a -um *adj* (-bur-) oak

rōbor·ō -āre -āvī -ātus *tr* to strengthen

rōb·ur *or* rōb·us -oris *n* hardwood; oak; prison *(at Rome, also called Tullianum);* objects made of hardwood: lance, club, bench; physical strength, power, toughness; power *(of mind);* best part, flower, choice, cream, élite; stronghold

rōb·us -a -um *adj* red

rōbust·us -a -um *adj* hardwood; oak; robust, strong, tough *(body);* firm, solid *(character)*

rō·dō -dere -sī -sus *tr* to gnaw, gnaw at; to rust, corrode; to say nasty things about, slander, run down

rogāl·is -is -e *adj* of a funeral pyre

rogāti·ō -ōnis *f* proposal, bill *(in the Roman assembly);* request, invitation; *(rhet)* question; rogātiōnem antiquāre to reject a bill; rogātiōnem ferre to introduce a bill; rogātiōnem perferre to pass a bill; rogātiōnem per vim perferre to push through a bill; rogātiōnem suādēre to back, push, *or* speak in favor of a bill; rogātiōnī intercēdere to veto a bill

rogātiuncul·a -ae *f* inconsequential bill; minor question

rogāt·or -ōris *m* proposer *(of a bill to the Roman assembly);* poll clerk *(who collects and counts votes);* beggar

rogāt·us -ūs *m* request

rogitāti·ō -ōnis *f (pol)* bill

rogit·ō -āre -āvī -ātus *tr* to keep asking (for)

rog·ō -āre -āvī -ātus *tr* to ask, ask for, beg, request; to question; to invite; to nominate for election; to bring forward for approval, introduce, propose *(bill); (w. double acc)* to ask *(s.o. for s.th.);* lēgem rogāre to introduce a bill; mīlitēs sacrāmentō rogāre to swear in soldiers; senātōrem sententiam rogāre to ask a senator for his opinion, ask a senator how he votes; **sententiās rogāre** to call the roll *(in the Senate);* **populum rogāre** to ask the people about a bill, to propose *or* introduce a bill; **prīmus sententiam rogārī** to have the honor of being the first *(senator)* to be asked his view, be the first to vote

rog·us -ī *m or* **rog·um -ī** *n* funeral pyre; *(fig)* grave, destruction

Rōm·a -ae *f* Rome; Roma *(goddess of Rome)*

Rōmān·us -a -um *adj* Roman **‖** *mpl* Romans

Rōmule·us -a -um *adj* of Romulus; Roman

Rōmulid·ae -ārum *mpl* descendants of Romulus, Romans

Rōmul·us -a -um *adj* of Romulus; Roman **‖** *m* Romulus *(son of Rhea Silvia and Mars, twin brother of Remus, and founder as well as first king of Rome)*

rōrāri·ī -ōrum *mpl* skirmishers *(light-armed Roman troops who usually initiate an attack and then withdraw)*

rōrid·us -a -um *adj* dewy

rōrif·er -era -erum *adj* dewy, dew-bringing

rōr·ō -āre -āvī -ātus *tr* to drip, trickle, pour drop by drop; to moisten **‖** *intr* to drop dew, scatter dew

rōs rōris *m* dew; moisture; spray; water; teardrop; **rōs Arabus** perfume; **rōs marīnus** *(or* **maris)** rosemary *(see* **rōsmarīnum);** **rōrēs pluviī** drizzle; **rōrēs sanguineī** drops of blood

ros·a -ae *f* rose; rosebush; rose bed; wreath of roses

rosāce·us -a -um *adj (crown)* of roses; **oleum rosāceum** rose oil

rosār·ium -(i)ī *n* rose garden

rōscid·us -a -um *adj* wet with dew; consisting of dew; dewy *(conditions; as epithet of the moon, stars, associated with dew);* moistened, sprayed

Rōsc·ius -(i)ī *m* Lucius Roscius Otho *(Cicero's friend, whose law in 67 B.C. reserved 14 rows of seats in the theater for members of the equestrian order)* **‖** Quintus Roscius *(famous Roman actor and friend of Cicero, d. 62 B.C.)* **‖** Sextus Roscius *(of Ameria, defended by Cicero in a patricide trial in 80 B.C.)*

Rōse·a -ae *or* **Rōsi·a -ae** *f* fertile district between Reate and the Veline Lake

rosēt·um -ī *n* rose bed, rose garden

rose·us -a -um *adj* rose, made of roses; rosecolored *(covering a wide range of reds);* rosy, pink *(dawn, sunset, cheeks, skin)*

Rōse·us -a -um *adj* **(-si-)** of Rosea

rōsmarīn·um -ī *n* rosemary *(shrub used in medicines, in perfumes, and as a seasoning)*

rōstell·um -ī *n* little beak; pointed nose *(of a rodent)*

rōstrāt·us -a -um *adj* beaked; *(ship)* having a pointed bow; **columna rōstrāta** column adorned with the beaks of conquered vessels to commemorate a naval victory; **corōna rōstrāta** navy medal *(awarded to the first man to board an enemy ship)*

rōstr·um -ī *n* bill, beak; snout, muzzle; curved bow *(of ship)* **‖** *npl* rostrum *(in the Roman Forum, so called because it was adorned with the beaks of ships taken from the battle of Antium, 338 B.C.);* **prō rōstrīs ōrātiōnem habēre** to give a speech from the rostrum

rōsus *pp of* **rōdō**

rot·a -ae *f* wheel; potter's wheel; torture wheel; mill wheel; magic wheel; child's hoop; disk *(of a heavenly body);* chariot, car *(of sun, moon, time);* **aquārum rota** water wheel

rot·ō -āre -āvī -ātus *tr* to turn, whirl about **‖** *pass* to roll around; to turn, revolve

rotul·a -ae *f* little wheel

rotundē *adv* smoothly, elegantly

rotundit·ās -ātis *f* roundness

rotund·ō -āre -āvī -ātus *tr* to make round; *(fig)* round off *(numbers)*

rotund·us -a -um *adj* rolling, revolving; round, circular, spherical; rounded, perfect; well-turned, smooth, polished *(style)*

rube·faciō -facere -fēcī -factus *tr* to make red, redden

rub·ēns -entis *adj* red; blushing

rub·eō -ēre *intr* to be red, be ruddy; to be bloody; to blush

ru·ber -bra -brum *adj* red *(including shades of orange);* ruddy; **Saxa Rubra** village on the Via Flaminia N. of Rome; **Mare Rubrum** Red Sea

rub·ēscō -ēscere -uī *intr* to get red, redden; to blush

rubēt·a -ae *f* toad

rubēt·a -ōrum *npl* bramble bushes, thicket of brambles

rube·us -a -um *adj* bramble, of brambles

Rubic·ō(n) -ōnis *m* Rubicon *(small stream marking the boundary between Italy and Cisalpine Gaul)*

rubicundul·us -a -um *adj* reddish

rubicund·us -a -um *adj* red, reddish; ruddy, flushed *(complexion)*

rubid·us -a -um *adj* red; ruddy

rūbīg- = **rōbīg-**

rub·or -ōris *m* redness; blush; bashfulness, sense of shame; shame, disgrace

rubrīc·a -ae *f* red clay; red ochre; red chalk; chapter heading *(of book of law, painted red)*

rub·us -ī *m* bramble bush; blackberry bush; blackberry

rūctātr·īx -īcis *adj (fem only) (of foods)* that causes belching

rūct·ō -āre -āvī -ātus *or* **rūct·or -ārī -ātus sum** *tr* & *intr* to belch

rūct·us -ūs *m* belch, belching

rud·ēns -entis *m* rope **‖** *mpl* rigging

Rudi·ae -ārum *fpl* town in Calabria in S. Italy *(birthplace of Ennius)*

rudiār·ius -(i)ī *m* retired gladiator

rudīment·um -ī *n* first attempt, beginning; early training; **rudīmentum adulēscentiae pōnere** to pass the beginning of his youth; **rudīmentum mīlitāre** basic training **‖** *npl* first lessons; fruits of one's early training

Rudīn·us -ā -um *adj* of Rudiae *(a town in Calabria)*

rud·is -is -e *adj* in the natural state; raw, undeveloped, rough, wild, unformed; inexperienced, unskilled, ignorant; uncultured, uncivilized; unsophisticated; *(of land)* not yet cultivated, virgin; *(of wool)* uncombed; *(of artefacts)* crude, roughly fashioned; *(of movement)* awkward, clumsy; *(of fruit)* unripe; *(of animals)* unbroken; *(of recruits)* raw; *(of literary works)* crude, unpolished, rough; *(w. gen or abl, w.* **ad** + *acc or* **in** + *abl)* inexperienced in, ignorant of, awkward at

rud·is -is *f* stick; rod; practice sword; wooden sword *(presented to a retiring gladiator)*

rud·ō -ere -īvī -ītum *intr* (**rūd-**) to roar, bellow; *(of a donkey)* to bray; *(of inanimate things)* to creak loudly

rud·or -ōris *m* roar, bellow

rūd·us -eris *n* crushed stone; rubble; piece of brass

Rūful·ī -ōrum *mpl* military tribunes appointed by a general *(as opposed to military tribunes elected by the people)*

rūful·us -a -um *adj* reddish

rūf·us -a -um *adj* red; red-haired **‖ Rūfus** *m* frequent Roman family name *(cognomen)*

rūg·a -ae *f* wrinkle; crease, small fold; shallow groove

rūg·iō -īre *intr* to bellow, roar

rūg·ō -āre *intr* to become wrinkled, become creased

rūgōs·us -a -um *adj* wrinkled, shriveled; corrugated

ruīn·a -ae *f* tumbling down, fall; collapse; debris, ruins; crash; catastrophe, disaster, destruction; defeat; wrecker, destroyer; *(fig)* downfall, ruin; *(fig)* source of ruin *or* destruction; **ruīnam dare** *(or* **trahere)** to fall with a crash

ruīnōs·us -a -um *adj* liable to ruin, going to ruin, tumbling; ruined, dilapidated

Rull·us -ī *m* Roman family name *(cognomen)*, *esp.* Publius Servilius Rullus *(whose agrarian bill was defeated by Cicero in 63 B.C.)*

rum·ex -icis *mf* sorrel *(grown as a vegetable, used in salads)*

rūmifer·ō -āre *tr* to carry reports of

rūmific·ō -āre *tr* to report

Rūmīn·a -ae *f* Roman goddess who was worshiped near the fig tree under which the she-wolf had suckled Romulus and Remus

Rūmīnāl·is -is -e *adj* **fīcus Rūmīnālis** fig tree of Romulus and Remus

rūmināti·ō -ōnis *f* chewing the cud; *(fig)* rumination, thinking over

rūmin·ō -āre -āvī -ātus *tr* to chew again **‖** *intr* to chew the cud

rūm·or -ōris *m* rumor, hearsay; shouting, cheering, noise; popular opinion, current opinion; reputation, fame; notoriety; calumny; **adversō rūmōre esse** to be in bad repute, be unpopular

rumpi·a -ae *f* long Thracian javelin

rumpō rumpere rūpī ruptus *tr* to break, break down, break open; to burst, burst through; to tear, split; to cause to snap; to tear, rend *(hair, clothes);* to cause *(s.th.)* to break; to force, make *(e.g., a path)* by force; to break in on, interrupt, cut short; to break, violate *(a law, treaty);* to break out in, utter *(complaints, etc.);* **amōrēs rumpere** to break off a love affair; **nūptiās rumpere** to annul a marriage; **silentium** *(or* **silentia) rumpere** to break silence **‖** *refl* & *pass* to burst forth, erupt

rūmuscul·ī -ōrum *mpl* gossip

rūn·a -ae *f* dart

runc·ō -āre -āvī -ātus *tr* to weed, weed out

ru·ō -ere -ī -tus *tr* to throw down, hurl to the ground; to level *(e.g., sand dunes);* to destroy, overthrow, lay waste; to sweep headlong; to upturn, churn up **‖** *intr* to dash, rush, hurry; *(of vehicles)* to go fast; *(of buildings)* to fall down, collapse; *(of fortunes)* to go to ruin; *(of rain)* to come pouring down; *(of the sun)* to set rapidly; *(w.* **in** + *acc)* **1** to charge, swoop down on; **2** to proceed with haste *or* impatience to *(an action);* **currū in bella ruere** to go into battle on the double

rūp·ēs -is *f* cliff

rupt·or -ōris *m* breaker, violator

ruptus *pp of* **rumpō**

rūricol·a -ae *mf* rustic, peasant **‖** *m* ox

rūrigen·a -ae *m* one born in the country, farmer

rūr·ō -āre *intr* to live in the country

rūrsus *or* **rūrsum** *or* **rūsum** *adv* back, backwards; on the contrary, on the other hand; in turn; again, a second time; *(in the direction from which one has come)* back again; once more; **rūrsus rūrsusque** again and again; **rūrsum prōrsum** *(or* **rūrsus (ac) prōrsus)** back and forth, backward and forward

rūs rūris *n* the country, countryside, lands, fields; farm, estate; **rūre** from the country; **rūre redīre** to return from the country; **rūrī**

in the country, on the farm; **rūrī** *(or* **rūre)** **vītam agere** to live in the country; **rūs īre** to go into the country ‖ *npl* countryside
rūsc·um -ī *n or* **rūsc·us** -ī *m* broom *(of twigs)*
russāt·us -a -um *adj* red, ruddy; clothed in red
russ·us -a -um *adj* red, russet; red-haired
rūstic·a -ae *f* country girl
rūsticān·us -a -um *adj* rustic, country, rural
rūsticāti·ō -ōnis *f* country life
rūsticē *adv* like a farmer; plainly, simply; boorishly
rūsticit·ās -ātis *f* simple country ways, rusticity; boorishness, coarseness
rūstic·or -ārī -ātus sum *intr* to live *or* stay in the country
rūsticul·us -a -um *adj* of the country, in the country, rural; plain, simple, unspoiled, unsophisticated; coarse, boorish ‖ *m* farmer ‖ *f* country girl
rūstic·us -a -um *adj* of the country, rural, rustic, country; plain, simple, provincial, rough, gross, awkward, prudish ‖ *m* rustic; *(pej)* hick ‖ *f* country girl
rūsum *see* **rūrsus**
rūt·a -ae *f* rue *(bitter herb);* bitterness, unpleasantness
rūt·a -ōrum *npl* minerals; **rūta caesa** *(or* **rūta et caesa)** *(leg)* everything mined *or* cut down on an estate, timber and minerals
rutābul·um -ī *n* spatula; poker, fire shovel *(instrument with flattened end)*
rūtāt·us -a -um *adj* flavored with rue *(a bitter herb);* bitter
rutil·ō -āre -āvī -ātus *tr* to make red, color red, dye red ‖ *intr* to glow red
rutil·us -a -um *adj* red, reddish yellow; strawberry-blond
rutr·um -ī *n* shovel, spade
rūtul·a -ae *f* a bit of rue *(bitter herb)*
Rutul·ī -ōrum *mpl* ancient people of Latium whose capital was Ardea
rutus *pp of* **ruō**

S

S, s *(supply* littera) *f* eighteenth letter of the Latin alphabet; letter name: **es**
s. d. *abbr* **salūtem dīcere**
Sab·a -ae *f* town in Arabia Felix, famous for its incense
Sabae·a -ae *f (sc.* terra) *(country of the Sabaeans, modern Yemen)*
Sabae·us -a -um *adj* Arabian, Sabaean, of the Sabaeans ‖ *f see* **Sabaea** ‖ *mpl* the Sabaeans *(people of S.W. Arabia, modern Yemen)*

Sabāz·ius -(i)ī *m* Bacchus ‖ *npl* festival in honor of Bacchus
sabbat·a -ōrum *npl* Sabbath
sabbatāri·a -ae *f* Sabbath-keeper *(i.e., Jewish woman)*
Sabell·us -a -um *adj* Sabellian, Sabine ‖ *m* Sabine *(i.e., Horace)*
Sabīn·us -a -um *adj* Sabine; **herba Sabīna** *(bot)* savin *(a juniper, used to produce a drug);* **ōleum Sabīnum** oil derived from savin ‖ *m* Roman family name *(cognomen)* *(e.g.,* Flavius Sabinus, the father of the Emperor Vespasian) ‖ *mpl* an ancient people of central Italy ‖ *f* Sabine woman ‖ *n* Sabine wine; Horace's Sabine farm
sabul·um -ī *n or* **sabul·ō** -ōnis *m* gravel, coarse sand
saburr·a -ae *f* gravel; ballast
saburr·ō -āre -āvī -ātus *tr* to ballast; *(coll)* to gorge with food
Sac·ae -ārum *mpl* **(Sag-)** Scythian tribe
saccipēr·ium -(i)ī *n* pocket; purse
sacc·ō -āre -āvī -ātus *tr* to filter, strain
sacc·ō -ōnis *m (pej) (of a rich person)* moneybags
saccul·us -ī *m* little bag; pouch
sacc·us -ī *m* sack, bag; pouch; bag for straining liquids, strainer
sacell·um -ī *n* chapel, shrine
sa·cer -cra -crum *adj* sacred, holy, consecrated; devoted to a deity for destruction, accursed; detestable; criminal, infamous ‖ *n see* **sacrum**
sacerd·ōs -ōtis *m* priest ‖ *f* priestess
sacerdōtāl·is -is -e *adj* priestly
sacerdōt·ium -(i)ī *n* priesthood
sacrāment·um -ī *n* guarantee, deposit *(sum of money which each of the parties to a lawsuit deposits and which is forfeited by the loser);* civil lawsuit; dispute; oath; voluntary oath of recruits; military oath; **eum obligāre mīlitiae sacrāmentō** to swear him into the army; **iūstīs sacrāmentīs contendere** to argue on equal terms; **omnēs sacrāmentō adigere** *(or* **rogāre)** *(mil)* to swear them all in; **sacrāmentum dīcere** *(mil)* to sign up; **sacrāmentum dīcere** *(w. dat)* to swear allegiance to
Sacrān·us -a -um *adj* of the Sacrani *(a people from Reate in Italy)*
sacrār·ium -(i)ī *n* shrine, chapel; sacristy
sacrāt·us -a -um *adj* hallowed, consecrated, holy, sacred
sacrif·er -era -erum *adj* carrying sacred objects
sacrificāl·is -is -e *adj* sacrificial
sacrificāti·ō -ōnis *f* sacrificing

sacrific·ium -(i)ī *n* sacrifice; **sacrificium facere** (*or* **perpetrāre**) (*w. dat*) to offer a sacrifice to

sacrific·ō -āre -āvī -ātus *tr & intr* to sacrifice

sacrificul·us -ī *m* sacrificing priest

sacrific·us -a -um *adj* sacrificial

sacrileg·ium -(i)ī *n* sacrilege; temple robbing; violation of sacred rites

sacrileg·us -a -um *adj* sacrilegious; profane, impious, wicked ‖ *m* temple robber; wicked person ‖ *f* impious woman

sacr·ō -āre -āvī -ātus *tr* to consecrate; to dedicate; to set apart, devote, give; to doom, curse; to hallow, declare inviolable; to hold sacred, worship; to immortalize

sacrōsānct·us -a -um *adj* sacred, inviolable, sacrosanct

sacr·um -ī *n* holy object, sacred vessel; holy place, temple, sanctuary; religious rite, act of worship, religious service; festival; sacrifice; victim ‖ *npl* worship, religion; secret, mystery; inviolability; **sacra facere** to sacrifice; **sine sacrīs hērēditātis** (*fig*) godsend, windfall

saeclum *see* saeculum

saec(u)lār·is -is -e *adj* (sēc-) centennial

saec(u)l·um -ī *n* (sēc-) generation, lifetime; century; spirit of the age, fashion

saepe *adv* often

saepenumerō *or* saepe numerō *adv* oftentimes, on many occasions

saep·ēs -is *f* (sēp-) hedge, fence, enclosure

saepīment·um -ī *n* (sēp-) hedge, fence, enclosure

saep·iō -īre -sī -tus *tr* (sēp-) to fence in, hedge in, enclose; to surround, encircle; to guard, fortify, protect, strengthen

saepissimē *adv* very often

saepissim·us -a -um *adj* very frequent

saepius *adv* more frequently

saepsī *perf of* saepiō

saept·um -ī *n* (sēp-) fence, wall, enclosure; stake; sheepfold; voting booth ‖ *npl* enclosure; voting booths, polls

saeptus *pp of* saepiō

saet·a -ae *f* (sēt-) bristle, stiff hair

saetig·er -era -erum *adj* (sēt-) bristly ‖ *m* wild boar

saetōs·us -a -um *adj* (sēt-) shaggy, bristly

saevē *adv* savagely, fiercely

saevidic·us -a -um *adj* spoken in anger

saev·iō -īre -iī -ītum *intr* to be fierce, be savage, be furious; (*of persons*) to be brutal, be violent

saeviter *adv* savagely, cruelly

saeviti·a -ae *f* rage, fierceness; brutality, savageness (*of persons*)

saevitūd·ō -inis *f* savageness

saev·us -a -um *adj* raging, fierce, cruel; brutal, savage, barbarous

sāg·a -ae *f* fortuneteller; sorceress

sagācit·ās -ātis *f* sagacity, shrewdness; keenness

sagāciter *adv* keenly, with keen scent *or* sight; with insight

Sagan·a -ae *f* name of a witch

Sagar·is -is *m*, **Sangari·us -i** *m* river flowing from Phyrgia into the Black Sea

Sagarīt·is -idis *f* a nymph, daughter of the river-god Sagaris, loved by Attis

sagāt·us -a -um *adj* wearing a military cloak

sag·āx -ācis *adj* keen-scented; sharp, perceptive (*mind*)

sagīn·a -ae *f* stuffing, fattening up; food, rations; rich food; fattened animal; fatness (*from overeating*)

sagīn·ō -āre -āvī -ātus *tr* to fatten

sāg·iō -īre *tr* to perceive quickly

sagitt·a -ae *f* arrow ‖ **Sagitta** (*astr*) Sagitta (*constellation*); an arrow in the constellation Sagittarius

sagittāri·us -a -um *adj* of *or* for an arrow ‖ *m* archer ‖ **Sagittārius** *m* (*astr*) Sagittarius, the archer (*constellation*)

sagittāt·us -a -um *adj* barbed

sagittif·er -era -erum *adj* carrying an arrow

Sagittipot·ēns -entis *m* (*astr*) Sagittarius (*constellation*)

sagm·en -inis *n* tuft of sacred herbs (*plucked in the Capitol by the consul or praetor and worn by the Fetiales as a sign of inviolability*)

sagulāt·us -a -um *adj* wearing a military coat ‖ *m* soldier

sagul·um -ī *n* short military coat (*esp. that of general officers*)

sag·um -ī *n* coarse mantle; military uniform; **ad sagum īre** (*or* **sagum sūmere**) to get into uniform; **in sagīs esse** to be in uniform; to go to war

Saguntīn·us -a -um *adj & m* Saguntine

Sagunt·um -ī *n or* **Sagunt·us** *or* **Sagunt·os -ī** *f* Saguntum (*city on E. coast of Spain (modern Sagunto), which Hannibal attacked, thus bringing on the First Punic War*)

sāl salis *m* (*n*) salt; salt water, sea; seasoning; flavor; good taste, elegance; pungency (*of words*); wit, humor, sarcasm ‖ *mpl* wisecracks

Salaci·a -ae *f* a sea goddess

salac·ō -ōnis *m* show-off, braggart

salamandr·a -ae *f* salamander

Salamīni·us -a -um *adj* of Salamis ‖ *mpl* people of Salamis

Salam·is -īnos *or* -īnis (*acc:* **Salamīna;** (*abl:* **Salamīne**) *f* island in the Saronic Gulf near Athens, opposite Eleusis ‖ city in Cyprus

salapūt·ium -(i)ī *n* midget
Salāri·a -ae *f* Via Salaria *(from Porta Collina to the Sabine district)*
salāri·us -a -um *adj* salt, of salt; **annōna salāria** revenue from salt works; **Via Salāria** Salt Road *(from the Porta Collina to the Sabine district)* ‖ *m* salt-fish dealer ‖ *n* salary, allowance *(originally the allowance given to soldiers for salt); (fig)* meal
sal·āx -ācis *adj* lustful; salacious, provocative
salebr·a -ae *f* a jolting; rut; roughness *(of speech)*
salebrōs·us -a -um *adj* rough, uneven
Sālentīn·ī -ōrum *mpl* (Sall-) a people who occupied the S.E. extremity of Italy
Salern·um -ī *n* town on the Campanian coast S.E. of Naples *(modern Salerno)*
Saliār·is -is -e *adj* Salian, of the Salii; sumptuous
Saliāt·us -ūs *m* Salian priesthood
salict·um -ī *n* willow grove
salient·ēs -ium *fpl* springs, fountains
salign·us -a -um *adj* willow
Sali·ī -ōrum *mpl* college of twelve priests dedicated to Mars who went in solemn procession through Rome on the Kalends of March
salīll·um -ī *n* small salt shaker
salīn·ae -ārum *fpl* salt pits, salt works; **salīnae Rōmānae** salt works at Ostia *(a state monopoly)*
salīn·um -ī *n* salt shaker
sal·iō -īre -uī *or* -iī -tum *tr (of an animal)* to mount ‖ *intr* to jump, leap, hop
Salisubsil(i)·ī -ōrum *mpl* dancing priests of Mars
saliunc·a -ae *f* wild nard *(aromatic plant)*
Sal·ius -(i)ī *m* priest of Mars *(see* **Saliī***)*
salīv·a -ae *f* saliva; taste, flavor
sal·ix -icis *f* willow tree
Sallentīnī *see* **Sālentīnī**
Sallustiān·us -a -um *adj* of Sallust; **hortī Sallustiānī** park in the N. part of Rome owned by Sallust ‖ *m* imitator of Sallust's style ‖ *n* a Sallustian expression
Sallust·ius -(i)ī *m* Sallust *(Gaius Sallustius Crispus, Roman historian, 86–34 B.C.)* ‖ Gaius Sallustius Crispus *(his great-nephew and adopted son, an advisor to Augustus and Tiberius, d.* A.D. *20)*
Salmac·is -idis *f* fountain at Halicarnassus on the W. coast of Asia Minor, which made all who drank from it soft and effeminate
Salmōn·ēus -ēos *m* son of Aeolus who imitated lightning and was thrown by Jupiter into Tartarus
Salmōn·is -idis *or* -idos *f* Tyro *(daughter of Salmoneus)*
Sal·ō -ōnis *f* tributary of the River Ebro *(modern Jalon)*

Salōn·ae -ārum *fpl* city on the Illyrian coast *(near modern Split)*
salp·a -ae *f* saupe *(type of fish)*
salsāment·um -ī *n (usu. pl)* salted food *(esp. fish)*
salsē *adv* facetiously, humorously
salsipot·ēns -entis *adj* ruling the sea
salsūr·a -ae *f* (process of) pickling
sals·us -a -um *adj* salted; briny, salty; facetious, humorous, witty ‖ *npl* salty food; witty remarks, satirical writings
saltāti·ō -ōnis *f* dancing, dance
saltāt·or -ōris *m* dancer
saltātōri·us -a -um *adj* dance, for dancing
saltātr·īx -īcis *f* dancing girl
saltāt·us -ūs *m* dance
saltem *adv* at least, in any event, anyhow; **nōn** *(or* **neque***)* **saltem** not even
salt·ō -āre -āvī -ātus *tr & intr* to dance
saltuōs·us -a -um *adj* wooded, covered with forest
salt·us -ūs *m* defile, pass; wooded pasture; opening in the woods, glade; forest; jungle; ravine; *(vulg)* female pudenda
salt·us -ūs *m* jump, leap; *(fig)* step, stage; **saltum dare** to leap
salū·ber *or* salū·bris -bris -bre *adj* healthful, healthy, wholesome; *(w. dat or* **ad***)* good for, beneficial to
salūbrit·ās -ātis *f* healthiness, wholesomeness; health, soundness
salūbriter *adv* healthfully; healthily; beneficially; **emere salūbriter** to buy cheaply
saluī *perf of* **saliō**
sal·um -ī *n* billow; sea in motion; high seas; **aerumnōsō nāvigāre salō** *(poet)* to sail a sea of troubles; **tīrōnēs salō nauseāque cōnfectī** recruits, hit hard by seasickness
sal·ūs -ūtis *f* health; welfare; prosperity; safety; greeting, best regards; **salūtem dīcere** *(abbr:* **s.d.***)* to send greetings; *(at end of letter)* to say goodbye; **salūtem magnam dīcere** *(w. dat)* to send warm greetings to, bid fond farewell to, to say goodbye to; **salūtem plūrimam dīcere** *(abbr:* **s.p.d.***)* to send warmest greetings; *(at end of letter)* to give best regards
salūtār·is -is -e *adj* salutary, healthful, wholesome; beneficial, advantageous, useful; *(w.* **ad***)* good for, beneficial for; *(w. dat)* beneficial to; **ars salūtāris** art of healing; **salūtāris littera** vote of acquittal *(the letter* **A** *for* **Absolvō***)*
salūtāriter *adv* beneficially
salūtāti·ō -ōnis *f* greeting, salutation; formal morning reception at the house of an important person; callers; **ubi salūtātiō dēfluxit** when morning callers have dispersed

salūtāt·or -ōris *m,* salūtātr·īx -īcis *f* morning caller

salūtif·er -era -erum *adj* health-giving

salūtigerul·us -a -um *adj* bringing greetings

salūt·ō -āre -āvī -ātus *tr* to greet, wish well; to send greetings to; to pay respects to, pay a morning call on; to pay reverence to *(gods);* to welcome; *(w. double acc)* to hail as

salvē *impv of* salveō

salvē *adv* well; in good health; satine *(or* satisne) salvē? *(supply agis or agit or agitur) (coll)* everything O.K.?

salv·eō -ēre *intr* to be well, be in good health; to be getting along well; salvē, salvēte *(or* salvētō)! hello!, good morning!, good day!; goodbye!; salvēbis ā meō Cicerōne my son Cicero wishes to be remembered to you; tē salvēre iubeō I bid you good day; valē, salvē goodbye

salv·us (salv·os) -a -um *adj* well, sound, safe, unharmed; living, alive; *(w. noun or pronoun in an abl absolute)* without violation of, without breaking, *e.g.,* salvā lēge without breaking the law; salvos sum *(coll)* I'm O.K.

Samae·ī -ōrum *mpl* inhabitants of Cephallenia

sambūc·a -ae *f* triangular stringed instrument, small harp

sambūcistri·a -ae *f* harpist *(female)*

Sam·ē -ēs *or (less frequently)* Sam·os -ī *f* ancient name of the island of Cephallenia

Samiol·us -a -um *adj* of Samian ware

Sami·us -a -um *adj* of Samos, Samian; Iūnō Samia Juno worshiped at Samos; testa Samia Samian potsherd *(noted for its thinness);* vir Samius Pythagoras ‖ *mpl* Samians ‖ *npl* delicate Samian pottery

Samn·īs -ītis *adj* Samnite ‖ *m* gladiator armed with Samnite weapons ‖ *mpl* the Samnites

Samn·ium -(i)ī *n* country of central Italy, whose inhabitants were the offshoot of the Sabines

Sam·os *or* Sam·us -ī *(acc:* -on *or* -um) *f* an island off the W. coast of Asia Minor, famous as the birthplace of Pythagoras ‖ *see* Samē

Samothrāc·a -ae *f* Samothrace *(island off the Thracian coast)*

Samothrāc·es -um *mpl* Samothracians

Samothrāci·us -a -um *adj* Samothracian ‖ *f* Samothrace *(island in N. Aegean Sea)*

sam(p)s·a -ae *f* crushed olive

sānābil·is -is -e *adj* curable

sānāti·ō -ōnis *f* healing, curing

sanciō sancīre sānxī sānctus *tr* to fulfill *(a threat, prophecy);* to ratify *(laws, agreements, treaties);* to enact *(a law);* to sanction *(a policy, practice);* to confirm the possession of *(property);* to condemn; *(w. abl of the penalty)* to make *(an offense, a person)* punishable by law with; Solōn capite sānxit quī

in seditiōne nōn alterīus utrīus partis fuisset Solon condemned to death anyone who did not side with one party or the other in a revolution

sānctē *adv* solemnly, reverently, religiously, conscientiously, purely

sānctimōni·a -ae *f* sanctity, sacredness; chastity

sāncti·ō -ōnis *f* consecration; sanctioning; penalty clause *(that part of the law that provided for penalties against those breaking that law),* sanction

sānctit·ās -ātis *f* sanctity, sacredness, inviolability; integrity; purity

sānctitūd·ō -inis *f* sanctity

sānct·or -ōris *m* enactor *(of laws)*

sānct·us -a -um *adj* consecrated, hallowed, sacred, inviolable, holy; venerable, august, divine; chaste

Sanc·us -ī *m* epithet of Semo *(a god of Sabine origin)*

sandaliāri·us -a -um *adj* sandal-maker's; Apollō Sandaliārius Apollo of Shoemakers' Street

sandaligerul·ae -ārum *fpl* maids who brought slippers to their mistress

sandal·ium -iī *n* sandal, slipper *(one in which the toes were covered; cf.* solea)

sandapil·a -ae *f* simple coffin

sand·yx -ycis *f* vermilion, scarlet

sānē *adv* sanely, reasonably, sensibly; certainly, doubtless, truly, very; *(ironically)* of course, naturally; *(w. negatives)* really, at all; *(in concessions)* to be sure, however; *(in answers)* yes, of course; *(w. imperatives)* then; haud *(or* nōn) sānē not very; nihil sānē absolutely nothing; sānē quam extremely

sānēsc·ō -ere *intr* to get well; to heal

Sangari·us -a -um *adj* living near the Sagaris River *(in Phrygia)* ‖ *m* Sagaris River

sangu·en -inis *m see* sanguis

sanguin·āns -antis *adj* bleeding; bloodthirsty

sanguināri·us -a -um *adj* bloodthirsty

sanguine·us -a -um *adj* bloody; bloodstained; blood-red; sanguineus imber a rain of blood

sanguinolent·us -a -um *adj* bloody, blood-stained; blood-red; vindictive

sangu·is -inis *m* blood; descent, parentage, family; descendant; murder, bloodshed; *(fig)* lifeblood, source of vitality, life, strength; forcefulness, life, vigor *(of a speech);* sanguinem dare to bleed; sanguinem effundere *(or* profundere) to bleed heavily; sanguinem haurīre to shed *(s.o.'s)* blood; sanguinis missiō *(med)* bloodletting; sanguinem mittere *(of a physician)* to let blood, bleed

sani·ēs -ēī *f* blood *(from a wound);* gore; foam, froth; venom

sānit·ās -ātis *f* health; sanity; common sense, discretion; solidity, healthy foundation *(for victory, etc.)*; soundness, propriety *(of style)*
sann·a -ae *f* mocking grimace, sneer, face
sanni·ō -ōnis *m* clown
sān·ō -āre -āvī -ātus *tr* to cure, heal; to correct, repair; to allay, quiet, relieve
Sanquāl·is -is -e *adj* of Sancus *(Sabine deity);* Sanquālis avis osprey
Santon·ī -ōrum *mpl* Gallic tribe N. of the Geronne
Santonic·us -a -um *adj* of the Santoni; herba *(or* virga) Santonica wormwood *(bitter aromatic herb used as a tonic)*
Santr·a -ae *m* a grammarian of the time of Varro
sān·us -a -um *adj* sound, hale, healthy; sane, rational, sensible; sober; *(w.* ab) free from *(faults, etc.)*
sānxī *perf of* sanciō
sap·a -ae *f* (distilled) new wine
sāperd·a -ae *m* a fish *(from the Black Sea)*
sapi·ēns -entis *adj* wise, sensible, judicious, discreet ‖ *m* sensible person; sage, philosopher; man of discriminating taste, connoisseur; title given to jurisconsults
sapienter *adv* wisely, sensibly
sapienti·a -ae *f* wisdom; common sense; philosophy; knowledge *(of principles, methods),* science
sap·iō -ere -īvī *or* -iī *tr* to have the flavor of, taste of; to smell like; to understand ‖ *intr* to have the sense of taste; to have sense, be sensible, be discreet, be wise
sāp·ō -ōnis *m* pomade; soap
sap·or -ōris *m* taste, flavor; delicacy; refinement, sense of taste
Sapphic·us -a -um *adj* Sapphic; Mūsa Sapphica Sappho *(as a tenth Muse)*
Sapph·ō -ūs *f (acc:* Sapphō) Greek lyric poetess of Lesbos *(born c. 612 B.C.)*
sarcin·a -ae *f* package, bundle, pack; burden *(of a womb);* sorrow, trouble ‖ *fpl* luggage, gear; movable goods, chattels, belongings
sarcināri·us -a -um *adj* luggage, of luggage; iūmenta sarcināria pack animals
sarcināt·or -ōris *m* patcher, repairer
sarcināt·us -a -um *adj* loaded down
sarcinul·ae -ārum *fpl* small bundles, little trousseau
sar·ciō -cīre -sī -tus *tr* to patch; to fix, repair
sarcophag·us -ī *m* stone coffin
sarcul·um -ī *n* garden hoe
Sardanapāl·us -ī *m* last king of the Assyrian empire of Nineveh *(c. 9th cent.)* whose decadence was legendary
Sard·ēs *or* Sard·īs -ium *fpl* Sardis *(capital of Lydia)*

Sardiān·us -a -um *adj* Sardian ‖ *mpl* inhabitants of Sardis
Sardini·a -ae *f* Sardinia
Sardiniēns·is -is -e *adj* Sardinian
Sardīs *see* Sardēs
sardon·yx -ychis *or* -ychos *m (f)* sardonyx *(precious stone)*
Sardō·us *or* Sard·us -a -um *adj & m* Sardinian
sarg·us -ī *m* sar *(fish)*
sar·iō -īre -uī *intr* (sarr-) to hoe; to weed
sarīs(s)·a -ae *f* long Macedonian lance
sarīs(s)ophor·os -ī *m* Macedonian lancer
Sarmat·ae -ārum *mpl* Sarmatians *(barbarous people of S.E. Russia)*
Sarmati·a -ae *f* Sarmatia
Sarmaticē *adv* Sarmatian, in the Sarmatian language
Sarmatic·us -a -um *adj* Sarmatian
sarment·um -ī *n* brushwood ‖ *npl* twigs, faggots
Sarn·us -ī *n* river in Campania near Paestum *(modern Sarno)*
Sarpēd·ōn -onis *or* -onos *m* king of Lycia who was killed by Patroclus at Troy
Sarr·a -ae *f* old name of Tyre
sarrāc·um -ī *n* (serr-) wagon
Sarrān·us -a -um *adj* Tyrian, Phoenician; dyed (Tyrian) purple
sarriō *see* sariō
sarsī *perf of* sarciō
sartāg·ō -inis *f* frying pan; hodgepodge
sart·us *or* sarct·us -a -um *pp of* sarciō ‖ *adj (occurring only with* tēctus) in good repair; aedem Castoris sartam tēctam trādere to hand over the temple of Castor in good repair ‖ *npl* repairs; sarta tēcta exigere to complete the repairs
sat *adv* sufficiently, quite; sat sciō I am quite sure
sat *indecl adj* enough, sufficient, adequate ‖ *n* enough; sat agere *(w. gen)* to have enough of, have one's hands full with
sat·a -ae *f* daughter; *(w. abl* begotten of)
sat·a -ōrum *npl* crops
sat·agō -agere -ēgī *intr* to have trouble enough, have one's hands full
satell·es -itis *mf* bodyguard, attendant, follower; *(pej)* lackey; partisan; *(w. gen)* accomplice in *(crime)*
sati·ās -ātis *f* sufficiency; overabundance, satiety, satisfied desire
Saticul·us -ī *m* inhabitant of Saticula *(Samnite town)*
satiet·ās -ātis *f* sufficiency, adequacy; satiety, weariness, disgust
satin' *or* satine (= satisne) *adv* quite, really
sati·ō -āre -āvī -ātus *tr* to satisfy, appease; to avenge; to fill, glut; to saturate; to cloy

sati·ō -ōnis *f* sowing, planting ‖ *fpl* sown fields

satis *adv* enough, sufficiently, adequately; satis bene pretty well

satis *or* sat *indecl adj* enough, sufficient, adequate ‖ *n* enough; *(leg)* satisfaction, security, guarantee; satis accipere to receive a guarantee; satis dare *(w. dat)* to give a guarantee to; satis facere *(w. dat)* to satisfy; to pay *(a creditor);* to make amends to *(by word or deed),* apologize to; satis facere *(w. dat of person and acc & inf)* to satisfy *(s.o.)* with proof that, demonstrate sufficiently to *(s.o.)* that; satis superque dictum est more than enough has been said

satisdati·ō -ōnis *f* putting up bail, giving a guarantee

satis·dō -dare -dedī -datum *intr* (also written as two words) see satis

satis·faciō -facere -fēcī -factus *tr (also written as two words)* see satis

satisfacti·ō -ōnis *f* amends, satisfaction; apology, excuse

satius *(comp of* satis*) adj (neut only)* satius est *(w. inf)* it is better *or* preferable to

sat·or -ōris *m* sower, planter; father; promoter, author

satrapē·a *or* satrapī·a -ae *f* satrapy *(office or province of a satrap)*

satrap·ēs *or* satrap·a -ae *m* satrap *(provincial governor in the Persian empire)*

sat·ur -ura -urum *adj* full, well-fed, stuffed; plump; fertile; deep *(color)*

satur·a -ae *f* (satir-) dish of mixed ingredients; mixture, hodgepodge; medley, variety show; literary medley of prose and poetry; satire, satirical poem; in *(or* per) saturam at random; collectively, en block; per saturam ferre to propose as a rider to a bill

saturēi·a -ōrum *npl* savory *(seasoning)*

saturit·ās -ātis *f* satiety; plenty, overabundance

Sāturnāli·a -ium *npl* festival in honor of Saturn, beginning on the 17th of December and lasting several days; iō Sāturnālia! cry of merrymakers at this festival; nōn semper Sāturnālia erunt *(fig)* it won't be Christmas forever; hilara Sāturnālia! Merry Saturnalia!

Sāturni·a -ae *f* Juno *(daughter of Saturn)*

Sāturnīn·us -ī *m* Lucius Appuleius Saturninus *(demagogic tribune in 103 and 100 B.C.)*

Sāturni·us -a -um *adj* Saturnian; Sāturnius numerus Saturnian meter *(archaic Latin meter based on stress accent)* ‖ *m* Jupiter; Pluto

Sāturn·us -ī *m* Saturn *(Italic god of agriculture, equated with the Greek god Cronos, ruler of the Golden Age, and father of Jupiter, Neptune, Juno, and Pluto)*

satur·ō -āre -āvī -ātus *tr* to fill, satisfy, glut, cloy, saturate; to satisfy, content

sat·us -a -um *pp of* serō (to plant) ‖ *m* son *(w. abl:* begotten of); status Anchīsā son of Achises *(i.e.,* Aeneas) ‖ *f* daughter *(see* sata) ‖ *npl see* sata

sat·us -ūs *m* sowing, planting; begetting; race, stock; seed *(of knowledge)*

satyrisc·us -ī *m* little satyr

satyr·us -ī *m* satyr; satyr play *(in which chorus consisted of satyrs)*

sauciāti·ō -ōnis *f* wounding

sauci·ō -āre -āvī -ātus *tr* to wound

sauci·us -a -um *adj* wounded; *(fig)* smitten, offended, hurt; drunk, smashed; madly in love; melted *(snow)* ‖ *mpl* the wounded

saurocton·os -ī *m (as title of a statue)* lizard killer

Sauromat·ae -ārum *mpl* Sarmatians *(barbaric tribe of S. Russia)*

sāviāti·ō -ōnis *f* (suav-) kissing

sāviol·um -ī *n* (suav-) little kiss, peck

sāvi·or -ārī -ātus sum *tr* (suav-) to kiss

sāv·ium -(i)ī *n* (suav-) puckered lips; kiss

saxātil·is -is -e *adj* rock, living among rocks ‖ *m* saxatile *(fish)*

saxēt·um -ī *n* rocky place; stone quarry

saxe·us -a -um *adj* rocky, stony; umbra saxea shade of the rocks

saxific·us -a -um *adj* petrifying, changing objects into stone

saxifrag·us -a -um *adj* rock-breaking

saxōs·us -a -um *adj* rocky, stony

saxul·um -ī *n* small rock *or* crag

sax·um -ī *n* boulder, rock; Tarpeian Cliff *(W. side of the Capitoline Hill)*

s(c)irpe·us -a -um *adj* wicker, of wicker ‖ *f* wickerwork

s(c)irpicul·a -ae *f* wicker basket

s(c)irpicul·us -ī *m* wicker basket

s(c)irp·us -ī *m* bulrush

scabellum *see* scabillum

sca·ber -bra -brum *adj* itchy; rough, scurfy

scābī *perf of* scabō

scabi·ēs -ēī *f* itch; eczema; *(fig)* itch

scabill·um -ī *n* (-bell-) stool, footstool; castanet tied to the ankle

scabiōs·us -a -um *adj* itchy, mangy; moldy

scabō scabere scābī *tr* to scratch

Scae·a port·a -ae *f* Scaean gate *(W. gate of Troy)*

scaen·a -ae *f* (scēn-) stage; backdrop, scenery; scene; *(fig)* public view, publicity; melodramatic behavior; pretense; pretext; canopy *(of forest acting like a backdrop);* tibi scenae serviendum est you must keep yourself in the limelight

scaenicē *adv* (scēn-) like on the stage

scaenic·us -a -um *adj* (**scēn-**) of the stage, theatrical, scenic; **lūdī scaenicī** plays
scaev·a -ae *f* favorable omen
Scaevol·a -ae *m* Gaius Mucius Cordus Scaevola *(Roman hero who infiltrated Porsenna's camp to kill Porsenna, and on being discovered, burned off his own right hand)* ‖ Quintus Mucius Scaevola *(consul in 95 B.C. and pontifex maximus)*
scaev·us -a -um *adj* left, on the left; perverse ‖ *f* sign *or* omen appearing on the left *(hence, unfavorable)*
scāl·ae -ārum *fpl* ladder; flight of stairs, stairs
scalm·us -ī *m* oarlock; oar; boat
scalpell·um -ī *n* scalpel
scalp·ō -ere -sī -tus *tr* to carve; to scratch; to tickle, titillate
scalpr·um -ī *n* chisel; knife; penknife
scalpsī *perf of* **scalpō**
sculptōr·ium -(i)ī *n* back-scratcher
sculptūr·a -ae *f* engraving
scalpurr·iō -īre *intr* to scratch
Scaman·der -drī *m* river at Troy *(also called Xanthus)*
scamh·us -a -um *adj* bowlegged
scammōne·a -ae *f (bot)* scammony *(plant with trumpet-like flowers similar to the morning-glory, used as a laxative)*
scamn·um -ī *n* bench; stool; throne
scan·dō -dere -dī scānsus *tr* to climb, scale; to climb aboard; to mount ‖ *intr* to climb; *(of buildings)* to rise, tower
scandul·a -ae *f* shingle *(of a roof)*
Scantīni·us -a -um *adj* Roman clan name *(nomen);* **lēx Scantīnia** law against unnatural vice
scaph·a -ae *f* light boat, skiff
scaph·ium -iī *n* (**scaf-**) boat-shaped drinking cup; chamber pot
scapul·ae -ārum *fpl* shoulder blades; shoulders; back
scāp·us -ī *m* shaft *(of a column);* stalk *(of a plant)*
scarīf·ō -āre *tr* to scratch open
scar·us -ī *m* scar *(fish)*
scatebr·a -ae *f* bubbling spring
scat·eō -ēre -uī *or* **scat·ō -ere** *intr* to bubble up, gush out; to teem
scatur(r)īgi·ō -inis *f* spring
scaturr·iō -īre *intr* to bubble, gush; to bubble over with enthusiasm
scaur·us -a -um *adj* clubfooted
scāz·ōn -ontis *m* scazon *(iambic trimeter with a spondee in the last foot)*
scelerātē *adv* criminally, wickedly
scelerāt·us -a -um *adj* profaned, desecrated; outlawed; criminal, wicked, infamous; **campus scelerātus** open field near the Colline gate where unchaste Vestals were buried

alive; **vīcus scelerātus** street on Esquiline Hill where Tullia, daughter of Servius Tullius, drove over her father's corpse ‖ *m* criminal; rascal
sceler·ō -āre -āvī -ātus *tr* to defile
scelerōs·us -a -um *adj* steeped in wickedness
scelestē *adv* wickedly, criminally
scelest·us -a -um *adj* wicked, villainous, criminal; unlucky ‖ *m* rascal
scel·us -eris *n* wicked deed, crime, wickedness; calamity; *(pej)* rascal
scēn- = **scaen-**
scēptrif·er -era -erum *adj* sceptered
scēptr·um -ī *n* scepter ‖ *npl* kingship, dominion, authority; kingdom; **scēptra Āsiae tenēre** to hold sway in Asia
scēptūch·us -ī *m* scepter-bearer *(high officer of state in the East)*
sc(h)ēm·a -ae *f,* **sc(h)ēm·a -atis** *or* **-atos** *n* figure, form; style; figure of speech
sched·a *or* **scid·a -ae** *f* sheet, page
schid·a -ae *f* (**scid-**) sheet *(of papyrus);* one of the strips forming a sheet of papyrus
Schoenē·is -idos *f* daughter of Schoeneus *(Atalanta)*
Schoenēi·us -a -um *adj* of Schoeneus ‖ *f* Atalanta
Schoen·eūs -eī *m* king of Boeotia and father of Atalanta
schoenobat·ēs -ae *m* tightrope-walker
schoen·us -ī *m* cheap perfume
schol·a -ae *f* school; lecture hall; lecture; learned debate; sect, followers
scholastic·us -a -um *adj* school, scholastic ‖ *m* rhetoric teacher, rhetorician; grammarian
scida *see* **scheda**
scidī *perf of* **scindō**
sci·ēns -entis *adj* aware of a fact, cognizant; having full knowledge, with one's eyes wide open; *(w. gen)* cognizant of, familiar with, expert in; *(w. inf)* knowing how to
scienter *adv* wisely, expertly
scienti·a -ae *f* knowledge, skill, expertise; science; *(w. dē or in + abl)* expertise in, skill in
sciī *perf of* **sciō**
scīlicet *adv* of course, evidently, certainly; *(ironically)* naturally, of course; *(as an explanatory particle)* namely, that is to say
scill·a -ae *f* (**squi-**) squill *(seaside plant of the lily family)*
scīn = **scīsne**, *i.e.,* **scīs** + **ne** do you know?
scindō scindere scidī scissus *tr* to cut, split, tear apart, tear open; to divide, separate; to interrupt
scintill·a -ae *f* spark; speck
scintill·ō -āre *intr* to sparkle, flash
scintillul·a -ae *f* little spark

sciō scīre scīvī *or* sciī scītus *tr* to know; to realize, understand; to have skill in; *(w. inf)* to know how to

Scīpiad·ās -ae *m* (·ēs) one of the Scipio family, a Scipio

scīpi·ō -ōnis *m* ceremonial staff *or* baton *(generally made of ivory and carried by persons of rank, such as a seer or a general at his triumph)* ‖ Scīpiō family name *(cognomen)* in the famous gens Cornelia ‖ Publius Cornelius Scipio Africanus Maior *(victor in the Second Punic War, 236–184 B.C.)* ‖ Publius Cornelius Scipio Aemilianus Africanus Minor *(victor in Third Punic War, c. 185–132 B.C.)*

Scīr·ōn -ōnis *or* -ōnos *m* robber who waylaid travelers on the road near Megara *(killed by Theseus)*

scīscitāt·or -ōris *m* interrogator

scīscit·ō -āre *or* scīscit·or -ārī -ātus sum *tr* to ask, question, interrogate; to consult; *(w. acc of thing asked and* ex *or* ab *of person asked)* to ask *(s.th.) of (s.o.)*, check on *(s.th.)* with *(s.o.)* ‖ *intr* (w. dē + *abl*) to ask about

scīscō scīscere scīvī scītus *tr (pol)* to approve, adopt, enact, decree; to learn, ascertain

sciss·or -ōris *m* carver *(person cutting meat at the table)*

scissūr·a -ae *f* crack, cleft

sciss·us -a -um *pp of* scindō ‖ *adj* split, rent; furrowed *(cheeks);* shrill *(voice)*

scītāment·a -ōrum *npl* delicacies, choice tidbits

scītē *adv* expertly, tastefully

scīt·or -ārī -ātus sum *tr* to ask; to consult *(oracle); (w. acc of thing and* ab *or* ex) to ask *(s.th.) of (s.o.)* ‖ *intr* (w. dē + *abl*) to ask *or* inquire about

scītul·us -a -um *adj* neat, pretty

scīt·um -ī *n* statute, decree

scīt·us -a -um *adj* experienced, skillful; suitable, proper; judicious, sensible, witty; smart, sharp *(appearance); (w. gen)* skilled in, expert at

scīt·us -ūs *m* decree, enactment

sciūr·us -ī *m* squirrel

scīvī *perf of* sciō *and of* scīscō

-sc·ō -ere *vbl suf* normally used only in the present system with inchoative force, e.g., lūcēscō to begin to shine

scob·is -is *f* sawdust, scrapings, filings

scom·ber -brī *m* mackerel

scōp·ae -ārum *fpl* broom; ūnae scōpae one broom

Scop·ās -ae *m* Greek sculptor from the island of Paros *(4th cent. B.C.)*

scopulōs·us -a -um *adj* rocky, craggy

scopul·us -ī *m* rock, cliff, crag; promontory; archery target

scop·us -ī *m* target

scorpi·ō -ōnis *or* scorp·ius *or* scorp·ios -(i)ī *m* scorpion; *(mil)* catapult ‖ Scorpiō *(astr)* Scorpion *(constellation)*

scortāt·or -ōris *m* a john *(prostitute's customer)*

scorte·us -a -um *adj* leather

scort·or -ārī *intr* to associate with prostitutes

scort·um -ī *n* prostitute; sex fiend *(of either sex)*

scort·um -i *n* skin, hide

screāt·or -ōris *m* hawker, hemmer *(one who constantly clears his throat)*

screāt·us -ūs *m* clearing of the throat

scre·ō -āre *intr* to clear the throat, hawk, hem

scrīb·a -ae *m* clerk, secretary

scrib(i)līt·a -ae *f* cheese cake

scrībō scrībere scrīpsī scrīptus *tr* to write, draw; to write down; to write out, compose; to draw up, draft *(a law, treaty, decree);* to create *(characters, episodes in a play);* to lay down in writing, prescribe; to register *(a person);* to draft *(colonists to a place);* to name *(in a will);* to enlist *(soldiers); (w. double acc)* to appoint *(s.o.)* as ‖ *intr* to write

scrīn·ium -(i)ī *n* case for scrolls; letter case; portfolio

scrīpsī *perf of* scrībō

scrīpti·ō -ōnis *f* writing; composition; spelling; wording, text

scrīptit·ō -āre -āvī -ātus *tr & intr* to keep writing, write regularly

scrīpt·or -ōris *m* writer; scribe, secretary; author; rērum scrīptor historian

scrīptul·a -ōrum *npl* lines on a game board

scrīptūr·a -ae *f* writing; composing; written work, composition; tax paid on public pastures; testamentary provision

scrīpt·us -a -um *pp of* scrībō ‖ *n* composition, treatise, work, book; actual text *(of a law, document);* literal meaning, letter *(as opposed to spirit);* duodecim scrīpta a type of game board; ōrātiōnem dē scrīptō dīcere to read off a speech; voluntās lēgis, nōn tantum scrīptum the spirit of the law, not only the letter *(of the law)*

scrīpul·um -ī *n* (scrīpt-) small weight, smallest measure of weight, scruple *(one twenty-fourth of an uncia, or ounce)*

scrob·is -is *mf* ditch, trench; grave

scrōf·a -ae *f* breeding sow

scrōfipāsc·us -ī *m* pig breeder

scrūpe·us -a -um *adj* full of sharp rocks, made of jagged rocks, jagged

scrūpōs·us -a -um *adj* full of sharp rocks, jagged, rough

scrūpulōsē *adv* scrupulously, precisely, carefully

scrūpulōs·us -a -um *adj* full of sharp projections of rock, jagged; scrupulous, meticulous, precise
scrūpul·us -ī *m* uneasy feeling, scruple, worry, headache; thorny problem
scrūp·us -ī *m* rough *or* sharp stone; uneasiness
scrūt·a -ōrum *npl* trash, junk
scrūtāt·or -ōris *m* examiner
scrūt·or -ārī -ātus sum *tr* to scrutinize, examine
sculp·ō -ere -sī -tus *tr* to carve, chisel, engrave
sculpōne·ae -ārum *fpl* clogs, wooden shoes
sculpsī *perf of* **sculpō**
sculptil·is -is -e *adj* carved, engraved
sculpt·or -ōris *m* sculptor
sculptūr·a -ae *f* carving; sculpture
sculptus *pp of* **sculpō**
scurr·a -ae *m* jester, comedian; city slicker
scurrīl·is -is -e *adj* scurrilous, offensive
scurrīlit·ās -ātis *f* offensive humor, scurrility
scurrīliter *adv* with offensive humor, like a buffoon
scurr·or -ārī *intr* to clown around
scūtāl·e -is *n* thong of a sling
scūtār·ius -(i)ī *m* shield-maker
scūtāt·us -a -um *adj* carrying a shield ‖ *mpl* troops armed with shields
scutell·a -ae *f* saucer, shallow bowl
scutic·a -ae *f* whip
scūtigerul·us -a -um *m* shield-bearer
scutr·a -ae *f* pan, flat dish
scutul·a -ae *f* wooden roller
scutulāt·us -a -um *adj* diamond-shaped ‖ *npl* checkered clothing
scūtul·um -ī *n* small shield
scūt·um -ī *n* oblong shield; *(fig)* shield, defense, protection
Scyll·a -ae *f* female monster on Italian side of Strait of Messina, that snatched and devoured sailors from passing ships ‖ daughter of Nisus who betrayed her father by cutting off his purple lock of hair
Scyllae·us -a -um *adj* Scyllan
scymn·us -ī *m* cub, whelp
scyph·us -ī *m* goblet, cup
Scȳr·os *or* **Scȳr·us -ī** *f* island off Euboea
Scyth·a *or* **Scyth·ēs -ae** *m* Scythian *(member of nomadic tribe N. of the Black Sea)*
Scythi·a -ae *f* country N. of the Black Sea
Scythic·us -a -um *adj* Scythian
Scyth·is -idis *f* Scythian woman
sē *or* **sēsē** *(gen:* **suī;** *dat:* **sibi;** *acc & abl:* **sē** *or* **sēsē** *pron (refl)* himself, herself, itself, themselves; one another; **ad sē** *(or* **apud sē)** at home; **apud sē** in one's senses; **inter sē** each other, one another, mutually; **in sē** associated with each other, one another, together; **per sē** by himself *(herself, itself, etc.),* alone

sē- *pref (also* **sēd-, sō-)** *added to verbs, etc.:* **1** *in the sense of "apart," "aside," e.g.:* **sēdūcere** to take aside; **sēditiō** a going apart, mutiny; **2** *sometimes privative, e.g.:* **sōcors** lacking in vitality, inactive
sēb·um -ī *n* tallow, grease, suet
sē·cēdō -cēdere -cessī -cessum *intr* to withdraw; to depart; to rebel, go on a sit-down strike, secede; **in ōtium sēcēdere** to retire
sē·cernō -cernere -crēvī -crētus *tr* to separate; to dissociate; to distinguish; to reject, set aside
sēcessi·ō -ōnis *f* withdrawal; secession
sēcess·us -ūs *m* retirement, retreat; isolated spot; country retreat
sēclū·dō -dere -sī -sus *tr* to shut off, shut up; to shut out; to seclude, bar; to hide
sec·ō -āre -uī -tus *tr* to cut, cut off; to reap; to carve *(meat);* to split up *(in classification);* to cut through, traverse *(e.g., the sea);* to cut short; to settle, decide; to follow, chase; to castrate; *(med)* to operate on; *(med)* to cut out, excise, cut off, amputate; **viam secāre** to open up a path
sēcrēti·ō -ōnis *f* dividing, separating *(into constituent parts)*
sēcrētō *or* **sēcrētē** *adv* separately, individually, apart; secretly; in private; away from one's companions
sēcrēt·us -a -um *pp of* **sēcernō** ‖ *adj* separate; isolated, solitary; secret; *(w. gen or abl)* deprived of, in need of ‖ *n* secret, mystery; mystic rite, mystic emblem; secret nature *(of a business);* abstruseness *(of a subject);* private conversation *or* interview, audience; isolated spot; **ā sēcrētō** *(or* **in sēcrētō** *or* **in sēcrētum)** in private; **sēcrētō in occultō cum aliquō agere** to discuss *(s.th.)* with s.o. in a private conversation; **sēcrētum dare (petere)** to grant (ask for) a private conference
sect·a -ae *f* path; way, method, course; school of thought; political party; code of behavior; **secta (vītae)** way of life, occupation
sectāri·us -a -um *adj* followed (by the flock)
sectāt·or -ōris *m* follower, adherent
sectil·is -is -e *adj* cut, divided
secti·ō -ōnis *f* cutting; cut, division; section; dissection; auctioning off of confiscated property; a buying up of confiscated property in lots; right to confiscated property; things so to be sold, lots
sect·or -ārī -ātus sum *tr* to keep following, follow eagerly, run after; to hunt *(game);* to go about searching for; to imitate; to run after *(girls);* to avenge; to follow *(an example, practice);* to go regularly to, frequent; to aim continually at *(an objective)*

sect·or -ōris *m* speculator in confiscated estates *(one who buys up confiscated property with the intention of reselling);* **sector zōnārius** purse-snatcher

sectūr·a -ae *f* incision; stone quarry

sectus *pp of* secō

sēcubit·us -ūs *m* sleeping alone

sēcub·ō -āre -uī *intr* to sleep by oneself; to live alone

secuī *perf of* secō

sēcul- = saecul-

secund·a -ōrum *npl* success

secund·ae -ārum *fpl (theat)* secondary role in a play; *(fig)* second fiddle

secundān·ī -ōrum *mpl* soldiers of the second legion

secundāri·us -a -um *adj* secondary; second-rate, inferior

secundō *adv* secondly

secund·ō -āre -āvī -ātus *tr* to favor, further; to make *(conditions)* favorable for travel; **secundāns ventus** favorable wind, tail wind

secundum *adv* after, behind **‖** *prep (w. acc)* **1** *(of space)* beside, by, along, alongside: **īre secundum mē** to walk beside me; **legiōnēs secundum flūmen dūxit** he led the troops along the river; **2** *(of time)* immediately after: **secundum lūdōs** immediately after the games; **3** *(in rank or quality)* next to, after: **secundum deōs hominēs hominibus ūtilēs esse possunt** next to the gods, people can be helpful to people; **4** *(of agreement)* according to, in compliance with: **secundum nātūram vīvere** to live in accordance with nature; **5** *(leg)* in favor of, to the advantage of; **abscentibus secundum praesentēs facillimē dabat** when a party (to the suit) was absent, he would very readily decide in favor of the party present

secund·us -a -um *adj* following; next, second *(in time; in rank);* backing, favorable, supporting; secondary, subordinate, inferior, second-string; alternate *(heir); (w. dat or* **ab)** second only to; **annō secundō** the next year; **ā mēnsis fīne secunda diēs** the second-last day of the month; **in secundam aquam** with the current; **rēs secundae** success, prosperity; **secundae partēs** supporting role; **secunda mēnsa** dessert; **secundō flūmine** downstream, with the current; **secundō lūmine** on the following day; **secundō marī** with the tide; **secundō populō** with the backing of the people; **secundus pānis** stale bread; **secundus ventus** tailwind, fair wind **‖ Secundus** *m* Roman first name *(praenomen)* **‖** *fpl see* **secundae ‖** *npl see* **secunda**

sēcūrē *adv* securely, safely

sēcūricul·a -ae *f* hatchet

secūrif·er -era -erum *adj* carrying an ax, ax-carrying

secūrig·er -era -erum *adj* carrying an ax, ax-wielding

secūr·is -is *f (acc: usu.* **secūrim)** ax, hatchet; *(fig)* blow, mortal blow; *(fig) (from the ax in the fasces, usu.* pl) power of life and death, supreme authority, sovereignty; **graviōrem reī pūblicae īnflīgere secūrim** to inflict a more serious blow on the State

sēcūrit·ās -ātis *f* freedom from care, unconcern, composure; freedom from danger, security, safety; false sense of security; carelessness

sēcūr·us -a -um *adj* carefree; secure, safe; cheerful; careless; offhand

secus *adv* otherwise, differently; **haud** *(or* **haut** *or* **nōn) secus ac** *(or* **nōn secus quam)** not otherwise than, just as, exactly as; **haud** *(or* **haut** *or* **nōn) secus sī** exactly as if, just as though; **sī secus accidet** if it turns out otherwise *(than expected),* if it turns out badly

secus *indecl n* sex; **secus muliebre** females; **secus virīle** males

secūt·or -ōris *m* chaser *(gladiator who fought against the net-man)*

secūtus *pp of* sequor

sed *or* set *conj* but; but also

sēdātē *adv* sedately, calmly

sēdāti·ō -ōnis *f* calming

sēdāt·us -a -um *adj* calm, composed

sēdecim *indecl adj* sixteen

sēdēcul·a -ae *f* little seat, low stool

sedentāri·us -a -um *adj* sedentary

sedeō sedēre sēdī sessum *intr* to sit, remain seated; *(of magistrates, esp. judge)* to sit, preside, hold court, be a judge; *(of an army)* to remain encamped; to keep the field; to settle down to a blockade; to be idle, be inactive; *(of clothes)* to fit; *(of buildings, towns)* to be located; *(of places)* to be low-lying; to sink, settle; to be firm, be fixed, be established; to stick fast, be stuck; to be determined

sēd·ēs -is *f* seat, chair, throne; residence, home; last home, burial place; base, foundation, bottom; **sēdēs bellī** theater of war

sēdī *perf of* sedeō

sedīl·e -is *n* seat, chair **‖** *npl* seats in the theater; rowers' benches

sēditi·ō -ōnis *f* sedition, insurrection, mutiny; dissension, quarrel, disagreement; warring *(of elements)*

sēditiōsē *adv* seditiously, in mutiny

sēditiōs·us -a -um *adj* seditious, mutinous; quarrelsome; troubled

sēd·ō -āre -āvī -ātus *tr* to calm, settle, still

sē·dūcō -dūcere -dūxī -ductus *tr* to take aside, draw aside, lead off, withdraw; to carry off; to lead astray; to put aside; to divide, split

sēducti·ō -ōnis *f* taking aside
sēduct·us -a -um *pp of* sēdūcō ‖ *adj* distant, remote
sēdulit·ās -ātis *f* application, earnestness; officiousness
sēdulō *adv* diligently; intentionally
sēdul·us -a -um *adj* diligent, busy; officious
sēdūxī *perf of* sēdūcō
seg·es -etis *f* grainfield; crop; arable land
Segest·a -ae *f* town in N.W. Sicily
Segestān·us -a -um *adj* of Segesta ‖ *mpl* people of Segesta ‖ *n* territory of Segesta
segmentāt·us -a -um *adj* trimmed with a flounce *(decorative border)*
segment·um -ī *n* section, segment; slice, trimming, flounce; zone *(of the earth)*
sēgnip·ēs -edis *adj* slow-footed
sēgn·is -is -e *adj* slow; inactive; sluggish, lazy
sēgniter *adv* slowly; lazily
sēgniti·a -ae *or* sēgniti·ēs -ēī *f* slowness; inactivity; laziness
sēgreg·ō -āre -āvī -ātus *tr* to segregate, separate; to dissociate; **ad sēsē sēgregandōs ā cēterīs** for the purpose of dissociating themselves from the rest; **sermōnem sēgregāre** to break off a conversation; **suspiciōnem ā sē sēgregāre** to ward off suspicion from oneself
Sēiāniān·us -a -um *adj* of Sejanus ‖ *mpl* partisans of Sejanus
Sēiān·us -ī *m* Roman family name *(cognomen) (esp. Lucius Aelius Sejanus, the notorious praetorian prefect under the Emperor Tiberius)*
sēiugāt·us -a -um *adj* separated, detached
sēiug·is -is *m* six-horse chariot
sēiug·ō -āre -āvī -ātus *tr (w. ab)* to separate from, detach from
sēiūnctim *adv* separately
sēiūncti·ō -ōnis *f* separation, division
sē·iungō -iungere -iūnxī -iūnctus *tr* to separate, part, sever; *(fig)* to sever, part, disconnect; to distinguish
sēlēcti·ō -ōnis *f* choice, selection
sēlēctus *pp of* sēligō
sēlēgī *perf of* sēligō
Seleucī·a -ae *f* name of several towns in Asia
Seleuc·us -ī *m* name of a line of six kings of Syria, whose ancestor, Seleucus Nicator, was a general under Alexander the Great and founded the Syrian monarchy *(c. 358–280 B.C.)*
sēlībr·a -ae *f* half pound
sē·ligō -ligere -lēgī -lēctus *tr* to select
Selīn·ūs -untis *f* town on the S.W. coast of Sicily ‖ town on the coast of Cilicia
sell·a -ae *f* chair, stool *(normally without back or armrests);* portable chair, sedan chair; **sella curūlis** magistrate's chair

sellāriol·us -a -um *adj (place)* for sitting *or* lounging
sellār·ius -(i)ī *m* lecher, lewd person
sellistern·ium -(i)ī *n* sacred banquet in honor of goddesses
sellul·a -ae *f* stool; sedan chair
sellulāri·us -a -um *adj* sedentary; **artifex sellulārius** craftsman who sits at his job ‖ *mpl* sedentary craftsmen
sēmanimis *see* sēmianimis
semel *adv* once, one time; but once, once and for all; the first time; ever, at some time, at any time; **semel aut iterum** once or twice
Semel·ē -ēs *or* Semel·a -ae *f* Semele *(daughter of Cadmus and mother of Bacchus by Jupiter)*
Semelēi·us -a -um *adj* of Semele
sēm·en -inis *n* seed; seedling, young plant, shoot: offspring; race, stock; *(in physics)* particle; *(fig)* instigator, root: **sēmen omnium malōrum** root of all evils
sēmēnstris *see* sēmēstris
sēmentif·er -era -erum *adj* seed-bearing, fruitful
sēment·is -is *f* sowing, planting; young crops; **ut sēmentem fēceris, ita metēs** *(prov)* as you sow, so shall you reap
sēmentīv·us -a -um *adj* at seed time, of the sowing season
sēmerm·is -is -e *adj* half-armed
sēmēstr·is -is -e *adj* (-mēns-) for six months, half-yearly, semi-annual
sēmēs·us -a -um *adj* half-eaten
sēmet = *emphatic form of* sē
sēmi- *pref before nouns and adjectives with the sense of* "half-" *(sometimes* sēm- *before vowels, e.g.:* **sēmēsus** half-eaten; **sēm(i)animus** half-alive; *also reduced to* sē- *e.g.:* **sēlībra** half pound
sēm(i)erm·is -is -e *or* sēm(i)erm·us -a -um *adj* half-armed
sēm(i)ēs·us -a -um *adj* half-eaten
sēm(i)ūstilāt·us -a -um *adj* (-tul-) half-burned
sēmiadapert·us -a -um *adj* half-open
sēmianim·is -is -e *or* sēm(i)anim·us -a -um *adj* half-alive, half-dead
sēmiapert·us -a -um *adj* half-open
sēmib·ōs -ōvis *adj (masc only)* half-ox; **sēmibōs vir** the Minotaur
sēmica·per -prī *m (masc only)* half-goat *(i.e., Pan or Faunus)*
sēmicrem(āt)·us -a -um *adj* half-burned
sēmicubitāl·is -is -e *adj* half-cubit long *or* wide
sēmide·us -a -um *adj* semidivine ‖ *m* demigod
sēmidoctus -a -um *adj* half-educated
sēmifact·us -a -um *adj* half-finished
sēmifer·us -a -um *adj* half-beast; half-savage ‖ *m* centaur

sēmifult·us -a -um *adj* half-propped
sēmigermān·us -a -um *adj* half-German
semigraec·us -a -um *adj* half-Greek
sēmigrav·is -is -e *adj* half-drunk
sēmigr·ō -āre -āvī -ātum *intr* (w. **ab**) to go away from, move away from
sēmihi·āns -antis *adj* half-open
sēmihom·ō -inis *adj (masc only)* half-man, half-beast; subhuman
sēmihōr·a -ae *f* half hour
sēmi·lacer -lacera -lacerum *adj* half-mangled
sēmilaut·us -a -um *adj* half-washed
sēmilīb·er -era -erum *adj* half-free
sēmilix·a -ae *f (pej) (of a commander)* sad sack, little more than a camp follower
sēmimarīn·us -a -um *adj* half-submerged
sēmim·ās -aris *adj* half-male, gelded, castrated **ǁ** *m* hermaphrodite
sēmimortu·us -a -um *adj* half-dead
sēminār·ium -(i)ī *n* nursery garden; *(fig)* breeding ground
sēmināt·or -ōris *m* originator
sēmi·n(ex) -necis *adj* half-killed, half-dead
sēmin·ium -(i)ī *n* breeding; stock
sēmin·ō -āre *tr* to sow; to beget, procreate; to produce
sēminūd·us -a -um *adj* half-naked
sēmipāgān·us -ī *m* little clown
sēmiplēn·us -a -um *adj (forces)* at half-strength; *(ships)* half-manned
sēmiputāt·us -a -um *adj* half-pruned
Semīram·is -idis *f* famous queen of Assyria, builder of Babylon and consort and successor of King Ninus
Semīrami·us -a -um *adj* of Semiramis; Babylonian
sēmirās·us -a -um *adj* half-shaven
sēmireduct·us -a -um *adj* bent back halfway
sēmirefect·us -a -um *adj* half-repaired
sēm·is -issis *m* half; half an **as** *(small coin);* ½% per month *or* 6% per annum; **nōn semissis homō** worthless fellow
sēmisen·ex -is *m* elderly gent
sēmisepult·us -a -um *adj* half-buried
sēmisomn·is -is -e *or* sēmisomn·us -a -um *adj* half-asleep
sēmisupīn·us -a -um *adj* half-prone
sēmit·a -ae *f* path, lane, track
sēmitāl·is -is -e *adj* of byways, backroad
sēmitāri·us -a -um *adj* back-alley
sēmi·vir -virī *adj* half-man, half-beast; unmanned; unmanly **ǁ** *m* half-man; eunuch
sēmivīv·us -a -um *adj* half-alive, half-dead
sēmod·ius -iī *m* half a peck
sēmōt·us -a -um *adj* remote, distant; private, intimate **ǁ** *npl* faraway places
sē·moveō -movēre -mōvī -mōtus *tr* to separate, remove, exclude
semper *adv* always, ever

sempitern·us -a -um *adj* everlasting
Semprōnius *see* **Gracchus**
sēmūnci·a -ae *f* half ounce *(one twenty-fourth of a Roman pound);* trifle
sēmūnciāri·us -a -um *adj* half-ounce; **faenus sēmūnciārium** interest at the rate of one twenty-fourth of the capital *(i.e., about 5% per annum)*
sēmūst·us -a -um *adj* half-burned
senācul·um -ī *n* open-air meeting place of the Senate in the Forum
sēnāriol·us -ī *m (pros)* trifling trimeter
sēnāri·us -a -um *adj (pros)* six-foot *(verse)* **ǁ** *m (pros)* iambic trimeter
senāt·or -ōris *m* senator
senātōri·us -a -um *adj* senatorial; in the Senate; of a senator
senāt·us -ūs *m* Senate; Senate session; **senātūs cōnsultum** decree of the Senate; **senātum dare** *(or* **praebēre)** to grant an audience with the Senate; to give *(s.o.)* the floor
Senec·a -ae *m* Lucius Annaeus Seneca *(Stoic philosopher and instructor of Nero, 4 B.C.–A.D. 65)*
senect·us -a -um *adj* aged, old **ǁ** *f* old age, senility
senect·ūs -ūtis *f* old age; old person
sen·eō -ēre *intr* to be old
sen·ēscō -ēscere -uī *intr* to get old; to decline, become feeble, lose strength; to wane, draw to a close
sen·ex -is *adj* aged, old **ǁ** *m* old man
sēn·ī -ae -a *adj* six each, in groups of six, six at a time; *(used in multiplication):* **aspicē bis sēnōs cycnōs!** see those twelve swans!; **sēnī dēnī** sixteen each
senīl·is -is -e *adj* of old people, of an old man; aged; senile
sēni·ō -ōnis *m* a six *(on dice)*
seni·or -or (-us) *(comp of* **senex)** *adj* older, elder; more mature *(years)* **ǁ** *m* elderly person, an elder *(over 45 years of age)*
sen·ium -iī *n* feebleness of age, decline, senility; decay; grief, trouble; gloom; crabbiness; old man
sēns·a -ōrum *npl* thoughts, sentiments, ideas
sēnsī *perf of* **sentiō**
sēnsicul·us -ī *m* petty aphorism
sēnsif·er -era -erum *adj* producing a sensation
sēnsil·is -is -e *adj* capable of sensation, sentient
sēnsim *adv* gropingly; tentatively; carefully; gradually, gently
sēns·us -a -um *pp of* **sentiō** **ǁ** *npl see* **sēnsa**
sēns·us -ūs *m* capacity for feeling, sensation; sense *(of hearing, etc.);* self-awareness, consciousness; awareness *(of conditions, situations);* feeling, emotion, sentiment; attitude, frame of mind; idea, thought; understanding, judgment, viewpoint; meaning, sense *(of a*

*word); intent, plan of action; self-contained expression, sentence; **commūnēs sēnsūs** commonplaces, trite topics; **cum sēnsū** with taste; **sēnsus commūnis** civic pride, concern for the common good

sententi·a -ae *f* opinion, view, judgment; purpose, intention; *(in the Senate)* motion, proposal; meaning, sense; plan of action; sentence; maxim; *(leg)* verdict, sentence; **dē sententiā** *(w. gen)* in accordance with the wishes of; **ex animī (meī) sententiā** *(in an oath)* to the best of (my) knowledge; **ex meā sententiā** in my opinion; to my liking; **in sententiam alicūius pedibus īre** to vote in favor of s.o.'s proposal *(literally, to go on foot to s.o.'s proposal);* **sententiam dīcere** *(in the Senate)* to express a view; **sententia est** *(w. inf)* I intend to; **sententiam prōnūntiāre** *(or* **dīcere)** to pronounce *or* give the verdict

sententiol·a -ae *f* phrase; maxim

sententiōsē *adv* sententiously, in moralizing style

sententiōs·us -a -um *adj* full of meaning, pregnant, sententious

senticēt·um -ī *n* thorny bush

sentīn·a -ae *f* bilge water; cesspool; bilge; *(fig)* dregs, scum, rabble

sentiō sentīre sēnsī sēnsus *tr* to perceive with the senses, feel, hear, see, smell; to realize; to observe, notice; to experience; to think, judge ‖ *intr (leg)* to vote, decide

sent·is -is *m* thorny bush, briar

sentīsc·ō -ere *tr* to begin to realize; to begin to observe, perceive

sent·us -a -um *adj* rough, rugged; untidy *(person)*

seorsum *or* **seorsus** *or* **sōrsum** *or* **sōrsus** *adv* apart, separately; *(w. abl or* **ab)** apart from

sēparābil·is -is -e *adj* separable

sēparātim *adv* apart, separately

sēparāti·ō -ōnis *f* severing, separation

sēparātius *adv* less closely, more widely

sēparāt·us -a -um *adj* separate, distinct, different

sēpar·ō -āre -āvī -ātus *tr* to separate, divide, part; to distinguish

sepelībil·is -is -e *adj* that may be buried

sepel·iō -īre -īvī *or* **-iī sepultus** *tr* to bury; *(fig)* to overwhelm, ruin, destroy, suppress

sēpēs *see* **saepēs**

sēpi·a -ae *f* **(saep-)** cuttlefish

sēpīment·um *see* **saepīmentum**

sēpio *see* **saepiō**

sēpiol·a -ae *f* little cuttlefish

sē·pōnō -pōnere -posuī -positus *tr* to set aside, drop, discard; to banish; to disregard, forget; to separate, pick out, select; to reserve; to remove, take away, exclude; to distinguish

sēposit·us -a -um *adj* remote, distant; select; distinct; private

sēps sēpis *mf* a poisonous snake

sēpse = *emphatic* **sē**

septem *indecl adj* seven

Septem·ber -bris -bre *adj* September, of September; **mēnsis September** September *(seventh month of the old Roman calendar until 153 B.C.)* ‖ **Septem·ber -bris** *m* September

septemdecim *indecl adj* (**-ten-**) seventeen

septemflu·us -a -um *adj* seven-mouthed *(Nile)*

septemgemin·us -a -um *adj* sevenfold

septempedāl·is -is -e *adj* seven-foot, seven-foot-high

septempl·ex -icis *adj* sevenfold

septem·vir -virī *m* septemvir *(member of a board of seven, established in 44 B.C. to distribute land to veterans)* ‖ *mpl* board of seven officials; **septemvirī epulōnum** college of priests responsible for sacred feasts

septemvirāl·is -is -e *adv* of the septemvirs, septemviral ‖ *mpl* septemvirs

septemvirāt·us -ūs *m* office of the septemvirs

septemvirī *see* **septemvir**

septēnār·ius -(i)ī *m* (*pros*) heptameter *(verse of seven feet)*

septendecim *indecl adj* (**septem-**) seventeen

septēn·ī -ae -a *adj* seven each, in groups of seven; **septēnī dēnī** seventeen each, seventeen in a group

septentri·ō -ōnis *m* the North; **ad** *or* **in septentriōnem** to the north, northward

septentriōnāl·is -is -e *adj* (**septem-**) northern; **Oceanus septentriōnālis** the North Sea ‖ *npl* northern regions, the North

septentriōn·ēs -um *mpl* (**septem-**) *(seven stars near the North Pole belonging to the Great Bear)* Great Bear; *(the seven stars of the Little Bear)* Little Bear; northern regions, the North; north wind

septiēns *or* **septiēs** *adv* seven times

septimān·us -a -um *adj* of *or* on the seventh ‖ *mpl* soldiers of the seventh legion

septimum *adv* for the seventh time

septim·us -a -um *adj* (**-tum-**) seventh

septim·us decim·us -a -um *adj* seventeenth

septingentēsim·us -a -um *adj* seven hundreth

septingent·ī -ae -a *adj* seven hundred

septuāgēsim·us -a -um *adj* seventieth

septuāgintā *indecl adj* seventy

septuenn·is -is -e *adj* seven-year-old

sēptum *see* **saeptum**

septūn·x -cis *m* seven ounces; seven-twelfths

sēptus *pp of* **sēpiō** *(see* **saepiō**)

sepulc(h)rāl·is -is -e *adj* of a tomb, sepulchral, funeral

sepulc(h)rēt·um -ī *n* grave, tomb

sepulc(h)r·um -ī *n* grave, tomb

sepultūr·a -ae f burial
sepultus pp of sepeliō
Sēquan·us -a -um adj of the Sequani ‖ mf the Seine River ‖ mpl the Sequani (a tribe of E. Gaul)
sequ·āx -ācis adj following, pursuing; penetrating (fumes); eager
sequ·ēns -entis adj next, following
seques·ter -tra -trum (or -ter -tris -tre) adj intermediate; negotiating; pāce sequestrā under the protection of a truce ‖ m trustee (with whom money or property is deposited); agent, go-between ‖ n sequestrō dare (or pōnere) to put in trust
sequius or secius (comp of secus) adv less; worse, more unfavorably; differently, otherwise; nec eō secius nonetheless; nihilō (or nīlō) sequius nevertheless
sequor sequī secūtus sum tr to follow; to escort, accompany, go with; to chase, pursue; to come after (in time); to go after, aim at; to head for ‖ intr to go after, follow, come next; (of words) to come naturally
Ser. abbr Servius (Roman first name, praenomen)
ser·a -ae f bolt, bar (of door)
Serāp·is -is or -idis m (Sar-) Egyptian god of healing
serēnit·ās -ātis f fair weather; serenity; favorableness
serēn·ō -āre -āvī -ātus tr to make fair, clear up, brighten
serēn·us -a -um adj clear, bright, fair; cloudless; cheerful, serene ‖ n clear sky, fair weather
Sēr·es -um mpl Chinese
serēsc·ō -ere intr to dry off
Sergi·us -(i)ī m Roman clan name (nomen) esp. Lucius Sergius Catilina (praetor in 68 B.C. and leader of the conspiracy put down by Cicero in 63 B.C.)
sēri·a -ae f large jar
sēri·a -ōrum npl serious matters, serious business
Sēric·us -a -um adj Chinese ‖ npl silks
seri·ēs -ēī f series, row, succession; train, sequence, order, connection; lineage
sēriō adv seriously, in all sincerity
sēri·us -is -e adj serious, earnest ‖ n serious matter; seriousness, earnestness ‖ npl see sēria
sērius adv later; too late; sērius ōcius sooner or later
serm·ō -ōnis m conversation, talk; discussion, discourse; common talk, rumor, gossip; language; diction; prose, everyday language
sermōncin·or -ārī -ātus sum intr to talk, converse, chat, chitchat

sermuncul·us -ī m small talk, gossip, chitchat; brief talk, chat
sērō adv (comp: sērius; superl: sērissimē) late; too late
ser·ō -ere -uī -tus tr to join, connect; to entwine, wreathe; to compose, combine, contrive
serō serere sēvī satus tr to sow, plant; (fig) to sow the seed of
serp·ēns -entis mf (large) snake, serpent, dragon ‖ Serpēns m (astr) Draco (constellation); Serpens (constellation, in the hand of Ophiuchus)
serpentigen·a -ae m dragon offspring
serpentip·ēs -edis adj dragon-footed
serperastr·um -ī n splint (for straightening the crooked legs of children); (mil) officer who keeps his soldiers in check
serpillum see serpyllum
serp·ō -ere -sī intr to creep, crawl; to wind; to move along slowly, spread slowly
serpyll·um -ī n (-pill-, -pull-) wild thyme (used for seasoning)
serr·a -ae f saw
serrāc·um -ī n (sarr-) large wagon
serrāt·us -a -um adj serrated, toothed (like a saw); notched
serrul·a -ae f small saw
sert·a -ae f wreath
sert·a -ōrum npl wreathes; festoons
Sertōriān·ī -ōrum mpl partisans of Sertorius
Sertōr·ius -(i)ī m general of Marius, assassinated in Spain by Perperna (c. 122–72 B.C.)
sert·us -a -um pp of serō (to join) ‖ f see serta ‖ npl see serta
seruī perf of serō (to join)
ser·um -ī n whey (milk serum, the watery liquid separating from curds)
sēr·us -a -um adj late; too late; occurring at a late hour; advanced, far gone; annī sērī ripe years; ulmus sēra slow-growing elm ‖ n late hour; in sērum rem trahere to drag out the matter until late
serv·a -ae f slave (female)
servābil·is -is -e adj retrievable
serv·āns -antis adj keeping; (w. gen) observant of
servāt·or -ōris m, servātr·īx -īcis f savior, preserver, deliverer
servīl·is -is -e adj slave, servile
servīliter adv slavishly
serv·iō -īre -īvī or -iī -ītum intr to be a servant or slave; to be obedient; (of buildings, land) to be mortgaged; (w. dat) 1 to be a slave to, be subservient to; 2 to serve; 3 to comply with, conform to; 4 to humor; 5 to be devoted to; 6 to work at; 7 to serve, be of use to
servit·ium -(i)ī n slavery; slaves
servitūd·ō -inis f servitude, slavery

servit·ūs -ūtis *f* slavery; slaves; property liability, easement
Serv·ius Tull·ius -(i)ī *m* sixth king of Rome *(credited with building the Servian Wall of tufa around Rome)*
serv·ō -āre -āvī -ātus *tr* to watch over, preserve, protect; to store, preserve; to keep, retain; to serve; to keep to, continue to dwell in
servol·a -ae *f* (-ula) young slave girl
servolicol·a -ae *f* slave of a slave *(female)*
servol·us -ī *m* (-ulus) young slave
serv·us *or* serv·os -a -um *adj* slave, servant ‖ *mf* slave, servant
sēscēnār·is -is -e *adj* (sexc-) a year and a half old
sēscēnāri·us -a -um *adj* six-hundred-man *(cohort)*
sēscēn·ī -ae -a *adj* six hundred each, in groups of six hundred
sēscentiēns *or* sēscentiēs *adv* (sexc-) six hundred times
sēsē *see* sē
sēsquī *adv* (-que) more by a half, one and a half times
sēsqui- *pref indicating that a quantity is multiplied by one and a half, e.g.,* sēsquihōra an hour and a half; sēsquilībra a pound and a half; *with ordinal numbers, it gives a number consisting of a unit and the fraction indicated by the numeral, e.g.,* sēsquitertius one and a third times as big; sēsquioctāvus one and an eighth times as big
sēsquialt·er -era -erum *adj* (sēsque-) one and a half times
sēsquihōr·a -ae *f* an hour and a half
sēsquilībr·a -ae *f* one and a half pounds
sēsquimod·ius -(i)ī *m* a peck and a half
sēsquioctāv·us -a -um *adj* (sēsque-) one and one-eighth times as big
sēsquiop·us -eris *n* the work of a day and a half
sēsquipedāl·is -is -e *adj* one and a half feet long *(or high, wide, thick, square, etc.)*
sēsqui·pēs -pedis *m* distance *or* length of one and a half feet
sēsquiplāg·a -ae *f* a stroke and a half
sēsquipl·ex -icis *adj* one and a half times as much
sēsquipl·us -a -um *adj* (sēscupl·us) one and a half times as big ‖ *n* one and a half times as much
sēsquiterti·us -a -um *adj* (sēsque-) one and a third times as big
sessibul·um -ī *n* seat, chair
sessil·is -is -e *adj (of the back of a centaur)* for sitting on; *(of plants)* low-growing
sessi·ō -ōnis *f* sitting; session; loafing

sessit·ō -āre -āvī -ātum *intr* to sit a lot, keep sitting, rest
sessiuncul·a -ae *f* small group *(sitting down together for a discussion)*
sess·or -ōris *m* spectator; resident
sessōr·ium -iī *n* sitting room
sēstertil·um -ī *n (coll)* a mere 100,000 sesterces
sēstert·ium -(i)ī *n (or declined as gen pl)* 100,000 sesterces
sēstert·ius -iī *(gen pl:* sēstertium) *(abbr:* HS) *m* sesterce *(small silver coin, equal to about one-fourth of a denarius, i.e., about 25¢, and used as the ordinary Roman unit in accounting; sums below 2000 sesterces are expressed by a cardinal number, e.g.,* ducentī sēsteriī; *sums from 2000 upwards are expressed by* mīlia sēstertium *(or* sēstertia, *with the distributives, or group-numbers* (bīna, quīnquāgēna, *etc.); sums of 1,000,000 and upwards are expressed by the numeral adverb in* -iēns (-iēs) *with* sēstertium *(taken as a gen pl or declined as a neuter singular noun:* deciēns *(i.e.,* deciēns centēna mīlia) sēstertium = *one million sesterces)*
Sest·os *or* Sest·us -ī *f* city on the Hellespont
sēt- = saet-
Sēti·a -ae *f* town in Latium famous for its wine *(modern Sezza)*
Sētīn·us -a -um *adj* Setine ‖ *n* Setine wine, wine from Setia
sētius *comp adv* (sēc-) later, more slowly; to a lesser degree, less readily; otherwise; nihilō sētius just the same, nonetheless; quō sētius *(w. subj)* so as to delay *or* prevent *(s.th. from happening):* impedīmentō est Caepiō quō sētius lēx ferātur Caepio is an impediment to having the law passed
seu *conj* or if; or; seu ... seu whether ... or
sevērē *adv* severely, sternly; seriously, in earnest; solemnly; sevēre dīcere to speak plainly
sevērit·ās -ātis *f* severity, sternness; self-discipline; seriousness
sevēritūd·ō -inis *f* severity, sternness; seriousness *(of expression)*
sevēr·us -a -um *adj* severe, strict, austere; serious, grave; ruthless, grim; plain, unadorned *(style of writing, architecture)*
sēvī *perf of* serō (to plant)
sēvoc·ō -āre -āvī -ātus *tr* to call aside, call away; to remove, withdraw; to separate; to appropriate *(from the common fund)*
sēv·um -ī *n* tallow, grease, suet
sex *indecl adj* six
Sex. *abbr* Sextus *(Roman first name, praenomen)*
sexāgē(n)sim·us -a -um *adj* sixtieth

sexāgēnāri·us -a -um *adj* sixty-year-old
sexāgēn·ī -ae -a *adj* sixty each; sixty at a time; sixty
sexāgiēns *or* sexāgiēs *adv* sixty times
sexāgintā *indecl adj* sixty
sexangul·us -a -um *adj* hexagonal
sexcēn- = sēscen-
sexcēnāri·us -a -um *adj* six-hundred-man *(cohort)*
sexenn·is -is -e *adj* six-year-old; sexennī diē in a six-year period
sexenn·ium -(i)ī *n* six-year period, six years
sexiēns *or* sexiēs *adv* six times
sexprīm·ī *or* sex prīm·ī -ōrum *mpl* six-member council *(in provincial towns)*
sextadecimān·ī -ōrum *mpl* soldiers of the sixteenth legion
sext·āns -antis *m* one-sixth; small coin *(one-sixth of an* as*)*; one-sixth of a pint
sextār·ius -(i)ī *m* pint
Sextīl·is -is -e *adj* of Sixtilis *(the sixth month of the old Roman year, which began in March; Sextilis was afterwards called August in honor of Augustus)*
sextul·a -ae *f* sixth of an ounce
sextum *adv* for the sixth time
sext·us -a -um *adj* sixth
sext·us decim·us -a -um *adj* sixteenth
sex·us -ūs *m* sex; *(gram)* gender
sī *conj* if; ō sī *(expressing a wish)* if only!; sī forte if by any chance, in the hope that; sī maximē however much; sī minus if not; sī modo provided that; sī vērō *(expressing scepticism)* if really
sibī *see* sē
sībil·a -ōrum *npl* hisses, hissing
sībil·ō -āre -āvī -ātus *tr* to hiss at; to whistle at ‖ *intr* to hiss; to whistle
sībil·us -a -um *adj* hissing; whistling ‖ *m & n* hissing; whistling; rustling
Sibyll·a -ae *f* (Sibu-) Sibyl *(esp. the Sibyl at Cumae)*
Sibyllīn·us -a -um *adj* Sibylline
sīc *adv* thus, so, in this way; thus, as follows; in these circumstances; in such a way, to such a degree; *(in assent)* yes
sīc·a -ae *f* (curved) dagger
Sicān·ī -ōrum *mpl* ancient people of Italy who migrated to Sicily
Sicāni·a -ae *f* Sicily
Sicān·is -idis *adj* Sicilian
Sicāni·us -a -um *adj* Sicilian ‖ *f* Sicily
Sicān·us -a -um *adj* Sicilian ‖ *mpl see* Sicānī
sīcār·ius -(i)ī *m* murderer, assassin; inter sīcāriōs accūsāre (dēfendere) to prosecute (defend) on a murder charge
siccē *adv* dryly; *(fig)* firmly, *(rhet)* plainly
siccit·ās -ātis *f* dryness; drought; firmness, solidity; plainness *(of style)*

sicc·ō -āre *tr* to dry, dry up; to drain; cruōrēs siccāre to stanch the blood
siccocul·us -a -um *adj* dry-eyed
sicc·us -a -um *adj* dry; thirsty; sober; firm, solid *(body);* solid *(argument);* dry, insipid *(style)*
Sicili·a -ae *f* Sicily
sicilicissit·ō -āre *intr* to act like a Sicilian
sīcīlicul·a -ae *f* sickle
Siciliēns·is -is -e *adj* Sicilian
sīcine *adv* is this how ... ?
sīcubi *adv* if anywhere, wheresoever
sīcul·a -ae *f* little dagger; *(vulg)* penis
Sicul·ī -ōrum *mpl* ancient Italic people who migrated to Sicily; Sicilians
sīcunde *conj* if from some place
sīcut *or* sīcutī *conj* as, just as; *(in elliptical clauses)* just as, like; *(introducing a comparison)* as it were, so to speak; *(introducing an example)* as for instance; *(of condition)* as, in the same condition as; as if, just as if; sīcut ... ita although ... yet
sīcutī *adv* *(archaic form of* sīcut*)*
Sicy·ōn -ōnis *mf* town in the N. Peloponnesus
Sicyōni·us -a -um *adj* Sicyonian ‖ *mpl* Sicyonians
sīdere·us -a -um *adj* starry; star-spangled; heavenly, divine
sīdō sīdere sīdī *or* sēdī sessum *intr* to sit down; to settle; *(of birds)* to land; to sink; to settle down, subside; *(of ships)* to be grounded
Sīd·ōn -ōnis *f* city of Phoenicia
Sīdōn·is -idis *adj* Phoenician ‖ *f* Dido; Europa; Anna
Sīdōni·us -a -um *adj* Sidonian, Phoenician; Theban ‖ *mpl* Sidonians
sīd·us -eris *n* constellation; star, heavenly body; sky, heaven; light, glory, beauty, pride; season; climate, weather; *(in astrology)* star, destiny
Sigambr·ī -ōrum *mpl* German tribe
Sīgē(i)·us -a -um *adj* Sigean; Trojan
Sīgē·um *or* Sīgē·on -ī *n* promontory near Troy
sigillār·ia -ium *or* -iōrum *npl* small objects of pottery stamped in relief with figures *or* ornamentation ‖ art market in Rome ‖ festival forming the final day of the Saturnalia
sigillāt·us -a -um *adj* adorned with little figures *or* patterns in relief
sigill·um -ī *n* statuette, figurine; stamped *or* embossed figure, a relief; seal *(made by a seal ring);* figure woven in tapestry
sigm·a -atis *n* semicircular couch *(for reclining at table)*
signāt·or -ōris *m* sealer, signer; witness
signāt·us -a -um *adj* marked with a stamp, coined

signif·er -era -erum *adj* bearing the constellations, starry ‖ *m* standard-bearer; chief, leader

signific·āns -antis *adj* clear, distinct, expressive; significant, meaningful

significanter *adv* clearly, graphically; meaningfully, significantly

significāti·ō -ōnis *f* signal, indication, sign, mark; meaning, sense, signification; emphasis; expression of approval, applause

signific·ō -āre -āvī -ātus *tr* to show, indicate, express, point out; to intimate; to notify, publish; to portend; to mean, signify ‖ *intr* to make signs, indicate

Signīn·us -a -um *adj* of *or* from Signia *(town in Latium, modern Segni, famous for its astringent variety of wine)*

signipot·ēns -entis *adj* ruling over the constellations

sign·ō -āre -āvī -ātus *tr* to mark, stamp, impress, imprint; to seal, seal up; to coin; to signify, indicate, express; to adorn; to distinguish, note

sign·um -ī *n* sign; indication, proof; military standard, banner; password; cohort, maniple; omen; symptom; shop sign; statue; a figure *(in a relief, picture, or embroidery);* device on a seal, seal; heavenly sign, constellation; **ab signīs dīscēdere** to break ranks, disband; **signa cōnferre** to engage in close combat; to concentrate troops; **signa cōnstituere** to halt; **signa conversa ferre** to wheel around and attack; **signa ferre** to break camp; **signa movēre in hostem** to advance against the enemy; **signa prōferre** to march forward; **signa servāre** to keep the order of battle; **signa sequī** to march in rank; **signa subsequī** to keep the order of battle; **signa trānsferre** to desert, join the other side; **signīs collātīs** in regular battle formation

sīlān·us -ī *m* waterspout *(originally designed as a head of Silenus*

Silar·us -ī *m* **(Siler-)** Sele River *(forming the boundary between Lucania and Campania and flowing by the town of Paestum)*

sil·ēns -entis *adj* silent, calm, quiet ‖ *mpl* the dead

silent·ium -(i)ī *n* silence; inactivity; **silentium facere** to obtain silence; to keep silent; **silentium significāre** to call for silence

Sīlēn·us -ī *m* teacher and companion of Bacchus, usually drunk; a Silenus *(wood-spirit)*

sil·eō -ēre -uī *tr* to leave unmentioned, say nothing about ‖ *intr* to be silent, be still; to keep silent; to be hushed; to rest, cease

sil·er -eris *n* willow

silēsc·ō -ere *intr* to become silent, fall silent, become hushed

sil·ex -icis *mf* flint stone, lava stone *(used in road paving and other construction);* cliff, crag; *(fig)* hardheartedness

silicern·ium -(i)ī *n* funeral meal; *(coll)* old fossil

silīg·ō -inis *f* winter wheat; wheat flour

siliqu·a -ae *f* pod, husk ‖ *fpl* pulse *(the edible seeds of certain leguminous plants, as lentils, peas)*

sillyb·us -ī *m* label *(giving the title of the scroll and author's name)*

sīl·ō -ōnis *m* snub nose

silua *see* **silva**

siluī *perf of* **sileō**

silūr·us -ī *m* European catfish

sīl·us -a -um *adj* snub-nosed

silv·a *or* **silŭ·a -ae** *f* woods, forest; shrubbery, bush, foliage, crop, growth; mass, quantity; material, supply

Silvān·us -ī *m* god of woods ‖ *mpl* woodland gods

silvēsc·ō -ere *intr (of a vine)* to run wild

silvestr·is -is -e *adj* wooded, overgrown with woods; woodland, living in the woods; wild, growing wild; rural, pastoral ‖ *npl* woodlands

silvicol·a -ae *mf* denizen of the forest

silvicultr·īx -īcis *adj (fem only)* living in the woods

silvifrag·us -a -um *adj (of the wind)* forest-smashing

silvōs·us -a -um *adj* wooded

sīmi·a -ae *f* monkey, ape; *(pej)* monkey

simil·is -is -e *adj* similar; *(w. gen, mostly of persons, or dat, mostly of things)* similar to, resembling, like; **hominēs inter sē similēs** people resembling one another; **vērī similis** probable, likely, realistic ‖ *n* comparison, parallel

similiter *adv* similarly; **similiter atque** *(or* **ac)** just as; **similiter ut sī** just as if

similitūd·ō -inis *f* likeness, resemblance; imitation; analogy; comparison, simile; monotony; *(w. gen or dat)* similarity to; **est hominī cum deō similitūdō** there is a resemblance between man and a god

sīmiol·us -ī *m (also pej)* little monkey

simītū *adv* at the same time; *(w.* **cum** + *abl)* together with

sīm·ius -iī *m (also pej)* monkey, ape

Simo·īs -entis *m* stream at Troy

Simōnid·ēs -is *m* lyric poet of the Greek island of Ceos *(fl 500 B.C.)* ‖ iambic poet of the Greek island of Amorgos *(7th cent. B.C.)*

simpl·ex -icis *adj* single, simple; unmixed; plain, ordinary, natural, without elaboration; frank; naive; in single file

simplicit·ās -ātis *f* simplicity; candor, frankness

simpliciter *adv* simply, plainly; frankly, candidly

simpl·us -a -um *adj* simple **ǁ** *n* the simple sum *or* number *(opp:* **duplum)**

simpul·um -ī *n* small ladle

simpuv·ium -(i)ī *n* libation bowl

simul *adv* together, at the same time; likewise; *(w. abl or* **cum)** together with; **simul atque** *(or* **ac** *or* **et)** as soon as; **simul ... simul** both ... and **ǁ** *conj* as soon as

simulācr·um -ī *n* image, likeness; portrait; form, shape, phantom, ghost; conception; sign, emblem; mere shadow; portraiture, characterization; **simulācra cērea** dolls

simulām·en -inis *n* imitation, copy

simul·āns -antis *adj* imitating; *(w. gen)* imitative of, able to imitate

simulātē *adv* insincerely, deceitfully

simulāti·ō -ōnis *f* faking, bluffing, bluff, pretense; **simulātiōne** *(w. gen)* under the pretense of

simulāt·or -ōris *m* imitator; pretender, phoney

simul·ō -āre -āvī -ātus *tr* **(simil-)** to imitate, copy; to represent; to put on the appearance of, simulate

simult·ās -ātis *f* enmity, rivalry, feud; jealousy; grudge

sīmul·us -a -um *adj* rather snub-nosed

sīm·us -a -um *adj* snub-nosed

sīn *conj* if however, if on the other hand, but if; **sīn aliter** but if not

sināp·i *or* **sināp·e -is** *n,* **sināp·is -is** *f* (white) mustard

sincērē *adv* sincerely, honestly

sincērit·ās -ātis *f (physical)* soundness; purity; sincerity, integrity

sincēr·us -a -um *adj* sound, whole, clean; untainted; sincere, real, genuine

sincip·ut -itis *or* **sincipitāment·um -ī** *n* half a head *(as food);* cheek, jowl *(of a hog);* brain

sind·ōn -ōnis *f* fine cotton *or* linen fabric, muslin

sine *prep (w. abl)* without

singillātim *or* **singulātim** *adv* singly

singlāriter *see* **singulāriter**

singulār·is -is -e *adj* single, alone, one at a time; specific, peculiar, special; individual; unique; *(gram)* singular **ǁ** *mpl* crack troops

singulāriter *adv* singly; particularly; *(gram)* in the singular

singulāri·us -a -um *adj* single, separate; unique

singulātim *adv* singly, individually

singul·ī -ae -a *adj* single, one at a time, one by one, individual; one each, one apiece; **in singulōs diēs** on each successive day; every day, daily *(w. comp or words denoting increase or decrease):* **crēscit in diēs singulōs hostium numerus** the number of the enemy increases

daily; **in singulōs hominēs** per man **ǁ** *mpl* individuals

singultim *adv* sobbingly, with sobs

singult·iō -īre *intr* to hiccup; to throb

singult·ō -āre -āvī -ātus *tr* to gasp out; to utter with sobs **ǁ** *intr* to gasp, sob

singult·us -ūs *m* sob, gasp; squirt *(of water, etc.);* death rattle

sinis·ter -tra -trum *adj* left, on the left; *(because in Roman augury the augur faced south, having the East on the left)* favorable, auspicious, lucky; *(because in Greek augury the augur faced north, having the East on his right)* unfavorable, inauspicious, unlucky; wrong, perverse, improper **ǁ** *mpl* soldiers on the left flank **ǁ** *f* left, left hand; left side; **a sinistrā** on the left **ǁ** *n* left side

sinisterit·ās -ātis *f* awkwardness

sinistrē *adv* badly, wrongly

sinistrōrsum *or* **sinistrōrsus** *adv* to the left

sinō sinere sīvī *or* **siī situs** *tr* to allow; **sine modo** only let, just let, if only

Sin·ōn -ōnis *m* Greek soldier who talked the Trojans into dragging the wooden horse into Troy

Sinōp·a -ae *or* **Sinōp·ē -ēs** *f* Sinope *(Greek colony on the S. coast of the Euxine or Black Sea)*

Sinuess·a -ae *f* **(Sino-)** city near the border between Latium and Campania

sīn·um -ī *n* large drinking cup

sinu·ō -āre -āvī -ātus *tr* to wind, curve; to fill out *(sails)*

sinuōs·us -a -um *adj* winding, sinuous, serpentine

sīn·us -ī *m* large drinking cup

sin·us -ūs *m* indentation, curve, fold, hollow; fold of the toga about the breast, pocket, purse; breast, bosom, lap; bay, gulf, lagoon; winding coast; valley, hollow; heart *(e.g., of a city),* interior; intimacy; **in sinū meō est** he *or* she is dear to me

sīpar·ium -(i)ī *n (theat)* curtain; **post sīparium** behind the scenes

sīp(h)·ō -ōnis *m* siphon; fire engine

sīphuncul·us -ī *m* small pipe

Sipyl·us *or* **Sipyl·os -ī** *m* mountain in Lydia on which Niobe was changed into a rock

sīquandō *or* **sī quandō** *conj* if ever

sīquidem *conj* if in fact

siremps *or* **sirempse = sī rem ipsam** *adj* the same; **sirempse lēgem iussit esse Iuppiter** Jupiter ordered the law to be the same

Sīr·ēn -ēnis *f* Siren *(sea nymph that had the power of charming sailors to their death with her song)*

Sīri·us -a -um *adj* of Sirius, of the Dog Star **ǁ** *m* Sirius, Dog Star *(in the constellation Canis Maior)*

sirp·e -is *n (bot)* silphium *(from which gum was extracted)*
sīr·us -ī *m* underground silo
sīs = **sī vīs** please, if you please
sistō sistere stitī *or* **stetī status** *tr* to cause to stand, make stand, put, place, set; to set up *(monument);* to establish; to stop, check, arrest; to put an end to; to produce in court; **pedem** *(or* **gradum) sistere** to halt, stop; **vadimōnium sistere** to answer bail, show up in court **ǁ** *refl* to present oneself, appear, come **ǁ** *pass* **sistī nōn potest** the crisis cannot be met, the case is hopeless **ǁ** *intr* to stand, rest; to stop, stay; to stand firm, last, endure; to show up in court; *(w. dat or* **contrā** + *acc)* to stand firm against
sistrāt·us -a -um *adj* with a tambourine
sistr·um -ī *n* tambourine, rattle
Sīsyphid·ēs -ae *m* descendant of Sisyphus *(Ulysses)*
Sīsyphi·us -a -um *adj* of Sisyphus; **sanguine crētus Sīsyphiō** born of the stock of Sisyphys *(i.e., Ulysses)*
Sīsyph·us *or* **Sīsyph·os -ī** *m* Sisyphus *(son of Aeolus, king of Corinth, whose punishment in Hades was to roll a rock repeatedly up a hill)*
sitell·a -ae *f* lottery urn
Sīth·ōn -onis *adj* Thracian
Sīthon·is -idis *or* **-idos** *adj* Thracian **ǁ** *f* Thracian woman
Sīthoni·us -a -um *adj* Thracian **ǁ** *mpl* Thracians
sitīculōs·us -a -um *adj* thirsty, dry
siti·ēns -entis *adj* thirsting, thirsty; arid, parched; parching; *(w. gen)* thirsting for, eager for
sitienter *adv* thirstily, eagerly
sit·iō -īre *tr* to thirst for **ǁ** *intr* to be thirsty
sit·is -is *f* thirst; *(w. gen)* thirst for
sitīt·or -ōris *m* thirsty person; **sitītor aquae** one who thirsts for water
sittyb·us -ī *m* label *(giving the title of the scroll and author's name)*
situl·a -ae *f* bucket; basin, urn
sit·us -a -um *pp of* **sinō ǁ** *adj* situated, located, lying; founded; *(w.* **in** + *abl)* resting on, dependent on
sit·us -ūs *m* position, situation, site, location; structure; neglect; mustiness; dust, dirt; idleness, inactivity, lack of use
sīve *or* **seu** *conj* or if; or; **sīve … sīve** whether … or
sīvī *perf of* **sinō**
smaragd·us *or* **smaragd·os -ī** *f (m)* emerald
smar·is -idis *f* a small sea fish
smīl·ax -acis *adj (bot)* smilax *(an evergreen climbing plant)*
Sminth·eüs -eī *m* epithet of Apollo
Smyrn·a -ae *f* town on W. coast of Asia Minor

sobol- = **subol-**
sōbriē *adv* soberly, moderately; sensibly
sōbriet·ās -ātis *f* sobriety
sobrīn·a -ae *f* cousin *(female, on the mother's side)*
sobrīn·us -ī *m* cousin *(on the mother's side)*
sōbri·us -a -um *adj* sober; temperate; sensible, reasonable
soccul·us -ī *m* small slipper
socc·us -ī *m* slipper; low shoe *(worn by actors in comedy); (fig)* comedy
soc·er *or* **soc·erus -erī** *m* father-in-law
soci·a -ae *f* associate, companion, ally, partner *(female)*
sociābll·is -ls -e *adj* compatible, intimate
sociāl·is -is -e *adj* allied, confederate; nuptial, conjugal; sociable
sociāliter *adv* sociably
socienn·us -ī *m* buddy; partner
societ·ās -ātis *f* companionship, fellowship; association, society; partnership; alliance, confederacy
soci·ō -āre -āvī -ātus *tr* to unite, associate; to share
sociofraud·us -ī *m* double-crosser, heel
soci·us -a -um *adj* joint, allied, confederate; held in common, common **ǁ** *m* associate, companion, ally, partner **ǁ** *f see* **socia**
sōcordi·a -ae *f* silliness, stupidity; apathy, laziness
sōcordius *adv* too apathetically
sōc·ors -ordis *adj* silly, stupid; apathetic, lazy, inactive
Sōcrat·es -is *m* Athenian philosopher *(469–399 B.C.)*
Sōcratic·ī -ōrum *mpl* Socratics
socr·us -ūs *f* mother-in-law
sodālici·us -a -um *adj* of companionship **ǁ** *n* companionship, intimacy; society, secret society
sodāl·is -is *m* companion, fellow, buddy, crony; member *(of a society, priestly college, etc.);* accomplice; **sodālis Augustālis** member of a fraternity associated with the cult of Augustus
sodālit- = **sodālic-**
sodālit·ās -ātis *f* companionship, fellowship; society, club, association; secret society
sōdēs = **sī audēs** if you will, please
sōl sōlis *m* sun; sunlight, sunshine; day
sōlāciol·um -ī *n* a bit of comfort
sōlāc·ium -(i)ī *n* (sōlāt-) comfort, relief
sōlām·en -inis *n* comfort
sōlār·is -is -e *adj* sun; **lūmen sōlāre** sunlight, sunshine
sōlār·ium -(i)ī *n* sundial; clock; sunny spot, balcony
sōlāt- = **sōlāc-**
sōlāt·or -ōris *m* comforter

soldūri·ī -ōrum *mpl* retainers *(of a chieftain)*
soldus *see* solidus
sole·a -ae *f* sole; sandal *(with toes exposed; cf.*
  sandalium); fetter; sole *(flatfish)*
soleār·ius -(i)ī *m* sandal-maker
soleāt·us -a -um *adj* wearing sandals
soleō solēre solitus sum *intr (w. inf)* to be in
  the habit of, be used to; usually: *e.g.,* solet
  cēnāre sērō he usually eats late; *(w.* cum +
  abl) to have sex with
sol(i)d·us -a -um *adj* solid, firm, dense; whole,
  entire; genuine; trustworthy; resolute ‖ *n*
  entire sum, total; a solid; mass, substance;
  solid earth
solidē *adv* solidly; thoroughly, downright;
  firmly
solidit·ās -ātis *f* solidity
solid·ō -āre -āvī -ātus *tr* to make firm; to make
  dense; to strengthen
sōliferre·um -ī *n* all-iron spear
sōlistim·us -a -um *adj* (-umus) perfect, complete; tripudium sōlistimum perfectly auspicious omen
sōlitāri·us -a -um *adj* solitary, lonely
sōlitūd·ō -inis *f* loneliness; deprivation; solitude; wilderness; *(w. gen)* state of being forsaken by ‖ *fpl* desert, wilderness
solit·us -a -um *adj* usual, customary, characteristic ‖ *n* the usual, the customary;
  formōsior solitō more handsome than usual;
  magis *(or* plūs) solitō more than usual
sol·ium -(i)ī *n* seat, chair; throne; dominion,
  sway; bathtub; stone coffin
sōlivag·us -a -um *adj* roaming alone; single,
  solitary
sollemn·is -is -e *adj* annual, periodic; solemn,
  religious; usual ‖ *n* usage, practice; solemn
  rite, solemnity, ceremony; feat; sacrifice; festival, games *(in honor of Roman holy days)*
sollemniter *adv* solemnly, religiously
soll·ers -ertis *adj* (sōl-) skilled, skillful, expert,
  clever
sollerti·a -ae *f* (sōl-) skill, shrewdness; clever
  plan; *(w. gen)* skill in
sollicitāti·ō -ōnis *f* vexation; anxiety; incitement, instigation
sollicitē *adv* anxiously, with solicitude; diligently
sollicit·ō -āre -āvī -ātus *tr* to shake, disturb; to
  disquiet, annoy, molest; to worry, make anxious; to provoke, tempt; to stir up, incite to
  revolt
sollicitūd·ō -inis *f* anxiety, uneasiness; worry;
  solicitude; *(w. gen)* anxiety over
sollicit·us -a -um *adj* stirred up, stormy *(sea);*
  tossed *(by the waves);* troubled, disturbed,
  restless; solicitous, anxious, worried; incited
  to revolt
sollif- = sōlif-

sollist- = sōlist-
soloecism·us -ī *m* mistake in grammar, sole-
  cism
Sol·ō(n) -ōnis *m* Solon *(famous Athenian leg-*
  islator c. 640–560 B.C.)
sōl·or -ārī -ātus sum *tr* to console; to relieve,
  mitigate *(fear, etc.)*
sōlstiāl·is -is -e *adj* of the summer solstice;
  midsummer's; solar
sōlstit·ium -(i)ī *n* summer solstice, midsummer, summer heat
sōlum *adv* only, merely, barely; nōn
  sōlum ... sed etiam not only ... but also
sol·um -ī *n* bottom, ground, floor; soil, land,
  country; sole *(of foot, shoe)*
sōl·us -a -um *adj* only, single, sole, alone;
  lonely, solitary
solūtē *adv* loosely, freely, without hindrance;
  negligently; without vigor
solūti·ō -ōnis *f* loosening; payment
solūt·us -a -um *adj* loose, untied, unbandaged;
  negligent; free; fluent; unrhythmical; uncontrolled; exempt, free; unbiased; unbridled
sol·vō -vere -vī *or* -uī -ūtus *tr* to loosen, untie
  (a cord); to release, untie, free; to dissolve,
  break up; to detach, disengage; to unlock,
  open; to melt; to relax *(the body);* to smooth,
  soothe; to impair, weaken, destroy; to acquit;
  to accomplish, fulfill; to pay, pay off; to
  solve, explain; to break *(a siege);* to break
  down *(a barrier);* to undergo *(punishment);*
  to get rid of *(feelings);* to loosen *(the bow-*
  els); to remove *(surgical dressings);* to
  unharness, unyoke *(animals);* to disperse into
  the atmosphere, dissipate; to enervate, sap the
  strength of *(a person);* crīnēs solvere to let
  down the hair *(in mourning);* nāvem *(or*
  rātem) solvere to cast off, set sail; ōra solvere to open the mouth *(to speak)* ‖ to melt,
  dissolve ‖ *intr* to weigh anchor, set sail
Solym·a -ōrum *npl* Jerusalem
Solym·us -a -um *adj* of Jerusalem ‖ *mpl*
  mountain tribe, supposed to have given its
  name to Jerusalem
somniculōsē *adv* sleepily, drowsily
somniculōs·us -a -um *adj* sleepy, drowsy
somnif·er -era -erum *adj* soporific, sleep-
  inducing; deadly *(poison)*
somni·ō -āre -āvī -ātus *tr* to dream of; to daydream about, imagine; somnium somniāre
  to have a dream ‖ *intr* to dream; to daydream
somn·ium -(i)ī *n* dream, vision; day-dream
somn·us -ī *m* sleep; night; sleep of death; indolence
sonābil·is -is -e *adj* noisy
sonip·ēs -edis *adj* loud-hoofed ‖ *m* steed
sonit·us -ūs *m* sound, noise, clang
sonivi·us -a -um *adj* noisy

son·ō -āre -uī -itus *tr* to utter, say, sound, express; to denote, mean; to sound like **ǁ** *intr* to sound; to ring, resound, make a noise; to be spoken of as

son·or -ōris *m* sound, noise, clang

sonōr·us -a -um *adj* sonorous, loud, noisy, clanging

sōns sontis *adj* guilty, criminal; *(w. abl of the crime)* guilty of **ǁ** *m* guilty one, criminal

sontic·us -a -um *adj* serious, critical

sonuī *perf of* **sonō**

-son·us -a -um *adjl suf denotes "sounding,"* e.g.: **raucisonus** hoarse-sounding

son·us -ī *m* sound, noise; tone

sophi·a -ae *f* wisdom

sophist·ēs -ae *m* sophist

Sophocl·ēs -is *or* **-ī** Greek writer of tragedies *(c. 495–406 B.C.)*

Sophoclē·us -a -um *adj* Sophoclean

soph·us -a -um *adj* wise **ǁ** *m* wise man, sage

sōp·iō -īre -īvī *or* **-iī -ītus** *tr* to put to sleep; to stun, knock unconscious; *(fig)* to calm, settle, lull

sop·or -ōris *m* deep sleep; stupor; apathy; sleeping potion

sopōrāt·us -a -um *adj* stupefied; unconscious; buried in sleep; allayed *(grief);* soporific

sopōrif·er -era -erum *adj* sleep-inducing

sopōr·us -a -um *adj* drowsy

Sōract·e -is *n* mountain in Etruria about 25 miles N.E. of Rome

sōrac·um -ī *n* chest, hamper

sorb·eō -ēre -uī -itus *tr* to suck in, gulp down; to absorb; *(fig)* to swallow

sorbil(l)·ō -āre -āvī -ātus *tr* to sip

sorbilō *adv* drop by drop, bit by bit

sorbiti·ō -ōnis *f* broth

sorb·um -ī *n* **(sorv-)** Juneberry

sorb·us -ī *f* **(sorv-)** Juneberry tree

sord·eō -ēre *intr* to be dirty, be shabby; to appear worthless

sord·ēs -is *f* dirt, filth; shabbiness, squalor; greed, stinginess; moral turpitude; meanness *(of behavior);* low rank, low condition; rabble, scum; **sordēs verbōrum** vulgarity **ǁ** *fpl* rags, dark clothes *(often worn as a sign of mourning)*

sord·ēscō -ēscere -uī *intr* to become dirty, become soiled

sordidāt·us -a -um *adj* in shabby clothes *(esp. as sign of mourning)*

sordidē *adv* vilely; greedily

sordidul·us -a -um *adj* rather soiled, rather shabby; *(fig)* low

sordid·us -a -um *adj* dirty, filthy; shabby; soiled, stained; dressed in mourning clothes; low *(rank);* vulgar

sorditūd·ō -inis *f* dirt, filth

sōr·ex -icis *m* shrewmouse

sōricīn·us -a -um *adj* squealing like mice

sōrīt·ēs -ae *m* sorites *(logical conclusion drawn from cumulative arguments)*

sor·or -ōris *f* sister; cousin; companion, playmate; **sorōrēs doctae** Muses; **sorōrēs trēs** three Fates; **sorōrēs trīstēs** gloomy Fates

sorōricīd·a -ae *m* murderer of a sister

sorōri·us -a -um *adj* sister's, of a sister; sisterly; **stuprum sorōrium** incest with a sister

sors sortis *f* lot; casting of lots, decision by lot; prophecy; fate, destiny, lot in life; portion, share; sort, kind

sōrsum *see* **seōrsum**

sortileg·us -a -um *adj* prophetic **ǁ** *m* soothsayer, fortuneteller

sort·iō -īre -īvī *or* **-iī -ītus** *or* **sort·ior -īrī -ītus sum** *tr* to cast lots for; to allot, assign by lot, appoint by lot; to obtain by lot; to choose, select; to share, divide; to receive, get by chance **ǁ** *intr* to cast *or* draw lots

sortīti·ō -ōnis *f* drawing lots, determining by lots

sortītō *adv* by lot; by fate

sortīt·us -ūs *m* lottery

Sosi·ī -ōrum *mpl* the Sosii *(two brothers famous as booksellers in Rome at the time of Horace)*

sōsp·es -itis *adj* safe and sound; auspicious, lucky

sōspit·a -ae *f* preserver *(epithet of Juno)*

sōspitāl·is -is -e *adj* beneficial

sōspit·ō -āre *tr* to preserve, protect

sōt·ēr -ēris *m* savior, protector

sōtēri·a -ōrum *npl* party for a person recovering from an illness

Sp. *abbr* **Spurius** *(Roman first name, praenomen)*

spād·īx -īcis *m* chestnut-brown horse

spad·ō -ōnis *m* eunuch

spar·gō -gere -sī -sus *tr* to scatter, sprinkle, strew; to disperse; to disseminate; to spot, dapple

sparsi·ō -ōnis *f* sprinkling

spars·us -a -um *pp of* **spargō ǁ** *adj* freckled, spotty

Spart·a -ae *or* **Spart·ē -ēs** *f* Sparta *(capital of Laconia)*

Spartac·us -ī *m* Thracian gladiator who led a revolt of gladiators against Rome in 73–71 B.C.

Spartān·us -a -um *adj* Spartan **ǁ** *m* a Spartan

Spartiāt·ēs -ae *m* Spartan

Spartiātic·us *or* **Spartic·us -a -um** *adj* Spartan

spart·um *or* **spart·on -ī** *n* Spanish broom *(fibrous plant used in making ropes, nets, etc.)*

sparul·us -ī *m* bream *(fish)*

spar·us *m or* **spar·um -ī** *n* hunting spear

spath·a -ae *f* spatula; broad two-edged sword
spati·or -ārī -ātus sum *intr* to stroll, take a walk; to walk solemnly; to spread out
spatiōsē *adv* extensively; long
spatiōs·us -a -um *adj* extensive; spacious; wide; *(of time)* long, lengthy; *(of vowel)* long; *(w. advl force)* with its *(his, etc.)* great size
spat·ium -(i)ī *n* space, room, extent; open space, public square; distance *(between two points);* walk, promenade *(place);* lap *(of a race);* racetrack; interval, period; time, opportunity; *(pros)* measure, quantity
speci·ēs -ēī *f* sight, view; outward appearance; outline, shape; fine appearance, beauty; deceptive appearance, show, semblance, pretense, pretext; resemblance; display, splendor; apparition; image, statue; idea, notion; reputation; species, sort; *(leg)* specific legal situation *or* case; **ad** *(or* **in) speciem** for show; **in speciem** *(or* **per speciem)** as a pretext, for the sake of appearances; **prīmā speciē** at first sight; **speciē** outwardly, to all appearances; **speciē** *(w. gen)* **1** in the guise of; **2** on the pretext of
specill·um -ī *n* probe *(surgical instrument)*
specim·en -inis *n* mark, sign, proof; example; model, ideal
speciō specere spexī spectus *tr* to look at
speciōsē *adv* splendidly
speciōs·us -a -um *adj* handsome, good-looking, beautiful; plausible; specious
spectābil·is -is -e *adj* visible; remarkable
spectāc(u)l·um -ī *n* sight, spectacle; public performance, show; stage play; theater
spectām·en -inis *n* sign, proof
spectāti·ō -ōnis *f* observation, view; examining, testing
spectāt·or -ōris *m* observer; spectator; critic, judge ‖ *mpl* audience
spectātr·īx -īcis *f* onlooker, observer; spectator *(female)*
spectāt·us -a -um *adj* tried, tested, proved; esteemed, distinguished
specti·ō -ōnis *f* observing the auspices; right to take the auspices
spect·ō -āre -āvī -ātus *tr* to observe, watch; to face in the direction of; to consider; to bear in mind; to aim at, tend toward; to examine, test
spectr·um -ī *n* specter, apparition
specul·a -ae *f* lookout, watchtower; summit; **in speculīs** on the lookout
spēcul·a -ae *f* slight hope; glimmer of hope
speculābund·us -a -um *adj* on the lookout
speculār·is -is -e *adj* transparent ‖ *n* windowpane *(of mica)*, window
specul·or -ōris *m* spy; explorer
speculātōri·us -a -um *adj* for spying, for reconnaissance ‖ *f* reconnaissance ship
speculātr·īx -īcis *f* spy *(female)*

specul·or -ārī -ātus sum *tr* to reconnoiter, observe, watch for
specul·um -ī *n* mirror *(made of polished metal)*
spec·us -ūs *m (n)* cave, cavern; grotto; *(any artificial excavation)* hole, pit, tunnel, ditch; cavity *(of a wound, etc.)*
spēlae·um -ī *n* (**-lē-**) den, cave
spēlunc·a -ae *f* cave
spērābil·is -is -e *adj* to be hoped for
spērāt·us -a -um *adj* hoped for, desired ‖ *f* fiancée
Sperchē·is -idos *adj (fem only)* of the Spercheus River
Sperchē·us -ī *m* (**-chi-**) Spercheus *(large river in Thessaly)*
spernō spernere sprēvī sprētus *tr* to spurn, scorn, reject; to speak disdainfully of; to separate, dissociate
spēr·ō -āre -āvī -ātus *tr* to hope for, expect, look forward to; to trust, trust in; to anticipate, await in fear; *(w. acc & inf; also w. nom & inf in imitation of the Greek; also w.* **ut** + *subj)* I hope that; **id quod nōn spērō** I hope that is not the case, I hope not ‖ *intr* to hope; **bene spērāre** to be optimistic; **nōn spērō** I hope not; **ut spērō** hopefully
spēs speī *f* hope; expectation; anticipation; apprehension *(of evil);* person *or* thing on which hopes are based, *e.g.:* **Gāius Marius spēs subsidium patriae** Gaius Marius, the hope and safeguard of our country; *(applied to one's offspring)* one's hopes for the future, *e.g.:* **mea cārissima fīliola et spēs reliqua nostra** my dearest little daughter and our only remaining hope; **in spē** in prospect; **in spē** *(w. gen)* with the prospect of; **in spem** *(w. gen)* so as to give the promise of; **praeter spem** beyond all expectation
sp(h)aer·a -ae *f* sphere, globe; ball; one of the imaginary spheres in which the heavenly bodies were supposed to travel around the earth; working model of the universe
sphaeristēr·ium -iī *n* ball field, ball court, tennis court
Sphin·x -gis *or* **-gos** *f* sphinx *(esp. the Sphinx of Boeotia whose riddle Oedipus was able to solve);* the Sphinx of Egypt at Giza
spīc·a -ae *f* point; ear *(of grain);* tuft, top, head *(of plants)*
spīce·us -a -um *adj* made of ears of grain
spīcul·um -ī *n* point; sting; dart, arrow
spīc·um -ī *n* ear *(of grain)*
spīn·a -ae *f* thorn; thornbush; prickle *(of animals);* spike *(of asparagus);* backbone, spine; *(fig)* thorny question
spīnēt·um -ī *n* thorn hedge, thorny thicket
spīne·us -a -um *adj* made of thorns
spīnif·er *or* **spīnig·er -era -erum** *adj* prickly, thorny

spīnōs·us -a -um *adj* thorny, prickly; *(fig)* thorny, difficult; obscure *(style)*

spint·ēr -ēris *m* bracelet

Spinth·ēr -ēris *m* Roman family name *(cognomen)*

spintri·a -ae *m* male prostitute *(given to particularly perverted acts)*

spinturnīc·ium -iī *n* bird of ill omen

spīn·us -ī *or* -ūs *f* thornbush

spīr·a -ae *f* coil *(of serpent);* chin strap

spīrābil·is -is -e *adj* good to breathe, life-giving *(air)*

spīrācul·um -ī *n* pore; vent

spīrāment·um -ī *n* vent; air hole; windpipe; breathing space, pause; animae spirāmenta lungs

spīrit·us -ūs *m* breathing, breath; breeze, wind; air, air current; wind of the bowels; breath of life, life; inspiration; spirit, soul; character, courage; enthusiasm, vigor; pride, arrogance; morale; *(gram)* aspiration; extrēmus *(or* ultimus) spīritus one's last breath; spīritum dūcere to take a breath

spīr·ō -āre -āvī -ātus *tr* to breathe, blow; to exhale; to give off the odor of, smell of; to aspire to, aim at ‖ *intr* to breathe; to be alive; to breathe after exertion, recover one's breath; *(of the wind)* to blow, blow auspiciously, be favorable; *(of things)* to give off an odor; *(of a quality)* to emanate; to have poetic inspiration

spissāment·um -ī *n* stopper, plug

spissāt·us -a -um *adj* condensed, concentrated

spissē *adv* thickly, closely, tightly; with effort, slowly

spissēsc·ō -ere *intr* to condense, become thick, become more compact

spissigrad·us -a -um *adj* slow-paced

spiss·ō -āre -āvī -ātus *tr* to condense, concentrate; to pack tightly; to intensify *(efforts)*

spiss·us -a -um *adj* thick; tight; dense; solid, compact; slow, sluggish; late; closely-woven, thick; packed, crowded; *(of blows, kisses)* coming thick and fast

splēn splēnis *m* spleen

splend·eō -ēre *intr* to be clear and bright; to shine, gleam; to become glossy; to be illustrious, be glorious; to be resplendent

splendēsc·ō -ere *intr* to become bright, begin to shine; *(w. abl)* to take on luster from

splendidē *adv* splendidly, brilliantly

splendid·us -a -um *adj* clear and bright; gleaming, glistening, sparkling; spotless, noble *(character);* splendid; sumptuous; showy; illustrious

splend·or -ōris *m* splendor; brightness, brilliance; clearness

splēniāt·us -a -um *adj* wearing a patch

splēn·ium -iī *n* patch

spoliāti·ō -ōnis *f* stripping, plundering; unjust deprivation *(of honor, dignity);* ousting *(from office)*

spoliāt·or -ōris *m*, spoliātr·īx -īcis *f* despoiler, robber

spoliāt·us -a -um *adj* stripped, robbed

spoli·ō -āre -āvī -ātus *tr* to strip; to pillage, plunder, rob; to take away *(possessions)*

spol·ium -iī *n* hide, skin; spoils, booty, loot ‖ *npl* arms, equipment, etc., stripped from an enemy; spolia opīma the spoils taken by a Roman general from the enemy leader he had killed in single combat; spolia secunda lesser spoils

spond·a -ae *f* bedframe, sofa frame; bed, sofa

spondā(u)l·ium -(i)ī *n* ritual hymn accompanied by a flute

spondeō spondēre spopondī spōnsus *tr* to promise solemnly, pledge, vow; to promise in marriage; to vouch for, back up ‖ *intr (leg)* to give a guarantee, put up bail; *(w.* prō + *abl)* to vouch for

spondē·us -ī *m (pros)* spondee *(foot consisting of two long syllables)*

spondyl·us -ī *m* a kind of shellfish, mussel

spongi·a -ae *f* (-ge-) sponge; sponge eraser; quilted corslet

spōns·a -ae *f* fiancée

spōnsāl·ia -ium *npl* engagement; engagement party

spōnsi·ō -ōnis *f* solemn promise; guarantee; bet; *(leg)* agreement between two parties that the loser pay a certain sum to the winner

spōns·or -ōris *m* guarantor, surety; Ammonius spōnsor prōmissōrum Cleopatrae Ammon, who backs up the promises of Cleopatra

spōns·us -a -um *pp of* spondeō ‖ *m* fiancé, bridegroom ‖ *f* fiancée ‖ *n* agreement, engagement

spōns·us -ūs *m* contract

sponte *(abl only) f (of persons, mostly with poss adj)* of one's own accord, voluntarily, deliberately, purposely; by oneself, unaided; *(of things)* of itself, spontaneously; on its own account, for its own sake; meā (suā, etc.) sponte of my own *(his own, her own, etc.)* accord; sponte aetātis as a consequence of one's years; sponte nātūrae (suae) of its own nature, naturally, spontaneously; suā sponte considered in itself, inherently, essentially

spopondī *perf of* spondeō

sport·a -ae *f* plaited basket

sportell·a -ae *f* little basket

sportul·a -ae *f* little basket *(in which gifts of food were given by the patron to his clients);* dole, present *(of food or money);* gift

sprēt·or -ōris *m* despiser, scorner

sprētus *pp of* spernō
sprēvī *perf of* spernō
spūm·a -ae *f* foam, froth; hair dye; spūmās agere ōre to froth at the mouth
spūmāt·us -a -um *adj* covered with foam
spūmēsc·ō -ere *intr* to grow foamy
spūme·us -a -um *adj* foaming
spūmif·er *or* spūmig·er -era -erum *adj* foaming
spūm·ō -āre -āvī -ātum *intr* to foam, froth; *(of places, things)* to be covered with foam; equī terga spūmantia the back of the horse soaked with sweat
spūmōs·us -a -um *adj* full of foam, foaming; bombastic
spuō spuere spuī spūtus *tr* to spit, spit out ‖ *intr* to spit
spurcāt·us -a -um *adj* foul, filthy
spurcē *adv* filthily; offensively; in filthy language
spurcidic·us -a -um *adj* foul-mouthed, smutty, obscene
spurcific·us -a -um *adj* smutty
spurciti·a -ae *or* spurciti·ēs -ēī *f* filth, smut
spurc·ō -āre -āvī -ātus *tr* to make filthy, foul up; to defile
spurc·us -a -um *adj* filthy, nasty, impure, unclean; foul *(weather)*
spūtātilic·us -a -um *adj* deserving to be spit on, contemptible, disgusting
spūtāt·or -ōris *m* spitter
spūt·ō -āre -āvī -ātus *tr* to spit, spit out; to avert *(by spitting)*
spūt·um -ī *n* spit, sputum
squāl·eō -ēre -uī *intr* to be rough, be scaly; to be coated, be clotted, be stiff; to be covered with filth, be caked with mud; *(of clouds, shade)* to be dark, be murky; *(of places)* to be covered with weeds, be overgrown; *(of land)* to lie waste *(from neglect, barrenness); (of persons)* to wear mourning clothes
squālidē *adv* harshly, roughly
squālid·us -a -um *adj* rough, scaly; stiff, caked with dirt; squalid; in mourning; coarse *(speech);* barren, waste *(land)*
squāl·or -ōris *m* squalor, dirtiness; desolation; uncouthness *(of style);* squalid clothes *(as a sign of mourning)*
squal·us -ī *m* a type of sea fish
squām·a -ae *f* scale *(of fish, serpent, etc.);* scale armor; scale-like yellow band on the abdomen of a bee
squāme·us -a -um *adj* scaly
squāmif·er *or* squāmig·er -era -erum *adj* scaly ‖ *mpl* fish
squāmōs·us -a -um *adj* covered with scales, scaly
squill·a -ae *f* (scill-) shrimp, crayfish
st *interj* shhh!, ssst!

stabilīment·um -ī *n* support, prop; *(fig)* mainstay
stabil·iō -īre -īvī -ītus *tr* to stabilize; to establish firmly
stabil·is -is -e *adj* stable, firm, steady; steadfast, unwavering, immutable
stabilit·ās -ātis *f* stability, firmness, steadiness, durability
stabiliter *adv* firmly; steadfastly
stabul·ō -āre -āvī -ātus *tr* to stable *or* house *(animals)* ‖ *intr* to have a stall
stabul·um -ī *n* stable, stall; lair; hut; brothel; *(coll)* flea bag, cheap lodgings
stact·a -ae *or* stact·ē -ēs *f* myrrh oil
stad·ium -iī *n* furlong; running track, stadium; stade *(= 625 feet)*
Stagīr·a -ōrum *npl* town in Macedonia, birthplace of Aristotle
Stagīrīt·ēs -ae *m* Aristotle
stāgn·ō -āre -āvī -ātus *tr* to overflow, inundate ‖ *intr* to form a pool; to be inundated
stāgn·um -ī *n (expanse of water, natural or artificial)* pool, lake, lagoon, swamp, straits; alloy of silver and lead ‖ *npl* the depths
stalagm·ium -(i)ī *n* eardrop, earring *(w. pendant)*
stām·en -inis *n* vertical threads of a loom, warp; thread; string *(of an instrument);* fillet *(worn by priests)*
stāmine·us -a -um *adj* consisting of threads; wrapped in threads
stann·um -ī *n* tin
Stat·a -ae *f* a goddess who gave protection against fire
statāri·us -a -um *adj* standing, stationary; *(of plays, actors, speakers)* free from violent action, calm, quiet ‖ *mpl* actors in a refined type of comedy ‖ *f* refined comedy
statēr·a -ae *f* scales; statēra aurificis goldsmith's scales
staticul·us -ī *m* pose
statim *adv* at once, on the spot
stati·ō -ōnis *f* standing still, stationary position; station, post; position; residence; anchorage; in statiōne at one's post, on guard ‖ *fpl* sentries
Stāt·ius -(i)ī *m* Publius Papinius Statius *(poet of the Silver Age of Latin literature, c. A.D. 40–96)*
statīv·us -a -um *adj* stationary; castra statīva bivouac ‖ *npl* bivouac; cum diē statīvōrum with a rest-day *(on the march)*
stat·or -ōris *m* attendant *(of provincial governor, later of the emperor)* ‖ Stator *m* cult title of Jupiter *(the Stayer from flight)*
statu·a -ae *f* statue
statūm·en -inis *n* rib *(of a hull)*
stat·uō -uere -uī -ūtus *tr* to cause to stand; to bring to a stop; to fix in the ground, plant; to

erect, build; to set up *(a statue)*, set up a statue of; to found *(a city);* to establish *(a practice, precedent, principle, state of affairs);* to decide, settle *(matters);* to decree; to strengthen, support; to appoint *(a time, place); (w. double acc)* to appoint *(s.o.)* as; to determine, fix, set *(a price, payment; penalty, punishment);* to draw up, arrange *(a battle line); (w.* **utrum)** to make up one's mind whether, decide whether; *(w. inf)* to decide to, resolve to; *(w.* **ut** + *subj)* to decide that; *(w. pred. noun or adj)* to judge, deem; **statuere fīnem** *(w. dat)* set a limit to

statūr·a -ae *f* stature, height; **brevis (longae) statūrae homō** a person of short (tall) stature

stat·us -a -um *pp* of **sistō** ‖ *adj* fixed, set *(times, places, seasons);* regular, average, normal

stat·us -ūs *m* position; posture; social standing, rank, prestige; state of affairs, situation, condition, status; *(gram)* mood of the verb; *(leg)* legal position *(in regard to rights, obligations); (mil)* position; *(rhet)* point at issue; **status reī pūblicae** type of government, form of constitution

statūt·us -a -um *adj* upstanding

steg·a -ae *f (naut)* deck

stel(l)i·ō -ōnis *m* newt, lizard *(with spotted back)*

stell·a -ae *f* star; constellation; starfish; **stella comāns** *(or* **crīnīta)** comet; **stella diurna** Lucifer; **stella errāns** planet; **stella dē caelō lāpsa** shooting star; **stella marīna** starfish; **stellae quīnque** the five *(recognized)* planets *(i.e., Mars, Mercury, Venus, Jupiter, Saturn)*

stell·āns -antis *adj* starry; star-shaped, starlike

stellāt·us -a -um *adj* set with stars, starry; made into a star; **stellātus Argus** *(fig)* Argus with bright eyes

stellif·er *or* **stellig·er -era -erum** *adj* star-bearing, starry

stemm·a -atis *n* genealogical tree, family tree, lineage ‖ *npl* antiquity, history

stercore·us -a -um *adj (vulg)* full of shit

stercor·ō -āre -āvī -ātus *tr* to fertilize, manure

sterculīnum *see* **sterquilīnium**

sterc·us -oris *n* manure, dung

steril·is -is -e *adj* sterile, barren; causing barrenness, blighting; empty, bare; unprofitable; unrequited; wild *(tree)*

sterilit·ās -ātis *f* sterility

stern·āx -ācis *adj* bucking *(horse)*

sternō sternere strāvī strātus *tr* to strew, spread; to cover *(couch, horse)* with a cloth; to pave *(a road, floor);* to strike down, lay low, slay; to raze; to overwhelm, defeat utterly; to flatten, smooth; to calm, calm down; **trīclīnium sternere** to set the table; ‖ *pass* to stretch out *(on the ground)*

sternūment·um -ī *n* sneeze

sternu·ō -ere -ī *tr* to give *(an omen)* by sneezing ‖ *intr* to sneeze

Sterop·ē -ēs *f* one of the Pleiades

Sterop·ēs -ae *m* a Cyclops working in Vulcan's blacksmith shop

sterquilīn·ium -(i)ī *or* **sterquilīn·um -ī** *or* **sterculīn·um -ī** *n* manure pile

stert·ō -ere *intr* to snore

Stēsichor·us -ī *m* Greek lyric poet of Himera in Sicily *(c. 640–555 B.C.)*

stetī *perf* of **stō**

Sthenel·us -ī *m* king of Mycenae, son of Perseus, and father of Eurystheus ‖ king of the Ligurians and father of Cycnus, who was changed into a swan

stibad·ium -(i)ī *n* semicircular seat *or* couch

stigm·a -atis *n* mark, brand; stigma *(of disgrace)*

stigmati·ās -ae *m* branded runaway slave

stigmōs·us -a -um *adj* branded

still·a -ae *f* drop; mere drop

stillicid·ium -(i)ī *n* drip, dripping

still·ō -āre -āvī -ātus *tr & intr* to drip

stil·us -ī *m* stylus *(pointed instrument for writing);* composition; style

stimulāti·ō -ōnis *f* stimulation, incitement

stimulātr·īx -īcis *f* a tease *(female)*

stimule·us -a -um *adj* of goads

stimul·ō -āre -āvī -ātus *tr* to goad, torment; to spur on, incite, excite

stimul·us -ī *m* goad, prick; *(fig)* stimulus, incentive, spur; *(mil)* pointed stake concealed below the ground

stingu·ō -ere *tr* to extinguish

stīpāti·ō -ōnis *f* crowd, throng

stīpāt·or -ōris *m* attendant, bodyguard ‖ *mpl* retinue

stīpendiāri·us -a -um *adj* liable to taxes, tributary ‖ *mpl* tributary peoples; mercenary troops

stīpend·ium -(i)ī *n* tax, tribute, tariff; *(mil)* pay; military service; year's service; campaign; **ēmerērī stīpendia** to have served out one's term; **ēmeritīs stīpendiīs** at the end of one's military service, at discharge; **merēre** *(or* **merērī) stīpendia** to serve in the army

stīp·es -itis *m* log; trunk; branch, tree; *(pej)* blockhead

stīp·ō -āre -āvī -ātus *tr* to pack, cram, crowd; to crowd around, accompany in a groups

stips stipis *f* donation, gift; alms

stipul·a -ae *f* stalk, blade; stubble; *(mus)* reed pipe

stipulāti·ō -ōnis *f* agreement, bargain; *(leg)* formal promise

stipulātiuncul·a -ae *f* insignificant promise

stipulāt·us -a -um *adj* promised

stipul·or -**ārī** -**ātus sum** *tr (of a buyer)* to demand a guarantee from *(the seller that the purchase is fair by asking the formal question "spondēsne? dabisne?," i.e., "do you promise? will you give?")* ‖ *intr (leg)* to make a solemn promise *(by answering "spondeō, dabō," i.e., "I promise, I shall give")*
stīri·a -**ae** *f* icicle
stirpitus *adv* by the roots
stirp·s *or* **stirp·ēs** *or* **stirp·is** -**is** *f (m)* stock, stem, stalk; root; plant, shrub; race, lineage; offspring, descendant; character, nature; source, origin, beginning, foundation
stīv·a -**ae** *f* plow handle
stlattāri·us -**a** -**um** *adj* imported
stō stāre stetī statum *intr* to stand; *(of buildings, cities)* to remain standing; to last, endure; to stand firm; to stand upright; *(of hair)* to stand on end; *(of eyes)* to remain fixed; *(of battle)* to continue; *(of a ship)* to be moored, ride at anchor; to be motionless; to be stuck; *(w.* **ex)** to consist of; *(w. abl or in* + *abl)* to depend on, rest with; *(w.* **per** + *acc of person)* to depend on, be due to, be the fault of, thanks to; **per mē stetit quīn** *(or* **nē** *or* **quōminus) proeliō dīmicārētur** it was due to me that there was no battle; thanks to me, there was no battle; **per mē stetit ut** it was due to me that ‖ *v impers (w. inf)* it is a fixed resolve; **mihi stat** *(w. inf)* it is my fixed resolve to, I have made up my mind to
Stōic·a -**ae** *f* Stoic philosophy
Stōicē *adv* stoically, like a Stoic
Stōic·us -**a** -**um** *adj & m* Stoic
stol·a -**ae** *f* dress *(female outer garment, counterpart of the male toga); ceremonial gown (worn by musicians)*
stolāt·us -**a** -**um** *adj* wearing a **stola;** *(fig)* ladylike
stolidē *adv* stupidly, brutishly
stolid·us -**a** -**um** *adj* dull, stupid, slow, insensitive; *(of things)* inert
stomach·or -**ārī** -**ātus sum** *tr* to be indignant at ‖ *intr* to be angry, fume
stomachōsē *adv* irritably
stomachōsius *adv* rather angrily
stomachōs·us -**a** -**um** *adj* irritable
stomach·us -**ī** *m* stomach; esophagus, gullet; taste; appetite; irritation, annoyance; **stomachum movēre** *(or* **facere)** to cause annoyance; **stomachus bonus** good appetite; good humor, patience
store·a *or* **stori·a** -**ae** *f* straw mat
strab·ō -**ōnis** *m* squinter ‖ **Strabō** *see* **Pompēius**
strāg·ēs -**is** *f* devastation; heap; pile of debris; havoc; massacre

strāgul·us -**a** -**um** *adj* covering, serving as a covering ‖ *n* rug, carpet; bedspread; horse blanket
strām·en -**inis** *n* straw
strāment·um -**ī** *n* straw; covering; saddlecloth; **strāmentum agreste** straw bed
strāmine·us -**a** -**um** *adj* straw, made of straw
strangul·ō -**āre** -**āvī** -**ātus** *tr* to strangle; to suffocate; to constrict; to stifle
strangūri·a -**ae** *f* strangury *(difficulty with urinating)*
stratēgēm·a -**atis** *n* stratagem; ruse
stratēg·us -**ī** *m* commander, general
stratiōtic·us -**a** -**um** *adj* soldierly
strāt·um -**ī** *n* quilt, blanket; bed, couch; horse blanket, saddlecloth; pavement; **strāta viārum** paved streets
strātūr·a -**ae** *f* paving *(of roads)*
strāt·us -**a** -**um** *pp of* **sternō** ‖ *n see* **strātum**
strāvī *perf of* **sternō**
strēn(u)·a -**ae** *f* good-luck omen; lucky gift sent at the New Year; **strēnuārum commercium** exchange of gifts
strēnuē *adv* briskly, quickly, actively, strenuously
strēnuit·ās -**ātis** *f* briskness, vigor, liveliness
strēnu·us -**a** -**um** *adj* brisk, vigorous, active; fast *(ship);* restless
strepit·ō -**āre** *intr* to be noisy; to clatter; to rustle
strepit·us -**ūs** *m* noise, din, racket; crash, bang, clank; rumble; rustle; creak, squeak
strep·ō -**ere** -**uī** -**itus** *tr* to shout ‖ *intr* to make a noise *(of any kind);* to rattle, clatter, clang; to rumble; to rustle; to creak, squeak; to roar; to hum; to murmur; *(of muscial instruments)* to sound, blare; *(of places)* to ring, resound, be filled
stri·a -**ae** *f* groove, channel, furrow
striāt·us -**a** -**um** *adj* grooved, fluted, furrowed ‖ *f* scallop *(marine mollusk)*
strictim *adv* superficially, cursorily
strictūr·a -**ae** *f* mass of hardened iron
strict·us -**a** -**um** *pp of* **stringō** ‖ *adj* close, tight, narrow
strīd·eō -**ēre** -**ī** *or* **strīd·ō** -**ere** -**ī** *intr* to make a high-pitched noise; to hiss, whistle; to whizz; to shriek, scream; to grate; to buzz; *(of a wound)* to gurgle; *(of wings)* to whirr
strīd·or -**ōris** *m* shrill *or* high-pitched sound *(e.g. of elephants, apes, monkeys, witches, rigging);* hiss *(of a snake, roasting meat);* whizzing; shriek, scream; whine *(of a saw);* harsh noise, grating *(of teeth, chain, etc.);* creak, squeak *(of door);* whirring *(of wings);* whistle *(of wind);* chirping *(of locusts, crickets, cicadas)*
strīdul·us -**a** -**um** *adj* shrill, strident; hissing; whistling; creaking

strigil·is -is *f* scraper, strigil *(used by athletes to scrape off oil, mud, etc.)*

strig·ō -āre *intr* to stop *(in ploughing);* to give out

strigōs·us -a -um *adj* lean, shriveled; bald *(style)*

stringō stringere strīnxī strictus *tr* to strip, clip; to draw *(a sword);* to draw tight, tie tight; to string *(a bow);* to pick *(fruit);* to strip off *(leaves);* to press together, compress; to graze, scratch; to border on; to touch lightly on *(a subject); (of a river)* to erode

string·or -ōris *m* (**strīg-**) twinge, shock

strix strigis *f* owl, screech owl

stroph·a -ae *f* (**strof-**) trick, feat of skill

Strophad·es -um *fpl* island home of the Harpies

strophiār·ius -(i)ī *m* bra-maker

stroph·ium -iī *n* brassiere, bra; head band

Stroph·ius -(i)ī *m* king of Phocis and father of Pylades

structil·is -is -e *adj* for building; **caementum structile** concrete

struct·or -ōris *m* builder, mason, carpenter; carver *(at table)*

structūr·a -ae *f* construction; structure

structus *pp of* **struō**

stru·ēs -is *f* pile, heap; row of sacrificial cakes

stru·īx -īcis *f* heap, pile

strūm·a -ae *f* tumor, swollen gland

strūmōs·us -a -um *adj (med)* scrofulous

stru·ō -ere -xī -ctus *tr* to build, erect; to deploy *(troops);* to arrange, regulate; to occasion; to compose; to contract *(words);* to plot, design, aim at; to load with

strūt(h)e·us -a -um *adj* **mālum strūtheum** *n (a small variety of)* quince

strūthocamēl·us -ī *m* ostrich

struxī *perf of* **struō**

Strȳm·ōn -onis *or* **-onos** *m* river on the Macedonian-Thracian border

Strȳmon·is -idis *f* Thracian woman

Strȳmoni·us -a -um *adj* of the Strymon, Thracian

stud·eō -ēre -uī *tr* to desire, be eager for; to make *(s.th.)* one's concern ‖ *intr (w. dat)* **1** to be eager for, be keen on, be interested in, be enthusiastic about; **2** to take pains with, busy oneself with, apply oneself to; **3** to pursue; **4** to study; **5** to be a partisan of

studiōsē *adv* eagerly, enthusiastically, diligently

studiōs·us -a -um *adj* eager, keen, enthusiastic; studious; *(w. gen)* partial to *(a person or cause); (w. gen or dat)* eager for, keen on, interested in, enthusiastic about, devoted to, fond of, desirous of; **litterārum studiōsus** studious

stud·ium -(i)ī *n* eagerness, keenness, enthusiasm; devotion *(to a person);* support, good-

will *(esp. in a political sense),* party spirit; study; *(w. gen)* eagerness for, enthusiasm for; *(w. ad or in + acc)* enthusiasm for ‖ *npl* studies; **studia contrāria** opposite parties

stultē *adv* foolishly

stultiloquenti·a -ae *f or* **stultiloqu·ium -(i)ī** *n* silly talk

stultiloqu·us -a -um *adj* talking foolishly

stultiti·a -ae *f* foolishness, silliness

stultivid·us -a -um *adj (foolishly)* seeing things that are not there

stult·us -a -um *adj* foolish, silly

stūp·a -ae *f* tow, coarse flax, hemp

stupe·faciō -facere -fēcī -factus *(pass:* **stupe·fīō -fierī -factus sum)** *tr* to stupefy, stun, shock

stup·eō -ēre -uī *tr* to be amazed at, marvel at ‖ *intr* to be knocked senseless, be stunned, be astounded, be amazed; to be stopped in one's tracks

stup·ēscō -ēscere -uī *intr* to become amazed, become bewildered

stūpe·us -a -um *adj* of tow, hempen

stupidit·ās -ātis *f* stupidity

stupid·us -a -um *adj* amazed, astounded; stupid

stup·or -ōris *m* numbness; stupor; bewilderment, confusion; dullness, stupidity

stupp·a -ae *f* hemp, coarse flax

stuppe·us -a -um *adj* hempen

stupr·ō -āre -āvī -ātus *tr* to have illicit sex with; to ravish, rape; to defile; **struprum īnferre** *(w. dat)* to have sex with; to violate

stupr·um -ī *n* immorality; illicit sex; fornication *(as distinct from adultery);* rape

stupuī *perf of* **stupeō**

sturn·us -ī *m* starling

Stygi·us -a -um *adj* Stygian; hellish; deadly; dismal, melancholy

Stymphāli(c)·us -a -um *adj* Stymphalian

Stymphāl·um -ī *n or* **Stymphāl·us** *or* **Stymphāl·os -ī** *m* district in Arcadia famous for its vicious birds of prey which were killed by Hercules as one his Twelve Labors

Sty·x -gis *or* **-gos** *f* chief river in the lower world; river in Arcadia

suādēl·a -ae *f* persuasion

suā·deō -dēre -sī -sus *tr* to recommend, suggest, propose; to urge, impel, induce ‖ *intr (w. dat)* to advise, urge, suggest to, propose to; **sibi suādēre** *(w. acc & inf)* to satisfy *or* convince oneself that

suāsi·ō -ōnis *f* recommendation; support, backing *(a proposal);* persuasive eloquence

suās·or -ōris *m* adviser; advocate, supporter

suāsōri·a -ae *f* rhetorical exercise *(giving of advice based on historical situations)*

suāsōri·us -a -um *adj* concerned with advice

suās·um -ī *n* dirty grey color

suāsus *pp of* **suādeō**

suās·us -ūs *m* advice

suāveol·ēns -entis *adj* sweet-smelling, fragrant

suāviātiō *see* **sāviātiō**

suāvidic·us -a -um *adj* smooth *(verses);* smooth-talking

suāviloqu·ēns -entis *adj* smooth-talking, charming

suāviloquenti·a -ae *f* charming way of talking, smooth talk

suāviolum *see* **sāviolum**

suāvior *see* **sāvior**

suāv·is -is -e *adj* charming, pleasant, agreeable, attractive, nice

suāvit·ās -ātis *f* charm, pleasantness, attractiveness

suāviter *adv* charmingly, pleasantly, attractively, sweetly

suāvitūd·ō -inis *f (term of endearment)* honey, sweetie

suāvium *see* **sāvium**

sub *(prep) (w. abl)* **1** under, beneath, underneath: **sub sōle ārdente** under the blazing sun; **sub dīvō** under the sky, in the open; **2** under the surface of *(the earth, water):* **sub terrā** below ground; **3** down in *(a depression, valley):* **urbs sub vallibus sita est** the city is located down in the valley; **4** close behind: **sub ipsō ecce volat Diorēs** look, Diores comes flying close behind him; **5** close (up) to: **ager noster sub urbe** our land close to town; **6** close by: **sub dextrā (sinistrā)** on the right (left); **sub manū** close at hand; **7** at the foot of, close to, near, right under *(mountain, wall):* **sub rādīcibus montium** at the foothills of the mountains; **sub mūrō stāre** to stand close to the wall; **8** immediately before, at the approach of: **sub vespere** at the approach of evening; **9** in the reign of, during the term of office of, under: **sub Tiberiō Caesare** in the reign of Tiberius Caesar; **10** at the hands of: **māiōre sub hoste** at the hands of a greater enemy; **11** under the name *or* title of: **quī Caesareō iuvenēs sub nōmine crēscunt** these young men are growing up under Caesar's name; **12** on the pretext of: **sub excūsātiōne valitūdinis** on the pretext of poor health ‖ *(w. acc)* **1** to a position below, under, beneath: **ēius exercitum sub iugum mīserat** he had sent his army under the yoke; **sub lectum rēpere** to crawl under the bed; **2** to a point at the foot of: **succēdunt sub montem in quō** they advance to the foot of the mountain on which; **3** up *(walls, mountains):* **subīre sub montem** to go up the mountain; **4** just before *(a point of time, event),* on the eve of: **sub idem tempus** at almost the same time; **sub ipsum spectāculum gladiātōrium** on the eve of the

gladiatorial show; **sub occāsum sōlis** just before sunset; **5** directly after: **sub eās litterās statim recitātae sunt tuae** your letter was read aloud right after that letter; **6** in response to: **sub hanc vōcem fremitus multitūdinis fuit** at this statement a roar went up in the crowd; **7** into a state of subjection: **Nīnus tōtam Asiam sub sē redēgit** Ninus subjected all of Asia to his control

sub- *pref* **1** *(before adjectives and verbs, giving the sense of reduced intensity):* **subamārus** somewhat bitter; **subrīdēre** to smile; **2** *(compounded with verbs it gives the senses of the preposition):* **2a** *(position underneath):* **subscrībere** to write underneath *or* below; **2b** *(movement up from below):* **subīre** to go up, climb; **2c** *(movement down):* **succīdere** to cut down; **2d** *(movement close to):* **subsequī** to follow close behind; **2e** *(substitution):* **sublegere** to substitute; **2f** *(secret activity and removal):* **subnotāre** to observe secretly; **subdūcere** to remove, steal; **3** *(before nouns, indicating lower rank):* **subcenturiō** assistant centurion

subabsurdē *adv* a bit absurdly

subabsurd·us -a -um *adj* a bit absurd

subaccūs·ō -āre *tr* to blame, find some fault with

subācti·ō -ōnis *f* working *(of the soil);* development *(of the mind)*

subāctus *pp of* **subigō**

subaerāt·us -a -um *adj (of gold)* having an inner layer of bronze

subagrest·is -is -e *adj* rather uncouth

subālār·is -is -e *adj* carried under the arms

subalb·us -a -um *adj* whitish, off-white

subamār·us -a -um *adj* somewhat bitter

subaquil·us -a -um *adj* somewhat dark *(complexion)*

subarroganter *adv* **(subadro-)** rather arrogantly

subauscult·ō -āre *tr* to eavesdrop on ‖ *intr* to eavesdrop

subbasilicān·us -ī *m* loafer *(hanging around the basilicas)*

subbib·ō -ere -ī *tr* to drink a little

subbland·ior -īrī *intr (w. dat)* to flirt with

subc- = **succ-**

subcoll·ō -āre -āvī -ātus *tr* to carry on one's shoulders

subdifficil·is -is -e *adj* rather difficult, a bit difficult

subdiffīd·ō -ere *intr* to be a little distrustful

subditīci·us -a -um *adj* phoney

subditīv·us -a -um *adj* substituted, spurious

subditus *pp of* **subdō**

subdiū *adv* by day

sub·dō -dere -didī -ditus *tr* to put under; to subdue; to substitute; to forge, make up; to

spread *(a rumor); (w. dat)* **1** to put *or* apply *(s.th.)* to, add *(s.th.)* to; **2** to subject *(s.o.)* to ‖ *refl* **sē aquīs subdere** to plunge into the water
subdoc·eō -ēre *tr* to instruct *(as an assistant instructor)*
subdolē *adv* rather cunningly
subdol·us -a -um *adj* underhand, sly, cunning
subdom·ō -āre *tr* to tame somewhat
subdubit·ō -āre *intr* to be rather undecided
sub·dūcō -dūcere -dūxī -ductus *tr* to draw up from below; to pull up, raise; to remove, take away, steal; to haul up, beach *(a ship);* to withdraw *(troops);* to balance *(accounts)*
subducti·ō -ōnis *f* drydocking, beaching; calculation, computation
sub·edō -edere *or* **-ēsse -ēdī -ēsus** *tr* to eat away below *or* eat away at the bottom of; **scopulum unda subēdit** water wore away the bottom of the cliff
sub·eō -īre -īvī *or* **-iī -itus** *tr* to enter *(a place; the mind);* to approach, attack; to undergo *(danger, punishment, etc.);* to help, support; to climb; to slip under; to dodge *(a blow)* ‖ *intr* to come *or* go up, climb; to follow; to advance, press forward; *(w. ad or in + acc)* **1** to come up against, attack; **2** to climb *(a mountain);* **3** to approach, enter
sūb·er -eris *n* cork tree, cork
subf- = **suff-**
subg- = **sugg-**
subhorrid·us -a -um *adj* rather coarse, rather uncouth
subiac·eō -ēre -uī *intr* to lie nearby; *(w. dat)* to lie under, lie close to; **montī subiacēre** to lie at the foot of the mountain
sub·iciō -icere -iēcī -iectus *tr* to throw up, fling up; to bring up; to bring up close, expose; to suggest; to add, append; to suborn; to substitute; to forge; *(w. dat or sub + acc)* **1** to put, place *(s.th.)* under; **2** to subject *(s.o.)* to; **3** to classify *(s.th.)* under; **4** to submit *(s.th.)* to *(one's judgment)*
subiecti·ō -ōnis *f* subjection; substitution; forgery
subiectissimē *adv* most humbly
subiect·ō -āre -āvī -ātus *tr* to toss up *(from below);* **stimulōs subiectāre** *(w. dat)* to prod s.o. on
subiect·or -ōris *m* forger
subiect·us -a -um *pp of* **subiciō** ‖ *adj (w. dat)* **1** located near, bordering (on); **2** subject to; **subiecta māteria** subject matter ‖ *m* subject, subordinate, underling
subigitāti·ō -ōnis *f (sl) (sexually)* fondling, feeling up
subigitātr·īx -īcis *f (sl)* a tease
subigit·ō -āre -āvī -ātus *tr (sl)* to arouse sexually by fondling, feel up

sub·igō -igere -ēgī -āctus *tr* to turn up, till, plow *(the soil);* to knead *(dough);* to grind, reduce to a powder: **farīna in pollinem subācta** flour reduced to a fine powder; to work *(wool into a smooth thread);* to rub down, massage *(the body, also in the erotic sense);* to tame, break in *(an animal);* to train, discipline *(the mind);* to conquer, subdue *(a country);* to row, propel *(a boat);* to make smooth *(by rubbing, polishing);* to lubricate; to whet, sharpen: **subigunt in cōte secūrīs** they sharpen their axes on a whetstone; to suppress, quell *(hostilities);* to subdue the spirit of, break the spirits of *(people);* *(w. inf or ut + subj)* to force, constrain *(s.o.)* to; *(w. ad)* to drive to: **subēgit nōs ad necessitūdinem dēdendī rēs** he drove us to the necessity of giving up our property
subimpud·ēns -entis *adj* rather shameless
subinān·is -is -e *adj* rather empty, rather pointless
subinde *adv* immediately afterwards; promptly; from then on; from time to time, now and then
subīnsuls·us -a -um *adj* rather insipid
subinvid·eō -ēre *intr (w. dat)* to envy *(s.o.)* a little
subinvīs·us -a -um *adj* rather disliked, somewhat unpopular
subinvīt·ō -āre *tr* to invite unenthusiastically
subīr·āscor -āscī -ātus sum *intr* to be annoyed; *(w. dat)* to be peeved at
subitāri·us -a -um *adj* requiring prompt action; *(of troops)* hastily called up *(to meet an emergency); (of buildings)* hastily erected; **rēs subitāria** emergency
subitō *adv* suddenly, unexpectedly, at once; **subitō dīcere** to speak extempore
subit·us -a -um *adj* coming on suddenly, sudden, unexpected; rash *(person);* emergency *(troops)* ‖ *n* emergency; **dē subitō** *(or* **per subitum)** suddenly
sub·iungō -iungere -iūnxī -iūnctus *tr (w. dat)* **1** to yoke *or* harness to; **2** to join to, connect with, add to; **3** to make subject to
sub·lābor -lābī -lāpsus sum *intr* to sink, fall down, collapse; to glide imperceptibly; to fall back, fail
sublātē *adv* loftily, in lofty tones
sublāti·ō -ōnis *f* elevation, raising
sublāt·us -a -um *pp of* **sufferō** *and of* **tollō** ‖ *adj* elated
sublect·ō -āre *tr* to coax, cajole
sub·legō -legere -lēgī -lēctus *tr* to gather up, pick up; to steal; to kidnap; to substitute; to overhear, pick up
sublest·us -a -um *adj* weak; trifling
sublevāti·ō -ōnis *f* alleviation

sublev·ō -āre -āvī -ātus *tr* to lift up, raise, support; to assist; to encourage; to promote, further *(an activity);* to lighten, alleviate; to make up for *(a fault)* ‖ *refl* to get up

sublic·a -ae *f* stake, pile *(esp. for a bridge)*

sublici·us -a -um *adj* resting on piles; **pōns sublicius** wooden bridge *(across the Tiber, built by Ancus Marcius, third king of Rome)*

subligācul·um -ī *n* loincloth, shorts; apron

sublig·ar -āris *n* loincloth, shorts; apron

sublig·ō -āre -āvī -ātus *tr (w. dat)* to tie *or* fasten *(e.g., a sword)* to *or* below

sublīmē *adv* aloft, on high

sublīmen *adv* upwards, on high

sublīm·is -is -e *adj* high, raised up, lifted high; *(of ideas)* lofty, grand, exalted; borne aloft, through the sky; aspiring; having lofty ideals; exalted in rank, eminent, distinguished; lofty, majestic *(style)* ‖ *npl* the heights

sublīmit·ās -ātis *f* loftiness, sublimity

sublīmius *comp adv of* **sublīmē**

sublingi·o -ōnis *m (hum)* dish-licker

sublingul·ō -ōnis *m (hum)* dish-licker, dish-washer

sub·linō -linere -lēvī -litus *tr* to smear over, coat *(a surface);* to smear the underside of; **ōs sublinere** *(w. dat)* to pull a practical joke on

sublūc·eō -ēre *intr* to shine faintly; *(w. dat)* to shine through

sub·luō -luere -luī -lūtus *tr* to wash underneath; to flow at the foot of *(a mountain);* to wash *(the underside of the body);* **quid solium sublūtō pōdice perdis?** why do you ruin the bathtub with washing your behind?

sublūstr·is -is -e *adj* dimly lighted; throwing some light, glimmering, flickering

subm- = summ-

sub·nāscor -nāscī -nātus sum *intr (w. dat)* to grow up underneath

sub·nectō -nectere -nexuī -nexus *tr* to fasten, tie *(s.th.)* underneath; to confine; *(w. dat)* to fasten *or* tie *(s.th.)* below *(s.th. else)*

subneg·ō -āre -āvī -ātus *tr* to half-refuse

subni·ger -gra -grum *adj* blackish

subnīsus -a -um *adj* (**-nix-**) propped up; *(w. dat)* **1** propped up on, resting on, leaning on; **2** relying on, confiding in; **3** elated by

subnot·ō -āre -āvī -ātus *tr* to note down, record, register; to observe secretly

subnub·a -ae *f* rival *(female)*

subnūbil·us -a -um *adj* somewhat cloudy, overcast

sub·ō -āre *intr* to be in heat

subobscēn·us -a -um *adj* somewhat obscene, shady, off-color

subobscūr·us -a -um *adj* somewhat obscure

subodiōs·us -a -um *adj* rather tiresome, rather annoying

suboffend·ō -ere *intr* to give some offense

subol·ēs -is *f* offspring; children; the young *(of animals);* race, stock

subolēsc·ō -ere *intr* to grow up

subol·et -ēre *v impers* there is a faint smell; **mihi subolet** I have an inkling, I have a sneaking suspicion

subor·ior -īrī -tus sum *intr* to rise up in succession, arise, proceed

subōrn·ō -āre *tr* to equip, supply, provide; to employ as a secret agent, induce secretly, suborn; to dress up *(in a costume, disguise);* to prepare, instruct *(for some underhand purpose)*

subp- = supp-

subr- = surr-

sub·scrībō -scrībere -scrīpsī -scrīptus *tr* to write underneath; to sign; to write down, record, register ‖ *intr (leg)* to sign an accusation, act as prosecutor; *(w. dat)* **1** to add in writing to; **2** to agree to; *(leg) (w. in + acc)* to sign an accusation against, indict

subscrīpti·ō -ōnis *f* inscription underneath; signature; s.th. written under a heading; recording *(of an offense by the censor);* record, register; *(leg)* specification *(of crimes)* in an indictment, a count, charge

subscrīpt·or -ōris *m (leg)* signer, co-signer *(of an accusation)*

subscrīptus *pp of* **subscrībō**

subsc·ūs -ūdis *f* (**sups-**) tenon of a dovetail

subsecīvus *see* **subsicīvus**

subsec·ō -āre -uī -tus *tr* to clip, trim, cut off; to pare, clip *(nails)*

subsecūtus *pp of* **subsequor**

subsell·ium -(i)ī *n* seat, bench; stool; seat *or* bench on a lower level; seat in the Senate; *(leg)* seat in the court *(usu. where the judge, prosecution, or the defense and their witnesses sat);* *(fig)* the bench, tribunal, court; seat *(in the theater);* **versātus in utrīsque subsellīs** experienced as lawyer and judge ‖ *npl* the courts; bleachers *(where the poor people sat);* *(fig)* occupants of the bleachers

subsen·tiō -tīre -sī -sus *tr* to have some inkling of

sub·sequor -sequī -secūtus sum *tr* to follow close after; to pursue; to back up, support; to imitate; to adhere to, conform to; to come after, succeed *(in time or order)* ‖ *intr* to ensue

subserv·iō -īre *intr (w. dat)* **1** to be subject to; **2** to accommodate oneself to, humor; **3** to support, aid

subsicīv·us *or* **subsecīv·us -a -um** *adj* (**sup-**) *(of land)* left over *(after an allotment);* extra, spare *(time);* extra, overtime *(work)*

subsidiāri·us -a -um *adj* in reserve; *(mil)* reserve ‖ *mpl (mil)* reserves

subsid·ium -(i)ī *n* aid, support; mainstay; place of refuge; protection; *(mil)* reserves; military support, relief; **ad** *(or* **in) subsidium** for support; **subsidiō esse** *(w. dat)* to be of help to ‖ *npl (mil)* reserves, reinforcements

sub·sīdō -sīdere -sēdī *tr* to lie in wait for ‖ *intr* to sit down, crouch down, settle down; to sink, subside, settle; to settle down, establish residence; *(of female animals) (w. dat)* to crouch under

subsignān·us -a -um *adj (mil)* special reserve *(troops)*

subsign·ō -āre -āvī -ātus *tr* to endorse, subscribe to *(an opinion);* to register, enter, record; to guarantee

subsil·iō -īre -uī *intr* **(suss-) (sups-)** to jump up

sub·sistō -sistere -stitī *tr* **(sups-)** to hold out against ‖ *intr* to stand up; to take a firm stand; to come to a standstill, stop; to stay behind; *(w. dat)* **1** to take a stand against, oppose, fight; **2** to meet *(an expense)*

subsort·ior -īrī -ītus sum *tr* to choose as a substitute by lot ‖ *intr* to choose a substitute by lot; *(in a passive sense)* to be chosen as a substitute

subsortīti·ō -ōnis *f* substitution by lot

substanti·a -ae *f* substance, essence; means, wealth, property

sub·sternō -sternere -strāvī -strātus *tr* to spread underneath; to cover; *(w. dat)* to put at the disposal of, make subservient to; **rem pūblicam libīdinī suae substernere** to misuse high office to serve one's lust

substit·uō -uere -uī -ūtus *tr* to submit, present; to substitute; *(w. dat or* **in locum** *w. gen)* to substitute for *or* in place of; **animō** *(or* **oculīs) substituere** to imagine

subst·ō -āre *intr* to stand firm, hold out; *(w. dat)* to stand up to

substrātus *pp of* **substernō**

substrāvī *perf of* **substernō**

substrict·us -a -um *adj* tight, narrow, small

sub·stringō -stringere -strīnxī -strictus *tr* to tie up, draw up; to restrain, control; *(w. dat)* to press *(s.th.)* close to

substructi·ō -ōnis *f* substructure, foundation

substru·ō -ere -xī -ctus *tr* to lay *(a foundation);* **viās glareā substruere** to lay a foundation of gravel on the roads

subsult·ō -āre *intr* to jump up and down

sub·sum -esse *intr* **(sup-)** to be near, be at hand; *(w. gen) (of feelings, qualities, underlying cause or meaning)* to form the foundation for, be at the bottom of; *(w. dat)* **1** to be below *or* underneath, be under; **2** to be at the foot of; **3** to be (located) at the edge of *(the sea);* **4** to be concealed in; **5** to be (worn) under *(e.g., a tunic);* **6** to be attached to *(a document);* **7** to be subject to, be subservient to

subsūt·us -a -um *adj* trimmed at the bottom

subtē(g)m·en -inis *n* weft, woof *(horizontal threads woven in between the warp threads in a loom);* yarn

subter *adv* **(sub-)** below, underneath ‖ *prep (w. abl)* beneath, below, underneath, under ‖ *(w. acc)* underneath, beneath; up to, close to, close beneath

subter·dūcō -dūcere -dūxī -ductus *tr* **(sup-)** to remove secretly ‖ *refl* to steal away, sneak away

subter·fugiō -fugere -fūgī *tr* **(sup-)** to evade, avoid ‖ *intr* to run off secretly

subter·lābor -lābī *tr* to glide *or* flow under ‖ *intr* to slip away

sub·terō -terere -trīvī -trītus *tr* **(sup-)** to wear away underneath

subterrāne·us -a -um *adj* subterranean, underground

subtex·ō -ere -uī -tus *tr* to sew on; to veil, cover; *(fig)* to work up, compose; *(w. dat)* **1** to sew onto; **2** to throw *(a covering)* over; **3** to work *(s.th.)* into *(a story or plot)*

subtīl·is -is -e *adj* **(sup-)** finely woven; delicate; subtle; discriminating, refined; precise, matter-of-fact; simple, unadorned *(style)*

subtīlit·ās -ātis *f* **(sup-)** fineness, minuteness; slenderness; exactness, precision; simplicity *(of style)*

subtīliter *adv* **(sup-)** finely, delicately; accurately; plainly, simply

subtim·eō -ēre *intr* to be a bit afraid

sub·trahō -trahere -trāxī -tractus *tr* **(sup-)** to drag up from beneath, drag out, draw off; to withdraw, remove; to withhold; to misappropriate, steal; to undermine; to avert *(eyes);* *(w. dat)* to drag *(s.th.)* away from; *(w. abl)* to rescue *(s.o.)* from the threat of, snatch *(s.o.)* from *(impending danger, ruin);* **oculīs subtrahere** to remove from sight ‖ *refl (w. ab)* to withdraw from, dissociate oneself from *(an activity, responsibility)*

subtrīst·is -is -e *adj* rather sad

subtrītus *pp of* **subterō**

subtrīvī *perf of* **subterō**

subturpicul·us -a -um *adj* somewhat disgraceful

subturp·is -is -e *adj* rather disgraceful, somewhat scandalous

subtus *adv* below, underneath

subtūs·us -a -um *adj* somewhat bruised

subūcul·a -ae *f* undertunic *(worn by both sexes)*

subulc·us -ī *m* swineherd

Subūr·a -ae *f* noisy business and nightlife district in Rome, N.E. of the Forum between the Esquiline and Quirinal Hills

Subūrān·us -a -um *adj* of the Subura
suburbānit·ās -ātis *f* proximity to Rome
suburbān·us -a -um *adj* suburban, near Rome
‖ *m* suburbanite ‖ *n* suburban Rome
suburb·ium -(i)ī *n* suburb
suburg·eō -ēre *tr (w.* ad*)* to keep *or* turn *(a ship)* close to
subvecti·ō -ōnis *f* transportation
subvect·ō -āre -āvī -ātus *tr* to bring up regularly; to transport regularly
subvect·us -ūs *m* bringing up; transportation
sub·vehō -vehere -vexī -vectus *tr* to carry *or* bring up; to transport
sub·veniō -venīre -vēnī -ventum *intr (w.* dat*)* to come up to aid, reinforce
subvent·ō -āre *intr (w.* dat*)* to rush to the aid of
subver·eor -ērī *intr* to be a bit apprehensive
subvers·ō -āre *tr* (-vors-) to ruin completely
subvers·or -ōris *m* one who overthrows *(a law)*
subver·tō -tere -tī -sus *tr* (-vort-) to turn upside down, upset, overthrow, subvert
subvex·us -a -um *adj* sloping upward
subvol·ō -āre *intr* to fly up
subvolturi·us -a -um *adj* vulture-like
subvolv·ō -ere *tr* to roll up(hill)
subvor- = **subver-**
suc(c)īdi·a -ae *f* leg *or* side of meat; *(fig)* extra income
succav·us -a -um *adj* hollow underneath
succēdāne·us -a -um *adj* (succī-) killed as a substitute
suc·cēdō -cēdere -cessī -cessus *tr* to climb; to march on *or* against, advance as far as ‖ *intr* to come up, climb; to come next, follow in succession; to turn out well, turn out successfully; *(w.* ad, in, *or* sub + *acc)* to climb, climb up; *(w.* dat*)* **1** to succeed, follow; **2** become a successor to; **3** to succeed in *(an undertaking);* **4** to yield to, submit to; **5** to relieve *(e.g., tired troops);* **6** to enter, go below to *(e.g., a shelter, a tomb); (w.* ad *or* in + *acc) (fig)* to attain *(e.g., high honors),* enter upon *(an inheritance);* **bene succēdere** to turn out well
succen·dō -dere -dī -sus *tr* to set on fire, set fire to; to light *(a fire); (fig)* to inflame, enkindle
succēns·eō -ēre -uī *intr* (sūsc-) *(w.* dat*)* to be enraged at
succēnsus *pp of* **succendō**
succenturiāt·us -a -um *adj* (subc-) in reserve
succenturi·ō -āre -āvī -ātus *tr* (subc-) to receive *(s.o.)* as a substitute into a *centuria*
succenturi·ō -ōnis *m* (subc-) assistant centurion, substitute for a centurion
successi·ō -ōnis *f* succession
success·or -ōris *m* successor

success·us -ūs *m* approach, advance uphill; outcome; success
succīdāneus *see* **succēdāneus**
suc·cīdō -cīdere -cīdī -cīsus *tr* (subc-) to cut down, cut off, mow down
suc·cidō -cidere -cidī *intr* (subc-) to sink, give way; to collapse, fail
succid·us -a -um *adj* (sūci-) juicy; *(coll)* plump *(girl)*
succidu·us -a -um *adj* sinking, falling, collapsing, giving way
succīnct·us -a -um *adj (of a person)* with clothes tucked up; *(of a statement)* concise; *(of a book)* compact; *(fig)* in a state of readiness; *(fig) (w.* abl*)* equipped with *(a means of defense, military strength);* **cultrō succīnctus** carrying a knife in his belt
suc·cingō -cingere -cīnxī -cīnctus *tr* to tuck up; to put on *(a sword);* to equip, arm; to surround closely ‖ *refl & pass (w.* abl*)* to gather up one's clothes with
succingul·um -ī *n* belt
succin·ō -ere *tr* to recite in a droning voice ‖ *intr* to chime in *(in conversation); (w.* dat*)* to accompany *(in singing or playing)*
succīsus *pp of* **succīdō**
succlāmāti·ō -ōnis *f* shouting in reply
succlām·ō -āre -āvī -ātus *tr* (subc-) to shout out after; to interrupt with shouts, heckle; *(w.* dat*)* to shout out *(words)* at
succontumēliōsē *adv* (subc-) rather insolently
suc·crēscō -crēscere -crēvī *intr* (subc-) to grow up; to be replenished; *(w.* dat*)* to attain to
succrētus *pp of* **succernō**
succrīsp·us -a -um *adj* (subc-) rather curly
succulent·us -a -um *adj* (subc-) succulent
suc·cumbō -cumbere -cubuī -cubitum *intr* (subc-) to fall back, sink back; to succumb, yield, submit
suc·currō -currere -currī -cursum *intr (w.* dat*)* **1** to run up to; **2** to run to help; **3** to occur to, enter the mind of; **4** *(topog)* to extend to the foot of ‖ *v impers* the thought occurs
succ·us *or* **sūc·us -ī** *m* sap, juice; taste, flavor; *(fig)* vitality
succuss·us -ūs *m* shaking, jolt
succust·ōs -ōdis *m* (subc-) assistant guard
suc·cutiō -cutere -cussī -cussus *tr* to toss up; to jolt *(a rider, vehicle)*
sūcidus *see* **succidus**
sūcin·us -a -um *adj & n* amber
sūctus *pp of* **sūgō**
sucul·a -ae *f* little pig
sucul·a -ae *f* winch, windlass
Sūcul·ae -ārum *fpl (astr)* Hyades
sūculent·us -a -um *adj* juicy, succulent
sūc·us -ī *m* juice; *(of the soil)* moisture; *(fig)* sap, vitality

sūdār·ium -(i)ī *n* handkerchief; towel
sūdātōri·us -a -um *adj* sweat, for sweating **ǁ** *n* sweat room, sauna
sūdātr·īx -īcis *adj* causing sweat
sud·is -is *f* stake, pile; pike *(weapon);* sharp projection, spike
sūd·ō -āre -āvī -ātus *tr* to sweat, exude; to soak with sweat; *(fig)* to sweat at, sweat over **ǁ** *intr* to sweat; to drip
sūd·or -ōris *m* sweat; moisture; *(fig)* hard work
sūducul·um -ī *n (hum)* sweat-maker *(i.e., a whipping post)*
sūd·us -a -um *adj* dry; clear, cloudless **ǁ** *n* clear weather, bright sky
Suēb·ī -ōrum *mpl* (Suēv-) generic name of a group of German tribes
Suēbi·a -ae *f* district E. of the Elbe
suēscō suēscere suēvī suētus *tr* to accustom, familiarize **ǁ** *intr (w. dat or inf)* to become accustomed to
Suētōn·ius -(i)ī *m* Roman clan name *(nomen) (esp. that of Gaius Suetonius Tranquillus, biographer, born c.* A.D. *69)*
suēt·us -a -um *pp of* suēscō **ǁ** *adj* usual, familiar
Suēvī *see* Suēbī
sūf·es *or* suff·es -etis *m* chief magistrate in Carthage
suffarcināt·us -a -um *adj* (subf-) stuffed, padded
suffarcin·ō -āre -āvī -ātus *tr* (subf-) to stuff, cram
suffect·us -a -um *pp of* sufficiō **ǁ** *adj* substitute; cōnsul suffectus substitute consul *(appointed to complete an unexpired term of another consul)*
sufferō sufferre sustulī sublātus *tr* (subf-) to suffer, bear, endure; to place at s.o.'s disposal, offer
suf·ficiō -ficere -fēcī -fectus *tr* to lay the foundation for; to dip, tinge, dye; to appoint to a vacancy; to yield, supply, afford **ǁ** *intr* to be sufficient; *(w. dat)* to suffice for
suf·figō -figere -fīxī -fīxus *tr* to nail up, fasten
suffīm·en -inis *n* incense
suffīment·um -ī *n* incense
suff·iō -īre -īvī *or* -(i)ī -ītus *tr* to fumigate; to perfume
suffīxus *pp of* suffīgō
sufflām·en -inis *n* brake *(on a vehicle)*
sufflāmin·ō -āre -āvī -ātus *tr* to apply the brakes to
sufflāt·us -a -um *adj* puffed up, bloated; *(fig)* bombastic; *(fig)* fuming *(w. anger)*
suffl·ō -āre -āvī -ātus *tr* to blow up, inflate **ǁ** *intr* to blow, puff
suffōc·ō -āre -āvī -ātus *tr* to choke, suffocate
suf·fodiō -fodere -fōdī -fossus *tr* (subf-) to stab, pierce; to dig under *(walls)*

suffrāgāti·ō -ōnis *f* (subf-) voting *(in s.o.'s favor)*, support
suffrāgāt·or -ōris *m* (subf-) voter; supporter *(at the polls)*, partisan
suffrāgātōri·us -a -um *adj* (subf-) partisan
suffrāg·ium -(i)ī *n* (subf-) ballot, vote; right to vote, franchise; decision, judgment; applause, approbation; suffrāgium ferre to cast a ballot; suffrāgium ferre *(w.* dē *or* in + *abl)* to vote on
suffrāg·or -ārī -ātus sum *intr* to cast a favorable vote; *(w. dat)* to vote in favor of, support, vote for; fortūnā suffrāgante with luck on our side
suffring·ō -ere *tr* (subf-) to break
suffug·ium -(i)ī *n* shelter, cover
sufful·ciō -cīre -sī -tus *tr* to prop up, underpin, support
suf·fundō -fundere -fūdī -fūsus *tr* (subf-) to pour in, fill; to suffuse, spread; to tinge, color; to infuse; virgineum ōre rubōrem suffundere *(w. dat)* to make *(s.o.)* blush like a girl
suffūr·or -ārī *tr* to filch, snitch
suffūsc·us -a -um *adj* (subf-) darkish
suffūsus *pp of* suffundō
Sugambr·ī -ōrum *mpl* a German tribe living to the E. of the Lower Rhine, above the Ubii
sug·gerō -gerere -gessī -gestus *tr* (subg-) to supply, add; to suggest
suggest·um -ī *n* platform; stage
suggestus *pp of* suggerō
suggest·us -ūs *m* platform; stage
suggrand·is -is -e *adj* (subg-) rather huge
sug·gredior -gredī -gressus sum *tr & intr* (subg-) to approach
sūgillāti·ō -ōnis *f* (suggill-, subgill-) bruise; affront
sūgill·ō -āre -āvī -ātus *tr* to beat black-and-blue; to affront, insult
sūgō sūgere sūxī sūctus *tr* to suck
suī *perf of* suō
suī *see* sē
suill·us -a -um *adj* of swine; carō suilla pork; grex suillus herd of swine **ǁ** *f* pork
sulc·ō -āre -āvī -ātus *tr* to furrow; to plow; to score, make a line in
sulc·us -ī *m* furrow; ditch, trench *(for plants);* track *(of a wheel or meteor);* wrinkle; plowing; wake *(of a ship)*
sulf·ur -uris *n* sulfur
Sull·a -ae *m* (Syll-) Sulla *(Cornelius Sulla Felix, Roman general, dictator, and political reformer, 138–78* B.C.*)*
Sullān·ī -ōrum *mpl* (Syll-) partisans of Sulla
sullātur·iō -īre *intr* to wish to be a Sulla
Sulm·ō -ōnis *m* town c. 90 miles E. of Rome, and birthplace of Ovid
Sulmōnēns·is -is -e *adj* of Sulmo

sulp(h)·ur *or* sulf·ur -uris *n* sulfur
sulp(h)urāt·us -a -um *adj* saturated with sulfur
sulp(h)ure·us -a -um *adj* sulfurous
sultis = sī vultis if you please
sum esse fuī futūrus *intr* to be; to exist; *(w. gen of possession)* to belong to, pertain to, be characteristic of, be the duty of; *(w. gen or abl of quality)* to be of, be possessed of, have; *(w. gen or abl of value)* to be valued at, cost; *(w. dat)* to belong to; *(w.* ab) to belong to; *(w.* ad) to be designed for; *(w.* ex) to consist of; est *(w. inf)* it is possible to, it is permissible to; est *(w.* ut) it is possible that; sunt quī there are those who, there are people who, they are of the type that
sumbolus *see* symbolus
sūm·en -inis *n* breast; teat, udder; breeding sow
summ- = subm-
summ·a -ae *f* main thing; chief point, gist, summary; sum, amount; contents, substance; sum of money; sum-total *(of hopes, etc.);* the whole issue, the whole case; *(phil)* totality of matter, the universe; ad summam in short; generally, on the whole; as the crowning touch, to complete it all; in summā in all; in summam taken as a whole; ad *(or* in) summam prōdesse *(or* prōficere) to be of general good; summa honōrāria honorarium, voluntary payment to a lawyer; summa rērum the world; supreme power; general welfare; summa summārum the whole universe
summān·ō -āre *intr* (subm-) to drip a bit
Summān·us -ī *m* Roman god of night lightning
summ·ās -ātis *adj* aristocratic, first-class
summātim *adv* on the surface; generally, summarily
summē *adv* very, extremely, intensely
summer·gō -gere -sī -sus *tr* (subm-) to sink, submerge, drown
summers·us -a -um *adj* (subm-) sunken; living underwater; *(sunk)* below the horizon
summer·us -a -um *adj* (subm-) nearly straight, nearly pure
sumministr·ō -āre -āvī -ātus *tr* (subm-) to furnish
summissē *or* summissim *adv* (subm-) in a low voice, softly; modestly, humbly
summissi·ō -ōnis *f* lowering, dropping
summiss·us -a -um *adj* lowered, stooping; lowered, soft *(voice);* humble, unassuming; submissive; too submissive, abject; *(of hair)* worn long, let down
sum·mittō -mittere -mīsī -missus *tr* (subm-) to let down, lower, sink, drop; to let *(hair)* grow long; to lower, reduce, moderate, relax, lessen; to humble; to rear, produce, put forth; to send secretly; to send as a reinforcement;

to send as a substitute; animum summittere *(w. dat)* to yield to ‖ *refl* to bend down, stoop over; to condescend; *(w. dat)* to give in to
summolestē *adv* (subm-) with some annoyance
summolest·us -a -um *adj* (subm-) rather annoying
summon·eō -ēre -uī -itus *tr* to give *(s.o.)* a gentle reminder, remind privately; patrēs salūtāvit nōminātim nūllō summonente he greeted senators by name, with no one prompting him
summopere *or* summō opere *adv* with the greatest diligence, with utmost effort
summōt·us -a -um *adj* secluded, distant
sum·moveō -movēre -mōvī -mōtus *tr* (subm-) to move up, advance; to clear *(e.g., the court);* to remove; to expel, banish; to deny admission to, keep off; to clear from the path of a magistrate; to dispense with *(a procedure);* to ward off *(heat, cold); (fig)* to drive away, forget about *(e.g., worries); (mil)* dislodge
summul·a -ae *f* small sum of money
summum *adv* *(w. numbers)* at most; at latest; ūnō aut summum alterō proeliō in one or at most two battles
summ·us -a -um *adj* highest, uppermost; the top of, the surface of; last, latest, the end of; greatest, best, top, consummate; finest, first-rate; at the height of *(a season);* perfect *(peace, tranquility);* closest, best *(friend);* most distinguished; middle *(finger); (of affairs, concerns)* most important, of highest importance; *(of a diner)* farthest to the left on the couch *(from the viewpoint of those dining); (of a couch)* to the left of the middle couch; omnia summa facere to do one's utmost; rēs summa *(or* rēs summae) critical situation; rēs summa *(or* respūblica summa) the welfare of the state, the general welfare; summa cēna main course; summa manus finishing touches; summa mēnsa main course; summa rudis head instructor in a gladiatorial school *(literally, top practice-sword);* summō iūre with the full force of the law ‖ *m* head of the table; ‖ *f see* summa ‖ *n* top, surface; highest place, head of the table; ab summō aut ab īmō at the top or the bottom of the page ‖ *npl* extremities *(of the body or its parts);* general purport *(of a writing)*
sūmō sūmere sūmpsī sūmptus *tr* to take up; to put on, dress oneself in, wear; to exact, inflict *(penalty);* to take up, begin, enter upon; to eat, consume; to assume, suppose, take for granted; to cite, adduce, mention; to assume, appropriate *(a title, name);* to embrace *(a practice, way of life);* to borrow *(words,*

ideas from other people); to select; to purchase, buy; to adopt *(a child);* **aliquid mūtuum sūmere** to borrow s.th.; **arma sūmere** to take up arms; **in manūs sūmere** to take in hand, take up *(for reading);* **in sē sūmere** to take upon oneself, assume; **mortem** *(or* **exitium)** *(usu. w.* **sponte) sūmere** to commit suicide; **supplicium sūmere** to exact punishment

sūmpti·ō -ōnis *f* assumption, premise

sūmptuāri·us -a -um *adj* expense, relating to expenses; *(of laws)* sumptuary, against extravagance

sūmptuōsē *adv* sumptuously, expensively

sūmptuōs·us -a -um *adj* costly, expensive; lavish, wasteful

sūmptus *pp of* **sūmō**

sūmpt·us -ūs *m* cost, expense; **sūmptui esse** *(w. dat)* to be expensive for; **sūmptum suum exercēre** to earn one's keep; **sūmptū tuō** at your expense

Sūn·ium *or* **Sūn·ion -iī** *n* S.E. promontory of Attica

suō suere suī sūtus *tr* to sew, stitch, tack together

suōmet = *emphatic form of* **suō**

suōpte = *emphatic form of* **suō**

suovetaurīl·ia -ium *npl* **(suovi-)** sacrifice of a pig, sheep, and bull

supell·ex -ectilis *f* furniture, household utensils; tableware; outfit, equipment

super *adv* on the top, on the surface, above; besides, moreover; in addition to what has been said; **satis superque** enough and to spare; **super esse** to be left over II *prep (w. acc)* over, above; upon, on top of; *(w. numbers)* over, more than; besides, over and above; **alius super alium** one on top of another, one after another; **super cēnam** *(or* **mēnsam)** over dinner, at table *(i.e., during the meal);* **super omnia** *(or* **cūncta)** above all, more than anything II *(w. abl)* above, over, upon, on; concerning, about, in the matter of; besides, in addition to; at *(e.g., midnight)*

sup·er -era -erum *adj see* **superus**

superā *adv* above

super·a -ōrum *npl* upper world, sky; heaven; heavenly bodies

superābil·is -is -e *adj* surmountable, climbable; conquerable

superad·dō -dere -didī -ditus *tr* to add besides, add to boot

super·āns -antis *adj* predominant; outstanding, remarkable

superāt·or -ōris *m* conqueror

superbē *adv* arrogantly, haughtily, snobbishly

superbi·a -ae *f* arrogance, haughtiness, snobbishness; pride

superbiloquenti·a -ae *f* haughty tone, arrogant speech

superb·iō -īre *intr* to be haughty; to be proud; to be superb, be magnificent; *(w. abl)* to take pride in

superb·us -a -um *adj* arrogant, haughty, snobbish; proud; overbearing, tyrannical; fastidious, disdainful; superb, magnificent; *(of an honor)* that is a source of pride; *(w. abl)* proud of; **āles superba** the phoenix

supercil·ium -(i)ī *n* eyebrow; frown, will *(of Jupiter);* stern looks; summit, brow *(of a hill);* arrogance, superciliousness; artificial eyebrow

superēmin·eō -ēre *tr* to tower over, top

superfici·ēs -ēī *f* top, surface; *(leg)* fixtures, improvements, buildings *(i.e., anything upon the property but not the land itself)*

super·fīō -fierī *intr* to be over and above; to be left over

superfīx·us -a -um *adj* stuck *or* impaled on top of; **rumpiīs superfīxa capita** heads stuck on top of long spears

superflu·ō -ere -xī *intr* to overflow; to be superfluous

superfuī *perf of* **supersum**

super·fundō -fundere -fūdī -fūsus *tr (w. abl)* to shower *(s.th.)* with; *(w. dat)* to pour *(s.th.)* upon II *refl & pass* to spread, spread out, extend

super·gredior -gredī -gressus sum *tr* to walk *or* step over; to surpass

super·ī -ōrum *mpl* the gods above; men on earth; mortals; upper world

super·iaciō -iacere -iēcī -iectus *or* **-iactus** *tr* to throw on top; to overshoot *(a target);* **fidem superiacere** to exceed the bounds of credibility; **natāre superiectō aequore** to swim in the flood waters

superimmin·eō -ēre *intr (w. dat)* to stand over *(s.o. in a threatening manner)*

superimpend·ēns -entis *adj* overhanging, towering overhead

superim·pōnō -pōnere -posuī -positus *tr* to place on top, place overhead

superimposit·us -a -um *adj* superimposed

superincid·ēns -entis *adj* falling from above

superincub·āns -antis *adj* lying above *or* on top

superin·cumbō -cumbere -cubuī *intr* to lean over; *(w. dat)* to lay oneself down on

superindu·ō -ere -ī *tr* to put on over one's other clothes

superin·iciō -icere -iēcī -iectus *tr* to throw on top

superin·sternō -sternere -strāvī -strātus *tr (w. abl)* to cover *(w. s.th.)*

superi·or -or -us *(comp of* **superus)** *adj* higher, upper; the upper part of; past, previous, preceding; older, elder, more advanced; superior, stronger; victorious, conquering; greater; **dē locō superiōre dīcere** to speak from the tribunal, handle a case in court; to speak from the rostra; **ex locō superiōre pugnāre** to fight from a vantage point

superiūmentār·ius -(i)ī *m* one charged with looking after the beasts of burden

superius *adv (e.g., mentioned)* above

superlāt·us -a -um *adj* exaggerated

supernē *adv* above, from above; on top; **dē supernē** from above

supern·us -a -um *adj* upper; situated high up; supernal, celestial

super·ō -āre -āvī -ātus *tr* to go over, pass over, rise above; to pass, go past, go beyond; to sail past, double; to outdo, surpass; to surmount *(difficulties);* to live past, live beyond; to overcome, vanquish; to arrive before *or* ahead of; **vītā superāre** to survive, outlive ‖ *intr* to mount, ascend; to be superior, have the advantage; to be left over, survive; to be superfluous; to be abundant; to remain to be done; *(w. dat)* to pass over, pass above

superobru·ō -ere *tr (also written as two words)* to cover completely, smother

superoccup·ō -āre *tr* to pounce on

superpend·ēns -entis *adj* towering overhead

super·pōnō -pōnere -posuī -positus *tr (w. dat)* to put *(s.th.)* upon; *(w.* **in** *+ acc)* to put *(s.o.)* in charge of

superquam quod *conj* in addition to the fact that

superscand·ō -ere *tr* to step over, climb over

superscrībō -scrībere -scrīpsī -scrīptus *tr* to write over *or* on top of

super·sedeō -sedēre -sēdī -sessum *tr (-sid-)* to sit on top of ‖ *intr* to sit on top; *(w. dat)* **1** to sit on *(e.g., an elephant);* **2** to preside over; **3** to refrain from, desist from; *(w. abl)* to refrain from, give up, steer clear of; *(w. inf)* to stop *(doing s.th.)*

superstagn·ō -āre -āvī *intr (of a river)* to overflow and form swamps

superst·es -itis *adj* standing by as a witness; surviving; posthumous; *(w. gen or dat)* outliving, surviving *(s.o.);* **superstes esse** to live on; **superstes esse** *(w. gen or dat)* to outlive *(s.o.)*

superstiti·ō -ōnis *f* superstition; blind adherence to rules

superstitiōsē *adv* superstitiously

superstitiōs·us -a -um *adj* superstitious; ecstatic; blindly adhering to rules

superstit·ō -āre *intr* to be left

superst·ō -āre -stetī *tr* to stand over ‖ *intr (w. dat)* to stand on, stand over

superstrāt·us -a -um *adj* spread over *(as a covering)*

superstru·ō -ere -xī -ctus *tr* to build upon

super·sum -esse -fuī -futūrus *intr* to be left over, still exist, survive; to abound; to overflow; to be excessive; to be superfluous; to be adequate, suffice; *(w. dat)* to outlive, survive *(s.o.)*

super·tegō -tegere -tēxī -tēctus *tr* to cover over

superurg·ēns -entis *adj* putting on pressure, adding pressure

super·us *or* **super -a -um** *adj* upper; of this world, of this life; northern; **ad aurās superās redīre** to come back to life; **mare superum** Adriatic Sea ‖ *mpl see* **superī** ‖ *npl see* **supera**

supervac(u)āne·us -a -um *adj* superfluous

supervacu·us -a -um *adj* superfluous

supervād·ō -ere *tr* to go over, climb over

super·vehor -vehī -vectus sum *tr* to sail, ride, *or* drive by *or* past

super·veniō -venīre -vēnī -ventus *tr* to come upon, come on top of; to overtake; to come over, close over, cover; to surprise ‖ *intr* to arrive suddenly; *(w. dat)* to come upon by surprise

supervent·us -ūs *m* sudden arrival, unexpected arrival

super·vīvō -vīvere -vixī *intr (w. dat)* to outlive

supervolit·ō -āre -āvī *tr* to hover over

supervol·ō -āre -āvī *tr* to fly over ‖ *intr* to fly across

supīn·ō -āre -āvī -ātus *tr* to turn over *(by plowing)*

supīn·us -a -um *adj* face-up; lying on one's back; turned upwards; sloping, sloping upwards; *(of streams)* flowing upwards *(to their source);* on one's back; lazy, careless, indifferent

supp- = subp-

suppāctus *pp of* **suppingō (subp-)**

suppaenitet -ēre *v impers* **(subp-)** *(w. acc of person and gen of thing regretted), e.g.,* **illum furōris suppaenitet** he somewhat regrets the outburst

suppalp·or -ārī *intr* **(subp-)** *(w. dat)* to coax *(s.o.)* a little

supp·ār -aris *adj* nearly equal

supparasīt·or -ārī *intr (w. dat)* to flatter *(s.o.)* a little like a parasite

suppar·um -ī *n or* **suppar·us -ī** *m* linen dress; small sail

suppeditāti·ō -ōnis *f* **(subp-)** good supply

suppedit·ō -āre -āvī -ātus *tr* **(subp-)** to supply, furnish ‖ *intr* to stand by; to be on hand, be in stock, be available; *(w. dat)* to be at hand for; *(w.* **ad** *or* **in** *+ acc)* to be adequate for

suppēd·ō -ere *intr (vulg)* to fart quietly

suppernāt·us -a -um *adj* hamstrung

suppeti·ae -ārum *fpl* assistance

suppeti·or -ārī -ātus sum *intr* (subp-) *(w. dat)* to help, assist
suppet·ō -ere -īvī *or* -**iī** -**ītum** *intr* to be at hand, be in stock, be available; *(w. dat)* **1** to be at hand for, be available to; **2** to be equal to, suffice for; **3** to correspond to
suppīl·ō -āre -āvī -ātus *tr* (subp-) to filch, snitch
sup·pingō -pingere -pēgī -pāctus *tr* (subp-) to fasten underneath
supplant·ō -āre -āvī -ātus *tr* (subp-) to trip up, cause to stumble
supplēment·um -ī *n* (subp-) *(mil)* reinforcement(s)
suppl·eō -ēre -ēvī -ētus *tr* (subp-) to fill up; to make good *(losses, damage, etc.); (mil)* to bring to full strength
suppl·ex -icis *adj* kneeling, on one's knees, in entreaty; humble, submissive ‖ *mf* suppliant
supplicāti·ō -ōnis *f* public thanksgiving, day of prayer; thanksgiving for victory; day of humiliation
suppliciter *adv* suppliantly, humbly
supplic·ium -(i)ī *n* (subp-) kneeling down, bowing down, humble entreaty; public prayer, supplication; *(because criminals were beheaded kneeling)* execution, death penalty; punishment, torture; suffering, pain; **supplicium dare** to atone; **supplicium dare** *(or* **pendere,** *or* **expendere,** *or* **luere)** to pay the penalty, suffer punishment; **supplicium sūmere** *(or* **exigere)** to exact punishment; to accept reparation; *(w.* **ab, ex, ex** + *abl)* to exact punishment from, put *(s.o.)* to death
supplic·ō -āre -āvī -ātum *intr* (subpl) *(w. dat)* to go on one's knees to, entreat, beg
supplōd·ō -dere -sī -sus *tr* (subp-) to stamp *(the foot)*
supplōsi·ō -ōnis *f* (subp-) stamping *(one's foot)*
sup·pōnō -pōnere -posuī -positus *tr* (subp-) *(w. dat)* **1** to put, place, set *(s.th.)* under; **2** to put *(s.th.)* next to, add *(s.th.)* to; **3** to substitute *(s.th.)* for; **potentiam in grātiae locum suppōnere** to substitute power for influence
support·ō -āre -āvī -ātus *tr* (subp-) to bring up, transport
suppositīci·us -a -um *adj* (subp-) spurious
suppositi·ō -ōnis *f* substitution
suppositus *pp of* **suppōnō**
suppostr·īx -īcis *f* unfair substituter *(female)*
suppressi·ō -ōnis *f* holding back *(of money),* embezzlement
suppress·us -a -um *adj* soft *(voice);* soft-spoken *(person)*
sup·primō -primere -pressī -pressus *tr* (subp-) to press down *or* under; to sink; to repress, stop; to suppress, keep secret; to stifle *(an utterance);* to detain in one's private

custody; to retain *(another's money)* in one's possession; to suppress *(feelings)*
supprōm·us -ī *m* (subp-) assistant butler
suppud·et -ēre *v impers* (subp-) to cause *(s.o.)* a slight feeling of shame; *(w. acc of person and gen of cause), e.g.:* **eōrum mē suppudet** I am a bit ashamed of them
suppūr·ō -āre -āvī -ātum *intr* to fester
supp·us -a -um *adj* lying on one's back, supine; upside down
supput·ō -āre -āvī -ātus *tr* to trim off the lower branches of; to count, compute
suprā *adv* on top, above; up above; earlier; beyond, more; **suprā quam** more than ‖ *prep (usu. w. acc; also w. abl) (sometimes following its object or separated from it by intervening words)* on, on top of; over, above; beyond; *(of time)* before, earlier than; north of; to the far side of; *(of amount)* over, beyond; in charge of; *(w. reference to position at the dining table, from the standpoint of those eating)* on the left of; **Atticus suprā mē, īnfrā Verrius accubēbat** Atticus sat to the left of me, Verrius to the right of me; **gallīnāceus suprā virī umerum deinde in capite astitit** the rooster stood on the man's shoulder and then on his head; **suprā caput** *(in a threatening way)* (hanging) over one's head; **suprā terram** above ground
suprālāti·ō -ōnis *f* exaggeration
suprālāt·us -a -um *adj* exaggerated
suprāscand·ō -ere *tr* to climb over
suprāscrīpt·us -a -um *adj* written above *(as a correction)*
suprēmum *adv* for the last time; as a final tribute
suprēm·us -a -um *(superl of* **superus)** *adj* last, latest, final; highest; greatest, supreme, extreme; critical, desperate *(time);* closing, dying, final; **suprēma manus** finishing touches; **suprēma multa** maximum fine; **suprēmum iūdicium** last will and testament; **suprēmum supplicium** death penalty; **suprēmus mōns** mountain top ‖ *n* last moment ‖ *npl* moment of death; funeral rites
supt- = **subt-**
Sur- = **Syr-**
sūr·a -ae *f (anat)* calf
surcul·us -ī *m* shoot, sprout, twig; slip, graft
surdas·ter -tra -trum *adj* somewhat deaf
surdit·ās -ātis *f* deafness
surd·us -a -um *adj* deaf; silent, noiseless; unheeding; dull, faint
Sūrēn·a -ae *m* grand vizier *(in Parthia)*
surgō surgere surrēxī surrēctum *intr* to get up; to stand up; to rise; to spring up and grow tall
surr- = **subr-**

surrancid·us -a -um *adj* **(subr-)** somewhat rancid *or* spoiled

surrauc·us -a -um *adj* **(subr-)** somewhat hoarse

surrēctus *pp of* **surgō** *and* **surrigō**

surrēmig·ō -āre *intr* to row along

Surrentīn·us -a -um *adj* of Surrentum *(modern Sorrento)*

sur·rēpō -rēpere -rēpsī -rēptum *tr* **(subr-)** to creep under, crawl under II *intr* to creep up; *(w. dat)* to creep up on

surreptīci·us -a -um *adj* **(subr-)** surreptitious; secretive

surreptus *pp of* **surripiō**

surrēptus *pp of* **surrēpō**

sur·rīdeō -rīdēre -rīsī *intr* **(subr-)** to smile

surrīdiculē *adv* **(subr-)** rather humorously

sur·rigō -rigere -rēxī -rēctus *tr* **(subr-)** to raise, lift up, erect

surring·or -ī *intr* **(subr-)** to grimace, make a face; to be somewhat annoyed

sur·ripiō -ripere -ripuī -reptus *tr* **(subr-)** to snatch secretly, pilfer; *(w. dat)* to pilfer *(s.th.)* from

surrīsī *perf of* **surrīdeō**

surrog·ō -āre -āvī -ātus *tr* **(subr-)** to propose as a substitute

surrostrān·ī -ōrum *mpl* **(subr-)** loafers around the Rostra *(in the Forum)*

surrub·eō -ēre *intr* **(subr-)** to blush slightly

surrūf·us -a -um *adj* **(subr-)** reddish

sur·ruō -ruere -ruī -rutus *tr* **(subr-)** to dig under; to loosen at the base; to tear down, demolish; *(fig)* to undermine, subvert

surrūstic·us -a -um *adj* **(subr-)** rather unsophisticated

surrutil·us -a -um *adj* **(subr-)** reddish

surrūtus *pp of* **surruō**

sūrsum *adv* **(sūrsus, sūsum, sūsus)** upwards, high up; **sūrsum deorsum** up and down

sūs suis *m* pig, hog; boar II *f* sow

Sūs·a -ōrum *npl* capital of Persia

sūscēnseō *see* **succēnseō**

sūscepti·ō -ōnis *f* undertaking

sūscept·um -ī *n* enterprise, undertaking

sus·cipiō -cipere -cēpī -ceptus *tr* to catch *(s.th. before it falls);* to support; to pick up, resume *(conversation);* to bear *(children);* to accept, receive *(under one's protection);* to take up, undertake; to acknowledge, recognize *(a child)* as one's own

sūscit·ō -āre -āvī -ātus *tr* to stir up, shake up; to build, erect; to cause *(s.th.)* to rise; to wake *(s.o.)* up; to encourage; to stir up *(rebellion, love, etc.);* to rouse *(from inactivity);* to have *(s.o.)* stand up in court *(as witness)*

suspect·ō -āre -āvī -ātus *tr* to gaze up at; to suspect

suspect·us -a -um *pp of* **suspiciō** II *adj* suspect, suspected, mistrusted

suspect·us -ūs *m* view from below; respect, esteem

suspend·ium -(i)ī *n* hanging; hanging oneself

suspen·dō -dere -dī -sus *tr* to hang up, hang; to prop up, support; to keep in suspense; to check *(temporarily);* to interrupt II *pass (w. ex)* to depend on

suspēns·us -a -um *adj* hanging, balanced; raised, poised; in suspense, uncertain, hesitant; marked by uncertainty; vague *(language); (w. ex)* dependent upon; **in suspēnsō** in suspense, on tenterhooks; undecided

suspic·āx -ācis *adj* suspicious; mistrustful

suspici·ō -ōnis *f* suspicion, mistrust; inkling; faint indication, trace, suggestion; *(w. gen)* suspicion *(of); (w. acc & inf or* **quasi)** suspicion that; **in suspiciōnem cadere** to fall under suspicion; **in suspiciōnem venīre** to come under suspicion; **Tarentīnōrum dēfectiō iam diū in suspiciōne Rōmānīs fuerat** the revolt of the Tarentines long been suspected by the Romans

suspiciō suspicere suspexī suspectus *tr* to look up at; to look up to, admire; to mistrust, suspect II *intr* to look up; *(w. in + acc)* to look up at *or* into

suspīciōsē *adv* suspiciously

suspīciōs·us -a -um *adj* mistrustful, suspicious; suspicious-looking; *(w. in + acc)* suspicious of

suspic·ō -āre *or* **suspic·or -ārī -ātus sum** *tr* to mistrust, suspect; to suppose, surmise, believe

suspīrāt·us -ūs *m* deep breath, sigh; labored breathing

suspīr·ium -(i)ī *n* deep breath, sigh; **suspīrium dūcere** *(or* **repetere** *or* **trahere)** to take a deep breath, sigh

suspīr·ō -āre -āvī -ātus *tr* to sigh for II *intr* to sigh, heave a sigh

susque dēque *adv* up and down; **dē Octāviō susque dēque est** it's all one *(i.e., of no consequence)* as far as Octavian is concerned

suss- = subs-

sustentāti·ō -ōnis *f* delay

sustent·ō -āre -āvī -ātus *tr* to build up; to hold upright; to support; to sustain *(w. food);* to maintain; to provide *(s.o. w. food, money, etc.),* support, maintain; to uphold *(the law);* to endure, hold up against; to hold back, keep in check; to delay, put off

sus·tineō -tinēre -tinuī *tr* to hold up, support; to hold back, hold in check; to uphold *(the law);* to sustain, support *(w. food, etc.);* to bear, endure *(trouble);* to hold up, delay, put off

sustoll·ō -ere *tr* to lift up, raise; to kidnap

sustulī *perf of* tollō
sūsum *see* sūrsum
susurrāt·or -ōris *m* mutterer, whisperer
susurr·ō -āre *tr & intr* to mutter, murmur, whisper
susurr·us -a -um *adj* whispering
susurr·us -ī *m* low, gentle noise; murmur, whisper, buzz, hum
sūt·a -ōrum *npl* coat of mail; joints
sūtēl·ae -ārum *fpl* patches; tricks
sūtil·is -is -e *adj* sewn together; **cumba sūtilis** boat made of skins; **rosae sūtilēs** a wreath of roses
sūt·or -ōris *m* shoemaker
sūtōri·us -a -um *adj* shoemaker's **‖** *m (hum)* Shoemaker Emeritus
sūtrīn·us -a -um *adj* shoemaker's **‖** *f* shoemaker's shop
Sūtr·ium -(i)ī *n* town in Etruria
sūtūr·a -ae *f* stitch; seam
sūt·us -a -um *pp of* suō **‖** *npl* joints
su·us -a -um *or* su·os -a -om *adj* his own, her own, its own, their own, one's own; due, proper, peculiar **‖** *pron masc pl* one's own people, one's own family, one's own friends **‖** *pron neut pl* one's own property
Sybar·is -is *f* town in S. Italy noted for its luxurious living **‖** *m* Sybaris *(boy's name, suggestive of decadence)*
Sybarīt·a -ae *m* Sybarite
Sybarītic·us -a -um *adj* Sybarite; *(fig)* erotic
Sȳchae·us -ī *m* husband of Dido
sȳcophant·a -ae *m* swindler; slanderer; cunning parasite
sȳcophanti·a -ae *f* deceptive trickery
sȳcophantiōsē *adv* deceitfully
sȳcophant·or -ārī -ātus sum *intr* to cheat; *(w. dat)* to pull a fast one on
Syēn·e -ēs *f* town in Egypt *(modern Aswan)*
Sylla *see* Sulla
syllab·a -ae *f* syllable
syllabātim *adv* syllable by syllable
Symaethē·us -a -um *adj* of the River Symaethus
Symaeth·is -idis *f* daughter of the river-god Symaethus
Symaeth·us -ī *m* River Symaethus in Sicily near Catana
symbol·a -ae *or* symbol·ē -ēs *f* contribution *(of money to a feast); (coll)* blows
symbol·us -ī *m* (sumb-) symbol, mark, token
symphōni·a -ae *f* harmony; symphony, band *(of singers or musicians)*
symphōniac·us -a -um *adj* concert, musical; **puerī symphōniacī** choristers **‖** *mpl* musicians
Symplēgad·es -um *fpl* two islands in the Black Sea which floated about and dashed against each other until they were fixed in place a split second after the *Argo* sailed by them

symplegm·a -atis *n* tangled group *(of persons embracing or wrestling)*
syngraph·a -ae *f* promissory note, I.O.U.
syngraph·us -ī *m* written contract; pass *(for safe-conduct)*
syn(h)od·ūs -ontos *m* bream *(fish)*
synhedr·us -ī *m* senator *(in Macedonia)*
Synnad·a -ōrum *npl or* Synn·as -adis *f* town in Phrygia, famous for its colored marble
synthesin·a -ae *f* dinner shirt
synthes·is -is *f* a set of matching articles; dinner service; *(matching)* dinner clothes
Syph·āx -ācis *m* (Syf-) king of Numidia at the time of the Second Punic War, siding with Carthage *(d. 203 b.c.)*
Syrācosi·us -a -um *adj* (-cūs) Syracusan **‖** *mpl* Syracusans
Syrācūs·ae -ārum *fpl* Syracuse *(chief city of Sicily)*
Syrācūsān·us *or* Syrācūsi·us -a -um *adj* Syracusan
Syri·a -ae *f* (Sur-) Syria *(usu. including Phoenicia and Palestine)*
Syriac·us -a -um *adj* Syrian; from Syria; produced in Syria
Syriātic·us -a -um *adj* Syrian
Sȳr·inx -ingos *f* nymph who was pursued by Pan and changed into a reed
Syri·us -a -um *adj* Syrian; of Syros in the Cyclades **‖** *m* Syrian
syrm·a -atis *n* robe with a train *(worn esp. by actors in tragedies);* tragedy
Syrophoen·īx -īcis *m* Syrophoenician *(Phoenicia was regarded as part of Syria)*
Sȳr·os -ī *f* Syros *(island in the Cyclades between Delos and Paros, modern Syria)*
syrt·is -is *f* sand bank, sand dune, quicksand **‖** Syrtis *f* Gulf of Sidra in N. Africa **‖** Gulf of Gabes **‖** *fpl* name of an area of sand dunes on the coast between Carthage and Cyrene
Syr·us -a -um *adj* (Sur-) Syrian **‖** *mf* Syrian; proper name of a slave

T

T, t *(supply* littera) *f* nineteenth letter of the Latin alphabet; letter name: **te**
T. *abbr* Titus *(Roman first name, praenomen)*
tabān·us -ī *m* horsefly
tabell·a -ae *f* small board, panel; plaque; writing tablet; page *(of a bound notebook);* ballot; picture, painting; votive tablet; game board; placard, notice; door panel **‖** *fpl* notebook
tabellāri·us -a -um *adj (leg)* regulating voting by secret ballot **‖** *m* mail carrier, courier

tāb·eō -ēre *intr* to waste away; to melt; to decay; to drip; **tābentēs genae** sunken cheeks
tabern·a -ae *f* hut; booth, stall, shop; inn; **taberna dīversōria** *(or* **meritōria)** inn
tabernācul·um -ī *n* tent; **tabernāculum capere** *(of an augur)* to set up a tent in which to take the auspices
tabernār·ius -(i)ī *m* shopkeeper
tāb·ēs -is *f* melting; wasting, decay; dwindling, shrinking; decaying matter, rot; disease; moral corruption; means of corruption
tāb·ēscō -ēscere -uī *intr* to begin to decay; to begin to melt; to rot
tābidul·us -a -um *adj* rotting; wasting
tābid·us -a -um *adj* wasting, decaying; melting; corrupting; infectious
tābific·us -a -um *adj* wasting; melting; *(fig)* gnawing
tabul·a -ae *f* plank, board; writing tablet; painting *(on a panel of wood)*; game board; votive tablet; door panel; placard, advertisement; auction notice; will; record; counting board **‖** *fpl* account books, records, register, lists; **tabulae novae** clean slate *(i.e., cancellation of debts)*
tabulār·ium -(i)ī *n* archives; archives building
tabulār·ius -(i)ī *m* accountant, bookkeeper
tabulāti·ō -ōnis *f* flooring; floor, story
tabulāt·us -a -um *adj* boarded **‖** *n* floor, story; layer; deck *(of a ship)*; row *(of trees)*
tāb·um -ī *n* rot, putrid matter; infectious disease, plague
tac·eō -ēre -uī -itus *tr* to be silent about, pass over in silence **‖** *intr* to be silent, be still
tacitē *adv* silently; secretly, privately; without publicity; tacitly, without express statement; imperceptibly, quietly
taciturnit·ās -ātis *f* taciturnity; silence; failure to communicate
taciturn·us -a -um *adj* taciturn, silent; noiseless, hushed, quiet
tacit·us -a -um *adj* silent; mute; unmentioned; secret; *(leg)* tacit; **per tacitum** in silence
Tacit·us -ī *m* Gaius(?) Cornelius Tacitus *(Roman historian, c. A.D. 55–115)*
tāctil·is -is -e *adj* tangible
tācti·ō -ōnis *f* touch, touching; feeling, sense of touch
tāctus *pp of* **tangō**
tāct·us -ūs *m* touch; handling; *(fig)* contact, influence
taed·a -ae *f* pine wood; pitch; pine board; pine tree; torch; wedding torch; *(fig)* wedding
tae·det -dēre -sum est *v impers* it irks; *(w. acc of person and gen of the cause)*, e.g., **mē taedet sermōnis tuī** I am sick of your talk, your talk irks me
taedi·fer -fera -ferum *adj* carrying a torch, torch-bearing

taed·ium -(i)ī *n* tediousness; weariness, boredom; feeling of disgust; object of disgust; nuisance
Taenarid·ēs -ae *m* man from Taenarus, Spartan *(esp. Hyacinthus)*
Taenar·is -idis *adj (fem only)* Spartan **‖** *f* Spartan woman
Taenari·us *or* **Taenare·us** -a -um *adj* of Taenarus, Taenarian; *(poet)* Spartan, Laconian
Taenar·um *or* **Taenar·on** -ī *n, or* **Taenar·os** *or* **Taenar·us** -ī *mf* Taenarus *(promontory at the S. tip of the Peloponnesus, near which a cavern was thought to lead to the lower world)*; Hades
taeni·a -ae *f* band, ribbon; string
taesum est *see* **taedet**
tae·ter -tra -trum *adj* (tet-) offensive, revolting, loathsome; hideous; *(of actions)* monstrous, horrible
taetrē *adv* foully, hideously
taetricus *see* **tētricus**
tag·āx -ācis *adj* light-fingered *(thief)*
Tag·ēs -is *m* Etruscan god, originator of divination and grandson of Jupiter
tālār·is -is -e *adj* ankle-length **‖** *npl* ankle-length clothes; sandals; winged sandals; *(fig)* means of getting away
tālāri·us -a -um *adj* of dice; **lūdus tālārius** game of dice
talāsiō *interj* (-lass-) wedding cry
tāle·a -ae *f* rod, bar, stake
talent·um -ī *n* talent *(Greek weight, varying from state to state, but equal to about 50 lbs.; also a unit of currency, consisting of 60 minae, or about 600 denarii, or about $600)*; **talentum magnum** Attic talent *(so called to distinguish it from talents from other cities of lower value)*
tāli·ō -ōnis *f (leg)* punishment in kind, exaction of compensation in kind
tāl·is -is -e *adj* such, of that kind; so great, so excellent; **tālis … quālis** such … as
tāliter *adv* in such a way
tālitr·um -ī *n* fillip *(flick with the tip of the middle finger and the thumb)*
talp·a -ae *mf* mole *(animal)*
Talthyb·ius -(i)ī *m* herald of Agamemnon
tāl·us -ī *m* ankle; anklebone; foot; knucklebone *(used in playing dice)*; **tālīs lūdere** to play dice; **tālōs iacere** to roll the dice
tam *adv* to such an extent, to such a degree, so, so much; **tam … quam** the … the; **tam magis … quam magis** the more … the more
tamar·īx -īcis *f* tamarisk *(ornamental shrub or short tree)*
tamdiū *or* **tam diū** *adv* so long, how long; **tamdiū quam** *(or* **tamdiū dum)** as long as

tamen *adv* yet, nevertheless, still, just the same

tamendem *adv* all the same

tamenetsī *conj* even though **ǁ** *adv* all the same, nevertheless

Tames·is -is *m or* **Tames·a -ae** *f* Thames River

tametsī *conj* even if, although

tamquam *conj* **(tan-)** as, just as, as much as; just as if; **tamquam sī** just as if

Tana·ger -grī *m* river in Lucania

Tanagr·a -ae *f* town in Boeotia

Tana·is -is *m* river of Sarmatia *(modern River Don)*

Tanaqu·il -ilis *f* wife of the elder Tarquin

tandem *adv* at last, in the end, finally; *(expressing urgency or impatience)* now, tell me, please, just; **quoūsque tandem** just how long?

tangō tangere tetigī tāctus *tr* to touch; to handle, meddle with; to taste; to come to, reach; to border on; to hit, beat; to wash; to anoint; to gall; to move to pity; to dupe; to touch upon, mention; to touch, be related to; to undertake; **dē caelō** *(or* **fulmine) tangere** to strike with lightning

tanquam *see* **tamquam**

Tantale·us -a -um *adj* of Tantalus

Tantalid·ēs -ae *m* descendant of Tantalus *(e.g., Atreus, Aegisthus, Agamemnon, Menelaus)*

Tantal·is -idos *f* female descendant of Tantalus *(e.g., Niobe, Hermione)*

Tantal·us -ī *m* son of Jupiter and father of Pelops and Niobe; he was punished in Hades with constant hunger and thirst

tantill·us -a -um *adj* so small, so little **ǁ** *n* a bit; **tantillō minus** a little less

tantisper *adv* just so long *(and no longer);* just for the moment

tantopere *or* **tantō opere** *adv* so much, so greatly, to such a degree, so earnestly, so hard

tantulum *adv* so little, in the least

tantul·us -a -um *adj* so little, so small **ǁ** *n* so little, such a trifle; **tantulō vēndere** to sell for such a trifling amount

tantum *adv (see also the neut of* **tantus)** so much, so greatly, to such a degree, so far, so long, so; only, just, but just; hardly, scarcely; **nōn tantum** all but, almost; **nōn tantum omnēs opitulārī voluērunt** almost all wished to be of assistance; **nōn tantum . . . sed etiam** not only . . . but also; **tantum modo** only

tantummodo *adv* only

tantundem *adv* just as much, just as far, to the same extent

tant·us -a -um *adj* of such size, so big, so great; so much; so little; so important **ǁ** *pron neut* so much; so little; so small an amount, so small a number; to such an extent *or*

degree; **alterum tantum** twice the amount; **in tantum** to such an extent; **tantī** of such value, worth so much, at so high a price; of little account, of such small importance; **tantō** *(as abl of price)* at such a price, for so much; *(w. comparatives)* by so much, so much the; **tantō ante (post)** so much earlier (later); **tantō melior!** so much the better!; **tantō nequior!** so much the worse!; **tantum est** that is all; **tantum abesse ut** to be so far (from being the case) that; **tantum āfuit ut perīculōsum reī pūblicae putāret exercitum ut** (+ *subj)* so far was he from thinking that the army was a threat to the country that . . . ; **ter (quater) tantum** three (four) times as much

tant·usdem -adem -undem *adj* just as big, just as large, just as great **ǁ** *n* the same quantity, just as much; *(w. advl force)* to the same degree, just as much; **tantīdem** at the same price; **tantundem est** it comes to the same thing

tap·ēs -ētis *m,* **tapēt·e -is** *n,* **tapēt·um -ī** *n* carpet; tapestry; coverlet

tapēt·ia -ium *npl* tapestry

taratantara *n* sound produced by the trumpet; **at tuba taratantara dīxit** but the trumpet went "taratantara"

tardē *adv* slowly; with difficulty; late; **cum tardissimē** at the latest

tardēsc·ō -ere *intr* to become slow; to falter

tardip·ēs -edis *adj* limping

tardit·ās -ātis *f* tardiness; slowness; procrastination; dullness, stupidity

tarditūd·ō -inis *f* tardiness; slowness

tardiuscul·us -a -um *adj* rather slow, slowish, dragging

tard·ō -āre -āvī -ātus *tr* to slow down, delay, hinder; to check *(emotions);* to dull *(the senses)* **ǁ** *intr* to go slow, take it easy; to hold back

tard·us -a -um *adj* tardy, slow; lingering; mentally slow, mentally retarded; deliberate; crippling; *(of events)* long drawn out, making slow progress

Tarentīn·us -a -um *adj* Tarentine **ǁ** *mpl* Tarentines

Tarent·um -ī *n* Tarentum *(town on S. coast of Italy, modern Taranto)* **ǁ** a section on the west side of the Campus Martius

tarm·es -itis *m* termite

Tarpēi·us -a -um *adj* Tarpeian; **mōns Tarpēius** *(or* **Tarpēia rūpēs** *(or* **Tarpēium saxum)** Tarpeian cliff *(on the Capitoline Hill from which criminals were thrown)* **ǁ** *f* Roman girl who treacherously opened the citadel to the Sabine attackers

tarpezīt·a -ae *m* **(trap-)** banker, moneychanger

Tarquiniān·us -a -um *adj* of the Tarquins

Tarquiniēns·is **-is** **-e** *adj* of the town of Tarquinii **‖** *mpl* inhabitants of Tarquinii
Tarquini·ī **-ōrum** *mpl* Tarquinii *(important Etruscan city on the W. coast of Italy, about seventy miles N. of Rome, modern Tarquinia)*
Tarquini·us **-a** **-um** *adj* Tarquinian **‖** *m* Tarquinius Priscus *(fifth king of Rome, c. 616–579 B.C.)* **‖** Tarquinius Superbus *(seventh and last king of Rome, c. 534–510 B.C.)*
Tarracīn·a **-ae** *f or* **Terracīn·ae** **-ārum** *fpl* Terracina *(town in Latium)*
Tarrac·o **-ōnis** *f* Tarraco *(now Terragona, ancient town on the East coast of Spain, which Augustus made the capital of one of the three Spanish provinces)*
Tarracōnēns·is **-is** **-e** *adj* of Terragona, Tarragonian; **Hispānia Tarracōnēnsis** Tarragonian Spain
Tartar·a **-ōrum** *npl or* **Tartar·us** *or* **Tartar·os** **-ī** *m* Tartarus *(lower level of Hades reserved for notorious criminals)*
Tartare·us **-a** **-um** *adj* of Tartarus, infernal
tat *or* **tatae** *interj* uhoh! *(expression of surprise)*
tat·a **-ae** *m (coll)* daddy; grandpa
Tat·ius **-(i)ī** *m* Titus Tatius *(king of the Sabines who later ruled jointly with Romulus until the latter had him killed)*
tau *indecl n* the Greek letter tau
taure·us **-a** **-um** *adj* bull's, of a bull; **terga taurea** bulls' hides; drums **‖** *f* rawhide, whip
Taur·ī **-ōrum** *mpl* inhabitants of Chersonesus Tauricus *(modern Crimea)*
Tauric·us **-a** **-um** *adj* Tauric **‖** *mpl* the Tauri
taurif·er **-era** **-erum** *adj (of regions)* bull-producing
tauriform·is **-is** **-e** *adj* bull-shaped
taurīn·us **-a** **-um** *adj* bull's; made of bull's hide; bull-like **‖** **Taurīn·us** **-a** **-um** of the Taurini *(a Ligurian tribe)* **‖** *mpl* the Taurini
Tauri·us **-a** **-um** *adj* Roman clan name *(nomen);* **lūdī Tauriī** games held in the Circus Flaminius in honor of the gods of the lower world
taur·us **-ī** *m* bull; bronze bull made as an instrument of torture **‖** **Taurus** *(astr)* Taurus *(constellation)* **‖** **Taurus** the Taurus mountain range in S.E. Asia Minor
taxāti·ō **-ōnis** *f* evaluation, assessment; *(leg)* maximum sum
taxill·us **-ī** *m* small die *(for playing dice)*
tax·ō **-āre** **-āvī** **-ātus** *tr* to touch repeatedly, handle; to appraise, assess the value of; to reproach; to tease
tax·us **-ī** *f* yew tree
Tāyget·ē **-ēs** *f (astr)* one of the seven Pleiads forming the constellation of the Pleiades
Tāyget·us **-ī** *m* mountain range in Laconia, separating it from Messenia to the W.

-te = *suf for* **tū** *and* **tē**
tē *pron, acc & abl of* **tū**
Teān·um **-ī** *n* town in Campania *(modern Teano)* **‖** town in Apulia *(modern Civitate)*
techn·a *or* **techin·a** **-ae** *f* trick
technyph·ion **-iī** *n* a little workroom
Tecmess·a **-ae** *f* mistress of Ajax son of Telamon
tēctē *adv* cautiously, guardedly
tēct·or **-ōris** *m* plasterer
tēctōriol·um **-ī** *n* bit of plasterwork
tēctōri·us **-a** **-um** *adj* plaster, of plaster; **opus tēctōrium** plasterwork, stucco **‖** *n* plaster, stucco; fresco painting; beauty preparation ·
tēct·um **-ī** *n* roof; ceiling; canopy; cover, shelter; house
tēct·us **-a** **-um** *pp of* **tegō** **‖** *adj* concealed; secret; guarded *(words);* reserved, secretive *(person)* **‖** *n see* **tēctum**
tēcum = **cum tē**
tēd- = **taed-**
Tege·a **-ae** *f* town in S.E. Arcadia
Tegeae·us **-a** **-um** *adj* Tegean, Arcadian **‖** *m* Pan **‖** *f* Arcadian maiden *(esp. Atalanta and Callisto)*
Tegeāt·ēs **-ae** *m* inhabitant of Tegea
teg·es **-etis** *f* mat *(used for lying on or as a covering)*
tegetīcul·a **-ae** *f* small mat
tegill·um **-ī** *n* hood, cowl
tegim·en *or* **teg(u)m·en** **-inis** *n (applied to clothing, armor, skin of an animal or of fruit)* cover, covering; vault *(of heaven)*
tegiment·um *or* **teg(u)ment·um** **-ī** *n (applied to clothing, armor, skins, shells)* cover, covering
tegō **tegere** **tēxī** **tēctus** *tr* to cover; to protect, shelter; to hide; to bury; **tegere lātus** *(w. gen)* to escort *(s.o.)*
tēgul·a **-ae** *f* tile **‖** *fpl* roof tiles, tiled roof; siding for walls
tegumen *see* **tegimen**
tegumentum *see* **tegimentum**
tēl·a **-ae** *f* web; warp *(horizontal threads of a loom);* yarn beam; loom; *(fig)* design, plan
Telam·ōn **-ōnis** *m* son of Aeacus, brother of Peleus, king of Salamis, and father of Ajax and Teucer
Telamōniad·ēs **-ae** *m* son of Telamon *(esp. Ajax)*
Telamōn·ius **-(i)ī** *m* Ajax *(son of Telamon)*
Tēlegon·us **-ī** *m* son of Ulysses and Circe
Telemach·us **-ī** *m* son of Ulysses and Penelope
Tēleph·us **-ī** *m* king of Mysia, wounded by the spear of Achilles and later cured by its rust
tēlin·um **-ī** *n* perfume made of fenugreek
tell·ūs **-ūris** *f* the earth; ground, earth; land, country; dry land

tēl·um -ī *n* missile, weapon; spear, javelin, dart; sword, dagger; ax; shaft *(of light);* **cum tēlis** *(or* **tēlō)** armed

temerāri·us -a -um *adj* casual, accidental; rash, thoughtless

temere *adv* by chance, without cause; at random; rashly, thoughtlessly; **nōn temere** not lightly; not easily; hardly ever; **nūllus diēs temere intercessit quō nōn scrīberet** hardly a day ever went by without his writing

temerit·ās -ātis *f* chance, accident; rashness, thoughtlessness ‖ *fpl* foolhardy acts

temer·ō -āre -āvī -ātus *tr* to darken, blacken; to violate, disgrace, defile

Temes·ē -ēs *f or* **Temes·a -ae** *f* town in Bruttium noted for its copper mines

tēmēt·um -ī *n* (intoxicating) liquor

temn·ō -ere *tr* to slight

tēm·ō -ōnis *m* pole, tongue *(of a carriage or plow);* wagon

Tempē *indecl npl* scenic valley between Mt. Olympus and Mt. Ossa in Thessaly

temperāment·um -ī *n* blend; moderation; temperate heat; restraint, balance

temper·āns -antis *adj* self-controlled

temperanter *adv* moderately

temperanti·a -ae *f* self-control, moderation

temperātē *adv* moderately

temperāti·ō -ōnis *f* blending; composition; proportion, symmetry; temperament; organization, constitution; control, controlling power

temperāt·or -ōris *m* controller; moderator; governor

temperāt·us -a -um *adj* tempered; self-controlled; moderate

temperī *or* **temporī** *adv* in time, on time; in due time, at the right time

temperi·ēs -ēī *f* blending; climate; mild climate, moderate temperature

temper·ō -āre -āvī -ātus *tr* to compound, combine, blend, temper; to regulate, modify *(in regard to temperature);* to adjust; to tune; to govern, control, rule; to control *(by steering)* ‖ *intr* to be moderate, exercise restraint; *(w. dat)* to exercise control over; *(w. abl or* **ab** + *abl, w.* **quīn, quōminus, nē,** *w. inf)* to refrain from

tempest·ās -ātis *f* time, period, season, occasion; stormy weather, storm; misfortune, disaster; hail *(of weapons)*

tempestīvē *adv* at the right time

tempestīvit·ās -ātis *f* right time, timeliness

tempestīvō *adv* at the right time

tempestīv·us -a -um *adj* timely, seasonable, fit; ripe, mature; in good time, early

templ·um -ī *n* temple, shrine, sanctuary; space marked off in the sky *or* on the earth for the observation of omens; open space, quarter; site for a temple

temporāl·is -is -e *adj* temporary; temporal

temporāri·us -a -um *adj* temporary; changeable *(character)*

tempore *or* **temporī** *adv* in time, on time; in due time, at the right time

temptābund·us -a -um *adj* making constant attempts, trying

temptām·en -inis *n* attempt, effort; *(w. gen)* test of

temptāment·um -ī *n* attempt, effort; temptation, trial

temptāti·ō -ōnis *f* trial; attack *(of sickness, of un enemy);* *(w. gen)* attack on

temptāt·or -ōris *m* assailant, attacker

tempt·ō -āre -āvī -ātus *tr* **(tent-)** to test, feel, probe; to attempt; to attack; to try to influence, tamper with, tempt, try to induce; to urge, incite, sound out; to worry, distress

temptus *pp of* **temnō**

temp·us -oris *n* time; period, season; occasion, opportunity; right time, good time, proper period; times, condition, state, position; need, emergency; *(anat)* temple; *(pros)* measure, quantity, cadence; **ad tempus** *(or* **temporis causā)** to suit the occasion; **ante tempus** before time, too soon; **ex tempore** on the spur of the moment; **idem temporis** at the same time; **id temporis** at that time; **in ipsō tempore** in the nick of time; **in tempore** at the right moment; just in time; as occasion offers; **in tempus** temporarily, for a time; **per tempus** just in time; **prīmum tempus** spring; **prō tempore** as time permits; according to circumstances; to suit the occasion; **tempore** at an opportune time; **temporī cēdere** to yield to circumstances; **tempus in ultimum** to the last extremity; **tunc tempus** for the time, at the time

tēmulent·us -a -um *adj* intoxicated

tenācit·ās -ātis *f* tenacity; miserliness

tenāciter *adv* tightly, firmly

ten·āx -ācis *adj* holding tight, gripping, clinging; sticky; firm; obstinate; stingy; *(w. gen)* clinging to

tendicul·ae -ārum *fpl* little snare, little noose, little trap

tendō tendere tetendī tentus *or* **tēnsus** *tr* to stretch, stretch out, hold out, spread; to strain; to head for; to aim, shoot *(an arrow);* to bend *(a bow);* to tune *(an instrument);* to pitch *(a tent)* ‖ *intr* to pitch tents, be encamped; to travel, sail, move, march; to endeavor; to contend, fight; to exert oneself; *(w. inf)* to try to; *(w.* **ad) 1** to tend toward, be inclined toward; **2** to move toward, travel to, aim for; *(w.* **contrā** + *acc)* to fight against

tenebr·ae -ārum *fpl* darkness; night; blindness; dark place, haunts; unconsciousness; death; lower world; obscurity, low station; ignorance; gloomy state of affairs

tenebricōs·us -a -um *adj* dark, gloomy; hidden, concealed *(lust)*

tenebric·us -a -um *adj* dark, gloomy

tenebrōs·us -a -um *adj* dark, gloomy

Tened·os *or* **Tened·us -ī** *f* Tenedos *(island off the coast of Troy)*

tenellul·us -a -um *adj* tender little, dainty little

tenell·us -a -um *adj* dainty

ten·eō -ēre -uī -tus *tr* to hold, hold tight; to keep; to grasp, comprehend; to comprise; to possess, occupy, be master of; to hold back, restrain, repress; to charm, amuse; to have control of, get the better of; to interest; to keep, detain; to hold to, stick to, insist on *(an opinion); (w. inf)* to know how to; **cursum** *(or* **iter** *or* **viam) tenēre** to continue on a course; **‖** *refl* to remain *(in a place)*, stay put **‖** *intr* to hold out, last, keep on; to continue, persist; to continue on a course; *(w.* **quīn, quōminus, nē** *or inf)* to refrain from; *(w.* **ut, nē)** to make good one's point (that, that not)

ten·er -era -erum *adj* tender, soft, delicate; young, youthful; impressionable; weak; effeminate; voluptuous

tenerāsc·ō *or* **tenerēsc·ō -ere** *intr* to grow weak; to become flabby

tenerē *adv* softly

tenerit·ās -ātis *f* weakness

teneritūd·ō -inis *f* tender age

tēnesm·os -ī *m* straining to defecate

ten·or -ōris *m* uninterrupted course; continuity; **ūnō tenōre** uninterruptedly

Tēn·os -ī *f* island of the Cyclades

tēns·a -ae *f* car carrying images of the gods in procession, float

tēns·us -a -um *pp* of **tendō ‖** *adj* stretched, drawn tight; stretched out

tentīg·ō -inis *f* lust

tentō *see* **temptō**

tentōr·ium -iī *n* tent

tent·us -a -um *pp* of **tendō** *and* **teneō ‖** *adj* stretched, drawn tight

Tentyr·a -ōrum *npl* town in Upper Egypt

tenuī *perf* of **teneō**

tenuicul·us -a -um *adj* poor, paltry

tenu·is -is -e *adj* thin; fine; delicate; precise; shallow *(groove, etc.);* slight, puny, poor, insignificant; plain, simple; small, narrow; shallow *(water)*

tenuit·ās -ātis *f* thinness, fineness; leanness; simplicity; precision; poverty; simpleness *(of style)*

tenuiter *adv* thinly; slightly; poorly, indifferently; exactly, minutely; superficially

tenu·ō -āre -āvī -ātus *tr* to make thin; to contract; to dissolve; to lessen; to weaken; to rarefy; to make *(the voice)* shrill; to emaciate *(the body)*

ten·us -oris *n* trap, snare

tenus *prep (w. gen; more frequently, w. abl, always placed after the noun)* as far as, up to, down to; **nōmine** *(or* **verbō) tenus** as far as the name goes, nominally

Te·os *or* **Te·us -ī** *f* town on the coast of Asia Minor, the birthplace of Anacreon

tepe·faciō -facere -fēcī -factus *tr* to warm up

tepefact·ō -āre *tr* to be in the habit of warming

tep·eō -ēre -uī *intr* to get warm; to grow lukewarm; to glow with love; to be cool, be indifferent; **tepēre puellā** to be in love with the girl

tep·ēscō -ēscere -uī *intr* to grow warm; to grow lukewarm, grow indifferent

tepid·us -a -um *adj* warm, lukewarm, tepid

tep·or -ōris *m* warmth; coolness, lack of heat *(in a bath);* lack of fire *(in a speech)*

tepuī *perf* of **tepeō** *and* **tepēscō**

ter *adv* three times

-ter *advl suf of third-declension adjectives:* **audācter** boldly; *stems in* -nt- *drop* -t-: **prūdenter** prudently; *also of second-declension adjectives:* **hūmāniter** kindly

-ter -terī *or* **-trī** *m* **-tera -terum** *or* **-tra -trum** *adjl suf* often *used to forming pairs:* **magister** master, **minister** servant; **noster** our, **vester** your

terdeciēns *or* **terdeciēs** *adv* thirteen times

terebinth·us -ī *f* terebinth, turpentine tree

terebr·a -ae *f* drill

terebr·ō -āre -āvī -ātus *tr* to bore, drill a hole in, pierce

terēd·ō -inis *f* grubworm

Tēreid·ēs -ae *m* Itys *(son of Tereus)*

Terentiān·us -a -um *adj* of the Terentian clan; *esp.* written, portrayed, *etc.,* by the poet Terence

Terent·ius -(i)ī *m* Terence *(Marcus Terentius Afer, Roman comic poet, c. 190–159 B.C.)*

ter·es -etis *adj* smooth, well-rounded; polished, shapely; round, cylindrical; *(fig)* fine, elegant

Tēr·eus -eī *or* **-eos** *m* evil king of Thrace, husband of Procne, and father of Itys

tergemin·us -a -um *adj* triplet, triple

ter·geō -gēre -sī -sus *or* **terg·ō -ere** *tr* to wipe off, wipe dry; to scour; to clean, cleanse

tergīn·um -ī *n* rawhide; scourge

tergiversāti·ō -ōnis *f* refusal; evasion, subterfuge

tergivers·or -ārī -ātus sum *intr* to turn one's back; to be shifty

tergō *see* **tergeō**

terg·um -ī *n or* terg·us -oris *n* back; back part, rear; ridge; hide; leather; leather objects: bag, shield, drum; *(mil)* rear; ā tergō in the rear, from behind; in tergum backward; tergum dare *or* vertere to turn tail, run away, flee
terment·um -ī *n* sore caused by friction
term·es -itis *m* branch, bough
Termināl·ia -ium *or* -iōrum *npl* festival in honor of Terminus *(god of boundaries, celebrated on February 23)*
termināti·ō -ōnis *f* the marking of the boundaries of a territory *(esp. w. boundary stones or posts);* boundary; tract of land along a boundary; end, goal *(of an activity);* decision, determining; *(rhet)* arrangement, ending *(of a sentence)*
termin·ō -āre -āvī -ātus *tr* to mark off with boundaries, bound, limit; to fix, determine, define; to terminate, conclude; to settle *(an issue); (rhet)* to round out *(a sentence)*
termin·us -ī *m* boundary, limit, bound ‖ Terminus god of boundaries
tern·ī -ae -a *adj* three apiece, three each, three at a time; three in a row
terō terere trīvī trītus *tr* to rub; to wear down; to wear out *(by constant handling);* to make *(words, expressions)* trite *(by repetition),* run into the ground; to travel *(a road)* repeatedly; to trample, crush; to spend, waste *(time);* to smooth, polish; to sharpen; to thresh *(grain);* to grind *(grain);* ōtium terere to waste time in idleness
Terpsichor·ē -ēs *f* Muse of dancing, of lyric poetry; *(fig)* poetry
ter(r)ūnc·ius -(i)ī *m* copper coin *(weighing three* ūnciae *= three-twelfths of an* as *or one-fortieth of a* dēnārius, *i.e., less than 1¢);* hērēs ex terūnciō heir to one fourth of an estate
terr·a -ae *f* the earth; land; earth, ground, soil; country, region, territory; in terrā *(or* terrīs) in the world, in existence; *(as contrasted with heaven)* on earth; *(astr)* the planet earth; terrā ortus sprung from the earth, indigenous; terrae fīlius a nobody; terrae *(or* terrārum) mōtus earthquake; ubi terrārum where in the world
terrāneol·a -ae *f* crested lark
terrēn·us -a -um *adj* earthly, terrestrial; earthen ‖ *n* land, ground
terr·eō -ēre -uī -itus *tr* to frighten, scare, terrify; to deter
terrestr·is -is -e *adj* of the earth, on the earth; land, earth; terrestrial; proelium terrestre land battle
terre·us -a -um *adj* earth-born
terribil·is -is -e *adj* terrible, frightful
terricul·a -ae *f* bogey; scary thing
terrific·ō -āre *tr* to terrify

terrific·us -a -um *adj* terrifying, awe-inspiring, alarming
terrigen·a -ae *m* earth-born creature
terriloqu·us -a -um *adj* ominous, alarming
terripav·ium -(i)ī *n* (-pud·ium, -puv·ium) *(etymologizing forms of* tripudium) *see* tripudium
territ·ō -āre -āvī *tr* to keep frightening; to try to scare, intimidate
territōr·ium -(i)ī *n* land around a town, territory, suburbs
terr·or -ōris *m* terror, alarm, dread
terruī *perf of* terreō
ters·us -a -um *pp of* tergeō ‖ *adj* clean, neat; terse; polished *(writing)*
tertiadecimān·ī -ōrum *mpl* soldiers of the thirteenth legion
tertiān·us -a -um *adj* recurring every three days, *(in our system: every other day),* tertian *(fever)* ‖ *mpl* soldiers of the third legion
tertiō *adv* in the third place, thirdly; the third time
tertium *adv* for the third time
terti·us -a -um *adj* third
terti·us decim·us -a -um *adj* thirteenth
terūnci·us -ī *m* three-fifth of an as, a quarter-as; *(fig)* a mere trifle; hērēs ex terūnciō heir to one-fourth
tervenēfic·us -ī *m (term of abuse)* three-time killer, absolute villain
tesqu·a -ōrum *npl* wilderness, wilds
tesselāt·us -a -um *adj* tessellated, mosaic
tessell·a -ae *f* cubed mosaic stone
tesser·a -ae *f* cube; die; watchword, countersign; tally, token; ticket *(for the distribution of money or grain)*
tesserār·ius -(i)ī *m (mil)* officer of the day
tesserul·a -ae *f* small cube; ticket
test·a -ae *f* brick, tile; jug, crock; potsherd; shellfish; shell *(of a crustacean, snail, etc.);* fragment, splinter *(esp. of a broken tooth or bone)*
testāmentāri·us -a -um *adj* pertaining to a will, testamentary ‖ *m* forger of wills
testāment·um -ī *n* testament, will
testāti·ō -ōnis *f* testifying to a fact; *(leg)* deposition
testāt·or -ōris *m* testator *(one who makes a will)*
testāt·us -a -um *adj* well-attested; witnessed
testicul·us -ī *m* testicle
testificāti·ō -ōnis *f* testifying; proof, evidence
testific·or -ārī -ātus sum *tr* to give as evidence, give proof of; to testify to; to vouch for; to invoke *(e.g., a god)* as one's witness; *(fig)* to give proof of
testimōn·ium -(i)ī *n* testimony
test·is -is *mf* witness ‖ *m* testicle

test·or -**ārī** -**ātus sum** *tr* to give as evidence; to show, prove, vouch for; to call to witness, appeal to **‖** *intr* to be a witness, testify; to make a will

test·ū -**ūs** *n see* **testum**

testūdine·us -**a** -**um** *adj* of a tortoise; made of tortoise shell

testūd·ō -**inis** *f* tortoise; tortoise shell; lyre, lute; arch, vault; *(mil)* protective shed *(for besiegers)*

testul·a -**ae** *f* potsherd

test·um -**ī** *n* earthenware lid; pot with a lid

tēte = *emphatic form of* **tē**

tetendī *perf of* **tendō**

Tēth·ys -**yos** *f* wife of Oceanus and mother of the sea nymphs; ocean, sea

tetigī *perf of* **tangō**

tetradrachm·um -**ī** *n* (-**trach-**) Greek silver coin *(worth four drachmas or four denarii or $4)*

tetra·ō -**ōnis** *m* game bird *(black grouse?)*

tetrarch·ēs -**ae** *m* tetrarch *(ruler of one fourth of a country); petty prince*

tetrarchi·a -**ae** *f* tetrarchy

tetrastich·on -**ī** *n* four-line poem

tetric·us -**a** -**um** *adj* stern, gloomy, crabby; harsh, rough

tetrissit·ō -**āre** *intr* to quack

Teu·cer *or* **Teu·crus** -**crī** *m* son of Telamon and half-brother of Ajax **‖** son of Scamander of Crete, father-in-law of Dardanus, and later king of Troy

Teucri·a -**ae** *f* Troy, land of the Teucrians

Teucr·us -**a** -**um** *adj* Teucrian, Trojan **‖** *mpl* Trojans

Teuthrantē·us -**a** -**um** *adj* Mysian

Teuthranti·us -**a** -**um** *adj* of Teuthras; **turba Teuthrantia** fifty daughters of Thespius

Teuthr·ās -**antis** *m* ancient king of Mysia, father of Thespius

Teuton·ēs -**um** *or* **Teuton·ī** -**ōrum** *mpl* Teutons

Teutonic·us -**a** -**um** *adj* Teutonic

tex·ō -**ere** -**uī** -**tus** *tr* to weave; to plait; to build; to compose

textil·is -**is** -**e** *adj* woven; brocaded **‖** *n* fabric

text·or -**ōris** *m* weaver

textrīn·um -**ī** *n* weaving; weaving room

textr·īx -**īcis** *f* weaver *(female)*

textūr·a -**ae** *f* texture; web; fabric

text·us -**a** -**um** *pp of* **texō** **‖** *n* woven cloth, fabric; web

text·us -**ūs** *m* texture

texuī *perf of* **texō**

Thā·is -**idis** *or* -**idos** *f* notorious Athenian prostitute

thalam·us -**ī** *m* woman's room; bedroom; marriage bed; marriage

thalassic·us *or* **thalassin·us** -**a** -**um** *adj* sea-green, aquamarine

Thal·ēs -**ae** *m* Thales *(early Ionian philosopher of Miletus, regarded as one of the Seven Sages, fl 575 B.C.)*

Thalī·a *or* **Thalē·a** -**ae** *f* Muse of comedy and light verse **‖** one of the Graces **‖** a Nereid, sea nymph

thall·us -**ī** *m* green bough; green stem

Thaps·os -**ī** *f* city of N. Africa where Caesar defeated the Pompeians *(46 B.C.)*

Thasi·us -**a** -**um** *adj* of Thasos; **Thasius lapis** Thasian marble

Thas·os -**ī** *f* island in the Aegean Sea, off the coast of Thrace

Thaumantē·us -**a** -**um** *adj* descended from Thaumas *(a Titan)*

Thaumanti·as -**adis** *or* **Thaumant·is** -**idis** *f* Iris *(daughter of the Titan Thaumas)*

theātrāl·is -**is** -**e** *adj* theatrical

theātr·um -**ī** *n* theater

Thēb·ae -**ārum** *fpl* Thebes *(capital of Boeotia, founded by Cadmus)* **‖** Thebes *(city of Upper Egypt)* **‖** Thebes *(city in Mysia, home of Eetion, destroyed by Achilles)*

Thēba·is -**idis** *or* -**idos** *adj (fem only)* Boeotian Thebes; of Thebes in Mysia; of Egyptian Thebes; **Thēbais nūpta** Theban bride *(i.e., Andromache)* **‖** *f* Theban woman; district around Egyptian Thebes, the Thebaid

Thēbān·us -**a** -**um** *adj & mf* Theban *(of Boeotia, Egypt, or Mysia)*

thēc·a -**ae** *f* case, box

them·a -**atis** *n* position of the planets *or* stars at one's birth, horoscope; *(rhet)* theme, topic proposed for debate in a school of rhetoric

Them·is -**is** *f* goddess of justice and of prophecy

Themistocl·ēs -**is** *m* Themistocles *(Athenian admiral and statesman, c. 528–459 B.C.)*

Themistoclē·us -**a** -**um** *adj* Themistoclean

thēnsaurāri·us -**a** -**um** *adj* of treasure

thēnsaurus *see* **thēsaurus**

Theocrit·us -**ī** *m* founder of Greek pastoral poetry, born at Syracuse *(3rd cent. B.C.)*

theologūmen·a -**ōn** *npl* essays on the gods

theolog·us -**ī** *m* theologian

therm·ae -**ārum** *fpl* hot baths, public baths *(which included rooms for social activities, lecture halls, theater, restaurants, workout rooms)*

Thermōd·ōn -**ontis** *m* river in Pontus, around which the Amazons were said to have lived

Thermōdontiac·us -**a** -**um** *adj* of the River Thermodon *(often applied to Amazons, esp. Hippolyta and Penthesilea, or to things connected with them)*

thermopōl·ium -**(i)ī** *n* hot-drink shop

thermopot·ō -āre *tr* to supply with warm drinks

Thermopyl·ae -ārum *fpl* (**-pul-**) Thermopylae *(famous pass in Thessaly, defended by Leonidas and his 400 Spartans in 480 B.C.)*

thermul·ae -ārum *fpl* small hot bath

Thersīt·ēs -ae *m* Greek soldier at Troy notorious for his ugliness

thēsaur·us -ī *m* (**thēns-**) storehouse; store, treasure, hoard

Thēs·eūs -eī *or* **-eos** *m* king of Athens, son of Aegeus and husband *(or* lover) first of Ariadne and later of Phaedra

Thēsē·us -a -um *adj* of Theseus

Thēsīd·ae -ārum *mpl* Athenians

Thēsīd·ēs -ae *m* Hippolytus *(son of Theseus)* ‖ *mpl* Athenians

thes·is -is *f (rhet)* general question *(opp:* a particular case)

Thespiad·es -um *fpl* descendants of Thespius *(fifty sons of Thespius's fifty daughters)*

Thespi·ae -ārum *fpl* town in Boeotia near Mt. Helicon

Thesp·is -is *m* traditional founder of Greek tragedy *(his first presentation was in 535 B.C.)*

Thespi·us -a -um *adj* Thespian ‖ *m* a king of Mysia who had fifty daughters; *see* **Thespiades** ‖ *fpl* town in Boeotia near Mt. Helicon

Thessali·a -ae *f* Thessaly *(most northerly district of Greece)*

Thessalic·us -a -um *adj* Thessalian

Thessal·is -idis *or* **-idos** *adj (fem only)* Thessalian ‖ *f* Thessalian woman *(esp. a witch)*

Thessal·us -a -um *adj* Thessalian ‖ *mpl* people of Thessaly

Thestorid·ēs -ae *m* Calchas *(son of Thestor and famous Greek seer in the Trojan War)*

thēta *indecl n* the Greek letter theta *(written on tablets by jurors voting for the death sentence)*

Thet·is -idis *or* **-idos** *f* sea nymph, daughter of Nereus and Doris, wife of Peleus, and mother of Achilles

thias·us -ī *m* Bacchic dance; troupe of Bacchic dancers

Thisb·ē -ēs *f* girl in Bablyon, loved by Pyramus ‖ small town in Boeotia

Thoantē·us -a -um *adj* of Thoas

Tho·ās -antis *m* king of the Taurians, slain by Orestes ‖ king of Lemnos and father of Hypsipyle

thol·us -ī *m* rotunda

thōr·āx -ācis *m* breastplate

Thrāc·a -ae *or* **Thrāc·ē -ēs** *f* Thrace *(country N. of the Aegean)*

Thrāci·us -a -um *adj* Thracian ‖ *f* Thrace

Thraex *see* **Thrēx**

Thr·āx -ācis *m* Thracian

Thre(i)ss·a -ae *f* Thracian woman

Thr·ēx -ēcis *or* **Thr·aex -aecis** *m* Thracian gladiator *(i.e., armed like a Thracian with saber and small shield)*

thron·us -ī *m* throne

Thūcȳdid·ēs -is *or* **-ī** *m* Thucydides *(Greek historian of the Peloponnesian War, c. 456–400 B.C.)*

Thūl·ē *or* **T(h)ȳl·ē -ēs** *f* island located in the far north, perhaps Iceland or part of Scandinavia

thunn·us -ī *m* tuna

thūr- = tur-

Thūri·ī -ōrum *mpl* Thurii *(Greek city on the Tarentine Gulf in S. Italy)*

Thūrīn·us -a -um *adj & m* Thurian

thū·s -ris *n* incense, frankincense

Thybris *see* **Tiberis**

Thyēn·ē -ēs *f* nymph who nursed Bacchus

Thyest·ēs -ae *or* **-is** *m* son of Pelops, brother of Atreus, and father of Aegisthus

thymbr·a -ae *f (bot)* savory *(used as a spice in cooking)*

thym·um -ī *n (bot)* thyme *(common garden herb used as seasoning)*

Thȳni·a -ae *f* Bithynia *(country of Asia Minor on the S. coast of the Black Sea)*

Thȳniac·us -a -um *adj* Bithynian

thynn·us -ī *m* tuna

Thȳn·us -a -um *adj & m* Bithynian

Thyōn·eūs -eī *m* Bacchus

thyrs·us -ī *m* Bacchic wand twined with vine leaves and ivy, and crowned with a pine cone

Ti. *abbr* **Tiberius** *(Roman first name, praenomen)*

tiār·a -ae *f or* **tiār·ās -ae** *m* tiara

Tiberīn·is -idis *or* **-idos** *adj (fem only)* of the Tiber

Tiberīn·us -a -um *adj* of the Tiber River ‖ *m* eponymous hero of the Tiber River

Tiber·is *or* **Tibr·is** *or* **Thybr·is -is** *m* Tiber River

Tiber·ius -(i)ī *m* Tiberius *(Roman first name, praenomen); esp.* Tiberius Claudius Nero Caesar *(successor of Augustus, 42 B.C.–A.D. 37, ruling from A.D. 14–37)* ‖ Tiberius Sempronius Gracchus *(socialist reformer, killed in 133 B.C.)*

tībi·a -ae *f* shinbone, tibia; flute

tībiāl·e -is *n* stocking

tībīc·en -inis *m* flutist; prop; pillar

tībīcin·a -ae *f* flutist *(female)*

Tibull·us -ī *m* Albius Tibullus *(Roman elegiac poet, c. 54–19 B.C.)*

Tīb·ur -uris *n* town of Latium on the Anio *(modern Tivoli)*

Tīburn·us -a -um *adj* of Tibur ‖ *m* legendary founder of Tibur
Tībur·s -tis *adj* of Tibur ‖ *mpl* inhabitants of Tibur ‖ *n* estate at Tibur
Tīburtīn·us -a -um *adj* of Tibur; travertine *(stone)* ‖ *n* estate at Tibur
Tīburt·us -ī *m* legendary founder of Tibur *(see* Tiburnus)
Tīcīn·us -ī *m* tributary of the Po
Tigellīn·us -ī *m* notorious favorite of Nero
tigill·um -ī *n* beam; log
tignāri·us -a -um *adj* carpenter's; faber tignārius carpenter; officīna tignāria carpenter's shop
tign·um -ī *n* beam, plank; lumber
tigr·is -is *mf* tiger
tigr·is -is *or* -idis *f* tigress
Tigr·is -is *or* -idis *m* Tigris River
tīli·a -ae *f* linden tree, lime tree
Tīmae·us -ī *m* Greek historian of Sicily *(c. 346–250 B.C.)* ‖ Pythagorean philosopher of Locri in S. Italy *(after whom Plato named one of his dialogues, 5th cent. B.C.)*
Tīmāgen·ēs -is *m* brilliant rhetorician in the time of Augustus
Timāv·us -ī *m* river which flows into the gulf of Trieste
timefact·us -a -um *adj* frightened
tim·eō -ēre -uī *tr* to fear, be afraid of ‖ *intr* to be afraid; *(w. dat or dē or prō + abl)* to fear for; *(w. ab + abl of source of fear)* to fear harm from
timidē *adv* timidly, fearfully
timidit·ās -ātis *f* timidity, fearfulness, cowardice
timid·us -a -um *adj* timid, fearful, cowardly; *(w. gen)* afraid of
tim·or -ōris *m* fear; alarm, dread
tīnctil·is -is -e *adj* obtained by dipping
tīnctus *pp of* tingō
tine·a -ae *f* moth *(destructive of clothes, books),* bookworm
tingō (tinguō) tingere tīnxī tīnctus *tr* to dip, soak; to dye, color; to tinge; to imbue
tinnīment·um -ī *n* ringing
tinn·iō -īre -īvī *or* -iī -ītus *tr & intr* to ring
tinnīt·us -ūs *m* ring, ringing; tinkling, jingling
tinnul·us -a -um *adj* ringing, tinkling; shrill
tintin(n)ābul·um -ī *n* bell; doorbell; cowbell
tintin(n)·ō -āre *or* tintin(n)·iō -īre *intr* to ring
tintinnācul·us -a -um *adj* jingling ‖ *mpl* chain gang
-tin·us -a -um *adjl suf* forms adjectives from adverbs denoting time, e.g.: crāstinus tomorrow's; prīstinus antique, ancient
tīn·us -ī *f* laurustinus *(evergreen shrub having white or pinkish flowers)*
-ti·ō -ōnis *fem suf* forms verbal nouns to denote the action of the verb, e.g.: āctiō act, action;

appears as -siō *from verbs which form the supine in* -sum, *e.g.:* cursiō running
Tīph·ys -yos *m* pilot of the *Argo*
tippūl·a -ae *f* water spider
Tīresi·ās -ae *m* famous blind seer at Thebes at the time of Oedipus
Tīridāt·ēs -ae *m* name of three kings of Parthia
tīr·ō -ōnis *m* novice, beginner; young man who has just come of age; *(mil)* recruit ‖ Tīrō Marcus Tullius Tiro *(Cicero's secretary)*
tīrōcin·ium -(i)ī *n* apprenticeship; beginning, first try; *(mil)* first campaign; *(mil)* military inexperience; *(mil)* body of raw recruits
tīruncul·us -ī *m* beginner, recruit
Tīryn·s -thos *f* town in the Argolid where Hercules was raised
Tīrynthi·us -a -um *adj* Tirynthian ‖ *m* Hercules ‖ *mpl* the people of Tiryns ‖ *f* Alcmena
Tīsamen·us -ī *m* son of Orestes and king of Argos
tisan·a -ae *f* pearl barley
tisanār·ium -(i)ī *n* (pti-) gruel; tisanārium oryzae rice gruel
Tīsiphon·ē -ēs *f* one of the three Furies who haunted murderers
Tīsiphonē·us -a -um *adj* belonging to Tisiphone; *(fig)* deserving of punishment by the Furies, guilty
Tīt·ān -ānos *or* Tītān·us -ī *m* Titan; sun; Prometheus ‖ *mpl* Titans *(giant sons of Uranus and Ge who rebelled against Uranus and put Cronus on the throne)*
Tītāni·us -a -um *adj* of the Titans, Titanic *(esp. of the sun, moon, or Prometheus)* ‖ *m* sun-god ‖ *f* Latona *(mother of Apollo and Diana)* ‖ Diana ‖ Pyrrha *(as descendant of Prometheus)* ‖ Circe *(as daughter of Sol or Helios)*
Tīthōni·us -a -um *adj* Tithonian ‖ *f* Aurora *(wife of Tithonus)*
Tīthōn·us -ī *m* son of Laomedon and husband of Aurora from whom he received the gift of immortality without eternal youth
Titiēns·is -is -e *adj* of the Tities tribe
Tit·iēs -ium *mpl* one of the three original Roman tribes
tītillāti·ō -ōnis *f* tickling, titillation;
tītill·ō -āre *tr* tickle, titillate
Titi·us -a -um *adj* Roman clan name *(nomen)*
tittibilīc·ium -(i)ī *n* trifle
titubanter *adv* falteringly
titubanti·a -ae *f* stumbling *(in speech)*
titubāti·ō -ōnis *f (lit & fig)* stumbling
titub·ō -āre -āvī -ātum *intr* to stagger, reel, totter; to falter, waver; to stumble, slip up *(in speech)*
titul·us -ī *m* inscription; label; title, heading *(of a book, chapter);* chapter *(of a book);* person-

al title; identification tag; notice, advertisement; pretext, ostensible motive; claim to fame; title of honor; renown; *(w. gen)* 1 honor *or* distinction arising from; 2 reputation for

Tit·us -ī *m* Roman first name *(praenomen); esp.* Titus Tatius *(a Sabine king who is said to have ruled with Romulus until the latter had him killed)* ‖ the Emperor Titus *(Titus Flavius Vespasianus, son of Vespasian; ruled* A.D. *79–81)*

Tity·os *or* **Tity·us -ī** *m* Tityus *(giant slain by Apollo for attempting to rape Latona and thrown into Tartarus)*

Tītyr·us -ī *m* shepherd in Vergil's pastorals, sometimes identified with Vergil himself

Tlēpolem·us -ī *m* son of Hercules

Tmar·os -ī *m* mountain in Epirus

Tmōlīt·ēs -is *adj (masc only)* of Mt. Tmolus ‖ *m* wine from Mt. Tmolus

Tmōli·us -a -um *adj* of Mt. Tmolus

Tmōl·us -ī *m* **(Tim-)** Tmolus *(mountain in Lydia famous for its wines)*

toculli·ō -ōnis *m* loan shark

todill·us -ī *m* type of small bird

tōfīn·us -a -um *adj* made of tufa

tōf·us -ī *m* **(toph-)** tufa *(porous volcanic rock, used extensively in Republican Rome as building stone)*

tog·a -ae *f* toga *(outer garment of a Roman citizen);* **toga ātra** dark toga *(unwhitened toga worn as sign of mourning);* **toga candida** white toga *(treated with chalk and worn by candidates for office);* **toga picta** brocaded toga *(worn by triumphant generals);* **toga praetexta** crimson-bordered toga *(worn by magistrates and freeborn children);* **toga pulla** dark-gray toga *(worn by mourners);* **toga pūra** *(or* **virīlis** *or* **lībera)** toga of manhood *(worn by young men from about the age of sixteen);* **ā togā pūrā** from boyhood

togāt·a -ae *f* Latin comedy *(on Roman themes and in Roman dress)*

togātār·ius -(i)ī *m* actor in a *fabula togata*

togātul·us -ī *m (pej)* miserable Roman *(of clients paying duty calls)*

togāt·us -a -um *adj* wearing a toga, true Roman; having a civilian occupation *or* status, civilian; peacetime; **fābula togāta** *(theat)* Latin comedy *(written on a native theme and presented in Roman dress);* **Gallia Togāta** Cisalpine Gaul *(between the Alps and the Po River)* ‖ *m* Roman citizen; civilian; humble client ‖ *f* prostitute; *see* **togāta**

togul·a -ae *f (pej)* little toga

tolerābil·is -is -e *adj* tolerable; patient

tolerābiliter *adv* without stress

toler·āns -antis *adj* tolerant; *(w. gen)* tolerant of, enduring

toleranter *adv* patiently

toleranti·a -ae *f* toleration, endurance

tolerāti·ō -ōnis *f* toleration, endurance

tolerāt·us -a -um *adj* tolerable, endurable

toler·ō -āre -āvī -ātus *tr* to tolerate, endure; to support, maintain, sustain

tollēn·ō -ōnis *m* crane, lift, derrick

tollō tollere sustulī sublātus *tr* to lift, raise; to raise *(the voice);* to draw *(lots);* to have *(a child);* to acknowledge *(a child);* to raise, educate; to weigh *(anchor); (of a ship)* to take on board; *(of a ship)* to have the capacity of; *(of a vehicle)* to pick up, take as a passenger; to win, carry off *(a prize);* to reap *(a profit);* to remove; to do away with, destroy; to cancel, abolish, abrogate; to lift, steal; to uplift, cheer up, excite; to erect, build up; to waste *(time);* **amīcum tollere** to cheer up a friend; **animōs tollere** to boost morale; **deōs tollere** to deny the existence of the gods; **dē mediō tollere** to kill; **diēm tollere** to take a day off *(from work);* **in crucem** *(or* **in furcam) tollere** to crucify ‖ *refl (of plants)* to grow high; **in caelum sē tollere** to ascend *or* climb into the sky ‖ *pass* to climb up, rise

Tolōs·a -ae *f* city in Narbonese Gaul *(modern Toulouse)*

Tolōsān·us -a -um *adj* **(Toloss-)** of Tolosa ‖ *mpl* people of Tolosa

Tolōs·ās -ātis *adj* produced in Tolosa ‖ *mpl* people of Tolosa

tolūtim *adv* at a trot, jogging

tomāc(u)l·um -ī *n* sausage

tōment·um -ī *n* pillow stuffing

Tom·ī -ōrum *mpl or* **Tom·is -is** *f* Tomi *(town on the Black Sea in modern Romania, where Ovid spent his years in exile)*

Tomīt·ae -ārum *mpl* people of Tomi

Tomītān·us -a -um *adj* of Tomi

tom·us -ī *m* a length of papyrus, sheet

Ton·āns -antis *m* Thunderer *(epithet of several gods, esp. Jupiter)*

tondeō tondēre totondī tōnsus *tr* to clip, shear, shave; to prune; to reap, mow; to crop, browse on; *(fig)* to fleece, rob; **ūsque ad cutem tondēre** *(fig)* to swindle, fleece *(literally, the clip right down to the skin)*

tonitrāl·is -is -e *adj* thunderous

tonitr·us -ūs *m or* **tonitr·um -ī** *n* thunder ‖ *mpl or npl* claps of thunder

ton·ō -āre -uī -itūrus *tr* to thunder forth *(words)* ‖ *intr* to thunder

tōns·a -ae *f* oar

tōnsil·is -is -e *adj* clipped

tōnsill·a -ae *f* **(tōs-)** tonsil

tonsit·ō -āre *tr* to shear regularly

tōns·or -ōris *m* **(tōs-)** shearer; barber

tōnsōri·us -a -um *adj* shaving; barber's

tōnstrīcul·a -ae *f* little hairdresser, little barber *(female)*

tōnstrīn·a -ae f barbershop

tōnstrīn·um -ī *n* trade of a barber, barbering

tōnstr·īx -īcis *f* hairdresser, barber *(female)*

tōnsūr·a -ae *f* clipping, shearing; **capillōrum tōnsūra** haircut

tōns·us -a -um *pp of* **tondeō** ‖ *f* oar

tōns·us -ūs *m* haircut; hairdo

tonuī *perf of* **tonō**

tōph·us -ī *m* (**tōf-**) tufa *(porous volcanic rock, used as building material esp. in the Republican period)*

topiāri·us -a -um *adj* garden, landscape ‖ *m* gardener, landscaper ‖ *f* landscaping

topic·a -ōrum *npl* "commonplaces" *(title of work by Aristotle on which Cicero based his work on this topic)*

topic·ē -ēs *f (rhet)* resourcefulness in finding topics for speeches

-t·or -ōris *masc suf, formed from verbs to denote the doer of the action of the verb, e.g.:* **amātor** lover; *becomes* **-sor** *from verbs which form the past participle in* **-sus**, *e.g.:* **tōnsor** shearer, barber

tor·al -ālis *n* valance; coverlet

torcul·ar -āris *or* **torcul·um -ī** *n* wine press, oil press

toreum·a -atis *n* embossed work, relief

-tōr·ium -(i)ī *neut suf often denoting places, e.g.*, **praetōrium** headquarters of the praetor *or* commander

torment·um -ī *n* windlass; catapult, artillery piece; shot; torture rack; *(lit & fig)* torture ‖ *npl* artillery

tormin·a -um *npl* colic, bowel trouble

torminōs·us -a -um *adj* suffering from colic, colicky

torn·ō -āre -āvī -ātus *tr* to turn on a lathe

torn·us -ī *m* lathe

torōs·us -a -um *adj* brawny, muscular

torpēd·ō -inis *f* numbness, lethargy, listlessness; stingray *(fish)*

torp·eō -ēre -uī *intr* to numb; to be stiff; to be stupefied; to be groggy

torp·ēscō -ēscere -uī *intr* to grow numb; to grow listless

torpid·us -a -um *adj* numbed, paralyzed; groggy

torp·or -ōris *m* torpor, numbness; grogginess

torpuī *perf of* **torpeō** *and* **torpēscō**

torquāt·us -a -um *adj* wearing a collar *or* necklace ‖ **Torquātus** *m* Titus Manlius Torquatus *(legendary Roman hero who wore a necklace taken from a gigantic Gaul he had slain)*

tor·queō -quēre -sī -tus *tr* to twist, turn, wind; to bend out of shape; to hurl; to wind up *(catapult)*; to turn *(so as to face in the opposite*

direction); to roll *(eyes);* to crane *(neck);* to divert the course of; to spin; to curl *(hair);* to wreathe *(the head);* (fig) to torment; **aliquem torquēre** (w. **in** *or* **adversus, contrā** + *acc)* to torture s.o. to give evidence against *(s.o.)*

torqu·ēs *or* **torqu·is -is** *m(f)* necklace; collar *(of twisted metal, as military decoration)*

torr·ēns -entis *adj* burning, seething; rushing, roaring *(stream);* fiery *(speech)* ‖ *m* torrent; current

torr·eō -ēre -uī tostus *tr* to roast, bake; to burn, scorch; to parch

torr·ēscō -ēscere -uī *intr* to become burned; to become parched

torrid·us -a -um *adj* baked, parched; dried up; frostbitten

torr·is -is *or* **torr·us -ī** *m* firebrand

torruī *perf of* **torreō**

torsī *perf of* **torqueō**

tortē *adv* crookedly

tortil·is -is -e *adj* twisted, winding, spiral, coiled

tort·ō -āre *tr* to twist, coil ‖ *pass* to writhe

tort·or -ōris *m* torturer

tortuōs·us -a -um *adj* tortuous, winding; *(fig)* complicated

tort·us -a -um *adj* bent, crooked, curved; coiled, twisted; curly *(hair);* winding *(road, labyrinth)*

tort·us -ūs *m* twist, coil; **tortūs dare** *(of a serpent)* to form loops

torul·us -ī *m* headband; tuft *(of hair)*

tor·us -ī *m* knot; bulge; muscle, brawn; bed, couch; mattress; cushion; mound; boss; flowery expression; **torus geniālis** conjugal bed

torvit·ās -ātis *f* grimness

torv·us -a -um *adj* grim

tostus *pp of* **torreō**

tot *indecl adj* so many, as many; **tot ... quot** as many ... as

totiēns *or* **totiēs** *adv* so often, so many times

totondī *perf of* **tondeō**

tōt·us -a -um *adj* the whole, all, entire; **totūs in illīs** totally absorbed in those matters ‖ *n* the whole matter, all; **ex tōtō** totally; **in tōtō** on the whole, in general; **in tōtum** totally

toxic·um -ī *n* poison *(originally, a poison in which arrowheads were dipped)*

trabāl·is -is -e *adj* of *or* for beams; **clāvus trabālis** spike; **tēlum trabāle** beam-like shaft

trabe·a -ae *f* ceremonial robe *(with purple stripes and worn by magistrates, augurs, and as dress uniform of the equites)*

trabeāt·us -a -um *adj* wearing a *trabea*

trab·s -is *f* beam, plank; timber; tree; object made of beams: roof, shaft, table, battering ram

Trāch·īn -īnis or **Trāch·ȳn -ȳnos** f Trachis (*town in Thessaly on Mount Oeta, where Hercules had himself cremated*)
Trāchīni·us -a -um adj of Trachin (Trachis) ‖ m Ceyx (*king of Trachin*) ‖ fpl "Women of Trachis" (*title of a play by Sophocles*)
tractābil·is -is -e adj tractable, manageable; (*of weather*) fit for navigation
tractāti·ō -ōnis f handling, management; discussion, treatment (*of a subject*); lesson (*in a class*)
tractātr·īx -īcis f masseuse
tractāt·us -ūs m touching, handling; management; treatise
tractim adv little by little, slowly; in a drawn out manner
tract·ō -āre -āvī -ātus tr to drag around, haul, pull; to touch, handle; to deal with, treat; to manage, control; to wield; to conduct, carry on, transact; to practice; to discuss; (*of an actor*) to play the role of; to examine, consider; **male tractāre** to mistreat ‖ refl to behave, conduct oneself ‖ intr to carry on a discussion
tract·us -a -um pp of **trahō** ‖ adj fluent; lengthy, continuous (*discourse*)
tract·us -ūs m dragging; dragging out, extension (*e.g., of a war*); track, trail; tract, expanse, extent, distance; region, district
trādidī perf of **trādō**
trāditi·ō -ōnis f handing over, surrender; transmission; item of traditional belief, custom, tradition
trādit·or -ōris m betrayer, traitor
trā·dō -dere -didī -ditus tr to hand over, surrender, deliver; to betray; to hand down, bequeath, transmit, pass on; to relate, recount; to teach; to introduce (*a person*) ‖ refl (*w. dat*) **1** to surrender to; **2** to devote oneself to
trā·dūcō -dūcere -dūxī -ductus tr to bring across or over, transfer; to convert, bring over; (*w. ad* or *in* + *acc*) to cause (*s.o.*) to change (*from one attitude, habit, etc.*) (*another*); to exhibit, display; to disgrace; to pass, spend; (*gram*) to derive; **trādūcere equum** (*of a member of the equestrian order who passed the censor's inspection*) to lead one's horse in the parade
trāducti·ō -ōnis f transference; passage (*of time*); metonymy; use of homonyms or homophones
trāduct·or -ōris m conveyor
trāductus pp of **trādūcō**
trād·ux -ucis mf vine branch (*trained across the space between trees in a vineyard*)
trādūxī perf of **trādūcō**
tragicē adv as in tragedy
tragicocōmoedi·a -ae f melodrama

tragic·us -a -um adj of tragedy, tragic; in the tragic style, grand, solemn; of a tragic nature, tragic ‖ m writer of tragedies
tragoedi·a -ae f tragedy
tragoed·us -ī m tragic actor
trāgul·a -ae f javelin
trag·us or **trag·os -ī** m body odor of the armpits; a fish (*of unknown type*)
trah·āx -ācis adj greedy
trahe·a -ae f sledge, drag (*used as a threshing device*)
tra·hō -here -xī -ctus tr to draw, drag, trail; (*in a temporal sense*) to bring in its wake; to draw out, pull out, extract; to drag out, protract; to lead, to come leading (*an animal*); (*of a river*) to carry along; to carry off (*as plunder*); to rob (*persons*); to take along (*on a trip*); to contract, wrinkle (*the brow*); to pull toward one; (*of physical forces*) to attract; to attract, lure, fascinate (*persons*); to draw (*water*); to draw (*conclusions*); to take on, assume; to acquire, get; to spin, manufacture; to win over (*to the other side*); to refer, ascribe; to distract; to keep on considering, ponder; **animam** (*or* **spīritum**) **trahere** to draw in breath; **pedem trahere** (*of a lame person*) to drag one foot
Trāiān·us -ī m Trajan (*Marcus Ulpius Trāiānus, Roman emperor, A.D. 98–117*)
trā·iciō -icere -iēcī -iectus tr to throw (*a weapon*) across; (*of a weapon*) to pierce, pass through; to place (*a bridge, a bar*) across; to pass through, break through; to move, shift (*s.th. from one place to another*); (*w. double acc*) to bring (*e.g., troops*) across (*e.g., a river, mountain*); (*w.* **trāns** + *acc*) to lead across; (*w.* **in** + *acc*) to lead over into; to shift (*words from one part of the sentence to another*) ‖ intr to cross over
trāiecti·ō -ōnis f crossing, passage; transposition (*of words*); shift of meaning; exaggeration
trāiectus pp of **trāiciō**
trāiect·us -ūs m crossing over, passage
trālāt- = **trānslāt-**
Trall·ēs -ium fpl Tralles (*town in Lydia on the Menander River, variously set in Caria and Lydia*)
Tralliān·us -a -um adj of Tralles
trāloqu·or -ī tr to talk over, enumerate, recount
trālūceō see **trānslūceō**
trām·a -ae f woof, warp (*in some form of weaving*)
trūm·es -itis m path, track, trail
trāmi- = **trānsmi-**
trānatō = **trānsnatō**

trān·ō *or* trānsn·ō -āre -āvī -ātus *tr* to swim across; to pass through, permeate **ǁ** *intr* to swim across; to pass through
tranquillē *adv* quietly, calmly
tranquillit·ās -ātis *f* tranquillity, stillness, calmness
tranquill·ō -āre -āvī -ātus *tr* to calm, quiet, compose
tranquill·us -a -um *adj* tranquil, calm, quiet **ǁ** *n* calm, quiet, tranquillity; calm sea
Tranquill·us -ī *m* Gaius Suetonius Tranquillus *(biographer of the emperors, born c.* A.D. *69)*
trāns- *pref (used with verbs or verbal derivatives in the sense of the preposition)*
trāns *prep (w. acc)* across, over, beyond
trānsab·eō -īre -īvī *or* -iī *tr* to pierce, pass right through *(and go some distance beyond)*
trānsācti·ōnis *f* business transaction, business deal
trānsāct·or -ōris *m* manager, negotiator
trānsāctus *pp of* trānsigō
trānsad·igō -igere -ēgī -āctus *tr* to pierce; to run *(s.o.)* through; *(w. double acc)* to run *(e.g., a sword)* through *(s.o.)*
Trānsalpīn·us -a -um *adj* Transalpine
trānsbīt·ō -ere *intr* to come *or* go across
trānscen·dō *or* trānsscen·dō -dere -dī -sus *tr* to climb *or* step over, surmount; to overstep, transgress **ǁ** *intr* to climb *or* step across
trāns·cīdō -cīdere -cīdī -cīsus *tr* to flog thoroughly
trāns·currō -currere -(cu)currī -cursum *tr & intr* to hurry, run *or* dash over; to run through; to run past; *(in writing)* to pass over quickly; to skim *(in reading)*
trānscurs·us -ūs *m* running through, passage; cursory mention, cursory treatment *(of a subject)*
trānsd- = trād-
trānsenn·a -ae *f* (trās-) lattice work; lattice window; fowler's net
trāns·eō -īre -īvī *or* -iī -itus *tr* to cross; to desert; to pass *(in a race);* to pass over, make no mention of; to treat cursorily; to overstep; to surpass **ǁ** *intr* to go over, go across, pass over; to pass by, go by; to shift *(to another opinion, topic, etc.);* *(of time)* to pass by; to pass away; *(w.* ad + *acc)* **1** to cross over to *(a place);* **2** to desert to; *(w.* in + *acc)* to change into; *(w.* per + *acc)* to penetrate, permeate
trāns·ferō -ferre -tulī -lātus *(or* trālātus) *tr* (trāf-) to carry *or* bring across; to transfer *(by writing);* to copy; to shift; to transform; to postpone; to translate; to use figuratively
trāns·fīgō -fīgere -fīxī -fīxus *tr* to pierce; to run *(s.o.)* through
trānsfigūr·ō -āre -āvī -ātus *tr* to transform
trānsfīxus *pp of* trānsfīgō

trāns·fodiō -fodere -fōdī -fossus *tr* to stab, pierce, run through
trānsfōrm·is -is -e *adj* transformed
trānsfōrm·ō -āre -āvī -ātus *tr* to transform
trānsfossus *pp of* trānsfodiō
trānsfret·ō -āre -āvī -ātum *intr* to cross the sea
trānsfug·a -ae *m* deserter, turncoat
trāns·fugiō -fugere -fūgī *intr* to go over to the enemy, desert
trānsfug·ium -(i)ī *n* desertion
trāns·fundō -fundere -fūdī -fūsus *tr* to transfuse; to pour; *(w.* in + *acc)* to pour *(a liquid)* into; *(w.* ad + *acc) (fig)* to shift *(affection, allegiance)* to
trānsfūsi·ō -ōnis *f* pouring from one vessel into another; *(fig)* intermarriage
trānsfūsus *pp of* trānsfundō
trāns·gredior -gredī -gressus sum *tr* to cross, pass over; to exceed **ǁ** *intr* to go across; to cross over *(to another party)*
trānsgressi·ō -ōnis *f* crossing; transition; transposition *(of words)*
trānsgressus *pp of* trānsgredior
trānsgress·us -ūs *m* crossing
trānsiciō *see* trāiciō
trānsiect- = trāiect-
trāns·igō -igere -ēgī -āctus *tr* to pierce, run through; to finish; to settle, transact; to accomplish, perform, conclude; to pass, spend **ǁ** *intr* to come to an agreement, reach an understanding
trānsil·iō *or* trānssil·iō -īre -uī *tr* to jump over, jump across; to overstep; to skip, omit **ǁ** *intr* to jump across
trānsit·āns -antis *adj* passing through
trānsiti·ō -ōnis *f* crossing, passage; switching *(to another party);* contagion, infection; passageway
trānsitōri·us -a -um *adj* affording a passage *(from one place to another)*
trānsitus *pp of* trānseō
trānsit·us -ūs *m* crossing, passage; passing; traffic; crossing over, desertion; change, period of change, transition; transference of possession *(of);* fading *(of colors);* **in trānsitū** in passing; **per trānsitum** by way of transition
trānslātīci·us -a -um *adj* (trāl-) transmitted, traditional, customary; usual, common
trānslāti·ō -ōnis *f* (trāl-) transfer, shift; transporting; translation; metaphor, figure
trānslātīv·us -a -um *adj* (trāl-) transferable
trānslāt·or -ōris *m* middleman *(in a transfer)*
trānslātus *pp of* trānsferō
trānsleg·ō -ere *tr (w. dat)* to read out to *(s.o.)*
trānsloqu·or -ī *tr* (trāl-) to recount from the beginning
trānslūc·eō -ēre *intr* (trāl-) to shine through; to be reflected

trānsmarīn·us -a -um *adj* from beyond the seas, foreign, overseas

trānsme·ō -āre *tr & intr* **(trām-)** to cross, pass through

trānsmigr·ō -āre -āvī -ātum *intr* **(trām-)** to move, change residence; to migrate, emigrate

trānsmin·eō -ēre *intr* to stick out on the other side

trānsmissi·ō -ōnis *f* crossing, passage

trānsmissus *pp of* **trānsmittō**

trānsmiss·us -ūs *m* passing over, crossing, passage

trāns·mittō -mittere -mīsī -missus *tr* **(trām-)** to send across; to transmit; to let pass; to hand over, entrust; to pass over, leave unmentioned; to endure; *(w.* in + *acc)* to send *(s.o.)* across to or into; *(w.* per + *acc)* to let *(s.o.)* pass through ‖ *intr* to cross over, cross, pass *(from one place to another)*

trānsmontān·ī -ōrum *mpl* people living across the mountains

trāns·moveō -movēre -mōvī -mōtus *tr* to move, transfer

trānsmūt·ō -āre -āvī -ātus *tr* to change, shift

trānsnat·ō -āre -āvī -ātus *tr* **(trān-)** to swim (across) ‖ *intr* to swim across

trānsnō *see* **trānō**

trānsnōmin·ō -āre -āvī -ātus *tr (w. double acc)* to rename as

Trānspadān·us -a -um *adj* beyond *or* N. of the Po River

trānspect·us -ūs *m* view, prospect

trāns·pōnō -pōnere -posuī -positus *tr* to transfer, move across

trānsport·ō -āre -āvī -ātus *tr* to transport

trānspositus *pp of* **trānspōnō**

trānsrhenān·us -a -um *adj* beyond the Rhine, E. of the Rhine

trānss- = trāns-

trāns(s)pic·iō -ere *tr* to look through

trān(s)·scrībō -scrībere -scrīpsī -scrīptus *tr* to transcribe, copy off; *(leg)* to transfer, convey

trānstiberīn·us -a -um *adj* across the Tiber

trānstin·eō -ēre *intr* to provide a link *(from one side to the other)*

trānstr·um -ī *n* crossbeam; rower's seat, thwart

trānsult·ō -āre *intr* to jump across

trānsūt·us -a -um *adj* pierced through *(w. a pointed object)*

trānsvecti·ō -ōnis *f* **(trāv-)** transportation; riding past *(in review)*

trāns·vehō -vehere -vexī -vectus *tr* **(trāv-)** to transport; to carry past *(in a parade)* ‖ *pass* to ride by *(in a parade); (of time)* to elapse

trānsverber·ō -āre *tr* to pierce through and through, transfix

trānsversāri·us -a -um *adj* lying crosswise ‖ *n* crosspiece

trānsversē *adv* crosswise; across one's course

trānsvers·us *or* **trānsvors·us -a -um** *adj* **(trāv-)** lying across, lying crosswise; inopportune; astray; in the wrong direction ‖ *n* wrong direction; **dē trānsversō** unexpectedly; **ex trānsversō** unexpectedly; sideways

trānsvolit·ō -āre *tr* to flit through, fly through

trānsvol·ō -āre -āvī -ātus *tr & intr* **(trāv-)** to fly over, fly across, fly by

trānsvorsus *see* **trānsversus**

trapēt·um -ī *n or* **trapēt·us -ī** *m* oil press

trapezīt·a -ae *m* banker, money-changer

trapezophor·um -ī *n* ornate table

Trapez·os -untis *or* **-untos** *f* city in Pontus on the Black Sea

Trasimēn·us -ī *m* **(-menn-)** Lake Trasimene *(lake in Etruria, modern Trasimeno, where Hannibal defeated the Romans in 217 B.C.)*

trāv- = trānsv-

trāxī *perf of* **trahō**

Trebi·a -ae *f* river which flows into the Po near Placentia *(modern Trebbia River, near which Hannibal defeated the Romans in 218 B.C.)*

Trebulān·us -a -um *adj* of Trebula *(town in central Campania);* **ager Trebulānus** district of Trebula

trecēn·ī -ae -a *adj* three hundred each; three hundred each time ‖ *mpl* lots of three hundred *(men)*

trecentēsim·us -a -um *adj* three-hundredth

trecent·ī -ae -a *adj* three hundred

trecentiē(n)s *adv* three hundred times

trechedīpn·um -ī *n* light garment worn to dinner *(by parasites)*

tredecim *indecl adj* thirteen

tremebund·us -a -um *adj* trembling, shivering

treme·faciō -facere -fēcī -factus *tr* to shake, cause to shake

tremend·us -a -um *adj* **(-mi-)** awe-inspiring; terrible

trem·ēscō -ēscere -uī *tr* to (begin) tremble at ‖ *intr* to (begin) tremble

trem·ō -ere -uī *tr* to tremble at ‖ *intr* to tremble, shiver, quake

trem·or -ōris *m* trembling, shivering; dread; cause of fright, terror

tremuī *perf of* **tremō** *and* **tremēscō**

tremul·us -a -um *adj* trembling, quivering, tremulous, shivering

trepidanter *adv* tremblingly, nervously

trepidāti·ō -ōnis *f* nervousness, alarm; trembling

trepidē *adv* nervously, in alarm

trepid·ō -āre -āvī -ātus *tr* to start at, be startled by ‖ *intr* to be nervous, be jumpy, be alarmed; *(of a flame)* to flicker; *(of streams)* to rush along

trepid·us -a -um *adj* nervous, jumpy; restless; bubbling; perilous, critical, alarming; **in rē trepidā** in a ticklish situation

trēs trēs tria *adj* three; *(denoting a small number)* a couple of

tress·is -is *m* sum of three *"pennies"*; mere trifle

trēsvirī *(gen:* **triumvirōrum)** *mpl* triumvirs, board of three commissioners; commissioners for distributing land among colonists; **trēsvirī Epulōnēs** superintendents of sacrifices and banquets of the gods

Trēver·ī *or* **Trēvir·ī -ōrum** *mpl* people E. of Gaul

tri- *pref* consisting of three of the things named, *e.g.,* **tricuspis** having three prongs

triangul·us -a -um *adj* triangular ‖ *n* triangle

triāri·ī -ōrum *mpl* soldiers of the third rank in a battle line, reserves

trib·as -adis *f* female sexual pervert

Triboc·ī -ōrum *mpl* tribe which settled on the Rhine in the region of modern Alsace

tribuāri·us -a -um *adj* tribal

tribuī *perf of* **tribuō**

tribūl·is -is *m* fellow tribesman

tribul·um -ī *n* threshing sledge *(wooden platform with iron teeth underneath)*

tribul·us -ī *m* caltrop *(thistle)*

tribūn·al -ālis *n* platform; tribunal, judgment seat; *(in camp)* general's platform; cenotaph; **prō tribūnālī** *(or* **in** *or* **ē tribūnālī)** officially

tribūnāt·us -ūs *m* tribuneship

tribūnici·us -a -um *adj* tribunician, tribune's ‖ *m* ex-tribune

tribūn·us -ī *m* tribune; **tribūnus aerārius** paymaster; **tribūnus mīlitāris** *(or* **mīlitum)** military tribune *(six in each legion, serving under the legatus, and elected by the people or at times appointed by the commander);* **tribūnus plēbis** tribune of the people *(initially two, eventually ten in number, serving in the interests of the plebeians)*

trib·uō -uere -uī -ūtus *tr* to divide; to distribute, bestow, confer, assign; to give, present; to concede, grant, allow; to ascribe, impute; to devote, spend

trib·us -ūs *f* tribe *(orginally three in number and eventually increased to thirty-five)*

tribūtāri·us -a -um *adj* tributary, subject to tribute; **tribūtāriae tabellae** letters of credit

tribūtim *adv* by tribes, tribe by tribe

tribūti·ō -ōnis *f* distribution

tribūt·um -ī *n or* **tribūt·us -ī** *m* tribute, tax; contribution

tribūt·us -a -um *pp of* **tribuō** ‖ *adj* arranged by tribes

trīc·ae -ārum *fpl* tricks; nonsense

trīcēn·ī -ae -a *adj* thirty each; thirty at a time, in groups of thirty

tric·eps -ipitis *adj* three-headed

trīcēsim·us -a -um *adj* (**-cēns-**) thirtieth

trichil·a *or* **tricli·a** *or* **tricle·a -ae** *f* bower, arbor; summer house

trīciēns *or* **trīciēs** *adv* thirty times

triclea *see* **trichila**

triclia *see* **trichila**

trīclīn·ium -(i)ī *n* dining couch *(running around three sides of a table);* dining room

trīc·ō -ōnis *m* schemer

trīc·or -ārī *intr* to cause trouble; to pull tricks

tricorp·or -oris *adj* triple-bodied

tricusp·is -idis *adj* three-pronged

trid·ēns -entis *adj* three-pronged ‖ *m* trident

Tridentif·er *or* **Tridentig·er -erī** *m* Trident Bearer *(epithet of Neptune)*

tridu·um -ī *n* three-day period, three days

trienn·ia -ium *npl* triennial festival *(celebrated every three years)*

trienn·ium -(i)ī *n* three-year period, three years

tri·ēns -entis *m* one third; coin *(one third of a "penny");* third of a pint

trientābul·um -ī *n* land given by the State to those from whom the State had borrowed, equivalent to one third of the sum which the state owed

trienti·us -a -um *adj* sold for a third

triērarch·us -ī *m* captain of a trireme

triēr·is -is -e *adj* having oars *or* rowers arranged in threes ‖ *f* trireme

trietēric·us -a -um *adj* triennial, recurring every three years ‖ *npl* festival of Bacchus

trietēr·is -idis *or* **-idos** *f* three-year period; triennial festival in honor of Bacchus

trifāriam *adv* in three places, on three sides; under three headings

tri·faux -faucis *adj* triple-throated

trifid·us -a -um *adj* three-forked; split into three parts

trifīl·is -is -e *adj* having three threads *or* strands of hair

Trifolīn·us -a -um *adj* belonging to the district of Trifolium near Naples

trifol·ium -(i)ī *n* clover

trifōrm·is -is -e *adj* triple-form *(of the goddess having the three aspects of Luna, Diana, and Hecate; of three-headed Geryon; of the Chimera as composed of a lion, snake, and goat)*

tri·fūr -fūris *m* archthief

trifurcif·er -erī *m* archvillain, hardened criminal

trigemin·us -a -um *adj* (**terg-**) threefold, triple ‖ *mpl* triplets

trīgintā *indecl adj* thirty

trig·ō(n) -ōnis or **-ōnos** m game of catch *(played with three players standing to form a triangle);* ball *(used in this game)*
trigōnāl·is -is -e *adj* pila trigōnālis ball used in the game of catch
trilībr·is -is -e *adj* three-pound
trilingu·is -is -e *adj* three-tongued
tril·īx -īcis *adj* three-ply, triple-stranded
trimē(n)str·is -is -e *adj* of three months
trimetr·us -ī m *(pros)* trimeter *(metric line consisting of three double feet, e.g., iambic trimeter, or a line consisting of six iambic feet)*
trimod·ius -iī m measure of three pecks
trīmul·us -a -um *adj* three-year-old
trīm·us -a -um *adj* three-year-old
-trīn·a -ae f *suf* denoting the place where an activity is conducted: **tōnstrīna** barbershop *(from* **tondēre** to cut, shear, clip)
Trīnacr·is -idis *fem adj* Sicilian
Trīnacri·us -a -um *adj* Sicilian ‖ m Empedocles ‖ f Sicily
trīn·ī -ae -a *adj* threefold, triple; three each, three at a time; *(w. nouns occurring only in pl)* three: **trīnae litterae** three letters, three epistles
Trinobant·ēs -um *mpl* a British tribe near Essex
trinoctiāl·is -is -e *adj* occurring on three successive nights
trinōd·is -is -e *adj* triple-knotted
trinumm·us -ī m popular name for a newly introduced coin of high value ‖ **Trinummus** title of a play by Plautus
triōbol·us -ī m three-obol coin, half-dramcha or half-denarius piece *(c. 50¢)*
triōn·ēs -um *mpl* team of three oxen used in plowing ‖ **Triōnēs** Great and Little Bear *(constellations)*
Triop·ās -ae *adj (masc & fem only)* of Erysichthon
Triopē·is -idos f Mestra *(daughter of Erysichthon and granddaughter of Triopas, king of Thessaly)*
Triopē·ius -(i)ī m Erysichthon *(son of Triopas, king of Thessaly)*
triparc·us -a -um *adj* extremely stingy, triply stingy
tripartītō *adv* **(-pert-)** in three parts, into three parts
tripartīt·us -a -um *adj* **(-pert-)** divided into three parts, threefold
tripector·us -a -um *adj* triple-bodied, triple-chested
tripedāl·is -is -e *adj* three-foot
tripertītus *see* **tripartītus**
trip·ēs -edis *adj* three-legged, three-footed
tripl·ex -icis *adj* threefold, triple ‖ n three times as much, triple portion

tripl·us -a -um *adj* triple, threefold
Triptolem·us -ī m son of Celeus the king of Eleusis, favorite of Ceres, inventor of agriculture and one of the judges in the lower world
tripudi·ō -āre -āvī -ātum *intr* to perform a ritual dance *(tripudium)*
tripud·ium -(i)ī n war dance *(ritual dance in triple time, originally performed by priests in honor of Mars);* favorable omen *(when the sacred chickens ate hungrily, letting some grains fall to the ground in the process)*
trip·ūs -odis or **-odos** m tripod *(three-footed caldron);* oracle, Delphic oracle
triquetr·us -a -um *adj* triangular; Sicilian
trirēm·is -is -e *adj* having three banks of oars ‖ f trireme
trīs *see* **trēs**
trīscel·um -ī n triangle
trīscurri·a -ōrum *npl* fantastic nonsense
trīsticul·us -a -um *adj* somewhat sad
trīstific·us -a -um *adj* saddening
trīstimōni·a -ae f or **trīstimōn·ium -(i)ī** n sadness
trīst·is -is -e *adj* sad, sorrowful; bringing sorrow, saddening; gloomy, sullen; stern, harsh; disagreeable, offensive *(odor);* bitter, sour *(taste);* unpleasant *(sound)*
trīstiter *adv (to cry)* bitterly; distressingly
trīstiti·a -ae or **trīstiti·ēs -ēī** f sadness, gloom, gloominess, depression; severity, sternness
trisulc·us -a -um *adj* with three furrows or grooves; three-pronged; three-fold, triple; three-forked
tritavi·a-ae f great-great-great-great-grandmother
tritav·us -ī m great-great-great-great-grandfather
trīticei·a -ae f facetious name of a fish invented to make a pun with *hordeia*
trītice·us -a -um *adj* wheat
trītic·um -ī n wheat
Trīt·ōn -ōnis m son of Neptune who blows through a shell to calm the seas ‖ river flowing through Lake Tritonis in N. Africa where Minerva was said to be born
Trītōniac·us -a -um *adj* Tritonian, associated with Minerva
Trītōn·is -idis or **-idos** f Minerva
Trītōni·us -a -um *adj* Tritonian ‖ f Tritonia *(i.e., Minerva)*
trīt·or -ōris m grinder
trītūr·a -ae f threshing; kneading
trīt·us -a -um *pp* of **terō** ‖ *adj* worn, well-worn; beaten *(path);* experienced, expert; common, trite
trīt·us -ūs m rubbing, friction

triump(h)e *interj* a cheer shouted in the parade of triumphing generals *or* in the procession of the Arval Brothers

triumphāl·is -is -e *adj* triumphal; having had a triumph **‖** *npl* triumphal insignia *(without the actual triumph)*

triumph·ō -āre -āvī -ātus *tr* to triumph over, vanquish **‖** *intr (w.* **dē** *or* **ex** + *abl)* to celebrate a triumph *(over a people)*

triumph·us -ī *m* triumph, victory parade; victory; **triumphum agere** *(w.* **dē** *or* **ex** + *abl)* to celebrate a triumph over *(a conquered people)*

trium·vir -virī *m* triumvir, commissioner; mayor *(of a provincial town)* **‖** *mpl* triumvirs; **triumvirī capitālēs** superintendents of prisons and executions

triumvirāl·is -is -e *adj* triumviral, of the triumvirs

triumvirāt·us -ūs *m* triumvirate *(appointed at various times to serve various purposes)*

trivenēfic·a -ae *f* nasty old witch

trīvī *perf of* **terō**

Trivi·a -ae *f* epithet of Diana

triviāl·is -is -e *adj* appropriate for the street corners, common, vulgar

triv·ium -(i)ī *n* crossroads, intersection; public street; the "gutter"

trivi·us -a -um *adj of* or at the crossroads; worshiped at the crossroads **‖** *f see* **Trivia**

-tr·īx -īcis *fem suf corresponding to the masc suf* **-tor** *and denoting female agents, e.g.,* **tōnstrīx** hairdresser, barber

Trō·as *or* **Trō·ias -adis** *or* **-ados** *adj (fem only)* Trojan **‖** *f* Troad, district of Troy; Trojan woman

trochae·us -ī *m (pros)* trochee *(metrical foot)* (— ˇ), tribrach *(metrical foot)* (ˇ ˇ ˇ)

trochle·a *f* block and tackle

troch·us *or* **troch·os -ī** *m* hoop

Troez·ēn -ēnis *or* **-ēnos** *f* town in the Argolid on the E. shore of the Peloponnesus

Troezēni·us -a -um *adj* of Troezen

Trōi·a -ae *f* Troy

Trōiān·us -a -um *adj & m* Trojan

Trōic·us -a -um *adj* Trojan

Trōil·us -ī *m* son of Priam, killed by Achilles

Trōiugen·a *adj (masc & fem only)* Trojan-born, born at Troy, of Trojan descent, Trojan **‖** *m* Trojan

Trōi·us -a -um *adj* Trojan **‖** *f see* **Trōia**

Tromentīn·us -a -um *adj* name of one of the rustic tribes of early Rome

tropae·um -ī *n* trophy, war memorial *(originally armor taken from the enemy and hung on a stake, but later a permanent war monument, set up to mark the defeat of an enemy)*

Trophōn·ius -(i)ī *m* Boeotian oracular god with a shrine at Lebadea

Trōs Trōis *m* Tros *(son of Erichthonius and grandson of Dardanus and king of Phrygia after whom Troy was named)* **‖** a Trojan

trucīdāti·ō -ōnis *f* slaughter, massacre, butchery

trucīd·ō -āre *tr* to slaughter, massacre, cut down

trucil·ō -āre *intr (of a thrush)* to chirp

truculentē *or* **truculenter** *adv* grimly, fiercely

truculenti·a -ae *f* ferocity, savagery; harshness; **truculentia caelī** harsh weather

truculent·us -a -um *adj* grim, fierce

trud·is -is *f* pointed pole, pike

trū·dō -dere -sī -sus *tr* to push, shove; to thrust; to force, drive; to put forth *(buds)*

trull·a -ae *f* dipper, ladle, scoop, trowel; brazier; wash basin

-tr·um -ī *neut suf denoting instrument, e.g.:* **arātrum** plow

trunc·ō -āre -āvī -ātus *tr* to lop off, maim; to amputate

trunc·us -a -um *adj* lopped; stripped *(of branches and leaves)*, trimmed; maimed, mutilated; imperfect, undeveloped **‖** *m* tree trunk; trunk, body *(of a human being)*; chunk of meat; blockhead

trūsī *perf of* **trūdō**

trūs·ō -āre *intr (w. dat)* to keep ramming *(s.o.)* *(i.e., have sexual intercourse with a girl)*

trūsus *pp of* **trūdō**

trutin·a -ae *f* pair of scales; criterion

trutin·or -ārī -ātus sum *tr* to weigh, balance

tru·x -cis *adj* savage, grim, fierce

trybl·ium -(i)ī *n* plate, bowl

trȳgōn·us ī *m* stingray

tū *pron* you *(singl)*

tuātim *adv* in your manner, as is typical of you

tub·a -ae *f* trumpet *(with a straight tube, as opposed to the* **cornū**) *used in war, at religious ceremonies, at the start of public shows, at weddings, funerals, etc.)*

tub·er -eris *f* exotic type of fruit tree **‖** *m* exotic kind of fruit

tūb·er -eris *n* lump, hump, swelling; **tūber terrae** *(bot)* truffle *(underground fungus used as food)*

Tūbert·us -ī *m* Roman family name *(cognomen), esp.* Aulus Postumius Tubertus *(dictator in 431 B.C. and conqueror of the Aequi at Algidus)*

tubic·en -inis *m* trumpeter

tubilūstr·ium -(i)ī *n* festival of trumpets *(celebrated on March 23 and May 23 and including a ritual cleaning of the trumpets)*

tuburcin·or -ārī -ātus sum *tr (coll)* to gobble up

tub·us -ī *m* tube, pipe

tuccēt·um _or_ **tūcēt·um -ī** _n_ sausage

Tucci·us -a -um _adj_ Roman clan name _(nomen), esp._ Tuccia _(a Vestal Virgin who vindicated her chastity by carrying water in a sieve)_

tudit·ō -āre _tr_ to keep hitting

-tūd·ō -inis _fem suf forms abstract nouns, chiefly from adjectives, e.g.:_ **fortitūdō** bravery, _from_ **fortis** brave

tueor _or_ **tuor tuērī tuitus sum** _or_ **tūtus sum** _tr_ to look at, gaze at, watch, observe; to took after, take care of; to guard, defend, protect; to keep in good order, maintain; to keep up _(practice);_ to preserve the memory of

tugur·ium -(i)ī _n_ hut, hovel

tuiti·ō -ōnis _f_ protection, support; upkeep, maintenance; **tuitiō suī** self-defense

tulī _perf of_ **ferō**

Tulli·a -ae _f_ Roman female name

Tulliān·um -ī _n_ state dungeon at the foot of the Capitoline Hill, said to have been added by Servius Tullius to the _Carcer Mamertinus_

Tulliol·a -ae _f_ little Tullia

Tull·ius -(i)ī _m_ Roman clan name _(nomen), esp._ Marcus Tullius Cicero _(Roman orator and politician, 106-43 B.C.)_ ‖ Servius Tullius _(6th king of Rome)_

Tull·us -ī _m_ early first name _(praenomen), esp._ Tullus Hostilius _(the third king of Rome)_

tum _adv_ then, at that time; at that moment; in those days; next; moreover, besides; **cum ... tum** both ... and especially, not only ... but also, if ... then surely; **tum cum** at the point when, at the time when, just then when; **tum ... tum** first ... then, at one time ... at another, now ... now, both . . . and, partly ... partly

tume·faciō -facere -fēcī -factus _tr_ to cause to swell; _(fig)_ to puff up _(with pride)_

tum·eō -ēre -uī _intr_ to be swollen, swell up; to be inflated; _(of language or speaker)_ to be bombastic; _(of a person)_ to be excited, be in a dither, be in a rage; to be proud

tum·ēscō -ēscere -uī _intr_ to begin to swell (up); _(of wars)_ to brew; to grow excited; to become enraged; to become inflated

tumid·us -a -um _adj_ swollen, swelling; bloated; rising high; proud, puffed up; arrogant; incensed, enraged, exasperated; bombastic

tum·or -ōris _m_ tumor, swelling; protuberance, bulging; elevation _(of the ground);_ commotion, excitement; anger, rage; vanity, pride

tumuī _perf of_ **tumeō** _and_ **tumēscō**

tumul·ō -āre -āvī -ātus _tr_ to bury

tumulōs·us -a -um _adj_ hilly, rolling

tumultuāri·us -a -um _adj_ confused, disorderly; makeshift; _(mil)_ emergency, drafted hurriedly to meet an emergency; **exercitus tumultuārius** emergency army; **pugna**

tumultuāria irregular battle _(i.e., not fought in regular battle formation)_

tumultuāti·ō -ōnis _f_ commotion

tumultu·ō -āre _or_ **tumultu·or -ārī -ātus sum** _intr_ to make a disturbance; to be in an uproar; _(mil)_ to fight in a disorganized way

tumultuōsē _adv_ disorderly, in confusion; in panic

tumultuōs·us -a -um _adj_ boisterous, turbulent; panicky; **somnium tumultuōsum** nightmare

tumult·us -ūs _m_ commotion, uproar; insurrection, rebellion, civil war; confusion _(of the mind);_ outbreak _(of crime);_ _(mil)_ sudden attack

tumul·us -ī _m_ mound; rising; ground swell; burial mound; **tumulus inānis** cenotaph

tūn = **tūne (tū + ne)** do you?

tunc _adv (of time past)_ then, at that time; _(of future time)_ then, in that event; _(of succession in time)_ thereupon; _(in conclusion)_ consequently, in that case; **tunc cum** then when, just when; only when; **tunc dēmum** not until then, then finally; **tunc maximē** just then; **tunc prīmum** then for the first time; **tunc quandō** whenever; **tunc quoque** then too; **tunc vērō** then to be sure, exactly then

tundō tundere tutudī tūnsus _or_ **tūsus** _tr_ to beat, pound, hammer, thump; to buffet; to thresh; _(fig)_ to harp on

tunic·a -ae _f_ tunic _(ordinary half-sleeved knee-length garment worn by both sexes);_ military tunic _(made of mail or hides as armor);_ skin, peel, husk, coating; _(anat, bot)_ tunic; **tunica molesta** tunic with inflammable material, in which criminals were burned alive; **tunica rēcta** _(woven on a warp-weighted loom)_ bridal tunic; **tunica palmāta** tunic embroidered with palm-leaf design, worn by triumphing generals and by magistrates presiding over games

tunicāt·us -a -um _adj_ wearing a tunic; in shirt sleeves; coated; covered with (hard) skin, tunicate

tunic(u)l·a -ae _f_ short tunic; thin skin; thin coating

tūnsus _pp of_ **tundō**

tuor _see_ **tueor**

turb·a -ae _f_ turmoil, disorder, uproar, commotion; brawl; crowd, mob, gang; multitude; common crowd, masses; a large number; _(coll)_ rumpus, to-do

turbāment·a -ōrum _npl_ means of disturbance

turbātē _adv_ in confusion

turbāti·ō -ōnis _f_ confusion, disorder

turbāt·or -ōris _m_ ringleader, rabble-rouser, demagogue

turbāt·us -a -um _adj_ confused, disorderly; disturbed, annoyed

turbell·ae -ārum *fpl* stir, row; **turbellās facere** to cause quite a row
turben *see* **turbō** *m*
turbidē *adv* confusedly, in disorder
turbid·us -a -um *adj* confused, wild, boisterous; muddy, turbid; troubled, perplexed; vehement; disheveled *(hair);* stormy *(weather, sky)*
turbine·us -a -um *adj* cone-shaped; gyrating like a spinning-top
turb·ō -āre -āvī -ātus *tr* to throw into confusion, disturb, agitate; to break, disorganize *(ranks in battle),* cause to break ranks; to confuse; to alarm; to muddy; to stir *(a liquid in order to thicken it);* to stir up *(ingredients; emotions);* to jumble up *(sounds);* to wipe out *(tracks, clues);* to tamper with *(documents);* to squander *(a fortune)* ‖ *intr* to behave in a disorderly manner, go wild; to be in a state of commotion; to riot, revolt
turb·ō -inis *m or* **turb·en -inis** *n* whirl, twirl; eddy; spinning, revolution; coil; spinning top; reel; spindle; wheel; tornado, whirlwind; wheel of fortune; *(fig)* whirlwind, storm
turbulentē *or* **turbulenter** *adv* boisterously, tumultuously, confusedly
turbulent·us -a -um *adj* turbulent, wild, stormy; disturbed, confused; seditious, trouble-making
turd·a -ae *f or* **turd·us -ī** *m* thrush
tūre·us -a -um *adj* of frankincense
tur·geō -gēre -sī *intr* to be swollen, be puffed up; to be bombastic
turgēsc·ō -ere *intr* to begin to swell (up); to begin to blow up *(in anger)*
turgidul·us -a -um *adj* poor swollen *(eyes)*
turgid·us -a -um *adj* swollen, puffed up; inflated; turgid, bombastic
tūribul·um -ī *n* censer
tūricrem·us -a -um *adj* incense-burning
tūrif·er -era -erum *adj* producing incense
tūrileg·us -a -um *adj* incense-gathering
turm·a -ae *f* troop, squadron *(of cavalry, originally consisting of 30 men);* crowd, group
turmāl·is -is -e *adj* of a squadron; equestrian ‖ *mpl* troopers
turmātim *adv* by troops, by squadrons, squadron by squadron
Turn·us -ī *m* king of the Rutuli, killed by Aeneas
turpicul·us -a -um *adj* ugly little; somewhat indecent
turpificāt·us -a -um *adj* corrupted, degenerate
turpilucricupid·us -a -um *adj (coll)* eager to make a fast buck
turp·is -is -e *adj* ugly, deformed; foul, filthy, nasty; disgraceful, shameless; dirty, obscene, indecent

turpiter *adv* repulsively; disgracefully, scandalously, shamelessly
turpitūd·ō -inis *f* ugliness, deformity; foulness; disgrace; moral turpitude
turp·ō -āre -āvī -ātus *tr* to disfigure; to soil, defile, pollute; to disgrace
turrif·er -era -erum *adj see* **turriger**
turrig·er -era -erum *adj* turreted; *(of Cybele)* wearing a turreted crown *(representing earth with its cities)*
turr·is -is *f* turret, tower; howdah *(on an elephant); (fig)* castle, mansion
turrīt·us -a -um *adj* turreted; fortified with turrets; crowned with turrets, adorned with a turret crown
turt·ur -uris *m* turtledove
tūs tūris *n* incense, frankincense
Tūsculānēns·is -is -e *adj* Tusculan
Tūsculān·us -a -um *adj* Tusculan ‖ *n* Tusculan estate *(esp. Cicero's)*
tūscul·um -ī *n* a little incense
Tūscul·um -a -um *adj* Tusculan ‖ *n* Tusculum *(town in Latium near Alba Longa, about 12 miles S. of Rome)*
Tūsc·us -a -um *adj* Etruscan
tussicul·a -ae *f* slight cough
tuss·iō -īre *intr* to cough, have a cough
tuss·is -is *(acc:* **tussim;** *abl singl:* **tussī)** *f* cough
tūsus *pp of* **tundō**
tūtām·en -inis *or* **tūtāment·um -ī** *n* means of protection; protector
tūte = **tū** + **te** *emphatic form of* **tū**
tūtē *adv* safely
tūtēl·a -ae *f* care, charge, protection, defense; guardianship; charge, thing protected; support, maintenance *(of persons);* upkeep *(of buildings);* guardian, keeper; **in suam tūtēlam (per)venīre** *(or* **tūtēlam accipere** *or* **suae tūtēlae fierī)** *(of a minor)* to become capable of managing one's own affairs
tūtemet = **tū** + **te** + **met** *emphatic form of* **tū**
tūtō *adv* safely, securely, without risk of harm; **tūtō esse** to exist safely
tūt·ō -āre *or* **tūt·or -ārī -ātus sum** *tr* to guard, protect, defend; to keep safe, watch, preserve; to ward off, avert; *(w.* **ab** + *abl or w.* **ad** *or* **adversus** + *acc)* to protect *(s.o.)* from, guard *(s.o.)* against
tūt·or -ōris *m* protector; *(leg)* guardian *(of minors, of women of any age, etc.)*
tutudī *perf of* **tundō**
tūt·us -a -um *pp of* **tueor** ‖ *adj* safe, secure; cautious, prudent ‖ *n* safe place, shelter, security; **ex tūtō** from a safe place, in safety
tu·us -a -um *(also* **tu·os -a -om)** *adj* your; your dear *(friend, etc.),* dear to you; typical of you; devoted to you; *(of circumstances)* favorable to you ‖ *pron* yours; **dē tuō** at your expense;

in tuō on your land; **quid tua?** what business is it of yours?; **tua** your girlfriend, your sweetheart; **tuā interest** (or **tuā rēfert** it is of importance to you); **tuī** your friends, your people, your family, your soldiers; **tuum est** (w. inf) it is your duty to, it's up to you to; **tuum est quod** it is thanks to you that

tuxtax adv (a word meant to imitate the sound of blows) whack, wham; **tuxtax meō tergō erit** (coll) it's going to be wham, whack all over my back

Tȳd·eūs -eī or **-eos** m Tydeus (son of Oeneus, one of the Seven against Thebes, and father of Diomedes)

Tȳdīd·ēs -ae m Diomedes (son of Tydeus)

tympaniz·ō -āre intr to play the drum

tympanotrīb·a -ae m timbrel player, drummer

tympan·um or **typan·um -ī** n drum, revolving cylinder; solid circular wheel (used on carts and wagons); dentated wheel (used as a waterwheel); (mus) drum, timbrel (esp. used in the worship of Cybele or Bacchus)

Tyndar·eūs -eī or **Tyndar·us -ī** m king of Sparta, husband of Leda, father of Castor and Clytemnestra, and reputed father of Pollux and Helen

Tyndarid·ēs -ae m descendant of Tyndareus (esp. Castor and Pollux)

Tyndar·is -idis f descendant of Tyndareus (esp. Helen and Clytemnestra)

Typhō·eūs -eī or **-eos** or **Tȳph·ōn -ōnis** m giant who was struck by Jupiter with lightning and buried under Mt. Etna

Typhōe·us -a -um adj of the monster Typhoeus

Tȳph·ōn -ōnis m see **Typhōeus**

typ·us -ī m figure, image, bas-relief (on the wall)

tyrannicē adv tyrannically

tyrannicīd·a -ae m assassin of a tyrant

tyrannic·us -a -um adj tyrannical

tyrann·is -idis or **-idos** f tyranny, despotism

tyrannocton·us -ī m tyrannicide, assassin of a tyrant

tyrann·us -ī m monarch, sovereign; (in a Greek city-state) unconstitutional (absolute) ruler

Tyrianthin·a -ōrum npl clothes of a violet color

Tyri·us -a -um adj Tyrian, Phoenician; Carthaginian; Theban; crimson (because of the famous dye produced at Tyre) ‖ mpl Tyrians; Carthaginians

Tȳr·ō -ūs or **-ōnis** f daughter of Salmoneus and mother of Pelias and Neleus by Poseidon

Tyr·os or **Tyr·us -ī** f Tyre (commercial city of Phoenicia, famous for its crimson dye, or "Tyrian purple"; its dye works were active until destroyed by the Crusaders)

tȳrotarīch·os -ī m dish of salted fish and cheese (as an example of a plain diet)

Tyrr(h)ēnic·us -a -um adj Etrurian, Etruscan

Tyrr(h)ēn·us -a -um adj Etrurian, Etruscan; **mare Tyrrhēnum** Tyrrhenian Sea (lying between the W. coast of Italy, Sardinia, and Sicily); **Tyrrhēnae volucrēs** the Sirens ‖ mpl Etruscans (Pelasgian people who migrated to Italy, perhaps from Lydia in Asia Minor)

Tyrrhēni·a -ae f Etruria

Tyrtae·us -ī m Spartan poet (7th cent. B.C.)

Tyrus see **Tyros**

U

U, u (supply littera) f twentieth letter of the Latin alphabet; letter name: **u**

ūb·er -eris adj rich, fertile; fruitful, productive; plentiful; plenty of; valuable; copious (tears); (of things) rich in content; imaginative (writer, style); (fig) productive ‖ n (woman's) breast, nipple; udder; bosom (of the earth); fertility; fertile soil, fruitful field

ūberius adv more fully, in greater abundance; more fruitfully; with greater exuberance

ūbert·ās -ātis f richness; fertility; productiveness; abundance; richness of content

ūbertim adv copiously; **ūbertim flēre** to cry bitterly

ubi or **ubī** adv (interrog) where; **ubi gentium** (or **terrārum**) (coll) where in the world ‖ conj where, in which; whereby; with whom, by whom; when, whenever

ubicumque conj wherever, wheresoever ‖ adv anywhere, everywhere

Ubi·ī -ōrum mpl German tribe on the Lower Rhine

ubinam adv just where?, wherever?; **ubinam gentium** where in the world

ubiquāque adv everywhere

ubīque adv everywhere, anywhere

ubiubi conj wherever

ubivīs adv anywhere, everywhere, wherever you please; **ubivīs gentium** (coll) anywhere in the world

ūd·ō -ōnis m felt slipper

ūd·us -a -um adj wet, moist; humid

Ūf·ēns -entis m river in Latium

-ūg·ō -inis fem suf formed from names of materials to denote a superficial film, e.g.: **ferrūgō** (iron) rust; formed from nouns, e.g.: **vesperūgō** the Evening Star

-ul·a -ae fem suf forms diminutives, e.g.: **arcula** small box or chest

ulcer·ō -āre -āvī -ātus tr to cause to fester; (fig) to wound

ulcerōs·us -a -um *adj* ulcerous
ulcīscor ulcīscī ultus sum *tr* to avenge oneself on, take revenge on, punish; to avenge, requite
ulc·us -eris *n* ulcer, sore
-ulent·us -a -um *adjl suf forms adjectives meaning "abounding in," "full of," e.g.:* **vīnulentus** full of wine, intoxicated
ūlīg·ō -inis *f* moisture, dampness
Ulix·ēs -is *or* **-eī** *or* **-ī** *m* Ulysses *(king of Ithaca, son of Laertes, husband of Penelope, and father of Telemachus and Telegonus)*
ūll·us -a -um *adj* any
ulme·us -a -um *adj* elm, made of elm; *(hum)* elm-whipped
ulmitrib·a -ae *m (coll)* slaphappy *(from being flogged with elm whips)*
ulm·us -ī *f* elm tree **‖** *fpl* elm whips
uln·a -ae *f* elbow; arm; *(as measure of length, span of the outstretched arms, c. 45 inches)* ell
ulpic·um -ī *n* type of garlic
ulteri·or -or -us *adj* farther, on the farther side, more remote; further, additional, more; longer; in a higher degree; worse; **Gallia Ulterior** Transalpine Gaul; **Hispānia Ulterior** the western of the two provinces of the Iberian peninsula **‖** *mpl* more remote people, those beyond **‖** *npl* things beyond
ulterius *adv* to a more distant place, farther away; to a further extent, further, more than that; **ulterius quam** further than
ulterius *prep (w. acc)* beyond
ultimō *adv* finally, last of all
ultimum *adv* finally; for the last time
ultim·us -a -um *adj* (**-tum-**) farthest, most distant, extreme; earliest; latest, final, last; greatest; lowest; meanest **‖** *n* last thing, end; **ad ultimum** to the end; to the extreme; in the highest degree; to the last degree, utterly; *(in an enumeration)* finally; **in ultimō** finally **‖** *npl* extremes; the worst
ulti·ō -ōnis *f* vengeance, revenge
ult·or -ōris *m* avenger, punisher
ultrā *adv* beyond, farther, besides **‖** *prep* **1** *(w. acc) (in a physical sense)* on the farther side of, beyond, past: **nihil est ultrā altitūdinem montium quō pertimendum est** there is nothing beyond *(i.e., except)* the heights of the mountains that needs to be feared; **2** *(in the temporal sense)* to a point later than, at a later time than, after, past; to a time further back than, earlier than: **ultrā mediam noctem** till past midnight; **3** *(of number, measure, degree)* over, beyond, more than, over and above: **nōn ultrā trēs versūs** not more than three verses; **4** *(in negative sentences, indicating the limit of an activity)* **nihil ultrā nervōs atque cutem mortī**

concēderat ātrae he had conceded to dark death nothing but sinews and skin *(i.e., his body)*
ultr·īx -īcis *adj (fem only)* avenging *(esp. of the Furies and other agents of retribution)* **‖** *f* avenger
ultrō *adv* to the farther side, beyond; on the other side; on both sides, in both directions; at the opposite end of the scale, conversely; besides, moreover, too; into the bargain, to boot; of one's own accord, without being asked; without being spoken to; unprovoked; **bella īnferre ultrō** to go to war (although) unprovoked; **ultrō et citrō** back and forth; **ultrō tribūta** expenditure incurred by the government for public works
ultus *pp of* **ulcīscor**
ulul·a -ae *f* owl
ululāt·us -ūs *m* howling *(esp. of dogs and wolves);* ulutation, wailing *(esp. of mourners);* war cry
ulul·ō -āre -āvī -ātus *tr* to howl out, howl at **‖** *intr* to howl; to ululate, wail; *(of places)* to resound
-ul·um -ī *neut suf forming diminutive neuter nouns:* **speculum** mirror
-ul·us *m and* **-ul·a** *f suf* **1** *forming diminutives:* **calculus** little stone; **2** *adjectives denoting repeated action:* **crēdulus** regularly believing, credulous; **3** *adjectives denoting diminished intensity:* **ūmidulus** dampish; **4** *nouns denoting instruments:* **furculus** pitchfork; **5** *nouns denoting endearment:* **uxorcula** dear wife
ulv·a -ae *f (bot)* sedge, rush
umbell·a -ae *f* umbrella, parasol
Um·ber -bra -brum *adj* Umbrian, of Umbria **‖** *m* Umbrian
umbilīc·us -ī *m* navel, bellybutton; midriff; middle, center; projecting end of dowels *or* cylinders on which scrolls were rolled; cockle, sea snail; **ad umbilīcum** *(or* **ad umbilīcōs)** to the end of the scroll *or* book
umb·ō -ōnis *m* boss *(of a shield);* shield; elbow
umbr·a -ae *f* shade; shadow; phantom, ghost; mere shadow *(of one's former self);* semblance; darkness, gloom; shelter, cover; privacy, retirement; umber *(fish);* **rhētorica umbra** rhetorician's school **‖** *fpl* darkness of night; lower world
umbrāc(u)l·um -ī *n* shade; bower, arbor; school; umbrella, parasol
umbrāticol·a -ae *mf* lounger *(in the shade)*
umbrātic·us -a -um *adj* too fond of the shade, lazy, inactive; secluded; private; **umbrāticus doctor** private tutor; pedant
umbrātil·is -is -e *adj* carried out in the shade, private, retired; academic
Umbri·a -ae *f* Umbria *(district in central Italy)*

umbrif·er -era -erum *adj* shady
umbr·ō -āre -āvī -ātus *tr* to shade, cast a shadow on; to overshadow
umbrōs·us -a -um *adj* shady
ūmect·ō -āre -āvī -ātus *tr* (**hūm-**) to wet, moisten
ūmect·us -a -um *adj* (**hūm-**) moist, damp
ūm·eō -ēre *intr* to be moist, be damp, be wet
umer·us -ī *m* (**hum-**) shoulder
ūmēsc·ō -ere *intr* to become moist, become wet
ūmidul·us -a -um *adj* dampish
ūmid·us -a -um *adj* (**hūm-**) moist, damp, wet; green, unseasoned *(lumber)* ‖ *n* wet place
ūmif·er -era -erum *adj* laden with moisture
ūm·or -ōris *m* (**hūm-**) moisture; liquid, fluid
umquam *or* **unquam** *adv* ever, at any time
ūnā *adv* together; **ūnā cum** together with; **ūnā venīre** to come along
ūnanim·āns -antis *adj* of one mind, of one accord
ūnanimit·ās -ātis *f* unanimity
ūnanim·us -a -um *adj* (**ūnian-**) unanimous; of one mind, of one heart
ūnci·a -ae *f* one-twelfth; ounce *(one-twelfth of a pound or* **lībra**); *(of interest rate)* 1% a year; *(in length)* inch *(25 mm, one twelfth of a foot or* **pēs**)
ūnciāri·us -a -um *adj* containing one-twelfth; one-ounce; one-inch
ūnciātim *adv* ounce by ounce, little by little
uncīnāt·us -a -um *adj* hooked, barbed
uncīn·us -ī *m* hook
ūnciol·a -ae *f* a mere twelfth
unc·ō -āre *intr* *(of a bear)* to grunt
ūncti·ō -ōnis *f* rubdown with oil; *(fig)* wrestling
ūnctit·ō -āre *tr* to keep rubbing with oil, keep oiling
ūnctiuscul·us -a -um *adj* somewhat too oily; unctuous
ūnct·or -ōris *m* anointer, rubdown man, masseur
ūnct·um -ī *n* sumptuous dinner
ūnctūr·a -ae *f* anointing
ūnct·us -a -um *pp of* **ung(u)ō** ‖ *adj* greasy; resinous; sumptuous
ūncul·us -a -um *adj* any at all
unc·us -a -um *adj* hooked, barbed; crooked ‖ *m* hook, clamp; grappling iron
und·a -ae *f* water; stream, river; wave; sea, seawater; current *(of air); (fig)* stream, tide, agitated mass
unde *adv* from where, whence; from whom; **unde unde** *(or* **undeunde**) by hook or by crook
ūndeciēns *or* **ūndeciēs** *adv* eleven times
ūndecim *indecl adj* eleven
ūndecim·us -a -um *adj* (**-decum-**) eleventh

undecumque *adv* (**-cun-**) from whatever place, from whatever source
ūndēn·ī -ae -a *adj* eleven in a group, eleven each, eleven
ūndēnōnāgintā *indecl adj* eighty-nine
ūndēoctōgintā *indecl adj* seventy-nine
ūndēquadrāgēsim·us -a -um *adj* thirty-ninth
ūndēquadrāgintā *indecl adj* thirty-nine
ūndēquīnquāgēsim·us -a -um *adj* forty-ninth
ūndēquīnquāgintā *indecl adj* forty-nine
ūndēsexāgintā *indecl adj* fifty-nine
undētrīcēsim·us -a -um *adj* twenty-ninth
ūndētrīgintā *indecl adj* twenty-nine
ūndēvīcēsimān·ī -ōrum *mpl* soldiers of the nineteenth legion
ūndēvīcēsim·us -a -um *adj* nineteenth
ūndēvīgintī *indecl adj* nineteen
undique *adv* from all directions, on all sides, everywhere; in all respects, completely
undison·us -a -um *adj* of roaring waves; **undisonī deī** gods of the roaring waves
und·ō -āre -āvī -ātum *intr* to move in waves, undulate; to billow; to overflow
undōs·us -a -um *adj* full of waves, billowy; wave-washed *(shore)*
ūnetvīcē(n)sim·us -a -um *adj* twenty-first
ūnetvīcēsimān·ī -ōrum *mpl* soldiers of the twenty-first legion
ungō *or* **unguō ung(u)ere ūnxī ūnctus** *tr* to oil, grease, anoint
ungu·en -inis *n* fat, grease; ointment
unguentāri·us -(i)ī *m* perfumer
unguentāt·us -a -um *adj* anointed; perfumed, wearing perfume
unguent·um -ī *n* ointment; perfume
unguicul·us -ī *m* fingernail; toenail; **ā tenerīs unguiculīs** from earliest childhood
ungu·is -is *m* fingernail; toenail; claw, talon; hoof; **ad unguem** to a tee, complete, perfect; **dē tenerō unguī** from earliest childhood
ungul·a -ae *f* hoof; claw, talon; *(fig)* horse
unguō *see* **ungō**
ūnicē *adv* singularly; particularly; **ūnicē ūnus** one and only
ūnicol·or -ōris *adj* of one and the same color, monochrome
ūnicorn·is -is -e *adj* one-horned
ūnic·us -a -um *adj* one and only, sole; singular, unique; uncommon
ūnifōrm·is -is -e *adj* uniform, having only one shape
ūnigen·a -ae *adj* (*masc & fem only*) only-begotten, only; of the same parentage
ūniman·us -a -um *adj* one-handed
ūni·ō -ōnis *f* single large pearl
ūnisubsell·ium -(i)ī *n* seat for one
ūniter *adv* jointly
ūniversāl·is -is -e *adj* universal
ūniversē *adv* generally, in general

ūniversit·ās -ātis *f* aggregate, whole; whole world, universe

ūnivers·us -a -um *adj* (-vors-) all, all together; all taken collectively; whole, entire ‖ *n* the whole; whole world, universe; in ūniversum on the whole, in general

ūnocul·us -ī *m* one-eyed person

ūnomammi·a -ae *adj (fem)* single-breasted *(Amazon)*

unquam *or* umquam *adv* ever, at any time

ūnumquicquid *pron* every little thing

ūn·us -a -um *adj* one, single, only, sole; one and the same; *(indefinite)* one, some; ūnae scōpae one broom; ūnus et alter one or two; ūnus quisque each one, every single one ‖ *pron* someone, a mere individual; ad ūnum to a man

ūnxī *perf of* ung(u)ō

ūpili·ō -ōnis *m* shepherd

upup·a -ae *f* hoopoe *(bird with fan-like crest and downward-curving bill);* hoe, mattock

-ūr·a -ae *fem suf forms nouns from nouns ending in* -tor *to denote office:* praetūra praetorship *(from* praetor); *forms nouns mainly from verbal derivatives in* -tus: nātūra nature *(from* nātus)

Ūrani·a -ae *or* Ūrani·ē -ēs *f* Muse of astronomy

urbānē *adv* politely, courteously; with sophistication; wittily

urbānit·ās -ātis *f* living in the city, city life; refinement; politeness; sophistication; wit; raillery

urbān·us -a -um *adj* of the city, city; courteous; sophisticated; witty; brash, forward ‖ *m* city dweller; *(pej)* city slicker

urbicap·us -ī *m* conqueror of cities

urbic·us -a -um *adj* city, of the city

urbi·us -a -um *adj* urbius clīvus slope on the Esquiline Hill

ur·bs *or* ur·ps -bis *f* city; the city of Rome

urceol·us -ī *m* little pitcher, little pot

urce·us -ī *m* pitcher, water pot

urc·ō -āre *intr (of a lynx)* to snarl

ūrēd·ō -inis *f* blight *(on plants)*

urgeō urgēre ūrsī *tr* to prod on, urge forward; to pressure, put pressure on *(s.o.);* to crowd, hem in; to follow up, keep at, stick by ‖ *intr* to be urgent; to be insistent

ūrīn·a -ae *f* urine

ūrīnāt·or -ōris *m* diver

ūrīn·ō -āre *or* ūrīn·or -ārī *intr* to dive

-ur·iō -īre -īvī *or* -iī *suf forming desideratives:* cēnāturīre to wish to eat

Ūrī·ōn -ōnis *m* Orion

Ūr·ios -iī *m* cult title of Zeus, as the sender of favorable winds

urn·a -ae *f* pot, jar; water pot; voting urn; urn of fate; cinerary urn; money jar; liquid measure *(= one half of an amphora)*

urnul·a -ae *f* small urn

ūrō ūrere ūssī ūstus *tr* to burn; to burn up, reduce to ashes, consume; to scorch, parch, dry up; to sting, pain; to nip, frostbite; to rub sore; to corrode; to annoy, gall, burn up, make angry; to inflame *(w. love)*

urps *see* urbs

urs·a -ae *f* she-bear ‖ Ursa Māior *(astr)* Great Bear *(constellation);* Ursa Minor *(astr)* Little Bear *(constellation)*

ūrsī *perf of* urgeō

ursīn·us -a -um *adj* bear, bear's

urs·us -ī *m* bear

urtīc·a -ae *f (bot)* stinging nettle *(causing a burning rash upon contact);* desire, itch

ūrūc·a *or* ūrīc·a -ae *f* caterpillar

ūr·us -ī *m* wild ox

Ūsīpet·ēs -um *mpl* German tribe on the Rhine

ūsitātē *adv* in the usual way, as usual

ūsitāt·us -a -um *adj* usual, customary, familiar; ūsitātum est *(w. inf)* it is customary to

ūspiam *adv* anywhere, somewhere, in some place or other

ūsquam *adv* anywhere *(in any place or to any place)*

ūsque *adv* all the way, right on; all the time, continuously; even, as much as; *(without addition of an adv or prep)* to the fullest extent, completely; ūsque ab *(w. abl)* all the way from; ever since; ūsque ad *(w. acc)* all the way to; all the way back in time to; ūsque adeō *(or* ūsque eō) ut to such an extent that; ūsque quāque every moment, continually; on all occasions, in everything ‖ *prep (w. acc)* up to, as far as, right until

ūsquequāque *or* ūsque quāque *adv* everywhere, as far as one can go in either direction; *(fig)* in every conceivable situation; in every possible respect, wholly

ūssī *perf of* ūrō

ūsti·ō -ōnis *f* burning

ūst·or -ōris *m* cremator

ūstul·ō -āre -āvī -ātus *tr* to scorch, singe

ūstus *pp of* ūrō

ūsū·capiō -capere -cēpī -captus *tr (leg)* to acquire ownership of *(by long use)*

ūsūcapi·ō -ōnis *f (leg)* acquisition of ownership *(through long use)*

ūsūr·a -ae *f* use, enjoyment; interest *(on capital)*

ūsūrāri·us -a -um *adj* for use and enjoyment; paying interest, interest-bearing

ūsurpāti·ō -ōnis *f* use; *(w. gen)* making use of, use of

ūsurp·ō -āre -āvī -ātus *tr* to use, make *(constant)* use of, employ; to exercise *(a right);* to put into practice *(a custom, operation);* to take possession of, acquire; to usurp; to name, call, speak of; to assume *(a title, honor, esp. arbitrarily);* to take up *(an inheritance);* to perceive *(with the senses),* observe, experience; **memoriam ūsurpāre** *(w. gen)* to invoke the memory of

ūsus *pp of* **ūtor**

ūs·us -ūs *m* use, enjoyment; practice, employment; experience, skill; usage, custom; familiarity; usefulness, advantage, benefit; occasion, need, necessity; **ex ūsū esse** *(or* **ūsuī esse)** *(w. dat)* to be useful to, be a good thing for; **in ūsū** in one's everyday experience; **in ūsū esse** to be in use; to be customary; **in ūsū (meō, tuō,** *etc.)* **est** it is to (my, your, *etc.)* advantage; **in ūsū habēre** *(or* **continēre)** to keep in use; **quis ūsus est?** *(w. gen)* what useful purpose is served by?; **scientia et ūsus** theory and practice; **sī ūsus veniat** if the need should arise, if the opportunity should present itself; **ūsus adest** a good opportunity comes along; **ūsus est** *(w. abl)* there is a need of; **ūsus et frūctus** use and enjoyment; **ūsū venit** it happens, it occurs; **ūsus venit** *(w. dat)* the need arises for

ūsusfrūctus *(gen:* **ūsūsfrūctūs)** *m* use and enjoyment, usufruct

ut *(or* **utī,** *an older form, increasingly rare after Cicero, but affected by archaizing authors) adv (in direct and indirect questions; in exclamations)* how; **ut miser est quī!** how pitiful is the man who! ‖ *conj (comparative)* as; *(adversative)* although; *(temporal)* when, while; *(purpose)* in order that; *(result, after* **adeō, eō, sīc, tālis, tam, tantus)** (to such a degree, so, such, so great) that; *(concessive)* granted that; *(introducing examples)* as, as for example; *(after verbs of fearing)* lest, that not; *(introducing an explanation or reason)* as, as being, inasmuch as; *(introducing indirect commands)* that; **ut maximē** at most; **ut perinde** *(or* **proinde)** according to the degree to which; **ut quī** (= **quippe quī)** as is natural for one who; **ut putā** *(indicating an example)* as say, for example

utcumque *or* **utcunque** *or* **utquomque** *adv* however; whenever; one way or another

ūt·ēns -entis *adj* well-off, well-to-do

ūtēnsil·is -is -e *adj* useful ‖ *npl* utensils, materials, provisions, similar things

u·ter -tra -trum *(gen:* **utrīus,** *dat:* **utrī)** *adj* which *(of the two)* ‖ *pron* which one *(of the two);* one or the other

ū·ter -tris *m* bag, skin, bottle; inflated bag to keep swimmers afloat

utercumque utracumque utrumcumque *adj* whichever *(of the two)* ‖ *pron* whichever one *(of the two)*

uterlibet utralibet utrumlibet *adj* whichever *(of the two)* you please ‖ *pron* whichever one *(of the two)* you please, either one *(of the two)*

uterque utraque utrumque *adj* each *(of the two),* both; **sermōnēs utrīusque linguae** conversations in both languages *(i.e., Greek and Latin)* ‖ *pron* each one *(of the two),* both; **uterque īnsāniunt** both are insane

uter·us -ī *m or* **uter·um -ī** *n* belly, abdomen; womb; potbelly *(of a man);* **uterum gerere** to be pregnant

utervīs utravīs utrumvīs *adj* whichever *(of the two)* you please, either ‖ *pron* whichever one *(of the two)* you please, either one

utī *see* **ut**

ūtibil·is -is -e *adj* useful, usable, practical

Utic·a -ae *f* city in Africa, N.W. of Carthage, where the younger Cato committed suicide in 46 B.C.

Uticēns·is -is -e *adj* of Utica ‖ *m* posthumous title of Cato

ūtil·is -is -e *adj* useful, profitable, practical; *(w. dat or* **ad** + *acc)* fit for, useful for, practical in

ūtilit·ās -ātis *f* usefulness, advantage

ūtiliter *adv* usefully, profitably

utinam *conj (introducing a wish)* if only, would that

utique *adv* anyhow, at least, at any rate; in particular, especially; without condition, absolutely; *(after negatives)* on any account; *(in obeying instructions)* without fail; **cūr utique** exactly why

ūtor ūtī ūsus sum *intr (w. abl)* **1** to use, make use of: **coquī hīs condīmentīs ūtuntur** cooks use these seasonings; **2** to enjoy: **valetūdine prosperā ūtī** to enjoy good health; **3** to practice, experience: **portīs patefactīs eō diē pāce prīmum ūsī sunt** as the gates were thrown open they experienced peace for the first time on that day; **4** to enjoy the friendship *or* companionship of: **multōs iam annōs tē ūsī sumus** for many years now we have enjoyed your friendship; **5** *(w. adv or abl of manner)* to treat: **omnibus sociīs clēmentiā ūtī** to treat all our allies with kindness; **familiāriter ūtēbar Caesare** I was on familiar terms with Caesar; **6** to hold *(office, military command):* **honōre ūtī** to hold office; **tribūnī mīlitēs et imperiō et īnsignibus cōnsulāribus ūsī sunt** the military tribunes held military commands and wore the consular insignia; **7** to handle, manage, control: **bene armīs, optimē equīs ūsus est** he managed arms well and horses very well; **8** to consume *(food or drink):* **quī vetere vīnō ūtuntur** who drink old wine; **9** to wear *(clothes):* **solūtīs vestibus ūtuntur Grātiae** the Graces wear loose dresses; **10** to live *or* spend one's time *(in a place):* **eō marī ūtī cōnsuērunt** they were used to living on (the coast of) that sea; **11** to play *(a musical instrument):* **quī fidibus aut tibiīs ūtī volunt** those who want to play the lyre or the flute

utpote *adv (reinforcing explanatory phrases or clauses)* as one might expect, as is natural, naturally, inasmuch as; **utpote cum** as you might expect since; **utpote quī** inasmuch as *(he is one)* who, inasmuch as he, because he

ūtrār·ius -(i)ī *m* water carrier, water boy

ūtric(u)lār·ius -(i)ī *m* bagpipe player

utrimque *or* **utrinque** *adv* from *or* on both sides, on either side; **utrimque cōnstitit fidēs** on both sides their word of honor held good

utrō *adv* to which of the two sides, in which direction

utrobīque *adv* on both sides, on either hand

utrōlibet *adv* to either side

utrōque *adv* to both sides, in both directions

utrōqueversum *adv* **(-vors-)** in both directions

utrubi *adv* at *or* on which of the two sides

utrubīque *adv* on both sides, on either hand

utrum *conj* whether

utut *adv* in whatever way, however

ūv·a -ae *f* grape; grapes; bunch of grapes; vine; swarm of bees; *(anat)* uvula; **ūva pāssa** raisin *(literally, grape spread out to dry)*

ūvēsc·ō -ere *intr* to become moist; *(fig)* to get drunk

ūvidul·us -a -um *adj* a little moist, dampish

ūvid·us -a -um *adj* wet, moist, damp; humid; drunk

ux·or -ōris *f* wife; mate *(of animals)*

uxorcul·a -ae *f* dear (little) wife

uxorcul·ō -āre -āvī *intr* to play the role of a wife

uxōri·us -a -um *adj* of a wife, wifely; very fond of a wife; henpecked

V

V, v *(supply* littera*)* *f* twenty-first letter of the Latin alphabet; letter name: **ve**

V, v is used in this dictionary to represent consonantal *u*

vac·āns -antis *adj* vacant, unoccupied; at leisure; unemployed; unattached, single; *(w. abl)* lacking, without; **puella vacāns** a single girl **‖** *npl* unoccupied estates

vacāti·ō -ōnis *f* freedom, exemption *(from duty, service, etc.);* exemption from military

service; payment for being exempted from military service; vacation, holiday, day off

vacc·a -ae *f* cow

vaccīn·ium -(i)ī *n (bot)* hyacinth

vaccul·a -ae *f* heifer

vacē·fīō -fierī *intr* to become empty, be emptied, be vacated

vacerr·a -ae *f* fence post

vacerrōs·us -a -um *adj (pej)* cracked, crazy

vacillāti·ō -ōnis *f* tottering

vacill·ō -āre -āvī -ātum *intr* **(vacc-)** to stagger, reel; to vacillate, waver; to be untrustworthy

vacīvē *adv* at leisure

vacīvit·ās -ātis *f* want, lack

vacīv·us -a -um *adj* **(voc-)** *(of a place)* unoccupied, vacant; *(w. gen)* free of, devoid of, free from

vac·ō -āre -āvī -ātum *intr* **(voc-)** to be empty, be vacant; to be unoccupied; to be ownerless; to be without, not to contain; to be free, be carefree; to be at leisure, have free time; *(of things)* to lie idle; to be *(romantically)* unattached; *(w. abl or* **ab) 1** to be free from; **2** to be devoid of; **3** to abstain from; **4** to be exempt from *(duty, responsibility); (w. dat or* w. **ad** *or* **in** + *acc)* to be free for, have time for, have spare time for; *(w. inf)* to have leisure to, have time to; **populō vacāre** to remain aloof from the people; **rēs pūblica et mīlite et pecūniā vacat** the country is relieved from furnishing an army and money; **semper philosophiae vacō** I always have time for philosophy **‖** *v impers (w. dat)* there is time for, there is room for; *(w. inf)* there is time to *or* for

vacuāt·us -a -um *adj* empty

vacuē·faciō -facere -fēcī -factus *tr* to empty, clear, free

vacuit·ās -ātis *f* freedom, exemption; emptiness; empty space; vacancy *(in an office); (w. gen or* w. **ab)** freedom from *(s.th. undesirable)*

Vacūn·a -ae *f* Sabine goddess, later identified with Victory

Vacūnāl·is -is -e *adj* of the goddess Vacuna

vacu·ō -āre -āvī -ātus *tr* to empty, clear, free; to strip *(a place of defenders, inhabitants)*

vacu·us -a -um *adj* empty, clear, free; vacant; worthless, useless; single, unmarried; widowed; at leisure; carefree; *(w. gen or abl or* w. **ab)** free from, devoid of, without; *(w. dat)* free for

vadimōn·ium -(i)ī *n (leg)* promise *(to appear in court),* bail *(given as a guarantee of one's appearance in court);* **vadimōnium dēserere** to default, jump bail; **vadimōnium differre** to postpone appearance in court, grant a continuance; **vadimōnium facere** to put up bail; **vadimōnium sistere** to appear in court

vadis *genit of* **vas**

vādō vādere vāsī *intr* to go, make one's way, advance

vad·or -ārī -ātus sum *tr (of a plaintiff)* to demand that *(s.o.)* put up bail; to sue

vadōs·us -a -um *adj* shallow

vad·um -ī *n or* **vad·us -ī** *m* shallow place, shallow, ford; shallow part of the sea, shoal; bottom *(of the sea)*, depths; sea, waters

vae *interj* woe!; *(w. acc or dat)* woe to

va·fer -fra -frum *adj* sly, cunning; subtle; ingenious

vafrē *adv* slyly, cunningly

vagē *adv* far and wide

vāgīn·a -ae *f* sheath, scabbard; hull *(of ear of grain); (anat)* vagina

vāg·iō -īre -īvī *or* **-iī** *intr (esp. of an infant)* to cry, bawl; *(of hares)* to squeal

vāgīt·us -ūs *m* cry

vag·or -ārī -ātus sum *or* **vag·ō -āre** *intr* to wander, range, roam

vāg·or -ōris *m* cry *(of a baby)*

vag·us -a -um *adj* wandering, roaming; shifting, inconstant; rambling *(speech);* roundabout *(explanation);* haphazard, erratic; fickle; *(of lovers)* changing from one partner to another; **stella vaga** planet

vāh *interj (expressing dismay, pain, annoyance, contempt, or surpise)* ah!, oh!; *(expressing unexpected admiration or surprise)* wow!

vaha *interj (expressing pleasant surprise)* aha!, wow!

valdē *adv* greatly, intensely; *(w. adj or adv)* very; *(as affirmative reply)* yes, certainly, to be sure

valē *interj* goodbye!

val·ēns -entis *adj* strong, powerful; healthy, well; coarse *(fabrics);* strong *(medicine);* vigorous *(plants);* potent, effective *(remedies; arguments)*

valenter *adv* strongly; energetically

valentul·us -a -um *adj* sturdy, robust

val·eō -ēre -uī valitūrus *intr* to be strong; to be vigorous; to be powerful; to be effective; to prevail, succeed; to be influential; to be valid; to be strong enough, be adequate, be capable, be able; to be of value, be of worth; to mean, signify; **tē valēre iubeō** I bid you farewell, goodbye to you; **valē** *(pl:* **valēte)** goodbye; **valē dīcere** to say goodbye, take leave

Valeriān·us -a -um *adj* belonging to Valerius

Valeri·us -a -um *adj* Roman clan name *(nomen), esp.* Publius Valerius Publicola *(recorded as one of the first two consuls in 509 B.C.)*

valēsc·ō -ere *intr* to grow strong, thrive; to grow powerful

valētūdinār·ium -(i)ī *n* hospital

valētūd·ō -inis *f* state of health; good health; ill health, illness; **bona** *(or* **commoda** *or* **firma** *or* **prospera** *or* **secunda) valētūdō** good health; **adversa** *(or* **īnfirma** *or* **mala)** poor health; **valētūdinis causā** for reasons of (poor) health

Valgi·us -a -um *adj* Roman clan name *(nomen), esp.* Gaius Valgius Rufus *(an Augustan poet and grammarian)*

valg·us -a -um *adj* knock-kneed

validē *adv* strongly, vehemently; *(in replies)* of coursc, ccrtainly, definitely

valid·us -a -um *adj* strong, powerful, able; healthy; robust; fortified; influential; efficacious

vallār·is -is -e *adj* of a rampart; **corōna vallāris** crown awarded to the first soldier to scale the enemy's rampart

vall·ēs *or* **vall·is -is** *f* valley

vall·ō -āre -āvī -ātus *tr* to fortify with a rampart, wall in; to protect, defend

vall·um -ī *n* palisade of stakes on top of an embankment; rampart

vall·us -ī *m* stake, pale; rampart with palisades, stockade; tooth *(of a comb)*

valv·ae -ārum *fpl* folding doors, double doors

vānēsc·ō -ere *intr* to vanish, fade

vānidic·us -a -um *adj* lying; boasting **ǁ** *m* liar; boaster

vāniloquenti·a -ae *f* empty talk, mere talk

vāniloquidōr·us -ī *m* liar, windbag

vāniloqu·us -a -um *adj* talking nonsense; lying; bragging

vānit·ās -ātis *f* falsity, unreality, deception, untruth; bragging; lying; vanity; worthlessness; frivolity

vānitūd·ō -inis *f* falsehood

vann·us -ī *f* winnowing fan

vān·us -a -um *adj* empty, vacant; groundless; pointless; hollow, unreal; lying, false; boastful; conceited, vain **ǁ** *n* emptiness; uselessness; deceptive appearance

vapidē *adv* poorly, badly

vapid·us -a -um *adj* flat, vapid, spoiled, bad; morally corrupt

vap·or -ōris *m* vapor, steam; warmth *(of the sun)*

vapōrār·ium -(i)ī *n* steam room

vapōr·ō -āre -āvī -ātus *tr* to steam up; to warm, heat **ǁ** *intr* to steam

vapp·a -ae *f* sour wine; *(pej)* brat, good-for-nothing

vāpulār·is -is -e *adj* in for a flogging

vāpul·ō -āre *intr* to get a beating; *(of savings, etc.)* to take a beating

vārē *adv* in a straddling manner

variantia 442 **Vēdiovis**

varianti·a -ae *f* diversity, variety

Vāriān·us -a -um *adj* of Varus *(i.e., Publius Quintilius Varus, whose legions were cut to pieces in Germany)*

variāti·ō -ōnis *f* diversification; variation; divergence

vāric·ō -āre -āvī -ātus *intr* to spread the legs, stand with legs spread apart

varicōs·us -a -um *adj* varicose

vāric·us -a -um *adj* with legs wide apart

variē *adv* variously; in different degrees; differently; severally, respectively; in a varied style; with changing colors

variet·ās -ātis *f* variety, difference, diversity; vicissitudes; inconstancy

vari·ō -āre -āvī -ātus *tr* to vary, diversify, change, make different; to give variety to; to variegate ‖ *intr* to change color; to vary, differ, change; to be diversified; to differ in opinion; to waver; **bellum variante fortūnā** a war with varying success, a war with ups and downs ‖ *v impers* **sī variāret** if there were a difference of opinion

vari·us -a -um *adj* variegated, of different colors; varied; composed of different elements, motley; many-sided *(personality);* conflicting *(opinions, reports);* changing, fluctuating *(conditions, fortunes);* versatile; inconstant, unsteady; untrustworthy, fickle *(character)*

Var·ius -(i)ī *m* Lucius Varius Rufus *(epic and tragic poet and friend of Vergil and Horace, died c. 12 B.C.)*

var·ix -icis *mf* varicose vein

Varr·ō -ōnis *m* Roman family name, *(cognomen),* esp. Gaius Terentius Varro *(consul in 216 B.C. and joint commander at Cannae)* ‖ Marcus Terentius Varro *(antiquarian, philologist, and librarian, 116–27 B.C.)* ‖ Publius Terentius Varro Atacinus *(born 82 B.C., poet, translator of Apollonius Rhodius' "Argonautica")*

vār·us -a -um *adj* knock-kneed; bent, crooked; opposed, contrary

vas vadis *m (leg)* bondsman *(person who provides surety or bail)*

vās vāsis *or* **vās·um -ī** *(pl:* **vās·a -ōrum)** *n* vessel, dish; utensil, implement ‖ *npl* equipment, gear; **vāsa colligere** *(mil)* to pack up one's gear; **vāsa conclāmare** *(mil)* to give the signal to pack the gear; **vāsa coquitātōria** pots and pans

vāsār·ium -(i)ī *n* allowance for furnishings *(given to a provincial governor)*

vāsculār·ius -(i)ī *m* metal worker; seller of housewear items

vāscul·um -ī *n* small vessel

vastāti·ō -ōnis *f* devastation

vastāt·or -ōris *m* devastator

vastē *adv* vastly, widely; coarsely, harshly; violently

vastific·us -a -um *adj* devastating

vastit·ās -ātis *f* wasteland, desert; state of desolation, emptiness; devastation, destruction; vastness, immensity; great open spaces

vastiti·ēs -ēī *f* ruin, destruction

vast·ō -āre -āvī -ātus *tr* to leave desolate; to lay waste; to cut *(troops)* to pieces

vast·us -a -um *adj* desolate; devastated; vast, enormous; uncouth; clumsy; unrefined *(pronunciation)*

vāt·ēs *or* **vāt·is -is** *m* seer, prophet; bard, poet ‖ *f* prophetess; poetess

Vāticān·us -a -um *adj* Vatican; **mōns** *(or* **collis)** **Vāticānus** hill in Rome on the right bank of the Tiber

vāticināti·ō -ōnis *f* prophesying, soothsaying, prophecy

vāticināt·or -ōris *m* prophet, seer

vāticin·ium -(i)ī *n* prophecy

vāticin·or -ārī -ātus sum *tr* to foretell, prophesy; to keep harping on ‖ *intr* to prophesy; to rant and rave, talk wildly

vāticin·us -a -um *adj* prophetic

vatill·um -ī *n* brazier

vātis *see* **vātēs**

vat·us -a -um *adj* knock-kneed

-ve *conj (enclitic)* or; **-ve ... -ve** either ... or

vēcordi·a -ae *f* (vae-) senselessness; madness

vēc·ors -ordis *adj* (vae-) senseless; insane

vectāti·ō -ōnis *f* riding *(on horseback or in a carriage)*

vectīg·al -ālis *n* tax; revenue; duty; tariff; private income; produce providing personal income; payment given to a magistrate *or* provincial governor; private income *or* revenue; **vectīgal aedīlicium** payment exacted by an aedile to finance games

vectīgāl·is -is -e *adj (of persons, cities, etc.)* subject to taxation, taxed, taxable; *(of land, etc.)* yielding taxes; **pecūnia vectīgālis** money raised by taxes

vecti·ō -ōnis *f* conveyance, transporting

Vect·is -is *f* Isle of Wight

vect·is -is *m* crowbar, lever; bar, bolt *(on a door or gate)*

vect·ō -āre -āvī -ātus *tr* to carry, transport *(by an habitual agent or means of conveyance)* ‖ *pass* to ride, drive, travel; **equō vectārī** to ride a horse; **nāve vectārī** to sail

vect·or -ōris *m* bearer, carrier; rider; passenger

vectōri·us -a -um *adj* of transportation; **nāvigia vectōria** cargo ships

vectūr·a -ae *f* transportation, conveyance; freight costs; fare

vectus *pp of* **vehō**

Vēdiov·is *or* **Vēiov·is -is** *m* Anti-Jove *(Etruscan divinity of the lower world, identi-*

fied with the Jupiter of the lower world) ‖ Little Jove *(identified with the infant Jupiter)*
veget·ō -āre *tr* to invigorate
veget·us -a -um *adj* vigorous; lively *(rhythm, time, mind, thoughts)* vivacious, energetic; bright *(eyes);* invigorating; vivid *(colors);* **intervallum temporis vegetissimum agricolīs** a period of time extremely busy for the farmers
vēgrand·is -is -e *adj* not huge, puny
vehem·ēns -entis *adj* (**vēm-**) vehement; intense *(heat, cold);* strong, powerful *(force);* strong *(taste, flavor);* potent *(drink, medicine);* severe *(pain);* serious *(illness);* drastic *(actions);* forceful, strongly expressive, tremendous *(writing, speech);* imperious, overmastering; forceful *(arguments);* violent *(men, animals, natural phenomena);* vigorous, active *(person);* ardent, great *(love)*
vehementer *adv* (**vēm-**) vehemently, impetuously; with great force, violently; firmly, strongly, energetically; in an impassioned manner; *(w. reference to feelings)* strongly, overpoweringly; *(modifying adjectives)* immensely, tremendously
vehic(u)l·um -ī *n* vehicle, wagon, cart; means of transportation; **praefectus vehiculōrum** director of the imperial post
veh·is -is *m (f)* wagonload
vehō vehere vexī vectus *tr* to carry, convey, transport ‖ *pass* to travel, ride, sail, be borne along
Vēi·ēns -entis *or* **Vēientān·us -a -um** *adj* of Veii
Vēi·ī -ōrum *mpl* old Etrurian city about 12 miles from Rome, captured by Camillus *(396 B.C.)*
Vēiov·is -is *or* **Vēdiovis -is** *m* ancient deity worshiped on the Capitoline Hill in Rome, considered to be the lower-world counterpart of Jupiter
vel *adv* even, actually; perhaps; for instance; *(with superlatives)* to the utmost ‖ *conj* either, or, as you wish, take your pick; **vel ... vel** either ... or
Vēlābrēns·is -is -e *adj* of the Velabrum
Vēlābr·um -ī *n* Velabrum *(low ground between the Capitoline and Palatine where a market was located)*
vēlām·en -inis *n* drape, covering, veil; clothing, robe; olive branch wrapped in wool *(symbol carried by a suppliant)*
vēlāment·um -ī *n* covering, wrapping; a wrap; olive branch wrapped in wool *(symbol carried by a suppliant); (fig)* screen, cover-up
vēlār·ium -(i)ī *n* awning *(over the open-air theater)*
vēlāt·ī -ōrum *mpl (mil)* reserves
vēl·es -itis *m* light-armed soldier, skirmisher

Veli·a -ae *f* the Velia *(elevated portion of the Palatine Hill in Rome)* ‖ town and port in Lucania
Veliēns·is -is -e *adj* of the Velia in Rome ‖ of Velia *(Lucanian town)*
vēlif·er -era -erum *adj* sail, sailing; **carīna vēlifera** sailboat, sailing ship
vēlificāti·ō -ōnis *f* sailing
vēlific·ō -āre -āvī -ātus *or* **vēlific·or -ārī -ātus sum** *tr* to sail through ‖ *intr* to sail; *(w. dat)* **1** to be under full sail toward, set one's course for; **2** to be hell-bent on *(e.g., high office)*
Velīn·us -a -um *adj* of Velia *(Lucanian town and port);* of the River Velinus; **lacus Valīnus** Valinc Lakc *(fed by the Veline river);* **tribus Velīna** one of the 35 Roman tribes, belonging to that region
Velīn·us -ī *m* river and lake in the Sabine territory
vēlitār·is -is -e *adj* of light-armed troops
vēlitāti·ō -ōnis *f* skirmishing
Velitern·us -a -um *adj* of Velitrae
vēlitēs = *pl of* **vēles**
vēlit·or -ārī -ātus sum *or* **vēlit·ō -āre** *intr* to make an irregular attack, skirmish; *(fig)* to indulge in a verbal skirmish
Velitr·ae -ārum *fpl* Volscian town in Latium on the S. side of the Alban Hills
Vēli·us -a -um *adj* Roman clan name, *(nomen), esp.* Velius Longus *(a grammarian of the age of Trajan)*
vēlivol·us -a -um *adj* speeding along under sail; sail-covered *(sea)*
velle *inf of* **vōlō**
vellic·ō -are *tr* to pluck, pinch, nip; to carp at, rail at
vellō vellere vellī *or* **vulsī** *or* **volsī vulsus** *or* **volsus** *tr* to pluck, pull, tear at, tear away, tear out; to tear up, tear down, destroy
vell·us -eris *n* fleece, skin, pelt; wool ‖ *npl* fleecy clouds
vēl·ō -āre -āvī -ātus *tr* to veil, wrap, envelop; to cover, clothe; to encircle, crown; to cover up, hide; to adorn *(temples, etc., ritually);* **vēlātus** sail-clad, fitted with sails
vēlōcit·ās -ātis *f* velocity, speed
vēlōciter *adv* speedily, swiftly
vēl·ōx -ōcis *adj* speedy, swift
vēl·um -ī *n* sail; veil; curtain, awning, covering; **plēnīs vēlīs** full speed ahead; **rēmīs vēlīsque** *(fig)* with might and main; **(ventīs) vēla dare** to set sail; **vēla facere** to spread one's sails
velut *or* **velutī** *adv* as, just as, even as; as for example; *(to introduce a simile)* as, as it were; *(in elliptical clauses)* like; **velut** *(or* **velut sī)** just as if, just as though, as if, as though
vēmēns *see* **vehemēns**

vēn·a -ae *f* blood vessel *(whether vein or artery); (contrasted with* **artēria**) vein; artery *(believed to conduct air or food and drink to the body);* duct *(in the body);* penis; vein, streak *(in wood, stone, minerals);* vein *(of ore);* channel, trench; watercourse; store of talent *or* ability; natural disposition; strength; **vēna aquae** streamlet ‖ *fpl (fig)* heart, core
vēnābul·um -ī *n* hunting spear
Venā·fer -fra -frum *or* Venāfrān·us -a -um *adj* of Venafrum
Venāfr·um -ī *n* Samnite town in S. central Italy
vēnālici·us -a -um *adj* for sale ‖ *m* slave dealer ‖ *npl* merchandise, imports and exports
vēnāl·is -is -e *adj* for sale; open to bribe ‖ *mf* slave offered for sale
vēnātic·us -a -um *adj* hunting
vēnāti·ō -ōnis *f* hunt, hunting; wild-beast show; game
vēnāt·or -ōris *m* hunter
vēnātōri·us -a -um *adj* hunter's
vēnātr·īx -īcis *f* huntress
vēnātūr·a -ae *f* hunting
vēnāt·us -ūs *m* hunting; *(fig)* game, bag
vēndibil·is -is -e *adj* marketable; on sale; attractive, popular, acceptable
vēnditāti·ō -ōnis *f* advertising; showing off
vēnditāt·or -ōris *m* hawker, self-advertiser
vēnditi·ō -ōnis *f* sale
vēndit·ō -āre -āvī -ātus *tr* to try to sell; to sell *(regularly);* to advertise; to give as a bribe ‖ *refl (w. dat)* to ingratiate oneself with
vēndit·or -ōris *m* vendor, seller; recipient of a bribe
vēnd·ō -ere -idī -itus *tr* to put up for sale; to sell, vend; to sell *(s.o.)* out, betray; to advertise; to praise, recommend
venēfic·a -ae *f* poisoner; sorceress, witch; *(term of abuse)* hag, witch
venēfic·ium -(i)ī *n* poisoning; poison; magical herb; magic, supernatural influence; dye; *(fig)* pernicious moral influence, malicious speech
venēfic·us -a -um *adj* poisoning, poisonous; magic ‖ *m* poisoner; sorcerer, magician
venēnāt·us -a -um *adj* poisonous, venomous; filled with poison; magic; bewitched, enchanted; *(fig)* venomous, bitter
venēnif·er -era -erum *adj* poisonous, venomous
venēn·ō -āre -āvī -ātus *tr (lit & fig)* to poison
venēn·um -ī *n* poison; drug, potion; magic charm; sorcery; ruin; dye; virulence *(of speech)*
vēn·eō -īre -iī -itūrus *intr* to go up for sale, be sold
venerābil·is -is -e *adj* venerable, revered

venerābund·us -a -um *adj* reverend; reverential, worshiping
venerand·us -a -um *adj* venerable, august
venerāti·ō -ōnis *f* veneration, reverence, deep respect
venerāt·or -ōris *m* respecter, adorer; admirer
Venere·us *or* Veneri·us -a -um *adj* of Venus; of sexual love, erotic; **rēs Veneriae** sexual intercourse ‖ *m* Venus throw *(best throw of the dice, when each of the four dice turns up a different number)* ‖ *mpl* attendants in Venus' temple
vener·or -ārī -ātus sum *or* vener·ō -āre *tr* to venerate, revere, worship, pray to; to implore, beg; to pray for
Venet·ī -ōrum *mpl* a people in N.E. Italy in the region of modern Venice ‖ a tribe in Gallia Lugdunensis
Veneti·a -ae *f* district of the Veneti in W. Gaul
Venetic·us -a -um *adj* of the Veneti *(of Gallia Lugdunensis)*
Venet·us -a -um *adj* Venetian; bluish ‖ *m* Venetian; a Blue *(i.e., a member of one of the racing factions in Rome)*
veni·a -ae *f* kindness, favor, goodwill; permission; pardon, forgiveness; **veniam dare** *(w. dat)* **1** to grant forgiveness to; **2** to do a favor to; **3** to grant permission to; **veniam petere** to ask permission; **veniā vestrā** with your leave
Venīli·a -ae *f* Italian nymph *(wife of Faunus or of Janus)*
veniō venīre vēnī ventum *intr* to come; to be coming, be on the way; to appear in court; to come to dinner; *(of plants)* to come up; *(w. in + acc)* **1** to come into; **2** to enter into *(an agreement, friendship, etc.);* **3** to fall into *(e.g., trouble, disgrace, etc.);* **in buccam venīre** to be on the tip of the tongue; **in mentem venīre** to come to mind
vēn·or -ārī -ātus sum *tr & intr* to hunt
vent·er -ris *m* stomach, belly; womb; embryo, fetus, unborn child; belly, protuberance; appetite, gluttony
ventil·ō -āre -āvī -ātus *tr* to fan, wave; to display, show off
venti·ō -ōnis *f* coming
ventit·ō -āre -āvī -ātum *intr* to keep coming, come regularly
ventōs·us -a -um *adj* windy, full of wind; of the wind; wind-like, swift as the wind; conceited; fickle
ventricul·us -ī *m* belly; ventricle *(of the heart)*
ventriōs·us -a -um *adj* pot-bellied
ventul·us -ī *m* breeze
vent·us -ī *m* wind; intestinal wind; *(fig)* storm; **ventum ēmittere** to break wind
vēnūcul·a -ae *f* grape *(of the type well suited for preserving)*

vēn·um *(gen not in use; dat:* **vēnō)** *n* sale, that which is for sale; for sale; **vēnum** *(or* **vēnō) dare** to put up for sale, sell; to sell as a slave; **vēnum** *(or* **vēnō) darī** to be sold; **vēnum** *(or* **vēnō) īre** to go up for sale, be sold

vēnum·dō -dare -dedī -datus *tr* **(-und-)** to put up for sale, sell

ven·us -eris *f* beauty, charm; sexual intercourse, sex; mating; beloved, love ‖ **Venus** Venus *(goddess of love and beauty; planet);* Venus-throw *(see* **Venereus)**

Venusi·a -ae *f* town in Apulia *(birthplace of Horace, modern Venosa)*

Venusīn·us -a -um *adj* of Venusia

venust·ās -ātis *f* beauty, charm, attraction

venustē *adv* prettily, charmingly

venustul·us -a -um *adj* cute, pretty

venust·us -a -um *adj* charming, attractive; interesting *(writing, writer)*

vēpallid·us -a -um *adj* very pale

veprēcul·a -ae *f* little brier bush

vepr·ēs -is *m (f)* brier, bramble bush

vēr vēris *n* spring, springtime; youth

vērātr·um -ī *n (bot)* hellebore *(used as a drug to treat insanity)*

vēr·āx -ācis *adj* truthful

verbēn·a -ae *f (bot)* verbena *(plant with clusters of flowers of various colors)* ‖ *fpl* sacred branches worn by heralds and priests

verb·er -eris *n* scourge, rod, whip; flogging, scourging; thong *(of a sling and similar weapon)* ‖ *npl* strokes, flogging

verberābilissum·us -a -um *adj* altogether deserving of a flogging

verberābund·us -a -um *adj* flogging all the way

verberāti·ō -ōnis *f* flogging

verberetill·us -a -um *adj* deserving of a flogging

verbere·us -a -um *adj* deserving of a flogging

verber·ō -āre -āvī -ātus *tr* to flog, scourge, whip; to batter, beat

verber·ō -ōnis *m* rascal *(deserving of flogging)*

verbivēlitāti·ō -ōnis *f* verbal skirmish

verbōsē *adv* verbosely

verbōs·us -a -um *adj* verbose

verb·um -ī *n* word; verb; saying, expression; proverb; mere talk, mere words; formula; **ad verbum** word for word, verbatim; literally, actually; **verba dare** *(w. dat)* to cheat *(s.o.),* feed *(s.o.)* a line; **verba facere** to speak, make a speech; **verbī causā** *(or* **verbī grātiā)** for instance; **verbō** orally; in a word, briefly; nominally, in name only; in theory; **verbō dē verbō** *(or* **verbum prō verbō** *or* **verbum verbō)** word for word

Vercell·ae -ārum *fpl* town in N.W. Gaul *(modern Vercelli)*

Vercingetor·ix -igis *m* famous leader of the Arverni in the Gallic War

vērcul·um -ī *n (term of endearment)* sweet springtime

vērē *adv* really, truly

verēcundē *adv* bashfully, modestly

verēcundi·a -ae *f* bashfulness, shyness, modesty; respect, awe, reverence; sense of shame; feeling of disgrace, disgrace, shame

verēcund·or -ārī *intr* to be bashful, be shy, feel ashamed

verēcund·us -a -um *adj* bashful, shy, modest, reserved

verēd·us -ī *m* fast hunting horse

verend·us -a -um *adj* inspiring respect, venerable; awesome ‖ *npl* sexual organs

ver·eor -ērī -itus sum *tr* to revere, have respect for; to fear ‖ *intr* to feel uneasy, be anxious, be afraid; *(w. gen)* to stand in awe of, be afraid of; *(w. dat)* to be afraid for; *(w.* **dē** + *abl)* to be apprehensive about; *(w.* **ut)** to be afraid that not; *(w.* **nē)** to be afraid that

verētr·um -ī *n* male sexual organ

Vergili·ae -ārum *fpl (astr)* Pleiades *(constellation)*

Vergil·ius *or* **Virgil·ius -(i)ī** *m* Roman clan name *(nomen),* esp. Vergil *(Publius Vergilius Maro, epic poet of the Augustan Age, 70–19 B.C.)*

Vergīni·us -a -um *adj* Roman clan name *(nomen),* esp. Lucius Verginius *(said to have killed his daughter to save her from the lust of Appius Claudius and thus to have brought about the overthrow of the decemvirs in 449 B.C.)* ‖ *f* his daughter

verg·ō -ere *tr* to cause to move in a downward direction, incline; to tilt down ‖ *intr* to turn, incline; to slope back *or* away; to decline; to lie, be situated; *(w.* **ad)** **1** to verge toward; to extend to; **2** to face (toward); **3** to incline toward, tend toward *(usu. a worse condition);* *(w.* **in** + *acc)* to sink into, lapse into *(lethargy, old age)*

vēridic·us -a -um *adj* truthful, speaking the truth; truly spoken

vēriloqu·ium -(i)ī *n* argument based on the true meaning of a word

vērīsimil·is -is -e *adj* probable, likely; realistic

vērīsimilitūd·ō -inis *f* probability, likelihood

vērit·ās -ātis *f* truth, truthfulness; real life, reality; honesty, integrity; correctness *(in eytmology and grammar);* **ex vēritāte** in accordance with the truth

vēriverb·ium -(i)ī *n* truthfulness

vermiculāt·us -a -um *adj* inlaid with wavy lines, vermiculated

vermicul·us -ī *m* grubworm, maggot; **in vermiculō** in the larval state

vermin·a -um *npl* stomach cramps

verm·is -is *m* worm

vern·a -ae *mf* home-born slave *(born in the master's house);* native

vernācul·us -a -um *adj* of home-born slaves; home-grown, native, domestic; of the neighborhood; indigenous; proletarian; *(of troops)* levied locally; *(w. gen)* native to *(a place)* ‖ *mf* home-born slave

vernīl·is -is -e *adj* servile; obsequious

vernīlit·ās -ātis *f* slavishness; rude behavior, impudence

vernīliter *adv* slavishly

vērn·ō -āre *intr* to show signs of spring; to burgeon, break into bloom; to be young

vernul·a -ae *mf* young slave *(born in the master's house);* native

vērn·us -a -um *adj* spring, of spring; **tempus vērnum** springtime

vērō *adv* in truth, in fact; certainly, to be sure; even; however

Vērōn·a -ae *f* city in N. Italy, birthplace of Catullus and Pliny the Elder

Vērōnēns·is -is -e *adj* Veronese ‖ *mpl* the people of Verona

verp·a -ae *f* penis *(as protruded from the foreskin)*

verp·us -a -um *adj* circumsized; having the foreskin drawn back

verr·ēs -is *m* pig, boar ‖ **Verrēs** Gaius Cornelius Verres *(notorious governor of Sicily in 73–70 B.C.)*

verrīn·us -a -um *adj* of a boar, of a pig, pork-

ver·rō -rere -rī -sus *tr* (vor-) to pull, drag, drag away, carry off; to sweep, scour, brush; *(of the wind)* to whip across, sweep *(the land)*

verrūc·a -ae *f* wart *(on the body);* small failing, minor blemish

verrūcōs·us -a -um *adj* full of warts; *(fig)* full of blemishes

verrunc·ō -āre *intr* to turn out well

versābil·is -is -e *adj* shifting, movable

versābund·us -a -um *adj* revolving

versātil·is -is -e *adj* capable of turning, revolving, movable; versatile

versicapill·us -a -um *adj* having hair that has turned grey, greying

versicol·or -ōris *adj* changing colors, of various colors

versicul·us -ī *m* short line, single line *(of verse or prose),* versicle ‖ *mpl* poor little verses

versificāti·ō -ōnis *f* versification

versificāt·or -ōris *m* versifier

versific·ō -āre *tr* to put into verse ‖ *intr* to write verse

versipell·is -is -e *adj* (vors-) changing appearance at will; sly ‖ *m* werewolf

vers·ō -āre -āvī -ātus *tr* (vor-) to keep turning, spin, whirl; to twist, bend, wind *(material in order to change its shape);* to turn *(the eyes)*

this way and that *(in uncertainty);* to keep shifting *(the limbs in restlessness);* to keep turning, maneuver *(a vehicle, a horse);* to swing *(a weapon)* in all directions; to stir *(the contents of a vessel, esp. the lots in an urn);* to keep turning over *(the ground, as in plowing); (fig)* to influence, sway *(a person in one direction or another); (fig)* to turn over in the mind, ponder, consider; *(pej)* to manipulate *(a person); (w. in + acc)* to focus *(the mind)* on; *(rhet)* to vary the expression *(of an idea)* ‖ *refl* to keep going around, keep on revolving; to spin around *(so as to face in the opposite direction)*

vers·or -ārī -ātus sum *intr* (vor-) to come and go frequently; to live, stay; to be, be in operation, obtain; *(w. adverbs)* to behave *(in a certain way);* to revolve; to spin around *(so as to face in the opposite direction);* to toss, writhe; *(w. in + abl)* **1** to be involved in, be engaged in, be busy with; **2** to stay in, live in, pass one's time in *(a place, among persons, or in surroundings);* **3** *(of things)* to be concerned with, have to do with; **4** to be subject to; **5** *(of an idea, mental image)* to be constantly present in *(the mind);* **6** *(of a speaker)* to dwell on; **in ōre vulgī versārī** to be constantly on people's lips

versōri·a -ae *f (naut)* rope used to set sail at an angle in order to tack

versum *adv* (vor-) *(usu. after another adv of direction)* back; **rūsum versum** backward; **sūrsum versum** up and down

versūr·a -ae *f* (vor-) rotation; loan *(of money to pay another debt);* **versūram facere** *(w. ab)* to get a loan from *(s.o. to pay another);* **versūrā solvere** to pay off *(another debt)* with borrowed money

versus *or* **versum** *adv* (vor-) *(w. ad)* toward, in the direction of; *(w. in + acc)* into, in toward; **sī in urbem versus ventūrī erunt** if they intend to come into the city; **sūrsum versus** upwards

versus *pp of* **verrō** *and* **vertō**

vers·us -ūs *m* (vor-) turning; furrow; line, row; turn, step *(in a dance); (in prose and poetry)* line, verse

versūtē *adv* (vor-) cunningly

versūti·ae -ārum *fpl* cunning, tricks

versūtiloqu·us -a -um *adj* smooth-talking, sly

versūt·us -a -um *adj* (vors-) clever, shrewd, ingenious; sly, cunning, deceitful

vert·ex -icis *m* (vor-) whirlpool, eddy, strong current; whirlwind, tornado; crown *or* top of the head; head; top, summit *(of mountain);* pole *(of the heavens);* **ex vertice** from above

verticōs·us -a -um *adj* swirling, full of whirlpools

vertīg·ō -inis *f* turning, whirling; dizziness

vert·ō -ere -ī versus *tr* **(vor-)** to turn, turn around, spin; to reverse; to invert, tilt; to change, alter, transform; to turn over, plow; to overturn, knock down; to destroy; to subvert, ruin; to ascribe, impute; to translate; *(w. ab)* to deflect from **‖** *refl* to turn; *(w. in + acc)* to change into **‖** *pass* to turn; *(w. in + acc)* to turn into; *(w. in + abl)* **1** to be in *(a place or condition);* **2** to be engaged in, be involved in **‖** *intr* to turn; to change; to turn out; *(w. in + abl)* to center on, depend upon

vertrag·us -ī *m* Gallic greyhound

Vertumn·us -ī *m* **(Vor-)** god of the changing seasons

ver·ū -ūs *n* spit *(for roasting);* javelin, dart

veruīn·a -ae *f* spit; small javelin

vērum *adv* truly; yes; *(in responses)* true but, yes but; but in fact; but yet, but even; yet, still; **nōn sōlum** *(or* **modo** *or* **tantum)** . . . **vērum** *(usu. followed by* **et, etiam** *or* **quoque)** not only . . . but also

vērumtamen *adv* nevertheless

vēr·us -a -um *adj* true, actual, genuine, real; fair, reasonable **‖** *n* truth, reality; honor, duty, right; **vērī similis** probable, likely; realistic; **vērī similitūdō** probability, likelihood

verūt·um -ī *n* dart, javelin

verūt·us -a -um *adj* armed with a javelin *or* dart

verv·ēx -ēcis *m* wether, castrated hog; *(term of abuse)* muttonhead

vēsāni·a -ae *f* **(vae-)** insanity, madness

vēsāni·ēns -entis *adj* raging

vēsān·us -a -um *adj* **(vae-)** insane; furious, savage, raging

vēsc·or -ī *intr (w. abl)* to feed on, eat; to feast on, enjoy

vēsc·us -a -um *adj* nibbled off; little, feeble; corroding, consuming

Veser·is -is *m* stream in Campania where Publius Decius Mus and Titus Manius Torquatus defeated the Latins in 340 B.C.

vēsīc·a -ae *f* bladder; bombast; objects made of bladder: purse, cap, football, lantern

vēsīcul·a -ae *f* little bladder; little bag

vesp·a -ae *f* wasp

Vespāsiān·us -ī *m* Vespasian *(Titus Flavius Vespasianus Sabinus, Roman Emperor,* A.D. *70–79)*

Vespāsi·us -a -um *adj* Roman clan name *(nomen), esp.* Vespasia Polla *(mother of Emperor Vespasian)*

vesp·er -erī *or* **-eris** *(acc usu.* **vesperum)** *m* evening; supper; the West; **ad vesperum** toward evening; **prīmō vespere** early in the evening; **sub vespere** toward evening; **tam vesperī** so late in the evening; **vespere** *or* **vesperī** in the evening

vesper·a -ae *f* evening; **prīma vespera** twilight; **prīmā vesperā** at twilight, at dusk

vesper·āscō -āscere -āvī *intr* to grow toward evening; **vesperāscente diē** as the day was getting late **‖** *v impers* evening is coming

vespertili·ō -ōnis *m* bat

vespertīn·us -a -um *adj* evening, in the evening; western

vesperūg·ō -inis *f* evening star

vespill·ō -ōnis *m* mortician

Vest·a -ae *f* Roman goddess of the hearth

Vestāl·is -is -e *adj* Vestal, of Vesta; **virgō Vestālis** Vestal virgin

ves·ter -tra -trum *adj* **(vos-)** your *(pl);* **‖** *pron* yours; **vestrī** your friends, your relatives, your soldiers, your school, your party; **vestrum est** *(w. inf)* it is up to you to; **voster** your master

vēstibul·um -ī *n* entrance, forecourt; beginning

vestīg·ium -(i)ī *n* footstep, step; footprint; track; trace, vestige; moment, instant

vestīg·ō -āre *tr* to track, trace; to check, find out

vestīment·um -ī *n* clothing; garment; blanket

Vestīn·us -a -um *adj* of the Vestini **‖** *mpl* the Vestini *(Oscan-speaking tribe of the central Apennines)*

vest·iō -īre -īvī *or* **-iī -ītus** *tr* to dress, clothe; to adorn, array, attire; *(fig)* to dress, clothe

vestiplic·a -ae *f* laundress, folder *(employed in ironing and folding clothes)*

vest·is -is *f* garment, dress; clothing; coverlet; tapestry; blanket; slough, skin *(of a snake);* **vestem mūtāre** to change one's clothes; to put on mourning clothes; **vestis longa** full dress including the full-length stola

vestispic·a -ae *f* female servant in charge of clothes

vestīt·us -ūs *m* clothing, clothes, dress, apparel; ornament *(of speech);* **mūtāre vestītum** to put on mourning clothes; **redīre ad suum vestītum** to end the mourning period

Vesuvi·us -a -um *adj* of Mt. Vesuvius; **mōns Vesuvius** Mt. Vesuvius

veter·a -um *npl* tradition, antiquity

veterāmentāri·us -a -um *adj* dealing in second-hand clothes

veterān·us -a -um *adj* & *m* veteran

veter·āscō -āscere -āvī *intr* to grow old

veterāt·or -ōris *m* old hand, expert; sly old fox

veterātōriē *adv* cunningly, slyly

veterātōri·us -a -um *adj* cunning

veter·ēs -um *mpl* the ancients; ancient authors

veterīn·us -a -um *adj* of burden **‖** *fpl* & *npl* beasts of burden

veternōs·us -a -um *adj* lethargic; sleepy, drowsy

vetern·us -ī *m* lethargy; old age; drowsiness; listlessness *(of old age)* vetit·um -ī *n* prohibition

vetitus *pp of* vetō

vet·ō -āre -uī -itus *tr* (vot-) to forbid, prohibit, oppose; to veto; *(w. inf, w.* nē, quōminus) to prevent from; *(w. inf, w. acc & inf, w.* nē, *w.* quīn) to forbid *(s.o. to do s.th.)*

vetul·us -a -um *adj* poor old

vet·us -eris *adj* old, aged; long-standing ‖ *mpl see* veterēs ‖ *npl see* vetera

vetust·ās -ātis *f* age; ancient times, antiquity; long duration, great age

vetust·us -a -um *adj* old, ancient; old-time, old-fashioned, good old *(days, etc.);* antiquated

vexām·en -inis *n* shaking, quaking

vexāti·ō -ōnis *f* shaking, jolting, tossing; distress

vexāt·or -ōris *m* jostler; harasser; troublemaker

vexī *perf of* vehō

vexillār·ius -(i)ī *m* standard-bearer ‖ *mpl* special reserves

vexillāti·ō -ōnis *f* (mil) detachment

vexill·um -ī *n* standard, flag, banner *(esp. the red flag hoisted above the general's tent as the signal for battle);* replica of the military banner, awarded for distinguished service; detachment of troops; vexillum praepōnere to hoist the red flag *(as the signal for battle)*

vex·ō -āre *tr* to shake, toss; to vex, annoy; to harass *(troops)*

vi·a -ae *f* way, road, street, highway; march, journey; method; right way, right method; path *(of an arrow);* inter viās on the road; in viā *(frontage)* on the road; sēsē in viam dare to hit the road, get on one's way; trīduī via a three-days' march; viam mūnīre to build a road; *(fig)* to pave the way; isle *(in the theater);* viā rēctā by a direct route; via vītae pathway of life

viāl·is -is -e *adj* of the highway

viāri·us -a -um *adj* for highway maintenance

viāticāt·us -a -um *adj* provided with traveling money

viātic·us -a -um *adj* for the trip, for traveling, travel ‖ *n* travel allowance, provisions for the journey; *(mil)* soldier's saving fund

viāt·or -ōris *m* traveler; passenger; attendant *(of a magistrate); (leg)* bailiff

vīb·ix -īcis *f* welt *(from a blow)*

vibr·ō -āre *tr* to brandish, wave around; to hurl ‖ *intr* to vibrate, quiver; *(of the tongue)* to flick

vīburn·um -ī *n (bot)* viburnum *(ornamental shrub, the bark of which was used in medicine)*

Vic·a Pot·a *(gen:* Vic·ae Pot·ae) *f* a goddess of victory

vīcān·us -a -um *adj* village ‖ *mpl* villagers

vicāri·us -a -um *adj* substitute ‖ *m* substitute, deputy, proxy; under-slave *(kept by another slave)*

vīcātim *adv* from street to street; from village to village; in hamlets

vice *prep (w. gen)* on account of; like, after the manner of

vicem *adv* in turn ‖ *prep (w. gen)* instead of, in place of; on account of; like, after the manner of

vīcēnāri·us -a -um *adj* of the number twenty

vīcēn·ī -ae -a *adj* twenty each, twenty apiece, twenty at a time, twenty in a group

vīcēsimān·ī -ōrum *mpl* soldiers of the twentieth legion

vīcēsimāri·us -a -um *adj* derived from the 5% tax

vīcēsim·us -a -um *adj* (vīcēns-) twentieth ‖ *f* 5% tax

vīcess·is -is *m* copper coin, worth about twenty cents

vici·a -ae *f* vetch *(grown for its edible seeds and used as fodder for animals)*

vīciē(n)s *adv* twenty times

vīcināl·is -is -e *adj* neighboring, nearby

vīcīni·a -ae *f* neighborhood; nearness, proximity

vīcīnit·ās -ātis *f* neighborhood, proximity; the neighborhood *(i. e., the neighbors)*

vīcīn·us -a -um *adj* neighboring, nearby, near; imminent ‖ *mf* neighbor ‖ *n* neighborhood; ex vīcīnō of a similar nature; in vīcīnō in close proximity

vicis *(gen; the nom singl and gen pl do not occur; acc singl:* vicem; *abl singl:* vice) *f* change, interchange, alternation; succession; exchange; interaction; return, recompense, retaliation; fortune, misfortune, condition, fate; plight, lot; changes of fate; duty, office, position; function, capacity, office; ad vicem *(w. gen)* after the manner of; in vicem *(or in* vicēs *or per* vicēs) in turn, alternately; in vicem *(or* invicem) *(w. gen)* instead of, in place of; legendī vicem suscipere to take one's turn in reading; vice in return; vice *(w. gen) or* vicem *(w. gen)* in place of, as a substitute for; vice versā *(or* vicibus versīs) vice-versa, conversely; vicibus in return

vicissim *or* vicissātim *adv* in turn, again

vicissitūd·ō -inis *f* change, interchange; regular succession, alternation; reversal, vicissitude; reciprocation

victim·a -ae *f* (-tum-) victim; sacrifice

victimār·ius -(i)ī *m* (-tum-) assistant at sacrifices

victit·ō -āre -āvī -ātum *intr* to live, subsist; *(w. abl)* to live on, subsist on

vict·or -ōris *m* victor; *(in apposition)* victor exercitus victorious army

victōri·a -ae *f* victory; **victōriam ferre** *or* **parere** *or* **reportāre dē** *or* **ex** to win a victory over

victōriāt·us -ī *m* victory coin *(of silver, stamped with the image of victory)*

Victōriol·a -ae *f* figurine of Victory

victr·īx -īcis *adj (fem & neut only)* victorious, triumphant

victus *pp of* vincō

vict·us -ūs *or* -ī *m* living, means of livelihood; way of life; food, sustenance

vīcul·us -ī *m* hamlet

vīc·us -ī *m* village, hamlet; ward, quarter *(in a city);* street, block

vidēlicet *adv* clearly, evidently; *(in irony)* of course, naturally; *(in explanations)* namely

vidēn = vidēsne? do you see?, do you get it?

videō vidēre vīdī vīsus *tr* to see, look at; to know; to consider; to understand, realize; *(w. ut)* to see to it that, take care that ‖ *pass* to seem, appear ‖ *v impers pass* it seems right, it seems good; **dīs vīsum est** the gods decided *(literally, it seemed (right) to the gods)*

vidu·a -ae *f* widow; spinster

viduit·ās -ātis *f* bereavement; want, lack; widowhood

vīdul·us -ī *m* leather travel bag, suitcase, knapsack

vidu·ō -āre -āvī -ātus *tr* to deprive, bereave; *(w. gen or abl)* to deprive of; **viduāta** left a widow

vidu·us -a -um *adj* bereft, destitute; unmarried; *(w. abl or* **ab***)* bereft of, destitute of, without ‖ *f see* vidua

Vienn·a -ae *f* chief city of the Allobroges in Gallia Narbonensis *(modern Vienne)*

viēt·or -ōris *m* cooper

viēt·us -a -um *adj* shriveled

vig·eō -ēre -uī *intr* to thrive, be vigorous, flourish

vig·ēscō -ēscere -uī *intr* to become vigorous, gain strength, become lively

vīgēsim·us -a -um *adj* twentieth

vig·il -ilis *adj* awake, wakeful; alert, on one's toes ‖ *m* watchman, guard, sentinel; fireman, policeman

vigil·āns -antis *adj* watchful, alert; disquieting *(worries)*

vigilanter *adv* vigilantly, alertly

vigilanti·a -ae *f* wakefulness; vigilance, alertness

vigil·āx -ācis *adj* alert; disquieting, sleep-disturbing *(worries)*

vigili·a -ae *f* wakefulness, sleeplessness, insomnia; vigil; vigilance, alertness; watch *(one of the four divisions of the night for keeping watch); (mil)* standing guard; *(mil)* guards, sentinels; **vigiliās agere** *(or* **agitāre** *or* **servāre)** to keep watch

vigil·ō -āre -āvī -ātus *tr* to spend *(the night)* awake; to make, do, perform, write *(s.th.)* while awake at night ‖ *intr* to stay awake; to be watchful; to be alert; *(w. dat)* to be attentive to

vīgintī *indecl adj* twenty

vīgintī·vir -virī *m* member of a board of twenty *(appointed by Caesar in 59 B.C. to distribute parcels of land in Campania)* ‖ member of a board of twenty in municipal administration

vīgintīvirāt·us -ūs *m* membership on the board of twenty

vig·or -ōris *m* vigor, liveliness

vīlic·a -ae *f* (vill-) foreman's wife, manager's wife

vīlic·ō -āre -āvī -ātum *intr* (vill-) to be a foreman, be a manager *(of an estate);* to be an overseer *(in the state)*

vīlic·us -ī *m* (vill-) foreman, manager *(of an estate)*

vīl·is -is -e *adj* cheap, inexpensive; common, worthless, contemptible; **vīlī** at a cheap price, cheaply

vīlit·ās -ātis *f* lowness of price, cheapness, low price; worthlessness

vīliter *adv* cheaply, at a low price

vīll·a -ae *f* country home; farmhouse; **vīlla rūstica** farmhouse, homestead; **vīlla urbāna** *(also in the country, with no farm attached)* country villa

vīllic- = vīlic-

vīllōs·us -a -um *adj* hairy, shaggy, bushy

vīllul·a -ae *f* small farmhouse; small villa

vīll·um -ī *n* drop of wine

vīll·us -ī *m* hair; fleece; nap *(of cloth)*

vīm·en -inis *n* osier; basket

vīment·um -ī *n* osier

Vīmināl·is -is -e *adj* Viminal; **Vīminālis Collis** Viminal Hill *(one of the seven hills of Rome)*

vīmine·us -a -um *adj* made of osiers

vīn *or* vīn' = vīsne? do you wish?, ya' wanna? *(fam)*

vīnāce·us -a -um *adj* grape, of grape ‖ *n* grape seed

Vīnāl·ia -ium *npl* wine festival; **Vīnālia priōra** earlier wine festival *(celebrated on April 23, when libations of wine from the previous year were poured to Jupiter);* **Vīnālia rūstica** country wine festival *(celebrated on August 19 and 20 in honor of Jupiter in thanksgiving for the successful harvest)*

vīnāri·us -a -um *adj* wine ‖ *m* wine dealer; vintner ‖ *npl* wine flasks

vincibil·is -is -e *adj* easily won

vinciō vincīre vīnxī vīnctus *tr* to bind, tie; to wrap; to encircle, surround; to restrain; *(med)* to bandage; *(med)* to ligature; *(rhet)* to link together, arrange rhythmically

vinc·ō vincere vīcī victus *tr* to conquer; to get the better of, beat, defeat; to outdo; to convince, refute, persuade; to prove, demonstrate; to outlast, outlive **‖** *intr* to win, be victorious; to prevail; to succeed

vīnct·us -a -um *pp of* **vinciō ‖** *adj* fettered, in bonds

vincul·um *or* **vincl·um -ī** *n* chain; fetter, cord, band; sandal strap; thong, rope; mooring cable; tether **‖** *npl* bonds, fetters; imprisonment; prison; **vincula pūblica** chains worn by a state prisoner; **aliquem in vincula conicere** to put s.o. in chains

Vindelic·us -a -um *adj* of the Vindelici **‖** *mpl* people living between the Rhaetian Alps and the Danube

vīndēmi·a -ae *f* vintage

vīndēmiāt·or -ōris *m* grape picker

vīndēmiol·a -ae *f* small vintage; minor sources of income

Vindēmit·or -ōris *m (astr)* a star in Virgo

vind·ex -icis *adj* avenging **‖** *m (leg)* claimant; defender, protector, champion; liberator; avenger, punisher

Vind·ex -icis *m* Roman family name *(cognomen), esp.* Gaius Julius Vindex *(leader of a rebellion in Gaul against Nero in* A.D. *69)*

vindicāti·ō -ōnis *f* avenging, punishment; *(leg)* claim

vindici·ae -ārum *fpl* legal claim; things *or* persons claimed; championship, protection; **vindiciās dare** *(or* **dīcere** *or* **dēcernere)** to hand over the things *or* persons claimed

vindic·ō -āre -āvī -ātus *tr* to lay legal claim to; to protect, defend; to appropriate; to demand; to demand unfairly; to claim as one's own; to avenge, punish; **in lībertātem vindicāre** to set free, liberate *(literally, to claim for freedom)*

vindict·a -ae *f* rod used in the ceremony of setting slaves free; defense, protection; vengeance, revenge, satisfaction

vīne·a *or* **vīni·a -ae** *f* vineyard; vine; *(mil)* shed *(used to defend besiegers against enemy missiles)*

vīnēt·um -ī *n* vineyard

vīnipoll·ēns -entis *adj* powerful through wine

vīnit·or -ōris *m* vine dresser

vinnul·us -a -um *adj* charming

vīnolenti·a -ae *f* **(vīnul-)** wine drinking, intoxication

vīnolent·us -a -um *adj* **(vīnul-)** drunk

vīnōs·us -a -um *adj* addicted to wine; tasting *or* smelling of wine

vīn·um -ī *n* wine

viol·a -ae *f* violet *(flower; color; dye)*

violābil·is -is -e *adj* vulnerable

violār·ium -(i)ī *n* bed of violets

violār·ius -(i)ī *m* dyer of violet

violāti·ō -ōnis *f* violation, profanation

violāt·or -ōris *m* violator, profaner

viol·ēns -entis *adj* violent, raging

violenter *adv* violently, vehemently

violenti·a -ae *f* violence

violent·us -a -um *adj* violent

viol·ō -āre -āvī -ātus *tr* to violate; to outrage, harm by violence

vīper·a -ae *f* viper; *(poisonous)* snake

vīpere·us -a -um *adj* viper's; snake's

vīperīn·us -a -um *adj* viper's, snake's

Vipsāni·us -a -um *adj* Roman clan name *(nomen);* **porticus Vipsānia** Vipsanian portico *(forming part of the Pantheon built by Agrippa in the Campus Martius)* **‖** Agrippa *(Marcus Vipsanius Agrippa, Augustus' friend and successful admiral)* **‖** *f* Vipsania *(esp. Vipsania Agrippina, daughter of Agrippa and the first wife of Emperor Tiberius)*

vir virī *m* man; he-man, hero; husband; lover; manhood, virility; *(mil)* infantryman

virāg·ō -inis *f* female warrior; heroine

Virb·ius -(i)ī *m* local deity, the reincarnation of Hippolytus, worshipped with Diana at Aricia **‖** son of Hippolytus

virēct·um -ī stretch of green

vir·eō -ēre -uī *intr* to be green; to be fresh, be vigorous, flourish

vīrēs = *pl of* **vīs**

vir·ēscō -ēscere -uī *intr* to turn green

virg·a -ae *f* twig, sprout; graft; rod, switch *(for flogging);* wand; walking stick, cane; colored stripe in a garment; branch of a family tree

virgāt·or -ōris *m* flogger

virgāt·us -a -um *adj* made of twigs *or* osiers; striped

virgēt·um -ī *n* osier thicket

virge·us -a -um *adj* of twigs, of kindling wood

virgi(n)dēmi·a -ae *f (hum)* harvest of birch rods *(i.e., a sound flogging)*

virgināl·is -is -e *adj* maiden's, girl's, girlish **‖** *n* female genitals

virgināri·us -a -um *adj* girl's

virgine·us *or* **virgini·us -a -um** *adj* virgin, of *or* for a virgin; proper to a virgin; of virgins

virginit·ās -ātis *f* girlhood; virginity

virg·ō -inis *f (marriageable)* girl, maiden; virgin **‖** **Virgō** Virgo *(constellation; aqueduct constructed by Marcus Vipsanius Agrippa)*

virgul·a -ae *f* little twig; wand; **virgula dīvīna** divining rod

virgult·um -ī *n* thicket; shrub **‖** *npl* brushwood; firewood; slips *(of trees)*

virgult·us -a -um *adj* covered with brushwood

virguncul·a -ae *f* lass, young girl

Vir(i)domar·us -ī *m* Insubrian leader killed in battle by Marcus Claudius Marcellus, 222 B.C., who thereby won the *spolia opima*
Viriāt(h)·us -ī *m* Lusitanian who led a guerrilla war against Rome *(147–140 B.C.)*
virid·āns -antis *adj* turning green; green
viridār·ium -(i)ī *n* garden
virid·is -is -e *adj* green; fresh, young ‖ *npl* greenery
viridit·ās -ātis *f* greenness; freshness
virid·ō -āre *tr* to make green ‖ *intr* to turn green
virīl·is -is -e *adj* male, masculine; adult; manly; *(gram)* masculine; **pars virīlis** male sexual organ; **prō virīlī partc** *(or* **portiōne)** to the best of one's ability ‖ *npl* manly *or* heroic deeds; male sexual organs
virīlit·ās -ātis *f* manhood, virility
virīliter *adv* manfully, like a man
virīpot·ēns -entis *adj* almighty
virītim *adv* man by man; per man; individually
virōs·us -a -um *adj* slimy; strong-smelling, fetid, stinking
virt·ūs -ūtis *f* manliness, manhood, virility; strength; valor, gallantry; excellence, worth; special property; moral excellence, goodness, virtue; good quality, high quality *(of persons, animals, things);* potency, effectiveness *(of drugs, medications);* **virtūte** *(w. gen)* through the good services of, thanks to ‖ *fpl* achievements; gallant deeds
vīr·us -ī *n* venom; slime; stench, pungency; saltiness
vīs *(gen not in use; dat & abl:* **vī;** *acc:* **vim;** *pl:* **vīr·ēs -ium)** *f* power, strength, force; influence; energy; hostile force, violence, attack; amount, quantity; meaning, force *(of words);* binding force *(of a law);* value, amount; **magna vīs** *(w. gen)* a large number of, a large amount of; **omnis vīs** *(w. gen)* the whole range of, the sum total of; **per vim** forcibly; **suā vī** in itself, intrinsically; **summā vī** with utmost energy; **vī** by force; **vim adferre** *(w. dat)* **1** to do violence to; **2** to rape; **3** to kill; **vim adferre sibī** *(or* **vītae suae)** to take one's own life; **vim facere** to make an assault; **vim habēre** *(w. gen)* to be equivalent *(in amount)* to ‖ **vīrēs** *fpl* strength; resources; potency, power *(of herbs, drugs);* *(mil)* military strength, fighting power; control, influence; financial resources, assets; powers of intellect, capability; meaning *(of words);* value, amount; **prō vīribus** with all one's might
viscāt·us -a -um *adj* smeared with birdlime
viscer·a -um *npl* fleshy parts of the body *(as distinct from skin and bones);* viscera, internal organs; womb; heart, vitals, bowels; *(fig)* innermost part, bowels, heart; center *(esp. of*

the earth); *(fig)* bosom friend, favorite; *(fig)* person's flesh and blood *(family, offspring)*
viscerāti·ō -ōnis *f* public distribution of meat
visc·ō -āre -āvī -ātus *tr* to catch in birdlime
visc·um -ī *n or* visc·us -ī *m* mistletoe; birdlime
visc·us -eris *n (anat)* organ; entrails ‖ *npl see* viscera
vīsend·us -a -um *adj* worth going to see, worth visiting ‖ *npl* the sights
vīsī *perf of* vīsō
vīsi·ō -ōnis *f* appearance, apparition; notion, idea
vīsit·ō -āre -āvī -ātus *tr* to keep seeing; to visit, go to visit
vīs·ō -ere -ī *tr* to look at with attention, view; to come *or* go to look at; to find out; to go and see, visit; to look in on *(the sick)* ‖ *intr* to go and look; *(w. ad)* to go to visit, call on *(esp. an invalid)*
vispillō *see* vespillō
viss·iō -īre *intr (sl)* to fart softly
vīs·um -ī *n* sight, appearance
Visurg·is -is *m* river in N. Germany *(modern Weser)*
vīsus *pp of* videō
vīs·us -ūs *m* (faculty of) sight; thing seen, sight, vision
vīt·a -ae *f* life; way of life; means of living, livelihood; manner of life; course of life, career; biography
vītābil·is -is -e *adj* undesirable, deserving to be shunned
vītābund·us -a -um *adj* taking evasive action
vītāl·is -is -e *adj* of life, vital; life-giving; likely to live, staying alive; able to survive; living, alive ‖ *npl (anat)* vital parts
vītāliter *adv* vitally
vītāti·ō -ōnis *f* avoidance
Vitell·ius -(i)ī *m* Vitellius *(Aulus Vitellius, Roman Emperor, from January 2 to December 22, A.D. 69)*
vitell·us -ī *m* little calf; yolk *(of egg)*
vīte·us -a -um *adj* of the vine
vīticul·a -ae *f* little vine
vītif·er -era -erum *adj* producing vines, vine-producing
vītigen·us -a -um *adj* produced from the vine
viti·ō -āre -āvī -ātus *tr* to spoil, corrupt, violate, mar; to falsify
vitiōsē *adv* faultily, badly, corruptly; **vitiōsē sē habēre** to be defective
vitiōsit·ās -ātis *f* corrupt *or* bad condition
vitiōs·us -a -um *adj* faulty, defective; (morally) corrupt, bad, depraved
vīt·is -is *f* vine; vine branch; centurion's staff; centurionship
vītisāt·or -ōris *m* vine planter
vit·ium -(i)ī *n* fault, flaw; defect, disorder; sin, offense, vice; flaw in the auspices; injurious

quality, disadvantage; augural impediment, unfavorable augury; *(leg)* legal defect, technicality; *(med)* lesion; **in vitiō esse** to be in a defective state, be defective; **meō vitiō pereō** I am ruined through my own fault; **vitiō** *(w. gen)* through the fault of; **vitiō dare** *(or* **vertere)** to regard as a fault; **vitium capere** *(or* **facere)** to develop a defect; **vitium dīcere** *(w. dat)* to insult s.o.

vīt·ō -āre -āvī -ātus *tr* to avoid, evade

vīt·or -ōris *m* basket-maker

vitre·us -a -um *adj* glass, of glass; glassy **‖** *npl* glassware

vītric·us -ī *m* stepfather

vitr·um -ī *n* glass; blue dye

vitt·a -ae *f* headband, fillet

vittāt·us -a -um *adj* wearing a fillet

vitul·a -ae *f* heifer

vitulīn·us -a -um *adj & f* veal

vītul·or -ārī *intr* to celebrate a festival; to be thankful and joyful; to shout for joy

vitul·us -ī *m* calf, young bull; foal; seal

vituperābil·is -is -e *adj* blameworthy

vituperāti·ō -ōnis *f* blaming, censuring; blame; scandalous conduct, blameworthiness

vituperāt·or -ōris *m* censurer

vituper·ō -āre -āvī -ātus *tr* to criticize, find fault with; to declare *(an omen)* invalid

vīvācit·ās -ātis *f* will to live; life-force; vitality

vīvār·ium -(i)ī *n* game preserve, zoo; fish pond

vīvāt·us -a -um *adj* animated, lively

vīv·āx -ācis *adj* long-lived; long-lasting, enduring; quick to learn

vīvē *adv* in a lively manner

vīverād·īx -īcis *f* rooted cutting *(i.e., having roots)*

vīvēscō *or* **vīvīscō vīvēscere** *intr* to become alive, come to life; to grow lively, get full of life

vīvid·us -a -um *adj* teeming with life, full of life; true to life, vivid, realistic; quick, lively *(mind);* vivid *(expression)*

vīvirād·īx -īcis *f see* **vīverādīx**

vīvīscō *see* **vīvēscō**

vīvō vīvere vixī victum *intr* to be alive, live; to be still alive, survive; to reside; *(w. abl or* **dē** *+ abl)* to live on, subsist on

vīv·us -a -um *adj* alive, living; lively; fresh; natural *(rock);* speaking *(voice);* **argentum vīvum** quicksilver; **calx vīva** lime; **mē vīvō** as long as I am alive **‖** *n (com)* capital; **ad vīvum resecāre** to cut to the quick

vix *adv* scarcely; hardly, with difficulty, barely

vixdum *adv* hardly then, scarcely yet

vocābul·um -ī *n* word, term; name, designation; noun; common noun

vōcāl·is -is -e *adj* having a voice, gifted with speech, speaking; gifted with song, singing; tuneful **‖** *f (gram)* vowel

vocām·en -inis *f* name, designation

vocāti·ō -ōnis *f* invitation *(to dinner); (leg)* summons

vocāt·or -ōris *m* inviter, host

vocāt·us -ūs *m* summons, call

vōciferāti·ō -ōnis *f* loud cry, yell

vōcifer·ō -āre *or* **vōcifer·or -ārī -ātus sum** *tr & intr* to shout, yell

vocit·ō -āre -āvī -ātus *tr* to call habitually, keep calling, usually call, name; to shout out again and again

voc·ō -āre -āvī -ātus *tr* to call, name; to summon; to call upon, invoke *(the gods);* to invite *(to dinner); (w. double acc)* to call *(s.o. s.th.);* to call for, require; *(w.* **dē** *+ abl)* to name *(s.o., s.th.)* after; *(mil)* to challenge; **ad sē vocāre** to summon; **aliquem ex iūre manum cōnsertum vocāre** *(leg)* to call out of court to settle the issue by physical combat; **in arma vocāre** to call to arms; **in dubium vocāre** to call into question; **in iūs vocāre** to summon to court; **in odium vocāre** to bring into disfavor; **in perīculum vocāre** to lead into danger

vōcul·a -ae *f* weak voice; soft note, soft tone; whisper, gossip

volaem·um -ī *n* (volē-) type of large pear

Volāterr·ae -ārum *fpl* old Etruscan hill town *(modern Volterra)*

Volāterrān·us -a -um *adj* of Volaterrae

volātic·us -a -um *adj* flying, winged; transitory, passing; inconstant

volātil·is -is -e *adj* able to fly; rapid; transitory

volāt·us -ūs *m* flight

Volcānāl·ia -ium *npl* (**Vulc-**) festival of Vulcan *(August 23)*

Volcāni·us -a -um *adj* (**Vulc-**) of Vulcan; **aciēs Vulcānia** Vulcan's battleline *(i.e., fire spreading in a line);* **arma Vulcānia** arms made by Vulcan *(for Achilles)*

Volcān·us -ī *m* (**Vul-**) Vulcan *(god of fire, son of Jupiter)*

vol·ēns -entis *adj* willing; permitting; ready; favorable **‖** *m* well-wisher

Voles·us -ī *m* Roman family name *(nomen),* esp. the father of Publius Valerius Publicola

volg- = vulg-

volit·āns -antis *m* winged insect

volit·ō -āre -āvī -ātum *intr* to flit about, fly about, flutter; to move quickly; to hover, soar

vol·ō -āre -āvī -ātum *intr* to fly

volō velle voluī *tr* to wish, want; to propose, determine; to hold, maintain; to mean; to prefer **‖** *intr* to be willing

Vologēs·us -ī *m* name of several Arsacid kings of Parthia

volōn·ēs -um *mpl* volunteers *(slaves who enlisted after the battle of Cannae, 216 B.C.)*

volpēs *see* **vulpēs**

Volsc·us -a -um *adj* Vulscan ‖ *mpl* Volscians *(ancient people in S. Latium, subjugated by the Romans in 5th & 4th cent. B.C.)*
volsell·a -ae *f* tweezers
Volsini·ī -ōrum *mpl* Etruscan city
volsus *pp of* **vellō**
volt = *older form of* **vult** he *(or* she *or* it) wishes
voltis = *older form of* **vultis** you wish
Voltumn·a -ae *f* Etruscan goddess in whose temple the twelve Etruscan states met
Volt·ur -uris *m* (**Vul-**) mountain of Apulia near the border of Samnium
Volturn·um -ī *n* town at the mouth of the Volturnus river ‖ old name of Capua
Volturn·us -ī *m* river flowing from the Apennines to the coast of Campania ‖ name for a S.E. wind
voltus *see* **vultus**
volūbil·is -is -e *adj* turning, spinning, revolving, swirling; voluble, rapid, fluent; changeable
volūbilit·ās -ātis *f* whirling motion; roundness; volubility; fluency; mutability
volūbiliter *adv* rapidly; fluently
volu·cer -cris -cre *adj* flying, winged; rapid, speedy
volu·cer -cris *m* bird
volucr·is -is *f* bird; fly. insect; **volucris Iūnōnis** the bird of Juno *(i.e., a peacock)*
voluī *perf of* **volō**
volūm·en -inis *n* roll, book; chapter; whirl, eddy; coil; fold
Volumni·us -a -um *adj* Roman clan name *(nomen)*
voluntāri·us -a -um *adj* voluntary ‖ *mpl* volunteers
volunt·ās -ātis *f* will, wish, desire, purpose, aim, intention; inclination; goodwill, sympathy; willingness, approval; choice, option; last will and testament; attitude *(good or bad);* meaning *(of words);* **ad voluntātem** *(w. gen)* according to the wishes of; **dē** *(or* **ex**) **voluntāte** *(w. gen)* at the desire of; **voluntāte** *(w. gen)* with the consent of
volup *adv* to one's satisfaction, with pleasure; **volup esse** to be a source of pleasure; **volup facere** *(w. dat)* to cause *(s.o.)* pleasure
voluptābil·is -is -e *adj* agreeable, pleasant
voluptāri·us -a -um *adj* pleasant, agreeable; voluptuous ‖ *m* voluptuary
volupt·ās -ātis *f* pleasure, enjoyment, delight ‖ *fpl* sensual pleasures; games, sports, public performances
voluptuōs·us -a -um *adj* pleasant, agreeable; giving pleasure
Volusi·us -a -um *adj* Roman clan name *(nomen), esp.* name of a Roman epic poet, mocked by Catullus

volūtābr·um -ī *n* wallow *(for swine)*
volūtābund·us -a -um *adj* wallowing about
volūtāti·ō -ōnis *f* rolling about, tossing about; wallowing; restlessness
volūt·ō -āre -āvī -ātus *tr* to roll about, turn over; to engross; to think over ‖ *pass* to wallow, luxuriate
volūtus *pp of* **volvō**
volva *see* **vulva**
vol·vō -vere -vī -ūtus *tr* to roll, turn about, wind; *(of a river)* to roll *(e.g., rocks)* along; to breathe; to unroll, read *(books, scrolls);* to pour out, utter fluently; to consider, weigh; *(of time)* to bring on, bring around; to form *(a circle);* to undergo *(troubles)* ‖ *pass* to roll, tumble; to revolve ‖ *intr* to revolve; to roll on, elapse
vōm·er *or* **vōm·is -eris** *m* plowshare; *(vulg)* penis
vomic·a -ae *f* sore, boil, abscess, ulcer; annoyance
vōmis *see* **vōmer**
vomiti·ō -ōnis *f* vomiting
vomit·ō -āre *intr* to vomit *(frequently)*
vomit·us -ūs *m* vomiting; vomit
vom·ō -ere -uī -itus *tr & intr* to vomit, throw up
vorāg·ō -inis *f* deep hole, abyss, chasm, depth
vor·āx -ācis *adj* swallowing, devouring; greedy, ravenous
vor·ō -āre -āvī -ātus *tr* to swallow, devour; *(fig)* to devour *(by reading)*
vors- = **vers-**
vort- = **vert-**
vōs *pron* you *(pl); (refl)* yourselves
vōsmet *pron (emphatic form of* **vōs**) you yourselves
voster *see* **vester**
vōtīv·us -a -um *adj* votive, promised in a vow
vot·ō -āre *see* **vetō**
vōt·um -ī *n* solemn vow *(made to a deity);* votive offering *(made for a prayer answered);* prayer, wish; thing wished for, wish; **compos vōtī** *(or* **vōtō**) **esse** to have had one's prayer answered; **in vōtō est** *(w. inf)* it is *(my)* wish to; **in vōtō est** *(w. ut + subj or w. acc & inf)* it is *(my)* wish that; **vōtī reus** obligated to fulfill a vow; **vōtō māior** surpassing one's fondest hopes; **vōtum est** *(w. inf)* it is *(my)* hope to; **vōtum est** *(w. ut + subj or w. acc & inf)* it is *(my)* hope that
voveō vovēre vōvī vōtus *tr* to vow, promise solemnly, pledge, devote *(to a deity);* to wish, wish for
vōx vōcis *f* voice; sound, tone, cry, call; word *(written or spoken);* utterance, saying, expression; proverb; language; accent
Vulcānus *see* **Volcānus**

vulgār·is -is -e *adj* **(vol-)** common, general, usual, everyday; low-class; unimportant, routine *(business)*; well-known, often repeated *(story)*

vulgāriter *adv* **(vol-)** in the usual way; commonly

vulgāt·or -ōris *m* **(vol-)** divulger

vulgāt·us -a -um *adj* **(vol-)** common, general; well-known; notorious

vulgivag·us -a -um *adj* roving; promiscuous

vulgō *adv* **(vol-)** generally, publicly, everywhere

vulg·ō -āre -āvī -ātus *tr* **(vol-)** to spread, publish, broadcast; to divulge; to prostitute; to level, make common

vulg·us -ī *n* **(vol-)** masses, public, people; crowd; herd, flock; rabble, populace; **in vulgus** *(or* **in vulgum)** to the general public, publicly

vulnerāti·ō -ōnis *f* **(vol-)** wounding, wound

vulner·ō -āre -āvī -ātus *tr* **(vol-)** to wound; to damage

vulnific·us -a -um *adj* inflicting wounds

vuln·us -eris *n* **(vol-)** wound; blow, stroke; blow, disaster

vulpēcul·a -ae *f* **(vol-)** little fox, sly little fox

vulp·ēs -is *f* **(vol-)** fox; craftiness, cunning

vuls·us *or* **vols·us -a -um** *pp of* **vellō** ‖ *adj* plucked, beardless, effeminate

vulticul·us -ī *m* **(vol-)** mere look

vult·um *see* **vultus**

vultuōs·us -a -um *adj* **(vol-)** full of airs, affected, stuck-up

vult·ur -uris *m* **(vol-)** vulture ‖ **Vultur** *m* mountain in Apulia

vulturīn·us -a -um *adj* **(vol-)** vulture-like, of a vulture

vultur·ius -(i)ī *m* **(vol-)** vulture

Vulturn·us -ī *m* **(Vol-)** principal river of Campania *(modern Volturno)*

vult·us -ūs *m* **(vol-)** face; looks, expression, features; look, appearance

vulv·a -ae *f* **(vol-)** wrapper, cover; womb; female genitalia, vulva; sow's womb *(as a delicacy)*

X

X, x *(supply* littera) *f* twenty-second letter of the Latin alphabet; letter name: **ix**

X = decem ten

Xanth·ō -ūs *f* a sea nymph *(daughter of Nereus and Doris)*

Xanthipp·e -ēs *f* wife of Socrates

Xanthipp·us -ī *m* father of Pericles ‖ Spartan commander of the Carthaginians in the First Punic War

Xanth·us -ī *m* river at Troy, identified with the Scamander River ‖ river and town of the same name in Lycia ‖ name applied by Vergil to a river in Epirus

xen·ium -iī *n* gift, present *(given by a guest to a host or by a host to a guest)*

Xenocrat·ēs -is *m* Greek philosopher, a disciple of Plato

Xenophan·ēs -is *m* early Greek philosopher from Colophon *(c. 565–470 B.C.)*

Xenoph·ōn -ontis *m* Greek historian and pupil of Socrates *(c. 430–354 B.C.)*

xērampelin·ae -ārum *fpl* reddish-purple clothes

Xerx·ēs -is *m* Persian king, defeated at Salamis *(c. 519–465 B.C.)*

xylospong·ium -(i)ī *n* a sponge attached to a stick, used in the same way as toilet paper is used today

xiphi·ās -ae *m* swordfish

xyst·us -ī *m or* **xyst·um -ī** *n* open colonnade *or* portico, walk, planted with trees and shrubs

Y

Y, y *(supply* littera) *f* twenty-third letter of the Latin alphabet; letter name: **ipsilon**

Y, y letter adopted from Greek into the Latin alphabet for the transliteration of words containing an upsilon *(for which u was used earlier),* and pronounced approximately as German ü. It appears to have been in use by the time of Cicero; but its use was restricted to foreign words.

Z

Z, z *(supply* littera) *f* twenty-fourth letter of the Latin alphabet; letter name: **zeta**

Zacynth·us *or* **Zacynth·os -ī** *f* island off W. Greece ‖ name for Saguntum, supposed to have been colonized by people from Zacynthus

Zaleuc·us -ī *m* traditional lawgiver of the Locrians

Zam·a -ae *f* town in Numidia where Scipio defeated Hannibal and brought the Second Punic War to an end *(202 B.C.)*

zāmi·a -ae *f* harm, damage, loss

Zanclae·us -a -um *adj* of Zancle

Zancl·ē -ēs *f* old name of Messina in N. Sicily
Zanclēi·us -a -um *adj* of Zancle
zēlotypi·a -ae jealousy
zēlotyp·us -a -um *f* jealous
Zēn·ō(n) -ōnis *m* Zeno the Stoic *(founder of Stoic philosophy and native of Citium in Cyprus, 335–263 B.C.)* ‖ Zeno *(Epicurean philosopher, the teacher of Cicero and Atticus, born c. 150 B.C.)*
Zephyr·us *or* **Zephyr·os -ī** *m* zephyr; west wind; wind
Zēt·ēs -ae *m* one of the two sons of Boreas *(Aquilo)*
Zēth·us *or* **Zēt·os -ī** *m* son of Jupiter and Antiope and brother of Amphion

Zeux·is -idis *m* Greek painter of Heraclea in Lucania *(fl c. 400 B.C.)*
zinzi·ō -āre *intr (of a blackbird)* to sing
zmaragd·us -ī *f (m)* emerald
zōdiac·us -a -um *adj* of the zodiac; **zōdiacus circulus** *(or* **orbis)** the zodiac ‖ *m* zodiac
Zōil·us -ī *m* a native of Amphipolis, proverbially stern critic of Homer, Plato, and others *(called Homeromastix = scourge of Homer)*
zōn·a -ae *f* belt, sash, girdle; money belt; zone, region; *(med)* shingles
zōnāri·us -a -um *adj* of a belt *or* girdle ‖ *m* belt maker, girdle maker
zōnul·a -ae *f* little belt *or* girdle
zōthēc·a -ae *f* niche, alcove
zōthēcul·a -ae *f* little alcove

A

a *indef article (when modifying a substantive, is unexpressed in Latin);* — **little carelessly** parum attente; — **little later** paulo post; **ten denari** — **pound** decem denari per libras; **twice** — **year** bis in anno
aback *adv* **taken** — attonit·us -a -um
abandon *tr* (de)relinquere
abandonment *s* derelicti·o -onis *f*
abashed *adj* erubesc·ens -entis
abate *tr (to lower)* imminuere; *(to slacken)* laxare; *(price)* remittere **II** *intr (to lessen)* imminuere; *(to decline)* decedere; *(of passion)* defervescere
abbey *s* abbati·a -ae *f*
abbot *s* abb·as -atis *m*
abbreviate *tr* breviare
abbreviation *s* not·a -ae *f*
ABC's *spl* primae litter·ae -arum *fpl;* **to know one's** — **litteras scire**
abdicate *tr* abdicare **II** *intr* se abdicare
abdication *s* abdicati·o -onis *f*
abdomen *s* abdom·en -inis *n*
abduct *tr* abducere; *(a girl)* rapere
abduction *s* rapt·us -ūs *m*
aberration *s (departure from right)* err·or -oris *m; (deviation from straight line)* declinati·o -onis *f*
abet *tr* adiuvare; **to** — **a crime** minister in maleficio esse
abeyance *s* **to be in** — iacēre
abhor *tr* abhorrēre ab *(w. abl)*
abhorrence *s* detestati·o -onis *f*
abhorrent *adj* **(to)** alien·us -a -um *(abl or* ab *w. abl)*
abide *intr* manēre; — **by** stare in *(w. abl)*
abiding *adj* mansur·us -a -um
ability *s (power)* potest·as -atis *f; (mental capacity)* ingen·ium -(i)i *n;* **ability to read and write** legendi scribendique facultas; **to the best of one's** — pro suā parte
abject *adj* abiect·us -a -um
abjectly *adv* abiecte, humiliter
ablative *s* ablativ·us -i *m; in the* — **case** casu ablativo
able *adj (having the power)* pot·ens -entis; *(having mental ability)* ingenios·us -a -um; **not** — **to fight** non pugnae potēns; **not to be** — **to** nequire *(w. inf);* **to be** — **to** posse *(w. inf)*
able-bodied *adj* valid·us -a -um
ablution *s* abluti·o -onis *f*
ably *adv* ingeniose
abnormal *adj* enorm·is -is -e

aboard *adv* in nave: **to go** — **a ship** navem conscendere
abode *s* domicil·ium -(i)i *n*
abolish *tr* tollere, abolēre
abolition *s* aboliti·o -onis *f*
abominable *adj* detestabil·is -is -e
abominably *adv* execrabiliter, odiose
abominate *tr* abominari, detestari
abomination *s* detestati·o -onis *f; (terrible crime)* flagit·ium -(i)i *n*
aborigines *spl* aborigin·es -um *mfpl*
abortion *s* abort·us -ūs *m;* **to perform an** — partum abigere
abortive *adj* abortiv·us -a -um; *(unsuccessful)* irrit·us -a -um
abound *intr* abundare, superesse; **to** — **in** abundare *(w. abl)*
abounding *adj* — **in** abund·ans -antis *(w. abl)*
about *adv (almost)* fere, ferme; *(approximately)* circa, circiter; **in** — **ten days** decem circiter diebus
about *prep (of place)* circa, circum *(w. acc); (of number)* circa, ad *(w. acc); (of time)* circa, sub *(w. acc); (concerning)* de *(w. abl)*
above *adv* supra, insuper; **to be** — *(e.g., bribery)* indignari *(w. acc);* **from** — desuper, superne
above *prep* supra, super *(w. acc);* — **all** ante omnia; — **all others** praeter omnes ceteros; **to be** — *(e.g., bribery)* indignari *(w. acc)*
abrasion *s* attrit·us -ūs *m*
abreast *adv* pariter; **to walk** — **of s.o.** latus alicui tegere
abridge *tr* breviare, contrahere; **to** — **a book** in compendium redigere
abridgment *s* epitom·e -es *f*
abroad *adv (in a foreign land)* peregre; *(of motion, out of doors)* foras; *(of rest, out of doors)* foris; **from** — extrinsec·us -a -um; *(w. verbs)* peregre; **to be** *or* go *or* live — peregrinari; **to get** — *(of news)* divulgari
abrogate *tr* abrogare, rescindere
abrupt *adj (sudden)* subit·us -a -um; *(rugged)* praerupt·us -a -um
abruptly *adv* subito, repente
abruptness *s* rapidit·as -atis *f*
abscess *s* vomic·a -ae *f*
absence *s* absenti·a -ae *f; in my* — me absente
absent *adj* abs·ens -entis; — **without leave** *(mil)* infrequ·ens -entis
absent *tr* **to** — **oneself** se removēre; *(not show up)* non comparēre
absentee *s* abs·ens -entis *mf*
absolute *adj* absolut·us -a -um, summ·us -a -um; *(unlimited)* īnfinit·us -a -um; — **power**

dominat·us -ūs *m*, tyrann·is -idis *f;* — **ruler** domin·us -i *m*, tyrann·us -i *m*

absolutely *adv (unconditionally)* praecise; *(completely)* utique, prorsus; — **nothing** nihil prorsus; **to rule — over** dominari *(w. in w. acc)*

absolution *s* absoluti·o -onis *f*

absolve *tr* veniam dare *(w. dat);* **to — from** absolvere ab *(w. abl)*

absorb *tr* absorbēre, (com)bibere; *(fig)* tenēre

absorbent *adj* bibul·us -a -um

abstain *intr* **(from)** se abstinēre *(w. abl)*

abstemious *adj* abstemi·us -a -um

abstinence *s* abstinenti·a -ae *f; (from food)* inedi·a -ae *f*

abstract *tr* **(from)** abstrahere (ab *w. abl); (an idea)* separare

abstract *s* compend·ium -(i)i *n;* **in the —** in abstracto

abstract *adj (idea)* mente percept·us -a -um; *(quantity)* abstract·us -a -um; — **noun** appellati·ō -ōnis *f*

abstraction *s* separati·o -onis *f; (idea)* noti·o -onis *f*

abstruse *adj* abstrus·us -a -um

absurd *adj* absurd·us -a -um

absurdity *s* inepti·a -ae *f*

abundance *s* abundanti·a -ae *f*, copi·a -ae *f*

abundant *adj* abund·ans -antis, larg·us -a -um; **to be —** abundare

abundantly *adv* abundanter, copiose

abuse *s (wrong use)* abus·us -ūs *m; (insult)* iniuri·a -ae *f*, convic·ium -(i)i *n;* **to heap — on** contumeliosissime maledicere *(w. dat)*

abuse *tr (to misuse)* abuti *(w. abl); (sexually)* stuprare; *(w. words)* maledicere *(w. dat)*

abusive *adj* **(toward)** contumelios·us -a -um (in *w. acc); (person)* maledic·us -a -um; **to be — to** abuti *(w. abl)*

abusively *adv* contumeliose

abyss *s* profund·um -i *n; (fig)* barathr·um -i *n*

academic *adj* academic·us -a -um

academy *s* academi·a -ae *f*

accede *intr* **to — to** assentire *(w. dat)*

accelerate *tr & intr* accelerare

acceleration *s* accelerati·o -onis *f*

accent *s* accent·us -ūs *m*, vo·x -cis *f; (peculiar tone of a people)* son·us -i *m;* **a Greek —** son·us -i *m* linguae Graecae; **to place an acute (grave, circumflex) — on a word** acutam (gravem, circumflexam) vocem in verbo ponere

accent *tr (in speaking)* acuere; *(in writing)* fastigare

accent mark *s* fastig·ium -(i)i *n*

accentuation *s (in speaking)* accent·us -ūs *m; (in writing, expr. by gerundive):* **careful in the — of syllables** in syllabis acuendis diligens

accept *tr* accipere, recipere; *(to approve of)* probare

acceptable *adj* **(to)** accept·us -a -um, probabil·is -is -e *(w. dat);* **to be — to** placēre *(w. dat)*

acceptably *adv* apte

acceptance *s* accepti·o -onis *f; (approval)* probati·o -onis *f*

access *s* adit·us -ūs *m*, access·us -ūs *m;* — **to books** copi·a -ae *f* librorum; **to gain — to** penetrare ad *(w. acc);* **to have — to** admitti *(w. dat)*

accessible *adj (of places)* pat·ens -entis; *(of persons)* facil·is -is -e; **to be — to** patēre *(w. dat)*

accession *s (addition)* accessi·o -onis *f;* — **to the throne** regni princip·ium -(i)i *n*

accessory *adj* adiunct·us -a -um; *(to a crime)* consci·us -a -um

accessory *s* affin·is -is *mf;* — **to this crime** affinis *mf* huic facinori

accident *s* cas·us -ūs *m;* calamit·as -atis *f* (autocinetica); **by —** casu

accidental *adj* fortuit·us -a -um; *(non-essential)* adventici·us -a -um

accidentally *adv* casu, forte

acclamation *s (shouts of applause)* clam·or -oris *m*, acclamati·o -onis *f; (oral vote)* conclamati·o -onis *f*

accommodate *tr (adapt)* **(to)** accommodare *(w. dat); (w. lodgings)* hospitium parare *(w. dat); (of an auditorium, etc.)* capere

accommodation *s* accommodati·o -onis *f; (convenience)* commodit·as -atis *f;* —**s** deversor·ium -(i)i *n*

accompaniment *s* concinenti·a -ae *f;* **to sing to the — of the flute** ad tibiam concinere

accompany *tr* comitari; *(mus)* concinere *(w. dat)*

accomplice *s* **(in)** partic·eps -itis *m (w. gen* or in *w. abl)*

accomplish *tr* efficere, perficere

accomplished *adj (skilled)* erudit·us -a -um; *(of a speaker)* disert·us -a -um

accomplishment *s (completion)* peracti·o -onis *f;* —**s** re·s -rum *fpl* gestae

accord *s* consens·us -ūs *m;* **of one's own —** suā sponte, ultro; **to be in — with** convenire *(w. dat);* **with one —** unanimiter

accordance *s* **in — with** secundum *(w. acc),* pro *(w. abl),* ex *(w. abl)*

accordingly *adv* proinde, itaque

according to *prep* secundum *(w. acc)*

accordion *s* harmonic·a -ae *f* diductilis

accost *tr* appellare, compellare; *(sexually)* lenare

account *s (financial)* rati·o -onis *f; (statement)* memori·a -ae *f; (story)* narrati·o -onis *f; (esteem)* reputati·o -onis *f;* **of little —** parvi preti; **of no** — nullius preti; **on** — **of** ob, propter *(w. acc);* **on that** — propterea; **the** — **balances** ratio constat; **to audit accounts** rationes dispungere; **to balance accounts** rationes conferre; **to be entered into an** — rationibus inferri; **to call to** — rationem poscere; **to give an** — rationem reddere; **to take** — of rationem habēre *(w. gen)*

account *tr (to consider)* ducere; *(to esteem)* aestimare; **to** — **for** rationem reddere *(w. gen);* **to** — **for his absence** rationem adferre cur absit

accountable *adj* **(for)** re·us -a -um *(w. gen)*

accountant *s* ratiocinat·or -oris *m,* ratiocinat·rix -ricis *f*

account books *spl* tabul·ae -arum *fpl* (accepti et expensi)

accounting *s* confecti·o -onis *f* tabularum; **to keep (accounting) books** tabulas conficere

accredited *adj* aestimat·us -a -um

accrue *intr* accrescere; **to** — **to** accedere *(w. dat),* redundare in *(w. acc)*

accumulate *tr* accumulare **‖** *intr* crescere, augēri

accumulation *s* congest·us -ūs *m; (pile)* cumul·us -i *m*

accuracy *s (pains bestowed)* cur·a -ae *f; (exactness)* subtilit·as -atis *f*

accurate *adj* exact·us -a -um; *(of a definition, observation)* subtil·is -is -e

accurately *adv* exacte; subtiliter

accusation *s* accusati·o -onis *f; (charge)* crim·en -inis *n;* **to bring an** — **against** accusare

accusative *s* accusativ·us -i *m;* **in the accusative (case)** casu accusativo

accuse *tr* **(of)** accusare *(w. gen or de w. abl);* **to** — **falsely** calumniari; **to** — **s.o. of a capital offense** aliquem rei capitalis re·um (-am) facere

accused *s* re·us -i *m,* re·a -ae *f*

accuser *s* accusat·or -oris *m,* accusatr·ix -icis *f*

accusingly *adv* accusatorie

accustom *tr* **(to)** assuefacere *(w. abl, dat or* ad *w. acc, or inf);* **to** — **oneself** *or* **become** —**ed to** assuescere *(w. dat),* ad, in *(w. acc);* **to be** —**ed to** solēre *(w. inf)*

ache *s* dol·or -oris *m*

ache *intr* dolēre; **I** — **all over** totus (-a) doleo; **my head** —**s** caput mihi dolet

achieve *tr* conficere; *(to win)* consequi

achievement *s* res, rei *f* gesta

acid *s* acid·um -i *n*

acid *adj* acid·us -a -um

acknowledge *tr* agnoscere; *(a child)* tollere

acknowledgement *s* confessi·o -onis *f; (money receipt)* apoch·a -ae *f*

acorn *s* glan·s -dis *f*

acoustics *spl* acustic·a -orum *npl*

acquaint *tr* **(with)** certiorem facere (de *w. abl);* **to** — **oneself with** cognoscere

acquaintance *s* familiarit·as -atis *f; (person)* familiar·is -is *mf*

acquainted *adj* not·us -a -um; — **with** gnar·us -a -um *(w. gen);* **to become** — **with** cognoscere

acquiesce *intr* **(in)** acquiescere (in *w. abl),* stare *(w. abl or* in *w. abl)*

acquiescence *s* assens·us -ūs *m*

acquire *tr* adipisci, nancisci

acquisition *s* quaest·us -ūs *m; (thing acquired)* quaesit·um -i *n*

acquit *tr* **(of)** absolvere (de *w. abl);* **to** — **oneself** se gerere

acquittal *s* absoluti·o -onis *f*

acre *s* iuger·um -i *n (actually .625 of an acre)*

acrid *adj* a·cer -cris -cre

acrobat *s* petauristari·us -i *m* (·a -ae *f);*

across *adv* in transversum

across *prep* trans *(w. acc)*

act *s (deed, action)* fact·um -i *n; (decree)* decret·um -i *n; (theat)* act·us -ūs *m;* **caught in the** — manifestari·us -a -um; **in the very** — in flagranti; **public** —**s** act·a -orum *npl*

act *tr (role)* agere **‖** *intr* agere; **to** — **as a friend** amicum agere; **to** — **as a servant** servile officium tueri; **to** — **badly** se turpiter gerere

acting *s* acti·o -onis *f*

action *s* acti·o -onis *f,* act·us -ūs *m; (deed)* fact·um -i *n; (leg)* acti·o -onis *f; (mil)* pugn·a -ae *f; (of speaker)* gest·us -ūs *m;* **to bring an** — **against** actionem intendere in *(w. acc)*

active *adj (life)* actuos·us -a -um; *(mind)* veget·us -a -um; *(busy)* impi·ger -gra -grum; *(gram)* activ·us -a -um; — **voice** gen·us -eris *n* activum; **be** — in versari in *(w. abl);* **be on active service** stipendia facere; **verb in the** — **voice** verbum agendi modi

actively *adv* impigre; *(energetically)* gnaviter

activity *s* agitati·o -onis *f; (energy)* industri·a -ae *f,* gnavit·as -atis *f*

actor *s* histri·o -onis *m,* act·or -oris *m; (in comedy)* comoed·us -i *m; (in tragedy)* tragoed·us -i *m*

actress *s* actr·ix -icis *f; (in Roman times)* mim·a -ae *f* [*Note: females did not normally act in regular Roman dramas*]

actual *adj* ver·us -a -um

actuality *s* verit·as -atis *f*

actually *adv* re verā

acumen *s* acum·en -inis *n*

acute *adj (angle, pain)* acut·us -a -um; *(vision, intellect)* a·cer -cris -cre

acutely *adv* acute, acriter

acuteness *s (of senses, intellect)* aci·es -ei *f*

adage *s* proverb·ium -(i)i *n*

ad *s* praeconium -(i)i *n*

adamant *adj* obstinat·us -a -um
Adam's apple *s* nod·us -ī *m* gutturis
adapt *tr* accommodare, aptare
adaptation *s* accommodati·o -onis *f*
adapted *adj* apt·us -a -um
add *tr* **(to)** addere, adicere *(w. dat or* ad *w. acc); (in speaking)* superdicere; *(in writing)* subscribere; **to — up** computare; **to be —ed to** accedere *(w. dat or* ad *w. acc)*
addict *tr* **to be —ed to** se tradere *(w. dat)*
addicted *adj* **— to** dedit·us -a -um *(w. dat)*
adding machine *s* machin·a -ae *f* additionalis
addition *s* accessi·o -onis *f,* adiecti·o -onis *f;* **in — praeterea,** insuper; **in — to** praeter *(w. acc),* super *(w. acc)*
additional *adj* additici·us -a -um
additionally *adv* accedit quod *(w. indic)*
address *s* alloqu·ium -(i)i *n; (on an envelope)* inscripti·o -onis *f* cursualis; *(comput)* inscripti·o -onis *f* electronica; *(speech)* conti·o -onis *f,* orati·o -onis *f*
address *tr (to speak to)* alloqui, compellare; *(a letter)* inscribere
address book *s (comput)* lib·er -ri *m* inscriptionum electronicarum
adduce *tr (witness, evidence)* producere; *(arguments)* afferre
adept *adj* **(in)** perit·us -a -um *(w. gen or abl or* in *w. abl)*
adequacy *s* sufficienti·a -ae *f*
adequate *adj* suffici·ens -entis; **to be — suffi-cere**
adequately *adv* satis, apte
adhere *intr* **(to)** haerēre, cohaerēre *(w. dat, abl, or* in *w. acc);* **to — to** *(fig)* stare in *(w. abl)*
adherence *s* adhaes·us -ūs *m*
adherent *s* assectat·or -oris *m*
adhesion *s* adhaesi·o -onis *f*
adhesive *adj* ten·ax -acis
adhesive *s* glut·en -inis *n*
adhesive tape *s* taeni·a -ae *f* adhaesiva
adjacent *adj* confin·is -is -e; **to be — to** adiacēre *(w. dat,* ad *w. acc),* contermin·us -a -um esse *(w. dat)*
adjective *s* adiectiv·um -i *n*
adjectival *adj* adiectival·is -is -e
adjectively *adv* pro apposito; **the word is used — vocabulum pro apposito ponitur**
adjoin *tr* adiacēre *(w. dat)*
adjoining *adj* coniunct·us -a -um, iunct·us -a -um; **— rooms** iuncta cubicula
adjourn *tr* differre; *(leg)* ampliare ‖ *intr* diferri
adjournment *s* dilati·o -onis *f; (leg)* amplificati·o -onis *f*
adjudicate *tr* addicere
adjunct *s* adiunct·um -i *n*

adjust *tr* **(to)** aptare, accommodare *(w. dat or* ad *w. acc); (to put in order)* componere ‖ *intr* **(to)** se accommodare *(w. dat or* ad *w. acc)*
adjustment *s* accommodati·o -onis *f; (of a robe)* structur·a -ae *f*
adjutant *s* opti·o -onis *m*
administer *tr (to manage)* administrare; *(medicines)* adhibēre; *(oath)* adigere; **to — justice** ius dicere
administration *s* administrati·o -onis *f;* **— of justice** iurisdicti·o -onis *f;* **— of public affairs** procurati·o -onis *f* reipublicae
administrative *adj* ad administrationem pertin·ens -entis
administrator *s* administrat·or -oris *m,* procurat·or -oris *m*
admirable *adj* admirabil·is -is -e
admiral *s* classis praefect·us -i *m*
admiration *s* admirati·o -onis *f*
admire *tr* admirari
admirer *s* admirat·or -oris *m; (lover)* am·ans -antis *mf*
admiringly *adv (use participle:)* admir·ans -antis
admissible *adj* accipiend·us -a -um
admission *s* confessi·o -onis *f; (being let in)* adit·us -ūs *m,* access·us -ūs *m;* **by his own — confessione suā**
admission ticket *s* tesser·a -ae *f* aditialis
admit *tr (to allow to enter)* admittere; *(e.g., into the senate)* asciscere; *(to grant as valid)* dare; *(to acknowledge)* agnoscere; **it is —ed** cōnstat; **to — flatly** profiteri palam
admittedly *adv* sane
admonish *tr* admonēre
admonition *s (act)* admoniti·o -onis *f; (words used)* monit·um -i *n*
adolescence *s* adulescenti·a -ae *f*
adolescent *adj* adulesc·ens -entis
adolescent *s* adulescentul·us -i *m*
adopt *tr (a child)* adoptare; *(an adult)* arrogare; *(customs, laws)* asciscere; *(a plan)* capere, inire
adoption *s* adopti·o -onis *f; (of an adult)* arrogati·o -onis *f; (of a custom)* assumpti·o -onis *f*
adoptive *adj* adoptiv·us -a -um
adorable *adj* adorand·us -a -um
adoration *s* adorati·o -onis *f*
adore *tr* adorare; *(fig)* demirari
adorn *tr* decorare, ornare
adornment *s (act)* exornati·o -onis *f; (object)* ornament·um -i *n*
Adriatic *adj* Adriatic·us -a -um
adrift *adv* **to be —** fluctuare; **to set —** aperto mari committere
adroit *adj* callid·us -a -um; *(dexterous)* dex·ter -tra -trum

adroitness *s* callidit·as -atis *f;* dexterit·as -atis *f*

adulation *s* adulati·o -onis *f*

adult *adj* adult·us -a -um; — **population** *(not including the aged)* pub·es -is *f*

adult *s* adult·us -i *m;* pub·es -eris *m*

adulterate *tr* adulterare

adulteration *s* adulterati·o -onis *f*

adulterer *s* adult·er -eri *m*

adulteress *s* adulter·a -ae *f*

adulterous *adj* adulterin·us -a -um

adultery *s* adulter·ium -(i)i *n;* **to commit** — adulterare

advance *tr (to more forward)* promovēre; *(money)* in antecessum solvere; *(a cause)* fovēre; *(to promote)* provehere; *(an opinion)* praeferre **‖** *intr (to go forward)* procedere; *(of steady movement on foot)* incedere; *(in riding or sailing)* provehi; *(to progress)* proficere; *(mil)* gradum *(or* pedem*)* inferre; **as the day —ed** die procedente

advance *s* progress·us -ūs *m;* **in** — ante; **to pay in** — pecuniam nondum debitam solvere

advanced *adj* provect·us -a -um; **at an — age** provectā aetate; **— in years** grand·is -is -e natu *(or* aevo*)*

advance man *s* praecurs·or -oris *m*

advancement *s* promoti·o -onis *f*

advantage *s (benefit)* commod·um -i *n; (a real good)* bon·um -i *n; (profit)* emolument·um -i *n; (usefulness)* utilit·as -atis *f;* **to be of —** prodesse; **to have an — over** praestare *(w. dat);* **to take — of** uti *(w. abl); (pej)* sibi quaestui habēre; **to take — of an opportunity** occasionem nancisci

advantageous *adj* util·is -is -e

advantageously *adv* utiliter

advent *s* advent·us -ūs *m*

adventure *s* cas·us -ūs *m*

adventurer *s* periclitat·or -oris *m*

adventurous *adj* aud·ax -acis

adverb *s* adverb·ium -(i)i *n*

adverbial *adj* adverbial·is -is -e

adverbially *adv* adverbialiter

adversary *s* adversar·ius -(i)i *m,* adversatr·ix -icis *f*

adversative *adj* adversativ·us -a -um

adverse *adj (mostly winds)* advers·us -a -um; *(times)* asp·er -era -erum; **— circumstances** re·s -rum *fpl* asperae

adversely *adv* male, infeliciter

adversity *s* re·s -rum *fpl* adversae; *(fig)* re·s -rum *fpl* asperae

advertise *tr* proscribere, divulgare

advertisement *s* praeconi·um -ī *n; (poster)* proscripti·o -onis *f*

advice *s* consil·ium -(i)i *n;* **to ask s.o. for —** aliquem consulere, aliquem consilium roga-

re; **to give good — to** rectum consilium dare *(w. dat)*

advisable *adj* **it is — to** expedit *(w. inf)*

advise *tr* suadēre *(w. dat)*

advisedly *adv* consulto

adviser *s* consult·or -oris *m*

advocate *s (leg)* advocat·us -i *m; (fig)* patron·us -i *m*

advocate *tr* suadēre

aedile *s* aedil·is -is *m*

aedileship *s* aedilit·as -atis *f*

aegis *s* aeg·is -idis *f; (fig)* tutel·a -ae *f*

aerial *adj* aëri·us -a -um

affable *adj* affabil·is -is -e

affably *adv* affabiliter

affair *s* negot·ium -i(i) *n,* res, rei *f; (love)* am·or -oris *m;* **to have an — with** consuetudinem habēre cum

affect *tr (to influence)* afficere; *(to move)* movēre; *(to pretend)* simulare

affectation *s* affectati·o -onis *f*

affected *adj* simulat·us -a -um; *(style)* putid·us -a -um

affection *s* am·or -oris *m*

affectionate *adj* am·ans -antis

affectionately *adv* amanter

affidavit *s* per tabulas testimon·ium -(i)i *n*

affiliated *adj* **to be — with a college** in collegio cooptari

affinity *s* affinit·as -atis *f;* **to have no — with** longe remot·us -a -um esse ab *(w. abl)*

affirm *tr* affirmare

affirmative *adj* affirm·ans -antis; **I reply in the —** aio; **to give an — answer** fateri ita se rem habere

affix *tr* affigere

afflict *tr* affligere; **to be —ed with** conflictari *(w. abl)*

affliction *s (cause of distress)* mal·um -i *n; (state of distress)* miseri·a -ae *f*

affluence *s* diviti·ae -arum *fpl*

affluent *adj* div·es -itis

afford *tr (opportunity, etc.)* praebēre; **I cannot —** res mihi non suppetit ad *(w. acc)*

affront *s* contumeli·a -ae *f*

afield *adv* **in** agro; *(astray)* vag·us -a -um, err·ans -antis

afloat *adj* nat·ans -antis; **to get a ship —** navem deducere

afoot *adv* pedibus; **to be —** *(fig)* geri; **what is —?** quid geritur?

aforementioned *adj* supra dict·us -a -um

afraid *adj* timid·us -a -um; **to be — of** timēre *(w. acc),* metuere *(w. acc);* **to make — terrēre; what are you afraid of?** quid est quod metuis?

afresh *adv* de integro, de novo

Africa *s* Afric·a -ae *f*

African *adj* African·us -a -um

African *s* Af·er -ri *m*

after *prep* post *(w. acc)*, ab, ex *(w. abl); (in rank or degree)* secundum *(w. acc);* **(and) — all** (et) re verā; **— an interval** interposito deinde spatio; **— that** deinde, subinde; **— this** post hac; **a little —** paulo post; **immediately —** statim ab *(w. abl);* **named — his father** a patre nominat·us -a -um: **right — sub** *(w. acc);* **the day —** postridie (quam)**; to be —** s.o. *(romantically)* aliquem petere **after** *conj* postquam

afternoon *s* postmeridian·um -i *n;* **in the —** post meridiem, postmeridie; **this —** hodie post meridiem

afternoon *adj* postmeridian·us -a -um

afterthought *s* posterior cogitati·o -onis *f*

afterwards *adv* postea

again *adv* iterum, rursus; *(hereafter)* posthac; *(in turn)* invicem; *(further)* porro; **— and —** identidem; **once —** denuo; **over —** denuo

against *prep* contra *(w. acc); (in a hostile manner)* adversus *(w. acc),* in *(w. acc);* **— the current** adverso flumine; **to lean — a tree** se ad arborem applicare; **to be —** adversari *(w. dat)*

age *s (time of life)* aet·as -atis *f; (era)* saecul·um -i *n,* aet·as -atis *f;* **don't ask me my —** noli me percontari meum aevum; **of the same —** aequaev·us -a -um; **old —** senect·us -utis *f;* **to be of —** sui iuris esse; **to be under twelve years of age** minor viginti annorum esse; **twelve years of —** duodecim annos nat·us -a -um; **under —** inpub·is -is -e **age** *tr* aetate conficere **‖** *intr* maturescere; *(to grow old)* senescere

aged *adj* annos·us -a -um, aetate provect·us -a -um; **a man — forty** vi·r -i *m* annos quadraginta natus

agency *s* acti·o -onis *f; (means)* oper·a -ae *f; (office)* procurati·o -onis *f;* **through the — of** per *(w. acc)*

agent *s (doer)* act·or -oris *m; (com)* procurat·or -oris *m,* negotiorum curat·or -oris *m;* **man is a free —** homo sui iuris est

aggravate *tr (to make worse)* aggravare; *(a wound)* ulcerare; *(to annoy)* vexare; **to become —d** ingravescere

aggravating *adj* molest·us -a -um

aggravation *s (annoyance)* vexati·o -onis *f*

aggregate *adj* tot·us -a -um; **in the —** in toto

aggression *s* incursi·o -onis *f;* **to commit — against** incursionem hostiliter facere in *(w. acc)*

aggressive *adj* hostil·is -is -e

aggressor *s* qui bellum ultro infert

aggrieved *adj* qui iniuriam accepit

aghast *adj* stupefact·us -a -um; **to stand —** obstupescere

agile *adj* agil·is -is -e; *(mind)* veget·us -a -um

agility *s* agilit·as -atis *f*

agitate *tr (to move rapidly to and fro)* agitare; *(to excite)* agitare; *(to disturb)* perturbare

agitated *adj (sea)* tumultuos·us -a -um; *(fig)* turbulent·us -a -um

agitation *s (violent movement)* agitati·o -onis *f; (mental or political disturbance)* commoti·o -onis *f*

agitator *s* vulgi turbat·or -oris *m*

ago *adv* abhinc; **a short time —** haud ita pridem; **a short while —** paulo ante; **how long —?** quam pridem?; **long —** iamdudum, multo ante; **not so long ago** haud ita pridem; **some time —** pridem; **three years —** abhinc tres annos

agonize *intr* (ex)cruciari

agonizing *adj* cruciabil·is -is -e

agony *s* acerbissimus dol·or -oris *m;* **to be in —** dolore angi

agrarian *adj* agrari·us -a -um

agree *intr* **— with** consentire cum *(w. abl); (to make a bargain)* pascisci cum *(w. abl); (of facts)* constare, convenire; **it had been —ed** convenerat; **it is generally —ed** fere convenit; **to — with s.o. about** assentire alicui de *(w. abl)*

agreeable *adj (pleasing)* grat·us -a -um; *(of persons)* commod·us -a -um; *(acceptable)* accept·us -a -um

agreeably *adv* grate, accommode

agreement *s* consens·us -ūs *m; (pact)* pacti·o -onis *f,* pact·um -i *n; (proportion)* symmetri·a -ae *f;* **according to the —** ex pacto: **there is general —** fere convenit

agricultural *adj* rustic·us -a -um; **the Latins were an — people** Latini agriculturae studebant

agriculture *s* agricultur·a -ae *f*

ah *interj* ah!; *(of grief, indignation)* vah!; *(of admiration)* eia!; **— me** eheu!

aha *interj* attat!

ahead *adv use verb with prefix* prae- *or* pro-; **— of time** ante tempus; **to get — of s.o.** aliquem praevenire; **go —, tell me!** agedum, dic mihi!; **to walk — of s.o.** aliquem praecedere

aid *s* auxil·ium -(i)i *n*

aid *tr* adiuvare

aide-de-camp *s* opti·o -onis *m*

ail *tr* dolēre *(w. dat);* **what —s you?** quid tibi est?

ailment *s* mal·um -i *n*

aim *s (mark)* scop·us -i *m; (fig)* fin·is -is *m,* proposit·um -i *n*

aim *tr* (in)tendere **‖** *intr* **to — at** *(a target)* destinare; *(to try to hit)* petere; *(to try to attain)* affectare; *(virtue, renown)* spectare

aimless *adj* van·us -a -um

aimlessly *adv* sine ratione

air s a·ër -eris *(acc:* aëra) *m; (upper air)*
aeth·er -eris *m; (air in motion)* aur·a -ae *f;*
(attitude) habit·us -ūs *m;* — **shaft**
aestuar·ium -(i)i *n;* **in the open** — sub divo;
to let in fresh — auras admittere; **to put on**
—**s** se iactare; **up in the** — *(fig)* in medio
relict·us -a -um
air *tr* ventilare; *(to disclose)* patefacere
airbag s aërius foll·is -is *m*
air conditioner s instrument·um -ī *n* aëri tem-
perando
aircraft carrier s nav·is -is *f* aëroplanigera
airhead s *(coll)* cucurbit·a -ae *f*
airily *adv* hilare
airing s ventilati·o -onis *f; (of an idea)* praedi-
cati·o -onis *f*
airline s tram·es -itis *m* aërius
airplane s aëroplan·um -i *n*
air pressure s pressi·o -onis *f* aëria
aisle s al·a -ae *f*
ajar *adj* semiapert·us -a -um
akimbo *adv* **to stand with arms** — ansat·us -a
-um stare
akin *adj* **(to)** finitim·us -a -um *(w. dat)*
alabaster s alabas·ter -tri *m*
alarm s *(loud notice of danger)* clam·or -oris
m; (sudden fright) pav·or -oris *m; (on a
clock)* suscitabul·um -i *n;* **the** — **went off**
suscitabulum sonuit; **to set the alarm for
(six o'clock)** obicem ad (horam sextam)
infigere; **to sound the** — signum monitorium
dare; *(mil)* classicum canere
alarm *tr* perturbare; **to become** —**ed**
expavescere
alarm clock s horologi·um -i *n* suscitatorium
alas *interj* eheu!
albumen s album·en -inis *n*
alcohol s spirit·us -ūs *m* vini
alcoholic *adj* alcoholic·us -a -um
alcoholic s bibos·us -i *m*, (·a -ae *f)*
alcove s zothec·a -ae *f*
ale s cerevisi·a -ae *f*
alert *adj* intent·us -a -um; — **mind** erecta
men·s -tis *f*
alert s monitorium sign·um -i *n;* **on the** —
intent·us -a -um; **to sound the** — signum
monitorium dare
alert *tr (to warn)* praemonēre; *(to rouse)*
excitare
alertness s alacrit·as -atis *f*
alias s nom·en -inis *n* mentitum
alibi s *(excuse)* speci·es -ei *f;* **to have an** —
dicere se alibi fuisse; *(fig)* se excusare
alien *adj* peregrin·us -a -um
alien s alienigen·a -ae *mf*
alienate *tr* alienare
alienation s alienati·o -onis *f*
alike *adj* simil·is -is -e
alike *adv* pariter

alimony s alimon·ium -(i)i *n*
alive *adj* viv·us -a -um; *(fig)* ala·cer -cris -cre
all *adj* omn·is -is -e, cunct·us -a -um; *(whole,
entire)* tot·us -a -um; *(denoting a unity of
parts in a body)* univers·us -a -um; — **the
most learned** doctissimus quisque
all *pron* omn·es -ium *mpl* & *fpl*, omn·ia -ium
npl; **in** — in summā; *(with numbers)* omnino;
not at — haudquaquam; **nothing at** — nihil
omnino; **one's** — propr·ium -(i)i *n;* **write** —
you can scribe quantum potes
all *adv* — **over** undique; — **along** usque ab initio; — **but** tantum non; — **powerful**
omnipot·ens -entis; — **the better** tanto
melius; — **the more** eo magis; — **too late**
immo iam sero
allay *tr* sedare; **to be** —**ed** temperari
allegation s affirmati·o -onis *f*
allege *tr* arguere; —**ing that** tamquam *(w. subj)*
allegiance s fid·es -ei *f;* **to pledge** — **to** fidem
obligare *(w. dat);* **to swear** — sacramentum
dicere
allegorical *adj* allegoric·us -a -um
allegory s allegori·a -ae *f*
allergic *adj* **(to)** obnoxi·us -a -um *(w. dat)*
allergy s allergi·a -ae *f*
alleviate *tr* levare
alleviation s levati·o -onis *f*
alley s angiport·us -ūs *m*
alliance s *(by marriage)* affinit·as -atis *f; (of
states)* foed·us -eris *n*, societ·as -atis *f;* **to
conclude an** — **with** foedus icere cum *(w.
abl),* **societatem facere cum** *(w. abl)*
allied *adj (pol)* foederat·us -a -um, soci·us -a
-um; *(related)* finitim·us -a -um
alligator s crocodil·us -i *m*
alliteration s alliterati·o -onis *f*
allocate *tr (funds)* attribuere; *(to assign)* distribuere
allocation s *(of funds)* attributi·o -onis *f;
(money)* attribut·um -i *n*
allot *tr* assignare
allotment s assignati·o -onis *f;* **an** — **of land**
ag·er -ri *m* assignatus
allow *tr* concedere *(w. dat),* sinere; **it is** —**ed**
licet; **it is** —**ed by Caesar** licet per
Caesarem; **to** — **for** indulgēre *(w. dat)*
allowable *adj* licit·us -a -um; **it is** — fas est
allowance s *(permission)* permissi·o -onis *f;
(concession)* veni·a -ae *f; (portion)* porti·o
-onis *f; (money)* stipend·ium -(i)i *n; (food)*
diari·a -orum *npl*
alloy s mixtur·a -ae *f; (of metals)* temperati·o
-onis *f*
all right *adv* licet; **it's all right** recte est; bene
habet
all-seeing *adj* omnitu·ens -entis
all-time *adj* post hominum memoriam
allude *intr* **to** — **to** attingere

allure *tr* allicere
allurement *s* blandiment·um -i *n*
alluring *adj* bland·us -a -um
allusion *s* significati·o -onis *f*
allusive *adj* obliqu·us -a -um
allusively *adv* oblique
ally *s* soc·ius -(i)i *m,* soci·a -ae *f*
ally *tr* sociare
almanac *s* fast·i -orum *mpl*
almighty *adj* omnipot·ens -entis
almond *s* amygdal·a -ae *f*
almond tree *s* amygdal·us -i *f*
almost *adv* paene, fere
alms *spl* stip·s -is *f*
aloft *adv (motion & rest)* sublime
alone *adj* sol·us -a -um; *(only)* un·us -a -um;
  all — persol·us -a -um; **to leave —** deserere;
  to let — mittere
alone *adv* solum
along *adv* porro, protinus; **all —** iamdudum;
  iam inde a principio; **— with** unā cum *(w.*
  abl); **to bring —** afferre; **to get — with** consentire cum *(w. abl)*
along *prep* per *(w. acc),* praeter *(w. acc)* secundum *(w. acc)*
aloof *adv* procul; **to keep — from the senate**
  curiā abstinēre; **to stand —** abstare
aloud *adv* clare
alphabet *s* element·a -orum *npl,* alphabet·um
  -i *n*
alphabetical *adj* litterarum ordine
alphabetically *adv* **to arrange —** in litteram
  digere
Alpine *adj* Alpin·us -a -um
Alps *spl* Alp·es -ium *fpl*
already *adv* iam
also *adv* etiam, et, necnon
altar *s* ar·a -ae *f*
alter *tr* mutare, commutare
alterable *adj* mutabil·is -is -e
alteration *s* mutati·o -onis *f*
altercation *s* altercati·o -onis *f*
alternate *adj* altern·us -a -um
alternate *tr & intr* alternare
alternately *adv* invicem, per vices
alternation *s* vicissitud·o -inis *f*
alternative *adj* alt·er -era -erum, alternat·us
  -a -um
alternative *s* alternata condici·o -onis *f,* opti·o
  -onis *f*
although *conj* quamquam *(w. indic),* quavis
  (w. subj), cum *(w. subj)*
altitude *s* altitud·o -inis *f*
altogether *adv* omnino
altruism *s* beneficenti·a -ae *f*
always *adv* semper
amass *tr* cumulare
amateur *s* idiot·a -ae *m*
amatory *adj* amatori·us -a -um

amaze *tr* obstupefacere
amazed *adj* (at) stupefact·us -a -um (cum
  w. abl)
amazement *s* stup·or -oris *m*
amazing *adj* mir·us -a -um
amazingly *adv* mirabiliter
Amazon *s* Amaz·on -onis *f*
ambassador *s* legat·us -i *m*
amber *s* electr·um -i *n*
ambidextrous *adj* aequiman·us -a -um
ambiguity *s* ambiguit·as -atis *f*
ambiguous *adj* ambigu·us -a -um
ambition *s* ambiti·o -onis *f*
ambitious *adj* laudis *(or* gloriae) studios·us -a
  -um; *(worker)* assidu·us -a -um; *(self-seek-*
  ing) ambitios·us -a -um
amble *intr* ambulare
ambrosia *s* ambrosi·a -ae *f*
ambulance arcer·a -ae *f*
ambush *s* insidi·ae -arum *fpl*
ambush *tr* insidiari *(w. dat)*
ameliorate *tr* corrigere, meliorem *or* melius
  facere ‖ *intr* melior *or* melius fieri
amenable *adj* (to) tractabil·is -is -e *(w. dat)*
amend *tr* emendare ‖ *intr* proficere
amendment *s* emendati·o -onis *f*
amends *spl* satisfacti·o -onis *f;* **to make —** satisfacere
amenity *s* amoenit·as -atis *f; (comfort)* com-
  mod·um -i *n*
America *s* Americ·a -ae *f;* **Central —**
  America Media; **North —** America
  Septentrionalis; **South —** America Australis
American *adj* American·us -a -um
American *s* American·us -i *m* (·a -ae *f)*
amethyst *s* amethyst·us -i *f*
amiable *adj* amabil·is -is -e
amiably *adv* suaviter
amicable *adj* amic·us -a -um
amicably *adv* amice
amid *prep* inter *(w. acc)*
amiss *adv* perperam; **to take —** aegre ferre
ammunition *s* missilium copi·a -ae *f*
amnesty *s* veni·a -ae *f*
among *prep* inter *(w. acc),* apud *(w. acc);* **from**
  — ex *(w. abl)*
amorous *adj* amatori·us -a -um; *(sexual)*
  libidinos·us -a -um
amount *s* summ·a -ae *f*
amount *intr* **to — to** efficere ad *(w. acc),* esse
  ad *(w. acc);* **it —s to the same thing** tantundem est; **to — to something** bonum exitum
  umquam factur·us -a -um esse; **what does it**
  — to? quid istuc valet?
amphitheater *s* amphitheatr·um -i *n*
ample *adj* ampl·us -a -um
amplification *s* amplificati·o -onis *f*
amplify *tr* amplificare
amply *adv* ample

amputate *tr* amputare
amputation *s* amputati·o -onis *f*
amuck *adv* **to run —** delirare
amulet *s* amulet·um -i *n*
amuse *tr* oblectare; **to — oneself (with)** se oblectare *(w. abl)*
amusement *s* oblectati·o -onis *f; (that which amuses)* oblectament·um -i *n*
amusement park *s* hort·i -orum *mpl* publici oblectarii
amusing *adj* festiv·us -a -um
an *indef article, unexpressed in Latin*
anachronism *s* temporum inversi·o -onis *f*
analogous *adj* analog·us -a -um
analogy *s* analogi·a -ae *f*
analysis *s* enodati·o -onis *f;* **to make an — of a compound substance** compositum in principia redigere
analytical *adj* analytic·us -a -um
analytically *adv* per analysin
analyze *tr* in principia redigere; *(words)* subtiliter enodare
anapest *s* anapaestus pe·s -dis *m*
anapestic *adj* anapaestic·us -a -um
anarchy *s* effrenata licenti·a -ae *f;* **to cause —** turbare omnia et permiscēre; **to have —** nullum omnino imperium habēre
anatomical *adj* anatomic·us -a -um
anatomy *s* anatomi·a -ae *f*
ancestor *s* proav·us -i *m;* **—s** maior·es -um *mpl*
ancestry *s* gen·us -eris *n*
anchor *s* ancor·a -ae *f;* **to weigh —** ancoram tollere
anchor *tr* ad ancoram deligare ‖ *intr* in ancorā stare
anchorage *s* stati·o -onis *f*
ancient *adj* antiqu·us -a -um, vetust·us -a -um; **in — times** antiquitus; **the —s** veter·es -um *mpl; (authors)* antiqu·i -orum *mpl*
and *conj* et, ac, atque, -que; **— so forth** et perinde; **— then** deincepsque
anecdote *s* fabell·a -ae *f*
anemic *adj* exsangu·is -is -e
anew *adv* denuo
angel *s* angel·us -i *m* (·a -ae *f*)
angelic *adj* angelic·us -a -um
anger *s* ir·a -ae *f*
anger *tr* irritare
angle *s* angul·us -i *m*
angler *s* piscat·or -oris *m*
angrily *adv* irate
angry *adj* irat·us -a -um; **to be — (with)** succensere, irasci *(w. dat);* **to get — with** irascari *(w. dat);* **to make —** irritare
anguish *s* ang·or -oris *m*
angular *adj* angular·is -is -e
animal *s* anim·al -alis *n; (wild beast)* besti·a -ae *f,* fer·a -ae *f; (domestic)* pec·us -udis *f*

animate *adj* animal·is -is -e
animate *tr* animare; *(fig)* excitare
animated *adj* veget·us -a -um
animosity *s* acerbit·as -atis *f*
ankle *s* tal·us -i *m*
ankle-length *adj* talar·is -is -e
anklet *s* periscel·is -idis *f*
annalist *s* annalium script·or -oris *m*
annals *spl* annal·es -ium *mpl*
annex *tr (nations)* adicere, adiungere
annexation *s* adiecti·o -onis *f*
annihilate *tr* delēre, ex(s)tinguere
annihilation *s* exstincti·o -onis *f*
anniversary *adj* anniversari·us -a -um
anniversary *s* festus di·es -ei *m* anniversarius
annotate *tr* annotare
annotation *s* annotati·o -onis *f*
announce *tr* nuntiare, indicere; *(to report)* renuntiare; *(officially)* denuntiare; *(laws, etc.)* proscribere
announcement *s* denuntiati·o -onis *f; (report)* renuntiati·o -onis *f*
announcer *s* annuntia·tor -toris *m* (·trix -tricis *f*)
annoy *tr* vexare, male habēre; **to be —ed at** stomachari ob *(w. acc),* moleste ferre
annoyance *s* molesti·a -ae *f*
annoying *adj* molest·us -a -um
annual *adj* annu·us -a -um
annually *adv* quotannis
annuity *s* annua pecuni·a -ae *f*
annul *tr (contract, law)* infirmare; *(a law)* abrogare; **to — a marriage** dirimere nuptias
annulment *s* infirmati·o -onis *f;* abrogati·o -onis *f*
anoint *tr* ung(u)ere
anointing *s* uncti·o -onis *f*
anomalous *adj* enorm·is -is -e; *(gram)* anomal·us -a -um
anomaly *s* enormit·as -atis *f; (gram)* anomali·a -ae *f*
anonymous *adj* sine nomine
anonymously *adv* sine nomine
another *adj* ali·us -a -ud; **—'s** alien·us -a -um; **at — time** alias; **in — place** alibi; **one after —** alius ex alio; **one —** inter se; **one ... —** ali·us -a -ud ... ali·us -a -ud; **to — place** alio
answer *tr* respondēre *(w. dat); (by letter)* rescribere *(w. dat); (to correspond to)* congruere cum *(w. abl)* **to — a question** ad interrogatum respondēre ‖ *intr* **to — for** rationem reddere *(w. gen);* **to — to the name of** vocari
answer *s* respons·um -i *n; (solution)* explicati·o -onis *f;* **that's not an — to my question** aliud te rogo
answerable *adj* re·us -a -um; **to be — for** praestare *(acc)*
answering machine *s* responstr·um -ī *n* telephonicum

ant *s* formic·a -ae *f*
antagonism *s* adversit·as -atis *f*
antagonist *s* adversar·ius -(i)i *m,* adversatr·ix -icis *f*
antarctic *adj* antarctic·us -a -um
antecedent *adj* anteced·ens -entis
antecedent *s* anteced·ens -entis *n; (gram)* nom·en -inis *n* antecedens
antechamber *s* atriol·um -i *n*
antedate *tr* diem vero antiquiorem ascribere *(w. dat); (to precede in time)* aetate antecedere *(w. dat or acc)*
antelope *s* tarandr·us -i *m*
antenna *s* antcnn·a -ae *f*
antepenult *s* syllab·a -ae *f* antepaenultima
anterior *adj* anter·ior -ior -ius
anteroom *s* atriol·um -i *n*
anthem *s* hymn·us -i *m* elatior; **national —** patrium carm·en -inis *n*
anthology *s* anthologi·a -ae *f*
anthropologist *s* anthropolog·us -i *m* (·a -ae *f*)
anthropology *s* anthropologi·a -ae *f*
anticipate *tr* anticipare; *(to expect)* spectare; *(mentally)* praesumere
anticipation *s* anticipati·o -onis *f,* praesumpti·o -onis *f*
anticlimax *s* clim·ax -acis *f* inversa
antics *spl* mot·us -uum *mpl* ridiculi
antidote *s* antidot·ium -(i)i *n*
antipathy *s* antipathi·a -ae *f*
antiquarian *adj* antiquari·us -a -um
antiquarian *s* antiquar·ius -(i)i *m* (·a -ae *f*)
antiquated *adj* antiquat·us -a -um
antique *adj* prisc·us -a -um; **— statues** sign·a -orum *npl* operis antiqui
antique *s* antiqui artificis op·us -eris *n*
antiquity *s* antiquit·as -atis *f; in —* antiquitus *[adv]*
anti-Semitic *adj* Iudaeis avers·us -a -um
anti-Semitism *s* Iudaeorum od·ium -(i) *n*
antithesis *s* contrar·ium -(i)i *n*
antler *s* corn·u -us *n*
anus *s* an·us -i *m*
anxiety *s* anxiet·as -atis *f*
anxious *adj* anxi·us -a -um; *(eager)* **(for)** studios·us -a -um *(w. gen)*
anxiously *adv* anxie; *(eagerly)* avide
any *adj* ull·us -a -um; *(after si, ne, nisi, num)* quis, quid; **at — time** aliquando
any *adv* **— longer** diutius; **— more** amplius
anybody *pron* aliquis; *(after si, nisi, ne, num)* quis; *(interrog)* ecquis, numquis; *(after negative)* quisquam; **— else?** ecquis alius?; **— you wish** quisvis, quislibet
anyhow *adv* quoquomodo; *(in any event)* utique; *(just the same)* nec eo setius
anyone *see* **anybody**
anything *pron* aliquid, quicquam; *(after si, nisi, ne, num)* quid; *(interrog)* ecquid,

numquid; *(after negative)* quiquam; **— else? aliquid** amplius, quicquam aliud; **— you wish** quidlibet; **hardly —** nihil fere
anyway *adv* quoquomodo; *(at least, in any event)* utique
anywhere *adv (in any place)* alicubi; *(frequently after* si) uspiam; *(usu. w. negative)* usquam; *(anywhere you please)* ubivis; *(to any place, usu. w.* si, ne, num) quo
aorta *s* grandis ven·a -ae *f* cordis
apart *adv* seorsum, separatim; **— from** praeter *(w. acc);* **to be —** distare; **to fall —** dilabi; **to set —** seponere; **to stand —** distare
apartment *s* diaet·a -ae *f*
apartment building *s* insul·a ae *f*
apathetic *adj* lent·us -a -um
apathy *s* lentitud·o -inis *f*
ape *s* sim·ius -(i)i *m,* simi·a -ae *f*
ape *tr* imitari
Apennines *spl* Apenninus mon·s -tis *m*
aperture *s* foram·en -inis *n*
apex *s* cacum·en -inis *n*
aphorism *s* sententi·a -ae *f*
aphrodisiac *s* sature·um -i *n*
apiece *adv no exact Latin equivalent, but its sense is expressed by distributive numerals, e.g.:* **they went out with two garments —** cum binis vestimentis exierunt; **he stationed one legion — at Brindisium and Tarentum** legiones singulas posuit Brindisi, Tarenti
apocalypse *s* apocalyps·is -is *f*
apocryphal *adj* apocryph·us -a -um
apologetic *adj* se excus·ans -antis
apologize *intr* satis facere, se excusare; **I — to you** me tibi excuso; **to — for s.o.** aliquem excusare
apology *s* excusati·o -onis *f;* **please accept my apologies** quaeso, accipe excusationes; **to make an — for** excusare
apoplectic *adj* apoplectic·us -a -um
apostle *s* apostol·us -i *m*
apostolic *adj* apostolic·us -a -um
apostrophe *s* apostroph·e -es *f; (gram)* apostroph·us -i *f*
apothecary *s (drugstore)* tabern·a -ae *f* medicina; *(druggist)* medicamentar·ius -(i)i *m* (·a -ae *f*)
appall *tr* exterrēre
apparatus *s* apparat·us -ūs *m*
apparel *s* vestit·us -ūs *m*
apparel *tr* vestire
apparent *adj* manifest·us -a -um; *(seeming)* fict·us -a -um
apparently *adv* specie, per spcciem; ut videtur
apparition *s* speci·es -ei *f*
appeal *intr (leg) (to a magistrate)* appellare *(acc); (to the people)* provocare (ad *w. acc);* **to — to** *(to be attractive to)* allicere; *(to the gods)* obtestari

appeal *s (leg)* appellati·o -onis *f; (to the people)* provocati·o -onis *f; (entreaty)* obtestati·o -onis *f; (attractiveness)* suavit·as -atis *f*
appealing *adj* suav·is -is -e; *(imploring)* suppl·ex -icis
appear *intr (to be visible)* apparēre; *(to show up)* comparēre; *(to arise suddenly)* oriri; *(to seem)* vidēri; *(in public, on the stage)* prodire; **to begin to** — patescere
appearance *s (becoming visible)* aspect·us -ūs *m; (outward show)* speci·es -ei *f; (likelihood)* similitud·o -inis *f; (vision)* vis·um -i *n;* **for the sake of** —s ad speciem; **to all** —s ut videtur; **to keep up** —s speciem gerere; **to make one's** — **in public** in publicum prodire; **to make one's** — **on the stage** in proscaenium prodire
appease *tr* placare
appeasement *s* placati·o -onis *f*
append *tr* subscribere
appendage *s* append·ix -icis *f*
appendicitis *s* appendicit·is -idis *f*
appendix *s* append·ix -icis *f; (anat)* append·ix -icis *f* coli
appetite *s* appetit·us -ūs *m; (for food)* cibi appetenti·a -ae *f;* **lack of** — inedi·a -ae *f;* **to control the** —s appetitūs regere
appetizer *s* gustati·o -onis *f*
applaud *tr* applaudere *(w. acc or dat); (to praise)* approbare **ǁ** *intr* plaudere
applause *s* plaus·us -ūs *m;* **to look for** — plausūs captare
apple *s* mal·um -i *n;* — **of my eye** meus ocell·us -i *m*
applecart *s* **to upset the** — plaustrum percellere
apple peel *s* malicor·ium -(i)i *n*
apple pie *s* mala *npl* in crusto cocta
apple tree *s* mal·us -i *f*
appliance *s* instrument·um -i *n*
applicable *adj* (**to**) commod·us -a -um *(w. dat)*
applicant *s* petit·or -oris *m*
application *s (act of requesting)* petiti·o -onis *f; (act of applying)* adhibiti·o -onis *f; (industry)* sedulit·as -atis *f; (med)* foment·um -i *n*
apply *tr (to put on or to)* (**to**) adhibēre *(w. dat or ad w. acc); (to wounds)* inponere *(w. dat or in w. acc);* **to** — **oneself to** se conferre ad *(w. acc);* **to** — **the mind to** animum adhibēre ad *(w. acc)* **ǁ** *intr* **to** — **to** pertinēre ad *(w. acc),* cadere in *(w. acc);* **to** — **for** petere
appoint *tr* designare, creare, dicere
appointment *s* creati·o -onis *f; (agreement to meet)* constitut·um -i *n; (order)* mandat·um -i *n;* **I have an** — **with you** constitutum tecum habeo; **to keep an** — ad constitutum venire
apportion *tr* dividere
apportionment *s* divisi·o -onis *f*

apposition *s* appositi·o -onis *f;* **a noun in** — **with** vocabulum appositum *(w. dat)*
appraisal *s* aestimati·o -onis *f; (com, fin)* taxati·o -onis *f*
appraise *tr* aestimare; *(com, fin)* taxare
appraiser *s* aestimat·or -oris *m; (com, fin)* taxat·or -oris *m*
appreciable *adj* aestimabil·is -is -e, haud exigu·us -a -um
appreciate *tr (to esteem)* magni aestimare; *(to discern)* cognosere
appreciation *s* aestimati·o -onis *f; (gratitude)* grati·a -ae *f;* **to show** — **to s.o. for** gratiam alicui referre ob *(w. acc)*
apprehend *tr (to arrest; to grasp)* apprehendere
apprehension *s (arrest; understanding)* apprehensi·o -onis *f; (fear)* tim·or -oris *m,* sollicitud·o -inis *f*
apprehensive *adj* sollicit·us -a -um
apprentice *s* tir·o -onis *m*
apprenticeship *s* tirocin·ium -(i)i *n*
approach *tr* appropinquare *(w. dat); (to approximate)* accedere *(w. dat or ad w. acc)* **ǁ** *intr* appropinquare, accedere; *(of an event)* appetere
approach *s* access·us -ūs *m; (of time)* appropinquati·o -onis *f; (by sea)* appuls·us -ūs *m*
approachable *adj (person)* facil·is -is -e; *(place)* pat·ens -entis
approbation *s* approbati·o -onis *f*
appropriate *adj* conveni·ens -entis, apt·us -a -um, idone·us -a -um; **it is** — **to** convenit *(w. inf or acc & inf)*
appropriate *tr (to claim)* vindicare; *(to claim presumptuously)* arrogare; *(money)* (**to**) dicere *(w. dat)*
appropriately *adv* apte, congruenter
appropriateness *s* convenienti·a -ae *f,* congruenti·a -ae *f*
appropriation *s* vindicati·o -onis *f; (of money)* (**for**) destinati·o -onis *f* (in *w. acc*)
approval *s* approbati·o -onis *f*
approve *tr* approbare; *(a law)* sciscere **ǁ** *intr* **to** — **of** probare
approved *adj* probat·us -a - um
approximate *adj* proxim·us -a -um
approximate *tr* accedere ad *(w. acc)*
approximately *adv* prope, propemodum; *(w. numbers)* ad *(w. acc)*
apricot *s* armeniac·um -i *n*
apricot tree *s* armeniac·a -ae *f*
April *s* April·is -is *m or* mens·is -is *m* Aprilis; **in** — mense Aprili; **on the first of** — Kalendis Aprilibus
apron *s* sublig·ar -aris *n*
apt *adj* apt·us -a -um; **to be** — **to** *(w. inf)* solēre *(w. inf)*

aptitude s **(for)** ingen·ium -(i)i n (ad w. acc)

aptly adv apte

aptness s *(fitness)* convenienti·a -ae f; *(talent)* ingen·ium -(i)i n; *(tendency)* proclivit·as -atis f

aqueduct s aquaeduct·us -ūs m

arable adj arabil·is -is -e; **— land** arv·um -i n

arbiter s arbit·er -ri m

arbitrarily adv ad arbitrium

arbitrary s libidinos·us -a -um; *(imperious)* imperios·us -a -um

arbitrate tr & intr disceptare

arbitration s arbitr·ium -(i)i n

arbitrator s arbi·ter -tri m

arbor s umbracul·um -i n

arc s arc·us -ūs m

arcade s portic·us -ūs f

arch s arc·us -ūs m, forn·ix -icis f

arch tr arcuare, fornicare

arch adj *(chief)* summ·us -a -um; **— enemy** summus (·a) adversar·ius -(i)i m (·a -ae f)

archaeological adj archaeologic·us -a -um

archaeologist s archaeolog·us -i m (·a -ae f); **—s excavated this site** archaeologi hunc situm excaverunt

archaeology s archaeologi·a -ae f

archaic adj prisc·us -a -um

archaism s locuti·o -onis f obsoleta

archbishop s archiepiscop·us -i m

archer s sagittar·ius -(i)i m; *(astr)* Arciten·ens -entis m

archery s ar·s -tis f sagittandi

architect s architect·us -i m (·a -ae f)

architectural adj architectonic·us -a -um

architecture s architectur·a -ae f

archives spl tabul·ae -arum fpl; *(place)* tabular·ium -(i)i n

arctic adj arctic·us -a -um

ardent adj ard·ens -entis

ardently adv ardenter

ardor s ard·or -oris m

arduous adj ardu·us -a -um

area s *(open space; in geometry)* are·a -ae f; *(region)* regi·o -onis f

area code (telephonicus) numer·us -i m pralectorius

arena s (h)aren·a -ae f

Argonaut s argonaut·a -ae m

argue tr *(to reason)* arguere; *(to discuss)* disceptare de *(w. abl)*; **to — a case** causam agere ‖ intr disputare; *(to wrangle)* altercari; **stop arguing** desine *(pl:* desinite) altercari

argument s *(discussion)* disputati·o -onis f; *(heated)* altercati·o -onis f; *(reason in support of a position)* argument·um -i n; **the force of his —** vis f argumenti eius; **to get into an —** in litem ambiguam descendere; **to put up an —** recusare

argumentative adj litigios·us -a -um

arid adj arid·us -a -um; *(fig)* ieiun·us -a -um

aright adv recte

arise intr surgere; *(of a group)* consurgere; *(of a storm, etc.)* oriri, cooriri; *(suddenly)* exoriri; *(to come into existence)* exsistere; *(to originate)* **(from)** nasci (ex w. abl)

aristocracy s *(class)* optimat·es -ium mpl; *(government)* optimatium dominat·us -ūs m

aristocrat s optim·as -atis m; f

aristocratic adj patrici·us -a -um

arithmetic s arithmetic·a -ae f

ark s arc·a -ae f

arm tr armare

arm s bracch·ium -(i)i n; *(upper arm)* lacert·us -i m; *(of the sea)* sin·us -ūs m; *(of a chair)* anc·on -onis m; **at —'s length** eminus [adv]; **to carry in one's —s** in manibus gestare; **to carry under one's —s** sub alā portare; **with —s akimbo** ansat·us -a -um; **with folded —s** compressis manibus; **with open —s** sinu complexuque ‖ spl arm·a -orum npl; **by force of —** vi et armis; **to be under —** in armis esse; **to lay down —** ab armis discedere; **to take up —** arma sumere

armaments spl apparat·us -ūs m belli

armchair s anconibus fabrefacta sell·a -ae f

armed adj armat·us -a -um

armistice s induti·ae -arum fpl; **to break off an —** indutias tollere

armlet s bracchiol·um -i n; *(bracelet)* armill·a -ae f

armor s arm·a -orum npl

armory s armamentar·ium -(i)i n

armpit s al·a -ae f

arms see arm

army s exercit·us -ūs m; *(in battle)* aci·es -ei f; *(on the march)* agm·en -inis n; **to join the —** ad militiam ire; **to raise an —** exercitum comparare

aroma s arom·a -atis n; *(of wine)* flo·s -ris m

aromatic adj aromatic·us -a -um

around adv circum, circa; **all —** undique

around prep circum *(w. acc)*; *(approximately)* circa, ad *(w. acc)*

arouse tr *(feelings)* suscitare, exagitare; *(to wake up)* e somno excitare; *(fig)* excitare; **to — suspicion** suspicionem movēre

arraign tr accusare

arraignment s accusati·o -onis f

arrange tr *(to set in order)* ordinare; *(the hair)* componere, comere; *(a plan, meeting)* constituere; *(matters, a cloak to hang properly)* collocare; *(to agree)* pacisci; *(to put each thing separately in its place)* digerere; **—ed in a circle** in orbe disposit·us -a -um

arrangement s ord·o -inis m; *(of the year, of elections)* ordinati·o -onis f; *(of matters, of a garment)* collocati·o -onis f; *(of a speech, of*

books) context·us -ūs *m; the — was that* convenit ut
array *s* vestit·us -ūs *m; (mil)* aci·es -ei *f*
array *tr* vestire; *(mil)* instituere
arrears *spl* reliqu·a -orum *npl,* residuae pecuni·ae -arum *fpl;* **to be in —** relinqui
arrest *s* prehensi·o -onis *f*
arrest *tr* (ap)prehendere; *(movement)* tardare; **to — the attention of all** omnes in se convertere
arrival *s* advent·us -ūs *m; (by sea)* appuls·us -ūs *m*
arrive *intr* advenire; *(by ship or on horseback)* advehi; *(of a ship)* appelli; **to — at** pervenire ad *(w. acc);* **to — before the messengers** nuntios praevenire; **to — in** *(a place, country)* pervenire in *(w. acc)*
arrogance *s* arroganti·a -ae *f*
arrogant *adj* arrog·ans -antis
arrogantly *adv* arroganter
arrow *s* sagitt·a -ae *f*
arrowhead *s* spicul·um -i *n*
arsenal *s* armamentar·ium -(i)i *n; (naval)* naval·ia -ium *npl*
arsenic *s* arsenic·um -i *n*
arson *s* incend·ium -(i)i *n* malo dolo
arsonist *s* incendiar·ius -(i)i *m* (·a -ae *f)*
art *s* ar·s -tis *f; (practice of some craft)* artific·ium -(i)i *n;* **fine —s** art·es -ium *fpl* elegantes; **to study —** artis studēre
artery *s* arteri·a -ae *f*
artful *adj* callid·us -a -um
artfully *adv* callide
art gallery *s* pinacothec·a -ae *f*
arthritis arthrit·is -idis *f,* articulorum dol·or -oris *m*
artichoke cinar·a -ae *f*
article *s (object)* res rei *f; (ware)* mer·x -cis *f; (term)* condici·o -onis *f; (in newspaper or magazine)* commentariol·us -i *m,* commentati·o -onis *f; (clause in a law)* cap·ut -itis *n; (gram)* articul·us -i *m;* **— of faith** decretum -i *n* fidei; **definite (indefinite) —** finitus (infinitus) articulus
articulate *tr* articulatim dicere
articulate *adj* dilucid·us -a -um
articulately *adv* articulate
articulation *s (distinct utterance)* explanati·o -onis *f; (anat)* commissur·a -ae *f*
artifice *s* artific·ium -(i)i *n*
artificial *adj (produced by human hands)* artificios·us -a -um; *(not genuine)* factici·us -a -um
artificially *adv* arte; *(by human hands)* manu
artillery *s* torment·a -orum *npl*
artisan *s* opif·ex -icis *mf; (usu. in hard material)* fa·ber -bri *m*
artist *s (of any of the fine arts)* artif·ex -icis *mf; (painter)* pict·or -oris *m* (·rix -ricis *f)*

artistic *adj* artif·ex -icis
artistically *adv* artificiose
as *conj & adv* ut; *(while)* ut, dum, cum; *(as article of comparison, denoting equality)* atque, ac; *(for example)* velut, ut, sicut; *(because)* cum; **— ... —** *(degree)* tam ... quam, aeque ... atque; **— far —** quo(a)d; **— far — I know** quod scio; **— for instance** ut puta; **— good —** aeque bonus atque; **— great —** tantus ... quantus; **— if** quasi; **— is** ut est; **— it were** tamquam; **— long —** tamdiu, tantisper dum, quam diu; **— many —** totidem; **— much** tantum; **— often —** toties ... quoties; **— soon —** cum primum; **— soon as possible** quam primum; **— though** quasi; **— well —** ac, atque; **— yet** adhuc; **just — if** perinde ac si; **not — yet** nondum
ascend *tr & intr* ascendere
ascendency *s (superior influence)* potenti·a -ae *f;* **to gain the —** superior fieri
ascension *s* ascensi·o -onis *f*
ascent *s* ascensi·o -onis *f,* ascens·us -ūs *m;* **during the — to the summit** dum in summum ascenditur
ascertain *tr* comperire
ascetic *adj* ascetic·us -a -um
ascribe *tr* ascribere
ash *s* cin·is -eris *m; (tree)* fraxin·us -i *f;* **—es** cin·is -eris *m; (esp. ashes of the dead)* ciner·es -um *mpl*
ashamed *adj* pudibund·us -a -um; **I am — of** pudet me *(w. gen);* **I am — to tell** pudet me referre; **there is nothing to be — of** non est quod pudeatur
ashen *adj* pallid·us -a -um
ashore *adv (motion)* in terram; *(rest)* in litore; **to go —** in terram egredi
Asia *s* Asi·a -ae *f*
Asian *adj* Asian·us -a -um
Asiatic *adj* Asiatic·us -a -um
aside *adv* seorsum; **to call —** evocare; **to set** *or* **put —** seponere; **to take —** seducere; **to turn —** deflectere
aside from *prep* praeter *(w. acc)*
asinine *adj* asinin·us -a -um
ask *tr* rogare; *(esp. to seek information)* quaerere; *(to beg, petition for, esp. of a request made to a superior)* petere; *(to demand)* poscere, postulare; quaerere; **he —ed me whether** quaesivit a me *(or* de me *or* ex me) num; **he —ed you a question** ille te interrogavit; **I — you this question** hoc te rogo; **to — a few questions** pauca quaerere; **to — further questions** quaerere ultra; **to — many questions** multa quaerere *or* rogare; **— one question after another** aliud ex alio quaerere; **to — questions** interrogare; **to — s.o. for s.th.** aliquem aliquid rogare; **to — that (that not)** rogare *(w.* ut *or* ne *w. subj);*

to — this question hoc quaerere; to — why requirere quamobrem ‖ *intr* to — about *(s.o., s.th)* de aliquo rogare; to — for petere
askance *adv* to look — (at) limis oculis aspicere
asleep *adj* dormi·ens -entis; half — semisomn·us -a -um; to be (sound) — (arte) dormire; to fall — obdormiscere
asparagus *s* asparag·us -i *m*
aspect *s* aspect·us -ūs *m*
asphalt *s* bitum·en -inis *n*
asphyxiation *s* asphyxi·a -ae *f*
aspirant *s* (to) appetit·or -oris *m (w. gen)*
aspiration *s* affectati·o -onis *f;* to have lofty —s magna spectare
aspire *intr* to — to appetere, affectare
aspiring *adj* (after) appet·ens -entis *(w. gen)*
ass *s* asin·us -i *m,* asin·a -ae *f; (fool)* asin·us -i *m; (anat)* clun·es -ium *mpl*
assail *tr* appetere; *(mil)* oppugnare
assailable *adj* expugnabil·is -is -e
assailant *s* oppugnat·or -oris *m*
assassin *s* percuss·or -oris *m,* parricid·a -ae *m*
assassinate *tr* per insidias interficere
assassination *s* caed·es -is *f* per īnsidias
assault *s* oppugnati·o -onis *f;* aggravated — *(leg)* vis *f;* — and battery vis *f* inlata; sexual — stuprati·o -onis *f;* to take by — expugnare
assault *tr (a person)* manūs inferre *(w. dat); (sexually)* stuprum īnferre *(w. dat); (mil)* oppugnare
assemblage *s* congregati·o -onis *f*
assemble *tr* cogere; *(to call together)* convocare ‖ *intr* convenire
assembly *s* coet·us -ūs *m; (mil, pol)* conti·o -onis *f; (electoral)* comiti·a -orum *npl;* in the — pro contione; to hold an — comitia *(or* contionem) habēre
assent *s* assens·us -ūs *m*
assent *intr* (to) assentiri *(w. dat);* to — to a request petenti annuere
assert *tr* affirmare, confirmare; *(to maintain, claim)* asserere
assertion *s* affirmati·o -onis *f; (claim)* asserti·o -onis *f*
assess *tr* taxare; *(for tax purposes)* censēre
assessment *s* taxati·o -onis *f; (for tax purposes)* cens·us -ūs *m*
assessor *s* cens·or -oris *m*
assets *spl* bon·a -orum *npl*
assiduous *adj* assidu·us -a -um
assiduously *adv* assidue
assign *tr* attribuere; *(land, duties)* assignare; *(time)* praestituere; *(task)* delegare; *(to allege)* afferre; *(in writing)* praescribere
assignment *s* attributi·o -onis *f; (of land, duties)* assignati·o -onis *f; (in school)*

pens·um -i *n;* to do the — pensum *(or* praescriptum) perigere
assimilate *tr* assimulare; *(food)* digerere; *(knowledge)* concipere
assimilation *s* digesti·o -onis *f*
assist *tr* adesse *(w. dat),* adiuvare
assistance *s* auxil·ium -(i)i *n;* to be of — to auxilio esse *(w. dat)*
assistant *s* adiut·or -oris *m,* adiutr·ix -icis *f*
associate *s* soc·ius -(i)i *m (·a -ae f)*
associate *adj* soci·us -a -um
associate *tr* consociare, adiungere ‖ *intr* to — with familiariter uti *(w. dat)*
association *s* societ·as -atis *f;* — with s.o consociati·o -onis *f (w. gen)*
assort *tr* digerere
assortment *s (arrangement)* digesti·o -onis *f;* a large — of jewelry gemm·ae -arum *fpl* plurimae et cuiusve generis
assuage *tr* allevare
assume *tr* assumere; *(a task)* suscipere; *(improperly)* arrogare; *(to take for granted in argument)* ponere; *(a role)* induere
assumption *s* assumpti·o -onis *f; (improper)* arroganti·a -ae *f; (hypothesis)* sumpti·o -onis *f*
assurance *s* fiduci·a -ae *f; (confidence)* confidenti·a -ae *f; (guarantee)* fid·es ei *f*
assure *tr (to promise)* confirmare, affirmare; to be *or* feel —ed confidere
assured *adj (e.g, victory)* explorat·us -a -um
assuredly *adv* profecto
asterisk *s* asterīsc·us -i *m*
asthma *s* asthm·a -atis *n;* to have — suspirio laborare
asthmatic *adj* asthmatic·us -a -um
astonish *tr* stupefacere
astonished *adj* attonit·us -a -um; to be — at obstupescere *(w. dat)*
astonishing *adj* mir·us -a -um
astonishingly *adv* admirabiliter
astonishment *s* admirati·o -onis *f; (speechlessness)* stup·or -oris *m*
astound *tr* (ob)stupefacere; to be —ed stupēre
astray *adv* vag·us -a -um; to go — errare; to lead s.o. — aliquem transversum agere
astrologer *s* astrolog·us -i *m,* mathematic·us -i *m*
astrology *s* astrologi·a -ae *f*
astronaut *s* astronaut·a -ae *m,* astronautri·a -ae *f*
astronomer *s* astrolog·us -i *m (·a -ae f)*
astronomical *adj* astronomic·us -a -um
astronomy *s* astronomi·a -ae *f*
astute *adj* astut·us -a -um
asylum *s* asyl·um -i *n*
at *prep (of place)* ad *(w. acc); (strictly, near)* apud *(w. acc); (usu. with names of towns, harbors, villas)* in *(w. abl), or* locative case;

(at the house of) apud *(w. acc); (of time)* use abl case; — **all** omnino, prorsum; — **first** primo, initio; — **home** domi; — **least** duxtaxat, utique; — **most** summum; — **once** momento, continuo; — **present** in praesentiā; — **the right time** in tempore
atheism *s* deos esse negare *(used as a neuter noun)*
atheist *s* athe·os -i *m* (·a -ae *f*)
Athenian *adj* Athenae·us -a -um
Athenian *s* Atheniens·is -is *mf*
Athens *s* Athen·ae -arum *fpl*
athlete *s* athlet·a -ae *mf*
athletic *adj* athletic·us -a -um
athletics *spl* ar·s -tis *f* athletica
atlas *s* orbis terrarum descripti·o -onis *f*
atmosphere *s* cael·um -i *n*
atmospheric *adj* caeli *(gen)*
atom *s* atom·us -i *f*
atomic *adj* atomic·us -a -um; — **bomb** pyrobol·um -i *n* atomicum; — **energy** vis *f* atomica; — **theory** atomorum doctrin·a -ae *f*
atone *intr* **to** — **for** (ex)piare
atonement *s* expiati·o -onis *f*
atrocious *adj* atro·x -ocis
atrocity *s (atrociousness)* atrocit·as -atis *f; (deed)* atrox facin·us -eris *n*
attach *tr (to fasten to)* annectere, adiungere; *(e.g., meaning)* subicere; **to** — **importance to s.th.** aliquid magni aestimare; **to** — **oneself to s.o.** se alicui adiungere; **to be —ed to s.o.** adhaerēre *(w. dat)*
attachment *s (contact)* iunctur·a -ae *f; (devotion)* stud·ium -(i)i *n;* **my** — **to the Roman people** studium meum in populum Romanum
attack *s* impet·us -ūs *m; (usu. on a town)* oppugnati·o -onis *f; (by cavalry)* incurs·us -ūs *m; (of a disease)* tentati·o -onis *f; (verbal)* petiti·o -onis *f*
attack *tr* aggredi; *(esp. w. physical force)* adoriri, vim īnferre *(w. dat); (towns)* oppugnare; *(of a disease)* tentare, invadere; *(verbally)* petere; **—ed by a sudden illness** corrept·us -a -um subitā valetudine
attacker *s* aggress·or -oris *m; (mil)* oppugnat·or -oris *m*
attain *tr* adipisci, cōnsequi; **to** — **to** pervenire ad *(w. acc)*
attainable *adj (by request)* impetrabil·is -is -e; **to be** — patēre
attempt *s* conat·us -ūs *m*
attempt *tr* conari, temptare, moliri
attend *tr (to accompany)* comitari; *(to escort)* prosequi; *(school, wedding, senate session)* frequentare; *(to be present at, e.g., a meeting)* adesse *(w. dat)*, interesse *(w. dat); (of a doctor)* assidēre *(w. dat);* **to** — **to** procurare, animadvertere, operam dare *(w. dat)*

attendance *s (in great numbers)* frequenti·a -ae *f; (of a doctor)* assiduit·as -atis *f*
attendant *adj* adiunct·us -a -um; — **circumstances** adiunct·a -orum *npl*
attendant *s (to officials)* apparit·or -oris *m; (servant)* minist·er -ri *m*, ministr·a -ae *f; (of a temple)* aeditu·us -i *m*
attention *s* attentus anim·us -i *m*, animi attenti·o -onis *f;* **pay attention!** attende! *(pl:* attendite!) *or* animum attende! *(pl:* animos attendite!); **pay** — **to what I am saying!** dictis meis attende! *(pl:* attendite!) **to attract** — animos hominum ad se convertere; **to call** — **to** indicare; **to call for** — animadverti iubēre; **to hold our** — animos nostros tenēre; **to pay** — **to** operam dare *(w. dat)*
attentive *adj* attent·us -a -um
attentively *adv* attente
attest *tr* testificare
attestation *s* testificati·o -onis *f*
attic *s* cenacul·um -i *n*
Attic *adj* Attic·us -a -um
Attica *s* Attic·a -ae *f*
attire *s* vestit·us -ūs *m*
attitude *s* habit·us -ūs *m; (of the body)* stat·us -ūs *m*
attorney *s* cognit·or -oris *m* (·rix -ricis *f*)
attorney general *s* advocat·us -i *m* (·a -ae *f*) fīsci
attract *tr (lit & fig)* trahere; **to** — **a buyer** emptorem adducere; **to** — **the attention of all** oculos omnium in se convertere
attraction *s* vis *f* attractionis; *(fig)* illecebr·a -ae *f*
attractive *adj* illecebros·us -a -um; *(esp. in looks)* specios·us -a -um, venust·us -a -um
attractively *adv* blande
attractiveness *s* lep·os -oris *m*
attributable *adj* ascribend·us -a -um
attribute *s* propr·ium -(i)i *n*, qualit·as -atis *f*
attribute *tr* (at)tribuere; *(to attribute wrongly)* affingere
attrition *s* attrit·us -ūs *m*
attune *tr* modulari
auburn *adj* fulv·us -a -um
auction *s* aucti·o -onis *f; (by the state)* hast·a -ae *f;* **to hold an** — auctionem habēre
auction *tr* **to** —**off** auctione vendere; *(by the state)* sub hastā vendere
auctioneer *s* praec·o -onis *m*
audacious *adj* aud·ax -acis
audaciously *adv* audacter
audacity *s* audaci·a -ae *f*
audible *adj* clar·us -a -um
audibly *adv* clarā voce
audience *s* auditor·es -um *mpl*, spectator·es -um *mpl; (bystanders)* coron·a -ae *f;* **to ask for a private** — secretum petere
audiocasette *s* phonocaset·a -ae *f*

audiotape s phonotaeni·a -ae f
audiovisual aid s audivisificum subsid·ium -(i)i n
audit s rationum inspecti·o -onis f
audit tr īnspicere; (educ) extra ordinem audire
auditory adj auditori·us -a -um
Augean adj Augiae (gen)
augment tr augēre, ampliare ‖ intr augēri
augmentation s increment·um -i n
augur s aug·ur -uris m; —'s **staff** litu·us -i m
augur intr augurari
augury s augur·ium -(i)i n
August s August·us -i m or mens·is -is m Augustus; **on the first of** — Kalendis Augustis
Augustan adj Augustal·is -is -e
aunt s (pateral) amit·a -ae f; (maternal) materter·a -ae f
auricle s auricul·a -ae f
auspices spl auspic·ium -(i)i n; **to take the** — auspicari; **under the** — **of** sub clientela (w. gen); **without taking the** — inauspicato
auspicious adj fel·ix -icis
auspiciously adv feliciter
austere adj auster·us -a -um
austerely adv austere
austerity s austerit·as -atis f
authentic adj genuin·us -a -um
authenticate tr recognoscere
authenticity s auctorit·as -atis f
author s (originator) auct·or -oris mf; (writer) script·or -oris m (·rix -ricis f); (inventor) condit·or -oris m
authoritative adj grav·is -is -e; (reliable) cert·us -a -um; (imperious) imperios·us -a -um
authority s auctorit·as -atis f; (leave) licenti·a -ae f; (power of a magistrate) imper·ium -(i)i n; (expert) auct·or -oris m; **on good** — gravi auctore; **the authorities** magistrat·ūs -uum mpl
authorization s auctorit·as -atis f
authorize tr **to** — **s.o. to** auct·or -oris m esse alicui (w. gerundive)
authorship s (origin) auct·or -oris m
autobiography s lib·er -ri m de vitā suā
autocracy s dominati·o -onis f
autocrat s domin·us -i m
autocratic adj tyrannic·us -a -um
autograph s chirograph·um -i n
autograph tr manu suā scribere
automatic adj automatari·us -a -um
automobile s autocinet·um -ī n
autumn s autumn·us -i m
autumn(al) adj autumnal·is -is -e
auxiliaries spl auxili·a -orum npl
auxiliary adj auxiliar·is -is -e

avail tr prodesse (w. dat); **to** — **oneself of** uti (w. abl); **what do laws** —? quid leges faciunt? ‖ intr valēre
avail s **but to no** — sed frustra; **to be of no** — usui non esse
available adj in promptu; **to be** — praesto [indecl] esse
avalanche s nivis ruin·a -ae f
avarice s avariti·a -ae f
avaricious adj avar·us -a -um
avariciously adv avare
avenge tr ulcisci, vindicare
avenger s ult·or -oris m, vind·ex -icis mf
avenging adj ultr·ix -icis
avenue s vi·a -ae f
average s med·ium -(i)i n; **on the** — peraeque
average adj peraeque duct·us -a -um, modic·us -a -um
average tr (to calculate) peraeque ducere; (to amount to) peraequare
aversion s fastid·ium -(i)i n; **to have an** — **for** fastidire
avert tr avertere
avid adj avid·us -a -um
avidly adv avide
avocation s stud·ium -(i)i n
avoid tr evitare; (a blow) declinare
avoidable adj evitabil·is -is -e
avoidance s vitati·o -onis f
await tr exspectare, manēre
awake adj vigil·ans -antis, desomn·is -is -e; **to be** — vigilare; **to be** — **all night** pervigilare
awaken tr somno excitare ‖ intr expergisci
award s praem·ium -(i)i n
award tr tribuere; (leg) addicere
aware adj gnar·us -a -um; **to be** — **of** scire
awareness s cōnscienti·a -ae f
away adv use verbs with prefix ab-; — **with you!** abi hinc!; **far** — procul; **to be** — abesse; **to fly** — avolare; **to go** — abire
awe s reverenti·a -ae f; **to stand in** — **of** verēri
awesome adj verend·us -a -um; (coll) mirific·us -a -um
awful adj terribil·is -is -e
awfully adv terribiliter
awhile adv paulisper, aliquamdiu
awkward adj inept·us -a -um; (unwieldly) inhabil·is -is -e
awkwardly adv inepte
awkwardness s inepti·a -ae f
awning s velar·ium -(i)i n
awry adj oblique; **to go** — perquam evenire
ax s secur·is -is f
axiom s proloqu·ium -(i)i n
axis s ax·is -is m
axle s ax·is -is m
azure adj caerule·us -a -um

B

babble *s* garrulit·as -atis *f*
babble *intr* blatire; **to — on about** effutire
babbler *s* blater·o -onis *m*
babbling *adj* garrul·us -a -um
babe *s* inf·ans -antis *mf*
baby *s* inf·ans -antis *mf*
baby *tr* indulgēre *(w. dat)*
babyish *adj* infantil·is -is -e
bacchanal *s* bacch·ans -antis *m*, bacch·a -ae *f*
Bacchanalia *spl* bacchanal·ia -ium *npl*
bacchanalian *adj* bacchanal·is -is -e
Bacchic *adj* bacchic·us -a -um
Bacchus *s* Bacch·us -i *m*
bachelor *s* caeleb·s -is *m; (degree)* bacchelau-
    re·us -i *m*
bachelorhood *s* caelibat·us -ūs *m*
back *s* terg·um -i *n*, dors·um -i *n;* **at one's —**
    a tergo; **— of the classroom** posterior par·s
    -tis *f* scholae; **— of the head** occipit·ium -(i)i
    n; **get off my —!** apage te a dorso meo!;
    lying on one's — resupin·us -a -um; **to**
    climb on his — super dorsum eius ascen-
    dere; **to turn one's — on** contemnere
back *adv* retro, retrorsum; *or use verbs with*
    prefix re- *or* retro-
back *tr* favēre *(w. dat)* ‖ *intr* **to — away from**
    refugere; **to — down** recedere; **to — out** se
    recipere; **to — up** retrogradi; *(of water)*
    refluere
backboard *s* plute·us -i *m*
backbone *s* spin·a -ae *f*
back door *s* postic·um -i *n*
backer *s* faut·or -oris *m; (pol)* suffragat·or
    -oris *m*
background *s (in paintings)* abscedent·ia -ium
    npl; (causes) ort·ūs -ūs *m; (of a person)* prior
    aet·as -atis *f*
backpack *s* manic·a -ae *f*
back seat *s* sed·es -is *f* posterior
backside *s (anat)* clun·es -ium *mpl*
backstairs *spl* posticae scal·ae -arum *fpl*
backstroke *s* natati·o -onis *f* resupina; **to do**
    the — natare resupin·us -a -um
backward *adv* retro, retrorsum
backward *adj (reversed)* supin·us -a -um;
    (slow) tard·us -a -um; **to be —** cunctari
backwardness *s* tardit·as -atis *f*
bacon *s* lard·us -i *m;* **to bring home the —**
    habēre panem
bad *adj* mal·us -a -um; *(usu. morally bad)*
    improb·us -a -um; *(health, weather)*
    advers·us -a -um; *(harmful)* noxi·us -a -um;
    (road) iniqu·us -a -um; *(rotten)* putid·us -a
    -um; **— news** acerbum nunt·ium -(i)i *n;* **it is**
    — to *(w. inf)* alienum est *(w. inf);* **to go —**
    corrumpi; **too bad about Cicero** male de

Cicerone; **wine is — for you** alienum tibi
    vinum est
badge *s* insign·e -is *n*
badger *tr* vexare
badly *adv* male; improbe; **to want —** valde
    cupere
badminton *s* lud·us -i *m* pilae pinnatae; **to**
    play — pilā pinnatā ludere
badness *s* maliti·a -ae *f; (moral)* improbit·as
    -atis *f*
baffle *tr* eludere
bag *s* sacc·us -i *m; (dim.)* saccul·us -i *m;*
    (handbag) bulg·a -ae *f*
baggage *s* sarcin·ae -arum *fpl; (mil)* impedi-
    ment·a -orum *npl*
bagpipes *s* utricular·ium -(i)i *n;* **to play the —**
    utriculario ludere
bail *s* vadimon·ium -(i)i *n;* **to be out on —**
    vadari; **to put up — for** spondēre pro
    (w. abl)
bail *tr* **to — s.o. out** *(leg)* aliquem vadari; *(fig)*
    aliquem e periculo servare; **to — out the**
    boat sentinam e navicula egerere; **to — out**
    water sentinam egerere
bailiff *s (in a courtroom)* viat·or -oris *m; (man-*
    ager of an estate) villic·us -i *m*
bait *s* esc·a -ae *f; (fig)* incitament·um -i *n;* **to**
    put the — on the hook escam hamo
    imponere
bait *tr* inescare; *(to tease)* lacessere
bake *tr* coquere
baker *s* pist·or -oris *m*, pistr·ix -icis *f*
bakery *s* pistrin·a -ae *f*
balance *s (pair of scales)* trutin·a -ae *f; (equi-*
    librium) aequilibr·ium -(i)i *n; (in bookkeep-*
    ing) reliqu·a -orum *npl; (fig)* compensati·o
    -onis *f*
balance *tr* librare; **to — accounts** rationes dis-
    pungere; **to — joy with grief** laetitiam cum
    doloribus compensare ‖ *intr* constare; **the**
    account —s ratio constat
balance sheet *s* rati·o -onis *f* accepti et expēnsi
balancing *s* **— of accounts** dispuncti·o -onis *f*
balcony *s* maenian·um -i *n*
bald *adj* calv·us -a -um; *(style)* arid·us -a -um;
    — head *(person)* calvit·ium -(i)i *n;* **to be —**
    calvēre
baldhead *s* calv·us -i *m*
baldness *s* calvit·ium -(i)i *n; (of style)* aridit·as
    -atis *f*
bale *s* fasc·is -is *m*
bale *tr (hay)* in fasces colligere
balk *tr* frustrari
ball *s* globul·us -i *m; (for playing)* pil·a -ae *f*,
    (inflated) foll·is -is *f;* **—s** *(anat) (sl) (lit &*
    fig) cole·i -orum *mpl;* **to play —** pilā ludere
    to throw the — follem *or* pollem coniecere
ballad *s* carm·en -inis *n*
ballet *s* saltati·o -onis *f*

ballet dancer *s* pantomim·us -i *m,* (·a -ae *f)*
ball field *s* camp·us -i *m* lusorius
ball game *s* lus·us -us *m* pilae *or* follis
ballot *s* suffrag·ium -(i)i *n;* **to cast a —** suffragium ferre
ballot box *s* suffragiorum cist·a -ae *f*
ballpoint pen *s* stil·us -i *m* sphaeratus
balm *s* balsam·um -i *n*
baloney *s* farcim·en -inis *n;* **baloney!** fabulae!
bamboo *s* arund·o -inis *f* Indica
bamboozle *tr* verba dare *(w. dat)*
ban *s* interdict·um -i *n*
ban *tr* interdicere
banana *s* arien·a -ae *f*
band *s (group)* man·us -ūs *f; (gang)* caterv·a
-ae *f; (for the head)* influ·a -ae *f; (of musicians)* symphoni·a -ae *f*
band *intr* **to — together** coniungi; *(pej)* coniurare
bandage *s* fasci·a -ae *f*
bandage *tr (a wound)* astringere; *(an arm, etc.)*
deligare
bandit *s* latr·o -onis *m*
banditry *s* latrocin·ium -(i)i *n*
bang *s* sonit·us -ūs *m,* crepit·us -ūs *m*
bang *tr* verberare; **to — together** concrepare ‖
intr sonitum facere; **to — on the door** fores
pulsare
bangs *(of hair)* anti·ae -arum *fpl*
banish *tr (from the confines of a state)* exterminare; *(usual formula in time of Cicero)*
aquā et igni interdicere; *(temporarily)* relegare; *(to some island)* deportare; *(cares, etc.)*
pellere, eximere
banishment *s (act)* relegati·o -onis *f,* interdic-
ti·o -onis *f* aquā et igni; *(state)* exil·ium
-(i)i *n*
banister *s* epimed·ion -(i)i *n*
bank *intr* **to — on** niti *(w. abl)*
bank *s (of river)* rip·a -ae *f; (of earth)* agg·er
-eris *m; (com)* argentari·a -ae *f*
bank account *s* rati·o -onis *f* argentaria
bank book *s* libell·us -i *m* comparsorum
banker *s* argentar·ius -(i)i *m* (·a -ae *f)*
banking *s* argentaria negotiati·o -onis *f;* **to be
engaged in —** argentariam facere
bank manager *s* argentariae modera·tor -toris
m (·trix -tricis *f)*
bankrupt *adj* (creditoribus) decoct·us -a -um;
(fig) in·ops -opis; **to be —** decoquere; **to go
— foro** cedere, conturbare
bankruptcy *s* decocti·o -onis *f;* **to declare —**
bonam copiam eiurare
bank teller *s* argentari·us -i *m* (·a -ae *f)*
bank window *s* ostiol·um -i *n* argentarium
banner *s* vexill·um -i *n*
banquet *s* conviv·ium -(i)i *n; (religious)*
epul·ae -arum *fpl;* **to go to** *or* **attend a —**
convivium inire

banter *s* cavillati·o -onis *f*
banter *intr* cavillari
bantering *s* cavillati·o -onis *f*
baptism *s* baptism·a -atis *n*
baptize *tr* baptizare
bar *s* vect·is -is *f; (of door)* ser·a -ae *f; (of gate)*
ob·ex -icis *m; (ingot)* lat·er -eris *m; (legal
profession)* for·um -i *n; (barroom)* oec·us -i
m potorius; *(of chocolate or soap)* quadrul·a
-ae *f; (of a cage)* clathr·i -orum *mpl;* **of
the —** forens·is -is -e; **to practice at the —**
causas agere
bar *tr (the door)* obserare; *(to keep away)* prohibēre; **to — s.o. from campaigning** submovēre aliquem petitione; **to — s.o.'s way**
obstare alicui
barb *s* ham·us -i *m; (sting)* acule·us -i *m*
barbarian *adj* barbar·us -a -um
barbarian *s* barbar·us -i *m,* barbar·a -ae *f*
barbaric *adj* barbaric·us -a -um
barbarism *s* barbari·a -ae *f; (in speech)* bar-
barism·us -i *m*
barbarity *s* ferocit·as -atis *f*
barbarous *adj* barbar·us -a -um
barbed *adj* hamat·us -a -um
barbecue *tr* in craticulā assare
barbecue grill *s* craticul·a -ae *f*
barber *s* tons·or -oris *m,* tonstr·ix -icis *f*
barber chair *s* sell·a -ae *f* tonsoria
barbershop *s* tōnstrin·a -ae *f*
bard *s* vat·es -is *m*
bare *adj* nud·us -a -um; *(style)* press·us -a -um
bare *tr* nudare
barefaced *adj (shameless)* impud·ens -entis;
(unconcealed) evidentissim·us -a -um
barefoot *adj & adv* nudis pedibus
bareheaded *adj* nudo capite
barely *adv* vix, aegre
bargain *s* pret·ium - (i)i *n* speciale; **a good —**
empti·o -onis *f* secunda; **to buy at a —** bene
emere; **to strike a —** pacisci
bargain *intr* pacisci; **to — for** depacisci
barge *s* lint·er -ris *f*
barge *intr* **to — in** *(coll)* intervenire
baritone *s* cant·or -oris *m* vocis gravis
bark *s (of tree)* cort·ex -icis *m; (of dog)*
latrat·us -ūs *m; (ship)* rat·is -is *f*
bark *intr* latrare; **to — at** allatrare
barking *s* latrat·us -ūs *m*
barley *s* horde·um -i *n*
barley *adj* hordeac·us -a -um; **— flour** hordea-
ca farin·a -ae *f*
barmaid *s* cauponae ministr·a -ae *f*
barn *s* horre·um -i *n*
barnyard *s* cohor·s -tis *f*
barometer *s* barometr·um -i *n*
barometric *adj* barometric·us -a -um
baron *s* bar·o -onis *m*
barracks *spl* castr·a -orum *npl* stativa

barrel *s* cup·a -ae *f*
barren *adj* steril·is -is -e
barrenness *s* sterilit·as -atis *f*
barricade *s* claustr·a -orum *npl,* agg·er -eris *m; (of logs)* concaed·es -ium *fpl*
barricade *tr* obsaepire
barrier *s* sept·um -i *n; (fig)* claustr·a -orum *npl*
barrister *s* causidic·us -i *m* (·a -ae *f*)
bar stool *s* seliquastr·um -ī *n* praealtum
bartender *s* caup·o -onis *m,* inservit·or -oris *m*
barter *s* permutati·o -onis *f* mercium
barter *tr* mutare *(w. acc of thing given and abl of thing received);* **to — booty for wine** praedam vino mutare **‖** *intr* **(with)** merces mutare *(cum w. abl)*
base *adj* humil·is -is -e; *(morally)* turp·is -is -e; *(coinage)* adulterin·us -a -um
base *s (groundwork; of a column)* bas·is -is *f; (mil)* castr·a -orum *npl;* **first (second, third, home) —** basis prima (secunda, tertia, summa); **to play first (second, third) —** apud primam (secundam, tertiam) basim ludere
base *tr* fundare; **to — the country on laws** civitatem legibus fundare
baseball *s (the ball)* basipil·a -ae *f; —* **game** basipilae lus·us -us *m;* **to play —** basipilā lūdere
baseless *adj* van·us -a -um
basement *s* hypoge·um -i *n*
bash *tr (coll)* percutere; **to — in** perfringere; **to — in a man's head** alicui caput perfringere
bashful *adj* verecund·us -a -um
bashfully *adv* verecunde
bashfulness *s* verecundi·a -ae *f*
basic *adj* prim·us -a -um
basics *spl* element·a -orum *npl*
basic training *s* rudimenta *npl* militaria
basilica *s* basilic·a -ae *f*
basin *s* pelv·is -is *f; (reservoir)* lac·us -ūs *m*
basis *s* bas·is -is *f*
bask *intr* **to — in the sun** apricari
basket *s* corb·is -is *f; (money basket)* fisc·us -i *m; (for flowers, fruit)* calath·us -i *m; (small food basket)* sportell·a -ae *f*
basketball *s* corbifoll·is -is *m;* **to play —** corbifolle ludere
bas-relief *s* anaglypt·a -orum *npl; (on plates, vessels)* toreum·a -atis *n*
bass *s (fish)* perc·a -ae *f* fluvialis; *(mus)* son·us -i *m* gravissimus; **to sing —** voce imā cantare
bassinet *s* cun·ae -arum *fpl*
bass viol *s* contrabass·um -i *n*
bastard *adj* spuri·us -a -um
bastard *s* noth·us -i *m*
baste *tr* lardo perfundere; *(in sewing)* suturam *(w. gen)* solute suere
bat *s (bird)* vespertili·o -onis *m; (club)* clav·a -ae *f*

bat *tr & intr* clavo pulsare
batch *s* mass·a -ae *f; (pile)* cumul·us -i *m*
bath *s* balne·um -i *n; (public)* balne·a -orum *npl; (bath and community center)* therm·ae -arum *fpl;* **to take a cold (hot) —** frigidā (calidā) aquā lavari
bathe *tr* lavare; *(face, sore limb)* fovēre **‖** *intr* lavari
bather *s* qui *(or* quae*)* lavat; *(swimmer)* natat·or -oris *m* (·rix -ricis *f*); **—s** lavant·es -ium *mpl*
bathing *s* lavati·o -onis *f; (swimming)* natati·o -onis *f*
bathroom *s* balneol·um -i *n; (toilet)* loc·us -i *m* secretus; *(public toilet)* foric·a -ae *f*
bath towel *s* gausapin·a -ae *f*
bathtub *s* sol·ium -(i)i *n*
baton *s* virg·a -ae *f*
battalion *s* cohor·s -tis *f*
batter *s* farin·a -ae *f* lacte ovisque mixta
batter *s (in baseball)* clava·tor -toris *m* (·trix -tricis *f*)
batter *tr* verberare; *(to shake by battering)* percutere; **to — down** ariete deicere
battering ram *s* ari·es -etis *m*
battery *s* accumulatr·um -i *n*
battle *s (general & mil)* pugn·a -ae *f; (mil)* proel·ium -(i)i *n;* **naval — off** pugna navalis ante *(w. acc);* **the — of** *(at or near a town)* proelium apud *or* ad *(w. acc);* **to fight a —** proelium facere
battle *tr* certare **‖** *intr* proeliari
battle-ax *s* bipenn·is -is *f*
battle-cry *s* clam·or -oris *m* militum; *(of barbarians)* barit·us -ūs *m*
battlefield *s* aci·es -ei *f*
battle formation *s* aci·es -ei *f*
battlement *s* pinn·a -ae *f*
baubles *spl* tric·ae -arum *fpl*
bawl *intr* clamitare; *(to cry)* flēre; *(of babies)* vagire
bawling *s* vociferati·o -onis *f; (crying)* flet·us -ūs *m; (by a baby)* vagit·us -ūs *m*
bay *s (of the sea)* sin·us -ūs *m; (tree)* laur·us -i *f;* **at —** obsess·us -a -um; **to keep at —** arcēre
bay *adj (light-colored)* helv·us -a -um; *(horse)* spad·ix -icis; *(of bay tree)* laure·us -a -um
bay *intr* ululare
bayonet *s* pugi·o -onis *m*
bayonet *tr* pugione fodere
bazaar *s* for·um -i *n* rerum venalium
be *intr* esse; *(of a situation)* se habēre, versari; **— gone!** apage!; **that is the situation** sic res se habent; **to — absent** abesse; **to — against** adversari; **to — among** interesse *(w. dat);* **to — fine** bene se habēre; valēre; **to — for** favēre *(w. dat),* stare cum *(w. abl);* **to — present** adesse, interesse; **to — up for sale**

vēnire; **to — up in years** aetate provect·us -a
-um esse; **to — up to a task** operi par esse
beach *s* act·a -ae *f,* lit·us -oris *n*
beach *tr (a ship)* subducere
beach chair *s* sell·a -ae *f* litoralis *(or* cubitoria)
beacon *s* ign·is -is *m* in specula; *(lighthouse)*
phar·us -i *f*
bead *s* bac·a -ae *f*
beagle *s* parvus can·is -is *m* venaticus
beak *s* rostr·um -i *n*
beaked *adj* rostrat·us -a -um
beaker *s (cup)* pocul·um -i *n; (decanter)* obb·a
-ae *f*
beam *s (of wood)* trab·s -is *f; (of light)* iub·ar
-aris *n; (ray)* rad·ius -(i)i *m*
beaming *adj* nit·ens -entis
bean *s* fab·a -ae *f; (kidney bean)* phasel·us
-i *mf*
bear *tr (to carry)* portare, ferre; *(to endure)*
ferre, pati; *(to produce)* ferre; *(to beget)*
parere; **to — away** auferre; **to — in mind**
recordari; **to — out** *(to confirm)* arguere; **to
— witness** testari ‖ *intr* **to — down on** *(to
approach)* appropinquare *(w. dat); (to press)*
inniti in *(w. acc); (to oppress)* opprimere; **to
— with** indulgēre *(w. dat)*
bear *s* urs·us -i *m,* urs·a -ae *f;* **—s grunt** ursi
grunniunt
bearable *adj* tolerabil·is -is -e
bear cub *s* ursae catull·us -i *m*
beard *s* barb·a -ae *f; (of grain)* arist·a -ae *f;* **to
cut his first —** barbatorium facere; **to grow
a —** barbam summittere
bearded *adj* barbat·us -a -um
beardless *adj* inberb·is -is -e
bearer *s (porter)* baiul·us -i *m; (of litter)* lec-
ticar·ius -(i)i *m; (of letter)* tabellar·ius -(i)i
m; (of news) nunt·ius -(i)i *m*
bearing *s (posture)* gest·us -ūs *m; (direction)*
regi·o -onis *f;* **to get one's —s** regionem
reperire; **to have a — on** pertinēre ad *(w.
acc)*
beast *s* besti·a -ae *f,* belu·a -ae *f; (brutish person)* belu·a -ae *f*
beastly *adj* beluin·us -a -um
beast of burden *s* iument·um -i *n*
beat *tr (to punish)* verberare; *(to knock on)* pulsare; *(to conquer)* vincere; *(the breast, drum)*
plangere; **to — back** repellere; **to — down**
demoliri; **to — in** perfringere; **to — the daylights out of** pulchre percopolare ‖ *intr* palpitare; **to — upon** *(of rain)* impluere in *(w.
acc); (of waves)* illidere; **to — around the
bush** circuitu uti, schemas loqui
beat *s (blow)* plag·a -ae *f,* ict·us -ūs *m; (of the
heart)* palpitati·o -onis *f; (mus)* ict·us -ūs *m;
(patrol area)* circuiti·o -onis *f*
beaten *adj (defeated)* vict·us -a -um; *(worn)*
trit·us -a -um

beating *s* verberati·o -onis *f; (defeat)* repuls·a
-ae *f; (of the heart)* palpitati·o -onis *f;* **to get
a —** vapulare
beautician *s* orna·trix -tricis *f*
beautiful *adj* pul·cher -chra -chrum; *(shapely)*
formos·us -a -um
beautifully *adv* pulchre
beautify *tr* ornare
beauty *s* pulchritud·o -inis *f*
beaver *s* fi·ber -bri *m*
because *conj* quod, quia, quoniam
because of *prep* ob, propter *(w. acc)*
beck *s* nut·us -ūs *m;* **at the — and call** ad arbitrium
beckon *tr* nutu vocare
become *tr* decēre ‖ *intr* fieri; **to — friends
with me once again** in gratiam mecum redire
becoming *adj* dec·ens -entis
becomingly *adv* decenter
bed *s* lect·us -i *m; (small)* lectul·us -i *m; (in the
garden)* areol·a -ae *f; (of a river)* alve·us -i
m; **— of roses** rosar·ium -(i)i *n;* **to be confined to —** lecto teneri; **to get out of —** e
lecto surgere; **to go to —** cubitum ire; **to
make the —** lectum sternere
bedbug *s* sciniph·is -is *m*
bedding *s* stragul·um -i *n*
bed frame *s* spond·a -ae *f*
bedlam *s* tumult·us -ūs *m*
bedpost *s* fulcr·um -i *n*
bedraggled *adj* sordid·us -a -um
bedridden *adj* valetudinari·us -a -um; **to be —**
lecto tenēri
bedroom *s* (dormitorium) cubicul·um -i *n*
bedspread *s* opertor·ium -(i)i *n*
bedstead *s* spond·a -ae *f*
bedtime *s* hor·a -ae *f* somni
bee *s* ap·is -is *f;* **—s buzz** apes bombilant
beech tree *s* fag·us -i *f*
beef *s* bubul·a *f;* **roast —** bubula assa
beefsteak *s* frust·um -i *n* bubulum
beehive *s* alve·us -i *m*
beeline *s* **to make a — for** directā viā contendere ad *(w. acc)*
beer *s* cer(e)visi·a -ae *f*
beer glass *s* hyal·us -i *m* cervisarius
beer mug *s* urce·us -i *m* cervisarius
beet *s* bet·a -ae *f*
beetle *s* scarabae·us -i *m*
befall *tr* contingere *(w. dat)* ‖ *intr* accidere,
contingere
befit *tr* decēre
befitting *adj* dec·ens -entis; **it is —** decet
before *prep (in front of)* ante *(w. acc),* pro *(w.
abl); (in time)* ante *(w. acc); (in the presence
of)* coram *(w. abl); (leg)* apud *(w. acc);* **— all
things** imprimis; **— long** propediem,
iamdudum; **— now** antehac
before *conj* antequam, priusquam

beforehand *adv* antea
befriend *tr* in amicitiam recipere
beg *tr* petere, orare **‖** *intr* mendicare; **to — for** deprecari; *(alms)* mendicare; **to — s.o. to** aliquem deprecari ut *(w. subj);* **to — from door to door** ostiatim mendicare
beget *tr* gignere
beggar *s* mendic·us -i *m* (·a -ae *f)*
begging *s* mendicit·as -atis *f;* **to go** — mendicare
begin *tr* & *intr* incipere; *(without finishing)* inchoare; *(to initiate)* instituere; **to — at** incipere ab *(w. abl);* **to — to bloom** florescere; **to — with** primum (omnium)
beginner *s* tir·o -onis *mf*
beginning *s (the act of starting)* incepti·o -onis *f; (the start itself)* init·ium -(i)i *n; (origin)* orig·o -inis *f;* **at the — of winter** ineunte *or* primā hieme; **at the — of the year** ineunte anno, principio anni; **from the very** — iam inde a principio; **in the** — inter initia; **—s** principi·a -orum *npl*
begrudge *tr* **to — my enemy his victory** amici victoriae invidēre
beguile *tr* fraudare
behalf *s* **on — of** pro *(w. abl)*
behave *intr* se gerere; **to — oneself** se probe gerere; **to — toward** uti *(w. abl);* **well-behaved** bene morat·us -a -um
behavior *s* mor·es -um *mpl;* **your — towards me was unfriendly** inimice te in me gessisti
behead *tr* decollare
beheading *s* decollati·o -onis *f*
behind *adv* pone, a tergo; **to be left — relinqui**
behind *prep* post *(w. acc); (esp. w. verbs of motion)* pone *(w. acc); (in support)* pro *(w. abl);* **from** — a tergo; **to talk about a friend — his back** absentem amicum rodere
behind *s (coll)* clun·es -ium *mpl,* postic·um -i *n*
behold *tr* conspicere
behold *interj* ecce!, en!
behoove *tr* **it behooves you to** *(w. inf)* oportet te *(w. inf)*
beige *adj* rav·us -a -um
being *s* en·s -tis *n;* **human — hom·o** -inis *m*
belabor *tr (to thrash)* verberare; *(to harp on)* cantare
belch *s* ruct·us -ūs *m*
belch *tr* **to — forth** eructare **‖** *intr* ructare
belfry *s* turr·is -is *f* campanis instructa
belie *tr (to prove false)* refellere; *(to disappoint)* frustrari; *(to disguise)* dissimulare
belief *s* fid·es -ei *f; (conviction) (in)* opini·o -onis *f (w. gen or* de *w. abl)*
believe *tr (thing)* credere; *(person)* credere *(w. dat); (to suppose)* existimare; **to make — simulare**
believer *s* cred·ens -entis *mf*

bell *s (large)* campan·a -ae *f; (small)* tintinnabul·um -i *n*
belle *s* bella puell·a -ae *f*
belligerent *adj (at war)* belliger·ans -antis; *(scrappy)* pugn·ax -acis
bellow *intr* mugire, boare
bell pepper *s* pip·er -eris *n* rotundum
bell tower *s* campanil·e -is *n*
belly *s* ven·ter -tris *m; (womb)* uter·us -i *m*
bellyache *s* tormin·a -um *npl;* **to have a — dolēre a torminibus**
belong *intr* **to — to** esse *(w. dat); (to be related)* pertinēre ad *(w. acc); (to be a member of)* in numero *(w. gen)* esse
belongings *spl* bon·a -orum *npl*
below *adj* infer·us -a -um
below *adv* infra
below *prep* infra *(w. acc)*
belt *s* cingul·um -i *n; (of women's clothes)* zon·a -ae *f; (sword belt)* balte·us -i *m; (area)* zon·a -ae *f;* **to tighten one's — sumptui parcere**
bemoan *tr* deplorare
bench *s* scamn·um -i *n; (esp. for senators and judges)* subsell·ium -(i)i *n; (for rowers)* transtr·um -i *n*
bend *tr* flectere, curvare; *(to cause to lean)* inclināre; *(the bow)* intendere, flectere; *(to persuade)* īnflectere; **to — back** reflectere; **to — down** deflectere **‖** *intr (e.g., of iron)* se inflectere; *(to give in)* cedere; **to — down** *or* **over** *(to stoop)* se inclinare, se demittere
bend *s* curvam·en -inis *n;* **— of the river** flex·us -ūs *m* fluminis; **— in the road** flex·us -ūs *m* viae infract·us -ūs *m*
bending *s* inclinati·o -onis *f*
beneath *adv* subter
beneath *prep* sub *(w. acc or abl);* **he thinks these matters are — him** arbitratur has res infra se positas
benefactor *s* largit·or -oris *m,* patron·us -i *m*
benefactress *s* patron·a -ae *f*
beneficence *s* beneficenti·a -ae *f*
beneficent *adj* benefi·cus -a -um
beneficial *adj* util·is -is -e, commod·us -a -um; **to be — prodesse**
benefit *s (deed)* benefic·ium -(i)i *n; (advantage)* commod·um -i *n;* **to have the — of** frui *(w. abl);* **to whose — is it?** cui bono est?
benefit *tr* prodesse *(w. dat),* iuvare **‖** *intr* proficere; *(financially)* lucrari; **to — from** utilitatem capere ex *(w. abl)*
benevolence *s* benevolenti·a -ae *f*
benevolent *adj* benevol·us -a -um
benevolently *adv* benevole
benign *adj* benign·us -a -um
bent *adj* flex·us -a -um, curv·us -a -um; **— backwards** recurv·us -a -um; **— forwards**

pron·us -a -um; — **inwards** camur·us -a
-um; — **on** *(fig)* attent·us -a -um ad *(w.*
acc)
bent *s* curvatur·a -ae *f; (inclination)* inclinati·o
-onis *f*
bequeath *tr* legare
bequest *s* legat·um -i *n*
bereave *tr* orbare
bereavement *s* orbit·as -atis *f*
bereft *adj* — **of** orbat·us -a -um *(w.*
abl or gen)
berry *s* bac·a -ae *f*
berth *s (cabin)* diaet·a -ae *f; (space for ship at*
anchor) stati·o -onis *f;* **to give wide** — **to**
devitare
beseech *tr* obsecrare
beset *tr* urgēre; *(mil)* obsidēre
beside *prep* ad *(w. acc),* iuxta *(w. acc);* — **the**
point nihil ad rem; **to be** — **oneself** delirare;
to sit — **s.o.** assidēre alicui; **to walk** — **s.o.**
alicui latus tegere
besides *adv* praeterea, ultro
besides *prep* praeter *(w. acc)*
besiege *tr* obsidēre; *(fig)* circumsedēre
best *adj* optim·us -a -um; *(most advantageous)*
commodissim·us -a -um; *(friend)* summ·us
-a -um; **it is** — **to** optimum est *(w. inf),*
maxime prodest *(w. inf)*
best *s* flo·s -ris *m;* **to do one's** — pro virili
parte agere; **to have the** — **of it** praevalēre;
to make the — **of it** aequo animo ferre; **to**
the — **of one's ability** pro viribus
best *tr* exsuperare
bestir *tr (to move)* ciēre; **to** — **oneself** *(to wake*
up) expergisci
best man *s* pronub·us -i *m*
bestow *tr* (**on**) tribuere, deferre *(w. dat)*
bestowal *s* largiti·o -onis *f*
bet *s* sponsi·o -onis *f; (the stake)* pign·us -eris
n; **to lose a** — sponsionis condemnari; **to win**
a — sponsione vincere
bet *tr* ponere; **I** — **he has taken off** pono eum
abivisse; **I** — **you he doesn't win** te sponsione provoco illum non esse victurum; **to** —
that ... spōnsionem facere *(w. acc & inf)*
betray *tr* prodere; *(feelings)* arguere
betrayer *s* prodit·or -oris *m*
betroth *tr* despondēre
betrothal *s* sponsal·ia -ium *npl*
betrothed *adj* spons·us -a -um
better *adj* mel·ior -ior -ius; *(preferable)* praes-
tant·ior -ior -ius; — **half** *(fig)* alter·a -ae *f;*
for the — in melius; **it is** — **to** *(w. inf)* com-
modius est *(w. inf);* **there, that's** — em istuc
rectius; **to be** — *(in health)* melius esse; **to**
get — convalescere; **to get the** — **of** praevalēre *(w. abl);* **where is your** — **half?** ubinam est tua altera?
better *adv* melius, potius
better *tr* meliorem *(or* melius) facere, corrigere; **to** — **oneself** proficere

betterment *s* correcti·o -onis *f*
betters *spl* melior·es -um *mpl*
between *prep* inter *(w. acc)*
bevel *tr* obliquare
beverage *s* pot·us -ūs *m*
bewail *tr* deplorare
beware *intr* cavēre; **to** — **of** cavēre
bewilder *tr* confundere
bewildered *adj* confus·us -a -um
bewilderment *s* confusi·o -onis *f*
bewitch *tr* fascinare; *(to charm)* demulcēre
beyond *adv* ultra
beyond *prep* ultra *(w. acc),* extra *(w. acc);*
(motion) trans *(w. acc);* **to go** — **the limits**
egredi extra terminos
bias *s (prejudice)* inclinati·o -onis *f; (line)*
line·a -ae *f* obliqua
bias *tr* inclinare
Bible *s* Bibli·a -orum *npl*
Biblical *adj* Biblic·us -a -um
bibliography *s* bibliographi·a -ae *f*
bicker *intr* altercari
bickering *s* altercati·o -onis *f*
bicycle *s* birot·a -ae *f;* **to ride a** — birotā vehi
bicyclist *s* birotari·us -i *m* (·a -ae *f*)
bid *tr (to order)* iubēre; *(to invite)* invitare; *(at*
auction) licitari; **to** — **farewell** valedicere
bid *s* licitati·o -onis *f;* **to make a** — licita-
tionem facere
bidder *s* licitat·or -oris *m* (·rix -ricis *f*)
bidding *s (command)* iuss·um -i *n; (at auction)*
licitati·o -onis *f;* **at his** — iussu eius; **to do**
s.o.'s — iussum alicuius exsequi
bide *tr* **to** — **one's time** tempus idoneum
opperiri
biennial *adj* biennial·is -is -e
bier *s* feretr·um -i *n; (euphem)* vitalis lect·us -i
m
big *adj* magn·us -a -um, ing·ens -entis; — **with**
child gravida; — **with young** praegn·ans
-antis; **to talk** — ampullari
bigamist *s* bimarit·us -i *m*
bigamy *s* bigami·a -ae *f*
big-hearted magnanim·us -a -um
bigmouth *s* bigmouth! os durum!; **to be a** —
(coll) durae buccae esse
bigot *s* qui suae opinioni nimium fidit
bigoted *adj* obstinate suae opinioni de partibus
(or de religione *or* de genere) dedit·us -a -um
bigotry *s* nimia suae de partibus *(or* de religione *or* de genere) opinioni fiduci·a -ae *f*
big toe *s* poll·ex icis *m*
bile *s* bil·is -is *f*
bilk *tr* fraudare
bill *s (of bird)* rostr·um -i *n; (proposed law)*
rogati·o -onis *f; (of money owed)* rati·o -onis
f debiti; *(paper money)* numm·us -i *m* chartarius; **ten-dollar** — nummus chartarius
decem dollarorum; — **of indictment** sub-

scripti·o -onis *f;* **to introduce a** — legem ferre; **to pass a** — legem perferre; **to turn down a** — legem *or* rogationem antiquare

bill collector *s* flagitat·or -oris *m* (·rix -ricis *f*)

billion *s* billi·o -onis *f*

billow *s* fluct·us -ūs *m*

bin *s (in wine cellar)* locul·us -i *m; (for grain)* lac·us -ūs *m*

bind *tr* ligare; *(wounds)* stringere; *(to obligate)* obligare; *(books)* conglutinare; **to** — **fast** devincere; **to** — **together** colligare; **to** — **up** alligare; *(med)* astringere

binding *adj* obligatori·us -a -um; *(law)* rat·us -a -um

binding *s* religati·o -onis *f*

binoculars *spl* binocular·es -um *mpl*

biographer *s* vitae scrip·tor -toris *m* (·trix -tricis *f*), biograph·us -i *m* (-a -ae *f*)

biographical *adj* ad memoriam vitae pertinens

biography *s* vit·a -ae *f*

biological *adj* biologic·us -a -um; — **warfare** bellum biologicum

biology *s* biologi·a -ae *f*

biologist *s* biologic·us -i *m*

birch *adj* betulin·us -a -um

birch tree *s* betul·a -ae *f*

bird *s* av·is -is *f;* —**s of a feather flock together** pares cum paribus facillime congregantur

birdcage *s* cave·a -ae *f*

bird's nest *s* nid·us -i *m*

birth *s* part·us -ūs *m; (lineage)* gen·us -eris *n*

birthday *s* di·es -ei *m* natalis *(or simply* natalis); **Happy** —! Felicem Natalem (tibi exopto)!

birthday cake *s* lib·um -i *n* (natalicium)

birthday party *s* natalici·a -ae *f;* **to throw a** — nataliciam agitare

birthday present *s* natalic·ium -(i)i *n*

birthplace *s* patri·a -ae *f*

birthright *s* iu·s -ris *n* e genere ortum

biscuit *s* crustul·um -i *n*

bisect *tr* in duas partes aequales secare

bishop *s* episcop·us -i *m*

bison *s* bis·on -ontis *m*

bit *s (for horse)* fren·um -i *n; (small amount)* aliquantul·um -i *n; (of food)* off·a -ae *f;* **a** — **of peace** aliquid quietis; — **by** — minutatim; **to cut (chop) to** —**s** minutatim secare (concidere)

bitch *s* can·is -is *f*

bite *s* mors·us -ūs *m; (by an insect, snake)* ict·us -ūs *m*

bite *tr* mordēre; *(of pepper, frost)* urere; *(of an insect)* icere

biting *adj (apt to bite)* mord·ax -acis; *(cutting)* asp·er -era -erum

bitter *adj (lit & fig)* amar·us -a -um; *(hatred)* asp·er -era -erum *(painful, sharp)* acerb·us -a

-um; — **taste in the mouth** amarum o·s -ris *n*

bitterly *adv (denoting wounded feeling)* amare; *(implying anger or harshness)* aspere; *(implying hostility)* infense; **to complain** — graviter queri; **to cry** — ubertim flēre, graviter lacrimare

bitterness *s (esp. of taste)* amarit·as -atis *f; (fig)* acerbit·as -atis *f; (wounded feeling)* amaritud·o -inis *f*

bitters *spl* absinth·ium -(i)i *n*

bivouac *s* excubi·ae -arum *fpl*

bivouac *intr* excubare

blab *tr* blaterare; **to** — **out** effutire ‖ *intr* deblaterare

black *adj (shiny black)* ni·ger -gra -grum; *(dull black)* a·ter -tra -trum; *(looks)* tru·x -cis

black *s (color)* nigr·um -i *n; (person)* Aethi·ops -opis *m;* **dressed in** — pullat·us -a -um

black-and-blue *adj* livid·us -a -um; — **mark** liv·or -oris *m*

blackberry *s* mor·um -i *n*

blackbird *s* merul·a -ae *f*

blackboard *s* tabul·a -ae *f* atra, tabula scriptoria

blacken *tr* nigrare

black eye *s* ocul·us -i *m* sugillatus

blacklist *s* proscripti·o -onis *f*

blacklist *tr* proscribere

black magic *s* magicae art·es -ium *fpl*

blackness *s* nigriti·a -ae *f*

blacksmith *s* ferrarius fa·ber -bri *m*

bladder *s* vesic·a -ae *f*

blade *s (edge)* lamin·a -ae *f; (of grass)* herb·a -ae *f; (of oar)* palm·a -ae *f*

blamable *adj* culpabil·is -is -e

blame *tr* culpare; **to** — **s.o. for** aliquem culpare ob *(w. acc);* **I am to** — ego in culpā sum; **you are to** — in culpā es

blame *s* culp·a -ae *f;* **to push the** — **on s.o.** culpam conferre in *(w. acc)*

blameless *adj* inte·ger -gra -grum

blame-worthy *adj* vituperabil·is -is -e

bland *adj (food)* len·is -is -e

blank *adj* inan·is -is -e; *(expression)* stolid·us -a -um

blanket *s* lod·ix -icis *f; (dim.)* lodicul·a -ae *f;* — **of snow** tegim·en -inis *n* niveum

blare *s* strepit·us -ūs *m*

blare *intr* strepare

blaspheme *tr* blasphemare

blasphemous *adj* blasphem·us -a -um

blasphemy *s* blasphemi·a -ae *f*

blast *s (of wind)* flam·en -inis *n; (of musical instrument)* flat·us -ūs *m;* — **of wind** flat·us -ūs *m*

blast *tr* discutere

blaze *s (glare)* fulg·or -oris *m; (fire)* incend·ium -(i)i *n;* **go to —s** *(coll)* i in malam rem!

blaze *tr* **to — a trail** semitam notare **‖** *intr* ardēre; **fires were —ing** ignes flagrabant; **to — up** exardescere

bleach *tr* dealbare

bleachers *spl* for·i -orum *mpl*

bleak *adj* immit·is -is -e; *(outlook, hope)* incommod·us -a -um

bleary-eyed *adj* lipp·us -a -um; **to be —** lippire

bleed *intr* sanguinem fundere

bleeding *adj* crud·us -a -um

bleeding *s* sanguinis profusi·o -onis *f; (bloodletting)* sanguinis missi·o -onis *f*

blemish *s (flaw)* vit·ium -(i)i *n; (on the body)* mend·um -i *n; (moral)* macul·a -ae *f*

blemish *tr* maculare

blend *tr* commiscēre; **to — in** immiscēre **‖** *intr* **to — in with** se immiscēre *(w. dat)*

blend *s* mixtur·a -ae *f; (proportionate)* temperi·es -ei *f*

blender machin·a -ae *f* concisoria

bless *tr* beare; *(consecrate)* consecrare; *(w. success)* secundare; *(eccl)* benedicere; — **you!** *(after s.o. has sneezed)* salve! *or* salutem!; — **you!** *or* — **your little heart!** di te ament!

blessed *adj* beat·us -a -um; *(of dead emperors)* div·us -a -um

blessing *s (thing)* bon·um -i *n; (eccl)* benedicti·o -onis *f*

blight *s* robig·o -inis *f; (fig)* tab·es -is *f*

blight *tr* robigine afficere; *(fig)* nocēre *(w. dat)*

blind *adj (lit & fig)* caec·us -a -um

blind *tr (lit & fig)* occaecare

blind alley *s* fundul·a -ae *f*

blindfold *tr* oculos obligare *(w. dat)*

blindfolded *adj* oculis obligatis

blindly *adv* temere

blindness *s* caecit·as -atis *f*

blinds *spl (on window)* transenn·a -ae *f;* **to close (open) the —** transennam aperire (demittere)

blink *intr* connivēre

bliss *s* beatitud·o -inis *f*

blissful *adj* beat·us -a -um

blissfully *adv* beate

blister *s* pustul·a -ae *f*

blister *intr* pustulare

bloated *adj* sufflat·us -a -um

block *s (of wood)* stip·es -itis *f; (of marble, stone)* mass·a -ae *f; (in a city)* vic·us -i *m; (obstruction)* impediment·um -i *n;* — **by —** vicatim

block *tr (e.g., the road)* obstruere; *(to choke up)* opplēre; **to — s.o.'s way** obstare alicui; **to — up** *(e.g. a window)* obstruere

blockade *s* obsidi·o -onis *f;* **to lift a —** obsidionem solvere; **to undergo a —** in obsidione teneri

blockade *tr* obsidēre

block and tackle *spl* trochle·a -ae *f*

blockhead *s* caud·ex -icis *m*

blond *adj* flav·us -a -um

blonde *s* flava femin·a -ae *f*

blood *s* sangu·is -inis *m; (outside the body)* cru·or -oris *m; (lineage)* gen·us -eris *n;* **there was bad — between him and Caesar** huic simultas cum Caesare intercedebat; **to stain with —** cruentare

bloodless *adj* exsangu·is -is -e; *(without bloodshed)* incruent·us -a -um

blood pressure *s* pressur·a -ae *f* sanguinis; **high —** hypertoni·a -ae *f*

blood-red *adj* sanguine·us -a -um

blood relative *s* consanguine·us -i *m* (·a -ae *f)*

bloodshed *s* caed·es -is *f*

bloodshot *adj* — **eyes** cruore suffusi ocul·i -orum *mpl*

bloodstained *adj* cruent·us -a -um

bloodthirsty *adj* sanguinari·us -a -um

blood vessel *s* ven·a -ae *f*

bloody *adj* sanguine·us -a -um

bloom *s* flo·s -ris *m;* **to be in —** florid·us -a -um esse

bloom *intr* florēre; **to begin to —** florescere

blooming *adj* flor·ens -entis

blossom *s* flo·s -ris *m;* **to shed its —s** deflorēre

blossom *intr* florēre

blot *s* macul·a -ae *f*

blot *tr* maculare; **to — out** delēre; *(to erase)* oblit(t)erare

blotch *s (stain)* macul·a -ae *f; (on the skin)* var·us -i *m*

blotchy *adj* maculos·us -a -um

blouse *s* pelusi·a -ae *f*

blow *s (stroke)* plag·a -ae *f; (blow which wounds)* ict·us -ūs *m; (w. the fist)* colaph·us -i *m; (fig)* plag·a -ae *f*

blow *tr* flare; *(a horn)* inflare; **to — out** *(candle)* ex(s)tinguere; **to — the nose** se emungere; **to — up** pulvere nitrato destruere **‖** *intr* flare; **to — hard** perflare; **to — over** *(of a storm)* cadere; **to — up** *(to get angry)* irasci

blowing *s* sufflati·o -onis *f*

blue *adj* caerule·us -a -um; *(dark blue)* cyane·us -a -um; *(pale blue)* subcaerule·us -a -um; *(melancholy)* melancholic·us -a -um

blue *s* caeruleus col·or -oris *m; (concrete)* caerule·um -i *n;* —**s** melancholi·a -ae *f;* **to have the —s** melancholic·us -a -um esse

blue-grey *adj (eyes)* caesi·us -a -um

blueprint *s* form·a -ae *f*

bluff *s* rup·es -is *f; (false threat)* simulata audaci·a -ae *f*

bluff *tr* decipere **‖** *intr* simulatā audaciā uti

blunder *s* err·or -oris *m; (in writing)* mend·um
-i *n*
blunder *intr* errare
blunderer *s* hom·o -inis *mf* ineptus (-a)
blunt *adj (dull)* heb·es -itis; *(person)*
inurban·us -a -um; *(speech)* impolit·us
-a -um
blunt *tr* hebetare
bluntly *adv* liberius
bluntness *s* hebetud·o -inis *f; (fig)* rusticit·as
-atis *f*
blur *s* macul·a -ae *f*
blur *tr* obscurare
blurred *adj* **the eyes are** — oculi caligant; **to
have** — **vision** quasi per caliginem vidēre
blurt *tr* **to** — **out** effutire
blush *s* rub·or -oris *m*
blush *intr* erubescere
bluster *intr (to swagger)* declamare, se iactare;
(of the wind) saevire
bluster *s (boasting)* iactati·o -onis *f; (din)*
strepit·us -ūs *m*
blustery *adj* ventos·us -a -um
boar *s* a·per -pri *m*
board *s (of wood)* tabul·a -ae *f; (food)* vict·us
-ūs *m; (council)* colleg·ium -(i)i *n; (judicial)*
quaesti·o -onis *f; (for games)* alve·us -i *m*
board *tr (vehicle, plane)* inscendere; *(ship)*
conscendere; **to** — **up** contabulare ‖ *intr (to
be a boarder)* victitare; **to** — **with** devertere
apud *(w. acc)*
boarder *s* deversit·or -oris *m*
boarding house *s* deversor·ium -(i)i *n*
boarding school *s* oecotrophe·um -i *n*
boardwalk *s* ambulacr·um -i *n* in litore
boast *intr* gloriari, se iactare
boast *s* iactanti·a -ae *f*
boastful *adj* glorios·us -a -um
boasting *s* gloriati·o -onis *f*
boat *s* navicul·a -ae *f*
boatman *s* naviculari·us -i *m*, lintrari·us -i *m*
bode *tr* portendere
bodiless *adj* incorporal·is -is -e
bodily *adj* corporis [*gen*]
body *s* corp·us -oris *n; (corpse)* cadav·er -eris
n; (person) hom·o -inis *m; (of troops)*
man·us -ūs *f; (of cavalry)* turm·a -ae *f;
(frame)* compag·es -ium *fpl;* **to come in a** —
agmine facto occurrere
bodyguard *s (single)* satell·es -itis *mf*
satellit·es -um *mpl; (of the emperor)* cohor·s
-tis *f* praetoria
bog *s* pal·us -udis *f*
bog *tr* **to** — **down** mergere; **to get** —**ed down**
in luto haesitare; *(fig)* haesitare
bogus *adj (counterfeit)* adulterin·us -a -um;
(sham) simulat·us -a -um; *(fictitious)* com-
mentici·us -a -um

boil *tr (to cause to boil)* fervefacere; *(to cook)*
coquere; **to** — **down** *(food)* decoquere;
(facts) coartare ‖ *intr* fervēre; *(fig)* bullire; **it
makes my blood** — facit ut sanguis ab irā
fervescit; **to** — **over** effervescere; **to** — **with
indignation** indignatione bullire
boil *s (med)* furuncul·us -i *m*
boisterous *adj (noisy)* turbid·us -a -um;
(stormy) procellos·us -a -um
bold *adj* aud·ax -acis
bold-faced *adj* impud·ens -entis
boldly *adv* audacter
boldness *s* audaci·a -ae *f*
bolster *tr* fulcire
bolt *s (of a door)* pessul·us -i *m*, ser·a -ae *f; (of
lightning)* ful·men -inis *n; (pin)* clav·us -i *m;
(screw)* cochle·a -ae *f*
bolt *tr* obserare; —**ed doors** oppessulatae
for·es -ium *fpl;* **to** — **down** *(food)* devorare ‖
intr (of a horse) se proripere; *(pol)* a factione
deficere
bomb *s* missil·e -is *n* dirumpens, bomb·a -ae *f;*
atomic — bomba atomica; **nuclear** —
bomba nuclearis
bomb *tr* missilibus dirumpentibus concutere
bombard *tr* tormentis verberare; *(fig)* lacessere
bombardment *s* tormentis verberati·o -onis *f*
bombastic *adj* tumid·us -a -um; **to be** —
ampullari
bomber *s* aëroplan·um -i *n* bombiferum
bond *s* vincul·um -i *n; (legal document)* syn-
graph·a -ae *f; (of love)* copul·a -ae *f*
bondage *s* servit·us -utis *f; (captivity)* captiv-
it·as -atis *f*
bondsman *s (slave)* famul·us -i *m; (leg)*
spōns·or -oris *m*
bone *s* os, ossis *n; (of fish)* spin·a -ae *f*
bone *adj (of bone)* osse·us -a -um
bone *tr (to remove bones from)* exossare
boneless *adj* ex·os -ossis
bonfire *s* ign·es -ium *mpl* festi
bonnet *s* redimicul·um -i *n*
bonus *s* praem·ium -(i)i *n, (mil)* donativ·um
-i *n*
bony *adj* osse·us -a -um
boogieman *s* larv·a -ae *f*
book *s* li·ber -bri *m;* **by the** — *(fig)* pro modo;
to write a — librum componere
book bag *s* manic·a -ae *f* libraria
bookbinder *s* glutinat·or -oris *m*
bookcase *s* forul·i -orum *mpl*
bookish *adj* libris dedit·us -a -um
bookkeeper *s* tabular·ius -(i)i *m* (·a -ae *f*) ,
dispēnsat·or -oris *m* (·rix -ricis *f*)
bookshelf *s* plute·us -i *m*, pegm·a -atis *n* librar-
ium
bookstore *s* librari·a -ae *f*
bookworm *s* tine·a -ae *f; (fig)* librorum hellu·o
-onis *m*

boom *s (of ship)* longur·ius -(i)i *m; (of harbor)* repagul·um -i *n; (sound)* sonit·us -ūs *m; (of waves)* frag·or -oris *m*
boor *s* rustic·us -i *m* (·a -ae *f*)
boorish *adj* rustic·us -a -um
boorishness *s* rusticit·as -atis *f*
boost *tr* efferre
boot *s* calce·us -i *m; (soldier's)* calig·a -ae *f; (of rawhide, reaching to the calf)* per·o -onis *m; (tragic)* cothurn·us -i *m*
boot *tr (coll)* calce petere ‖ *intr* prodesse; **to —** insuper
booth *s* tabern·a -ae *f*
booting up *s (comput)* initiati·o -onis *f* systematis
boot up *intr (comput)* initiare systema
booze *s* temet·um -i *n*
border *s (edge)* marg·o -inis *mf; (seam)* fimbri·a -ae *f; (boundary)* fin·is -is *m; (frontier)* lim·es -tis *m;* **to mark the —** finem discernere
border *tr* attingere ‖ *intr* **to — on** attingere
bordering *adj* finitim·us -a -um
bore *tr* terebrare; *(a person)* obtundere; **to — a hole in** excavare; **to — a hole through s.th.** aliquid perforare
bore *s (tool)* terebr·a -ac *f; (fig)* molest·us -i *m* (·a -ae *f*); **don't be a —** ne sis odios·us -a
born *adj* nat·us -a -um; **to be —** nasci; *(fig)* oriri
borough *s* municip·ium -(i)i *n*
borrow *tr* mutuari; *(fig)* imitari
borrowed *adj* mutu·us -a -um
bosom *s* sin·us -ūs *m; (of female)* mammill·ae -arum *fpl*
bosom friend *s* intimus(-a) familiar·is -is *mf*
boss *s (owner)* domin·us -i *m* (·a -ae *f*); *(coll)* ipsim·us -i *m; (ornamental fixture)* bull·a -ae *f; (on a shield)* umb·o -onis *m*
boss *tr* dominari in *(w. acc)*
botanical *adj* herbari·us -a -um
botanist *s* herbar·ius -(i)i *m* (·a -ae *f*)
botany *s* ar·s -tis *f* herbaria
botch *tr* male gerere
both *adj* amb·o -ae -o; *(of pairs)* gemin·us -a -um; *(each of two)* ut·erque, -raque, -rumque; **— parents** uterque par·ēns -entis *m;* **in — directions** utroque; **on — sides** utrimque
both *pron* amb·o -ae -o; *(w. singular verb)* ut·erque, -raque, -rumque
both *conj* **— ... and** et ... et
bother *tr* vexare ‖ *intr* **to — about** operam dare *(w. dat)*
bother *s* negot·ium -(i)i *n*
bothersome *adj* molest·us -a -um
bottle *s* ampull·a -ae *f; (large)* lagoen·a -ae *f*
bottle *tr* in ampullas infundere
bottom *s* fund·us -i *m; (of a ship)* carin·a -ae *f; (of a mountain)* rad·ix -icis *m;* **the — of**

im·us -a -um; **the — of the sea** imum mar·e -is *n*
bottom *adj* im·us -a -um
bottomless *adj* profund·us -a -um
bough *s* ram·us -i *m*
boulder *s* sax·um -i *n*
bounce *tr* repercutere; *(coll)* eicere ‖ *intr* resilire
bounce *s (leap)* salt·us -ūs *m; (energy)* vig·or -oris *m*
bound *adj* alligat·us -a -um; **it is — to happen** necesse est accidat; **to be — for** tendere ad *or* in *(w. acc)*
bound *s (leap)* salt·us -ūs *m;* **to set —s** modum facere
bound *tr* terminare, continēre; **they are —ed on one side by the Rhine** unā ex parte flumine Rheno continentur ‖ *intr (to leap)* salire
boundary *s* fin·is -is *m; (esp. fortified)* lim·es -itis *m*
boundless *adj* infinit·us -a -um
bountiful *adj* larg·us -a -um
bounty *s* largit·as -atis *f*
bouquet *s* corollar·ium -(i)i *n; (of wine)* flo·s -ris *m*
bout *s* certam·en -inis *n*
bow *s* arc·us -ūs *m; (in a ribbon)* plex·us -ūs *m*
bow *s (of ship)* pror·a -ae *f; (bending)* capitis summissi·o -onis *f;* **to take a —** caput summittere
bow *tr* flectere; *(one's head)* demittere ‖ *intr* se demittere; **to — to** *(to accede to)* obtemperare *(w. dat)*
bowels *spl* alv·us -i *f*
bower *s* umbracul·um -i *n*
bowl *s* crater·a -ae *f; (large with handles)* catin·us -i *m; (smaller)* catill·us -i *mf (for libations)* pater·a -ae *f*
bowl *intr* conis ludere
bowling *s* conorum lus·us -us *m*
bowling alley *s* oec·us -i *m* conorum lusūs
bowling ball *s* glob·us -i *m* lusorius
bowling pin *s* con·us -i *m* lusorius
bowlegged *adj* valg·us -a -um
bowstring *s* nerv·us -i *m*
box *s (chest)* arc·a -ae *f; (for books)* caps·a -ae *f; (for clothes, etc.)* cist·a -ae *f; (for perfume, medicine)* pyx·is -idis *f*
box *tr (to enclose in a box)* includere; *(an opponent)* pugillare cum *(w. abl);* **to — s.o. on the ear** alicui alapam adhibēre ‖ *intr* pugillare
boxer *s* pug·il -ilis *mf*
boxing *s* pugillat·us -ūs *m*
boxing glove *s* caest·us -ūs *m*
boxing match *s* pugillat·us -ūs *m*
boy *s* pu·er -eri *m; (dim.)* puerul·us -i *m*
boyfriend *s* am·ans -antis *m*
boyhood *s* pueriti·a -ae *f;* **from — a** puero

boyish *adj* pueril·is -is -e
bra *s* stroph·ium -(i)i *n*
brace *s (strap)* fasci·a -ae *f; (pair)* pa·r -ris *n; (prop)* fulment·um -i *n*
brace *tr (to bind)* ligare; *(to strengthen)* firmare; *(to prop)* fulcire; **to — oneself for** se comparare ad *(w. acc)*
bracelet *s* armill·a -ae *f*
bracket *s* mutul·us -i *m;* **—s** *(in writing)* unc·i -orum *mpl*
brag *intr* se iactare; **to — about** iactare
braggart *s* iactat·or -oris *m* (·rix -ricis *f)*
bragging *s* iactanti·a -ae *f*
braid *s* limb·us -i *m; (of hair)* spir·a -ae *f*
braid *tr* plectere
brain *s* cerebr·um -i *n;* **—s** *(talent)* ingen·ium -(i)i *n;* **to have (no) —s** cor (non) habēre
brain *tr (sl)* caput elidere *(w. dat)*
brainless *adj* soc·ors -ordis
brainstorm *s* inflat·us -ūs *m* spiritūs
brain trust *s* consil·ium -(i)i *n* sapientium
brake *s (on wagon)* sufflam·en -inis *n; (thicket)* dumet·um -i *n;* **to apply (step on) the —** rotam sufflaminare
brake pedal pedal·e -is *n* sufflaminis
bramble *s* dum·us -i *m; (thorny bush)* sent·is -is *m*
branch *s (of tree)* ram·us -i *m; (of pedigree)* stemm·a -atis *n; (of knowledge)* disciplin·a -ae *f; (of medicine, etc.)* par·s -tis *f*
branch *intr* **to — out** ramos porrigere; *(fig)* scindi, diffundi
branch office *s* officin·a -ae *f* auxiliaria
brand *s (mark)* stigm·a -atis *n; (com)* not·a -ae *f; (type)* gen·us -eris *n; (of fire)* fa·x -cis *f*
branding iron *s* caut·er -eris *m*
brandish *tr* vibrare
brandy *s* vini spirit·us -ūs *m*
brash *adj* temerari·us -a -um
brass *s* orichalc·um -i *n*
brassiere *s* stroph·ium -(i)i *n*
brat *s* procax pusi·o -onis *mf*
brave *adj* fort·is -is -e
brave *tr* sustinēre
bravely *adv* fortiter
bravery *s* fortitud·o -inis *f*
bravo *interj* macte!
brawl *s* rix·a -ae *f*
brawl *intr* rixari
brawler *s* rixat·or -oris *m* (·rix -ricis *f)*
brawling *adj* iurg·ans -antis
brawn *s* lacert·us -i *m*
brawny *adj* lacertos·us -a -um
bray *intr* rudere
braying *s* rudit·us -ūs *m*
brazen *adj* aëne·us -a -um; *(fig)* impud·ens -entis
breach *s* ruin·a -ae *f; (of treaty)* dissid·ium -(i)i *n;* **— in the wall** ruin·a -ae *f* muri; **to**

commit a — of promise fidem frangere; **to make a small — in the wall** aliquantulum muri discutere
bread *s* pan·is -is *m; (fig)* vict·us -ūs *m;* **loaf of — panis** *m;* **to earn one's —** sibi victum quaerere
bread basket *s* panar·ium -(i)i *n*
breadcrumb *s* mic·a -ae *f* panis
breaded *adj* saligne·us -a -um
breadth *s* latitud·o -inis *f;* **in — in** latitudinem
break *tr (arm, dish, treaty, one's word)* frangere; *(the law)* violare; *(leg, ankle)* suffringere; *(silence)* rumpere; *(camp)* movēre; *(in several places)* diffringere; **to — a fall** casum mitigare; **to — apart** diffringere; **to — a treaty** foedus frangere; **to — down** *(to demolish)* demoliri; **to — down into** *(categories)* deducere in *(w. acc);* **to — formation** ordinem solvere; **to — in** *(a horse)* domare; **to — in pieces** confringere; **to — off** *(e.g., a branch)* praefringere; *(friendship or action)* dirumpere; *(a meeting, conversation)* interrumpere; **to — one's word** fidem frangere; **to — open** effringere; **to — up** dissolvere ‖ *intr* frangi, rumpi; *(of day)* illucescere; *(of strength)* deficere; **to — forth** erumpere; **to —into** *(e.g., a house)* irrumpere *(w. acc or* intra *w. acc); (e.g., a city)* invadere *(w. acc or* in *w. acc);* **to — loose from** se eripere ex *(w. abl);* **to — off** *(to stop short)* repente desinere; **to — out** erumpere; *(of trouble)* exardescere; *(of war)* exoriri; *(of fire)* grassari; **to — up** dissolvi, dilabi; *(of a meeting)* dimitti; **to — with** dissidēre ab *(w. abl)*
break *s (of a limb)* ruptur·a -ae *f; (interruption)* intercaped·o -inis *f; (for rest)* intervall·um -i *n,* vacati·o -onis *f; (escape)* effug·ium -(i)i *n;* **— of day** prima lu·x -cis *f*
breakage *s* fractur·a -ae *f*
breakdown *s (of health)* debilit·as -atis *f; (mechanical)* defect·us -ūs *m; (division)* deducti·o -onis *f*
breaker *s* fluct·us -ūs *m* a saxo fractus
breakfast *s* ientacul·um -i *n;* **for — in** ientaculum; **to eat —** ientare
breakfast *intr* ientare
breakneck *adj* praec·eps -ipitis
breakup *s* dissoluti·o -onis *f*
breakwater *s* mol·es -is *f* lapidum in mari structa
breast *s* pect·us -oris *n; (of a woman)* mamm·a -ae *f; (when filled with milk)* ub·er -eris *n; (fig)* praecord·ia -ium *npl;* **to make a clean — of it** confiteri omnia
breast-feed *tr* uberibus alere
breastplate *s* loric·a -ae *f*
breath *s* spirit·us -ūs *m,* anim·a -ae *f;* **— of air** aur·a -ae *f;* **deep —** anhelit·us -ūs *m;* **out of — anhel·us** -a -um; **to catch one's —** respi-

rare; **to draw a** — spiritum trahere; **to hold one's** — animam continēre; **to take a** — animam *or* spiritum ducere; **to take one's** — **away** exanimare; **to waste one's** — operam perdere

breathe *tr* ducere, spirare; *(to whisper)* susurrare; **to** — **fire** flammas exspirare; **to** — **one's last** animam exspirare **II** *intr* spirare, respirare; **to** — **upon** inspirare *(w. dat)*

breather *s (breathing space)* spat·ium -(i)i *n*

breathing *s* respirati·o -onis *f*

breathless *adj* exanim·is -is -e

breeches *spl* brac·ae -arum *fpl*

breed *s* gen·us -eris *n*

breed *tr* parere, gignere; *(to cause)* producere; *(to raise)* educare, alere; **familiarity** —**s contempt** conversatio parit contemptum

breeder *s (man)* generat·or -oris *m; (animal)* matr·ix -icis *f; (fig)* nutr·ix -icis *f*

breeding *s* fetur·a -ae *f;* **good** — humanit·as -atis *f*

breeze *s* aur·a -ae *f*

breezy *adj* ventos·us -a -um

brethren *spl* fratr·es -um *mpl*

brevity *s* brevit·as -atis *f*

brew *s* cerevisiae ferment·um -i *n*

brew *tr* concoquere **II** *intr* excitari

brewer *s* cerevisiae coct·or -oris *m*

brewery *s* officin·a -ae *f* ad cerevisiam concoquendam

bribe *s* pret·ium -(i)i *n,* praem·ium -(i)i *n,* pecuni·a -ae *f*

bribe *tr* (pecuniā) corrumpere

briber *s* corrupt·or -oris *m* (·rix -ricis *f)*

bribery *s* corrupti·o -onis *f; (pol)* ambit·us -ūs *m*

brick *s* lat·er -eris *m*

brick *adj* laterici·us -a -um

bricklayer *s* laterum struct·or -oris *m*

bridal *adj* nuptial·is -is -e; — **bed** genialis tor·us -i *m;* — **suite** thalam·us -i *m;* — **veil** flamme·um -i *n*

bride *s* nupt·a -ae *f*

bridegroom *s* marit·us -i *m*

bridesmaid *s* pronub·a -ae *f*

bridge *s* pon·s -tis *m*

bridge *tr* pontem imponere *(w. dat)*

brief *adj* brev·is -is -e; **make it** —! in pauca confer!

brief *tr* edocēre

brief *s (leg)* commentar·ius -(i)i *m*

briefing *s* mandat·a -orum *npl*

briefly *adv* breviter, paucis (verbis); **to put if** — ut breviter dicam

brigade *s (infantry)* legi·o -onis *f; (cavalry)* turm·a -ae *f*

brigadier *s* tribun·us -i *m* militum

brigand *s* latr·o -onis *m*

bright *adj* clar·us -a -um; *(day, sky)* seren·us -a -um; *(stars, gems)* lucid·us -a -um; *(beaming)* nitid·us -a -um; *(smart)* a·cer -cris -cre; — **eyes** oculi vegeti

brighten *tr* illuminare **II** *intr* lucescere, clarēscere; **his face** —**ed up** vultus eius in hilaritatem solutus est

brightly *adv* clare, lucide

brightness *s* nit·or -oris *m,* cand·or -oris *m; (of sky)* serenit·as -atis *f*

brilliance *s* splend·or -oris *m; (ability)* lu·x -cis *f;* — **of style** nit·or -oris *m* orationis

brilliant *adj* splendid·us -a -um; *(esp. fig: achievement, speech, battle, etc.)* luculent·us -a -um

brilliantly *adv* splendide, luculente

brim *s (rim)* or·a -ae *f; (border)* marg·o -inis *mf;* **to fill to the** — ad summam oram implēre

brimful *adj* ad summum plen·us -a -um

brimstone *s* sulf·ur -uris *n*

bring *tr* (**to**) afferre (ad *w. acc); (by carriage, etc.)* advehere; *(letters, report, news)* perferre; **to** — **about** efficere, perficere; **to** — **along** afferre; **to** — **(s.o.) around** circumagere (aliquem); **to** — **back** referre, reducere; *(to recall)* revocare; *(by force, authority)* redigere; **to** — **before a court of law** producere in iudicium; **to** — *(a matter)* **before the senate** ad senatum referre de *(w. abl);* **to** — **credit to** fidem ferre *(w. dat);* **to** — **down** deferre; *(e.g., a tower)* deicere; **to** — **forth** prodere, depromere; *(to yield)* ferre; **to** — **forward** proferre; **to** — **in** inferre; *(on a vehicle)* invehere; *(money, profit)* efficere; **to** — **it about that** efficere ut; **to** — **on** afferre; *(illness, fever)* adducere; *(fig)* obicere; **to** — **oneself** to animum inducere ut *(w. subj);* **to** — **out** *(to reveal)* proferre; *(to elicit)* elicere; *(the wine)* (ex)promere; *(a book)* prodere; **to** — **over** perducere; *(fig)* perducere, conciliare; **to** — **to** adducere; **to** — **together** cōnferre; *(to assemble)* cogere, contrahere; *(esp. forces)* comparare; *(estranged persons)* conciliare; **to** — **to order** in ordinem cogere; **to** — **to pass** efficere; **to** — **under one's control** subigere; **to** — **up** subducere; *(children)* educare; *(to vomit)* evomere; *(a topic)* mentionem facere de *(w. abl)*

brink *s* marg·o -inis *mf;* **on the** — **of death** morti vicin·us -a -um; **to be on the** — **of disaster** in summo discrimine versari

brisk *adj (lively)* ala·cer -cris -cre; *(wind)* vehement·ior -ior -ius; *(weather)* frigid·us -a -um; **to be** — vigēre

briskly *adv* alacriter

briskness *s* alacrit·as -atis *f,* vig·or -oris *m*

bristle *s* saet·a -ae *f*

bristle *intr* horrēre

Britain *s* Britanni·a -ae *f*
British *adj* Britannic·us -a -um
brittle *adj* fragil·is -is -e
broach *tr* in medium proferre
broad *adj* lat·us -a -um; *(grin)* solut·us -a -um; *(general)* commun·is -is -e; **in — daylight** *(fig)* propalam; **to sleep till — daylight** ad multum diem dormire
broadcast *s* emissi·o -onis *f*
broadcast *tr* divulgare; *(a program)* emittere
broadcast station *s* emistr·um -i *n*
broaden *tr (to widen)* dilatare; *(to enlarge)* ampliare ‖ *intr* in latitudinem crescere, latescere
brocade *s* seric·um -i *n* aureo *(or* argento) filo intertextum
broccoli *s* brassic·a -ae *f* oleracea Botyrtis
brochure *s* libell·us -i *m*
broil *s* rix·a -ae *f*
broil *tr* torrēre ‖ *intr* torrēri
broke *adj* **to be —** solvendo non esse
broken *adj* fract·us -a -um; *(by age, hard times)* confect·us -a -um; *(faltering)* infract·us -a -um; **— in** domit·us -a -um
broken-hearted *adj* deiect·us -a -um
broker *s* arillat·or -oris *mf*
bronze *s* ae·s -ris *n*
bronze *adj* aëne·us -a -um
brooch *s* fibul·a -ae *f*
brood *s* prol·es -is *f; (of birds, etc. hatched together)* fetur·a -ae *f*
brood *intr* **to — over** *(lit & fig)* incubare *(w. dat),* parturire
brook *s* rivul·us -i *m*
brook *tr* tolerare, pati
broom *s* scop·ae -arum *fpl*
broth *s* iu·s -ris *n*
brothel *s* lupan·ar -aris *n*
brother *s* fra·ter -tris *m*
brotherhood *s* fraternit·as -atis *f; (organization)* sodalit·as -atis *f*
brother-in-law *s* lev·ir -iri *m*
brotherly *adj* fratern·us -a -um
brow *s* fron·s -tis *f; (of a hill)* dors·um -i *n;* **to knit the —** frontem contrahere
browbeat *tr* minis et terrore commovēre
brown *adj (w. a dash of yellow)* fulv·us -a -um; *(chestnut color)* spad·ix -icis; *(of skin)* adust·us -a -um
browse *intr* depasci; *(comput) (the Web)* navigare; *(text documents)* perlustrare
browser *s (comput) (Web viewer)* navigatr·um -i *n; (viewer of text documents)* perlustratr·um -i *n*
bruise *tr* contundere; *(to make black-and-blue)* sugillare
bruise *s* contusi·o -onis *f; (black-and- blue)* suggillati·o -onis *f*
bruise mark *s* liv·or -oris *m*

brunette *s* puell·a -ae *f* subfusca
brunt *s* tota vis *f*
brush *s (scrub brush)* penicul·us -i *m; (painter's)* penicill·us -i *m; (skirmish)* aggressi·o -onis *f; (bushes)* vigult·a -orum *npl*
brush *tr (lightly)* verrere; *(teeth)* purgare; *(shoes)* detergēre; **to — aside** spernere; **to — away** *or* **out** detergēre ‖ *intr* **to — past s.o.** aliquem praetereundo leviter terere
brutal *adj* imman·is -is -e
brutality *s* immanit·as -atis *f*
brutally *adv* immaniter
brute *adj* brut·us -a -um
brute *s* belu·a -ae *f*
brutish *adj* imman·is -is -e
bubble *s* bull·a -ae *f*
bubble *intr* bullire, bullare; *(of a spring)* scatēre
bubbling *s* bullit·us -ūs *m; (of a spring)* scatebr·a -ae *f*
bubbly *adj (person)* argutis scat·ens -entis
buck *s* cerv·us -i *m; (he-goat)* hirc·us -i *m*
bucket *s* situl·a -ae *f;* **to kick the —** *(coll)* animam ebullire
buckle *s* fibul·a -ae *f*
buckle *tr* fibulā nectere ‖ *intr (to bend)* flecti; *(to collapse)* collabi; **to — down** se applicare; **to — up** se fibulā nectere, se accingere
buckler *s* parm·a -ae *f*
bucolic *adj* bucolic·us -a -um
bud *s* gemm·a -ae *f; (of a flower)* cal·yx -ycis *m;* **to nip s.th. in the —** aliquid maturum occupare
bud *intr* gemmare
buddy *s* conger·o -onis *m*
budge *tr* ciēre, movēre ‖ *intr* se movēre, loco cedere
budget *s* pecuniae rati·o -onis *f*
buffalo *s* ur·us -i *m*
buffet *s (sideboard)* abac·us -i *m; (slap)* alap·a -ae *f*
buffoon *s* scurr·a -ae *f;* **to play the —** scurrari
bug *s* cim·ex -icis *mf*
buggy *s (two-wheeled)* carpent·um -i *n; (four-wheeled)* pertorrit·um -i *n*
bugle *s* bucin·a -ae *f,* corn·u -ūs *n*
bugle call *s* classic·um -i *n*
bugler *s* bucinat·or -oris *m*
build *tr (house, ship)* aedificare; *(house, walls)* (ex)struere; *(bridge)* fabricare; *(wall, rampart)* ducere; *(road)* munire; *(hopes)* ponere; **to — up** exstruere
builder *s* aedificat·or -oris *m,* struct·or -oris *m*
building *s (act)* aedificati·o -onis *f,* exstructi·o -onis *f; (structure)* aedific·ium -(i)i *n*
building site *s* are·a -ae *f*
bulb *s* bulb·us -i *m*

bulge *intr (swell)* tumēre; *(to stand out)* prominēre
bulge *s* tub·er -eris *n*
bulk *s* amplitud·o -inis *f; (mass)* mol·es -is *f; (greater part)* maior par·s -tis *f*
bulkiness *s* magnitud·o -inis *f*
bulky *adj (huge)* ing·ens -entis; *(difficulty to handle)* inhabil·is -is -e
bull *s* taur·us -i *m; (sl)* fabul·ae -arum *fpl;* **to sling the —** *(sl)* confabulari
bulldog *s* can·is -is *m* Moloss·us
bulldozer *s* machin·a -ae *f* aggerandi
bullet *s* glan·s -dis *f* plumbea
bulletin *s* libell·us -i *m; (news)* nunt·ius -(i)i *m*
bulletin board *s* tabul·a -ae *f* publica
bullfrog *s* ran·a -ae *f* ocellata
bullock *s* iuvenc·us -i *m*
bull's eye *s* scop·us -i *m* medius; **hit the —** scopum medium ferire
bully *s* scordal·us -i *m*
bully *tr* procaciter lacessere
bulwark *s (wall)* moen·ia -ium *npl; (any means of defense)* propugnacul·um -i *n; (fig)* ar·x cis *f*
bump *s (swelling)* tub·er -eris *n; (thump)* plag·a -ae *f,* sonit·us -ūs *m*
bump *tr* pulsare, pellere ‖ *intr* **to — against** offendere; **to — into s.o.** *(meet accidentally)* alicui occurrere
bumper *s* cont·us -i *m* tutorius
bumpy *adj* tuberos·us -a -um; *(road, ground)* iniqu·us -a -um
bun *s (roll)* lib·um -i *n,* collyr·is -idis *f*
bunch *s* fascicul·us -i *m; (of grapes)* racem·us -i *m; (group)* glob·us -i *m*
bunch *intr* **to — together** glomerari
bundle *s* fasc·is -is *m; (of straw)* manipul·us -i *m*
bundle *tr* **to — up** *(with clothes)* coöperire
bungle *tr (a job)* inscite gerere, inscite agere ‖ *intr* errare
bungler *s* imperit·us -i *m* (·a -ae *f*)
burden *s* on·us -eris *n*
burden *tr* onerare
burdensome *adj* oneros·us -a -um
bureau *s* minister·ium -(i)i *n; (chest)* armar·ium -(i)i *n; (for clothes)* vestiar·ium -(i)i *n*
burglar *s* effractar·ius -(i)i *m* (·a -ae *f*)
burglary *s* (domūs) effractur·a -ae *f*
burial *s (act)* sepultur·a -ae *f; (ceremony)* fun·us -eris *n*
burlesque *s* ridicula imitati·o -onis *f*
burly *adj* corpulent·us -a -um
burn *tr* urere, cremare; **to — down** deurere; **to — out** exurere; **to — up** comburere ‖ *intr* flagrare, ardēre; **to — down** deflagrare; **to — out** exstingui; **to — up** conflagrare
burn *s* adusti·o -onis *f; (injury)* ambust·um -i *n*
burner *s* disc·us -i *m* coctorius

burning *adj* ard·ens -entis
burn-out *s* defecti·o -onis *f* virium
burrow *intr* defodere
bursar *s* dispensat·or -oris *m* (·rix -ricis *f*)
burst *s (spurt)* impet·us -ūs *m; (noise)* frag·or -oris *m; — of anger* iracundiae impet·us -ūs *m; — of applause* clamor·es -um *mpl*
burst *tr* rumpere; *(with noise)* displodere; **to — asunder** dirumpere; **to — open** effrangere ‖ *intr* rumpi; **to — forth** prorumpere; **to — in** irrumpere; **to — out** erumpere; **to — out laughing** risum effundere
bury *tr* sepelire; *(to hide)* abdere; **to — the sword in his side** lateri abdere ensem
bus *s* raed·a -ae *f* longa
bus driver *s* raeda longae gubernat·or -oris *m* (·rix -ricis *f*)
bush *s* frut·ex -icis *m; (thorny bush)* dum·us -i *m;* **to beat around the —** circuitione uti
bushel *s* medimn·us -i *m*
bushy *adj (full of bushes)* dumos·us -a -um; *(full of branches)* ramos·us -a -um; *(tail)* villos·us -a -um
busily *adv* impigre, sedulo
business *s* negot·ium -(i)i *n; (trade, calling)* ar·s -tis *f; (matter)* res, rei *f; (establishment)* officin·a -ae *f;* **I always made it my — to be present** ego id semper egi ut adessem; **to mind one's own —** negotium suum agere; **what — do you have here?** quid negoti tibi hic est?; **what — is it of his?** quid illius interest?
business agent *s* negotiorum curat·or -oris *m* (·rix -ricis *f*)
business card *s* chartul·a -ae *f* negotialis
business district *s* empori·um -i *n*
business establishment *s (w. its premises)* negotiati·o -onis *f*
businessman *s* negotiat·or -oris *m*
businesswoman *s* negotiat·rix -ricis *f*
buskin *s* cothurn·us -i *m*
bust *s* imag·o -inis *f; (bosom)* pect·us -oris *n; (woman's)* mammill·ae -arum *fpl*
bustle *s (hurry)* festinati·o -onis *f; (running to and fro)* discurs·us -ūs *m*
bustle *intr* festinare; **to — about** discurrere
busy *adj* occupat·us -a -um; *(time)* operos·us -a -um; *(w. business matters)* negotios·us -a -um; **be — with** versari in *(w. abl)*
busy *tr* **to — oneself with** versari in *(w. abl)*
busybody *s* ardali·o -onis *mf*
but *prep* praeter *(w. acc)*
but *adv* modo, tantum
but *conj* sed; *(stronger)* at; **— if** quodsi; sin; **— if not** sin aliter
butcher *s* lan·ius -(i)i *m; (fig)* carnif·ex -icis *m*
butcher *tr (animals)* caedere; *(people)* contrucidare
butcher shop *s* lanien·a -ae *f*

butchery s trucidati·o -onis f
butler s prom·us -i m
butt s (mark) met·a -ae f; (backside) clun·es -ium mpl; — **of ridicule** ludibr·ium -(i)i n
butt tr arietare ‖ intr **to — in** interpellare
butter s butyr·um -i n
butter tr butyrum adhibēre ad (w. acc); **to — s.o. up** blandiri (w. dat)
butterfly s papili·o -onis m
buttermilk s lactis ser·um -i n
buttock s clun·is -is mf
button s globul·us -i m vestiarius; (comput) plectr·um -i n
button tr globulo (or globulis) stringere
buttress s anter·is -idis f
buttress tr suffulcire
buxom adj ampl·us -a -um
buy tr (from) emere, mercari de (w abl); **to — back** or **off** redimere; **to — up** coëmere
buyer s empt·or -oris m (·rix -ricis f)
buying s empti·o -onis f
buzz s bomb·us -i m
buzz intr bombilare
by prep (agency) a, ab (w. abl); (of place) (near) apud (w. acc); (along) secundum (w. acc); (past) praeter (w. acc); (in oaths) per (w. acc); — **and —** mox; — **means of** per (w. acc); — **oneself** per se; (alone) sol·us -a -um
bye vale! (pl: valete!)
bygone adj praeterit·us -a -um; (olden) prisc·us -a -um
bylaw s praescript·um -i n
bypass s circuit·us -ūs m
bypass tr ambire
bystander s spectat·or -oris m (·rix -ricis f)
byway s deverticul·um -i n
byword s proverb·ium -(i)i n

C

cab s (for hire) raed·a -ae n meritoria
cabbage s brassic·a -ae f; (head of cabbage) caul·is -is m
cabin s (cottage) cas·a -ae f; (on a ship) daiet·a -ae f
cabinet s armar·ium -(i)i n; (pol) consil·ium -(i)i n principis
cabinet member s consilia·tor -toris m (·trix -tricis f)
cable s rud·ens -entis m; (for anchor) ancoral·e -is n
cablecar s curr·us -i m funalis
cackle intr (of hens) gracillare; (of geese) gingrire
cackle s gingrit·us -ūs m

cactus s cact·us -i m
cad s hom·o -inis mf rudis
cadaver s cadav·er -eris n
cadaverous adj cadaveros·us -a -um
cadence s numer·us -i m
cadet s discipul·us -i m (·a -ae f) militaris
cafe s cafe·um -i n
cafeteria s refector·ium -(i)i n
cage s cave·a -ae f
cage tr in caveā includere
caged adj caveat·us -a -um
cagey adj callid·us -a -um
cahoots spl **be in — with** colludere cum (w. abl)
cajole tr lactare
cake s placent·a -ae f; (birthday cake) lib·um -i n; (wedding cake) mustace·us -i m
calamitous adj calamitos·us -a -um
calamity s calamit·as -atis f; **to suffer —** calamitatem perferre
calcium s calc·ium -(i)i n
calculate tr computare; (fig) existimare
calculated adj subduct·us -a -um
calculation s computati·o -onis f; (fig) ratiocinati·o -onis f
calculating adj (pej) versut·us -a -um
calculator s machinul·a -ae f calculatoria
caldron s cortin·a -ae f; (of copper) ahen·um -i n
calendar s calendar·ium -(i)i n; (in Roman period) fast·i -orum mpl
calends spl Kalend·ae -arum fpl
calf s vitul·us -i m (·a -ae f); (anat) sur·a -ae f
caliber s (fig) ingen·ium -(i)i n
call s vocati·o -onis f; (shout) clam·or -oris m; (visit) salutati·o -onis f; (summons) accit·us -ūs m; **social —** offic·ium -(i)i n; **to make** or **pay a social —** officium peragere
call tr (to summon) ad se vocare; (to name) appellare, vocare; **to — aside** sevocare; **to — away** avocare; **to — back** revocare; **to — down** devocare; **to — forth** evocare; (to cause) provocare; (fig) elicere; **to — in** (money) cogere; (for advice) advocare; (a doctor) accersere; **to — off** (to cancel) revocare, tollere; (to read) citare; **to — out** (to call forth) evocare; (to shout) exclamare; **to — to account** (to upraid) compellere; **to — together** convocare; **to — to mind** recordari; **to — to witness** testari; **to — up** (mil) evocare ‖ intr **to — for** (to demand) poscere; (to require) requirere; **to — on** (to invoke) invocare; (for help) implorare; (to visit) visere
caller s saluta·tor -toris m (·trix -tricis f)
calling s (profession) ar·s -tis f; (station) stat·us -ūs m
callous adj callos·us -a -um; (fig) dur·us -a -um; **to become —** occallescere; (fig) obdurescere

callus *s* call·um -i *n*

calm *adj (unruffled)* tranquill·us -a -um; *(sleep, sea, speech, old age)* placid·us -a -um; *(mentally)* aequ·us -a -um

calm *tr* sedare, tranquillare

calming *s* sedati·o -onis *f*

calmly *adv* tranquille, placide; *(of a person)* aequo animo

calmness *s (lit & fig)* tranquillit·as -atis *f;* **with —** aequo animo

calumny *s (abuse)* maledict·um -i *n; (slander)* calumni·a -ae *f*

camel *s* camel·us -i *m*

cameo *s* imag·o -inis *f* ectypa

camera *s* photomachinul·a -ae *f*

camouflage *s* dissimulati·o -onis *f*

camouflage *tr* dissimulare

camp *s* castr·a -orum *npl;* **summer —** aestiv·a -orum; *npl* **winter —** hibern·a -orum *npl*

camp *adj* castrens·is -is -e

camp *intr* castra ponere

campaign *s (mil)* expediti·o -onis *f,* stipend·ium -(i)i *n; (pol)* **(for)** petiti·o -onis *f (w. gen)*

campaign *intr (mil)* stipendium merēre; *(pol)* ambire, prensare

campaigning *s (pol)* ambiti·o -onis *f; (corruptly)* ambit·us -ūs *m*

camp follower *s* cal·o -onis *m*

can *s* vascul·um -i *n* stanneum

can *tr (to store)* condere ‖ *intr* posse; *(to have the power)* pollēre; **I — not** nequeo, non possum

canal *s* foss·a -ae *f* navigabilis

canary *s* fringill·a -ae *f* Canaria

cancel *tr* tollere; *(to cross out)* cancellare, delēre

cancellation *s* deleti·o -onis *f; (fig)* aboliti·o -onis *f*

cancer *s* can·cer -cri *m,* carcinom·a -atis *n*

cancerous *adj* canceros·us -a -um

candid *adj* apert·us -a -um

candidate *s (for)* candidat·us -i *m* (·a -ae *f) (w. gen);* **to announce oneself as —** profiteri

candidly *adv* aperte, libere

candied *adj* succharo condit·us -a -um

candle *s* candel·a -ae *f*

candlestick *s* candelabr·um -i *n*

candor *s* cand·or -oris *m*

candy *s* cuppedi·ae -arum *fpl;* **piece of —** dulciol·um -i *n*

cane *s (walking stick)* bacul·us -i *m; (reed)* harund·o -inis *f*

cane *tr* baculo verberare

canine *adj* canin·us -a -um

canister *s* pyx·is -idis *f*

cannibal *s* anthropophag·us -i *m*

cannon *s* torment·um -i *n*

cannonball *s* glob·us -i *m* missilis

canoe *s* scaph·a -ae *f*

canoe *intr* scapham impellere; **to go —ing** scaphā gestari

cannon *s* torment·um -i *n*

cannon ball *s* glob·us -i *m* tormenti

canon *s (eccl)* can·on -onis *m*

canonical *adj* canonic·us -a -um

canonize *tr* in numerum sanctorum referre

canon law *s* ius, iuris *n* canonicum

canopy *s* aulae·um -i *n*

canteen *s (flask)* laguncul·a -ae *f; (mil)* caupon·a -ae *f* castrensis

canter *s* lenis quadrupedans grad·us -ūs *m*

canter *intr* leniter currere

canton *s* pag·us -i *m*

canvas *s* linte·um -i *n* crassum; *(for painting)* textil·e -is *n*

cap *s* pille·us -i *m; (worn by certain priests)* galer·us -i *m*

capability *s* facult·as -atis *f*

capable *adj (skilled)* soller·s -tis, perit·us -a -um; **(of)** cap·ax -acis *(w. gen);* **— of enduring** *(cold, hunger, etc.)* pati·ens -entis *(w. gen);* **— of holding 500 spectators** cap·ax -acis quingentorum spectatorum

capably *adv* scite

capacity *s (extent of space)* capacit·as -atis *f; (extent of mental power)* mensur·a -ae *f; (ability)* ingen·ium -(i)i *n*

cape *s* promontor·ium -(i)i *n; (garment)* humeral·e -is *n*

caper *s (leap)* exsultati·o -onis *f; (prank)* ludibr·ium -(i)i *n; (bold criminal act)* scel·us -eris *n;* **to pull a —** scelus patrare

capital *adj (chief)* praecipu·us -a -um; *(offense, punishment)* capital·is -is -e; *(letters)* uncial·is -is -e

capital *s (chief city)* cap·ut -itis *n; (archit)* capitul·um -i *n; (com)* cap·ut -itis *n,* sor·s -tis *f*

capital punishment *s* supplic·ium -(i)i *n* capitis; **to suffer —** supplicio capitis affici

capitol *s* capitol·ium -(i)i *n*

capitulate *intr* se dedere

capitulation *s* dediti·o -onis *f*

capon *s* cap·o -onis *m*

caprice *s* libid·o -inis *f*

capricious *adj* inconst·ans -antis

capriciously *adv* inconstanter

Capricorn *s* Capricorn·us -i *m*

capsize *tr* evertere ‖ *intr* everti

capsule *s* capsul·a -ae *f; (bot)* vascul·um -i *n*

captain *s (in infantry)* centuri·o -onis *m; (in cavalry)* praefect·us -i *m; (in navy)* navarch·us -i *m; (of merchant ship)* navis magis·ter -tri *m*

caption *s* capitul·um -i *n; (leg)* praescripti·o -onis *f*

captious *adj (tricky)* captios·us -a -um; *(carping)* moros·us -a -um
captivate *tr* capere
captive *adj* captiv·us -a -um
captive *s* captiv·us -i *m* (·a -ae *f)*
captor *s* capt·or -oris *m; (of a city)* expugnat·or -oris *m*
capture *s* comprehensi·o -onis *f; (of a city)* expugnati·o -onis *f; (of animals)* captur·a -ae *f*
capture *tr* capere, excipere; *(city)* expugnare; *(by surprise)* opprimere
car *s (chariot)* curr·us -ūs *m; (carriage)* raed·a -ae *f,* carr·us -i *m; (modern)* autocinet·um -i *n,* raed·a -ae *f;* **to drive a** — raedam gubernare *or* agere; **to go by** — raedā ire; **to go for a ride in a** — gestationem raedā facere; **to stop the** — raedam sistere; **to take s.o. by** — aliquem raedā ducere
caravan *s* commeat·us -ūs *m*
carbon *s* carbon·ium -(i)i *n*
carcass *s* cadav·er -eris *n*
card *s* chart·a -ae *f; (playing card)* chartul·a -ae *f* lusoria; **birthday** — charta natalicia; **calling** — charta salutatoria; **to cut (deal, shuffle) the** —s chartulas seponere (distribuere, miscēre); **to play** —s chartulis (lusoriis) ludere;
cardboard *s* chart·a -ae *f* crassior
cardinal *adj* principal·is -is -e; *(color)* ru·ber -bra -brum; *(numbers)* cardinal·is -is -e
cardinal *s (eccl)* cardinal·is -is *m*
car door *s* raedae ostiol·um -i *n*
card table *s* mens·a -ae *f* lusoria
care *s (anxiety, oversight, attention)* cur·a -ae *f,* oper·a -ae *f; (diligence)* diligenti·a -ae *f; (charge)* tutel·a -ae *f; (watching over)* custodi·a -ae *f;* — **was taken by the senate to** *(w.inf)* opera a senatu data est ut; **take** — **of yourself!** cura ut valeas!; **to take** — **not to** cavēre ne; **to take (good)** — **of** (diligenter) curare
care *intr* curare; **for all I** — meā causā; **I don't** — **nil** moror; **I don't** — **for wine** ego vinum nihil moror; **to** — **for** *(to look after)* curare; *(to like)* amare, diligere; *(to be fond of, with negatives)* morari; **what do I** — **?** quid mihi est?
career *s* curricul·um -i *n; (pol)* curs·us -ūs *m* honorum
carefree *adj* secur·us -a -um
careful *adj (attentive)* dilig·ens -entis, curios·us -a -um; *(cautious)* caut·us -a -um; *(watchful)* vigil·ans -antis; *(of work)* accurat·us -a -um; **careful!** cave!
carefully *adv* diligenter; caute
carefulness *s* cur·a -ae *f,* diligenti·a -ae *f,* cauti·o -onis *f*

careless *adj* negleg·ens -entis, incurios·us -a -um
carelessly *adv* neglegenter
carelessness *s* incuri·a -ae *f; (stronger)* neglegenti·a -ae *f*
caress *s* amplex·us -ūs *m*
caress *tr* fovēre, palpare; *(to embrace)* amplecti
caretaker *s* cust·os -odis *mf*
carfare *s* vectur·a -ae *f* currūs
cargo *s* on·us -eris *n;* **to put a ship's** — **aboard** navem onerare
cargo plane *s* aëroplan·um -i *n* onerarium
cargo ship *s* nav·is -is *f* oneraria
caricature *s (picture)* gryll·us -i *m; (fig)* ridicula imitati·o -onis *f*
caricature *tr* imaginem *(w. gen)* in peius fingere; *(fig)*, detorquēre
car key *s* clav·is -is *f* accensiva
carnage *s* strag·es -is *f*
carnal *adj* carnal·is -is -e; — **pleasure** volupt·as -atis *f* libidinosa
carnival *s* feri·ae -arum *fpl* ante quadragesimam
carnivorous *adj* carnivor·us -a -um
carol *s* cant·us -ūs *m*
carouse *intr* comissari
carp *s* cyprin·us -i *m*
carp *intr* **to** — **at** carpere
carpenter *s* fa·ber -bri *m* tignarius
carpentry *s* materiatur·a -ae *f* fabrilis
carpet *s* tapet·e -is *n*
carriage *s* vehicul·um -i *n,* raed·a -ae *f; (esp. women's)* carpent·um -i *n*
carrier *s* baiul·us -i *m*
carrot *s* carot·a -ae *f*
carry *tr* ferre; *(of heavier things)* portare; *(by vehicle)* vehere; *(a law)* perferre; **to get carried away with enthusiasm** studio efferri; **to** — **away** auferre; evehere; **to** — **in** importare; invehere; **to** — **off** auferre; *(by force)* rapere; **to** — **on** *(to conduct)* exercēre; *(war)* gerere; **to** — **out** efferre; evehere; *(to perform)* exsequi; **to** — **through** perferre; **to** — **weight** auctoritatem habēre ‖ *intr (of sound)* audiri; **to** — **on** pergere; *(to behave)* se gerere
cart *s* plaustr·um -i *n; (dim.)* plostell·um -i *n; (two-wheeled, drawn by oxen)* carr·us -i *m;* **putting the** — **before the horse** praeposteris consiliis
cart *tr* plaustro vehere; **to** — **off** plaustro evehere
carve *tr* sculpere; *(to engrave)* caelare; *(at table)* secare
carver *s (engraver)* caelat·or -oris *m; (at table)* sciss·or -oris *m*
carving *s* caelatur·a -ae *f*
carving knife *s* cultell·us -i *m*

case *s* *(leg)* caus·a -ae *f;* *(matter, circumstances, condition)* res, rei *f;* *(instance)* exempl·um -i *n;* *(container)* involucr·um -i *n;* *(patient)* aeg·er -ri *m,* aegr·a -ae *f;* *(gram)* cas·us -ūs *m;* **if that's the** — si res sic habet; **in any** — utcumque; **in no** — nequaquam; **in the** — **of Priam** in Priamo; **since that's the** — quae cum ita sint

cash *s* pecuni·a -ae *f* praesens *(or* numerata), numm·i -orum *mpl,* numerat·um -i *n;* **in** — numerato; **in cold** — calidis nummis; **in hard** — in nummis: **to pay** — praesenti *(or* numeratā) pecuniā solvere

cash box *s* arc·a -ae *f*
cashier *s* dispensa·tor -toris *m* (·trix -tricis *f)*
cash payment *s* repraesentati·o -onis *f*
cash register *s* machin·a -ae *f* accepto et expenso numerando
casing *s* *(cover)* tegim·en -inis *n*
casino *s* aleator·ium -(i)i *n*
cask *s* cad·us -i *m*
casket *s* capul·us -i *m*
Caspian Sea *s* Caspium mar·e -is *n*
casserole *s* *(dish)* coctor·ium (i)i *n;* *(food)* miscellane·a -orum *npl*
cassette *s* caset·a -ae *f;* *(for video)* caseta magnetoscopica
cassette recorder *s* casetophon·um -i *n*
cast *s* *(throw)* iact·us -ūs *m;* *(mold)* typ·us -i *m;* — **of characters** distributi·o -onis *f* partium in singulos actores
cast *tr* iacere; *(metal)* fundere; *(a vote)* ferre; **to** — **aside** abicere; **to** — **a vote** suffragium ferre; **to** — **down** deicere; **to** — **in** inicere; **to** — **off** *(skin)* exuere; *(fig)* ponere; **to** — **out** eicere, expellere; **to** — **upon** superinicere; *(fig)* aspergere ‖ *intr* **to** — **off** navem solvere
caste *s* ord·o -inis *m*
castigate *intr* castigare
cast iron *s* ferr·um -i *n* fusum
castle *s* castell·um -i *n;* *(chess)* turr·is -is *f*
castrate *tr* castrare
castration *s* castrati·o -onis *f*
casual *adj* fortuit·us -a -um; *(person)* negleg·ens -entis
casually *adv* fortuito, casu, forte
casualty *s* cas·us -ūs *m;* *(mil)* bello caduc·us -i *m* (·a -ae *f)*
cat *s* fel·es -is *f,* catt·a -ae *f,* catt·us -i *m*
cataclysm *s* cataclysm·os -i *m*
catacombs *spl* catacumb·ae -arum *fpl*
catalogue *s* catalog·us -i *m*
cataract *s* cataract·a -ae *f;* *(of the eyes)* glaucom·a -atis *n*
catastrophe *s* calamit·as -atis *f*
catcall *s* irrisi·o -onis *f*
catch *s* *(of fish)* praed·a -ae *f;* *(fastening)* fibul·a -ae *f;* **to think s.o. a great** — aliquem

magni facere; **what's the** — ? quid est captio?
catch *tr* capere; *(unawares)* excipere; *(to surprise)* deprehendere; *(to hear)* exaudire; *(falling object)* excipere, suscipere; *(in a net)* illaquēre; *(fish)* captare; *(birds)* excipere; **to** — **a cold** gravedine affligi; **to** — **fire** ignem *or* flammam concipere; **to** — **hell** convicium habēre; **to** — **his eye** experimentum oculorum eius capere; **to** — **red-handed** deprehendere; **to** — **one's breath** respirare; **to** — **sight of** conspicere ‖ *intr* **to** — **at** arripere; **to** — **on** comprehendere; **to** — **up to** *(or* with) consequi
catcher *s* excep·tor -oris *m* (·trix -tricis *f)*
catching *adj* *(contagious)* contagios·us -a -um; *(fig)* grat·us -a -um
categorical *adj* categoric·us -a -um
categorically *adv* categorice
category *s* categori·a -ae *f*
cater *intr* cibum suppeditare; **to** — **to** indulgēre *(w. dat)*
caterer *s* obsona·tor -toris *m* (·trix -tricis *f)*
caterpillar *s* eruc·a -ae *f;* *(mech)* vehicul·um -i *n* catenarium
cathedral *s* ecclesi·a -ae *f* cathedralis
Catholic *adj* Catholic·us -a -um
catnap *s* lenis *(or* brevis) somn·us -i *m;* **to take a** — somno brevi uti
cattle *s* pec·us -oris *n,* bov·es -um *mpl*
cauliflower *s* brassic·a -ae *f* Pompeiana; *(plant)* brassica oleracea botryitis
causal *adj* causal·is -is -e
cause *s* caus·a -ae *f;* *(motive)* rati·o -onis *f*
cause *tr* facere, efficere; *(pain, swelling, war)* movēre; **to** — **a quarrel** litem facere; **to** — **him to leave** facere ut abeat; **to** — **trouble** malum facere
causeway *s* agg·er -eris *m*
caustic *adj* caustic·us -a -um; *(fig)* mord·ax -acis
cauterize *tr* adurere
caution *s* cauti·o -onis *f;* **to use great** — diligenter circumspicere; **with** — pedetemptim
caution *tr* (ad)monēre
cautious *adj* caut·us -a -um
cautiously *adv* caute
cavalcade *s* pomp·a -ae *f*
cavalry *s* equitat·us -ūs *m,* equit·es -um *mpl*
cave *s* spec·us -ūs *m*
cave *intr* **to** — **in** corruere, collabi
caveat *s* monit·um -i *n*
cavern *s* cavern·a -ae *f*
cavernous *adj* cavernos·us -a -um
caviar *s* ov·a -orum *npl* acipenseris
cavity *s* cav·um -i *n;* *(anat)* lacun·a -ae *f;* *(in tooth or bone)* cari·es -ei *f*
cavort *intr* exsultare
caw *intr* crocire, crocitare

CD *s* compactus disc·us -i *m*
CD player *s* discophon·um -i *n*
CD-ROM *s* orbicul·us -i *m* opticus
CD-ROM drive *s* instrument·um -i *n* orbiculis legendis
cease *tr & intr* desinere; *(temporarily)* intermittere
cease-fire *s* induti·ae -arum *fpl;* **to call for a —** indutias poscere
ceaseless *adj* perpetu·us -a -um
ceaselessly *adv* perpetuo
cedar *s* cedr·us -i *f*
cedar *adj* cedre·us -a -um
cede *tr & intr* (con)cedere
ceiling *s* tect·um -i *n; (arched or vaulted)* camer·a -ae *f; (panelled)* lacun·ar -aris *n*
celebrate *tr* celebrare; *(in song)* canere
celebrated *adj* cele·ber -bris -bre
celebration *s* celebrati·o -onis *f; (of rites)* sollemn·e -is *n*
celebrity *s* celebrit·as -atis *f; (person)* hom·o -inis *mf* illustris
celery *s* heleoselin·um -i *n*
celestial *adj* caelest·is -is -e
celibacy *s* caelibat·us -ūs *m*
celibate *adj* caeleb·s -is
cell *s (room)* cell·a -ae *f; (biol)* protoplasm·a -atis *n*
cellar *s* hypoge·um -i *n*
cell phone *s* telephon·ium -(i)i *n* portabile
cellophane *s* membran·a -ae *f* pellucida
cement *s (concrete)* ferrum·en -inis *n; (glue)* ferrumen
cement *tr* ferruminare; *(to glue)* conglutinare ‖ *intr* coalescere
cemetery *s* sepulcret·um -i *n*
censer *s* turibul·um -i *n*
censor *s* cens·or -oris *m*
censorship *s* censur·a -ae *f; (of literature)* literarum censur·a -ae *f*
censure *s* vituperati·o -onis *f*
censure *tr* animadvertere; *(officially)* notare
census *s* civium enumerati·o -onis *f; (in the Roman sense)* cens·us -ūs *m;* **to conduct a —** recensum populi agere
cent *s* centesim·a -ae *f;* **I don't owe anyone a red —** assem aerarium nemini debeo
centaur *s* centaur·us -i *m*
centennial *adj* centenari·us -a -um
centennial *s* centesimus ann·us -i *m*
center *s* med·ium -(i)i *n; (math)* centr·um -i *n;* **in the — of the town** in medio oppido
center *tr* in centrum ponere ‖ *intr* **to — on** niti *(w. abl)*
central *adj* medi·us -a -um, central·is -is -e
central heating *s* calefacti·o -onis *f* centralis
centralize *tr (authority)* ad unum deferre
centurion *s* centuri·o -onis *m*

century *s* saecul·um -i *n; (mil, pol)* centuri·a -ae *f;* **— old** saecular·is -is -e
ceramic *adj* fictil·is -is -e
ceramics *s* ar·s -tis *f* figlina; *(objects)* fictil·ia -ium *npl*
cereal *s* cere·al -alis *n*
cerebellum *s* cerebell·um -i *n*
cerebrum *s* cerebr·um -i *n*
ceremonial *adj* sollemn·is -is -e
ceremonial *s* sollemn·e -is *n; (religious)* rit·us -ūs *m*
ceremonious *adj* solemn·is -is -e; *(person)* officios·us -a -um
ceremoniously *adv* rite
ceremony *s* caerimoni·a -ae *f; (pomp)* apparat·us -ūs *m;* **religious ceremonies** religion·es -um *fpl*
certain *adj (sure)* cert·us -a -um; *(indefinite)* quidam quaedam quoddam; **for —** certe, pro certo; **it is certain that** constat *(w. acc & inf);* **to make —** explorare
certainly *adv* profecto; *(in answers)* sane
certainty *s* cert·um -i *n; (belief)* fid·es -ei *f*
certificate *s* testimon·ium -(i)i *n*
certification *s* testificati·o -onis *f*
certified *adj* affirmat·us -a -um; *(of credentials)* testimonium hab·ens -entis, testimonial·is -is -e
certify *tr* confirmare; *(to attest)* testificari
cessation *s* cessati·o -onis *f; (temporary)* intermissi·o -onis *f;* **— of hostilities** induti·ae -arum *fpl*
chafe *tr* urere; *(w. the hand)* fricare; *(to excoriate)* atterere; *(to vex)* irritare ‖ *intr* stomachari
chagrin *s* stomach·us -i *m*
chagrined *adj* **to be —** stomachari
chain *s* caten·a -ae *f; (necklace)* torqu·es -is *mf; (fig)* seri·es -ei *f;* **dog on a —** can·is -is *m* catenis vinctus
chain *tr* catenas inicere *(w. dat)*
chain store *s* tabern·a -ae *f* societatis
chair *s* sell·a -ae *f; (w. rounded back)* arcisell·ium -(i)i *n; (of a teacher)* cathedr·a -ae *f; (of a Roman magistrate)* sella *f* curulis
chair *tr (a meeting)* praesidēre *(w. dat),* praeesse *(w. dat)*
chairperson *s* praes·es -idis *mf*
chalice *s* cal·ix -icis *m*
chalk *s* cret·a -ae *f*
chalk *tr* cretā notare; *(cover with chalk)* cretā illinere; **to — up** notare
chalky *adj (chalk-like)* cretace·us -a -um; *(full of chalk)* cretos·us -a -um
challenge *s* provocati·o -onis *f; (leg)* reiecti·o -onis *f,* recusati·o -onis *f*
challenge *tr* provocare; *(a claim)* vindicare; *(validity)* recusare; *(leg)* reicere

challenger *s* provoca·tor -toris *m* (·trix -tricis *f*)

challenging *adj* provoc·ans -antis

chamber *s (room)* conclav·e -is *n; (bedroom)* cubicul·um -i *n; (pol)* curi·a -ae *f*

chambermaid *s* ancill·a -ae *f* cubicularia

chamber pot *s* lasan·um -i *n*

champ *tr & intr* mandere; **to — on the bit** frena dente premere

champagne *s* vin·um -i *n* effervescens

champion *s (sports)* summ·us (-a) athlet·a -ae *mf; (defender)* propugna·tor -toris *m* (·trix -tricis *f*)

championship *s* titul·us -i *m* victoriae

chance *s (accident)* cas·us -ūs *m; (opportunity)* potest·as -atis *f; (risk)* pericul·um -i *n; (prospect)* sp·es -ei *f; (fig)* ale·a -ae *f;* **by —** casu, forte; **by some — or other** nescio quo casu; **game of —** ale·a -ae *f;* **to give s.o. a — to** potestatem alicui facere *(w. inf);* **to stand a —** potestatem habēre; **to take a —** periculum adire

chance *tr* periclitari ‖ *intr* accidere; *often expressed by the adverb* forte: **I —ed to see the aedile** aedilem forte conspexi; **to — on** occurrere *(w. dat)*

chance *adj* fortuit·us -a -um

chancellor *s (pol)* princ·eps -ipis *mf* consilii

chandelier *s* lampadum corymb·us -i *m*

change *s* mutati·o -onis *f; (complete)* commutati·o -onis *f,* permutati·o -onis *f; (variety)* variet·as -atis *f; (of fortune)* vicissitud·o -inis *f; (coins)* numm·i -orum *mpl* minores; **— of clothes** mutati·o -onis *f* vestis; **— of heart** animi mutati·o -onis *f;* **for a —** varietatis causā

change *tr* mutare; *(completely)* commutare; **to — into** convertere in *(w. acc);* **to — one's mind** sententiam mutare ‖ *intr* mutari, variare; *(of the moon)* renovari; **the wind changed** ventus se vertit; **to — for the better (worse)** in meliorem (peiorem) partem mutari; **to — into** verti in *(w. acc)*

changeable *adj* mutabil·is -is -e; *(fickle)* inconst·ans -antis

changeless *adj* immutabil·is -is -e

channel *s (TV)* televisorius canal·is -is *m; (of rivers)* alve·us -i *m; (arm of the sea)* fret·um -i *n; (groove)* stri·a -ae *f*

channel *tr* sulcare, excavare; *(to guide)* ducere

chant *s* cant·us -ūs *m*

chant *tr* cantare

chaos *s* cha·os -i *n; (confusion)* perturbati·o -onis *f*

chaotic *adj* confus·us -a -um

chap *s* fissur·a -ae *f; (person)* hom·o -inis *m; (boy)* pu·er -eri *m*

chap *tr* diffindere; **—ed lips** fissur·ae -arum *fpl* labrorum ‖ *intr* scindi

chapel *s* sacell·um -i *n*

chapter *s* cap·ut -itis *n*

char *tr* amburere

character *s* mor·es -um *mpl; (inborn)* indol·es -is *f,* ingen·ium -(i)i *n; (repute)* existimati·o -onis *f; (type)* gen·us -eris *n; (letter)* litter·a -ae *f; (theat)* person·a -ae *f;* **to assume the — of a plaintiff** petitoris personam capere

characteristic *s* propr·ium -(i)i *n*

characteristic *adj* propri·us -a -um; **it is — of a father to protect his family** patris est familiam suam tegere

characteristically *adv* proprie

characterize *tr* describere, pingere

character witness *s* advocat·us -i *m* (·a -ae *f*)

charade *s* mim·us -i *m;* **—s** aenigm·a -atis *n* syllabicum

charcoal *s* carb·o -onis *m*

charge *s* accusati·o -onis *f; (leg)* lis, litis *f,* crim·en -inis *n; (mil)* impet·us -ūs *m; (into enemy territory)* incurs·us -ūs *m; (command)* mandat·um -i *n; (trust)* cur·a -ae *f,* custodi·a -ae *f; (office)* mun·us -eris *n; (cost)* impens·a -ae *f;* **capital —** lis capitis; **free of —** gratis; **to be in — of** praeesse *(w. dat);* **to bring —s against** litem intendere *(w. dat);* **to put in — of** praeficere *(w. dat);* **to take — of** curare

charge *tr* indicare *(with gen of indefinite price or abl of definite price), e.g.,* **to — a lot for the meal** cenam multi indicare; **to — ten dollars for the meal** cenam decem dollaris indicare; *(to attack)* incurrere *(w. dat or acc); (to enjoin upon)* mandare *(w. dat of person and* ut *w. subj);* **to — a certain price for goods** pretium statuere merci; **to — a fixed price** pretium certum constituere; **to — an expense to the citizens** sumptum civibus inferre; **to — s.o. with** *(a crime)* arguere aliquem *(w. gen or abl of the charge)* ‖ *intr (to make a charge)* irruere

charger *s* bellat·or -oris *m*

chariot *s* curr·us -ūs *m; (for racing)* curricul·um -i *n; (for war)* essed·um -i *n*

charioteer *s* aurig·a -ae *m; (combatant in a chariot)* essedar·ius -(i)i *m*

charitable *adj* benign·us -a -um; *(lenient in judgment)* mit·is -is -e

charitably *adv* benigne

charity *s* liberalit·as -atis *f; (Christian love)* carit·as -atis *f*

charlatan *s* ostentat·or -oris *m* (·rix -ricis *f*); *(quack doctor)* pharmacopol·a -ae *mf*

charm *s (attractiveness)* venust·as -atis *f,* lep·os -oris *m; (spell)* carm·en -inis *n; (amulet)* amulet·um -i *n*

charm *tr (to bewitch)* incantare; *(to delight)* capere; **to lead a —ed life** vitam divinitus munitam gerere

charmer *s (fig)* delici·ae -arum *fpl*
charming *adj (esp. to the eye)* amoen·us -a -um; *(in manner)* lepid·us -a -um; *(beautiful)* venust·us -a -um
chart *s* tabul·a -ae *f; (nautical)* nautica tabul·a -ae *f*
chart *tr* designare
charter *tr (to hire)* conducere; *(to grant a charter to)* diploma donare *(w. dat)*
charter *s (instrument conferring privileges)* diplom·a -atis *n*
chartreuse *adj* chlorin·us -a -um
chase *s (hunt)* venati·o -onis *f; (pursuit)* insectati·o -onis *f*
chase *tr (to hunt)* venari; *(to engrave)* caelare; *(romantically)* petere; **to — away** abigere ‖ *intr* **to — after** petere
chasm *s* hiat·us -ūs *m*
chaste *adj* cast·us -a -um
chastely *adv* caste
chasten *tr (to chastise)* castigare
chastise *tr* castigare
chastisement *s* castigati·o -onis *f*
chastity *s* castit·as -atis *f*
chat *s* familiaris serm·o -onis *m;* **to have a —** fabulari
chat *intr* fabulari
chattel *s* res, rei *f* mancipi; **—s** bon·a -orum *npl*
chatter *s* clang·or -oris *m; (idle talk)* garrulit·as -atis *f; (of teeth)* crepit·us -ūs *m*
chatter *intr* balbutire; *(of birds)* canere; **my teeth —** dentibus crepito
chatty *adj* garul·us -a -um
cheap *adj* vil·is -is -e; **to be — as dirt** pro luto esse; **to sell —er** minoris vendere
cheaply *adv* bene, vili (pretio); **to live — parvo** sumptu vivere
cheapen *tr* pretium minuere *(w. gen)*
cheapness *s* vilit·as -atis *f*
cheat *tr* fraudare; **to — s.o. out of his money** aliquem pecuniā fraudare ‖ *intr (in school)* furtim exscribere
cheat *s* plan·us -i *m,* frau·s -dis *f*
cheater *s* frauda·tor -toris *m* (·trix -tricis *f*)
check *tr (to restrain, e.g., an onset, flow of blood, eager horses)* inhibēre; *(to slow down)* retardare; *(accounts)* dispungere; *(to verify)* comprobare; *(to mark with a check mark)* virgulā notare; **to — luggage** sarcinas mandare; **to — off** *(to make a check mark at)* notare; **to — out** *(to inquire into)* inquirere in *(w. acc)* ‖ *intr (to balance, be correct)* constare; **to — up on** exquirere
check *s* syngraph·a -ae *f,* perscripti·o -onis *f; (bill)* rati·o -onis *f* nummaria; *(restraint)* coërciti·o -onis *f;* **to cash a —** arcario syngrapham praebēre; **to hold in — supprimere; to write a — for** argentum perscribere *(w. dat)*

checkbook *s* cod·ex -icis *f* syngrapharum
checker *s* latruncul·us -i *m;* **—s** *(game)* latrunculorum lud·us -i *m;* **to play —s** latrunculis ludere
checkered *adj* vari·us -a -um
checklist *s* ind·ex -icis *m*
check mark *s* virgul·a -ae *f;* **to put a — at** annotare, virgulā notare
checkup *s* inspecti·o -onis *f*
cheek *s* gen·a -ae *f; (when puffed out by eating, blowing)* bucc·a -ae *f*
cheekbone *s* maxill·a -ae *f*
cheer *s* clam·or -oris *m;* **to be of good —** bono animo esse
cheer *tr* hortari; **to — up** exhilare; **— up!** bono animo es!
cheerful *adj* hilar·us -a -um
cheerfully *adv* hilariter
cheerfulness *s* hilarit·as -atis *f*
cheerless *adj* illaetabil·is -is -e
cheese *s* case·us -i *m*
cheese cake *s* savill·um -i *n*
chef *s* archimagir·us -i *m* (·a -ae *f*)
chemical *adj* chemic·us -a -um
chemical *s* chemic·um -i *n*
chemist *s* chemic·us -i *m* (·a -ae *f*)
chemistry *s* chemi·a -ae *f*
cherish *tr* fovēre; *(fig)* colere
cherry *s* ceras·um -i *n*
cherry pie *s* cerasa *npl* in crusto cocta
cherry-red *adj* cerasin·us -a -um
cherry tree *s* ceras·us -i *f*
chess *s* lud·us -i *m* scacorum, scacilud·ium -(i)i *n;* **to play — scacis** ludere
chessboard *s* scacar·ium -(i)i *n*
chest *s (anat)* pect·us -oris *n; (box)* arc·a -ae *f,* armar·ium -(i)i *n; (for clothes)* vestiar·ium -(i)i *n*
chestnut *s* castane·a -ae *f*
chestnut tree *s* castane·a -ae *f*
chew *tr* manducare; **to — the cud** ruminare; **to — out** *(coll)* pilare
chewing gum *s* cumm·is -is *f* masticabilis
chicanery *s* praevaricati·o -onis *f*
chick *s* pull·us -i *m; (term of endearment)* pull·a -ae *f*
chicken *s* pull·us -i *m* gallinaceus, gallin·a -ae *f; (meat)* gallinace·a -ae *f*
chicken-hearted *adj* muricid·us -a -um
chicory *s* cichore·um -i *n*
chide *tr* increpitare
chief *adj* princ·eps -ipis; *(first in rank)* primari·us -a -um; **— justice** summus iud·ex -icis *m*
chief *s* princ·eps -ipis *m; (ringleader)* cap·ut -itis *n*
chiefly *adv* praecipue, inprimis
chief of police *s* praefect·us -i *m* (·a -ae *f*) vigilum

chieftain *s* du·x -cis *m*
child *s* inf·ans -antis *mf*, fil·ius -(i)i *m;* children liber·i -orum *mpl;* to bear a — parturire; with — gravida
childbearing *s* part·us -ūs *m*
childbirth *s* part·us -ūs *m*
childhood *s* infanti·a -ae *f*, pueriti·a -ae *f;* from — a puero *or* a pueris
childish *adj* pueril·is -is -e; *(fig)* inept·us -a -um
childishly *adv* pueriliter; *(fig)* inepte
childless *adj* orb·us -a -um
childlike *adj* pueril·is -is -e
chill *s* frig·us -oris *n; (of the body)* horr·or -oris *m;* to have the —s algēre
chill *tr* refrigerare
chilly *adj* frigidul·us -a -um; *(susceptible to cold)* alsios·us -a -um; it's getting — aër frigescit
chime *s* son·us -i *m*
chime *intr* concinere; to — in succinere; *(to interrupt)* interpellare
chimera *s* chimaer·a -ae *f*
chimney *s* camin·us -i *m*
chimpanzee *s* satyr·us -i *m*
chin *s* ment·um -i *n;* to drop the — labrum demittere
China *s* Ser·es -um *mpl*
china *s* murrin·a *(or* myrrhin·a) -orum *npl*
Chinese *adj* Seric·us -a -um
chink *s* rim·a -ae *f; (sound)* tinnit·us -ūs *m*
chink *intr* tinnire
chip *s* assul·a -ae *f; (of pottery)* fragment·um -i *n*
chip *tr (wood)* ascio dedolare; *(to break off a piece of)* praecidere; to — in *(money)* conferre
chipper *adj* ala·cer -cris -cre
chirp *s (of birds)* pipat·us -ūs *m; (of crickets)* strid·or -oris *m*
chirp *intr (of birds)* pipilare; *(of crickets)* stridēre
chisel *s* scalpr·um -i *n*
chisel *tr* scalpro caedere; *(to cheat)* emungere; *(to borrow)* mutuare
chivalrous *adj* magnanim·us -a -um
chivalry *s (knighthood)* equestris dignit·as -atis *f; (spirit)* magnanimit·as -atis *f*
chocolate *s* socolat·a -ae *f: (drink)* pot·us -ūs *m* socolatae
chocolate *adj* socolate·us -a -um
chocolate bar *s* tabell·a -ae *f* socolatae
chocolate pudding *s* erne·um -i *n* socolateum
chock-full *adj* refert·us -a -um
choice *s* electi·o -onis *f; (power of choosing)* opti·o -onis *f; (diversity)* variet·as -atis *f*
choice *adj* elect·us -a -um
choir *s* chor·us -i *m*
choke *tr* strangulare || *intr* strangulari

choking *s* strangulati·o -onis *f*
choose *tr* eligere; to — to *(to prefer to)* malle *(w. inf)*
chop *s* ofell·a -ae *f;* pork — ofella *f* porcina
chop *tr (wood)* dolabrā caedere; to — off praecidere; to — up minutatim concidere
choral *adj* symphoniac·us -a -um
chord *s* nerv·us -i *m*
chore *s* pens·um -i *n;* to do —s pensa facere
chorus *s* chor·us -i *m*
chorus girl *s* ambubai·a -ae *f*
Christ *s* Christ·us -i *m*
christen *tr* baptizare
Christendom *s* cuncti Christian·i -orum *mpl*
Christian *adj* Christian·us -a -um
Christian *s* Christian·us -i *m* (·a -ae *f*)
Christianity *s* Christianism·us -i *m*
Christmas *s* fest·um -i *n* nativitatis Christi; it won't be — forever *(fig)* non semper Saturnalia erunt; Merry —! Fausta Festa Natalicia Christi (tibi exopto!); to celebrate — all year long *(fig)* semper Saturnalia agere
Christmas carol *s* cantic·um -i *n* de Christi natali
Christmas day *s* Christi di·es -ei *m* natalis
Christmas Eve *s* vigili·a -ae *f* nativitatis Christi
Christmas gift *s* natalicium munuscul·um -i *n;* to give (exchange, receive, wrap) —s offerre (inter se dare, accipere, involvere) natalicia munuscula
Christmas Holidays *spl* feri·ae -arum *fpl* nataliciae; to spend the — ferias natalicias agere
Christmas tree *s* arb·or -oris *f* natalicia; to decorate the — with lights, balls, and tinsel arborem nataliciam igniculis et globulis et laminis ornare
chronic *adj* long·us -a - um
chronicle *s* annal·es -ium *mpl*
chronological *adj* in — order servato temporis ordine
chronology *s* temporum ord·o -inis *m*
chubby *adj* crass·us -a -um
chuckle *intr* pressā voce cachinnare
chum *s* familiar·is -is *mf*, sodal·is -is *mf*
chummy *adj* familiar·is -is -e
chunk *s* frust·um -i *n*
church *s* ecclesi·a -ae *f*
chute *s* decliv·e -is *n*
cicada *s* cicad·a -ae *f*
cider *s* hydromel·um -i *n*
cigar *s* sigar·um -i *n*
cigarette *s* sigarell·um -i *n;* pack of —s capsell·a -ae *f* sigarellorum; to smoke a — fumum sigarelli sugere
cigarette lighter *s* ignitabul·um -i *n*
cinch *s (coll)* res, rei *f* facilis factu
cinder *s* favill·a -ae *f*

cinema *s* cinemate·um -i *n*

cinnamon *s* cinnamom·um -i *n*

cipher *s* *(code)* not·a -ae *f;* *(a nobody)* numer·us -i *m;* *(zero)* nihil *n*

circle *s* circul·us -i *m;* *(social)* coet·us -ūs *m; (movement)* gyr·us -i *m; (anything round)* orb·is -is *m;* **family** — coron·a -ae *f* domi; **to form a** — *(to stand in a circle)* in orbem consistere

circle *tr* circumdare, cingere; *(to draw)* circumducere **‖** *intr* circumagi

circuit *s* circuit·us -ūs *m;* **short** — dissoluti·o -onis *f* vis eletricae; **to make a** — circumire, circumagi

circuit court *s* convent·us -ūs *m*

circuitous *adj* flexuos·us -a -um; **by a** — **route** circuitu; **to take a** — **route** circumagi

circular *adj* rotund·us -a -um

circular *s* litter·ae -arum *fpl* passim dimissae

circulate *tr (to spread)* in vulgum spargere **‖** *intr (of money)* in usum venire; *(to flow)* circumfluere; *(of news, rumors)* percrebescere

circulation *s (of blood)* circulati·o -onis *f;* **to be in** — *(e.g., of books)* in manibus esse

circumcise *tr* circumcidere

circumcised *adj* recutit·us -a -um, curt·us -a -um

circumcision *s* circumcisi·o -onis *f*

circumference *s* ambit·us -ūs *m; (geom)* peripheri·a -ae *f*

circumflex *s* circumflexus accent·us -ūs *m*

circumlocution *s* ambit·us -ūs *m*

circumscribe *tr* circumscribere

circumspect *adj* circumspect·us -a -um

circumspection *s* circumspecti·o -onis *f*

circumstance *s* res, rei *f; (circumstances collectively)* temp·us -oris *n;* **according to** —**s** pro re, pro tempore; **as** —**s arise** e re natā; **in humble** —**s** tenui re; **to yield to** — tempori cedere; **under no** —**s** nequaquam; **under the** —**s** quae cum ita sint

circumstantial *adj (incidental)* adventici·us -a -um; **to rest on** — **evidence** coniecturā contineri

circumvent *tr* circumscribere

circumvention *s* circumscripti·o -onis *f*

circus *s* circ·us -i *m; (performance)* circens·es -ium *mpl*

cistern *s* cistern·a -ae *f*

citadel *s* ar·x -cis *f*

citation *s (summons)* vocati·o -onis *f; (quotation)* loc·us -i *m* allatus; *(act of quoting)* prolati·o -onis *f*

cite *tr (leg)* evocare, citare; *(to quote)* proferre; *(in writing)* ponere

citizen *s* civ·is -is *mf; (of a municipality)* munic·eps -ipis *mf;* **private** — privat·us -i *m* (·a -ae *f)*

citizenship *s* civit·as -atis *f*

city *adj* urban·us -a -um

city *s* urb·s -is *f*

city council *s* decurion·es -um *mpl*

civic *adj* civil·is -is -e

civil *adj* civil·is -is -e; *(polite)* urban·us -a -um; — **rights** iu·s -ris *n* civile; **to deprive s.o. of** — **rights** aliquem capite deminuere; **loss** **(taking away) of** — **rights** diminuti·o -onis *f* capitis

civilian *s* togat·us -i *m,* privat·us -i *m* (·a -ae *f)*

civilian *adj* togat·us -a -um, privat·us -a -um

civility *s* comit·as -atis *f*

civilization *s* (humanus) cult·us -ūs *m*

civilize *tr* excolere

civilized *adj* human·us -a -um

clad *adj* indut·us -a -um

claim *s (demand)* postulati·o -onis *f; (leg)* vindici·ae -arum *fpl; (land)* a·ger -gri *m* assignatus; *(assertion)* affirmati·o -onis *f;* **to lay** — to vindicare

claim *tr (to demand)* postulare; *(esp. leg)* vindicare; *(to assert)* affirmare; **to** — **the thing as ours** rem nostram vindicare

claimant *s* peti·tor -toris *m* (·trix -tricis *f)*

clam *s* my·ax -acis *m*

clamber *intr* scandere; **to** — **down** descendere; **to** — **up** *(e.g., a mountain)* scandere

clammy *adj* umid·us -a -um

clamor *s* clam·or -oris *m*

clamor *intr* vociferari; **to** — **for** flagitare

clamp *s* confibul·a -ae *f*

clamp *tr* constringere; **to** — **down on** *(fig)* compescere

clam shell *s* nyacis test·a -ae *f*

clan *s* gen·s -tis *f*

clandestine *adj* clandestin·us -a -um

clandestinely *adv* clam, furtim

clang *s* clang·or -oris *m*

clang *intr* clangere

clank *s* crepit·us -ūs *m*

clank *intr* crepare

clap *s (of hands)* plaus·us -ūs *m; (of thunder)* frag·or -oris *m;* **a loud** — **of thunder** gravis fragor *m*

clap *tr* **to** — **the hands** manūs complodere **‖** *intr* plaudere

claptrap *s* iactati·o -onis *f*

clarification *s* explicati·o -onis *f*

clarify *tr* deliquare; *(fig)* explicare

clarity *s* clarit·as -atis *f*

clash *s* concurs·us -ūs *m; (sound)* crepit·us -ūs *m; (fig)* dissonanti·a -ae *f; (of colors)* repugnanti·a -ae *f*

clash *intr (to collide)* concurrere; *(to make a noise by striking)* concrepare; *(disagree)* discrepare

clasp *s* fibul·a -ae *f; (embrace)* amplex·us -ūs *m*

clasp *tr (to embrace)* amplecti; *(to grasp)* comprehendere

class *s (pol)* class·is -is *f,* ord·o -inis *m; (of pupils)* class·is -is *f; (kind)* gen·us -eris *n;* **lower** — ordo inferior; **middle** — ordo medius; **upper** — ordo superior; **working** — ordo operarius

class *tr (e.g., according to wealth)* describere; **to** — **as** in numero *(w. gen)* habēre

classical *adj* classic·us -a -um

classics *spl* scriptor·es -um *mpl* classici

classification *s* descripti·o -onis *f*

classify *tr* describere

clatter *s* strepit·us -ūs *m*

clatter *intr* strepare, crepitare

clause *s (gram)* articul·us -i *m,* membr·um -i *n; (leg)* cap·ut -itis *n*

claw *s* ungu·is -is *m; (of birds)* ungul·a -ae *f; (of a crab)* bracch·ium -(i)i *n*

claw *tr* lacerare

clay *s* lut·um -i *n; (white potter's clay)* argill·a -ae *f*

clay *adj* fictil·is -is -e

clean *adj* mund·us -a -um; *(lit & fig)* pur·us -a -um

clean *tr* purgare; *(to make tidy)* mundare; **to** — **s.o. out** *(of money)* aliquem excatarissare

cleaning rag *s* drapp·us -i *m*

cleanliness *s* munditi·a -ae *f*

cleanly *adv* omnino, penitus

cleanse *tr* purgare; *(by washing)* abluere; *(by rubbing)* detergēre

clear *adj* clar·us -a -um; *(unclouded)* seren·us -a -um, sud·us -a -um; *(liquids)* limpid·us -a -um; *(transparent)* pellucid·us -a -um; *(voice)* liquid·us -a -um; *(style)* lucid·us -a -um; *(explanation)* illustr·is -is -e; *(manifest)* conspicu·us -a -um; *(conscience)* rect·us -a -um; *(mind)* sag·ax -acis; — **of** exper·s -tis *(w. gen);* **it is** — manifestum est; *(leg)* liquet; **to keep** — **of** evitare

clear *tr* purgare; *(to make open)* expedire; *(to acquit)* absolvere; *(land)* exstirpare; *(the table)* mundare; *(profit)* lucrari; **to** — **away** detergēre, amovēre; *(by force)* amoliri; **to** — **out** emundare; **to** — **up** enodare ‖ *intr (of weather)* disserenare; — **out!** apage!

clearance *s* purgati·o -onis *f; (space)* interval·lum -i *n*

clearly *adv* clare; *(obviously)* aperte

clearness *s* clarit·as -atis *f; (of sky)* serenit·as -atis *f; (of style)* perspicuit·as -atis *f*

clear-sighted *adj* **to be** — clare decernere

cleave *tr* findere ‖ *intr* **to** — **to** adhaerere *(w. dat)*

cleaver *s* dolabr·a -ae *f*

cleft *s* rim·a -ae *f,* fissur·a -ae *f*

clemency *s* clementi·a -ae *f*

clement *adj* clem·ens -entis

clench *tr* comprimere; **to** — **the fist** manum comprimere

clergy *s* cler·us -i *m*

cleric *s* cleric·us -i *m*

clerk *s* scrib·a -ae *mf; (in a shop)* tabernari·us -i *m (·a -ae f)*

clever *adj* callid·us -a -um

cleverly *adv* callide

cleverness *s* callidit·as -atis *f*

cliché *s* verb·um -i *n* tritum

click *s* crepit·us -ūs *m*

click *tr (comput)* deprimere, pulsare; **double-click** bis deprimere *(or* pulsare); **left-click** sinistrorsum deprimere; **right-click** dextrorsum deprimere ‖ *intr* crepitare; *(to succeed)* bene vertere

client *s* cli·ens -entis *mf*

cliff *s* rup·es -is *f*

climate *s* cael·um -i *n;* **cold (hot, temperate, warm)** — fervens (frigidum, temperatum, tepidum) caelum; **mild** — temperi·es -ei *f*

climax *s (fig)* culm·en -inis *n; (rhet)* gradati·o -onis *f*

climb *tr* ascendere; *(to the top)* conscendere; **to** — **(up) a tree** in arborem inscendere, *(to the top)* arborem conscendere; **to** — **the stairs** pers scalas ascendere ‖ *intr* ascendere

climb *s* ascens·us -ūs *m*

clinch *vt (to settle)* confirmare ‖ *intr (in boxing)* amplecti

cling *intr (to)* adhaerēre *(w. abl or dat or ab w. abl);* **to** — **together** cohaerēre

clip *s* fibul·a -ae *f*

clip *tr (to cut)* tondēre; *(words, tail)* mutilare

clipping *s* tonsur·a -ae *f;* —**s** resegmin·a -um *npl*

cloak *s* pall·ium -(i)i *n; (cape with hood for travel)* paenul·a -ae *f; (mil)* sag·um -i *n; (general's)* paludament·um -i *n;* **wearing a** — palliat·us -a -um

cloak *tr* dissimulare, tegere

clock *s* horolog·ium -(i)i *n;* **at three o'clock** tertiā horā; **the** — **keeps good time** horologium recte metitur; **to set (wind) the** — horologium temperare (intendere)

clock *tr* horologio metiri

clog *tr (to hinder, fetter)* impedire; *(to block up)* obstruere

clogs *spl* sole·ae -arum *fpl*

cloister *s* portic·us -ūs *f; (eccl)* monaster·ium -(i)i *n*

close *adj (near)* propinqu·us -a -um; *(dense)* dens·us -a -um; *(tight)* art·us -a -um; *(intimate)* intim·us -a -um; *(shut)* occlus·us -a -um; *(atmosphere)* crass·us -a -um; **at** — **quarters** comminus *[adv];* — **attention** anim·us -i *m* attentissimus; — **friend** familiar·is -is *mf;* **to be on the** —**est possible terms with s.o.** aliquo familiarissime uti; **to**

be — at hand adesse, instare; to keep — to adhaerēre *(w. dat)*

close *adv* prope, iuxta; — to *(near)* prope *(w. acc)*, iuxta *(w. acc); (almost)* paene

close *tr* claudere; *(eyes, lips)* premere; *(to end)* finire; *(comput)* concludere; in —ing denique; to — down claudere; to — a bargain pascisci; to — up praecludere ‖ *intr* coïre, claudi; to — in on the enemy undique fauces hostium premere

close *s* fin·is -is *m;* at the — of the year exeunte anno; to bring to a — finire; to draw to a — terminari

closely *adv* prope; *(attentively)* attente

closet *s* armar·ium -(i)i *n; (for clothes)* vestiar·ium -(i)i *n* (parieti insertum)

closing *adj* ultim·us -a -um

closing *s* conclusi·o -onis *f*

clot *s* concretus cru·or -oris *m*

clot *intr* concrescere

cloth *s* pann·us -i *m; (linen)* linte·um -i *n; (as fabric)* text·um -i *n*

clothe *tr* vestire, induere

clothes *spl* vestiment·a -orum *npl*

clothes hanger *s* fulcim·en -inis *n* vestiarium

clothes hook *s* unc·us -i *m* vestiarius

clothing *s* vestit·us -ūs *m;* an article of — vestiment·um -i *n*

clothing store *s* tabern·a -ae *f* vestiaria

cloud *s* nub·es -is *f; (dark storm cloud)* nimb·us -i *m;* small — nubecul·a -ae *f*

cloud *tr* nubibus velare; *(fig)* obscurare ‖ *intr* to — up nubescere

cloudburst *s* maximus im·ber -bris *m;* I arrived in Capua in a — maximo imbri Capuam veni

cloud-capped *adj* nubif·er -era -erum

cloudless *adj* seren·us -a -um, sud·us -a -um

cloudy *adj* nubil·us -a -um; somewhat — subnubil·us -a -um; to get — nubilare

clout *s* ict·us -ūs *m;* to have — *(coll)* plurimum posse

clove *s (of garlic)* nucle·us -i *m*

cloven *adj* bisulc·us -a -um; — hoofs ungul·ae -arum *fpl* spissae

clover *s* trifol·ium -(i)i *n*

clown *s* scurr·a -ae *m*

clown *intr* to — around scurrari

clownish *adj* scurril·is -is -e

club *s (cudgel)* clav·a -ae *f; (society)* sodalit·as -atis *f*, sodalic·ium -(i)i *n*

club *tr* clavā dolare

cluck *intr* glocidare, singultire

cluck *s* singult·us -ūs *m*

clue *s* indic·ium -(i)i *n*

clump *s* mass·a -ae *f;* — of trees arbust·um -i *n*

clumsily *adv* inscite, rustice

clumsiness *s* insciti·a -ae *f*, rusticit·as -atis *f*

clumsy *adj* inscit·us -a -um, incomcinn·us -a -um; *(of things)* inhabil·is -is -e

cluster *s (of fruit, flowers, berries)* corymb·us -i *m; (of grapes)* uv·a -ae *f; (of people)* coron·a -ae *f*

cluster *intr* congregari; to — around stipare

clutch *s* ungul·a -ae *f;* from one's —es e manibus; in one's —es in suā potestate

clutch *tr* arrigere

clutch *s (of a car)* pedal·e -is *n* iunctionis

clutter *s* congeri·es -ei *f*

clutter *tr* to — up conturbare

coach *s (four-wheeled)* raed·a -ae *f; (two-wheeled, closed in, with arched top, for women)* carpent·um -i *n; (trainer)* exerci·tor -toris *m (·trix -tricis f); (of gladiators)* lanist·a -ae *m*

coach *tr* exercitare; *(a student)* admonēre, docēre

coagulate *intr* coïre

coal *s* carb·o -onis *m;* lapis gagas *(gen:* lapidis gagatis) *m*

coalesce *intr* coalescere

coalition *s* coniuncti·o -onis *f*

coal mine *s* fodin·a -ae *f* carbonaria

coal miner *s* carbonum foss·or -oris *m*

coarse *adj (materials)* crass·us -a -um; *(unfinished)* rud·is -is -e; *(manners)* incult·us -a -um

coarseness *s* crassitud·o -inis *f; (of manners)* rusticit·as -atis *f*

coast *s* or·a -ae *f* maritima; the — is clear nihil obstat

coast *intr* to — along the shore oram praetervehi

coastguard *s* custod·es -um *mpl* orae maritimae

coastal *adj* maritim·us -a -um

coastline *s* or·a -ae *f* maritima

coat *s* amicul·a -ae *f*, paenul·a -ae *f; (of animals)* pell·is -is *f; (of paint, plaster)* inducti·o -onis *f*

coat *tr* illinere, obducere; —ed tongue lingu·a -ae *f* fungosa

coating *s* inducti·o -onis *f*

coat of arms *s* insign·ia -ium *npl*

coat rack *s* sustentacul·um -i *n* vestium

coax *tr* blandiri

coaxing *s* blandiment·a -orum *npl*

coaxing *adj* bland·us -a -um

coaxingly *adv* blande

cobbler *s* sut·or -oris *m*

cobweb *s* arane·um -i *n*

cock *s* gall·us -i *m*

cock-a-doodle-do *interj* cocococo!

cockeyed *adj* — person strab·o -onis *m*

cock fight *s* rix·a -ae *f* gallorum

cockpit *s* cell·a -ae *f* aëroplani

cockroach *s* blatt·a -ae *f*

cocksure *adj* omnino confid·ens -entis
cocktail *s* propom·a -atis *n*
cocky *adj* iact·ans -antis
cocoa *s* coco·a -ae *f*
cocoanut *s* nu·x -cis *f* palmae Indicae
cocoon *s* globul·us -i *m*
coddle *tr* indulgēre *(w. dat)*
code *s (laws)* leg·es -um *fpl; (rules)* praecept·a -orum *npl; (system of symbols)* not·ae -arum *fpl;* **in —** per notas
co-ed *s (coll)* condiscipul·a -ae *f*
codicil *s* codicill·i -orum *mpl*
codify *tr* digerere; **to — the law** ius *(or* leges) digerere
coerce *tr* coercēre, cogere
coercion *s* coerciti·o -onis *f*
coexist *intr* simul exsistere
coffee *s* caffe·um -i *n;* **cup of —** pocill·um -i *n* caffei
coffee maker *s* machin·a -ae *f* caffearia
coffeepot *s* hinnul·a -ae *f* caffei
coffee set *s* synthes·is -is *f* caffearia
coffer *s* arc·a -ac *f*
coffin *s* capul·us -i *m*
cog *s* den·s -tis *m*
cogent *adj* grav·is -is -e
cognate *adj* cognat·us -a -um
cognition *s* cogniti·o -onis *f*
cognizance *s* cogniti·o -onis *f;* **to take — of** cognitionem tractare de *(w. abl)*
cognizant *adj* **(of)** consci·us -a -um *(w. gen)*
cohabit *intr* consuescere
cohabitation *s* consuetud·o -inis *f*
cohere *intr* cohaerēre
coherence *s* context·us -ūs *m*
coherent *adj* cohaer·ens -entis
coherently *adv* constanter
cohesion *s* cohaerenti·a -ae *f*
cohesive *adj* ten·ax -acis
cohort *s* cohor·s -tis *f*
coil *s* spir·a -ae *f*
coil *tr* glomerare **‖** *intr* glomerari
coin *s* numm·us -i *m;* **gold —** aure·us -i *m;* **silver —** argent·um -i *n*
coin *tr (to mint)* cudere; *(to stamp)* signare; *(words)* fingere, novare
coinage *s* monet·a -ae *f*
coincide *intr* **(with)** congruere (cum *w. abl)*
coincidence *s* concursati·o -onis *f*
coincidental *adj* fortuit·us -a -um
cold *adj* frigid·us -a -um; *(icy)* gelid·us -a -um; **to be —** frigēre; **to become —** frigescere; **to turn —** frigescere
cold *s* frig·us -oris *n; (med)* graved·o -inis *f;* **to catch a —** gravedinem contrahere; **to have a —** gravedine laborare
cold-blooded *adj (fig)* crudel·is -ie -e
cold spell *s* frigor·a -um *npl*
coldly *adv (fig)* frigide

coldness *s* frig·us -oris *n*
cold wave *s* frigor·a -um *npl*
coleslaw *s* acetari·a -um *npl* e brassica facta
colicky *adj* colic·us -a -um
coliseum *s* amphitheatr·um -i *n*
collaborate *intr* adiu·tor -toris *m* (·trix -tricis *f)* esse; **to — with the enemy** hostibus subvenire
collapse *s* ruin·a -ae *f*
collapse *intr* collabi
collar *s* collar·e -is *n*
collar *tr* collo comprehendere
collarbone *s* iugul·um -i *n*
collate *tr* conferre
collateral *adj (lines of descent)* transvers·us -a -um; *(effect)* adiunct·us -a -um
collateral *s (com)* sponsi·o -onis *f*
colleague *s* colleg·a -ae *mf*, consor·s -tis *mf*
collect *tr* conferre, colligere; *(to assemble)* convocare; *(money)* exigere; **to — oneself** mentem *or* animum colligere; **to — paintings and statues** tabulas signaque comparare **‖** *intr (of water)* colligi
collected *adj* **to be —** praesentis animi esse
collection *s (act)* collecti·o -onis *f; (pile or group collected)* congeri·es -ei *f; (literary)* corp·us -oris *n*
collective *adj* commun·is -is -e; *(gram)* collectiv·us -a -um
collectively *adv* communiter, unā
college *s* colleg·ium -(i)i *n*
collegiate *adj* collegial·is -is -e
collide *intr* confligere, collidi
collision *s* conflicti·o -onis *f*, concurs·us -ūs *m;* **a — of ships with one another** concurs·us -ūs *m* navium inter se
colloquial *adj* cotidian·us -a -um; **— language** serm·o -onis *m* cotidianus
collusion *s* collusi·o -onis *f;* **to be in — with** colludere cum *(w. abl)*
colon *s (anat)* col·um -i *n; (gram)* col·on -i *n*
colonel *s* tribun·us -i *m* militum
colonial *adj* colonic·us -a -um
colonist *s* colon·us -i *m* (·a -ae *f)*
colonize *tr* coloniam deducere in *(w. acc)*
colonnade *s* portic·us -ūs *f*
colony *s* coloni·a -ae *f*
color *s* col·or -oris *m;* **—s** vexill·um -i *n;* **with flying —s** magnā cum gloriā
color *tr* colorare; *(to dye)* tingere
colossal *adj* imman·is -is -e
colossus *s* coloss·us -i *m*
colt *s* equul(e)·us -i *m*
column *s* column·a -ae *f; (line)* agm·en -inis *n*
comb *tr* pectere; **to — back** repectere; **to — out** expectere
comb *s* pect·en -inis *m*

combat *s* pugn·a -ae *f,* dimicati·o -onis *f;* **in hand-to-hand combat** comminus [*adv*]; — **with wild beasts** venati·o -onis *f*
combat *tr* pugnare cum *(w. abl)*
combatant *s* pugnat·or -oris *m*
combative *adj* pugn·ax -acis
combination *s (act)* coniuncti·o -onis *f; (result)* iunctur·a -ae *f; (of various ingredients)* compositi·o -onis *f;* **a syllable is a — of letters** syllaba est comprehensi·o -onis *f* litterarum
combine *tr* coniungere, miscēre, componere; *(in due proportion)* temperare **‖** *intr* coïre, coniungi
combined *adj* coniunct·us -a -um, in unum coact·us -a -um
combustible *adj* igni obnoxi·us -a -um
combustion *s* combusti·o -onis *f;* **during —** dum comburitur
come *intr* venire; *(to arrive)* pervenire; *(to happen)* fieri; *(of sleep)* accedere; **— here!** huc accede!; **— on!** agedum!; **— what may** quod fors feret; **to — about** evenire, fieri; **to — across** occurrere *(w. dat);* **to — after** (sub)sequi; **to — again** revenire; **to — along** procedere; *(to accompany)* comitari; **to — apart** solvi; **to — at** *(in a hostile manner)* petere; **to — away** abscedere; **to — back** revenire, redire; **to — before** praevenire; **to — between** intervenire; **to — by** praeterire; *(to get)* acquirere; **to — down** *(to descend)* descendere; *(e.g., to the sea)* devenire; **to — down from antiquity** ex antiquitate tradi; **to — down with an illness** morbo corripi; **to — first** antevenire; **to — forth** exire; *(fig)* exoriri; **to — forward** prodire; **to — from** venire ab *((w. abl),* derivari ab *(w. abl);* **to — in** introire; **to — into play** accedere; **to — near** appropinquare, accedere; **to — off** *(e.g., stem comes off the apple)* recedere ab *(w. abl);* **to — off victorious** victor discedere; **to — off without a loss** sine detrimento discedere; **to — on** pergere; *(to progrèss)* proficere; **to — on top of** *(s.th. else)* supervenire *(w. dat);* **to — out (of)** exire (ex *w. abl); (to be published)* edi, emitti; *(of teeth)* cadere; *(of evidence)* emergere; *(to end)* evenire; **to — over** supervenire; *(to a different part)* transgredi; *(of feelings, conditions)* obire, occupare; **to — round** *(fig)* transgredi; **to — to** advenire ad *or* in *(w. acc); (to cost)* vēnire *(w. gen of price); (after fainting)* resipiscere; **to — to a head** concoqui; **to — to one's senses** ad se redire; **to — to pass** evenire, fieri; **to — to the assistance of** subvenire *(w. dat);* **to — together** convenire; **to — up** subvenire; *(to occur)* provenire; **to — up to** *(to approach)* accedere ad *(w. acc);* **to — upon** *(to find)* invenire; *(to attack, as dis-*

eases) ingruere *(w. dat);* **whatever —s into s.o.'s head** quae cuique libuissent
comedian *s* scurr·a -ae *m; (theat)* comoed·us -i *m* (·a -ae *f)*
comedy *s* comoedi·a -ae *f*
comely *adj* venust·us -a -um
comet *s* comet·es -ae *m*
comfort *s* solat·ium -(i)i *n;* **—s** commod·a -orum *npl*
comfort *tr* consolari
comfortable *adj* commod·us -a -um; **make yourselves —** rogo ut vobis suaviter sit
comfortably *adv* commode
comforter *s* consolat·or -oris *m* (·rix -ricis *f); (for bed)* stragul·um -i *n*
comforting *adj* consol·ans -antis
comic *adj* comic·us -a -um
comical *adj* ridicul·us -a -um
comics *spl* libell·i -orum *mpl* pictographici
comic strip *s* gryli·i -orum *mpl*
coming *adj* ventur·us -a -um; **he's got what's coming to him** habet quod sibi debetur
coming *s* advent·us -ūs *m*
comma *s* comm·a -atis *n*
command *s (order; comput)* iuss·um -i *n; (mil)* imper·ium -(i)i *n; (jurisdiction)* provinci·a -ae *f;* **— of language** copi·a -ae *f* verborum; **to be in — of** praesse *(w. dat);* **to give a — to** imperare *(w. dat);* **to hold supreme military —** summam imperi tenēre; **to put s.o. in — of** aliquem praeficere *(w. dat)*
command *tr (to order)* iubēre; *(to control)* imperare *(w. dat); (to require)* exigere
commander *s* du·x -cis *m,* praefect·us -i *m*
commander-in-chief *s* imperat·or -oris *m;* **to be —** imperii summam tenēre
commanding officer *s* dux, ducis *mf*
commandment *s* mandat·um -i *n;* **the Ten —s** decalog·us -i *m*
commemorate *tr* celebrare
commemoration *s* celebrati·o -onis *f,* memori·a -ae *f;* **in — of** in memoriam *(w. gen)*
commence *tr & intr* incipere; **to — hostilities** belli initium facere
commencement *s* init·ium -(i)i *n; (educ)* admissi·o -onis *f* ad gradum academicum
commend *tr* approbare; *(to recommend; to commit)* commendare
commendable *adj* probabil·is -is -e
commendation *s* commendati·o -onis *f,* lau·s -dis *f*
commensurate *adj* **(with)** par, adaequat·us -a -um *(w. dat);* **to be — with** congruere *(w. dat or cum w. abl)*
comment *intr* **(on)** sententiam dicere *(or* scribere) (de *w. abl)*
comment *s* commentar·ius -(i)i *m,* sententi·a -ae *f; (note)* annotati·o -onis *f*
commentary *s* commentari·i -orum *mpl*

commentator *s* interpr·es -etis *mf*
commerce *s* commerc·ium -(i)i *n;* to engage
in — negotiari
commercial *adj* mercatori·us -a -um
commercial *s* praecon·ium -(i)i *n*
commiserate *intr* to — with misereri *(w.
gen)*
commission *s* mandat·um -i *n;* *(group)*
consil·ium -(i)i *n;* out of — ex usu; to do
business on — ex mandato negotiari
commission *tr* delegare, mandare
commissioner *s* curat·or -oris *m* (·trix -tricis
f); highway — viarum curator *m;* police —
praefect·us -i *m* vigilum; water — aquarum
curator *m*
commit *tr (crime)* admittere; *(to entrust)* committere; to — an error errare; to — a sin
peccare; to — to memory memoriae mandare; to — to prison in carcerem conicere; to
— to writing litteris mandare
commitment *s* pign·us -oris *n*
committee *s* consil·ium -(i)i *n*
commodity *s* mer·x -cis *f*
common *adj (shared)* commun·is -is -e, pub-
lic·us -a -um; *(ordinary)* cotidian·us -a -um,
vulgar·is -is -e; *(well-known)* vulgat·us -a
-um; — noun nom·en -inis *n* appellativum;
— people vulg·us -i *n;* to have — sense cor
habēre
common *s* in — communiter; *(for all)* in medium
commoner *s* plebei·us -i *m* (·a -ae *f);* —s
pleb·s -is *f*
commonly *adv* vulgo, fere
commonplace *adj* vulgar·is -is -e
commonwealth *s* res, rei *f* publica
commotion *s* tumult·us -ūs *m*
commune *s* pag·us -i *m;* *(people)* commun·e
-is *n*
commune *intr* confabulari, colloqui
communicate *tr* communicare; *(information)*
impertire ‖ *intr* to — with communicare *(w.
dat)*
communication *s* commerc·ium -(i)i *n;* *(talk)*
communicati·o -onis *f;* *(message)* litter·ae
-arum *fpl,* nunt·ius -(i)i *m*
communicative *adj* affabil·is -is -e
communion *s* communi·o -onis *f*
community *s* civit·as -atis *f*
commutation *s* mutati·o -onis *f;* *(reduction)*
remissi·o -onis *f*
commute *tr* commutare; his death sentence
was —d to exile capitis damnato exilium ei
permissum est ‖ *intr (travel)* ultro citroque
commeare
commuter *s* commeat·or -oris *m* (·trix -tricis *f)*
compact *adj* spiss·us -a -um, dens·us -a -um
compact *s* pact·um -i *n;* *(esp. public)* foed·us
-eris *n;* to abide by the — in pacto manēre;

to make a — *(of two parties)* foedus inter se
facere
compact *tr* densare
compact disk (CD) *s* compactus disc·us -i *m*
compactly *adv* spisse, confertim
companion *s* com·es -itis *mf;* *(mil)* contuber-
nal·is -is *m*
companionship *s* sodalit·as -atis *f;* to enjoy
s.o.'s — aliquo familiariter uti
company *s* *(com)* societ·as -atis *f;* *(guests)*
conviv·ium -(i)i *n;* *(mil)* centuri·o -onis *f;*
(theat) gre·x -gis *m;* to keep each other —
inter se colere
company commander *s* centuri·o -onis *m*
comparable *adj* comparabil·is is e, aequiper-
abili·is -is -e
comparative *adj* comparativ·us -a -um, alio-
rum ratione habitā; *(gram)* comparativ·us -a
-um
comparative *s* *(gram)* comparativ·um -i *n,*
grad·us -ūs *m* comparativus; in the — comparative, in comparatione
comparatively *adv* comparative
compare *tr* (with) comparare, conferre (cum
w. abl); —ed with adversus *(w. acc)* ‖ *intr*
aequiparare; *(to be on a level with s.o.)*
aliquem aequiperare
comparison *s* comparati·o -onis *f;* in — with
adversus *(w. acc)*
compartment *s* locul·us -i *m;* *(in a train,
plane)* diaet·a -ae *f*
compass *s* *(instrument)* circin·us -i *m;* *(magnetic)* ac·us -ūs *f* magnetica
compassion *s* misericordi·a -ae *f*
compassionate *adj* misericor·s -dis
compassionately *adv* misericorditer
compatibility *s* congruenti·a -ae *f*
compatible *adj* congru·us -a -um
compatriot *s* civ·is -is *mf*
compel *tr* compellere, cogere
compendium *s* summar·ium -(i)i *n*
compensate *tr* compensare ‖ *intr* to — for
repensare, rependere
compensation *s* *(act)* compensati·o -onis *f;*
(pay) merc·es -edis *f;* *(for damages)* poen·a
-ae *f*
compete *intr* certare
competence *s* facult·as -atis *f;* *(legal capacity)*
iu·s -ris *n*
competent *adj* perit·us -a -um; *(leg)* locupl·es
-etis
competently *adv* satis idoneë
competition *s* certam·en -inis *n*
competitor *s* competi·tor -toris *m* (·trix
-tricis *f)*
compilation *s* *(act)* collecti·o -onis *f;* *(result)*
collectane·a -orum *npl*
compile *tr* componere
compiler *s* composi·tor -toris *m* (·trix -tricis *f)*

complacency s am·or -oris m sui
complacent adj sibi placens
complain intr (about) queri (de w. abl)
complaint s querel·a -ae f; (leg) crim·en -inis n; (med) vit·ium -(i)i n; **to raise** —s querelas facere
complement s complement·um -i n; (mil) numer·us -i m; **to give the legions their full** — **of men** complēre legiones
complete adj (entire) plen·us -a -um; (untouched) integ·er -ra -rum; (finished) perfect·us -a -um; (set) iust·us -a -um
complete tr (to accomplish) perficere, peragere, conficere; (years) explēre; (to finish) absolvere; (to make whole) complēre
completely adv plane, prorsus
completion s completi·o -onis f; (accomplishment) perfecti·o -onis f, confecti·o -onis f
complex adj multipl·ex -icis
complexion s col·or -oris m; **having a healthy complexion** colorat·us -a -um
complexity s multiplex natur·a -ae f
compliance s obtemperati·o -onis f; **in** — **with an agreement** ex pacto et convento
compliant adj obsequ·ens -entis
complicate tr implicare
complicated adj implicat·us -a -um
complication s implicati·o -onis f
complicity s conscienti·a -ae f
compliment s blandiment·um -i n; **as a** — honoris gratiā; **to pay s.o. a** — gratulari (w. dat)
compliment tr gratulari (w. dat)
complimentary adj honorific·us -a -um
comply intr **to** — **with** obsequi (w. dat), morem gerere (w. dat)
component s element·um -i n
compose tr componere; (verses) condere; (to calm) sedare; **to** — **oneself** se colligere
composed adj tranquill·us -a -um; **to be** — **of** constare ex (w. abl)
composer s scrip·tor -toris m (·trix -tricis f); (mus) musicorum modorum script·or -oris m
composite adj composit·us -a -um
composition s (act) compositi·o -onis f; (in literature) scripti·o -onis f; (work composed) script·um -i n
composure s tranquillit·as -atis f; **to bear with** — aequo animo ferre; **to lose one's** — perturbari
compound adj composit·us -a -um
compound s compositi·o -onis f; (noun) compositum verb·um -i n
compound tr componere, duplicare
compound interest s anatocism·us -i m
comprehend tr continēre; (to understand) comprehendere
comprehensible adj perspicu·us -a -um

comprehension s (act of grasping) comprehensi·o -onis f; (power of understanding) intellect·us -ūs m
comprehensive adj ampl·us -a -um
compress tr comprimere; (to abridge) coartare
compress s (med) foment·um -i n
compression s compressi·o -onis f
comprise tr continēre; **to be** —**d of** constare ex (w. abl)
compromise s (bilateral) compromiss·um -i n; (unilateral) accommodati·o -onis f
compromise tr compromittere; (to imperil) in periculum ac discrimen vocare ‖ intr pacisci
compulsion s vis f, necessit·as -atis f; **by** — per vim
compulsory adj necessari·us -a -um
computation s computati·o -onis f
compute tr computare
computer s ordinatr·um -i n
computer adj ordinatral·is -is -e
computer game s lus·us -us m ordinatralis; **to play a** — lusum ordinatralem ludere
comrade s sodal·is -is m; (mil) contubernal·is -is m
comradery s societ·as -atis f
con tr (coll) verba dare (w. dat); defraudare; **to** — **s.o out of his money** aliquem pecuniā defraudare
con artist s (coll) plan·us -i m
concave adj concav·us -a -um
conceal tr celare, occultare, abdere
concealed adj celat·us -a -um
concealment s (act) occultati·o -onis f; (place) latebr·ae -arum fpl; **to be in** — latebras agere
concede tr concedere
conceit s superbi·a -ae f
conceited adj superbiā tum·ens -entis
conceivable adj quod fingi potest
conceive tr concipere ‖ intr **to** — **of** fingere
concentrate tr in unum locum contrahere ‖ intr **to** — **on** animum intendere in (w. acc)
concentrate s (by boiling) decocti·o -onis f
concentration s in unum locum contracti·o -onis f; (fig) animi intenti·o -onis f
concentric adj concentric·us -a -um; — **circles** orb·es -ium mpl orbibus impeditae
concept s sententi·a -ae f
conception s (in womb) concept·us -ūs m; (idea) informati·o -onis f
concern s (affair) res, rei f, negot·ium -(i)i n; (interest, worry) cur·a -ae f; (importance) moment·um -i n; **it is of** — **to me** mihi curae est
concern tr attinēre or pertinēre ad (w. acc); (to worry) sollicitare; **as far as I'm** —**ed** per me; **how does that** — **you?** quid id ad te attinet?; **it** —**s me (you)** meā (tuā) rēfert; **to** — **oneself** animum agitare, curare

concerned *adj (about, for)* sollicit·us -a -um de (pro) *(w. abl);* **I am concerned** mihi curae est; **I'm not terribly — about** laboro non valde de *(w. abl)*

concerning *prep* de *(w. abl)*

concert *s (mus)* concent·us -ūs *m,* symphoni·a -ae *f; (fig)* consens·us -ūs *m;* **in — ex** composito; **to attend a —** concentui adesse

concession *s* concessi·o -onis *f; (thing)* concess·um -i *n; (com)* conducti·o -onis *f;* **to make a —** concedere

conch *s* conch·a -ae *f*

conciliate *tr* conciliare

conciliation *s* conciliati·o -onis *f*

conciliatory *adj* pacific·us -a -um

concise *adj* press·us -a -um, brev·is -is -e

concisely *adv* presse

conciseness *s* brevit·as -atis *f*

conclave *s* conclav·e -is *n*

conclude *tr (to end)* terminare; *(to infer)* colligere; **I must — my speech** mihi perorandum est; **to — a treaty** foedus icere

conclusion *s (end)* fin·is -is *m,* conclusi·o -onis *f; (of speech)* perorati·o -onis *f; (inference)* conclusi·o -onis *f;* **in —** ad ultimum; **they came to the — that** eis placuit ut; **to draw the —** colligere

conclusive *adj* firm·us -a -um, cert·us -a -um

concoct *tr* concoquere; *(to contrive)* fingere, conflare

concoction *s* pot·us -ūs *m; (fig)* machinati·o -onis *f*

concomitant *adj* adiunct·us -a -um

concord *s* concordi·a -ae *f*

concourse *s (act)* concurs·us -ūs *m; (crowd)* frequenti·a -ae *f*

concrete *adj* concret·us -a -um; **— noun** vocabul·um -i *n (opp:* appellatio); **in the —, not in the abstract** re, non cogitatione

concrete *s* concret·um -i *n*

concubine *s* concubin·a -ae *f*

concur *intr* consentire

concurrence *s* consensi·o -onis *f*

concussion *s (med)* quassatur·a -ae *f*

condemn *tr* damnare; **to — to death** capitis damnare

condemnation *s* damnati·o -onis *f*

condensation *s* densati·o -onis *f*

condense *tr* (con)densare ‖ *intr* densari

condescend *intr* se summittere

condescending *adj* fastidios·us -a -um

condescendingly *adv* fastidiose

condescension *s* comit·as -atis *f*

condition *s (state)* stat·us -ūs *m,* condici·o -onis *f; (stipulation)* condici·o -onis *f,* le·x -gis *f;* **in bad (good) —** male (bene) habit·us -a -um; **in excellent —** habitissim·us -a -um; **on — that** eā lege ut; **physical —** corporis habit·us -ūs *m*

condition *tr* informare

conditional *adj* condicional·is -is -e

conditionally *adv* condicionaliter

condolence *s* consolati·o -onis *f;* **I gave him my — doloris** eius particeps factus sum; **letter of —** litter·ae -arum *fpl* consolatoriae

condone *tr* condonare

conducive *adj* util·is -is -e ad *(w. acc)*

conduct *s (behavior)* mor·es -um *mpl; (management)* administrati·o -onis *f*

conduct *tr (to lead)* adducere; *(to manage)* administrare

conductor *s* (symphoniacorum) magis·ter -tri *m; (on a train)* traminis curat·or -oris *m*

conduit *s* canal·is -is *m*

cone *s* con·us -i *m*

confederacy *s (treaty)* foed·us -eris *n; (allied states)* civitat·es -um *fpl* foederatae

confederate *adj* foederat·us -a -um

confederate *s* soci·us -i *m* (·a -ae *f*)

confederation *s* civitat·es -um *fpl* foederatae

confer *tr* deferre, tribuere ‖ *intr* colloqui, conferre

conference *s* colloqu·ium -(i)i *n; (gathering)* congress·us -ūs *m*

confess *tr* confiteri; *(a fault)* fateri

confessedly *adv* ex confesso

confession *s* confessi·o -onis *f*

confidant *s* consci·us -i *m* (·a -ae *f*)

confide *tr* committere ‖ *intr* **to — in** confidere *(w. dat)*

confidence *s* fid·es -ei *f; (assurance)* fiduci·a -ae *f; (esp. self-confidence)* confidenti·a -ae *f;* **to have — in** fidem habēre *(w. dat);* **to inspire — in** fidem facere *(w. dat)*

confident *adj* (con)fid·ens -entis; **to be —** confidere; **to be — that** pro certo scire *(w. acc w. inf)*

confidential *adj (worthy of confidence)* fid·us -a -um; *(secret)* secret·us -a -um

confidently *adv* fidenter

configuration *s* figur·a -ae *f*

confine *tr* includere; *(to restrain)* cohibēre; *(to limit)* circumscribere

confined *adj* art·us -a -um, angust·us -a -um; **to be — to bed** lecto teneri

confines *spl* confin·ium -(i)i *n; (boundary)* fin·es -ium *mpl;* **on the — of** finitim·us -a -um *(w. dat);* **within the — of** in confinio *(w. gen)*

confirm *tr* confirmare; *(to prove)* comprobare; *(to ratify)* sancire

confirmation *s* confirmati·o -onis *f*

confirmed *adj* (con)firmat·us -a -um; *(habitual)* inveterat·us -a -um; *(proved)* comprobat·us -a -um

confiscate *tr* publicare

confiscation *s* publicati·o -onis *f*

conflagration *s* incend·ium -(i)i *n*

conflict *s* pugn·a -ae *f;* **to be in** — *(fig)* inter se repugnare
conflict *intr* inter se repugnare
conflicting *adj* repugn·ans -antis
confluence *s* conflu·ens -entis *m;* **at the** — **of the Tiber and the Anio** inter confluentes Tiberim et Anionem
conform *intr (to)* obtemperare *(w. dat),* se accommodare ad *(w. acc)*
conformity *s* convenienti·a -ae *f;* **in** — **with** secundum *(w. acc)*
confound *tr (to confuse)* confundere; *(to disconcert)* exanimare
confounded *adj* nefand·us -a -um
confront *tr* obviam ire *(w. dat); (to oppose)* obstare *(w. dat)*
confrontation *s* obstanti·a -ae *f*
confuse *tr* confundere, turbare
confused *adj* confus·us -a -um, turbat·us -a -um
confusedly *adv* confuse
confusion *s* confusi·o -onis *f*
confutation *s* refutati·o -onis *f*
confute *tr* confutare
congeal *tr* congelare ‖ *intr* concrescere, se congelare
congenial *adj* consentane·us -a -um
congenital *adj* nativ·us -a -um
congested *adj* refert·us -a -um
congestion *s (traffic)* frequenti·a -ae *f,* concurs·us -ūs *m;* **nasal** — stillati·o -onis *f*
congratulate *tr* gratulari *(w. dat)*
congratulations *spl* gratulation·es -um *fpl;* —! gratulationes *or* macte virtute esto *(pl:* estote)!
congratulatory *adj* gratulabund·us -a -um
congregate *tr* congregare ‖ *intr* congregari
congregation *s* coët·us -ūs *m*
congress *s* congress·us -ūs *m*
conical *adj* conic·us -a -um
conjectural *adj* coniectural·is -is -e
conjecturally *adv* ex coniecturā
conjecture *s* coniectur·a -ae *f*
conjecture *tr* coniectare
conjugal *adj* coniugal·is -is -e
conjugate *tr* declinare
conjugation *s* declinati·o -onis *f*
conjunction *s* concurs·us -ūs *m; (gram)* coniuncti·o -onis *f*
conjure *tr (to beseech solemnly)* obtestari; **to** — **up** *(ghosts)* elicere; *(fig)* excogitare, effingere
con man *s* plan·us -i *m*
connect *tr* connectere; *(in a series)* serere
connected *adj* coniunct·us -a -um; *(by marriage)* affin·is -is -e; *(of buildings)* (**to**) adfict·us -a -um *(w. dat);* **to be closely** — **with** inhaerēre *(w. dat);* **to be** — **with s.o. by**

blood and race aliquem sanguine ac genere contingere
connection *s* coniuncti·o -onis *f,* nex·us -ūs *m; (kin)* necessitud·o -inis *f; (by marriage)* affinit·as -atis *f*
connivance *s* indulgenti·a -ae *f*
connive *intr* connivēre
connoisseur *s* doct·us -a existima·tor -toris *m* (·trix -tricis *f)*
connotation *s* significati·o -onis *f* latens
conquer *tr* vincere; — **a country** terrā potiri
conqueror *s* vict·or -oris *m,* victr·ix -icis *f*
conquest *s* victor·ia -ae *f*
conscience *s* conscienti·a -ae *f;* **good conscience** mens conscia recti; **guilty** — mala conscientia *f;* **to have no** — nullam religionem habēre
conscientious *adj* pi·us -a -um, religios·us -a -um
conscientiously *adv* diligenter
conscious *adj* consci·us -a -um
consciously *adv* sciens, de industriā
consciousness *s (awareness)* conscienti·a -ae *f;* **to lose** — animum relinquere; **to regain** — resipiscere
conscript *s* tir·o -onis *mf*
consecrate *tr* consecrare
consecration *s* consecrati·o -onis *f*
consecutive *adj* continu·us -a -um
consecutively *adv* continenter
consent *intr* assentiri
consent *s* assens·us -ūs *m;* **to give one's** — permittere; **with the** — **of the people** secundo populo; **without my** — me invito
consequence *s* consecuti·o -onis *f,* event·us -ūs *m;* **a man of** — hom·o -inis *m* auctoritate praeditus; **as a** — ex eo; **it is of great** — magni interest; **it is of no** — nihil refert; **thing of no** — parva res, rei *f*
consequent *adj* consequ·ens -entis
consequently *adv* igitur, itaque
conservation *s* conservati·o -onis *f*
conservative *adj* a rebus novandis abhorr·ens -entis; *(pol)* reipublicae statūs conservandi studios·us -a -um; — **party** optimat·es -um *mpl*
conserve *tr* conservare
consider *tr* considerare; *(to deem)* aestimare, ducere; *(to respect)* respicere; **to** — **it already done** istuc iam pro facto habēre
considerable *adj* aliquantul·us -a -um; *(of persons)* illustr·is -is -e; *(of size)* ampl·us -a -um
considerably *adv* aliquantum; *(w. comp)* multo, aliquanto
considerate *adj* human·us -a -um
consideration *s* considerati·o -onis *f; (regard)* respect·us -ūs *m; (ground, motive)* rati·o -onis *f; (payment)* pret·ium -(i)i *n;* **out of** — **for** ob *(w. acc);* **to have** — **for the wound-**

ed; sauciorum rationem habēre; **to show —
for s.th.** alicuius rei respectum habēre
considering *prep* pro *(w. abl)*
consign *tr* mandare
consignment *s* **goods given** (*or* **sent**) **on —**
merc·es -ium *fpl* ex perscriptione traditae *(or*
missae)
consist *intr* **to — of** constare ex *(w. abl),* consistere ex *(w. abl)*
consistency *s* constanti·a -ae *f*
consistent *adj* const·ans -antis
consistently *adv* constanter
consolation *s* consolati·o -onis *f; (thing)*
solac·ium -(i)i *n*
console *tr* consolari
consolidate *tr* solidare, stabilire
consonant *s* conson·ans -antis *f*
consort *s* coniu·x -gis *mf*
consort *intr* **to — with** familiariter uti *(w. abl),*
se associare cum *(w. abl)*
conspicuous *adj* conspicu·us -a -um
conspicuously *adv* insigniter
conspiracy *s* coniurati·o -onis *f*
conspirator *s* coniurat·us -i *m* (·a -ae *f)*
conspire *intr* coniurare
constable *s* viat·or -oris *m*
constancy *s* constanti·a -ae *f*
constant *adj (fixed)* const·ans -antis; *(loyal)*
fid·us -a -um; *(incessant)* perpetu·us -a -um
constantly *adv* assidue, perpetuo
constellation *s* sid·us -eris *n*
consternation *s* consternati·o -onis *f;* **to be in
—** trepidare; **to throw into —** perterrēre
constipated *adj* **he is —** venter eius est astric-
tus
constipation *s* alv·us -i *f* astricta
constituent *s (part)* element·um -i *n;* **—s** *(pol)*
suffragator·es -um *mpl*
constitute *tr* constituere
constitution *s (physical)* habit·us -ūs *m; (pol)*
reipublicae leg·es -um *fpl*
constitutional *adj* legitim·us -a -um
constitutionally *adv* legitime
constrain *tr* cogere
constraint *s* vis *f;* **by —** per vim
construct *tr* construere; *(esp. things of
mechanical kind)* fabricare
construction *s* constructi·o -onis *f,* fabricati·o
-onis *f; (of a road)* muniti·o -onis *f; (interpretation)* interpretati·o -onis *f; (gram)* con-
structi·o -onis *f*
construe *tr* interpretari; *(gram)* construere
consul *s* cons·ul -ulis *m;* **— elect** consul *m* des-
ignatus
consular *adj* consular·is -is -e; **a man of —
rank** consular·is -is *m*
consulship *s* consulat·us -ūs *m;* **during my —**
me consule; **in the — of Caesar and
Bibulus** Caesare et Bibulo consulibus; **to**

hold the — consulatum gerere; **to run for
the —** consulatum petere
consult *tr* consultare **‖** *intr* deliberare
consultation *s* consultati·o -onis *f*
consume *tr* consumere
consumer *s* emp·tor -toris *m* (·trix -tricis *f)*
consuming *adj* ed·ax -acis
consummate *adj* summ·us -a -um
consummate *tr* consummare
consummation *s* consummati·o -onis *f; (end)*
exit·us -ūs *m*
consumption *s* consumpti·o -onis *f; (disease)*
tab·es -is *f*
contact *s* contact·us -ūs *m; (connection)* neces-
situd·o -inis *f;* **to come in — with** contingere
contagious *adj* contagios·us -a -um
contain *tr* continēre; *(to hold, as a vessel)*
capere
container *s* receptacul·um -i *n,* va·s -sis *n*
contaminate *tr* contaminare
contamination *s* contaminati·o -onis *f*
contemplate *tr* contemplari; *(some action)*
considerare
contemplation *s* contemplati·o -onis *f; (of an
action)* considerati·o -onis *f*
contemplative *adj* contemplativ·us -a -um
contemporaneous *adj* aequal·is -is -e
contemporaneously *adv* simul
contemporary *s* aequaev·us -i *m* (·a -ae *f)*
contempt *s* contempt·us -ūs *m;* **to feel — for**
comtemnere; **to hold s.o. in —** aliquem
despicatum habēre
contemptible *adj* contempt·us -a -um
contemptibly *adv* abiecte
contemptuous *adj* **— of** despici·ens -entis *(w.
gen)*
contend *tr (to aver)* affirmare **‖** *intr* contendere; *(to dispute)* verbis certare; **to —
against** adversari
contending *adj* avers·us -a -um
content *adj* **(with)** content·us -a -um *(w. abl)*
content *s* **to your heart's —** arbitratu tuo
content *tr* satisfacere *(w. dat)*
contented *adj* content·us -a -um
contentedly *adv* aequo animo
contention *s* contenti·o -onis *f*
contentious *adj* pugn·ax -acis; *(litigious)* liti-
gios·us -a -um
contentment *s* aequus anim·us -i *m*
contents *spl* quod inest, quae insunt; *(of a
book)* argument·um -i *n; (see* **table of contents)**
contest *s* certam·en -inis *n*
contest *tr (to dispute)* resistere *(w. dat); (leg)*
lege agere de *(w. abl)*
contestant *s* peti·tor -toris *m* (·trix -tricis *f)*
context *s* context·us -ūs *m*
contiguous *adj* contigu·us -a -um
continence *s* continenti·a -ae *f*

continent _s_ par·s -tis _f_ mundi [_not_ continens, _which means "mainland"_]

contingent _s_ man·us -ūs _f_

contingent _adj_ adventici·us -a -um; **to be — on** dependēre ex _(w. abl)_

continual _adj_ continu·us -a -um; _(lasting)_ perpetu·us -a -um

continually _adv_ assidue, continenter

continuance _s_ continuati·o -onis _f; (leg)_ prolati·o -onis _f_

continuation _s_ continuati·o -onis _f_

continue _tr_ continuare; _(leg)_ proferre ‖ _intr_ pergere; _(to last)_ persistere

continuity _s_ continuit·as -atis _f_

continuous _adj_ continu·us -a -um, perpetu·us -a -um

continuously _adv_ continenter

contortion _s_ contorti·o -onis _f_

contour _s_ lineament·um -i _n_

contraband _s_ interdict·a -orum _npl_

contraception _s_ conceptionis inhibiti·o -onis _f_

contraceptive _adj_ conceptionem inhibit·ens -entis

contraceptive _s_ atoc·ium -(i)i _n_

contract _tr_ contrahere ‖ _intr_ contrahi; **to — for** pacisci, locare; _(of the party undertaking the work)_ conducere; **to — for the making of a statue** statuam faciendam locare

contract _s_ pact·um -i _n; (on the part of the hirer)_ locati·o -onis _f; (on the part of the one hired)_ redempti·o -onis _f_

contraction _s_ contracti·o -onis _f; (of a word)_ compend·ium -(i)i _n_

contractor _s_ conduct·or -oris _m_

contradict _tr_ contradicere; **to — oneself** pugnantia loqui

contradiction _s_ contradicti·o -onis _f; (inconsistency)_ repugnanti·a -ae _f_

contradictory _adj_ contradictori·us -a -um, repugn·ans -antis

contraption _s_ machin·a -ae _f_

contrary _adj (opposite)_ contrari·us -a -um; _(fig)_ repugn·ans -antis; **— to** contra _(w. acc)_

contrary _s_ contrar·ium -(i)i _n;_ **on the —** contra

contrast _s_ comparati·o -onis _f_, oppositi·o -onis _f_

contrast _tr_ comparare, opponere ‖ _intr_ discrepare

contribute _tr_ contribuere, conferre ‖ _intr_ **to — towards** conferre ad _or_ in _(w. acc)_

contribution _s_ contributi·o -onis _f; (money)_ stip·s -is _f; (gift)_ don·um -i _n_

contributor _s_ colla·tor -toris _m_ (·trix -tricis _f_)

contributory _adj_ contribu·ens -entis

contrite _adj_ paenit·ens -entis

contrition _s_ paenitenti·a -ae _f; (eccl)_ contriti·o -onis _f_

contrivance _s (act)_ machinati·o -onis _f; (thing)_ machin·a -ae _f_

contrive _tr_ excogitare, machinari

control _s (restraint)_ continenti·a -ae _f; (power)_ moderati·o -onis _f_, potest·as -atis _f_

control _tr_ continēre; _(to govern)_ imperare _(w. dat)_

controller _s_ modera·tor -toris _m_ (·trix -tricis _f_)

controversial _adj_ controvers·us -a -um

controversy _s_ controversi·a -ae _f_

convalesce _intr_ convalescere

convalescent _adj_ convalesc·ens -entis

convene _tr_ convocare ‖ _intr_ coïre

convenience _s_ commodit·as -atis _f; (thing)_ commod·um -i _n;_ **at your —** commodo tuo; **at your earliest —** commodissime

convenient _adj_ commod·us -a -um; _(time, occasion)_ opportun·us -a -um

conveniently _adv_ commode, opportune

convention _s_ convent·us -ūs _m; (custom)_ consuetud·o -inis _f_

conventional _adj_ vulgat·us -a -um

converge _intr_ in medium vergere, in unum locum coïre

conversant _adj_ perit·us -a -um; **to be — with** versari in _(w. abl)_

conversation _s_ colloqu·ium -(i)i _n;_ **to engage in — with** sermones cum _(w. abl)_ conferre

conversational _adj_ in colloquio usitat·us -a -um

converse _intr_ colloqui

converse _s_ convers·us -ūs _m_

conversely _adv_ e converso

conversion _s_ conversi·o -onis _f_

convert _tr_ convertere

convert _s_ neophyt·us -i _m_ (·a -ae _f_)

convertible _adj_ commutabil·is -is -e

convertible _s_ autoraed·a -ae _f_ tecto plicatile

convex _adj_ convex·us -a -um

convey _tr_ convehere, advehere; _(to impart)_ significare; _(leg)_ abalienare

conveyance _s (act)_ advecti·o -onis _f; (vehicle)_ vehicul·um -i _n; (leg)_ abalienati·o -onis _f_

convict _s_ qui ad poenam damnatus est

convict _tr (of)_ convincere _(w. acc of the person and gen of the offense);_ **—ed of a lie** mendaci manifest·us -a -um

conviction _s (leg)_ damnati·o -onis _f; (belief)_ persuasi·o -onis _f;_ **it is my firm —** mihi persuasissimum est

convince _tr_ persuadēre _(w. dat)_

convinced _adj_ **I am firmly — that** plen·us (-a) persuasionis sum _(w. acc & inf)_

convincing _adj_ ad persuadendum apt·us -a -um; **there is — proof that** magno argumento est _(w. acc & inf)_

convivial _adj_ hilar·is -is -e

conviviality _s_ hilarit·as -atis _f_

convocation _s_ convocati·o -onis _f_

convoke *tr* convocare
convoy *s (naut)* praesidiaria class·is -is *f*
convulse *tr* convellere
convulsions *spl* spasm·us -i *m;* to have —
spasmo vexari
convulsive *adj* spastic·us -a -um
coo *intr* canere; *(of a pigeon)* gemere
cooing *s* cant·us -ūs *m;* gemit·us -ūs *m*
cook *s* coqu·us -i *m,* coqu·a -ae *f*
cook *tr* coquere; to — up *(fig)* excogitare ‖ *intr*
coquere
cooked *adj* elix·us -a -um
cookie *s* crustul·um -i *n*
cool *adj* frigidul·us -a -um; *(fearless)*
impavid·us -a -um; *(indifferent)* frigid·us -a
-um
cool *s* to keep one's — mentem compescere
cool *tr* refrigerare ‖ *intr* refrigerari; *(fig)* defervescere; to — off intepescere
cooling *adj* frigoric·us -a -um
coolness *s* frig·us -oris *n; (indifference)* lenti-
tud·o -inis *f; (calmness)* aequus anim·us -i *m*
coop *s (for chickens)* cave·a -ae *f*
coop *tr* to — up includere; to be cooped up in
the house in aedibus coartat·us (-a) esse
cooperate *intr* unā agere
cooperation *s* adiument·um -i *n,* coöperati·o
-onis *f*
coordinate conjunction *s* coniuncti·o -onis *f*
copulativa
cope *intr* to — with certare cum *(w. abl);* to be
able to — with par *(w. dat)* esse; to be
unable to — with impar *(w. dat)* esse
copier *s* polygraph·um -i *n*
copious *adj* copios·us -a -um
copiously *adv* copiose
copper *s* cupr·um -i *n,* ae·s -ris *n*
copper *adj* cuprin·us -a -um
copulate *intr* coïre
copulation *s* coït·us -ūs *m*
copulative *s (gram)* copulativ·us -a -um
copy *s* exempl·ar -aris *n,* exempl·um -i *n*
copy *tr (to imitate)* imitari; *(in writing)* (from)
exscribere (ex *w. abl)*
copycat *s* simi·a -ae *mf*
copyright *s* ius, iuris *n* proprium scriptoris
cord *s* funicul·us -i *m*
cordial *adj* benign·us -a -um; *(sincere)* sin-
cer·us -a -um; to give s.o. a — welcome
aliquem benigne excipere
cordiality *s* comit·as -atis *f*
cordially *adv* benigne, ex animo
cordon *s* coron·a -ae *f*
cordon *tr* to — off saepire
corduroy *s* textil·e -is *n* crassum et striatum
core *s (of fruit)* volv·a -ae *f; (fig)* nucle·us -i *m*
Corinth *s* Corinth·us -i *f;* gulf of — Sin·us -us
m Corthiniacus
Corinthian *adj* Corinthi·us -a -um

cork *s* cort·ex -icis *m; (stopper)* obtura-
ment·um -i *n*
corkscrew *s* extracul·um -i *n*
corn *s* maiz·ium -(i)i *n; (on toe)* call·us -i *m;*
— on the cob maizium in spicā
corned beef *s* bubul·a -ae *f* muriatica
corner *s* angul·us -i *m; (of street)* compit·um -i
n; (tight spot) angusti·ae -arum *fpl*
corner *tr* impedire; *(com)* coëmere ad quaestum
cornice *s* coron·a -ae *f*
cornucopia *s* corn·u -ūs *n* copiae
corollary *s* corollar·ium -(i)i *n*
coronation *s* coronati·o -onis *f*
coronet *s* diadem·a -atis *n*
corporal *adj* corporal·is -is -e, corporis [*gen*];
— punishment verber·a -orum *npl*
corporal *s* decuri·o -onis *mf*
corporate *adj* corporat·us -a -um
corporation *s* colleg·ium -(i)i *n*
corporeal *adj* corporeal·is -is -e
corps *s* legi·o -onis *f*
corpse *s* cadav·er -eris *n*
corpulent *adj* corpulent·us -a -um
corpuscle *s* corpuscul·um -i *n*
correct *adj* rect·us -a -um *(opp:* pravus); *(in*
the sense of "corrected") correct·us -a -um;
(free from faults) emendat·us -a -um
correct *tr* corrigere; *(esp. mistakes in writing)*
emendare; *(to chastise)* castigare
correction *s* correcti·o -onis *f;* emendati·o
-onis *f;* castigati·o -onis *f*
corrective *adj* ad corrigendum apt·us -a -um
corrective *s* remed·ium -(i)i *n*
correctly *adv* recte *(opp:* prave); emendate; to
speak (spell) — recte loqui (scribere)
correlation *s* mutua rati·o -onis *f*
correspond *intr* congruere; *(to each other)*
inter se congruere; *(by letter)* epistularum
commercium habēre
correspondence *s* congruenti·a -ae *f;*
(exchange of letters) epistularum
commerc·ium -(i)i *n*
correspondent *s* epistularum scrip·tor -toris *m*
(·trix -tricis *f)*
corridor *s* andr·on -onis *m*
corroborate *tr* confirmare
corrode *tr* erodere
corrosion *s* rosi·o -onis *f; (rust)* robig·o -inis *f;*
(on iron) ferrug·o -inis *f; (on copper)* aerug·o
-inis *f*
corrosive *adj* corrosiv·us -a -um; *(fig)* mord·ax
-acis
corrupt *tr* corrumpere
corrupt *adj* corrupt·us -a -um, putrid·us -a
-um; *(accessible to bribery)* venal·is -is -e;
(text) depravat·us -a -um
corrupter *s* corrup·tor -toris *m* (·trix -tricis *f)*
corruption *s* corrupti·o -onis *f*

corsage *s* fascicul·us -i *m* florum
corselet *s (mil)* loric·a -ae *f*
cortege *s* comitat·us -ūs *m*
cosily *adv* commode
cosmetic *s* offucin·a -ae *f*, medicam·en -inis *n; (rouge-like)* fuc·us -i *m*
cost *s (price)* pret·ium -(i)i *n; (expense)* impens·a -ae *f*; **—** **of living** anon·a -ae *f*
cost *intr* constare *(w. gen of indefinite price and abl of definite price or w. advs);* **how much does it —?** quanti constat?; **the victory — the lives of many** victoria morte multorum constitit; **to — 200 denari** ducentis denariis constare; **to — a lot (little, nothing, more, less)** multi (parvi, gratis, pluris, minoris) constare; **to — very much** carissime constare; **to — very little** vilissime constare
costliness *s* carit·as -atis *f*
costly *adj* pretios·us -a -um; *(extravagant)* sumptuos·us -a -um
costume *s* habit·us -ūs *m,* cult·us -ūs *m*
cosy *adj* commod·us -a -um
cot *s* grabat·us -i *m*
cottage *s* cas·a -ae *f*
cotton *s* gossyp·ium -(i)i *n*
cotton *adj* gossypin·us -a -um
couch *s* lectul·us -i *m* tomento fartus; *(esp. for dining)* lect·us -i *m*
cough *s* tuss·is -is *(acc:* tussim) *f;* **to have a bad —** male tussire
coughss *tr* **to — up** extussire ‖ *intr* tussire
council *s* concil·ium -(i)i *n*
councilor *s* consiliar·ius -(i)i *m*
counsel *tr* consulere
counselor *s* consilia·tor -toris *m* (·trix -tricis *f)*
count *s* com·es -itis *m; (leg)* crim·en -inis *n*
count *s* computati·o -onis *f; (total)* summ·a -ae *f; (of indictment)* cap·ut -itis *n*
count *tr* numerare, computare; *(to regard)* habēre, ducere; **to — out** *or* **up** enumerare; **— out to** annumerare *(w. dat)* ‖ *intr* aestimari, habēri; **to — upon** confidere *(w. dat);* **you can — on it that** erit tibi perspectum *(w. acc & inf)*; **you can — on me** potes niti me [*abl*]; **you don't — extra** numerum es mihi
countdown *s* denumerati·o -onis *f* inversa
countenance *s* vult·us -ūs *m*
countenance *tr* indulgēre *(w. dat)*
counter *s (of shop, kitchen)* abac·us -i *m; (in games)* calcul·us -i *m*
counteract *intr* obsistere *(w. dat); (a sickness)* medēri *(w. dat)*
counterattack *s* impet·us -ūs *m* contra hostium impetum
counterattack *intr* impetum contra hostium impetum facere
counterfeit *tr (to pretend)* simulare; *(money)* adulterare

counterfeit *s* monet·a -ae *f* adulterina
counterfeit *adj* simulat·us -a -um; *(money)* adulterin·us -a -um
counterfeiter *s* falsari·us -i *m* (·a -ae *f)*
counterpart *s (person)* pa·r -ris *n; (thing)* res, rei *f* gemella
countersign *tr* contrascribere
countless *adj* innumerabil·is -is -e
country *s* terr·a -ae *f; (territory)* fin·es -ium *mpl; (not city)* ru·s -ris *n; (native)* patri·a -ae *f; (pol)* res publica *(gen* rei publicae) *f;* **of what —** cui·as -atis; **of what — are you?** cuiates estis?
country *adj* rustic·us -a -um
country estate *s* suburban·um -i *n*
country-fresh *adj* agrest·is -is -e
country house *s* vill·a -ae *f* urbana
countryman *s* civ·is -is *m*
country road *s* vi·a -ae *f* regionalis
countryside *s* agr·i -orum *mpl*
couple *s* pa·r -ris *n; (married couple)* marit·i -orum *mpl;* **a couple of** aliquantul·i -ae -a
couple *tr* copulare ‖ *intr (of animals)* coïre
courage *s* virt·us -utis *f,* anim·us -i *m;* **to lose — animum** demittere; **to take — bono** animo esse
courageous *adj* fort·is -is -e
courageously *adv* fortiter
courier *s* curs·or -oris *m,* cursr·ix -icis *f; (letter carrier)* tabellari·us -i *m* (·a -ae *f)*
course *s (movement, of ship, of river, of stars; in school)* curs·us -ūs *m; (of life)* rati·o -onis *f; (of water)* duct·us -ūs *m; (route)* it·er -ineris *n; (at table)* fercul·um -i *n; (order)* seri·es -ei *f; (for racing)* circ·us -i *m,* stad·ium -(i)i *n;* **in due —** mox; **in the — of** inter *(w. acc);* **in the — of time** procedente tempore; **of —** nempe, profecto; *(sarcastically)* scilicet; **to be driven off —** cursu excuti; **to change —** iter flectere
court *s (leg)* for·um -i *n,* iudic·ium -(i)i *n; (open area)* are·a -ae *f; (inner court of a house)* cavaed·ium -(i)i *n; (palace)* aul·a -ae *f; (retinue)* comitat·us -ūs *m;* **court of appeal** iudicium appellatorium; **to hold — ius** dicere; **to take to — in** iudicium vocare
court *tr* colere, ambire; *(a woman)* petere; *(danger)* se offerre *(w. dat)*
court costs *spl* litis impens·ae -arum *fpl*
courteous *adj* com·is -is -e
courteously *adv* comiter
courtesan *s* meretr·ix -cis *f*
courtesy *s* comit·as -atis *f;* **— of** beneficio *(w. gen)*
courtesy call *s* offic·ium -(i)i *n*
courthouse *s* basilic·a -ae *f*
courtier *s* aulic·us -i *m*
courtly *adj* aulic·us -a -um
court-martial *s* iudic·ium -(i)i *n* castrense

court-marshal *tr* in iudicium castrense vocare

courtroom *s* iudici·um -i *n*

courtship *s* procati·o -onis *f*

courtyard *s* are·a -ae *f; (in a Roman house)* peristyl·ium -(i)i *n*

cousin *s (on mother's side; used also for cousin in general)* consobrin·us -i *m* (·a -ae *f); (on father's side)* patruel·is -is *mf*

cove *s* sin·us -ūs *m*

covenant *s* pact·um -i *n*

covenant *intr* pacisci

cover *s (for concealment and shelter)* tegment·um -i *n; (lid)* opercul·um -i *n; (mil)* praesid·ium -(i)i *n; (pretense)* speci·es -ei *f;* **to take —** suffugere; **under — of darkness** nocte adiuvante

cover *tr* tegere, operire; *(to hide)* celare; **to — up** obtegere; *(against the cold)* bene operire

coverlet *s* stragul·um -i *n; (for bed or couch)* toral·e -is *n*

covet *tr* concupiscere

covetous *adj* appet·ens -entis

covey *s* gre·x -gis *m*

cow *tr* domare

coward *s* hom·o -inis *mf* ignav·us (-a)

cowardice *s* ignavi·a -ae *f*

cowardly *adj* ignav·us -a -um

cowboy *s* bubulc·us -i *m* (Americanus)

cower *intr* subsidere

coy *adj* verecund·us -a -um

coyly *adv* verecunde

coyness *s* verecundi·a -ae *f*

cozily *adv* commode

cozy *adj* commod·us -a -um

crab *s* can·cer -cri *m*

crabbiness *s* morosit·as -atis *f*

crabby *adj* moros·us -a -um

crack *s* rim·a -ae *f; (noise)* crepit·us -ūs *m;* **at the — of dawn** primā luce

crack *tr* findere; *(nuts, etc.)* perfringere; *(a code)* enodare; **to — jokes** ioca dicere **ǁ** *intr* rimas agere; *(to sound)* crepitare; *(of the voice)* irraucescere; **to — down on** compescere

cracked *adj* rimos·us -a -um; *(crazy)* cerrit·us -a -um

cracker *s* crustul·um -i *n*

crackle *intr* crepitare

crackling *s* crepit·us -ūs *m*

crack troops *spl* copi·ae -arum *fpl* electissimae

cradle *s* cunabul·a -orum *npl*

cradle *tr* fovēre

craft *s (trade)* artific·ium -(i)i *n; (skill)* ar·s -tis *f; (cunning)* dol·us -i *m; (naut)* navig·ium -(i)i *n*

craftily *adv* callide

craftsman *s* artif·ex -icis *m*

craftsmanship *s* artific·ium -(i)i *n*

crafty *adj* callid·us -a -um

cram *tr* farcire; **to — together** constipare **ǁ** *intr (for an examination)* cuncta confertim menti inculcare

cramp *s* spasm·us -i *m*

cramp *tr* comprimere; **to be —ed for space** in angusto sedēre

crane *s (bird)* gru·s -is *mf; (machine)* tollen·o -onis *m*

crank *s (mech)* unc·us -i *m; (person)* moros·us -i *m* (·a -ae *f)*

crank *tr* volvere

crash *s* frag·or -oris *m*

crash *intr* fragorem dare; *(comput)* corruere; **to come —ing down** corruere

crass *adj* crass·us -a -um

crate *s* cist·a -ae *f*

crater *s* crat·er -eris *m*

crave *tr* concupiscere

craven *adj* ignav·us atque abiect·us -a -um

craving *s* desider·ium -(i)i *n*

crawl *intr* repere; *(esp. of snakes)* serpere

crawl *s (of babies)* reptati·o -onis *f*

crayon *s* cerul·a -ae *f*

craze *s* fur·or -oris *m*

craziness *s* dementi·a -ae *f*

crazy *adj (person)* dem·ens -entis; *(idea)* insuls·us -a -um; **he's — about her** eam deperit; **he's — about sports** morbosus est in athleticas; **to drive s.o. —** mentem *(w. gen)* alienare

creak *s* strid·or -oris *m*

creak *intr* stridēre

creaking *s* strid·or -oris *m*

creaking *adj* stridul·us -a -um

cream *s* crem·um -i *n*, spum·a -ae *f* lactis; *(fig)* flo·s -ris *m*

crease *s* plicatur·a -ae *f*

crease *tr* plicare **ǁ** *intr* plicari

create *tr* creare; *(in the mind)* fingere

creation *s (act)* creati·o -onis *f; (world)* summ·a -ae *f* rerum, mund·us -i *m; (fig)* op·us -eris *n*

creative *adj* creatr·ix -icis; *(able)* ingenios·us -a -um

creator *s* creat·or -oris *m; (originator)* auc·tor -toris *m* (·trix -tricis *f)*

creature *s (living)* anim·al -alis *n; (tool)* minis·ter -tri *m*

credence *s* fid·es -ei *f;* **to gain —** fidem habēre; **to give — to** credere *(w. dat)*

credentials *spl* testimoni·a -orum *npl*

credibility *s* fid·es -ei *f*

credible *adj* credibil·is -is -e; *(of persons)* locupl·es -etis

credit *s (faith)* fid·es -ei *f; (authority)* auctorit·as -atis *f; (reputation)* existimati·o -onis *f; (com)* fid·es -ei *f; (recognition)* lau·s -dis *f;* **to buy on —** in diem emere; **to have —** fide stare

credit *tr* credere *(w. dat); (com)* acceptum referre *(w. dat);* **to — my teacher with my success** successum meum magistro ascribere
creditable *adj* honest·us -a -um
credit card *s* tabell·a -ae *f* tributaria
creditor *s* credit·or -oris *m*
credulity *s* credulit·as -atis *f*
credulous *adj* credul·us -a -um
creed *s* fid·es -ei *f*
creek *s* riv·us -i *m*
creep *s (pej)* larv·a -ae *f*
creep *intr* repere; **it makes my skin —** facit ut horream
crescent *s* lun·a -ae *f* crescens
crescent-shaped *adj* lunat·us -a -um
crest *s (of a hill)* iug·um -i *n; (of an animal or helmet)* crist·a -ae *f*
crew *s* gre·x -gis *m; (naut)* naut·ae -arum *mpl; (rowers)* remig·es -um *mpl*
crib *s (manger)* praesep·e -is *n; (for a baby)* lectul·us -i *m*
cricket *s* gryll·us -i *m;* **—s chirp** grylli strident
crime *s* scel·us -eris *n,* facin·us -eris *n*
criminal *adj* scelest·us -a -um, facineros·us -a -um
criminal *s* sons, sontis *mf*
criminally *adv* nefarie
crimp *tr* crispare
crimson *adj* coccine·us -a -um
crimson *s* cocc·um -i *n*
cringe *intr* abhorrēre; *(to behave servilely)* se demittere, adulari
cripple *s* claud·us -i *m* (·a -ae *f*)
cripple *tr* debilitare; *(fig)* frangere
crippled *adj (in the hands)* manc·us -a -um; *(lame)* claud·us -a -um
crisis *s* discrim·en -inis *n*
criterion *s* norm·a -ae *f*
critic *s* reprehens·or -oris *m* (·rix -ricis *f); (literary)* cens·or -oris *m* (·rix -ricis *f*)
critical *adj (relating to criticism; crucial)* critic·us -a -um; *(blaming)* censori·us -a -um; **the situation is —** res est in summo discrimine
criticism *s* reprehensi·o -onis *f; (literary)* iudic·ium -(i)i *n,* ar·s -tis *f* critica
criticize *tr* reprehendere; *(literature)* iudicare
croak *intr* coaxare; *(of ravens)* crocitare; *(to die) (coll)* animam ebullire
croaking *s* vox, vocis *f* rauca
crock *s* oll·a -ae *f*
crocodile *s* crocodil·us -i *m*
crook *s (shepherd's)* ped·um -i *n; (thief)* fur, furis *mf*
crook *tr* curvare
crooked *adj* curvat·us -a -um; *(fig)* dolos·us -a -um
crop *s (of grain)* seg·es -itis *f; (of a bird)* inglu·vi·es -ei *f*

crop *tr (to cut)* tondēre; *(to harvest)* metere **‖** *intr* **to — up** exsistere, surgere
cross *s (structure)* cru·x -cis *f; (mark)* decuss·is -is *m; (fig)* cruciat·us -ūs *m*
cross *adj (across)* transvers·us -a -um; *(contrary)* contrari·us -a -um; *(peevish)* acerb·us -a -um; *(hybrid)* mixt·us -a -um
cross *tr* transire; *(a river)* traicere; *(a mountain)* transcendere; *(to thwart)* frustrari, adversari; *(hybrids)* miscēre; **to — one's mind** alicui in mentem venire; **to — one's path** alicui obviam venire; **to — the legs** poplites alternis genibus imponere; **to — out** expungere
crossbar *s* tign·um -i *n* transversum
crossbreed *s* hibrid·a -ae *mf*
crossbreed *tr* miscēre
cross-examination *f* interrogati·o -onis *f*
cross-examine *tr* interrogare
cross-eyed *adj* strab·us -a -um
crossing *s* transit·us -ūs *m; (of a river)* traiect·us -ūs *m; (of roads)* biv·ium -(i)i *n; (of three roads)* triv·ium -(i)i *n; (of four roads)* quadriv·ium -(i)i *n*
cross reference *s* indic·ium -(i)i *n* translatum
crossroads *spl* quadriv·ium -(i)i *n; (esp. in the country)* compit·um -i *n*
crosswise *adv* in transversum
crotch *s (anat)* bifurc·um -i *n*
crouch *intr* subsidere
crouch *s* in a **—** subsid·ens -entis
crow *s (bird)* corn·ix -icis *f; (of rooster)* gallicin·ium -(i)i *n;* **as the — flies** mensurā currente [*lit: in a running measurement*]; **—s craw** cornices crocitant
crow *intr (of roosters)* cucurire, canere; *(to boast)* gloriari
crowbar *s* vect·is -is *m*
crowd *s* frequenti·a -ae *f; (mob)* turb·a -ae *f; (of people flocking together)* concurs·us -ūs *m; (common people)* vulg·us -i *n*
crowd *tr* frequentare **‖** *intr* **to — around** stipare, circumfundi *(w. dat);* **to — together** congregari
crowded *adj* frequ·ens -entis; **— together** confert·us -a -um
crowing *s* cant·us -ūs *m*
crown *s (of king)* insign·e -is *n* regium; *(wreath)* coron·a -ae *f; (power)* regn·um -i *n; (top)* vert·ex -icis *m; (fig)* ap·ex -icis *m*
crown *tr* coronare; insigne regium capiti *(w. gen)* imponere
crucifix *s* imag·o -inis *f* Christi crucifixi
crucifixion *s* crucis supplic·ium -(i)i *n*
crucify *tr* crucifigere
crude *adj* rud·is -is -e, incult·us -a -um
crudely *adv* inculte
cruel *adj* crudel·is -is -e
cruelly *adv* crudeliter

cruelty *s* crudelit·as -atis *f*
cruise *intr* circumvectari, navigare
cruise *s* navigati·o -onis *f*
cruiser *s* nav·is -is *f* longa
crumb *s* mic·a -ae *f*
crumble *tr* friare ‖ *intr* friari; *(to fall down)* corruere
crumbling *adj* friabil·is -is -e
crumple *tr* corrugare
crumpled *adj* corrugat·us -a -um
crunch *tr* dentibus frangere
crush *tr* contundere; *(fig)* opprimere
crush *s* contusi·o -onis *f; (crowd)* frequenti·a -ae *f* densissima
crust *s* crust·um -i *n*
crusty *adj* crustos·us -a -um; *(fig)* cerebros·us -a -um
crutch *s* bacul·um -i *n; (fig)* fultur·a -ae *f*
cry *s (shout)* clam·or -oris *m; (of a baby)* vagit·us -ūs *m*
cry *tr* clamare; **to — out** exclamare ‖ *intr (to shout)* clamare; *(to shout repeatedly)* clamitare; *(to weep)* lacrimare, flēre; *(of infants)* vagire; **to — over** flere
crying *s* flet·us -ūs *m; (of a baby)* vagit·us -ūs *m*
crypt *s* crypt·a -ae *f*
cryptic *adj* occult·us -a -um
crystal *adj* crystallin·us -a -um
crystal *s* crystall·um -i *n*
crystal-clear *adj* pellucid·us -a -um
cub *s* catul·us -i *m*
cube *s* cub·us -i *m*
cubic *adj* cubic·us -a -um
cubit *s* cubit·um -i *n*
cuckoo *s* cucul·us -i *m*
cucumber *s* cucum·is -eris *m*
cud *s* rum·en -inis *n;* **to chew the —** ruminare
cudgel *s* fust·is -is *m*
cue *s (hint)* nut·us -ūs *m,* indic·ium -(i)i *n; (theat)* verb·um -i *n* monitorium
cuff *s (of sleeve)* extrema manic·a -ae *f; (blow)* colaph·us -i *m*
culminate *intr* ad summum venire
culmination *s* fastig·ium -(i)i *n*
culpable *adj* culpand·us -a -um
culprit *s* re·us -i *m,* re·a -ae *f*
cultivate *tr (land, mind, friendship)* colere
cultivation *s* cultur·a -ae *f*
cultivator *s* cult·or -oris *m*
culture *s* cultur·a -ae *f*
culvert *s* cloac·a -ae *f*
cumbersome *adj* inhabil·is -is -e
cunning *adj (clever)* callid·us -a -um; *(sly)* astut·us -a -um
cup *s* pocul·um -i *n*
cupboard *s* armar·ium -(i)i *n* in parieti insertum
Cupid *s* Cupid·o -inis *m*

cupidity *s* cupidit·as -atis *f*
cupola *s* thol·us -i *m*
cur *s (coll)* can·is -is *m* nothus; *(fig)* scelest·us -i *m*
curable *adj* sanabil·is -is -e
curative *adj* medicabil·is -is -e
curator *s* cura·tor -toris *m* (·trix -tricis *f*)
curb *s (& fig)* fren·um -i *n; (of the road)* crepid·o -inis *f*
curb *tr* frenare; *(fig)* refrenare
curbstone *s* crepid·o -inis *m*
curdle *tr* coagulare ‖ *intr* coïre
cure *s (remedy)* remd·ium -(i)i *n; (process)* sanati·o -onis *f*
cure *tr* sanare; *(to pickle)* salire
curiosity *s* curiosit·as -atis *f; (thing)* miracul·um -i *n*
curious *adj* curios·us -a -um; *(strange)* mirabil·is -is -e
curiously *adv* curiose
curl *s (natural)* cirr·us -i *m; (artificial)* cincinn·us -i *m*
curl *tr* crispare ‖ *intr* crispari; *(of smoke)* volvi
curler, curling iron *s* calamistr·um -i *n*
curly *adj* crisp·us -a -um, cirrat·us -a -um
currency *s* monet·a -ae *f; (use)* us·us -ūs *m;* **to gain —** percrebrescere
current *adj (opinion)* vulgar·is -is -e; *(in general use)* usitat·us -a -um
current *s* vis *f* fluminis *n; (of air)* afflat·us -ūs *m; (electrical)* electricum fluent·um -i *n;* **against the —** adverso flumine; **with the —** secundo flumine
curriculum *s* studiorum curricul·um -i *n*
curse *s* maledict·um -i *n; (fig)* pest·is -is *f*
curse *tr* maledicere *(w. dat)* ‖ *intr* maledicere
cursed *adj* exsecrabil·is -is -e
cursing *s* convic·ium -(i)i *n*
cursor *s (comput)* curs·or -oris *m*
cursorily *adv* strictim
cursory *adj* lev·is -is -e, brev·is -is -e
curt *adj* abrupt·us -a -um
curtail *tr (to cut off a part of)* praecidere; *(to diminish)* minuere
curtain *s (on a window or shower)* vel·um -i *n; (theat)* aulae·um -i *n;* **to draw the —s** vela obducere
curvature *s* curvatur·a -ae *f*
curve *s (of road)* anfract·us -ūs *m; (of river)* flex·us -ūs *m*
curve *tr* incurvare, flectere ‖ *intr* incurvari
curved *adj* curv·us -a -um; *(as a sickle)* falcat·us -a -um
cushion *s* pulvin·us -i *m; (fig)* levam·en -inis *n*
custard *s* artolagan·us -i *m*
custodian *s* cust·os -odis *mf*
custody *s* tutel·a -ae *f,* custodi·a -ae *f;* **to keep in —** custodire; **to take into —** in vincula conicere

custom *s* mo·s -ris *m,* consuetud·o -inis *f;* **according to the — of the Roman people** more populi Romani

customary *adj* consuet·us -a -um; *(regularly occurring)* sollemn·is -is -e

customer *s* cli·ens -entis *mf; (buyer)* emp·tor -toris *m* (·trix -tricis *f)*

customs *spl (tax)* portor·ium -(i)i *n*

customs officer *s* porti·tor -toris *m* (·trix -tricis *f)*

cut *tr* secare; *(hair)* tondēre; *(to fell)* caedere; *(to mow)* resecare; **cut it out!** desiste! *(pl:* desistite!); **cut the talk!** segrega sermonem!; **to — and paste** *(comput)* secare et glutinare; **to — apart** dissecare; **to — away** recidere, abscindere; **to — down** caedere; *(to kill)* occidere; **to — in pieces** concidere; **to — off** praecidere; *(to intercept)* intercludere; **to — open** incidere; **to — out** exsecare; *(out of a rock, etc.)* excidere; **to — short** intercidere; *(to abridge)* praecidere; *(to interrupt)* interpellare; **to — short the school day** ludum artare; **to — to pieces** concidere; **to — up** minutatim concidere; *(the enemy)* trucidare

cute *adj* bell·us -a -um, bellul·us -a -um

cutlery *s* instrument·a -orum *npl* escaria

cutlet *s* frust·um -i *n*

cutthroat *s* sicar·ius -(i)i *m*

cutting *adj (sharp)* acut·us -a -um; *(fig)* acerb·us -a -um

cutting *s (act)* secti·o -onis *f; (thing)* segm·en -inis *n; (for planting)* taleol·a -ae *f*

cyberspace *s* cyberspat·ium -(i) *n*

cycle *s* orb·is -is *m; (of events)* ord·o -inis *m*

cylinder *s* cylindr·us -i *m*

cylindrical *adj* cylindrat·us -a -um

cymbal *s* cymbal·um -i *n*

cynic *adj* cynic·us -a -um

cynic *s* cynic·us -i *m* (·a -ae *f)*

cynical *adj* acerb·us -a -um

cynicism *s* acerbit·as -atis *f*

cypress *s* cypress·us -i *f*

D

dab *s* massul·a -ae *f*

dab *tr* **to — on** illinere

dabble *intr* **to — in** leviter attingere

dad, daddy *s* tat·a -ae *m*

dactyl *s* dactyl·us -i *m*

dactylic *adj* dactylic·us -a -um

daffodil *s* asphodel·us -i *m*

daffy *adj (coll)* delir·us -a -um

dagger *s* pugi·o -onis *m*

daily *adj* cotidian·us -a -um

daily *adv* cotidie

dainties *spl* cuppedi·a -orum *npl*

dainty *adj* delicat·us -a -um

daisy *s* bell·is -idis *f*

dale *s* vall·is -is *f*

dally *intr (to linger)* morari; *(to trifle)* nugari; *(amorously)* blandiri

dam *s* mol·es -is *f; (of animals)* mat·er -ris *f*

dam *tr* **to — up** (operibus) obstruere

damage *s (loss)* damn·um -i *n; (injury)* nox·a -ae *f*

damage *tr* laedere; *(a person)* fraudi esse *(w. dat);* **to — s.o.'s reputation** aestimationem alicuius violare

dame *s* domin·a -ae *f; (girl)* puell·a -ae *f*

damn *tr* damnare, exsecrari

damnable *adj* damnabil·is -is -e

damnably *adv* damnabiliter

damnation *s* damnati·o -onis *f*

damp *adj* (h)umid·us -a -um

dampen *tr* humectare; *(fig)* restringere

dampness *s* ulig·o -inis *f*

damsel *s* puell·a -ae *f*

dance *s* saltati·o -onis *f*

dance *tr* **to — a number** canticum desaltare ‖ *intr* saltare

dance band *s* symphonicac·i -orum *mpl* saltationis

dancer *s* salta·tor -toris *m* (·trix -tricis *f)*

dancing *s* saltati·o -onis *f*

dandelion *s* aphac·a -ae *f*

dandruff *s* porrig·o -inis *f*

dandy *adj* bell·us -a -um

dandy *s* hom·o -inis *m* bellus

danger *s* pericul·um -i *n;* **to be in — of** periclitari *(w. abl);* **to be in grave — in** praecipite esse

dangerous *adj* periculos·us -a -um

dangerously *adv* periculose; *(seriously)* graviter

dangle *tr* suspendere ‖ *intr* pendēre

dank *adj* (h)umid·us et frigid·us -a -um

Danube River *s* Davuvi·us -i amn·is -is *m*

dare *tr* provocare ‖ *intr* audēre

daredevil *s* parabol·us -i *m*

daring *adj* aud·ax -acis

daring *s* audaci·a -ae *f*

dark *adj* obscur·us -a -um; *(in color)* fusc·us -a -um; *(gloomy)* a·ter -tra -trum; *(stern)* atr·ox -ocis; **—est night** spississima no·x -ctis *f;* **— eyes** nigri ocul·i -orum *mpl;* **it is growing —** advesperascit

dark *s* tenebr·ae -arum *fpl;* **after —** de nocte; **in the —** *(i.e., secretly)* clam et occulte; **I am in the —** *(i.e., mentally)* mihi tenebrae sunt; **to keep in the —** celare

darken *tr* obscurare; *(colors)* fuscare

dark horse *s* canditat·us -i *m* (·a -ae *f)* inopinat·us (-a)

darkness *s* tenebr·ae -arum *fpl;* — **fell** tenebrae factae sunt
darling *adj* suavissim·us -a -um
darling *s* delici·ae -arum *fpl*, ocell·us -i *m;* **my darling** *(in address)* mi ocelle
darn *tr* resarcire
darn *interj* (me) hercule!
darn *s* **I don't give a** — **about that (him, them)** id (eum, eos) non flocci facio
darned *adj* **I'll be** — **if ...** male mi sit, si ...
dart *s* spicul·um -i *n*
dart *intr (to move quickly)* provolare; *(of snake's tongue)* vibrare; **to** — **out** emicare
dash *tr (to splash)* aspergere; *(hopes)* frustrari; **to** — **against** allidere ad *(w. acc);* **to** — **off** *(letter)* scriptitare; **to** — **to pieces** discutere; **to** — **to the ground** affligere ‖ *intr* ruere
dash *s* impet·us -ūs *m; (animation)* alacrit·as -atis *f; (small amount)* mensur·a -ae *f* duorum digitorum
dashboard *s* tabul·a -ae *f* indicatoria
dashing *adj* ala·cer -cris -cre; *(showy)* nitid·us -a -um
data *spl* dat·a -orum *npl*
database *s (comput)* datorum repositor·ium -(i)i *n*
date *s* di·es -ei *f; (appointment)* constitut·um -i *n; (fruit)* palmul·a -ae *f;* **by what** —? quam ad diem?; **out of** — obsolet·us -a -um; **to** — adhuc; **to have a** — **with** consitutum habere cum *(w. abl);* **up to** — rec·ens -entis
date *tr* diem ascribere *(w. dat); (a girl)* constitutum habere cum *(w. abl)* ‖ *intr* **to** — **from** originem trahere ab *(w. abl)*
dative *s* dativ·us -i *m*, cas·us -ūs *m* dativus
daub *tr* oblinere
daughter *s* fili·a -ae *f*
daughter-in-law *s* nur·us -i *f*
daunt *tr* perterrēre
dauntless *adj* impavid·us -a -um
dauntlessly *adv* impavide
dawdle *intr* cessare
dawn *s* auror·a -ae *f;* **at** — primā luce; **before** — anteluculo
dawn *intr* dilucescere; **to** — **on** *(fig)* occurrere *(w. dat)*
day *s* di·es -ei *m;* **any** —**now** propediem; **by** — interdiu; — **after** — diem de die, in singulos dies; — **by** — in dies; — **and night** diem noctemque, et dies et noctes; **every** — cotidie; **from** — **to** — in dies; **from that** — **on** ex eo die; **just the other** — nuper quidem; **next** — postridie; **one** — *(in the past)* quodam die; **some** — olim; **the** — **after** postridie; **the** — **after that** postridie eius diei; **the** — **after tomorrow** perendie; **the** — **before** pridie; **the** — **before yesterday** nudiustertius [*adv*]; **the following** — postero die;

these —**s** his temporibus; **till late in the** — ad multum diem; **three** —**s after that** post quartum eius diei
day *adj* diurn·us -a -um
daybreak *s* dilucul·um -i *n; at* — primā luce; **before** — antelucio; **till** — in primam lucem
daydream *s* hallucinati·o -onis *f*
daydream *intr* hallucinari
daydreamer *s* hallucina·tor -toris *m* (·trix -tricis *f*)
daylight *s* lu·x -cis *f*, dies, diei *m;* **to let in the** — diem admittere
daytime *s* temp·us -oris *n* diurnum; **in the** — interdiu
daze *s* stup·or oris *m*
daze *tr* obstupefacere
dazzle *tr* praestringere
dazzling *adj* fulgid·us -a -um
DCD *s* digitalis compactus disc·us -i *m*
deacon *s* diacon·us -i *m*
dead *adj* mortu·us -a -um; *(without sensation)* sine sensu; **I'm** —! *(coll)* interii! *or* perii!
dead *s* — **of night** media no·x -ctis *f;* — **of winter** brum·a -ae *f;* **the** — man·es -ium, mortu·i -orum *mpl*
dead *adv* omnino, prorsus
deaden *tr* obtundere
dead end *s* fundul·a -ac *f; (fig)* cessati·o -onis *f*
dead-end street *s* fundul·a -ae *f*
deadline *s* praestituta di·es -ei *f;* **to meet the** — diem praestitutam obire; **to set the** — diem praestituere
deadly *adj* mortif·er -era -erum; *(hatred)* capital·is -is -e
deaf *adj* surd·us -a -um; **to be** — **to** non audire; **to go** — obsurdescere; **to turn a** — **ear** obsurdescere; **you're preaching to deaf ears** ad surdas aures cantas
deafen *tr* exsurdare
deaf-mute *adj* surd·us idemque mut·us -a -um
deafness *s* surdit·as -atis *f*
deal *s (quantity)* copi·a -ae *f*, vis *f; (pact)* pacti·o -onis *f; (com)* negot·ium -(i)i *n;* **a good** — **longer** multo diutius; **a good** — **of** aliquantum *(w. gen);* **it's a deal!** pactam rem habeto *(pl:* habetote)!
deal *tr* partiri; *(cards)* distribuere; **to** — **him a blow in the stomach** pugnos in ventrem ingerere ‖ *intr (com)* negotiari; **easy to** — **with** tractabil·is -is -e; **I'll** — **with you later** tecum mihi res erit serius; **to** — **with** *(a topic)* agere *(w. abl)*, tractare; **(a person)** uti *(w. abl)*
dealer *s* negotia·tor -toris *m* (·trix -tricis *f); (of cards)* distribu·tor -toris *m* (·trix -tricis *f)*
dealings *spl (com)* negotiati·o -onis *f; (relations)* commerc·ium -(i)i *n;* **to have** —**s with** commercium habēre cum *(w. abl)*

dean *s* decan·us -i *m* (·a -ae *f*)

dear *adj (highly valued; high-priced)* car·us -a -um; **my — friend!** mi amice!

dear *interj* **O —!** *(in dismay)* hei!; *(in embarrassment)* au au!

dearly *adv (intensely)* valde; *(at high cost)* magni

dearness *s* carit·as -atis *f*

dearth *s* inopi·a -ae *f*

death *s* mor·s -tis *f; (in violent form)* ne·x -cis *f;* **to condemn s.o. to —** aliquem capitis damnare; **to meet one's —** mortem obire; **to put s.o. to —** aliquem ad mortem dare, supplicium de aliquo sumere

deathbed *s* tor·us -i *m* extremus

deathless *adj* immortal·is -is -e

deathlike *adj* mortuos·us -a -um

deathly *adj* pallid·us -a -um

death penalty *s* supplic·ium -(i)i *n* capitis

death sentence *s* **to receive the —** capitis damnari

debase *tr* depravare; *(coinage)* adulterare; **to — oneself** se demittere

debasement *s* adulterati·o -onis *f*

debatable *adj* controversios·us -a -um, ambigu·us -a -um

debate *s* disceptati·o -onis *f*

debate *tr* disceptare de *(w. abl)* ‖ *intr* disserere, disputare

debater *s* disputa·tor -toris *m* (·trix -tricis *f*)

debauchery *s* licenti·a -ae *f*

debilitate *tr* debilitare

debit *s* expens·um -i *n*

debit *tr* in expensum referre

debt *s* ae·s -ris *n* alienum; *(fig)* debit·um -i *n;* **to be in —** aere alieno esse; **to pay off a —** aes alienum persolvere; **to run up a —** aes alienum conflare

debtor *s* debi·tor -toris *m* (·trix -tricis *f*)

decade *s* dec·as -adis *f*

decadence *s* occas·us -ūs *m*

decadent *adj* degen·er -era -erum

decalogue *s* decalog·us -i *m*

decamp *intr* castra movēre

decapitate *tr* detruncare

decathlon *s* decathl·um -i *n*

decay *s* tab·es -is *f; (fig)* defecti·o -onis *f*

decay *intr* putrescere, tabescere

decease *s* decess·us -ūs *m*

deceased *adj* defunct·us -a -um

deceit *s* frau·s -dis *f*, dol·us -i *m*

deceitful *adj* fall·ax -acis

deceitfully *adv* fallaciter

deceive *tr* decipere, fallere

December *s* Decem·ber -bris *m or* mens·is -is *m* December; **in —** mense Decembri; **on the first of —** Kalendis Decembribus

decency *s* decor·um -i *n*

decent *adj* dec·ens -entis; *(adequate)* rect·us -a -um

decently *adv* decenter

deception *s* fallaci·a -ae *f*

deceptive *adj* fall·ax -acis

decide *tr & intr* decernere; **the Senate decided** senatui placuit; **to — to** constituere *(w. inf)*

decided *adj* cert·us -a -um

decimate *tr* decimare; *(fig)* depopulari

decipher *tr* enodare

decision *s* sententi·a -ae *f; (of deliberative body)* decret·um -i *n; (of Senate)* auctorit·as -atis *f; (leg)* iudic·ium -(i)i *n; (a win in sports)* praevalenti·a -ae *f* punctorum; **to make a (wise) —** (sapienter) decernere

decisive *adj* cert·us -a -um; **— battle** decretoria pugn·a -ae *f*

deck *s (naut)* pon·s -tis *m;* **ship with a —** nav·is -is *f* constrata

deck *tr* ornare; *(tables)* sternere

deck chair *s* sell·a -ae *f* cubitoria

decked out *adj (in)* subornat·us -a -um *(w. abl)*

declaim *intr* declamare

declamation *s* declamati·o -onis *f*

declamatory *adj* declamatori·us -a -um

declaration *s* declarati·o -onis *f; (of war)* denuniati·o -onis *f*

declarative *adj* declarativ·us -a -um

declare *tr* declarare; *(to say out plainly)* edicere; *(war)* indicere ‖ *intr* **to — for** favēre *(w. dat)*

declension *s* declinati·o -onis *f*

declinable *adj* declinabil·is -is -e

decline *s (slope)* decliv·e -is *n; (of strength, etc.)* deminuti·o -onis *f;* **to cause a — in prices** pretia levare

decline *tr (to refuse)* recusare; *(gram)* declinare, flectere; **to — battle** pugnam detrectare ‖ *intr* inclinare; *(to decay, fail)* deficere, decrescere; *(of prices)* laxare

decode *tr* enodare

decompose *tr* resolvere ‖ *intr* putrescere, dissolvi

decomposition *s* dissoluti·o -onis *f*

decorate *tr* ornare

decoration *s (act)* ornati·o -onis *f; (ornament)* ornament·um -i *n; (distinction)* dec·us -oris *n*

decorator *s* exorn·ator -toris *m* (·trix -tricis *f*)

decorum *s* decor·um -i *n*

decoy *s* ill·ex -icis *mf*

decoy *tr* allicere

decrease *s* imminuti·o -onis *f*

decrease *tr* imminuere ‖ *intr* decrescere; *(of prices)* retro abire

decreasingly *adv* in minus

decree *s* decret·um -i *n; (of the Senate)* senatūs consult·um -i *n; (of the assembly)* scit·um -i *n;* **to pass a — of the senate** senatūs consultum facere

decree *tr* decernere; **the people —d** populus iussit

decrepit *adj* decrepit·us -a -um

decry *tr* vituperare

dedicate *tr (book, etc.)* dedicare; **to — oneself** to se dedere *(w. dat)*

dedication *s* dedicati·o -onis *f; (of a book)* nuncupati·o -onis *f; (devotion)* stud·ium -(i)i *n*

deduce *tr (to infer)* colligere

deduct *tr* deducere; **to — from the capital what has been paid in interest** de capite deducere quod usuris pernumeratum est

deduction *s* deducti·o -onis *f; (inference)* conclusi·o -onis *f*

deed *s* fact·um -i *n; (pej)* facin·us -oris *n; (leg)* instrument·um -i *n;* **good —** benefic·ium -(i)i *n*

deem *tr* ducere, habēre

deep *adj* alt·us -a -um; *(very deep)* profund·us -a -um; *(of sounds)* grav·is -is -e; *(of color)* satur -a -um; *(sleep)* art·us -a -um; *(recondite)* recondit·us -a -um; **— silence fell** ingens silentium factum est; **in — thought** cogitabund·us -a -um

deep *s* alt·um -i *n*

deepen *tr* defodere; *(e.g., affection)* augēre ‖ *intr* alt·ior -ior -ius fieri

deepfreezer *s* arc·a -ae *f* gelatoria

deeply *adv* alte; *(inwardly)* penitus; *(fig)* graviter, valde; **to be — grieved** graviter dolēre; **to be — in love** graviter amare

deep red *adj* coccine·us -a -um

deep-seated *adj* insit·us -a -um

deep-sunk *adj (eyes)* concav·us -a -um

deer *s* cerv·us -i *m,* cerv·a -ae *f*

deface *tr* deformare

defaced *adj* deform·is -is -e

defacement *s* deformit·as -atis *f*

defamation *s* obtrectati·o -onis *f*

defamatory *adj* probros·us -a -um

defame *tr* diffamare, infamare

default *s* delict·um -i *n*

defeat *s (pol)* repuls·a -ae *f; (mil)* clad·es -is *f; (sports)* adversum certam·en -inis *n;* **a — at the polls** comitiis repulsa; **— in running for the consulship** consulatūs repulsa; **to suffer a —** *(pol)* repulsam ferre; *(mil)* cladem accipere

defeat *tr* vincere, superare; *(to baffle)* frustrari; **to — a bill** rogationem antiquare

defect *s* vit·ium -(i)i *n*

defect *intr (to desert)* deficere

defection *s* defecti·o -onis *f; (to the enemy)* transfug·ium -(i)i *n*

defective *adj* vitios·us -a -um; *(gram)* defectiv·us -a -um

defend *tr* defendere; *(leg)* patrocinari *(w. dat)*

defendant *s* re·us -i *m,* re·a -ae *f*

defender *s* defens·or -oris *m (·trix -tricis f); (leg)* patron·us -i *m (·a -ae f)*

defense *s (act)* defensi·o -onis *f; (means)* praesid·ium -(i)i *n; (leg)* patrocin·ium -(i)i *n; (speech)* defensi·o -onis *f*

defense lawyer *s* defens·or -oris *m (·trix -tricis f)*

defenseless *adj* infens·us -a -um; *(unarmed)* inerm·is -is -e

defensible *adj* defensibil·is -is -e

defensive *adj* **— and offensive alliance** societ·as -atis *f* ad bellum defendendum atque inferendum facta; **— and offensive weapons** tela ad tegendum et ad nocendum; **to put s.o. on the —** aliqucm ad sua defendenda cogere

defer *tr* differre ‖ *intr* **to — to** obsequi *(w. dat)*

deference *s* observanti·a -ae *f;* **out of —** reverenter

deferential *adj* **(to)** observ·ans -antis *(w. gen)*

defiance *s* contempti·o -onis *f;* **in — of the law** invitis legibus

defiant *adj* insol·ens -entis

deficiency *s* defect·us -ūs *m; (of supplies, water, money)* penuri·a -ae *f*

deficient *adj* **(in)** in·ops -opis *(w. gen);* **to be —** deesse

deficit *s* lacun·a -ae *f;* **there is a —** deficit; **to make up the —** lacunam explēre

defile *s* fauc·es -ium *fpl*

defile *tr* inquinare; *(usu. fig)* contaminare

defilement *s* contaminati·o -onis *f*

define *tr* definire

definite *adj* definit·us -a -um *(opp:* infinitus)

definitely *adv* certe

definition *s* definiti·o -onis *f*

definitive *adj* definitiv·us -a -um

definitively *adv* definite

deflect *tr* deflectere

deflection *s* deflecti·o -onis *f*

deflower *tr* devirginare

deform *tr* deformare

deformed *adj* deform·is -is -e

deformity *s* deformit·as -atis *f*

defraud *tr* fraudare

defray *tr* suppeditare; **to — the costs** sumptūs suppeditare

deft *adj* agil·is -is -e, habil·is -is -e

deftly *adv* scite

defunct *adj* defunct·us -a -um

defy *tr* contemnere

degeneracy *s* mor·es -um *mpl* deteriores

degenerate *adj* degen·er -eris

degenerate *s* hom·o -inis *mf* degen·er (-eris)

degradation *s* ignomini·a -ae *f*

degrade *tr (to lower rank)* in ordinem redigere; *(fig)* dehonestare

degrading *adj* indign·us -a -um

degree *s* grad·us -ūs *m; (diploma)* studiorum diplom·a -atis *n;* **by —s** gradatim; **in some**

— aliquatenus; **positive (comparative, superlative)** — gradus positivus (comparativus, superlativus); **third** — quaesti·o -onis *f* severissia; **to such a — that** adeo ut
deification *s* consecrati·o -onis *f*
deify *tr* inter deos referre
deign *tr* dignari, curare
deism *s* deism·us -i *m*
deity *s* num·en -inis *n*
dejected *adj* demiss·us -a -um
dejection *s* animi abiecti·o -onis *f*
delay *s* mor·a -ae *f*
delay *tr* demorari ‖ *intr* morari
delectable *adj* delectabil·is -is -e
delegate *s* legat·us -i *m* (·a -ae *f*)
delegate *tr (to depute)* delegare; *(to entrust)* demandare
delegation *s (act)* mandat·us -ūs *m; (group)* legati·o -onis *f*
delete *tr* eradere; *(comput)* delēre
deleterious *adj* noxi·us -a -um
deliberate *adj* deliberat·us -a -um
deliberate *intr* deliberare, consulere
deliberately *adv* de industriā
deliberation *s* deliberati·o -onis *f*
delicacy *s* subtilit·as -atis *f; (food)* matte·a -ae *f;* **delicacies** cuppedi·a -orum *npl*
delicate *adj (of fine texture)* subtil·is -is -e; *(e.g., girl)* delicat·us -a -um; *(taste, work of art)* eleg·ans -antis; *(health)* infirm·us -a -um; *(matter)* lubric·us -a -um
delicious *adj* sapid·us -a -um
delight *s* delectati·o -onis *f; (cause of delight)* delici·ae -arum *fpl*
delight *tr* delectare ‖ *intr* **to — in** delectari *(w. abl)*
delighted *adj* (**with**) delectat·us -a -um *(w. abl)*
delightful *adj* suav·is -is -e
delightfully *adv* suaviter
delineate *tr* delineare, describere
delineation *s* descripti·o -onis *f*
delinquency *s* delict·um -i *n*
delinquent *adj* noxi·us -a -um
delinquent *s* noxi·us -i *m* (·a -ae *f*)
delirious *adj* delir·us -a -um
delirium *s* delir·ium -(i)i *n*
deliver *tr (to hand over)* tradere; *(to free)* liberare; *(to surrender)* prodere; *(a speech)* habēre, dicere; *(sentence)* dicere; *(message)* referre; *(blow)* intendere; *(child)* obstetricari; *(a letter)* reddere
deliverance *s* liberati·o -onis *f*
deliverer *s* libera·tor -toris *m* (·trix -tricis *f*)
delivery *s (freedom)* liberati·o -onis *f; (of goods)* traditi·o -onis *f; (of a speech)* acti·o -onis *f; (childbirth)* part·us -ūs *m*
delude *tr* deludere
deluge *s* diluv·ium -(i)i *n*
deluge *tr* obruere, inundare

delusion *s* delusi·o -onis *f*
demagogue *s* publicol·a -ae *m*
demand *s* postulati·o -onis *f,* postulat·um -i *n*
demand *tr* postulare, flagitare
demanding *adj* **to be** — multa exigere
demarcation *s* confin·ium -(i)i *n*
demean *tr* **to — oneself** se demittere
demeanor *s* gest·us -ūs *m*
demented *adj* dem·ens -entis
demerit *s* vit·ium -(i)i *n; (mark)* vitii not·a -ae *f*
demigod *s* her·os -oïs *m*
demise *s* decess·us -ūs *m*
democracy *s* civit·as -atis *f* popularis
democrat *s* civ·is -is *m* popularis
democratic *adj* popular·is -is -e; **— party** part·es -ium *fpl* populares
democratically *adv* populi voluntate
demolish *tr* demoliri
demolition *s* demoliti·o -onis *f*
demon *s* daem·on -onis *m*
demonstrable *adj* demonstrabil·is -is -e
demonstrably *adv* manifeste
demonstrate *tr (to show)* monstrare; *(to prove)* demonstrare
demonstration *s (proof)* demonstrati·o -onis *f; (display)* ostent·us -ūs *m; (popular display of opinion)* protestati·o -onis *f* popularis
demonstrative *adj* demonstrativ·us -a -um
demoralization *s* depravati·o -onis *f*
demoralize *tr (to corrupt)* depravare; *(to discourage)* percellere
demote *tr* loco movēre
demotion *s* a gradu moti·o -onis *f*
demure *adj* modest·us -a -um
demurely *adv* modeste
den *s* latibul·um -i *n; (in a home)* tablin·um -i *n*
denarius *s* denari·us -i *m (worth about one dollar)*
deniable *adj* infitiand·us -a -um
denial *s* negati·o -onis *f; (refusal)* repudiati·o -onis *f;* **to give s.o. a flat —** praecise alicui negare
denomination *s (name)* denominati·o -onis *f; (sect)* sect·a -ae *f*
denominator *s* numer·us -i *m* dividens
denotation *s* denotati·o -onis *f*
denote *tr* significare
denounce *tr (to inform against)* deferre; *(to condemn)* reprehendere
dense *adj* dens·us -a -um; *(crowded)* spiss·us -a -um; *(stupid)* crass·us -a -um
densely *adv* dense, crebro; **— populated region** regi·o -onis *f* uberrimae multitudinis
density *s* densit·as -atis *f*
dent *s* not·a -ae *f*
dent *tr* imprimere, cavare
dented *adj* collis·us -a -um

dentist *s* medic·us -i *m* dentarius, medic·a -ae *f* dentaria

dentistry *s* dentium medicin·a -ae *f*

denture *s* prostes·is -is *f* dentalis

denude *tr* nudare

denunciation *s (by informer)* delati·o -onis *f; (condemnation)* reprehensi·o -onis *f*

deny *tr* negare, infitiari; *(to refuse)* (de)negare, abnuere

depart *intr* abire; *(to die)* obire; **to — for his province** abire in provinciam

departed *adj* defunct·us -a -um

department *s (of administration)* provinci·a -ae *f,* administrati·o -onis *f; (branch)* gen·us -eris *n; (academic)* facult·as -atis *f;* **— of classics** litterarum classicarum facultas

department store *s* pantopol·ium -(i)i *n*

departure *s* abit·us -ūs *m,* abscess·us -ūs *m; (death)* obit·us -ūs *m*

depend *tr* **to — on** dependēre de *(w. abl),* niti *(w. abl);* **it —s on you** in te positum est; **it — a lot on whether** plurimum refert num

dependable *adj* fid·us -a -um

dependant *s* cli·ens -entis *mf*

dependence *s* fiduci·a -ae *f*

dependency *s* provinci·a -ae *f*

dependent *adj* obnoxi·us -a -um

depict *tr (to paint)* pingere; *(in words)* describere, depingere

deplete *tr* deminuere

depletion *s* deminuti·o -onis *f*

deplorable *adj* miserabil·is -is -e

deplore *tr* deplorare

deploy *tr (mil)* expedire, instruere

deponent *s* depon·ens -entis *n,* verb·um -i *n* deponens

depopulate *tr* vacuefacere

deportment *s* gest·us -ūs *m*

depose *tr* summovēre; *(leg)* testificari

deposit *s* deposit·um -i *n; (earnest money)* arrhab·o -onis *m; (of fluids)* sedim·en -inis *n;* **to put down 10 denari as a —** decem denarios arrhaboni dare

deposit *tr* **to — money in a bank** pecuniam in argentariā deponere

deposition *s (leg)* testimon·ium -(i)i *n*

depositor *s* deposi·tor -toris *m (·trix -tricis f)*

depot *s (com)* empor·ium -(i)i *n; (mil)* armamentar·ium -(i)i *n*

depraved *adj* prav·us -a -um

depravity *s* pravit·as -atis *f*

deprecate *tr* deprecari

deprecation *s* deprecati·o -onis *f*

depreciate *tr* detrectare

depreciation *s* detrectati·o -onis *f; (of price)* vilit·as -atis *f*

depredation *s* spoliati·o -onis *f*

depress *tr* deprimere; *(fig)* infringere

depressed *adj* abiect·us -a -um; **to be —** abiecto animo esse

depressing *adj* trist·is -is -e

depression *s (emotional)* anim·us -i *m* fractus; *(fin)* res adversae

deprivation *s (act)* privati·o -onis *f; (state)* inopi·a -ae *f*

deprive *tr* privare; **to — s.o. of** aliquem privare *(w. abl)*

depth *s* altitud·o -inis *f;* **a hundred feet in —** *(as opposed to frontage)* centum pedes in agrum; **the —s** profund·um -i *n*

deputation *s* legati·o -onis *f*

deputy *s* legat·us -i *m (·a -ae f)*

derange *tr* conturbare

deranged *adj* mente capt·us -a -um

derangement *s (of mind)* mentis alienati·o -onis *f*

dereliction *s* derelicti·o -onis *f*

deride *tr* irridēre

derision *s* irrisi·o -onis *f*

derisive *adj* irrid·ens -entis

derivation *s* derivati·o -onis *f*

derivative *adj* derivativ·us -a -um

derive *tr* (de)ducere; *(words)* derivare; **to — pleasure from** voluptatem capere ex *(w. abl)* ‖ *intr* procedere

derogatory *adj* indign·us -a -um

descend *intr* descendere; **to — on** *(to attack)* irrumpere in *(w. acc)*

descendant *s* progeni·es -ei *f;* **the —s** poster·i -orum *mpl*

descent *s* descens·us -ūs *m; (slope)* cliv·us -i *m; (lineage)* gen·us -eris *n*

describe *tr* describere

description *s* descripti·o -onis *f*

desecrate *tr* profanare

desecration *f* violati·o -onis *f*

desert *s* desert·a -orum *npl*

desert *tr* deserere, relinquere ‖ *intr* deserere; *(esp. mil)* transfugere

deserter *s* transfug·a -ae *mf*

desertion *s (abandonment)* deserti·o -onis *f; (esp. mil)* transfug·ium -(i)i *n*

deserts *spl* merit·a -orum *npl;* **he got his —** habet quod sibi debebatur

deserve *tr* merēre, merēri

deservedly *adv* merito, iure

deserving *adj (of)* dign·us -a -um *(w. abl)*

design *s (of a building, etc.)* descripti·o -onis *f; (drawing)* adumbrati·o -onis *f; (plan)* form·a -ae *f*

design *tr* designare; *(to draw in lines)* delineare; *(to sketch)* adumbrare; *(fig)* machinari

designate *tr* designare

designation *s (appointment)* designati·o -onis *f; (name)* nom·en -inis *n*

designer *s (of s.th. new)* invent·or -oris *m (·trix -tricis f); (as an architect)* designa·tor -toris *m* (·trix -tricis *f*); *(of a stratagem)* fabrica·tor -toris *m* (·trix -tricis *f*)

designing *adj* callid·us -a -um

desirable *adj* desiderabil·is -is -e

desire *s* cupidit·as -atis *f; (longing)* desider·ium -(i)i *n; (sexual)* libid·o -inis *f*

desire *tr* cupere, optare; *(to long for what is lacking)* desiderare

desirous *adj* (of) cupid·us -a -um *(w. gen)*

desist *intr* (from) desistere *(w. abl or de w. abl)*

desk *s* mens·a -ae *f* scriptoria; *(teacher's)* pulpit·um -i *n*

desolate *adj* desolat·us -a -um; *(of persons)* afflict·us -a -um

desolation *s* solitud·o -inis *f*

despair *s* desperati·o -onis *f*

despair *intr* desperare; **to — of** desperare *(w. acc or de w. abl)*

desperado *s* sicar·ius -(i)i *m*

desperate *adj* *(hopeless)* desperat·us -a -um; *(dangerous)* periculos·us -a -um; **in their — situation** in extremis rebus suis; **to take — measures** ad extrema descendere

desperately *adv* vehementer; **to be — in love** perdite amare

desperation *s* desperati·o -onis *f*

despicable *adj* despicat·us -a -um

despise *tr* despicere, spernere

despite *prep* contra *(w. acc)*

despoil *tr* spoliare

despondency *s* animi abiecti·o -onis *f*, tristiti·a -ae *f*

despondent *adj* abiect·us -a -um; **to be —** animo demisso esse

despondently *adv* animo demisso

despot *s* tyrann·us -i *m*

despotic *adj* tyrannic·us -a -um

despotically *adv* tyrannice

despotism *s* dominati·o -onis *f*

dessert *s* secunda mens·a -ae *f*, bellari·a -orum *npl*

destination *s* loc·us -i *m* destinationis

destine *tr* destinare

destiny *s* fat·um -i *n*, sor·s -tis *f*

destitute *adj* (of) inop·s -is *(w. gen or abl)*, eg·ens -entis *(w. gen)*

destitution *s* inopi·a -ae *f*

destroy *tr* destruere, delēre; **to be —ed** interire

destroyer *s* dele·tor -toris *m* (·trix -tricis *f*)

destruction *s* exit·ium -(i)i *n*

destructive *adj* exitial·is -is -e

desultory *adj* inconst·ans -antis

detach *tr* seiungere; *(by breaking)* abscindere; *(by pulling)* avellere

detached *adj* seiunct·us -a -um

detachment *s* *(act)* seiuncti·o -onis *f; (mil)* man·us -ūs *f; (aloofness)* secess·us -ūs *m*

detail *s* **—s** singul·a -orum *npl;* **in —** singulatim, diligenter; **to go into —** per singula ire

detail *tr* exsequi, enarrare

detain *tr* morari, retinēre

detect *tr* detegere, deprehendere

detection *s* deprehensi·o -onis *f*

detective *s* inquisi·tor -toris *m* (·trix -tricis *f*), indiga·tor -oris *m* (·trix -tricis *f*)

detention *s* retenti·o -onis *f*

deter *tr* deterrēre

detergent *s* smegm·a -atis *n*

deteriorate *tr* deteri·orem -orem -us facere ‖ *intr* deteri·or -or -us fieri

determination *s* *(resolution)* constanti·a -ae *f; (decision)* consil·ium -(i)i *n*

determine *tr* *(to fix)* determinare; *(to decide)* constituere

determined *adj* *(resolute)* firm·us -a -um; *(fixed)* cert·us -a -um

detest *tr* detestari

detestable *adj* detestabil·is -is -e

detestation *s* detestati·o -onis *f*

dethrone *tr* regno depellere

detonate *intr* crepare

detonation *s* frag·or -oris *m*

detour *s* circumit·us -ūs *m;* **to take a —** circumire

detract *tr* detrahere ‖ *intr* **to — from** obtrectare

detraction *s* obtrectati·o -onis *f*

detractor *s* obtrecta·tor -toris *m* (·trix -tricis *f*)

detriment *s* detriment·um -i *n*

detrimental *adj* damnos·us -a -um; **to be — to** detrimento esse *(w. dat)*

devastate *tr* vastare

devastating *adj* damnos·us -a -um

devastation *s* *(act)* vastati·o -onis *f; (state)* vastit·as -atis *f*

develop *tr* *(character, mind)* confirmare; *(to improve)* excolere; ‖ *intr* crescere; *(to advance)* progredi; **to — into** evadere in *(w. acc)*

development *s* *(unfolding)* explicati·o -onis *f; (advance)* progress·us -ūs *m; — of events* event·us -ūs *m;* **to attain full —** adolescere

deviate *intr* (from) se declinare (de *w. abl); (to act in violation of)* (from) discedere (ab *w. abl);* **not to — from the course** cursum tenēre

deviation *s* declinati·o -onis *f*

device *s* artific·ium -(i)i *n*, machin·a -ae *f; (plan)* consil·ium -(i)i *n; (emblem)* sign·um -i *n*

devil *s* diabol·us -i *m;* **go to the —!** abi in malam crucem!; **those —s!** istae larvae!

devilish *adj* diabolic·us -a -um; *(fig)* nefand·us -a -um

devious *adj* devi·us -a -um; *(person)* astut·us -a -um, versut·us -a -um

devise *tr* excogitare
devoid *adj* exper·s -tis *(w. gen or abl);* **to be —** **of** carēre *(w. abl)*
devolve *intr* **to — upon** cedere in *(w. acc); (by inheritance)* pervenire ad *(w. acc)*
devote *tr* devovēre, consecrare; **to — oneself to** se dedere *(w. gen)*
devoted *adj* **(to)** dedit·us -a -um *(w. dat),* studios·us -a -um *(w. gen)*
devotee *s* cul·tor -toris *m* (·trix -tricis *f*)
devotion *s* devoti·o -onis *f;* **—s** prec·es -um *fpl*
devour *tr* vorare; *(fig)* haurire
devout *adj* pi·us -a -um
devoutly *adv* pie
dew *s* ro·s -ris *m*
dewy *adj* roscid·us -a -um
dexterity *s* callidit·as -atis *f*
dexterous *adj* callid·us -a -um
dexterously *adv* callide
diabolical *adj* diabolic·us -a -um
diadem *s* diadem·a -atis *n*
diagnose *tr* discernere
diagnosis *s* diagnos·is -is *f*
diagonal *adj* diagonal·is -is -e
diagonally *adv* in transversum
diagram *s* form·a -ae *f,* descripti·o -onis *f*
diagram *tr* describere
dial *s* *(of clock)* tabul·a -ae *f* horaria; *(of a telephone)* tabula selectoria
dial *tr* seligere ‖ *intr* numerum seligere
dialect *s* dialect·us -i *f*
dialectic *adj* dialectic·us -a -um
dialectics *s* dialectic·a -ae *f*
dialogue *s* serm·o -onis *m; (written discussion)* dialog·us -i *m*
diameter *s* diametr·os -i *f*
diamond *s* adam·as -antis *m*
diaper *s* fasci·ae -arum *fpl*
diaphragm *s* sept·um -i *n* transversum, diaphragm·a -atis *n*
diarrhea *s* alvi defusi·o -onis *f*
diary *s* diar·ium -(i)i *n*
diatribe *s* convic·ium -(i)i *n*
dice *spl* ale·ae -arum *fpl; (the game)* ale·a -ae *f;* **to roll the —** aleas iactare; **to play —** aleā ludere
dictate *tr* dictare; *(to prescribe)* praescribere
dictate *s* praescript·um -i *n*
dictation *s* dictati·o -onis *f;* **to take —** dictata exscribere
dictator *s* dictat·or -oris *m*
dictatorial *adj* dictatori·us -a -um
dictatorship *s* dictatur·a -ae *f*
diction *s* dicti·o -onis *f*
dictionary *s* glossiar·ium -(i)i *n,* lexic·on -i *n*
didactic *adj* didascalic·us -a -um
die *s* ale·a -ae *f;* **the — is cast** alea iacta est
die *intr* mori; **to — laughing** risu emori; **to — off** demori; **to — out** emori

Diesel *adj* Diselian·us -a -um
diet *s* *(food)* victūs rati·o -onis *f; (dietary regime)* diaet·a -ae *f;* **to be on a —** victūs rationem observare
diet *intr* victūs rationem inire
dietary *adj* diatetic·us -a -um
differ *intr* differre; *(in opinion)* dissentire; *(to disagree)* discrepare
difference *s* differenti·a -ae *f; (wide difference)* distanti·a -ae *f; (disagreement)* discrepanti·a -ae *f;* **— of opinion** dissensi·o -onis *f;* **how much — does it make?** quantum interest?; **it makes no (a lot of) — to me (you) whether ... or** nil meā (tuā) interest *or* rēfert utrum ... **an; there is no — between god and god** nihil inter deum et deum interest; **there isn't the slightest — between them** ne minimum quidem inter eos interest; **what — does it make whether ... ?** quid refert utrum ... ?
differentiate *tr* discernere
differently *adv* aliter; *(variously)* varie, diverse
differing *adj* disson·us -a -um
difficult *adj* difficil·is -is -e; *(blocked up, e.g., a road)* impedit·us -a -um; **it is a — thing to** magnum est *(w. inf)*
difficulty *s* difficult·as -atis *f;* **with —** aegre
diffidence *s* *(distrust)* diffidenti·a -ae *f; (modesty)* verecundi·a -ae *f*
diffident *adj* diffid·ens -entis; *(modest)* verecund·us -a -um
diffuse *adj* diffus·us -a -um; *(verbally)* verbos·us -a -um
diffuse *tr* diffundere
diffusely *adv* effuse
diffusion *s* diffusi·o -onis *f*
dig *tr* *(garden, well)* fodere; **to — a hole in the ground** terram excavare; **to — a hole in the wall (wood)** parietem (lignum) perfodere; **— up** *(e.g., the garden, the earth)* confodere; **to — up s.th. about** *(fig)* quicquam eruere de *(w. abl)*
digest *s* summar·ium -(i)i *n*
digest *tr* concoquere
digestion *s* concocti·o -onis *f*
digestive *adj* peptic·us -a -um
digging *s* fossi·o -onis *f*
digit *s* numer·us -i *m*
digital *adj* digital·is -is -e; **— clock** horolog·ium -(i)i *n* digitale
dignified *adj* grav·is -is -e
dignify *tr* honestare
dignitary *s* vir -i *m* amplissimus, femina -ae amplissima
dignity *s* dignit·as -atis *f,* gravit·as -atis *f*
digress *intr* digredi
digression *s* digressi·o -onis *f*
dike *s* agg·er -eris *m*
dilapidated *adj* ruinos·us -a -um
dilate *tr* dilatare ‖ *intr* dilatari

dilatory *adj* cunctabund·us -a -um
dilemma *s (difficulty)* angusti·ae -arum *fpl; (logical)* dilemm·a -atis *n;* **to be in a —** haerēre in salebrā
diligence *s* diligenti·a -ae *f*
diligent *adj* dilig·ens -entis
diligently *adv* diligenter
dilute *tr* diluere
dilution *s* mixtur·a -ae *f*
dim *adj* heb·es -etis, obscur·us -a -um; **to be —** hebēre; **to become —** hebescere
dim *tr* hebetare ‖ *intr* hebescere
dimensions *spl* mensur·a -ae *f;* **to take the —s of** mensuram *(w. gen)* agere
diminish *tr* minuere; *(weight, value, authority)* levare ‖ *intr* minui
diminutive *adj* exigu·us -a -um; *(gram)* deminutiv·us -a -um
diminutive *s (gram)* deminutiv·um -i *n*
dimness *s* hebetud·o -inis *f*
dimple *s* gelasin·us -i *m*
din *s* strepit·us -ūs *m;* **to make a —** strepare
dine *intr* cenare; **to — out** foris cenare
diner *s* conviv·a -ae *mf*
dingy *adj* squalid·us -a -um
dining car *s* curr·us -ūs *m* cenatorius
dining couch *s* tor·us -i *m*
dining room *s* cenati·o -onis *f,* triclin·ium -(i)i *n*
dining table *s* mens·a -ae *f* escaria
dinner *s* cen·a -ae *f;* **over —** per cenam; **to eat —** cenare, cenam sumere; **what did you have for —** quid in cenā habuisti?
dinner clothes *spl* cenatori·a -orum *npl*
dinner guest *s* conviv·a -ae *mf*
dinner party *s* conviv·ium -(i)i *n*
dinner time *s* hor·a -ae *f* cenandi
dinosaur *s* dinosaur·us -i *m*
dint *s* **by — of** per *(w. acc)*
diocese *s* dioeces·is -is *f*
dip *tr* immergere; *(to wet by dipping)* ting(u)ere ‖ *intr* mergi; **to — into** *(fig)* attingere
dip *s (decrease)* deminuti·o -onis *f; (slope)* declivit·as -atis *f; (food)* embamm·a -atis *n;* **to take a —** *(short swim)* natare
diphthong *s* diphthong·us -i *f*
diploma *s* studiorum diplom·a -atis *n;* **to get a —** studiorum diploma merere
diplomacy *s* **to settle matters by —** rem legationibus componere
diplomatic *adj (fig)* sag·ax -acis
dipper *s* trull·a -ae *f;* **Big Dipper** Urs·a -ae *f* Maior; **Little Dipper** Urs·a -ae *f* Minor
dire *adj* dir·us -a -um
direct *adj* (di)rect·us -a -um
direct *vt* dirigere; *(to manage)* administrare; *(to order)* iubēre; *(a weapon)* intendere; *(a let-*

ter) inscribere; **to — attention to** animum attendere ad *(w. acc)*
direction *s (act)* directi·o -onis *f; (quarter)* par·s -tis *f; (management)* administrati·o -onis *f; (instruction)* mandat·um -i *n; (order)* praecept·um -i *n;* **in all —s** in omnes partes; **in a southerly —** in meridiem versus; **in both —** utroque; **in every —** quoquoversus; **in the — of Gaul** in Galliam versus; **in the — of Rome** Romam versus
directive *s* mandat·um -i *n*
directly *adv* directe, rectā; *(immediately)* statim; **to go —** ire rectā
director *s* rect·or -oris *m,* rec·trix -tricis *f*
directory *s (office of director)* magister·ium -(i)i *n; (list, catalog)* ind·ex -icis *m; (comput)* plicarum ind·ex -icis *m*
dirge *s* neni·a -ae *f*
dirt *s* sord·es -is *f (usu. pl); (mud)* lut·um -i *n*
dirt-cheap *adj* pro luto
dirtiness *s* spurciti·a -ae *f*
dirty *adj* sordid·us -a -um, spurc·us -a -um; *(fig)* obscen·us -a -um; **— old man** salax sen·ex -is *m;* **— talk** serm·o -onis *m* obscenus; **to give s.o. a — look** aliquem minus familiari vultu respicere
dirty *tr* spurcare, foedare
disability *s* imbecillit·as -atis *f*
disable *tr (to weaken)* debilitare; *(to cripple)* mutilare; *(a ship)* afflictare
disabled *adj* invalid·us -a -um; *(maimed)* manc·us -a -um; **totally —** omnibus membris capt·us -a -um
disadvantage *s* incommod·um -i *n*
disadvantaged *adj* incommodat·us -a -um
disadvantageous *adj* incommod·us -a -um, iniqu·us -a -um
disagree *intr (with)* dissentire (ab *w. abl);* **the food —d with me** cibus stomachum offendit; **to strongly —** vehmenter dissentire
disagreeable *adj* iniucund·us -a -um; *(smell)* graveol·ens -entis; *(person)* importun·us -a -um
disagreement *s* dissensi·o -onis *f*
disallow *tr* vetare
disappear *intr* evanescere; **to — from sight** oculis subduci, abire ex oculis
disappearance *s* exit·us -ūs *m*
disapppoint *tr* fallere, frustrari; **I'll not — you** opinionem tuam non fallam
disappointment *s (act)* frustrati·o -onis *f; (result)* incommod·um -i *n*
disapproval *s* improbati·o -onis *f*
disapprove *tr* improbare ‖ *intr* **to — of** improbare
disarm *tr* exarmare
disarrange *tr* turbare
disarray *s* perturbati·o -onis *f*
disaster *s* calamit·as -atis *f; (mil)* clad·es -is *f*

disastrous *adj* calamitos·us -a -um
disastrously *adv* calamitose
disavow *tr* diffitieri, infiteri
disavowal *s* infitiati·o -onis *f*
disband *tr* dimittere **‖** *intr* dimitti
disbelief *s* incredulit·as -atis *f*
disbeliever *s* incredul·us -i *m* (·a -ae *f*)
disburse *tr* expendere, erogare
disbursement *s* erogati·o -onis *f*, impens·a -ae *f*
disc *s* orb·is -is *m*
discard *tr* abicere
discern *tr* *(to distinguish)* discernere; *(to see clearly)* perspicere
discernible *adj* dignoscend·us -a -um
discerning *adj* perspic·ax -acis
discernment *s* *(faculty)* discrim·en -inis *n*; *(act)* perspicienti·a -ae *f*
discharge *s* *(release)* liberati·o -onis *f*; *(mil)* missi·o -onis *f*; *(of missiles)* coniect·us -ūs *m*, emissi·o -onis *f*; *(of duty)* perfunct·io -onis *f*; *(bodily)* defluxi·o -onis *f*; **dishonorable —** missio *f* cum ignominiā; **honorable —** missio honesta
discharge *tr* *(to perform)* perfungi *(w. abl)*; *(mil)* dimittere; *(debt)* exsolvere; *(defendant)* absolvere; *(missiles)* immittere, conicere
disciple *s* discipul·us -i *m*
disciplinarian *s* **a strict —** exac·tor -toris *m* (·rix -ricis *f*) gravissimus (-a) disciplinae
discipline *s* disciplin·a -ae *f*; *(punishment)* castigati·o -onis *f*
discipline *tr* disciplinā instituere; *(to punish)* castigare
disclaim *tr* infitiari
disclaimer *s* infitiati·o -onis *f*
disclose *tr* *(to reveal)* patefacere, detegere; *(to tell)* promere; *(to divulge)* enuntiare
disclosure *s* patefacti·o -onis *f*
discolor *tr* decolorare **‖** *intr* decolorari; *(to fade)* pallescere
discomfit *tr* profligare
discomfort *s* incommod·um -i *n*
discomfort *tr* incommodare
disconcerting *adj* molest·us -a -um
disconnect *tr* disiungere
disconsolate *adj* maest·us -a -um
discontent *s* offensi·o -onis *f*
discontent *tr* offendere
discontented *adj* parum content·us -a -um
discontentedly *adv* animo iniquo
discontinue *tr* intermittere **‖** *intr* desinere
discord *s* discordi·a -ae *f*; *(mus)* dissonanti·a -ae *f*
discordant *adj* discor·s -dis; *(mus)* disson·us -a -um
discotheque *s* discothec·a -ae *f*
discount *tr* deducere; *(to disregard)* praetermittere

discount *s* *(com)* decessi·o -onis *f*; **a five- (ten-, twenty-) percent —** quinarum (denarum, vicesimarum) centesimarum decessio
discourage *tr* animum (animos) *(w. gen)* infringere; *(to dissuade)* dehortari; **to be —d** animo (animis) deficere, animum (animos) demittere
discouragement *s* animi infracti·o -onis *f*
discouraging *adj* advers·us -a -um
discourse *s* serm·o -onis *m*; *(written)* libell·us -i *m*
discourse *intr* (on) disserere *(w. abl)* de
discourteous *adj* inurban·us -a -um
discourteously *adv* inurbane
discourtesy *s* inurbanit·as -atis *f*
discover *tr* invenire; *(to explore)* explorare
discoverable *adj* indagabil·is -is -e
discoverer *s* inven·tor -toris *m* (·rix -ricis *f*)
discovery *s* inventi·o -onis *f*; *(thing discovered)* invent·um -i *n*
discredit *s* dedec·us -oris *n*; macul·a -ae *f*; **to be a — to one's family** familiae suae dedecori esse; **to bring — upon oneself** maculam suscipere *(w. abl of cause)*
discredit *tr* *(to disbelieve)* non credere *(w. dat)*; *(to disgrace)* labem inferre *(w. dat)*
discreet *adj* caut·us -a -um, prud·ens -entis
discrepancy *s* discrepanti·a -ae *f*
discretion *s* *(tact)* iudic·ium -(i)i *n*; *(entire control)* arbitr·ium -(i)i *n*; **at one's —** ad arbitrium suum
discretionary *adj* lib·er -era -erum; **to give s.o. — power** liberum arbitrium alicui permittere
discriminate *tr* distinguere
discriminating *adj* discern·ens -entis
discrimination *s* *(act of distinguishing)* distincti·o -onis *f*; *(discernment)* discrim·en -inis *n*; *(prejudice)* opini·o -onis *f* praeiudicata
discuss *tr* disputare de *(w. abl)*, disceptare de *(w. abl)*
discussion *s* disputati·o -onis *f*; **there was a long — about** diu disputatum est de *(w. abl)*
disdain *tr* fastidire
disdain *s* fastid·ium -(i)i *n*; **to treat with —** dedignari
disdainful *adj* fastidios·us -a -um
disdainfully *adv* fastidiose
disease *s* morb·us -i *m*
diseased *adj* aegrot·us -a -um
disembark *tr* e nave exponere **‖** *intr* e nave exire
disengage *tr* expedire, eximere
disentangle *tr* explicare
disfavor *s* invidi·a -ae *f*, offens·a -ae *f*; **to be in great — with s.o.** magnā in offensā esse apud aliquem; **to fall into — with s.o.** suscipere invidiam apud aliquem
disfigure *tr* deformare

disfranchise *tr* civitatem adimere *(w. dat)*

disgorge *tr* evomere

disgrace *s* dedec·us -oris *n*, ignomini·a -ae *f*; *(thing)* flagit·ium -(i)i *n*; *(public disgrace)* ignomin·ia -ae *f*; **that's a darn —!** edepol facinus improbum est!; **to become a — to** dedecori esse *(w. dat)*

disgrace *tr* dedecorare

disgraceful *adj* dedecor·us -a -um

disgracefully *adv* turpiter

disguise *s* vestit·us -ūs *m* alienus; *(fig)* person·a -ae *f*; **in —** mutatā veste

disguise *tr* dissimulare

disgust *s* taed·ium -(i)i *n*

disgust *tr* stomachum movēre *(w. dat)*; **I am — ed with** me taedet *(w. gen)*, me piget *(w. gen)*

disgusting *adj* foed·us -a -um

disgustingly *adv* foede

dish *s* *(open and flat)* patin·a -e *f*; *(small)* catill·us -i *m*; *(large)* lan·x -cis *f*; *(course)* fercul·um -i *n*; **to wash the —es** vasa coquinatoria eluere

dishearten *tr* animum (animos) *(w. gen)* infringere; **to be —ed** animum (animos) demittere

disheveled *adj (hair)* pass·us -a -um

dishonest *adj* fraudulent·us -a -um; *(lying)* mend·ax -acis

dishonestly *adv* dolo malo

dishonesty *s* frau·s -dis *f*

dishonor *s* dedec·us -oris *n*

dishonor *tr* dedecorare

dishonorable *adj* dedecor·us -a -um, inhonest·us -a -um; **— discharge** missi·o -onis *f* cum ignominiā

dishonorably *adv* inhoneste

dishpan *s* labr·um -i *n* (ad vasa coquinatoria eluenda)

dishwasher *s* machin·a -ae *f* elutoria

disillusion *tr* errorem adimere *(w. dat)*

disinclination *s* declinati·o -onis *f*

disinfect *tr* contagia depellere de *(w. abl)*

disinfectant *s* remed·ium -(i)i *n* ad contagia depellenda aptum

disinherit *tr* exheredare

disintegrate *intr* dilabi

disinter *tr* effodere

disinterested *adj* inte·ger -gra -grum

disinterestedly *adv* integre

disjoin *tr* disiungere

disjointed *adj* incomposit·us -a -um

disjointedly *adv* incomposite

disk *s* orb·is -is *m*; *(comput)* disc·us -i *m*; **floppy —** discus flexibilis

disk drive *s (comput)* instrument·um -i *n* disculis legendis

diskette *s (comput)* discul·us -i *m*

dislike *s* od·ium -(i)i *n*

dislike *tr* aversari

dislocate *tr* luxare

dislocation *s* luxatur·a -ae *f*

dislodge *tr* depellere

disloyal *adj* perfid·us -a -um

disloyally *adv* perfide

disloyalty *s* perfidi·a -ae *f*

dismal *adj* maest·us -a -um

dismally *adv* maeste

dismantle *tr* diruere

dismay *s* consternati·o -onis *f*

dismay *tr* percellere

dismember *tr* membratim dividere

dismemberment *s* mutilati·o -onis *f*

dismiss *tr* dimittere; *(fear)* mittere

dismissal *s* dimissi·o -onis *f*

dismount *intr* ex equo desilire

disobedience *s* inobedienti·a -ae *f*

disobedient *adj* parum obedi·ens -entis

disobey *tr* non obedire *(w. dat)*

disorder *s* confusi·o -onis *f*; *(of mind)* perturbati·o -onis *f*; *(med)* mal·um -i *n*; *(pol)* tumult·us -ūs *m*

disordered *adj* turbat·us -a -um; *(of mind or body)* aegrot·us -a -um

disorderly *adj* inordinat·us -a -um; *(of troops)* effus·us -a -um; *(unruly)* turbulent·us -a -um

disorganization *s* dissoluti·o -onis *f*

disorganize *tr* conturbare

disorganized *adj* dissolut·us -a -um

disown *tr (statement)* infitiari; *(heir)* abdicare; *(thing)* repudiare

disparage *tr* obtrectare

disparagement *s* obtrectati·o -onis *f*

disparaging *adj* obtrect·ans -antis

disparity *s* discrepanti·a -ae *f*

dispassionate *adj* frigid·us -a -um

dispassionately *adv* frigide

dispatch *tr* mittere; *(to finish)* perficere; *(to kill)* interficere

dispel *tr* dispellere, depellere

dispensary *s* medicamentaria tabern·a -ae *f*

dispensation *s* distributi·o -onis *f*; *(exemption)* immunit·as -atis *f*

dispense *tr* distribuere; *(to release)* solvere ‖ *intr* **to — with** remittere

dispenser *s* dispensa·tor -toris *m* (·trix -tricis *f*)

disperse *tr* dispergere, dissipare ‖ *intr* diffugere; *(gradually)* dilabi

dispersion *s* dispersi·o -onis *f*

dispirited *adj* animo fract·us -a -um

displace *tr* summovēre; **—ed person** profug·us -i *m*, profug·a -ae *f*

displacement *s* amoti·o -onis *f*

display *s (exhibit)* ostent·us -ūs *m*; *(ostentation)* ostentati·o -onis *f*

display *tr* ostendere; *(to show off)* ostentare

displease *tr* displicēre *(w. dat)*

displeased *adj* offens·us -a -um; **to be — at** aegre ferre

displeasing *adj* ingrat·us -a -um

displeasure *s* offens·a -ae *f*

disposable *adj* in promptu

disposal *s* dispositi·o -onis *f;* **at your —** penes te

dispose *tr* disponere, ordinare; *(to incline)* inclinare ‖ *intr* **to — of** *(to settle)* componere; *(to sell)* abalienare; *(to get rid of)* tollere

disposed *adj* inclinat·us -a -um; *(pej)* pron·us -a -um

disposition *s* *(character)* indol·es -is *f;* *(arrangement)* dispositi·o -onis *f;*

dispossess *tr (of)* pellere *(w. abl)*

disproportion *s* inconcinnit·as -atis *f*

disproportionate *adj* inaequal·is -is -e

disproportionately *adv* inaequaliter

disprove *tr* refellere, redarguere

disputable *adj* disputabil·is -is -e

dispute *s* *(debate)* disputati·o -onis *f;* *(argument)* altercati·o -onis *f;* **beyond —** indisputabil·is -is -e; **that is a matter of —** id disputari potest

dispute *tr & intr* disputare

disputed *adj* controvers·us -a -um

disqualify *tr* excipere; **to — s.o. from** aliquem excipere ex *(w. abl) or* ne *or* quominus

disquiet *tr* inquietare

disquieted *adj* inquiet·us -a -um

disregard *s* *(for)* incuri·a -ae *f (w. gen),* neglegenti·a -ae *f (w. gen)*

disregard *tr* neglegere, omittere

disreputable *adj* infam·is -is -e

disrepute *s* infami·a -ae *f*

disrespect *s* neglegenti·a -ae *f*

disrespectful *adj* **(toward)** negleg·ens -entis (in *w. acc*)

disrespectfully *adv* parum honorifice

disrupt *tr* disturbare

disruption *s* discid·ium -(i)i *n*

dissatisfaction *s* displicenti·a -ae *f*

dissatisfied *adj* parum content·us -a -um

dissatisfy *tr* male satisfacere *(w. dat)*

dissect *tr* insecare

dissection *s* incisi·o -onis *f*

dissemble *tr & intr* dissimulare

disseminate *tr* disseminare

dissension *s* dissensi·o -onis *f*

dissent *s* dissensi·o -onis *f*

dissent *intr* dissentire

dissertation *s* commentati·o -onis *f*

dissimilar *adj* dissimil·is -is -e

dissimiliarity *s* dissimilitud·o -inis *f*

dissipate *tr* dissipare ‖ *intr* dissipari

dissipation *s* dissipati·o -onis *f*

dissolute *adj* dissolut·us -a -um

dissolution *s* dissoluti·o -onis *f*

dissolve *tr* dissolvere; *(to melt)* liquefacere; *(meeting)* dimittere ‖ *intr* liquescere; *(to break up)* dissolvi

dissonance *s* dissonanti·a -ae *f*

dissuade *tr* dissuadēre *(w. dat)*

distance *s* distanti·a -ae *f,* spat·ium -(i)i *n;* *(long way)* longinquit·as -atis *f;* **at a —** procul, longe

distant *adj* dist·ans -antis; *(remote)* longinqu·us -a -um; *(fig)* parum familiar·is -is -e; **to be — from** abesse *or* distare ab *(w. abl)*

distaste *s* **(for)** fastid·ium -(i)i *n (w. gen)*

distasteful *adj (of food)* tet·er -ra -rum; *(fig)* odios·us -a -um

distend *tr* distendere; *(sails)* tendere

distil *tr & intr* stillare, destillare

distinct *adj (different)* divers·us -a -um; *(clear)* distinct·us -a -um

distinction *s* *(act of distinguishing)* distincti·o -onis *f;* *(the thing distinguished)* discrim·en -inis *n;* *(mark, badge)* insign·e -is *n;* *(honor)* hon·or -oris *m;* *(status)* amplitud·o -inis *f;* *(decoration)* praem·ium -(i)i *n;* **a man of —** vir -i *m* illustris; **without —** promiscue

distinctive *adj* propri·us -a -um

distinguish *tr* distinguere, discernere; **to — oneself** enitēre

distinguishable *adj* spectand·us -a -um

distinguished *adj* insign·is -is -e; *(of high rank)* ampl·us -a -um; **to be —** cnitēre

distort *tr* distorquēre; *(words)* detorquēre; *(to misinterpret)* male interpretari

distortion *s* distorti·o -onis *f;* *(fig)* depravati·o -onis *f*

distract *tr* distrahere, vocare

distracted *adj* distract·us -a -um; *(distraught)* vecor·s -dis

distraction *s* *(cause)* avocament·um -i *n;* *(state)* distracti·o -onis *f* animi; *(w. verbs of loving, etc.)* **to —** efflictim

distraught *adj* vecor·s -dis

distress *s* miseri·a -ae *f,* dol·or -oris *m;* *(difficulty)* angusti·ae -arum *fpl*

distress *tr* angere, afflictare

distressed *adj* sollicit·us -a -um

distressing *adj* importun·us -a -um

distribute *tr* distribuere

distributer *s* distribu·tor -toris *m* (·trix -tricis *f*)

distribution *s* distributi·o -onis *f*

district *s* *(esp. in a city)* regi·o -onis *f;* *(an extent of country)* tract·us -ūs *m*

distrust *s* **(of)** diffidenti·a -ae *f (w. gen)*

distrust *tr* diffidere *(w. dat)*

distrustful *adj* **(of)** diffid·ens -entis *(w. dat)*

distrustfully *adv* diffidenter

disturb *tr* perturbare; *(to render anxious)* sollicitare; *(to upset)* commovēre; *(s.o.'s sleep)* inquietare

disturbance *s* perturbati·o -onis *f;* *(pol)* tumult·us -ūs *m*

disturber *s* — **of the peace** turba·tor -toris *m* (·trix -tricis *f*) oti

disuse *s* desuetud·o -inis *f*

ditch *s* foss·a -ae *f*

ditty *s* cantilen·a -ae *f*

divan *s* lectul·us -i *m*

dive *s* (*of a swimmer*) salt·us -ūs *m;* (*coll*) popin·a -ae *f*

dive *intr* praeceps desilire; (*e.g. of a submarine*) urinari

diver *s* urina·tor -toris *m* (·trix -tricis *f*)

diverge *intr* deflectere, declinare; (*of view*) discrepare

diverse *adj* divers·us -a -um

diversification *s* variati·o -onis *f*

diversify *tr* variare

diversion *s* (*recreation*) oblectament·um -i *n;* (*of a river*) derivati·o -onis *f;* (*pastime*) avocati·o -onis *f*

diversity *s* diversit·as -atis *f*

divert *tr* (*rivers*) avertere, divertere; (*attention*) avocare; **to — s.o.'s anger and turn it on oneself** iram alicuius in se derivare

divest *tr* exuere, nudare; **to — oneself of** exuere, ponere

divide *tr* dividere; (*to distribute*) partiri; **to — the year into 12 months** annum in duodecim menses discribere **‖** *intr* se scindere

divination *s* divinati·o -onis *f*

divine *adj* divin·us -a -um

divine *tr* divinare; (*to guess*) conicere

divinely *adv* divinitus

diviner *s* aug·ur -uris *m,* harusp·ex -icis *m*

diving board *s* tabul·a -ae *f* desultoria

divinity *s* divinit·as -atis *f;* (*god*) num·en -inis *n*

divisible *adj* dividu·us -a -um

division *s* divisi·o -onis *f;* (*part*) par·s -tis *f;* (*mil*) legi·o -onis *f;* — **of opinion** dissensi·o -onis *f*

divorce *s* divort·ium -(i)i *n*

divorce *tr* divortium facere cum (*w. abl*)

divulge *tr* vulgare, divulgare

dizziness *s* vertig·o -inis *f*

dizzy *adj* vertiginos·us -a -um

do *tr* agere, facere; (*to carry out, succeed in doing*) efficere; **to — a hitch in the army** stipendia facere; **to — a kindness** beneficium facere; **to — one's best to** (*w. inf*) operam dare ut (*w. subj*); **to — s.o. in** aliquem pessum dare; **to have enough to —** satagere; **what am I to —?** quid faciam?; **what have I to — with you?** quid mihi et tibi est? **‖** *intr* agere; (*for emphatic auxiliary, use* vero: **I — wish to go** cupio vero ire); (*when* **I —.** *is used to answer a question, repeat the verb in the question:* **— you believe? I —.** credisne? credo.); **how — you —?** quid agis?; **it will — you (a lot of, no) good** (multum, nihil)

proderit tibi; **it won't — to** non satis est (*w. inf*); **that'll —!** satis est!; **to — away with** tollere, perdere; **to — well** (*to make out well*) recte facere; (*to have good health*) bene valēre; **to — without** carēre (*w. abl*); **what's doing?** quid agitur?; **will this —?** satin(e) est?

docile *adj* docil·is -is -e, tractabil·is -is -e

dock *s* naval·e -is *n;* (*leg*) cancell·i -orum *mpl*

docket *s* memnisc·us -i *m*

dockyard *s* naval·ia -ium *npl*

doctor *s* medic·us -i *m* (·a -ae *f*); (*academic title*) doc·tor -toris *m* (·trix -tricis *f*)

doctorate *s* doctoris grad·us -ūs *m*

doctrine *s* doctrin·a -ae *f,* dogm·a -atis *n*

document *s* instrument·um -i *n*

documentary *s* documentar·ium -(i)i *n*

dodge *s* dol·us -i *m*

dodge *tr* eludere; (*to shift aside and so avoid*) declinare; **to — the draft** sacramentum detrectare

doe *s* cerv·a -ae *f*

dog *s* can·is -is *mf;* **to go to the —s** (*coll*) pessum ire

dogged *adj* pervic·ax -acis

doggedness *s* pervicaci·a -ae *f*

doggerel *s* inepti versicul·i -orum *mpl*

dog house, dog kennel *s* canis cubil·e -is *n*

dogma *s* dogm·a -atis *n*

dogmatic *adj* dogmatic·us -a -um; (*pej*) arrog·ans -antis

dogmatism *s* arroganti·a -ae *f*

dog star *s* canicul·a -ae *f,* Siri·us -i *m*

doing *s* facin·us -eris *n;* **what's —?** quid agitur?

dole *s* sportul·a -ae *f*

dole *tr* **to — out** parce dare

doleful *adj* lugubr·is -is -e

dolefully *adv* maeste

doll *s* pup·a -ae *f*

dollar *s* dollar·us -i *m*

dolphin *s* delphin·us -i *m*

dolt *s* caud·ex -icis *m*

domain *s* (*kingdom*) regn·um -i *n;* **public —** ag·er -ri *m* publicus

dome *s* thol·us -i *m*

domestic *adj* domestic·us -a -um

domestic *s* famul·us -i *m,* famul·a -ae *f*

domesticate *tr* domare

domicile *s* domicil·ium -(i)i *n*

dominant *adj* praeval·ens -entis; **to be —** auctoritate pollēre; **to become —** potent·ior -ior -ius fieri

dominate *intr* (**over**) dominari (in *w. acc*)

domination *s* domin·ium -(i)i *n*

domineer *intr* dominari

domineering *adj* imperios·us -a -um

dominion *s* imper·ium -(i)i *n*

don *tr* induere

donation *s* donati·o -onis *f*
done *adj* I'm — for! nullus sum! *or* perii!; have — with fear! omitte timorem!; no sooner said than — dictum factum; well done! macte virtute!
donkey *s* asin·us -i *m*, asell·us -i *m*
donor *s* dona·tor -toris *m*, dona·trix -tricis *f*
doom *s* fat·um -i *n*
doom *tr* damnare
door *s* ianu·a -ae *f*, ost·ium -(i)i *n*; *(double doors)* for·es -ium *fpl*; *(folding doors)* valv·ae -arum *fpl*; **back** — postic·um -i *n*; **from** — **to** —— ostiatim; **out of doors** *(position)* foris; *(direction)* foras; **there's the** — *(turning a person out)* exeundum hinc foras
doorbell ostii tintinabul·um -i *n*; **the** — **is ringing** ostii tintinabulum tinnit; **to ring the** — pulsabulum comprimere
doorkeeper *s* ostiar·ius -(i)i *m*
doorknob *s* ianuae manubr·ium -(i)i *n*
doorpost *s* post·is -is *m*
doorstep *s* lim·en -inis *n*
doorway *s* ost·ium -(i)i *n*
Doric *adj* Doric·us -a -um
dormant *adj* res·es -idis; *(hidden)* lat·ens -entis; **to lie** — iacēre
dormitory *s* dormitor·ium -(i)i *n*
dorsal *adj* dorsal·is -is -e; — finn·a -ae *f* dorsalis
dose *s* porti·o -onis *f*; **small** — portiuncul·a -ae *f*
dot *s* punct·um -i *n*
dot *tr* punctum imponere *(w. dat)*
dotage *s* sen·ium -(i)i *n*
dote *tr* **to** — **on** deamare
doting *adj* deam·ans -antis
double *adj* dupl·ex -icis; *(of pairs)* gemin·us -a -um; *(as much again)* dupl·us -a -um; *(meaning)* ambigu·us -a -um; — **"i" as in "armarii"** i littera gemminata, ut armarii
double *s* dupl·um -i *n*; —**s** *(in tennis)* lud·us -i *m* bis binorum; **on the** — curriculo
double *tr* duplicare; *(a cape)* praetervehi ‖ *intr* duplicari
double-dealing *s* frau·s -dis *f*
double-dealing *adj* versut·us -a -um
double-edged *adj* bipenn·is -is -e
double home *s* dom·us -ūs *f* duplex
double room *s* cubicul·um -i *n* duorum lectorum
double-talk *s* simulati·o -onis *f* et fallaci·a -ae *f*
doubly *adv* dupliciter
doubt *s* dub·ium -(i)i *n*; *(distrust)* suspici·o -onis *f*; **there is no** — **that** non dubium est quin *(w. subj)*; **without** — sine dubio
doubt *tr* dubitare *(w. acc of neuter pronoun only; otherwise use* de *w. abl)*; **I do not** — **that** non dubito quin *(w. subj)*

doubtful *adj* *(of persons)* dubi·us -a -um; *(of things)* incert·us -a - um, anc·eps -ipitis
doubtfully *adv* dubie; *(hesitatingly)* dubitanter
doubtless *adv* haud dubie, sine dubio
dough *s* farin·a -ae *f* ex aquā subacta
douse *tr* *(to put out)* exstinguere; *(to drench)* madefacere
dove *s* columb·us -i *m* (·a -ae *f*)
down *s* plum·a -ae *f*; *(of hair)* lanug·o -inis *f*; *(of plants)* papp·us -i *m*
down *adv* deorsum; *(often expressed by the prefix* de-: **to flow** — defluere); **to pay money** — repraesentare pecuniam; **to run** — decurrere; — **from** de *(w. abl)*; — **to** usque ad *(w. acc)*
down *prep* de *(w. abl)*
down *adj* decliv·is -is -e; *(depressed)* demiss·us -a -um; *(financially)* ad inopiam redact·us -a -um; **to feel** — **and out** infractum animum gerere **to hit a man when he is** — iacentem ferire
downcast *adj* *(in low spirits)* demiss·us -a -um; **with** — **eyes** deiectis in terram oculis
downfall *s* occas·us -ūs *m*
downgrade *tr* in ordinem redigere
downhearted *adj* animo fract·us -a -um
downhill *adj* decliv·is -is -e, pron·us -a -um; **it was all** — **after that** proclivia omnia erant postilla; **the last part of the road is** — ultima via est prona
downhill *adv* per declive; **as his business went** — inclinatis rebus suis
download *tr* *(comput)* ex rete prehendere, ex rete expromere
downpour *s* im·ber -bris *m* maximus
down pat *adv* **you have the whole thing** — ordine omnem rem tenes
down payment *s* arrab·o -onis *f*; **to make a** — **of $100** centum dollaros arraboni dare
downright *adj* direct·us -a -um; *(unmixed)* mer·us -a -um
downright *adv* prorsus, plane
downstairs *adv* *(direction)* deorsum; *(position)* in imo tabulato; **to go** — per scalas descendere
downstream *adv* secundo flumine
downward *adj* decliv·us -a -um, pron·us -a -um
downwards *adv* deorsum
downy *adj* plume·us -a -um
dowry *s* do·s -tis *f*
doze *intr* dormitare; **to** — **off** in somnium delabi
dozen *adj & pron* duodecim *(indecl)*
drab *adj* cinere·us -a -um
draft *s* *(drink)* haust·us -ūs *m*; *(mil)* dilect·us -ūs *m*; *(breeze)* aur·a -ae *f*; *(first copy)* exempl·ar -aris *n*; *(money)* syngraph·a -ae *f*; *(of*

net) iact·us -ūs *m; (of ship)* immersi·o -onis *f;* **to hold a —** *(mil)* dilectum habēre

draft *tr (mil)* conscribere

draft-dodger *s* qui militiam subterfugit

drag *s (fig)* impediment·um -i *n;* **to be a — on s. o.** aliquem retardare

drag *tr* trahere; *(w. suddenness or violence)* rapere; **to — away** abstrahere; **to — down** detrahere; **to — out** protrahere **‖** *intr* trahi; **to — on** protrahi

dragnet *s* tragul·a -ae *f*

dragon *s* drac·o -onis *m*

drain *s* cloac·a -ae *f; (loss)* defecti·o -onis *f*

drain *tr (marshland)* siccare; *(a cup, the treasury, strength)* exhaurire

drainage *s* exsiccati·o -onis *f*

drainage ditch *s* incil·e -is *n*

drainpipe *s* canal·is -is *m*

drama *s (single play)* fabul·a -ae *f; (genre)* dram·a -atis *n*

dramatic *adj* scaenic·us -a -um; *(fig)* animum mov·ens -entis

dramatics *s* histrioni·a -ae *f*

dramatist *s* poet·a -ae *m* scaenicus

dramatize *tr* ad scaenam componere

drape *s* aulae·um -i *n*

drape *tr (to wrap)* amicire; *(to cover)* velare

drapery *s* aulae·a -orum *npl*

drastic *adj* ultim·us -a -um; severissim·us -a -um

draw *tr (to pull)* trahere; *(a picture)* delineare; *(a line)* ducere; *(inference)* colligere; *(bow)* adducere; *(sword)* educere; *(water)* haurire; *(breath)* ducere; *(geometrical figures)* describere; **to — aside** seducere; **to — apart** diducere; **to — away** avertere; **to — back** retrahere; **to — blood** cruorem ducere; **to — off** detrahere, abducere; *(wine)* depromere; **to — out** extrahere; *(fig)* elicere; **to — the conclusion** colligere; **to — together** contrahere; **to — up** subducere; *(to write)* componere; *(mil)* instituere **‖** *intr* **to — back** pedem referre; *(fig)* recedere; **to — near** appropinquare; **to — up to** *(of ships)* appetere

drawback *s* impediment·um -i *n*

drawbridge *s* pon·s -tis *m* versatilis

drawer *s* locul·us -i *m*

drawing *s* pictur·a -ae *f* linearis

drawl *s* lentior pronuntiati·o -onis *f*

drawl *intr* voces lentius pronuntiando trahere

dread *s* formid·o -inis *f*

dread *tr* formidare

dread *adj* dir·us -a -um

dreadful *adj* terribil·is -is -e

dreadfully *adv* horrendum in modum

dream *s* somn·ium -(i)i *n;* **in a —** in somnio

dream *tr & intr* somniare; **to — about** somniare de *(w. abl)*

dreamer *s (fig)* nuga·tor -toris *m* (·trix -tricis *f)*

dreamy *adj* somniculos·us -a -um

drearily *adv* triste

dreary *adj (place)* vast·us -a -um; *(person)* trist·is -is -e

dredge *tr* machinā alveum *(w. gen)* perfodere

dregs *spl* fae·x -cis *f; (fig)* sentin·a -ae *f*

drench *tr* madefacere

dress *s* vest·is -is *f* muliebris; *(ankle-length)* vestis talaris; *(Roman)* stol·a -ae *f*

dress *tr* vestire, induere; *(to deck out)* exornare; *(wounds)* curare; *(the hair)* comere; **—ed in a (fancy) coat** subornat·us -a -um aliculā; **—ed in white** amict·us -a -um veste albā; **to — down** *(to chew out)* pilare; **to get —ed** amiciri; *(in fancy clothes)* se exornare **‖** *intr* se induere; **to — up** se exornare

dresser *s* vestiar·ium -(i)i *n*

dressing *s* ornati·o -onis *f; (stuffing)* fart·um -i *n; (med)* foment·um -i *n; (on salad)* embamm·a -atis *n;* **Caesar (Blue Cheese, French, Italian, Russian, Thousand Island) —** embamma Caesarianum (Casei Caerulei, Gallicum, Italicum, Russicum, Mille Insularum)

dressing room *s (at a bath)* apodyter·ium -(i)i *n*

dressing table *s* mens·a -ae *f* comatoria

dressmaker *s* vestific·a -ae *f*

dress shoes *spl* socc·i -orum *mpl; (for women, of different colors)* soccul·i -orum *mpl*

dribble *tr (basketball)* repercutitare **‖** *intr* stillare

dribbling *s (basketball)* repercuti·o -onis *f*

drift *s (intent)* proposit·um -i *n*

drift *intr* fluitare

drifter *s* larifug·a -ae *mf*

drill *s (tool)* terebr·a -ae *f; (mil)* exercitati·o -onis *f; (school)* exercit·ium -(i) *n*

drill *tr (to bore)* terebrare; *(mil)* exercēre; *(students)* instituere

drink *tr* bibere, potare; **to — in** *(fig)* haurire; **to — up** epotare **‖** *intr* bibere; **to — to** propinare *(w. dat)*

drink *s* pot·us -ūs *m,* poti·o -onis *f*

drinkable *adj* potabil·is -is -e

drinker *s* po·tor -toris *m* (·trix -tricis *f); (habitual)* potat·or -oris *m*

drinking *s* poti·o -onis *f*

drinking *adj* bibos·us -a -um

drinking cup *s* scyph·us -i *m*

drinking straw *s* siph·o -onis *m*

drip *s* stillicid·ium -(i)i *n*

drip *intr* destillare

drive *tr* agere, pellere; *(to force)* compellere; *(a vehicle)* agitare, gubernare; *(to convey)* vehere; **to — away** abigere; *(fig)* depellere; *(in confusion)* deturbare; **to — back** repellere; **to — home** *(in a car)* domum autoraedā adducere; *(fig)* animo infigere; **to**

— in *(sheep, etc.)* cogere; *(nails)* infigere; **to — mad** dementem facere; **to — off** abigere; **to — on** impellere; **to — out** expellere; **to — out of one's mind** infuriare; **to — up** subigere ‖ *intr (in a carriage)* vehi; **to — off** *(in a carriage)* avehi; **to — on** *or* **past** praetervehi

drive *s (in carriage)* vectur·a -ae *f; (energy)* vis *f,* impigrit·as -atis *f*

drivel *s* saliv·a -ae *f; (fig)* inepti·ae -arum *fpl*

drivel *intr (fig)* delirare

driver *s* raedari·us -i *m* (·a -ae *f); agita·tor -toris *m* (·trix -tricis *f); (of a chariot)* aurig·a -ae *m*

driver's license *s* raedarii diplom·a -atis *n*

drizzle *s* pluvi·a -ae *f* rara et minuta

drizzle *intr* leniter pluere

drone *s (bee)* fuc·us -i *m; (buzz)* bomb·us -i *m; (person)* cessat·or -oris *m*

drone *intr* murmurrare

droop *tr* demittere ‖ *intr* languēre

drooping *adj* languid·us -a -um

drop *s* gutt·a -ae *f; (a drop as falling)* still·a -ae *f, (fall)* cas·us -ūs *m,* laps·us -ūs *m; (decrease)* deminuti·o -onis *f; (a little bit)* paulul·um -i *n;* **— by — by** stillatim

drop *tr (purposely)* demittere, deicere; *(to let slip)* omittere; *(to lay low)* sternere; *(a hint)* emittere; *(anchor)* iacere; *(work)* desistere ab *(w. abl);* **— it!** *(no more of that)* missa istaec fac!; **let's — the subject** missa haec faciamus ‖ *intr (to lessen)* cadere, concidere; *(to trickle)* (de)stillare; *(to fall)* decidere; *(esp. from the sky)* delabi, decidere; **to — behind** cessare; **to — down** decidere; **to — in on** visere; **to — off to sleep** obdormiscere; **to — out of** excidere de *(w. abl)*

drop-out *s* desti·tor -toris *m* (·trix -tricis *f)* de scholā

droppings *spl* merd·ae -arum *fpl*

drought *s* siccit·as -atis *f*

drove *s* gre·x -gis *m*

drown *tr* demergere; *(fig)* opprimere; **to — out** obscurare ‖ *intr* submergi

drowsily *adv* somniculose

drowsy *adj* somniculos·us -a -um

drub *tr* pulsare, verberare

drudge *s (slave)* mediastin·us -i *m* (·a -ae *f)*

drudgery *s* oper·a -ae *f* servilis

drug *s* medicam·en -inis *n; (narcotic)* medicament·um -i *n* psychotropicum

drug addict *s* medicamentis psychotropicis dedit·us -i *m* (·a -ae *f)*

druggist *s* medicamentar·ius -(i)i *m* (·ia -iae *f)*

drugstore *s* medicamentari·a -ae *f*

Druids *spl* Druid·ae -arum *mpl*

drum *s* tympan·um -i *n;* **to play the —** tympanum pulsare

drum *tr* **to — up** exquirere ‖ *intr* tympanum pulsare; **to — on the table** mensam digitis pulsare

drummer *s* tympanist·a -ae *m* (·ria -riae *f)*

drunk *adj* ebri·us -a -um; *(habitually)* ebrios·us -a -um

drunk, drunkard *s* ebrios·us -i *m* (·a -ae *f)*

drunken *adj* ebri·us -a -um

drunkenness *s* ebriet·as -atis *f; (habitual)* ebriosit·as -atis *f*

dry *adj* arid·us -a -um, sicc·us -a -um; *(thirsty)* sicc·us -a -um; *(wine)* auster·us -a -um; *(boring)* ieiun·us -a -um

dry *tr* siccare; **to — out** exsiccare; **to — up** arefacere ‖ *intr* arescere

dryad *s* dry·as -adis *f*

dry cleaner *s* full·o -onis *m; (shop)* fullonic·a -ae *f*

drydock *s* siccum naval·e -is *n*

dryer *s (for hair)* instrument·um -i *n* siccatori·um; *(for clothes)* machin·a -ae *f* siccatoria

dry land *s* arid·um -i *n*

dryness *s* siccit·as -atis *f*

dry run *s* simulacr·um -i *n*

dual *adj* dual·is -is -e

dub *tr* appellare

dubious *adj* dubi·us -a -um; *(shady)* anc·eps -ipitis

duck *s* an·as -atis *f; (as food)* anatin·a -ae *f;* **—s quack** anates tetrinniunt

duck *tr (in the water)* deprimere; **to — the issue** rem evitare ‖ *intr* se inclinare

duckling *s* anaticul·a -ae *f*

duct *s* tub·us -i *m*

due *adj (owed)* debit·us -a -um; *(merited)* merit·us -a -um, iust·us -a -um; **— honors** meriti honor·es -um *mpl;* **— to** propter *(w. acc),* causā *(w. gen);* **to be — to** fieri ab *(w. abl);* **to fall — on the fifth day** in quintum diem cadere

due *s* debit·um -i *n;* **—s** stipendi·a -orum *npl;* **to give everyone his —** suum cuique tribuere

due *adv* rectā; **— east** rectā ad orientem

duel *s* singulare certam·en -inis *n*

duel *intr* viritim pugnare

duet *s* bicin·ium -(i)i *n*

duffel bag *s* sarcinul·a -ae *f*

duke *s* du·x -cis *m*

dull *adj* heb·es -itis; *(mind)* tard·us -a -um; *(uninteresting)* frigid·us -a -um

dull *tr* hebetare

dullness *s (of minds)* tardit·as -atis *f*

duly *adv* rite, recte

dumb *adj* mut·us -a -um; *(fig)* stupid·us -a -um

dumbfounded *adj* obstupefact·us -a -um; *(speechless)* elingu·is -is -e

dummy *s* effigi·es ei *f; (stupid person)* bar·o -onis *m*

dumpling *s* farinae subactae globul·us -i *m*

dumpy *adj* brev·is -is -e et obes·us -a -um
dunce *s* bar·o -onis *m*
dung *s* sterc·us -oris *n; (of birds)* merd·ae -arum *fpl*
dungeon *s* rob·ur -oris *n*
dupe *tr* decipere
duplicate *adj* dupl·ex -icis
duplicate *s* exempl·ar -aris *n*
duplicate *tr* duplicare
duplicity *s* duplicit·as -atis *f*
durability *s* firmit·as -atis *f*
durable *adj* durabil·is -is -e
duration *s (period of time itself)* spat·ium -(i)i *n; (lastingness)* diurnit·as -atis *f;* **of long —** diuturn·us -a -um; **of short —** brev·is -is -e
during *prep* inter *(w. acc)*, per *(w. acc)*
dusk *s* crepuscul·um -i *n*
dusky *adj* fusc·us -a -um
dust *s* pulv·is -eris *m*
dust *tr* detergēre
dustpan *s* vatill·um -i *n*
dusty *adj* pulverulent·us -a -um
dutiful *adj* pi·us -a -um, officios·us -a -um
duty *s (social or moral)* offic·ium -(i)i *n; (task)* mun·us -eris *n; (tax)* portor·ium -(i)i *n;* **to be on —** *(mil)* stationem agere; **when I do my —** *(coll)* cum mea facio
DVD *s* digitalis discul·us -i *m* magnetoscopi-cus
dwarf *s* pumili·o -onis *mf*
dwarfish *adj* pumil·us -a -um
dwell *intr* habitare; **to — upon** commorari in *(w. abl)*
dweller *s* incol·a -ae *mf*
dwelling place *s* sed·es -is *f*
dwindle *intr* imminui, decrescere
dye *s* tinctur·a -ae *f*
dye *tr* ting(u)ere, inficere
dying *adj* moribund·us -a -um; **I am — to know** valde aveo scire
dynamic *adj (fig)* vehem·ens -entis
dynamics *spl* dynamic·a -ae *f*
dynasty *s* dom·us -ūs *f* regnatrix; **under the Flavian —** potiente rerum Flaviā domu
dysentery *s* dysenteri·a -ae *f*
dyspepsia *s* dyspepsi·a -ae *f*

E

each *adj & pron* quisque, quidque; *(of two)* uterque, utraque utrumque; *(individually)* singul·i -ae -a; **— and every** unusquisque, unaquaeque, unumquodque; **— day** cotidie; **— other** inter se, invicem; **he stationed one legion — in Brundisium, Tarentum, and Sepontum** legiones singulas posuit Brindisi, Tarenti, Seponti
eager *adj* **(for)** cupid·us -a -um *(w. gen)*, avid·us -a -um *(w. gen)*, studios·us -a -um *(w. gen)*
eagerly *adv* cupide, avide
eagerness *s* avidit·as -atis *f*
eagle *s* aquil·a -ae *f;* **—s screech** aquilae strident
ear *s* aur·is -is *f; (outer ear)* auricul·a -ae *f; (of corn)* spic·a -ae *f;* **to give an — to** aurem praebēre *(w. dat)*
earache *s* auris dol·or -oris *m;* **to have an —** ab aure laborare
earl *s* com·es -itis *m*
earlobe *s* lann·a -ae *f* auris
early *adj (in the morning)* matutin·us -a -um; *(coming naturally early)* matur·us -a -um; *(before its time)* praematur·us -a -um, praec·ox -ocis; *(of early date)* antiqu·us -a -um; *(beginning)* prim·us -a -um; **from — youth** a primā adolescentiā; **in — spring** primo vere; **in — times** antiquitus
early *adv (in the morning)* (bene) mane; *(too soon)* praemature; *(in good time)* mature; **as — as possible** quam maturrime; **— enough** satis temperi; **— in life** ab ineunte aetate **— in the morning** bene mane; **his father died —** pater eius decessit mature
earmark *tr* destinare
earn *tr* merēre, merēri; **to — a living** quaestum facere
earnest *adj (eager)* intent·us -a -um; *(serious)* seri·us -a -um; **— money** arrab·o -onis *m*
earnest *s* **in —** ex bonā fide, serio
earnestly *adv* intente, valde
earnestness *s* gravit·as -atis *f*
earnings *spl* quaest·us -ūs *m*
earrings *spl* inaur·es -ium *fpl; (of several pearls)* crotali·a -orum *npl*
earth *s (land)* terr·a -ae *f; (planet)* tell·us -uris *f; (globe)* orb·is -is *m* terrarum; **of —, made of —** terren·us -a -um, terre·us -a -um; **why on —** quidnam
earthen *adj* terren·us -a -um; *(pottery)* fictil·is -is -e
earthenware *s* fictil·ia -ium *npl*
earthly *adj (made of earth)* terren·us -a -um; *(opposed to heavenly)* terrestr·is -is -e; **for what — reason** quare tandem
earthquake *s* terrae mot·us -ūs *m*
earthy *adj (humor)* terren·us -a -um
earthworm *s* lubric·us -i *m*
ease *s (leisure)* ot·ium -(i)i *n; (easiness)* facilit·as -atis *f;* **at one's —** otios·us -a -um; **to live in —** in otio vivere; **to set s.o.'s mind at —** alicuius animum tranquillum reddere; **to speak with —** solute loqui
ease *tr* levare, laxare; *(to assuage)* mitigare

easily *adv* facile

east *adj* oriental·is -is -e

east *s* ori·ens -entis *m;* **from — to west** ab oriente ad occidentem; **on the —** ab oriente; **to sail —** ad *or* in orientem navigare; **to the —** in orientem versus [*versus is an adverb*]

Easter *s* Pasch·a -ae *f,* Pasch·a -atis *n*

Easter *adj* Paschal·is -is -e

easterly *adj* oriental·is -is -e

eastern *adj* oriental·is -is -e

Eastertime *s* temp·us -oris *n* Paschale

eastward *adv* ad orientem

east wind *s* Eur·us -i *m*

easy *adj* facil·is -is -e; *(graceful)* lepid·us -a -um; *(without obstacles, e.g., a road)* expedit·us -a -um; *(life)* otios·us -a -um; **— to understand** intellectu facil·is -is -e; **take it —!** *(farewell)* i *(or* ambula otiose!; **to take it — otiari**

easy chair *s* arcisell·ium -(i)i *n* tomento fartum

easy-going *adj* secur·us -a -um, facil·is -is -e

eat *tr* edō edere *or* ēsse; *(to live on)* vesci *(w. abl);* **to — away** corrodere; **to — breakfast** ientare, ientaculum sumere; **to — dinner** cenare; **to — lunch** prandēre; **to — up** comēsse ‖ *intr* ēsse, cenare; **to — and drink** cibum et potionem adsumere; **to — out** foris cenare

eatable *adj* esculent·us -a -um

eating *s* es·us -ūs *m*

eaves *spl* suggrund·a -ae *f*

eavesdrop *intr* subauscultare; **— on** subauscultare

eavesdropper *s* auc·eps -ipis *mf*

ebb *s* recess·us -ūs *m;* **— and flow** aestūs recess·us -ūs *m* et access·us -ūs *m;* **to be at a low —** *(fig)* iacēre

ebb *intr* recedere, refluere; *(fig)* decrescere

ebony *s* eben·um -i *n*

ebony *adj* ebenin·us -a -um

eccentric *adj* abnorm·is -is -e

ecclesiastic *adj* ecclesiastic·us -a -um

echo *s* repercuss·us -ūs *m,* ech·o -us *f; (poet)* imag·o -inis *f*

echo *tr* repercutere; *(to repeat what s.o. has said)* subsequi; **to — a sound** sonum referre ‖ *vi* resonare

echoing *adj* reson·us -a -um

eclectic *adj* eclectic·us -a -um

eclipse *s* defecti·o -onis *f*

eclipse *tr* obscurare

eclogue *s* eclog·a -ae *f*

economic *adj* economic·us -a -um, ad opes publicas pertin·ens -entis

economical *adj* frugi *(indecl),* parc·us -a -um

economically *adv* parce

economics *s* publicarum opum scienti·a -ae *f*

economist *s* qui *or* quae rei publicae opes exponit

economize *intr* **(on)** parcere *(w. dat); (of the state)* publicos sumptūs minuere

economy *s* frugalit·as -atis *f;* **public —** publicarum opum administrati·o -onis *f*

ecstasy *s* *(trance)* ecstas·is -is *f; (rapture)* elati·o -onis *f* voluptaria; **to be in —** laetitiā gestire

eddy *s* vort·ex -icis *m*

eddy *intr* (in se) volutari

edge *s* *(very often expressed by* extrem·us -a -um *modifying the substantive); (margin)* marg·o -inis *mf; (of knife, etc.)* aci·es -ei *f; (of forest)* or·a -ae *f;* **on —** anxi·us -a -um; **on the —** in praecipiti

edge *tr* *(garment)* practexcrc; *(to sharpen)* acuere ‖ *intr* **to — away** sensim abscedere; **to — closer** sensim appropinquare

edgewise *adv* **to get in a word —** vocem in sermonem insinuare

edging *s* *(fringe)* limb·us -i *m; (gold border)* patag·ium -(i)i *n*

edible *adj* edul·is -is -e

edict *s* edict·um -i *n;* **to issue an —** edictum proponere

edification *s* humanit·as -atis *f*

edifice *s* aedific·ium -(i)i *n*

edify *tr* ad humanitatem excolere

edit *tr* edere; *(to correct)* emendare

edition *s* editi·o -onis *f*

editor *s* edi·tor -toris *m* (·trix -tricis *f)*

educate *tr* erudire, instituere

educated *adj* erudit·us -a -um

education *s* eruditi·o -onis *f*

educational *adj* scholastic·us -a -um; *(teaching)* praeceptiv·us -a -um

educator *s* praecep·tor -toris *m* (·trix -tricis *f)*

eel *s* anguill·a -ae *f*

eerie *adj* prodigios·us -a -um

efface *tr* delēre

effect *s* effect·um -i *n; (show)* iactati·o -onis *f;* **cause and —** caus·a -ae *f* et consecuti·o -onis *f;* **—s** bon·a -orum *npl;* **for mere —** ad iactationem; **in —** reapse; **to go into —** valēre; **to have an —** valēre; *(med)* pollēre; **to have a beneficial — on** prodesse *(w. dat);* **to have a harmful** *or* **negative — on** obesse *(w. dat);* **to put into —** efficacem reddere; **to take —** operari, efficax fieri; **to the same —** in eandem sententiam; **to this —** huiusmodi; **without —** frustra

effect *tr* conficere, efficere

effective *adj* profici·ens -entis, effic·ax -acis, habil·is -is -e

effectively *adv* efficienter; **to speak —** plurimum in dicendo valēre

effectual *adj* effic·ax -acis

effeminate *adj* effeminat·us -a -um

effeminately *adv* effeminate

effete *adj* effet·us -a -um

efficacious *adj* effic·ax -acis
efficaciously *adv* efficaciter
efficacy *s* virt·us -utis *f,* efficacit·as -atis *f*
efficiency *s* efficienti·a -ae *f*
efficient *adj (competent)* habil·is -is -e
efficiently *adv* diligenter, perite
effigy *s* effigi·es -ei *f*
effort *s* nis·us -ūs *m;* to be worth the —
pretium operae esse; to make an — eniti;
with great — enixe
effortless *adj.* facil·is -is -e
effortlessly *adv* sine labore
effrontery *s* os oris *n;* you have the — to *(w. inf)* os tibi inest ut *(w. subj)*
effusion *s* effusi·o -onis *f*
effusive *adj* effus·us -a -um
effusively *adv* effuse
egg *s* ov·um -i *n;* fried —s ova *npl* fricta;
hard-boiled — ovum *n* durum excoctum;
scrambled —s ova *npl* permixta; soft-boiled
— ovum molliter coctum *n;* to lay an —
ovum parere
egg *tr* to — on incitare
egghead *s* hom·o -inis *mf* ingeniosus (-a)
eggplant *s* melongen·a -ae *f*
egg-shaped *adj* oval·is -is -e
eggshell *s* ovi putam·en -inis *n*
egg white *s* ovi alb·um -i *n*
egotism *s* am·or -oris *m* sui
egotist *s* sui ama·tor -toris *m* (·trix -tricis *f)*
egotistical *adj* sibi soli consul·ens -entis
egress *s* egress·us -ūs *m*
egress *intr* egredi
eight *adj* octo [*indecl*]; — times octies
eighteen *adj* duodeviginti [*indecl*]
eighteenth *adj* duodevicesim·us -a -um
eighth *adj* octav·us -a -um
eighth *s* octava par·s -tis *f*
eightieth *adj* octogesim·us -a -um
eighty *adj* octoginta [*indecl*]
either *adj & pron* u·ter -tra -trum
either *conj* — ... or vel ... vel; *(where the alternatives are mutually exclusive)* aut ... aut
eject *tr* eicere
ejection *s* eiecti·o -onis *f*
eke *tr* to — out a livelihood victum aegre parare
elaborate *adj* elaborat·us -a -um, exquisit·us -a -um
elaborate *tr* elaborare ‖ *intr* (on) singillatim loqui (de *w. abl*)
elaboration *s* lim·a -ae *f*
elapse *intr* praeterire, intercedere
elastic *adj* elastic·us -a -um
elasticity *s* elasticit·as -atis *f*
elated *adj* to be — efferri
elation *s* anim·us -i *m* elatus

elbow *s* cubit·um -i *n;* resting on one's — in
cubitum erect·us -a -um; to lean one one's
— cubito inniti; to rub —s with conversari
cum *(w. abl)*
elbow *tr* cubitis pulsare; to — one's way
through the crowd cubitis turbam depulsare
de viā
elbowroom *s* spat·ium -(i)i *n* satis laxum
elder *adj* mai·or -or -us natu
elderberry *s (bush)* sambuc·us -i *f; (berry)*
sambuc·um -i *n;* — wine vin·um -i *n* sambuceum
elderly *adj* aetate provect·ior -ior -ius
eldest *adj* maxim·us -a -um natu
elect *tr* creare, eligere
elect *adj (office)* designat·us -a -um; *(elite)*
lect·us -a -um
elect *npl* the — *(eccl)* elect·i -orum *mpl*
election *s (act of choosing)* electi·o -onis *f;*
—s *(pol)* comiti·a -orum *npl;* to hold —s
comitia habēre
election day *s* di·es -ei *m* comitialis
electioneering *s* ambiti·o -onis *f*
elective *adj (pol)* suffragiis creat·us -a -um; *(of choice)* elegend·us -a -um
elective *s* disciplin·a -ae *f* electa
electoral *adj* suffragatori·us -a -um
electorate *s* suffragator·es -um *mpl*
electric(al) *adj* electric·us -a -um
electrical appliances *spl* electrica instrument·a -orum *npl*
electrical engineer *s* machinat·or -oris *m* electricus
electrical engineering *s* machinati·o -onis *f* electrica
electric bulb *s* globul·us -i *m* electricus
electric chair *s* sell·a -ae *f* electrica interficiendi
electric cord *s* funicul·us -i *m* electricus
electric current *s* fluent·um -i *n* electricum
electric fan *s* machin·a -ae *f* ventigena
electrician *s* electridis opif·ex -icis *mf*
electricity *s* vis *f* electrica, electr·is -idis *f*
electric light lum·en -inis *n* electricum; to
turn on (turn off) the light lumen accendere
(extinguere)
electric razor *or* shaver *s* rasor·ium -(i)i *n* electricum
electric stove *s* focul·us -i *m* electricus
electric wire *s* fil·um -i *n* electricum
electrify *tr* electricā vi afficere; *(to thrill)* vehementer excitare
electrocute *tr* vi electricā interficere
electrocution *s* interit·us -ūs *m* electricus
electronic *adj* electronic·us -a -um
elegance *s* eleganti·a -ae *f*
elegant *adj* eleg·ans -antis
elegantly *adv* eleganter

elegiac *adj* elegiac·us -a -um; — **verse** eleg·i -orum *mpl*

elegy *s* elegi·a -ae *f*

element *s* element·um -i *n;* —**s** principi·a -orum *npl* rerum; *(fig)* rudiment·a -orum *npl;* **to be out of one's** — peregrin·us (·a) et hospes esse

elemental *adj* primordi·us -a -um

elementary *adj* simpl·ex -icis; — **instruction** element·a -orum *npl*

elementary school *s* lud·us -i *m* litterarius

elementary school teacher *s* litterari·us -i *m* (·a -ae *f*)

elephant *s* elephant·us -i *m;* —**s trumpet** elephanti barriunt

elevate *tr* levare, (at)tollere; *(fig)* efferre

elevated *adj* edit·us -a -um

elevation *s* elati·o -onis *f; (height)* altitud·o -inis *f; (hill)* loc·us -i *m* editus

elevator *s* cellul·a -ae *f* scansoria

eleven *adj* undecim [*indecl*]

eleventh *adj* undecim·us -a -um

elf *s* num·en -inis *n* pumilum

elicit *tr* elicere

elide *tr* elidere

eligible *adj (pol)* qui *or* quae per leges deligi potest; *(bachelor)* optabil·is -is -e

eliminate *tr* amovēre, tollere

elimination *s use a verbal paraphrase or* amoti·o -onis *f*

elision *s* elisi·o -onis *f*

elite *adj* elect·us -a -um

elite *s* flo·s -ris *m*

elk *s* alc·es -is *f*

ellipsis *s* ellips·is -is *f*

elliptical *adj* elliptic·us -a -um

elm *s* ulm·us -i *f*

elocution *s* pronuntiati·o -onis *f*

elongate *tr* producere, longius facere

elongated *adj* praelong·us -a -um

elope *intr* insciis atque invitis parentibus cum amatore *(or* amatrice) domo fugere

elopement *s* clandestina fug·a -ae *f* et nupti·ae -arum *fpl*

eloquence *s* eloquenti·a -ae *f; (natural)* facundi·a -ae *f*

eloquent *adj* eloquens, disert·us -a -um

eloquently *adv* eloquenter, diserte

else *adj* **anyone** — quivis alius; **anything** —? aliquid amplius?; **no one** — nem·o -inis *m* alius; **nothing** — nihil aliud; **who** —? quis alius?

else *adv (besides)* praeterea; *(otherwise)* aliter; **or** — alioquin; **somewhere** — *(position)* alibi; *(direction)* alio

elsewhere *adv (position)* alibi; *(direction)* alio

elucidate *tr* illustrare, explicare

elucidation *s* explicati·o -onis *f*

elude *tr* eludere

elusive *adj (difficult to grasp)* fug·ax -acis; *(difficult to describe)* recondit·us -a -um

Elysian *adj* Elysi·us -a -um; — **Fields** Camp·i -orum *mpl* Elysii

emaciate *tr* macerare

emaciated *adj* ma·cer -cra -crum; **to become** — emacrescere

emaciation *s* maci·es -ei *f*

e-mail *s* litter·ae -arum *fpl* electronicae; *(the system)* curs·us -ūs *m* electronicus

e-mail *tr* litteras electronicas mittere ad *(w. acc)*

e-mail address *s* inscripti·o -onis *f* electronica

emanate *intr* emanare

emanation *s (gas)* exspirati·o -onis *f; (issue)* emissi·o -onis *f*

emancipate *tr (a son)* emancipare; *(a slave)* manumittere

emancipation *s (of a son)* emancipati·o -onis *f; (of a slave)* manumissi·o -onis *f*

emasculated *adj (lit & fig)* effeminat·us -a -um

embalm *tr* condire

embankment *s* agg·er -eris *m*

embargo *s (on goods)* prohibiti·ō -onis *f* commercii; *(on ships)* retenti·o -onis *f* navium; **to lay an — on ships** naves ab exitu prohibēre; **to lift the — on ships** naves dimittere

embark *tr* imponcrc ‖ *intr* (in navem) conscendere; **to — upon** *(fig)* ingredi

embarkation *s* conscensi·o -onis *f; (usu. expressed by the verb: after the — of the army* exercitu in naves imposito)

embarrass *tr* perturbare; **to be** —**ed** erubescere

embarrassing *adj* erubescund·us -a -um

embarrassment *s* conturbati·o -onis *f; (financial)* angusti·ae -arum *fpl*

embassy *s* legati·o -onis *f*

embellish *tr* exornare; **to — facts rather than report them accurately** res gestas magis exornare quam fideliter narrare

embellishment *s (act)* exornati·o -onis *f; (result)* ornament·um -i *n*

ember *s* favill·a -ae *f*

embezzle *tr* (pecuniam) avertere

embezzlement *s* peculat·us -ūs *m*

embezzler *s* pecula·tor -toris *m* (·trix -tricis *f*), avers·or -oris *m* (·rix -ricis *f*)

embitter *tr* exacerbare

embittered *adj* exacerbat·us -a -um

emblazon *tr* insignire

emblem *s* indic·ium -(i)i *n; (badge)* insign·e -is *n*

emblematic *adj* symbolic·us -a -um

embodiment *s* effigi·es -ei *f*, form·a -ae *f*

embody *tr* includere, informare, effingere

emboss *tr* caelare

embrace *s* amplex·us -ūs *m*

embrace *tr* amplect·or -ī amplexus sum

embroider *tr* acu pingere
embroidered *adj (w. colors)* pict·us -a -um
embroidery *s (art)* ar·s -tis *f* acu pingendi; *(product)* pictur·a -ae *f* in textili (facta); picta vest·is -is *f*
embroil *tr* implicare
embroilment *s* implicati·o -onis *f*
embryo *s* part·us -ūs *m* inchoatus
emend *tr* emendare
emendation *s* emendati·o -onis *f*
emerald *s* smaragd·us -i *f (m)*
emerald *adj* smaragdin·us -a -um
emerge *intr* emergere; *(to arise)* existere
emergency *s* discrim·en -inis *n*
emergency *adj* subitari·us -a -um
emigrant *s* emigr·ans -antis *mf*
emigrate *intr* (**to**) emigrare (in *w. acc)*
emigration *s* emigrati·o -onis *f*
eminence *s* praestanti·a -ae *f; (rise in the ground)* loc·us -i *m* editus
eminent *adj* emin·ens -entis, egregi·us -a -um, ornatissim·us -a -um
eminently *adv* insigniter
emissary *s* legat·us -i *m (·a -ae f)*
emission *s* emissi·o -onis *f*
emit *tr* emittere; *(to utter)* proferre; *(scent)* exhalare
emotion *s* animi mot·us -ūs *m;* affect·us -ūs *m;* **strong —** permoti·o -onis *f;* **to express —s** animi emotūs exprimere
emotional *adj* affectūs animi mov·ens -entis
emperor *s* imperat·or -oris *m; (title chosen by Augustus)* princ·eps -ipis *m*
emphasis *s* vis *f; (gram)* impressi·o -onis *f*
emphasize *tr (a word)* premere; *(idea)* exprimere
emphatic *adj* grav·is -is -e
emphatically *adv* graviter
empire *s* imper·ium -(i)i *n*
empirical *adj* empiric·us -a -um
empirically *adv* ex experimentis
empiricism *s* empiric·e -es *f*
employ *tr (to use)* uti *(w. abl),* adhibēre; *(to hire)* conducere **to — precaution** uti observatione
employee *s* conduct·us -i *m (·a -ae f)*
employer *s* conduc·tor -toris *m (·trix -tricis f)*
employment *s (act)* us·us -ūs *m; (as a means of livelihood)* quaest·us -ūs *m; (hiring)* conducti·o -onis *f*
empower *tr* potestatem *(w. dat)* facere; *(to enable)* facultatem dare *(w.dat)*
empress *s* impera·trix -tricis *f*
emptiness *s* inanit·as -atis *f; (fig)* vanit·as -atis *f*
empty *adj* vacu·us -a -um, inan·is -is -e; *(street)* desert·us -a -um; *(fig)* van·us -a -um; *(stomach)* ieiun·us -a -um

empty *tr (contents)* vacuefacere; *(bottle, stomach)* exhaurire; *(to strip bare)* exinanire ‖ *intr (of river)* se effundere
empty-handed *adj* inan·is -is -e; *(without a gift)* immun·is -is -e
empty-headed *adj* frivol·us -a -um
emulate *tr (to rival)* aemulari; *(to imitate)* imitari
emulation *s* aemulati·o -onis *f; (imitation)* imitati·o -onis *f*
emulous *adj* (**of**) aemul·us -a -um *(w. gen)*
enable *tr* facultatem *(w. dat)* dare
enact *tr* sancire; *(of the plebs)* sciscere; *(of the Roman people)* iubēre; *(of a absolute ruler)* imponere
enactment *s (of senate)* senatūs consult·um -i *n; (of the plebs)* plebis scit·um -i *n;* sancti·o -onis *f*
enamel *s* smalt·um -i *n*
enamel *adj* smaltin·us -a -um
enamored *adj* **to be — of** deamare
encamp *intr* castra ponere, (in castris) considere
encampment *s* castr·a -orum *npl*
encase *tr* includere
enchant *tr* fascinare; *(fig)* capere
enchanted *adj* incantat·us -a -um, capt·us -a -um
enchanting *adj (fig)* venust·us -a -um
enchantment *s* incantament·um -i *n; (fig)* illecebr·ae -arum *fpl*
enchantress *s* mag·a -ae *f*
encircle *tr* circumdare
enclitic *s* enclitic·um -i *n*
enclose *tr* includere; *(with a fence)* saepire; **to — a document in a letter** libellum litteris subicere
enclosure *s (fence)* saept·um -i *n; (mail)* res *f* epistulae subiecta
encompass *tr (to surround)* cingere; *(to include)* complecti
encore *s* revocati·o -onis *f;* **he received an —** revocatus est
encounter *s (meeting)* congress·us -ūs *m; (fight)* pugn·a -ae *f*
encounter *tr (unexpectedly)* occurrere *(w. dat),* offendere; *(the enemy)* obviam ire *(w. dat);* **to — death** mortem oppetere
encourage *tr* (ad)cohortari; *(of one cast down)* animum *or* animos *(w. gen)* confirmare
encouragement *s* hortat·us -ūs *m;* confirmati·o -onis *f*
encroach *intr* invadere; **to — upon** occupare; *(rights)* imminuere; **to — upon a neighbor's land** terminos agri proferre
encroachment *s* usurpati·o -onis *f; (on rights)* imminuti·o -onis *f*
encumber *tr* impedire
encumbrance *s* impediment·um -i *n*

encyclical *s* litter·ae -arum *fpl* publicae pontificales
encyclopedia *s* orb·is -is *m* doctrinae
end *s* fin·is -is *m,* termin·us -i *m; (termination of life)* exit·um -i *n; (aim)* proposit·um -i *n; (of a speech)* perorati·o -onis *f;* **at the — of the day** extremo die; **at the — of the letter** in extremis litteris; **at the — of the year** exeunte anno; **in the —** ad extremum, denique; **that's the — of me** actum est de me; **to come to an —** finem capere; **to make both —s meet** aegre intra modum nummorum vivere; **to put an — to** finem imponere *(w. dat); to the — of spring* ad ultimum ver; **toward the — of his life** tempore extremo; **to what — ?** quo?, quorsum?
end *tr* finire, terminare ‖ *intr* desinere, finem capere; *(of time)* exire; **to — up** evenire, evadere
endanger *tr* in periculum vocare
endear *tr* carum (-am) reddere, devincire
endearing *adj* car·us -a -um, bland·us -a -um
endearment *s* blanditi·ae -arum *fpl*
endeavor *s* conat·us -ūs *m*
endeavor *intr* conari, niti
ending *s* fin·is -is *m,* exit·us -ūs *m*; *(gram)* terminati·o -onis *f*
endless *adj* infinit·us -a -um; *(time)* aetern·us -a -um
endlessly *adv* sine fine
endorse *tr* comprobare; *(a check)* chirographum a tergo *(w. gen)* inscribere
endorsement *s* fav·or -oris *m; (com)* subscripti·o -onis *f*
endow *tr* donare
endowed *adj* **(with)** praedit·us -a -um *(w. abl)*
endowment *s (of body or mind)* do·s -tis *f; (financial)* dotati·o -onis *f*
endurable *adj* tolerabil·is -is -e
endurance *s* patienti·a -ae *f; (duration)* durati·o -onis *f*
endure *tr* tolerare ‖ *intr* durare
enduring *adj* toler·ans -antis; *(lasting)* durabil·is -is -e
enemy *s (public)* host·is -is *m; (private)* inimic·us -i *m* (·a -ae *f*)
enemy *adj* hostic·us -a -um, infest·us -a -um; inimic·us -a -um
energetic *adj* impi·ger -gra -grum
energy *s* vis *f;* **atomic energy** vis atomica
enervate *tr* enervare
enforce *tr (the law)* exercēre, exsequi
enforcement *s* exsecuti·o -onis *f*
enfranchise *tr* civitate donare; *(a slave)* manumittere; *(to vote)* suffragium dare *(w. dat)*
enfranchisment *s* civitatis donati·o -onis *f; (of a slave)* manumissi·o -onis *f; (right to vote)* suffragii ius, iuris *n*

engage *tr (to hire)* conducere; *(to employ)* adhibēre; *(attention)* occupare; *(to involve)* implicare; *(enemy)* proelium facere cum *(w. abl),* dimicare cum *(w. abl)* ‖ *intr* **to — in** suscipere, ingredi; **to — in battle** proeliari; **to — in conversation** sermonem instituere *(or* serere*)*
engaged *adj (to marry)* spons·us -a -um; **to be — in** versari in *(w. abl)*
engagement *s (to marry)* pacti·o -onis *f* nuptialis; *(business)* occupati·o -onis *f; (mil)* proel·ium -(i)i *n;* **to break off the —** sponsum repudiare
engagement party *s* sponsal·ia -ium *npl*
engaging *adj* suav·is -is -e
engender *tr* gignere
engine *s* machin·a -ae *f*
engineer *s* machina·tor -toris *m* (·trix -tricis *f*); *(mil)* fa·ber -bri *m*
engineering *s* machinalis scienti·a -ae *f*
England *s* Angli·a -ae *f,* Britanni·a -ae *f*
English *adj* Anglic·us -a -um
English *s* **to know —** Anglice scire; **to speak —** Anglice loqui; **to teach —** Anglice docēre
engrave *tr* caelare
engraver *s* caelat·or -oris *m*
engraving *s* caelatur·a -ae *f*
engross *tr* **(in)** animum occupare in *(w. abl);* **to be —ed in** tot·us -a -um esse in *(w. abl)*
engulf *tr* devorare, mergere
enhance *tr* amplificare
enhancement *s* amplificati·o -onis *f*
enigma *s* aenigm·a -atis *n*
enigmatic *adj* ambigu·us -a -um
enigmatically *adv* per aenigmata
enjoin *tr* iubēre
enjoy *tr* frui *(w. abl); (to have the benefit of, e.g., good health, friendship, company)* uti *(w. abl)*
enjoyment *s* fruct·us -ūs *m; (the sense of pleasure itself)* delectati·o -onis *f*
enlarge *tr* amplificare
enlargement *s* amplificati·o -onis *f*
enlighten *tr (physically)* illustrare; *(mentally)* illuminare; *(to instruct)* erudire
enlightened *adj* erudit·us -a -um
enlightenment *s* humanit·as -atis *f*
enlist *tr (support)* conciliare; *(mil)* conscribere; *(to swear in)* sacramento adigere ‖ *intr (mil)* sacramentum dicere, nomen dare
enlistment *s* conscripti·o -onis *f*
enliven *tr* excitare
enmity *s* simult·as -atis *f;* **to be at — with** in simultate esse cum *(w. abl);* **to feel — toward** simultatem habēre cum *(w. abl)*
ennoble *tr* honestare, nobilitare
ennui *s* taed·ium -(i)i *n*
enormity *s* immanit·as -atis *f*
enormous *adj* imman·is -is -e

enormously *adv* praeter modum

enough *adj* satis [*indecl*]; **— trouble** satis laboris; **time —** satis temporis

enough *adv* satis; **— of this!** haec hactenus!; **more than —** satis superque

enrage *tr* infuriare

enrapture *tr* oblectare; **to be —d** gaudio efferri

enrich *tr* locupletare, ditare

enroll *tr* ascribere; **to — s.o. in the patrician order** aliquem inter patricios asciscere ‖ *intr* ascribi, nomen dare

enshrine *tr* consecrare

ensign *s (banner)* sign·um -i *n; (officer)* signif·er -eri *m*

enslave *tr* in servitutem redigere

enslavement *s* servit·us -utis *f,* servit·ium -(i)i *n*

ensnare *tr* illaquēre; *(fig)* illicere

ensue *intr* insequi

ensuing *adj* insequ·ens -entis

entail *tr* adferre

entangle *tr* implicare

entanglement *s* implicati·o -onis *f*

enter *tr* intrare, ingredi, inire; *(office)* inire; *(to pierce)* penetrare in *(w. acc); (comput)* in ordinatrum referre; **to — in a memorandum** in libellum referre; **to — in an account book** in rationem inducere; **to — politics** rem publicam inire ‖ *intr* intrare, ingredi, inire; **to — into an alliance with s.o.** societatem cum aliquo facere; **to — upon** *(to undertake)* suscipere; *(a magistracy)* inire

enterprise *s (undertaking)* incept·um -i *n; (project)* op·us -eris *n; (venture)* aus·um -i *n; (enterprising disposition)* alacer ac promptus anim·us -i *m*

enterprising *adj* ala·cer -cris -cre et prompt·us -a -um

entertain *tr (a guest)* excipere; *(idea)* admittere; *(to amuse)* oblectare

entertainer *s* ludi·o -onis *m; (host)* hosp·es -itis *mf*

entertaining *adj* festiv·us -a -um

entertainment *s (amusement)* oblectati·o -onis *f; (cultural, esp. at a dinner party)* acroam·a -atis *n; (by the host)* hospit·ium -(i)i *n;* **public —s** spectacul·a -orum *npl*

enthrall *tr* captare

enthusiasm *s* stud·ium -(i)i *n*

enthusiastic *adj* **(about)** studios·us -a -um *(w. gen)*

enthusiastically *adv* studiose

entice *tr* allicere

enticement *s* illecebr·a -ae *f*

enticing *adj* illecebros·us -a -um

entire *adj* tot·us -a -um, univers·us -a -um

entirely *adv* omnino

entirety *s* expressed by univers·us -a -um: **to look at the matter in its —** rem universam contemplari

entitle *tr (a book, essay)* inscribere; *(to name)* appellare; *(to give title to)* potestatem dare *(w. dat);* **to be —d to do anything** ius aliquid faciendi habēre; dignus esse qui aliquid faciat

entity *s* en·s -tis *n*

entomb *tr* sepulchro condere

entomologist *s* entomologic·us -i *m* (·a -ae *f*)

entomology *s* entomologi·a -ae *f*

entourage *s* comitat·us -ūs *m*

entrails *spl* ext·a -orum *npl*

entrance *s* adit·us -ūs *m,* introit·us -ūs *m; (act)* ingressi·o -onis *f; (doorway)* osti·um -i *n;* **at the — to the theater** in aditu theatri

entrance *tr* rapere

entrance hall *s* vestibul·um -i *n*

entrance way *s* ost·ium -(i)i *n*

entreat *tr* obsecrare

entreaty *s* obsecrati·o -onis *f*

entree *s* cen·a -ae *f* altera

entrench *tr (lit & fig)* vallare; **to — oneself** subsidere

entrenchment *s* muniment·um -i *n*

entrepreneur *s* negotia·tor -toris *m* (·trix -tricis *f*)

entrust *tr* committere

entry *s (act)* ingressi·o -onis *f,* introït·us -ūs *m; (of house)* ost·ium -(i)i *n; (in accounts)* nom·en -inis *n*

entwine *tr* implicare, implectere

enumerate *tr* enumerare

enumeration *s* enumerati·o -onis *f*

enunciate *tr* exprimere

enunciation *s (of sounds)* explanati·o -onis *f; (setting forth)* enuntiati·o -onis *f*

envelop *tr* involvere

envelope *s* involucr·um -i *n* (epistulare)

enviable *adj* invidios·us -a -um

envious *adj* invid·us -a -um; **to be — of** invidēre *(w. dat)*

environment *s* circumiect·a -orum *npl*

environs *spl* vicinit·as -atis *f*

envision *tr* fingere

envoy *s* legat·us -i *m* (·a -ae *f*)

envy *s* invidi·a -ae *f*

envy *tr* invidēre *(w. dat)*

enzyme *s* enzym·a -ae *f*

eons *spl* plurima saecul·a -orum *npl*

ephemeral *adj (brief)* brev·is -is -e; *(perishable)* caduc·us -a -um

epic *adj* epic·us -a -um

epic *s* epos *n (only in nom & acc),* poem·a -atis *n* epicum

epicure *s* hellu·o -onis *m*

Epicurean *adj (of Epicurus)* Epicure·us -a -um; *(fig)* voluptari·us -a -um

Epicurean *s* Epicure·us -i *m; (hedonist)* voluptari·us -i *m* (·a -ae *f*)
epidemic *adj* epidem·us -a -um
epidemic *s* pestilenti·a -ae *f*
epidermis *s* epiderm·is -is *f,* summa cut·is -is *f*
epigram *s* epigramm·a -atis *n*
epilepsy *s* morb·us -i *m* comititalis
epilogue *s* epilog·us -i *m*
episcopal *adj* episcopal·is -is -e
episode *s* event·us -ūs *m,* cas·us -ūs *m*
epistle *s* epistul·a -ae *f*
epitaph *s* titul·us -i *m* (sepulchri)
epithet *s* epithet·on -i *n*
epitome *s* empitom·a -ae (·e -es) *f*
epoch *s* saecul·um -i *n*
equal *adj* aequ·us -a -um; *(matching)* pa·r -ris; **to be — to the task** muneri par esse
equal *s* pa·r -ris *mf & n;* **to be on an — with the gods** in aequo dis stare
equal *tr* aequare
equality *s* aequalit·as -atis *f;* **to be on — with** in aequo *(w. dat)* stare
equalization *s (act)* exaequati·o -onis *f; (state)* aequalit·as -atis *f*
equally *adv* aeque
equanimity *s* aequus anim·us -i *m*
equate *tr* **(with)** aequiparare (cum *or* ad *or dat)*
equation *s* aequati·o -onis *f*
equator *s* aequinoctialis circul·us -i *m*
equestrian *adj* equestr·is -is -e
equestrian *s* equ·es -itis *m*
equidistant *adj* **to be —** aequo intervallo inter se distare
equilibrium *s* aequilibr·ium -(i)i *n*
equinox *s* aequinoct·ium -(i)i *n*
equip *tr* ornare; *(with arms)* armare
equipment *s* instrument·um -i *n,* apparat·us -ūs *m*
equitable *adj* aequ·us -a -um
equitably *adv* aeque
equity *s* aequ·um -i *n*
equivalence *s* aequalit·as -atis *f*
equivalent *adj* pa·r -ris, aequ·us -a -um; **one gold coin is — to ten silver ones** pro decem argenteis aureus unus valet; **to be —** valēre
equivalent *s* quod idem valet
equivocal *adj* ambigu·us -a -um
equivocate *intr* tergiversari
era *s* temp·us -oris *n,* saecul·um -i *n*
eradicate *tr* eradicare, exstirpare
eradication *s* exstirpati·o -onis *f*
erase *tr* eradere, delēre
eraser *s* deletil·e -is *n,* cumm·is -is *f* deletilis
erasure *s* litur·a -ae *f*
ere *conj* priusquam
ere *prep* ante *(w. acc);* **— long** mox; **— now** ante hoc tempus, antehac
erect *adj* erect·us -a -um

erect *tr (to raise)* erigere; *(to build)* exstruere; *(statue)* ponere, statuere
erection *s (building)* exstructi·o -onis *f; (setting up)* erecti·o -onis *f*
erode *tr* erodere
erosive *adj* erod·ens -entis
erotic *adj* libidinos·us -a -um
err *intr* errare, peccare
errand *s* mandat·um -i *n,* mun·us -eris *n*
erratic *adj* inconst·ans -antis
erroneous *adj* fals·us -a -um; **to be —** in erratis esse
erroneously *adv* perperam
error *s (of opinion)* err·or -oris *m;(instance)* errat·um -i *n; (in writing, clerical)* mend·a -ae *f,* mend·um -i *n; (in grammar)* vit·ium -(i)i *n;* **to commit an —** mendum admittere; **to make many —s** multa errare
erudite *adj* erudit·us -a -um
erudition *s* eruditi·o -onis *f*
erupt *intr* erumpere
eruption *s* erupti·o -onis *f*
escalate *tr (to increase)* augēre; *(to intensify)* intendere **‖** *intr* (in)crescere, ingravescere
escalator *s* scal·ae -arum *fpl* mobiles
escapade *s* facin·us -oris *n* temerarium
escape *s* effug·ium -(i)i *n*
escape *tr* fugere; *(in a quiet way)* subterfugere; **to — the notice of** fallere **‖** *intr* effugere
escort *s* comitat·us -ūs *m; (protection)* praesid·ium -(i)i *n*
escort *tr* prosequi
esophagus *s* gul·a -ae *f*
especially *adv* praecipue, potissimum, maxime; *(w. clauses)* praesertim
espresso *s* caffe·a -ae *f* expressa
essay *s (treatise)* libell·us -i *m*
essence *s* essenti·a -ae *f*
essential *adj* necessari·us -a -um; *(basic)* prim·us -a -um
essentially *adv* necessario
establish *tr* constituere; *(to settle firmly)* stabilare; *(to prove)* probare
establishment *s (act)* constituti·o -onis *f; (com)* negot·ium -(i)i *n*
estate *s (landed property)* fund·us -i *m,* praed·ium -(i)i *n; (state)* stat·us -ūs *m*
esteem *s* aestimati·o -onis *f;* **to hold s.o in high (highest) —** aliquem magni (maximi) facere
esteem *tr* aestimare; **to — highly (more, very highly)** magni (pluris, maximi) facere
estimate *s (valuation)* aestimati·o -onis *f; (judgment)* iudic·ium -(i)i *n;* **to form an —** iudicium facere; **to give an —** modum impensarum explicare
estimation *s* aestimati·o -onis *f*
estrange *tr* alienare; **to become —ed from s.o.** aliquem a se alienare
estrangement *s* alienati·o -onis *f*

estuary *s* aestuar·ium -(i)i *n*
eternal *adj* aetern·us -a -um
eternally *adv* in aeternum
eternity *s* aeternit·as -atis *f*
ether *s* aeth·er -eris *m*
ethereal *adj* aethere·us -a -um
ethical *adj* moral·is -is -e
ethics *spl* ethic·e -es *f; (of an individual)*
mor·es -ium *mpl*
Ethiopia *s* Aethiopi·a -ae *f*
Etruria *s* Etruri·a -ae *f*
etiquette *s* regim·en -inis *n* morum
etymological *adj* etymologic·us -a -um
etymology *s* etymologi·a -ae *f*
eulogist *s* lauda·tor -toris *m* (·trix -tricis *f*)
eulogize *tr* laudare
eulogy *s* laudati·o -onis *f*
eunuch *s* eunuch·us -i *m; (pej)* spad·o -onis *m*
euphemism *s* euphemism·us -i *m*
euphemistic *adj* — **expression** vo·x -cis *f* per
euphemismum usurpata
euphony *s* vocalit·as -atis *f*
Europe *s* Europ·a -ae *f*
European *adj* Europae·us -a -um
evacuate *tr* vacuefacere; *(people)* deducere;
(bowels) exonerare
evacuation *s (mil)* deducti·o -onis *f;* — **of the**
bowels alvi purgati·o -onis *f*
evade *tr* eludere
evaluate *tr* aestimare
evaluation *s* aestimati·o -onis *f*
evangelical *adj* evangelic·us -a -um
evangelist *s* evangelist·a -ae *m* (·ria -riae *f*)
evangelize *tr* evangelizare
evaporate *tr* evaporare ‖ *intr* evaporari
evaporation *s* evaporati·o -onis *f*
evasion *s (avoidance)* fug·a -ae *f; (dodging)*
tergiversati·o -onis *f; (round-about speech)*
ambag·es -um *fpl;* **to practice** — tergiversari
evasive *adj* ambigu·us -a -um
evasively *adv* ambigue
eve *s* vesp·er -eri *m; (of a feastday)* vigili·ae
-arum *fpl;* **on the** — **of** sub *(w. acc),* pridie
(eius diei)
even *adj* aequal·is -is -e; *(level)* plan·us -a -um;
(of numbers) pa·r -ris; **to get** — **with s.o.**
aliquem ulcisci
even *adv* etiam; *(esp. to emphasize single*
words) vel; — **if,** — **though** etsi, etiamsi; —
so nihilominus; **not** — ne ... quidem
evening *s* vesp·er -eri *m,* vesper·a -ae *f;* **all** —
totā vesperā; **early in the** — primo vespere;
in the — vespere, vesperi; — **falls** ves-
perascit; **good** —! salve!, *(pl:* salvete!); **last**
— heri vesperi; **on Saturday** — die Saturni
vesperi; **this** — hodie vesperi; **toward** — sub
vesperum; **in the early** — primo vespere;
very late in the — pervespere; **yesterday** —
heri vesperi

evening *adj* vespertin·us -a -um
evening star *s* Hesper·us -i *m*
evenness *s* aequalit·as -atis *f*
event *s* res, rei *f; (adverse)* cas·us -ūs *m; (out-*
come) event·us -ūs *m;* **at all** —s saltem; **in**
any — utique; **in the** — **that** si forte
eventful *adj* memorabil·is -is -e
eventual *adj* ultim·us -a -um
eventuality *s* event·us -ūs *m*
eventually *adv* aliquando, denique
ever *adv (always)* semper; *(at any time)*
umquam; *(after* si, nisi, num, ne) quando; —
since ex quo (tempore); **for** — in aeternum;
greater than — maior quam umquam; **more**
than — magis quam umquam
evergreen *adj* semperviv·us -a -um; — **tree**
arbor quae semper viret
everlasting *adj* sempitern·us -a -um
evermore *adv* **for** — in aeternum
every *adj* omn·is -is -e, quisque, quaeque,
quodque; — **day** cotidie, in dies; — **night**
per singulas noctes; — **now and then** interdum; — **other day** alternis diebus; — **year**
quotannis
everybody *pron (each one)* quisque; *(all)*
omn·es -ium *mpl; (stronger)* nem·o -inis *m*
non; — **for himself** pro se quisque
everyday *adj* co(t)tidian·us -a -um; *(ordinary)*
usitat·us -a -um
everyone *pron see* **everybody**
everything *pron* omn·ia -ium *npl,* nihil non
everywhere *adv* ubique
evict *tr* expellere, detrudere
eviction *s* expulsi·o -onis *f*
evidence *s* testimon·ium -(i)i *n; (information*
given) indic·ium -(i)i *n;* **to give** — testari; **to**
give — **against s.o.** testimonium dare in
aliquem; **on what** — **will you convict me?**
quo me teste convinces?; **to turn state's** indicium profiteri
evident *adj* manifest·us -a -um; **it is** —
apparet, manifestum est, constat
evidently *adv* manifeste
evil *adj* mal·us -a -um
evil *s* mal·um -i *n*
evil-minded *adj* malevol·us -a -um
evince *tr* praestare
evoke *tr* evocare, excitare
evolution *s* progress·us -ūs *m,* evoluti·o -onis *f*
evolve *tr* evolvere per gradūs ‖ *intr* evolvi per
gradūs
exact *adj* exact·us -a -um, accurat·us -a -um;
(persons) dilig·ens -entis; **at the** — **time**
when ipso tempore quo
exact *tr* exigere
exaction *s* exacti·o -onis *f*
exactly *adv* accurate; — **as** sic ut
exactness *s* accurati·o -onis *f*

exaggerate *tr* in maius extollere; *(numbers)* augēre; **to — the facts** excedere actae rei modum

exaggeration *s* superiecti·o -onis *f* veri; **false-hoods and —s** falsa et maiora vero; **he is given to —** omnia in maius extollere solet

exalt *tr* amplificare, efferre

exaltation *s* elati·o -onis *f*

exam *s* probati·o -onis *f;* **to flunk an —** probatione cadere; **to pass an —** probationem sustinere, e probatione feliciter evadere; **to take an —** probationem obire; **tough —** probatio rigorosa

examination *s* investigati·o -onis *f;* *(leg)* quaesti·o -onis *f, (in school)* probati·o -onis *f*

examine *tr* investigare, scrutari; *(witnesses)* interrogare; *(students)* probare

examiner *s* investiga·tor -toris *m* (·trix -tricis *f*); *(leg)* inquisi·tor -toris *m* (·trix -tricis *f*)

example *s* *(illustration)* exempl·um -i *n; (lesson)* document·um -i *n;* **for —** exempli gratiā; **to set an —** exemplum praebēre

exasperate *tr* exasperare

exasperated *adj* irat·us -a -um

exasperation *s* irritati·o -onis *f*

excavate *tr* excavare

excavator *s* *(person)* foss·or -oris *m; (machine)* machin·a -ae *f* fossoria

excavation *s* excavati·o -onis *f*

exceed *tr* excedere, superare

exceedingly *adv* magnopere, valde, nimium

excel *tr* superare **ll** *intr* excellere, praestare

excellence *s* excellenti·a -ae *f*

Excellency *s* *(eccl)* Eminentissim·us -i *m*

excellent *adj* optim·us -a -um, excell·ens -entis; *(excelling others)* praest·ans -antis

excellently *adv* egregie, optime

except *tr* excipere

except *prep* praeter *(w. acc);* **— that** nisi quod

exception *s* excepti·o -onis *f;* **with the — of** praeter *(w. acc);* **with this — hoc** excepto; **without a single —** ne uno quidem excepto; **without —** omnes ad un·um -am -um

exceptional *adj* praest·ans -antis

exceptionally *adv* praeter modum

excess *s* nim·ium -(i)i *n;* **to be in —** superesse; **to —** nimis; **to go to — in anything** nimium esse in aliqua re

excess *adj* nimi·us -a -um

excessive *adj* (**in**) immodic·us -a -um *(w. gen or abl)*

excessively *adv* immodice, nimis

exchange *s* *(of goods)* permutati·o -onis *f; (of money)* collyb·us -i *m;* **in — for** pro *(w. abl);* **rate of —** collyb·us -i *m*

exchange *tr* (**for**) permutare *(w. abl);* **to — greetings** consalutare; **to — letters** commercium epistulare habēre; **to — prisoners** capitivos inter se permutare

excise *tr* exsecare, excidere

excision *s* exsecti·o -onis *f*

excitable *adj* percit·us -a -um; *(irritable)* irritabil·is -is -e

excite *tr* excitare; *(to provoke)* incitare

excited *adj* commot·us -a -um, excitat·us -a -um

excitement *s* commoti·o -onis *f; (that which excites)* incitament·um -i *n;* **to feel —** excitari

exclaim *tr* exclamare; *(as a group)* conclamare; *(in reply)* succlamare

exclamation *s* exclamati·o -onis *f*

exclamation point *s* sign·um -i *n* exclamationis

exclude *tr* excludere

exclusion *s* exclusi·o -onis *f*

exclusive *adj* propri·us -a -um; **— of** praeter *(w. acc)*

exclusively *adv* solum

excommunicate *tr* excommunicare

excommunication *s* excommunicati·o -onis *f*

excrete *tr* emittere

excrement *s* excrement·um -i *n*

excretion *s* *(act)* excreti·o -onis *f; (result)* excrementr·um -i *n*

excruciating *adj* cruci·ans -antis

excursion *s* it·er -ineris *n* voluptatis causā susceptum

excusable *adj* excusabil·is -is -e

excuse *s* excusati·o -onis *f; (pretext)* praetext·um -i *n*

excuse *tr* ignoscere *(w. dat);* **— me!** ignosce mihi!; **please excuse me** obsecro, mihi ignoscas; **to — oneself** se excusare

execute *tr* *(a criminal)* supplicio capitis afficere; *(to perform)* exsequi, efficere

execution *s* exsecuti·o -onis *f; (capital punishment)* supplic·ium -(i)i *n* capitis

executioner *s* carnif·ex -icis *m*

executive *adj* ad administrationem pertin·ens -entis

executive *s* administra·tor -toris *m* (·trix -tricis *f*)

executor *s* curat·or -oris *m* testamenti

executrix *s* cura·trix -tricis *f* testamenti

exemplary *adj* eximi·us -a -um

exemplify *tr* exemplum *(w. gen)* exponere

exempt *tr* eximere

exempt *adj* (**from**) vacu·us -a -um (ab *w. abl);* *(from tribute)* immun·is -is -e, lib·er -era -erum; **to be — from military service** militiae vacationem habēre

exemption *s* immunit·as -atis *f; (from military service)* vacati·o -onis *f* militiae

exercise *s* *(bodily)* exercitati·o -onis *f; (athletic)* palaestr·a -ae *f; (written; mil)* exercit·ium -(i)i *n; (literary)* them·a -atis *n; (use)* us·us -ūs *m*

exercise *tr* exercēre; *(to use)* uti, adhibēre ‖ *intr* se exercēre
exert *tr* adhibēre; **to — oneself** viribus eniti
exertion *s* contenti·o -onis *f,* nis·us -ūs *m*
exhalation *s* exhalati·o -onis *f*
exhale *tr* exhalare ‖ *intr* exspirare
exhaust *s* emissar·ium -(i)i *n*
exhaust *tr (to drain)* exhaurire; *(to tire out)* defatigare, conficere; **to — a subject** totam rem acuratissime plenissimeque tractare
exhausted *adj* fatigat·us -a -um, defess·us -a -um; **to be** *or* **become —** a viribus deficere
exhausting *adj* laborios·us -a -um
exhaustion *s* defecti·o -onis *f* virium
exhibit *tr* exhibēre; *(games)* ēdere
exhibition *s* exhibiti·o -onis *f; (display)* ostentati·o -onis *f; (public performance)* lud·i -orum *mpl; (gladiatorial show)* mun·us -eris *n*
exhilarate *tr* exhilare
exhilarating *adj* animum exhilar·ans -antis; **the morning air is —** exhilarant animos aurae matutinae
exhilaration *s* hilarit·as -atis *f*
exhort *tr* hortari
exhortation *s* hortam·en -inis *f; (act)* hortati·o -onis *f*
exhume *tr* exhumare
exigency *s* necessit·as -atis *f*
exile *s (temporary)* ex(s)il·ium -(i)i *n; (for life)* deportati·o -onis *f; (person)* exs·ul -ulis *mf*
exile *tr* exterminare; *(for a time)* relegare; *(for life)* deportare
exist *intr* esse, ex(s)istere; *(to be extant)* exstare; *(of human beings)* vivere
existence *s (of human beings)* vit·a -ae *f;* **he denies the — of gods** negat deos esse
exit *s* exit·us -ūs *m*
exonerate *tr* absolvere, culpā liberare
exorbitant *adj* immodic·us -a -um; **to make — demands** immodice postulare
exotic *adj* mirific·us -a -um
expand *tr* expandere, extendere ‖ *intr* expandi, se extendere
expanse *s* spat·ium -(i)i *n*
expansion *s* prolati·o -onis *f; (fig)* auct·us -ūs *m*
expatriate *tr* exterminare
expatriate *s* exs·ul -ulis *mf*
expect *tr* exspectare; **not —ing** necopin·ans -antis; **sooner than —ed** opinione celerius; **what do you —?** quid vis fieri?
expectancy *s* spe·s -i *f*
expectation *s* exspectati·o -onis *f;* **contrary to —** praeter opinionem
expectorate *tr & intr* exspuere
expediency *s* utilit·as -atis *f*
expedient *adj* util·is -is -e; **it is — that** exped-it *(w. acc & inf)*

expedient *s* mod·us -i *m*
expedite *tr* expedire, maturare
expedition *s (mil)* expediti·o -onis *f; (speed)* celerit·as -atis *f;* **to lead troops on an —** copias educere in expeditionem
expeditious *adj* cel·er -eris -ere
expeditiously *adv* celeriter; **as — as possible** quam celerrime
expel *tr* expellere
expend *tr* impendere, expendere
expenditure *s* impens·a -ae *f*
expense *s (cost)* pret·ium -(i)i *n; (outlay)* impens·a -ae *f,* sumpt·us -ūs *m;* **at great —** magno sumptu; **at my own —** meo sumptu
expensive *adj* car·us -a -um, pretios·us -a -um, sumptuos·us -a -um
expensively *adv* sumptuose
experience *s* us·us -ūs *m,* experienti·a -ae *f;* **military —** usus *m* in re militari; **political —** usus *m* in republicā; **a man of long —** vi·r -ri *m* longā experientiā
experience *tr* experiri, cognoscere, subire
experienced *adj* **(in)** perit·us -a -um *(w. gen)*
experiment *s* experiment·um -i *n*
experimental *adj* usu comparat·us -a -um
expert *s* **(in)** peritissim·us -i *m (·a -ae f) (w. gen)*
expert *adj* **(in)** perit·us -a -um *(w. gen)*
expertly *adv* scienter, callide
expertness *s* callidit·as -atis *f*
expiate *tr* expiare, luere
expiation *s* expiati·o -onis *f*
expiration *s* exit·us -ūs *m;* **at the — of the fifth year** quinto anno exeunte
expire *intr (to die)* exspirare; *(of time)* exire
explain *tr* explanare, explicare
explainable *adj* explicabil·is -is -e
explanation *s* explanati·o -onis *f,* explicati·o -onis *f*
expletive *s* explement·um -i *n*
explicit *adj* apert·us -a -um
explicitly *adv* aperte, plane
explode *tr* displodere; *(fig)* explodere ‖ *intr* displodi
exploit *s* facin·us -oris *n;* **—s** re·s -rum *fpl* gestae
exploit *tr* uti *(w. abl); (pej)* abuti *(w. abl)*
exploration *s* explorati·o -onis *f,* indagati·o -onis *f*
explore *tr* explorare, indagare
explorer *s* explorat·or -oris *m*
explosion *s* dirupti·o -onis *f; (sound)* frag·or -oris *m*
exponent *s* interpr·es -etis *mf*
export *tr* exportare, evehere
exporter *s* exportat·or -oris *m*
exports *spl* merc·es -ium *fpl* quae exportantur

expose *tr* exponere; *(to bare)* nudare; *(to uncover)* detegere; *(to danger)* obicere; **to be —ed to** patēre *(w. dat)*
exposition *s* expositi·o -onis *f*
exposure *s (to cold)* expositi·o -onis *f; (of guilt)* deprehensi·o -onis *f*
expound *tr* exponere, interpretari
express *adj* express·us -a -um
express *tr* exprimere; *(to show)* significare; **to — oneself** loqui, dicere
expression *s* verb·um -i *n; (of the face)* vult·us -ūs *m;* **joy beyond —** gaudia maiora quam quae verbis exprimi possint
expressive *adj* signific·ans -antis; *(eyes)* argut·us -a -um; *(fig)* loqu·ax acis; **— of** ind·ex -icis *(w. gen)*
expressly *adv* plane
express train *s* tram·en -inis *n* citissimum
expressway *s* vi·a -ae *f* citissima
expulsion *s* expulsi·o -onis *f,* exacti·o -onis *f*
expunge *tr* oblitterare
expurgate *tr* expurgare
exquisite *adj* exquisit·us -a -um
exquisitely *adv* exquisite
extant *adj* superst·es -itis; **to be —** exstare
extempore *adv* ex tempore
extemporaneous *adj* extemporal·is -is -e
extemporaneously *adv* ex tempore
extemporize *intr* ex tempore dicere
extend *tr (time)* extendere, producere; *(a hand)* porrigere; **to — the empire** ampliare imperium; **to — the governor's term** prorogare imperium ‖ *intr* extendi; *(of land, body of water)* tendere, patēre, pertinēre; **to — to** tendere ad *(w. acc);* **to extend over** *(to cover)* obtinēre
extension *s* extenti·o -onis *f; (lengthening)* producti·o -onis *f; (e.g., of the fingers)* porrigi·o -onis *f; (of size, of time)* prolati·o -onis *f;* **— of the term of office** prorogati·o -onis *f* imperii
extensive *adj* lat·us -a -um
extensively *adv* late
extent *s* spat·ium -(i)i *n; (of a country)* fin·es -ium *mpl;* **to a great —** magnā ex parte; **to some —** aliquā ex parte; **to this —** hactenus
extenuating *adj* **— circumstances** eae res quibus culpa minuitur
exterior *adj* exter·ior -ior -ius
exterior *s* speci·es -ei *f*
exterminate *tr* ad internecionem delēre
extermination *s* interneci·o -onis *f*
external *adj* extern·us -a -um
externally *adv* extrinsecus
extinct *adj* exstinct·us -a -um; **to become —** obsolescere
extinction *s* exstincti·o -onis *f*
extinguish *tr* exstinguere
extol *tr* laudibus efferre

extort *tr* extorquēre
extortion *s* res *fpl* repetundae
extortionist *s* extor·tor -toris *m (·*trix -tricis *f)*
extra *adj* addit·us -a -um; **— charge** additament·um -i *n* pretii
extra *adv* insuper, praeterea
extract *s (chemical)* expressi·o -onis *f; (literary)* excerpt·um -i *n; (synopsis)* compend·ium -(i)i *n*
extract *tr* extrahere; *(to squeeze out)* exprimere; *(teeth)* evellere; *(from a literary source)* excerpere
extraction *s (act)* evulsi·o -onis *f; (descent)* stirp·s -is *f;* **of German —** oriund·us -a -um a Germanis
extracurricular *adj* extraordinari·us -a -um
extraneous *adj* alien·us -a -um
extraordinarily *adv* praeter modum
extraordinary *adj* extraordinari·us -a -um, insolit·us -a -um; *(outstanding)* eximi·us -a -um
extravagance *s* sumpt·us -ūs *m*
extravagant *adj (exceeding bounds)* immodic·us -a -um; *(in expenditure)* sumptuos·us -a -um; *(spending)* prodig·us -a -um
extravagantly *adv* immodice; *(expensively)* sumptuose; *(lavishly)* profuse, prodige
extreme *adj* extrem·us -a -um
extreme *s* extrem·um -i *n;* **from one — to another** ab imo ad summum; **in the — ad** extremum; **to go to —s** descendere ad extrema
extremely *adv* summe, perquam
extremist *s* assecta·tor -toris *m (·*trix -tricis *f)* rerum novarum
extremity *s* extremit·as -atis *f,* extrem·um -i *n;* **extremities of the body** eminentes part·es -ium *fpl* corporis; **we have been reduced to extremities** ad extrema perventum est
extricate *tr* expedire, extrahere
extrinsic *adj* extrari·us -a -um
extrude *tr* extrudere ‖ *intr* extrudi
exuberance *s (of growth)* luxuri·es -ei *f; (of spirit)* redundanti·a -ae *f*
exuberant *adj (growth)* luxurios·us -a -um; *(unrestrained)* effus·us -a -um; **to be —** *(of style)* redundare
exude *tr* exudare ‖ *intr* emanare
exult *intr* exsultare, gestire
exultant *adj* laetabund·us -a -um
exultantly *adv* laete
exultation *s* exsultati·o -onis *f*
eye *s* ocul·us -i *m; (of needle)* foram·en -inis *n; (of plant)* gemm·a -ae *f;* **blind in one —** lusc·us -a -um; **keep your — on that guy!** adserva *(pl:* adservate) istum!; **keep your —s open!** cave circumspicias!; **look me in the —!** aspicedum contra me!; **to be in the public —** scaenae servire; **to keep an — on**

cavēre, in oculis habēre; **to shut one's —s to** conivēre; **with —s wide open** hiantibus oculis
eye *tr* aspicere
eyeball *s* orb·is -is *m* oculi, ocul·us -i *m*
eyebrow *s* supercil·ium -(i)i *n*
eyeglasses *spl* perspicill·a -orum *npl;* **to wear — perspicillis uti
eyelash *s* palpebrae pil·us -i *m;* **—s** palpebrarum pil·i -orum *mpl*
eyelid *s* palpebr·a -ae *f*
eyesight *s* aci·es -ei *f,* vis·us -ūs *m;* **to lose one's — oculos perdere
eyesore *s (fig)* res, rei *f* taetra
eyewitness *s* oculat·us (-a) test·is -is *mf*

F

fable *s* fabul·a -ae *f*
fabled *adj* fabulos·us -a -um
fabric *s (pattern of weaving)* text·us -us *m; (framework)* fabric·a -ae *f;* **coarse (sheer, thin; thick) —** crassus (tenuis; pinguis) textus
fabricate *tr* fabricare; *(fig)* fingere
fabrication *s* fabricati·o -onis *f; (fig)* comment·um - *n*
fabulous *adj* mirabil·is -is -e
fabulously *adv* perquam
face *s* faci·es -ei *f,* o·s -ris *n; (forward part of anything)* fron·s -tis *f;* **— to —** coram; **— to — with** coram *(w. abl);* **on the — of it** primā facie; **to lose —** honestatem amittere; **to make a — os ducere; **to one's —** coram; **to save — dignitatem conservare
face *tr (to look towards)* aspicere; *(to withstand, e.g., danger)* obviam ire *(w. dat); (to confront)* se opponere *(w. dat)* **∥** *intr* spectare; **to — about** *(mil)* signa convertere; **to — north (south,** *etc.)* ad *or* in septentrionem (in meridiem, *etc.)* spectare
face powder *s* fuc·us -i *m*
facet *s* gemmae superfici·es -ei *f; (fig)* aspect·us -ūs *m*
facetious *adj* facet·us -a -um
facetiously *adv* facete
face value *s (com)* nom·en -inis *n; (fig)* speci·es -ei *f*
facilitate *tr* facilius reddere
facility *s (skill)* facult·as -atis *f; (ease)* facilit·as -atis *f;* **facilities** commod·a -orum *npl*
facing *s (archit)* tector·ium -(i)i *n*
facing *adj* adversus *(w. acc)*
facsimile *s* imag·o -inis *f*

fact *s* fact·um -i *n,* res, rei *f;* **as a matter of —** enimvero; **in —** vero, quidem; **the — that ... — quod *(w. indic);* **the —s speak for themselves** res ipsa indicat *or* res pro se loquitur
faction *s* facti·o -onis *f; (party)* part·es -ium *fpl*
factory *s* officin·a -ae *f*
faculty *s* facult·as -atis *f; (educ)* ord·o -inis *m* professorum
fade *intr (of colors)* pallēre; *(of strength, etc.)* marcescere; **to — away** evanescere
fag, faggot *s (sl)* cinaed·us -i *m*
fail *tr (to disappoint)* deficere; *(to desert)* deserere, destituere; **time, voice, lungs — me** me dies, vox, latera deficiunt; **to — a test** probatione cadere; **words — me** quid dicam non invenio **∥** *intr* deficere; *(educ)* cadere; *(com)* decoquere
fail *s* **without —** certo, omnino
failing *s (deficiency)* defect·us -ūs *m; (fault)* vit·ium -(i)i *n; (ceasing)* remissi·o -onis *f*
failure *s (of strength, breath, supplies)* defecti·o -onis *f; (lack of success)* offensi·o -onis *f; (com)* ruin·a -ae *f* fortunarum; *(person)* hom·o -inis *mf* perditus (-a); *(fault)* vit·ium -(i)i *n*
faint *adj (weary)* fess·us -a -um; *(drooping)* languid·us -a -um; *(sight, etc.)* heb·es -itis; *(sound)* surd·us -a -um; *(colors)* pallid·us -a -um; *(courage)* timid·us -a -um
faint *intr* collabi, animo linqui
faint-hearted *adj* ignav·us -a -um
faintness *s (of impression)* levit·as -atis *f; (of body)* langu·or -oris *m*
fair *adj (handsome)* pul·cher -chra -chrum; *(complexion)* candid·us -a -um; *(hair)* flav·us -a -um; *(weather)* seren·us -a -um; *(cloudless)* sud·us -a -um; *(wind)* secund·us -a -um; *(impartial)* aequ·us -a -um; *(ability)* mediocr·is -is -e; **— and square** sine fuco ac fallaciis; **I think that's — id aequi facio; **that's not — of you** non aequum facis
fair *s* nundin·ae -arum *fpl*
fairground *s* prat·um -i *n* festivum
fairly *adv* aeque; *(somewhat)* aliquantulum; *(moderately)* mediocriter
fair-minded *adj (just)* iust·us -a -um; *(impartial)* aequ·us -a -um
fairness *s (justice)* aequit·as -atis *f; (of complexion)* cand·or -oris *m*
fairy *s* num·en -inis *n; (water fairy)* nymph·a -ae *f; (wood fairy)* dry·as -adis *f; (homosexual) (sl)* cinaed·us -i *m*
fairytale *s* fabul·a -ae *f*
faith *s* fid·es -ei *f;* **in bad — de fide malā; **in good — ex bonā fide; **to have — in** credere *(w. dat)*
faithful *adj* fid·us -a -um, fidel·is -is -e
faithfully *adv* fideliter

faithfulness *s* fidelit·as -atis *f*
faithless *adj* infidel·is -is -e
faithlessly *adv* perfide
fake *s* simulati·o -onis *f; (person)* simula·tor -oris *m* (·trix -tricis *f)*
fake *adj* fucos·us -a -um, fall·ax -acis
fake *tr* simulare
falcon *s* falc·o -onis *m*
fall *s (drop)* cas·us -ūs *m; (by slipping)* laps·us -ūs *m; (autumn)* autumn·us -i *m; (e.g., of a tower)* ruin·a -ae *f; (of a town)* excid·ium -(i)i *n; (decrease)* deminuti·o -onis *f; (moral)* laps·us -ūs *m;* the —s desiliens aqu·a -ae *f*
fall *intr* cadere; *(several together)* concidere; *(to die)* occidere; *(to abate)* decrescere; *(violently)* corruere; *(to occur)* accidere, incidere; *(by lot)* contingere; to — apart dilabi; to — at the feet of procubare ad pedes *(w. gen);* to — asleep in somnum decidere, obdormiscere; to — away desciscere; to — back recidere; *(to retreat)* pedem referre; to — back on recurrere ad *(w. acc);* to — down on *(e.g., the bed)* decidere in *(w. acc);* to — due cadere; to — for *(a person)* amore perdi in *(w. acc); (a trick)* falli *(w. abl);* to — forwards procidere, prolabi; to — in love with amare, coepisse amare; to — into incidere in *(w. acc);* to — in with *(to meet)* incidere in *(w. acc); (to agree)* congruere cum *(w. abl);* to — into a trap in plagas incidere; to — into the hands of in manūs *(w. gen)* incidere, in potestatem *(w. gen)* devenire; to — off *(e.g., a wagon)* decidere de *or* ex *(w. abl); (fig)* in deterius mutari; to — on *(a certain day)* incidere in *(w. acc);* to — on one's sword in gladium incumbere; to — on top of incidere super *(w. acc);* to — out *(mil)* ordine egredi; to — out of excidere de *(w. abl);* — out with *(in disagreement)* dissentire ab *(w. abl);* to — short of non contingere; to — over *(to topple over)* cadere; *(to stumble over)* pedem offendere ad *(w. acc);* to — short deficere; to — short of the goal metam non contingere; to — sick in morbum incidere; to — to *(of inheritances, etc.)* obvenire *(w. dat);* to — to the ground in terram decidere; to — under *(to be listed under)* cadere sub *(w. acc);* to — under s.o.'s sway in ditionem alicuius venire, in potestatem alicuius cadere; to — upon incidere ad *(w. acc); (to assail)* incidere in *(w. acc);* to let — demittere
fallacious *adj* fall·ax -acis
fallacy *s* capti·o -onis *f*
fallible *adj* errori obnoxi·us -a -um
fallow *adj (land)* noval·is -is -e; to lie — cessare
false *adj* fals·us -a -um; *(counterfeit)* adulterin·us -a -um

falsehood *s* comment·um -i *n*
falsely *adv* falso
falsify *tr (documents)* corrumpere; *(to tamper with)* vitiare
falsity *s* fals·um -i *n*
falter *intr (to stammer)* haesitare; *(to totter)* titubare
falteringly *adv* titubanter
fame *s* fam·a -ae *f,* clarit·as -atis *f*
famed *adj* clar·us -a -um
familiar *adj* (with) familiar·is -is -e *(w. dat); (well known)* not·us -a -um; to be on — terms with familiariter uti *(w. abl)*
familiarity *s* familiarit·as -atis *f;* to be on terms of — with familiariter uti *(w. abl)*
familiarize *tr* (with) assuefacere *(w. dat)*
family *s (parents and children)* dom·us -ūs *f; (household and domestics)* famili·a -ae *f;* — on the father's (mother's) side paternum (maternum) gen·us -eris *n;* to come from a good — honesto loco nat·us -a -um esse
family *adj* familiar·is -is -e; — inheritance heredit·as -atis *f* gentilicia; — name gentile nom·en -inis *n;* — secrets arcan·a -orum *npl* domūs; — tree gen·us -eris *n,* stemm·a -atis *n*
famine *s* fam·es -is *f*
famished *adj* famelic·us -a -um
famous *adj* (prae)clar·us -a -um; — for inclut·us -a -um *(w. abl)*
famously *adv* insigniter
fan *s* flabell·um -i *n; (admirer)* fau·tor -toris *m* (·trix -tricis *f); (winnowing)* vann·us -i *m*
fan *tr* ventilare; *(fire)* accendere; *(fig)* excitare
fanatic *adj* fanatic·us -a -um
fanaticism *s* fur·or -oris *m* (religiosus)
fancied *adj* fict·us -a -um
fanciful *adj* commentici·us -a -um
fancy *adj* sumptuos·us -a -um, pretios·us -a -um
fancy *s* imaginati·o -onis *f; (caprice)* libid·o -inis *f; (liking)* prolub·ium -(i)i *n*
fancy *tr* imaginari
fang *s* den·s -tis *m*
fantastic *adj (unreal)* van·us -a -um; *(wonderful)* mirific·us -a -um
far *adj* longinqu·us -a -um; on the — side of the Po ultra Padum
far *adv* procul; *(of degree)* longe; as — as quantum, quatenus; *(up to)* tenus *(always after the governed word) (w. abl or gen);* as — as I'm concerned per me; as — as the neck cervicibus tenus; by — longe, multo; by — the wealthiest state longe opulentissima civit·as -atis *f;* — away procul; — near longe lateque; — be it from me to say equidem dicere nolim; — from it! minime!; — off procul; — otherwise longe aliter; how — quoad, quousque; so — hactenus; so — so

good belle adhuc; **thus —** hactenus; **to be — away (from)** longe abesse (ab *w. abl); **to be very — from the truth** longissime abesse a vero

faraway *adj (distant)* longinqu·us -a -um

farce *s (lit & fig)* mim·us -i *m*

farcical *adj* mimic·us -a -um

fare *s (food)* vict·us -ūs *m; (money)* vectur·a -ae *f; (passenger)* vec·tor -toris *m* (·trix -tricis *f)*

fare *intr* agere, se habēre

farewell *interj* vale! *(pl:* valete!)

far-fetched *adj* arcessit·us -a -um, quaesit·us -a -um; **— idea** quisitum consil·ium -(i)i *n*

far-flung *adj* late pat·ens -entis

farm *s* fund·us -i *m*, rus, ruris *n;* **on the —** ruri

farm *tr (to till)* arare, colere; *(taxes)* redimere; **to — out** locare

farm animals *spl* pecor·a -um *npl*

farmer *s* agricol·a -ae *m*

farm house *s* vill·a -ae *f* (rustica)

farming *s* agricultur·a -ae *f*

farm worker *s* colon·us -i *m*

far-off *adj* longinqu·us -a -um

far-reaching *adj* grav·is -is -e

farsighted *adj* provid·us -a -um

fart *s (sl)* pedit·um -i *n*

fart *intr (sl)* pedere

farther *adj* ulter·ior -ior -ius

farther *adv* longius, ulterius; **no — than** non ultra quam; **to advance —** procedere ulterius

farthermost *adj* ultim·us -a -um

farthest *adj* ultim·us -a -um

fasces *spl* fasc·es -ium *fpl*

fascinate *tr* capere

fascinating *adj* mirific·us -a -um, bland·us -a -um

fascination *s* blanditi·a -ae *f*

fashion *s* mod·us -i *m*, mo·s -ris *m;* **to be in —** more fieri; **to come into — in** morem venire; **to go out of — obsolescere

fashion *tr* fabricare; *(to form a figure of)* effingere

fashionable *adj* eleg·ans -antis; **it is — moris est

fashionably *adv* ad morem

fast *adj (swift)* cel·er -eris -ere; *(firm)* firm·us -a -um; *(tight)* astrict·us -a -um; *(shut)* occlus·us -a -um; *(color)* stabil·is -is -e; *(talk)* expedit·us -a -um

fast *adv (swiftly)* celeriter; *(firmly)* firmiter; **to be — asleep** arte dormire

fast *s* ieiun·ium -(i)i *n;* **to break the — ieiunium solvere; **to keep the — ieiunium servare

fast *intr* ieiunare, cibo abstinēre

fasten *tr* affigere, astringere; *(to tie)* ligare; **to — down** defigere; **to — to** *(w. nails, rivets)* affigere *(w. dat or* ad *w. acc); (by tying)* annectere, illigare *(w. dat or* ad *w. acc);* **to —

together *(w. nails, etc.)* configere; *(by tying)* connectere, colligare ‖ *intr* **to — upon** arripere

fastener *s (clip)* fibul·a -ae *f*

fastening *s (act)* colligati·o -onis *f; (device)* vincul·um -i *n*

fastidious *adj* fastidios·us -a -um

fastidiously *adv* fastidiose

fasting *s* ieiun·ium -(i)i *n*

fat *adj* pingu·is -is -e; **to get — pinguescere

fat *s* ad·eps -ipis *mf*

fatal *adj* fatal·is -is -e, letal·is -is -e

fatality *s* cas·us -ūs *m* fatalis

fatally *adv* fataliter

fate *s* fat·um -i *n; (lot)* sor·s -tis *f*

fated *adj* fatal·is -is -e

fateful *adj* fatal·is -is -e

Fates *spl* Parc·ae -arum *fpl*

fathead *s (sl)* fatu·us -i *m* (·a -ae *f)*

father *s* pa·ter -tris *m;* **— of the family** paterfamilias *(gen:* patrisfamilias) *m;* **on the —'s side** patri·us -a -um

fatherhood *s* paternit·as -atis *f*

father-in-law *s* soc·er -eri *m*

fatherless *adj* orb·us -a -um

fatherly *adj* patern·us -a -um; *(kind)* patri·us -a -um

fathom *s* uln·a -ae *f*

fathom *tr* penitus cognoscere

fathomless *adj* profund·us -a -um

fatigue *s* (de)fatigati·o -onis *f*

fatigue *tr* (de)fatigare

fatigued *adj* (de)fatigat·us -a -um

fatten *tr* saginare ‖ *intr* **to — up** pinguescere

fatty *adj* pingu·is -is -e; **all — substances** omnia quae adipis naturam habent

fatuous *adj* fatu·us -a -um

faucet *s* epitom·ium -(i)i *n;* **to turn on (off) the — epitomium versare (reversare)

fault *s* culp·a -ae *f*, delict·um -i *n;* **I am at — in** culpā sum, penes me culpa est; **not to be at — extra culpam esse; **to be at — *(leg)* in noxā esse; **to find — with** vituperare

faultless *adj* inte·ger -gra -grum; *(without blemish)* emendat·us -a -um

faultlessly *adv* emendate

faulty *adj* vitios·us -a -um; *(having errors)* mendos·us -a -um

faun *s* faun·us -i *m*

favor *s* fav·or -oris *m; (good will of a party or nation)* grati·a -ae *f; (good turn)* benefic·ium -(i)i *n*, grat·um -i *n*, grati·a -ae *f;* **to ask s.o. a — gratiam ab aliquo petere; **to be in — of** favēre *(w. dat);* **to be in — with s.o.** cum aliquo in gratiā esse; **to do s.o. a — gratum alicui facere; **to do s.o. a bigger — gratius alicui facere; **to return s.o. a — gratiam alicui referre; **to restore s.o. to — aliquem in gratiam restituere; **to show — gratiam facere

favor *tr* favēre *(w. dat)*, secundare; **to — severer measures** asperiora suadēre
favorable *adj* prosper·us -a -um; *(wind, circumstances, auspices, gods)* secund·us -a -um; *(suitable)* idone·us -a -um
favorably *adv* benigne; **to be — disposed toward s.o.** bono animo esse in aliquem
favored *adj* grat·us -a -um
favorite *adj* dilect·us -a -um
favorite *s* delici·ae -arum *fpl*
favoritism *s* iniquit·as -atis *f*
fawn *s* hinnule·us -i *m*
fawn *intr* **to — on** adulari
fawning *adj* bland·us -a -um
fax *s* telecopi·a -ae *f*
fax *tr* per telecopiam mittere
fax machine telecopiatr·um -i *n*
fear *s* met·us -ūs *m; (timidity, as a variety of* metus) tim·or -oris *m;* **he put the — of God into them** curavit ut illis Iuppiter iratus esset; **out of —** prae metu; **to be in — in** metu esse; **to be in — of** metuere; **to be inspired with — metum** capere
fear *tr & intr* timēre; *(as a constant condition)* metuere
fearful *adj* **(of)** timid·us -a -um *(w. gen or* ad *w. acc); (dreadful)* terribil·is -is -e, dir·us -a -um
fearless *adj* impavid·us -a -um
fearlessly *adv* impavide, intrepide
feasibility *s* possibilit·as -atis *f*
feasible *adj* possibil·is -is -e
feast *s* epul·ae -arum *fpl; (religious)* di·es -ei *m* festus
feast *tr* pascere; **to — one's eyes on** oculos pascere *(w. abl)* ‖ *intr* epulari
feat *s* facin·us -oris *n; — of arms* facinus *n* militare; **—s** re·s -rum *fpl* gestae
feather *s* penn·a -ae *f; (downy)* plum·a -ae *f*
feather *tr* **to — one's nest** *(fig)* opes accumulare
feathered *adj* pennat·us -a -um
feathery *adj* plumos·us -a -um
feature *s* lineament·um -i *n; (fig)* propriet·as -atis *f*
February *s* Februar·ius -(i)i *m or* mens·is -is *m* Februarius; **in —** mense Februario; **on the first of —** Kalendis Februariis
federal *adj* foederat·us -a -um
federalize *tr* confoederare
federation *s* consociati·o -onis *f*
fee *s* merc·es -edis *f; (for tuition)* Minerv·al -alis *n; (for membership)* honorar·ium -(i)i *n*
feeble *adj* *(infirm)* imbecill·us -a -um; *(frail)* infirm·us -a -um; *(senses, impression made)* heb·es -etis; **to grow —** languescere
feebleness *s* imbecillit·as -atis *f*
feebly *adv* infirme

feed *tr* pascere; *(to nourish)* alere, nutrire; *(of streams, etc.)* servire *(w. dat)* ‖ *intr* **(on)** pasci *(w. abl)*, vesci *(w. abl)*
feed *s* pabul·um -i *n*
feel *tr* *(hunger, pain, heat, cold, etc.)* sentire; *(with hands)* tentare; **to — compassion for** misereri *(w. gen);* **to — grief** dolēre; **to — one's way** viam tentare; *(fig)* caute et cogitate rem tractare; **to — pain** dolore affici; **to — pity for** misereri *(w. gen);* **to — the pulse** *(med)* pulsum venarum attingere, venas tentare ‖ *intr* **because I felt like it** quia mihi libitum est; **I wasn't —ing well** ego me non belle habebam; **to — annoyed** gravari; **to — bad (good)** *(physically)* se male (bene) habēre; **to — better** *(physically)* melius se habēre; **to — fine** se bene habere; **to feel glad** laetari; **to — happy** gaudēre; **to — really bad about** valde dolere; **to — sad** maest·us -a -um esse
feel *s* tact·us -ūs *m*
feeler *s* experiment·um -i *n;* **to send out —s** tentare
feeling *s* *(touch, sensation)* tact·us -ūs *m; (sensibility)* sens·us -ūs *m; (emotion)* affect·us -ūs *m; (taste)* iudic·ium -(i)i *n; (compassion)* misericordi·a -ae *f;* **to hurt s.o.'s —s** aliquem offendere
feign *tr* fingere, dissimulare
feint *s* simulati·o -onis *f*
felicitous *adj* fel·ix -icis
feline *adj* felin·us -a -um
fell *tr* *(trees)* caedere; *(person)* sternere
fellow *s* *(companion)* soc·ius -(i)i *m; (coll)* hom·o -inis *m;* **my good —, what have you there?** mi homo, quid istuc est?; **young —** adulescentul·us -i *m*
fellow citizen *s* civ·is -is *mf*
fellow countryman *s* civ·is -is *m*
fellow creature *s* hom·o -inis *m*
fellow man *s* alt·er -erius *m*
fellow member *s* sodal·is -is *mf*
fellow passenger *s* convec·tor -toris *m* (·trix -tricis *f*)
fellow soldier *s* commilit·o -onis *m*
fellow student *s* condiscipul·us -i *m* (·a -ae *f*)
fellowship *s* sodalit·as -atis *f; (award)* stipend·ium -(i)i *n* in sumptūs studiosorum
fellow townsman *s* munic·eps -ipis *m*
fellow worker *s* soci·us -i *m* (·a -ae *f*) operum
felon *s* scelest·us -i *m* (·a -ae *f*)
felonious *adj* scelest·us -a -um
felony *s* scel·us -eris *n*
felt *adj* coact·us -a -um
felt *s* coact·a -orum *npl*
female *adj* muliebr·is -is -e
female *s* muli·er -eris *f*
feminine *adj* muliebr·is -is -e; *(gram)* feminin·us -a -um

fence *s* saep·es -is *f*
fence *tr* **to — in (off)** saepire ‖ *intr* batuere
fencing *s* gladii ar·s -tis *f*
fend *tr* **to — off** arcēre ‖ *intr* **to — for oneself** sibi consulere
fender *s* luticipul·um -i *n*
ferment *s* ferment·um -i *n;* *(fig)* aest·us -ūs *m*
ferment *tr* fermentare; *(fig)* excitare ‖ *intr* fermentari; *(fig)* fervēre
fermentation *s* fermentati·o -onis *f*
fern *s* fil·ix -icis *f*
ferocious *adj* saev·us -a -um
ferociously *adv* saeve
ferocity *s* saeviti·a -ae *f*
ferret *tr* **to — out** eruere
ferry *s* nav·is -is *f* traiectoria
ferry *tr* traicere
ferryboat *s* cymb·a -ae *f*
ferryman *s* portit·or -oris *m*
fertile *adj* fertil·is -is -e
fertility *s* fertilit·as -atis *f*
fertilize *tr* laetificare
fertilizer *s* laetam·en -inis *n*
fervent *adj* ard·ens -entis
fervently *adv* ardenter
fervid *adj* fervid·us -a -um
fervidly *adv* fervide
fervor *s* ferv·or -oris *m*
fester *intr* suppurare
festival *s* fest·um -i *n*
festive *adj* festiv·us -a -um
festivity *s* *(celebration)* solemn·ia -ium *npl; (gaiety)* festivit·as -atis *f*
fetch *tr* *(to summon)* arcessere; *(to go to get)* petere
fetid *adj* foetid·us -a -um
fetter *s* comp·es -edis *m*
fetter *tr* compedes inicere *(w. dat); (fig)* impedire
feud *s* simult·as -atis *f*
fever *s* febr·is -is *f;* **high —** ardens febris *f;* **slight —** febricul·a -ae *f;* **to have (or to run) a —** febricitare
feverish *adj* febriculos·us -a -um
few *adj* pauc·i -ae -a; **a — aliquot** *[indecl];* **in a — words** paucis
fiasco *s* calamit·as -atis *f*
fiber *s* fibr·a -ae *f*
fickle *adj* mobil·is -is -e
fickleness *s* mobilit·as -atis *f*
fiction *s* ficti·o -onis *f;* narrati·o -onis *f* fabulosa
fictitious *adj* fict·us -a -um
fictitiously *adv* ficte
fiddle *s* fid·es -ium *fpl*
fiddle *intr* fidibus canere
fiddler *s* fidic·en -inis *m,* fidicin·a -ae *f*
fiddlesticks *spl (coll)* nugae!
fidelity *s* fidelit·as -atis *f*

fidget *intr* trepidare
fidgety *adj* inquiet·us -a -um
field *s* ager, agri *m; (plowed)* arv·um -i *n; (undeveloped)* camp·us -i *m; (sports)* are·a -ae *f; (mil)* aci·es -ei *f; (of studies)* disciplin·a -ae *f*
fiend *s* diabol·us -i *m*
fiendish *adj* diabolic·us -a -um
fierce *adj* atr·ox -ocis; *(intensive)* fer·ox -ocis
fiercely *adv* atrociter; ferociter
fierceness *s* atrocit·as -atis *f;* ferocit·as -atis *f*
fiery *adj* igne·us -a -um; *(fig)* ard·ens -entis
fife *s* tibi·a -ae *f*
fifteen *adj* quindecim *[indecl];* **— times** quindecies
fifteenth *adj* quint·us decim·us -a -um
fifth *adj* quint·us -a -um; **for the — time** quinto
fifth *s* quinta par·s -tis *f*
fiftieth *adj* quinquagesim·us -a -um
fifty *adj* quinquaginta *[indecl]*
fig *s* *(fruit, tree)* fic·us -i *f*
fight *s* pugn·a -ae *f; (battle)* proel·ium -(i)i *n; (brawl)* rix·a -ae *f; (boxing)* pugilati·o -onis *f*
fight *tr* pugnare cum *(w. abl)* ‖ *intr* pugnare; *(to brawl)* rixari; *(to box)* pugilari; *(w. sword)* digladiari; **to — it out** depugnare; **to — hand to hand** cominus pugnare
figment *s* **— of the imagination** figment·um -i *n*
figurative *adj* translat·us -a -um
figuratively *adv* per translationem
figure *s* figur·a -ae *f; (any form)* form·a -ae *f; (in a painting)* imag·o -inis *f;* **female —** forma muliebris
figure *tr* *(to think)* putare; **to — out** excogitare ‖ *intr* **to — on** niti *(w. abl)*
figured *adj* *(adorned w. figures)* sigillat·us -a -um
figure of speech *s* figur·a -ae *f* orationis
figure skating *s* patinati·o -onis *f* artificiosa
filament *s* fil·um -i *n*
filbert *s* nu·x -cis *f* avellana
file *s* *(for iron)* lim·a -ae *f; (for woodwork)* scobin·a -ae *f; (for papers)* scap·us -i *m; (cabinet)* scrin·ium -(i)i *n; (row)* ord·o -inis *m; (comput)* document·um -i *n;* **—s** document·a -orum *npl,* act·a -orum *npl;* **in single —** singul·i -ae -a per ordinem
filial *adj* pi·us -a -um
filibuster *intr* legem latam orationibus protractis retardare
filings *spl* scob·is -is *f*
fill *s* **to have one's —** se replēre
fill *tr* implēre; *(office)* fungi *(w. abl);* **to — up** complēre, explēre ‖ *intr* **to — up on** se implēre *(w. abl)*
filly *s* equul·a -ae *f*

film *s (haze)* calig·o -inis *f; (for camera)* tae-niol·a -ae *f,* pellicul·a -ae *f;* **documentary** — taeniola documentaria; **movie** — taeniola cinematographica; **photographic** — taeniola photographica; **to show a** — taeniolam (cin-ematographicam) exhibēre

filter *s* col·um -i *n*

filter *tr* percolare **‖** *intr* percolari

filtering *s* percolati·o -onis *f*

filth *s* sord·es -ium *fpl*

filthiness *s* squal·or -oris *m; (fig)* obscenit·as -atis *f*

filthy *adj* sordid·us -a -um; *(fig)* obscen·us -a -um

filtration *s* percolatı·o -onis *f*

fin *s* pinn·a -ae *f*

final *adj* ultim·us -a -um

finally *adv* denique, postremo

finance *s (private)* res, rei *f* familiaris; *(public)* rati·o -onis *f* aeraria

finance *tr* faenerare

financial *adj* pecuniari·us -a -um

find *tr* invenire, reperire; *(to hit upon)* offend-ere; **to** — **out** cognoscere

finder *s* reper·tor -toris *m* (·trix -tricis *f)*

findings *spl* compert·a -orum *npl*

fine *adj (thin)* tenu·is -is -e; *(opp. of coarse)* subtil·is -is -e; *(superior)* perbon·us -a -um; *(nice)* bell·us -a -um; *(weather)* seren·us -a -um; — **arts** art·es -ium *fpl* elegantiores *(or* ingenuae); **that's** — bene hoc est; **to feel** — se bene habēre; **you did** — probe fecisti

fine *s* mul(c)t·a -ae *f*

fine *tr* mul(c)tare *(w. abl of the fine)*

finery *s* munditi·ae -arum *fpl*

finesse *s* arguti·ae -arum *fpl;* **with** — argute

finger *s* digit·us -i *m; (of glove)* digital·e -is *n;* **index** — index digitus *m;* **little** — minimus digitus *m;* **middle** — medius digitus *m; (as an obscene gesture)* digitus inpudicus *or* infamis *or* obscenus; **not lift a** — pressis manibus sedēre; **ring** — minimo proximus digitus; **to point the** — **at** digitum intendere ad *(w. acc);* **to snap the** —**s** digitis concre-pare

finger *tr (to handle)* attrectare; *(to inform on)* deferre; *(mus)* pulsare

fingernail *s* ungu·is -is *m*

fingertip *s* digit·us -i *m* primoris

finicky *adj* fastidios·us -a -um; — **appetite** fastid·ium -(i)i *n*

finish *s* fin·is -is *m; (in art)* perfecti·o -onis *f; (polish)* politur·a -ae *f*

finish *tr* conficere; *(to put an end to)* terminare; **to** — **off** conficere; *(to use up)* consumere; *(to destroy)* perdere; *(to kill)* occidere; **to add the** —**ing touch to** ultimam manum afferre *(w. dat);* **to** — **speaking** sermonem finire; **to**

— **writing** *(a book, etc.)* absolvere **‖** *intr* desinere

finish line *s (sports)* calx, calcis *f,* cret·a -ae *f*

finite *adj* finit·us -a -um

fire *s* ign·is -is *m; (conflagration)* incend·ium -(i)i *n; (of artillery)* coniect·us -ūs *m; (fig)* ard·or -oris *m;* **by** — **and sword** ferro ignique; **on** — flagr·ans -antis; **to be on** — ardēre; **to catch** — ignem concipere; **to put out a** — incendium exstinguere; **to set on** — incendere, inflammare

fire *tr* accendere; *(missile)* conicere; *(to dis-miss)* amovēre

fire alarm *s* sign·um -i *n* monitorium incendii

fire chief *s* praefect·us -i *m* vigilum

fire engine *s* siph·o -onis *m*

firefighter *s* vig·il -is *mf*

fireplace *s* foc·us -i *m*

fireproof *adj* ignibus impervi·us -a -um

fireside *s* foc·us -i *m*

fire station *s* stati·o -onis *f* vigilum

firewood *s* lign·a -orum *npl*

fireworks *s* spectacul·um -i *n* pyrotechnicum

firm *adj* firm·us -a -um; *(foundation)* stabil·is -is -e; **to stand** — perstare

firm *s (com)* societ·as -atis *f*

firmament *s* cael·um -i *n*

firmly *adv* firme; *(w. firm hold)* tenaciter

firmness *s* firmit·as -atis *f*

first *adj* prim·us -a -um; *(of two)* pri·or -or -us; **among the** — in primis; **for the** — **time** pri-mum; **he was the** — **to enter** primus intravit

first *adv* primum; **at** — primo; — **of all** imprimis

first aid *s* prima curati·o -onis *f*

firstborn *adj* primogenit·us -a -um

first-class *adj* eximi·us -a -um; *(masterly)* graphic·us -a -um; — **seat** sed·es -is *f* primae classis

first fruits *spl* primiti·ae -arum *fpl*

fiscal *adj* aerari·us -a -um; *(belonging to the emperor's finances)* fiscal·is -is -e

fish *s* pisc·is -is *m; (as food)* piscat·us -ūs *m;* **little** — *(lit & fig)* piscicul·us -i *m;* **to catch** — pisces captare

fish *tr* piscari; **to** — **for** *(fig)* expiscari; **to go fishing** piscatum ire

fisher *s* pisc·ator -toris *m* (·trix -tricis *f)*

fishhook *s* ham·us -i *m*

fishing *s* piscat·us -ūs *m*

fishing line *s* lin·um -i *n*

fishing rod *s* (h)arund·o -inis *f* (piscatoria)

fishing tackle *s* instrument·um -i *n* piscatorium

fish market *s* for·um -i *n* piscarium

fish pond *s* piscin·a -ae *f*

fishy *adj* pisculent·us -a -um; *(fig)* suspicios·us -a -um

fissure *s* fissur·a -ae *f*

fist *s* pugn·us -i *m;* **to make a —** pugnum facere

fistfight *s* **to have a —** pugnis certare

fistula *s* fistul·a -ae *f*

fit *s (of anger, etc.)* impet·us -ūs *m;* **a good —** vestiment·um -i *n* bene factum; **by —s and starts** carptim; **fainting —** defecti·o -onis *f;* **—s** morb·us -i *m* comitialis; **to have the —s** *(fig)* delirare; *(in anger)* furere

fit *adj* **(for)** apt·us -a -um, idone·us -a -um *(w. dat); (healthy)* san·us -a -um

fit *tr* accommodare; *(to apply)* applicare; **to — out** instruere, ornare ‖ *intr* convenire; **to — in with** congruere cum *(w. abl);* **to — together** inter se cohaerēre

fitful *adj (sleep)* inquiet·us -a -um

fitly *adv* apte

fitness *s* convenienti·a -ae *f; (of persons)* habilit·as -atis *f*

fitting *adj* dec·ens -entis; **it is —** convenit, decet

five *adj* quinque [*indecl*]; *(distributives)* quin·i -ae -a, *modifying nouns which have no singular, e.g.,* **five camps** quina castr·a -orum *npl;* **— times** quinquies; **— years** quinquenn·ium -(i)i *n*

fix *s* **a quick —** praesens remed·ium -(i)i *n;* **to be in a —** *(coll)* in angustiis versari

fix *tr (to repair)* reficere, corrigere; *(to patch)* resarcire; *(to arrange)* disponere; *(to adjust)* accommodare; *(meals)* parare; *(to fasten)* figere; *(the eyes)* intendere; *(time, place, limits)* statuere; *(to avenge)* ulcisci ‖ *intr* **to — upon** inhaerēre *(w. dat)*

fixed *adj (day, boundaries)* cert·us -a -um; **— resolve** men·s -tis *f* solida; **— stars** stell·ae -arum *fpl* inerrantes; **— upon** *(intent upon)* intent·us -a -um *(w. dat)*

fixture *s* affix·um -i *n*

fizz *intr* sibilare

fizzle *intr* sibilare; *(coll)* deficere, cadere

flabbergast *tr* conturbare

flabbiness *s* molliti·a -ae *f*

flabby *adj* flacc·us -a -um

flaccid *adj* flaccid·us -a -um

flag *s* vexill·um -i *n;* **to wave the —** vexillum quassare

flag *tr* signo indicare ‖ *intr* languescere; *(to lose interest)* refrigescere

flagrant *adj* nefari·us -a -um

flagship *s* nav·is -is *f* praetoria

flail *s* pertic·a -ae *f*

flail *tr* fustibus cudere

flake *s* squam·a -ae *f;* **snow —s** plumeae niv·es -ium *fpl*

flaky *adj (sl)* delir·us -a -um

flame *s (of fire; sweetheart)* flamm·a -ae *f*

flame *intr* flammare; **to — up** scintillare; *(fig)* exardescere

flank *s (of animal)* il·ia -ium *npl; (mil)* lat·us -eris *n;* **on the —** a latere

flank *tr* tegere latus *(w. gen)*

flap *s (of dress)* lacini·a -ae *f*

flap *tr* plaudere *(w. abl);* **to — the wings** alis plaudere ‖ *intr (to hang loosely)* fluitare

flare *s* fulg·or -oris *m; (torch)* fa·x -cis *f*

flare *intr (to blaze)* coruscare; **to — up** *(of diseases)* urgēre; *(of anger, passions)* exardescere

flash *s* fulg·or -oris *m;* **— of lightning** fulg·ur -uris *n;* **in a —** ictu temporis

flash *tr* ostentare ‖ *intr* fulgēre, coruscare

flashback *s* veteris memoriae recordati·o -onis *f*

flashlight *s* instrument·um -i *n* micans

flashy *adj* specios·us -a -um

flask *s* laguncul·a -ae *f*

flat *adj (level)* plan·us -a -um; *(not mountainous)* campes·ter -tris -tre; *(on one's back)* supin·us -a -um; *(on one's face)* pron·us -a -um; *(insipid)* vapid·us -a -um; **to fall —** *(e.g., of a play, speech)* frigēre

flatfooted *adj* plaut·us -a -um

flatly *adv* palam

flatness *s* planiti·es -ei *f*

flatten *tr* complanare; *(to prostrate)* prosternere

flatter *tr* blandiri

flatterer *s* adula·tor -toris *m* (·trix -tricis *f*)

flattering *adj* bland·us -a -um

flattery *s* blanditi·a -ae *f*

flatulence *s* inflati·o -onis *f*

flatware *s* instrument·a -orum *npl* escaria

flaunt *tr* iactare

flaunting *adj* glorios·us -a -um

flaunting *s* iactati·o -onis *f*

flavor *s* sap·or -oris *m; (substance)* condiment·um -i *n*

flavor *tr* condire

flaw *s (defect)* vit·ium -(i)i *n; (chink)* rimul·a -ae *f*

flawless *adj* sine vitio

flax *s* lin·um -i *n*

flea *s* pul·ex -icis *m*

flea market *s* for·um -i *n* rerum venalium

fleck *s* macul·a -ae *f*

fledgling *s* pull·us -i *m*

flee *intr* effugere ‖ *intr* fugere; **to — to** confugere ad *or* in *(w. acc)*

fleece *s* vell·us -eris *n*

fleece *tr (fig)* spoliare

fleecy *adj* lanig·er -era -erum

fleet *s* class·is -is *f*

fleet *adj* cel·er -eris -ere

fleet-footed *adj* celerip·es -edis

fleeting *adj* fug·ax -acis

flesh *s* car·o -nis *f;* **in the —** viv·us -a -um

flesh wound *s* car·o -nis *f* vulnerata

fleshy *adj* corpore·us -a -um; *(fat)* corpulent·us -a -um

flexibility *s* flexibilit·as -atis *f; (fig)* molliti·es -ei *f*

flexible *adj (lit & fig)* flexibil·is -is -e

flick *s* crepit·us -ūs *m; (of the finger)* talitr·um -i *n*

flick *tr* **to — away** excutere

flicker *intr (of a flame)* trepidare

flickering *adj* tremul·us -a -um; **— lamps** occidentes lucern·ae -arum *fpl*

flier *s (circular)* libell·us -i *m*

flight *s (flying)* volat·us -ūs *m; (escape)* effug·ium -(i)i *n; (covey)* gre·x -gis *m;* **— of steps** gradati·o -onis *f;* **to put to —** fugare; **to take to —** terga vertere

flighty *adj* lev·is -is -e

flimsy *adj* praetenu·is -is -e; *(trivial)* frivol·us -a -um

flinch *intr* tergiversari; *(to start)* absilire

fling *s* iact·us -ūs *m;* **to have a —** ingenio indulgēre

fling *tr* conicere; **to — away** abicere; **to — down** deicere; **to — open** reicere, patefacere

flint *s* sil·ex -icis *mf*

flinty *adj* silice·us -a -um

flippancy *s* protervit·as -atis *f*

flippant *adj* prompt·us -a -um atque lev·is -is -e

flippantly *adv* temere ac leviter

flirt *s* lup·us -i *m,* lup·a -ae *f*

flirt *intr* **to — with** *(a person)* subblandiri *(w. dat); (an idea)* ludere cum *(w. abl)*

flirtation *s* leves amor·es -um *mpl*

flit *intr* volitare

float *s (raft)* rat·es -is *f; (on fishing line)* cort·ex -icis *m;* **a — in a parade** fercul·um -i *n* in pompā

float *tr (to launch)* deducere ‖ *intr* fluitare; *(in the air)* volitare

flock *s (of birds, goats, sheep)* gre·x -gis *m;* **in —s** gregatim

flock *intr* **to — around** circumfluere *(w. acc);* **to — to** affluere ad *(w. acc);* **to — together** congregari

floe *s* fragment·um -i *n* glaciei natans

flog *tr* verberare

flogging *s* verberati·o -onis *f;* **to get a —** vapulare

flood *s (deluge)* diluv·ium -(i)i *n; (of tears, words)* flum·en -inis *n;* **the Flood** inundanti·a -ae *f* terrarum

flood *tr (lit & fig)* inundare ‖ *intr* inundare

floodgates *spl* cataract·ae -arum *fpl;* **to open the — of** *(fig)* effundere habenas *(w. gen)*

floodtide *s* access·us -ūs *m*

floor *s (ground)* sol·um -i *n; (paved)* paviment·um -i *n; (story)* tabulat·um -i *n;* **to have the —** veniam dicendi habēre; **to lay the —** pavimentum facere; *(on an upper story)* contabulare; **to throw on the —** in pavimentum proicere

floor *tr (to knock down)* sternere; *(to shock, make a deep impression on)* percutere

flooring *s* contabulati·o -onis *f*

flop *s (failure)* naufrag·ium -(i)i *n*

flop *intr* deficere; *(business)* decoquere; *(theat)* frigēre; **to — down** corruere

floppy disk *s (comput)* discul·us -i *m* flexibilis

floral *adj* flore·us -a -um

florist *s* vendi·tor -toris *m* (·trix -tricis *f*) florum

flotilla *s* classicul·a -ae *f*

flounce *s* instit·a ae *f*

flounder *s (fish)* pass·er -eris *m*

flounder *intr* volutari; *(in speech)* haesitare

flour *s* farin·a -ae *f; (finest)* poll·en -inis *m*

flourish *s (mus)* taratantara *n* [*indecl*]

flourish *tr* vibrare; *(to sound)* canere ‖ *intr* florēre; *(mus)* praeludere

flour mill *s* pistrin·um -i *n*

flout *tr (to scorn)* spernere; *(to mock)* deridēre

flow *s* fluxi·o -onis *f; (of the tide)* access·us -ūs *m; (of words)* flum·en -inis *n*

flow *intr* fluere; **to — by** adluere; **to — down from** defluere de *(w. abl);* **to — into** influere in *(w. acc);* **to — past** praeterfluere

flower *s (lit & fig)* flo·s -ris *m*

flower *intr* florescere

flower bed *s* are·a -ae *f* floribus consita

flowery *adj* florid·us -a -um

flower shop *s* tabern·a -ae *f* floralis

flu *s* graved·o -inis *f;* **to suffer from the —** gravedine loborare

fluctuate *intr* fluctuare; *(fin)* iactari, se iactare

fluctuation *s* fluctuati·o -onis *f; (variation)* mutati·o -onis *f*

flue *s* cunicul·us -i *m* fornacis

fluency *s* volubilit·as -atis *f*

fluent *adj* volubil·is -is -e, perflu·ens -entis

fluently *adv* volubiliter

fluid *adj* fluid·us -a -um

fluid *s* um·or -oris *m*

fluke *s (of anchor)* den·s -tis *m; (luck)* fortuit·um -i *n*

flunk: to — a test in probatione cadere

fluorescent light tubul·us -i *m* florescens

flurry *s* commoti·o -onis *f;* **— of activity** festinati·o -onis *f*

flush *s (blush)* rub·or -oris *m; (onrush)* impet·us -ūs *m*

flush *tr (to purge)* proluere; **to — out** *(game)* excitare ‖ *intr* erubescere

fluster *tr* turbare, inquietare

flute *s* tibi·a -ae *f; (archit)* stri·a -ae *f*

fluting *s (archit)* striatur·a -ae *f*

flutist *s* tibic·en -inis *m; (female)* tibicin·a -ae *f*

flutter *s (of wings)* plaus·us -ūs *m; (bustle)* festinati·o -onis *f; (vibration)* trem·or -oris *m; (of the heart)* palpitati·o -onis *f*
flutter *intr (of a heart)* palpitare; *(of a bird)* volitare; *(of a flag)* fluitare; *(w. alarm)* trepidare
flux *s* flux·us -ūs *m;* **to be in a state of —** fluere
fly *s* musc·a -ae *f;* **a — buzzes** musca bombilat
fly *tr* **to — a plane** aëroplanum gubernare ‖ *intr* volare; *(to flee)* fugere; **to — apart** dissilire; **to — away** *or* **off** avolare; **to — in the face of** lacessere; **to — off the handle** exardescere; **to — open** dissilire, patēre; **to — out** evolare, provolare; **to — under** subtervolare; **to — up** subvolare
flyer *s see* **flier**
flying *adj* volatil·is -is -e
flying *s* volat·us -ūs *m*
foal *s* pull·us -i *m; (of horse)* equul·us -i *m; (of asses)* asell·us -i *m*
foal *tr & intr* pario parere peperi
foam *s* spum·a -ae *f*
foam *intr* spumare; *(of sea)* aestuare
foaming *adj* spum·ans -antis
foamy *adj* spume·us -a -um
focus *tr* **to — attention** *(or* **mind***)* **on** animum attendere ad *(w. acc)*
fodder *s* pabul·um -i *n*
foe *s (public)* host·is -is *m; (private)* inimic·us -i *m* (·a -ae *f)*
fog *s* nebul·a -ae *f*
foggy *adj* nebulos·us -a -um
foible *s* vit·ium -(i)i *n*
foil *s (for fencing)* rud·is -is *f; (leaf of metal)* lamin·a -ae *f; (very thin)* bracte·a -ae *f; (fig)* umbr·a -ae *f*
foil *tr* eludere, frustrari
fold *s* sin·us -ūs *m; (wrinkle)* rug·a -ae *f; (for sheep; the Church)* ovil·e -is *n*
fold *tr* plicare; **to — up** complicare
folder *s* integument·um -i *n* astrictorium; *(comput)* coöpercul·um -i *n*
foliage *s* fron·s -dis *f*
folio *s* li·ber -bri *m* maximae formae
folk *s* homin·es -um *mpl;* **common — vulg·us** -i *n,* pleb·s -is *f*
folk music *s* music·a -ae *f* vulgaris
folk song *s* carm·en -inis *n* vulgare
follow *tr* sequi; *(closely)* instare *(w. dat),* assequi; *(immediately after)* subsequi; *(instructions)* parēre *(w. dat); (to understand)* intellegere; **to — up** *(to the end)* persequi ‖ *intr* insequi; **it —s that** sequitur ut; **to — up on** persequi; **to — upon** supervenire *(w. dat)*
follower *s* secta·tor -toris *m* (·trix -tricis *f); (hanger-on)* assec(u)l·a -ae *mf*
following *s (attendants)* comitat·us -ūs *m; (pol)* facti·o -onis *f*

following *adj* sequ·ens -entis, proxim·us -a -um, poster·us -a -um
folly *s* stultiti·a -ae *f*
foment *tr* fovēre
fond *adj* **(of)** am·ans -antis *(w. gen),* studios·us -a -um *(w. gen);* **to be — of** amare
fondle *tr* mulcēre, fovēre
fondly *adv* amanter
fondness *s* **(for)** *(persons, country)* carit·as -atis *f* (erga *w. acc);* **(for)** *(things)* stud·ium -(i)i *n (w. gen)*
food *s* cib·us -i *m*
food processor *s* machin·a -ae *f* coquinaria
fool *s* stult·us -i *m* (·a -ae *f); (idiot)* fatu·us -i *m* (·a -ae *f);* **to make a — of** ludificare; **to make a — of oneself** fatuari, ineptire
fool *tr* fallere
foolhardily *adv* temere
foolhardy *adj* temerari·us -a -um
foolish *adj* stult·us -a -um
foolishly *adv* stulte; **to act —** ineptire
foolishness *s* stultiti·a -ae *f*
foot *s (of men, animals, tables, chairs)* pe·s -dis *m; (of mountain)* rad·ix -icis *m; (of pillar)* bas·is -is *f;* **on — pedibus; to set — in** pedem ponere in *(w. abl);* **to tread under — calcare**
foot *tr* **to — a bill** impensam sumere
football *s (ball)* pedifoll·is -is *m; (game)* pedifoll·ium -i *n,* pedilud·ium -(i)i *n;* **to kick (pass) the —** pedifollem pulsare (transmittere); **to play —** pedifolle ludere
football player *s* pedilus·or -oris *m*
foothills *spl* radic·es -um *mpl* montis
foothold *s* grad·us -ūs *m* stabilis
footing *s* grad·us -ūs *m;* **on an equal —** ex aequo; **to be on an equal — with** in aequo stare *(w. dat);* **to get one's —** locum capere; **to lose one's —** de gradu labi
footnote *s* annotati·o -onis *f* imae paginae
footpath *s* semit·a -ae *f*
footprint *s* vestig·ium -(i)i *n*
footrace *s* curs·us -ūs *m*
foot soldier *s* ped·es -itis *m*
footstool *s* scabell·um -i *n*
footwear *s* calceament·um -i *n*
for *prep (extent of time or space)* render by *acc; (price)* render by *gen* or *abl; (on behalf of; in place of; instead of; in proportion to, in consideration of)* pro *(w. abl); (purpose)* ad *(w. acc); (cause)* causā *(w. gen) (always after the governed word),* ob *(w. acc); (after negatives)* prae *(w. abl); (toward)* erga *(w. acc); (out of, for, e.g., joy, fear)* prae *(w. abl); (to denote the appointment of a definite time)* in *(w. acc);* **as for** quod attinet ad *(w. acc);* — **all that** nec eo setius; — **nothing** gratis, gratuito; *(in vain)* frustra; — **the last three months** in ternos novissimos menses; — **the rest of the year** in reliquum anni tempus; —

these reasons his de causis; **good — nothing** ad nullam rem util·is -is -e; **to be —** *(to be in favor of)* studēre *(w. dat),* favēre *(w. dat);* **to live — the day** in diem vivere; **what —?** quare?

for *conj (generally first in a clause)* nam, siquidem, *(never first)* enim

forage *s* pabul·um -i *n*

forage *intr* pabulari

foray *s* incursi·o -onis *f*

forbear *intr* desistere

forbearance *s* patienti·a -ae *f*

forbid *tr* vetare, prohibēre

forbidding *adj* odios·us -a -um

force *s* vis *(acc:* vim; *abl:* vi; *pl:* vires) *f;* **by —** vi; **large (small) force** magnae (exiguae) copi·ae -arum *fpl;* **—s** *(mil)* vir·es -ium *fpl,* copiae *fpl;* **to be in —** *(of laws)* valēre; **to use — vim** adhibēre

force *tr* cogere, impellere; *(a door)* rumpere; **to — back** repellere; **to — down** detrudere; **to — out** extrudere, extorquēre; **to — s.o. to surrender** aliquem in dicionem redigere

forced *adj (unnatural)* quaesit·us -a -um; **— march** magnum *or* maximum it·er -ineris *n*

forceful *adj* valid·us -a -um, val·ens -entis

forceps *spl* forc·eps -ipis *mf*

forcible *adj* per vim fact·us -a -um

forcibly *adv* per vim, vi

ford *s* vad·um -i *n*

ford *tr* vado transire

fore *adj* pr·ior -ior -ius

forearm *s* bracch·ium -(i)i *n*

forearm *tr* praemunire; **to be —ed** praecavēre

forebears *spl* maior·es -um *mpl*

forebode *tr* portendere

foreboding *s* portent·um -i *n; (feeling)* praesensi·o -onis *f*

foreboding *adj* presag·us -a -um

forecast *s* coniectur·a -ae *f,* praedicti·o -onis *f; (of weather)* (caeli) praenuntiati·o -onis *f*

forecast *tr* praedicere, praenuntiare

forecastle *s* pror·a -ae *f*

foredoom *tr* praedestinare

forefather *s* atav·us -i *m;* **—s** maior·es -um *mpl*

forefinger *s* index digit·us -i *m*

forego *tr* dimittere

foregone conclusion *s* praeiudicat·um -i *n;* **to take it as a —** id pro praeiudicato ferre

foregoing *adj* pr·ior -ior -ius

forehead *s* fron·s -tis *f*

foreign *adj (of another country)* extern·us -a -um; *(opposite of home-produced)* adventici·us -a -um; *(coming from abroad)* peregrin·us -a -um; *(not pertaining to)* alien·us -a -um; **to live (travel) in a — country** peregrinari

foreigner *s* peregrin·us -i *m* (·a -ae *f)*

foreknowledge *s* providenti·a -ae *f*

forelady *s* procura·trix -tricis *f*

foreman *s* procura·tor -toris *m; (on an estate)* villic·us -i *m*

foremost *adj* prim·us -a -um; *(of chief importance)* princ·eps -ipis

forenoon *s* antemeridianum temp·us -oris *n;* **in the —** ante meridiem

forensic *adj* forens·is -is -e

foreground *s* prior par·s -tis *f*

forerunner *s* praenunt·ius -(i)i *m,* praecurs·or -oris *m*

foresee *tr* providēre

foreseeing *adj* provid·us -a -um

foresight *s* providenti·a -ae *f; (precaution)* provisi·o -onis *f*

forest *adj* silvestr·is -is -e

forest *s* silv·a -ae *f*

forestall *tr* praeoccupare

foretell *tr* praedicere

forethought *s* providenti·a -ae *f*

forever *adv* in perpetuum

forewarn *tr* praemonēre

forfeit *s* mult·a -ae *f*

forfeit *tr* multari *(w. abl)*

forfeiture *s* amissi·o -onis *f*

forge *s* forn·ax -acis *f* ferraria

forge *tr* excudere; *(a document)* corrumpere; **to — a signature on** *(a document)* signo adulterino obsignare

forged *adj* fals·us -a -um

forger *s (of wills)* subiec·tor -toris *m* (·trix -tricis *f);* **(of any document)** falsari·us -i *m* (·a -ae *f)*

forgery *s* fals·um -i *n*

forget *tr* **(about)** oblivisci *(w. gen);* **— about it!** eice id ex animo!

forgetful *adj* oblivios·us -a -um

forgetfulness *s* oblivi·o -onis *f*

forgive *tr* ignoscere *(w. dat)*

forgiveness *s* veni·a -ae *f*

forgiving *adj* ignosc·ens -entis

forgo *tr* dimittere; **to — a triumph** triumphum dimittere

fork *s* furc·a -ae *f; (small fork)* furcill·a -ae *f; (in the road)* biv·ium -(i)i *n*

fork *tr* **to — over** *(coll)* persolvere; **— over!** cedo! *(pl)* cette!

forlorn *adj* destitut·us -a -um

form *s* form·a -ae *f; (document)* formul·a -ae *f; (gram)* figur·a -ae *f;* **in due —** rite

form *tr* formare; *(to produce)* efficere; *(a plan, partnership, alliance)* inire; **to — a long line** agmen longum facere; **to — an opinion** iudicium facere; **to — such bitter enmities** tam graves simultates excipere; **to — the imperative** imperativum facere ‖ *intr* nasci, fieri

formal *adj* iust·us -a -um; *(stiff)* composit·us -a -um

formality *s* rit·us -ūs *m;* **formalities** iust·a -orum *npl;* **with due —** rite

formation *s* conformati·o -onis *f; in —* instruct·us -a -um

former *adj* pr·ior -ior -ius; *(immediately preceding)* super·ior -ior -ius; *(original, olden)* pristin·us -a -um; **the — ... the latter** ille ... hic

formerly *adv* antehac, antea

formidable *adj* formidabil·is -is -e

formless *adj* inform·is -is -e

formula *s* formul·a -ae *f; (leg)* acti·o -onis *f*

forsake *tr* deserere

forswear *tr* adiurare

fort *s* castell·um -i *n*

forth *adv (often expressed in Latin by a prefix, e.g.,* **to go —** exire); **and so —** et cetera; **from that day —** inde, ex eo (die)

forthcoming *adj* futur·us -a -um; **to be —** praesto esse

forthright *adj* apert·us -a -um

forthwith *adv* protinus, extemplo

fortieth *adj* quadragesim·us -a -um

fortification *s* muniment·um -i *n*

fortify *tr* munire

fortitude *s* fortitud·o -inis *f*

fortress *s* castell·um -i *n*

fortuitous *adj* fortuit·us -a -um

fortuitously *adv* fortuito

fortunate *adj* fortunat·us -a -um

fortunately *adv* feliciter

fortune *s* fortun·a -ae *f; (estate)* op·es -ium *fpl,* res, rei *f;* **bad —** fortuna *f* adversa; **good —** fortuna *f* prospera; **to make a —** rem facere; **to squander one's —** rem dissipare; **to tell —s** hariolari

fortuneteller *s* hariol·us *m* (·a -ae *f*)

fortunetelling *s* hariolati·o -onis *f*

forty *adj* quadraginta [*indecl*]

forum *s* for·um -i *n*

forward *s (sports)* oppugna·tor -toris *m* (·trix -tricis *f*)

foreward *tr (mail, e-mail)* deferre

forward *adv* prorsus, prorsum; *(often expressed by the prefix* pro-, *e.g.,* **to move —** promovēre)

forward *adj (cocky)* proterv·us -a -um; **— motion** progress·us -ūs *m*

foster *tr* alere, fovēre

foster brother *s* collacte·us -i *m*

foster child *s* alumn·us -i *m* (·a -ae *f*)

foster father *s* alt·or -oris *m*

foster mother *s* altr·ix -icis *f*

foster sister *s* collacte·a -ae *f*

foul *s* **to commit a —** *(sports)* poenaliter agere

foul *adj (dirty)* foed·us -a -um; *(language)* obscen·us -a -um; *(weather)* turbid·us -a -um; *(deed)* foed·us -a -um; *(smell)* te·ter -tra

-trum; **— play** dol·us -i *m* malus; **to run — of** inruere in *(w. acc)*

foul *tr* inquinare; *(morally)* contaminare; **to — up** *(coll)* conturbare

foully *adv* foede

foul-mouthed *adj* maledic·us -a -um

found *tr* fundare, condere

foundation *s* fundament·um -i *n;* **to lay the — for** *(lit & fig)* fundamenta iacere *(w. gen)*

founder *s* condi·tor -toris *m* (·trix -tricis *f*)

founder *intr (lit & fig)* pessum ire

foundling *s* expositici·us -i *m* (·a -ae *f*)

fountain *s* fon·s -tis *m*

fountainhead *s* cap·ut -itis *n* fontis

fountain pen *s* graph·ium -(i)i *n* replebile

four *adj* quattuor [*indecl*] **— each** quatern·i -ae -a; **— times** quater; **— years** quadrenn·ium -(i)i *n;* **on all —** rep·ens -entis

fourfold *adj* quadrupl·us -a -um

four-footed *adj* quadrup·es -edis

fourscore *adj* octoginta [*indecl*]

fourteen *adj* quattuordecim [*indecl*]

fourteenth *adj* quart·us decim·us -a -um

fourth *adj* quart·us -a -um; **for the — time** quartum

fourth *s* quarta par·s -tis *f;* **three —s** tres part·es -ium *fpl*

fourthly *adv* quarto

fowl *s* av·is -is *f; (domestic)* gallin·a -ae *f*

fox *s* vulp·es -is *f;* **an old —** *(coll)* veterat·or -oris *m;* **foxes yelp** vulpes genniunt

foyer *s* vestibul·um -i *n*

fracas *s (brawl)* rix·a -ae *f; (quarrel)* iurg·ium -(i)i *n*

fraction *s* par·s -tis *f* exigua; *(math)* fracti·o -onis *f*

fracture *s* fractur·a -ae *f*

fracture *tr* frangere

fragile *adj* fragil·is -is -e

fragility *s* fragilit·as -atis *f*

fragment *s* fragment·um -i *n*

fragrance *s* suavis od·or -oris *m*

fragrant *adj* suaveol·ens -entis

frail *adj* infirm·us -a -um

frailty *s* infirmit·as -atis *f*

frame *s (of a picture)* form·a -ae *f; (of the body)* figur·a -ae *f; (of buildings, etc.)* compag·es -is *f; (of bed)* spond·a -ae *f;* **— of mind** anim·us -i *m;* **to be in a good — of mind** bono animo esse

frame *tr* fabricari; *(to contrive)* moliri; *(a picture)* in formā includere; *(a person)* falso insimulare; *(to draw up a form of words)* concipere

framework *s* compag·es -is *f; (of wood)* contignati·o -onis *f*

France *s* Galli·a -ae *f*

franchise *s* iu·s -ris *n* suffragii

frank *adj* lib·er -era -erum, simpl·ex -icis

frankincense *s* tus, turis *n*
frankly *adv* aperte, candide
frankness *s* libert·as -atis *f*
frantic *adj* fur·ens -entis
frantically *adv* furenter
fraternal *adj* fratern·us -a -um
fraternally *adv* fraterne
fraternity *s* sodalit·as -atis *f*
fraternize *intr* conversari
fratricide *s (doer)* fratricid·a -ae *mf; (deed)* fratris parricid·ium -(i)i *n*
fraud *s* frau·s -dis *f; (leg)* dol·us -i *m* malus
fraudulent *adj* fraudulent·us -a -um
fraudulently *adv* fraudulenter
fraught *adj (with)* plen·us -a -um *(w. abl)*
fray *s* rix·a -ae *f; (contest)* certam·en -inis *n*
freak *s* monstr·um -i *n; (whim)* libid·o -inis *f;* — **of nature** lus·us -ūs *m* naturae
freakish *adj* monstruos·us -a -um
freckle *s* lentig·o -inis *f*
freckled *adj* lentiginos·us -a -um
free *adj* lib·er -era -erum; *(disengaged) (from)* vacu·us -a -um *(w. abl); (generous)* liberal·is -is -e; *(from duty, taxes)* immun·is -is -e; *(unencumbered)* expedit·us -a -um; — **of charge** gratuito; **for** — gratis; **if you are** — si vacabis; **to be** — **from** vacare *(w. abl)*
free *tr* liberare; *(slave)* manumittere; *(son)* emancipare
freeborn *adj* ingenu·us -a -um
freely *adv* libere; *(of one's own accord)* sponte, ultro; *(frankly)* aperte; *(generously)* large
freedman *s* libert·us -i *m*
freedom *s* libert·as -atis *f*
freedwoman *s* libert·a -ae *f*
free-style swimming *s* natati·o -onis *f* libera
free will *s* volunt·as -atis *f;* **of one's own** — suā sponte
freeze *tr & intr* gelare; **to** — **up** congelare
freezer *s* caps·a -ae *f* frigorifica
freezing *adj* gelid·us -a -um
freezing, freezing mark *s* punct·um -i *n* glaciale; **three degrees above** — tres gradūs supra punctum glaciale
freight *s (cargo)* on·us -eris *n; (cost)* vectur·a -ae *f*
freighter *s* nav·is -is *f* oneraria
freight train *s* tram·en -inis *n* onerarium
French *adj* Gallic·us -a -um; **in** — Gallice; **to speak** — Gallice loqui
French fries *spl* pom·a -orum *npl* (terrestria) fricta
frenzied *adj* fur·ens -entis
frenzy *s* fur·or -oris *m*
frequency *s* crebrit·as -atis *f*
frequent *adj* cre·ber -bra -brum; **to become** — crebrescere
frequent *tr* frequentare

frequenter *s* frequenta·tor -toris *m* (·trix -tricis *f*)
frequently *adv* crebro; **more** — crebrius; **most** — creberrime
fresco *s* op·us -eris *n* tectorium
fresh *adj (food, flowers, etc.)* rec·ens -entis; *(cool)* frigidul·us -a -um; *(not tired)* inte·ger -gra -grum; *(forward)* proterv·us -a -um; *(green)* virid·is -is -e; *(water)* dulc·is -is -e; — **air** aur·a -ae *f*
freshen *tr* recreare, renovare **‖** *intr (of wind)* increbrescere; **to** — **up** se recreare
freshly *adv* recenter
freshman *s* tir·o -onis *mf*
freshness *s* viridit·as -atis *f*
fret *intr* angi, stomachari
fretful *adj* stomachos·us -a -um
fretting *s* sollicitud·o -inis *f*
friction *s* fricti·o -onis *f*
Friday *s* di·es -ei *m* Veneris
fried *adj* frict·us -a -um; — **eggs** ov·a -orum *npl* in oleo fricta
friend *s* amic·us -i *m* (·a -ae *f*), familiar·is -is *mf; (of a thing)* ama·tor -toris *m* (·trix -tricis *f*); **best** — summus amicus, summa amica
friendless *adj* amicorum in·ops -opis
friendliness *s* benevolenti·a -ae *f*
friendly *adj* amic·us -a -um; **in a** — **manner** amice
friendship *s* amiciti·a -ae *f*
frieze *s* zoöphor·us -i *m*
fright *s* terr·or -oris *m*
frighten *tr* terrēre; **to** — **away** absterrēre
frightening *adj* terrific·us -a -um
frightful *adj* terribil·is -is -e
frightfully *adv* foede
frigid *adj* frigid·us -a -um
frigidity *s* frig·us -oris *n*
frigidly *adv* frigide
frill *s (plaited border)* instit·a -ae *f;* —**s** *(fig)* tric·ae -arum *fpl*
fringe *s (trim)* fimbri·ae -arum *fpl; (border)* marg·o -inis *m*
fringe *adj (outer)* ultimus -a -um; *(secondary)* secundari·us -a -um
fringed *adj* fimbriat·us -a -um
frisk *tr* scrutari **‖** *intr* lascivire
fritter *s* lagan·um -i *n*
fritter *tr* **to** — **away** terere
frivolity *s* levit·as -atis *f; (thing)* nug·ae -arum *fpl*
frivolous *adj* frivol·us -a -um
frivolously *adv* nugatorie
frizzle *tr* crispare
frizzled *adj* calamistrat·us -a -um
fro *adv* **to and** — huc (et) illuc
frog *s* ran·a -ae *f;* —**s croak** ranae coaxant
frolic *intr* lascivire

from *prep* a(b) *(w. abl); (denoting strictly descent from above, but used in other senses; subtraction; source)* de *(w. abl); (from within, out of)* e(x) *(w. abl); (cause)* ob *(w. acc);* — **above** desuper; — **a to z** *(fig)* ab acia et acu; — **day to day** diem de die; — **here** hinc; — **there** illinc; — **where** unde; — **within** intrinsecus; — **without** extrinsecus

front *s* fron·s -tis *f; (on the march)* primum agm·en -inis *n; (appearance)* speci·es -ei *f;* **in** — a fronte, adversus; **in** — **of** *(in the presence of)* coram *(w. abl); (position)* pro *(w. abl);* **the** — **of the classroom** prior par·s -tis *f* conclavis scholaris; **the** — **of the house** frons aedium

front *adj* pr·ior -ior -ius; *(feet)* prim·us -a -um; — **door** antic·um -i *n;* — **hall** vestibul·um -i *n,* fauc·es -ium *fpl;* — **seat** sed·es -is *f* anterior; — **teeth** dent·es -ium *mpl* primores

frontage *s* fron·s -tis *f;* **a hundred feet of** — centum pedes in fronte

frontal *adj* advers·us -a -um; — **attack** impet·us -ūs *m* ex adverso

frontier *s* lim·es -itis *m; (fig)* termin·us -i *m*

frontline *s (mil)* aci·es -ei *f*

frost *s* pruin·a -ae *f*

frostbitten *adj* frigore ambust·us -a -um

frosty *adj* pruinos·us -a -um

froth *s* spum·a -ae *f*

froth *intr* spumare

frothy *adj* spume·us -a -um

frown *s* contracti·o -onis *f* frontis

frown *intr* frontem contrahere; **to** — **on** improbare

frozen *adj* frigore *(or* glacie) concret·us -a -um

frugal *adj* frugi [*indecl*]

frugality *s* frugalit·as -atis *f*

frugally *adv* frugaliter

fruit *s* fruct·us -ūs *m; (esp. orchard fruit)* pom·um -i *n; (of tree)* mal·a -orum *npl;* —**s of the earth** frug·es -ium *fpl*

fruitful *adj* fecund·us -a -um; *(actually yielding fruit)* frugif·er -era -erum

fruitfully *adv* fecunde

fruitfulness *s* fecundit·as -atis *f*

fruit juice suc·us -i *m* pomarius

fruitless *adj* steril·is -is -e; *(fig)* irrit·us -a -um

fruitlessly *adv* frustra

fruit stand *s* tabern·a -ae *f* pomaria

fruit tree *s* pom·us -i *f*

frustrate *tr (to break off, e.g., an undertaking)* dirimere, ad irritum redigere; *(to baffle)* frustrari

frustrating *adj* incommod·us -a -um

frustration *s* frustrati·o -onis *f*

fry *s (dish of things fried)* frix·a -ae *f*

fry *tr* frigere

frying pan *s* sartag·o -inis *f*

fuel *s* aliment·um -i *n,* materi·a -ae *f* propulsoria; **to add** — **to the flames** *(fig)* oleum addere camino

fuel oil *s* ole·um -i *n* incendiarium

fuel tank *s* olei receptacul·um -i *n*

fugitive *s (from country or home)* profug·a -ae *mf; (pej)* fugitiv·us -i *m (·a -ae f)*

fugitive *adj* fugitiv·us -a -um

fulcrum *s (of lever)* pressi·o -onis *f*

fulfill *tr (a duty)* explēre, praestare; *(prophecy)* implēre; **to** — **a promise** promissum exsolvere

fulfilled *adj (prayer, hope)* rat·us -a -um

fulfillment *s (carrying out)* exsecuti·o -onis *f; (of a prophecy, etc.)* perfecti·o -onis *f*

full *adj (of)* plen·us -a -um *(w. gen or abl); (filled up)* explet·us -a -um; *(entire)* solid·us -a -um; *(satisfied)* sat·ur -ura -urum; *(dress)* fus·us -a -um; **at** — **speed** citato gradu; **in** — **swing** in mediis rebus

full-blown *adj (flowers)* apert·us -a -um; *(mature)* adult·us -a -um

full-grown *adj* adult·us -a -um

full-length *(dress)* talar·is -is -e

fully *adv (completely)* plene, funditus; *(quite)* penitus, prorsus

full moon *s* plenilun·ium -(i)i *n*

fumble *tr (the ball)* demittere ‖ *intr* haesitare; **to** — **for** explorare

fume *s* halit·us -ūs *m*

fume *intr* exaestuare

fumigate *tr* fumigare, suffire

fumigation *s* suffit·us -ūs *m*

fun *s* ioc·us -i *m;* **pure** — mera hilar·ia -ium *npl;* **to have** — se oblectare; **to make** — **of** *(or* **poke** —at) eludere; **to say it for** — id per iocum dicere

function *s* mun·us -eris *n,* offic·ium -(i)i *n; (gram)* potenti·a -ae *f*

function *intr* fungi, munus implēre

functionary *s* magistrat·us -ūs *m*

fund *s* pecuni·a -ae *f* collecta; *(store of anything)* copi·a -ae *f;* —**s** pecunia *f,* op·es -um *fpl*

fundamental *adj* prim·us -a -um

fundamentally *adv* funditus, penitus

funeral *s* fun·us -eris *n; (funeral procession and obsequies)* exsequi·ae -arum *fpl;* **to attend a** — (con)venire in funus

funeral *adj* funere·us -a -um; **to perform the** — **rites** parentare

funereal *adj* funebr·is -is -e

fungus *s* fung·us -i *m*

funnel *s* infundibul·um -i *n*

funny *adj* ridicul·us -a -um; *(humorous)* festiv·us -a um

fur *s* pell·is -is *f*

furious *adj* furios·us -a -um

furiously *adv* furiose

furl *tr* complicare; *(sail)* legere
furlough *s* commeat·us -ūs *m; on* — in com-
meatu; **to get a** — commeatum impetrare; **to**
grant a — commeatum dare
furnace *s* forn·ax -acis *f*
furnish *tr* suppeditare; *(to fit out)* ornare,
instruere; **to** — **a home (an apartment)**
supellectile instruere
furnished *adj* (supellectile) instruct·us -a -um
furniture *s* supell·ex -ectilis *f;* **piece of** —
par·s -tis *f* supellectilis
furrow *s* sulc·us -i *m*
furry *adj* villos·us -a -um
further *adj* ulter·ior -ior -ius; **without** — **ado**
sine morā; sine ullo tumultu
further *adv* ultra, longius
further *tr (to serve)* servire *(w. dat); (to pro-*
mote) promovēre; *(to aid)* adiuvare; **to** —
our own interests nostris commodis servire
furtherance *s* progress·us -ūs *m*
furthermore *adv* porro, praeterea
furthest *adj* ultim·us -a -um
furthest *adv* longissime
furtive *adj* furtiv·us -a -um
furtively *adv* furtim, furtive
fury *s* fur·or -oris *m*
fuse *tr* fundere ‖ *intr* coalescere
fusion *s* fusur·a -ae *f*
fuss *s* perturbati·o -onis *f;* **to make a great** —
over nothing laborare in angusto, *(coll)* de
lanā caprinā rixari
fuss *intr* satagere, tumultuari
fussy *adj* fastidios·us -a -um
futile *adj* futil·is -is -e
futility *s* futilit·as -atis *f*
future *adj* futur·us -a -um; **for all** — **time** in
posterum; — **perfect tense** temp·us -oris *n*
futurum perfectum; — **tense** tempus futurum
future *s* futur·a -orum *npl,* posterum temp·us
-oris *n;* **in the** — posthac; **for the** — in
posterum

G

gab *s* garrulit·as -atis *f*
gab *intr* garrire
gabby *adj* garrul·us -a -um
gable *s* fastig·ium -(i)i *n*
gadfly *s* taban·us -i *m*
gag *s (joke)* ioc·us -i *m*
gag *tr* os obstruere *(w. dat)* ‖ *intr* nauseare
gaiety *s* hilarit·as -atis *f*
gaily *adv* hilare
gain *s* lucr·um -i *n*
gain *tr* consequi, acquirere; *(victory)* consequi,
adipisci; *(by asking)* impetrare; *(office, mili-*

tary command) capere; **to** — **access to a per-**
son penetrare ad aliquem; **to** — **ground** *(fig)*
increbrescere; **to** — **possession of** potiri
(w. abl)
gainful *adj* lucros·us -a -um
gainsay *tr* contradicere *(w. dat)*
gait *s* incess·us -ūs *m*
gala *adj* festiv·us -a -um
gala *s* festivit·as -atis *f*
galaxy *s* ingens coët·us -ūs *m* stellarum; vi·a
-ae *f* lactea
gale *s* procell·a -ae *f*
gall *s* bil·is -is *f; (insolence)* insolenti·a -ae *f*
gall *tr* urere, mordēre
gallant *adj* fort·is -is -e; *(polite)* officios·us
-a -um
gallantly *adv* fortiter
gallantry *s* fortitud·o -inis *f*
gall bladder *s* fel, fellis *n*
gallery *s* portic·us -ūs *f; (open)* peristyl·ium
-(i)i *n; (for paintings)* pinacothec·a -ae *f*
galley *s* nav·is -is *f* longa; *(two banks of oars)*
birem·is -is *f; (three banks of oars)* trirem·is
-is *f; (kitchen)* culin·a -ae *f*
Gallic *adj* Gallic·us -a -um
galling *adj* mord·ax -acis
gallon *s* cong·ius -(i)i *m*
gallop *s* citissimus curs·us -ūs *m; at a* — citato equo
gallop *intr (of a horse)* quadrupedare; *(of the*
rider) citato equo contendere
gallows *s* patibul·um -i *n*
gallstone *s* calcul·us -i *m*
galore *adv* satis superque
galvanize *tr* incitare
gamble *tr* **to** — **away** in aleā perdere ‖ *intr*
aleā ludere
gambler *s* alea·tor -toris *m* (·trix -tricis *f*)
gambling *s* ale·a -ae *f*
game *s* lud·us -i *m; (w. dice)* ale·a -ae *f; (veni-*
son) praed·a -ae *f;* **to make** — **of** ludificari;
to play a — lusum ludere
gamecock *s* gall·us -i *m* rixosus
game show *s* spectacul·um -i *n* lusorium
gamut *s* tota rerum seri·es -ei *f;* **to run the** —
omnia amplecti
gander *s* ans·er -eris *m;* **to take a** — **at** *(coll)*
strictim aspicere
gang *s* gre·x -gis *m,* man·us -ūs *f; (of ruffians)*
grex grassatorum
gang *intr* **to** — **together** coniurare; **to** — **up on**
conspirare in *(w. acc)*
gang member *s* praed·o -onis *m* gregalis
gangplank *s (naut)* pon·s -tis *m*
gangrene *s* gangren·a -a *f*
gangster *s* grassat·or -oris *m*
gangway *s (naut)* for·us -i *m*
gap *s* hiat·us -ūs *m*

gape *intr* hiare; **to — at** attonito animo inhiare *(w. dat)*

gaping *adj* hi·ans -antis

garage *s* autocineti *(or* autocinetorum) receptacul·um -i *n*

garb *s* vestit·us -ūs *m*, cult·us -ūs *m*

garbage *s* quisquili·ae -arum *fpl*; **— in, — out** ex quisquiliis fiunt quisqiliae

garble *tr* corrumpere, detorquēre

garden *s* hort·us -i *m*

gardener *s* hortulan·us -i *m; (ornamental)* topiar·ius -(i)i *m*

gardening *s* hortorum cult·us -ūs *m; (ornamental)* topiaria ar·s -tis *f*

gargle *intr* gargarizare

gargling *s* gargarizati·o -onis *f*

garland *s* coron·a -ae *f*, sert·a -ae *f*

garlic *s* al(l)·ium -(i)i *n*

garment *s* vestiment·um -i *n*

garner *tr* colligere

garnish *tr* ornare

garret *s* cenacul·um -i *n*

garrison *s* praesid·ium -(i)i *n*

garrison *tr (a post w. troops)* praesidium collocare in *(w. abl)*

garter *s* periscel·is -idis *f*

gas *s (anat)* inflati·o -onis *f; (gasoline)* benzin·um -i *n;* **step on the — !** *(coll)* matura *(pl:* maturate)!; **to step on the —** pedale benzinarium deprimere

gash *s* patens plag·a -ae *f*

gash *tr* caesim ferire

gasp *s* anhelit·us -ūs *m*

gasp *intr* anhelare; **to — for breath** singultare animam

gas pedal *s* pedal·e -is *n* benzinarium

gas pump *s* antli·a -ae *f* benzinaria

gas station *s* stati·o -onis *f* benzinaria

gas stove *s* focul·us -i *n* gaseus

gas tank *s* immissar·ium -(i)i *n* benzinarium

gastric *adj* stomachi [*gen*]

gastronomy *s* ars, artis *f* coquinaria

gate *s* port·a -ae *f*

gateway *s* adit·us -ūs *m*

gather *tr (to assemble)* colligere; *(fruit, nuts, flowers)* legere; *(to infer)* colligere, conicere; *(to suspect)* suspicari; **to — up** colligere ‖ *intr* convenire

gathering *s* convent·us -ūs *m; (collecting)* collecti·o -onis *f*

gaudily *adv* laute

gaudiness *s* lautiti·a -ae *f*

gaudy *adj* laut·us -a -um

gauge *s* modul·us -i *m*

gauge *tr* metiri

gaunt *adj* ma·cer -cra -crum

gauntlet *s* digital·ia -ium *npl;* **to throw down the —** provocare

gauze *s* co·a -orum *npl*

gawk *intr* **(at)** stupide spectare

gawky *adj* inept·us -a -um

gay *adj* hilar·is -is -e; *(homosexual)* cinaed·us -a -um

gay *s* cinaed·us -i *m*

gaze *s* conspect·us -ūs *m; (fixed look)* obtut·us -ūs *m*

gaze *intr* tueri; **to — at** intueri

gazelle *s* dorc·as -adis *f*

gear *s* apparat·us -ūs *m*

gearshift *s* iuncti·o -onis *f* velocitatum

gee *interj* hercle!; edepol!

geez *interj* eu hercle!; eu edepol!

gem *s* gemm·a -ae *f*

gender *s* gen·us -eris *n*

genealogy *s* propagin·es -um *fpl*

general *adj (as opposed to specific)* general·is -is -e; *(wide-spread)* vulgar·is -is -e; *(shared by all)* commun·is -is -e, public·us -a -um; **in — ad summum,** generatim

general *s* du·x -cis *mf*, impera·tor -toris *m* (·trix -tricis *f*)

generalize *intr* in summam loqui

generally *adv (opp: specifically:* membratim) generatim; *(for the most part)* plerumque, fere

generalship *s* duct·us -ūs *m*

general store *s* pantopol·ium -(i)i *n*

generate *tr* generare

generation *s (act of producing)* generati·o -onis *f; (age)* aet·as -atis *f*

generic *adj* general·is -is -e

generosity *s* liberalit·as -atis *f*

generous *adj* liberal·is -is -e

generously *adv* liberaliter

genesis *s* orig·o -inis *f*

genial *adj* com·is -is -e

geniality *s* comit·as -atis *f*

genially *adv* comiter

genitals *spl* genital·ia -ium *npl; (female)* muliebr·ia -ium *npl*

genitive *s* genitiv·us -i *m*, cas·us -ūs *m* genitivus

genius *s* ingen·ium -(i)i *n*

genteel *adj* urban·us -a -um

gentile *adj* gentil·is -is -e

gentile *s* gentil·is -is *mf*

gentility *s* nobilit·as -atis *f*

gentle *adj* clem·ens -entis, mit·is -is -e; *(gradual)* moll·is -is -e; *(wind, etc.)* len·is -is -e; *(tame)* mansuet·us -a -um

gentleman *s* vi·r -ri *m* honestus

gentleness *s* clementi·a -ae *f; (gradualness)* lenit·as -atis *f; (tameness)* mansuetud·o -inis *f*

gently *adv* leniter, clementer; *(gradually)* sensim

gentry *s* optimat·es -um *mpl*

genuine *adj* sincer·us -a -um

genuinely *adv* sincere
genus *s* gen·us -eris *n*
geographer *s* geograph·us -i *m* (·a -ae *f*)
geographical *adj* geographic·us -a -um
geography *s* geographi·a -ae *f*
geological *adj* geologic·us -a -um
geologist *s* geolog·us -i *m* (·a -ae *f*)
geology *s* geologi·a -ae *f*
geometric(al) *adj* geometric·us -a -um
geometry *s* geometri·a -ae *f*
germ *s* germ·en -inis *n*
German *adj* Germanic·us -a -um
German *s* German·us -i *m* (·a -ae *f*); **to speak** — Germanice loqui
germane *adj* affin·is -is -e
Germany *s* Germani·a -ae *f*
germinate *intr* germinare
germination *s* germinat·us -ūs *m*
gerund *s* gerund·ium -(i)i *n*
gesticulate *intr* gesticulari
gesture *s* gest·us -ūs *m*
gesture *intr* gestu indicare
get *tr* (*to acquire*) nancisci; (*to receive*) accipere; (*by purchase*) parare, comparare; (*by entreaty*) impetrare; (*to fetch*) afferre; (*to understand*) tenēre, comprehendere; (*a cold*) incidere in (*w. acc*); **I can't** — **him to talk** non quco orare ut loquatur; **now** — **this** nunc cognosce rem; **to** — **back** recuperare, repetere; **to** — **down** depromere; **to** — **hold of** prehendere; **to** — **in** (*crops*) condere; **to** — (*a defendant*) **off** expedire, servare; **to** — **out** (*a spot*) oblitterare; (*to extort*) extorquēre; **to** — **ready** parare; **to** — **rid of** tollere; (*a person*) amoliri; **to** — **the better of** superare; **to** — **together** cogere ‖ *intr* (*to become*) fieri; — **out of my way!** de via mea decede (*pl*: decedite)!; **to** — **abroad** palam fieri; **to** — **along well** bene se habēre; **to** — **along with** concorditer congruere cum (*w. abl*); **to** — **away** aufugere, evadere; **to** — **at** ulcisci; **to** — **back** reverti; **to** — **down** descendere; **to** — **dressed** amiciri; **to** — **even with** malum vicissim dare (*w. dat*); **to** — **in** pervenire; **to** — **off** aufugere; (*a bus, plane, ship, train*) egredi de (*w. abl*); **to** — **on** procedere; (*a horse*) conscendere; (*a bus, plane, ship, train*) inscendere in (*w. acc*); **to** — **on well** bene se habēre; (*to succeed*) bene succedere; **to** — **out** exire; (e curru) descendere; **to** — **out of** (*a situation*) evadere; **to** — **over** (*a wall*) transcendere; (*difficulty*) superare; (*a sickness*) convalescere ex (*w. abl*); **to** — **ready** sese parare; **to** — **rid of** (*that pest*) (istum molestum) amoliri; **to** — **somewhere** aliquid consequi; **to** — **through** (*to complete*) conficere; **to** — **to** (*a place*) prevenire; **to** — **together** congregari, convenire; **to** — **up** surgere; (*as a group*) consurgere; (*from sleep*) expergisci; (*out of respect due s.o.*) assurgere

ghastly *adj* (*deadly pale*) lurid·us -a -um; (*shocking*) foed·us -a -um
ghost *s* umbr·a -ae *f*; (*haunting spirit*) larv·a -ae *f*; **to give up the** — animam ebullire
ghost town *s* urb·s -is *f* deserta
giant *s* gig·as -antis *m*
gibberish *s* nug·ae -arum *fpl*
gibbet *s* patibul·um -i *n*
gibe *s* irrisi·o -onis *f*
gibe *tr & intr* irridēre
giblets *spl* gingeri·a -orum *npl*
Gibraltar *s* Calp·e -es *f*; **strait of** — fret·um -i *n* Gaditanum
giddiness *s* vertig·o -inis *f*
giddy *adj* vertiginos·us -a -um; (*light-minded*) lev·is -is -e
gift *s* don·um -i *n*, mun·us -eris *n*; (*e.g., of beauty*) do·s -tis *f*
gifted *adj* ingenios·us -a -um; (*endowed*) praedit·us -a -um
gig *s* (*carriage*) cis·ium -(i)i *n*
gigantic *adj* praegrand·is -is -e
giggle *intr* summissim cachinnare
gild *tr* inaurare
gilded *adj* inaurat·us -a -um
gilding *s* (*art*) auratur·a -ae *f*; (*gilded work*) aur·um -i *n* inductum
gills *spl* branchi·ae -arum *fpl*
gilt *adj* inaurat·us -a -um
gin *s* iunipero infectus spirit·us -ūs *m*
ginger *s* zingi·ber -beris *n*
gingerly *adv* pedetemptim
giraffe *s* camelopardal·is -is *f*
gird *tr* cingere; **to** — **oneself** cingi
girder *s* tign·um -i *n*
girdle *s* stropp·i -orum *mpl*
girdle *tr* cingere
girl *s* puell·a -ae *f*; (*unmarried girl*) virg·o -inis *f*
girlfriend *s* amicul·a -ae *f*
girlhood *s* puellaris aet·as -atis *f*
girlish *adj* puellar·is -is -e
girth *s* (*measure around*) ambit·us -ūs *m*; (*of a horse*) cingul·a -ae *f*
gist *s* summ·a -ae *f*
give *tr* dare; (*as a gift*) donare; (*to deliver*) tradere; **give it here!** cedo (*pl*: cette)! [*an old imperative; can take a direct object*]; — **it to 'em!** adhibe! (*pl*: adhibite!); **not** — **a hoot about s.o.** aliquem dupundi non facere; **to** — **in marriage** in matrimonium dare; **to** — **away** donare; (*to betray*) prodere; **to** — **back** reddere; **to** — **forth** emittere; **to** — **oneself up to** se addicere (*w. dat*); **to** — **off** emittere; **to** — **out** ēdere; **to** — **s.o. a dirty look** respicere aliquem minus familiari vultu; **to** — **s.o. the slip** alicui subterfugere; **to** — **up**

(hope, power) deponere; *(to abandon)* dimittere; **to — up the ghost** animam ebullire; **to — way** *(to yield)* cedere; *(to comply)* obsequi; *(mil)* pedem referre ‖ *intr* **to — in to** cedere *(w. dat);* **to — up** *(to surrender)* se dedere; *(to stop)* desistere

giver *s* da·tor -toris *m* (·trix -tricis *f*)
giving *s* dati·o -onis *f*
glacial *adj* glacial·is -is -e
glacier *s* mol·es -is *f* conglaciata
glad *adj* laet·us -a -um; **I am — to hear that** libenter audio *(w. acc & inf);* **to be —** gaudēre
gladden *tr* laetificare
glade *s* nem·us -oris *n*
gladiator *s* gladiat·or -oris *m*
gladiatorial *adj* gladiatori·us -a -um; **— show** mun·us -eris *n*
gladiola *s* gladiol·us -i *m*
gladly *adv* libenter
gladness *s* gaud·ium -(i)i *n*
glamor *s* nit·or -oris *m*
glamorous *adj* nitid·us -a -um; **to be —** nitēre
glance *s* aspect·us -ūs *m;* **at a —** primo aspectu; **to cast a — at** strictim aspicere
glance *intr* **to — at** strictim aspicere; *(in reading)* strictim legere; **to — off** stringere
gland *s* glandul·a -ae *f*
glare *s* fulg·or -oris *m*
glare *intr* fulgēre; **to — at** torvis oculis tueri
glaring *adj* fulg·ens -entis; *(striking)* manifest·us -a -um
glass *s* *(material)* vitr·um -i *n; (for drinking)* cal·ix -icis *m* vitreus, pocill·um -i *n* vitreum; **—es** perspicill·a -orum *npl;* **to wear —es** perspicillis uti
glass *adj* vitre·us -a -um
glassware *s* vitre·a -orum *npl*
glaze *tr* vitrum illinere *(w. dat)*
gleam *s* fulg·or -oris *m; (fig)* aur·a -ae *f;* **slight — of hope** levis aur·a -ae *f* spei
gleam *intr* coruscare
gleaming *adj* corusc·us -a -um
glean *tr* colligere
gleaning *s* spicileg·ium -(i)i *n*
glee *s* laetiti·a -ae *f*
gleeful *adj* laet·us -a -um
gleefully *adv* laete
glib *adj* volubil·is -is -e
glibly *adv* volubiliter
glide *intr* labi
glider *s* anemoplan·um -i *n*
glimmer *s* lu·x -cis *f* dubia; **— of hope** specul·a -ae *f*
glimmer *intr* sublucēre
glimpse *s* aspect·us -ūs *m* brevis; **to have a — of** dispicere
glisten *tr* nitēre
glistening *adj* nitid·us -a -um

glitter *s* fulg·or -oris *m*
glitter *intr* fulgēre
gloat *intr* oculos pascere; **to — over** oculos pascere *(w. abl)*, exsultare *(w. abl)*
globe *s* glob·us -i *m; (earth)* orb·is -is *m* terrarum
globule *s* globul·us -i *m*
gloom *s* tenebr·ae -arum *fpl; (fig)* maestiti·a -ae *f*
gloomily *adv* maeste
gloomy *adj* tenebros·us -a -um; *(fig)* maest·us -a -um
glorification *s* glorificati·o -onis *f*
glorify *tr* glorificare
glorious *adj* glorios·us -a -um
gloriously *adv* gloriose
glory *s* glori·a -ae *f*
glory *intr* **(in)** gloriari (in *w. abl*)
gloss *s* *(on a word)* interpretati·o -onis *f; (sheen)* nit·or -oris *m*
gloss *tr* annotare; **to — over** colorare
glossary *s* glossar·ium -(i)i *n*
glossy *adj* nitid·us -a -um
glove *s* chirothec·a -ae *f; (for work)* digitabul·um -i *n*
glow *s* ard·or -oris *m*
glow *intr* ardēre
glowing *adj* ard·ens -entis; *(w. heat)* cand·ens -entis; **to speak in — terms about** ornatissime loqui de *(w. abl)*
glowingly *adv* ferventer
glue *s* glut·en -inis *n*
glue *tr* glutinare; **to — together** conglutinare
glum *adj* maest·us -a -um, trist·is -is -e
glut *tr* satiare
glutton *s* hellu·o -onis *m;* **to be a —** helluari
gluttonous *adj* gulos·us -a -um
gnarled *adj* nodos·us -a -um
gnash *tr* **to — the teeth** dentibus frendere
gnat *s* cul·ex -icis *m*
gnaw *tr & intr* rod·o -ere rosi rosus; **to — at** arrodere
gnawing *adj* mord·ax -acis
go *s* *(try)* conat·us -ūs *m;* **to have a — at** tentare; **to make a — of it** rem bene gerere; **on the —** nav·us -a -um
go *intr* eo ire ii *or* ivi iturus; **to — about** *(work)* aggredi; **to — abroad** peregre exire; **to — after** petere; **to — against** obstare, adversari *(w. dat);* **to — along with** assentire *(w. dat);* **to — around** circumire; **to — aside** discedere; **to — astray** errare; **to — back** reverti; **to — back on one's word** fidem fallere; **to — before** praeire *(w. dat);* **to — between** intervenire; **to — beyond** egredi; *(fig)* excedere; **to — by** *(to pass)* praeterire; *(the rules)* servare; *(promises)* stare *(w. abl);* **to — down** descendere; *(of sun)* occidere; *(of ship)* mergi; *(of price)* laxari; *(of swelling)* se

summittere; **to — for** petere; *(to fetch a person)* adducere; *(a thing)* adferre; *(the bait)* appetere; **to — forth** exire; **to — in** introire; **to — into** inire; **to — off** abire; *(as gun)* displodere; **to — on** *(to continue)* pergere; *(to happen)* fieri, agi; **to — out** exire; *(of fire)* exstingui; **to — out ahead** antecedere; **to — out of doors** prodire; **to — over** *(to cross)* transire; *(a subject)* percurrere; *(to examine)* perscrutari; *(to repeat)* repetere; **to — straight** rectum iter vitae insistere; **to — through** *(to travel through)* obire; *(to suffer)* perferre; **to — through with** pertendere; **to — to** adire, accedere ad; **to — to and fro** commeare; **to — to the aid of** succurrere *(w. dat);* **to — towards** petere; **to — under** submergi; **to — up** subire *(w. acc);* *(of prices)* ingravescere; **to — with** comitari; **what's going on?** quid agitur?; **what's going on here?** quid rei hic est?

goad *s* stimul·us -i *m*

goad *tr* instigare; *(fig)* stimulare; *(to exasperate)* exasperare

goal *s* fin·is -is *m; (at the racetrack)* cal·x -cis *f; (sports)* port·a -ae *f;* **to score a —** *(in soccer)* follem in portam pede pulsare

goal keeper *s* portari·us -i *m* (·a -ae *f*)

goal line *s* calx, calcis *f,* cret·a -ae *f*

goal post *s* pal·us -i *m* portae

goat *s* ca·per -pri *m,* capr·a -ae *f;* **—s bleat** capri balant

gobble *tr* devorare

gobbler *s* hellu·o -onis *m*

go-between *s* internunti·us -i *m* (·a -ae *f*)

goblet *s* pocul·um -i *n*

goblin *s* larv·a -ae *f*

god *s* de·us -i *m;* **God** De·us -i *m;* **God bless you!** tibi di bene faciunt!; *(to s.o. sneezing)* salve! *or* salutem!; **— forbid!** Deus averruncet!; **— willing** Deo volente; **thank —** Deo gratias!; **ye —s!** di superi!

god-awful *adj* taeterrim·us -a -um

goddess *s* de·a -ae *f*

godfather *s* spons·or -oris *m* loco infantis, patrin·us -i *m*

godhead *s* deit·as -atis *f*

godless *adj* impi·us -a -um

godlike *adj* divin·us -a -um

godliness *s* piet·as -atis *f*

godmother *s* spons·trix -tricis *f* loco infantis, matrin·a -ae *f*

going *s* iti·o -onis *f;* **good —!** bene factum!

gold *adj* aure·us -a -um

gold *s* aur·um -i *n*

golden *adj* aure·us -a -um

goldfinch *s* cardel·is -is *f*

goldfish *s* hippur·us -i *m*

gold leaf *s* auri bracte·a -ae *f*

gold mine *s* aurifodin·a -ae *f*

gold-plated *adj* aurat·us -a -um

goldsmith *s* aurif·ex -icis *m*

good *adj* bon·us -a -um; *(morally)* prob·us -a -um; *(useful)* util·is -is -e; *(beneficial)* salutar·is -is -e; *(kindhearted)* benevol·us -a -um; *(fit)* idone·us -a -um; **— and proper** plane et probe; **— for you!** *(said in praise)* macte virtute esto! *(pl:* estote!); **— going!** bene factum!; **— —!** euge, euge!; **— job!** bene *(or* recte) factum!; **— thinking!** bene putas!; **— turn** benefic·ium -(i)i *n;* **I am having a — time** mihi pulchre est; **it is — to** *(w. inf)* commodum est *(w. inf);* **it is not — to** *(w. inf)* non convenit *(w. inf);* **to be — for** prodesse *(w. dat); (to be valid)* valēre; **to do s.o. —** alicui prodesse; **to have a — time** *(to celebrate)* genio indulgēre; **to make —** compensare; **to seem —** videri

good *n* bon·um -i *n; (profit)* lucr·um -i *n;* **for — in** perpetuum; **—s** bon·a -orum *npl; (for sale)* merc·es -cium *fpl;* **it does no —** non prodest; **to do s.o. —** alicui prodesse

good *interj* bene!; **very —** bene sane!

goodbye *interj* vale! *(pl:* valete!); **to say —** vale iubēre

good-for-nothing *s* **to be a —** nihil hominis esse

good-for-nothing *adj* nequam [*indecl*]

good-hearted *adj* benevol·us -a -um

goodly *adj (amount)* ampl·us -a -um; **a — number of** nonnull·i -ae -a

good-natured *adj* facil·is -is -e

goodness *s* bonit·as -atis *f; (moral)* probit·as -atis *f; (generosity)* benignit·as -atis *f*

goodwill *s* **(toward)** benevolenti·a -ae *f* (in *w. acc*)

goose *s* ans·er -eris *m;* **geese cackle** anseres gingriunt

gooseberry *s* acin·us -i *m* grossulae

gore *s* cru·or -oris *m*

gore *tr* cornibus confodere

gorge *s* angusti·ae -arum *fpl*

gorge *tr* **to — oneself** se ingurgitare

gorgeous *adj* laut·us -a -um

gorgeously *adv* laute

Gorgon *s* Gorg·o -onis *f*

gory *adj* cruent·us -a -um

gospel *s* evangel·ium -(i)i *n*

gossamer *s* arane·a -ae *f*

gossip *s (talk)* gerr·ae -arum *fpl,* fam·a -ae *f; (person)* garrul·us -i *m* (·a -ae *f*)

gossip *intr* garrire

gouge *tr* **to — out s.o.'s eye** oculum alicui eruere; *(to swindle)* fraudare

gourd *s* cucurbit·a -ae *f*

gout *s* arthrit·is -idis *f; (in the feet)* podagr·a -ae *f; (in the hands)* chiragr·a -ae *f*

govern *tr* imperare *(w. dat),* gubernare; *(to control)* moderari; *(a province)* praeesse *(w. dat); (gram)* iungi *(w. dat)*

governess *s* magistr·a -ae *f*

government *s* res *f* publica *(gen:* rei publicae) [*also written as one word*]

governor *s (of a province)* praes·es -idis *m; (of an imperial province)* legat·us -i *m; (of a Roman province)* procons·ul -ulis *m; (of a smaller province)* procurat·or -oris *m*

governorship *s* praefectur·a -ae *f*

gown *s* vest·is -is *f* talaris; *(of a Roman woman)* stol·a -ae *f*

grab *tr* rapere; **to — hold of** invadere; **to — with both hands** inicere utramque manum *(w. dat)*

grace *s* grati·a -ae *f; (pardon)* veni·a -ae *f;* to say **— (before meals)** consecrationem recitare; *(after meals)* gratias agere

grace *tr (to adorn)* decorare; *(to add honor and distinction)* honestare

graceful *adj* decor·us -a -um

gracefully *adv* decore

graceless *adj* illepid·us -a -um

Graces *spl* Grati·ae -arum *fpl*

gracious *adj* benign·us -a -um

graciously *adv* benigne

gradation *s* grad·us -ūs *m; (rhet)* gradati·o -onis *f*

grade *s* grad·us -ūs *m; (mark or letter for performance)* not·a -ae *f*

grade *tr (papers)* notare; *(to evaluate students' work)* aestimare

gradient *s* proclivit·as -atis *f*

gradual *adj* per gradus

gradually *adv* gradatim, sensim

graduate *tr* ad gradum admittere **‖** *intr* gradūs suscipere, diploma studiorum adipisci

graduate *s* graduat·us -i *m* (·a -ae *f)*

graft *s* surcul·us -i *m; (pol)* ambit·us -ūs *m*

graft *tr* inserere

grain *s (single)* gran·um -i *n;* frument·um -i *n; (in wood)* fibr·a -ae *f;* **against the —** transversis fibris; *(fig)* invitā Minervā; **with a — of salt** cum grano salis

grammar *s* grammatic·a -ae *f; (book)* ars, artis *f*

grammarian *s* grammatic·us -i *m*

grammatical *adj* grammatic·us -a -um

granary *s* horre·um -i *n*

grand *adj* grand·is -is -e; **— old style of oratory** grandis orati·o -onis *f*

grandchild *s* nep·os -otis *m,* nept·is -is *f*

granddaughter *s* nept·is -is *f*

grandeur *s* maiest·as -atis *f*

grandfather *s* av·us -i *m*

grandiloquent *adj* grandiloqu·us -a -um

grandmother *s* avi·a -ae *f*

grand piano *s* clavicord·ium -(i)i *n* aliforme

grandson *s* nep·os -otis *m*

grant *tr (to bestow)* concedere; *(usu. s.th. that is due)* tribuere; *(to acknowledge)* fatēri; *(in geometry)* dare; **—ed, he himself is nothing** esto, ipse nihil est; **— that** sit quidem ut; **to take for —ed** sumere

grant *s* concessi·o -onis *f;* **to make anyone a — of anything** aliquid alicui concedere

granular *adj* granos·us -a -um

grape *s* uv·a -ae *f,* acin·us -i *m;* **bunch of —s** uva

grape picker *s* vindemit·or -oris *m*

grapevine *s* vit·is -is *f; (fig)* fam·a -ae *f*

graphic *adj (fig)* express·us -a -um

graphically *adv (fig)* expresse

grapnel *s* unc·us -i *m*

grapple *intr* luctari

grasp *s (act of grasping; comprehension)* comprehensi·o -onis *f;* **he escaped my —** manus meas effugit; **to wrest from one's —** de manibus extorquēre; **within one's —** inter manūs

grasp *tr* prehendere; *(mentally)* comprehendere **‖** *intr* **to — at** *(lit & fig)* captare

grasping *adj* avar·us -a -um

grass *s* gram·en -inis *n,* herb·a -ae *f*

grasshopper *s* grill·us -i *m;* **—s chirp** grilli fritinniunt

grassy *adj* graminos·us -a -um

grate *s* clathr·i -orum *mpl; (hearth)* camin·us -i *m*

grate *tr* conterere **‖** *intr* stridēre; **to — upon s.o.** alicuius animum offendere

grateful *adj* grat·us -a -um; **I am deeply — to you for** tibi gratiam habeo maximam quod *(w. indic)*

gratefully *adv* grate

gratification *s* gratificati·o -onis *f; (pleasure, delight)* volupt·as -atis *f,* delectati·o -onis *f;* **— of natural desires** expleti·o -onis *f* naturae

gratify *tr* gratificari *(w. dat)*

gratifying *adj* grat·us -a -um

grating *s* cancell·i -orum *mpl; (sound)* strid·or -oris *m*

gratis *adv* gratis

gratitude *s* grati·a -ae *f;* **to feel —** gratiam habēre; **to show —** gratiam referre

gratuitous *adj* gratuit·us -a -um

gratuitously *adv* gratuito

gratuity *s* stip·s -is *f*

grave *adj* grav·is -is -e; *(stern)* sever·us -a -um

grave *s* sepulcr·um -i *n*

gravel *s* glare·a -ae *f*

gravely *adv* graviter

gravestone *s* monument·um -i *n,* cipp·us -i *m*

graveyard *s* sepulcret·um -i *n*

gravitate *intr* vergere

gravitation *s* ponderati·o -onis *f*

gravity *s (importance; gravitational pull)* gravit·as -atis *f; (personal)* severit·as -atis *f*
gravy *s* iu·s -ris *n*
gravy bowl *s* vascul·um -i *n* iuris
gray *adj* can·us -a -um; **to become —** canescere
gray-eyed *adj* caesi·us -a -um
gray-headed *adj* can·us -a -um
grayish *adj* canesc·ens -entis
grayness *s* caniti·es -ei *f*
graze *tr (cattle)* pascere; *(to touch lightly)* perstingere ‖ *intr* pasci
grease *s* ad·eps -ipis *m; (lubricant)* axungi·a -ae *f*
grease *tr* ungere, illinere
grease job *s* uncti·o -onis *f* autocineti
greasy *adj* unct·us -a -um
great *adj* magn·us -a -um; *(thirst)* ing·ens -entis; **as — as** tant·us ... quant·us -a -um; **— amount of money** ingens pecuni·a -ae *f;* **— big** grand·is -is -e; **it was really —!** bene fuit mehercule!; **how — quant·us -a -um; so — tant·us -a -um; very —** permagn·us -a -um, maxim·us -a -um
great *interj* eu!; papae! *(expression of surprise and delight)*
great-aunt *s (on father's side)* proamit·a -ae *f; (on mother's side)* promaterter·a -ae *f*
great-granddaughter *s* pronept·is -is *f*
greater *adj* mai·or -or -us *(gen:* maioris)
greatest *adj* maxim·us -a -um
great-grandfather *s* prova·us -i *m*
great-grandmother *s* proavi·a -ae *f*
great-grandson *s* pronep·os -otis *m*
great-great-grandfather *s* abav·us -i *m*
great-great-great-grandfather *s* atav·us -i *m*
greatness *s* magnitud·o -inis *f*
great-uncle *s* avuncul·us -i *m* maior
greaves *spl* ocre·ae -arum *fpl*
Grecian *adj* Graec·us -a -um
Greece *s* Graeci·a -ae *f*
greed *s* avariti·a -ae *f*
greedily *adv* avide
greediness *s* avariti·a -ae *f*
greedy *adj* avid·us -a -um
Greek *adj* Graec·us -a -um
Greek *s* Graec·us -i *m;* **to know (read, speak, teach) —** Graece scire (legere, loqui, docēre)
green *adj* virid·is -is -e; *(dark-green)* prasin·us -a -um; *(fresh)* rec·ens -entis; *(unripe, e.g., apples)* crud·us -a -um; **to become —** virescere
green *s* col·or -oris *m* viridis; *(lawn)* loc·us -i *m* herbidus; **—s** holer·a -um *npl*
greenhouse *s* viridar·ium -(i)i *n* hibernum
greenish *adj* subvirid·is -is -e
greenness *s* viridit·as -atis *f; (fig)* crudit·as -atis *f*
green pepper *s* piperit·is -idis *f*

greet *tr* salutare, salutem dicere *(w. dat)*
greeting *s* salutati·o -onis *f;* **to return a —** resalutare
gregarious *adj* gregal·is -is -e; *(person)* social·is -is -e
grenade *s* pyrobol·us -i *m*
grey *see* gray
greyhound *s* vertag·us -i *m* (·a -ae *f*)
gridiron *s* craticul·a -ae *f*
grief *s* dol·or -oris *m*, maer·or -oris *m;* **good —!** mehercules!; **to come to —** perire; **to be overwhelmed with —** in maerore iacēre; **to feel — (over)** dolorem capere (ex *w. abl*)
grievance *s* querell·a -ae *f*
grieve *tr* dolore afficere ‖ *intr* maerēre, dolēre
grievous *adj* grav·is -is -e
grievously *adv* graviter
griffin *s* gryp·s -is *m*
grill *s* craticul·a -ae *f*
grill *tr* super craticulum assare; *(w. questions)* percontari
grim *adj* torv·us -a -um; *(e.g., winter)* deform·is -is -e
grimace *s* vult·us -ūs *m* distortus
grimly *adv* torve
grin *s* subris·us -ūs *m* distortus
grin *intr* distorto vultu subridēre
grind *tr (grain)* molere; *(in mortar)* contundere; *(on whetstone)* exacuere; **to — out a song** canticum extorquēre; **to — the teeth** dentibus frendere
grindstone *s* co·s -tis *f*
grip *s* comprehensi·o -onis *f*
grip *tr* comprehendere
gripping *adj* mov·ens -entis
grisly *adj* horrend·us -a -um
gristle *s* cartilag·o -inis *f*
gristly *adj* cartilaginos·us -a -um
grit *s* haren·a -ae *f*
gritty *adj* harenos·us -a -um
grizzly *adj* can·us -a -um
grizzly bear *s* urs·us -i *m* horridus
groan *s* gemit·us -ūs *m*
groan *intr* gemere
grocer *s* olitari·us -i *m* (·a -ae *f*)
groceries *spl* obsoni·a -orum *npl;* **to shop for —** obsonare
grocery store *s* tabern·a -ae *f* cibaria
groggy *adj* titub·ans -antis
groin *s* ingu·en -inis *n*
groom *s* novus marit·us -i *m*
groom *tr* curare
groove *s* stri·a -ae *f*
groove *tr* striare
grope *intr* praetentare
gropingly *adv* pedetentim
gross *adj (corpulent)* crass·us -a -um; *(indelicate)* indecor·us -a -um; *(coarse)* rud·is -is

-e; *(inordinate)* nimi·us -a -um; *(ignorance, folly)* ing·ens -entis
grossly *adv* nimium
grotesque *adj* distort·us -a -um
grotto *s* antr·um -i *n*
ground *s* sol·um -i *n,* hum·us -i *m,* terr·a -ae *f; (level ground)* sol·um -i *n; (reason)* rati·o -onis *f; (place)* loc·us -i *m;* **on the — ** humi; **to be burnt to the — ** ad solum exuri; **to fall to the — ** ad terram decidere; **to gain — ** proficere; **to level with the — ** solo adaequare; **to lose — ** recedere; *(mil)* pedem referre
ground *tr* fundare; *(to teach)* imbuere; *(a ship)* subducere; ‖ *intr (naut)* haerēre
ground beef *s* bubul·a -ae *f* concisa
ground floor *s* pedeplan·a -orum *npl*
groundless *adj* van·us -a -um; *(false)* fals·us -a -um
groundwork *s* substructi·o -onis *f; (fig)* fundament·um -i *n;* **to lay the — ** fundamentum iacēre *(or* agere)
group *s (band)* man·us -ūs *f; (class)* gen·us -eris *n; (crowd)* glob·us -i *m*
group *tr* disponere ‖ *intr* **to — around** circulari, stipari
grouping *s* dispositi·o -onis *f*
grouse *s (bird)* tetra·o -onis *m*
grove *s* nem·us -oris *n; (sacred grove)* luc·us -i *m*
grovel *intr* repere, se prosternere
grow *tr* colere, serere ‖ *intr* crescere; *(to become)* fieri; *(of vegetables)* nasci; *(to shoot up)* se promittere; **to let the hair, beard — long** capillam, barbam promittere; **to — back** renasci; **to — old** senescere; **to — out** excrescere; **to — out of** *(e.g., a wall)* innasci *(w. dat or* in *w. abl); (fig)* oriri ex *(w. abl);* **to — over** *(e.g., of a skin over a wound)* induci *(w. dat);* **to — silent** tacēre; **to — up** adolescere; *(to arrive at puberty)* pubescere
grower *s* cult·or -oris *m*
growl *s* fremit·us -ūs *m*
growl *intr* fremere; **to — at** ogganire
grown-up *adj* adult·us -a -um
growth *s* increment·um -i *n; * **full — ** maturit·as -atis *f*
grub *s* vermicul·us -i *m; (food)* vict·us -ūs *m*
grub *intr* effodere
grudge *s* invidi·a -ae *f;* **to hold a — against** succensēre *(w. dat)*
grudgingly *adv* invit·us -a -um *(adj in agreement with the subject)*
gruelling *adj* (de)fatig·ans -antis
gruesome *adj* tae·ter -tra -trum
gruff *adj* asp·er -era -erum
gruffly *adv* aspere
gruffness *s* asperit·as -atis *f*

grumble *intr* murmurare; *(in a suppressed tone)* mussare; **to — about** queri de *(w. abl)*
grumbling *s* increpati·o -onis *f*
grumpy *adj* stomachos·us -a -um
grunt *s (of a bear, pig)* grunnit·us -ūs *m*
grunt *intr (of a bear, pig)* grunnire
guarantee *s* fid·es -ei *f; (money)* sponsi·o -onis *f; (person who guarantees)* va·s -dis *m; (in legal contracts)* satisdati·o -onis *f;* **to give, receive a — ** fidem dare, accipere
guarantee *tr* fidem dare *(w. dat),* spondēre
guaranteed *adj* spons·us -a -um
guarantor *s* spons·or -oris *m* (·rix -ricis *f)*
guard *s* custodi·a -ae *f; (mil)* praesid·ium -(i)i *n; (person)* cust·os -odis *mf;* **to be on one's — against** praecavēre; **to mount — ** custodiam agere
guard *tr* custodire ‖ *intr* **to — against** cavēre
guarded *adj* caut·us -a -um
guardedly *adv* caute
guardhouse *s* carc·er -eris *m* militaris
guardian *s* cust·os -odis *mf; (of minor or orphan)* tut·or -oris *m*
guardianship *s* custodi·a -ae *f; (of minor or woman)* tutel·a -ae *f*
guess *s* coniecti·o -onis *f*
guess *tr & intr* conicere, divinare
guest *s* hosp·es -itis *mf; (at dinner)* conviv·a -ae *mf*
guest room *s* hospit·ium -(i)i *n*
guidance *s* duct·us -ūs *m; (advice)* consil·ium -(i)i *n;* **under the — of the deity** deo ducente
guidance counselor *s* consiliat·or -oris *m* academicus, consiliatr·ix -icis *f* academica
guide *s* dux, ducis *mf;* itineris dux *mf*
guide *tr (as a local guide)* ducere; *(to manage, control)* regere
guidebook *s* itinerar·ium -(i)i *n*
guided missile *s* missil·e -is *n* directum
guild *s* colleg·ium -(i)i *n*
guile *s* dol·us -i *m*
guileful *adj* dolos·us -a -um
guileless *adj* simpl·ex -icis
guilt *s* culp·a -ae *f*
guilty *adj* son·s -tis; **— of** noc·ens -entis *(w. gen or abl);* **the — one** sons, sontis *mf;* **to be found — of** noxi·us -a diiudicari *(w. gen or abl);* **to be — in culpā esse; **to punish the — ** sontes punire
guise *s* speci·es -ei *f; (features, dress)* habit·us -ūs *m;* **under the — of** sub specie *(w. gen)*
guitar *s* cithar·a -ae *f* Hispanica
gulf *s* sin·us -ūs *m*
gull *s* merg·us -i *m*
gullet *s* gul·a -ae *f*
gullibility *s* credulit·as -atis *f*
gullible *adj* credul·us -a -um
gulp *s* singult·us -ūs *m*
gulp *tr* **to — down** obsorbēre ‖ *intr* singultare

gum *s* gummi *n* [*indecl*], gumm·is -is *f; (anat)* gingiv·a -ae *f*

gumption *s* alacrit·as -atis *f*

gun *s* sclopet·um -i *n;* **to fire the —** sclopetare; **to jump the —** signum praevertere; **to stick to one's —s** in sententiā stare

gurgle *intr* singultare; *(of a stream)* murmurare

gurgling *s* singult·us -ūs *m; (of a stream)* murmurati·o -onis *f*

gush *s* effusi·o -onis *f,* erupti·o -onis *f; (of water)* scatebr·a -ae *f;* **with a — of tears** profusis lacrimis

gush *intr* scaturire; **to — out** prorumpere; *(of blood from a wound)* emicare

gust *s* flam·en -inis *n,* flat·us -ūs *m*

gusto *s* stud·ium -(i)i *n*

gusty *adj* procellos·us -a -um

gut *s* intestin·um -i *n*

gut *tr* exenterare; *(a building)* amburere

gutted *adj (by fire)* ambust·us -a -um

gutter *s* canal·is -is *m,* riv·us -i *m;* **to clean out the —** rivos deducere

guttural *adj* guttural·is -is -e

guy *s* **poor —** homuncul·us -i *m;* **that —** iste

guzzle *tr & intr* potare gulose

guzzler *s* po·tor -toris *m,* (·trix -ricis) *f*

gym *s* gymnas·ium -(i)i *n*

gym instructor exercita·tor -oris *m* (·trix -tricis *f*)

gym shoes *spl* calce·i -orum *mpl* gymnici

gymnasium *s* gymnas·ium -(i)i *n*

gymnastic *adj* gymnastic·us -a -um

gymnastics *spl* palaestric·a -ae *f*

gynecology *s* gynaecologi·a -ae *f*

gypsum *s* gyps·um -i *n*

gyrate *intr* gyrare

H

habit *s* consuetud·o -inis *f; (dress)* habit·us -ūs *m;* **to be in the — of** consuescere *(w. inf);* **to break the — of** abscedere ab usu; **to get into the — of** se assuefacere *(w. inf)*

habitation *s* habitati·o -onis *f*

habitual *adj* usitat·us -a -um

habitually *adv* de more, ex more

habituate *tr* assuefacere

hack *s (cut)* plag·a -ae *f; (taxicab) (coll)* raed·a -ae *f* meritoria

hack *tr* caedere; **to — to pieces** concidere

hacker *s (comput)* effractar·ius -(i)i *m* electronicus, effractari·a -ae *f* electronica

hackneyed *adj* trit·us -a -um

haddock *s* gad·us -i *m*

hag *s* an·us -ūs *f*

haggard *adj* ma·cer -cra -crum

haggle *intr (to bargain)* licitari; *(to wrangle)* altercari

ha-ha-ha *interj* hahhahae!

hail *s* grand·o -inis *f*

hail *intr* **it is —ing** grandinat

hail *tr* appellare

hail *interj* salve! *(pl:* salvēte!)

hailstone *s* grandinis gran·um -i *n*

hailstorm *s* grandin·es -um *fpl*

hair *s (of head or beard)* capill·us -i *m, (or* capill·i -orum *mpl); (in locks or dressed)* crin·is -is *m; (hair as an ornament, of men or women)* com·a -ae *f; (single)* pil·us -i *m; (of an animal)* saet·a -ae *f;* **he was within a —'s breadth of** nil propius est factum quam ut; **long — (left uncut)** capilli promissi; **to split —s** cavillari

hairbrush *s* penicul·us -i *m* comatorius

haircut *s* tons·us -ūs *m;* **to get a —** facere ut capilli tondeantur

hairdo *s* compt·us -ūs *m*

hairdresser *s* tons·trix -tricis *f*

hair dryer *s* favoni·us -i *m*

hairless *adj (of head)* calv·us -a -um; *(of body)* gla·ber -bra -brum

hairnet *s* reticul·um -i *n*

hair oil *s* capillar·e -is *n*

hairpin *s* crinal·e -is *n*

hairstyle *s* compt·us -ūs *m*

hairy *adj* pilos·us -a -um; *(chest)* saetos·us -a -um, hirsut·us -a -um

hale *adj* **— and hardy** salv·us et valid·us -a -um

half *s* dimidia par·s -tis *f*

half *adv* dimidio; *(partly)* partim; **— and —** pro parte semissā

half *adj* dimidiat·us -a -um, dimidi·us -a -um; **— the drinks** dimidiae potion·es -um *fpl*

half alive *adj* semiviv·us -a -um

half asleep *adj* semisomn·us -a -um

halfbreed *s* hybrid·a -ae *mf*

half brother *s (on mother's side)* fra·ter -tris *m* uterin·us; *(on father's side)* fra·ter -tris *m* consanguineus

half-burnt *adj* semiust·us -a -um

half-cooked *adj* semicoct·us -a -um

half-dead *adj* semianim·us -a -um

half-eaten *adj* semes·us -a -um

half-finished *adj* semiperfect·us -a -um

half-full *adj* semiplen·us -a -um

half-hour *s* semihor·a -ae *f*

half-moon *s* lun·a -ae *f* dimidiata; *(shape)* lunul·a -ae *f*

half-open *adj* semiapert·us -a -um

half pint *s (sl)* homuncul·us -i *m*

half pound *s* selibr·a -ae *f*

half sister *s (on mother's side)* sor·or -oris *f* uterina; *(on father's side)* sor·or -oris *f* consanguinea

halftime *s (sports)* dimidium temp·us -oris *n*
halfway *adj* medi·us -a -um
half-year *adj* semestr·is -is -e
hall *s (large room)* atr·ium -(i)i *n,* aul·a -ae *f; (corridor)* andr·on -onis *m; (building for meetings)* curi·a -ae *f,* basilic·a -ae *f*
hallo *interj* heus!
hallucinate *intr* alucinari
hallucination *s* alucinati·o -onis *f*
hallway *s* andr·on -onis *m; (at front of house)* fauc·es -ium *fpl*
halo *s* coron·a -ae *f*
halt *s* paus·a -ae *f,* mor·a -ae *f;* **to come to a —** consistere
halt *tr* sistere ‖ *intr* consistere; *(to limp)* claudicare
halter *s* capistr·um -i *n*
halting *adj* claud·us -a -um; *(fig)* haesitabund·us -a -um
halve *tr* ex aequo dividere
ham *s* pern·a -ae *f; (back of the knee)* popl·es -itis *m;* **smoked —** perna fumosa
hamburger *s* bubul·a -ae *f* concisa
hamlet *s* vic·us -i *m*
hammer *s* malle·us -i *m*
hammer *tr* malleo tundere
hamper *s* corb·is -is *m*
hamper *tr* impedire
ham sandwich *s* pastill·um -i *n* pernā fartum
hamstring *s* poplitis nerv·us -i *m*
hamstring *tr* poplitem succidere *(w. dat); (fig)* impedire
hand *s* man·us -ūs *f; (handwriting)* chirograph·um -i *n; (of dial)* gnom·on -onis *n; (worker)* operar·ius -(i)i *m;* **at —** praesto, ad manum; **by —** manu; **from — to —** de manu in manum; **— in —** iunctis manibus; **—s off!** noli *(pl:* nolite) tangere!; aufer(te) manūs!; **—s up!** tolle *(pl:* tollite) manus!; **left —** laev·a -ae *f,* sinistr·a -ae *f;* **old —** veterat·or -oris *mf;* **on the one —, on the other** unā ex parte ... alterā ex parte; *or use* hic ... ille; **on the other —** contra; **right —** dext(e)r·a -ae *f;* **these things are not in our —s** haec non sunt in nostra manu; **to be near at —** subesse; **to have a — in s.th.** interesse alicui rei; **to have clean —s** manūs pecuniae abstinentes habēre; **to have in —** in manibus habēre; **to have one's —s full** satagere; **to lay —s on** manum inicere *(w. dat);* **to live from — to mouth** in horam vivere; **to pass a thing from — to —** aliquid de manu in manum tradere; **to shake —s** dextram dextrae iungere; **to sit on one's —s** *(fig)* compressis manibus sedēre; **to take in —** suscipere
hand *tr* tradere, porrigere; **to be —ed over to** *(by a judge)* adiudicari *(w. dat);* **to — around** circumferre; **to — down** tradere; **to**

— in reddere; **to — over** tradere; *(to betray)* prodere
handbag *s* bulg·a -ae *f; (for traveling)* vidul·a -ae *f*
handbook *s* enchirid·ion -(i)i *n,* manual·e -is *n*
handbrake *s* sufflam·en -inis *n* manuale
handcuff *tr* manicas inicere *(w. dat)*
handcuffs *spl* manic·ae -arum *fpl*
handful *s* manipul·us -i *m*
handicraft *s* artific·ium -(i)i *n*
handiwork *s* opific·ium -(i)i *n*
handkerchief *s* sudar·ium -(i)i *n,* mucinn·ium -(i)i *n*
handle *s* manubr·ium -(i)i *n; (of a cup)* ansul·a -ae *f*
handle *tr* tractare
handlebars *spl* manubr·ium -(i)i *n*
handling *s* tractati·o -onis *f*
hand luggage *s* sarcinul·ae -arum *fpl* manuales
handsome *adj* pul·cher -chra -chrum
handsomely *adv* pulchre; *(liberally)* liberaliter
handsomeness *s* pulchritud·o -inis *f*
handwriting *s* chirograph·um -i *n*
handy *adj (of things)* habil·is -is -e; *(of persons)* soller·s -tis; *(at hand)* praesto
hang *tr* suspendere; *(by a line)* appendere; *(the head)* demittere; **go — yourself!** abi in malam crucem! ‖ *intr* pendēre; **—ing down** demiss·us -a -um; **to — around with** frequens adesse cum *(w. abl);* **to — down** dependēre; **to — on to** haerēre *(w. dat);* **to — out with** *(coll)* morari cum *(w. abl);* **to — over** imminēre *(w. dat)*
hangar *s* receptacul·um -i *n* aëroplani *(or* aëroplanorum)
hanger-on *s* assecl·a -ae *mf*
hanging *adj* pensil·is -is -e
hanging *s (execution)* suspend·ium -(i)i *n;* **—s** aulae·a -orum *npl*
hangman *s* carnif·ex -icis *m*
hangout *s* desidiabul·um -i *n*
hangover *s* crapul·a -ae *f;* **to sleep off a —** crapulam obdormire
hanker *intr* **for** desiderare
haphazard *adj* fortuit·us -a -um
happen *intr* accidere, fieri, contingere; **I happened to spot** forte conspexi; **it happens that** contingit ut; **to — to s.o.** alicui contingere; **to — upon** incidere in *(w. acc);* **what happened?** quid factum est?
happily *adv* feliciter, beate
happiness *s* felicit·as -atis *f*
happy *adj* felix, beat·us -a -um
harangue *s* conti·o -onis *f;* **to give a —** contionem habēre
harangue *tr & intr* contionari
harass *tr* vexare
harassment *s* vexati·o -onis *f*
harbinger *s* praenunti·us -i *m* (·a -ae *f*)

harbor *s* port·us -ūs *m*
harbor *tr* excipere; **to — hopes, thoughts** portare spes, cogitationes
hard *adj* dur·us -a -um; *(difficult)* difficil·is -is -e; *(severe)* a·cer -cris -cre; **— on** dur·us -a -um in *(w. acc);* **— to please** difficil·is -is -e; **— work** op·us -eris *n* arduum; **it is — to do** est difficile factu; **to become —** durescere
hard *adv* valde, sedulo, summā vi; **to take s.th. —** aliquid aegre ferre
hardback *or* **hardcover book** li·ber -bri *m* lino contectus
hard drive *s (comput)* stati·o -onis *f* dura
harden *tr* durare; *(fig)* indurare **‖** *intr* durescere; *(fig)* obdurescere
hardhearted *adj* dur·us -a -um
hardiness *s* rob·ur -oris *n*
hardly *adv* vix, aegre; **— any** null·us -a -um fere
hardness *s* duriti·a -ae *f; (fig)* acerbit·as -atis *f*
hardship *s* lab·or -oris *m*
hardware *s* ferrament·a -orum *npl; (comput)* apparat·us -ūs *m* ordinatralis *(or* computatralis)
hardware store *s* tabern·a -ae *f* ferraria
hardworking *adj* laborios·us -a -um
hardy *adj* robust·us -a -um
hare *s* lep·us -oris *m*
harem *s* gynaece·um -i *n*
hark *interj* heus!
harken *intr* audire; **to — to** auscultare *(w. dat)*
harlot *s* meretr·ix -icis *f*
harm *s* iniuri·a -ae *f,* noxi·a -ae *f;* **to come to —** detrimentum accipere
harm *intr* nocēre *(w. dat),* laedere
harmful *adj* noxi·us -a -um
harmless *adj* innocu·us -a -um
harmonica *s* homonic·a -ae *f* inflatilis
harmonious *adj* canor·us -a -um; *(fig)* concor·s -dis
harmoniously *adv* consonanter; *(fig)* concorditer
harmonize *tr* componere **‖** *intr* concinere; *(fig)* consentire
harmony *s* harmoni·a -ae *f; (fig)* concordi·a -ae *f*
harness *s* equi ornament·a -orum *npl*
harp *s* lyr·a -ae *f;* **to play the —** lyrā ludere
harp *intr* **(on)** cantare; **to — on the same theme** cantilenam eandem canere
harpist *s* psalt·es -ae *m*
harpoon *s* iacul·um -i *n* hamatum
harpoon *tr* iaculo hamato transfigere
Harpy *s* Harpyi·a -ae *f*
harrow *s* irp·ex -icis *m*
harrow *tr* occare
harsh *adj* asp·er -era -erum; *(sound)* rauc·us -a -um; *(fig)* dur·us -a -um, sever·us -a -um; **— towards** dur·us -a -um in *(w. acc)*

harshly *adv* aspere, severe
harshness *s* asperit·as -atis *f,* duriti·a -ae *f*
harvest *s (reaping)* mess·is -is *f; (the crops)* provent·us -ūs *m*
harvest *tr* met·o -ere messui messus
hash *s* minut·al -alis *n*
hash *tr* comminu·o -ere -i -tus
haste *s* festinati·o -onis *f;* **in —** propere, festinanter; **to make —** properare
hasten *tr & intr* properare
hastily *adv* propere, raptim; *(without reflection)* temere
hastiness *s* celerit·as -atis *f; (without reflection)* temerit·as -atis *f*
hasty *adj* temerari·us -a -um
hat *s* petas·us -i *m*
hatch *s (naut)* foram·en -inis *n*
hatch *tr (fig)* coquere; *(of chickens)* ex ovis excludere
hatchet *s* asci·a -ae *f*
hate *s* od·ium -(i)i *n*
hate *tr* od·i -isse [*v defect*]
hateful *adj* odios·us -a -um, invis·us -a -um; **to be — to** odio esse *(w. dat)*
hatefully *adv* odiose
hatred *s* **(of, toward)** od·ium -(i)i *n* (in *w. acc)*
haughtily *adv* superbe
haughtiness *s* superbi·a -ae *f*
haughty *adj* superb·us -a -um
haul *s (catch)* captur·a -ae *f; (transport)* vectur·a -ae *f*
haul *tr* trahere, vehere; **to — off to prison** rapere in carcerem; **to — up** *(a boat)* subducere
haunch *s* clun·is -is *f* et cox·a -ae *f*
haunt *s* loc·us -i *m* frequentatus; *(of animals)* latebr·ae -arum *fpl*
haunt *tr* frequentare; *(to disturb)* inquietare
haunted *adj* a larvis frequentat·us -a -um
have *tr* habēre; *(to be obliged)* debēre; **— it your way!** esto ut libet; **I — confidence** fiducia est mihi; **to — a tough time of it** valde laborare; **to — it in for s.o.** alicui periculum denuntiare; **what do you — to do with her?** quid rei tibi est cum illā?
haven *s* port·us -ūs *m*
have-not *s* paup·er -eris *mf*
havoc *s* strag·es -is *f;* **to wreak —** stragem dare
hawk *s* accipi·ter -tris *mf;* **—s caw** accipitres crocitant
hawk *tr* venditare; **to — up phlegm** pituitam exsecrare per tussim
hawker *s* circulat·or -oris *m*
hawk-eyed *adj* lynce·us -a um
hawser *s* retinacul·um -i *n*
hay *s* faen·um -i *n; (fig)* **make — while the sun shines!** occasionem amplectere!; carpe diem!; **to make —** faenum secare
hayloft *s* faenil·ia -ium *npl*

haystack *s* faeni met·a -ae *f*
hazard *s* pericul·um -i *n*
hazard *tr* to — a guess coniecturam tentare
hazardous *adj* periculos·us -a -um
haze *s* nebul·a -ae *f*
hazelnut *s* nu·x -cis *f* avellana
hazy *adj* nebulos·us -a -um; *(fig)* obscur·us -a -um
he *pron* hic, is; *(male)* ma·s -ris *m*
head *s* cap·ut -itis *n; (mental faculty)* ingen·ium -(i)i *n; (fig)* princ·eps -ipis *m;* back of the — occipit·um -i *n;* from — to foot ab imis unguibus usque ad verticem summum; — first praec·eps -cipitis; — of state rec·tor -toris *m* (·trix -tricis *f*) civitatis; — over heels in love tot·us -a -um in amore; it all came to a — in discrimen summa rerum adducta est; to be a — taller than toto vertice supra *(w. acc)* esse; to come into s.o.'s — alicui in buccam venire; to come to a — *(of a boil)* caput facere; to have a good — cor habēre; to put —s together capita conferre; use your — ! cogita! *(pl:* cogitate!); wine goes to my — vinum in cerebrum mihi abit
head *adj* prim·us -a -um
head *tr* praesse *(w. dat),* ducere ‖ *intr* to — for tendere ad *(w. acc)*
headache *s* capitis dol·or -oris *m*
headband *s* inful·a -ae *f*
headfirst *adv* prae·ceps -cipitis
headgear *s* capitis tegm·en -inis *n*
heading *s* titul·us -i *m*
headland *s* promuntur·ium -(i)i *n*
headless *adj* trunc·us -a -um
headlight *s* (autocineti) luminar·e -is *n;* to turn on (turn off) the (bright) —s luminaria (praecandentia) accendere (exstinguere)
headlong *adv* praec·eps -itis
headmaster *s* scholae rect·or -oris *m*
headmistress *s* scholae rec·trix -tricis *f*
headquarters *spl* sed·es -is *f; (mil)* praetor·ium -(i)i *n*
head start *s* to get a — iter praecipere; *(fig)* aliquantum temporis praecipere
headstrong *adj* contum·ax -acis
headway *s* to make — proficere; to make no — nihil proficere; we are making some — proficimus aliquantum
headwind *s* vent·us -i *m* adversus
heady *adj (of wine)* fervid·us -a -um
heal *tr* mederi *(w. dat),* sanare ‖ *intr* sanescere; *(of wounds)* coalescere
healer *s* medic·us -i *m* (·a -ae *f*)
healing *adj* salutar·is -is -e
healing *s* sanati·o -onis *f*
health *s (good or bad)* valetud·o -inis *f;* bad (delicate, good, ill) — adversa (infirma,

secunda, incommoda) valetudo; for reasons of (bad) — valetudinis causā; to be in good — bene valēre; to drink to the — of propinare *(w. dat);* to enjoy excellent — optima valitudine uti
healthful *adj* salubr·is -is -e
healthily *adv* salubriter
healthy *adj* san·us -a -um; *(places)* salubr·is -is -e
heap *s* cumul·us -i *m,* acerv·us -i *m*
heap *tr* acervare; to — up accumulare, exstruere; to — *(blows, favors, abuse)* upon congerere (plagas, beneficia, maledicta) *(w. dat or* in *w. acc)*
hear *tr* (from) audire (ex *w. abl); (to learn)* (from) cognoscere, accipere (ex *w. abl)*
hearing *s (act)* auditi·o -onis *f; (sense)* audit·us -ūs *m; (leg)* cogniti·o -onis *f;* hard of — surdas·ter -tra -trum; to hold a — cognitionem habēre
hearken *intr* auscultare; to — to auscultare *(dat)*
hearsay *s* auditi·o -onis *f*
heart *s* cor, cordis *n; (fig)* anim·us -i *m;* by — ex memoria; from the — ex animo; — and soul toto pectore; my — was in my throat anima mihi in naso erat; to learn by — ediscere; to love with all one's — toto pectore amare; to take to — cordi habēre
heartache *s (fig)* cur·a -ae *f,* cordol·ium -(i)i *n*
heart attack *s* impet·us -ūs *m* cordiacus
heartbreak *s* ang·or -oris *m*
heartbroken *adj* ae·ger -gra -grum animo
heartburn *s* praecordiorum dol·or -oris *m*
heart failure *s* defecti·o -onis *f* cardiaca
heart-felt *adj* haud simulat·us -a -um
hearth *s* foc·us -i *m*
heartily *adv* cum summo studio
heartiness *s* alacrit·as -atis *f*
heartless *adj* inhuman·us -a -um
heartlessly *adv* inhumane
heartsick *adj* animo ae·ger -gra -graum
heart-to-heart *adj* intim·us -a -um
hearty *adj* sincer·us -a -um; *(meal)* laut·us -a -um
heat *s* cal·or -oris *m,* ard·or -oris *m; (fig)* ferv·or -oris *m;* — of the day aest·us -ūs *m*
heat *tr* cal(e)facere ‖ *intr* calescere
heathen *adj* pagan·us -a -um
heathen *s* pagan·us -i *m* (·a -ae *f*)
heating *s* calefacti·o -onis *f*
heave *tr* attollere; to — a sigh (of relief) gemitum (levationis) ducere ‖ *intr (to swell)* fluctuare; *(of the chest)* anhelare
heaven *s* cael·um -i *n; for* —'s sake obsecro *[lit: I pray];* good —s! pro divum fidem!; — s above! O di immortales!; — forbid! di melius faxint!; I'm in seventh — digito caelum attingo; in —'s name pro deum

fidem; **thank** — dis gratia; **to move — and
earth** caelum ac terras miscēre
heavenly *adj* caelest·is -is -e
heavily *adv* graviter; *(slowly)* tarde
heaviness *s* gravit·as -atis *f*
heavy *adj* grav·is -is -e; *(sad)* maest·us -a -um;
(rain) magn·us -a -um
Hebraic *adj* Hebraic·us -a -um
Hebrew *adj* Hebrae·us -a -um
Hebrew *s* Hebrae·us -i *m* (·a -ae *f*); *(language)*
lingu·a -ae *f* Hebraea; **to know (read, speak)**
— Hebraice scire (legere, loqui)
hecatomb *s* hecatomb·e -es *f*
heck *s & interj* — no! minine vero!; **to give
s.o.** — aliquem verbis malis obiurgare; **who
the heck are they?** qui, malum, isti sunt?
heckle *tr* interpellare
heckler *s* convicia·tor -toris *m* (·trix -tricis *f*)
hectic *adj* febriculos·us -a -um
hedge *s* saep·es -is *f*
hedge *tr* **to — in** saepire; **to — off** intersaepire
‖ *intr* tergiversari
heed *s* cur·a -ae *f;* **to take —** curare
heed *tr* curare, observare; *(to obey)* parēre
(w. dat)
heedless *adj* incaut·us -a -um; **— of** immem·or
-oris *(w. gen)*
heedlessness *s* neglegenti·a -ae *f*
heel *s* cal·x -cis *mf; (of a shoe)* fulment·um -i
n; (sl) nequam hom·o -inis *mf;* **to take to
one's —s** se in pedes conicere
hefty *adj* robust·us -a -um; *(thing)* ing·ens
-entis
heifer *s* iuvenc·a -ae *f*
height *s* altitud·o -inis *f; (of person)* procerit·as
-atis *f; (top)* culm·en -inis *n; (fig)* fastig·ium
-(i)i *n*
heighten *tr* amplificare, augēre
heinous *adj* atr·ox -ocis
heir *s* her·es -edis *mf*
heir apparent *s* her·es -edis *mf* legitim·us (-a)
heiress *s* her·es -cdis *f*
heirloom *s* res, rei *f* hereditaria
helicopter *s* helicopter·um -i *n;* **to fly a —** heli-
copterum gubernare; **to fly in a —** helcoptero
vehi
hell *s* infer·i -orum *mpl,* Orc·us -i *m; (eccl)*
Gehenn·a -ae *f;* **go to —!** *(sl)* i *(pl:* ite) in
malam crucem!; **to catch —** *(sl)* convicium
habēre
Hellenic *adj* Hellenic·us -a -um
Hellenism *s* Hellenism·us -i *m*
hellish *adj* infern·us -a -um
hello *interj* salve *(pl:* salvete)!; **— there!** eho
istic!; **Terentia says — to you** Terentia tibi
salutem dicit
helm *s* gubernacul·um -i *n*
helmet *s (of leather)* gale·a -ae *f; (of metal)*
cass·is -idis *f*

helmsman *s* gubernat·or -oris *m*
help *s* auxil·ium -(i)i *n*
help *tr* opem ferre *(w. dat)*, iuvare, adiuvare
helper *s* adiu·tor -toris *m* (·tr·ix -icis *f*)
helpful *adj* util·is -is -e
helpless *adj* inop·s -is
helplessness *s* inopi·a -ae *f*
hem *interj* hem!, ehem!
hem *s* or·a -ae *f,* limb·us -i *m*
hem *tr* circumsuere; **to — in** *(to surround)* circumdare; *(by entrenchments)* circumvallare;
(to restrain) cohibēre
hemisphere *s* hemisphaer·ium -(i)i *n*
hemlock *s* cicut·a -ae *f*
hemorrhage *s* sanguinis profluv·ium -(i)i *n*
hemorrhoids *spl* haemorrhoid·a -ae *f*
hemp *s* cannab·is -is *f*
hempen *adj* cannabin·us -a -um
hen *s* gallin·a -ae *f*
hence *adv* hinc; *(consequently)* igitur
henceforth *adv* posthac, dehinc
henchman *s* adiut·or -oris *m*
henpecked *adj* uxori·us -a -um
her *pron* eam, illam, hanc
her *adj* eius, illius, huius; **— own** su·us -a -um
herald *s (pol)* fetial·is -is *m; (crier)* praec·o
-onis *m*
herald *tr* (prae)nuntiare
herb *s* herb·a -ae *f*
herd *s (of animals)* gre·x -gis *m; (of oxen and
large animals)* arment·um -i *n; (pej)* vulg·us
-i *n*
herd *tr* **to — together** congregare ‖ *intr* **to —
together** congregari
herdsman *s* armentar·ius -(i)i *m*
here *adv* hic; **— and now** depraesentiarium
[*adv*]; **— and there** passim; **— I am!** ecce
me!; **— with it!** cedo *(pl:* cette)! [*can take an
object, e.g.,* **— with that book!** cedo illum
librum!]
hereabouts *adv* hic alicubi
hereafter *adv* posthac
hereafter *s* vit·a -ae *f* post mortem
hereby *adv* ex hoc, hinc
hereditary *adj* hereditari·us -a -um
heredity *s* gen·us -eris *n;* **by —** iure heredi-
tario, per successiones
herein *adv* in hoc, in hac re, hic
heresy *s* haeres·is -is *f*
heretical *adj* haeretic·us -a -um
hereupon *adv* hic
herewith *adv* unā cum hac re
heritage *s* heredit·as -atis *f*
hermaphrodite *s* androgyn·us -i *m*
hermit *s* eremit·a -ae *m*
hermitage *s* eremitae cell·a -ae *f*
hernia *s* herni·a -ae *f*
hero *s* vi·r -ri *m; (demigod)* her·os -oïs *m*

heroic *adj (age)* heroïc·us -a -um; fortissim·us -a -um
heroically *adv* fortissime
heroin *s* heroin·um -i *n;* **to use —** heroino uti
heroine *s* virag·o -inis *f; (myth)* heroïn·a -ae *f*
heroism *s* virt·us -utis *f*
heron *s* arde·a -ae *f*
herring *s* hareng·a -ae *f*
hers *pron* eius, illius
herself *pron (refl)* se; *(intensive)* ipsa; **by —** per se; **to —** sibi; **with —** secum
hesitant *adj* dubi·us -a -um
hesitantly *adv* cunctanter
hesitate *intr* dubitare
hesitation *s* dubitati·o -onis *f; (in speaking)* haesitati·o -onis *f*
heterogeneous *adj* divers·us -a -um
hew *tr* dolare, caedere
hey *interj* ohe!; **— you!** heus tu!
hi *interj* salve *(pl:* salvete)!
hiatus *s* hiat·us -ūs *m*
hiccup *s* singult·us -ūs *m*
hiccup *intr* singultire
hidden *adj* occult·us -a -um; **to lie —** latēre
hide *s* cor·ium -(i)i *n; (pelt)* pell·is -is *f;* **to be after s.o.'s —** corium alicuius petere; **to risk one's own —** corio suo ludere; **to save one's own —** corium servare
hide *tr* abdere, celare ‖ *intr* latēre
hide and seek *s* **to play —** per lusum latitare et quaeritare
hideous *adj* foed·us -a -um
hideously *adv* foede
hideousness *s* foedit·as -atis *f*
hiding *s* occultati·o -onis *f; (whipping)* verberati·o -onis *f*
hiding place *s* latebr·a -ae *f*
hierarchy *s* hierarchi·a -ae *f*
high *adj* alt·us -a -um; *(rank)* ampl·us -a -um; *(price)* magn·us -a -um; *(wind)* vehem·ens -entis; *(fever)* ard·ens -entis; *(note)* acut·us -a -um; *(expensive)* car·us -a -um; *(ground)* edit·us -a -um; *(virtue, good, etc.)* summ·us -a -um; **at a — price** magni (pretii) *or* magno pretio; **— and dry** auxilii exper·s -tis; **— and low** ubique; **— and mighty** superb·us -a -um; **— noon** meridi·es -ei *m;* **— blood pressure** hypertoni·a -ae *f;* **— opinion** magna opini·o -onis *f;* **— seas** alt·um -i *n;* **— tide** maximus aest·us -ūs *m;* **to be — on drugs** a medicamentis psychotropicis inebriare
high *adv* alte; **to aim —** magnas res appetere; **from on —** desuper; **on —** sursum versum
highball *s* aqu·a -ae *f* vitae aquā effervescenti commixta
highborn *adj* generos·us -a -um
high-class *adj* praest·ans -antis; *(goods)* laut·us -a -um

high-flown *adj* inflat·us -a -um
highhanded *adj* insol·ens -entis
highhandedly *adv* insolenter
high jump *s* salt·us -ūs *m* in altum
highlander *s* montan·us -i *m* (·a -ae *f)*
highlands *spl* regi·o -onis *f* montuosa
highlights *spl* praecipu·a -orum *npl* rerum
highly *adv (value)* magni; *(intensity)* vehementer, valde
high-minded *adj (noble)* magnanim·us -a -um
high-pitched *adj* acut·us -a -um
high priest *s* pontif·ex -icis *m,* sacerd·os -otis *m* maximus
highrise (building) *s* multizon·ium -(i)i *n*
high school *s* schol·a -ae *f* superior
high treason *s* maiest·as -atis *f* (laesa); **convicted of —** de maiestate damnat·us -a -um
highway *s* strat·a -ae *f* autocinetica
hijack *tr vi* abducere
hijacker *s* latr·o -onis *m*
hike *s* ambulati·o -onis *f;* **to go for a —** ambulatum ire
hike *tr (to increase)* augēre, efferre ‖ *intr* ambulare
hilarious *adj* hilar·us -a -um
hilariously *adv* hilare
hilarity *s* hilarit·as -atis *f*
hill *s* coll·is -is *m*
hillock *s* tumul·us -i *m*
hillside *s* cliv·us -i *m*
hilly *adj* clivos·us -a -um
hilt *s* capul·us -i *m*
him *pron* eum, illum, hunc; **of —** eius, illius huius
himself *pron (refl)* se; *(intensive)* ipse; **to —** sibi; **with —** secum
hind *s* cerv·a -ae *f*
hind *adj* poster·ior -ior -ius; **— end** *(coll)* postic·um -i *n*
hinder *tr* impedire, prohibēre; *(to block)* obstare *(w. dat)*
hindmost *adj* postrem·us -a -um
hindrance *s* impediment·um -i *n*
hindsight *s* posteriores cogitation·es -um *fpl*
hinge *s* card·o -inis *m*
hinge *intr* **to — on** *(fig)* niti *(w. abl)*
hint *s* significati·o -onis *f,* indic·ium -(i)i *n;* **to throw clear —s** nec dubias significationes iacere
hint *tr* suggerere, innuere
hip *s* cox·a -ae *f*
hippie *s* anticonformist·a -ae *m* (·ria -riae *f)*
hippodrome *s* hippodrom·os -i *m*
hippopotamus *s* hippopotam·us -i *m*
hire *s* merc·es -edis *f; (act)* conducti·o -onis *f*
hire *tr* conducere; **to — oneself out** auctorari; **to — out** locare
hired *adj* conduct·us -a -um, mercenari·us -a -um

hireling *s* mercenari·us -i *m* (·a -ae *f*)
his *adj* eius, illius, huius; — **own** su·us -a -um,
propri·us -a -um
hiss *s* sibil·us -i *m*
hiss *tr* & *intr* sibilare
historian *s* historic·us -i *m* (·a -ae *f*)
historical *adj* historic·us -a -um
history *s* histori·a -ae *f;* **ancient** — antiqua historia *f;* **modern** — recentioris aetatis historia *f;* **to write a** — **of the Roman people** res (gestas) populi Romani perscribere
histrionic *adj* histrional·is -is -e
hit *s* plag·a -ae *f,* ict·us -ūs *m; (success)* success·us -ūs *m*
hit *tr* icere, ferire; *(a baseball)* pulsare; *(of an illness)* affligere, occupare; **to** — **it off with** concordare cum *(w. abl);* **to** — **s.o. for a loan** ferire aliquem mutuo argento; **you've** — **the nail on the head** acu rem tetigisti ‖ *intr* **to** — **upon** offendere
hitch *s* nod·us -i *m;* **there is a** — haeret res (in salebrā); **without a** — sine difficultate
hitch *tr* coniungere
hitchhike *intr* alienis vect·us (-a) iter facere
hither *adv* huc
hither *adj* citer·ior -ior -ius
hitherto *adv (of time)* adhuc; *(of place)* huc usque
hive *s* alve·us -i *m*
hmmm *interj* hem!
hoard *s* acerv·us -i *m*
hoard *tr* coacervare, recondere
hoarder *s* accumula·tor -toris *m* (·trix -tricis *f*)
hoarse *adj* rauc·us -a -um; **to get** — irraucescere
hoarsely *adv* raucā voce
hoary *adj* can·us -a -um
hoax *s* frau·s -dis *f*
hobble *intr* claudicare
hobby *s* avocament·um -i *n*
hobnob *intr* (**with**) conversari (cum *w. abl*)
hock *tr (to pawn) (coll)* pignernare
hock *s* **in** — pignerat·us -a -um
hockey *s* lud·us -i *m* hocceius; **field** — ludus hocceius campestris; **ice** — ludus hocceius glacialis; **to play** — hocceio ludere
hockey puck *s* discul·us -i *m*
hockey stick *s* ferul·a -ae *f* repanda
hoe *s* sarcul·um -i *n*
hoe *tr* sarculare
hog *s* porc·us -i *m,* sus suis *mf;* —**s oink** sues grunniunt
hogwash *s* **that's** — quisquiliae!
hoist *tr* sublevare
hold *s (of ship)* cavern·a -ae *f;* **to get** *or* **take** — **of** prehendere; *(with both hands)* comprehendere
hold *tr* tenēre; *(to contain)* capere; *(to think)* habēre; *(elections, meeting, discussions)*

habēre; *(office, consulship, etc.)* gerere; **able to** — *(e.g., of a theater)* cap·ax -acis *(w. gen);* — **it!** *(stop!)* asta!; — **it please!** mane obsecro!; **to** — **back** retinēre; *(laughter, tears)* tenēre; **to** — **court** *(leg)* quaerere; **to** — **forth** *(e.g., hands)* porrigere; *(to offer)* praebēre; **to** — **in** inhibēre, cohibēre; **to** — **in high (highest) esteem** magni (maximi) facere; **to** — **in honor** in honore habēre; **to** — **off** arcēre; **to** — **one's breath** animam comprimere; **to** — **one's tongue** tacēre; **to** — **out** *(e.g., hands)* protendere; **to** — *(e.g., a compress)* **to** *(e.g., one's cheek)* admovēre (fomentum) ad (malam); **to** — **up** attollere; *(to detain)* detinēre, impedire; **to** — **up one's head** mentum tollere ‖ *intr* **to** — **back** cunctari; **to** — **forth** *(to speak)* contionari; **to** — **on to** tenēre; **to** — **out** *(to last)* durare, permanēre; **to** — **together** cohaerēre
holder *s* possess·or -oris *m; (instrument)* receptacul·um -i *n*
holding *s* possessi·o -onis *f*
hole *s* foram·en -inis *n; (of mice, etc.)* cav·um -i *n;* **to dig a** — **in the ground** locum in terra excavare; **to dig a** — **in the wall** parietem perfodere
hole-in-the-wall *s (cheap lodgings)* stabul·um -i *n*
holiday *s* di·es -ei *m* festus; fest·um -i *n; (from school)* dies feriatus; —**s** feri·ae -arum *fpl;* **public** — di·es -ei *m* sollemnis
holiness *s* sanctit·as -atis *f*
hollow *adj* cav·us -a -um; *(fig)* inan·is -is -e
hollow *s* cav·um -i *n; (depression)* lacun·a -ae *f;* — **of the hand** cava man·us -ūs *f*
hollow *tr* **to** — **out** excavare
holly *s* il·ex -icis *n* aquifolium
holocaust *s* holocaust·um -i *n*
holy *adj* sanct·us -a -um
homage *s* cult·us -ūs *m;* **to pay** — **to** colere
home *s* aed·es -ium *fpl,* dom·us -ūs *f;* **at** — domi; **at my** — domi meae, apud me; **at your** — domi tuae, apud te; **from** — domo; **to make oneself at** — se intimum facere; **to my** — ad me
home *adv (motion)* domum; *(place where)* domi
home *adj* domestic·us -a -um
home appliance *s* electricum instrument·um -i *n* domesticum; —**s** electrica utensil·ia -ium *npl* domestica
homebody *s* hom·o -inis *mf* umbratilis
home front *s* **on the** — **and on the war front** domi et militiae
home invader *s* effractari·us -i *m* (·a -ae *f*)
home invasion *s* effractur·a -ae *f*
homeland *s* patri·a -ae *f*
homeless *adj* tecto car·ens -entis
homelike *adj* familiar·is -is -e

homeliness *s* rusticit·as -atis *f*
homely *adj* inspecios·us -a -um
homemade *adj* domestic·us -a -um
homemaker *s* materfamilias *(gen:* matrisfamilias) *f*
home page *(comput)* pagin·a -ae *f* domestica
home plate *s* bas·is -is *m* summa
home run *s* circuit·us -ūs *m* basium; **to hit a —** circuitum basium facere
homesick *adj* appet·ens -entis tecti sui; **to be —** ex desiderio tecti sui laborare
homesickness *s* tecti sui desider·ium -(i)i *n*
homestead *s* fund·us -i *m*
hometown *s* patri·a -ae *f*
homeward *adv* domum
homework *s* pens·um -i *n* domesticum; *(written)* praescript·um -i *n* domesticum
homicidal *adj* cruent·us -a -um
homicide *s (person)* homicid·a -ae *mf; (deed)* homicid·ium -(i)i *n*
homily *s* tractat·us -ūs *m* moralis
homogeneous *adj* pari naturā praedit·us -a -um
homosexual *adj* cinaed·us -a -um; **— partner** *(euphem)* fra·ter -tris *m*
homosexual *s* cinaed·us -i *m*
hone *tr* acuere
honest *adj* prob·us -a -um; *(truthful)* ver·ax -acis; **— to God, — to goodness** mediusfidius
honestly *adv* **tell me —** dic bonā fide
honesty *s* probit·as -atis *f*
honey *s* mel, mellis *n; (term of endearment)* melill·a -ae *f*, mel, mellis *n*, melcul·um -i *n*
honeycomb *s* fav·us -i *m*
honeysuckle *s* clymen·us -i *m*
honor *s* hon·or -oris *m; (mark of distinction)* dignit·as -atis *f;* **on my —** meā fide; **on your —** per fidem; **sense of —** pud·or -oris *m;* **word of —** fid·es -ei *f*
honor *tr* honorare; *(to respect)* colere
honorable *adj* honest·us -a -um
honorably *adv* honeste
honorary *adj* honorari·us -a -um, honoris causā
hood *s* cucull·us -i *m; (of a car)* ploxen·um -i *n*
hoodlum *s* grassat·or -oris *m*
hoof *s* ungul·a -ae *f*
hook *s* unc·us -i *m; (esp. for fishing)* ham·us -i *m;* **by — or by crook** quocumque modo
hook *tr (to catch w. a hook)* inuncare; *(fig)* capere
hooked *adj* hamat·us -a -um; *(crooked)* adunc·us -a -um
hookey *s* **to play —** insciis parentibus a scholā abesse
hoop *s* circul·us -i *m; (toy)* troch·us -i *m; (shout)* clam·or -oris *m*

hoot *s* cant·us -ūs *m;* **not give a — about** pili facere *(w. acc)*, flocci non facere *(w. acc)*
hoot *tr* explodere ‖ *intr* obstrepere; *(of owls)* bubulare
hop *s* salt·us -ūs *m*
hop *intr* salire, subsaltare
hope *s* spes spei *f;* **glimmer of —** specul·a -ae *f;* **to give up all —** desperare
hope *intr* sperare; **to — for** exspectare; **to — that** sperare *(w. acc & inf)*
hopeful *adj* bonae spei
hopefully *adv* ut spero [*as I hope*]
hopefuls *spl (persons)* spe·s -rum *fpl*
hopeless *adj* desperat·us -a -um
hopelessly *adv* desperanter
hopelessness *s* desperati·o -onis *f*
hopper *s (in a restroom)* sell·a -ae *f* familiarica; *(funnel-shaped container)* infundibul·um -i *n*
horde *s* turb·a -ae *f; (wandering)* vaga multitud·o -inis *f*
horizon *s* fini·ens -entis *m*
horizontal *adj* librat·us -a -um
horizontal bar *s* ferr·um -i *n* transversum
horizontally *adv* per libram
hormone *s* hormon·um -i *n*
horn *s (of an animal)* corn·u -ūs *n; (mus)* bucin·a -ae *f;* **to blow the —** bucinā clangere
horned *adj* cornig·er -era -erum
hornet *s* crab·o -onis *m*
horny *adj* sal·ax -acis
horoscope *s* horoscop·us -i *m;* **to cast a —** horoscopare; **to have the same —** uno astro esse
horrible *adj* horribil·is -is -e
horribly *adv* horribili modo
horrid *adj* horrid·us -a -um
horrify *tr* horrificare
horror *s* horr·or -oris *m; (strong aversion)* od·ium -(i)i *n*
hors d'oeuvres *spl* promuls·is -idis *f*
horse *s* equ·us -i *m,* equ·a -ae *f;* **to beat a dead —** asellum currere docēre
horseback *s* **on — in** equo; **to fight on — ex** equo pugnare; **to ride — in** equo vehi
horsehair *s* pil·us -i *m* equinus
horsefly *s* taban·us -i *m; —s buzz** tabani bombilant
horseman *s* equ·es -itis *m*
horserace *s* curricul·um -i *n* equorum; **—s** equirri·a -orum *npl*
horseradish *s* armoraci·a -ae *f*
horseshoe *s* sole·a -ae *f* (equi)
horsewhip *s* scutic·a -ae *f*
horsewhip *tr* scuticā verberare
horticultural *adj* ad hortorum cultum pertin·ens -entis
horticulture *s* hortorum cult·us -ūs *m*

hose *s (tube)* tubul·us -i *m; (stocking)* tibial·e -is *n;* **rubber** — tubulus cummeus
hosiery *s* feminal·ia -ium *npl*
hospitable *adj* hospital·is -is -e
hospitably *adv* hospitaliter
hospital *s* valetudinar·ium -(i)i *n*
hospitality *s* hospitalit·as -atis *f*
host *s (entertainer)* hosp·es -itis *m; (army)* copi·ae -arum *fpl; (immense number)* multi-tud·o -inis *f; (wafer)* hosti·a -ae *f*
hostage *s* obs·es -idis *mf;* **to exchange —s** obsides inter se permutare
hostess *s* hospit·a -ae *f; (at an inn)* cop·a -ae *f*
hostile *adj* infens·us -a -um; *(forces, soil)* hostil·is -is -e; **in a — manner** hostiliter, infense
hot *adj* calid·us -a -um; *(boiling)* ferv·ens -entis; *(seething, sultry)* aestuos·us -a -um; *(of spices)* a·cer -cris -cre; *(fig)* ard·ens -entis; **— weather** aest·us -ūs *m;* **it is (very) — today** hodie (maxime) caletur; **to be — calēre; to become —** calescere; **to be in — water** *(coll)* in angustiis versari
hotbed *s* seminar·ium -(i)i *n*
hotdog *s* hill·a -ae calens *(gen:* hillae calentis) *f*
hotel *s* deversor·ium -(i)i *n;* **to stay at a — in** deversorio morari
hot-headed *adj* cerebros·us -a -um
hotel manager *s* deversorii direc·tor -toris *m* (·trix -tricis *f*)
hot pants *spl* brac·ae -arum *fpl* brevissimae
hot plate *s* disc·us -i *m* coctorius
hot-tempered *adj* stomachos·us -a -um
hound *s* catul·us -i *m*
hound *tr* instare *(w. dat)*
hour *s* hor·a -ae *f;* **a half —** semihora; **an — and a half** sesquihora; **a quarter of an —** quadr·ans -antis *m* horae; **at all —s** omnibus horis; **every —** singulis horis; **from — to —** in horas; **three quarters of an —** dodr·ans -antis *m* horae
hourly *adv* in horas
hourly *adj* in horas; *(output)* in horā
house *s* dom·us -ūs *m,* aed·es -ium *fpl; (family)* dom·us -ūs *m,* gen·s -tis *f;* **at the — of** apud *(w. acc)*
house *tr* domo excipere; *(things)* condere
house arrest *s* custodi·a -ae *f* libera
housebreaker *s* effractari·us -i *m* (·a -ae *f*)
housebroken *adj* domit·us -a -um
household *adj* familiar·is -is -e
household *s* famili·a -ae *f*
household gods *spl* Lar·es et Penat·es -um *mpl*
housekeeper *s* dispensa·tor -toris *m* (·trix -tricis *f*)
housekeeping *s* rei familiaris cur·a -ae *f*
housemaid *s* ancill·a -ae *f*
housewife *s* materfamilias *(gen:* matrisfamil-ias) *f*

hovel *s* tugur·ium -(i)i *n*
hover *intr* pendēre; **to — over** impendēre *(w. dat)*
how *adv* quomodo, quo pacto; *(chiefly after verbs of hearing, telling, etc.)* ut *w. subj); (to what degree)* quam; **— are you? (— are you doing?)** quid agis? *(pl:* quid agitis?); **— come?** qui fit? *or* qui istuc?; **— far is ... from ... ?** quantum distat *(or* abest) ... ab *(w. abl)?;* **— goes it?** qui fit?; **— long** quamdiu, quousque; **— long ago** quam pridem, quam dudum; **— many** quot *[indecl];* **— many times** quotiens, quoties; **— much** quantus -a -um; **— much** *(at what price)* quanti; **how much did this sell for?** quanti hoc venit? **— much does this cost?** quanti hoc constat? **— much is this?** hoc quanti constat? **— often** quotiens; **— old are you?** quot annos nat·us (-a) es? **— so?** quid ita?; **— soon** quam dudum; **—'s that?** *(what did you say?)* quidum? *or* qui iam?
however *adv (nevertheless)* tamen, autem; *(in whatever way)* quoquomodo; *(to whatever degree)* quamvis *(esp. w. adj or adv; followed by subj);* **— great** quant·uscumque -acumque -umcumque; **— many** quotquot; **— often** quotiescumque
howl *s* ululat·us -ūs *m*
howl *intr (lit & fig)* ululare
hub *s* ax·is -is *m*
hubbub *s* tumult·us -ūs *m; (noise of brawling)* convic·ium -(i)i *n*
huckster *s* instit·or -oris *m*
huddle *intr* coacervari, stipari; **—ed together** confert·i -ae -a
huddle *s* coron·a -ae *f; (sports)* symplegm·a -atis *n*
hue *s* col·or -oris *m;* **to raise a — and cry** conclamare; *(to complain)* conqueri
huff *s* offensi·o -onis *f;* **to be in a —** stomachari
huff *intr* stomachari
hug *s* complex·us -ūs *m*
hug *tr* complecti, amplecti; **to — each other** inter se amplecti
huge *adj* ing·ens -entis; *(of monstrous size)* imman·is -is -e; **— sum of money** ingens pecuni·a -ae *f*
hugeness *s* immanit·as -atis *f*
hulk *s (hull of unseaworthy ship)* alve·us -i *m* desertus; *(heavy ship)* nav·is -is *f* oneraria
hulking, hulky *adj* grav·is -is -e
hull *s* alve·us -i *m*
hum *s* murm·ur -uris *m; (of bees)* bomb·us -i *m*
hum *intr* murmurare; *(of bees)* bombilare
human *adj* human·us -a -um; **— feelings** humanit·as -atis *f;* **— race** gen·us -eris *n* humanum
human being *s* hom·o -inis *mf*

humane *adj* human·us -a -um
humanely *adv* humane
humanity *s* humanit·as -atis *f; (people)* homin·es -um *mpl*
humanize *tr* excolere
humble *adj (modest)* summiss·us -a -um; *(obscure)* humil·is -is -e
humble *tr* deprimere; **to — oneself before s.o.** se summittere alicui
humbly *adv* summisse
humdrum *adj (dull)* molest·us -a -um; *(banal)* trit·us -a -um
humid *adj* umid·us -a -um
humidity *s* um·or -oris *m*
humiliate *tr* deprimere
humiliating *adj* humil·is -is -e
humiliation *s* dedec·us -oris *n*
humility *s* humilit·as -atis *f*
humor *s* festivit·as -atis *f; (mood)* anim·us -i *m;* **he is in bad —** stomachosus est; **he is in good —** festivus est; **sense of —** festivit·as -atis *f*
humor *tr* indulgēre *(w. dat),* morem gerere *(w. dat)*
humorous *adj* festiv·us -a -um
humorously *adv* festive
hump *s* gibb·er -eris *m*
humpbacked *adj* gibb·er -era -erum
hunch *s* opini·o -onis *f;* **to have a —** opinari
hundred *adj* centum [*indecl*]; **— times** centie(n)s
hundredfold *adj* centupl·ex -icis
hundredfold *s* centupl·um -i *n*
hundredth *adj* centesim·us -a -um
hunger *s* fam·es -is *f; (voluntary)* inedi·a -ae *f*
hunger *intr* esurire; **to — for** cupere
hung jury *s* **to be acquitted by a —** sententiis paribus absolvi
hungrily *adv* avide, voraciter
hungry *adj* esuri·ens -entis; **to be —** esurire
hunt *s* venati·o -onis *f*
hunt *tr* venari **‖** *intr* **to — for** quaerere
hunter *s* vena·tor -toris *m* (·trix -tricis *f); (horse)* equ·us -i *m* venaticus
hunting *s* venat·us -ūs *m;* **to go —** venari
hunting *adj* venatic·us -a -um; **— dog** can·is -is *m* venaticus; **— gear** instrument·um -i *n* venatorium; **— spear** venabul·um -i *n*
huntress *s* venatr·ix -icis *f*
hurdle *s (obstacle)* ob·ex -icis *mf*
hurl *tr* conicere
hurray *interj* euax!, io!
hurricane *s* ingens procell·a -ae *f*
hurried *adj* praeproper·us -a -um; *(too hasty)* praec·eps -ipitis
hurriedly *adv* raptim; *(carelessly)* negligenter
hurry *tr* rapere; **to — away** abripere **‖** *intr* properare, festinare; *(to rush hurriedly)*

ruere; **to — along** se agere; **— up!** matura! *(pl:* maturate!)
hurry *s* festinati·o -onis *f; in a —* festinanter; **to be in a —** festinare, properare
hurt *s* iniuri·a -ae *f*
hurt *adj* sauci·us -a -um; *(emotionally)* sauci·us -a -um, offens·us -a -um
hurt *tr* nocēre *(w. dat),* laedere; *(fig)* offendere **‖** *intr* dolēre; **to — a lot** vehementer dolēre
husband *s* marit·us -i *m*
husbandry *s* agricultur·a -ae *f*
hush *s* silent·ium -(i)i *n*
hush *tr* comprimere; *(a secret)* celare **‖** *intr* tacēre
hush *interj* st!
husk *s* follicul·us -i *m; (of beans, etc.)* siliqu·a -ae *f; (of grain)* glum·a -ae *f*
husky *adj* robust·us -a -um; *(of voice)* rauc·us -a -um
hustle *tr* trudere **‖** *intr* inter se trudere
hustler *s* hom·o -inis *mf* strenu·us (-a)
hut *s* tugur·ium -(i)i *n*
hyacinth *s* hyacinth·us -i *m*
hybrid *s* hybrid·a -ae *f*
Hydra *s* Hydr·a -ae *f*
hydraulic *adj* hydraulic·us -a -um
hydrophobia *s* hydrophobi·a -ae *f*
hyena *s* hyaen·a -ae *f*
hygiene *s* salubrit·as -atis *f,* hygien·e -es *f;* **to practice —** hygienen exercēre
hygienic *adj* salubr·is -is -e, hygienic·us -a -um
hymn *s* hymn·us -i *m*
hyperbole *s* hyperbol·e -es *f*
hypercritical *adj* nimis sever·us -a -um
hypertext *s* hypertext·us -ūs *m*
hypertext *adj* hypertextual·is -is -e
hyphen *s* hyphen [*indecl*] *n*
hypenate *tr* hypen ponere
hypochondriac *s* melancholic·us -i *m* (·a -ae *f)*
hypocrisy *s* simulati·o -onis *f*
hypocrite *s* simula·tor -toris *m* (·trix -tricis *f)*
hypocritical *adj* simulat·us -a -um
hypothesis *s* hypothes·is -is *m*
hypothetical *adj* hypothetic·us -a -um
hysteria *s* delirati·o -onis *f*
hysterical *adj* delir·us -a -um

I

I *pron* ego; **— myself** egomet
iamb *s (pros)* iamb·us -i *m*
iambic *adj (pros)* iambe·us -a -um
ice *s* glaci·es -ei *f*
iceberg *s* glaciei niviumque concreta mol·es -is *f*

icebound *adj* glacie consaept·us -a -um
ice cream *s* gelidum crem·um -i *n*
ice hockey *s see* **hockey**
ice rink *s* stad·ion -(i)i *n* glaciale
ice skate *s* patin·us -i *m*
ice skate *intr* patinare
ice skater *s* patina·tor -toris *m* (·trix -tricis *f*)
ice skating *s* patinati·o -onis *f*
ice water *s* nivata aqu·a -ae *f*
icicle *s* stiri·a -ae *f*
icon *s* (*comput*) ic·on -onis *f*
icy *adj* glacial·is -is -e
idea *s* (*notion*) consil·ium -(i)i *n*; (*thought*) sententi·a -ae *f*; **it's a good — to** expedit (*w. lnf*)
ideal *adj* perfect·us -a -um
ideal *s* exempl·ar -aris *n*
idealist *s* hom·o -inis *mf* summae virtutis
idealistic *adj* omnibus virtutibus ornat·us -a -um
identical *adj* idem eadem idem, unus atque idem
identify *tr* agnoscere
identity *s* identit·as -atis *f*
idiocy *s* fatuit·as -atis *f*
idiom *s* propriet·as -atis *f* linguae (Latinae *or* Anglicae)
idiomatic expression *s* vox quae linguae (Latinae *or* Anglicae) propria est
idiosyncrasy *s* propr·ium -(i)i *n*
idiot *s* fatu·us -i *m* (·a -ae *f*)
idiotic *adj* fatu·us -a -um
idle *adj* vacu·us -a -um; (*pointless*) van·us -a -um; (*lazy*) ignav·us -a -um; **to be —** cessare
idle *tr* **to — away** terere ‖ *intr* cessare, vacare
idleness *s* cessati·o -onis *f*
idler *s* cessa·tor -toris *m* (·trix -tricis *f*)
idle talk *s* nug·ae -arum *fpl*
idly *adv* segniter
idol *s* simulacr·um -i *n*; (*eccl*) idol·um -i *n*; (*fig*) delici·ae -arum *fpl*
idolater *s* idololatr·es -ae *mf*
idolatrous *adj* idololatric·us -a -um
idolatry *s* idololatri·a -ae *f*
idolize *tr* venerari
idyl *s* idyll·ium -(i)i *n*
if *conj* si; **as —** quasi, tamquam; **and —, but — quodsi; even — etiamsi; — not** ni, si minus; **— only** si modo; (*to express a wish*) utinam (*w. subj*)
iffy *adj* (*coll*) dubi·us -a -um
igneous *adj* igne·us -a -um
ignite *tr* accendere ‖ *intr* flammam concipere, exardescere
ignoble *adj* ignobil·is -is -e; (*base*) turp·is -is -e
ignobly *adv* turpiter
ignominious *adj* ignominios·us -a -um
ignominiously *adv* ignominiose

ignominy *s* ignomini·a -ae *f*
ignoramus *s* nesapi·us -i *m* (·a -ae *f*)
ignorance *s* ignoranti·a -ae *f*, insciti·a -ae *f*
ignorant *adj* ignar·us -a -um, inscit·us -a -um; (*unlearned*) indoct·us -a -um; **to be — of** ignorare
ignorantly *adv* inscienter
ignore *tr* praeterire; (*to omit*) neglegere
Iliad *s* Ili·as -adis *f*
ill *adj* (*used of body or mind*) ae·ger -gra -grum; (*used of body*) aegrot·us -a -um; (*evil*) mal·us -a -um; **to be —** aegrotare; **to fall — in** morbum incidere
ill *adv* male; **to be — at ease** sollict·us -a -um esse
ill *s* mal·um -i *n*
ill-advised *adj* inconsult·us -a -um
ill-boding *adj* infaust·us -a -um
ill-bred *adj* inurban·us -a -um
ill-disposed *adj* (**toward**) malevol·us -a -um (*w. dat*)
illegal *adj* illicit·us -a -um
illegitimate *adj* haud legitim·us -a -um; (*of birth*) noth·us -a -um
illegitimately *adv* contra legem
ill-fated *adj* infel·ix -icis
ill-gotten *adj* male part·us -a -um
ill health *s* valetud·o -inis *f* adversa; **for reasons of —** valetudinis causā
illiberal *adj* illiberal·is -is -e
illicit *adj* illicit·us -a -um
illicitly *adv* illicite
illiteracy *s* ignorati·o -onis *f* legendi scribendique
illiterate *adj* illiterat·us -a -um
ill-mannered *adj* male morat·us -a -um
illness *s* morb·us -i *m*
illogical *adj* absurd·us -a -um
illogically *adv* absurde
ill-omened *adj* infel·ix -icis
ills *spl* mal·a -orum *npl*
ill-starred *adj* infel·ix -icis
ill-tempered *adj* iracund·us -a -um
ill-timed *adj* intempestiv·us -a -um
illuminate *tr* illuminare; (*to enlighten*) excolere
illumination *s* illuminati·o -onis *f*
illusion *s* err·or -oris *m*; **optical —** oculorum ludibr·ium -(i)i *n*
illusive *adj* van·us -a -um
illusory *adj* fall·ax -acis
illustrate *tr* (*to shed light on*) illustrare; (*to exemplify*) exempla (*w. gen*) adducere; (*to draw*) delineare; (*to picture*) in tabulis depingere
illustration *s* (*example*) exempl·um -i *n*; (*picture*) tabul·a -ac *f*
illustrious *adj* illustr·is -is -e
ill will *s* malevolenti·a -ae *f*

image *s* sign·um -i *n; (esp. a portrait or bust)* imag·o -inis *f; (esp. a figure of a god)* simulacr·um -i *n*

imagery *s* imagin·es -um *fpl*

imaginary *adj* commentici·us -a -um, imaginari·us -a -um

imagination *s (faculty)* imaginati·o -onis *f;* cogitati·o -onis *f*

imaginative *adj* ingenios·us -a -um

imagine *tr* (animo) fingere, imaginari

imbecile *s* fatu·us -i *m* (·a -ae *f)*

imbecile *adj* fatu·us -a -um

imbedded *adj* (**in**) infix·us -a -um (in *w abl)*

imbibe *tr* imbibere

imbue *tr* imbuere

imitate *tr* imitari

imitation *s (act)* imitati·o -onis *f; (thing)* imag·o -inis *f*

imitator *s* imita·tor -toris *m* (·trix -tricis *f)*

immaculate *adj* immaculat·us -a -um

immaterial *adj* incorporal·is -is -e; *(unimportant)* nullius momenti

immature *adj* immatur·us -a -um

immaturity *s* immaturit·as -atis *f*

immeasurable *adj* immens·us -a -um

immediate *adj* proxim·us -a -um

immediately *adv* statim, confestim; — **after** sub *(w. acc)*

immemorial *adj* antiquissim·us -a -um; **from time** — ex omni memoriā aetatum

immense *adj* immens·us -a -um

immensely *adv* vehementer

immensity *s* immensit·as -atis *f*

immerse *tr* (im)mergere

immersion *s* immersi·o -onis *f*

imminent *adj* immin·ens -entis; **to be** — instare

immobile *adj* immobil·is -is -e

immobility *s* immobilit·as -atis *f*

immoderate *adj* immodic·us -a -um

immoderately *adv* immodice

immodest *adj* impudic·us -a -um

immodesty *s* immodesti·a -ae *f*

immolate *tr* immolare

immolation *s* immolati·o -onis *f*

immoral *adj* prav·us -a -um

immorality *s* perditi mor·es -um *mpl*

immortal *adj* immortal·is -is -e

immortality *s* immortalit·as -atis *f*

immortalize *tr* immortalitati tradere

immovable *adj (lit & fig)* immobil·is -is -e

immune *adj* immun·is -is -e

immunity *s* immunit·as -atis *f,* vacati·o -onis *f;* **promise of** — fid·es -ei *f* publica

immutability *s* immutabilit·as -atis *f*

immutable *adj* immutabil·is -is -e

imp *s* pu·er -eri *m* protervus

impact *s* impuls·us -ūs *m*

impair *tr* imminuere

impale *tr* palo infigere

impart *tr* impertire, communicare

impartial *adj* aequ·us -a -um

impartiality *s* aequit·as -atis *f*

impartially *adv* aequabiliter; **to judge** — aequo (animo) iudicare

impassable *adj* impervi·us -a -um

impassioned *adj* vehem·ens -entis; **with** — **gestures** ardenti motu gestuque

impassive *adj* sensu car·ens -entis

impatience *s* impatienti·a -ae *f*

impatient *adj* impati·ens -entis; iniquo animo; **to be** — **with** iniquo animo ferre

impatiently *adv* iniquo animo

impeach *tr* criminari, accusare

impeachment *s* accusati·o -onis *f*

impede *tr* impedire

impediment *s* impediment·um -i *n; (in speech)* haesitati·o -onis *f*

impel *tr* impellere

impending *adj* immin·ens -entis

impenetrable *adj* impenetrabil·is -is -e; *(fig)* occult·us -a -um

impenitence *s* impaenitenti·a -ae *f*

imperative *adj* inst·ans -antis; *(gram)* imperativ·us -a -um; — **mood** mod·us -i *m* imperativus

imperceptible *adj* tenuissim·us -a -um

imperceptibly *adv* sensim

imperfect *adj (not completed)* imperfect·us -a -um; *(faulty)* vitios·us -a -um; — **tense** temp·us -oris *n* praeteritum

imperfection *s* vit·ium -(i)i *n*

imperfectly *adv* vitiose

imperial *adj* imperiatori·us -a -um; *(of an emperor)* principal·is -is -e

imperil *tr* in periculum adducere

imperious *adj* imperios·us -a -um

imperiously *adv* imperiose

imperishable *adj* incorrupt·us -a -um

impermeable *adj* impervi·us -a -um

impersonal *adj (detached)* incurios·us -a -um; *(gram)* impersonal·is -is -e

impersonally *adv (gram)* impersonaliter

impersonate *tr* sustinēre partes *(w. gen),* simulare

impersonation *s* simulati·o -onis *f*

impertinence *s* protervit·as -atis *f*

impertinent *adj* proterv·us -a -um; *(not to the point)* nihil ad rem

impertinently *adv* proterve

impervious *adj* impervi·us -a -um

impetuosity *s* violenti·a -ae *f*

impetuous *adj* viol·ens -entis

impetus *s* impet·us -ūs *m*

impiety *s* impiet·as -atis *f*

impinge *intr* — **on** incidere *(w. dat)*

impious *adj* impi·us -a -um; *(stronger)* nefari·us -a -um

impiously *adv* impie; *(stronger)* nefarie
impish *adj* proterv·us -a -um
implacable *adj* implacabil·is -is -e
implacably *adv* implacabiliter
implant *tr* inserere, ingenerare
implement *s* instrument·um -i *n; (iron tool)* ferrament·um -i *n*
implement *tr* exsequi
implicate *tr* implicare
implication *s* indic·ium -(i)i *n; (act)* implicati·o -onis *f;* **by —** tacite
implicit *adj* tacit·us -a -um; *(absolute)* summ·us -a -um
implicitly *adv* tacite
implied *adj* tacit·us -a -um; **to be — in** incsse in *(w. abl)*
implore *tr* implorare
imply *tr* innuere, indicare; *(to mean)* significare
impolite *adj* inurban·us -a -um
impolitely *adv* inurbane
impoliteness *s* inurbanit·as -atis *f*
impolitic *adj* inconsult·us -a -um
import *tr* importare, invehere
import *s (meaning)* significati·o -onis *f;* **—s** importatici·a -orum *npl*
importance *s* moment·um -i *n;* **it is of the greatest — to me** permagni meā interest; **of — grav·is** -is -e; **to be a person of great —** plurimum pollēre; **to be of great —** magni esse
important *adj* magn·us -a -um; *(weighty)* grav·is -is -e; **an — and wealthy city** gravis atque opulenta civit·as -atis *f;* **it is — to me (to you, to us)** meā (tuā, vestrā, nostrā) refert; **it's not all that — to me** mihi tanti non est; **to be — magni** (momenti *or* negoti) esse; **to be very — maximi** (momenti *or* negoti) esse
importune *tr* flagitare, sollicitare
impose *tr* imponere; *(to enjoin)* iniungere; **to — a fine (a punishment) on s.o.** alicui multam (poenam) irrogare **‖** *intr* **to — upon** abuti *(w. abl)*
imposition *s (excessive burden)* importunit·as -atis *f; (act) use* imponere
impossibility *s* impossibilit·as -atis *f*
impossible *adj* impossibil·is -is -e; **it is —** non fieri potest
imposter *s* frauda·tor -toris *m* (·trix -tricis *f*)
impotence *s* infirmit·as -atis *f; (sexual)* sterilit·as -atis *f*
impotent *adj* infirm·us -a -um; *(sexually)* steril·is -is -e
impound *tr* publicare; *(animals)* includere
impoverish *tr* in egestatem redigere
impoverished *adj* eg·ens -entis
impractical *adj* inutil·is -is -e
impregnable *adj* inexpugnabil·is -is -e
impregnate *tr* gravidam facere

impregnation *s* fecundati·o -onis *f*
impress *tr (on the mind; to imprint)* imprimere; *(a person)* commovēre; **to — s.th. on s.o.** aliquid alicui inculcare
impression *s (on a person)* animi mot·us -ūs *m; (print)* impressi·o -onis *f; (copy)* exempl·ar -aris *n; (idea)* opini·o -onis *f;* **to make a (deep) — on** (maxime) commovēre *(w. acc)*
impressive *adj* grav·is -is -e
impressively *adv* graviter
imprint *s* impressi·o -onis *f*
imprint *tr* imprimere; **to be —ed on the mind** in animum imprimi
imprison *tr* in vincula conicere
imprisonment *s* custodi·a -ae *f*
improbable *adj* haud credibil·is -is -e, haud probabil·is -is -e
impromptu *adj* subit(ari)·us -a -um
impromptu *adv* ex tempore
improper *adj* indecor·us -a -um
improperly *adv* indecore
improve *tr* mel·iorem -iorem -ius facere; *(where a fault exists)* emendare; *(soil)* laetificare **‖** *intr* mel·ior -ior -ius fieri; *(med)* convalescere
improvement *s* emendati·o -onis *f; (condition)* mutati·o -onis *f* in meliorem statum; *(progress made)* profect·us -ūs *m;* **to make — proficere**
improvise *tr* ex tempore dicere *or* componere
imprudence *s* imprudenti·a -ae *f*
imprudent *adj* imprud·ens -entis
imprudently *adv* imprudenter
impudent *adj* impud·ens -entis
impugn *tr* inpugnare, in dubium vocare
impulse *s* animi impet·us -ūs *m*
impulsive *adj* temerari·us -a -um
impulsively *adv* impetu quodam animi
impunity *s* impunit·as -atis *f;* **with — impune**
impure *adj* immund·us -a -um; *(morally)* impur·us -a -um
impurely *adv* impure
impurity *s* immunditi·a -ae *f; (moral)* impurit·as -atis *f*
impute *tr* imputare
in *prep in (w. abl); (in cities, use locative); (in the writings of)* apud *(w. acc); (of time)* render by abl; *(denoting rule, standard or manner)* in *(w. acc), e.g.,* **— the manner of slaves** servilem in modum; **— all** ex toto; **— that** quod; **— the course of the night** de nocte; **— the course of the third watch** de tertiā vigiliā; **— the likeness of** ad similitudinem *(w. gen);* **— the month of September** (de) mense Septembri; **— the same manner** ad eundem modum, eodem modo

in *adv (motion)* intro; *(rest)* intra, intus; **is your father** — estne pater intus?

inability *s* impotenti·a -ae *f,* nulla facult·as -atis *f*

inaccessible *adj* inacess·us -a -um; **to be** — *(of a person)* rari aditūs esse

inaccuracy *s* indiligenti·a -ae *f,* incuri·a -ae *f; (error)* err·or -oris *m*

inaccurate *adj* parum accurat·us -a -um; *(in error)* vitios·us -a -um

inaccurately *adv* parum accurate

inactive *adj* iner·s -tis

inactivity *s* inerti·a -ae *f*

inadequate *adj* im·par -paris

inadequately *adv* parum, haud satis

inadmissible *adj* illicit·us -a -um

inadvertent *adj* imprud·ens -entis

inadvertently *adv* imprudenter; *more frequently expressed by the adjective* imprud·ens -entis

inalienable *adj* quod alienari non potest

inane *adj* inan·is -is -e

inanimate *adj* inanim·us -a -um

inapplicable *adj* **to be** — non valēre

inappropriate *adj* haud apt·us -a -um

inappropriately *adv* parum apte

inarticulate *adj* indistinct·us -a -um

inasmuch as *conj* quandoquidem

inattention *s* indiligenti·a -ae *f*

inattentive *adj* haud attent·us -a -um

inattentively *adv* neglegenter

inaudible *adj* **to be** — audiri non posse

inaugurate *tr (an official)* inaugurare; *(to begin)* incipere

inauguration *s* inaugurati·o -onis *f;* init·ium -(i)i *n*

inauspicious *adj* infaust·us -a -um

inauspiciously *adv* malo omine

inborn, inbred *adj* innat·us -a -um

incalculable *adj* inaestimabil·is -is -e; *(fig)* immens·us -a -um

incantation *s* incantament·um -i *n*

incapable *adj* incap·ax -acis; **to be** — **of** non posse *(w. inf)*

incapacitate *tr* debilitare

incarcerate *tr* in carcerem conicere

incarnate *adj* incarnat·us -a -um

incarnation *s* incarnati·o -onis *f*

incautious *adj* incaut·us -a -um

incautiously *adv* incaute

incendiary *adj* incendiari·us -a -um

incense *s* tus, turis *n*

incense *tr* ture fumigare; *(to anger)* incendere

incentive *s* incitament·um -i *n*

incessant *adj* assidu·us -a -um

incessantly *adv* assidue

incest *s* incest·us -ūs *m*

incestuous *adj* incest·us -a -um

inch *s* unci·a -ae *f;* — **by** — unciatim; **not to yield an** — non tranversum digitum discedere

incident *s* cas·us -ūs *m,* res, rei *f*

incidental *adj* fortuit·us -a -um

incidentally *adv* casu, inter alias res

incinerate *tr* cremare

incinerator *s* receptacul·um -i *n* cremandi

incipient *adj* incipi·ens -entis

incision *s* incisur·a -ae *f*

incisive *adj* a·cer -cris -cre

incisors *spl* dent·es -ium *mpl* primores

incite *tr* incitare

incitement *s* incitament·um -i *n*

incivility *s* rusticit·as -atis *f*

inclemency *s* inclementi·a -ae *f; (of weather)* asperit·as -atis *f*

inclement *adj* asp·er -era -erum

inclination *s (act, propensity)* inclinati·o -onis *f; (slope)* proclivit·as -atis *f*

incline *s* acclivit·as -atis *f*

incline *tr & intr* inclinare

inclined *adj* propens·us -a -um; **I am** — **to believe** crediderim

include *tr (to contain)* continēre; *(to enclose)* includere; *(to comprise)* comprehendere; —**ing me** me haud excepto; —**ing your brother** in his frater tuus

inclusive *adj expressed by* adnumerare: **from the 1st to the 10th** — a primo die ad decimum adnumeratum *(or* ipso decimo adnumerato)

incognito *adv* alienā indutā personā

incoherent *adj* perturbat·us -a -um; **to be** — non cohaerēre

incoherently *adv* **to speak** — male cohaerentia loqui

income *s* quaest·us -ūs *m,* merc·es -edis *f*

incomparable *adj* incomparabil·is -is -e

incomparably *adv* unice

incompatibility *s* repugnanti·a -ae *f*

incompatible *adj* repugn·ans -antis

incompetence *s* insciti·a -ae *f*

incompetent *adj* inscit·us -a -um

incomplete *adj* imperfect·us -a -um

incomprehensible *adj* quod mente non comprehendi potest

inconceivable *adj* incredibil·is -is -e

inconclusive *adj* anc·eps -ipitis

incongruous *adj* male congru·ens -entis, inconveni·ens -entis

inconsiderable *adj* exigu·us -a -um

inconsiderate *adj* inconsiderat·us -a -um

inconsistency *s* discrepanti·a -ae *f*

inconsistent *adj* inconst·ans -antis; **to be** — **with** abhorrēre ab *(w. abl)*

inconsistently *adv* inconstanter

inconsolable *adj* inconsolabil·is -is -e

inconstancy *s* inconstanti·a -ae *f*

inconstant *adj* inconst·ans -antis
incontestible *adj* non contendend·us -a -um
incontinence *s* incontinenti·a -ae *f; (of sex)* licenti·a -ae *f*
incontinent *adj* incontin·ens -entis; *(sexually)* libidinos·us -a -um
incontrovertible *adj* quod refutari non potest
inconvenience *s* incommod·um -i *n*
inconvenience *tr* incommodare
inconvenient *adj* incommod·us -a -um
inconveniently *adv* incommode
incorporate *tr* adicere; *(to unite, esp. politically)* contribuere; *(to form into a corporation)* constituere
incorporeal *adj* incorporal·is -is -e
incorrect *adj* mendos·us -a -um, vitios·us -a -um
incorrectly *adv* perperam
incorrigible *adj* perdit·us -a -um
incorrupt *adj* incorrupt·us -a -um
incorruptible *adj* incorruptibil·is -is -e; *(upright)* inte·ger -gra -grum
increase *s* increment·um -i *n; (act)* accreti·o -onis *f*
increase *tr* augēre, ampliare ‖ *intr* augeri, crescere
incredible *adj* incredibil·is -is -e
incredibly *adv* incredibiliter
incredulity *s* incredulit·as -atis *f*
incredulous *adj* incredul·us -a -um
increment *s* increment·um -i *n*
incriminate *tr* criminari
incubate *tr* incubare
incubation *s* incubati·o -onis *f*
inculcate *tr* inculcare
inculcation *s* inculcati·o -onis *f*
incumbent *adj* it is — on oportet *(w. acc)*
incumbent *s* qui *(or* quae) honorem gerit
incur *tr* subire; *(guilt)* admittere
incurable *adj* insanabil·is -is -e
incursion *s* incursi·o -onis *f*
indebted *adj* obaerat·us -a -um; *(obliged)* obnoxi·us -a -um; **to be — to s.o. for a sum of money** pecuniam alicui debēre
indecency *s* impudiciti·a -ae *f*
indecent *adj* impudic·us -a -um
indecently *adv* impudice
indecision *s* haesitati·o -onis *f*
indecisive *adj (battle)* anc·eps -ipitis; *(person)* dubi·us -a -um
indeclinable *adj* indeclinabil·is -is -e
indeed *adv* vere, profecto; *(concessive)* quidem; *(reply)* certe, vero; *(interrog)* itane?
indefatigable *adj* indefatigabil·is -is -e
indefensible *adj (an action)* non excusand·us -a -um; *(mil)* parum firm·us -a -um; **to be —** defendi non posse

indefinite *adj* incert·us -a -um; *(vague)* anc·eps -ipitis; *(gram)* infinit·us -a -um *(opp: finitus)*
indelible *adj* indelibil·is -is -e
indelicate *adj* inurban·us -a -um
indemnify *tr* damnum restitutere *(w. dat),* compensare
indemnity *s* indemnit·as -atis *f,* damni restituti·o -onis *f*
indent *tr (to notch)* incisuris signare; *(a line)* a margine movēre
indentation *s* incisur·a -ae *f*
indented *adj* incis·us -a -um; *(serrated)* serrat·us -a -um
independence *s* libert·as -atis *f*
Independent *adj* lib·er -era -erum; *(one's own master)* sui pot·ens -entis; *(leg)* sui iuris
independently *adv* libere, suo arbitrio
indescribable *adj* inenarrabil·is -is -e
indescribably *adv* inenarrabiliter
indestructible *adj* indelebil·is -is -e
indeterminate *adj* indefinit·us -a -um
index *s* ind·ex -icis *m*
Indian *adj* Indic·us -a -um
Indian *s* Ind·us -i *m* (·a -ae *f*)
indicate *tr* indicare, significare; **to — that** docēre *(w. acc & inf)*
indication *s* indic·ium -(i)i *n*
indicative *s (gram)* indicativus mod·us -i *m*
indict *tr* nomen *(w. gen)* deferre
indictment *s* nominis delati·o -onis *f;* **bill of —** libell·us -i *m*
indifference *s* aequus anim·us -i *m; (apathy)* lentitud·o -inis *f,* neglegenti·a -ae *f*
indifferent *adj (apathetic)* indiffer·ens -entis; *(mediocre)* mediocr·is -is -e; **to be — to s.th.** aliquid nil morari
indifferently *adv* indifferenter
indigenous *adj (home-grown)* vernacul·us -a -um; *(of people)* indigen·a -ae; **the — Latins** indigenae Latini
indigent *adj* eg·ens -entis
indigestible *adj* crud·us -a -um
indigestion *s* crudit·as -atis *f*
indignant *adj* indignabund·us -a -um; **— at** indign·ans -antis *(w. gen);* **to be —** indignari
indignantly *adv* indignanter
indignation *s* indignati·o -onis *f*
indignity *s* indignit·as -atis *f*
indirect *adj* indirect·us -a -um; **— discourse** obliqua orati·o -onis *f*
indirectly *adv* indirecte
indiscreet *adj* inconsult·us -a -um
indiscreetly *adv* inconsulte
indiscretion *s* imprudenti·a -ae *f;* **driven by youthful —** licentiā iuvenali impuls·us -a -um
indiscriminate *adj* promiscu·us -a -um
indiscriminately *adv* sine discrimine

indispensable *adj* omnino necessari·us -a -um
indisposed *adj* (**to**) avers·us -a -um (ab *w. abl*);
  (sick) aegrot·us -a -um
indisputable *adj* cert·us -a -um, haud dubi·us
  -a -um
indissoluble *adj* indissolubil·is -is -e
indistinct *adj* parum clar·us -a -um
indistinctly *adv* parum clare
individual *adj (of one only)* singular·is -is -e;
  (of more than one) singul·i -ae -a; *(particular)* quidam quaedam, quoddam; *(peculiar)*
  propri·us -a -um
individual *s* hom·o -inis *mf;* —s singul·i -ae
  -a; **to benefit the country or** —s civitati aut
  singulis civibus prodesse
individually *adv* singulatim
individuality *s* proprium ingen·ium -(i)i *n*
indivisible *adj* indivisibil·is -is -e
indolence *s* inerti·a -ae *f*
indolent *adj* in·ers -ertis
indomitable *adj* indomit·us -a -um
indorse *tr* ratum facere
indubitable *adj* indubitabil·is -is -e
indubitably *adv* sine dubio
induce *tr* adducere
inducement *s* incitament·um -i *n*
indulge *tr* indulgēre *(w. dat)*
indulgent *adj* indulg·ens -entis
indulgently *adv* indulgenter
industrial *adj* ad frabricationem et vendi-
  tionem mercium pertin·ens -entis
industrialist *s* magis·ter -tri *m* officinarum
industrious *adj* industri·us -a -um
industriously *adv* industrie
industry *s (effort)* industri·a -ae *f; (com)* fabri-
  cati·o -onis *f* et venditi·o -onis *f* mercium
inebriated *adj* ebri·us -a -um
ineffable *adj* ineffabil·is -is -e
ineffective *adj* irrit·us -a -um, ineffic·ax -acis;
  to be — effectu carēre
ineffectual *adj* ineffic·ax -acis
ineffectually *adv* frustra
inefficient *adj* ineffic·ax -acis
inelegant *adj* ineleg·ans -antis
ineligible *adj* non eligend·us -a -um
inept *adj* inept·us -a -um
ineptitude *s* inepti·ae -arum *fpl*
inequality *s* inaequalit·as -atis *f; (social)* iniq-
  uit·as -atis *f*
inequitable *adj* iniqu·us -a -um
inert *adj* in·ers -ertis
inertia *s* inerti·a -ae *f*
inevitable *adj* inevitabil·is -is -e
inevitably *adv* necessario
inexact *adj* haud accurat·us -a -um; *(of persons)* indilig·ens -entis
inexcusable *adj* inexcusabil·is -is -e
inexhaustible *adj* infinit·us -a -um, copios·us
  -a -um

inexorable *adj* inexorabil·is -is -e
inexpensive *adj* vil·is -is -e
inexperience *s* imperiti·a -ae *f*
inexperienced *adj* (**in**) imperit·us -a -um
  (w. gen)
inexplicable *adj* inexplicabil·is -is -e
inexpressible *adj* inenarrabil·is -is -e
inextricable *adj* inextricabil·is -is -e
infallibility *s* erroris immunit·as -atis *f*
infallible *adj* qui *or* quae errare non potest
infamous *adj (ill-famed)* infam·is -is -e;
  (wicked) nefand·us -a -um, nefari·us -a -um
infamously *adv* cum infamiā
infancy *s* infanti·a -ae *f*
infant *s* inf·ans -antis *mf*
infanticide *s (deed)* infanticid·ium -(i)i *n;
  (person)* infanticid·a -ae *mf*
infantile *adj* infantil·is -is -e
infantry *s* peditat·us -ūs *m*, pedit·es -um *mpl*
infantry man *s* ped·es -itis *m*
infatuated *adj* mente capt·us -a -um; **to be** —
  with s.o. aliquem afflictim amare
infatuation *s* dementi·a -ae *f*
infect *tr* inficere; *(fig)* contaminare
infection *s* contagi·o -onis *f*
infectious *adj* contagios·us -a -um
infer *tr* colligere, conicere; **I — from what
  you say that** ... ex verbis tuis colligo *(w.
  acc & inf)*
inference *s* coniectur·a -ae *f*, deducti·o -onis *f;
  (logic)* conclusi·o -onis *f*
inferior *adj* deter·ior -ior -ius
infernal *adj* infern·us -a -um; *(fig)* nefand·us
  -a -um
infertile *adj* steril·is -is -e
infertility *s* sterilit·as -atis *f*
infest *tr* infestare
infidel *s* infidel·is -is *mf*
infidelity *s* infidelit·as -atis *f*
infiltrate *tr* se insinuare in *(w. acc)*
infinite *adj* infinit·us -a -um
infinitely *adv* infinite; *(coll)* infinito
infinitive *s* infinitiv·um -i *n*
infinity *s* infinit·as -atis *f*
infirm *adj* infirm·us -a -um
infirmary *s* valetudinar·ium -(i)i *n*
infirmity *s* infirmit·as -atis *f*
inflame *tr (lit & fig)* inflammare; *(fig)* incendere
inflammable *adj* ad exardescendum facil·is
  -is -e
inflammation *s* inflammati·o -onis *f*
inflammatory *adj* turbulent·us -a -um
inflate *tr* inflare
inflated *adj* inflat·us -a -um
inflation *s* inflati·o -onis *f*
inflect *tr (gram)* declinare
inflection *s* declinati·o -onis *f*

inflexible *adj* inflexibil·is -is -e; *(fig)* obstinat·us -a -um
inflexibly *adv* obstinate
inflict *tr* infligere, inferre; **to — a deadly blow** mortiferam plagam infligere; **to — punishment on s.o.** aliquem supplicio afficere; **to — wounds on** vulnera inferre *(w. dat)*
influence *s* grati·a -ae *f;* **to have — on** valēre apud *(w. acc);* **to have (great, more, very great, little, no) influence on** magnum (plus, plurimum. paulum, nihil) posse apud *(w. acc)*
influence *tr* movēre
influential *adj* auctoritate grav·is -is -e, gratios·us -a -um
influenza *s* catarrh·us -i *m*
influx *s* influxi·o -onis *f*
inform *tr* certiorem facere, docēre; **having been —ed about this** his rebus cognitis ‖ *intr* **to — against** deferre de *(w. abl)*
informal *adj (casual)* familiar·is -is -e, facil·is -is -e; *(unofficial)* privat·us -a -um
informality *s* familiarit·as -atis *f*
informant *s* ind·ex -icis *mf*
information *s* re·s -rum *fpl,* nunt·ius -(i)i *m; (leg)* indic·ium -(i)i *n;* **having received this — his** rebus cognitis
informer *s* dela·tor -toris *m* (·trix -tricis *f)*
infraction *s* infracti·o -onis *f*
infrequency *s* rarit·as -atis *f*
infrequent *adj* rar·us -a -um
infrequently *adv* raro
infringe *tr* violare ‖ *intr* **to — upon** usurpare
infringement *s* violati·o -onis *f; (of rights)* imminuti·o -onis *f*
infuriate *tr* efferre, exasperare
infuse *tr* infundere; *(fig)* inicere
infusion *s* infusi·o -onis *f*
ingenious *adj* ingenios·us -a -um, soll·ers -ertis
ingeniously *adv* sollerter
ingenuity *s* sollerti·a -ae *f*
ingest *tr* ingerere
inglorious *adj* inglori·us -a -um
ingloriously *adv* sine gloriā
ingot *s* lat·er -eris *m*
ingrained *adj* insit·us -a -um
ingratiate *tr* **to — oneself with** gratiam inire ab *(w. abl)*
ingratitude *s* ingratus anim·us -i *m*
ingredient *s (generally not expressed by a noun)* element·um -i *n;* **a composition, the —s of which** compositio quae habet; **the medication consists of the following —s** medicamentum constat ex his
inhabit *tr* incolere
inhabitable *adj* habitabil·is -is -e
inhabitant *s* incol·a -ae *mf*
inhale *tr* haurire, ducere ‖ *intr* spiritum ducere
inharmonious *adj* disson·us -a -um

inherent *adj* inhaer·ens -entis; **to be — in** inhaerēre in *(w. abl),* inesse in *(w. abl)*
inherit *tr* hereditate excipere
inheritance *s* heredit·as -atis *f;* **to come into an —** hereditatem adire
inhospitable *adj* inhospital·is -is -e
inhuman *adj* inhuman·us -a -um
inhumanly *adv* inhumane
inhumanity *s* inhumanit·as -atis *f*
inimical *adj* inimic·us -a -um
inimitable *adj* inimitabil·is -is -e
iniquitous *adj* improb·us -a -um
iniquity *s* improbit·as -atis *f*
initial *adj* prim·us -a -um
initial *s* prima nominis litter·a -ae *f*
initial *tr* primis litteris nominis signare
initiate *tr* initiare
initiation *s* initiati·o -onis *f*
initiative *s* vis *f;* **on my own —** meā sponte
inject *tr* inicere, immittere
injection *s* iniecti·o -onis *f*
injudicious *adj* inconsult·us -a -um
injudiciously *adv* inconsulte
injunction *s* mandat·um -i *n;* **to get an —** ad interdictum venire
injure *tr* nocēre *(w. dat),* laedere
injurious *adj* noxi·us -a -um
injury *s* nox·a -ae *f,* iniuri·a -ae *f*
injustice *s* iniustiti·a -ae *f; (act of injustice)* iniuri·a -ae *f*
ink *s* atrament·um -i *n*
inkling *s* obscura significati·o -onis *f;* **to have an —** suspicari
inland *adj* mediterrane·us -a -um
inland *adv* intus; **towns — from Tarentum** oppida per continentem a Tarento
in-law *s* affin·is -is *mf*
inlay *tr* inserere; *(with mosaic)* tessellare
inlay *s* caelatur·a -ae *f*
inlet *s* aestuar·ium -(i)i *n*
inmate *s* (carceris) inquilin·us -i *m* (·a -ae *f)*
inmost *adj* intim·us -a -um
inn *s* deversor·ium -(i)i *n, (esp. of an inferior type)* caupon·a -ae *f*
innate *adj* innat·us -a -um
inner *adj* inter·ior -ior -ius
innermost *adj* intim·us -a -um
inning *s (of baseball)* miss·us -ūs *m*
innkeeper *s* caup·o -onis *m; (female)* caupon·a -ae *f,* cop·a -ae *f*
innocence *s* innocenti·a -ae *f*
innocent *adj* (of) innoc·ens -entis *(w. gen)*
innocently *adv* innocenter
innocuous *adj* innocu·us -a -um
innocuously *adv* innocue
innovate *tr* novare
innovation *s* novit·as -atis *f,* re·s -ei *f* nova
innovative *adj* multa nov·ans -antis
innovator *s* qui *(or* quae) multa novat

innumerable *adj* innumer·us -a -um
inoculate *tr* serum inserere *(w. dat)*
innoculation *s* seri insiti·o -onis *f*
inoffensive *adj* innoxi·us -a -um
inopportune *adj* intempestiv·us -a -um
inopportunely *adv* parum in tempore
inordinate *adj* immoderat·us -a -um
inordinately *adv* immoderate
input *s (comput)* (datorum) init·us -ūs *m;* — and output (datorum) initus exitusque
inquest *s* inquisiti·o -onis *f; (leg)* quaesti·o -onis *f;* **an — was held on the cause of death** quaesitum est quae mortis causa fuisset
inquire *intr* (into) inquirere (in *w. acc)*
inquiry *s* quaesti·o -onis *f*
inquisition *s* inquisiti·o -onis *f*
inquisitive *adj* curios·us -a -um
inquisitor *s* quaesit·or -oris *m*
inroad *s* incursi·o -onis *f;* **to make —s into territory** incursiones in fines facere
insane *adj* insan·us -a -um
insanely *adv* insane
insanity *s* insanit·as -atis *f*
insatiable *adj* insatiabil·is -is -e
inscribe *tr* inscribere
inscription *s* inscripti·o -onis *f*
inscrutable *adj* occult·us -a -um
insect *s* insect·um -i *n*
insecure *adj* haud tut·us -a -um
insecurity *s* **feeling of —** sollicitud·o -inis *f*
insensible *adj* insensil·is -is -e; *(fig)* dur·us -a -um
insensitive *adj* dur·us -a -um
insensitivity *s* duriti·a -ae *f*
inseparable *adj* inseparabil·is -is -e
insert *tr* inserere, interponere; *(in writing)* ascribere
insertion *s* interpositi·o -onis *f*
inside *adj* inter·ior -ior -ius; **— of** *(time)* intra *(w. acc);* **— out** inversus
inside *adv* intus; **go —!** i *(pl:* ite) intus!
inside *prep* intro *(w. acc)*
inside *s* interior par·s -tis *f;* **—s** viscer·a -um *npl*
inside of *prep* intra *(w. acc)*
insidious *adj* insidios·us -a -um
insidiously *adv* insidiose
insight *s* cogniti·o -onis *f;* **to have a profound — into human character** mores hominum atque ingenia penitus perspecta habēre
insignia *spl* insign·ia -ium *npl*
insignificance *s* exiguit·as -atis *f*
insignificant *adj* exigu·us -a -um, nullius momenti, parv·us -a -um
insincere *adj* insincer·us -a -um
insincerely *adv* haud sincere
insincerity *s* ingen·ium -(i)i *n* haud sincerum
insinuate *tr (to hint)* operte significare

insinuation *s* significati·o -onis *f*
insipid *adj* insuls·us -a -um
insipidly *adv* insulse
insist *intr* instare; **I — that** certum est mihi *(w. acc & inf);* **to — on** urgēre, postulare
insistence *s* pertinaci·a -ae *f*
insistent *adj* pertin·ax -acis; *(urgent)* urg·ens -entis
insolence *s* insolenti·a -ae *f*
insolent *adj* insol·ens -entis
insoluble *adj* insolubil·is -is -e; *(fig)* inexplicabil·is -is -e
insolvent *adj* decoct·us -a -um; **I am insolvent** solvendo non sum
inspect *tr* inspicere; *(mil)* recensēre
inspection *s* inspecti·o -onis *f; (mil)* recensi·o -onis *f*
inspector *s* cura·tor -toris *m* (·trix -tricis *f)*
inspiration *s (divine)* afflat·us -ūs *m; (prophetic)* fur·or -oris *m; (idea)* noti·o -onis *f*
inspire *tr* inspirare; **divinely —d** divino spiritu instinct·us -a -um; **to — s.o. with courage** animos alicui addere; **to — s.o. with fear** alicui formidinem inicere
instability *s* instabilit·as -atis *f*
install *tr (mechanically)* instruere; *(w. augural solemnity)* inaugurare
installation *s* inaugurati·o -onis *f; (mechanical)* constructi·o -onis *f; (mil)* castr·a -orum *npl* stativa
installment *s (com)* pensi·o -onis *f;* **to pay in five —s** quinque pensionibus solvere
instance *s* exempl·um -i *n;* **for —** exempli gratiā; **for — when** ut enim cum; **in this —** in hac re
instant *adj* praes·ens -entis; **this —** statim
instantaneous *adj* praes·ens -entis
instantaneously *adv* continuo
instantly *adv* confestim, statim
instead *adv* potius, magis
instead of *prep* pro *(w. abl); (w. verb)* non ... sed
instigate *tr* instigare, concitare
instigation *s* instigati·o -onis *f;* **at your —** te auctore
instigator *s* auct·or -oris *mf,* instiga·tor -toris *m* (·trix -tricis *f)*
instill *tr* instillare
instinct *s* natur·a -ae *f*
instinctive *adj* natural·is -is -e
instinctively *adv* naturā
institute *tr* instituere
institute *s* institut·um -i *n*
institution *s (act)* instituti·o -onis *f; (thing instituted)* institut·um -i *n*
instruct *tr (to teach)* instituere, docēre; *(to order)* mandare *(w. dat or* ut, ne); **to — s.o. in s.th.** aliquem aliquo instruere

instruction *s* instituti·o -onis *f,* doctrin·a -ae *f;*
—**s** praecept·a -orum *npl; (orders to do s.th.)*
mandat·a -orum *npl;* **to give —s to** mandare
(w. dat)
instructive *adj* ad docendum apt·us -a -um
instructor *s* doc·ens -entis *mf,* praecep·tor
-toris *m* (·trix -tricis *f)*
instrument *s* instrument·um -i *n; (mus)*
organ·um -i *n; (leg)* syngraph·a -ae *f*
instrumental *s* util·is -is -e; **you were — in**
bringing s.th. to pass tuā operā factum est;
(in negative sentences) **you were instrumen-**
tal in not ... per te stetit quominus ...
instrumentality *s* oper·a -ae *f*
insubordinate *adj (mutinous)* seditios·us -a
-um; *(disobedient)* male par·ens -entis
insubordination *s (mutiny)* sediti·o -onis *f;* **to**
be guilty of — per licentiam ducibus non
parēre
insufferable *adj* intolerand·us -a -um
insufficiency *s* inop·ia -ae *f*
insufficient *adj* haud suffici·ens -entis
insufficiently *adv* haud satis
insular *adj* insulan·us -a -um
insulate *tr* segregare
insult *s* contumeli·a -ae *f*
insult *tr* contumeliā afficere
insulting *adj* contumelios·us -a -um
insultingly *adv* contumeliose
insuperable *adj* insuperabil·is -is -e
insurance *s* cauti·o -onis *f* indemnitatis, asse-
curati·o -onis *f;* **car —** assecuratio vehicularia; **casualty —** assecuratio indemnitatis;
health — assecuratio valetudinaria; **life —**
vitae assecuratio, pro vita cautio
insurance company *s* eran·us -i *m*
insurance policy *s* cauti·o -onis *f* indemnitatis
insure *tr* praecavēre de damnis
insurgent *adj* rebell·is -is -e
insurgent *s* rebell·is -is *mf*
insurmountable *adj* inexsuperabil·is -is -e
insurrection *s* rebelli·o -onis *f; (civil strife)*
sediti·o -onis *f*
intact *adj* incolum·is -is -e
intangible *adj* intactil·is -is -e
integer *s* numer·us -i *m* integer
integral *adj* ad totum necessari·us -a -um;
(entire) integ·er -ra -rum
integrity *s* integrit·as -atis *f*
intellect *s* intellect·us -ūs *m*
intellectual *adj* intelleg·ens -entis
intelligence *s* intellegenti·a -ae *f; (information)*
nunt·ius -(i)i *m*
intelligent *adj* intelleg·ens -entis
intelligently *adv* intellegenter
intelligible *adj* intellegibil·is -is -e
intelligibly *adv* intellegibiliter
intemperance *s* intemperanti·a -ae *f*
intemperately *adv* intemperanter

intend *tr* in animo habēre, destinare, in animo
esse *(w. dat of the subject)*
intended *adj* destinat·us -a -um; *(of future*
spouse) spons·us -a
intense *adj* extrem·us -a -um, summ·us -a -um;
(vigorous) a·cer -cris -cre; *(emotions)*
grand·is -is -e; *(heat, cold)* magn·us -a -um;
(excessive) nimi·us -a -um
intensely *adv* valde, vehementer
intensify *tr* intendere
intensity *s* vehementi·a -ae *f,* vis *f*
intensively *adv* vehementer
intensive pronoun *s* pronom·en -inis *n* inten-
tionis
intent *adj* intent·us -a -um; **to be — on** animum intendere in *(w. acc)*
intently *adv* intente
intention *s* consil·ium -(i)i *n; (meaning)* signi-
ficati·o -onis *f;* **with the best —s** optimo
animo utens
intentionally *adv* de industriā
inter *tr* inhumare
intercede *intr (on behalf of)* deprecari (pro *w.*
abl)
intercept *tr* intercipere
interception *s* intercepti·o -onis *f*
intercession *s* deprecati·o -onis *f; (of a trib-*
une) intercessi·o -onis *f*
intercessor *s* depreca·tor -toris *m* (·trix
-tricis *f)*
interchange *s* permutati·o -onis *f; (of a high-*
way) coniuncti·o -onis *f* viarum
interchange *tr* permutare
intercourse *s (sexual)* coït·us -ūs *m; (social;*
sexual) consuetud·o -inis *f*
interdict *tr* interdicere *(w. acc of person and*
abl of thing; dat of person and acc of thing)
interdiction *s* interdicti·o -onis *f*
interest *s (attention)* **(in)** stud·ium -(i)i *n (w.*
gen); (advantage) us·us -ūs *m; (fin)* faen·us
-oris *n,* usur·a -ae *f;* **compund —** anato-
cism·us -i *m;* **it is in my —** meā interest; **rate**
of — usur·ae -arum *fpl;* **simple —** perpetuum faenus; **to have an — in painting** studium pinguendi habere; **to lend money at —**
pecuniam faenori dare; **to take an — in s.th.**
studio alicuius teneri
interest *tr (to affect the mind)* tenēre; *(to*
delight) delectare; **sports don't — me** athlet-
icae me non tenent
interested *adj* **— in** studios·us -a -um *(w. gen),*
attent·us -a -um *(w. dat);* **children are —ed**
in games liberi ludis tenentur; **I am — in**
music musicae *[dat]* studeo; **I am not the**
least bit — in races circensibus ne levissime
quidem tencor
interesting *adj* iucund·us -a -um; **this books is**
— hic liber me tenet

interfere *intr* se interponere *(w. dat); (to prevent s.th.)* intercedere; **the tribunes will not — with the praetor's making a motion** tribuni non praetori intercessuri sunt, quominus referat

interference *s* intercessi·o -onis *f*

interim *s* intervall·um -i *n;* **in the —** interim

interior *adj (inner)* inter·ior -ior -ius; *(inland)* mediterrane·us -a -um

interior *s* interior par·s -tis *f; (region)* mediterrane·a -orum *npl;* **in the —** in mediterraneo, intus; **toward the —** intus

interjection *s* interiecti·o -onis *f*

interlinear *adj* interscript·us -a -um

interlude *s (pause, break, intermission)* dilud·ium -(i)i *n,* intercaped·o -inis *f; (theat)* embol·ium -(i)i *n*

intermarriage *s* co(n)nub·ium -(i)i *n*

intermarry *intr* matrimonio inter se coniungi

intermediary *s* internunti·us -i *m* (·a -ae *f*)

intermediate *adj* medi·us -a -um

interment *s* sepultur·a -ae *f*

interminable *adj* infinit·us -a -um

intermission *s* intercaped·o -inis *f*

intermittent *adj* intermitt·ens -entis

intermittently *adv* interdum

internal *adj* intestin·us -a -um, intern·us -a -um

internally *adv* intus, interne

international *adj* inter gentes; **— law** ius, iuris *n* gentium

internet *s* interret·e -is *n*

internet *adj* interretial·is -a -um

interpolate *tr* interpolare

interpolation *s* interpolati·o -onis *f*

interpret *tr* interpretari

interpretation *s* interpretati·o -onis *f*

interpreter *s* interpr·es -etis *mf*

interrogate *tr* interrogare

interrogation *s* interrogati·o -onis *f*

interrogative *adj* interrogativ·us -a -um

interrupt *tr* interrumpere; *(speech)* interpellare

interruption *s* interrupti·o -onis *f; (of a speaker)* interpellati·o -onis *f*

intersect *tr* intersecare

intersection *s* intersecti·o -onis *f; (of roads)* compit·um -i *n,* quadriv·ium -(i)i *n*

intersperse *tr* immiscēre

interstate *adj* inter civitates

intertwine *tr* intertexere

interval *s* intervall·um -i *n*

intervene *intr (to be between)* interiacēre, interesse; *(to come between)* intercedere, intervenire

intervening *adj* medi·us -a -um

intervention *s* intervent·us -ūs *m*

interview *s* colloqu·ium -(i)i *n* interrogatorium

interview *tr* percontari

interviewer *s* perconta·tor -toris *m* (·trix -tricis *f*)

interweave *tr* intertexere

intestinal *adj* ad intestina pertin·ens -entis

intestine *adj* intestin·us -a -um

intestine *s* intestin·um -i *n;* **the large —** intestinum crassius; **the small —** intestinum tenue

intimacy *s* familiarit·as -atis *f,* consuetud·o -inis *f,* nessitud·o -inis *f; (sexual)* consuetudo

intimate *adj* familiar·is -is -e; *(stronger than preced.)* intim·us -a -um

intimately *adv* familiariter, intime

intimate *tr* indicare, innuere

intimation *s* indic·ium -(i)i *n*

intimidate *tr* (per)terrēre

intimidation *s* min·ae -arum *fpl*

into *prep* in *(w. acc)*

intolerable *adj* intolerabil·is -is -e

intolerably *adv* intoleranter

intolerance *s* intoleranti·a -ae *f*

intolerant *adj* intoler·ans -antis

intonation *s (chant)* cant·us -ūs *m; (stress)* accent·us -ūs *m*

intone *tr* cantare

intoxicate *tr* ebrium *(or* ebriam*)* reddere

intoxicated *adj* ebri·us -a -um

intoxication *s* ebriet·as -atis *f*

intractable *adj* intractabil·is -is -e

intramural *adj* intramuran·us -a -um

intransigence *s* obstinati·o -onis *f*

intransigent *adj* obstinat·us -a -um

intransitive *adj (gram)* intransitiv·us -a -um

intrepid *adj* intrepid·us -a -um

intrepidly *adv* intrepide

intricate *adj* contort·us -a -um

intricately *adv* contorte

intrigue *s* consil·ium -(i)i *n* clandestinum

intrigue *tr* tenēre, capere

intriguing *adj (engaging)* illecebros·us -a -um; *(baffling)* nodos·us -a -um

intrinsic *adj* ver·us -a -um, per se; **it has no — worth** res ipsa per se nullius pretii est

intrinsically *adv* vere

introduce *tr (e.g., a custom, theory)* introducere; *(a person)* tradere

introduction *s (preamble)* praefati·o -onis *f; (of a speech, book)* exord·ium -(i)i *n; (a bringing in)* inducti·o -onis *f*

introspection *s* sui contemplati·o -onis *f*

introspective *adj* se ipsum inspici·ens -entis

introvert *s* hom·o -inis *mf* umbratic·us (-a)

intrude *intr* se interponere; **to — on** se imponere *(w. dat)*

intruder *s* intervent·or -oris *m; (into a home)* effrac·tor -toris *m* (·trix -tricis *f*)

intrusion *s* irrupti·o -onis *f*

intuition *s* intuit·us -ūs *m*

intuitive *adj* intuitiv·us -a -um

intuitively *adv* mentis propriã vi ac naturã

inundate *tr* inundare

inundation *s* inundati·o -onis *f*

invade *tr* invadere in *(w. acc)*

invader *s* invas·or -oris *m*

invalid *adj* irrit·us -a -um

invalid *s* aegrot·us -i *m* (·a -ae *f*)

invalidate *tr* irrit·um -am -um facere

invaluable *adj* inaestimabil·is -is -e

invariable *adj* immutabil·is -is -e

invariably *adv* semper

invasion *s* incursi·o -onis *f; (fig)* violati·o -onis *f*

invective *s* convic·ium -(i)i *n*

inveigh *intr* **to — against** invehi in *(w. acc),* insectarı

invent *tr* invenire; *(to contrive)* excogitare, fingere

inventive *adj* ingenios·us -a -um

invention *s (act)* inventi·o -onis *f; (thing invented)* invent·um -i *n*

inventor *s* inven·tor -toris *m* (·trix -tricis *f*)

inventory *s* bonorum ind·ex -icis *m,* inventar·ium -(i)i *n*

inverse *adj* invers·us -a -um

inversely *adv* inverso ordine

inversion *s* inversi·o -onis *f*

invert *tr* invertere

invest *tr (money)* collocare; *(to besiege)* obsidēre

investigate *tr* investigare; *(leg)* quaerere, cognoscere

investigation *s* investigati·o -onis *f; (leg)* cogniti·o -onis *f*

investigator *s* investiga·tor -toris *m* (·trix -tricis *f*) *(leg)* quaesi·tor -toris *m* (·trix -tricis *f*)

investment *s (of money)* collocati·o -onis *f; (money invested)* locata pecuni·a -ae *f; (mil)* obsessi·o -onis *f*

inveterate *adj* inveterat·us -a -um

invigorate *tr* corroborare

invigorating *adj* apt·us -a -um ad corpus firmandum

invincible *adj* insuperabil·is -is -e, invict·us -a -um

inviolable *adj* sacrosanct·us -a -um

inviolate *adj* inviolat·us -a -um

invisible *adj* invisibil·is -is -e

invitation *s* invitati·o -onis *f*

invite *tr* invitare; **to — to dinner** ad cenam vocare

inviting *adj* suav·is -is -e

invitingly *adv* suaviter

invocation *s* invocati·o -onis *f*

invoice *s* tabul·a -ae *f* mercium

invoke *tr* invocare

involuntarily *adv* sine voluntate

involuntary *adj* haud voluntari·us -a -um; **— bodily action** naturalis acti·o -onis *f* corporis

involve *tr* implicare, *(to comprise)* continēre

involved *adj (intricate)* involut·us -a -um; *(occupied)* implicat·us -a -um; **to be — in debt** aere alieno laborare; **to be — in many errors** multis erroribus implicari; **to be — in war** illigari bello

invulnerable *adj* invulnerabil·is -is -e

inward *adj* inter·ior -ior -ius

inwardly *adv* intus, intrinsecus

inwards *adv* introrsus

Ionian *adj* Ionic·us -a -um

irascible *adj* iracund·us -a -um

Ireland *s* Hiberni·a -ae *f*

iris *s* ir·is -idis *f*

Irish *adj* Hibernic·us -a -um

irk *tr* incommodare; **I am —ed, it —s me** me taedet

irksome *adj* molest·us -a -um

iron *s (metal; for clothes)* ferr·um -i *n*

iron *adj* ferre·us -a -um

iron *tr (clothes)* premere, (ferro) levigare

ironical *adj* ironic·us -a -um

ironically *adv* per ironiam

irony *s* ironi·a -ae *f*

irradiate *tr* illustrare **‖** *intr* effulgēre

irrational *adj* irrational·is -is -e

irrationally *adv* absurde

irreconcilable *adj* implacabil·is -is -e; *(incompatible)* omnino inter se contrari·i -ae -a

irrecoverable *adj* irreparabil·is -is -e

irrefutable *adj* certissim·us -a -um

irregular *adj (having no regular form)* enorm·is -is -e; *(not uniform)* inaequal·is -is -e; *(fever)* incert·us -a -um; *(gram)* anomal·us -a -um; **— army** exercit·us -ūs *m* tumultuarius; **— verb** verb·um -i *n* inaequale

irregularity *s* enormit·as -atis *f; (gram)* anomali·a -ae *f;* **to be guilty of some —** peccare aliquid

irregularly *adv* inaequaliter; **"duo" is — declined** "duo" inaequaliter declinatur

irrelevant *adj* alien·us -a -um; **it is —** nil ad rem pertinet

irreligious *adj* impi·us -a -um erga deos; *(actions)* irreligios·us -a -um

irremediable *adj* insanabil·is -is -e

irreparable *adj* irreparabil·is -is -e

irreproachable *adj* inte·ger -gra -grum

irresistible *adj* invict·us -a -um; *(enticing)* blandissim·us -a -um

irresolute *adj* incert·us -a -um (sententiae); *(permanent characteristic)* parum firm·us -a -um

irresolutely *adv* dubitanter

irresolution *s* dubitati·o -onis *f,* anim·us -i *m* parum firmus

irresponsibility *s* incuri·a -ae *f*

irresponsible *adj* incurios·us -a -um

irretrievable *adj* irreparabil·is -is -e

irreverence *s* irreverenti·a -ae *f*
irreverent *adj* irrever·ens -entis (deorum)
irrevocable *adj* irrevocabil·is -is -e
irrigate *tr* irrigare
irrigation *s* irrigati·o -onis *f*
irritability *s* iracundi·a -ae *f*
irritable *adj* iracund·us -a -um
irritate *tr* irritare; *(a wound)* inflammare
irritation *s* irritati·o -onis *f*
island *s* insul·a -ae *f*
islander *s* insulan·us -i *m* (·a -ae *f*)
islet *s* parva insul·a -ae *f*
isolate *tr* secernere
issue *s (result)* event·us -ūs *m; (question)* res, rei *f; (offspring)* prol·es -is *f; (of a book)* editi·o -onis *f; (of money)* emissi·o -onis *f*
issue *tr (to distribute)* distribuere; *(orders)* edere, promulgare; *(money)* erogare; *(book)* edere **‖** *intr* emanare, egredi; *(to turn out, result)* evenire
isthmus *s* isthm·us -i *m*
it *pron* id
Italian *adj* Italic·us -a -um, Ital·us -a -um
italics *spl* litter·ae -arum *fpl* inclinatae
Italy *s* Itali·a -ae *f*
itch *s* prurig·o -inis *f*
itch *intr* prurire; *(fig)* gestire; **to have —ing ears** auribus prurire
itchy *adj* pruriginos·us -a -um
item *s* res, rei *f; (news)* nunt·ius -(i)i *m; — of merchandise* merx, mercis *f*
itinerant *adj* circumforane·us -a -um
itinerary *s* itinerar·ium -(i)i *n*
its *pron* eius; **— own** su·us -a -um
itself *pron (refl)* se, sese; *(intensive)* ipsum
ivory *s* eb·ur -oris *n*
ivory *adj* eburne·us -a -um
ivy *s* heder·a -ae *f*

J

jab *s* puls·us -ūs *m*
jab *tr* fodicare
jabber *intr* blaterare, garrire
jabbering *s* garrulit·as -atis *f*
jack *s* machin·a -ae *f* ad levandum; *(cards)* scurr·a -ae *m*
jackass *s* asin·us -i *m*
jacket *s* iacc·a -ae *f;* **leather —** iacca scortea
jack-of-all-trades *s* hom·o -inis *m* omnis Minervae
jackpot *s* **to hit the —** Venerem iacere; *(fig)* magnum lucrum facere
jaded *adj* defess·us -a -um
jagged *adj* serrat·us -a -um; *(of rocks)* praerupt·us -a -um

jail *s* carc·er -eris *m*
jail *tr* in carcere includere
jailbird *s* furcif·er -eri *m*
jailer *s* carcerari·us -i *m* (·a -ae *f*)
jam *s* baccarum conditur·a -ae *f;* **to be in a —** *(fig)* in angustiis versari
jam *tr* frequentare; *(to obstruct)* obstruere
jamb *s* post·is -is *m*
jangle *tr* & *intr* crepitare
janitor *s* ianit·or -oris *m*
January *s* Ianuar·ius -(i)i *m or* mens·is -is *m* Ianuarius; **in —** mense Ianuario; **on the first of —** Kalendis Ianuariis
jar *s* oll·a -ae *f; (large, with two handles)* amphor·a -ae *f*
jar *tr (to shock)* offendere; *(of sound)* strepere **‖** *intr* discrepare
jargon *s* confusae voc·es -ium *fpl*
jarring *adj* disson·us -a -um
jaundice *s* morb·us -i *m* regius
jaundiced *adj* icterici·us -a -um; **to see things with — eyes** omnia in deteriorem partem interpretari
jaunt *s* excursi·o -onis *f;* **to take a —** excurrere
jaunty *adj* veget·us -a -um
javelin *s* iacul·um -i *n;* **to hurl a —** iaculari
jaw *s (upper)* mal·a -a *f; (lower)* maxill·a -ae *f;* **—s** fauc·es -ium *fpl*
jawbone *s* maxill·a -ae *f*
jay *s* gracul·us -i *m*
jealous *adj* zelotyp·us -a -um
jealousy *s* zel·us -i *m*, zelotypi·a -ae *f*
jeans *spl* bracc·ae -arum *fpl* Genuenses
jeer *s* irris·us -ūs *m*
jeer *tr* deridēre **‖** *intr* deridēre; **to —at** irridēre
jello *s* sorbill·um -i *n* concretum
jelly *s* cyl·on *(also* quil·on) -i *n*
jellyfish *s* pulm·o -onis *m*
jeopardize *tr* periclitari
jeopardy *s* pericul·um -i *n*
jerk *s* mot·us -ūs *m* subitus; *(person)* hom·o -inis *mf* nequam
jerk *tr (to push)* subito trudere; *(to pull)* subito revellere
jerky *adj* salebros·us -a -um
jest *s* ioc·us -i *m;* **in —** iocose
jest *intr* iocari
jester *s* ioculat·or -oris *m; (buffoon)* scurr·a -ae *m*
jestingly *adv* per iocum
Jesus *s* Ies·us -u *(dat, abl, voc:* Iesu; *acc:* Iesum) *m*
jet *s* scatebr·a -ae *f*
jet-black *adj* nigerrim·us -a -um
jet engine *s* machin·a -ae *f* pyraulocinetica
jet plane *s* aëroplan·um -i *n* pyraulocineticum
jetty *s* mol·es -is *f*
Jew *s* Iudae·us -i *m*
jewel *s* gemm·a -ae *f*

jeweler *s* gemmari·us -i *m* (·a -ae *f*)

jewelry *s* gemm·ae -arum *fpl*

jewelry store *s* gemmari·a -ae *f*

Jewess *s* Iudae·a -ae *f*

Jewish *adj* Iudae·us -a -um

jilt *tr* repudiare

jingle *s* tinnit·us -ūs *m*

jingle *intr* tinnire

jitters *spl* scrupul·us -i *n;* **to give s.o. the —** scrupulum alicui inicere

jittery *adj* scrupulos·us -a -um

job *s (piece of work)* op·us -eris *n; (as a means of livelihood)* quaest·us -ūs *m; (task)* pens·um -i *n,* mun·us -eris *n;* **a tough —** spissum opus ct opcrosum; **good —!** recte factum!; **to get a —** quaestum impetrare

jobless *adj* quaestūs exper·s -tis

jockey *s* agas·o -onis *m*

jocular *adj* iocular·is -is -e

jog *intr* tolutim currere

join *tr (to connect)* coniungere, connectere; *(to come into the company of)* se iungere *(w. dat); (to join as a companion)* supervenire *(w. dat); (to go over to)* transire; **—ing hands** manibus nex·i -ae -a ‖ *intr* coniungi; **to — in** particeps esse *(w. gen);* **to — together** inter se coniungi

joint *adj* commun·is -is -e

joint *s (anat)* articul·us -i *m; (of a plant)* genicul·um -i *n,* nod·us -i *m; (of a structure)* compag·es -inis *f;* **to smoke a —** fumum cannabis sugere

jointly *adv* unā, communiter

joist *s* tign·um -i *n*

joke *s* ioc·us -i *m;* **as a —** per iocum; **to make a — of** iocum risumque facere de *(w abl);* **to play a — on** ludibrio habēre

joke *intr* iocari; **now you're —ing** iocaris nunc tu; **to be —ing** iocari

joker *s* iocula·tor -toris *m* (·trix -tricis *f); (cards)* chartul·a -ae *f* fortunans

joking *s* iocati·o -onis *f;* **all — aside** ioco remoto

jokingly *adv* per iocum

jolly *adj* hilar·is -is -e, hillar·us -a -um

jolt *s* (im)puls·us -ūs *m*

jolt *tr* iactare; *(fig)* percellere ‖ *intr* iactari

jolting *s* iactati·o -onis *f*

jostle *tr* pulsare

jot *s* hil·um -i *n;* **not a —** minime; **to care not a — for** non flocci facere

jot down *tr* breviter scribere *(or* notare*)*

journal *s (magazine)* ephemer·is -idis *f; (diary)* diar·ium -(i)i *n*

journalist *s* scrip·tor -toris *m* (·trix -tricis *f*) actorum

journey *s* it·er -ineris *n;* **to take a —** iter facere

journey *intr* iter facere; **to — abroad** peregrinari

journeyman *s* opif·ex -icis *m*

Jove *s* Iuppiter, Iovis *m*

jovial *adj* hilar·is -is -e

jowl *s* bucc·a -ae *f*

joy *s* gaud·ium -(i)i *n;* **to feel —** gaudēre

joyful *adj* laet·us -a -um

joyfully *adv* laete

joyless *adj* illaetabil·is -is -e

joystick *s (comput)* vectul·us -i *m*

jubilant *adj* laetitiā exsult·ans -antis

jubilation *s* exsultati·o -onis *f*

jubilee *s* ann·us -i *m* anniversarius

Judaic *adj* Iudaïc·us -a -um

Judaism *s* Iudaïsm·us -i *m*

judge *s* iud·ex icis *mf; (in criminal cases)* quaesi·tor -toris *m* (·trix -tricis *f);* **to sit as —** *(to hold court)* ius dicere

judge *tr* iudicare; *(to think)* existimare; *(to value)* aestimare; *(to decide between)* diiudicare

judgment *s* iudic·ium -(i)i *n,* sententi·a -ae *f;* **against my better —** adversum ingenium meum; **in my —** iudicio meo; **to pronounce —** ius dicere; **to sit in — over** ius dicere inter *(w. acc)*

judgment seat *s* tribun·al -alis *n*

judicial *adj* iudicial·is -is -e; **— proceedings** iudici·a -orum *npl;* **— system** rati·o -onis *f* iudicialis

judicially *adv* iure

judicious *adj* sapi·ens -entis

judiciously *adv* sapienter

judo *s* luct·a -ae *f* iudoïca

jug *s* urce·us -i *m*

juggle *tr (figures)* vitiare, interpolare ‖ *intr* praestigias agere

juggler *s* praestigiat·or -oris *mf*

juice *s* suc·us -i *m*

juicy *adj* sucos·us -a -um

July *s* Iul·ius -(i)i *or* mens·is -is *m* Iulius; **in —** mense Iulio; **on the first of —** Kalendis Iuliis

jumble *s* congeri·es -ei *f*

jumble *tr* permiscēre

jump *s* salt·us -ūs *m*

jump *tr* transalire; **to — rope** ad funem salire ‖ *intr* salire; **to —at** *(opportunity)* captare; **to — for joy** dissilire gaudimonio, exsultare; **to — up** exsurrigere

junction *s* coniuncti·o -onis *f; (roads)* compit·um -i *n*

juncture *s* temp·us -oris *n;* **at this —** hic

June *s* Iun·ius -(i)i *m or* mens·is -is *m* Iunius; **on the first of —** Kalendis Iuniis

jungle *s* silv·a -ae *f* densa

junior *adj* min·or -or -us natu

junior *s* iuni·or -oris *m*

juniper *s* iuniper·us -i *f*

junk *s* scrut·a -orum *npl*

jurisdiction *s* iurisdicti·o -onis *f*

jurisprudence *s* iurisprudenti·a -ae *f*
jurist *s* iurisconsult·us -i *m* (·a -ae *f*)
juror *s* iud·ex -icis *m,* iudiatr·ix -icis *f*
jury *s* iudic·es -um *mpl*
just *adj* iust·us -a -um; *(fair)* aequ·us -a -um; *(deserved)* merit·us -a -um
just *adv (only)* modo; *(exactly)* prorsus; *(w. adv)* demum, denique; — **about** *(pretty well, virtually)* propemodum; — **after** sub *(w. acc);* — **a moment ago** modo; — **as** *(comparison)* perinde ac, sic ut; *(temporal)* cum maxime; — **before** sub *(w. acc);* — **in time** tempori; — **now** modo; — **so** ita prorsus; — **then** tunc maxime; — **what?** quidnam?; — **when** cum proxime — **who?** quisnam?
justice *s* iustiti·a -ae *f; (just treatment)* ius iuris *n; (person)* praet·or -oris *m*
justifiable *adj* excusat·us -a -um
justifiably *adv* iure
justification *s* excusati·o -onis *f*
justify *tr* excusare, expurgare
jut *intr* prominēre; **to — out** procurrere; **to — out into the sea** in aequor procurrere
juvenile *adj* iuvenil·is -is -e; — **delinquent** adulesc·ens -entis *mf* noxi·us (-a)
juvenile *s* adulesc·ens -entis *mf*
juxtaposition *s* propinquit·as -atis *f;* **to put in** — apponere

K

kale *s* cramb·e -es *f*
kangaroo *s* halmatur·us -i *m*
karate *s* luct·a -ae *f* caratica
keel *s* carin·a -ae *f*
keel *intr* **to — over** collabi
keen *adj* a·cer -cris -cre
keenly *adv* acriter
keenness *s (of scent)* sagacit·as -atis *f; (of sight)* aci·es -ei *f; (of pain)* acerbit·as -atis *f; (enthusiasm)* stud·ium -(i)i *n*
keen-scented *adj* sagacissim·us -a -um
keep *tr* tenēre; *(to preserve)* servare; *(to celebrate)* agere; *(to guard)* custodire; *(to obey)* observare; *(to support)* alere; *(animals)* alere, pascere; *(to store)* condere; *(to detain, hold back)* detinēre; — **a stiff upper lip!** fac ut animo forti sis!; — **your cool!** compesce mentem!; **to — annoying** subinde molestare; **to — apart** distinēre; **to — at bay** sustinēre; **to — away** arcēre; **to — back** retinēre, cohibēre; *(to conceal)* celare; **to — back nothing** nihil reticēre; **to — back tears** lacrimas tenēre; **to — company** comitari; **to — down** reprimere; **to — from** prohibēre; **to — hands off** manum abstinēre; **to — in**

cohibēre; **to — in custody** asservare; **to — in line the wavering Senate** confirmare labantem ordinem; **to — in mind** in memoriā habēre *or* tenēre; **to — off** arcēre, defendere; **to — to oneself** secum habēre; **to — pace with** pariter ire cum *(w. abl);* **to — secret** celare; **to — the company waiting** convivas morari; **to — together** continēre; **to — under control** compescere; **to — under lock and key** clavi servare; **to — up** sustinēre; **to — up one's courage** animo erecto esse; **to — (a person) waiting** detinēre, demorari; **to — your eyes on** oculos intentare in *(w. acc);* **what kept you?** quid tenuit quominus venires? **‖** *intr (to last)* durare; **to — away from** abstinēre ab *(w. abl);* **to — up with** *(to keep pace with)* subsequi; *(to equal)* aequare, aemulari
keep *s* custodi·a -ae *f; (support)* aliment·um -i *n*
keeper *s* cust·os -odis *mf*
keeping *s* tutel·a -ae *f;* **in — with** pro *(w. abl)*
keepsake *s* monument·m -i *n*
keg *s* cad·us -i *m*
kennel *s* stabul·um -i *n* caninum
kerchief *s* sudar·ium -(i)i *n*
kernel *s* nucle·us -i *m; (fig)* medull·um -i *n*
ketchup *s* ketsup·um -i *n*
kettle *s* leb·es -etis *f*
kettledrum *s* tympan·um -i *n* aeneum
key *s* clav·is -is *f; (pitch)* voculati·o -onis *f; (clue)* ans·a -ae *f; (on a piano)* plectr·um -i *n; (on the keyboard)* malleol·us -i *m;* **to hit the** — malleolum pulsare
keyboard *s (of a computer or typewriter)* plectrolog·ium -(i)i *n; (on a piano or organ)* clavitur·a -ae *f*
keyhole *s* claustell·um -i *n*
kid *s (coll)* frust·um -i *n* pueri *or* puellae
kid *tr* ludere, ludificare, jocari
kick *s* cal·x -cis *mf*
kick *tr* calce ferire; *(a ball)* pede pulsare; **to — the bucket** *(coll)* animam ebullire **‖** *intr* calcitrare
kid *s* haed·us -i *m; (child)* parvul·us -i *m* (·a -ae *f*)
kid *tr & intr* ludificari
kidnap *tr* surripere
kidnapper *s* plagiar·ius -(i)i *m* (·a -ae *f*)
kidnapping *s* plag·ium -(i)i *n*
kidney *s* ren, renis *m*
kidney bean *s* phasel·us -i *m*
kill *s* nex, necis *f; (prey)* praed·a -ae *f*
kill *tr* interficere; *(by cruel means)* necare; *(by wounds or blows)* caedere; **to — time** tempus perdere *(or)* fallere; **you're —ing me!** me enicas!
killer *s* interfec·tor -toris *m* (·trix -tricis *f*)
kiln *s* forn·ax -acis *f*

kilogram *s* chilogramm·a -atis *n*
kilometer *s* chilometr·um -i *n*
kin *s* cognat·i -orum *mpl;* **next of —** proxim·i -orum *mpl*
kind *adj* benign·us -a -um; **— to** *or* **toward** benevol·us -a -um erga *(w. acc)*
kind *s* gen·us -eris *n; that —* **of war** eius modi bell·um -i *n;* **what — of** qual·is -is -e, qui quae quod
kindergarten *s* paedotrophe·um -i *n*
kindhearted *adj* benign·us -a -um, benevol·us -a -um
kindle *tr* incendere, accendere
kindly *adj* human·us -a -um
kindly *adv* benigne
kindness *s* benignit·as -atis *f; (deed)* benefic·ium -(i)i *n;* **to bestow a — on s.o.** beneficium apud aliquem collocare; **to do (return) an act of —** beneficium dare (reddere)
kindred *adj* consanguine·us -a -um
kindred *s* consanguinit·as -atis *f; (relatives)* consanguine·i -orum *mpl* (·ae -arum *fpl*)
king *s* re·x -gis *m*
kingdom *s* regn·um -i *n*
kingfisher *s* alced·o -inis *f*
kingly *adj* regi·us -a -um; *(worthy of a king)* regal·is -is -e
king-sized *adj* imman·is -is -e
kinsman *s* necessar·ius -(i)i *m*
kinswoman *s* necessari·a -ae *f*
kiss *s* oscul·um -i *n; (passionate)* bas·ium -(i)i *n*
kiss *tr* osculari; *(passionately)* basiare
kissing *s* osculati·o -onis *f,* basiati·o -onis *f*
kit *s* apparat·us -ūs *m*
kitchen *s* culin·a -ae *f*
kitchen knife *s* cul·ter -tri *m* coquinaris
kitchen utensils *spl* instrument·a -orum *npl* coquinatoria
kite *s (bird)* milv·us -i *m; (toy)* milvus papyraceus; **to fly a —** facere ut milvus papyraceus volet
kith and kin *spl* propinqu·i -orum et adfin·es -ium *mpl*
kitten *s* catul·us -i *m* felinus
knack *s* sollerti·a -ae *f*
knapsack *s* sacciper·ium -(i)i *n* dorsuale
knave *s* scelest·us -i *m*
knead *tr* subigere
knee *s* gen·u -us *n;* **on bended —** duplicato poplite; **to fall at s.o.'s —s** *(in entreaty)* se ad genua alicuius proicere; **to fall on one's —s to** genua ponere *(w. dat of person so honored)*
kneecap *s* patell·a -ae *f*
knee-deep *adj* genibus tenus alt·us -a -um
kneel *intr* genibus niti; **to — down** ad genua procumbere

knell *s* campan·a -ae *f* funebris
knife *s* cul·ter -tri *m; (small)* cultell·us -i *m; (for surgery)* scalpell·um -i *n*
knight *s* equ·es -itis *m*
knighthood *s* equestris dignit·as -atis *f*
knightly *adj* eques·ter -tris -tre
knit *tr* texere; **to — the brow** frontem contrahere
knob *s* tub·er -eris *n; (on door)* bull·a -ae *f*
knock *s* puls·us -ūs *m*
knock *tr* **knock it off!** *(coll)* parce! *(pl:* parcite!);* **to — down** deicere; *(in boxing)* sternere; *(fig) (at auction)* addicere; **to — in** impellere; **to — one's head against the wall** caput ad parietem offendere; **to — out** *(in boxing)* consternere; **to — out s.o.'s brains** cerebrum alicui excutere ‖ *intr* **to — about** *(to ramble)* vagari; **to — at** pulsare, percutere
knocking *s* pulsati·o -onis *f*
knock-kneed *adj* var·us -a -um
knoll *s* tumul·us -i *m*
knot *s* nod·us -i *m; (of people)* turbul·a -ae *f;* **to tie a —** nodum facere; **to untie a —** nodum expedire
knot *tr* nodare
knotty *adj* nodos·us -a -um; *(fig)* spinos·us -a -um
know *tr* scire; *(a person, place)* novisse; **let me — how you are doing** fac ut sciam *(or* fac me certiorem) quid agas; **to get to —** noscere; **not to —** ignorare, nescire; **to — for sure** certum *(or* certo) scire; **to — how to** scire *(w. inf)*
know-how *s* sollerti·a -ae *f*
knowing *adj* callid·us -a -um
knowingly *adv* scienter, prudens
knowledge *s* scienti·a -ae *f; (of s.th.)* cogniti·o -onis *f;* **without the — of** clam *(w. abl);* **without your —** clam vobis
known *adj* not·us -a -um; **it is well — that** nobile est *(w. acc & inf);* **— to me by sight** familiar·is -is -e oculis meis; **to become —** enotescere; **to make —** divulgare, palam facere; **well —** notissim·us -a -um
knuckle *s* articul·us -i *m* digiti
knuckle *intr* **to — down to** incumbere in *(w. acc);* **to — under to** cedere *(w. dat)*
knucklehead *s (coll)* bar·o -onis *m*
kowtow *intr* **(to)** adulari *(w. dat)*
kudos *s* laus, laudis *f*

L

label *s* pittac·ium -(i)i *n*
label *tr* pittacium affigere *(w. dat); (fig)* notare

labor _s_ lab·or -oris _m; (manual work)_ oper·a -ae _f; (work done)_ op·us -eris _n;_ **to be in —** laborare in utero; **woman in —** puerper·a -ae _f_

labor _intr_ laborare, eniti; **to — under** laborare _(w. abl)_

laboratory _s_ officin·a -ae _f_ experimentis agendis

labored _adj_ affectat·us -a -um

laborer _s_ operar·ius -(i)i _m,_ oper·a -ae _f_

labor union _s_ colleg·ium -(i)i _n_

labyrinth _s_ labyrinth·us -i _m_

lace _s_ op·us -eris _n_ reticulatum

lace _tr (to tie)_ nectere; _(to tighten)_ astringere

lacerate _tr_ lacerare

laceration _s_ lacerati·o -onis _f_

lack _s_ inopi·a -ae _f;_ **for — of** inopiā _(w. gen)_

lack _tr_ carēre _(w. abl)_ ‖ _intr_ **to be —** deficere; _(to be missing)_ deesse

lackadaisical _adj_ remiss·us -a - um

lackey _s_ pedisequ·us -i _m; (fig)_ assecl·a -ae _mf_

laconic _adj_ brev·is -is -e

lacrosse _s_ lud·us -i _m_ lacrossensis; **to play —** ludo lacrossensi ludere

lacrosse stick _s_ coroci·a -ae _f;_ **to cradle the —** corociam agitare

lad _s_ pu·er -eri _m_

ladder _s_ scal·ae -arum _fpl; (fig)_ grad·us -ūs _m;_ **one —** unae scalae

laden _adj_ onust·us -a -um

ladle _s_ ligul·a -ae _f; (for wine)_ trull·a -ae _f_

ladle _tr_ ligulā fundere

lady _s_ domin·a -ae _f_

lady-like _adj_ liberal·is -is -e

lag _intr_ morari; **to — behind** cessare

laggard _s_ cessa·tor -toris _m_ (·trix -tricis _f)_

lagoon _s_ lacun·a -ae _f_

laid up _adj (sick)_ lecto affix·us -a -um

lair _s_ cubil·e -is _n_

laity _spl_ laïc·i -orum _mpl_

lake _s_ lac·us -ūs _m_

lamb _s_ agn·us -i _m,_ agn·a -ae _f; (meat)_ agnin·a -ae _f_

lame _adj_ claud·us -a -um; **— in one leg** claud·us -a -um altero pede; **to be —** claudicare

lamely _adv (fig)_ inconcinne

lameness _s_ claudit·as -atis _f_

lament _s_ lament·um -i _n; (complaint)_ querel(l)·a -ae _f_

lament _tr_ lamentari ‖ _intr_ deplorare

lamentable _adj_ lamentabil·is -is -e

lamentation _s_ lamentati·o -onis _f_

lamp _s_ lucern·a -ae _f,_ lamp·as -adis _f_

lampoon _s_ libell·us -i _m_ ad infamiam

lampoon _tr_ diffamare

lamppost _s_ pil·a -ae _f_ lanternā affixa

lamprey _s_ muren·e -es _f_

lance _s_ lance·a -ae _f_

lance _tr_ incidere, pungere

land _s_ terr·a -ae _f; (soil)_ sol·um -i _n; (territory)_ fin·es -ium _fpl; (as a possession)_ a·ger -gri _m;_ **on — and sea** terrā marique; **piece of —** ager; **public —** ager publicus _(or_ agri publici)

land _tr_ in terram exponere; _(to get) (coll)_ adipisci ‖ _intr (of a person)_ in terram egredi; _(of a ship)_ (ad terram) appellere; _(of a plane)_ deorsum appellere; _(of flying creatures)_ **(on)** considere in _(w. abl),_ insidere _(w. dat)_

land _adj (animals, route)_ terren·us -a -um; _(animals, route, troops)_ terrestr·is -is -e; _(battle)_ pedes·ter -tris -tre

landholder _s_ agrorum possess·or -oris _m_ (·rix -ricis _f)_

landing _s_ egress·us -ūs _m; (of a plane)_ appuls·us -ūs _m; (on stairs)_ scalar·ium -(i)i _n_

landing place _s_ appuls·us -ūs _m_

landlady _s_ (insulae) domin·a -ae _f_

landlord _s_ (insulae) domin·us -i _m_

landmark _s_ lap·is -idis _m_ terminalis

landscape _s_ regionis sit·us -ūs _m_

landslide _s_ terrae laps·us -ūs _m_

land tax _s_ vectig·al -alis _n_

lane _s_ semit·a -ae _f; (for planes)_ aëria vi·a -ae _f_

language _s_ lingu·a -ae _f,_ serm·o -onis _m; (diction)_ orati·o -onis _f;_ **abusive and insulting — against s.o.** maledice contumelioseque dict·a -orum _npl_ in aliquem; **the Latin —** lingua Latina, sermo Latinus

language lab _s_ officin·a -ae _f_ loquelaris

languid _adj_ languid·us -a -um

languish _intr_ languēre

languishing _adj_ languid·us -a -um

languor _s_ langu·or -oris _m_

lanky _adj_ prolix·us -a -um

lantern _s_ la(n)tern·a -ae _f_

lap _s_ sin·us -ūs _m; (fig)_ grem·ium -(i)i _n; (in a race)_ spat·ium -(i)i _n_

lap _tr_ lambere; **to — up** haurire, absorbēre

lapse _s_ laps·us -ūs _m; (error)_ peccat·um -i _n;_ **after a — of one year** interiecto anno; **the — of time** lapsus temporum

lapse _intr_ labi; **to — into** recidere in _(w. acc)_

laptop computer _s_ ordinatrul·um -i _n_ portabile

laquer _s_ resin·a -ae _f_ temeto soluta

laquer _tr_ resinā obducere

larceny _s_ furt·um -i _n_

lard _s_ ad·eps -ipis _mf; (from bacon)_ lar(i)d·um -i _n_

large _adj_ magn·us -a -um; **to a — extent** magnā ex parte

largely _adv_ plerumque

largess _s_ largiti·o -onis _f;_ **to give a — to** largiri _(w dat)_

lark _s_ alaud·a -ae _f_

larynx _s_ gutt·ur -uris _n_

lascivious *adj* lasciv·us -a -um
lasciviously *adv* lascive
lash *s (blow)* verb·er -eris *n; (whip)* flagell·um -i *n*
lash *tr* verberare, flagellare; *(to censure severely)* castigare; *(to fasten)* annectere, alligare **ǁ** *intr* **to — out at** castigare
lashing *s* verberati·o -onis *f*
lass *s* puell·a -ae *f*
lassitude *s* lassitud·o -inis *f*
last *adj* postrem·us -a -um, ultim·us -a -um; *(immediately preceding)* proxim·us -a -um; *(in line)* novissim·us -a -um; **at — demum; for the — time** postremo; **— but one** paenultim·us -a -um; **— night** heri vesperi, proximā nocte; **the night before —** superiore nocte; *(adj used where English uses an adv, e.g.,* **Cicero spoke last** Cicero novissimus locutus est)
last *intr* durare; **to — for some time** aliquod tempus habēre; **to — long** *(of a fever, etc.)* diu permanēre
lasting *adj* diuturn·us -a -um
lastly *adv* denique, postremo
latch *s* pessul·us -i *m*
latch *tr* oppessulare
late *adj* ser·us -a -um; *(loitering behind time)* tard·us -a -um; *(far advanced)* mult·us -a -um; *(recent in date)* rec·ens -entis; *(deceased)* demortu·us -a -um; *(of an emperor)* divus; **Homer was not —r than Lycurgus** Homerus non infra Lycurgum fuit; **it was — in the day** serum erat diei; **till — at night** ad multam noctem
late *adv* sero; **all too — immo iam sero; — at night** multā nocte; **— in life** seri anni; **not till — in the day** multo denique die; **too — serius; very — serissime**
lately *adv* nuper
latent *adj* lat·ens -entis, occult·us -a -um
later *adv* postea; **a little — postea aliquanto; many years — multis post annis; sooner or — ocius serius; to postpone till —** differre in aliud tempus
lateral *adj* lateral·is -is -e
latest *adv* **at — summum; perhaps tomorrow, at latest, the day after that** fortasse cras, summum perendie
Latin *adj* Latin·us -a -um; **the Latin people** Latin·i -orum *mpl* **ǁ** *s* lingu·a -ae *f*, Latina, serm·o -onis *m* Latinus; **in first year Latin** primo anno Latinitatis; **to learn — Latine** discere; **to know (understand) — Latine** scire; **to speak — Latine** (loqui); **to teach — Latine** docēre; **to translate into — Latine** reddere; **to translate from Greek into Latin** ex Graeco in Latinum (con)vertere *(or* transferre); **to understand — Latine** scire; **to write — Latine** scribere

Latinity *s* Latinit·as -atis *f*
Latin teacher *s* Latinitatis magis·ter -tri *m* (·tra -trae *f)*
latitude *s* latitud·o -inis *f; (fig)* libert·as -atis *f*
Latium *s* Lat·ium -(i)i *n*
latter *adj* poster·ior -ior -ius; **the — hic**
lattice *s* cancell·i -orum *mpl*
laudable *adj* laudabil·is -is -e
laudably *adv* laudabiliter
laudatory *adj* laudativ·us -a -um
laugh *s* ris·us -ūs *m*
laugh *intr* ridēre; **to — at** ridēre; *(to mock)* irridēre
laughable *adj* ridicul·us -a -um
laughingstock *s* ludibr·ium -(i)i *n*
laughter *s* ris·us -ūs *m; (loud, indecorous)* cachinnati·o -onis *f*
launch *tr* deducere; *(to hurl)* iaculari **ǁ** *intr* **to — out** proficisci
launder *tr* lavare
laundress *s* lotr·ix -icis *f*
laundry *s* lavator·ium -(i)i *n; (Roman)* fullonic·a -ae *f; (dirty clothes)* lavandari·a -orum *npl*
laureate *adj* laureat·us -a -um
laurel *adj* laure·us -a -um
laurel tree *s* laur·us -i *f*
lava *s* liquefacta mass·a -ae *f*
lavender *s* lavandulace·us -a -um
lavish *adj* prodig·us -a -um
lavish *tr* prodigere, profundere
lavishly *adv* prodige
law *s* lex, legis *f; (right; the entire body of law)* ius, iuris *n; (divine)* fas *n* [indecl]; **against the law** contra ius; *(against a specific law)* contra legem; **by — lege; in accordance with the — lege; to break a — legem** violare; **to lay down the —** *(to scold)* vehementer obiurgare; **to introduce a — legem** ferre; **to pass a — legem** perferre; **unwritten — mos moris** *m*
law-abiding *adj* bene morat·us -a -um, legi obsequ·ens -entis
law court *s* iudic·ium -(i)i *n; (building)* basilic·a -ae *f*
lawful *adj* legitim·us -a -um; **it is — fas est**
lawfully *adv* legitime
lawless *adj* ex·lex -legis
lawlessness *s* licenti·a -ae *f*
lawmaker *s* legisla·tor -toris *m* (·trix -tricis *f)*
lawn *s* pratul·um -i *n;* **to mow the —** pratulum resecare
lawnmower *s* herbisectr·um -i *n*
lawsuit *s* lis, litis *f,* caus·a -ae *f;* **to bring** *or* **file a — against s.o.** litem alicui intendere
lawyer *s* iurisconsult·us -i *m* (·a -ae *f);* **defense — advocat·us -i** *m* (·a -ae *f);* **trial — causidic·us -i** *m* (·a -ae *f)*

lax *adj (person)* remiss·us -a -um; *(discipline)* lax·us -a -um
laxity *s* remissi·o -onis *f*
lay *tr (to put)* ponere; *(eggs)* parere; *(foundations)* iacere; *(bricks)* struere; *(hands)* inicere; **to — a finger on s.o.** aliquem uno digito attingere; **to — an ambush** insidiari; **to be laid up** cubare; **to — aside** ponere; *(cares, fear)* amovēre; **to — before** proponere; **to — claim to** arrogare, vindicare; **to — down** deponere; *(rules)* statuere; **to — down arms** ab armis discedere; **to — hands on s.th.** aliquid invadere; **to — hold of** prehendere; **to — it on the line** *(coll)* directum loqui; **to — out** *(money)* expendere; *(plans)* designare; **to — siege to** obsidēre; **to — the blame on** culpam conferre in *(w. acc);* **to — up** condere; **to — waste** vastare **‖** *intr* — **off!** *(coll)* desine! *(pl:* desinite!); **to — for** insidiari; **to — over** *(on a trip)* commorari
lay *s (mus)* cantilen·a -ae *f*
layer *s* lamin·a -ae *f; (stratum)* cor·ium -(i)i *n*
layer *tr* **to — the hair** comam in gradūs frangere
layover *s* commorati·o -onis *f*
lazily *adv* ignave, pigre
laziness *s* pigriti·a -ae *f*
lazy *adj* ignav·us -a -um, pi·ger -gra -grum
lead *s (metal)* plumb·um -i *n*
lead *adj* plumbe·us -a -um
lead *s* primus loc·us -i *m; (theat)* primae part·es -ium *fpl;* **to take the —** praeesse; *(theat)* primas partes suscipere
lead *tr* ducere; *(life)* agere; **to — about** circumducere; **to — astray** in errorem inducere; **to — away** abducere; **to — off** divertere; **to — on** conducere, illicere **‖** *intr (of a road)* **to — to** ducere ad *(w. acc);* **to — up to** tendere ad *(w. acc)*
leaden *adj* plumbe·us -a -um
leader *s* du·x -cis *mf,* princ·eps -ipis *mf*
leadership *s* duct·us -ūs *m;* **under my — me** duce
leading *adj* princ·eps -cipis, primari·us -a -um; **— man (lady)** *(theat)* histri·o -onis *mf* primarum partium
leaf *s* fol·ium -(i)i *n; (of vine)* pampin·us -i *m; (of paper)* sched·a -ae *f; (of metal)* bracte·a -ae *f;* **to turn over a new —** ad bonam frugem se recipere
leafless *adj* fronde nudat·us -a -um
leafy *adj* frondos·us -a -um
league *s* foed·us -eris *n*
leak *s* rim·a -ae *f*
leak *tr (information)* divulgare; **‖** *intr* rimas agere, perfluere
leaky *adj* rimos·us -a -um
lean *adj (meat, person)* ma·cer -cra -crum

lean *tr* inclinare **‖** *intr* inclinare, niti; **—ing forward** inclinat·us -a -um; **to — against** se applicare *(w. dat);* **to — back** se inclinare, reclinare; **to — on** inniti in *(w. abl)*
leap *s* salt·us -ūs *m*
leap *intr* salire; **to — for joy** exsultare
leap year *s* bisextilis ann·us -i *m,* intercalaris annus
learn *tr* discere; *(from elders)* accipere; **to — by heart** ediscere; **to — thoroughly** perdiscere **‖** *intr* — **about** cognoscere; *(to be informed about)* certior fieri de *(w. abl)*
learned *adj* doct·us -a -um, erudit·us -a -um
learnedly *adv* docte
learner *s* disc·ens -entis *mf*
learning *s* doctrin·a -ae *f,* eruditi·o -onis *f*
lease *s* conducti·o -onis *f; (act on part of proprietor)* locati·o -onis *f*
lease *tr* conducere; **to — out** locare
leash *s* cingul·um -i *n*
leash *tr* cingulo alligare
least *adj* minim·us -a -um
least *adv* minime; **at —** utique; *(emphasizing a particular word)* saltem
least *n* minim·um -i *n;* **not in the —** ne minimum quidem
leather *s (tanned or untanned)* cor·ium -(i)i *n; (tanned)* alut·a -ae *f*
leather *adj* ex corio, scorte·us -a -um; **— raincoat** scortea paenul·a -ae *f*
leathery *adj* lent·us -a -um
leave *tr* relinquere; *(to entrust)* mandare, tradere; *(legacy)* legare; **— me alone!** omitte *(pl:* omittite) me!); **to — behind** relinquere; **to — it up to s.o.** alicui mandare ut *(w. subj);* **to — no stone unturned** nullo loco deesse; **to — out** omittere **‖** *intr (to depart)* discedere, abire; **to — off** desinere
leave *s* permissi·o -onis *f;* **— of absence** commeat·us -ūs *m;* **to ask —** veniam petere; **to obtain —** veniam impetrare; **to take — of** valēre iubēre; **with your —** pace tuā (vestrā)
leaven *s* ferment·um -i *n*
lecherous *adj* libidinos·us -a -um
lectern *s* lector·ium -(i)i *n*
lector *s* lec·tor -toris *m (·*trix -tricis *f)*
lecture *s* lecti·o -onis *f; (public)* acroas·is -is *f; (less formal)* schol·a -ae *f; (explaining an author)* praelecti·o -onis *f;* **to give a — on** acroasin facere de *(w. abl); (less formally)* scholam habēre de *(w. abl)*
lecture *tr (to reprove)* obiurgare **‖** *intr* acroases facere; *(less formally)* scholas habēre
lecture hall *s* auditor·ium -(i)i *n*
lecturer *s* lec·tor -toris *m (·*trix -tricis *f)*
ledge *s* proiectur·a -ae *f; (of a cliff)* dors·um -i *n*
ledger *s* cod·ex -icis *m* (accepti et expensi)
leech *s* sanguisug·a -ae *f*

leer *intr* limis oculis spectare
leering *adj* lim·us -a -um
left *adj* laev·us -a -um, sinis·ter -tra -trum; **on the** — a sinistrā; **to the** — sinistrorsum
left-handed *adj* laev·us -a -um
leftover *adj* reliqui·us -a -um
leftovers *spl* reliqui·ae -arum *fpl*
leg *s* cru·s -ris *n;* *(of table, etc.)* pes pedis *m*
legacy *s* legat·um -i *n*
legal *adj* legitim·us -a -um
legally *adv* legitime, lege *or* legibus
legalize *tr* sancire
legate *s* legat·us -i *m* (·a -ae *f)*
legation *s* legati·o -onis *f*
legend *s* fabul·a -ae *f; (inscription)* titul·us -i *m*
legendary *adj* fabulos·us -a -um, commenti·ci·us -a -um,
legging *s* ocre·a -ae *f*
legible *adj* legibil·is -is -e
legion *s* legi·o -onis *f*
legionary *s* mil·es -itis *m* legionarius
legislate *intr* leges dare *or* ferre
legislation *s (act)* legum dati·o -onis *f; (the laws)* leg·es -um *fpl*
legislator *s* legum la·tor -toris *m* (·trix -tricis *f)*
legitimate *adj* legitim·us -a -um
legitimately *adv* legitime
leisure *s* ot·ium -(i)i *n;* **at** — otios·us -a -um; **to be at** — vacare, otiari
leisure *adj* otios·us -a -um, vacu·us -a -um; — **activity** op·us -eris *n* subsicivum
leisure time *s* temp·us -oris *n* vacuum
leisurely *adj* lent·us -a -um
lemon *s* pom·um -i *n* citreum
lemonade *s* aqu·a -ae *f* limonata
lend *tr* **to** — **money** pecuniam mutuam dare *or* commodare; *(at interest)* pecuniam faenerare; **to** — **one's ear to** aures praebēre *(w. dat)*
length *s* longitud·o -inis *f; (of time)* longinquit·as -atis *f;* **at** — tandem; **in** — in longitudinem
lengthen *tr (space)* extendere; *(vowels)* producere *(opp:* corripere); *(time)* protrahere ‖ *intr* longior fieri
lengthwise *adv* in longitudinem
lengthy *adj* long·us -a -um
leniency *s* lenit·as -atis *f*
lenient *adj* len·is -is -e
leniently *adv* leniter
lens *s* len·s -tis *f* optica
lentil *s* len·s -tis *f*
leopard *s* (leo)pard·us -i *m*
leper *s* lepros·us -i *m* (·a -ae *f)*
leprosy *s* lepr·ae -arum *fpl*
less *adj* min·or -or -us
less *adv* minus
lessee *s* conduc·t·or -toris *m* (·trix -tricis *f)*
lessen *tr* (im)minuere ‖ *intr* decrescere

lesson *s* document·um -i *n; (in school)* lecti·o -onis *f,* praecept·um -i *n;* **to be a** — **to** documento esse *(w. dat);* **to give** —**s in** docēre; **to give** —**s in grammar** grammaticam docēre
lessor *s* loca·tor -toris *m* (·trix -tricis *f)*
lest *conj* ne
let *tr (to allow)* sinere, permittere; *(to lease)* locare; — **me see** licet (ut) videam; **let's go** eamus; **to** — **alone** omittere; **to** — **down** *(to disappoint)* deësse *(w. dat);* **to** — **fall** e manibus mittere; **to** — **fly** emittere; **to** — **go** (di)mittere; **to** — **in** admittere; **to** — **off** absolvere; **to** — **out** emittere; **to** — **pass** omittere; **to** — **slip an opportunity** occasionem amittere ‖ *intr* **to** — **up** residēre; **the rain is letting up** imber detumescit
lethal *adj* morti·fer(us) -fera -ferum
lethargic *adj* lethargic·us -a -um
lethargy *s* letharg·us -i *m*
letter *s (of alphabet)* litter·a -ae *f; (epistle)* litter·ae -arum *fpl,* epistul·a -ae *f;* **by** — per litteras; **capital** — littera grandis; —**s form syllables** litterae faciunt syllabas; **to the** — ad verbum
letter carrier *s* tabellari·us -i *m* (·a -ae *f)*
lettered *adj* litterat·us -a -um
letterhead *s* titul·us -i *m*
lettering *s* titul·us -i *m,* litter·ae -arum *fpl*
letter opener *s* ensicul·us -i *m* epistularis
lettuce *s* lactuc·a -ae *f*
leukemia *s* leukaemi·a -ae *f*
levee *s* agg·er -eris *m*
level *adj* plan·us -a -um
level *s* planiti·es -ei *f; (tool)* libr·a -ae *f;* **to be on a** — **with** par esse *(w. dat)*
level *tr* (ad)aequare; *(to destroy)* diruere; **to** — **to the ground** solo aequare
lever *s* vect·is -is *m*
levity *s* levit·as -atis *f*
levy *s* delect·us -ūs *m*
levy *tr (troops)* conscribere; *(tax)* exigere
lewd *adj* incest·us -a -um
lewdly *adv* inceste
lewdness *s* impudiciti·a -ae *f*
liable *adj* obnoxi·us -a -um; *(inclined)* inclinat·us -a -um
liar *s* mend·ax -acis *mf*
libation *s* libati·o -onis *f;* **to pour a** — libare
libel *s* calumni·a -ae *f*
libel *tr* calumniari
libelous *adj* famos·us -a -um
liberal *adj* liberal·is -is -e; *(free)* lib·er -era -erum; *(in giving)* larg·us -a -um; — **arts** art·es -ium *fpl* liberales, artes bonac, artes ingenuae
liberality *s* liberalit·as -atis *f*
liberally *adv* liberaliter, large
liberate *tr* liberare; *(a slave)* manumittere
liberation *s* liberati·o -onis *f*

liberator *s* libera·tor -toris *m* (·trix -tricis *f*)
libertine *s* hom·o -inis *mf* dissolutus (-a)
liberty *s* libert·as -atis *f;* **at** — lib·er -era
-erum; **to be at** — licet *(w. dat of English
subject);* **to take liberties with s.o.** liberius
se in aliquem gerere
librarian *s* bibliothecari·us -i *m* (·a -ae *f*)
library *s* bibliothec·a -ae *f*
license *s (permission)* copi·a -ae *f,* potest·as
-atis *f; (freedom)* licenti·a -ae *f; (to drive)*
diplom·a -atis *n* gubernationis
license *tr* potestatem dare *(w. dat)*
license plate *s* notacul·um -i *n* autocineti
licentious *adj* dissolut·us -a -um
licentiously *adv* dissolute
lick *tr* lambere; *(daintily)* ligurrire; *(to thrash)*
verberare; *(to defeat)* (de)vincere **to** — **the
plate** catillare; **to** — **out** elingere; **to** — **up**
delingere
licking *s (spanking)* verberati·o -onis *f;* **to get
a** — vapulare
lictor *s* lict·or -oris *m*
lid *s* operiment·um -i *n*
lie *s* mendac·ium -(i)i *n;* **to give the** — **to**
redarguere; **to tell a** — mendacium dicere
lie *intr (to tell a lie or lies)* mentiri; *(to be lying
down)* iacēre; *(in bed)* cubare; *(to be situated)*
sit·us -a -um esse; **to** — **down** iacēre; *(to
rest)* decumbere; **to** — **in the direction of**
vergere ad *(w. acc);* **to** — **in wait for**
insidiari *(w. dat);* **to** — **on** *or* **upon** incubare
(w. dat); **to** — **on one's back** resupin·us -a
-um iacēre; **to** — **on one's left (right) side** in
latus sinistrum (dextrum) cubare; **to** — **on
one's stomach** pron·us -a -um iacēre
lieu *s* **in** — **of** loco *(w. gen)*
lieutenant *s* legat·us -i *m; (mil)* centuri·o -onis
m; (modern) locumten·ens -entis *mf*
life *s* vit·a -ae *f; (age)* aet·as -atis *f; (fig)*
alacrit·as -atis *f;* **but such is** — sed vita fert;
it's not a question of — **or death** non capitis res agitur; **on my** —! ita vivam!; **spark of**
— animul·a -ae *f;* **to come to** — reviviscere;
to lead the — **of Riley** vitam Chiam gerere;
to lose one's — animam amittere; **true to** —
veri simil·is -is -e
life blood *s* suc·us -i *m* et sangu·is -inis *m*
lifeboat *s* navicul·a -ae *f* ad servandum
life-giving *adj* alm·us -a -um
lifeguard *s* cust·os -odis *mf* nantium
life imprisonment *s* **he was given** — carceri
quoad vivat damnatus est; **to give s.o.** —
aliquem damnare carceri quoad vivat
life insurance *s* vitae assecurati·o -onis *f*
lifeless *adj* inanim·us -a -um, exanim·is -is -e;
(fig) exsangu·is -is -e, frigid·us -a -um
lifelessly *adv* frigide
life style *s* vitae proposit·um -i *n*

lifetime *s* aet·as -atis *f;* **once in a** — singulis
aetatibus
lift *tr* tollere; **to** — **her hand to her face**
manum ad faciem suam admovēre; **to** — **up**
attollere; **to** — **weights** libramenta tollere
ligament *s* ligament·um -i *n*
ligature *s* ligatur·a -ae *f*
light *s* lu·x -cis *f,* lum·en -inis *n* (electricum);
(lamp) lucern·a -ae *f;* — **and shade** *(in painting)* lum·en -inis *n* et umbr·ae -arum *fpl;* **to
bring to** — in lucem proferre; **to come to** —
apparēre; **to throw** — **on** lumen adhibēre *(w.
dat);* **to turn on (off) the** — lumen (electricum) accendere (expedire)
light *adj (in weight)* lev·is -is -e; *(bright)*
lucid·us -a -um; *(of colors)* candid·us -a -um;
(easy) facil·is -is -e; *(nimble)* agil·is -is -e;
(wine) tenu·is -is -e, len·is -is -e; *(food)* lev·is
-is -e; **to grow** — lucescere; **to make** — **of** in
levi habēre
light *tr* accendere; *(to illuminate)* illuminare **‖**
intr flammam concipere; **to** — **up** *(fig)*
hilar·is -is -e fieri; **to** — **upon** offendere
light bulb *s* globul·us -i *m* electricus
lighten *tr (to illumintate)* illustrare; *(weight)*
allevare, exonerare **‖** *intr (in the sky)* fulgu-
rare
lighter *s* ignitabul·um -i *n*
light-hearted *adj* hilar·is -is -e
lighthouse *s* phar·us -i *f (m)*
lightness *s* levit·as -atis *f*
lightning *s* fulg·ur -uris *n; (in its destructive
effects)* fulm·en -inis *n;* **struck by** — fulmine
ict·us -a -um
likable *adj* amabil·is -is -e, grat·us -a -um
like *adj* simil·is -is -e *(w. dat); (equal)* par *(w.
dat),* aequ·us -a -um *(w. dat);* **in** — **manner**
similiter
like *prep* instar *(w. gen);* tamquam, ut; **he said
s.th.** — **this** haec fere dixit; **that's more** — **it**
propemodum est
like *tr* amare, curare; **he** —**s to paint** libentis-
sime pingit; **I** — **this (best)** hoc mihi (potissimum) placet; **I'd like to** velim *(w. inf);* **I** —
to do this me iuvat hoc facere; **I** — **to watch
the races** libenter circenses specto; **stay if
you** — mane *(pl:* menēte) si libet
likeable *adj see* **likable**
likelihood *s* verisimilitud·o -inis *f*
likely *adj* verisimil·is -is -e, probabil·is -is -e;
it is more — **that** verisimilius est *(w. acc &
inf);* **it is most** — **that** proximum est *(w. acc
& inf)*
likely *adv* probabiliter; **more** — probabilius
liken *tr* comparare
likeness *s* similitud·o -inis *f; (portrait)*
effigi·es -ei *f,* simulacr·um -i *n*
likewise *adv* pariter, similiter, item

liking *s* am·or -oris *m; (fancy)* libid·o -inis *f;*
according to one's — ex libidine; **to my** —
ex meā sententiā; **to their** — ad arbitrium
lilac *s* syring·a -ae *f* vulgaris
lily *s* lil·ium -(i)i *n*
lily of the valley *s* convallaria maial·is -is *f*
limb *s* art·us -ūs *m,* membr·um -i *n; (of tree)*
ram·us -i *m*
limber *adj* flexil·is -is -e
limbo *s (eccl)* limb·us -i *m*
lime *s* cal·x -cis *f; (fruit)* mal·um -i *n* citreum
limestone *s* cal·x -cis *f*
lime tree *s* tili·a -ae *f*
limit *s* fin·is -is *m,* mod·us -i *m;* **to set** —**s to**
finire
limit *tr* finire, terminare; *(to restrict)* circumscribere
limitation *s* circumscripti·o -onis *f*
limited *adj* finit·us -a -um; *(time)* brev·is -is -e;
(resources) exigu·us -a -um
limp *s* claudicati·o -onis *f*
limp *intr* claudicare
limp *adj* flaccid·us -a -um
linden tree *s* tili·a -ae *f*
line *s (drawn)* line·a -ae *f; (row)* seri·es -ei *f,*
agm·en -inis *n; (lineage)* stirp·s -is *f,* gen·us
-eris *n; (mil)* aci·es -ei *f; (of poetry or prose)*
vers·us -ūs *m; (cord)* fun·is -is *m;* **drop me a**
— **when you have time** scribe aliquid litterarum quando vacas; **he's feeding you a** —
verba tibi iste dat; **in a straight** — rectā
līneā; **I will write a few** —**s in answer to**
your letter pauca ad tuas litteras rescribam;
— **of work** *or* **business** quaest·us -ūs *m;* **the**
front — *(mil)* principi·a -orum *npl;* **to draw**
a — lineam ducere; **to form a long** — agmen
longum facere; **to keep s.o. in** — imperare
(w. dat); **to lay it on the** — *(fig)* directum
loqui
line *tr (the streets)* saepire; **to** — **a garment**
with wool vestem introrsum lanā obducere
lineage *s* gen·us -eris *n*
lineal *adj* linear·is -is -e
lineally *adv* rectā līneā
lineament *s* lineament·um -i *n*
linear *adj* linear·is -is -e
linen *s* linte·um -i *n,* lin·um -i *n*
linen *adj* linte·us -a -um; — **cloth** linteol·um
-i *n*
linesman *s (sports)* iud·ex icis *m* linearius
linger *intr* morari, cunctari
lingering *adj* cunctabund·us -a -um
lingering *s* cunctati·o -onis *f*
linguist *s* linguarum perit·us -is -i *m (·a -ae f)*
linguistics *s* linguistic·a -ae *f*
liniment *s* leniment·um -i *n*
link *s (of chain)* anul·us -i *m; (bond)*
vincul·um -i *n; (comput)* conex·us -ūs *m*
link *tr* coniungere; *(comput)* conectere

linking *s (comput)* conecti·o -onis *f*
linseed oil *s* ex lini semine ole·um -i *n*
lint *s* linament·um -i *n*
lintel *s* lim·en -inis *n* superum
lion *s* le·o -onis *m;* —**s roar** leones rugiunt
lioness *s* leaen·a -ae *f*
lip *s* labr·um -i *n; (edge)* or·a -ae *f;* **keep a stiff**
upper — fac ut animo forti sis; **lower**
(upper) — interius (superius) labrum; **to be**
on everyone's —**s** in ore esse omni populo
lip service *s* obseq·ium -(i)i *n* falsum
liquefy *tr* liquefacere
liquid *adj* liquid·us -a -um
liquid *s* um·or -oris *m*
liquidate *tr* removēre, dimittere; *(accounts)*
persolvere; *(convert into cash)* in pecuniam
vertere
liquor *s* temet·um -i *n*
lisp *s* balbutire
lisping *adj* blaes·us -a -um
list *s* numer·us -i *m; (naut)* inclinati·o -onis *f;*
— **of charges** subscripti·o -onis *f; (e-mail*
list) grex, gregis *m* (interretialis)
list *tr* enumerare; **to** — **among the murderers**
habēre sicariorum numero ‖ *intr (naut)*
inclinare
listen *intr* auscultare; **to** — **to** auscultare *(w.*
dat); — **to me!** ausculta mihi!
listless *adj* languid·us -a -um; des·es -idis
listlessly *adv* languide
list owner *s (comput)* gregis modera·tor -toris
m (·trix -tricis f)
litany *s* litani·a -ae *f*
liter *s* litr·a -ae *f*
literal *adj* propri·us -a um *(opp:* translativus)
literally *adv* ad verbum, proprie *(opp:* figurate)
literary *adj (person)* litterat·us -a -um; — **pur-**
suits studi·a -orum *npl* litterarum; — **style**
scribendi gen·us -eris *n,* stil·us -i *m*
literature *s* litter·ae -arum *fpl; (printed matter)*
libr·i -orum *mpl* editi
litigant *s* litig·ans -antis *mf*
litigate *intr* litigare
litigation *s* li·s -tis *f*
litter *s (vehicle)* lectic·a -ae *f; (of straw, etc.)*
strament·um -i *n; (brood)* fet·us -ūs *m;*
(refuse) reiect·a -orum *npl*
litter *tr* spargere; **to** — **the streets** scruta viis
spargere ‖ *intr* reiecta dispergere
little *adj* parv·us -a -um; **for a** — **while**
paulisper; — **brother** fratercul·us -i *m;* —
sister sororcul·a -ae *f*
little *adv* parum, paulum; **a** — paululum, pusil-
lum; **a** — **bigger** paulo amplior; — **by** —
paulatim
little *s* aliquantul·um -i *n*
little people *spl (coll)* popul·us -i *m* minutus
live *tr* **to** — **a good life** vitam bonum agere; **to**
— **it up** ferias agere ‖ *intr* vivere, vitam

agere; *(to reside)* habitare, incolere; **to —
near** accolere; **to — in the city** urbem incolere; **to — in the Subura** habitare in Suburā;
to — on *(food)* vesci *(w. abl);* **to — on borrowed time** de lucro vivere; **to — up to**
aequiparare
live *adj* viv·us -a -um
livelihood *s* vict·us -ūs *m;* **to gain a —** victum
quaeritare
liveliness *s* alacrit·as -atis *f*
lively *adj* veget·us -a -um
liver *s* iec·ur -oris *n*
livestock *s* pec·us -oris *n*
livid *adj* livid·us -a -um; **to be —** livēre
living *adj* viv·us -a -um; **as long as Hannibal
was living** Hannibale vivo
living *s (livelihood)* vict·us -ūs *m,* quaest·us
-ūs *m;* **to make a —** quaestum facere *or* victum quaeritare
living room *s* sessor·ium -(i)i *n*
lizard *s* lacert·us -i *m* (·a -ae *f*)
load *s* on·us -eris *n*
load *tr* onerare
loaded *adj (rich)* bene nummat·us -a -um,
pecuniosissim·us -a -um; *(drunk)* uvid·us
-a -um
loaf *s* **(of bread)** pan·is -is *m*
loaf *intr* cessare
loafer *s* cessa·tor -toris *m* (trix -tricis *f*)
loafing *s* cessati·o -onis *f*
loam *s* lut·um -i *n*
loan *s* (argenti) mutu·um -i *n;* **to hit s.o. for a
—** aliquem mutuo ferire
loan *tr* faenerari
loathe *tr* fastidire
loathing *s* fastid·ium -(i)i *n*
loathsome *adj* tae·ter -tra -trum
lobby *s* vestibul·um -i *n*
lobe *s* lob·us -i *m*
lobster *s* astac·us -i *m*
local *adj* loci [*gen*], regionis [*gen*]
locality *s* loc·us -i *m*
local number *s* numer·us -i *m* localis
local train *s* tram·en -inis *n* commune
located *adj* sit·us -a -um
lock *s (of door)* ser·a -ae *f; (of hair)* crin·is -is
m; **—, stock, and barrel** cum porcis, cum
fiscinā; **to be kept under — and key** esse
sub clavi
lock *tr* obserare, oppessulare; **to — in** includere; **to — out** excludere; **to — up** occludere;
(in prison) in carcerem compingere
locker *s* loculament·um -i *n*
locket *s* capsell·a -a *f; (worn by boys, of
leather, silver, or gold)* bull·a -ae *f;* **to wear
a — around the neck** capsellam de cervice
gerere; **wearing a —** bullat·us -a -um
lockjaw *s* tetan·us -i *m*

locomotive *s* (vaporaria) machin·a -ae *f* tractoria
locust *s* locust·a -ae *f;* **—s chirp** locustae
strident
lodge *tr* **to — a complaint against s.o.** nomen
alicuius deferre ‖ *intr* **(with)** deversari (apud
w. acc); (to stick) inhaerēre
lodger *s* hosp·es -itis *mf; (in a tenement)* insu-
lari·us -i *m* (·a -ae *f*)
lodging *s* hospit·ium -(i)i *n;* **to take up —** hospitium accipere
loft *s* tabulat·um -i *n*
lofty *adj* (ex)cels·us -a -um; *(fig)* sublim·is
-is -e
log *s* stip·es -itis *m*
loggerheads *spl* **to be at —** rixari
logic *s* dialectic·a -orum *npl*
logical *adj* logic·us -a -um; *(reasonable)*
rational·is -is -e
logically *adv* ex ratione
log in *intr (comput)* inire
log out *intr (comput)* exire
loin *s* lumb·us -i *m*
loiter *intr* cessare
loiterer *s* cessa·tor -toris *m* (·trix -tricis *f*)
loll *intr* recumbere
lone *adj* sol·us -a -um
loneliness *s* solitud·o -inis *f*
lonely *adj* solitari·us -a -um
lonesome *adj* solitari·us -a -um
long *adj* long·us -a -um; *(of time)* diuturn·us -a
-um; *(lengthened; syllable)* product·us -a
-um; *(opp:* brevis, correptus); **a — way off**
longinqu·us -a -um; **for a — time** iam diu;
ten miles long decem milia passuum in longitudinem
long *adv* diu; **a little —er** paulo longius; **—
how long?** quamdiu?; **how much —er?**
quamdiu etiam; **— after** multo post; **— ago**
iamdudum, iampridem; **— before** multo
ante; **it would take too — to ...** longum
erat *(w. inf);* **—er** diutius; **too —** nimium diu
long *intr* avēre; **to — for** desiderare
long-distance number *s* numer·us -i *m* longin-
quus
longed-for *adj* expectat·us -a -um
longevity *s* longaevit·as -atis *f*
longing *s* desider·ium -(i)i *n*
longing *adj* avid·us -a -um
longingly *adv* avide
longitude *s* longitud·o -inis *f*
long jump *s (sports)* salt·us -ūs *m* in longum
long-lasting *adj* diutin·us -a -um
long-lived *adj* viv·ax -acis, longaev·us -a -um
long-sleeved *adj* manicat·us -a -um
long-standing *adj* vetustissim·us -a -um
long-suffering *adj* pati·ens -entis
long-winded *adj* long·us -a -um

look s *(act of looking)* aspect·us -ūs *m; (facial expression)* vult·us -ūs *m; (appearance)* speci·es -ei *f;* —s *(general appearance)* habit·us -ūs *m*
look *intr* aspicere; *(to seem)* videri; **he** —s **stern** severitas inest in vultu eius; **I don't know what he (she)** —s **like** quā sit facie nescio; **it** —s **that way to me** ita mihi videtur; — **!** aspice!; — **here, you!** eho, tu! **to** — **about** circumspicere; **to** — **after** curare; **to** — **after oneself** sibi consulere; **to** — **around** respicere, circumspicere; **to** — **around for** prospicere; **to** — **at** intueri, aspicere; *(to study)* considerare; **to** — **back** respicere; **to** — **down** despicere; **to** — **down on** despicere *(w. acc);* **to** — **for** quaerere; **to** — **forward to** exspectare; **to** — **glad** laetitiam vultu aperte ferre; **to look into** *(lit & fig)* inspicere; *(to examine)* perscrutari; **to** — **into one's own mind** introspicere in mentem suam; **to** — **on** intueri, observare; **to** — **out** prospicere; **to** — **out for** quaerere; **to** — **out of the window** ex fenestrā prospicere; **to** — **s.o. in the face** rectis oculis aliquem aspicere; **to** — **towards** spectare; **to** — **up** suspicere, oculos erigere; *(to research)* inquirere in *(w. acc);* **to** — **up at** suspicere; **to** — **up to** *(implying respect)* suspicere; **to** — **up to heaven** in caelum suspicere; **to** — **upon** *(to regard)* habēre
looker-on s specta·tor -toris *m* (·trix -tricis *f)*
look-out s *(person)* specula·tor -toris *m* (·trix -tricis *f); to keep a careful* — omnia circumspectare
loom s tel·a -ae *f*
loom *intr* in conspectum prodire
loop s sin·us -ūs *m*
loophole s *(in a law)* rim·a -ae *f*
loose *adj* lax·us -a -um; *(flowing, slack)* flux·us -a -um; *(not chaste)* dissolut·us -a -um; — **bowels** fusa alv·us -i *f*
loose-leaf folder s collector·ium -(i)i *n*
loose-leaf tablet s codicill·us -i *m* chartarum
loosely *adv* laxe; *(dissolutely)* dissolute
loosen *tr* solvere, laxare **‖** *intr* solvi
lop *tr* **to** — **off** praecidere; *(in pruning)* amputare
lop-sided *adj* inaequal·is -is -e
loquacious *adj* loqu·ax -acis
lord s domin·us -i *m*
Lord s Domin·us -i *m*
lord *intr* **to** — **it over** dominari in *(w. acc)*
lordly *adj* imperios·us -a -um
lordship s dominati·o -onis *f*
lore s doctrin·a -ae *f*
lose *tr (mostly unintentionally)* amittere, *(mostly blamably)* perdere; **to** — **one eye** altero oculo capi; **to** — **heart** deficere; **to** — **one's way** (ab)errare, viā decedere

loss s *(act)* amissi·o -onis *f; (damage sustained)* damn·um -i *n; (com, fin)* iactur·a -ae *f; (mil)* adversa pugn·a -ae *f; (pol)* repuls·a -ae *f;* **to incur some** — aliquid damni contrahere; **to suffer a** — damnum *(or* repulsam) ferre, iacturam facere
lost *adj* perdit·us -a -um; **to be** — perire; **to get** — aberrare
lot s sor·s -tis *f; (destiny)* fat·um -i *n; (piece of land)* agell·us -i *m;* **a** — *(coll)* multum; **a better** *(coll)* multo melior; **casting of** —s sortiti·o -onis *f;* —s **of people** mult·i -orum *mpl;* **to draw** —s **for** sortiri
lotion s liniment·um -i *n*
lottery s sortiti·o -onis *f*
loud *adj* magn·us -a -um **‖** *adv* magnā voce, clare
loudmouth s clama·tor -toris *m* (·trix -tricis *f)*
loudspeaker s magaphon·um -i *n*
lounge s *(room)* exedr·ium -(i)i *n; (couch)* lectul·us -i *m*
lounge *intr* otiari
louse s pedicul·us -i *m; (pej)* lubric·us -i *m*
lousy *adj* pediculos·us -a -um; *(coll)* foed·us -a -um
lout s rustic·us -i *m*
loutish *adj* rustic·us -a -um
lovable *adj* amabil·is -is -e
love s am·or -oris *m; to be in love with* amare; **to fall in** — **with** in amorem *(w. gen)* incidere
love *tr* amare, diligere
love affair s am·or -oris *m*
loveliness s venust·as -atis *f*
lovely *adj* venust·us -a -um
love potion s philtr·um -i *n*
lover s am·ans -antis *mf; (homosexual partner)* fra·ter -tris *m*
loveseat s bisell·ium -(i)i *n* (tomento fartum)
lovesick *adj* amore ae·ger -gra -grum
loving *adj* am·ans -antis
low *adj (close to the ground; in status)* humil·is -is -e; *(of price)* vil·is -is -e; *(of birth)* obscur·us -a -um; *(low-pitched)* grav·is -is -e; *(not loud)* summiss·us -a -um; *(depressed)* trist·is -is -e; *(vile)* turp·is -is -e; **at** — **tide** ubi aestus recessit; — **interest** leve faen·us -oris *n*
low *adv* humiliter; summissā voce
low *intr* mugire
lowborn *adj* degen·er -eris
lower *tr* demittere, deprimere; *(price)* imminuere
lower *adj* infer·ior -ior -ius; — **jaw** mandibul·a -ae *f; of the* — **world** infer·us -a -um; **the** — **world** infer·i -orum *mpl*
lowermost *adj* infim·us -a -um
lowing s mugit·us -ūs *m*
lowlands *spl* campestr·ia -ium *npl*

lowly *adj* humil·is -is -e
loyal *adj* fidel·is -is -e, fid·us -a -um; **to remain —** in fide manēre
loyally *adv* fideliter
loyalty *s* fidelit·as -atis *f*
lube job *s* uncti·o -onis *f* autocineti
lubricate *tr* unguere
lucid *adj* lucid·us -a -um
Lucifer *s* Lucif·er -eri *m*
luck *s* fortun·a -ae *f;* **bad —** fortun·a -ae *f,* infortun·ium -(i)i *n;* **good —** fortun·a -ae *f;* **good —! feliciter!
luckily *adv* feliciter
luckless *adj* infel·ix -icis
lucky *adj* fel·ix -icis; **— stiff** Fortunae fil·ius -(i)i *m*
lucrative *adj* lucrativ·us -a -um
lucre *s* lucr·um -i *n*
ludicrous *adj* ridicul·us -a -um
ludicrously *adv* ridicule
lug *tr* trahere
luggage *s* sarcin·ae -arum *fpl*
luggage rack *s* retinacul·um -i *n* sarcinale
luggage tag *s* pittac·ium -(i)i *n* sarcinale
lukewarm *adj* tepid·us -a -um; *(fig)* segn·is -is -e, frigid·us -a -um
lukewarmly *adv* segniter
lull *s* qui·es -etis *f*
lull *tr* sopire; *(to calm, as a storm)* sedare; *(fig)* demulcēre
lullaby *s* lall·um -i *n*
lumber *s* materi·a -ae *f*
luminary *s* lum·en -inis *n*
luminous *adj* lucid·us -a -um; *(fig)* dilucid·us -a -um
lump *s* glaeb·a -ae *f,* mass·a -ae *f; (on the body)* tub·er -eris *n*
lump *tr* **to — together** coacervare; **to — s.o. together with** aliquem accudere *(w. dat)*
lumpy *adj* glaebos·us -a -um
lunacy *s* alienati·o -onis *f* mentis
lunar *adj* lunar·is -is -e
lunatic *s* insan·us -i *m* (·a -ae *f)*
lunch *s* prand·ium -(i)i *n;* **to eat (have) —** prandium sumere; **to have for —** in prandium habēre
lunch *intr* prandēre
luncheon *s* prand·ium -(i)i *n*
lung *s* pulm·o -onis *m*
lunge *s* ict·us -ūs *m*
lunge *intr* prosalire
lurch *s* propuls·us -ūs *m;* **to leave in a —** derelinquere
lurch *intr* titubare
lure *s* illecebr·a -ae *f; (bait)* esc·a -ae *f*
lure *tr* allicere; *(an animal)* inescare
lurid *adj* horrend·us -a -um
lurk *intr* latēre, latitare
luscious *adj* praedulc·is -is -e, suav·is -is -e

lush *adj* luxurios·us -a -um
lust *s* libid·o -inis *f; (for power, etc.)* cupidit·as -atis *f*
lust *intr* **to — after** concupiscere
luster *s* splend·or -oris *m*
lustful *adj* libidinos·us -a -um
lustfully *adv* libidinose, lascive
lustily *adv* valide
lusty *adj* valid·us -a -um
luxuriance *s* luxuri·es -ei *f*
luxuriant *adj* luxurios·us -a -um; *(fertile, rich)* laet·us -a -um
luxuriate *intr* luxuriare
luxurious *adj* sumptuos·us -a -um
luxuriously *adv* sumptuose
luxury *s* luxuri·a -ae *f*
lye *s* lixivi·a -ae *f*
lying *adj* mend·ax -acis, falsiloqu·us -a -um
lying *s* mendacit·as -atis *f*
lymph *s* lymph·a -ae *f*
lynx *s* lyn·x -cis *mf*
lyre *s* lyr·a -ae *f*
lyric *adj* lyric·us -a -um
lyric *s* (lyricum) carm·en -inis *n*

M

macaroni *s* collyr·a -ae *f,* past·a -ae *f* tubulata
mace *s* virg·a -ae *f*
machination *s* dol·us -i *m*
machine *s* machin·a -ae *f*
machinery *s* machinament·um -i *n*
machinist *s* machinat·or -oris *m*
mackerel *s* scom·ber -bri *m*
mad *adj* insan·us -a -um, furios·us -a -um; *(angry)* irat·us -a -um; **to be —** furere; **to be — about s.o.** *(to be madly in love with)* aliquem deperire; **to be — at s.o.** suscensēre *(w. dat);* **to go —** mente alienari
madam *s* domin·a -ae *f*
madden *tr* mentem alienare *(w. dat); (fig)* furiare
maddening *adj* molest·us -a -um, exacerb·ans -antis
madly *adv* furiose; **to be — in love** insane amare
madman *s* hom·o -inis *m* furiosus
madness *s* fur·or -oris *m*
magazine *s* *(journal)* commentari·i -orum *mpl* periodici imaginei; *(storehouse)* horre·um -i *n*
maggot *s* verm·is -is *m*
magic *adj* magic·us -a -um; **to perform — tricks** praestigiari
magic *s* magica ar·s -tis *f*
magically *adv* velut magicā quādam arte et vi

magician *s* mag·us -i *m*, mag·a -ae *f*
magisterial *adj* ad magistratum pertin·ens -entis
magistracy *s* magistrat·us -ūs *m*
magistrate *s* magistrat·us -ūs *m*
magnanimity *s* magnanimit·as -atis *f*
magnanimous *adj* magnanim·us -a -um
magnet *s* magn·es -etis *m*
magnetic *adj* magnetic·us -a -um
magnificence *s* magnificenti·a -ae *f*
magnificent *adj* magnific·us -a -um
magnificently *adv* magnifice
magnify *tr* amplificare
magnitude *s* magnitud·o -inis *f*
maid *s* ancill·a -ae *f*
maiden *s* virg·o -inis *f*
maidenhood *s* virginit·as -atis *f*
maidenly *adj* virginal·is -is -e
mail *s* res, rerum *fpl* cursuales; *(letters)* epistul·ae -arum *fpl; (postal system)* curs·us -ūs *m* publicus; *(armor)* loric·a -ae *f;* **to deliver (forward) the —** res cursuales reddere (deferre); **stack of —** multiiugae litterae *fpl*
mail *tr* dare
mailbox *s* capsul·a -ae *f* tabellaria
mailman *s* tabellar·ius -(i)i *m*
maim *tr* mutilare
maimed *adj* manc·us -a -um
main *adj* praecipu·us -a -um; **the — point** cap·ut -itis *n;* **in the —** magnā ex parte
main *s* pelag·us -i *m*
mainland *s* contin·ens -entis *f*
mainly *adv* praecipue
main road *s* vi·a -ae *f* principalis
maintain *tr (to keep)* tenēre; *(to keep alive)* alere; *(to defend)* sustinēre; *(to argue)* affirmare
maintenance *s (support)* sustentati·o -onis *f; (means of living)* vict·us -ūs *m*
majestic *adj* august·us -a -um; **how — was his address!** quanta fuit in oratione maiestas!
majesty *s* maiest·as -atis *f*
major *adj* ma·ior -ior -ius
major *s (mil)* tribun·us -i *m* militaris; *(in logic)* maior praemiss·a -ae *f; (educ)* disciplin·a -ae *f* primaria
major in *intr* operam primariam *(cuidam disciplinae)* dare
majority *s* maior par·s -tis *f*
make *s* form·a -ae *f,* figur·a -ae *f*
make *tr* facere; *(to render by molding, shaping)* fingere; *(to render)* reddere; *(to construct)* fabricare; *(to appoint)* creare; *(to force)* cogere; **to — amends for** corrigere; **to — believe (that)** assimulare quasi *(w. subj),* simulare *(w. acc & inf);* **to — fun of** eludere; **to — haste** festinare; **to — light of** parvi facere; **to — money** pecuniam facere; **to — much of** magni facere; **to — over** transferre;

to — peace pacem parere; **to — public** publicare; **to — the bed** lectum sternere; **to — up *(story)*** fingere; **to — up for lost time** cessata tempora corrigere; **to — up with (s.o)** reverti in gratiam cum *(w. abl);* **to — use of** uti *(w. abl);* **to — way for** cedere *(w. dat),* viam dare *(dat)* ‖ *intr* **to — away with** amovēre; **to — do** suppetere; **to — for** petere
make-believe *adj* fict·us -a -um
maker *s* fabrica·tor -toris *m* (·trix -tricis f)
make-up *s* compositi·o -onis *f; (disposition)* indol·es -is *f; (cosmetics)* fuc·us -i *m*
maladministration *s* mala administrati·o -onis *f*
malady *s* morb·us -i *m*
malaria *f* malari·a -ae *f*
malcontent *adj* dissid·ens -entis
male *adj* masculin·us -a -um
male *s* ma·s -ris *m*
malevolence *s* malevolenti·a -ae *f*
malevolent *adj* malevol·us -a -um
malice *s* malevolenti·a -ae *f*
malicious *adj* malevol·us -a -um
maliciously *adv* malevolo animo
malign *tr* obtrectare
malignant *adj* malevol·us -a -um; *(med)* malign·us -a -um
mall *s* for·um -i *n*
mallet *s* malle·us -i *m*
malnutrition *s* aliment·um -i *n* tenue
malpractice *s* delict·a -orum *npl*
maltreat *tr* vexare, abuti *(w. abl); (w. blows, etc.)* mulcare
mama *s* mamm·a -ae *f*
man *s (human being)* hom·o -inis *m; (male)* vir, viri *m*
man *tr (ships)* complēre; *(the walls)* praesidio firmare
manage *tr* curare; *(a bank)* moderari; *(esp. on large scale)* administrare, gerere; **if you can — it** si id conficere poteris
manageable *adj* tractabil·is -is -e
management *s* cur·a -ae *f,* administrati·o -onis *f*
manager *s* cura·tor -toris *m* (·trix -tricis *f); (steward)* procurat·or -oris *m; (of an estate)* villic·us -i *m; (of a bank)* modera·tor -toris *m* (·trix -tricis *f)*
mandate *s* mandat·um -i *n*
mane *s* iub·a -ae *f*
maneuver *s (mil)* decurs·us -ūs *m; (trick)* dol·us -i *m*
maneuver *intr (mil)* decurrere; *(fig)* machinari, tractare
manger *s* praesep·e -is *n*
mangle *tr* lacerare, dilaniare
manhood *s* virilit·as -atis *f; (period of puberty)* pubert·as -atis *f*
mania *s* insani·a -ae *f*

maniac *s* furios·us -i *m* (·a -ae *f*)
manifest *adj* manifest·us -a -um
manifest *tr* manifestare, declarare
manifestation *s* patefacti·o -onis *f*
manifestly *adv* manifeste
manifesto *s* edict·um -i *n*
manifold *adj* vari·us -a -um
maniple *s* manipul·us -i *m*
manipulate *intr* tractare
manipulation *s* tractati·o -onis *f*
mankind *s* gen·us -eris *n* humanum
manliness *s* virt·us -utis *f;* **to act with —** viriliter agere
manly *adj* viril·is -is -e
manner *s* mod·us -i *m; (custom)* consuetud·o -inis *f;* **after the — of** ritu *(w. gen),* more *(w. gen);* **bad —s** rusticit·as -atis *f;* **good —s** urbanit·as -atis *f;* **in a cruel —** crudelem in modum
mannerism *s* mala affectati·o -onis *f*
mannerly *adj* urban·us -a -um
mannikin *s* homuncul·us -i *m* (·a -ae *f*)
man-of-war *s* nav·is -is *f* longa
manor *s* praed·ium -(i)i *n*
man servant *s* serv·us -i *m*
mansion *s* dom·us -ūs *f*
manslaughter *s* homicid·ium -(i)i *n*
mantel *s* plute·us -i *m* fornacis
mantle *s (women's outdoor wear)* pall·a -ae *f; (fig)* velament·um -i *n*
mantle *tr* tegere, dissimulare
manual *adj* manual·is -is -e; **— labor** oper·a -ae *f* quae manibus exercetur
manual *s* enchiridi·on -onis *n,* ars, artis *f*
manufacture *s* fabric·a -ae *f*
manufacture *tr* fabricari
manufacturer *s* fabrica·tor -toris *m* (·rix -ricis *f*)
manure *s* sterc·us -oris *n*
manure *tr* stercorare
manuscript *s* cod·ex -icis *m*
many *adj* mult·i -ae -a; **a good —** nonnull·i -ae -a; **as — ... as** quot ... tot; **how —** quot [*indecl*]; **in — ways** multifariam; **so —** tot [*indecl*]
many-colored *adj* multicol·or -oris
many-sided *adj* multipl·ex -icis; *(fig)* versatil·is -is -e
map *s* tabul·a -ae *f* geographica; **— of the world** orb·is -is *m* terrarum pictus
map *tr* **to — out** designare
maple *adj* acern·us -a -um
maple tree *s* ac·er -eris *n*
mar *tr* foedare; *(esp. fig)* deformare
marauder *s* praedat·or -oris *m*
marauding *s* praedati·o -onis *f*
marble *adj* marmore·us -a -um
marble *s* marm·or -oris *n*

March *s* Mart·ius -(i)i *m or* mens·is -is *m* Martius; **in — mense** Martio; **on the first of — Kalendis** Martiis
march *s* iter, itineris *n*
march *tr* ducere **‖** *intr* iter facere, incedere; **to — on** signa proferre
mare *s* equ·a -ae *f*
margarine *s* margarin·um -i *n*
margin *s* marg·o -inis *mf*
marginal *adj* margini ascript·us -a -um
marigold *s* calth·a -ae *f*
marijuana *s* cannab·is -is *f;* **to smoke —** fumum cannabis sugere
marine *adj* marin·us -a -um
marine *s* mil·es -itis *mf* classic·us (-a); **the —s** classiari·i -orum *mpl*
mariner *s* naut·a -ae *m*
maritime *adj* maritim·us -a -um
mark *s* not·a -ae *f; (sign, token)* indic·ium -(i)i *n; (brand)* stigm·a -atis *n; (blemish)* macul·a -ae *f; (target)* scop·us -i *m; (of wound)* cicatr·ix -icis *f; (characteristic)* expressed with gen after verb esse, *e.g.,* **it is the — of a small mind** pusilli animi est
mark *tr (to draw or make a mark on anything)* notare; *(to observe)* animadvertere; *(with pencil, etc.)* designare; **— my words!** animum intende *(pl:* animos intendite) in mea dicta!; **to — down** scribere; **to — down the price** pretium circumcidere; **to — off** metiri
marked *adj* distinct·us -a -um, manifest·us -a -um
markdown *s* pretii deminuti·o -onis *f*
marker *s* ind·ex -icis *m; (tombstone)* monument·um -i *n*
market *s* macell·um -i *n; (demand)* desider·ium -(i)i *n;* **on the open —** promercal·is -is -e
marketable *adj* venal·is -is -e
market day *s* nundin·ae -arum *fpl*
marketplace *s* for·um -i *n*
market town *s* empor·ium -(i)i *n*
marmalade *s* quil·on -onis *n* ex aurantis confectum
maroon *tr* derelinquere
marriage *s* matrimon·ium -(i)i *n;* **to give a daughter in —** filiam in matrimonio collocare
marriageable *adj (girl)* nubil·is -is -e
marriage alliance *s* affinit·as -atis *f*
marriage contract *s* pacti·o -onis *f* nuptialis
married *adj (of a woman)* nupta; *(of a man)* maritus; **to get —** matrimonio coniungi
marrow *s* medull·a -ae *f*
marry *tr (said of a man)* in matrimonium ducere, uxorem ducere; *(said of a woman)* nubere *(w. dat)*
marsh *s* pal·us -udis *f*
marshal *s* du·x -cis *m*

marshal *tr* disponere
marshy *adj* palus·ter -tris -tre
mart *s* empor·ium -(i)i *n*
martial *adj* bellicos·us -a -um
martyr *s* mart·yr -yris *mf*
martyrdom *s* martyr·ium -(i)i *n*
marvel *s* miracul·um -i *n*
marvel *intr* to — at mirari
marvelous *adj* mir·us -a -um
marvelously *adv* mire
masculine *adj* mascul·us -a -um; *(gram)* masculin·us -a -um
mash *s* mixtur·a -ae *f; (for cattle)* forag·o -inis *f*
mash *tr* commiscēre; *(to bruise)* contundere
mask *s* person·a -ae *f*
mask *tr (fig)* dissimulare
mason *s* lapidar·ius -(i)i *m*
masonry *s* op·us -eris *n* caementicium
mass *adj* tot·us -a -um; *(large-scale)* magnari·us -a -um
mass *s* mol·es -is *f; (large amount)* copi·a -ae *f; (of people)* turb·a -ae *f; (eccl)* miss·a -ae *f;* the —es vulg·us -i *n*
mass *tr* congerere, coacervare ‖ *intr* congeri, coacervari
massacre *s* trucidati·o -onis *f*
massacre *tr* trucidare
massage *s* iatraliptic·e -es *f*
massage *tr* fricare
masseur *s* iatralipt·es -ae *m*
masseuse *s* iatralipt·es -ae *f*
massive *adj* solid·us -a -um, ing·ens -entis
mast *s (of ship)* mal·us -i *m; (for cattle)* glan·s -dis *f*
master *s* domin·us -i *m; (teacher)* magis·ter -tri *m; (controller)* arbi·ter -tri *m;* to be — of potens esse *(w. gen)*, compos esse *(w. gen);* not be — of impotens esse *(w. gen)*
master *tr* superare; *(to learn)* perdiscere; *(passion)* continēre
masterful *adj* pot·ens -entis, imperios·us -a -um
master key *s* clav·is -is *m* complures ianuas aperiens
masterly *adj* perit·us -a -um
master of ceremony *s* magis·ter -tri *m* convivii
masterpiece *s* magnum op·us -eris *n*
master's degree *s* grad·us -us *m* magistralis
mastery *s* dominati·o -onis *f;* having — of pot·ens -entis *(w. gen)*
masticate *tr* mandere
mastiff *s* Moloss·us -i *m*
mat *s* teg·es -etis *f*
match *s (marriage)* nupti·ae -arum *fpl; (contest)* certam·en -inis *n; (an equal)* par paris *mf; (to light)* rament·um -i *n* flammiferum; a — for par *(w. dat);* not a — for impar *(w. dat)*

match *tr* adaequare ‖ *intr* quadrare
matchless *adj* incomparabil·is -is -e
match maker *s* nuptiarum concilia·tor -toris *m* (·trix -tricis *f)*
mate *s* soc·ius -(i)i *m (·a -ae f); (spouse)* coniu·(n)x -gis *mf*
mate *intr* coïre
material *adj* corpore·us -a -um; *(significant)* haud lev·is -is -e
material *s* materi·a -ae *f; (cloth)* textil·e -is *n*
materially *adv* magnopere
maternal *adj* matern·us -a -um; — aunt materter·a -ae *f;* — uncle avuncul·us -i *m*
maternity dress *s* puerperae vest·is -is *f*
mathematical *adj* mathematic·us -a -um
mathematician *s* mathematic·us -i *m (·a -ae f)*
mathematics *s* mathematic·a -ae *f*
matrimony *s* matrimon·ium -(i)i *n*
matrix *s* form·a -ae *f*
matron *s* matron·a -ae *f*
matronly *adj* matronal·is -is -e
matter *s (substance)* materi·a -ae *f; (affair)* res, rei *f; (med)* pus, puris *n;* for that — adeo; no — nihil interest; no — how ... quamvis *(w. subj);* what on earth's the —? quidnam est?; what's the — with you? quid est tibi *(or* tecum)?
matter *intr impers* refert; it does not — nihil interest; nihil refert; it —s a lot multum *or* magnopere refert; what does that — to me (to you)? quid refert meā (tuā)?
matting *s* teget·es -um *fpl*
mattress *s* culcit·a -ae *f;* air — culcita inflatilis
mature *adj* matur·us -a -um
mature *intr* maturare
maturely *adv* mature
maturity *s* maturit·as -atis *f*
maul *tr* mulcare
mausoleum *s* mausole·um -i *n*
maw *s* ingluvi·es -ei *f*
mawkish *adj* putid·us -a -um
mawkishly *adv* putide
maxim *s* axiom·a -atis *n; (rule, precept)* praecept·um -i *n*
maximum *adj* quam maxim·us -a -um
maximum *s* maxim·um -i *n,* summ·um -i *n*
May *s* Mai·us -i *m or* mens·is -is *m* Maius; in — mense Maio; on the first of — Kalendis Maiis
may *intr* posse; — I leave? licetne mihi abire? *or* licetne mihi (ut) abeam?; *(possibility, expressed by subj):* I — go eam; perhaps s.o. may say fortasse quispiam dixerit
maybe *adv* forsitan, fortasse
mayhem *s* iniuri·a -ae *f* violenta corporis; *(havoc)* strag·es -is *f*
mayonnaise *s* liquam·en -inis *n* Nagonicum
mayor *s* praefect·us -i *m (·a -ae f)* urbi
mayoralty *s* praefectur·a -ae *f* urbi

maze *s* labyrinth·us -i *m*
me *pron* me; **by** — a me; **to** — mihi; **with** — mecum
mead *s (drink)* muls·um -i *n*
meadow *s* prat·um -i *n*
meager *adj* exil·is -is -e; *(insufficient)* exigu·us -a -um
meagerly *adv* exiliter
meagerness *s* exilit·as -atis *f*
meal *s* cib·us -i *m; (flour)* farin·a -ae *f;* **to eat a** — cibum sumere
mealymouthed *adj* blandiloqu·us -a -um
mean *adj (middle)* medi·us -a -um; *(low)* humil·is -is -e; *(cruel)* vil·is -is -e
mean *s* med·ium -(i)i *n*
mean *tr* significare; *(after s.th. has been mentioned)* dicere, *e.g.,* **of course, you** — **Plato** Platonem videlicet dicis; *(to intend)* velle, in animo habēre; **do you** — **me?** mene vis?; **Yes, I do** aio; **how do you** — **that?** qui istuc vis?; **now you know what I** — scis iam quid loquar; **what does this** — quid hoc sibi vult?; **what do you** — **by that?** quid istuc est verbi?; **what I** — **is** *(in correcting a misunderstanding)* at enim; **what does my father** —**?** quid sibi vult pater?
meander *intr* sinuoso cursu labi
meaning *s* sens·us -ūs *m,* significati·o -onis *f;* **basic** — princeps significatio
meaningful *adj* signific·ans -antis
meanness *s (lowliness)* humilit·as -atis *f; (cruelty)* crudelit·as -atis *f*
means *spl (way, method)* rati·o -onis *f,* mod·us -i *m;* **by all** — maxime, omnino; **by fair** — recte; **by** — **of** *render by abl or* per *(w. acc);* **by no** — haudquaquam
meantime *adv see* **meanwhile**
meanwhile *adv* **in the** — interea, interim
measles *spl* morbill·i -orum *mpl*
measurable *adj* mensurabil·is -is -e
measure *s* mensur·a -ae *f; (proper measure)* mod·us -i *m; (course of action)* rati·o -onis *f; (leg)* rogati·o -onis *f;* **beyond** — supra modum; **in some** — aliquā ex parte; **to take** —**s** consulere *(w. dat of that on behalf of which;* in *w. acc of person against whom)*
measure *tr* metiri; **to** — **off** metari **‖** *intr* patēre, colligere; **measuring ten miles in circumference** patens *(or* colligens*)* decem milia passuum circuitu
measurement *s* mensur·a -ae *f*
meat *s* car·o -nis *f*
meatball *s* globul·us -i *m* carneus
meat grinder *s* machin·a -ae *f* carnaria
meat tray *s* carnar·ium -(i)i *n*
meaty *adj (fig)* sententios·us -a -um
mechanic *s* opif·ex -icis *m*
mechanical *adj* mechanic·us -a -um; — **engineer** mechinat·or -oris *m*

mechanics *s* mechanica ar·s -tis *f*
mechanism *s* mechinati·o -onis *f,* instrument·um -i *n*
medal *s* **(gold, silver, bronze)** insign·e -is *n* (aureum, argenteum, aereum)
medallion *s* nomism·a -atis *n* sollemne
meddle *intr* **(in)** se interponere (in *w. acc)*
meddler *s* ardali·o -onis *mf*
meddlesome *adj* curios·us -a -um
medial *adj* medi·us -a -um
median *adj* dimidi·us -a -um
median *s* mediocrit·as -atis *f*
mediate *tr* conciliare **‖** *intr* se interponere ad componendam litem; **to** — **between estranged friends** aversos amicos componere
mediation *s* intercessi·o -onis *f*
mediator *s* interces·sor -soris *m (·rix* -ricis *f)*
medical *adj* medic·us -a -um; — **practice** medicin·a -ae *f*
medicate *tr* medicare
medication *s* medicament·um -i *n*
medicinal *adj* medicat·us -a -um
medicine *s (science)* medicin·a -ae *f; (remedy)* medicament·um -i *n;* **to practice** — medicinam exercēre
medieval *adj* medii aevi *(gen used as adj)*
mediocre *adj* mediocr·is -is -e
mediocrity *s* mediocrit·as -atis *f*
meditate *intr* cogitare, meditari
meditation *s* cogitati·o -onis *f,* meditati·o -onis *f*
meditative *adj* cogitabund·us -a -um
Mediterranean *s* mar·e -is *n* internum, mar·e -is *n* nostrum
medium *s (middle)* med·ium -(i)i *n; (expedient)* mod·us -i *m; (agency)* concilia·tor -toris *m (·trix* -tricis *f)*
medium *adj* mediocr·is -is -e
medley *s* farrag·o -inis *f*
meek *adj* mit·is -is -e; *(unassuming)* summiss·us -a -um
meekly *adv* summisse
meekness *s* anim·us -i *m* summissus
meet *tr* convenire, obviam ire *(w. dat); (danger, death, etc.)* obire **‖** *intr* convenire; *(to converge)* confluere; *(to cross)* intersecare; **to** — **half way** compromittere; **to** — **with** offendere, subire
meet *s (contest)* certam·en -inis *n*
meeting *s (of two or many individuals)* congress·us -ūs *m; (assembly)* convent·us -ūs *m; (for consultation)* consil·ium -(i)i *n;* **to hold a** — conventum habēre; consilium habēre
megaphone *s* megaphon·um -i *n*
melancholy *s* maestiti·a -ae *f*
melancholy *adj* maest·us -a -um
melee *s* turb·a -ae *f,* tumult·us -ūs *m*

mellow *adj* matur·us -a -um; *(from drinking)* temulent·us -a -um
melodious *adj* canor·us -a -um
melodiously *adv* canore, modulate
melodramatic *adj* **to be** — paratragoedare
melody *s* mel·os -i *n,* melodi·a -ae *f,* cant·us -ūs *m*
melt *tr* liquefacere, dissolvere; **to** — **down** conflare ‖ *intr* liquescere
melting *s* liquati·o -onis *f*
melting pot *s* mixtur·a -ae *f* multarum gentium
member *s (of the body)* membr·um -i *n; (part)* pars, partis *f; (of an organization)* sodal·is -is *mf*
membership *s (the members)* sodal·es -ium *mpl;* **to be admittted to** — sodalis ascribi *or* cooptari
membrane *s* membran·a -ae *f*
memento *s* monument·um -i *n*
memoirs *spl* commentari·i -orum *mpl*
memorable *adj* memorabil·is -is -e
memorandum *s* not·a -ae *f*
memorial *adj* memoral·is -is -e; — **service** rit·us -ūs *m* memoralis
memorial *s* monument·um -i *n*
memorize *tr* memoriae mandare, ediscere
memory *s* memori·a -ae *f; from* — ex memoriā, memoriter; **if** — **serves me right** si ego satis commemini; **in** — **of** in memoriam *(w. gen);* **to commit to** — memoriae mandare; **to have a good** — esse memoriā bonā; **within the** — **of man** post hominum memoriam
menace *s* min·ae -arum *fpl*
menace *tr* minari, minitari; *(of things)* imminēre *(w. dat)*
menacing *adj* min·ax -acis; *(only of persons)* minitabund·us -a -um
mend *tr* emendare; *(clothes)* sarcire ‖ *intr (to improve in health)* melior fieri
mendicant *s* mendic·us -i *m* (·a -ae *f)*
menial *adj* servil·is -is -e
menial *s* serv·us -i *m,* serv·a -ae *f*
menses *spl* menstru·a -orum *npl*
mental *adj* mente concept·us -a -um
mentally *adv* mente, animo
mention *s* menti·o -onis *f;* **to make** — **of** mentionem facere *(w. gen)*
mention *tr* commemorare; *(by name)* nominare; **not to** — silentio praeterire; **not to** — **the fact that** ... ut mittam quod *(w. indic);* **not to** — **the others** ne de alteris referam
menu *s* ciborum tabell·a -ae *f; (comput)* iussorum tabella *f*
mercantile *adj* mercatori·us -a -um
mercenary *adj* mercenari·us -a -um
mercenary *s* mil·es -itis *m* mercenarius
merchandise *s* merc·es -ium *fpl*
merchant *s* mercat·or -oris *m; (in a market)* macellari·us -i *m* (·a -ae *f)*

merchant ship *s* nav·is -is *f* mercatoria
merciful *adj* misericor·s -dis
mercifully *adv* misericorditer
merciless *adj* immisericor·s -dis
mercilessly *adv* immisericorditer
mercurial *adj* a·cer -cris -cre
Mercury *s* Mercur·ius -(i)i *m*
mercury *s* argent·um -i *n* vivum
mercy *s* misericordi·a -ae *f*
mere *adj* mer·us -a -um
merely *adv* tantummodo, solum
meretricious *adj* meretrici·us -a -um
merge *tr* confundere ‖ *intr* confundi
meridian *s* meridianus circul·us -i *m*
merit *s* merit·um -i *n*
merit *tr* merēre, merēri
meritorious *adj* laudabil·is -is -e
mermaid *s* nymph·a -ae *f* marina
merrily *adv* festive, hilare
merry *adj* hilar·us -a -um, festiv·us -a -um, fest·us -a -um; **Merry Christmas** fausta festa Natalici·a -ae *f* Christi
merry-go-round *s* orb·is -is *m* volubilis lusorius
merrymaking *s* festivit·as -atis *f*
mesh *s (of net)* macul·a -ae *f*
mess *s (dirt)* squal·or -oris *m; (confusion)* rerum perturbati·o onis *f;* **geez, what a** —! eu edepol res turbulentas!; **to make a** — turbas conciēre
mess *tr* inquinare, foedare; **to** — **up** *(to upset)* conturbare, confundere
message *s* nunt·ius -(i)i *m*
messenger *s* nunti·us -i *m* (·a -ae *f)*
mess hall *s* cenati·o -onis *f*
metal *adj* metallic·us -a -um
metal *s* metall·um -i *n*
metallurgy *s* metallurgi·a -ae *f*
metamorphosis *s* metamorphos·is -is *f,* transfigurati·o -onis *f*
metaphor *s* translati·o -onis *f*
metaphorical *adj* translat·us -a -um
metaphorically *adv* per translationem
metaphysical *adj* metaphysic·us -a -um
metaphysics *s* metaphysic·a -ae *f; (as a title)* metaphysic·a -orum *npl*
meteor *s* fa·x -cis *f* caelestis
meteorology *s* meteorologi·a -ae *f*
mete out *tr* emetiri
meter *s (unit of measure; verse)* metr·um -i *n*
method *s* rati·o -onis *f*
methodical *adj* disposit·us -a -um
methodically *adv* disposite
meticulous *adj* accurat·us -a -um
meticulously *adv* accurate
metonymy *s* metonymi·a -ae *f*
metrical *adj* metric·us -a -um
metropolis *s* cap·ut -itis *n,* metropol·is -is *f*
metropolitan *adj* metropolitan·us -a -um

mettle *s* anim·us -i *m*
miasma *s* noxius halit·us -ūs *m*
microphone *s* microphon·um -i *n*
microscope *s* microscop·ium -(i)i *n*
microwave oven *s* furnul·us -i *m* undarum brevium
mid *adj* medi·us -a -um
midday *adj* meridian·us -a -um
midday *s* meridi·es -ei *f*
middle *adj* medi·us -a -um; — **age** aet·as -atis *f* media
middle *s* med·ium -(i)i *n;* **in the middle of the road** in mediā viā
middle class *s* ord·o -inis *m* medius; *(Roman)* equit·es -um *mpl*
middle school *s* schol·a -ae *f* media
midget *s* pumili·o -onis *mf*
midnight *s* media no·x -ctis *f;* **around** — mediā circiter nocte; **at** — (de) media nocte
midriff *s* diaphragm·a -atis *n*
midst *s* med·ium -(i)i *n;* **in the** — **of** inter *(w. acc)*
midsummer *s* summa aest·as -atis *f*
midway *adv* medi·us -a -um; **he stood** — **between the lines** stabat medius inter acies
midwife *s* obstetr·ix -icis *f*
midwinter *s* brum·a -ae *f*
midwinter *adj* brumal·is -is -e
might *s* vis *f;* **with all one's** — summā ope; **with** — **and main** manibus pedibusque
might *intr* render by imperfect subjunctive: **he might say** diceret
mightily *adv* valde
mighty *adj* validissim·us -a -um
migraine *s* hemicrani·a -ae *f;* **to have a** — **headache** dolere ab hemicraniā
migrate *intr* migrare
migration *s* migrati·o -onis *f*
migratory *adj* migr·ans -antis; — **birds** volucr·es -um *fpl* advenae
mild *adj* mit·is -is -e; *(esp. of weather)* clem·ens -entis; **to grow** — mitescere
mildew *s* muc·or -oris *m*
mildewed *adj* **to become** — mucorem contrahere
mildness *s* lenit·as -atis *f; (of weather)* clementi·a -ae *f*
mile *s* mille *n* passūs; **three** —**s** tria milia *npl* passuum
milestone *s* milliar·ium -i(i) *n; (fig)* gradati·o -onis *f*
militant *adj* milit·ans -antis
military *adj* militar·is -is -e; — **age** aet·as -atis *f* militaris; — **command** imper·ium -(i)i *n;* — **service** militi·a -ae *f;* **to perform** — **service** militare
military *s* militi·a -ae *f*
militia *s* militi·a -ae *f* domestica
milk *s* lac, lactis *n*

milk *tr* mulgēre
milky *adj* lacte·us -a -um
Milky Way *s* Vi·a -ae *f* Lactea
mill *s* mol·a -ae *f; (factory)* fabric·a -ae *f*
mill *intr* — **around** circumfundi, tumultuari
millennium *s* mille ann·i -orum *mpl*
miller *s* pist·or -oris *m*
million *adj* decies centena milia *(w. gen)*
millionaire *s* hom·o -inis *mf* praedives
millstone *s* mol·a -ae *f*
mime *s* mim·us -i *m*
mimic *s* imita·tor -toris *m* (·trix -tricis *f*)
mimic *tr* imitari
mimicry *s* imitati·o -onis *f*
mince *tr* concidere; **not to** — **words** Latine loqui; **without mincing words** sine fuco ac fallaciis
mind *s (most general)* anim·us -i *m; (strictly intellectual)* men·s -tis *f;* **it slipped my** — **to write to you** fugit me ad te scribere; **I was out of my** — **when** ... desipiebam mentis cum ... ; **set your** — **at ease** habe animum lenem et tranquillum; **to bear in** — meminisse *(w. gen);* **to be in one's right** — compo·s -tis mentis suae esse; **to be of sound** — comp·os -otis mentis esse; **to be out of one's** — a se alienat·us -a -a esse; **to call to** — cum animo suo recordari; **to change one's** — mentem *(or* sententiam) mutare; **to come to** — in mentem venire, *(coll)* in buccam venire; **to have in** — in animo habēre; **to make up one's** — **to** ... constituere *(w. inf);* **to show presence of** — schemas non loqui; **what's on your** —? quid tibi in animo est
mind *tr (to look after)* curare; *(to regard)* respicere; *(to object to)* aegre ferre; — **your manners!** mores tuos respice!; **never** — **what he says** mitte *(pl:* mittite) quod dicit; **to** — **one's own business** suum negotium agere ‖ *intr* gravari; **I don't** — nil moror; **never** —! sine!
mindful *adj* mem·or -oris
mine *s* fodin·a -ae *f,* metall·um -i *n; (fig)* thesaur·us -i *m*
mine *tr* effodere
mine *adj* me·us -a -um
miner *s* foss·or -oris *m,* metallic·us -i *m*
mineral *s* metall·um -i *n*
mineral *adj* metallic·us -a -um
mineralogist *s* metallorum perit·us -i *m*
mineralogy *s* metallorum scienti·a -ae *f*
mineral water *s* aqu·a -ae *f* mineralis
mingle *tr* commiscēre ‖ *intr* se immiscēre
miniature *s* minuta tabul·a -ae *f*
miniature *adj* minut·us -a -um
minimum *adj* quam minim·us -a -um
minimum *s* minim·um -i *n*
minion *s* clien·s -tis *mf*

miniskirt s castul·a -ae f brevissima (or decurtata)

minister s adminis·ter -tri m; (eccl) minis·ter -tri mf, sacerd·os -otis mf

minister intr ministrare

ministry s ministrati·o -onis f

minor s pupill·us -i m, pupill·a -ae f

minor adj min·or -or -us

minority s minor par·s -tis f

minstrel s (vagus) fidic·en -inis m

mint s (for making money) monet·a -ae f; (bot) menth·a -ae f

mint tr cudere

minute s temporis moment·um -i n, minut·a -ae f; any — now iam iamque; in a — momento temporis; the — I saw you extemplo ubi ego te vidi; this — (right now) iam; (immediately) actutum; to keep —s acta diurna conficere; wait a —! mane dum!

minute adj (small) minut·us -a -um; (exact) accurat·us -a -um

minutely adv minute, subtiliter

miracle s miracul·um -i n

miraculous adj miraculos·us -a -um

miraculously adv miraculose

mirage s imag·o -inis f ficta

mire s lut·um -i n

mirror s specul·um -i n; to look at oneself in the — se in spectaculo tueri; to look into the — in speculum inspicere

mirth s hilarit·as -atis f

mirthful adj hilar·is -is -e

misadventure s infortun·ium -i(i) n

misapply tr abuti (w. abl)

misapprehend tr male intellegere

misapprehension s falsa concepti·o -onis f

misbehave intr indecore (or male) se gerere

misbehavior s morum pravit·as -atis f

miscalculate tr male iudicare ‖ intr errare

miscalculation s err·or -oris m

miscarriage s abort·us -ūs m; (fig) malus success·us -ūs m

miscarry intr abortum facere; (fig) male succedere

miscellaneous adj miscellane·us -a -um

mischance s infortun·ium -i(i) n

mischief s malefic·ium -i(i) n; (of children) lascivi·a -ae f; to refrain from doing any — ab iniuria et maleficio temperare

mischievous adj malefic·us -a -um; (playful) lasciv·us -a -um

misconceive tr perperam intellegere

misconception s falsa opini·o -onis f

misconduct s delict·um -i n; to be guilty of — delictum in se admittere

misconstrue tr perperam interpretari

misdeed s delict·um -i n

misdemeanor s levius delict·um -i n

misdirect tr fallere

miser s avar·us -i m (·a -ae f)

miserable adj mis·er -era -erum

miserably adv misere

miserly adj avar·us -a -um

misery s miseri·a -ae f

misfortune s infortun·ium -(i)i n

misgiving s sollicitud·o -inis f; to have —s about diffidere (w. dat)

misgovern tr male administrare, male regere

misguide tr seducere

misguided adj (fig) dem·ens -entis

mishap s incommod·um -i n

misinform tr falsa docēre (w. acc)

misinterpret tr perperam interpretari

misinterpretation s prava interpretati·o onis f

misjudge tr & intr male iudicare

mislay tr amittere, alieno loco ponere

mislead tr seducere, decipere

mismanage tr male gerere

mismanagement s mala administrati·o -onis f

misnomer s falsum nom·en -inis n

misplace tr alieno loco ponere; confidence in such persons is —ed is male creditur

misprint s errat·um -i n typographicum, mend·um -i n

misquote tr aliis verbis ponere

misquotation s falsa prolati·o -onis f

misrepresent tr detorquēre

misrepresentation s sinistra interpretati·o -onis f

misrule s prava administrati·o -onis f

miss s err·or -oris m; (term of respect) domin·a -ae f

miss tr (to overlook) omittere; (one's aim) aberrare (w. abl), non attingere; (to feel the want of) desiderare; to — the mark destinato aberrare ‖ intr (to fall short) errare

misshapen adj deform·is -is -e

missile s missil·e -is n

missing adj abs·ens -entis; (lost) amiss·us -a -um; to be — deësse

mission s (delegation, sending) missi·o -onis f; (goal) fin·is -is m

misspell tr perperam scribere

misspend tr prodigere

misstate tr parum accurate memorare

misstatement s fals·um -i n

mist s nebul·a -ae f

mistake s err·or -oris m, errat·um -i n; (esp. in writing) mend·um -i n; by — perperam; full of —s mendos·us -a -um; to make a — errare; you're making a big — erras perverse

mistake tr to — (s.o. or s.th.) for habēre pro (w. abl)

mistaken adj fals·us -a -um; to be — falli; unless I am — ni fallor

mistletoe s visc·um -i n

mistress *s* domin·a -ae *f,* her·a -ae *f; (paramour)* concubin·a -ae *f; (teacher)* magistr·a -ae *f*
mistrust *s* diffidenti·a -ae *f*
mistrust *tr* diffidere *(w. dat)*
mistrustful *adj* diffid·ens -entis
mistrustfully *adv* diffidenter
misty *adj* nebulos·us -a -um
misunderstand *tr* perperam intellegere
misunderstanding *s* falsa opini·o -onis *f; (disagreement)* dissid·ium -(i)i *n*
misuse *s* abus·us -ūs *m;* **that is a — of the term** id est verbum alieno loco adhibēre
misuse *tr* abuti *(w. abl); (to revile)* conviciari
mite *s (bit)* parvul·us -i *m; (coin)* sext·ans -antis *m*
miter *s* mitr·a -ae *f*
mitigate *tr* mitigare
mitigation *s* mitigati·o -onis *f*
mix *tr* miscēre; **to — in** admiscēre; **to — up** commiscēre; *(fig)* confundere
mixed *adj* mixt·us -a -um; *(undistinguished)* promiscu·us -a -um; **— salad** commixta acetari·a -orum *npl*
mixer *s* machin·a -ae *f* mixtoria
mixture *s* mixtur·a -ae *f*
moan *s* gemit·us -ūs *m*
moan *intr* gemere
moat *s* foss·a -ae *f*
mob *s* turb·a -ae *f,* vulg·us -i *n*
mob *tr* stipare
mobile *adj* mobil·is -is -e
mobile home *s* domuncul·a -ae *f* subrotata
mobility *s* mobilit·as -atis *f*
mock *tr* irridēre
mock *adj* mimic·us -a -um; **— death** mimica mor·s -tis *f;* **— sea battle show** naumachiae spectacul·um -i *n*
mockery *s* irrisi·o -onis *f*
mode *s* mod·us -i *m,* rati·o -onis *f; (fashion)* us·us -ūs *m;* **— of life** vitae rati·o -onis *f*
model *s* exempl·ar -aris *n; (of clothes)* vestimentorum monstra·trix -tricis *f (or* monstra·tor -toris *m);* **on the — of** ad simulacrum *(w. gen)*
model *tr* formare; *(e.g., a statue)* fingere; **to — oneself after** imitari
modem *s (comput)* transmodulatr·um -i *n*
moderate *adj (of persons)* moderat·us -a -um; *(of things)* modic·us -a -um; **of — size** modic·us -a -um
moderate *tr* moderari, temperare
moderately *adv* moderate
moderation *s* moderati·o -onis *f*
moderator *s* praes·es -idis *mf*
modern *adj* rec·ens -entis
modest *adj (restricted)* modest·us -a -um, verecund·us -a -um; *(slight)* modic·us -a -um
modestly *adv* verecunde

modesty *s* modesti·a -ae *f,* verecundi·a -ae *f*
modification *s* mutati·o -onis *f*
modify *tr* (im)mutare; *(gram)* adici *(w. dat);* **which noun does "bonus" —?** cui nomini "bonus" adicitur?
modulate *tr* flectere
modulation *s* flexi·o -onis *f*
moist *adj* (h)umid·us -a -um
moisten *tr* (h)umectare
moisture *s* hum·or -oris *m*
molar *s* den·s -tis *m* molaris
molasses *s* sacchari fae·x -cis *f*
mold *s* form·a -ae *f; (mustiness)* muc·or -oris *m*
mold *tr* formare, fingere **II** *intr* mucescere
molder *intr* putrescere
moldiness *s* muc·or -oris *m*
moldy *adj* mucid·us -a -um
mole *s (animal)* talp·a -ae *f; (sea wall)* mol·es -is *f; (on skin)* naev·us -i *m*
molecule *s* particul·a -ae *f*
molehill *s* **to make mountains out of —s** e rivo flumina magna facere
molest *tr* vexare
molt *intr* plumas ponere
molten *adj* liquefact·us -a -um
mom *s* mamm·a -ae *f*
moment *s* temporis moment·um -i *n;* **at any —** omnibus momentis; **at the —** nunc, isto tempore; **at the very —** ipso tempore; **at the very same —** puncto temporis eodem; **for a —** paulisper; **in a —** momento temporis; *(presently)* statim;; **just a — ago** modo
momentarily *adv* statim
momentary *adj* brev·is -is -e
momentous *adj* magni momenti *(gen, used adjectively)*
monarch *s* rex, regis *m*
monarchical *adj* regi·us -a -um
monarchy *s* regn·um -i *n*
monastery *s* monaster·ium -(i)i *n*
Monday *s* di·es -ei *m* Lunae; **every —** singulis diebus Lunae
monetary *adj* pecuniari·us -a -um
money *s* pecuni·a -ae *f,* argent·um -i *n; (of paper)* monet·a -ae *f* chartacea
money belt *s* ventral·e -is *n; (of cloth)* zon·a -ae *f*
moneychanger *s* numular·ius -(i)i *m*
moneylender *s* faenerat·or -oris *m*
money order *s* (nummorum) mandat·um -i *n* cursuale
mongrel *s* hybrid·a -ae *m*
monitor *m* admoni·tor -toris *m* (·trix -tricis *f); (comput)* monitor·ium -(i)i *n*
monk *s* monach·us -i *m*
monkey *s (also as term of abuse)* sim·ius -(i)i *m,* simi·a -ae *f;* **—s chatter** simii strident
monogram *s* monogramm·a -atis *n*
monologue *s* monologi·a -ae *f*

monopolize *tr* monopolium exercēre in *(w. acc)*
monopoly *s* monopol·ium -(i)i *n*
monosyllabic *adj* monosyllab·us -a -um
monosyllable *s* monosyllab·um -i *n*
monotonous *adj* semper idem (eadem, idem); *(sing-song)* canor·us -a -um
monotony *s* taed·ium -(i)i *n*
monster *s* monstr·um -i *n*
monstrosity *s* monstr·um -i *n*
monstrous *adj* monstros·us -a -um
monstrously *adv* monstrose
month *s* mens·is -is *m;* **on the first of the —** Kalendis
monthly *adj* menstru·us -a -um
monthly *adv* singulis mensibus
monument *s* monument·um -i *n*
monumental *adj (huge)* ing·ens -entis; *(important)* grav·is -is -e
moo *intr* mugire
mood *s* animi habit·us -i *m; (gram)* mod·us -i *m;* **imperative (indicative, subjunctive) —** modus imperativus (indicativus, subiunctivus); **to be in a good —** bonum animum habēre; **to get over one's —** animum superare
moodiness *s* morosit·as -atis *f*
moody *adj* moros·us -a -um
moon *s* lun·a -ae *f;* **full —** luna plena; **new —** luna nova; **the — is shining** luna nitescit; **time of full —** plenilun·ium -(i)i *n;* **time of new —** novilun·ium -(i)i *n*
moonlight *s* lunae lum·en -inis *n;* **by —** per lunam
moonshine *s (coll)* temet·um -i *n* illicitum
moonstruck *adj* lunatic·us -a -um
Moor *s* Maur·us -i *m*
moor *tr* religare, ancoris retinēre
moor *s* tesc·a -orum *npl*
moose *s* alc·es -is *f*
mop *s* penicul·us -i *m*
mop *tr* detergēre; **to — up** *(mil)* vestigia hostium amoliri
mope *intr* languescere; *(to be in a gloomy mood)* maerēre
moped *s* autobirot·a -ae *f*
moral *adj (relating to morals)* moral·is -is -e; *(morally proper)* honest·us -a -um, prob·us -a -um
moral *s (of story)* document·um -i *n*
morale *s* anim·us -i *m; (of several)* anim·i -orum *mpl;* **— is low** animi deficiunt
morality *s* boni mor·es -um *mpl,* integrit·as -atis *f*
moralize *intr* de moribus disserere
morals *spl* mor·es -um *mpl*
morass *s* pal·us -udis *f*
morbid *adj* morbid·us -a -um

more *adj* plus *(w. gen); (pl)* plur·es -es -ia; *(denoting greater extent of space or time)* amplius: **for — than four hours** amplius quattuor horis; **— money, strength, power** plus pecuniae, virium, potentiae; **— of this at another time** de hoc alias pluribus; **— than** plus quam; **— than enough** ultra quam satis; **and what's —, he even comes into the senate** immo vero etiam in senatum venit
more *adv* magis; **— and —** magis magisque; **— or less** plus minus; **no — non** diutius; **once —** iterum, denuo
moreover *adv* praeterea
morning *s* mane *n (indecl),* temp·us -oris *n* matutinum; **early in the —** bene mane; **from — till evening** a mane usque ad vesperam; **good —!** salve!; **in the — mane; the next —** mane postridie; **this — hodie** mane; **to sleep all — totum** mane dormire
morning *adj* matutin·us -a -um
morning star *s* Lucif·er -eri *m*
morose *adj* moros·us -a -um
morosely *adv* morose
moroseness *s* morosit·as -atis *f*
morsel *s* off·a -ae *f*
mortal *adj* mortal·is -is -e; *(deadly)* mortif·er -era -erum
mortal *s* mortal·is -is *mf*
mortality *s* mortalit·as -atis *f*
mortally *adv* mortifere; **to be — wounded** mortiferum vulnus accipere
mortar *s* mortar·ium -(i)i *n*
mortgage *s* hypothec·a -ae *f;* **to pay off a —** hypothecam liberare; **to take out a —** hypothecam obligare
mortgage *tr* obligare
mortify *tr (to vex)* offendere
mosaic *s* tessellatum op·us -eris *n*
mosaic floor *s* tesselatum et sectile paviment·um -i *n*
mosquito *s* cul·ex -icis *m*
moss *s* musc·us -i *m*
mossy *adj* muscos·us -a -um
most *adj* plurim·us -a -um, plerusque, -aque, -umque; **for the — part** maximā ex parte; **— people** plerique
most *adv (w. verbs)* maxime; *(w. adjectives and adverbs, expressed by superl., or w. adjectives ending in -ius, expressed w.* maxime *w. positive);* **— enthusiastically** animosissime
mostly *adv (principally, for the most part)* maximam partem; *(generally)* plerumque
motel *s* deversor·ium -(i)i *n* vehicularium
moth *s* blatt·a -ae *f*
moth-eaten *adj* blattis peres·us -a -um
mother *s* ma·ter -tris *f*
motherhood *s* matris stat·us -ūs *m*
mother-in-law *s* socr·us -ūs *f*

motherless *adj* matre orb·us -a -um
motherly *adj* matern·us -a -um
motion *s* mot·us -ūs *m; (proposal of a bill)*
rogati·o -onis *f;* **to make a — regarding**
referre (de *w. abl); to oppose a —* rogationi
obsistere; **to set in —** ciēre, movēre
motion *intr* significare; *(to nod)* innuere
motionless *adj* immot·us -a -um
motivate *tr* concitare
motivation *s* **(for)** rati·o -onis *f (w. gen),* inci-
tament·um -i *n (w. gen); —* **to study** incita-
mentum studiendi
motive *s* rati·o -onis *f; he had a strong —* ratio
magna ei erat
motive *adj* mov·ens -entis
motley *adj* vari·us -a -um
motor *s* motor·ium -(i)i *n,* motr·um -i *n*
motor boat *s* scaph·a -ae *f* automaria
motor oil *s* ole·um -i *n* motorii
motorcycle *s* autobirot·a -ae *f*
motorcyclist *s* autobirotari·us -i *m* (·a -ae *f)*
motorist *s* autoraedari·us -i *m* (·a -ae *f),*
autocinetist·es -ae *mf*
mottled *adj* maculos·us -a -um
motto *s* sententi·a -ae *f,* dict·um -i *n*
mound *s (round)* tumul·us -i *m; (reaching*
lengthwise) agg·er -eris *m*
mount *s* mon·s -tis *m*
mount *tr* conscendere **ǁ** *intr* ascendere
mountain *s* mon·s -tis *m*
mountain chain *s* mont·es -ium *mpl* perpetui
mountaineer *s* montan·us -i *m* (·a -ae *f)*
mountainous *adj* montan·us -a -um
mountain top *s* culm·en -inis *n* summi montis
mounted *adj (on horse)* equestr·is -is -e
mourn *tr & intr* lugēre
mourner *s* plora·tor -toris *m* (·trix -tricis *f)*
mournful *adj* lugubr·is -is -e
mournfully *adv* maeste
mourning *s* maer·or -oris *m; (outward expres-*
sion) luct·us -ūs *m; (dress)* vest·is -is *f*
lugubris; **in —** pullat·us -a -um; **to go into —**
vestitum mutare
mouse *s (animal & comput)* mu·s -ris *m; mice*
squeak mures mintriunt
mouse clicker *s (comput)* muris pulsabul·um
-i *n*
mousetrap *s* muscipul·um -i *n*
mouth *s* os, oris *n; (of beast)* fau·x -cis *f; (of*
river) ost·ium -(i)i *n; (of bottle)* lur·a -ae *f;*
shut your —! obsera os tuum!
mouthful *s* bucc·a -ae *f*
mouthpiece *s* interpr·es -etis *mf*
movable *adj* mobil·is -is -e
movables *spl* mobil·ia -ium *npl*
move *tr* movēre; *(emotionally)* commovēre; *(to*
propose) ferre **ǁ** *intr* movēri, se movēre;
(to change residence) migrare;
to — on progredi

movement *s* mot·us -ūs *m*
movie *s* taeniol·a -ae *f* cinematographica,
fabul·a -ae *f* cinematographica; **to go to see a**
— ludum cinematographicum visere; **to**
show a — taeniolam cinematographicam
exhibēre
movie camera *s* machinul·a -ae *f* cinematographica
movie projector *s* proiectr·um -i *n* cinematographicum
movie screen *s* linte·um -i *n* late extentum
movie theater *s* cinemate·um -i *n;* **to go to the**
— *(or* **to the movies)** in cinemateum ire
moving *adj* flebil·is -is -e, flexanim·us -a -um
mow *tr* resecare; **to — the lawn** pratulum resecare
mower *s* herbisectr·um -i *n*
mowing *s* herbisic·ium -(i)i *n*
much *adj* mult·us -a -um; **as — ... as** tantus ... quantus; **how —** quant·us -a -um;
how — does this cost? quanti hoc constat?;
— less nedum; **so —** tant·us -a -um; **too —**
nimi·us -a -um; **very —** plurim·us -a -um
much *adv* multum; *(w. comparatives)* multo;
very — plurimum
muck *s* sterc·us -oris *n*
mucous *adj* mucos·us -a -um
mucus *s* muc·us -i *m*
mud *s* lut·um -i *n,* lim·us -i *m*
muddle *tr* turbare; *(fig)* perturbare
muddle *s* turb·a -ae *f*
muddy *adj* lutulent·us -a -um; *(troubled)* tur-
bid·us -a -um
muffin *s* scriblit·a -ae *f*
muffle *tr (to wrap up)* involvere; *(to weaken)*
hebetare, diluere; **to — up** obvolvere
muffled *adj* surd·us -a -um
mug *s (cup)* pocul·um -i *n; (face)* vult·us -ūs *m*
mug *tr* mulcare
mugger *s* percuss·or -oris *m*
muggy *adj* humid·us -a -um
mulberry *s* mor·um -i *n*
mulberry tree *s* mor·us -i *f*
mule *s* mul·us -i *m; —s bray* muli rudiunt
mulish *adj* obstinat·us -a -um
mull *intr* **to — over** aestuare in *(w. abl)*
multifarious *adj* vari·us -a -um
multiplication *s* multiplicati·o -onis *f*
multiply *tr* multiplicare **ǁ** *intr* augēri
multitude *s* multitud·o -inis *f; (crowd)* turb·a
-ae *f*
mumble *tr & intr* murmurare
mumps *spl* parotit·is -idis *f*
munch *tr* manducare
mundane *adj* mundan·us -a -um
municipal *adj* municipal·is -is -e
municipality *s* municip·ium -(i)i *n*
munificence *s* munificenti·a -ae *f*
munificent *adj* munific·us -a -um

munificently *adv* munifice
munitions *spl* apparat·us -ūs *m* belli
mural *adj* mural·is -is -e
mural *s* pictur·a -ae *f* muralis
murder *s* (*active in sense*) caed·es -is *f;* (*passive in sense*) nex, necis *f*
murder *tr* caedere, necare, interficere; **to — a song** lacerare canticum
murderer *s* homicid·a -ae *mf;* (*of father, mother, or near relative*) parricid·a -ae *mf*
murderous *adj* cruent·us -a -um
murky *adj* caliginos·us -a -um
murmur *s* murm·ur -uris *n*
murmur *tr & intr* murmurare
murmuring *s* admurmurati·o -onis *f*
muscle *s* muscul·us -i *m;* **to pull a —** musculum distorquēre
muscular *adj* musculos·us -a -um
Muse *s* Mus·a -ae *f*
muse *intr* secum agitare
museum *s* muse·um -i *n*
mushroom *s* bolet·us -i *m*
music *s* music·a -ae *f;* (*of instruments and voices*) cant·us -ūs *m*
musical *adj* (*of persons, things*) music·us -a -um; (*of sound*) canor·us -a -um; **— instrument** instrument·um -i *n* musicum
musician *s* music·us -i *m* (·a -ae *f*); (*of stringed instrument*) fidic·en -inis *m;* (*female*) fidicin·a -ae *f;* (*of wind instruments*) tibic·en -inis *m;* (*female*) tibicin·a -ae *f*
musket *s* scoplet·um -i *n*
must *s* must·um -i *n*
must *intr* **I — go** mihi eundum est, me oportet ire, debeo ire, necesse est (ut) eam
mustache *s* sub·ium -(i)i *n*
mustard *s* sinap·is -is *f*
muster *tr* (*mil*) lustrare; (*fig*) cogere; **to — up courage** animum sumere ‖ *intr* coïre
muster *s* (*mil*) copiarum lustrati·o -onis *f*
musty *adj* mucid·us -a -um
mutable *adj* mutabil·is -is -c
mute *adj* mut·us -a -um
mutilate *tr* mutilare, truncare
mutilated *adj* mutil·us -a -um
mutilation *s* mutilati·o -onis *f*
mutineer *s* seditios·us -i *m* (·a -ae *f*)
mutinous *adj* seditios·us -a -um
mutiny *s* sediti·o -onis *f*
mutiny *intr* seditionem facere
mutter *s* murmurati·o -onis *f*
mutter *tr & intr* mussare
mutton *s* ovillin·a -ae *f*
mutual *adj* mutu·us -a -um
mutually *adv* mutuo, inter se
muzzle *s* capistr·um -i *n*
muzzle *tr* capistrare
my *adj* me·us -a -um; **— own** propri·us -a -um
myriad *adj* (*innumerable*) sescent·i -ae -a

myrrh *s* myrrh·a -ae *f*
myrtle *s* myrt·us -i *f*
myself *pron* (*refl*) me; (*intensive*) ipse, egomet; **by —** sol·us -a; **to —** mihi
mysterious *adj* arcan·us -a -um
mysteriously *adv* arcane
mystery *s* myster·ium -(i)i *n;* (*fig*) res, rei *f* occultissima
mystical *adj* mystic·us -a -um
mystically *adv* mystice
mystify *tr* confundere
myth *s* myth·os -i *m,* fabul·a -ae *f*
mythical *adj* fabulos·us -a -um, fabular·is -is -e
mythological *adj* fabulos·us -a -um
mythology *s* histori·a -ae *f* fabularis, mythologi·a -ae *f*

N

nab *tr* prehendere
nadir *s* fund·us -i *m*
nag *s* (*horse*) caball·us -i *m;* (*woman*) oblatra·trix -tricis *f*
nag *tr* obiurgitare
nagging *adj* obiurgatori·us -a -um; (*annoying*) molest·us -a -um
naiad *s* naï·as -adis *f*
nail *s* clav·us -i *m;* (*of finger, toe*) ungu·is -is *m;* **to cut the —s** ungues resecare; **to drive in a —** clavum figere; **you hit the — on the head** tu rem acu tetigisti
nail *tr* clavīs (con)figere (*w. dat of that to which*); **to — (boards) together** (tabulas) inter se clavīs configere; **to — to the cross** cruci figere
naive *adj* simpl·ex -icis
naively *adv* simpliciter
naiveté *s* simplicit·as -atis *f*
naked *adj* nud·us -a -um; **the — truth** verit·as -atis *f* plana; **with the — eye** sine amplificatione visus
nakedly *adv* (*fig*) aperte
name *s* nom·en -inis *n;* (*a significant designation*) appellati·o -onis *f;* (*good name, reputation*) fam·a -ae *f;* (*term*) vocabul·um -i *n;* **by —** nominatim; **her — is Maria** Maria appellatur *or* illi nomen est Maria *or* illi nomen est Mariae; **in — only** sub nomine; **family —** cognom·en inis *n;* **first —** praenom·en -inis *n;* **middle —** nomen; **to have a bad —** male audire; **to have a good —** bene audire
name *tr* (*to call by a name; to mention by name*) nominare; (*to enumerate*) nuncupare; (*to appoint*) dicere; **named Tiberius** nomine

Tiberius; **to be named after one's father** nominari a patre

nameless *adj* nominis exper·s -tis

namely *adv* scilicet

namesake *s* person·a -ae *f* cognominis

nap *s* brevis somn·us -i *m; (of cloth)* vill·us -i *m;* **to take a** — brevi somno uti

nap *intr* breviter obdormiscere; meridiare

nape *s* — **of the neck** cerv·ix -icis *f*

napkin *s* mapp·a -ae *f*

Naples *s* Neapol·is -is *f*

narcissus *s* narciss·us -i *m*

narcotic *s* medicament·um -i *n* psychotropieum

nard *s* nard·um -i *n*

narrate *tr* narrare

narration *s* narrati·o -onis *f*

narrative *s* narrati·o *f,* fabul·a -ae *f,* histori·a -ae *f*

narrator *s* narra·tor -toris *m* (·trix -tricis *f)*

narrow *adj* angust·us -a -um; *(fig)* art·us -a -um; **to have a** — **escape** aegre periculum effugere

narrow *tr* coar(c)tare ‖ *intr* coar(c)tari

narrowly *adv* vix, aegre

narrow-minded *adj* animi angusti *or* parvi *(gen used adjectively);* **to be** — angusti animi esse

narrowness *s* angusti·ae -arum *fpl*

narrows *spl* angusti·ae -arum *fpl,* fauc·es -ium *fpl*

nasal *adj* ad nares pertin·ens -entis; **to have a** — **voice** de naribus loqui

nasty *adj (foul)* foed·us -a -um; *(mean)* turp·is -is -e, taetric·us -a -um

natal *adj* natal·is -is -e

nation *s* gen·s -tis *f,* nati·o -onis *f; (organized political community)* popul·us -i *m*

national *adj (expr. by gen of* gens *or* natio *or* populus):* — **customs** gentis mor·es -um *mpl;* — **assembly** concil·ium -(i)i *n* populi

nationality *s* civit·as -atis *f*

nationalize *tr* publicare, in usum publicum vertere

native *adj* indigen·a -ae *mf;* — **land** patri·a -ae *f;* — **language** patrius serm·o -onis *m*

native *s* indigen·a -ae *mf;* **he is a** — **of Athens** Athenis natus est

nativity *s* ort·us -ūs *m,* genitur·a -ae *f*

natural *adj (history, law, daughter, death)* natural·is -is -e; *(not man-made)* nativ·us -a -um; *(innate; opp:* traditus) innat·us -a -um; *(unaffected)* incomposit·us -a -um, simplex

natural disposition *s* indol·es -is *f*

naturalization *s* civitatis donati·o -onis *f*

naturalize *tr* civitate donare

naturally *adv* naturā, naturaliter; *(unaffectedly)* simpliciter; *(of its own accord)* sponte; *(of course)* nempe, utpote

natural science *s* physic·a -ae *f*

nature *s (of a specific thing)* natur·a -ae *f; (universal nature)* rerum natur·a -ae *f; (mostly of persons)* ingen·ium -(i)i *n;* **second** — altera natur·a -ae *f;* **beauties of** — amoenitat·es -um *fpl* locorum

naught *s* nihil; **to come to** — deficere; **to set at** — nihili facere

naughty *adj* improbul·us -a -um; *(saucy)* petul·ans -antis

nausea *s* nause·a -ae *f; (fig)* fastid·ium -(i)i *n*

nauseate *tr (fig)* fastidium movēre *(w. dat);* **to be** —**ed** fastidire

nautical *adj* nautic·us -a -um

naval *adj* naval·is -is -e

nave *s (archit)* nav·is -is *f*

navel *s* umbilic·us -i *m*

navigable *adj* navigabil·is -is -e

navigate *tr* gubernare ‖ *intr* navigare

navigation *s* navigati·o -onis *f; (as a field)* re·s -rum *fpl* nauticae

navigator *s* guberna·tor -toris *m* (·trix -tricis *f)*

navy *s* copi·ae -arum *fpl* navales; **to have a powerful** — navibus plurimum posse

navy yard *s* naval·ia -ium *npl*

nay *adv* non ita, immo

near *prep* prope *(w. acc); (esp. to denote a battle site)* ad *(w. acc),* apud *(w. acc); (in the vicinity, e.g., of a city)* apud *(w. acc)*

near *adj* propinqu·us -a -um; *(of relation)* proxim·us -a -um; *(neighboring)* vicin·us -a -um *(w. dat),* prope *(w. acc);* — **at hand** in promptu, praesto; **nearer** propr·ior -ior -ius; **nearest** proxim·us -a -um

near *adv* prope, iuxta

near *tr* accedere *(w. acc or* ad *w. acc),* appropinquare *(w. dat or* ad *w. acc)*

nearby *adv* in proximo

nearly *adv* prope, fere, ferme

nearness *s* propinquit·as -atis *f*

nearsighted *adj* myop·s -is

neat *adj (clean, elegant)* mund·us -a -um; *(properly groomed)* compt·us -a -um; *(in good taste)* concinn·us -a -um

neat *interj* optime!

neatly *adv* munde; concinne

neatness *s* munditi·a -ae *f*

necessarily *adv* necessario

necessary *adj* necessari·us -a -um; **consultation is** — consulto opus est; **if it is** — **for your health** si opus est ad tuam validtudinem; **if it is** — **for you to stay** si opus est te commorari; **it is** — necesse est

necessitate *tr* cogere

necessity *s* necessit·as -atis *f; (want)* egest·as -atis *f; (thing)* res necessaria *f;* — **is the mother of invention** ingeniosa est rerum egestas

neck *s (of body or bottle)* cerv·ix -icis *f (often pl. without change of meaning); (of animal)* coll·um -i *n;* **— and —** cursu aequo

necklace *s* monil·e -is *n; (of precious stones)* monile gemmatum

necktie *s* focal·e -is *n*

nectar *s* nect·ar -aris *n*

need *s (necessity)* necessit·as -atis *f; (want)* inopi·a -ae *f;* **there is — of** opus est *(w. abl)*

need *tr* egēre *(w. abl, more rarely w. gen),* indigēre *(w. abl); (to require)* requirere; **I (you, we) — money** opus est mihi (tibi, nobis) argento [*abl*]

needle *s* ac·us -ūs *f*

needle *tr* instigare, stimulare

needless *adj* minime necessari·us -a -um; **— to say** quid multa?, quid quaeris?

needlessly *adv* sine causā

needy *adj* egen·s -tis, in·ops -opis

nefarious *adj* nefari·us -a -um

negation *s* negati·o -onis *f*

negative *adj* negativ·us -a -um

negative *s* negati·o -onis *f;* **to answer in the —** negare

neglect *tr* neglegere

neglect *s* neglect·us -ūs *m*

neglectful *adj* neglegen·s -tis

negligence *s* negligenti·a -ae *f,* incuri·a -ae *f*

negligent *adj* neglig·ens -entis

negligible *adj* tenu·is -is -e, lev·is -is -e

negotiable *adj* mercabil·is -is -e

negotiate *tr* agere de *(w. abl);* **to — a peace de** pacis condicionibus agere ‖ *intr* negotiari

negotiation *s* transacti·o -onis *f;* **to settle disputes by —** controversias per colloquia componere

negotiator *s* concilia·tor -toris *m* (·trix -tricis *f*)

Negro *s* Aethiop·s -is *mf*

neigh *intr* hinnire; **to — at** adhinnire

neigh *s* hinnit·us -ūs *m*

neighbor *s (in the neighborhood)* vicin·us -i *m* (·a -ae *f*); *(next door)* proxim·us -i *m* (·a -ae *f*). *(on the border)* finitim·us -i *m* (·a -ae *f*)

neighborhood *s* vicini·a -ae *f*

neighboring *adj* vicin·us -a -um; *(next-door)* proxim·us -a -um

neighborly *adj* benign·us -a -um

neither *pron* neu·ter -tra -trum

neither *conj* nec, neque; **— ... nor** neque ... neque; **that's — here nor there** *(matter of indifference)* susque deque est

neophyte *s* tir·o -onis *mf*

nephew *s* fratris *(or* sororis*)* fil·ius -(i)i *m*

nepotism *s* nimius in necessarios fav·or -oris *m*

nerd *s* inconcinn·us -i *m* (·a -ae *f*)

Nereid *s* Nere·is -idos *f*

nerve *s* nerv·us -i *m; (fig)* audaci·a -ae *f;* **to get on one's —s** irritare; **what nerve!** O audaciam!

nervous *adj* trepid·us -a -um

nervously *adv* trepide

nervousness *s* trepidati·o -onis *f*

nest *s* nid·us -i *m;* **to build a —** nidificare

nest *intr* nidificare

nestle *intr* recubare

net *s (also comput)* ret·e -is *n*

net *tr (to catch in a net)* irretire; *(com)* lucrari sumptibus deductis

netting *s* reticul·um -i *n*

nettle *tr* vexare

network *s* op·us -eris *n* reticulatum

neuter *adj (gram)* neu·ter -tra -trum, neutral·is -is -e; **in the —** neutraliter

neutral *adj* medi·us -a -um; **to be — medium** se gerere; neutri parti favēre

neutrality *s* nullam in partem propensi·o -onis *f*

neutralize *tr* aequare

never *adv* numquam; **— mind!** sine! *(pl:* sinite!*);* **— yet** nondum

nevermore *adv* numquam posthac

nevertheless *adv* nihilominus, tamen

new *adj* nov·us -a -um

newfangled *adj* novici·us -a -um

newly *adv* nuper, modo

newlyweds *spl* coniug·es -um *mpl* recentes

newcomer *s* adven·a -ae *mf*

news *s (no single Latin counterpart exists) (message)* nunt·ium -(i)i *n,* nunt·ius -(i)i *m;* **any — ?** num quidnam novi?; **good — boni** nuntii *mpl;* **I just got — that ...** modo mihi nuntiatum est *(w. acc & inf);* **if you have to have any — about** si quid forte novi habes de *(w. abl);* **is there any — ?** numquid novi?; **— came** nuntiatum est; **no other —?** nihil praeterea novi?; **to bring good —** gaudium nuntiare; **when he heard this — his** auditis

news broadcast *s* nunti·i -orum *mpl* (radiophonici, televisifici)

newscast *s* telediar·ium -(i)i *n*

newscaster *s* radiophonic·us -a *or* televisific·us -a annuntia·tor -toris *m* (·trix -tricis *f*)

newspaper *s* act·a -orum *npl* diurna; **morning (evening, weekly) —** acta diurna matutina (vespertina, hebdomadalia)

newsstand *s* tabernul·a -ae *f* actorum diurnorum

New Testament *s* Testament·um -i *n* Novum

New Year *s* ann·us -i *m* novellus; **—'s Day** Kalend·ae -arum *fpl* Ianuariae; **—'s Eve** pridi·es -ei *m* Kalendarum Ianuariarum

next *adj* proxim·us -a -um; *(of time)* insequen·s -tis; **— best** secund·us -a -um; **— day** postridie; **— to** proxim·us -a -um *(w. dat),* iuxta *(w. acc)*

next *adv (place)* proxime; *(time)* deinde, mox

next of kin *spl* proxim·i -orum *mpl*

nibble *tr* arrodere; *(fig)* carpere ‖ *intr* rodere; **to — at** arrodere

nice *adj (dainty)* delicat·us -a -um; *(pleasant)* suav·is -is -e; *(cute)* bell·us -a -um; *(exact)* accurat·us -a -um; *(weather)* seren·us -a -um; **it was — of you to invite me** bene me vocas; **to say s.th. nice** aliquid belli dicere

nicely *adv (well)* bene; *(exactly)* subtiliter; *(prettily)* belle

nicety *s* subtilit·as -atis *f*

niche *s* aedicul·a -ae *f; (fig)* loc·us -i *m* proprius

nick *s* incisur·a -ae *f;* **in the very — of time** in ipso articulo temporis

nick *tr* incidere

nickname *s* agnom·en -inis *n*

niece *s* fratris *(or* sororis) fili·a -ae *f*

niggardly *adj* parc·us -a -um

nigh *adj* propinqu·us -a -um

night *s* no·x -ctis *f;* **at —, by —** nocte, noctu; **every —** per singulas noctes; **good —!** bene valeas et quiescas!; **last —** proximā nocte; **late at —** multā de nocte; **— after —** per singulas noctes; **— and day** *(continually)* noctes et dies; **one —** quādem nocte; **on the following —** insequente nocte; **(on) the — before** last superiore nocte; **till late at —** ad multam noctem; **to spend the —** pernoctare

nightcap *s (drink)* embasiocoet·as -ae *m*

nightclub *s* discothec·a -ae *f*

nightfall *s* prim·ae tenebr·ae -arum *fpl;* **at —** sub noctem, primis tenebris; **till —** usque ad noctem

nightingale *s* luscini·a -ae *f*

nightly *adj* nocturn·us -a -um

nightly *adv* de nocte

nightmare *s* tumultuosum somn·ium -(i)i *n;* **to have —s** per somnium exterrēri, somnium turbulentum pati

night owl *s (bird)* noctu·a -ae *f; (person)* noctis av·is is *mf*

night watch *s* vigili·a -ae *f; (guard)* vig·il -ilis *m*

night table *s* mensul·a -ae *f* cubicularis

nil *s* nihil *n* [*indecl*]

nimble *adj* agil·is -is -e

nine *adj* novem [*indecl*]; **— times** noviens

nineteen *adj* undeviginti [*indecl*]

nineteenth *adj* undevicesim·us -a -um

ninetieth *adj* nonagesim·us -a -um

ninety *adj* nonaginta [*indecl*]

ninth *adj* non·us -a -um

nip *tr* vellicare; *(of frost)* urere; **— the thing in the bud!** principiis obsta!; **to — off** desecare

nippers *spl* for·ceps -cipitis *m*

nipple *s* papill·a -ae *f*

nitwit *s (sl)* barcal·a -ae *mf*

no *adj* null·us -a -um; **by — means** nequaquam, haud; **he has — more money**

non plus pecuniae habet; **— doubt** nempe; **— more than three times** ter nec amplius; **— parking!** cave statuas vehiculum!; **— passing!** cave praeveharis! **— stopping!** ne sistito!; **— trouble** nihil negotii; **— way!** nullo modo!, nequiquam!; **there is — news** nihil novi est

no *adv* non, minime; **— indeed** minime vero; **— longer** non iam; **no, thank you** benigne; **to say —** negare

nobility *s* nobilit·as -atis *f; (the nobles as a group)* nobil·es -ium *mpl*

noble *adj* nobil·is -is -e; *(morally)* honest·us -a -um

noble *s* hom·o -inis *mf* nobilis

nobleman *s* vir! -i *m* nobilis

nobly *adv* praeclare

nobody *pron* nem·o -inis *m;* **some — or other** nescio qui terrae filius

nocturnal *adj* nocturn·us -a -um

nod *s* nut·us -ūs *m*

nod *intr* nutare; *(to doze)* dormitare; *(in assent)* annuere

noise *s* strepit·us -ūs *m; (high-pitched)* strid·or -oris *m; (crash)* frag·or -oris *m; (crackling, rattling)* crepit·us -ūs *m; (esp. of people talking loud)* convic·ium -(i)i *n;* **to make —** strepere, crepitare

noise *tr* **to — abroad** evulgare

noiseless *adj* tacit·us -a -um

noiselessly *adv* tacite

noisily *adv* cum strepitu

noisy *adj* strep·ens -entis; *(clamorous)* clamos·us -a -um, turbulent·us -a -um

nomad *s* nom·as -adis *mf*

nomadic *adj* vag·us -a -um

nominal *adj (not in fact)* simulat·us -a -um; *(slight)* exigu·us -a -um

nominally *adv* nomine, verbo

nominate *tr* nominare

nomination *s* nominati·o -onis *f*

nominative *adj* nominativ·us -a -um; **— case** cas·us -ūs *m* nominativus *or* rectus

nominee *s* hom·o -inis *mf* designat·us (-a)

nonchalant *adj* **to be —** aequo animo esse

nonchalantly *adv* aequo animo

noncomittal *adj* anc·eps -ipitis

nondescript *adj* non describend·us -a -um

none *pron* nem·o -inis *m*

nonentity *s* nihil·um -i *n*

nones *spl* Non·ae -arum *fpl (on the 7th day in March, May, July, and October; in all other months, on the 5th day)*

nonessential *adj* supervacane·us -a -um

nonplussed *adj* perplex·us -a -um

nonsense *s* nug·ae -arum *fpl;* **cut out the —!** omitte *(pl:* omittite) nugas!; **—! nugas!; no —!** ne nugare!; **that's a lot of —** nugae sunt istae magnae; **to talk** — (nugas) garrire, nugari

nonsensical *adj* inept·us -a -um

noodle *s* collyr·a -ae *f*

noodle soup *s* ius iuris *n* collyricum

nook *s* angul·us -i *m*

noon *s* meridi·es -ei *m;* **at** — meridie; **before** — ante meridiem

noonday *adj* meridian·us -a -um

no one *pron* nem·o -inis *m;* — **else** nemo alius

noose *s* laque·us -i *m; (knot)* nod·us -i *m*

nor *conj* nec, neque, neve

norm *s (rule, standard)* norm·a -ae *f; (average)* med·ium -(i)i *n; (pattern)* exempl·um -i *n*

normal *adj* solit·us -a -um

normally *adv* usitate, ex more; *(usually)* plerumque

north *s* septentrion·es -um *mpl;* **on the** — a septentrionibus; **to face** — in septentriones spectare

north *adv* ad septentriones; — **of** supra *(w. acc)*

north *adj* septentrional·is -is -e; — **of** supra *(w. acc)*

northeast *adj & adv* inter septentriones et orientem solem

northern *adj* septentrional·is -is -e

northern lights *spl* auror·a -ae *f* Borealis

north pole *s* arct·os -i *m*

northwards *adv* (ad) septentriones versus [versus *is an adverb*]

north wind *s* aquil·o -onis *m*

nose *s (as a feature of the face)* nas·us -ūs *m; (of animal)* rostr·um -i *n; (as a function of smell)* nar·es -ium *fpl;* **by a** — aegre, vix; **having a large** — nasut·us -a -um; **to blow the** — emungere; **to have a good** — **for** festive odorari; **to look down one's** — **at** contemnere; **to turn up one's** — **at** naso adunco suspendere *(w. acc);* **under his very** — ante oculos eius

nosebleed *s* sanguinis profluv·ium -(i)i *n* per nares

nostril *s* nar·is -is *f*

nosey *adj* curios·us -a -um; **I don't want to be** — **but** ... non libet curios·us (-a) esse sed ...

not *adv* non; *(more emphatic and used chiefly before adjs and advs)* haud, *e.g.,* **I do** — **quite understand** haud sane intellego; *(less than should be)* parum, minus, *e.g.,* **Terentia has not been feeling well** Terentia minus belle habuit; **and** — nec, neque; — **at all** non omnino, haudquaquam; — **bad** non male; — **even** ne ... quidem; — **including** sine *(w. abl),* praeter *(w. acc);* — **including you** te excepto; — **only** ... **but also** non solum

... sed etiam; — **that** non quod *(w. subj);* — **yet** nondum

notable *adj* notabil·is -is -e

notably *adv* insigniter

notary *s* scrib·a -ae *mf*

notation *s* notati·o -onis *f*

notch *s* incisur·a -ae *f*

notch *tr* incidere

note *s (mark)* not·a -ae *f; (comment)* annotati·o -onis *f; (brief letter)* litterul·ae -arum *fpl; (sound)* son·us -i *m,* vo·x -cis *f; (com)* chirograph·um -i *n;* **a brief** — scriptur·a -ae *f* brevis; **to make** — **of** in commentarios referre; **to take** —**s** enotare

note *tr* notare; *(to notice)* animadvertere

notebook *s* libell·us -i *m,* pugillar·es -ium *mpl*

noted *adj (well-known)* not·us -a -um; *(famous)* praeclar·us -a -um

notepad *s* pugillar·es -ium *mpl*

noteworthy *adj* notabil·is -is -e

nothing *pron* nihil, nil; **for** — *(free)* gratis, gratuito; *(in vain)* frustra; **good for** — nequam [*indecl*]; — **but** nihil nisi; **to think** — **of** nihili facere

notice *s (act of noticing)* notati·o -onis *f; (announcement)* denuntiati·o -onis *f; (sign)* proscripti·o -onis *f,* titul·us -i *m;* **to escape** — latēre; **to escape the** — **of** fallere; **to give** — **of** denuntiare

notice *tr* animadvertere

noticeable *adj* insign·is -is -e

noticeably *adv* insigniter

notification *s* denuntiati·o -onis *f*

notify *tr* certiorem facere, denuntiare

notion *s* noti·o -onis *f; (whim)* libid·o -inis *f*

notoriety *s* fam·a -ae *f; (bad)* infami·a -ae *f*

notorious *adj* infam·is -is -e

notwithstanding *adv* nihilominus

notwithstanding *prep expr. by various participles, e.g.,* **notwithstanding the auspices** neglectis auspiciis

nought *pron* nihil

noun *s* nom·en -inis *n;* **proper and common** —**s** nomina propria et appellativa

nourish *tr* alere, nutrire

nourishing *adj* frugi [*indecl*], salubr·is -is -e

nourishment *s* aliment·um -i *n*

novel *adj* novici·us -a -um, inaudit·us -a -um

novel *s* histori·a -ae *f* commenticia, op·us -eris *n* fabulosum

novelist *s* scrip·tor -toris *m* (·trix -tricis *f)* operis fabulosi

novelty *s* novit·as -atis *f*

November *s* Novem·ber -bris *m or* mens·is -is *m* November; **in** — mense Novembri; **on the first of** — Kalendis Novembribus

novice *s* tir·o -onis *mf; (eccl)* novici·us -i *m* (·a -ae *f)*

now *adv* nunc; *(denoting urgency and emphasis)* iam; *(transitional, esp. in argumentation; never the first word in the sentence)* autem; **even —** etiam nunc; **from — on** ab hoc tempore, iam inde; **just —** *(a moment ago)* modo; **— and then** iterdum; **— at last** nunc tandem; **— ... —** modo ... modo; **— that** posteaquam *(w. indic);* **— what?** quid nunc?; **right —** iam iam; **ten years from —** ad decem annos

nowadays *adv* his temporibus

nowhere *adv* nusquam

noxious *adj* noxi·us -a -um

nozzle *s* ans·a -ae *f*

nuclear *adj* nuclear·is -is -e; **— energy** vis *f* nuclearis

nude *adj* nud·us -a -um

nudge *tr* fodicare

nudity *s* nudati·o -onis *f*

nugget *s* mass·a -ae *f*

nuisance *s* molesti·a -ae *f;* **what a — it is!** quam molestum est!

null *adj* **— and void** irrit·us -a -um; **to be — and void** cessare; **to render —** infringere

nullification *s* abrogati·o -onis *f*

nullify *tr* irritum facere, abrogare

numb *adj* torpid·us -a -um; **to become —** torpescere; **to be —** torpēre

number *s (gram & math)* numer·us -i *m;* **a — of** aliquot; **relying on their superior —s** multitudine fret·us -a -um; **to assemble in large —s** frequentissimi convenire; **without — innumerabil·is -is -e

number *tr* numerare; **a fleet —ing 1000 ships** classis mille numero navium; **to be —ed among** adnumerat·us -a -um *(w. dat)*

numberless *adj* innumer·us -a -um

numbness *s* torp·or -oris *m;* *(fig)* stup·or -oris *m*

numeral *s* nom·en -inis *s* numerale

numerator *s* numerat·or -oris *m*

numerical *adj* numeral·is -is -e

numerically *adv* numero

numerous *adj* cre·ber -bra -brum

numismatics *s* doctrin·a -ae *f* nummorum

numskull *s* bar·o -onis *mf*

nun *s* nonn·a -ae *f*

nuncio *s* nunt·ius -(i)i *m*

nuptial *adj* nuptial·is -is -e

nuptials *spl* nupti·ae -arum *fpl*

nurse *s* nutr·ix -icis *f;* *(med)* nosocom·a -ae *f;* *(male)* nosocom·us -i *m*

nurse *tr (a baby)* nutrire; *(the sick)* curare; *(fig)* fovēre

nursery *s (for children)* infantium diaet·a -ae *f;* *(for plants)* seminar·ium -(i)i *n*

nursing home *s* nosocom·ium -(i)i *n*

nurture *tr* nutrire, colere

nut *s* nu·x -cis *f;* **a hard — to crack** *(fig)* quaesti·o -onis *f* nodosa; **he is a —** *(pej)* nuga iste est; **to be —s** a se alienat·us -a esse; **to be —s about** (amore) deperire *(w. acc);* **you're —s** deliras

nutcracker *s* nucifrangibul·um -i *n*

nutriment *s* nutriment·um -i *n*

nutrition *s* nutriti·o -onis *f*

nutritious *adj* alibil·is -is -e

nutshell *s* nucis putam·en -inis *n;* **in a —** *(fig)* paucis verbis

nutty *adj (coll)* vecor·s -dis, baceol·us -a -um

nymph *s* nymph·a -ae *f*

O

oaf *s* stult·us -i *m* (·a -ae *f*)

oak *adj* querce·us -a -um

oak *s* querc·us -ūs *f;* *(esp. timber)* rob·ur -oris *n*

oar *s* rem·us -i *m;* **to pull the —s** remos ducere

oarsman *s* rem·ex -igis *m*

oasis *s* fertilis regi·o -onis *f* in desertis

oath *s* iusurandum *(gen:* iurisiurandi*) n;* *(mil)* sacrament·um -i *n;* **false —** periur·ium -(i)i *n;* **to take an —** iurare; *(mil)* sacramentum dicere

oats *spl* aven·a -ae *f*

obdurate *adj* obstinat·us -a -um

obdurately *adv* obstinate

obedience *s* oboedienti·a -ae *f*

obedient *adj* (to) oboedien·s -tis *(w. dat)*

obediently *adv* oboedienter

obeisance *s* **to make — to** *(fig)* venerari

obelisk *s* obelisc·us -i *m*

obese *adj* obes·us -a -um

obesity *s* obesit·as -atis *f*

obey *tr* parēre *(w. dat)*, oboedire *(w. dat)*

obfuscate *tr* confundere; *(to darken)* obscurare

obituary *s* Libitinae rati·o -onis *f*, denuntiati·o -onis *f* mortis

object *s* obiect·um -i *n*, res, rei *f;* *(aim)* proposit·um -i *n;* *(gram) expressed by the verb* adiungi, *e.g.,* **"the man" is the object of the verb** "hic homo" verbo adiungitur

object *intr (to feel annoyance)* gravari; *(to make objections)* recusare; **to — to** aegre ferre; **I do not —, provided that ...** non repugno dummodo ... ; **I do not — to your leaving** non recuso quominus abeas

objection *s* oppositi·o -onis *f;* **if you have no —** si per te licet; **I have no —** per me licet; **to raise many —s** multa in contrariam partem afferre

objectionable *adj* improbabilis -is -e

objective *adj (real)* ver·us -a -um; *(unbiased)* aequ·us -a -um; *(gram)* accusativ·us -a -um
objective *s* proposit·um -i *n*
object lesson *s* document·um -i *n*
obligation *s* obligati·o -onis *f; (duty)* offic·ium -(i)i *n;* **be under** — debēre
obligatory *adj* necessari·us -a -um
oblige *tr (to force)* cogere; *(to put under obligation)* obligare; *(to do a favor for)* morigerari *(w. dat);* **to be —ed to** debēre *(w. inf); (to feel gratitude toward)* gratiam habēre *(w. dat)*
obliged *adj* **I am much — to you for sending me your book** fecisti mihi pergratum quod librum ad me misisti
obliging *adj* officios·us -a -um, commod·us -a -um
obligingly *adv* officiose
oblique *adj* obliqu·us -a -um
obliquely *adv* oblique
oblong *adj* oblong·us -a -um
obnoxious *adj* invis·us -a -um
obscene *adj* obscen·us -a -um
obscenely *adv* obscene
obscenity *s* obscenit·as -atis *f*
obscure *adj* obscur·us -a -um
obscure *tr* obscurare
obscurely *adv* obscure
obscurity *s* obscurit·as -atis *f; (of birth)* humilit·as -atis *f,* ignobilit·as -atis *f; (of speech)* ambiguit·as -atis *f*
obsequies *spl* exsequi·ae -arum *fpl*
obsequious *adj* nimis obsequ·ens -entis
obsequiousness *s* obsequ·ium -(i)i *n*
observable *adj* notabil·is -is -e
observance *s* observanti·a -ae *f; (rite)* rit·us -ūs *m*
observant *adj* attent·us -a -um; — **of** dilig·ens -entis *(w. gen)*
observation *s* observati·o -onis *f; (remark)* notati·o -onis *f*
observe *tr (to watch, keep, comply with)* observare; *(to remark)* dicere
observer *s* specta·tor -toris *m* (·trix -tricis *f*)
obsess *tr* occupare; **I am obsessed by** tot·us -a sum in *(w. abl)*
obsession *s* mentis prehensi·o -onis *f*
obsolescent *adj* obsolesc·ens -entis; **to be —** obsolescere
obsolete *adj* obsolet·us -a -um; **to become —** exsolescere
obstacle *s* impediment·um -i *n; (barrier)* ob·ex -icis *m*
obstinacy *s* obstinati·o -onis *f*
obstinate *adj* obstinat·us -a -um
obstinately *adv* obstinate
obstreperous *adj* tumultuos·us -a -um, clamos·us -a -um
obstruct *tr* obstare *(w. dat)*

obstruction *s* impediment·um -i *n*
obtain *tr* adipisci; *(by asking)* impetrare; **to — pardon** veniam impetrare
obtainable *adj* impetrabil·is -is -e
obtrude *intr* intervenire
obtrusive *adj* molest·us -a -um, importun·us -a -um
obtuse *adj* obtus·us -a -um
obviate *tr* praevertere
obvious *adj* apert·us -a -um; **it was — that** apparebat *(w. acc & inf)*
obviously *adv* aperte, manifeste
occasion *s* occasi·o -onis *f,* facult·as -atis *f; (reason)* caus·a -ae *f; (time)* temp·us -oris *n;* **if the — should arise** si occasio fuerit; **for the —** *(temporary)* ad tempus
occasion *tr* locum dare *(w. dat)*
occasional *adj* rar·us -a -um
occasionally *adv* interdum, per occasionem
occidental *adj* occidental·is -is -e
occult *adj* occult·us -a -um
occupant *s* habita·tor -toris *m* (·trix -tiricis *f*)
occupation *s* possessi·o -onis *f; (employment)* occupati·o -onis *f,* quaest·us -ūs *m;* **what is your —** quem quaestum facis?
occupy *tr* occupare; *(to possess)* possidēre; *(to take by force)* capere; *(space)* complēre; *(time)* uti *(w. abl)*
occur *intr (to take place)* accidere; *(to show up, appear)* nasci; *(to the mind)* in mentem venire; **it occurred to me** mihi in mentem venit; **to — at the right time** competere
occurrence *s* cas·us -ūs *m,* event·us -ūs *m*
ocean *s* ocean·us -i *m*
oceanic *adj* oceanens·is -is -e
ochre *adj* silace·us -a -um
octave *s (mus)* intervall·um -i *n* octavum
October *s* Octo·ber -bris *m or* mens·is -is *m* October; **in —** mense Octobri; **on the first of —** Kalendis Octobribus
ocular *adj* ocular·is -is -e
oculist *s* oculari·us (-a) medic·us -i *m* (·a -ae *f*)
odd *adj (of number)* im·par -paris; *(quaint)* insolit·us -a -um; *(remaining)* reliqu·us -a -um; **how —!** quam ridiculum!
oddity *s* rarit·as -atis *f; (thing)* mir·um -i *n*
oddly *adv* mirum in modum
odds *spl* — **and ends** quisquili·ae -arum *fpl;* **the — are against us** impares sumus; **the — are that** probabilitas est ut *(w. subj);* **to be at — with** dissidēre ab *(w. abl);* **to lay — that not** pignore certare ne *(w. subj)*
odious *adj* odios·us -a -um
odium *s* od·ium -(i)i *n,* invidi·a -ae *f*
odor *s* od·or -oris *m*
odorous *adj* odorat·us -a -um
Odyssey *s* Odysse·a -ae *f; (fig)* it·er -ineris *n* operosum

of *prep (possession) rendered by gen; (origin)* de *(w. abl),* ex *(w. abl); (concerning)* de *(w. abl); (denoting description or quality) expr. by gen or abl:* **a man — of highest talents** vir summi ingeni *(or* summo ingenio);* **one — them** unus de illis *(or* ex illis);* **statue of bronze** statua ex aere facta

off *adv* procul, longe; **far — procul; to be a long way — longe abesse; to be — to hinc** abire ad *(w. acc),* se hinc agere ad *(w. acc);* **— with you!** aufer te modo!; **well — *(rich)*** bene nummerat·us -a -um; **where are you — to?** quo te agis?

off *prep* de *(w. abl); (said of an island)* ante *(w. acc);* **— (the coast of) Italy** ante Italiam

offend *tr* offendere ‖ *intr* **to — against** violare

offender *s* re·us -i *m* (·a -ae *f),* sons sontis *mf*

offense *s (fault)* offens·a -ae *f,* delict·um -i *n; (insult)* iniuri·a -ae *f; (displeasure)* offensi·o -onis *f;* **to give — to** offendere

offensive *adj* iniurios·us -a -um; *(odors, etc.)* odios·us -a -um, foed·us -a -um; *(language)* malign·us -a -um; *(aggressive)* bellum inferens; **to go on the — bellum inferre**

offer *tr* offerre, praebēre; **to — help to** opem ferre *(w. dat);* **to — violent resistance to** vim afferre *(w. dat)*

offer *s* propositi·o -onis *f; (of marriage)* condici·o -onis *f*

offering *s* don·um -i *n*

offhand *adj* incurios·us -a -um; **— remark** dict·um -i *n* incuriosum; obiter dictum

offhand *adv* confestim, ex tempore; **to say —** de summo pectore dicere

office *s (place of work)* officin·a -ae *f; (pol)* hon·or -oris *m; (duty)* offic·ium -(i)i *n;* **through the good —s of** per *(w. acc);* **to reach high — ad honorem pervenire**

officer *s* magistrat·us -ūs *m; (mil)* sagat·us -i *m* (·a -ae *f); (police)* vig·il -ilis *mf*

officiold maid *s* an·us -ūs *f* innupta

al *adj* public·us -a -um; **— residence** dom·us -ūs *f* publica

official *s* magistrat·us -ūs *m*

officiate *intr* officio *(or* munere) fungi; *(of a clergyman)* rem divinam facere

officious *adj* importun·us -a -um

officiously *adv* importune

offing *s* **in the —** in promptu

offset *tr* compensare

offshoot *s* surcul·us -i *m; (fig)* consequ·ens -entis

offshore *adj* litore dist·ans -antis

offside *adj* **to be — seorsum stare**

offspring *s* prol·es -is *f*

offstage *adj & adv* in postscaenio

often *adv* saepe; **very — persaepe**

ogle *tr* oculis amatoriis tuēri

ogre *s* larv·a -ae *f*

oh *interj* oh!, ohe!; **— boy!** eu!; **— my!** vae mihi!

oho *interj* eho!

oil *s* ole·um -i *n*

oil *tr* ung(u)ere

oil press *s* torcul·ar -aris *n*

oily *adj* oleos·us -a -um; *(like oil)* oleace·us -a -um; **to have an — taste** oleum sapere

ointment *s* unguent·um -i *n*

old *adj* vet·us -eris [*single ending*]; *(aged)* sen·ex -is, aetate provect·us -a -um; *(out of use)* obsolet·us -a -um; *(worn)* trit·us -a -um; *(ancient)* antiqu·us -a -um; **good — days** prisca tempor·a -um *npl;* **of — olim, quondam; —er** ma·ior -ior -ius (natu); *(among old people)* sen·ior -ior -ius; **—est** maxim·us -a -um (natu); **to be no more than ten years — non plus quam decem annos habēre; to be ten years —** decem annos nat·us -a -um esse; **to grow — senescere**

old age *s* senect·us -utis *f*

old-age home *s* gerontocom·ium -(i)i *n*

old-fashioned *adj* prisc·us -a -um

old maid *s* an·us -ūs *f* innupta

old lady *s* an·us -ūs *f;* **little — anicul·a -ae *f***

old man *s* sen·ex -is *m*

old woman *s* an·us -ūs *f*

oldster *s* sen·ex -icis *mf*

oldtimer *s* sen·ex -icis *mf*

oligarchy *s* paucorum gubernati·o -onis *f* civitatis; *(members of the oligarchy)* opimat·es -um *mpl*

olive *s* ole·a -ae *f,* oliv·a -ae *f*

olive grove *s* olivet·um -i *n*

olive oil *s* ole·um -i *n*

olive tree *s* oliv·a -ae *f*

Olympia *s* Olympi·a -ae *f*

Olympiad *s* Olympi·as -adis *f*

Olympic *adj* Olympic·us -a -um

omelet *s* lagan·um -i *n* de ovis confectum

omen *s* om·en -inis *n; bad* — omen malum *(or* infaustum); **good — bonum *(or* secundum) omen; to announce unfavorable —s** obnuntiare; **to get favorable —s** litare

ominous *adj* ominos·us -a -um

omission *s* omissi·o -onis *f,* praetermissi·o -onis *f; (thing)* mend·um -i *n*

omit *tr* (o)mittere, praetermittere

omnipotence *s* omnipotenti·a -ae *f*

omnipotent *adj* omnipoten·s -tis

omniscient *adj* omnia sci·ens -entis

omnivorous *adj* omnivor·us -a -um

on *prep (place)* in *(w. abl); (about, concerning)* de *(w. abl); (ranged with)* ab *(w. abl); (depending, hanging on)* de *(w. abl); (close to, e.g., a river)* iuxta *(w. acc),* ad *(w. acc); (on the side of, in the direction of)* ab *(w. abl):* **— me** meā impensā; **— my side** cum me; — **the east** ab oriente; — **the west** ab occidente

on *adv* porro; *(continually)* usque; **and so** — et cetera; **from then** — ex eo (tempore); — **and** — continenter; **to drink** — **till daylight** potare usque ad primam lucem; **to go** — pergere; **to move**— procedere

once *adv (one time)* semel; *(formerly)* olim, quondam; **at** — statim, illico, continuo; **for** — demum; — **and for all** semel (et) in perpetuum; — **I get started, I can't stop** quando incipio, desinere non queo; — **more** iterum; — **or twice** semel iterumque; — **upon a time** olim

onceover *s* conspect·us -ūs *m* brevis

one *adj* un·us -a -um; — **day** *(in the past)* quodam die; *(in the future)* aliquando; **at** — **time** simul; — **ladder** unae scal·ae -arum *fpl;* **to have** — **and the same wish** idem velle

one *pron* un·us -a -um; *(a certain person)* quidam, quaedam, quoddam; **it is all** — perinde est; — **and the same** unus et idem; — **after another** ali·us -a -um ex alio; — **another** inter se, alius alium; — **by** — singulatim; — **house** unae aed·es -ium *fpl;* — **or the other** alterut·er alterut·ra alterut·rum; — **or two** un·us -a -um et alt·er -era -erum *(w. pl verb);* —**'s own** propri·us -a -um; — **would think that time stood still** putes stare tempus; **only** — unic·us -a -um

one-eyed *adj* lusc·us -a -um

onerous *adj* oneros·us -a -um; *(hard)* difficil·is -is -e

oneself *pron (refl)* se; **by** — per se; **to keep to** — se secludere; **to** — sibi; **with** — secum

one-sided *adj* inaequal·is -is -e

onetime *adj* prisc·us -a -um; *(outdated)* obsolet·us -a -um

one-track mind *s* anim·us -i *m* angustus

one-way street *s* vi·a -ae *f* unici cursūs

onion *s* caep·a -ae *f*

onlooker *s* specta·tor -toris *m* (·trix -tricis *f*)

only *adj* sol·us -a -um, unic·us -a -um, un·us -a -um

only *adv* solum, tantum, dumtaxat; **not** — ... **but also** non solum ... sed etiam

only-begotten *adj* unigenit·us -a -um

onrush *s* irrupti·o -onis *f*

onset *s* impet·us -ūs *m*

onslaught *s* oppungnati·o -onis *f,* incurs·us -ūs *m*

onward *adv* porro

onyx *s* on·yx -ychis *m*

ooze *intr* manare

opal *s* opal·us -i *m*

opaque *adj* haud translucid·us -a -um

open *adj (not shut)* apert·us -a -um, paten·s -tis; *(evident)* manifest·us -a -um; *(sincere)* candid·us -a -um; *(public)* public·us -a -um;

(of a question, undecided) inte·ger -gra -grum; **in the** — **(air)** sub divo; **to be** — **to** *(e.g, bribery, disease)* patēre *(w. dat);* **to lie** — patēre

open *tr* aperire; *(to uncover)* retegere; *(letter)* resignare; *(book)* evolvere; *(conversation)* exordiri; *(w. ceremony)* inaugurare; *(mouth)* diducere; *(door)* recludere; **to** — **up a hole** foramen laxare ‖ *intr* patescere, se pandere; *(gape)* dehiscere; *(of a wound)* recrudescere

open-handed *adj* larg·us -a -um

open-hearted *adj* ingenu·us -a -um

opening *s (act)* aperti·o -onis *f; (aperture)* foram·en -inis *n; (e.g., of a cave)* os, oris *n; (opportunity)* loc·us -i *m*

opening night *s* prima nox *f*

openly *adv* (pro)palam

open-minded *adj* docil·is -is -e, liberal·is -is -e

opera *s* melodram·a -atis *n;* **to go to see an** — melodrama visere

opera house *s* theatr·um -i *n* melodramaticum

operate *tr* agere; *(to manage, e.g., a business)* exercēre ‖ *intr* operari; **to** — **on** *(surgically)* secare

operating system *s (comput)* system·a -atis *n* internum

operation *s (act of doing or working)* effecti·o -onis *f; (surgical)* secti·o -onis *f; (business)* negot·ium -(i)i *n;* **to conduct military** —**s** res gerere

operative *adj* effica·x -cis

operator *s* opif·ex -icis *mf*

operetta *s* melodramat·ium -(i)i *n*

opinion *s* opini·o -onis *f,* sententi·a -ae *f;* **good** — **of** aestimati·o -onis *f* de *(w. abl);* **in my** — meā sententiā, meo iudicio, meo animo; **public** — fam·a -ae *f;* **to ask s.o. for his** — aliquem sententiam rogare; **to be of the** — opinari; **to express an** — sententiam dicere; **to form an** — iudicium facere; **to hold the** — **that** opinionem habēre *(w. acc & inf)*; **to stick to one's** — in sententiā perstare; **what is your** — **about** ... ? quid opinaris de *(w. abl)?*

opinion poll *s* interrogati·o -onis *f* publica, rogati·o -onis *f* sententiarum

opium *s* op·ium -(i)i *n*

opponent *s* adversari·us -i *m* (·a -ae *f*); *(pol)* competi·tor -toris *m* (·trix -tricis *f*)

opportune *adj* opportun·us -a -um

opportunist *s* indaga·tor -toris *m* (·trix -tricis *f*) occasionis

opportunity *s* occasi·o -onis *f,* potest·as -atis *f;* **as** — **offered** ex occasione; **to give s.o. the** — **to** alicui potestatem dare *(w. gen of gerundive);* **to take** *or* **get the** — occasionem nancisci

oppose *tr* adversari *(w. dat); (w. words)* contra dicere *(w. dat);* **to — the idea that** adversari ne *(w. subj)*

opposite *adj* advers·us -a -um, contrari·us -a -um

opposite *prep* contra *(w. acc);* versus *(w. acc)* [*often postpositive*]; **— of** exadverso *(w. gen)*

opposition *s* oppositi·o -onis *f; (obstacle)* impediment·um -i *n;* **— party** par·s -tis *f* diversa

oppress *tr* opprimere, gravare

oppression *s* oppressi·o -onis *f,* iniuri·a -ae *f; (harsh rule)* dominati·o -onis *f*

oppressive *adj* praegrav·is -is -e; **to become — ** ingravescere

oppressor *s* oppress·or -oris *m,* tyrann·us -i *m*

opprobrium *s* ignomini·a -ae *f*

optic *adj* ocular·is -ie -e

optical *adj* opticus -a -um

optician *s* fab·er -ri *m* opticus

option *s* opti·o -onis *f;* **you have the — either to ... or** tibi optio datur utrum ... an

or *conj* vel, aut, —ve; *(in questions)* an; **either ... or** *(mutually exclusive)* aut ... aut; *(optional)* vel ... vel; *(in uncertainty)* sive ... sive **— else** alioquin; **— not** annon; *(in indirect questions)* necne

oracle *s* oracul·um -i *n*

oracular *adj* fatidic·us -a -um

oral *adj* verbal·is -is -e, verbo tradit·us -a -um

orally *adv* voce, verbis

orange *s* mal·um -i *n* aurantium; *(color)* col·or -oris *m* luteus

orange *adj (color)* lute·us -a -um, aurant·us -a -um

orangeade *s* mali aurantii poti·o -onis *f*

orange juice *s* aurantii suc(c)·us -i *m*

oration *s* orati·o -onis *f;* **to deliver an —** orationem habēre

orator *s* orat·or -oris *m (·trix -tricis f)*

oratorical *adj* oratori·us -a -um

oratory *s* oratoria ar·s -tis *f*

orb *s* orb·is -is *m*

orbit *tr* **to — the earth** orbem terrae circumagere

orbit *s (astr)* orbit·a -ae *f,* ambit·us -ūs *m;* **to go into —** in orbitam ire

orchard *s* pomar·ium -(i)i *n*

orchestra *s* symphoni·a -ae *f; (part of theater)* orchestr·a -ae *f*

orchid *s* orch·is -is *m*

ordain *tr* decernere, edicere; *(eccl)* ordinare

ordeal *s* discrim·en -inis *n*

order *s (class, arrangement, sequence)* ord·o -inis *m; (command)* iuss·um -i *n; (mil)* imperat·um -i *n;* **to call to —** convocare; **— to** ut *(w. subj);* **in — not to** ne *(w. subj);* **in short —** brevi; **made to —** proprie fact·us -a -um; **out of —** ex usu, inordinat·us -a -um;

(unruly) effrenat·us -a -um; **out of the regular —** extra ordinem; **to arrange in —** ordinare; **to draw up an army in — of battle** aciem ordinare

order *tr (to command)* imperare *(w. dat),* iubēre; *(to arrange)* disponere, ordinare; *(to ask for)* postulare, poscere

orderly *adj* composit·us -a -um; *(well behaved)* modest·us -a -um

orderly *s* accens·us -ūs *m; (mil)* tessarari·us -i *m (·a -ae f)*

ordinal *adj* ordinal·is -is -e

ordinance *s* edict·um -i *n,* decret·um -i *n*

ordinarily *adv* plerumque, fere

ordinary *adj* usitat·us -a -um, solit·us -a -um; *(everyday)* cotidian·us -a -um; *(traditional, not novel)* tralatici·us -a -um

ordnance *s (mil)* apparat·us -ūs *m* belli; *(artillery)* torment·a -orum *npl*

ore *s* ae·s -ris *n;* **iron —** ferr·um -i *n* infectum

organ *s (anat)* par·s *f* corporis, visc·us -eris *n; (mus)* organ·um -i *n;* **the internal —s** viscer·a -um *npl;* **to play the —** organo canere

organic *adj* pertinen·s -tis ad partem corporis

organism *s* compag·es -is *f*

organist *s* organic·en -inis *m,* organicin·a -ae *f*

organize *tr* ordinare, instituere, componere

organizer *s* auc·tor -toris *m (·trix -tricis f)*

organization *s* structur·a -ae *f; (society)* sodalit·as -atis *f*

orgy *s* comissati·o -onis *f*

Orient *s* orien·s -tis *m*

oriental *adj* oriental·is -is -e

origin *s* orig·o -inis *f; (birth)* gen·us -eris *n; (source)* fon·s -tis *m*

original *adj* primitiv·us -a -um, prim·us -a -um; *(one's own)* propri·us -a -um; *(new)* inaudit·us -a -um

original *s* archetyp·um -i *n,* exempl·ar -aris *n; (writing)* autograph·um -i *n*

originality *s* propriet·as -atis *f* ingenii

originally *adv* initio, principio

originate *tr* instituere **‖** *intr* oriri

originator *s* auc·tor -toris *m (·trix -tricis f)*

ornament *s* ornament·um -i *n*

ornamental *adj* decor·us -a -um

ornate *adj* ornat·us -a -um

ornately *adv* ornate

orphan *s* orb·us -i *m (·a -ae f)*

orphaned *adj* orbat·us -a -um

orphanage *s* orphanotroph·ium -(i)i *n*

orthodox *adj* orthodox·us -a -um

orthodoxy *s* rati·o -onis *f* orthodoxa

orthography *s* orthographi·a -ae *f*

oscillate *intr* ultro citroque se inclinare; *(fig)* dubitare

oscillation *s* ultro citroque inclinati·o -onis *f; (fig)* dubitati·o -onis *f*

ostensible *adj* simulat·us -a -um

ostensibly *adv* per speciem
ostentation *s* ostentati·o -onis *f*
ostentatious *adj* specios·us -a -um
ostracism *s* relegati·o -onis *f; (Athenian custom)* testarum suffragi·a -orum *npl*
ostrich *s* struthiocamel·us -i *m*
other *adj (different)* ali·us -a -ud; *(remaining)* reliqu·us -a -um; *(additional)* ceter·us -a -um; **all the** —**s** omnes alii *(or* aliae); **every** — **day** tertio quoque die; **on the** — **hand** contra; **the** — alt·er -era -erum; **the** — **day** nuper; **to attend to** — **people's affairs** aliena curare
other *adv* aliter; — **than** praeter *(w. acc)*, extra *(w. acc)*
otherwise *adv* aliter; *(in the contrary supposition)* alioquin; **to think** — aliter sentire; **you didn't do it yet;** — **you would have told me** nondum id fecisti; alioquin mihi narasses
otter *s* lutr·a -ae *f*
ouch *interj* au!; ei!; oeei!
ought *intr* **I** — **to** debeo *(w. inf)*, oportet me *(w. inf)*
ounce *s* unci·a -ae *f*
our *adj* nos·ter -tra -trum; — **men** nostr·i -orum *mpl*
ours *pron* nos·ter -tra -trum
ourselves *pron refl* nos(met); **by** — per nos; **to** — nobis; **we** — *(intensive)* nosmet ips·i -ae
oust *tr* eicere
out *adv (outside)* foris; *(motion)* foras; **get** —**!** apage!; — **with it!** *(tell me!)* cedo! *(pl:* cette!) *[an old imperative]*; **the book is not yet** — liber nondum in manibus est; **the fire is** — incendium est extinctum; **the secret is** — arcanum est palam; **to dine** — foris cenare; **to go all** — se extendere
out of *prep (from)* ex *(w. abl); (esp. after verbs denoting material; also selection from a number)* de *(w. abl); (on account of)* ob *(w. acc)*, propter *(w. acc); (beyond)* extra *(w. acc)*, praeter *(w. acc);* **I am** — **money** argento expers sum; **if it is not** — **place** nisi alienum est; — **doors** foris; — **the way** devi·us -a -um; — **wood** de ligno; **to be** — **country** peregrinari
out-and-out *adv* tot·us -a -um
outbreak *s* erupti·o -onis *f; (disturbance)* sediti·o -onis *f*
outburst *s* erupti·o -onis *f;* **in an** — **of anger** impoten·s -tis irae
outcast *s* ex·sul -sulis *mf*
outcome *s* event·us -ūs *m*
outcry *s* clam·or -oris *m; (noisy shouting)* convic·ium -(i)i *n*
outdo *tr* superare
outdoors *adv* foris; *(motion)* foras
outer *adj* exter·ior -ior -ius; — **space** intermundi·a -orum *npl*

outermost *adj* extrem·us -a -um
outfielder *s* extern·us -a cust·os -odis *mf*
outfit *s* apparat·us -ūs *m; (dress)* habit·us -ūs *m*, synthes·is -is *f; (costume)* cult·us -ūs *m*
outfit *tr* ornare
outflank *tr* circumire
outflow *s* effluv·ium -(i)i *n*
outgrow *tr* excedere ex *(w. abl)*, staturā superare
outing *s* excursi·o -onis *f*
outlandish *adj* absurd·us -a -um
outlast *tr* diutius durare *(w. abl)*, durando superare
outlaw *s* proscript·us -i *m* (·a -ae *f)*
outlaw *tr* aquā et igni interdiccre *(w. dat)*, proscribere
outlay *s* impens·a -ae *f*
outlet *s* exit·us -ūs *m; (for water)* emissar·ium -(i)i *n; (com)* mercat·us -ūs *m;* **electrical** — electrica capsul·a -ae *f* contactūs
outline *s* adumbrati·o -onis *f*, delineati·o -onis *f;* **to draw the** — **of a thing** primas modo lineas alicuius rei ducere
outline *tr* delineare, adumbrare
outlive *tr* supervivere *(w. dat)*, superst·es -itis esse *(w. dat)*
outlook *s* prospcct·us -ūs *m; (prospect)* expectati·o -onis *f; (chance)* fortun·a -ae *f*
outlying *adj* extern·us -a -um; *(just outside)* circumiect·us -a -um; *(far out)* remot·us -a -um
outmoded *adj* obsolet·us -a -um, desuet·us -a -um
outnumber *tr* multitudine superare
out-of-date *adj* obsolet·us -a -um
out-of-doors *adj & adv* sub divo
out-of-the-way *adj* devi·us -a -um, remot·us -a -um
outpost *s* stati·o -onis *f*
outpouring *s* effusi·o -onis *f*
output *s* fruct·us -ūs *m; (comput)* exit·us -ūs *m*
outrage *s* iniuri·a -ae *f*, flagit·ium -(i)i *n*
outrage *tr* iniuriā afficere
outrageous *adj* flagitios·us -a -um
outrageously *adv* flagitiose
outrank *tr* dignitate antecedere *(w. dat)*
outright *adj* manifest·us -a -um
outright *adv* prorsus; *(at once)* statim
outrun *tr* cursu superare
outset *s* init·ium -(i)i *n;* **from the** — a principio
outshine *tr* praelucēre *(w. dat)*
outside *s* par·s -tis *f* exterior; *(appearance)* speci·es -ei *f;* **on the** — extrinsecus
outside *prep* extra *(acc)*
outside *adv (position)* foris; *(motion)* foras; **from** — extrinsecus
outside *adj* extern·us -a -um

outsider s advem·a -ae *mf; (from abroad)* peregrin·us -i *m* (·a -ae *f*)

outskirts *spl* circumiect·a -orum *npl;* suburb·ium -(i)i *n; just on the — of the province* fere ad extremum provinciae finem

outspoken *adj* liberius dic·ax -acis

outspread *adj* patul·us -a -um

outstanding *adj* praest·ans -antis; *(of debts)* residu·us -a -um

outstretched *adj* porrect·us -a -um

outstrip *tr (in running)* cursu superare; *(excel)* excellere *(w. dat of person outstripped)*

outward *adj* extern·us -a -um

outwardly *adv* extrinsecus

outweigh *tr* praeponderare; *(fig)* praevertere *(w. dat)*

outwit *tr* deludere, dolis vincere

oval *adj* ovat·us -a -um

oval *s* ovata form·a -ae *f*

ovation *s* plaus·us -ūs *m; (second-class triumph)* ovati·o -onis *f*

oven *s* furn·us -i *m*

over *adv (excess)* nimis; *all — (everywhere)* ubique; *it's all —! (coll)* actum est!; *— and — identidem; — there* illic, in illo loco; *(motion)* illuc; *when the battle was —* confecto proelio

over *prep (motion over, above)* super *(w. acc); (across)* trans *(w. acc); (in position above)* supra *(w. acc); (w. verbs of motion, denoting space traversed)* per *(w. acc); (w. numbers)* plus quam; *— and above* super *(w. acc); — sixty years old* maior (quam) annos sexaginta annos nat·us -a -um; *the water was — a man's head* humanā magnitudine maior erat fluminis altitudo

overabundant *adj* supervacane·us -a -um

overall *adj* tot·us -a -um

overall *adv* in toto

overalls *spl* encombom·a -atis *n*

overawe *tr* (de)terrēre

overbalance *tr* praeponderare

overbearing *adj* superb·us -a -um, insol·ens -entis

overboard *adv* ex nave (in mare); *to go — for* nimis studēre *(w. dat); to throw —* iacturam facere *(w. gen of person or thing thrown)*

overburden *tr* nimis onerare

overcast *adj* obnubil·us -a -um, nubilos·us -a -um

overcharge *tr* plus aequo exigere ab *(w. abl)*

overcoat *s* paenul·a -ae *f,* superindument·um -i *n*

overcome *tr* superare, vincere

overconfident *adj* nimis confid·ens -entis

overcooked *adj* percoct·us -a -um

overdo *tr* exaggerare, in maius extollere; *to — it* se supra vires extendere

overdose *s* medicament·um -i *n* supra modum

overdose *intr* medicamentum supra modum (con)sumere

overdraw *tr — one's account* amplius scribere quam apud argentariam pecuniae praesto sunt

overdue *adj (money)* residu·us -a -um

overeat *intr* immodice ēsse, heluari

overestimate *tr* maioris aestimare

overflow *s* inundati·o -onis *f*

overflow *tr* inundare **||** *intr* abundare, redundare

overgrown *adj* obsit·us -a -um; *(too big)* praegrand·is -is -e

overhang *tr* impendēre *(w. dat)*

overhanging *adj* impend·ens -entis

overhasty *adj* praeproper·us -a -um

overhaul *tr* reficere; *(to pass)* consequi

overhead *adv* desuper, insuper

overhead *adj* super·us -a -um, immin·ens -entis

overhead *s (fin)* impens·a -ae *f* negotii

overhead projector *s* proiector·ium -(i)i *n* supracapitale

overhear *tr* auscultare, excipere

overheat *tr* percalefacere

overindulge *intr* immodice indulgēre

overjoyed *adj* I am —! *(coll)* immortaliter gaudeo!; *to be — at the sight of a son* ad conspectum filii laetitiā exsultare

overladen *adj* praegravat·us -a -um

overland *adj* per terram

overlap *tr* excedere **||** *intr (to coincide)* convenire, congruere

overlay *tr* inducere, illinere

overlay *s* tegim·en -inis *n,* obducti·o -onis *f*

overload *tr* nimis onerare

overlook *tr (not to notice)* praetermittere; *(to pardon)* ignoscere *(w. dat),* omittere; *(a view)* prospicere, spectare

overlord *s* domin·us -i *m*

overnight *adv* nocte, per noctem; *to stay —* pernoctare

overpass *s* transit·us -ūs *m*

overpopulated *adj* confert·us -a -um

overpower *tr* opprimere, subigere

overpowering *adj* praeval·ens -entis

overrate *tr* nimis magni aestimare; *to be an — ed man* famā minor esse

overreach *tr* circumvenire

overriding *adj* praecipu·us -a -um

overripe *adj* permatur·us -a -um

overrun *tr* occupare

overseas *adj* transmarin·us -a -um

overseas *adv* trans mare

oversee *tr* praeesse *(w. dat),* procurare

overseer *s* cura·tor -toris *m* (·trix -tricis *f*)

overshadow *tr* obumbrare; *(fig)* obscurare

overshoot *tr* excedere; **to — the mark** ex orbitā ire; **don't — the mark** ne ultra quam est opus contendas

oversight *s* *(superintendence)* cur·a -ae *f;* *(carelessness)* incuri·a -ae *f*

oversleep *intr* diutius dormire

overspread *tr* obducere

overstate *tr* in maius extollere

overstep *tr* transgredi

overstock *tr* **to — a shop** tabernam super quam est opus rebus venalibus instruere

overt *adj* apert·us -a -um

overtake *tr* consequi

overtax *tr* *(fig)* abuti *(w. abl)*

overthrow *s* eversi·o -onis *f*

overthrow *tr* evertere, deicere

overtime *adj* — **work** oper·a -ae *f* subsiciva

overtime *s* *(in a game)* additicium temp·us -oris *n*

overtly *adv* palam

overture *s* *(proposal)* condici·o -onis *f;* *(mus)* exord·ium -(i)i *n* (melodramatis); **to make —s** **to** agere cum *(w. abl)*

overturn *tr* evertere; **—ed tables** eversae mens·ae -arum *fpl* ‖ *intr* everti

overwhelm *tr* obruere, opprimere; **to be —ed** **with work** obrui tamquam fluctu, sic opere

overwork *tr* immodico labore onerare; **to — oneself** plus aequo laborare

overwrought *adj* perturbat·us -a -um

owe *tr* debēre

owing to *prep* propter *(w. acc)*

owl *s* bub·o -onis *m;* **— hoot** bubones bubilant

own *adj* propri·us -a -um; **one's — su·us -a -um**, propri·us -a -um

own *tr* tenēre, possidēre; *(to acknowledge)* confitēri

owner *s* domin·us -i *m* (·a -ae *f*)

ownership *s* domin·ium -(i)i *n*

ox *s* bos, bovis *m;* **oxen bellow** boves boant

oyster *s* ostre·a -ae *f*

oyster bed *s* ostrear·ium -(i)i *n*

oyster shell *s* ostreae test·a -ae *f*

P

pace *s* *(step)* pass·us -ūs *m,* grad·us -ūs *m;* *(measure of length; five Roman feet)* pass·us -ūs *m;* *(speed)* velocit·as -atis *f;* **to keep — with** pariter ire cum *(w. abl)*

pace *tr* **to — off** passibus emetiri ‖ *intr* gradi; **to — up and down** inambulare

pacific *adj* pacific·us -a -um

pacification *s* pacificati·o -onis *f*

pacifist *s* imbell·is -is *mf*

pacify *tr* placare

pack *s* *(bundle)* sarcin·a -ae *f;* *(of animals, of people)* gre·x -gis *m;* *(throng)* turb·a -ae *f;* **— of cigarettes** capsell·a -ae *f* sigarellorum

pack *tr* *(items of luggage)* colligere; *(a theater)* stipare; *(to fill completely)* frequentare, complēre; *(to compress)* stipare; **to — up the luggage** sarcinas *(or* vasa*)* colligere

package *s* sarcin·a -ae *f*

packet *s* fascicul·us -i *m*

pact *s* pact·um -i *n;* **to make a —** pacisci

pad *s* pulvill·us -i *m*

pad *tr* suffarcinare

padding *s* fartur·a -ae *f*

paddle *s* rem·us -i *m*

paddle *intr* remigare

paddock *s* saept·um -i *n*

pagan *adj* pagan·us -a -um

pagan *s* pagan·us -i *m* (·a -ae *f*)

paganism *s* paganit·as -atis *f*

page *s* *(of book)* pagin·a -ae *f;* *(boy)* pu·er -eri *m;* *(messenger)* nunt·ius -(i)i *m;* **at the top (bottom) of the —** in summā (imā) paginā

page *tr* arcessere

pageant *s* pomp·a -ae *f*

pail *s* situl·a -ae *f*

pain *s* dol·or -oris *m;* *(fig)* ang·or -oris *m;* **— in the neck** *(coll)* molest·us -i *m;* **severe —** ingens *or* vehemcns dolor; **stop being a —in the neck** molest·us (-a) ne sis; **to be in —** dolēre; **to feel —** dolore affici; **to take —s to** operam dare (ut *w. subj or w. inf*); **to take great —s to** in magno negotio habēre *(w. inf)*

pain *tr* dolore afficere ‖ *intr* dolēre

painful *adj* molest·us -a -um; *(bitter, distressful)* acerb·us -a -um; **to be extremely —** dolores magnos movēre

painfully *adv* magno cum dolore

painkiller *s* medicament·um -i *n* anodynum

painless *adj* doloris exper·s -tis

painstaking *adj* operos·us -a -um

paint *s* pigment·um -i *n*

paint *tr & intr* ping·o -ere pinxi pictus

paintbrush *s* penicill·us -i *m*

painter *s* pic·tor -toris *m* (·trix -tricis *f*)

pair *s* par, paris *n;* *(of oxen)* iug·um -i *n*

pair *tr* coniungere ‖ *intr* coïre

pajamas *spl* synthes·is -is *f* dormitoria

palace *s* regi·a -ae *f,* aul·a -ae *f*

palatable *adj* sapid·us -a -um

palate *s* palat·um -i *n;* *(sense of taste)* gustat·us -ūs *m*

palatial *adj* regi·us -a -um

pale *adj* pallid·us -a -um; **to be —** pallēre; **to grow —** pallescere

pale *s* pal·us -i *m;* *(enclosure)* saept·um -i *n*

paleography *s* palaeographi·a -ae *f*

palette *s* pictoris tabul·a -ae *f*

palisade *s* vall·um -i *n*

palliative *s* leniment·um -i *n*

pallid *adj* pallid·us -a -um
pallor *s* pall·or -oris *m*
palm *s* *(of the hand; palm tree; palm branch, as token of victory)* palm·a -ae *f;* **to grease s.o.'s** — aliquem pecuniā corrumpere; **to win the** — palmam ferre
palm off *tr* **(on)** imponere *(w. dat)*
palpable *adj* tractabil·is -is -e; *(fig)* manifest·us -a -um
palpitate *intr* palpitare
palpitation *s* palpitati·o -onis *f*
palsy *s* paralys·is -is *f*
paltry *adj* vil·is -is -e
pamper *tr* indulgēre *(w. dat)*
pamphlet *s* libell·us -i *m*
pan *s* patin·a -ae *f;* *(for frying)* sartag·o -inis *f*
pan *intr* **to** — **out** *(coll)* bene evenire
panacea *s* panace·a -ae *f*
pancake *s* lagan·um -i *n*
pandemic *adj* evagat·us -a -um
pandemic *s* evagata pestilenti·a -ae *f*
pandemonium *s* tumult·us -ūs *m*
pander *intr* lenocinari; **to** — **to** indulgēre *(w. dat)*
panderer *s* len·o -onis *m*
pandering *s* lenocin·ium -(i)i *n*
panegyric *s* laudati·o -onis *f*
panel *s* *(of wall)* abac·us -i *m;* *(of ceiling)* lacun·ar -aris *n;* *(of door)* tympan·um -i *n;* *(of jury)* iudic·es -um *mpl;* *(discussion group)* colleg·ium -(i)i *n*
paneled *adj* laqueat·us -a -um
pang *s* dol·or -oris *m*
panic *s* pav·or -oris *m*
panicky, panic-stricken *adj* pavid·us -a -um
panoply *s* arm·a -orum *npl*
panorama *s* prospect·us -ūs *m*
pant *intr* anhelare; **to** — **after** *(fig)* gestire
pantheism *s* pantheism·us -i *m*
pantheist *s* pantheist·a -ae *m* (·ria -riae *f*)
Pantheon *s* Panthe·um -i *n*
panther *s* panther·a -ae *f*
panting *adj* anhel·us -a -um
panting *s* anhelit·us -ūs *m*
pantomime *s* *(play; actor)* mim·us -i *m;* *(actress)* mima -ae *f*
pantry *s* cell·a -ae *f* penaria
pants *spl* brac·ae -arum *fpl;* **hot** — perbreves bracae femineae
pantyhose *spl* tibial·ia -ium *npl* bracaria
papa *s* tat·a -ae *m*
paper *s* *(stationery)* chart·a -ae *f;* *(newspaper)* act·a -orum *npl* diurna; **packing** — charta emporetica; **—s** script·a -orum *npl*
paper *adj* chartace·us -a -um
paper clip *s* fibicul·a -ae *f* chartarum
paperback *s* lib·er -ri *m* chartā contectus
paperhanger *s* tapetar·ius -(i)i *m,* parietum exornat·or -oris *m*

paprika *s* capsic·um -i *n*
papyrus *s* papyr·us -i *f*
par *s* **to be on a** — **with** par esse *(w. dat)*
parable *s* parabol·a -ae *f*
parachute *s* decidicul·um -i *n*
parachute *intr* decidiculo descendere
parade *s* pomp·a -ae *f;* *(mil)* decurs·us -ūs *m*
parade *tr* ostentare ‖ *intr* in pompā incedere; *(mil)* decurrere
paradise *s* paradis·us -i *m*
paradox *s* paradox·um -i *n*
paragon *s* specim·en -inis *n*
paragraph *s* cap·ut -itis *n*
parallel *adj* parallel·us -a -um; *(fig)* consimil·is -is -e
parallel *tr* exaequare
paralysis *s* paralys·is -is *f*
paralytic *adj* paralytic·us -a -um
paralyze *tr* enervare; *(fig)* percellere
paralyzed *adj* per omnia membra resolut·us -a -um
paramount *adj* suprem·us -a -um
paramour *s* *(male)* moech·us -i *m;* *(female)* meretr·ix -icis *f*
parapet *s* plute·us -i *m*
paraphernalia *s* apparat·us -ūs *m*
paraphrase *s* paraphras·is -is *f*
paraphrase *tr* laxius liberiusque interpretari
parasite *s* parasit·us -i *m*
parasol *s* umbell·a -ae *f*
parcel *s* fascicul·us -i *m* (cursualis); *(plot of land)* agell·us -i *m*
parcel *tr* **to** — **out** dispertire
parch *tr* torrēre
parched *adj* torrid·us -a -um
parchment *s* membran·a -ae *f*
pardon *s* veni·a -ae *f;* **to obtain a** — veniam impetrare; **to grant a** — **to** *(leg)* absolvere
pardon *tr* ignoscere *(dat);* condonare *(w. acc of thing & dat of person);* *(leg)* absolvere; **after being —ed** post impetratam veniam; **— me for what I said** ignosce mihi, quod dixero
pardonable *adj* ignoscend·us -a -um
pare *tr* *(vegetables)* deglubere; *(the nails)* resecare
parent *s* paren·s -tis *mf*
parentage *s* gen·us -eris *n,* stirp·s -is *f*
parental *adj* parental·is -is -e
parenthesis *s* interclusi·o -onis *f*
pariah *s* sentin·a -ae *f* reipublicae
parity *s* parit·as -atis *f*
park *s* hort·i -orum *mpl* publici
park *tr* *(a car)* statuere ‖ *intr* vehiculum statuere
parking meter *s* statimetr·um -i *n;* **to put a coin into the** — nummum in statimetrum immittere
parking fee *s* tax·a -ae *f* stativa

parking garage *s* multizon·ium -(i)i *n* stativum
parking lot *s* are·a -e *f* stativa
parking-lot attendant *s* cust·os -odis *mf* areae stativae
parley *s* colloqu·ium -(i)i *n*
parley *intr* colloqui
parliament *s* parliament·um -i *n;* **member of** — parliamentari·us -i *m* (·a -ae *f*)
parlor *s* sessor·ium -(i)i *n*
parody *s* parodi·a -ae *f*
parole *s* fid·es -ei *f* data; **on** — custodiae immun·is -is -e (per bonos mores)
parole *tr* fide interpositā demittere
paroxysm *s* access·us -ūs *m*
parricide *s (murder)* parricid·ium -(i)i *n; (murderer)* parricid·a -ae *mf*
parrot *s* psittac·us -i *m*
parse *tr* proprietates *(w. gen)* describere
parsimonious *adj* parc·us -a -um
parsimoniously *adv* parce
parsley *s* petroselin·um -i *n*
part *s* par·s -tis *f; (role)* part·es -ium *fpl; (duty)* offic·ium -(i)i *n;* **for the most** — maximā ex parte; **in** — partim; **on the** — **of** ab *(w. abl);* **to act the** — **of** sustinēre partes *(w. gen);* **to take** — **in** interesse *(w. dat)*
part *tr* separare, dividere; **to** — **company** discedere ‖ *intr* discedere, abire; *(to go open)* dehiscere; **to** — **with** dimittere
partial *adj (unfair)* iniqu·us -a -um; *(incomplete)* manc·us -a -um, per partes
partiality *s* fav·or -oris *m; (unfairness)* iniquit·as -atis *f*
partially *adv* aliquā ex parte, partim
participant *s* parti·ceps -cipis *mf*
participate *intr* **to** — **in** interesse *(w. dat)*, particeps esse *(w. gen)*
participation *s* societ·as -atis *f*
participial *adj (gram)* participial·is -is -e
participle *s* particip·ium -(i)i *n;* **future** — futuri temporis participium; **perfect** — praeteriti temporis participium; **present** — praesentis temporis participium
particle *s (faint trace)* vestig·ium -(i)i *n; (tibit)* particul·a -ae *f; (gram)* particul·a -ae *f*
particular *adj (special)* praecipu·us -a -um; *(fussy)* fastidios·us -a -um; **in** — potissimum
particularly *adv* praecipue, praesertim
particularize *tr* exsequi, enumerare
particulars *spl* singul·a -orum *npl*
parting *s* discess·us -ūs *m*
partisan *s* fau·tor -toris *m* (·trix -tricis *f; (guerilla)* factiosus armig·er -eri *m*
partition *s* partiti·o -onis *f; (between rooms)* pari·es -etis *m; (compartment)* loculament·um -i *n; (section)* pars, partis *f*
partition *tr* dividere
partitive *adj (gram)* partitiv·us -a -um

partly *adv* partim
partner *s* soc·ius -(i)i *m,* soci·a -ae *f,* partic·eps -ipis *mf; (in office)* colleg·a -ae *mf; (in marriage)* con·iu(n)x -iugis *mf*
partnership *s* societ·as -atis *f;* **to dissolve a** — dissociari; **to form a** — societatem inire
partridge *s* perd·ix -icis *mf*
party *s (for entertainment)* conviv·ium -(i)i *n; (side)* pars, partis *f; (pol)* facti·o -onis *f,* part·es -ium *fpl; (detachment)* man·us -ūs *f;* **opposite** — partes diversae; **to give a** — convivium dare; **to join a** — parti se adiugere; **to throw a** — convivium agitare
pass *s (defile)* angusti·ae -arum *fpl,* salt·us -ūs *m, (basketball, football)* follis transmiss·us -ūs *m; (free ticket)* tesser·a -ae *f* gratuita; **things have come to such a** — **that** eo rerum ventum erat ut *(w. subj)*
pass *tr (to go by)* praeterire; *(exceed)* excedere; *(to approve)* probare; *(time)* degere; *(a law)* perferre; *(by the assembly)* iubēre; *(basketball, football, lacrosse)* transmittere; **he tried to** — **himself off for Philip** se Philippum ferebat; — **me the vegetables** porrige mihi holera; **to** — **around** circumferre; **to** — **down** tradere; **to** — **a test** probationem sustinere; **to** — **out** distribuere; **to** — **sentence** ius dicere; **to** — **the test** approbari; **to** — **up** praetermittere ‖ *intr (of time)* transire; *(to walk by)* praeterire; *(to ride by)* praetervehi; **to come to** — fieri, evenire; **to let** — praetermittere; **to let an army** — **through the country** exercitum per fines transmittere; **to** — **away** *(to die)* perire, decedere; *(to come to an end)* transire; **to** — **by** *(e.g.,* **a park)** praeterire *(hortos); (in a carriage or ship)* praetervehi; **to** — **for** habēri; **to** — **on** *(to go forward)* pergere; *(to die)* perire; **to** — **out** collabi, intermori; **to** — **over** *(e.g., of a storm)* transire; *(to make no mention of)* praeterire; **to** — **over the fact that** mittere quod *(w. subj);* **to** — **through** *(e.g.,* **a town)** transire; *(of an arrow, spear)* ire per *(w. acc);* **to** — **through enemy lines** per hostes vadere
passable *adj (of road)* pervi·us -a -um; *(tolerable)* tolerabil·is -is -e
passably *adv* tolerabiliter
passage *s (act)* transit·us -ūs *m; (by water)* traiecti·o -onis *f; (road)* it·er -ineris *n; (in a book)* loc·us -i *m (pl:* loc·i -orum); **to allow anyone a** — **through the province** alicui transitum dare per provinciam
passbook *s (bank book)* argentariae libell·us -i *m*
passenger *s* vec·tor -toris *m* (·trix tricis *f)*
passenger train *s* tram·en -inis *n* commune
passer-by *s* praeter·iens -euntis *mf*

passing s obit·us -ūs m; **no —!** cave praeveharis!

passion s (strong desire of any kind, esp. lust) cupidit·as -atis f; (strong emotion) animi permoti·o -onis f; (lust) libid·o -inis f; (violent anger) iracundi·a -ae f; **to fly into a —** exardescere iracundiā et stomacho

passionate adj ard·ens -entis; (given to bursts of anger) iracund·us -a -um

passionately adv ardenter; iracunde

passive adj toler·ans -antis, iner·s -tis; (gram) passiv·us -a -um

passively adv toleranter; (gram) passive

Passover s Pascha [indecl], Pasch·a -atis n

passport s (commeatūs) diplom·a -atis n

password s (also comput) tesser·a -ae f

past adj praeterit·us -a -um; (immediately preceding) proxim·us -a -um, super·ior -ior -iŭs; **— participle** praeteriti temporis particip·ium -(i)i n

past s praeterit·um -i n; (past tense) praeteritum temp·us -oris n

past prep praeter (w. acc)

pasta s collyr·a -ae f

paste s glut·en -ineris n

paste tr glutinare; (to strike) ferire

pasteboard s chart·a -ae f crassa

pastime s oblectament·um -i n; **by way of —** oblectamenti causā

pastoral adj (poetry) bucolic·us -a -um; (of shepherds) pastoral·is -is -e

pastoral s bucolic·um -i n

pastry s crustul·a -orum npl; **pastries** cuppedi·a -orum npl

pastry shop s cuppedinari·a -ae f

pasture s (grazing land) pascu·um -i n; (feeding of animals) past·us -ūs m

pasture tr pascere **‖** intr pasci; **to go out to —** pastum ire

pat s plag·a -ae f lenis; **— on the back** (fig) approbati·o -onis f

pat tr demulcēre

patch s pann·us -i m

patch tr resarcire; **to — up** (fig) refovēre

patchwork s cent·o -onis m; **to make —** (out of old clothes) centones facere

patent adj manifest·us -a -um

patent s ius, iuris n praecipuum

patently adv manifesto

paternal adj patern·us -a -um; (like a father) patri·us -a -um

paternity s paternit·as -atis f

path s semit·a -ae f, call·is -is m

pathetic adj flebil·is -is -e

pathless adj invi·us -a -um

pathos s vis f ad misericordiam movendam

pathway s semit·a -ae f; **the — of life** vitae semita

patience s patienti·a -ae f

patient adj pati·ens -entis

patient s ae·ger -gri m (·gra -grae f)

patiently adv aequo animo, patienter

patriarch s patriarch·a -ae m

patriarchal adj patriarchic·us -a -um

patrician adj patrici·us -a -um

patrician s patric·ius -(i)i m

patrimony s patrimon·ium -(i)i n

patriot s am·ans -antis mf patriae

patriotic adj am·ans -antis patriae

patriotism s am·or -oris m patriae

patrol s circuitor·es -um mpl

patrol tr & intr circumire

patron s patron·us -i m

patronage s patrocin·ium -(i)i n

patroness s patron·a -ae f

patronize tr favēre (w. dat); (a shop) frequentare

patter s crepit·us -ūs m; **the — of feet** mollis puls·us -ū m pedum

pattern s exempl·ar -aris n; (of weaving) text·us -ūs m; **— of behavior** indol·es -is f

pattern tr **— after** imitari

paucity s paucit·as -atis f

paunch s ven·ter -tris m obesus; **to have a —** ventre obeso esse

pauper s pau·per -eris mf

pause s paus·a -ae f; (break) intercaped·o -inis f, intermissi·o -onis f; (music) caesur·a -ae f

pause intr subsistere; (to halt) insistere; **to — in speaking** in dicendo subsistere

pave tr sternere; **to — the way to** (fig) viam facere ad (w. acc)

pavement s paviment·um -i n

pavilion s tentor·ium -(i)i n

paving stone s sax·um -i n quadratum

paw s pe·s -dis m

paw tr pedibus pulsare

pawn s pign·us -oris n

pawn tr pignerare

pawnbroker s pignerna·tor -toris m (·trix -tricis f)

pay s merc·es -edis f; (mil) stipend·ium -(i)i n

pay tr (money) solvere; (in full) persolvere, pendere; (a person) pecuniam (mercedem) solvere (dat); (mil) stipendium numerare (w. dat); **to — back** restituere; (to avenge) vindicare; **to — in cash** numerare; **to — off a debt** nomen exsolvere, aes alienum persolvere; **to — on time** ad tempus or ad diem dictam solvere; **to — out (money) to** denumerare (nummos) (w. dat); **to — s.o. a compliment** aliquem laudare; **to — s.o. a visit** aliquem invisere; **to — (s.o.) for** solvere (w. acc of thing and dat of person); **to — respects to** salutare; **to — the penalty** poenam dare **‖** intr it **—s to ...** operae pretium est (w. inf); **to — for** (merchandise) emere; (a misdeed) poenas dare ob (w. acc)

payable *adj* solvend·us -a -um
payday *s* di·es -ei *f* pecuniae
paymaster *s* dispensat·or -oris *m*
payment *s (act)* soluti·o -onis *f; (sum of money)* pensi·o -onis *f*
pay phone *s* telephon·um -i *n* nummarium
pea *s* pis·um -i *n*
peace *s* pa·x -cis *f;* in a state of — pacat·us -a -um; in — and in war domi et militiae *(or* in militiā); to break the — pacem frangere; to bring about — between pacem conciliare inter *(w. acc);* to conclude — on these terms pacem his legibus constituere; to conduct — negotiations with s.o. cum aliquo de pace agere; to hold one's — tacēre; to live in — pacem agitare; to make — with pacificare cum *(w. abl)*
peaceably *adv* cum bonā pace
peaceful *adj* tranquill·us -a -um
peacefully *adv* tranquille, cum bonā pace
peace-loving *adj* pacis am·ans -antis
peacemaker *s* pacifica·tor -toris *m* (·trix -tricis *f)*
peace offering *s* placam·en -inis *n*
peacetime *s* ot·ium -(i)i *n*
peach *s* persic·um -i *n*
peach *adj (color)* punice·us -a -um
peacock *s* pav·o -onis *mf*
peak *s* vert·ex -icis *m; (of a mountain)* cacum·en -inis *n*
peal *s (of thunder)* frag·or -oris *m; (of bells)* concent·us -ūs *m*
peal *intr* resonare
peanut *s* arach·is -idis *f* hypogea
peanut butter *s* butyr·um -i *n* ex arachidibus
peanut butter sandwich *s* pastill·um -i *n* butyro ex arachidibus fartum
pear *s* pir·um -i *n*
pearl *s* margarit·a -ae *f*
pearl earrings *spl* inaur·es -ium *fpl* ex margaritis
pearl necklace *s* monil·e -is *n* ex margaritis
pearly *adj* gemme·us -a -um
pear tree *s* pir·us -i *f*
peasant *s* rustic·us -i *m* (·a -ae *f)*
peasantry *s* agrest·es -ium *mpl*
pea soup *s* ius, iuris *n* ex pisis
pebble *s* calcul·us -i *m*
peck *s* mod·ius -(i)i *m; (perfunctory kiss)* basiol·um -i *n*
peck *tr* vellicare
peculiar *adj* peculiar·is -is -e; *(belonging to one person or thing only)* propri·us -a -um; *(odd)* inusitat·us -a -um, absurd·us -a -um
peculiarity *s* propriet·as -atis *f*
pedagogue *s* paedagog·us -i *m*
pedal *s* pedal·e -is *n*
pedant *s* hom·o -inis *mf* moros·us (-a)
pedantic *adj* moros·us -a -um

pedantry *s* morosit·as -atis *f*
peddle *tr* venditare
peddler *s* instit·or -oris *m;* door-to-door — qui *(or* quae) merces suas ostiatim venditat
pedestal *s* bas·is -is *f*
pedestrian *adj* pedes·ter -tris -tre; — crossing transit·us -ūs *m* peditum
pedestrian *s* ped·es -itis *mf*
pedigree *s* stemm·a -atis *n*
pediment *s* fastig·ium -(i)i *n*
pedophile *s* pedica·tor -toris *m* (·a -ae *f)*
pee *intr (coll)* facere *(for* aquam facere)
peel *s* cut·is -is *f; (rind, thick skin)* cor·ium -(i)i *n;* apple — mali cutis; orange peel corium mali aurantii
peel *tr* resecare cutem *(w. gen)*
peep *s* conspect·us -ūs *m* fugax
peep *intr* furtim conspicere
peephole *s* conspicill·um -i *n*
peer *s* par, paris *mf*
peer *intr* to — at intuēri
peerless *adj* incomparabil·is -is -e
peevish *adj* stomachos·us -a -um
peevishly *adv* stomachose
peg *s* paxill·us -i *m*
pelican *s* pelican·us -i *m*, onocrotal·us -i *m*
pellet *s* globul·us -i *m*
pell-mell *adv* turbate
pelt *s* pell·is -is *f*
pelt *tr (to hurl)* conicere; to — s.o. with stones aliquem lapidare
pen *s* calam·us -i *m; (enclosure)* saept·um -i *n; (for pigs)* suil·e -is *n; (for sheep)* ovil·e -is *n*
pen *tr* scribere; to — in includere, saepire
penal *adj* poenal·is -is -e
penalize *tr* mul(c)tare
penalty *s* poen·a -ae *f; (fine)* mul(c)t·a -ae *f;* to pay the — poenas dare *or* (per)solvere
penance *s* satisfacti·o -onis *f; (eccl)* expiati·o -onis *f;* to do — for expiare
pencil *s* graph·is -idis *f*
pencil sharpener *s* instrument·um -i *n* cuspidarium
pendant *s* ornament·um -i *n* pensile
pending *adj* suspens·us -a -um; *(leg)* sub iudice
pending *prep* inter *(acc)*
pendulum *s* librament·um -i *n; (of clock)* oscill·ium -(i)i *n*
penetrate *tr* penetrare ad *(w. acc)* ‖ *intr* penetrare
penetrating *adj (cold)* acut·us -a -um *(keen-sighted)* perspic·ax -acis
penetration *s* introit·us -ūs *m;* aci·es -ei *f* mentis
penguin *s* aptenodyt·es -is *f*
peninsula *s* paeninsul·a -ae *f*
penitence *s* paenitenti·a -ae *f*
penitent *adj* paenit·ens -entis

penitentiary *s* ergastul·um -i *n*
penknife *s* cultell·us -i *m*
penmanship *s* man·us -ūs *f*
pennant *s* vexill·um -i *n*
penniless *adj* in·ops -opis
penny *s* as, assis *m*
pension *s* annu·a -orum *npl*
pensive *adj* meditabund·us -a -um
pentathlon *s* pentathl·um -i *n;* **to win the —** pentathlo vincere
penult *s* paenultima syllab·a -ae *f*
penultimate *adj* paenultim·us -a -um
people *s* homin·es -um *mpl; (as political entity)* popul·us -i *m; (of a country)* gen·s -tis *f;* **common —** vulg·us -i *n;* **— say** aiunt; **— who say** qui aiunt, qui dicunt
people *tr* frequentare
pep *s* alacrit·as -atis *f*
pep rally *s* convent·us -ūs *m* hortatorius
pep talk *s* conti·o -onis *f;* **to give a —** contionem habēre
pepper *s* pip·er -eris *n*
pepper *tr* pipere condire; *(w. blows)* verberare
peppermint *s* menth·a -ae *f*
pepper shaker *s* piperin·um -i *n*
perceive *tr* percipere
percent *s* per centum, centesim·a -ae *f*
percentage *s* porti·o -onis *f*
perceptible *adj* percipiend·us -a -um
perceptibly *adv* sensim
perch *s (for birds)* pertic·a -ae *f; (fish)* perc·a -ae *f*
perch *intr* **(on)** insidēre *(w. dat)*
perchance *adv* forte
percolate *tr* percolare ‖ *intr* permanare
percussion *s* percuss·us -ūs *m*
percussion instrument *s* percussionale instrument·um -i *n* musicum
perdition *s* interit·us -ūs *m*
peremptory *adj* arrogan·s -tis
perennial *adj* perenn·is -is -e
perfect *adj* perfect·us -a -um; *(utter, total)* tot·us -a -um; **the perfect tense** tempus praeteritum perfectum; **to enjoy almost — health** inlaesā prope valetudine uti
perfect *s (gram)* praeterit·um perfect·um -i *n*
perfect *tr* perficere
perfection *s (act)* perfecti·o -onis *f; (excellence)* summ·a -ae *f*
perfectly *adv* perfecte; *(totally)* plane
perfidious *adj* perfid·us -a -um
perfidy *s* perfidi·a -ae *f*
perforate *tr* perforare
perforation *s* foram·en -inis *n*
perform *tr* perficere, peragere; *(duty)* fungi *(w. abl),* praestare; *(theat)* agere
performance *s* perfuncti·o -onis *f; (work)* op·us -eris *n; (of a play)* acti·o -onis *f; (play)* fabul·a -ae *f*

performer *s* ac·tor -toris *m* (·trix -tricis *f); (theat)* histri·o -onis *mf*
perfume *s* od·or -oris *m*, ungent·um -i *n*
perfume *tr* odoribus imbuere
perfunctorily *adv* parum diligenter
perfunctory *adj* parum dilig·ens -entis
perhaps *adv* fortasse, forsitan
peril *s* pericul·um -i *n*
perilous *adj* periculos·us -a -um
perilously *adv* periculose
perimeter *s* circinati·o -onis *f; (geom)* perimetr·os -i *f*
period *s (span of time, class period)* spat·ium -(i)i *n; (chronological)* temp·us -oris *n; (punctuation mark)* punct·um -i *n; (complete phrase or sentence)* period·us -i *m*, ambit·us -ūs *m;* **I'm not going. period!** non ibo, dixi!; **— of life** aet·as -atis *f;* **over a long — of time** in diuturno spatio
periodic *adj* recurr·ens -entis
periodical *s* commentar·ium -(i)i *n*
periodically *adv* temporibus statis
periphery *s* peripheri·a -ae *f*
periphrastic *adj* periphrastic·us -a -um
perish *intr* interire, perire
perishable *adj* quae cito corrumpuntur
peristyle *s* peristyl·ium -(i)i *n*
perjure *tr* **to — oneself** periurare
perjured *adj* periur·us -a -um
perjury *s* periur·ium -(i)i *n;* **to commit —** periurare
perk up *tr* erigere; **to — the spirits** animum demissum erigere ‖ *intr* **to —** reviviscere
perky *adj* ala·cer -cris -cre
permanence *s* stabilit·as -atis *f*
permanent *adj* perpetu·us -a -um
permanently *adv* perpetuo
permeable *adj* pervi·us -a -um
permeate *tr* permanare, permeare
permissible *adj* **it is — for me to** licet mihi ire *(or* licet eam)
permission *s* permiss·um -i *n;* **to grant — to** permittere *(w. dat);* **with your —** bonā tuā veniā; **without your father's —** invito patre; **you have my — to leave** per me licet ut abeas
permit *tr* permittere *(w. dat)*
permutation *s* permutati·o -onis *f*
pernicious *adj* pernicios·us -a -um; *(deadly)* letal·is -is -e
perniciously *adv* perniciose
peroration *s* perorati·o -onis *f*
perpendicular *adj* perpendicular·is -is -e
perpendicular *s* line·a -ae *f* perpendicularis
perpendicularly *adj* ad perpendiculuum
perpetrate *tr* perficere, peragere
perpetrator *s* auc·tor -toris *m* (·trix -tricis *f)*
perpetual *adj* perpetu·us -a -um
perpetually *adv* perpetuo

perpetuate *tr* perpetuare
perpetuity *s* perpetuit·as -atis *f*
perplex *tr* distrahere, turbare
perplexing *adj* perplex·us -a -um
perplexity *s* dubitati·o -onis *f,* perturbati·o -onis *m*
persecute *tr* insectari
persecution *s* insectati·o -onis *f*
persecutor *s* insecta·tor -toris *m* (·trix -tricis *f*)
perseverance *s* perseveranti·a -ae *f*
persevere *intr* perseverare, perstare
persevering *adj* persever·ans -antis
persist *intr* perseverare, perstare
persistence *s* perseveranti·a -ae *f*
persistent *adj* pertin·ax -acis
persistently *adv* pertinaciter
person *s* hom·o -inis *mf,* person·a -ae *f; (gram)* persona *f;* **in —** ips·e -a -um
personable *adj* com·is -is -e
personage *s* hom·o -inis *mf* praestabilis
personal *adj* privat·us -a -um; *(gram, leg)* personal·is -is -e; **— appearance** form·a -ae *f* et habit·us -ūs *m;* **— computer** ordinatr·um -i *n* domesticum; **— finances** res, rei *f* familiaris
personality *s* indol·es -is *f*
personally *adv* *rendered by* ips·e -a -um
personification *s* prosopopei·a -ae *f*
personify *tr (inanimate objects)* vitam sensumque tribuere *(dat);* **to — evil** malum in personam suam constituere
personnel *s* operari·i -orum *mpl;* soci·i -orum *mpl*
perspective *s* *(viewpoint)* conspect·us -ūs *m* animi; *(in drawing)* scaenographi·a -ae *f*
perspiration *s* *(sweating)* sudati·o -onis *f; (sweat)* sud·or -oris *m*
perspire *intr* sudare
persuade *tr* persuadēre *(w. dat)*
persuasion *s* persuasi·o -onis *f*
persuasive *adj* persuasibil·is -is -e
persuasively *adv* persuabiliter
pert *adj* proc·ax -acis
pertain *intr* **(to)** pertinēre (ad *w. acc)*
pertinence *s* congruenti·a -ae *f*
pertinent *adj* apposit·us -a -um; **to be — ad** rem pertinēre
perturb *tr* perturbare
perusal *s* perlecti·o -onis *f*
peruse *tr* perlegere
pervade *tr* permanare per *(w. acc)*
pervasive *adj* undique circumfus·us -a -um
perverse *adj* pervers·us -a -um
perversely *adv* perverse
perversion *s* perversit·as -atis *f*
perversity *s* perversit·as -atis *f*
pervert *s* hom·o -inis *mf* pervers·us (-a)
pervert *tr* depravare; *(words)* detorquēre
pessimist *s* hom·o -inis *mf* moros·us (-a)
pessimistic *adj* moros·us -a -um

pest *s* vexa·tor -toris *m* (·trix -tricis *f*)
pester *tr* vexare
pestilence *s* pestilenti·a -ae *f*
pestle *s* pistill·um -i *n*
pet *s* delici·ae -arum *fpl;* **to have a dog as a —** canem in deliciis habēre
pet *tr (to stroke)* permulcēre; *(to fondle)* subigitare **‖** *intr* inter se subigitare
petal *s* floris fol·ium -(i)i *n*
petition *s* petiti·o -onis *f; (pol)* libell·us -i *m*
petition *tr* supplicare
petitioner *s* suppl·ex -icis *mf*
petrify *tr* in lapidem convertere; *(fig)* perterrēre **‖** *intr* lapidescere
petticoat *s* inducul·a -ae *f*
pettiness *s* anim·us -i *m* angustus
petty *adj* minut·us -a -um et angust·us -a -um
petulance *s* petulanti·a -ae *f*
petulant *adj* petul·ans -antis
pew *s* subsell·ium -(i)i *n*
phantasy *s* phantasi·a -ae *f*
phantom *s* larv·a -ae *f,* spectr·um -i *n*
pharmacist *s* medicamentari·us -i *m* (·a -ae *f*)
pharmacy *s* tabern·a -ae *f* medicamentaria
phase *s* lunae faci·es -ei *f; (fig)* vic·es -ium *fpl*
pheasant *s* phasian·us -i *m* (·a -ae *f*)
phenomenal *adj* singular·is -is -e
phenomenon *s* res, rei *f; (s.th. remarkable)* miracul·um -i *n*
phew *interj (gratified surprise or relief)* ehem!; *(at a bad odor)* fi!
philanthropic *adj* human·us -a -um
philanthropy *s* humanit·as -atis *f*
philologist *s* philolog·us -i *m* (·a -ae *f*)
philology *s* philologi·a -ae *f*
philosopher *s* philosoph·us -i *m*
philosophical *adj* philosophic·us -a -um
philosophically *adv* philosophice; *(calmly)* aequo animo
philosophize *intr* philosophari
philosophy *s* philosophi·a -ae *f; (theory)* rati·o -onis *f*
phlegm *s* phlegm·a -atis *n*
phobia *s* formid·o -inis *f*
phone *s* telephon·um -i *n*
phone *tr* per telephonum loqui cum *(w. abl)*
phoney *adj* affectat·us -a -um
phosphorus *s* phosphor·us -i *m*
photo *s* *see* **photograph**
photo shop *s* officin·a -ae *f* photographica
photocopier *s* machin·a -ae *f* phototypica
photocopy *s* exempl·ar -aris *n* phototypicum
photograph *s* imag·o -inis *f* photographica; **to take —s** imagines luce exprimere
photograph *tr* photographice reddere
photographer *s* photograph·us -i *m* (·a -ae *f*)
photographic film *s* taeniol·a -ae *f* photographica
photography *s* photographi·a -ae *f*

phrase *s* locuti·o -onis *f*
phrase *tr* verbis exprimere
phraseology *s* loquendi rati·o -onis *f*
physical *adj (relating to nature)* physic·us -a -um; — **condition** corporis habit·us -ūs *m;* — **strength** corporis vir·es -ium *fpl*
physical therapist *s* iatralipt·es -ae *mf*
physical therapy *s* iatraliptic·e -es *f*
physician *s* medic·us -i *m* (·a -ae *f)*
physicist *s* physic·us -i *m* (·a -ae *f)*
physics *s* physic·a -orum *npl*
physiognomy *s* physiognomi·a -ae *f*
physiological *adj* physiologic·us -a -um
physiologist *s* physiolog·us -i *m* (·a -ae *f)*
physiology *s* physiologi·a -ae *f*
physique *s* corporis habit·us -ūs *m*
pianist *s* clavic·en -inis *m* (·ina -inae *f)*
piano *s* clavicord·ium -(i) i *n;* **to play the —** clavicordio canere
pick *tr (to choose)* eligere; *(to pluck)* carpere; *(to gather)* legere; **to — a quarrel** iurgi causam inferre; **to — out** eligere; **to — pockets** manticulari; **to — the teeth** dentes perfodere; **to — up** *(to raise)* tollere; *(a language)* perbibere ‖ *intr* **to — on s.o.** aliquem carpere
pick *s (tool)* dolabr·a -ae *f; (the best)* flo·s -ris *m*
pickax *s* dolabr·a -ae *f*
picked *adj* elect·us -a -um
picket *s (mil)* stati·o -onis *f*
pickle *s (brine)* muri·a -ae *f; (vegetable)* oxycucum·er -eris *m;* **to be in a —** in angustiis versari
pickled *adj* muriā condit·us -a -um; *(drunk)* madid·us -a -um; **— olives** oxycomin·a -orum *npl*
pickpocket *s* sacculari·us -i *m* (·a -ae *f)*
picnic *s* conviv·ium -(i)i *n* sub divo
picnic basket *s* panar·ium -(i)i *n*
pictorial *adj* pictori·us -a -um
picture *s* tabul·a -ae *f* picta
picture *tr* effingere
picture gallery *s* pinacothec·a -ae *f*
picturesque *adj* amoen·us -a -um
pie *s* crust·um -i *n;* **apple —** mal·a -orum *npl* in crusto cocta; **cherry —** ceras·a -orum *npl* in crusto cocta
piece *s* par·s -tis *f; (of food)* frust·um -i *n; (broken off)* fragment·um -i *n; (drama)* fabul·a -ae *f; (very often not expressed by a separate word, e.g.,* **a —** *of* **bread** pan·is -is *m;* **a — of cheese** case·us -i *m;* **a — of ground** agell·us -i *m;* **a — of meat** car·o -nis *f;* **a — of paper** chart·a -ae *f); to break in —s* confringere; **to cut in —s** minute concidere; **to fall to —s** dilabi; **to tear to —s** dilaniare; *(e.g., paper)* conscindere
piece *tr* **to — together** fabricari *or* fabricare

piecemeal *adv* frustillatim, separatim
pier *s* mol·es -is *f*
pierce *tr* perforare; *(w. a sword)* perfodere; *(fig)* pungere
piercing *adj* acut·us -a -um
piety *s* piet·as -atis *f*
pig *s* porc·us -i *m;* **—s oink** porci grunniunt
pigeon *s* columb·a -ae *f;* **—s coo** columbae gemunt
pigeon coop *s* columbar·ium -(i)i *n*
pigheaded *adj* obstinat·us -a -um
pigment *s* pigment·um -i *n*
pigsty *s* suil·e -is *n*
pike *s* hast·a -ae *f; (fish)* lup·us -i *m*
pilaster *s* parastatic·a -ae *f*
pile *s* acerv·us -i *m; (nap of cloth)* vill·us -i *m; (for cremation)* rog·us -i *m*
pile *tr* **(on)** congerere *(w. dat);* **to — up** exstruere ‖ *intr* **to — up** crescere
pilgrim *s* peregrina·tor -toris *m* (·trix -tricis *f)* religionis causā
pilgrimage *s* peregrinati·o -onis *f* religionis causā
piling *s* sublic·a -ae *f*
pill *s* pilul·a -ae *f*
pillage *s* rapin·a -ae *f*
pillage *tr* diripere ‖ *intr* praedari
pillar *s* pil·a -ae *f*
pillow *s* cervic·al -alis *n*
pillowcase *s* cervicalis tegim·en -inis *n*
pilot *s* guberna·tor -toris *m* (·trix -tricis *f)*
pilot *tr* gubernare
pimp *s* len·o -onis *m*
pimp *tr* & *intr* lenocinari
pimple *s* pustul·a -ae *f*
pin *s* ac·us -ūs *f; (peg)* clav·us -i *m*
pin *tr* acu figere; **to — down** defigere; *(fig)* devincire
pincers *spl* forc·eps -ipis *mf*
pinch *tr* vellicare ‖ *intr (of cold; of shoe)* (ad)urere
pinch *s (e.g., of salt)* mensur·a -ae *f* duorum *(or* trium) digitorum; **in a —** *(fig)* in angustiis; *(in a doubtful situation)* in re dubiā
pine *s* pin·us -i *f*
pine *intr* **to — away** tabescere; **to — for** desiderare
pineapple *s* pom·um -i *n* pineum
pink *adj* punice·us -a -um, rose·us -a -um; **to be in the — of health** optimā valetudine uti
pinnacle *s* fastig·ium -(i)i *n*
pint *s* sextar·ius -(i)i *m*
pioneer *s* praecurs·or -oris *m; (originator)* auc·tor -toris *m* (·trix tricis *f)*
pious *adj* pi·us -a -um, prob·us -a -um
piously *adv* pie, religiose, sancte
pipe *s* tub·us -i *m;* fistul·a -ae *f* aquaria; *(conduit)* canal·is -is *m; (mus)* fistul·a -ae *f*
pipe organ *s* organ·um -i *n* fistuli instructum

pique *tr* offendere
piracy *s* latrocin·ium -(i)i *n*
pirate *s* pirat·a -ae *m*
piratical *adj* piratic·us -a -um
pistachio *s* pistac·ium -(i)i *n*
pit *s* fove·a -ae *f; (quarry)* fodin·a -ae *f; (theat)* cave·a -ae *f*
pit *tr* **to — one against another** alium cum alio committere
pitch *s* pi·x -cis *f; (sound)* son·us -i *m; (degree)* grad·us -ūs *m; (slope)* fastig·ium -(i)i *n;* **to such a — of** eo *(w. gen)*
pitch *tr (to fling)* conicere; *(camp)* ponere; *(tent)* tendere
pitcher *s* urce·us -ı *m; (baseball)* coniec·tor -toris *m* (·trix -tricis *f)*
pitcher's mound *s* coiectoris (coniectricis) grum·us -i *m*
pitchfork *s* furc·a -ae *f*
piteous *adj* miserabil·is -is -e
piteously *adv* miserabiliter
pitfall *s (& fig)* fove·a -ae *f*
pith *s* medull·a -ae *f*
pithy *adj* sententios·us -a -um
pitiable *adj* miserand·us -a -um
pitiful *adj* flebil·is -is -e; *(contemptible)* abiect·us -a -um
pitifully *adv* misere
pitiless *adj* immisericor·s -dis
pitilessly *adv* immisericorditer
pittance *s* mercedul·a -ae *f*
pity *s* misericordi·a -ae *f; it is a — that ...* male accidit *(w. acc & inf);* **to feel — for** commiserescere *(w. gen)*
pity *tr* miserēre *(w. gen),* miserēri *(w. gen);* **I — him** miseret me eius
pivot *s* ax·is -is *m; (fig)* card·o -inis *m*
placard *s* titul·us -i *m*
place *s* loc·us -i *m (pl:* loc·a -orum *npl);* **at your —** apud te; **from that —** illinc; **from this —** hinc; **in — of** *(in stead of)* pro *(w. abl);* **in — of parents** in locum parentum; **in the first —** primum; **in the last —** postremo; **in the same —** ibidem; **out of —** alien·us -a -um; **this is not the — to ...** non est hic locus ut *(w. subj);* **to take —** fieri; **to take s.o.'s —** locum alicuius usurpare; **to that —** eo; **to the same —** eodem
place *tr* ponere, locare; *(pointing to the placing of an object in connection with other objects)* (col)locare; *(to identify)* (re)cognoscere
placement *s* collocati·o -onis *f*
placid *adj* placid·us -a -um
placidly *adv* placide
plagiarism *s* furt·um -i *n* litterarium
plagiarist *s* fu·r -ris *mf* litterari·us (-a)
plagiarize *tr* furari, compilare
plague *s* pestilenti·a -ae *f; (fig)* pest·is -is *f*
plague *tr* vexare

plain *s* planiti·es -ei *f,* camp·us -i *m;* **open —s** campi latentes
plain *adj (clear)* manifest·us -a -um; *(unadorned)* simpl·ex -icis; *(of one color)* unicol·or -oris; *(frank)* sincer·us -a -um; *(homely)* invenust·us -a -um
plainly *adv* plane; simpliciter
plaintiff *s* peti·tor -toris *m* (·trix -tricis *f)*
plaintive *adj* flebil·is -is -e
plaintively *adv* flebiliter
plan *s* consil·ium -(i)i *n; (for a building)* form·a -ae *f;* **to form a —** consilium inire; **to make —s for a trip** de itinere consilium facere
plan *tr* destinare, in animo habēre; *(to scheme)* meditari ‖ *intr* **to — on** in animo habēre
plane *s (tool)* runcin·a -ae *f; (level surface)* planiti·es -ei *f; (airplane)* aëroplan·um -i *n*
plane *tr* runcinare
planet *s* planet·a -ae *f*
plank *s* tabul·a -ae *f; (builder's term)* ax·is -is *m*
plant *s* plant·a -ae *f; (industrial)* fabric·a -ae *f*
plant *tr* serere; **hls feet are —ed on** pedes stipantur in *(w. abl);* **to — a field** agrum conserere; **to — one's feet on the ground** pedes in terram deferre
plantation *s* plantar·ium -(i)i *n*
planter *s* sat·or -oris *m*
planting *s* sat·us -ūs *m*
plaster *s* tector·ium -(i)i *n*
plaster *tr* tectorium inducere *(w. dat)*
plasterer *s* tect·or -oris *m*
plaster of Paris *s* gyps·um -i *n*
plastic *adj* plastic·us -a -um
plastic *s* materi·a -ae *f* plastica
plate *s* patin·a -ae *f,* catin·us -i *m; (small dish)* patell·a -ae *f,* catill·us -i *m; (sheet)* lamin·a -ae *f*
plate licker *s* catill·o -onis *m*
plateau *s* aequ·um -i *n*
platform *s* suggest·us -ūs *m; (in train station)* crepid·o -inis *f* (ferriviaria)
platitude *s* trita sententi·a -ae *f*
Platonic *adj* Platonic·us -a -um
platoon *s* manipul·us -i *m*
platter *s* lan·x -cis *f*
plaudits *spl* plaus·us -ūs *m*
plausible *adj* verisimil·is -is -e
play *s* lud·us -i *m; (theat)* fabul·a -ae *f;* **to be at —** ludere
play *tr* ludere; *(radio, television, records, tapes)* usurpare; *(instrument)* canere *(w. abl);* **stop —ing games!** desiste ludos facere!; **to — ball** pilā ludere; **to — a trick on** ludificari; **to — the lead role** primas partes agere; **to — the role of a parasite** parasitum agere ‖ *intr* **to — up to** adulari

player *s* lus·or -oris *m,* lus·rix -ricis *f; (theat)* histri·o -onis *mf; (on wind instrument)* tibic·en -inis *m,* tibicin·a -ae *f; (on stringed instrument)* fidic·en -inis *m,* fidicin·a -ae *f*

playful *adj* ludibund·us -a -um; *(frolicsome)* lasciv·us -a -um

playfully *adv* per ludum

playfulness *s* lascivi·a -ae *f*

playground *s* are·a -ae *f* lusoria

playing cards *spl* chartul·ae -arum *fpl* lusoriae

playing field *s* camp·us -i *m* lusorius

playmate *s* collus·or -oris *m* (·rix -ricis *f*)

plaything *s* ludibr·ium -(i)i *n*

playwright *s* fabularum scrip·tor -toris *m* (·trix -tricis *f*)

plea *s* supplicati·o -onis *f; (law)* excepti·o -onis *f;* **to enter a — against s.o.** exceptionem obicere alicui; **well-founded —** iusta exceptio *f*

plead *tr (ignorance)* causari; **to — a case before the court** causam pro tribunali agere ‖ *intr* **to — for** petere; **to — with s.o.** aliquem supplicare

pleasant *adj* iucund·us -a -um; *(to sight)* amoen·us -a -um

pleasantly *adv* iucunde

pleasantry *s* iocosa dicacit·as -atis *f*

please *tr* placēre *(w. dat); anyone you —* quilibet, quaelibet; **anything you —** quidlibet; **if you —** si placet; si videtur; **—!** sis (= si vis); amabo te *(coll);* **pleased to meet you!** mihi pergratum est te convenire!; **— God!** Deo volente

pleasing *adj* grat·us -a -um

pleasurable *adj* iucund·us -a -um

pleasure *s* volupt·as -atis *f;* **at their own —** suo arbitrio; **it is my —** libet; **to derive (great) — from** (magnam) voluptatem capere de *(w. abl);* **with — libemter

pleat *s* plicatur·a -ae *f*

pleat *tr* plicare

pleated *adj* plicat·us -a -um

plebeian *adj* plebei·us -a -um

plebeians *spl* pleb·s -is *f*

plebiscite *s* plebiscit·um -i *n*

plebs *spl* plebs, plebis *f*

pledge *s* pign·us -oris *n; (proof)* testimon·ium -(i)i *n*

pledge *tr* (op)pignerare, obligare; **to — one's word** fidem obligare

Pleiades *spl* Pleiad·es -um *fpl*

plenary *adj* plen·us -a -um

plentiful *adj* larg·us -a -um, copios·us -a -um

plenty *s* copi·a -ae *f;* **to have — of** abundare *(w. abl)*

plethora *s* redundanti·a -ae *f*

pleurisy *s* pleurit·is -idis *f*

pliable *adj* tractabil·is -is -e

pliant *adj* lent·us -a -um

pliers *spl* for·ceps -cipis *mf*

plight *s* discrim·en -inis *n;* **in a sorry —** male perdit·us -a -um; **what a sorry —!** O rem miseram!

plod *intr* assidue laborare

plodder *s* sedul·us (-a) hom·o -inis *mf*

plodding *adj* sedul·us -a -um

plot *s (conspiracy)* coniurati·o -onis *f; (of ground)* agell·us -i *m; (of a play)* argument·um -i *n*

plot *intr* coniurare, moliri

plow *s* aratr·um -i *n*

plow *tr* arare; **to — under** inarare; **to — up** exarare

plowing *s* arati·o -onis *f*

plowshare *s* vom·er -eris *m*

pluck *s* anim·us -i *m*

pluck *tr (flowers, fruit)* carpere; *(feathers)* vellere; **to — off** decerpere; **to — out** evellere; **to — up one's courage** animo esse

plug *s* obturament·um -i *n; (electrical)* spin·a -ae *f* contactūs electrici; *(a boost)* verb·a -orum *npl* suadentia

plug *tr* obturare; **to — in** adnectere, inserere ‖ *intr* **to — away at** assidue laborare

plum *s* prun·um -i *n*

plumage *s* plum·ae -arum *fpl*

plumber *s* plumbar·ius -(i)i *m*

plume *s* crist·a -ae *f*

plummet *s* perpendicul·um -i *n*

plummet *intr* praecipitare

plump *adj* pingu·is -is -e

plum tree *s* prun·us -i *f*

plunder *s (act)* rapin·a -ae *f; (booty)* praed·a -ae *f*

plunder *tr* praedari

plunderer *s* praedat·or -oris *m*

plundering *s* rapin·a -ae *f*

plundering *adj* praedatori·us -a -um

plunge *tr* mergere; *(sword, etc.)* condere ‖ *intr* se mergere; **to — into the midst of the enemy** inter mucrones hostium se immergere

pluperfect (tense) *s* plus quam perfectum temp·us -oris *n*

plural *adj* plural·is -is -e

plural *s* numer·us -i *m* multitudinis; **in the —** pluraliter

plurality *s* multitud·o -inis *f; (majority)* maior par·s -tis *f*

plush *adj* laut·us -a -um

plus *s* **consider it a —** id deputa esse in lucro

plus *conj* **2 plus 2 are 4** duo et duo sunt *(or* fiunt) quattuor

plus sign *s* crucicul·a -ae *f*

ply *tr* exercēre, urgēre

poach *tr (eggs)* frigere ‖ *intr* illicitā venatione uti

poacher *s* vena·tor -toris *m* (·trix -tricis *f*) illic·it·us (-a)

pocket *s* saccul·us -i *m;* **to line one's —s** ditescere

pocket *tr* in sacculo condere

pocketbook *s (small book)* pugillar·es -ium *mpl; (purse)* marsup·ium -(i)i *n*

pocket knife *s* cultell·us -i *m* plicabilis

pockmark *s* cicatr·ix -icis *f*

pod *s* siliqu·a -ae *f*

podium *s* pod·ium -(i)i *n,* pulpit·um -i *n*

poem *s* poëm·a -atis *n;* **to write a —** poema condere

poet *s* poët·a -ae *m*

poetess *s* poëtri·a -ae *f*

poetic *adj* poëtic·us -a -um

poetically *adv* poëtice

poetics *s* ar·s -tis *f* poëtica

poetry *s (art)* poëtic·e -es *f; (poems)* poës·is -is *f,* carm·en -inis *n*

poignant *adj* acerb·us -a -um

poinsettia *s* euphorbi·a -ae *f*

point *s* punct·um -i *n; (pointed end)* acum·en -inis *n; (of sword, etc.)* mucr·o -onis *m; (of a spear)* cusp·is -idis *f; (point in dispute)* quaesti·o -onis *f; (gram, sports)* punct·um -i *n; (in time)* articul·a -ae *f* temporis; **at this very —** hoc ipso in loco; **beside the —** ab re, nihil ad rem; **but to return to the —** sed ad propositum; **from this — on** posthac, hinc; **get the —?** tenesne *(pl:* tenetisne) rem?; **get to the —!** veni ad rem!; **main — cap·ut -itis *n;* **now here's the —** nunc cognosce rem; **on that —** hac de re; **— of view** sententi·a -ae *f,* opini·o -onis *f;* **to come to a —** acui; **to be on the — of** in eo esse ut, *e.g., he was on the point of being arrested (or* haud abfuit) ut comprehenderetur; **the —is that I no longer care about such things** quod caput est, iam ista non curo; **to score a —** punctum ferre; **to such a —** that eo ut; **to the — ad rem; **up to this —** hactenus; **what's your —?** *(what are you driving at?)* quo evadis?; **what was your — in writing to me?** quid retulit te mittere ad me litteras?; **you miss the —** nihil ad rem pertinet

point *tr (to sharpen)* acuere; **to — out** monstrare, indicare; **to — the finger at** digitum intendere ad (*w. acc*) ‖ *intr* **to — at** digito monstrare

point-blank *adv* **to turn down —** omnino repudiare

pointed *adj* acut·us -a -um; *(fig) (stinging)* aculeat·us -a -um

pointer *s* ind·ex -icis *mf; (comput)* (muris) index

pointless *adj* supervacu·us -a -um

poise *s* urbanit·as -atis *f*

poise *tr* librare

poison *s* venen·um -i *n*

poison *tr* venenare; *(fig)* vitiare

poisoning *s* venefic·ium -(i)i *n*

poke *tr (to jab)* fodicare, pungere; *(w. the elbow)* cubito pulsare; *(fire)* fodere; **to — fun at** eludere

poker *s* rutabul·um -i *n*

polar *adj* arctic·us -a -um

pole *s* ass·er -eris *m; (short pole)* asserul·us -i *m; (long pole)* longur·ius -(i)i *m; (of the earth)* pol·us -i *m;* **North (South) Pole** ax·is -is *m* septentrionalis (meridianus)

pole vaulting *s* salt·us -ūs *m* perticarius

police *s* vigil·es -um *mpl*

police officer *s* vig·il -ilis *mf*

policy *s* rati·o -onis *f; (document)* chirograph·um -i *n; (contract)* pact·um -i *n;* **insurance — cauti·o -onis *f* indemnitatis

polish *s (shine)* nit·or -oris *m; (refined manners)* urbanit·as -atis *f; (for shoes)* cerom·a -atis *n*

polish *tr* polire; **to — up** expolire

polite *adj* urban·us -a -um; **(to)** com·is -is -e (*w. dat or* erga *w. acc)*

politely *adv* urbane, comiter

politeness *s* urbanit·as -atis *f,* comit·as -atis *f*

politic *adj* prud·ens -entis

political *adj* civil·is -is -e; **for — reasons** rei publicae causā; **from — motives** per ambitionem; **— affairs (matters)** res, rerum *fpl* civiles; **— career** curs·us -ūs *m* publicus; **— science** scienti·a -ae *f* civilis; **— supporter** suffraga·tor -toris *m* (·trix -tricis *f)*

politician *s* vir, viri *m,* (femin·a -ae *f)* civilium rerum perit·us (-a)

politics *s* respublica *(gen:* reipublicae) *f;* **to be (involved) in —** in republicā versari **to enter —** rempublicam inire; **to talk — at table** ad mensam res publicas crepare

polka *s* saltati·o -onis *f* Bohemica; **to dance the —** Bohemice saltare

poll *s* diribitor·ium -(i)i *n; (survey)* rogati·o -onis *f* sententiarum; **the —s** suffragi·a -orum *npl;* comiti·a -orum *npl*

polling booth *s* saept·um -i *n*

poll tax *s* capitum exacti·o -onis *f*

pollute *tr* polluere

pollution *s* polluti·o -onis *f*

polo *s* alsulegi·a -ae *f* equestris

polo shirt *s* subucul·a -ae *f* cum curtis manicis

polygamy *s* polygami·a -ae *f*

polysyllabic *adj* polysyllab·us -a -um

polytheism *s* multorum deorum cult·us -ūs *m*

pomegranate *s* mal·um -i *n* Punicum, mal·um -i *n* granatum

pommel *tr* pulsare, verberare

pomp *s* apparat·us -ūs *m*

pompous *adj* magnific·us -a -um, glorios·us -a -um

pompously *adv* magnifice

pond *s* stagn·um -i *n*

ponder *tr* animo volutare
ponderous *adj* ponderos·us -a -um
pontiff *s* pontif·ex -icis *m*
pontifical *adj* pontifical·is -is -e
pontificate *s* pontificat·us -ūs *m*
pontificate *intr* ex cathedrā loqui
pontoon *s* pont·o -onis *m*
pony *s* mannul·us -i *m*
pool *s* (*of water*) lacun·a -ae *f;* (*for swimming*) piscin·a -ae *f;* (*billiards*) lud·us -i *m* tudicularis; **to shoot —** globulos eburneos clavā tudiculari super mensam impellere
pool *tr* conferre
poor *adj* (*impoverished*) paup·er -eris: (*pitiable*) mis·er -era -erum; (*meager*) exil·is -is -e; (*soil*) ma·cer -cra -crum; **poor guy** mis·er -eri *m*
poorly *adv* parum, mediocriter
pop *s* crepit·us -ūs *m;* (*father*) pap·a -ae *m,* tat·a -ae *m*
pop *intr* crepare; **to — out** exsilire
popcorn *s* maiz·ium -(i)i *n* inflatum
pope *s* pap·a -ae *m*
poplar *s* popul·us -i *f*
pop music *s* music·a -ae *f* popularis
poppy, poppyseed *s* papav·er -eris *n*
populace *s* vulg·us -i *n*
popular *adj* popular·is -is -e; **be — with** gratios·us -a -um esse apud (*w. acc*); **— feeling** sens·us -ūs *m* populi
popularity *s* grati·a -ae *f,* fav·or -oris *m* populi; **to enjoy — among** gratiam habēre apud (*w. acc*); **to seek —** favorem populi sectari
populate *tr* frequentare
population *s* multitud·o -inis *f*
populous *adj* frequ·ens -entis
porcelain *s* fictil·ia -ium *npl* elegantia
porch *s* pergul·a -ae *f*
porcupine *s* hystr·ix -icis *f*
pore *s* foram·en -inis *n*
pore *intr* **to — over** diligenter scrutari
pork *s* porcin·a -ae *f*
pork chop *s* off·a -ae *f* porcina
porpoise *s* porcul·us -i *m* marinus
porridge *s* pul·s -tis *f*
port *s* (*also comput*) port·us -ūs *m*
portal *s* port·a -ae *f*
portend *tr* portendere
portent *s* portent·um -i *n*
portentous *adj* prodigios·us -a -um
porter *s* atriens·is is *m;* (*carrier*) baiul·us -i *m*
portfolio *s* scrin·ium -(i)i *n*
portico *s* portic·us -ūs *f*
portion *s* porti·o -onis *f*
portion *tr* partire; **to — out** dispertire
portly *adj* **to be —** opimo corporis habitu esse
portrait *s* imag·o -inis *f*
portray *tr* depingere, exprimere
pose *s* stat·us -ūs *m*

pose *intr* statum sumere
position *s* positi·o -onis *f;* (*of the body*) gest·us -ūs *m;* (*office*) hon·or -oris *m;* (*rank*) dignit·as -atis *f;* (*state*) condici·o -onis *f;* (*sports*) loc·us -i *m;* **what — do you play?** quo loco ludis?
positive *adj* cert·us -a -um; (*opp: negative*) affirmativ·us -a -um; (*gram*) positiv·us -a -um; **are you — that ...** scisne pro certo (*w. acc & inf*); **— degree** grad·us -ūs *m* positivus
positively *adv* certo, praecise
possess *tr* possidēre
possession *s* possessi·o -onis *f;* **in the — of** penes (*w. acc*); **to gain — of** potiri (*w. abl*)
possessive *adj* quaestuos·us -a -um; (*gram*) possessiv·us -a -um
possessor *s* possess·or -oris *m,* possestr·ix -icis *f*
possibility *s* facult·as -atis *f*
possible *adj* possibil·is -is -e; **as quickly as —** quam celerrime; **is it really possible that you are telling the truth?** numquid vera dicis?; **it is —** fieri potest; **it is — for me to** possum (*w. inf*)
possibly *adv* (*perhaps*) fortasse; **as carefully as I — can** quam diligentissime possum; **I may — go to Sicily** fieri potest ut in Siciliam proficiscar
post *s* (*stake*) post·is -is *m,* pal·us -i *m;* (*station*) stati·o -onis *f;* (*in a race*) met·a -ae *f*
post *tr* (*a notice*) in publicum proponere; (*to station*) collocare: **to — a letter** litteras dare
postage *s* vectur·a -ae *f* litterarum; **to pay the —** pro vecturā epistulae solvere
postage stamp *s* pittac·ium -(i)i *n* cursuale
postal delivery *s* perlati·o -onis *f* cursualis
postcard *s* chartul·a -ae *f* cursualis; (*with a picture*) photochartul·a -ae *f* cursualis
postdate *tr* diem seriorem scribere (*w. dat*)
poster *s* fol·ium -(i)i *n* murale; **to put up a — folium** murale proponere
posterior *adj* poster·ior -ior -ius
posterity *s* posterit·as -atis *f;* (*descendants*) poster·i -orum *mpl*
posthaste *adv* quam celerrime
posthumous *adj* postum·us -a -um
postman *s* tabellar·ius -(i)i *m*
post office *s* diribitor·ium -(i)i *n* cursuale
post office window ostiol·um -i *n* cursuale
postpone *tr* differre
postponement *s* dilati·o -onis *f*
postscript *s* adiecti·o -onis *f* litterarum
posture *s* stat·us -ūs *m*
pot *s* (*of clay*) oll·a -ae *f;* (*of bronze*) ahen·um -i *n;* (*chamber pot*) matell·a -ae *f;* (*marijuana*) cannab·is -is *f;* **—s and pans** vas·a -orum *npl* coquinaria; **to go to — (*fig*)** pessum ire; **to smoke —** fumum cannabis sugere

potato *s* pom·um -i *n* terrestre; **baked** — pomum terrestre in furno coctum; **fried potatoes** poma terrestria fricta; **mashed potatoes** pulticul·a -ae *f* ex pomis terrestribus
potato chips *s* lamin·ae -ae *fpl* pomorum terrestrium
pot-bellied *adj* ventrios·us -a -um
pot belly *s* vent·er -ris *m* obesus *or* poriectus; **to have a** — ventre obeso esse
potentate *s* tyrann·us -i *m*
potential *adj* cap·ax -acis, futur·us -a -um
potential *s* potenti·a -ae *f* latens
potholder *s* bascaud·a -ae *f*
potion *s* poti·o -onis *f*
potroast *s* ass·a -ae *f*
potsherd *s* test·a -ae *f*
potshot *s* ict·us -ūs *m* reperticius
potter *s* figul·us -i *m;* —'s **wheel** rot·a -ae *f* figularis
pottery *s* fictil·ia -ium *npl*
potty *s* matell·a -ae *f*
pouch *s* saccul·us -i *m*
poultry *s* av·es -ium *fpl* cohortales
poultry *s* av·es -ium *fpl* cohortales
pounce *intr* **to** — **on** insilire *(w. dat or in w. acc)*
pound *s* libr·a -ae *f (w.* pondo *sometimes added);* **a half** — selibr·a -ae *f;* **a** — **and a half** sesquilibr·a -ae *f;* **a** — *(or* **per** —) in libras; **a quarter** — quadran·s -tis *f* pondo
pound *s (for animals)* saept·um -i *n*
pound *tr* contundere; **to** — **the pavement** *(fig)* vicatim ambulare
pour *tr* fundere; **to** — **into** infundere *(in w. acc);* **to** — **out** effundere; **to** — **water on his hands** aquam in eius manūs infundere; **to** — **water on his head** caput illi aquā perfundere ‖ *intr* fundi, fluere; **to come** —**ing out** *(of people)* se effundere; **to** — **down** *(of rain)* ruere; **to** — **into** *(of people)* se infundere in *(w. acc)*
pouring *adj (rain)* effus·us -a -um
pout *intr* labellum extendere
poverty *s* paupert·as -atis *f; (inadequacy)* egest·as -atis *f*
poverty-stricken *adj* inop·s -is
powder *s* pulv·is -eris *m*
powder *tr* pulvere conspergere
powder puff *s* pulvill·us -i *m* ad fucandum
power *s (strength)* vis *f; (ability)* copi·a -ae *f; (control, dominium)* potest·as -atis *f; (excessive; non-constitutional)* potenti·a -ae *f; (mil, pol)* imper·ium -(i)i *n;* **as far as is in our** — quantum in nobis est; — **of the mind** vir·es -ium *fpl* ingenii; **to have great** — multum posse
power drill *s* terebr·a -ae *f* machinalis

powerful *adj (physically)* valid·us -a -um; *(kings, etc.)* pot·ens -entis; *(e.g., medicine)* effic·ax -acis
powerfully *adv* valde
powerless *adj* invalid·us -a -um, impot·ens -entis; **to be** — nil valēre
power saw *s* serr·a -ae *f* machinalis
practical *adj* util·is -is -e; *(sensible)* prud·ens -entis; *(philosophy)* effectiv·us -a -um
practically *adv* usu; *(almost)* fere
practice *s (actual employment or experience)* us·us -ūs *m; (repeated action)* exercitati·o -onis *f; (rehearsal)* meditati·o -onis *f; (custom)* consuetud·o -inis *f;* **to have a large** — **as a doctor** medicus praecipuae celebritatis esse; **to make a** — **of** factitare
practice *tr (medicine, patience)* exercēre; *(to rehearse)* meditari
practice session *s* spat·ium -(i)i *n* exercitationis *(or* meditationis)
practitioner *s* exercita·tor -toris *m (·*trix -tricis *f); (medical)* medic·us -i *m (·*a -ae *f)*
praetor *s* praet·or -oris *m*
praetorship *s* praetur·a -ae *f;* **to hold the** — praeturam gerere
pragmatic *adj* pragmatic·us -a -um
prairie *s* camp·us -i *m* latissime patens herbisque obsitus
praise *s* lau·s -dis *f*
praise *tr* laudare
praiseworthy *adj* laudabil·is -is -e
prance *intr* exsilire
prank *s* lud·us -i *m*
prankster *s* lus·or -oris *m (·*rix -ricis *f)*
pray *intr* precari, orare; **to** — **for** petere, precari; **to** — **to** adorare; **to** — **to the gods for peace** deos pacem precari
prayer *s* pre·x -cis *f*
preach *tr & intr* praedicare
preacher *s* praedica·tor -toris *m (·*trix -tricis *f)*
preamble *s* exord·ium -(i)i *n*
precarious *adj* precari·us -a -um; **in a most** — **position** in summo discrimine
precariously *adv* precario
precaution *s* cauti·o -onis *f;* **to take** —**s** praecavēre
precede *tr* antecedere *(w. acc or dat)*
precedence *s* prior loc·us -i *m;* **to take** — **over** antecedere
precedent *s* exempl·um -i *n*
preceding *adj* pr·ior -ior -ius
precept *s* praecept·um -i *n*
preceptor *s* praecep·tor -toris *m (·*trix -tricis *f)*
precinct *s* termin·i -orum *mpl; (pol)* regi·o -onis *f*
precious *adj* pretios·us -a -um; — **stone** gemm·a -ae *f*
precipice *s* praec·eps -ipitis *n;* **down a** — **in** praeceps; **over the** — per praecipitia

precipitate *tr* praecipitare
precipitious *adj* praec·eps -ipitis
precise *adj (exact)* exact·us -a -um; *(particular)* accurat·us -a -um
precisely *adv* subtiliter
precision *s* accurati·o -onis *f*
preclude *tr* praecludere
precocious *adj* praec·ox -ocis
preconceive *tr* praecipere; —d idea praeiudic·ium -(i)i *n*
preconception *s* praeiudicata opini·o -onis *f*
precursor *s* praenuntia·tor -toris *m* (·trix -tricis *f*)
predatory *adj* praedatori·us -a -um
predecessor *s* deces·sor -soris *m* (·rix -ricis *f*)
predestine *tr* praedestinare
predicament *s* discrim·en -inis *n*
predicate *s* praedicat·um -i *n*
predict *tr* praedicere
prediction *s* praedicti·o -onis *f*
predilection *s* (for) stud·ium -(i)i *n (w. gen)*
predispose *tr* inclinare
predisposed *adj* (to) obnoxi·us -a -um *(w. dat)*
predisposition *s* inclinati·o -onis *f*
predominant *adj* praeval·ens -entis
predominate *intr* praevalēre
preeminent *adj* praecipu·us -a -um, praest·ans -antis
preempt *tr* praeoccupare
preexist *intr* antea exsistere *or* esse
preexistent *adj* anteced·ens -entis
preface *s* praefati·o -onis *f*
prefatory *adj* to make a few — remarks pauca praefari
prefect *s* praefect·us -i *m*
prefecture *s* praefectur·a -ae *f*
prefer *tr* praeponere, praeferre, malle; *(charges)* deferre; I — to *(would rather)* malo *(w. inf)*
preferable *adj* pot·ior -ior -ius, praestant·ior -ior -ius; *(when more than two are compared)* potissim·us -a -um
preference *s* fav·or -oris *m; in* — to potius quam; to give — to s.o. over aliquem anteponere *(w. dat)*
prefix *s* praepositi·o -onis *f* (per compositionem)
prefix *tr* (to) praeponere *(dat)*
pregnancy *s* gravidit·as -atis *f*
pregnant *adj* gravid·us -a -um; *(of language)* press·us -a -um
prejudge *tr* praeiudicare
prejudice *s* praeiudicata opini·o -onis *f*
prejudice *tr* to be —d against praeiudicatam opinionem habēre in *(w. acc)*; to — the people against studia hominum inclinare in *(w. acc)*
prejudicial *adj* noxi·us -a -um

preliminary *adj* pr·ior -ior -ius; to make a few — remarks pauca praefari
prelude *s (mus)* praecenti·o -onis *f; (fig)* praelusi·o -onis *f*
premature *adj* praematur·us -a -um
prematurely *adv* ante tempus
premeditate *tr* praemeditari
premeditated *adj* praemeditat·us -a -um
premeditation *s* praemeditati·o -onis *f*
premier *s* princ·eps -ipitis *mf*
premise *s (major)* propositi·o -onis *f; (minor)* assumpti·o -onis *f;* —s praed·ium -(i)i *n*
premium *s* praem·ium -(i)i *n; at a* — car·us -a -um
premonition *s* praemonit·us -ūs *m*
preoccupation *s* nescio qua de re sollicitati·o -onis *f*
preoccupied *adj* nescio qua de re sollicit·us -a -um
preoccupy *tr* distringere
preparation *s* praeparati·o -onis *f;* to make careful —s diligentem praeparationem adhibēre
prepare *tr (to make ready)* parare; *(to make ready beforehand)* praeparare; *(a medicine)* componere; *(a speech, case)* meditari; to — to parare *(w. inf)* ‖ *intr* to — for se (prae)parare ad *(w. acc)*
preponderance *s* praestanti·a -ae *f*
preposition *s* praepositi·o -onis *f;* —s take either the accusative or the ablative praepositiones aut accusativo aut ablativo casui serviunt
preposterous *adj* absurd·us -a -um
prerogative *s* iu·s -ris *n* praecipuum
presage *tr* praesagire
prescribe *tr* mandare; *(a medicine)* praescribere
prescription *s (med)* praescript·um -i *n;* to write a — medicinam praescribere
presence *s* praesenti·a -ae *f; in my* — me praesente; in the — of coram *(w. abl);* — of mind praesenti·a -ae *f* animi
present *adj* praesen·s -tis; at — hoc tempore; for the — in praesentiā; — tense praesens temp·us -oris *n;* to be — (at) adesse *(w. dat); (of fever, infection)* inesse
present *s* don·um -i *n*
present *tr (to give)* donare; *(to introduce)* introducere; *(to bring forward)* praebēre, offerre; an opportunity —s itself occasio obvenit; to — evidence testimonium dicere
presentable *adj* dec·ens -entis, idone·us -a -um, spectabil·is -is -e
presentation *s (of gifts)* donati·o -onis *f; (show)* spectacul·um -i *n; (introduction)* introducti·o -onis *f*
presentiment *s* praesensi·o -onis *f*
presently *adv* mox, statim

preservation *s* conservati·o -onis *f*
preserve *tr* conservare, tuēri; *(fruit)* condire
preserves *spl* conditur·a -ae *f*
preserver *s* conserva·tor -toris *m* (·trix -tricis *f*)
preside *intr* **(over)** praesidēre *(w. dat)*; **to — at a trial** iudicio praeesse, ius dicere
presidency *s* praefectur·a -ae *f; (term of office)* magister·ium -(i)i *n*
president *s* praes·es -idis *mf*
presidential *adj* praesidial·is -is -e
press *s (for wine)* prel·um -i *n; (press)* prelum typographicum; *(the journalists)* diurnari·i -orum *mpl; (printed matter)* script·a -orum *npl* typis edita; **freedom of the —** licenti·a -ae *f* scribendi; **hot off the —** modo ex prelo typographico; **to send to the —** prelo subicere
press *tr* primere; *(clothes)* levigare; *(a typewriter key)* deprimere *(fig)* urgēre; **to — down** deprimere; **to — together** comprimere || *intr* **to — forward** anniti; **to — on** pergere, instare
press conference *s* congress·us -ūs *m* diurnariis docendis
pressing *adj* urg·ens -entis, inst·ans -antis
pressure *s* pressur·a -ae *f; (strain)* ang·or -oris *m*
pressure *vt* urgēre
prestige *s* auctorit·as -atis *f*
presumably *adv* sane
presume *tr* inferre, sumere, conicere; *(to take liberties)* sibi arrogare
presumption *s* praesumpti·o -onis *f*
presumptuous *adj* praesumptios·us -a -um
presuppose *tr* praesumere
pretend *tr (to pretend what is not, followed by acc & inf)* simulare, fingere; *(to hide what is by pretending)* dissimulare; **I'll — I don't know him** dissimulabo me eum novisse; **I'll — I'm leaving** simulabo quasi abeam; **to — to be shocked** fingere se inhorrescere
pretender *s* simula·tor -toris *m* (·trix -tricis *f*); *(to the throne)* petit·or -oris *m*
pretense *s* simulati·o -onis *f;* **under false —s** dolo malo; **under the — of** per speciem *(w. gen);* **without —** sine fuco
pretension *s (claim)* postulati·o -onis *f; (display)* ostentati·o -onis *f;* **to make —s to** affectare, sibi arrogare
pretentious *adj* jact·ans -antis; *(showy)* specios·us -a -um
preterite *s* temp·us -oris *n* praeteritum
preternatural *adj* praeter naturam
pretext *s* praetext·um -i *n,* speci·es -ei *f;* **a — for war** praetextum belli; **he left under the pretext that …** hinc abiit quasi *(w. subj);* **under the — of** (sub) specie *(w. gen)*
pretor *see* **praetor**

prettily *adv* belle
pretty *adj* bell·us -a -um, bellul·us -a -um
pretty *adv* satis, admodum; **a — considerable quantity** aliquantul·um -i *n; —* **well** mediocriter; *(just about)* propemodum
pretzel *s* pretiol·a -ae *f*
prevail *intr (to be prevalent)* obtinēre, praevalēre; *(to win)* vincere; **to — upon** persuadēre *(w. dat)*
prevalent *adj* (per)vulgat·us -a -um; **to become —** increbrescere
prevaricate *intr* praevaricari
prevent *tr* prohibēre; **to — s.th. from happening** prohibēre ne *(or* quominus) quid fiat
prevention *s* impediti·o -onis *f*
preventive *adj* **to adopt all — measures** omnia providēre et curare
previous *adj* pri·or -or -us
previously *adv* antehac, antea, prius
prey *s* praed·a -ae *f*
prey *intr* **to — on** praedari
price *s* pret·ium -(i)i *n;* **at a high (low, very low, exorbitant) —** magni (parvi, minimi, nimii); **at any —** quanticumque prctii; **to set the —** pretium constituere
priceless *adj* inaestimabil·is -is -e
price list *s* pretiorum ind·ex -icis *m*
price tag *s* pretii pittac·ium -(i)i *n*
prick *tr* pungere; *(fig)* stimulare; **to — up the ears** aures arrigere
prick *s (puncture)* punct·um -i *n; —* **of conscience** ang·or -oris *m* conscientiae
prickle *s* acule·us -i *m*
prickly *adj* spinos·us -a -um
pride *s* superbi·a -ae *f; (source of pride)* dec·us -oris *n;* **to take — in** gloriari de *or* in *(w. abl)*
pride *tr* **to — oneself on** iactare
priest *s* sacerd·os -otis *mf; (of a particular god)* flam·en -inis *m*
priestess *s* sacerd·os -otis *f*
priesthood *s (office)* sacerdot·ium -(i)i *n*
priestly *adj* sacerdotal·is -is -e
prim *adj* (nimis) dilig·ens -entis
primacy *s* primat·us -ūs *m*
primarily *adv* praecipue, principio
primary *adj* principal·is -is -e; *(chief)* praecipu·us -a -um
prime *s* flo·s -ris *m;* **to be in one's —** aetate florēre
prime *adj* prim·us -a -um, optim·us -a -um
prime minister *s* minis·ter -tri *m* (·tra -trae *f*) primari·us (-a)
primer *s* libell·us -i *m* elementarius
primeval *adj* pristin·us -a -um
primitive *adj* primitiv·us -a -um
primordial *adj* primordi·us -a -um
primrose *s* primul·a -ae *f* vulgaris
prince *s* regis fil·ius -(i)i *m*
princely *adj* regi·us -a -um

princess *s* regis fili·a -ae *f*

principal *adj* principal·is -is -e, praecipu·us -a -um; — **parts** part·es -ium *fpl* principales

principal *s (of a school)* scholae rec·tor -toris *m* (·trix -tricis *f); (fin)* cap·ut -itis *n;* **assistant** *or* **vice** — scholae rec·tor -toris *m* vicarius, scholae rec·trix -tricis *f* vicaria; —'**s office** rectoris (rectricis) officin·a -ae *f*

principality *s* principat·us -ūs *m*

principally *adv* praecipue

principle *s* princip·ium -(i)i *n; (rule of conduct)* praecept·um -i *n;* **a man of** — vi·r -ri *m* gravis et severus

print *s* not·a -ae *f* impressa; *(cloth)* pann·us -i *m* imaginibus impressus

print *tr* imprimere; *(with type)* typis imprimere

printer *s (person)* typograph·us -i *m; (mechanical device)* machin·a -ae *f* typographica, impressor·ium -(i)i *n*

printing *s* typographi·a -ae *f*

printing press *s* prel·um -i *n* typographicum

print shop *s* officin·a -ae *f* typographica

prior *adj* pr·ior -ior -ius

priority *s* primat·us -ūs *m,* ius, iuris *n* praecipuum

prism *s* prism·a -atis *n*

prison *s* carc·er -eris *m;* **to throw into** — in carcerem conicere

prisoner *s (leg)* re·us -i *m,* re·a -ae *f; (of war)* captiv·us -i *m,* captiv·a -ae *f; (for debt)* nex·us -i *m;* **to exchange** —s captivos inter se permutare

pristine *adj* pristin·us -a -um; *(unspoiled)* inte·ger -gra -grum

privacy *s (seclusion)* secess·us -ūs *m; (secrecy)* secret·um -i *n*

private *adj (secluded)* secret·us -a -um; *(person)* privat·us -a -um; *(tutor)* domestic·us -a -um; *(one's own)* propri·us -a -um; *(mil)* gregari·us -a -um; **in** — in privato, secreto

private *s* mil·es -itis *mf* gregari·us (·a)

privately *adv* clam, secreto; *(in a private capacity)* privatim

privation *s* egest·as -atis *f; (loss)* privati·o -onis *f*

privilege *s* privileg·ium -(i)i *n*

privy *adj* privat·us -a -um; — **to** consci·us -a -um *(w. gen)*

privy *s* loc·us -i *m* secretus, latrin·a -ae *f*

prize *s (reward)* praem·ium -(i)i *n; (prey)* praed·a -ae *f;* **first** — primar·ium -(i)i *n;* **second** — secundar·ium -(i)i *n;* **to win a** — praemium auferre

prize *tr* magni aestimare

prize fighter *s* pug·il -ilis *m* mercenarius

pro *adj* affirmativ·us -a -um; *(professional)* veteran·us -a -um; **pro vote** confirmativ·um -i *n*

pro *s (professional)* veteran·us -i *m* (·a -ae *f);* **to weigh the** —s **and cons** dubitare (in) diversitate rationum

pro *prep* pro *(w. abl)*

probability *s* veri similitud·o -inis *f*

probable *adj* verisimil·is -is -e

probably *adv* probabiliter

probation *s* probati·o -onis *f;* **on** — in liberā custodiā

probe *s* indagati·o -onis *f; (med)* specill·um -i *n*

probe *tr* scrutari

problem *s* quaesti·o -onis *f,* aerumn·a -ae *f; (math)* problem·a -atis *n;* **to have stomach (heart, back)** —s stomacho (corde, tergo) dolēre; **the** — **is** ... quaeritur ... ; **what's the** — ? quid est negotii?

problematical *adj* anc·eps -ipitis

procedure *s* mod·us -i *m* operandi, rati·o -onis *f*

proceed *intr* procedere; *(to go on)* pergere; **to** — **against** persequi; **to** — **from** oriri ex *(w. abl)*

proceedings *spl* act·a -orum *npl; (leg)* acti·o -onis *f*

proceeds *spl* redit·us -ūs *m*

process *s* rati·o -onis *f; (leg)* acti·o -onis *f*

processor *s (comput)* editor·ium -(i)i *n*

proclaim *tr* pronuntiare

proclamation *s (act)* pronuntiati·o -onis *f;* pronunt·ium -(i)i *n*

proclivity *s* proclivit·as -atis *f*

proconsul *s* procons·ul -ulis *m*

proconsular *adj* proconsular·is -is -e

proconsulship *s* pronconsulat·us -ūs *m*

procrastinate *intr* procrastinare

procrastination *s* procrastinati·o -onis *f*

procreate *tr* procreare

procreation *s* procreati·o -onis *f*

proctor *s* procura·tor -toris *m* (·trix -tricis *f)*

procurable *adj* comparand·us -a -um

procure *tr* comparare

procurement *s* comparati·o -onis *f*

prodigal *adj* prodig·us -a -um

prodigality *s* dissipati·o -onis *f*

prodigious *adj* imman·is -is -e

prodigy *s* prodig·ium -(i)i *n; (fig)* miracul·um -i *n*

produce *s* fruct·us -ūs *m*

produce *tr (to bring forward)* producere, proferre; *(to bring into existence)* parere, gignere; *(to cause)* efficere, movēre; *(a play)* docēre; *(public games)* edere; *(crops)* ferre

producer *s* chorag·us -i *m*

product *s* op·us -eris *n; (result)* exit·us -ūs *m*

production *s (act)* fabricati·o -onis *f; (work)* op·us -eris *n*

productive *adj* efficien·s -tis; *(fertile)* fer·ax -acis, fertil·is -is -e productivity *s (of fields, mines, etc.)* fertilit·as -atis *f*

profanation *s* violati·o -onis *f*

profane *adj* profan·us -a -um

profanity *s* verb·a -orum *npl* profana

profess *tr* profitēri

professed *adj* manifest·us -a -um

profession *s (learned occupation; declaration)* professi·o -onis *f*

professional *adj* ad professionem pertin·ens -entis; veteran·us -a -um; *(expert)* perit·us -a -um

professor *s* profess·or -oris *m,* profes·trix -tricis *f;* **to be a** — profiteri

proffer *tr* promittere

proficiency *s* progress·us -ūs *m,* periti·a -ae *f*

proficient (in) *adj* perit·us -a -um (*w. gen*)

profile *s* faci·es -ei *f* obliqua; *(portrait)* imag·o -inis *f* obliqua; *(description)* descripti·o -onis *f*

profit *s (financial)* lucr·um -i *n; (benefit)* emolument·um -i *n* bonum; **to make a** — lucrum facere

profit *tr* prodesse *(w. dat)* ‖ *intr* **to** — **by** uti *(w. abl);* **to** — **from** proficere *(w. abl)*

profitable *adj* fructuos·us -a -um; *(fin)* quaestuos·us -a -um; **to be** — **for s.o.** prodesse alicui

profitably *adv* utiliter

profitless *adj* inutil·is -is -e, van·us -a -um

profound *adj* alt·us -a -um; *(recondite)* abstrus·us -a -um

profoundly *adv* funditus

profundity *s* altitud·o -inis *f*

profuse *adj* profus·us -a -um

profusely *adv* profuse

profusion *s* profusi·o -onis *f*

progeny *s* progeni·es -ei *f*

prognosis *s* praedict·um -i *n* (medici *or* medicae)

prognosticate *tr* praedicere

prognostication *s* praedicti·o -onis *f*

program *s* institut·um -i *n,* rati·o -onis *f; (booklet)* libell·us -i *m; (comput)* programm·a -atis *n*

program *tr (comput)* programmare

programmer *s (comput)* programma·tor -toris *m* (·trix -tricis *f*)

progress *s* progress·us -ūs *m;* **in** — in motu, in progressu; **to make** — proficere

progress *intr* progredi

progression *s* progress·us -ūs *m*

progressive *adj* profici·ens -entis

progressively *adv* gradatim

prohibit *tr* vetare

prohibition *s* interdicti·o -onis *f*

project *s* proposit·um -i *n*

project *tr* proicere ‖ *intr* prominēre, exstare; *(of land)* excurrere

projectile *s* missil·e -is *n*

projecting *adj* emin·ens -entis

projection *s* proiectur·a -ae *f*

projector *s* proiector·ium -(i)i *n;* **overhead** — proiectorium supracapitale

proletarian *adj* proletari·us -a -um

proletariat *s* pleb·s -is *f*

prolific *adj* fecund·us -a -um

prologue *s* prolog·us -i *m*

prolong *tr* producere; *(term of office)* prorogare

prolongation *s* dilati·o -onis *f; (of term of office)* prorogati·o -onis *f*

promenade *s (walk)* ambulati·o -onis *f; (place)* ambulacr·um -i *n*

promenade *intr* spatiari

prominence *s* eminenti·a -ae *f*

prominent *adj* promin·ens -entis

promiscuous *adj* promiscu·us -a -um

promiscuously *adv* promiscue

promise *s* promiss·um -i *n;* **I am not making any definite** —**s** nihil certi polliceor; — **of immunity** fid·es -ei *f* publica; **to break a** — (made to) fidem (datam *w. dat)* fallere; **to keep a** — promissum servare; **to make a** — fidem dare, promissum facere; **to make many** —**s** multa promittere

promise *tr* promittere, pollicēri; *(in marriage)* despondēre

promising *adj* bonā (maximā, summā) spe *(abl used adjectively);* **less** — min·or -or -us opinione

promissory note *s* chirograph·um -i *n,* syngraph·a -ae *f*

promontory *s* promuntur·ium -(i)i *n,* ligul·a -ae *f*

promote *tr (in rank)* promovēre; *(a cause, the arts, etc.)* favēre *(w. dat); (in school)* in superiorem classem *(or* gradum) pronovēre; **to** — **to a higher rank** in ampliorem gradum promovēre

promoter *s* fau·tor -toris *m* (·trix -tricis *f*)

promotion *s (act)* promoti·o -onis *f; (result)* amplior grad·us -ūs *m*

prompt *s (comput)* monit·us -ūs *m*

prompt *adj* prompt·us -a -um

prompt *tr* subicere, suggerere; *(incite)* commovēre

promptly *adv* statim, extemplo

promulgate *tr* promulgare

promulgation *s* promulgati·o -onis *f*

prone *adj* (to) pron·us -a -um (ad *or* in *w. acc)*

prong *s* den·s -tis *m*

pronominal *adj* pronominal·is -is -e

pronoun *s* pronom·en -inis *n*

pronounce *tr (to declare)* pronuntiare; *(a word, judicial sentence)* dicere; **to** — **a vowel short or long** vocalem correpte aut pruducte pronuntiare

pronunciation *s* pronuntiati·o -onis *f*
proof *s* document·um -i *n;* *(indication)* indic·ium -(i)i *n*
proof *adj* — **against** impervi·us -a -um *(w. dat)*
proofread *tr* legere et emendare
proofs *spl (from the press)* plagul·ae -arum *fpl;* **to correct** —s plagulas corrigere
prop *s* fulcr·um -i *n*
prop *tr* fulcire; **to** — **oneself up on** se fulcire *(w. dat)*
propaganda *s* re·s -rum *fpl* ad animos hominum movendos
propagate *tr* propagare; *(information)* disseminare
propagation *s* propagati·o -onis *f;* disseminati·o -onis *f*
propel *tr* propellere
propeller *s* propulsr·um -i *n*
propensity *s* propensi·o -onis *f*
proper *adj (becoming)* decor·us -a -um, dec·ens -entis; *(suitable)* idone·us -a -um; **it is** — **for an orator to speak** decet oratorem loqui; — **noun** proprium nom·en -inis *n (opp:* appellativum nomen)
properly *adv (in the strict sense)* proprie; *(fitly)* apte, commode
property *s* bon·a -orum *npl; (characteristic)* virt·us -utis *f,* propriet·as -atis *f;* **private** — res, rei *f* familiaris
prophecy *s* vaticinati·o -onis *f*
prophesy *tr* vaticinari
prophet *s* vat·es -is *mf; (Biblical)* prophet·a -ae *m*
prophetess *s* vat·es -is *f*
propitiate *tr* propitiare
propitiation *s* propitiati·o -onis *f*
propitious *adj* propiti·us -a -um
proportion *s* proporti·o -onis *f;* **in** — pro ratā parte; **in** — **to** pro *(w. abl)*
proportionately *adv* pro portione
proposal *s* propositi·o -onis *f,* condici·o -onis *f;* **to accept a** — condicionem accipere; **to make a** — **that** condicionem ferre ut
propose *tr* proponere; *(esp. a law)* ferre; *(esp. of the tribunes)* rogare; **to** — **a toast to** propinare *(w. dat)*
proposition *s (offer)* condici·o -onis *f; (logic)* propositi·o -onis *f*
propound *tr* proponere, exponere
proprietor *s* domin·us -i *m*
proprietress *s* domin·a -ae *f*
propriety *s* decor·um -i *n*
propulsion *s* propulsi·o -onis *f*
prosaic *adj* ieiun·us -a -um, frigid·us -a -um
proscribe *tr* proscribere
proscription *s* proscripti·o -onis *f*
prose *s* pros·a -ae *f*

prosecute *tr (to carry out)* exsequi; *(leg)* litem intendere *(w. dat),* iudicio persequi; **to** — **offenses** delicta exsequi
prosecution *s* exsecuti·o -onis *f; (leg)* accusati·o -onis *f*
prosecutor *s* accusa·tor -toris *m* (·trix -tricis *f*)
prospect *s* prospect·us -ūs *m; (hope)* spes, spei *f;* **his** —s **are good** is in bonā spe est
prospective *adj* futur·us -a -um
prosper *intr* vigēre
prosperity *s* re·s -rum *fpl* secundae
prosperous *adj* prosper·us -a -um
prosperously *adv* prospere
prostitute *s* meretr·ix -icis *f,* prostitut·a -ae *f;* **to be a** — prostare
prostitute *tr* prostituere
prostrate *tr* sternere; **to** — **oneself at the feet of** se proicere ad pedes *(w. gen)*
prostrate *adj* prostrat·us -a -um; *(fig)* fract·us -a -um; **to fall** — se proicere
prostration *s (act)* prostrati·o -onis *f; (state)* anim·us -i *m* fractus
protect *tr* (pro)tegere
protection *s* praesid·ium -(i)i *n; (protecting power)* tutel·a -ae *f*
protective *adj* proteg·ens -entis
protector *s* tu·tor -toris *m,* tu·trix -tricis *f*
protest *s* obtestati·o -onis *f*
protest *tr (to assert positively)* asseverare, declarare ‖ *intr* contra dicere; **to** — **against** contra dicere *(w. dat)*
prototype *s* exempl·ar -aris *n*
protract *tr* producere
protracted *adj* product·us -a -um
protrude *intr* prominēre, eminēre
proud *adj* glorios·us -a -um; *(haughty)* superb·us -a -um; **to be** — **of** superbire *(w. abl),* gloriari *(w. acc or* de *or* in *w. abl)*
proudly *adv* superbe
prove *tr (by evidence, argument)* probare; **this** —s **that ...** documento est *(w. acc & inf)* ‖ *intr (of persons)* se praebēre, se praestare; *(of a thing, event)* evadere, fieri, exire
proverb *s* proverb·ium -(i)i *n*
proverbial *adj* proverbial·is -is -e
provide *tr (to get ready)* parare; *(to furnish)* suppeditare; *(to equip)* ornare; **to** — **by law that** sancire ut ‖ *intr* **to** — **for** providēre *(w. dat); (of laws)* iubēre
provided *adj* instruct·us -a -um; **well** — refert·us -a -um
provided (that) *conj* dummodo *(w. subj)*
providence *s* providenti·a -ae *f*
provident *adj* provid·us -a -um
providential *adj* divin·us -a -um
providentially *adv* divinitus
provider *s* provis·or -oris *m* (·(t)rix -(t)ricis *f*)
province *s* provinci·a -ae *f*

provincial *adj* provincial·is -is -e; *(pej)* rustic·us -a -um

provision *s (stipulation)* condici·o -onis *f;* **—s** vict·us -ūs *m; (mil)* commeat·us -ūs *m;* **with the added** — exceptione adiectā

provisional *adj* temporari·us -a -um

provisionally *adv* ad tempus

proviso *s* condici·o -onis *f;* **with the** — **that** eā condicione ut, hac lege ut

provocation *s* irritament·um -i *n*

provocative *adj (language)* molest·us -a -um; *(enticing)* ill·ex -icis

provoke *tr (to cause)* (com)movēre; *(to irritate)* irritare, movēre

provoking *adj* molest·us -a -um

provost *s* praeposit·us -i *m* (·a -ae *f)*

prow *s* pror·a -ae *f*

prowess *s* vir·es -ium *fpl,* virt·us -utis *f*

prowl *intr* vagari, grassari

prowler *s* praeda·tor -toris *m* (·trix -tricis *m)*

proximity *s* propinquit·as -atis *f*

proxy *s* vicari·us -i *m* (·a -ae *f)*

prude *s* tetric·a -ae *f*

prudence *s* prudenti·a -ae *f*

prudent *adj* prud·ens -entis

prudently *adv* prudenter

prudish *adj* tetric·us -a -um

prune *s* prun·um -i *n* passum

prune *tr* (am)putare

pruning *s* putati·o -onis *f*

pruning shears *spl* fal·x -cis *f*

pry *intr* perscrutari; **to** — **into** investigare

prying *adj* curios·us -a -um

pseudonym *s* falsum nom·en -inis *n*

psychiatric *adj* psychiatric·us -a -um

psychiatrist *s* psychiat·er -ri *m* (·ria -riae *f)*

psychiatry *s* psychiatri·a -ae *f*

psychic *adj* psychic·us -a -um

psychoanalysis *s* psychoanalys·is -is *f*

psychoanalyst *s* psycholanalyst·a -ae *m* (·ria -riae *f)*

psychological *adj* de animo, psychologic·us -a -um

psychologist *s* psycholog·us -i *m* (·a -ae *f)*

psychopath *s* psychopathic·us -i *m* (·a -ae *f)*

puberty *s* pubert·as -atis *f*

public *adj* public·us -a -um; *(known)* vulgat·us -a -um; **in a** — **capacity** publice; — **affairs** respublica *(gen:* reipublicae) *f*

public *s* public·um -i *n,* vulg·us -i *n;* **in** — propalam; *(outdoors)* foris; **to appear in** — prodire in publicum; **to open** *(e.g., a road)* **to the** — publicare

publican *s* publican·us -i *m*

publication *s* publicati·o -onis *f; (of a book)* editi·o -onis *f; (book)* li·ber -bri *m*

publicity *s* celebrit·as -atis *f*

publicly *adv* propalam

publish *tr* publicare, patefacere; *(book)* edere

publisher *s* edi·tor -toris *m* (·trix -tricis *f; (publishing house)* dom·us -ūs *f* editoria

pucker *intr* **to** — **up the lips** osculari

pudding *s* erne·um -i *n*

puddle *s* lacun·a -ae *f*

puerile *adj* pueril·is -is -e

puff *s* flat·us -ūs *m*

puff *tr* inflare; **to be** —**ed up** tumēre ‖ *intr (to pant)* anhelare; **to** — **up** intumescere

puffy *adj* sufflat·us -a -um; *(swollen)* tum·ens -entis

pull *tr (to drag)* trahere, tractare; **to** — **a fast one on s.o.** os alicui sublinere; **to** — **apart** distrahere; **to** — **away** avellere; **to** — **down** detrahere; *(buildings)* demoliri, destruere; **to** — **oneself together** se colligere; **to** — **out** extrahere; *(hair)* evellere; *(e.g., a weapon, tooth)* eximere; **to** — **out by the roots** exstirpare; *(weeds)* eruncare; **to** — **the wool over s.o.'s eyes** sobdol·us (-a) esse adversus aliquem ‖ *intr* **to** — **at** vellicare; **to** — **through** pervincere; *(from an illness)* convalescere

pull *s (act)* tract·us -ūs *m; (influence)* grati·a -ae *f;* **to have** — **with** gratiam habēre apud *(w. acc)*

pulley *s* trochle·a -ae *f*

pullman car *s* curr·us -ūs *m* dormitorius

pulmonary *adj* pulmone·us -a -um; *(disease)* pulmonari·us -a -um

pulp *s* pulp·a -ae *f*

pulpit *s* pulpit·um -i *n; (eccl)* cathedr·a -ae *f*

pulsate *intr* palpitare

pulse *s* puls·us -ūs (venarum) *m;* **fast (weak)** — venarum pulsus vegetus (languidior); **to feel s.o.'s** — venas *(or* pulsum venarum) alicuius tentare

pulverize *tr* pulverare, contundere

pump *s* antli·a -ae *f*

pump *tr* haurire; **to** — **out,** — **dry** exhaurire; **to** — **with questions** percontari

pumpkin *s* pep·o -onis *m*

pun *s* verborum lus·us -ūs *m*

punch *s (tool)* verucul·um -i *n; (blow)* pugn·us -i *m; (drink)* poti·o -onis *f* ex fructuum suco; **to give s.o. a** —, **land a** — **on s.o.** pugnum alicui ducere

punch *tr* pugnum ducere *(w. dat),* pugno *(or* pugnis) caedere; **to** — **a hole in** pungere

punch-drunk *adj* stupefact·us -a -um

punching bag *s* coryc·us -i *m*

punctual *adj* dilig·ens -entis, prompt·us -a -um; **to be** — ad tempus venire

punctually *adv* ad tempus, tempori

punctuate *tr* interpungere

punctuation *s* interpuncti·o -onis *f*

punctuation mark *s* interpunct·um -i *n*

puncture *s (act)* puncti·o -onis *f; (small hole)* punct·um -i *n*

puncture *tr* pungere
pungent *adj* acut·us -a -um
Punic *adj* Punic·us -a -um
punish *tr* punire, animadvertere in *(w. acc),* poenā afficere, supplicium sumere de *(w. abl);* **to — with loss of one half of one's property** multare dimidiā parte; **to — with loss of the priesthood and dowry** multare sacerdotio et uxoris dote
punishable *adj* puniend·us -a -um
punishment *s (act)* puniti·o -onis *f; (penalty)* poen·a -ae *f,* supplic·ium -(i)i *n;* **— for crimes** poena facinorum; **to inflict — on s.o.** aliquem poenā afficere; **without —** impune
puny *adj* pusill·us -a -um
pup *s* catul·us -i *m,* catell·a -ae *f;* **—s whimper** catuli ganniunt; **to have —s** catulos parere
pupil *s* discipul·us -i *m* (·a -ae *f); (of the eye)* pupill·a -ae *f*
puppet *s* pup·a -ae *f,* neuropast·um -i *n; (fig)* minist·er -tri *m*
puppy *s* catul·us -i *m,* catell·a -ae *f*
purchase *s (act)* empti·o -onis *f; (merchandise)* mer·x -cis *f*
purchase *tr* emere, comparare, mercari
purchase price *s* pret·ium -(i)i *n; (of grain)* annon·a -ae *f*
purchaser *s* emp·tor -toris *m* (·trix -tricis *f*)
pure *adj* pur·us -a -um; *(unmixed)* mer·us -a -um; *(morally)* cast·us -a -um
purely *adv* pure; *(quite)* omnino; *(solely)* solum
purge *tr* purgare, mundare
purge *s* purgati·o -onis *f; (pol)* proscripti·o -onis *f*
purification *s* purificati·o -onis *f*
purify *tr* purificare; *(fig)* expiare
purity *s* purit·as -atis *f; (moral)* castit·as -atis *f*
purple *s* purpur·a -ae *f;* **dressed in —** purpurat·us -a -um
purple *adj* purpure·us -a -um
purport *s* significati·o -onis *f,* sententi·a -ae *f;* **a communication to the same —** tabell·ae -arum *fpl* in eandem fere sententiam
purport *tr* significare
purpose *s (aim, end)* proposit·um -i *n,* fin·is -is *m; (wish)* men·s -tis *f;* **on —** consulto; **to no —** frustra, nequaquam; **to what —** quorsum
purpose *tr* in animo habēre
purposely *adv* consulto, de industriā
purr *intr* murmurare
purr *s (of a cat)* murm·ur -uris *n*
purring *s* murmurati·o -onis *f*
purse *s* marsupp·ium -(i)i *n*
purse *tr (to pucker up)* astringere
pursuance *s* exsecuti·o -onis *f;* **in — of** secundum *(w. acc),* ex *(w. abl)*
pursuant to *prep* secundum *(w. acc)*

pursue *tr (an enemy)* insequi; *(a course, plan)* insistere *(w. acc or dat);* **I will not — this subject further** quod non prosequar longius; **to — one's studies** studiis insistere; **to — an advantage** utilitatem sequi; **to — wealth and power** opes et potentiam consectari
pursuit *s* insectati·o -onis *f; (striving after)* consectati·o -onis *f; (eager desire for and aiming at; occupation)* stud·ium -(i)i *n*
pus *s* pu·s -ris *n*
push *tr* trudere, impellere; **to — away** *or* **back** repellere ‖ *intr* **to — on** contendere, iter facere
push *s* puls·us -ūs *m; (strong effort)* nis·us -ūs *m; (mil)* impet·us -ūs *m*
pushy *adj* aud·ax -acis, proc·ax -acis
pussy *s* cat·us -i *m,* fel·es -is *f*
put *tr* ponere, collocare; **— yourself in my place** fac qui ego sum, te esse **to — an end to** finem facere *(w. dat);* **to — aside** ponere; **to — away** seponere, abdere; *(in safety)* recondere; **to — back** reponere; **to — down** deponere; *(to suppress)* supponere, sedare; *(in writing)* scribere; **to — his hand to his mouth** manum ad os apponere; **to — in** inserere; **to — in order** ordinare; **to — in prison** in custodiam tradere; **to — off (to another time)** differre (in aliud tempus); **to — on** imponere *(w. dat); (to add)* addere; *(clothes)* se induere *(w. abl); (a ring)* (anulum) digito aptare; *(a cap)* (pilleum) capiti suo imponere; *(a sword)* cingere latus (gladio); **to — on the table** ponere super mensam; **to — out** *(the hand)* proferre; *(to remove, e.g., from office)* submovēre; *(a fire)* exstinguere; **to — out of one's mind** ex animo delēre; **to — out of the way** demovēre; *(to murder)* de medio tollere; **to — together** componere, conferre; **to — up** *(to erect)* statuere, erigere; *(to build)* aedificare; *(to raise, e.g., hands)* erigere; **to — up for sale** venum dare; ‖ *intr* **to — in** *(of ships)* appellere; **to — in to port** portum petere; **to — out to sea** solvere; **to — up with** tolerare
putrefy *intr* putrescere
putrid *adj* putrid·us -a -um
putty *s* glut·en -inis *n* vitrariorum
puzzle *s* aenigm·a -atis *n*
puzzle *tr* confundere
puzzled *adj* confus·us -a -um
puzzling *adj* perplex·us -a -um
pygmy *s* pygmae·us -i *m*
pyjamas *spl* synthes·is -is *f* dormitoria
pylon *s* colum·en -inis *n*
pyramid *s* pyram·is -idis *f*
pyre *s* rog·us -i *m*
pyrrhic *adj* pyrrhichi·us -a -um; **— foot** ped·es -is *m* pyrrhichius

Pythagorean *adj* Pythagorae·us -a -um
Pythian *adj* Pythi·us -a -um

Q

quack *s (phoney)* circulat·or -oris *m; (bad physician)* pharmacopol·a -ae *m; (of a duck)* tetrissitat·us -ūs *m*
quack *intr* tetrissitare
quadrangle *s* quadriangul·um -i *n; (of a college)* are·a -ae *f*
quadrangular *adj* quadriangul·us -a -um
quadruped *s* quadrup·es -edis *mf*
quadruple *tr* quadruplicare
quadruple *adj* quadrupl·us -a -um, quadrupl·ex -icis
quadruplets *spl* quattuor liber·i -orum *mpl* gemini
quaestor *s* quaest·or -oris *m*
quaestorship *s* quaestur·a -ae *f;* **to hold the —** quaesturam gerere
quagmire *s* pal·us -udis *f*
quail *s* coturn·ix -icis *f*
quaint *adj* insolit·us -a -um
quake *intr* tremere
quake *s* trem·or -oris *m*
qualification *s (endowment)* indol·es -is *f; (limitation)* excepti·o -onis *f*
qualified *adj (competent)* perit·us -a -um; *(limited)* modic·us -a -um; **— for** apt·us -a -um ad *(w. acc),* habil·is -is -e ad *(w. acc)*
qualify *tr* aptum *or* idoneum reddere; *(to limit)* temperare **‖** *intr* apt·us -a -um esse, idone·us -a -um esse
quality *s* qualit·as -atis *f; (excellence)* virt·us -utis *f*
qualm *s* fastid·ium -(i)i *n;* **— of conscience** scrupul·us -i *m*
quantity *s* numer·us -i *m,* quantit·as -atis *f;* **a large —** frequenti·a -ae *f*
quarantine *s* separati·o -onis *f* per pestilentiam
quarantine *tr* segregare, separare
quarrel *s* iurg·ium -(i)i *n; (stronger)* rix·a -ae *f;* **to pick a — with** iurgio contendere cum *(w. abl)*
quarrel *intr* iurgare, altercari; rixari; **to — with one another about** inter se iurgare de *(w. abl)*
quarrelsome *adj* iurgios·us -a -um
quarry *s* lapicidin·ae -arum *fpl; (prey)* praed·a -ae *f*
quart *s* duo sextari·i -orum *mpl*
quarter *s (fourth part)* quarta par·s -tis *f,* quadran·s -tis *m; (side, direction)* par·s -tis *f; (district)* regi·o -onis *f;* **at close —s** comminus [*adv*]; **—s** *(dwelling)* tect·um -i *n; (tempo-*

rary abode) hospit·ium -(i)i *n;* **neither giving nor asking for —** sine missione
quarter *tr* in quattuor partes dividere; *(to give lodgings to)* hospitium praebēre *(w. dat)*
quarterly *adj* trimestr·is -is -e
quarterly *adv* tertio quoque mense
quartermaster *s* castrorum praefect·us -i *m*
quash *tr (rebellion)* opprimere; *(a law)* rescindere
quatrain *s* tetrastich·on -i *n*
quavering *adj* tremul·us -a -um
queasy *adj* nauseabund·us -a -um; **to feel —** nauseare
queen *s* regin·a -ae *f*
queen bee *s* rex, regis *m* apium
queer *adj* insolit·us -a -um; *(strange)* inept·us -a -um; *(eccentric)* inconcinn·us -a -um; *(effeminate)* effeminatus
queer *s* effeminat·us -i *m*
quell *tr* sedare
quench *tr* exstinguere; **to — a thirst** sitim sedare
querulous *adj* querul·us -a -um
query *s* quaesti·o -onis *f*
query *tr & intr* quaerere
quest *s* inquisiti·o -onis *f;* **to be in — of** requirere; **to go in — of** investigare
question *s* quaesti·o -onis *f,* interrogati·o -onis *f;* **I ask you this —** hoc te rogo; **many —s are raised** multa quaeruntur; **no —, he's at fault** nempe in culpā est; **out of the —** haud licit·us -a -um; **that's a loaded —** captiosum interrogatum est; **there is no — that** non dubium est quin *(w. subj);* **to ask a —** interrogare, quaerere; **to answer the question** ad rogatum *(or* interrogatum*)* respondēre; **to ask a loaded —** captiose interrogare; **to ask many —s** multa interrogare; **to call into —** in dubium vocare; **to keep asking —s** rogitare; **why do you ask such —s?** cur ista quaeris? **without —** sine dubio
question *tr* interrogare, percontari; *(to doubt)* dubitare, in dubium vocare; *(to examine)* scrutari
questionable *adj* dubi·us -a -um
questioning *s* interrogati·o -onis *f,* indagati·o -onis *f*
question mark *s* not·a -ae *f* interrogativa
queue *s (line)* ord·o -inis *m*
queue up *intr* se in ordinem adducere
quibble *s* capti·o -onis *f*
quibble *intr* cavillari
quibbler *s* cavilla·tor -toris *m* (·trix -tricis *f*)
quibbling *s* cavillati·o -onis *f*
quick *adj* cel·er -eris -ere; *(agile)* agil·is -is -e; *(mentally)* astut·us -a -um; *(w. hands)* facil·is -is -e; *(w. wits)* argut·us -a -um
quicken *tr* accelerare
quick lime *s* calx, calcis *f* viva

quickly *adv* cito

quickness *s* celerit·as -atis *f; (of mind)* acum·en -inis *n; (agility)* agilit·as -atis *f*

quicksand *s* syrt·is -is *f*

quicksilver *s* argent·um -i *n* vivum

quick-tempered *adj* iracund·us -a -um

quiet *adj* quiet·us -a -um; *(silent)* tacit·us -a -um; **quiet!** fac *(pl:* facite) silentium!; **to keep** — quiescere; *(to refrain from talking)* silēre

quiet *s* qui·es -etis *f; (leisure)* ot·ium -(i)i *n; (silence)* silent·ium -(i)i *n*

quiet *tr* tranquillare, sedare

quill *s* penn·a -ae *f*

quilt *s* culcit·a -ae *f*

quince *s* cydon·ium -(i)i *n*

quintessence *s* medull·a -ae *f; (fig)* summ·a -ae *f*

quip *s* faceti·ae -arum *fpl*

quip *tr & intr* per iocum dicere

quirk *s* propr·ium -(i)i *n*

quit *tr (to leave)* relinquere, deserere; *(a position, job)* se abdicare *(w. abl); (to stop)* cessare, desinere; **— laughing!** noli *(pl:* nolite) ridēre! ‖ *intr* cessare; *(to resign)* se abdicare

quite *adv* omnino, admodum; **not —** parum, aegre; *(not yet)* nondum

quiver *s* pharetr·a -ae *f;* **wearing a —** pharetrat·us -a -um

quiver *intr* tremere

quivering *s* trem·or -oris *m*

Quixotic *adj* ridicul·us -a -um

quizz *s* probatiuncul·a -ae *f (see* **exam)**

quoit *s* disc·us -i *m;* **to play —s** disco ludere

quota *s* rata par·s -tis *f*

quotation *s (act)* prolati·o -onis *f; (words quoted)* loc·us -i *m* allatus

quote *tr* ponere, afferre

R

rabbi *s* rabbi *m* [*indecl*]

rabbit *s* cunicul·us -i *m*

rabble *s* turb·a -ae *f,* vulg·us -i *n*

race *s (lineage)* gen·us -eris *n; (foot race)* certam·en -inis *n* cursūs; *(horse race)* curs·us -ūs *m* equorum; *(of chariots)* curricul·um -i *n; (of cars)* certamen autocinetorum

race *intr* certare; *(running)* pedibus certare; *(on horseback)* cursu equestri certare

race car *s* autocinet·um -i *n* currile

racecourse *s* stad·ium -(i)i *n*

racehorse *s* cel·es -etis *m*

racer *s* curs·or -oris *m*

racetrack *s* curricul·um -i *n; (for horses)* hippodrom·us -i *m*

rack *s (shelf)* plute·us -i *m; (for punishment)* equule·us -i *m;* **to put to the —** equuleo torquēre

rack *tr* **to be —ed with pain** dolore distinēri; **to — one's brains about s.th.** aliquā re scrutandā fatigari

racket *s (noise)* strepit·us -ūs *m; (shouting)* clam·or -oris *m; (for tennis)* reticul·um -i *n;* **to raise a —** clamorem tollere

racketeer *s* circula·tor -toris *m* (·trix -tricis *f)*

radiance *s* fulg·or -oris *m*

radiant *adj* fulgid·us -a -um

radiate *tr* emittere ‖ *intr* radiare

radiation *s* radiati·o -onis *f*

radiator *s* caloris radiatr·um -i *n*

radical *adj* innat·us -a -um; *(thorough)* tot·us -a -um

radical *s* rerum novarum cupid·us -i *m* (·a -ae *f)*

radically *adv* penitus

radio *s* radiophon·um -i *n;* **to turn down (up) the —** vim radiophoni remittere (amplificare); **to turn on (turn off) the —** radiophonum excitare *or* accendere (expedire)

radio broadcast *s* emissi·o -onis *f* radiophonica

radio station *s* stati·o -onis *f* radiophonica

radish *s* raphan·us -i *m*

radius *s* rad·ius -(i)i *m*

raffle *s* ale·a -ae *f,* sortiti·o -onis *f*

raffle *tr* **to — off** aleā vendere, sortiri

raft *s* rat·is -is *f*

rafter *s* trab·s -is *f*

rag *s* pannicul·us -i *m*

rage *s* fur·or -oris *m,* ir·a -ae *f;* **to fly into a —** irā efferri

rage *intr* furere, saevire

ragged *adj* pannos·us -a -um

raid *s* incursi·o -onis *f*

raid *tr* praedari

raider *s* praedat·or -oris *m*

rail *s* longur·ius -(i)i *m*

rail *intr* **to — at** insectari

railing *s (fence)* saepiment·um -i *n; (abuse)* convic·ium -(i)i *n*

railroad *s* ferrivi·a -ae *f*

railroad car *s* curr·us -ūs *m* ferriviarius

railroad station *s* stati·o -onis *f* ferriviaria

raiment *s* vestit·us -ūs *m*

rain *s* pluvi·a -ae *f; (stormy)* imb·er -ris *m;* **heavy, steady —** magni et assidui imbres; **the — is letting up** *or* **tapering off** imber detumescit

rain *impers* pluit pluere pluit; **it is —ing** pluit; **to — buckets** urceatim pluere; **to — hard** vehementer pluere

rain basin *s (in the atrium)* impluv·ium -(i)i *n*

rainbow *s* arc·us -ūs *m* pluvius

rain cloud *s* nimb·us -i *m*

raincoat *s* scorte·a -ae *f; (hooded)* paenul·a -ae *f*

rainy *adj* pluvi·us -a -um

raise *tr (to lift up)* tollere; *(finger, ladder, eyes)* erigere; *(to build)* exstruere; *(money)* expedire; *(an army)* (con)scribere, comparare; *(siege)* solvere; *(children, crops, animals)* educare; *(to stir up)* excitare; *(to promote)* provehere; *(prices)* augēre; *(crops)* colere; *(beard)* demittere; **to — the curtain** aulaea premere; **to — the head (eyes)** caput (oculos) attollere

raisin *s* (uva) pass·a -ae *f*

rake *s* rastell·us -i *m*

rake *tr* radere; **to — in money** pecuniam corradere

rally *s* conti·o -onis *f*

rally *tr (mil)* in ordines revocare **ǁ** *intr* se colligere; *(after a retreat)* se ex fugā colligere; *(from sickness)* convalescere

ram *s* ari·es -etis *m;* **—s bleat** arietes balant

ram *tr* fistucare; *(to cram)* infercire

RAM *(comput)* memori·a -ae *f* volatilis

ramble *s* vagati·o -onis *f*

ramble *intr* vagari, errare; **to — on** *(in speech)* garrire

rambling *adj* err·ans -antis; *(fig)* vag·us -a -um

ramification *s* ramificati·o -onis *f*

ramp *s* agg·er -eris *m*

rampage *s* **to go on a —** ferocire

rampage *intr* furere

rampant *adj* effrenat·us -a -um; *(widespread)* divulgat·us -a -um

rampart *s* vall·um -i *n*

ranch *s* latifund·ium -(i)i *n*

rancher *s* pecuar·ius -(i)i *m*

rancid *adj* rancid·us -a -um

rancor *s* iracundi·a -ae *f*

random *adj* fortuit·us -a -um; **at —** temere

range *s (row)* ord·o -inis *m; (of mountain)* iug·um -i *n; (reach)* iact·us -ūs *m; (extent)* fin·es -ium *mpl;* **to be in —** intra teli iactum esse; **to be out of —** extra teli iactum abesse; **the enemy were just within —** non longius hostes aberant quam quo telum adici posset

range *tr* ordinare, disponere **ǁ** *intr (to rove at large)* pervagari; *(to vary)* discrepare

rank *s* ord·o -inis *m,* grad·us -ūs *m; (high rank)* dignit·as -atis *f;* **in close — *(mil)*** firmis ordinibus; **the — and file** *(i.e., ordinary soldiers)* manipular·es -ium *mpl*

rank *tr* in numero habēre **ǁ** *intr* in numero haberi; **to — first** primatum obtinēre

rank *adj (extreme)* summ·us -a -um; *(of smell)* foetid·us -a -um

ransack *tr* diripere; *(to search thoroughly)* exquirere

ransom *s (act)* redempti·o -onis *f; (money)* pret·ium -(i)i *n*

ransom *tr* redimere

rant *intr* ampullari; **to — and rave** debacchari

rap *s (slap)* alap·a -ae *f; (blow)* ict·us -ūs *m; (at door)* pulsati·o -onis *f; (w. knuckles)* talitr·um -i *n;* **not to give a — about** non flocci facere *(w. acc)*

rap *tr (to criticize)* exagitare **ǁ** *intr* **to — at** *(a door)* pulsare

rapacious *adj* rap·ax -acis

rape *s* stupr·um -i *n* per vim

rape *tr* per vim stuprare, stupro violare

rapid *adj* rapid·us -a -um

rapidity *s* rapidit·as -atis *f*

rapidly *adv* rapide

rapids *spl* vad·um -i *n* candicans

rapine *s* rapin·a -ae *f*

rapist *s* constuprat·or -oris *m*

rapture *s* exsultati·o -onis *f;* **to be in —s of delight** gaudio efferi

rapturous *adj* exsult·ans -antis

rare *adj* rar·us -a -um; *(meat)* semicoct·us -a -um *(opp: percoctus)*

rarefied *adj* rarefact·us -a -um

rarely *adv* raro

rarity *s* rarit·as -atis *f,* paucit·as -atis *f; (thing)* res, rei *f* rara

rascal *s* scelest·us -i *m* (·a -ae *f*)

rascally *adj* scelest·us -a -um

rash *adj* temerari·us -a -um

rash *s* impetig·o -inis *f*

rashly *adv* temere

rashness *s* temerit·as -atis *f*

raspberry *s* mor·um -i *n* Idaeum

raspberry bush *s* mor·a -ae *f* Idaea

rat *s* mus, muris *m; (person)* transfug·a -ae *m;* **I smell a —** aliquid mihi subolet; **like drowned —s** tamquam mures udi; **—s squeak** mures mintriunt

rat *intr* **to — on s.o.** aliquem deferre

rate *s* proporti·o -onis *f; (price)* pret·ium -(i)i *n; (scale)* norm·a -ae *f;* **at any —** utique; **— of exchange** collyb·us -i *m;* **— of interest** faen·us -oris *n*

rate *tr* aestimare, taxare; **to — s.o. highly** aliquem magni facere

rather *adv* potius, prius; *(somewhat)* aliquanto, paulo, *or render by comparative of adjective or adverb*

ratification *s* sancti·o -onis *f*

ratify *tr* sancire, comprobare

rating *s* aestimati·o -onis *f*

ratio *s* proporti·o -onis *f*

ration *s (portion)* demens·um -i *n;* **—s** *(mil)* cibari·a -orum *npl*

ration *tr* demetiri

rational *adj* ratione praedit·us -a -um; sapi·ens -entis; *(sane)* san·us -a um; **to be —** sapere

rationalize *intr* ratiocinari, rationaliter explicare

rationally *adv* ratione, sapienter
rattle *s* crepit·us -ūs *m;* *(toy)* crepitacul·um -i *n*
rattle *tr* crepitare *(w. abl);* **to — off** cito volvere ‖ *intr* crepare, crepitare; **to — on** garrire
rattlesnake *s* crotal·us -i *m* horridus
raucous *adj* rauc·us -a -um
ravage *tr* vastare, populari
ravages *spl* vastati·o -onis *f*
rave *intr* furere, saevire
raven *s* corv·us -i *m;* **—s croak** corvi crocitant
ravenous *adj* vor·ax -acis
ravenously *adv* voraciter
ravine *s* vall·is -is *f* praerupta
raving *adj* furios·us -a -um; **to be — mad** plane furere
ravish *tr* stuprare
ravishing *adj* suavissim·us -a -um
raw *adj* crud·us -a -um; *(weather)* asp·er -era -erum; *(jokes)* incondit·us -a -um
ray *s* rad·ius -(i)i *m;* **— of hope** specul·a -ae *f*
raze *tr* solo aequare
razor *s* novacul·a -ae *f;* **electric —** rasor·ium -(i)i *n* electricum
reach *s* *(grasp, capacity)* capt·us -ūs *m;* *(of weapon)* iact·us -ūs *m;* **out of my —** extra ictum meum; **within my —** sub meo ictu
reach *tr* *(e.g., a high branch)* contingere, attingere; *(of space)* pertinēre ad *(w. acc),* extendi ad *(w. acc);* *(to come up to)* assequi; *(to arrive at)* pervenire ad *or* in *(w. acc);* *(to hand)* porrigere; *(to attain to, e.g., old age)* adipisci; **to — out the hand** manum porrigere
react *intr* affici; **to — to** referre
reaction *s* affect·us -ūs *m;* **what was his — to ... ?** quo animo tulit ... ?
reactionary *s* qui *or* quae pristinum rerum statum revocare vult
read *tr & intr* legere; **to — aloud** recitare, clare legere; **to — over** translegere; **to — through** perlegere; **to — well** commode legere
readable *adj* lectu facil·is -is -e
reader *s* lec·tor -toris *m* (·trix -tricis *f);* *(book)* lib·er -ri *m*
readily *adv* *(willingly)* libenter; *(easily)* facile
readiness *s* facilit·as -atis *f;* **in —** in promptu
reading *s* lecti·o -onis *f;* *(public recital)* recitati·o -onis *f*
reading lamp *s* lamp·as -adis *f* lectoria
reading room *s* oec·us -i *m* lectorius
ready *adj* **(for)** parat·us -a -um, prompt·us -a -um (ad *w. acc)*
real *adj* ver·us -a -um
real estate *s* re·s -rum *fpl* soli *(opp:* re·s -rum *fpl* mobiles); **piece of —** praed·ium -(i)i *n*
real estate broker *s* praedia·tor -toris *mf*
realistic *adj* verisimil·is -is -e
reality *s* res, rei *f,* verit·as -atis *f;* **in —** re vērā

realization *s* *(e.g., of plans)* effect·us -ūs *m;* *(of ideas)* comprehensi·o -onis *f*
realize *tr* sentire; *(to effect)* efficere, ad exitum perducere; **to — great profits from** magnas pecunias facere ex *(w. abl)*
really *adv* vero, profecto, re vērā; *(surely)* sane, certe
realm *s* regn·um -i *n*
reap *tr* metere; *(fig)* percipere; **to — the reward for** fructum percipere ex *(w. abl)*
reaper *s* mess·or -oris *m;* machin·a -ae *f* messoria
reappear *intr* redire, revenire; *(from below)* resurgere
rear *tr* educare ‖ *intr* *(of horses)* arrectum se tollere
rear *s* terg·um -i *n;* *(sl)* clun·es -ium *mpl or fpl;* *(mil)* novissimum agm·en -inis *n;* **on the — a tergo; to bring up the —** agmen cogere
rear (end) *s* *(sl)* postic·um -i *n*
rearing *s* educati·o -onis *f*
reason *s* *(faculty; reasonable ground)* rati·o -onis *f;* *(cause)* caus·a -ae *f;* *(moderation)* mod·us -i *m;* **for good —s** iustis de causis; **for that —** ideo, idcirco, eā de causā; **for this —** hāc de causā, itaque, quamobrem; **for —s of poor health** valetudinis causā; **for various —s** multis de causis; **there is no — why** nihil causae est, cur; **to give a — why** adferre rationem, quamobrem; **what's the — why** quid est enim, cur; **with —** cum causā
reasonable *adj* *(fair)* aequ·us -a -um; *(moderate)* modic·us -a -um; *(judicious)* prud·ens -entis
reasonably *adv* ratione, iuste; modice
reasoning *s* ratiocinati·o -onis *f;* *(discussing)* disceptati·o -onis *f*
reassemble *tr* recolligere, rursus cogere
reassert *tr* iterare
reassurance *s* confirmati·o -onis *f*
reassure *tr* confirmare, redintegrare
rebate *s* deminuti·o -onis *f*
rebel *s* rebell·is -is *mf*
rebel *intr* rebellare, desciscere
rebellion *s* rebelli·o -onis *f*
rebellious *adj* rebell·is -is -e; *(disobedient)* contum·ax -acis
rebirth *s* novus ort·us -ūs *m*
reboot *tr* *(comput)* redinitiare
rebound *s* result·us -ūs *m*
rebound *intr* resultare, resilire
rebuff *s* repuls·a -ae *f,* reici·o -onis *f*
rebuff *tr* repellere, reicere
rebuild *tr* reficere
rebuke *s* reprehensi·o -onis *f*
rebuke *tr* reprehendere, vituperare
rebut *tr* refutare, redarguere
rebuttal *s* refutati·o -onis *f*
recall *s* revocati·o -onis *f*

recall *tr* revocare; *(to remember)* recordari; **as I —** ut mea memoria est; **to — to mind** in memoriam redigere

recant *tr* recantare, retractare

recapitulate *tr* summatim colligere

recapitulation *s* repetiti·o -onis *f,* compend·ium -(i)i *n*

recapture *s* recuperati·o -onis *f*

recapture *tr* recuperare

recede *intr* recedere

receipt *s (act)* accepti·o -onis *f; (document)* apoch·a -ae *f;* **—s and expeditures** accept·a -orum *npl* et dat·a -orum *npl*

receive *tr* accipere

receiver *s* recep·tor -toris *m* (·trix -tricis *f); (of a telphone)* auscultabul·um -i *n*

recent *adj* rec·ens -entis

recently *adv* nuper

receptacle *s* receptacul·um -i *n*

reception *s (act)* accepti·o -onis *f; (social event)* hospit·ium -(i)i *n*

receptionist *s* salutatr·ix -icis *f*

receptive *adj* docil·is -is -e; **to be — to treatment** recipere curationem

recess *s (place)* recess·us -ūs *m; (in a wall)* adyt·um -n; *(intermission)* intermissi·o -onis *f,* paus·a -ac *f; (vacation)* feri·ae -arum *fpl; (leg)* iustit·ium -(i)i *n*

recipe *s* praescript·um -i *n*

recipient *s* accep·tor -toris *m* (·trix -tricis *f)*

reciprocal *adj* mutu·us -a -um

reciprocally *adv* mutuo, invicem

reciprocate *tr* reddere ‖ *intr* reciprocare

recital *s* recitati·o -onis *f*

recitation *s* recitati·o -onis *f*

recite *tr* recitare

reckless *adj* temerari·us -a -um

recklessly *adv* temere

recklessness *s* temerit·as -atis *f*

reckon *tr* aestimare ‖ *intr* **to — on** confidere *(w. dat)*

reckoning *s* numerati·o -onis *f; (account to be given)* rati·o -onis *f; —* **of time** ratio *f* temporis

reclaim *tr* reposcere, repetere

recline *intr* recubare; *(at table)* accumbere, recumbere; *(said of several guests)* discumbere

recluse *s* solitari·us -i *m* (·a -ae *f)*

recognition *s* agniti·o -onis *f*

recognizance *s* vadimon·ium -(i)i *n*

recognize *tr* agnoscere; *(to acknowledge)* noscere; *(to admit)* accipere

recoil *intr* resilire; *(in horror)* **(from)** refugere (ab *w. abl); (fig)* fastidire *(w. acc)*

recoil *s* recessi·o -onis *f*

recollect *tr* recordari

recollection *s* recordati·o -onis *f*

recommence *tr* redintegrare ‖ *intr* redire

recommend *tr* commendare

recommendation *s* commendati·o -onis *f;* **letter of —** litter·ae -arum *fpl* commendaticiae

recompense *s* remunerati·o -onis *f*

recompense *tr* remunerare; *(to indemnify)* compensare

reconcilable *adj* placabil·is -is -e; *(of things)* conveni·ens -entis

reconcile *tr* reconciliare, componere; **to be — ed** in gratiam restitui

reconciliation *s* reconciliati·o -onis *f*

reconnaissance *s* speculati·o -onis *f*

reconnoiter *tr* perspeculari

reconquer *tr* revincere

reconsider *tr* reputare, revolvere

reconstruct *tr* restituere, renovare

reconstruction *s* restituti·o -onis *f,* renovati·o -onis *f*

record *s* monument·um -i *n;* orb·is -is *m* phonographicus; *(top performance)* palm·a -ae *f;* **—s** act·a -orum *npl,* annal·es -ium *mpl; (in bookkeeping)* tabul·ae -arum *fpl;* **to break the —** gradum praestitutum superare; **to play (listen to) —s** orbes phonographicos exhibēre (audire)

record *tr* referre *or* scribere in tabulas; *(sounds)* (voces, musicam) per machinam phonographice imprimere

recorder *s* procura·tor -toris *m* (·trix -tricis *f)* ab actis; *(machine)* machinul·a -ae *f* phonographica, discophon·um -i *n*

recording *s* impressi·o -onis *f (w. gen)* per discophonum

recording secretary *s* ab actīs *mf*

record player *s* machinul·a -ae *f* phonographica; discophon·um -i *n*

recount *tr* enarrare

recoup *tr* recuperare

recourse *s* refug·ium -(i)i *n;* **to have — to** fugere ad; *(to resort to)* descendere ad

recover *tr (to regain)* recuperare ‖ *intr (from an illness)* convalescere; *(to come to one's senses)* ad se redire

recoverable *adj* reparabil·is -is -e; *(of persons)* sanabil·is -is -e

recovery *s* recuperati·o -onis *f; (from illness)* recreati·o -onis *f*

recreate *tr* recreare

recreation *s* oblectati·o -onis *f*

recriminate *tr* invicem accusare

recrimination *s* mutua accusati·o -onis *f*

recruit *s* tir·o -onis *mf;* **raw —** tiro rudis

recruit *tr (mil)* conscribere; *(one's strength)* reficere

recruiting *s* delect·us -ūs *m*

recruiting officer *s* conquisi·tor -toris *m* (·trix -tricis *f)*

recruitment *s* dilect·us -ūs *m*

rectify *tr* corrigere, emendare

rectitude *s* probit·as -atis *f*
rector *s* rect·or -oris *m*
rectum *s* an·us -i *m*
recur *intr* redire
recurrence *s* redit·us -ūs *m*
recurrent *adj* recurr·ens -entis, assidu·us -a -um
red *adj* ru·ber -bra -brum; *(hair)* ruf·us -a -um; *(ruddy)* rubicund·us -a -um; **to be —** rubēre; **to grow —** rubescere
red cent *s* **I don't owe anyone a —** assem aerarium nemini debeo; **I haven't a —** assem aerarium habeo nullum
redden *tr* rubefacere, rutilare ‖ *intr* rubescere; *(to blush)* erubescere
reddish *adj* subru·ber -bra -brum; *(hair)* subruf·us -a -um
redeem *tr* redimere
redeemer *s* liberat·or -oris *m; (eccl)* Redempt·or -oris *m*
redemption *s* redempti·o -onis *f*
redhead *s* ruf·us -i *m* (·a -ae *f)*, rutil·us -i *m* (·a -ae *f)*
red-hot *adj* cand·ens -entis
redness *s* rub·or -oris *m*
redouble *tr* ingeminare
redound *intr* redundare
redress *s* satisfacti·o -onis *f;* **to demand —** res repetere
redress *tr* restituere, emendare
reduce *tr* minuere; *(to a condition)* redigere; *(mil)* expugnare
reduction *s* deminuti·o -onis *f; (mil)* expugnati·o -onis *f*
redundancy *s* redundanti·a -ae *f*
redundant *adj* supervacu·us -a -um
reed *s* harund·o -inis *f*
reef *s* scopul·us -i *m*
reek *intr* fumare; **to — of** olēre
reeking *adj* putid·us -a -um
reel *s* fus·us -i *m*
reel *tr* **to — off** recitare volubiliter ‖ *intr (to stagger)* titubare
reelect *tr* iterum eligere *or* creare
reenter *tr* iterum intrare in *(w. acc)*
reentry *s* redit·us -ūs *m; (of a missile)* reditus in aërem terrae
reestablish *tr* restituere
reestablishment *s* restituti·o -onis *f*
refashion *tr* renovare, restituere
refectory *s* cenati·o -onis *f*
refer *tr* referre, remittere ‖ *intr* **to — to** attingere, alludere
referee *s* arbi·ter -tri *m* (·tra -trae *f)*
reference *s* rati·o -onis *f; (place in a book)* loc·us -i *m; (as to character)* commendati·o -onis *f;* **in — to s.th.** ex relatione ad aliquid; **letter of —** litterae commendaticiae; **with —**

to our annals ad nostrorum annalium rationem
refine *tr* expolire; *(metals)* excoquere; *(manners)* excolere
refined *adj* urban·us -a -um, human·us -a -um
refinement *s (of liquids)* purgati·o -onis *f; (fig)* urbanit·as -atis *f,* humanit·as -atis *f*
reflect *tr* repercutere ‖ *intr* **to — on** considerare, reputare
reflection *s* repercussi·o -onis *f; (thing reflected)* imag·o -inis *f; (thinking over)* siderati·o -onis *f;* **without —** inconsulte
reflective *adj* cogitabund·us -a -um
reflexive *adj* reciproc·us -a -um
reform *tr* reficere; *(to amend)* corrigere, emendare ‖ *intr* se corrigere
reform *s* correcti·o -onis *f*
reformation *s* correcti·o -onis *f*
Reformation *s* Reformati·o -onis *f*
reformer *s* correc·tor -toris *m* (·trix -tricis *f)*
refract *tr* refringere
refraction *s* refracti·o -onis *f*
refractory *adj* contum·ax -acis
refrain *s* vers·us -ūs *m* intercularis
refrain *intr* **to — from** abstinēre ab *(w. abl);* **I — from speaking** abstineo quin dicam; **he will not — from boasting** non temperabit quin iactet
refresh *tr* recreare, reficere; *(the memory)* redintegrare
refreshing *adj* iucund·us -a -um
refreshment *s (food)* cib·us -i *m; (drink)* pot·us -ūs *m*
refrigerate *tr* refrigidare
refrigerator *s* frigidar·ium -(i)i *n*
refuge *s* refug·ium -(i)i *n;* **to take — with** confugere in *(w. acc)*
refugee *s* profug·us -i *m* (·a -ae *f)*, ex(s)·ul -ulis *mf*
refulgent *adj* fulgid·us -a -um
refund *tr* restituere
refund *s* pecuni·a -ae *f* restituta
refusal *s* recusati·o -onis *f*
refuse *tr* recusare, negare
refutation *s* refutati·o -onis *f*
refute *tr* refutare, redarguere
regain *tr* recuperare
regal *adj* regal·is -is -e
regally *adv* regaliter
regard *s* rati·o -onis *f; (concern)* cur·a -ae *f; (esteem)* grati·a -ae *f;* **give him (her) my best —s** dicito ei plurimam meis verbis salutem; **give my —s to your brother** fratrem tuum iube salvēre; **to have — for** rationem *(w. gen)* habēre; **to send best —s to** salutem plurimam ascribere *(w. dat)*
regard *tr (to look at)* respicere, intueri; *(to concern)* spectare ad *(w. acc); (to esteem)* aesti-

mare; *(to consider)* habēre; **to — his word as law** pro legibus habēre quae dicat
regarding *prep* de *(w. abl)*
regardless *adj* — **of** negleg·ens -entis *(w. acc);* — **of order of preference** omisso ordine
regardless *adv* quidquid accedat
regatta *s* curs·us -ūs *m* navium
regency *s* interregn·um -i *n*
regenerate *tr* regenerare
regeneration *s* regenerati·o -onis *f*
regent *s* inter·rex -regis *m*
regicide *s (murderer)* regis occis·or -oris *m; (deed)* caed·es -is *f* regis
regime *s* administrati·o -onis *f*
regimen *s* vict·us -ūs *m*
regiment *s* legi·o -onis *f*
regimental *adj* legionari·us -a -um
regimental commander *s* legat·us -i *m* legionis
region *s* regi·o -onis *f;* **in the — of** circa *(w. acc)*
regional *adj* regional·is -is -e; *(characteristic)* peculiar·is -is -e
register *s (list)* tabul·ae -arum *fpl; (public records)* act·a -orum *npl*
register *tr* perscribere, in tabulas referre; *(emotions)* ostendere ‖ *intr* nomen dare, nomen in tabulas referre
registrar *s* tabulari·us -i *m* (·a -ae *f)*
registration *s* in tabulas relati·o -onis *f,* perscripti·o -onis *f*
registry *s* tabular·ium -(i)i *n*
regret *s* paenitenti·a -ae *f*
regret *tr* **I —** me paenitet *(w. gen)*
regretful *adj* paenit·ens -entis
regrettable *adj* paenitend·us -a -um
regular *adj (common)* usitat·us -a -um; *(proper)* iust·us -a -um; *(consistent)* const·ans -antis; *(arranged, coming in order)* ordinari·us -a -um; **— army** exercit·us -ūs *m* permanens
regularity *s (orderly arrangement)* ord·o -inis *m; (evenness, unbroken succession)* constanti·a -ae *f*
regularly *adv* ordine, constanter, assidue
regulate *tr* ordinare, disponere; *(to control)* moderari *(w. dat); (to adjust)* temperare, accommodare
regulation *s (act)* ordinati·o -onis *f; (rule)* praecept·um -i *n,* iuss·um -i *n*
rehabilitate *tr* restituere
rehearsal *s* meditati·o -onis *f; (theat)* prolusi·o -onis *f*
rehearse *tr* meditari; *(theat)* proludere
reign *s* regn·um -i *n,* imper·ium -(i)i *n;* **during his —** eo rege; **— of terror** *(fig)* tempor·a -um *npl* violenta
reign *intr* regnare; **to — over** regnare in *(w. abl),* dominari in *(w. acc)*

reimburse *tr* rependere
reimbursement *s* pecuniae restituti·o -onis *f*
rein *s* haben·a -ae *f;* **to give free —** to frena dare *(w. dat);* **to give full —** to habenas immittere *(w. dat);* **to loosen the —s** frena dare; **to tighten the —s** habenas adducere
reindeer *s* tarandr·us -i *m*
reinforce *tr* firmare, supplēre
reinforcement *s* subsid·ium -(i)i *n;* **—s** *(mil)* supplement·um -i *n; (fresh troops)* subsidiari·i -orum *mpl*
reinstate *tr* restituere
reinstatement *s* restituti·o -onis *f*
reinvest *tr* iterum locare
reiterate *tr* iterare
reiteration *s* iterati·o -onis *f*
reject *tr* reicere; **to — a bill** regationem antiquare
rejection *s* reiecti·o -onis *f,* repuls·a -ae *f*
rejoice *intr* gaudēre
rejoin *tr* redire ad *(w. acc)* ‖ *intr* respondēre
rejoinder *s* respons·um -i *n*
rekindle *tr* resuscitare
relapse *s* recidiv·a -ae *f;* **to have a —** recidere
relapse *intr* recidere
relate *tr* referre, narrare ‖ *intr* **to — to** pertinēre ad
related *adj* propinqu·us -a -um; *(by birth)* **(to)** cognat·us -a -um *(w. dat); (by marriage)* **(to)** affin·is -is -e *(w. dat)*
relation *s* narrati·o -onis *f; (reference)* rati·o -onis *f; (relative)* cognat·us -i *m* (·a -ae *f); (relationship)* cognati·o -onis *f*
relationship *s (by blood)* consanguinit·as -atis *f,* cognati·o -onis *f; (by marriage; connection)* affinit·as -atis *f*
relative *adj* cum ceteris comparat·us -a -um; *(gram)* relativ·us -a -um; **— to** de *(w. abl)*
relative *s* cognat·us -i *m* (·a -ae *f)*
relatively *adv* comparate; **not absolutely but —** non simpliciter sed comparatione
relax *tr* remittere, relaxare ‖ *intr* se remittere, se laxare
relaxation *s* relaxati·o -onis *f,* remissi·o -onis *f*
relaxing *adj* remissiv·us -a -um
release *s* liberati·o -onis *f*
release *tr* solvere; *(a prisoner)* liberare
relegate *tr* relegare
relent *intr* mitescere
relentless *adj* inexorabil·is -is -e, dir·us -a -um; *(unending)* continu·us -a -um
relentlessly *adv* sine missione
relevant *adj* **to be —** ad rem attinēre
reliable *adj* cert·us -a -um; *(person)* fid·us -a -um
reliance *s* fiduci·a -ae *f*
reliant *adj* **(on)** fret·us -a -um *(w. abl)*
relic *s* reliqui·ae -arum *fpl; (trace)* vestig·ium -(i)i *n*

relief *s (alleviation)* levati·o -onis *f; (comfort)* lenim·en -inis *n; (help)* auxil·ium -(i)i *n; (in sculpture)* toreum·a -atis *n; (of sentries)* mutati·o -onis *f;* **to be a —** levamento esse

relieve *tr* levare, mitigare; *(to aid)* succurrere *(w. dat); (a guard)* succedere *(w. dat),* excipere; **to — oneself** *(to urinate)* vesicam exonerare; *(coll)* facere; *(to have a bowel movement)* ventrem exonerare

religion *s* religi·o -onis *f;* **regard for —** religi·o -onis *f*

religious *adj* religios·us -a -um; **— ceremonies, — rites** religion·es -um *fpl*

relinquish *tr* relinquere; *(office)* se abdicare ab *(w. abl)*

relish *s (flavor)* sap·or -oris *m; (enthusiasm)* stud·ium -(i)i *n; (seasoning)* condiment·um -i *n*

relish *tr* gustare, non male appetere

reluctance *s* aversati·o -onis *f;* **with —** invite

reluctant *adj* invit·us -a -um, luct·ans -antis

reluctantly *adv* invite

rely *intr* **to — on** confidere *(w. dat),* niti *(w. abl);* **—ing on** fret·us -a -um *(w. dat or abl)*

remain *intr* manēre, permanēre; *(of things)* restare; *(to be left over)* superesse; **it —s that ...** restat ut *(w. subj);* **to — in that condition** subsistere in eo habitu

remainder *s* reliqu·um -i *n*

remaining *adj* reliqu·us -a -um

remains *spl* reliqui·ae -arum *fpl*

remark *tr* dicere

remark *s* dict·um -i *n*

remarkable *adj* notabil·is -is -e

remarkably *adv* mire, egregie

remedial *adj* remedial·is -is -e; *(med)* medicabil·is -is -e

remedy *s* **(for)** remed·ium -(i)i *n* (contra *w. acc); (a healing drug)* medicament·um -i *n;* **a quick (powerful, efficacious) —** praesentaneum (strenuum, praesentissimum) remedium; **to apply a — to** remedium adhibēre *(w. dat)*

remedy *tr* corrigere; *(med)* mederi *(w. dat)*

remember *tr* meminisse *(w. gen),* recordari, memoriā tenēre; **if I — right** si bene memini

remembrance *s* recordati·o -onis *f*

remind *tr* (ad)monēre

reminder *s* admoniti·o -onis *f;* **as a —** memoriae causā

reminisce *intr* meditari; **to — about** recordari

reminiscence *s* recordati·o -onis *f*

remiss *adj* negleg·ens -entis

remission *s* remissi·o -onis *f,* veni·a -ae *f*

remit *tr* remittere

remittance *s* remissi·o -onis *f,* pecuni·a -ae *f* transmissa

remnant *s* reliqu·um -i *n;* **—s** reliqui·ae -arum *fpl*

remodel *intr* reformare, transfigurare

remonstrate *intr* **to — with** obiurgare

remorse *s* paenitenti·a -ae *f*

remorseless *adj* immisericor·s -dis

remote *adj* remot·us -a -um

remote control *s* moderatr·um -i *n* remotum

remotely *adv* procul

remoteness *s* longinquit·as -atis *f*

removable *adj* mobil·is -is -e

removal *s* amoti·o -onis *f; (of fear, pain)* depulsi·o -onis *f*

remove *tr* amovēre, tollere

remunerate *tr* remunerari

remuneration *s* remunerati·o -onis *f*

rend *tr* lacerare, scindere; *(to split)* findere

render *tr* reddere; *(to translate)* vertere; **to — thanks** gratias reddere

rendezvous *s (meeting)* constitut·um -i *n; (meeting place)* loc·us -i *m* praestitutus

renegade *s* transfug·a -ae *mf*

renew *tr* renovare, redintegrare; **to — one's strength** recipere ex integro vires

renewal *s* renovati·o -onis *f*

renown *s* fam·a -ae *f*

renowned *adj* praeclar·us -a -um

rent *s* merc·es -edis *f; (tear)* scissur·a -ae *f;* **to pay the — for this room** mercedem huic cubiculo dare

rent *tr (to let out)* locare; *(to hire)* conducere; **to — out** locare

renunciation *s* repudiati·o -onis *f*

reopen *tr* iterum aperire; **the discussion was —ed** res retractata est

reorganize *tr* denuo constituere

repair *tr* reparare, reficere; *(clothes)* resarcire

repair *s* refecti·o -onis *f;* **in bad —** ruinos·us -a -um; **in good —** bene reparat·us -a -um

repairman *s* refect·or -oris *m*

repair shop *s* officin·a -ae *f* reparatoria

reparation *s* satisfacti·o -onis *f;* **to make —s** satisfacere

repay *tr* remunerari; *(money)* reponere, retribuere

repayment *s* remunerati·o -onis *f*

repeal *tr* abrogare, tollere

repeal *s* abrogati·o -onis *f*

repeat *tr* iterare, repetere; *(a ritual)* instaurare; **— after me** eisdem verbis mihi redde *(pl:* reddite)

repeatedly *adv* identidem

repel *tr* repellere; *(fig)* aspernari

repent *tr* **I — me** paenitet *(w. gen)* ‖ *intr* **I — me** paenitet

repentance *s* paenitenti·a -ae *f*

repentant *adj* paenit·ens -entis

repercussion *s* repercuss·us -ūs *m*

repetition *s* iterati·o -onis *f,* repetiti·o -onis *f*

replace *tr* reponere

replant *tr* reserere

replenish *tr* replēre
replete *adj* replet·us -a -um
reply *s* respons·um -i *n*
reply *tr & intr* respondēre
report *s* (*rumor*) fam·a -ae *f;* (*official*) renuntiati·o -onis *f;* (*noise*) frag·or -oris *m;* **the —spread** fama percrebuit
report *tr* (**to**) referre, nuntiare, (*officially*) renuntiare (*w. dat*); **it is —ed** fama est; **to —for duty** in promptu operae se habēre
reporter *s* rela·tor -toris *m* (·tris -tricis *f*); (*for a newspaper*) diurnari·us -i *m* (·a -ae *f*)
repose *s* qui·es -etis *f*
repose *intr* quiescere
repository *s* receptacul·um -i *n*
reprehend *tr* reprehendere
reprehensible *adj* vituperabil·is -is -e, improb·us -a -um
represent *tr* (*to portray*) repraesentare; (*to stand in the place of another*) personam (*w. gen*) gerere; in loco (*w. gen*) stare; (*a character*) partes (*w. gen*) agere
representation *s* (*act*) repraesentati·o -onis *f;* (*likeness*) imag·o -inis *f*
representative *s* vicari·us -i *m* (·a -ae *f*)
repress *tr* reprimere, cohibēre
repression *s* cohibiti·o -onis *f*, continenti·a -ae *f*
reprieve *s* supplicii dilati·o -onis *f;* **to grant a —** supplicium differre
reprimand *s* reprehensi·o -onis *f*
reprimand *tr* reprehendere
reprint *tr* denuo imprimere
reprint *s* altera editi·o -onis *f*
reprisal *s* ulti·o -onis *f;* **to make —s** retaliare
reproach *s* exprobrati·o -onis *f;* (*disgrace*) opprobr·ium -(i)i *n*
reproach *tr* opprobrare, vituperare
reproachful *adj* obiurgatori·us -a -um, contumelios·us -a -um
reprobate *s* perdit·us -i *m* (·a -ae *f*)
reproduce *tr* regenerare, propagare; **to — a play** iterum fabulam referre
reproduction *s* regenerati·o -onis *f;* (*likeness*) effigi·es -ei *f*
reproductive *adj* genital·is -is -e; **— organs** genital·ia -ium *npl*
reproof *s* obiurgati·o -onis *f*
reprove *tr* obiurgare
reptile *s* besti·a -ae *f* serpens
republic *s* respublica (*gen:* reipublicae) *f;* (*modern form*) civit·as -atis *f* popularis
republican *adj* optimatibus addict·us -a -um
republicans *spl* optimat·es -ium *mpl*
repudiate *tr* repudiare
repudiation *s* repudiati·o -onis *f*
repugnance *s* aversati·o -onis *f*
repugnant *adj* avers·us -a -um

repulse *s* depulsi·o -onis *f;* (*political defeat*) repuls·a -ae *f*
repulse *tr* repellere
repulsive *adj* odios·us -a -um, foed·us -a -um
reputable *adj* honest·us -a -um
reputation *s* fam·a -ae *f;* **bad —** infami·a -ae *f;* **good —** honest·as -atis *f*
repute *s* fam·a -ae *f*
request *s* petiti·o -onis *f;* **to deny a —** negare roganti; **to grant a —** satisfacere petenti
request *tr* petere, rogare
require *tr* poscere, postulare; (*to need*) egēre (*w. gen*); (*to call for*) requirere, desiderare
requirement *s* necessar·ium -(i)i *n*
requisite *adj* necessari·us -a -um
requisition *s* postulati·o -onis *f*
requital *s* retributi·o -onis *f*
requite *tr* compensare, retribuere; (*for a favor*) remunerari
rescind *tr* rescindere
rescue *s* liberati·o -onis *f;* **to come to s.o.'s —** subvenire alicui
rescue *tr* (*to snatch away*) (**from**) eripere (*dat or* ab, de, ex *w. abl*); (*to free*) liberare
research *s* investigati·o -onis *f*, indagati·o -onis *f*
research *tr* investigare, indagare
resemblance *s* similitud·o -inis *f*
resemble *tr* simil·is -is -e esse (*w. gen, esp. of persons, or w. dat*)
resembling *adj* simil·is -is -e (*w. gen, esp. of persons, or w. dat*)
resent *tr* aegre ferre, indignari
resentful *adj* iracund·us -a -um, indign·ans -antis
resentment *s* iracundi·a -ae *f*, indignati·o -onis *f*
reservation *s* reservati·o -onis *f*, retenti·o -onis *f;* **mental —s** exception·es -um *fpl* animo conceptae
reserve *s* (*restraint*) pud·or -oris *m;* (*stock*) copi·a -ae *f;* (*mil*) subsid·ium -(i)i *n;* **in —** seposit·us -a -um; **—s** (*mil*) subsidiari·i -orum *mpl*
reserve *adj* (*mil*) subsidiari·us -a -um
reserve *tr* reservare
reserved *adj* (*of seat*) assignat·us -a -um; (*of disposition*) taciturn·us -a -um; (*discreet*) modest·us -a -um
reservoir *s* lac·us -ūs *m;* (*of an aqueduct*) castell·um -i *n*
reset *tr* reponere
reside *intr* habitare, colere; **to — in** inhabitare, incolere
residence *s* sed·es -is *f*, domicili·ium -(i)i *n*
resident *s* incol·a -ae *mf*
residue *s* residu·um -i *n*

resign *tr (an office)* se abdicare ab *(w. abl);* **to — oneself to** animum summittere *(w. dat)* **‖** *intr* **(from)** se abdicare *(w. abl)*

resignation *s* abdicati·o -onis *f; (fig)* aequus anim·us -i *m*

resigned *adj* summiss·us -a -um; **to be —** aequo animo esse; **to be — to** aequo animo ferre

resilience *s* molliti·a -ae *f*

resilient *adj* resili·ens -entis

resin *s* resin·a -ae *f*

resist *tr* resistere *(w. dat),* obstare *(w. dat),* repugnare *(w. dat)*

resistance *s* repugnanti·a -ae *f;* **to offer — to** obsistere *(w. dat)*

resolute *adj* const·ans -antis, confirmat·us -a -um

resolutely *adv* constanter

resolution *s (determination)* constanti·a -ae *f; (decision, decree)* decret·um -i *n; (of Senate)* consult·um -i *n*

resolve *s* constanti·a -ae *f*

resolve *tr* constituere; *(to reduce, convert)* resolvere, dissolvere

resonance *s* resonanti·a -ae *f*

resonant *adj* reson·us -a -um

resort *s* loc·us -i *m* celeber; **last —** ultimum auxil·ium -(i)i *n*

resort *intr* **to — to** *(to frequent)* frequentare; *(to have recourse to)* confugere ad *(w acc.); (to lower oneself)* descendere ad *(w. acc.)*

resource *s* subsid·ium -(i)i *n;* **—s** op·es -ium *fpl*

respect *s (high esteem)* observanti·a -ae *f,* hon·or -oris *m; (regard)* respect·us -ūs *m; (religious awe)* religi·o -onis *f, e.g,* **— for an oath** religio iuris iurandi; **in every —** ex omni parte; **in other —s** ceterum; **in — to knowledge** scientiā; **to mention s.o. out of —** aliquem honoris causā nominare

respect *tr (to esteem highly)* observare; *(to esteem with fear)* verēri

respectability *s* honest·as -atis *f*

respectable *adj* honest·us -a -um

respectably *adv* honeste

respectful *adj* rever·ens -entis, observ·ans -antis

respectfully *adv* reverenter

respecting *prep* de *(w. abl)*

respective *adj* propri·us -a -um

respectively *adv* proprie

respiration *s* respirati·o -onis *f*

respite *s* intermissi·o -onis *f*

resplendent *adj* splendid·us -a -um

respond *tr & intr* respondēre

respondent *s (leg)* re·us -i *m* (·a -ae *f)*

response *s* respons·um -i *n*

responsibility *s* **(for)** cur·a -ae *f (w. gen);* **it is my — to** est mihi curae *(w. inf);* **it is the —**

of a father to say this patris est haec dicere; **sense of —** piet·as -atis *f*

responsible *adj* obnoxi·us -a -um; *(reliable)* fid·us -a -um; **to be — for** praestare *(w. acc);* **to hold anyone —** rationem reposcere ab aliquo

rest *s* qui·es -etis *f; (support)* fulcr·um -i *n; (remainder)* reliqu·um -i *n;* **the — of the men** ceter·i -orum *mpl*

rest *tr (to lean)* reclinare **‖** *intr* (re)quiescere; *(to pause)* cessare; **to — on** inniti in *(w. abl),* niti *(w. abl);* **—ing on his elbow** reclinatus in cubitum

restaurant *s* caupon·a -ae *f*

restitution *s* restituti·o -onis *f;* **to demand —** res repetere; **to make —** restituere

restive *adj* contum·ax -acis

restless *adj* inquiet·us -a -um

restlessly *adv* inquiete

restlessness *s* sollicitud·o -inis *f*

restoration *s* restaurati·o -onis *f*

restore *tr* restituere, reddere; *(to rebuild)* restaurare, reficere; **to — to health** recurare; **to — to order** in integrum reducere

restrain *tr* coërcēre; *(tears, laughter)* tenēre; *(emotions)* cohibēre

restraint *s* fren·um -i *n; (moderation)* moderati·o -onis *f*

restrict *tr* restringere; *(to limit)* **(to)** definire *(w. dat)*

restriction *s* mod·us -i *m; (limitation)* excepti·o -onis *f*

restrictive *adj (gram)* restring·ens -entis

restroom *s* loc·us -i *m* secretus; *(public)* foric·a -ae *f*

result *s* exit·us -ūs *m,* event·us -ūs *m;* **without —** nequiquam

resume *tr* resumere

resumé *s* summar·ium -(i)i *n*

resumption *s* resumpti·o -onis *f*

resurrection *s* resurrecti·o -onis *f*

resuscitate *tr* resuscitare

retail *tr (sell retail)* divendere

retailer *s* propol·a -ae *mf*

retain *tr* retinēre

retainer *s (adherent)* assectat·or -oris *m; (fee)* arrab·o -onis *m*

retake *tr (e.g. a town)* recipere

retaliate *intr* ulcisci

retaliation *s* ulti·o -onis *f*

retard *s* heb·es -etis *mf*

retard *tr* tardare

retarded *adj* heb·es -etis

retch *intr* sine vomitu nauseare

retention *s* retenti·o -onis *f*

retentive *adj* ten·ax -acis

reticence *s* taciturnit·as -atis *f*

reticent *adj* taciturn·us -a -um

retinue *s* comitat·us -ūs *m*

retire *intr* recedere; *(from work)* in otium venire; *(from office)* abire; *(for the night)* dormitum ire
retired *adj* emerit·us -a -um
retirement *s (act)* recess·us -ūs *m; (state)* ot·ium -(i)i *n;* to go into — in otium venire
retiring *adj* modest·us -a -um
retort *s* respons·um -i *n*
retort *tr* & *intr* respondēre
retrace *tr* repetere
retract *tr (words)* retractare; *(a promise)* revocare
retraction *s* retractati·o -onis *f*
retreat *s (act; place)* recess·us -ūs *m; (mil)* recept·us -ūs *m;* to sound the — *(mil)* receptui canere
retreat *intr* recedere, se recipere
retribution *s* retributi·o -onis *f*
retrieve *tr* recuperare, recipere
retrievable *adj (loss)* pensabil·is -is -e
retrospect *s* in — respici·ens -entis
retrospective *adj* respici·ens -entis
return *s (coming back)* redit·us -ūs *m; (gain)* redit·us -ūs *m,* quaest·us -ūs *m; (profit)* fruct·us -ūs *m*
return *tr (to give back)* reddere; *(to send back)* remittere; to — a favor gratiam referre ‖ *intr (to go back)* redire; *(to come back)* reverti
reunion *s* readunati·o -onis *f; (social)* comitum convent·us -ūs *m*
reunite *tr* iterum coniungere; *(to reconcile)* reconciliare ‖ *intr* reconciliari
reveal *tr* retegere, recludere; *(to unveil)* revelare
revel *s* comissati·o -onis *f*
revel *intr* comissari, debacchari
revelation *s* patefacti·o -onis *f*
reveler *s* comissa·tor -toris *m* (·trix tricis *f*)
revelry *s* comissati·o -onis *f*
revenge *tr* ulcisci
revenge *s* ulti·o -onis *f,* vindict·a -ae *f;* to seek — ultionem petere; to take — for s.th. small vindictam parvae rei quaerere; to take — on se vindicare in *(w. acc)*
revengeful *adj* ulciscendi cupid·us -a -um
revenue *s (of both private and public income)* vectig·al -alis *n*
reverberate *intr* resonare
reverberation *s* resonanti·a -ae *f*
revere *tr* revereri, venerari
reverence *s* reverenti·a -ae *f;* — due to the gods deorum caerimoni·a -ae *f*
reverend *adj* reverend·us -a -um
reverent *adj* rever·ens -entis
reverential *adj* venerabund·us -a -um
reverently *adv* reverenter
reversal *s* reversi·o -onis *f*
reverse *s* contrar·ium -(i)i *n; (change)* conversi·o -onis *f; (defeat)* clad·es -is *f;* to suffer a

— *(mil)* cladem accipere; *(pol)* repulsam ferre
reverse *tr* invertere, (com)mutare; *(decision)* rescindere, abrogare
revert *intr* reverti
review *s* recogniti·o -onis *f; (e.g., of a lesson)* retractati·o -onis *f; (of a book)* censur·a -ae *f; (mil)* recensi·o -onis *f*
review *tr* recensēre; *(a lesson)* retractare
reviewer *s* cens·or -oris *m* (·rix -ricis *f*)
revile *tr* maledicere *(w. dat)*
revise *tr* corrigere, emendare; *(laws)* retractare
revision *s* emendati·o -onis *f; (literary)* recensi·o -onis *f*
revisit *tr* revisere, revisitare
revival *s* redanimati·o -onis *f; (fig)* renovati·o -onis *f*
revive *tr* resuscitare; *(to renew)* renovare; *(strength)* refovēre ‖ *intr* reviviscere
revocation *s* revocati·o -onis *f*
revoke *tr* revocare; *(a law)* rescindere, abrogare
revolt *s* rebelli·o -onis *f; (civil discord)* sediti·o -onis *f;* to rise in — against s.o. coöriri in aliquem
revolt *tr* offendere ‖ *intr* deficere
revolting *adj* tae·ter -tra -trum
revolution *s (e.g., of a wheel)* conversi·o -onis *f; (change)* commutati·o -onis *f; (of planets)* ambit·us -ūs *m; (pol)* res novae *fpl*
revolutionary *adj* nov·us -a -um, inusitat·us -a -um; *(pol)* seditios·us -a -um
revolutionary *s* hom·o -inis *mf* rerum novarum cupidus (-a)
revolutionize *tr* novare
revolve *tr (in mind)* volutare ‖ *intr* revolvi
revulsion *s* revulsi·o -onis *f*
reward *s* praem·ium -(i)i *n*
reward *tr* praemio afficere
rewrite *tr* rescribere
rhapsody *s* rhapsodi·a -ae *f*
rhetoric *s* rhetoric·a -ae *f;* to practice — declamare
rhetorical *adj* rhetoric·us -a -um; — question quaesti·o -onis *f* non respondenda
rhetorician *s* rhet·or -oris *m*
rheumatism *s* dol·or -oris *m* artuum, rheumatism·us -i *m*
rhinoceros *s* rhinocer·os -otis *m*
rhubarb *s* rad·ix -cis *f* Pontica
rhyme *s* homoēoteleut·on -i *n*
rhythm *s* numer·us -i *m*
rhythmical *adj* numeros·us -a -um
rib *s* cost·a -ae *f*
rib *tr (to taunt)* taxare
ribbon *s* taeni·a -ae *f; (as badge of honor)* ·nul·a -ae *f*
rice *s* oryz·a -ae *f*

rich *adj* div·es -itis; *(of soil)* opim·us -a -um; *(food)* pingu·is -is -e; *(costly)* laut·us -a -um
rich buck *s (sl)* sacc·o -onis *mf*
riches *spl* diviti·ae -arum *fpl*
richly *adv* copiose, laute
rickety *adj* instabil·is -is -e
rid *tr* liberare; **to get — of** *(worries)* diluere; *(persons)* amoliri
riddle *s* aenigm·a -atis *n*
riddle *tr* confodere
ride *tr* **to — a horse (bike)** equo (birotā) vehi ‖ *intr* equitare, equo vehi; **to — off** avehi
ride *s* vecti·o -onis *f;* **to go for a —** gestationem autocineto facere
rider *s (on horse)* rec·tor -toris *m* (·trix -tricis *f); (in carriage)* vec·tor -toris *m* (·trix -tricis *f); (attached to documents)* adiecti·o -onis *f*
ridge *s* iug·um -i *n,* dors·um -i *n*
ridicule *s* (de)ridicul·um -i *n*
ridicule *tr* irridēre
ridiculous *adj* ridicul·us -a -um
ridiculously *adv* ridicule
riding *s* equitati·o -onis *f; (in a carriage)* vectati·o -onis *f*
rife *adj* **(with)** frequ·ens -entis *(w. abl)*
riffraff *s* fae·x -cis *f* populi
rifle *tr* expilare
rifle *s* sclopet·um -i *n* striatum; **automatic —** sclopetum automatum; **to fire a —** sclopetare
rifleman *s* sclopetat·or -oris *m*
rig *tr* adornare; *(ship)* ornare
rigging *s* fun·es -ium *mpl*
right *adj (correct)* rect·us -a -um; *(opp. of left)* dex·ter -tra -trum; *(just)* iust·us -a -um; *(suitable)* idone·us -a -um, apt·us -a -um; *(true, reasonable)* ver·us -a -um; **all —** recte, probe; **on the —** a dextrā; **that's —** sic *(or* ita) est; **to do the — thing** frugem facere; **to the —** dextrorsum; **you're —** probe dicis, bene dixisti, vera dicis
right *adv (correctly)* recte; **— away** statim, continuo; **— from the start** in principio ilico; **— now** nunciam; **to turn —** dextrorsum se vertere
right *s (hand)* dextr·a -ae *f; (leg)* ius, iuris *n; (what is permitted by God or conscience)* fas *n* [indecl]; **by what —** quo iure; **on the — as you come in** dextrā introeunti; **the — *(of knights and senators)* **to wear the gold ring** ius anuli; **to waive one's —s** iure suo decedere; **you have every — to ...** omne fas tibi est *(w. inf)*
right *tr (to correct)* emendare, corrigere; *(a fallen statue)* restituere; *(to avenge)* vindicare
righteous *adj* iust·us -a -um
righteousness *s* iustiti·a -ae *f*
rightful *adj* legitim·us -a -um
rightfully *adv* iuste

right-hand *adj* dex·ter -tra -trum; **— man** dextell·a -ae *f*
rigid *adj* rigid·us -a -um
rigidity *s* rigidit·as -atis *f*
rigidly *adv* rigide
rigor *s* rig·or -oris *m*
rigorous *adj* sever·us -a -um, dur·us -a -um
rim *s* or·a -ae *f,* marg·o -inis *f; (of a jar)* labr·um -i *n; (of a wheel)* canth·us -i *m*
rind *s (thick skin of fruit)* cor·ium -(i)i *n*
ring *s* anul·us -i *m; (of people)* coron·a -ae *f; (for fighting)* aren·a -ae *f; (for boxing)* suggest·us -ūs *m* pugilatorius; *(sound)* sonit·us -ūs *m; (of bells)* tinnit·us -ūs *m;* **engagement —** anulus pronubus; **to take off a —** anulum detrahere; **to wear a —** anulum gestare; **wedding —** anulus nuptialis
ring *tr* **to — a bell** tintinnabulum tractare ‖ *intr* tinnire, resonare
ringing *s* tinnit·us -ūs *m*
ringleader *s* instiga·tor -toris *m* (·trix -icis *f*)
rinse *tr* colluere; **to — out** eluere
rinsing *s* colluvi·es -ei *f*
riot *s* tumult·us -ūs *m;* **to run —** luxuriari
riot *intr* tumultuari, seditionem movēre
rioter *s* seditios·us -i *m* (·a -ae *f*)
riotous *adj* seditios·us -a -um; **— living** luxuri·a -ae *f*
rip *tr* scindere; **to — apart** discindere; *(fig)* discerpere
ripe *adj* matur·us -a -um
ripen *tr* maturare ‖ *intr* maturescere
ripple *intr* trepidare
ripple *s* flucticul·us -i *m,* undul·a -ae *f*
rise *intr (from a seat, from sleep; of the sun)* surgere; *(in a body)* consurgere; *(out of respect)* assurgere; *(of heavenly bodies)* oriri; *(of a river, have its source)* exoriri *(of the voice)* crescere; **to — again** resurgere; **to — up against** adoriri
rise *s* ort·us -ūs *m; (to higher office)* ascens·us -ūs *m; (slope)* cliv·us -i *m;* **— in the ground** loc·us -i *m* editus; **to give — to** parere, gignere, excitare
riser *s* **early —** tempestiv·us -i *m* (·a -ae *f*)
rising *s* ort·us -ūs *m*
rising *adj* ori·ens -entis; **gently — ground** loc·us -i *m* paulatim ab imo acclivis; **— star** *(fig)* adolescen·s -tis *mf* summā spe et animi et ingenii praedit·us (-a)
risk *s* pericul·um -i *n;* **at your own —** tuo periculo; **to be at —** periclitari; **to run the —** periculum subire, periculum facere; **to take a —** periculum adire
risk *tr* in periculum vocare, periclitari
risky *adj* an·ceps -cipitis, periculos·us -a -um
rite *s* rit·us -ūs *m,* caeremoni·a -ae *f*
ritual *adj* ritual·is -is -e
ritual *s* rit·us -ūs *m*

rival *s* rival·is -is *mf; (pol)* competi·tor -toris *m* (·trix -tricis *f*)

rival *adj* aemul·us -a -um

rival *tr* aemulari

rivalry *s* aemulati·o -onis *f; (among lovers)* rivalit·as -atis *f*

river *s* flum·en -inis *n,* amn·is -is *m*

rivet *s* clav·us -i *m*

river bed *s* alve·us -i *m*

rivet *tr (eyes, attention)* defigere

rivulet *s* rivul·us -i *m*

road *s* vi·a -ae *f; (route)* it·er -ineris *n;* **on the — in itinere; paved —** strat·a -ae *f;* **to build a —** viam munire

roadside *s* **by the —** secundum viam

roam *intr* errare, vagari

roar *s (of tigers)* fremit·us -ūs *m; (of lions)* rugit·us -ūs *m***; *(noise, as of a river)* strepit·us -ūs *m*

roar *intr (of lions)* fremere, rugire; *(of tigers)* fremere; *(to laugh hard)* cachinnare

roast *adj* ass·us -a -um

roast *s* ass·um -i *n*

roast *tr* torrēre; *(esp. meat)* assare

roast beef *s* bubul·a -ae *f* assa

roast chicken *s* gallinace·a -ae *f* assa

roast pork *s* porcin·a -ae *f* assa

roast veal *s* vitulin·a -ae *f* assa

rob *tr* rapere, eripere; *(to deprive)* privare; **to — s.o. of** spoliare aliquem *(w. abl)* ‖ *intr* latrocinari

robber *s* latr·o -onis *mf; (home invader)* perfoss·or -oris *m*

robbery *s* latrocin·ium -(i)i *n*

robe *s* vest·is -is *m; (of kings, augurs, knights)* trabe·a -ae *f; (of tragic actors)* pall·a -ae *f*

robe *tr* vestire

robin *s* rubecul·a -ae *f;* **—s chirp** rubeculae pipilant

robust *adj* robust·us -a -um

rock *s* sax·um -i *n; (cliff)* rup·es -is *f;* **between a — and a hard place** inter sacrum saxumque

rock *tr* movēre, motare; **to — the cradle** cunas agitare ‖ *intr* vibrare; **to — from side to side** in utramque partem toto corpore vacillare

rocket *s* missil·e -is *n,* rochet·a -ae *f*

rocking chair *s* sell·a -ae *f* oscillaris

rocky *adj* saxos·us -a -um

rod *s* virg·a -ae *f,* ferul·a -ae *f*

rodent *s* mus, muris *mf*

rogue *s* furcif·er -eri *m*

roguish *adj* nequam [*indecl*]

role *s* part·es -ium *fpl;* **to take the lead —** primas partes suscipere

role model *s* exempl·ar -aris *n*

roll *tr* volvere; **to — back** revolvere; **to — out** extendere, pandere; **to — over** evolvere; **to — over and over** pervolvere; **to — the dice**

talos mittere; **to — together** *(to twist)* convolvere; **to — up** convolvere; *(from below)* subvolvere ‖ *intr* volvi

roll *s (book)* volum·en -inis *f; (of names)* catalog·us -i *m; (leg)* alb·um -i *n; (bun)* collyr·a -ae *f; (sweet roll)* pastill·us -i *m;* **to call —** nomina recitare

roll call *s* nominum recitati·o -onis *f*

roller *s* cylindr·us -i *m,* orbicul·us -i *m*

rollerblade *intr* pedirotis labi

rollerblades *spl* pedirot·ae -arum *fpl*

Roman *adj* Roman·us -a -um

Roman *s* Roman·us -i *m* (·a -ae *f*)

romance *s* fabul·a -ae *f* amatoria; *(affair)* amor·es -um *mpl*

romantic *adj* amatori·us -a -um

Romeo *s* agag·a -ae *m*

romp *intr* lascivire

roof *s* tect·um -i *n;* **— of the mouth** palat·um -i *n*

roof *tr* contegere

roof tile *s* tegul·a -ae *f*

room *s (of house)* conclav·e -is *n,* cubicul·um -i *n; (small room)* cell·a -ae *f; (tiny room)* cellul·a -ae *f; (space)* loc·us -i *m,* spat·ium -(i)i *n;* **— with bath** cubiculum balneo instructum

room *intr* manēre

roominess *s* laxit·as -atis *f*

roommate *s* soci·us -i *m* (·a -ae *f*) cubicularis

roomy *adj* lax·us -a -um

roost *s* pertic·a -ae *f*

roost *intr* cubitare, insistere

rooster *s* gall·us -i *m* gallinaceus; **—s crow** galli canunt, cucuriunt

root *s* rad·ix -icis *f; (fig)* fon·s -tis *m;* **to take — coalescere**

root *tr* **to become —ed** *(lit & fig)* radices agere; **to be —ed** inhaerēre; **to — out** eradicare ‖ *intr* **to — for** acclamare

rope *s* fun·is -is *m,* rest·is -is *f*

rosary *s* rosar·ium -(i)i *n*

rose *s* ros·a -ae *f*

rosebed *s* rosar·ium -(i)i *n*

rosebud *s* rosae cal·yx -ycis *m*

rosebush *s* frut·ex -icis *f* rosae

rose garden *s* roset·um -i *n*

rosemary *s* ro·s -ris *m* marinus

rosin *s* resin·a -ae *f*

rostrum *s* rostr·a -orum *npl;* **to speak from the —** pro rostris loqui

rosy *adj* rose·us -a -um; *(fig)* festiv·us -a -um

rot *intr* putrescere, tabescere

rot *s* putred·o -inis *f,* tab·es -is *f*

rotate *intr* volvi

rotation *s* rotati·o -onis *f;* **in —** per *or* in orbem; **— of command** vicissitud·o -inis *f* imperitandi

rote *s* **by —** memoriter

rotten *adj* putrid·us -a -um
rotunda *s* thol·us -i *m*
rouge *s* fuc·us -i *m*
rough *adj* asp·er -era -erum; *(of character)* dur·us -a -um; *(weather)* inclem·ens -entis, turbid·us -a -um; *(shaggy)* hirsut·us -a -um; *(masonry)* impolit·us -a -um; — **guess** informata cogitati·o -onis *f*
rough-and-ready *adj* prompt·us -a -um
roughen *tr* asperare
roughly *adv* aspere, duriter; *(approximately)* fere
roughneck *s (coll)* rup·ex -icis *m*
roughness *s* asperit·as -atis *f; (brutality)* ferit·as -atis *f*
round *adj* rotund·us -a -um
round *s (in boxing)* congress·us -ūs *m;* **to give a — of applause** plausum dare; — **of beef** fem·ur -oris *n* bubulum transverse sectum; —**s of applause** plaus·us -ūs *m* multiplex; **to go the —s** *(of a policeman)* vigilias circumire; **to make the —s of** circumire *(w. acc)*
round *tr (a corner)* circumire; *(a cape)* superare; **to — off** concludere; **to — out** complere; **to — up** cogere
roundabout *adj* **in a — way** per ambages, circuitu; — **route** circuit·us -ūs *m;* **to tell a — story to** ambages narrare *(w. dat)*
rouse *tr* excitare
rousing *adj* vehem·ens -entis; **a — harangue** incitata et vehemens conti·o -onis *f*
rout *s* fug·a -ae *f; (defeat)* clad·es -is *f; (rabble)* vulg·us -i *n;* **to put to —** in fugam convertere
rout *tr* fugare, fundere
route *s* it·er -ineris *n*
routine *s* ord·o -inis *m;* **daily —** cotidianus ordo *m*
routinely *adv* ex consuetudine
rove *intr* errare, vagari
rover *s* err·o -onis *m*
row *s* ord·o -inis *m,* seri·es -ei *f;* **in a row** continu·us -a -um; **for seven days in a —** per septem continuos dies; — **of seats** grad·us -ūs *m;* — **of trees** ordo arborum; **three days in a —** triennio continuo
row *tr* remis propellere ‖ *intr* remigare; **to — hard** remis contendere
rowboat *s* scaph·a -ae *f* remigera
rower *s* rem·ex -igis *mf*
row home *s* aed·es -ium *fpl* seriales
rowing *s* remig·ium -(i)i *n*
royal *adj* regi·us -a -um; *(worthy of a king)* regal·is -is -e; — **power** regn·um -i *n*
royally *adv* regie, regaliter
royalty *s* regn·um -i *n*
rub *tr* fricare; **to — away** detergēre; **to — down** defricare; **to — in** infricare

rub *s* fricat·us -ūs *m;* **and that's the —** hoc opus, hic labor est
rubbing *s* frici·o -onis *f*
rubbish *s (lit & fig)* quisquili·ae -arum *fpl*
rubble *s* rud·us -eris *n*
rubric *s* rubric·a -ae *f*
ruby *s* carbuncul·us -i *m*
ruckus *s* clam·or -oris *m;* **why are you raising such a —?** quid istum clamorem tollis?
rudder *s* gubernacul·um -i *n*
ruddy *adj* rubicund·us -a -um
rude *adj* rud·is -is -e; *(impolite)* inurban·us -a -um; *(character)* asp·er -era -erum
rudeness *s* inhumanit·as -atis *f,* inurbanit·as -atis *f*
rudiment *s* element·um -i *n*
rudimentary *adj* elementari·us -a -um
rue *tr* **I rue** me paenitet *(w. gen)*
rueful *adj* maest·us -a -um
ruffian *s* rup·ex -icis *m*
ruffle *s* limb·us -i *m*
rug *s* stragul·um -i *n,* tapet·e -is *n*
rugby *s* harpast·um -i *n;* **to play —** harpasto ludere
rugged *adj* asp·er -era -erum, dur·us -a -um; *(terrain)* praerupt·us -a -um
ruin *s* exit·ium -(i)i *n;* —**s** rud·us -eris *n;* **to go to —** ruere, pessum ire, perire
ruin *tr* perdere, corrumpere; *(morally)* depravare
ruinous *adj* exitios·us -a -um
rule *s (instrument; regulation)* regul·a -ae *f; (government)* regim·en -inis *n;* **absolute —** dominati·o -onis *f;* **to break the —** regulam frangere; **to follow (observe) the —** regulam servare; **to lay down the —s** regulas instituere
rule *tr* regere ‖ *intr* regnare, dominari; **to — out** excludere, excipere; **to — over** imperare *(w. dat),* dominari in *(w. acc)*
ruler *s* rec·tor -toris *m (·trix -tricis f); (instrument)* regul·a -ae *f*
ruling *s* sententi·a -ae *f*
rum *s* sicer·a -ae *f,* vin·um -i *n* Indicum
rumble *s* murm·ur -uris *n*
rumble *intr* murmurare; **my stomach is rumbling** sonat mihi circum stomachum
rumbling *s* murm·ur -uris *n*
ruminate *intr* ruminare
rummage *intr* **to — through** perscrutari
rummage sale *s* venditi·o -onis *f* scrutaria
rumor *s* rum·or -oris *m;* **there's a — going around** rumor pervagatur
rump *s* clun·es -ium *fpl*
rumple *s (in garment)* rug·a -ae *f*
rumple *tr* corrugare
rump roast *s* ass·um -i *n* posterius
rumpus *s* **to raise a —** turbas dare

run *tr (to manage)* exercēre; **to — a fever** febricitare; **to — a program** programma administrare; **to — down** *(to disparage)* detrectare; *(w. vehicle)* obterere; **to — her hand over my hair** ducere capillos meos lentā manu; **to — up** *(increase)* augēre; **to — up bills** aes alienum conflare ‖ *intr* currere; *(to flow)* fluere; **the program is running** programma operatur; **to — about** discurrere; **to — after** petere; **to — around** discurrere; **to — around the table** discurrere circa mensam; **to — away** aufugere; **to — aground** offendere; **to — down** decurrere; *(of water)* defluere; **to — for office** honorem petere; **to — foul of** impingcre; **to — high** *(of a river, sea)* tumēre; **to — into** *(to meet)* occurrere *(w. dat)*, incidere in *(w. acc)*, offendere; **to — low** deficere; **to — off** aufugere; *(of water)* defluere; **to — on** percurrere, continuare; **to — out** excurrere; *(of time)* exire; *(of supplies)* deficere; **to — over** *(of fluids)* superfluere; *(details)* percurrere; **to — short** deficere; **to — through** *(to dissipate)* dissipare; **to — through a list of** exsequi; **to — together** concurrere; **to — up and down** modo huc modo illuc currere; **to — up to s.o.** accurrere ad aliquem

run *s* curs·us -ūs *m;* **in the long —** in exitu; **on the —** cursim; **to have the —s** citā alvo laborare

runaway *s* transfug·a -ae *mf*
rundown *s* compend·ium -(i)i *n*
run-down *adj* defatigat·us -a -um; *(dilapidated)* ruinos·us -a -um
rung *s (of ladder)* grad·us -ūs *m*
run-in *s* altercati·o -onis *f*
runner *s* curs·or -oris *m* (·rix -ricis *f*)
runner-up *s* competi·tor -toris *m* (·trix -tricis *f*) iuxta victorem *(or* victricem*)*
running *s* cursur·a -ae *f;* **— for office** petiti·o -onis *f* honoris; **— of the government** administrati·o -onis *f* rei publicae
runny nose *s* distillation·es -um *fpl*
run-off *s* certam·en -inis *n* ultimum
runt *s* pumili·o -onis *mf*
runway *s* aërdrom·os -i *m*
rupture *s (of relations)* discid·ium -(i)i *n;* *(med)* herni·a -ae *f*
rupture *tr* rumpere ‖ *intr* rumpi
rural *adj* rural·is -is -e
ruse *s* dol·us -i *m*
rush *s (plant)* iunc·us -i *m;* *(charge)* impet·us -ūs *m;* *(of people)* **(on)** concurs·us -ūs *m* (ad *w. acc.);* *(hurry)* festinati·o -onis *f*
rush *tr (to attack)* oppugnare; *(to do in a hurry)* festinare; *(to cause to hurry)* urgēre ‖ *intr* festinare, ruere; **to — away** avolare; **to — by** praeterlabi; **to — forth** se proripere; **to — in**

irruere; **to — into** irruere in *(w. acc);* **to — out** evolare, erumpere
rust *s* rubig·o -inis *f;* *(of iron)* ferrug·o -inis *f*
rust *intr* rubiginem trahere
rustic *adj* rustic·us -a -um
rustic *s* rustic·us -i *m* (·a -ae *f*)
rustle *intr* crepitare
rustle *s* crepit·us -ūs *m*
rusty *adj* rubiginos·us -a -um; **to become —** rubigine obduci; *(fig)* desuescere
rut *s* orbit·a -ae *f*
ruthless *adj* immisericor·s -dis
ruthlessly *adv* immisericorditer
rye *s* secal·e -is *n*

S

Sabbath *s* sabbat·a -orum *npl;* **to keep the —** sabbatizare, sabbata observare; **to break the —** sabbata violare *(or* neglegere*)*
saber *s* acinac·es -is *m*
sabotage *s* eversi·o -onis *f (or* vastati·o -onis *f)* occulta
sabotage *tr* occulte evcrtere
saboteur *s* evers·or -oris *m* (·trix - tricis *f*)
saccharin *s* sacchar·on -i *n*
sack *s* sacc·us -i *m;* *(of leather)* culle·us -i *m;* *(mil)* direpti·o -onis *f*
sack *tr* in saccos condere; *(mil)* diripere; *(coll) (to fire)* amovēre
sackcloth *s* cilic·ium -(i)i *n;* **in — and ashes** sordidat·us -a -um
sacrament *s (eccl)* sacrament·um -i *n*
sacred *adj* sa·cer -cra -crum
sacrifice *s (act)* sacrific·ium -(i)i *n;* *(victim)* hosti·a -ae *f;* *(fig)* iactur·a -ae *f;* **to offer (perform) a —** sacrificium agere (facere), rem divinam facere
sacrifice *tr* sacrificare, immolare; **to — an eye for** oculum impendere pro *(w. abl);* **to — one's life for another** vitam pro aliquo profundere
sacrilege *s* sacrileg·ium -(i)i *n*
sacrilegious *adj* sacrileg·us -a -um
sacristan *s* neocor·us -i *m,* aeditu·us -i *m*
sad *adj* trist·is -is -e *(showing grief on one's face)* maest·us -a -um
sadden *tr* contristare
saddle *s* ephipp·ium -(i)i *n*
saddle *tr (fig)* imponere *(w. acc of thing and dat of person);* **to — a horse** equum sternere
sadly *adv* maeste
sadness *s* tristiti·a -ae *f;* *(outer display)* maesti·ti·a -ae *f*
safe *adj* tut·us -a -um; *(unharmed)* incolum·is -is -e; *(harmless)* innocu·us -a -um; *(sure)*

cert·us -a -um; — **and sound** salv·us -a -um; — **from danger** tutus a periculo

safe *s* arc·a -ae *f*

safe-conduct *s* **under** — publicā fide interpositā

safe-deposit box *s* depositor·ium -(i)i *n* syngrapharum

safeguard *tr* tueri

safeguard *s* cauti·o -onis *f;* **there is but one — against these troubles** horum incommodorum cautio una est *(followed by* ut *or* ne)

safekeeping *s* **for** — in fidem

safely *adv* tute, tuto

safety *s* sal·us -utis *f;* **in** — tuto

safety pin *s* fibul·a -ae *f*

safety valve *s* spirament·um -i *n*

saffron *s* croc·us -i *m*

saffron *adj* croce·us -a -um

sag *intr* prave dependēre; *(to decline in value)* decrescere; *(to lose vigor)* languēre

sagacious *adj* sag·ax -acis

sagacity *s* sagacit·as -atis *f*

sage *s (wise person)* hom·o -inis *mf* sapi·ens -entis

sage *adj* sapi·ens -entis

sail *s* vel·um -i *n;* **to set** — vela dare

sail *intr* nave vehi, navigare; **to** — **down to** devehi ad *or* in *(w. acc);* **to** — **up to** subvehi ad *or* in *(w. acc)*

sail boat *s* scaph·a -ae *f* velifera

sailing *s* navigati·o -onis *f*

sailor *s* naut·a -ae *m,* nautri·a -ae *f*

saint *s* sanct·us -i *m* (·a -ae *f)*

saintly *adj* sanct·us -a -um

sake *s* **for heaven's** — ! pro deum fidem! **for the** — **of** causā *or* gratiā *(w. gen);* **for the** — **of glory** gloriae causā *(or* gratiā); **for your** — tuā *(pl:* vestrā) causā

salable *adj* vendibil·is -is -e

salacious *adj* sal·ax -acis

salad *s* acetari·a -orum *npl*

salad dressing embamm·a -atis *n (see* **dressing)**

salamander *s* salamandr·a -ae *f*

salary *s* mer·ces -cedis *f,* salar·ium -(i)i *n;* **to pay s.o. a fair** — mercedem aequam alicui solvere

sale *s* venditi·o -onis *f;* **for** — venal·is -is -e; **this house is for** — haec aedes sunt venales; **to advertise a house for** — aedes venales inscribere; **to go up for** — venum ire; **to put up for** — venum dare, prostare

saleslady *s (in a shop)* tabernari·a -ae *f; (in a clothing store)* vestiari·a -ae *f*

salesman *s (in a shop)* tabernar·ius -(i)i *m;* **traveling** — instit·or -oris *m*

salient *adj* promin·ens -entis; *(chief)* prin·ceps -cipis

saline *adj* sals·us -a -um

saliva *s* saliv·a -ae *f*

sallow *adj* pallid·us -a -um

sally *intr* eruptionem facere

sally *s* procurs·us -ūs *m (or* erupti·o -onis *f)* (militum)

salmon *s* salm·o -onis *m*

saloon *s* caupon·a -ae *f,* tabern·a -ae *f* potoria

salt *s* sal, salis *m*

salt *tr* salire, sale condire; **to** — **away** *(coll)* seponere

saltless *adj* insals·us -a -um

salt mine *s* salin·ae -arum *fpl*

salt shaker *s* salin·um -i *n*

salt water *s* aqu·a -ae *f* marina *(or* salsa)

salty *adj* sals·us -a -um

salubrious *adj* salu·ber -bris -bre

salutary *adj* salutar·is -is -e

salutation *s* salutati·o -onis *f*

salute *s* sal·us -utis *f*

salute *tr* salutare

salvage *tr* (con)servare, redimere

salvage *s (act)* conservati·o -onis *f; (objects)* reliqu·um -i *n*

salvation *s* sal·us -utis *f*

salve *s* unguent·um -i *n*

same *adj* idem, eadem, idem *(gen:* eiusdem *for all genders);* **at the** — **place** ibidem; **at the** — **time** simul, eodem tempore; **in the** — **way** eodem modo; **it's all the** — **to me** meā nihil interest; **the** — **thing** idem; **the very** — ipsissim·us -a -um

sameness *s* similitud·o -inis *f*

sample *s* exempl·um -i *n*

sample *tr* tentare; *(food, drink)* libare

sanctify *tr* sanctificare

sanctimonious *adj* sanctitatem affect·ans -antis

sanction *s* auctorit·as -atis *f; (approval)* approbati·o -onis *f;* **with the** — **of the people** iussu populi; **without the** — **of the people** iniussu populi

sanction *tr* ratum facere

sanctity *s* sanctit·as -atis *f*

sanctuary *s* sanctuar·ium -(i)i *n; (refuge)* asyl·um -i *n*

sand *s* (h)aren·a -ae *f*

sandal *s (simplest form, with sole fastened to feet with thongs)* sole·a -ae *f; (w. covered toes)* sandal·ium -(i)i *n*

sandbag *s* sacc·us -i *m* harenae

sandbank *s* syrt·is -is *(or* -idis) *f*

sandpile *s* cumul·us -i *m* harenae

sandstone *s* lap·is -idis *m* (h)arenaceus

sand trap *s (golf)* harenari·a -ae *f*

sandwich *s* pastill·um -i *n* fartum; **ham** — pastillum pernā fartum

sandy *adj* (h)arenos·us -a -um

sandy-haired *adj* ruf·us -a -um

sane *adj* san·us -a -um

sanguine *adj* plen·us -a -um spei
sanitarium *s* valetudinar·ium -(i)i *n*
sanitary *adj* salubr·is -is -e
sanitation *s* purgati·o -onis *f*
sanity *s* sanit·as -atis *f*
sap *s* suc·us -i *m*
sap *tr* (ex)haurire
sapling *s* surcul·us -i *m*
Sapphic *adj* Sapphic·us -a -um
sapphire *s* sapphir·us -i *f*
sarcasm *s* dicacit·as -atis *f*
sarcastic *adj* dicacul·us -a -um, dic·ax -acis
sarcastically *adv* acerbe
sarcophagus *s* sarcophag·us -i *m*
sardine *s* sard·a -ae *f*
sardonic *adj* amar·us -a -um
sash *s* zon·a -ae *f*
Satan *s* Satan *m* [*indecl*]
Satanic *adj* Satanic·us -a -um, diabolic·us -a -um
satchel *s* per·a -ae *f*
satellite *s* satell·es -itis *mf; (astr)* stell·a -ae *f* minor
satiate *tr* satiare
satiated *adj* sat·ur -ura -urum
satire *s* satir·a, satur·a -ae *f*
satirical *adj* satiric·us -a -um; *(biting)* mord·ax -acis
satirist *s* script·or -oris *m* saturarum
satirize *tr* arripere
satisfaction *s* volupt·as -atis *f; (amends)* satisfacti·o -onis *f;* **my house gives me great —** domus mea mihi valde placet; **to derive the greatest — from** incredibilem voluptatem capere ex *(w. abl);* **to your —** ex tuā sententiā
satisfactorily *adv* satis bene
satisfactory *adj* idone·us -a -um
satisfied *adj* content·us -a -um; *(repaid)* compensat·us -a -um
satisfy *tr* satisfacere *(w. dat); (thirst, hunger, expectation)* explēre; *(creditors)* satisfacere *(w. dat)*
saturate *tr* saturare
Saturday *s* di·es -ei *m* Saturni
Saturn *s* Saturn·us -i *m;* **feast of —** Saturnal·ia -ium *npl (Dec. 17-23)*
satyr *s* satyr·us -i *m*
sauce *s* condiment·um -i *n,* ius, iuris *n*
saucepan *s* cacub·us -i *m,* sartag·o -inis *f*
saucer *s* patell·a -ae *f*
saucily *adv (fig)* petulanter
saucy *adj (fig)* petul·ans -antis
sauna *s* sudator·ium -(i)i *n*
saunter *intr* vagari
sausage *s* farcim·en -inis *n*
savage *adj (wild, untamed)* fer·us -a -um; *(cruel)* saev·us -a -um
savage *s* hom·o -inis *mf* ferox

savagely *adv* atrociter
save *tr* **(from)** servare (ex *w. abl);* **to — up** reservare
save *prep* praeter *(w. acc)*
saving *s* conservati·o -onis *f;* **—s** pecul·ium -(i)i *n*
savings account *s* comput·us -i *m* conditorius
savings bank *s* argentari·a -ae *f* peculiis asservandis
savior *s* serva·tor -toris *m* (·trix -tricis *f)*
Savior *s* Salvat·or -oris *m*
savor *s* sap·or -oris *m*
savor *tr* sapere
savory *adj* sapid·us -a -um
saw *s (tool)* serr·a -ae *f; (saying)* proverb·ium -(i)i *n*
saw *tr* serrā secare **‖** *intr* serram ducere
sawdust *s* scob·is -is *f*
saxophone *s* saxophon·um -i *n*
say *tr* dicere; **as they say** ut aiunt; **needless to — quid** multa?; **no sooner said than done** dictum (ac) factum; **— hello to Rose** iube *(pl:* iubete) Rosam salvēre; **so they — ita** aiunt; **that is to —** scilicet; **they —** dicitur; **to — that … not** negare *(w. acc & inf)*
saying *s* dict·um -i *n;* **as the — goes** ut aiunt
say-so *s* auctorit·as -atis *f;* **on your —** te auctore
scab *s* crust·a -ae *f*
scabbard *s* vagin·a -ae *f*
scaffold *s* fal·a -ae *f*
scald *tr* urere
scale *s (for weighing)* trutin·a -ae *f; (of fish)* squam·a -ae *f; (gradation)* grad·us -ūs *m; (mus)* diagramm·a -atis *f;* **pair of —s** stater·a -ae *f*
scale *tr (fish)* desquamare; **to — a wall** murum per scalas ascendere
scallop *s (shellfish)* pect·en -inis *m; (curve)* sin·us -ūs *m*
scalp *s* pericran·ium -(i)i *n*
scaly *adj* squamos·us -a -um
scam *s* frau·s -dis *f*
scam artist *s* plan·us -i *m* (·a -ae *f)*
scammer *s* frauda·tor -toris *m* (·trix -tricis *f)*
scamp *s* furcif·er -eri *m*
scamper *intr* cursare; **to — about** cursitare, discurrere; **to — away** aufugere
scan *tr* examinare; *(to read over)* perlegere; *(verse; comput)* scandere
scandal *s* opprobr·ium -(i)i *n;* **to be a — to the community** opprobrio esse civitati
scandalize *tr* offendere
scandalous *adj* probros·us -a -um, flagitios·us -a -um
scanner *s (comput)* scansor·ium -(i)i *n*
scansion *s* syllabarum enarrati·o -onis *f*
scant *adj* exigu·us -a -um
scantily *adv* exigue

scantiness *s* exiguit·as -atis *f*
scanty *adj* exigu·us -a -um
scapegoat *s* piacul·um -i *n*
scar *s* cicatr·ix -icis *f*
scar *tr* cicatricibus foedare; *(fig)* maculare
scarce *adj* rar·us -a -um
scarcely *adv* vix; *(with effort)* aegre
scarcity *s* rarit·as -atis *f*, inopi·a -ae *f*
scare *tr* terrēre; **to — off** absterrēre
scarecrow *s* terricul·um -i *n*
scared *adj* territ·us -a -um; **I'm — to death** exanimat·us (-a) metu sum
scarf *s* amictor·ium -(i)i *n* (collare)
scarlet *adj* coccin·us -a -um
scarlet fever *s* febr·is -is *f* purpurea
scathing *adj* aculeat·us -a -um
scatter *tr* spargere, dispergere ‖ *intr* dilabi, diffugere
scavenger *s* cloacar·ius -(i)i *m* (·a -ae *f*)
scene *s (vista)* prospect·us -ūs *m; (picture)* pictur·a -ae *f; (theat)* scaen·a -ae *f;* **behind the —s** post siparium; **Italy, the — of the civil war** Italia, arena belli civilis; **on the — in re** praesenti; **to make a — convicium** facere
scenery *s (theat)* scenae apparat·us -ūs *m; (of nature)* speci·es -ei *f* regionis
scent *s (sense)* odorat·us -ūs *m; (of dogs)* sagacit·as -atis *f; (fragrance)* od·or -oris *m*
scent *tr* odorari
scented *adj* odorat·us -a -um
scepter *s* sceptr·um -i *n*
sceptic *s* sceptic·us -i *m* (·a -ae *f*)
sceptical *adj* **to be —** dubitare
schedule *s* schedul·a -ae *f; (timetable)* horar·ium -(i)i *n;* **bus — horarium** autoraedarum longarum; **class — horarium** academicum; **flight -** horarium aëroplanorum; **train — horarium** traminum
schedule *tr* tempus *(w. gen)* constituere
scheme *s* consil·ium -(i)i *n; (pej)* dol·us -i *m*
scheme *intr* moliri
scholar *s* philolog·us -i *m* (·a -ae *f*), erudit·us -i *m* (·a -ae *f*)
scholarly *adj* erudit·us -a -um, doct·us -a -um
scholarship *s* eruditi·o -onis *f*, litter·ae -arum *fpl; (grant)* pecuni·ae -arum *fpl* quae scholari alendo praebentur
scholastic *adj* scholastic·us -a -um
school *s* lud·us -i *m; (advanced school)* schol·a -ae *f; (group holding like opinions)* sect·a -ae *f; (of fish)* grex, gregis *m;* **elementary — lud·us -i** *m* litterarius; **to attend — scholam** frequentare; **to go to — in scholam** itare; **to skip — insciis** parentibus a scholā abesse
school book li·ber -bri *m* scholaris
schoolboy *s* discipul·us -i *m*
school building *s* aedific·ium -(i)i *n* scholare
schoolgirl *s* discipul·a -ae *f*
schoolmaster *s* ludi magis·ter -tri *m*

schoolmate *s* condiscipul·us -i *m* (·a -ae *f*)
school mistress *s* ludi magistr·a -ae *f*
schoolroom *s* schol·a -ae *f*
school supplies *spl* instrument·um -i *n* scholare
science *s* scienti·a -ae *f*, disciplin·a -ae *f;* **natural — rati·o** -onis *f* physica
scientific *adj* physic·us -a -um
scientifically *adv* ratione
scientist *s* physic·us -i *m* (·a -ae *f*)
scion *s* edit·us -i *m*
scissors *spl* forf·ex -icis *f*
scoff *s* cavillati·o -onis *f*
scoff *intr* cavillari; **to — at** irridēre
scoffer *s* irris·or -oris *m* (·(t)rix -(t)ricis *f*)
scold *tr* obiurgare
scolding *s* obiurgati·o -onis *f;* **to get a — ob·iurgari**
scoop *s* trull·a -ae *f; (news)* nunti·us -i *m* proprius
scoop *tr* **to — out** excavare
scoot *intr* provolare; *(to run off)* celeriter fugere
scooter *s* birot·a -ae *f* pede pulsa; **motor — motoria** birota pede pulsa
scope *s (extent)* spat·ium -(i)i *n; (range)* aspect·us -ūs *m*
scorch *tr* adurere
scorching *adj (sun, day, etc.)* flagrantissim·us -a -um; **— heat** aest·us -ūs *m* flagrantissimus
score *s (total)* stat·us -ūs *m*, summ·a -ae *f; (twenty)* viginti *[indecl];* **(reckoning)** rati·o -onis *f;* **final — status** finalis; **the — is tied** summae punctorum sunt pares; **to even the — with** *(fig)* ulcisci; **to keep — rationem** notare; **to know the —** *(fig)* scire quid agatur
score *tr* notare; **to — a goal** *(soccer)* follem per portam pede pulsare; *(lacrosse)* pilam per portam iacere; **to — a point** punctum ferre; **to — a touchdown** calcem *(or* cretam) attingere
scorn *s* contempti·o -onis *f*
scorn *tr* contemnere
scornful *adj* fastidios·us -a -um
scornfully *adv* contemptim
scorpion *s* scorpi·o -onis *m;* **—s sting** scorpiones icunt
Scot *adj* Scotic·us -a -um
Scot *s* Scot·us -i *m*
Scotch *adj* Scotic·us -a -um; *(tight with money)* (*sl*) sordid·us -a -um
scot-free *adj* **to get off — impunit·us** -a -um dimitti
Scotland *s* Scoti·a -ae *f*
scoundrel *s* furci·fer -feri *m*, propud·ium -(i)i *n*
scour *tr (to rub clean)* tergēre; *(to roam over)* pervagari
scourge *s* flagell·um -i *n; (fig)* pest·is -is *f*

scourge *tr* flagellare
scourging *s* flagellati·o -onis *f*
scout *s* explorat·or -oris *m*
scout *tr* explorare
scowl *s* contracti·o -onis *f* frontis
scowl *intr* frontem contrahere
scowlingly *adv* fronte contractā
scram *interj* apage!
scramble *s (hurried climbing)* ascens·us -ūs *m* rapidus; *(scuffle, struggle)* nix·us -ūs *m*, contenti·o -onis *f*
scramble *tr (eggs)* commiscēre ‖ *intr (to climb hurriedly)* scandere operose; *(to scuffle)* eniti, turbare; **to — for** diripere, certatim captare; **to — up** scandere
scrap *s (small piece)* frust·um -i *n; (brawl)* rix·a -ae *f; (junk)* metall·um -i *n* scrutarium, scrut·a -orum *npl;* **to get into a — in** rixam iri
scrap *tr* reicere ‖ *intr (to brawl)* rixari
scrape *s (scratch)* rasur·a -ae *f,* levis inscisur·a -ae *f; (fig)* difficult·as -atis *f; (quarrel)* rix·a -ae *f*
scrape *tr* radere; **to — together** *(money, etc.)* corradere
scraping *s* rasur·a -ae *f*
scratch *tr* radere; *(the head)* scabere; **to — up** *(e.g., the earth)* scalpere
scratch *s* levis incisur·a -ae *f*
scrawl *s* mala scriptur·a -ae *f*
scrawl *tr & intr* male scribere
scrawny *adj* strigulos·us -a -um
scream *s* ululat·us -ūs *m,* clam·or -oris *m; (of child)* vagit·us -ūs *m*
scream *intr* ululare; *(of child)* vagire
screech *s* strid·or -oris *m*
screech *intr* stridēre
screen *s* umbracul·um -i *n; (on TV or comput)* quadr·um -i *n* visificum; *(movie screen)* linte·um -i *n* cinematicum; **the — ars,** artis *f* cinematica
screen *tr (to shelter)* (pro)tegere; *(to test)* probare
screen play *s* script·um -i *n* scaenarium
screw *s* cochle·a -ae *f*
screw *tr* torquēre; *(to defraud)* defraudare; *(sexually) (vulg)* debattuere
screwdriver *s* cochleatorstr·um -i *n*
scribble *tr & intr* conscribillare
scribe *s* scrib·a -ae *m*
script *s* script·um -i *n; (hand)* man·us -ūs *f*
scroll *s* volum·en -inis *n*
scroll *intr (comput)* volvere; **to — down** devolvere
scrub *tr* (de)tergēre
scruple *s* scrupul·us -i *m; (misgiving)* diffidenti·a -ae *f*
scrupulous *adj* scrupulos·us -a -um
scrupulously *adv* diligenter

scrutinize *tr* (per)scrutari
scrutiny *s* (per)scrutati·o -onis *f*
scuffle *s* rix·a -ae *f*
scuffle *intr* rixari
sculptor *s* sculpt·or -oris *m*
sculptress *s* sculptr·ix -icis *f*
sculpture *s (art)* sculptur·a -ae *f; (work)* sign·um -i *n* (marmoreum)
sculpture *tr* sculpere
scum *s (foam)* spum·a -ae *f; (fig)* sentin·a -ae *f*
scurrilous *adj* scurril·is -is -e
scurry *intr* volitare, properare
scuttle *tr* pertundere ac deprimere
scythe *s* fal·x -cis *f*
sea *s* mar·e -is *n,* **by —** mari, navc
seacoast *s* or·a -ae *f* maritima
seafaring *adj* maritim·us -a -um
seafood *s* vict·us -ūs *m* maritimus
sea gull *s* lar·us -i *m*
sea horse *s* hippocamp·us -i *m*
seal *s* sigill·um -i *n; (animal)* phoc·a -ae *f*
seal *tr* signare; **to — up** obsignare
seam *s* sutur·a -ae *f*
seaman *s* naut·a -ae *m*
seamanship *s* nauticarum rerum us·us -ūs *m*
seamstress *s* sarcinatr·ix -icis *f*
seaport *s* port·us -ūs *m*
sear *tr* adurere
search *s* investigati·o -onis *f,* indagati·o -onis *f*
search *tr* investigare; *(to shake down a person)* excutere; **to — out** exquirere ‖ *intr* quaerere; **to — for** quaerere
searchlight *s* luminar·e -is *n*
seashore *s* act·a -ae *f*
seasick *adj* nauseabund·us -a -um; **to be —** nauseare
seasickness *s* nause·a -ae *f*
season *s* anni temp·us -oris *n; (proper time)* opportunit·as -atis *f,* tempus *n;* **in due — (in)** tempore; **in —** tempestiv·us -a -um
season *tr* condire; *(fig)* assuefacere
seasonable *adj* temptestiv·us -a -um
seasoned *adj (spicy)* condit·us -a -um; *(inured)* inveterat·us -a -um
seasoning *s* condiment·um -i *n*
seat *s* sed·es -is *f,* sell·a -ae *f; (on a fixed bench or chair)* sedil·e -is *n; (in school)* subsell·ium -(i)i *n; (fixed abode)* domicil·ium -(i)i *n;* **back (front) —** sedes posterior (anterior); **reserved —** sedes reservata; **— of honor** *(in dining room)* loc·us -i *m* praetorius; **to take one's —** considere
seat *tr* sede locare; **to — oneself** considere
seatbelt *s* cinctur·a -ae *f* securitatis; **to fasten (unfasten) the —** cincturam securitatis accingere (laxare)
seawater *s* aqu·a -ae *f* marina
seaweed *s* alg·a -ae *f*
secede *intr* secedere

secession *s* secessi·o -onis *f*
seclude *tr* secludere
secluded *adj* seclus·us -a -um, secret·us -a -um
seclusion *s* secess·us -ūs *m*, solitud·o -inis *f*
second *adj* secund·us -a -um; **a — ** alt·er -era -erum; **a — time** iterum; **in the — place** deinde; **ranking — to** s.o. alter ab aliquo; **— to Achilles** ab Achille secundus; **to play — fiddle** secundas partes agere
second *s (handler)* adiu·tor -toris *m* (·trix -tricis *f); (of time)* moment·um -i *n* temporis, secund·a -ae *f*
second *tr* adesse *(w. dat),* favēre *(w. dat);* **to — a motion** in sententiam alicuius dicere
secondary *adj* secundari·us -a -um
secondhand *adj* trit·us -a -um
second nature *s* consuetud·o -inis *f*
second-rate *adj* secundari·us -a -um
secrecy *s* secret·um -i *n; (keeping secret)* silent·ium -(i)i *n*
secret *adj* secret·us -a -um; **to keep — ** celare
secret *s* secret·um -i *n;* **and he makes no — of it** neque id occulte fert; **in — ** clam; **keep this a —!** haec tu tecum habeto! **to keep a — ** commissum celare; **to reveal a — ** commissum enuntiare
secretary *s* scrib·a -ae *mf,* amanuens·is -is *mf; (corresponding)* ab epistulis; *(pol)* (ad)minist·er -ri *m* (·ra -ae *f),* praefect·us -i *m* (·a -ae *f),* e.g., **— of agriculture** agriculturae provehendae praefectus (-a); **— of commerce** commercii praefectus (-a); **— of education** eruditionis praefectus (-a); **— of the interior** rerum interiorum praefectus (-a); **— of state** *or* **of foreign affairs** rerum externarum praefectus; **— of the treasury** aerarii praefectus (-a)
secrete *tr (to hide)* abdere; *(med)* secernere, distillare
secretion *s* secreti·o -onis *f,* distillati·o -onis *f*
sect *s* sect·a -ae *f*
section *s* secti·o -onis *f,* pars, partis *f;* **(of a city)** regi·o -onis *f*
sector *s (math)* sect·or -oris *m; (mil)* par·s -tis *f* aciei
secular *adj* profan·us -a -um; *(laic)* laic·us -a -um, secular·is -is -e
secure *adj* tut·us -a -um
secure *tr (to make safe)* munire; *(to obtain)* comparare; *(to fasten)* religare, affigere; **to — oneself against fraud** muniri contra fraudes
securely *adv* tuto
security *s* securit·as -atis *f; (pledge)* satisdati·o -onis *f,* pign·us -oris *n*
sedate *adj* sedat·us -a -um
sedate *tr* sedare
sedentary *adj* sedentari·us -a -um
sedge *s* ulv·a -ae *f*

sediment *s* sediment·um -i *n*
sedition *s* sediti·o -onis *f*
seditious *adj* seditios·us -a -um
seduce *tr (to entice)* illicere, pellicere; *(to ravish)* stuprum inferre *(w. dat),* stuprare
seducer *s* corrupt·or -oris *m,* ill·ex -icis *mf*
seduction *s* corruptel·a -ae *f*
seductive *adj* illecebros·us -a -um
see *tr* vidēre; *(to distinguish w. the eyes)* cernere; *(to look at)* aspicere; *(to spot from afar)* prospicari; **I see** *(understand)* teneo; **to go to — ** visere; **II** *intr* vidēre; **see to it that you ...** fac ut *(w. subj),* cura *(or* da curam) ut *(w. subj);* **to — about** investigare, inquirere; **to — after** curare; **to — eye to eye with** consentire cum *(w. abl);* **to — off** deducere, comitari usque ad profectum; **you see** *[parenthetical]* enim
see *interj* ecce!
see *s* sed·es -is *f*
seed *s* sem·en -inis *n; (offspring)* progeni·es -ei *f; (in fruit)* acin·um -i *n*
seedbed *s* seminar·ium -(i)i *n*
seedling *s* surcul·us -i *m*
seedy *adj (unkempt)* sordidat·us -a -um
seek *tr* quaerere, petere; *(to strive after)* consectari; **to — to** conari *(w. inf)*
seem *intr* videri; **as it —s** ut videtur; **it —s to me** meā sententiā
seeming *adj* specios·us -a -um
seemingly *adv* ut videtur
seemly *adj* decor·us -a -um
seep *intr* manare; **to — through** permanare
seer *s* vat·es -is *m*
seethe *intr* aestuare
segment *s* segment·um -i *n*
segregate *tr* segregare, separare
segregation *s* separati·o -onis *f*
seismograph *s* apparat·us -ūs *m* ad terrae motum observandum
seize *tr* prehendere, arripere; *(mil)* occupare; *(fig)* afficere
seizure *s* comprehensi·o -onis *f; (med)* accessi·o -onis *f*
seldom *adv* raro; **very — ** perraro
select *tr* seligere, eligere
selection *s (act)* selecti·o -onis *f; (things chosen)* elect·a -orum *npl*
self *pron* ips·e -a -um; **he was never again his old — ** coloris sui numquam fuit
self-appointed *adj* sibi arrog·ans -antis
self-assurance *s* confidenti·a -ae *f*
self-assured *adj* fid·ens -entis
self-centered *adj* sibi dedit·us -a -um
self-confidence *s* fiduci·a -ae *f*
self-confident *adj* sibi fid·ens -entis
self-conscious *adj* diffid·ens -entis
self-control *s* continenti·a -ae *f*
self-controlled *adj* comp·os -otis sui

self-defense *s* sui defensi·o -onis *f;* **in —** sui defendendi causā
self-denial *s* abstinenti·a -ae *f*
self-esteem *s* sui approbati·o -onis *f*
self-evident *adj* manifest·us -a -um
self-government *s* ius, iuris *n* sui gubernandi
self-indulgent *adj* intemper·ans -antis
self-interest *s* sui utilit·as -atis *f*
selfish *adj* avar·us -a -um
selfishness *s* avariti·a -ae *f*
self-made *adj* **he is a — man** de nihilo crevit
self-respect *s* pud·or -oris *m,* dignit·as -atis *f*
self-righteous *adj* prave sanct·us -a -um
self-sufficient *adj* per se suffici·ens -entis
sell *tr* vendere; *(as a practice)* venditare; **to — for 3000 sesterces per pound** vendere ternis milibus nummum in libras; **to — short** *(fig)* levi momento aestimare **‖** *intr* venire, venum ire
seller *s* vendi·tor -toris *m* (·trix -tricis *f*)
semblance *s* speci·es -ei *f,* umbr·a -ae *f;* **under the — of a just treaty** sub umbrā *(or* sub specie) foederis aequi
semester *s* semestr·e -is *n*
semicircle *s* semicircul·us -i *m*
semicircular *adj* semicircul·us -a -um
semicolon *s* punct·um et caes·um -i *n*
seminar *s* seminar·ium -(i)i *n* academicum
seminary *s* seminar·ium -(i)i *n*
semivowel *s* semivocal·is -is *f (supply* littera)
senate *s* senat·us -ūs *m; (building)* curi·a -ae *f;* **— session** senatus *m;* **a — session was held on that very day** senatus eo ipso die agebatur
senatorial *adj* senatori·us -a -um
send *tr* mittere; *(on public business)* legare; **to — away** dimittere; **to — back** remittere; **to — forward** praemittere; **to — into** intromittere in *(w. acc);* **to — out** emittere **‖** *intr* **to — for** arcessere
sender *s* qui (quae) mittit
senile *adj* senil·is -is -e
senility *s* sen·ium -(i)i *n*
senior *adj* (natu) mai·or -or -us; *(in school)* seni·or -oris *mf*
seniority *s* aetatis praerogativ·a -ae *f*
sensation *s* sens·us -ūs *m; (fig)* mir·um -i *n;* **a painful —** doloris sensus; **to make a —** conspici
sensational *adj* mirabil·is -is -e
sense *s (faculty; meaning)* sens·us -ūs *m; (understanding)* prudenti·a -ae *f; (meaning)* vis *f,* significati·o -onis *f;* **— of duty, of responsibility** piet·as -atis *f*
sense *tr* sentire
senseless *adj* absurd·us -a -um; *(unconscious)* omni sensu car·ens -entis
sensible *adj* prud·ens -entis; **to be —** sapere
sensibly *adv* prudenter

sensitive *adj* sensil·is -is -e; *(touchy, sore)* moll·is -is -e
sensual *adj* voluptari·us -a -um; **— pleasure** corporis volupt·as -atis *f*
sensuality *s* libid·o -inis *f*
sentence *s (gram)* sententi·a -ae *f,* orati·o -onis *f; (leg)* iudic·ium -(i)i *n; (decision of an arbiter)* arbitr·ium -(i)i *n;* **to pass — on s.o.** arbitrium de aliquo agere; *(leg)* iudicium facere de aliquo
sentence *tr* damnare, condemnare; **to — to death** capitis damnare
sententious *adj* sententios·us -a -um
sentiment *s (opinion)* sententi·a -e *f,* opini·o -onis *f, (feeling)* sens·us -ūs *m*
sentimental *adj* moll·is -is -e, sensu affect·us -a -um
sentimentality *s* animi molliti·es -ei *f*
sentinel, sentry *s* cust·os -odis *mf,* vig·il -is *mf; (collectively)* stati·o -onis *f;* **to be on sentry duty** in statione esse
separable *adj* separabil·is -is -e
separate *tr* separare, disiungere **‖** *intr* separari, disiungi
separate *adj* separat·us -a -um
separately *adv* separatim
separation *s* separati·o -onis *f*
September *s* Septem·ber -bris *m or* mens·is -is *m* September; **in — mense** Septembri; **on the first of —** Kalendis Septembribus
sepulcher *s* sepulcr·um -i *n*
sequel *s* sequel·a -ae *f,* postprincip·ium -(i)i *n*
sequence *s* ord·o -inis *m*
serenade *tr* occentare
serenade *s* nocturnus concent·us -ūs *m*
serene *adj* seren·us -a -um
serenely *adv* serene
serenity *s* serenit·as -atis *f*
serf *s* serv·us -i *m*
serfdom *s* servit·ium -(i)i *n*
sergeant *s* opti·o -onis *mf*
series *s* seri·es -ei *f*
serious *adj* seri·us -a -um, grav·is -is -e; **are you —?** serione dicis tu?
seriously *adv* serio, graviter; **to take — in** serium convertere
seriousness *s* gravit·as -atis *f; (of things)* ser·ium -(i)i *n*
sermon *s* homili·a -ae *f;* **to give a —** homiliam habēre
serpent *s* angu·is -is *mf,* serp·ens -entis *mf;* **—s hiss** serpentes sibilant
servant *s* famul·us -i *m* (·a -ae *f*), serv·us -i *m* (·a -ae *f*)
serve *tr (to be a servant to)* servire *(w. dat); (food)* apponere; *(to be useful)* prodesse *(w. dat);* **to — a sentence** poenam subire; **to — a summons on** diem dare *(dat);* **to — one's country** de re publica merēre **‖** *intr (mil)*

(stipendia) merēre; *(to suffice)* sufficere; *(tennis)* deicere; **the trunk — the elephant as a hand** proboscis elephanto pro manu est; **to — as a soldier or sailor** (ut) miles aut nauta merēre
service *s (favor)* offic·ium -(i)i *n; (mil)* militi·a -ae *f,* stipendi·a -orum *npl; (work)* minister·ium -(i)i *n;* **to be at s.o.'s** — alicui praesto esse; **to be of — to** prodesse *(w. dat)*
serviceable *adj* util·is -is -e
serviceman *s* militar·is -is *m*
service station *s* stati·o -onis *f* benzinaria
servile *adj* servil·is -is -e
servitude *s* servit·us -utis *f*
sesame *s* sesam·um -i *n*
session *s* sessi·o -onis *f;* **to be in** — sedēre
sesterce *s* sestert·ius -(i)i *m (used in smaller sums; large sums are expressed by the collective form* sestertium = mille sesterti, *usually with the distributive numeral, e.g.,* **hundred thousand sesterces** centena sestertia, *but also with the cardinal, as,* septem sestertia **seven hundred thousand sesterces)**
set *tr (to place)* ponere; *(to make to stand)* sistere, statuere; *(diamonds, etc.)* includere; *(a broken limb)* collocare; *(course)* dirigere; *(date)* constituere; *(example)* praebēre; *(limit)* imponere; *(table)* instruere; *(plants)* serere; *(clock)* constituere; **to — apart** seponere; **to — a price** pretium statuere; **to — aside** ponere; *(to rescind)* rescindere; **to — a trap** insidias tendere; **to — bounds to** modum *(w. gen)* habēre; **to — down** deponere; *(in writing)* perscribere; **to — foot in** attingere; **to — forth** exponere, proponere; **to — free** liberare; **to — in motion** ciēre; **to — in order** componere; **to — off** *(to adorn)* adornare; **to — on fire** incendere; **to — one's hopes on** spem collocare in *(w. abl);* **to — s.o. over** aliquem praeficere *(w. dat);* **to — up** statuere **‖** *intr (of stars, sun)* occidere; **to — about waging wars** bella incipere; **to — in** *(to begin)* incipere; **to — out** proficisci
set *adj (fixed)* cert·us -a -um; *(prescribed, e.g., day, sacrifice)* stat·us -a -um; *(prepared)* parat·us -a -um; **in — terms** composite; **— speech** declamati·o -onis *f*
set *s (a set of two)* par, paris *n; (gear, set of tools)* instrument·um -i *n; (number of persons customarily associated)* glob·us -i *m;* **a — of tools for one's trade** artis instrumentum *n*
setback *s* **to suffer a —** *(mil)* adversum casum experiri; *(pol)* repulsam ferre
setting *s (of sun)* occas·us -ūs *m; (situation)* res, rerum *fpl*
settle *tr* statuere; *(business)* transigere; *(colony)* deducere; *(people, e.g., on public*

lands) constituere; *(disagreement)* componere; *(debt)* expedire; **to — accounts with** rationes putare cum *(w. abl)* **‖** *intr (to the bottom)* subsidēre; *(to alight, land)* **(on)** insidere *(w. dat); (to fix one's home)* **(in)** considere *or* insidere (in *w. abl);* **we —d among ourselves to** constituimus inter nos ut
settled *adj (sure, certain)* cert·us -a -um
settlement *s (of a colony)* deducti·o -onis *f; (the colony itself)* coloni·a -ae *f; (of an affair)* compositi·o -onis *f; (terms)* pact·um -i *n*
settler *s* colon·us -i *m,* adven·a -ae *mf*
seven *adj* septem *[indecl];* **— times** septies
sevenfold *adj* septempl·ex -icis
seventeen *adj* septendecim *[indecl]*
seventeenth *adj* septim·us decim·us -a -um
seventh *adj* septim·us -a -um; **to be in — heaven** in caelo esse
seventieth *adj* septuagesim·us -a -um
seventy *adj* septuaginta *[indecl]*
sever *tr* separare **‖** *intr* disiungi
several *adj* aliquot *[indecl]*
severally *adv* singulatim
severe *adj (rigorous, strict)* sever·us -a -um; *(wound, punishment)* grav·is -is -e; *(winter)* a·cer -cris -cre; *(cold, pain)* dur·us -a -um
severely *adv* severe, graviter
severity *s* severit·as -atis *f,* gravit·as -atis *f*
sew *tr* suere; **to — up** consuere
sewer *s* cloac·a -ae *f*
sewing *s* sutur·a -ae *f*
sewing machine *s* machin·a -ae *f* sutoria
sex *s (gender)* sex·us -ūs *m; (intercourse)* Ven·us -eris *f,* coït·us -ūs *m;* **to have illicit — with** stuprum inferre *(w. dat)*
sextant *s* sext·ans -antis *m*
sexton *s* aditu·us -i *m*
sexual *adj* sexual·is -is -e; **— desire** libid·o -inis *f;* **— intercourse** coït·us -ūs *m*
sh-h-h *interj* st! st!
shabbily *adv* sordide
shabbiness *s* sord·es -ium *fpl*
shabby *adj* sordid·us -a -um; *(worn out, torn)* obsolet·us -a -um
shackle *tr* compedibus constringere
shackles *spl* vincul·a -orum *npl; (on the legs)* comped·es -um *fpl*
shade *s* umbr·a -ae *f;* **—s** *(of the dead)* man·es -ium *mpl*
shade *tr* opacare, adumbrare
shadow *s* umbr·a -ae *f*
shadowy *adj* umbros·us -a -um; *(fig)* inan·is -is -e, exil·is -is -e
shady *adj* opac·us -a -um; *(pej)* infam·is -is -e
shaft *s (arrow)* sagitt·a -ae *f; (of spear)* hastil·e -is *n; (of a mine)* pute·us -i *m*
shaggy *adj* villos·us -a -um
shake *tr* quatere, concutere; *(violently)* quassare; *(head)* nutare; *(to get rid of)* amoliri; **to**

— **hands** (**with**) dextram iungere (cum *w. abl*); (*when campaigning*) manus prensare; **to — off a bad reputation** infamiam discutere; **to — the head** nutare; (*in dissent*) abnutare; **to — up** (*fig*) commovēre, perturbare ‖ *intr* tremere; (*to totter*) vacillare; **her sides shook with laughter** eius latera commoverunt risu; **to begin to —** intremescere

shakedown *s* extorsi·o -onis *f*

shake-up *s* magna commutati·o -onis *f*

shaking *s* quassati·o -onis *f*; (*w. cold, fear*) trem·or -oris *m*

shaky *adj* tremul·us -a -um; (*weak*) debil·is -is -e; (*unreliable*) instabil·is -is -e

shallow *adj* (*river, sea*) tenu·is -is -e; (*trench*) humil·is -is -e; (*well*) brev·is -is -e; (*fig*) lev·is -is -e; **quite —** minime alt·us -a -um

shallows *spl* vad·a -orum *npl*

sham *s* dol·us -i *m*

sham *adj* simulat·us -a -um

shambles *spl* turb·a -ae *f*, confusi·o -onis *f*

shame *s* pud·or -oris *m*; (*disgrace*) dedec·us -oris *n*; **— on our Senate and morals!** pro senatu et moribus! **— on you!** sit pudor!; **that's a darn shame!** edepol facinus improbum!; **to have lost all sense of —** omnem pudorem exuisse; **to put s.o. to —** ruborem alicui incutere; **what a —!** facinus indignum!; O rem indignam!

shame *tr* ruborem incutere (*w. dat*)

shamefaced *adj* verecund·us -a -um

shameful *adj* probros·us -a -um, ignominios·us -a -um

shamefully *adv* probrose, turpiter

shameless *adj* impud·ens -entis

shamelessly *adv* impudenter

shampoo *s* loment·um -i *n* capillare

shamrock *s* trifol·ium -(i)i *n*

shank *s* cru·s -ris *n*

shanty *s* tugur·ium -(i)i *n*

shape *s* form·a -ac *f*, figur·a -ae *f*; **to be in good (bad) —** boni (mali) habitūs esse

shape *tr* figurare, formare

shapeless *adj* inform·is -is -e

shapely *adj* formos·us -a -um; (*limbs*) ter·es -etis

shard *s* test·a -ae *f*

share *s* par·s -tis *f*, porti·o -onis *f*; (*stock*) acti·a -ae *f*

share *tr* partire; (*to enjoy with, have in common with*) (**with**) communicare (cum *w. abl*) ‖ *intr* **to — in** particeps esse (*w. gen*)

shark *s* pistr·ix -icis *f*, pistr·is -is *f*

sharp *adj* acut·us -a -um; (*abrupt*) prae·ceps -cipis; (*mind*) ac·er -ris -re, sag·ax -acis; (*taste*) acerb·us -a -um

sharpen *tr* (ex)acuere

sharply *adv* acriter

sharpness *s* aci·es -ei *f*; **— of vision** oculorum acies; (*of mind*) acum·en -inis *n*

shatter *tr* quassare, confringere; (*to knock apart*) discutere

shave *tr* radere; **to — off** deradere ‖ *intr* barbam (*or* faciem) radere

shave *s* rasur·a -ae *f*; **to have a close —** (*fig*) aegre effugere

shaven *adj* adras·us -a -um

shavings *spl* rament·a -orum *npl*

shawl *s* amicul·um -i *n*

she *pron* ea, illa, haec

sheaf *s* fasc·is -is *m*

shear *tr* tondēre

shearing *s* tonsur·a -ae *f*

shears *spl* forf·ex -icis *f*

sheath *s* vagin·a -ae *f*

sheathe *tr* in vaginam recondere

shed *tr* (*tears, blood, etc.*) fundere, effundere; (*to cast off*) exuere, spargere; (*feathers, leaves*) ponere; **to — light on a subject** lumen alicui rei adhibēre ‖ *intr* (*of plants*) deflorescere

shed *s* tugur·ium -(i)i *n*; (*mil*) vine·a -ae *f*

sheep *s* ov·is -is *f*

sheepfold *s* ovil·e -is *n*

sheepish *adj* pudibund·us -a -um

sheepishly *adv* pudenter

sheepskin *s* pell·is -is *f* ovilla

sheer *adj* (*pure, utter*) mer·us -a -um; (*steep*) praerupt·us -a -um

sheet *s* (*for the bed*) stragul·um -i *n* linteum; (*of paper*) sched·a -ae *f*; (*of metal*) lamin·a -ae *f*; **— of papyrus** chart·a -ae *f*

shelf *s* plute·us -i *m*

shell *s* (*of clam or oyster*) conch·a -ae *f*, test·a -ae *f*; (*of a turtle*) testud·o -inis *f*; (*of nuts, eggs*) putam·en -inis *n*

shellac *s* malth·a -ae *f*

shellfish *s* conch·a -ae *f*

shelter *s* tegm·en -inis *n*; (*refuge*) refug·ium -(i)i *n*; (*lodgings*) hospit·ium -(i)i *n*

shelter *tr* tegere; (*refugees*) excipere

shepherd *s* past·or -oris *m*

sheriff *s* geraif·a -ae *mf*

shield *s* (*round*) parm·a -ae *f*; (*oblong*) scut·um -i *n*

shield *tr* protegere

shift *tr* (*to change*) mutare; (*transfer*) transferre ‖ *intr* mutari; **to — for oneself** sibi providēre

shift *s* (*change*) mutati·o -onis *f*; (*period of work*) laboris spat·ium -(i)i *n*

shifting *adj* (*wind, weather*) vari·us -a -um

shiftless *adj* pi·ger -gra -grum

shifty *adj* mobil·is -is -e; (*untrustworthy*) prav·us -a -um

shimmer *intr* micare, tremere

shimmer *s* lum·en -inis *n* tremulum

shin *s* tibi·a -ae *f*

shinbone _s_ tibi·a -ae _f_
shine _s_ nit·or -oris _m,_ fulg·or -oris _m_
shine _intr_ lucēre; _(with a bright light)_ fulgēre; _(to excel)_ praestare; **to — forth** elucēre, enitēre; **to — on** affulgēre _(w. dat)_
shingle _s_ tegul·a -ae _f_
shiny _adj_ fulgid·us -a -um, nitid·us -a -um
ship _s_ nav·is -is _f; —'s captain_ navarch·us -i _m_
ship _tr_ navi invehere, devehere; _(to send)_ mittere
shipbuilder _s_ naupeg·us -i _m_
ship owner _s_ navicular·ius -(i)i _m_
shipwreck _s_ naufrag·ium -(i)i _n;_ **to suffer —** naufragium facere
shipwrecked _adj_ naufract·us -a -um
shipyard _s_ naval·ia -ium _npl_
shirk _tr_ abhorrēre ab _(w. abl),_ evitare
shirt _s_ subucul·a -ae _f,_ camisi·a -ae _f_
shiver _intr_ horrēre, tremere
shiver _s_ horr·or -oris _m,_ trem·or -oris _m_
shoal _s_ _(of fish)_ exam·en -inis _n;_ _(shallow)_ vad·um -i _n_
shock _s_ offensi·o -onis _f;_ electricus ict·us -ūs _m_
shock _tr_ _(emotionally)_ percutere, attonere; **to be —ed** inhorrescere
shocked _adj_ attonit·us -a -um
shocking _adj_ tae·ter -tra -trum, horrend·us -a -um
shoe _s_ _(worn with toga)_ calce·us -i _m;_ _(oxfords)_ calceus subtalaris; _(fancy low shoe, of different colors, decorated with pearls, etc.)_ socc·us -i _m,_ soccul·us -i _m;_ _(red shoes of a senator)_ calceus mulleus
shoe polish _s_ cerom·a -atis _n_ sutorium
shoemaker _s_ sut·or -oris _m_
shoe store _s_ tabern·a _f_ sutrina
shook up _adj_ consternat·us -a -um; **all —** vehmenter perturbat·us -a -um
shoot _tr_ _(missile)_ conicere; _(person)_ sclopeto transfigere; **I shot myself in the foot** mihi asciam in crus impegi ‖ _intr_ volare; **to — up** crescere; _(to sprout)_ germinare; _(sl)_ medicamentum psychotropicum infundere
shoot _s_ surcul·us -i _m_
shooting star _s_ fae·x -cis _f_ caelestis
shop _s_ tabern·a -ae _f;_ _(workshop)_ officin·a -ae _f_
shop _intr_ mercari; _(for groceries)_ obsonare; **to — for** mercari; _(groceries)_ obsonare; **to go shopping** emptum ire; **I shopped for clothes** per tabernas lustravi ut vestes emerem
shopkeeper _s_ tabernari·us -i _m_ (·a -ae _f_)
shopper _s_ emp·tor -toris _m_ (·trix -tricis _f_); _(for groceries)_ obsona·tor -toris _m_ (·trix -tricis _f_)
shopping _s_ empti·o -onis _m;_ _(for groceries)_ obsonat·us -ūs _m_
shopping spree _s_ emacit·as -atis _f;_ **to go on a — effundi in emacitate**
shore _s_ lit·us -oris _n,_ or·a -ae _f_

shore _tr_ **to — up** fulcire
short _adj_ brev·is -is -e; **a — vowel** vocal·is -is _f_ correpta; **in a — time** brevi; **in —** ad summam; **to make — shrift of** dimittere; **to run — deficere**
short _s_ _(electrical)_ defectus curs·us -ūs _m_ electricus
shortage _s_ inopi·a -ae _f,_ exiguit·as -atis _f_
shortchange _tr_ non satis pecuniae reddere; _(fig)_ fraudare _(w. dat)_
shortcoming _s_ defect·us -ūs _m_
shortcut _s_ compendiari·a -ae _f;_ **to take a — compendariā ire**
shorten _tr_ curtare, imminuere; contrahere; _(to limit)_ coarctare; _(a syllable)_ corripere ‖ _intr_ contrahi, minui
shorthand _s_ not·ae -arum _fpl;_ **to take down in — notis excipere**
short-lived _adj_ brev·is -is -e, fug·ax -acis
shortly _adv_ brevi, mox
shortness _s_ brevit·as -atis _f;_ **— of breath** asthm·a -atis _n_
shorts _spl_ breves brac·ae -arum _fpl;_ _(underwear)_ subligacul·um -i _n_
shortsighted _adj_ my·ops -opis; _(fig)_ improvid·us -a -um
shortstop _s_ intermedius basiari·us -i _m,_ intermedia basiari·a -ae _f_
shorttempered _adj_ iracund·us -a -um
short-winded _adj_ anhel·us -a -um
shorty _s_ pumili·o -onis _mf_
shot _s_ _(of a gun)_ scopleti crepit·us -ī _m;_ _(of liquor)_ mera poti·o -onis _f;_ _(guess)_ coniectur·a -ae _f;_ **long —** dubia ale·a -ae _f;_ **— in the arm** _(fig)_ instigati·o -onis _f;_ **to take a — at it** _(fig)_ id periclitari
shot _adj_ _(worn out)_ attrit·us -a -um
shotgun _s_ focil·e -is _n_ (bifistulatum)
should _intr_ _(ought)_ debēre; **I — go** mihi eundum est; **if I — say no** si negem
shoulder _s_ umer·us -i _m;_ _(of animals)_ arm·us -i _m;_ **to give s.o. the cold —** aliquem reicere; **to shrug the —s** umeros allevare
shoulder _tr_ suscipere
shoulder bag _s_ per·a -ae _f_
shoulder blade _s_ scapul·a -ae _f_
shout _s_ clam·or -oris _m;_ _(of approval)_ acclamati·o -onis _f_
shout _tr_ clamare, acclamare; **to — s.o. down** alicui obstrepere; **to — out** exclamare ‖ _intr_ clamare; _(continuously)_ clamitare
shove _tr_ trudere, pulsare; **to — the book under the bed** mittere librum subter lectum ‖ _intr_ **to — off** _(to depart)_ proficisci; _(naut)_ terram repellere
shove _s_ impulsi·o -onis _f,_ impuls·us -ūs _m_
shovel _s_ rutr·um -i _n_
shovel _tr_ rutro tollere; **to — out** rutro eicere

show *tr* monstrare, ostendere; *(to display)* exhibēre; *(to explain)* docēre; **this —s that ...** indicio est *(w. acc & inf);* **to — off** ostentare ‖ *intr* manifest·us -a -um esse; **to — off** se iactare; **to — up** apparēre

show *s (appearance)* speci·es -ei *f; (display)* ostentati·o -onis *f; (pretense)* simulati·o -onis *f; (public entertainment)* spectacul·um -i *n;* **for —** ad speciem; **to put on a public —** spectaculum edere

shower *s (rain)* im·ber -bris *m; (of stones, darts)* vis *f,* multitud·o -inis *f; (for bathing)* balne·um -i *n* pensile; **bridal —** conviv·ium -(i)i *n* nuptiale; **to take a —** balneo pensili uti

shower *tr* fundere; **to — down arrows on** infundere sagittas *(w. dat)*

showy *adj* specios·us -a -um

shred *s* segment·um -i *n* panni; **in —s** sciss·us -a -um, pannos·us -a -um; **not a — of evidence** nihil omnino testimonii; **to tear to —s** discindere

shred *tr* discindere, concidere

shrewd *adj* astut·us -a -um; *(calculating)* callid·us -a -um

shrewdly *adv* astute, callide

shrewdness *s* acum·en -inis *n;* callidit·as -atis *f*

shriek *s* strid·or -oris *m*

shriek *intr* stridēre

shrill *adj* peracut·us -a -um

shrimp *s* squill·a -ae *f; (person)* pumili·o -onis *mf*

shrine *s* delubr·um -i *n,* fan·um -i *n*

shrink *tr* contrahere ‖ *intr* contrahi; *(to withdraw)* refugere; **to — from** abhorrēre *or* refugere ab *(w. abl)*

shrink *s (coll)* pyschiat·er -ri *m* (·ria -riae *f*)

shrivel *tr* corrugare ‖ *intr* corrugari

shriveled *adj* rugos·us -a -um

shroud *s* vestiment·um -i *n* funebre; *(cover)* integument·um -i *n*

shroud *tr* involvere

shrub *s* frut·ex -icis *m*

shrubbery *s* fruticet·um -i *n*

shrug *tr* **to — the shoulders** umeros allevare

shrug *s* umerorum allevati·o -onis *f*

shudder *intr* horrēre; **to — at the sight** horrēre visu

shudder *s* horr·or -oris *m*

shuffle *tr (cards)* permiscēre ‖ *intr* claudicare

shun *tr* (de)vitare, evadere; **to — publicity** forum ac lucem fugere

shut *tr* claudere; **to — down** *(comput)* claudere; **to — in** includere; **to — off** occludere; **to — one's eyes** to connivēre in *(w. acc);* **to — out** excludere; **to — up** concludere ‖ *intr* **to — down** cessare **to — up** conticescere; **— up!** obsera os tuum!; **why don't you just — up?** quin tu taces modo?

shutdown *s* cessati·o -onis *f*

shutter *s* foricul·a -ae *f*

shy *adj* verecund·us -a -um; *(timid)* timid·us -a -um

shy *intr (of horses)* consternari; **to — away from** abhorrēre ab *(w. abl)*

shyly *adv* verecunde, timide

shyness *s* verecundi·a -ae *f*

shyster *s* legulei·us -i *m* (·a -ae *f*)

sibyl *s* sibyll·a -ae *f*

sibylline *adj* Sibyllin·us -a -um

sic *tr* **to — the dog on** instigare canem in *(w. acc)*

Sicily *s* Sicili·a -ae *f*

sick *adj (mentally or physically)* ac·ger -gra -grum; *(physically)* aegrot·us -a -um; **I am — and tired of** me valde pertaedet *(w. gen);* **to be —** aegrotare; **to fall —** in morbum incidere; **to feel —** nauseare

sickbed *s* lect·us -i *m* aegrotantis

sicken *tr* fastidium movēre *(w. dat)* ‖ *intr* in morbum incidere; *(to feel disgust)* fastidire

sickening *adj* tae·ter -tra -trum

sickle *s* fal·x -cis *f*

sickly *adj* morbos·us -a -um, infirm·us -a -um

sickness *s* morb·us -i *m,* aegritud·o -inis *f*

side *s (of a body, hill, camp, ship, etc.)* lat·us -eris *n; (quarter, direction)* par·s -tis *f; (faction)* part·es -ium *fpl; (kinship)* gen·us -eris *n;* **at the — of** a latere *(w. gen);* **from all —s** undique; **having heard only one —, he condemned her** alterā tantum parte auditā condemnavit eam; **on all —s** undique; **on both —s** utrimque; **one — of the island** unum latus insulae; **on one —** unā ex parte; **on that —** illinc; **on the one — ... on the other** hinc ... illinc; **on their —** pro illa parte; **on the right —** of latere dextro *(w. gen);* **on the mother's —** materno genere; **on this —** hinc; **on this — of** cis *(w. acc),* citra *(w. acc);* **— by —** alius alium iuxta, contigu·us -a -um; **to be on the — of** stare ab *(w. abl),* sentire cum *(w. abl);* **to leave s.o.'s —** a latere alicuius discedere; **to lie on his —** in latus cubare; **to take —s** favēre; **to walk at s.o.'s —** tegere latus alicui

side *adj* lateral·is -is -e

side *intr* **to — with** partes sequi *(w. gen),* stare ab *(w. abl),* sentire cum *(w. abl)*

sideboard *s* abac·us -i *m*

sided *adj* **many-sided** multilater·us -a -um; **one-sided** unilter·us -a -um

sidekick *s (coll)* contubernal·is -is *mf*

sideline *s (sports)* line·a -ae *f* lateralis; **on the —s** *(fig)* remot·us -a -um, non partic·eps -itis

sidelong *adj* obliqu·us -a -um

sidestep *tr* (e)vitare, effugere

side street *s* deverticul·um -i *n,* vi·a -ae *f* lateralis

sideswipe *tr* obliquo ictu concutere
sidetrack *tr* deflectere, divertere
sidewalk *s* crepid·o -inis *f*
sideways *adv* in obliquum, oblique
siege *s* obsidi·o -onis *f;* **to lay — to** obsidēre
siesta *s* meridiati·o -onis *f;* **to take a —** meridiare
sieve *s* cribr·um -i *n; (little sieve)* cribell·um -i *n*
sift *tr* cribrare; *(fig)* scrutari **‖** *intr* **to — through** (per)scrutari
sigh *s* suspir·ium -(i)i *n*
sigh *intr* suspirare; **to — for** desiderare
sight *s (sense)* vis·us -ūs *m; (act of seeing)* aspect·us -ūs *m; (range)* conspect·us -ūs *m; (appearance)* speci·es -ei *f; (show)* spectacul·um -i *n;* **at first —** *(on the first appearance of a person or thing)* primā specie; *(looking at it subjectively)* primo aspectu; **at —, by —** aspectu. **in —** in conspectu, ante oculos; **out of —** e conspectu; **to catch — of** conspicere; **to lose — of** e conspectu amittere
sight *tr* conspicari, conspicere
sightseeing *s* spectati·o -onis *f* visendorum
sightseer *s* specta·tor -toris *m* (·trix -tricis *f*) visendorum
sign *s* sign·um -i *n,* indic·ium -(i)i *n; (mark)* not·a -ae *f; (distinction)* insign·e -is *n; (omen)* portent·um -i *n*
sign *tr (document)* subscribere; *(to ratify by signature and seal)* signare; **to — one's name to a letter** nomen epistulae notare
signal *intr* signum dare; *(by a nod)* annuere
signal *s* sign·um -i *n; (mil)* classic·um -i *n*
signal *adj* insign·is -is -e
signature *s* subscriptum nom·en -inis *n,* subscripti·o -onis *f*
signer *s* signa·tor -toris *m* (·trix -tricis *f*)
signet *s* sigill·um -i *n*
signet ring *s* annul·us -i *m* signatorius
significance *s (meaning)* significati·o -onis *f; (importance)* moment·um -i *n*
significant *adj* signific·ans -antis, magni momenti
signify *tr* significare
silence *s* silent·ium -(i)i *n;* **—!** tace! *(pl:* tacete!);* **to call for —** silentium facere; **to pass over in —** silentio praeterire
silence *tr* comprimere; *(by argument)* refutare
silent *adj* tacit·us -a -um; **be! —** tace! *(pl:* tacete!);* **to become —** conticescere; **to be —** tacēre; **to keep s.th. —** aliquid tacēre; **to keep — about s.th.** de aliquo silēre
silently *adv* tacite
silk *s* seric·um -i *n*
silk *adj* seric·us -a -um
silkworm *s* bomb·yx -ycis *mf*
sill *s* lim·en -inis *n* inferum
silliness *s* inepti·a -ae *f*

silly *adj* desipi·ens -entis; **don't be —** noli ineptire; **to be —** desipere, ineptire
silver *s* argent·um -i *n*
silvermine *s* argentifodin·a -ae *f*
silversmith *s* fa·ber -bri *m* argentarius
silverware *s* argente·a -orum *npl,* vas·a -orum *npl* argentea
silvery *adj* argente·us -a -um; *(of hair)* can·us -a -um
similar *adj* simil·is -is -e
similarity *s* similitud·o -inis *f*
similarly *adv* similiter, pariter
simile *s* translat·um -i *n*
simmer *intr* leniter fervēre
simple *adj* simpl·ex -icis; *(easy)* facil·is -is -e; *(weak-minded)* inept·us -a -um; *(frank)* sincer·us -a -um
simpleton *s* inept·us -i *m* (·a -ae *f*), caud·ex -icis *m*
simplicity *s* simplicit·as -atis *f*
simplify *tr* facil·iorem -iorem -ius reddere
simply *adv (in a simple manner)* simpliciter; *(only)* tantummodo; **I — don't know what he is thinking of** plane quid cogitet nescio
simulate *tr* simulare
simulation *s* simulati·o -onis *f*
simultaneous *adj* eodem tempore
simultaneously *adv* simul, unā
sin *s* peccat·um -i *n*
sin *intr* peccare
since *prep* ex *(w. abl),* ab *(w. abl),* post *(w. acc);* **ever —** usque ab *(w. abl),* ex quo tempore
since *adv* abhinc; **long —** iamdudum
since *conj (temporal)* ex quo tempore, postquam, cum; *(causal)* quod, quia, quoniam, cum
sincere *adj* sincer·us -a -um
sincerely *adv* sincere
sincerity *s* sincerit·as -atis *f*
sinew *s* nerv·us -i *m*
sinful *adj* prav·us -a -um
sing *tr & intr* canere, cantare
singe *tr* adurere, amburere
singer *s* canta·tor -toris *m* (·tr·ix -icis *f*)
singing *s* cant·us -ūs *m*
single *adj* sol·us -a -um, unic·us -a -um; *(unmarried male)* caeleb·s -is; *(ummarried female)* innupta; **in — combat** vir unus cum viro congrediendo; **not a — one** ne un·us -a -um quidem; **— room** cubicul·um -i *n* unius lecti
single *tr* **to — out** eligere
singly *adv* singulatim
singsong *s* cantic·um -i *n*
singsong *adj* canor·us -a -um
singular *adj (only one; outstanding; gram)* singular·is -is -e; **in the —** singulariter
singularly *adv* singulariter, unice

sinister *adj* malevol·us -a -um

sink *tr* submergere; *(as a hostile act)* deprimere; *(money)* collocare ‖ *intr (to settle at the bottom)* (de)sidere; *(of ships)* mergi; *(of morale)* cadere; **to — in the mud** limo se immergere

sink *s (in kitchen)* fusor·ium -(i)i *n; (in bathroom)* labell·um -i *n*

sinless *adj* peccati exper·s -tis

sinner *s* pecca·tor -toris *m* (·trix -tricis *f*)

sip *tr* sorbillare

sip *s* sorbiti·o -onis *f*

siphon *s* siph·o -onis *m*

sir *interj (to a master)* ere! *(to an equal)* bone vir! *(to a superior)* domine!

sire *s* genit·or -oris *m*

siren *s* sir·en -enis *f; (alarm)* classic·um -i *n*

sister *s* sor·or -oris *f;* **little —** sororcul·a -ae *f*

sisterhood *s* sororum societ·as -atis *f*

sister-in-law *s* glo·s -ris *f; (sister of husband)* sor·or -oris *f* mariti; *(wife of brother)* ux·or -oris *f* fratris

sisterly *adj* sorori·us -a -um

sit *intr* sedēre; **to — as judge** ius dicere; **to — beside** assidēre *(w. dat);* **to — down (on)** considere *(super w. acc);* **to — on** insidēre *(w. dat);* **to — up** *(to stay awake)* vigilare; *(straight)* recte sedēre; **to — up all night** pervigilare

site *s* sit·us -ūs *m; (for building)* are·a -ae *f*

sitting *s* sessi·o -onis *f*

sitting duck *s (coll)* facilis praed·a -ae *f*

sitting room *s* sessor·ium -(i)i *n*

situated *adj* sit·us -a -um; **— near, on** apposit·us -a -um *(w. dat)*

situation *s* sit·us -ūs *m; (circumstances)* res, rei *f;* **that's the —** res sic se habet; **you see what the — is** vides quo in loco haec res sit

situps *spl* **to do —** identidem residere

six *adj* sex [*indecl*]; **— times** sexies

sixfold *adj* sextupl·us -a -um

sixteen *adj* sedecim [*indecl*]

sixteenth *adj* sext·us decim·us -a -um

sixth *adj* sext·us -a -um

sixth *s* sexta par·s -tis *f*

sixtieth *adj* sexagesim·us -a -um

sixty *adj* sexaginta [*indecl*]

size *s* magnitud·o -inis *f,* amplitud·o -inis *f;* **of huge —** ing·ens -entis

skate *intr* (rotulis) patinare

skate *s* calce·us -i *m* subrotatus

skateboard *s* tabul·a -ae *f* subrotata

skater *s* patina·tor -toris *m* (·trix -tricis *f*)

skating *s* patinati·o -onis *f*

skein *s* glom·us -i *m*

skeleton *s* scelet·us -i *m*

skeleton key *s* adultera clav·is -is *f*

sketch *s* adumbrati·o -onis *f*

sketch *tr* adumbrare, delineare; *(in words)* describere

ski *intr* nartare

ski *s* nart·a -ae *f;* **— boot** *s* calig·a -ae *f* nartatoria; **— jump** *s* suggest·us -us *m* desultorius; **— jumping** *s* desultur·a -ae *f* nartatoria; **— lift** *s* anabathr·um -i *n* nartatorium; **— lodge** *s* deversor·ium -(i)i *n* nartatorium; **— pole** *s* bacul·um -i *n* nartatorium; **— slope** *s* cliv·us -i *m* nartatorius **to put on —** nartas pedibus aptare, nartas adstringere; **to take off the —s** nartas destringere

skier *s* narta·tor -toris *m* (·trix -tricis *f*)

skiing *s* nartati·o -onis *f*

skiff *s* scaph·a -ae *f*

skill *s* sollerti·a -ae *f; (derived from experience)* periti·a -ae *f*

skilled *adj* perit·us -a -um

skillful *adj* sol·ers -ertis, scit·us -a -um; *(w. hands)* habil·is -is -e

skillfully *adv* sollerter, scite

skillet *s* cucumell·a -ae *f*

skim *tr (milk)* despumare; *(glance through)* cursim legere, percurrere

skim milk *s* lac, lactis *n* despumatum

skimp *intr* parcere, sumptūs concidere; **to — on** parce uti *(w. abl)*

skimpy *adj* parc·us -a -um, exigu·us -a -um

skin *s (of man)* cut·is -is *f; (of animals)* pell·is -is *f;* **(pale** pallida; **dry** arida; **tough** dura; **wrinkled** rugosa**)**

skin *tr* pellem detrahere *(w. dat)*

skinny *adj* mac·er -era -erum

skip *tr* praeterire, praetermittere ‖ *intr* subsultare; **to — over** transilire

skipper *s* nauarch·us -i *m*

skirmish *s* leve certam·en -inis *n*

skirmish *intr* levia proelia conserere

skirt *s* gunn·a -ae *f,* castul·a -ae *f*

skirt *tr* tangere

skit *s* parodi·a -ae *f*

skittish *adj (restive)* contum·ax -acis; *(shy)* verecund·us -a -um

skull *s* calvari·a -ae *f;* **fractured —** cap·ut -itis *n* fractum; **to break s.o.'s —** *(coll)* caput dirumpere

skunk *s* viverr·a -ae *f* putoria; *(person) (sl)* propud·ium -(i)i *n*

sky *s* cael·um -i *n;* **under the open —** sub divo

sky-blue *adj* caerule·us -a -um

skylark *s* alaud·a -ae *f*

skylight *s* compluv·ium -(i)i *n*

skyscraper *s* multizon·ium -(i)i *n*

slab *s* tabul·a -ae *f,* quadr·a -ae *f*

slack *adj* lax·us -a -um

slacken *tr* remittere, laxare ‖ *intr* remitti, minui

slain *adj* occis·us -a -um

slake *tr (thirst)* exstinguere

slalom *s* decursi·o -onis *f* flexuosa

slam dunk *s* tuxtax-immissi·o -onis *f*
slander *s* calumni·a -ae *f*
slander *tr* calumniari
slanderer *s* obtrecta·tor -toris *m* (·trix -tricis *f*)
slanderous *adj* calumnios·us -a -um
slang *s* vulgaria verb·a -orum *npl*
slant *tr* acclinare; *(fig)* detorquēre ‖ *intr* proclinari
slanted *adj* transvers·us -a -um; *(news)* distort·us -a -um
slanting *adj* obliqu·us -a -um
slap *s* alap·a -ae *f;* — in the face *(fig)* repuls·a -ae *f*
slap *tr* alapam dare *(w. dat);* to — s.o. in the face os alicuius palmā pulsare
slaphappy *adj (dazed from blows)* torpid·us -a -um; *(happy-go-lucky)* secur·us -a -um
slash *s (cut)* caesur·a -ae *f; (blow)* ict·us -ūs *m; (wound)* vuln·us -eris *n*
slash *tr* caedere, vulnerare; *(to reduce)* imminuere
slat *s* tigill·um -i *n*
slate *s* tegul·a -ae *f; (pol)* ind·ex -icis *m* candidatorum; clean slate tabul·a -ae *f* rasa
slaughter *s* trucidati·o -onis *f*
slaughter *tr* trucidare, mactare
slaughterhouse *s* carnar·ium -(i)i *n*
slave *s* serv·us -i *m* (·a -ae *f*)
slave *intr* sudare, laborare operose
slave dealer *s* mang·o -onis *m*
slavery *s* servitud·o -inis *f*
slave labor *s* op·us -eris *n* servile
slave trade *s* venalic·ium -(i)i *n*
slavish *adj* servil·is -is -e
slavishly *adv* serviliter
slay *tr* interficere
slayer *s* interfec·tor -toris *m* (·trix -tricis *f*)
sled *s* trahe·a -ae *f* (lusoria)
sledge *s* trahe·a -ae *f*
sledgehammer *s* marc·us -i *m*
sleek *adj* nitid·us -a -um
sleep *s* somn·us -i *m;* deep — sop·or -oris *m;* sound — somnus artus
sleep *tr* to — off a hangover crapulam edormire ‖ *intr* dormire, quiescere; to go to — dormitum ire; *(to doze off)* obdormiscere; to put to — in sumnum collocare, consopire; to — over indormire *(w. abl)*
sleepily *adv* somniculose
sleeping bag *s* sacc·us -i *m* dormitoria
sleeping car *s* curr·us -ūs *m* dormitorius
sleeping pill *s* catapot·ium -(i)i *n* somniferum
sleepless *adj* insomn·is -is -e
sleeplessness *s* insomni·a -ae *f*
sleepwalk *intr* dormiens ambulare
sleepwalker *s* somnambul·us -i *m* (·a -ae *f*)
sleepy *adj* semisomn·is -is -e, somniculos·us -a -um
sleet *s* nivosa grand·o -inis *f*

sleeve *s* manic·a -ae *f*
sleeveless *adj* sine manicis
sleigh *s* trahe·a -ae *f;* to go — riding traheā vehi
sleight of hand *s* praestigi·ae -arum *fpl*
slender *adj (slim)* gracil·is -is -e; *(meager)* exigu·us -a -um
slice *s* segment·um -i *n*
slice *tr* secare; to — off desecare
slick *adj (smooth, slippery)* lubric·us -a -um; *(shrewd)* callid·us -a -um; *(wily)* cat·us -a -um
slide *intr* labor labi lapsus sum
slide *s* laps·us -ūs *m; (photo)* imag·o -inis *f* translucida; to show —s imagines translucidas exhibēre
slide projector *s* proiector·ium -(i)i *n* imaginum translucidarum
slight *adj* exigu·us -a -um; *(of small account)* lev·is -is -e
slight *s* neglegenti·a -ae *f*
slight *tr* neglegere; *(to offend)* aspernari
slightly *adv* parum
slily *adv* astute, callide
slim *adj* gracil·is -is -e; — hope specul·a -ae *f*
slime *s* lim·us -i *m*
slimy *adj* limos·us -a -um
sling *s* fund·a -ae *f; (med)* fasci·a -ae *f*
sling *tr* iaculari
slingshot *s* fund·a -ae *f*
slink *intr* to — away furtim se subducere
slip *s* laps·us -ūs *m; (of paper)* schedul·a -ae *f; (error)* peccat·um -i *n; (in grafting)* surcul·us -i *m; (underdress)* subucul·a -ae *f;* — of the tongue lapsus -ūs *m* linguae; — of the pen mend·um -i *n;* to give s.o. the — aliquem fallere
slip *tr (to give furtively)* furtim dare ‖ *intr* labi; to let — amittere, praetermittere; to — away elabi; *(to leave furtively)* furtim se subducere; to — out of elabi ex *(w. abl); (to escape from)* excidere ex *(w. abl)*
slipper *s* sole·a -ae *f;* wearing —s soleat·us -a -um
slippery *adj* lubric·us -a -um; *(deceitful)* subdol·us -a -um
slipshot *adj* negleg·ens -entis
slit *s* incisur·a -ae *f*
slit *tr* incidere, insecare
sliver *s* schidi·a -ae *f; (small piece)* frustul·um -i *n*
slobber *intr* to — on conspuere
slop *s* quisquili·ae -arum *fpl*
slope *s* cliv·us -i *m;* steep (gentle) — arduus (lenis) clivus
slope *intr* proclinari, vergere; —ing toward the sea vergens ad mare
sloping *adj* decliv·is -is -e; *(upwards)* accliv·is -is -e

sloppy *adj (roads)* lutulent·us -a -um; *(weather)* spurc·us -a -um; *(person, work)* negleg·ens -entis

slot *s* rim·a -ae *f*

sloth *s* pigriti·a -ae *f*

slothful *adj* pi·ger -gra -grum

slot machine *s* machin·a -ae *f* aleatoria; **to play a —** machinam aleatoriam impellere

slouch *intr* languide incedere; **to — down** *(in a chair)* parum erecte sedēre

slouch *s (loafer)* cessa·tor -toris *m* (·trix -tricis *f*)

slough *s (of snake)* exuvi·ae -arum *fpl*

slovenly *adj* incompt·us -a -um

slow *adj* tard·us -a -um; *(physically, mentally)* lent·us -a -um; **— to learn** segn·is -is -e

slow down *tr* retardare, impedire ‖ *intr (of rain)* detumescere; *(walk, run)* cursum reprimere

slowly *adv* tarde, lente

slowpoke *s* cuncta·tor -toris *m* (·trix -tricis *f*)

slug *s* lim·ax -acis *mf*; *(of a bullet)* glans, glandis *f* plumbea

slug *tr (to hit)* percut·io -ere percussi percussus

sluggish *adj* pi·ger -gra -grum, heb·es -etis; **to be —** hebēre

sluggishly *adv* pigre

sluggishness *s* pigriti·a -ae *f*

slumber *s* somn·us -i *m*, sop·or -oris *m*

slumber *intr* dormitare

slur *s* macul·a -ae *f*

slur *tr (words)* balbutire

slush *s* niv·es -ium *fpl* solutae

slush fund *s* largition·es -um *fpl*

slut *s* meretr·ix -icis *f*

sly *adj* astut·us -a -um; **on the —** clam

slyness *s* astuti·a -ae *f*

smack *s (flavor)* sap·or -oris *m*; *(blow)* alap·a -ae *f*; *(kiss)* bas·ium -(i)i *n*

smack *tr* ferire; *(to kiss)* basiare; **to — one's lips** labra claudere cum strepitu ‖ *intr* **to — of** sapere *(w. acc)*

small *adj* parv·us -a -um

smaller *adj* min·or -or -us

smallest *adj* minim·us -a - um

small-minded *adj* pusilli animi, soc·ors -ordis; **to be —** angusti *(or* pusilli*)* animi esse

smallpox *s* variol·ae -arum *fpl*; **to have —** variolis laborare

small talk *s* sermuncul·us -i *m*

smart *adj (clever)* callid·us -a -um, soll·ers -ertis; *(talented)* ingenios·us -a -um; *(elegant)* eleg·ans -antis; *(stylish)* laut·us -a -um; *(impertinent)* insol·ens -entis; *(of pace)* vel·ox -ocis; **don't talk — to me** noli male mihi dicere

smart *s* dol·or -oris *m*

smart *intr* dolēre

smart aleck *s* hom·o -inis *mf* impudens

smart-ass *s (sl)* impud·ens -entis *mf*

smartly *adv* callide; eleganter

smash *s* concussi·o -onis *f*

smash *tr (also —* **up)** confringere

smashup *s* collisi·o -onis *f*

smattering *s* cogniti·o -onis *f* manca

smear *s* macul·a -ae *f*

smear *tr* oblinere, illinere; *(to vilify)* inquinare

smell *s (sense)* odorat·us -ūs *m*; *(odor)* od·or -oris *m*; **to have a keen sense of —** bene olēre

smell *tr* olfacere ‖ *intr* olēre; **to — bad** male olēre, obolēre; **to — good** bene olēre, iucunde olēre; **to — like** *or* **of** olēre *(w. acc)*

smelly *adj* olid·us -a -um

smelt *tr* liquefacere, fundere

smile *s* subris·us -ūs *m*; **with a —** subrid·ens -entis

smile *intr* subridēre; **to — at** arridēre *(w. dat)*

smirk *s* molestus subris·us -ūs *m*

smirk *intr* moleste subridēre

smite *tr* ferire, percutere

smock *s* tunic·a -ae *f*

smoke *s* fum·us -i *m*; **where there's — there's fire** flamma fumo est proxima

smoke *tr (meat)* infumare; *(cigar, cigarette, marijuana)* fumum (sigari, sigarelli, cannabis) sugere ‖ *intr* fumare

smoker *s* fuma·tor -toris *m* (·trix -tricis *f*

smoky *adj* fumos·us -a -um

smooth *adj* lēv·is -is -e; *(hairless)* gla·bcr -bra -brum; *(polished)* ter·es -itis; *(calm)* placid·us -a -um; *(of talk)* bland·us -a -um

smoothly *adv* lēviter; blande

smooth *tr* lēvare; *(to file)* limare; **to — the path to** viam facere ad *(w. acc)*

smoothness *s* lev·or -oris *m*

smooth-talking *adj* blandiloqu·us -a -um

smother *tr (flames, tears, anger)* opprimere; *(to choke)* suffocare

smudge *s* lab·es -is *f*, macul·a -ae *f*; *(smear)* litur·a -ae *f*

smudge *tr* inquinare, maculare

smug *adj* sui content·us -a -um, confid·ens -entis

smuggle *tr f* furtim sine portorio exportare *or* importare

smuggler *s* vec·tor -toris *m* (·trix -tricis *f*) vetitae mercis

smugness *s* confidenti·a -ae *f*

smut *s (soot)* fulig·o -inis *f*; *(foul language, writing)* obscenit·as -atis *f*

smutty *adj* fumos·us -a -um; *(obscene)* obscen·us -a -um

snack *s* merend·a -ae *f*; **to have a —** merendam capere

snack *intr* adedere

snack bar *s* voratrin·a -ae *f*

snafu *adj* confus·us -a -um

snag *s (stumbling block)* impediment·um -i *n;* **to hit a —** impedimento occurrere

snail *s* cochle·a -ae *f; (without shell)* lim·ax -acis *f*

snake *s* angu·is -is *mf;* **— in the grass** *(fig)* amic·us -i *m* perfidus, amic·a -ae *f* perfida

snap *s (noise)* crepit·us -ūs *m; (bite)* mors·us -ūs *m; (easy task)* op·us -eris *n* facile; **cold —** frigor·a -um *npl*

snap *tr (to break off suddenly)* praefrangere; **to — the fingers** digitis concrepare; **to — up** corripere ‖ *intr (to break with a sharp noise)* dissilire; *(to make a sharp sound)* crepare; *(to go mad)* subito furere; **to — at** *(w. teeth)* morsu petere; *(in speaking)* increpare; **to — out of it** repente resipiscere

snappy *adj (brisk)* ala·cer -cris -cre, veget·us -a -um; *(chic)* eleg·ans -antis; **make it —!** matura! *(pl:* maturate!)

snapshot *s* imag·o -inis *f* photographica

snare *s* laque·us -i *m;* **to lay —s for a rival** rivali laqueos disponere

snare *tr* illaquēre; **to — wild animals** feras laqueis captare

snarl *s (of a dog)* rict·us -ūs *m,* hirrit·us -ūs *m; (of a person)* gannit·us -ūs *m*

snarl *tr* increpare ‖ *intr (dog)* ringi, hirrire; *(person)* gannire

snatch *tr* rapere, arripere; *(to steal)* surripere; **to — away** eripere; **to — up** corripere

sneak *s* lucifug·us -i *m* (·a -ae *f*)

sneak *intr* correpere; **to — away** clam se seducere; **to — away from (s.o.)** clam se subducere *(w. dat);* **to — into** correpere in *(w. acc);* **to — off** clanculum abire; **to — out of** correpere ex *(w. abl);* **to — up on** obrepere *(w. dat)*

sneakers *spl* calce·i -orum *mpl* gymnici

sneer *s* rhonch·us -i *m*

sneer *intr* irridēre; **to — at** irridēre, aspernari

sneeze *s* sternument·um -i *n*

sneeze *intr* sternuere

snicker *s* ris·us -ūs *m* insulsus

snicker *intr* ridēre inepte

snide *adj* maledic·us -a -um, mord·ax -acis; **to make a — remark** mordaciter dicere

sniff *s* **to get a — of** olfacere

sniff *tr* naribus captare; *(cocaine)* naribus ducere; *(e.g., trouble)* odorari

sniffle *intr* mucum inspirare; *(to weep lightly)* leviter flēre

sniffles *spl* **to have the —** gravedine laborare

snip *tr* **to — off** praecidere

snippy *adj* insol·ens -entis

snivel *s* muc·us -i *m*

snivel *intr* mucum resorbēre; *(to whine)* queri

snob *s* hom·o -inis *mf* fastidios·us (-a)

snobbish *adj* fastidios·us -a -um

snore *s* r(h)onch·us -i *m*

snore *intr* stertere, r(h)onchare

snort *s* fremit·us -ūs *m*

snort *intr* fremere

snout *s* rostr·um -i *n*

snow *s* nix, nivis *f*

snow *tr* **to — in** nive obruere ‖ *v impers* ningit ningere ninxit; **it is —ing** ningit

snowball *s* pil·a -ae *f* nivis

snowball *intr* percrebescere

snowbank *s* cumul·us -i *m* nivis

snowbound *adj* nivibus obrut·us -a -um

snowdrift *s* niveus agg·er -eris *m*

snowed under *adj* **I am — with** *(fig)* obruor, tamquam nive, sic ego *(w. abl)*

snowfall *s* nivis cas·us -ūs *m*

snowflakes *spl* ningu·es -um *fpl*

snowstorm *s* ning·or -oris *m*

snow-white *adj* nive·us -a -um

snowy *adj* nival·is -is -e

snub *tr* neglegere

snub *s* repuls·a -ae *f*

snuff *tr* inhalare; **to — out** exstinguere

snug *adj* commod·us -a -um

snugly *adv* commode

so *adv* sic, ita, *(before adjectives)* tam; **and — forth** et cetera; **— far** eatenus, adhuc; **— help me** mehercules; **how —** quid ita?; **is that —?** itane?; **— far — good** belle adhuc; **— many** tot *[indecl];* **— much** tant·us -a -um; *(so greatly)* tantopere; **— much for that** eatenus; **— often** totiens; **— slight a** *(e.g., fever)* tantul·us -a -um; **— so** *(tolerably well)* sic tenuiter; **— that** ut; **— that not** ne; **— then** quapropter; **— to speak** ut ita dicam; **that's not —** haud ita est; **— what?** quid ergo?

so *pron* **— and —** ille et ille

soak *tr* madefacere; *(to soften while soaking)* macerare ‖ *intr* madēre

soap *s* sap·o -onis *m;* **bar of —** saponis quadrul·a -ae *f;* **liquid —** sapo liquidus

soar *intr* in sublime ferri; *(of birds)* subvolare

sob *s* singult·us -ūs *m*

sob *intr* singultare

sober *adj* sobri·us -a -um *(opp;* ebrius); *(fig)* moderat·us -a -um

soberly *adv* sobrie; moderate

sobriety *s* sobriet·as -atis *f*

so-called *adj* sub nomine, supposatici·us -a -um

soccer *s* pedifoll·ium -(i)i *n;* **to play —** pedifolle ludere

soccer ball *s* pedifoll·is -is *m*

soccer field *s* camp·us -i *m* pedifollii, camp·us -i *m* lusorius

soccer player *s* lus·or -oris *m* (lusr·ix -icis *f*) pedifollii

soccer shoes *spl* calceament·a -orum *npl* pedifollii

sociable *adj* sociabil·is -is -e; *(pleasant in society)* facil·is -is -e
social *adj* *(companionable)* social·is -is -e; *(life)* commun·is -is -e; *(institutions, laws, customs, duties)* civil·is -is -e; — **call** offic·ium -(i)i *n*
social security *s* assecurati·o -onis *f* socialis
social science *s* disciplin·a -ae *f* civilis
society *s* societ·as -atis *f;* **high** — optimat·es -ium *mpl; secret* — sodalit·as -atis *f;* — **as a whole** omnes homin·es -um *mpl*
sock *s* pedal·e -is *n,* ud·o -onis *m; (blow)* ict·us -ūs *m*
sock *tr (coll)* percutere, icere
socket *s* contact·um -i *n* electricum; *(anat)* cav·um -i *n*
sod *s* caesp·es -itis *m*
soda *s (soft drink)* aqu·a -ae *f* Selterana; *(in natural state)* nitr·um -i *n*
sofa *s* lectul·us -i *m* tomento fartus
soft *adj* moll·is -is -e; *(fruit)* mit·is -is -e; *(fig)* delicat·us -a -um
soften *tr* mollire; *(fig)* lenire ‖ *intr* mollescere; *(of fruit)* mitescere; *(fig)* mitescere
softhearted *adj* miseric·ors -ordis
softly *adv* molliter; *(noiselessly)* leniter; *(opp. of loudly)* summissā voce
software *s (comput)* part·es -ium *fpl* programmationis
soil *s* sol·um -i *n,* hum·us -i *f*
soil *tr* inquinare, spurcare
sojourn *s* commorati·o -onis *f*
sojourn *intr* commorari
solace *s* solat·ium -(i)i *n*
solace *tr* consolari
solar *adj* solar·is -is -e; — **eclipse** solis defecti·o -onis *f*
solder *s* ferrum·en -inis *n*
solder *tr* ferruminare
soldier *s* mil·es -itis *mf*
soldierly *adj* militar·is -is -e
sole *adj* sol·us -a -um, unic·us -a -um
sole *s (of shoe)* sol·um -i *n; (anat)* plant·a -ae *f; (fish)* sole·a -ae *f*
solely *adv* solum, tantummodo
solemn *adj* sollemn·is -is -e
solemnity *s* sollemnit·as -atis *f*
solemnly *adv* sollemniter; **to swear** — religiosissimis verbis iurare
solemnize *tr* celebrare
solicit *tr* flagitare; **to** — **sex from s.o.** aliquem stuprum rogare
solicitation *s* flagiti·o -onis *f*
solicitor *s* flagita·tor -toris *m* (·trix -tricis *f); (leg)* iurisperit·us -i *m* (-a -ae *f)*
solicitous *adj* anxi·us -a -um
solicitude *s* anxiet·as -atis *f,* sollicitud·o -inis *f*
solid *adj* solid·us -a -um; *(food)* plen·ior -ior -ius; *(real, true)* firm·us -a -um; **men of** —

character homin·es -um *mpl* probati; — **gold** totum aur·um -i *n*
solidly *adv* solide, firme
soliloquize *intr* secum loqui
soliloquy *s* soliloqu·ium -(i)i *n*
solitary *adj* solitari·us -a -um
solitude *s* solitud·o -inis *f*
solstice *s* solstit·ium -(i)i *n*
soluble *adj* dissolubil·is -is -e
solution *s* dilut·um -i *n; (solving)* soluti·o -onis *f,* explicati·o -onis *f*
solve *tr* (dis)solvere
solvency *s* facult·as -atis *f* solvendi
some *adj* ali·qui -qua -quod; *(a certain)* quidam quaedam quoddam; *(several)* nonnull·i -ae -a; *(a few)* aliquot [*indecl*]; *(some amount of)* aliquid *(w. gen);* — **twenty days later** aliquos viginti dies post; — **... or other** nescio qui, nescio quae, nescio quod; — **war or other** nescio quod bellum; **to drink** — **wine** aliquid vini bibere
some *pron* aliqu·i -ae -a; *(several)* nonnull·i -ae -a; *(certain people)* quidam, quaedam, quaedam; — **... others** alii ... alii
somebody *pron* aliquis; — **or other** nescio quis
somebody *s* hom·o -inis *mf* (-a) amplissimus
someday *adv* olim, aliquando
somehow *adv* aliquā (viā); — **or other** nescio quomodo
someone *pron* aliquis; — **else** ali·us -a
somersault *s* **to do a** — cernuare
somersault *intr* cernuare
something *pron* aliquid; — **else** aliud ultra; — **or other** nescio quid
sometime *adv* aliquando; — **ago** dudum, pridem
sometimes *adv* interdum, nonnumquam; — **... — modo ... modo**
somewhat *adv* aliquantum; *(w. comparatives)* aliquanto, paulo; **to feel** — **better** meliuscul·us -a -um esse
somewhere *adv* alicubi; *(w. motion)* aliquo; — **else** alibi; *(w. motion)* alio
somnolence *s* somnolenti·a -ae *f*
somnolent *adj* somnolent·us -a -um
son *s* fil·ius -(i)i *m*
song *s* cant·us -ūs *m*
son-in-law *s* gen·er -eri *m*
sonorous *adj* sonor·us -a -um
soon *adv* mox, brevi (tempore); *(in a minute)* iam; *(at any moment)* iam iam; **as** — **as** simulatque, cum primum; **as** — **as possible** quam primum; **how** — **?** quam mox?; — **thereafter** mox deinde; **too** — nimium cito; **very** — perbrevi tempore
sooner *adv* prius; *(preference)* potius; **no** — **said than done** dicto citius *or* dictum factum; — **or later** serius ocius

soot *s* fulig·o -inis *f*
soothe *tr* mulcēre, lenire
soothsayer *s* vat·es -is *m*
soothsaying *s* vaticinati·o -onis *f*
sooty *adj* fuliginos·us -a -um
sop *s* offul·a -ae *f*
sop *tr* **to sop up** absorbēre
sophism *s* sophism·a -atis *n*
sophist *s* sophist·es -ae *m*
sophisticated *adj* urban·us -a -um
sophistry *s* capti·o -onis *f*
sophomore *s* sophomor·us -i *m* (·a -ae *f*)
soprano *s* supranist·a -ae *f*
sorcerer *s* mag·us -i *m*
sorceress *s* mag·a -ae *f*
sorcery *s* magae art·es -ium *fpl*
sordid *adj* sordid·us -a -um
sordidly *adv* sordide
sore *adj (aching)* dol·ens -entis; *(angry)* irat·us -a -um; **— throat** exasperatae fauc·es -ium *fpl*
sore *s* ulc·us -eris *n*
sorely *adv* vehementer
soreness *s* dol·or -oris *m*
sorority *s* sodalit·as -atis *f* alumnarum
sorrow *s* dol·or -oris *m*
sorrow *intr* dolēre
sorrowful *adj* maest·us -a -um
sorrowfully *adv* maeste
sorry *adj* mis·er -era -erum; **I am — about** me paenitet *(w. gen);* **I (you) feel — for** me (te) miseret *(w. gen)*
sort *s* gen·us -eris *n;* **that — of man** eius generis *(or* modi) vi·r -ri *m*
sort *tr* digerere; *(ballots, mail)* diribēre
sot *s* fatu·us -i *m;* *(drunkard)* potat·or -oris *m*
soul *s (principle of life)* anim·a -ae *f; (principle of intellection and sensation)* anim·us -i *m;* **not a —** nem·o -inis *m; (human being)* mortal·is -is *m*
sound *adj (healthy)* san·us -a -um; *(strong)* valid·us -a -um; *(unimpaired, e.g., apple)* inte·ger -gra -grum; *(true, genuine)* ver·us -a -um; *(sleep)* art·us -a -um; *(stomach)* firm·us -a -um; **a — mind in a —body** mens sana in corpore sano; **to be of — mind** comp·os -otis mentis esse
sound *s* son·us -i *m;* *(noise)* strepit·us -ūs *m;* *(of trumpet)* clang·or -oris *m;* *(strait)* fret·um -i *n;* **loud —** frag·or -oris *m*
sound *tr* **to — the alarm** classicum canere; **to — the signal for battle** bellicum canere; **to — the retreat** receptui canere; **to — the trumpet** bucinam inflare ‖ *intr* sonare; *(to seem)* videri; **to — off** clamitare
soundly *adv (of beating)* egregie; *(of sleeping)* arte

soundness *s* sanit·as -atis *f; (firmness)* firmit·as -atis *f; (correctness)* integrit·as -atis *f*
soup *s* iu·s -ris *n;* **noodle —** ius collyricum
soup bowl *s* magid·a -ae *f*
soup ladle *s* trull·a -ae *f*
soup spoon *s* cochle·ar -aris *n*
sour *adj* acid·us -a -um, acerb·us -a -um; *(fig)* amar·us -a -um, moros·us -a -um; **I have a — stomach** cibus mihi acescit; **to turn —** acescere
source *s* fon·s -tis *m,* orig·o -inis *f*
souse *s (sl)* pota·tor -toris *m* (·trix -tricis *f*)
soused *adj (sl)* uvid·us -a -um
south *s* meridi·es -ei *m;* **in the —** a meridie; **to face —** in meridiem spectare
south *adv* ad *(or* in) meridiem
south *adj* meridian·us -a -um; **— of** infra *(w. acc)*
southeast *adv* inter meridiem et solis ortum
southern *adj* austral·is -is -e, meridional·is -is -e
southward *adv* in meridiem
southwest *adv* inter solis occasum et meridiem
south wind *s* aus·ter -tri *m*
souvenir *s* monument·um -i *n*
sovereign *adj* suprem·us -a -um
sovereign *s* princ·eps -ipis *m,* rex, regis *m*
sovereignty *s* principat·us -ūs *m*
sow *s* porc·a -ae *f,* sus, suis *f;* **—s oink** sues grunniunt
sow *tr* serere; *(a field)* conserere
sower *s* sat·or -oris *m*
space *s* spat·ium -(i)i *n; (of time)* intervall·um -i *n*
spacious *adj* ampl·us -a -um
spaciousness *s* amplitud·o -inis *f*
spade *s* pal·a -ae *f;* **to call a — a —** quamque rem suo nomine appellare
spaghetti *s* spacell·i -orum *mpl*
Spain *s* Hispani·a -ae *f*
spam *s (comput)* saginati·o -onis *f*
span *s (extent)* spat·ium -(i)i *n; (measure)* palm·us -i *m;* **brief — of life** exigua brevit·as -atis *f* vitae
Spaniard *s* Hispan·us -i *m* (·a -ae *f*)
Spanish *adj (esp. people)* Hispan·us -a -um; *(esp. things)* Hispanic·us -a -um; *(esp. foreign things connected with Spain)* Hispaniens·is -is -e; **to speak —** Hispanice loqui
spank *tr* ferire palmā
spanking *s* **to get a —** vapulare
spar *s* tign·um -i *n*
spar *intr* dimicare; *(fig)* digladiari
spare *tr* parcere *(w. dat)*
spare time *s* temp·us -oris *n* subsicivum
sparing *adj* parc·us -a -um
sparingly *adv* parce

spark *s* scintill·a -ae *f; (fig)* ignicul·us -i *m*
sparkle *intr* scintillare
sparkling *adj* corusc·us -a -um
spark plug *s* candel·a -ae *f* accensiva
sparrow *s* pass·er -eris *m*
sparse *adj* rar·us -a -um
Spartan *adj* Laconic·us -a -um
spasm *s* distenti·o -onis *f* nervorum; **to have a muscle** — a musculi spasmo laborare
spasmodically *adv* interdum
spatter *tr* aspergere; **—ed with rain and mud** imbre lutoque aspers·us -a -um
spatula *s* spath·a -ae *f*
spawn *s* ov·a -orum *npl*
spawn *intr* ova parere
speak *tr* loqui, dicere; **to — Latin** Latine loqui **‖** *intr* loqui; **so to** — ut ita dicam; **— of the devil** lupus in fabulā; **to — of** dicere de *(w. abl);* **to — to** alloqui *(w. acc);* **to — up** eloqui; **to — with** colloqui cum *(w. abl);* **well, speak up!** quin tu eloquere!
speaker *s* dic·ens -entis *mf; (speech maker)* ora·tor -toris *m* (·trix -tricis *f); (device)* megaphon·um -i *n*
spear *s* hast·a -ae *f*
spear *tr* hastā transfigere
special *adj* praecipu·us -a -um; **— delivery letter** epistul·a -ae *f* accelerata
speciality *s* propriet·as -atis *f*
specially *adv* praecipue
species *s* speci·es -ei *f*
specific *adj* cert·us -a -um
specify *tr* subtiliter enumerare
specimen *s* exempl·um -i *n*, speci·men -inis *n*
specious *adj* specios·us -a -um
speck *s* macul·a -ae *f*
speckled *adj* maculos·us -a -um
spectacle *s* spectacul·um -i *n*
spectator *s* specta·tor -toris *m* (·trix -tricis *f*)
specter *s* larv·a -ae *f*
spectral *adj* larval·is -is -e
spectrum *s* spectr·um -i *n*
speculate *intr* coniecturam facere; *(com)* foro uti
speculation *s (guess)* coniectur·a -ae *f; (com)* ale·a -ae *f*
speculative *adj* coniectural·is -is -e
speculator *s* contempla·tor -toris *m* (·trix -tricis *f); (com)* dardanar·ius -(i)i *m* (·a -ae *f*)
speech *s (faculty of speech; address)* orati·o -onis *f;* **to make a** — verba facere, orationem habēre
speechless *adj* elingu·is -is -e; **he was struck** — mutus erat ilico, obstupefactus est
speed *s* celerit·as -atis *f; (haste)* festinati·o -onis *f;* **at full** — magno cursu
speed *tr* prosperare, secundare; **to — up** accelerare **‖** *intr* properare, festinare; *(in a car)* velociter gubernare

speedboat *s* nav·is -is *f* velox
speedily *adv* celeriter
speedy *adj* cit·us -a -um
spell *tr* scribere; **to — correctly** recte scribere; **to spell with** scribere per *(w. acc) e.g.:* **some** — **"cum" with a "q"** if it signifies time quidem scribunt "cum" per "q" litteram, si tempus significat
spell *s (charm)* incantament·um -i *n; (period)* spat·ium -(i)i *n* temporis
spellbound *adj* fascinat·us -a -um
spelling *s* orthographi·a -ae *f*
spend *tr (money, time, effort)* impendere; *(time)* agere, consumere; *(w. the idea of waste)* terere; **to — effort, money (on)** operam, pecuniam impendere (in *w. acc or w. dat);* **to — the night** pernoctare; **to — the summer** aestivare; **to — the winter** hiemare
spendthrift *s* nep·os -otis *mf*, prodig·us -i *m* (·a -ae *f*)
spent *adj (weary)* fess·us -a -um; *(worn out)* effet·us -a -um
sperm *s* sem·en -inis *n*
spew *tr* vomere
sphere *s* sphaer·a -ae *f; (fig)* provinci·a -ae *f*
spherical *adj* sphaeric·us -a -um
sphinx *s* sphin·x -gis *f*
spice *s* condiment·um -i *n*
spice *tr* condire
spicy *adj* condit·us -a -um, a·cer -cris -cre; *(racy)* sal·ax -acis
spider *s* arane·a -ae *f*
spider web *s* arane·um -i *n*, araneae tel·a -ae *f*
spigot *s* epistom·ium -(i)i *n*
spike *s* clav·us -i *m* trabalis
spike *tr* pungere; **to — a drink** potioni temetum adicere
spill *tr* effundere; **to — blood** sanguinem fundere **‖** *intr* effundi, effluere
spill *s ((coll)* laps·us -ūs *m*, cas·us -ūs *m;* **to take a** — labi, cadere
spin *tr* versare; *(thread)* nēre; **to — a top** turbinem versare; **to — a web** telam texere **‖** *intr* versari
spinach *s* spinace·a -ae *f* oleracea
spinal *adj* spinae [*gen*]
spine *s (anat)* spin·a -ae *f* dorsi
spineless *adj* enervat·us -a -um
spinster *s* innupt·a -ae *f*
spiral *adj* spiral·is -is -e
spiral *s* spir·a -ae *f*
spirit *s* spirit·us -ūs *m;* anim·us -i *m; (temper, disposition)* ingen·ium -(i)i *n; (ghost)* larv·a -ae *f*, umbr·a -ae *f;* **full of** — animos·us -a -um; **— of the law** volunt·as -atis *f* legis; **—s of the dead** man·es -ium *fpl;* **that's the right** — now nunc tu frugi bonae es; **to be in high —s** hilar·us -a -um esse; **to be in low —**

s demiss·us -a -um esse; **to defend with such — ** tam enixe defendere

spirited *adj* animos·us -a -um

spiritless *adj* ignav·us -a -um

spiritual *adj* animi [*gen*]; *(incorporeal)* incorporeal·is -is -e; *(devout)* religios·us -a -um

spit *s (for cooking)* ver·u -us *n; (spittle)* sput·um -i *n*

spit *tr* spuere; *(frequentative)* sputare; **to — out** exspuere ‖ *intr* spuere; **to — in s.o.'s face** in faciem *(w. gen)* inspuere

spite *tr* offendere

spite *s* malevolenti·a -ae *f; * **for —** consulto; **in — of** *(no exact Latin equivalent, sometimes expressed by an abl. absolute, e.g.,* **in — of all the arguments of his opponent, he stuck to this guns** contemptis omnibus adversari rationibus, in sententiā suā perseveravit

spiteful *adj* malevol·us -a -um

splash *tr* aspergere; **to — the face with warm water** faciem aquā tepidā fovēre

splash *s* sonit·us -ūs *m* undae; *(display)* ostentati·o -onis *f*

spleen *s* splen, splenis *m; * **to vent one's —** iram effundere

splendid *adj* splendid·us -a -um; **— !** euge!

splendidly *adv* splendide

splendor *s* splend·or -oris *m*

splint *s (med)* ferul·a -ae *f*

splinter *s* assul·a -ae *f;* **bone —** fragment·um -i *n* ossis

splinter *tr* assulatim findere

split *s* fissur·a -ae *f*

split *tr* findere; **to — one's sides laughing** ilia sua risu dissolvere ‖ *intr* findi; *(to depart) (sl)* abire, discedere

splotch *s* macul·a -ae *f*

splotch *tr* maculare

spoil *tr (to mar)* vitiare; *(to ruin)* perdere; *(a child)* depravare; *(food)* corrumpere ‖ *intr (of food)* corrumpi

spoils *spl* spoli·a -orum *npl*

spoke *s* rad·ius -(i)i *m*

spokesman *s* interpr·es -etis *m*

spondee *s* sponde·us -i *m*

sponge *s* spongi·a -ae *f*

sponge *tr* **to — a meal** cenam captare

sponge stick *s (used by Romans in place of toilet paper)* xilospong·ium -(i)i *n*

sponsor *s* auct·or -oris *m,* faut·or -oris *m; (godparent)* spons·or -oris *m* (·rix -ricis *f*)

sponsor *tr* favēre *(w. dat); (a law)* proponere, ferre; **to — games** ludos edere

sponsorship *s* auctorit·as -atis *m; * **under my —** me auctore

spontaneity *s* alacrit·as -atis *f*

spontaneous *adj* automat·us -a -um, subitari·us -a -um

spontaneously *adv* sponte, ultro

spool *s* fus·us -i *m*

spoon *s* cochle·ar -aris *n*

spoonful *s* cochlearis mensur·a -ae *f*

sporadic *adj* rar·us -a -um

sporadically *adv* dispersim

sport *s* lud·us -i *m,* athletic·a -ae *f,* disport·us -ūs *m; (person)* hom·o -inis *mf* genialis

sport *tr* ostentare

sportive *adj* iocos·us -a -um

sport shirt *s* camisi·a -ae *f* campestris

sportsman *s* venat·or -oris *m; (fig)* aequus lus·or -oris *m*

sportswear *s* vest·is -is *f* campestris

spot *s* macul·a -ae *f; (stain)* lab·es -is *f; (place)* loc·us -i *m; * **on the —** *(immediately)* ilico; *(in trouble)* in angustiis, in artibus rebus; **to hit the —** oblectare; **to the same —** eodem

spot *tr (to espy)* conspicere, conspicari; *(to stain)* maculare

spotless *adj* immaculat·us -a -um

spotlight *s* lumin·a -um *npl* scaenica; **be in the —** scaenae servire

spotted *adj* maculos·us -a -um

spouse *s* coniu(n)x, coniugis *mf*

spout *s (jet)* torr·ens -entis *m; (rain spout)* os, oris *n* canalis; *(of jug)* os, oris *n*

spout *tr* eiaculari; *(speeches)* declamare ‖ *intr* emicare

sprain *tr* luxare; **to — an ankle** talum luxare

sprain *s* luxatur·a -ae *f*

sprawl *intr* insulse recumbere; *(to extend)* late extendi

spray *s* asperg·o -inis *f*

spray *tr* aspergere

spread *tr (to unfold)* pandere; *(to stretch)* extendere; *(to smear on)* oblinere; *(to scatter)* dispergere; *(to make known)* divulgare; **to — a blanket on the floor** extendere lodiculam in pavimento ‖ *intr* patēre, patescere; *(of rumor)* percrebrescere; *(of disease)* serpere

spread *s (expanse)* spat·ium -(i)i *n; (dissemination)* divulgati·o -onis *f; (ranch)* latifund·ium -(i)i *n; (feast)* cen·a -ae *f* lautissima

spreading *adj (tree)* patul·us -a -um; *(epidemic)* evag·ans -antis

spread sheet *s (comput)* chart·a -ae *f* computativa

spree *s* **drinking —** commissati·o -onis *f; * **shopping —** effrenata empti·o -onis *f*

sprig *s* ramul·us -i *m,* surcul·us -i *m*

sprightliness *s* alacrit·as -atis *f*

sprightly *adj* veget·us -a -um, ala·cer -cris -cre

spring *s (season)* ve·r -ris *n; (leap)* salt·us -ūs *m; (of water)* scaturg·o -inis *f,* fon·s -tis *m*

spring *adj* vern·us -a -um

spring *tr* **to — a leak** rimas agere ‖ *intr (to come from)* oriri, enasci; *(of rivers, etc.)* exoriri; *(to leap)* salire; **to — down** desilire; **to — forth** *(to sprout)* pullulare; **to sudden-**

ly — **open** subito se pandere; **to — up** subito crescere

springboard *s* petaur·us -i *m*

spring break *s* feri·ae -arum *fpl* vernae; **to spend the —** ferias vernas agere

springtime *s* vernum temp·us -oris *n*

sprinkle *tr* spargere; **to — s.th. on** inspergere aliquid *(w. dat or super w. acc)* ‖ *intr* leviter pluere

spr inkle *s* levis pluvi·a -ae *f*

sprinkling *s* aspersi·o -onis *f;* *(small number)* rarae personae

sprinkling can *s* nassitern·a -ae *f*

sprint *s* curs·us -ūs *m* brevis

sprint *intr* breviter currere

sprout *s* pull·us -i *m*

sprout *intr* pullulare, germinare

spruce *s* *(tree)* abi·es -etis *f*

spruce *adj* laut·us -a -um

spruce *tr* **to — up** mundare ‖ *intr* **to — up** se mundare

spry *adj* agil·is -is -e

spunk *s* alacrit·as -atis *f*

spunky *adj* ala·cer -cris -cre

spur *s* calc·ar -aris *n;* *(fig)* incitament·um -i *n;* **on the — of the moment** de improviso

spur *tr* *(a horse)* calcaribus concitare; *(fig)* urgēre, stimulare

spurious *adj* spuri·us -a -um

spurn *tr* spernere

spurt *intr* emicare

sputter *tr & intr* *(spit)* spuere; *(words, sounds)* balbutire

spy *s* specula·tor -toris *m* (·trix -tricis *f*)

spy *tr* *(to catch sight of)* conspicari ‖ *intr* speculari; **to — on** speculari, explorare

squabble *s* rix·a -ae *f*

squabble *intr* rixari

squad *s* manipul·us -i *m,* turm·a -ae *f*

squadron *s* *(of cavalry)* turm·a -ae *f; (of ships)* class·is -is *f*

squalid *adj* squalid·us -a -um

squall *s* procell·a -ae *f*

squalor *s* squal·or -oris *m*

squander *tr* dissipare, prodigare

squanderer *s* prodig·us -i *m* (·a -ae *f*)

square *adj* quadrat·us -a -um; *(fig)* honest·us -a -um; **— foot** quadratus pe·s pedis *m;* **— meal** largior cib·us -i *m*

square *s* quadrat·um -i *n; (open, four-sided space)* are·a -ae *f; (tool)* norm·a -ae *f*

square *tr* *(math)* quadrare; **to — accounts** rationem habēre ‖ *intr* convenire, congruere; **this simply does not —** non sane quadrat; **to — off** pugnis minitari

squash *tr* conterere

squash *s* cucurbit·a -ae *f*

squat *intr* subsidere

squat *adj* parv·us atque obes·us -a -um

squeak *intr* stridēre; *(of mice, rats)* mintrire

squeak *s* strid·or -oris *m*

squeamish *adj* fastidios·us -a -um; **to feel —** fastidire

squeeze *tr* comprimere; **to — out** exprimere; **to — the flesh** *(when campaigning)* prensare

squint *intr* limis oculis aspicere

squint-eyed *adj* strab·us -a -um

squirrel *s* sciur·us -i *m*

squirt *tr* proicere, effundere ‖ *intr* emicare

squirt *s* coniect·us -ūs *m; (coll)* pu·er -eri *m* procax

stab *s* ict·us -ūs *m,* punct·a -ae *f*

stab *tr* pungere, fodere, perforare

stability *s* stabilit·as -atis *f*

stabilize *tr* stabilire, firmare

stable *adj* stabil·is -is -e

stable *s* stabul·um -i *n; (for horses)* equil·e -is *n; (for cows, oxen)* bubil·e -is *n; (of boxers, gladiators)* famili·a -ae *f*

stack *s* acerv·us -i *m,* stru·es -is *f*

stack *tr* coacervare

stadium *s* stadi·um -i *n*

staff *s* *(scepter)* scipi·o -onis *m; (personnel)* operari·i -ōrum *mpl; (mil)* contubernal·es -ium *mpl,* legat·i -orum *mpl*

staff member, staff officer *s* legat·us -i *m,* contubernal·is -is *mf*

stag *s* cerv·us -i *m*

stage *s* *(theat)* scaen·a -ae *f; (degree)* grad·us -ūs *m;* **during the early —s of** inter initia *(w. gen);* **— of life** par·s -tis *f* aetatis; **to go on the —** in scaenam prodire

stage play *s* lud·us -i *m* scaenicus

stagger *tr* obstupefacere ‖ *intr* titubare

stagnant *adj* stagn·ans -antis; *(fig)* in·ers -ertis

stagnate *intr* stagnare; *(fig)* torpēre, cessare

stagnation *s* *(fig)* cessati·o -onis *f*

stag party *s* conviv·ium -(i)i *n* sine feminis

stain *s* lab·es -is *f,* macul·a -ae *f*

stain *tr* maculare; *(to dye)* tingere

stainless *adj* immaculat·us -a -um

stair *s* grad·us -ūs *m;* **—s** scal·ae -arum *fpl,* grad·ūs -uum *mpl;* **to climb the —** per gradūs ascendere

staircase *s* scal·ae -arum *fpl*

stairway *s* scal·ae -arum *fpl*

stairwell *s* scalar·ium -(i)i *n*

stake *s* pal·us -i *m; (wager)* deposit·um -i *n;* **to be at —** agi; **to burn at the —** ad palum igni interficere

stake *tr* *(to wager)* deponere

stale *adj* vet·us -eris; *(bread)* secund·us -a -um, hestern·us -a -um

stalk *s* *(of plant)* stirp·s -is *m,* caul·is -is *m; (of grain)* calam·us -i *m;* **— of asparagus** stirps asparagi

stalk *tr* *(game)* venari; *(a person)* insidiis persequi

stall *s* stabul·um -i *n; (small shop)* tabern·a -ae *f*

stall *tr* sistere, impedire ‖ *intr* morari, cunctari

stallion *s* admissar·ius -(i)i *m*

stamina *s* vir·es -ium *fpl,* firmit·as -atis *f*

stammer *tr & intr* balbutire

stammering *adj* balb·us -a -um

stammering *s* balbuti·es -ei *f*

stamp *s (mark)* not·a -ae *f; (impression made)* impressi·o -onis *f; (on a letter)* pittac·ium -(i)i *n* cursuale; — **of the foot** supplosi·o -onis *f* pedis

stamp *tr* imprimere, notare; *(money)* cudere; *(feet)* supplodere; **to — out** conterere; *(fig)* supprimere, exstinguere

stampede *s (of animals)* erupti·o -onis *f,* fug·a -ae *f; (fig)* tumult·us -us *m*

stampede *intr* aufugere, discurrere

stance *s* stat·us -ūs *m;* **to take the — of a fighter** statum proeliantis componere

stand *s (halt)* stati·o -onis *f,* mor·a -ae *f; (platform)* suggest·us -ūs *m; (point of view)* sententi·a -ae *f;* **to make a — against** restare adversus *(w. acc);* **to take the —** testificari

stand *tr (to set upright)* statuere; *(to tolerate)* tolerare, ferre; **I can't — him** istum ferre non queo; **I can't — the cold** frigoris impatiens sum; **to — one's ground** perstare; **to — one's ground against** subsistere *(w. dat)* ‖ *intr* stare; **how do matters — ?** quomodo res se habent?; **to keep —ing** perstare; **to — aloof** abstare; **to — at the door** adsistere ad fores; **to — by** adesse *(w. dat),* favēre *(w. dat);* **to — by one's promises** promissis manēre; **to — by one's word** in fide stare; **to — close to** adsistere ad *(w. acc);* **to — fast** consistere; **to — for** significare, indicare; *(to put up with)* tolerare; **to — for office** honorem petere; **to — in awe of** in metu habēre; **to — in for** in loco *(w. gen)* esse; **to — in the way of** obstare *(w. dat);* **to — in need of** indigēre *(w. abl);* **to — on end** *(of hair)* inhorrescere; **to — out** exstare, eminēre; **— still** consistere; **to — up** surgere; **to — up for s.o.** alicui adesse; **to — up to anyone** coram alicui resistere

standard *adj* solit·us -a -um; **— author** script·or -oris *m* classicus

standard *s* norm·a -ae *f,* mensur·a -ae *f; (mil)* vexill·um -i *n*

standard-bearer *s* vexillar·ius -(i)i *m*

standard of living *s* consuetud·o -inis *f* victūs

stand-in *s* vicar·ius -(i)i *m (·a -ae f)*

standing *s* stat·us -ūs *m;* **of long —** vet·us -eris

standing *adj* perpetu·us -a -um

standing ovation *s* **to give s.o. a —** alicui stantes plaudere

stands *spl (bleachers)* for·i -orum *mpl*

standstill *s* **to be at a —** haerēre; **to come to a —** consistere

stanza *s* vers·ūs -uum *mpl; (of four lines)* tetrastich·on -i *n*

staple *adj* necessari·us -a -um; *(chief)* praecipu·us -a -um; **—s** vict·us -ūs *m*

staple *s* uncinul·us -i *m* (metallicus)

staple *tr* consuere

stapler *s* uncinator·ium -(i)i *n,* consutor·ium -(i)i *n* (chartarum)

star *s* stell·a -ae *f,* sid·us -eris *n; (fig)* lum·en -inis *n*

star *intr (theat)* primas partes agere

starch *s* amyl·um -i *n*

starch *tr* amylare

stare *s* obtut·us -ūs *m*

stare *intr* stupēre; **to — at** intueri

starfish *s* stell·a -ae *f*

stark *adj* rigid·us -a -um

stark *adv* omnino, penitus

starlight *s* siderum lum·en -inis *n*

starling *s* sturn·us -i *m*

starry *adj* sidere·us -a -um, stellat·us -a -um

start *s (beginning)* init·ium -(i)i *n,* incip·ium -(i)i *n; (startled reaction)* trepidati·o -onis *f; (sudden movement)* salt·us -ūs *m; (of journey)* profecti·o -onis *f;* **at the — of the year** anno ineunte; **from the —** a principio; **to get a head —** on antecedere; **to get a — on s.o.** aliquem occupare; **to get off to a bad —** initia male ponere; **to have a two-day — on s.o.** biduo antecedere aliquem; **to make a —** initium capere; **you've made a good —** bene se habent tibi principia

start *tr* incipere, instituere ‖ *intr* incipere, (ex)ordiri; *(to take fright)* resilire; **to — out** proficisci; **to — with** incipere ab *(w. abl)*

starter *s (of a car)* incitatr·um -i *n;* **for —s** principio

starting gate *s* carcer·es -um *mpl*

startle *tr* terrēre

starvation *s* fam·es -is *f;* **to die of —** fame enecari *or* mori; **to go on a — diet** abstin·ax -acis esse

starve *tr* fame interficere ‖ *intr* fame confici, fame consumi

starved *adj* **I'm —** fame enectus sum

state *s* stat·us -ūs *m; (pol)* civit·as -atis *f,* respublica *(gen:* reipublicae) *f;* **— of affairs** re·s -rum *fpl;* **— of mind** affecti·o -onis *f* animi; **to be in a better —** in meliore loco esse; **to be in a worse —** deteriore statu esse; **to restore s.th. to its former —** in pristinum statum aliquid restituere

state *tr* declarare, affirmare; *(of writers)* auctor esse; *(in writing)* scribere

statement *s* dict·um -i *n,* affirmati·o -onis *f; (of a witness in court)* testimon·ium -(i)i *n;* **to make a —** profiteri

statesman *s* vir, viri *m* reipublicae administrandae peritus, vir civilis

statesmanship *s* ar·s -tis *f* reipublicae administrandae

station *s* stati·o -onis *f*

station *tr* locare, disponere

stationary *adj* stabil·is -is -e, immot·us -a -um

stationery *s* re·s -rum *fpl* scriptoriae, chart·a -ae *f* epistularis

stationery store *s* tabern·a -ae *f* chartaria

statistics *spl* cens·us -ūs *m,* breviar·ium -(i)i *n*

statue *s* statu·a -ae *f,* sign·um -i *n*

stature *s* statur·a -ae *f; (fig)* amplitud·o -inis *f*

status *s* stat·us -ūs *m;* **the — quo** praesens status

statute *s* constitut·um -i *n,* lex, legis *f* scripta

staunch *adj* fid·us -a -um, firm·us -a -um

staunch *tr* **to — the flow of blood** sanguinem cohibēre

stave *tr* **to — off** arcēre

stay *tr* detinēre; *(to curb)* coercēre **‖** *intr* manēre; *(temporarily)* morari, commorari; **to — at home** se continēre; **to — away from** abstinēre *(w. abl)*

stay *s (sojourn)* mansi·o -onis *f; (delay)* mor·a -ae *f; (prop)* fulcr·um -i *n; —* **of execution** prolati·o -onis *f* supplicii extremi

steadfast *adj* const·ans -antis

steadfastly *adv* constanter

steadily *adv* firme, constanter

steadiness *s* constanti·a -ae *f*

steady *adj* stabil·is -is -e, firm·us -a -um; *(fig)* const·ans -antis; **— weather** aequales tempestat·es -um *fpl*

steak *s* off·a -ae *f* bubula

steal *tr* furari, surripere **‖** *intr* furari; **to — away** se subducere, clam aufugere; **to — over** subrepere *(w. dat)*

stealth *s* furt·um -i *n;* **by —** furtim

stealthily *adv* furtim, clam

stealthy *adj* furtiv·us -a -um

steam *s* vap·or -oris *m (coll)* vis *f;* **to let off —** *(coll)* motūs animi effundere

steam *intr* vaporare, fumare

steam bath *s* sudator·ium -(i)i *n*

steamboat *s* nav·is -is *f* vapore acta

steam engine *s* vaporia machin·a -ae *f* vectoria

steed *s* equ·us -i *m* bellator

steel *s* chalyb·s -is *m*

steel *adj* chalybei·us -a -um

steel *tr* **to — oneself against** obdurescere contra *(w. acc)*

steel mill *s* fabric·a -ae *f* chalybeia

steep *adj* ardu·us -a -um

steep *tr* madefacere; **—ed in crime** inquinat·us -a -um sceleribus

steeple *s* turr·is -is *f* campanaria

steepness *s* arduit·as -atis *f*

steer *s* iuvenc·us -i *m*

steer *tr* gubernare, dirigere

steering *s* gubernati·o -onis *f*

steering wheel *s* gubernacul·um -i *n*

stem *s* stirp·s -is *f; (of a ship)* pror·a -ae *f*

stem *tr* obsistere *(w. dat)*

stench *s* put·or -oris *m,* foet·or -oris *m*

stenographer *s* notari·us -i *m* (·a -ae *f)*

stenography *s* scripti·o -onis *f* notaria

step *s* pass·us -ūs *m,* grad·us -ūs *m; (measure)* rati·o -onis *f;* **flight of —s** scal·ae -arum *fpl;* **— by —** gradatim; **—s** *(of stairs)* grad·ūs -uum *mpl;* **out of —** *(fig)* abson·us -a -um; **to keep in —** *(march)* presso gradu incedere; *(fig)* congruere; **to take —s** *(to take measures)* rationem inire; **to watch one's —** cavēre

step *intr* grad·ior -i gressus sum; **to — down** degredi; *(fig)* se abdicare; **to — in** ingredi; *(fig)* intervenire, intercedere; **to — on** calcare; **to — up** *(increase)* augēre, accelerare; **— on it!** matura! *(pl:* maturate!)

stepbrother *s (on father's side)* vitrici fil·ius -(i)i *m; (on mother's side)* novercae fil·ius -(i)i *m*

stepdaughter *s* privign·a -ae *f*

stepfather *s* vitric·us -i *m*

stepmother *s* noverc·a -ae *f*

stepping stone *s (fig)* facult·as -atis *f* procedendi

stepsister *s (on father's side)* vitrici fili·a -ae *f; (on mother's side)* novercae filia

stepson *s* privign·us -i *m*

stereo *s* stereophon·ium -(i)i *n*

stereophonic *adj* stereophonic·us -a -um

stereotype *s (fig)* res, rei *f* trita

stereotyped *adj* trit·us -a -um

sterile *adj* steril·is -is -e

sterility *s* sterilit·as -atis *f*

sterling *adj* argente·us -a -um; *(genuine)* ver·us -a -um; *(upright)* prob·us -a -um

stern *adj* sever·us -a -um

sternly *adv* severe

sternness *s* severit·as -atis *f*

stew *s* carn·es -ium *fpl* cum condimentis elixae; **to be in a —** turbid·us -a -um animi esse; **to be in a — over** aestuare *(w. causal abl or* in *w. abl)*

stew *tr* lento igne coquere **‖** *intr* **I —ed over it for a long time** in eo aestuavi diu

steward *s* procurat·or -oris *m; (of country estate)* villic·us -i *m; (in a plane)* hosp·es -itis *m* aërius

stewardess *s* hospit·a -ae *f* aëria

stewardship *s* procurati·o -onis *f*

stewed *adj* iurulent·us -a -um; *(drunk)* elix·us -a -um

stick *s (twig)* ramul·us -i *m; (for striking)* fust·is -is *m; (cane)* bacul·um -i *n*

stick *tr* figere; **to — one's neck in the noose** cervices nodo condere; **to — up** *(to rob)* latrocinari *(w. dat)* ‖ *intr* haerēre, haesitare; **to — out** eminēre, prominēre; **to — to the usual order** ordinem conservare; **to — to the truth** in veritate manēre; **to — to one's guns** in sententiā stare

sticky *adj* viscos·us -a -um

stiff *adj* rigid·us -a -um; *(knee)* content·us -a -um; *(formal)* frigid·us -a -um

stiffly *adv* rigide; frigide

stiffen *tr* durare, rigid·um -am -um facere; *(w. starch)* amylare ‖ *intr* obdurescere

stiffness *s* rig·or -oris *m; (of joints)* articulorum dol·or -oris *m*

stifle *tr* suffocare; *(fig)* opprimere

stigma *s* stigm·a -atis *n,* not·a -ae *f; (stain)* dedec·us -oris *n*

stigmatize *tr* notare

still *adj* quiet·us -a -um; immot·us -a -um; **to be —** silēre, tacēre; **to hold —** non movēre

still *adv (adversative)* tamen; *(till now)* adhuc, etiamnum; *(w. comparatives)* etiam, etiamnum

still *tr* pacare, sedare

stillborn *adj* abortiv·us -a -um

stillness *s (silence)* silent·ium -(i)i *n; (quiet)* qui·es -etis *f*

stilted *adj* arcessit·us -a -um

stilts *spl* grall·ae -arum *fpl;* **a walker on —** grallat·or -oris *mf*

stimulant *s* irritament·um -i *n*

stimulate *tr* stimulare

stimulus *s* stimul·us -i *m*

sting *s (on an insect)* acule·us -i *m; (bite)* ict·us -ūs *m; (of conscience)* ang·or -oris *m*

sting *tr (of a bee)* icere; *(fig)* mordēre ‖ *intr (to hurt)* dolēre

stinginess *s* sord·es -ium *fpl*

stingray *s* pastinac·a -ae *f*

stingy *adj* sordid·us -a -um

stink *s* put·or -oris *m,* fet·or -oris *m*

stink *intr* putēre, fetēre; **to — of garlic** obolēre allium

stinky *adj* fetid·us -a -um

stint *s* **without —** sine modo

stint *tr* coercēre ‖ *intr* parcere, frugi [*indecl*] esse

stipend *s* salar·ium -(i)i *n*

stipulate *tr* stipulari

stipulation *s* stipulati·o -onis *f,* condici·o -onis *f;* **with the — that** eā condicione ut *(w. subj)*

stir *s* tumult·us -ūs *m*

stir *tr* excitare ‖ *intr* se movēre

stirring *adj* ad movendos animos apt·us -a -um

stirrup *s* staped·ium -(i)i *n*

stitch *tr* suere

stitch *s* tract·us -ūs *m* acūs; **— in the side** subitus lateris dol·or -oris *m;* **to be in —es** in cachinnum effundere

stock *s (supply)* copi·a -ae *f; (race)* gen·us -eris *n; (handle)* lign·um -i *n; (fin)* acti·a -ae *f* **to take — of** permetiri

stock *tr (to provide with)* instruere; *(to store)* condere

stockade *s* vall·um *n*

stocking *s* tibial·e -is *n*

stock broker *s* collybist·a -ae *m* (·ria -riae *f)*

stock exchange *s* collyb·us -i *m*

stock market *s* chrematister·ium -(i)i *n,* burs·a -ae *f*

Stoic *adj* Stoic·us -a -um

Stoic *s* Stoic·us -i *m*

stoical *adj* dur·us -a -um, pati·ens -entis

Stoicism *s* Stoica disciplin·a -ae *f*

stole *s* amict·us -ūs *m*

stolen *adj* furtiv·us -a -um; **— goods** furt·a -orum *npl*

stomach *s* stomach·us -i *m; to have — trouble* a stomacho laborare

stomach *tr* tolerare

stomachache *s* stomachi dol·or -oris *m*

stone *s* lap·is -idis *m,* sax·um -i *n; (of olive, peach)* os, ossis *n; to leave no — unturned* nihil praetermittere

stone *tr* lapidare, lapidibus obruere

stoned *adj (drunk)* elix·us -a -um

stonecutter *s* lapicid·a -ae *m*

stone quarry *s* lapidicin·a -ae *f*

stony *adj (full of stones)* lapidos·us -a -um

stool *s (bench)* scabell·um -i *n; (for sitting or mounting)* scamn·um -i *n; (feces)* alv·us -i *f;* **when the — is not passed** ubi alvus non descendit

stoolpigeon *s* ind·ex -icis *mf*

stoop *s (posture)* inclinati·o -onis *f,* curvatur·a -ae *f; (of a house)* pergul·a -ae *f*

stoop *intr* se inclinare *or* proclinare; **to — to** descendere in *(w. acc)*

stop *tr* sistere; *(to desist from)* desinere *(w. inf);* **to — up** obturare ‖ *intr* consistere; *(to cease)* desistere; **—!** asta!; **— right there!** sta ilico!; **— talking** desine *(pl:* desinite) loqui!; **they finally —ed talking** finem loquendi demum fecerunt; **to — off at** deversari apud *(w. acc)*

stop *s* mor·a -ae *f;* **to come to a —** consistere; **to put a — to** comprimere

stopgap *s* tibic·en -inis *m*

stop-over *s* commorati·o -onis *f;* **to make a —** commorari

stoppage *s* obstructi·o -onis *f*

stopper *s* obturament·um -i *n; (halt)* cessati·o -onis *f*

stop sign *s* sign·um -i *n* subsistendi

stop watch *s* chronoscop·ium -(i)i *n*

store *s (supply)* copi·a -ae *f; (shop)* tabern·a -ae *f;* **in —** prompt·us -a -um, in expedito; **to set great — by** magni facere
store *tr* condere, reponere; **to — away** recondere; **to — up** reponere
storehouse *s* promptuar·ium -(i)i *n; (for grain)* horre·um -i *n; (fig)* thesaur·us -i *m*
storekeeper *s* tabernari·us -i *m* (·a -ae *f)*
storeroom *s* cellar·ium -(i)i *n*
stork *s* ciconi·a -ae *f*
storm *s* tempest·as -atis *f,* procell·a -ae *f;* **a — arose** tempestas coörta est; **a — of protests** tempestas querelarum; **to take by —** expugnare
storm *tr* expugnare ‖ *intr* desaevire; **to come —ing in** se infundere
stormy *adj* turbid·us -a -um, procellos·us -a -um; *(fig)* tumultuos·us -a -um
story *s* fabul·a -ae *f; (rumor)* fam·a -ae *f; (of a building)* tabulat·um -i *n,* contignati·o -onis *f;* **to make a long — short** ne long·us -a sim *or* ne longam faciam
storyteller *s* fabula·tor -toris *m* (·trix -tricis *f)*
stout *adj* corpulent·us -a -um, plen·us -a -um; *(brave)* fort·is -is -e; *(strong)* valid·us -a -um
stoutly *adv* fortiter
stove *s* foc·us -i *m,* focul·us -i *m;* **electric (gas) —** focus electricus (gaseus)
stow *tr* condere ‖ *intr* **to — away** in navi delitescere
stowaway *s* vec·tor -toris *m* (·trix -tricis *f)* clandestin·us -a
straddle *tr* cruribus varicatis insistere super *(w. acc)*
straggle *intr* palari; **to — over the country-side** palari per agros
straggler *s* palat·us -i *m* (·a -ae *f)*
straggly *adj* **— beard** horrida barb·a -ae *f*
straight *adj* rect·us -a -um, direct·us -a -um; **— as a line** lineae modo rect·us -a -um
straight *adv* directo, rectā
straighten *tr* rect·um -am -um facere; **to — out** corrigere, explicare; **to — up** ordinare
straightforward *adj* apert·us -a -um, simpl·ex -icis
straightlaced *adj* sever·us -a -um
straightway *adv* statim, prorsus
strain *tr* contendere; *(muscle)* luxare; *(to filter)* percolare ‖ *intr* enit·or -i enixus sum
strain *s (tension)* contenti·o -onis *f; (effort)* lab·or -oris *m,* nis·us -ūs *m; (wrench)* lux·us -ūs *m; (mus)* mod·us -i *m*
strained *adj (style)* arcessit·us -a -um
strainer *s* col·um -i *n*
strait *s* fret·um -i *n;* **Strait of Messina** Fretum Siculum; **to be in dire —s** in angustiis esse
strand *s (of hair)* flocc·us -i *m; (of rope)* fil·um -i *n*
strand *tr* vadis illidere

stranded *adj (ship)* vadis illis·us -a -um; *(fig)* sol·us -a -um et in·ops -opis
strange *adj* mir·us -a -um, *(unfamiliar)* inusitat·us -a -um, insolit·us -a -um; *(incongruous)* abson·us -a -um; *(foreign)* peregrin·us -a -um; **— to say** mirabile dictu
strangely *adv* mirum in modum
strangeness *s* novit·as -atis *f*
stranger *s* peregrin·us -i *m* (·a -ae *f);* **a perfect —** omnino ignot·us -i *m* (·a -ae *f)*
strangle *tr* strangulare
strap *s* lor·um -i *n; (for shoe or sandal)* obstragul·um -i *n*
strap *tr* ligare, astringere; **to be —ed for money** in artibus rebus esse
strapping *adj* robust·us -a - um
stratagem *s* stratagem·a -atis *n; (trick)* dol·us -i *m*
strategic *adj* bene ordinat·us -a -um; *(advantageous)* commod·us -a -um; *(mil)* apportun·us -a -um
strategy *s (artfulness)* astuti·a -ae *f; (mil)* rati·o -onis *f* militaris
straw *adj* stramentici·us -a -um
straw *s* strament·um -i *n; (a single stalk)* culm·us -i *m; (for drinking)* siph·o -onis *m;* **cottages thatched with —** cas·ae -arum *fpl* stramento tectae; **to clutch at —s** ultimam spem capere
strawberry *s* frag·um -i *n*
strawberry-blond(e) *adj* fulv·us -a -um
stray *intr* errare, aberrare
stray *adj* err·ans -antis; *(dog, cat)* extrari·us -a -um
streak *s* line·a -ae *f; (of character)* ven·a -ae *f; (tendency)* proclivit·as -atis *f; (spell)* curs·us -ūs *m* brevis; **— of lightning** fulg·or -oris *m;* **yellow —** ignavi·a -ae *f*
streak *tr* lineis distinguere; maculare ‖ *intr (to dash)* ruere
stream *s* riv·us -i *m;* **down the —** secundo flumine; **—s of sweat** rivi *mpl* sudoris; **up the —** adverso flumine
stream *intr* se effundere
streamer *s* vexill·um -i *n*
street *s* vi·a -ae *f; (in city)* vic·us -i *m; (with houses)* plate·a -ae *f; (very narrow)* tram·es -itis *m*
streetcar *s* curr·us -ūs *m* electricus
streetcleaner *s* purgat·or -oris *m* viarum
street clothes *spl* forens·ia -ium *npl*
street map *s* tabul·a -ae *f* viaria
streetwalker *s* muli·er -eris *f* secutuleia
strength *s* vir·es -ium *fpl*
strengthen *tr* confirmare
strenuous *adj (brisk)* strenu·us -a -um; *(unremitting)* sedul·us -a -um; *(arduous)* laborios·us -a -um
strenuously *adv* strenue

stress *s (accent)* ict·us -ūs *m; (emphasis)* vis *f,* pond·us -eris *n;* (**tension**) tensi·o -onis *f; (importance)* pond·us -eris *n;* **not to lay much — upon a matter** aliquid levi momento aestimare; **to lay — on trifles** addere pondus nugis

stress *tr* exprimere, in mentem imprimere

stretch *tr* tendere; *(to tighten what is already stretched)* contendere; *(in different directions)* distendere; *(to elongate, e.g., the skin)* producere; **to — or relax the muscles** nervos intendere aut remittere; **to — out the hand to** *(to help s.o.)* manum intendere *(w. dat);* **to — the legs** crura in longitudinem extendere ‖ *intr* extendi, distendi; *(geog)* tendere; *(of a person while yawning)* pandiculari; **to — out on the couch** se extendere super torum

stretch *s (expanse)* tract·us -ūs *m,* spat·ium -(i)i *n; (extension)* extensi·o -onis *f*

stretcher *s* lecticul·a -ae *f*

strew *tr* spargere, sternere

stricken *adj* afflict·us -a -um

strict *adj (severe)* sever·us -a -um; *(accurate)* dilig·ens -entis; *(person in authority)* acerb·us -a -um; **according to the — letter of the law** summo iure; **— meaning of the word** verbi sens·us -ūs *m* proprius; **— truth** verit·as -atis *f* ipsa

strictly *adv* severe; *(carefully)* diligenter; **— speaking** proprie, immo

strictness *s* severit·as -atis *f*

stricture *s* vituperati·o -onis *f*

stride *s* pass·us -ūs *m* grandis; **to make —s** procedere

stride *intr* procedere passibus grandibus

strife *s* iurg·ium -(i)i *n,* discordi·a -ae *f; (struggle)* contenti·o -onis *f*

strike *tr* ferire, percutere, icere; **I was struck by his boldness** miratus sum audaciam eius; **struck blind** oculis capt·us -a -um; **struck by lightning** de caelo percuss·us -a -um; **to — a bargain, deal** pacisci; **to — fear into s.o.** incutere timorem in *(w. acc)* ‖ *intr (of workers)* opere faciendo cessare

strike *s* cessati·o -onis *f* operis, operistit·ium -(i)i *n; (blow)* ict·us -ūs *m;* **to go on —** opus intermittere; **to make a —** *(in bowling)* omnes conos simul prosternere

striking *adj* insign·is -is -e

strikingly *adv* mirum in modum

string *s* funicul·us -i *m; (thread)* fil·um -i *n; (for bow)* nerv·us -i *m; (mus)* chord·a -ae *f; (comput)* seri·es -ei *f;* **— of pearls** line·a -ae *f* margaritarum

string *tr (a bow)* intendere; **to — together** colligare

stringent *adj* sever·us -a -um

stringy *adj* fibrat·us -a -um

strip *tr* (de)nudare, spoliare; **to — off** *(clothes)* exuere; *(e.g., a tribune of power)* privare; *(of rights)* nudare ‖ *intr* se exuere vestibus

strip *s (of cloth; of land)* lacini·a -ae *f; (of paper)* sched·a -ae *f; (e.g., of bacon)* segment·um -i *n*

stripe *s (streak)* lim·es -itis *m; (welt)* vib·ex -icis *m; (blow)* ict·us -ūs *m; (line)* lineament·um -i *n; (on toga)* clav·us -i *m*

strive *intr* (**after, for**) nit·or -i nisus *(or* nixus) sum (ad *or* in *w. acc)*

striving *s* contenti·o -onis *f,* nis·us -ūs *m*

stroke *s* ict·us -ūs *m,* plag·a -ae *f; (of oars)* verb·er -eris *m; (in swimming)* mot·us -ūs *m* bracchiorum; *(med)* apoplexi·a -ae *f;* **— of luck** lus·us -ūs *m* fortunae mirabilis; **— of the oars** verber remorum; **— of the pen** pennae duct·us -ūs *m*

stroke *tr* (per)mulcēre

stroll *s* ambulati·o -onis *f* otiosa; **to take a —** spatiari

stroll *intr* spatiari

stroller *s* lecticul·a -ae *f* rotalis infantium; *(person)* spatia·tor -toris *m* (·trix -tricis *f)*

strong *adj (body, remedy)* valid·us -a -um *(opp:* imbecillus); *(smell)* grav·is -is -e; *(powerful)* pot·ens -entis; *(feeling)* a·cer -cris -cre; *(language)* vehem·ens -entis

strongly *adv* valide, vehementer

strongbox *s* arc·a -ae *f*

stronghold *s* castell·um -i *n*

structure *s (disposition, arrangement, building)* structur·a -ae *f; (makeup)* compositi·o -onis *f,* natur·a -ae *f*

struggle *s* certam·en -inis *f,* pugn·a -ae *f; (fig)* luctati·o -onis *f*

struggle *intr* contendere, luctari

strum *tr* pulsare

strumpet *s* scort·um -i *n*

strut *s* incess·us -ūs *m* magnificus

strut *intr* magnifice incedere

stub *tr* offendere

stub *s* segment·um -i *n,* reliqu·um -i *n*

stubble *s* stipul·a -ae *f*

stubborn *adj* obstinat·us -a -um; *(defiant and unyielding)* contum·ax -acis

stubbornly *adv* obstinate, contumaciter

stubbornness *s* obstinati·o -onis *f,* contumaci·a -ae *f*

stucco *s* tector·ium -(i)i *n*

stuck *adj* **to be —** *(out of ideas)* haerēre; **to be — on someone** in amore haerēre erga aliquem

stuck-up *adj* vultuos·us -a -um, fastidios·us -a -um; **to be —** fastidire

stud *s* clav·us -i *m; (horse)* admissar·ius -(i)i *m*

student *s* discipul·us -i *m* (·a -ae *f); (at university)* scholastic·us -i *m* (·a -ae *f);* **a law —**

iuris studios·us -a; **a medical —** medicinae studios·us -a

studied *adj* meditat·us -a -um

studies *spl* studi·a -orum *npl*

studio *s* officin·a -ae *f* artificis

studious *adj* studios·us -a -um discendi

study *s* stud·ium -(i)i *n;* (*room*) tablin·um -i *n*

study *tr* studēre (*w. dat*); (*to scrutinize*) perscrutari **‖** *intr* studēre; (*at night*) lucubrare; **to — under a teacher of rhetoric** operam dare dicendi magistro

study period *s* spat·ium -(i)i *n* ad studiendum

stuff *s* materi·a -ae *f;* (*goods*) bon·a -orum *npl,* res, rerum *fpl;* (*junk*) scrut·a -orum *npl*

stuff *tr* farcire; (*w. food*) saginare; **to — it down s.o.'s throat** saginare aliquem recusantem

stuffed *adj* fart·us -a -um, refert·us -a -um; (*gorged*) saturat·us -a -um

stuffed shirt *s* (*coll*) hom·o -inis *mf* tumid·us (-a)

stuffing *s* (*in cooking*) fart·um -i *n;* (*in pillow, upholstery*) toment·um -i *n*

stuffy *adj* (*air*) crass·us -a -um

stultify *tr* ad irritum redigere

stumble *intr* offendere; **to — over new words** nova verba offendere; **to — upon** incidere in (*w. acc*)

stumbling block *s* offensi·o -onis *f*

stump *s* caud·ex -icis *m*

stun *tr* stupefacere; (*fig*) obstupefacere

stunned *adj* attonit·us -a -um

stunt *s* aus·um -i *n*

stunted *adj* curt·us -a -um

stupefy *tr* obstupefacere

stupendous *adj* permir·us -a -um

stupid *adj* stupid·us -a -um

stupidity *s* stupidit·as -atis *f*

stupidly *adv* stupide

stupor *s* stup·or -oris *m*

sturdiness *s* firmit·as -atis *f*

sturdy *adj* firm·us -a -um

sturgeon *s* acipens·er -eris *m*

stutter *intr* balbutire

stutterer *s* balb·us -i *m* (·a -ae *f*)

stye *s* suil·e -is *n*

style *s* (*kind*) gen·us -eris *n;* (*manner*) mod·us -i *m;* (*fashion*) mos, moris *m,* consuetud·o -inis *f;* (*of writing*) stil·us -i *m;* (*literary*) scribendi genus *n;* (*rhetorical*) dicendi genus *n;* (*architectural*) structurae genus *n;* (*of dress*) habit·us -ūs *m;* **in the new —** novo more; **to go out of —** exolescere

style *tr* vocare, nominare

stylish *adj* specios·us -a -um

subdirectory *s* (*comput*) plicarum subind·ex -icis *m*

subdivide *tr* iterum dividere

subdivision *s* subdivisi·o -onis *f;* (*of land*) segment·um -i *n* agri

subdue *tr* (*to conquer*) subicere; (*to overcome*) superare; (*to soften*) domare, placare

subject *adj* subiect·us -a -um; **— to** subiectus (*w. dat*); (*to disease*) obnoxi·us -a -um (*w. dat*)

subject *tr* subicere, subigere; **to — to** (*to expose to*) obicere (*w. dat*)

subject *s* (*e.g., English, math*) disciplin·a -ae *f;* (*one under the rule of others*) subiect·us -i *m,* civ·is -is *m,* cli·ens -entis *mf;* (*topic*) res, rei *f,* argument·um -i *n;* (*gram*) subiect·um -i *n;* **to change the —** in aliā aquā navigare

subjection *s* servit·us -utis *f*

subjective *adj* propri·us -a -um

subject matter *s* materi·a -ae *f*

subjugate *tr* subigere

subjunctive *adj* subiunctiv·us -a -um; **— mood** mod·us -i *m* subiunctivus

subjunctive *s* subiunctiv·us -i *m*

sublime *s* sublimit·as -atis *f,* summ·a -ae *f*

sublime *adj* sublim·is -is -e

sublimely *adv* excelse

submarine *s* nav·is -is *f* submarina

submerge *tr* demergere, inundare **‖** *intr* se demergere

submission *s* (*yielding*) dediti·o -onis *f;* (*humbleness*) obsequ·ium -(i)i *n*

submissive *adj* summiss·us -a -um

submissively *adv* summisse

submit *tr* (*e.g., a proposal*) referre **‖** *intr* se submittere; **to — to** obtemperare (*w. dat*)

subordinate *tr* subicere, supponere

subordinate *adj* subiect·us -a -um; **— conjunction** coniuncti·o -onis *f* subiunctiva

subordinate *s* subiect·us -i *m* (·a -ae *f*), inferi·or -oris *mf*

suborn *tr* subornare

subscribe *intr* **to —** (*to agree with*) assentiri (*w. dat*); (*a magazine*) praescribere

subscriber *s* subscrip·tor -toris *m* (·trix -tricis *f*)

subscription *s* subscripti·o -onis *f;* (*magazine*) praescript·um -i *n*

subsequent *adj* sequ·ens -entis

subsequently *adv* deinde, postea

subservient *adj* obsequios·us -a -um

subside *intr* (*of panic, the sea, wind*) desidere; (*of passion*) defervescere

subsidiary *adj* subsidiari·us -a -um

subsidy *s* subsid·ium -(i)i *n*

subsist *intr* subsistere

subsistence *s* vict·us -ūs *m*

substance *s* substanti·a -ae *f;* (*wealth*) res, rei *f;* (*gist*) summ·a -ae *f*

substantial *adj* solid·us -a -um; (*real*) ver·us -a -um; (*rich*) opulent·us -a -um; (*important*) magn·us -a -um; (*meal*) plen·us -a -um

substantially *adv* magnā ex parte

substantiate *tr* confirmare
substantive *s* substantiv·um -i *n*
substitute *adj* vicari·us -a -um, suppositi·us -a -um
substitute *s* vicari·us -i *m* (·a -ae *f); as a —* in vicem; **I will go as a — for you** ibo pro te
substitute *tr* **(for)** substituere (pro *w. abl),* supponere (pro *w. abl)* **‖** *intr (for)* in locum *(w. gen)* succedere
substitution *s* substituti·o -onis *f*
subterfuge *s* perfug·ium -(i)i *n*
subterranean *adj* subterrane·us -a -um
subtle *adj (e.g., definition)* subtil·is -is -e; *(crafty)* astut·us -a -um; **a — distinction** tenuis et acuta distincti·o -onis *f;* **a — plan** rati·o -onis *f* astuta
subtlety *s* subtilit·as -atis *f*
subtract *tr* detrahere, **to — the interest paid from the capital** de capite deducere quod usuris pernumeratum est
subtraction *s* deducti·o -onis *f*
suburb *s* suburb·ium -(i)i *n*
suburban *adj* suburban·us -a -um
subversion *s* eversi·o -onis *f*
subversive *adj* seditios·us -a -um
subvert *tr* evertere
succeed *tr* succedere *(w. dat),* insequi **‖** *intr (of persons)* rem bene gerere; *(of activities)* prospere evenire
success *s* success·us -ūs *m; (person)* hom·o -inis *mf* beat·us (-a); *(thing)* bene res, rei *f* gesta
successful *adj (of persons)* fel·ix -icis; *(of things)* prosper·us -a -um
successfully *adv* prospere, fortunate
succession *s* successi·o -onis *f; (series)* seri·es -ei *f*
successive *adj* continu·us -a -um; **on five — nights** quinque continuis noctibus
successor *s* success·or -oris *m* (·rix -ricis *f)*
succinct *adj* press·us -a -um
succinctly *adv* presse
succulence *s* suc·us -i *m*
succulent *adj* suculent·us -a -um
succumb *intr* succumbere
such *adj* tal·is -is -e; **as —** per se; **in — a way** tali modo; **— a big** tant·us -a -um; **— ... as** talis ... qualis; **— is the case** res se ita habent
such *adv (coll)* tantopere
suck *tr* sugere; **to — dry** ebibere; **to — in** sorbēre; **to — up** exsorbēre
sucker *s (fool)* barcal·a -ae *mf; (bot)* surcul·us -i *m;* **to take s.o. for a —** alicui os sublinere
suckle *tr* alere, mammam dare *(w. dat)*
suction *s* suct·us -ūs *m*
suction cup *s* cucurbitul·a -ae *f*
sudden *adj* subit·us -a -um, repentin·us -a -um; **all of a —** de improviso

suddenly *adv* subito, repente
suddenness *s* impet·us -ūs *m*
suds *spl* aqu·a -ae *f* sapone infecta
sue *tr* litem intendere *(dat)* **‖** *intr (leg)* litem inferre; **to —for** petere, poscere
suffer *tr* pati, tolerare; **to — the punishment** poenam dare, supplicium dare **‖** *intr* pati; **to — from** laborare *(w. abl);* **—ing from** oppress·us -a -um *(w. abl)*
sufferable *adj* tolerabil·is -is -e
suffering *s* dol·or -oris *m,* ang·or -oris *m*
suffice *intr* sufficere, satis esse
sufficient *adj* satis *(w. gen)*
sufficiently *adv* satis, affatim
suffocate *tr* suffocare **‖** *intr* suffocari
suffocation *s* suffocati·o -onis *f*
suffrage *s* suffrag·ium -(i) *n*
sugar *s* sacchar·um -i *n*
sugar *tr* saccharo condire
sugar bowl *s* vascul·um -i *n* sacchari
sugar cane *s* arund·o -inis *f* sacchari
sugarcoat *tr (fig)* lenire
suggest *tr* suadere; *(to propose)* proponere; **as you —** quemadmodum suades
suggestion *s (act)* (ad)moniti·o -onis *f; (proposal)* monit·um -i *n; (inkling)* indicati·o -onis *f*
suggestive *adj* indic·ans -antis
suicide *s* mor·s -tis *f* voluntaria; **to commit —** sibi mortem consciscere
suit *s (of clothes)* synthes·is -is *f; (leg)* lis, litis *f,* acti·o -onis *f;* **to bring a — against** actionem intendere *(w. dat)*
suit *tr* accommodare, convenire *(w. dat);* **not — displicēre** *(w. dat)*
suitable *adj* apt·us -a -um, idone·us -a -um
suitcase *s* vidul·us -i *m*
suite *s (apartment)* diaet·a -ae *f; (retinue)* comitat·us -ūs *m*
suitor *s* proc·us -i *m*
sulfur *s* sulf·ur -uris *n*
sulk *intr* aegre ferre, moros·us -a -um esse
sulky *adj* moros·us -a -um
sullen *adj* contum·ax -acis
sullenly *adv best expressed by the adjective*
sully *tr* inquinare
sultry *adj* aestuos·us -a -um
sum *s* summ·a -ae *f;* **for a large —** magni *or* magno; **for a small —** parvi *or* parvo; **— and substance of a letter** cap·ut -itis *n* litterarum; **— total** summ·a -ae *f* summarum
sum *tr* **to — up** computare; *(to summarize)* summatim describere; **to — up** ad summum, in summā
summarily *adv* summatim
summarize *tr* summatim describere
summary *s* summar·ium -(i)i *n,* breviar·ium -(i)i *n*
summation *s* perorati·o -onis *f*

summer *s* aest·as -atis *f;* **to spend the —** aestivare

summer *adj* aestiv·us -a -um; **— resort** aestiv·a -orum *npl;* **— vacation** feri·ae -arum *fpl* aestivae; **to spend the — vacation** ferias aestivas agere

summit *s* culm·en -inis *n; (fig)* fastig·ium -(i)i *n;* **the — of the mountain** summus mon·s -tis *m*

summit conference *s* colloqu·ium -(i)i *n* primorum civitatum

summon *tr* arcessere; *(meeting)* convocare; **— ed as a witness** citat·us -a -um testis; **to — to an inquiry** vocare ad disquisitionem; **to — up courage** animum erigere

summons *s (leg)* vocati·o -onis *f;* **to issue s.o. a —** diem dicere *(w. dat)*

sumptuary *adj* sumptuari·us -a -um

sumptuous *adj* sumptuos·us -a -um

sumptuously *adv* sumptuose

sun *s* sol, solis *m*

sun *tr* **to — oneself** apricari

sunbathe *intr* apricari

sunbathing *s* apricati·o -onis *f*

sunbeam *s* rad·ius -(i)i *m* solis

sunburnt *adj* adust·us -a -um

Sunday *s* di·es -ei *m* solis; *(eccl)* Dominic·a -ae *f*

Sunday school *s* schol·a -ae *f* Dominicis habita

sundial *s* solar·ium -(i)i *n*

sundown *s* solis occas·us -ūs *m*

sundried *adj* pass·us -a -um

sundry *adj* divers·i -ae -a, aliquot [*indecl*]

sunflower *s* helianth·us -i *m*

sun glasses *spl* perspicill·a -orum *npl* solaria (*or* infuscata)

sunken *adj* depress·us -a -um

sunlight *s* sol, solis *m*

sunny *adj* apric·us -a -um

sunrise *s* solis ort·us -ūs *m;* **at —** sole orto

sunset *s* solis occas·us -ūs *m;* **at —** sole occidente

sunshine *s* sol, solis *m*

suntan *s* adustus col·or -oris *m;* **to get a —** colorare

suntanned *adj* colorat·us -a -um

superabundant *adj* nimi·us -a -um

superabundantly *adv* satis superque

superb *adj* magnific·us -a -um

superbly *adv* magnifice

superficial *adj (fig)* lev·is -is -e; **— wound** vuln·us -eris *n* quod in summa parte est

superfluous *adj* supervacane·us -a -um; **to be regarded as —** pro supervacuo haberi; **to be — redundare**

superhuman *adj* divin·us -a -um; *(fig)* incredibil·is -is -e; **— form** form·a -ae *f* maior humanā

superintend *tr* praeesse *(w. dat)*

superintendence *s* cur·a -ae *f*

superintendent *s* (pro)cura·tor -toris *m* (·trix -tricis *f*); *(of an apt. bldg.)* procurat·or -oris *m* insulae

superior *adj* super·ior -ior -ius; **to be — in cavalry** plus valēre equitatu

superior *s* praeposit·us -i *m* (·a -ae *f*)

superiority *s* praestanti·a -ae *f*

superlative *adj* eximi·us -a -um; *(gram)* superlativ·us -a -um

superlative *s* grad·us -ūs *m* superlativus; **in the superlative; give me "laetus" in the —** dic "laetus" superlative

supermarket *s* superinstitor·ium -(i)i *n*

supernatural *adj* divin·us -a -um; supra naturam

supersede *tr* succedere *(w. dat)*

superstition *s* superstiti·o -onis *f*

superstitious *adj* superstitios·us -a -um

supervise *tr* (pro)curare

supervision *s* cur·a -ae *f*

supine *adj* supin·us -a -um

supine *s* supin·um -i *n*

supper *s* cen·a -ae *f;* **after —** cenat·us -a -um; **for — in** cenam; **to eat —** cenare

supplant *tr* supponere, praevertere

supple *adj* flexibil·is -is -e, moll·is -is -e

supplement *s* supplement·um -i *n*

supplement *tr* amplificare

suppliant *s* suppl·ex -icis *mf*

supplicate *tr* supplicare

supplication *s* supplicati·o -onis *f*

supplied *adj* **well — with** copios·us -a -um *(w. abl)*

supply *s* copi·a -ae *f;* **supplies** *(mil)* commeat·us -ūs *m (used both as collective singular and in the plural);* **to cut off the enemy's —** intercludere hostes commeatibus

supply *tr (to furnish)* praebēre, suppeditare; *(to fill up)* supplēre; **to be supplied with** suppeditare *(w. abl)*

support *s (prop)* fulcr·um -i *n; (help)* subsid·ium -(i)i *n; (maintenance)* aliment·um -i *n; (backing)* stud·ium -(i)i *n*

support *tr (to hold up)* fulcire, sustinēre; *(to maintain)* alere; *(children) (leg)* exhibēre; *(to help)* adiuvare; *(to back)* favēre *(w. dat)*

supportable *adj* tolerabil·is -is -e

supporter *s* fau·tor -toris *m* (·trix -tricis *f*)

suppose *tr & intr* opinari, putare; **I — (parenthetical)** ut opinor

supposition *s* opini·o -onis *f*

suppress *tr* comprimere; *(for a time)* reprimere; *(information)* opprimere

suppression *s* suppressi·o -onis *f*

supremacy *s* dominat·us -ūs *m; (supreme power)* imper·ium -(i)i *n;* **to exercise —** dominari

supreme *adj* suprem·us -a -um, summ·us -a -um

supremely *adv* unice, maxime

sure *adj* cert·us -a -um; *(faithful)* fid·us -a -um; **be — to come** facito *(or* fac) modo ut venias; **for —** pro certo; **I am —** mihi persuadeo; **I am — that** ... certus (-a) sum *(w. acc & inf);* **to be —** nempe; **to know for —** certum *(or* pro certo) scire

surely *adv* certe, profecto, quidem

surf *s* aest·us -ūs *m*

surf *tr (comput)* navigare ‖ *intr* tabulā fluctivagā per summas undas prolabi

surface *s* superfici·es -ei *f;* **— of the sea** summum mar·e -is *n*

surfboard *s* tabul·a -ae *f* fluctivaga

surge *s* aest·us -ūs *m*

surge *intr* surgere, tumescere; **to — forward** proruere

surgeon *s* chirurg·us -i *m* (·a -ae *f);* **the — operated on her** chirurgus eam secuit

surgery *s (the art)* chirurgi·a -ae *f; (practice)* man·us -ūs *f;* **to use — on** manum adhibēre *(w. dat)*

surgical *adj* chirurgic·us -a -um

surly *adj* moros·us -a -um et difficil·is -is -e

surmise *s* coniectur·a -ae *f;* **to make —s** opinari

surmise *tr* conicere, opinari

surmount *tr* superare

surmountable *adj* superabil·is -is -e

surname *s* cognom·en -inis *n*

surpass *tr* superare, excedere

surplus *s* residu·um -i *n*

surplus *adj* subsiciv·us -a -um

surprise *s (feeling)* mirati·o -onis *f; (thing)* mir·um -i *n;* **to catch by —** deprehendere; **to feel —** mirari; **to the — of all, he says** ... cunctis improvisis ait ... ; **to take s.o. by —** excipere aliquem incaut·um -am

surprise *tr* de improviso excipere; *(pleasantly)* admirationem movēre *(w. dat); (mil)* opprimere; **to be —d at** mirari, admirari; **to be —d that** ... mirari *(w. acc & inf)*

surprise attack *s* subita incursi·o -onis *f*

surprising *adj* mir·us -a -um

surprisingly *adv* mire, mirabiliter

surrender *s* traditi·o -onis *f; (leg)* cessi·o -onis *f; (mil)* dediti·o -onis *f*

surrender *tr* tradere, dedere ‖ *intr* se dedere, se tradere; **to force a people to —** populum in deditionem venire cogere

surreptitious *adj* furtiv·us -a -um

surreptitiously *adv* furtim

surround *tr* circumdare, cingere

surroundings *spl* vicini·a -ae *f*

survey *s* inspecti·o -onis *f; (of land)* mensur·a -ae *f*

survey *tr* oculis lustrare; *(land)* permetiri

surveyor *s* agrimens·or -oris *m*

survival *s* sal·us -utis *f*

survive *tr* supervivere *(w. dat),* superesse *(w. dat)* ‖ *intr* superst·es -itis esse

surviving *adj* superst·es -itis

survivor *s* superst·es -itis *mf*

susceptible *adj* moll·is -is -e; **— to** obnoxi·us -a -um *(w. dat)*

suspect *s* suspect·us -i *m* (·a -ae *f)*

suspect *tr* suspicari; *(to surmise)* opinari; **to be —ed of** in suspicionem venire quasi *(w. subj)*

suspend *tr* suspendere, differre; **to be — ed from office** summoveri administratione rei publicae

suspense *s* exspectati·o -onis *f; in —* suspens·us -a -um; **to end the —** exspectationem discutere

suspension *s* interrupti·o -onis *f,* intermissi·o -onis *f*

suspicion *s* suspici·o -onis *f;* **to come under — in** suspicionem venire; **to throw — on** suspicionem adiungere ad *(w. acc)*

suspicious *adj* suspic·ax -acis; *(suspected)* suspect·us -a -um

suspiciously *adv* suspiciose

sustain *tr* sustinēre; *(hardships, loss, injury, etc.)* ferre

sustenance *s* vict·us -ūs *m*

suture *s* sutur·a -ae *f*

swab *s* spongi·a -ae *f; (brush)* penicul·us -i *m*

swab *tr* detergēre

swaddling clothes *spl* incunabul·a -orum *npl*

swagger *intr* se iactare

swallow *s* haust·us -ūs *m; (bird)* hirund·o -inis *f*

swallow *tr* vorare; *(liquids)* sorbēre; **to — up** devorare, absorbēre

swamp *s* pal·us -udis *f*

swamp *tr* demergere

swampy *adj* paludos·us -a -um

swan *s* cycn·us -i *m*

swank *adj* laut·us -a -um

swap *tr* permutare; **to — places** loca inter se permutare

swap *s* permutati·o -onis *f*

swarm *s* exam·en -inis *n*

swarm *intr (of bees)* examinare; *(of people)* congregari, frequentare

swarthy *adj* fusc·us -a -um

swathe *s* fasci·a -ae *f*

sway *s* dici·o -onis *f,* imper·ium -(i)i *n;* **to hold — regnare**

sway *tr (to influence)* suadēre *(w. dat)* ‖ *intr* vacillare

swear *tr* iurare; **to — in** sacramento adigere ‖ *intr* iurare; **to — off** eiurare

sweat *s* sud·or -oris *m;* **no —!** non laboro!; **to break a —** insudare

sweat *intr* sudare

sweat suit *s* vest·is -is *f* gymnica
sweep *tr* verrere; **to — s.o. off his feet** aliquem captare; **to — out** everrere ‖ *intr* **to — by** *(to dash by)* praetervolare
sweeper *s (soccer)* lus·or -oris *m* liber, lusr·ix -icis *f* libera
sweet *adj* dulc·is -is -e; *(fig)* bland·us -a -um
sweeten *tr* dulcem *(or* dulce) reddere; *(fig)* lenire
sweetheart *s* delici·ae -arum *fpl,* volupt·as -atis *f,* ocell·us -i *m; (in address)* mea voluptas, mi ocelle
sweetly *adv* dulce; *(fig)* suaviter
sweetness *s* dulced·o -inis *f*
sweets *spl* cuppedi·a -orum *npl*
swell *s* aest·us -ūs *m*
swell *tr* tumefacere ‖ *intr* tumēre; **to — (up)** *(of limbs)* turgēre, se attollere *(opp.* se summittere)
swelling *s* tum·or -oris *m*
swelter *intr* aestu laborare
sweltering *adj* aestuos·us -a -um
swerve *intr* aberrare
swift *adj* cel·er -eris -ere
swiftness *s* celerit·as -atis *f*
swim *intr* natare; **to — across** tranare
swimmer *s* nata·tor -toris *m* (·trix -tricis *f*)
swimming *s* natati·o -onis *f; (of the head)* vertig·o -inis *f*
swimming meet certam·en -inis *n* natatorum
swimming pool *s* piscin·a -ae *f*
swimsuit *s* vest·is -is *f* balnearis
swindle *s* frau·s -dis *f*
swindle *tr* fraudare
swindler *s* frauda·tor -toris *m* (·trix -tricis *f*)
swine *s* sus, suis *mf*
swing *s* oscill·um -i *n*
swing *tr* librare ‖ *intr* oscillare
swipe *tr (to steal)* surripere
Swiss *adj* Helveti·us -a -um
switch *s (whip)* virgul·a -ae *f,* verb·er -eris *n; (change)* transit·us -ūs *m,* commutati·o -onis *f; (electrical)* epitol·ium -(i)i *n* electricum
switch *tr (to whip)* verberare; *(to change)* commutare; **to — off** disiungere ‖ *intr* transire; **to — from wine to water** transire a vino ad aquam; **to — over to the plebs** transire ad plebem
Switzerland *s* Helveti·a -ae *f*
swivel *tr & intr* vertere, volvere
swivel chair *s* sell·a -ae *f* volvens
swollen *adj* tumid·us -a -um
swoon *s* defecti·o -onis *f* animi
swoon *intr* intermor·ior -i -tuus sum
swoop *s* impet·us -ūs *m*
swoop *intr* **to — down on** involare in *(w. acc); to — upon** petere
sword *s* glad·ius -(i)i *m,* ens·is -is *m;* **with fire and —** ferro ignique

swordfish *s* glad·ius -(i)i *m,* xyphi·as -ae *m*
sycamore *s* sycamor·us -i *f*
sycophant *s* sychophant·a -ae *mf*
syllabic *s* syllabic·us -a -um
syllable *s* syllab·a -ae *f;* **—s form words** syllabae faciunt dictiones
syllogism *s* syllogism·us -i *m*
symbol *s* symbol·us -i *m,* sign·um -i *n,* indic·ium -(i)i *n*
symbolic *adj* **to be — of s.th.** signum esse alicuius
symbolically *adv* symbolice
symbolize *tr* repraesentare
symmetrical *adj* congru·ens -entis
symmetry *s* symmetri·a -a *f,* proporti·o -onis *f*
sympathetic *adj* misericor·s -dis
sympathy *s* misericordi·a -ae *f;* **to show — for** commiserari *(w. acc)*
symphony *s* symphoni·a -ae *f,* concent·us -ūs *m*
symposium *s* convent·us -ūs *m; (lit)* collectane·a -orum *npl*
symptom *s* sign·um -i *n,* indic·ium -(i)i *n*
synagogue *s* synagog·a -ae *f*
synchronize *tr* congruentem reddere ‖ *intr* congruere
syndicate *s* societ·as -atis *f*
synod *s* synod·os -i *f*
synonym *s* verb·um -i *n* idem declarans, synonym·um -i *n*
synonymous *adj* idem declaran·s -tis; **a Latin word — with the Greek** verb·um -i *n* Latinum quod idem Graeco valet
synopsis *s* synops·is -is *f,* breviar·ium -(i)i *n*
syntax *s* syntax·is -is *f,* constructi·o -onis *f* verborum
synthesis *s* compositi·o -onis *f; (phil)* rati·o -onis *f* consectaria
synthetic *adj* artificios·us -a -um
syringe *s* clyst·er -eris *m*
system *s* rati·o -onis *f; (phil)* doctrin·a -ae *f*
systematic *adj* ordinat·us -a -um
systematically *adv* certā ratione
systematize *tr* in ordinem redigere

T

tab *s* pittac·ium -(i)i *n; (coll)* rati·o -onis *f* (debiti), impens·a -ae *f;* **to keep —s on** caute obscrvarc; **to pick up the —** rem solvere
tab *tr* designare, notare
tabernacle *s* tabernacul·um -i *n*
table *s* mens·a -ae *f; (list)* ind·ex -icis *m,* tabul·a -ae *f;* **at —** apud mensam; **to clear the —** mensam mundare; *(Roman)* mensam

auferre; **to set the —** mensam ponere; **to sit down at the —** mensae assidere; **to wait on —s** ad mensas ministrare
tablecloth *s* mantil·e -is *n*
table of contents *s* ind·ex -icis *m* capitum; *(often expressed by the passive verb:* —: **Earthquakes; Chasms, etc.** continenter in hoc libro: De Terrae Motibus; De Terrae Hiatibus, etc.)
tablespoon *s* ligul·a -ae *f*
tablet *s* tabul·a -ae *f; (med)* catapot·ium -(i)i *n*
tableware *s* mensae vas·a -orum *npl*
tabulate *tr* in ordinem disponere
tacit *adj* tacit·us -a -um; *(leg)* licit·us -a -um
tacitly *adv* tacite
taciturn *adj* taciturn·us -a -um
tack *s* clavul·us -i *m*
tack *tr* **to — on** *(in sewing)* assuere; *(to add on)* subicere **‖** *intr (of ships)* reciprocari
tackle *tr* obsistere *(w. dat); (to deal with)* tractare
tackle *s (gear)* .apparat·us -ūs *m; (naut)* rudent·es -ium *mpl*
tact *s* urbanit·as -atis *f*
tactful *adj* urban·us -a -um
tactician *s* rei militaris perit·us -i *m*
tactics *spl* belli gerendi rati·o -onis *f; (methods)* rati·o -onis *f* rei gerendae
tadpole *s* ranuncul·us -i *m*
tag *s* appendicul·a -ae *f,* pittac·ium -(i)i *n*
tag *tr* appendiculam *(or* pittacium) affigere *(w. dat); (to touch)* tangere **‖** *intr* **to — along** (con)sequi
tail *s* caud·a -ae *f;* **to turn —** tergum vertere
tail *tr* insequi
taillight *s* lum·en -inis *n* posticum
tailor *tr (to adapt)* aptare, accommodare
tailor *s* vestit·or -oris *m,* vestific·us -i *m* (·a -ae *f)*
tailor shop *s* vestificin·a -ae *f*
taint *s* contagi·o -onis *f; (blemish)* vit·ium -(i)i *n*
taint *tr* inficere; *(fig)* corrumpere
take *tr (in nearly all senses of the English word)* capere; *(w. eagerness or haste)* arripere; *(what is offered)* accipere; *(to require)* requirere; *(to grasp, take hold of)* comprehendere; *(food, drink, poison)* sumere; *(to suppose)* opinari; *(to regard, consider)* accipere, habēre, ducere; *(to endure)* pati; **I can't — it anymore** pati nequeo amplius; **— it easy!** parce *(pl:* parcite)!; **to — a bath** balneo uti; **to — a dislike to** capere odium *(w. gen);* **to — as a certainty** sumere pro certo; **to — aside** seducere; **to — a trip** iter facere; **to — a walk** spatiari; **to — away (from)** adimere *(w. dat),* auferre *(w. dat or*

abl or ab *w. abl);* **to — back** recipere, repetere; **to — by the hand** manu prehendere; **to — captive** capere; **to — charge of** curare; **to — credit for** capere gratiam *(w. gen);* **to — down** *(words of a speaker)* excipere; *(posters, signs)* refigere; **to — flight** fugam capere; **to —** *(a dog)* **for a walk** ducere; **to — for granted** praesumere; **to — from** adimere *(w. dat);* **to — great pains to** in magno negotio habēre *(w. inf);* **to — hold of** *(to grasp)* (com)prehendere; *(of a disease)* capere; **to — in** *(as guest)* recipere; *(to deceive)* decipere, fallere, verba dare *(w. dat);* **to — in hand** suscipere; **to — into consideration** respicere; **to — it hard that** ... graviter ferre *(w. acc & inf);* **to — its name from** nomen capere ex *(w. abl);* **to — leave of your senses** a te exire; **to — notice of** observare; **to — off** *(clothes, shoes, ring, locket)* detrahere; **to — on** suscipere; **to — over** *(a position)* occupare; **to — pains to** in magno negotio habēre *(w. inf);* **to — part in** capessere partem *(w. gen);* **to — place** fieri; **to — pleasure in** capere laetitiam ex *(w. abl);* **to — out** *(to produce)* proferre; *(from storage)* promere; **to — out a loan** pecuniam mutuam sumere; **to — out of his pocket** de sinu proferre; **to — pity on** capere misericordiam *(w. gen);* **to — possession of** occupare; **to — the opportunity** capere occasionem; **to — the place of** occupare locum *(w. gen);* **to — to task** exprobrare; **to — up** *(a day)* consumere; *(a task)* suscipere; *(space)* occupare; *(to snatch up)* corripere; *(arms)* capere; **to — (it) upon oneself** sibi sumere, in se conferre; **to — vengeance on** vindicare **‖** *intr* **I'm —ing off** apoculo *(coll);* **it would — too long to** longum esset *(w. inf);* **to — after** similis esse *(w. gen, esp. of persons; w. dat, esp. of things);* **to — off** abire, proficisci; *(coll)* apoculare; *(of a plane)* avolare; **to — off from** *(e.g., work)* absistere *(w. abl);* **to — over completely** plane tenēre
take *s* praed·a -ae *f; (earnings, profits)* captur·a -ae *f*
take-off *s* avolati·o -onis *f*
tale *s* fabul·a -ae *f; (short tale)* fabell·a -ae *f;* **to tell —s** blaterare
talent *s* talent·um -i *n; (fig)* ingen·ium -(i)i *n*
talented *adj* ingenios·us -a -um, ingenio praedit·us -a -um
talk *s* serm·o -onis *m;* **idle —** nug·ae -arum *fpl;* **small —** sermuncul·us -i *m*
talk *intr* loqui; **to — back (to)** insolenter respondēre *(w. dat);* **to — tough** durae buccae esse; **to — with** colloqui cum *(w. abl)*
talkative *adj* loqu·ax -acis

talker *s (idle)* blater·o -onis *mf*

talk show *s* spectacul·um -i *n* disputativum

tall *adj* alt·us -a -um, cels·us -a -um; *(person)* procer·us -a -um, long·us -a -um; **to be —** procerā staturā esse, longus esse

tally *s* rati·o -onis *f; (scorecard)* tesser·a -ae *f*

tally *intr* convenire, congruere

tambourine *s* tympan·um -i *n*

tame *adj* mansuet·us -a -um

tame *tr* mansuefacere, domare

tamely *adv* mansuete; *(fig)* ignave

tamer *s* domi·tor -toris *m* (·trix -tricis *f*)

taming *s* domit·us -ūs *m*

tamper *intr* **to — with** *(e.g., the jury)* sollicitare; *(writings)* depravare; *(to falsify)* vitiare

tan *tr* colorare; *(by sun)* adurere ‖ *intr* colorari, fuscare

tan *s* adustus col·or -oris *m;* **to get a —** colorari

tangent *s* line·a -ae *f* tangens

tangible *adj* tractabil·is -is -e; *(actual)* solid·us -a -um

tangle *s* nod·us -i *m; (fig)* implicati·o -onis *f*

tangle *tr* nodare, implicare ‖ *intr* **to — with** se implicare in *(w. abl)*

tank *s* lac·us -ūs *m; (mil)* autocurr·us -ūs *m* armatus

tankard *s* canthar·us -i *m*

tanned *adj* adust·us -a -um, colorat·us -a -um

tantalize *tr* vexare

tantamount *adj* pa·r -ris

tantrum *s* acessi·o -onis *f* irae; **to throw a —** accessione irae efferi

tap *s* levis ict·us -ūs *m,* plag·a -ae *f* mollis

tap *tr* leviter ferire; *(wine, etc.)* relin·o -ere relevi; **to — s.o.'s phone** alicuius sermonem telephonicum clam sublegere

tape *s (adhesive)* taeni·a -ae *f* adhaesiva; *(audiotape)* phonotaeniol·a -ae *f; (audiocasette)* phonocaset·a -ae *f*

tape *tr* in phonotaeniolā imprimere, in phonocasetā imprimere

taper *s* cere·us -i *m*

taper *tr* fastigare ‖ *intr* decrescere, fastigari

tape measure *s* taeni·a -ae *f* mensuralis

tape recorder *s* magnetophon·um -i *n*

taper off *intr* decrescere; *(of rain)* detumescere

tapestry *s* tapet·e -is *n*

tapeworm *s* taeni·a -ae *f*

taproom *s* cauponul·a -ae *f*

tar *s* pix, picis *f*

tardily *adv* tarde, lente

tardiness *s* tardit·as -atis *f*

tardy *adj* tard·us -a -um

target *s* scop·us -i *m*

tariff *s* portor·ium -(i)i *n*

tarnish *tr* infuscare ‖ *intr* infuscari

tarpaulin *s* stragul·um -i *n*

tarry *intr* commorari

tart *adj* acerb·us -a -um, ac·er -ris -re

tart *s* scriblit·a -ae *f*

task *s* pens·um -i *n;* **to take to —** exprobrare

taste *s (sense)* gustat·us -ūs *m; (flavor)* sap·or -oris *m; (fig)* iudic·ium -(i)i *n;* **lack of good —** deformit·as -atis *f;* **this is not to my —** hoc non mei stomachi est

taste *tr* gustare ‖ *intr* sapere; **to — bad, good** male, bene sapere; **to — like** reddere saporem *(w. gen),* sapere *(w. acc)*

tasteful *adj* eleg·ans -antis; *(neat in arrangement)* concinn·us -a -um

tastefully *adv* eleganter

tasteless *adj* insipid·us -a -um; *(fig)* insuls·us -a -um

tastelessly *adv* insulse

tasty *adj* sapid·us -a -um

tattered *adj* pannos·us -a -um

tatters *spl* pann·i -orum *mpl;* **to be in —** pannos·us -a -um esse

taunt *s* convic·ium -(i)i *n*

taunt *tr* conviciari; **to — s.o. with his low birth** ignobilitatem alicui obicere

taut *adj* intent·us -a -um

tavern *s* caupon·a -ae *f*

tavern keeper *s* caup·o -onis *m*

tawdry *adj* vil·is -is -e

tax *s* vectig·al -alis *n;* **to impose a — on** victigal imponere *(w. dat);* **to pay —es** vectigalia pensitare

tax *tr* vectigal imponere *(w. dat);* **to — oneself to the utmost** contendere omnes nervos

taxable *adj* vectigal·is -is -e

tax collector *s* exac·tor -toris *m* (·trix -tricis *f*), publican·us -i *m*

taxi *s* raed·a -ae *f* meritoria

tea *s* the·a -ae *f;* **teacup** pocill·um -i *n* theanum; **teapot** hirni·a -ae *f* theana

teach *tr (w. double acc)* docēre; **to — Latin** Latine docēre

teachable *adj* docil·is -is -e

teacher *s* docen·s -tis *mf,* ludi magis·ter -tri *m* (·tr·a -trae *f*)

teaching *s* doctrin·a -ae *f;* **— assistant** *s* hypodidascul·us -i *m* (·a -ae *f*); **— method** rati·o -onis *f* docendi

team *s (sports)* turm·a -ae *f; (of animals)* iug·um -i *n*

tear *s* lacrim·a -ae *f; (a rent)* scissur·a -ae *f;* **to shed —s** lacrimas profundere

tear *tr* scindere; **I can't — myself away from my books** in libris haereo; **to — apart** discindere; **to — down** revellere; *(a building)* diruere; **to — off** abscindere; **to — open** rescindere; **to — out** evellere; **to — to pieces**

(di)laniare, discerpere; **to — up** *(trees, shrubs)* convellere; *(paper)* discindere **‖** *intr (to rush)* volare, ruere; **to — along a road** viam vorare

tease *tr* taxare

teaspoon *s* parvum cochle·ar -aris *n*

teat *s* mamm·a -ae *f*

technical *adj* artificios·us -a -um, technic·us -a -um; **— term** verb·um -i *n* proprium unius disciplinae

technique *s* ar·s -tis *f*, technica rati·o -onis *f*

technology *s* officinarum art·es -ium *fpl*, technologi·a -ae *f*

tedious *adj* lent·us -a -um, taedios·us -a -um; **it would be — to** longum est *(w. inf)*

tedium *s* taed·ium -(i)i *n*

teem *intr* scatēre, redundare

tee shirt *s* colob·ium -(i)i *n*

teenager *s* adulesc·ens -entis *mf*

teeth *spl* dent·es -ium *mpl;* **back —** dentes posteriores; **front —** dentes primores

teethe *intr* dentire

teething *s* dentiti·o -onis *f*

telephone *adj* telephonic·us -a -um; **— book** *s* telephonicus ind·ex -icis *m;* **— call** *s* telephonem·a -atis *n;* **— number** numer·us -is *m* telephonicus; **— receiver** auscultabul·um -i *n*

telephone *s* telephon·um -i *n;* **by —** telephonice; **to call s.o. on the —** aliquem per telephonum vocare; **to speak with s.o. on the —** cum aliquo telephonice colloqui; **the — is ringing** telephonum tinnit; **to use a pay —** telephono monetali uti

telephone *tr* per telephonum vocare *(or* compellare*)*

telephone booth *s* cell·a -ae *f* telephonica

telescope *s* telescop·ium -(i)i *n*

television *s* televisi·o -onis *f; (set)* televisor·ium -(i)i *n;* **to turn on (turn off) the —** televisorium excitare (exstinguere); **to turn down (turn up) the —** vim televisorii remittere (augēre); **to watch —** televisionem spectare

television audience televisor·es -um *mpl*

television broadcast *s* emissi·o -onis *f* televisifica

television channel *s* canal·is -is *m* televisificus

television program *s* programm·a -atis *n* televisificum

television screen *s* quadr·um -i *n* televisificum

television series *s* seri·es -ei *f* televisifica

tell *tr* narrare, referre; *(to show, indicate)* docēre; **— me the truth!** dic mihi verum!; **to — s.o. off** aliquem castigare; **to — s.o. to** *(w. inf)* imperare alicui ut *(w. subj);* **to — you**

the truth ut verum dicam **‖** *intr (to be effective)* pollēre, valēre

teller *s* numera·tor -toris *m* (·trix -tricis *f*)

telltale *adj* partefaci·ens -entis

temerity *s* temerit·as -atis *f*

temper *s (anger)* iracundi·a -ae *f;* **to have a bad —** summā iracundiā esse; **to keep one's — iram** tenēre; **to lose one's —** iracundiā efferri

temper *tr* temperare

temperament *s* indol·es -is *f*

temperamental *adj* instabil·is -is -e; *(excitable)* fervid·us -a -um

temperance *s* temperanti·a -ae *f*

temperate *adj* temperat·us -a -um

temperature *s* temperatur·a -ae *f;* **the — fell below 32 degrees** temperatura lapsa est subter duos et triginta gradūs; **to run a —** febricitare; **what is the —?** quo gradu stat temperatura?

tempest *s* tempest·as -atis *f*, procell·a -ae *f*

tempestuous *adj* procellos·us -a -um

temple *s* templ·um -i *n; (anat)* temp·us -oris *n*

temporal *adj (earthly)* profan·us -a -um

temporarily *adv* ad tempus

temporary *adj* temporari·us -a -um; **— stadium** stadi·um -i *n* ad tempus exstructum

tempt *tr* temptare; **to — fate** experiri casūs

temptation *s* tentati·o -onis *f*

ten *adj* decem [*indecl*]: **— times** decies

tenable *adj* defensibil·is -is -e

tenacious *adj* ten·ax -acis

tenaciously *adv* tenaciter

tenacity *s* tenacit·as -atis *f*

tenant *s* conduc·tor -toris *m* (·trix -tricis *f*); *(of an apartment)* insulari·us -i *m* (·a -ae *f*)

tend *tr* curare **‖** *intr (to be wont)* solēre; **I — to believe** crediderim [*perf subj*]

tendency *s* inclinati·o -onis *f*

tender *adj* ten·er -eris -ere, moll·is -is -e; *(affectionate)* indulg·ens -entis, am·ans -antis; *(sore)* dol·ens -entis

tender *tr* deferre

tenderly *adv* tenere

tenderness *s (softness)* tenerit·as -atis *f; (affection)* indulgenti·a -ae *f*

tendon *s* nerv·us -i *m*

tendril *s (of vine)* pampin·us -i *m; (of plants)* clavicul·us -i *m*

tenement *s* conduct·um -i *n*, insul·a -ae *f*

tenet *s* dogm·a -atis *n*

tenfold *adj* decempl·ex -icis

tennis *s* tenisi·a -ae *f*, tenilud·ium -(i)i *n;* **to play —** tenisiā ludere

tennis ball *s* pil·a -ae *f* tenisiae

tennis court *s* sphaerister·ium -(i)i *n*

tennis match *s* certam·en -inis *f* tenisiae

tennis player *s* teniludi·us -i *m* (·a -ae *f*)

tennis racket *s* reticul·um -i *n* manubriatum

tenor *s (purport)* sens·us -ūs *m; (singer)* cant·or -oris *m* vocis mediae

tense *adj (stretched)* tent·us -a -um; *(anxious)* anxi·us -a -um

tense *s (gram)* temp·us -oris *n*

tension *s* intenti·o -onis *f; (mental strain)* anxiet·as -atis *f*

tent *s* tentor·ium -(i)i *n*

tentative *adj* tent·ans -antis

tenth *adj* decim·us -a -um

tenterhooks *spl* **to be on** — animi pendēre

tenuous *adj* tenu·is -is -e

tenure *s (fixed period)* spat·ium -(i)i *n; (possession)* possessi·o -onis *f; (pol)* imperii temp·us -oris *n; (of a professor)* mun·us -eris *n* perpetuum

tepid *adj* tepid·us -a -um

term *s (word)* appellati·o -onis *f; (limit)* termin·us -i *m; (length of time)* spat·ium -(i)i *n; (semester)* studiorum spatium *n; (math)* termin·us -i *m;* — **of office** spatium (temporis) magistratūs; **on these** —**s** his condicionibus, his legibus; **to accept (dictate, propose, reject)** —**s of peace** condiciones pacis accipere (dicere, ferre, repudiare); **to be on friendly** —**s with a country** in amicitiā populi esse; **to be on good** —**s with** in gratiā esse cum *(w. abl);* **to come to** —**s** pacisc·or -i pactus sum; **to stick by the** —**s** in condicionibus manēre

terminal *adj* extrem·us -a -um

terminal *s* stati·o -onis *f* ultima; *(comput)* terminal·e -is *n*

terminate *tr* terminare **‖** *intr* terminari; *(of words)* cadere

termination *s* terminati·o -onis *f*

termite *s* tered·o -inis *f*

terrace *s* agg·er -eris *m; (patio)* xyst·us -i *m*

terrain *s* locorum sit·us -ūs *m*

terrestrial *adj* terrestr·is -is -e

terrible *adj* terribil·is -is -e

terribly *adv* horrendum in modum

terrific *adj* terrific·us -a -um; *(great)* festiv·us -a -um; —**! euge!**

terrify *tr* terrēre, terrificare

territory *s* a·ger -gri *m,* territor·ium -(i)i *n; (country)* fin·es -ium *mpl*

terror *s* terr·or -oris *m*

terse *adj* press·us -a -um

tersely *adv* presse

test *s* experiment·um -i *n; (exam)* probati·o -onis *f;* **to flunk a** — in probatione cadere; **to pass a** — probationem sustinēre

test *tr* experiri; probare

testament *s* testament·um -i *n;* **New (Old) Testament** Novum (Vetus) Testamentum

testamentary *adj* testamentari·us -a -um

testator *s* testa·tor -toris *m* (·trix -tricis *f*)

testicle *s* testicul·us -i *m*

testify *tr* testificari

testimonial *s* laudati·o -onis *f*

testimony *s (proof)* indicati·o -onis *f; (leg)* testimon·ium -(i)i *n*

test tube *s* catin·us -i *m*

testy *adj* stomachos·us -a -um

tetanus *s* tetan·us -i *m*

tether *s* retinacul·um -i *n*

tether *tr* religare

text *s* verb·a -orum *npl* scriptoris; *(comput)* text·us -ūs *m*

textbook *s* enchirid·ion -(i)i *n,* ars, artis *f*

textile *adj* textil·is -is -e

textile *s* textil·e -is *n*

texture *s* textur·a -ae *f*

than *adv* quam; **less** — minus quam; **more** — plus quam; **other** — alius ac; **sooner** — prius quam

thank *tr* gratias agere *(w. dat);* **no,** — **you** benigne; **no,** — **you just the same** tam gratia est; — **heaven!** sit dis gratia!; — **you for** gratias tibi ago ob *(w. acc)*; — **you for helping me** gratias tibi ago quod me iuvisti

thankful *adj* **to be** — **to** gratiam habere *(w. dat)*

thankfully *adv* grate

thankless *adj* ingrat·us -a -um

thanks *spl* grati·ae -arum *fpl;* — **a lot!** multas gratias!; — **a million!** sescentas gratias!; — **to Caesar, I am free** beneficio Caesaris liber sum; — **to me (you,** *etc.)* meā (tuā, *etc.)* operā; **to give** — gratias agere

thanks *interj* gratias!

thanksgiving *s* gratulati·o -onis *f; (public act)* supplicati·o -onis *f*

Thanksgiving Day Di·es -ei *m* Gratulationis

that *adj* ill·e -a -ud; is, ea id; *(sometimes contemptuous)* ist·e -a -ud

that *pron demonstrative* ill·e -a -ud; is, ea, id; ist·e -a -ud; **that is, if Aquila will allow me** si tamen per Aquilam licerit; — **is to say** videlicet; — **was the life!** illud erat vivere!

that *conj (purpose, result, command)* ut; *(after verbs of fearing)* ne

thatch *s* strament·um -i *n*

thatch *tr* stramento tegere

thaw *tr* (dis)solvere **‖** *intr* tabescere

the *article not expressed in Latin; however to express celebrity, use* ill·e -a -ud: — **Hercules of Xenophon** Hercules Xenophontius ille

the *adv* — ... — quo ... eo; — **less he pursued glory,** — **more it followed him** quo minus gloriam petebat eo magis eum sequebatur

theater *s* theatr·um -i *n;* — **of war** sed·es -is *f* belli

theatrical *adj* theatral·is -is -e

thee *pron* te; **of** — de te; **to** — tibi; **with** — tecum

theft *s* furt·um -i *n*

their *adj* illorum, illarum, illorum; eorum, earum, eorum; — **own** su·us -a -um

them *pron* eos, eas, ea; ill·os -as -a; ist·os -ae -a; **to** — eis, illis, istis

theme *s* (*topic*) materi·a -ae *f,* argument·um -i *n; (essay)* tractat·us -ūs *m*

themselves *pron refl* se; **to** — sibi

themselves *pron intensive* ips·i -ae -a

then *adv (at that time)* tum, tunc; *(after that)* deinde; *(therefore)* igitur, ergo; **now and** — interdum; — **and there** ilico

thence *adv* inde, illinc

thenceforth *adv* dehinc

theologian *s* theolog·us -i *m* (·a -ae *f*)

theological *adj* theologic·us -a -um

theology *s* theologi·a -ae *f*

theoretical *adj* rational·is -is -e

theorizing *s* ratiocinati·o -onis *f*

theory *s* rati·o -onis *f;* **the** — **and practice of war** ratio et usus belli

therapist *s* therapeut·a -ae *m* (·ria -riae *f*)

therapy *s* therapi·a -ae *f*

there *adv* ibi; *(thither)* illuc; — **are** sunt; — **is** est

thereabouts *adv* circa, circiter, fere

thereafter *adv* deinde

thereby *adv* eā re, eo

therefore *adv* itaque, igitur, ergo

therefrom *adv* exinde, ex eo

thereupon *adv* subinde

thermometer *s* thermometr·um -i *n*

thesis *s* thes·is -is *f*

they *pron* ei eae ea; illi illae illa; isti istae ista

thick *adj* crass·us -a -um; *(closely packed)* dens·us -a -um, spiss·us -a -um; **through** — **and thin** per invia

thicken *tr* densare, spissare **‖** *intr* crassescere

thicket *s* frutect·um -i *n*

thickly *adv* dense

thickness *s* crassitud·o -inis *f*

thick-headed *adj* obtus·us -a -um

thick-skinned *adj* callos·us -a -um; *(fig)* dur·us -a -um

thief *s* fur, furis *mf;* **an out and out** — tri·fur -furis *mf*

thievery *s* furt·um -i *n*

thigh *s* fem·ur -oris *n;* **to slap the** — femur percutere

thigh bone *s* cox·a -ae *f*

thimble *s* digital·e -is *n*

thin *adj* tenu·is -is -e, exil·is -is -e; *(lean)* ma·cer -cra -crum; **to become** — macrescere

thin *tr* attenuare; **to** — **out** rarefacere

thine *adj* tu·us -a -um

thing *s* res, rei *f;* **of all** —**s!** edepol!

think *tr* cogitare; *(to believe, imagine, etc.)* putare, credere, opinari; *(upon mature reflection)* aestimare; *(to give one's opinion on)* censēre; *(to surmise)* suspicari; **that is exactly what I** — ita prorsus existimo; **to** — **over** reputare, in mente agitare; **to** — **up** excogitare; **what do you** —**?** quid censes? **‖** *intr* cogitare, putare; **to** — **better of** sententiam mutare de *(w. abl);* **to** — **highly of** magni habēre; **to** — **ill of Crassus** male opinari de Crasso; **to** — **of** memorare, recordari

thinker *s* philosoph·us -i *m*

thinking *s* cogitati·o -onis *f*

thinness *s* tenuit·as -atis *f*

third *adj* terti·us -a -um

third *s* tertia par·s -tis *f*

thirdly *adv* tertio

thirst *s* sit·is -is *f*

thirst *intr* sitire; **to** — **for** *(fig)* appetere

thirstily *adv* sitienter

thirsty *adj* siti·ens -entis

thirteen *adj* tredecim [*indecl*]

thirteenth *adj* terti·us decim·us -a -um

thirtieth *adj* tricesim·us -a -um

thirty *adj* triginta [*indecl*]

this *adj* hic, haec, hoc

thistle *s* cardu·us -i *m*

thither *adv* illuc, eo

thong *s* lor·um -i *n*

thorn *s* spin·a -ae *f;* **crown of** —**s** coron·a -ae *f* spinea

thorn bush *s* vepr·es -is *m*

thorny *adj* spinos·us -a -um; *(fig)* nodos·us -a -um

thorough *adj* perfect·us -a -um

thoroughly *adv* penitus, prorsus, omnino

thoroughbred *adj* generos·us -a -um

thoroughfare *s* perv·ium -(i)i *n*

those *adj* see **that**

thou *pron* tu

though *conj* quamquam, quamvis

though *adv* tamen

thought *s* *(act, faculty)* cogitati·o -onis *f; (product of thinking)* cogitat·um -i *n;* **on second** — cum ego recogito

thoughtful *adj* *(reflecting)* cogitabund·us -a -um; *(careful)* provid·us -a -um; *(kind)* human·us -a -um

thoughtless *adj* inconsult·us -a -um
thoughtlessly *adv* inconsulte, temere
thousand *adj* mille [*indecl*]; **a — times** millies
thousandth *adj* millesim·us -a -um
thrash *tr* verberare
thrashing *s* verber·a -orum *npl*
thread *s* fil·um -i *n; (comput)* seri·es -ei *f* (epistularum electronicarum); **to hang by a — ** *(fig)* filo pendēre
thread *tr* inserere
threadbare *adj* pannos·us -a -um; *(worn-out)* detrit·us -a -um
threat *s (act)* minati·o -onis *f;* **—s** min·ae -arum *fpl*
threaten *tr* minari *(w. acc of thing and dat of person);* **to — s.o. with death** comminari necem alicui ‖ *intr* imminēre, impendēre
threatening *adj* min·ax -acis, minitabund·us -a -um
three *adj* tres, tres, tria; **— times** ter
threefold *adj* tripl·ex -icis
three-headed *adj* tric·eps -itis
three-legged *adj* trip·es -edis
thresh *tr* terere
thresher *s* tribul·um -i *n*
threshing *s* tritur·a -ae *f*
threshing floor *s* are·a -ae *f*
threshold *s* lim·en -inis *n*
thrice *adv* ter
thrift *s* parsimoni·a -ae *f*
thriftily *adv* frugaliter
thriftiness *s* frugalit·as -atis *f*
thrifty *adj* parc·us -a -um, frugal·is -is -e
thrill *s (delight)* delectati·o -onis *f*
thrill *tr* commovēre
thrilling *adj* mirific·us -a -um
thrive *intr* vigēre, virēre; *(to prosper)* se bene habēre
thriving *adj* veget·us -a -um, prosp·er -era -erum
throat *s* fauc·es -ium *fpl*
throb *s* palpitati·o -onis *f*
throb *intr* palpitare; *(of a vein)* agitare
throes *spl* dol·or -oris *m*, ang·or -oris *m*
throne *s* sol·ium -(i)i *n; (fig) (regal power)* regn·um -i *n;* **to restore to the —** restituere in regnum; **to succeed to the —** recipere regnum; *(of emperors)* recipere imperium
throng *s* frequenti·a -ae *f*
throng *intr* **to — around** stipare
throttle *tr* strangulare
throttle *s* epitom·ium -(i)i *n*
through *prep* per *(w. acc); (on account of)* ob *(w. acc)*
through *adv render by compound verb with* trans- *or* per-, *e.g.,* **to read —** perlegere; **— and —** omnino

throughout *adv* prorsus
throughout *prep* per *(w. acc)*
throw *tr* iacere, conicere; *(freq)* iactare; *(to hurl)* conicere; *(esp. missiles)* mittere; **to — an apple at s.o.** aliquem malo petere; **to — a stone at s.o.** impingere lapidem alicui; **to — at** conicere ad, in *(w. acc);* **to — away** abicere; **to — back** reicere; **to — down** deicere; **to — food to the dogs** cibum canibus obicere; **to — in the way of** obicere *(w. dat);* **to — into the fire** proicere in ignem; **to — off** *(a rider)* eicere, excutere; *(clothes, bonds)* exuere; *(to mislead)* auferre; **to — oneself at the feet of s.o.** ad pedes alicuius se proicere; **to — oneself down** *(from a height)* se praecipitare; **to — open** patefacere; **to — out** eicere; **to — out of the game** a campo relegare; **to —** *(e.g., a cloak)* **over s.o.** inicere (pallium) alicui; **to — the book at s.o.** *(fig)* summo iure cum aliquo agere; **to — together** conicere in unum; **to — up** evomere ‖ *intr* **to — up** vomere
throw *s* iact·us -ūs *m*
thrush *s* turd·us -i *m*
thrust *s* impet·us -ūs *m*, ict·us -ūs *m*
thrust *tr* trudere, impellere; **to — back** retrudere; **to — off** detrudere; **to — out** extrudere; **to — together** contrudere
thumb *s* poll·ex -icis *m*
thumb tack *s* cuspidiol·a -ae *f* pollice infixa
thump *s* percussi·o -onis *f;* grav·is sonit·us -ūs *m*
thump *tr* tundere
thunder *s* tonitr·us -ūs *m*
thunder *intr* tonare
thunder bolt *s* fulm·en -inis *n*
thunderstruck *adj* attonit·us -a -um
Thursday *s* di·es -ei *m* Iovis
thus *adv* ita, sic; **and —** itaque
thwart *tr* obstare *(w. dat)*
thy *adj* tu·us -a -um
tiara *s* diadem·a -atis *n*
Tiber *s* Tiber·is -is *(acc: -im) m*
tick *s (insect)* ricin·us -i *m; (clicking)* levis ict·us -ūs *m*
ticket *s* tesser·a -ae *f; (label)* pittac·ium -(i)i *n;* **one-way —** tessera unius cursūs; **round-trip —** tessera itūs reditūsque
ticket agent *s* tesserari·us -i *m* (·a -ae *f)*
ticket window *s* ostiol·um -i *n* tesserarium
tickle *tr & intr* titillare
tickling *s* titillati·o -onis *f*
ticklish *adj* titillatione affect·us -a -um; *(delicate)* periculos·us -a -um, lubric·us -a -um
tide *s* aest·us -ūs *m;* **high —** aestūs access·us -ūs *m;* **low —** aestūs recess·us -ūs *m*
tidiness *s* munditi·a -ae *f*

tidings *spl* nunt·ius -(i)i *m;* **to bring** — **of joy** gaudium nuntiare

tidy *adj* mund·us -a -um

tidy up *tr* mundare, ordinare

tie *s* vincul·um -i *n; (necktie)* focal·e -is *n; (of blood, kinship)* necessitud·o -inis *f; (of a score)* aequalit·as -atis *f* punctorum; **it's a** — *(in sports)* pares sunt

tie *tr* (al)ligare; *(in a knot)* nodare; *(to equal)* aequare; **to be tied down** *(e.g., w. business)* impediri; **to** — **one's hair in a knot** colligere capillos in nodum; **to** — **back** revincire; **to** — **up** alligare; *(a wound)* deligare; *(money)* occupare; *(in work, etc.)* impedire

tier *s* ord·o -inis *m*

tie-up *(on highway)* affluenti·a -ae *f* vehiculorum

tiger *s* tigr·is -is *mf;* —**s roar** tigres fremunt

tight *adj (knot, clothes)* strict·us -a -um, art·us -a -um; *(shoe)* restrict·us -a -um; *(tense)* intent·us -a -um; *(stingy)* sordid·us -a -um; **to be in a** — **spot** in angustiis esse; **to get** — **on wine** se vino devincire

tighten *tr* adstringere

tight-fisted *adj* adstrict·us -a -um

tightly *adv* arte; **too** — **bandaged** nimis adstrict·us -a -um

tigress *s* tigr·is -is *(or* -idis) *f*

tile *s* lamin·a -ae *f* fictilis; *(on roof)* tegul·a -ae *f*

till *conj* dum, donec

till *prep* usque ad *(w. acc);* — **late at night** ad multm noctem; — **late in the day** ad multum diem; **till the month of July** in mensem Iulium

till *tr (the soil)* colere

tillage *s* agricultur·a -ae *f*

tiller *s (person)* agricol·a -ae *m; (helm)* gubernacul·um -i *n*

tilt *tr* proclinare

timber *s* materi·a -ae *f*

time *s* temp·us -oris *n; (age, period)* aet·as -atis *f; (leisure)* ot·ium -(i)i *n; (opportunity)* occasi·o -onis *f; (interval)* invervall·um -i *n; (of day)* hor·a -ae *f;* **after so long a** — tanto intervallo; **ahead of** — ante tempus; **a long** — **already** iamdudum, e.g., **I've been here a long** — **already** iamdudum adsum; **another** — alias; **around the** — **of the battle** sub tempus proelii; **at about the same** — sub idem tempus; **at one** — ... **at another** alias ... alias; **at that** — *(at that hour)* ad id temporis; *(in the past)* tum; **at the right** — ad tempus, tempestive; **at the same** — simul; **at the wrong** — intempestive; **at** —**s** interdum; **a very short** — **ago** modo; **before** — *(prematurely)* ante tempus; **for all future** — in posterum; **for a long** — diu; **for a short** — brevi tempore, paulisper; **for a** — parumper; **for some** — aliquamdiu; **for the first** — primum; **for the** — **being** in tempus; **from that** — **on** ex eo (tempore); **from** — **to** — interdum; **I have no** — non est mihi tempus; **in a short** — brevi; **in** — ad tempus, temperi; **it is high** — to tempus maxime est *(w. inf);* **many** —**s** saepius; **once upon a** — olim; **on** — tempestive, tempori; **there is no** — **to cry** non vacat flēre; **there is no** — **to lose** maturato opus est; **there was a** — **when** tempus erat cum; **to ask what** — **it is** horas quaerere *or* inquirere; **to have** — **for** vacare *(w. dat);* **to make up for lost** — cessata tempora corrigere; **to say what** — **it is** quotas horas nuntiare; **to see what** — **it is** horas inspicere; **to waste** — tempus perdere; **to while away the** — tempus fallere; **what** — **is it?** quota hora est?; **you couldn't have come at a better** — non potuisti magis per tempus advenire

time *tr* clepsydrā *(or* horologio) metiri

timeliness *s* tempestivit·as -atis *f*

timely *adj* tempestiv·us -a -um

timepiece *s* horolog·ium -(i)i *n*

times *(used with numeral adverbs)* e.g., **ten** — decies; **no more than three** — ter nec amplius

timetable *s* horar·ium -(i)i *n*

timid *adj* timid·us -a -um

timidity *s* timidit·as -atis *f*

tin *s* stann·um -i *n*

tin *adj* stanne·us -a -um

tincture *s* col·or -oris *m*

tinder *s* fom·es -itis *m*

tingle *intr* formicare

tinkle *intr* tinnire

tinsel *s* bracteol·a -ae *f*

tint *tr* tingere

tip *s* ap·ex -icis *m,* cacum·en -inis *n; (of sword, horn)* mucr·o -onis *m; (hint)* indic·ium -(i)i *n; (money)* stip·s -is *f;* **on the** — **of the tongue** in labris primoribus; — **of the nose** imus nas·us -i *m*

tip *tr (to make pointy)* praefigere; *(to give a tip to)* stipem dare *(w. dat);* **to** — **over** vergere

tippler *s* pot·or -oris *m*

tipsy *adj* ebriol·us -a -um

tiptoe *adv* in digitos errect·us -a -um

tiptoe *intr* erect·us -a in digitos ambulare

tire *tr* fatigare; **to** — **out** defatigare ‖ *intr* defatigari; **I** — **of** me taedet *(w. gen)*

tire *s* canth·us -i *m* cummeus; **to put air in the** — canthum cummeum inflare

tired *adj* fess·us -a -um; **I am sick and** — **of** me pertaedet *(w. gen);* — **out** defess·us -a -um

tireless *adj* assidu·us -a -um
tiresome *adj* molest·us -a -um
tissue *s* mucin·ium -(i)i *n* chartaceum
tit *(vulg)* *s* mamm·a -ae *f;* **to give s.o. — for tat** alicui par pari respondēre
titanic *adj* ing·ens -entis
tithe *s* decum·a -ae *f*
titillate *tr* titillare
title *s* titul·us -i *m; (of a book)* inscripti·o -onis *f; (of a person)* appellati·o -onis *f; (claim)* iu·s -ris *n*
title *tr* inscribere
title page *s* ind·ex -icis *m*
titter *s* lenis ris·us -us *m*
to *prep often rendered by the dative; (motion, except with names of towns, small islands)* ad *(w. acc),* in *(w. acc); (reaching to)* tenus *(always placed after the case) (w. gen);* **— and fro** huc illuc; **— my, your, his house** ad me, te, eum; **— the country** rus; **up —** usque ad *(w. acc)*
toad *s* buf·o -onis *m*
toast *s (bread)* pan·is -is *m* tostus; *(health)* propinati·o -onis *f;* **to drink a — to** propinare *(w. dat)*
toast *tr* torrēre; *(in drinking)* propinare *(w. dat)*
toaster *s* tostr·um -i *n*
toboggan *s* sclodi·a -ae *f*
toboggan run *s* decurs·us -ūs *m* sclodiae
today *adv* hodie
today *s* hodiernus di·es -ei *m*
toe *s* digit·us -i *m* pedis; **big —** poll·ex -icis *m* (pedis)
toga *s* tog·a -ae *f; (worn by magistrates and freeborn children)* toga praetexta; *(worn by a candidate for office)* toga candida; *(worn by young men on coming of age)* toga virilis *or* toga pura; **to receive the — of manhood** togam virilem sumere
together *adv* simul, unā
toil *s* lab·or -oris *m*
toil *intr* laborare
toilet *s* latrin·a -ae *f* loc·us -i *m* secretus; *(public)* foric·a -ae *f;* **to sit on the —** in sellā familiaricā sedēre
toilet bowl *s* labell·um -i *n* intimum
toilet paper *s* chartul·a -ae *f* hygienica
toilet seat *s* sell·a -ae *f* familiarica
token *s* sign·um -i *n; (memento)* pign·us -eris *n;* **by the same —** eandem ob rem
tolerable *adj* tolerabil·is -is -e; *(fair)* mediocr·is -is -e
tolerably *adv* mediocriter
tolerance *s* patienti·a -ae *f*
tolerant *adj* toler·ans -antis
tolerate *tr* tolerare
toleration *s* tolerati·o -onis *f*

toll *s* vectig·al -alis *n; (at ports)* portor·ium -(i)i *n*
toll booth *s* tabern·a -ae *f* vectigalis rotaris; rotar·ium -(i)i *n*
toll collector *s* exac·tor -toris *m (·trix -tricis f)* vectigalis rotaris
toll call *s* telephonem·a -atis *n* longinquum
toll road *s* vi·a -ae *f* vectigalis rotaris
tomato *s* lycopersic·um -i *n*
tomb *s* sepulcr·um -i *n*
tomboy *s* puell·a -ae *f* puerilis
tombstone *s* stel·a -ae *f*
tomorrow *adv* cras; **day after —** perendie; **— morning** cras mane; **— night** cras nocte; **until —** in crastinum
ton *s* duo milia libras; **to have —s of money** nummorum nummos habēre
tone *s* son·us -i *m; (in painting)* col·or -oris *m*
tongs *spl* for·ceps -cipis *mf*
tongue *s* lingu·a -ae *f; (of shoe)* ligul·a -ae *f;* **to hold one's —** linguam continēre; **his name was on the tip of my —** versabatur mihi nomen in primoribus labris
tonsils *spl* tonsill·ae -arum *fpl*
too *adv* nimis, nimium; *(also)* quoque *(always postpositive);* **— bad about Marcus** male de Marco
tool *s* instrument·um -i *n; (dupe)* minis·ter -tri *m;* **—s** *(comput)* instrumenta
toolbar *s (comput)* tabell·a -ae *f* instrumentorum
tooth *s* den·s -tis *m;* **— and nail** *(fig)* toto corpore et omnibus ungulis
toothache *s* dol·or -oris *m* dentium
toothbrush *s* penicul·us -i *m* dentibus purgandis
toothed *adj* dentat·us -a -um
toothless *adj* edentul·us -a -um
toothpaste *s* past·a -ae *f* dentaria
toothpick *s* dentiscalp·ium -(i)i *n*
top *adj* summ·us -a -um
top *s* ap·ex -icis *m; (of tree)* cacum·en -inis *n; (of house)* fastig·ium -(i)i *n; (toy)* turb·o -inis *m;* **at the — of the page** ab summā paginā; **on —** supra; **on — of that** insuper; **— of the head** vert·ex -icis *m;* **— of the mountain** summus mon·s -tis *m*
top *tr* superare; **to — it off** in summo
topcoat *s* superindument·um -i *n*
top-heavy *adj* praegrav·is -is -e a superiore parte
topic *s* res, rei *f,* argument·um -i *n*
topmost *adj* summ·us -a -um
topography *s* regionis descripti·o -onis *f*
topple *tr* evertere ‖ *intr* titubare

topsy-turvy *adv* everything was — omnia erant sursum deorsum; **to turn everything** — omnia sursum deorsum versare

torch *s* fax, facis *f*

torment *s* torment·um -i *n; (pain inflicted)* cruciat·us -ūs *m*

torment *tr* cruciare

tormentor *s* carnif·ex -icis *mf*

torn *adj* sciss·us -a -um

tornado *s* turb·o -inis *m*

torrent *s* torr·ens -entis *m*

torrid *adj* torrid·us -a -um

tortoise, tortoise shell *s* testud·o -inis *f*

torture *s* torment·um -i *n (almost always used in the plural); (pain inflicted by way of punishment or cruelty)* cruciat·us -ūs *m;* **instruments of** — torment·a -orum *npl;* **to question under** — tormentis quaerere

torture *tr* torquēre, cruciare

torturer *s* tort·or -oris *m*

toss *s* iact·us -ūs *m*

toss *tr* iactare; **to be —ed about** *(at sea)* fluitare ‖ *intr* iactari

total *adj* tot·us -a -um, univers·us -a -um

total *s* summ·a -ae *f*

totalitarian *adj* ab unā factione dominat·us -a -um

totalitarianism *s* dominati·o -onis *f* tyrannica civitatis ab unā factione

totally *adv* omnino, prorsus

totter *intr* titubare

touch *tr* tangere; *(to stir)* movēre; **to — deeply** commovēre ‖ *intr* inter se contingere; **to — on** attingere

touch *s* tact·us -ūs *m;* **to put the finishing —es to** ultimam *(or* summam) manum imponere *(w. dat)*

touch-and-go *adj* anc·eps -itis

touchdown *s* **to make a —** calcem *(or* cretam) attingere

touching *adj* flexanim·us -a -um

touchstone *s (fig)* obruss·a -ae *f*

touchy *adj (person)* stomachos·us -a -um; *(matter)* lubric·us -a -um

tough *adj* dur·us -a -um; *(hardy)* robust·us -a -um; *(difficult)* difficili·is -is -e

toupee *s* galericul·um -i *n;* **to wear a —** galericulo uti

tour *s (rounds)* circuit·us -ūs *m; (abroad)* peregrinati·o -onis *f;* **to complete a three-year — of duty** triennium militiae explēre

tour bus *s* coenautocinet·um -i *n* perigeticum

tour guide *s* mystagog·us -i *m* (·a -ae *f);* dux, ducis *mf* itinerari·us (-a)

tourist *s* peregrina·tor -toris *m* (·trix -tricis *f*)

tournament *s* certam·en -inis *n*

tow *s* stupp·a -ae *f*

tow *tr* remulco trahere

toward *prep* versus *(w. acc),* ad *(w. acc); (of feelings)* erga *(w. acc),* in *(w. acc); (of time)* sub *(w. acc)*

towel *s* gausapin·um -i *n,* mantel·e -is *n; (hand towel)* manuterg·ium -(i)i *n*

tower *s* turr·is -is *f*

tower *intr* **to — over** imminēre *(w. dat)*

towering *adj* excels·us -a -um

towline *s* remulc·um -i *n*

town *s* oppid·um -i *n; (small town)* oppidul·um -i *n*

town hall *s* curi·a -ae *f*

townsman *s* oppidan·us -i *m*

tow truck *s* remulcicarr·us -i *m*

toy *s* ludibr·ium -(i)i *n*

toy *intr* **to — with** ludere cum *(w. abl)*

trace *s* vestig·ium -(i)i *n; (for horses)* helc·ium -(i)i *n;* **no — of a wound** nulla suspici·o -onis *f* vulneris

trace *tr* indagare; *(to outline)* delineare; **to — back to** repetere ab *(w. abl)*

track *tr* indagare; **to — down** indagare; **to — up** *(e.g., a rug)* maculare

track *s* vestig·ium -(i)i *n; (path)* semit·a -ae *f,* call·es -is *m; (the sport)* cursur·a -ae *f; (course laid out for runners)* curricul·um -i *n; (of wheel)* orbit·a -ae *f; (of railroad)* orbit·a -ae *f* ferriviaria; **to keep — of** conspicere

trackless *adj* avi·us -a -um

tract *s (land; treatise)* tract·us -ūs *m*

tractor *s* tractr·um -i *m*

trade *s* commerc·ium -(i)i *n; (profession)* artific·ium -(i)i *n;* **to carry on — in** commercium *(w. gen)* facere

trade *tr* commutare ‖ *intr* mercaturas facere, negotiari

trader *s* merca·tor -toris *m* (·trix -tricis *f*)

tradesman *s* opif·ex -icis *m*

trademark *s* not·a -ae *f*

trade union *s* syndicat·us -ūs *m*

tradition *s* traditi·o -onis *f,* mo·s -ris *m* maiorum; **there is an old —** ab antiquis traditur

traditional *adj* a maioribus tradit·us -a -um

traffic *s* commerc·ium -(i)i *n; (on street)* transit·us -ūs *m,* commeat·us -ūs *m* vehiculorum; **heavy —** celebrit·as -atis *f* viae *(or* viarum); frequenti·a -ae *f* vehiculorum

traffic cop *s* vigil -is *mf* viatori·us (-a)

traffic jam *s* affluenti·a -ae *f* vehicularia

traffic light *s* semiphor·um -i *n* (**red** rubrum; **yellow** flavum; **green** viride)

tragedian *s (playwright)* tragoed·us -i *m; (actor)* tragicus act·or -oris *m*

tragedy *s* tragoedi·a -ae *f*

tragic *adj (lit & fig)* tragic·us -a -um

tragically *adv* tragice

trail *s* vestig·ium -(i)i *n;* *(path)* call·es -is *m*

trail *tr* investigare; *(to drag)* trahere **‖** *intr* trahi; *(to lag)* cunctari

trailer home *s* habitacul·um -i *n* remulcatum

train *s* *(sequence)* seri·es -ei *f,* ord·o -inis *m;* *(of robe)* peniculament·um -i *n;* *(retinue)* comitat·us -ūs *m;* *(rail)* tram·en -inis *n* (ferriviarium); **a through** — tramen directum

train *tr* instituere, exercēre; *(to habituate)* assuefacere **‖** *intr* se exercitare

trainer *s* exerci·tor -toris *m* (·trix -tricis *f); (of gladiators)* lanist·a -ae *m*

training *s* instituti·o -onis *f; (practice)* exercitati·o -onis *f*

train schedule *s* horar·ium -(i)i *n* traminum

train station *s* stati·o -onis *f* ferriviaria

train ticket *s* tesser·a -ae *f* ferriviaria

trait *s* mos, moris *m*

traitor *s* prodi·tor -toris *m* (·trix -tricis *f*)

traitorous *adj* perfid·us -a -um

tramp *s* vagabund·us -i *m* (·a -ae *f),* larifug·a -ae *m; (of feet)* puls·us -ūs *m*

tramp *intr* grad·ior -i gressus sum

trample *tr* proterere; **to** — **underfoot** conculcare **‖** *intr* **to** — **on** proterere

trampoline *s* desultor·ium -(i)i *n*

trance *s* stup·or -oris *m;* **in a** — in excessu mentis; **she fell into a** — cecidit super eam mentis excessus

tranquil *adj* tranquill·us -a -um

tranquility *s* tranquillit·as -atis *f*

tranquilize *tr* tranquillare

transact *tr* transigere, agere

transaction *s* negot·ium -(i)i *n*

transatlantic *adj* transatlantic·us -a -um

transcend *tr* superare, antecedere

transcendental *adj* sublim·is -is -e

transcribe *tr* transcribere

transcript *s* exempl·um -i *n*

transcription *s* transcripti·o -onis *f*

transfer *s* translati·o -onis *f; (of property)* alienati·o -onis *f*

transfer *tr* transferre; *(property)* abalienare **‖** *intr* — **to** *(another train, etc.)* transcendere in *(w. acc)*

transference *s* translati·o -onis *f*

transfigure *tr* transfigurare

transform *tr* vertere, commutare

transformation *s* commutati·o -onis *f*

transgress *tr* violare, perfringere

transgression *s* violati·o -onis *f; (deed)* delict·um -i *n*

transgressor *s* viola·tor -toris *m* (·trix -tricis *f*)

transient *adj* transitori·us -a -um

transition *s* transit·us -ūs *m*

transitive *adj* transitiv·us -a -um

transitively *adv* transitive

transitory *adj* transitori·us -a -um

translate *tr* (con)vertere, transferre; **to** — **into Latin** in Latinum (sermonem) convertere; **to** — **from Latin to English** ex Latino in Anglicum (con)vertere

translation *s* translat·a -orum *npl; (act of translating)* translati·o -onis *f*

translator *s* interpr·es -etis *mf*

transmission *s* transmissi·o -onis *f*

transmit *tr* transmittere

transmutation *s* transmutati·o -onis *f*

transparency *s* pagin·a -ae *f* pellucida

transparent *adj* pellucid·us -a -um; *(fig)* perspicu·us -a -um

transpire *intr (to happen)* fieri

transplant *tr* transferre, transponere; *(med)* inserere

transport *tr* transportare, transvehere

transport *s* vectur·a -ae *f; (ship)* nav·is -is *f* oneraria; *(rapture)* sublimit·as -atis *f*

transportation *s* vectur·a -ae *f*

transpose *tr* transponere

trap *s* laque·us -i *m,* pedic·a -ae *f; (fig)* insidi·ae -arum *fpl*

trap *tr* irretire; *(fig)* inlaqueare

trappings *spl* apparat·us -ūs *m; (of horse)* phaler·ae -arum *fpl*

trash *s* scrut·a -orum *npl; (fig)* nug·ae -arum *fpl*

trashy *adj (cheap)* vil·is -is -e; *(obscene)* obscen·us -a -um

travel *tr* **to** — **a road** viā ire **‖** *intr* iter facere; **to** — **abroad** peregrinari; **to** — **by car (train, plane, ship)** autoraedā (tramine, aëroplano, navi) vehor vehi vectus sum

travel agency *s* sed·es -is *f* perigetica

travel agent *s* itinerum procura·tor -toris *m* (·trix -tricis *f*)

traveler *s* viat·or -oris *mf; (abroad)* peregrina·tor -toris *m* (·trix -tricis *f*)

traverse *tr* peragrare, lustrare

travesty *s* perversa imitati·o -onis *f*

tray *s* fercul·um -i *n*

treacherous *adj* perfid·us -a -um; **to be on** — **ground** in lubrico versari

treacherously *adv* perfide

treachery *s* perfidi·a -ae *f*

tread *tr* calcare **‖** *intr* incedere; **to** — **on** insistere *(w. dat),* calcare

tread *s* incess·us -ūs *m*

treason *s* perduelli·o -onis *f,* maiest·as -atis *f*

treasonable *adj* perfid·us -a -um (contra civitatem)

treasure *s* thesaur·us -i *m,* gaz·a -ae *f*

treasure *tr* fovēre, magni aestimare

treasurer *s* aerari praefect·us -i *m* (·a -ae *f*)

treasury *s* arc·a -ae *f; (of the state)* aerar·ium -(i)i *n; (of the emperor)* fisc·us -i *m*

treat *s* oblectament·um -i *n;* **it's my —** meo sumptu convivium est

treat *tr* uti *(w. abl),* tractare; *(patient)* curare; *(topic)* tractare; *(to entertain)* impensam sumere pro *(w. abl)*

treatise *s* commentati·o -oni *f*

treatment *s* tractati·o -onis *f; (med)* **(for)** curati·o -onis *f (w. gen of illness)*

treaty *s* foed·us -eris *n;* **according to the terms of the —** ex pacto, ex foedere; **to break a —** foedus frangere; **to conclude a —** foedus icere; **to violate a —** foedus violare

treble *adj* tripl·ex -icis; *(of sound)* acut·us -a -um

tree *s* arb·or -oris *f*

treetop cacum·en -inis *n*

trellis *s* cancell·i -orum *mpl*

tremble *intr* tremere; **to — all over** contremere

trembling *adj* tremul·us -a -um

trembling *s* trem·or -oris *m*

tremendous *adj* imman·is -is -e

tremendously *adv* valde, vehementer

tremulous *adj* tremul·us -a -um

trench *s* foss·a -ae *f;* **to dig a —** fossam fodere

trend *s* inclinati·o -onis *f*

trespass *intr* in alienum fundum ingredi (sine domini permissu)

trespass *n* peccat·um -i *n*

tress *s* crin·is -is *m*

trestle *s* fulciment·um -i *n*

trial *s (attempt)* conat·us -ūs *m; (experiment)* experienti·a -ae *f; (test)* probati·o -onis *f; (suffering)* tribulati·o -onis *f; (leg)* quaesti·o -onis *f;* iudic·ium -(i)i *n;* **to be on — for** iudicium de *(w. abl)* subire; **to conduct a —** quaestionem exercēre; **to go to — in ius ire**

trial lawyer *s* ac·tor -toris *m* (·trix -tricis *f)* causarum

triangle *s* triangul·um -i *n*

triangular *adj* triquetr·us -a -um

tribe *s* trib·us -ūs *f*

tribulation *s* tribulati·o -onis *f*

tribunal *s (law court)* iudic·ium -(i)i *n; (platform)* tribun·al -alis *n;* **on the — pro tribunali**

tribune *s* tribun·us -i *m;* **plebeian — tribunus plebis**

tribuneship *s* tribunat·us -ūs *m*

tribunician power *s* tribunicia potest·as -atis *f*

tributary *adj* vectigal·is -is -e

tributary *s (river)* amn·is -is *m* in alium influens

tribute *s* vectig·al -alis *n,* tribut·um -i *n;* **to pay a — to s.o.** aliquem laudibus debitis efferre

trick *s* dol·us -i *m; (feat of skill)* stroph·a -ae *f;* **is this a — ?** num hoc est captio?; **to play a — on s.o.** aliquem ludificari

trick *tr* fallere, deludere

trickle *s* stillicid·ium -(i)i *n*

trickle *intr* stillare

trickster *s* veterat·or -oris *mf*

tricky *adj* dolos·us -a -um; *(difficult)* nodos·us -a -um

tricycle *s* trirot·a -ae *f*

trident *s* trid·ens -entis *m*

triennial *adj* trienn·is -is -e

trifle *s* res, rei *f* parva; *(a little)* paul·um -i *n; (somewhat)* paululum; **—s** nug·ae -arum *fpl*

trifle *intr* nugari

trifling *adj* parv·us -a -um, exigu·us -a -um

trigger *s* ligul·a -ae *f* (sclopeti)

trigger *tr (fig)* facessere

trigonometry *s* trigonometri·a -ae *f*

trill *tr* vibrare

trim *adj* compt·us -a -um

trim *tr* adornare; *(to prune)* putare; *(the hair)* tondēre

trim *s* **to be in — boni** habitūs esse

trimmings *spl* ornat·us -ūs *m*

trinket *s* ornament·um -i *n*

trio *s* trini·o -onis *f*

trip *s* it·er -ineris *n;* **to take a — iter facere**

trip *tr* pedem opponere *(w. dat); (fig)* fallere ‖ *intr* pedem offendere; *(fig)* errare, labi

tripartite *adj* tripartit·us -a -um

tripe *s* omas·um -i *n*

triple *adj* tripl·ex -icis

triple *tr* triplicare

triplets *s* trigemin·i -orum *mpl*

tripod *s* trip·us -odis *m* (photographicus)

trireme *s* trirem·is -is *f*

trisyllabic *adj* trisyllab·us -a -um

trite *adj* trit·us -a -um

triumph *s (victory)* victori·a -ae *f; (entry of victorious general)* triumph·us -i *m;* **to celebrate a — triumphum agere**

triumph *intr* triumphare; **to — over** devincere; *(of a general)* triumphare de *(w. abl)*

triumphal *adj* triumphal·is -is -e

triumphant *adj (masc)* vict·or -oris *m; (fem)* victr·ix -icis

trivial *adj* lev·is -is -e

triviality *s* nug·ae -arum *fpl*

trolley *s* curr·us -ūs *m* electricus

trombone *s* tub·a -ae *f* ductilis

troop *s* caterv·a -ae *f; (of cavalry)* turm·a -ae *f;* **—s** copi·ae -arum *fpl*

trooper *s (coll)* veteran·us -i *m*

trophy *s* tropae·um -i *n*

tropical *adj* torrid·us -a -um

tropics *spl* zon·a -ae *f* torrida

trot *intr* tolutim ire

trouble *s* mal·um -i *n,* lab·or -oris *m,* aerumn·a -ae *f; (annoyance)* molesti·a -ae *f; (effort, pains)* oper·a -ae *f;* **if it is no —** si grave non erit; **it's not worth the —** non est pretium operae; **to be in —** laborare; **to cause s.o. (big) —** alicui molestiam (gravem) adhibēre; **to get s.o. into —** in aliquem aerumnam obserere; **to have stomach —** stomacho laborare; **to make a heap of — for s.o.** magnum malum alicui dare; **to take the — to …** operam dare ut *(w. subj);* **what's the —?** quid negoti est?

trouble *tr* vexare, angere; **I don't want to — you** nolo tibi molest·us (-a) esse

troubled *adj* confus·us -a -um; *(times)* turbulent·us -a -um; **— face** vult·us -ūs *m* exercitatus; **to be — with** laborare ex *(w. abl)*

troublemaker *s* turba·tor -toris *m* (·trix -tricis *f)*

troublesome *adj* operos·us -a -um; *(person)* molest·us -a -um

trough *s* alve·us -i *m*

trounce *tr (to punish)* castigare; *(to defeat decisively)* devincere

troupe *s* grc·x -gis *m*

trousers *spl* brac·ae -arum *fpl*

trout *s* truct·a -ae *f*

trowel *s* trull·a -ae *f*

truant *s* cessa·tor -toris *m* (·trix -tricis *f);* **to play —** insciis parentibus a scholā abesse

truce *s* induti·ae -arum *fpl;* **during the —** per indutias; **to agree to a —** indutias cum hostibus pacisci; **to break off a —** indutias tollere

truck *s* autocarr·um -i *n*

truck driver autocarri gubernat·or -oris *m*

trudge *intr* repere; **to — over many places** plura loca calcare

true *adj* ver·us -a -um; *(genuine)* german·us -a -um; *(faithful)* fid·us -a -um; *(exact)* rect·us -a -um; **that's —** verum dicis *or* res ita est

truffle *s* tub·er -eris *n* (cibarium)

truism *s* ver·um -i *n* tritum

truly *adv* vere, profecto

trump *tr* **to — up** effingere

trumpet *s (mil)* tub·a -ae *f,* aes, aeris *n; (for civilian purposes)* buccin·a -ae *f; (of an elephant)* barrit·us -ūs *m*

trumpet *intr (of an elephant)* barrire

trumpeter *s* buccinat·or -oris *m*

truncheon *s* fust·is -is *m*

trundle *intr* volvere

trunk *s (of tree, of body)* trunc·us -i *m; (for clothes)* cist·a -ae *f; (of car)* receptacul·um -i *n* sarcinarum; *(of elephant)* probosc·is -is *f,* man·us -ūs *f*

trust *s* fiduci·a -ae *f,* fid·es -ei *f;* **to put one's — in** (con)fidere *(w. dat)*

trust *tr (persons or acts)* fidere *(w. dat); (esp. words spoken)* credere *(w. dat); (to entrust)* committere; **not — his eyes** fidem oculorum timēre ‖ *intr* **to — in** fidere *(w. dat)*

trustee *s* fiduciari·us -i *m* (·a -ae *f)*

trusteeship *s* tutel·a -ae *f*

trustful *adj* credul·us -a -um

trusting *adj* (con)fid·ens -entis

trustingly *adv* fidenter

trustworthiness *s* fid·es -ei *f*

trustworthy *adj* fid·us -a -um; *(witness)* locupl·es -etis

trusty *adj* fid·us -a -um

truth *s (abstract)* verit·as -atis *f; (concrete)* ver·um -i *n;* **in —** vero; **this is the —** haec sunt vera; **to speak the —** verum dicere; **to tell the —** ut verum *(or* vera) dicam *(or* loquar)

truthful *adj* ver·ax -acis

truthfully *adv* veraciter

try *tr* conari, tentare, temptare; *(to put to the test)* experiri; *(leg)* iudicare; *(to hold a judicial inquiry of)* cognoscere; **to — a case (of)** causam cognoscere (de *w. abl);* **to — one's best to (not to)** operam dare ut (ne) *(w. subj);* **to — one's patience** patientiā abuti; **to — to obtain** affectare

trying *adj* incommod·us -a -um, molest·us -a -um

tryout *s* prolusi·o -onis *f*

T-shirt *s* colob·ium -(i)i *n*

tub *s* labr·um -i *n*

tube *s* tubul·us -i *m,* fistul·a -ae *f*

tuberculosis *s* phithis·is -is *f*

tuck *s* plic·a -ae *f*

tuck *tr* **to — up** succingere; **with tunic —ed up** succinct·us -a -um

Tuesday *s* di·es -ei *m* Martis

tufa *s* tof·us *or* toph·us -i *m*

tuft *s* flocc·us -i *m*

tug *s* tract·us -ūs *m; (ship)* nav·is -is *f* tractoria

tug *tr* trahere ‖ *intr* **to — at** vellicare

tugboat *s* nav·is -is *f* tractoria

tuition *s* minerv·al -alis *n*

tumble *intr* volvi, corruere

tumbler *s* pocul·um -i *n* vitreum

tumor *s* tum·or -oris *m*

tumult *s* tumult·us -ūs *m*

tumultuous *adj* tumultuos·us -a -um

tuna *s* thunn·us -i *m*

tune *s* cant·us -ūs *m;* **in —** conson·us -a -um; **out of —** abson·us -a -um; **to be out of —** discrepare; **to change one's —** recantare; **to the — of** ad numerum *(w. gen)*

tuneful *adj* canor·us -a -um

tunic *s* tunic·a -ae *f;* **long-sleeved** — tunica *f* manicata; **small** — tunicul·a -ae *f;* — **reaching to the ankles** tunica *f* talaris; **wearing a** — tunicat·us -a -um

tunnel *s* cunicul·us -i *m;* *(for cars, trains)* spec·us -ūs *m* (autocineticus, ferriviarius)

turban *s* mitr·a -ae *f*

turbid *adj* turbid·us -a -um

turbulence *s* agitati·o -onis *f;* *(air)* flabr·a -orum *npl* violenta

turbulent *adj* turbulent·us -a -um

turf *s* caesp·es -itis *m*

turgid *adj* turgid·us -a -um

turkey *s* gallopav·o -onis *m;* **to talk** — *(coll)* Latine loqui

turmoil *s* perturbati·o -onis *f;* **mental** — animi commoti·o -onis *f*

turn *s* *(in the road)* flex·us -ūs *m* viae, anfract·us -ūs *m;* *(circuit)* circuit·us -ūs *m;* *(revolution)* conversi·o -onis *f;* *(change, course)* vicissitud·o -inis *f;* *(inclination of the mind)* inclinati·o -onis *f;* **a good** — benefic·ium -(i)i *n;* **at every** — omnibus ex partibus; **in** — invicem; **it's your** — **now** nunc te ordo vocat; **out of** — extra ordinem; **to take a** — **for the better, worse** in melius, in peius inclinari; **to take** —**s driving** invicem *(or* per vices, in vices) gubernare

turn *tr* (con)vertere; *(to twist)* torquēre; *(to bend)* flectere; **to** — **around** circumagere, volvere; **to** — **aside** deflectere; **to** — **away** avertere; **to** — **back** convertere; **to** — **down** *(to refuse)* recusare, detrectare; **to** — **into** vertere in *(w. acc);* **to** — **loose** liberare; **to** — **off** *(computer, light)* exstinguere; **to** — **on** *(light)* accendere; *(computer)* excitare; **to** — **over** *(to hand over)* tradere; *(property)* alienare; *(in the mind)* agitare; *(to upset)* evertere; **to** — **over a new leaf** se reformare; **to** — **over the pages of a book** librum evolvere; **to** — **one's attention to** animadvertere; **to** — **out** eicere; **to** — **up** *(w. hoe)* invertere; **to** — **up the nose** nares corrugare; **to** — **upside down** quod sursum est, deorsum facere **‖** *intr* verti, versari; **something will turn up, I hope** fiet aliquid, spero; **to** — **against** disciscere ab *(w. abl);* **to** — **around** converti; **to** — **aside** se declinare; **to** — **away** aversari; **to** — **back** reverti; **to** — **into** mutari in *(w. acc),* vertere in *(w. acc);* **to** — **out** evenire, evadere; **to** — **out fine** belle cadere; **to** — **up** *(to occur)* intervenire; *(to show up)* apparēre

turncoat *s* transfug·a -ae *mf*

turnip *s* rap·um -i *n*

turn-off *s* deverticul·um -i *n*

turnout *s* concurs·us -ūs *m*

turnpike *s* autocinetica vi·a -ae *f* quadripertita

turn signal *s* ind·ex -icis *m* directionis

turnstile *s* port·a -ae *f* volubilis

turpentine *s* terebinthina resin·a -ae *f*

turquoise *adj* turcic·us -a -um

turret *s* turricul·a -ae *f*

turtle *s* testud·o -inis *f*

tusk *s* den·s -tis *m*

tutelage *s* tutel·a -ae *f*

tutor *s* domesticus praecep·tor -toris *m,* domestica praecep·trix -tricis *f*

tutor *tr* privatim instituere

TV *(see* **television)**

TV room *s* conclav·e -is *n* televisorio instructum

tweezers *spl* volsell·a -ae *f*

twelfth *adj* duodecim·us -a -um

twelve *adj* duodecim [*indecl*]; — **times** duodecies

twentieth *adj* vicesim·us -a -um

twenty *adj* viginti [*indecl*]; — **times** vicies

twice *adv* bis

twig *s* ramul·us -i *m*

twilight *s* *(evening)* crepuscul·um -i *n;* *(early dawn)* dilucul·um -i *n*

twilight *adj* sublucan·us -a -um

twin *adj* gemin·us -a -um

twin *s* gemin·us -i *m* (·a -ae *f),* gemell·us -i *m* (·a -ae *f)*

twine *s* fil·um -i *n*

twine *tr* circumplicare **‖** *intr* **to** — **around** circumplecti *(w. acc)*

twinge *s* dol·or -oris *m;* **to suffer such** —**s of conscience that** ita conscientia mentem excitam vexat ut

twinkle *s* nit·or -oris *m,* scintill·a -ae *f;* *(in one's eyes)* nict·us -ūs *m*

twinkle *intr* micare

twinkling *s* *(of eye)* nict·us -ūs *m*

twirl *tr* versare, circumagere **‖** *intr* versari

twist *tr* torquēre **‖** *intr* se torquēre

twit *tr* obiurgare

twitch *s* vellicati·o -onis *f*

twitch *tr* vellicare **‖** *intr* formicare

twitter *s* pipul·um -i *n*

twitter *intr* pipilare

two *adj* duo, duae, duo; — **at a time, two each** bin·i -ae -a; — **camps** bina castr·a -orum *npl;* — **times** bis

two-bit *adj (worthless)* sestertiari·us -a -um

two-edged *adj* anc·eps -ipitis; — **ax** bipenn·is -is *f*

two-faced *adj (pej)* bilingu·is -is -e

twofold *adj* dupl·ex -icis

two-footed *adj* bip·es -edis

two-headed *adj* bic·eps -ipitis

two hundred *adj* ducent·i -ae -a

two-pronged *adj* bid·ens -entis

twosome *s* par, paris *n*
two-time *tr* fraudare
two-timer *s* infidel·is is *mf*
two-way *adj* bivi·us -a -um
tycoon *s* magnat·us -i *m*
type *s* exempl·um -i *n; (class)* gen·us -eris *n; (print)* typ·i -orum *mpl;* **that — of person** istius generis homo; **this — of speech** huius generis orati·o -onis *f*
type *tr* dactylographare
typesetter *s* typothet·a -ae *m* (·ria -riae *f*)
typewriter *s* dactylograph·ium -(i)i *n*
typewriter key *s* malleol·us -i *m*
typing *s* dactylphraphica ar·s -tis *f*
typist *s* dactylograph·us -i *m* (·a -ae *f*)
typhoon *s* turb·o -inis *f* violenta
typical *adj* typic·us -a -um
typically *adv* per typum
typify *tr* repraesentare, imaginem *(w. gen)* fingere
typist *s* scrib·a -ae *mf*
tyrannical *adj* tyrannic·us -a -um
tyrannically *adv* tyrannice
tyrannicide *s (act)* tyrannicid·ium -(i)i *n; (person)* tyrannicid·a -ae *m*
tyrant *s* tyrann·us -i *m*
tyranny *s* tyrann·is -idis *f*
tyro *s* tir·o -onis *mf*
Tyrrhenian *adj* Tyrrhenic·us a um

U

ubiquitous *adj* ubique praes·ens -entis
udder *s* ub·er -eris *n*
ugh *interj* vah!; heu!
ugliness *s* deformit·as -atis *f*
ugly *adj* deform·is -is -e; **to make —** deformare
uh-oh *interj (when taken by surprise)* attat!; attatae!
ulcer *s* ulc·us -eris *n*
ulcerate *intr* ulcerari
ulcerous *adj* ulceros·us -a -um
ulterior *adj (place)* ulter·ior -ior -ius; *(time)* poster·us -a -um; **— motive** rati·o -onis *f* recondita
ultimate *adj* ultim·us -a -um
ultimately *adv* ad ultimum, denique
ultimatum *s* propositi·o -onis *f* ultima
umbilical cord *s* umbilic·us -i *m*
umbrage *s* **to take — at** aegre ferre
umbrella *s* umbell·a -ae *f*
umpire *s* arbi·ter -tri *m* (·tra -trae *f*)

unabashed *adj* intrepid·us -a -um; *(pej)* impud·ens -entis
unabated *adj* continu·us -a -um
unable *adj* **(to)** nequi·ens -entis *(w. inf);* **— to control his anger** impot·ens -entis irae; **— to keep up with the words of the speaker** male subsequ·ens -entis verba dicentis; **to be — to** non posse *or* nequire *(w. inf)*
unabridged *s* complet·us -a -um
unaccented *adj* accentu car·ens -entis, sine ictu
unacceptable *adj* **(to)** invis·us -a -um *(w. dat)*
unaccompanied *adj* incomitat·us -a -um
unaccomplished *adj* infect·us -a -um
unaccountable *adj* inenodabil·is -is -e
unaccountably *adv* praeter opinionem
unaccustomed *adj* insuet·us -a -um
unacquainted *adj* **— with** ignar·us -a -um *(w. gen)*, exper·s -tis *(w. gen)*
unadorned *adj* inornat·us -a -um
unadulterated *adj* mer·us -a -um
unaffected *adj* simpl·ex -icis
unafraid *adj* impavid·us -a -um
unaided *adj* non adiut·us -a -um
unalterable *adj* immutabil·is -is -e
unaltered *adj* immutat·us -a -um
unanimous *adj* unanim·us -a -um
unanimously *adv* consensu omnium, unā voce
unanswerable *adj* irrefragabil·is -is -e
unappeased *adj* implacat·us -a -um
unappreciative *adj* ingrat·us -a -um
unapproachable *adj* inaccess·us -a -um
unarmed *adj* inerm·is -is -e
unasked *adj* iniuss·us -a -um
unassailable *adj* inexpugnabil·is -is -e
unassuming *adj* modest·us -a -um
unattached *adj* vacu·us -a -um, solut·us -a -um; *(unmarried)* cael·eb·s -ebis
unattainable *adj* ardu·us -a -um, inaccess·us -a -um
unattended *adj (unaccompanied)* sine comitatu; *(not cared for)* neglect·us -a -um; **— by pain** privat·us -a -um dolore
unattractive *adj* invenust·us -a -um
unauthorized *adj* illicit·us -a -um
unavailable *adj* non expedit·us -a -um
unavailing *adj* inutil·is -is -e
unavenged *adj* inult·us -a -um
unavoidable *adj* inevitabil·is -is -e
unaware *adj* insci·us -a -um
unbearable *adj* intolerabil·is -is -e
unbeaten *adj* invict·us -a -um
unbecoming *adj* indecor·us -a -um; **it is —** dedecet
unbefitting *adj* indecor·us -a -um
unbend *intr* animum remittere
unbending *adj* inflexibil·is -is -e

unbiased *adj* sine ira et studio
unbidden *adj* iniuss·us -a -um
unbind *tr* revincire
unbleached *adj* crud·us -a -um
unblemished *adj* intact·us -a -um
unblest *adj* infortunat·us -a -um
unbolt *tr* reserare
unborn *adj* nondum nat·us -a -um
unbounded *adj* infinit·us -a -um
unbridled *adj (lit & fig)* infren·is -is -e
unbroken *adj* irrupt·us -a -um; *(of horses)* indomit·us -a -um
unbuckle *tr* refibulare
unburden *tr* exonerare
unburied *adj* inhumat·us -a -um
unbutton *tr* diloricare
uncalled-for *adj* alien·us -a -um
uncanny *adj* mir·us -a -um
uncared-for *adj* neglect·us -a -um
unceasing *adj* assidu·us -a -um
unceasingly *adv* assidue, sine fine
uncertain *adj* incert·us -a -um; **to be —** haerēre, vacillare
uncertainty *s* dubitati·o -onis *f*
unchangeable *adj* immutabil·is -is -e
unchanged *adj* immutat·us -a -um
unchanging *adj* immutat·us -a -um
uncharitable *adj* immisericor·s -dis
unchaste *adj* parum cast·us -a -um
uncivil *adj* inurban·us -a -um
uncivilized *adj* incult·us -a -um
unclasp *tr* refibulare
uncle *s (father's brother)* patru·us -i *m; (mother's brother)* avuncul·us -i *m;* **great —** magnus patruus *(or* avunculus) *m*
unclean *adj* immund·us -a -um
uncombed *adj* inpex·us -a -um
uncomfortable *adj* incommod·us -a -um
uncommon *adj* rar·us -a -um; *(outstanding)* egregi·us -a -um
uncommonly *adv* praeter solitum
uncomplaining *adj* pati·ens -entis
unconcerned *adj* incurios·us -a -um
unconditional *adj* sine exceptione
unconditionally *adv* nullā condicione
unconnected *adj* disiunct·us -a -um
unconquerable *adj* invict·us -a -um
unconscionable *adj* iniqu·us -a -um
unconscious *adj* omni sensu car·ens -entis; **— of** ignar·us -a -um *(w. gen)*, insci·us -a -um *(w. gen)*
unconstitutional *adj* illicit·us -a -um
uncontrollable *adj* impot·ens -entis
uncontrolled *adj* effrenat·us -a -um
unconventional *adj* insolit·us -a -um
unconvinced *adj* **I am — that** non adductus sum ut credam *(w. acc & inf)*

unconvincing *adj* non verisimil·is -is -e
uncooked *adj* crud·us -a -um
uncorrupted *adj* incorrupt·us -a -um
uncouth *adj* inurban·us -a -um
uncover *tr* detegere
uncritical *adj* credul·us -a -um
uncultivated *adj* incult·us -a -um
uncut *adj (hair)* intons·us -a -um; *(wood)* incaedu·us -a -um
undamaged *adj* incolum·is -is -e
undaunted *adj* intrepid·us -a -um
undecided *adj* anc·eps -ipitis; **— whether ... or** cunctat·us -a -um utrum ... an
undefended *adj* indefens·us -a -um
undefiled *adj* incontaminat·us -a -um
undeniable *adj* haud dubi·us -a -um
under *adv* subter, infra
under *prep (position)* sub *(w. abl); (motion)* sub, subter *(w. acc); (less than)* infra *(w. acc);* **— the appearance of** sub specie *(w. gen);* **— the pretense of** per simulationem *(w. gen)*
underage *adj* impub·es -is
underbid *tr* minoris faciendum conducere
underbrush *s* frutect·um -i *n,* dumet·a -orum *npl*
undercover *adj* abdit·us -a -um, secret·us -a -um
undercover agent *s* emissari·us -i *m* (·a -ae *f)*
undercurrent *s* torr·ens -entis *m* subterfluens; **— of feeling** intimus animi sens·us -ūs *m*
underdone *adj* semicrud·us -a -um
underestimate *tr* minoris aestimare
underfoot *adv* obvi·us -a -um
undergarment *s* subucul·a -ae *f; (worn chiefly by women)* suppar·um -i *n*
undergo *tr* subire; **to — change** se mutare; **to — punishment** poenam dare
underground *adj* subterrane·us -a -um
undergrowth *s* virgult·a -orum *npl*
underhanded *adj* clandestin·us -a -um
underhandedly *adv* clam, furtim
underline *tr* subnotare
underling *s* minis·ter -tri *m*
undermine *tr* subruere; *(fig)* labefactare
underneath *adv* infra, subter
underneath *prep (position)* infra *(w. acc),* sub *(w. abl); (motion)* sub *(w. acc)*
underpants *spl* brac·ae -arum *fpl* interiores
underpass *s* viaeduct·us -ūs *m*
underpin *tr* fulcire
underpinnings *spl* fulciment·a -orum *npl*
underrate *tr* minoris aestimare
undershirt *s* subucul·a -ae *f*
understand *tr* intellegere; *(a language or art)* scire; **do you — now?** iam tenes?; **I don't quite —** non satis intellego; **"ego" is under-**

stood **if I should say: "sum philosophus"** subauditur "ego" si dicam "philosophus sum"; **to — Latin** Latine scire
understanding *adj* prud·ens -entis
understanding *s* intellect·us -ūs *m; (agreement)* consens·us -ūs *m; (condition)* condici·o -onis *f*
undertake *tr* adire ad *(w. acc),* suscipere; *(to begin)* incipere
undertaker *s* pollinc·tor -toris *m* (·trix -tricis *f*)
undertaking *s* incept·um -i *n*
undervalue *tr* minoris aestimare
underwear *s* subucul·a -ae *f*
underworld *s* infer·i -orum *mpl; (criminals)* inhonest·i -orum *mpl*
undeserved *adj* immerit·us -a -um
undeservedly *adv* immerito
undeserving *adj* **(of)** indign·us -a -um *(w. abl)*
undeveloped *adj* incult·us -a -um
undignified *adj* indecor·us -a -um
undiminished *adj* imminut·us -a -um
undiscernible *adj* impercept·us -a -um
undiscerning *adj* heb·es -etis
undisciplined *adj* immoderat·us -a -um; *(mil)* inexercitat·us -a -um
undisguised *adj* apert·us -a -um
undismayed *adj* interrit·us -a -um
undisputed *adj* cert·us -a -um; **since this is —** cum hoc constet
undistinguished *adj* ignobil·is -is -e
undisturbed *adj* imperturbat·us -a -um; **— peace** immota pa·x -cis *f*
undivided *adj* indivis·us -a -um
undo *tr (knot)* solvere; *(fig)* infectum reddere, irritum facere; *(to ruin)* perdere; **you have undone everything** omnia irrita fecisti
undone *adj (ruined)* perdit·us -a -um; **to be —** *(to be ruined)* perire
undoubted *adj* haud dubi·us -a -um
undoubtedly *adv* haud dubie, nimirum
undress *tr* exuere; **to get undressed** vestimenta exuere **‖** *intr* se exuere
undue *adj (excessive)* nimi·us -a -um; *(unfair)* iniqu·us -a -um
undulate *intr* undare, fluctuare
undulating *adj* undulabund·us -a -um
undulation *s* undarum agitati·o -onis *f*
unduly *adv* nimis, plus aequo
undying *adj* aetern·us -a -um
unearth *tr* effodere; *(fig)* detegere
unearthly *adj* haud mortal·is -is -e, caelest·is -is -e
uneasily *adv* turbate; **to sleep —** male dormire
uneasiness *s* sollicitud·o -inis *f*
uneasy *adj* sollicit·us -a -um
uneducated *adj* indoct·us -a -um

unemployed *adj* otios·us -a -um; **to be —** cessare
unemployment *s* cessati·o -onis *f*
unencumbered *adj* expedit·us -a -um
unending *adj* infinit·us -a -um, perpetu·us -a -um
unendurable *adj* intolerand·us -a -um
unenjoyable *adj* iniucund·us -a -um
unenlightened *adj* inerudit·us -a -um
unenviable *adj* non invidend·us -a -um
unequal *adj* inaequal·is -is -e; **— to** im·par -paris *(w. dat)*
unequalled *adj* singular·is -is -e
unequally *adv* impariter
unerring *adj* cert·us -a -um
unerringly *adv* certe
uneven *adj* iniqu·us -a -um; *(rough)* asp·er -era -erum
unevenness *s* iniquit·as -atis *f*
unexpected *adj* inopinat·us -a -um; *(unforeseen)* improvis·us -a -um
unexpectedly *adv* de improviso
unexplored *adj* inexplorat·us -a -um
unfading *adj* semper rec·ens -entis; *(fig)* perenn·is -is -e
unfailing *adj (friend)* cert·us -a -um; *(waters)* perenn·is -is -e
unfair *adj* iniqu·us -a -um
unfairly *adv* inique
unfaithful *adj* infid·us -a -um; *(adulterous)* adult·er -era -erum
unfamiliar *adj* ignot·us -a -um
unfamiliarity *s* **(with)** imprudenti·a -ae *f (w. gen)*
unfashionable *adj* obsolet·us -a -um, non ad morem
unfasten *tr* resolvere, laxare
unfavorable *adj* iniqu·us -a -um; **— and favorable omens** omin·a -um *npl* tristia et laeta
unfavorably *adv* male, inique
unfed *adj* impast·us -a -um
unfeeling *adj* dur·us -a -um
unfetter *tr* vincula demere *(w. dat)*
unfinished *adj* imperfect·us -a -um; *(crude)* rud·is -is -e
unfit *adj* inept·us -a -um; *(not qualified)* inhabil·is -is -e
unfold *tr* explicare; *(story)* enarrare **‖** *intr* patescere
unforeseen *adj* improvis·us -a -um
unforgiving *adj* inexorabil·is -is -e
unfortified *adj* immunit·us -a -um
unfortunate *adj* infel·ix -icis
unfortunately *adv* infeliciter; **—, it rained** male accidit quod pluit
unfounded *adj* van·us -a -um

unfriendliness s inimiciti·a -ae f
unfriendly adj parum amic·us -a -um,
inimic·us -a -um; **in an — manner** inimice
unfruitful adj infecund·us -a -um; (ineffective)
irrit·us -a -um
unfurl tr pand·o -ere -i pansus or passus
unfurnished adj imparat·us -a -um, nud·us
-a -um
ungainly adj inhabil·is -is -e
ungenerous adj illiberal·is -is -e
ungentlemanly adj inurban·us -a -um
ungird tr dis·cingo -cingere -cinxi -cinctus
ungodly adj impi·us -a -um; (wicked)
nefand·us -a -um; (coll) immoderat·us -a -um
ungovernable adj intractabil·is -is -e
ungraceful adj inconcinn·us -a -um
ungracious adj illepid·us -a -um
ungrateful adj ingrat·us -a -um
ungratefully adv ingrate
ungrudging adj non invit·us -a -um
ungrudgingly adv sine invidia
unguarded adj incustodit·us -a -um; (of
words) inconsult·us -a -um
unhandy adj inhabil·is -is -e
unhappily adv infeliciter
unhappiness s infelicit·as -atis f
unhappy adj infel·ix -icis
unharness tr disiungere
unhealthiness s mala valetud·o -inis f; (of a
place) gravit·as -atis f
unhealthy adj infirm·us -a -um, morbos·us -a
-um; (place, season, wind) grav·is -is -e
unheard-of adj inaudit·us -a -um
unheeded adj neglect·us -a -um
unheroic adj ignav·us -a -um
unhesitating adj prompt·us -a -um
unhindered adj expedit·us -a -um
unhinge tr de cardine detrahere; (fig) perturbare
unholy adj impi·us -a -um
unhoped-for adj insperat·us -a -um
unhurt adj incolum·is -is -e
unicorn s monocer·os -otis m
uniform adj aequabil·is -is -e, const·ans -antis
uniform s ornat·us -ūs m; (mil) ornat·us -ūs m
militaris; **in —** subornat·us -a -um
uniformed adj subornat·us -a -um
uniformity s aequabilit·as -atis f
uniformly adv aequabiliter
unify tr coniungere, solidare
unilateral adj de uno latere tantummodo
unimaginable adj supra animi vires
unimaginative adj heb·es -etis
unimpaired adj inte·ger -gra -grum
unimpeachable adj probatissim·us -a -um
unimportant adj parv·us -a -um
uninformed adj indoct·us -a -um

uninhabitable adj inhabitabil·is -is -e
uninhabited adj desert·us -a -um
uninjured adj incolum·is -is -e
uninspired adj non inspirat·us -a -um
unintelligible adj incomprehensibil·is -is -e,
obscur·us -a -um
uninteresting adj ieiun·us -a -um, frigid·us
-a -um
uninterrupted adj continu·us -a -um
uninviting adj iniucund·us -a -um
union s (act) coniuncti·o -onis f; (social) soci-
et·as -atis f; (agreement) consens·us -ūs m;
(marriage) coniug·ium -(i)i n; (of workers)
syndicat·us -ūs m
unique adj unic·us -a -um
unison s concent·us -ūs m; **to sing in —** unā
voce canere
unit s unit·as -atis f, mon·as -adis f
unite tr coniungere; (to make into one) unire ‖
intr coīre, coalescere
united adj consociat·us -a -um; **— opposition**
(pol) conspirati·o -onis f
United States (of America) Uniti Statūs
(Americae) (gen: Unitorum Statuum);
Civitat·es -um fpl Foederat·ae -arum
(Americae)
unity s unit·as -atis f
universal adj universal·is -is -e
universally adv universe
universe s universit·as -atis f
university s (studiorum) universit·as -atis f
unjust adj uniust·us -a -um
unjustly adv iniuste
unjustifiable adj quod nihil excusationis habet
unkempt adj incompt·us -a -um
unkind adj inhuman·us -a -um
unkindly adv inhumane
unknowingly adv inscienter
unknown adj ignot·us -a -um; **— to his wife**
clam uxorem
unlawful adj contra ius, illicit·us -a -um; (w.
reference to state law) contra legem; **it is —
to** nefas est (w. inf)
unlawfully adv contra legem (or leges)
unleavened adj non fermentat·us -a -um; **—
bread** pan·is -is m azymus, panis sine fer-
mento
unless conj nisi
unlike adj dissimil·is -is -e; **it is not — going**
non est dissimile atque ire
unlimited adj infinit·us -a -um
unload tr exonerare
unlock tr reserare; **with the door unlocked**
reseratis foribus
unlooked-for adj inopinat·us -a -um
unluckily adv infeliciter

unlucky *adj* infel·ix -icis; *(omen)* infaust·us -a -um; — **day** di·es -ei *m* ater

unmanageable *adj* intractabil·is -is -e

unmanly *adj* moll·is -is -e

unmannerly *adj* male morat·us -a -um, inurban·us -a -um

unmarried *adj (man)* cael·ebs -ibis; *(woman)* innupta

unmask *tr* detegere

unmatched *adj* singular·is -is -e

unmerciful *adj* immisericor·s -dis

unmercifully *adv* immisericorditer

unmistakable *adj* evid·ens -entis, cert·us -a -um

unmistakably *adv* sine dubio

unmoved *adj* immot·us -a -um

unnatural *adj* contra naturam; *(event)* monstruos·us -a -um; *(deed)* imman·is -is -e

unnaturally *adv* contra naturam

unnecessarily *adv* ex supervacuo

unnecessary *adj* haud necessari·us -a -um

unnerve *tr* debilitare

unnoticed *adj* praetermiss·us -a -um; **to go —** **by** latēre inter *(w. acc)*

unobjectionable *adj* culpā exper·s -tis

unoccupied *adj* vacu·us -a -um; *(land)* apert·us -a -um; **to be —** vacare

unofficial *adj* privat·us -a -um

unpack *tr* e cistis eximere

unpaid *adj (of money)* debit·us -a -um; *(of service)* gratuit·us -a -um

unpalatable *adj* insuav·is -is -e

unparalleled *adj* singular·is -is -e

unpardonable *adj* cui ignosci non potest, inexcusabil·is -is -e

unpatriotic *adj* immem·or -oris patriae

unpaved *adj* instrat·us -a -um

unpleasant *adj* iniucund·us -a -um

unpleasantly *adv* iniucunde

unpolished *adj* impolit·us -a -um

unpolluted *adj* impollut·us -a -um; *(fig)* intact·us -a -um

unpopular *adj* invis·us -a -um

unpopularity *s* invidi·a -ae *f*

unpracticed *adj* inexpert·us -a -um

unprecedented *adj* inaudit·us -a -um

unprejudiced *adj* aequ·us -a -um

unpremeditated *adj* inconsult·us -a -um, subit·us -a -um

unprepared *adj* imparat·us -a -um

unpretentious *adj* demiss·us -a -um

unprincipled *adj* improb·us -a -um

unproductive *adj* infecund·us -a -um

unprofitable *adj* inutil·is -is -e, van·us -a -um

unprofitably *adv* nullis fructibus

unprotected *adj* indefens·us -a -um

unprovoked *adj* ultro

unpunished *adj* inpunit·us -a -um; **to allow a** **crime to go —** maleficium impune habēre

unqualified *adj* haud idone·us -a -um; *(complete)* consummat·us -a -um

unquenchable *adj* inexstinct·us -a -um

unquestionable *adj* certissim·us -a -um

unquestionably *adv* facile

unquestioning *adj* credul·us -a -um

unravel *tr* retexere; *(fig)* enodare

unreasonable *adj* absurd·us -a -um

unreasonably *adv* absurde

unrefined *adj* crud·us -a -um

unrelenting *adj* inplacabil·is -is -e

unremitting *adj* assidu·us -a -um

unrepentant *adj* impaenit·ens -entis

unrest *s (outbreak of disorder)* inquietud·o -inis *f*

unrestrained *adj* effrenat·us -a -um

unrighteous *adj* iniust·us -a -um

unripe *adj* immatur·us -a -um

unrivaled *adj* incomparabil·is -is -e

unroll *tr* evolvere

unruffled *adj* immot·us -a -um

unruliness *s* impotenti·a -ae *f*

unruly *adj* impot·ens -entis, turbulent·us -a -um

unsafe *adj* intut·us -a -um

unsalted *adj* insals·us -a -um

unsatisfied *adj* inexplet·us -a -um

unsatisfactory *adj* non idone·us a um

unsavory *adj* insipid·us -a -um; *(disreputable)* foed·us -a -um

unscrew *tr* retorquēre

unseal *tr (letter)* resignare; *(a jar)* relinere

unseasonable *adj* intempestiv·us -a -um

unseemly *adj* indecor·us -a -um

unseen *adj* invis·us -a -um

unselfish *adj* suae utilitatis immem·or -oris

unselfishly *adv* liberaliter

unsettle *tr* sollicitare

unsettled *adj* incert·us -a -um; *(of mind)* sollicit·us -a -um

unsettling *adj* sollicit·ans -antis

unshaken *adj* immot·us -a -um

unshaved *adj* irras·us -a -um

unsheathe *tr* destringere

unsightly *adj* turp·is -is -e

unskillful *adj* imperit·us -a -um

unskillfully *adv* imperite

unskilled *adj* imperit·us -a -um

unsophisticated *adj* simpl·ex -icis

unsound *adj* infirm·us -a -um; *(of mind)* insan·us -a -um; *(ill-founded)* van·us -a -um

unsparing *adj (merciless)* inclem·ens -entis; *(lavish)* larg·us -a -um

unsparingly *adv* inclementer; *(lavishly)* large

unspeakable *adj* ineffabil·is -is -e

unstable *adj* instabil·is -is -e; *(fig)* lev·is -is -e, inconst·ans -antis
unstained *adj* pur·us -a -um; *(honor)* intaminat·us -a -um
unsteadily *adv* inconstanter
unsteady *adj* inconst·ans -antis; *(tottering)* caduc·us -a -um
unsubscribe *intr (comput)* cessare
unsuccessful *adj* infel·ix -icis
unsuccessfully *adv* infeliciter
unsuitable *adj* incommod·us -a -um
unsuited *adj* haud idone·us -a -um
unsullied *adj* intaminat·us -a -um
unsuspected *adj* non suspect·us -a -um, praeter suspicionem
untamed *adj* indomit·us -a -um
untasted *adj* ingustat·us -a -um
untaught *adj* indoct·us -a -um
unteachable *adj* indocil·is -is -e
untenable *adj* infirm·us -a -um, quod defendi non potest
unthankful *adj* ingrat·us -a -um
untie *tr* solvere
until *conj* dum, donec, quoad
until *prep* usque ad *(w. acc)*, in *(w. acc);* **to put off — tomorrow** differre in crastinum; **— late at night** in multam noctem; **— now** adhuc
untimely *adj* intempestiv·us -a -um; *(premature)* praematur·us -a -um
untiring *adj* assidu·us -a -um
untold *adj (numberless)* innumer·us -a -um; *(story)* immemorat·us -a -um
untouched *adj* intact·us -a -um; *(fig)* immot·us -a -um
untrained *adj* inexercitat·us -a -um
untried *adj* intemptat·us -a -um
untrodden *adj* non trit·us -a -um
untroubled *adj* tranquill·us -a -um
untrue *adj* fals·us -a -um; *(disloyal)* infid·us -a -um
untrustworthy *adj* infid·us -a -um
unusual *adj* inusitat·us -a -um
unusually *adv* praeter solitum
unutterable *adj* infand·us -a -um
unvarnished *adj (fig)* nud·us -a -um
unveil *tr* revelare; *(fig)* patefacere
unversed *adj* **— in** imperit·us -a -um *(w. gen)*
unwanted *adj* ingrat·us -a -um; *(superfluous)* supervacane·us -a -um
unwarranted *adj* iniust·us -a -um
unwary *adj* incaut·us -a -um
unwelcome *adj* ingrat·us -a -um
unwieldy *adj* inhabil·is -is -e
unwilling *adj* invit·us -a -um
unwillingly *adv* invite
unwind *tr* revolvere

unwise *adj* imprud·ens -entis
unwisely *adv* imprudenter
unworthily *adv* indigne
unworthiness *s* indignit·as -atis *f*
unworthy *adj* **(of)** indign·us -a -um *(w. abl)*
unwrap *tr* explicare, evolvere
unwritten *adj* non script·us -a -um
unyielding *adj* inflexibil·is -is -e, dur·us -a -um
unyoke *tr* disiungere
up *adv* sursum; (**up** *is often expressed in Latin by the prefix* con-, com- cor-, ex-, sub- *combined with the verb:* **— in the air** *(in uncertaintiy)* in medio relict·us -a -um; **to be — in the air** *(to be undecided)* pendēre; **to eat —** comesse; **to finish —** conficere; **to snatch —** corripere; **to rise —** exsurgere; **to lift —** sublevare; **to charge — the hill** erigere aciem per adversum collem; **to go — the mountains** ire in adversos montes; **to rise — against us** exsurgere adversus *(or* in*)* nos; **— and down** sursum deorsum; **to run — and down** modo huc modo illuc cursare; **— to** tenus *(w. abl) (always placed after its case, e.g.,* **the water came up to the waist** umbilico tenus aqua erat*);* **—s and downs** modo sic, modo sic; **— till now** antehac
upbraid *tr* castigare verbis
upbringing *s* educati·o -onis *f*
upheaval *s* eversi·o -onis *f*
uphill *adj* accliv·is -is -e; *(fig)* difficil·is -is -e; **to have an — struggle** clivo laborare
uphill *adv* adversus clivum, in collen
uphold *tr* servare, sustentare
upkeep *s* impens·a -ae *f*
uplift *tr* sublevare
upon *prep (position)* super *(w. abl)*, in *(w. abl); (motion)* super *(w. acc)*, in *(w. abl); (directly after)* ex *(w. abl)*, sub *(w. abl); (converning)* de *(w. abl);* **— my word** fidem do
upper *adj* super·ior -ior -ius; *(world, air)* super·us -a -um; **an — room** superius cenacul·um -i *n;* **the — classes** superiores *(or* ampliores*)* ordin·es -um *mpl;* **to get the — hand** superare, vincere
uppermost *adj* summ·us -a -um
upright *adj* erect·us -a -um; *(of character)* honest·us -a -um, inte·ger -gra -grum
uproar *s* tumult·us -ūs *m;* **to be in an —, to cause an —** tumultuari
uproot *tr* eradicare, erurere
ups and downs *spl* **he has his —** ei modo bene, modo male est; **there are —** est modo sic, modo sic
upset *tr* evertere, subvertere; *(to worry)* perturbare, commovēre

upset *adj* perculs·us -a -um, commot·us -a -um; **don't be** — noli *(pl:* nolite) perturbari

upset *s (setback)* offensi·o -onis *f; (at polls)* repuls·a -ae *f;* **to suffer an** — offensionem *(or* repulsam) ferre

upside down *adv* **everything was** — omnia erant sursum deorsum; **to turn** — sursum deorsum versare

upstairs *adv (direction)* sursum; *(position)* in superiore tabulato; **to go** — per scalas ascendere

upstairs *s* dom·us -ūs *f* superior

upstairs bedroom *s* cubicul·um -i *n* superius

upstart *s* novus hom·o -inis *m; (pej)* terrae fil·ius -(i)i *m*

upstream *adv* adverso flumine

up to *prep* usque ad *(w. acc),* tenus *(postpositive, w. abl or gen);* **it is** — **you** ex te pendet

upwards *adv* sursum; — **of** *(of number)* plus quam

urban *adj* urban·us -a -um

urge *tr* urgēre, impellere; **to** — **on** stimulare, incitare; *(horses)* admittere

urge *s* impuls·us -ūs *m,* animi impet·us -ūs *m*

urgency *s* necessit·as -atis *f*

urgent *adj* inst·ans -antis; grav·is -is -e; **whose need was most** — quibus summa necessitudo erat; **to be** — instare

urgently *adv* vehementer

urging *s* stimul·us -i *m;* **at the** — **of the consul** consule auctore

urinal *s* matell·a -ae *f,* lasan·um -i *n*

urine *s* urin·a -ae *f*

URL *s (comput)* Universale Rerum Locatr·um -i *n,* inscripti·o -onis *f* interretialis

urn *s* urn·a -ae

us *pron* nos; **of** — nostri; *(partitive)* nostrum; **to** — nobis; **with** — nobiscum

usage *s* us·us -ūs *m; (custom)* consuetud·o -inis *f*

use *s* us·us -ūs *m;* **no** —! frustra!; **in common** — usitat·us -a -um; **it is no** — nihil opus est; ilicet; **to be in** — in usu esse; **to be of** — usui esse; **to be of no** — inutile esse, usum nullum habēre; **to come into** — invalescere, in morem *(or* in usum) venire; **to make** — **of** uti *(w. abl);* **what's the** —? quid opus est?

use *tr* uti *(w. abl); (to take advantage of)* abuti *(w. abl);* **to** — **in a sentence** in sententiā ponere; **to** — **s.th. for** aliquid adhibēre *(w. dat);* **to** — **up** consumere, exhaurire ‖ *intr* **I used to** solebam *(w. inf)*

used *adj* usitat·us -a -um; *(second-hand)* trit·us -a -um; — **to** *(accustomed to)* assuet·us -a -um *(w. dat)*

useful *adj* util·is -is -e; **to be** — usui esse

usefully *adv* utiliter, commode

useless *adj* inutil·is -is -e

uselessly *adv* frustra

usher *n (in theater)* dissignat·or -oris *m*

usual *adj* solit·us -a -um; **as** — ut solet; **more than** — plus solito; **you were wrong as** — errabas ut solebas *(or* ex consuetudine tuā)

usually *adv* plerumque, fere

usurp *tr* invadere *(w. acc or* in *w. acc),* usurpare

usurpation *s* usurpati·o -onis *f*

usurper *s* usurpa·tor -toris *m* (·trix -tricis *f)*

usury *s* immodica usur·a -ae *f*

utensils *spl* untensil·ia -ium *npl;* **household** — suppel·ex -ectilis *f;* **kitchen** — coquinatori·a -orum *npl*

utility *s* utilit·as -atis *f*

utilize *tr* uti *(w. abl),* adhibēre

utmost *adj* summ·us -a -um

utmost *n* **to do one's** — omnibus viribus contendere

utter *adj* tot·us -a -um

utter *tr* emittere; *(to reveal what is a secret)* proloqui; **she never —ed a word** nullum verbum emisit

utterance *s* dict·um -i *n;* **to give** — **to one's feelings** exprimere dicendo sensa

utterly *adv* omnino, funditus

uttermost *adj* extrem·us -a -um

uvula *s* uvul·a -ae *f*

V

vacancy *s* vacuit·as -atis *f; (in hotel)* cubicul·um -i *n* vacans

vacant *adj* vacu·us -a -um; *(look, stare)* inan·is -is -e; **to be** — vacare

vacate *tr* vacuefacere

vacation *s* feri·ae -arum *fpl;* **at the beginning (the end of)** — feriis ineuntibus (feriis peractis); **summer** — feriae aestivae; **to be on** — feriat·us -a -um esse; **to spend the** — ferias agere

vaccinate *tr* vaccinum inserere in *(w. acc)*

vaccination *s* vaccinati·o -onis *f*

vaccine *s* vaccin·um -i *n*

vacillate *intr* vacillare

vacillating *adj* vacill·ans -antis

vacuum *s* inan·e -is *n*

vacuum cleaner *s* pulveris hauritor·ium -(i)i *n*

vagabond *s* larifug·a -ae *mf*

vagary *s* libid·o -inis *f*

vagina *s* vagin·a -ae *f*

vagrancy *s* vagati·o -onis *f*

vagrant *adj* vag·us -a -um

vagrant *s* err·o -onis *mf*
vague *adj* vag·us -a -um; *(not fixed)* incert·us -a -um; *(ambiguous)* ambigu·us -a -um
vaguely *adv* incerte
vagueness *s* obscurit·as -atis *f,* abiguit·as -atis *f*
vain *adj (empty)* van·us -a -um; *(proud)* superb·us -a -um; **in —** frustra
vainly *adv* frustra
vainglorious *adj* glorios·us -a -um
valedictorian *s* valedic·ens -entis *mf*
valedictory *s* orati·o -onis *f* valedicens
valentine *s* chartul·a -ae *f* amatoria
valet *s* cubicular·ius -(i)i *m*
valiant *adj* fort·is -is -e
valid *adj* firm·us -a -um
valley *s* vall·es *(or* vall·is) -is *f*
valor *s* fortitud·o -inis *f*
valuable *adj* pretios·us -a -um; **to be —** pretium habēre
valuables *spl* res, rerum *fpl* pretiosae
valuation *s* aestimati·o -onis *f*
value *s* pret·ium -(i)i *n*
value *tr* aestimare; **to — highly** magni aestimare; **to — s.o. for his prowess** aliquem probare a viribus
valueless *adj* vil·is -is -e
valve *s* epistom·ium -(i)i *n*
vampire *s* vespertili·o -onis *m; (fig)* hirud·o -inis *f*
vandal *s* evers·or -oris *m*
vanguard *s (mil)* primum agm·en -inis *n*
vanish *intr* (e)vanescere, diffugere
vanity *s* vanit·as -atis *f*
vanquish *tr* profligare, devincere
vantage *s* commod·um -i *n; —* **point** superior loc·us -i *m*
vapor *s* vap·or -oris *m*
variable *adj* vari·ans -antis
variance *s* differenti·a -ae *f;* **at — with** dissid·ens -entis ab *(w. abl);* **to set the state at —** serere civiles discordias
variation *s* variet·as -atis *f*
varicose vein *s* var·ix -icis *f*
variety *s* variet·as -atis *f*
various *adj* vari·i -ae -a; **in — ways** varie
variously *adv* varie
vary *tr* variare, mutare ‖ *intr* variare, mutari
vase *s* vascul·um -i *n*
vast *adj* vast·us -a -um
vastly *adv* valde, maxime
vastness *s* immensit·as -atis *f*
vat *s* cup·a -ae *f*
vault *s (archit)* camer·a -ae *f; (leap)* salt·us -ūs *m; (for valuables)* thesaur·us -i *m*
vault *intr* salire
vaunt *tr* iactare ‖ *intr* se iactare

VCR *s* magnetoscop·ium -(i)i *n*
veal *s* vitulin·a -ae *f*
veer *intr* se vertere
vegetable *s* hol·us -eris *n* [*also collective for vegetables*]
vegetable *adj* holitari·us -a -um
vegetable garden *s* hort·us -i *m* holitorius
vegetarian *adj* holerari·us -a -um
vehemence *s* vehementi·a -ae *f*
vehement *adj* vehem·ens -entis; *(violent)* violent·us -a -um
vehemently *adv* vehementer
vehicle *s* vehicul·um -i *n*
Veii *spl* Vei·i -orum *mpl*
veil *s* ric·a -ae *f; (bridal)* flamme·um -i *n; (fig)* integument·um -i *n*
veil *tr* velare
vein *s (anat)* ven·a -ae *f;* **in a similar —** ad similem sententiam
velocity *s* velocit·as -atis *f*
velvet *s* velvet·um -i *n*
vend *tr* vendere
vendetta *s* simult·as -atis *f*
vendor *s* vendi·tor -toris *m* (·trix -tricis *f*)
veneer *s* ligni bracte·a -ae *f; (fig)* speci·es -ei *f*
venerable *adj* venerabil·is -is -e
venerate *tr* venerari
veneration *s* venerati·o -onis *f*
venereal *adj* venere·us -a -um
Venetian blinds *spl* transenn·a -ae *f;* **to open, (close, let down, raise) the —** transennam aperire (claudere, demittere, subvolvere)
vengeance *s* ulti·o -onis *f;* **to take — on s.o.** se vindicare ab *(w. abl);* **with a —** valde, vehementer
venison *s* ferin·a -ae *f*
venom *s* venen·um -i *n*
venomous *adj* venenat·us -a -um
vent *s* spirament·um -i *n*
vent *tr* aperire; **to — one's wrath on** iram erumpere in *(w. acc)*
ventilate *tr* ventilare
ventriloquist *s* ventriloqu·us -i *m* (·a -ae *f*)
venture *s* facin·us -eris *n;* **to risk a —** periculum subire
venture *tr* periclitari; **to — all** dare summam rerum in aleam
venturesome *adj* aud·ax -acis
veracity *s* veracit·as -atis *f*
veranda *s* subdial·ia -ium *npl*
verb *s* verb·um -i *n*
verbal *adj* verbal·is -is -e
verbally *adv* verbo
verbatim *adv* ad verbum
verbose *adj* verbos·us -a -um
verdict *s* sententi·a -ae *f;* **to deliver the —** sententiam pronuntiare; **to give a guilty —** con-

demnatoriam sententiam ferre; **to give a —
of acquittal** absolutoriam sententiam ferre
verge *s* marg·o -inis *m;* **to be on the — of** non
procul abesse ut *(w. subj)*
verge *intr* **to — on** non multum distare ab
(w. abl)
verification *s* confirmati·o -onis *f*
verify *tr* comprobare, confimare
vermilion *adj* minian·us -a -um
vermilion *s* min·ium -(i)i *n*
vermin *spl* bestiol·ae -arum *fpl*
vernacular *s* patrius serm·o -onis *m*
versatile *adj* versatil·is -is -e
verse *s* vers·us -ūs *m*
versed *adj* (**in**) versat·us et exercitat·us -a -um
(in *w. abl)*
versification *s* versificati·o -onis *f*
versify *intr* versificare
version *s* translati·o -onis *f;* **to give a literal —
of** plane vertere
vertebra *s* vertebr·a -ae *f*
vertex *s* vert·ex -icis *m*
vertical *adj* rect·us -a -um; **a — line** perpen-
dicul·um -i *n*
vertically *adv* ad perpendiculum
very *adj* ips·e -a -um; **on the — day on which**
ipso die quo
very *adv* valde, admodum, perquam, maxime,
per- *(w. adj or adv);* **— good** optim·us -a
-um; **— good!** optime!; **— well!** *(in agreement)* fiat!
vessel *s* vas, vasis *n; (ship)* navig·ium -(i)i *n*
vest *s* thor·ax -acis *m*
vestal virgin *s* virg·o -inis *f* vestalis
vestibule *s* vestibul·um -i *n*
vestige *s* vestig·ium -(i)i *n*
vestment *s* vestiment·um -i *n*
veteran *s* veteran·us -i *m* (·a -ae *f)*, emerit·us -i
m (·a -ae *f)*
veterinarian *s* veterinari·us -i *m* (·a -ae *f)*
veterinary *adj* veterinari·us -a -um
veto *s* intercessi·o -onis *f;* **to interpose a —**
intercedere
veto *tr* intercedere *(w. dat)*
vex *tr* vexare
vexation *s* vexati·o -onis *f*
via *prep* per *(w. acc)*
vial *s* phial·a -ae *f*
vibrate *intr* vibrare
vibration *s* vibrat·us -ūs *m*
vicar *s* vicar·ius -(i)i *m; (eccl)* sacerd·os
-otis *m*
vicarious *adj* vicari·us -a -um
vice *s (shameful deed)* flagit·ium -(i)i *n; (flaw)*
vit·ium -(i)i *n; (tool)* retinacul·um -i *n*
vice admiral *s* classis subpraefect·us -i *m* (·a
-ae *f)*

vice chancellor *s* procancellar·ius -(i)i *m* (·ia
-iae *f)*
vice president *s* praesidis vicar·ius -(i)i *m* (·ia
-iae *f)*
vice principal *s* (scholae) rect·or -oris *m* vicarius, rectr·ix -icis *f* vicaria
viceroy *s* subregul·us -i *m*
vicinity *s* vicini·a -ae *f;* **in the — of** circum
(w. acc)
vicious *adj* crudel·is -is -e
viciously *adv* crudeliter
vicissitude *s* vicissitud·o -inis *f*
victim *s* victim·a -ae *f;* **to fall — to** obire
(w. dat)
victimize *tr (to swindle)* circumvenire; *(to
assault, kill)* vim inferre *(w. dat)*
victor *s* vict·or -oris *m,* victr·ix -icis *f*
victorious *adj* vict·or -oris, *(of a female)*
victr·ix -icis [*used appositively*]; **to be —**
vincere
victory *s* victori·a -ae *f;* **news of —** litter·ae
-arum *fpl* victrices; **to win a —** victoriam
consequi *or* adipisci; **to gain a — over the
enemy** ab hoste victoriam reportare
video cassette *s* caset·a -ae *f* magnetoscopica
video cassette recorder (VCR) *s* magneto-
scop·ium -(i)i *n*
video game lus·us -ūs *m* magnetoscopicus; **to
play —s** lusūs magnetoscopicos ludere
videotape *s* taeniol·a -ae *f* magnetoscopica; **to
play** *or* **show a —** taeniolam mangetoscopi-
cam exhibēre
vie *intr* certare, contendere
view *s* aspect·us -ūs *m,* conspect·us -ūs *m;
(from above)* despect·us -ūs *m; (from a window)* prospect·us -ūs *m; (opinion)* sententi·a
-ae *f;* **almost in — of the city** paene in conspectu urbis; **in my — ** meo iudicio; **in — of**
pro *(w. abl);* **this is my point of —** hoc sic
mihi videtur; **to come into —** apparēre; **to
enjoy a — of** conspectu *(w. gen)* uti; **to get a
bird's eye — of the city** omnem urbem sub
uno aspectu despicere
view *tr* visere, spectare; *(to regard)* intueri
vigil *s* vigili·ae -arum *fpl; (lasting all night)*
pervigil·ium -(i)i *n*
vigilance *s* vigilanti·a -ae *f*
vigilant *adj* vigil·ans -antis
vigilantly *adv* vigilanter
vigor *s* vig·or -oris *m*
vigorous *adj* ala·cer -cris -cre
vigorously *adv* alacriter
vile *adj* vil·is -is -e
vilify *tr* infamare
villa *s* vill·a -ae *f;* **my — at Formiae** meum
Formian·um -i *n*
village *s* pag·us -i *m,* vic·us -i *m*

villager *s* pagan·us -i *m* (·a -ae *f*)
villain *s* scelest·us -i *m* (·a -ae *f*)
villany *s* nequiti·a -ae *f; (deed)* scel·us -eris *n*
vindicate *tr* vindicare; *(to justify)* probare; *(person)* defendere
vindication *s* vindicati·o -onis *f*
vindictive *adj* ultionis cupid·us -a -um
vine *s* vit·is -is *f*
vine arbor *s* pergul·a -ae *f*
vinegar *s* acet·um -i *n*
vinegar bottle *s* acetabul·um -i *n*
vineyard *s* vine·a -ae *f*
vintage *s* vindemi·a -ae *f*
violate *tr* violare
violation *s* violati·o -onis *f*
violator *s* viola·tor -toris *m* (·trix -tricis *f*)
violence *s* violenti·a -ae *f*
violent *adj* violent·us -a -um
violently *adv* violenter
violin *s* fidicul·a -ae *f;* **to play the —** fidiculā canere
virgin *adj* virg·o -inis *f (used appositively);* **— forest** silv·a -ae *f* intacta
virgin *s* virg·o -inis *f*
virile *adj* viril·is -is -e
virility *s* virilit·as -atis *f*
virtually *adv* fere
virtue *s* virt·us -utis *f; (power)* vis *f;* **by — of** per *(w. acc),* ex *(w. abl)*
virtuous *adj* prob·us -a -um, virtute praedit·us -a -um
virtuously *adv* cum virtute, honeste
virulence *s* vis *f,* gravit·as -atis *f*
virulent *adj* virulent·us -a -um
viscera *spl* viscer·a -um *npl*
visible *adj* visibil·is -is -e; *(striking, noticeable)* manifest·us -a -um
visibly *adv* manifeste
vision *s (sense)* vis·us -ūs *m; (apparition)* visi·o -onis *f*
visionary *s* somni·ans -antis *mf*
visit *s (formal)* salutati·o -onis *f;* **to pay s.o. a — aliquem visere
visit *tr* visere, visitare; **to go to —** visere
visitor *s* hosp·es -itis *mf*
visor *s* buccul·a -ae *f*
vista *s* prospect·us -ūs *m*
visual *adj* ad visum pertinens, oculorum *[gen)]*
visualize *tr* fingere
visually *adv* oculis
vital *adj* vital·is -is -e; *(essential)* necessari·us -a -um
vitally *adv* praecipue
vitality *s* vis *f* vitalis
vitamin *s* vitamin·um -i *n*
vitiate *tr* vitiare, corrumpere
vivacious *adj* viv·ax -acis

vivaciously *adv* vivaciter
vivid *adj* vivid·us -a -um
vividly *adv* vivide
vivify *tr* vivificare
vocabulary *s* verborum copi·a -ae *f; (list of words)* vocabulorum ind·ex -icis *m*
vocal *adj* vocal·is -is -e
vocation *s* vocati·o -onis *f*
vocative *s* vocativ·us -i *m,* cas·us -ūs *m* vocativus
vociferous *adj* clamos·us -a -um
vogue *s* mos, moris *m;* **to be in —** moris esse
voice *s* vox, vocis *f; (of a verb)* gen·us -eris *n;* **what — is "audimur"? it is passive**. cuius generis est "audimur"? est passivi generis [Note: "genus" *in connection with nouns and adjectives means "gender," and in connection with verbs means "voice"*]
void *adj* inan·is -is -e; **— of** vacu·us -a -um *(w. abl)*
void *s* inan·e -is *n*
volatile *adj* volatic·us -a -um, lev·is -is -e
volcanic *adj* vulcani·us -a -um
volcano *s* mon·s -tis *m* flammas et vaporem eructans
volition *s* volunt·as -atis *f*
volley *s* coniect·us -ūs *m; (fig)* tempest·as -atis *f*
volleyball *s* foll·is -is *m* volatilis; *(game)* lus·us -ūs *m* follis volatilis; **to play —** folle volatili ludere
volt *s* volt·ium -(i)i *n*
volume *s (book)* volum·en -inis *n; (quantity)* copi·a -ae *f; (of voice)* magnitud·o -inis *f*
voluminous *adj* voluminos·us -a -um; **— writer** scrip·tor -toris *m* (·trix -tricis *f*) per multa diffusus volumina
voluntarily *adv* suā voluntate, ultro
voluntary *adj* voluntari·us -a -um; *(unpaid)* gratuit·us -a -um
volunteer *s* voluntari·us -i *m* (·a -ae *f); (mil)* mil·es -itis *mf* voluntari·us (-a)
volunteer *intr (mil)* sponte nomen dare; **to — to do s.th.** aliquid ultro facere
voluptuous *adj* voluptari·us -a -um
vomit *tr & intr* vomere
vomit *s* vomit·us -ūs *m*
voracious *adj* vor·ax -acis
voraciously *adv* voraciter
vortex *s* vort·ex -icis *m*
vote *s* suffrag·ium -(i)i *n; (fig) (judgment)* sententi·a -ae *f;* **to cast a —** suffragium ferre
vote *tr* **to — down** antiquare ‖ *intr* suffragium ferre; *(of a judge)* sententiam ferre; *(of a senator)* censēre; **to — for** suffragari *(w. dat)*
voter *s* suffraga·tor -toris *m* (·trix -tricis *f*)
voting booth *s* saept·um -i *n*

votive *adj* votiv·us -a -um; — **offering** vot·um -i *n*

vouch *intr* **to — for** testificari, affirmare

voucher *s* testimon·ium -(i)i *n* (per tabellas)

vouchsafe *tr* concedere

vow *s* vot·um -i *n*

vow *tr* vovēre ‖ *intr* spondēre

vowel *s* vocal·is -is *f*

voyage *s* it·er -ineris *n; (by sea)* navigati·o -onis *f*

voyage *intr* iter facere; *(abroad)* peregrinari; *(by sea)* navigare

voyager *s* peregrina·tor -toris *m* (·trix -tricis *f*); *(by sea)* naviga·tor -toris *m* (·trix -tricis *f*)

vulgar *adj* vulgar·is -is -e; *(low)* vil·is -is -e

vulgarity *s* obscenit·as -atis *f,* dicti·o -onis *f* obscena

Vulgate *s* Bibli·a -orum *npl* editionis vulgatae

vulnerable *adj* qui (quae, quod) vulnerari potest; *(of a fortress)* expugnabil·is -is -e

vulture *s* vult·ur -uris *m; (fig)* hom·o -inis *mf* rapax

W

wad *s* fascicul·us -i *m*

waddle *intr* anatis in modum incedere

wade *intr* per vada ire; **to — across** vado transire

waffle *s* vafl·um -i *n*

wag *tr (the tail)* movēre

wage *tr* **to — war** bellum gerere

wager *tr* deponere

wager *s* sponsi·o -onis *f*

wages *spl* merc·es -edis *f;* **to receive (fair, good, low, unfair)** — (aequam, magnam, parvam, iniquam) mercedem accipere

wagon *s* carr·us -i *m; (for agricultural purposes)* plaustr·um -i *n; (toy)* plostell·um -i *n*

wail *intr* plorare

wailing *s* plorat·us -ūs *m*

waist *s* media par·s -tis *f* corporis

wait *intr* exspectare, opperiri; *(not to depart)* manēre; **to — for** exspectare, opperiri; **to — on** ministrare *(w. dat);* **to — on tables** ministrare

wait *s* mor·a -ae *f;* **to lie in — for** insidiari *(w. dat)*

waiter *s* minis·ter -tri *m*

waiting room *s* oec·us -i *m* praestolatorius

waitress *s* ministr·a -ae *f*

waive *tr* remittere

wake *tr* (e somno) excitare ‖ *intr* **to — up** expergisci, evigilare

wake *s* tract·us -ūs *m* aquarum a tergo navis; **in the — of** post *(w. acc)*

wakeful *adj* vig·il -ilis

walk *s (act)* ambulati·o -onis *f; (place)* ambulacr·um -i *n,* xyst·us -i *m; (covered)* portic·us -ūs *f; (gait)* incess·us -ūs *m;* **to go for a —** demabulatum ire

walk *intr* ambulare, incedere; **to — out on** *(coll)* deserere; **to — up and down** deambulare; **to — up to** accedere ad *(w. acc)*

wall *s (inner or outer wall of a house)* pari·es -etis *m; (exterior)* mur·us -i *m;* **—s** *(of town)* moen·ia -ium *npl,* mur·us -i *m*

wall *tr* **to — in** moenibus munire; **to — up** *(w. stones, bricks)* concludere (saxis, lateribus)

wall clock *s* horolog·ium -(i)i *n* parietarium

walled *adj* moenibus munit·us -a -um

wallet *s* per·a -ae *f*

wallop *tr (coll)* percolopare; **to get —ed** vapulare

wallow *intr* volutari

walnut *s* iugl·ans -andis *f*

walnut tree *s* iugl·ans -andis *f*

walrus *s* odoben·us -i *m*

waltz *s* saltati·o -onis *f* in gyrum

waltz *intr* saltare in gyrum

wan *adj* pallid·us -a -um

wander *intr* errare, vagari; **to — about** pervagari; **to — over** pererrare

wanderer *s* err·o onis *mf*

wandering *s* errati·o -onis *f*

wane *intr* decrescere

want *s (scarcity)* penuri·a -ae *f; (opp:* copia) inopi·a -ae *f; (extreme want)* egest·as -atis *f;* **to be in —, suffer —** egēre

want *tr* velle, cupere; *(to lack)* egēre *(w. abl);* **now what do you —?** quid nunc tibi vis?

wanting *adj (defective)* vitios·us -a -um; *(missing)* abs·ens -entis; **to be —** deficere, deesse

wanton *adj (lewd)* libidinos·us -a -um; *(unwarranted)* iniqu·us -a -um

war *s* **(against, with)** bell·um -i *n* (contra *or* adversus *w. acc);* **civil —** bellum civile *or* domesticum; **foreign —** bellum externum; **in —** bello, belli tempore; **in — and in peace** pace belloque; **offensive —** *(of war yet to be begun)* bellum ultro inferendum; *(of war already begun)* bellum ultro illatum; **to be involved in —** bello implicari; **to bring a — to a successful conclusion** bellum conficere; **to carry on — with** bellum gerere cum *(w. abl);* **to cause a —** bellum movēre; **to conduct a —** *(of a general)* bellum administrare; **to declare — on** bellum indicere *(w. dat);* **to fight a —** bellum gerere; **to go to — with** bellum inferre *(w. dat);* **to settle a — by diplomacy** bellum componere; **to start a —**

with bellum inire cum *(w. abl);* **to take part in a** — bellum capessere; **to wage a** — bellum gerere; — **against pirates** bellum piraticum; — **against slaves** bellum servile; — **of extermination** bellum internecium; — **breaks out** bellum exardescit

war *intr* **(against)** bellare (adversus *w. acc)*

warble *intr* canere; *(to twitter)* fritinnire

war cry *s* ululat·us -ūs *m*

ward *s (minor)* pupill·us -i *m* (·a -ae *f); (of a city)* regi·o -onis *f;* — **by** — regionatim

ward *tr* **to** — **off** arcēre, avertere

warden *s* carcerar·ius -(i)i *m* (·ia -iae *f)*

wardrobe *s (place to keep clothes)* vestiar·ium -(i)i *n; (clothes)* vestiment·a -orum *npl*

warehouse *s* horre·um -i *n*

wares *spl* merc·es -ium *fpl*

warfare *s* res, rei *f* bellica, bell·um -i *n*

war-horse *s* equ·us -i *m* bellator

warily *adv* caute

warlike *adj* bellicos·us -a -um

warm *adj* calid·us -a -um; *(just warm)* tepid·us -a -um; *(fig)* fervid·us -a -um; **to be** — calēre; **to become** — calescere, tepescere

warm *tr* calefacere, tepefacere; **to** — **up** *(food)* recoquere; *(by exercise)* exercēre

warm-hearted *adj* am·ans -antis

warmly *adv* ardenter; *(kindly)* benigne; — **dressed** spissis vestibus involut·us -a -um

warmth *s* cal·or -oris *m; (fig)* ferv·or -oris *m*

warm-up *s* exercitati·o -onis *f*

warn *tr* monēre

warning *s* monit·um -i *n; (lesson)* document·um -i *n*

warp *s* stam·en -inis *n*

warp *tr* torquēre **‖** *intr (of wood)* pandere

warped *adj* pand·us -a -um

warping *s* pandati·o -onis *f*

warrant *tr (to guarantee)* praestare; *(to justify, call for)* probare

warrant *s* mandat·um -i *n;* — **for arrest** praemandat·a -orum *npl*

warranty *s* satisdati·o -onis *f*

warrior *s* bellat·or -oris *m*

warship *s* nav·is -is *f* longa

wart *s* verruc·a -ae *f*

wary *adj* caut·us -a -um

wash *tr* lavare; **to** — **away** abluere; **to** — **out** eluere **‖** *intr* lavari

wash *s* lavandari·a -orum *npl;* **to send to the** — ad lavandum dare

wash basin *s* aqual·is -is *m*

wash cloth *s* drapp·us -i *m* lavatorius

washer, washmachine *s* machin·a -ae *f* lavatoria

washing *s* lavati·o -onis *f*

wasp *s* vesp·a -ae *f*

waste *s* detriment·um -i *n; (of time, money)* iactur·a -ae *f*

waste *tr* effundere; *(time, effort)* perdere, terere; **I'm wasting my time** frustra tempus contero; **to** — **one's breath** *(fig)* operam perdere **‖** *intr* **to** — **away** tabescere

waste *adj* vast·us -a -um; **to lay** — vastare

waste basket *s* scirpicul·us -i *m* chartarius

wasteful *adj* prodig·us -a -um

wastefully *adv* prodige

wasteland *s* solitud·o -inis *f*

watch *s (timepiece)* horolog·ium -(i)i *n; (guard)* vigili·a -ae *f; (sentry)* excubi·ae -arum *fpl;* **to keep** — excubare; **to keep** — **over** invigilare *(w. dat),* custodire

watch *tr (to observe)* observare, spectare; *(to guard)* custodire **‖** *intr* cavēre; **hey you,** — **out!** heus tu, cave!; **to** — **out for** cavēre *(w. abl or dat or* ab *w. abl);* — **out that you don't** … cave ne …

watchful *adj* vigil·ans -antis

watchman *s* vig·il -ilis *m*

watchtower *s* specul·a -ae *f*

watchword *s* tesser·a -ae *f*

water *s* aqu·a -ae *f;* **fresh** — aqua dulcis; **in deep** — *(fig)* artibus in rebus; **rain** — aqua pluvialis; **running** — proflu·ens -entis *f;* **salt** — aqua salsa

water *tr* irrigare; *(animals, plants)* adaquare

water bottle *s* lagoen·a -ae *f* aquaria

water boy *s* aquar·ius -(i)i *m,* aquat·or -oris *m*

water clock *s* clepsydr·a -ae *f*

water closet *s* latrin·a -ae *f,* loc·us -i *m* secretus

watercolor *s* pigment·um -i *n* aquā dilutum

waterfall *s* cataract·a -ae *f*

waterfront *s* lit·us -oris *n; (of city)* naval·ia -ium *npl*

watering can *s* nassitern·a -ae *f*

waterlogged *adj* aquā gravid·us -a -um

watermelon *s* melopep·o -onis *m*

water pipe *s* fistul·a -ae *f* aquaria

waterproof *adj* aquae impervi·us -a -um

waterski *s* nart·a -ae *f* aquaria

waterski *intr* per summas undas natare

watertight *adj* aquae impervi·us -a -um; *(fig)* absolut·us -a -um

watery *adj* aquos·us -a -um

watt *s* vatt·ium -(i)i *n*

wave *s* und·a -ae *f,* fluct·us -ūs *m*

wave *tr (hands, arms)* iactare; *(weapon, flag)* quassare; *(hair)* crispare

waver *intr* labare, nutare, vacillare

wavering *adj* nut·ans -antis, vacill·ans -antis

wavy *adj* und·ans -antis; *(hair)* crisp·us -a -um

wax *s* cer·a -ae *f*

wax *adj* cere·us -a -um

wax *tr* incerare ‖ *intr* crescere
way *adv (coll)* longe, multo
way *s* vi·a -ae *f; (route)* it·er -ineris *n; (manner)* mod·us -i *m; (plan, system, method)* rati·o -onis *f; (habit)* mo·s -ris *m;* **all the —** from usque ab *(w. abl);* **all the — to** usque ad *(w. acc);* **a long — off** longinqu·us -a -um; **by the —** *(incidentally)* obiter; **by — of** per *(w. acc),* viā *(w. gen);* **get out of the —!** abi, apage!; **have it your —!** esto ut lubet!; **if it is not too much out of your —** si tibi non sane devium erit; **I'm in a bad —** mihi male est; **in every —** omnibus modis; **in no —** nullo modo; **in the same —** eodem modo; **in the —** obvi·us -a -um; **in this —** ad hunc modum; **to be a long — off** longe distare; **to be in the — of** obesse *(w. dat);* **to be out of the —** devi·us -a -um esse; **to get in the — of** intervenire *(w. dat);* **to get under —** ancoram solvere; **to give —** *(of a structure)* labare; *(to yield)* concedere; *(mil)* pedem referre; **to get one's own —** pervincere; **to give — to** indulgēre *(w. dat);* **to have one's own —** res pro arbitrio gerere; **to stand in the — of** obstare *(w. dat);* **under —** proced·ens -entis; **— in** ingress·us -ūs *m;* **— out** exit·us -ūs *m;* **what is the quickest (best) — to … ?** quae est brevissima (optima) via ad *(w. acc)?*
wayfarer *s* viat·or -oris *mf*
waylay *tr* insidiari *(w. dat)*
wayward *adj* inconst·ans -antis
we *pron* nos; **— ourselves** *(masc)* nosmet ipsi; *(fem)* nosmet ipsae
weak *adj (in body, mind, resources)* infirm·us -a -um; *(from defects)* debil·is -is -e; *(argument, light, constitution)* tenu·is -is -e; *(senses)* heb·es -etis; *(voice)* exil·is -is -e
weaken *tr* infirmare, debilitare ‖ *intr* hebescere, labare
weakly *adv* infirme
weakness *s* infirmit·as -atis *f,* debilit·as -atis *f; (of mind)* imbecillit·as -atis *f; (flaw)* vit·ium -(i)i *n; (of arguments)* levit·as -atis *f*
wealth *s* diviti·ae -arum *fpl; (resources)* op·es -um *fpl; (store, plenty)* copi·a -ae *f*
wealthy *adj* div·es -itis
wean *tr* ab ubere depellere; *(fig)* **(from)** desuefacere ab *(w. abl)*
weapon *s* tel·um -i *n,* ferr·um -i *n*
wear *tr (clothes)* gerere, gestare; *(to wear regularly)* uti *(w. abl);* **to — out** *(clothes, a person)* conterere ‖ *intr* durare; *(to last)* perferre; **to — out** dilabi
wear *s* trit·us -ūs *m;* **— and tear** intertriment·um -i *n*
weariness *s* lassitud·o -inis *f*

wearisome *adj* operos·us -a -um
weary *adj* fess·us -a -um
weary *tr* fatigare
weasel *s* mustel·a -ae *f; (pej)* hom·o -inis *mf* lucifugus (-a)
weather *s (good or bad)* tempest·as -atis *f,* cael·um -i *n;* **beautiful (clear, cloudless, cloudy, fine, foul, lousy, rainy) —** egregia (clara, suda, nebulosa, serena, foeda, spurca) tempestas; **— conditions** tempestatum habit·us -ūs *m;* **types of —** gener·a -um *npl* tempestatum, tempestat·es -um *fpl*
weather *tr* **to — a storm** procellam durare; *(fig)* res adversas superare
weatherbeaten *adj* tempestate afflict·us -a -um
weather forecast *s* praenuntiati·o -onis *f* tempestatis
weather report *s* renuntiati·o -onis *f* tempestatis
weave *tr* texere
web *s (spider's)* arane·um -i *n; (on a loom)* tel·a -ae *f;* **the Web** Tel·a -ae *f (see* **World Wide Web)**
web site *s* sit·us -ūs *m* interretialis
wed *tr (a woman)* ducere; *(a man)* nubere *(w. dat)* ‖ *intr (of bride)* nubere; *(of groom)* uxorem ducere
wedding *s* nupti·ae -arum *fpl*
wedding *adj* nuptial·is -is -e; **to set the — day** diem nuptiis dicere; **— day** dies -ei *m* nuptiarum; **— gown** vest·is -is *f* nuptialis; **— present** don·um -i *n* nuptiale; **— reception** conviv·ium -(i)i *n* nuptiale; **— ring** anul·us -i *m* nuptialis
wedge *s* cune·us -i *m*
wedlock *s* matrimon·ium -(i)i *n*
Wednesday *s* di·es -ei *m* Mercurii
weed *s* herb·a -ae *f* mala
weed *tr* eruncare
week *s* hebdom·as -adis *f,* septiman·a -ae *f*
weekday *s* di·es -ei *m* profestus
weekend *s* fin·is -is *m* hebdomadis; **on the —** exeunte hebdomade
weekly *adj* hebdomadal·is -is -e
weekly *adv* septimo quoque die, singulis hebdomadibus
weep *intr* flēre, lacrimare; **to — for** flēre, deplorare
weeping *s* flet·us -ūs *m*
weigh *tr* pendere; *(fig)* examinare; **to — down** degravare; *(fig)* opprimere; **to — out** expendere ‖ *intr* **to — much** magni ponderis esse
weight *s* pond·us -eris *n; (heaviness)* gravit·as -atis *f; (influence)* auctorit·as -atis *f; (importance)* moment·um -i *n*
weight lifting *s* sublati·o -onis *f* libramentorum

weighty *adj* grav·is -is -e
welcome *s* salutati·o -onis *f;* **I gave him a warm —** eum amantissime excepi
welcome *adj* opportunissim·us -a -um; **you're —!** *(after a person says "thank you)* libenter!
welcome *tr* benigne excipere
welcome *interj* salve!; *pl:* salvete!
weld *tr* (con)ferruminare
welfare *s* sal·us -utis *f; (charity)* carit·as -atis *f*
well *s* pute·us -i *m*
well *adj (healthy)* san·us -a -um, salv·us -a -um; **all's —** salva res est; **it is — to** convenit *(w. inf);* **to be —** valēre; **to get —** convalescere
well *adv* bene, recte; **he is — off** bene se habet; *(fin)* bene aeratus est; **I am doing —** mihi bene est; **very —** optime; **— done!** macte virtute esto!
well *interj* immo; *(all right)* licet; **— now** age ergo; **— —!** enim vero!
well-behaved *adj* bene morat·us -a -um
well-being *s* sal·us -tis *f*
well-born *adj* generos·us -a -um
well-bred *adj* bene educat·us -a -um
well-deserved *adj* rite merit·us -a -um
well-done *adj* optime fact·us -a -um; *(cooking)* percoct·us -a -um; **— done!** macte virtute esto!
well-heeled *adj* bene aerat·us -a -um
well-known *adj* nobil·is -is -e, not·us -a -um
well-mannered *adj* bene morat·us -a -um
well-off *adj* bene aerat·us -a -um
well-read *adj* litterat·us -a -um
well-spoken *adj* disert·us -a -um
well-supplied *adj* copiosissim·us -a -um
well-timed *adj* opportun·us -a -um
welter *s* congeri·es -ei *f*
werewolf *s* versipell·is -is *m*
west *s* occas·us -ūs *m* (solis); **in the —** ab occidente; **toward the —** in occasum
western *adj* occidental·is -is -e
westward *adv* in occasum, in occidentem versus [versus *is an adverb*]
west wind *s* Zephyr·us -i *m*
wet *adj* uvid·us -a -um; *(through and through)* madid·us -a -um; **to get —** madefieri
wet *tr* madefacere
wet-nurse *s* nutr·ix -icis *f*
whack *tr (coll)* percolopare
whack *s* colaph·us -i *m;* **to give s.o. a —** colaphum alicui ducere
whale *s* balaen·a -ae *f*
wharf *s* naval·e -is *n*
what *adj interrog* qui, quae quod; **— kind of, — sort of** qual·is -is -e
what *pron interrog* quid, quidnam; **— about me?** quid de me?; **— do you take me for? a**

fool? pro quo me habēs? pro stulto?; **— else?** quid amplius?; quid aliud?; **— else can I do for you?** quid est quod tibi efficere possum amplius?; **— for?** quam ob rem?; **— is it?** *(what's the trouble?)* quid est negoti?; **— is it? out with it!** quid id est? cedo!; **— is this all about?** quid enim?; **— next?** quid deinde?; **—'s that?** *(what did you say?)* quid id est?; **—'s that to you?** quid ad te attinet?; **—'s the matter?** quid est?; **— is the reason why ... ?** quid est quod *(w. indic);* **—'s up?** quid rei est?; **—'s wrong?** quid est?
whatever *pron* quicquid; **—!** quidvis!
whatever *adj interrog* quicumque, quaecumque, quodcumque
wheat *s* tritic·um -i *n*
wheedle *tr* blandiri; **to — out of s.o.** eblandiri ex aliquo
wheel *s* rot·a -ae *f;* **the — turns** rota revolvitur
wheelbarrow *s* pab·o -onis *m*
wheelchair *s* sell·a -ae *f* rotalis
when *adv (interrog)* quando
when *conj* cum, ubi, ut; **— first** cum primum; **— joking** inter iocos
whence *adv* unde
whenever *adv* quandocumque, utcumque
where *adv* quā, ubi; *(motion)* quo; **from —?** unde?; **— are you from?** unde es?; **— on earth** ubinam gentium
whereabouts *s* positi·o -onis *f,* loc·us -i *m* quo
whereas *conj* quandoquidem
whereby *adv* quā viā, quo
wherever *adv (position)* ubicumque, quo in loco; *(direction)* quocumque
wherefore *adv* quare, quamobrem
wherein *adv* in quo, in quibus, ubi
whereof *adv* de quo, de quibus
whereupon *adv* quo facto; *(then)* deinde
wherever *conj* quacumque, ubicumque, sicubi
wherewithall *s* **to have the — to** unde habēre *(w. inf)*
whet *tr* acuere; **to — the appetite** exacuere appetentiam (cibi)
whether *conj (in single indir. ques.)* num, -ne, an; **— ... or** *(in multiple indir. ques.)* utrum ... an, -ne ... an, *or ...* an; *(in disjunctive conditions)* sive ... sive, seu ... seu; **— ... or not** utrum ... necne
whetstone *s* co·s -tis *f*
which *pron interrog* quis, quid; *(of two)* ut·er -ra -rum **‖** *pron rel* qui, quae, quod
which *adj interrog* qui, quae, quod; *(of two)* u·ter -tra -trum **‖** *adj rel* qui, quae, quod
whichever *pron* quicumque, quaecumque, quodcumque; *(of two)* utercumque, utracumque, utrumcumque

whiff *s (slight smell)* od·or -oris *m* exiguus; **to get a — of** subolēre; **— of air** aur·a -ae *f*
while *s* temp·us -oris *n,* spat·ium -(i)i *n;* **after a —** paulo post; **a good — after** aliquanto post; **a long —** diu; **a short — ago, a short — before** paulo ante; **for a short —** paulisper; **for a —** aliquamdiu; **in a little —** in brevi spatio; **once in a —** interdum
while *conj* dum, quoad, donec
while *tr* **to — away the time** tempus fallere
whim *s* arbitr·ium -(i)i *n;* **according to their — and pleasure** ad eorum arbitrium et nutum
whimper *s* vagit·us -ūs *m*
whimper *intr* vagire
whimsical *adj* mobil·is -is -e
whine *intr* plorare
whinny *s* hinnit·us -ūs *m*
whinny *intr* hinnire
whip *s* flagell·um -i *n,* ver·ber -beris *n*
whip *tr* flagellare; *(coll)* superare; **to — out** eripere
whipped cream *s* crem·um -i *n* battutum
whippersnapper *s* frust·um -i *n* pueri
whipping *s* verberati·o -onis *f;* **to get a —** vapulare
whirl *tr* torquēre, rotare **ll** *intr* torquēri, rotari
whirl *s* turb·o -inis *m*
whirlpool *s* vert·ex -icis *m,* gurg·es -itis *m*
whirlwind *s* turb·o -inis *m*
whirr *intr* stridēre, increpare
whisk *tr (to brush lightly)* verrere; **to — away** everrere, eripere **ll** *intr* **to — about** *(to move about quickly)* circumvolitare
whiskbroom *s* scopul·a -ae *f*
whisker *s (of animal)* saet·a -ae *f;* **by a — vix;** **—s** barb·a -ae *f*
whiskey *s* aqu·a -ae *f* vitae
whisper *s* susurr·us -i *m*
whisper *tr & intr* susurrare
whistle *s (sound)* sibil·us -i *m; (pipe)* fistul·a -ae *f; (of wind)* strid·or -oris *m*
whistle *tr* **to — some tune** exsibilare nescio quid **ll** *intr* sibilare; *(of the wind)* stridēre
whit *s* **every — as good** omnino par; **not a — better** nihilo melius
white *adj* alb·us -a -um; *(brilliant)* candid·us -a -um; *(hair)* can·us -a -um; **to be —** albēre, albicare; **to turn —** albescere; *(face)* pallescere; **— bread** pan·is -is *m* candidus
white *s (the color; of an egg, of the eye)* alb·um -i *n;* cand·or -oris *m*
whiten *tr* dealbare, candefacere **ll** *intr* albescere, canescere
whitewash *s* albar·ium -(i)i *n; (fig)* fuc·us -i *m*
whitewash *tr* dealbare; *(fig)* fucare
whither *adv* quo, quorsum

whithersoever *adv* quocumque
whitish *adj* subalb·us -a -um
whittle *tr & intr* ad fastigium secare; *(to carve)* sculpere
whiz *intr* stridēre, increpare; **to — by** praetervolare
whiz *s (sound)* strid·or -oris *m; (brilliant person)* ingen·ium -(i)i *n*
who *pron interrog* quis; **— are you?** quis tu homo es?; **— says so?** quis hoc dicit factum? **— the devil** quis malum **ll** *pron rel* qui, quae
whoa *interj* eho!
whoever *pron* quicumque, quaecumque
whole *adj* tot·us -a -um, cunct·us -a -um, univers·us -a -um; *(unimpaired)* incolum·is -is -e, inte·ger -gra -grum
whole *s* tot·um -i *n;* **on the —** plerumque, ex toto; **taken as a —** in summam
wholehearted *adj* sincer·us -a -um
wholesale *adj* magnari·us -a -um; **to carry on — business** magnariam mercaturam facere
wholesale *adv* acervatim
wholesaler *s* magnarius (-a) negotia·tor -toris *m* (·trix -tricis *f*)
wholesome *adj* salutar·is -is -e
whole-wheat bread *s* autopyr·us -i *m*
wholly *adv* omnino, prorsus
whom *pron* quem; **of —** cuius; **to —** cui; **with — quocum,** cum quo
whoop *s* ululat·us -ūs *m*
whoop *intr* ululatum tollere
whore *s* scort·um -i *n*
whorehouse *s* lupan·ar -aris *n*
whoremonger *s* scortat·or -oris *m*
whose *pron* cuius; *pl:* quorum, quarum, quorum
why *adv* cur, quamobrem, quare; **just —** cur tandem; **that's — ...** quo fit ut *(w. subj);* **— is it that ...** quid est quod *(w. indic);* **— not?** quid ita non?; *(as an expression of assent; of course)* quippini *or* quidni?; **— say more?** quid plura?; **— so? because ...** quid ita? quia ... ; **— the devil** cur malum
wick *s* fil·um -i *n*
wicked *adj* improb·us -a -um
wickedly *adv* improbe, sceleste
wickedness *s* improbit·as -atis *f*
wicker *adj* vimine·us -a -um
wicker basket *s* scirpul·us -i *m*
wide *adj* lat·us -a -um; *(spread out)* pass·us -a -um, porrect·us -a -um; **to be — of** aberrare ab *(w. abl)*
wide *adv* late; **far and —** longe et late
wide-awake *adj (fig)* ala·cer -cris -cre
wide-eyed *adj* oculis apertis; *(surprised)* attonit·us -a -um
widely *adv* late; *(among people)* vulgo

widen *tr* dilatare **‖** *intr* dilatari; *(of a country)* se pandere

widespread *adj* divulgat·us -a -um

widow *s* vidu·a -ae *f*

widower *s* vidu·us -i *m*

width *s* latitud·o -inis *f;* **ten feet in —** decem pedes in latitudinem

wield *tr (weapon)* tractare, vibrare; **to — supreme power** plurimum pollēre

wife *s* ux·or -oris *f; (of a slave)* contubernal·is -is *f*

wifely *adj* uxori·us -a -um

wig *s* capillament·um -i *n*

wiggle *tr* torquēre **‖** *intr* se torquēre; *(of a woman)* crisare

wild *adj* fer·us -a -um; *(desolate)* vast·us -a -um; *(mad)* insan·us -a -um; *(uncontrolled)* efferat·us -a -um; *(of trees, plants)* silvestr·is -is -e; *(of land)* incult·us -a -um; *(of disposition)* fer·ox -ocis; **— beast** fer·a -ae *f,* fera besti·a -ae *f*

wild *s* **growing in the —** silvestr·is -is -e; **the —s** incult·a -orum *npl*

wildcat *s* lynx, lyncis *mf*

wildcat *adj (unauthorized)* illicit·us -a -um

wilderness *s* desert·a -orum *npl; (fig)* vastit·as -atis *f*

wild-goose chase *s* vanum incept·um -i *n*

wildly *adv* saeve, ferociter

wildness *s* ferit·as -atis *f*

wile *s* dol·us -i *m*

wiliness *s* callidit·as -atis *f*

will *s* volunt·as -atis *f,* anim·us -i *m; (intent)* proposit·um -i *n; (testament)* testament·um -i *n; (of gods)* nut·us -ūs *m;* **against one's —** invit·us -a -um; **at —** ad libidinem suam; **of one's own free —** suā sponte; **to make a —** testamentum facere

will *tr (a legacy)* legare

willful *adj* consult·us -a -um

willfully *adv* consulto

willing *adj* lib·ens -entis; **to be —** velle

willingly *adv* libenter

willingness *s* volunt·as -atis *f*

willpower *s* vis *f* mentis

willy-nilly *adv* nolens volens

wily *adj* va·fer -fra -frum

win *s* victori·a -ae *f;* **a — on points** praevalenti·a -ae *f* punctorum

win *tr (to attain)* adipisci, consequi; *(to gain)* potiri; *(victory)* reportare, adipisci; **to — a battle** proelio vincere; **to — a bet** sponsione vincere; **to — a court case** iudicio vincere; **to — friends** amicos acquirere; **to — highest honors** amplissimos honores consequi; **to — the hearts of the people** conciliare animos

plebis; **to — over** conciliare **‖** *intr* vincere; **to — out** *(to prevail)* praevalēre

wince *intr* **to — with sudden pain** prae dolore subito horrēre

winch *s* sucul·a -ae *f*

wind *s* vent·us -i *m;* **head (tail) —** ventus adversus (secundus); **I got — of it long ago** iam pridem id mihi subolebat

wind *tr* circumvolvere; *(a clock)* intendere; **the plant wound itself around the tree** herba arbori se circumvolvit; **to — up** *(a speech)* concludere, perorare; **to — up one's affairs** res domesticas et familiares in ordinem redigere

winded *adj* anhel·ans -antis

windfall *s (fig)* lucr·um -i *n* insperatum

winding *adj* flexuos·us -a -um

windmill *s* mol·a -ae *f* vento acta

window *s* fenestr·a -ae *f; (of glass)* fenestra vitrea; *(comput)* fenestell·a -ae *f*

windowpane *s* specular·e -is *n,* fenestrae vitr·um -i *n*

window seat *s* sed·es -is *f* fenestralis

windpipe *s* arteri·a -ae *f* aspera

windshield *s* vitr·um -i *n* antiaërium

windshield wiper *s* vitriterg·ium -(i)i *n*

windstorm *s* procell·a -ae *f*

windup *s* fin·is -is *m,* termin·us -i *m; (of a speech)* perorati·o -onis *f*

windy *adj* ventos·us -a -um

wine *s* vin·um -i *n; (undiluted)* mer·um -i *n; (cheap wine)* vapp·a -ae *f;* **dry (light, red, sweet, white) —** austerum (tenue, sanguineum, dulce, album) vinum

wine cellar *s* cellar·ium -(i)i *n* vinarium

wined and dined *adj* prans·us et pot·us -a -um

wine glass *s* hyal·us -i *m* vinarius

wing *s* al·a -ae *f; (of a building)* lat·us -eris *n; (mil)* corn·u -ūs *n*

winged *adj* alat·us -a -um

wink *intr* nictare, connivēre; **to — at** nictare *(w. dat)*

winner *s* vic·tor -toris *m* (·trix -tricis *f*)

winning *adj (fig)* amoen·us -a -um

winnings *spl* lucr·um -i *n*

winter *s* hiem·s -is *f;* **at the beginning (end) of —** ineunte (exeunte) hieme; **in the dead of —** mediā hieme; brumā; **to spend the —** hiemare

winter *intr* hiemare, hibernare

winter *adj* hibern·us -a -um, hiemal·is -is -e; **— clothes** hiberna vestiment·a -orum *npl;* **— time** hiemale temp·us -oris *n*

winter quarters *spl* hibern·a -orum *npl*

wintry *adj* hiemal·is -is -e, brumal·is -is -e

wipe *tr* tergēre; *(lips)* abstergēre; **to be —ed out** *(of a debt)* deperire; **to — away**

abstergēre; *(tears)* extergēre; **to — off** *or* **clean** detergēre; **to — out** *(writing)* delēre; **to — the nose** emungere

wire *s* fil·um -i *n* ferreum; *(of silver)* filum argenteum; *(of copper)* filum aëneum

wisdom *s* sapienti·a -ae *f*

wise *adj* sapi·ens -entis, prud·ens -entis

wise *s (way)* mod·us -i *m;* **in no — ** nequaquam

wise guy *s* impud·ens -entis *m;* **don't be a —!** ne sis impudens!

wisely *adv* sapienter, prudenter

wish *s (act of wishing)* optati·o -onis *f; (thing wished)* optat·um -i *n; (prayer)* vot·um -i *n;* **according to one's —es** de sententiā; **according to your —es** secundum voluntatem tuam; **best —es to your brother** salutem plurimam fratri tuo; **I give you three —es** tres optationes tibi do

wish *tr* optare, velle, cupere; **to — earnestly** exoptare || *intr* **to — for** exoptare, expetere

wishing *s* optati·o -onis *f*

wisp *s (of hair, grass, etc.)* manipul·us -i *m*

wistful *adj* desiderii plen·us -a -um

wistfully *adv* oculis intentis

wit *s (intellect)* ingen·ium -(i)i *n; (humor)* facceti·ae -arum *fpl; (person)* hom·o -inis *mf* facet·us (·a -ae); **to be at one's —s' end** delirare; **to —** scilicet

witch *s* strig·a -ae *f,* mag·a -ae *f*

witchcraft *s* ar·s -tis *f* magica

with *prep* cum *(w. abl); (at the house of)* apud *(w. acc)*

withdraw *tr* seducere, avocare; *(words)* revocare || *intr* recedere

wither *tr* torrēre || *intr* marcēre

withered *adj* marcid·us -a -um

withhold *tr* retinēre; *(to suppress)* supprimere

within *adv* intus, intra; *(on the inside)* intrinsecus; **— and without** intrinsecus et extrinsecus

within *prep (place, time, the law)* intra *(w. acc); (during a definite period)* inter *(w. acc);* **— a few days** paucis diebus

without *adv* extra, exterius; *(out of doors)* foris; **from —** extrinsecus

without *prep* sine *(w. abl),* absque *(w. abl);* **I could in no way enter — their seeing me** nullo modo introire poteram quin me viderent; **to be —** carēre *(w. abl)*

withstand *tr* resistere *(w. dat),* obsistere *(w. dat)*

witness *s* test·is -is *mf; (to a signature)* obsigna·tor -toris *m* (·trix -tricis *f);* **to bear — ** testificari; **to be called as a —** contestari; **to call to —** testari; **trustworthy witness** testis locuples *(gen:* testis locupletis) *mf*

witness *tr* testificari; *(to see)* interesse *(w. dat),* spectare

witticism *s* faceti·a -ae *f*

wittily *adv* facete, festive

witty *adj* facet·us -a -um

wizard *s* mag·us -i *m*

woe *s* luct·us -ūs *m;* **—s** mal·a -orum *npl*

woeful *adj* luctuos·us -a -um

woefully *adv* misere, flebiliter

wolf *s* lup·us -i *m,* lup·a -ae *f;* **wolves howl** lupi ululant

wolf cub *s* lupae catul·us -i *m*

woman *s* muli·er -eris *f,* femin·a -ae *f;* **old —** an·us -ūs *f;* **young —** muliercul·a -ae *f*

womanly *adj* muliebr·is -is -e

womb *s* uter·us -i *m*

wonder *s* admirati·o -onis *f; (astonishing object)* miracul·um -i *n;* **and no —** nec mirum; **seven —s of the world** septem miracula mundi; **to excite —** mirationem facere

wonder *intr* mirari; **I wonder what's up** miror quid hoc sit negoti; **to — at** admirari

wonderful *adj* (ad)mirabil·is -is -e

wonderfully *adv* mirabiliter

wont *adj* **to be — to** solēre *(w. inf)*

woo *tr* petere

wood *s* lign·um -i *n;* **—s** silv·a -ae *f*

wooded *adj* silvos·us -a -um

wooden *adj* ligne·us -a -um

wooden spoon *s* cochle·ar -aris *n* coquinarium

woodland *s* salt·us -ūs *m*

wood nymph *s* Dry·as -adis *f*

woodpecker *s* pic·us -i *m*

woods *spl* silv·a -ae *f*

woody *adj (full of wood fibers)* lignos·us -a -um; *(covered with woods)* silvos·us -a -um, silvestr·is -is -e

wooer *s* proc·us -i *m*

wool *s* lan·a -ae *f;* **to pull the — over s.o.'s eyes** subdol·us (-a) esse adversus aliquem

woolen *adj* lane·us -a -um

word *s (in context)* verb·um -i *n; (out of context)* vocabul·um -i *n; (gram)* dicti·o -onis *f; (spoken)* vox vocis *f,* dict·um -i *n; (promise)* fid·es -ei *f; (news)* nunt·ius -(i)i *m;* **in a —** ad summam; **I want a — with you** paucis te volo; **to break one's —** fidem fallere; **to give one's —** fidem dare; **to keep one's —** fidem praestare; **to send —** muntiare; **why should I take your — for it?** cur tibi credam?; **— for —** ad verbum; **— of honor** fid·es -ei *f;* **—s fail me** mihi verba desunt; quid dicam non invenio; **you took the —s right out of my mouth** tu quidem ex ore orationem mihi eripuisti; **upon my —** meā fide; **— of honor** fid·es -ei *f*

wordy *adj* verbos·us -a -um

work *s (labor, pains)* oper·a -ae *f; (act of working and thing completed; literary work)* op·us -eris *n; (labor, trouble)* lab·or -oris *m; (employment)* occupati·o -onis *f,* negot·ium -(i)i *n;* **at —** occupat·us -a -um, negotios·us -a -um; **good —s** recte et honeste fact·a -orum *npl;* **one day's work** una opera *f;* **to throw out of —** de negotio deicere

work *tr (to exercise)* exercēre; *(to till)* colere; *(a machine)* administrare; **to — one's way up** proficere; **to — out** solvere; **to — up** elaborare; *(emotion)* efferre; *(fig)* excitare, perturbare ‖ *intr* laborare, operari; *(to function)* fung·or -i functus sum; **to — at** *(or* **on)** operam dare *(w. dat);* **to — out** *(to exercise)* exercitare

worker *s (unskilled)* operari·us -i *m (·a -ae f); (skilled)* opif·ex -icis *mf; (day laborer)* oper·a -ae *f* [*mostly in the pl*]

workmanship *s* op·us -eris *n,* artific·ium -(i)i *n*

workout *s* exercitati·o -onis *f*

workshop *s* officin·a -ae *f*

world *s (universe)* mund·us -i *m,* summ·a -ae *f* rerum; *(earth)* orb·is -is *m* terrarum; *(mankind)* homin·es -um *mpl;* **next —** vit·a -ae *f* futura; **where in the —** ubi terrarum, ubi gentium; **worst poet in the —** pessimus poeta omnium

worldly *adj* profan·us -a -um

world war *s* bell·um -i *n* mandanum

worldwide *adj* univers·us -a -um, per orbem terrarum pat·ens -entis

World Wide Web (WWW) Tel·a -ae *f* Totius Terrae (TTT)

worm *s* verm·is -is *m;* **earth worm** lumbric·us -i *m*

worm *tr* **to — one's way into** se insinuare in *(w. acc)*

worm-eaten, wormy *adj* vermiculos·us -a -um

worn out *adj (person)* fatigat·us -a -um; *(clothes)* trit·us -a -um

worrisome *adj* molest·us -a -um

worry *s* sollicitud·o -inis *f; (cause)* molesti·a -ae *f*

worry *tr* sollicitare; **don't — yourself to death** ne te crucia ‖ *intr* sollicitari; **don't —!** noli *(pl:* nolite) sollicitari!

worse *adj* pe·ior -ior -ius, deter·ior -ior -ius; **to get —** ingravescere; **to make matters —** res exasperare; **to make —** peiorem reddere, deteriorem reddere; **to turn out for the —** in peius evenire

worse *adv* peius, deterius

worsen *intr* ingravescere

worship *s* cult·us -ūs *m,* venerati·o -onis *f*

worship *tr* colere, venerari

worshipful *adj* rever·ens -entis

worshipper *s* cul·tor -toris *m (·trix -tricis f)*

worst *adj* pessim·us -a -um, deterrim·us -a -um; **— of all** maxime alien·us -a -um

worst *adv* pessime

worst *tr* vincere

worth *s (value)* pret·ium -(i)i *n,* aestimati·o -onis *f; (merit)* dignit·as -atis *f; (prestige)* auctorit·as -atis *f;* **man is of little —** hom·o -inis *m* parvi preti est; **of great —** pretios·us -a -um; **of little —** vil·is -is -e

worth *adj* dign·us -a -um *(w. abl);* **a slave — any price** serv·us -i *m* quantivis preti; **he is — a lot of money** divitias maximas habet; **he is — nothing** nihil est; **how much are pigs — here?** quibus hic pretis porci veneunt?; **it is — knowing** est operae pretium cognoscere; **this is — s.th. to me** hoc mihi in lucro est; **to be — a lot** multum valēre

worthless *adj* vil·is -is -e; *(of persons)* nequam [*indecl*]; **completely — fellow** nequissimus hom·o -inis *m*

worthlessness *s* inanit·as -atis *f*

worthwhile *adj* **to be —** operae pretium esse

worthy *adj* **(of)** dign·us -a -um *(w. abl)*

wound *s* vuln·us -eris *n; (fig)* offensi·o -onis *f*

wound *tr* vulnerare; *(fig)* offendere

wounded *adj* sauci·us -a -um

wow *interj (expressing amazement, surprise)* vah!; hui!

wrangle *intr* rixari, altercari

wrangling *s* discordi·a -ae *f*

wrap *tr (to wind)* involvere; **to — oneself** se amicire; **to — the head in his toga** caput obvolvere togā; **to — up** complicare; *(against the cold)* involvere; *(to finish)* conficere, finem facere *(w. dat)*

wrap *s (cloak)* amict·us -ūs *m*

wrapper *s* involucr·um -i *n*

wrapping paper *s* chart·a -ae *f* emporetica

wrath *s* ir·a -ae *f,* iracundi·a -ae *f*

wrathful *adj* iracund·us -a -um

wreak *tr* **to — havoc** stragem dare; **to — vengeance on** ulcisci

wreath *s* sert·um -i *n,* coron·a -ae *f*

wreathe *tr (to twist)* torquēre; *(to adorn with wreathes)* nectere

wreck *s* ruin·a -ae *f; (of ship)* naufrag·ium -(i)i *n;* **he is a —** naufragus est

wreck *tr* frangere; *(fig)* delēre

wren *s* regul·us -i *m*

wrench *s (tool)* forf·ex -icis *f; (twist)* luxati·o -onis *f*

wrench *tr (a limb)* detorquēre, luxare; **to — away** eripere

wrest *tr* extorquēre, eripere

wrestle *intr* luctari

wrestler *s* luct·or -oris *m*
wrestling *s* luctati·o -onis *f*
wrestling match *s* certam·en -inis *n* luctation-
is
wretch *s* mis·er -eri *m,* miser·a -ae *f*
wretched *adj* mis·er -era -erum
wretchedly *adv* misere
wretchedness *s* miseri·a -ae *f*
wring *tr* contorquēre; **to — the neck** gulam
frangere; **—ing his hands** manibus inter se
constrictis; **to — out a cloth** linteolum
exprimere
wrinkle *s* rug·a -ae *f*
wrinkle *tr* corrugare; **to — the forehead** frontem contrahere
wrinkled *adj* rugos·us -a -um
wrist *s* primoris man·us -ūs *f;* **sleeves reaching
all the way down to the —s** manicae prolix-
ae usque in primores manūs
wrist bone *s* carp·us -i *m*
writ *s* mandat·um -i *n*
write *tr* scribere; *(a book)* conscribere; *(poetry,
book)* componere; *(history)* perscribere; **to —
a program** *(comput)* programma componere;
to — Latin Latine scribere
writer *s* scrip·tor -toris *m* (·trix -tricis *f)*
writhe *intr* torquēri
writing *s* *(act)* scripti·o -onis *f; (result)*
script·um -i *n,* scriptur·a -ae *f;* **in the —s of
Cicero** apud Ciceronem; **—s** script·a
-orum *npl*
wrong *s* nefas *n (indecl),* iniuri·a -ae *f,* mal·um
-i *n;* **to do —** peccare, male facere
wrong *adj (opp:* erectus) prav·us -a -um;
(incorrect, mistaken) fals·us -a -um; *(unfair)*
iniqu·us -a -um; *(unsuitable)* alien·us -a -um;
(faulty) vitios·us -a -um; *(morally)* nefas
[*indecl*]; **if I have done anything —, I'm
sorry** si quid perperam feci, me paenitet; **to
be — errare; what's — with you?** quid est
tecum?
wrong *tr* iniuriam inferre *(w. dat),* offendere
wrongdoing *s* probr·um -i *n,* malefact·um -i *n*
wrongly *adv* perperam, male
wrought *adj* confect·us -a -um
wrought iron *s* ferr·um -i *n* temperatum
wry *adj* contort·us -a -um; *(sharp)* mord·ax
-acis, sals·us -a -um

Y

yacht *s* phasel·us -i *m; (smaller model)* cel·ox
-ocis *f*
yank *tr (coll)* vellere

yap *intr (to prattle)* garrire; *(to grumble)* gannire
yapping *s (prattle)* garrit·us -ūs *m;* gannit·us
-ūs *m*
yard *s* are·a -ae *f* domūs; *(measure)* tres pedes
mpl; **back yard** area (domūs) postica
yardarm *s* antenn·a -ae *f*
yarn *s (of linen)* fil·um -i *n* lini; *(of wool)*
fil·um -i *n* laneum; *(story)* fabul·a -ae *f*
yawn *s* oscitati·o -onis *f*
yawn *intr* oscitare, hiare; *(to gape open)* dehiscere
year *s* ann·us -i *m;* **at the beginning (end) of
the —** ineunte (exeunte) anno; **a — from
now** ad annum; **a hundred —s from now** ad
centum annos; **every —** quotannis; **five —s**
quinquenn·ium -(i)i *n;* **for a — in annum;
four —s** quadrenn·ium -(i)i *n;* **he is twenty
—s old** viginti annos natus est; **in his later
—s** tempore extremo; **in the — of our Lord**
anno Domini; **it's ten —s since the law was
passed** decem anni sunt quum lata lex est; **I
wish you a happy New Year** Novum
Annum laetum tibi exopto; **last —** anno
superiore; **next —** anno proximo; **three —s**
trienn·ium -(i)i *n;* **twice a —** bis (in) anno;
two —s bienn·ium -(i)i *n;* **up in —s** aetate
provect·us -a -um
yearly *adj* annu·us -a -um
yearly *adv* quotannis
yearn *intr* **to — for** desiderare
yearning *s* **(for)** desider·ium -(i)i *n (w. gen)*
yeast *s* ferment·um -i *n*
yell *s* clam·or -oris *m,* ululat·us -ūs *m*
yell *tr* clamāre ‖ *intr* ululare; *(in pain)* eiulare
yellow *adj (hair, gold, sand, grainfields,
honey)* flav·us -a -um; *(teeth)* lurid·us -a
-um; *(hair, sand)* fulv·us -a -um
yellowish *adj* subflav·us -a -um
yelp *intr (like a dog)* gannire; *(in pain)* eiulare;
what's he —ing for? quid ille gannit?
yelp *s* gannit·us -ūs *m; (in pain)* eiulat·us -ūs *m*
yes *adv* ita, sic, sane, oppido *(but the most frequent way in Latin to express a simple yes is
to repeat the word emphasized in the question):* **do you want me? Yes.** visne me? Te.;
has he sold her? Yes. eam vendidit?
Vendidit.
yes-man *s* assecl·a -ae *m*
yesterday *adv* heri; **the day before —**
nudiustertius [*adv*]; **— evening** heri vesperi;
— morning heri mane
yet *adv (contrast, after adversative clause)*
tamen; *(time)* adhuc; *(w. comparatives)*
etiam; **as — adhuc; not — nondum**
yew *s* tax·us -i *f*

yield *tr (to produce)* ferre, parere; *(to surrender)* concedere ‖ *intr* cedere; **to — to** cedere *(w. dat)*

yield *s* fruct·us -ūs *m; (profit)* quaest·us -ūs *m*

yipes *interj (to express surprise, fear, dismay)* eheu!

yippee *interj (to express joy, elation)* ehem!

yoke *s* iug·um -i *n; (fig)* servit·us -utis *f*

yoke *tr* coniungere

yokel *s* rustic·us -i *m* (·a -ae *f*)

yolk *s* vitell·us -i *m*

yonder *adv* illic

yonder *adj* ill·e -a -ud

you *pron* tu; *(ye)* vos; **to —** tibi; vobis; **with —** tecum; vobiscum; **— know** [*parenthetical*] enim

young *adj (children)* parv·us -a -um (natu), parvul·us -a -um (natu); *(goat, vine)* novell·us -a -um; **— boy** puerul·us -i *m;* **— bride** nova nupt·a -ae *f;* **— daughter** filiol·a -ae *f;* **— girl** puellul·a -ae *f;* **— lady** muliercul·a -ae *f;* **— man** adulescentul·us -i *m,* adulesc·ens -entis *m; (between the ages of 20 and 40)* iuven·is -is *m*

younger *adj* iun·ior -ior -ius, min·or -or -us (natu)

youngster *s* adulescentul·us -i *m* (·a -ae *f*)

your *adj* tu·us -a -um; *pl:* ves·ter -tra -trum

yourself *pron refl* te; **by —** per te; **to —** tibi; **with —** tecum ‖ *pron intensive* **you —** *(masc)* tu ipse; *(fem)* tu ipsa

yourselves *pron refl* vos; **to —** vobis; **with —** vobiscum ‖ *pron intensive* **you —** *(masc)* vos ipsi; *(fem)* vos ipsae

youth *s (age)* adulescenti·a -ae *f; (collectively)* iuvent·us -utis *f; (young person)* iuven·is -is *mf,* adulesc·ens -entis *mf*

youthful *adj* iuvenil·is -is -e

youthfully *adv* iuveniliter

Z

zany *adj* delir·us -a -um

zeal *s* stud·ium -(i)i *n,* ferv·or -oris *m*

zealot *s* fanatic·us -i *m* (·a -ae *f*)

zealous *adj* studios·us -a -um

zealously *adv* studiose, enixe

zebra *s* zebr·a -ae *f*

zenith *s* vert·ex -icis *m; (fig)* fastig·ium -(i)i *n*

zephyr *s* Zephyr·us -i *m*

zero *s* nihil *n,* nil *n* [*indecl*]

zest *s* sap·or -oris *m; (fig)* gustat·us -ūs *m;* **— for true praise** gustatus *m* verae laudis

zig-zag *adj* tortuos·us -a -um; **— streets** anfract·ūs -uum *mpl* viarum

zip code *s* numer·us -i *n* cursualis

zipper *s* clausur·a -ae *f* tractilis

zither *s* cithar·a -ae *f*

zodiac *s* Zodiac·us -i *m,* signifer orb·is -is *m*

zone *s* zon·a -ae *f,* regi·o -onis *f*

zoo *s* vivar·ium -(i)i *n,* hort·i -orum *mpl* zoölogici

zoology *s* zoölogi·a -ae *f*

Abbreviations

abbr	abbreviation	*geog*	geography	*pej*	pejorative
abl	ablative	*geol*	geology	*perf*	perfect
acc	accusative	*gram*	grammar	*phil*	philosophy
adj	adjective	*hum*	humorous	*pl*	plural
adjl	adjectival	*imperf*	imperfect	*poet*	poetry
adv	adverb	*impers*	impersonal verb	*pol*	politics
advl	adverbial	*impv*	imperative	*pp*	past participle
anat	anatomy	*indecl*	indeclinable	*pref*	prefix
archit	architecture	*indef*	indefinite	*prep*	preposition
astr	astronomy	*indic*	indicative	*pres*	present
bot	botany	*inf*	infinitive	*pron*	pronoun
c.	circa, about	*interj*	interjection	*pros*	prosody
cf.	confer, compare	*interrog*	interrogative	*prov*	proverb
cent.	century	*intr*	intransitive	*refl*	reflexive
coll	colloquial	*leg*	legal	*rel*	relative
com	commerce	*lit*	literal	*relig*	religion
comp	comparative	*loc*	locative	*rhet*	rhetoric
conj	conjunction	*m*	masculine noun	*s*	substantive
d.	died	*masc*	masculine	*S.*	South(ern)
dat	dative	*math*	mathematics	*singl*	singular
defect	defective verb	*med*	medicine	*sl*	slang
dim.	diminutive	*mf*	masculine or feminine noun	*s.o.*	someone
E.	East(ern)			*s.th.*	something
eccl	ecclesiastical	*mil*	military	*subj*	subjunctive
educ	education	*mpl*	masculine plural noun	*suf*	suffix
euphem	euphemism			*superl*	superlative
esp.	especially	*mus*	music	*theat*	theater
expr.	expressed	*n*	neuter noun	*topog*	topography
f	feminine noun	*N.*	North(ern)	*tr*	transitive verb
fem	feminine	*naut*	nautical	*usu.*	usually
fig	figurative	*neg.*	negative	*vbl*	verbal
fin	finance	*neut*	neuter	*v defect*	defective verb
Ē	floruit, flourished	*nom*	nominative	*v impers*	impersonal verb
fpl	feminine plural noun	*npl*	neuter plural noun	*vulg*	vulgar
		opp	opposite of	*w.*	with
fut	future	*p*	participle	*W.*	West(ern)
gen	genitive	*pass*	passive		

JOHN C. TRAUPMAN, Ph.D. in Classics, Princeton University, was chairman of the Department of Classics, St. Joseph's University (Philadelphia). He is the author of *The New College German & English Dictionary; Latin Is Fun, Books I and II; Lingua Latina, Books 1 and II;* and *Conversational Latin for Oral Proficiency.* He was associate editor of *The Scribner-Bantam English Dictionary* and Editor-in-Chief for the Wimbleton Publishing Co., Ltd., London. He has served as President of the Philadelphia Classical Society, the Pennsylvania Classical Association, and the Classical Association of the Atlantic States, and is a member of the American Advisory Board of Lexus, Ltd., Glascow, Scotland.

Dictionaries in the Series

Edwin B. Williams, General Editor

The New College French & English Dictionary
 by Roger J. Steiner

The New College German & English Dictionary
 by John C. Traupman

The New College Italian & English Dictionary
 by Robert C. Melzi

The New College Latin & English Dictionary
 by John C. Traupman

The New College Spanish & English Dictionary
 by Edwin B. Williams,
 revised by Roger J. Steiner

AMSCO SCHOOL PUBLICATIONS, INC.